THE COMPLETE
BIBLE
COMMENTARY

George Williams
FOREWORD BY T. W. WILSON

The Complete Bible Commentary by George Williams.

Foreword by T. W. Wilson copyright © 1994 by Kregel Publications.

Published by Kregel Publications, a division of Kregel Inc., 2450 Oak Industrial Dr. NE, Grand Rapids, MI 49505.

Cover Photograph: Julie A. Richardson

Library of Congress Cataloging Card Number 75-13929

ISBN 978-0-8254-4104-2

5 6 7 8 / 26 25 24 23 22 21

Printed in the United States of America

CONTENTS

FOREWORD

George Williams was an outstanding Christian of the nineteenth century. In addition to seven languages, including Hebrew and Greek, he knew the Scriptures and Him of whom the Scriptures speak.

It is an unique work, containing much valuable material not to be found anywhere else, and is uncompromisingly loyal to the Virgin Birth and to the deity, atonement, and resurrection of Christ. The writer stands upon the absolute authority of the Scriptures. Each doctrine of Scripture is emphatically presented.

My first introduction to this work was when it was first published in America under the title *The Student's Commentary on the Holy Scriptures* by Kregel Publications.

I have recommended it to many preachers as one of the finest collection of nuggets I have ever come across. It is deep, it is biblical, and it is practical. I don't believe there is a one-volume commentary in my library that is more effective than this work.

Billy Graham, who has taken this work with him around the world, says:

> "Williams' *Complete Bible Commentary* is a valued volume in my library. I have always appreciated its basic commitment to the authority and inspiration of the Scriptures and found its insights to be an excellent source for sermon preparation or personal Bible study.
>
> It is an excellent addition to any pastor's or Bible student's library. Your knowledge of the Word will greatly increase, and your heart will be blessed as it ministers to you."

As with any commentary, one would not agree with everything the author suggests; however, I would wholeheartedly recommend this one to any Christian who wants to increase his or her knowledge of the Scriptures and be effective in witnessing to others

T.W. WILSON

Montreat, North Carolina

BIOGRAPHICAL NOTE

My brother-in-law, George Williams, was one of the Paymasters in Dublin Castle, then the center of the British Government in Ireland. He was first awakened to spiritual realities about the age of sixteen and went with his family to the parish church of Stillorgan when Dr. Chadwick, afterwards Bishop of Londonderry, was the minister.

His close association with the evangelical revivals of the nineteenth century, especially that associated with D. L. Moody, brought him into touch with the outstanding Bible students of his day. He lived a most active, practical Christian life. In his combination of gifts as a Bible expositor, open-air preacher, and worker among young people, his retentive memory, musical talent, and his power of telling a story well all made him welcome in public-school camps, student gatherings, and children's services.

His open-air campaigns for five years in the South and West of Ireland will be long remembered. He was a champion of free speech, and in this spirit he proclaimed the Free Gospel; he suffered sorely in health from the effects of these strenuous days until the end of his life.

The first editions of the *Commentary* appeared anonymously. In the third edition the author's wife wrote:

> The compiler, George Williams, suppressed his name because he felt physically unable for correspondence, but in December 1928 he was called to Higher Service—in his seventy-eighth year. His life from the age of sixteen had been devoted to the Master, to whom he had early dedicated himself. He was born in Dublin in 1850, and as a young man he received a nomination to the Treasury, Dublin Castle, and there, among an . . . aristocratic circle, he became familiarly known as "Christian." He was an untiring worker in spite of indifferent health, and besides his official duties he found time for Christian service of many kinds. His vacations were spent in evangelistic work at home and abroad. He had a familiar knowledge of French, German, Italian and Spanish and preached in these languages at many mission centers.
>
> After his marriage and retirement from the Civil Service, he lived at Bessbrook in the North of Ireland. Always a diligent student of the Bible, for the last twenty years of his life he studied Hebrew and renewed his knowledge of Greek and Latin in preparation for the work of this *Commentary*.

H. Stephens Richardson

NOTES ON GENESIS i. 1, and i. 5.

The Law of the number 7, which appears throughout the entire Bible, first occurs in Gen. i. 1, and may be shown, though not exhaustively, in the subjoined note —

Verse Order	Numeric Value	Alphabet Place	Name
1	2	2	Beth
2	200	20	Resch
3	1	1	Aleph
4	300	21	Shin
5	10	10	Yod
6	400	22	Tau
7	2	2	Beth
8	200	20	Resch
9	1	1	Aleph
10	1	1	Aleph
11	30	12	Lamed
12	5	5	He
13	10	10	Yod
14	40	13	Mem
15	1	1	Aleph
16	400	22	Tau
17	5	5	He
18	300	21	Shin
19	40	13	Mem
20	10	10	Yod
21	40	13	Mem
22	6	6	Vau
23	1	1	Aleph
24	400	22	Tau
25	5	5	He
26	1	1	Aleph
27	200	20	Resch
28	90	18	Tzade

" In Hebrew this verse has 7 words.

The 7 words contain 28 letters (4 × 7).

The subject and predicate have 14 letters (2 × 7). and the objects 14 letters (2 × 7).

The first object "the heavens" has 7 letters, and the second object "the earth" has 7 letters.

God, heavens, and earth have 14 letters (2 × 7).

Numeric value of these 3 words is 777 = 111 × 7.

Place value is 147, or 21 × 7 = 7 × 7 × 3.

Words 3 and 4 begin with vowel letters and have 7 letters.

Words 1, 2, 5, 6, and 7 begin with consonants and have 21 letters, and their sum is 21.

The first and last letters of each of the 7 words have a *total* value of 1526 = 218 × 7.

Of which the numeric value is 1393 = 199 × 7, and the place value 133 = 19 × 7.

Of this place value the first, middle and last words have 70 = 7 × 2 × 5 whose sum is 14.

The numeric value of 1393 is also divided thus : the first and last letters of the first and last of the 7 words have 497 = 71 × 7, the remaining letters have 896 = 128 × 7.

Or 7 × 2 + 7, whose sum is 21 = 3 × 7.

The numeric value of the first, middle and last letters of the verse is 133 = 19 × 7.

Of which the first 2 letters have 42 = 6 × 7, and the last 2 letters have 91 = 13 × 7.

Of the 28 letters, 3 occur only once, their numeric values being 126 = 18 × 7.

The numeric value of the first and last letters of the first 4 words is 847 = 121 × 7, and of the last 3 words 546 = 78 × 7.

The 3 final letters of the first 3 words have a numeric value of 441 = 63 × 7, or 9 sevens of sevens.

The only verb " created " has a numeric value of 203 = 29 × 7.

The first letter of " God," and the last letter of " earth " have numeric value of 91 = 13 × 7.

The first syllable of the verse has a numeric value of 203 = 29 × 7.

The place value of the first, middle and last syllables of the verse is 84 = 12 × 7.

The Hebrew alphabet consists of 22 letters, of which exactly *half* or 11 are used. Their numeric values are, 1, 2, 5, 6 : 10, 30, 40, 90 ; 200, 300, 400.

Their place values are 1, 2, 5, 6 ; 10, 12, 13, 18 ; 20, 21, 22.

Thus they consist of 3 classes. Places 1, 2, 5, 6, have unit values ; places 10, 12, 13, 18, have tens ; and places 20, 21 and 22 have hundreds.

But 6 + 1 are 7 = 1 × 7..

10 + 18 are 28 = 4 × 7.

20 + 22 are 42 = 6 × 7.

their sum being 77 = 11 × 7.

Of the 3 classes the first and last have 7 numbers.

Whose sum 1, 2, 5, 6, 20, 21, 22 is 77 = 11 × 7.

Divided thus the units have 14 = 2 × 7, and the hundreds 63 = 9 × 7.

These 7 numbers are divided into 4 for the units, and 3 for the hundreds ; the units are thus divided, 1 + 6 = 7, and the middle ones 2 + 5 = 7.

The 3 numbers for the hundreds are also divided, the first and last 20 + 22 = 42 or 6 × 7, and the middle one 21 = 3 × 7.

The *only* other verse in the Pentateuch which has 7 words of 28 letters is Exodus xx. v. 1, which begins the Ten Commandments."

This Law of 7 may also be recognised in Physics, Astronomy, Geology, Colour, Music, Botany and Medicine. It links heaven and earth, and testifies to the Divine inspiration of the Scriptures.

Could any one of the greatest scientists either ancient or modern, make in seven words a statement of corresponding grandeur with that of the first verse of the Bible and exhibit in its structure the same mysterious force and beauty of this mystic number ?

Verse 5. The formula " the evening and the morning " of verses 5, 8, 13, 19, 23, and 31 explains Matt. xii. 40, and xvi, 21, thus Thursday evening and Friday morning were the first day, Friday evening and Saturday morning the second day, and Saturday evening and Sunday morning the third day, so making three days and three nights. In British law a man sentenced to one day's imprisonment, is released the day he is sentenced, and may therefore spend only five minutes in jail.

GENESIS

GENESIS I—GENESIS II. 3.—These thirty-four verses form an Introduction to Genesis, and indeed to the whole Bible.

" In the beginning, God," Gen. i. 1.

" And God," Gen. i. 3.

" Then cometh the end, God," 1 Cor. xv. 24.

God begins the Christian life in the soul, God sustains the Christian life in the soul and God perfects the Christian life in the soul. It is all God ! (Phil. i. 6, R.V.)

The first page of the Bible corresponds to the last page, all is blessing and light and love and rest, because all is God.

" Beginning " is the subject of this book ; it teaches that God is the Beginner of the visible and invisible universe, as He is the Beginner of salvation in the soul of the sinner. See note on page 43.

The first verse of the chapter reveals God as the Creator of the heavens and the earth at some unknown period in the past.

The second verse points to a stupendous convulsion that affected the earth, for it says the earth was, that is became, without form and void, sunk in the deep, and wrapped about with darkness. See notes on Isaiah xlv.

The remainder of the chapter describes the renewing power of the Spirit of God in producing light and life and beauty from out of this ruin. The creative energy of that Holy Spirit operates to-day in a similar manner in the ruined nature of man. Believers are new creations (2 Cor. v. 17) and are created unto good works (Eph. ii. 10). Thus the ruin revealed in the second verse pictures the sinner prior to regeneration, and the order, beauty, and rest of chapter ii. 1-3, set forth the perfection of the Spirit's work in him.

The words " created " and " made " (ii. 3) close this first chapter and should be distinguished when it is being read. The difficulties which science, imperfect and limited, here finds have been satisfactorily discussed by able commentators, and their arguments need not be repeated, except to draw attention to these important and distinctive words, " Create " and " Made " (ii.3). For example, He " created " the sun, moon, and stars at some unknown period of time " in the beginning " (i. 1), and afterwards, when preparing the earth for man, He " made," i.e., appointed (iv. 14-18) them in relation to the earth as light-holders (Heb.), as measurers of time, and as vehicles of revelation (Ps. xix). Modern science admits that light is indefinable; that it exists independently of the sun ; and that the astronomy of this chapter is superhuman. See note on page 43.

The important word " and " occurs 102 times, and is designed to fasten attention upon the 102 separate actions of God in this Introduction.

In chapter i. 26, 27, the Divine purpose is announced, and in chapter ii. 7, the Divine action is described in the creation of man.

The word " man " in verse 26 means mankind ; hence the word " them." The word " man " in verse 27 should have the definite article, and should read " the man ", that is, Adam—" the same man Adam " spoken of in chapter ii. 7. These are not therefore, two accounts of the creation of man, but one Divine statement.

There is no evening to the Sabbath Day, it has no evening, it is eternal. It foretells Christ, the true Sabbath, in whom God rests and in whom believers rest. This is " God's own rest " of Heb. iv.

" Blessing " is stamped upon this Introduction to the history of God's interest in man and His creatures. He blessed the living creatures, verse 22 ; He blessed man, verse 28, and He blessed the seventh day.

GENESIS II. 4-25.—The expression, "these are the generations," occurs eleven times in this first book of the Bible (Gen. xxv. 12 and 13 counting as one), and mark its Divine divisions. They occur altogether fourteen times in the Bible. Thus, Gen. 11 times, and Num. iii, 1 ; Ruth iv. 18-22 ; and Matt. i, 1.

"Generation" means family history.

This chapter reveals Christ as Jehovah Elohim, man's Redeemer. The first chapter reveals Him as Elohim, man's Creator. He first prepares the beauteous world in which man is to dwell and then He creates man, and, as Jehovah, enters into covenant with him. These two great titles of Christ are distinguished throughout the entire Bible, and finally appear in its two closing chapters, which treat of redeemed man and a new earth. If, therefore, the first two chapters of the Bible are the work of two editors, as some suppose, then, by a parity of reasoning, so are the last two !

The tree of death (verse 17), appears at the opening of the Bible, the tree of Calvary (1 Pet. ii. 24), in the middle of the Bible and the tree of life (Rev. ii. 7), at the end of the Bible.

Verse 20, together with verse 26 of the prior chapter, show that man before the fall possessed intuitive knowledge and a real government over the works of God's hands. (Ps. viii, Heb. ii.).

"Thou shalt be sentenced to death" expressed the doom of verse 17.

Verse 24 was spoken by God. The words, "And God said" should be supplied. (See note on Matt. xix. 5).

GENESIS III.—Five great periods embrace Bible History : Innocence, Conscience, Law, Grace, and Righteousness. Declension, not progress, is stamped upon all. Each period opens hopefully but ends in Judgment. This chapter narrates the ruin and judgment of the first period.

Satan first questions the inspiration of the Bible (v. 1), (" hath God said "), then he denies its teaching, (v. 4), (" ye shall not surely die "), and finally substitutes his own gospel—the immanence of God (v. 5), (" ye shall be as Elohim ").

Eve misquotes the Word of God, and adds to it one addition and two misquotations, the addition " neither shall ye touch it," the two misquotations, " we may eat " instead of " we may freely eat " and " lest we die " instead of " ye shall surely die." Thus Satan's triple cunning contrasts with man's triple simplicity.

Contrast verse 6 with Luke iv. 3-13. Both present the three temptations, " the lust of the flesh," " the lust of the eyes " and " the pride of life." The First man falls, the Second man conquers.

"Where art thou," is the first question in the Old Testament, " Where is he," is the first question in the New (Matt. ii. 2). The Old Testament : God seeking the sinner ; the New Testament, the sinner seeking God.

Adam hides from God, not because of any change in God, but because of the change in himself, wrought by the entrance of sin. The clothing he provided for himself did very well until God appeared and was then found to be worthless. Sinners clothe themselves with morality, sacraments and religious ceremonies ; they are as worthless as Adam's apron of fig leaves.

God questions Adam and his wife, He promises them a Saviour and He clothes them. He asks the serpent no question, He judges him, and it is in listening to this judgement that the guilty pair hear the First Great Promise respecting Christ. See Notes on Hebrews xi.

There are seven such great promises in the Old Testament : four in Genesis and three in the remaining books. They predicted that the Redeemer should be of the Human Race (Gen. iii. 15) ; of a section of that race, Shem, (Gen. ix. 26) ; of a nation belonging to that section, the Hebrew (Gen. xii. 3) ; of a tribe in that nation, Judah (Gen. xlix. 10) ; of a family in that tribe, David (2 Sam. vii. 16) ; of a member of that family, a woman, the Virgin (Isa. vii. 14) ; and lastly in a village belonging to that woman, Bethlehem (Mic. v. 2). Thus these Great Prophetic Circles are narrowed, and finally close around the Lamb and Son of God.

The Holy Spirit in 1 Tim. ii. 14 teaches that Adam sinned more deeply than his wife. She is condemned in verse 16 to subjection to him ; prior to that condemnation she was his helpmeet or equal. 1 Cor. xiv. 34 includes this subjection in " the Law "

Man is expelled from the garden lest by

eating of the tree of life he should perpetuate his misery, but God's love for him, though fallen and guilty, is so strong that He accompanies him into exile, making His dwelling place with him at the east of the Garden between the Cherubim, a sword, made of flame, forbidding access to the tree of life. Verse 24 should read " and He made His dwelling place at the east of the garden between the cherubim, the fierce flame—the Shechinah—turning every way to guard the way of the tree of life." Chapter iv. verses 3, 7, 14, and 16 are made intelligible by this translation.

The sense of verse 22 is : " Behold the man (thinks) he is become as one of us," etc.

" Thistles " (v. 18). The Hebrew words may include noxious insects.

GENESIS IV.—Eve is mentioned four times in the Bible, Gen. iii. 20, iv. 1, 2 Cor. xi. 3, and 1 Tim. ii, 13. She names her sons " Cain," that is begotten, and " Abel," that is vanity, thus illustrating the ignorance into which she was plunged because she had trusted Satan for knowledge. At Cain's birth she joyfully cries " I have gotten the man promised by Jehovah ! " Very soon she learns that he was out of the Evil One (1 John iii. 12) and when his brother is given to her she exclaims with anguish, "Vanity !"

The brothers dress their altars at the " door " (v. 7) of the mysterious Tabernacle in which God dwells, and attached to which is the flaming sword. There is no difference between the brothers, but an eternal difference between their sacrifices. They are both corrupt branches of a decayed tree, both born outside Eden, both guilty, both sinners, no moral difference, and both sentenced to death. The words " by faith " (Heb. xi. 4) teach that God had revealed a way of approach to Him (Rom. x. 17). Abel accepts this way, Cain rejects it. Abel's altar speaks of repentance, of faith, and of the precious blood of Christ, the Lamb of God without blemish. Cain's altar tells of pride, unbelief, and self-righteousness.

Abel's altar is beautiful to God's eye and repulsive to man's. Cain's altar, beautiful to man's eye and repulsive to God's. These " altars " exist to-day, around the one, that is, Christ and His atoning work, few are gathered, around the other many. God accepts the slain lamb and rejects the offered fruit ; and the offering being rejected so of necessity is the offerer. Heb. xi. 4 says God " testified over " (R.V.) Abel's gifts, that is, by fire from heaven—possibly the flaming sword—(Lev. ix. 24, Judges vi. 21, 1 Kings xviii. 38, 1 Chron. xxi. 26). See Notes on Heb. xi. 24.

God loves Cain, and wishing to bless him also, He tells him that if he will make an offering similar to his brother's it will be accepted, that the lamb for the sin-offering was close at hand, lying at the door entrance (Heb.) of the Tabernacle before which the brothers were standing, adding that He would give him, if obedient, dominion over the whole earth and dispose his brother to willingly accept that government, as He had disposed Eve (ch. iii. 16) to willingly accept subjection to Adam. This would appear to be the force of the word " desire " in both passages. Amazing grace ! Cain rejects this love, invites his brother into the field and murders him. Adam sins against God and Cain sins against man. In their united conduct we have sin in all its forms, and that on the first page of human history.

Cain's religion was too refined to slay a lamb, but not too cultured to murder his brother. God's way of salvation fills the heart with love ; man's way of salvation inflames it with hatred. " Religion " has ever been the greatest cause of bloodshed. Cain (v. 13) accepting lightly the vengeance of God dreads that of man. God in added grace gives him a pledge (sign) so that no one shall slay him. The Tabernacle of God and its flaming sword are now impossible, and Cain becomes a wanderer in the far-off land of Nod. Nod means " land of the wanderers."

The second question in the Bible is : " What hast thou done ? " This concerns man's sins, the fruit of his sinful nature. " Where art thou ? " points to the fact of that sinful nature in man.

Cain makes himself as comfortable as possible in the earth, he builds a city, adorns it with the arts and sciences, and cheers its homes with music. His posterity is detailed ; and, remarkable fact, not one of them is stated to have died ! The children of the promise, however, in the next chapter, all die.

Lust and lawlessness quickly appear in Lamech ; he takes two wives, and he murders two men ; but he need not be disquieted threat, because if God forbad anyone to punish Cain who was so great a sinner, how much safer was he as being less guilty than Cain ! The first poem, therefore, in human history, like most poetry ever since, glorifies immorality and murder, and denies coming wrath. Lamech, in effect, says that God would be to blame if aught happened to him, i.e., that there is no future punishment. See Notes on Num. xxiii. 10 and Luke xiv. 15.

Abel having been murdered, God raises up Seth and Enoch as depositaries of the Messianic promise. Their birth closes the first section of this book. As already stated there are eleven sections each introduced by the words " these are the generations." This first section gives the " generations of the heaven and of the earth," that is, the family history of the Heavenly Seed—the children of Seth, and of the Earthly Seed—the children of Cain. So soon then as these two families definitely appeared, the men, that is, the sons of Cain, began to fasten upon the others, that is, the sons of Seth—but in contempt and hatred—the name of Jehovah : This would appear to be the meaning of the words : " Then began men to call upon the name of Jehovah." Eve " called " her son by the name of Seth ; Seth " called " his son by the name of Enoch, but the family of Cain " called " them, contemptuously, by the name of Jehovah. So it was at Antioch, believers were contemptuously called by the name of Christ.

The sense of verse 13 may be : Is my sin so great that it cannot be forgiven ? i.e., Why so great a stir about a matter so small ! Thus the son spoke as the father, for Cain was morally born of the Wicked One (1 John iii. 12).

GENESIS V.—This second division of the Book of Genesis is introduced by the words : " This is the book of the generations of Adam," not, " these are the generations of Adam," as in the ten other divisions, but " This is *the book* of the generations of Adam." Why is this ? Matt. i. 1 gives the answer " The book of the generation of Jesus Christ." He is the last Adam.

The family history of this, the heavenly race, is marked by death. What a contradiction ! No matter how long a member of this family lived, yet three words attend his name : " and he died." As before noticed

no such fact is recorded in connection with Cain's family.

Three statements are made in the Bible respecting Enoch : he walked with God (Gen. v), he witnessed for God (Jude), he pleased God (Heb. xi). Prior to the Fall, God walked with man ; subsequent to it man walked with God. Apparently, Enoch was 65 years of age when he was converted and entered into this Divine fellowship. To-day, if a man walks with God thirty years after conversion, it is felt to be an encouraging proof of the power of Christ to save and to keep, but here is a man who walked with God three hundred years ! The possibility and power of this life of victory is made the more remarkable by the statement that he did not live a life of isolation (though he did live a life of separation), for he was a married man with a family.

The word Methuselah means : " It (the Deluge) shall be sent " when he is dead ; and so it came to pass. A few weeks after his death the flood destroyed the world of the ungodly. From the time he was a little boy, Methuselah must have heard his father speak of this coming flood.

The heavenly Lamech, like his earthly cousin and namesake, sings, but how different is the song ! The earthly Lamech, as already learned, sang of lust and vileness, the heavenly Lamech sings of comfort and peace. He calls his child " Noah," that is, rest, comfort, consolation. He finds consolation and rest in the gift of this child when dwelling in a sin-cursed earth. A beauteous picture of the believer, who, though surrounded by the toils and sorrows of this life, and affected by them, yet finds a satisfying comfort in Christ, the true Child of Consolation. The heavenly Lamech refuses to make his home in this sin-blighted earth, and looking forward to the Promised Child, the true Noah, he finds in Him a true peace. The earthly Lamech makes this world his home and comforts his heart in a false peace, as has been already noticed in the fourth chapter.

As stated in chapter x. verses 2 and 21, Shem was the youngest son of Noah. He and his ancestor Seth illustrate the principle, so often met with in the Bible, that the last shall be first, and the younger preferred to the elder.

GENESIS VI, 1-8—The close of this second section of the Book of Genesis and of the world that then was, synchronize. The heavenly and the earthly families unite, the fruit of that union seemed exceedingly fair in man's judgment, for it says they became mighty men, men of renown. How different was God's judgment! He drowned them one and all in the flood. Satan's efforts are always put forth to bring about a union between the "Sons of God" and the "children of this present evil world"; but this union to-day, as in the days of Noah, "grieves Him at His heart."

This expression "it grieved Him at His heart" reveals the tender pitying love of God. A heart of stone cannot be grieved, only a heart that loves. But only one man is found amid the millions of mankind to respond to that love. It was Noah; but if Noah was saved, it was not because of any moral excellence discovered by God in him but, as stated in verse 8, because of the energy of grace in the heart of God. The eyes of God looked upon him in grace; and if in the next verse it states that he was a righteous man, that he was perfect in his generations and that he walked with God he had nought whereof to boast. His perfect pedigree was his by natural birth, and his righteousness was his by spiritual birth (Heb. xi. 7).

GENESIS VI. 9-22.—The third section of this "Book of the Beginnings" opens with the words "These are the generations of Noah." The word "generations" occurs twice in the ninth verse. Hebrew scholars point out in the original text the use of different words here, and that the first means "pedigree" and the second "contemporaries." Not only was Noah of pure descent from Adam but he was also pure in his conduct, for he walked habitually with God (see vii. v.). The one word points to his natural birth; the other to his spiritual birth (Heb. xi. 7).

All stands now in contrast with Eden. That was a realm of life with the tree of death in its midst. This, a realm of death with the "Tree of Life" (Christ) in the midst. For of a smitten tree was the ark made. Then there was death in the tree; now life in the ark. God then said "away from the tree!" Satan said "Hasten to it!" God now says "Hasten to the ark and live!"; Satan says "Keep away from it!" Conscience drove Adam from God. Revelation draws

Noah to God. Conscience convicts the sinner of what he is. Revelation assures him of what an all-sufficient Saviour Christ is. He is as sure a Saviour to the sinner as the ark was to Noah.

The designed distinction in the Divine Titles is observable in verse 13 and in vii. 1, 9 and 16. In relation to the living creatures at large, and to man, and to the earth He is Elohim. But in relation to Noah and the clean beasts He is Jehovah. This proves unity and not duality of authorship.

In verse 18 the word "covenant" appears for the first time in the Scripture.

Ship-builders point out that the dimensions of the ark were exactly those of an ocean-going ship designed for safety.

GENESIS VII.—The human race owes its existence to the fact that one man was terror-stricken. The epistle to the Hebrews states that Noah prepared this ark because he believed the Divine warning. (See note on Heb. xi. 7). The bearer of this warning may have been Enoch. When first warned Noah was directed to "bring" with him into the ark the living creatures in pairs. One hundred and twenty years later, when about to enter the ark, he is commanded to "take" to him the clean by sevens. The first command provided for propagation; the second for sacrifice—and this second and added command was naturally not given till the last moment. The word "take" suggests that the clean animals would present themselves at the door of the ark in sevens. This would have perplexed Noah had he not been told immediately beforehand to accept them.

Elohim broke up the great deep; Jehovah shut Noah into the ark (v. 16).

Those who dwelt upon the tops of the loftiest mountains perished equally with those who lived in the deepest valleys. There was no difference. Many who live upon the mountains of morality think themselves secure from the judgment of fire that is now coming, and pity the certain fate of those who live in the depths of vice. But as in the judgment of water so in the judgment of fire, all will alike perish who are out of Christ.

Noah illustrates the Scripture terms "lost" and "saved." Standing without the door of the ark he was lost, that is, exposed to the coming judgment and sure to perish. Standing inside the door he was saved, that is, sheltered from the coming doom and sure not to perish. To pass from the one condition to the other he had but to take one step—a step into the ark—and he was in immediate safety.

Noah was saved through the baptism of the ark. The ark was sinless, Noah sinful, the ark suffered the fierceness of Divine anger—a baptism into death—but not one wave of that judgment reached Noah. He was absolutely safe. Noah could not perish because the ark could not perish. The ark could not perish because Jehovah was in the ark; that ark was Christ-God in Christ reconciling man unto Himself. He did not say " go into the ark " but " come into the Ark." The apostle Peter in the third chapter of his first epistle points out that this is how sinners are saved—the baptism into death and the resurrection out of death of Jesus Christ. He says that the baptism and resurrection of the ark was a type of the death and resurrection of Christ ; and declares that that antitype-baptism saves believers.

Thus closed in baptism and death the second period of human history. The dispensation of conscience, like the prior period, the dispensation of innocence, began in sunshine and ended in blackest night. The three remaining periods of history reveal the same characteristics.

GENESIS VIII.—The Ark rested on the top of the mountains on the day that Christ rose from the dead. On the 27th day of the second month God spake to Noah saying " Go forth," not " Come forth." The invitation " Come thou into the Ark " shows that God was the first person to enter the Ark ; the command " Go forth out of the Ark " shows that He was the last to leave it. Noah and God had dwelt together in the Ark for a full solar year, that is from the 17th day of the 2nd month until the 22nd day of the corresponding month in the following year—365 days.

Noah builds an altar and worships, not the Ark but God. The Ark was the instrument of his salvation as the cross was of Paul's. But the apostle did not worship the cross as multitudes do to-day, but worshipped Him who died upon it.

The capacity of the Ark to hold the animals is evidenced by a Museum at Paris. Its cubical content is much smaller than the Ark and yet it contains more than 4000 animal specimens of full size.

The cubical content of the Ark was nearly 3,000,000 feet. Scientists declare the distinct species of four-footed animals to be 250. If this number be doubled and a certain proportion multiplied by seven for the clean animals, and if an equal number of birds be added and twelve cubic feet allotted to each animal and to each bird, the total number of cubic feet would be about 1,000,000, leaving 2,000,000 cubic feet for provisions. Thus it has been scientifically ascertained that there was abundance of room in the Ark for its inhabitants.

GENESIS IX. — Man fails in every position in which he is put by God. Scarcely is Noah placed by God in the renewed earth than he falls into the shameful sin of drunkenness ; but as always, so here, man's sin provides an occasion for the overabounding grace of God and at the same time the sure expression of His abhorrence of evil. Japheth is promised dominion in the earth, and so it has come to pass. To Shem is given the glory of being the progenitor of the promised Redeemer, and Canaan is doomed to abject servitude. And yet, perhaps, the words " Canaan shall be his servant " may contain a gracious prophecy and may read " Canaan shall become Jehovah's servant." This would accord with the present day partial fulfilment of this great triple prophecy. The sons of Japheth govern the world, the sons of Shem enrich it with the Bible, and the sons of Canaan, after millenniums of slavery, are to-day becoming servants of Jehovah Jesus. The grace that much more abounds where sin abounds, and that in this triple prophecy foretells a Saviour for all men, as represented in these three great heads of the three families that compose mankind—that grace appears in the conversion of the Ethiopian (Ham) (Acts viii.), the conversion of Paul (Shem) (Acts ix.), and the conversion of Cornelius (Japheth) (Acts x.).

The prediction respecting Canaan must have in the days of Moses, upheld the faith of those who loved the word of the Lord, and excited the ridicule of those who despised it. For the political position of affairs in the world at that time contradicted the prophecy. The sons of Shem, that is the Israelites, were slaves ; the sons of Canaan, that is the Egyptians, were the masters of the world ! But to-day the truthfulness of prediction is established ; and in the day of blessing that awaits Israel, and through her the nations, the full glory of this great promise and prophecy will be displayed. As already pointed out the conversion of the Ethiopian, of Saul and of Cornelius, foretell the introduction of Shem, Ham and Japheth into a brighter world than their fore-fathers looked out upon when leaving the Ark.

The note on Luke iii. 36, should be read in connection with verses 22-25.

Prior to the Flood Noah was probably mocked and opposed, but he did not shame-fully sin as after the Flood when he was King of the whole earth. The Christian is in greater moral danger when in prosperity than when in adversity ; and this principle is true in the spiritual realm as in the material.

The covenant made with Noah and with the living creatures re-appears in Rev. iv. 3. See Notes on that chapter.

It is reasonable to believe that neither rain, nor clouds, existed before the Flood. (See ii. 5 and 6, with 2 Peter iii. 5 and 6). The rain must, therefore, have caused great terror. The rainbow was consequently a new object of beauty and wonder.

GENESIS X.—The Fourth division of this book is marked by the words " These are the generations of the sons of Noah," that is, the family history of the sons of Noah. Their order is thus given, Shem, Ham and Japheth, but the following verses reverse this order : Japheth and his sons being placed first, Ham and his sons second, Shem and his sons third.

Japheth means enlargement ; so has it come to pass. His sons practically govern the world. Ham's sons are degraded and oppressed. Shem means "Name of Renown." He was the father of the Eastern races —nations famous for philosophy and religion, but most of all because out of Shem sprang Jesus, the Plant of Renown (Ezek. xxxiv. 29).

This chapter sets out the nations as divided in the earth ; the following chapter gives the cause of that division. This is an instance of one of the " Laws " or principles to be noticed throughout the whole Bible, exhibiting design on the part of the

Holy Spirit in recording facts out of chrono-logical order in order to make prominent a spiritual lesson, or to hold the attention of the reader to the main subject of the sixty-six books of the Bible, which is " Sin and Salvation."

The great figure of this chapter is Nimrod, and the great city of the chapter is Babylon. He and his city foreshadow the coming AntiChrist and his city. Nimrod was a son of Ham, not of Shem. He may be assumed to have counselled and built the tower of Babel of the next chapter. He was practically king of the whole earth (v. 8). He was a mighty slave-hunter against the face of Jehovah (v. 9), that is, in defiance of Jehovah. Babylon was the beginning of his kingdom (v. 10). He invaded Assyria and built Nineveh with its broad avenues (Rehoboth) (v. 11)—a city of great splendour.

GENESIS XI. 1-9.—This chapter reveals the cause of the divisions recorded in the prior one. The cause was rebellion against the Divine command to replenish the earth. Men resolved to keep together, to build a city and to establish a great temple worship. Nimrod, whose name means " rebel," headed, according to tradition, this rebellion. God called their city "Babel," that is "confusion ; " He confounded their language ; and scattered them abroad on the face of all the earth.

This prince Nimrod, and his city Babylon, and the plain on which it was erected, Shinar, all claim attention. They represent Satan's efforts, using man as his agent, to oppose and destroy God's plans. God has his Prince and his City ; so has Satan. And these opposing princes with their cities occupy most of the pages of the Bible—the closing pages of the Book revealing the triumph of Emmanuel and Jerusalem over AntiChrist and Babylon. In order to man's blessing God set apart for Himself one day (the Sabbath), one land (Palestine), one peo-ple (Israel), and wrote one book (the Bible). Satan's purpose is to degrade the Book, to destroy the People, to ruin the Land and to desecrate the Day. His first agent raised up after the Flood was Nimrod, and the weapon he placed in Nimrod's hand was idolatry. Before the Flood idolatry was impossible. The Garden of Eden, the mysterious Tabernacle at its eastern entrance, with the cherubim and the sword of flame, made the worship of idols hopeless. After the Flood, these no longer existed on the earth. It was easy, therefore, for Satan to introduce idols and heroes as representing God. Nimrod, after his death, was worshipped under many names. These names constantly appear in ancient history.

This was man's first attempt to form a religious association. It contrasts with the association that God formed at Pentecost. The one ended in confusion ; the other established concord.

This Third Period of human history, that is, the dispensation of Law, began with the confounding of tongues. The next period, the Dispensation of Grace, opened with the gift of tongues ; and the future Dispensation of Glory (Rev. vii. 9) will restore the harmony of tongues (Zeph. iii. 9).

Man's City had its foundations in the earth, and sought to ascend from earth to heaven. God's City will descend from heaven to earth.

GENESIS XI. 10—XII. 3.—The Fifth division of Genesis opens by setting out the family history of Shem. This places the reader of the Bible upon what may be termed Messiah's Highway ; for He was to spring out of Shem.

The early verses of this chapter record man's effort to establish himself in the earth and to make for himself a name ; the verses now under consideration show God calling a man out of the earth—Abraham—and giving him a name. Man said " Let us make us a name." God said to Abraham, " I will make thee a name."

Abraham's appearance necessitates the next division of the Book of Genesis, the sixth division : the generations of Terah.

Abraham was the youngest son, but the grace that chose Abel, Shem, Jacob, and Ephraim—all younger sons—chose him.

He was an idolator (Joshua xxiv. 2), possessing no moral claim upon God, he was " a Syrian ready to perish." (Deut. xxvi. 5). But He who said to the Publican " Follow me " (Luke v. 27), said " Come with me and I will bless thee, and thou shalt be a blessing."

With the family history of Shem, of Terah and with the call of Abraham, is introduced the Divine purpose of blessing families, as such, and bringing them into God's Kingdom upon earth. This explains why the apostles in the book of the Acts received whole families into the church of the " Kingdom " by baptism.

GENESIS XII. 4–XIII. 4.—Encouraged by the seven promises of the 2nd and 3rd verses of this chapter, with which may be compared the seven promises made in Exodus vi. 6–8 to Moses, Abraham starts for the better land.

This was his first surrender : there were five of them in all. He here surrenders his native land ; then the vale of the Jordan ; then the riches of Sodom ; then Ishmael ; and, lastly, Isaac. Each painful surrender was followed by increased spiritual wealth, as though in return for yielding up a sixpence to God he received £10,000.

This chapter is important, for it records the first steps of this great believer in the path of faith. There were believers before him, but the Scripture speaks of him as the father of believers. God said to him : " Come with me unto a land that I will show thee." He went out not knowing whither he went, but faith was rewarded, for verse 5 says " into the land of Canaan he came." He actually found himself in the promised land. Thus is it to-day. The Holy Spirit says "Believe on the Lord Jesus Christ and thou shalt be saved." The sinner believes and he is saved. Into " the land of Canaan " he comes. This is the first step in the life of faith. See notes on Acts vii.

But what an unexpected experience for Abraham l He finds the hateful, impure, and hostile Canaanite in God's land (v. 6). This was faith's first trial ; his heart would be tempted to question the fact that this was God's land, for how could the Canaanite be in God's land ! So in the present day the young believer expects after conversion to find nothing in his nature hostile to Christ, but is distressed and perplexed very soon to painfully learn that, alas, the Canaanite is in the land, and that he is now commencing a life-long battle with what the New Testament calls " The Flesh."

But if the Canaanite is in the land, so also is Jehovah. Directly Abraham reaches Sychem the Lord appears unto him, and promises him a son who was to be the progenitor of the Redeemer of all nations. To enjoy these conscious " appearings " of Jesus to the soul, the believer must keep in the path of faith and take the succeeding steps of obedience in that path.

In the eighth verse Abraham reaches the highest level of spiritual experience at this period. It may be described as the Epistle to the Ephesians. He reaches a mountain top, that is the heavenly places, he pitches his tent there, thus confessing himself a pilgrim in a land that belonged to him, and builds an altar. He is both a pilgrim and a worshipper. It was faith that enabled him to claim this land as his own, and yet it was the same faith that enabled him to live in it as though it were not his own !

Happy would it have been for Abraham had he remained upon that mountain top. Alas, he leaves it and is very soon found in Egypt. A famine comes and his faith breaks down in the presence of this trial. It was indeed a mystery that Abraham could not solve why there should be the Canaanite and a famine in God's own chosen land. His heart must have whispered to him that he was under a delusion ; how could such things be found in a land that God had led him into ? But God always tests faith ; and as with Abraham so with all young converts. Soon after they have entered upon the path of faith comes the test, that is, a famine. When the first glow of the new found joy begins to moderate, and the dull realities of the daily life depress the spirit, the heart of the unbeliever feels a famine and the tempta-tion offers itself to go down into Egypt for food, that is to seek companionship and interest amongst the unconverted ! Abraham should have resolved rather to die of starva-tion on the mountain top in fellowship with God, than to feast on the choice meals of Egypt in fellowship with Pharaoh.

This was one of the thirteen famines recorded in the Bible, and its Satanic purpose was undoubtedly to prevent the birth of the Messiah. It was so very near being successful that on this occasion, as on others, God had to specially intervene to defeat the plot. Sarah is taken into Pharaoh's house in order that she might become the mother of a child by the Egyptian king, thus defeating the Messianic promise made to Abraham. Defeated on this occasion, Satan renewed the effort later on in the case of Abimelech, king of Gerar

Abraham in Egypt presents a repulsive picture of contemptible and abject cowardice. To save himself, he denies his wife, and places her in the home of another man to be his wife. Such is the deep depth to which the Christian readily falls directly he leaves the path of faith. God had said to Abraham on the day of his conversion, " I will bless thee

and thou shalt be a blessing," but in the land of Egypt he is a curse. Because of him, Pharaoh and his family are plagued with great plagues, and this heathen prince hurries this man of God out of his land as he would chase away a pestilence.

In the path of faith the Christian is a blessing to the world, but in the path of self-will a curse.

If Abraham went " down " into Egypt in verse 10, grace brings him " up " out of Egypt in chapter xiii. 1 ; and then, famine or no famine, led him to that mountain top where his tent had been at the beginning, " unto the place of the altar which he had made there at the first," and there, doubtless with tears and shame, he called, by sacrifice, on the name of the Lord ; that is, on the saving name of Jesus. His backslidings were forgiven, his soul was restored, and he resumes his true life as a pilgrim and a worshipper with his tent and his altar ; neither of which he had in Egypt.

In this chapter there are two indirect testimonies to its truthfulness, and these testimonies are the more interesting because, prior to recent discovery, they seemed to deny accuracy. The one statement is found in verse 14, recording that the Egyptians noticed the beauty of Sara. Eastern women being always veiled, this statement appeared to mark an error in the Bible. Recent discovery, however, proves that at this period women in Egypt went about unveiled.

The second undesigned evidence of accuracy may be noticed in verse 16. Egypt is famous in the Bible for horses, why therefore did Pharaoh give none to Abraham ? Recent discovery reveals there were no horses in Egypt till the 18th dynasty.

GENESIS XIII. 5-18.—The faith that hangs upon an Abraham fails to give victory over the world, and so Lot chooses the plain of Jordan, though well knowing the character of the men of Sodom. He lifts up his eyes, and noticing how the plain resembled the land of Egypt, he chooses him that fertile vale, separates himself from God's acknow-ledged king and priest, and pitches his tent " toward Sodom." In chapter xviii. 22, the angels of wrath go " toward Sodom " and in chapter xix. 27, Abraham looked " toward Sodom." Here is sin desired, sin discovered, and sin doomed.

How did Lot know that the plain of Sodom resembled the land of Egypt ? Alas, he had been there.   Who brought him there ? Abraham ;   and it was the wealth that Abraham got in Egypt by falsehood that led to the breach with Lot and incited him " toward Sodom." An elder Christian often leads a younger one into worldly circles that give the younger a taste for a life in fellowship with the unconverted.

Wealth whether gotten legitimately or illegitimately often causes strife amongst Christians ; poverty rarely does so. Abraham says to Lot, " let there be no strife between us for we are brethren." And this request is introduced by the statement that the Canaanite and the Perizzite were then in the land. The apostle Paul in writing to the Philippians begs them not to engage in disputes because they dwelt in the midst of a crooked and perverse nation—among whom they were to shine as lights in the world (Phil. ii. 14, 15).

There are six steps in Lot's downward course, viz : he " strove " (xiii. 7) ; he " beheld " (xiii. 10) ; he " chose " (xiii. 11) ; he " pitched toward ". Sodom (xiii. 12) ; he " dwelt " in Sodom (xiv. 12) ; and he " sat in the gate " of Sodom (xix. 1).

This was Abraham's second surrender. It was more difficult than the first. It is a hard thing for an uncle to give way to a nephew. But if the eye of faith is filled with the glory of the city which hath the foundations, such surrenders are made possible.

Directly Lot departs, God draws near to Abraham saying, " Lift up now thine eyes and look northward and southward and eastward and westward : for all the land which thou seest, to thee will I give it, and to thy seed for ever; and I will make thy seed as the dust of the earth." This is a triple promise. First, a grant of the land to Abraham personally, thus ensuring his resurrection. Second, the resurrection and perpetual endowment of his children ; and third, that they should be as numberless as the dust of the earth. In xv. 5, his children are promised to equal the stars of the heaven in multitude. (See Note on xvii. 3). Heb. xi. 9–16 speak of these two great families of which Abraham was the head—the redeemed nations, numerous as the dust of the earth ; Israel glorious and multitudinous as the stars of the heaven.

It is much better to let God choose than for the Christian to choose. Lot lifts up his eyes in self-will and obtains a few acres ; Abraham lifts up his eyes in self-renunciation and is given the whole land.

Obedient to the Divine command in verse 17, Abraham removes his tent to Hebron and builds an altar there. His spiritual life from this time onward was influenced by four " Looks," as Peter's was by two, but with this difference, the apostle's looks were looks that he received, that in John i. which saved him, and that in Luke xxii. which restored him. The Patriarch's "looks" were those which he directed toward the earth (Gen. xiii. 14) ; toward heaven (Gen. xv. 5) ; toward Jehovah (Gen. xviii. 2) ; and toward the Divinely given substitute (Gen. xxii. 13).

GENESIS XIV.–XV. 1.—Recent discoveries attest the existence of these kings at this time. These are the first battles recorded in history.

The number " thirteen " occurs here ; it is its first occurrence in Scripture, and is the number of rebellion. Its subsequent occurrences in the Scriptures present the same feature.

Contrast in verses 12 and 13 the words " Lot, he dwelt as a citizen in Sodom," " Abraham, the Hebrew, *he* dwelt as a passenger in the plain of Mamre." To dwell in " Sodom " involves a Christian in its fortunes with its consequent misery, suffering and captivity (Gen. xiii. 13). To dwell as a pilgrim and a worshipper in the plain of Mamre ensures peace, wealth, dignity, victory, and the power to help and deliver others. Lot could neither deliver Sodom nor himself. Abraham could deliver both. The only way to help and bless the world is to live apart from it, in fellowship with God. But, genuine separation from the world can only result from true fellowship with God. Isolation is not separation. Isolation chills ; separation warms. Isolation makes self the centre ; ˙separation makes Christ the centre. Isolation produces indifference to the need of others ; separation fills the heart with love and interest for the needy and perishing. So soon then as Abraham hears of the captivity of his relative (" brother "), he immediately sets out to save him. Such is the energy of love. Abraham's was the faith that not only overcomes the world, but that works by love.

Such is the nature of Divine faith. It purifies the heart; it rescues the perishing; and it puts kings to flight!

There is no time so dangerous to the Christian as the morrow after a great spiritual victory. Abraham gains two victories, one over the king of Elam, the other over the king of Sodom. Abraham pursues the king of Elam, but the king of Sodom pursues Abraham. Melchizedek, recognising the danger which threatens Abraham, steps between him and the oncoming temptation, and makes a fresh revelation of God to his soul. Abraham's ear at once catches the glorious truth that he is blessed, that is, enriched, by a God who is at once the most High God, and, also, the possessor of heaven and earth; and consequently, in the power of this revelation, he sets his believing foot upon all the wealth of Sodom as though it were dust. This was his third surrender.

A man-made priest has no power to step between the soul and approaching temptation. Christ, the Melchizedek priest, alone can do this. Strange as it may appear, yet it is true, and often to be observed in the Scriptures, that a liability to fall deeply, closely follows a period of exceptional spiritual elevation. Hence Christian people should watch and pray with increased vigilance immediately after periods of revival.

What the Scripture says about Melchizedek will be found in the comments made upon Heb. vii.; here it may be suggested that Melchizedek was Shem. He was alive at this time and lived for 60 years more. He died when Abraham was 150 years of age. Melchizedek, as Shem, is a type of Christ the righteous king, firstly, in History (Gen. xiv.), secondly, in Prophecy (Ps. 110), and lastly, in fulfilment (Heb. vii).

The faith that energized this third surrender was rewarded and enlarged by the revelation of an unconditional covenant based upon and confirmed by Christ's death, which secured to Abraham righteousness, sonship and heirship. The next chapter sets these out in their Divine perfection.

In the house of faith and separation, 318 servants were born and trained and armed. In the house of Lot not one. Abraham saved many; Lot saved no one.

Lot preferred the impure gold of Sodom to the bread of Hebron, and the companionship of the loathsome citizens of Gomorrha to fellowship with holy Abraham. Thus he flouted and despised Abraham. And yet directly Lot was in need, Abraham, at the risk of his life, hastened to save him! Such is Christ on whom Abraham believed.

Four lessons are taught in this story.

1. Life and limb should be risked for undeserving people.

2. Victory only possible if born, trained, and armed in the house of faith.

3. Separation, not isolation, helps the world.

4. After victory comes depression and danger.

So the chapter contrasts the two first missionary societies, Satan's (v. 1-12) and Immanuel's (v. 13-16).

GENESIS XV.—The great victory over the king of Sodom is followed by a period of depression. But He who in the wondrous depths of His love knows our thoughts afar off, hastens to the side of His despondent servant and with exquisite sympathy says, " Fear not, Abraham, I am thy shield and thy exceeding great reward!" Poor Abraham's confused heart answers, " but what canst thou give me, I continue childless!" And now appear upon the dark background of Abraham's dejection the three great truths of Righteousness, Sonship and Heirship.

Abraham asks two questions: "What wilt thou give me?" and, " Whereby shall I know?" Christ is the answer to the first question; the Covenant, to the second.

The only basis upon which a Holy God can establish blessing for sinful men is the person and work of Christ, dead for their sins but risen for their justification. In reply to Abraham's first question God promises him a son out of death and invites him to look upon the countless stars as picturing the glory and multitude of the children of the Divine Seed. Had Abraham looked upon his own dead body he would have found it impossible to believe such a promise, but he looked upon the stars, believed what God said, and his faith was reckoned to him for righteousness. Because he believed God, God declared him a righteous man (Rom. iv., Gal. iii.).

Directly the sinner believes God's testimony about His beloved Son, He is not only declared righteous, but he is made a son and an heir.

Sonship is introduction into the family; heirship, into the kingdom. Hence therefore, when Abraham asks " How shall I know that I shall inherit (not merit) the kingdom," he is not only given this unconditional covenant, but he is caused to experience the suffering which the heirs of the kingdom must know. The apostle says, " If we suffer with him we shall also reign with him." Sonship and glory, heirship and hardship are mutually related.

The covenant was unconditional, God was the one and only contracting party (Gal. iii. 20), but its foundation was grace, for five living creatures are sacrificed to establish it. Five in the scripture is the number of grace; and these five sacrifices set out the fulness of the great sacrifice of Calvary.

The great horror that descended upon Abraham foretold the suffering of the heirs of promise. The furnace of fire that passed between the parted sacrifices expressed the burning trials that the sons of the kingdom must suffer at the hands of Satan and men, but the lamp of fire symbolises the perpetual presence and sustaining grace of the Spirit of God in those trials.

The period of 400 years does not mean, as appears at first sight, that the Egyptians were to afflict the Israelites for that length of time, but that Abraham's children, beginning with Isaac, would be sojourners for 400 years, and that, within that period, they would experience servitude and suffering; and so it came to pass, for they were sojourners, servants and sufferers.

Levi, Kohath, Amram and Moses fulfilled the prediction of verse 16: they were four generations.

This same verse illustrates 2 Peter iii. 9, for God not willing that any should perish, granted to the Amorites a day of grace that lasted four centuries. This grace to the Amorite was the more striking because it entailed suffering upon Israel. The argument of 2 Peter iii. 9, is that Christian people must not impatiently murmur at their sufferings in this long drawn-out day of grace, for it is motived by God's long-suffering compassion toward the perishing.

Up to this day in Abraham's life, God was wont to say to him, " I will give thee this land," but from the hour of this blood-sealed covenant, He says, " I have given thee this land "; for promises based upon the precious blood of Christ are so absolutely sure that faith can claim them as already possessed. Hence the believer in the Lord Jesus Christ is neither ashamed nor afraid to say, " I am saved."

Up to the close of this chapter attention is directed to God's plans with respect to the blessing of man. From this chapter on, God's ways in carrying out these plans are recorded.

To Abraham's first question (v. 2) there was no answer, for God wanted him to continue speaking. He says " Sweet is thy voice " (Cant. ii, 14); and so great is His love to His people that he would rather hear their voice in complaint than not at all !

GENESIS XVI.—Chapter xv. sets out the faithfulness of God, chapter xvi. the faithlessness of Abraham. The covenant that secured to Abraham riches far exceeding the wealth of Sodom was the more amazing because it neccessitated the death of Him who made it ! Such was the faithful love to which Abraham responded with unbelief and impatience. The apostle says ye have need of patience that ye may inherit the promises. The " flesh " can neither believe nor wait for a Divine promise.

The path of faith is full of dignity, the path of unbelief full of degradation. Abraham, finding that God has failed to give him a son, and tired of waiting, no longer sets his hope upon God but upon an Egyptian slave girl. The natural heart will trust anything rather than God. Abraham thinks that he can, by his clever plan, hasten and bring to pass the Divine promise. The result is misery. He succeeds in his plan, Ishmael is born; but better were it for Abraham and the world had he never been born ! It is disastrous when the self-willed plans of the Christian succeed.

It is interesting to know that Abraham's marriage with Hagar, Sarah's treatment of her, and her subsequent expulsion from the household were all strictly legal actions, as now appears from the recently discovered code of laws in existence at that time in Palestine.

The Epistle to the Galatians declares that Sarah and Hagar represent the two principles of law and grace. Hagar represents salvation by works; Sarah, salvation by faith. These principles are opposed to one another. Ishmael is born as the result of man's planning and energy. Isaac is born as the result of God's planning and energy. In the birth of Ishmael, God had nothing to do, and as regards the birth of Isaac man was dead. So is it to-day, salvation by works entirely depends on man's capacity to produce them ; salvation by faith upon God's ability to perform them. Under a covenant of works, God stands still in order to see what man can do. Under the covenant of grace, man stands still to see what God has done. The two covenants are opposed ; it must be either Hagar or Sarah. If Hagar, God has nothing to do with it ; if Sarah, man has nothing to do with it.

The Angel of Jehovah, that is Jesus himself, meets Hagar upon the road to her native land, promises to bless her, tells her He has heard her affliction and comforts her. Alas, that later on, she should have by her conduct despised this grace and sought to murder the Divinely given child. She calls the name of the well where she met Jesus the Lord, " The well of living after seeing," for she said, " Do I live after seeing God ? " She did live, but not as that other woman whom Jesus met at Sychar's well. These wells and these women are here contrasted.

GENESIS XVII.—Two words give the keynote to this chapter. They are " circumcision " and " promise,"—that is, " death," and " grace."

Fourteen years of silence on the part of God follow upon Abraham's folly in the matter of Ishmael; but man's foolish plannings cannot undo God's eternal counsels. The time is fulfilled and the child of promise must be born. But faith must be energised if Isaac is to be begotten ; and accordingly there is a new and abrupt revelation made of Jehovah to Abraham's soul as " El-Shaddai." This is the first occurrence of this great Divine title. It assured Abraham that what God had promised, He was almighty to perform. The first occurrence of this title in the New Testament (2 Cor. vi. 18) expresses the same truth. Throughout the chapter therefore, man is dead and God is the actor ; and it is not so much what God was for Abraham, but what He was Himself—not " I am thy shield," but " I am El-Shaddai." Hence the third verse in contrast with xv. 2, 3, pictures the Patriarch as a silent worshipper listening to Elohim who talks with him.

The three persons of the Godhead appear in this passage as the reader moves backward from the 3rd verse to the 1st verse : Elohim, El-Shaddai, and Jehovah.

In verses 3, 9, 15, 18, 22, and 23, is found the title " Elohim," that is Creator, because in these verses He creates new names, a new sign of covenant, and a new vessel of grace, Isaac.

In the first verse God, as El-Shaddai, says, " Walk before me and be thou perfect." " Perfect " here means " guileless " ; that is, God says, be simple, leave all to me, let me plan for you. I am Almighty. No longer scheme to beget an Ishmael, but trust me to give you an Isaac. This is the meaning of " perfect " in this passage. It does not mean that Abraham could be sinlessly perfect, for he could not. This word " perfect " occurs four times in the New Testament : Matt. v. 48 ; Matt. xix. 21 ; Phil. iii. 12 ; and Heb. x. 1. These four passages treat of benevolence, self-denial, glory and assurance of salvation. None of them teach sinless perfection.

The name Isaac is a divinely given name bestowed before birth, and Isaac himself is a type of the Blessed One, also divinely named prior to his birth, Matt. i. 21.

It is not an exaggeration to compare Abraham's children to sand and stars; they are but feeble figures, for what natural objects could effectively illustrate the fulness of divine power in resurrection ? In the plenitude of this power, God could say to this " dead " man, " I will make "—" I will establish "—" I will give "—" I will bless," and could set before him three engagements. First, that He would be a God to him and his children ; second, that the land of Canaan should be their perpetual possession ; and third, that kings and nations should be born of him.

The fifth letter of the Hebrew alphabet is introduced into the names of Abram and Sarai. The number 5 in the Scriptures is the number of grace, The principle thus appears in these new names, that not human merit but divine love is the base of earthly and heavenly blessing.

Romans iv. makes it clear that Abraham's laughter in verse 17 was the laughter of faith and not of unbelief. It was the joyful laughter of a worshipper when Abraham fell upon his face. His words in effect were, " oh what joy, Sarah and I, though so aged, are to have a child ! " The Lord in John viii. 56 no doubt pointed to this occasion when he said that Abraham rejoiced to see His day and was glad. The exclamation, "Oh that Ishmael might live before thee" was not the cry of unbelief—as is plain from verse 20— nor was it a prayer that Ishmael should be the child of promise, but it was a cry of faith that Ishmael might receive some measure of Divine blessing, though he was to be set aside in favour of the unseen child now promised.

The great subject of the chapter, therefore, is the expansion of the covenant already revealed in chapters xii. and xv. The new features here introduced are the purposes of God in electing Israel and the Gentiles to salvation. Both these countless multitudes of redeemed men spring from Abraham as the first vessel of promise and the root of all who should after him believe unto life everlasting. At the same time the chapter sets out the two principles upon which these divine purposes are founded. These principles are death and grace. The sign of circumcision expressed the one, the Divine promise the other. Man must have the sentence of death written upon his flesh, and grace brings to this dead man life and ever-enduring riches. The sign of circumcision, therefore, declared man to be absolutely without moral value, and justly, as a sinner, sentenced to death. Grace takes up Abraham who was by nature an idolator, declares him to be a righteous man because he believed the testimony of God, and makes him the root out of which Israel and the redeemed nations should proceed.

The alacrity of Abraham's obedience to this new revelation is very lovely. He and all his are circumcised forthwith ; but it is to be noted that Isaac was circumcised on the eighth day, Ishmael in the thirteenth year. He that was born after the flesh is by his natural birth a rebel, though he may enter into an outward covenant, but he that was born after the spirit is a child of the resurrection.

The Epistles to the Romans, to the Galatians and to the Colossians teach that Christians are circumcised in the cross of Christ, baptised in the death of Christ, and raised in the resurrection of Christ.

Circumcision, a compound Latin word, meaning to " cut-around," is the removal of the fore-skin. This holy commandment, though not binding on Christian parents, if observed, will help their sons to be stronger in body and purer in mind. God, by this ordinance, stamped with the sign of death the organ of man's highest physical power, and thus taught, and teaches him, his ruin as born of the first Adam, his incapacity to produce sinless life, and the truth that only by connection with the Prince of Life can he bring forth fruit unto God. Abraham's spiritual life, as a circumcised man, now immediately enters upon a higher plane, as the next chapter shows.

At this point in studying his life it may be suggested that he and his sons illustrate different aspects of Christian living. Abraham, the life of faith ; Isaac, of sonship ; Jacob, of planning ; Joseph, of victory.

The Scriptures continually present Abraham as a pattern of faith. Isaac pictures the happy life of sonship in the father's house, where all things were provided for him. Jacob schemed and managed, but never became a prince of God until the sun rose upon him as a cripple ; and, finally, Joseph is led through suffering to victory.

Circumcision teaches, not only the death of self as essential to a life of fruit bearing, but it also reveals how high, and holy, and precious to God are love, and marriage, and parenthood. Man had, and has, deeply degraded these. Israel was now taught by this sacred ordinance, given by infinite love and wisdom, to honour that which the nations dishonoured.

GENESIS XVIII.—The first verse of this chapter confirms the experience of the Christian that a fresh revelation of the Lord to the soul follows upon obedience to a Divine command.

God now being better known, Abraham enters upon a higher experience, and instead of asking gifts for himself intercedes for others. This is the fruit of the faith and obedience of the prior chapter. He stands upon the mountain-top with God, looks down upon the cities of the plain and pleads for them. Lot on the other hand, though a righteous man, enjoys no such communion, and is by angel hands with difficulty saved.

The energy and intelligence of the Divine life in Abraham's soul is seen in his conduct. He sits, not sleeps, in the heat of the day; he looks, he recognises his Divine visitant accompanied by His angelic servants, he runs to meet Him, he bows himself to the ground, he urges a rest, he hastens into the tent, he presses Sarah to make ready quickly cakes upon the hearth, he himself runs unto the herd and fetches a calf, he commands the servant to hasten to dress it, he himself as a servant places the food before his guests, and as a slave ready for further service, stands while they eat. All is activity, for not only is he active himself but he makes everybody else active. Here is a great principle that can be a great teacher. Spiritual activity in the heart of one servant of Christ's stirs up activity in the hearts of other servants.

" And they did eat "—this is a mystery. Psalm lxxviii speaks of angel's food, and Luke xxiv. and Acts x. state that Christ ate after His resurrection. He here eats that which Abraham provided, and the angels eat with Him.

Unbelief makes men cowards and liars. Sarah laughs with unbelief, and then, through fear, denies the fact. In spite, however, of her incredulity, and in spite of Satan's seeming success in having retarded the birth of a child till it was impossible to nature—in spite of all, the mighty words of grace and promise are spoken—" Sarah shall have a son ! "

There is in the Scripture the laughter of faith and the laughter of unbelief. Unbelief in Matt. ix. 24, " laughed Him to scorn," but faith in Ps. cxxvi. 2, fills the mouth with laughter.

Abraham now appears as the friend of God. He is left alone with Him, and God tells him, not what concerns himself, but what concerns the world. A friend speaks to a friend of that which he has upon his heart. Thus God with Abraham. It is a beautiful scene—Abraham, a stranger in the Land of Promise, communing with God on high, looking down upon a doomed world—and God communing with him, because all the nations should be blessed in him.

GENESIS XIX.—That principle of evil, which the Bible calls " sin," and which has wrought such ruin in human nature, painfully appears in this chapter. Its inhuman loathsomeness in the conduct of the men of Sodom, its incredible shame in the action of Lot toward his daughters, and of theirs afterward toward him, by which originated two shameful nations, Moab and Ammon—for, begotten in shame, both had a shameful history, (Deut. xxiii. 3, Judges x. 10, Num. xxi. 29, 2 Chron. xx. 1, Zeph. ii. 8) ; and its incurable rebellion in Lot's wife.

Men may mock at relatives who are the servants of Christ, but it is no disadvantage to have such relatives, for verse 29 says, " God remembered Abraham and saved Lot."

In Lot's reception of the two angels there is not that warmth and activity in him as was seen in Abraham ; for living in Sodom had sapped those springs of spiritual power which abounded in the patriarch. The angels, on their part, had to be pressed to accept hospitality from the nephew which they at once accepted from the uncle. Fellowship with the world hinders and limits communion, and makes the soul lethargic.

It is not to be wondered at that the young men who were engaged to be married to Lot's daughters (verse 14 should read : " which were to marry." R.V. Margin) refused to believe him. He seemed to them as one that talked nonsense ; and they were justified in thinking so, for his conduct nullified his testimony. Christian ministers cannot expect to win their congregations from the wrath to come, if they themselves live as though there were no such wrath to be feared !

The loving violence of the angels with this unhappy procrastinator was most touching. Its cause is revealed in the words " the Lord being merciful unto him." His folly in lingering, and, further, in preferring his own place of safety to that proposed by the angels, illustrates the deep unbelief of the heart. Living in Sodom gave him a distaste for the mountain proposed by the angels, and so he pleads for permission to settle down in Zoar, urging the smallness of the town as an argument in its favour. But little cities that are godless are as dangerous to the Christian as big ones ; and, ultimately, he had to seek safety from the people of Zoar in the very mountain that he at the first refused to flee to.

The brimstone and fire, that is, burning brimstone, which destroyed the cities, did not burst upon them from hell beneath but from heaven above. The language is very terrible, " Jehovah rained burning brimstone from Jehovah out of heaven." The repetition of the dread title " Jehovah," together with the fact that the burning brimstone came from heaven, adds to the horror of the judgment. The doom of these cities is referred to in : Deut. xxix. 23, Isa. xiii. 19, Jer. xlix. 18, Zeph. ii. 9, Matt. x. 15, 2 Pet. ii. 6, and Jude 7.

GENESIS XX.—Sin is just as hateful in a man of God as in a man of the world, and its guilt is greater. Abraham must have been shocked at the power of unbelief in the several actors of the prior chapter, but was he equally shocked at the power of evil in himself in this chapter ? The sin and misery that resulted years before from journeying " toward the south country " should have taught him never again to move in that direction. But man, as such, never learns nor can learn spiritual lessons. Abraham once more forsakes the path of faith; and in denying his wife sinks to a depth of moral degradation that is contemptible in the extreme. His fall on this occasion was deeper than on the prior one ; for he now had the Divine promise that within that very year Sarah should become the mother of a miraculous child. So long as the Christian walks in the path of faith, he is clothed with dignity and ennobled with courage. But, directly he leaves that path, he falls lower than the children of the Evil One. Nothing but faith can impart true elevation to a man's character, because it alone connects the soul with God.

There is in the confession of Abraham to Abimelech this painful feature revealed in his character. He starts upon his course with a falsehood, and compels his wife to be the degraded sharer of the lie.

These facts revealed by unsparing truth, make it plain' that Abraham by natural disposition and character was cowardly and false. He was only noble when energized by faith. Sad as all this is, there is encouragement in it for the weakest ; for it teaches that the most abject and contemptible man may become noble and strong, if by faith he surrenders his broken humanity to Him who can subdue all things unto Himself. Thus we find Abraham, so abject here before this heathen prince, reproving him later on with dignity and boldness (xxi. 25).

" Abimelech " was the official title of the kings of Gerar, as " Pharaoh " was of the kings of Egypt. Hence considerable periods of time elapsed between the occurrence of these titles, but the same king is not thereby intended in every instance.

If it be objected that this whole occurrence is incredible, because no heathen prince would desire to marry a woman upwards of 90 years of age, or to conceive such a passion for her that, to secure her, he would murder her husband—the very fate which Abraham feared for himself—it may be replied that, first, this was Satan's second effort to bring about the birth of the Messiah by the intervention of a heathen father, and that therefore he would, and could, incite Abimelech to this action ; and, in the second place, it is not unreasonable to believe, from the fact that Sarah nourished Isaac from his birth until he was between 3 and 5 years of age, that God must have miraculously renewed her youth, so that she became sufficiently youthful in appearance to suitably become the wife of Abimelech.

So successful was Satan in his planning that, but for the special intervention of God there would have been a catastrophe. Sarah is delivered through a dream. Twenty such are recorded in the Scriptures.

A divine principle, however, shines forth in this sad chapter, and, that is, that God in His amazing grace is not ashamed to be called the God of a poor, feeble, imperfect, and stumbling man, if there is, in spite of all the weakness, faith and love in the heart. This principle appears again in the prophecy of Balaam, when Jehovah's word is " I have not seen perverseness in Israel "; and, again, as to Joshua the high priest (Zech. iii.), God answers Satan, not by pointing to any moral beauty in Joshua, but to what He Himself had done for him in snatching him as a brand from the fire. Similarly, on this occasion, He owns Abraham as His prophet ; and if the patriarch by his own faithlessness had deeply degraded himself, so as to be justly rebuked by the heathen prince, yet God, in His faithfulness, clothes him with dignity, and honours him in the presence of Abimelech.

In calling Abraham her brother, Abimelech, by the irony, rebuked Sarah. She was responsible at all costs to be loyal to Isaac who was, at the time, present to faith. She was reproved by the irony. She is a type of Israel, as Isaac was of Christ, the Divine seed (Gal. iii.) ; and the Gentile, as typified by Abimelech, returns her to her true position with the cutting reproof that she at least ought to have known and maintained her relationship to Christ.

The words " Thou art but a dead man " of verse 3 mean " Thou shalt surely be struck dead," that is, " if thou seekest to make Sarah thy wife."

Contrast here the innocent Abimelech and the guilty Abraham. The contrast heightens and deepens the mystery of the Divine election when the words are contrasted, " Thou art a dead man," " he is a prophet and he shall pray for thee." Thus is it emphasized that natural goodness and integrity, as in the case of Abimelech, do not necessarily make a man a child of God, and, on the other hand, a temporary moral lapse through fear does not unmake the believer a member of the household of faith. The apostle Peter's case is also an illustration of this truth.

The closing verses of this chapter contain a solemn lesson for all Christian people. Because of Abraham's abandonment of the path of faith, and for so long as he failed to walk in that path, so long were no children born to Abimelech and to his household. This physical fact illustrates a spiritual reality in Christian experience. It is not unreasonable to learn from all this that the birth of spiritual children in the Gospel is hindered or delayed by the inconsistent conduct of prominent Christian people.

GENESIS XXI.—In spite of all Satan's efforts Isaac, the progenitor and type of the Messiah is born ; and born at the " set time," that is, the " exact time " of which God had spoken to Abraham. The fourfold repetition of Sarah's name in the first three verses is emphatic ; the Holy Spirit impressing the fact that Sarah was in very truth the mother of this miraculous child. His birth was a miracle ; but at the same time it must not be forgotten that human life at that period was very much longer than to-day, so that a woman of 90 was not at all so aged as would appear in present times. Sarah's father lived for 200 years ; at the time of Isaac's birth Shem was about 560 years of age ; and there must have been many thousands of persons at the time who had already lived through two or three centuries.

The chapter presents a new creation, hence the Divine title " Elohim " and not " Jehovah " appears throughout it, until verse 33 is reached. In this verse God is " Jehovah " because it touches His covenant relationship as a Saviour. In Mary's song (Luke i. 37, 38, 46 and 47) both titles are united ; and in verses 54 and 55 she connects the mercy shown to her with that which signalised the wondrous birth of Isaac.

Isaac means " laughter." His advent filled the mouth of Sarah with laughter, and caused all that heard to laugh with her. So the birth of the Divine child in the soul of the believer sets him a-singing, and he, in his turn, becomes a channel of joy to others.

The facts recorded in verses 7 and 8 support the belief, already expressed in commenting upon the prior chapter, that Sarah's youth was miraculously renewed, and she made so fair that a king desired her. This may be expressed to-day in spiritual terms. The birth of Christ in the soul of an aged person effects a renewing of the moral nature so strikingly that the aged convert is loved and admired by even prominent unconverted men.

The effect of the birth of Isaac was to make manifest the character of Ishmael. Ishmael hated him, and so did his mother. Prompted by her he sought to murder Isaac (Gal.iv. 29), and with his mother was justly expelled. Both merited the severer sentence of death. Thus the birth of Isaac which filled Sarah's heart with mirth, filled Hagar's with murder.

Isaac and Ishmael symbolize the new and the old nature in the believer. Sarah and Hagar typify the two covenants of works and grace, of bondage and liberty (Gal. iv.). The birth of the new nature demands the expulsion of the old. It is impossible to improve the old nature. The Holy Spirit says in Rom. viii. that " it is enmity against God, that it is not subject to the law of God, neither indeed can be." If therefore it cannot be subject to the law of God, how can it be improved ? How foolish therefore appears the doctrine of moral evolution ! The Divine way of holiness is to " put off the old man " just as Abraham " put off " Ishmael. Man's way of holiness is to improve the " old man," that is, to improve Ishmael. The effort is both foolish and hopeless. Of course the casting out of Ishmael was " very grievous in Abraham's sight," because it always costs a struggle to cast out this element of bondage, that is, salvation by works. For legalism is dear to the heart. Ishmael was the fruit, and to Abraham the fair fruit of his own energy and planning. But the Epistle to the Galatians states that Hagar, the bondwoman, represents the covenant of the law, and that her son represents all who are of " works of law," that is, of all who seek righteousness on the principle of works of righteousness. But the bondswoman cannot bring forth a free man ! The Son alone makes free, and He makes free indeed. Sarah, the free-woman, symbolizes the covenant of grace and liberty. " So then, we are not children of the bondswoman but of the free."

The weaning of the son and heir of an Eastern chieftain is a great event. It oftentimes does not take place till the boy is upwards of 5 years of age. This is especially the case if the mother believes that he will be her only child. Eastern women are of the opinion that the longer they nourish a child the stronger he will be when a man. It is reasonable therefore to conclude that Isaac was sufficiently grown so as to make it possible for Ishmael to seek his life. The word " persecuted " in Gal. iv. 29, is understood by some Greek scholars to imply murder. and Scripture confirms it (See Gen. iii. 15, Rom. viii. 7).

At this feast the young chieftain is presented to the tribe in the special dress appropriate to him as heir and priest. It must therefore have become evident to Hagar that her son was definitely displaced, and this fact no doubt engendered the anger which incited Ishmael's action. Both mother and son merited death ; the milder punishment of banishment was commanded by God ; and it was in keeping with the custom of the time, directly a son reached 17 years of age, to send him forth to seek his own fortune. Because he was Abraham's son God guarded his footsteps, heard his prayer (v. 17), and caused his mother to see a well.

The lad grows, and becomes the founder of the great Arabian nation.

This was Abraham's fourth surrender, it was very grievous in his sight, but he hastens to instantly obey. He rises early, not late, in the morning, and with a breaking heart dismisses his wife and his son. But his wounded heart is comforted by the tender words of sympathy and promise spoken to him by God.

The mighty words " in Isaac shall thy seed be called " are explained in Gal. iii. 16, as referring to Christ. The birth of Isaac marks a distinct advance in the spiritual experience of Abraham. From this moment onwards all is strength and victory. He casts out the bond-woman and her son ; he no longer fears the prince of this world (Abimelech), but reproves him ; and now that the heir is come, Christ in type, he knows himself to be the possessor of heavenly as well as earthly promises. The heathen prince confesses that God is with him. The well of the oath is witness to Abraham's title in the earth and to Abimelech's confession of the fact. Accordingly he takes possession of the land, plants a tree, not a " grove " (Heb.) and worships Jehovah as the Everlasting God ; for the God that gave Isaac must be in truth the Everlasting God. So Abraham now dwells where the power of the world had been ; Abimelech as well as Ishmael withdraw from his land. All this is a pledge of what Israel shall have and of the glory and dominion that will be hers in Christ, and with Christ as the Everlasting God. This is the Divine definition of Jehovah (v. 33) i.e. " Jesus Christ, the same yesterday and to-day and for ever."

Ishmael was 20 years of age when expelled, and Isaac was 5. Shem was 580. The words translated " son " and " lad " are distinctive in the Hebrew text. The former is relative ; the latter, descriptive. The former might read " child," and the latter " young man." In relation to Hagar Ishmael was her child ; as descriptive of himself, he was a young man. Similarly, in the next chapter Isaac is termed a lad, although he was 25 years of age at the time of his symbolic death and resurrection.

GENESIS XXII.—The first mention of love in the Bible is here found in the second verse. The next occurrence appears in xxiv. 67.

The words " after these things " are significant, for a new scene now opens. The heir of the promise is sacrificed and raised again, and all the promises are confirmed in, and to him. The whole chapter is Christ in His death and resurrection, and the world-wide redemption which results therefrom.

This was Abraham's fifth, and greatest, and last surrender. In response to it God seems to find human language inadequate, as a vehicle, to express the fulness of the heavenly wealth with which He now enriches His beloved servant. How full of dignity are the words " God did test Abraham."

There is no verse which says " God did test Lot." It is a high honour to be tested by God. There are various kinds of trial, trial from circumstances or trial from the hand of Satan, but the highest character of trial, and it is full of dignity, is that which comes from God Himself.

As in the prior chapter, so here, there is prompt obedience. Abraham rises early in the morning. There was also faith ; he can say to the question of his dearly-loved child, " God will Himself provide Himself the lamb," and the Holy Spirit says in Hebrews xi. that the patriarch fully believed that God would raise him up from the dead ; " from whence also he received him in a figure."

The calmness of Abraham's faith, as contrasted with human religious excitement appears in the seven statements of verse 3 : the last of these actions occupying three days journey. The deliberate activity of faith in his soul is seen in that he rises early in the morning, with his own hands saddles the ass, cleaves the wood, not commanding the servants to do either of these things, and with his son and the two servants journeys day after day, and on the third day offers up his son, his only son, whom he loved, upon one of the mountains where God offered up His dearly-beloved Son eighteen hundred years later.

The word " Moriah " is a Hebrew word, and means " foreseen by Jehovah." Here was the threshing floor that David bought, and here Solomon built the temple. The verse 14 should read thus : " In this mount Jehovah shall be seen." This was fulfilled in 2 Sam. xxiv. 25, 1 Chron. xxi. 26, and 2 Chron. vii. 1–3.

The " third day " in verse 4 points to the resurrection of Christ. The words " and come again," in verse 5, have the verb in the plural, thus—" we will come again." This was a proof of Abraham's faith (Heb. xi.) " And they went both of them together," verses 6 and 8, beauteous picture of the Father and the Son in the antitype (2 Cor. v. 19).

Isaac, as the unresisting burnt-offering, is a striking type of Him who said, " I delight to do Thy will, O my God."

He who said "Abraham, Abraham " (v. 11), was the mighty God who said : " Martha, Martha," " Simon, Simon," " Saul, Saul."

" In the stead of his son," here is the doctrine of substitution clearly stated.

" The second time " (verse 15). The first time was for substitution (verse 11) ; the second time, for revelation. Reading Abraham's actions in verse 13 as following upon verse 12, and noticing the reading as given by some scholars thus : " Behold, behind him a solitary ram caught in the thicket," and, further, " Abraham took the ram "—it may reasonably be deduced that God told him of this burnt-offering, and directed him to offer it up in the stead of Isaac.

The oath of verse 16 is the foundation of Israel's blessings. David's " sure mercies " are all founded on it. (Gen. xxiv. 7, Exod. xiii. 5, Ps. cxxxii, 11, Luke i. 73).

As before pointed out, the comparison of Abraham's natural and spiritual children to the stars of heaven and the sand that is upon the sea shore is not an exaggeration ; for no natural figure could exaggerate the resurrection power of God.

The promise that all the nations of the earth should be blessed in the Promised Seed (v. 18) predicts primarily the salvation of the Gentiles, as such. This is a proof that the " mystery " revealed in the Epistle to the Ephesians, and revealed there for the first time, is not the blessing of the Gentile nations, but the " mystery " i.e. the secret concerning Christ and the church ; which is another thing altogether. See Rom. xi. 12.

The closing verses of the chapter are introduced here to lead up to Rebecca, the future wife of Isaac.

GENESIS XXIII.—Sarah is the only woman in the Bible whose age and death and burial are recorded. This is significant, partly, no doubt, because she is the mother of the Hebrew nation, and partly because the promised heir having come, the vessel of the promise, that is, Sarah, i.e. the first covenant, necessarily passes away.

Abraham now appears as a mourner, and as a merchant. A striking elevation of conduct appears in each character. Faith gave that dignity of speech and carriage. The Christian who walks by faith in the heavenly places is, like Abraham, not only perfectly straight in business transactions, but also deeply affectionate in natural relationships. His love for Sarah demands an honoured tomb for her precious dust, and faith in respect of her furnishes a testimony as to her resurrection. Love bent down over her sleeping face, and faith "stood up" from before its dead. The sons of Heth offer him the choicest of their sepulchres, but in death as in life the man of faith would be a pilgrim, would have no fellowship with the children of darkness, would not be indebted to them even for a grave, and accordingly insisted on this purchase. They had no idea that Abraham was looking forward to the possession of the whole land ; and because he did so look forward, the possession of a grave was by no means a small matter to him. Heb. xi. states " These all died, not having received the promise " ; but in dying as in living they found the promises real and satisfying. His purchase of this tomb was not only a proof of his love for Sarah but a testimony to his belief that she would rise again and with him possess the whole land.

The cave with the field cost £50. The show of generosity on the part of Ephron was only a show. Abraham did not bargain with him but immediately paid him the full price that he ultimately demanded. The word " dwelt " in verse 10 means that Ephron was sitting at the moment in the gate of the city among his fellow citizens (see R.V.) ; and the argument of verse 11 is, the field and the cave are only worth the trifling sum of £50. What is that between rich men like us ! Take them both ; I give them to you. This was pretence, as similar language between the Arab chieftains is at the present day in like circumstances.

The legal language, and definite description of the property, of verse 17, is all strictly in conformity with the laws then in existence as shown by the most recent discoveries.

This field and sepulchre are situated at Hebron ; they are there to-day ; and doubtless the sepulchre contains at this moment the bodies of these mighty dead.

GENESIS XXIV.—The decline in parental authority and government which is so painfully evident in the present day, is illustrated by the patriarchs. Abraham, cherishing the promises, takes early steps to obtain from the family of Shem a wife for his son. The energy of this faith is less vigorous in the soul of Isaac, he does not exercise the same care, but yet he has sufficient spiritual life tó be grieved because Esau marries a Canaanite. Jacob, in his turn, has not even that measure of Divine concern in his heart, and allows his sons to act in this matter as

they pleased without it causing him any pain. Such is the fatal downward course that marks family and church life.

There is not a more beautiful story in the Bible than this of Eliezer winning a bride for his master's son. Many see in the story an illustration of the mission of the Holy Spirit going forth after the death and resurrection of the Son of God's love to seek the Church, to win her heart, by a disclosure to her of the unsearchable riches of Christ, and to present her as a chaste virgin to Him. But it can only be an illustration, for the Epistle to the Ephesians teaches that the church is never mentioned in the Old Testament. The story very well pictures the Gospel messenger winning, by his testimony, one afar off and leading the listener to Jesus.

Abraham was about 140 years of age when he sought a wife for his son.

It is assumed that this eldest servant of his house was Eliezer. He modestly calls himself " Abraham's servant." He suppressed himself and his name and continually exalted Isaac. So should the Christian messenger hide himself and exalt Christ.

Abraham's outcry at the proposed return of Isaac to Haran (verses 5, 6, 8), and his fear lest his son should marry a daughter of the Canaanite, reveal how deep and true was the Divine life in his soul.

The words " wondering at her " (v. 21) mean " eagerly watching her."

It was when Laban saw the jewelry upon his sister's hands, that he showed kindness to Eliezer ; but Rebecca showed him kindness before she saw. This was characteristic of Laban.

In verses 42–44 Eliezer repeats his prayer from memory, but inexactly. Who could have written the actual prayer and Eliezer's imperfect remembrance of it but the Holy Spirit ? This is a remarkable illustration of inspiration.

Verse 63 joined with the closing words of verse 67, suggest, that Isaac went out into the field to meditate upon his beloved mother and indulge his grief at her loss. A father's love foresees the sorrow and provides for it. Isaac loves Rebecca and is consoled. This is the second mention of love in the Bible.

GENESIS XXV.—Sarah having waxed old and vanished away (Heb. ix. 13), that is, the Jewish covenant of works and exclusive.

salvation having determined, Keturah, the Gentile, now appears with her sons. Thus is the future pictured. Isaac, slain and raised to life again (Christ) takes to himself a bride, Rebekah (Israel). He brings her into his mother's tent who had been the depositary of the promises. So will Israel, in a future happy day, be brought by Christ in the new marriage covenant into all that was promised to her under the old, and over Jerusalem and all the land will be a covering of nuptial glory (Isa. iv. 5).

This having been accomplished, the nations of the earth (Keturah and her sons) will be raised up as children to Abraham and receive their inheritance.

Note that Isaac first made Rebekah his wife and then loved her, or, having loved her from the moment he met her, he continued to love her after he had married her. This is not always so amongst men.

Midian was a half-brother of Ishmael's. They were confederates. The angel had said to Hagar that her child was to dwell in the presence of all his brethren. Verse 18 of this chapter states that " he died in the presence of all his brethren." This verse should read, " he dwelt in the midst of all his brethren " (R.V.), that is, of all his half brothers the children of Keturah. Judges viii. 24, 25, solves the difficulty of Gen. xxxvii. 25, and harmonizes with Gen. xxv. 18, as showing that the Ishmaelites and the Midianites might be spoken of as one people, just as the English, the Scotch and the Welsh are known as the British people.

Abraham now dies and passes off the scene, making way for the heir of promise. Jacob was 15 years of age when Abraham died. Eber the grandson of Shem was 460 years of age at this time. Abraham was born only two years after the death of Noah and was 150 years of age when Shem died. He was, therefore, in a position to receive from many witnesses the facts affecting the ante-diluvian world. He was born of the Spirit at 75 years of age and departed to be with Christ at 175. He was, therefore, a sojourner for 100 years. It is pleasant to read in verse 9 that Isaac and Ishmael stood side by side at their father's grave.

The words " these are the generations of Ishmael " open the seventh section of this first book of the Bible. It is a very short section because it deals with the son of the bond-maid. The words " And these are the

generations of Isaac " introduce the eighth section of the book. Note the language of verses 12 and 19. Compare the words " Ishmael, Abraham's son " and " Isaac, Abraham's son," but observe what follows in each case. In the one case, " whom Hagar, the Egyptian, the slave, bare." In the other case the majestic words " Abraham begat Isaac." The word " begat " is important, it is the same form of the verb as in the case of the birth of Seth, i.e. the godly seed.

Satan hindered the birth of Jacob for twenty years. But God overruled his malice to emphasize once more the great truth that He displays the riches of His grace and glory where nature is dead. This is a principle in the spiritual life which nature is unwilling to learn.

Rebecca's language in verse 22 appears obscure. It may be paraphrased thus : " if in answer to prayer God is about to give me the joy of being a mother why am I so physically oppressed that I am in danger of death ? " It must indeed have appeared perplexing to her that such an answer to prayer should be accompanied by such mysterious suffering. Many Christians have had, in their spiritual life, in union with answered prayer, spiritual sorrows which Rebecca's experience illustrate. And, further, two energies, the one believing and the other unbelieving, struggled within her ; like the two natures within the believer. How fortifying is the statement that the one should be stronger than the other, and that it was the younger should be the stronger. So the two boys may represent the two natures in the Christian. The Divine nature is the younger but it is to have the victory.

Isaac loved Esau, but it was because he did eat of his venison ; this is characteristic of a man, for men love eating. Rebecca loved Jacob, not because of any personal enjoyment he brought to her, but she loved him for his own sake. This is characteristic of a woman ; and the more characteristic because it may be assumed from their subsequent history that Esau was personally superior to Jacob.

But the Holy Spirit in the Epistle to the Hebrews calls him a " profane person," and, this, because he sold his birthright. He bartered future and eternal wealth for present and temporary need. Jacob, on the other hand, gave up present things, poor things no doubt, only pottage ; but poor as they were, they had power over Esau's heart. The Birthright included (1) the Father's Blessing involving Supremacy; (2) a Double Portion of the family estate; and (3) the Domestic Priesthood. Jacob, deplorable as was his character, valued Divine and Eternal blessing ; and had he placed himself in God's hands, the prophecy, made to his mother before he was born, would have been fulfilled to him, and without the degradation and suffering which his own scheming brought upon him.

The Domestic Priesthood meant that the eldest son acted as priest for the family, and offered the sacrifices which God had commanded Adam and his sons to offer. These are the priests, without doubt, spoken of in Exod. xix. 22, and also in Exod. xxiv. 5. With this priesthood were joined the ten commandments and the simple laws connected with them ; but Israel having rejected this high honour, saying to Moses " speak thou to us, but let not God speak to us"— this peculiar glory was taken from them and vested in the tribe of Levi.

The four " ands " of verse 34 marking the deliberateness of Esau's acts are very solemn ; " and he did eat, and drink, and rose up, and went his way ! " With deep pathos and sorrow, and with indignation, the Holy Spirit adds, " Thus Esau despised his birthright ! "

As Satan moved Cain to murder Abel so as to prevent the birth of the promised Redeemer (1 John iii. 8–12), so he moved Ishmael to murder Isaac (Gal. iv. 29), and Esau, before his birth, to murder Jacob (v. 22). This last instance is very mysterious ; and the more so when contrasted with Luke i. 44. John the Baptist, prior to his birth, welcomed the Deliverer ; Esau, prior to his birth, hated Him. Compare John ix. 2 and see Notes on Ezek. xxxv.

Had Esau killed his mother before his birth as well as Jacob and himself, Satan would have rejoiced ; for, as in the case of Judas, into whom he entered, he has no compassion for his agents.

GENESIS XXVI.—It is not difficult for Satan to break down the faith of a believer. So small a matter as a famine is sufficient. A famine sent Abraham into Egypt where he denied Sarah, who was the vessel of the promises. A similar weapon is used to push Isaac into Gerar, where he also denies his wife ! It is evident from the second verse that in spite of the lesson taught him by his father's experience he would have gone down into Egypt, had not the Lord appeared to him and prevented him, saying, " Go not down into Egypt ; dwell in the land which I shall tell thee of." But it would seem from verse 3 that he had not faith to dwell in that part of the land that God promised to tell him of, and accordingly God condescended to his fears saying in effect : very well, sojourn, if you will, in this land, that is, the land of the Philistine, only do not go down into Egypt, and I will be with thee, and will bless thee, etc. Accordingly it is stated in verses 12, 13 and 14 that Jehovah did bless him in that land in material wealth, but he suffered spiritually, was a moral injury to the Philistines, was continually contending with them, had anything but a life of peace and, finally, was asked by them to go away !

If it is disastrous to the spiritual life for the Christian to go down into " Egypt," it is dangerous to go down unto " Gerar," for it is a halfway house to Egypt. A man may, like Isaac, become very rich in "Gerar," but it is not recorded that Jehovah appeared to Isaac in Gerar. He appeared to him before he went there and the very night of the day that he left.

It is instructive to mark the progress in Isaac's soul He " departed thence " (v. 17) ; " he removed from thence " (v. 22) ; " he went up from thence " (v. 23) ; " Jehovah appeared unto him " (v. 24) ; " he builded an altar " (v. 25) ; " he called upon the name of the Lord " (v. 25) ; " he pitched his tent " (v. 25) ; and " he digged a well " (v. 25). Passing through this valley of Baca, he made it a well, for he went from strength to strength. This was an undisputed well which the Philistines could not stop because they were not there. In this land of Beersheba he finds peace and refreshment and fellowship with God. So long as he dwelt at Gerar there was nothing but strife and contention.

The patriarch's gentleness in not resisting evil and in yielding to the violence of the herdmen of Gerar shows how placid was his character. Such was his life—his consenting to be slain, his meekness in betrothal, his mourning for his mother, and his refusal to hold the wells which he himself digged—all suggest the meekness and gentleness of Christ

It is when Isaac definitely separates himself from the men of Gerar that they come to him seeking blessing through him from God. All the time that he dwelt amongst them it is not recorded that they approached him in this way. This is one of the many lessons in the Bible which teach the Christian that he best helps the world when living in separation from it.

The promise in verse 3 of the land to Isaac personally, as in the case of each Patriarch, involves resurrection.

The word " my " occurs five times in verse 5. A voice to be heard, a charge to be kept, commandments to be obeyed, statutes to be loved, and laws to be followed.

Beersheba is so named in verse 33 by Isaac. It had already been similarly named by Abraham. This is one of the instances in the Bible of the same name being reimposed, and in each case for a new and added reason. Compare Bethel, and the name Israel as illustrating this point.

Esau's profanity in selling his birthright was quickly followed by his double marriage with the Hittite. So is it ever, the heart that despises heavenly things very quickly becomes doubly yoked to this present evil world.

Esau and Jacob were 20 years of age when Eber died. He (Eber) was 280 years of age when Noah died. He was therefore able to fully instruct Jacob as to the facts of the flood and of the world that then was.

GENESIS XXVII.—The history of Jacob is a treasure house of spiritual instruction for the people of God. It sets out God's electing grace and man's hopeless depravity. It was grace that elected Jacob to be a prince of God ; for he was a most ignoble character. He, his father, his mother and his brother, all form a dark background to the brightness of God's amazing love. In them is found a humbling picture of sensuality, deceit, cunning, falsehood, hate and murder ! Jacob was the most unlovely member of the family ; yet grace chose him to be the Head of all the nations of the earth. Grace banishes all human pretensions and asserts God's right to act as He will. Grace heaps everything upon those who deserve nothing. God loved Jacob because of some sufficient reason in Himself, known to Himself, and not because Jacob was lovable. Thus the history of this patriarch illustrates the saving power of Divine grace, and for this reason, that

Jacob himself is a sad illustration of the destructive power of fallen human nature. How full of comfort, therefore, is the last verse of Psalm xlvi ! Here are brought together into the one verse the two great titles " The Lord of Hosts " and " God of Jacob." The one title presents Him as the God of countless hosts of sinless angels ; the other title proclaims Him as the God of one stumbling, sinning, scheming, planning and broken man ! These Divine titles link Almighty power with infinite grace.

Jacob's history teaches the lesson, which the natural will is so unwilling to learn, that planning for self instead of resting in the hand of God brings sorrow. Hence Jacob's miserable testimony to Pharaoh : " Few and evil have been the years of my life " (ch. xlvii. 9) ; and, again, his wail " all these things are against me ! " How different the apostle Paul's testimony ! " But none of these things move me " ; and, again, " I have fought the good fight, I have finished the course, I have kept the faith. Henceforth, etc " And yet with all his weakness Jacob was a believer and God answered his faith but chastened himself.

Isaac pictures the elect nation of Israel living by faith within the Land of Promise and waiting for its possession : Jacob, the same elect people, heir of the promises, wandering among the Gentiles because of their own misconduct, an outcast, and yet watched over by God. He had then no altar (see xxxiii. 20), for self-planning took him out of the path of communion. It is one thing to be watched over by God ; it is a higher experience to walk with God.

If Esau was ready to sell the birthright for a mess of pottage ; his father was prepared to sell it for a dish of venison ! Humbling picture of a man of God under the power of his lower sensual nature ! " He trembled very exceedingly " (v. 33) and no wonder, for he had been told by God at the time of Jacob's birth that he was to possess the birthright. His conscience is now aroused, and he trembles very exceedingly under a just fear. This fear brings him back into the path of faith, and directly he returns to that path he steps from sensuality to dignity. He blesses with all the consciousness of having power to bless. He says : " I have blessed him, yea, and he shall be blessed." He speaks as if he possessed the earth and all its treasures. This is faith ! Faith ennobles ; nature degrades ! How noble the figure of Isaac in verses 33–40 ; how ignoble in verses 1–4 !

Isaac was 137 years of age at this time. His step-brother Ishmael had died at that age. Perhaps it was the fact of his death that made Isaac think that he also was about to die ; but he lived for 43 years longer (ch. xxxv. 28).

" The will of the flesh " made him wish to bless Esau, but faith in the end conquered (Heb. xi. 20), and he cries respecting Jacob : " I have blessed him, and he shall be blessed." Heb. xii. 17 recalls Esau's bitter weeping, when he found that he had lost the birthright, and how he failed with his tears to cause his father to change his mind. He found no place of repentance in his father's will. That is the meaning of the language in this passage.

The prediction in verse 40, that Esau should break Jacob's yoke from off his neck was fulfilled upwards of 900 years later, as recorded in 2 Kings viii.

Isaac was mistaken as to the proximity of his death (v. 2) ; Esau was mistaken as to an early opportunity for murdering his brother (v. 41) ; and Rebecca was mistaken (v. 44) in her expectation to see Jacob soon again, for she died before he returned home.

GENESIS XXVIII.—How impossible it is for the natural man to understand the word of God and the life of faith, is here evidenced in Esau. He tries to enter the way of life and obedience by marrying a daughter of Ishmael ! But such wisdom is folly with God !

Feeble as was Jacob's faith yet was it a Divine faith ; and therefore it is that the added blessing of his father in verses 3 and 4 God endorses in verses 14 and 15. A wanderer, he is promised the guardianship and companionship of El-Shaddai. This great title, declaring God to be the Almighty One, assured Jacob beforehand of the sufficiency and ability of Jehovah to meet and provide for all his needs. This is the more instructive when it is noticed that God promises to bless him in going obediently to Haran just as he had promised to bless his grandfather Abraham if obediently leaving Haran. This illustrates how the life of faith appears a life of contradictions to human wisdom.

A lonely wanderer, hated by his brother, and obliged to flee from his home in order to save his life, Jacob learns the very first night of his exile that he is the object of heaven's love and care, and that the angels of God were busily employed passing and repassing from heaven to earth in ministering to him. He learnt that earth and heaven were united, and united in his interest and for his temporal and eternal welfare. This wondrous " ladder " united him to Jehovah the God of his grandfather and the God of his father ; for not only did the angels descend by it to him, but God Himself descended this stairway of glory and, standing beside him, said : " Behold I am with thee and will keep thee in all places whither thou goest." Jacob merited nothing and God promised him everything. Such is grace ! The words " above it " in verse 13 should be understood as " beside him " (R.V. margin).

Thus Jacob learned in spirit that Christ makes heaven and earth one (John i. 51), and that a day would come, as here promised to him, when the heavens and the earth would sing harmoniously together ; and that he and his countless children, and all the nations of the earth should be the happy inhabitants of that blissful world. (Hos. ii. 21–23)

The promise " I will not leave thee " (v. 15) first occurs here. It may be termed " Salvation Grace." Then " Pilgrimage Grace " (Deut. xxxi. 6). Then " Fighting Grace " (Jos. i. 5, 8). Then " Missionary Grace," i.e. building the spiritual temple (1 Chron. xxviii. 20). Then " Daily Contentment Grace " (Heb. xiii. 5).

The " House of God " and the " Gate of Heaven " now becomes a place of intelligent and reverential worship for Jacob's heart. How happy and free from care would Jacob's life have been had he let God plan for him !

Jacob " vowed a vow," that is, he made a solemn vow. This is the first recorded vow in the Bible. There is much to make it appear that the word " if " in this passage means " since." Personal salvation is not a matter of education, but of revelation (Matt. xi. 27). And Jacob no doubt had received a good religious education from his parents ; but, now, for the first time, Jehovah reveals Himself to him. In that night was Jacob born from above ! His language, therefore, expresses the faith of a young convert. He believes the exceeding great and precious promises made to him, he receives Jesus as his Saviour and he yields himself as a slave to Him. So real is his conversion that the strongest appetite in his nature— cupidity—is affected, and he consecrates a large portion of his yearly gains to the Lord. Such is the moral effect of real conversion ! The like power showed itself later on in the soul of Zacchæus, when he cried : " Behold, Lord, the half of my goods I give to the poor."

Luz now becomes Bethel ! Luz means " separation " ; Bethel means the " House of God." " Ye who were afar off," says the apostle, " are now made the habitation of God through the Spirit."

Isaac and Esau refused subjection to God ; Rebecca and Jacob refused co-operation with God. The rebellion of the human will is seen in the first pair and its wickedness in the second pair.

GENESIS XXIX.—Grace forgave Jacob, and confirmed to him the promises ; yet must he reap the bitter fruit of his sin. He is at the outset of his life deceived, exactly as he deceived his father, and deeply wounded in the deepest affections of his heart. Leah is dressed up to represent Rachel, and, when too late, he discovers the deception !

It is a popular mistake to suppose that Jacob did not marry Rachel till the end of the second 7 years, for Joseph was born during the first seven. He had already served his seven years for Rachel in verse 20. The week he fulfilled in verse 27 means the week for Leah. The little word " also " in verse 28 helps to make this fact the clearer.

The tender love of the Heavenly Father's heart for a slighted wife is beautifully shown in the fact that He gave six sons to Leah.

The title Jehovah is used in connection with five sons (verses 31–35 and ch. xxx. 24). The title Elohim is used with six sons (ch. xxx. 2, 6, 17, 18, 20, 23). No title is used with Benjamin (ch. xxxv. 16). Leah had six sons, the others two apiece.

The word " hated " in verse 31 means " loved less" (Deut. xxxi. 15, Mal. i. 3, Matt. vi. 24, Luke xiv. 26). The name "Levi" in verse 34 is believed by many scholars to mean " honour," " Now this time will my husband honour me," is the gladsome cry of this joyful mother of children.

GENESIS XXX.—Rachel pictures Israel ; Leah, the nations. Rachel is first loved, but not possessed—sorrowful and childless ; Leah, blessed with children and triumphant. But Rachel has children afterwards on the earth, Joseph and Benjamin. Joseph, a beauteous type of Christ rejected by his brethren but glorified among the Gentiles.

Benjamin, a type also of Christ, the son of his mother's sorrow, but of his father's right hand ; that is, the Messiah was to be born of Israel, and that is why Israel had to drink so great a cup of sorrow ; but He becomes the Lord Messiah reigning in power in the heavens at the right hand of God.

There is a mystic law which brings a man into connection with men morally similar to himself, and, accordingly, bargain-loving Jacob meets with bargain-loving Laban, and they now appear doing their utmost to out-wit each other ! But how sad is Jacob's conduct as contrasted with Laban's, for Laban had never been at Bethel , he had seen no open heaven, nor the ascending and descending angels ; and, most solemn of all, he had not seen Jesus the Lord and received mighty promises from Him. No wonder he was grasping and worldly ! But to find Jacob after all he had seen and heard, acting in this way, is very humbling, and is not uncommon to-day.

GENESIS XXXI.—At Bethel Jacob was to learn what God was ; at Haran, what man was. And what a difference ! At Bethel, God enriched him : at Haran, man robbed him ! His learning what man really was was a needed lesson for such a pupil as Jacob ; for, had he not schemed and shuffled and planned for himself, but trusted God to plan for him, how dignified and noble and beautiful would have been his life ! He secures wealth by exceptional knowledge of natural law in the breeding of sheep ; and finally steals away as though he were a thief.

In the third verse God directs Jacob to return home and promises to be with him. But so unwilling is the natural heart to trust God and wait for Him to arrange the journey, that the patriarch immediately takes matters into his own hands, with the result that he nearly lost his life. Had he waited for God to go before him, how different would have been his experience !

The principle already noticed of the use of the Divine titles reappears in this chapter, in the third and twenty-fourth verse : "Jehovah said unto Jacob," and, " Elohim came to Laban."

The River in verse 21 is the River Euphrates. In verses 27–30 Laban adds hypocrisy to idolatry.

It is a humbling picture of the depth to which man has fallen, that, let the evidence of the existence and the goodness of God be never so overwhelming yet will he cling to idolatry ! Laban acknowledged in the prior chapter that God had manifestly prospered Jacob ; and in this chapter God Himself actually appears to him in a dream ! These facts should have taught him that idols were vain and wicked inventions of man's folly, and yet he clings to them !

The word " furniture " in verse 34 should read " saddle " ; and the word " searched " means " felt with his hands." Deceit begets deceit, and therefore it is that Rachel deceives her father.

The expression " the Fear of Isaac " in verse 42 means the God whom Isaac feared.

The two names in verse 47 belong to two languages, and have the same meaning, i.e. " heap of witness." The word " Mizpeh " means " watch-tower."

The "Fear of his father Isaac" in verse 53 as in verse 42, means the God whom Jacob worshipped.

The parting of Laban and Jacob sadly illustrates the mutual suspicion which grips men's hearts when governed by the spirit of the world.

GENESIS XXXII.—The second vision corresponds to that at Bethel in chapter xxviii. Laban and his hostile host withdraw, and the angels of God appear to comfort Jacob and assure him of God's overruling care for him. These, no doubt, were the same angels that twenty years back had guarded him as he slept upon his stone pillow at Bethel. Then his possessions consisted of a staff, but now he has become a host ; and he calls this place Mahanaim, i.e., two camps—his feeble camp and the encircling camp of God's mighty angels.

But, although the angels visibly appear to him in order to convince him of the loving care which watched over him, yet he at once schemes how he may protect himself from his brother's just anger. Yet some spiritual progress may be seen, for now he prays as well as schemes. But like many to-day, he first makes his plans and then he prays ! He should have reversed the action. But the sense of having acted wrongly fills the heart with a thousand fears, and robs the Christian of confidence toward God and dignity before man. Though he had prayed for deliverance from Esau, he had no real confidence in his prayer being heard, and he says : " I will appease him with a present ; " and as to

dignity before man—his language is : " My lord Esau "—and " Thy servant Jacob."

" And Jacob was left alone, and there wrestled a man with him." In this chapter, and in Hos. xii, this Man is called God, the Angel, Elohim Sabaoth, and Jehovah.

The passage in Hosea helps to explain this crisis in Jacob's life. God had a controversy with Israel because of her disobedience. She finds herself faced by great danger; this danger was God's instrument of discipline for her, and the hand that was wounding her was, in effect, the Divine hand; but instead of clinging with weeping and supplication to that faithful God who would surely have delivered her, she sends for help to Syria and to Egypt. The prophet points back to Jacob, and reminds the nation that he did not act as they now are doing. When God had a controversy with him because of his faulty life ; and when as a consequence Jacob found himself in deadly peril and realized that God Himself was behind that peril, and that it was not with Esau his brother that he had to contend, but with the Angel of Jehovah Himself ; and when sore broken by that mighty hand he ceased to wrestle and clung with weeping and supplication to the very God that wounded him, then it was he got the victory and the glorious name of Israel.

The great principle that God cannot give victory to " the flesh," appears in this night scene. It is the broken heart that begins to experience what Divine power means. Better for the sun to rise upon a limping Israel than to set upon a lying Jacob.

Jacob, for his misconduct was exiled from the promised land, having nothing but his staff. He returns a wealthy prince, but lamed. So Israel cast out of Jehovah's land because of her sin will return with abundance, but broken and contrite in spirit.

GENESIS XXXIII.—The action of Esau shows how groundless were Jacob's fears, and how needless his plans. The straight path of faith and obedience is free from the tormenting apprehensions which wear out the doubting heart.

Jacob's thigh is disjointed, but his will remains unbroken and so immediately he begins to plan how he may deceive Esau. He engages to follow him to Mount Seir, but at once sets out for Succoth ! This gives a further insight into the depths of unbelief and evil in the heart of man and of the exceeding riches of grace in the heart of God. Notwithstanding the vision of the Angels, and the night of wrestling with God Himself, he resumes his evil schemings for self-conservation, and distrusts the promises of Divine preservation.

The folly of following his own thoughts is seen in his building a house at Succoth. It became a memorial of sin and shame. This is the first mention of a " house " in connection with the patriarchs. The life of pilgrimage is only easy to him who keeps his eye upon the promises. God was the God of Bethel. He had said to him : " I am the God of Bethel " : He had not said : " I am the God of Succoth," and if he moves from Succoth it is to buy land in a country in which he was to be a pilgrim. No doubt he erects an altar there, for the conscience is uneasy without religious forms, but the Divinely chosen place for the altar was Bethel and not Shechem.

Verse 18 should read as in R.V., " Jacob came in peace to Shechem."

GENESIS XXXIV.—Jacob is delivered out of Shechem, but under circumstances of shame, anguish, and terror. The sin and dishonour and deceit and murder narrated in this chapter would never have happened, had he ceased his perpetual planning, and walked as a little child with God. How great a place in his heart " self " had is shown by his language in the 30th verse. He speaks only of the danger to himself and his family from the enraged Canaanite. He expressed no horror at the treachery and bloodshed of which his sons were guilty. He does so years afterwards ; but his action and his language here are deplorable. He seems to have quite forgotten the Divine assurance of safety which had been repeated to him again and again ; he takes his eyes off God, he looks only at the violence of Simeon and Levi, and he cries out : " I shall be destroyed ! " Such is the miserable experience of all who, though true Christians, live as citizens in Shechem when they ought to be pilgrims at Bethel. Verse 23. Many are willing to join the church for the sake of its Dinahs and diamonds.

Jacob is here personally responsible for the conduct of his children. This principle operates to-day. The misconduct of the children of Christ's servants is oftentimes due to the disobedient action of their parents in living in fellowship with the world. Dinah goes out to see the daughters of the land. That seemed very innocent. But these daughters led to a companionship of shame. The Christian who walks with his Lord escapes this snare.

GENESIS XXXV.—About ten years had now passed since God had said to Jacob, " Return unto thy land, I am the God of Bethel." But how slow was he to obey this command ! Had he gone swiftly to Bethel, and had he " dwelt " there, as commanded, what sin and sorrow would have been avoided! Now at last he goes " up " to Bethel. Physically and morally it was indeed a going-up. Shechem lies on low ground, Bethel amid the mountains about 30 miles distant. It was also a moral ascent. At Shechem, God is known as God, the God of Israel ; but at Bethel, He reveals Himself as El-Shaddai ; and Jacob recognizes him as God of the House of God. It is vital to know God as a personal Saviour, but it is a higher spiritual experience to know Him as " Son over His own house." At Shechem he kept this Saviour and his salvation to himself, and permitted his family and household to retain their idols. But this cannot be suffered if God is to be recognized and publicly confessed as the God of Bethel, that is, the God of the House of God ; for the elect are His House, and " judgment must begin at the House of God," and " Holiness becometh thy House O Lord for ever ! " When therefore he learns that he is to meet God publicly at Bethel, he at once feels that idols cannot be brought into fellowship with that House, and accordingly he commands the surrender of all the strange gods that were in their hands and in their ears, and he buried them beneath the oak which is in Shechem. How much better if he had burned them ! Many Christians at a time of revival bury their idols, and, like Jacob, bury them in a spot where they can easily find them again and dig them up ! Few Christians burn them.

The Divine command to Jacob ten years back, and now renewed, was " to go up to Bethel and dwell there." Disobedience preceded this command and followed it. In Bethel itself there was victory, but before Bethel was Shechem, and after Bethel, Edar. The one, the scene of Dinah's dishonour; the other, of Reuben's incest.

Better is the house of weeping than the house of rejoicing, and Jacob was therefore happier in his soul when weeping beneath the oak for the aged Deborah than when sitting in his self-built house on the plains of Succoth. The introduction of this aged servant here is very affecting, and Jacob's excessive grief reveals an affectionate nature. What no doubt sharpened his grief was, that though he might close the eyes of his mother's servant, he, by his own misconduct, was not to see that mother herself !

The great name of " Israel," promised to him in chapter xxxii. at Penuel, is now given at Bethel ; and, with it, is revealed the glorious title El-Shaddai, i.e. God Almighty— the God who was able to fulfil to him the promises here made. To Jacob personally, as to Isaac and Abraham, resurrection is assured ; for He says : " to thee will I give this land." Note : (xxxii. 28) " Thy name shall be " ; (xxxv. 10) " He called his name." Compare John i. " Thou art Simon " ; " Thou shalt be Peter." See Notes on Matt. xvi.

In verse 14 is found the first mention of a drink-offering. When God first revealed Himself to Jacob at this spot, Jacob poured oil upon the pillar ; now he pours both oil and wine. Then, there was godly fear, now, there is joy as well as fear. This stone figures Christ the Rock of Ages, anointed with the Holy Spirit and filled with the joy of God.

Benjamin is born   Sorrowing nature calls him " Ben oni," i.e. " child of my sorrow." Faith calls him " Benjamin," i.e. " son of the right hand." Prophetic picture of Him who was to be at first the " Man of Sorrows," and then the " Man at God's right hand."

Throughout the chapter the patriarch is called Jacob, excepting in verses 21 and 22 where three times the Holy Spirit names him Israel. How strange this contradiction appears to human wisdom ! Jacob is his name of weakness, Israel, of strength, and yet is he only named Israel in connection with wandering and dishonour ! So is it at all times ! Bitter earthly sorrows may often closely follow sweet spiritual experiences.

The Holy Spirit in the last verse of the chapter records the death of Isaac. But this did not occur till Joseph was fifteen years of age. It is here given so as to make way for the commanding figure of Joseph—beauteous type of Christ, rejected by his brethren but exalted among the Gentiles.

How striking are the three statements respecting Isaac's decease : " he gave up the ghost, and died, and was gathered to his people." Why not the one expression " he died " ?

GENESIS XXXVI.—Esau and his sons, as the men of the world, who have their portion in this life (Ps. xvii. 14), established themselves in power, with their kings and their dukes, and their riches and their possessions, while the Heirs of Promise, that is, Jacob and his sons, are still pilgrims and strangers. This furnishes a prophetic picture.

The first eight verses of the chapter contain the Generations, i.e. the Family History of Esau personally ; verses 9-43 the Generations of Esau politically. The one section deals with him in Canaan ; the other, in Mount Seir.

Esau's sons were born in Canaan and went out of it ; Jacob's sons were born out of it and went into it.

Verse 31 is brought forward by many as proving that the Book of Genesis was composed when kings reigned over the children of Israel, or even later. But this is no proof whatever ; for the same person that wrote this verse was manifestly the same who wrote verse 6 of chapter xvii., verse 11 of chapter xxxv., and Deut. xvii. 14-20.

GENESIS XXXVII. 2-36.—This chapter opens the eleventh and last division of the Book of Genesis. This is shown by the expression " These are the Generations," i.e. the Family History of Jacob. And the very next word is " Joseph ! " · Thus, abruptly, is this exceptionally beautiful character brought forward. He forms a remarkable type of Christ. Loved by his father ; clothed so as to show his equality with his father ; testifying of heavenly things to his brethren ; repeating that testimony in spite of their opposition and hatred ; as the faithful servant testifying of them to Jacob ; going with alacrity, when sent, to seek them in Shechem, the scene of their treachery and bloodshed ; sold by them for twenty pieces of silver (i.e. thirty shekels) to Gentiles, and by these cast into dungeons of darkness ; brought out therefrom and exalted to Pharaoh's right hand ; blessing the Gentiles ; and finally, forgiving, and enriching his brethren —he presents in all a striking and prophetic picture of the Lord Jesus Christ.

This is a powerful testimony to the inspiration of Scripture; for no man, either before or after the writing of the New Testament, could have composed such a story.

The opening verse in this chapter sets Joseph forward as a shepherd, seventeen years of age. His mother was still living but died within the year, his father was 108 years of age, and his grandfather Isaac 168. The verse suggests that Joseph was placed by his father in a position of responsibility. The statement " he was the son of his old age " may be translated that he possessed the wisdom of an old man though so young. The coat he wore was that worn by Eastern chieftains and was given to the son for whom the birthright was designed. This pictured the equality of the father and of the son.

The mention of Joseph's mother in verse 10 is thought by some to be a mistake in the text, Rachel being already dead. But she was still living at the time, and died shortly afterwards.

The absence of population in Palestine at this time is a proof of the truthfulness of the history. The most recent discoveries in Egypt testify to the historic accuracy of the domestic and public structure of Egyptian society at this period.

The merchants who bought Joseph are called Midianites and Ishmaelites. They were sons of Abraham by Hagar and Keturah. Judges viii. 24, 25, shows how they were mixed together, and how they were distinguished one from the other. Egyptian records show that these people traded in spices, balm, myrrh, and slaves. A Judas sold Joseph for 20 pieces of silver, i.e. 30 silver shekels, and a Judas sold Christ for 30 pieces of silver.

Jacob was deceived by the blood of a kid, as he had himself deceived his father with the skin of a kid. The sorrowing father says, " I will go down into the grave unto my son," not into a sepulchre but into the grave, i.e. " Sheol." This is the first occurrence of this word in the Bible; it means the spirit world.

GENESIS XXXVIII.—This chapter is a parenthesis introduced here as an actual picture of the sin, darkness, corruption and self-will of Joseph's brethren during the whole period of his absence from them, and as the certain fruit of their rejection of him. It is a fore-picture of the moral condition of the Jews to-day as the result of their rejection of the Messiah.

The chapter is also placed here in order to show the connection between Christ and his predecessor Judah. Chapter i. of Matthew shows how truly Christ made Himself of no reputation and by being born a member of the tribe of Judah, humbled Himself. For in that genealogy the names, Tamar and Bathsheba appear. But He in no wise inherited from these any taint of sin, for He was conceived of the Holy Spirit, and though born of a woman was wholly free from moral corruption.

Judah marrying a Canaanite sinned with his eyes open, for he must have known the will of God in that matter (Gen. xxiv. 3, xxvi. 35, xxvii. 46, xxviii. 1). The law of marrying a brother's widow (v. 8) is an old and present Eastern law. There are about thirty-four laws appearing in the Book of Genesis which were afterwards confirmed by God to Moses. This was one of them.

Judah, an unnatural brother, was punished in his own children.

Tamar did not degrade herself, as is popularly thought, to the level of a public and abandoned woman, but assumed to be a virgin devoted to the worship of the Phallus. This is shown by the word Kesedah which only appears here and in Hos. iv. 14.

GENESIS XXXIX.—Recent discoveries harmonize with the political and social conditions of Egypt at this remote period. An Eastern race governed the country, this explains why Potiphar is three times declared to be an " Egyptian " (vs. 1, 2, 5). Otherwise it would seem strange that an officer in the Egyptian government service should be stated to be " an Egyptian." These discoveries have also demonstrated that at this time it was the custom to place a confidential slave in command of a large household; that the Egyptians ate apart from foreigners; that Egyptian women were not secluded in a harem, but mixed in general society, and were licentious; and that houses were constructed so that to reach the store-room the confidential slave would have to pass through the main house. Thus the facts here related are shown to be real, and not the imaginative composition of men hundreds of years later.

It is five times stated, verses 2-5, that Divine blessing accompanied Joseph. Verse 2 states that " Jehovah was with Joseph and he was (that is, he " became ") a prosperous man " ; and the other statements are added respecting the prosperity of everything that was under his hand. The words in verse 4 " he served him," mean that Joseph became Potiphar's personal servant

As to Joseph's person, two statements are made similar to those made with respect to his mother Rachel—his figure was handsome and his face beautiful. His action in resisting the temptation pressed upon him showed him to be the true first-born ; for his chastity rebuked the unchastity of Reuben who was the natural firstborn. His language to his master's wife was very fine. He urged three reasons against wrong-doing. First, gratitude to his master who had put everything into his hands ; second, respect for her seeing that she was his wife ; and third, fear of God.

This is the second occasion that the Sacred History speaks of Joseph's garment. His brothers took the one; Potiphar's wife the other. They tried to hide their sin with that garment ; she tried to hide hers with this.

In one moment Joseph exchanged a palace for a prison. Psalm cv. states that he was laid in iron and his feet hurt with fetters. But Jehovah was with him as much in the prison as in the palace ; and this Divine companionship, and its prosperity is three times emphasized. The Governor of the prison, as was the case with Potiphar, relieved himself of all anxiety, and did so reasonably, because he recognized that Divine blessing rested upon Joseph and upon all that he did. As to Potiphar, it states in verse 6 that " he left all that he had in Joseph's hand and he knew not ought he had;" that is, he cared about nothing that he had, that is, as to its safety ; but it adds truthfully that he did care about that which he ate, for the Egyptian tablets make it clear that the people at that time were very much given to good living.

GENESIS XL.—One very lovely feature in Joseph's character was that he never murmured; and another yet more beautiful one was, his unselfish interest in the needs and sorrows of others. These two evidences of the Divine life in his soul appear in the quickness of his eye in noticing the sadness of his fellow prisoners, and in the gentleness of his words in begging the chief cupbearer to do something for his liberation.

But the Divine discipline permitted that he should be tempted in all points, and so the chief cupbearer forgat him, although he knew his innocence, and that he possessed a mysterious relationship to God.

All these facts helped to build up Joseph as a very striking type of Israel's Saviour and the world's Redeemer.

It is an interesting and profitable study to examine all the passages in the Sacred Scriptures which speak of dreams, and of how God used them as a channel of communication to men, whether inside or outside the Covenant of Grace.

Joseph " served " the prisoners, and, no doubt, with gentle sympathy ; he pleased his master ; and he preached faithfully the Word of the Lord whether it announced grace or wrath. As a lamb he opened not his mouth ; and in response to his goodness he met only ingratitude, forgetfulness and indifference. See Amos vi. 6. He did not accuse his brothers but simply said he had been stolen. He gently pleaded : " Remember me ! " but was forgotten.

Some scholars deny that Egypt had birthdays and vines but recent excavations prove the contrary.

GENESIS XLI.—Joseph, whilst yet in humiliation, becomes the interpreter of the thoughts and counsels of God ; and in his elevation executes with power those counsels, and subjects all Egypt to him who sat upon the throne. In all this was Joseph a wonder-fully full type of Christ, who, in the humilia-tion of His first Advent, revealed the counsels and affections of God's heart, and who will, in the glory of His second Advent, establish the Kingdom of God in power over the whole earth. Thus is Jesus both Joseph, i.e. " Jehovah shall add," and also, Zaphnath-paaneah, i.e. " life more abundant."

Pharaoh dreams of seven cattle, and seven ears of corn. The Egyptian " Book of the Dead " (now in the British Museum) with its sacred cows and mystic number " seven " —a book beyond doubt well known to Pharaoh—must have helped to convince the king that this double dream was supernatural. The magicians failing to interpret the double dream, the chief cupbearer acknowledged his fault in forgetting Joseph; the latter is fetched from the dungeon, and having been shaved (the first mention of shaving in human history), stands before Pharaoh, and not only interprets the dream, but proposes a statesman-like scheme for profiting by it.

Recent discoveries at the First Cataract, and at El-Kab record the fact of this seven years famine. The date is given as 1700 B.C. This date accords with accepted Bible chronology.

The dream was doubled, in order, as Joseph says in verse 32, to denote its Divine certainty. This explanation of the word " double " in this verse, furnishes perhaps, the key to the meaning of the same word in Isa. xl. 2, lxi. 7, Jer. xvi. 18, xvii. 18, Zech. ix. 12, Rev. xviii. 6. Some Bible scholars, however, place the definite article before the word " double," thus giving the word the significance of " acquittance " or " receipt."

Joseph, rejected by his brethren, is given by God a Gentile wife and two sons, Manasseh and Ephraim, i.e. " forgetfulness " and " fruitfulness " ; and so soon as this elect family is complete the famine comes. This famine was designed by God, not only to bless and instruct Egypt, but mainly, to be the means of bringing Joseph's brothers in repentance to his feet. It is all, possibly, a picture of present and future facts. The true Joseph in His present rejection by His brethren takes to Himself an election from among the Gentiles. The completion of that election, if this picture may be so interpreted; will be followed by " the time of Jacob's trouble " the effect of which trouble will be to cause the Sons of Israel to recognize Him whom they had pierced, and to mourn and weep. Verse 13 illustrates John xx. 23. See Note on that passage.

The accusation " Ye are spies " was morally true ; for the men who were guilty of the treachery, cruelty and cupidity of xxxiv. 25-29 would have acted similarly in Egypt if they had had the power.

An interpreter was necessary, for after 20 years' absence from the homeland, though the power to understand the language of childhood may remain, yet the power to speak it is largely lost. Also, it was necessary that the state officers in attendance upon Joseph should be privy to the conversation. God spoke through the Urim stone and the Bethesda pool, and no doubt through Joseph's divining cup. Satan imitates this Divine action.

GENESIS XLII, XLIII, XLIV, XLV.—
Joseph's skill—that skill which only love

can give—in leading his brothers step by step to a confession of their sin against him, and to a sense of its blackness in the sight of God, is a picture of the future action of the Lord Jesus Christ in bringing Israel to recognize her sin in rejecting Him, and the consequent enormity of that sin against God. Had Joseph thought of his own dignity and of his own affection, he would have revealed himself at once to his brothers. Such a revelation would have produced confusion, but not repentance. He loved them, and therefore sought their spiritual welfare. He acted so as to bring their sin to remembrance, to make them confess it with their own lips, and not just to him and in his presence, for he still concealed himself from them, but to God and in His presence. His detention of Simeon, and, afterwards of Benjamin, was skilfully designed so as to find out if they still were indifferent to the cries of a captive brother and the tears of a bereaved father. His plan succeeded admirably, his sternness and his kindness both conspired to disquiet them ; and his goodness helped to lead them to repentance. Judah exclaims : " God hath found out the iniquity of thy servants ! " They had been guilty of many dreadful sins, and these are recorded in the Sacred Text, but they only think of this one great commanding sin, the rejection of their brother Joseph. And so when at last he recognizes the success of his action, and that their hearts are truly broken before God and converted, and that, therefore, his making himself known to them would be a spiritual advantage to them, he cries out : " I am Joseph whom ye sold ! " It is a lovely scene ! Thus true affection keeps self in the background, and makes use of circumstances to secure the spiritual welfare of even those who have most deeply sinned against that affection.

Possibly Simeon devised this evil and, therefore, was bound and placed in prison.

The union of Benjamin with Joseph points forward to the day when Christ, as Benjamin, will be the son of the right hand to Israel, and, as Joseph, king over all the earth.

The distress of Judah and the others, shows that they were no longer, in heart, the men of twenty years back. They declared that they loved their father too much to be indifferent to his tears, and their brother Benjamin too much to consent to his captivity.

Joseph's grace in covering up their sin

directly they confessed it ; in hiding it from Pharaoh, and in hasting to acknowledge them before Pharaoh as his brothers, illustrates the richer grace of Him who says, " Your sins and iniquities will I remember no more."

Joseph's heart beat true to God and to his brothers. He kept pressing upon them that it was God who had taken him out of the pit and placed him upon the throne ; and his action led them to feel that it was against God they had sinned, rather than against himself ; and yet he assured them that God loved them and overruled all for their salvation.

GENESIS XLVI.—The two names, Jacob and Israel are here used by the Holy Spirit with great emphasis. When he does not believe (xlv. 26) he faints and is called " Jacob " ; when he does believe (xlv. 28 and xlvi. 1), he takes courage and boldly steps out and is called " Israel."

God spake to him in the visions of the night as " Israel," but addressed him as " Jacob, Jacob " ; just as afterwards he spoke to Peter, and said, " Simon, Simon." To arrest attention He repeats the name; and to kindle affection and confidence He uses the personal name and not the official title.

God forbade Abraham and Isaac to go down into Egypt, He now encourages Jacob to go, saying : " I will go down with thee." When God promises His company there need be neither hesitation nor fear.

The tenderness of God's love to Jacob shines out wonderfully in verse 4. He couples Joseph with Himself, saying : " I will go with thee, and Joseph shall put his hand upon thine eyes," i.e., shall close thine eyes in peace. Well did God know how true Jacob's heart was to Himself and to Joseph.

The difference in the numbers between verses 26 and 27 and Acts vii. 14, is at once removed by noticing that the one passage speaks of Jacob's " kindred," the other of those " which came out of his loins."

God said : " Fear not to go down into Egypt ! " This showed that Jacob did fear to go down. Love for Joseph prompted him to go, but love for God made him hesitate ; for God had forbidden his fathers to go. He, therefore, at Beersheba, sought for guidance, and got it. This anxiety, not to be misled by natural affection, evidenced spiritual growth.

GENESIS XLVII.—The moment when Joseph revealed himself in his glory to his brethren was when Judah took the sorrow of the aged Israel to heart, and put himself into it. It is a wonderful picture of Christ's revelation of Himself, when Judah, in the latter day, will voice the sorrow of Israel in connection with the rejection of Jesus, the true Joseph.

Joseph is not ashamed of his brethren. He presents them to the great king. Jacob, although he has to confess a short and troubled life, and is himself a despised shepherd, yet blesses the mighty monarch ; " and without contradiction, the less is blessed of the greater." The least and most faltering of God's children is superior to the mightiest monarch ; and is conscious of the superiority.

The commanding facts that now appear in this chapter, and the prior one, are as follows : God appears to Jacob as the God of Isaac, not of Abraham, i.e., the God of the risen Christ. Joseph, raised from the pit to the throne, another type of Christ, enriches his brethren with all the promises, which they by their rejection of him had forfeited, but which are now, upon the ground of grace, restored to them. At the same time they are given the richest province in Egypt. The Egyptians, themselves representative of all the Nations of the earth, are saved from death by Joseph, made by him the willing slaves of the throne, and their future assured to them. All this is a striking picture of what has yet to come to pass. This is the subject of Rom. ix, x, and xi, in which chapters it is pointed out that Israel and the Gentile will inherit the promises, in fellowship, solely upon the ground of pure grace.

Joseph was the greatest benefactor Egypt ever had. In one day, by Divine wisdom, he destroyed slavery and landlordism. He set up only one master, and one landlord, in the nation, and that was the nation itself, as physically embodied in Pharaoh. Were all nations wise they would learn from him. His non-purchase of the land belonging to the priests was reasonable, for they already were civil servants ; and his charging a state rent of one-fifth part of the increase was a very low charge. Herodotus records a confirmatory statement with respect to these Temple lands ; and Turkish law to-day fixes four-fifths of the increase as an agricultural rent, if the landlord supplies cattle and seed.

In verse 27, the nation is for the first time called " Israel."

Feeble as was his body, and imperfect his faith, yet did Jacob esteem God's land, and the promises connected therewith, as unspeakably superior to Egypt with all its glory! He begs Joseph—he makes him swear—that he will put his bones where his heart was—in the land of Palestine. Confusion is caused by connecting Heb. xi. 21 with the last verse of this chapter. The comments upon the next chapter will show that Jacob worshipped twice; once upon the head of his bed, as here; and, the second time, when leaning on his staff.

GENESIS XLVIII.—The Holy Spirit in Heb. xi. 21 points to Jacob's action in this chapter as the great faith action of his life. Feeble and dying, and having nothing except the staff on which he leant and worshipped, he yet bestowed vast and unseen possessions on his grandsons. He first recited the gift of the land of Canaan to him by God (verses 3 and 4), then, making Joseph his firstborn (v. 22), he adopts his two sons as his own (" even as Reuben and Simeon they shall be mine "), and, setting the younger above the elder, endowed them with the firstborn's double portion. It is a beauteous picture of a faith that was Divine, intelligent, and triumphant.

The double portion given to Joseph as the firstborn was a conquered portion (v. 22). The possession given by God to the Divine Firstborn among many brethren is also a conquered possession, i.e., His people redeemed out of the hand of the enemy—the Amorite.

This statement of verse 22 is an instance of the Law of Subsequent Mention. Acts xx. 35 is another instance, and Jude 14 yet another. This is one of the Laws peculiar to the vast library known as " the Bible."

Jacob's faith overcame Joseph's will, i.e., the " will of man " (v. 19); just as Isaac's faith overcame the " will of the flesh " (Gen. xxvii). See Note on Heb. xi. 20, 21.

Esau sold his birthright, and Reuben forfeited his. Jacob therefore could bestow it on whom he would. Joseph had a double claim; he merited the birthright; and, also, he was the firstborn of Rachel who was Jacob's true wife.

It was on this occasion that Jacob worshipped leaning on the top of his staff. The incident may thus be paraphrased : The aged patriarch sits upon the side of his bed, and leans upon his staff. Joseph brings forward his sons. Jacob lays the staff aside, the two boys are placed between his knees, and the aged pilgrim kisses them and embraces them. The boys are now withdrawn by their father, who recognizes that Israel, overcome with emotion, is about to worship. The aged patriarch retakes his staff, and leaning upon it, so as not to fall upon his face, bows in grateful worship before God (v. 12). Strengthening himself once more upon the bed, he bids his grandsons yet again to come near him, and, crossing his hands, he blesses them. It was no empty blessing but rich with eternal wealth ; as faith very well knew.

Thus was Jacob a worshipper in chapter xlvii and in chapter xlviii. In chapter xlvii he worshipped " leaning upon the top of his bed " ; and in chapter xlviii he worshipped " leaning upon the top of his staff." In the one chapter he worshipped as a stranger; in the other as a pilgrim. His heart was not set upon the wealth of his luxurious bedchamber, but was far away in God's chosen land, and if he, for the moment, lay upon a costly couch, such as Joseph, as viceroy over all Egypt, without doubt provided for him, yet was he a worshipper thereon. On the second occasion he worshipped as a pilgrim, leaning as a wanderer upon his staff, and speaking of the treasures that he saw by faith.

The anxiety of Jacob's faith throbs in the chapter. He fears the influence of Egypt upon his sons. His nature led him all his life long to grasp at wealth and position, but now faith shines brightly, and he earnestly points Joseph and his sons to the true riches promised by God. They were in great danger. Joseph was viceroy, and brilliant prospects in Egypt were within his reach for his children. The aged patriarch urges him not to make his home in Egypt, but to set his heart in Canaan. He tells him that it is a doubly precious land ; first, because God gave it to him ; and, second, because there he buried Rachel. In effect, he said to Joseph : " That land should be doubly precious to thee, because of these two facts." It is a scene of touching tenderness ! The aged eyes of the dying patriarch glow once more with the love of early manhood. He looks eagerly into Joseph's eyes, as much as to say: " Joseph, I loved her ; and she was thy mother." Thus he laid these two great pleas upon the heart of Joseph so that they should save him from making Egypt his country.

GENESIS XLIX.—This chapter forms one of the great dispensational prophecies of the Word of God. It concerns the " latter days " and the " last days " (v. 1). This is the first occurrence of this expression : " the last days." It occurs fourteen times in the Old Testament. In ten passages the Hebrew term is rendered " latter days," and in four, " last days." The term, therefore, embraces the First and Second Advents of the Messiah. This distinction between the " latter days " and the " last days " reappears in 1 and 2 Tim.

The prophecy may be thus divided : Reuben, Simeon, and Levi, the moral history of Israel up to the First Advent ; Judah, the apparition of the Messiah and His rejection ; Zebulon and Issachar, the dispersion and subjugation of the Jews among the Gentiles ; Dan, the appearing and kingdom of the Anti-Christ · verse 18, the cry of anguish of the elect sons of Israel for the Second Coming of Christ ; Gad, Asher, and Naphtali, the moral character of that election as victorious, royally nourished, and true witnesses with goodly words ; Joseph and Benjamin together predict the Second Coming, in glory, of Israel's Messiah.

As sons they stood before " Jacob "; as listeners, before " Israel." This expressed the difference of their standing in nature and in election.

No prophet, ruler, or great man sprang out of Reuben.

Simeon and Levi were scattered and divided as here predicted. The curse upon Levi was afterwards turned into a blessing (Exod. xxxii, Deut. x).

The seemingly opposing statements between verse 10 and Ezek. xxi. 27, may be thus resolved :

The sceptre departed from Judah when Shiloh (Christ) came. It departed at His birth. St. Luke states expressly that Mary was compelled by the Roman Government to go to Bethlehem to be enrolled in a census ; and the Holy Spirit points out that this census was then *first* made ! Again, the sceptre departed from Judah at the death of Christ ; for He being the only member of that tribe entitled to hold the sceptre, it consequently departed when He died.

But Shiloh was not like earthly kings, for He rose three days later from the grave.

And the Holy Spirit tells us in Acts ii. 36 that the sceptre was then handed to Him by God.

Thus when Shiloh came the sceptre departed from Judah, and yet was it, at the same time, given to Shiloh, whose " right it was."

The words, " *The* Sceptre," in verse 10, stand for Him who holds it, and may, therefore, be understood as a Messianic Title. There are six Messianic titles in the Pentateuch, each commencing with the letter S : Seed, Gen. iii. 15 ; Shiloh, Gen. xlix. 10 ; Sceptre, Gen. xlix. 10 ; Shepherd, Gen. xlix. 24 ; Stone, Gen. xlix. 24 ; and Star, Num. xxiv. 17.

The expression " from between his feet " (v. 10) is an idiom, and means, " from among his children."

Although Dan should be a tribe of Israel and bear rule as such, yet should he become a treacherous serpent ; and this prediction causes a break in the stream of the prophecy to permit of the cry " I have waited for thy salvation, O Jehovah ! " This was the first tribe to beguile the tribes into idolatry. It is omitted in Rev. vii. This prediction and these facts suggest that the Anti-Christ will be a member of this tribe.

" Benjamin shall ravin as a wolf." Judges iii, 1 Sam. xi, and 1 Sam. xiv illustrate this ; but most of all the Apostle Paul, who was a Benjamite, and, as such, prior to his conversion, hungered to devour his fellow men, and, after his conversion, hungered to save them (Acts vii. 58, viii. 1, 3, ix. 1, 13, 14, 21, xxii. 4-8, 1 Tim. i. 13).

The prophecy concluded, the patriarch charges his sons to surely bury him in the land of Canaan. He would not that even his bones should remain in Egypt. He had now lived in that land for seventeen years in ease and splendour. He had had the gratification of seeing his son set, practically, upon its throne ; but all the splendour and ease failed to wreck his faith, it burned brightly to the end, and he says to his sons, " Bury me with my fathers in the land of Canaan."

The sense of verses 3 and 4 may be thus expressed : " The excellency of dignity and the excellency of power shall pass away as water ; thou shalt not have the excellency," i.e., the birthright. See 1 Chron. v. 1.

GENESIS L.—Joseph closed his father's eyes, as predicted in chapter xlvi. 4.

The fact that Joseph did not speak personally to Pharaoh in verse 4 accords with the most recent discoveries which show that mourners at this time did not shave, and, therefore, could not enter the royal presence.

Verse 4 is one of the very many in the Pentateuch which evidence the immense antiquity of these five books.

The incurable unbelief of the heart is illustrated by the cruel thoughts of Joseph's brothers as to his affection for them. This unbelief moved Joseph to tears ; and in his action and language he once more stands forth as, perhaps, the most remarkable type of Christ in the whole Bible.

Heb. xi. 22 draws attention to the double testimony of Joseph's faith when dying, that is : that God would surely redeem them out of Egypt ; and that they were to carry his bones out with them when leaving. Faith comes by hearing Joseph heard and believed what God had said to Abraham, to Isaac, and to Jacob as to the gift of Canaan to the Nation ; and in verse 24 he unites these three names in connection with this great promise. So they embalmed him and carried up his bones and buried them in the pleasant land (Exod. xiii. 19, Joshua xxiv. 32).

Thus the Book of Genesis begins with a living God and ends with a dead man. The subject of its first chapter is creation ; that of its last chapter, a coffin !

The sentences : " the greater light to rule the day," and " the lesser light to rule the night " are formed of Hebrew letters whose numerical values, and all their combinations express, respectively, solar and lunar numbers. This shows a knowledge of astronomy equal to, if not indeed superior to, that of the present day.

The Holy Spirit tells the story of Creation in one chapter, but that of the Tabernacle in nineteen. Why? Because every whit of the latter sets out the glory of the Person and Work of Christ in Atonement, and that glory (Rev. v.) is greater than His glory as Creator (Rev. iv.). See notes on Rev. iv. and v.

EXODUS

EXODUS I.—As the subject of Genesis is man's ruin, so that of Exodus is man's redemption. The Hebrew title for the book is " These are the names." This accords with the subject of the book, for redemption is an individual matter. The book teaches that this redemption can only be effected by blood. It opens with Israel as a helpless slave in the power of the enemy, and doomed by him to destruction ; it closes with Israel redeemed, enriched, and free. The method of this deliverance was the death of the Paschal Lamb. The book, therefore, teaches that where there is no blood there is no salvation.

The wise planning of the Egyptian monarch was very sagacious, so long as he left God outside. But the entrance of God into these plans turned their wisdom to folly. All schemes which ignore God illustrate human folly.

The ruins of the great treasure cities, Pithom and Raamses, exist to-day, and are well known.

Satan, in order to make impossible the birth of the promised Redeemer, energized Pharaoh to order the destruction of all the male children. He was, however, defeated by woman ; and this made his defeat the more striking, for he won his first victory by deceiving a woman.

The names of mighty monarchs have perished, but the names of Shiphrah and Puah stand eternal on the Sacred page. They no doubt were the two head nurses, for in verse 19 they account to the Egyptian government for the conduct of their colleagues.

The faith of these brave women, for they risked their own lives, is recognized by God, and He dealt well with them. It must not be assumed that they were guilty of falsehood. There is no reason to suppose that what they stated was not perfectly true. The statement in verse 21, coupled with the statements of the prior verses, means that God protected them from being put to death by Pharaoh ;

and, that because of their faith, He made them houses ; that is, He gave them large families.

The Egyptian Government finding their plan of destroying the male children useless, issued a general proclamation ordering the people at large to throw every Hebrew male infant into the river wherever found.

EXODUS II.—Moses was a member of the tribe of Levi. He was the seventh from Abraham, Abraham was the seventh from Heber, and Enoch the seventh from Adam. Miriam and Aaron were already born.

The action of his mother was, without doubt, that of a Divinely given faith. She placed the infant in an Ark made water-tight with pitch. It was in an Ark daubed with pitch that Noah was saved. So great was her faith in placing the child in God's hands that she did not stay to watch over him ; but she was quickly fetched to become nurse to him ! It is a beauteous story. It shows how God is even in little things, and overrules them as well as great things to help forward His purposes. Little did this Egyptian princess think that day as she walked by the river that the God of gods was directing her footsteps. And thus Moses was nourished in the palace and seated at the table of the very monarch who commanded his destruction !

Great events have hung upon a tear, but never greater than those which were brought to pass by the tears of this babe ! The defeat of Satan, the salvation of Israel and of the Nations, the trustworthiness of God's Word, and the Salvation of the world through an incarnate Saviour—all these lay hidden in the tears that wetted that infant cheek upon that day.

From the language of Hebrews xi. 24, it is clear that a time came when Moses had the choice of accepting or refusing the throne of Egypt. He refused, and cast in his lot with the hated and oppressed Hebrews. Moved by indignation, compassion, and a consciousness of personal fitness for the enterprise, he resolved to deliver them from their cruel bondage. But God cannot give victories to the "flesh"; and Moses must spend forty long years, as a shepherd, in the deserts of Arabia, in order to fit him to be a shepherd to Israel.

An important principle appears in this chapter. It is, that providence and faith must not be confounded. Providence gave Moses what faith taught him to surrender. Earthly wisdom counselled him to use his position in the Egyptian court as a means for liberating his people. This would have spared him much affliction; but it would have recognized Pharaoh's lordship, and wholly failed to separate Israel from Egypt and bring her into fellowship with, and dependence upon, God. Faith led Moses to give up the throne and to identify himself with God and His people, but his nourishment and education in the court of Pharaoh were of priceless value. They were providential. They helped to form and fashion him for his future ministry. Thus Providence shapes the vessel, but Faith imparts the necessary intelligence and power. To move forward, therefore, in dependence upon the shapings of providence without the intelligence and energy of faith, is to advance to failure. The opposite to this is seen in Christ.

Moses, like Joseph, was rejected by his brethren; but, like Joseph, he continued to love them. Stephen, in Acts vii., sought by this double rejection to awaken the Sanhedrin to its guilt in rejecting Christ.

The priest of Midian had three names, Reuel, Jethro and Raguel. This latter name means "a friend of God." He was a descendant of Abraham by Keturah. He no doubt, like Job and Melchisedek, was king and priest to his tribe. He was a worshipper of the true God. It is interesting to reflect that the original knowledge of God, although corrupted, seems never to have been lost in Arabia. Here Job, Jethro, Balaam, and Mahomet lived, and here Moses saw the burning bush and was called to his life work.

Judges iv. 11, states that Hobab was the father-in-law of Moses. Numbers x. 29, describes him as the brother-in-law of Moses. This presents a difficulty to many; but there is none, for the Hebrew word means relative as well as father-in-law.

Joseph and Moses, as already remarked, are types of Christ. Joseph was rejected because of hatred to his person; Moses, because of unbelief as to his mission. The former was personally hated: the latter, officially refused.

The glorious name "Elohim" occurs five times in verses 23-25. As yet He was not known to Israel as "Jehovah." Five is the number of grace. No moral excellence in Israel attracted God's love; it was their misery that drew out His heart to them. He gave audience to their cry; He heard their groaning; He remembered His covenant, He looked upon them; and He had respect unto them.

EXODUS III-IV. 17.—God not only gave to Moses the faith that led him to identify himself with His people; but also endowed him with the power to deliver them. Forty years in the desert was needed to humble the strength of the "flesh" and destroy its hope. The possible king of Egypt was now an obscure shepherd. This putting of man and his resources to death opened the door for God to come in with His Almighty power. The flame of fire in the lowly desert bush—emblem of the Deity and Humanity of Christ —and the great name "I am" proceeding out from the fire revealed this Almighty power to Moses. It was the same fire, there called a lamp, that Abraham saw (Gen. xv. 17). The Voice that called "Moses, Moses," was the very same Voice that said "Martha, Martha" and the love that said, "I have surely seen," and "I have heard," and "I know," and "I am come down to deliver," and "I am come to bring up"—that was the same love that shines forth in John xiii. 1!

The carnal mind is not subject to the law of God, neither indeed can be. The very Moses who in chapter ii. 11-13 stepped forward with energy to champion his people, is the very same Moses who in chapter iii. 11-13 steps back and declares himself unequal to the enterprise. Faith neither steps forward nor backward, but holds His hand who says: "Certainly I will be with thee."

The glorious name "I am," i.e. "Jehovah," was now first made known to Israel. To Abraham, to Isaac, and to Jacob, He revealed Himself as "El-Shaddai," that is "God, the Almighty"; for that was the revelation they needed. But to Israel, enslaved and helpless, a further revelation was necessary;

and the glorious name " I am " was given to her as a blank cheque, so that she could write after these two words whatever her need demanded. For example, she needed a deliverer, and at once she had the answer, " I am the Deliverer " ; she needed a comforter and again came the response, " I am the Comforter " ; she needed all kinds of provision—needs immeasurably beyond human skill to meet—and at once her faithful God says, " I am the Provider." Moses was commanded, verses 15-22, to tell the Children of Israel that this mighty God, Jehovah, was the God of Abraham, the God of Isaac, and the God of Jacob, that that was His name for ever and His memorial to all generations. He changes not, He is the same yesterday, and to-day, and for ever. His name is Jesus ; and that is God's greatest name !

The glad tidings of great joy that Moses was to carry to Israel were these : " I will bring you up out of the affliction of Egypt into a land flowing with milk and honey." This was the message ; and Moses' faith in delivering it was strengthened beforehand by the Divine assurance that it would be believed.

The three days journey of verse 18 was not deceitfully proposed by God, but furnished as a test for Pharaoh.

The word " borrow " in verse 22 is correctly translated " ask " in the R.V. See note on chapter xii. 35.

The hesitating and timid Moses of Mount Horeb was the same courageous and self-reliant Moses who smote the Egyptian dead ! His strength then unfitted him as a Divine instrument, and now his weakness unfitted him. God can use neither one nor the other, if the strength is trusted, or if the weakness is sheltered behind as an excuse. Weakness, as in the case of Moses, budded into unbelief, and blossomed into rebellion. But how tenderly God dealt with him ! The burning flame proclaimed His holiness; the spoken word, His grace. What Moses saw, taught him that God was holy ; what he heard, that God was gracious.

To assure him God gave him two promises and three signs. The promises were : " I will be with thee "; and " Ye shall serve God upon this mountain " (Horeb). The three signs were : the serpent, leprosy, and blood. The serpent, Satan and his power ; leprosy, sin introduced by him ; blood poured out, the wrath of God. These three signs taught Moses that the Divine power which was to

fit him for his mission could make Satan as helpless as the rod in his hand, and use him in the accomplishment of God's counsels. Further, that Divine power could cleanse away sin—a malady as loathsome and incurable as leprosy ; and, lastly, that that same Almighty power would judge with death those who despised that grace.

The word translated " caught it " i.e. stiffened (ch. iv. 4), is the same word in Hebrew as " hardened " when used with respect to Pharaoh.

In spite of these promises and signs the unbelief of Moses' heart ripened into rebellion, and he refused to go; but he immediately consented on being promised the companionship of his brother Aaron. Such is man's heart ! Promised the companionship of God, Moses refuses to go, but willingly volunteers if accompanied by a feeble fellow-creature. He would feel safer leaning on the arm of Aaron than leaning on the arm of Jehovah ! And yet Aaron was no real help to him, but the contrary ; for he made the golden calf. But how full of tender pity was God ! He provided this companion, and bade Moses take " this rod " in his hand wherewith he was to do " the signs " R.V.

" And thou shalt put the words in his mouth " R.V., Here is a definition of inspiration.

Aaron was to be Moses' " spokesman " i.e. " prophet " (ch. vii. 1). God's prophet is God's spokesman. He tells him what to say—He puts " the words " into his mouth.

EXODUS IV. 18-31.—Moses courteously asked leave of Jethro to return to Egypt, for, in a sense, he was Jethro's servant.

The Midian in which Jethro lived was not the Midian of the Dead Sea region, but of the eastern shore of the Gulf of Akaba. The town of Madyan stands there to-day ; and the Mohammedans of the town welcome pilgrims on the way to Mecca shouting, " Come into the city of the brother-in-law of Moses."

Moses took his wife and his two sons Gershom and Eliezer, and, with the rod of God in his hand, departed for Egypt.

The rod of God must be carefully distinguished from the rod of Aaron. The one symbolized the wrath of God; the other His grace. (See Notes on Num. xx).

God told Moses beforehand that He would harden, i.e. embolden, or make courageous, Pharaoh's heart. The Holy Spirit comments on this in Rom. ix. It was a just judgment upon Pharaoh ; he hardened his own heart seven times, and then God, in a just judgment, hardened, or suffered to be hardened, his heart. It would not be just that men should' resist the pleadings of God's Holy Spirit, and then fancy to escape judgment by yielding when they found escape impossible. God has but to withdraw His gracious Spirit and man's heart remains hard. The citizens of the Southern States of America hardened their hearts when God pleaded with them on behalf of the slaves, and then He, in just wrath, hardened their hearts so that they resolved upon war ; and thus He compelled them to drink a deep cup filled with blood.

Moses was commanded to announce to Pharaoh that Jehovah, the God of Israel, was about to slay his son. But Moses had to learn that disobedience and rebellion in him was just as hateful as in Pharaoh ; and that God, because of His nature, must judge with death sin wherever found. On approaching Egypt therefore this holy God sought to judge his little boy, Eliezer, because of Moses' disobedience in not having had him circumcised, as God had commanded. The passage throws a great light upon the inner life of Moses. It may be assumed, from what is related, that he yielded to the wishes of his wife in this matter, though he knew he was disobeying God. The particulars are not fully given because the Holy Spirit did not think this necessary, but evidently, in order to save the child's life, and urged to it by Moses, she circumcised him herself, and then with anger and passion declared that her husband's religion was a religion of blood, i.e. of blood-stained rites.

Thus Moses had to learn that God would judge him before He judged Pharaoh, and that rebellion in the one was the same as rebellion in the other ; and this lesson must have enabled Moses to proclaim this dreadful truth with the force of a personal experience.

This is a moral principle which Rom. vi, Col. ii, and many other scriptures teach. Christians, under the New Covenant, are circumcised in the death of Jesus Christ; that is, they "die" as to their old nature. They then go forth with a message of death and of life ; but they must have a personal experience of the bitterness, to the natural will, of that spiritual circumcision. They must consent to "die," if they would be effective messengers of the Cross.

The Israelites hearing that God had visited them, bowed the head and worshipped.

It is affecting the meeting of Moses and Aaron at the foot of Mount Horeb. They kiss each other. Forty years later they stand upon Mount Horeb ; and, again, they kiss each other, but for the last time !

Most people understand that the agent of the Divine wrath sought to kill Moses himself ; but the Angel was to slay Pharaoh's son because of Pharaoh's rebellion, and Moses was to learn the terror of this judgment by the Angel being commanded to slay his son because of his rebellion.

EXODUS V-VI. 1.—The close of chapter iv. presents the people worshipping in believing joy. The close of this chapter sets before the reader the same people filled with unbelieving bitterness. The glad tidings of salvation is one thing ; the struggle against the power that keeps the soul in bondage is another. Satan will not let his captive go free ; and God permits the bitter experience of his power in order to exercise and strengthen faith. It is good for a man to learn painfully the nature of sin's dominion, and his absolute helplessness in the grip of that monarch.

The first move of Israel toward deliverance plunged her into deeper misery so that the people would have preferred being left quiet in their slavery. This is oftentimes the spiritual experience of awakened sinners.

The first verse illustrates the Gospel. It is a feast with the Lord Jesus (" unto Me ") ; and it is enjoyed in " the wilderness."

The second sentence in verse 22 should read thus : " Lord, wherefore hast Thou suffered Thy people to be so evil entreated ? "

It is better to feast in the wilderness with Christ than to labour in the brick-kilns with Pharaoh.

The opposition of Pharaoh, and the unbelief and anger of Israel, were a double discouragement for Moses. The first effort of a Christian to do good is often chilled by similar unbelief on the part of the church, and by opposition on the part of the world.

EXODUS VI. 2-27.—Instead of turning away from so unbelieving and petulant a people, God, in His love, and pity, and grace encourages them and Moses, by telling them what He was, and what He would do. In His message to them, through Moses, He bids them look at the strength of the Divine hand that would surely deliver them (v. 1). Five times He declares that He is " Jehovah " (vs. 2, 3, 6, 7, 8,) ; and seven times He utters the great words " I will " (vs. 6, 7, 8) ; and three times He declares " I have " (vs. 4, 5). This was all a revelation of the Almighty power and unchanging faithfulness of Him who was come down to deliver them ; and the numbers 3, 5, and 7, harmonize with the revelation. But nothing can cure the unbelief of the natural heart : the people hearkened not ; and Moses, looking at himself instead of at God, doubted his ability to persuade Pharaoh (vs. 9-12).

The grace that gave the promises of the first half of the chapter, records the names of those whom Pharaoh declared to be his slaves, God numbers those that belong to Himself, He calls them " My people " though they still were in the power of the enemy. To make this grace more amazing the three tribes of Reuben, Simeon, and Levi are chosen as representing the whole nation.

The power of the Divine life in the heart of Moses appears in his recording that Aaron was his elder brother, and in his faithfully relating his own unbelief and faults.

For explanation of " Know " (v. 3) see notes on Psalm lxxxiii.

EXODUS VI. 28, VII.—Moses having declared that he was of " uncircumcised lips," that is, that he was wanting in eloquence, grace once more pities his fears, and Aaron is appointed to be his prophet, i.e. his spokesman.

The magicians, Jannes and Jambres (2 Tim. iii. 8), by the power of Satan imitate the power of God ; but Aaron's rod swallowed up their rods, thus inflicting the first blow on the gods of Egypt. The rods are still called rods, in verse 12, though they had become serpents.

Verse 13 should read : " and it " i.e. the miracle, " hardened Pharaoh's heart."

The Nile—like the serpent—was one of the great gods of the Egyptians. It was turned into blood, as well as all the streams and rivers and ponds fed by it. Verse 15 suggests that this plague took place at the moment that Pharaoh arrived upon the bank of the river in order to worship it.

The nine plagues that preceded the destruction of the first-born form three groups of three plagues each. The first two plagues of each group were threatened beforehand ;

the last plague of each group, i.e. the lice, the boils, and the darkness, fell without warning. Further, Aaron inflicted the first group of three, and Moses the last group of three.

The sense of verses 3-5, as illustrated by verse 13, is that the effect of the plagues on Pharaoh's heart would be to harden it. Such is the incurable hatred of the natural heart that Divine judgments harden instead of subduing it. See Rev. ix. 20, 21 and xvi. 21.

EXODUS VIII.—The frog was an Egyptian god. It was worshipped as the symbol of fecundity.

The sense of verse 9 is " command me as a master and I will obey you. When shall I " etc.,

The unannounced plague of lice compelled Jannes and Jambres to say " this is the finger of God." They could, perhaps by Satanic power, imitate God, but they could not create life.

The fourth plague was specially severe to idolators. Beelzebub was the god of flies, but he was now proved to be impotent.

Pharaoh said first : " Sacrifice in the land " (ch. viii. 25) ; then : " Go not very far away," (ch. viii. 28) ; then : " Let your men go " (ch. x. 11) ; and then : " Go, but leave your flocks behind " (ch. x. 24). Satan's efforts always are directed to prevent a definite breach between the Church and the World.

It was possible to Jannes and Jambres, as some think, and as may be seen to-day in the east, by sleight of hand to turn rods into serpents, water into blood, and bring up frogs out of a river, but it was impossible to them to turn dust into lice. The only other living creature that the Bible says is made out of dust is man. Singular conjunction ! Was it this fact that compelled the magicians to the great confession : " This is the finger of God ! "

EXODUS IX.—The fifth plague struck at the Egyptian adoration of animals. Their three popular gods were the bull, the cow, and the ram.

The statement in verse 6 that " all the cattle of Egypt died," means, as stated in verse 3, " all the cattle which is in the field " for cattle were affected by the next plagues as shown in verses 9 and 19. Further, the expression " all cattle " means " cattle of every kind."

The sixth plague very possibly was aimed at their great god Typhon, i.e. the Devil. The furnace was where human victims to this god were burnt alive. Pharaoh possibly was standing before this furnace. Moses, not Aaron, in the sight of Pharaoh casts the ashes up toward heaven. If the sacrifices were being offered to avert the plagues, the ashes, instead of doing so, brought a fresh one.

The seventh plague was directed against the two gods Isis and Osiris. The message announcing this plague is full of marvels. Two of these are very prominent. One, the grace that did not at once destroy Pharaoh, for such is the sense of verse 15, but gave him warning, and urged him to bring all his people and cattle under cover so that they should escape ; the other, the Divine purpose in raising Pharaoh up to resist these Divine judgments. See note on Rom. ix. 17.

Verses 20 and 21 illustrate salvation by faith.

Verse 31 is important as helping to show that the ten plagues occupied from three to four months.

EXODUS X.—The god Serapis was believed by the Egyptians to protect from locusts. This eighth plague struck at that belief. Locusts were so dreaded by the Egyptians that Pharaoh's ministers roughly urge him to let Israel go. The king consents, provided the little ones are left behind. He knew if they were, their parents' hearts would compel them to return. Mark x. 14 and Ephesians vi. 4, together with verse 9 of this chapter, teach that God will have little children in His kingdom, and that they must not be left outside.

The word " evil " in verse 10, means the death threatened in verse 28.

Locusts are brought by the east wind and carried away by the west wind now, as in the days of Moses.

The ninth plague robbed the Egyptians of their supreme god, the Sun, and proved Jehovah to be the God of gods. The plagues deepened in intensity, and affected property as well as persons.

In reply to Pharaoh's proposal that Israel should leave their flocks and herds in Egypt, Moses replied that not only would they take every beast with them, but that also Pharaoh himself, must provide them with cattle for the burnt-offerings.

The statement at the close of verse 26

points a lesson true at all times. The second step in the spiritual life is not revealed until the first is taken (John vii. 17). " Egypt " must be left, that is the first step, before the nature of spiritual worship can be learned.

Chapter xi. 1-3 is a parenthesis. Verse 4 continues the last interview between Pharaoh and Moses.

EXODUS XI, XII.—The tenth plague may be said to have destroyed all the gods of Egypt. It introduced the Passover. The Holy Spirit states in 1 Cor. v. 7, that the Passover pictured Christ's sacrifice of Himself in order to save sinners sentenced to die.

Two great facts appear in the Passover, the certain doom of the first-born, and his certain salvation. He was doomed to death by God, not because of his conduct, but because of his birth. This latter fact he could not alter ; and he was, therefore, hopelessly lost. He was, however, absolutely saved, because of the value of the life sacrificed for him. He knew he was saved because God had pledged Himself to most certainly save all who sprinkled the shed blood upon their door posts.

All sinners are justly doomed by God to death. But he loves them as He loved the firstborn, and therefore the Lamb of God has suffered that death. His precious blood, that is, His priceless life, poured out, attests the fact. The Word of God promises eternal safety to whoever will seek salvation in that atoning Saviour. The believer in Christ knows therefore that he shall never perish ; and this knowledge is based on two facts outside of himself : these are, the preciousness of Christ's blood to God; and, the faithfulness of God to His own promise.

The words " borrowed " and " lent," verses 35 and 36, should read " asked " and " gladly gave," i.e. pressed them to take.

The " sojourning " and the " dwelling " of the Children of Israel must be carefully distinguished. They sojourned in Canaan ; they dwelt in Egypt. The dwelling in Egypt lasted 215 years ; the sojourning, a similar period. The total period from the promise to Abraham to the Exodus was therefore 430 years. From the birth of Isaac it was 400 years.

Every verse in these two chapters is rich with instruction respecting Christ as the true Paschal Lamb ; the absolute and conscious safety that those enjoy who believe upon Him ; and their consequent separation from, and deliverance out of, this present evil world. It was reasonable that Israel should demand the jewels of the Egyptians, for they owed the Israelites an immense sum of money as pay for public works executed by Israel during the period of her enforced servitude.

The "one law" of circumcision (v.41) in order to obtain entrance into God's family, i.e. the new birth, was a necessity to both home-born and stranger. So regeneration is a necessity to both the child of Christian parents and the child of infidels.

EXODUS XIII.—The Israelites ceased to be slaves to Pharaoh, but it was in order that they should become slaves to Jehovah. Moses (v. 1 and 2), was directed to tell the people that they now were God's people, for He had bought them ; and that they were therefore to be holy. This double injunction was given in the two commandments respecting the first-born and the unleavened bread.

Immediately that Israel was redeemed out of Egypt, instructions were given respecting the annual observance of the Passover. That is to say, Israel was to perpetually confess to the world that her salvation out of Egypt, and her settlement in Canaan, was wholly due to the preciousness of the blood of the Paschal Lamb. The people of God to-day give a like testimony.

Compare the expression in verse 5, " and it shall be," with the similar expression in verse 11 ; and the expression " with a strong hand " in verse 9, with a similar expression in verse 16. Following verse 5 the reader notes that certain days were to be set aside (v. 6 and 7) ; an explanation of this was to be given to the children (v. 8) ; a sign was provided (v. 9) ; and the reason stated, i.e. what the strong hand of Jehovah had done.

Following verse 11 directions are given as to the separation of the first-born ; the explanation therefore to be given to the children ; the token to be provided (v. 16) ; and the reason stated, i.e. what God's strong hand had done.

The " sign " of verse 9, and the " token " of verse 16 figuratively mean that what is done by the hand, desired by the eye, and spoken by the mouth, is all to be subject to the Word of God.

Verse 13 legislated for the redemption of a man and of an ass by the death of a lamb. This is humbling to human pride. The ass was an unclean animal ; and with its broken neck fitly pictured the true moral condition of the most highly cultivated man. But the death of the lamb obtained redemption. Only thus can sinners be saved.

Verses 17 and 18 reveal the tender pity of God in condescending to the weakness of His people. The title " Elohim " and not " Jehovah " occurs three times in these two verses. This is characteristic. Elohim in pity as Creator. Jehovah in power as Redeemer.

God did not tell His people to " go " to Canaan, but to " come " ; for verses 21, 22, show that He was their Travelling Companion. By day, the cloud sheltered them from the heat of the sun, and by night it gave them light so that there was no darkness at all. This cloud remained with them up to the death of Moses. The Ark then went before them (Josh. iii).

Moses in the baptism of the Red Sea " shook off " the powers and principalities of Egypt ; so Christ in the baptism of Calvary. Exod. xiv. 27, 28 illustrates Col. ii. 15. Connect 1 Cor. x. 2. The " third day " of Josh. i. 2 and 11 and of iii. 2 and 7 illustrate Christ arising from the baptism into which He, in type, descended at the Red Sea. There the redeemed were baptized into Him, in type, as the Leader and Commander of His people, and at the Jordan, as the Captain of their salvation leading the many sons to glory. See notes on Col. i. and ii.

EXODUS XIV.—The New Biblical Guide (by the Rev. John Urquhart) should be read in all its volumes ; but particularly those dealing with the times of Joseph and Moses. The lover of the Scriptures will there find a spiritual and scientific feast, and effective explanations of the supposed difficulties in the sacred Text covering that period.

The fear, unbelief, and anger of the very people who had witnessed God's wonders in the land of Egypt would appear incredible but that each Bible student finds these evils in his own heart, and learns, by sad experience, that great depression of mind usually follows exceptional spiritual triumphs. So was it with Israel at the Red Sea. Unbelief cried out : " the wilderness will become our grave "; but the result was that the Sea became Pharaoh's grave. David cried out: " I shall one day perish by the hand of Saul "; but Saul fell down slain on Mount Gilboa, and David ascended his throne at Jerusalem. Elijah fled from the face of Jezebel; but she was dashed to earth, and he rode up to heaven.

Hebrews xi. suggests that Israel had to keep believing while passing through the sea that the waters would not overwhelm them. The Egyptians had not to exercise any faith; for they saw the open road before them. Yet they were drowned; for the Holy Spirit says " there remained not so much as one of them."

The way of faith is life to the redeemed but death to the rebellious.

EXODUS XV.—The Red Sea and the Jordan typify the death and resurrection of Christ. The Red Sea pictures death to sin— the Jordan, death to self. The one separates from Egypt; the other, from the wilderness.

Moses began and ended his wilderness life with a song. That of Deut. xxxii. is the one referred to in Rev. xv. 3.

There was no singing in Egypt; there was groaning. Singing only follows redemption.

This is the oldest song of praise in existence. The greatest poets unite in admiration of its surpassing beauty and sublimity. It is a song of praise; its theme is Jehovah Jesus; and it praises Him for His destruction of the enemy. It begins with Redemption and ends with Glory.

There were two companies of singers—one formed of men, led by Moses; the other of women, led by Miriam. She and her choir " answered them " i.e. the men; and what they sang (v. 21) appears to be the chorus, which most probably was sung after each statement of the song.

This is the first of the ten songs of praise recorded in the Bible; the last is Rev. xiv. 3.

" Self " is absent from the song; it is all about Jehovah, and His power to save.

Miriam, i.e. Mary, is the first prophetess mentioned in the Bible.

The first affections of the new heart may be expressed by the words " praise " and " fellowship." Hence there stands at the beginning of the chapter " *Then* sang Moses,"

and " He is my God, I will prepare Him an habitation " (Ps. xxii. 3). God did not dwell either with Adam in innocence, or with Abraham in promise. But when Redemption, in type, was accomplished, He descended from heaven in a cloud and abode with Israel.

The absence of the conjunction " and " in verse 9, is a beautiful instance of the Law of Omission. The reader is swiftly carried through verse 9 to the grand climax in verse 10. Verse 13 is a fine illustration of the nature of faith. It makes promised blessing a present fact. Israel had many long and weary miles to travel before she reached Zion, the habitation of Jehovah's glory. But faith makes present " things hoped for," and therefore this verse says " Thou hast guided them to Thy holy habitation."

Verses 14-17 (R.V.) further illustrate the nature of a Divine faith. The song declares that all the enemies shall become still as a stone, and that Israel shall pass triumphantly over and enter the promised land.

This first song in the Bible was sung on a shore heaped with dead men—an appalling scene of Divine wrath—and the last song in the Bible will be sung in a scene of yet greater wrath and destruction (Rev. xix). These inspired records of God's ways on earth, and of His action toward sin, anger the self-righteous heart.

Israel was baptized into Moses at the Red Sea. (See notes on 1 Cor. x.), and into Joshua at the Jordan. Both baptisms expressed union, the one to Moses, the other to Joshua. (See note on Jude 9).

From the Red Sea to Sinai Israel was under grace. This helps to explain God's action toward them. At Sinai they, alas, put themselves under Law. A recognition of this makes clear the purpose of the legislation given prior to Sinai. See note on Jer. vii. 22.

God tests faith in order to strengthen and enrich it. This test comes always shortly after conversion. Israel journeys three days in the Wilderness and finds no water. When water is found there is an added trial—the water is bitter. But the smitten tree being cast therein the waters become sweet. Thus trial may surely be sweetened, if, in the energy of faith, a crucified Saviour is introduced into it, and so Jesus found to be Jehovah— Rophi. (See notes on Ps. xxiii).

Not to be thankful (Rom. i. 21), and to murmur lead to greater sins. Israel murmured, and their unbelief deepened as they murmured.

The refreshment enjoyed at Elim suggests that supplied by the Christian mimstry. The Lord sent out twelve apostles and seventy others to revive His wearied inheritance with the tidings that the Kingdom of Heaven was at hand.

Chapters xv.-xl. may be parted into two divisions. The whole section begins with the journeys to Sinai (ch. xv. 22–xix. 2) and closes with the journeys from Sinai (ch. xl. 36–38) The giving of the Law and the making of the Tabernacle form the subject of the first and second sections respectively ; and the two divisions are bound together by the six ascents and descents of Moses.

The redeeming blood of Christ delivers from the power of Satan (Heb. ii. 14) and brings into the paradise of God (Rev. vii. 14, 15).

EXODUS XVI.—The Manna prefigured the descent of the True Bread, of which if a man eat he shall live for ever (John vi. 51). It was a test of appetite and of obedience (v. 4). In Egypt, Israel had slave food; in the desert, angels' food ; and the test quickly revealed that the natural man has no appetite for heavenly things. The people soon called it " light food."

The Manna was so precious that it could not bear contact with the earth. It fell upon the dew, and had to be gathered ere the sun was up ; and freshly every morning. Yesterday's Manna did not do for to-day, nor to-day's for to-morrow (Num. ix). Thus must the Christian feed upon Christ every day, as He reveals Himself in the Scriptures.

Israel in the desert presents a striking picture ! Egypt behind them, Canaan before them, the Wilderness around them, and the Manna above them. They were a heaven-born people, and a heaven-bound people, and ate a heaven-baked bread.

When looking back toward Egypt they murmured, when looking forward toward the Wilderness they saw the glory of the Lord.

Amid the milk and honey of Canaan Israel was to remember this heavenly bread (vs. 32–34). It was a record of a Divine provision that never failed ; and it remained ever sweet and fresh. Remarkable illustration of the Bible.

With the Manna is linked the Sabbath.

The day of rest here suddenly reappears after a silence of more than two thousand years. Redemption being accomplished, the Sabbath is gifted to Israel. But man has no heart for God's rest (v. 27–29). His nature is bad. He can neither rest with, nor work for, God. If God makes a rest for him, he will not keep it ; and if God tells him to work, he will not do it. In this chapter Israel refused the Sabbath as a gift, and in Num. xv. disobeyed it as a law.

Seven facts characterized the Manna, viz : small, round, white, sweet, hard, melting, heavenly. This was Israel's daily bread (Matt. vi. 11).

Verse 36 is not to be confused with Ezek. xlv. 11. Two different measures are intended—an " omer " and a " homer." An omer is the tenth part of an ephah, and an ephah is the tenth part of a homer.

In verses 34 and 35 are found two illustrations of the " Law of Prior Mention " of a subsequent matter, i.e., the " Testimony," or Ark, not at that time yet made, and the forty years (v. 35) then still future.

" Manna " is a compound Hebrew word and means : " What is it ? " This explains the seeming difficulty in verse 15 of naming what was unknown.

EXODUS XVII.—It seemed strange that God, who professed to love them, should lead Israel into a desert, both foodless and waterless. But love led them there that they might learn the desperate unbelief of their own hearts, and the unfailing faithfulness of God's heart. Only in a desert could God reveal what He can be to those that trust Him ; for only there was Israel dependent upon Him for everything. Without God— nothing ; with God—everything.

The water from the smitten Rock foretold the living water, the Holy Spirit, to be sent forth by the smitten Saviour. The Holy Spirit was shed forth as the fruit of Christ's sacrifice (1 Cor. x. 4). The Rock was smitten by the very same rod of judgment that smote the land of Egypt.

The reception of the Holy Spirit immediately causes war. " *Then* came Amalek and fought with Israel." Up to this point God had fought for them. Israel was to stand still and see His salvation ; but the command now is to go out and fight (v. 9). There is an immense difference between justification and sanctification. The one is Christ fighting for us ; the other, the Holy Spirit fighting in us. The entrance of the new nature is the beginning of warfare with the old. Amalek pictures the old carnal nature. He was the grandson of Esau, who before and after birth tried to murder Jacob, and who preferred the mess of 'pottage to the birthright. This carnal nature wars against the Spirit, " it is not subject to the law of God neither indeed can be " ; and God has decreed war against it for ever (v. 16). The victory over Amalek hung upon the intercession of Moses, and upon the wisdom and valour of Joshua. Christ is both Moses and Joshua to His people—excepting that His hands never grow weary.

God did not destroy Amalek, but determined to have war with him from generation to generation. He was to dwell in the land, but not to reign in it. Romans vi. says, " Let not sin therefore reign in your mortal bodies." This command would be unmeaning if sin were not existing in the Christian. Sin dwells in a believer, but dwells and reigns in an unbeliever. Compare Rom. vii. 20 with viii. 11, and note the word " dwelleth."

Thus the manna, the sabbath, the water, and Amalek foretold the great spiritual facts of Christ the Bread from heaven ; of the rest of God into which believers enter ; of the gift of the Holy Spirit ; and of the unending war with the " flesh."

Joshua here first appears—now 53 years of age. A slave in Egypt he becomes a victor in Horeb.

Verse 14 is the birth of the Bible as a written Book. The command was " write this in the Book," not in a book. This was the Book given to Joshua ; to Solomon (1 Kings ii. 1-4) ; to Joash (11 Chron. xxiii. 11) ; it was the Book found by Hilkiah (11 Kings xxii) ; later on obeyed by Nehemiah (ch. viii. and xiii); declared by Malachi (ch. iv.) to have been given to Moses; used by the Lord in preaching and teaching(Luke xxiv. 27-44); and declared by Him to be God's Word. (Mark vii. 10 and 13).

Recent discoveries prove that writing was fully developed before the time of Moses.

It is remarkable that the first mention of the Bible should be in connection with the hostility of the natural man (Amalek) to the spiritual man (Israel). War has ever since accompanied the Book. The Pagans, the Papists, the Sceptics, and the Critics have all warred against it. No book has been so hated, and so loved.

An invaluable analysis of Israel's first battle will be found in " The New Biblical Guide."

EXODUS XVIII.—This chapter is a parenthesis. It occurred between verses 10 and 11 of Numbers x.

The events narrated give a prophetic picture of the coming millennial kingdom. Jehovah up to this point having given " grace," now gives " glory." The Gentiles, represented by Jethro, unite with Israel, now redeemed and triumphant, in worshipping Jehovah as the God of Gods, and in feasting together before Him. At the same time an orderly government is established so that all things should be subjected to God.

Thus will it be in that happy day so often imaged by the prophets, when Jesus, the Divine Jeshurun, shall judge in righteousness the Gentiles brought into the Kingdom of God with Israel.

Some lovers of the Word of God regard Zipporah and her children as representing the Church of God in this beauteous scene ; but the language of the apostle Paul in Ephesians respecting " the Mystery " makes this difficult to accept.

Israel's first battle assures her last battle (Rev. xix). It will be fought by the Divine Joshua, and be immediately succeeded by the setting up of the Millennial Kingdom. So this parenthetic chapter brings these two battles prophetically together. Moral rather than chronological order is one of the peculiar features of Bible history. The healing of Bartimæus illustrates this law. See notes on Luke xviii. 31 to xix. 10.

EXODUS XIX.—The feast of the Passover witnessed Israel's departure from Egypt, and that of Pentecost, fifty days later, their arrival at Horeb, i.e. Sinai, the mountain of chapter iii. 12. (See Companion Bible, Appendix 50). So Exod. xvii. 6 and Acts ii. synchronize. The water was a fore-picture of the poured forth Spirit (Acts ii. 33, R.V.).

Moses' ascents and descents at Sinai were as follows :

Ascents		Descents
xix. 3-6	First	xix. 7, 8
xix. 8-13	Second	xix. 14-19
xix. 20-24	Third	xix. 25
xxiv. 9-xxxii. 14	Fourth	xxxii. 15-30
xxxii. 31-33	Fifth	xxxii. 34-xxxiv. 3
xxxiv. 4-28	Sixth	xxxiv. 29-35

They emphasize the Divine origin of the Law, and of the Tabernacle.

Chapter iii. 4: " Elohim called unto him out of the bush " ; chapter xix. 3 : " Jehovah called unto him out of the mountain."

The salvation of verse 4 was an accomplished salvation, wholly of God, and therefore unconditional. He could say, " I have brought you unto Myself."

But the special glory proposed in verses 5 and 6 was conditional upon obedience.

To this message the people replied : " All that Jehovah hath spoken we will do."

Had they known their own hearts they would have replied that such a condition was impossible to them ; and they would have cast themselves upon God that He should give them new hearts capable of such an obedience. This would have been granted, and the Feast promised in chapter v. enjoyed.

Instead of the Feast there was fear and judgment.

To awaken the people to a consciousness of their inability, without this new heart, to draw near to God and do all that He commanded, the terrific scene of verses 9-25 was designed and displayed. But even that failed to instruct people so dull of hearing. As a consequence God's action toward them, and with them, now changed. Up to Sinai Grace reigned ; from Sinai, and onward—Law.

The words " and God answered him " may be translated " and God kept answering him by a voice." This explains how the following chapters were given to Moses

The priests spoken of in verses 22 and 24, were the first-born. They were superseded by the Sons of Levi.

If the section (vs. 20-25) be understood as following chronologically the close of chapter xxiii, then there will appear no difficulty between it and the section verses 18-21 in chapter xx. That is to say, these sections show that, at first, the people stood afar off, but, later, began to press too near. This illustrates man's fallen nature, he stands afar off when he should draw nigh, and he presses to the front when he should keep back.

EXODUS XX. 1-21.—The first verse of this chapter follows verse 19 of the prior chapter. In both verses God is named " Elohim." This shows that the ten commandments are of universal application. Their function was to make man conscious

that he was a sinner, that he could not save himself, and that he needed a Saviour (Rom. vii. 7). These commandments were like a mirror let down from heaven in which man could see his own vileness.

The Lord Christ divided these ten commandments into two groups (Matt. xxii. 37-40). There are five commandments in each group. The first five have as a connecting keynote the words : " Jehovah thy God." This group begins with honouring God and closes with honouring parents given by God. The second group of commandments have as a connecting keynote the word : " Thou." This group enjoins love to others, as the first commanded love to God.

The command " Thou shalt not kill " is correctly translated in the R.V. " thou shalt do no murder." God in His Holy Word commands magistrates to put evil men to death (Rom. xiii. 4). That is not murder. To " kill " and to " commit murder " are two different verbs in the Hebrew Text.

" And all the people saw the thunderings " (compare Rev. i. 12). This use of the verb " saw " is peculiar to the Holy Scriptures, and makes very real to the reader the " thunderings " of this chapter and the " voice " of Rev. i.

The verbal inspiration of the Ten Commandments is affirmed in the statement of verse 1—" God spake all these Words saying." The commandments were not partly Divine and partly Mosaic. Faith recognizes this verbal inspiration in the whole Bible as confidently as in the Ten Words.

EXODUS XX. 22—XXIII. 33. — Man, conscious that he was a sinner, stood afar off directly God manifested Himself. But God loved him and desired to be near him, and therefore instructed him as to the altar of verse 24, and said " I will come unto thee, and I will bless thee."

This altar pictured Jesus. The earth, His humanity ; the stone, His Deity ; the shed blood, His priceless life sacrificed to put away sin and bring the sinner back to God (1 Peter iii. 18). No tool was to embellish the altar ; it was perfect in its beauty to the eye of God. And such was Jesus, As well seek to paint the lily or adorn the rose, as for man to attempt to add to the beauty of Him who is altogether lovely. The altar was to stand on a level with the people. Such was Jesus. He was accessible to all, even little children could come to Him. See notes on Deut. xxvii. and Joshua viii. 30. There were to be no steps up to the altar. When man exalts himself before God he only exposes his own moral nakedness (v. 26).

The legislation that followed in connection with this altar, and which fills chapters xxi–xxiii., alternates between worship and conduct. God and man stand revealed in these alternate passages. The amazing love of God, and the shocking depravity of man. It is humiliating to learn that such laws had to be made to protect men from the appalling evil which prompted them to oppress one another. On the other hand the tender love of God shines forth like the sun in this legislation. That mighty love even thought upon the tooth of a little slave girl, and enacted that she should be set free if so slightly injured.

The true Christian life is here set out under three feasts, four commands and one promise.

First feast: Passover, i.e., Forgiveness.

Second feast: First fruits, i.e. righteousness.

Third Feast: Tabernacles, i.e. Glory.

These three feasts are fulfilled in Christ. They foreshadowed His Crucifixion, His Resurrection and His Coronation.

The foundation of all blessing is Grace (Passover) and its completion is Glory (Tabernacles): Its maintenance is Power (First-fruits) i.e. Pentecost—the Holy Spirit.

First command: Leaven, i.e. Corruption: man's corrupt doctrine is not to be added to the fact of atonement. Hence the importance and sweetness of the expressions " My Sacrifice " and " Feasts unto Me." Heathen atonement conceives man propitiating an angry God. Christian atonement, The God of Love making a propitiation on behalf of sinful man.

Second Command: No interval to be permitted between the death of the lamb and the eating of its fat. The joys of salvation are not to be dissevered from their Author and His atoning death. That death is the one and only source of all spiritual blessing.

Third Command: God first.

Fourth Command: No violation of natural affection to be committed when putting God first.

The One Promise: "He shall keep thee." This one promise embraces all the exceeding great and precious promises, and assures a happy issue to the pilgrim life.

The legislation of these chapters proves how incompetent is the conscience as a monitor and guide to man. Paul had not known sin except the law had said " thou shalt not covet." Conscience is a moral agent on which the word of God acts—without that Word it is like to a lantern without a candle in it.

In connection with chapter xxi. 6, see notes on Psalm xl. and Hebrews x.

EXODUS XXIV.—Hebrews ix. 15–23 is the comment of the Holy Spirit upon verses 3–8 of this chapter. This was the first Covenant, the Covenant of Works. God and Israel were the covenanting parties. Israel promised a perfect obedience and God promised them temporal and eternal felicity. The Covenant was established in the blood of the slain lamb. Half of the blood was sprinkled on the Altar, thus pledging God to His engagement; the other half was sprinkled upon the people, so pledging them. Moses having read from the Bible the ten commandments, and the judgments based thereon, i.e., chapters xxi–xxiii., he then sprinkled the blood also upon the Bible. (See note on I Peter i. 2).

" *Then* went up Moses " etc. Before the invitation of verse 1 could be accepted the blood of the burnt and peace offerings must be shed. Sinners, even though they be as distinguished as these princes, cannot approach God in their own persons: they can only draw near through the blood of Jesus.

The men who in verse 1 are styled " elders," are named " nobles " in verse 11. Why? Because in verse 10 they saw the God of Israel. To have fellowship with God ennobles men.

John 1. 18 says " No man hath seen God at any time." This statement does not oppose verse 10. The Hebrew verb " to see " in this latter verse means "to see in vision"; that in the former verse means to see with the bodily eyes.

The sapphire stone expressed the purity of God. " And upon the nobles He laid not His hand," that is, to destroy them (Gen. xxii. 12; I Sam. v. 9 etc.); but, on the contrary, they saw God, and did eat and drink," that is, they lived." (See note on Gen. xvi. 13).

Sinai pictured the Temple. The foot of the mountain, with its great altar of burnt-offering and the multitude, formed the outer court. Higher up the mountain, the nobles worshipped in the inner court ; and on the summit, Moses in the Holiest of All.

Before being called into the midst of the cloud, in which cloud he spent 40 days and 40 nights, Moses had to wait 6 days in the presence of the cloud.

This was the first recorded " Breaking of Bread," as a religious feast in the Bible (v. 11). It was the Fellowship of Access ; Acts x. 41, was the Fellowship of Testimony ; and Luke xxii. 30, the Fellowship of Glory. Horeb, Galilee, and Zion. The other communal meals recorded in the Scriptures under this title were rather social actions, e.g. Luke xxiv. 30, Acts ii. 42, and xx. 7, 1 Cor. x. and xi. etc.

Moses would need 40 days to write in " the Book " from the Mouth of God all that appears in the following directions respecting the Tabernacle and its ministry.

Grace furnished the table of Exod. xxiv. 11 as it will furnish that of Luke xxii. 30. The elders did not bring their lunch up the mountain with them. They were made nigh by the blood of Christ (Eph. ii). All the guests of the King of Kings are nobles (Luke xxii. 30).

Eating and drinking spiritual food with Him gives power for testimony.

Only those who continue with Him in His rejection will feast on thrones with Him.

EXODUS XXV.—Man's inability to keep the Law being foreknown and demonstrated (Exod. xxxii. 1 and Deut. xxxi. 21), God committed it to the Tabernacle, i.e. to Christ in type.

So the making of the Tabernacle is the subject of chapters xxv.–xxx. This section contains two parts. The first : Christ descending from the Ark, that is, His throne, to the brazen altar, that is, Calvary. The second : Christ ascending from the brazen altar with His own blood, and resuming His seat upon His throne. Chapters xxv. xxvi. and xxvii. picture, in symbol, this gracious outcoming of God to meet the sinner. Chapters xxviii. xxix. and xxx. present man, in symbol, drawing near to God in the person of the Great High Priest. Thus the first half of this section of Exodus begins with the Ark and moves outward to the brazen altar ; the second, begins with the brazen altar and moves inward to the Ark.

The materials, the furniture, the vessels, and everything within and without the Tabernacle symbolize the person, the atoning work, the ministries, the glories and the perfections of Christ as Jehovah's Perfect Servant, and as the Saviour and High Priest of His people. The keynote of the building is grace. " Five " is the number of grace. This number appears perpetually in connection with the Tabernacle. Access to God is the lesson it teaches. Solomon's Temple was different. Fellowship and glory are its keynotes ; not grace and access.

The Tabernacle, therefore, is a manifestation of the glory of the grace of the Lord Jesus Christ, and of His relationship with sinners who draw nigh unto Him. It was founded upon the silver of the redemption money, thus showing forth that man can only have access to God and a standing before Him on the foundation of Christ's accomplished Redemption. The Tabernacle pictured grace ; the Temple, glory.

The Tabernacle, as also the Temple of Solomon, were copies of patterns in the heavens (Heb. viii. 2 and ix. 23). Nothing was left to the imagination of either Moses, David, or Solomon. All was Divine.

To understand, in detail, the teaching of the Tabernacle and its ministries, " Notes on Exodus and Leviticus " by C. H. M. (Morrish, London) should be read.

In this twenty-fifth chapter the Holy Spirit describes the Ark, the Table, and the Lampstand. All were of pure gold. They proclaimed Christ as the Light of the World, the Life of the World, and the Saviour of the World.

The cover of the Ark formed the Mercy Seat ; on it was sprinkled the atoning blood. The Cherubim looked down upon the Mercy Seat. In Solomon's Temple they looked out upon the Millennial earth. It was of this blood-sprinkled Mercy Seat that God spoke when He said : " There will I meet with thee." Here, in type, was the only meeting place between God and the sinner. Here, righteousness and peace kissed each other. God demands, and the sinner needs, a spotless righteousness. This is found in the Cross of Jesus. At this blood-sprinkled Mercy Seat God is perfectly glorified, and the believer eternally saved.

The Cherubim are celestial beings about whom the Bible gives no information ; except that they appear to have some connection with creation, its ruin, and its ultimate restoration.

The Ark had a crown of gold, so had the Table, and also the Altar of Incense (ch. xxx. 3). These three crowns belong to Jesus as Saviour, as King and as High Priest.

" Over against it " (v. 37) i.e. the Table of Shew Bread. See xxvi. 35. Thus the Holy Spirit reveals the sufficiency of Christ as the bread of His people day by day, and always fresh.

EXODUS XXVI.—The Tabernacle was one. It pictured the person and work of Christ. Grace was its keynote. This was expressed by the number " five " and its multiples. There were fifty boards, fifteen bars, one hundred sockets, four roof coverings each fifteen yards in length. Three coverings were formed of ten curtains each, coupled together with fifty loops and fifty taches of gold and fifty taches of brass, and one covering had eleven curtains.

The fifty boards were of common desert wood overlaid with gold, as was also the Ark, i.e. the Humanity and Deity of Christ. The boards were based on redemption silver and crowned with the same. The crown was visible, the foundation not. The Redemption work of Christ reaches from the depths of the sinner's need to the heights of God's throne. Every several board set out some moral glory in the nature and life of Christ. The boards were held in position by the fifteen bars, five on the south side, five on the north and five on the west, or hinder part of the house. The middle bar of each five was a single bar, and ran from one end of the building to the other. There were therefore three such bars. " Three " in the Holy Scriptures is the number of Deity. All the bars together witnessed to Divine grace that linked together into unity all the perfections of Christ, as revealed in the four Gospels.

There were four coverings to the Tabernacle corresponding to the four Gospels. The outermost covering, Christ as Servant and Prophet (Mark) ; the next covering, ram skins dyed red, Christ as King (Matt.) ; the third covering, goats' hair, pure white, Christ as Priest (Luke) ; the innermost covering, Christ as God (John).

" Every curtain shall have one measure " (v. 2). In Christ's nature as God and Man this harmony is everywhere visible in the Gospels.

Many Christian people think that the Tabernacle symbolizes the House of God, i.e., the Church, the one Body ; that the boards represent individual members of the Church, and the central bar the Divine life that makes them one. But the Holy Spirit's statement in Ps. xxix. 9, that every whit of this building uttered Christ's praise, militates against that interpretation.

The Tabernacle contained two chambers, the Holy and the Most Holy. At the western extremity of the inner chamber was placed the Ark. Israel therefore worshipped with their backs to the sun. There were two veils, the first hung upon five pillars ; these stood on sockets of brass and were overlaid with gold. This hanging with its pillars pictured Christ ; the five pillars, His grace ; the shittim wood, His humanity ; the gold, His Deity ; the brass, His faithfulness ; the hanging itself, the glorious mystery of His being in His incarnation.

Inside this hanging were placed the Lampstand and the golden Table.

The veil itself hung upon four pillars of shittim wood overlaid with gold, and stood upon sockets of silver. This inner veil was ornamented with cherubim, the outward not. Hebrews ix. states that this veil pictured Christ's flesh rent in expiation.

Verses 23 and 24 speak of the corners of the Tabernacle. Each corner was formed by two boards. These boards were coupled together beneath by the silver socket of redemption money, and coupled together above. Thus the corners of the Tabernacle were as beauteous and harmonious as the rest of the building. Such, alas, is not the case in the " corners " of ordinary Christian people.

EXODUS XXVII. 1-19.—The great brazen altar represented Jesus and Calvary. The brass pictured judgement and the enduring strength of His atoning sacrifice ; its polished surface, His sinlessness ; its measurements, three by five, His Deity and His Grace ; its shape, foursquare, expressed its provision and sufficiency for the four quarters of the earth ; and its position, in front of the entrance to the House, that the crucified Lamb of Calvary is the one and only way to God. It was borne by staves, thereby accompanying the people in their pilgrim way to Canaan, so teaching the lesson, that there never comes a period in the Christian life where the atoning blood of Christ can be dispensed with.

The Tabernacle was to stand in the Court ;

the court was formed by pillars socketed in brass. hooked and filleted with silver. Upon these pillars hung fine twined linen. The numbers " three " and " five " appear in all the measurements of this court—except that the gate of the court, similar to the entrance to the Most Holy Place, had four pillars. What spiritual lessons do these two sets of four pillars teach ?

On approaching the Tabernacle the eye saw the white curtains of the court enriched with brass and silver. Such was Jesus in His nature and life—sinless, and adorned with Divine beauties. The hangings of the gate, in all the wealth of their Divinely chosen embroidery, proclaimed the ten thousand perfections of Him who said, " I am the Door."

The polished brass of the Tabernacle and its brazen vessels expressed the discovery and the judgement of sin ; the polished brass of Solomon's Temple, foreshadowed the purity, power, and glory of Christ's millennial government. Placed in conjunction they proclaimed grace and glory.

The Tabernacle had three courts. There are three heavens ; of these the Earth is the first or outward court. Man consists of three courts of which the body is the outward. The Bible contains three courts. The Tabernacle had three doors, giving admission to the outer court, the Holy Place and the Most Holy. The curtain that formed the door at each entrance was in each case similar. This curtain pictured the Deity and Humanity of Christ, and the three doors teach that He is the only doorway into the Kingdom of God whether on earth, in heaven or above the heavens.

Inside the Tabernacle everything was gold ; outside, brass. The gold within declared Christ's essential Godhead ; the burnished brass without, His governmental power. Thus He appeared to John in Rev. i.

The absence of the Golden Altar of Incense, and the seeming interruption of the narrative by the introduction of Aaron and his sons, will be found profitably explained in " Notes on Exodus " by C. H. M. (Morrish, London).

The precious name of Jesus is written, therefore, upon the Tabernacle itself,and upon everything connected with it, within and without. It all sets out also the infinite perfection of His atonement and ministry on behalf of fallen man. At the brazen altar sin is judged and annihilated ; at the laver a new moral nature is imparted ; at the golden table, bread from heaven, revealed by the light of the golden lampstand, is feasted upon ; at the altar of incense, worship in the sweet name of Jesus is enjoined, and, finally, in The Most Holy Place there is fellowship with God in the light of the Shechinah through the cleansing power of the precious blood (1 John i. 7).

The golden and brazen altars were foursquare, the offerings were four—burnt, meal, peace and sin—the meal offering had four ingredients and four forms ; and so, in correspondence, the Holy Spirit gives a foursquare record of the Great Antitype in the Four Gospels.

EXODUS XXVII. 20—XXVIII. 43.—The subject of this section is the raiment of the High Priest ;   that of the next section, his sacrifices.

Aaron and his priestly garments and his sacrifices form a beauteous picture of the Person, the graces, and the ministries of the Great High Priest who has passed into the heavens.

Five priests were chosen from among the children of Israel (v. 1). Thus " grace " is the foundation and energy of priesthood. Aaron was the chief ; he pictured Christ ; his sons represented the Jewish election. They are popularly supposed to picture the church. But St Paul's language about the " Mystery " disaccords with that interpretation. Aaron was to minister unto God (v. 3) in holy garments for glory and for beauty (v 2). The garments numbered eight. Eight is the Dominical number, and also the number of resurrection. The Lord Christ in His shining garments upon the Mount of Transfiguration, appears there as the True Aaron. He had five sinners grouped around Him. These were His spiritual sons ; and they represented elect Israel, the kingdom of priests and an holy nation.

" Notes on Exodus " by C. H. M. suggest helpful spiritual lessons symbolized by these garments.

The ephod was essentially the priestly garment. It was worn by Aaron the priest, Samuel the prophet, and David the king. Christ combines all three offices. It was made of the same materials as the veil, but with threads of gold and no cherubim. The golden thread in the ephod declared the Divine righteousness of the priest ; the cherubim on the veil, the judicial authority of the Son of Man. Christ, as priest, is the Divine Righteousness ; Christ, as man, the Divine Judgment.

Aaron's robes pictured the needs of the people ; his sacrifices, the claims of God. The ephod with its shoulder pieces and breast plate was the principal vestment. Thus arrayed Aaron symbolized Christ in the mystery of His Divine Manhood, bearing His people on His shoulders, the place of strength, and, bound upon His heart, the place of love. On the shoulders the names were according to their birth (v. 10), but on the heart according to the tribes, as God chose them (v. 21) ; but all the names were engraved on precious stones ; that is, stones which shine the more brightly when more intensely shone upon.

In the pocket of the mysterious stones, were placed the mysterious stones, known as Urim and Thummim, by means of which the Divine judgement of a matter was made known to Israel. Thus robed, Aaron bore the judgment of the congregation before the Lord, and communicated the judgment of the Lord to the congregation (vs. 29, 30).

The precious stones upon the shoulders and upon the heart of Aaron were so securely bound to the ephod that they could not be detached from it. " Who shall separate us from the love of Christ ? "

The embroidered girdle of the ephod suggested service. John xiii. records that " He girded Himself."

The robe, all of blue, and carrying on its extremity bells of gold and pomegranates of blue, purple, and scarlet is actualized in Christ as a priest in heaven (Heb. viii. 4), in whom profession (bells) and fruit · (pomegranates) are equally proportioned.

The linen vest and breeches symbolized the inward personal purity of the Great High Priest. Aaron's sons were to wear similar underclothing ; but Aaron's vest was to be embroidered. No one saw this embroidered linen vest but God. His eye alone could estimate and enjoy its beauty. Such was Jesus. None but God sees the exquisite perfections of His hidden sinless Manhood, and the absolutely pure affections which energize Him as a Heavenly Priest.

As symbolized by the pure linen, Aaron and his sons stood and ministered in the one righteousness. The sons were also girded and crowned for service—a beauteous picture of

the happy day to come when Israel's true Priest, with His many sons, will appear, as a kingdom of priests, to minister on behalf of the redeemed nations.

Aaron's crown was to carry on its front a golden plate, bearing the words, " Holiness to the Lord." In the Millennium this engraving will appear on the bells of the horses (Zech. xiv). This golden plate and its engraving pictured Israel as an election before God. Imperfect as Israel was in herself, as thus represented by Aaron and his crown, she was Holiness itself.

" Upon his heart before the Lord continually " and " upon his forehead before the Lord continually " (vs. 30, 38). These statements united together reveal the untiring activity of the heart and mind of the Greater than Aaron on behalf of His people.

The brazen altar, the golden altar, and the throne pictured Christ's activities as the Good Shepherd, as the Great Shepherd, and as the Chief Shepherd ; as also His offices as Prophet, Priest, and King.

EXODUS XXIX—The consecration of Aaron and his sons furnishes " shadows of good things to come "—but only shadows. Water, blood, and oil in this chapter symbolize judgment, atonement, and the Holy Spirit. Shed blood was the foundation of all. There was the bullock for the sin offering, the ram for the burnt-offering, and a second ram for the peace-offering. Upon the flesh of the second ram Aaron and his sons feasted. This explains John vi. 53. Everything here is Jesus. He is Aaron ; He is also the burnt-offering, the sin-offering, and the peace-offering. Aaron, however, was but a " shadow." He had to offer for his own sins. Christ offered Himself for the world's sins.

Priestly service in the House of God is based upon the blood of Jesus ; its energy is the Holy Spirit; and its requirement, the death of self. Aaron's sons were first washed—that meant death to sin and self ; they were then sprinkled with the atoning blood ; after that anointed with the oil ; and then strengthened with the holy food.

Aaron, being a type of Christ, was anointed with oil directly after his baptism—his sons anointed with blood, and then with oil. Immediately after Christ's baptism in the Jordan He was anointed with the Holy Spirit. He needed no atonement personally.

For notes on the sacrifices see Lev. viii.

EXODUS XXX.—When Aaron and his sons were anointed, the sons were anointed with him, and not he with them. Everything is connected with Jesus. His precious blood had first to be poured out before the Spirit could be poured forth; and sinners must first be washed from their sins in that precious blood before they can receive the Holy Spirit. Thus cleansed and sanctified, worship at the golden altar of incense is possible; but not otherwise.

God having brought His people out of Egypt established the brazen altar outside the Tabernacle and the golden altar inside; and appointed a Mediator to maintain relationship with Him in order that He might dwell among them. The brazen altar symbolized the perfection of Christ's sacrifice for sin; the golden altar, the preciousness of His person. The altar itself spoke of Jesus. The wood and the gold pre-figured His humanity and Deity; it was crowned (see note on chapter xxv. 24); and it had staves to bear it so as to be the day and night companion of a pilgrim people. The incense burned upon it spoke of Him. Aaron himself, in his robes of glory, pictured Him; and the light of the golden lampstand foretold Him, who being the light of that world that needs no sun came into this world to be its Light.

The fire of verse 7, and the blood of verse 10, teach that there can be no acceptable worship apart from atonement.

Verses 11-16 show that the people were identified with this Divinely appointed worship as having been redeemed. Every man's soul was to be ransomed. All were to be ransomed in the one way. All were to pay alike. In the matter of atonement all worshippers stand on one common ground. As to Christian service, there is necessarily a distinction to be recognized, because the question of capacity enters. This appears in the last chapter of Leviticus, where Moses (Law) estimated a man "according to the sanctuary," and the priest (Grace) valued him "according to his ability."

The word "atonement" means in the Hebrew text "a cover"; it is not the English word "at-one-ment." "Now our sins may all be covered with the precious blood He shed" (Ps. xxxii. 1).

The brazen altar was for the sinner; the brazen laver for the saint. The former testified of the blood of Christ; the latter, of the Word of God; the former cleansed the conscience; the latter, the conduct. The sons of Aaron, already cleansed and clothed and crowned, had, nevertheless, to wash their hands and feet in the laver before entering the Tabernacle, or approaching the altar. To maintain conscious fellowship with God, and to be effective ministers in priestly service for man, the daily washing of the Word must never be neglected lest death enter the soul (v. 21).

The laver was made of mirrors (ch. xxxviii. 8). This, perhaps, put an end to a form of Egyptian idolatry; but it certainly ennobled the use to which the metal was put. It is better that "self" should be humiliated by looking into the pure mirror of God's Word, than that it should be gratified by beholding its natural face in a glass.

The ointment (v. 25), and the perfume (v. 35), set out the spiritual and personal perfections of Christ. The ointment was not to be imitated, nor poured upon man's flesh Spiritual graces cannot be imitated, nor can they be given to men "in the flesh." The perfume, when beaten "very small," was offered to God. The minutest emotions of Christ's nature, as a Man, were perfect; and all was "of like weight" in His sinless nature

EXODUS XXXI.—Tubal-Cain and Bezaleel, may be contrasted. The one used his skill to adorn the kingdom of Satan; the other his wisdom to beautify the House of God. But Bezaleel did not, like Tubal-Cain, use iron (see note on 11 Chron. xxiv. 12). Christians should be careful that their talents are engaged in building up the spiritual temple.

Bezaleel and his companions were wise-hearted, it does not say wise-headed (v. 6) They did not appoint themselves to this ministry; this appears from the expressions: " I have called," " I have filled," " I have given," " I have put," " I have commanded."

"My sabbaths ye shall keep." What distinguishes God's people is participation in God's rest. Christ is God's rest (Heb. iv). The honour, or dishonour, done to the Sabbath was the test under Law. The honour, or dishonour, done to Christ, the test under grace. Death was the penalty of dishonouring the Sabbath; a similar penalty attaches to dishonouring Christ. Unitarians should consider this.

The Sabbath was associated with the Manna, (ch. xvi.), with the giving of the Law (ch. xx.), and with the making of the Tabernacle (ch. xxxi).

Zeal in building the Tabernacle, enthusiasm in observing the Law, and energy in gathering the Manna, were not permitted to disturb God's rest.

EXODUS XXXII.—On the top of the mount Moses was sitting, in spirit where Mary sat (Luke x. 39), and feasting his eyes upon " patterns of heavenly things," whilst at the foot of the mount Aaron and the people sat at the feet of Satan, admiring the Golden Calf, and dancing and singing around it. Fifteen hundred years later Moses sat at the feet of Jesus upon the Mount of Transfiguration, whilst Satan at the foot of the mount tortured an unhappy boy. The Devil can make men dance and sing, or writhe and scream if either action can oppose or dishonour Christ.

The calf was the great god of the Egyptians. It was carried in the vanguard of their processions. Sacrifices were offered to it, and lascivious dances executed in its honour. It was worshipped as the generator of life.

People who are ignorant of the brutishness of fallen man's heart think it incredible that men and women who had passed through the Red Sea, who daily looked upon the pillar of fire, who heard the voice of God, and who witnessed the sublime terrors of Mount Sinai, could possibly have fallen, in so short a time, into such gross idolatry The apostle Paul did not share this incredulity, for he declares that these facts admonish the Christian Church (1 Cor. x).

Moses had gone up on high, and because he delayed to return, Israel made a god that they could see. So is it to-day. Christendom prefers a human priest, and a little piece of bread that may be seen and handled, to the Divine Priest who is passed into the heavens.

One of the depths of Satan is not to abolish God but to represent Him by something visible. Hence the feast of verse 5 was proposed as a feast to Jehovah. Also he can through a religious teacher like Aaron associate idolatry with Christ, recognize the good in all religions, and provide a worship that appeals to man's natural heart. Everything was done by Aaron under the cover of " religion." The people offered the sacrifices, then sat down to eat them and to drink the libations, and then rose up for the impure dancing (vs. 6 and 19). They were very

comfortable without Moses; they did not need him at all (1 Cor. x. 7).

The word " gods " (v. 4) is the Plural of Majesty. It means : " This is the great God that brought thee up out of the land of Egypt."

The character of Moses shines here with much beauty. On the top of the mount he pleads with God for the people; at the foot of the' mount he pleads with the people for God. God's glory was the great concern of his heart in both positions.

Israel's greatest prophets were Moses and Paul (compare verse 32 with Rom. ix. 3).

It was impossible to associate the Tables of the Law written with the finger of God with the Golden Calf fashioned with the finger of man. Moses broke them. He burned the calf, ground it to powder, mixed it with water, and compelled the people to drink it. Modern science has discovered the secret of treating gold in this fashion, and so accredits Moses as a Master Chemist.

Israel lost that day the priesthood, and Levi won it (Deut. xxxiii. 8).

Moses descended from on high with the Law. Confronted with man's sin, he broke both tables, and then returned with a cheerless " peradventure " on his lips to seek an uncertain forgiveness. He failed. Christ descended from on high, fulfilled the Law ; and having, on behalf of sinners, suffered its full penalty, returned to heaven with His precious blood, the sign of His accomplished atonement, to obtain an absolutely certain forgiveness.

EXODUS XXXIII —" I have seen the affliction of my people " (ch. iii. 7)'; " I have seen this people and behold it is a stiff-necked people " (ch. xxxii. 9, and xxxiii. 3, 5). Grace meets the cry of need, but judgment must deal with rebellion ; and accordingly " an angel " is to accompany the people. Mercy, however, rejoices against judgment, and so this angel was to be the " Presence Angel," or " my Angel " (ch. xxxii. 34, xxxiii. 14).

The repentance of the people, and the intercession of Moses (v. 4, 6, 16), made it possible for God to bless (v. 17). Grace clothes naked sinners; but a sinner decked in ornaments must be stripped.

The " tent " of this chapter is not the Tabernacle. The Hebrew text distinguishes between them. The camp having been defiled by the golden calf, Moses pitches this tent as a meeting place with God. It was pitched outside the camp, and became a place for individual worship (v. 7). Hebrews xiii. directs similar action wherever there has been corporate departure from God.

Loyalty to truth led Moses out to this tent (v. 8), and love to the sinner brought him back into the camp (v. 11). Joshua, a much younger man, deemed it wiser for him to remain in the tent. Christians ought to be strong enough to return into the camp as Moses did ; but if they have not that spiritual strength, it is wiser for them to imitate Joshua.

The cloud descended from the top of Sinai to the door of the tent (v. 9), and there Jehovah talked " face to face with Moses as a man speaketh unto his friend." This was amazing love !

Moses seizes upon the word " grace " (v. 12), and with wonderful spiritual intelligence pleads that God should continue to accompany them because they were a stiff-necked people ! (ch. xxxiv. 9). The fact that they were a stiff-necked people is urged as an argument ; for it was just such people that grace, and only grace, could bless.

The nation, having apostatized, lost its priesthood ; Levi obtained it by his faithfulness ; and Moses was appointed Mediator. It was, as such, that God spoke with him face to face (v. 11) ; and, as Mediator, Moses asked who was to accompany him (v. 12) ; and he also asked that God's way to Canaan might be shown to him (v. 13). He did not wish to take his own way; and he pointed out, (vs. 15 and 16), that the enterprise was impossible without the companionship of God ; and that it was that companionship, and nothing else, that separated Israel from the surrounding nations.

God, retiring into His freedom of action in sovereignty and grace, granted these petitions; and Moses, having asked in verse 13 " Show me thy way," now prayed " Show me thy glory " (v. 18). To this was replied, " I will make all my goodness pass before thee." Grace comes first, then glory. Moses could not have endured the glory. Joined with the grace proclaimed in verse 19 is the liberty God reserves to Himself to show mercy to whom He wills (Rom. ix. 15). Law blots out the sinner ; Grace blots out the sin.

Moses' heart was painfully lonely. Excepting Joshua, he at this time had no companion but God. He clung to Him. His entreaties not to be left alone but, on the contrary, to be permitted to enjoy a fuller and closer companionship, is pathetic.

EXODUS XXXIV.—" Grace " is the keynote of this chapter. Whenever man fails God retires into Christ in whom is no failure. The ten commandments were re-given, but they were to be committed to the Ark—symbol of Him who said " Thy word have I hid in my heart."

The name of Jehovah was proclaimed in the cloud, and that name was " Love."

Moses, in the power of that revelation, urges as a motive for God's presence with them, the very reason that God gave for His destruction of them, i.e., their stiffneckedness ; and he added : " Take us for Thine inheritance."

This new covenant was based upon Moses as Mediator. It is touching to recognize the love which repeated the ten commandments and the sacrifices and feasts connected therewith. This was not mere repetition ; it was loving instruction. It taught Israel that although there was a change of relationship, there was no change of affection or of foundation truth. Redemption by blood, surrender of self, sabbath rest for the soul, enjoyment of the feasts, and a compassion for all living things so great that it would not seethe a kid in its mother's milk—all this revealed how unchangeable and eternal are the foundations of justification and sanctification.

The love that repeated these commandments surely promised to give Israel the good land, and to perform marvels for their benefit—marvels, the fulfilment of which is predicted in the book of Revelation.

In verse 13 is found the first mention of Phallic worship in the Bible. For such was the object of worship here described as a " grove," or Ashera.

The wondrous revelation of God in this chapter is declared in II Cor. iii. to have been the ministration of death ; for as the people were still under Law, the more gracious God was the more guilty they were.

Moses being now Mediator, his face shone because God had spoken with him. " He wist not that his face shone." Samson wist not that the Lord was departed from him (Judges xvi. 20). Peter wist not that he was delivered (Acts xii. 9).

Israel was afraid to come nigh, so Moses had to put a veil on his face. (See notes on II Cor. iii). Amazing grace that joined glory with the second giving of the Law after that Israel had so deeply sinned.

Moses' face did not shine at the first giving of the Law; for Israel, as yet, had not apostatized. Grace abounds superlatively where sin abounds; hence the glory upon the face of the Mediator.

What would have been the Divine relationships with Israel if the Golden Calf apostasy had not taken place, is not revealed in the Bible. God spoke directly to the people from Sinai. They refused such intimacy through fear, and quickly afterwards set up the Golden Calf. God, in His love, refused to forsake them (Neh. ix.), and resumed relationship with them through sacrifice and mediatorship. Moses (type of Christ, Heb. iii) was appointed Apostle and High Priest; the Tabernacle was pitched; and, at the Mercy Seat, the promise was given to Moses, "There will I meet with thee" (ch. xxv. 22); and, at the door of the Tabernacle, that to the people, in connection with the continual burnt-offering, "There will I meet with you" (ch. xxix. 42, 43). God now spoke out of the Tabernacle; not from Sinai. This introduces Leviticus.

EXODUS XXXV–XL.—The minute repetition in these chapters of the materials used in the construction of the Tabernacle, and of the vessels and furniture of that place of worship, is tiresome to a secular reader, but precious to a spiritual eye. Why this minute repetition? Because the Tabernacle, its curtains, its boards, its hooks, its sockets its pins, its spoons—everything connected with it, displayed to God's heart the infinite perfections and glories of His Dearly Beloved Son. The fourfold movement from the Mercy Seat to the brazen altar, and always in this order, necessitated four Gospels (xxxvii. 1; xxxix. 35; xl. 3; and xl. 20).

God's rest (the Sabbath) opens the section, and His resting place (the Tabernacle) closes it. In the greatness of His love He invites man into His own rest, and then comes and dwells with him (Heb. iv). Even when building the Tabernacle the Sabbath Rest was to be observed (ch. xxxv. 2); and, similarly, when eating the Manna, no fire was to be kindled on the Sabbath Day to boil or bake it; it was to be eaten as prepared by the Lord of the Sabbath (ch. xxxv. 3).

All was accomplished "as the Lord commanded Moses." The frequent repetition of these words should be noted. Nothing was left to man's ingenuity or taste (xxxix. 42, 43).

The "willing hearted," the "wise hearted,' and the "stirred hearted" offered themselves, and their gifts, to the Lord. Thus willingness and obedience characterized the people.

The Tabernacle, therefore, having been made according to the Divine pattern, was filled with the Divine Glory; but, not until sprinkled with precious blood, and anointed with holy oil. Only in a crucified and anointed Saviour can God dwell with man.

The words Splendour, xxxvii. 1, xxxviii. 21; Service, xxxix. 32-43; Sacrifice, xl. 1-16; and Sonship, xl. 17-38 express the four Gospel glories of the Messiah, in these four repeated movements from the golden throne of glory to the brazen altar of suffering. The distinguishing feature of the first passage is costliness (xxxviii. 24-31)—the splendour of the King (Matt.); that of the second, service —(xxxix. 32-43 and its tenfold "all"), the humility of the Servant (Mark); that of the third, Sacrifice and anointing (xl. 2 and 9 for the time was Passover)—the sacrifice of the anointed Lamb of God (Luke); and that of the fourth, the indwelling of the glory (xl. 34)—the Godhead of the Messiah (John).

The precious objects that mark this passage are thus associated: the golden throne and the golden altar (see note on Heb. ix. 4 and Exod. xl. 5 etc.); the lampstand and the table; and the altar of brass and the laver—i.e., Christ as Prince and Priest; as Light and Life; and as Saviour and Sanctifier.

The Holy Spirit is mentioned twelve times in the Gospel by Luke but only six times in Matthew, four times in Mark, and seven times in John.

LEVITICUS

LEVITICUS I.—The Hebrew Title for this Book is " And He called." It is therefore the Book of the Tabernacle, that is, worship. Its subject is : Christ and the perfection of His offering and Priesthood. The Holy Spirit is not named, because His office is ˙to speak, not of Himself, but of Christ (John xvi. 14). The first word is " And," thus connecting the book with Exodus ; the same word connects Exodus with Genesis, and Numbers with Leviticus.

There are four great offerings : the Burnt Offering, the Meal Offering, the Peace Offering and the Sin Offering, chapters i-vi. 7.

In the " Law " of the Offerings, chapters vi. 8-vii. 34, this order is changed.

Priesthood is the subject of chapters viii-x.

The foundations of Atonement and Priesthood being laid, the remainder of the Book deals with ceremonial Laws, the Great Day of Atonement, the Feasts, and legislation affecting the worshippers.

God only accepted such offerings as He Himself ordained. The worshipper, imperfect and sinful in himself, was accepted in the perfection of the offering. The conscience being a reflection of the sacrifice remained imperfect because the Leviticus sacrifices were imperfect. Christ's sacrifice being perfect gives a perfected conscience ; and, therefore, a peace that nothing can destroy.

The burnt-offering typified Christ offering Himself without spot to God. It was a voluntary offering. So Christ delighted to do God's will. He laid down His life of Himself. Therefore it is that the victim was a male without blemish. This signified the spotless perfection of Christ's manhood. The entire sacrifice was burnt on the altar; that is, it was wholly for God. Such was the devotion of Christ's heart. The skin of the sacrifice was given to the priest. Only the mere surface of Christ's offering up of Himself to God can be apprehended by the believer.

The infinite depths of that great surrender are beyond human understanding.

The inwards were washed with water, so Christ's emotions, as well as His ways and words, when judged by the Word of God, were found to be sinless. With respect to Him, all within and without was without blemish.

The worshipper laid his hand upon the head of the burnt offering to make an atonement for himself, that is, to cover himself and his sin. It was then accepted for him ; that is, all the spotless perfection of the offering was transferred to him. In the sin offering, on the other hand, the guilt of the sinner was transferred to the victim. The sinner's sins are placed upon Christ, and Christ's sinlessness, upon the sinner. These are the two wonders of substitution. (See notes on chapter iv. 4).

Whether the offering were a costly bullock or a little turtle-dove, such as a rich man or a poor man might respectively bring, in either case was it " an offering made by fire of a sweet savour unto the Lord." However great or little may be the intelligence in relation to the atonement of Christ, all is precious to God, if Christ indeed is the object of the heart.

Of the humble offering of verse 15, it is said, with touching grace, that the priest should bring it unto the altar. This action of the priest is not recorded in connection with the more costly offerings of verses 10 and 3.

LEVITICUS II.—The meal offering prefigured Christ's spotless humanity. The flour, not merely ground corn, but flour, revealed Him as perfect and ready for God's service. The fineness of the flour predicted that in Him there should be no unevenness or roughness. The flour was to be mingled with oil, and oil poured upon it. Such was the man Christ Jesus. He was born of the Holy Spirit, and afterwards anointed by the Holy Spirit.

Aaron and his sons ate the meal offering, but all the frankincense was burnt, together with a portion of the flour and oil, for a sweet savour unto the Lord. The highest Christian energy (which the Sons of Aaron represent) may partially apprehend the perfection and beauty of Christ's life as a man, but the frankincense of that life was for God. Jesus, as a man, said, and did, and thought, and felt, and desired, everything to the glory of God. God alone could understand, and value, and enjoy such frankincense.

There was neither leaven nor honey, but there was salt in the meal offering. Honey causes fermentation. There was neither error nor corruption in Jesus, but in Him was very visible the salt of the incorruptible, preservative and faithful Word of God.

Whether the meal offering were broken in pieces, baked in an oven, on a griddle, or in a frying-pan, it and all its pieces were alike precious.

LEVITICUS III.—The infinite fulness of the atoning Sacrifice of Christ needed many offerings to show forth, even faintly, its plenitude. The burnt offering pictured Christ dying; the meal offering, Christ living; and this chapter presents Him as making peace by the blood of His cross, and so establishing for man communion with God.

The burnt offering was a male; the peace offering, a male or female. In either case, without blemish. The peace offering being concerned with communion, a female was permitted as expressive of the incapacity of the worshipper to fully comprehend the unsearchable riches of Christ's nature and work. There was no such limitation on the part of God; hence in the burnt offering it was a male of the first year.

The peace offering was to be offered "before the Lord" (v. 1), "unto the Lord" (v. 3), and "a sweet savour to the Lord" (v. 5). The worshipper laid his hand upon the head of the offering, and its blood was sprinkled on the altar round about; for fellowship is encircled by atonement, and only exists within it. Thus God and the worshipper were brought into fellowship. Peace was established. Its eternal and unshakeable foundation was not the worthfulness of the worshipper but the preciousness of the sprinkled blood.

All the fat was wholly burnt upon the altar as a sweet savour. The fat and the blood

symbolized the priceless life and the precious inward affections of the Lamb of God. The infinite value of these God alone can estimate; whilst to the worshipper were given the wave breast and the heave shoulder (see chapter vii). The poor man's goat was as precious, and received the same ceremony, as the rich man's heifer.

LEVITICUS IV-V. 13.—The burnt offering, the meal offering, and the peace offering were sweet-savour offerings. The sacrifices for sin were not sweet-savour offerings; these sacrifices formed two classes, "sin offerings" and "trespass offerings." The sin offering was made for a priest, for the whole congregation, for a ruler, and for one of the common people. When offered for a priest or for the congregation, it secured relationship, for the blood was sprinkled seven times before the veil; it founded worship, for the blood was sprinkled upon the altar of incense; and it gave boldness to the worshippers, for the blood was poured out at the door of the Tabernacle.

As regards a ruler, or one of the common people, the blood was all poured out at the brazen altar because theirs was a question merely of individual sin, not of congregational guilt. A ruler, however, had to sacrifice a male; one of the common people, a female; in either case, without blemish. An exceptional sinner needs a stronger view of the efficacy of the death of Christ to consciously put away his sin than an ordinary sinner does.

Grace (ch. v. 11-13) furnished a handful of flour as a sin offering to a poor man, as it provided a bullock for a ruler. Flour, not wheat, for the sacrifice of life alone could atone for sin.

The words "through ignorance" (vs. 2, 13, 22, 27) prove that man, whether he be a chief priest or a "common person," cannot know what sin is. This is humbling, and comforting. It reveals that the efficacy of Christ's atonement for sin is not to be measured by man's consciousness of sin, but by God's measurement of it. To believe this fact fills the heart with a Divine peace.

The sin offering was wholly burnt outside the camp, but the blood and the fat were offered to God. This double action illuminates the cross. Jesus suffered "outside the camp," thereby showing how abhorrent to God is sin; yet, at the same time, was His blood precious, and the fat, i.e. His inward personal excellence, " most holy." The incense, the showbread, the sin offering, and the meal offering, are all named " most holy." Thus the Spirit of God, when speaking of Jesus, as a man, or, as an offering for sin, repeats with emphasis, that He was in His entire being " most holy."

Directly the sinner laid his hand upon the substitute it was put to death (v. 4) ; but in the burnt offering it was not so (ch. i. 4). The burnt offering was indeed also put to death ; but before being killed the words " it shall be accepted for him to make an atonement, i.e. a covering for him," are introduced. These two passages explain substitution. In the burnt offering the sinlessness of the victim is transferred to the worshipper ; in the sin offering the sinfulness of the sinner is transferred to the victim. Personal identification with Christ brings peace ; for it means the taking away of sin and the reception of righteousness.

This section (vs. 27–31) illustrates the efficacy of the death of Christ to deliver the sinner justly sentenced to death because of his failure to keep the law perfectly. The four words, " sin " (v. 27), " guilty " (v. 27), " blood " (v. 30), " forgiven " (v. 31), illumine the Gospel. A man sins, he is pronounced guilty ; and, therefore, doomed to die ; the blood of a spotless victim, i.e. its life, is poured out on behalf of the man, and he is pronounced thereby forgiven.

The man is not sentenced to death because of some great sin, but because of a very little sin committed through ignorance, yet is the sin so great in God's sight that to expiate its guilt all the blood of the spotless sacrifice must be poured out at the bottom of the altar. So, to atone for, i.e. to cover, the smallest conceivable departure from absolute sinlessness, and that through ignorance, the whole of Christ's blood must be shed. This shows how desperate a disease is sin

In order to obtain forgiveness for his sin the man said nothing, and did nothing, except to lay his hand upon the head of the spotless substitute, thus transferring his guilt and its doom to the substitute. The law claimed the man's life as the just penalty for his sin. The sin being transferred, the law then claimed the life of the substitute ; and directly that life was surrendered, the full claim of the law was satisfied and the man thereby saved. The knowledge that he was saved was founded upon two facts outside of himself, i.e.

the value of the blood shed for him, and the trustworthiness of the word spoken to him. On this Divine foundation the Christian's peace rests. The knowledge that Christ's blood is of infinite value to cleanse all sins ; and the conviction that the Word of God, which declares that whoever trusts that Saviour shall never be confounded, is trustworthy—this double knowledge establishes assurance of salvation.

In the redemption of the transgressor the priest did everything ; the man, nothing. He stood, he looked, he listened, he believed ! Like action to-day in relation to Christ on the cross ensures conscious salvation.

The fat of the sin offering for a " common person " (v. 27) was burned upon the altar for a " sweet savour." This is not said of the offering for the priest, for the congregation, or for the ruler. If Christ's death for a multitude is sweet to God, His death for an individual sinner of the common people is especially sweet. Such is grace !

The first five verses of chapter v. declare to be sins meriting death, actions or non-actions regarded by man as trivial, if not innocent. Such persons had to confess that they had sinned in these things, and they had to bring as a sin offering either a lamb, or a turtledove, or an ephah of fine flour. The priest made an atonement, and the sinner was forgiven. To " forgive " is to unbind. Forgiveness means the unbinding from off the soul of the death sentence bound upon it by the committed sin.

Life surrendered could alone unbind this sentence. In the slain lamb, or the crushed wheat, this judgment appears. The priest, the lamb, the crushed breadcorn—all symbolized Christ and His atoning work (Isa. liii. 5).

" The voice of swearing " (v. 1) was the action of the Hebrew judge in adjuring by God a prisoner, or a witness, to " utter " the truth. To refuse to answer was to sin against Jehovah. In obedience to this command Micaiah before Ahab (1 Kings xxii. 16) and Jesus before Caiaphas (Matt. xxvi. 63) at once replied. This is the Divine method of swearing a witness.

LEVITICUS V. 14—VI. 7. — The trespass offering was provided to atone for trespass against God, and trespass against man. In trespass against God, sacrifice came first and restitution afterwards ; in trespass against man, this order was reversed. In either case one-fifth more was added to the defaulting principal. Christ, as the trespass offering, not only restored to God that which He took not away, but He added the one-fifth thereto. In Redemption He brought greater glory to God than the glory lost at Creation.

" The holy things of the Lord " (v. 15) refer to first-fruits, first-born, etc., i.e. failure in fulfilling such ordinances.

Verses 15 and 16 legislate for sins of omission ; verse 17, of commission.

The expressions "through ignorance" (v. 15) and " wist it not " (v. 17, 18) dispose of the popular fallacy that sincerity secures salvation.

The words " against the Lord " (ch. vi. 2) reaffirm, what so often appears in the Bible, that, to sin against a neighbour is to sin against God. He makes human sorrows His own ; hence David cried : " I have sinned against the Lord."

A fifth part is twenty per cent. Zacchæus gave much more. The blood of the cross restores the conscience ; the holiness of the cross hands back the defrauded property, and adds a fifth part thereto.

Unregenerate man does not delight in the holiness of God. He, with pleasure, thinks of the love and goodness and mercy and grace of God ; but his thoughts respecting these are unholy thoughts.

LEVITICUS VI. 8—VII. 38.—This section sets out the Laws connected with the Burnt Offering, the Meal Offering, the Sin Offering, and the Peace Offering. Also the Law in relation to the High Priests' Consecration Offering.

The order in which the offerings are placed does not here correspond with that found in the opening chapters of the book. There, the sin offering comes last ; here, the peace offering. This shows design. Only an absolutely perfect Victim could put away sin by the sacrifice of Himself ; hence the sin offering is placed last ; but only a fully accomplished atonement can give peace to the conscience, and therefore in the Laws affecting the sacrifices the peace offering is put last.

The Burnt Offering was to burn all night, and in the morning, dressed in his clean linen garments, the priest was to gather its ashes and place them beside the altar, and then, in his garments of beauty, bring them with befitting glory unto a clean place, i.e. the cleansed Millennium earth. Through this night of mystery the fragrance of Christ's offering up of Himself to God ascends continually. " In the morning " He will appear to His people Israel in His double glory as the White-robed Priest, and the Glory-crowned Mediator ; and it will then be demonstrated to the world, as here fore-shadowed by the honourable treatment of the ashes, that His Person and His work have been accepted of God.

The fire that consumed the burnt offering originally came from heaven (ch. ix. 24), and was maintained perpetually burning by the unwearied ministry of the priest. It was lacking in the second Temple. It testified on the one hand to the unceasing delight of God in the sacrifice of Christ, and on the other hand, to His unceasing hatred of sin. False teachers to-day put this fire out by denying the doctrines of the atonement and of the wrath to come.

The Meal Offering, as the other offerings, was first for God and His glory, and then for man and his need. A memorial of it (v. 15), with all the frankincense, was burnt on the altar for a sweet savour, and the remainder eaten by Aaron and his sons in the Holy Place. As the sin offering, and the trespass offering, so was it " most holy." Thus the Holy Spirit testifies to the sinlessness of Christ as a man, and at the moment in which He was " made sin " upon the cross.

Verses 19–23 form a parenthesis. It treats of the special relationship of the High Priest to the meal offering. His meal offering was to be offered morning and evening. It was to be " baked " i.e., " well kneaded " (v. 21), and wholly burnt, not eaten. (See Heb. vii. 27). Aaron, though High Priest, was a sinner, and twice every day had to shelter himself, in type, behind a sinless Saviour.

No leaven was permitted with the meal offering. It was to be eaten in a holy place, and only by the male children of the High Priest. These Laws clothed with dignity the Meal offering. They teach the necessity of holiness of heart and conduct, and that energy of spiritual intelligence is needed to feed upon Christ as the Bread from Heaven.

The Sin Offering was killed in the place where the Burnt Offering was slain, and its body burned outside the camp. If the blood were brought into the Sanctuary, the flesh of the offering was not eaten, but if not brought in, the flesh was eaten (Heb. xiii. 11).

So desperate a malady is sin that anything that came in contact with the sin offering had to be washed, broken, or scoured.

The Sin Offering, whose blood was brought

into the sanctuary, symbolizes Christ bearing before God the sin of the whole world. The Sin Offering whose blood was not so brought in, but whose flesh was eaten by the priest, presents Christ as making His own the sins of the individual sinner who believes upon Him.

The Burnt Offering and the Sin Offering being slain upon the one spot sets out the unity of the death of Christ in its two aspects. At Golgotha He was at one and the same moment, accursed of God as the Sin Offering, and beloved of the Father as the Burnt Offering.

The Law of the Peace Offering commanded unleavened cakes (v. 12) and leavened bread (v. 13). The one symbolized the sinless humanity of Christ; the other, the sinful humanity of the worshipper. The One had sin on Him but not in Him; the other, had sin in him but not on him.

The Peace Offering for thanksgiving was eaten the same day that it was offered; the Peace Offering for a vow, the same day or the next day—because a vow, or a voluntary offering, necessarily affected the heart more than an ordinary thanksgiving. This law taught the offerer to closely associate the death and sufferings of the slain lamb with the blessing that he gave thanks for. It teaches men to-day the same lesson. To dis-associate worship and thanksgiving from the anguish and bloodshedding of the Lord Jesus is to offer to God an abomination (v. 18), and to bring death into the soul and into the church.

Ceremonial cleanliness was obligatory before eating the peace offering (vs. 20, 21). Disobedience in this matter entailed death (vs. 20, 21). To profess faith in the Person and atonement of Christ, and claim fellowship with Him, and be secretly unclean, ensures the wrath of God.

The fat of the peace offering was to be wholly given to God, because it symbolized the excellent affections of His dearly-beloved Son. The fat of any animal that died, or was accidentally killed, might be used for other purposes, but not eaten. Similarly was the blood precious.

The wave breast and the heave shoulder were to be eaten. The one was "heaved," i.e., lifted up, before God as expressive of its preciousness and acceptability to Him; the other "waved," i.e., presented to the four quarters of the earth as setting forth the sufficiency of this offering to give life to the world. Further, Christ's shoulder upholds, and His breast consoles, all those who trust in Him; and they nourish those who serve Him in any form of Christian ministry to others.

Verses 35 to 38 sum up chapters i–viii. The reverence due to the person and to the work of Messiah was enjoined by the two laws respecting the fat and the blood. They expressed excellency and efficiency. "This is my beloved Son" declared the one; and "peace through the blood of His cross" (Col. i. 20) proclaimed the other.

LEVITICUS VIII.—The subject of Leviticus is a Sacrifice, a Priest, and a Place of Worship. Chapters viii., ix. and x. are concerned with priesthood. Sacrifice is the foundation. The sinner needs a sacrifice; the worshipper, a priest. Christ is both. The Place of Worship is the heavens.

These three chapters make prominent the authority of the Bible, the preciousness of the Blood, and the power of the Holy Spirit.

The words "This is the thing which the Lord commanded," and, "Moses did all that the Lord commanded," etc., proclaimed the authority of the Word.

The value and necessity of the blood are revealed in the words "and he killed it" "and he slew it " etc., etc., " and took of the blood," " and put it," " and sprinkled it " etc., etc.

The power of the Spirit was symbolized in the anointing oil poured upon Aaron, and sprinkled upon his sons, and upon the Tabernacle.

Three words may express the contents of chapters viii. ix. and x. They are: Consecration, Mediation, Sanctification.

The whole congregation was gathered to the door of the Tabernacle to witness the Sanctification, i.e., the setting apart, of Aaron to the priesthood. Thus the smallest child learnt that he had a share in the love and ministry of this great priest. So the feeblest Christian is assured of the personal interest which the True Aaron has for him.

In verse 5 Moses makes known to the people what God had revealed to him (Exod. xxviii).

The anointing oil was "poured" upon Aaron, but only "put" upon his sons; and even this, not upon them till after they had been cleansed by the blood.

The Tabernacle was sanctified with oil at the same moment that Aaron was anointed.

The Tabernacle pictured Christ as the Dwelling place of God, and it, as such, like Aaron as a type of Christ as High Priest, needed no atonement.

The four great offerings were then sacrificed; but in this order : The Sin Offering first, followed by the Burnt Offering, the Meal Offering and the Peace Offering.

Cleansed, clothed, and crowned though they were, yet the moment their hands touched the sacrifice the sinless victims were slain. Such is the nature and the doom of sin.

The ear, the hand, and the foot were first cleansed with blood, and then anointed with oil. The cleansing of the precious blood, and the energizing of the Holy Spirit, alone fit even the noblest character for entry into God's service.

Beautiful and costly as was the raiment of Aaron, yet had it to be sanctified by oil and blood. The religious sensibilities of an unregenerate man are shocked at such a command.

For seven days Aaron and his sons dwelt at the door of the Tabernacle, and feasted upon the results of accomplished atonement as foreshadowed in the unleavened bread of the meal offering, and the heave-shoulder and wave-breast of the peace offering.

LEVITICUS IX.—This chapter describes the mediation of Aaron the High Priest.

On " the eighth day " he, robed in linen and anointed, came forth out of the Tabernacle to offer up the four great sacrifices for the people, i.e. the Sin Offering, the Burnt Offering, the Meal Offering, and the Peace Offering ; and a public proclamation was made that God would accept him and his sacrifice by a special manifestation of his glory. This came to pass.

Aaron, on that day, was a fore-picture of Christ sanctified, anointed with the Holy Spirit, and sent into the world in order to put away its sin by the sacrifice of Himself. " The glory of the Father " raised Him from the dead, thus accepting His person and His work.

But on " the eighth day," that is, the future millennial day, Israel will see the true Priest coming forth from the heavenly sanctuary, and then the glory of the Lord will fill the whole earth.

Aaron having consummated the fourfold sacrifice, lifted up his hands (R.V.) and blessed the people, and then retired into the Tabernacle. The Lord Jesus having finished His sacrificial work lifted up His hands and blessed the disciples (Luke xxiv. 50), and was parted from them and carried up into heaven. And He will so come again in like manner with uplifted hands.

All this is pictured in verses 22, 23, 24. The atonement made, Aaron blesses the people, and, accompanied by Moses, as king and priest, he secretes himself for a little while, then reappears in his twofold character; and, now robed in his garments of beauty and glory, with hands uplifted, he blesses the people once again. Thus will it be when Messiah comes.

What some might think to have been a mistake, was, on the contrary, fully in harmony with the significance of the prophetic teaching of this scene. The blood of the sin offering was not brought into the sanctuary in order to be sprinkled on the golden altar and before the veil. That action secured the presence of God as dwelling in the midst of an erring and sinful people, and recognized the existence of God as inhabiting the Most Holy Place. But in this chapter the blood is shed and sprinkled at the brazen altar, and Aaron appears as God manifest in flesh in the midst of His people. Thus will it be in the day foreshadowed in the chapter, Christ will appear to His people, and the door of the Tabernacle, with the brazen altar, will become the meeting-place and dwelling-place of God with man.

" Fire came out from before Jehovah and consumed the burnt offering "—not fire from heaven but fire from out of the Most Holy Place. It consumed the offering but it did not consume the Tabernacle. God accepted the offering up of the body of Jesus Christ ; but that holy body saw no corruption.

In the sacrifices of Leviticus there are two different Hebrew words for the verb " to burn." One word is used in relation to the burnt offering, etc., and it means a flame of acceptance. The other is used in respect of the sin offering and it signifies a devouring fire.

The robes of beauty and of glory pictured Christ's deity ; the linen garments in which he offered the sacrifice, His humanity. The words " Holiness to Jehovah " were not removed from Aaron's head when he laid aside his robe of glory, for Christ's humanity was as sinless as His deity. His nature was as holy at the carpenter's bench at Nazareth as upon the throne of glory in heaven.

LEVITICUS X. — Nadab and Abihu illustrate the great Bible truth that man always and immediately fails when placed in any position of responsibility and glory. Adam, Noah, Moses, Solomon, the Apostles, etc., and the Hebrew and Christian Churches are sad proofs of this fact.

" And there went out a fire from the Lord and devoured them." As to the burnt offerings there " came out a fire and consumed them "—a great contrast ! When all was done as the Lord commanded, the result was glory ; when something was done which man devised, the fruit was judgment. Sin and death entered while yet the people were worshipping and rejoicing.

The strange fire that was offered must have been fire not taken from off the brazen altar. It had therefore no connection with the atonement. It was the sin of Cain. It is a sin largely committed to-day. Jesus said : " I am the Way, no man cometh unto the Father but by Me." Acceptable worship can only be in the energy of the Holy Spirit, in the truth of the shed blood, and in obedience to the inspired word. The fire of the Holy Spirit associates itself alone with the blood of the crucified Saviour ; all other fire is " strange fire."

Nadab and Abihu were " devoured " by the fire ; but their priestly raiment was not burnt, like as the Tabernacle was not burnt (v. 5).

In Nadab and Abihu is seen the presumption of the " flesh " ; in Aaron and his two remaining sons, the timidity of the "flesh." They had to be urged by Moses to maintain their high position and to eat the precious things connected therewith (vs. 6, 7, and 12-15) ; and it is noteworthy that on this dreadful day the daughters of Aaron were permitted to partake of the wave-breast and heave-shoulder. So incurably darkened is man's natural will that whenever God manifests His judgments men seek refuge in a false humility ; as here, and as in the case of David and the Ark.

Many think that the commandment of verse 9 proves that Nadab and Abihu were intoxicated at the time of their death. David desired to dwell in the House of the Lord all the days of his life. Of necessity, therefore, he would have had to be a life-long total abstainer. Anything that excites nature must be avoided if God would be acceptably worshipped. What, therefore, the unregenerate man finds to be a help to worship the spiritual man finds to be a hindrance.

Verses 10 and 11 following immediately upon verse 9 make certain that intoxicating liquor impairs the judgment in moral questions, and weakens the intelligence in spiritual matters.

Nadab and Abihu, at the opening of this chapter, sinned positively ; their brothers, at the close of the chapter, sinned negatively. Divine judgment dealt with the first sin ; Divine forbearance with the second.

Aaron should have eaten the goat of the sin offering ; so making the sins of the people his own. But his personal grief unfitted him for bearing their sorrows. How different the True Aaron in John xvi. 22. He laid His own immeasurable griefs aside, and His loving heart engaged itself with those of His disciples. It was not disobedience on Aaron's part but human infirmity and sorrow.

LEVITICUS XI.—Priesthood having been established, to it was now committed the judgment of that which defiled. The priest stood nearest to God. Thus the lesson was taught, and it still operates, that to exercise a right judgment in moral and doctrinal matters, continuous and close fellowship with God is absolutely necessary.

This section of Leviticus contains chapters xi-xv. Its laws were not only a test of obedience, and a loving provision for the health and happiness of the people, but they also give a humbling picture of the weakness and corruption of fallen human nature.

It should be noted that the Word of the Lord was the one and only judge in all these matters. That Word, the Holy Spirit declares in 2 Tim. iii, thoroughly furnishes to all good works, and makes the man of God perfect. It must therefore of necessity be an infallible rule of Christian living, for how could imperfection produce perfection ?

In this eleventh chapter, the God of Israel entered with amazing detail into the daily food of His people, in order to teach them to make a difference between the unclean and the clean (v. 47). Love was the basis of this legislation.

With respect to animals, those only that chewed the cud and divided the hoof were to be eaten. Outward holiness of conduct and inward digestion of all Holy Scripture are clearly suggested by this ; and they must not be divorced, as is clear from verse 26.

Fish that had both fins and scales were clean. Fins to enable them to move through the water, and scales to resist its action. A Christian is to be in the world, but he must not let the world be in him. He is to resist its influence and swim against its current. Spiritual life and energy can alone give this resistance and progression.

Birds that flew, and that had legs above their feet to leap withal, were clean; but those that could not so leap, or that fed upon flesh, were unclean. The native air of the Christian is the upper air. On the wings of faith he is to mount up thither; his food is not to be carnal; and when, of necessity, he must touch earth, he is to touch it as lightly as possible, and not to rest thereon.

As to creeping things, those that had many feet, and that dragged the body along the earth, were unclean. The apostle says that minding earthly things is an evidence of hostility to the cross of Christ.

An unclean animal, fish, bird, or reptile, when dead, defiled whatsoever it touched; excepting an abundant spring of water, and seed-corn. Christ the Lord, as man, was undefiled by contact with sinners and with sin. He was, and is, the living water that springeth up into everlasting life, and He is the corn of wheat that bringeth forth much fruit (John xii).

The word " more " in verse 42 should read " many."

The eater (v. 40) ate ignorantly; for Num. xv. 30, and Deut. xiv. 21, commanded death for whoever did so presumptuously.

Because Israel was elected to be a peculiar treasure to God, therefore she was to cleanse herself from all filthiness of the flesh and spirit, and to be holy, for God was holy (vs. 44, 45).

LEVITICUS XII.—This chapter humbles and comforts. It humbles, because it declares that man by nature is defiled, and needs cleansing. It comforts, because it provides a redemption without money and without price—for two young pigeons could be had for nothing.

The birth of a child recalled the sin and disobedience of Eden, and that woman was the instrument of that rebellion. Hence, after the birth of a boy, the mother was shut out of the Tabernacle for forty days, and, in the case of a girl, for eighty days; nor was she permitted to touch any hallowed thing.

The extreme poverty of the Lord's earthly parents was evidenced by their bringing two pigeons, the one for a sin offering, the other for a burnt offering (Luke ii, 24).

Thus tender love and amazing grace shine forth in this chapter—amazing grace, for He, the Lord of Glory, condescended to be made of so poor a woman; and tender love, for He commanded that women during the time of their greatest weakness should be protected from visitors. Disobedience to this law has occasioned many deaths and much suffering.

The Virgin Mary knew she was a sinner and needed the cleansing of atoning blood, for she brought the two pigeons, as here commanded.

LEVITICUS XIII, XIV.—Sins are the fruit of sin. The sacrifices for the cleansing of the leper foreshadowed the efficacy of the sacrifice of Christ to deal with sin in the nature. The trespass and sin offerings signified the power of the same sacrifice to atone for sins in the conduct. Further, in the cleansing of the leper, first, justification, and then, sanctification were pictured. This is the theme of Romans i–viii.

Leviticus xiii. is leprosy discovered; Leviticus xiv., leprosy cleansed.

Leprosy was discoverable in persons, in garments, and in houses.

A leper, white all over, was clean. He was a leper, but the disease was not active in him, it was, in a sense, dead. Thus " sin " should be " dead " in the Christian (Rom. vi).

Leprosy vividly illustrates sin. It is loathsome, contagious, incurable, and fatal.

The minute directions given in the chapter, and the care and patience enjoined upon the priest, show how God distinguishes between sin and infirmity. A man might have a form of skin disease in appearance like leprosy, but the priest was skilled to pronounce it other than leprosy. The Heavenly High Priest is a Priest for infirmity as well as for sin; and the instructed Christian will not confound these (Heb. iv., v., ix).

The legislation of the chapter reveals how tenderly, faithfully, and patiently Jesus the Lord acts towards the sinner.

On four occasions Christ endorsed Leviticus as having been written by Moses. The Modernist says the book was forged by Ezra. The Christian believes the Master and not the Modernist.

Lev. xii. 3,   John vii. 22, 23.
Lev. xiv. 3–32.   Matt. viii. 4.
Lev. xx. 9.   Mark vii. 10.
Lev. xxiv. 5–9.   Matt. xii. 4.

The priest alone could judge whether a man were a leper or no. Directly a person was declared to be a leper, he was placed without the camp, and compelled, by voice and clothing, to confess himself a leper.

Leprosy in a garment is a type of sin in a man's circumstances, or habits. The priest was commanded to show the same patience and care in judging a garment as in judging a man. If only a " spot," the garment was washed. If the spot changed, and ceased spreading, the piece affected was torn out. But if, after having been washed, the plague remained unchanged, or spread, the entire garment was burnt.

Sometimes a Christian must abandon part of his business, because of evil attaching to it, and sometimes he must abandon it altogether. This is a principle which affects the whole Christian life.

One "bright spot" revealed the disease as surely as an extensive and revolting eruption. So one pleasing sin reveals the ·fact of corruption in human natue as certainly as an hundred revolting vices. There is, as to the nature, no moral difference.

The carnal mind finds this chapter tiresome uninteresting and unpleasant. To the spiritual mind it is humbling and comforting. Love untiring and infinite wisdom are the foundation of these statutes. The reader finds himself as a moral leper in the tender, patient, wise and loving hands of the heavenly Priest ; and, accordingly, he studies every word with humiliation and adoration.

The triple cleansing of the next chapter illustrates the justification, the purification, and the sanctification of Romans i. to viii. Chapters i–iii. 20 : the leprosy of sin declared ; chapters. iii. 21 to v. 11: the sinner justified by the death of Christ ; chapters v. 12 to vi. 23 : the believer washed in the baptism of Christ ; and chapters vii. and viii. : the Christian sanctified by the Spirit of Christ. Sanctification progresses in the soul as the Spirit reveals the riches of the atonement, as symbolized in the four offerings of chapter xiv. 10–20.

LEVITICUS XIII. and XIV.—continued.—
The leper was cleansed by blood, by water, and by oil. These symbolized the blood of Christ, the Word of God, and the Holy Spirit. This triple cleansing restored him to the camp, to the family, and to the Tabernacle. All was based upon the preciousness and efficacy of the shed blood. Apart from the blood of Jesus moral reformation and spiritual power are impossible. Excepting the washing of himself in water, the leper did nothing for his cleansing ; the priest did everything. The leper is the sinner, the priest is Jesus. The priest " went forth " out of the camp to where the leper was, and the leper was "brought " to him. So Christ came down from Heaven to where the sinner is, and the Holy Spirit brings the sinner to Him. See note on 1 Cor. vi. 9–11.

Having been thus brought together, the priest led the leper to running, i.e. living water (beauteous image of the Holy Spirit), and proceeded to the first of the three cleansings.

He was cleansed by blood, that is by the sacrifice of a sinless life. The " earthen vessel " pointed onward to Christ's spotless humanity ; the slain bird, Christ crucified ; the living bird, Christ resurrected and ascended into Heaven. The living bird mounted heavenward with the blood of the slain bird upon its wings ; and the same blood having been sprinkled seven times upon the leper, the priest pronounced him clean. At the same time, cedar wood, scarlet, and hyssop were dipped in the blood of the slain bird, because, not only does the precious blood of Christ cleanse the defiled creature, but it also cleanses the defiled creation. This latter fact awaits a future happy demonstration.

One single bright " spot " just as truly as one thousand great spots proved a man to be a leper, and excluded him from the kingdom of God, i.e., the camp. One sin, as certainly as one thousand sins, excludes from heaven.

The precious blood that cleanses the sinner is the same blood with which Christ entered into the Holy Place, having obtained eternal Redemption (Heb. ix. 12). Christ, as High Priest, and the believer have one and the same title to enter heaven. That title, is the precious blood shed at Calvary. The leper and the living bird were both sprinkled with the blood of the slain bird.

The second stage in the cleansing of the leper is described in verse 8. He washed himself and his clothes in water. He then entered the camp, but had to remain outside of his own tent and of God's Tent for seven days. Directly the repentant sinner is cleansed by the precious blood of Christ, he is called upon to " cleanse himself " from all defilement of the flesh and spirit. This cleansing is effected by the washing of water by the Word. That is, he judges himself, and his habits (" his clothes "), by the infallible standard of the Holy Scriptures, and he resolutely turns away from everything that that standard condemns. Thus he cleanses himself.

The third and final cleansing was then operated by the priest eight days after the first cleansing. A trespass offering, a sin offering, a meal offering, and a burnt offering were required to make atonement for him. The blood of the trespass offering was put upon the ear, the hand, and the foot of the leper, and upon that blood was sprinkled the holy anointing oil. These things being accomplished the leper was pronounced finally clean, and was permitted to enter God's House and his own house.

Two great facts shine here with exceptional lustre ; and both were of grace. First, the uniting together of God's House with the leper's house ; and, second, the placing side by side of the High Priest and the leper ; for these two were sprinkled with . blood and anointed with oil. Only Aaron's sons were similarly consecrated ; and thus, ceremonially, was the leper " put among the sons."

The priest represented the Great High Priest passed into the heavens. His double cleansing of the leper illustrated justification and sanctification. The first cleansing pictured Christ's atoning work for the sinner ; the second cleansing, the Holy Spirit's work in the believer, giving him assurance of salvation, deliverance from his sins, and power to enter into the presence of God. The blood was his title, and the Spirit (oil) his capacity.

Verses 21–32 legislated, in grace, for those who were too poor to provide the more costly sacrifices ; but in such cases it was absolute that the sacrifice must be a sacrifice of blood. (See notes on Heb. ix., x).

To cleanse leprosy in a house the priest was commanded to take the earthen vessel and the two birds, as in the case of the leper. The careful, patient, action of the priest in this section of the chapter reveals the tenderness and long-suffering which the Heavenly Priest again exercises in connection with sin in a family, or in a religious society—here pictured by a " house " ; and the lesson is also thus repeated, that there is but one cure for sin, whether in an individual or a community or in nature, and that one cure is the cleansing blood of Christ.

" The priest shall pronounce him clean " (v. 7). This expresses justification, and illustrates Rom. i. to v. 11. " The priest shall make him clean " (v. 11). This is sanctification, and corresponds to Rom. v. 12 to viii. See notes on Rom. i–viii., and 1 John v. 8.

LEVITICUS XV.—The lessons of this chapter are : First, the Holiness of God and of His Dwelling-place ; Second, the loving and minute interest that He takes in the habits of His children. Nothing was too small or too private for Him. Their clothing and their health concerned Him deeply. Third, the corruption of fallen nature ; it defiled. Waking or sleeping, sitting, standing, or lying, its every touch conveyed pollution —a painful lesson for proud humanity. Fourth, the cleansing power of the shed blood, and the sanctifying virtue of the Word of God as the only way of cleansing and holiness.

Thus the nature of sin is exhibited in the chapter. Even that which was unavoidable defiled. But these unavoidable pollutions were less morally serious than leprosy ; and hence the provision made for restoration to communion with God was a sin offering, a burnt offering, and a washing with water.

The saliva from the sinner's lip defiled (v. 8) ; that from the Saviour's lip healed (Mark viii. 23).

Defilement is cleansed by the blood (1 John i. 7), by the Spirit (Titus iii. 3–5) and by the Word (Eph. v. 26). See notes on prior chapter.

Justification assures of salvation from the guilt of sin (Rom.) ; sanctification effects separation from the filth of sin (Heb.). A simple knowledge of Christ as the slain and living bird suffices to assure the conscience as to justification, but a fuller knowledge of Him as the burnt, the meal, the trespass, and the sin offering is needed to cleanse the conduct and effect sanctification.

LEVITICUS XVI.—This chapter describes the Great Day of Atonement. It occurred once a year. There was no other day like it. It dealt with the sins of the whole nation for twelve months. It foreshadowed the Lamb of God taking away the sins of the world. Abel's lamb redeemed one man ; the Paschal lamb, one family ; the Day of Atonement lamb, one nation ; the Lamb of Calvary, the whole world !

This was the only day in the year that the High Priest entered the Most Holy Place. Enveloped in a cloud of incense he presented the blood of the burnt offering and of the sin offering, which he sprinkled once upon the golden Mercy-seat—for God, knowing its value, needed but the one presentation—and seven times before the Mercy-seat—for a seven times repeated sprinkling of the blood, where the worshipper stood, was needed to give him assurance, and to help him to understand its preciousness. See note on 1 John i. 7.

The Tabernacle, and all connected therewith, was cleansed, as well as the nation. The atoning sacrifice of Calvary not only redeems man, so that he can dwell with God, but redeems the Creation, so that it can become the Dwelling-place of God.

See notes upon the Epistle to the Hebrews. The fourth verse foreshadows the spotless humanity of the Divine High Priest. The seventeenth verse illustrates the truth that man has no part in the great work of making an atonement, either for himself or for others.

The two goats set out the death and victory of Christ, thus furnishing a complete salvation. The one goat was for Jehovah, the other for Azazel. The goat for Jehovah was slain, and its blood sprinkled upon the Mercy Seat, thus making atonement ; the goat for Azazel, that is for Satan the Adversary, was sent out into the desert as the living one to challenge and put to silence that Accuser, and all accusers. The one is Rom. iii., i.e., every sin covered ; the other, Rom. viii, every accuser silenced. See notes on Zech. iii.

Verses 29–34 point to the great day of Zech. xii. and Rev. i. On that day Israel will see her Great High Priest. She will afflict her soul, she will recognize the plenitude of the atonement made by Him for her, and she will enter a blissful Sabbath of Rest.

The solemn ritual of the Great Day of Atonement declared that entrance into the presence of God was barred to the sinner, and that the blood of bulls and of goats could not rend the veil that shut men out from God. It further declared, that atoning blood was the basis of God's throne ; hence the nearer the

worshipper approached to that throne the greater was the value attached to the blood shed at the brazen altar. The entire way from the brazen altar by the brazen laver, the golden altar, and the veil, and up to the throne, was a blood-sprinkled way. Without the veil, the blood was precious ; but it was within the veil that its preciousness was fully revealed. The great factors within the veil were, the blood and the incense. The one expressed the fragrance of the Person of Christ, the other, the efficacy of His work.

No " meal " or " peace offering " appeared on this day, because atonement, and not fellowship, was the business of that day.

LEVITICUS XVII.—The first nine verses of this chapter determined the one and only place where sacrifice was to be offered, i.e., the door of the Tabernacle.. This law guarded the people from sacrificing to demons, and asserted God's ownership of life. Thus God was honoured, and His People's relationship with Him maintained.

In verse 2 occurs for the first time the phrase : "And unto all the children of Israel." This marked the solemnity of the command ; and the words : " This is the thing which Jehovah has commanded," drew attention to the penalty which followed disobedience.

There is no contradiction between these verses and Deut. xii. 15, 21. The context there shows that only food is in question ; the context here, specially verse 7, treats of offering sacrifice.

The words, " no more," in verse 7, make it clear that the people had sacrificed to demons in the land of Egypt. In Isa. xiii. 21, xxxiv. 14, the word is translated " satyrs " i.e., half man, half goat. It was the great goat-god Pan ; afterwards worshipped by the Greeks and Romans. Compare Joshua xxiv. 14, 2 Chron. xi. 15 R.V., Ezek xx. 7, xxiii. 3.

Verses 10–16 denounce death upon anyone that ate blood. Verse 11, together with Luke xxiv. 39, 1 Cor. xv. 50 and Heb. xiii. 20, destroys the foundation on which the Romish mass stands.

Thus the chapter teaches how precious is the blood of Christ to God ; and that the only meeting place between God and man is Calvary. The chapter insists that it is the blood, and the blood alone, that makes an atonement for sinners. It was Christ's death that rent the veil, it is His blood that procures forgiveness of sins and boldness to enter into the Holiest.

LEVITICUS XVIII., XIX., XX.—In the first five verses God reminded Israel that He was a holy God, and that having called them into fellowship with Himself they must be a holy people. They were not to do after the abominations of the Egyptians or the Canaanites. God was to be their standard of holiness. And with what dignity did He clothe them ! Twice here He says, " I am Jehovah your God." It was this relationship that demanded a separation from all that defiled. Again, in verse 30, He repeats, " I am Jehovah your God," and frequently in chapters xix. and xx.

In chapter xix. seven groups of laws end with the words, " I am Jehovah your God," and eight groups with the words, " I am Jehovah."

This section of the book sets forth the appalling degradation of man apart from God, and the pity of God for little children, widows, and the poor. The little children were not to be burnt in the fire to Moloch. Food in the harvest field and the vineyard was to be purposely left for the widow, the poor, and the stranger. The day labourer was to receive his pay each evening. What exquisite thought for so humble a member of society ! The deaf, the blind, the afflicted, were all to be treated with the deepest compassion. Marriage and family relationships were to be had in honour ; and integrity in business together with impartiality in judgment, was to be observed because Jehovah was their God.

The association of the family with the sabbath, and the precedence given to the mother (xix. 3), are noteworthy. The sabbath when rightly observed, unites the family, and, together, they form the foundation of society. In the East the mother is despised. God commands her to be honoured.

LEVITICUS XXI., XXII.—This section contains two divisions : The First (ch. xxi. 1–xxii. 16), commanded that the priests should be undefiled ; the Second (ch. xxii. 17–33), that the offerings should be without blemish. The foundation of this legislation was laid in the fact and the purpose stated in chapter xxii. 32, 33.

That holiness becometh God's House for ever, is true in all periods of time. God demanded an unblemished priest and an unblemished sacrifice (ch. xxi. 21 and xxii. 20). Such was Christ as Priest and Sacrifice.

Law forbade a priest who was physically imperfect to exercise his office (ch. xxi. 16–21), but grace furnished him his daily bread (v. 22).

In the Christian life God must have the first place, then will the nearest and dearest relatives have their right place. Further, to beget souls for God, and nourish them in the Word of His grace, the believer must be equipped with full spiritual energy, and stand apart from everything that defiles. In xxi. 4 the sense is, the priest may not defile himself in mourning for the dead as the nobleman may.

In the life of separation unto God there must be holiness, but not hardness (ch. xxii. 26–28) ; and as enjoined in chapter vii. 15, spiritual or physical wealth was not to be separated from the precious blood that bought it (ch. xxii. 29, 30 with Rom. viii. 32).

It is not to be supposed that the priest's daughter of chapter xxi. 9 was to be burnt alive. She was to be " burnt up " as the sacrifices were burnt up. They were not burnt alive, but first put to death and then burnt ; so in chapter xx. 14 and in this case ; and in all cases in the Scriptures where it is commanded to burn transgressors.

LEVITICUS XXIII.—Israel's sacred year contained one weekly and seven annual feasts, but the annual feasts were related to the weekly feast. The weekly feast was the Sabbath ; the seven annual feasts were : Passover, Unleavened Bread, First-fruits, Pentecost, Trumpets, Atonement, and Tabernacles.

Verse 2 declares these to be the " Feasts of Jehovah," and the words, " even these are my feasts," are added for emphasis. Alas, when He came in flesh they had ceased to be " Feasts of Jehovah " and had become " Feasts of the Jews " (John ii. 13, v. 1, vi. 4, xi. 55). A similar change may be witnessed to-day in what professes to be the Kingdom of God.

The feast of the Sabbath stood apart as being God's rest. It was a prophecy and a promise of the rest in Christ that remaineth to the people of God. See notes on Heb. iii and iv.

The foundation of the seven feasts was Grace ; the top-stone, Glory ; for the Passover proclaimed redemption through the blood, and the last feast—Tabernacles, pictured the Millennium. Between these two feasts came the sheaf of the First-fruits, i.e., the Resurrection of Christ ; Pentecost, i.e., the Descent of the Holy Spirit upon the First-fruits themselves ; and the Great Day of Atonement when they shall look upon Him whom they have pierced, and, repentant, receive the new heart predicted by Ezekiel.

The command to do no servile work is repeated ten times in connection with these feasts. Man's activities were forbidden to intrude themselves into a salvation which was Divine and perfect. God desired happy redeemed children in His family, and not slaves. See notes on Heb. ii–iv.

The words " at even " (v. 5) should read " between the evenings," i.e., at any time from sunset of one day to sunset of the next.

The apostle Paul states, " Christ our Pass-over has been (R.V.) sacrificed for us, therefore let us keep the feast—with the unleavened bread of sincerity and truth "—not with material bread, as is the custom in almost all the churches of Christendom.

The sheaf of first-fruits was to be waved on the morrow after the Sabbath. That was the day that Christ rose from the grave. No sin offering accompanied the sheaf, for Jesus was sinless. See notes on James i.

The bread for the Feast of Pentecost was to be baked with leaven because that bread represented the redeemed. But with this leavened bread seven lambs, one young bullock, and two rams, and a meal offering, and one kid for a sin offering, and two lambs for a peace offering, were to be offered unto the Lord ; thus proclaiming that an infinite Saviour has been provided by God to engrace weak and erring men.

God would have the Gentile also at His festival board, and hence the command of verse 22.

The Feast of Trumpets proclaimed the coming of the Day of Atonement, and drew the attention of the whole nation to that great feast.

The words " afflict your souls " (v. 27) mean " humble yourselves " (1 Peter v. 6) and bow to God's way of Salvation and rest.

Thus these seven feasts formed a Great Sabbatic Week of feasting, rest, and gladness. Such are the joys offered to sinners in the Gospel.

The Sheaf of the First-fruits appears in 1 Cor. xv. 23, the First-fruits themselves in Rev. xiv. 4 Israel and the nations in Millennial blessing will be the harvest.

LEVITICUS XXIV.—The first nine verses of this chapter are repetitions from the book of Exodus—the reason for that appears in the legislation now made concerning the man who dishonoured the name of Jehovah.

The golden lampstand with its sacred flame, and the pure table with its Presence Bread, were figures, as already noted, of Christ as the Bread of Life and the Light of the World. They are here inserted designedly by the Holy Spirit between the Feasts of Jehovah and the blasphemer of Jehovah, between the feasting of the one chapter and the fighting of the other. The " Feasts of Jehovah " would become " Feasts of the Jews " ; and the nation itself, represented by the son of the Israelitish woman, would seek to kill the true man of Israel (v. 10), but there would be no failure in the Son of God's love. The sons of Israel might fail to present Jehovah with the food of their peace-offerings, but the Divine Bread would unfailingly remain as the Presence Bread in the true Tabernacle ; and the earthly Israel might fail to be a light to the nations, but the Divine Israel would never fail as The Light of the world.

The subjection of mind that appears in verse 12, and the anxiety to do what God wished, and not to act in the heat of their own judgment, is very lovely.

The Gentile (v. 22) was to have an equal place with the Hebrew within the goodness and severity of the righteous law decreed in verses 17-23.

Thus this chapter contrasts with the previous one. The despiser of the glad and glorious Gospel of chapter xxiii. suffers the doom of chapter xxiv.

The Light of verse 2 shines back on chapter xxiii. revealing the love of God's heart, and shines forward on chapter xxiv. exposing the hatred of man's heart. The Bread of verse 5 has an appropriate relation also to both chapters. The Bread furnished the tables and the Light flooded the feasts with sun-shine, but the rebel got stones instead of bread. In Palestine stones often resemble bread.

LEVITICUS XXV-XXVI. 2.—The doctrine of this chapter is that the people of Israel and the land of Israel belonged to Jehovah, and that He, as the Divine Goel, i.e., Redeemer, had redeemed them both at the expense of His own precious blood.

The legislation of the chapter affected the Sabbatic year and the Jubilee year. These, together with the weekly Sabbath, pointed onwards to the Millennial rest that awaits Israel. Infinite wisdom, amazing love, and a health-giving test of faith, appear in these commandments. For it was a real test of faith not to plant any crops either in the sixth or forty-ninth years.

The principles that these laws expressed are singular to the Bible. Private property in land was forbidden—it belonged to Jehovah. Usury upon money, or a percentage upon goods, was not permitted in respect of loans to needy neighbours. All the food produced by the earth in the Sabbatic and Jubilee years was common property, to be eaten but not to be stored. Land, or its fruits, might be mortgaged, but the mortgage became void at the Jubilee ; and, at any time prior to the Jubilee, either might be redeemed at the option of the borrower. A distinction was made between property created by man's industry (as for instance a house in a walled city), and property created by God, i.e., land. The house could be sold in perpetuity ; and consequently bequeathed by will ; land, never. A house in a village was deemed to be an agricultural asset, and could not therefore become personal property. The Jubilee voided all contracts and released all slaves.

The Sabbatic year was to be kept unto Jehovah (v. 2).

The trump of Jubilee which proclaimed liberty to all was to be sounded on the Great Day of Atonement. The cancellation of all debts and the liberation of all slaves was effected by the death of the atoning lamb. Thus was foreshadowed the world-wide redemption purchased by the spotless Lamb of God.

The nearness or remoteness of the Jubilee increased or diminished the value of a sale or mortgage. As the Christian realizes the nearness or remoteness of the coming of the Lord, so does he place a low or a high value on earthly things.

Only a relative could redeem a bondman and his inheritance. To redeem the slaves of sin it therefore was necessary that Christ should become man.

In verses 38, 42 and 55 of this chapter, and verse 13 of the next chapter, are found the words, " brought forth." Israel was brought forth out of Egypt to be free, to be rich, and to be Jehovah's servant.

The first two verses of chapter xxvi. close the section of this book dealing with weekly, annual, and Jubilee Sabbaths. A double injunction was given forbidding idolatry and enjoining true Sabbatic worship. The command respecting idolatry most probably was addressed to Israelites bound to heathen masters (ch. xxv. 47-55). These were in danger of this sin during the period of their servitude.

The legislation of chapters xxv-xxvii. was given from Sinai, not from the Tabernacle— (xxv. 1 ; xxvi. 46 ; xxvii. 34)—but it appears in this book and not in Exodus, because it relates to communion rather than to government, and is only possible in a life of priestly power in the Holy Spirit.

LEVITICUS XXVI. 3-46.—In chapter xxvi are recorded God's singular vows to His people, and in chapter xxvii His people's singular vows to Him. In these latter there might be failure, but never in the former.

The four occurrences of " If " and " Then " should be noted in this chapter.

Verses 3-13 promised blessing for obedience. Verses 40-45 assured restoration upon repentance.

Between these sections of the chapter, i.e., from verse 14 to verse 39, are set out the five great judgments denounced upon disobedience. Compare with these the five visitations in wrath of Isa. v. 25 ; ix. 12, 17, 21 ; x. 4 ; and also the five lamentations of Amos iv. 6-12.

The " seven times " of these judgments predicted the seventy years (5×7×2) in Babylon (Jeremiah xvi. 18) ; and possibly the 2520 (360×7) of Gentile rule over Israel, commencing with Nebuchadnezzar.

Palestine still enjoys her Sabbaths (v. 43), because she lieth desolate without the sons of Jacob. But the fulfilment of this last section of the chapter is at hand.

The last 1800 years of Jewish history are accurately foretold in the predictions of verses 32-39.

David and his mighty men illustrate the truth of verse 8.

The judgment declared upon the idols in verse 30 showed the helplessness of the gods worshipped.

" If they shall confess their iniquity " (v. 40). This is the one condition for personal and national restoration.

LEVITICUS XXVII.—The singular vows affected persons, animals, houses and fields; together with property designated as " devoted things " and " tithes."

The land was Emmanuel's land ; and He by a singular vow offered Himself and the land to God. He therefore fulfilled all the conditions of this chapter. He is the True Priest pointed to in verse 21. Israel valued Him at 30 pieces of silver, but He valued Israel and the land at the price of His own blood.

In the case of a person devoting himself or his property, Moses was to make an estimation of the value of the vow. As to atonement (Ex. xxx. 15), all stood upon one platform. But in the matter of a vow it was not so. Spiritual energy and experience must be measured by righteousness. Moses represented righteousness.

But if a man were poor then his vow was to be estimated by the priest. The priest was the exponent of grace. Israel at Mount Horeb made a " singular vow," which, when tested by the standard of righteousness, failed. But the True Aaron, the Great High Priest, will estimate her in grace, and will fulfil for her all the righteous requirements of a vow.

Death (v. 29) was denounced upon the violator of the law governing " devoted " things (v. 28). Hence the doom of Achan and Ananias and Sapphira ; and, indirectly, of Samson and Saul (1 Sam. xv. 23). Everything devoted was entrusted to the custody of the high priest (Num. xviii. 14). Samuel, as a living sacrifice, was handed over to Eli (1 Sam. i. 25) and remained so devoted till death. Believers are " devoted " to Christ (Rom. xii. 1). Violation of that surrender brings death into the soul, in harmony with the principle of verse 29 of this chapter.

NUMBERS

NUMBERS I.—The Divine Title for this book is " In the Wilderness." Its subject therefore is pilgrimage and warfare. It is the fourth book of the Pentateuch, and is connected with the three prior books by its first word " and." The number " four " is the number of the earth. This book therefore contains four types of Christ as Son of man on earth :

1. The Bread of Life   Chapter xi. 7–9.
2. The Water of Life   Chapter xx. 11.
3. The Serpent on the Pole Chapter xxi. 9.
4. The Star out of Jacob   Chapter xxiv. 17.

The theme of Leviticus is worship ; that of Numbers is warfare. Spiritual Israelites are to be warriors as well as worshippers. The ministry of the priest in the prior book is followed in the latter by the service of the Levite and the soldier. Communion and service in the Christian life should be related and balanced.

The opening scene of this book touches the heart. Israel is in the wilderness. God has brought her there so that being wholly dependent upon Him for food, clothing, health, protection and all things, she might learn what He can be to the heart that trusts Him. Such lessons could not be learnt either in Egypt or Canaan. In this first chapter He gathered His people around Himself and numbered them exactly. Here were both sweetness and dignity—to be so recognized by God and drawn to His side.

But this entailed warfare : and hence fourteen times in this chapter occur the words, " all that were able to go forth to war." Fellowship with God means warfare with the world.

This fourth book opens and closes with a census of these men of war. Thirty-eight years separate the one census from the other. In the first census they numbered 603,550, in the second 601,730, showing a total decrease of 1820. In Egypt they increased ;

in the wilderness they decreased. Of the first census all perished except two (see ch. xxvi. 24). The Holy Spirit in 1 Cor. x. says that these facts are recorded to admonish those who think they stand to take heed lest they fall.

To be a soldier in the army of Israel a man should be born an Israelite. He had " to declare his pedigree " (v. 18). Failure to do so secured rejection. To be a Christian soldier the new birth is essential. The Christian soldier must be born a Christian. This birth takes place when the Holy Spirit reveals Christ to the soul. This is the Christian's " pedigree " ; and it is his duty to " declare " it. It is impossible to be an effective soldier for Jesus Christ if there is any uncertainty upon this point. People who are doubtful as to whether they are children of God or not, make poor soldiers on the battlefield. Christian conflict is not a warfare with personal doubts and fears as to one's salvation, but it is a succession of battles with enemies of God within and without. (See Gal. v. and Eph. vi). Compare notes on 1 Cor. ix. 24.

The Christian is a priest, a levite, and a soldier, i.e., a worshipper, a worker, and a warrior.

NUMBERS II.—Directly an Israelite declared his pedigree he took up a position beneath his standard. Each standard was pitched " far off," that is, over against the Tabernacle. The position of the standard was determined by the position of the Tabernacle. Thus birth and obedience characterized each soldier. He declared his pedigree, and he paraded beneath his standard. To be an effective Christian soldier, not only is it necessary that there should be absolute certitude as to the reality of a personal experience of being " born from above," but there must be a full subjection of will to the Word of God, and of heart to the Temple of God, i.e., the standard and the tent of verse 2 (R.V.)—that is, to Christ, for He is both.

God is not the author of confusion but of order. This is illustrated by the regulations of this chapter.

The Tabernacle occupied the centre of the camp. At its eastern door Moses, Aaron and his sons pitched their tents. On the South side the Kohathites, on the West the Gershonites, and on the North the Merarites respectively encamped.

Then outside these the twelve tribes were thus grouped : On the East, Judah, Issachar and Zebulon beneath the standard of Judah ; on the South, Reuben, Simeon, and Gad beneath the standard of Reuben ; on the West, Ephraim, Benjamin, and Manasseh beneath the standard of Ephraim ; and on the North, Dan, Naphtali, and Asher beneath the standard of Dan.

When marching, Judah, with his two tribes, led the van ;   Reuben followed with his brothers ;   then the Levites with the Tabernacle ;   and, behind them, marched the two great divisions of Ephraim and Dan.

Thus the vanguard was " praise," the rearguard, " judgment " ; and at the centre, " communion " inspired the one and instructed the other.

Hebrew writers say that the sign on each of these four great standards were the signs of the Zodiac ; and that the colours of the standards corresponded to the colours of the four rows of precious stones in the high-priest's breast-plate. If this be so, then these standards have a relationship to Ezek. i. 10, and Revelation iv. 7.

As to the Levites, the order of their camping is shown in chapter iii. ; their marching, in chapter x.

When encamped, or on the march, Ephraim, Benjamin, and Manasseh were nearest to the mercy-seat. Hence their being named in Ps. lxxx. 3.

On the march the positions of greatest danger were the van and the rear ; accordingly Judah and Dan were numerically the strongest ;   the divisions of Reuben and Ephraim were weaker as to numbers.

The last verse of the chapter is pleasant to read. As Jehovah commanded so they encamped, and so they marched !

" Every man in his place " (v. 17). If Christ (the Ark) be " in the midst " and every one takes a right position to Him, then Christian fellowship will naturally result.

NUMBERS III. AND IV.—In the first ten verses of this chapter Aaron and his priestly house are introduced, because the Levites were to be wholly given to him for the service of the Tabernacle. Their service in the Tabernacle was only of value as it was subject to Aaron, and executed in fellowship with him. Christians are wholly given to the Heavenly Priest, and their life is to be one of subjection to Him, and fellowship with Him. The Levite was redeemed by the blood of the Lamb ;   claimed absolutely by God as representing the first-born (vs. 12, 13) ;   and entirely given to Aaron for service (v. 9). Every Christian should make these three facts true in his own experience ; and remember that his service is only effective as it is rendered in fellowship with Jesus.

Levi by nature was self-willed, treacherous, and fierce ;   instruments of cruelty were in his habitation (Gen. xxxiv. xxxix). Because of his taking his stand on the Lord's side on the day of the golden calf, grace brought him into the habitation of God—though God could not enter his habitation—and placed the holy vessels of that Tabernacle in the very hands that once held the instruments of cruelty. He was then, in type, put to death in chapter viii, cleansed and anointed, and so appointed to his ministry. Thus, grace chose him, and holiness fitted him for service in the Tabernacle of Witness (see ch. viii.), so that he could say : To me to live is the Tabernacle !

The Levites were arranged in three divisions, Gershon, Kohath and Merari. The burden of the sons of Gershon is given in verses 25, 26 ; that of Kohath in verses 30, 31 ; that of Merari in verses 36, 37.

The ministry of Aaron and his sons is described in verse 38 as " keeping the burden of the sanctuary, even the burden of the children of Israel." (Compare 1 Tim. i. 18).

All the males of the Levites, according to verse 39, numbered 22,000, but if the numbers recorded in verses 22, 28, and 34 are added together, 22,300 results. This is supposed to be a mistake, but it is not so : for the 300 in question must represent the first-born of the Levites themselves, and being the first-born of their own tribe they could not become representatives of the first-born of other tribes.

The command to Moses and Aaron (ch. iv. 20) instructed them so to control the Kohathites, that they should not bring death upon themselves by looking upon the Ark.

The command implies that the guilt of their death would be charged to Moses and Aaron.

The next chapter omits noticing the laver as one of the vessels to be carried by the Kohathites. This is designed because the laver did not symbolize any personal or ministerial grace, peculiar to Christ, such as the other vessels of the sanctuary did.

The broken number in ch. iii. 43, in 2 Sam. xxiii. 39, and in John xxi. 11 attest how precious to God is the individual believer in every relationship.

Spiritual vigour is a necessity in Christian service (ch. iv. 3).

Only hands that were cleansed by the atoning blood and anointed by the holy oil could touch the symbolic vessels of the sanctuary. Aaron and his sons alone were so cleansed and anointed. This principle operates to-day in the handling of the Word of God (2 Cor. iv. 2, and 1 John i. 1).

The divine law of order should govern the life, the family, the business, and the church.

NUMBERS III. AND IV.—continued.— Grace entrusted the Levites with the Tabernacle and its vessels when on the march, and love apportioned to each the load suited to his strength. Thus it was that the heaviest portions of the sanctuary were given to the sons of Merari who numbered 3,200 (v. 44), whilst the lightest articles were given to the sons of Gershon, who only numbered 2,630 (v. 40). To everyone was given his service according to his burden (v. 49); so that whether the burden was one of the pins or one of the golden bowls of the tent of meeting, the bearer knew that grace honoured him, and love thought for him. Hence, it was a greater dignity to carry a pin of the Tabernacle than to wield the sceptre of Egypt !

The disposition of the coverings that hid the ark, the table, the lampstand, the altar of incense, the vessels of ministry and the brazen altar, set forth the sufferings of Christ and the glories that should follow. These coverings were : the veil of the Temple, badger-skins, and cloths of blue, scarlet, and purple. The outward covering in each case was badger-skin, except the Ark, i.e., the throne of Jehovah. Its outermost covering was a cloth of blue, to illustrate possibly the heavenly character of the kingdom which was proposed then to be set up upon earth ; and which will be introduced at the Second Advent. The other vessels, beauteous symbols of the nature and ministries of Christ Himself, were hidden externally by the same covering that was outmost upon the Tabernacle. Outwardly He had no beauty that men should desire Him (Isa. liii. 2).

Verse 20 reads thus in the R.V.: " They (the Kohathites) shall not go in to look on the holy things even for a moment, lest they die " (2 Sam. vi. 7). When God dwells in power in the camp it is as when a wire is charged with electricity. Hence, when He withdrew men could look on, and handle these holy things with impunity. The carnal curiosity which would analyse Christ's human nature brings death into the soul.

NUMBERS V.—Israel's shepherd having in this orderly way disposed this flock around Himself, was not unmindful of the physical and moral health of His sheep ; hence the legislation of this chapter. These are not repetitions of previous commandments but complementary statutes, mainly applicable to Israel when on their way through the Wilderness. It must have been an affecting sight to see this company of lepers marching parallel with the host, or behind it.

The sin of stealing (vs. 5-10) could easily be committed during a march continued from year to year. How wonderful the grace that spoke of it as " a trespass against Jehovah ! " The sentence " and that person be guilty " (v. 6) means : " becomes consciously convicted of their guilt." If no relative of the injured person were discoverable, then the stolen property, and the added fifth, was to be recompensed, i.e., handed back to the Lord i.e., to the priest.

The water of jealousy was a loving provision made by God for the protection of helpless women.

Sin whether passive (" leper "), active (" issue ") or relative (" dead ") defiled and therefore excluded from the camp because Jehovah was there (vs. 2 and 3). Such was the righteous function of law. When in grace He returned to the camp, He cleansed the leper, staunched the issue, and raised the dead, and thus removed all defilement (Luke v. 13 ; vii. 15 ; and viii. 44).

As the entrance into the faithless wife of the divinely-prepared test revealed in her body the corruption that was in her heart, so the entrance of Messiah into Jerusalem brought its evil to the surface. She was the unfaithful wife intended in this chapter. But, as in verses 1-4, so here grace contrasts with law, for the one sentenced to death (v. 31); the other ordains to life (Hos. ii. Rev. i. 5).

The earthen vessel containing the cleansing water of the laver, and the sacrificial dust from the foot of the brazen altar symbolized Messiah's prepared body (Heb. x. 5) indwelt by the Word of God (John i. 1, and xiii. 5), and brought into the dust of death (Ps. xxii. 15). He redeems by His blood; for His love is from everlasting to everlasting.

The record of Israel's shame and sin (v. 23) was blotted out in the bitter waters of Calvary (Col. ii. 14, and Isa. xliii. 25).

NUMBERS VI. AND VII.—Separation and Dedication are the key-notes of these chapters. They may be thus subdivided : Separation, chapter vi. 1-12 ; Humiliation, chapter vi. 13-21 ; Benediction, chapter vi. 22-27 ; Dedication, chapter vii. Thus these two chapters idealise the Spirit-filled life.

The word " Nazarite " means " a separated one." He drank no wine, he wore long hair, and he approached no dead person.

Wine symbolizes earthly joy and fictitious strength. The joy of the Lord and the filling of the Spirit are the strength of the true Nazarite.

Long hair is a shame to a man (1 Cor. xi). The meekness and gentleness of Christ compose the Christian's crown ; but to the natural man that meekness has the appearance of effeminacy, and is regarded with contempt. But it was when Samson's hair was cut that he began to be " afflicted " by a woman !

Natural affection was not to have the first claim in the life of separation to God, or even to interrupt it. A want of natural affection is to characterize the last days (2 Tim. iii. 3). It must have its place, but not His place !

Thus the Nazarite was, and is, an enigma to the children of this world. To be joyful, he withdrew from joy ; to be strong, he became weak ; and, in order to love his relatives, he " hated " them (Luke.xiv. 26) !

Contact with that which defiled determined this vow of consecration ; and so this life of separation had to be resumed afresh. In the Christian life it is impossible to live upon a past experience. Confession and reconsecration beneath the Cross of Jesus must be present realities (vs. 11, 12) if the joy and power of Nazariteship are to be spiritual facts.

This vow might be temporary, or for life. John the Baptist was a life, the apostle Paul a temporary Nazarite (Acts xviii. 18).

His vow observed faithfully to the end, the Nazarite was forbidden to boast of his goodness, but, on the contrary, reminded that he was a sinner, so great that four sacrifices were necessary to cover his sins ; and his long hair, which he might be tempted to keep as a proud memorial of his consecration, he had himself to throw into the fire to be burnt up !

In the midst of this life of Separation (ch. vi.) and Dedication (ch. vii) is placed the triple blessing of Father, Son and Holy Spirit. Verse 24, Jehovah the Father, the source of all blessing ; verse 25, Jehovah the Son, the channel of all blessing ; verse 26, Jehovah the Spirit, the imparter of all blessing.

Dedication gifts (ch. vii.) must follow, and not precede separation (ch. vi). Compare 2 Cor. viii. 5. But in both cases the cleansing sacrifice was needed to sanctify the gifts however sincere the self—or wealth—surrender (vi. 14 and vii. 16) ; otherwise they must be rejected, as were Cain's gifts.

The understanding love of iv. 24-33 is repeated in vii. 7 and 8. Outward service to Christ may need mechanical help, but the burdens of inward communion (Kohath) must be borne on the heart.

The human historian would compress the offerings of these princes into one verse—for they were all similar ; but to God they were so precious that they are minutely detailed and repeated. A corresponding affection appears in the names and actions recorded in 2 Sam. xxiii. and Rom. xvi. Christ loves His servants and so sees to it that countless millions through many centuries shall read of them. Thus little Benjamin and his gifts are given as much importance as great Judah and his offerings.

The last verse illustrates inspiration. The Voice that issued from the flame of the burning bush and from the flame of the mercy-seat and from the glory of Rev. i. 12 was the Voice that said, " Learn of Me " (Matt. xi. 29).

NUMBERS VIII.—The consecration of Levi is the subject of this chapter, and its doctrine is that the cleansing blood of Christ and the illumination of the Holy Spirit alone admit to the life of Christian service.

Read in connection with the third chapter,

three facts appear : His election, his equipment, and his appointment. Grace elected him, holiness equipped him, and love appointed him.

For notes on his election see chapter iii.

His consecration was sacrificial (v. 8), and it was practical (v. 7).

Three actions appear in each verse.

In verse 7 the water and ashes of the red heifer were sprinkled upon him (ch. xix.) ; all his flesh was shaved ; and, lastly he washed his clothing, and so made himself clean. These actions symbolize a purged conscience, a crucified will, and a cleansed life.

The Divine foundation for this practical cleansing appears in verse 8 : the burnt-offering, the sin-offering, and the meal-offering, i.e., the full atonement perfected at Calvary. There was no peace-offering ; for the subject here was not worship and fellowship, as in Leviticus, but the service and warfare of the Wilderness, as in Numbers (vs. 24, 25, 26. R.V. margin).

The service to which love appointed Levi was to carry the Tabernacle, and to serve it in the Wilderness.

Every Christian should be a Levite—elected, equipped, and appointed. Constrained by love he bears and exalts Christ in his life, and serves Him in His members, the spiritual temple.

The chapter opens with the Golden lampstand. Ministry to be acceptable, and effective, must be done in the light of the Holy Spirit.

NUMBERS IX.—The first fourteen verses of this chapter suggest the confession of the mouth ; the last nine the surrender of the will. Delivered from the power of the enemy by the blood of the lamb they yielded themselves to God to be led as He pleased.

The Scriptures record ten passovers ; of these, five are especially significant : Egypt (Ex. xii.) ; the Wilderness (Num. ix.) ; the Land (Joshua v.) ; the Reformation (2 Chron. xxxv.) ; and the Restoration (Ezra vi. 19).

Redemption by blood is the foundation of all Christian experience. It cleanses the conscience, restores the soul, and inspires the songs and feasts of Canaan. Never in this world, nor in that which is to come, will redeemed men reach a degree of holiness that will permit them to dispense with the precious blood of Christ.

The Paschal Lamb, i.e., Christ crucified (1 Cor. v. 7) met Israel in Egypt, accompanied her through the desert, planted her in the land, and, when she sinned restored her to its milk and honey.

The practical life of the wilderness necessitated the legislation of verses 6-14. Hence, this law is not found in Ex. xii. Hezekiah's obedience to this passage is a fine illustration of the subjection of his heart to the Word of God.

But the grace that permitted this condescension to wilderness weakness forbade any lowering of the standard of holiness ; and it is therefore significant the absence of detail in verse 3, and the fullness of detail in verses 11, 12, 13, Weakness in a church does not allow of any departure from the Word of the Lord, or the lowering of the standard of holy living.

The closing nine verses of the chapter give a lovely picture of true liberty, because of absolute dependence. God protected them by day and by night. He planned for them, He chose their camping ground, He decided when they were to march and when they were to rest. According to the Word of the Lord they journeyed, and according to the Word of the Lord they abode in their tents—whether it were by day or by night, or whether it were two days, or a month or a year. Thus Israel's shepherd led his flock by the hand of Moses and Aaron.

NUMBERS X.—The two silver trumpets illustrate the Old and New Testaments. They were made of one piece ; and their testimony to the host of Israel, however varied the message, was one. Their ministry was : First, to gather the people together around the Tabernacle ; and, Second, to set them in motion for Canaan.

The trumpets also sounded an alarm for war, and a joyful sound for Festival.

The sounding of the trumpets was the privilege of the sons of Aaron.

All Christian people should live as priests in nearness to God, and should use the Old and New Testaments to gather people around Jesus ; to set them in motion for Heaven ; and when on that journey, to acquaint them with the testimony of the Scriptures respecting warfare against evil, and the sufficiency of the grace provided in Christ for His members—pictured by the feasts of Jehovah—so that they may rejoice in the Lord alway.

2 Chron. xiii. records a faith that reposed upon verse 9 of this chapter ; and 2 Chron. xxix. a faith that recalled and obeyed verse 10.

Israel rested an entire year at Mount Sinai. The tender love which planned such rest after the excitement of the coming out of Egypt, and the march to Horeb, showed how real was the care and affection that God had for His ancient people.

The host of Israel, when on the march, formed a column of five divisions.

In the centre of this column marched Levi in three Divisions—the first two bearing the Tabernacle, the third, preceded by the camp of Reuben, carrying the vessels of the sanctuary. The first two divisions marched sufficiently ahead of the third division to enable them to have the Tabernacle pitched by the time that the Kohathites arrived with their burden.

The statement in verse 33 that the Ark went before them seems to conflict with verse 21 ; but uniting Ex. xiv. 19 with Num. ix. 18, and remembering that the Ark and the cloud were one, it is quite simple to understand that when the Tabernacle was taken down the cloud moved to the forefront of the host (v. 11) and so led them. Verse 33, therefore, might read thus : " And the cloud of the Ark, etc., went before them."

Hobab, Moses' brother-in-law the Kenite, foolishly refused to join the people of God. His descendants (1 Sam. xv. 6) nearly perished as the result of their ancestor's folly.

Thus Israel's shepherd did not tell His sheep to " go " through the great and terrible desert, but invited them to " come "—He was their travelling Companion.

If Hobab heard the testimony of the people, as given in the next chapter, it is not to be wondered at that he disbelieved Moses' enthusiastic words about the advantage of going with them to Canaan. Murmuring church members neutralize a minister's appeals to the undecided to enter the Christian life.

NUMBERS XI.—In verse 1 of this chapter the reader steps out of sunshine into darkness. Up to this point the love and wisdom of God fill the scene ; now man and his ingratitude and folly appear. Such is man's history. Placed in Eden, or in the renewed earth after the deluge, or in the miracle-filled Wilderness after Egypt, or in the land of milk and honey, or under a new covenant at Pentecost, or in the future millennial earth, he sins the moment he moves.

Chapter x. closes with a beautiful picture of the tender love of Jehovah going out before them an easy three days journey in the Wilderness to search out a resting-place for them, and chapter xi. opens with the murmurs of the people complaining of the fatigue of the journey and the discomfort of the resting place ! The result was death ; for murmuring means unbelief, and unbelief always occasions spiritual death ; and further, the companionship of God is death to a man except he be " born from above."

It only needed the test of the Wilderness to make visible the incurable unbelief and ignorance of their heart. Forgetting the lash of the taskmaster, they recall the perishing bread of Egypt and turn away with loathing from the manna ! To a heart not in communion with God, Christ, the true manna, becomes distasteful, and nourishment is sought in " the world " which holds in bondage those who go down to it.

The " mixed multitude that was among them " (v. 4) originated this lusting after Egypt ; so was it in apostolic days (Gal. ii. 4, and Jude 4). " Mixed " companionship and " mixed " principles lead the Christian into weakness and sin.

Unbelief and discontent are terribly contagious. Moses adds to the gloom of this chapter ; verses 10-15 record his impatience, and verses 21-23, his unbelief. Like Elijah, he petulantly calls upon God to kill him out of hand ! (v. 15). And yet these two men appeared with the God of glory upon the Mount of Transfiguration ! A pitying grace relieved him of the weight of his charge, whilst upbraiding him. But Moses was, in truth, no whit less burdened, for the spiritual power granted to the 70 elders was taken from him (v. 17).

The meekness of Moses in wishing that all were prophets (v. 29) and in getting into the camp (v. 30), no doubt to listen to the prophesying of Eldad and Medad, is very lovely.

How living is the interest of these records when it is remembered that Moses himself wrote these sad facts of his own weakness and sin !

Egypt's table contained six dishes (v. 5), Canaan's, seven (Deut. viii. 8).

The murmurers of Ex. xiv. 11 were not consumed with fire, as were those of this chapter ; because at that time Israel was not under Law but under grace.

The quails were not piled upon the ground to a height of two cubits (v. 31), but they flew at that height ; and so were easily captured.

Israel desired God's gifts but had no heart for the Giver. To accept the gifts of that bountiful Hand, and to seek to enjoy them independently of It, brings death into the soul.

" My wretchedness " (v. 15), i.e., the misery of my people.

Israel worshipped in Egypt the great god of the Egyptians (Joshua xxiv. 14, Acts vii. 42, 43). This suggests that they declared that he treated them better (v. 5) than Jehovah did ; and, further, that that god, and not Jehovah, sent the quails. If this be so, then the repeated judgment (v. 1 and 33) is made more solemn.

NUMBERS XII.—In this chapter the darkness continues and deepens. In the prior chapter the people murmured, and Moses murmured ; now Miriam murmurs, and Aaron murmurs. When people are annoyed they quickly find a cause of complaint ; but in such circumstances it is never just.

Verse 10, and her name coming first in verse 1, make it clear that Miriam led in this rebellion.

The Ethiopian, i.e., Cushite wife, was Zipporah. The Bible forbidding marriage with a Gentile (Gen. xxiv. 3), Miriam had apparently a just ground for condemning Moses.

But she forgot that God, in grace, reserved freedom of action to Himself ; and had, therefore, revealed to Abraham His purpose of uniting all nations to him and blessing them.

Moses' action was dispensational and prophetic. Rejected by his brethren he turned in grace to the Gentile ; and then, as king in Jeshurun, brought her into the family of Israel. Such is, and will be, the gracious purpose of Messiah the Lord God of Israel.

Miriam's exclusion for seven days pictures the present position of the nation.

But it is most probable that Moses in listening to the advice of his father-in-law Jethro with respect to the seventy magistrates, and in proposing a chieftainship to his brother-in-law Hobab, originated this outbreak on the part of Miriam and Aaron. They

were being overlooked, and Moses' wife's family unduly considered. It was a family quarrel. Had Moses waited only upon God this cause of dissension would not have been furnished to his brother and sister. It is a serious thing for a Christian to be influenced by human wisdom, for he not only makes mistakes himself, but he provides stumbling-blocks for others.

And thus the onward march of the church of God was delayed for a whole week because one woman objected to the person whom her brother married.

It is an instructive light upon the nature of inspiration to picture Moses declaring himself, in verse 3, to be the meekest man in the earth ; just as he had recorded himself in chapter xi. 21–23, as the greatest sceptic in the camp.

" The form of Jehovah shall he behold " (v. 8 R.V.). (Compare Col. i. 15). This prophecy was fulfilled on the Mount of Transfiguration. Prior to that he, and others, saw Jehovah in angelic form.

Miriam and Aaron, as prophetess and priest, rebelled against Moses who was " faithful in all God's house " (Heb. iii. 2). They ought to have been afraid to do so. Such was Israel's action as prophetess and priest to Christ as Son over His own house ; and therefore is she smitten with leprosy. The intercession of the Divine Mediator will, however, secure her future restoration. See notes on 2 Sam. vi.

NUMBERS XIII. AND XIV.—The new Biblical Guide (Urquhart) throws most interesting light upon these two chapters.

The chapters continue the sad story of unbelief, idolatry (ch. xiv. 33 with Lev. xvii. 7), and rebellion.

Deut. i. 19–22 shows that the command to send out the spies was given in response to the people's request. They also asked for and got the quails, the Law and a King. Had they let God plan for them how different would have been their history !

Deut. viii. 7–9 declared that God had spied out the land for them. Had they believed this they would never have made the request of Deut. i. 22.

The ten spies walked by sight and not by faith (" we saw ") (vs. 28, 32, 33). Caleb and Joshua walked by faith and not by sight, saying, " Jehovah, He will bring us into this land " (ch. xiv. 8).

Unbelief and folly and falsehood are bound up together. In chapter xiii. 27 they declared that the land flowed with milk and honey, and in verse 32 that it ate up the inhabitants thereof! And in verse 33 they reported that they were in the sight of the Anakim as grasshoppers! How did they know that?

At the Red Sea they lifted up their voice and sang; but at Kadesh-barnea they lifted it up to weep. Then they had their eye upon God, and so faith sang; here they looked at the giants, and so unbelief wept.

God is now blamed (ch. xiv. 3) whereas before they had only blamed Moses.

At Horeb they said, " let us make a calf," here, " let us make a captain " (ch. xiv. 4). The calf was made because it had brought them out of the land of Egypt; the captain was to be made in order to lead them back to Egypt!

Faith and truth are never popular (ch. xiv. 10).

Moses' renunciation of self accords with that of the Apostle Paul. They are the two greatest and noblest men in the Bible.

The prayer of Moses (ch. xiv. 13-19) reveals love for the Name of Jehovah and love for guilty sinners. His plea that these should be forgiven was based upon the power of God and the greatness of His mercy. Compare Ps. xxv. 11, where the argument for pardon is not the smallness but the greatness of the iniquity.

Grace forgave the sin but Government caused their carcases to fall in the Wilderness. The one forgives, the other fore-dooms. Gal. vi. 7.

The ten temptations of chapter xiv. 22 were:

Red Sea	Exodus xiv.
Marah	Exodus xv.
Sin	Exodus xvi.
The Manna	Exodus xvi. 20.
The Manna	Exodus xvi. 27.
Rephidim	Exodus xvii.
Horeb	Exodus xxxii.
Taberah	Numbers xi.
Kibroth	Numbers xi.
Kadesh	Numbers xiv.

Chapter xiv. 39-45 illustrate the presumption of the natural heart, just as the closing verses of chapter xiii. illustrate its cowardice. The carnal mind (Rom. viii.) cannot serve God; it is timid when it should be bold, and bold when it should be timid. It advances when it should stand still; and it stands still when it should advance

NUMBERS XV.—The holy God who said, " Surely they shall not see the land " (ch. xiv. 23) was the gracious God who said, " when ye be come into the land " (ch. xv. 2). Thus was the earth to be filled with the glory of His severity and the glory of His goodness!

In spite of human sin and weakness, God's counsels of glory and of grace have, and shall have, their accomplishment. Here, therefore, He speaks of Israel's possession of the Promised Land; of the offerings of righteousness which they would then voluntarily bring; of the wine of joy which was to accompany those offerings (vs. 3-12); and, grace being the foundation of all this felicity, the Gentile (vs. 13-16) is made a sharer in the great salvation. One sacrifice was to be for the congregation, and also for the stranger (v. 15); and so Christ offered up Himself, not only to redeem Israel, but also to save the world.

Verses 17-21 taught the people that the bread that came up out of the ground for their nutriment was as great a miracle as the bread that came down from heaven; and hence the perpetual heave-offering of verse 21 acknowledged that Jehovah not only gave them the land but also was the Creator of the " bread of the land " (v. 19).

Verses 22-28 provided the sweet-savour-offering for the sin of omission, i.e., ignorance, whether committed by the people, or by an individual. The burnt-offering, and the sin-offering, and the meal-offering, and the drink-offering typified the infinite sacrifice of the Lamb of God as being necessary to cover even so small a sin as the sin of omission.

But for a presumptuous sin there was no atonement; and therefore the Sabbath-breaker (v. 32) was destroyed from out of the congregation.

He was put in ward till it was made known what should be done to him, i.e., how he was to be put to death; for Ex. xxxi. 15 had already commanded that he should be put to death.

The commandment of the closing verses of the chapter made it visible to Israel that they were a heavenly people, and that this great fact should especially be present to their hearts when necessarily coming in closest touch with the earth. This Divine institution was speedily degraded (Matt. xxiii. 5).

Provision was made for the sin of ignorance in connection with obedience to the Word of the Lord, but there was no offering commanded for the sin of indifference. That sin is very visible to-day in Christendom. Human opinion is set above Divine injunction.

NUMBERS XVI.—The sad story of man and his ways—interrupted by chapter xv.—is now resumed. It is a humbling story, for it reveals what human nature is ; and it is instructive, for it reveals what God is.

Korah was first cousin to Moses and Aaron (1 Chron. vi. 2, 3). He was encamped close to Reuben ; and hence their association in this rebellion.

God chose Aaron to be high Priest. Korah " gainsayed " that. The princes of Reuben attacked the kingship given to Moses by God.

The spirit therefore of the rebellion was to cast down the Blessed One—Christ—whom God has appointed both King and Priest. The apostle Jude speaks of the continuous energy of this hatred of man's heart against the Lord and against His Christ.

Moses fell on his face, that is, he stepped aside so that the rebels should stand face to face with God. Christian workers, when unjustly attacked by fellow-workers, should act similarly.

Moses did not attempt to defend himself and Aaron. He left all to the judgment of God. That judgment was terrible. Fire came out from the Tabernacle and destroyed the two hundred and fifty princes, at the same time that the earth opened her mouth and swallowed all that appertained to them.

As to the rest of the congregation, who in heart sympathized with the rebellion (v. 41), the very priesthood that they sought to destroy saved them (vs. 47, 48).

To bring a sinning people through a wilderness, a Divine Priest is necessary. Of Him Aaron was a type.

NUMBERS XVII. 1-11.—Christ is God's High Priest. In Him is life, beauty, perfume, health, and food. These were pictured by the buds, the blossoms, and the almonds on Aaron's rod. None of these are found in a priest made by man.

Each rod of the twelve bore a mighty name. Through the night in which they lay hidden within the Tabernacle the sons of Israel might have expressed confidence in such and such a name, as to-day members of the Greek and Roman churches repose confidence in the names of Mary, Peter, Paul, etc. But in the morning all the rods were found to be dead sticks, notwithstanding the names they bore, except the rod of Aaron. It, alone, was living, beauteous and accepted.

All through the Wilderness journey that rod of grace was ever before the Lord. Heb. ix. recalls that it and the Manna accompanied Israel in the Tabernacle through the Wilderness.

That was the rod that Moses was told to take and, holding it in his hand, to " speak to the rock." Alas, he smote the rock (see notes on chapter xx. 8).

This living Rod is Jesus. Those who trust Him, and Him alone, will be safely brought through the Wilderness of this world to the heavenly Canaan.

The brazen plates (xvi. 39 and 40) without the Tabernacle, and the budded rod within, taught the double lesson that certain death awaited those who presumed to approach God in their own person, but certain life those who drew near through the accepted person, and precious blood of the Great High Priest.

NUMBERS XVII. 12—XVIII. 32.—Man understands neither holiness nor grace. In chapter xvi. 3 the people claimed the right to enter the Tabernacle because all the congregation was holy. In chapter xvii. 12, 13, they cried out for the suppression of the Tabernacle because it was an agent of death to them ! The flesh presumes where it ought to retire, and distrusts where it ought to confide.

God's gracious answer to this pride and folly was, in type, to reveal still more of the glory and power of the High-Priesthood of Christ. In response to the cry of alarm, " shall we be consumed with dying ? " God answered, Aaron shall bear the iniquity of the sanctuary that there be no wrath any more upon the children of Israel. Thus they found security in that very priest whom they despised and rejected.

The first nineteen verses of chapter xviii concern priesthood ; the remaining, ministry.

Aaron and his sons were to make the sins of the people so truly their own that they were to eat the sin-offerings, as already commanded in Leviticus. The Levites also in doing the service of the Tabernacle were to bear the iniquity of the congregation (v. 23).

The true Priest and Levite, Jesus Christ, alone satisfies the requirements of this chapter.

The love that appointed this ministry provided for its maintenance by granting to it all the best of the oil, and all the best of the wine, and of the wheat.

NUMBERS XIX.—This chapter being found in Numbers and not in Leviticus shows inspiration. Had this sacrifice of the red heifer been invented by Jewish priests, as some affirm, they would have placed it in the Book of Leviticus.

The sacrifices of Leviticus concerned worship. This provision for sin in Numbers was made for pilgrimage, and therefore the Holy Spirit places it in this book.

The chapter contains four sections :

1st   The purge provided.
2nd The persons to be purged.
3rd   The mode of application.
4th   The warning.

The heifer symbolized Christ. It was spotless externally and without blemish internally. It was free from any bondage whatever. It was a female, and it was red Christ in His humanity was spotless within and without ; He was gentle as a woman ; He was never in bondage to any sin ; the Law had no claim upon Him as a debtor ; and He robed Himself with the red earth of manhood.

Eleazar led the heifer forth without the camp ; and there was she slain. So was Christ led of the Spirit to Calvary, where He offered up Himself.

It does not say that Eleazar was to slay the heifer, it simply provided that the heifer must die if sin was to be purged.

The creation, represented by cedar wood, hyssop, and scarlet, shall be redeemed ; but, being defiled, it must first be judged (v. 6).

The blood of the heifer is only once mentioned in the chapter (vs. 4, 5). So Christ was once offered. It needed not that the heifer should be re-slain—its ashes sufficed.

Purification from the defilements unavoidable during pilgrimage was effected by an application of the ashes of the burnt heifer with running, i.e., living water. Christ's death need not be repeated, as the sacerdotalists teach, in order to the forgiveness of the daily sins of the celestial pilgrim. It only needs that the meaning and perfection of His death, typified by the burnt ashes, should be effectively applied to the conscience by the living Spirit, symbolized by the running water, and the sense of forgiveness and cleansing is enjoyed.

The last twelve verses reveal the malignity of sin, and its enduring contagion and defilement. Accidentally touching a bone, even though it were a thousand years old, defiled and procured exclusion from the camp. Restoration was only possible after an application of the ashes of the heifer on the third day and on the seventh day. The three days prior to the first purging fastened on the conscience the hatefulness of sin to God ; the four days prior to the second and final application of the ashes and running water, instructed the conscience as to the perfection of the purge and the wonders of the grace that provided it.

Possibly the third day pointed to the resurrection of Christ ; the seventh day to His return in glory. During the first period only an imperfect sense of the fulness of His sacrifice is possible ; but in the coming glorious seventh day there will be a perfected consciousness of this fulness.

But to enjoy this perfect salvation on the seventh day it must be appropriated on the third (v. 12).

" At even " (v. 19) the defiled person was pronounced clean. The preciousness of Christ's atoning blood, and its sufficiency to cleanse from all sin, speak with special sweetness to the heart and conscience at even, when life is closing and the shadows of death are about to fall.

The presence of death in a house defiled everything in the house, except a covered vessel. The Christian pilgrim necessarily comes in contact with " death " every day, i.e., with that which defiles, but he escapes defilement if he is a " covered vessel," that is, if he lives under the covering of the Holy Spirit.

The warning, duplicated in verses 13 and 20, predicts the doom of those who deny the need of Christ's atoning death.

These commands were opposed to the Egyptian customs respecting the dead. They struck at idolatry and superstition ; and, at the same time, established an admirable sanitary law.

NUMBERS XX-XXI. 3.—The first month in verse 1 was the first month of the fortieth year after they had come out of Egypt (v. 28 with chapter xxxiii. 38 and Deut. ii. 1-7). There is a blank of nearly thirty-eight years between the occurrences of this chapter and the mission of the spies. It is important to notice this.; for it is the new generation that now chides with Moses.

It did seem strange that a God who professed to love them should bring them into an " evil place " (v. 5) ; but He brought them there because He loved them, and because only there, and neither in Egypt nor in Canaan, could He reveal to them the inexhaustible resources treasured in His hand for them.

They thirsted for water. Close at hand was a rock. They judged of God as they judged of that rock ; they deemed Him to be as insensible as it to their need. They thought that God, like that rock, had neither eyes to see their misery, ears to hear their cry, a heart to pity them, nor resources to relieve them. But the message came : " Speak to the rock " ; and when the rock was appealed to the response was immediate and overflowing.

Thus were they taught that they were not to judge God by the natural sense as they judged that rock.

The first resource of nature is to murmur against God (v. 3-5) ; the first resource of faith is to hasten to God (v. 6).

This rod was not the rod of God's wrath that smote Egypt and the first rock at the first Meribah. This was Aaron's rod (v. 9), the rod of priesthood and not of judgment. Nor was this rock to be smitten, but to be spoken to. Alas, Moses did not speak to the rock, he spoke to the people—unadvisedly— and he struck the rock. But where sin abounded grace did much more abound ; and the rock gave forth its water abundantly. Judgment, however, fell upon Moses ; he was forbidden to lead the people into the promised land. It is the priesthood of Christ that brings His people through the Wilderness and into Canaan. This is the argument of the Epistle to the Hebrews.

Miriam and Aaron both die in this fortieth year ; she preceding him by about four months.

It affects the heart to picture the farewell of Moses and Aaron upon Mount Hor. Better would it have been for Moses in Exodus iv., and better would it have been for Aaron, if they had let God plan for them.

The correspondence between Israel and Edom shows the gentleness of the one and the hatred of the other. Just as God would not let Esau injure Jacob, so now He forbade Jacob to injure Esau (Deut. ii. 4, 5).

The violence of the Canaanite quickly followed upon the suffering caused by thirst (ch. xx. 2) and the sorrow occasioned by the death of Miriam and Aaron (ch. xxi. 1-3). But trial and sorrow temper the soul to a whole-hearted consecration, and so victory was granted to Israel.

NUMBERS XXI. 4-35.—The four words : Salvation, Pilgrimage, Refreshment, and Victory outline the facts of this chapter.

Salvation engages verses 4-9 ; Pilgrimage, verses 10-15 and 19, 20 ; Refreshment, verses 16-18 ; and Victory, verses 21-35.

To help Nicodemus to understand the way of salvation, the Lord used the first section of this chapter.

Only living men can be pilgrims. Directly Israel obtained life by a look, they journeyed. The words "they journeyed," "they pitched" (R.V.) set out this life of pilgrimage. It was in truth a delightsome life of liberty and freedom from care. Each evening they pitched their moving tents a day's march nearer home.

Men of the world think the pilgrim path to heaven devoid of happiness. They err. Right in the midst of this pilgrim way is the well whereof Jehovah spake—an unseen well. This well symbolizes Jesus and the inexhaustible and satisfying treasures of joy and strength found in Him.

The scene pictured in verses 16, 17, 18, illustrates faith. At God's command the people form an immense circle upon the dry sand. The nobles, by direction of the lawgiver, dig in the sand with their pilgrim staves. It was contrary to reason to expect water in a sand-heap ; and foolish to attempt to dig a well in sand with sticks. Meanwhile the people sing of the well which apparently does not exist and which they cannot see ! But they believed the promise : " Gather the people together and I will give them water " ; and therefore they digged, and sang, and the hidden refreshment was opened to them.

Strengthened by the waters of this hidden well Israel entered upon a life of continuous victory. Sihon, himself a victor, fell before these celestial pilgrims. Then the Amorites were driven out ; and, finally, Og, the king of Bashan, and his people were destroyed until there were none left alive. They had been given four hundred years in which to repent (Gen. xv. 16), but in vain. And God in His love to the human family ordained the total destruction of these unspeakably depraved people.

Men condemn the God of the Bible because He commanded the slaughter of children ; but the Christian cleaves to Him all the more because of that command. A right-minded father, who loved his children, would refuse admission to their table to a little child afflicted with a deadly and contagious disease just as sternly as to a man or a woman suffering from the same disease ; and the knowledge that all three had been by him shut out would lead his children to love and trust him all the more.

The men represent coarse sins ; the women, pretty sins ; the children, innocent sins. Sin cannot be improved ; there is but one way of dealing with it, and that is death. These three sins appear in the temptation of Eve. " She saw that the tree was good for food," that is, the gross sin ; that " it was pleasant to the eyes," that is, the pretty sin ; and that " it was desirable to make one wise," that is, the innocent sin.

Similarly was the Lord tempted. " Make these stones bread " ; " All this glory will I give thee " ; and, " Come suddenly to thy Temple " as predicted by Malachi. But Jesus slew these three sins with the sword of the Spirit.

NUMBERS XXII.—The Holy Spirit in the Epistles of Jude and 2 Peter says that Balaam loved money. He loved it so much that he was willing for its sake to place his prophetic gift at the disposition of Satan in order to curse those whom God had blessed.

It is one of the great mysteries of the Bible, that a gift of prophecy can be possessed apart from moral character.

Balaam uttered four prophecies concerning Israel. Four words express their import : Separation, Justification, Sanctification, Exaltation.

When beneath the language of piety the heart is set on evil, it only needs a very little test to expose the evil. God said to Balaam " If the men come to call thee, rise up, and go with them " (v. 20). Balaam did not wait for the men to call him ; and hence God's anger ; and his action shows he was determined to go whether or not.

The angel of Jehovah with a sword in his hand (v. 23) was also seen by David (1 Chron. xxi. 16).

Balaam desired by enchantments to turn that sword against Israel, but he found it turned against himself. Jehovah opened the mouth of the ass (v. 28), and the eyes of the prophet (v. 31). The latter was more difficult than the former.

Self-will refuses to be instructed by circumstances, but a will yielded to God is careful to observe them. Three times Balaam refused to learn from the animal on which he rode ; and so blinded was he by the love of money that the dumb beast, speaking with man's voice, failed to make him hesitate.

To-day, as on that day, disobeying God degrades man below the brute beast.

Pharaoh, Balaam, Achan, Saul, David and Judas, said respectively, " I have sinned " ; but only David said this sincerely.

NUMBERS XXIII.—" And Jehovah put a message in Balaam's mouth " (v. 5). This is inspiration. The word " defy " in verses 7 and 8 means " be wrath against " (see R.V.).

The doctrine of Balaam's first parable is that of Rom. ix. x. xi. It is that God had chosen, and numbered, and separated, and blessed the children of Israel.

This is the unshakeable foundation of God's eternal salvation. It defeats Satan ; for how can he destroy a people whom God has chosen, not because of their merit, but because He has thus willed ?

To " die the death of the righteous " (v. 10), and to receive his " last end," that is, his reward, the righteousness of the righteous must be possessed. That righteousness is a spotless, i.e., a Divine righteousness. Balaam meant that God would be to blame if he did not so die. (See note on Luke xiv. 15, and Gen. iv. 23).

A nation or an individual may not be as admirable upon one side of their character as upon another. Balak brought Balaam to where he had another view of the camp of Israel. But it was useless to do so ; for Israel, as the Divine election, was accepted before God in Christ ; and no matter from what point of view Christ is viewed, nought meets the eye but perfection.

This great foundation truth of the Gospel appears in Balaam's second parable. Neither iniquity in Jacob, nor perverseness in Israel were visible to the Divine eye because that eye rested on the perfections of Him in whom Israel was chosen. Who could lay anything to the charge of those whom God justified, i.e., declared righteous ?

Verses 18-21 express God's immutable purposes, and verses 22-24, Israel's immutable privileges.

NUMBERS XXIV.—Verse 1 of this chapter shows that the prophet in his " madness " was willing to listen to the voice of the devil, though unwilling to listen to the voice of the ass. The corruption, depravity, and rebellion of man's will is fearfully and mysteriously illustrated in Balaam. Even at the time of being consciously subject to the afflatus of the Holy Spirit, in his thirst for money he sought by enchantments to become inspired of an Unclean Spirit. So knowledge of spiritual things is not spiritual knowledge.

The word " open " in verse 3 reads " closed " in the R.V. It means both—closed physically, but open spiritually ; that is, in a trance, or ecstasy ; as suggested by the italics in verse 4.

This third vision under the similitude of gardens, valleys, trees, water-springs, and further, unicorns and lions, pictures Israel as Jehovah's consecrated servant adorned with spiritual graces, strengthened with all might, and enriching all nations with " water poured out of his buckets " (v. 7). These predictions will be fulfilled in the millennium.

Compare the " latter days " and the " last days" of the Apostle Paul's letters to Timothy with the " latter days " of verse 14.

In the fourth parable the Messiah Himself appears as the " Star " and " Sceptre " (v. 17) : His should be the dominion (v. 19). Israel redeemed by Him should do valiantly ; and all His, and their enemies be destroyed (vs. 17, 18, 19).

Total destruction awaited Amalek " the first of the nations " that opposed Israel (v. 20) ; and the Assyrian should carry the Kenite into captivity ; and this occasions the question, who shall live when God establisheth him ? i.e., the Assyrian ; for he would leave none alive (vs. 21-23).

But the Greeks and the Romans would come and humble Assyria and the Hebrews ; but he, i.e., the last Roman monarch, the Anti-Christ who sent these ships should perish for ever.

NUMBERS XXV.—The three prior chapters concerned Israel's " standing " ; this chapter revealed her " state."

In those chapters the reader viewed Israel from the top of Pisgah, and listened to God's testimony concerning her, and his purposes for her—and this testimony was given while yet she was in the Wilderness (ch xxi . 1) Viewed from Pisgah all was perfection because all was Divine ; and repeated efforts to curse only gave occasion for the revelation of fresh glories.

But in this chapter the standpoint is the plain, and all is changed   Their imperfections become painfully apparent. The opening and closing of 2 Cor. xii. present a similar contrast between the perfection of God's people as to their standing in Christ, and the imperfection of their state as to their conduct in the Wilderness. Balaam's parables give God's estimate of the former ; the javelin of Phinehas His judgment upon the latter.

The Wilderness journey was now over, and the people abode in Shittim till after the death of Moses and until the passage of the Jordan (v. 1).

The judgment of this chapter was brought about by the cunning of Balaam (ch. xxxi. 16, Rev. ii. 14).

The deadly subtilty of Balaam's teaching is evidenced by his being mentioned ten times in the Bible, outside of these chapters.

As to-day in parts of India, so at that day women were dedicated to the national idol ; and sexual intercourse with them was, by the cunning of Satan, as an angel of light, consecrated as the highest action of religious worship. These are the women spoken of in verses 1 and 2.

It opened the way for actual marriage as in verse 6, for when Satan fails in a religious attack (xxii.–xxiv.) he often succeeds through a worldly marriage.

Twenty-four thousand died in the plague (v. 9). 1 Cor. x. 8, says 23,000 : the added words, " in one day " remove the difficulty. Those slain, verses 4, 5, doubtless numbered 1,000.

NUMBERS XXVI.—Their pilgrimage ended, Israel was now about to enter the Promised Land. The remaining chapters of this book are occupied therefore with matters proper to that great event : and accordingly in this chapter God numbers afresh His people, and counts them by name as heirs ready to take possession of the inheritance.

" But among these there was not a man of them whom Moses numbered in the Wilderness of Sinai, save Caleb the son of

Jepnunneh and Joshua the son of Nun "
(vs. 64, 65).

The Holy Spirit in Heb. iii. and iv. states
that these perished because the word preached
did not profit them for they were not united
with the faith of those who did hear, i.e.,
Caleb and Joshua.

Effectual salvation results from believing
the Word of God. Listening to the Gospel
avails nothing. Power to realize salvation,
to overcome sin, to grow in grace comes as
the Word of God is grasped by faith. Faith
takes possession of all that God offers.

A comparison of this census with that of
chapter i. shows that some tribes increased
while others decreased. The details of this
comparison will be found in the " Companion
Bible."

Reuben (v. 7), as predicted in Gen. xlix. 4,
shows a decrease of 2730. This is one of the
many undesigned evidences in the Bible
of inspiration.

The children of Korah did not perish
with their father. Their descendants were
prominent in Solomon's Temple. Samuel
and Heman were of them ; and two groups of
Psalms are associated with them—xlii–xlix
and lxxxiv–lxxxviii.

The total decrease was 1820. In Egypt
they multiplied exceedingly; in the Wilderness they decreased.

NUMBERS XXVII.—The faith of the
daughters of Zelophehad presents a striking
contrast to the unbelief of those who fell in
the desert. While yet in the Wilderness they
claimed by faith the unseen fields of Canaan ;
and, further, their faith leaped a barrier
which both nature and Law set before them.

This was precious and refreshing to the
heart of God ; and, accordingly, special legislation was given to meet their faith. This
new law secured the marriage of Mary with
her cousin Joseph ; and, accordingly, her
Child, legally adopted by Joseph, was, and
is, the only lawful king and possessor of
Canaan.

The names of these daughters of faith are
for ever inscribed by the Holy Spirit. See
Josh. xvii. 3. See chapter xxxvi, where they
were commanded to marry their cousins so that
the land-marks which guarded the inheritance
of their fathers should not be removed. Here
is a great principle. A vigorous faith must not
override the claims of others, but wait upon
God for direction in all cases where that faith,

in its activities, might, if undisciplined,
impoverish relatives or neighbours.

The Divine faith that enabled these noble
women to claim the promised land, enabled
Moses to accept exclusion from it ; and, with
exquisite meekness, to stand aside and let
another, and a younger man, lead the hosts
of Jehovah over Jordan.

Base as was his conduct toward him, he
loved the people to the end (vs. 15, 16, 17).
He was permitted to see the goodly land, on
one of whose mountains, the Mount of
Transfiguration, he was later on to stand
with the God of Israel.

NUMBERS XXVIII., XXIX.—These two
chapters are not mere repetitions of Lev.
xxiii.

The doctrine of these offerings and those
of Leviticus is the same, i.e. life and righteousness through an atoning Saviour : and that
doctrine was as fresh and as precious to
Moses at the close as at the beginning of his
ministry.

The sacrifices in Leviticus mainly provided
for the life of the Wilderness ; these in
Numbers for that of the Promised Land.

The Levitical sacrifices rather set out, in
type, the results of Christ's atonement in the
blessing of sinners ; the offerings of these
two chapters direct attention to the glory
and perfection of Him who accomplished the
atonement.

But it will be noted throughout these two
chapters that no matter what the day or
feast, when in Canaan, the sin-offering was
never to be omitted ; for no spiritual attainment negatives the need of the atoning
death of Christ.

The possession of Canaan, with these
offerings as a testimony to the sufficiency
of the Redeemer who brought Israel there,
point forward to the coming Millennium.

Thus the great lesson is taught that
salvation from Egypt, maintenance in the
Desert, and rest in the Promised Land are
based upon the precious blood of Christ ;
and that the glory of the coming Millennium
will not obscure this doctrine, but, on the
contrary, double it (v. 9).

In these commands, therefore, the Spirit
of God pointed the Israelites to the rest into
which they were about to enter, and
instructed them as to the testimony to Christ
which they were to set up publicly, and
sustain, when placed therein.

The character of these two chapters is, therefore, millennial, and foreshadows the rest and joy which God will then publicly find in His Dearly Beloved Son. Hence the language of verse 2, " My offering," " My bread," " My sacrifices," " offered unto Me," as a " sweet savour unto Me."

There are 71 verses in this section ; thirteen concern the sin-offering—it is never absent—and fifty-eight the sweet savour offerings. The special theme, therefore, is God's delight in Christ publicly to be made known in Christ's coming earthly kingdom.

The offerings commanded in this section to be observed in the land were : Daily, Weekly, Monthly and Yearly.

The yearly feasts were to be Passover, Pentecost and Tabernacles, with their related feasts of Unleavened Bread, Trumpets and Great Day of Atonement.

The Sabbath offering was doubled, as already pointed out, because when the true Sabbath dawns its light will double the glory of Calvary's cross.

Thus day by day, week by week, month by month and year by year there was to be a national and unbroken testimony to the preciousness of Christ as God's beloved Son in whom His soul delighted ; and a confession that their possession of that land, and its milk and honey, was wholly due to the preciousness of the blood shed by that Saviour for the remission of their sins.

Upon the first day of the Feast of Tabernacles (ch. xxix. 12) thirteen bullocks were to be offered by fire as a sweet savour, and on each of the following days of the feast one bullock less, until, on the seventh day, seven bullocks were to be offered, whilst on the eighth day but one bullock. On these seven days fourteen lambs, two rams, and one kid, for a sin-offering were to be daily sacrificed ; but on the eighth day but one ram, seven lambs and the sin-offering.

Why thirteen bullocks, and not fourteen, on the first day ? and why only one on the eighth day ? Perhaps because the first seven days foreshadowed the imperfect knowledge of the Millennium—the number thirteen suggesting imperfection—whilst the " eighth day " points forward to the perfect day. But through the seven days there were always the fourteen lambs, the two rams, and the sin-offering. In Christ's work is no imperfection.

NUMBERS XXX.—A vow made by a man was irrevocable ; but that made by a woman could be disallowed by her father, or husband.

But a husband, having by silence confirmed a vow made by his wife, and yet wishing to release her from it, could only do so by bearing her iniquity, i.e., the punishment occasioned by it (v. 15).

Such was the law. There was no relief for the man ; hence when the Man Christ Jesus said, " I will pay my vows unto Jehovah," and, " I delight to do Thy will Oh my God," there was no release for Him. The bitter cup of Gethsemane had to be drained.

There was release for a woman, but she could not effect it herself ; only one that was related to her, and that loved her, could do so. Such was Israel. She vowed at Sinai to perform all that Jehovah commanded. Her Divine Bridegroom and Husband permitted the vow ; but she, having failed to keep it, came, therefore, under sentence of death. To redeem her from this doom, her Husband, in grace, took it upon Himself (v. 15), and so delivered her from her vow. She could not deliver herself.

Thus in these statutes and commandments Christ is found everywhere ; His sufficiency is revealed, and man's sinfulness and inability to save himself declared.

NUMBERS XXXI.—The sin of chapter xxv. occasioned this war. Christians make wars for themselves by forming fellowships with the world. The warfare to which they are called is that of Ephesians vi ; and their wisdom, and their obedience, is to pass through this world as strangers and pilgrims, having no relations whatever, except those of Gospel testimony and natural sympathy with those whom they must necessarily meet as they journey. War was to characterize Canaan ; faith and patience, the Wilderness.

However, if, because of that forbidden union, war results, God gives a complete victory ; provided that which seduced be utterly destroyed.

God said : " Avenge the children of Israel of the Midianites," and Moses said : " Avenge Jehovah of Midian," i.e., execute the vengeance of Jehovah upon Midian. These are remarkable sentences. Israel was to be Jehovah's instrument of vengeance upon Midian ; but Israel was to be a willing instrument, and thus clear herself thoroughly from all the defilement, which by her disobedience, she had contracted. Nothing was to be excused, nothing spared, and all the spoil passed through the fire, or purified with the water and ashes of the red heifer (ch. xix).

All Israel having sinned in this matter, a thousand men from each tribe were enlisted for the war ; and the command was not given to Joshua, girded with a sword, but to Phinehas, bearing in his hands the holy instruments and the trumpets.

This is to be noted. The avengement of an evil relationship being in question, a priest with the holy vessels, appears at the head of the soldiery, and that priest, the self-same man who first struck at that very evil which was now to be destroyed (ch. xxv. 7).

This substitution of Joshua by Phinehas, made more evident the fact that this was a war that Israel would not have had to wage if she had not forsaken the straight road of obedience to the Word of the Lord.

Balaam did not die the death of the righteous, but perished fighting against the people of God (v. 8).

Moses was the meekest of all men when his personal importance was questioned ; but he had a godly jealousy when Jehovah's name was concerned (v. 14).

The wholesale destruction of a hopelessly depraved people is an evidence of the wisdom and love of God. (See notes on ch. xxi).

The division of the spoil between the combatants and non-combatants accords with the grace of Him who will reward the desire to battle for His name as though the desire became fact.

The thank-offering given by the soldiers, because not one had fallen in the battle, amounted to about £90,000.

Through this great conflict the 12,000 came without the loss of one man, and through the greater conflict of Rev. vii.-xiv. the 144,000 (12,000 × 12) will also triumphantly come, and stand, not one missing, with the Lamb upon Mount Zion. See notes on those chapters.

The 32,000 female children were not reserved for immoral purposes, as some suppose, but for domestic service. The Law punished the former with death but permitted a Hebrew soldier to marry a captive woman, but only on the condition of strictly observing the legislation made in her favour, designed so as to make immorality and slavery impossible ; and she could at any moment become a member of the Family of Israel and claim her freedom after one to seven years

NUMBERS XXXII.—The highway of " His will " is straighter and safer than the bye-way of " My will." The path of self-will is never so smooth as that of faith and obedience. God's plan for Israel was, first, to conquer Canaan, and then, the vast region between the Jordan and the Euphrates. Reuben and his allies elected to reverse this ; the result was present suffering and future loss. They had immediately to bid farewell to their wives and children and march away to a seven years war, in which many of them would probably lose their lives ; and, later on, they were the first tribes to be carried into captivity and exile, where they still remain.

The cause that originated this action was the possession of wealth (v. 1).

There is always a tendency in the heart to find a resting place in the blessings on the Wilderness side of Jordan rather than to desire eagerly, as the apostle Paul did the richer inheritance beyond Jordan. If the Christian would enjoy the highest possible life, there must be a passing out of the Wilderness of a stunted Christian life into the Canaan of a life of joy and of power in the Holy Spirit. There must be a definite frontier set between the Wilderness and Canaan ; and there is no frontier like the Jordan—it symbolizes the death of self. See notes on Joshua xxii.

These men knew that Moses was not to enter the promised land (ch. xxvii. 12). Then, why did they say : " Bring us not over Jordan ? " It was because they knew well that Moses' heart was already there, and there because it was Emmanuel's land ; and thus their own language emphasized the contrast between the affection of his heart for the land which their hearts so little desired to possess.

NUMBERS XXXIII.—The love that led Israel through the great and terrible Wilderness for forty years so that they lacked nothing, commanded Moses to minutely record their wanderings. This command, and this record, reveal the tenderest love, and prove that their Divine Shepherd accompanied them every step of the way from Egypt to Canaan. In all their afflictions He was afflicted ; He cherished them as a nurse her children ; He suffered not their garments to wax old, nor their feet to swell (Neh. ix). The chapter shows that He never lost sight of them for a single day.

When reading this record of their journeyings it is impossible not to be affected by the memories which gather around the names : Rameses, Pi-hahiroth, The Red Sea, Marah, Elim, Rephidim, etc.

The chapter is exceedingly precious to the Christian pilgrim. It assures him of the Unchanging Love that watches over each day's journey ; and that there is not a difficulty, or sorrow, in that journey unnoticed by that Love.

The chapter further suggests that when the Ransomed of the Lord enter the heavenly Zion with everlasting joy upon their heads, they will find a similar record of their wanderings awaiting them there ; and, admiring the grace and faithful love that kept the record, will praise Him, who, having loved His own which were in the world, loved them to the end.

The closing verses of the chapter assured the people of the possession of Canaan ; but upon the condition that they drove out all the inhabitants and utterly destroyed their idols. Failing to do so, the spared inhabitants would become pricks in their eyes and thorns in their sides. Compromise with evil injures the eyesight and weakens the heart.

Verse 4 reads thus (R.V.) " While the Egyptians were burying," etc.

NUMBERS XXXIV.—The Hand of Love that guided the sons of Israel through the Desert, in this chapter fixed the bounds of their habitation. It was only a very real and tender love that could occupy itself with such details. But the people were Jehovah's people—the land, Emmanuel's land—and to love, nothing is small or unimportant.

In all periods of time God's people, through unbelief and spiritual indolence, have failed to take possession of that which God provided for them. So was it with Israel. Love provided and portioned out to them a land flowing with milk and honey ; but they only took a part of it, and quickly lost what they conquered.

A brighter day, however, is to dawn, when Israel, redeemed and blessed under the New Covenant, will be brought by the Divine Joshua into Jehovah's pleasant land, and established there in righteousness for ever.

NUMBERS XXXV.—The tender love that portioned out a goodly heritage to each tribe —to the weakest as well as to the strongest— did not fail to provide a fitting maintenance

for Levi. Forty-eight cities were given to him in all Israel. Thus the prediction of Gen. xlix. 7 was fulfilled, and, at the same time, turned into honour and blessing because of the faithfulness of Ex. xxxii. 26. Jehovah became Levi's inheritance, they were His personal servants, and therefore wholly cast upon Him for their daily bread. They were to concern themselves about His service, He having undertaken to concern Himself about their maintenance.

" Make thou His service thy delight,"
" He'll make thy wants His care."

God gifted the land to the Nation ; the Nation gifted forty-eight cities to the Levites ; the Levites gifted six of these cities to the man-slayer.

The measurements of verses 4 and 5 are to be thus understood : one thousand cubits were measured from the wall of the city outwards. This was called the " suburb of the city." A further measure of two thousand cubits was granted outside, and in addition to, the first thousand, as common pasture land. Buildings on the inner one thousand suburb might be sold, as in Leviticus, but none of the two thousand cubit pasture land.

The cities of refuge were six in number ; three westward of Jordan, and three eastward. They were placed thus :

Kedesh over against Golan, i.e., Holiness over against Happiness.

Shechem over against Ramoth, i.e., Strength over against Exaltation.

Hebron over against Bezer, i.e., Fellowship over against Fortress.

These names set out the sufficiency of Jesus as the Refuge of sinners. In Him is found Holiness, Strength, Fellowship, a Fortress, Uplifting, and Happiness. God puts Holiness first and Happiness last. Man reverses this order.

In the City of Refuge the man-slayer found safety, and in the death of the High Priest, liberty. The Avenger of Blood symbolized the Law. It demanded the death of the man-slayer. The death of the High Priest satisfied this claim and liberated the man-slayer. Christ's death, not His life, rent the veil, and frees the sinner from the curse of the Law. Similarly the death of the lamb, and not its spotlessness, redeemed the Law-breaker of Leviticus iv. The man-slayer was then at liberty to return to his possession. When Israel shall look upon Him whom they have pierced, it will be then revealed to them that

His death restores them to the land and family of God.

Thus a city of refuge stood almost at every man's door ;· but to enjoy its safety the manslayer had to flee thither. Had such a man said, " If I am to be saved I shall be saved," etc., and not fled to the nearest city, he would have perished.

There was one man who found neither refuge in the city nor liberty in the death of the High Priest. It was the murderer by intention. Sinners who flee to Jesus, by doing so prove that they are not willingly guilty of His blood ; and they therefore find in Him both safety and liberty. But sinners who refuse thus to seek mercy in Him, demonstrate by their refusal that they are verily guilty of His death ; and for these men there is no salvation

The Holy Spirit writes of these cities of refuge in Ex. xxi., Num. xxxv., Deut. iv., Deut. xix., and Joshua xx.

The statement in verse 33 that "blood defileth a land," means blood unlawfully shed defiled a land.

The command in verse 30, that the murderer should be put to death does not conflict with the command, " Thou shalt not kill." This latter command correctly reads in the R.V., " Thou shalt do no murder."

NUMBERS XXXVI.—To the notes on chapter xxvii. may be added that, as necessities arose in the Wilderness journey, or in the conquest of Canaan, there were additions made to the Civil Law, as for instance in this chapter, but never any change in the legislation respecting atonement and worship.

A Divine faith, in its triumphs and activities, moves within the revealed will of God. He, having revealed His will as to the allotment of the Promised Land in tribal sections, these noble daughters of Zelophehad and of faith, accept that will, and consent to marry their cousins, so that the land of their possession should not, because of a marriage with the member of another tribe, become the property of that tribe. (1 Cor. vii. 39).

DEUTERONOMY

DEUTERONOMY I.—" The Words " is the Hebrew Title for this book.

They were spoken by Moses to the new generation of the children of Israel one month previous to his death.

The theme of the Book is that possession of Canaan was dependent upon the keeping of the Law given at Sinai.

Sinai was one of the peaks of a mountain mass named Horeb.

Nothing but prosperity was promised upon fidelity to that Law, and nothing but misery if unfaithful thereto.

A lesson of the book is the impossibility of the natural man taking hold upon and keeping Divine privileges.

The Book contains three sections :

1. Chapters i-xi. 2. Chapters xii-xxix., 3. Chapters xxx.-xxxi.

The first section : God and the Wilderness —Wilderness.

The second section : Law and the Land— Word.

The third section : Grace and the Kingdom —World.

Satan's three temptations of the Lord were based on these three sections. Jesus was the true Israel, the Son called out of Egypt, and as such He appeared to fulfil the righteousness demanded by this book. He was found in the Wilderness hungry and without bread. The first temptation was therefore, " Make thyself bread," that is, " Be independent of God." The second temptation was, " Come suddenly to Thy Temple and Land," as predicted by the prophet Malachi, " do not fear to cast Thyself down, the angels have been charged to bear thee up." The third temptation was, " To obtain the kingdom, it is not necessary to suffer and die ; I will give it Thee."

Jesus answered each temptation by a verse from the first section of this book. This fact shows that God's One Book covers all periods of Israel's history, and therefore of man's history.

The word " declare " in verse 5 means " explain " or " make plain," and especially in writing.

Exodus and Deuteronomy illustrate the two great steps of the Christian life—the steps " out of " and " into "—out of the House of bondage into the Land of corn and wine.

The second step demands a greater energy of faith than the first. To enjoy salvation by faith is a vital and great experience, but to claim, and consciously possess, all spiritual blessings in the heavenlies demands a deeper and richer faith. In both experiences there must be the obedience of faith.

The blessings set out in this book, and the exemption from sickness and sorrow promised, symbolize the spiritual health and wealth and happiness which are the property of the church of God.

Israel was promised exemption from disease and poverty, because they were an earthly people. The Church of God, being heavenly, is promised earthly tribulation, but victory by faith in that tribulation. This is a greater salvation than that promised to Israel.

The life of obedience and consecration is a joyful life. Chapters xii. 7, xiv. 26, xvi. 14, 15, xxvi. 11.

The most prominent lesson in the book is that there is but one God—the great God and Saviour Jesus Christ (Titus ii. 13, R.V., 2 Peter i. 1, R.V.).

The Holy Spirit says (John i. 17) that God gave the Law to man through Moses. " Modern Thought " asserts it was invented by Ezra and his companions. Scholarship destroys this theory, for it points to the total absence of Persian and Grecian words, and of the Divine Titles peculiar to later Hebrew history and literature, in the Pentateuch, and to many other textual and religious features. " Is the Higher Criticism Scholarly " by

R. D. Wilson, Professor of Semitic Languages, may, for example, be consulted. (Marshall, London, 1/-).

DEUTERONOMY II.—Because Esau was to be afraid of Israel (v. 4), therefore the children of Israel were to " take heed unto themselves." The Christian is to be on his guard in the presence of a timid enemy just as much as when confronted with a bold one.

Esau refused to let Israel pass through their land ; but sold food to them (vs. 6 and 29). Compare Num. xx. 18-21.

Moab was forbidden to be distressed ; but God afterwards judged both Moab and Esau (2 Chron. xx. Amos i).

Israel lay for thirty and eight years in the Wilderness paralysed by unbelief, like the man at the Pool of Bethesda (John v. 5). He pictured the nation ; and Jesus, the true Joshua, brought him over the unseen Jordan into the goodly land. But the Pharisees and scribes of that day were as blind to such wonders as are the Pharisees and scribes of to-day (v. 16).

See notes on Num. xxi. in explanation of verse 34.

The reason that no one city was too strong for Israel (v. 36) was because God gave them all into their hand.

DEUTERONOMY III.—The word " bedstead " in verse 11 means probably " tomb " ; and its measurement here corresponds to that of the tomb of Marduk in Babylon. Rabbath was the capital city of the children of Ammon where the Temple of Milchom was. and where Og's tomb would naturally be

The utter destruction of verse 6 is justified in the notes on Num. xxi.

The sea of Chinnereth (v. 17) was doubtless so called from its shape, which resembled a harp. The two words appear related in the Hebrew text. In the New Testament this sheet of water is called the Sea of Tiberias, and the Sea of Galilee, and the Lake of Gennesaret.

The prayer of verse 24 is not related elsewhere.

Beth-peor, i.e., the house of Peor, where Baal was worshipped, became the burial place of Moses (ch. xxxiv.).

DEUTERONOMY IV.—The injunction of verse 2 corresponds to Rev. xxii. 18, 19. Compare chapter xii. 32. The Psalms and the Prophets are not additions to the Word which Moses commanded Israel from the mouth of the Lord, but entreaties and exhortations to return to that Word, and obey it.

Those who did cling to that word found it to be a Life-giving Word (v. 4) ; but those who forsook it perished (v. 3). Verse 9 declares what so often appears in the Holy Scriptures, that fallen man is incapable of knowing God and learning spiritual lessons. It would appear incredible that people who saw such marvels, and heard such statutes from out of the burning mountain, could ever have made a calf and declared it to be God, but every new-born person knows it to be possible, and a thousand facts prove its truth.

The apostle Peter warns professors under the New Covenant of a similar disposition to forget spiritual wonders (2 Peter i. 9).

This repeated lapsing of Israel into idolatry destroys the theory that Jehovah was a creation of the religious emotions of the Israelites ; for history proves that nations cleave to the gods that they invent, whereas Jehovah and Israel were perpetually at war.

The Voice that spake out of the midst of the fire (v. 12) was the Voice that John heard in Rev. i. 10, 12. This is made clear by the use of the verb " saw " in both passages. John turned to " see the Voice " that was speaking to him. Moses says, " you saw no similitude only a voice." Man's voice is so lifeless and empty that no one would turn to " see " it.

" He will not forsake thee " (v. 31). This is the first occurrence of this promise. See chapter xxxi. 6, Joshua i. 5, 1 Chron. xxviii. 20, Heb. xiii. 5.

DEUTERONOMY V.—The argument of this chapter is that God, and not Moses, is the Author of the Law. Moses insists again and again upon this great fact. See 2 Peter i. 20.

The word " only " may be supplied after the word " fathers " in verse 3.

The observance of the Sabbath (vs. 14, 15), which in Ex. xx. is urged because of God's creation rest, is here commanded in the interest of slaves. This shows God's tender pity for the defenceless. Israel is here enjoined to remember that she herself was a slave in the land of Egypt.

In the tenth commandment in Exod. xx. property precedes a wife, but here the wife preceaes property. This variation, together with that respecting the Sabbath, harmonises with the differing actualities of life in the Wilderness and in the land. In the luxurious life of the land wives and slaves were to have a fitting place in the home.

Verses 22 to 33 relate the origin and cause of the mediatorship of Moses.

The title "living God," in verse 26 here first occurs. It stands in contrast with idols and idolatry (Acts xiv. 15, 1 Thess. i. 9, etc.).

DEUTERONOMY VI.—The Lord Jesus Christ in Matt. xxii. 35-40 pointed to verses 4 and 5 of this chapter as being the first and great commandment of the Law.

There are two Hebrew words for the English word "one." The first means a single, or only one; the second, a compound unity. It is the second that is used in verse 4, so this verse implies the Trinity.

The Hebrews accepting verses 7 to 9 literally, invented the phylacteries, or front-lets, which the Pharisees made broad.

Prosperity often occasions forgetfulness of God (v. 12).

"To swear by God's name" means to worship God (v. 13).

Israel was never to forget two great facts in her past history, and was never to be ashamed to point them out, viz.: slavery and salvation (vs. 20-23).

Verse 16 was quoted by the Lord to Satan in the temptation in the Wilderness.

The righteousness of verse 25 was the righteousness offered under the first Covenant. It stands in contrast with the righteousness offered to faith under the second Covenant.

DEUTERONOMY VII.—Israel was God's sword for the destruction of the Seven Nations of Canaan. God could have Himself destroyed them, as He destroyed the Antidiluvians and the people of Sodom and Gomorrah, but the employment of Israel as His instrument in this just judgment (see notes on Num. xxi.) was designed to write upon her heart a horror of idolatry and of the unspeakable wickedness which it sanctioned and sanctified (vs. 1-5).

When executing the Divine wrath upon these corrupt nations they were not to assume themselves morally superior to them, but to remember that they owed everything to the electing love of God—God chose to love them because of a sufficient reason which he discovered in Himself, but not in them (vs. 6-11).

The salvation promised to Israel was an earthly salvation, including material wealth, exemption from disease, and supremacy over all other nations. The salvation peculiar to the spiritual "Israel" is heavenly; and hence these material blessings and exemptions cannot be claimed by Christian people now—although of course God reserves to Himself liberty of action to act as He pleases with His children at all times.

"Chosen unto salvation" 2 Thess. ii. 13, is the keynote of this chapter.

The vehement and repeated appeals to the Hebrews in this book against idolatry destroy the theory that it was composed by Ezra; for in his day Israel was pure from idol worship. The unclean spirit of idolatry had been cast out, and the house was swept and garnished, but, alas, empty. See note on Matt. xii. 43.

DEUTERONOMY VIII.—These chapters teach that as to God all was electing love, faithfulness, grace, and almighty power. As to Israel, standing as she did upon a covenant of works, all depended upon obedience and holding fast. Their possession of the land entirely rested upon their observance of the Law.

As a reason why they should fully trust Him, He reminded them of how He had led them and taught them.

The motives why they should observe all the commandments of verse 1 are given in verses 2-5; and the motives why they should walk in the ways of verse 6 are given in verses 7-9. Verses 2-5 recall Divine preservation; verses 7-9 Divine provision.

They were to be watchful lest prosperity caused them to forget the Redeemer who delivered them from the bondage of Egypt (vs. 10-16); and they were to guard against thinking that that prosperity was due to their own intelligence and power.

DEUTERONOMY IX. 1—X. 11.—As the keynote of chapter viii. was "Preservation," so the keynote of this chapter is "Perverseness." Faithful and tender as was the love of chapter viii., it was responded to with perverseness.

The first six verses of the chapter are Prospective. Their future victories would not result because of their righteousness, but because of the wickedness of the nations that God justly condemned to extermination.

Verses ix. 7 to x. 11, are Retrospective. They were to remember and forget not how they had provoked Jehovah their God continually.

Modern religious thought, recognizing good in all religions, would have applauded Aaron's conduct in the matter of the golden calf as wise and gentle and large-minded and sympathetic, and Moses' action as narrow and ill-tempered and disastrous, but God's judgment was otherwise ; for He would have killed Aaron had not Moses interceded for him (v. 20). The Apostle Paul's language and conduct in the Epistle to the Galatians (ii. 11–16) would similarly receive the approbation of God and the condemnation of man.

Israel having proved incapable as the custodian of the Law, God retired into Christ, and under the figure of the Ark, committed it to Him (x. 1, 5). He hid it in His heart and perfectly, as Man, obeyed it and glorified it (Psa. cxix. 11).

DEUTERONOMY X. 12—XI. 32.—Two motives were given in this section to encourage Israel to obedience : " for thy good " (v. 13), and " that ye may be strong " (xi. 8).

The reasons enjoining circumcision of heart (v. 16) are the universal power of God (v. 14), and His electing grace (v. 15) ; and the motives urging love to the stranger, the fatherless, and the widow (x. 18, 19) are the irresistible power of God (v. 17) and His impartiality as Judge.

Because of the fulfilment of the Divine promises to the fathers (x. 22) they were to love and obey their Great Shepherd (xi. 1) ; and because of the fierceness of His judgments upon their enemies (vs. 2–7), they were to keep all His commandments.

To water with the foot (v. 10) is peculiar to countries in which the crops are matured by irrigation. The water is turned on or off a field by the action of the foot in opening or closing a small wooden sluice.

The " first or early rain " and the " latter rain " fall respectively in October and April (v. 14).

The blessing and the curse set before them in verses 26 to 32 close the first section of this Book.

DEUTERONOMY XII.—The second section of this book begins here and runs, as already stated, to the end of chapter xxix. Its keynote is Jehovah and the Land, and it treats of the conditions under which God and Israel could dwell in fellowship in that Land. Separation from all evil ; worship ; family and national relationships ; and the prosperity that would follow obedience, and the misery that would result from disobedience, form the contents of the section.

These commands were not a repetition of the old ordinances, but a restatement of the conditions necessary to companionship with God in the land of their possession. These commandments claimed them as a people belonging to Him ; they were to give up every other relationship in order to be only His. They were utterly to destroy everything having even a remote connection with idolatry ; and they were to have but one place of worship ; and that place He Himself would choose. Moses was careful never to name the place that God would choose.

The theme of this book being direct relationship with God, the priests and Levites are only introduced in order to be commended to the love and care of Israel.

The one centre for national worship foreshadowed Calvary, to which, in spirit, all must go in order to meet God, and worship Him.

One centre for worship secured purity of doctrine and national unity.

This centre is repeatedly presented as a scene of rejoicing ; even slaves were to have their share in the joy.

Israel was to turn to God from idols (1. Thess. i.) ; and consequently He was to be the Companion and centre of their joys and worship. He gave them the land and its abounding fruits ; they were to eat and rejoice before Him when they went to the place which He should choose. It was that they might meet Him and feast with Him. His love to them was so deep and tender that He could not consent to stand outside of their joys, but in the very midst of them.

There is no contradiction between verse 13 and verse 21. The former verse deals with burnt-offerings offered congregationally at Jerusalem ; the latter verse with personal, or family sacrifices, such as Exod. xx. 24–26, and 1 Sam. xvi. 5. In this latter passage the verb " sacrifice " is the same word in Hebrew as " kill " in verse 21, i.e., " kill in sacrifice."

The word " holy " in verse 26 means " set apart." In addition to the tithes commanded to be given, voluntary tithes and vows and free-will offerings were invited.

DEUTERONOMY XIII.—Chapters xiii. to xxvi. are occupied with Moses' fourth address. See chapter i.

Seduction to idolatry is the subject of this chapter. There are three sections: Seduction by a preacher (vs. 1–5); Seduction by a relative (vs. 6–11); and Seduction by a community (vs. 12–18).

In the first section, verses 1 and 2 describe the seduction, verses 3 and 4 its prohibition, and verse 5 its excision. Similarly in the second section, verses 6 and 7 describe the seduction, verse 8 its prohibition, and verses 9 and 10 its excision; and in the last section, verse 13 narrates the seduction, verse 14 its inquisition, and verses 15 and 16 its excision.

The last clause of verse 5, with verses 11 and 17 and 18, assured the success of this severity, i.e., its fruition.

Every trace of idol worship was to be utterly destroyed : for what men do not see does not tempt them so powerfully as what they do see.

A surgeon is to be esteemed equally with a physician. The Lord Jesus Christ is both ; and is to be loved and trusted equally in both relations.

DEUTERONOMY XIV.—Because Jehovah would dwell with them in the land of their possession, therefore they were to look nice (vs. 1, 2); they were to eat food that was nice (vs. 3–21); they were to have feelings that were nice (vs. 21 and 27–29); and they were to enjoy, without fear or hesitation, all the good things that God would give them (vs. 23–26), having made, on their part, abundant provision for the needy and for the stranger (v. 28).

See notes on Leviticus xi. in regard to clean and unclean animals, and the spiritual lessons suggested by the legislation respecting them.

The permission in verse 26 to purchase wine and strong drink and drink them before the Lord at the place that He should choose is difficult of explanation. There are eight Hebrew words in the Bible for fermented liquor, and their use shows that they were all intoxicating. That there is such a thing in the Scriptures as unfermented wine is evidenced in the office and action of the cup-bearer of Gen. xl. 11, Neh. ii. 1, and

John ii. 8 ; and total abstinence from wine is written in the Scriptures from one end to the other.

As to the permission of verse 26, the liquors were to be drunk before the Lord. This fact would make excess and drunkenness impossible. His presence will legitimatise many joys which in His absence are too dangerous to be indulged. Hence the apostle Paul, though himself a total abstainer from wine, because it, owing to the Lord's absence, was abused, could, in harmony with the Scriptures, recommend it to Timothy as a medicine (Rom. xiv. 21, xv. 1, 1 Cor. viii. 13, Acts xviii. 18, 1 Tim. v. 23).

Compare John ii. 1–11 and Luke xxii. 12–20.

The objection that the legislation of verse 21 was immoral because permitting strangers to do what was wrong in itself, is removed by observing the force of the Infinite Absolute in the Hebrew text. Professor Mason of Cambridge translates the verse :

" Ye shall not eat any carcase ; shouldst thou give it to the sojourner who is in thy gates *he* would indeed eat it ; or shouldst thou sell even to the foreigner (he would not object to buy) but *thou* art an holy people," etc.

DEUTERONOMY XV.—The seventh year, beauteous promise of the future Millennium, was to be a year of joy and gladness for debtors and for slaves.

The unchanging motive, perpetually repeated, why they should be compassionate to the necessitous and the strangers, was the remembrance of their own bondage in Egypt and the grace that delivered them from it (v. 15). They were not to receive the grace of God in vain ; they were to show that grace to others in order that no discredit should attach to their Redeemer's name. See 2 Cor. vi. 1, and 3.

There is no conflict between v. 4 and v. 11. Two Hebrew words are used, that in v. 11, meaning the afflicted—such as widows and orphans for example.

DEUTERONOMY XVI. 1–20.—The Three great annual feasts of Passover, Pentecost and Tabernacles were to be feasts of Jehovah, and feasts to Jehovah. Joy was to be the keynote of them all. See notes on Lev. xxiii.

They were to be observed at the place which He should choose ; for they were designed to set forth the person and work of the Lord Jesus Christ.

The distinctive teaching of Leviticus and Deuteronomy should never be lost sight of. The priest is very prominent in Leviticus, but scarcely seen in Deuteronomy ; and this, not because he and his work are superseded by the latter book, but because the one book teaches how the sinner may draw near to God and receive forgiveness, life, and righteousness ; whilst the theme of the other book is the gladness of the pardoned sinner in the possession of a conscious salvation, and the enjoyment of personal and direct relationships with God as a Father and a Saviour.

It was in order to the maintenance of this direct relationship between the people and God that the judges and officers of verses 18-20 were to be appointed.

As to the feasts, God surrounded Himself with joy, He invited His people to share that joy, and He urged them to bring the stranger and the needy into that joy. Christ and His fulness were pictured in these gladsome feasts.

But there was an interesting distinction between the joy of Pentecost and the joy of Tabernacles. The one was associated with redemption from Egypt, and its joy was to be joined with watchfulness. But the joy of Tabernacles was to be without care, for it foreshadowed the kingdom.

DEUTERONOMY XVI. 21 — XVII. 20. Purity of worship and, in type, the perfection of Christ's person are all-important. At the mouth of two witnesses the seducer to idolatry was to be put to death. The Hebrew Rabbins bring forward this passage as justifying the condemnation and death of Jesus of Nazareth. But He did not invite the people to become idolators (vs. 1-7).

Matters of controversy (vs. 8-13) were not to be decided independently of God, but, on the contrary, in direct connection with Him. If all Christian people would be careful to bring God in upon the scene of their bickerings, how swift and satisfactory would be the settlement !

Should Israel desire a king he was to obey the instructions of verses 14-20. He was, with his own hand, to write a copy of the Bible (v. 18) ; he was to read it every day (v. 19) ; he was to obey it (v. 19) ; he was not to deviate from it in any particular (v. 20) ; he was not to multiply horses lest doing so should excite a desire on the part of the people to return to Egypt (v. 16) ; he was not to be a polygamist because that would lead to idolatry (v. 17) ; and he was not to heap up gold, for the love of money is a root of all evil.

The wisest Christian professor cannot do without the Bible. Solomon, the wisest of all kings, disobeyed these commandments ; and, so far as it is revealed, died a wicked old man.

Death was alike the doom of whoever disobeyed either the civil or the sacred law (vs. 5 and 12). God could have judged such persons directly, but, as in 1 Cor. v. 5, He tests and teaches His people by committing this judgment to them.

DEUTERONOMY XVIII.—Judges, chapter xvi., kings, chapter xvii., and priests, chapter xviii—all would fail in keeping the nation in touch with God, but a Prophet, promised at Sinai, like unto Moses, God would raise unto them (vs. 15-19) ; and in Him would be no failure !

Opposition prophets would arise from amongst the Heathen (vs. 9-14), and from among the Hebrews (vs. 20-22) ; but they were not to be regarded, for they would be false prophets.

The word " perfect " in verse 13 means single-hearted, that is, pure from idolatry.

All that Christ taught, and the very words He used in His teaching, were from God (v. 18). There was no misgiving in the Divine Mind as to that certitude. Seven times He asserted that all His words and statements were given to Him by God ; and in His last prayer He pleaded that it was God's word, and God's words, that He gave to the disciples—He did not speak from Himself as Man, but from God. See notes on John vii. 16, 17 and xvii. 8. How wicked and daring, therefore, is the teaching of those who say that He was an ignorant Jew of His day ; and that He taught what was not in every particular true.

DEUTERONOMY XIX.—For notes upon the Cities of Refuge see Num. xxxv.

Landmarks (v. 14) were not to be removed —stumbling blocks will be for ever removed (Matt. xiii. 41, R.V.).

False witnesses were to suffer the punishment which by their perjured evidence they designed the accused to suffer (v. 21).

Life (vs.1-13), property (v.14) and character (vs. 15, 21) are here all safe-guarded by Divine law.

Verse 21 is supplemented and not contradicted by Matt. v. 38, 39. A brutal man who destroyed the eye of even a child was justly condemned (Exod. xxi. 23) to have his eye destroyed—and present-day justice approves this law for it orders criminals who maltreat their victim to be flogged—but the child instructed in Matt. v. by Him who ordained Exod. xxi. learns to offer forgiveness to the aggressor upon his confession of his fault. Thus would she be perfect as her Father in heaven, for He forgives all manner of sin provided it is repented of.

DEUTERONOMY XX.—War was not to be entered upon, or waged, in self-will, but in fellowship with God, and under the government of His Word and Spirit.

The allegation that the women of verse 14 were reserved for immoral purposes is refuted by the laws governing domestic slavery, and condemning to death any one guilty of immorality.

The Christian life is a war and it must be waged under the government of the Holy Spirit and in fellowship with God ; otherwise there will be no victory.

Some energies in the moral realm must be put to death (v. 16) and others brought into subjection, their reproductive power being first destroyed (vs. 13 and 14).

DEUTERONOMY XXI.—The legislation of this chapter provided for the case of the man found slain ; that of the child of the unloved wife ; that of the rebellious son ; and that of the beautiful captive.

God was to be brought into touch with all these : thus showing His tender solicitude for individuals as well as for nations, and the regard He had for family life.

The confession of verses 7 and 8 will be that of Israel in the latter day, when, in the light of Calvary (vs. 4–6), they will clear themselves from the murder of the Messias.

Meanwhile the unbelieving members of the nation will suffer the doom of the stubborn and rebellious son (vs. 18–21).

The hardness of heart of the priests in quoting verse 23 to Pilate is appalling.

Thus the legislation of verses 1–9 shows how precious human life is to God.

DEUTERONOMY XXII.—The statutes here commanded concerned benevolence, mercy, and all that would strike against the sensibilities of nature, whether human nature,

or animal (v. 10), or vegetable (v. 9). Wives were to be protected from brutish husbands, and unfaithfulness on her part to be punished with death.

Three commands in verses 9–11 express three principles, antagonistic to modern religious thought and action.

Divers Seeds   Mixed Teaching
Ox and Ass   Mixed Service
Woollen and Linen Mixed Conduct

Mixed teaching, like mixed seeds, produces sterility. At creation (Gen. i), there was no mixture ; and, hence, fertility. Every seed was " after his kind," and was pronounced by God to be " good." The seed that Christian workers and ministers are to sow must be the unmixed Word of God. His Word is not to be mixed with man's philosophy. Christ, the True Minister, said " I have given them thy Word," " I have not spoken from Myself."

The ox was " clean," the ass, " unclean." Together they formed an unequal yoke. When Christian people join with the unconverted in Christian work, or marriage, or business, it is an unequal yoke, and can never have Divine approval.

Clothing in Scripture figures conduct. White linen represents the righteous acts of saints (Rev. xix. 8 R.V.). Christian action is to be unmixed ; it is to be absolutely clean and sincere.

" Defiled " (v. 9) i.e. consigned (R.V.) to the refuse fire (1 Cor. iii. 12, 13).

DEUTERONOMY XXIII.—The prohibitions of verses 1 and 2 struck at idolatry and cupidity. Eastern parents mutilated in various ways their children, either in honour of their gods, or else to get higher wages for them as servants ; and many children were born, not in wedlock, but as a result of idolatrous licentious ceremonies.

These prohibitions illustrate two great spiritual principles, viz. : spiritual birth, and not ceremonial professions, introduces into the family of God ; and, second, true spiritual life has the power of reproduction. Hence if there is no fruit unto God there can be no admission into the congregation of the Lord.

Only those soldiers who were ceremonially clean were permitted to go forth to war (v. 9). The reason for this is found in verse 14.

DEUTERONOMY XXIV. — The minute regulations of these chapters show how God came into the most intimate concerns of His people. To those who loved Him this was a deep joy, but to those who did not love Him, an intolerable and irritating intrusion. But it was a love both deep and tender that interested itself in soldiers, escaped slaves, physical emotions, divorce, the poor, the pay of the day-labourer, etc.

The spirit of all these ordinances is very touching as showing the goodness and pity of God, who deigns to take knowledge of all these things, and to teach His people delicacy, propriety, consideration for others, sensitive-ness—in a word, Christ-likeness.

The regulations respecting divorce checked and limited that evil—an evil which could not be removed at the time owing to the hardness of their hearts; as the Lord Himself pointed out (Matt. xix. 8).

DEUTERONOMY XXV.—The legislation of this chapter, like that of those that precede it, shows how God honours man. Idolatry dishonours him.

Merited punishment was not to be inhuman. The condemned was not to receive more than forty stripes; and these were not to be inflicted by some heartless official in private, but by an officer of the court in the presence of the judge.

The apostle Paul five times received these forty stripes save one (2 Cor. xi. 24); but unjustly.

God's care of animals (v. 4), of a childless wife (v. 5), of family property (vs. 7-10), of personal dignity (vs. 11 and 12), and of honesty in trade (vs. 13-16), shines brightly in these ordinances.

Amalek was to be utterly destroyed; not so the Egyptian. The Egyptian pictures man, as such; the Amalekite, man as the willing agent of evil. The Christian's attitude to ordinary men of the world is necessarily different from that towards the willing and determined enemies of goodness and justice.

The God who condemned Amalek to utter extinction was the very same God who tenderly sheltered the little bird of chapter xxii. 6. The same God appeared in flesh and in Luke xii. 5, 6, taught that the hand that upholds the little sparrow thrusts wicked men into hell.

DEUTERONOMY XXVI.—The Divine principles that govern worship in spirit and in truth appear in this chapter.

The Place, the Priest, the Worshipper, and the character of his worship all foreshadowed Calvary, the Great High Priest, salvation by grace, and the thankfulness and holiness that are the fruits of grace.

The worshipper confessed that he was by nature a " Syrian ready to perish "; that grace had brought him into the good land promised to the fathers; and that the same grace had filled his cup to overflowing, the bounty of which the basket of first-fruits was the evidence.

At the same time he declared that he had walked in the statutes and judgments of the Lord; and he prayed for blessing upon the people and church of God (v. 15).

In this service of singular beauty Jehovah avouched the worshipper to be His peculiar treasure, and the worshipper avouched Jehovah to be his God.

The worship of the chapter illustrates the unity, and yet the diversity of, and between, Leviticus and Deuteronomy. The worship in Deuteronomy is the enjoyment in the Land of Promise of a relationship already estab-lished in the Wilderness. It was a joying before Him in the enjoyment of what He had given—not the drawing near to Him in the Holiest. It pictured the confidence, joy, nearness and fellowship of the coming Millennial kingdom. But all the joy of Deuteronomy was purchased, and based upon redemption by blood in Exodus and Leviticus; just as all the happiness of the Millennium will be the fruit of the precious blood shed on Calvary.

The worshipper as here described was to come with joy bearing his basket of first-fruits to the place of the burnt and sin-offering chosen by God. The basket testified that God was the author of all the worshipper's happiness.

There was then to be a declaration that the land promised was now possessed. This declaration was to be made to the priest (Christ in type).

Then there was the confession that the worshipper was born of a Syrian ready to perish (Jacob); that he had no personal merit; that he was a member of a nation of slaves; that he had been redeemed by grace; and that he was now saved and happy in the land flowing with milk and honey.

But the grace that showed such pity to him he was enjoined (v. 11) to show to others —not only to his relatives and fellow country-men, but to the Gentile stranger.

God's House being holy, worship there should be sincere ; and hence the declarations of verses 13 and 14.

Following this declaration as to obedience, prayer was offered for the whole nation ; and the crown was set upon all this lovely scene of worship by the mutual avouchment of verses 17 and 18.

These principles form the Divine basis of true worship.

Thus God and His gifts were recognised. God first ; for His blessings turn the heart away from Him if their first effect is not to turn it to Him.

This lovely scene of happiness and worship closes the teaching of the book. All is sunshine ; the people are in possession of the goodly land ; they rejoice and feast therein with Jehovah ; and their consciousness of salvation and security is based upon free grace and redeeming blood. They share their riches with the widows, the fatherless, and the stranger, the poor and the slaves. Every third year they give the special tithe of that year (v. 12) to the necessitous within their gates. They did not rob God by withholding these gifts from His poor (v. 13) ; they did not make an excuse of domestic affliction, or personal interest, and so withhold this bounty ; and thus they were in truth a holy people unto Jehovah their God (v. 19).

Had Israel observed these commandments and these statutes they would have been a nation of holy and happy worshippers, and Palestine would have been a Paradise of felicity, peace, and love.

DEUTERONOMY XXVII.—Possession of the Land depended on obedience to the Law. On the Canaan side of Jordan that Law was to be made visible to all upon a monument of great stones plastered with plaster. This pillar was to be set up in Mount Ebal, and, with it, an altar of unhewn stone. Half the tribes were to take their stand by this altar and by this engraved Law, the other tribes were to take their place upon Mount Gerizim. Those upon Mount Gerizim were " to bless the people " ; those upon Mount Ebal " to stand for the curse "—it does not say they were to curse the people.

Burnt-offerings and peace-offerings were commanded ; but no sin-offering ; for the action of that day presupposed a redeemed people, but placed under the curse if they should break the Law.

The apostle Paul based his argument in Gal. iii., upon this chapter. (See notes upon that chapter).

The blessings of Gerizim are entirely omitted, for the subject here was the judgment that would surely follow upon failure in a full obedience to the commandments engraved upon the stones.

The altar was erected on Ebal, not on Gerizim ; and, as pointed out, sin-offerings are not mentioned. The burnt-offerings and peace-offerings were to be presented by those who had fulfilled the righteousness of the Law. Only one Man accomplished that ; and He on the mount of cursing erected an altar upon which He offered up Himself as a sin-offering for all those who by disobedience had brought upon themselves the doom of the Law, that is, death. At the same time in thus offering up Himself, He became on behalf of these guilty Law-breakers, the burnt-offering and the peace-offering which their sin and failure made it impossible for them to bring to God. See notes on Exodus xx. 24 and Joshua viii. 30.

DEUTERONOMY XXVIII.—The principles of God's government of His ancient people, under a Covenant of works, are set out in this chapter. History demonstrates the justice of that government ; and the fulfilment of these dread predictions makes absolute the fact that the Name of Jehovah Elohim is both fearful and glorious.

The joy of serving God (v. 47) is contrasted with the anguish of serving self (v. 48).

The word " fray " (v. 26) means "frighten.'

The words in verse 68 " Ye shall be sold " mean, " ye shall be offered for sale."

This last verse was fulfilled after the destruction of Jerusalem by the Romans. Multitudes of the prisoners were carried to Egypt in ships and offered for sale in the slave-market ; but no man buying them, they were driven in thousands into the desert, where they miserably perished. This fulfilment of a prophecy fifteen hundred years old is one of the many proofs that the Bible is superhuman.

Verses 33 and 36 point to the Chaldeans, and verse 49 to the Romans.

DEUTERONOMY XXIX.—This chapter closes the second section of Deuteronomy. (See notes on chapter i).

The close of this section is the personal application to the conscience of the people, individually and collectively, of all that precedes. It is the last message to the people as they are about to take possession of Emmanuel's land, under the Covenant of works (v.29). The people are to remember that they are the children of those who perished in the desert ; they are reminded of the visible miracles then present before their eyes—the manna, the water, the fiery cloud, the enduring clothing, the unswollen foot ; and they are plainly told in verse 19 that a secret and bitter root of sin would expel them out of the good land, whilst on the other hand obedience would establish them therein (v. 13).

The import of the last verse will better appear if it be thus read :—" The secret purposes of Jehovah our God, and the things that are revealed, concern us and our children for ever (they are our eternal property) in order that we may perform all the words of this law."

This verse is much misunderstood. It does not mean that the secret things belong to God, and the revealed things to His people ; but it does mean that God's purposes, whether secret or revealed, all belong to Israel. The things revealed were the consequences that would follow upon obedience or disobedience ; and these carry the reader up to the close of this chapter ; the secret counsels of God are the purposes of God in grace to Israel, notwithstanding her disobedience, these form the subject of the remaining chapters of this book. These purposes are therefore revealed, and are of deep interest. They could not be a rule of conduct ; that rule was found in the ordinance of the Law. It was failure to keep that rule that opened the door to these hidden counsels of grace.

DEUTERONOMY XXX.—This last section of this Book, chapters xxx. to xxxiv., has as its keynote, the secret counsels of Jehovah respecting His ancient people. Things to come ; the Land possessed on the principle of faith and not merit (Rom. x) ; the blessing of the Tribes ; and the death of Moses—illustrating that Law could not bring Israel into the promised possession—these are the materials of these four chapters.

The section opens by supposing the people already driven out of the Land because of disobedience and therefore unable to practise the requirements of the Law. A new principle is thereupon introduced, the principle of salvation by faith as opposed to the principle of salvation by works. Here is one of the secret purposes of God revealed. Canaan was to be possessed, and enjoyed, on the principle of grace as opposed to law, of believing as against doing. This is the doctrine of Rom. x. Upon this principle of grace a new moral nature (v. 6) will be given to them which will enable them to keep all the commandments and statutes as spiritually interpreted by Jehovah Himself in the Sermon on the Mount. Righteousness by Law being impossible because they were cast out of the Land, where alone that righteousness could be won—if that were possible—God, in this chapter, reveals His secret purpose of bringing them back to that land, and establishing them there in the righteousness that the Law aimed at ; but this restoration was to be on the principle of faith, and not of legal observance.

DEUTERONOMY XXXI.—The Law, as represented by Moses, being unable, because of the feebleness of man's moral nature, to bring the people into Canaan, Joshua, as typifying the living Saviour, now appears, and is presented to the people as the great captain who would, without fail, bring them over Jordan (vs. 1–8).

At the same time the Law was written and given in charge to the priests, who were commanded to read it all, in the year of release, to the men, the women, and the children. It was to be read during the Feast of Tabernacles so that they should perpetually remember that the Land, and all the bounties it produced for them, belonged to Jehovah, and the Book was to be a witness that these riches would continue to be theirs if they were obedient (vs. 9–13 and 24–29).

Moses was dismissed to his grave, and Joshua appointed to his captaincy under the shadow of a prophecy predicting the apostasy of the nation and the terrific judgments which would, consequently, fall upon them.

Were this a history of human imagination the inventor would never dream of closing the service of one great chieftain, and beginning the exploits of another, in such a cloud of gloom and depression.

Jehovah foreknowing this apostasy, Moses was commanded to write a song that was to be a witness for God against it (vs. 19–22). The words of the song occupy the next chapter.

The promise, " I will not forsake thee," is repeated seven times in the Scripture, viz. : Gen. xxviii, 15 ; Deut. iv. 31, xxxi. 6, 8 ; Joshua i. 5 ; Heb. xiii. 5 ; 1 Chron. xxviii. 20.

DEUTERONOMY XXXII. — The first reference to the song of Moses is found in verse 19 of the previous chapter ; the last reference, in Rev. xv. 3. (See notes on that chapter).

Five times in the song Jehovah is praised as the Rock (vs. 4, 15, 18, 30, 31). The occurrences in verses 31 and 37 ironically refer to the false rocks of the nations. Five is the number of grace.

The first six verses proclaim the Divine name, and nature, and perfect work, and righteous ways. The titles " Jehovah," " Elohim," " Rock," " El," and " Father," appear in this introduction.

Verses 7–14 celebrate His goodness and bounty during the period of the Pentateuch. Verses 15–19 record Israel's evil response to that goodness during the period of their kings.

Verse 20 contemplates the period between the Captivity in Babylon and the Advent of the Messiah.

Verse 21 relates to the period of the Acts of the Apostles (Rom. x. 11).

The section verses 22–33 relates to Israel's present dispersion, and verses 34–43 to their sufferings under the future Anti-Christ, and their final restoration.

Four great facts are specially noticeable in the Song. First : That God in His secret counsels respecting the earth appointed Israel (v. 8), as the chief nation at the centre, or navel, of the earth, i.e., Palestine, and disposed all other nations in relation thereto. Second : that the Gentiles shall partake of the grace laid up for Israel (vs. 21, 43). Third : that all Israel shall be saved (v. 43) ; and lastly : that these facts are based upon, and secured by, the glory connected with the name of the Lord, i.e., both Hebrews and Gentiles must have perished for ever but that God abides true to His nature and promises.

DEUTERONOMY XXXIII. — This was Moses' last and tenth address.

The blessing of the Tribes in this chapter contemplates them as dwelling in the land in fellowship with Jehovah their King (v. 5), and so harmonizes with the teaching and character of this Book. The blessing of the Tribes in Gen. xlix. harmonizes with that Book, and is future and historical.

The first five verses picture God as King in Jeshurun, i.e., among the upright, attended with thousands of angels, and having His people Israel guarded by His hand and seated at His feet, whilst He makes known to them His fiery law.

It is to be remarked that the blessing here is, in each instance, according to grace, and not to the rights of nature, as in Genesis.

The meaning of the name of each tribe, that which is said respecting each, and the order in which they are placed illustrate the facts of the spiritual life. Therefore it is that the first blessing that grace bestows is life (v. 6). Then follows power (v. 7) ; consecration and worship (vs. 8–11) ; communion (v. 12) ; the fruit of the Spirit (vs. 13–17) ; service and prayer (vs. 18 and 19) ; judgment of evil (vs. 20 and 21) the overcoming life (vs. 22 and 23) ; and, the final result, a multitude of spiritual children, an acceptable ministry to brethren, and a Christian walk in the unction of the Holy Spirit, and in the strength of revealed truth.

The last four verses, like the first four, set forth the perfections of Israel's Saviour, and declare that her greatest glory is that she is the saved of Jehovah.

Jeshurun, meaning the upright ones, was God's tender name for His people Israel as chosen in Christ. See Deut. xxxii. 15, xxxiii. 5 and 26, and Isa. xliv. 2. Compare the term " the upright " in the Psalms and in Proverbs, and also " the Upright One," i.e., Messiah.

DEUTERONOMY XXXIV.—Travellers declare that it is quite possible to see from the top of the mountains opposite Jericho the whole extent of the countries described in verses 1–4.

Moses, as the servant of Jehovah, and the Mediator of the First Covenant, could not bring Israel into the resurrection life beyond Jordan ; so he died in the Wilderness and was buried there. God buried him. Of none other is this recorded ; but He raised him for the Transfiguration.

Man is so insensate and idolatrous that Israel would, without doubt, have given Divine honours to the Great Leader, when dead, who, while living, they treated with ingratitude, and more than once set about to murder ! Such is man, and such is his nature !

Many prophetic students think that Moses will be Elijah's companion in the future testimony against Anti-Christ.

As to Satan and " the body of Moses " see notes on Zech. iii. and Jude 9.

God spoke to Joshua as He spoke to Moses (Joshua i. 1, 5) and so the details of Moses death and burial appear in this chapter.

JOSHUA

JOSHUA I.—The name Joshua means "Jesus the Saviour." This book is a fore-picture of the time when the true Joshua will rapture his people to the Heavens, without dying (1 Thess. 4), and, with them, war against the evil spirits and their Prince, who now possess those heavenly places (Eph. vi.), eject Satan and his hosts (2 Thess. ii. 7), and cast them down to the earth (Rev. xii. 7-12).

The book also illustrates the Christian life of rest (Heb. iv.) and of victory (Rom. viii.) possible to the Christian who, by faith, in the energy of the Holy Spirit, lives in the Heavenlies in Christ (Eph. ii).

Moses, as representing the Law, could not bring Israel into the Promised Land; he must die, for he had made one failure under that Law, and possession of Canaan by Law, could only be by a perfect obedience to it. Man, being a sinner, cannot give this perfect obedience. Joshua, type of the risen Saviour, brought Israel into the goodly Land. Grace, operating in the power of the Holy Spirit, can bring men into the enjoyment of that which the Law, because of man's moral weakness, on which it acts, can never do.

Moses was a servant in the Wilderness, Joshua a son in the Land. The subject of Deuteronomy is the Wilderness; that of Joshua is the Land. Most Christian people are satisfied to be servants in the Wilderness; few ambition to be sons in the Land.

Joshua's success depended upon his obedience to his two companions — the Eternal Word (v. 5) and the Written Word (v. 8); that is Jesus and the Bible. Obedience to such companionship alone gives a victorious Christian experience. The question is often asked by Sacerdotalists : " What is the rule of faith ? " Their answer is : " The Catholic Church and its teaching." God's answer in this chapter, and in many other chapters, is, " The Bible."

Promise is one thing, possession another; God said, " I, even I, do give you the Land " (v. 2). Such was the promise; but the one condition of possession was the placing of the foot upon it (v. 3). So God promises to all men forgiveness, life, righteousness and glory in Christ, upon the condition of believing on Him. Only those, therefore, become the possessors of these realities who do believe upon Him.

Meditating upon the Word of God, and not the mere reading of it, nourishes and instructs the Christian. The best commentary on the Scriptures is obedience.

Had the two tribes and the half tribe permitted God to choose for them how much happier and safer they would have been ! But they chose for themselves land on the wrong side of Jordan, and brought upon themselves many sorrows and early captivity (1 Kings xxii. 3). Such is the sad experience of Christian people who plan for themselves and do not have fellowship with the thoughts of God. His plan was, first to conquer Canaan and then the land stretching from the Jordan to the Euphrates. The two tribes and a half thought the reverse would be the better plan. God's plan to-day is—first, to gather out an election from the Nations and then to save the world (Acts xv. 14-18). Many Christian workers wish to reverse this.

Verse 18 illustrates the disobedience and folly of the natural heart. Man is always willing to obey a human rather than a Divine law. These men who now condemned to death any who refused to obey Joshua, themselves refused to obey Jehovah. Multitudes at the present moment strictly honour Friday as a fast day, which is an ordinance of man, but dishonour Sunday, to honour which is a commandment of God.

The third day of verse 11 with iii. 2 and 7, predicts the resurrection of Christ—for God powerfully magnified Him on that day (Rom. i. 4)—and it connects the baptism of the Jordan with that of the Red Sea. See notes on Exod xiii. xiv., and Col. i. and ii.

The worthlessness of man's protestations of fidelity at the close of the chapter contrasts with the worthfulness of God's promises of faithfulness at the opening of the chapter. " I will be with thee " (v. 5). See note on Deut. iv. 31.

JOSHUA II.—Rahab was a debauched member of a doomed race. Yet grace saved her. She based her plea for salvation upon the fact that she was justly ordained by God to destruction. Many people refuse to bestir themselves in the matter of personal salvation because of the belief that if they are ordained to be saved, they will be saved, and if ordained to be lost they will be lost. But all sinners are justly ordained to be lost (Rom. v. 12) and therefore, all sinners may be saved. Rahab prefaced her plea for salvation by declaring that she knew all were doomed to destruction, and because of this Divine Judgment she asked for a true token that would assure her of her safety in the Day of Wrath that was coming.

She was immediately provided with a way of salvation. It was a very simple way. She had but to bind some scarlet thread in a window. A child could do that. Salvation to-day from the Wrath to come is equally simple. Trusting in the Lord Jesus Christ, and in his precious blood, secures eternal salvation.

Rahab lost not a moment in making her calling and election sure. She bound the scarlet thread in the window. And directly she did so she was saved—that is, she was in safety, and assured of safety. Prior to binding the scarlet line in the window she was ordained to destruction, but from the moment she trusted that " true token " she was ordained to salvation.

Rahab's assurance of salvation was not founded upon an inward experience, but upon an outward evidence—that is, the scarlet line. In it was perfection; in herself imperfection. Looking upon that " true token," and believing the testimony respecting it, she was assured of deliverance in the Day of Doom that was coming. Thus the outward token gave an inward peace. The believer in Jesus enjoys a similar peace. The preciousness of Christ's blood, and the testimony of the Holy Scriptures concerning it, is the outward token which brings assurance of salvation to the heart that trusts Christ. It was vain for Rahab to seek for salvation upon the ground of personal worthiness; for she

was vile indeed. It is equally vain for the most moral to claim salvation to-day, for all have sinned, none are righteous, and all are under sentence of death (Rom. v. 12).

A faith that is born of God always evidences itself by seeking the salvation of others. Rahab pleads for her father, her mother, her brothers, her sisters and all belonging to them ; and they were all saved.

The moral effect of a Divine Faith is further seen in Rahab. She became a good woman, joined the people of God, married one of its princes, and her name shines in the genealogy of Jesus Christ (Matt. i).

An incidental proof of the accuracy of this story is the statement that stalks of flax were spread upon the roof. The flooding of Jordan, the eating of the Passover, and the ripening of the flax harvest, all occurred at the end of March or commencement of April.

The spies may not have known Rahab's character, for the Hebrew text suggests that she was an innkeeper, whilst the Greek text of Heb. xi. 31 proves that she was an harlot. It is to this day a sad truth that in foreign countries innkeepers are sometimes private prostitutes.

JOSHUA III.—The crossing of the Red Sea was salvation out of Egypt; the passage of Jordan, salvation into Canaan. The believer is saved from the kingdom of Satan to the Kingdom of God. Egypt pictures the one kingdom ; Canaan the other. The death and resurrection of Christ, symbolized by the Paschal Lamb, the Red Sea and the Jordan delivered from the one kingdom and translated into the other (Col. i. 13). The passage of the Jordan illustrates a personal experience of that death and resurrection. Those who passed through the Red Sea perished in the Wilderness. It was necessary that their children should learn by a personal experience that the salvation that brought them into Canaan was the same that brought them out of Egypt—that is, the Red Sea and Jordan both picture the death and resurrection of Christ. See notes on Col. ii. and Exod. xiii., xiv.

But Israel might have entered Canaan forty years earlier at Kadesh-barnea in the power of Red Sea truth. Then the representation of that truth would not have been necessary, as afterwards, at the Jordan. They could have learned that the salvation that delivered them from Egypt translated them into the " Land of Promise." But unbelief condemned them to the Wilderness. Similar failure marked the early Christians. The Epistle to the Romans teaches salvation from Egypt ; that to Ephesians, salvation to Canaan. But unbelief, hindering an immediate passage from the one epistle to the other, the Wilderness epistles of Corinthians and Galatians intervene—the one dealing with moral failure, the other with doctrinal error. In a word, a wilderness experience. Were the Gospel preached to-day in apostolic power, intelligence, and fulness, converts would pass swiftly from Egypt to Canaan ; but because of defective teaching many have, in later years, to go through a definite " Jordan " experience of a kind of second conversion, called " Keswick " teaching.

The Priests were to bear the Ark, lifting it up above themselves ; the officers were to pass through the midst of the camp urging the people to look upon it and to follow it— not to follow the priests but to follow " it." Every Christian has this double privilege. As a priest, he is to exalt Christ in his life, and, as an officer, he is to preach Christ.

A space of about a mile was to intervene between the Ark and the Host. The Ark moved from the midst of the Host, its usual position, to a point a mile in advance. Israel was to tread an unknown way—an impossible way—and, therefore, the Ark of the Covenant was to be placed where all could see it and follow it. Further, this great intervening space taught the people that the waters of Jordan did not flee before Israel but before the Ark. So once more in the Scriptures the great doctrine is taught—that Christ by Himself conquered death for His people ; and that, in that great and perfected redemption, there is, and can be, no such thing as human co-operation.

The moment the priest's feet touched the waters they fled ! Such is the power of Christ over death.

The repetition of the word " and " in verse 10 is one of the vast number of instances of the use of this important word in the Sacred Scriptures. Its repetition is designed by the Holy Spirit. Compare Luke xiv. verses 13 and 21.

JOSHUA IV.—There were two distinct memorial , each one constructed of twelve stones. The one was buried by Joshua in the midst of Jordan (v. 9), the other set up at Gilgal (v. 20). The stones buried in Jordan were no doubt Wilderness stones ; those set up at Gilgal, Jordan stones. These two monuments illustrate Rom. vi., vii. and viii. The twelve stones buried in Jordan signified the death and burial of Israel's forty years of unbelief and sinning in the Wilderness ; the stones set up at Gilgal, her new life of resurrection power and victory. Four facts are stated about these stones. They were taken, they were carried, they were laid down, and they were set up (v. 8 and 20). The origin of these stones was the deep bed of Jordan ; their purpose was to testify that Israel owed her entrance into the goodly land only and wholly to Divine grace and power. The stones " set up " in unity and beauty at Gilgal were the very same stones that had lain scattered and hidden beneath the waters of Jordan before the Ark of the Covenant had delivered them from their tomb and brought them into the glad sunshine. These two monuments, therefore, express the great truths of Romans and Ephesians, i.e., that in the Baptism of Christ the Believer dies to his old life and rises into a new life ; and he is reminded that, as to his moral origin, he was buried beneath the waters of the wrath of God ; that, as to his present position, he is now set up upon resurrection ground ; and that his duty is to testify daily to the glory of Christ, the one and only Saviour. The Lord Jesus Christ said to the Pharisees that if the children were silent the very stones would cry out ! These stones set up at Gilgal cried out day and night !

The twelve men chosen to take up these stones out of the midst of Jordan represented the nation. They were the twelve men spoken of in chapter iii. verse 12.

There was but one way into Canaan and that was the Divine way made by the Ark of the Covenant. There is but one way into heaven. Jesus says, " I am the way." The Ark typified Him—its precious wood His humanity, its gold His Deity, its blood-sprinkled cover His Atonement. As the Ark descended into the depths of Jordan and rolled back its waters, so Christ descended into the deep waters of the wrath of God and opened the one way into everlasting life. So long as the Ark remained in the midst of Jordan the one way into Canaan was open and safe. Directly the Ark left the river, the waters returned in their strength, and the day of grace closed.

Israel's action in crossing the river illustrates salvation by faith. In the bed of the river stood the Ark, behind it the mountain of mighty waters, before it a passage into the Promised Land.

Israel believing that the Ark could keep back the flood, trusted herself to the passage of the river, and was saved. Faith, exercising the same trust in Christ, brings the believer safely into heaven.

The crossing took place on the tenth day of the first month, thus giving opportunity for choosing the lamb which, four days later, was to be slain at the Passover.

JOSHUA V.-VI. 5.—The strong fortress of Jericho barred Israel's entrance to the land. Its conquest was impossible to Israel, for its walls were great and high. God cannot give victories to " the flesh," i.e., to " self." Hence " the flesh " must be " put to death"— the " old man " must die and the " new man " enjoy a life of victory in Christ and with Christ. Jordan meant : " Ye have died." Gilgal : " Make dead therefore."

Accordingly the Holy Spirit presents in this chapter four foundation principles characterizing a life of victory, and necessary to the gaining of even one victory. These four principles are : The death of self ; testimony to the blood of the Lamb ; feeding on the Word of God ; and subjection to Christ as Lord.

Israel was about to smite the Seven Nations of Canaan with the Sword of the Lord. This was the dreadful ministry to which they were called by God. But before they were fitted to use that sword on others, they must themselves feel its sharpness and " die " beneath its stroke. This was illustrated in Circumcision. Only those are fitted to use the Sword of the Spirit, which is the Word of God, who have themselves experienced the death-stroke which it gives to " Nature "—that is to the natural man, his wisdom and his goodness. It is most bitter to a man to learn that all his goodness must be slain with the Sword of the Lord just as much as all his badness. But to the Christian this is most sweet ; for it brings him into a resurrection life, and the power of that life takes all strength from Satan. Man, as man, let him be never so religious, has no strength against Satan. Jericho's walls never fall before him ! But if death be suffered it becomes a shelter ; for what can Satan do with a dead man ?

Can he overcome one who having died is alive again ! Hence the Apostle writes : " We are the circumcision, and have no confidence in the flesh."

By the public eating of the Passover Israel proclaimed that her redemption out of Egypt, and her position in the Land of Promise, were alike due to the preciousness of the blood of the Paschal Lamb. True spiritual victories can only be won where there is this testimony to the person and work of the Lord Jesus Christ.

Manna was angels' food—it suited the Wilderness and its defective spiritual life. The "old corn of the land," that is, the deep and precious things of the Scriptures—the "strong meat of the Word"—accords with the full life of the heavenly places, and is a necessity of the strength needed for spiritual conquests there.

An absolute condition of victory is full surrender to Christ as Lord. He must be accepted as captain, be permitted to plan, and be fully obeyed. When Joshua recognized who the mysterious Visitor was, he at once yielded up his position as commander-in-chief, and surrendered his sword. The Lord Christ handed back the sword to Joshua saying, " I have given Jericho into thy hand." That city belonged to Him, though its inhabitants were unaware of the fact, and, therefore, He could say : " I have given."

Joshua had to put his shoes from off his feet and show the same reverence to Christ in the likeness of a man, that Moses had shown to Him as God in the Burning Bush. He who is called " a man " in v. 13, is declared to be "Jehovah" in vi. 2. Thus is Christ very God and very man.

The reproach of Egypt (ch. v. 9) was dual. So long as Israel wandered in the Wilderness Egypt reproached them with the taunt that Jehovah could not bring them into the Promised Land ; and, further, all of Egypt that attaches to a servant of God is a reproach to him. Would that Christians recognised this fact to-day ! This double reproach was " rolled away " at Gilgal.

Israel's two passovers, Exod. xii. and Joshua v., and their two baptisms, Exod. xiv. and Joshua iv, illustrate the doctrine of Col. i. and ii. See notes on these chapters.

JOSHUA VI. 6-27.—The four principles, necessary to victory in the spiritual life, set out in the previous chapter, i.e., the making dead of self; testimony to the Atonement; meditation on the Word; and subjection to Christ as Lord—these are, in this chapter, followed by six further principles which must be brought into exercise in the actual winning of victories in the Christian life. These six principles are: 1. The intelligence of faith; 2. The obedience of faith; 3. The exercise of faith; 4. The "folly" of faith; 5. The patience of faith; and 6. The victory of faith.

The intelligence of faith puts Jesus in the midst, just as Israel, at God's command, put the Ark in the midst.

The obedience of faith observes exactly the Word of the Lord, as Israel, in this chapter, minutely obeyed the many Divine directions.

The exercise and patience of faith are here illustrated in that Israel had to march silently round the city day after day for seven days. Such exercise developes faith. Naaman, the Syro-phenician woman, and Martha and Mary, and many others, had their faith so exercised. The Apostle rejoiced that his converts, faith "grew exceedingly"; and it grew because exercised by "much affliction."

The "folly" of faith is here evidenced by Israel's silent march day by day round the city; and by their using, instead of battering rams, trumpets made of the horns of rams! The soldiers on the walls must have greatly mocked them.

The victory of faith is seen in the fact that the wall fell down without the use of means that could account for its fall.

The wall of Jericho was its strength; the wealth of Jericho, its joy. Israel was to have no fellowship with either. As to the wall, faith was to destroy it; as to the wealth, faith was to devote it. At Jericho God and Satan were face to face. It was the first great battle in the Land. It was a crisis. Therefore God must be everything; the victory must be entirely wrought by Him; and the spoil must be wholly His. He cannot misuse wealth, but His children can— and especially at the beginning of their Christian life. Later on, when further trained and taught, Israel shared the spoil with God, and in fellowship with Him. So is it in the divine life. Gifts which, at the beginning, would be a snare may, later on, be sources of legitimate joy; but only so if shared in fellowship with God. Fellowship in that which was the joy of Jericho would have brought Israel into bondage to the world; just as accepting the wealth of Sodom would have robbed Abraham of his independence. The believer's joy is to be spiritual if he would win spiritual victories; and his confidence is not to be in the might and wisdom of man—i.e., the wall of Jericho—but in the Word which says, "I have given Jericho into thine hand."

This was Israel's first battle in the Land. It should be contrasted with her first battle in the Wilderness (Exod. xvii). These two battles illustrate the difference between conflict in the Christian life of Wilderness experience and that of "Ephesian" experience. Battles in the Heavenly places are so much easier than those in the Wilderness, because Christ does all the fighting, and He gives to faith the privilege of claiming the victory as her own. In the "Wilderness" there is much struggling and frequent defeat.

Grace elected Rahab and her kindred out of the abomination and its judgment. The words "She dwelleth in Israel unto this day," show that this history was written during Rahab's lifetime, and that the life which that believer receives is a life that is eternal. Rahab was a believer; she lived, in her children, up to the birth of the Messiah, of whom she was an ancestress; and she lives still

Israel's victory of faith brought about the salvation of Rahab. This fact is both solemn and cheering. A life of victory procures blessing for the perishing; not living a life of victory means spiritual loss to the world.

Salvation by the scarlet line was not only simple, it was also sure. When the day of wrath came the safety it promised it gave. Thus will it be in the Day of the Wrath to come. That day will prove how sure is the salvation which follows upon simply trusting Jesus.

Recent excavations have exposed the ruined walls of Jericho. They lie in great masses overturned, and of incredible thickness. One section of the wall remains unbroken. Here Rahab's house must have stood; and so on the completion of the final circuit the priests with the Ark halting there, it would not be necessary for that part of the wall to fall, for there were among the Levites no soldiers to go up every man straight before him.

JOSHUA VII.—The morrow of a great victory in the spiritual life is especially dangerous to the Christian. He is tempted to be thrown off his guard, to be over-confident, and to forget prayer. Had Joshua prayed about Ai, sin would have been immediately discovered and defeat avoided.

A hidden sin was the cause of Israel's defeat. In the life of victory God is the one and only strength of the Christian. He has no other strength. But God cannot give that strength if sin be indulged. If He did, He would deny His own nature, which is holiness. When He acts in power in the midst of His people He must act in harmony with His own nature ; and hence He must judge sin in the camp of Israel with the same " fierce anger " (v. 26) with which He judged it in the city of Jericho. That judgment in both cases was death.

But if the discovery and judgment of sin be painful, and if there be faithfulness in dealing with it, then grace gives both blessing and victory, and the valley of Achor becomes a Door of Hope (Hos. ii. 5). Sin should be feared, but neither its bitterness nor its punishment should be dreaded ; for it is at this point that God resumes His victory-giving fellowship with His child.

Babylon and money have a hateful attraction for the Christian. He finds these things among the unconverted around him, as Achan found them in Jericho, and his heart covets them. This explains the weakness of the Christian church to-day. These sins are indulged instead of being confessed and forsaken. God has therefore withdrawn His power, and there is universal weakness and defeat. Fellowship with God can only be enjoyed if resolute separation from all evil be observed.

Achan involved his family in the like ruin with himself. The use of the plural in the Hebrew text, and the adoption of the same word in the Greek translation of the Bible in verse 1 of this chapter and in Acts v. 1 and 2, suggest that they, like Sapphira, were privy to the theft ; but the moral principle was true that day, as it is now, that a man, in sinning, destroys his family as well as himself. The drunkard illustrates this terrible fact.

To be " burned with fire " does not mean to be burned alive in a fire. The guilty, under God's law, were first to be stoned to death, and then " burned up " with fire. Hebrew scholars recognize this in the original text.

The animals were burned up in sacrifice, but not burned alive.

JOSHUA VIII.—Victories are easily won in the path of simplicity and faith ; but if sin has been indulged it costs considerable pain to win even small victories. To overcome Ai what trouble was necessary ! All the people had to be mustered, an ambushment had to be set, Israel had to pretend to flee ! Nothing of this was seen in the capture of Jericho. Those to-day who walk the path of faith are undisturbed by the popular ferment about Biblical inspiration for they find the historic facts of the Scriptures to be present spiritual realities.

However, Israel having returned to Him who was her strength, victory resulted ; and grace gave her the spoils of the victory (v. 27). Such is God ! Where sin abounds grace doth much more abound.

For a vindication of God's action in utterly destroying all the inhabitants of Jericho and Ai, see notes on Num. xxi.

Joshua's action in burying the king of Ai the same day that he was put to death (Deut. xxi. 22), and his erection of an altar upon Mount Ebal (Deut. xxvii.), not only shows that he possessed the Book of Deuteronomy, but it furnished a public testimony to the fact that Canaan was Jehovah's Land, though at the moment in the possession of the enemy ; that therefore it was not to be defiled ; and that its tenure by Israel was founded upon the person and work of the Lord Jesus Christ.

As to this altar—its form, its material, its purpose, and its position—see notes on Exod. xx. 24 and Deut. xxvii.

It was placed on Mount Ebal, the mount of the curse, and not upon Mount Gerizim, the mount of blessing. Christ, who alone perfectly obeyed the Law, had, therefore, enjoyed, as a man, its blessing, yet, voluntarily, in love for those who, by sinning, had incurred its curse, ascended the hill of malediction, and, in His own person, suffered the judgment, and thus brought out from under the curse those who were sentenced to death. See notes on Deut. xxvii.

The heap of stone (v. 29), the pillar of stone (v. 32), and the altar of stone (v. 30) witnessed to the thoughts of God about sin, righteousness and atonement— the hatefulness of sin, the holiness of law, and the loveliness of Christ.

Visitors to these two mountains say that it is quite easy to speak across the intervening valley and be perfectly heard.

JOSHUA IX.—At Ai Israel trusted her own strength, and did not pray, and was defeated. At Gibeon she trusted her own wisdom, and did not pray and was defeated ! The sharp lesson taught at Ai was forgotten immediately. Such is the natural heart !

Satan is more to be dreaded as a humble suppliant than as a roaring lion. To make him flee he only needs to be resisted ; but to stand against his wiles, the whole armour of God must be employed. Had Joshua asked counsel at the mouth of the Lord instead of putting the mouldy bread of the Gibeonite into his own mouth, he would not have fallen into this snare. Satan, through the mouth of the Gibeonite, abundantly quoted the Bible to Joshua (vs. 6, 9, 10, 24), just as afterwards he did to the greater than Joshua, but the Lord defeated him with three verses out of the Law.

Had Joshua so acted he would have got the victory.

Satan can only deceive the Christian when he takes the management into his own hands instead of consulting the Lord. Communion with God gives a spiritual instinct which discerns an enemy, and refuses to make him an ally. To do so is to lose a victory ; to impair single-eyed dependence upon God ; to limit independence ; and to set up a perpetual snare. Four centuries later, in the days of Saul, the presence of the Gibeonites occasioned both sin and sorrow.

But grace triumphs over man's folly. The Gibeonites become the Nethinim. This word means " given," i.e., devoted to the Sanctuary of Jehovah. Their lives were spared because the princes of Israel had taken an oath to them in the name of Jehovah, but, because of their deceit, they were condemned to be drawers of water to the House of the Lord. They were not condemned to domestic slavery to the Israelites, but to bondage to " the congregation." Grace, therefore, brought them into the glory and joy of Ps. lxxxiv. 10, and instructed David to appoint them to high position in the Temple (Ezra viii. 20). Later on they were carried away captive with Israel ; they were among the first to return with Ezra and Nehemiah, pledging themselves to keep the statutes given by God to Moses (Ezra ii., 43-58),

Nehemiah vii. 60) ; and they are last read of in Nehemiah iii. 26, x. 28, and xi. 21, as making their home outside the water-gate of Jerusalem Why the water-gate ? Because, being near the water supply, they could the more readily discharge the honourable bondage to which Joshua had condemned them of being drawers of water to the Temple of Jehovah. Thus a curse, justly pronounced by Law, becomes, by Grace, a blessing.

JOSHUA X. 1-15.—When anyone makes peace with the Divine Joshua he brings upon himself the anger of his companions. Thus was it with Gibeon. But Joshua was able to protect and deliver the Gibeonites ; and Jehovah Jesus is able to deliver from their enemies those who know Him as their peace.

Joshua needed a fresh revelation (v. 8). He was perhaps discouraged and anxious because of his foolish action in the matter of Gibeon. But this word from the Lord so energized him that he marched in one night twenty-six miles. In the prior chapter the same journey occupied three days. When self and its wisdom govern the heart, rapidity and energy in the work of God are impossible. John outran Peter to the sepulchre, for Peter was weighted with a heavy heart and a guilty conscience.

Hailstones in Palestine are often as big as a man's two fists, and strike dead both men and cattle.

The supposed conflict between the Bible and Science found in this chapter does not exist. The phenomenon observed every year in Northern Europe occurred that day at Gibeon. It was a miracle, but it could be effected by the earth moving very slightly on its axis, thus causing the sun to remain above the horizon, as it does every summer in Norway. That this was so is confirmed by the State documents of Egypt, China and Mexico which record this double-day ; for such a declination of the earth would keep those three countries in the sunlight. Herodotus, Lord Kingsborough in his history of the Mexicans, and the Chinese philosopher Huai-nan-Tzu quote these records.

Hebrew scholars point out that the words " stand still " and " midst " are defective translations. The word " sun " is to be understood as " sunlight " ; as in many other passages in the Bible. " Stand-still " should be translated " remain ", and " midst " means the " half-of " i.e., " the horizon," for so the Easterns are accustomed to speak, and this word is frequently thus translated in the Bible. The Hill of Gibeon at the moment when Joshua spoke was behind him to the east, and the Sun was setting in front of him to the west. It was evening, and a continuance of the daylight was needed in order to complete the victory. What Joshua said may, therefore, be thus expressed in modern English : " Sun, keep shining upon Gibeon, and thou Moon in the valley of Ajalon ! And the sunlight remained, and the moonlight continued, until the nation had avenged themselves on their enemies. So the sun lingered upon the horizon and hasted not to go down an entire day." Thus the western face of the mountains of Gibeon was lit up so as to make possible this great victory.

JOSHUA X. 16-43.—There is but one way to deal with sin, and that is to place the triumphant foot of faith upon its neck, and to put it to death. It is impossible to improve sin, just as, in the judgment of God, it was impossible for Israel to improve these five kings. Man, in his folly, tries to improve what is opposed to God; but the failure of his effort ever reveals its foolishness.

Gilgal is mentioned five times in this chapter. This is very important. Verse 15 is thought by many people, either to be a quotation from the Book of Jasher, or an error in transcription , for it seems to interrupt the historic current of the chapter. But those who experience the spiritual realities corresponding to these historic facts, know the importance and necessity of this fifteenth verse ; for not only must Gilgal, i.e., the circumcision of self, be the centre from whence the Christian is to go forth to victory and to which he is to return after the triumph, but—and this is very important—he must, in spirit, abide there during the course of the battle, because the activities of the conflict, and its triumphs, tend to draw the heart away from God and divide its attention. True strength is always to be had at Gilgal ; there self is judged and mortified, and God and His power realized and enjoyed. The repeated mention, therefore, of Gilgal in this chapter, and the apparently needless interruption of the statement of verse 15, express an important principle which must be true in the experience of the Christian if he is to win victories over sin.

JOSHUA XI.—The victory at the waters of Merom made Joshua master of the north of Palestine, as that at Beth-horon made him master of the south.

The objection that it was cruel to command that the horses should be houghed has both a military and an agricultural answer. The Israelites, being Infantry, and making a surprise attack (v. 7), it was sound generalship to make the chariots useless by hamstringing the horses before they could be yoked. This made them useless for war, but not for agriculture. Many thousands of horses are mutilated every year so as to make them more fit for domestic purposes, and nobody accuses the veterinary surgeons of cruelty.

The frequent mention of Hazor (v. 1, 10, 10, 11, 13) introduces a great principle. Hazor was the world's centre of power. Natural wisdom would propose to make it the seat of government so that it should be that for God which before it had been for the world—" for Hazor beforetime was the head of all those kingdoms." But God will in no wise allow the world's seat of power to become that of His people. They were to depend exclusively on Him, and to dwell with Him at Gilgal. Accordingly Hazor is totally destroyed. Not a vestige of its former power must remain to compete with Gilgal. The centre and source of power must be all Divine.

Thus Joshua at God's command totally destroyed the Nephelim and the Anakim. Mysterious verses in the Bible suggest that these unhappy people were the offspring of union with wild beasts. Their total destruction, therefore, was necessary in love to man ; and God is love.

JOSHUA XII.—Where there was faithfulness there was rest, but where Israel was disobedient and did not utterly destroy all that breathed, there was compromise and defeat. This is an ever present principle in Christian experience. To a mind governed by the spirit of this world chapters in the Bible which contain lists of names are uninteresting, but not so to those who sit where Mary sat. They hang with appetite over every word that the Holy Spirit has written ; and to such students the list of victories in this chapter is full of interest.

On the Wilderness side of Jordan Israel conquered only two kings, on the Canaan side thirty-and-one. So is it in the Christian life.

Those who are satisfied to stop short of claiming and enjoying all the exceeding great and precious promises of the new Covenant win but few victories over sin and self and the world, but those who go on unto perfection (Heb. vi. 1) win many victories.

It is encouraging and touching to read of these thirty-and-one victories so definitely and individually recorded. There were not just thirty victories, but thirty-and-one. Each several victory was important in the eye of God and precious to the heart of God, however uninteresting and small they might appear to man. No victory over the enemy is small to God's mind. The broken numbers in Scripture, as for instance the number of the first-born of Israel, the number of David's mighty men, the number in the net of John xxi. etc., etc., form a profitable Bible subject for study.

Recent excavations have brought to light letters respecting Gezer dated 1400-700 B.C.

JOSHUA XIII.—Joshua was now one hundred and one years of age.

The first seven, and, perhaps, the first twelve verses of the chapter, are the very words of Him who said, " In my Father's House are many mansions." He here pointed out to His people " the very much land " that He had prepared for them. He desired to make them understand and know all that He had given them. He had a perfect plan for them, as He has for His own to-day. There was nothing uncertain in His arrangements, but, on the contrary, everything was orderly and well defined. The fact that these verses are the very words of the Lord Jesus Christ make them especially precious to the Christian, whilst, to the ordinary reader, they are uninteresting.

The sad word "nevertheless " (v. 13) expresses man's response to the exceeding great and precious promises of the preceding verses. Such is also the sad condition of the Christian Church to-day. All spiritual blessings are hers in the heavenlies in Christ, but how few of these are really possessed and enjoyed ! There is a difference between the gifts of God and the enjoyment of those gifts ; and, accordingly, how many enemies remain unsubdued in the hearts of Christian people.

Many times it is stated in the chapter that Moses gave the land east of the Jordan to the two tribes and a half. When dealing with the possessions west of the Jordan it is repeated with emphasis that God gave them.

Twice in the chapter (vs. 14 and 33) the special glory which was Levi's is recorded ; that is, that he had no inheritance other than Jehovah the God of Israel; that was his inheritance.

JOSHUA XIV.—This is a sunshine chapter. Amid the darkness of the unbelief of the tribes Caleb's faith shines like a sun. His was a Divine faith. Such a faith overcomes the world ; and, accordingly, he claims the great mountains for a possession, and not only expels the giants from thence, but even Arba the greatest of the giants ! (v. 15 R.V.). Such was the energy of faith in the heart of this beloved man ! The result was that Kirjath-Arba—that is the city of Arba—became Hebron—that is " fellowship " ; and the land had rest from war, for whenever there is faithfulness there is rest.

Thus Caleb who was a slave in the plains of Egypt became a prince upon the mountains of Hebron, and illustrates Ps. lxviii. 13.

Giant sins entrenched on strong mountains are helpless before a faith that is born of God. This fact may be experienced by Christian people if they will but wholly follow the Lord as Caleb did.

JOSHUA XV.—Judah, being the royal tribe, and Joseph having the birthright, which was forfeited by Reuben, were the first to receive their portions in the goodly Land.

It is delightful to read of this apportionment. When God enriches his people everything is real, substantial, and definite. He gives largely ; and his blessings may, without fear of disappointment, be counted just as this chapter records the 116 cities given to Judah.

But a life of blessing with God has definite borders, just as the lot of Judah had its divinely marked boundaries. It is important that God should choose a lot in life for each one of His people, and that they should be satisfied with that lot and its limitations.

Achsah's faith and intelligence were admirable. So sure was she that the South Land given to her by her father was really hers, and would not be taken from her by the Canaanite, that she asked for springs of water to make that land fertile. Her father, gladdened by such faith and intelligence, gave her more than she asked. Even a South

Land needs springs of water, and therefore it is that without the Holy Spirit the most happily circumstanced life, or a gifted ministry, must be alike barren ; and if men give good gifts unto their children, as Caleb did to Achsah, how much more will the Heavenly Father give the Holy Spirit to them that ask him ?

Man, however valiant, is never perfect, and therefore Jerusalem remained in the power of the Jebusite (v. 63) until David, type of Israel's mighty king, captured it. In how many lives is found a fortress opposed to Christ's government which ought to have been conquered at the beginning.

Caleb, Achsah, and Othniel illustrate the energies of a Divine faith. Such a faith (1) Claims the promise ; (2) Lays hold upon the promise ; and (3) Enjoys the promise.

Caleb "claimed the promise" of Deut. i. 36 (Joshua xiv. 9) notwithstanding the giants of verse 12.

Achsah "laid hold upon the promise" (ch. xv. 19) by asking for springs of water in addition to the field. Faith asked for a spring, and Love, in response, gave both the upper and nether springs.

Othniel showed boldness in battle ; Achsah boldness in petition. He was Israel's first deliverer and ruler ; his faith grew exceedingly (Judges iii. 9, and 2 Thessalonians i. 3). The Land had rest from war, and Faith "enjoyed the Promise."

So precious is such faith to God that the lovely story is repeated in Judges i. 12, 15. See notes on that chapter.

JOSHUA XVI and XVII.—-The words " lot " " line " " part " and " portion " all mean the same thing in Hebrew. Joseph (chapter xvii, 14) was dissatisfied with his lot ; but the true Joseph, in Psalm xvi. 6, declared that the lines had fallen to Him in pleasant places, and that he had a goodly heritage; and he added, in Psalm cxxv. 3, that the rod of the wicked should not rest upon the lot of the righteous.

The two tribes and a half chose for themselves. They did not wait for God to give them their portion ; and therefore the rod of the wicked very soon rested upon their self-chosen lot.

The whole land was, in effect, first given to Judah and Joseph, the other tribes receiving their portions according as they stood in relationship to the Royal and First-born sons of Jacob. These sons, united, typify Christ, to whom the whole land is promised (Psalm ii and cx).

All was according to the Word of the Lord. The casting of lots, the men who were to cast them, the divisions by families, by tribes, and by names—all was Divine— nothing was left either to the will or wisdom of man.

The portions were allotted " according to their families." This expressed the measure of their need ; and it was richly supplied. In Ephesians, the believer's " lot " is given not in proportion to either faith or need " but according to His riches." Compare the four " accordings " of Ephesians i. 4-7. with Numbers xxvi. 54.

The meanings of the Hebrew names of the towns and mountains, etc., which on the one side separated a tribe from the world, and on the other side, from a brother-tribe, are full of valuable teaching for the Christian. They plainly show how fellowship with evil on the one hand, or a lack of fellowship with truth on the other hand, sap faith and rob the servant of God of power to drive out the inhabitants of the Land.

The children of Manasseh could not drive out the inhabitants of those cities, but the Canaanite would dwell in the Land ; but the day will come when Israel's mighty King will take possession of the Land, and then there will be " no more the Canaanite in the House of the Lord " (Zech. xiv. 21).

The action of the five daughters of Zelophehad was very fine. When faith is in action it matters not how weak nature may be ; and the Holy Spirit here with joy recounts, not only the faith of these intelligent women, but their names ; and this He does twice (see Num. xxvii. 1).

The boasting, discontent, unbelief, selfishness, and cowardice of the children of Joseph was, with fine scorn, rebuked by Joshua ; who was himself of the tribe of Joseph. Where there is obedience and faith there is abundance of blessing ; and this principle is true at all times and in all ages.

The portion of Joseph stretched from the Jordan to the Mediterranean. The one extremity suggests the death of self ; the other, the love of God. The border marked the contact with the other tribes. In the daily intercourse with fellow-Christians a putting of self to death, and a consciousness of the depth and breadth of the love of God, are needed to make that fellowship sweet and profitable.

JOSHUA XVIII.—To enjoy peace with God and to claim and possess the promises of God are differing experiences in the Christian life. Israel was quite willing to enjoy a Meeting for Worship in the peaceful vale of Shiloh, but not disposed to take possession of the Land which God had subdued before her. This inactivity of soul is as true to-day as it was then.

The Tabernacle remained at Shiloh and Gibeon for three hundred years, and ceased to be used when superseded by Solomon's Temple. It symbolized Grace—the Temple foreshadowed Glory. Both are found in Jesus the God of grace and glory.

Benjamin's lot, as predicted by Moses in Deut. xxxiii, rested upon the shoulders of Mount Zion and Mount Moriah.

The expression "according to their families" is very sweet. God provided a lot for Benjamin sufficiently large to amply provide for each family. No one family, therefore, needed to be apprehensive as to the supply of its necessities. All were provided for ; and the three-fold repetition of the fact (vs. 11, 21, 28) attests its reality.

JOSHUA XIX.—However unfaithful man may prove himself to be, God ever remains faithful, for He cannot deny Himself. Therefore He did not fail to point out in detail to His people all that belonged to them. It is very beautiful to learn from these chapters how minutely, patiently, and repeatedly He described to His people the goodly land which He had given them ; and to notice how He divided it to them by families so that all should share alike, and no one family be preferred before another.

The last verse of this chapter is especially important. Whenever the Holy Spirit repeats a statement particular attention should be given to what is stated. So here the fact is emphasized that God distributed the land to Israel ; that He employed Eleazar, Joshua and the Chiefs as His agents ; that the distribution was by lot ; that the lots were drawn at the door of the Tabernacle ; and that all took place in Shiloh.

The ordered solemnity of these proceedings, and the fact that God decided the portion for each tribe, effectually prevented any challenge as to the justness of the distribution.

From this the lesson may be learned that they are happy, and well provided for, who allow God to choose for them.

Joshua in not choosing for himself until all the others had received their portions, furnishes another pleasing proof of the beauty of his character. His character may be said to be almost perfect. There is nothing recorded to his disparagement except that he objected to "lay"-preaching, for which Moses reprimanded him (Num. xi. 27-29). But he chose according to the commandment of the Lord. There is no previous record of this command. It is an instance of the Law of Subsequent Mention.

Simeon got no definite portion, and thus was fulfilled the prediction of Gen. xlix. 7.

Zebulun and Issachar were placed as neighbours between the Sea of Galilee and the Mediterranean, thereby fulfilling the prophecy of Deut. xxxiii. 18 and 19.

Judah (i.e., Praise) got a portion " too much for them " (v. 9). God always gives more than the praising heart can contain. Thus, in Canticles, the portion is too large for the heart that finds, in Ecclesiastes, the heart too large for the portion.

Accordingly Judah shares the inheritance with Simeon. Simeon, because of his misconduct (Gen. xlix.), was under a curse. Judah shares her abounding grace with the outcast brother, and thus doubles her joy. Halving Divine blessing with others doubles it. This is a great principle ; and it should stimulate the missionary spirit.

Thus it was that Simeon, justly doomed to wrath, was taken up in grace—the curse being turned into a blessing—and given a seat among the sons at the King's table ; for the Lord sprang out of Judah (Heb. vii. 14).

Simeon was saved by grace, not by works. The name means " Hearing." The Holy Spirit in Gal. iii. 2 contrasts salvation by doing and salvation by hearing, and teaches that only upon the latter principle can sinners be given a portion in the Heavenly Canaan.

JOSHUA XX.—For notes on this chapter see comments on Num. xxxv.

The provision of cities of Refuge instructed Israel as to the sacredness of human life to God, whilst the command to utterly destroy the inhabitants of the land taught her the hatefulness of sin to God. There is no contradiction here, for the one command is the complement of the other.

Heb. vi. 18 sets forth Christ as the City of Refuge for sinners guilty of His blood ; and the six cities appointed by Joshua display, by the meaning of their names, something of the sufficiency of that Saviour ; for in Him is found " Holiness " (Kedesh) " Strength " (Shechem) " Fellowship " (Hebron) " Safety" (Bezer) " Uplifting " (Ramoth) and " Happiness " (Golan).

God puts holiness first and happiness last. Man reverses this.

The man-slayer, restored to his possession upon the death of the High Priest, after his temporary exile because of his deed, is a figure of Israel in the latter day restored to the Promised Land from which she has been exiled as the slayer of the Messiah ; and His appearing as the dead yet living High Priest (" I am He that liveth and was dead ") will be the occasion of that restoration.

JOSHUA XXI.—The faithfulness and love that gave to each tribe a goodly heritage did not fail to provide richly for the scattered sons of Levi. Judgment scattered them in Israel, but grace made them a Kingdom of Priests and gave them forty-eight cities with their pasture-lands. This gift is three times declared in the chapter to have been according to the commandment of the Lord (vs. 2, 3, and 8).

Six of these cities were Cities of Refuge for the man-slayer ; and this fact is especially recorded of five of them. But one city, Bezer, though a city of refuge, is not, in this chapter, so distinguished. Why does the Holy Spirit omit here this distinction with reference to this city ? The answer may, perhaps, be found in xxii. 10–34. (See notes on that chapter).

That altar of man's rebellious imagination was set up close to Bezer, for both were opposite to Jericho, and, morally, neutralized it as a city of refuge. God had but one centre of blessing, in type, Calvary ; any other centre—even an exact pattern—denied that Divine centre ; and Bezer's sufficiency as a refuge being based upon Shiloh's atoning sacrifices and High Priest, the erection of the Reubenite altar destroyed that sufficiency because it destroyed that base. So to-day man's imitations of Christ's atoning work, and his addition of other centres of spiritual blessing, attack the uniqueness of God's only

refuge for sinners. Only at Shiloh was the Book that accredited Bezer as a refuge to the man-slayer, and only at Shiloh was the priest whose death satisfied the demand of the avenger of blood.

Thus in this chapter, and in the preceding one, does the Divine Author record the riches and honours poured upon the guilty tribes of Simeon and Levi.

The chapter closes with the testimony that " there failed not aught of any good thing which Jehovah had spoken to Israel."

JOSHUA XXII.—Self-pleasing and self-easing both bring trouble and defeat. This is the lesson of this chapter and of the next.

A self-chosen path is a path of trouble, anxiety, dissension, and danger. A path chosen by God is straight and simple, and furnished with peace. Had Reuben and his brethren not planned for themselves they would have been much happier. But as the result of pleasing " self " they had seven years of hard fighting as the vanguard of the armies of Israel ; they had, during this long period, daily anxiety for their defenceless families and flocks in the Wilderness beyond Jordan ; and, returning home, they were filled with fear as to the future. This fear induced them to set up " a pattern " of the altar which was at the door of the Tabernacle of the Congregation. This was sternly forbidden by God ; for it opened the door to idolatry ; and therefore were the children of Israel so alarmed, and, when remonstrating with the Reubenites, recalled the judgments that fell upon them because of the idolatry of Baal-Peor (Num. xxv.), and the rebellion of Achan.

Religious man can set up imposing buildings—the Altar was " a great altar to see to " (v. 10) and can use very vehement and orthodox language (v. 22), and can be very " careful " and full of " purpose " (v. 24 R.V.). The children of Israel, and their chiefs, were " well-pleased " (vs. 30 and 33) with the action and the words of the Reubenites ; but the chapter does not say that God was well-pleased ; nor does it say that Joshua asked counsel of God in the matter. Had he done so a happier issue would have no doubt followed. See notes on the previous chapter.

JOSHUA XXIII.—The " long time " (v. 1), was eight years.

Joshua told the Israelites what God had told him in chapter i, that prosperity depended upon fidelity to the Bible (v. 6), affection to Him who wrote it (v. 8), and separation from the nations (v. 12).

These Divine principles secure spiritual prosperity to-day.

The fidelity of God to His people forms the fine testimony of verse 14; and Israel's tenure of the land on the condition of obedience is set out in verses 15 and 16. They failed in that obedience and perished quickly, as predicted, from off the goodly land.

JOSHUA XXIV.—Joshua was a prophet. This appears from verses 2 and 27. In the former verse occurs the usual definite pronouncement as to the Divine origin and authority of the message which is peculiar to every prophet in the Scriptures, i.e., " Thus saith the Lord," and in the latter verse it is stated that the words spoken on this occasion by Joshua were all of them the very words of the Lord.

In this latter verse two remarkable statements appear. First, that Joshua knew that he spoke under inspiration; and, second, that the stone heard and registered all the Divine words—suggesting that, if necessary, it could, as a witness, repeat them. Thus the Lord told the Pharisees that the very stones were prepared to give their testimony to His Person and mission.

Joshua reminded the people that Abraham was an idolator when grace found him (v. 2); that they themselves were idolators in Egypt (v. 14); and added that they were still idolators, though secretly, at the moment he was speaking to them (v. 23).

Idolatry is incurably naturalized in man's heart. Three forms of it were pointed to by Joshua—one being worse than the other. The idolatry of Chaldea was impure, that of Egypt was worse, but that of Canaan was unspeakable.

People who have idols in their hearts and homes can yet use very brave religious language. The people protested again and again their determination to serve Jehovah. But Joshua, being a prophet, and, consequently, aware of the existence of their secret idols, tells them : " Ye cannot serve the Lord " (v. 19). And no man can serve God until he becomes re-born (Rom. viii. 7).

All the days of Joshua's government (v. 31) were only fourteen years, and all the days of the Elders that outlived him only three years ; and then came Israel's swift lapse into the abominations of idolatry.

The bones of Joseph were buried in the " field " that Jacob bought from the Shechemites. Abraham bought a "sepulchre" from the same tribe (Acts vii. 16). This is an instance of the Law of Subsequent Mention ; and there is no contradiction between Moses and Stephen. The purchase of a " sepulchre " and the purchase of a " field " are distinct transactions.

Israel's dwelling-place was designed to be in God's pleasant land, having His dwelling-place in their midst, i.e., the Tabernacle. But the limit of their government was to be the Euphrates. The Jordan was the boundary of their home—the Euphrates the border of their government. This is all a figure of things to come, both as respects Israel and the Church. Israel, under the Divine Joshua, will dwell in the Promised Land, but will be clothed with a power which will govern the whole world. As to the church, her home is in the heavenlies and the heavenly things are properly hers, but the Apostle says, " All things are yours," and hence the spiritual Israel, though domiciled in the heavenlies, has possessions embracing these " all things."

The argument of verses 19-23 is that God will not accept the worship and service of idolators ; nor will He forgive the sin of continuance in idolatry. There must be total separation from it.

JUDGES

JUDGES I.—Joshua was a book of victory —Judges is a book of defeat. Defeat resulted from unbelief and disobedience. It is true Joshua died, but God remained ; and hence there was no reason for defeat. But they looked at the chariots of iron (v. 19) instead of looking at the Arm of the Lord, and so became the miserable bondmen of those whom they should have utterly destroyed. They first permitted to remain in their midst the inhabitants of the land, and then, very soon, became insensible of the existence of these sources of evil and misery. Such is the sad history to-day of many a Christian, and many a church. The faith of a weak woman, Achsah, and the courage of her cousin, Othniel (v. 12-15), are here again recorded by the Holy Spirit, and stand out in contrast to the cowardice and unbelief of the tribes. All should have been, and might have been, as true-hearted and victorious as these young people. See notes on Joshua xvi.

In the victories given to Judah, Simeon and Manasseh, God showed what He could do for the heart that trusted Him. But the ground won by faith can only be held by faith ; and very soon, therefore, the Canaanite and the Philistine recovered possession of what they had lost.

In His love to His people God from time to time raised up Judges to shepherd them. The Hebrew word for Judge means : one who sets right what has been put wrong. These Judges were all distinguished by some disability, as will appear when each one's history is studied, and they will be found to illustrate the principle that God uses weak things to confound the mighty (1 Cor. i. 27). With these Judges God gave gracious revivals ; but after each revival the nation fell into deeper sin and bondage. The most perilous time in the believer's life is the morrow of a revival. At such a time increased watchfulness and prayerfulness are necessary.

God raised up these Judges because " His heart was grieved for the misery of Israel," and " yet they would not hearken unto their Judges " but corrupted themselves more and more with their idols. This fact contradicts the belief of those who say that Jehovah was invented by the Israelites, and was their tribal God, just as Chemosh was invented by the Moabites. But people always remain faithful to the god whom they invent, whereas there was perpetual contention between Jehovah and Israel. This fact is one of the many demonstrations that God is the one, true and only God, and that man's heart is incurably diseased by sin.

Thirteen judges appear in this book : twelve were chosen by God, and one was a usurper.

The Book of Joshua records the inheritance possessed : the Book of Judges the inheritance despised. The Book contrasts the faithfulness of God and the faithlessness of Israel. Chapter xxi. 25 is the keynote to the Book.

Public victories (vs. 1-12) depend upon secret supplies (vs. 13-15).

God did not command the mutilation of Adoni-bezek. He commanded his destruction. Religious energy, when not in fellowship with God and in obedience to His word, ever tends to excess. But yet the king admitted the justice of his punishment.

There is no confusion between verses 7 and 21 because one half of Jerusalem, i.e., Mount Zion, belonged to Judah while the other half, i.e., Mount Moriah, belonged to Benjamin ; and both tribes only obtained temporary possession of the city. See xix. 10-12.

It is foolish to put to task-work those whom God commanded to be put to the sword, for very soon the slaves put their masters to task-work. This principle is true to-day. There is but one way to deal with anything in the heart, or life, which is opposed to Christ and that one way is to put it to death, and not to try and just keep it in subjection.

The deep-seated hostility of man's heart to God is illustrated in verses 23-26. The one man and his family saved out of the doom of Luz, untaught by the fearful lesson, refused to join the people of God, removed far off to the idolatrous Hittites, builded a city there, and called it Luz. He set up again what he had seen God destroy. He re-names it Luz and the Holy Spirit adds with solemnity, " which is the name thereof unto this day " ; and this is true, for, to this day, men so act.

Rahab's action was the reverse. She and her family were the only ones saved out of the doom of Jericho. But grace changed her heart, and she joined the Church of God.

Luz became Bethel. The word " Luz " means " separation." " Bethel " means " the House of God." That which was far off was brought nigh—and brought nigh through judgment. Sinners are brought nigh through judgment ; but the judgment falls not on them ; it fell on their Substitute.

JUDGES II–III. 6.—Verse 1 should read " The Angel of Jehovah " i.e.. the Lord Jesus Christ.

The doctrine of the chapter is that God cannot give victories to the " flesh."

The Divine Angel " came up from Gilgal." Israel had left that centre of power, but He had not left it ; and He was the strength of Israel. It was at Gilgal that Israel got the power by which she overcame the Canaanite. The inward exercises of the heart, the putting to death of the members which are upon the earth, i.e., true circumcision, has no outward glory ; it is little in the eyes of man, and it makes man little in his own eyes, but it fills the soul with power, and makes the presence of God real. So strength was not shewn at Gilgal—it was shewn at Jericho ; but it was gathered at Gilgal. This principle is the secret of overcoming.

But when Gilgal was forsaken it was discovered that the Angel of the Covenant with His almighty power had been there, and was still there. He comes up from Gilgal. The result of leaving Gilgal was to weep in the valley of Bochim. The tears were shed for lost blessing. The people had sufficient life in their souls to weep and to worship (v. 4 and 5) ; and God accepted their tears and their worship, but withheld His strength and the light of His countenance, for they did not return to Gilgal. All this pictures the feeble spiritual condition of many of God's people to-day. This change from Gilgal to Bochim explains the servitudes of this Book. Praise and power at Gilgal were exchanged for weeping and weakness at Bochim.

The statement about Joshua and the elders (vs. 6–10) is repeated here designedly. by the Holy Spirit to justify the righteous indignation and words of The Angel of Jehovah.

As the Hebrew Church directly the elders died joined the surrounding nations, and corrupted herself, so did the Christian Church immediately after the death of the Apostles.

Six times in this Book is it recorded that the children of Israel did evil in the sight of the Lord. The definite article should be used in these six passages, i.e., " the evil " ; it means, idolatry. The passages are iii. 7 and 12, iv. 1., vi. 1, x. 6, xiii. 1.

The religion of fallen man is not a gradual ascent to what is higher and better but a declension to what is lower (ii. 12).

The two special commandments—not to intermarry with the nations and to utterly destroy all idols—were at once disobeyed (ch. iii. 6).

Defeat results from unbelief, and from the want of a definite experience (ch. ii. 7). Those who had had the definite experience, as children, of the Passover and the Red Sea, and, later on, of the Manna and the smitten Rock, the Jordan Passage, and the fallen walls of Jericho, these followed the Angel of the Covenant and were faithful to His Word. But a new generation arose that had no such definite experience ; and God, knowing what the heart is, left within the borders of the land the Philistines, and others, in order to put that new generation to the proof, that they might learn their own feebleness, and God's ability to keep and bless them.

Thus the wisdom of God turned their unfaithfulness into blessing ; and, by means of trials, He rebuked their unbelief ; for prosperity without trial deadens the soul.

JUDGES III. 7 – 31.—Idolatry leads to slavery (v. 7 and 8). There was first bondage to Baal, and then, as a result, bondage to Chushan. This is the experience of men in all ages.

Every time that they cried unto Jehovah He raised up a Saviour for them (vs. 9 and 15). When they cried, He delivered—no matter how guilty they were. There was no delay. " If we confess our sins He is faithful and just to forgive us our sins." Forgiveness immediately follows upon confession.

The saviours whom God raised up illustrate the teaching of 1 Cor. i. 27. Each one expressed some form of weakness. Othniel was the son of a younger brother; Ehud was left-handed; Shamgar had but an ox-goad; Deborah was a woman; Gideon was the least in the poorest family in Manasseh; Jephthah was the son of an harlot; and Samson was a Nazarite.

The word "quarries" (v. 19 and 26) should read, as in the margin of the Revised Version, "graven images." How sad to learn from verse 19 that these idols had been set up at Gilgal—an outrage upon the hallowed associations of that sacred spot. It was the dwelling-place of the Angel· of Jehovah, or had been (ch. ii. 1). Gilgal pictures the broken and contrite heart in which God dwells. If He be grieved away from such an heart, very quickly it becomes the home of graven images.

God can use feeble instruments as well as feeble persons. The rod in Moses' hand; Ehud's left hand; the ox-goad; a nail; a piece of a mill-stone; a pitcher and trumpet; and the jaw-bone of an ass. Most of the great heroes of the Christian Church were men of very humble birth—such as the Apostles and Luther and Calvin and Livingstone and Moody, etc.

" To cover the feet " (v. 24) means to sleep. Most men to-day when they lie down to sleep in the afternoon, whether indoor or outdoor, cover the lower limbs with a rug. See note on 1 Sam. xxiv. 3.

The R.V. gives the true sense of verse 22. Ehud thrust the sword with such force into the King's body that he transfixed him.

JUDGES IV.—This chapter and the following form one chapter and may be cited as the women's chapter. A woman's faith (Deborah) wins a great victory, and a woman's fidelity (Jael) destroys a great tyrant, and saves thousands of her sex from a fate worse than death (ch. v, verses 7, 11, 24, 30).

There was one heart that did not tremble before Sisera and his nine hundred chariots of iron. She " sat as judge " under a palm tree near Bethel (v. 5). Her namesake, Rebecca's nurse, was buried there four hundred years back. Many Christian people are shocked at Deborah's conduct in preaching and ruling in the Church of God, and at Jael's conduct in striking down the enemies of God. But both women were raised up and energized by God for their respective

ministries; as were also the great women of the Pauline Epistles. If the Scriptures be read apart from traditional teaching no surprise will be felt at the honours and ministries given to woman in the churches of the First and Second Covenants.

Two of Deborah's prophesies are found in this chapter (v. 7 and 9).

Barak obeyed the summons; but his want of faith to go alone robbed him of the honour of the victory. He wanted someone near and visible upon whom he could lean. To such a feeble faith the arm even of a woman gives more confidence than the Arm of God. God did not honour him, because he did not honour God. God is best honoured by being trusted; and Barak having had no direct relationships with God had not the consciousness of God's presence with him such as direct communications give. Fear does not honour God. He cannot associate His glory with the terrors of unbelief; and consequently the faith and courage of Deborah and Jael stand in fine contrast with the unbelief and timidity of Barak.

Jehovah " discomfited " Sisera and all his host. The Hebrew word implies supernatural discomfiture.

God who energized Shamgar to destroy the Philistine with an ox-goad, strengthened Jael to slay the Syrian with a tent-peg. Her conduct in so doing is unjustly condemned by many. But the Holy Spirit points, in the Scriptures, to only two women as pre-eminently " blessed amongst women "; the one was Jael, and the other the Virgin Mary. The latter is associated with the advent of Israel's Redeemer; the former with the judgment of Israel's Oppressor.

Jael by her righteous and courageous act saved her life, defended the honour of her absent husband, her own honour and that of many hundreds of her sex (ch. v. 30). By going into the woman's tent (v. 22 Heb.) Sisera was guilty of a most cruel action, and it was a very base return for the kindness and hospitality shewn to him. He knew well that Desert Law condemned to death a woman into whose part of the tent a man entered. She could only save herself by, if possible, putting him to death. Such was the Law of the Desert; and Jael was a daughter of the Desert and not of Israel.

But the Law of that time, and of the present day, commanded an Arab woman to shew the greatest hospitality to a visitor. This

Jael did. Sisera's cowardly conduct in then entering her apartment in order to secrete himself the more securely, was the action of a man not fit to live. The poor woman bravely did her duty—she put him to death. Thus was fulfilled the Word of the Lord as spoken by the prophetess Deborah (v. 9).

Every right-minded woman acts on the same principle to-day. If an evil-doer enters her house when she is alone, her wisdom is to receive him courteously and set an abundant meal before him. Her duty is to immediately telephone to the police. The man is arrested and punished, and society praises the woman. There being neither police nor telephones in the days of Jael she had to take matters into her own hand ; and this she did with skill and courage. When she said " Fear not " (v. 18) she never can have anticipated that he would have rewarded her kindness by intruding into her private tent. That it was into that forbidden part of the tent he intruded is clear from the Hebrew text.

JUDGES V.—This song should be read with the assistance of the Revised Version and the Companion Bible. They make clear the obscure passages.

" Then sang Deborah and Barak on that day." Victory must precede singing. Miriam sang on the Red Sea shore covered with the bodies of the drowned Egyptians. At Bochim they wept, for weeping follows defeat.

In verse 2 (R.V.) praise to God is called for : First, because leaders, such as Barak, placed themselves at the head of the troops ; and, second, because the soldiers enlisted willingly for the war.

The kings and princes addressed in verse 3 are those who in verse 19 were confederate with Sisera. They are invited in verses 4 and 5 to remember the wondrous acts and the mighty power of the God of Israel in the great and terrible Desert through which He led His people.

The song then contrasts the then present miserable condition of the nation (vs. 6-8) ; and points out that this condition of war, defencelessness, depopulation, and insecurity resulted from idolatry (v. 8).

" My heart saith to the leaders," i.e., to the princes, magistrates, and merchants (v. 10), " that willingly offered themselves among the people : Bless ye the Lord." This is, perhaps, the true translation of the original text.

But they were not only to bless the Lord, they were also to speak ; and what they were to speak about is set out in verse 11. This verse may be thus translated : " Instead of the shouting of the archers (of Sisera) in the places of drawing water, there shall they rehearse the righteous acts of Jehovah." This rehearsal was to be shared in by the ordinary people who walked by the way and not confined to princes who rode on white asses and sat on rich carpets (v. 10).

The conduct of the tribes is contrasted (v. 13-18). First, reference is made to the fact that only a minority of the chiefs and of the people volunteered for the enterprize, but that that did not discourage Deborah, for Jehovah " came down " for her against the mighty (v. 13).

Ephraim, although noted among the Amalekites, and therefore in personal jeopardy, is honourably mentioned as the first who helped in the war. They, with Benjamin, Zebulon and Issachar, charged valiantly into the valley after Barak (" at his feet "). Compare chapter iv (v. 10 and 14)

Reuben, Dan and Asher stood aside and attended to their business affairs. By their inaction they lost both blessing and honour. But the inhabitants of Meroz, in allowing the fugitives to escape in the day of battle itself, when, without any risk to themselves, they could have destroyed these cruel oppressors, were accursed, and the doom was pronounced by the Angel of Jehovah Himself, i.e., the Lord Jesus Christ. If when the Holy Spirit is acting in energy, either in opposition to some great evil or in promoting a religious revival, Christian people take up a neutral position, they lose the manifestation and the experience of the power of God. But if, like the people of Meroz, they are so placed that they can effectually come to the help of the Lord, and don't do so, then they bring death upon their souls.

The Virgin Mary was blessed " among women " (Luke i. 42) . Jael was also blessed " of, or among women " (v. 24 R.V.). Both these statements are made by the Holy Spirit, and in each case, through the mouth of a woman. The one was Deborah ; the other Elizabeth. The meaning in each case is that their fellow-women would account these women signally fortunate and happy.

JUDGES VI.—Once more the children of Israel relapse into " the evil," i.e., idolatry. In response to their cry of consequent distress a prophet is sent; but his call to repentance is unheeded. This appears from the fact that the men of his village wished to kill Gideon because he destroyed their idols.

But there was one ear that listened to the Divine message. The Angel of Jehovah appeared to Gideon and said: "Mighty man of valour, go in thy might and save Israel." Gideon was strong because he knew himself to be weak (v. 15), and because he believed Jehovah to be mighty (v. 13); and the misery that he was in because of the Midianites caused him to lift his heart to God instead of accepting, as others did, the tyranny of the oppressor.

He was threshing wheat *in* the wine-press (v. 11 R.V.). A threshing-floor could be easily seen because exposed to view, but a wine-press was sunk in the ground. Christ the Lord usually manifests himself to his servants when engaged in their ordinary business. Compare Moses at the burning bush (Exod. iii.), and the Apostles by the lake-shore (John xx.).

The Angel when speaking to Gideon used the word "thee" but Gideon, in his reply, used the word "us." This showed his sympathy with, and for, the people; and revealed the searchings of heart—product of faith—which recognized that the mighty God who had done such great things for them in the past was He who had delivered them into the hand of the enemy.

As in Gideon's day so now, reading the Scriptures instructs an exercised heart respecting sin and its bitter consequences, and respecting God and His ability to save.

The apparition of the Angel caused, first, fear (vs. 22 and 23), and then, peace (v. 24). Jesus, as Jehovah-Shalom, "made peace," "is our peace," and "gives peace" (Ephes. ii. 14, 15. John xiv. 27). .

Where God reveals Himself to the soul there always follows a public testimony to His Person and Glory. Such is the moral effect of true conversion. Gideon destroyed the idols in his own home.

Public victories cannot be won in the absence of private victories; and therefore was Gideon tested by the command of verse 25. Obedience to this command led to the enduement with power. The Spirit of Jehovah "clothed Himself with Gideon" (v. 34 R.V. margin). The Angel of Jehovah, gave the command; and, upon obedience, the Spirit of Jehovah, bestowed the power; and men recognized that enduement, and they gathered around Gideon.

The double test with the fleece made plain to Gideon that God could withhold and grant blessing. He could bless Gideon, and no one else; and, on the other hand, He could bless everybody else, but not Gideon. Rahab and Jericho illustrate the one action and Nineveh and Jonah the other.

JUDGES VII.—In accordance with Deut. xx. verse 8, the cowardly were given the option of returning home, and twenty-two thousand did so. When faith is growing-love abounds; and, accordingly, Gideon's faith having been nourished by the miracle of the fleece, he did not bitterly reproach these men for their cowardice.

God who knows the heart planned so that Israel could not say "My own hand hath saved me." Man always wants to have a hand in his own salvation; hence religious teachers, who have never experienced the new birth, bitterly oppose the doctrine taught in the hymn:

Nothing either great or small,
Nothing sinner, no,
Jesus did it, did it all,
Long, long ago!

A further test dismissed 9,700 men. They by laying their swords aside, and going down with deliberation upon their knees to drink, showed that they were concerned about their own needs and comforts. The three hundred on the other hand, showed by their action that God and the fortunes of His Kingdom had the first place in their hearts; and that they would not let even necessary needs hinder them in getting to work.

Yesterday's faith will not win to-day's battle; and therefore the dream of the barley cake was a fresh channel of strength to Gideon's heart. Barley-bread was the poorest of all bread; but yet one cake of barley-bread, with God behind it, could overturn the greatest tent in the camp of Midian. (v. 13 R.V.).

To the Midianite He was "God" (v. 14) to the Israelite He was "Jehovah" (v. 15).

In the battle the weapons of their warfare were not carnal but spiritual; and, therefore, mighty. The trumpets and the torches had but one purpose, and that was to announce the presence of God. The light of that Presence always puts the enemy to flight.

The burning torch shone within the earthen vessel; but, that it might shine unhindered, the vessel had to be broken. The Apostle Paul compares the Gospel testimony committed to the Christian to treasure in an earthen vessel. He says: " We have this treasure in earthen vessels that the excellency of the power may be of God and not of us."

The names " Oreb " and " Zeeb " mean " Raven " and " Wolf." At that day, as in the present time, men truthfully pictured themselves and their governments as wild beasts, or birds of prey.

A faith that leans upon the faith of another cannot stand a test which first-hand-faith in God can stand. The thirty-one thousand seven hundred men who for a time followed Gideon, because moved by his faith, failed in the day of battle. This moral principle is true to-day.

All that Gideon desired to be assured of was the companionship of God. In that consciousness he would have gone single-handed against the hosts of the Midianites.

The multitude of Israel (v. 23) joined in the triumphs of the victory. Without faith themselves they were quite willing to profit by the faith of another; and this measure of religious energy may be witnessed in the present day.

JUDGES VIII.—The pride and jealousy of the " flesh " (v. 1); its cowardice and time-serving (vs. 6 and 8); and its incurable idolatry (v. 27), are here sadly pictured, together with its corruption (vs. 30 and 31), and its forgetfulness and ingratitude (vs. 34 and 35).

The men of Ephraim were taught with tenderness (vs. 2 and 3); the men of Succoth with thorns (v. 16). Grace dealt with Ephraim; righteousness with Succoth. Gideon, in the energy of a Divine faith, acted toward both with moral elevation and power. He was as admirable toward the men of Ephraim as toward those of Succoth. It is sad when petulance is shown because of a seeming slight in connection with the Lord's work, but it is very much sadder when sympathy is shown to the enemy, and help refused to the servants of God, who, though faint, are yet pursuing. Such action, though overlooked for the moment, yet, later on, is chastised with righteous indignation.

Gideon's moral elevation in setting himself on one side was very fine. The secret of the Lord and of faith in Him was with Gideon. It would have been useless for him to try and explain this to the men of Ephraim; and it would have been wrong for him to contend with them. Such is often the experience of God's best servants. Their faith defeats the enemy, and others enjoy the victory and its fruits. The man of faith is satisfied with having done the work committed to him; the others are satisfied with the spoils of the pursuit; they make that a victory unto themselves, and it must be allowed them. And indeed they did shew some energy on behalf of the God of Israel, and, so far, stand in contrast with the men of Succoth and Penuel.

Satan, as an angel of light, and a minister of righteousness, knows how to set a snare for the foot of God's truest servants; and he knows that the best time to set the snare is during the excitement that follows a great victory. What more commendable and pleasing to the religious mind than to use the wealth of the enemy—more than three thousand pounds (v. 26)—in making an ephod? Was not an ephod a Bible garment? Was it not of Divine ordination? And Gideon put his foot in the snare; and the very man who had destroyed a gross form of idolatry in his home, set up a refined form of the same evil in his kingdom.

The parenthesis in verse 24 explains the difficulty of Gen. xxxvii. v. 25, 28, 36, and xxxix. v. 1. Ishmael and Midian were half-brothers, and so their descendants might justly be called by either name.

JUDGES IX.—The truth that he that soweth to the flesh shall of the flesh reap corruption is illustrated repeatedly in this chapter. Abimelech was a natural son of Gideon; he therefore was born of the will of the flesh, and he became a channel and an instrument of evil to Israel. Good were it for the nation had he never been born! Little did Gideon think at the time of his birth that the child would become a source of sin and calamity to the people of God. A wrong action, which, at the time, seems harmless, bears bitter fruit in after years. Abimelech brought destruction upon the men of Shechem, and they, and their neighbours, brought destruction upon Abimelech.

Abimelech's success with his mother's relatives was one of the evil fruits of polygamy. He never should have been born.

Although he only slew sixty-nine persons yet was he justly charged with the guilt of having slain seventy, for that was the desire of his heart ; and God reads the heart, and apportions the guilt accordingly (Matt. v. 28, Acts vii. 52).

The House of Baal-berith, i.e., the Lord of the Covenant, (v. 4), and the House of Millo (v. 6), and the oak shaped as a pillar (v. 6, R.V.) show how fully re-established was idolatry (compare chapter viii. vs. 27 and 33).

Jotham's allegory was both a parable and a prophecy. It had an immediate fulfilment ; for the men of Shechem elected the bramble to rule over them, and mutual destruction was the result.

But the allegory had a wider significance. In the Scriptures Israel is figured as a fig tree, an olive tree, and a vine. These symbolize National blessing, covenant blessing, and spiritual blessing. The bramble is a fore-picture of Anti-christ. In the future dark day of Israel's rebellion she will turn aside from all this Divine fulness and put her trust in the rule of Anti-Christ ; and mutual destruction will be the result.

What God permits He is stated in the Bible to perform (v. 23).

The god Berith (v. 46) was unable to protect his worshippers, and so they all miserably perished in the flames.

It was not " a piece of a mill stone " but " an upper mill stone " that the woman dropped upon Abimelech's head. (v. 53 R.V.).

JUDGES X.—Untaught by repeated judgments and miseries Israel once more did " the evil " in the sight of the Lord : and with more determination than ever, for the nation greedily wallowed in seven gross and hateful forms of idolatry which existed amongst their heathen neighbours (v. 6). This appears to be the lowest point of debasement that they touched at this period of their history.

The Philistines on the west and the Ammonites on the east " vexed and oppressed them." These words may be translated " broke and crushed them." In earlier days when serving one false god they were oppressed but on one side, but now, serving a multitude of idols, they are oppressed on both sides. This fact is as true for men and nations to-day as it was then.

But there was sufficient energy of life in Israel to bring out the cry of confession (v. 10). To be conscious of misery is a sign

of life (v. 9). Because of the deceitfulness of the heart, and because of the deceitfulness of sin, bondage is accepted after a slight struggle, and then, after a time, the slave becomes unconscious of the slavery.

The confession " We have sinned against Thee " showed true repentance, for it showed a sense of injury done to God, and not merely sorrow because of the miseries that lay upon themselves. Remorse is not repentance— mental distress because of the painful results of sin is not repentance ; but a sense of the grief and dishonour occasioned to God, and sorrow because He has been sinned against, that is repentance. David and Simon Magus illustrate true and false repentance. The one cried out, " I have sinned against the Lord." His first thought was God and His Glory. The other said, " Pray for me that none of these things come upon me." His first thought was himself and how to secure exemption from punishment.

JUDGES XI.—Jephthah was a man of base birth, and was despised, rejected, and hated by his brethren (vs. 2 and 7). Such are the instruments, as already noticed, that God uses to rebuke His people, and confound man's wisdom and power.

Vain, i.e., broken or bankrupt men, gathered unto Jephthah in his exile, as, in later years, a similar class joined David in the Cave of Adullam.

Jephthah's skill and courage as a guerilla chief becoming known unto the elders of Gilead they invited him to be their head and captain ; and Jephthah, after a dignified reproof because of their past conduct to him, and a solemn religious ceremony at Mizpeh, accepted the position.

Like many able and brave generals Jephthah was averse to bloodshed, and, therefore, did his best to dissuade the King of Ammon from making war. He rehearsed Israel's history for three hundred years, and pointed out how God had given them the land which they possessed, and that Ammon had no title to it. The Ammonite King would not, however, be dissuaded ; he risked a battle, and was totally defeated.

It is not to be assumed that Jephthah put his daughter to death and offered up her body as a burnt-sacrifice to Jehovah, for such sacrifices were sternly forbidden in the Law (Lev. xviii. 21 and xx. 2–5). The word "and" in verse 31 is frequently translated in, the

Scriptures " or." (See Marg.). The vow contained two parts ; Dedication or Immolation, in accordance with Lev. xxvii. He, accordingly, dedicated his daughter to Jehovah by a perpetual virginity (vs. 36, 39, and 40). This is conclusive from the statement in verse 39 that after her father had performed his vow " she knew no man," that is, she never was married ; and, further, that yearly, for four days, the daughters of Israel went " to talk with " or " rehearse " with (ch. v. 11—the same word in Hebrew) or to " celebrate in song " this willing dedication of this noble daughter of a brave father. Thus they " rehearsed " this great act of her life rather than, as popularly supposed, lamented the horror of her death.

JUDGES XII.—Christian people must not be discouraged nor weakened in their confidence in God's overruling hand, if in their successful efforts to do good to others they experience sorrow and opposition. Jephthah's success in saving his countrymen from a cruel oppressor was followed by the loss of the companionship of his only child, and by the murderous hatred of the men of Ephraim. These men, cowardly (v. 2) jealous, and vainglorious (ch. viii. vs. 1-3), set out for Jephthah's home in order to burn him alive in his own house (v. 1) ; and in response to Jephthah's elevated and modest appeal (vs. 2 and 3) replied with gross insults (v. 4) ; and brought upon themselves a just punishment (vs. 5 and 6).

Forty-and-two thousand may not mean 42,000 but 40 plus 2,000, i.e., 2,040.

Just as his lips unmasked the pretended Gileadite and showed him to be an Ephraimite—for he could not pronounce the word Shibboleth aright, so mere professors of religion expose themselves to be such when they vainly try to use spiritual language. " Shibboleth " means a "stream" ; " Sibboleth " a " burden."

Jephthah and Abdon present a contrast. The one risked his life, won a great victory, and delivered Israel ; and after a childless life was buried in an unknown grave. Such is the gratitude of man ! The other risked nothing that is recorded, he had forty sons and thirty grandsons (v. 14), and his grave is described with great minuteness. But the Holy Spirit in Heb. xi. 32 places Jephthah's valorous name upon the golden tablets of the eternal records and ignores Abdon. God never forgets those who trust and serve Him, however much they may be forgotten by man.

JUDGES XIII.—The Philistines now became prominent, and continued to be so up to the time of David, when they were finally subdued.

The Philistine represents a fact : Samson a principle.

The fact is , that there are enemies within the Christian's heart, for the Philistine was an inward, and not an outward, foe. The principle is : that this inward enemy can only be defeated by full consecration to God.

With respect to the meaning of Nazariteship see notes on Num. vi.

Nazariteship is the one and only source of strength against enemies in the heart. This principle gives peace and victory ; for it means the putting of self to death, and a thorough-going and definite separation from all that upon which man leans for joy and strength.

Israel had at this time fallen so completely into the power of the enemy that only a Nazarite could be used by God to deliver them. But as always, so in this case, man failed. Christ was the true Nazarite. The source of His strength was a secret unknown to the world. In His day Israel was in a worse bondage than that of the Philistine ; and He, in the power of full consecration, walked amongst sinners separate from them —separate from evil—and yet He was in the midst of them as their Light and their Salvation. So, as Samson, He began to save His people from the Philistine in His first Advent, and, as David, He will complete His saving work in His second Advent.

The world, and worldly Christians, cannot understand this principle of separation and victory ; and those who do know it only retain their strength so long as they abide in this state of complete separation.

The Angel of Jehovah (v. 3) was the same Angel that appeared to Gideon (i.e., the Lord Jesus Christ in Angelic form).

The faith of Manoah was very admirable (vs. 8 and 12) and his ignorance very deplorable (v. 17) ; for if not rebuked he would have given Divine honour to a person whom he believed to be a creature and not the Creator (v. 16).

When asked what was His name the Angel replied. " Wonderful." This, in the Hebrew text, is the same word as in Isaiah ix. 6. His doing wondrously in ascending up to Heaven in the flame of fire proved Him to be entitled to this Great Name.

Christ is a wonderful Saviour. He is Wonderful for what He is to sinners, and Wonderful because of what He does for saints.

The Divine directions respecting the child having been given to the mother is a striking instance of the fact that a boy's future largely depends upon a mother's training.

The woman's reasoning in verse 23 was sound. The fact that the Angel accepted the sacrifice was an evidence of salvation and life and not of condemnation and death; for the Angel was God (v. 22). Sinners are saved, not by their acceptance of Christ, but by God's acceptance of Christ on their behalf; but sinners must accept this Saviour in order to profit by the Divine acceptance of His Person and Work (John i. 12).

JUDGES XIV.—Samson's history illustrates the tendency of the Christian to fall at any moment from this position of whole-hearted separation unto God into all that in which the world finds its joy and strength. Such a tendency does not always, and to the same extent, produce the same evil fruits, but invariably leads, as in Samson's case, to the loss of both strength and sight. God, in His sovereignty and freedom of action, may overrule such failure in order to execute just judgment upon a guilty world, but He does not safeguard His disobedient child from the painful consequences of unbelief and disobedience. Hence it is remarkable that whenever the world draws away by its allurements those whom God has separated unto Himself, it brings down the wrath of God upon the world. Sarah in the houses of Pharaoh and Abimelech, and Samson in his marriage with a Philistine, are instances of this Divine principle. God made use of Samson's marriage with a Philistine to punish that people; but that did not excuse Samson's folly and disobedience; for had he yielded himself unto God, and his members as instruments of righteousness (Rom. vi. 13), how much greater and more glorious would have been the victories granted to him! His conduct showed an ignorance of Bible-teaching as to marriage, but his heart was true to the Lord; and in the freshness of that strength he could rend the lion (v. 6) and slay the Philistine (v. 19).

Though there may be features in a Christian's conduct and worship not sanctioned by the Word of the Lord, yet when the heart cleaves to Him God oftentimes grants the power of His Spirit; but, as in Samson's case, that power was granted not in connection with his marriage but quite the contrary; for it was its mis-adventure which led to the punishment and death of the Philistines (v. 19).

The depths of Satan may be recognized in his action toward Israel in connection with the Philistines. The other nations " mightily oppressed " Israel, but it is not stated that the Philistines did so. They simply " ruled " Israel; and so insensible had Israel become to slavery that they accepted this yoke. This is the sad history of many a Christian life. Bondage to some inward form of evil is submitted to, its rule accepted, and spiritual insensibility results (ch. xv. 11).

Satan therefore introduced this new form of rule and bondage as distinct from the former violence and cruelty; and Samson's countrymen were satisfied with it. He therefore could not get them to join him in a general revolt, as was the case with former judges; and, therefore, it was necessary that a private cause of quarrel should arise. His proposed marriage furnished such an occasion, and God used it to that end (v. 4).

In the East a year usually elapsed between betrothal and marriage. Hence there was in all probability that interval between verses 7 and 8. The marriage feast lasted seven days; the bridegroom entertaining his thirty companions in one house—the bride, her friends in another. The proposing of riddles was, and is, a favourite pastime on such occasions. The bride grossly deceived Samson, and did not, after all, marry him but his companion. This was in accordance with the recently discovered laws of Khammurabi.

JUDGES XV.—The life is usually marked by folly when self-will is the spring of action. On the contrary, when God's will governs the life, prudence and prosperity result. Accordingly Samson foolishly returned to the woman who so basely betrayed him. His action in doing so was magnanimous and forgiving, but it was foolish. The woman's father was guilty of insult and falsehood (v. 2); but the end of it all was that he and his daughter suffered the horrid doom which she by her

treachery to Samson sought to escape
(ch. xiv. 15 and ch. xv. 6).

The destruction of the Philistines' harvest
—it was the month of May—was a just
retribution because of their unjust conduct
to Samson.

Jackals and not foxes (R.V. margin) were
the instruments of that destruction. If it
be objected that Samson's action was cruelty
to animals it may be replied; first, that,
assuming the jackals perished, their death
would be an advantage to the country; and,
second, that it is quite possible that the
animals suffered nothing beyond fright, for
they continually ran away from the fire which
they created, and, directly the flame of the
burning torch reached their tails, it burned
the fastenings and set them free.

The Revised reading of verse 7 sets forth
Samson's conduct as wonderfully noble. He
placed himself between this treacherous
woman, who was so unworthy of being
defended, and her enraged neighbours, and
told them that if they put her to death in this
horrid manner he would take a terrible
vengeance upon them. Apparently he
arrived too late to save her and her father;
but he smote them with a great slaughter.

The opposition of the world is bitter to the
Nazarite Christian, but the opposition of the
Church is more bitter. The men of Judah
say to Samson: "Knowest thou not that the
Philistines rule over us?" They wished to
live in peace under that government; and
they did not wish to have a Nazarite in their
midst who would disturb that peace and
excite the world against them. They were
quite ready to hand Samson over to a cruel
death in order to maintain peace. This condition of spiritual degradation marks, and has
marked, the history of the Christian Church.

But just as the lion had no strength
against Samson so the Philistine had no
strength against him. In this Samson is a
type of Christ who destroyed him that had
the power of death, that is, the Devil, and
thus food and sweetness are brought out of
death as the honey out of the conquered lion.

God's victories are usually won with
despised instruments. The feeblest instrument is destruction to the enemy if God be
behind it!

The well that refreshed the fainting
Samson was not found in the jaw-bone but
in Lehi, i.e., the hollow place. It was a
depression in the ground, and was so named;

and from that day the well was called
"Enhakkore," that is, "the well of him
that called." The Divine titles should here
be noticed. Samson called on "Jehovah,"
i.e., the Covenant Saviour, and "Elohim",
i.e. the Creator, provided the well.

JUDGES XVI.—Samson could rend lions
and conquer Philistines, but he could not rend
his lusts nor conquer his appetites.

He went down to Gaza to have guilty
fellowship with a degraded woman, and used
his Divinely-given strength to bear away the
doors and bars that would have imprisoned
him, but without bringing any moral profit
to the fallen Philistine or to her compatriots.
Christ, the true Nazarite, descended to earth,
not to have guilty union with its fallen
inhabitants, but to redeem them; and at the
dawning of the day he burst the bars of the
tomb and ascended to the heavenly Hebron
(v. 3); thereby securing eternal life for the
degraded sons of men.

Samson's betrothed (ch. xiv. 17), and
Delilah (v. 18) having both deceived him, it
may be assumed that it was this woman at
Gaza who informed the Philistines of his
visit to her house (v. 2).

A Christian, when governed by self-will,
can fall deeper into folly and sin than a man
of the world. This explains Samson's
incredible conduct with Delilah. It is plain
from the facts of the chapter that she was a
debauched woman. Moral strength is not the
same thing as intellectual or physical
strength.

Compare the eleven hundred pieces of
silver of this chapter with those of the next
chapter, and note the evil wrought by them
in each case.

Samson "wist not that Jehovah was
departed from him"; but he very soon
found it to be so when a crisis came. Fellowship with the world had robbed him of his
strength. Such is the position of many a
Christian minister to-day.

The Philistines put his eyes out and
degraded him to the abject position of
provider of bread and sports (vs. 21 and 25).
Such is ever the moral result of association
with the world—it obtains the mastery, the
Christian loses his eyesight and liberty, and
becomes a mere purveyor of entertainments
to the church.

The enemy could cut off Samson's hair but
could not destroy its life. The world may rob

the Christian of the secret of his strength, but it cannot destroy the source of that strength.

Samson died with the Philistines. It was not suicide. He recognized that the association with them which his self-will had brought about involved him in the judgment which was to fall upon them. This principle is always in operation. Association with the world necessitates sharing its calamities and judgments; though this does not of course touch the question of eternal salvation.

Recent excavations at Gaza have laid bare the two stone bases on which the pillars stood that Samson displaced.

Samson's history presents a mystery, also found elsewhere in the Scriptures, that an imperfect moral character may accompany great spiritual gifts—as for example Balaam and Judas Iscariot; but sorrow and failure mark all such histories.

JUDGES XVII.—The death of Samson closes the Book of Judges historically. In the remaining five chapters the Holy Spirit discloses the inward moral condition of the nation during the period covered by the entire book. Phinehas was High Priest at the time that the events in the last chapter occurred.

It is all a sad picture of confusion, idolatry, sin, and violence; and it all resulted from neglect of the Bible. Had they read and obeyed the Five Books of Moses they would have been a holy and a happy people. But they were self-willed; and four times in this section of the book it states " every man did that which was right in his own eyes."

" The love of money is a root of all evil " (R.V.). The eleven hundred shekels of silver of this chapter are connected with idolatry, as those of the last chapter were with immorality. Money readily becomes an idol.

Idolatry in Israel had a fitting birth. It was born in dishonesty (vs. 2 and 3).

The images of verse 4 must have been small—corresponding to domestic crucifixes and crosses of the present day—for two hundred shekels of silver would be worth only about twenty-three pounds.

These images, together with the ephod and teraphim and priest of verse 5, suggest that this domestic chapel was a corrupt imitation of the Tabernacle.

All was, however, contrary to the Word of God. It commanded only one place of Worship. It forbade images; and it permitted none to be priests but the sons of Aaron.

Micah called his Chapel a " House of God " (R.V. margin) but the Holy Spirit called it a house of idols (v. 5). The true House of God was neglected and as hard to find then as it is to-day (xxi. 19); and when found amusements rather than worship characterised it (xxi. 21-23).

Had Phinehas and the nation obeyed the Scriptures this Levite (v. 7) would not have had to rove about looking for a situation.

He was to be a " father " as well as a " priest " to Micah in return for his board, his clothes, and his salary of 25s. a year. To the present day many enjoy both these titles of " father " and " priest " and the associated salary.

The young man became " his priest " (v. 12) not Jehovah's priest, and officiated in Micah's house, not in God's House.

Micah said " Now know I that Jehovah will do me good seeing I have a Levite to my priest "; but the " good," as in all such cases, never came; for he was afterwards robbed of both his idols and his priest. He had, like some people in the present-day, a little knowledge of Scriptural Worship, but only sufficient to make him idolatrous and superstitious.

Micah no doubt was a well-to-do county magnate. Such persons think it very proper to have domestic chapels. They furnish them with altars and pictures and crosses and candles and call them " Houses of God." They would be deeply pained, or greatly angered, if their chapels were called " houses of gods " (v. 5).

JUDGES XVIII.—The events of this chapter probably occurred in the time that Othniel judged Israel. The Danites should have taken from the Philistines the " lot " which had been given them by God (Joshua xix. 40). But not having faith sufficient to attack and overcome that nation, they undertook an expedition against a small and defenceless people in the extreme north of Palestine, built a city there, which they called " Dan "—thus originated the expression " from Dan even to Beer-sheba " —and publicly established idolatry. This shameful action explains the subsequent calamities that fell upon that tribe, and the omission of their name in Rev. vii.

Men always like to have their self-made plans sanctioned by religion (v. 5).

The ambiguous answer of the Levite in no wise committed him ; and was as delusive as that of a heathen oracle.

The action of the Danite spies in asking this Levite to divine for them—no doubt by means of the teraphim or the ephod—shows how far at this early date the Word of God was departed from. They ought to have been shocked and grieved at a Levite assuming priestly functions ; and they should have been indignant at the existence of a house of idols in rivalry with the Tabernacle of Jehovah.

Ceremonial religion and violence, robbery, and plunder readily accord ; and the richer the ceremonial the feebler and poorer becomes the moral consciousness. Mankind has religious affections. He must have objects on which to exercise these affections, and hence the passion for images, pictures, crosses, and symbols in what is popularly called " worship."

The Danites evidently expected to be attacked, for they put their families in the front, thus placing the armed men between them and danger (v. 21).

The Holy Spirit, in verse 29, uses the great name " Israel " and not the feeble name " Jacob." This is very affecting and solemn. It is to emphasize the depth of Dan's guilt in setting up idolatry. The Holy Spirit says : " And he was a son of Israel ! " and he adds, with equal sadness : " They set them up Micah's graven image which he made " ; and, as a climax, this was done at the very time that the House of God was in Shiloh ! and continued all the time that it remained there.

Verse 30 gives the name of this Levite, and mentions that he was a grandson of Moses. As in the Christian Church so in the Jewish, corruption appeared at the very beginning. So ashamed were the Jews of this Levites' near relationship to Moses, and so unwilling to dishonour Moses by publicly reading aloud his name in this verse that they used the name " Manasseh " instead, and hence that name appears in the margin of the Revised and Authorised Bibles.

JUDGES XIX.—The internal condition of Israel, as revealed by the Holy Spirit in this and the two succeeding chapters, becomes the darker when it is remembered that the High Priest at that time was Phinehas the son of Aaron ; and that thousands were still living who witnessed the passage of the Jordan, the capture of Jericho and the many other evidences of the existence, the power, and the holiness of God.

The Lord said that Moses because of the hardness of their heart suffered them to have more than one wife, but that in the beginning it was not so. The Levite, therefore, in having a secondary wife—they were called concubines—did not stand in a dishonourable relation to her.

The unhappy woman in sinning against her husband little dreamt of the dreadful doom that would result from her action. The Devil pays hard wages. The terrible story pictures the misery, shame, and ruin that come upon the heart that, unfaithful to the True Husband, lives in guilty union with the world. The night in such a heart is dark indeed ; and all the world gives is abuse and not honour (v. 25).

How painful it must have been to the Spirit of God—who is the Holy Spirit—to record such vileness !

It would have been better for the Levite to have spent the night with the heathen than with the professed children of God (vs. 10-15); for the latter had already become viler than the former although Joshua was not long dead !

The baseness and cowardice of the Levite and his host, who ought to have given their lives in defence of the woman, and the horrible vileness of the men of the city, prove the truth of the Scriptural doctrine that man's heart is desperately wicked, and his nature thoroughly corrupt.

Lot's last night in Sodom gives a similar illustration of the loathsome depths to which men sink when they cease to retain God in their knowledge (Rom. i. 18-32).

The black crimes of this black night became historical in Israel, and worse than historical ; for in Hosea ix. 9 and x. 9 the Prophet sadly cries that the nation was still deeply corrupting itself as in the days of Gibeah ; that they were still guilty of the same abominations ; and still refusing to believe in any punishment, just as the men of Gibeah had confidently stood in the day of battle.

These closing chapters of the Book of Judges picture the moral darkness that settles down upon a nation, or a church, when the Bible is disregarded and men follow the religious and social teachings of their own hearts.

The terrible message of the Levite was necessary to awaken the nation, so deep was the impure sleep into which it had fallen

JUDGES XX.—The men of Israel were shocked at the fruits of the " flesh " in the men of Gibeah but they were blind to the activities and power of that same principle of evil in themselves. They were filled with anger because of the conduct of these men against a Levite and his wife, but there is no record of their sense of the sin against God, and of the evil of idolatry which at the time existed in their midst. So is it to-day. A sin against God is lightly regarded, but a sin against society is mercilessly judged.

Had the children of Israel acted at the beginning (v. 8–11) as they did later on in verse 26, they would have not suffered the two defeats of verses 21 and 25. Their planning without God was one of the fruits of that fallen nature which they shared in common with the men of Gibeah. It is true that, after they had made their plans, they prayed (v. 18), but it was to ask, not whether they were to go to battle or not, but who was to go first, and the Divine reply was Judah. And, prior to the second defeat, in response to their prayer, they are again permitted to go up against Benjamin.

There is instruction in this for Christian people at all times. Before the tribes were fitted to judge evil in others they needed a sharp discipline to teach them to judge evil in themselves. The nation was self-willed— there was no king—no restraint—everyone did that which was right in his own eyes. There was national departure from God. The result was seen in the disorder and violence of these chapters. The patience and love of God in maintaining relationships with such a people excite admiration and worship. So dead in their souls had the people become that they never thought of asking God how the matter was to be dealt with ; nor were they conscious that they themselves were guilty of sins which cried out for the Divine wrath.

It was necessary, therefore, that they should learn a deep moral lesson ; for God cannot give victories to man's natural will. The forty thousand who perished in the first two battles were no doubt men who deserved to perish ; and the effect of the sharp lesson

is seen in verse 26. The nation at last draws near to God in repentance and sorrow, and, confessing themselves to be sinners, they offered burnt-offerings and peace-offerings. As interpreted by the New Testament, they confessed their own guilt, they declared themselves worthy of the wrath of God, and they pleaded the person and work of Christ the Lamb of God for pardon and acceptance ; and, their souls now humbled and taught, they were in a fit moral state to go up against Gibeah. It indeed deserved wrath, but Israel merited wrath herself, and had in a figure to suffer it in and with Christ before drawing the sword against Benjamin.

The " Shall I go," of verse 28 should have displaced the " which of us shall go " of verse 18. Living at a distance from God blunts the spiritual sense ; and it often needs trouble and sorrow to restore that sense, and to bring the soul back into fellowship with God.

JUDGES XXI.—When people are governed by excitement and not by the Word of God, they bind themselves by oaths which lead to difficulty and to bloodshed (vs. 3, 10, and 21).

It is true that the men of Jabesh-Gilead merited punishment, because their refusal to judge the evil at Gibeah shewed that they thought little of it, or that they sympathized with it. But had Israel followed the Word of the Lord from the beginning, and not bound themselves by rash vows (v. 5), and had they waited upon God for direction with respect to Jabesh-Gilead, how different would be the history of this chapter !

There was, however, some life and intelligence in their souls, for, after the victory (v. 4), as before the victory (ch. xx. 26), they in a figure, betook themselves to Calvary. In the life of Spiritual Warfare the soul needs a fresh baptism of confession and forgiveness at Calvary after victories as before them ; and it is the neglect of this return to Calvary, after a victory, which causes so many Christian people to be thrown off their guard and to fall.

It gives a sad picture of the condition of the nation at this time that, although the Benjamites lived within a short distance of Shiloh where the Tabernacle was pitched, yet so complete was their neglect of it that the minute directions of verse 19 had to be given them to enable them to find it ; and, further, the mention of only one yearly feast —God having commanded three—was an added proof of departure from His Word ; and, finally, " *the* dances " of verse 21 (R.V.) showed how heathen customs had invaded the House of God ; for no such dancing was ordained in the Book of Leviticus. It is all a mournful illustration of that to-day which professes to be the House of God. Amusement displaces worship.

Verse 22 should be read as in the Revised Version.

The last verse gives the Divine explanation of the condition of license and bloodshed which this Book records. The disobedience of chapter i. 27-36 was the commencement of all the' evil.

The lessons of the book are painful but needful. They teach that there never comes a point in the Christian life when prayer, and watching, and the Bible, may be laid aside. No position in grace—no height of Christian experience—no succession of spiritual victories —can keep the soul from falling. Only daily fellowship with God, meditation upon and obedience to His Holy Word, and the ever-present power of the in-dwelling Holy Spirit, can preserve the Christian from backsliding. It is a solemn truth that a past experience of Divine blessing—no matter how rich and wonderful—is useless to the heart that is out of fellowship with God. Israel's history abundantly illustrates this fact. There must be no compromise with evil either in Egypt, in the Wilderness, or in the Land. The Christian's wisdom is to seek refuge in " death " (Rom. vi.) ; for how can sin deceive or conquer a person who is " dead "—but this refuge must be a " daily dying," and a spiritual reality.

The incurable opposition of the heart, and its insensibility to the Divine teaching and discipline of the previous chapter are illustrated once more in this last chapter (for planning before praying is practised) and violence and confusion result.

RUTH

RUTH I.—Two Books in the Bible are named after women—Ruth and Esther. In the one, a Gentile woman marries a Hebrew, and, in the other, a Hebrew woman marries a Gentile. Both marriages predict, as foretold in Gen. xii. 3, xviii. 18, xxii. 18, xxvi. 4, Ps. lxxii. 17, Acts iii. 25 and many other Scriptures, that the Gentiles, as such, are to be brought into the Kingdom of God in connection with Israel. This of course has no relation to the Church of God, which is quite a distinct thing.

Most Christian people accept Ruth as a type of the Church. But the facts of the Book do not authorize this. Naomi typifies Israel in the latter day—an exile from Canaan, a widow, impoverished, and having no heir. She returns to the Land of Promise bringing Ruth, that is, the Gentile, with her. They and their property are redeemed by Boaz, i.e., Christ ; the nearer kinsman, i.e., the Law, being unable to do so, and unwilling, because it necessitated union with the Gentile, i.e., Ruth. Israel having departed from God, and the Gentile being far off from God and outside of the Promises, the Law had no power to establish either of them in blessing.

In this Book is recorded the operations of grace in blessing those who merited no grace ; and of the prosecution of God's purposes in spite of the sin and disorder which marked that time ; for God never fails to act even in the midst of evil ; and having decreed that Ruth the Gentile should be an ancestress of the Messiah, He bent every circumstance to the accomplishment of that purpose.

Elimelech means " God is my King," Naomi signifies " Pleasant," her sons " Sickly " and " Pining " and Ruth " Beautiful."

Just as Abraham should have stayed with God in the Land of Promise in spite of the famine rather than go down into Egypt and sin there against God, so had it been better for Naomi to have done than to beg bread from the Moabite. The result was she found herself a widow childless and poor

It is not surprising that there was a famine in the land, for every man did that which was right in his own eyes (Judges xxi. 25). It would be the natural result of the moral state of the nation at the time.

No doubt she only contemplated a brief sojourn in Moab, but verse 2 says she " continued " there. When the Christian goes down into the world to seek entertainment there he generally ends by " continuing" there.

The news reaching Naomi (v. 6) that there was bread in Bethlehem, she set out to return home, but she had so little faith in the promises of God, and such a poor experience as the result of her own disobedience, that she discouraged her daughters-in-law from returning with her. Christians like Naomi give a false testimony respecting God and His action with His people (vs. 20 and 21). God had not dealt " very bitterly " with her. All would have been quite otherwise had she trusted Him.

But on returning she found a well-spread table (v. 22) and the precious blood of the Pascal Lamb, for it was barley harvest, that is, the Passover. This is what the backslider ever finds on coming home to God—the Precious Blood to cleanse and heal his backslidings, and a well-spread table to meet and satisfy his necessities.

It was not forbidden in the Law to a Hebrew to marry a Moabite woman, but a Moabite was forbidden to enter the congregation of the Lord (Deut. xxiii. 3).

It was commanded by God that a surviving brother should marry his widowed sister-in-law (vs. 11–13).

There is in no language under the sun a more beautiful or more pathetic passage than Ruth's address to Naomi.

This beautiful story illustrates redemption by Christ and union with Christ. There is one Hebrew word for kinsman and redeemer for he only had the " right to redeem " who was a kinsman.   Hence it was necessary that the Lord Jesus Christ should become man in order to redeem man.   Ruth's marriage, and the wealthy home into which she was brought, picture the satisfying joy and fulness of blessing which union with Christ secures for the heart that trusts Him.

A contrast between Samson and Ruth illustrates Fellowship with the World versus Fellowship with Christ.

When the Christian goes " down " to the world, as Samson "went down" to the Philistine (Judges xiv. 1) the result is that the world gains nothing—as the Philistine gained nothing spiritually—but that the Christian, like Samson, loses wisdom, strength eyesight and life. " He wist not that Jehovah was departed from him."   Like many to-day he could go out and shout ; but there was no power behind the shout.

But when the Gentile, Ruth, "went up" to Bethlehem she found food, home, honour, and love ; and the world gained everything ; for she, as ancestress of the Messiah, linked Christ with it !

RUTH II.—When Ruth forsook her people and her native land to put her trust under the wing of Jehovah the God of Israel (vs. 11 and 12), and when, as a gleaner, she sought her daily bread from the Hand of that Gracious God who had made this provision for the widow and stranger (Lev. xix. 9), she little thought that she was to find a bridegroom among the Princes of Judah.   Such is the experience of everyone who turns the back upon the best the world can offer, and seeks in Christ, and in the fellowship of His " field " and " servants " spiritual daily bread.   These little conceive the measure of the grace of Him " who takes knowledge " of them (v. 10), and " lets fall handfuls on purpose for them " (v. 16), and who reaches out the choicest dainties for them that they may eat (v. 1).

Boaz in his instructions to the reapers directed them to give Ruth greater liberty than that commanded by the Law (vs. 15 and 16).

The word " left " in verse 14 means " left thereof " (R.V.) ; that is, Boaz gave her far more than she could eat.

Naomi's advice to Ruth (v. 22) was wise and astute.   She pointed out that Boaz was

a redeemer ; that, as such, he had the right to redeem their property, which, through poverty, they had lost ; that such a redemption involved marriage with Ruth ; that his singular kindness to her in the harvest field suggested something more than kindness: and that, therefore, Ruth would be wise to abide by his maidens and seek no other field.

RUTH III.—Boaz, whose name means " in him is strength," typifies Christ Risen.

This chapter is one of exquisite beauty and deep spiritual teaching.

Ruth for a time was satisfied with the gifts that flowed from the hand of Boaz, but the sweeter and deeper joy of union with Boaz himself was suggested to her by Naomi. This marks an important stage in Christian experience, and underlies John i. 29 as contrasted with John i. 36.   At first the forgiveness that Christ gives, together with His other gifts, satisfies the heart ; but, later, a deeper desire is awakened to be occupied with the Giver rather than with His gifts, and the soul hungers for the closest intimacy with Himself.   This higher Christian experience is often suggested by an older Christian to a younger, as Naomi suggested union with Boaz to Ruth.

The boldness of faith and love is very precious to the Lord Jesus Christ.   He commands " boldness " in drawing near to Him (Heb. iv. 16).   To be timid, therefore, is to be disobedient, and it grieves His Heart. Ruth's boldness in drawing nigh unto Boaz made her all the more precious in his eyes (v. 10).

There was no impropriety in Ruth's action. It was the Law and custom of the time.   To draw a portion of a kinsman's mantle over one was the legal way of claiming protection and redemption.   Ruth effected this with great delicacy and skill.   She chose a public place such as the threshing-floor where many persons were present ; but not to embarrass Boaz, but to give him liberty to act as he wished, she made her claim under the cover of darkness.

In the East grain is winnowed at night, partly because of the heat during the day, but mainly because there is at night sufficient wind to make the operation possible.   The winnowers when tired lie down in their clothes on the threshing-floor and take some sleep.   So important is the business that the proprietor himself assists.   A frequent posture for a slave on such an occasion would be to lie at the master's feet. Ruth took that humble place, but at the same time, with admirable boldness, gently drew the skirt of the master's mantle over herself ; and when he, "startled," asked "who is that ?" She answered " I am Ruth thy slave ; spread therefore thy skirt over me for thou art my kinsman, and hast the right to redeem me." She first drew the garment herself, and then she asked him to place it over her. She thus, with perfect refinement, claimed his protection ; asked him to recover her property ; and to marry herself. This affecting ceremony of the mantle is still observed in connection with marriage in the East.

Boaz, whose character commands admiration, immediately responded to her faith and love ; declared that her actions toward him were " kindness " (v. 10) ; that this latter kindness of desiring himself rather than his gifts was greater than the former ; that there was a nearer " kinsman " (v. 13) who had a claim to her and her land ; and that if he were unable to redeem her, Boaz himself would do so. Laden with his gifts (v. 15) and cheered with his promises Ruth returned to Naomi.

RUTH IV.—Ruth found it to be good to " sit still " and let Boaz do everything. When there is anything important to be done the person interested cannot " sit still " unless assured that the successful execution of the matter rests in hands that are competent, and faithful. Herein lies the principle of salvation by faith. The second chapter of Galatians contrasts two principles for the obtaining of life and righteousness—the one principle : works of law, i.e., religious ceremonies and personal moral efforts ; the other principle : the hearing of faith, i.e., " sitting still." The Holy Spirit teaches in that chapter that nothing can be had upon the first principle, but everything upon the second. So Ruth " sat still," wholly trusted Boaz, and, as a result, obtained what her heart had never conceived of when leaving Moab. From the position of a pauper she was, in one day, raised to the dignity of a princess. The love of an husband, the joy of motherhood, and the dignity of a palace were the fruits of " sitting still." This is all a lovely picture of the satisfying joys that fill the hearts of those who give up trying to save themselves, and who rest wholly in the hands of a Redeemer and Kinsman, greater than Boaz, but typified by him, who has already accomplished the entire work of redemption.

In the Christian life there is a great need of this " sitting still." Christian people are too restless. They do not wait sufficiently upon God and for God. Saul was willing to wait " upon God " but not " for God " and so lost the Kingdom (1 Sam. xiii). There is usually an abundance of thinking, planning, and scheming, and a neglect of prayer and sitting still and permitting God to act and plan, and the result is trouble and spiritual loss.

Boaz had to purchase Ruth from a kinsman who had a prior claim, but who declared that he could not redeem her (v. 6). The Law has a prior claim to sinners, but it cannot redeem them. Christ, the Divine Kinsman, became Man in order to redeem. It cost Boaz nothing to redeem Ruth, beyond the setting aside of himself and his own interests, but it cost Christ everything to redeem sinners.

Thus Ruth, a " wild olive tree," was grafted into, and became a partaker of, " the root and fatness of the olive tree, i.e., Israel ; but she could not boast that this was due to any commanding personal claim, all she could say was " Why have I found grace in thine eyes (ch. ii. 10) seeing I am a Gentile."

This is a beautiful fore-picture of that future day when the Redeemer shall bring the Gentile nations into the Covenant made with Abraham.

After the sin and confusion of the Book of Judges it is refreshing to read this precious story of faith and peace and love ; setting out, as it does, a very lovely picture of union with Christ ; and it teaches that in a time of outward departure from God a remedy is to be found, not in going back to the murmuring of the Wilderness, or the servitude of Egypt, but in a nearer and deeper union with Christ.

I SAMUEL

1 SAMUEL I.—The two Books of Samuel and the two Books of Kings record the history of the kingdom in its outward aspect ; the two Books of Chronicles disclose its inward history as commented on by the Holy Spirit.

In the Hebrew Bible " Chronicles " forms one book, and " Kings " and " Samuel " two books.

Samuel was the first of the Prophets (Acts iii. 24).

The history of Man invariably shows moral failure, and never shows the opposite. This is a fact denied by fashionable religious teachers. God, in order to maintain relationship with His people, set up Priests, but they defiled His Courts ; He raised up Judges but they became idolators ; He commissioned prophets but they, apart from inspiration, like Samuel, Elijah and Jonah showed partiality, self-will, or rebellion ; and He introduced Kings, but they rebelled against Him and burnt the Bible. Finally he sent Him Who was both Prophet, Priest, and King, and they nailed Him to the tree ! As the result, Israel has been cast out of the goodly land, and remains under wrath until the day when with broken and contrite heart they shall look on Him Whom they have pierced. In that day a Government will be founded impossible of failure.

Elkanah was a Levite (1 Chron. vi.), but not untouched by the corruption of his day, for he had two wives. Domestic misery was the result.

The title " Jehovah Sabaioth " (v. 3) is here the first occurrence of this Divine Title. It occurs two hundred and eighty-one times. It is characteristic of the Books of the Kingdom ; it has a special relationship to Israel.

The Tabernacle of Moses was at this time pitched in Shiloh, and, later on, at Gibeon (2 Chron. i. 3). It remained there up to the completion of Solomon's Temple, when, no doubt, it was taken down.

Hophni and Phinehas were priests " unto Jehovah " (v. 5 R.V.). This is very solemn ! They were evil men, and yet occupied, officially, a certain relationship to God. Under the Covenant of Law, and its divinely appointed Priesthood, such a position was possible, but under the Covenant of Grace, where there is no earthly Priesthood, it is impossible. But, men not recognizing the distinction between these two Covenants, have invented an order of priests, and clothed them with the sacramental powers of the Sons of Aaron !

There are seven Temples mentioned in the Scriptures (v. 9) 1, the Tabernacle (1 Sam i. 9) ; 2, Solomon's (1 Kings vi. 5) ; 3, Zerubbabel's (Ezra iv. 1) ; 4, Herod's (John ii. 20); 5, The Remnant's (2 Thess. ii. 4) ; 6, The Millennial Temple (Ezek. xli.) and 7, The Heavenly Temple (Rev. xxi.). Believers in the New Testament are compared seven times to a Temple (1 Cor. iii. 9, 1 Cor vi. 19, 2 Cor. vi. 16, Eph, ii. 20, Heb. iii. 6, 1 Peter ii. 5, and 1 Peter iv. 17).

Eli's supposing Hannah to be drunk, throws a sad light upon the corruption of that time, for it suggests that drunkenness, even among women, and during public worship, was common.

Hannah accepted the words of Eli (v. 17) as a divine answer to her prayer ; for she was no more sad.

The words " a bullock " (v. 25) should read as in the R.V. " the bullock," thus according with ver 24, which should read " a bullock of three years " instead of " three bullocks."

The R.V. margin reads " And they worshipped Jehovah there " (v. 28). It is a sweet picture ! the little boy, and his father and mother, worshipping Jehovah !

In the East when a woman has an only son, and thinks it probable that she will have no other, she does not wean him till he is seven or eight years of age. It is their belief, and many competent medical authorities share it, that the later a boy is weaned, the stronger he will afterwards be as a man (see notes on Gen. xxi. 9 with Gal. iv. 29).

It was bitter to the flesh but sweet to the spirit to part with the little boy, yet the faith that secured him was the self-same faith that surrendered him.

Faith asked this one child from the Lord of Hosts. What a remarkable conjunction ! As the gloom deepens God gives fresh revelations of Himself for faith to lean upon and prove.

1 SAMUEL II.—In this chapter the Holy Spirit contrasts Hophni and Phinehas with Hannah—a feeble woman, with two proud priests. In the one is seen the fruit of the Spirit ; in the other, the works of the Flesh. Her testimony revealed the faith and love of the feeble remnant then existing in the nation ; their conduct the general corruption into which the people had sunk. God rebuked the nation through this feeble woman. Such has been, and is, one of the great principles of His Government. She testified that "the pillars of the earth are Jehovah's " : that is, that everything hangs upon God, and God alone. This is a fact of Divine Government which is distasteful to man.

The Song of Hannah should be read together with the Song of Mary (Luke i. 46). The theme of both is one and the same : i.e. Christ, His glory as King and Priest : and God's action in government in raising up the meek and casting down the proud.

The Song of this chapter is constructed in Sections which alternate ; thus contrasting Jehovah and His enemies as follows :—

Verse 2   Jehovah, His holiness.
Verse 3   The enemy, his arrogancy.
Verse 3   Jehovah, His knowledge.
Verse 4   The enemy, his ignorance.
Verse 6-9 Jehovah, His power.
Verse 10   The enemy, his weakness.
Verse 10   Jehovah, His glory.

All who rejoice in God's salvation will, like Hannah, have their " mouths enlarged," that is—will have something big to testify of (v. 1).

A " horn " is part of a woman's head-dress in the East. To it the veil is attached, and then thrown back over the shoulders. The " horn " is set more upright on the head after the birth of a child.

The divine title " Christ," or " Anointed " (v. 10.) here first occurs in the Bible ; and the Holy Spirit used the lips of a woman to frame the word.

It forms a great prophecy, and points forward to the time when the Son of Man, as King and Priest (Zech. vi. 12. 13.) will sit upon the throne of His glory in Jerusalem, and so usher in His Millennial Reign.

The duty of Hophni and Phinehas, as commanded by God in Leviticus was, 1, to burn the fat of the peace offering upon the Altar ; 2, to accept the breast and shoulder as their portion ; and, 3, to eat them sodden, that is boiled. The remainder of the animal was partaken of by the worshipper (See notes on Leviticus). Their violence, impiety, and greed caused men to abhor the Sacrifices of the Lord.

The word " presently " (v. 16.) means " immediately," " without delay," " at once."

Eli's blessing (v. 20.) had a double result— Hannah gave birth to five more children, and Samuel " grew before the Lord."

Eli, in obedience to the Law, should have put his sons to death ; but, too indulgent as a father, he merely feebly remonstrated with them, pointing out 1, Their guilt in provoking a public scandal (v. 23) ; 2, In leading others to do wrong (v. 24) ; and 3, In themselves sinning against God.

If it be asked : " Why did not God slay these two priests as He slew Nadab and Abihu ? " the answer is : because He was then dwelling in power in the camp, but in Eli's day He had withdrawn Himself because of Israel's apostasy. There is a great difference in an electric wire when charged and not charged.

The answer to all the questions in verses 27 and 28 is " Yes."

In the East, old age is regarded as a sign of Divine favour ; and a family without aged members is despised.

This prophecy was partially fulfilled in Israel's bondage to the Philistine, in the capture of the Ark, and in the death of Hophni and Phinehas on one day (ch. iv.) ; but its complete fulfilment will not take place till after Israel's future restoration (v. 35).

When the moral perception is darkened by evil there is an inability to recognize the approaching judgments of God. So was it with Israel at this time ; and because of this moral condition God decreed a just judgment upon them. The word " because " (v. 25) should read " therefore."

1 **SAMUEL III.**—It is possible to minister unto the Lord and yet not to know the Lord : compare verses 1 and 7 with Matt. vii. 22.

The Word of the Lord was precious in those days. Note the precious things of the Old Testament, and the precious things of the New Testament.

There was no " open vision " : that is, God had not at that time so manifestly accredited a messenger to Israel as to secure a universal acceptance of the fact.

The first three verses picture the moral condition of the nation. Night reigned ; the lamp of God was going out in the Temple ; the High Priest's eyes were grown dim so that he could not clearly see ; and both he and Samuel were asleep !

It was at this dark moment that God chose to reveal Himself ; yet not to some influential personage, but to a little boy !

The statement in verse 7 that Samuel did not yet know the Lord is very solemn. He was born of godly parents, and was engaged in the Temple Service ; he was occupied with the things of God but did not know God ; and, what is of terrible import, the Holy Spirit, as to this ignorance of God, places Samuel alongside of Hophni and Phinehas ! (ch. ii. 12). Many no doubt at the present day are equally strangers to God and yet are ministers in the Church of God !

Verse 10 is one of the ten thousand proofs in the Bible that the Jehovah of the Old Testament and the Jesus of the New Testament, are the one Person, God over all blessed for ever ! For He Who said, " Samuel, Samuel " was the very same who said, " Martha, Martha," " Simon, Simon." Just as in human literature the style reveals the author, so here.

Many people say that it is wrong to speak to a child about the wrath of God. This belief shows how even religious teachers are fallen from God's moral likeness ; for His first message to little Samuel was an appalling one !

The sentence " made themselves vile " (v. 13), is better translated in the Revised Version, " brought a curse upon themselves," i.e., the wrath of God.

Eli's submission to God's righteous judgment is the one bright spot in his feeble character. Though his sons were more precious to him than the Law of God, i.e., the Bible, yet was his heart true to Jehovah ;

and grief at the loss of that, viz., the Ark, which symbolized the Presence of God with Israel, caused his death. He is a type of many good men who fail in energy and faithfulness, who have not firmness enough to boldly rebuke evils in the Church, and yet whose personal piety cannot be questioned.

In raising up Samuel as the first of the prophets God introduced a new channel of communication with His people. Samuel was, at the same time, the last of the Judges.

God's method of revealing Himself to man is the same to-day as in the days of Samuel. It is by the Word of the Lord (v. 21). He speaks in His Son (Heb. i.) who is the Incarnate Word of God, and He speaks in the Bible which is the Written Word of God (2 Pet. i. 19-21, 2 Tim. iii. 15, 16, and Mark vii. 13).

" And the word of Samuel came to all Israel " (iv. 1). This sentence belongs to verse 21. Thus are bound together in the one verse the expressions : " The Word of Jehovah," and : " The word of Samuel." The mouth that uttered the words was Samuel's ; the words that were uttered were God's.

1 **SAMUEL IV.**—This is a dark and sorrowful chapter. Eli was physically blind (v. 15), the elders were spiritually blind (v. 3), the people were grossly superstitious (v. 5), Israel was defeated and enslaved by the Philistine (vs. 9 and 10), Hophni and Phinehas were slain (v. 11), and the Ark of God was taken !

Whenever God reveals Himself the hostility of the enemy is aroused. Directly God revealed Himself in Shiloh (ch. iii. 21) the Philistine revealed himself in Aphek (ch. iv. 1)

It is very striking that the Holy Spirit states (v. 1) that the Israelites " pitched beside Ebenezer." It was not so named until twenty years later (ch. vii. 12). This is designed. On that day of defeat faith looked forward to the future day of victory ; and set up, in anticipation. upon the stricken field, the " Stone of Help," i.e., " Ebenezer." This fact is full of comfort at this present time when the moral condition of the Christian Church so closely resembles that of the Hebrew Church at that day.

Instead of disobeying the Bible in violating the Most Holy Place and fetching the Ark of God to themselves, they should have betaken themselves to the Ark of God, i.e., the Throne of God, and, at the door of the

Tabernacle of the Congregation, confessed their sins, broken their idols, and thus returned to God. Victory would have been the sure result.

Hophni and Phinehas boldly intruded into the Most Holy Place, into which none were permitted to enter except the High Priest, and that but once a year, and not without blood (Heb. ix. 7).

No swift judgment smote these impious men, for God had withdrawn Himself from His Dwelling-Place.

The further the heart departs from God and His Word, the greater is the importance attached to Symbols and Ceremonies (v. 5). The people, no doubt, remembered how the Jordan fled before the Ark, and they expected the same fear would put the Philistine to flight. But the Ark was but the Symbol of the Divine Presence. Now, when confronted by the enemy, the symbol was made to displace the Substance. This sad feature is only too visible to-day in Christendom, where, as in the Latin and Greek Churches, the bread that perisheth displaces the Bread that endureth unto everlasting life, and, in some sections of the Protestant Church, the table of the Lord excites more loyalty than the Person of the Lord.

Eli's "seat" (v. 13 and 18) was the Judges' seat. It was placed by the wayside at the gate of a city, and was the place of judgment. Some of these "seats" have been recently dug up and found to be elaborately carved in stone, and *without a back*! This is a witness to the truth of the Bible.

Eli judged Israel forty years. Had he judged in fellowship with God, and in obedience to the Scriptures, the disasters that befel on the day of his death would never have happened; and yet, in his death, he showed that the interests of God's Kingdom had a true place in his heart.

The last four verses of the chapter throw a shaft of light across the darkness; and the detail into which the Holy Spirit enters in the narrative shows how precious to Him was the measure of Divine life in the soul of this true-hearted woman. She is here placed upon the face of the Divine record with great vividness. The Holy Spirit recalls her affection for her aged father-in-law, and for her godless and faithless husband, but points with emphasis to the fact that grief for God's Kingdom swallowed up the joy of motherhood (John xvi. 21).

1 SAMUEL V.—It is a touching proof of the faithfulness of God to His sinning people that the title, " Ark of Jehovah " rather than " Ark of God " is so often used in this and the following chapter.

" Jehovah " was His Covenant Name to Israel ; and therefore the faithfulness that judged sin in His people equally judged sin against His people. It was as Jehovah, and because He was Jehovah, that He withheld at Aphek the power which He showed at Ashdod. Had He manifested that power at Aphek Israel would have been glorified, and not God ; but manifesting it against the oppressor of His people, and in the very heart of the Temple of their god, He vindicated His own glory, and judged the enemy.

Had God overthrown the Philistine at Aphek He would thereby have associated Himself with the evil of His people. God can make no compromise with evil ; and a victory granted that day to Israel would have shewn that God thought lightly of sin ; and that He was willing to identify Himself with the moral condition of a people living in willing bondage to the grossest evils.

The Philistine was a domestic, not a foreign enemy. He illustrates the power of the enemy inside the professing Christian Church, and is more to be dreaded than any enemy who stands outside.

Many images of the god Dagon have been recently discovered. He is supposed to represent Noah. The head and the arms were those of a man ; the body that of a fish. His first fall before the Ark could no doubt have been kept secret by the priests ; but his mutilated members upon the threshold on the following day was a public proof that all the idols of the heathen are vanity ; and the fact could not be hidden. Poor man, in his superstitious religion, tried to compromise the matter by over-stepping the threshold of Dagon's temple ; and at the present day he makes somewhat similar physical movements in order to guard himself against the supposed malevolence of unseen divinities.

It is not at all a pleasant thing for the people of this world to have God in their midst. He keeps up a perpetual controversy with their sins and their idolatries ; and as the Philistines were not willing to become

His people, they determined that the best thing they could do was to get rid of Him. This is the attitude of human society to-day.

The plague that broke out upon the Philistines was, most likely, the present bubonic plague of the East. Large tumours appear in the cavities of the body; and it first makes its appearance among such rodents as rats and mice. The Revised Version reads " that tumours brake out upon them "; and this, together with the gift of golden mice in the next chapter, points to the nature of the disease.

The Bible in the Critics' Temple does as much damage to-day as the Ark in the Philistines' Temple did in that day.

The Ark symbolized Christ in the mystery and glory of His nature. (See notes on Exod. xxv). The Philistine associated Him with idols; the Israelite subjected Him to criticism (see next chapter). Upon both people fell the wrath of God. These men have their successors to-day in the sacerdotal and Socinian churches, and the anger of God will surely strike them.

1 **SAMUEL VI.–VII.** 1.—In this chapter Israel had to learn that God must be reverenced by His people (Lev. xix. 30, Ps. lxxxix. 7). In the prior chapter the Philistines had to learn that He is a God greatly to be feared. Heb. x. 31, says, " It is a fearful thing to fall into the hands of the living God "; and the facts of these two chapters illustrate the truth of this statement.

The deep ignorance and incurable rebellion of man's heart appear in verse 6. Although aware of all this yet these Philistine priests worshipped the false god Dagon !

The lowing kine upon the highway to Beth-shemesh (v. 12) had more spiritual intelligence. Untaught to such labour, and resisting their strongest instincts, they, whilst calling out for their young, yet took the straight way to the land of Judah. This test made it absolutely clear to the Philistines that the God of Israel was the one true God; and yet such a demonstration failed to turn that nation from its sins and its idols. A similar result followed in Jerusalem (Jno ii. 23) when the same Mighty God personally demonstrated His Power before the eyes of the multitude. They were convinced by the evidence, but not converted ! Men proudly declare that they would become Christians if convinced by evidence. They deceive themselves. They are by nature Philistines, and Philistines they will remain in spite of the most overwhelming proofs of God's Being and Power, until the Holy Spirit is pleased to reveal Christ to them and cause them to be re-born.

The offering of golden models of the tumours and the mice as votive offerings to God, for a guilt-offering (v. 8), is still observed; and a visitor to any one of the so-called " holy places " in Roman Catholic and Heathen countries will see models of diseased limbs, etc., consecrated as thank-offerings.

The Philistines being ignorant of the requirements of the law (Num. iv. 15, vii. 9, x. 21), no judgment fell upon them because of their " new cart." But David's " new cart " produced sad results (2 Sam. vi).

The word " it " in verse 9 means the Ark and not the cart, as is clear from the word " his " in the same sentence; and from the use in the Hebrew text of the masculine gender, " Ark " being masculine and " cart " feminine. Thus God and His Throne form a Unity.

This unity appears very solemnly in the judgment that fell upon the Israelites because of their inquisitive irreverence in respect of that Throne. God had commanded that it should be veiled by the curtains of the Tabernacle and only approached through a divinely appointed High Priest, with confession of sin, and the presentation of atoning blood. These people, like many to-day, pushed all this Bible-teaching aside, and, assisted even by Levites (v. 15), exposed the Throne to public view; and went so far as to criticize its contents. The Ark was not only the Throne of God but was also, as revealed in the Books of Exodus and Leviticus, a beauteous symbol of Christ in His essential Deity and sinless Humanity. But ever since He arose from the dead many who profess to be His disciples. not only deny Him in His office as the Atoning Mediator between God and men, but, with bold impiety, try to subject His mysterious nature to the demonstrations of human wisdom, impelled by the same spirit which urged the men at Beth-shemesh to look into the Ark.

Many people assume that the numbers recorded in verse 19 must be erroneous. On the contrary, they are most probable; and the Christian student believes they are accurate. There are two slaughters mentioned in the verse ; first, " He smote the men of Beth-shemesh." Seventy men perished under that stroke. And second, " He smote of the people of the land ; " and in that slaughter fifty thousand perished. Nothing is more reasonable to assume than that the people gathered from all sides to Beth-shemesh directly the wonderful news reached them of the recovery of the Ark. Multitudes of them must never have seen the Ark, because hidden in the Tabernacle ; and therefore its public exhibition would powerfully excite the popular interest, and attract people from far and near ; and, accordingly, remembering the thousands who perished from time to time in the Wilderness under the wrath of God because of rebellion, the death of fifty thousand on this occasion is not disproportionate.

Some Hebrew scholars read the Hebrew text of verse 19 thus : " Seventy men, two fifties, and one thousand." That is, 70 +50 + 50 +1000 = 1170.

The word " thousand " and the word " chief " are similar in Hebrew. Hence verse 19 may also read.: " He smote of the people seventy men "—50 chief men. That is to say of the seventy men 50 were heads of families. This word " thousand " or " prince " (see Micah v. 2, and Matt. ii. 6) may perhaps apply to 1 Kings xx. 30, and 2 Chron. xxxii. 21.

" Israel lamented after Jehovah for the time was long, for it was twenty years " (ch. vii. 2). How often has this been the experience of God's people ! His Presence not having been appreciated, He withdraws the consciousness of that Presence, and the proofs of that Presence ; and, as the result, His absence causes His value to be felt. To His heart also twenty years was " a long time "—though nineteen hundred years is " a little while "—showing how He feels the loss of His people's fellowship.

1 SAMUEL VII. 2.—This chapter is like a beam of sunshine upon a dark and cloudy day. It records a great revival. This revival was doubtless the result of Samuel's faithful preaching. He preached for twenty years (v. 2). His preaching, doctrinally, was reconciliation to God by the death of His Son (v. 9 with Rom. v. 10), and, ethically, a turning to God from all idols to serve the living and the true God (v. 3 with 1 Thess. 1. 9).

Israel had not ceased to worship Jehovah, but she had associated other gods with Him. This has ever been Satan's object as an angel of light ; and, accordingly, multitudes to-day worship Jesus Christ and the Virgin Mary giving to Him a higher form of worship than to her ; just as Israel gave a lesser worship to Ashtaroth, the Queen of Heaven, the Mother of the Divine Child, than they did to Jehovah.

But God will not accept such worship, nor the association of other gods with Himself, for He said (Exod. xx. 3) : " Thou shalt have none other gods together with me."

God's true servants always preach as Samuel preached. They arouse people to a consciousness of their sinful condition before God ; they set forth the Lamb of God evidently crucified among them (Gal. iii. 1 with v. 9 and v. 17) as the Divine Way of pardon and righteousness ; and they denounce all compromise with evil.

Water poured out upon the ground (v. 6 with 2 Sam. xiv. 14) expresses utter helplessness. Water is power ; but when poured upon the ground the power is lost, and can never be recovered again. Such was Israel's condition. They had lost all their strength, and it was impossible to them to recover it. But God never fails the heart that cries to Him, and that hangs upon Him, and so He ministers limitless strength through the seeming weakness and defeat of Calvary (for such is Calvary to man) just as He clothed His people with power directly they offered up the sucking lamb—a striking symbol of weakness, but to faith, of power.

A victory resulted which glorified God, delivered Israel, and banished the Philistine (v. 13).

The stone of victory (v. 12) succeeded, but did not precede, the lamb of sacrifice. And Samuel " took a lamb " (v. 9). Then Samuel " took a stone " (v. 12). God cannot give victories to fallen man—" He gives them to His dearly beloved Son ; and hence His people " overcome by the Blood of the Lamb" (Rev. xii. 11) ; and they overcome in no other way.

Samuel was a Levite, and accordingly (1 Chron. xxiii. 27-32) he could offer a burnt-offering ; though he could not enter the Tabernacle, not being a son of Aaron.

The Tabernacle, at this time, was useless as a centre of worship ; for the Throne of God, that is, the Ark, had been removed from it. It was not until a king reigned in righteousness—a type of Him Who is to come—that that throne was restored to its divinely appointed centre (1 Kings. viii. 6–11).

But when, because of the weakness of the flesh (Rom. viii. 3), a divinely-ordered service breaks down, then faith always finds her refuge in God ; and so was it with Samuel. He returned, in spirit, to the patriarchal life of Abraham ; for He lived as a pilgrim in the land of promise and built there an altar unto the Lord (v. 17). He dwelt at Ramah. This word may be translated "rejected, yet exalted." That is the true home in this world of every true servant of God.

So the conditions of a revival are : A sense of need (v. 2) ; a destruction of idols (v. 3) ; prayer (v. 5) ; confession of weakness and sin (v. 6) ; and faith in the cleansing blood of the Lamb of God (v. 9). The result is they overcome by the blood of the Lamb (Rev. xii. 11).

1 SAMUEL VIII.—A father cannot transmit faith to his sons, nor can he make prophets out of them. Samuel's sons were no better as judges than Eli's sons as priests.

Israel had no faith to lean immediately upon God. A king whom they could see, although he was only a feeble, foolish, and dying man, was preferred to an unseen king Almighty, Wise and Eternal. The nation wished to be like unto the surrounding nations (v. 5 and v. 20), forgetting that their glory and happiness consisted in being unlike these nations. Multitudes of professing Christians are, to-day, in the same condition of spiritual feebleness. Not possessing a faith that hangs immediately upon God, they demand so-called priests or pastors whom they can see and lean upon ; and they are continually fearful lest they should in any way be diverse from the world, conformity to which is forbidden in Rom. xii. 2.

Samuel was about sixty years of age at this time, and about one hundred years old at the time of his death, which preceded that of Saul by about two years. He practically lived right through the forty years of Saul's reign. This fact adds to Saul's guilt in living a life of almost continuous rebellion against the Word of the Lord (1 Chron. x. 13, 14, 1 Chron. xiii. 3).

The request for a king was evil in the eyes of Samuel (v. 6), because of the rebellion and impatience of the people in not waiting for the King whom God had promised (Gen. xvii. 6 and 16, xxxv. 11, xlix. 10, Num.xxiv. 17, Deut. xvii. 14–20).

God in His tender love plainly told them of the treatment they would receive from the king of their own choice. Six times is the fact repeated : " He will take " (vs. 11, 13, 14, 15, 16, 17). Contrast the action of God's King in the prophecies of Isaiah and Jeremiah where the expression " I will give " occurs directly seven times, and, indirectly, many times. Compare also the first and last occurrences of this expression in the Bible (Gen. xvii. 8 with Rev. xxi. 6).

This earnest warning was unheeded, and the righteous judgment of verse 18 was the bitter experience of their self-will. This action of a Wisdom, which is both loving and perfect, may be recognized in all periods of human history. How often and how lovingly God by His Holy Spirit, through His word, and through His servants, warns His children of the bitter consequences sure to follow if in self-will they pursue a desired path. What misery and sorrow fill the cup of many a young Christian who persists in marrying a drunkard ! As with Israel, so in such a case, God permits self-will to have its own way. But how much happier would it have been for Israel to have placed themselves and their difficulties in God's hands and asked Him to plan for them !

The history of the Kings affords abundant instances in fulfilment of Samuel's predictions. 1 Sam. xiv. 52 began these fulfilments.

Just as impoverishment and servitude resulted, as predicted by Samuel, from Israel's self-willed establishment of a human government, so spiritual poverty and loss of liberty follow in the Christian life when there is subjection to the commandments and doctrines of men, instead of to the authority of the Word of God.

1 SAMUEL IX.—To satisfy the carnal wishes of the people God gave them a king such as they desired. He had a handsome presence and was about seven feet in stature (v. 2). He forms a contrast to the Apostle Paul. Both men had the same name ; both were members of the same tribe ; but the one exhibits the power of the "flesh" ; the other, the power of the Spirit. As to physical strength, and a personal attractive appearance, Saul of Tarsus was wholly unlike

King Saul, for his "bodily presence was weak" (2 Cor. x. 10).

There are three genealogies given to Saul, 1 Sam. ix. 1, 1 Sam. xiv. 51, 1 Chron. viii. 33 with ix. 39. The supposed difficulties in these genealogies will be found resolved in "The Companion Bible."

David, who had charge of his father's sheep, "kept" them; but Saul lost his father's asses, and could not find them!

Beauty and height of stature distinguished the son of Kish, but his life illustrates the fruitless effort of the "old man" to live as the "new man" (Rom. vii.).

His reign is a demonstration of how the "flesh", i.e., the natural will of man, however cultivated and religious, is wholly a stranger to the springs and energies of the spiritual life. The "flesh" can never do anything aright. It is either too courageous or too cowardly, too forward or too backward, too weak or too strong, too wise or too foolish. All this appears in the history of King Saul.

To man's eye this gigantic Benjamite was one upon whom they could lean with confidence. But in reality he was nothing but weakness; for he "enquired not of the Lord" (1 Chron. x. 14), but trusted his own heart, i.e., his own wisdom, and was consequently a fool (Prov. xxviii. 26); and just as the people leaned upon him so he leaned upon them; for when Saul saw "any strong man" he took him (ch. xiv. 52); and before going out to battle "he gathered an host."

Samuel by the Spirit of God could read the heart of Saul and see there the greed and ambition of which Saul was, perhaps, at the time unconscious. The Revised Reading of verse 20 suggests this. It reads: "And for whom is all that is desirable in Israel? Is it not for thee?" Samuel hinted: "Why spend your time looking for a few asses when the wealth of the nation is at your command?" Saul's reply of affected modesty failed to hide from Samuel the secret pleasure with which he received the hint.

Samuel placing Saul in the chiefest place (v. 22) among the nobles at the public banquet, and commanding the choicest dish to be set before him, was a public action of marked significance, and plainly told the Chiefs that Saul was the elected King.

The entire passage from verses 3 to 27 illustrates the Gospel message. It pictures a wanderer vainly seeking a lost possession. So man vainly seeks lost innocence. His

servant tells him of the Great Prophet. Many masters are as wholly ignorant of the Saviour as Saul was of Samuel, and they first hear of Him from a servant. Next, Saul thought to purchase the grace of the Prophet with a quarter shekel, i.e., sixpence! Just as sinners conceive it possible to purchase salvation by their religious emotions and efforts—which are absolutely valueless. Verses 12 and 13 show how effectively young women can point seekers to the Saviour. Verses 14 and 19 show how accessible Christ is, and that He is on the look-out for those who are coming to Him. Samuel was watching for Saul, as Jesus, at Sychar's well, was watching for the woman. The result of meeting with Samuel is set out in verses 19 to 27. Saul received Honour, for he was told to "go up" (v. 19); and Maintenance, for he was to "eat bread"; and Noble Fellowship ("with me"); and A Crown (x. 1).

1 SAMUEL X.—First the private and then the public appointment of Saul as the First King of Israel is the subject of the opening and the closing verses of this chapter. The intervening verses detail the lessons which were designed to teach him upon what principle, and by what power, he was to govern the nation; but he failed to learn these lessons.

Samuel "kissed" Saul (v. 1). This in the East, as also to-day in the West, is the mode of expressing homage to a Sovereign. In the East, the face is kissed; in the West, the hand. So Pharaoh commanded his subjects "to kiss Joseph"; and, in the second Psalm, the Holy Spirit counsels sinners to "kiss the Son," i.e., the Messiah; that is, to become His subjects, for a refusal to do so would bring upon them His wrath.

The fulfilment of the three signs given by Samuel to Saul were no doubt designed to confirm in Saul's mind the conviction that Samuel was indeed the Prophet of the Lord; for it must not be forgotten, that although but a few miles separated their homes, yet chapter ix. 6 makes it clear that Saul was such a stranger to God and His Kingdom that he did not know even of the existence of this mighty prophet (v. 18). But there was a deeper design in the appointment of these three lessons for Saul.

How often is there a language, intelligible to a spiritual mind, but which the natural heart cannot read ? Thus was it with Saul. And yet with him, as with all men, his entire future hung upon his learning these lessons. If " the flesh " could please God and serve Him (Rom. viii. 8). Saul was fully equipped to demonstrate the fact ; but in spite of his physical and religious equipment, he failed at the first real test (chs. x. 21, and xiii. 8). Samuel was recognized by God as the link between Him and Israel. So long as Saul maintained relationship with Samuel he was " another man." He was to wait for Samuel. He was to publicly confess that divine blessing was connected with the prophet, and not with himself ; and he was to refuse to seek for victory apart from God. In all this there was nothing but failure. He could indeed gain an easy victory over the Ammonite (ch. xi.), but the Philistine was the one enemy who put faith to the proof. There are in the Christian life enemies who do not necessarily really test faith. But there always is one particular foe—some moral Philistine—that does put faith to the proof ; and a conflict with him quickly makes clear whether his antagonist is a real Christian or only a professing one ; for, in the latter case, defeat is sure. The Ammonite was an external foe—the Philistine an internal, and therefore much more difficult to conquer ; and although two years elapsed between the proposal of the test and its application (unite chs. x. 8 and xiii. 1), yet, whatever may have been the delay, the moral character of the test itself had not been altered ; and the intermediate successes granted by God to Saul should have prepared him for the test had he had a heart to learn spiritual lessons.

The first lesson—that of Rachel's tomb and his meeting with his father's two messengers there—should have taught him that the child of his mother's sorrow (for he was himself by descent a son of Rachel), became " the son of the right hand " ; that the path to power lay through weakness, and sorrow, and death ; that Jacob's love for Rachel, and his own father's anxiety for himself (v. 2), taught him that sympathy was the first essential in the art of government ; and, coupled with it, that death of self enriches another's joy, and that human life is more valuable than property. Kings, as a rule, deny these principles.

The second lesson revealed to him that God had still a few in Israel—" three men " who loved and served Him in spite of the national corruption and the dominion of the Philistine. Saul was to identify himself with such, and not with the rich and proud of the land. In such companionship he would find real strength : for they gave him to eat (v. 4). Their God was the God of Bethel—that gracious God who had there revealed Himself to sinful, stumbling Jacob, and turned him, weak as he was, into the victorious Israel ; not through natural power—for he crippled that—(Gen. xxxii. 32), but through the energy of faith. These memories should have been full of meaning for Saul as pointing out to him the true road to success and victory.

The third sign was most significant. The hill of God, the Seat of God's authority, was in the power of the Philistine ! (v. 5). But yet there was a band of young men there prophesying and praising, that is, testifying for God and singing to His Name. Meeting this company the Spirit of God (v. 10) not of " Jehovah " came mightily upon Saul's " flesh " and he joined them, but he very soon left them. This company, and the mysterious power that clothed them, loudly announced to Saul that the only energy that could dispossess the Philistine from God's hill was a spiritual energy, and not a carnal. But this lesson he also failed to learn. So his eyes were opened to present facts—the hill of God in the power of the Philistines, a few who remembered the God of Bethel and sought Him, and the power of the Holy Spirit manifesting itself in the very face of the Philistine foe ; as it afterwards did in apostolic days in the presence of the Devil and the opposition of his servants.

The name of " God " is significant in verses 9 and 10. It is His name as Creator in relationship to His creatures, as such ; and not involving, as the Name " Jehovah " does, a spiritual and covenanted union.

The question (v. 12) : " But who is their father ? " i.e., Master or teacher (compare ch. xix. 20, 2 Kings ii. 3 and iv. 38 with Acts iii. 24) is important. The question was not : " Who are these very clever young men ? " But it was : " Who is their master and teacher ? " This question showed that the people were just as much strangers to God and His Kingdom as Saul was. Samuel was the first of the prophets (Acts iii.) so he was the master of these singers ; but the people knew it not. However, the preaching and praising of his disciples compelled public attention to the master ; and Christian people to-day should live such lives of praise and testimony—now that the Church of God is in the hand of " the Philistine "—that they will not attract attention to themselves but to their Divine Master. Men will take knowledge of them that they have been with Jesus.

Verses 14 to 16 show that Saul, as is always the case when anyone proposes to live for God, was not to find sympathy among his relatives.

Once more Samuel pointed out to the people their sin in not waiting for God's king ; and Saul exhibited by his conduct (v. 22) the cowardice of the " flesh " as chapter ix. 21 revealed its ambition.

1 **SAMUEL XI.**—Verse 12 of the next chapter states that it was anxiety because of the threatened Ammonite invasion that influenced the people to demand a king. Their conduct illustrates the unbelief and rebellion of man's heart. They would rather lean upon a king whom they could see, and who was mortal, than upon a king unseen and almighty. And when God did give them such a king as they desired, they despised him (ch. x. 27). But when they saw Saul victorious, that was a fact that suited nature, and they confirmed him in the kingdom (v. 15). But faith is not of nature.

All went well with Saul until he was tested. The test proved that he had no spiritual life in reality. If it were possible for man, as man, to know and serve God then Saul was fully fitted to do so. He was magnanimous, generous, politic, wise, courageous, handsome, and physically powerful. To these natural gifts God added spiritual energies ; and more than once it is mentioned that they came mightily upon him. But the reception of the nature of the Holy Spirit, i.e., the new birth—is distinct from temporary energetic visitations of the Spirit.

Had the Reubenites not chosen for themselves a home on the Wilderness side of Jordan, then they would not have had the suffering and anxiety of the opening verses of this chapter. Anxiety and loss must result when self plans displace God's plans.

To destroy the right eye would not only be a reproach to the nation, as evidence of its impotency, but it would also make the victims unfit for military service, because the shield borne in war covered the left eye. But this inhuman mutilation would not make the men of Jabesh Gilead unfitted to be hewers of wood and drawers of water to the Ammonite.

Christian people who live a life half in the world and half in the kingdom, are the slaves of the Ammonite ; they have defective spiritual vision, and are useless in the wars of the Lord.

Saul's fierce message (v. 7) ; his skilful disposition of his army into three brigades ; his swift night march and sudden onslaught upon the enemy, were all admirable ; whilst his generosity toward those who had despised him (v. 13) was worthy of the noblest character.

But Samuel, a man of faith and having spiritual instincts, recognized that these natural endowments in Saul's character, however lovely, would never stand the test of conflict with a domestic foe, and hence he invited Saul to accompany him to Gilgal, there to have fellowship with God beneath the cross of Jesus—as typified by the peace offerings. Gilgal, as before pointed out, symbolized crucifixion with Christ, i.e., the putting to death of self-will, and the secret of power for war—as illustrated by Joshua's starting from and returning to that centre—a war in which the weapons are spiritual and not carnal. Saul could physically accompany Samuel thither, and also " rejoice greatly " (v. 15), and yet remain a stranger to the real and inward significance of the place.

1 **SAMUEL XII.**—The testimony which the people were compelled to give to the righteousness of Samuel's government as God's appointed judge, was a condemnation of themselves in desiring a king ; and the thunderstorm, in a serene harvest day in June, was a divine evidence of the just anger of God because of their rejection of Him. But grace, based upon election, and upon the work and person of Christ (v. 22), engaged itself (vs. 14 and 23) to continually pray for them notwithstanding their folly, and assured them that if they, and their king, only feared Jehovah and served Him with their hearts, they should personally prove the truth of the statement in verse 22 that Jehovah would not forsake His people ; but that, if disobedient, they should surely perish (v. 25).

Unlovely as the people were, and grossly ungrateful to him, yet Samuel loved them ! Beautiful picture of a heart near to God

which, forgetting self, loves a sinning people !
Samuel now retired and Saul began his
government ; and had he, influenced by the
lessons of the three signs of chapter x., and
committing himself to the dominion of that
mighty Spirit which at the hill of God, and in
the presence of the Philistine, clearly showed
him the true and only power that could give
him victory, all would have been well with
him !

1 SAMUEL XIII.—In the first two verses
of this chapter there are three difficulties which
puzzle some people. The first two difficulties
are found in the Hebrew text, which reads
thus : " Saul was one year old when he began
to reign, and he reigned two years." It is
asked, " How could it be true that he was
but one year old, when, according to
chronology, he was between twenty and
thirty ; and, again, it cannot be the case that
he reigned but two years for he reigned forty
(Acts xiii. 21) ? But these difficulties are
removed by chapter x. verse 6. One year
after he became " another man " his reign
commenced ; and it only really continued two
years, for the Philistines quickly recovered
their great defeat under Samuel and established their dominion over the entire land,
and so effectually disarmed the Israelites
that there was neither sword nor spear found
in the hand of any one of them—the only
iron instrument permitted being a file with
which to sharpen their smaller farming
implements.

The Apostle Paul did not say that Saul
"reigned" forty years ; he said that God gave
them a king "for the space of forty years."
There is a difference between a people having
a king and a prince reigning as a king.

The statement in verse 1 is the sad record
by the Holy Spirit that Saul only "reigned"
two years ; for that was the brief period of his
government in fellowship with God. See
2 Chron. xxii. 2.

The third difficulty is met by the fact that
upwards of twenty years elapsed between
verses 1 and 2 ; they are passed over in
silence by the Spirit of God.

Jonathan (" given of God ") is a fine
illustration of the possibilities and energies of
a divinely-given faith in the face of hostile
circumstances both of parentage and environment

It is instructive to contrast the son with
the father. Jonathan acted in the energy of

faith ; Saul in the energy of nature. Jonathan
would call his people " Israelites," as God
called them ; Saul called them " Hebrews " as
the Philistines called them (v. 3). Saul, as
a natural man, and as God's officially-
appointed king, could follow the impulse of
faith in the heart of Jonathan, but he did not
personally possess it. That which seeks its
strength in the wisdom and energy of man can
never go beyond the source from which it
springs ; and hence the moral and inward
movements of faith are wholly unknown to it.
But whenever there was any measure of
obedience on the part of Saul to the will of
God, He lent him His aid ; for God loved
His people.

But that which energized the heart of
Jonathan was the divine gift of faith, and,
because divine, it was victorious over the
world, in spite of the universal ruin which
met Jonathan's eye on every side ; for that
which is born of God overcomes the world
(1 Jno v. 4). Thus Jonathan here stands as an
animating figure for the servants of God to-
day. Saul represents Christendom as officially
the visible kingdom of God upon earth, but
corrupted and enslaved ; yet within this
broken kingdom it is still possible for faith
to win her victories as Jonathan won his.

But whenever faith acts the world opposes ;
and hence the Philistines are found quickly
encamped at Michmash (v. 5) ; and Satan,
who knows and dreads the power of faith,
brought up his agents as the sand which is on
the seashore in multitude. All that poor
man could do was to hide himself in holes,
and pits, and thickets, and rocks !

It is plain from verses 8 and 13 that
Samuel, from the mouth of the Lord, commanded Saul to summon the people to Gilgal,
and there to wait seven days for him ; and
this was purposely designed by God as a test
as to whether Saul would subject himself to
God's Will or act in the energy of his own.
The test demonstrated that he was willing to
wait on God but not willing to wait for God ;
and so he lost the kingdom. To wait till the
opening of the seventh day could satisfy
conscience ; but only faith could wait till the
close of that day. In making himself a priest,
and offering the sacrifice, he knew he was
disobeying the Bible (v. 12) ; but he had, as
men have to-day, a religious argument in
mitigation of his disobedience (v. 12). He
had his eyes upon the people (v. 11) and not
upon God and His commandments

Saul did not lose the throne because of the power of the Philistine. The fault was between his heart and God. The Philistine did not attack him. Satan is satisfied if he can keep the soul off the path-way of faith. The picture here is truly sad! Those who professed to be the people of God and heirs of the promises, are found unarmed in the presence of enemies who despoil them. But faith in God may be exercised no matter what the condition of the people of God may be ; and God will ever honour it ; and this the facts of the next chapter illustrate.

Recent excavations remove the obscurities in the Hebrew text of verses 20 and 21, and show that a payam and three killeshon were exorbitant prices to charge for such services. This is the true translation :

" And all Israel went down to the Philistines to forge every man his ploughshare and his *'eth*, and his axe and his goad ; and the inducement was a payam for the ploughshares and for the *'ethim*, and three *killeshon* for the axes, and to put a point on the goad ; so that in the day of battle no sword or spear was found in the hand of the people."

1 SAMUEL XIV.—If the last chapter shows the folly and effects of unbelief, this chapter shows the wisdom and results of faith ; for wherever faith is found God displays His strength. Thus the ugliness of unbelief in Saul is contrasted with the beauty of faith in Jonathan.

Faith neither lessens (v. 4) nor creates (v. 9) difficulties. Her path is open, very narrow, and made difficult by sharp rocks on either hand. But these are not difficulties to God ! Jonathan did not think of himself ; and his words to his armour-bearer (v. 6) do not express doubt as to God's ability to overcome them, but assurance. Faith's fair flower looks never so fair as when blooming in such a rocky and savage defile, beset with enemies, such as is pictured here.

Jonathan's faith was based upon God and His covenanted relationship to His people Israel. He did not say (v. 12) "Jehovah hath delivered them into my hand," but, " into the hand of Israel." He was to be nothing—the God of Israel was to be everything. It was quite true that Israel at this time was a moral ruin ; but faith forgets, or nullifies, circumstances and builds upon divine promises. This characterizes faith. Though broken and sinful yet was God with,

and for, His people, and not with, and for, the uncircumcised Philistine (v. 6). Thus there was no boasting in Jonathan, his expectation was from God ; and he went forth to witness for God in the very stronghold of the enemy. If they are foolish enough to come down, he will wait for them ; for faith does not create difficulties for itself (v. 9). If they bid him come up, they will, by doing so, foolishly open his path into their very fortress. Their folly in either event would be a sign to Jonathan that God had struck their sword out of their hand ; and this was proved to be the case.

Faith's great passion ever is that God should manifest Himself ; and great therefore must have been Jonathan's joy at the supernatural terror that seized the Philistines, and the convulsion that shook the earth (v. 15) : for it was manifest that God and not Jonathan was the author of these preternatural manifestations.

Faith confers not with flesh and blood—not even with a father—(v. 1 with Gal. i. 16), but the first act of the " flesh " is " to number the people " (v. 17) !

In Jonathan is seen the quietness and confidence of the " New Man " ; in Saul the fussiness, excitement, folly, and impotence of the " old man." Unbelief never knows what to do ; but it can furnish itself with the accessories of religious ceremonial. It can build an altar (v. 35), call for the Ark (v. 18) and lean upon the priestly member of a condemned house (v. 19). But it never knows what to do. It is all excitement. It cries out : " Bring hither the Ark of God ! " when it meant the " ephod of God " (ch. xxiii. 6, 9, xxx. 7, 8), for the Ark of God was at Kirjath Jearim where it was placed after its recovery from the Philistines ; the " flesh " can order the priest to pray, and the next moment, in its fussiness, order him to stop praying (v. 19). Unbelief, however good its intentions in trying to help the work of faith, can do nothing but spoil it. It makes man very great and God very small. Saul speaks of avenging himself on his enemies. In this section of the chapter the words " I " and " Me " and " My " fill Saul's mouth. Contrast this with Jonathan's language in the first part of the chapter. Carnal zeal hinders or limits victory (vs. 24 and 46) ; for when man intrudes himself into the work of God—bringing his own strength into it—he stops it. His foolish command to put to death those who failed to obey his laws only made more visible the disobedience of his own heart to obey God's Laws (ch. xv. 19). But the people rescued Jonathan from the insensate hands of his excited father ; and God's action in refusing to answer (v. 37) only helped to make more manifest the folly of the king.

Thus faith can act by itself—unbelief, never ! With the one, there is neither haste nor excitement, only victory. With the other, there is planning, and commanding, and counter-commanding, and running about, and defeat !

In the path of faith there is honey (v. 26) ; in the path of unbelief, there is hunger (v. 31). God furnishes ample refreshment upon the heavenly way so that there was "a stream of honey" (v. 26 R.V.) upon the very battle-field. But that which is an invitation of faith made it a duty, under sentence of death, to partake of it. The corrupt Christian Church is a sad illustration to-day of the same intrusion of man's will into God's Kingdom. But there are those to-day who, like happy Jonathan, live and fight with God (v. 45), and whose faith in Him leads them so far ahead on the celestial road that they neither hear nor heed the senseless laws which poor men, holding official office in Christendom, make.

So long as Jonathan, i.e., faith, took the lead, everything prospered; but when Saul, that is, unbelief, put himself at the head, the effect was to lose the full fruit of the victory.

Except in verse 21, the Holy Spirit gives the heavenly name of "Israelite" even to the most timorous of those who companied with Saul and Jonathan (ch. xiii. 6) ; but in verse 21 refuses it to those who lived at peace with the Philistines. This lesson conflicts with the accepted teaching of many professing Christians to-day who condemn hostility to the agents of evil within the church, urge compromise with them, and speak eloquently of "the sweetness of peace."

Foolish and carnal as Saul was, yet God helped him against Israel's enemies on every side (vs. 47, 48, 52), for He loved His people ; and as yet Saul had not been put to a final proof, nor had he as yet turned in hatred against the king whom God had chosen, and who was after His own heart.

1 SAMUEL XV.—Saul was tested twice and failed under each test. The Philistine was God's instrument in the first test ; the Amalekite, in the second. The first test proved him to be carnal, for he waited on God, but not for God. The second test showed him to be disobedient, for he set his own will above God's will. In the first test he failed to trust God ; in the second test, to obey God. These two words "trust" and "obey" are keynotes in the Christian life, and are impossible to those outside that life.

With this final proof of Saul's unfitness to be King over Israel, the history of his reign, as a connected history, ceases, and God's chosen king, David, appears.

The words "I remember" (v. 2) contrast with the words "Thou shalt not forget" (Deut. xxv. 19). The Amalekites were the determined and cruel enemies of the People of God. They were the first to attack them in the Desert (Exod. xvii.) (See notes on that chapter). When Israel was faint and weary they attacked the feeble among them (Deut. xxv. 18). Because of this hatred God commanded their extinction, and urged His People not to forget that duty so soon as they were settled in Canaan (Deut. xxv. 19). They did forget it ; but God did not forget it (v. 2) ! He loved His People ; yet He gave Amalek five hundred years respite for repentance ; but in vain. That nation, like the Seven nations of Canaan, resisted every Divine impulse, and finally became so corrupt that, in the interests of humanity, Love decreed its absolute extinction. For a vindication of this action on the part of God see notes on Num. xxi. This just doom on Amalek was predicted by Balaam in Num. xxiv. verse 20.

The Holy Spirit says that "Saul and the people" spared Agag and the best of the spoil (v. 9) but Saul said that it was "the people that spared them" (v. 15). God said : "Saul hath not performed my commandment" (v. 11). Saul said : "I have performed the commandment of Jehovah" (v. 13), adding that the spoil was spared in order to offer sacrifice unto Jehovah (vs. 15 and 21). All these statements were falsehoods. His professions of repentance (vs. 24 and 30) were false, for he thought only of the threatened punishment, and his own honour (vs. 23 and 30). True repentance is toward God—and hence David said, "I have sinned against Jehovah" (see notes on 2 Sam. xii).

It is true that Saul betook himself to Gilgal,

as was meet; but, before doing so, he marched to Carmel and set up a vainglorious monument to himself there, having a hand as a token of victory upon it (see R.V.). But Samuel said to him that He that gave victory to Israel was the "Strength of Israel" (see R.V. margin).

Although Samuel turned again after Saul it does not say that he joined him in his act of official worship, for as soon as possible he left him for ever. Yet he mourned for him continually, as at the first he spent a sleepless night of sorrow on his account (v. 11); but there is no record that Saul mourned for himself.

A righteous judgment fell upon Saul and Agag. The one King was rejected; the other, slain.

1 SAMUEL XVI.—In this chapter, in that which precedes, and in that which follows, there are four supposed difficulties easy of explanation.

The first is found in chapter xv. verses 29 and 35. These verses state that God repents and that He does not repent. To "repent" means to change one's mind. God alters His action because of failure in man, but He never changes His mind because of failure in Himself; for there never was, is, nor can be any failure in God!

The second difficulty is found in the opening verses of chapter xvi. where God tells Samuel, as some think, to deceive the people of Bethlehem. There was no deceit, but, on the contrary, the exquisite skill and tender pity with which God teaches His pupils in the School of Faith—the very same God who, centuries afterwards, said to Peter: "Thrust out a little from the shore" and then said, (the minor commandment having been obeyed) "Launch out into the deep." Thus was Samuel gently taught and encouraged. Afraid to obey the command to anoint David, he is commissioned to offer up a sacrifice—his Loving Master well knowing that in obeying this lesser command, and thus, in type, betaking himself to Calvary, his faith would be strengthened, and he would, in the presence of a goodly company of witnesses, boldly do what he feared to perform; and then, not run away and hide, but return to his home as much as to say: Let Saul come and kill me if he will (v. 13). The School of Faith has many such pupils in it to-day; they are being taught by the same wise, loving and patient Teacher; and they, like Samuel, find the atmosphere of Calvary the best tonic for spiritual fears.

The third difficulty is found in contrasting the eight sons of Jesse (vs. 10 and 11) with his seven sons in 1 Chron. ii. 15. The answer is simple. The one passage is history: the other, genealogy. One of the sons evidently died without issue; and, therefore, would not of course appear in the family register.

The last difficulty is pointed to as existing between chapter xvi. verses 21 and 22 and chapter xvii. 55-58. This difficulty is removed when it is noticed that though David, his family, and his heroic conduct in fighting the lion and the bear, were all known to one of the pantry-boys at the Court (v. 18), and by him told to one of the privy-councillors (v. 17)—(the word "servant" in verses 17 and 18 is different in the Hebrew text)—yet there is nothing to show that all this information was imparted to Saul. Further, it is clear from chapter xvii. verses 31-39 that Saul and David were not strangers to each other; and, lastly, a king makes many more minute inquiries about the family and social position of a young man who is to be connected with him as a son-in-law than when appointed as a minstrel. Saul was really ignorant of David and his exploits; not so the servant! So is it to-day! The great and the rich are profoundly ignorant of Jesus, whilst those in low estate know Him well.

Samuel's continuing to mourn for Saul (v. 1) shows the great beauty of his affectionate and unselfish nature; but it was an evidence of failure in his public duty as a Prophet, and of a want of alacrity in accepting the will of God, who, in the exercise of His Sovereignty, rejected the one king and chose the other. This sovereignty appears in God choosing the youngest son; and in choosing him after His own heart—not after David's heart! It was not because of any moral beauty in David that God chose him, but he chose him because of what He found in Himself.

God did not at once set David upon the throne as He had done in the case of Saul. He had first to be tested, and humbled, and made to feel his dependence on God, and the sufficiency of God to uphold him and maintain him. Hence, at the outset of his career, he is brought face to face with Satan (v. 23). So was it with the Blessed One, of whom

David was a type. His public life began with an encounter with the Devil. It was thus, and by his subsequent sufferings, that David was moulded and trained to be the channel through which the Psalms were given to the world.

The word " armour-bearer " in verse 21 may mean " Attendant " or " Page." If Job had ten such attendants, (2 Samuel xviii. 15.) Saul would surely have several.

It is generally accepted that David was about fifteen years of age at the time of his first anointing. He was anointed as King three times.

Some Hebrew scholars translate v. 23 : And David played in order that Saul might be refreshed etc., and that the evil spirit might depart, etc. This translation would explain the seeming contradiction of chapter xviii. 11. In this case the prior verse does not say that the playing effected the purpose, but that it sought it.

I. SAMUEL XVII.—The number " six " is stamped upon Goliath (vs. 4-7). He was six cubits high and he had six pieces of armour. This number " six " was stamped upon Nebuchadnezzar's golden image, and it will identify the future Anti-christ ; the number of whose name will be 666 (Rev. xiii. 18).

David was sent by his father to his brothers to bless them and do them good, but, like Joseph's brothers when he was sent to bless them, he met with envy and hatred. Thus was it with God's Beloved Son. His brothers, Mary's sons, did not believe on Him (John vii. 5.), and, with her, sought to lay hold upon Him as being beside Himself (Mark iii. 32.) ; and His spiritual brethren. Israel, nailed Him to the Tree.

Verse 15. reads thus in the R.V. :— " Now David went to and fro from Saul to feed his father's sheep at Bethlehem " ; that is, it was his habit to go to and fro.

To take " a pledge " (v. 18.) means to bring back some letter or evidence of a brother's welfare.

David's question (v. 26. with chapter xviii. 23.) does not mean that he desired the King's daughter and her money—every man he spoke to had no higher thought than that— but was evidently intended as a rebuke, for he pointed out to them that the matter was much nobler and more serious, and this he did by bringing the Philistine and the

Living God face to face ; and what had a woman and her money to do with that ? David's heart was engaged with higher concerns.

God cannot give victories to " the flesh " and its armour (v. 38), nor can faith use them (v. 39); but by secret victories (vs. 34-37) He trains His servants for public triumphs. It is vain to hope for victory over the " Philistine " in public if, in private, the " lion " and the " bear " have not been vanquished. This is one of the fundamental principles governing the christian life.

David chose him five smooth stones out of the brook (v. 40). If the brook, with its living running water, pictures the Holy Spirit, then might the five smooth stones picture the Five Books of the Law ; for these were given forth of the Holy Spirit, just as the stones had been shaped and smoothed by the water. One of these stones, fresh from the brook's bed, and shot in faith, laid the Giant low ; and since that day many another giant has been similarly slain.

David running to meet the Philistine (v. 48) is one of the finest pictures in the Bible.

The return of David with the head of the Philistine in his hand, dismissed the terrors of the men of Israel and filled their hearts with peace. So Christ, returning from the grave, having vanquished death with his own Sword (Hebrews II. 14), as David cut off the Philistine's head with his own sword, delivers His people from the fear of death, and fills their hearts with the peace of God which passeth all understanding.

Saul, having promised exemption of taxation to the family of the victor, and the hand of his daughter in marriage with a handsome dowry, naturally asks Abner (v. 55) for information respecting David's father and his position in society (see notes on prior chapter). But here appears something deeper. Saul willingly accepted the relief that David's skill provided him (ch. xvi 23), but did not seek to know David personally ; and so when he comes forth to battle for the Lord and do His work he has to say, " Whose son art thou ? " Such is man and such is the " flesh ! " It is ever willing to accept Christ's gifts, and yet remain a stranger to Him ! In Jonathan (ch. xviii. 1) is seen the affection of faith. He loved David as his own soul ; he became the object of his whole affection ; and he stripped himself of his royal armour and gave all to David (v. 4). This is a lovely illustration of the unselfish power of a supreme affection.

It is possible that David, anticipating that the four that were born to the giant (2 Sam. xxi. 22) would help Goliath, or seek to avenge his death, chose the five stones. His action in so doing expressed faith and not fear. He believed that one stone sufficed to kill a giant. So one book of the Law vanquished Satan in the battle of Matt. iv.

1 SAMUEL XVIII.—Both David and Jonathan conquered the Philistines by faith ; but David's faith was the greater, for he met the great enemy of his people face to face, and destroyed him. David's was the faith of the Blessed One whom he typified ; Jonathan's, the faith of His people. They are quite willing to give Him everything, including the throne of their lives, and to set themselves aside in order that He may have the Kingdom. Saul pictures the unbelieving Jews who hated Him, and desired to have the inheritance for themselves (Matt. xxi. 38).

David not having clothing suitable for a Royal Court, Jonathan clothed him in his own raiment, even to his sword and his girdle. Thus, as noticed in the last chapter, love willingly gives up everything.

Saul as an instrument of Satan tried to kill David. This was another effort on his part to make impossible the Promise of Gen. iii. 15 and so thwart the advent of the Redeemer. This explains why so many of those who were the ancestors of Christ were the objects of Satan's peculiar cunning and hatred.

But the more Saul tried to destroy David the more did God prosper him (vs. 13–16).

The king's promise to give his daughter to the victor was not kept ; but, on the contrary, a snare was set for David's foot. Merab was indeed proposed, but upon the added condition that David should adventure his life and slay more of the Philistines, and thereby, as Saul hoped, lose his life (v. 17). But this plan having failed, the king laid another snare for him. He grossly insulted him by giving the bride, a day or two before the marriage, to another man. By this, no doubt, he hoped to sting David into some disloyal language or conduct that would justify his being put to death ; but it also failed.

In his envy and rage he hoped again to bring about the death of David at the hands of the Philistines, by demanding, as a dowry for his second daughter, one hundred of their fore-skins. David accepts the conditions and slays two hundred Philistines ; for they were God's enemies, and in slaying them David acted as God's servant and not as Saul's instrument. But here Saul illustrates the truth of Rom. viii. 5–8. Circumcision was a solemn, instructive, and significant ordinance of God that should mark His People as severed from the world, but Saul, with an appearance of religious zeal, made use of it to please himself and to destroy David. He made, so to speak, two hundred "converts" ; but they were dead converts. His plan is in operation at the present day ; and multitudes of dead converts have been made on the same principle, and secured for the outward Kingdom of God.

1 SAMUEL XIX.—This chapter records nine attempts made by Saul upon the life of David. Saul was not incapable of generous and just feelings. These showed themselves at times. But they were such as is possible to the " natural man," for God was not in them (vs. 4–7).

But a brilliant victory won by David over the Philistines (v. 8) revived, without doubt, the envy and murderous rage of Saul against him (v. 9). It is a deep and dreadful mystery that self-will, envy and passion appear to make possible the entrance of an evil spirit into a man's heart, and make him a helpless slave of the power of the demon.

In warring with the Philistine it is the power of faith which alone gives victory. This explains why, in that warfare, David always succeeded, and Saul always failed.

David did not seek to defend himself against Saul, nor to gather his friends together and head a revolt against him. He betook himself to Samuel, and sought, in fellowship with him, the sheltering wing of God, and the solace of spiritual communion. His doing so was a recognition by David of that Power which owned and clothed Samuel, and which had for some reason, unknown to David, set Saul as King over Israel. Therefore it was, though David could no longer dwell with Saul, he would not conspire against him, for he was Jehovah's Anointed officially, though privately rejected.

Saul and his messengers became subject to that same Power ; but it was only a physical subjection ; it did not affect their hearts, or change their moral natures or conduct.

Saul here presents a sad and terrible picture ! One moment generous and kind ; the next, murderous and cruel ! One moment controlled by the Spirit of God ; the next, by the spirit of the Demon ! A useless ruined vessel, his life was wrecked because he hated David. Apart from that hatred, nothing is recorded to lead to the belief that his public or private conduct was unworthy of a man and a king ; and men would not have known that there were such depths of malignity in his character had David never appeared. David's person and victories made manifest Saul's true character.

So was it with man when the Greater than David appeared. His apparition immediately made manifest fallen man's true nature ; just as Light makes manifest Darkness.

Saul launched his javelin with such fury at David that he drove it into the wall !

Michal was an idolatress (v. 13 R.V.) and, being such, she found it easy to be a liar (v. 17) ; for falsehood and idolatry go hand-in-hand.

It may be assumed that David did not know that there was an idol in his house ; for in all ages women have been more disposed to idolatry than men ; hence, to the present day, a rich woman who comes into possession of a furnished house, will remove from the walls the words of the Lord of Life and put in their place idolatrous pictures of dead saints.

The word " naked " (v. 24) here, as elsewhere in the Bible, means stripped of one's outward clothing.

1 SAMUEL XX.—David was now a wanderer, and continually pursued by man's king who sought his life. He was, and is, in this a type of the true King of Israel, now rejected and hated by the world, after having been actually betrayed and murdered by the official Israel (Acts iii. 14 and 15). But just as the kingdom came ultimately to David, and just as he gave high positions in that kingdom to those who had loved him when an outcast, so will Christ the Lord receive by-and-bye the dominion of the earth, and He will appoint to great honour those who now love and follow Him.

Saul threw off the last restraint : he sought to slay David even in the presence of Samuel (xix. 22-24); and he wilfully resisted the last mighty visitation of the Holy Spirit. David could not, therefore, now return to him. To do so would have been to unite himself with a declared enemy of Divine Truth. Jonathan appears to have clung to the hope that the scene of chapter xix. 23 and 24 made certain that his father was at last really born of the Holy Spirit (v. 2) ; but David knew better (v. 3). Yet still Jonathan was true to David ; and though now an exile, he loved him, if it were possible, even more deeply than when, radiant with youth and flushed with victory, he replied to Saul with a modesty that heightened the glory of his great deed (ch. xvii. 58). Had Jonathan not been governed by a false sense of filial duty he would have shared David's exile, and not returned to his father (v. 42).

There is nothing to oppose the belief that David did spend the three days (v. 19) at home (vs. 6 and 28).

Verse 17 is understood by some Hebrew scholars to mean that Jonathan caused David to hear him repeat the oath ; i.e., because he loved him so truly he repeated his engagement to David, and caused David to repeat his engagement to him.

The " business " of verse 19 was that spoken of in chapter xix. vs. 2 and 3.

The plan of shooting two arrows and linking the word " come " with the first and " make speed " with the second, was cleverly designed so as to protect all three from the possible vengeance of the frenzied King.

Affection necessitated a meeting, and love was fertile in planning it. Jonathan's going out to shoot with the lad was an ordinary circumstance that would not attract notice. David was evidently hidden, and only showed himself when the lad was gone away.

The path of faith is straight and simple ; that of unbelief, tortuous and untruthful. David should have done his duty, and trusted God to plan for him and to protect him.

Verse 30 should read thus : " Thou son of rebellious perversity ! " That is, Saul accused his son of being a rebel, as well as David ; and he added that Jonathan had chosen David to his own confusion and nakedness, and that of his mother, i.e., he was depriving himself of the throne, and disrobing his mother of the royal dignities which would attach to her ; for, in the East, the King's Mother is the greatest woman in the nation. The King in his rage pointed to this in expressive but coarse language.

1 **SAMUEL XXI.**—This chapter gives a humbling view of the weakness and falsehood of human nature even in the best of men.

It also teaches the bitter lesson that departure from the path of faith not only means loss of all personal dignity, but it involves injury to others. Thus as Abraham, when he left the path of faith, became the occasion of sickness and disease to the Egyptians (Gen. xii. 17), so David's conduct caused the death of the High Priest and eighty-five of his fellow-priests, together with their wives and children (ch. xxii. 18 and 19).

So long as the Christian " trusts and obeys " so long is he a blessing to the world, but he becomes a curse when he leaves that narrow but victorious path.

The contrast between David's scrabbling on the door of the Philistine (v. 13) and David with the head of the Philistine in his hand (ch. xvii. 57), helps to fasten upon the mind the fact that the life of the Christian is wholly different from that of the scientist or the philosopher. Experience gained in these latter realms can be retained and profited by ; but this is not so in the Christian life. In this life, directly fellowship with God is lost, all past experience is also lost ; and even the cleansing from old sins is forgotten (2 Pet. i. 9). This terrible truth is painfully illustrated many times in the Bible—notably by the children of Israel, who speedily forgat his works in Egypt and in the Desert (Ps. lxxviii. 11 and cvi. 13)—and by David when he said : " I shall one day perish by the hand of Saul " (1 Sam. xxvii. 1), although the promises of God, and his own past experiences, assured him to the contrary.

This forgetting and losing of past experiences as a characteristic of the spiritual life, explains many passages in Bible History which appear inexplicable to the ordinary historical student.

David, taking himself out of the Hand of God, fled to Nob, a village on the side of the Mount of Olives ; and he, in order to obtain bread for himself and his hungry followers (Matt. xii. 3), deceived the High Priest (v. 2). At that time. as at the present day, it was the common belief that it was lawful in certain circumstances to lie, provided no injury was done thereby unto others But David's falsehood occasioned the death of a great many innocent persons ; and he himself learned, later on, that all liars shall have their portion in the lake that burns with fire (Ps. xxxiv. 12, 13 with Rev. xxi. 8).

The hallowed bread that David and his men ate was the shewbread. Once a week its twelve loaves were removed from the Golden Table to make way for twelve fresh loaves. David's argument in verse 5 was that the bread had become unhallowed because removed from the " vessel " i.e., the Golden Table ; and, the more so, seeing the fresh loaves had been hallowed that very day and placed thereon. Further, that the " vessels ," i.e., the " wallets " of himself and his companions were " holy," that is, consecrated ; and, finally, that they all had lived apart from their wives for the three days as required in Exod. xix. 15, and, as will, in a future day, be repeated. (Zech. xii. 10-14.) These two latter passages illustrate Christ's teaching when He says that no earthly affection, however sweet, must be permitted to conflict in the heart with the Divine claims.

The following chapter (vs. 10 and 15) suggests that the High Priest was told by God to give the hallowed bread to David ; and that same Gracious God, afterwards in Matt. xii. 7, explained that He permitted this because He desired mercy rather than sacrifice ; that is, that works of mercy, such as feeding hungry men, are more pleasing to Him than ritualism, or asceticism. (Col. ii. 18-23).

One falsehood leads to another (v. 8) ; and trusting a human helper blinds the spiritual vision (v. 9). The sword of Goliath should have reminded David that it was powerless to deliver the Philistine, and would, therefore, fail to deliver him ; and, yet, he foolishly says " there is none like that ! "

The wisdom which led into the court of the Philistine (v. 10), became the shame of the feigned madness which led to an expulsion ; and so David was expelled, just as Abraham had been.

The old sword of the Philistine, and the new cart of the Philistine, illustrate war and worship after the flesh. David, in using both instead of living by faith and obeying the word of God, brought sorrow to himself and death to others.

1 **SAMUEL XXII.**—Restored in soul (Ps. xxxiv.) David now took his place outside the camp, and " the excellent in the earth " gathered around him (Ps. xvi. 3 and Heb. xi. 38). To him they were excellent ; to the world they were men distressed, indebted,

and dissatisfied (v. 2). The Prophet Gad (v. 5) and the Priest Abiathar (v. 20) both joined him ; so that, rejected as he was, yet was he God's elect King and the centre of a living testimony for Jehovah, whilst with Saul was the outward and official testimony —but it was dead. Such is the position to-day in Christendom. The outward form of a testimony for God exists, but its living reality is only found among those who know and love and serve their rejected Lord. Such persons are despised by the great and proud, but He ennobles them, He calls them " the excellent in the earth," and He says that in them is all His delight (Ps. xvi. 3).

This conjunction of David, Gad, and Abiathar is remarkable. They picture Christ as Prophet, Priest, and King awaiting, in seclusion, the day of His appearing, when to Him, as to David, the gathering of the people will be.

The destruction of the whole House of Eli, as predicted in chapters ii. 31 and iii. 12, was, with the exception of Abiathar, fulfilled by Saul (vs. 18 and 19). As to Abiathar, a just judgment expelled him from the priesthood. 1 Kings ii. 27 reads : " So Solomon thrust out Abiathar from being High Priest unto Jehovah ; that the word of the Lord might be fulfilled which He spake concerning the House of Eli."

1 SAMUEL XXIII.—Verse 6 states that Abiathar joined David at Keilah. This fact shows that verse 1 should read in the Hebrew text: "Now they had told David, saying ;" and it is thus translated by competent scholars.

The simplicity, brevity, and definiteness of David's prayer (vs. 2, 10. 11 and 12) is a model for all who believe that God hears and answers prayer.

David's gentleness with those who had not the same measure of faith as he had (v. 3) is also a model for all Christian people. He did not proudly and scornfully scold them for their want of faith, as many would do to-day, but he sympathized with their fears, and said he would again ask God for guidance.

David adventured his life to save the men of Keilah, and they, with base ingratitude, promptly prepared to betray him to Saul (v. 12) ; just as the men of Ziph (v. 20), to whom no doubt he had been a shield, hasted also to betray him. Thus was it with Him of whom David was a type. He came to redeem Israel and to save the Gentile, and they joined together to crucify Him. Such is fallen man !

It was true affection, and a real putting of self to death, that made Jonathan visit David in the wood (v. 16) and remind him of the Divine Promises. But had he had the same degree of intelligence as of affection, he would have thrown in his lot with David in the wood and not returned to his house (v. 18). He is never read of again in the Holy Scriptures till he appears slain by the Philistine on Mount Gilboa (ch. xxxi. 2).

Sometimes God in His wisdom does not deliver His servant until all appears lost and faith seems a deception. David was apparently lost—escape was impossible (v. 26) —but at the very last moment he was delivered. Satan's agents are not always under his control ; and from time to time they upset his plans (vs. 27, 28).

Christian tourists in the Holy Land visit this famous rock (v. 28) and find it good to read at its side the closing verses of this chapter.

Saul could promise wealth and position to his followers (ch. xxii. 7), whilst David could only offer hunger and hardship ; and yet the one King walked with God, and the other fought against Him ! This mystery continues still. The children of Faith are, as a rule, poor and few in number ; the children of rebellion, many and rich. But the inward contrast between Saul and David was as noteworthy as the outward. Saul made frightful progress inwardly in evil ; David, rapid progress in good. Outward progress in prosperity, joined with active inward progress in iniquity, is at once a snare to the mind and a trial to faith, for it seems to contradict the teaching of the Bible. David had neither home nor refuge, but he had the Word of God (the Prophet), and communion with God (the Priest) ; and this was his portion in his exile. Thus when the Church of the First Covenant fell into ruin David could, in the energy and intelligence of a faith that reached forward into a future day, eat the shewbread and take the Ephod (v. 9 with ch. xxi. 6). In all this he is a remarkable type of Christ, and a pattern to the confused children of God dwelling amid the ruins of Christendom. But their duty is not, as some think, to go forth and battle against Christendom, but it is to wage war against the Philistine ; just as David had no power against Saul, nor did he wage war against him, as he might have done, but he only had power against that which was hostile to them both, that is, the Philistine.

1 **SAMUEL XXIV.**—" The rocks of the wild goats " (v. 2) mean cliffs accessible to wild goats but dangerous of access to men. Saul, however, hated David so fiercely that he ventured his life upon these heights in the effort to reach and murder him. He, at the first, loved David " greatly " (ch. xvi. 21), but such is the power of jealousy that it changed that affection into murderous hatred. All Christian people should watch against the entrance of this enemy into their hearts ; and those most highly placed in the Kingdom of God should remember that they are in special danger of being enslaved by it.

The cave in which Saul lay down " to cover his feet "—that is, to rest from the heat of the day, is still, in the opinion of travellers, easy to recognize. The entrance is small, the interior very large, and capable of affording abundant room for David and his men to so " crouch down " in its sides that they would not be observed (v. 3).

The supposed promise of verse 4 had never been given by God. Such is man ! Promises that are given he lightly esteems, and promises that are not given he invents and believes.

David's heart " smote " him (v. 5) because in cutting off the lappet of Saul's robe while the King was, no doubt, asleep—the robe covering his feet—he felt he had been guilty of an action not worthy of a loyal subject and not respectful in a son-in-law. Hence in his apology (vs. 9-15) he first confessed the wrongfulness of his conduct as a subject (v. 10) and then as a son (v. 11). Whenever a Christian does anything boastful, or fails in his duty toward his fellow men, and in the respect and sympathy due to them, his heart " smites him," and peace does not return to his breast until he has confessed his failure, first to God, and then to man ; that is, to the person whom he has sinned against.

Saul was not yet wholly lost to right feelings, and so he wept (v. 16). But weeping does not change the moral nature ; and, accordingly, many days did not elapse till Saul once more started out with his three thousand men to seek and destroy David (v. 2 with ch. xxvi. 2). Therefore it was that David, who was born of the Spirit, did not " commit himself " to Saul but got him up into his stronghold (v. 22). Similarly, the Root and Offspring of David did not commit Himself to those in Israel

who professed a faith in Him because they saw the miracles which He did (John ii. 24), but, on the contrary, speaking to one of these " men "—a " man " of the Pharisees named Nicodemus—he told him that a faith based on evidence, and a repentance founded on reformation, were useless. Man, however religious, must be re-born.

" To cover the feet " is understood by many scholars as a euphemism for the meaning stated in the margin of Judges iii. 24 A.V. But it would scarcely be possible for David, in that case, to cut the King's robe, but quite possible if Saul were sleeping. See note on Judges iii. 24.

1 **SAMUEL XXV.**—The great figures of this chapter are Samuel, David and Abigail. They typify the Law, Christ and the true Israel. The Law and the Prophets were until John ; then the King appeared, but in rejection and hatred, yet loving hearts joined Him, shared His exile and sufferings, animated by the knowledge that those who suffered with Him should reign with Him (2 Tim. ii. 12).

Accordingly Samuel disappears and Abigail appears. In the intelligence of a true faith she accepted and confessed David as God's elect King—Saul being but " a man" (v. 29). She left her wealthy home to be an outcast and a wanderer with David ; and, like the thief on the cross, she looked forward to the coming Kingdom and said " Remember me " (v. 31). Jonathan truly loved David, but did not share his rejection and sufferings. He pictures those who will be in the Kingdom, but they will not reign. Abigail represents those who will reign with Him because they suffered with Him. David generously said that Jonathan's love to him surpassed the love of women (2 Sam. i. 26), but it did not surpass nor equal the love of Abigail.

David was entitled to a just payment from Nabal, for he had protected his property from the Desert robbers which abounded, and still abound, in that part of the country. There were two Carmels—this was the Southern one—the word means " fruitful." To the present day wealthy Arab Chieftains, when shearing their sheep, hold a festival, and make rich presents to the neighbouring chieftains. The word " Nabal " means " a fool " ; and it was foolish, as well as discourteous and unjust and insulting, to treat David as he did.

No man is perfect even though he be a type of Christ ; and David like the Apostle

Paul (Acts xxiii. 3), stung with the injustice of Nabal's language, started out to punish him ; but God delivered him from the snare. Abigail was the instrument of that deliverance.

Not only was she beautiful in person but she was yet more beautiful in character. Her faith and her intelligence were admirable. She judged both Nabal and Saul as God judged them. She recognized in David his title as King ; his personal perfection ; his valour in fighting God's battles ; and, where others only saw a rebel, she saw a redeemer ; and all this was not just merely the intelligence of the head, it was accompanied by the affection of the heart (vs. 23-31).

Had David kept closely to the teaching of the Bible he would have had but one wife ; for so was it ordained " from the beginning " (Matt. xix. 8).

I SAMUEL XXVI.—Two facts are illustrated in this chapter. One is, that " the natural man " is the helpless but willing tool of evil ; the other is, that " the spiritual man " never accustoms himself to evil. Saul illustrates the first fact ; David, the second. Saul knew well (ch. xxiv. 20) that David was God's chosen King, and that he would certainly reign ; and yet he, again and again, tried to destroy him ! Such is the power of evil ! Satan is also the helpless but willing agent of sin ; and though he knew that God's Elect King would surely be born, and will certainly reign, yet he strove to hinder the one event, and makes unceasing efforts to prevent the other. This fact respecting man's fallen nature proves the absolute necessity of a new moral creation—an unpopular doctrine uniformly taught in both the Old and New Testaments.

David illustrates the truth that the spiritual nature never accustoms itself to evil (vs. 9, 19, 20, 23, and 24). Man's nature does accustom itself to evil ; after a little time ceases to be shocked by its manifestations ; and, later on, gives way to them.

Between the spiritual and the natural natures there is, in this world, "a great space," just as there was between David and Saul (v. 13), and, in the next world, "a great gulf fixed " (Luke xvi. 26). They are eternally separated. It is impossible to cultivate the one so that it will develop into the other. Many believe this to be possible. It is known as the doctrine of Moral Evolution. But the great gulf fixed between these two natures make a transition from the one to the other impossible ; and hence the necessity of being " created anew in Christ Jesus " (Ephes. ii. 10) before the eternal world is entered ; for there everything is " fixed."

In this chapter David refused to act independently of God. He put himself entirely into Jehovah's hands. It is noteworthy the number of times he uses that precious Name (vs. 9, 10, 10, 11, 11, 16, 16, 19, 19, 19, 20, 23, 23, 23, 24). This is characteristic ; it is the Spirit of Christ in David in the Psalms ; for David was a Prophet (Acts ii. 30).

An Arab Chieftain sleeps on the ground, or in a tent, in the centre of a circular barricade formed by his men and their animals, having at his head a flask of water, and his spear fixed upright in the ground.

Abishai was David's nephew. His subsequent action shows him to have been a determined soldier void of compassion.

The configuration of the country where Saul camped permits of one person speaking with ease to another person, a deep valley effectually separating them. David (v. 19) humbly admitted the possibility of his having so sinned against God that Saul was the righteous instrument of God's just anger against him, but he pointed to a sin-offering as the Divine way of forgiveness.

The new nature never can trust the old ; so David went on his way (v. 25)—the way of faith—and Saul, like Judas, went to " his place." (Acts i. 25).

I SAMUEL XXVII.—David in this chapter sorrowfully illustrates the fact that all previous experience is lost directly the path of faith is left. Forgetting the sure promises made to him—promises that even Saul acknowledged (ch. xxiv. 20)—and disobeying the Divine command to dwell in the Land of Judah (ch. xxii. 5). he said in his heart, " I shall one day perish by the hand of Saul."

Forsaking the path of faith not only causes the loss of past experience but it leads into sin and sorrow. David's planning seemed for the moment successful (v. 4), but it quickly brought him to the sin of deception (vs. 9-12).

There is no half-way house between fellowship with God and fellowship with the Philistine. If the Philistine is made a refuge, then must David dwell in the midst of them, and declare himself ready to fight with them against the People of God (ch. xxix. 8). God.

it is true, in His love and pity for His servant, overruled all for his safety, but at the same time He sorely chastened him (ch. xxx.) ; and David's action in joining Achish not only delayed his possession of the Kingdom, but it became the occasion for teaching his six hundred men to sin against light and knowledge. There was but One who never cast aside entire dependence upon God, and He was the Author and Perfecter of Faith.

In actual Christian life, as in the Scriptures, despondency and unbelief quickly follow upon a great crisis of faith. It was so with Elijah (1 Kings xix.) as with David and Peter and others. It would seem as if an unusual effort of faith exhausted the heart, which is the vessel of that faith, with the result that fear and weakness result. But no such failure was ever seen in the Man Christ Jesus.

The destruction of the Amalekites and their neighbours was legitimate (ch. xv.).

Achish was probably a title, and hence the king of Gath of this chapter may have been a successor of the king of chapter xxi. But kings, for reasons of state, are willing to ally themselves to-day with a prince whom yesterday they regarded as a fool. Two years intervened between chapters xxi. and xxvii.

David could congratulate himself on the success of his plan, for he baffled Saul, he won Ziklag, he conquered Amalek, and he deceived Achish—but what would have been his experience had he sought to know and to follow God's plan ?

1 SAMUEL XXVIII.—When a Christian seeks the protection and patronage of a man of the world, he must place himself and his spiritual gifts at the disposition of his protector. A sad and degrading bondage ! This was David's unworthy and God-dishonouring relation with Achish. In such circumstances Satan does not fail to provide earthly honours, and, accordingly, Achish made David Captain of his Body-Guard (vs. 1 and 2 with chapter xxix).

David was in a false position. God in His faithful love delivered him from it ; but, as in the case of Jacob, chastened him severely. Had David let God plan for him he would have been saved from much shame and sin and sorrow.

But Saul was in a worse case. Samuel was dead (v. 3) ; the Philistines were pressing him (v. 4) ; and God had departed from him (v. 6). In his misery he sought direction from the demons ; though well knowing that the Word of God sternly forbade such unlawful intercourse. God permitted Samuel to appear (v. 14), with the result that the unhappy woman was terror-stricken, and the king stretched upon the ground paralysed with fear. His namesake, Saul of Tarsus, also " fell to the earth " (Acts ix. 4). But how great was the contrast ! The one rose and went away " that night " (v. 25), with a deeper night in his soul, to his doom ; the other rose and went *his* way, with the great Light in his heart, to receive the Crown of righteousness that was laid up for him.

1 SAMUEL XXIX.—This chapter records the lowest and most wretched point in David's history previous to his coming to the kingdom. He professes himself ready and eager to fight against God's beloved people, and to help Satan to destroy them ! He told many lies to Achish, but that of this chapter was the crowning one in his then life of duplicity and falsehood ; for while professing this devotion to the Philistine monarch, he must have been rejoicing secretly at escaping from so dreadful a position. All this shows how deeply a child of God can fall when he leans upon the hand of man and not upon the Hand of God. The path of faith is wearying to nature ; and there is an ever-present temptation to seek ease from the thorns through which that path sometimes leads. The persecution of professors of religion has oftentimes the effect of throwing the servant of God into the arms of the enemies of God ; just as Saul's hatred drove David to the Philistines. But this only happens when the Christian follows his own will, and thinks, by doing so, to avoid the very difficulties which, had he walked with God, would have become channels of teaching and refreshment to his soul. The more glorious a work there is for faith, the more sure is nature to weary if faith grows feeble. How dreadful it would have been for David had he actually fought against the Israel of God, and sought to slay the king whose life he had twice so touchingly saved !

It is refreshing to turn the eyes from David to God. With Him all here is faithfulness, and love, and compassion. He delivers his erring and sinful servant, using the jealousy of the lords of the Philistines as a means to this end ; but He sorely chastened David, as the next chapter shows.

1 **SAMUEL XXX.**—The folly of sheltering under the hand of man rather than under the Hand of God was quickly proved by David ; for the Amalekites, taking advantage of the expedition of the Philistines against Saul, invaded the land and burnt Ziklag with fire.

This bitter trial brought David back to the Lord, and effected a true restoration of his soul. Suffering and loss accompany departure from the Lord, and there must be chastisement in order to the restoration of communion. Chastening is grievous, but it yields the peaceable fruit of righteousness (Heb. xii. 11).

God was to David a present God, and a gracious and forgiving Saviour. Though he had so deeply sinned against Him, yet now in his distress he strengthened himself in Jehovah his God (v. 6). He enquired of Him, and God answered him as simply and definitely as David had simply and definitely prayed. In spite of David's sad falls he really knew God ; he held direct intercourse with Him ; and, when restored in soul, turned to Him for comfort and guidance.

The first resource of nature was seen in David's men—they murmured and grew angry. The first resource of faith appeared in David—he cast his burden upon the Lord (v. 6) ; and with the result that he recovered all (v. 19).

Directly communion with God is resumed, the life is clothed with victory and moral beauty. The Amalekites were totally defeated (v. 17) ; the Bible obeyed (v. 24 with Num. xxxi. 27) ; and a goodly portion given to David's friends (vs. 26-31). Thus companionship with God secures not only victory and obedience, but gives the power to deny self so that others may be enriched. By these gifts David demonstrated to the children of Israel that Jehovah was with him ; and so it ever is : blessing others with gifts won from the enemy proves to the world that God and the giver are in association.

The grace of David to the Egyptian (v. 11) pictures the love of Him who came to save the lost and the dying. The man was lost in the field ; he was sick and dying of hunger and thirst. He was a child of Ham ; the slave of an Amalekite ; and an enemy to David. This is a true picture of the sinner. By nature, a child of wrath (Eph. ii. 3) ; by practice, a slave to " the flesh " ; by action, an enemy to Christ ; and, by condition, lost, sick and dying. David's servants, filled with David's spirit, found the Egyptian and brought him to David and laid him at his feet. Happy place ! He there found bread, and water, and figs, and two clusters of raisins ; i.e., Life, Strength, Health, and Joy—the New Wine of the New Kingdom. The Epistles to the Romans, to the Hebrews, to the Ephesians, and to the Philippians unlock the preciousness of these four gifts of grace : the water, the bread, the figs, and the raisins. The Egyptian became the servant of David, having received the assurance from him of salvation from death and from his old master (v. 15), and shared with him the glory of the great victory. So will Christ associate with Himself in His Crowning Day those whom He came to seek and to save.

1. **SAMUEL XXXI.**—The sunny morn of Saul's reign ended in a black night of tempest and horror. Self-will wrecked his life (1 Chron. x. 13 and 14). Only a Spirit-born man can serve and please God. Saul was raised up, as a king after the people's heart, to deliver them from the Philistines ; and if it were possible for " the natural man " to do God's will, then Saul must have succeeded ; but he perished at the hands of the very enemies whom he set out to conquer ! Such must ever be the result when " the flesh " attempts to do battle for God.

The action of the men of Jabesh-Gilead was a pleasant proof of their gratitude to Saul for his deliverance of them from the Ammonites (chapter xi).

From Jabesh-Gilead to Beth-shan is about ten miles.

Saul stood in the strength of gift rather than in that of the Giver ; and instead of acting for God he acted instead of Him. The result was ruin to himself and bondage to his people.

Saul may be assumed to have been twenty at his Coronation ; he reigned forty years, and would therefore be sixty at the time of his death.

The account of his death in 1. Chronicles x. is not contradictory to this chapter ; it is complementary. The one is history, the other commentary. The one is esoteric, the other exoteric.

The principle of " trust and obey " was put aside by him in regard to the Philistine in the one (xiii. 9) and to the Amalekite in the other (xv. 11). David obeyed both in 2 Sam. v. 23, for he trusted for the movement in the tops of the trees, and obeyed when it came.

2 SAMUEL

2 SAMUEL I.—David the king is the great figure of this Book ; and, when walking in the Light, presents a rich type of Messiah the King. The first part of the Book records the victories which accompanied his life of faith and conflict ; the second part relates the defeats he suffered when prosperity had seduced him from the path of faith and had opened the door to self-will.

A life of conflict is bitter to the flesh but enriching to the spirit. Nature wearies of it. But a life of prosperity is full of snares to the soul. A contrast between David's "last words" in chapter xxiii. and his triumphant song of chapter xxii. is most marked. The song was written before prosperity had injured his spiritual life.

So long as he acted in the simplicity of faith, so much was his conduct beautified. Faith made him simple and satisfied whether as a shepherd boy or as a king ; whether loved by Saul or hated by him ; whether victorious in secret or in public. Faith elevated and dignified him ; and enabled him courageously to endure hardships against which nature can only murmur and grow impatient. Faith enabled him to look above and behind circumstances and people, and to see and trust the Great Shepherd upon whose all-sufficiency he rested. Faith was the most precious gift he had ; it bound his heart to God by a thousand bonds of affection. It gave him energy ; it gave him patience ; it made him willing to be a slave on earth because He whom he loved was in heaven ; and he would one day awake in His likeness !

But instead of faith being strengthened by victories, nature grows weary of the conflict, and rebels at circumstances. Self-will then leads into positions where God cannot be glorified. Thus David fell from his lofty estate and dishonoured, among the Philistines, the Master whom he loved ! But where sin abounded grace did much more abound ; and therefore it was that at this sad period of his life he was first chastened and then enthroned.

The Amalekite (v. 2) was justly judged ; for his own words showed the falsehood and evil of his heart. His whole story was a fabrication ; and he thought David was altogether such a man as himself !

Verse 18 (R.V.) does not mean that David profited by the lesson of the lost battle and introduced archery into his army, but that he taught this Lamentation to his fellow Tribesmen of Judah ; and the Lament was known as the "Lamentation of the Bow" ; that is, the bow of Jonathan (v. 22). Compare Luke xx. 37, R.V. where the entire record of God's appearing to Moses is called "The Bush."

2 SAMUEL II.—"The House of Saul" and "the House of David" stand in opposition one to the other. The one pictures the life as governed by Self ; the other, the life as governed by God. The latter life alone secures victory.

The simplicity, dependence, and obedience of David's faith at this crisis in his history were only possible to a heart that kept very close to God (v. 1). It was the subjection of his own will to God's Will, and the refusal to act on his own judgment and plan for himself.

Abner's action was that of "the natural man" (v. 8). Although he knew that David was God's elect King, yet, in self-will and ambition, he set up his cousin Ishbosheth, Saul's son, as King over Israel. That was rebellion against God.

David's message to the men of Jabesh-gilead was both generous and wise. It showed that he sincerely mourned the death of Saul ; it assured those brave men of his protection should the Philistines strike at them because of what they had done ; and it gently invited them to cast in their lot with him.

Active opposition to Christ and his Kingdom quickly follows upon the establishment of a rival kingdom in the heart. Abner, having set up his own king, very quickly took the further step of attacking God's King and Kingdom (v. 12).

The sharp swords which mutually destroyed the young men should have been used against the Philistine, and not against one another. The destructive energy which rival groups within the Christian Church employ against each other would accomplish great things if used against national evils.

Among the Arabs to the present day the capture, or killing, of a Commander-in-Chief, and the securing of his armour, is an object of eager ambition. So was it with Asahel (v. 22); and now, as then, the backward thrust of the spear-handle, furnished with a spike, is often effective in despatching a pursuer (v. 23).

Joab's point in verse 27 was that Abner's provocation of "that morning" (v. 14) originated the fraternal strife.

Abner and his men walked "all that night" (v. 29); and David's servants also marched "all that night"; but it was to Hebron, to God's elect King; and hence for them there was "the break of day" (v. 32). So is it now; and so will it be. The servants of man's kingdom and those of Emmanuel's kingdom are in deadly opposition. They march through "the night"; but there will be "a break of day" for the latter, and "the blackness of darkness forever" to the former!

2 SAMUEL III.—"The House of Saul" was opposed to, and persecuted the "House of David." Fellowship was impossible (v. 1). As then, he that was born after the flesh persecuted him that was born after the Spirit, so is it now (Gal. iv. 29). A carnal nature is the enemy of the spiritual; but victory is assured to the latter; and although it may not be the highest Christian experience, yet it would be well were it true for the church, and for the individual Christian, that "the House of David waxed stronger and stronger" and "the House of Saul weaker and weaker" (v. 1).

The simple, straight, sunlit, and victorious path of fellowship with God is exchanged, in this chapter, for the tortuous, crooked, and dark ways of man. David does not once ask counsel of God; on the contrary he accepts that of man, and plans and schemes for himself. Neglecting the teaching of the Book of Genesis he became a polygamist, making, what the world would applaud as politic, alliances with heathen princes and others—marriages which bore bitter fruit in Amnon, Absalom, Adonijah, etc. (vs. 2–5); he accepted Abner's treachery (v. 13), pronouncing it "good"; he recalled Saul's daughter to his side, without once enquiring of the Lord for direction in any of these matters; and instead of obeying the Word of the Lord and putting Joab to death for his most cruel murder of Abner (Gen. ix. 6), he tried to satisfy his conscience with weeping (v. 32), fasting (v. 35), a voluminous denunciation of the murderer, and a state funeral for the murdered. Had he at this period walked with God he would not have had to make the sad and bitter confession of his weakness, though anointed as king (v. 39). As a good man, he manifested his abhorrence of Abner's assassination; but he failed, as the Divinely appointed chief-magistrate of the nation, to do his duty.

Thus no type of Christ is perfect; and yet at this time was David a type of the Messiah bringing everything in subjection to Himself after He shall have taken His future throne. The prophecies of Zechariah and Micah suggest to some Bible prophetical students that Christ will establish His millennial reign in detail after His appearing, and not by one overwhelming and universal action.

Abner was related to Ishbosheth as Joab was to David. Joab was clever, ambitious, bloodthirsty, and heartless. He was an ungodly man who deemed it politic to affect a zeal for God (ch. xxiv. 3). Abner was morally superior to Joab; but he was a traitor to his master (v. 12) and a rebel to his God (v. 18). He had no real heart for David as God's king, but was moved to help him by wounded pride. He reaped as he sowed (v. 27).

To marry a king's widow was, in the East, to aspire to the throne (compare v. 7 with 1 Kings ii. 22).

Politically it strengthened David's claim to the throne to have Michal by his side; but did he not disobey in principle, Deut. xxiv. 4?

2 SAMUEL IV.—The fruits of man's carnal nature appear in the first part of this chapter, and stand in contrast with those of the spiritual nature, which shine forth in its last part. The lust of gold, as a reward, incited the two captains to treachery and murder (vs. 8-10). Such is man by natural birth! In David, on the other hand, is seen the just anger and righteous action of the spiritual nature ; of its attitude in relation to sin ; and its refusal to rejoice at the destruction of a rival.

The fact of Mephibosheth's lameness is introduced here to explain why he could not be a rival to David ; because, in the East, such an infirmity nullified his claim to the throne; and thus it is made clear in the chapter that the death of Ishbosheth removed the only obstacle in David's path to the kingdom.

In the East it is the custom for the officer to go to headquarters the day before and secure a wheat ration for his men. There was nothing, therefore, in the action of these captains to excite suspicion (v. 6).

David by promptly executing the murderers assured the nation that he had no part in the crime ; and he, at the same time, taught all men the fine moral lesson that the death of an enemy is to the Godly heart a grief and not a joy.

It would have been well for these captains had they lost their hands and their feet in early life, and so have become Mephibosheths! These members, when yielded to God, become instruments of righteousness (Rom. vi. 13), when yielded to sin, instruments of unrighteousness.

2 SAMUEL V.—Just as the murderers of Ishbosheth could use religious language (ch. iv. 8), so could the rebellious Elders of Israel to David ; but only when their own plans had failed (vs. 2 and 3). Thus can man drape all his actions in religious clothing.

The Elders of Israel condemned themselves by admitting their knowledge of God's election of David ; but they did not make any confession of their sin and rebellion, other than by anointing David King over all Israel. This was his third anointing as king.

Although marred by human infirmity, yet is David, in this chapter, a type of the Messiah when He will take possession of Jerusalem, expel the Canaanite from thence (Zech. xiv. 21), and establish His kingdom over the whole land. Hence the name " David " occurs twenty-eight times in the chapter — 4 × 7. So Jerusalem will be foursquare and perfect on every side.

It is easier to walk the path of faith as a poor shepherd boy than as a king. God had appointed David to be " Chief and Captain," and yet, through David's acting in the wisdom of his own heart, Joab was made chief because he climbed up by the water-channel (1 Chron. xi). In this appeared the man of energy, but not the man of God ; and thus he foolishly bound himself to Joab and to the natural claims which he had on him. But Joab's name does not appear in the list of David's mighty men.

Again, as a poor lad, David had obeyed the Bible, but, as a king, he disobeyed Deut. xvii. 17 and multiplied to himself wives in Jerusalem—the sacred dignity of the place making more painfully manifest the evil of his natural heart in doing as he liked and in following his own will.

Verse 6 may read thus : " Thou shalt not come in hither ; for the blind and the lame shall drive thee away by merely shouting : ' David shall not come in hither ! ' "

Zion was God's city, but it was so completely in the power of the enemy that even the blind and the lame were deemed sufficiently strong to garrison it against David. Such is the sad case with the Christian Church to-day! The spiritually blind and lame garrison its walls, and think, by loud words of false teaching, to exclude the true servants of the True King. There is a holy hatred ; and such enemies of Truth are justly hated by the Divine David and by all in whom His Spirit dwells ; and they, in in their turn, hate Him (v. 8, R.V. margin).

Directly David was established as King in Jerusalem, the Gentiles appeared bearing gifts (v. 11). So will it be in the morning of the millennium.

But as it will be then, so was it in David's experience ; and such is the experience of all who, in any age, make Jesus King in their hearts and lives—the Philistines at once attacked David (vs. 17-25). Many are discouraged and surprised on meeting with strong opposition directly upon the establishment of Christ's Kingdom in their hearts ; but it must ever be so till He comes in glory.

David was granted two victories. Awakened from his carnal sleep by the danger that threatened him, he resumed his true life of enquiring of the Lord (vs. 19 and 23), and learned that there must be fresh guidance and fresh power for fresh victories (vs. 19 and 23). Yesterday's faith will not win to-day's battle. See 1 Chron. xiv.

2 SAMUEL VI.—David, Uzzah, and Michal are the prominent figures in this chapter. They illustrate : The planning of the flesh ; the presumption of the flesh ; and the pride of the flesh ; and the anger, death, and barrenness that result respectively (vs. 3, 6, 20 and vs. 8, 7, and 23).

Had David inquired of the Lord, and consulted the Bible (Num. iv. 15), success, and not disaster, would have resulted. But he consulted man (1 Chron. xiii.), imitated the Philistine, and organized a great public function in which David and his plans largely obscured God and His glory ; and, consequently, the day ended in anger and fear (vs. 8 and 9). All this was the planning of the " flesh."

What man has set up he feels himself bound to sustain. But the God of Israel needed not, as the gods of the nations, a human hand to uphold Him. It was necessary that He should teach His people this lesson. He must be had in reverence of all them that are round about Him ; and all must learn that God judged the " flesh " in an Israelite as in a Philistine ; for there is no difference. Uzzah, no doubt, thought with exultation of how the Ark of God was death to the men of Ashdod, but he never anticipated its being death to himself ! But a living God is a consuming fire to the actings of the carnal nature whether inside or outside the family of Abraham. Thus did he judge the presumption of the flesh in both Miriam and Uzzah.

Miriam (Num. xii) belittled Christ ; Uzzah supported Him. This double dishonour is popular to-day. He is declared by some to be only one great teacher among many ; and others try to uphold Him with the carnal hand of modern scholarship.

Manifested spiritual energy excites the opposition and contempt of " Society." The Holy Spirit, in verses 16, 20, and 23, calls Michal " Saul's daughter," not " David's wife." This is designed. She was the daughter of man's king ; and, therefore, was irritated at an action which she thought belittled her royal dignity. David did not angrily dispute the matter, but immediately brought God in, saying : " It was before Jehovah I danced " (v. 21). So Michal had no children ; for the " flesh "—let it be never so dignified—" cannot bring forth fruit unto God." Such was the pride of the " flesh."

How often it happens that, on returning to his home from a scene of great spiritual feasting, the Christian only meets there hostility and contempt (vs. 19 and 20).

Of course Michal's statement in verse 20 was wholly untrue. See 1 Chron. xv. 27.

But David having on this second occasion consulted the Bible (1 Chron. xv. 13), the day was " a day of joy " to Israel (v. 12).

How may it be known that these things really happened ? Because they happen now !

Verse 23 states that Michal had no children. But chapter xxi. 8 says she had five sons. Sons and adopted sons are often synonymous in the Hebrew text. The verse says that Michal brought up these sons for Adriel. He was her brother-in-law (1 Sam. xviii. 19). It is to be presumed that their mother had died. It would be natural that Michal should adopt her nephews as her sons and bring them up as such. In this sense they would " be born to her." See Gen. l. 23 (Marg.).

When walking with God David feared God ; when walking with the world he was afraid of God.

2 SAMUEL VII.—As in Gen. xv. God promised the land to Abraham's Seed, so in this chapter, He promised the throne to David's Seed. The Seed is Christ ; and, therefore, in each instance the Covenant was unconditional, for there could be no failure on Christ's part.

Christ, as Melchisedek, will possess both the land and the throne. David, in spirit, and in the intelligence of faith, went forward into Melchisedek's day, and so acted from time to time, as king and priest ; but he being a man of war could not really typify Melchisedek, who is King of Peace ; this glory was reserved for Solomon.

David established the kingdom over which Solomon reigned. Christ will be both David and Solomon. As David, He will conquer the land, and, as Solomon, He will reign in peace.

The following Psalms, together with the Prophecy of Zechariah, should be read in this connection : Psalms viii., lxxii., lxxviii., lxxxix., cx., cxxxii. See notes on those Psalms.

In this chapter David is seen enthroned after suffering and rejection, and yet awaiting the establishment of his power in peace— the peace established in Solomon. This is the theme of the first part of the Book of Revelation, where Christ is seen, as Messiah, seated on the throne of God, but waiting for that of the Kingdom ; and He is seen there as having suffered.

When God makes deep revelations of Himself to the soul, the effect is to bless God rather than to praise Him.

In verse 1 David sat before himself in his own house ; in verse 18, he sat before God in His House. In the one house, his heart was inflated with the wonderful things he proposed to do for God ; but in the other House, his heart was amazed at the wonderful things God proposed to do for him ; for God revealed to him that of him the Messiah should be born ; and that the throne of His Kingdom should be established for ever. On hearing this astounding promise David exclaimed in amazement : " And is this the decree concerning The Man ? " (v. 19), or : " Is this Thy purpose respecting humanity ? "

The Prophet Nathan here first appears. The difference between inspiration and non-inspiration is illustrated by verses 3 and 5. The latter communication begins : " Thus saith Jehovah " and contains neither a mis-direction nor an imperfection. The former communication was : " Thus saith Nathan " and was exceedingly foolish. To tell a king to do all that was in his heart was anything but safe advice.

2 SAMUEL VIII.—Just as David settled his own house by first establishing the Ark in Zion, and then subduing the Gentiles, as recorded in this chapter, so will the Messiah do. Of Him David is here a type ; but an imperfect one. For there is a sad " but " in verse 4. The Bible forbade him to have horses and chariots. In Christ no such imperfection ever appeared, or can appear.

Metheg-ammah was Gath (1 Chron. xviii. 1). As a fortress it acted as a " bridle " upon Judah and Jerusalem.

Like the modern Kurds, all these Moabite marauders richly deserved death. David, however, spared one-third of them ; and they became his servants.

There is no contradiction between the statements in verse 4 and 1 Chron. xviii. 4 ; they are complementary and independent. The one record deals with the campaign connected with the effort to " recover " power in the Euphrates valley ; the other, to " establish " it. In the decisive battle of

the campaign seventeen hundred cavalry (Syrian) perished (v. 4, R.V.) ; but in the whole campaign itself, seven thousand horsemen lost their lives, and one thousand chariots were captured.

Horses may be skilfully houghed so as to make them useless for war but not for agriculture. It is not more cruel than castration.

Twice is it stated (vs. 6 and 14, R.V.) that " Jehovah gave victory to David whithersoever he went." David therefore could not vaunt himself of that which was " given " to him.

The spoils of these wars David set aside for the future Temple at Jerusalem (v. 11).

There is no conflict between verse 13 and 1 Chron. xviii. and Ps. lx. It is evident that the Syrians helped the Edomites. David defeated the former ; Abishai the latter ; and Joab (1 Kings xi. 16) completed the conquest by remaining six months in the country. Adding the recorded figures together the total number, forty-six thousand, indicates the completeness of the victory.

Meanwhile, at home, David set up an ordered government, and promoted to high positions those who had been his companions in the time of his rejection. Similarly will David's Greater Son appoint to high estate in His coming Kingdom those who now share His reproach.

2 SAMUEL IX.—The great truth that God pardons and blesses sinners " for Christ's sake " (Ephes. iv. 32) is illustrated in this chapter by David's action with Mephibosheth " for Jonathan's sake."

This principle of grace cannot be affected by either merit or de-merit on the part of the person engraced ; and therefore Mephibosheth could sit at the King's table though deformed (v. 13).

The chapter contrasts the personal beauty, the wealth, the dignity, and the grace of David with the deformity, the poverty, and the de-merit of Mephibosheth.

Mephibosheth was born of the rebellious and doomed " House of Saul " (vs. 1 and 3). Such was his nature. His name signified " out of my mouth proceeds reproach," i.e. hatred to God's King (Josh. v. 9. Psa. lxix. 9. Heb. xi. 26) ; and he lived in a land of " no pasture " (Lo-Debar) on the wilderness side of the Jordan " afar off." He was a cripple, and a " dog " (v. 8). Thus he aptly pictured man as a rebel by nature, a sinner by practice, morally deformed, self-convicted, and far from God.

Yet David, " for Jonathan's sake," sought him, and found him, and pardoned him, and enriched him, and gave him a place among his sons, and brought him into his banqueting house, unfolding over him his banner of love !

Mephibosheth's response to this grace was that he came, he believed, he accepted, and he loved (vs. 6, 8, and ch. xix. 24).

The one condition which Mephibosheth fulfilled, and which made real to him his translation from hungry Lo-Debar to the banqueting of Mount Zion, was that he surrendered unreservedly to David. A similar surrender on the part of the sinner to the Saviour, carries with it a consciousness of forgiveness, life, and glory.

When sitting at the King's table, Mephibosheth's eyes must have shone with admiration and affection when fixed on David ; but what self-abasement must have clothed his mind when his gaze fell upon his deformed feet ! Yet the knowledge that he was there " for Jonathan's sake," and not because of any personal worthfulness, must have continually assured him of his position ; and so " he did eat continually at the King's table " (v. 13).

Grace saved him ; the riches of that grace endowed him ; and its exceeding riches set him as a son at the King's table continually. (v. 7 with Ephes. ii. 4, 7).

2 SAMUEL X.—Mephibosheth accepted David's grace and was honoured ; Hanun despised it and was judged. It is folly to reject the grace, and madness to resist the power of God's chosen king.

For further notes on Hanun's conduct see 1 Chron. xix.

The campaign against the Syrians, as recorded in this chapter (vs. 15-19), appears to conflict with 1 Chron. xix.

It is objected that so vast an extent of country embraced between the Mediterranean Sea and the River Euphrates, must have produced a larger army than 40,000 men ; that the Syrian king would never venture to march against so great a general as David with so small an army ; that the one record describes the Syrian as attacking the Israelites, the other stating the reverse ; that the one passage details 700, the other, 7,000 chariots ; and, finally, that 2 Sam. declares the army to have consisted of 40,000 horse-men, whilst Chronicles declares them to have been footmen !

A popular answer to these difficulties may be sought by pointing out that the Hebrew characters for 700 and 7,000 are so similar that it is very difficult to distinguish between them, and that the soldiers were, at the same time, footmen and horsemen—that is, they were mounted infantry.

But if the passages are put together they will be found to fit into each other so neatly as to remove all difficulties.

It will be at once observed that the 700 chariots were brigaded with the cavalry and the 7,000 with the infantry.

In ancient times there were two classes of war-chariots (as with modern artillery), i.e. light and heavy. In these verses the light chariots accompany the cavalry, the heavy, the infantry ; and it will be observed that the proportion of the one to the other is as one to ten.

Competent military critics are of the opinion that this proportion of one to ten is the proportion that should be observed by a modern general when requisitioning light and heavy artillery for an expeditionary force ; the light artillery being attached to the cavalry, the heavy, to the infantry.

Adding, therefore, the two bodies of men and war-chariots together, an army appears proportionate to the territory from whence it was drawn, that is—80,000 men with 7,700 chariots—the total force being divided into two brigades of equal strength as to the personnel but unequal as to the artillery : that is, a cavalry brigade of 40,000 men with 700 light chariots, and an infantry brigade of the same number of men, but with 7,000 chariots.

The battle that took place on this occasion, if the two accounts are united, may be thus described. David hastily gets together as effective a striking force as he can. He makes a forced march, and a surprise attack upon the Syrians. The infantry and heavy war-chariots, not being mobile, are immediately engaged, and routed. But the cavalry brigade, with its park of light chariots, is enabled to draw itself up in battle array and attack David. This great general, with extraordinary skill, manages to get his men together, although thrown out of formation, as would naturally result from their victorious attack upon the infantry, and presents a front to this well-nigh overwhelming cavalry attack,

and wins a second victory. To a statesman
and a soldier, this victory over the cavalry
brigade would appear the more remarkable,
and hence would be recorded in the Book of
2 Samuel. But in the Divine judgment, the
energy of faith in David's heart that prompted
this swift march and bold attack upon the
Syrian host is fittingly recorded in 1 Chron.

This chapter closes the prosperous period
of David's reign. Sin and sorrow and shame
followed as the result of inactivity in warring
against evil, and of negligence in reading and
obeying the Bible.

2 SAMUEL XI.—This chapter testifies to
the inspiration of the Bible, for only the Holy
Spirit could have recorded so faithfully its
infamy and horror. It gives a true insight
into man's nature as sinful and fallen ; and it
teaches the reader the humbling lesson that
such is the nature he possesses, and that, if
Divine restraints are withheld, and temptations sufficiently attractive and skilful
proffered, there is no depth of evil and shame
and falsehood to which he will not fall.

Had David obeyed the Bible and put Joab
to death for the murder of Abner (ch. iii.) he
would, in all probability, have escaped the
snares and crimes of this chapter ; for he
would himself have gone forth to battle
against the Ammonites.

Again, had he kept under the government
of the Word of God which had made him
"Chief and captain" (ch. v. 2), he would have,
in the energy of the faith that destroyed
Goliath and the lion and the bear, himself
ascended the water-channel and captured the
Jebusite fortress. But in a moment of carnal
excitement and generosity he offered the
honour to another ; and Joab was not slow
to seize it ; and so this false step also led to the
moral wreckage of this chapter when David
further surrendered himself into the hands
of Joab.

The Christian has to watch and pray
against the noble and generous emotions of
his natural will just as much as against its
vile and ignoble passions ; for, as here in
David's case, the former may open the door
to the latter.

Indolence and ease were as fatal to David
in Jerusalem as they were to him in Gath,
where he sought rest and safety from the
hand of Saul, and, consequently, fell very
deeply.

The sunshine, which in the main, brightened
David's path up to this moment, now left it ;
and from this time onward to his
death, darkness and sorrow and judgment
were his experience. Contrast 2 Tim. iv. 7.

Uriah was one of David's seven-and-thirty
mighty men (xxiii. 39). To make him the
bearer of the letter arranging for his murder
was a depth of infamy which is appalling.

David's language in verse 25 contrasts
painfully with his eloquence in chapter iii. 29.
It is easy to eloquently denounce another's
conduct, but very lightly to touch one's own
evil actions.

David's efforts to shield Bathsheba form
the one redeeming feature in this sad history.
But his plans were his own ; and, unfortunately, they succeeded. Bitter fruit usually
follows from successful human plans. Had
David, directly that he sinned against God
and Uriah and Bathsheba, cast himself with
anguish of heart upon God, He would have
made a way of escape and forgiveness consistent with Himself and morally instructive
to David.

2 SAMUEL XII.—God raised up David
to witness, as a king, to the nature of Divine
government. David in this matter of Uriah
falsified that testimony, and, therefore, God
vindicated Himself by judging and chastening
David in the sight of all men (vs. 10-12). He
was, accordingly, disgraced by one son (xiii.
14), banished by another (xv. 19), rebelled
against by a third (1 Kings ii.), cursed by a
subject (xvi. 5), betrayed by his friends,
and deserted by his people. His child was
stricken with death ; the sword never
departed from his house ; and his whole
subsequent history was a succession of sorrows
and calamities. Thus God protects women,
honours marriage, and strikes with burning
judgments a sin which men lightly regard,
clothe with poisonous poetry, or treat as a
subject of humour and jesting.

David's anger in verse 5 is a remarkable
instance of how sensitive the moral judgment
may be at the very time when the heart is
blinded by sin ! This fact illustrates the
deceitfulness of sin (Heb. iii. 13).

The words "I gave" mean that God
permitted these things to happen ; but, as
He Himself said in Matt. xix. 4 and 8, "At
the beginning it was not so." In the East it
is the rule that the widows of a conquered
king enter the harem of the conqueror.

Forgiveness at once follows upon sincere

repentance (v. 13). Compare 1 John i. 9, Isa. vi. 6 (" then flew "). and Luke xv. 18. ("his father ran ").

David had a true knowledge of God, and, therefore, when charged with his sin, his first thought was, not the punishment that would surely follow, but the injury done to God. He at once thought of Him, and cried out, " I have sinned against Jehovah ! " Simon Magus (Acts viii. 24), on the other hand, thought first of himself, and of how to escape punishment, thus showing that he had no spiritual knowledge of God

As a penitent, David lay upon the ground (v. 16) ; as a worshipper he sat (vii. 18), and as a servant, he stood (1 Chron. xxviii. 2).

Psalm li. witnesses to the depth and sincerity of the king's repentance ; and his submission to the judgment that smote his child showed that, although more guilty than they, yet he had a spiritual knowledge of God which his courtiers did not possess. He laid open the tenderest emotions of his heart to God—the heart that God was wounding— but directly the Will of God was manifested, he at once submitted. This was the evident work of the Holy Spirit in him. But it was only seen in its perfection when the True David cried out " Let this cup pass from me ; yet not what I will."

David really loved Bathsheba ; and she was in many respects a woman of character. She only consented to enter his house as his wife and queen, and that her child should be the future king (1 Kings i. 17).

Rabbah was partly built on the riverside (v. 27) and partly on a mound. Joab captured the one city ; David, the other. (v. 29). Or verse 27 may mean that Joab had captured the water supply of the city.

The last verse means that the Ammonites were made agricultural slaves.

2 SAMUEL XIII.—Only two short years followed upon the death of David's child and then the judgments predicted by Nathan began their fulfilment.

At this time David was fifty-three years of age, Amnon twenty-two, Absalom twenty, Tamar fifteen, and Solomon two. Amnon was probably regarded by Absalom, and by the people, as the Crown Prince.

Had David followed the teaching of the Bible and married but one wife, chosen for him by God, he would have escaped the bitter sorrows that flow from polygamy.

In the East even King's daughters are proud of their skill in baking fancy bread. The word " meat " in verse 5 is the same as " cakes " in verses 6, 8 and 10.

It was not unknown in the East for brothers to marry their half-sisters—Sarah was half-sister to Abraham—but Tamar's words in verse 13 were, perhaps, only used by her in desperation as a door of escape from her immediate peril.

The indulgence of violent pleasures is often followed by violent hatreds (v. 15). Such is fallen human nature !

To put white wood-ashes on the head is, in the East, a sign of mourning, as is also the rending of the garments.

If David had done his duty as commanded by the Law, he would have put Amnon to death ; but his own misconduct paralysed his hand, and he tried to satisfy his conscience by being very angry (v. 21).

It is the custom for Eastern Princes to give sumptuous entertainments at the time of the annual sheep-shearing.

Absalom's pressing invitation to the king and all his sons, was designed to cloak his murderous intentions with regard to Amnon.

David's grief for the death of Amnon, and his affection for the exiled Absalom, coupled with his earnest entreaties for the life of Bathsheba's child, prove him to have been of a very affectionate nature. The same pleasing feature appeared in his ancestor Jacob.

Talmai, king of Geshur, was grandfather to Absalom and Tamar. Their mother was his daughter.

2 SAMUEL XIV.—When dependence upon God, and subjection to His Word, cease to govern the life, then is it easy for the wisdom of this world to entangle the heart. Therefore it was that the wise woman of Tekoah easily entrapped David to indulge his affection as a father rather than perform his duty as a ruler. The Law of God commanded the death of Absalom. The king should have obeyed that Law. Had he done so, many lives would have been saved, and much sin and suffering escaped. Had he obeyed the Word of the Lord and put Amnon to death still greater evil would have been thereby prevented. All this teaches the lesson, which man is so slow to learn, that a Christian embitters his days by acting independently of God. Amid all the movements of this chapter was God enquired of ? He does not once appear.

The argument of the woman was very clever. It dealt with the secret wish of the king to pardon his son, and with the hindrance thereto which public opinion and the Divine Law presented. She skilfully persuaded him that exceptional provocation justified a setting aside of the Law, and a defiance of the people ; and she got the king to pledge himself to this in the interest of her supposed son. Directly the king committed himself, she then asked him why would he not act toward his own son similarly ? The king could not deny the force of the argument : he recalled Absalom ; and, after an exclusion of two years from court to mark his abhorrence of the crime, forgave him.

David was encouraged to pardon Absalom when he found that Joab approved. Joab's design in favouring the matter was, no doubt, to make Absalom indebted to him, and thus to get both the present and future king into his power.

2 SAMUEL XV.—The unnatural rebellion and violent death of Absalom, were the greatest sorrows and trials of David's life. Psalms iii., xli., lv., lxix., cix., reveal the depth and greatness of these trials—but of course only the griefs and experiences of the Man of Sorrows could satisfy the language of these prophecies.

David was now fifty-six, Absalom twenty-four and Solomon six years of age.

A chariot and horses and fifty men to run before, i.e., to clear the way, were the accompaniments of royalty.

Absalom easily deceived the people by a profession of devotion to them (vs. 2-6), and as easily deceived his father by a profession of devotion to God vs. 7 and 8.

Because man has fallen from God's moral image, therefore he can readily deceive and be deceived (2 Timothy iii., 13).

The fact of his own birth at Hebron, and David's coronation there, and its nearness to Jerusalem, no doubt led Absalom to select it as the starting-point of the rebellion.

David's prompt decision to leave Jerusalem and place the Jordan between him and the rebels, was the action of a skilful soldier.

The loyalty of Ittai the Philistine, and the royal body-guard of six hundred Philistines which he commanded, here stand in contrast with the disloyalty of Absalom and the men of Israel, and they illustrate the present loyalty of the Gentile nations to the Son of David, when rejected by His own Nation.

The grace of God is the basis of all blessing (vs. 25 and 26). David was conscious that he merited only wrath ; and this he publicly confessed with bared foot, covered head, and tear-dimmed eye (v. 30).

The inability of the natural heart to learn spiritual lessons is here illustrated by David's scheme to deceive Absalom by means of Hushai's pretended loyalty.

David was willing to pray (v. 31) but he was not willing to trust ; so man's poor confused heart is always ready in times of stress and danger " to do something " ; and generally that " something " is evil, or foolish.

The period of forty years in verse 7 is assumed by many to be an error in transcription for four years. But that is not so. The history here is that of David, and not of Absalom, and deals with this great crisis in his life. He was now fifty-six years of age. He was sixteen when anointed King by Samuel (1. Samuel xvi.) ; and, accordingly, as here stated, it was now forty years since his public life began.

2. SAMUEL XVI.—It only needs a crisis to reveal the infirmity and corruption of fallen human nature, and to destroy the illusion that man is noble and divine. This chapter presents one such crisis, and, as a consequence, records the falsehood of Ziba (v. 3), the irritation and unjust judgement of David (v. 4), the imprecations of Shimei (vs. 7 and 8), the deceit of Hushai (vs. 18 and 19) the infamous counsel of Ahithophel, and Absalom's abominable obedience to it.

Shimei's denunciation of David as the murderer of Saul, was unjust ; but David could not resent it, for he was the murderer of Uriah.

The degradation of David's wives in the sight of all Israel, fulfilled the prophecy of Nathan ; and, doubtless, feelings of revenge against David for his treatment of Bathsheba excited Ahithophel—for he was her grand-father—to this horrid crime (ch. xii. 11).

Thus the conqueror of Goliath was hunted from his throne, and dishonoured in his home, by his own son ; and that in fulfilment of the Word of the Lord ! Such is God's holy wrath against sin ; and such the bitter fruit of sin. The sword—the sharp **two-edged** word of the Word of God—was unsheathed against David. How just is God ! But whom He loves He chastens ; and, accordingly, while thus revealing His righteous anger, He, at the same time, overruled these judgments to draw David into a closer fellowship with Himself ; to discipline and teach his heart so that his sorrows, the fruit of his sins, became occasions of spiritual enrichment to him. It was when burdened with these sorrows and conscious of their justice, and, yet, at the same time, in heart truly and eternally bound to God, that the Holy Spirit inspired him to write, in the Book of the Psalms, those confessions of sin and of integrity which Christ will cause repentant Israel, in the latter day, to utter, and which He, in sympathy with them, will utter with them and for them. Thus these special Psalms are characterized by integrity of heart and confession of sin, the Spirit of Christ using the language in the fulness of His sympathy. Therefore was He baptised of John ; for he hastened to connect Himself, not with Israel in their sin, but with the first movement of the Holy Spirit leading them to its confession and judgment.

Thus at this time David became a type of the Messiah suffering with His people, confessing their sins as His own, and baring His breast to the Sword of Jehovah (Zech. xiii. 7) as if He were the guilty one.

In all this there is great encouragement for Christian people in circumstances where faith might fail and the heart be discouraged. This chapter is a valuable testimony that God does not cast off His people when they sin against Him ; that He forgives them directly they confess their faults ; that He overrules all to enrich their knowledge of Himself ; and that He furnishes them with expressions and sentiments proper to restoration of soul.

The stones were aimed at David and at his servants (v. 6). So is it to-day. In his rejection these true servants followed " after " him (xv. 17) ; were " beside him " (v. 18) ; were " with him " (xvi. 14) ; and were " on his right hand and on his left " (xvi. 6). So they sheltered David from the stones.

2 SAMUEL XVII.—This chapter is a striking fore-picture of Israel's rejection of the Son of David. The chapter sets out the nation hating David, even to death, though he had saved them from all their enemies ; a few sharing his rejection (vs. 27–29) ; Ahithophel, like Judas, betraying him and then hanging himself ; and " the maid-servant " completes the picture (v. 17).

Ahithophel's personal hatred to David is shown in the words " I will arise," " I will come," " I will smite," " I will bring back," etc. (vs. 1–3).

The proposal to single out David and murder him " pleased Absalom well and all the Elders of Israel " ; and yet Absalom was his son, and all the Elders of Israel had received nothing from him but good ! How true is it that the heart is desperately wicked (Jer. xvii. 9).

Hushai's foolish counsel, given with an exuberance of Oriental colour and imagination, was just what would please an ambitious and vainglorious Arab prince.

The little maid and the great king are spoken of in the one verse (v. 17). This is an encouraging instance of how useful the most insignificant persons can be to the Prince of Princes in the interests of His Kingdom.

Many Eastern houses are built around an interior court containing a cistern. This is sometimes dry ; and when covered in with boards the top is frequently utilized for drying corn. In such a cistern the young men hid themselves ; and the woman's statement that they were gone over the brook of water, was, in a sense, true, if, as is often the case, a stream of water, not always running, supplied the cistern.

Mortified pride, as well as the conviction that the rebellion was doomed to failure, and a just vengeance sure to follow, no doubt decided Ahithophel to destroy himself.

David was probably half-brother to Zeruiah and Abigail ; Jesse being his father and Nahash theirs (v. 25).

Refreshing as were the gifts brought by Shobi and his companions to David, more refreshing to him must have been the affection which prompted the gifts. Precious to the Lord, while still rejected, is the love that expresses itself to Him by deeds and gifts however small or great.

It was at this period that David was inspired to write the forty-second and forty-third Psalms.

2 SAMUEL XVIII.—When natural affection displaces religious duty both are lost. David, loving Absalom with an overweening affection, disobeyed the commandment of God which sentenced him to death. But the result was disobedience to God, and a much more painful death for Absalom than the scriptural one by stoning.

Josephus writes that Absalom was entangled by his long hair in the boughs of the tree. The Bible simply says he was caught by his head. His death must, therefore, have been one of prolonged agony until terminated by the lances of his former friend Joab, and his young men.

The forest in which the battle took place still remains; and travellers state that, to the present day, it could well prove fatal to fugitive soldiery (v. 8), and that a rider's head, in the excitement of escaping, could easily be caught in the low-bending and twisted branches of the trees.

The forest was called "the Wood of Ephraim" although situated to the eastward of the Jordan. Ephraim means "fruitful," and the word, like "Carmel," may have been the name of more than one district; or Joshua xvii. 15-18 may have originated the name being given to this forest.

Joab's action in putting Absalom to a well-merited death, and then immediately ordering the pursuit to cease (vs. 15 and 16), showed sound judgment and great humanity.

The "pillar" of verse 18, and the heap of stones of verse 17, mark the aim and the end of ambition. The pillar was doubtless surmounted by "a hand" (Heb.) indicative of victory; but the grave was heaped with stones expressing infamy. Such must ever be the inglorious end of all who rebel against God's elect king, Jesus Christ.

Why Joab restrained Ahimaaz is difficult to say. Ahimaaz's affection for David is easy to recognize; but it was an affection that hurt truth (v. 29), just as David's affection weakened justice. Man's sweetest affections are imperfect and broken.

The last verse should read: "Would God I had died instead of thee, Oh, Absalom, my son, my son!"

David's bitter grief was no doubt deepened by the consciousness that his own sin originated Absalom's rebellion and death, and by the painful reflection that there was no hope in such a death. Hence his cry of anguish desiring that he might have died instead of him.

2 SAMUEL XIX.—Grace forgives sin, but the righteousness that ordains that "whatsoever a man soweth that shall he also reap" is inexorable. David's sin with Bathsheba was pardoned, but righteousness decreed that the sword should never depart from his house; and, in addition to that, sin itself, when committed, so weakens the moral judgment, and so degrades the mind and heart, that selfishness, injustice, forgetfulness of duty, and many similar evils result.

This chapter, as a mirror, exhibits these sad facts. David seems to have forgotten the use and meaning of prayer. Amid the incessant movement of the chapter it is not once mentioned that David "enquired of the Lord." The result was that he allowed his selfish and excessive affection for his rebellious son to smother the affection which he should have shewn for his brave and faithful soldiers; he pardoned Shimei, swearing unto him by Jehovah—an oath which he should not have taken (1 Kings ii. 8 and 9)—when he ought to have judged him; he condemned Mephibosheth when he should have done him justice; he rewarded Ziba when he should have punished him; and he hastened up to Jerusalem without giving time for the chiefs and soldiers of the Northern Tribes to assist in the Restoration, thus occasioning the bloodshed and misery that followed in the next chapter.

Joab's habitual insolence to the King might have been condoned, and his murder of Abner forgiven; but his having personally slaughtered Absalom finally turned David's heart against him. It was clear that Joab had no affection for David; at heart he was a rebel. This fact was manifested by Solomon, who executed a righteous judgment upon him.

Amasa was David's nephew. His murder is recounted in the next chapter.

Barzillai asked a question (v. 34) that can be answered, and that cannot be answered. It can be answered, for the believer is to live forever; and it cannot be answered, for he might be dead in an hour.

Doubtless David rewarded Chimham with an estate, as is suggested by Jeremiah xli. 17.

Had David at this time, like Nehemiah, formed the habit of ejaculatory prayer, he would, like Nehemiah, have proved that God hears such prayer; and he would have been saved from the faults and errors recorded in this chapter.

How refreshing to turn from David the type to Christ the anti-type ! The prophecies abundantly prove that at his restoration to the throne of Israel, He will execute righteous judgment—so righteous that the isles, that is, the Gentile nations, shall wait for His law (Isa. xlii. 4).

2 SAMUEL XX.—The painful lesson, and terrible fact, that sin begets sin, is repeated in this chapter. This fact is the more painful and terrible when a servant of God is the primal actor. How deeply painful the knowledge must have been to David's stricken heart that he was the guilty author of the crimes and bloodshed here recorded. Had he walked with God, in submission to His Word, and in the centre of the Narrow Way, the unhappy but innocent women of verse 3 would never have been dishonoured and imprisoned ; Sheba would not have become a rebel and lost his life ; Amasa would not have been murdered ; and Joab would not have become a murderer !

The words " from Jordan to Jerusalem " (v. 2) make it clear that the rupture between the tribes took place from the commencement of the royal journey from Gilgal (xix. 15).

Verse 4 shows that David fulfilled his promise (xix. 13), and made Amasa Commander-in-chief of the forces.

But Amasa's want of energy (v. 5) showed either incapacity or disloyalty.

David's appointment of Abishai, and not Joab (v. 6), to the command of the troops showed how deeply he was estranged from Joab.

The words " went before them " (v. 8) should read, as in the R.V., " came to meet them."

The Revised Reading of verse 8 supports Josephus who says that Joab allowed the sword to drop on the road so as to throw Amasa the more off his guard.

In the East to take a man by the beard with the right hand and kiss him is a marked action of courtesy and friendship.

It was easy for Joab, when thus holding Amasa with the right hand, with the left hand to sweep his sword from off the road and plunge it into Amasa's body.

The hold that Joab had upon the soldiers is here seen in that, not only did his own men follow him after this atrocious deed, but even Amasa's regiments.

One wise woman skilfully put an end to the rebellion, and so proved that wisdom is better than weapons of war. " A mother " (v. 19) i.e., " a mother city "—" an important city."

The last four verses evidence the ordered re-establishment of David's kingdom ; but the reappearance of Joab, as commander-in-chief, shadows the record. This re-appointment, coupled with the soldiers' words in verse 11, is a proof that, in public affairs, David could not do without Joab and Joab could not do without David. Had David continued in the Path of Faith he would himself, as already pointed out, have captured Jerusalem, retained his God-given position as captain and chief, and thus never have fallen into the hands of his crafty and ambitious nephew.

2 SAMUEL XXI.—It is possible to be zealous for God's people and yet not to fear God (v. 2). The fear of the word of God would have saved Saul from dishonouring the name of God. His action illustrates the mischief which the energy of the natural man causes when he essays to help spiritual interests. Multitudes of zealous men, for example, champion the Bible, some with bludgeons and pistols to impose its authority, and others with rationalistic efforts to make its statements and doctrines acceptable to human reason. The fruit of Saul's action was a physical famine (v. 1) ; the result of this double system of defending the Bible is a spiritual famine.

It mattered little how much discredit attached to Saul's name or to David's name, but God, acting at this time in government, had to vindicate His own name in relation to the Gibeonites, and to recall Israel to the duty of respecting the oath given to that people (Joshua ix. 15, 19 and 20). Their breach of this Covenant now brought the wrath upon them predicted by Joshua.

In this manner Saul once again demonstrated that the carnal mind is not subject to the Law of God, neither indeed can be ; and that they that are in the flesh cannot please God (Romans viii.).

Spiritual and physical weakness sadly appear in David in this chapter. A son of Goliath, but for Abishai's intervention, would have slain him, for " David waxed faint " (v. 15-17). David, as a shepherd boy, was stronger than David as a crowned king. Doing his own will, and following his lusts, robbed him of the power which he had when but a lad. A crown, backed by the flesh, is helpless against a giant that a sling, backed by God, can overthrow.

The weakness in David's soul is seen in that though in verse 1 he "enquired of the Lord," yet he did not continue in prayer, but trusted his own judgment, and handed over Saul's sons to death. Rizpah's beautiful and touching action awakened him somewhat, and he tried to soften his conduct by giving honourable sepulchre to these seven princes and to Saul and Jonathan (v. 10-14). If David had continued in prayer, God would, possibly, have shown him some happier way of executing judgement and vindicating His name (see 1 Sam. xxiv. 21, 22).

Four sons of the giant—the word " brother " in verse 19 should read " son," as is clear from v. 22—were slain by David's servants. It was the energy of the faith in David that slew the giant himself, that animated these mighty men to slay the sons.

It is refreshing and encouraging to learn from this that faith is contagious ; it must, however, be observed that it was easier to slay a giant when all Israel was flushed with victory than when trembling with terror, as was the case in the great day of David's victory.

2 SAMUEL XXII.—David's " song " (chapter xxii.) and David's " last words " (chapter xxiii.) point prophetically to the Messiah, who in His sufferings and the glories that are to follow, will fulfil and satisfy the language of these utterances. But as affecting David himself, what a difference appears between them ! The one, a song of triumph ; the other, the sad note that " his house was not so with God " (ch. xxiii. 5). The " song " was written at the close of his years of suffering and rejection—a song of praise—for he had learned what God was to him in all his necessities and dangers.

In his " last words " he celebrates his outward prosperity ; he describes what Israel's king ought to be, and will be ; he does this in language of most attractive beauty, but sorrowfully adds that it was not true of him.

The two poems teach the lesson that outward poverty and inward wealth is better than outward wealth and inward poverty ; and they are comments upon the two parts into which his life was divided—his days of adversity, which were happy days, and his days of prosperity, which were sad days.

Comments on this " song " will be found in notes on Ps. xviii., where the Holy Spirit repeats it with such variations as He was pleased to make ; just as the Lord, when repeating on the plain (Luke vi. 17) the sermon preached upon the Mount (Matt. v.), made such variations as pleased Him.

2 SAMUEL XXIII., 1-7.—These matchless verses contrast the infirmity of David as a type and shadow, with the perfection of the Messiah as the Anti-type and Substance.

The matter of the poem is the sure advent and perfect government of the wondrous Son promised to David.

They are David's " last words," because his heart conceived of nothing more to be desired than the appearing and kingdom of Israel's Promised King. Therefore it was that, when the Holy Spirit had given David the seventy-second Psalm setting out the glories of that government, David added the words : " The prayers of David the son of Jesse are ended," i.e., accomplished.

As " son of Jesse " (v. 1) these were his " last words," and as "son of Jesse" (Ps. lxxii. 20) the predictions of that psalm satisfied his last prayers ; for to him there could not possibly be any greater joy than the appearing and kingdom of the Blessed Lord Jesus Christ.

He had been a poor shepherd lad, but was raised to a throne and anointed as king ; but, best of all, inspired of the Holy Spirit to be the " sweet Psalmist of Israel."

Thus with his " last words " David solemnly declared that the Psalms he wrote were not composed by him, but by the Spirit of Jehovah. The tongue was David's (v. 2), but the words were God's (vs. 2 and 3).

He uses the title " God of Jacob " to express his belief that Divine grace, and not personal merit, was the originating cause of all the goodness shown to him, just as it was the foundation of all the goodness shown to Jacob ; for when he deserved only wrath, and had nothing, God shewed him only grace, and promised him everything.

The Revised Version margin helps to make plain the prophecy of verses 3 and 4. It foretold the advent of One who should rule men righteously, in the fear of God ; and that His rule, contrasted with man's, would be comparable to the cloudless sunshine of a beautiful morning following the black shadows of a dark night, and to the rich herbage produced by refreshing rain clothing a, till then, barren land.

That this righteous and perfect Ruler will certainly appear, is assured by the Holy Trinity titles given to the Author of the Prophecy. He is called Jehovah : " Jehovah spake," i.e., the Holy Spirit (v. 2) ; He is called God of Israel, i.e., Christ, " the God of Israel said " (v. 3) ; and He is called the Rock of Israel, i.e., God the Father, " the Rock of Israel spake " (v. 3).

David confesses (v. 5) that neither he, nor any member of his family, fulfilled, or could fulfil, the promises of this prophecy ; but he rejoices in the knowledge, that, in keeping with the terms of the Everlasting Covenant, ordered in all things and sure, made with him, there would be born in his family the Great King described in these last words, and in Psalm lxxii.

But he adds that the introduction of that Kingdom will be accompanied by the just and eternal punishment of all evil-doers (Matt. xiii. 14-42). Such men are here compared to thorns. Thorns cannot be cultivated. They can only be violently removed by violent instruments (vs. 6 and 7); and their end will be, as in Matt. xiii., a fiery doom " in their own place " (v. 7) ; just as Judas is said to have gone to " his own place." The Psalms—called by ignorant persons imprecatory—predict the just judgment of these wicked men. These Psalms do not belong to this dispensation—the dispensation of " the patience of Jesus Christ "—but they do belong to the next, which will be the dispensation of " the power of Jesus Christ " ; and so they destroy the doctrine of moral evolution, for no hand can evolve a fruit tree from a thorn.

2 SAMUEL XXIII., 8-39.—The notes on 1 Chron. xi. and Rom. xvi. should be read in connection with this chapter.

David's mighty men, and their exploits, should have a great place in the heart of the Bible student, because the Holy Spirit has been pleased to give a double record of them.

A similar double record may be expected when David's Son and Lord establishes His future Kingdom in Jerusalem.

The first record of His mighty men and women is found in the New Testament. How many of these names will appear in the second record ?

David's mighty men numbered thirty-and seven, and they were divided into three companies. The first company contained three : Adino, Eleazar, and Shammah. The second company numbered three : Abishai, Benaiah, and Asahel. The third company numbered thirty-one ; their names are given in verses 24-39.

The broken numbers of the Bible are very important. David's mighty men, Israel's first-born when redeemed from Egypt, the Levites, the hundred and fifty and three " great fish " of John xxi., the twenty-nine of Rom. xvi., etc., etc., emphasize the personal character of redemption, consecration, warfare, election, i.e., the Christian life—its commencement and its progress.

The chief of the first three had two names. The one, no doubt, was personal ; the other, titular.

This chapter seems to credit him with having slain eight hundred at one time. 1 Chron. xi. says, three hundred.

The Revised Version reconciles the two records. He boldly, single-handed, met the attack of eight hundred men, and slew three hundred of them ; the remainder perished on the same day. Stephen bravely facing his enemies (Acts vii.) was the Hachmonite of the New Testament.

Eleazar's courage was made the more admirable from the fact that his comrades had all run away. His hand clave to the sword ; and so did St. Paul's hand to the Sword of the Spirit, and, with equal courage, for he himself states that all in Asia forsook him, and that when brought before Nero no man stood by him (2 Tim. i. 15 and iv. 16 and 17). What victories would be won in the Gospel warfare if Christian people were so truly attached to the Bible as Eleazar's hand was to his sword, so that the sword and his arm became one weapon !

The brilliancy of Shammah's victory was heightened by the fact that he defended a small piece of ground of very little value. Putting the records together—and they are complementary—the ground contained nothing but barley and lentils ; and it might have been argued that it was not worth fighting for. But why should the Philistine have even one inch of Immanuel's Land, let it be never so poor an inch ? And so Shammah, although the army had taken to flight, stood in the field and successfully held it, thus illustrating Luther's translation of Eph. vi. 13, " and having overcome all, to hold the field."

The glory of these victories was given to Jehovah (vs. 10 and 12) ; and to that same gracious God were ascribed the victories in the Book of the Acts, notably in chapters xiv. and xv. where God is stated fifteen times to have been the Actor.

These three mighty men were those who drew the water from the well of Bethlehem. Three facts are here recorded showing their love for David. The first was, that they joined him in his gloomy cavern in " the time of harvest." That is, they did not wait to gather the fruit of their toil and outlay, but turned their back upon it all, constrained by love for David, though he was an outcast and a fugitive. The second was, that they kept so close to David's person that they caught his sigh, " Oh that one would give me drink," etc. ; and the third was, that they actually risked their lives to fetch the water. Those who live close to Jesus hear the longings of His heart for draughts of love from Africa and India and China ; and, like these mighty men, they turn their backs on home and wealth, and risk, or lay down, their lives to win for Christ the affection and service of nations held as hopelessly in the power of Satan as the well of Bethlehem was in the hand of the Philistine.

Verse 17 should read as in the Revised Version, " Shall I drink the blood," etc. The water represented the lives that were risked in fetching it.

If Abishai, like Adino, slew three hundred why had he not equal rank, or at least a place in the First Company ? Because Adino boldly faced eight hundred, slaying three hundred of them ; whereas Abishai most probably accomplished his exploit in the course of a battle, and possibly most of those he slew were fugitives.

The Egyptian, the Moabite, and the lion fell beneath the sword of Benaiah ; and victory over the world, the flesh, and the devil is assured to him who shares the power that animated Benaiah.

The " flesh " has a double personality, one repulsive, the other attractive, one moral, the other immoral—both lion-like, and both sprung from the one corrupt father. Both must die (Rom. vi.). Men applaud the putting to death of the repulsive " flesh,"

but they rebel against a like doom for the attractive " flesh " ; but that was the lesson that Job had to learn. He found that all his goodness had to be put to the sword as well as all his badness. This is a lesson that men refuse to learn ; for they are proud of their own goodness, and cannot understand that it must die beneath the wrath that at Calvary judged both the goodness and the badness of man.

The slothful saith, " there is a lion in the way " (Prov. xxii. 13 and xxvi. 13) and keeps indoors. But Benaiah sallied out in the bitter cold ; made the snow a helper; thereby tracked the lion to the pit ; went down into it ; and, with astonishing valour, despatched him. Thus to the man of faith stumbling-blocks become stepping-stones; obstacles, helping hands ; and secret sins are tracked out and put to the sword in their hiding-places.

That this was a well-known exploit is shown by the Hebrew text using the definite article, so that the verse reads : " he slew the lion in the pit in the time of snow."

The servants of David's Lord frequently to-day, as in the past, defeat the imposing champions of the world—especially the Rationalists—with their own weapons ; just as Benaiah slew the " goodly Egyptian " with his own spear.

Asahel was the third member of the second three, and, at the same time, captain of the thirty.

Joab's name appears in this list, but not himself, for time proved him to be a rebel ; but his faithful armour-bearer is found there. Ahithophel, another rebel, his name appears, but not himself ; his valiant son shines among these mighty dead. Love and loyalty to Christ will be the great test in the day of His appearing. (1 Cor. xvi. 22).

2 SAMUEL XXIV.—This chapter and 1 Chron. xxi., with the notes on them, should be read together.

Verse 1 may read : " And David was moved." 1 Chron. xxi. states by whom. God permitted this liberty to Satan in order to judge the pride and rebellion of Israel. Thus the natural desires of David's heart occasioned teaching and discipline to himself, and to the seventy thousand men, who, no doubt merited judgment as rebels and idolators.

The chapter reveals God in government and in grace. In point of time, its events preceded those of the previous chapter. This is designed. That chapter pre-figures the glories of Christ ; and records the names of the companions of that glory. This chapter speaks of the sufferings of Christ, as the sin-offering, which He should accomplish at Jerusalem. David foreshadowed this (v. 25), for no priest is mentioned. Frequently in the Scriptures —as for example Isa. lii. 13 and 14—the glories of Christ are made to precede the sufferings of Christ.

It is easy to detect the " flesh," in another ; and so Joab, a man of the world, readily recognized the folly of David (v. 3).

David's heart, as in chapter xii. 13, did not smite him until the sin was accomplished, though its pursuit occupied more than nine months. Sin, when accomplished, occasions disgust ; it is the pursuit of it which has such a hateful attraction for the heart. Directly the sin is committed, Satan no longer cares to hide its ugliness.

Exod. xxx. 12 explains the sin of David and the resulting plague. His action not only ministered to his self-importance— " that I may know " (v. 2)—but his not giving the ransom for the soul was a denial of the great truth that no man, woman, or child, whether moral or immoral,· can be a member of God's family apart from redemption by the precious blood of Christ. This redemption money was the foundation upon which the Tabernacle stood. Fellowship with God is based alone upon a like foundation.

Three statements in this chapter seem to conflict with 1 Chron. xxi.

The first concerns the threatened famine, the duration of which is given in the two chapters as " seven years " and " three years."

There are two simple answers to this difficulty. 2 Sam. xxi. records a three years famine as a judgment from God upon the nation because of its conduct towards the Gibeonites. When God offered three additional years of famine to David, He did so in the year intervening between these two periods, so that there would be seven years threatened. And if David had elected these three years, there would, therefore, have been in fact, seven such years. There is no difficulty in believing that the prophet mentioned both periods to the king. The accuracy of Scripture is here demonstrated in that it is 2 Sam. which mentions the three

years of famine that preceded David's numbering of the people, and that it is the same book which threatens the larger number of years of famine. On the other hand, 1 Chron., not relating the three years of famine in connection with the Gibeonites, appropriately, therefore, records the shorter period. Further, the actual wording of the two passages is interesting. 2 Sam. reads, " Shall seven years of famine come unto thee in thy land ? ", but 1 Chron. xxi reads, " Take which thou wilt : either three years of famine, etc." The expression, therefore, " come unto thee in thy land," harmonizes with the foregoing argument ; for it asks David if the country is to suffer such a lengthy period of famine, whilst the wording in 1 Chron. accords with the suggestion that the king was to " take" three additional years of misery to the wretchedness already suffered.

The second answer is that the number " seven " in the Scriptures expresses intensity, and that, therefore, what the prophet threatened was a " seven years famine " to last for three years. That is, the three years famine was not to be a partial or light affliction, but a very dreadful and intense one.

The next seeming discrepancy is one between 270,000 and 300,000, in the total of the census commanded by David.

1 Chron. xxvii. removes this difficulty. Here it appears that each tribe was bound to supply two thousand men a month for the service of the king, twenty-four thousand being the total of those on active duty in any one month. Multiplying this twenty-four thousand by twelve, the result gives two hundred and eighty-eight thousand. If the twelve thousand officers in the text be added, the full strength of the standing army reaches three hundred thousand. The thirty thousand men remaining to be deducted from this latter total in order to make the two records agree, can easily be accounted for by remembering that Judah was David's own tribe, and it was, therefore, a wise policy on his part to provide that half the officers, i.e., six thousand, should be of his tribe, and these, with their twenty-four thousand tribesmen, were for some good reason omitted.

Another explanation is found in comparing the actual wording of the two passages. Chronicles says " all Israel were 1,100,000 men that drew sword," while 2 Sam. says " there were in Israel 800,000 valiant men that drew sword." Evidently 300,000 were young soldiers that could not be justly deemed " valiant." Similar details appear with respect to Judah. Samuel states that "the men of Judah were 500,000" ; Chronicles recording the number of " the men that drew the sword " as 470,000. Evidently, therefore, the remaining 30,000 were either untrained men, or non-combatants.

The third conflicting statement respects the price paid for the threshing-floor of Araunah the Jebusite.

The difficulty is removed by observing that the smaller sum was paid for the "' threshing-floor and the oxen," the larger sum for the " place " upon which the threshing-floor stood. The total price paid, therefore, for the whole piece of ground, with the threshing-floor and the oxen, was six hundred shekels of gold and fifty shekels of silver.

1 KINGS

1 KINGS I.—The Books of the Kings give the outward history of the kingdom of Israel —its rise, its fall, and God's testimony in the midst of the apostasy.

The Books of the Chronicles reveal the inner history. For example, Kings apportions three verses to Hezekiah's Reformation ; Chronicles, three chapters.

Out of Christ nothing stands. Every type of Him failed. God's council from the beginning has been to set up man in blessing and clothe him with responsibility, and then He Himself to accomplish in grace the purposes of love which man's failure forfeited. Directly man was chosen he broke down ; and always has this been so, as the history of the successive Heads of the dispensations abundantly proves. These Heads were Adam, Noah, Abraham, Moses, David and Nebuchadnezzar. All failed immediately upon appointment. But God's purposes were not thereby defeated, for these men were but types of Christ. In Him is, and can be, no failure ; and He will perfectly accomplish all that grace has designed.

This principle of election and responsibility is finely set out in the promise made to David of a Son whom God would raise up to him, God being His Father, and He being His Son, Who should build the Temple of Jehovah and reign for ever and ever. This was the promise, and David himself knew that it referred to Christ.

But the words " If he commit iniquity," etc., express responsibility; and David understood that these concerned Solomon.

After Solomon's reign, a great part of the books of the Kings is occupied with the ministry of Elijah and Elisha.

Adonijah, Joab, and Abiathar, set up their kingdom in opposition to God's elect king. God had no place in their hearts ; and so Solomon did not suit them. God's choice never does suit man.

Moses, being a prophet, predicted the establishment of kings in Israel (Gen. xxxvi. 31, xvii. 6, xxxv. 11, Deut. xvii. 14-20). The great principle here appears of : First, that which is natural ; then, that which is spiritual (1 Cor. xv. 46). See notes on 1 Chron. 1.

Medical men, both ancient and modern, believe, and believed, that a young person can communicate electrical heat to an aged person (vs. 2-4). The following chapter (v. 22) shows that Abishag was legally married to David ; for to marry the widow of a king was to pretend to the throne.

The events of this and the following chapter are characteristically omitted in 1 Chron. Here are seen man's efforts to rule , there, God's resolve to overrule.

Adonijah the fourth son of David was now the eldest surviving. Amnon, Chileab (probably) and Absalom were dead. He was Absalom's half-brother, and, like him, very handsome and over-indulged by his father (vs. 5 and 6).

Men never make a common choice with God. Solomon was God's chosen king ; and the conspirators knew that well, for they were careful not to invite him to their feast (v. 10).

Nathan's loyalty to the Word of the Lord (2 Sam. vii. 12 with 1 Chron. xxii. 9) awakened David to energy (v. 28). Alas ! that he needed this awakening of soul ; but deadness and lethargy are the fruit of pleasing self. Yet faith, once more aroused to energy, recognized God's true King, Solomon, and suppressed the rebellion.

So close is En-rogel to Jerusalem (v. 9) that it was easy for the conspirators to hear the rejoicings of the city (v. 41).

Solomon's dignified dismissal of Adonijah to his house showed that already he possessed a wisdom which, after his prayer (ch. iii. 9), was greatly augmented.

Thus the Book of the Kings begins with Solomon and ends with Nebuchadnezzar.

It opens with the Temple built, and closes with the Temple burnt. It commences with deliverance from the Philistines and ends with captivity to the Chaldeans. Not David's moral conduct, but his fidelity to the Law, was held up before all his successors as a standard to be aimed at ; for, great as were his sins and his crimes—and they were neither excused nor covered up by God—yet was he, and is he, for all time, remarkable as an earnest lover of Divine Truth ; and his fame as the sweet Psalmist of Israel, will live for ever.

1 KINGS II.—Although David's faith was not energetic enough to judge the enemies of the kingdom, as established by God, yet was it intelligent enough to instruct Solomon to do what was proper. Many people are offended at these instructions, and condemn David strongly for, as they say, exhibiting such a cruel, vindictive, and treacherous spirit even on his death-bed. But this charge is unjust. Personal animus is altogether absent. On the contrary, with respect to Joab, he never mentions his murder of Absalom, but only of his having slain Abner and Amasa ; and, as the Revised Version makes clear (v. 5), these crimes he declares were committed against him, thus, in effect, eliminating himself personally, and, as in the case of Shimei (v. 44), making the interests of God's people his only concern. As to Shimei, Grace pardoned him (2 Sam. xvi.), but Righteousness judged him (1 Kings II). David pictures Christ acting in grace during the present Dispensation, that is, when rejected. Solomon represents Christ reigning in righteousness, establishing judgment and justice in all the earth. His action in casting out of his kingdom all evil doers, is a fore-picture of what will happen at Christ's coming (Matt. xiii. 41 and 42). He will unmask and judge all disaffected to His throne, just as Solomon did, guided by the Divine wisdom given to him. So was it with Shimei and Joab. Under the reign of Grace they were spared, but when Righteousness was enthroned in power, the treason that was in their hearts was manifested ; and, Grace no longer reigning, they were justly slain.

This death-bed charge of David to Solomon was, therefore, altogether admirable. It was not that of a revengeful private person, but it was the judicial act of a Chief Magistrate

conscious of his responsibility when handing over his office to his successor. Joab's crimes he vividly portrayed to Solomon, saying that he put the blood of his victims upon his girdle and in his shoes (v. 5).

But he prefaced these instructions by pointing out to Solomon that success lay only in close adherence and full subjection to the Written Word of God (v. 3). Such a doctrine always has aroused, and still arouses, the opposition, and excites the anger, of the natural heart whether moral or immoral.

The honours reserved for the sons of the Gileadite, point to the assured positions of glory which those will have in Christ's coming kingdom who now company with Him when despised and rejected of men.

The sentence of expulsion upon Abiathar and of death upon Joab, shows that these were associated with Adonijah in his second rebellion, as in his first, and that they were determined traitors.

As to Shimei, it only needed a very little test to manifest the state of his heart towards God's elect King, for in this matter of the runaway servants, he totally ignored him and his government.

As husband of the late Monarch's widow Abishag, and as the elder brother (v. 22), Adonijah could dispute the throne with Solomon. His asking for Abishag revealed his purpose and manifested his treason. He was justly put to death.

Adonijah's wisdom in seeking the intercession of the king's mother, and his success in gaining her interest, are pointed to by many as authorizing and illustrating the efficacy of prayer to the Virgin Mary ; and verses 13–21, especially verse 20, are quoted as confirmatory of such a doctrine and belief. But the result of Bath-sheba's intercession was the just anger of the king, and the destruction of the petitioner !

With respect to verse 9 it may be pointed out that the power of the negative in Hebrew construction may here apply, and that, consequently, the verse should read : " His hoar head bring thou not down to the grave with blood," i.e., because of his past conduct.

1 KINGS III.—Israel was forbidden to make affinity in marriage with the Canaanites; but with respect to the Egyptians such passages as Isa. xix. 21, 23, 25, Zech. xiv. 18, Deut. xxiii. 7, and Ezek. xxix. 13, suggest that they are vessels of mercy,

prepared unto millennial glory, in union with Israel, and, as such, are representative of the future redeemed Gentile nations. Solomon's marriage, therefore, with the daughter of Egypt, and her introduction into the city of David, where the Ark was—symbol of the Covenant and of God's relationship with His people—brought her into that Covenant (Ps. xlv. 8-16). The Covenant was not made with Pharaoh's daughter, but grace placed her where the Ark, the symbol of the Covenant, was hidden ; and thus was she safe-guarded and sheltered by Him who had made that Covenant with His people, and Who will, in the latter day, include in it all the nations of the earth (Jer. xii. 16.

The Brazen Altar was at Gibeon, where was the Tabernacle. The Ark was in the city of David. The Brazen Altar was visible ; the Ark was hidden. The Brazen Altar pictures Christ lifted up from the earth in suffering, rejection, and death ; the Ark, Christ hidden in the heavenlies awaiting the time of His manifestation in glory. In the sad days of the Judges and of Saul, the Tabernacle was forsaken, and the Ark, disrupted from the Brazen Altar, retired into the city of David, and was there hidden till the glory under Solomon was established. It was there that Solomon brought Pharaoh's daughter (v. 1), and not to Gibeon. Such is the grace which awaits the Gentile. Having at the Brazen Altar (Calvary) put away sin by the sacrifice of Himself, Christ has retired into the heavens, and Gentiles, like Pharaoh's daughter, shelter themselves in that hidden Saviour. He, like Solomon, will build them a House with many mansions and they, in union with Israel, will enter into the glory of His millennial kingdom.

As before noticed, every man whom God raised up and clothed with responsibility immediately failed. Solomon sacrificed in high places, contrary to the word of the Lord (Deut. xii. 11, etc.), and he only had sufficient energy in his soul to obey the statutes of David his father. How much better had he set before his soul, as his standard of conduct, the statutes of the Bible (vs. 2-4).

His prayer for wisdom was very good, and it pleased God. But a prayer for holiness would have been better. He asked that his head might be filled with wisdom, but a heart filled with love would have equipped him better for his lifework. The value and power of affection were taught him by the very first case he had to decide as a Judge. It was that of the two women and the living child. The one woman was clever ; the other, natural. The one was moved by her head ; the other, by her heart. Solomon should have learned that a loving heart is better than a clever head.

It is not said that these were Hebrew women. From the anxiety of the false mother to claim the child, it might be assumed they were sacred Virgins attached to a Canaanite temple, in which the highest act of worship was to become the unmarried mother of a male child, and so represent the promised Virgin and Child of Gen. iii. Men called them virgins ; God called them harlots. Rahab probably was one of these temple women.

As in Acts xxi. 24, so here, Solomon (vs. 4 and 15) offered at his personal cost the sacrifices for sin required by the law. It was a fore-picture of Messiah offering at the expense of His own blood, but without cost to man, a sacrifice for sin so great that it embraces humanity. How great, therefore, will be the punishment of those who neglect or despise it !

1 KINGS IV.—The prosperity, the eating and drinking and making merry (v. 20), the abundance (vs. 22 and 23), the peace and safety (vs. 24 and 25), the extended dominion (v. 21), the external honour (v. 34), and the internal dignity (v. 2) all resulted from the one fact that Solomon was king. The destruction of the rebels, and the enthronement of God's elect prince, originated this universal contentment and prosperity. It is a feeble fore-picture of the happy day that awaits the earth when the rebels who now govern it, and fill it with misery, will be overthrown, and the Prince of Peace, the greater than Solomon (Matt. xii. 42), will take unto Himself His great power and reign before His ancient people Israel gloriously. The present miseries that oppress the nations, and which they vainly try to remove by repeated efforts, would all be at once put an end to, and universal peace, happiness and prosperity secured, if men would invite Messiah to return and take the government of this world into His mighty hands.

The princes appointed by Solomon as his viceroys illustrate the promise of Luke xix. 17. One of these viceroys reigned in Bashan over the three score great cities having walls and brazen bars. The gigantic ruins of these cities attest the truthfulness of the record as to their number and strength.

A mistake is assumed to exist between verse 26 and 2 Chron. ix 25. Attention to the actual words of the Bible disposes of this assumption. 2 Chron. ix. deals with four thousand stalls for horses *and* chariots, whilst 1 Kings iv. draws attention to a different matter, viz. : forty thousand stalls of horses. The one passage points to the provision made by Solomon for four thousand chariots, and the trained horses needed for them, the other passage narrates the total number of horses ordinarily in his hands. Contrary to the teaching of the Bible, he was, alas, a wholesale horse-dealer. He bought horses and chariots from Egypt, and resold them at a profit to the kings of the Hittites and their neighbours. Nothing is, therefore, more reasonable than that he should have had four thousand stalls for horses and chariots, and also forty thousand stalls of horses. Assuming that there were, as was usual, two horses in each stall, the number of these horses would, therefore, be eighty thousand.

Solomon's disobedience to Deut. xvii. 16 was prepared by David's disobedience to Lev. xix. 19. David's mule (i. 33), which was a breach of Lev. xix. 19, prepared the way for Solomon's horse, which was a breach of Deut. xvii. 16. Thus it often happens that an elder Christian by disobedience to one command in the Bible, leads a younger Christian to boldly disobey another.

1 KINGS V.—The building of the Temple as God's dwelling-place and throne, was an earnest of the fulfilment of the promise, yet to be realized, of the establishment of Jehovah's house and government in the millennial earth ; and just as the willing Gentiles were at Solomon's disposition, and helped joyfully to further his designs, so will they be at the disposition of the Greater than Solomon, and will, with gladness, serve Him.

Thus the Temple with its many chambers (ch. vi. 5), may be viewed as a type of the Father's House with its many mansions (John xiv. 1). It is possible that the Lord alluded to this when speaking these words. It is touching to the heart to notice here that God surrounded Himself with dwellings in the very place where He established His House ;

and whilst His continuance in that habitation depended upon the obedience of Solomon, and, therefore, was temporal, His dwelling with His people under the new covenant, is dependent upon the faithfulness of the Divine Solomon ; and, that obedience being assured, the fellowship is, therefore, perpetual.

If the notes on 2 Chron. chapters ii-vii. be read in connection with 1 Kings v-viii. the typical outlines of this great Temple as Jehovah's home and throne, will be recognized, and the seeming inaccuracies will be found to be harmonious and independent statements true to fact, and prophetic of that which will surely come to pass.

This great house was characterized by gold and brass—figures of righteousness and government. The Tabernacle was founded on silver—emblem of redemption. Thus righteousness and judgment will characterize Christ's reign upon earth ; and harmonious therewith will be associated the Cherubim of Judgment (ch. vi. 23-28). His reign in the heavens will be associated with the seraphim, and the gold will be transparent as glass (Rev. xxi. 21) ; for the glory of the terrestrial is one and the glory of the celestial is another.

The bringing down of the timber (v. 9) and the bringing up of the stones (v. 17), present a double illustration of grace separating sinners from their standing in nature and in darkness, and, having beautified and perfected them, placing them as precious woods and costly stones in the spiritual House of God.

The provision of verse 11 was for Hiram's household ; that of 2 Chron. ii. 10 was for his workmen in Lebanon.

The "levy" of verse 13 was composed of freemen ; the burden-bearers and hewers of verse 15 were slaves. These, by consenting to circumcision, could become members of the family of Israel, and, therefore, free.

1 KINGS VI.—Verse 1 of this chapter illustrates the promise that God not only forgives but forgets sin ; for the years of Israel's bondage to the nations are omitted. The lesson is at the same time taught that years, or days, spent in bondage to the world are for ever lost. Thus what appears a chronological error in the text is found to be a designed message of comfort and warning.

For particulars of this supposed error the Companion Bible should be consulted.

The Temple consisted of the Porch, twenty cubits long, one hundred and twenty cubits high (see notes on 2 Chron.), and ten cubits deep (v. 3) ; the House, twenty cubits wide, sixty cubits long, and thirty cubits high (v 2); and the Oracle, i.e., the Most Holy Place, twenty cubits wide, twenty cubits long, and twenty cubits high (v. 20). The Great Brazen Altar (see 2 Chron. iv.) was also twenty cubits square ; for atonement and glory are one ; and hence the conversation in the Mount of Glory was about His decease which He should accomplish at Jerusalem (Luke ix. 31). Atonement is the theology of Heaven, and the entrance to God's Home is as wide and as high as the home itself ; but desirable as that doorway is—and David wished to dwell there all the days of his life—yet was it only half the depth of the Oracle, for double is the bliss of the Home of God to the Vestibule of that home.

The many Mansions rested upon three sides of the House (v. 10), but did not form a part of the House (v. 6). Thus is the distinction preserved between the essential Godhead of Christ and all that rests upon Him as a Saviour.

The House was built of stone, cedar, cypress, olive-wood, and gold. The instruments of its service were largely brass. These materials set forth the Deity, the precious and sinless humanity, and the strength, the grace, and the governmental power of Christ. Just as every whit of the Tabernacle symbolized the glories attaching to Him in His First Advent, so all the dazzling splendour of the Temple prefigured the glories of His Second Advent. Both buildings were designed by God ; nothing was left to the religious feeling or the taste or imagination of either Moses or Solomon (Heb. viii. 5 and 1 Chron. xxviii. 19).

The knops, the flowers, and the ornamentation prefigure the moral beauties and perfections that Christ will display in His future government of the world.

As this Temple was built without outward noise (v. 7), so was Christ, the True Temple, prepared of God without observation (Luke xvii. 20 and Heb. x. 5).

This same verse (v. 7) may also point to the noiseless formation of God's spiritual Temple, the Redeemed House of Israel—for in Heaven itself there is no temple (Rev. xxi. 22) because the City itself will be the Temple.

There is no vail mentioned, because the figure here is not that of access to God but of dwelling with God. (See 2 Chron. iii. and iv). There are folding doors which open ; for millennial fellowship will be real but partial. Full fellowship will only be enjoyed in the New Heavens and the New Earth.

The Cherubim symbolized judgment. Their wings met over the blood-sprinkled Mercy-seat and reached to either extremity of the Most Holy Place. God's Judgments have Calvary for their centre, and are as wide as His Home.

The Cherubim of Gold attached to the Mercy-seat, and made of the same mass of gold, looked downward upon the sprinkled blood ; the Cherubim made of olive-wood, looked outward. God's perfect judgments will, in the millennium, be enabled to look out from Calvary upon a kingdom wherein shall dwell Righteousness. This is not now possible, for Righteousness retreated to Heaven when Christ went to the Father (John xvi. 10).

The Cherubim were overlaid with pure gold, for righteousness will characterize judgment when the kingdoms of this world become the kingdoms of Jehovah and of His Christ. See note further on.

Thus the dwelling-place of God was resplendent with gold, and so expressed Divine Righteousness.

The massive door posts of the Oracle, and of the House, were made of olive-wood ; the double doors of the former were of olive ; those of the latter, of cypress. These precious woods symbolized the perfection and the acceptance of Christ as the new and living Way to God. He is the Door through which if any man enter in he shall be saved—saved because the gratified eye and heart of God rest with complacency upon the door and not upon the one who enters.

The doors were beautified with chased work in gold of Cherubim, palm trees, and open flowers. Such is, and was, and ever will be, Jesus the Lamb of God and the Son of God.

This was God's House and Throne, and, therefore, the Cherubim at once appear in the molten sea, the door, and the throne itself. See notes on Rev. iv. and v.

The wonders of these chapters are as uninteresting to human wisdom as the scene at Calvary to Plato if he had happened to pass by there that day.

1 KINGS VII.—The Temple, the House of the Forest of Lebanon, and the vessels of

brass are the great subjects of this chapter, and the preceding one. The Temple prefigured Christ in His personal millennial glory ; the House of the Forest of Lebanon, the home of Israel and the redeemed Gentile in union with the great King and Judge ; and the vessels of brass, the strength and glory of His government.

In a word, all is Christ in His perfection as God, as Redeemer, and as King ; and everything connected with Him expresses solidity, magnificence, and splendour both without and within. The Temple, the glory of His person; the House, the riches of His affections; and the Vessels of brass, the endurance of His government.

The narrative respecting the temple and its vessels is twice interrupted. Such breaks in a narrative should be noticed. They are designed by the Divine Writer. The first interruption is found in chapter vi. 11-13. Solomon was in danger of thinking that he was sure of God's presence and favour because he was building Him so magnificent a temple. Many people think so to-day when building costly churches. But God interrupted the enterprise by telling Solomon that His presence and favour would not be secured by building a House of Prayer, but by loving and obeying the Bible.

The second interruption is contained in the first twelve verses of this chapter. Its object is to introduce those who are to be the happy worshippers in this temple of glory. Solomon's " own house " (ch. vii. 1 and Heb. iii. 6) pictures the Redeemed House of Israel ; the house for Pharaoh's daughter, the redeemed Gentile. Both are here seen united to Christ, He being in the midst, they leaning upon Him, associated with Him in His glorious government, and lodged in equal splendour. His heart demanded this interruption, for it longs for the day when He will gather all the redeemed around Him.

The House of the Forest of Lebanon was no doubt so named because built and adorned with cedar-wood brought from Lebanon ; just as the East India House is so named though situated in London.

Because of human infirmity and ignorance it is not easy to understand clearly the description given in the chapter of this great palace, but it may be pictured as consisting of three palaces : that is, the Central Hall, Solomon's own house, and the house of Pharaoh's daughter. The Porch, in which was placed the Throne of Judgment, was situated in front of the central hall ; and the two houses, one on either side of it. This central court was embellished with forty-five magnificent pillars of cedar-wood, fifteen in a row. The three palaces formed a unity. They were all alike. They were equally splendid inwardly and outwardly ; the glory was not all on the outside, nor was it hidden, everything within was as glorious and costly and beautiful as everything without ; and all proclaimed the glory of him who built the whole. Everything manifested the splendour, the riches, and the power of the Great King—a figure of Messiah " in the midst," having on either side redeemed and glorified men. The costly materials with which this great palace was constructed, were similar to those used in the building of the Temple ; for God's moral nature and His public government, harmonize. See notes on Rev. vii.

As around the Temple Court, so around the Palace Court was built an enclosing wall (v. 12 R.V.). The wall was formed with three tiers of costly stone, and a coping of precious cedar-wood. Historians say it was about four feet high. The stone was white and polished, and the wall must have been exceedingly beautiful. Thus the holiness of the Palace corresponded to that of the Temple. The perfection and beauty of these buildings may be partly realised by noticing that even the stones which were hidden in the foundations were of costly marble, polished and bevelled. No eye but God's saw these ; but they were most precious to Him, for they pictured the inward spotlessness and moral glory of that Body (John ii. 19, 21) which to Him was without spot.

There is no confusion here with 2 Chron. ii. 14. Hiram's mother was of the tribe of Dan by birth, and of the tribe of Naphtali by marriage.

The pillars of brass are mentioned six times in the Bible, viz.: 1 Kings vii. 15, 2 Kings xxv. 13, 1 Chron. xviii. 8, 11 Chron. iii. 15, Jer. xxvii. 19, and lii. 17.

These Scriptures state that the brass was captured by David from the Syrians ; that the pillars were hollow ; that, with their capitals, they stood forty feet in height and eighteen in circumference ; that they weighed about twenty tons each ; that the capitals were of globular form, highly ornamented with fringes, network, foliage and pomegranates ; that they were placed at the entrance to the Temple ; that, because of national departure from the teaching of the Bible, their destruction and removal to Babylon was predicted by Jeremiah ; and that the prophecy was shortly after fulfilled.

The variations between some of these passages as to the dimensions of the pillars and their capitals mark accuracy and not disagreement. The statements are complementary. Each pillar was eighteen cubits high, inclusive of a socket half a cubit high, to which must have been jointed the capital. Omitting this socket, the total length of the two pillars, as recorded in 2 Chron., was thirty-five cubits. The capitals were each five cubits high, but, excluding the ornamental work, three cubits, and including the lily work, four cubits. There were, in all, 400 pomegranates (v. 42) that is, 200 upon each pillar (v. 20) disposed in two rows of a hundred each (2 Chron. iii. 16), or ninety-six " on a side "—the remaining four occupying what might be termed the turnings of the pillar (Jer. lii. 23). The one pillar was named Jachin ; the other, Boaz. See notes on Luke vi.

These notable pillars were peculiar to the Temple, as distinguished from the Tabernacle; for, in the Tabernacle, God was the Travelling Companion of His people, but, in the millennium, He will be a Resident among them.

The pillars were works of art, displaying a strength, beauty, and grace of surpassing splendour. They fore-shadowed the strength of Israel's future King, and the purity and stability of the government that He will establish. The Cherubim of olive wood (see 2 Chron. iii. 13 R.V.) from within the Most Holy Place looked out through these pillars, in anticipation, upon the order and perfection of that Divine Government.

These pillars, therefore, pictured Christ as Israel's Millennial King ; they voiced the strength, the grace, the beauty, the life and the varied fruit of the Spirit which will be seen in Him when He sets up His visible Kingdom over the earth. Their dazzling splendour of polished brass, illumined by the rising sun, prefigured the moral glory of Christ as the door into the House of God.

The Sermon on the Mount (Matt. v–vii) and the Sermon on the Plain (Luke vi.) illustrated these two resplendent pillars They disclosed the saving strength of the King,

and the stable moral principles of the kingdom which He proposed to establish. But men would have neither Him nor His Kingdom ; and so they nailed Him to the Tree. See notes on Luke vi. 17–49.

In the Tabernacle in the Wilderness there was one laver ; in the Temple of Solomon there were eleven. One, of immense size, was fixed ; the remaining ten were movable. These magnificent vessels of polished brass, highly ornamented, fore-shadowed the purity, the glory, the grace, the sufficiency, the perfection, and the power of the government which Immanuel will establish in the future millennial earth ; and they expressed the perfect adjustment which will be manifested between that future government and the spiritual power which will energize and cleanse it. It will be a pure government.

The oxen and the wheels may be assumed to be symbols of service (Ezek. i. and 1 Tim. v. 18) ; the water, to prefigure the Holy Spirit (Titus. iii. 5 and 6). The metal with which these vessels were made was highly polished so that they were, in effect, immense mirrors, and must have dazzlingly reflected the rays of the sun.

The oxen and the wheels were placed beneath the lavers containing the water. There was no disproportion. The strength of each was measured to the weight of the water. The Great Laver, when filled, must have weighed more than 100 tons. In the cleansed earth, Christ will act as the Servant of Jehovah. There will be no imperfection in that service. It will all be executed in the energy and under the power of the Holy Spirit. The service, and the power energizing it, will be exactly proportioned. The power will be above, and the service subject to it ; just as the oxen and the wheels were beneath the lavers. This great principle should be true of all Christian service. Real service can only be rendered when under the power, and animated by the energy, of the Holy Spirit.

All these lavers, their brims, their panels, their ledges, their borders, their oxen, their bases, and their wheels, were exquisitely ornamented, both within and without. That which was hidden was as perfectly ornamented as that which was seen. This will be fulfilled in the perfect government which Christ will present to the eye of man and to the eye of God.

The measurements of these lavers point to the sufficiency of the grace, wisdom, and power which Israel's Great King will furnish to meet the need of imperfect and sinful man. The numbers three, five, ten, and thirty express Divine fulness ; four and six, earthly need and human insufficiency. The Great Laver was five cubits high, ten cubits broad, and thirty cubits in circumference. Five is the number of grace, six of human imperfection, and ten of Divine perfection. One fifth of the external height of the laver was ornamented with knops fashioned like heads of oxen. These were ten in number, and surrounded the laver in two rows, five in a row ; suggesting the grace and the perfection of Christ's future government in the earth. The massive oxen beneath the laver were twelve in number, a trinity of them facing each of the four points of the compass. These numbers, three and four, predicted the Divine fulness which will equally bless the entire earth. The Cherubim, and the foliage enchased on the lavers, and everything connected with them, expressed the moral beauty of the future government which God will set up over the earth in Christ ; so the Cherubim appear in Rev. iv. and v.(see notes there).

The Great Laver was, as already stated, stationary ; the others movable. Christ's government will be both. Jerusalem will be its fixed centre ; the whole earth its sphere ; and all will be characterized, both at its centre and its extremities, by the same spiritual power.

This principle should be true in the inward and outward life of Christian service.

The ten bases, or carriages, upon which the smaller Lavers were placed, again presented the numbers three, four, and ten. The carriage was square. At each corner was a " support," " shoulder " or " undersetter," designed to receive, and hold in its place, the Laver placed upon the bronze platform of the carriage. As with the Great Laver, so with these, the panelling and ornamentation was equally beautiful whether seen or unseen.

The splendour and number of these Lavers in contrast with the one Laver of the Wilderness, foretold the perfection, splendour, and glory that will characterize Israel's future home as contra-distinguished from the path to it.

All the vessels of polished brass connected with the Temple displayed, as before stated, in type, the Glory of Christ and the splendour of His Kingdom. His Person and His Government will express power and magnificence. This being the subject-matter of this chapter, the Holy Spirit, designedly, omits any mention of the Veil and the great Brazen Altar ; for here attention is drawn to the King Himself, and not to the subject of access to Him ! Both the Veil and the Altar are appropriately introduced in 2 Chron ; for attention there is drawn to the Temple as the glorious Throne of the Great King, and to the approach, in grace, to that Throne ; and a veil is appropriate, for the full splendour of that Throne is to be reserved for the New Earth.

The Great Laver is stated in 1 Kings vii. 26 to have " contained " 2,000 baths of water, while 2 Chron. iv. 5 records that it " received and held " 3,000. This is assumed to be an inaccuracy. But what a vessel usually contains is not the same as what it could receive and hold. There is, therefore, no inaccuracy, but, on the contrary, completion.

A " spoon " (v. 50) was not as imposing as a " candlestick " (v. 49), but the temple would have been incomplete without it ; and both were of the same precious metal. A Sunday School Teacher should not be despised by a Bishop.

1 KINGS VIII.—One year, and, perhaps, three, elapsed between the completion of the Temple, and its dedication. This great event occurred in the Year of Jubilee, during the Feast of Tabernacles, and in connection with the Great Day of Atonement. The Feast of the Dedication lasted for seven days, then followed the Great Day of Atonement, and then the seven days of the Feast of Tabernacles. Thus are the circumstances of the dedication harmonized with the grace and the glory of the future kingdom which was foreshadowed.

The Ark of the Covenant was brought up from Zion the city of David, where it had been lodged in a tent, to the neighbouring hill of Moriah upon which the Temple was built ; and the Tabernacle of Moses was brought up from Gibeon, where it had been in the days of Saul. It may be assumed that the Tabernacle and its vessels were reverently laid up in " the treasuries of the House " (ch. vii. 51). The Ark, having the Tables of the Law within it, was placed within the Oracle. All was performed exactly as the Bible commanded, and consequently the glory of Jehovah filled the House of Jehovah (v. 11).

The magnitude of the peace-offerings sacrificed that day not only typified the fulness and sufficiency of future millennial glory, but were necessary to provide food for the millions of worshippers who were present. The amount of meat required by the city of London every day is extraordinarily great.

By God's command (1 Chron. xxviii. 19) there were variations made in the vessels of the Temple as contrasted with those of the Tabernacle. These changes harmonize with its purpose as an exposition of the coming glory, but there was no alteration in respect of the Ark, for it was God's one and only throne ; but its staves were withdrawn, and the Golden Pot of Manna, and Aaron's Rod that budded, which were associated with it in the Wilderness (Exod. xvi. 33, Num. xvii. 10 and Heb. ix. 4), are not mentioned. All this is harmonious. The Ark entered into its rest. The staves with which the Priests had borne it in the Wilderness, were withdrawn, and became the memorials of that time of pilgrimage, and testified to the grace and faithfulness which had brought them into God's rest. But Aaron's Rod and the Pot of Manna are not mentioned, for these, being types of that which would be substantial in the millennium, necessarily disappeared—they would be out of place in the glorious reign and rest of Canaan. Therefore it was that Solomon, as Priest and King, in the presence of a manifested glory, displaced Aaron and his priesthood ; for he, and not the High Priest, dedicated the Temple and blessed the people. Hence also the silence respecting the veil.

But the Ten Commandments remained ; for the Word of the Lord endureth forever. It is mentioned with emphasis (v. 9) that they, and nothing else, were in the Ark. And this had to be ; for the Law of God was hidden in Messiah's heart (Ps. cxix. 11), as it was hidden in the Ark ; and that Law will be the basis and rule of the righteousness which will govern the millennium.

The people being assembled as a nation, Solomon recalled their birth, as a nation, when redeemed out of Egypt (vs. 16 and 21), and did not go back to Abraham, to Isaac and to Jacob.

God by appearing on Horeb in thick darkness thus " spake " in action. It was to this, no doubt, that Solomon referred (v. 12).

The Person, the Posture, and the Petitions of the King should be kept before the heart when studying this prayer. The Person is Christ, in type ; His Posture, when standing, the King ; when kneeling, the Great High Priest ; His Petitions, individual, national, and universal.

The prayer contains seven petitions, divided into two sections. The first two petitions concern God and Solomon, i.e., His faithfulness (vs. 23 to 26), and His affections (vs. 27-30). A double plea is based upon these Divine characteristics ; first, that He would fulfil His promises ; and second, that He would grant the petitions now presented. The remaining five petitions were drawn from the Book of Deuteronomy ; the same Book which supplied the Lord with effective answers to Satan's temptations.

The first petition was based upon Deut. xxv. 1 ; the second, upon Deut. xxviii. 25, with Lev. xxvi. 40 ; the third, upon Deut. xxviii. 23 with Lev. xxvi. 19 ; the fourth, upon Deut. x. 19 and iv. 34, and was answered a thousand years later in Acts viii. 27, etc. ; the fifth was founded upon Deut. xxviii. 36 and practised by Daniel and Nehemiah.

The alleged inaccuracy between verses 22 and 54 is harmonized by 2 Chron. vi. 13. Solomon, as is the custom to-day, first stood before the congregation and then knelt before God.

The expression " the plague of his own heart " (v. 38) does not mean, as is popularly supposed, a man's besetting sin, or greatest grief, but the plague, i.e., the punishment striking him, and which he " knows," that is, recognizes, as a Divine chastisement because of the rebellion of his heart.

The " furnace of iron " (v. 51) does not mean a furnace having iron as its fuel, but a furnace so fiercely heated that it could melt iron. It was in " the midst " of such a furnace of suffering that God found His people ; and it was out of the midst of such a furnace that He redeemed them.

The prayer presented God as the people's one and sufficing resource when the consequences of their folly and rebellion would come upon them ; and, in harmony with the First Covenant, it set the people under the condition of obedience.

The blessing pronounced by Solomon upon the people was mainly thanksgiving. This spiritual fact may be recognised throughout the Bible. Blessing results from thanks-giving ; hence a life of thanksgiving to God secures blessing to man. Thanksliving should accompany thanksgiving.

Directly Solomon's prayer closed, fire fell from heaven and consumed the burnt-offering (2 Chron. vii. 1).

Thus the cloud (v. 10) and the fire (2 Chron. vii. 1) accredited the Temple, as they had the Tabernacle (Exod. xl. 35, and Lev. ix. 24). Fire from heaven attested Elijah's offering ; and, doubtless, a similar attestation dis-tinguished Abel's sacrifice from Cain's. Verses 22-54 precede, in time, verses 10-21. See 2 Chron. vii.

The language of verses 56 and 57 shows that Solomon was well acquainted with the Books of Genesis, Deuteronomy, and Joshua ; and verse 58 shows a similar familiarity with the Book of Leviticus.

The promise " I will not leave thee nor forsake thee " (v. 57) was first made to Jacob (Gen. xxviii. 15) for saving grace ; then to Israel (Deut. xxxi. 6) for preserving grace ; then to Joshua (Joshua i. 5 and 8) for over-coming grace ; then to Solomon (1 Chron. xxviii. 20) for serving and worshipping grace ; and, lastly, to the spiritual Israel (Heb. xiii. 5 and 6) for confiding grace for daily bread.

If in response to the faithfulness of God (v. 56) Israel had shown a like faithfulness to his Word (v. 58) the result would have been the salvation of the world (v. 60). It was to effect this purpose of grace that God chose Israel as a people unto Himself ; and Israel's unfaithfulness has postponed, but not defeated, that purpose. It will yet be accomplished ; for Christ is the true Israel, and in Him there cannot be failure.

Verse 60 should read : " Jehovah, He is the God (that is the only one God) ; and there is none else." Therefore, in verse 61, the nation was urged to be " perfect," that is, loyal to Him and to His Holy Book. No other god was to be associated with Him.

The food necessary for so vast a multitude (v. 63) was consecrated food, and accepted food. The people sat at the Lord's Table, and daily broke bread with Him during this double feast. As always, so here, there was on that Table royal abundance sufficient to meet, and surpass, the need of the hungry. This Israel proved in the Gospel Day when, all having eaten and been filled, twelve baskets-full of the fragments that remained proved the ability of the Great King to more

than satisfy the need of never so great a multitude.

The words " a Feast " (v. 65) should read " the Feast " ; i.e., the Feast of Tabernacles.

The first day of this seventh month was the Feast of Trumpets. Then followed, it may be assumed, the Seven Days of the Feast of the Dedication of the Temple. On the tenth day, was the Great Day of Atonement when the sin of the nation for the past year was covered by the blood of the lamb. On the fifteenth day of the month the Feast of Tabernacles began, closing on the twenty-second ; and on the eighth day, that is, the twenty-third of the month (v. 66 with 2 Chron. vii. 10), the people were dismissed to their homes praising God for all the goodness that He had shown to them.

Solomon took his stand at the brazen altar, i.e., at Calvary. There he knelt as a worshipper, spread forth his empty hands as a beggar, and prayed as a petitioner. Those he prayed for appear as defiled sinners, defeated soldiers, diseased sufferers, scattered strangers, and sorrowing slaves. Thus the prayer was based upon The Person (the Temple) and the atoning work (the brazen altar) of Christ. Only there can pardon and help be claimed and found.

For the correspondence with John xvii. see notes on that chapter, and on 2 Chron. vi. and vii.

The foundation of the prayer is shown by the displacement of verses 10 and 11 so as to relate them to verse 5, i.e., atonement made (v. 5), and accepted (v. 11). This appears in John xvii. 4 and 5. The duration of the prayer is seen in 2 Chron. vi. 12 and vii. 1, i.e., from Calvary to Advent. This appears in John xvii. 4 and 24.

1 KINGS IX., 1-25.—Verses 2-9 should be placed in a parenthesis. They record God's answer to Solomon's prayer, His acceptance of the Temple as His dwelling-place, and of the Oracle as His throne. This fact was of world-wide importance. It was the establish-ment upon earth of the Kingdom of Heaven. Jerusalem was to be the world centre, and the administration of the kingdom was to be committed to Israel and to her king. Accord-ingly Solomon is stated in 1 Chron. xxix. 23 to have " sat upon the throne of Jehovah in Jerusalem."

But this committal to Solomon and Israel was conditional upon obedience. That condition was violated, and, as a consequence, the government of the earth was taken out of the hand of Israel and placed in the hands of Nebuchadnezzar and the Gentiles, by whom Jehovah's Throne and House were cast down by God's just decree. But when the Greater than Solomon comes, that Throne will be re-established, and His kingdom shall have no end.

The path of safety pointed out by God to Solomon was obedience and attachment to the Bible (vs. 4-6). But Solomon, instead of obeying Deut. xvii. verses 16-20, occupied himself and his people with bricks and stones (vs. 15-24) rather than with multiplying copies of the Scriptures; and these bricks and stones occasioned the disruption of his kingdom (xii. 4).

Verse 8 is difficult of translation, not because, as popularly thought, of obscurity in the Hebrew text, but because of ignorance in the human head. The argument of the passage supports the reading: "And this House shall become conspicuous," etc. This is full of meaning. That Temple, which was designed to testify to the love of God, should become a testimony to the wrath of God because of departure from the Word of God. The Christian is a temple of God (1 Cor. vi. 19), and, as such, a testimony to the love of God; but if he turns aside from the Word of God, he becomes a testimony to the Wrath of God.

Omitting the parenthesis, verse 1 of the chapter reads on into verse 10 thus: " It came to pass when Solomon " etc. (v. 1) " it came even to pass " etc. (v. 10).

The word "Cabul" is unknown to scholars. It probably means "rubbish."

Six score talents of gold equals now about £2,000,000.

" The Millo " was a fortress on the wall of Jerusalem.

Recent excavations at Gezer have brought to light Egyptian correspondence of 1,450 B.C., and Assyrian of 647 B.C. This latter correspondence throws light upon 2 Chron. xxxiii. 11 as pointing to an Assyrian conquest of Palestine at that time.

Tadmor (v. 18) was afterwards called Palmyra because of its palms. Its stupendous ruins prove its past magnificence.

The three annual Feasts of verse 25 were Passover, Pentecost, and Tabernacles.

For an explanation of the supposed differences between this chapter and 2 Chron. viii. see notes on that chapter.

1 **KINGS IX. 26—X. 29.**—The words " riches " and " wisdom " (v. 23) furnish the key words of this chapter.

In it the riches and wisdom of Solomon alternate. His Riches, verses 26-28; his Wisdom, verses 1-10; his Riches, verses 11 and 12; his Wisdom, verse 13; his Riches, verse 14-29.

Ezion-geber means " the Giant's Backbone." It is a singularly-shaped reef of rocks outside that port at the top of the Gulf of Akaba. A similarly shaped mass of rock off the north coast of Ireland is called " the Giant's Causeway."

Sheba, a grandson of Cush, settled in Abyssinia. This chapter and Acts viii., show that Queens were not unusual in that land.

The Lord in Matt. xii. 42 predicts that the Queen of Sheba will reappear in the Resurrection. For comments upon her visit to Solomon see notes upon 2 Chron. ix.

For many years verse 29 was declared to be unhistoric because of its mention of Hittite kings. It was an " assured result " of historic study that no such nation ever existed; but recent excavations in Asia Minor have demonstrated the accuracy of the Bible.

God foresaw, and predicted, in Gen. xxxvi. 31 that Israel would have kings; and in Deut. xvii He forbade them to multiply wives, horses, and riches. This chapter faithfully records Solomon's disobedience to these commands. He multiplied all three. His wisdom did not save him from this folly. However richly God may bless His people, they can never with impunity forsake the path laid down for them in His Holy Book. He promised riches to Solomon, and He would have fulfilled that promise, whilst, at the same time, enriching Solomon's spiritual life. But he was not satisfied to wait for the realisation of the promise. He took matters into his own hands, with the result that he enriched himself but impoverished his soul; for the means he took to enrich himself, showed a heart at a distance from God, and, in the end, they procured his ruin (see notes on 2 Chron. viii).

Verse 28 should read as in the R.V.

1 **KINGS XI., 1-25.**—There is no sadder picture in the Bible than that of Solomon's fall. His extraordinary gift of wisdom did not save him from disobedience to the Law of God. His neglect of that Law, and his loss

of the fellowship with God which gives power to it, opened the door wide to the entrance of every form of evil. Had he clung to the Sacred Scriptures how bright would have been his life ! History records no fairer start and no sadder end, excepting Judas's. Deut. xvii. warned him against women, wealth, and weapons, and yet these proved his ruin ! His own mother Bath-sheba (Prov i. and xxxi.) had warned him in vain. He could not have been more than fifty years of age when he apostatized. It was upon the hallowed Mount of Olives that he built these temples to the false gods. The Holy Spirit calls them "Abominations," and "the abomination that maketh desolate," because idolatry desolates both heart and land, and begets the vilest sins.

Departure from God's Law brings trouble into the life ; and therefore the chapter tells of the adversaries who disturbed Solomon's kingdom. How often have Christian people sorrowfully proved this fact !

The perfection of David's heart toward God (vs. 4 and 6) was with respect to its faultlessness as to idolatry.

Olivet, because of Solomon's action, was afterwards called "the Mount of Corruption" (2 Kings xxiii. 13).

God did not judge Solomon without a previous warning, tempered with mercy (vs. 11-13). It is not stated who was the messenger, but it was probably Ahijah. One tribe was promised to Rehoboam, that is, one tribe in addition to his own tribe of Judah, i.e., the tribe of Benjamin ; Levi and Simeon largely joined him, but these could not be justly spoken of as formal tribes, because they were scattered in Israel, as predicted. (Gen. xlix. 5-7).

There is a special Hebrew verb used in the Bible for "to be angry." It is only used of Divine anger. It occurs fourteen times. Here, and in five other passages, a form of the verb is used expressing the forcing of oneself to be angry with a person who is loved.

David subdued Syria (2 Sam. viii.) ; Solomon, weakened by sin, lost it (v. 25).

It is to be understood (vs. 14-25) that Hadad joined Rezon, and, on the death or disappearance of that chieftain, became King of Syria and founder of the Dynasty afterwards known as Ben-hadad, and which brought such suffering upon Israel. The sin of to-day ensures the suffering of to-morrow, for Solomon's conduct originated Ben-hadad.

Solomon's third adversary was a domestic one. The two former adversaries were foreign. A life of self-will ensures trouble both within and without the home.

Jeroboam was an Ephraimite (v. 26 R.V.). This fact, because of the predictions in Gen. xlix. and in Deut. xxxiii. respecting Ephraim, may have been the reason why he fled to Egypt. His appointment to be Chief of the House of Joseph (v. 28) doubtless gave birth to the ambition to be Chief of the whole nation (v. 37), and Ahijah's prophecy confirmed it.

Solomon and Jeroboam illustrate the evil and unbelief of man's heart. Jeroboam would not wait for God to give him the kingdom, but tried to get it by his own efforts (v. 26). So fallen is man's nature that he will use Divine promises, and the daily gifts of God's love, for the accomplishment and gratification of his own unholy desires, and degrade the very gifts and promises of God to the service of the "flesh." Solomon sought to kill Jeroboam (v. 40) because God had chosen him ; and thus he also manifested the murderous hatred of the natural heart against God and His people.

This is the last statement made by the Holy Spirit about Solomon personally. It is a dreadful statement. The next fact recorded is his death ; and what a death ! There is not one word in the Sacred Record to lighten its gloom.

The prosperity promised to Jeroboam was conditional upon his obedience to the Law (v. 38). He made no attempt to fulfil this condition ; and, accordingly, his family perished beneath the just judgments of God.

The four last words of verse 39 are very important. They confirm the fact of the prophecies of Gen. xlix. and Deut. xxxiii. respecting the royal dignity of the tribe of Judah : and united with the word "chose" (vs. 32, 34, 36) prove that the Divine Election is the immutable base of man's salvation. God did not choose Judah, David, and Jerusalem because of their excellence, but because of some satisfactory and eternally unchanging reason found in Himself. Against such a purpose of grace, the Adversary can object nothing, but is put to silence (Zech. iii. 2).

1 KINGS XII., 1-24.—Two facts close the previous chapter, viz., that Solomon was one of

the worst of the kings, and that he reigned forty years. One word gives the one great fact of this chapter—disruption. Forty years of the rule of exceptional talent is immediately followed by the breaking up of the kingdom ! Why ? Because Solomon turned aside from the Bible. To draw away from God's precious book, produces disunion—to draw round it, secures union. Nehemiah viii. gives a most striking picture. The scattered sons of Israel gather themselves together as one man, and request Ezra to bring the Book which Jehovah commanded to Israel. " And all the people gathered together to give attention to the words of the Book." How often does family disunion result from the fact that the head of the family, professing like Solomon to be a servant of the Lord, lives a life of disobedience to the word of the Lord.

In the action of Rehoboam and of the people, is exhibited the folly of the natural heart, and its incurable hostility to God. In the difficulty in which they find themselves the king consults " man " instead of God ; and the people trust themselves into the cruel hands of one, i.e., Jeroboam, who had been the instrument of the " grievous yoke " which oppressed them (xi. 28), instead of into the pitiful hands of Emmanuel !

The " scorpion " of verse 11 corresponds to the " cat " of to-day. It was a scourge, and, therefore, more painful than a whip.

The subjection of Rehoboam to the Word of the Lord (v. 24) contrasted with the insubjection of Solomon to the same Word (v. 15 and xi. 11) is a remarkable instance of how a fool (Eccles. ii. 18, 19), when he obeys the Bible, is wiser than a Solomon who disobeys it.

1 KINGS XII. 25—XIII. 32.—Jeroboam makes Shechem his capital. Here was Abraham's first altar and Jacob's first home. Here the tribes met ; here Joseph was buried. But God chose Jerusalem as the capital ; hence the envy of Ephraim (Isa. xi. 13). Following still further the wisdom of his own heart, he restores Aaron's golden calf, and establishes a new centre of worship in opposition to the Throne that was in the Temple at Jerusalem. A sorrowful instance of how hundreds of years after a Christian is dead, his evil conduct may live and influence others. The last verse of chapter xiii. states that this action on the part of Jeroboam became *the* sin which brought about the destruction of his whole family. (In verse 34 the definite article should be supplied before sin).

All is now prosperous, and sanctioned, and strengthened by religion. But, suddenly, God enters and lays all in ruins. How comfortably man could get on without God ! The scene is very striking—Jeroboam, arrayed as king and priest, stands by his beauteous altar offering incense to God. The entire court assists, together with a vast multitude of worshippers. Nothing is wanting to win the admiration of the religious world. Suddenly a stranger steps forward ! The Word of the Lord sounds out like a trump denouncing the wrath of God upon all this popular piety. The King's arm is withered, the altar rent, and its sacrificial ashes scattered to the four winds. A prophetic picture of what is to come to pass in a yet future day. In the midst of wrath, however, God remembers mercy. The King's hand is healed, but not his heart. It remains unmoved by either the wrath of God or the grace of God. It is not terrified by the one nor tendered by the other. His restored hand holds on to its sin ; and his rebellious heart immediately plans to weaken, and discredit, the prophet's testimony by inviting him to partake of the hospitality of the royal palace, and thus to sanction the king and his government.

The prophecy against this false altar is remarkable in that it names the king who, 250 years later, was to destroy it. The prophet Isaiah, in his day, similarly names the heathen prince who was to restore the true altar at Jerusalem.

Both prophecies came to pass : Josiah, the Christian prince, destroyed the false altar of Bethel, and Cyrus, the heathen prince, restored the true altar at Jerusalem.

Disobedience to the Word of the Lord is more serious in a servant of God than in an enemy of God. The king loses his hand ; the prophet, his life ! He was commanded not even by drinking water to sanction the religious evil which he was commissioned to condemn. His heart should have recognized the need of such a testimony ; and he had sufficient light to direct him. To eat and to drink with such enemies of truth was to deny the reality of the terrific doom he had denounced upon these worshippers, and their worship. It was to make an alliance between truth and error, so that truth would cease to be truth, and lose its authority and obligation. But he listens to another voice, the voice of the old prophet— and he was a prophet—and thereby disobeys the Lord, destroys his testimony, and loses his life.

The old prophet, whose duty it was to have testified against the evil around him, bore with it, and, by his silence, sanctioned it, therefore, he was very anxious that the young prophet should approve his unfaithfulness, by association with it. The young prophet is ensnared. God, in love to Jeroboam and his guilty associates, confirms His word by judging the disobedient messenger, and punishes the old prophet by compelling him to pronounce sentence of death upon his youthful brother.

Great principles stand out in this sad history to instruct all Christian people. Their duty is to sound out the Word of the Lord, and, by separation from evil, to accredit their testimony against it. They are commanded by their Lord to warn men of the wrath to come ; and, by their conduct, they should make it plain that they themselves believe in the reality of this coming wrath. There are, however, old prophets, that is Christians who live in guilty fellowship with the world, and these are ever anxious to get faithful servants of the Word of God to sanction their unfaithfulness by a compromising intimacy with them. Young Christians have to be upon their guard with respect to these " old prophets " ; for the latter will use Scriptural arguments to seduce the former from the straight path of obedience, and will claim, as the old prophet did, to speak by the Word of the Lord. If these " old prophets " are listened to, the results will be that the listeners will nullify their testimony, and bring death into their souls.

A little judgment punished Jeroboam's great sin, but a great judgment punished the prophet's little sin. Such are the just ways of God; for to whom much is given much will be required. It is more solemn to be a minister than to be a magistrate.

The fierce lion and the timid ass were, unlike the prophet, obedient to the voice of God, for the one did not flee, and the other did not devour, as their natures respectively prompted them. They stood in the highway to testify to the wrath of God. Compare the prophet Balaam and his ass.

1 **KINGS XIII. 33 - XIV. 20.**—The determined unbelief and folly of the natural heart is illustrated by Jeroboam in these verses. The just anger of God in destroying his idolatrous altar, and the amazing grace of God in restoring his withered hand, are alike resisted by him—" he returns not from his evil way," but returns to it ; "and this thing became *the* sin unto his house." "Sin " in verse 34 should read " the sin."

The darkness of his heart is further seen in his asking the Queen to disguise herself lest the people should know her to be the Queen. The path of fellowship with God is straight, courageous and dignified. But how full of scheming and cowardice, the way of the transgressor ! To openly seek help from God on behalf of his son, would show the people that he himself had no faith in the idol he had set up, and would affect the stability of his kingdom. His folly is further to be seen in that his wife was to try and deceive the God of Israel, although she sought unto Him for truth !

The unhappy Queen is dispatched home with a terrific message of doom, and told (v. 14) that the instrument of the Divine wrath, that is Baasha, was even then being prepared by God to utterly destroy the Royal family. Directly her feet cross the threshold of the palace, her child dies.

This child was the only member of the doomed household in which some good was found ; and it is remarkable that he was taken away. Thus it may be learnt that the untimely death of a child may evidence the love of God.

1 **KINGS XIV. 21-31.**—Rehoboam was a fool. His father Solomon knew that he was a fool. In Ecclesiastes he says that it embitters the life of a wise king to know that he will be succeeded by a fool ; and that in the hands of this fool will be placed all the great works and institutions which he had laboriously brought into being !

On opening the books of the Kings and reading of the accession of each king, the Bible student looks quickly with nervous apprehension at the next verse, and a feeling of gladness warms his heart when he reads that the king did that which was good and right in the sight of the Lord, but a great sadness is the opposite feeling, when the verse says he did that which was evil. This sadness is the deeper when he observes that the nation imitated the king. Verse 22 states that Judah did that which was evil in the sight of the Lord. 2 Chron. xii. records that the nation joined in that rebellion ; nor did Rehoboam lead them in a half-hearted way, but into the most abominable forms of idolatrous worship.

The fruit of departure from the Bible appears—continual contention with his brethren of the Northern kingdom, and humiliating subjection to the triumphant king of Egypt, give a striking picture of the experience of the Christian when he refuses to subject his heart and life to the government of the written Word. At home, contention ; abroad, slavery. It is true he tries to keep up the appearance of wealth ; but it is only appearance, not reality. Thus the world robs the unfaithful Christian of spiritual wealth, as Shishak robbed Rehoboam of his golden shields. The poor king replaces them with shields of brass ! Had he walked with God he would never have lost the shields of gold.

1 KINGS XV. 1–32.—The force of the word " perfect " in Scripture is to be ascertained from the context. The command in Matt. v. 48, " Be ye therefore perfect as your Father who is in heaven is perfect," is explained by the context to mean that, just as God is kind to the unthankful and to the evil, so must His children be. Abijam's heart was not perfect as David's was. The context here shows that the perfection consisted in purity of worship and absolute separation from idolatry.

But if the Holy Spirit recalls David's perfection in the matter of doctrine He, with terrible fidelity to truth, recalls his abominable conduct with regard to Uriah the Hittite ; conduct made all the more black by the fact that Uriah was one of his own brave thirty and seven mighty men ! So here are found the sad words : " David did that which was right all the days of his life, *save only* in the matter of Uriah the Hittite." The Holy Spirit once more, in 2 Chron. xvii. 3, recalls this dark page in David's history, in that He records that Jehoshaphat walked in the *first ways* of his father David.

The expression " a lamp in Jerusalem " has doubtless relation to the fact, that a light is kept burning day and night in every eastern house ; and if the light, for any

reason, be extinguished, it is regarded as a great calamity. A son, therefore, in the home is as a lamp in the house ; so God gave David a lamp in Jerusalem, in setting up his son after him.

The king's mother is stated here to have been the daughter of Abishalom ; but in 2 Chron. xi. it is stated she was the daughter of Absalom, and, 2 Chron. xiii., that she was the daughter of Uriel. " Daughter " and " granddaughter " in the Bible are related terms ; so, putting these three passages together, it would appear from them that the king's mother was the daughter of the son-in-law of Absalom.

The statement, in verse 6, that there was war between Rehoboam and Jeroboam, and the statement, in verse 7, that there was war between Abijam and Jeroboam, is neither mere repetition nor a mistake. It is the Holy Spirit emphasizing the fact that the life of the Christian, whose heart is not perfect, is a life of contention. Therefore it is that we have these three statements, first : " There was war between Jeroboam and Rehoboam continually " (xiv. 30), second : " Now there was war between Jeroboam and Rehoboam all the days of his life," third : " and there was war between Abijam and Jeroboam " (xv. 6–7). The experience of the Christian, whose heart is perfect, is, " great peace have all they that love thy law."

In 2 Chron. xii. 16 the king's name is recorded as Abijah ; but the sacred affix " jah " was very quickly changed by the Holy Spirit into the word " jam." Such alas ! is the case in many a life ; there is a fair start, but a foul ending ! The first title means : " Jehovah is my Father ; " the second : " The sea is my Father." The heavenly contrasted with an earthly birth— the restless sea with the peace-filled heaven.

Asa started well but ended badly. George Müller of Bristol was wont to pray, " Lord ; let me not die a wicked old man." It is not, alas, unusual to meet with Christians who, in later years, have lost the divine energy which marked the first days of their spiritual life. Asa's loyalty to the Bible is such that he removes his grandmother from the court. He cuts down and burns the obscene idol that she had set up, and he put away out of the land the Sodomites ; that is, the men and the women devotees who practised the immoral religious rites connected with the Ashera. But later on in his government, when in a difficulty, he leans upon the arm of the king of Syria instead of leaning upon God. He bribes Benhadad to be false to his treaty with Baasha, and his plan succeeds. It is disastrous to a Christian when his " fleshly " schemes prosper. Not at once, but, surely, later on, the sad fruit of such action appears. Asa oppresses the people by forcing them to construct great fortresses on the frontier ; and this was another proof of the decline of spiritual life and confidence in God. And, in his old age, he is diseased in his feet. What originated this disease in his feet ? The arm of Benhadad on which he leant ! Had he leant on God's arm, his aged feet would have been as hind's feet. (Psa. xviii. 33).

Two solemn facts appear in Nadab's reign. The first : that the predicted wrath of God surely comes to pass ; and, second : that the judgment often falls at a time when circumstances deny its probability. The affairs of the kingdom are so prosperous that the king is enabled to carry the war into the Philistine country, and besiege one of their great cities. In the midst of this prosperity the Divine judgment strikes him, and he and the entire royal family perish. Had Nadab attacked idolatry instead of attacking the Philistines, how different would have been his end ! He knew well the doom pronounced against him by Ahijah the Shilonite ; but his doing evil in the sight of the Lord, and his walking in the way of his father, show that he did not believe in the threatened wrath of God. It pictures multitudes to-day, who, though they continually hear of the wrath that is coming, yet cover their sins, and prosperously pursue their worldly concerns. Like Nadab they will be suddenly cut off and that without remedy, and, like him, they will involve others in the same destruction.

1 KINGS XV. 33—1 KINGS XVI. 28.—The four kings, Baasha, Elah, Zimri, and Omri leave the one sad record upon the page of sacred history, viz. : that they did evil. Their wars and their acts are stated to be recorded in the Chronicles of the Kings of Israel. Where is this book ? It is lost. Why ? Because there is no profit to be had from the doings of the workers of iniquity.

The closing words of verse 7 are very solemn. God raised up Baasha to execute judgment upon Jeroboam's family, but because Baasha executed that judgment with personal and cruel delight, therefore,

God smote his family. Later on in the Bible this same principle reappears. The Babylonians were judged by God because they also mercilessly executed His wrath upon Israel. (Isa. xlvii. 6). Christian people should never indulge a personal satisfaction on witnessing, or hearing of, Divine chastisement upon others.

Two facts mentioned in this chapter should be fixed in the mind of the Bible student, first : that Omri was the father of Ahab ; the second : that he bought the Hill of Samaria for about £2,000 and founded that famous city on it.

1 KINGS XVI. 29-XVII. 24.—With striking solemnity Ahab is thus thrice introduced : " Ahab, the son of Omri, began to reign," and : " Ahab, the son of Omri, reigned," and : " Ahab, the son of Omri, did evil in the sight of Jehovah above all that were before him." Thus attention is called to the personality of this wicked man. He sets up a satanic Trinity, viz. : the Calf, Baal, and the Ashera. This last was an abominable object of worship, too obscene to be described. This triple worship was senseless, merciless and shameless. Confronting this evil king stands Elijah ; for, when evil comes to a head, God raises up an exceptional testimony against it. Thus the prophets in Judah worked no miracles ; those in Israel, very striking ones. Judah remained, on the whole, faithful to the Bible : hence miracles were not necessary. Israel having rejected the Sacred Book, God in His pity and grace, accredited His messengers to that section of the nation by very remarkable miracles. 2 Kings xx. 11 was an answer to prayer.

But between these two great figures, Ahab and Elijah, is placed Hiel the Bethelite. Ahab and Elijah should both have learned a lesson from him. Ignoring, or despising the Bible, he moves against the prediction of Joshua, now 500 years old, and rebuilds the walls which the judgment of God had thrown down. On the foundations being laid, his eldest son is smitten with death, his next son and his next die as the walls rise higher, and his youngest son descends into the grave on the completion of the work. Ahab should have learned from this how vain, and how deadly, is the result of opposing God ; and Elijah should have learnt, for his part, how impotent is punishment to turn away man from his purpose ; and this, not because of impotency in the punishment, but because of the incurable rebellion of man's *will*. He should have learnt that grace alone can break down the natural heart. He should have interceded for Israel and not "against" Israel. Rom. xi. 2 interprets his ministry and furnishes its keynote. God gave him liberty of action (v. 1) and so he resolved, by suffering, to force the nation back to the Law. Only in glory, (Luke ix. 31,) did he learn that grace in Atonement can accomplish this. In Elijah's history, therefore, the successive efforts made by God to teach him this great truth, and their failure, appear.

His second lesson was given him by the brook Cherith. The mighty prophet in his determination to force Israel back to Jehovah, and to His Holy Book, by means of suffering, is now compelled to accept his daily food from "unclean" birds; and, further, he is compelled to daily watch, for many days, the brook becoming shallower and shallower, thus impressing upon him the terrible suffering of the unhappy people, until at length it dries completely up. Thus was he designed to feel the misery that reigned on the east frontier of Israel.

He is now ordered to the extreme western frontier to learn his third lesson; and here his iron will again refuses to give way before equal misery; and here also his passionate zeal for the Law is wounded by being compelled to accept food from a Gentile. How extreme was the suffering upon the Gentile, as well as upon Israel, was made plain to him by the appalling destitution and approaching death of this poor woman and her son.

The little word "the" should be noticed in the Revised Version. The poor woman speaks of *the* barrel and *the* cruse (v. 12), Elijah speaks of "the" barrel and "the" cruse (v. 14) and the inspired writer (v. 16) states that: "the barrel of meal wasted not, neither did the cruse of oil fail, according to the Word of Jehovah."

The death of the woman's son brings her sin to remembrance. It is not stated what that sin was; but the woman's language shows anger and despair. On the other hand, the giving life to the boy causes her to joyfully exclaim: "now I know that Jehovah is truth." This was a fourth lesson to Elijah, teaching him that grace, and not judgment, wins the sinner to God; but he refused to learn it. See note on Rev. xvi. 11.

The expression "what have I to do with thee," occurs several times in the Bible. It means: "What have we in common?." The answer is, "nothing." David uses it twice with respect to his cousins, the sons of Zeruiah. How impossible it was for them to have anything in common with him in the spiritual life! Elisha uses it in 2 Kings iii. to express how deep was the gulf between him and Jehoram the son of Ahab. Three times the demons, by using the same expression, reveal how Satan has nothing in common with Christ, or Christ with Satan. And lastly the Lord used it to the Virgin Mary to show how impassable is the gulf between His sinless Deity and her sinful humanity, (see notes on John ii. 4), and that only One Voice had authority for His ear.

1 KINGS XVIII.—The word "many" in verse 1 sobs with a Divine anguish. What untold suffering lies under that little word! How it seems to throb with pity!

The apostle James states that Elijah prayed as earnestly for the rain to be given as he had prayed for it to be withheld. God yielded to the persistent cry of the prophet and permitted him to use this dreadful instrument to try to destroy idolatry; but it is easy to feel how willingly He answered the second prayer, and how He hastened to say in verse 1, "I will send rain upon the earth!"

Elijah and Obadiah confronting each other is an instructive picture for the Christian. In Elijah there is the dignity, strength, calmness and decision of a man who walks in fellowship with God. In Obadiah, on the other hand, the haste, the excuses, the ignorance of the spiritual life, and the anxiety to give evidence of being a true servant of God! How pitiable and poor is all this! What a noble figure Elijah makes, but Obadiah an almost abject one. He should not have helped to dull Ahab's conscience in sanctioning, by his presence, the abominations of his idolatrous court. And yet how kind and gracious God is! The moment Obadiah appears in the chapter, the Holy Spirit hastens to draw attention to the fact that he feared Jehovah greatly, and that he had indeed saved the lives of the prophets.

The four hundred and fifty prophets of Baal obeyed the king's command and came to Carmel, but the four hundred prophets of the Ashera remained away. Baal being the god of fire, Elijah's challenge made the issue decisive. The prophet, building his altar of twelve stones to represent the twelve tribes of Israel, is a fine instance of an intelligent faith acting upon, and confessing, a Divine promise and purpose in the face of human failure and folly. He remembers that Jehovah had said to broken Jacob, " Israel shall be thy name " ; and in the energy of this faith he constructs the altar with twelve stones.

The destruction of the prophets of Baal furnishes a striking illustration of acquaintance with the Bible, and of obedience to its teaching. The command to put all such prophets to death will be found in Deuteronomy.

Elijah, as the apostle James points out, had obtained the promise of rain prior to this great scene on Carmel : but the fulfilment of the promise is not given until after God is glorified. Therefore it is that the prophet ascends to the top of the mountain, and waits with bowed head for the promised rain.

But at the moment of his greatest triumph and apparent success, the Spirit, that is, the grace of the Lord Jesus Christ, takes commanding hold of the fiery prophet and forces him into a principle of grace which he was not willing to learn or practise. He is compelled to urge this impious king to eat and drink, and then made to run before his chariot along the storm-swept road the entire way to the gate of Jezreel. It was only the compelling grace of the Lord Jesus that could constrain a prophet of judgment and fire to be concerned about the physical needs of a blood-stained idolator like Ahab; and then to attend him as a slave ; for it was the duty of a slave thus to run before his master's chariot. How amazing is the love of God ! The excitement of the day, no doubt, had caused Ahab to forget to take necessary food. Guilty and abominable as he was, yet is he cared for by the Divine pity ; and, marvel of grace ! God's noblest servant is compelled to attend him as a slave.

This section of the chapter gives three striking pictures of Elijah. To man's judgment the first picture is the grandest ; the second, less impressive ; and, the third, abject. To the spiritual eye it is the reverse ! The first picture presents the triumphant prophet standing by his blazing altar ; the second pictures him on the lonely mountain top bowed in expectant prayer ; the third depicts him as a slave splashing through the mud of the highway before the chariot of Ahab. To the spiritual mind this is the noblest picture of the three, for it illustrates the grace of Him who came to minister to, and to give His life for, the most violent of His enemies (Luke xxii. 50, 51).

The Kishon (v. 40), the sea (v. 43), and a well which still exists, could severally, or collectively, supply the water needed to fill the trench (v. 35).

1 KINGS XIX.—The Christian is in most danger of a deep fall immediately after a great triumph. This fact appears in the lives of Abraham, and Samson, and Moses, and David and many others. Christian people should be specially watchful and prayerful immediately after a revival. Elijah could boldly face the 450 prophets of Baal, but he fled for his life the next day from one woman. Faith entirely failed at a mere threat from Jezebel. This resulted because law was the energy of his testimony, and not grace. Elijah's faith, like that of Moses at Meribah, was not based upon the grace which superabounds where sin abounds. Hence the one great prophet was forbidden entrance to the land, and the other dismissed from it. Both, however, subsequently appear together in the land on the mount of transfiguration with the promised Messiah, who is the God of all grace.

The prophet flees to the Wilderness. He who has not Divine strength has no power against evil, and is compelled to take refuge in isolation. Elijah's heart was true to God, but, his intelligence not being instructed by grace, he could not stand against Satan's power. He might have had this intelligence had he been willing, but his heart was far from such a state. When occupied with self, specially religious self, it is impossible to make others see what God really is. Self blinds even so mighty a prophet as Elijah. Angry and rebellious, he throws himself down to sleep in the desert. In himself a picture of the nation that he testified against, how touching the tender pity that twice refreshed him, saying with such exquisite love : " Eat, for the journey is too great for thee." This should have touched the prophet, and made him feel what he ought to have been in the midst of his people, since Jehovah was such a God as this ; for it was the Angel of Jehovah Himself who twice aroused him to eat the provided bread. Yet still untaught he reaches Horeb ; and, in reply to the solemn question : "What doest thou here Elijah ? "—a question which should have brought him to repentance and sorrow—he at once begins to speak well of himself and ill of the nation. He should have set himself aside and interceded for, and not against Israel, as Rom. xi. teaches. He was angry because the people would not listen to him and turn unto Jehovah. Christian people must watch and pray against religious irritability. It is often felt by a Christian worker when his efforts to induce people to attend gospel services are repulsed.

The angry prophet, crouching with embittered heart in the cavern, pictured the nation. The " flesh " in him was just as hateful as the " flesh " in them. He is invited to come forth and meet God. He refuses ; he must therefore be compelled to come forth. A tempest rends the mountains, an earthquake the rocks, and a fire follows. But Jehovah was not in these ; and Elijah could neither be burnt out nor forced out. Then comes the sudden objective stillness : he wraps his face in his mantle, and comes out, and stands in the entrance of the cave. Had his heart not been occupied with self he would have learned that tempests, earthquakes and fires cannot accomplish what the gentle voice of love can. He should have recognized that there was no difference between his heart and that of the nation ; and, that as coercion failed to make him leave his cave, so it failed, and must fail, to compel men to leave their sins.

But he will not learn. When asked again " What doest thou here Elijah ? " he repeats his angry and foolish words, and intercedes *against* Israel. Had he loved sinners as his Lord did, how different would have been his action and language !

God's answer is just and sorrowful. Judgment will be executed upon the guilty, but Elijah is dismissed ; and, sad mission for him, he is commissioned to prepare the instruments for that judgment. Elijah was true to the Law, and was consequently honoured, but he failed to understand the thoughts of love and grace that fill the heart of God for guilty men. He is gently rebuked by being told of the 7,000 who had not bowed the knee to Baal. Had he leant more upon God and crucified self, he would have known at least some of these 7,000.

So he leaves Horeb and finds one of these 7,000. i.e., Elisha. Elijah " passes over " unto him, that is, he crosses the Jordan, and casts his mantle upon him as he ploughs. At that time and since, casting the mantle upon the shoulders of another expressed his appointment as successor. The gentle-spirited lad accepts the office, only begging permission to kiss his father and his mother ; a beautiful instance of courage and love, a courage that boldly faced almost certain death, and a love that thought upon his parents.

Not far off there was a large Divinity School in which a body of students was being prepared for the prophetic office. Upon none of these did Elijah cast his mantle, but, guided by the Holy Spirit, he cast it upon a plough boy. How different are God's thoughts from man's ! He chooses an Amos, a Paul, or a Moody, and, through them rebukes, and refreshes, the official Ministry.

The twelve " I " and " me " and " my " etc., reveal the strength of the religious self in the prophet's heart. His purpose was right ; his spirit wrong. " They seek my life to destroy it " contrasts with the Apostle Paul's " I count not my life to be dear unto myself " (Acts xx. 24).

Elijah led Elisha to Gilgal, i.e. to Calvary (2 Kings ii. 1), for only there can the life of testimony and power begin, and only there can it be nourished. The church to-day is empty and powerless because the doctrine of the Atonement is avoided or denied. See notes on Joshua, iv. 19, v. 10, and Judges ii 1-5, and 2 Kings ii.

1 · KINGS XX. — This chapter, taken with the preceding, illustrates the truth that man, as man, always breaks down when charged by God with the execution of any matter. Elijah is called to proclaim the goodness of God, and Ahab chosen to express His severity. Self-will in both caused both to fail. Elijah smites the earth with a curse, instead of enriching it with a blessing, and Ahab hails the determined enemy of God as his " brother," and dismisses him in peace when he should have put him to death. Both prophet and King occupy positions of public responsibility in relation to God ; but the conduct of both, as public servants of God, shows that neither of them enjoyed that personal intimate fellowship with God which gives knowledge of the "mind of the Lord," which crucifies self, and which only thinks of God and His claims and honour

This is a fine principle; Moses illustrates it; in his conduct is seen the "goodness and severity" of God intelligently recognised—goodness to His people, but severity towards His enemies. He who, from love to the people, prayed to be blotted out from the Book of life, is he also who said in the presence of evil," Slay every man his brother." Ahab, to please and honour himself, sets the Syrian as a brother by his side, and honours the man whom God had justly sentenced to death. Judgment is accordingly denounced upon him, and he goes down to his house, heavy and displeased, as Elijah to his cave.

See notes on 1 Samuel vi. 19, in explanation of verse 30 ; though it is not impossible for the wall of a city to fall upon 27,000 men crowded in a confined space at its foot, and to kill them.

1 **KINGS XXI.**—The thoughts of man's heart toward God are thoughts of unbelief, rebellion, and hatred, whilst the thoughts of God's heart toward man are thoughts of pity and love. The chapter opens with Ahab refusing to listen to God's loving voice which had spoken to him so plainly in the remarkable victory given to him over the Syrians, but willingly listening to Jezebel's cruel voice prompting him to perhaps the blackest of his black crimes. In Naboth we see a beautiful instance of loyalty to the Bible. He does not refuse his vineyard to the King through selfishness or churlishness, but because God had forbidden private property in land and its consequent transference. (Lev. xxv. 23 and Num. xxxvi., 7).

But if the Christian is faithful to the Bible, Satan knows how to use the Bible as an instrument to rob him both of his property and his life. The history of the Holy Inquisition illustrates this. Accordingly, the religious charge of blasphemy is brought against Naboth, the Court is constituted, its judgment given, and the sentence executed strictly in conformity with the Scriptures.

What, therefore, could Naboth do but commit the keeping of his soul to Jehovah as unto a faithful Creator ?

But Israel's Shepherd saw it all, and with a terrific message wrecks the enjoyment Ahab promised himself. Yet, cruel and wicked as the guilty king was, upon his showing the feeblest evidence of repentance the God of Naboth promises an arrest of judgment. It was not true repentance, it was fear of judgment, but not sorrow for sin. Ahab's subsequent conduct proves this ; and yet how amazing is the grace of God ! He respects this repentance, shallow and earthly as it was.

These chapters exhibit God in government, in accordance with the principle revealed to Moses in the mountain, and afterwards more fully revealed by Jehovah Himself in the Sermon on the Mount, i.e., the great double principle of showing mercy and visiting iniquity. In reading the two books of Samuel, and the two Books of the Kings, this fact should never be lost sight of, that it is God in government ; this helps the reader to understand much that might otherwise be obscure.

Ahab continually illustrates the truth that fallen man cannot, and will not, know God and share His thoughts. What the king has (Benhadad) he lets go, and what he had not (the vineyard) he covets. How far was he from sharing the thoughts of God ! Such is the heart of every unconverted man ! How humiliating is the opening and closing picture of the king as given in the chapter ! Like a petulant child he refuses food because he cannot get the play-toy he covets, and, like a cowardly child, he denies himself food so as to avert punishment ! How contemptible are great kings when slaves to sin and self.

And Ahab was a great king, as his wars and his public works and palaces testify. He was a gifted and able prince, and far surpassed other kings of Israel in the energy, culture, and splendour of his reign.

1 **KINGS XXII. 1-40.**—Prosperity is more dangerous to the Christian life than adversity. Outwardly all was prosperous with Ahab—he had an ivory palace—but the secret of the Lord was with Elijah, and he knew the doom that was coming upon all this glory. There was also an outward reformation, the prophets of Baal do not appear in the chapter, but, on the contrary, 400 professed prophets of Jehovah ; and Jehovah's true servant Jehoshaphat is invited to sanction all this outward goodness, and, alas ! he does so. But Ahab's heart is all unchanged. What a difference lies between the judgment of God and the appearance of things !

Jehoshaphat goes "down" to Ahab ! Whenever the Christian unites with the world, even in what appears to be a laudable enterprise, he goes "down". If Ahab had

" gone up " to Jehoshaphat and recognized Jerusalem as God's city and the Temple as His throne, and sought forgiveness and life there, how different his end would have been ! But the world never " goes up " to the Christian ; it is ever and always the Christian who " goes down " to the world.

It is easy to trap an unwatchful servant of the Lord by what appears to be Christian duty. Ramoth Gilead belongs to Israel, but is in the power of the enemy ! What, therefore, could be more praiseworthy and Scriptural than to recover it for God ! But the world, that is, Ahab, was to reap all the profit, and Jehoshaphat nothing, except the danger and weakness which this unholy alliance brought to him. Few temptations are more dangerous to the Christian than when Satan, as a minister of righteousness, invites his assistance in winning something or other for God. At such a time the servant of the Lord must keep very close to his Master.

This alliance with Ahab revealed a secret root of spiritual weakness in Jehoshaphat's heart, the fruit of which was disastrous to his children. Jehoshaphat did not help Ahab to return to truth, but Ahab helped Jehoshaphat to be unfaithful to Jehovah ; and if afterwards Ahab's son joined Jehoshaphat, it was merely to get gold from Ophir !

The bravery of Micaiah condemns the cowardice of Jehoshaphat. Micaiah is the king and Jehoshaphat the slave. Jehoshaphat should have stepped down from his throne, thrown his mantle around the courageous prophet, and valiantly taken his stand at his side. There is no one more cowardly and contemptible than a Christian who walks in fellowship with the religious world. Micaiah is led away to prison and to torture, and Jehoshaphat raises neither hand nor voice on his behalf ! See notes on 2 Chron. xvii-xx.

Two royal fools at once meet us in these verses. Jehoshaphat was a fool to go into battle, at Ahab's suggestion, in his royal robes, and Ahab was a greater fool to propose to escape the Divine doom pronounced upon him by going into battle without his royal robes. God is not mocked ; the arrow of death, winged by wrath both just and holy, pierces him. His dead body is brought to Samaria, his chariot is washed at a loathsome pool where harlots were accustomed to wash themselves, and dogs lick up his blood. Such was the sordid and horrible end of Ahab ! As

a king, he was great, cultivated, courageous, a bold soldier, a successful general, a lover of art and refinement, but a blood-stained idolator. Contrast his end with that of his great enemy Elijah : the one mounts up to heaven in his chariot ; the other goes down to death from his chariot ! See notes on 2 Kings v. and Acts viii.

God loved Ahab and sought to save him again and again, but in vain.

1 KINGS XXII. 41 - 50. — Jehoshaphat's reign, in this book, is disposed of in ten verses, but one hundred and two verses are devoted to it in 2 Chron. This harmonizes with the character and purpose of these books. To the historian, Jehoshaphat's reign is not very interesting, but how intensely interesting to the man of faith !

The watchful love that records that he walked in all the ways of Asa his father ; that he turned not aside from it ; that he did that which was right in the eyes of the Lord ; that he refused association in commerce with the idolatrous Ahaziah ; and that he expelled the Sodomites out of the land, with equal fidelity records that he failed to abolish the high places.

Here is found a striking instance of how eagerly the Divine love points to all that can be commended in a Christian's character, and gently and sorrowfully prefaces any defect with a pitying " howbeit."

It is suggestive that the Holy Spirit brings together in this brief history Jehoshaphat's over-lordship of Edom, in which country he was represented by a deputy, that is, a viceroy, and his fitting out ships to gather gold ; but a hand of love broke his ships, and his son lost the kingdom of Edom. A lesson may be learnt here. The possession of property whets the natural appetite for amassing wealth. The Christian must watch and pray against this temptation, and not rebel if God upsets well-laid plans for gratifying it.

See notes on 2 Chron. xx. and Isa. xxxix.

1 KINGS XXII. 51-2 KINGS 1-18.—The energy of evil is seen in king Ahaziah in that " he walked in the way of his father, and in the way of his mother and in the way of Jeroboam." He sought healing from Baalzebub and not from God ; and, when rebuked by Elijah, he sent soldiers to arrest him in order to put him to death.

Elijah, like John, was clothed with camels'

hair fastened with a girdle. The Baptist, like the prophet, called Israel to repentance, and was indeed Elijah to that generation.

The fire that consumed the captains and their men was a just fire. This is shown by the words of the prophet, " if I be a man of God," for it makes plain that the language of the officers, and notably of the second, was contemptuous. The third captain behaves differently, and his life, and that of his men, is preserved.

Christ, as the Angel of Jehovah, appears in verses 3 and 15. Elijah's prompt obedience to both commands shows restoration of soul : but, alas, there could be no restoration of ministry. How often is this true in the history of servants of the Word The tender love of God, however, to His dear servant did not fail. He had in secret to judge him, but in public He honours him He did not make known to his contemporaries his petulance and weakness, but He makes them known to us for our instruction. Had He not intervened (v. 15) Elijah would have destroyed the third company, for the zealous " I " (v 10, 12) still animated him.

2 KINGS

2 KINGS II.—John the Baptist came neither eating nor drinking, and Israel said, " he hath a devil." The Son of Man came eating and drinking, and they said," Behold a winebibber ! " Such was Israel's response to Elijah and Elisha who were types of John and Christ. Elijah—" Jehovah is God " — figures law, and Elisha — " God is Salvation "—represents grace. The one prophet sought to drive Israel to God ; the other, to win her ; both failed, but with this difference, that failure angered Elijah, and that anger made him impossible as a channel of the true thoughts of God to Israel, which were thoughts of grace and not of anger. So he must be replaced by Elisha and not re-appointed, as many think ; but God honours the faithfulness of His loved servant by rapturing him with glory into the heavens without death. He is carried up in a chariot by a whirlwind, and attending him in his triumphant ascent are the chariots of God—chariots of fire and horses of fire. (R.V.) " The chariots of God are twenty thousand, even thousands of. thousands, Jehovah is among them " (Ps. lxviii. 17). It is per-missible, therefore, to believe the Lord accompanied these chariots, and personally escorted Elijah into heaven.

Elisha had now been ten years with his master—a testing time—and the last test now comes. He is bidden to tarry at Gilgal, or at Bethel, or at Jericho, but he refuses. He will not separate from Elijah until God parts them ! Here was fidelity and love ; and such was the instrument that God wanted for His work. Together they retrace the triumphant path of Joshua and the hosts of Israel. It befitted Elijah's last day of service to visit these scenes of former glory but present shame. The journey was also full of teaching for Elisha. Gilgal, speaking to him of Calvary, the source of victory ; Bethel, recalling the faithfulness of God ; Jericho, the scene of His might over all the power of the enemy. What memories gathered round these places ! but he wanted present realities, so he clung to Elijah.

Prior to the rapture of the mighty prophet, the sons of the prophets officiously intrude their needless knowledge ; and, after the rapture, with the same unspiritual officious-ness, they vex the anguished heart of Elisha with persistent suggestions to search for the body of his loved master. They could neither enter into the sorrow of the heart of Elisha, nor understand the thoughts of the Spirit of God. Their officiousness but sharpened the pain he suffered—a pain so sharp that he bade them not to speak about it.

As the master and the disciple are passing dry-shod through the parted waters of Jordan, Elijah asks, " What shall I do for thee before I be taken away from thee ? "—words full of tender love. Elisha asks for the portion of the first-born, and Elijah replies, " Thou hast asked a hard thing,"i.e. not a difficult thing, but," thou hast made a great claim." Such is the meaning of the word " hard " in the verse. It expresses the greatness of the appetite of the heart of Elisha for spiritual power.

The repetition of the word " father " in verse 12 signifies," my beloved father, my revered father." And he saw him no more !

Elisha begged for a double portion and he got it. His master wrought eight miracles ; he, sixteen.

The challenge " Where is Jehovah the God of Elijah ? " voiced the unbelief and desolation of the hearts of the sons of the prophets who were watching him, and the answer and demonstration " He is even here " (Heb.) taught them that if Elijah had left them, God remained. And these men were not slow to learn the lesson, for they said one to another, " the spirit of Elijah doth rest on Elisha."

The prophet of grace and truth, in all the power and glory of resurrection life, now enters the Land of Promise—his starting point being the heavens with its horses and chariots of fire. In this power he enters the city of the curse, and at once heals its barren waters. The new cruse—a beauteous symbol of the sinless body of the Lord Jesus, and the salt in it—a type of the incorruptible word of God that in its plenitude dwelt in Him, were the vehicles of the healing power. These descend into the bitter source of Jericho's barrenness, and life, beauty and fruit result—a striking picture of the moral effect in the life of a man when the Incarnate Word of God possesses his heart.

But if grace hastens to bless with life a death-doomed city that, repenting and believing, appeals to it, its rejection entails judgment and death. Forty two " young men," (not little children, deride) the prophet's testimony and bid him ascend up to heaven, as he absurdly says Elijah did, and they perish.

A double spirit rested upon him—grace and truth. Truth only energized Elijah, but grace and truth, Elisha. The one is seen in the healing of Jericho ; the other, in the death of the mockers.

Elisha did not ask for a double portion of Elijah's own spirit, or of his methods, but of the divine energy that clothed him.

The rapture of Enoch, of Elijah, of the saints (Matt. xxvii. 52), and of the Lord, were all secret. It is, therefore, reasonable to believe that the rapture of 1 Thess. iv. 16 may also be secret.

2 KINGS III.—The incurable insubjection of the natural will, even in a Christian, to the Word of the Lord, is seen in Jehoshaphat. In spite of two severe lessons from God, he, for the third time, unites with the religious world in a "laudable" enterprise. He joined Ahab to recover Ramoth Gilead, nearly lost his life, and was sharply rebuked by the prophet Jehu. He united with Ahab's son Ahaziah in shipbuilding, but his ships were broken ; and now he unites with Jehoram, Ahaziah's brother, in making war upon their neighbours, with the result that once again he nearly loses his life, and, in addition, helps to drive the Moabites into still deeper idolatry.

Jehoram removes the obscene idol erected by his father, but resolutely holds on to the great sin of Jeroboam, that is, to the golden calf. In the Books of the Kings, as in the first Epistle of John, " sin " principally means the substitution of a god other than the Lord Jesus, and " holiness " means fidelity to that God and Saviour.

In his misery Jehoram recognizes Jehovah, but only to blame Him as the author of his suffering. Jehoshaphat, however, casts himself upon God, and grace fills the thirsty valley with water. To obtain the water, and to retain it, faith must be in exercise, and must " fill " the valley with ditches in order that it may be filled with water. Such is the humbling toil that the soul must engage in when in a false position, and if it would obtain deliverance ! What painful experiences, both physical and spiritual, the apostle Paul brought upon himself when he joined with the Pharisees in defence of religious truth, and with the Romans on behalf of civil liberty ! Many a Christian, like Jehoshaphat, finds himself, as the result of self-will, in a waterless valley ; but, even there, if he humbles himself, grace will fill the valley with refreshment and victory.

Elisha, who provided water for Elijah's hands is honoured by God as His instrument to provide water for these kings and their armies. Public and brilliant ministries must be preceded by humble and hidden ones. To pour water on the hands of anyone is the action of a servant. The word " poured " in verse 11 may mean poured and " continues to pour", for Elijah was not necessarily dead at this time. This expedition may have occurred prior to his rapture (2 Chron. xxi. 12). John iii. 16, reads, " God so loved the world." He did love the world, and He loves it still.

The word " Nay " in verse 13 might be thus expressed, " Say not so."

How desirable to be under the hand of the Lord as a harp beneath the hand of the minstrel ! Its strings must be in tune, but they are silent till swept by the hand of the master. Such were Elisha's lips when touched by the hand of the Lord. This is a possibility to all Christian people ; were it realized there would be a great revival. Victory crowns the opening hours of the day of battle, but defeat darkens its close. The triumphant men of Israel break down the walls of the cities and cast the stones upon the fertile fields and into the wells of water. Success carries them beneath the walls of Kir-haraseth, the King's capital, and the only city left with stone walls. Battering engines are immediately set in position to make a breach. The king

of Moab, in desperation, tries to fight his way
to the king of Edom, doubtless in the hope
that that king might help him to escape. The
effort is vain ; so in a paroxysm of religious
frenzy he sacrifices his eldest son to the fire-
god, in effect, to Satan. The horrid deed
inflames with religious fury the Moabites,
terror-strikes the superstitious Israelites—
themselves idolators—and they hasten back
to their own land having accomplished
nothing, except to deluge their neighbour's
country with blood, and push its unhappy
people deeper into the black depths of devil-
worship. What a humbling and instructive
lesson for Christian people who help the
unconverted in their unholy schemes for
enriching themselves by the destruction of
their fellow creatures. The Liquor Traffic
furnishes a sad illustration.

Verse 19 is to be understood as a
prediction,and as a direction for Jehoshaphat,
and not as a command. Jehoshaphat should
have been instructed by it and left the field
directly the Moabites fled.

2 KINGS IV. 1-7.—The sufficiency of grace
in relation to man's folly and need, appears
in the miracles of Elisha. He is a saviour
to Israel and a healer to the Gentiles. In the
previous chapter living water is abundantly
given to the three kings who are about to
perish. The same grace now grants an overflowing provision of wealth to the impoverished widow. The succeeding miracles
strikingly prove that " grace upon grace "
is the measure of the grace that hastens to
the help of needy and sinful men. These
miracles characterize Elisha's ministry. The
thirsty are refreshed ; the poor and needy
provided for ; the childless made the joyful
mother of children ; the dead raised to life ;
the broken-hearted bound up ; the hungry
healed and fed ; the lepers cleansed ; and
victory given over all the power of the enemy.
Such is Christ to broken humanity.

Many a Christian is like this widow. There
is depression,poverty and bondage in the life,
instead of joy, wealth, and liberty. " In the
house,"—that is, " at hand "—is a secret
source of fulness and blessing—the pot of
oil, that is, the Holy Spirit ; and if that
source of life and power be drawn upon, it is
found to be more than sufficient to meet and
satisfy the needs of all the empty vessels
brought near to its fulness. The pot of oil,
so lightly regarded by human wisdom, or

overlooked, as the rock in the case of Israel
(Num. xx. 8),responds at once when appealed
to, and the house is filled with the " life more
abundant."

2 KINGS IV. 8-37.—The gift of a son by
natural birth, and the re-gift of that son by
resurrection birth, were the sixth and seventh
miracles of Elisha.

The Shunammite was not only a person of
position in society, but also of spiritual refinement and insight. She set a value upon
eternal realities, and so with great delicacy
she fitted up a room in the porch of her house ;
and, recognizing that the prophet's affections
were heavenly, she furnished it with extreme
simplicity. Owing to the situation of the
room, Elisha could enter and leave it freely.
To her faith and care a child is promised.
The promise is emphasized by the repetition
of the time when this miracle should take
place. Elisha says, " at this season when
the spring cometh thou shalt embrace a son."
The words " according to the time of life "
mean " when the spring cometh." The
words that burst from the lips of the
Shunammite reveal the wild joy of her heart.

She watches her little boy dying upon her
knees, and, when dead, lays him upon the
bed of the man of God ; but the prolonged
agony of that dreadful day, and the blackness of death that closed it, failed to quench
the feeble flame of faith that was in her heart,
or to provoke a word of complaint or anger.
In her anguish she turns to God and not
from Him, and as a result she learns that
that gracious God can not only give a child
to enfeebled nature, but can bring back that
child from out of the power of death. How
must her heart have oftentimes blessed Him
for having led her along such a path as this.
Just as to Martha and Mary He was a
mightier God and a greater Saviour because
He had permitted Lazarus to die, so was
He to this mother in her day.

To instruct and strengthen her faith, to
keep her hanging upon God, the prophet
teaches her that a dead staff laid upon a dead
face cannot give life. Religious ceremonies,
however scriptural, are paralysed in the
presence of death ; but when the prophet
bows himself down upon the child, then
walks in the house once hither and once
thither, and then taking up the child in his
arms, embraces him—a beauteous picture
of the true Elisha in the activities of His

love—then is the child revived, and placed all living in the arms of his mother, who, speechless with joy, receives him back from God.

Shunem was a village some miles from Mount Carmel.

2 KINGS IV. 38-44.—The lesson of Elisha's Eighth miracle is, that " Jesus saves," whilst that of the Ninth Miracle is, that " Jesus satisfies."

There is a famine in the land, one of the thirteen famines recorded in the Bible. The sons of the prophets are faced by hunger. God in His goodness and love provides abundantly for them. One of these men, not satisfied with the Divine provision, adds to it, and in so doing; introduces death. So was it at the beginning. A richly spread table was furnished to man in the Garden of Eden, but, dissatisfied with its abundance, he added to it, and thus brought death upon himself and upon his children.

The dying men in their despair turn to God for salvation, and once more the Divine grace responds to their need. The meal, similitude of the " Bread of God," descends into the pot of death, absorbs into itself and destroys the poison, expresses from itself life and healing, and the sons of the Prophets, invited by Elisha, eat of the pottage, and find life in death.

So Jesus, the Bread that cometh down from heaven, descended into death ; · by the sacrifice of Himself destroyed death ; and in His death sinners find life.

These poisoned and dying men, in order to be saved, had only to believe Elisha's testimony that there was life in the pottage, and take and eat. So death-doomed men, believing God's testimony that whosoever believeth upon His beloved Son shall never die, believe that testimony, trust Christ, and find life in Him.

But Jesus not only saves, He satisfies. The prophet's servant is bidden to place twenty barley cakes before one hundred men. The servant, astonished, exclaims, " What, should I set this before an hundred men ? " His master replies, " give the people that they may eat : for thus saith the Lord, they shall eat and leave thereof " ; and so it came to pass. The hundred men failed to exhaust the Divine abundance.

Men judge of Jesus Christ as the prophet's servant judged of the barley cakes. They do not believe that He can satisfy the hunger of their hearts. They think it impossible to satisfy their hunger with what He is, and provides, and that with Him, or apart from Him, all the resources of excitement and pleasure must be provided if life would be bright, satisfying and cheerful. But all that the world offers can never satisfy man's spirit ; for how can that which is matter satisfy that which is spirit ! Jesus does satisfy, and more than satisfy, just as these men proved how more than sufficient for their need were the barley cakes.

This was the first of the three miracles of feeding multitudes recorded in the Bible ; the other two are found in Matt. xiv. and xv. These three feasts are set over against the thirteen famines; the famines are connected with Satan ; the feasts with Jesus. Three in the Scriptures is the number of fulness, thirteen that of rebellion, disturbance and want.

2 KINGS V. 1-19.—Grace, of which Elisha is the instrument, having visited Israel, now reaches out to the Gentile, and Naaman is healed. This is a picture of the present dispensation, as the Lord Jesus Christ predicted in the synagogue at Nazareth.

This Tenth miracle is frequently used by preachers to illustrate the Gospel. The hopeless position of Naaman, though only slightly touched by the disease ; the simplicity of the remedy ; the worthlessness of the provision he made ; his anger when his plan of cure was rejected ; and his cleansing—all illustrate the Epistles to the Romans and to the Hebrews.

The first nineteen verses of this chapter sing of mercy ; the last eight, of judgment. The Psalmist desired to sing of both. Many preachers to-day desire to sing only of the first. A true preacher sings of both. Compare the last two songs in the Bible (Rev. xix).

The use of the Great Covenant Title, Jehovah, in the first verse makes it clear that Naaman, ere he knew it, was a vessel of mercy, chosen beforehand of God unto this grace. The Lord Jesus in John xvii. 6 speaks of the men given unto Him out of the world. While yet in the world they were in the Covenant of Grace though they did not know it. Thus was it with Naaman.

The little maid is a lovely character. She had good cause to hate her captor and to rejoice on hearing of the dreadful disease that afflicted him ; but she pitied him, and so she also, though a little slave child, became as well as the great prophet Elisha an instrument of grace.

Twenty-one lepers are mentioned in the Bible—Exod. iv. 6, Num. xii. 10, 2 Kings v. 1, 2 Kings v. 27, 2 Kings vii. 3, 2 Kings xv. 5, Matt. viii. 2, Matt. xxvi. 6, Luke xvii. 12 — the first of these lepers was Moses.

The command to Naaman was : " Go, wash ", the command to the woman of Samaria : " Go, call " (John iv. 16), and the command to the young ruler : " Go, sell " (Matt. xix 21).

In verse 11 Naaman says : " Behold I thought " ; in verse 15 he joyfully cries : " Behold now I know." Such is the experience of many when seeking spiritual health by a self-thought plan. Their plans, like their thoughts, are vain ; but, when they humble themselves to God's way of life and health, they possess Divine certitude.

Naaman is bidden to go into peace. Had the prophet said to him : " you may bow," he would have sanctioned idolatry. Had he said :" you must not bow," he would have placed himself between Naaman's soul and God, and brought Naaman's conscience into bondage to Elisha. He knew well the disturbance that bowing in the House of Rimmon would cause to Naaman's new found peace, and that that disquietude would throw Naaman upon God, and not upon any prophet. God's servants are not "directors of conscience," as some men claim to be, but ministers of the Truth.

2 KINGS V. 20—27.—It is a dreadful thing to sin against righteousness, but it is more dreadful to sin against grace, and in a day of grace. This adds to Gehazi's guilt, and marks the judgment that fell upon him as just. Man may judge it as unjust, but it was a Divine judgment ; and the man who pronounces it unjust sets himself up above God. Messiah sang of judgment (Ps. ci.) and the first (Ps. civ. 35) and last Hallelujahs (Rev. xix.) applaud the destruction of multitudes.

This was Elisha's Eleventh miracle. It accompanies in character the Third. Both miracles express the wrath of God ; the one, against unbelief of the gospel in a day of grace ; the other, against degradation of the gospel in the same age.

Gehazi hid his sin as Adam, Achan and Ananias did, and as multitudes have since done ; but in vain.

" Went not mine heart with thee when the man turned again to meet thee." Some Hebrew scholars translate this : " Did not my heart beat within me when the man turned to meet thee." This suggests the anguish that convulsed the prophet's bosom at the moment that his spiritual work was being wrecked by Gehazi's action. There is a throb of agony in the question " Is it a time to receive money and garments ? " A day of grace is a time to give and not to receive ; and Elisha evidently thought with trembling of the injury threatened to Naaman's faith by this action. That from which Naaman was freed is now bound upon Gehazi and his children for ever ; for a man by sinning not only brings damage to himself but also to his family. Gehazi goes out a leper as white as snow, that is, a leper completely diseased and incurably diseased. A sinner as white as snow means a sinner completely saved ; a leper as white as snow means a leper completely lost.

Gehazi as he stood before Elisha pictures Israel. For grace, overflowing the bounds of the covenant and reaching out to the Gentile awakened anger or covetousness in Israel's heart—anger when the Lord in the synagogue at Nazareth recalled the healing of Naaman ; and covetousness when the same Lord, in Elisha, refused Naaman's gifts. The elder son (Luke xv.) was made both covetous and angry by the grace that met the prodigal.

Gehazi was the ordained servant of the prophet, and doubtless would have succeeded to him as his master did to Elijah. Ministers of the Gospel must therefore watch against these two sins of anger and covetousness. Some are prone to anger when the grace of God goes out beyond the narrow limits of their own denomination and visits unrecognized " sects " (so called) ; others are tempted to profit by this abounding grace and to turn it to the enrichment of their own reputation or that of their church. These sins, if committed, bring into the minister's soul the deadness which binds the unconverted, just as Gehazi brought upon himself the malady which afflicted Naaman.

This fearful demonstration of the wrath of God for what men would think a very trivial offence, must have made Naaman's heart tremble in relation to idolatry— assuming that he heard the terrible report.

2 KINGS VI. 1-7.—This Twelfth miracle may be thus paraphrased. Elisha's house becomes too small for the divinity students. They plan therefore to descend to the Jordan valley and build a larger house with the wood which abounds there. Elisha says they may do so if they please. One of them, however, moved by personal love to the prophet, begs him to go with them. He, touched by this mark of affection, consents. On reaching the Jordan bank they fall to at cutting logs. Presently the young man who had urged Elisha to accompany them, utters a cry of distress—the axe head had slipped off its handle and fallen into the deep waters of the river. No longer can he take a share in the work ; and to add to his distress, the axe head was borrowed. He hurries to his loved master to tell him of his loss and embarrassment. Elisha asks to be led to the spot where the axe head sank, he proceeds to shape out a new axe handle, and, casting it upon the dark and rapid waters of the river, it overcomes the powerful current of the stream, remaining stationary on the surface of the water. The axe head immediately rises from the bottom, becomes firmly united to the handle, and the young workman, invited by the master, reaches out his hand and takes it.

The affection of this student for his master, and Elisha's love for them all, is touching. Had they been wiser they would have waited for him to plan for them in their difficulty. Had they done so, they would have been saved from the distress and anxiety which befell them. Most of the troubles which come upon Christian people come by not allowing God to plan for them. Difficulties and trials in Christian work arise oftentimes from the same cause. The gentle " I will go " of the prophet is, in the circumstances, very touching.

" But as the one (Hebrew) was felling a tree," that is, the student spoken of in verse 3.

" And he cut down a stick," the verb " to cut " in this verse is not the same as in verse 4. It is the same word that occurs in Can. iv. 2, and the passage may be translated, " He neatly fashioned a handle." Possibly the student had fashioned his own axe handle, for apparently it was only the axe head that was borrowed. It is not, therefore, a matter of surprise that it lost its hold of the iron. When God, as represented by his prophet, fashions a miraculous axe handle, how different the hold that it may be expected to have !

What the great lesson is which this miracle is intended to teach has not yet been discovered ; but minor lessons may be learned. One is, that love is as willing to work little miracles as great, and is ready to do as marvellous things in a pantry as in a palace. Nothing that affects a Christian is a matter of indifference to Christ, however small the matter may be. John Newton sings :

" Not one concern of ours is small
    If we belong to Him ;
To teach us this, the Lord of all
    Once made the axe to swim."

The prophet's stick cast into the waters of death (Jordan) resurrected the axe-head, but his staff, laid upon the face of the dead child, failed to resurrect him. The staff was most likely superior, as a work of art, to the stick, but it accomplished nothing. A highly cultured sermon is no doubt much above the simple testimony of an artisan, but the latter may be full of spiritual power, and produce spiritual results, while the former, wanting spiritual power, fails to impart life to dead souls.

Yet another simple lesson is suggested by this miracle. A possibly laudable energy incites these students to enlarge their spiritual borders ; but they make the mistake of descending into a death atmosphere—the Jordan valley. It had been better for them, surely, if they had sought some breezy height, as Abraham, Elijah, and their own master did. Doubtless Elisha's kind consenting to go with them was to secure them from the painful consequences of their self-taught lesson. So self-will in trying to do what in itself may be a Christian work, but in an atmosphere deadly to the soul, results in the loss of all spiritual power, as this student lost that which alone could fell the timber, that is, the axe-head. And then the Christian worker is faced with the hopeless task of shaping out beams for the house of God with an axe handle ! Many Christian people are thus engaged. They have lost the spiritual power that was " lent " to them from on high, and they foolishly try to produce with the handle the results which the head alone can bring to pass. When power is thus lost, in order to regain it the Christian worker must at once hasten to Jesus, as the student did to Elisha, and go with Him to the very place where the power was lost, and the power will be restored in that place of weakness and repentance ; and, not only restored, but given back to him with a new and Divinely fashioned axe handle, that is, a scriptural and experimental equipment that will retain its hold upon the power of God.

A preacher, being challenged as to whether he really believed that the axe-head was made to swim, replied, that he did, because God had made his heart, heavy with a sense of guilt, to swim, and that that was a greater miracle than the other.

These students in theology were about one hundred in number (2 Kings iv. 43) ; they were as insensible to the activity of the Holy Spirit (2 Kings ii. 16) as to the anguish of the prophet's heart (2 Kings ii. 3) ; and not upon one of them did Elijah cast his mantle, but upon the young ploughman (1 Kings xix. 19). They found the Bible-School of the man of God too " strait," so they planned to go to Jordan without him, and there build for themselves an imposing college. As possibly now in some schools, so then, only one per cent. of these divinity students were really loyal to the master, and clung to him.

2 KINGS VI. 8-23.—This portion opens with the hostility of the King of Syria and closes with the benevolence of the King of Israel. Between these two actions occur the Thirteenth, Fourteenth and Fifteenth miracles of Elisha. He first baffles, and then leads, the Syrians. He closes and opens their eyes, prior to which he opens the eyes of his servant.

The servant cries out, "Alas, my master! how shall we do ? " Before entering the service of the greater than Elisha, it is well to count the cost, for fellowship with Him is sure to bring His servant into conflict and trial. But such trials are precious, for the eyes may be opened, and the vision of the horses and chariots of fire, i.e., of the angels, enjoyed ! There is no falsehood in verse 19. It is evident that Elisha went out of the city to meet the bewildered Syrians and said truthfully to them, " This is not the way to the man that ye seek, neither is this the city." Both these statements were true at the moment of speaking. He then added, " Follow me and I will bring you to the man whom ye seek," so (not " but ") he led them to Samaria, where they found the man they

sought, that is, Elisha, and also the king for he was the man they really sought.

The Syrians are feasted right royally instead of being slaughtered, are dismissed to their homes, and the moral effect of this clemency is apparent in their subsequent conduct.

These men sought Elisha in order to destroy him ; he meets their hatred with love and seats them at the banqueting table of that love, and the result is a change of action on their part. Such is the wondrous love of the true Elisha to men in return for the hatred which made them His betrayers and murderers. Grace instead of putting them to death as, like these Syrians, they merited, seats them at the Royal table of heaven and fills them with good things. The moral effect of such grace is then evidenced in a definite break with evil.

2 KINGS VI. 24-VII. 2.—The previous verse says that " the bands of Syria came no more into the land of Israel," but verse 24 immediately says that they did. This seeming contradiction is removed by noticing the word " bands " and the words " all his host." The former means bands of marauders ; the latter, a disciplined army.

Had Ahab, as was his public duty, put Benhadad to death when he was in his power, the sufferings recorded in this passage would have been avoided. This siege and its horrors fulfil the prophecy then made to Ahab by the rebuking prophet.

Asses' flesh was unclean, and the worst part of the carcase was the head, and yet it was sold for upwards of £5, so severe was the famine in the city, and half a pint of guano (doves' dung) for twelve shillings and sixpence.

The killing of her son by this mother is one of the ten instances recorded in the Scriptures of death being occasioned by a woman. The first was Jael, whose action was most just, and the last, Herodias, whose conduct was most unjust.

This whole passage presents a striking illustration of the difference between the profession of a Divine faith and its possession. The statements here made lead to the belief that Elisha promised, on behalf of God, deliverance to Jehoram from the besiegers. Jehoram credits the promise, humbles himself and puts sackcloth on his flesh. But sackcloth on the flesh is not Divine light in the soul, nor is speaking of God with the lips the same thing as knowing God in the Holy Spirit. Jehoram, therefore, first indignantly protests against Elisha's testimony for God, and then despairingly exclaims that it is useless to wait for Him any longer. The words in verse 33, " Behold this evil is of the Lord ; why should I wait for the Lord ? " were no doubt spoken by the king. At the same time he resolves to murder Elisha. Such is the result of professing faith in Christ when the heart is all unchanged.

How amazing is the grace that, in response to the murderous unbelief of the king's heart, and the scornful unbelief of the courtier's, promised such an abundance of food, and so soon that it was to be had almost for nothing. A righteous judgment, however, forbids its enjoyment to the unbelieving captain.

2 KINGS VII. 3-20.—Undesigned co-incidences attesting the accuracy of the Scriptures are always interesting to the spiritual mind. Such a co-incidence is found in verses 7 and 10. An eastern camp is generally arranged with the tents in the centre and the animals tethered around them. Verse 7, therefore, describes the Syrians as leaving their tents, their horses and their asses, while verse 10 speaks of the lepers as reaching the asses, the horses and the tents. The terrified Syrian rushed out of his tent, ran through the animals, and fled. The lepers, on the other hand, passed through the animals, and entered the tents.

The apostle Paul in 1 Cor. i., teaches that God does not choose as messengers of the gospel many persons in high position, but, as a rule, those in a very humble station in life. Those four leprous men illustrate this Divine principle. They were the bearers of a gospel message to the famishing thousands of Samaria. This should encourage all Christian people, no matter how young or poor or ignorant, to be preachers of the gospel.

The lepers pointed out to one another that punishment would overtake them if in such a gladsome day they held their peace. The apostle Paul similarly said that punishment would overtake him if he preached not the gospel.

Grace furnished food to the famishing, and truth ordained death to the unbelieving (v. 20).

2 KINGS VIII. 1-15.—Little did this elect woman think that the love which had

given her back her child would now provide beforehand for her needs and that of her son through the seven years of famine ! But in the land of the Gentile, Israel's Shepherd guards her and keeps her ; and when the period of judgment upon the nation closes, all is given back into her hand that was originally hers, and the very enemies of the kingdom compelled to serve her interests.

Thus is it to-day, with the election of Israel, for this believing woman pictures that beloved election. Israel's Great Shepherd is maintaining her in the land of the Gentile ; and in a soon coming day, when the indignation is overpast, she will be restored to all her ancient glory.

Gehazi appears here as a court chaplain amusing and entertaining an idolatrous king and a corrupt court with stories about Elisha. What a fall from what he once had been ! The princes and courtiers of this world are always willing to listen to preaching that pleases them, but nothing must be said of righteousness, temperance, and judgment to come !

Elisha, obeying the Divine command given to Elijah, comes to Damascus to anoint Hazael king over Syria. In answer to the question respecting the king's illness, he truthfully replies, " he shall surely recover" (R.V.), that is, the illness is not fatal, and there is no reason why he should not recover, but he shall certainly die. Hazael reports the first part of the answer to the king, but not the whole of it.

The expression, " Is thy servant a dog," etc., does not mean, " am I so vile that I should be guilty of murdering my king," but : " can it be that I, who am only a dog, should mount the throne of Syria and accomplish such great deeds ! "

The murder was cleverly effected. In the east it is quite customary to place a wetted cloth upon the face of a fevered patient so as to reduce the fever. Hazael, however, placed it so as to suffocate the king ; and yet would it appear as though the king had died from natural causes.

If Hazael be contrasted with the Shunammite, the lesson appears that planning for self may lead into great evils, but that letting God plan, secures the restoration of all that seemed to have been hopelessly lost.

Hazael blushed ; Elisha wept. The prophet's penetrating eye showed Hazael that his murderous scheme had been revealed by

God to His servant ; but neither Elisha's tears nor words could turn the ambitious murderer from his purposes. So neither Jesus' tears nor words availed to turn the priests from their murderous determination to destroy Him, and bring ruin upon themselves and their city.

2 KINGS VIII. 16–29.—The words, " Jehoshaphat being then king of Judah " are important, because explaining the seeming discrepancy of seven years between this verse and 2 Kings i. 17. It proves, what so often appears in other reigns, that Jehoram governed jointly with his father prior to his father's death.

If 1 Kings xxii. be studied in connection with these facts, it will give ground to believe that Jehoshaphat, anticipating he might lose his life in the battle of Ramoth-Gilead, made his son Jehoram regent, and five or six years later, clothed him with full regal power.

The successful revolt of Edom (v. 20) fulfilled the prophecy of Gen. xxvii. 40.

The battle may be thus described. Joram —not " Jehoram " as in verse 16, for, doing evil in the sight of the Lord, the Holy Spirit elides from his name the Jehovah syllable—Joram with the captains of his chariots and his army, endeavouring to reduce the Edomites to obedience, is surrounded by the latter. Making a great effort, the king, with his force of chariots, breaks through the enemy, and the people, that is, the Israelitish soldiers, flee to their homes. This victory secured the independence of Edom.

The words " unto this day " in verse 22 show that the Holy Spirit caused these records to be written while the kingdom of Judah was yet in existence, and prior, therefore, to the captivity.

The supposed error of one year between verse 25 and chap. ix. 29, is removed by joining the two passages, and so making it clear, that Ahaziah began to reign as associate king with his father in the 11th year of King Jehoram of Israel, and as sole monarch in the following year.

2 Chron. xxii. 2, states that Ahaziah was 42 years of age when he began to reign ; this chapter gives his age as 22. The statements are reconciled by the words being added in 2 Chron., " his mother (Athaliah) was his counsellor to do wickedly." She was the great-grand-daughter of Omri, and her

family was 42 years of age, for Omri began to reign in 832, and 42 years later, that is in 790, Ahaziah ascended the throne. As representing the house of David he was 22 years of age ; as representing that of Omri, 42. The two ages express the distinction in him physically and morally. He was the agent of the 42-year-old house of Omri, but he was a willing and responsible agent, and hence justly credited with the age of that family. 'Hebrew scholars point out that the original text reads, " a son of 42 years was Ahaziah ", that is, the son of a family that at the time had practised evil for 42 years. God can add 20 years to the moral age of a king as he can deduct 20 from his physical age ; an example of this latter is recorded in 1 Samuel xiii. 1.

If all things are caused to work together for good to them that love God, so are they permitted to work together for evil to them that hate Him ; and therefore it was that in His providence circumstances were overruled, so that these two kings were brought together at Naboth's vineyard in order to their suffering a just and predicted doom.

2 KINGS IX.—The judgment of the house of Ahab now commences. Jehu is the Divine instrument chosen to execute that judgment. He illustrates how zealous an unconverted man can be for God when it suits his personal interests and ambitions to attack national evils. What he did on behalf of righteousness he did well and with energy. But his zeal was carnal ; he utterly destroyed Baal, but permitted the golden calves to exist. This fact shows that his heart was a stranger to a Divine faith. God recognises his zeal, for the chapter reveals God in outward government, and not in judgment of the secrets of Jehu's heart.

Elisha anoints Jehu and thus obeys the command given to Elijah. Some do not understand why this one action should be the action of two prophets. But Elijah and Elisha form a unity ; for only of Elisha, as a prophet, is it said he should be " in the room of " Elijah. Both prophets represent Christ. Elijah, Christ as a minister of the first covenant, prior to the cross ; and Elisha, Christ as a minister of the new covenant, subsequent to Pentecost.

The obedience and courage of the young prophet is striking. He takes his life in his hands in executing this command. Elisha in love to him commands him, directly he fulfils his commission, to flee and tarry not.

In verse 8 there are two figures of speech which occur frequently in the historic books and which need explanation. They are: " I will cut off from Ahab him,' etc., and " him that is shut up and left in Israel." The first means every male child, for boys of tender age in the east wear little or no clothing, and hence the action is that of a child ; the other expresses an able-bodied man, whether "shut up" in a garrison or " left " on patrol duty in the open country. The two sentences, therefore, give a vivid picture of the total destruction of the family of Ahab.

The conduct of the officers over whom Jehu was commander-in-chief, was similar to that of officers of the present day. They contemptuously call the servant of God a crack-brained fellow ; but directly they learn the substance of his message, their superstitious fears, uniting with their self-interests, prompt them to immediate action. They place their uniform coats on the topmost step of the outside stairway which led to the roof of the house, thus making a kind of throne ; they seat the commander-in-chief on it, so that he may be seen by all the soldiers ; and they proclaim him king.

The word " whoredoms " in verse 22 means " idolatries," and is to be so understood throughout the books of the Old Testament, except where the context clearly states otherwise ; and in the following verse the words "he turned his hands", means in order to wheel his chariot round ; and, further, the words in verse 24 " between his arms " mean " between his shoulders."

The latter part of verse 25 may read thus : " Remember, how that when I and thou rode together after Ahab his father, Jehovah pronounced this doom against him " (Ahab) ; saying, " Surely," etc. Jehu here paraphrases the terrible message given to Ahab by Elijah after the murder of Naboth. The fourfold repetition of the name " Jehovah," coupled with the sentence " according to the word of Jehovah," add to the solemnity of the action of casting the dead body of the king upon the very piece of ground which the vineyard of Naboth formerly occupied, and attest the fulfilment of the prophecy.

The death of the king of Judah is fancied by some to be otherwise here related than in 2 Chron. If, however, the two records be united, harmony results. Ahaziah flees in his chariot to Samaria ; hides there, but finding his hiding-place discovered, he flees again ; is overtaken ; brought back as a prisoner to Jehu ; is condemned by him to death ; is accordingly mortally wounded in his chariot ; his servants are permitted to take him away to Jerusalem ; and he expires on arriving at the village of Megiddo.

Jezebel heard of the murder of the king, her grandson, by Jehu, and accordingly dressing herself as the queen, she tries to over-awe Jehu, and at the same time by reminding him of Zimri and his fate, suggests to him the wisdom of coming to terms with her. But it is useless to appeal to an unconverted man inflamed with religious zeal and excited by personal interest. Jezebel is thrown down ; the horses are splashed with her blood ; the very dogs turn from the skull and hands and feet that had designed and executed such abominations ; and no tomb but infamy perpetuates her memory.

2 KINGS X.—Jezreel, the scene of the cruel murder of Naboth and his sons, becomes the theatre of the just wrath of God upon the murderers. Here may be learned something of how God regards sin and judges it ; and if in long-suffering grace He delays the judgment, yet does the long-suffering heighten the terror of the Divine anger. In harmony with this, how appalling is the expression in the book of Revelation, " the wrath of the Lamb !"—not the wrath of the Lion, but " the wrath of the Lamb."

Man can be very zealous for God and yet not know Him ; but this zeal only goes as far as it suits personal interests, or religious and political opinions. The Spanish Conquerors of South America illustrate the truth of this ; and to-day multitudes of Protestants are very zealous in promoting the expansion of the gospel, but are strangers personally to the converting grace of the Saviour presented in the gospel. Like Jehu, the zeal of such persons only lasts so long as it suits themselves.

Ahaziah, Joash, and Amaziah all died violent deaths ; and these three kings are omitted in the Lord's genealogy in Matt. i.

The term " sons " in verse 1, as is the case so often in the Bible, includes grandsons and great-grandsons.

Jehonadab was a Kenite, a descendant of the father-in-law of Moses. His descendants

honourably appear in Jer. xxxv. He gave
his hand to Jehu as a pledge of fidelity, and
not merely to be helped up into the chariot.

The word " city " in verse 25 means the
innermost part of a town or of a house. It
represents the citadel of the former or the
innermost chamber of the latter. The statement therefore is, that the captains, in order
that none of the priests or worshippers should
escape, penetrated even into the most sacred
chamber, of the Temple of Baal. The temple
was made a draught house, that is, a re-
ceptacle for the sewage of the city.

In fulfilment of the promise of verse 30,
Jehu was succeeded by Jehoahaz, Joash,
Jeroboam II and Zechariah. His was the
longest dynasty in all Israel.

An Assyrian inscription, now in the
British Museum, records that Jehu bought
off Shalmanezer II with bars of gold and
silver, and with golden goblets and pitchers
and a golden ladle. This testimony from
Assyria accords with the closing verses of
this chapter, which state that God began to
chasten Jehu because he took no heed to
walk in His law, and to destroy the golden
calves.

2 KINGS XI.—The facts related in this
chapter illustrate past, present, and future
prophecy. A false religious power (Athaliah)
obtains the mastery; the true king is slain; his
child is raised up from among the dead, then
hidden for six years in the Temple of God ; in
the seventh year he comes forth ; takes to
himself his kingdom ; the usurper is slain ;
peace reigns ;   and all the people rejoice.
This is Messianic history and promise. By
wicked men Christ was crucified and slain ;
God raised Him from the dead ; He is now
hidden in the heavens, the true Temple of
God ; in the morning of the seventh year,
that is, the millennium, He will appear, and
taking to Himself His great power which has
already been given to Him, but not yet
exercised by Him, He will ascend the throne
of Jehovah at Jerusalem and reign before His
ancients gloriously, having cast out of His
kingdom all things that cause stumbling
and them that work iniquity.

Athaliah, daughter of Jezebel, and equally
ambitious and able, destroyed, that is, she
believed she destroyed, the entire Royal
family. Jehosheba, wife of Jehoiada the
high priest, was sister to the late king, and
therefore, aunt to the infant Joash. She

must have been a woman of nerve and ability.
Verse 2 says that she stole the infant prince
from among the kings' sons that were slain.
It was a courageous act on her part to enter
such a slaughter-house. It may be assumed
that she did so to look with grief and horror
upon her murdered nephews and cousins.
The infant Joash lay among them apparently
dead ; she found him still living, stole him,
and hid him.

The words " from among " in verse 2 are
expressive, they are used of Christ. He was
raised " from among " the dead, and hidden
with God on high.

The Temple was the safest place in which
to hide the child, for 2 Chron. xxiv. 7 states
that it had been broken up, and everything
removed to the house of Baal. Hence the
Temple was quite deserted ; and the bedchamber, that is, the chamber in which the
bedding was stored, was the safest chamber
in this hiding-place. This was one of the
chambers built against the side of the House
of God by king Solomon.

The six years of Athaliah's reign and the
true king's absence, picture what the apostle
calls " man's day," as contrasted with " the
day of the Lord." The number six in the
Bible is associated with man. He was created
on the 6th day ; Goliath had six pieces of
armour ;   six instruments formed Nebuchadnezzar's band ;   and the name of Anti-
Christ will be a computation of three sixes.

The steps taken by Jehoiada to bring about
this royal revolution may be thus paraphrased. He sends for the officers of the
Royal bodyguard, the Carites (R.V.) ; these
mercenaries came from Caria in Asia Minor.
They are mentioned by Herodotus as forming
the bodyguard of Ptsammeticus, king of
Egypt. One regiment was ordered by the
high priest to surround the king's house, and
the two remaining regiments to parade in
front of the Temple. Any person attempting
to force their way through the troops, was
to be put to death. The guard relieved on
that morning (v. 9) was not to return to
barracks, but to fall in with the relieving
guard and join the main body in defence of
the king. The infant prince was then
brought forth, the crown put upon his head,
and the Bible placed in his hand. This was
the very book written by Moses himself
(Exod. xvii. 14, Deut. xvii. 18, 2 Chron.
xxxiv. 14).

The word " ranges " in verse 15 mean the

ranks of the soldiery ; and the words " they laid hands on her " in verse 16, mean that the soldiers with their hands made a way for her, and thus protected her from the people, who apparently would have lynched her. She reached the horse-entry to the royal palace and there was put most justly to death.

The king now cast out of his kingdom all things that caused stumbling ; that is, the altars and images and temples of Baal, breaking them thoroughly, and put to death him that worked iniquity, that is, Mattan, the priest of Baal. The city and the people of the land rejoiced. So will it be when the Prince of Peace appears. Till then, not-withstanding the Hague Court of Arbitration, the nations will never enjoy either peace or prosperity. He Himself states in Matt. xxiv. 7, that the entire period of His absence will be marked by war and misery.

2 KINGS XII.—Joash pictures one of those men who, so long as they have at their side a strong Christian personality like Jehoiada, appear to be really converted, but directly they lose this support, it is seen that they are destitute of personal spiritual life ; and sooner or later active hostility is shown. to faithful reprovers, just as this ungrateful king murdered the son of his benefactor. In 2 Chron. xxiv. 25 the word " sons " is found. For an explanation of this seeming discrepancy see the comments upon that chapter.

There was not sufficient energy in the soul of Jehoiada to abolish the worship upon the high places, as commanded by the Bible. It was not idolatrous worship, but it. was for-bidden by God for many reasons, one, no doubt, being that it militated against the unity of the nation, and also that it favoured a relapse to idolatry. There was to be but one centre of worship for Israel, as there is but one place of worship for the Christian, that is, Calvary. To Israel, Christ is " the Lamb slain from the foundation of the world " ; to the Church, He is " the Lamb slain from before the foundation of the world."

There are three sources of income pointed to in verse 4. First, " the money of everyone that passeth the account," that is, the poll tax of Exod. xxx. 12 ; second, " the money that every man is set at," that is, the re-demption money of Lev. xxvii. ; and third, " all the money that cometh into any man's

heart to bring," that is, the ordinary free-will-offerings legislated for in Leviticus. The " trespass money " and " sin money " (v. 16), was not used for the repairing of the Temple, but handed to the priests in obedience to Lev. xv. and Num. v.—a beautiful instance of knowledge of, and fidelity to, the Word of of God. How different Israel's history would. have been, and also the fortunes of this king, had that infallible Word been alway obeyed !

The chest spoken of in verse 9, is not the chest spoken of in 2 Chron. xxiv. 8. The one chest was placed inside the Temple by Jehoiada ; the other, outside, by the king. The one had a lid with holes in it for the reception of coined money ; the other was a large box to receive valuables of all kinds. That within the Temple was to hold the money spoken of in verse 4 ; that without the Temple, to receive gifts in kind, similar to those invited by Moses from the congrega-tion in the Wilderness (2 Chron. xxiv. 9).

Hazael, as the rod of God, smites Jerusalem twice : verses 17 and 18 record his first attack, and 2 Chron. xxiv. 23 his second.

In verse 18 the king is named Jehoash, that is, " the fire of Jehovah," but in verse 19 his name is degraded to Joash, i.e., " fire." Why ? The murder of Zechariah !

2 KINGS XIII.—The wrath of Jehovah is the subject of verse 3 ; the compassion of Jehovah, of verse 23 ; the gift of Jehovah (a saviour) verse 5 ; and the principle which turned away the wrath and provided a saviour, was not the existence of any moral worthiness in Israel, for she had none, but the unconditional covenant made with Abraham, as stated in verse 23. " For Abraham's sake," " for David's sake," " for Jonathan's sake," all illustrate the principle of Ephes. iv. 32, " for Christ's sake." This great principle of salvation gives all the glory to the Saviour and none to the person saved.

The saviour spoken of in verse 5, coupling that verse with the 25th, may be assumed to have been a skilful military general, doubtless Jeroboam ii. (xiv. 27).

The fidelity with which the ten tribes clung to the worship of the golden calf, rebukes and instructs the Christian. Rebukes, for, alas; how defective is the loyalty of even the most saintly person to Christ ; and instructs, for it makes clear that Jehovah Elohim was not a Divinity invented by the Israelites, as some think, for had that been so, then would they have served Him faithfully; but the fact that they were continually forsaking Him and turning to idols, and that there was perpetual contention between them and God, proves the testimony of the Bible that the God of Israel is God over all, blessed for ever.

The seeming discrepancy of one year between verse 10 of this chapter and the first verses respectively of chapters xii. and xiv. is at once removed by making Amaziah associate king in the 39th year of his father's reign; that is, one year before Joash died. The reason for this co-regency may be found in the " great diseases " of 2 Chron. xxiv. 25.

Elisha falls sick and dies of the sickness. This is how, as a rule, ordinary men die. Some excellent and most Christian people believe that true servants of God are never afflicted with sickness, and cannot be, because all sickness comes from the Devil. But Elisha was a true servant of God, and yet he fell sick and died of the sickness!

This great prophet's ministry lasted for about sixty-six years. The first twenty years appear to have been active years, closing with the anointing of Hazael. Then follows a long silence of forty-five years, and he now once more appears, but very sick, and dying. The grace that marked his ministry shines brightly in his last message of mercy and victory. He places his hands upon the king's hands to make it clear that the victory would be wholly of grace and from God, and that it would be absolutely certain. The faith, however, in the heart of the king, divided as it was between Jehovah and the golden calf, was necessarily feeble, and moved the grief and indignation of the mighty heart that loved the people and thirsted for their complete deliverance.

So great was the energy of life in Elisha's testimony, that he, though dead, restores life to a corpse. How often is this seen, in principle, to-day! A mighty prophet of the Lord—a Wesley or a Moody—dies, but years after they are dead, multitudes revive into life eternal through contact with that which remains of them—their books—or, as in this case, his, i.e., Elisha's bones.

The resurrection wrought by contact with Elisha's bones gives the comforting instruction that, while apparently dead to Israel, the true Elisha is still the vessel of life to that beloved people; and that He will in a future day, restore them to life, in a manner as unexpected and powerful, directly they come in contact with Him.

This was Elisha's sixteenth and last miracle. It was wrought after he was dead.

2 KINGS XIV.—See notes on 2 Chron. xxv.

The seeming discrepancy of one year that appears in verse 1 has been explained in the previous chapter. It may be added here that the Bible method of counting parts of years for complete years, must not be overlooked; and that the so-called chronological difficulties in the Holy Scriptures arise, not from imperfection in the text, but from the absence of fuller information.

Amaziah did that which was right in the sight of the Lord, yet not like his progenitor David, but like his father Joash; that is, he began well and ended badly.

His loyalty to the Bible, as narrated in verse 6, not only proves that the Law existed at this time, but is a beautiful instance of obedience to the written Word of God.

The Holy Spirit has given to man four histories of the life, death, and resurrection of Christ. This He did by design. He also has been pleased to inspire three records of the kings of Judah. These three records are found in the Books of Kings and of Chronicles and in the prophecies of Isaiah, Amos, and Hosea. The first record, that is, Kings, sets out the actions of these monarchs; the prophets contain the messages sent to them; and Chronicles is a Divine commentary upon their conduct in relation to those messages. Studying, therefore, the history of these kings upon that principle, rich lessons respecting God and His thoughts, and of His overruling man's plans and actions, may be learnt.

The spiritual lessons of this reign are too evident to need comment.

Amaziah's son, called Azariah and also Uzziah, both names having a similar meaning, was " made king " (v .21) when sixteen years old. He was three years old at the date of his father's murder. This appears plain from verse 1 of chapter xv. There was, therefore, a regency that lasted for thirteen years.

The prosperous reign of Jeroboam ii. seemingly conflicts with the fact that he worshipped the golden calf, but verses 25, 26, 27 and 28 reveal the profound depths of love and grace in the heart of God towards His erring children. Guilty and rebellious as they were, He promised them a saviour by the word of the prophet Jonah, " for He saw the affliction of Israel that it was very bitter." The promised saviour was doubtless Jeroboam ii. (xiii. 5), for under him the northern kingdom enjoyed very great prosperity.

" From the entering of Hamath unto the sea of the plain," means from a pass between Lebanon and Hermon to the Dead Sea.

" Shut up or left " may mean there was neither urban nor rural population (v. 26). See note on ix. 8.

2 KINGS XV.—The Syrian having been defeated, the Assyrian now appears. So has it ever been, and so is it to-day. There is a faith which can overcome one moral enemy, but the removal of that foe only makes room for the entrance of another. Such a faith is not a faith that is born of God, for whatsoever is born of God overcomes both the Syrian and the Assyrian.

It refreshes the heart to hear the Holy Spirit say " he did that which was right ; " but it saddens the heart to hear the sorrowful word " howbeit ! " Happy the Christian in whose record, as written on high, there is no " howbeit ! "

The fact of Uzziah's leprosy is here recorded ; the reason for it is given in 2 Chron. xxvi.

The death of this Royal leper taught Isaiah that he was a moral leper, and needed Divine cleansing. (See Notes on Isa. vi).

At this period the prophets Hosea, Joel, Amos, Micah, Isaiah and Jonah exercised their ministry. Their prophecies should be studied in connection with the history of these kings. They foretold the doom of both the Northern and Southern kingdoms. Hosea followed Elisha..

Between certain of these kings of Judah and Israel there were interregnums. Information as to these will be found in the " Companion Bible."

The statement, " Jeroboam . . . who made Israel to sin " occurs twenty-one times in the Holy Scriptures. How exceedingly solemn that the Holy Spirit should record this one fact twenty-one times ! It is possible for a professing Christian to set up in his life a sin which, hundreds of years after he is dead, will lead others into sin ; for the sin of Jeroboam gave birth to sins in his own life and in the lives of those who followed him.

Zachariah's enthronement and death fulfilled two prophecies ; the one is found in 2 Kings x. 30 ; the other in Amos vii. 9.

The Pul of verse 19 and the Tiglath-pileser of verse 29 are one and the same monarch. Hence 1 Chron. v. 26 should read thus : " The God of Israel stirred up the spirit of Pul, king of Assyria, even the spirit of Tiglath-pileser king of Assyria " etc. The first name Pul is possibly a throne name, similar to Czar ; the second, a personal and later name. Recently discovered tablets confirm this. These tablets also record the names of several of these Jewish kings, and help to determine the dates of their respective reigns.

Verse 33 states that Jotham reigned sixteen years, but verse 30 records the usurpation of Hosea in the twentieth year of Jotham. This seeming error is removed by the statement in verse 5 that Jotham judged the people during his father's dreadful illness.

2 KINGS XVI.—In all that the Holy Spirit says about King Ahaz in the Books of Kings, Chronicles, and Isaiah there is a throbbing of anguish which the reader can feel, and also a note of indignation ; as, for example, in the words " this is that king Ahaz " (2 Chron. xxviii. 22). His full name as appears in the Assyrian state records was Jehoahaz (i.e., the possession of Jehovah), but the Spirit of God strikes the Jehovah syllable out of his name, and invariably calls him " Ahaz," i.e., " possession." Such was his life, he was led and influenced and possessed by anyone or anything except God.

His history illustrates how disastrous it is for the spiritual profit of a man when his own plans succeed. God, through Isaiah, earnestly counselled him not to invite the king of Assyria to help him against the confederate kings of Israel and Damascus. He, however, followed his own counsel, and with success ; but the ultimate result was ruin.

Not only did he worship the golden calf of the kings of Israel, but he introduced the horrible religion of Moloch, the god of fire, the red-hot iron arms of whose image received and burned alive helpless little children in thousands. And he completed his apostasy by displacing the great brazen altar of God's appointment, and setting up in its stead a pagan altar inspired from Damascus.

The notes on Isaiah vii. and viii. should be read in connection with this chapter

So determined was Ahaz in his opposition to the Bible, that not only did he send to Urijah the high priest a sketch of the idolatrous altar that he saw at Damascus, but he also sent with it a model ; for that is the import of the words (v. 10) " the fashion of the altar and the pattern of it."

Urijah the priest was as guilty as Ahaz the king.

The words " the altar," (v. 14), means the new idolatrous altar, and in verse 15 it is called the " great altar." But the true altar, God's great altar of brass, was thrust aside " to enquire by "—that is, in time of need when help was needed, for heathen altars are voiceless (1 Kings xviii). When a false god is set up in the heart what room is there for anything that belongs to Jesus ?

The degradation of the laver in verse 17 illustrates the hostility of man's heart to the great Bible doctrine of the new birth. It is to this doctrine that the apostle Paul refers in Titus iii. 5, where he states that the sinner is saved and cleansed, not in a material laver of Solomon's Temple, but in the spiritual laver of a new birth operated by the Holy Spirit.

Verse 18 is a difficult one. It appears to mean that a building inside the Temple area, having some relation to the Temple itself, was divorced from that purpose and fitted up as a palace for the king of Assyria. This would harmonize with the following verse which speaks of the rest of the acts of Ahaz. And what was the principal one of these acts ? It was the shutting up of the House of God, as related in 2 Chron. So is it ever in the spiritual life. If provision be made for the world in connection with Divine worship, then in a short time that worship will cease. The building, that is, the outward form, will remain, but it will be a dead form.

There was more than one occasion upon which Judah went down to ally herself with Israel, but never one instance of Israel going up to ally herself with Judah. The reign of Ahaz shows the bitter fruit that follows from such a " going down." Friendship bought at the expense of truth gains nothing but contention and spiritual weakness.

A comparison of verse 2 of this chapter with verse 2 of chapter xviii. makes it clear that Ahaz was between ten and eleven when his son Hezekiah was born. There is no improbability in this to Eastern peoples, and even in Western nations the marriage of children occurs. Henry II. of France and his wife were married at fourteen years of age. This age in Europe would correspond to ten or eleven in Asia.

2 KINGS XVII.—Even a dull nature must feel the sorrow that speaks in this chapter. The long-suffering of God is forced to an end by twenty wicked kings, and two hundred and sixty-five years of national rebellion, after repeated messages of love and warning.

The ten tribes were carried away beyond Damascus, as predicted by Amos, and are exiles to the present day. The remaining tribes were temporarily exiled to Babylon, as predicted by Jeremiah, but ultimately carried away beyond Babylon, as foretold by Stephen (Acts. vii. 43).

There was anarchy for nine years between Pekah and Hoshea. This solves the difficulty which has been supposed to exist between verse 1 of chapter xvi. and verse 1 of chapter xvii.

From the statement in verse 2, coupled with his tacit permission of the invitation of 2 Chron. xxx. 5-11, it may be, perhaps, concluded that Hoshea took no interest in religious controversies, or was a sceptic.

Including the statements of chapter xviii. 9-12, and noticing the important word " they " in verse 10 of that chapter, the historic incidents of the present chapter may be thus understood : Shalmanezer, king of Assyria, and So, king of Egypt, contend for the over-lordship of Palestine. After some years of unrest, Hoshea becomes king of Samaria as vassal to Assyria. But, suspected of secretly treating with the king of Egypt, he is called to account by Shalmanezer, found guilty, and imprisoned for life. The Assyrian king then marches into Palestine, and, after a three years siege, captures Samaria. During the siege, Shalmanezer dies. He is succeeded by Sargon. The city being captured, "they" (xviii. 10), that is, the Assyrian generals, instructed by Sargon, carry the inhabitants captive to Armenia.

The justice of this judgment is set out in verses 7-23. The downward course of every backslider is indicated by the secret sins of verse 9, to be soon followed by the public abandonment of all the commandments of God.

The next section of the chapter occupies verses 24-33. It describes the five nations, with their five gods, that the Assyrian government placed in the north of Palestine and Samaria. In the Bible an idol is called a "lover," i.e., a "husband." Idolatry is, therefore, called "adultery." Samaria, together with an outward worship of Jehovah, was devoted to these five idols, or "husbands." It was to God a hateful medley. No wonder that the Lord said to the Samaritan woman, in John iv., that she worshipped she knew not what. Her actual and personal conduct illustrated the nation; for Jesus said to her: "Thou hast had five husbands, and he whom thou now hast is not thy husband, i.e., the God of "our father Jacob," whom the nation professed to worship. He then presents Himself to her heart as the true husband, and immediately a striking picture follows of a happy nuptial day that yet awaits the Samaritan. See notes on John iv.

The next section of the chapter, that is, verses 34–40, concerns the ten tribes; the last verse of the chapter, the Samaritans. This helps to remove the difficulty apparent between verses 33 and 34. Verse 33 states "they feared Jehovah," verse 34, "they fear not Jehovah." Verse 33 intends the Samaritans; verse 34, the Israelites. The last three words of verse 23, "unto this day," connect with the first three words of verse 34, "unto this day." This fact makes it clear that, even in captivity, the banished tribes retained the worship of the golden calf.

A Divine principle appears between verses 33 and 34. The Samaritan outwardly worshipped God, though still worshipping his national deity; and that worship of God is recognized. The Israelite outwardly worshipped God, but, at the same time, the golden calf. That worship of God is not recognized. This is striking and very solemn. God gave a revelation to Israel, the Bible; hence she was responsible, and was intended to share that revelation with the Gentile. She did not do so. The Gentile, therefore, not having received this revelation, did not stand in the same position of responsibility to God. Hence, God in His love and pity accepted the dim worship of the Samaritan and rejected the mixed worship of the Israelite. From this it may be deduced that, at the present day, God may accept the bewildered worship of a Mohammedan whilst rejecting the medley worship of a Roman or a Greek Catholic. Thus we have in this chapter the origin of the Samaritan nation that is so often met with in the New Testament.

The expulsion of the Israelites from God's pleasant land, and the introduction into it by God, of lions, shows that both the people and the land belonged to Him. Because the people were His people, therefore He carried them away; and because the land was His land, therefore He brought the lions in. It is quite true, as stated in Exodus xxiii. 29, that lions naturally multiply owing to the waste of a population, but the Holy Spirit states in verse 25 of this chapter that the lions were instruments of God's discipline and teaching. Thus this passage, which many find perplexing, presents no difficulties to an intelligent reader. On the contrary, it teaches him the faithfulness of God to the people and to the land, both which He chose for His peculiar treasure.

2 KINGS XVIII.—From the accession of Hezekiah to the Captivity, the Assyrian and the Babylonian overshadow the house of David, and call forth those exercises of heart which are painful to the flesh but profitable to the spirit. These enemies appeared because of Israel's unfaithfulness. So is it in the Christian life. Fidelity to the Lord, and to His precious Book, saves the Christian from those trials which a want of fidelity surely brings; and yet the pitying love and wisdom of God may use these very griefs as instruments of spiritual enrichment to those who, like Hezekiah and Josiah, really love Him, though that love be imperfect.

Hezekiah began his reign as a vassal of the king of Assyria, by whom he was placed upon the throne during the lifetime of his father Ahaz. In verse 7 it is recorded that he rebelled against that monarch, and defeated the Philistines. The completeness of his victory over these people is shown in the expression "from the tower of the watchman to the fenced city." The watchman's tower is placed in desolate districts; the fenced city is a populous centre. The expression therefore means that the entire country was smitten.

This victory over the Philistine, who was an internal enemy, and the later victory over the Assyrian, who was an external enemy, illustrate the fact that victory over both inward and outward temptation is promised to the overcomer.

The statement in verse 4 that the king brake in pieces the brazen serpent, calling it contemptuously "Nehushtan," that is, "a bit of brass," is very important. This bit of brass was already eight hundred and thirty-five years old, and though originally set up by God, as a symbol, had become an object of worship—so prone is the heart to idolatry. The Holy Spirit here records the action of Hezekiah with approval. Were this true man of God now living he would no doubt destroy in like manner the Paschal Supper, because it has become an idolatrous sacrament.

If it be objected that the words "unto those days," of verse 4 cannot be true, the answer is that Stephen in Acts vii pointed out to the Sanhedrin that the Israelites, from the commencement of their history right up to the captivity, were idolators, secretly or publicly—secretly, no doubt, when good kings such as David reigned, and publicly when such restraint was withdrawn.

In the following verse the same praise is given to him as to Josiah in chapter xxiii. 25. Some may regard these verses as conflicting with each other. The respective contexts, however, show there is no disagreement. Hezekiah exceeded all other kings as a believer, Josiah as a reformer. Attention is drawn to the one king because of the exercises of his heart under great trials; and to the other king, because of the energies of his hand in judging great evils.

The little word "they" in verse 10, already noticed in the prior chapter, is one of the many undesigned evidences of the accuracy of sacred history. Verse 9 states that Shalmanezer began the siege of Samaria, but that his generals captured the city. This harmonizes with recent excavations, which reveal that this Assyrian king died during the course of the siege. This passage from verse 9 to verse 12, repeating as it does information already given in the prior chapter, is no doubt introduced designedly by the Holy Spirit as a solemn reminder to the house of David, and to Christian people of to-day, that God has the same controversy with evil, and will judge it with a like judgment, whether it be practised by the followers of David or of Jeroboam.

Hezekiah's connection with Assyria, and his double victory over its king, may be thus outlined. Ahaz, having become a vassal of Assyria and sent presents, that is, paid tribute, associated Hezekiah with himself in the throne, a year prior to his death. Hezekiah in his time was also a vassal to the Assyrian ; but in the fourteenth year of his reign, he rebelled. On the approach, however, of the Assyrians on their way to conquer Egypt, he expressed regret to the king for his conduct and paid him the sum of £1,000,000 as tribute money. Sennacherib accepted the apology, and resumed his march toward Egypt. On hearing, however, that Hezekiah was strengthening the fortifications at Jerusalem (2 Chron. xxxii. 5), he dispatched his commander-in-chief with two other high officials and a great army to Jerusalem, not wishing doubtless to have a fortified city in his rear. This action was deemed by Isaiah (xxxiii. 1) a breach of faith. The Assyrian host encamped at Jerusalem, and with insulting language the city was called upon to capitulate. Hezekiah, being assured by Isaiah that if he confided in Jehovah he would be delivered, refused to surrender ; and just as all hope seemed to be gone, a message from Sennacherib reached the Assyrian army ordering it to rejoin him at all speed, for the king of Egypt was advancing to attack him with a great host. The Assyrian army accordingly struck camp, rejoined Sennacherib, defeated the Egyptians, and marched victoriously towards that land. In the meantime Sennacherib sent a violent letter to Hezekiah telling him it was folly to trust in his God, and that the Assyrians would speedily return and destroy him and his city. But on that very night a mysterious plague destroyed in his camp 185,000 men. Terrified by this crushing stroke, and dreading the vengeance of his enemies, he returned "by the way that he came," i.e., by the eastern bank of Jordan, to his own land, and was there murdered by his sons. It is not without interest to the Christian that the State Records of Egypt and Assyria, so far as they have been recovered, confirm the foregoing facts.

The repetition of Hezekiah's name in verse 16 emphasizes a lesson. The very Hezekiah who overlaid the pillars of the Temple of Jehovah with gold, was the very same Hezekiah who cut off the gold and sent it to the Assyrian king as tribute. Unbelief is costly, and compromise seldom delivers. Had Hezekiah trusted fully he would not have lost his wealth, and he would have been spared much anxiety.

The Assyrian captain added to Hezekiah's perplexity by pointing out to him (v. 25) the existence of a Divine prophecy authorizing the Assyrian king to destroy the land of Israel. This is very wonderful, for it shows that the message of Isaiah x. had reached as far as Assyria.

There is instruction to be had in verse 36. There are occasions when faith stands silent before human boasting and violence, content to lean back upon God and whisper all into His gracious ear. This brings victory, for in the multitude of words, even in Christian lips, there wanteth not sin.

2 KINGS XIX.—The prophet Isaiah here appears for the first time on the pages of the Bible.

Verse 7 reads in the R.V. : " Behold I will put a spirit in him," i.e., a spirit of cowardice and fear, so that the rumour, that is, the serious report that was to reach him, would unnerve him. The report in question was no doubt the approach of the Egyptian army, which necessitated the retirement of Rab-shakeh from Jerusalem. The prophecy of this verse overleaps the victory over the Egyptians, with the subsequent mysterious destruction of the Assyrian host, and foretells the hasty return of the king to Assyria, and his death there.

Satan caused two letters to be written to Hezekiah. The first, a violent one from the king of Assyria; the second, a kind one from the king of Babylon. The first drove him to the Lord, the second drew him from the Lord. Satan is much more to be feared as a kind friend than as a roaring lion.

Verse 15 is one of the very large number of verses in the Old Testament proving that, from the beginning of their history, Jehovah was not to Israel's consciousness and belief a Tribal God, as some learned men believe, but was the one and only and living God—the God not only of the whole earth, but also of the heavens.

The second message of the prophet Isaiah is a double one—verses 21-28 contain the message to Sennacherib, verses 29-34 the message to Hezekiah.

In the first message, God rebukes the boasting monarch by pointing out 'o him (v. 25) that, before he was born, God had purposed and planned to employ him as His rod of wrath against the nations whom he had conquered, and whose gods he had cast into the fire. This fact, therefore, deprived the king of any claim to self-congratulation.

Verse 25, though understood by many to refer to the Creation, may be thus read : " Hast thou not heard how, long ago, I planned it, and, before you were born, I purposed it. Now have I brought it to pass that thou shouldst," etc. (See Isa. x. 5, twenty-eight years earlier).

The message to Hezekiah in verse 29 foretold him that for two years public affairs would be so disturbed that it would be impossible to till the land, but that God would cause it to bring forth sufficient food to sustain them during that period, and that in the third year there would be such general security that they would be enabled both to sow and to reap.

The R.V. makes an interesting change in verse 32 of the word " into." The sentence accordingly reads : " He shall not come *unto* this city." This is repeated in verse 33. Thus Hezekiah was assured that the dreaded enemy, far from returning to Jerusalem as he had boasted, would not be permitted by God to come even in sight of it ; and so it came to pass.

The Divine principle, that God forgives sin for Christ's sake, and not because of any worthiness discoverable in the sinner, appears in verse 34. Not because of any moral beauty in Hezekiah did God deliver Jerusalem, but for His Own sake, and for David's sake, i.e., the true David, Christ. This principle reappears in verse 6 of chapter xx. The Bible does not set out to prove the existence of God, nor to explain the grace of God in election. It simply states these great facts.

The words in verse 35 : " when they arose early in the morning," and the words " dead corpses " in the same verse, perplex some people. For, if they were dead, how could they arise early in the morning ! and, further, what is a dead corpse ? The answer is simple, " when men (R.V.) arose in the morning, etc.", and the Hebrews have two words, one meaning an insensible corpse, the other, a dead corpse, or, as is said to-day, a dead body.

Ancient history records that Sennacherib bequeathed his throne to his youngest son Esarhaddon, and in order to gain the favour of his god, promised to sacrifice the two elder sons to that divinity. These sons, doubtless prompted by fear on the one hand and by jealousy on the other, murdered their father in the December of that year, but six months later were obliged to flee into Armenia, to escape the vengeance of Esarhaddon. Sennacherib's Will, bestowing the throne upon this son, has been recently discovered, and is now in the British Museum.

2 KINGS XX.—Chronologically, the events of this chapter precede those of chapters xviii. and xix. (beginning at verse 13 of chapter xviii.) This is a principle that constantly appears in the Holy Scriptures. For example, in the Gospel of Luke the healing of Bartimæus precedes the conversion of Zacchæus; in point of time it followed it. This is designed, because the purpose of the Bible is not to record historic facts, though the record of the facts is infallible, but to teach spiritual lessons. So is it here; and the lesson is both sweet and humbling. It is sweet, because it reveals the grace that hastens immediately to place before the reader the precious faith which Hezekiah had in God in days of darkness and fear—a faith that called forth the praise recorded in chapter xviii. 5; humbling, because the Holy Spirit does not fail to go back and record the weakness, and folly, and self-will of the king prior to these days of trust and victory.

Another example of this Divine principle of displacement is found in Isa. lii. 13, where the Holy Spirit overleaps the sufferings of Christ and hastens to point to His glories, afterwards returning to the subject of His sufferings.

It is difficult to gather from the sacred text why Hezekiah was unwilling to die. Putting together the statements of this chapter, of 2 Chron. xxxii. and of Isa. xxxviii., it might be concluded that he feared to die because he was a sinner, or that he refused to die because he was a successful revivalist, or that he was disappointed in dying because he was not to witness the Advent of the promised Redeemer. The language of Isa. xxxviii. 17 suggests that he feared to die because of his sins, and that he had been living in a false peace which the approach of death destroyed. His words in this chapter express possibly the petulance of a successful religious reformer, who, thinking himself necessary to the successful maintenance of a great revival, is taken aback and annoyed at so summary a dismissal; and, finally, verse 11 of Isa. xxxviii. bases the belief that the king, having no child, and living in a time of revival at home and threatened destruction abroad,

expected to witness the promised appearing of the Divine Son of David.

In verses 5 and 6 the foundation principle reappears of Divine blessing reaching sinners for Christ's sake. Hezekiah is promised recovery, and Jerusalem deliverance, not for Hezekiah's sake, for he had in truth no perfect holiness, being a sinner, "but for mine own sake and for my servant David's sake"; that is, Christ.

A poultice of figs was Divinely ordered for the recovery of the king. This is one of the many passages in the Bible showing that God uses medicine as a means for healing disease.

The impious king Ahaz, when offered a sign from God, with false piety declined, saying: "I will not tempt Jehovah!" The good king Hezekiah, in the energy of true faith, asked for a sign, and God, responding to that faith, brought the shadow of the sun ten degrees backward upon the sundial of that very king Ahaz!

It was a miracle, similar no doubt to that granted to Joshua. As in his case, so here, it was possible of execution by a very slight inclination of the earth, such as occurs every year in Northern Europe.

The wealth that Hezekiah showed to the Babylonian Ambassadors is that spoken of in 2 Chron. xxxii. 27, and which was afterwards sent as tribute to Sennacherib, as recorded in the previous chapter. The wealth described in 2 Chron. xxxii. 23, together with the remnant of the treasure spoken of in 2 Kings xx. 17, was carried to Babylon, as predicted by Isaiah. Daniel and his companions were eunuchs in the palace of the king of Babylon, as foretold in verse 18. In them is seen the beauty and power of Divine faith: they glorify the very God who, to human justice, was so unjustly punishing them for the folly of an ancestor. The whole prophecy of verses 17 and 18 was very remarkable, because at that time Babylon was a feeble kingdom.

Secular history relates that at this epoch the king of Babylon was seeking allies to strengthen him against the king of Assyria; hence his embassage to Hezekiah. No doubt they proposed a treaty, for verse 13 states that Hezekiah "hearkened unto them"; and it may justly be assumed that his object in showing them the house of his armour, and the house of his treasures, was to convince the ambassadors of the value of an ally who possessed such resources.

Hezekiah is a type of the true Emmanuel, of Him before whom "the Assyrian," i.e., the Anti-Christ, the desolator of Israel, will fall. The notes upon the opening chapters of Isaiah will elucidate this.

See notes on corresponding chapters in 2 Chronicle and in Isaiah.

2 KINGS XXI.—Manasseh was the worst king of Judah, just as Hezekiah was the best, and yet he reigned the longest. This is a proof of the truthfulness of these records; for, had they been imagined by man, Manasseh would have been accorded the shortest reign.

Not only did this king exceed his ancestors in idolatry, but he exceeded the debased Amorites whom God destroyed before the children of Israel.

There were three main objects of idolatrous worship which seduced Israel—the Golden Calf, Baal, and the Ashera. The calf, that is, a bull-calf, was worshipped as the symbol of life; Baal, the fire-god, that is, the sun, moon and stars, was adored as the originator of life; and the Ashera, i.e., the Phallus, was bowed down to as the author of life. The last was the most degrading, and it was that which the king placed in the Temple of God (v. 7). In this verse the words "a graven image of the grove" means a carved Ashera. It was removed by Josiah (ch. xxiii. 6). The word "Phallus" is a Greek word, and means the male organ of pro-creation. It was held to symbolize the giver of life. It was made of wood or stone or metal, and it was generally a tree trimmed into the shape of that organ, and intended to recall the Tree of Life, which stood in the Garden of Eden. It was the most debased of all forms of idolatry. It is without doubt to this that Ezekiel in chapter viii. refers when describing with indignation the abominable idolatry practised in the very Temple of God at Jerusalem. He exclaims in verse 17: "They put the branch to the nose," not "their nose," but "the nose," that is, God's face. In other words, they thrust the Ashera, that is, the Phallus, into the very face of God Himself. This they did by publicly placing it in the Temple. The Holy Spirit, when recording in verses 2-7 the abominations of Manasseh, reserves this abomination to the end, as being the climax. It is popularly termed "Phallic worship."

As recorded in 2 Chronicles, judgment fell upon Manasseh. He was carried away captive to Babylon. In his captivity he sought the Lord, who was gracious to him, and restored him to his throne.

. This king exceeded all others in wickedness; verse 9 says that he "seduced" men to evil, and "to do more evil" than did the incredibly debased Amorite. This is not said of any prior king.

"The line of Samaria and the plummet of the house of Ahab" is an expression signifying that the judgment of God, meted out to Samaria and her king, would be visited upon Jerusalem and her king, and even more exhaustively; for Jerusalem was to be as thoroughly denuded of her inhabitants as a dish is wiped of its contents and turned upside down. Prisoners were measured to capital punishment at that time with a line and a plummet.

From verse 16 it may be gathered that this king cruelly persecuted those who refused to forsake the Bible and its teaching. Tradition records that Isaiah was one of these martyrs.

The history of his wicked son is dismissed in five verses. It does not say of him, as it does even of Manasseh, that he slept with his fathers.

Neither Manasseh nor his son Amon was buried in the sepulchre of the kings.

The expression "familiar spirits," in verse 6, means demon spirits who were obedient to human mediums. The word "familiar" is from the Latin "familius," a servant.

The captivity and restoration of Manasseh are recorded in the Book of Chronicles. It is there stated that Manasseh was taken "among thorns." The margin of the R.V. says "taken with hooks." The Assyrian inscriptions picture royal captives being led before the Assyrian monarch by a chain fastened to a hook inserted in the lip.

The restoration of Manasseh to his throne two years before his death, was thought by learned men to be improbable owing to the historic character of the kings of Assyria. Recent excavations, however, reveal that at this very time the Princes of Tyre and of Egypt were restored to their governments by the Assyrian monarch, and loaded with many gifts. Similar clemency to Manasseh is not, therefore, to be wondered at, nor deemed improbable.

2 KINGS XXII.—Compare notes on 2 Chron. xxxiv. and xxxv.

Manasseh began to reign at twelve. He no doubt was brought up by his father Hezekiah in the fear of God. Josiah began his reign at eight. He was trained by his ungodly father in the worship of idols. And yet Manasseh was a bold servant of evil, and Josiah a determined disciple of righteousness ! Of him it is said, that " he turned not aside to the right hand or to the left " from doing that which was right in the sight of the Lord. He is the only king of whom this is recorded. He was predicted by name more than three hundred years before his birth (1 Kings xiii. 2). Compare Cyrus, John the Baptist, and Jesus.

The prophet Jeremiah stood in the same relation to Josiah as Isaiah to Hezekiah. It is pleasant to assume that he and the king were boys together, and that, possibly, Jeremiah helped in the conversion of Josiah. This conversion took place when the king was sixteen years of age (2 Chron. xxxiv. 3).

The great facts of this reign are : the conversion of the king, the discovery of the Bible, and the national reformation that followed. But the prophets record that it was only a reformation, and not a regeneration ; for the people quickly returned to idol-worship and its associated abominations and social corruptions.

The young king began the reformation at the house of God. This led to the discovery of the Bible. It was the original Pentateuch, written by the hand of Moses (2 Chron. xxxiv. 14, R.V.), and laid up by the side of the Ark (Deut. xxxi. 24-26).

It is easy for a man to know whether he has spiritual life or not. If, when reading the Bible, he is neither comforted nor terrified, then is it evident that his soul is dead. Josiah was truly born from above, for he trembled exceedingly when hearing words written by God more than eight hundred years before he was born.

The highest officers of the state were despatched to consult a woman preacher named Huldah. Why were they not commanded to go to the great men preachers Jeremiah and Zephaniah, who were at this time attached to the court ? There are other women preachers mentioned in the Bible : Miriam, Deborah, Noadiah, Isaiah's wife, Anna, and Philip's daughters ; together with the many women preachers for ever famed in the letters of the apostle Paul.

The word " college " in verse 14 means no doubt a district of the city. The word " college ", as denoting a district, is used at the present day by the Latin races in connection with parliamentary representation.

The message of verses 18 and 19 is thus translated by some : " Thus saith Jehovah the God of Israel . . . the words which thou hast heard [shall surely come to pass]. In that thy heart was tender . . . I also have heard thee, saith the Lord."

Huldah predicted that the king should die in peace. He died in war. But there was no error here. The word " peace " had reference to the postponement of the coming wrath of God, and not to the anger of an earthly monarch. So he died a death that he brought upon himself by his own self-will.

Comparing 2 Chron. xxxiv. 1 with xxxvi. 5, it appears that the king was only thirteen at marriage. This is quite common in the East where children mature rapidly.

2 KINGS XXIII. 1-35.—When prince or peasant begins to read the Bible he at once feels it to be his duty to read it to others. Accordingly Josiah, recognizing that the Bible is for the world and not just for a handful of priests, as some think, gathered all the people together, i.e., the elders, and all the men of Judah, and all the inhabitants of Jerusalem, and the priests, and the adults, and the children—seven great companies of people— and caused all the words of the Book to be read to them, inviting those who would receive and obey them to testify their decision by standing on their feet. Here is Scriptural warrant for similar action on the part of modern preachers. But then, as now, the resolution did not last long, as is proved by Jeremiah xi.

The king, having removed out of the Temple all idolatrous vessels and idols, burnt them in the fields of Kidron, and carried the ashes to Bethel, where Jeroboam had set up the bull-calf, and scattered them there in order to pollute that place of idolatrous worship.

As for the Ashera which Manasseh had, later on, when repentant, removed (2 Chron. xxxiii. 15), and which no doubt Amon restored (2 Chron xxxiii. 23), and placed in the temple itself, verse 6 specially points out the righteous fury which the king showed in its destruction and degradation. At the same time the houses—that is, the tents of the unhappy men and women who performed the licentious rites of this dreadful religion—he destroyed, together with the

embroidered curtains which veiled the Ashera.
Having cleansed Jerusalem, the king defiled
all the "high places" that were throughout
the entire kingdom, both North and South,
although God alone was worshipped upon
them. This he did in obedience to the Law
which commanded that incense and sacrifice
should be confined to the one altar at
Jerusalem ; and verse 9 evidently means
that he forbade the priests of these high
places to officiate at the altar of Jehovah, but
allowed them their maintenance among the
priests that were infirm, as commanded by
the Bible. Such subjection to the Word of
God was very lovely.

Topheth, now first mentioned, was the
place outside Jerusalem where children were
burnt alive in sacrifice to Moloch. Historians
think that the word is related to that for a
" drum," which instrument the priests loudly
struck so as to drown the cries of agony of the
unhappy children.

" The mount of corruption " means the
Mount of Olives, and was so called on account
of the idolatries connected with it.

The prediction, three hundred and sixty-
nine years old, respecting the altar at Bethel,
was now fulfilled, and it, and all similar altars,
for ever defiled by the bones of dead men.
Both Israelites and heathen regarded dead
men's bones as a perpetual defilement.

The greatest of the passovers was now
observed. Hezekiah's passover (2 Chron.
xxx. 26) is similarly described. Both statements are true. Hezekiah's was greater than
any before it ; but Josiah's was still greater.
Hezekiah's was held just before the captivity
of the Northern kingdom; Josiah's immediately preceded that of the Southern kingdom.

Josiah perished on the famous field of
battle where Barak defeated Sisera. Had he
been as subject to the Word of God in his
later years as in his former, he would not have
thus fallen by the sword.

The judgments denounced upon the nation
came to pass, in spite of this temporary
reformation. The Book of Jeremiah reveals
that even at the time that Josiah was destroying idolatry, the nation was secretly
planning its restoration, which restoration
was quickly effected.

The three months' reign of Jehoahaz is
briefly dismissed with the statement that
he did evil in the sight of the Lord, and that,
as predicted by Jeremiah, he was carried
captive into Egypt and died there.

2 KINGS XXIII. 36.—XXIV. 17.—The
spiritual poverty of a family or of a church
often results from the disobedience of the
father or the pastor. 2 Chron. xxxv. 22
states that Josiah "hearkened not unto the
words of Necho from the mouth of God."
This Divine message was the more solemn
because it was conveyed to him through this
heathen prince ; but he refused to obey, and
the result was that his son Jehoiakim was
compelled to begin his reign by handing a
great tribute, forced from the people, to the
king of Babylon. Had Josiah walked with
God in the obedience of His Word, his family
and his people would not have had to suffer
such loss.

Verse 36 states that Jehoiakim reigned
eleven years. This is true as an historical
fact, but, alas, not true as a spiritual reality.
For in Jeremiah xxii. 15 the Spirit of God,
addressing this impious king—a king who
had burned part of the Bible, and such an
action revealed a will that would have burnt
the entire volume—the Spirit of God
addressing him, says : " Shalt thou reign ? '
The answer is " No ; and accordingly his
son Jehoiachin, who in verse 8 is said to have
ascended the throne at eighteen years of age,
is stated in 2 Chron. xxxvi. 9 to have begun
to reign at eight years of age. From eight to
eighteen, both years included, is eleven years ;
the exact period that Jehoiakim reigned, and
yet did not reign.

In this connection it is interesting to learn
from verse 12 that Jehoiachin began to reign
in the eighth year of the king of Babylon ;
and, further, that Jeremiah xxxii. 1 and
lii. 29 speak of the eighth and the eighteenth
years of Nebuchadnezzar. In the Book of
Daniel God reveals the great fact that He
took the government of the world out of
Israel's hand and placed it in the hand of
Nebuchadnezzar, to whom it was said :
" Thou art this head of gold." It is, therefore,
remarkable that at the time of this tranfer-
ence these numbers, "eight" and "eighteen,"
should appear over against each other as
marking the evening of Israel's night, and the
dawn of Babylon's day.

A further interesting fact appears in connection with these numbers, which is, that
the king of Egypt and the king of Babylon
were contending for the over-lordship of
Jerusalem, and that the Egyptian monarch,
having carried away Jehoahaz captive and
placed his brother Jehoiakim on the throne,

induced the Babylonian monarch to refuse to recognize Jehoiakim as king, and, from motives of policy, to recognize instead his little son Jehoiachin, then eight years of age. Eleven years later the Babylonian king removed him, placing his uncle Zedekiah in possession of the kingdom. Any one or all of these solutions remove what appears to be a chronological difficulty.

The campaign of Nebuchadnezzar against Jerusalem is said in Jer. xxv. 1 and xlvi. 2 to have occurred in the fourth year of Jehoiakim. Daniel i. 1 says in the third year. Both statements are true. Daniel, who lived in Babylon, records the setting out of the king for Jerusalem ; Jeremiah, who lived in Jerusalem, points to the king's arrival beneath the walls of the city. The march from Babylon to Jerusalem must have occupied a very considerable time.

In this deportation were carried away Mordecai, Ezekiel, Daniel, and Nehemiah.

Jehoiakim is the only king whose burial is not recorded. Verse 6 states " he slept with his fathers," but the invariable addition " and was buried," etc., is wanting. This is remarkable and solemn, for Jeremiah had predicted that his dead body should be cast out in the day to the heat and in the night to the frost (Jer. xxxvi. 30) ; and that he should not have a funeral ; that mourners would not follow him lamenting his decease ; and that he should be buried with the burial of an ass, drawn and cast forth beyond the gates of Jerusalem (Jer. xxii. 18, 19).

Jehoiachin, in Jer. xxii. 24, and xxiv. 1, is also called Coniah and Jeconiah. The ennobling syllable " Jah " is elided from his name, in just indignation, by the Spirit of God.

2 KINGS XXIV. 18-XXV. 30.—The wrath of God, as predicted by Jeremiah, fell, and Judah was carried into captivity, and the last king died a blinded prisoner in Babylon. The prophets Jeremiah and Ezekiel (Ezek. xii. 13 ; Jer. xxxii. 4, xxxiv. 3) predicted that he should see the king of Babylon, that he should not see the city of Babylon, and yet that he should die there. So it came to pass. He saw the king of Babylon at Riblah ; his eyes were there put out. He was then carried to Babylon, which, being blind, he did not see ; and he died there.

On the very day of Nebuchadnezzar's arrival beneath the walls of Jerusalem, the prophet Ezekiel, exiled by the river Chebar, witnessed the fact in vision (Ezek. xxiv. 1, 2).

Verse 8 narrates the arrival of the Babylonian general at Jerusalem on the 7th day of the month. Jeremiah lii. 12 records the 10th day. There is no error here ; the one verse says " unto Jerusalem," the other ; " into Jerusalem."

The statements of verses 13-17 have no interest for the unspiritual mind, but to the heart that knows God how full of agony they appear ! These precious vessels, and all this gathered wealth, designed by God Himself to express the millennium glories of Christ as King and Priest, were broken, dishonoured, and carried to Babylon. Sad result of the unbelief of the elect nation to whom God had entrusted such glories !

The differences in the dimensions of the two pillars between this chapter and 1 Kings vii. 18, and 2 Chron. iii. 15, is reconciled by the two pillars being reckoned together in the one passage ; and the dimensions of the chapiters and the wreathen work being separately recorded or not, as designed by the Sacred Writer.

" So Judah was carried away." Thus ended that kingdom as Jeremiah had predicted (xx. 4).

In defiance of the Word of God (Jer. xlii. ; xliii., xliv.), the residue of the people retired to Egypt, and placed themselves under the protection of the king of that country. They forced Jeremiah to accompany them ; but, as foretold by him, they perished, and the Egyptian monarch was destroyed by Nebuchadnezzar.

The action of Nebuchadnezzar's son in showing kindness to Jehoiachin is a fore-picture of the favour which the kings of the earth will show to captive Israel in a future day.

The disasters of this chapter originated in the affinity which Jehoshaphat made with the house of Ahab. Three hundred years after the author of such disobedience was dead, its bitter fruit continued to reproduce itself. Here is a lesson for all Christian people. The displacement of one enemy, i.e., the Egyptian, only makes room for the entrance of another, the Babylonian. This kingdom represents the captivity to the world into which the disobedient Christian falls, just as Egypt pictures the state of nature out of which the believer is saved. The closing chapters of this book are especially solemn, because recording the contest between Egypt and Babylon as to which of them was to possess the land given by Jehovah to Israel ! Like Israel the Christian only stands by faith ; and directly he ceases so to stand he becomes the captive of one or other of these unbelieving powers. Ezekiel (ch. xvii.), with Hosea (x. 1), set forth the inward and outward history of the nation at this time, and the notes on these chapters should be studied.

Amid the Temple treasures carried to Babylon, special attention is directed to the two pillars of brass set up by Solomon at God's command at the door of the Temple. These pillars, as already noted, expressed the glory of Christ as the strength of His people and the source of their assurance of salvation. The other vessels symbolized other features of Emmanuel's fulness—something of the unsearchable riches of Christ expended by Him upon those who love Him. In like manner, as Babylon robbed Israel of all these treasures, so the world to-day robs the unfaithful Christian of the conscious enjoyment of what he has in Christ, and of the spiritual power (the pillars) which he experienced when walking in the path of obedience.

Thus Jehovah's throne at Jerusalem was cast down and man's throne at Babylon set up ; and, strange mystery, God recognized it, committed to it the government of the world, and with it commence the " Times of the Gentiles," which are to continue up to, and to close with, the reign of the last Great king of Babylon, the Anti-Christ.

The love, and patience, and pity of God to unbelieving and rebellious Israel up to the very capture of the city are most affecting. The prophets Jeremiah and Ezekiel must be read to learn how amazing that patient love was !

1 CHRONICLES

1 CHRONICLES I–IX. 34.—The history of the Kings, unhappily broken up by man into four books, is the Divine Record of the folly, faithlessness, and failure of Israel under their monarchs. The Chronicles, broken by human wisdom into two books, set out the faithfulness of God to the Election chosen by grace. Thus are there two books, i.e., " The Book of the Kings " and " The Words of the Days," or, in modern language, " The Diary." But how intensely interesting—a Diary kept by God ! And, what an added interest ! the purpose of the Diary is to record the actings of His grace toward those whom He had beforehand chosen as vessels of mercy unto salvation. " Kings," therefore, gives the external history of Israel; " Chronicles," the internal history of the elect portion of that nation. This Divine Diary begins with the First Adam, and carries on the story of Grace and election to the Second Adam ; hence this book is placed as the last in the Hebrew Bible, and the reader passes at once to the first chapter of Matthew.

The Two Great Families, that after the flesh, and that after the Spirit, appear on the opening pages of the Diary ; but only so much is noted respecting the First Family as suffices to make prominent that which concerns the Second. Hence, as the inspired apostle says, that which is " natural " is placed first, and then that which is "spiritual." In accordance with this, the family history of Japheth and of Ham precedes that of Shem. Joktan precedes Peleg ; Ishmael, Isaac ; the sons of Keturah have precedence over the sons of Isaac ; and the posterity of Esau, with its kings and dukes, engage the Record before Isaac's descendants had ever a king, (Gen. xvii. 6, xxxv. 11 ; Deut. xvii. 14-20 ; Gen. xxxvi.).

This Sacred Diary, on reaching in chapter ii the sons of Israel, hastens to trace the genealogy of the spiritual Israel through David onwards, prophetically, to the Messiah.

This section of the book closes at chapter ix. 34.

A minute study of these nine chapters, which appear so uninteresting to the mere scholar, yields considerable spiritual wealth to the Christian. The assumed inaccuracies are found not to exist ; as, for instance, the confounding of Caleb the son of Hezron with his descendant, Caleb the son of Jephunneh ; the omission by the Holy Spirit of the tribes of Dan and Zebulon ; the greater notice given to some families than to others ; the naming of some men after their properties rather than after their families ; the interruption of the narrative by references to the judgment of God or to the blessing of God ; His remembering mercy to the family of Saul ; the honourable mention of Levi and his ministry ; and much besides—all lit up with a Divine recognition of the faith which preserved, even in captivity, these titles to promised possessions. For unbelief would have cried out in Babylon " Of what use, or value, are these tiresome genealogies ! "

But triumphant faith records : " So all Israel were reckoned by genealogies ; and, behold, they are written in the book ! "

The great divisions of this section of the Scripture may be marked thus : chapter i. 1-4, Adam to Noah ; chapter i. 5-27, Noah to Abraham ; chapter i. 34-ii. 1, Abraham to Israel ; chapter ii. 1-iii. 1, Israel to David ; chapter iii. 1-ix. 1, David to the Captivity, together with the tribes, omitting Dan and Zebulon ; chapter ix. 2-ix. 34, the Israelites who returned from the Captivity to Jerusalem.

At verse 35 of chapter ix, the Holy Spirit returns to the time of Samuel, and takes up the genealogy of King Saul in order to introduce the history of David and his sons.

Amid the treasures of these nine chapters may be specially pointed out the following : chapter ii. 5, 21, 23 present Hezron as a son of Judah, but his grandson, Jair, is registered as a son of Manasseh (Num. xxxii. 41). This is not a mistake but, on the contrary an interesting illustration of the law of Num. xxvii, for Hezron married a daughter of Machir of the tribe of Manasseh, became the adopted son of Machir and, consequently a member of the tribe of Manasseh. Of Hezron, therefore, it could be accurately recorded that he was a son of Manasseh by adoption, but begotten of Judah. There are several other similar illustrations of the law of Num. xxvii. in the Bible. They are all important, because proving the claim of Jesus of Nazareth to the throne of David. Luke states that Mary was of the family of David, that her husband Joseph was "of Eli," Matthew stating that he was "begotten" of Jacob. Eli was the son of David through Nathan; Jacob, the son of David through Solomon. Joseph, therefore, like Hezron, is accurately recorded in the Bible as the son of Jacob by natural birth, and as the son of Eli by legal adoption. Mary was undoubtedly the daughter of Eli; and by her marriage with Joseph the only two families that could claim the throne coalesced. Her Son Jesus, legally adopted by Joseph, became the one and only heir to the throne of Israel; and, by His resurrection from the dead, is to-day, and remains for ever, the one and only king.

The prayer of Jabez (ch. iv. 10) may be expressed by four words: grace, growth, guidance and guardianship.

Chapter iv. 18 makes a woman immortal! She was an Egyptian, the daughter of Pharaoh. How very interesting! But she joins the people of God and receives a new name, Bithiah, i.e., the daughter of Jehovah! The proud daughter of the Egyptian monarch degrades herself by becoming the wife of a Hebrew slave; no doubt her name was, therefore, with ignominy, erased from the royal genealogy of Egypt, but—what eternal glory!—engrossed among the daughters of the Royal Family of heaven!

Verses 22 and 23 of this same chapter may be thus read: "Jokim and Saraph, who married in Moab, returned to Bethlehem (these records are ancient). These were the potters; these dwelt among plantations and hedges; there they dwelt with the king for his work." Like Ruth and Naomi (Ruth i. 19) they return from Moab to Bethlehem, and are employed on the Royal estate in a very humble position. But the Holy Spirit, with exquisite grace, adds that the work though lowly, was work "for the king," and, further, that they dwelt there "with the king!" No doubt the king dwelt in the palace and they in a cottage down in the plantations and hedges, but it is recorded of them that "they dwelt with the king!" Such is the grace that to-day appoints to some such hidden ministry those that were afar off, and ennobles them by recording that "they dwell with the king for His work." Recent excavations at this pottery site have revealed vessels bearing the names of the potters as given in these verses.

Chapter v. 18-26 reviews the history of the two and a half tribes who chose their inheritance on the wrong side of Jordan. Verses 23 and 24 appear to form a parenthesis, disposing of the half-tribe of Manasseh that chose God's side of the river. Those who chose the wrong side are here stated to have quickly fallen into idolatry, and to have been the first carried into captivity. The pity of this is increased by the recital, in verses 18-22, of the life of victory which they enjoyed when walking in the Truth. Their fate, like that of Lot, is a warning to those followers of Christ who live a life that borders upon the world.

The large space given (ch. vi.) to Levi and his ministry, and the affection with which the Holy Spirit points to the varied exercises of that ministry, help to remind sons and priests of the kingdom how precious to God are worship and service.

In ii. 15 David appears as the seventh son; in 1 Sam. xvi. 10 as the eighth. There is no conflict. One is history; the other, genealogy. In the latter, dead men, or childless men, do not necessarily appear.

1 CHRONICLES IX. 35-X. 14. — As already pointed out, the Holy Spirit, in the last ten verses of this chapter, returns to the days of Samuel, recites the pedigree of King Saul, and then, in chapter x., repeats the circumstances of that monarch's death, and thus presents an introduction to the kingdom of David.

In this introduction the causes which brought the wrath of God upon Saul are stated. In 1 Sam. the fact of this wrath is recorded. The older record therefore states the fact; the later record, the reason. This is an illustration of the characteristic difference between the Book of the Kings and the Book of the Chronicles.

The members of Saul's family who are

stated in verse 6 to have died with him were, it is plain, those only who accompanied him into the battle ; for, as it appears later on, Ishbosheth and Mephibosheth, and the others who remained at home, are not here included.

Idols, being senseless blocks of wood or stone, could not of themselves know of the Philistine victory ; so in verse 9 the Holy Spirit, with fine scorn, writes that the tidings of it were brought to them !

Verse 10, united with 1 Sam. xxxi. 10 (the one statement dealing with Saul's head, the other with his body), shows that the two books are independent and complementary. This is very important. There are many similar proofs of this fact in Chronicles ; and they show that the one book was not a copy, made by men, of the other, but that the two books, Kings and Chronicles, were written by the Spirit of God.

It is, therefore, very interesting to read verses 11 and 12 of this chapter together with chapter xxxi.. of 1 Sam., and to notice that the one passage states where the body of Saul was found, that is, at Beth-shan ; that the bones were burnt prior to burial ; and that the tree mentioned in the older record is stated in the newer to have been an oak-tree. These points are all of great value as showing independent composition by an infallible Author.

The three words, " So Saul died," occur in verse 6 and in verse 13. The one verse points to the fact ; the other, to the reason. The reason was dual : first, his disobedience in not destroying the Amalekites ; second, his impiety in seeking counsel from the devil. With deep solemnity verse 14 adds " he enquired not of Jehovah : therefore He slew him." Men could see the outward historic event, but only the Spirit of God could reveal the cause of the event.

Should it be objected that 1 Sam. xxviii. 6 contradicts this statement of verse 14, Hebrew scholars, in reply, point out that the verb " to enquire " used in 1 Sam. is a different verb from that used in 1 Chron. The one records an outward and formal action ; the other, an inward and deep emotion. Had Saul enquired of the Lord with the same intense earnestness with which he enquired of the witch, how prompt and gracious would have been the response !

1 CHRONICLES XI.—In this chapter we

have David's Coronation (vs. 1–3) ; David's Capital (vs. 4–9) ; and David's Captains (vs. 10–47).

The elders of Israel offer three reasons why they should make David king. First, he was nearly related to them ; second, he was a successful general ; third, the Bible commanded it. It is noticeable that they put God and His Word last, as men do to-day. These reasons, confessed by themselves, should have brought them to David's side long before ; but, as a rule, men will not do what they know to be their duty until self-interest impels them.

Thus David, the commanding figure of the First Book of Chronicles, is introduced. He is a type of his Greater Son ; and therefore it is that, characteristically, the first event of the book is the deliverance of Jerusalem from the Jebusite, and David's ascension on the throne of Jehovah at Zion. Such will be the action of Israel's Great King in a future happy day.

But all types fail. David, instead of personally capturing the city, offers to make chief and captain whoever does so, and thus fastens Joab, who at heart was a traitor, as a thorn in his side. God had appointed David both chief and captain (1 Sam. ix. 16).

The captains formed three companies : the First Three, the Second Three, and The Thirty. The First Three were Adino, Eleazar, and Shamma (2 Sam. xxiii.), the Second Three were Abishai, Benaiah, and the third is nameless—most probably Joab ; the Thirty captains with their chief are named in verses 26-47

The Three pointed to in verse 20, of whom Abishai was chief, are the Three who broke through the host of the Philistines and fetched the water for David.

In the comments made upon 2 Sam. xxiii. will be found some spiritual lessons suggested by the brave deeds of these captains ; but it may be here repeated that Joab's name does not appear in either of the lists. His two brothers and his armour-bearer are honourably recorded, thus making more conspicuous his non-appearance ; further, the one list is much longer than the other ; and, lastly, the shorter list, that is, the Samuel one, is placed at the close of David's reign, the other at its commencement. This is another evidence of the independence of these books, and of their accuracy ; for what is more natural than that, during the course of thirty-three years, some should have died, and some proved faithless. The " Overcomer," faithful to the Divine David, will enter with Him, as the Divine Solomon, into the glory of His kingdom of Peace ; and therefore it is that the final list is found in the one book at the close of David's reign. Not all who are good soldiers of Jesus Christ to-day will, alas, be found such, thirty years hence !

1 CHRONICLES XII.—The general subject of these chapters is not the personal history of David, but rather the establishment of the kingly power in the House of David, according to God's ordination. It pictures a kingdom of blessing—a prophecy of the kingdom to be established in blessing under the hand of the Divine David. The faults and sufferings of David, whether before or after his enthronement, are consequently unrecorded.

There is no mention of a High Priest. This is in keeping with the subject, for Messiah will be both King and Priest on his throne (Zech. vi. 13).

The chapter emphasizes the great fact— and it was prophetic—that this king was " according to the Word of Jehovah."

Then, the mighty men, who had shared his rejection, now share his glory ; and both their names and their deeds are entered upon the imperishable tablets of his kingdom : an encouragement for all those who now, suffering with Christ, shall presently reign with Him (2 Tim. ii. 12).

These men became mighty because of their companionship with David. Many of them had been with Saul, but they did not become mighty men till they left him and joined David. Companionship with David made heroes of men who had been formerly either ordinary men or cowards. History affords abundant instances of timid women and nerveless men performing the noblest deeds because of companionship with Jesus. The men in this chapter, so long as they were the servants of Saul, were, together with their master, overcome by the Philistines. But from the day they became the servants of David, they overcame the Philistines because their master overcame them. So is it to-day. Those who trust in the power of man's religion (Saul) are overcome by inward passions (the Philistines), but those who submit to God's salvation (David) prove that He can subdue all these appetites to Himself.

Nor was it to be wondered at that these men should conquer the Philistines, for, even in Saul's camp, when all Israel was terror-stricken, their Leader had slain *The* Philistine, and, thereby, assured the victory over all Philistines. After this, similar achievements became quite common, for David's bold spirit made all men valorous. When God acts in power, He gives strength to the weak and turns them into an army of warriors. This is an historic fact. Whenever God has raised up a mighty man, in a very short time mighty men showed themselves on all sides. Luther is an illustration ; for he with whom God is, attracts those in whose hearts the Spirit is speaking, and, presently, there is a great host like the host of God !

The Holy Spirit points, in the first place, to those who came to David at Ziklag while yet David was a fugitive, and then in verse 23 and the following verses, to those who, when David's fortunes had improved, joined him at Hebron ; but whether at Ziklag or Hebron, He delights to mention some of them by name, and relate their deeds. They were David's helpers in war.

And first among these heroes appear Saul's own relations. They could use with equal dexterity of right or left hand, the very weapons with which Saul himself was slain ! They gave both hands to David ; and they were skilful hands ! Here is a message for Christian men to-day !

The Gadites " separated themselves " from their tribesmen and from Saul, and, in their determination to stand in with David in his exile, they, first of all, defeat the servants of Saul eastward of Jordan ; then they ford the river while in flood ; then engage and defeat another of Saul's armies ; and, crowned with these three victories, join David at Ziklag.

Some of the men of Benjamin and Judah, following the example of Saul's relatives, essay to join themselves to David, but he suspects them. Learning, however, that God was bringing them, faith triumphs, and he makes them officers in his own regiment.

Finally, those of Manasseh—and this great name appears three times in verses 19 and 20—who came to David to Ziklag are honourably mentioned. They were all mighty men of valour ; they were captains in the host ; and they helped David against the rovers, i.e., the Amalekites, who had burnt Ziklag (1 Sam. xxx).

The troops who came to David to Hebron, are detailed in the second half of the chapter. They are all praised for some characteristic or other. In their resolve to make David king they came " ready armed to the war." They did not come to get ready for the war, but already armed for it. Of Judah it is said that they bore shield and spear. Of Manasseh, that they were expressed by name to come and make David king. As to Issachar, he had understanding of the times to know what Israel ought to do. What contentions about so-called sacraments would be avoided to-day if Christian men had understanding of the time, i.e., the dispensation, in which they are living !

As to the residue, they were expert in war ; or they could keep rank ; or they were of one heart ; or they had all manner of instruments of war ; and these instruments, and this knowledge, and this discipline, and these perfect hearts were all given to one great purpose—to make David king !

Specially is it to be noted that all the men of Issachar, the men who had understanding of the times, were at the commandment of their two hundred chiefs. And what were their chiefs commanding them to do ? To make David king !

So were they three days with David in Hebron feasting and rejoicing ; and there was abundance of all good things ! This has always been the experience when people come together with one heart to make Jesus king.

It has been objected that there must be a mistake in the numbers recited in verses 24 and 33. Only six thousand of Judah against fifty thousand of Zebulon ! The numbers, on the contrary, denote accuracy and fidelity to present-day spiritual facts. Although David was of Judah, yet that tribe with Benjamin and Simeon and Levi, held by Saul. These were the tribes that crucified the Son of David ; and at all times a Christian's nearest relations are those who are the last to acknowledge him as a man of God. Further, these were the tribes who suffered great losses in battles with Saul against the Philistines, especially on the fatal day at Gilboa, whilst those to the North and East had not their ranks thus reduced, and, therefore, could contribute these thousands of men to David's camp at Hebron.

But if these Southern tribes were faithful to Saul, they proved equally faithful to David from the day they joined him, whilst the Northern tribesmen who came in their thousands, with such blowing of trumpets and beating of drums, deserted with equal fickleness his cause and family in the day of Rehoboam. Not those who come with emotional readiness to the Saviour are always those who, later on, in a crisis, remain faithful to Him. Compare Acts xx. 37, 38 and 2 Tim. i. 15.

1 **CHRONICLES XIII.** — This chapter teaches the Christian to be on his guard against religious emotions which belong to nature, and to see to it that his worship and conduct are governed by the Word of God. David's hasting to bring up the Ark of God to the new centre of his kingdom was laudable, and had he obeyed the Bible nothing but blessing would have resulted. Instead, however, of blessing, there was death and fear. He consulted with the captains and every leader, saying : " If it seem good unto you let us bring the Ark of God to us," and then he adds " if it seem good to Jehovah our God." God was put second. David should have consulted the Bible, as he afterwards did in chapter xv. His second mistake was in imitating the Philistines in the matter of the new cart (Num. iv. 15, vii. 9, x. 21), and the third and great error was in assuming that God needs man's hand to steady and uphold His kingdom.

When God acts in power in the midst of His people that power can wreck their most elaborate religious programme. David gathers the captains, and the leaders, and the thousands, and all Israel from Sihor to Hamath, and the new cart, and the harps, and the cymbals, and the timbrels, and the trumpets, and everyone played with all his might ; but in one moment the trumpetings and the rejoicings are turned to sorrow and terror ! To touch an electric wire when " alive " is death ; and such is God to the " flesh." No doubt David thought with exultation of how Dagon was smitten before the Ark, but he is displeased because Uzza is smitten. He has to learn the lesson that the " flesh " in the Israelite is the same as the " flesh " in the Philistine.

The statement made in verse 3 respecting the Ark is characteristic of the Book of Chronicles, and throws a sad light upon the self-will which energized Saul's government. God accepted the " new cart " from the Philistines ; it expressed their faith. They left God to act, testifying that He was the God of all Creation. The Philistines had not the Bible, but Uzza had ; and, therefore, he was responsible.

David's joy was turned into sorrow and fear. The word " displeased " in verse II means " saddened." So the Ark was brought into the house of Obed-edom ; and that very God who was death and dread to the king, was life and joy to the servant.

The words " I," " me," " us," " our," and " we," sadly evidence how " self " was in reality the centre of this great religious ceremony. Chapter xv. will show how God and His Word formed the centre of that other day, and how " self " was covered with contempt.

The sentence in verse 6 : " whose name is called on it " means : " where His name is called upon," that is, where public worship was held.

1 CHRONICLES XIV.—The first two verses picture the coming day when Christ, the Shepherd of His people, shall be confirmed by God the Father as King over Israel, and when the Gentile Princes, here represented by Hiram, shall bring their offerings to His feet.

This action on the part of Hiram helped to assure David that God had established his kingdom ; but the teaching of the Holy Spirit in David's heart instructed him that his kingdom was lifted up on high and his throne confirmed, not because of his personal excellence, but because Israel was the flock of God. Grace elected that flock and chose David as its shepherd.

Alas, he was not a perfect type of the Great Shepherd. Can one such be found in the Scriptures ! What a fall there is here from the second verse into the third ! Yet the Holy Spirit faithfully records facts ; and " where sin abounded, grace did much more abound," and, consequently, this passage is here introduced to show, amongst other facts, that Nathan and Solomon were both born in Jerusalem, becoming thereby entitled to the throne, and the verse establishes their connection with Christ, for Nathan was the progenitor of Mary, and Solomon of Joseph.

A double victory over the Philistine closes the chapter. Directly David is made king over the whole land, the Philistines seek him in order to kill him. That is the meaning of the word " seek " in verse 8. Prior to this Saul had " sought " him with a like murder-

ous purpose. This is a present spiritual experience. The Philistines dwelt in the land. They illustrate the energies of sin that dwell in the Christian (Rom. vii. 17). So soon as Christ is enthroned as king over the whole life, these energies gather themselves together to crucify Him in the believer's heart. Where Divine faith and a child-like obedience have the upper hand, there is complete victory over them.

The victory of the first day, and the methods which grace counselled for the winning of it, are not to be rested in in order to secure victory for the next day. Upon the first day the Divine command was : " go up!" the next day the same voice said : " go not up, turn away from them." Had David thought it unnecessary to pray previous to the second battle he would no doubt have been defeated. He must learn that God cannot give victories to the " flesh " ; it must be humbled and made dead. So David is commanded to run away from the Philistines— and that was very humbling to so brave a soldier—then to hide, and wait, and listen for the power and leading of the Holy Spirit. No two victories are alike, hence there must be definite exercises of heart and prayer if the Philistine is to be defeated the second time. See notes on 2 Sam. v. 23. " Trust and obey " are words which express principles in the spiritual realm—one passive, the other active. David trusted while watching the tree-tops, and he obeyed when they moved. Saul did not trust in relation to the Philistine (1 Sam. xiii. 12), or obey in regard to the Amalekite (1. Sam. xv. 11).

David did not, like Jacob, bury the idols ; he burnt them !

The Divine titles, Elohim, and Jehovah appear here and in 2 Sam. v. Here, " Elohim," six times, " Jehovah," three times. In 2 Sam. " Jehovah," ten times, " Elohim," once. This harmonizes with the two books. Samuel emphasizes the faithfulness of Jehovah to the weak and erring David. Chronicles, the power of Elohim over the Philistine and his gods. The Holy Spirit read both titles in David's heart ; for " He maketh intercession for us with groanings which cannot be uttered."

1 CHRONICLES XV.-XVI. 3. — David, taught by the judgment upon Uzza, searched the Scriptures, and learning therefrom how the Ark should be carried (Num. iv. 15),

obeyed the Word of the Lord, and with singing and joy it was brought to Zion.

The action here is the setting up of the Throne of Jehovah, that is, the Ark, in Zion. David is the central figure. The High Priest is not seen. David, as King and Priest—like unto Melchizedek distributing bread and wine (xvi. 3)—appears in connection with the Throne, and blesses the people. Grace is the foundation upon which all is here established. The Tabernacle and the Brazen Altar are at a distance—at Gibeon. They represented the First Covenant, now passed away, and the Holy Spirit carries David and Israel forward into the liberty of the New Covenant, and the whole scene is prophetic of the day when the Son of David will establish His Throne in Zion and reign thereon as King and Priest before His ancients gloriously. There will be in that day the remembrance of the One Great Sacrifice once accomplished at Calvary, just as upon this day the blood once sprinkled upon the mercy seat of the Ark was the memorial of the atonement consummated at the brazen altar. Calvary will not be repeated in the day when Israel's King appears in Zion, but its remembrance, as being the foundation of all blessing, will be very prominent. So is it in this chapter. The brazen altar and the Tabernacle are at Gibeon ; the Ark is not brought there by David, but to Zion. In this connection the notes on Ps. lxxviii, lxviii, and cxxxii should be read.

The picture, therefore, is one of kingly power and grace. The Ark, that is, the Throne, is the visible sign of these glories. The king himself appears, and, as Melchizedek, blesses the people. The priests do not appear. Michal, the daughter of Saul, i.e., " the flesh," cannot understand this, and consequently is childless ; for how can the " flesh " bring forth fruit unto God ! Thus, prophetically, the placing of the Ark in Zion, and not at Gibeon, was a setting aside of the First Covenant and a setting up of the Second. The statements, therefore, of this chapter destroy the theory known as " The Priests' Code."

Reading Ps. lxviii. 11, 25, there would appear to have been three choirs upon this great day. The first contained three men, Heman, Asaph, and Ethan (v. 19). They sang, and accompanied the song with cymbals of brass. Then followed the maidens' choir with timbrels, and eight musicians, with psalteries, accompanied them (v. 20). The words " on Alamoth " in this verse should read " for the maidens," and the verb " were appointed " should be carried down from the prior verse, and the text would then accordingly read : Zechariah, etc., were appointed with psalteries for, i.e., to accompany Alamoth, that is, the maidens' choir. The third band of singers and musicians contained six men (v. 21). They played with harps on the Sheminith to excel, i.e., an octave above, and what is to-day called " counter tenor." Thus the instruments of music, that is, psalteries, harps, and cymbals (v. 16), sounding " with " (not " by ") lifting up the voice with joy, were in this way distributed. The first choir was accompanied by cymbals ; the second by psalteries ; the third by harps.

Obed-edom and Jeiel (v. 18), as doorkeepers, (not porters) marched behind the Ark, and Berechiah and Elkanah as doorkeepers before it

Verse 22 may read " and Chenaniah, chief of the Levites, famed for song, instructed about the song, because he was skilful "; that is, he was precentor, or choirmaster.

From verse 26 it may be gathered that the Levites that bare the Ark, mindful of Uzza's doom, feared to touch it ; but finding help, instead of death, they stopped, after taking a few steps, to offer sacrifices of joy.

Chapter xiii. 8 states that they played and sang with " all their might " ; but that was fleshly might. On this occasion this expression is absent, but its place is taken by offerings and a chastened joy.

The words of Moses (Num. x. 35, 36) may be here set in contrast with Ps. cxxxii. 8. In the Wilderness Israel sought her rest surrounded by enemies ; in Zion, she, typically, entered into God's rest. Israel, the camp and the priesthood, were no longer the rest of God.

1 CHRONICLES XVI. 4-43. —The song which the three choirs were to sing may be thus apportioned : verses 8-22, the first choir ; the subject being Israel in connection with Jehovah and His throne in Zion. The second choir, that is, the maiden chorus, sang verses 23-33, the subject being The Gentiles in connection with Jehovah in Zion. The third choir sang verses 34-36, the subject here being The Redemption of Israel from the Great Captivity, then still future, and predicted in Leviticus and Deuteronomy.

The words of this song reappear in Ps. xcvi., cv., cvi., cvii., cxviii., and cxxxvi. This is felt by some to be a difficulty; but here the Divine Author is pleased to repeat Himself, and to do so with variations. Human authors claim the same liberty.

This song was specially arranged for that occasion. The psalms in which it reappears are prophetic, and will be sung by Israel in a future day when Jehovah returns to Zion. It is, therefore, profitable to notice the variations between those psalms and this song; and to observe how these variations are necessary, because of the enlarged conditions which will characterize that coming day of glory.

Verse 7, therefore, may be understood thus: "then, on that day, David handed to Asaph and his brethren, as the principal thing, this psalm, to thank Jehovah."

In verse 4 and verse 6 the Ark, has two titles, i.e., "the Ark of Jehovah," and "the Ark of the Covenant of God." These two titles form the foundation of the song. Verses 8-22 connect with the Ark, or throne of Jehovah, for He was Jehovah to Israel. Verses 23-33 connect with the Ark of the Covenant of God, for God is Elohim to the Gentiles.

Israel, in the first section of the song, is called to praise Jehovah and to make known and proclaim His deeds and wondrous works to the Gentiles (vs. 8 and 9). The words "His strength" in verse 11 should read "The Ark of His strength"; for it is there that the seeker gets strength. Then the song recalls His faithfulness, His wondrous works, and His wondrous Book (v. 12), and His protection of Israel (vs. 21, 22) when they were but a little company of wanderers prior to their descent into Egypt.

The Gentiles, in their section of the song, are bidden to worship God alone because He made the heavens and established the earth (vs. 25, 26, and 30). His creative power is here contrasted with idols, which are things of nought; and in verse 29 the purity and beauty of Divine worship are contrasted with the impurity and horror of idolatry.

Following the last verse of the song, the people shouted the "Amen," and cried "Hallelujah." In the coming Crowning Day, as in Ps. cvi. 48, all the people shall say "Amen," "Hallelujah."

David, as the Melchizedek king, orders all the ministry both before the throne in Jerusalem and the altar in Gibeon. The Tabernacle was empty, the Throne of God, i.e., the Ark, being in Zion. But the New Covenant, here prefigured, not yet being come, provision is made at the brazen altar to condescend to the weakness and need of the people; and, connected with this, Zadok, the High Priest, appears. But it is his one appearance in these four great Davidic chapters.

1 CHRONICLES XVII.—As set out in the preceding four chapters, the settlement of the Ark upon Mount Zion pictures the 'day, yet future, when Christ, as Melchizedek and David, seats Himself upon His Throne of Grace and Righteousness in Jerusalem, and accepts the worship of Israel and the Gentiles. Then will the Kingdom Psalms be sung; then will the redeemed Sons of Jacob sing aloud unto God; and, invited by them, the ransomed Nations will join in the mighty anthem. Unitedly they will sing "His mercy endureth for ever." In that day Christ will appear as the true Ark of the Covenant upon Mount Zion. The song, therefore, of chapter xvi contains every subject which the presence of Christ in Zion would give occasion to celebrate, prior to the full display of His glory as the "Greater than Solomon."

David, having, by the prompting of the Holy Spirit, brought up the Ark to Zion, and not to Gibeon, now desires to build the House that was to set forth the millennial glory of the Messiah. But he learns, through Nathan, that that is to be accomplished by his son. This son was named Jedidiah and Solomon, i.e., "beloved of Jehovah" and "Prince of Peace." Such is, and will be, Jesus of Nazareth. David, subduing all his enemies, casting the Jebusite out of Zion, and setting up there the throne of Jehovah, is a type of the Messiah. He is stated in Exodus xv to be Jehovah the man of war, and Rev. xix states that He makes war righteously. As the great Captain of the Host, He will overcome all His enemies, establish His throne in Zion, redeem Israel, and make the Gentiles subject to His sceptre. Having accomplished all this, He will then, as the Divine Solomon, display the glory of His millennial reign. The Temple that Solomon built in minute obedience to the Divine plan (xxviii. 11 and 12) was designed to symbolize that glory. The Tabernacle in the Wilderness exhibited His grace; the Temple of Solomon, His glory.

The Tabernacle foretold His first Advent in humility; the Temple of Solomon, His second Advent in power and great glory. Hence David could not build that Temple, for he typified Messiah as a man of war, destroying His enemies and setting up His throne. Solomon, typifying Christ as the Prince of Peace, builds the glorious palace of Jehovah, and in doing so, gives a fore-picture of the time when the kingdoms of this world shall become the kingdom of our Lord and of His Christ, the Son of David, who shall reign for ever and ever.

The power of the Divine life in David's heart is evidenced by the character of his prayer. Self is abased, and God exalted. He believes, and gives thanks for, the wonderful revelation just made to him, but only speaks of that as setting out the glory, the grace, and the sufficiency of that faithful God the Giver of these promises. The Giver rather than His gifts engaged David's heart ; and love to Him clothed David's lips with praise.

The sentence in verse 5," I have gone from tent to tent," etc., may be thus translated : " I lived in a tent and tabernacle."

The revelation made to David was, that one of his sons should become king of Israel and build the Temple. This son was Solomon. But the language used respecting him will only be fulfilled at the Advent of the true Solomon ; and David's prayer recognizes this.

The words " mine " and " my " in verse 14 reveal the fact that the Temple and the kingdom were both God's, and that David and his sons were but viceroys and deputies. In 2 Sam. vii. 16, the words are " thine " and " thy." This is not contradictory but complementary. The one book records what God said to Nathan ; the other, Nathan's repeating the message to David. Hence the words " mine " and " my " are changed into " thine " and " thy."

The notes on 2 Sam. vii., and the several Psalms related therewith, should be read in connection with this chapter. These various passages will be seen to predict the Advent of one great final king of Israel, who would bring enduring glory, and who would be the Mighty God, who, when Israel was a slave, redeemed him ; when he sojourned in tents, sojourned in one also ; when attacked by enemies, became his Captain ; and when established in peace, dwelt with him in the House of His glory.

1 **CHRONICLES XVIII.**—The faults and sins of David, faithfully recorded in the Book of the Kings, are here passed over in silence, because the purpose of this book is to set out the ways and thoughts of God towards Israel ; and accordingly only so much of the history is given as is necessary to that purpose.

Christ, in type, i.e., the Ark, being now enthroned in Zion, the centre of the kingdom, David enjoys complete victories over all enemies both home and foreign. The Philistines, internal enemies, are first bridled, (see note on 2 Sam. viii. 1), and then the external foes are brought into subjection. This illustrates the moral fact, always true, that when Christ is set upon the throne of the heart, victory over both inward and outward enemies is assured. But the inward are first conquered, as in the case of David and the Philistines in this chapter.

The seeming disagreement between verse 4 of this chapter and verse 4 of 2 Sam. viii. has been explained in the notes upon that chapter.

Had David fully followed the Bible, he would not have reserved one hundred horses for military purposes, for the Scripture forbade him to multiply horses to himself.

David's houghing the chariot horses cannot justly be held to have been needless cruelty. His soldiers, having no chariots or cavalry, their only method of self-defence against, and over, the enemy's cavalry was by hough-ing the horses in the heat of the action. It was a military necessity. Further, houghing a horse, if skilfully done, only rendered it unfit for war; the animal remained useful for other service. And, lastly, it is not consistent for modern society to approve, as it does, of the castration of horses, and to condemn David's action in houghing them. The one mutilation is as cruel, if not more so, than the other, but is practised for the advantage of agriculture and commerce.

There were three campaigns against the Syrians :—David's, when he slew twenty-two thousand (v. 5) ; Abishai's, when he slew eighteen thousand (v. 12) ; and Joab's, when he slew twelve thousand, (Ps. lx. title).

When the Holy Spirit repeats a statement it claims especial attention. Verse 6 says that Jehovah gave David victory whither-soever he went. This is repeated in verse 13. The servants of God are, it is to be feared, few of whom this repetition may be made ! Some are victorious over one enemy, or at one period of their life, but how few are victorious over all enemies, and at all periods of their life ! but this is the Spirit's testimony to David in this chapter.

The affection of David's heart for the people and House of God is evidenced by his consecrating the entire spoil of these victories to Jehovah's treasury. He kept nothing for himself. It shows rich spiritual experience on the part of Christian people when all the glory and profit of spiritual victories are denied to self and willingly given to the enrichment of others, whether physically or spiritually ; for just as David's victorious spoils equipped Solomon for his service for God, so the spiritual victories of one servant of God may energize another for missionary effort at home or abroad.

Six officers of state are mentioned in verses 15-17 ; of these one is a recorder, and the other a scribe. This shows how highly the nation of Israel prized and guarded their state Records, and, above all, the Scriptures.

1 CHRONICLES XIX.—The Divine life in the heart of David was evidenced not only by his casting out of his kingdom all things that offended and them that did iniquity, but also by his shewing grace to those who, from of old, were outside the Divine promises, and had no claim to them. But his grace was despised, his servants shamefully entreated, and consequently judgment fell. In that day, to-day, and in days to come, this principle of judgment following upon rejected grace may be, and will be, recognized. The Ammonites hire the Syrians to help them against David, but in vain ; for, let the allied hosts be never so strong, yet can they not overcome the Divine energy which offered grace, and that, being rejected, decrees judgment.

David's servants had their beards shaven from off the one half of their faces, and their mantles cut off behind close to the girdle. In Egypt to wear a beard was a disgrace (Gen. xli. 14); in Palestine it was a disgrace to be without one ! The energy of evil in man's heart treats at all times the Ambassadors of the King of Kings with contumely. But· it is better to be a naked servant of Jesus than a robed prince of Satan.

The differing statements in the remainder of this chapter in relation to 2 Sam. x. will be found explained in the notes on that book.

1 CHRONICLES XX.—This chapter carries on the record of David's overcoming life—or, rather, the overcoming life that was in David—a life so strong that it energized others to slay even giants. The chapter is remarkable also because of its silence respecting David and Bathsheba. It was when David tarried at Jerusalem (v. 1) that that incident happened.

Thus three Divine principles are taught by the chapter. The first, that there is an overcoming life which gives continuous victory. Second, that that life may so powerfully operate in one servant of God that others are emboldened to attack the greatest evils and destroy them. Third, that when a Christian is forgiven, God, true to His promise, forgets the sin, and omits it from the later books of His remembrance.

There is no discrepancy in verse 2, for Joab summoned David to complete the capture of the city (2 Sam. xii. 27).

David did not torture his prisoners of war, as some suppose on reading verse 3. He condemned them to perpetual service in various trades. It is to these that David points in chapter xxii. 15.

1 CHRONICLES XXI.—When Satan fails to break down a servant of God by one plan he tries another, and generally succeeds. As a rule, his first plan is violence ;· his second plan, subtilty. He lays a semi-religious trap for the Christian's foot, and thus causes him to fall. So was it here with David ! What the Philistines, the Ammonites and the Syrians failed to effect, this mental weapon accomplished. What was more laudable than to verify the truthfulness of the promise made to Abraham, that his children should exceed the stars in multitude ! But to seek to carnally verify a Divine promise, brings deadness into the soul ; and such a desire leads not *to* the Bible but *from* the Bible. Hence in this action of David's there is no reference whatever to Exodus xxx. 12. On the contrary, he says " bring the number to *me* that *I* may know it." Had he obeyed the Scripture, the foundation of the Temple would have been laid, as that of the Tabernacle was, with the Redemption money of the thousands of Israel, instead of the blood of the seventy thousand that perished.

After a victory there is always a secret temptation in the heart of a Christian to search for a personal and carnal cause.

A preacher is tempted to think that the conversions reported during his ministry resulted from the clearness, or the force, or the eloquence of his preaching. Thus was it with David. Conqueror over all his enemies, he wishes to find out for himself the strength of the weapon, i.e., his standing army, which was his glory, and with which he gained his victories, and he took his eye off the strength of God from whom alone the victories came. This sin, and it is a great one, brings famine, defeat, or death into the soul.

" Where sin abounds grace doth much more abound." David's folly gives Divine grace the opportunity of fixing the spot where sin was to be atoned for, and fellowship with God maintained. The picture is striking. The wrath of God about to fall on the city, the guilty king confessing his sin, the spotless sacrifice slain, and the judgment of God vindicated and honoured. This grace is the more apparent and all-embracing, when it is noticed that the ground upon which this most satisfactory sacrifice was offered up belonged to a Gentile—Araunah, the Jebusite.

David here is a striking type of Christ—excepting that whilst David was personally guilty, Christ the true King and High Priest of Israel, was sinless. Here David takes all the sin upon himself, offers the sacrifice, intercedes for the people, satisfies Divine justice, and restores peace with God. Sovereign grace shines in every action of this scene. No priest is seen other than David. David could not go to the Tabernacle at Gibeon, for that represented the Covenant of Works, and there was no salvation for him there. If he is to be delivered from the avenging sword of the angel, God Himself must provide a salvation upon another principle, that is, salvation by grace ; and this is what is seen at the threshing-floor of the Jebusite.

Putting together verse 1 of this chapter with verse 1 of 2 Sam. xxiv., the doctrine, which so often appears in the Holy Scriptures, is once more taught, that God permits Satan a limited power as His agent for bringing merited judgment upon men.

Joab was a clever and far-seeing man. He recognized how impolitic was the king's proposal to number the people, and, the king being a religious man, he uses a religious argument in order to move him from his purpose. A man of the world has often better political eyesight than a self-willed Christian.

The difference between the results of the census here and in 2 Sam. xxiv. has been already explained in the notes on that chapter.

David repented of his sin prior to God's visit to him. He confessed he had sinned greatly against God. His admission that he had sinned, that he had sinned greatly, and that he had sinned against God, all reveal a heart that really knew God and loved Him.

In the notes upon 2 Sam. xxiv. will be found a solution of the difficulties felt by some with respect to the number of years of famine ; and also as to the price paid for the threshing-floor.

Chapter xxvii. 23, 24 shows a consciousness in David's heart that his numbering of the people was a carnal effort to verify a Divine promise.

The site for the Temple belonging to a Gentile, and the men employed in the building of the Temple being Gentiles, accord with the Lord's declaration that the House was to be a House of Prayer for all nations ; and such will it be in coming millennial days.

The Divine titles " Elohim " and "Jehovah " appear in verses 14-19, and their use should be noted by the reader.

1 **CHRONICLES XXII.** 2-19—The Angel of Jehovah having pointed out the spot where the Temple was to be built, and the prince—that is, Solomon—who was to build it, David immediately urges his son, and all the princes, to set their hearts and souls to the enterprise.

The house was to be " exceeding magnifical, of fame and of glory throughout all countries," because it was to show forth, in type, the millennial glory of the Messiah, just as the Tabernacle had set forth His mediatorial glory

The word "strangers" in verse 2 means the forced labourers and prisoners of war, spoken of in 2 Sam. xii., 1 Kings v. and ix., etc.

Verses 8, 9 and 10 repeat what has already been pointed out, that David typifies Christ as a man of war destroying his enemies, and Solomon as Christ, the Prince of Peace, reigning over a kingdom freed from these enemies.

Ishmael (Gen. xvi. 11), Isaac (Gen. xvii. 19), Solomon (v. 9), Josiah (1 Kings xiii. 2), Cyrus (Isa. xliv. 28), John the Baptist (Luke i. 13), and Jesus (Luke i. 31), were named by God previous to their birth. These names, their contexts, and their meanings, provide a profitable subject for Bible study. See notes on these Scriptures.

The words "in my trouble," verse 14, confirm what so often appears in the character of David, that all through his stormy life of warfare, his heart was true to one great purpose, i.e., the establishment of the House of God, and the Peace of God in the midst of the people of God.

The sum of money contained in verse 14 amounts to about £6,420,000,000 ; or, since the Great War of 1914-18, £10,000,000,000.

It is interesting to notice that the total of the census handed to David, taxed at the Divine rate of half a shekel per head, equals £70,000, and that seventy thousand men perished. God, who reads all hearts, doubtless knew that these were rebels.

1 CHRONICLES XXIII.—Chapters xxiii-xxvii. detail the Sacred and Civil appointments made by David in relation to the House of Glory now to be set up. The Sacred appointments are set out in chapters xxiii. 3-xxvi. 28, the Civil appointments in chapters xxvi. 29-xxvii. 34. The Levites engage chapter xxiii ; the sons of Aaron, chapter xxiv.

The enthronement of Solomon during the lifetime of David is twice recorded by the Holy Spirit, and designedly. This section is, therefore, introduced by the union of David and Solomon as king and priest. David orders everything as though he were the High Priest. So will it be by and by. The Great King and Priest, Christ Jesus, will, as David and Solomon in unison, build the Temple of Jehovah, and will not only bear the glory of it, but be the glory of it. This is why this chapter opens with the appointment of Solomon as king with David.

In verse 3 the Levites are numbered from thirty years and upward ; in verse 24, from twenty years and upward. The latter age was commanded by David (v. 27), the former age by Moses (Num. iv. 23) ; both by inspiration of God. The lowering of the age has a sweet message for the heart (vs. 25, 26). When the Tabernacle was a pilgrim, strong men of thirty years of age were needed to carry it, but now that God had given rest unto His people there was abundant service for younger and weaker men. So the lesson is learnt that higher Christian service embraces, rather than excludes, feebler natural abilities. The special Hebrew word used for "man" in verse 3, meaning "a strong man," helps to emphasize this lesson.

The Levites were to serve in companies of two thousand a month, the officers, porters, and singers being divided in a corresponding proportion.

The workers and the worshippers in verse 5 were equal in number. This principle should be true of every church, and of every believer. It is not so always. Many are willing to worship, but not to work ; and many to work, but not to worship. The instruments for praise had not to be chosen, or invented, by the worshippers, they were placed in their hands by David. Alas, that so soon must these harps be hung upon the willows of Babylon ! and hung by the very hands that should have awakened upon their strings the sweet songs of Zion !

The spiritual ministry of the Christian is illustrated in verse 13. First, separation to the ministry itself ; then, the duration of the ministry, "for ever " ; and lastly, the fellowship of the ministry, "he and his sons" ; i.e., Christ and His brethren." Then the activities of the ministry. They are three : to burn incense before the Lord ; to minister unto the Lord ; and to bless in the name of the Lord. The Christian's life is to be one of prayer, activity, and benediction.

The glorious title, "Man of God," belonging almost exclusively in the Bible to Moses, occurs in verse 14.

"Every morning and every evening" (v. 30) the sons of Levi were to thank and praise the Lord. The remainder of each day was to be busily spent in the service of the House of the Lord. This service necessarily placed in their hands a considerable amount of property daily ; and hence in verse 29 the standards of measure and size were committed to them. Honesty in business matters characterizes the true Christian minister, in sacred things as in secular.

1 CHRONICLES XXIV.—The sons of Aaron and their ministry form the subject of this chapter, as that of the Levites the prior one. David ordered everything. The Temple was not yet built, but its doors, its gates, its materials, its vessels, its ministries and all its activities existed in David's heart, and existed there by Divine inspiration, as he himself declared to Solomon (ch. xxviii. 19). So is Christ. In His book were all His members written while as yet there were none of them ; and the millennial and eternal glories will make visible what

exists, and has always existed, in His heart.

The R.V. translation of verse 5 illumines the text. The sons of Eleazar and Ithamar were " princes of the sanctuary, and princes of God " inscribed (v. 6) " in the presence of the king." Ithamar had but eight sons, but they were equally Princes of God. Together, these princes, with their sons, formed the four and twenty courses of the ministry within the Temple. Each priest served from Sabbath to Sabbath.

The chiefs of the four and twenty courses are given in verses 7-18. Each course was named after its chief. Zacharias (Luke i. 5) belonged to the eighth course, that is, the course of Abijah (v. 10). It is interesting to learn from Luke i. 5 how the Divine Son of David, through all the changes of Israel's history, watched over and maintained these courses of the priests.

If Christian people were as skilful in the word of righteousness as they should be, they would never find these lists of names dull, but, on the contrary, full of moral wealth. The Holy Spirit wrote these lists, and in so doing, designed the profit of God's people.

Verse 19 declares that all this ordered service was divinely appointed. The " lots " " came forth " to each prince by Divine decision, and this in the presence of the king, and the princes, and the High Priest, and the chief of the fathers, and the priests and Levites. Possibly the " lot " was that of Exod. xxviii. 30, (see notes upon that passage). What a dignity it gives to the minister of the heavenly sanctuary—and that minister may be but a kitchen-maid—to learn that she is a prince of the sanctuary (for "in Christ " there is neither male nor female), and that she exercises her ministry " in the presence of the King ! "

Verses 20-30 set out the names of the chiefs of the twenty-four courses of Levites enumerated in chapter xxiii. 6--23. Verse 31 records that these sons of Levi were appointed by God to their ministry as definitely and publicly as the sons of Aaron ; and it adds that no distinction was made between the " principal fathers " and " their younger brethren." The ministry of a " younger brother " is as precious to God as that of a " principal father," and vice versa. The words " over against " should be translated " equally with."

1 CHRONICLES XXV.—In the Tabernacle of the desert there was no such provision for song as in the Temple of Solomon ; and this because the former spoke of a provided redemption, but the latter of an accomplished salvation. Hence David, by the Spirit, composed " the songs of the Lord " (v. 7), and also the instruments which were to accompany these songs. As already seen, the singers numbered four thousand (ch. xxiii. 5). At the head of these came the two hundred and eighty-eight choristers of this chapter, and at their head stood Asaph, Heman, and Jeduthun, who " prophesied " respectively with harp, psaltery and cymbal. They did not, as is the case to-day, " perform " or " render " a sacred song, but they prophesied in the service of the House of God, "according to the king's order," singing in the House of Jehovah the songs of Jehovah. All was Divine.

The " host " of verse 1 means the Levites —their " captains " meaning their chiefs (Num. iv. 3, 23, 30, 35, 39, 43 ; viii. 24). The " service " of verse 1 means the service of praise ; and to that ministry the two hundred and eighty-eight singers of this chapter were " separated."

Shimei's name is omitted in verse 3, but appears in verse 17. The reader is to find out why.

The names of Heman's six sons form in Hebrew a sentence. This sentence glorified God for " lifting up the horn " (v. 5) i.e., blessed God for giving so many children to this inspired minstrel.

Thus the Temple was to be filled with song. Praise will characterize the millennium. So, to-day, an accomplished salvation fills the believer's mouth with singing.

1 CHRONICLES XXVI.—Just as worship at the Throne was the subject of the prior chapter, so service at the gate is the theme of this. Grace is its opening note. The sons of Korah are first chosen as door-keepers, their duty being to prevent the presumption of which their father was guilty. Such are the ways of God ! The sinful sons of a rebellious father are set on high by Him, and heavenly things are committed to their hands.

The ninety-three chiefs of this chapter, to verse 28, were the officers of the four thousand workers of chapter xxiii. 5. The two hundred and twelve officers of chapter ix. 22, were connected with the Tabernacle, not with the Temple.

Loyalty to Truth enriches the heart. Obed-edom illustrates this. God blessed him (v. 5) by giving him numerous sons and grandsons. These are declared to be " able men," " valiant men," and " mighty men of valour "—men " able in strength for the service."

But in this service, the " small " as well as the" great " had their place from God (v. 13), and that " for every gate " , thus teaching the lesson that every Christian, no matter how young or lowly, is responsible to guard every truth of the Gospel.

There were gates to be kept, and treasures to be guarded. Only " valiant men " (v. 7) and " discreet counsellors " (v. 14) could effectually undertake such service. Spiritual courage and wisdom are needed in order to contend earnestly for the faith once for all delivered to the saints.

This chapter proves how real to David's heart was the House of Glory that was to be built. He could see all its gates and its treasures and its storehouses (vs. 13, 15, 20). He could even see the causeways leading up to the gates ; and he could appoint the doorkeepers for the eastward gate as for the northward, southward, and westward. Every avenue was guarded, and every causeway and gate effectually protected. Such should be the fidelity of Christian people to-day to every department of revealed truth respecting the person, work, and glory of the Lord Jesus Christ, of whom this Temple was a symbol.

Verse 27 recalls the often forgotten lesson, that the Spiritual Temple of Jehovah must be built up with " spoils won in battle." There must be labour in prayer, battling with wicked spirits in heavenly places, and sharp encounters with the Devil and his human servants, if spoil, that is, souls, are to be won.

The marginal reading of Num. iv. 23, joined with 1 Tim. i. 18, gives the character of the " warfare " that is " to be warred." These verses illustrate this chapter. The soldiers here are grouped in two companies— Doorkeepers to exclude evil, and Treasure-keepers to guard wealth. This implies warfare. Timothy was a Doorkeeper, and a Treasure-keeper. This was the " warfare " that he was to war. His battling as a " Doorkeeper " is the theme of 1 Tim. i. 3 ; his warring as a " Treasure-keeper " appears in 1 Tim. vi. 20.

The last four verses of the chapter detail the civil appointments made by David, as contrasted with the sacred. Verse 29 defines these as made for the " outward business over Israel," that is, magisterial duties outside the Temple, as distinguished from ministerial service inside the Temple. These officers and judges were men of valour (v. 31), and of the tribe of Levi. The appointment of these officers by David, in unison with his appointment of the priests, shows how fully the Holy Spirit carried him forward into the day when Christ, as David and Solomon, and as king and priest, will make all sacred and civil nominations in His kingdom.

The variations in the spelling of some of the names in these chapters is an evidence of the accuracy of the records. Just as in English the name Helen, Ellen, and Eleanor, or Jos, and Joseph, appearing in lists of names would indicate, not inaccuracy but affectionate accuracy, so is it in these lists. The variations show that the persons really existed ; that they were well known ; and that they had a popular place in public knowledge.

1 CHRONICLES XXVII.—David's standing army, consisting of three hundred thousand men, served monthly at twenty-four thousand a month, their twelve thousand officers acting in a similar proportion. Six thousand of these officers were most probably drawn from David's own tribe, as pointed out in the notes on 2 Sam. xxiv. 9. In addition to these, David's own regiment of six hundred men (1. Sam. xxiii.), divided into three companies of two hundred each, and commanded by the " thirty," formed his body-guard.

Verses 23 and 24, as already noted, show how conscious David was of his sin in numbering the people.

Verses 25–34 detail the honourable positions held by David's household officers in his kingdom. To their hands was committed " the substance which was king David's " ; the education of his sons ; positions in his privy council ; and the highest appointments in his army. The names Ahithophel and Joab appear, illustrating the sad truth that it is possible to have a very high official position in the spiritual household of the King of Kings, and yet, at heart, be a rebel to Jesus !

1 **CHRONICLES XXVIII.**—There is a temptation to carry a religious matter through single-handed, when to do so there is a sufficiency of personal and material ability, a sense of mental and administrative power and a conviction of Divine direction. In such circumstances the energetic Christian omits, or forgets, or refuses to invite the fellowship of his Christian brethren. It was not so with David. He was mentally and financially able to provide everything necessary for the erection of the Temple. But his heart was filled with grace, and he invited and urged everybody, young and old, rich and poor, to take a share in the setting up of this House of Glory. It was true that their gifts were poor indeed compared with his, but they were precious to him and to God. Such is the grace of the Lord of Glory ! He could build His spiritual temple without human assistance, but in His wonderful grace He invites men to become fellow-labourers with Himself ; and in the coming day of His Kingdom He will acknowledge the efforts of such fellow-labourers as though they had done great things.

" God " was the keynote of David's address to his people, and to Solomon. He made nothing of himself—all was God and the Divine election. Verse 2 says " he stood up upon his feet." In 2 Sam. xii. he lay on the ground as a penitent ; in 2 Sam. vii. he " sat " i.e., crouched (Heb.), before God as a worshipper ; and in this chapter he stands on his feet as a servant. Hence it is that in this address obedience to God, and to His electing will, is the characteristic of the message. The king points to his election and to his rejection with equal subjection of heart. He first speaks of his rejection in being forbidden to build the Temple, and then humbly recalls his election as king over Israel. To his disciplined heart the one Divine action was as much to be accepted and admired as the other.

The closing verses of the chapter are most important, not only because they declare that the Temple of Solomon was wholly planned by God, and an absolutely full pattern of it and its vessels given to David—nothing being left to his or to Solomon's imagination—but it throws a great light upon the mode of inspiration. This appears in verses 12 and 19. Here David says that this Divine pattern was communicated to him by his being compelled by the Hand, i.e.,

the Spirit of Jehovah, to record it all in writing. The verse, therefore, pictures David drawing the pattern of every portion of the Temple, great or small, and of every article of its varied ministry, and writing notes explanatory of the drawings, and defining the woods and metals to be used, and the weight of the several metals, and he is seen to do all this when in a trance. Such is a Bible view of how the Bible was written.

Nothing was left to Solomon's genius or taste. All was " by the Spirit " (v. 12) ; all was Divine ! To worship God with acceptance men must worship " by the Spirit " and " in the Truth."

Verse 20—see note on Deut. iv. 31.

1 **CHRONICLES XXIX.**—The word " palace " in verse 1 is a Persian word, as is also the word " dram " in verse 7, and these words determine the date of this book.

The " house " of verse 3 means " the most holy place," the " houses " of verse 4 both the " holy," and " most holy place." David declares in verse 3 that of his " own proper good " i.e., his private property, he had given for the Temple upwards of £31,000,000. This money was to be spent in overlaying with gold the inner walls of the two chambers of worship (v. 4).

The princes' contribution amounted to more than £50,000,000, without estimating the value of the brass, the iron and the precious stones. If to the value of the gold and silver of this passage be added that of chapter xxii. 14, the total amount contributed in gold and silver amounted to about £1000,000,000. What was the value of the brass, the iron, the precious stones, and the costly woods is impossible to determine. Perhaps the gross total, adding all the gifts together, might be estimated at £2000,000,000. Many Bible students find it impossible to believe that such wealth existed at this time in the hands of David and of the princes of Israel. But why should it be deemed incredible ? It may, however, help to remove this difficulty when it is remembered that the Chronicles were written many years after the death of Solomon, and that the Babylonian talent was one half, the Syrian talent one-fifth the value of the Jewish coin, and that therefore it would be quite reasonable to divide this £2000,000,000 by two or by five.

David's ascription of praise, verses 10-19,

contains a thousand beauties. He makes nothing of himself and of his people ; he traces all to God's sovereign grace. They possessed nothing, they were beggars, and strangers, and creatures of a day ! But, as to God, with Him was greatness, power, glory, victory, majesty, dominion, lordship, riches, honour, continuance, wisdom, faithfulness and holiness !

Should the assertion be made that verse 20 authorizes worshipping God and the saints, the answer is twofold. First, what proves too much proves nothing ; and, second, the emphasis must be laid in the verse upon the words, " they bowed down their heads." That is, the physical action of worshipping God and doing homage to the king was similar, as indeed it is to-day, but the emotion of the heart was very different ! In the one case it was adoration ; in the other, loyalty.

Solomon was made king " the second time." This double consecration was necessary because he was Divinely designed to be a type of the Greater than Solomon. Two key-words unlock the significance of these two crownings. The key-words are " the altar of burnt-offering " (ch. xxii. 1), and the " throne of Jehovah " (ch. xxix. 23). The first symbolizes grace ; the second, glory. The first is connected with Calvary ; the second, with the New Jerusalem. The setting up of the altar of burnt-offering in the threshing-floor of Araunah the Jebusite was followed by the first coronation of Solomon. The completion of the material for the Temple occasioned the second crowning. So with Christ. Sacrificed upon Calvary, He is crowned in the heavens ; His spiritual Temple completed, He will ascend the throne of Jehovah at Jerusalem in the crowning day that is coming by and by.

2 CHRONICLES

2 CHRONICLES I.—This short chapter shows how quickly a public servant of God may fall, and what a broken vessel the wisest of men was! The opening verses present Solomon as a Christ confessor; the closing verses describe him as a horse dealer! This sad fall resulted from not reading and obeying the Bible. It forbade him to go down to Egypt for horses (Deut. xvii. 16). The Bible is necessary to holiness. Solomon's wisdom did not save him from Egypt's horses, nor from Egypt's idols! Disobedience to the Word of the Lord sets the feet on a downward and slippery path; first the horses, and then the idols! A union with the world in commerce quickly leads to social intercourse, and ends in idolatry (1 John v. 21).

Solomon's first public action was to confess, without shame, to the whole world, that he, and all Israel, owed everything to the blood of the Lamb. He sought to set out something of the infinite preciousness of that blood by offering a thousand burnt-offerings upon the brazen altar made by Bezaleel. But ten thousand times ten thousand offerings could never worthily exhibit the preciousness of that blood! It was, however, a fine testimony on the part of Solomon at the commencement of his reign. How happy Bible students would be had Solomon maintained this testimony, without fault, to the close of his reign!

Solomon having honoured and sought God in public, God enriched him in private. The king's prayer was a beautiful prayer, but he might have prayed a better. He should have asked for goodness rather than cleverness. He asked for wisdom to make him a successful ruler; how much better had he asked for grace to make him an obedient servant.

It is intensely interesting to learn here that this Tabernacle of the congregation where Solomon worshipped, was the very one that Moses made in the Wilderness. Once again Moses is called " the servant of the Lord "— a title of peculiar dignity, markedly given to him.

How sad and swift is the descent from verse 13 to 14! The words in verse 16, " and linen yarn " should read as in the R.V. " in droves." The king became a wholesale horse-dealer! His Egyptian agents bought the horses in droves, forwarded them to Jerusalem, and the king re-sold them to the neighbouring kings at a profit. It would appear incredible that a king of amazing wealth should descend to such a traffic; but it does not appear incredible to those who have been taught by the Spirit, through the Scriptures, something of the ignoble follies of the human heart, even in positions of great splendour.

2 CHRONICLES II.—Verse 2 records that Solomon personally resolved to build this house of glory, and that he was not merely prompted to do so by his father David. Verse 2 and the last verse of the chapter, state the number of persons employed in the execution of the work. These men were Gentiles, prisoners of war, justly condemned to hard labour for life; but any one of them, or all of them, by submitting to circumcision, could become free men. David, in making these men captives, instead of putting them to death, as he might justly have done, and Solomon in making them fellow-workers with himself in the building of the Temple, form together a picture of Him who saves men, makes them His captives, and His fellow-labourers in the building of His spiritual temple.

Solomon's letter to Hiram is singularly beautiful. With truth it may be said, that its keynote was Jesus and His fulness. It gives a pleasant picture of the condition of his soul at this time. He says that the House was to be for Jehovah, and that incense, shewbread, and burnt-offering were to express its daily worship. These three speak of Jesus. The incense: the sweetness of His name. The shewbread: the sufficiency of His grace. The burnt-offering: the perfection of His work.

There is no discrepancy between verse 10 and 1 Kings v. 11. There the allowance was for Hiram's household at Tyre ; here for Hiram's labourers in Lebanon. Nor is there any discrepancy between verse 14 and 1 Kings vii. 14. The woman was a daughter of Dan by birth, but a widow of Naphtali by marriage.

The three thousand and six hundred foremen of verses 2 and 18 were in verse 2 to oversee the work, and in verse 18 to keep the people at work. 1 Kings v. 16 divides these foremen into two companies of three thousand three hundred, and three hundred. These latter were " the chiefs " of the former. There is no conflict with 2 Chron. ii. 2 and 18.

Confirmation of this is found in comparing 1 Kings ix. 23 with 2 Chron. viii. 10 where these three hundred " chiefs " again appear, and these passages show the importance of the word " besides " in 1 Kings v. 16.

Solomon's testimony to Christ (v. 4) was honoured by God (ch. v. 14) and responded to by man (v. 12 and ix. 23). The plentitude and perpetuity of Christ's atoning sacrifice are taught typically in v. 6 and ii. 4.

2 CHRONICLES III. 1–V. 1.—As suggested when reading the First Book of Kings, the Temple of Solomon was a fore-picture of the millennial glory of Christ as Melchizedek, whilst the Tabernacle in the Wilderness set out His grace as a Saviour. Both structures were minutely designed by God. Nothing was left to the imagination of either Moses or Solomon. Grace was expressed by the Tabernacle ; glory, by the Temple. Hence, silver was prominent in the one ; gold, in the other. The Tabernacle spoke of access to God ; the Temple, of fellowship with God. The first building pictured Christ in His First Advent ; the later building, Christ in His Second Advent. The first building was paved with sand ; the second, with gold. The first was a tent ; the second, a temple ; but whether a tent or temple, the materials, the vessels and all the gathered wealth of each, were precious, and uttered His praise. Solomon's action in gathering all Israel to the door of the Tabernacle of Moses, and then, four years later, to the porch of the palace of Jehovah, brought these two Houses of Worship remarkably together, made manifest their relationship, and teaches the great lesson, that the way to fellowship with God

is through the Atonement of Christ. This great doctrine was expressed, as pointed out in the first chapter, by the sacrificial blood poured out at the brazen altar.

Thus Solomon and the Temple together picture Christ's glorious kingdom over the earth. Solomon in his glory, riches and wisdom, sets out the person of Christ. The Temple symbolises the nature of Christ— gold prefiguring His Deity, cedar His humanity ; but all has Grace in Atonement as its foundation ; for this palace of glory was built upon the threshing-floor of Ornan the Jebusite.

The Temple proper contained two chambers. The first, or Holy Place, was twenty cubits long, twenty cubits broad, and thirty cubits high. The second, or most Holy Place, was twenty cubits long, twenty cubits broad, and twenty cubits high. In front of these two chambers was the porch ; it was twenty cubits long and ten cubits broad (1 Kings vi. 3). Its height, by transposing the letters, was twenty cubits, not one hundred and twenty. The ground plan (" first measure " v. 3) was 60 cubits. Thus : the most Holy place 20 cubits, the Holy place 20 cubits, the Porch 10 cubits, and the Ascent to the Porch 10 cubits (2 Chron. ix. 4). See notes on 1 Kings vi.

The flooring, the ceiling, the walls, the ornamentation, the costly stones, the precious woods, the gold, the brass, the carved cherubim, the vails, the two pillars and all the vessels of the house, together with its golden doors, and the dedicated treasures— all pictured the glories, the perfections, the graces, the ministries, the activities and the offices of Christ in His Second Advent and millennial reign.

On entering either chamber of the sanctuary, nought was seen above, beneath, or on either side, but the purest gold, wrought by Divine inspiration into exquisite ornamentation—palm trees and wreathen work and cherubim.

The grace of the Holy Spirit in drawing attention to the nails used in the construction of this great Temple, touches the heart. He does not overlook such small and simple things when detailing all these dazzling splendours. He only saw them, for they were hidden, but they held all together, and are remembered and named by God. Were a golden lamp-stand to speak slightingly of the little golden nail, as great preachers are sometimes tempted so to treat a junior

Sunday School teacher, the nail could reply that it also was formed of pure gold, and had an indispensable office in the structure of this palace of Jehovah.

The word "inward" in verse 13 means "toward the house" (R.V.) i.e., outwards. In the Tabernacle, the cherubim looked down upon the blood-sprinkled mercy-seat, for only there could their eyes rest with satisfaction, all around being under the reign of sin and death. But here the new Cherubim look "outward" upon a kingdom governed in righteousness by the King of righteousness.

In 1 Kings the vail is not mentioned. The reason for this omission will be found in the notes upon that book. There also will be found interesting points concerning the pillars, Jachin and Boaz, together with a solution of the supposed contradiction between the two records as to their size. See notes on Matt. vii. and Luke vi.

In the notes upon 1 Kings vii. 26 will be found an explanation of the supposed mistake between that verse and here in chapter iv. 5.

The altar of brass, chapter iv. 1, was as long and as broad as the Most Holy Place, teaching that if sinners are to have fellowship with God it can only be brought to pass by an atonement as great as heaven itself, and which infinitely meets all the requirements of the holiness of God.

In the notes on 1 Kings vi and vii will be found comments upon the laver, the lampstands, and the other vessels of the sanctuary.

2 CHRONICLES V. 2–14.—A Feast, obedience to the Bible, the exalting of Messiah as Saviour and King, the song of worship proclaiming His ever-enduring goodness, and the descent of the cloud of glory, attesting the Divine recognition of this worship—these give the facts of the chapter.

The Feast was the Feast of Tabernacles.

Obedient to the Bible, the Levites bore the Ark (v. 4), and the priests (v. 7) placed it in the Holiest of All, beneath the wings of the Cherubim.

The staves, necessary for carrying the Ark while Israel was a pilgrim in the desert, now that Israel is entered into God's rest, are drawn out.

The objection that the statement "and there it is unto this day" (v. 9) is not true now, and could not have been true at the time that this book was written, can be doubly answered. First, it was true at the time this book was

written, there being no reason to doubt that this was the very Ark similarly placed in Ezra's Temple; and, second, it is true to-day, spiritually, as Heb. iv. and Rev. xi. prove.

The Ark of verse 7 and the altar of verse 12 symbolize the death and resurrection of the Lord Christ, and formed the foundation of the singing and feasting of the chapter. The Book of the Revelation predicts that this same Divine foundation will be the base of the world's bliss when Jesus comes.

Directly the worshippers were of one heart in proclaiming the goodness and enduring mercy of Jehovah, then it was that the glory-cloud filled the House. This is true to-day in the experience of Christian people. When the Christian heart is filled with thoughts of Jesus and His unsearchable riches, and when all that is within the man unites to praise that glorious Saviour, then the heart enjoys a wondrous consciousness of the presence and glory of God. This is equally true of a company of believers.

Because the glory of Jehovah filled the House of Elohim, the ministry appointed under a covenant of works became impossible. Those priests tried to "stand" in those heavenly surroundings, but they could not. The "priests," under the covenant of grace, are seated (not standing) in the heavenlies, they are at home, and at ease amidst these eternal glories.

It is, however, oftentimes true in a Christian congregation, that the Divine presence is so consciously felt, that it brings to a stop all outward ministry, and lifts the assembly into a rapture of silent worship.

It should be noted that, in the last verse, the glory was the glory of Jehovah, but the House was the House of Elohim. The Holy Spirit in thus distinguishing between these Divine Titles, invites the reader to the first two and last two chapters of the Bible.

2 CHRONICLES VI.—To understand the prophetic and dispensational value of Solomon's prayer, attention should be fixed upon four factors, viz.: Solomon, the Temple, Israel, and the Heathen.

It should also be recognized, as already pointed out, that chapters v. vi. and vii. are a fore-picture of the setting up of the millennial reign of Christ, who will, as the true Solomon, and as Melchisedek, ascend His throne at Jerusalem and sit thereon as king and priest (Zech. vi. 13).

It will be helpful to add a little respecting the four factors connected with this great prayer :

Solomon typifies Christ. He here appears as King and Priest. Hence the prayer.

The Temple in this book represents the Throne of God ; in " Kings," the Home of God. " Kings " therefore designedly omits mentioning the altar and the vail. The two pillars express not only the stability and strength of Christ Himself, but also the stability and strength of the government He will set up upon the earth. Toward that Earth the Cherubim now look " outwards " with complacency. In the Tabernacle, this outward look was to them impossible ; they only looked upon the Ark of the Covenant, for all else was under the curse.

Israel presents the twelve tribes now restored and replaced in their own land.

The Heathen, i.e., the " strangers," prefigured the Nations of the earth, who will be made one with Israel in the day when the Spirit will be poured out upon all flesh.

The time predicted in these three chapters is the millennium. In that day the double statement of " Kings " and " Chronicles " will come to pass : i.e., the glory, as in " Kings," will appear directly Christ (the Ark) enters into His millennial rest ; and as in " Chronicles," so soon as the song of praise ascends. That song will celebrate the untiring mercy of which Israel's blessing will be the proof in that day. Her deliverance and restoration will then demonstrate the truth of the words sung at the close of chapter v.

Two words, " Altar ", and " Feast ", are prominent in chapter vi. The " Altar " proclaims the atoning death of the Lamb of God, upon which all millennial blessing will be based ; and the Feast, i.e., the Feast of Tabernacles, announces the millennium, of which period of blessing that Feast is a type.

The cloud which was darkness to the Egyptians, which protected the Israelites from the heat in the desert, and which now descended upon the Temple, was, to Solomon, the voice of the Lord. Hence his language of verse 1 ; for there is no such written declaration in the Bible.

The platform, or pulpit, of verse 13 was made of brass ; as were also the altar and the laver. This fact and the dimensions " three " and " five " should be observed. " Three " is the number of Divine perfection; " five," of electing grace. Brass expresses strength and purity ; the altar, atoning blood ; the laver, regeneration. Such was the platform upon which Solomon stood to bless the people, and then knelt to pray for the people. All who would testify for God and help their fellow men must stand upon a like platform.

The king " stood," verses 1-12, and " knelt," verses 14-42. See notes on 1 Kings viii.

2 CHRONICLES VII.—The scene of this chapter is one of grandeur and awe. The king, with uplifted hands, kneeling in royal robes upon the brazen platform ; the vast multitude prostrate upon the ground ; the fire from heaven consuming the sacrifice upon the brazen altar ; and the cloud of the glory of Jehovah filling the House of Jehovah—all formed a scene of mysterious splendour such as the world has never witnessed.

The fact that this was the only Temple in the whole world in which the one true God was worshipped, adds to the moral grandeur of the scene ; and the inspired prayer of the great king and priest at its dedication, befits this fact. The spiritual knowledge revealed in that prayer, and the visible fire that burned upon the altar, came from heaven ; both originated there ; both were Divine. Man could not have created that miraculous fire, nor that equally miraculous knowledge. The fact of the existence of God was attested by the fire ; and that fire stamped with truth the religious teaching of the prayer, and the typical significance of the burnt-offering.

The prayer proclaimed the unity of God, His habitation the Heavens and not a Temple, and the moral perfections of His Being—His love, grace, goodness, holiness, providence, and power. No nation possessed this knowledge of God ; nor could any nation by reason, or culture, obtain such knowledge. It could only be had by revelation. Thus both the fire and the teaching of the prayer, came from heaven.

The sacrifice was first offered, i.e., its life surrendered to God as an atonement for sin and to make peace, and then, in the majority of cases, the flesh furnished food for the vast multitude who attended the festival. The number of animals slaughtered, sufficed therefore for the food of the assemblage : the Lamb of God is both the salvation and food of His people.

The Festival lasted fourteen days—the first

seven being the Feast of the Dedication, the second seven, the Feast of Tabernacles. The twenty-second day of the second month was the last day of this latter feast. The people were dismissed on the twenty-third day.

The words " by their ministry " (v. 6), arrest the attention. These instruments were in themselves voiceless, but the living hand or breath awoke them to praise. The worshipper should be such an instrument. When willingly yielded to the Lord, what wondrous music His skilful hand, or living breath, can awaken to the glory of God !

A comparison of 1 Kings vi. 37 and ix. 1, with 2 Chron. vii. 1 and viii. 1, would appear to show that thirteen years intervened between Solomon's prayer and its full answer. The fire from heaven was an immediate answer ; and this later answer is a comforting instance of how God does not forget prayer.

Yet there is, perhaps, here a note of sadness and Divine anxiety, and, alas, well founded ! For but a day or two (so to speak) afterwards, Solomon prostrated himself before idols, and became a wicked old man ! It may not be unreasonable to believe that this interval of thirteen years was permitted as a test ; and that God in His love, in order to save the king from his impending fall, then appeared to him, by night, with His message of assurance and warning. See notes on 1 Kings ix.

Two humbling facts appear in this history : First, man cannot of himself learn to know God—God must reveal Himself to him ; second, unless restrained by grace, man turns away from this glorious revelation and becomes a worshipper of devils.

The covenant with David, (v. 18), was unconditional, for it contemplated Christ ; that with Solomon and his sons (v. 19) was conditional.

The cloud of the glory of Jehovah which filled the House of Jehovah was the cloud of Exod. xiii. 21, 22, xl. 34, and Matt. xvii. 5, where it is described as " a bright cloud."

The fire that consumed the burnt-offering at the dedication of the Temple " came down from heaven," but the fire that consumed the burnt-offering at the dedication of the Tabernacle " came out from before the Lord," that is, came out from between the Cherubim within the Most Holy Place. But in coming out from, and passing through the Tabernacle, it did not burn it, for that tent was Christ. This is characteristic. The fire from the Tabernacle is Christ in His First Advent ; the fire from heaven, Christ in His Second Advent.

For the foundation and the duration of Solomon's prayer, and for its correspondence with the prayer of John xvii, see notes on 1 Kings viii.

2 CHRONICLES VIII.—This chapter faintly pictures the peace and plenty which will characterize the millennial earth. Fenced cities are built to protect the land, and store cities furnished to provide food for its people. At the same time the former enemies of Israel are made subject, and the king of Tyre, as representative of the Gentiles, contributes to the glory of the kingdom. All this was an earnest of the dominion promised to Israel, and which will surely yet be given to them.

But Solomon, like all other types, was a broken figure of Him who is to come. He builds chariot cities, and all that he " desired to build for his pleasure " in Jerusalem, in Lebanon, and in all the land of his dominion. The Bible forbade the chariot cities, and in the hands of the true Solomon the " pleasure of Jehovah " is to prosper, and not the king's own pleasure.

It is, however, pleasant to read of his fidelity to God's commandments as to public worship ; of how careful he was to obey that Word minutely ; and how, for at least some years, he daily and publicly proclaimed to the world that all his glory was founded upon atoning blood.

In the same spirit of obedience to the Bible, he observed the three great feasts of the Passover, Pentecost, and Tabernacles.

There are three statements in this chapter which are assumed by some to be inaccuracies; but they illustrate the accuracy, and not the inaccuracy, of the Sacred Scriptures. The first is found in verse 10, which compared with 1 Kings ix. 23, shows a difference of three hundred officers. These are independent matters. Five hundred and fifty officers were over the slaves " that wrought in the work " ; the two hundred and fifty were " chiefs " over the people ; which is quite another thing. The second is found in verse 18, for it is declared to be impossible that ships should pass from Tyre to Ezion-geber across the land. But why not ? Missionary Societies to-day send ships, in sections, over long distances in Africa ; and no shipbuilder in Hiram's day, or to-day, would find the matter impossible. The third supposed inaccuracy is also found in verse 18 ; for compared with 1 Kings ix. 28, there is a discrepancy of thirty talents. This shows accuracy. The one verse points to the gross value of the metal at Ophir ; the other, to its net value when handed to King Solomon. The difference in value would be a reasonable deduction for freight and refining.

2 CHRONICLES IX.—The glory of the Lord having now risen upon Israel (Isa. lx.), the kings of the Gentiles come to that light, bringing their riches with them, and find there a glory and a wisdom such as the world had never seen. None of these monarchs are mentioned particularly, except the Queen of Sheba, the Holy Spirit reserving that dignity for a woman. She is further honoured by the Lord Himself in Matt. xii. 42, where He predicts her reappearance in the resurrection.

This queen hears the fame of Solomon. At first she does not believe the report, but after a little, moved by its repetition, she determines to put the matter to the test. She undertakes a long, fatiguing, and expensive journey ; she finds that the report is true, but that the half had not been told her. The effect is the destruction of all her self-complacency, and that the surpassing glory of Solomon and his court makes her and her court of no value. She gives gifts to Solomon—gifts which could be measured. Solomon gives her gifts—gifts which could not be measured—and yet it is said that no spices ever were brought to him such as she brought ; and she returned to her land having learnt of the one and only true God.

How much nobler this African queen was than are the men of to-day ! Like her, they hear the fame of the " greater than Solomon," and, like her, they do not believe the report. But, unlike her, they do not bestir themselves to test what they have heard. If they did so bestir themselves, they would find that all that is said about the love and saving power of the Lord Christ, is true, and they would exclaim that the half had not been told them ! No more of the self-spirit would be left in them, and the unsearchable riches of Christ would be poured into their bosoms ; and although their gifts to Him, i.e., their hearts, their love, their trust, could all easily be measured, yet would He, in His grace, declare

that no such spices come into His treasury as those brought by pardoned sinners.

Verse 12 relates that Solomon gave to this queen not only all her desire, and further, whatsoever she asked, but also returned into her hand all the wealth that she had given to him. When men surrender themselves, their wills, and their wealth to the " greater than Solomon," He restores them all, sanctified and blessed ; and, with them, He gives new treasures never dreamt of !

The weight of gold paid each year to Solomon was six hundred and sixty-six talents ; and this number joined with the six steps to his throne (v. 18) stamps imperfection upon all his glory ; for " six " is the number of man, and just comes short of " seven," which is the number of perfection. Man was created on the sixth day. Goliath and Nebuchadnezzar's great image, present this number ; and finally it reappears in the Anti-Christ.

Two fleets are to be understood as described in verse 21. One fleet went to Tarshish that is, Spain, mainly to fetch silver. The other fleet, consisting of ships built after the model of Tarshish ships, sailed from Eziongeber to Africa, for ivory and gold, and to India for precious stones, gold and silver and apes and peacocks. Apes and peacocks appear in the Hebrew text as Tamil words.

In verses 24, 25, and 28, the Holy Spirit sorrowfully calls attention to Solomon's passion for horses. These were forbidden him by the Word of God. Later on, they were instruments in the Devil's hand for destroying Judah (2 Chron. xii. 3, 4, 9, Ps. xxxiii. 17).

The supposed mistake found in verse 25 and 1 Kings iv. 26, will be found explained in the notes on this latter passage.

Desires forbidden by the Word of God, if indulged, afterwards return, like Solomon's horses, as instruments of captivity to the soul.

Verse 29 makes it clear that God in His love to His wilful servant forewarned him as to Jeroboam ; but in vain.

The last dark days of Solomon's reign are as faithfully recorded by the infallible Spirit of God as the first bright ones. George Müller's prayer was, therefore, a Spirit-taught prayer : " Lord, do not let me die a wicked old man ! "

Solomon died at the early age of sixty. Had he not been a backslider, he might have lived to be one hundred and twenty.

As already stated, the Books of Chronicles record the counsels and the grace of God with respect to the House of David, and trace its connection with the Messiah. They only, therefore, mention such faults as require to be known in order to understand the activity of that grace and the accomplishment of those counsels. Hence, as in the case of David, the grave moral lapses of Solomon are, in this history, omitted. In "Kings" God faithfully writes history; in Chronicles, He graciously comments upon it. Compare Exod. ii. 15 with Heb. xi. 27.

2 CHRONICLES X.—In addition to the notes upon 1 Kings ix., it is instructive to point out how the dissatisfaction of the nation with the glorious reign of Solomon, and their election of his enemy Jeroboam as king, picture what is predicted in Rev. xix. There it is foretold that although Christ will maintain an absolutely perfect government over the whole earth for one thousand years, yet will the world be dissatisfied with that reign of glory and righteousness, will call back Satan from exile, as Israel called back Jeroboam, and enthrone him as prince over all the earth.

Shechem was the national sanctuary and capital before the Divine selection of Jerusalem (Jos. xxiv. 1). It was the site of Abraham's first altar, and was Jacob's first home. Here Joseph was buried, and here the tribes met. Here, alone in all the world, is the Paschal Lamb still slain.

The introduction of Jeroboam in verse 2, without any explanation of who he was, shows that acquaintance with him is assumed (1 Kings xi. 26-40). This introduction of a person into the narrative, occurring from time to time in Chronicles, and assuming acquaintanceship, shows that the Author of these books, and of the Books of the Kings, was one and the same; i.e., the Spirit of God. Verse 15 furnishes another instance of assumed acquaintanceship with the prophecy of Ahijah the Shilonite.

This fulfilment of the prediction of Ahijah affords an instance, similar to many others in the Scriptures, of prophecies being accomplished by the operation of human passions, and in the natural course of events. Men think that they are obeying their own wills, and carrying out their own plans, unconscious that the matter is of God, and permitted and overruled by Him for the performance of His Word.

The word "tribute" in verse 18 is rightly translated "levy" in the R.V. It means the forced labourers who were compelled to serve in the execution of public works. These labourers, as already learned, were prisoners of war; and it shows the moral decadence of the nation that its disruption was originated, and effected, by these idolatrous strangers.

Hadoram's courage in trying to quell the revolt was, alas, courage on behalf of a bad master. He was one of the nine persons stoned to death of whom the Scriptures speak. The notes on Lev. xxiv detail these nine persons.

Although only the three tribes of Judah, Benjamin, and Levi remained loyal to the House of David, and to Jehovah, yet are they frequently spoken of afterwards as the "People of Israel." Numerous passages in Ezra and Nehemiah, together with Acts iv. 27, illustrate this fact. Their loyalty explains the use of this language.

2 CHRONICLES XI.—In fulfilment of 1 Kings xi. 36 the tribe of Benjamin was given to David, that is, to Judah, by God. The tribe of Levi voluntarily joined, (verses 13, 14) and, after them, many out of the revolting ten tribes who remained true to Jehovah and the Scriptures.

The fifteen cities that the king fortified in Judah and in Benjamin were evidently intended for defence against Egypt. Th fact that Jeroboam established the national religion of Egypt in his dominions must have made that great empire more formidable to Rehoboam.

With great sagacity the king placed his sons as governors of the fenced cities; providing them with all necessary provision of food and money. To strengthen their position he married them to several wives apiece; and, if these wives were drawn from the foremost families of each city, as most likely they were, that fact would make the worldly wisdom of Rehoboam yet more conspicuous. The "many wives" of verse 23 were sought for his sons, and not for himself, as the R.V. shows.

For three years Rehoboam walked in subjection to the Word of God and prospered; but only for three years.

In verse 21 Maachah, also named Michaiah (ch. xiii. 2), is stated to have been the daughter of Absalom. but this later chapter describes her as the daughter of Uriel. The words " daughter " and " granddaughter " are synonymous. Josephus says that Uriel was the son-in-law of Absalom.

2 CHRONICLES XII.—But all Rehoboam's sagacity, and his fenced cities, failed to save him from the king of Egypt. Had he remained true to the Lord, he would have been absolutely safe from his Egyptian enemy ; but neither fenced cities, nor worldly wisdom, can protect a throne that is disloyal to truth.

Directly Rehoboam felt himself strong, he forsook the Law, the only shield that could protect him (Eph. vi. 16 " the faith "), that is, the Bible ; and, as a result, the unsearchable riches left him by David and Solomon were all carried off into Egypt. It is better to be weak and cling to the Bible, than to possess supposed strength and forsake it ; for forsaking the Bible entails the loss of the priceless truths bequeathed to the Church of God by the apostles of Jesus Christ.

Being placed by God in a public position carries with it great responsibility. Rehoboam " forsook the law of the Lord, and all Israel with him." Christian people, in every rank of life, exercise an influence. The higher their social position, the greater, therefore, is their responsibility. Those beneath them in position imitate them. The king leaves the narrow way that leads to life, and enters the broad road that ends in destruction, and the entire nation follows him into that way of death. This great and dreadful principle operates to-day as effectually as three thousand years ago.

When living in fellowship with the world the two tribes are named "Judah " (v. 5). But when walking in fellowship with God they are, because of that fellowship, recognized as " Israel " (vs. 1 and 6). The use, therefore, of this latter title is not an error in the text but a fact in the spiritual life.

Verse 8 contrasts the sweetness of Christ's service with the bitterness of man's.

The shields of gold borne by the king's bodyguard when the monarch went up to the house of the Lord were carried into Egypt. They were replaced by brazen shields. The world robs the Church of Divine realities in public worship, and the Church tries to hide the loss by substituting imitations.

The sentence in verse 12 " also in Judah things went well " may mean " also to Judah there were good words," i.e., from God. That is, there was a message of grace from Him, not only to Rehoboam, but also to Judah. The passage, may, however, be thus understood (as in the R.V.), " also in Judah there were good words," i.e., of repentance, similar to the repentant language of the king.

Verses 13 and 14 form a brief recapitulation of all the foregoing facts ; and the evil conduct of verse 14 is not to be understood as a backsliding from the repentance of verse 12, it is to be understood as an explanation. It records that the idolatry into which he fell (v. 1) was caused by the teaching of his idolatrous mother, and by the fact that he did not prepare, that is, fix his heart (Ps. lvii. 7) to keep seeking, that is, hanging upon God.

Thirty-five verses contain Rehoboam's history in the Book of Kings ; fifty-eight verses in Chronicles. His idolatrous mother is mentioned twice in Kings, once in Chronicles. Seventy-six words in 1 Kings record his lapse into idolatry, but only six words relate it in Chronicles. His repentance is a prominent feature in Chronicles, but not mentioned in Kings. These facts illustrate the difference between these two books.

The campaign of Shishak against Jerusalem is described on the wall of the famous Temple at Karnak near Thebes, and is illustrated with a portrait of Rehoboam.

2 CHRONICLES XIII.—The history of Abijah occupies eight verses in Kings, but twenty-three verses in Chronicles. Fidelity to fact, as to what he was personally, records in Kings the change of his name from Abijah to Abijam ; further, that his mother's name was Maachah ; that he walked in all the sins of his father Rehoboam ; and, that any prosperity he enjoyed was for the sake of David his father. Grace, in Chronicles, omits these sad personal facts ; names him Abijah ; gives to his mother the honourable title of Michaiah ; and describes at length his bold testimony for God and the Bible, and his valour and success in battle. The battle was won because he and his soldiers relied upon " Jehovah, the God of their fathers " (v. 18).

Abijah means " Jehovah is my Father " ; Abijam, " the sea," that is, tumult, " is my father." Fellowship with God, carries with it the enjoyment of a father's love. Turning aside to idols, fills the heart with restlessness

Maachah signifies " oppression " ; Michaiah " who is like Jehovah ? " In chapter xv. 16, the queen is named " Maachah " because there she is an idolatress. Serving idols brings the soul into bondage ; serving God leads it into a liberty so great that it gives the bold and joyful challenge, " who is like Jehovah ? "

The expression " a covenant of salt " in verse 5, means an irrevocable covenant. (See Lev. ii. 13 and Num. xviii. 19).

The size of these two armies, and the immense multitude slain in the battle, need cause no surprise when compared with the numbers shown in the census made by David ; and when it is remembered that in a hand to hand engagement many thousands can be slain in a few moments, and very many thousands in the subsequent rout. The steady increase of Judah and decrease of Israel may be learned from the number of their soldiers. Rehoboam had 180,000 ; Abjiah, eighteen years later, 400,000 ; Asa, still later, 580,000 ; Jehoshaphat, thirty-two years later, 1,160,000. On the other hand, Jeroboam assembled 800,000, while Ahab's army was likened to two little flocks of kids.

2 CHRONICLES XIV.—The reign of Asa in the Book of Kings is told in fifteen verses ; forty-eight verses describe it in the Book of Chronicles.

Asa did that which was good and right in the eyes of Jehovah his God ; and his heart was perfect all his days (xiv. 2 and xv. 17). " Perfect " does not here mean " sinless," but loyal to the teaching of the Bible, and hostile to idolatry.

As resulting from this loyalty, tranquillity was enjoyed. This is stated five times in verses 1-6.

There was hostility between Asa and Baasha all their days, but no campaigning.

The idolatry destroyed in verse 3 was no doubt that existing in the city of Jerusalem. This is suggested by the word " also " in verse 5, and the statement in chapter xv. 17 that, as to Israel, that is, in the country districts, the high places escaped demolition.

Idolatry brings in its train weakness and disquietude. Obedience to God's Word brings strength and peace (vs. 3-8).

The faith of one man frequently affects others and produces a revival. In a short time Asa is surrounded by 580,000 comrades. But in the battle with Zerah, his faith rest

not on them, but on God. Reading from the R.V., with the margin, the argument of verse 11 would appear, not to be that God can work with a strong or a weak instrument, which is quite true, but that He can give the victory to a helpless person as against a mighty enemy. The verse ,therefore, may be paraphrased thus : Lord, Thou art the only Saviour. Thou canst help him who hath no strength against the mighty. Help us, Oh Jehovah our God, for we rely on Thee."

The result of the battle was that every Ethiopian was slain, and great spoil obtained. Thus may it be in the Christian life. Jesus is a great Saviour, He can give the victory against one million sins and put them all to death, and then enrich the soul with exceeding much spoil.

The words " His host " are loving words. They mean that His peoples' battles are His own.

The word " fear," in verse 14, means that a great terror from Jehovah fell on them. (See chapter xix. 7, 9).

2 CHRONICLES XV.—The prophet Azariah is not mentioned elsewhere in the Bible.

His message to Asa was given as the king, with his victorious soldiers, returned from the slaughter of the Ethiopians. It was a message, and a prophecy. The message is contained in verses 2-7 ; the prophecy in the last six words of verse 7. The words " now for a long season " (v. 3) " and in those times" (v. 5) are connected. They mean, that from long ago every time that Israel departed from the Law, i.e., the Bible, " there was no peace but great vexations." The days of Gideon (Judges v. 6, and vi. 6), illustrate this.

Asa, encouraged by this message and prophecy, repaired the altar in front of the Temple ; destroyed the remaining idols in his kingdom ; gathered all his people to Jerusalem for the feast of Pentecost ; gifted to the Lord an immense portion of the spoil captured in his successful campaign ; induced everybody to enter into a covenant to serve the Lord ; decreed, in obedience to Deut. xvii. 2-6, the death of all idolators ; destroyed the monstrous Ashera of his grandmother, and removed her from being queen.

As before pointed out, the word " perfect " in verse 17 means pure from idolatrous worship, and not necessarily moral perfection. the word " reign " in verse 19 signifies " kingdom."

2 CHRONICLES XVI.—The victorious Asa of chapter xiv. becomes the defeated Asa of chapter xvi. Spiritual victories teach the natural heart nothing. New victories cannot be won by the remembrance of old faith ; there must be a fresh exercise of faith in every crisis.

The success of a self-made plan is a disaster. Asa's scheme in bribing the Syrian king to falsehood and treachery, succeeded for the moment ; but the real result was that he lost the opportunity of destroying both Baasha and Benhadad ; he involved himself in continual war ; he oppressed his own subjects; he persecuted God's prophet ; he became diseased in his feet, and died under the hands of charlatan physicians. Had he, in his later years, as in his first years, relied wholly on the mighty hand of God, his life would have been a going from strength to strength.

The word " reign " in verse 1 should be " kingdom." It was the sixteenth year of Asa's reigning, but the thirty-sixth year of the kingdom over which he reigned. Baasha was therefore alive at this time ; and not nine years dead as some suppose.

The words " Let there be " should be supplied at the beginning of verse 3.

The duplication of the words "behold," and " lo," (v. 11) is important. When the Holy Spirit speaks thus, special attention should be given to what is said. The word " behold " is really a verb. " Behold " is used by the Spirit, " Verily " by the Son, and " Yea " by the Father.

The physicians of verse 12 are not to be assumed to be such as Luke was, but superstitious priests who used charms. This is the first mention of them among the Hebrews.

The peculiar statement occurs in verse 13 that " Asa slept with his fathers, and died." This compared with the decease of other kings, suggests that his death was not natural, but a Divine chastisement.

The word " sepulchres " (v. 14) means " a great sepulchre." It is an instance of the use of the plural to express majesty.

The words in verse 12, " his disease became exceeding great " is translated by some Hebrew scholars, " mounted high up " ; that is, ascended from his feet into his body, and so caused his death by mortification. To hide this, his body was laid in a bed of odours, and a very great burning of spices made for him. But the odours could not hide the cause of his death.

Many servants of God become diseased in their feet in their old age ; that is, their Christian walk, i.e., their manner of life, dishonours, instead of adorns, the Gospel of Christ ; and in place of leaving behind them a sweet savour of Jesus' name, they leave an unpleasant memory, which " all the odours prepared by the apothecaries' art " fail to remove.

" How beautiful upon the mountains are the feet of him that publisheth peace." Continuance upon those " mountains " guarantees the preacher against this disease in the feet.

2 CHRONICLES XVII.—See notes on 1 Kings xxii and Isa. xxxvi–xxxix. Jehoshaphat strengthened himself against Israel. Israel was his most dangerous enemy because of the worship of Jehovah and the Golden Calf. That which claims to be connected with God, but is linked with evil, is the most dangerous enemy to the servants of God.

Ahab's daughter and feast secured Jehoshaphat's fall. Compare Hezekiah and the king of Babylon.

So long as Jehoshaphat walked in the first ways of David, and not after the doings of Israel, he prospered. But this prosperity became a snare to him, and made it worth while to others to seek alliance with him. He joined affinity with Israel. Alliance with the world prevents victory over the world. The heart, when not kept by God, can act generously with respect to evil which it does not fear ; but that is not true love. Jehoshaphat's faithfulness and generosity to Ahab meant unfaithfulness to God, and brought upon him the wrath of God (ch. xix. 2). Compare " against Israel " (v. 1) and " with Ahab " (xviii. 1).

The character, however, of Jehoshaphat is a fine one and refreshes the heart. In many respects his reign is more beautiful than that of any other king.

The words " lifted up " in verse 6 mean " encouraged." The double result of this encouragement was the destruction of idolatry, and the setting up of Bible-schools in his dominions. The Bible-schools were placed in charge of five princes, nine Levites, and two priests. They took with them the Book of the Law (v. 9), i.e., the Book written by Moses. (See notes on Exod. xvii). Loving and obeying the Bible makes the Christian spiritually strong, and equips him for the wars of the Lord.   It is therefore appropriate that this evidence of affection for God's Holy Book should be quickly followed by the appearing of an army of 1,600,000 men.

2 CHRONICLES XVIII.—Riches and honour are more dangerous to the spiritual life than contempt and poverty.   In verse 2 Satan kills sheep in abundance to feast Jehoshaphat ; in verse 31 he tries to kill Jehoshaphat himself.   This was one trap.   Jehoshaphat marries his son Jehoram to Athaliah, the daughter of Ahab (xxi. 6).   The world would call it a brilliant match ; but it drenched Jerusalem with blood.   This was a second trap.

When the Christian " goes down " to the world, he is received with great hospitality ; but immediately is made a tool of by the world (vs. 2 and 3).   Ramoth-Gilead belonged to Israel, and to recover it from the enemy was surely a good work.   But to undertake the matter in fellowship with Ahab was to do evil.

Three unequal yokes appear in this history :   marriage, war, and commerce.

Had this Book a human author, verses 18-21 would never have been composed. The Holy Spirit does not hesitate to record this scene in heaven.

There are three courts in this chapter. The reader is introduced into each, and permitted to hear what was said in them— the court of Ahab, the court of Heaven, and the Court of Syria.

God's message to Ahab through Micaiah was a message of love. He plainly told this blood-stained idolator that if he went up to the battle he would surely perish.   Ahab closed his ears to the gracious message, and thought to out-wit God by disguising himself ; but he perished.

Verse 31 illustrates the Divine titles of Genesis i. and ii.   To Jehoshaphat, God was Jehovah, that is, a covenanted Saviour : to the Syrians, He was Elohim, that is, the Creator.

2 CHRONICLES XIX.—Jehoshaphat returned to his house in peace, that is, in bodily peace, as contrasted with Ahab—but only in physical peace, for the message of the prophet Jehu must have added to the unrest that oppressed his heart.

This was the brave prophet that reproved Baasha (1 Kings xvi.), and here rebuked Jehoshaphat.

The message shows what God thinks as to joining with godless men in praiseworthy enterprises.

The wrath of God denounced upon the king, found its fulfilment in the events of the next chapter.

The three courts of justice established by the king, and the language used by him in connection with them, make it plain that Jehoshaphat read, and loved, and obeyed the Bible.   (See Deut. xvii.).

Local courts were in the first instance set up in the county towns.   Controversies undecided by these courts were returned to Jerusalem (vs. 8–10), where the higher court heard them.   This higher court was composed of both clergy and laity.   The third, or supreme court, formed the Court of Appeal, and had two Divisions, the Sacred and the Civil.   In all these courts the Levites acted as lawyers.

The " fear " of verse 7 means " dread," that is, the judges were to dread the just anger of God if they took bribes or respected persons in judgment.

The " fear " of verse 9 means reverential fear.   The English word " fear " in these two verses is a different word in the Hebrew text.

2 CHRONICLES XX.—Two foundation principles appear in this chapter.   First, God's fidelity to His Word, i.e., His wrath, and, second, His response to faith, i.e., His love.   The prophet announced the wrath of God because of Jehoshaphat's unholy alliance with Ahab, and the Ammonites and Moabites become the instruments of that wrath.   But in response to Jehoshaphat's cry of distress (v. 12), and his song of faith (v. 19), sung before the battle began, a complete victory was granted to him.   No doubt these enemies were encouraged to attack him because of the disastrous issue of the campaign against Ramoth-Gilead.   This is a fine instance of a guilty servant seeking refuge in the bosom of the very God who was justly smiting him. The words prayer (v. 3), promise (v. 17), praise (v. 21), and peace (v. 30) explain the secret of the victory and its fruit.

The assemblage of verse 4 was to ask help of the Lord.   The assemblage of verse 26 was to bless the Lord.   The " fear " that Moab inspired preceded the prayer meeting of verse 4 ;   the " joy " that God inspired

(v. 27) followed the praise meeting of verse 26. So God can give victory to faith but not to folly. Compare notes on Judges vii. and 1 Kings xxii.

The language of verses 6 and 9 repeats the words respectively of David and Solomon. They evidence that the Bible was kept written up to date ; and that it was loved, read, and obeyed, by the true servants of God. There is frequent evidence of this fact in the Scriptures.

Abraham is three times called " the Friend of God," viz. : in verse 7 of this chapter, in Isaiah xli. 8, and in James ii. 23.

The " beauty of holiness " (v. 21) is understood by many to mean the Temple. May it not rather mean the beauty of God's holy action ? The passage pictures Jehovah advancing against the disobedient Jehoshaphat with his rod of wrath (Moab) in His hand, and Jehoshaphat approaches God, not with words of anger or complaint, but with a cry of distress (v. 12) ; and then, assured of victory (v. 17), he raises a song of praise in which he proclaims all the ways of God, both in wrath and grace, to be holy and beautiful.

The command in verse 17, " stand still," should be read together with a similar command in other books of the Bible. A concordance will give all the instances. They, together, furnish a very profitable Bible-reading.

There is no contradiction between chapter xvii. 6 and verse 33 of this chapter. Jehoshaphat commanded the destruction of these high places, and, so far as he was individually responsible, he took them away ; but the people failed to carry out his commands.

" After this "—after the wonderful deliverance of this chapter, after the solemn warning of chapter xix. 2, after his experience in chapter xviii. 1 ! This was Jehoshaphat's third alliance with the guilty house of Ahab. It was fellowship in commerce. God in His love and wisdom broke it up. No amount of Christian experience guarantees against such folly. The Christian life is a daily one ; and watching and praying is as necessary to an experienced as to an inexperienced Christian.

Comparing verses 36 and 37 with 1 Kings xxii. 48, 49, two expeditions appear. The first, ships to go to Tarshish, that is, Spain ; the second, ships of Tarshish, ie., Tarshish ships, that is, ocean-going vessels, to sail to Ophir for gold. The one fleet sailed to the west, the other to the east. God broke them both.

2 CHRONICLES XXI.—The title " king of Israel " in verse 2, which some scholars think to be an error in transcription, illustrates the principle, so often met with in the Bible, that God recognizes a faithful remnant as His entire people. This principle appears in the action of the Lord when He disowned relationship to His mother and brothers and sisters who had come to take charge of Him as a lunatic, and declared that His disciples were His family. (Mark iii. 21 and 31.)

The slaughter of all the sons of Jehoshaphat by Jehoram was in conformity with Satan's design to prevent the birth of the Messiah. At this period of time, in order to carry out this purpose, he employed Jehoshaphat (ch. xviii. 1), Jehoram (ch. xxi. 4), the Arabians (ch. xxii. 1), and Athaliah (ch. xxii. 10). He nearly succeeded. The entire Messianic line was destroyed, except one infant—Joash, and on that one thread the hope of man's redemption hung.

Jehoram reigned two years in partnership with his father, and six years as sole king. (See notes on 2 Kings viii. 16).

Historical students point out that Elijah could not have written a letter to Jehoram, because he was already dead ; but verse 12 does not speak of a " letter." It says a " writing," of which Elijah was the author, was brought to king Jehoram. It was a prophecy. The verse does not say when it was written. God raised up Elijah to prophesy against the house of Ahab, and Jehoram being Ahab's son-in-law, there was nothing unusual in the utterance of this prophecy against him. By Divine design the prophecy was handed to Jehoram at the intended moment. Cyrus and Alexander the Great were also handed prophetic writings from Isaiah and Daniel.

Jehoram died " without being desired," that is, unregretted.

2 CHRONICLES XXII.—This king had three names, viz : Ahaziah, Azariah, and Jehoahaz. All have the same meaning in Hebrew, i.e., " Jehovah taketh hold." These variations in the name evidence accuracy, and not inaccuracy, as is also the case in English. Compare Harry, Hal, Henry.

For an explanation of the forty-two years in verse 2, see notes on 2 Kings viii. 26 ; and read the same notes for a reconciliation of the seemingly conflicting accounts of Ahaziah's death.

The destruction which overtook the house of David illustrates the disaster sure to come upon the spiritual life of an individual, or a church, when there is a connection formed with what professes to be of God, but which in reality is of Satan. Such was the house of Omri; and Jehoshaphat's false step in making affinity with it, bore bitter and blood-stained fruit.

2 CHRONICLES XXIII.—This chapter is complementary to 2 Kings xi. See notes on that chapter.

2 CHRONICLES XXIV.—See notes on 2 Kings xii.

At the commencement of his reign Joash leant on Jehoiada who was a good man, afterwards he leant on the Princes of Judah, who were wicked men. To lean on men, whether they be good or wicked, is disastrous. Had the king leant " only upon God " (Ps. lxii. 5), how different would have been his history !

Jehoiada was wanting in spiritual intelligence (v. 3), and in executive energy (v. 6).

As in other passages, so here, this remnant of the nation is called " Israel " (v. 5). Thus God honoured any devotedness to Himself.

Verse 7 reveals that the slaughter of Jehoram's brothers (ch. xxi. 4) was not unmerited.

In repairing the Temple iron was used (v. 12). It was not used in constructing the Tabernacle. It also appears in the great image of Nebuchadnezzar. Many to-day are trying to repair the spiritual temple with iron, that is, with human authority. Origen introduced this system of repairing the Christian Church. Compare 1 Chron. xxii. 3.

" Moses, the servant of Jehovah " (v. 6). This title occurs eighteen times in the Bible. " Moses, the servant of Elohim " (v. 9) occurs four times.

Jehoiada was born in Solomon's reign. He therefore lived through six reigns. Joshua died at 110. Jehoiada was buried among the kings (v. 16) ;—an honour denied to Joash (v. 25).

The first occurrence in literature of the word " protestant " is found in Jerome's Bible, in verse 19. It is interesting that this word should be found in the Roman Catholic Bible centuries prior to the Reformation.

The Lord in Luke xi. 50, 51, twice uses the verb " require " (v. 22).

The wrath of God predicted in verses 18 and 20 came to pass in verses 23 and 24.

The word " sons " in verse 25 is an instance of the grammatical form called the " plural of majesty " ; it means the great and brave and God-fearing son of Jehoiada.

The history of Joash illustrates how terrible and immediate are the judgments that fall upon those who are officially and closely connected with God and Truth.

2 CHRONICLES XXV.—See notes on 2 Kings xiv.

Four statements in verse 4 are important. The book was " *the* Book of Moses," not a copy of the book, but *the* book itself. It was a " written " book ; its content was the Law; and, lastly, God was the author of that Law. The book was, therefore, inspired.

Amaziah sought help from the " religious world." There is always a temptation to lean upon the arm of flesh. The disastrous result is seen in verse 13. When a Christian makes a false step, it brings injury to others as well as to himself. Ministers of the Gospel bring great spiritual damage upon their congregations when they buy the assistance of mere professors of religion in some worthy enterprise.

Success is dangerous. Victory over the Edomites was quickly followed by slavery to their idols. This often happens. The Northern European nations, victorious over the Papal Church, quickly set up their sacramental idols, and are enslaved by them to this day.

What Satan fails to do by violence he accomplishes by guile. The Edomites having failed to destroy Judah, their gods provoke the wrath of Jehovah, and defeat, poverty, and death overtake Amaziah. His reign opened with sunshine, but closed with darkest night. With God there is prosperity ; without God, ruin.

In verse 28 occurs the unique instance of the expression " the city of Judah." When a king turns away from the Lord (v. 27), the Holy Spirit declines to call his burial place by the lofty titles of " city of David " or " Jerusalem."

2 CHRONICLES XXVI.—Uzziah, named Azariah in 2 Kings, was four years of age at the time of his father's murder. He was sixteen years of age when crowned. There was, therefore, a regency for twelve or thirteen years. So long as he leant upon Zechariah (v. 5) he prospered. It is dangerous to lean upon even a good man.

The " engines " of verse 15, were called by the Romans " balista " ; they could throw stones, weighing three hundred pounds, a quarter of a mile. Pliny states that the " balista " was a Syrian invention. That statement has a curious relation to this verse.

Uzziah was " marvellously helped," that is, God prospered him so greatly that people marvelled. But when he was strong he entered the zone of real danger. " When we are weak, then are we strong " (2 Cor. xii). Strong Christians are in very great danger.

Uzziah, like Cain, claimed the right to personally worship God without the intervention of an atoning Saviour and High Priest. He was a Unitarian.

On the forehead of the High Priest was " Holiness to the Lord " (Christ). On the forehead of Uzziah was " sinfulness" (leprosy).
See notes on 2 Kings xvi. and Isa. vi.

2 CHRONICLES XXVII. — Jotham was twenty-five when he began to reign alone. He was twenty when he became co-regent with his father.

" He entered not into the House of the Lord." This probably means that, terrified by the fate of his father, he did not attend the Temple services. If this be so, then Uzziah, Jotham, and Ahaz illustrate how incurably diseased is the natural heart. The first king boldly intrudes into the Temple, the second, timidly stands away from it, and the third shuts it up !

Had Jotham, instead of building fortified cities and castles and towers in the mountains and in the forests, broken down the High Places at which the people did corruptly, he would have effectually protected himself against the afterwards victorious Syrians (see 2 Kings xv).

The Holy Spirit (vs. 1, 8) twice records his age and the length of his reign. Why ? A deeper spiritual knowledge of the Scriptures could furnish a satisfying answer ; but the repetition draws attention to two facts that affect the heart ; the one, that the king was very young ; the other, that he was true to God to the end.

2 CHRONICLES XXVIII.—See notes on 2 Kings xvi, to which chapter this is complementary.

An important principle appears in the verses 5–15. It also appears in connection with Babylon. When executing God's judgment upon transgressors, or delivering His messages of wrath to sinners, there must be no jubilation on the part of the messenger, nor excess of temper in the instrument. If called by God to such a service, the person, or persons, employed should be filled with self-judgment, humility and compassion.

Ahaz outdid all others in his apostasy to idols. Hence the words in verse 22 " This is that king Ahaz." Three other specially branded transgressors appear in Cain (Gen. iv. 15), and Dathan and Abiram (Num. xxvi. 9).

The word " kings " in verse 16 means " the great king." It is the Plural of Majesty. The gods of Damascus did not really smite Ahaz (v. 23), but he believed they did.

Ahaz is entitled " King of Israel " (v. 19), and his fathers are named " kings of Israel " (v. 27). These are not errors in transcription or intelligence, as some suppose, but touching illustrations of the amazing grace and faithfulness which recognized as " Israel " a remnant of the nation, however feeble and fallen.

2 CHRONICLES XXIX.—The reign of Hezekiah illustrates the designed difference between the Book of the Kings and the Book of the " Comments." In " Kings " three chapters are given to the Civil events of this king's reign and only three verses to the Religious. In Chronicles this is reversed. Three chapters are devoted to the Religious events and one to the secular.

The moral order in Chronicles differs from the chronological in Kings. (Compare 1 Cor. x. with Exodus, where the same principle appears).

These facts show that Chronicles is independent of, and complementary to, Kings ; that the authorship is one ; that the so-called discrepancies and exaggerations are designed ; that difficulties are created by assuming that the books ought to be alike ; and that both books were written by God for the instruction and admonition of His people.

The " east street " (v. 4) was the open space opposite the entrance to the Temple.
It is not stated if idolatrous objects existed

inside the Temple, but what was there is called "filthiness" in verse 5 and "uncleanness" in verse 16.

The words "for this" in verse 9 point back to the actions recited in verses 6 and 7. These actions detail the steps which the Enemy of Souls takes in all ages in turning sinners away from Jesus, in putting out the light of the Bible, in suppressing prayer, and in causing true worship to cease.

The king does not state in verse 10 that he himself put it into his own heart to effect this reformation, but that he found this holy desire there. It was put there by God.

The names of these fourteen Levites have no interest for the historians of this world, but such an interest for the Holy Spirit that they are here all set out, and they have been read already by hundreds of millions of people for more than two thousand years. Such is the estimation which lovers of Bible religion enjoy in Divine history.

The statement: "the commandment of the king by the words of the Lord," and the subsequent actions of the king, show that Hezekiah, in all that he did and commanded, confined himself to "the volume of the Book"(Ps. xl. 7),just as the singers in verse 30 confined themselves to the hymn book compiled by David and Asaph.

True cleansing begins in the "inner part" (v. 16), and proceeds outward. Man makes clean the outside and stops there.

The first day of the first month is specially pointed to in the Scriptures. (Gen. viii. 13, Exod. xii. 2, 2 Chron. xxix. 17, Ezra vii. 9, Ezra x. 17, Ezek. xlv. 18).

First, the sin-offering, and then the burnt-offering, were sacrificed. The sprinkling of the blood of the sin-offering upon the golden altar ; the laying, on the part of the king and the people, of their guilty hands upon the sacrifice ; the flaying of the burnt-offering (v. 34) ; and the singing and worship associated with it, and not with the sin-offering, show that the Book of Leviticus existed at that time, and that it was minutely obeyed by Hezekiah and Israel.

2 CHRONICLES XXX.—Hezekiah's Passover was one of the Ten Great Passovers of the Bible. Certain facts connected with its observance prove that the Pentateuch was read, loved, and obeyed by Hezekiah. He invited all Israel (Exod. xii.) ; he kept the feast in the second month instead of the first (Num. ix) ; he ordained that it should be observed "as it is written" (Lev. xxiii) ; he declared that their miseries were those predicted in Deuteronomy (v. 7) ; that God would have compassion upon them if they turned unto Him, as promised in Deuteronomy (v. 9) ; that all was to be regulated by the Word of the Lord, i.e., by the Bible (v. 12) ; that the priests should officiate according to the Law of Moses (v. 16) ; he pointed out to the people that many of them were not ceremonially clean according to the Scriptures (v. 17) ; learning that a multitude ate the Passover "otherwise than it was written" (v. 18), he prayed that they might be pardoned, thus showing his reverence for the Bible and his fear of disobeying it (Lev. xv. 31) ; he believed the threatened plague to be a reality (v. 20) ; he kept the feast of unleavened bread seven days, because so the Book of God ordained (v. 21) ; and, in a word, in the observance of the feast, he confined himself within the leaves of the Bible.

The state of anarchy in the Northern Kingdom, and the disposition of king Hoshea toward religious liberty (2 Kings xvii. 2), favoured the enterprise of the open-air preachers. They, however, had much abuse and little success.

Verse 26 does not contradict 2 Kings xxiii. 22: Josiah's passover was after Hezekiah's.

Verse 27 assumes inspiration ; for the information there given is superhuman.

2 CHRONICLES XXXI.—The home idols having been smashed, and fourteen happy days spent in spirit "at the feet of Jesus," (Luke x. 39) Hezekiah and his friends went out throughout the whole country and utterly destroyed all idolatry. Such is the power that obedience and communion give to the soul.

The public unrest caused by the threatened invasion of the Assyrians was availed of by these faithful men to advance the interests of the Kingdom of God. This is a fine lesson, and teaches that Christian people should take advantage of public troubles to testify for Christ, and not to come under the power of political passions.

Those who yielded themselves to God to be His instruments in this reformation were enriched and glorified—enriched by the abounding tithes, and glorified by their names being inscribed upon the Sacred Record

Such is God's way with His servants; they enjoy the blessing and share the glory. (1 Cor. ix. 13, 14).

So abundant was the provision made for the Temple Ministry that storehouses had to be built to warehouse the food for the approaching winter; and certain Levites were appointed to apportion therefrom daily bread for all the families of Levi then in Jerusalem. This " set office," i.e., office of trust (v. 15), was administered by men who " sanctified themselves in holiness," that is, devoted themselves with holy honesty to this ministry (v. 18).

" They utterly destroyed," (v. 1) i.e. The Divine Plan ; " The camp of Jehovah " (v. 2 R.V.), i.e., The Divine Place ; " The Law of Jehovah " (v. 3), i.e., The Divine Book ; and " The firstfruits of corn " (v. 5), i.e., The Divine Blessing. This last is certain if the three prior are living facts.

2 CHRONICLES XXXII.—Reading the first verse as in the R.V., the sentence appears : "After this faithfulness, Sennacherib." Faithfulness, i.e., fidelity to the Bible, is sometimes rewarded with outward prosperity, but always meets with Satanic hostility. Christian people, therefore, should not think it a strange experience if, when seeking to fully follow the Lord, they are suddenly confronted with sharp trials. If, like Hezekiah, they lean only upon God for deliverance, they will find, as he did, that the Angel of Jehovah is " mighty to save."

Recent discoveries at Jerusalem have revealed a water channel cut by Hezekiah through the solid rock, and so constructed at one point that the flow of water could be stopped by the insertion of a stone plug in the narrowed passage. The plug was found in the side of the channel ; and an inscription in ancient Hebrew engraved in the wall of the cutting, determined the age of the work.

Sennacherib sent two messages, one verbal (v. 9) ; the other, written (v. 17). The word " letters " in this latter verse is the plural of magnitude ; it means a big, blasphemous, and boastful letter.

Between verses 16 and 17 the occurrences took place which are detailed in the notes upon 2 Kings xviii, xix.

Verse 12 illustrates that wherever there is practical obedience to the teaching of the Bible it will be misinterpreted by people of the world. The written Word commanded there should be only one altar in Israel Man approves of many.

Reading in the book of the prophets it is abundantly clear that Hezekiah's revival was not permanent among the people ; and putting verses 25, 26, and 31 together, it may be assumed that Hezekiah, like Peter, said, that though all should prove faithless, yet would not he ! But God left him that he might learn what was in his own heart ; and thus was he humbled.

Had he kept close to Jehovah, he would have spoken to the ambassadors of Babylon of His unsearchable riches, and not of his own poor treasures of silver and gold ; and he would also have testified to them of " the wonder done in the land," i.e., the movement of the sunlight upon the dial of Ahaz.

The Babylonians, being ardent and skilled astronomers, were naturally very much interested in that matter. It was a miracle similar to that in the days of Joshua. By a slight declination of the earth the sun was made either to appear stationary in the sky, or else to appear to move backward. This phenomenon is witnessed every year in Europe between 3 p.m. on the 21st of December and the corresponding time on the 21st of the following June. The miracle in Joshua's day, as in Hezekiah's, consisted in this declination of the earth occurring in one day instead of in six months. It was a miracle ; and God alone could perform it. See notes on Mat. xv. 32.

2 CHRONICLES XXXIII.—Hezekiah, who was a blessing to his people, only reigned twenty-nine years, but Manasseh, who was a malediction to his people, reigned fifty-five.

This mysterious law still operates. It frequently happens that useful men and women die early, and useless people live long.

The sins which brought upon the Northern kingdom the judgment of " Lo-ruhamah," the same sins were now about to bring upon Judah the corresponding judgment of " Lo-ammi " (Hosea i).

Isa. xxii, Jer. iii, and all Amos reveal how seldom the heart—and it is that which God judges—corresponds with the semblance of fidelity to Truth which appears on the surface. The reformation which Hezekiah's faith and zeal effected, at once disappeared at the accession of Manasseh. He filled Jerusalem with shameful idols and with innocent blood ; and although God, who was always ready to pardon, forgave him, yet could He not forget this wickedness (2 Kings xxiv. 4).

Amon followed Manasseh in his iniquity, but not in his repentance ; and was murdered by his own servants.

In these histories each man may see his own heart reflected ; for, without God, what is the heart of man ? And in these histories may also be read the heart of God, and the grace which flowed therefrom, to bless men who refused to be blessed, and who, in their wilfulness, chose eternal ruin !

See notes on 2 Kings xxi.

Recent discoveries reveal that Babylon (v. 11) and not Nineveh, was at this time the residence of the Assyrian Monarch.

2 CHRONICLES XXXIV.—See notes on 2 Kings xxii and xxiii.

The three events of this chapter are the conversion of the king, the discovery of the Bible, and the reformation that resulted.

The king was sixteen at his conversion.

After his conversion, and prior to the discovery of the Bible, " he began to purge " Judah and Jerusalem from idolatry ; and six years later, when he had purged " the land and the House ", i.e., Judah and the Temple, the Bible was found.

Learning from it how defective the reformation was, he proceeded to a thorough one. A cleansing of the heart and life under the searchlight of the Word of God differs vastly from a reformation initiated by the feeble light of conscience, or tradition. But loyalty to conscience leads to the discovery of revealed Law. (Hosea vi. 3).

Verses 3, 4, 5, record the first and partial reformation.

Verses 6, 7, 33, together with 2 Kings xxiii, describe the greater and more thorough cleansing of the entire country, north and south.

Thus what appears to he a chronological discrepancy between 2 Kings and 2 Chronicles, disappears.

The words " with their mattocks round about " (v. 6) read in the R.V. " amid their ruins round about ". The Assyrians had reduced the northern towns to ruins, but left the idols and their altars unharmed. Josiah destroyed them ; and the Holy Spirit adds the solemn statement that they were destroyed in the midst of the ruins which they had occasioned.

Hilkiah, the high priest, who was, as high priest, an expert, said " I have found The Book " (v. 15). Shaphan, a mere scribe, said " a book " (v. 18).

2 CHRONICLES XXXV.—Three verses in Kings are given to Josiah's Passover—here, nineteen verses. This illustrates the difference between the two books.

Verse 3 makes plain that the Ark had been removed out of the Temple. Its restoration showed how the king knew, and loved, and obeyed the Bible.

Owing to the destruction wrought by the Assyrians, the mass of the people were very poor. The king and the princes, therefore, gave them animals for the burnt and peace-offerings, and lambs for the passover.

The passover being a family festival, the king followed the written instructions of David and Solomon under which the priests, the Levites, and the heads of families were so organized that, without confusion, the lamb for each family could be slain and its body roasted and eaten.

At the same time the other sacrifices were duly offered as commanded by God ; and, continuously throughout the day, the sons of Asaph sang, and the doorkeepers guarded the gates.

Thus the Holy Spirit with joy describes how closely Josiah kept to the written word of God in the observance of this passover.

Verse 6 records that Josiah believed that Moses wrote the Pentateuch ; and verse 12 showed his acquaintanceship with the Book of Exodus—especially chapter xii—which is there named " the Book of Moses "

Verse 18 does not contradict 2 Kings xxiii. 22. This Passover was subsequent to Hezekiah's, and greater. It was greater than all previous ones from the days of Samuel, not because it was larger, but because it conformed so closely to the Holy Scripture. Thus God in this record honoured Josiah because Josiah honoured Him. Hezekiah's Passover exceeded Solomon's (xxx. 26) ; Josiah's exceeded Samuel's, and Nehemiah's Feast of Tabernacles exceeded Joshua's (Neh. viii. 17).

After all this, that is, thirteen years after the king had restored the Temple worship, he foolishly lost his life at Megiddo, the scene of Barak's triumph. Those who, like Josiah, are famed for loyalty to the Bible, need prayerfully to cultivate the habit of daily believing dependance upon God—the life of faith—for, so deceptive is the heart that it will pride itself upon subjection to the Scriptures, and, because of that pride, refuse to accept a message from God because a heathen is the messenger (v. 22).

The " flesh " in Josiah was the same as the " flesh " in Ahab (v. 22). Both thought by disguising themselves to make void the Word of God. The " flesh " in the apostle Paul when he was coming down from the third heaven was exactly the same as when he was going up to Damascus to torture and murder the disciples of Jesus. Hence the necessity for the " stake ".

The expression " what have I to do with thee ? " (v. 21) means "what have we in common ? " the answer is, " nothing." It occurs three times. (See 2 Kings iii. 13, and John ii. 4).

Lamentations iv. 20, Jeremiah xxii. 10-18, and Zechariah xii. 11, illustrate verses 24 and 25.

Jeremiah was Josiah's father-in-law.

Two books are referred to in verses 26, 27. In verse 26, the Bible ; in verse 27, the record. The latter recited Josiah's actions ; the former, as a standard, measured his goodness. These two books exist to-day for every Christian.

2 CHRONICLES XXXVI.—Chronicles is the last book in the Hebrew Bible ; and this is, therefore, the last chapter. This fact adds solemnity to the words in verse 16 that " there was no remedy ". This ending to the Hebrew Bible led to the conversion of the famous Rabbi, Joseph Rabinovitch.

See notes on 2 Kings xxiii, xxiv, xxv.

The word " brother " in verse 10 means " relative," as frequently appears in the Bible. Zedekiah was uncle to Jehoiakim.

" From the mouth of Jehovah " (v. 12) ; " through the mouth of Jeremiah " (v. 21). These expressions illustrate inspiration. The words were from the mouth of Jehovah, that is, the words were God's words ; the instrument used for making them known to Israel was Jeremiah's mouth. The words did not originate in Jeremiah's mouth, but in Jehovah's mouth. (See note on 2 Peter i. 19-21).

The deportation of Israel, and the vessels of the House of God, to Babylon, has little interest for men of the world, but had an intense interest for the Spirit of God. Reading these verses—the closing words of the Hebrew Bible—the Christian heart feels the sob of anguish and love which pulsates in the text. Doubtless the Lord had this passage in mind when speaking the words recorded in Matthew xxiii. 23-39.

" The House of Jehovah " (v. 14) ; " their sanctuary " (v. 17). It was no longer Jehovah's. Compare " my Father's House " (John ii. 16), at the opening of the Lord's ministry, and, " your house " (Matthew xxiii. 28.), at its close.

" The God of Heaven." This is the first occurrence of this title. As the " God of Israel," He dwelt between the cherubim ; as " the God of Heaven "—Israel being Lo-ammi—He recognises " The Times of the Gentiles " ; and as " Lord of all the earth " He will reign in the Millennium.

The Chronology of the Books of Daniel, Ezra, Haggai, Zechariah, Esther, Malachi, and Nehemiah.

AS LEARNED FROM THE SCRIPTURES.

THE COMMENCING DATE, B.C., 520, IS THUS ARRIVED AT:

From the death of Christ to Cyrus (Dan. ix. 25)		483 years
From the death to the birth of Christ (Luke iii. 23 Jno. ii. 23, v. 1, vi. 4, xii. 1).	Deduct	33 years.
		450 years.
From Cyrus to Nebuchadnezzar (Jer. xxv. 1 and 11)		70 years.
	Total,	520 years.

The Proclamation of Cyrus closed the 70 years' servitude predicted by Jeremiah, and commenced the 483 years to the death of the Messiah—foretold by Daniel.

The names Ahasuerus and Artaxerxes are appellative and not personal. They correspond to Pharaoh, Cæsar, etc.

The commandment to restore Jerusalem pointed to in Dan. ix., 25, is the one predicted in Isaiah xlv. 13, and recorded in 2 Chron. xxxvi., 22, and Ezra, i. 1.

Isaiah predicted that Cyrus should restore Jerusalem (" he shall build My city") and lay the foundation of the Temple. Ezra relates the issue of the Proclamation and its ultimate accomplishment.

B.C.	Date.	EVENT.
520		Nebuchadnezzar began to reign (Jer. xxv. 1.)
518		Daniel's interpretation of the King's dream (Dan. ii.)
501		Jerusalem destroyed and the Temple burnt (2 Kings xxv.)
456		Daniel's vision of the Four Wild Beasts (Dan. vii. 1.)
454		Daniel's vision of the Ram and He-Goat (Dan. viii. 1.)
453		Belshazzar slain (Dan. v. 30.)
453		Darius Ahasuerus Artaxerxes, the Median, King of Persia, began to reign (Dan. v. 31.)
453		Daniel's vision of the 70 Heptads (Dan. ix. 1, 25.)
451		Cyrus Ahasuerus Artaxerxes commands the restoration of Jerusalem (Ezra i.)
451		The Exiles' return under Zerubbabel (Ezra ii.)
450		Restoration of the City and of the Temple begun (Ezra iii. 8), and stopped for 15 years till 435 (Ezra iv.)
449		Daniel's last vision and death (Dan. x. 1.; xii. 13).
444		Cambyses Ahasuerus Artaxerxes began to reign (Ezra iv. 6.)
444		The Samaritans petition him against Jerusalem (Ezra iv. 6.)
437		Smerdis Ahasuerus Artaxerxes began to reign (Ezra iv. 7.)
436		Darius Hystaspes Ahasuerus Artaxerxes, the Persian, began to reign (Hag. i.)
435		Haggai and Zechariah began to prophesy (Zech. i.)
435		Restoration of the City and Temple resumed (Ezra v.)
434		Queen Vashti deposed (Esther i.)
430		Completion of the Temple (Ezra vi. 15.)
429		Esther crowned Queen at Shushan (Esther ii. 16, 17.)
429		Ezra's journey to Jerusalem (Ezra vii. 1, 7.)
424		Death of Haman and deliverance of Israel (Esther iii. 7.)
417		Nehemiah's journey to Jerusalem (Neh. ii.)
405		Nehemiah's return to Babylon (Neh. xiii. 6.)
403		Nehemiah's second journey to Jerusalem (Neh. xiii. 7.)
403		The Prophet Malachi.

This Chronology conflicts with the Ptolemaic. That Chronology is based on the conjectural astronomy of the Ancients, and on the conflicting and uncertain estimates of Grecian Historians. It differs from Bible Chronology by 82 years. " The Romance of Bible Chronology," by Rev Martin Anstey, M.A., B.D., may be consulted in support of this statement.

EZRA

EZRA I.—As shewn on the preceding chart the Books of Esther, Ezra, and Nehemiah synchronize. These last two books form one in the Hebrew Scriptures. Their subject is the building of the Temple, and the repairing of the Wall of Jerusalem.

Israel having failed under the Priests, the Judges, and the Kings, God placed kingly power in the hand of the Gentile ; where it still resides. But He stirred up the heart of Cyrus to cause a remnant of His people to return to Jerusalem and to rebuild the Temple and the city, in order that, four centuries later, He might present to the remnant in that Temple the true King, His Dearly Beloved Son. His rejection resulted in the destruction of the city and the Temple by the Romans, and in the dispersion of the People.

The seventy years of captivity, predicted in Leviticus xxvi and Jeremiah xxix, having expired, Cyrus, as foretold in Isaiah xliv, was raised up by God to accomplish His work. Secular history records that he was shown these prophecies by Daniel, his aged Prime Minister, and thereby encouraged to befriend the Hebrews.

The Divine Titles in verses 2-4 should be noted. To the Gentile Cyrus, God was the " God of Heaven ", (v. 2) ; to the Captives, He was " Jehovah, the God of Israel " (v. 3) ; and to both, in common, He was " The God " (v. 3), i.e., the One, True, Living, and Only God.

" The chief of the fathers ", (v. 5.), are named in the next chapter.

Sheshbazzar, the Crown Prince of Judah, was Zerubbabel : He had two names. This Crown Prince did not recover the throne, nor could he, because of the judgment pronounced upon Jehoiachin. Jesus of Nazareth was not a descendant of Solomon and Jehoiachin, but of Solomon's elder brother, Nathan.

The basins, the dishes, the knives, and the other vessels possess no interest for the natural heart. But how often must the Lord, as man, have read and re-read these words ! They were all precious to His heart ; and they are precious to the heart that loves Him. There were only twenty-nine knives, and a knife is very small in comparison with a charger, but each knife was precious and counted.

The God of Heaven having placed kingly power in the hand of the Gentile, it was because of this that the Lord said, " Render unto Caesar the things that are Caesar's."

EZRA II.—Israel was carried into captivity to Babylon because of idolatry. A remnant returned cleansed from that greatest of all sins. Alas ! that that unclean spirit, having been cast out, should have returned later with other spirits more wicked than itself. It re-introduced idolatry under a worse form, and will yet perfect it in the worship of the Wild Beast and his image (Rev xiii. 8, 15).

The outstanding fact in this chapter is, there was faithfulness, though feebleness—feebleness, because there was no priest with Urim and Thummim (v. 61-63)—faithfulness, because they resolved that, so far as in them lay, the family of God should be a pure family, a numbered and recognised people. Hence, whoever could not produce his genealogy was set aside.

Judah, no longer a kingdom, became a Province of the Persian Empire (v. 1).

The word " Tirshatha " (v. 63) is a Persian word meaning Governor. Zerubbabel was a Tirshatha (v. 63), later, Nehemiah, (Neh. viii. 9).

Verse 23 should be read in connection with Jeremiah xi. 21-23. The sinners having been destroyed out of Anathoth, righteousness established a new generation.

This feeble body of returned exiles is called " all Israel " in verse 70. Thus God acknowledged and ennobled them because, though few and despised, they were faithful to His Word. This is an encouragement to faith in all times of public spiritual deadness.

EZRA III.—The Bible and the atonement are the two great facts of this chapter—the one recognised as authoritative, the other confessed as necessary. Everything was done as "it is written" (vs. 2, 4). Faith kept strictly to the Word of God. That Word had cleansed them from idolatry; this the physical marvels of Egypt and the Wilderness failed to do. Instructed by the Scriptures, they offered up the burnt-offerings and the sin-offerings, and thus publicly confessed themselves to be guilty sinners, and that only by the shedding of atoning blood could they be forgiven and brought back to God.

The seventh month was the month of the Blowing of Trumpets, and of the Feast of Tabernacles. That Feast pointed forward to, and promised, the Millennium, when all Israel shall be saved.

Dread of the surrounding nations did not cause them to seek safety in walls and battlements, but in burnt-offerings and sin sacrifices. They, in effect, and in spirit, sought refuge in a crucified Saviour. They placed themselves under the wings of the God of Israel. This was a beautiful testimony.

Joy and tears accompanied the foundation of the Second Temple. Both were acceptable to God. He rejoiced in their joy and understood their tears, putting them doubtless into His bottle (Psalm lvi. 8). "Afar off" (v. 13) "a noise was heard"; closer at hand, weeping. This latter suited nearness to God. They wept because they remembered the First House; and their tears confessed the truth, and testified what God had been to His people, and 'how far they had wandered from Him. Those who walk closely with God, and look at what the Christian Church is to-day, weep as they recall what it was in the days of the Apostle Paul.

EZRA IV.—Intelligence in the Scriptures is not always accompanied by the boldness which faith gives. Josiah was renowned for the former; Hezekiah, for the latter. The language of Zerubbabel and his colleagues in verse 3 showed great intelligence in the Word of God, but their action in verse 4, a sad breakdown in faith in God. Terrified by the people of the land. they ceased for

fifteen years from building the Temple. The word "troubled" in this verse means "stopped them by fear". They should not have stopped. The edict ordering them to stop (vs. 17-22) did not reach Jerusalem till two years later; and by that time the Temple might have been finished. It was a test of faith, and they failed. Later on, encouraged by Haggai and Zechariah, their faith revived; they dared to build although there was a royal decree forbidding them; and the effect of that faith was a decree in their favour brought about by the intervention of their enemies. It is good to trust God !

The Holy Spirit reveals in verse 1 the Samaritans as "adversaries". They appeared before Israel in the garb of piety, but in their own clothes before the great and noble Asnapper. It was a snare of Satan. His object was,, as always, to introduce the seed of the serpent in amongst the children of the Promise, and so prevent the birth of the Messiah. Having failed in that purpose, he has, since the birth and resurrection of the Lord Jesus, sought to mix up error with truth, and, as predicted in the parable, to sow tares among the wheat. These are some of the "depths" of Satan of which the Apostle writes. Hence he continually seeks, under the cover of a false charity, to induce Christian people to accept in spiritual efforts the co-operation of persons who are not true followers of Christ.

But Zerubbabel and Joshua held fast to the one Authority which taught them that God had separated Israel out from among the nations to be a witness for Truth; that he had forbidden marriage with them; and that it was largely owing to disobedience to this command that they had lost their glory.

EZRA V.—The building of the Temple ceased for fifteen years. It was then resumed as the result of a revival. This revival was caused by the preaching of Haggai and Zechariah. God's method of saving and helping men is by preaching. Israel's faith having been restored by this ministry, the building was resumed in spite of the Royal decree, and the opposition of the Samaritans. The prophecies of Haggai and Zechariah should be read in connection with this chapter.

Tatnai was a just governor-general of the vast regions to the westward of the River Euphrates. He personally visited Jerusalem rather then listen to the reports of Israel's adversaries. He asked who authorised the building of the Temple (v. 3) ; and what were the names of the leaders in the matter (v. 4), and, this information received, he forwarded the particulars to King Darius. In the meantime, through God's over-ruling, the people were not over-awed by the visit of these Imperial Commissioners, so that they asked and got permission to continue the enterprise (v. 5).

Verse 4 may read thus :—" Then said we unto them after this manner " (i.e., as set out in verses 11-15). And they said: " what are the names of the men that are erecting this building ? " (see v. 10).

The viceroy's letter to King Darius is not only a model of clearness and brevity, but is a striking testimony to the faithfulness and humility of Israel's confession of the true God, of her sin against Him, and of His grace in granting her a partial restoration.

The " great king " of verse 11 was Solomon ; and the " many years " of the same verse, were, at that time, nearly five hundred.

EZRA VI.—The facts of this chapter are :— The Triumph of Faith (v. 14) ; the overruling of God (v. 22) ; loyalty to the Bible (v. 18) ; the need of a sacrifice for sin (v. 17) ; the public confession that possession of Canaan was wholly due to the blood of the Paschal Lamb (v. 20) ; and the moral effect of obedience to the Word of God (vs. 21, 22.)

The unbelief of chapter iv. 4, was followed by the Royal decree of chapter iv. 21 forbidding the building of the Temple. The faith of chapter v. 5, was rewarded by the Royal decree of chapter vi. authorising it. Thus faith is the victory that overcometh the world.

The " Book of Moses " (v. 18) means the Pentateuch. This statement shows that the book existed at that time, and originated and authorised the burnt-offerings, the sin-offerings, the Passover and the feast of Unleavened Bread.

The sin-offering for the twelve tribes in verse 17 showed humility and intelligence. Although the cost and toil expended upon the Temple was mainly the fruit of Judah's faith, yet that tribe confessed themselves sinners on the same platform as the other tribes ; and instead of vaunting themselves of their religious superiority, they sought, in common with the others, atonement for their sins in the blood of the sin-offering.

The observance of the passover was a testimony to the whole world (similar to the passover of Joshua v. 10), that Israel owed her possession of the land of Canaan wholly and solely to the redeeming power of the sprinkled blood of the Paschal Lamb.

The New Testament gives the same double testimony to the efficacy of Christ's precious blood—it cleanses from all sin, and it admits to heaven, i.e., pardon and possession, (Rev. I. 5, and vii. 14, 15).

EZRA VII.—The word " Artaxerxes " (v. 1) is a title similar to Sultan, Pharaoh, Czar, etc. The personal name of this king is unknown, but he appears in history as Darius Hystaspes. Darius is also a title meaning " king " or " emperor ". This is the Artaxerxes of Nehemiah ii. 1, and Ezra vi. 14.

Ezra was a direct descendant of Aaron, and uncle to the high-priest Joshua. He was a skilful student of the Scriptures (v. 6). That verse states that God " gave " the Pentateuch and that Moses wrote it. The tenth verse adds that Ezra set his heart to seek to know the mind and will of God, i.e., God's revelation of Himself, and of the way of salvation. He sought this light, not in himself, but in the Law of God, i.e., the Pentateuch. Three facts are stated in this tenth verse :—first, his determination to know God's way of salvation ; second, his purpose to obey it ; and, third, his resolution to teach it to others. The New Testament commands men to hear the Gospel ; to obey it ; and to make it known to others. Any person who professes to believe the Gospel, but does not live the Gospel, and make it known to others, is self-deceived.

The king's testimony concerning Ezra is instructive and important—instructive, for it shows that Ezra was not ashamed to stand before the king, Bible in hand (v. 14), and make known to him the Word of God— and important, because revealing how greatly Ezra's teaching influenced this heathen prince. In verses 14 and 25 the Great King declares the book which Ezra held in his hand to be the Law of God, and the Wisdom of God ; he declares this God (vs. 12 and 23) to be the " God of Heaven ", and, in verse 15, to be the " God of Israel " ; and in verse 11, Ezra is further described as being " the scribe even a scribe ", i.e., a perfect scribe, that is, a most skilful and publicly recognised Bible student ; and, lastly, the Book is declared not merely to contain a Divine message, but to be the " commandments and " statutes " of Jehovah, and that Ezra was a minute student of the very " words " in which, and with which, those commandments were conveyed to men.

The Royal Councillors mentioned in verses 14, 15 were seven in number. Their names are found in Esther i. 10. It is interesting to find them joining the king in making costly gifts for the Temple at Jerusalem.

All persons attached to the Temple service were to be exempt from taxation ; and Ezra was authorised to appoint magistrates to the westward of the river Euphrates. These magistrates were only to judge those who acknowledged the authority of the Mosaic law (v. 25).

" The good hand of God " (vs. 6, 9, 28) is a reference to chapter viii. 21-23, 31, 32.

" In his hand " (vs. 6 and 14), i.e., he was the custodian of the original Pentateuch as written by Moses ; and he actually held the mighty roll in his hand from time to time when teaching the king.

EZRA VIII.—The four months journey of Ezra from Babylon to Jerusalem with probably six thousand men, women, and children (v. 21), and upwards of £500,000 in precious metals, along a road infested by bandits, murderers, and robbers, without the loss of a penny, or a life, although they were unprovided with military protection, is one of the most remarkable instances in the Bible of faith. Ezra's bold statement to the king that God's power is exercised for His people, and against His enemies, was finely supported by his refusal to accept an escort.

Lists of names in the Bible become intensely interesting if regarded as specimen pages from the Book of Life. Revelation xxi. 27 limits admission to " the city foursquare " to those only whose names are entered in that book. In Luke x. 20, the Lord tells the seventy that their names were written in it. To the Christian heart, therefore, these lists of names are never dull.

The Levites (v. 15) failed to take hold, at the first, on this great revival. They did so afterwards. The Levite of the Bible corresponds to the Christian worker of to-day; and it is not an uncommon experience to find the usefulness of a revival limited by the want, or indolence, of such workers.

Boldness in faith, and affliction in prayer, are spiritual companions. Compare verse 21 with verse 22.

Ezra's business-like action in numbering and weighing all the vessels of value, and committing them to trustees, who in their turn, had to hand them over, after being re-weighed, to the Temple authorities at Jerusalem, is an example that should be followed by all Christian people in money matters, both secular and religious.

On reaching Jerusalem they hasted to offer up burnt-offerings and sin-offerings in great number, that is, they proclaimed that, in spite of their faith, and their praying, and their fasting, and their costly donations to the Temple, yet were they great sinners needing a great Saviour. The greatness and sufficiency of that Saviour were typified in the multitude of the animals slain.

The " enemies " and " liers in wait " of verse 31, who failed to rob Ezra because protected by the God of Israel, correspond to the evil activities which beset the daily path of the Christian pilgrim. These seek to rob him of spiritual wealth, and of his soul ; but God can give daily victories on the road to the Heavenly Jerusalem as real, and as great, as those He gave Ezra on the road to the earthly Jerusalem

EZRA IX and X.—The arrival of Ezra at Jerusalem with the Bible in his hand at once made manifest the moral condition of the returned exiles ; for the Word of God is a discerner of evil (Hebrews iv. 12).

This chapter deals with a crisis. To understand it a few facts may be recalled :—

The Restoration from Babylon differed from the Redemption from Egypt. The whole nation was redeemed in the one case ; only a remnant in the other. Power characterized the Redemption ; the Bible, the Restoration. At the Redemption, kingly power was placed by God in the hand of Israel ; hence the opposition of Pharaoh. At the Restoration, kingly power had already been transferred by God to the hand of the Gentile, and, therefore, Artaxerxes was favourable. It was not power that the Remnant needed, it was a knowledge of the Bible. Artaxerxes himself recognised this (chapter vii. 25)'; and this heathen prince was God's minister through whom prosperity reached the exiles—for God could not overlook a throne which He had Himself established.

His stirring up the heart of this monarch, and His raising up Ezra, Nehemiah, Haggai, Zechariah and Malachi is a touching proof of His lovingkindness to this faithless and sinful remnant of His people. These prophets were sent forth by Him in order that, under the searchlight of His Word, the evil that still clung to them might be exposed and banished. Two other important facts should not be forgotten at this crisis. They are, that those who went up to Jerusalem did so voluntarily, and that the rebuilding of the Temple is more prominently recorded than the rebuilding of the wall. Restoration of soul must begin from the inside, and can be only enjoyed by those who willingly forsake the Babylon of worldly fellowship for the Jerusalem of Divine companionship.

Intermarriage with the Canaanite was forbidden by God so as to maintain a holy seed and effect the birth of the Messiah. Satan, to prevent that birth, brought about these marriages. Faithfulness to God and His word, and not human affection, formed the great crisis of Ezra's day. It is also the great question of this day (Luke xiv. 26).

Ezra's prayer teaches that it is worse to sin against love than to sin against law.

He chose the time of the evening sacrifice to confess his sin and the sin of the nation, for the poured-out blood of that sacrifice proclaimed forgiveness and atonement. Divinely inspired repentance always brings the soul to Calvary.

Ezra, with rent mantle, on his knees, in the public street, praying and weeping, aroused the people, not only to confession of their sin, but to the forsaking of it ; and, as a consequence, they found mercy. But three months were needed to purge the evil away (chapter x. 16, 17), it was so great.

The words of Ezra's prayer prove how well he was acquainted with the five books of Moses.

The guilt of the high priest's family (chapter x. 18, 19) is a proof of how quickly the Remnant responded with unfaithfulness to God's faithfulness. But, such is God, and such is man !

The theme of chapter ix. is "sin confessed ; " that of chapter x. is, "sin forsaken."

"Ezra" commands separation from evil ; "Nehemiah" forbids fellowship with unbelievers. This double principle characterized those in their day who were faithful to God, and to the Word of His grace. Similar principles should govern those to-day who, amid the confusion of a corrupt Christianity, seek to walk with God.

NEHEMIAH

NEHEMIAH I.—The word "Nehemiah" means "comforter given by Jehovah." He was a prince of Judah, and was appointed by Artaxerxes Governor of the Province of Judæa.

The palace at Shushan, modern Susa, has been recently excavated, and many important inscriptions found.

The number of times that Nehemiah prayed should be noted.

This, his first prayer recorded in this book, was intelligent, humble and scriptural. He addressed Jehovah as the "God of Heaven," not as the "God of Israel." This showed intelligence, for the Glory had left the Temple at Jerusalem and had withdrawn into heaven (Ezekiel xi. 22-24). He confessed that he himself, as well as his fellow country-men, had sinned; that was humility; and the prayer was scriptural, for it was woven together of words and promises taken from Lev. xxvi, Deut. iv, vii, xxx, and 1 Kings viii.

National repentance is the one great condition of national restoration (v. 9). Compare Acts iii and xxviii.

NEHEMIAH II.—Nehemiah, though a prince and holding the highest position in the Imperial court, did not set his heart upon the glorious city of Shushan, but on the ruined city of Jerusalem. He loved it and its people because both belonged to God Thus was it with Jacob, Joseph, and Moses. They occupied high positions in Egypt, but their hearts were in Canaan. It was God's land.

Nehemiah illustrates the confidence of faith; the perseverance of faith; the intelligence of faith; the obedience of faith; the courage of faith; and the wisdom of faith.

To be sad in the presence of the Persian monarch was punishable with death; hence Nehemiah's fear (v. 2).

Eastern Monarchs being in daily dread of poison, any appearance of agitation in the cup-bearer would be regarded as especially suspicious.

The words "Artaxerxes" and "Ahasuerus" being titles and not personal names, it is suggested that this monarch was Darius Hystaspes, the husband of Esther, and that she is the queen mentioned in verse 6. But he may have been Xerxes.

The statements in verse 3, respecting the condition of Jerusalem, would appear to show that the wall built by Zerubbabel had already fallen into ruin, or that the exiles had only had energy enough to build the Temple. The quick cry of believing prayer, shot up to heaven between the king's question and Nehemiah's answer, reveals the habit and atmosphere of prayer which characterized Nehemiah. The answer was as immediate as the prayer was swift.

"The good hand of God" (v. 8) is a term expressing His purpose (Acts iv. 28); His power (1 Chron. xxix. 12); His sovereignty (Psalm xxxi. 15); His providence (1 Chron. xxix. 16); His ability to supply every need (Psalm civ. 28); His overruling (Neh. ii. 8); and His guardianship (John x. 28).

The king's readiness to grant all Nehemiah's requests; his giving him, unasked, an escort of cavalry; and his anxiety that he should return to his service, are so many proofs of the nobility and beauty of Nehemiah's character.

All who venture, in any way, to forward the interests of the Kingdom of Heaven are sure to meet with opposition from the world, and discouragement from the church. Nehemiah found it to be so. The opposition was offered by Sanballat and his friends (v. 10), and the discouragement by the men of Judah (chapter iv. 10, vi. 10-19).

The opposition of Sanballat took six forms :—Irritation (chapter ii. 10); Contempt (chapter ii. 19); Anger (chapter iv. 1-3); Violence (chapter iv. 7, 8); Cunning (chapter vi. 1, 2); and compromise (chapter vi. 5-7).

The wisdom of Nehemiah's faith is seen in the skill and secrecy with which he began his great work of repairing the walls of the city. A Divine faith rather seeks to disarm opposition than to provoke it.

Recent excavations in Egypt have discovered letters written to the sons of Sanballat, who is described in them as governor of Samaria.

NEHEMIAH III.—This Jerusalem had twelve gates ; so shall the future city have.

The chapter begins and ends with the Sheep Gate ; thus showing how completely the walls were repaired.

It was called the " Sheep Gate " because through it entered the sheep destined for sacrifice.

The rebuilding of this gate, and its two towers, primarily fulfilled Jeremiah xxxi. 38. The future will complete the prophecy. It was built " to the Lord " ; hence the word " sanctified " twice found in verse 1.

Energy in church-work does not guarantee loyalty in spiritual work. Compare chapter iii. 1, with chapter xiii. 4, 7.

The people of each neighbouring city, or village, built a gate opposite to themselves through which to enter for refuge ; and each citizen of the city itself repaired the wall over against his own house, thus securing personal safety. Both actions express true principles in all evangelistic work.

The chapter may be regarded as a specimen page from God's book of remembrance. It is, therefore, to be noted, that Meremoth appears twice (vs. 4 and 21) ; that the nobles did not put their necks to the work (v. 5) ; that gold-refiners and perfumers and merchants can fortify " Jerusalem " (vs. 8 and 32) ; that magistrates and their daughters, contrary to modern religious opinion, were permitted to assist (v. 12) ; that Baruch, to his undying fame, is recorded to have repaired " earnestly " (v. 20) ; and that a lodger (v. 30), having only one room, may take his little share in the great work and not be forgotten of God.

Little did Baruch think, as amid the sneers and taunts of the enemy he zealously laboured that millions of men 2000 years later would read about him.

Acceptable service for God is never far to seek (v. 30).

NEHEMIAH IV.—Contempt and violence from the enemy, and cowardice from the men of Judah (vs. 3 and 8, and vs. 10 and 12) were defeated by praying and watching (vs. 4, 5, 9). All Christian workers must expect opposition from the world and discouragement from the church ; but prayer and watchfulness always bring victory. Nehemiah's prayer was a Holy Spirit prayer —it accorded with that dispensation ; nor was it a prayer for personal vengeance.

Verse 12 should read as in the R.V. Compare " ten times " with Gen. xxxi. 7.

The " higher places " in the Christian life need to be guarded as carefully as the " lower places " (v. 13) ; and the day is as perilous as the night (vs. 9, 21).

God, not Nehemiah, got the glory (v. 15). " From that time forth " (v. 16) half the people mounted guard fully armed and half " wrought in the work."

This latter half was again divided (vs. 17 and 18); half of them bore burdens (" hodmen ") and held a weapon in the free hand ; the other half were builders (" brick-layers ") and, needing both hands, had their swords girded by their sides. Whether a " builder " or a " burden-bearer," the Christian is in equal danger and cannot dispense with the " Sword of the Spirit."

" The men of the guard," i.e., the Persian guard (chapter ii. 6).

The last line of v. 23, may read :—" Each man went on guard with his weapon and water-bottle ". A modern soldier goes into action with a rifle, a spade, and a water-flask. The Christian soldier has his sword, his spade and his water-bottle.

NEHEMIAH V.—The opening verses of this chapter illustrate the deep evil of the natural heart ; the closing verses, the deeper love of the new heart. The one lesson humbles ; the other cheers.

God, in His love and pity, redeemed these men from slavery, but they, having some money, immediately used it to enslave their poorer brethren, and ruin them ; contrary to Lev. xxv. 35-38. The love of money makes man merciless.

In the presence of the priests they had to promise by oath to restore everything (v. 12). They kept their word (v. 13).

It was "the fear of God" that made Nehemiah to differ from other Governors. He used his princely wealth to feed 150 people every day, and he dined them generously (v. 18). Far from oppressing the people he did not even demand his legal salary of £2,000 a year (v. 15).

Tears without and troubles within failed to stay his zeal in repairing the wall (v. 16). Compare 2 Cor. vii. 5.

Nehemiah did not ask God to note his goodness, but begged to be enriched from God's goodness. He did not covet the praise of man, but the smile of God. Seeking the former embitters the mind; seeking the latter, sweetens the spirit.

NEHEMIAH VI.—Satan laid three traps in this chapter for Nehemiah's foot, but three spiritual energies delivered him from them. The first snare was treachery (v. 2); the second, compromise (v. 7); the third, religious falsehood (v. 10).

The three spiritual energies which saved Nehemiah from these snares were:—Full engagement in Christian work (v. 3); Prayer (vs. 9 and 14); and Obedience to the Bible (vs. 11-13).

This third snare was very subtle; but knowledge of the Scriptures broke it. That Divine Word forbade Nehemiah, being a prince of the tribe of Judah, and not a priest of the tribe of Levi, to enter the Temple. Thus was Shemaiah shown to be a false prophet. His message contradicted the Bible.

Some may escape a snare once set, but few when it is set four times (v. 4).

Compromise (v. 7) ensnares a vast number of ministers and Christian workers; but it always injures the work of God.

The mischief designed in verse 2 was, no doubt, murder.

In the East, to address an " open letter " to a state Governor is a designed insult. It is also a method of making public the assumed evil conduct of the person addressed.

The expression " shut up " (v. 10) (compare Jeremiah xxxvi. 5) may be understood to mean, " imprisoned by the Holy Spirit," i.e., under the afflatus of the Spirit. It may therefore be assumed that this false prophet caused Nehemiah to hear that he was so " shut up." Nehemiah hastened, as a thirsty man, to hear the Divine message; and would have been entrapped but for his knowledge of the Scriptures.

The snare was a double one. It was planned so that either God would slay him for entering the Temple (v. 11, R.V. margin), or that, if not so slain, his influence as a

keeper of the Law would be destroyed (v. 13).

Owing to Nehemiah's energy and faith the wall was finished in fifty-two days; and, as predicted in Daniel ix. 25, " in troublous times."

It is possible for the hands to be very busy in the outward work of the Gospel, and, at the same time, for the heart to be pledged to the enemies of the Lord. Such was Meshullam (Compare verse 18 with chapter iii. 4, 30).

NEHEMIAH VII.—Vigilance (vs. 1-4), Pedigree (vs. 5-69), and Worship (vs. 70-73), form the three harmonious keynotes of this chapter.

Nehemiah's leave of absence expiring, he handed over the custody of the city to his brother and to Hananiah, charging them to all vigilance against the enemy.

The treasury of verses 70 and 71 was the Temple treasury.

The chapter ends thus: " and all Israel dwelt in their cities." The next sentence begins the eighth chapter.

It is impossible to the natural man to watch and worship. A spiritual birth is absolutely necessary. Only those who could prove their birth as children of Israel were empowered to watch and worship and work. This fundamental principle stands out on every page of the Bible. They only who are children of God by a spiritual birth through faith in Christ Jesus can work and watch and worship.

When God and His Word have their due place, safety and rest result—" all Israel dwelt in their cities."

The supposed age discrepancies between the Register of this chapter and that in Ezra ii. are reconciled by the chronological table shown in the notes on Ezra.

NEHEMIAH VIII.—Love for God's Holy Book, and obedience to its teaching, are the two pleasant facts of this chapter.

The fifteenth day of the seventh month was the Feast of Tabernacles.

This feast was observed in obedience to Leviticus xxiii; and the Law was read to all the people because Deuteronomy xxxi. 9-13 so commanded.

The reading of the Bible was preceded by prayer and worship (v. 6).

The people wept, for they recognised how deeply they had sinned against so loving a God. It was hearing the words of the Book that awoke them to this consciousness.

But they were encouraged to rejoice because God was rejoicing in them (v. 10). " The joy of the Lord," that is, the joy that filled God's heart because of their obedience, meant both strength and safety to them. (Compare Numbers xiv. 8 and Zephaniah iii. 17).

The Bible-reading on the first day lasted six hours. All the people assisted at it. On the second day only the nobles, the priests, and the Levites attended, and, directly they came upon the commandment respecting the Feast of Tabernacles, they at once took steps to obey it.

The statement in verse 17 is quite true. The sacrifices commanded for that feast are stated in previous Scriptures to have been offered ; but there is no record of the people having dwelt in booths.

NEHEMIAH IX.—The people made great mirth because they understood the words declared unto them (chapter viii. 12). To understand the words of the Bible appears to worldly men a strange cause for mirth. But His commandments are not grievous ; and so, on the second day, they found written that they should dwell in booths and have a week's holiday !

On the twenty-fourth day of the month, that is, two days after the feast had closed, the great convention of this chapter was held. Three hours was given to Bible-reading, and three hours to confession, prayer, and worship.

Their confession shows how attentively they had read the Bible, and how well they had learned the lesson of man's total corruption and of God's amazing grace.

They confessed that that mercy was based upon election (v. 7), and not upon any moral excellence in man.

" He came down," " He spake," " He gave," " He revealed," " He commanded " (vs. 13, 14).

" True laws " (v. 13) mean laws of truth (John i. 17).

The " but " of verse 17 stands in contrast with the " but " of verse 16 ; and the " nevertheless " of verse 31 with the " nevertheless " of verse 26.

The four downward steps of unbelief, rebellion, Bible-hatred and murder, appear in verse 29.

The ministry of the prophets was designed to bring them back to the Bible (v. 29). The instrument that spoke was the prophet, but the Speaker was the Holy Spirit (v. 30).

True repentance leads to action. They signed a pledge to walk in God's law (chapter x. 29).

" Forsake " (v. 31) i.e. " did not fail to provide." Same word in LXX. and Heb xiii. 5.

NEHEMIAH X.—The important statement of this chapter is the acceptance by the restored Israelites of the written Word of God (vs. 29, 34), as the sole authority for conduct and worship.

They did not say that that Holy Book belonged to a past age and was out of date ; but, on the contrary, they confessed its teaching to be living and binding.

God honours those who honour His Book ; and accordingly a roll of honour opens this chapter.

None of these men dreamt that two thousand years after their death millions of people would read their names with praise to God.

Verses 32-39 show how willingly the people obeyed the legislation of the Bible providing for the maintenance of the Temple and its ministry. This legislation was found in the Books of Leviticus and Numbers, and was not forged by Ezra.

The words " we will not forsake " (verse 39) mean " we will not fail to provide for." Such is the meaning of the word used by the Greek translators of the Old Testament. The same Greek word occurs in Hebrews xiii. 5 ; which may therefore read thus :— " I will never leave thee nor fail to provide for thee."

Israel took an oath, adding to it a curse, not to fail to provide for the Temple ; but they quickly broke the pledge. Israel's Shepherd keeps His pledge, although given without an oath.

The Rule of Faith for the Church of God under the first Covenant was the Bible ; and it remains the Rule of Faith for the Church of God under the Second Covenant.

NEHEMIAH XI.—Jerusalem having been recovered from the enemy, and surrounded by a wall, it had now to be garrisoned and held against him. There is a spiritual energy which wins a position for God but which takes no steps to hold it for God.

Nehemiah recognised the necessity of holding what had been won.

Jerusalem was the point of greatest danger; and, therefore, the Holy Spirit honours in this chapter the brave men who garrisoned it.

This chapter, therefore, may be regarded as another specimen page from the Book of Life.

The garrison consisted of the nobles, the priests, the door-keepers, some of the Levites, a body of volunteers, and one in ten of the people, drawn by lot.

The sons of Perez (v. 6)—soldiers, were " valiant men," but the brethren of Amishai (vs. 13, 14)—priests, were " mighty men of valour." Nearness to God does not make men effeminate.

The outward business of the House of God (v. 16) was committed to two chieftains of Levi ; but the inward business of that House (v. 22) was given to the singers the sons of Asaph.

When in captivity (Psalm cxxxvii) the hand that should have awakened the song upon the pleasant harp was used to hang it upon the willow tree. But now, restored to Zion, Israel could sing !

The Christian life is outward and inward. The singing is to be inward. If the song of God is not in the heart there will be neither melody nor power in the life.

The grace that placed the singers within the House of God provided in tender love for their daily bread, and, accordingly, the Persian monarch was moved to apportion them a fitting maintenance. How admirable is the love of God in making a mighty king supply bread to an obscure psalm-singer ! (v. 23 and Ezra vi. 8., vii. 20).

For the first time in the Bible, Jerusalem is now called " the holy city " (vs. 1 and 18). It was not so called in the days of Israel's kingdom and glory. The Spirit of God delights to ennoble and to recognise fidelity to the Word of God, in circumstances of weakness, and fear, and danger.

The consecration of chapters viii. ix. and x. was followed by the deeper consecration of chapters xii. and xiii. ; but this deeper consecration was the fruit of the faith and obedience which animated them to garrison the city, and to sing there.

NEHEMIAH XII.—God and the Bible formed the centre around which the returned captives gathered. Hence the prominence given in the books of Ezra and Nehemiah to the priests and Levites. The priests with their sacrifices typified worship through the atonement and intercession of Christ ; the Levites were the public teachers of the Law.

Worship and meditation upon the Holy Scriptures form the foundation of the Christian life in the individual, the family or the church. If these be destroyed the church disappears.

The first twenty-six verses, therefore, of this chapter are very important, not only because of the spiritual fact just pointed out, but also because these registries secured the purity of the pedigree of the Aaronic priesthood; and because, the nation being no longer governed by kings, high priests marked the chronology of the people up to the advent of the Messiah.

The wall, having been completed, was now dedicated. The entire praise for its erection was given to God and none to the builders. The whole multitude was parted into two companies (v. 31), and each company, headed by a choir, moved; the one to the right, and the other to the left, to make, with sounding of cymbals and of song, the half-circuit respectively, of the walls, and the dual march was so planned that the two companies met again upon the wall opposite the Temple (v. 40), in which House of Prayer the united choirs " sang aloud," whilst the priests offered sacrifices. So all, even the little children, rejoiced, and " the joy of Jerusalem was heard afar off."

The words " that day " (vs. 43, 44, chapter xiii. 1) mark the singing, the giving, and the obeying that accompanied the building of the wall. When Christian people to-day take up a public definite position for God, encompassed by the completed wall of the apostolic faith once for all delivered to the saints, the graces of singing, giving, and obeying follow.

These people were few in number, had no influence, and were servants to a foreign monarch, but they had faith to claim the name of Israel, to grasp the promises associated with that name, and to confess publicly the Being and the Law of the gracious God who gave those promises ; and it is because they were so few and so feeble that two whole books in the Bible are given to them.

The words in verse 44 " Judah rejoiced for the priests and for the Levites that waited " mean, that Judah gave with joy the tithes for the priests etc. ; and the words. in verse 47, that " they sanctified for the Levites, and the Levites sanctified for the sons of Aaron " mean that the people gave tithes for the Levites, and that the Levites, in their turn, gave a tithe of these tithes to the priests (Numbers xviii).

To complete the circuit of the city, and to meet ultimately at the House of God, these children of faith had to part for a time one from another.   To maintain the entire wall of Christian doctrine against the enemy—and not apologetically, but with singing—Christian men at all periods have had to deny themselves the sweets of Christian fellowship temporarily, but in the certitude that the whole church of God is marching to a future blissful day of united praise in the eternal Home of God.

NEHEMIAH XIII.—On reaching Deuteronomy xxiii. in the course of the public reading of the Scriptures, the returned captives, directly they heard the command of verses 3-6, obeyed it (v. 3).

The " mixed multitude " had always been a snare (Numbers xi.) to the Israel of God under the First Covenant ; and this snare remains to the present day under the Second Covenant.

After the dedication ot the wall, Nehemiah returned to the Persian court. But after some time, possibly two years, he obtained leave of absence and returned to Jerusalem, because, it may be assumed, he had heard of the faithlessness of the High Priest and the nobles to the covenant they had subscribed (chapter x.). On reaching Jerusalem he was filled with grief and indignation. The High Priest himself had lodged Tobiah the Ammonite in the very chamber reserved for the Messiah, as typified by the meal-offering and the frankincense (v. 5). How often in the history of an individual, or a church, has " the great chamber " which should be filled with Christ and His preciousness, been fitted up for the Ammonite and his loathesomeness !

The Temple was cleansed ;   the priests and Levites restored ; the payment of tithes resumed ; Sunday trading abolished ; foreign wives removed ; and rebels exiled (v. 28).

Deadly cancers need faithful surgery (vs. 8, 11, 17, 21, 25, and 28).

Nehemiah did not ask his countrymen to remember him, to ·erect a statue to his honour, or recompense him 'for his public services. He sought the honour that cometh from God only (vs. 14, 22, 31). His plea for salvation, in verse 22, was based upon the greatness of God's mercy, and not upon the merit of his own works. " Remember me " etc., are, chronologically, the last words of the Old Testament.

It is important to remember that Ezra and Nehemiah are the last two books of the Old Testament ; and that the next event in Sacred History was the apparition of the Messiah 400 years later.

The providence of God is seen in these two books preparing Jerusalem and Judah for that apparition. The captives, purged from idolatry, were brought back to Immanuel's land. Under Nehemiah their civic position was assured by the Gentile monarchs, to whom God had committed the government of the world. Israel was to hold this position until the coming of Messiah, separate from the nations, faithful to the Law, without a king, and rendering unto Caesar the things that were Caesar's. The Messiah came and invited them to shelter beneath His wings ; but they would not !

He also, as Messenger of the Covenant, proposed to cleanse the Temple and place His glory there ; but they rejected Him, and still suffer the consequences of that rejection.

The distinction between these two books must be kept before the mind. " Nehemiah," because it deals with Israel's civic position, contains no Messianic prophecies or hopes. The restoration of the city is the theme. Ezra, on the other hand, having for its subject the Temple, and the prophecies of Haggai, Zechariah, and Malachi has, as its key-note, the promised presence of the King and Priest who was to purge their sins, and establish them as a kingdom in righteousness.

Israel being " Lo-ammi " (Hosea i. 9), the kingly power remained in the hands of the Gentiles, but the Royal family of David was divinely preserved till He came whose right it was to reign.

Satan, failing to detach the people from the Bible, and to bring them back to idols, tried to frustrate the Messiah's mission by imposing tradition upon the Bible. But he failed. (Matthew xxiii.)

ESTHER

ESTHER I.—Shushan the palace has been recently excavated and its marble pillars and pavements restored to view.

The book of Esther presents to the reader the captives of Israel scattered among the Gentiles under the just judgment of Hosea i. 9, and yet loved and cared for, in secret, by God. Being "Lo-ammi" He could not publicly recognise them. That recognition could only be given to the Gentile, to whom He had committed supreme power. Without revoking the judgment pronounced through Hosea, He secretly watched over them, and, without displaying Himself, shaped public affairs in their interest. They had lost all title to His protection, and, therefore, it is an extremely important and comforting study to observe in this Book how His hidden hand prepared and directed everything for a people, in themselves unlovely, but beloved for the fathers' sakes. Hence the Holy Spirit, with design, is careful not to let the name of God appear in the Book, though it lies concealed in the Hebrew Text (Companion Bible). The absence, therefore, of that name is a great encouragement to faith, for the argument and the lesson which its omission conveys is, that behind the visible events of history, there is an Almighty and Faithful Love that cherishes and protects the broken and scattered people of God.

The word "Ahasuerus" is a kingly title. Many scholars believe him to be the Artaxerxes of Nehemiah ii. 1, and Ezra vii. 1, i.e., Darius Hystaspes. The Chronological Chart at the opening of the Book of Ezra shows the credibility of this belief. Others think him to be Xerxes.

ESTHER II.—Chapter i. 3, with ii. 16, show that four years elapsed between the degradation of Vashti and the enthronement of Esther.

Mordecai was with Nehemiah, an exile in Shushan. He held a high position in the palace. Daniel and Ezekiel were exiled to Babylon (2 Kings xx. 16-18 ; 2 Kings xxiv. 14, 15 ; Daniel i. 3).

Haman was an Amalekite, a descendant of Agag the king of the Amalekites. Mordecai was a Benjamite, a descendant of Saul, the king of the Israelites. Haman's death ended God's war with Amalek. So Mordecai did what Saul failed to do (Exodus xvii. 16 ; 1 Samuel xv. ; Esther iii. 1 ; vii. 10 ; ix. 10).

Verse 20 reveals one of the many beauties of Esther's character. When placed upon the throne she loved and obeyed her adopted father as when she was a child in his house.

Thus in the providence of God, and by His overruling of human folly, Esther was seated upon the throne at the very time that Satan made a supreme effort to destroy every member of the tribe of Judah in particular, and the Israelites in general, so as to make impossible the advent of the promised Redeemer. He was defeated by the hidden hand of God. The judgment threatened in Deuteronomy xxxi. 16-18—" I will hide my face "—came to pass ; but though Israel proved faithless to Him, He abode faithful to her, for He could not deny Himself, and, though He hid Himself, yet was His care over them as real as ever. The natural heart finds it hard to trust in an unseen Care-taker ; but Esther and Mordecai hung upon His unseen Hand (chapter iv. 16).

Esther's action was admirable. She was ready not only to give up her throne in the interest of a despised body of slaves, but to sacrifice her very life in order to deliver them.

ESTHER III.—Mordecai explained to the palace officials that his not reverencing Haman was not due to discourtesy to Haman, or disobedience to the king, but because he was a Hebrew (v. 4) ; that is, he worshipped the one and only true and living God.

It was quite usual for Eastern monarchs,

as in later years for Roman Emperors, and, to-day, for the Japanese sovereign, to claim Divine homage, for themselves, or for their deputies.

Refusal to give this homage brought Daniel into the den of lions, and the three princes into the fiery furnace. It may justly, therefore, be assumed from Mordecai's statement in verse 4, that he was a worthy companion of Daniel and the princes.

Haman was an Amalekite. As such, he was an enemy to God, and Jehovah had sworn to have war with him for ever (Exodus xvii. 16) God's enemies were Mordecai's enemies, for Mordecai was a servant of God. This fact respecting Haman was an added reason why faithfulness to God demanded this seeming discourtesy to Haman.

Verse 7 does not mean that twelve months were employed in seeking, by means of the lot, a propitious day for the slaughter of the Jews. This is confirmed by verse 12. It means that the diviners sought for a favourable day, month by month, and at last chose the thirteenth day of the twelfth month as promising success.

The number "thirteen" is interesting in this book. (See verses 12 and 13 with chapter viii. 12). It is pointed out by some scholars that the number "thirteen" appears continuously in the numerical values of the names connected with Haman. A study of this number in Scripture will be found very profitable.

Satan never lacks money for his purposes. To indemnify the Persian Treasury against possible loss by the destruction of the Captives, Haman offered the king 10,000 talents, i.e., £5,000,000 (v. 9). History states that Darius Hystaspes loved money.

The inhuman plot fully planned, the king and Haman sat down to drink; but consternation filled the homes of the Persians (v. 15). The next chapter describes the bitter anguish that filled the homes of the Hebrews.

ESTHER IV.—Esther's marriage took place in the seventh year of the reign of Ahasuerus (chapter ii. 16). This murderous decree was issued five years later (chapter iii. 7).

Esther's pointing out that she had not been summoned to the Royal Presence for thirty days, was to suggest that, perhaps, the king had tired of her, and, therefore, her intercession would be valueless, if not fatal.

This noble woman resolved, however, to sacrifice her life for the sake of her people.

Her request that a prayer-meeting, lasting for three days and three nights, should be held outside the palace, in unison with a similar prayer-meeting inside, showed her belief that God hears prayer, and that He is a very present help in time of trouble.

ESTHER V.—Recent excavations at Shushan prove that the writer of this book intimately knew the royal palace. The "New Biblical Guide" (Urquhart) gives interesting details as to this, and shows how Esther could pass from the House of the Women into the Inner Court of the King's House in order to make her petition; and, later on, passed from the House of the Women into the Banqueting House without at any time leaving the palace.

Esther's intelligence and tact were admirable. Her life and that of her people hung on a thread. She was playing with edged tools, and the slightest mistake would have been fatal. To invite the king to a banquet was a master-stroke of policy; and to include his favourite minister in the invitation was not only an added evidence of skill and of a deep knowledge of human nature, but it was, at the same time, a clever plan for getting Haman into her power.

The repetition of her invitation showed extraordinary wisdom. At the first banquet the king rightly divined that some important matter lay behind the invitation; else why should Esther risk her life by coming un-invited into his presence? It was surely not merely to invite him and Haman to a dinner? Esther, by repeating the invitation, and postponing the secret petition, enhanced its importance, whilst, at the same time, she increased her personal interest in the king's affections, and more deeply excited his curiosity. Further, she more effectually threw Haman off his guard, and so secured his fall.

The gallows (v. 14) was immediately made, but none too soon for its fitted purpose of hanging its own constructor.

ESTHER VI.—God can use the sleeplessness of a king to the advantage and honour of His people. This fact is an encouragement to faith.

Had Mordecai complained at the time that he saved the king's life (chapter ii. 21, 23) of the non-recognition of his services, he would have lost the extraordinary honours recorded in this chapter. It is always better, and more dignified, not to seek for human recognition but to walk in fellowship with God, doing one's duty, and waiting for the honour that cometh from above ; and it will surely come, as this chapter proves. (See notes on Luke vii. 36).

The statement in verse 8 does not mean that the king's crown was to be placed upon Mordecai's head, but that he was to ride upon the horse which bore the emblem of royalty upon its head. This is the more evident from verse 9 and verse 10 which only mention the royal apparel and the horse.

The declaration of Haman's wife and friends in verse 13, is an evidence of the futility of Satan's efforts to destroy a testimony for God, however imperfect that testimony may be.

ESTHER VII.—The king asked Esther what was her petition and what was her request (v. 2), and Esther replied that she petitioned for her own life, and requested for that of her people ; and, with admirable wisdom, added, that if they had been merely condemned to slavery she would have remained silent, although even that injustice—and this was a clever argument to introduce—would have injured the king's revenues beyond the possibility of compensation.

The recently discovered palace at Shushan shows how possible it was for the incensed monarch to pass from the banquet into the palace garden, and back again. This is an evidence of the truthfulness of this history.

Thus Haman, the last of the Amalekite Royal family, perished, as the result of the faith, courage, and wisdom of Mordecai, a descendant of the Benjamite Royal family See 1 Samuel xv.

" Five " is the number of grace. Hebrew scholars point out that the name Jehovah occurs five times in this book (the last time in the form " I am ") hidden, in each occurrence, in an acrostic. The acrostics read backwards and forwards alternately ; thus showing the opposition of the enemy, and the over-ruling purpose of God.

Two of these acrostics occur in this chapter. " Who is he and where is he " (v. 5) contains the name " I am " read backwards ; and " that there was evil determined against him " (v. 7), shows the name " Jehovah " spelt forwards. Haman was Satan's agent against Jehovah, but Ahasuerus was God's minister for Jehovah.

ESTHER VIII.—The darkness and terror of " that night " (chapter vi. 1) contrast with the light and gladness of " that day " of the first verse of this chapter.

Haman is called " the Jew's enemy " four times in this book, viz :—chapters iii. 10, viii. 1, ix. 10, ix. 24.

Mordecai became prime minister. Joseph and Daniel were also prime ministers to heathen princes.

If God, in the pursuance of His purposes, places one of His servants in such a high position, He will give him grace and wisdom to glorify Him in that position. But an ambitious Christian, who by his energy and talent, and in order to gratify himself, grasps at such a post, cannot count upon God to deliver him from its snares and temptations.

The laws of the Medes and Persians being irrevocable, the king could not recall his decree ; but he could issue a fresh one authorising Esther's people to defend themselves against all that should attack them (v. 11).

The last clause of the seventeenth verse does not necessarily mean that many of the Persians joined the Hebrew church, but that they sided with the Jews. The word " became " may, therefore, be translated " made common cause with."

ESTHER IX AND X.—The number " thirteen " which is so feared by the superstitious children of this world, is a gladsome number to the people of God, for on that day of the month Adar, that is March, the Amalekite and all his allies were destroyed.

Esther's request that a second day should be granted in Shushan for the destruction of the evil men who abetted Haman and his sons, and who, in truth, were energised by Satan, was most wise and prudent. The Hebrews would have lived in daily fear of the vengeance of these men if they had not been destroyed. Esther's wise conduct gave perfect peace to her people, and, at the same time, punished with death men worthy of death.

When hung upon the gallows Haman's sons were already dead ; and this public confirmation of the fact exhibited the justice of the king and confirmed the tranquility of the people.

It is interesting to learn that the numerical value of the names of these ten sons (v. 7-9), together with that of their parents Haman and Zeresh, and the title the Agagite, form combinations of numerals all divisible by the number " thirteen."

Three times in this chapter (v. 10, 15, 16), it is pointed out that on the spoil they laid not their hand. No doubt they remembered the lesson of 1 Samuel xv.

To this day the feast of Purim is observed in obedience to the ordinance (v. 20-32).

The greatness of Ahasuerus closes the book (chapter x. 1) as it opens it (chapter i. 1) ; and thus ends the last historical volume of the Old Testament.

JOB

JOB I.—This is the oldest book in the World. It was written by Moses (Luke xxiv. 27, 44). It explains the problem why good men are afflicted. It is in order to their sanctification. See notes on chapter xlii. It is interesting that this difficult question should be the first taken up and answered in the Bible.

The books of Esther and of Job present two Eastern princes, Ahasuerus and Job, in the hands of God and of Satan ; and in each book the result is the same : God is glorified, Satan defeated, and man blessed.

Job was the greatest of the men of the East (v. 3), as Ahasuerus was the greatest of the kings of the East (Esther x. 1).

Esther exhibits God's hidden care of a nation ; Job, His hidden care of a man. Both books show Satan's hostility to individuals and to nations.

Esther closes the Historical books of the Bible ; Job begins the Emotional books. These are Job, Psalms, Proverbs, Ecclesiastes, and Canticles, and their several themes are— The Death of Self, The Life in God, The School of God, The Emptiness of Earth, and The Fulness of Christ.

Accepting the principle that the Bible is a self-contained and self-interpreting Book, and that it is not necessary to go outside of it for satisfactory information, it may be possible that Job the son of Issachar (Gen. xlvi. 13) is the person meant here ; that he went down to Egypt with his father, being about 20 years of age ; that he left Egypt later on for the land of Uz (see Gen. xxii. 20, Jer. xxv. 20) ; that he was seventy years of age at the time of his great trial ; and, assuming that the double blessing of chapter xlii. 10, included a double of his then age of seventy, he lived to be two hundred and ten (70 and 140) ; and Moses, at that time being 55 years of age, and already fifteen

years in Midian, was, therefore, competent to be the writer of this book, and, possibly, knew Job personally.

"Job," i.e., the discovery of the worthlessness of self, is the first step in Christian experience, and " Canticles," i.e., the worthfulness of Christ, the last step. But " Canticles " can never be reached until " Job " has been first passed through.

Job does not symbolise an unconverted but a converted man. It was necessary that one of God's children should be chosen for this trial ; for the subject of the book is not the conversion of the sinner, but the consecration of the saint. It is evident that an unconverted man needs to be brought to an end of himself ; but that a man who feared God, who was perfect, and who eschewed evil, should also need this, is not so clear. Here comes in the mystery of the Book. God uses Satan, calamity, and sickness to be His instruments in creating character and making men partakers of His holiness. Such were the instruments ; but the Hand that used them was God's ; and the facts of this book explain to Christian people, who, like Job, are conscious of personal integrity, why calamities, sorrows, and diseases are permitted to afflict them.

The effect of the Divine action was that Job " abhorred himself " (chapter xlii. 5, 6). This language shows that he had thought well of himself. His creed was orthodox, for he approached God through sacrifice, and his conduct was faultless, for he was a just man and eschewed evil. But these sharp trials, and especially the anger which the unjust accusations of his friends stirred up in his heart, revealed to himself unknown depths of moral ugliness ; and, finally, his being challenged to measure himself with God, made him conscious that in him, that is, in his " flesh," there dwelt no good thing.

This is a deep and painful experience which all Christian people have not reached. See last chapter.

The three friends show the impotence of human experience (Eliphaz), of human tradition (Bildad), and of human merit (Zophar). To elucidate the riddle of this book, Elihu pointed to God as just, and at the same time, the Saviour and Justifier of sinful men. His ministry, as Mediator, occupies the central position in the entire book, and it is preceded and followed by four corresponding members of a unique structure, thus :—

Introduction,	Conclusion,
Satan's assault,	Satan's defeat,
Arrival of friends,	Departure of friends,
Job and Elihu.	Job and God.

" Everyone his day " (v. 4) means, " everyone on his birthday "

The brothers inviting their sisters to their houses showed unity and affection in the family ; and was an evidence of what an admirable father Job was.

The words " gone about " (v. 5) mean " came round."

Job offering burnt-offerings on behalf of his children, revealed him as a true follower of Abel and Noah.

The expression " cursed God in their hearts " (v. 5), is translated in the R.V. " renounced God," i.e., put God outside of their feasting. It is easier to forget God, and be independent of Him, when merry than when sad.

The " sons of God " of verse 6 were the angels of His might. They appear again in chapter ii. 1. The expression in both verses " there was a day," that is, " there came to be a day," shows that these angelic ministers appeared at appointed seasons to give account to God of their actions. Satan's appearing among them is a solemn mystery.

This is the first instance in the Bible of this mighty angel being named " Satan," or " the Adversary." In other parts of the Scriptures he is called " The Accuser," " The Devil," " The Serpent," " Beelzebub," " The Prince of this World," " The God of this World," and " The Prince of the Power of the Air."

Verse 10 proves how absolutely secure from Satanic malignity are the children of God. Compare 1 John v. 18, 19.

Satan requests God to put forth His hand and touch, or hurt, Job. God would not do so, but gave Satan permission to put forth his hand.

The words " while he was yet speaking " repeated three times (vs. 16, 17, 18), show the rapidity and vehemence of Satan's assault.

The first and third calamities came from the hand of man, (the Sabeans and the Chaldeans). The second and the fourth were superhuman, (lightning and tempest).

Satan has permitted power over the hearts of men and the forces of the universe.

In each case the messengers place the loss of property above the sacrifice of life. The same feature may be recognised to-day in Parliamentary debates and newspaper reports.

But Job judged otherwise. He did not " arise," that is, " spring to his feet " (v. 20), until he had heard of the death of his children.

Job's first word in this book is the word " naked." His last is the word " dust." These two words accurately describe the noblest man that fallen humanity can idealise.

The " mother " of verse 21 means the earth.

The last verse should read " In all this Job sinned not, nor charged God with injustice."

JOB II.—" Skin for skin " (v. 4) is a contracted proverb, and means that to exchange one article for its equivalent costs nothing.

If the word " yea " be changed into " but," as many scholars affirm, the argument reads : " Skin for skin one will give, but all that a man hath will he give for his life. Put forth, however, Thy hand now and hurt his bone and his flesh, and he will curse Thee to Thy face. And Jehovah said unto Satan, Behold he is in thine hand ; but spare his life."

The " potsherd " of verse 8 was made of wood, and the " ashes " of the same verse were wood ashes, which being white and sprinkled upon the head, or sat among, expressed great grief.

The language of Job's wife was that of idolatry and scepticism. She said in effect :— " Why do you hold on to your religious profession ! Throw your idol god aside ; there is no eternity ; you need not be afraid to die ; there is nothing behind death. This religion of Abel, Noah, and Abraham is a fairy tale ! "

The word " evil " in verse 10 means " calamity."

Job did not sin with his lips, but he was filled with horror and self-abasement when he became conscious of how he was sinning in his heart. Chapter xxix. shows that the beauteous graces of God in him made him lovely to his own eyes, and satisfied with himself. He had never been in the presence of God, although obedient to the revealed will of God. But he was no hypocrite; he lost all to which Satan traced his piety, and it shone forth brighter then ever.

JOB III.—This chapter forms the first stanza of the greatest poem in the world. It contains three sections. Job laments his birth (vs. 2-9), and gives the reasons why (v. 10); he laments his infancy (vs. 11, 12), and gives the reasons why (vs. 13-19); and he laments his manhood (vs. 20-23), and gives the reasons why.

The third verse should read: "or the night in which it was said" etc, for Job did not know whether he was born at night or during the day.

The first verse should read:—"and cursed his birthday."

Verses 4 and 5 curse the day, and verses 6 to 9 the night in which he was born.

That word "solitary" in verse 7 better means "barren" (R.V.), i.e., he wished that no child had been born that night.

Verse 8 may read thus: "Let those who are skilful to bring up the great serpent curse the day." That is, "Let men (like Balaam), by enchantments, excite Satan to make that a day of ill omen."

The argument of verse 10 is, that had he never been born he had not known sorrow.

"Why did the knees receive me?" (R.V.). In the East a father places a new-born child upon his knees as accepting the child as his own, and pledging himself to provide for it.

The argument of verses 13-19 is, that had he died in infancy he would now be enjoying the quietude of the grave, in which world kings, counsellors, princes, prisoners, slaves and the weary are at rest.

The word "light" in verses 20 and 23 means "life."

JOB IV.—"Yet trouble came", or "is come" (R.V.); and Eliphaz and his two friends possibly brought "the trouble" that Job feared. That is, what Job "greatly feared" (chapter iii. 25) was, that the religious world would believe him to be a hypocrite, a secretly wicked man, because of these overwhelming calamities that had fallen upon him. Although silent, yet something in the bearing of the three princes probably convinced Job that they were the agents of this supreme trial.

Eliphaz represents the man of science. He argued from experience and from facts; and he, accordingly, satisfied himself that Job was undoubtedly a secret sinner. He laid down two propositions, and sought to prove them by the demonstration of experience, but as he and his two friends had no true knowledge of God, their arguments, though they said many things that, in themselves, were true, failed to explain the riddle why righteous men are afflicted.

The two propositions were: "Who ever perished being innocent?" or "Where were the righteous cut off?" (v. 7); and, second, "wrath killeth the foolish man, and envy slayeth the silly one" (V. 2).

The words "As I have seen" (v. 8), introduce the proofs in support of the proposition of verse 7. The proofs are found in verses 8 and 9; and verses 10 and 11 add that wicked men, even though they were as strong as lions figuratively, are helpless in the grip of Divine retributive justice.

Perhaps Eliphaz hinted that the lion, the lioness, and the young lions were Job, his wife, and his children.

The argument from experience is next fortified by the general statement, learnt in the night visions from a spectre, that the angels are untrustworthy, justly chargeable with folly, and, therefore, how much more men, who dwell in houses of clay, houses more frail than a moth's body, whose span of existence is only from morning to evening, and of so little value that their destruction is unworthy of notice; and as to the principle of life which inhabits this clay envelope, it is removed from them without their being able to prevent the removal, and death overtakes them before they have lived long enough to attain unto wisdom (vs. 12-21).

The "it" of verse 5 means calamity.

Verse 6 may be thus paraphrased:— "Ought not thy fear of God to be thy trust; and the uprightness of thy ways thy hope?"

The words "a little" in verse 12 mean a whisper.

"Crushed before the moth" (v. 19) means sooner, or easier, than a moth.

" From morning to evening " (v. 20) should read " twixt morning and evening " ; and they perish for ever without anyone having sufficient interest in them to save them.

JOB V.—Verse 1 is adduced by the Roman Church as authorising prayers to the saints. The argument, however, of the verse is to show the uselessness of such prayer. Job is here challenged to produce, if he can, any spiritual authority to " answer," i.e., to approve and deliver him ; and if he proposes to get help from the saints, i.e., the angels, that would be useless ; for they have been declared in verse 18 of the prior chapter to be untrustworthy and foolish.

Eliphaz' second proposition is contained in verse 2, which, paraphrased, reads thus :— " Vexation kills the godless man, and envy slays the senseless." The proofs in support of this proposition are found in verses 3 to 5.

These proofs are introduced by the formula " I have seen," (see ch. iv. 8), and the application of the argument is closed in verse 27 by the assertion " this we have found out by observation, and so it is."

The passage (vs. 3-5) may read thus :— I have seen the ungodly taking root, but at once I foretold the fate of his habitation, saying—" His children shall be far from safety ; they shall be condemned in the gate, i.e., by a court of justice ; no one shall be able to deliver them from death ; the hungry shall eat up their harvest though it be protected by a thorn hedge ; and, as for their substance, the thirsty shall drink it up."

Verses 6 to 26 contain an argument ; and, founded on it, an exhortation. All here is true, but Eliphaz used these truths to try to prove Job to be a secret sinner ; which was a falsehood.

The argument is found in verses 6 and 7, and it is :—that suffering originates from man's sinful nature, just as sparks originate from a fire ; and, accordingly, the origin of suffering is not to be sought in the operation of physical law (v. 6), but is the effect of moral corruption.

Based upon this argument appears the Greatness of God (vs. 9-16), and the Goodness of God (vs. 17-26).

The seven troubles of verse 19 are detailed as :—famine, war, slander, public insecurity, atmospheric disturbance, wild beasts, and damage to crops from animals and all noxious agencies (" stones ").

JOB VI.—The arguments in Job's reply to Eliphaz are :—That his bemoaning was very light in comparison with his affliction, even though his words of complaint were rash and .wild (vs. 2, 3) ; for his anguish was no ordinary one but an exceptional one of God's special infliction (v. 4) ; even animals (v. 5) complain when needing food, how much more justly he himself, when the food offered him was so uninviting that his nature refused to touch it (vs. 6, 7).

Therefore he desired that God's hand might be " loosed " upon him so as to put him to death (v. 8, 9) ; he should not fear to die, but, on the contrary, rejoice to die, for he had not denied the Holy One (v. 10). As to the prolongation of life suggested to him by Eliphaz, what would that advantage him, seeing he had no strength in himself or hope of deliverance from others (vs. 11-13). He pointed out that even had he forsaken the fear of God yet should his friends, even in such a case, pity his misery, but, alas, they were as deceitful streams in a burning desert (vs. 14-21). He challenged them to say if he had requested their sympathy or their help (vs. 22, 23) ; he asked them to point out what evil thing he had actually done worthy of being reproved (vs. 24, 25) ; he urged it to be absurd to reprove the mere words of a desperate man, and added that such persons would attack orphans and feast themselves on the disasters of a friend (vs. 26, 27) ; he invited them to look at his face and see if it were that of a hypocrite ; and he demanded that they " return," or retract, their unjust accusation of him, claiming that his tongue was as honest as his face, and his moral intelligence in detecting evil as acute as theirs (vs. 28-30).

JOB VII.—When reading the Book of Job the R.V. should be everywhere used. Here it helps to make clear the argument of the first four verses, which is, that life is a battle with misery comparable to that of the slave, or hireling, who longs for the conclusion of the day's toil. Job protests that he is in a worse state, for the slave enjoys the unconsciousness of refreshing sleep, but that his misery is greater at night than during the day (vs. 3, 4, 13, 14, 15, 16).

The argument of verses 5 to 21 is, that seeing that man is but a piece of clay (v. 17), and that the life therein is but for a moment (v. 6), why should God interest Himself so much in him as to make him the object of His afflictive blows (v. 20) and the victim of such sufferings (v. 5-10)? He, therefore, in verse 11 declares that he is justified in the utterance of this complaint.

Verse 8 may read thus : " The eye of him that seeth me (the human eye) shall see me no more ; but Thine eyes shall be upon me though I shall not be."

Verses 9 and 10 are not a denial of resurrection, but a statement that man cannot return to human society and resume his ordinary life therein after death.

The argument of verse 12 is :—I am confined within an experience of misery, and cannot escape therefrom, just as the sea is confined (Jer. v. 22) to its bed, and the sea-monster to its element.

Verse 17 may read thus :—" What is man that Thou shouldst make Him of so much importance, and that Thou shouldst expend so much thought upon him? It is the opposite of the query of Psalm viii. 4, which admires God's loving interest in man.

The expression in verse 19 " till I swallow down my spittle " is an idiom for " just for a moment "—as in English, " till I draw my breath."

The word " Preserver " in verse 20 should be " Watcher " (R.V.). To the natural will the thought is intolerable that God's watchful eye should scrutinise every action ; but to the will enlightened by, and subjected to, the Holy Spirit, the fact is delightful.

The petulant question :—" Why dost Thou not pardon my transgression ? " etc. (v. 21) expresses the popular belief of highly moral men, who, while admitting, like Job, that they have sinned, claim forgiveness as a right, and so remain in darkness. Compare the case of the Syro-Phoenician woman, who did not get what she wanted until she had abandoned that ground (Mark vii. 25).

Job's thought from verse 17 onwards was, if he had sinned against God, it would be much kinder of God to forgive him than to torment him. Why keep on tormenting a frail creature whose life was so brief that, when sought next morning, he is found to have ceased to exist.

JOB VIII.—Bildad's effort to prove Job a secret sinner and a hypocrite was based upon tradition. His language was rougher than that of Eliphaz.

He began by declaring Job's words to be like blustering wind (v. 2), and by hinting (v. 3) that it would be impossible for God to pervert judgment and justice. It was, therefore, evident that Job was a wicked man, because the magnitude of his sufferings demonstrated their Divine origin.

He then very cruelly said that Job's children perished because of their sins ; he asserted that if Job himself were pure and upright God would pardon him and make his home—formerly unholy—righteous and prosperous ; and he added that though that home might first be small yet would it ultimately become very large (vs. 4-7).

Arguing from tradition he then brought forward two objects, one nourished by moisture, the papyrus, the other by heat—perhaps a bramble—to prove Job's hidden wickedness.

The authors of this tradition are pointed to in verses 8-10. The hundreds of years that they personally lived, and which enabled them to acquire a vast store of wisdom, contrasted with the brevity of Job's life and that of his friends (v. 9). These aged and wise men spoke out of their heart, that is intelligently, and not like Job, out of the mouth, that is, foolishly.

That which these aged and wise men handed down by tradition, is contained in verses 11-19. The papyrus, nourished by moisture, flourishes for but a day, and pictures the hypocrite's hope. The bramble (v. 16), forced by the sun, covers a garden, and mounts its encircling wall (v. 17), but it is torn from its place (v. 18), the joy of its brief life ends (v. 19), better plants grow instead of it (v. 19), and the very garden in which it grew disowns it.

That God does not cast away a righteous man, or give a helping hand to an evil doer, is quite true ; but it had no application to the problem that confounded Job.

The words " then wait " supplied at the beginning of verse 21, and the word " till," read " until," complete the argument that the fact of verse 20 being so, tradition made it absolutely certain that an evil man may enjoy a brief prosperity, as Job had enjoyed, but that if he repents, and waits, God will fill his mouth with laughter and put to confusion his enemies.

JOB IX.—In the first four verses Job admits the truth of what Bildad stated in verse 20 of the previous chapter, but asks :—

" How may a sinner be justified, i.e., declared innocent, before God ?" adding that however wise that man may be, and however strong morally, yet could he not either brave God, or even dare to answer God, though he might have a thousand answers to God's one question ; or, if God put a thousand questions to him, he could not answer one of them.

The answer to verse 2 is found in Romans iii.

Job argues it is foolish to dispute with God, for His works are unsearchable (vs. 5-10), and His ways inscrutable (vs. 11, 12), and that man is incompetent to understand either (vs. 13-18) ; and he points out in verses 16-18 that if he had called upon God, as Bildad proposed, and God had answered him, yet he could not believe that he had answered him favourably, for he was still breaking him with calamities and sufferings so bitter that he had no respite so much as to take his breath.

In verse 9 the words " the stars which fill " should be supplied so that the second part of the verse may read :—" and the stars that fill the chambers of the south." This verse shows that the rotundity of the earth was known at that time.

Verses 19-31 contain two statements corresponding to those of verses 5-10, and 11 and 12. These statements are :—Job's helplessness in presence of the Justice of God (vs. 19-34), and of the actions of God (vs. 25-31). He says, in verse 19, that if he appealed to Justice, God was a powerful antagonist, and who could summon Him to a court ? and, in verse 20, that even there in trying to justify himself his own mouth would condemn him and his innocence be found perverseness. He adds (vs. 22, 24) that it was " all one," i.e., useless, impossible to understand the ways of Divine Justice, for the innocent and the guilty were punished alike, the earth was abandoned to the power of evil men, and the very ministers of justice were incompetent to discern between right and wrong ; and he asks (v. 24) if God is not the author of all this confusion and injustice, who then is the author ?

The statement in verses 25-31 deals with the action of God, and Job's helplessness in relation to it. He says (vs. 27-29), that it would be labour in vain to try to be cheerful, for two terrors from God, before both of which he is helpless, cause him to shudder—the one terror, the hideous disease that was destroying his body ; the other terror, the future judgment that would destroy his soul, for he knew that in that judgment he would not be found innocent (v. 28) ; and he adds that, in spite of all efforts at moral amendment (v. 30), yet in the light of that pitiless judgment-seat he, consciously innocent, would be exposed as being so guilty that his very clothes would abhor him.

The word " for " (v. 32) leads to the climax of the chapter, it gathers up the four preceding statements, viz :—Job's inability to understand the works and ways of God ; and his inequality as a litigant with God. These facts cause him to cry out for a Mediator who would be both God and man, and who would bring them together in peace. This Mediator is the Man Christ Jesus, Himself God.

Granted this Mediator, Job exclaims :— " Then would I speak and boldly plead my cause ; but now, alas, it is not so with me."

JOB X.—No " Daysman " being present, Job exclaims that he is weary of living ; he claims his right to vent his complaints about himself, and to demand from God the evidence of his assumed guilt (vs. 1 and 2).

He contrasts the power (vs. 3-7) and the action (vs. 14-17) of the Divine Judge with the helplessness (vs. 8-13) and weakness (vs. 18 and 19) of himself as the accused.

The power of the Judge is shown in verses 3 and 7 to be despotic—He favours the wicked and oppresses the good (v. 3), and from His decision there is no appeal (v. 7). He is not as a human judge, defective in knowledge (v. 4) and shortlived (v. 5), who must seek, by evidence and investigation, to find out the truth (v. 6), for He knew, being God, that Job was innocent (v. 7). The powerlessness of Job is described in verses 8 to 12—a description highly scientific—and this physical powerlessness is made the more complete by the statement in verse 13 that Job's creation and affliction were foreordained.

The action of the Judge is set out in verses 14 to 17. He treats the accused as guilty (v. 15) ; He brings forward host upon host of witnesses (v. 17, R.V. margin) ; and, like a lion, He hunts him down, and then returns to torture him by His wondrous strength (v. 16). The next two verses, corresponding to verses 8 to 12, contrast the weakness of Job.

The Judge therefore being God why such enquiry? Why such haste? Why not let Job alone for the few days that precede the eternal night? (vs. 20-22).

JOB XI.—Zophar was a moralist. He believed in salvation by merit, and thereby sought to prove that Job must be a wicked man.

His address may be subdivided thus:—

God's judgments on Job.	(vs. 1-6).
Job's ignorance.	(vs. 7-8).
God's Knowledge.	(vs. 9-12).
The efficacy of good works.	(vs. 13-14).
Their reward.	(vs. 15-19).
God's judgment on the wicked in general.	(v. 20).

The word "lies" in verse 3 means "babblings." or "boastings." (R.V.).

The word "mockest" in same verse means "upbraidest" God.

The argument in verse 6 is that the secrets of Divine Wisdom far exceed their visible effects; and that, therefore, Job's secret wickedness was much greater than its visible punishment.

The word "it" (v. 8), means the knowledge of the nature and the ways of God; these are undiscoverable by human reason.

The argument of verses 10-12 is based on the action of a judge who, passing through a country, calls up for judgment those who are shut up in prison, and from whose judgment there is no appeal. God knows men's wickedness, and needs not, as an earthly judge to enquire whether the accused be guilty or not, and verse 12 contrasts the ignorance of man, who is by birth and nature as ignorant and insubject as a wild ass's colt. (R.V.).

The expression "waters that pass away" (v. 16) means "dangerous waters," such as a flood; and Zophar's argument is, that if Job would give up his sins, and betake himself to prayer, (vs. 13, 14), God's afflictive judgments would cease, and he would forget his miseries, as men quickly forget the injury done by an inundation.

"The eyes of the wicked shall fail," means that the good fortune which they anticipate shall never materialize (v. 20).

JOB XII.—Job's reply to Zophar occupies Chapters xii., xiii., and xiv.

Its general argument is: that misfortunes equally afflict good men and bad men; and that this fact disproves the belief that adversity is an evidence of bad conduct.

The three chapters may be thus sectioned:—

Job not inferior to his friends,
(xii. 1-5., xiii. 1-5.)
His appeal to them
(xii. 6-12., xiii. 6-18.)
He recites God's actions.
(xii. 13-15.)
He appeals to God.
xiii. 19—xiv. 22.

The fourth verse of this chapter may read thus: "I am as one mocked of his neighbour, who saith, 'He professeth to call upon God, and to be answered by Him!' Thus am I, a just and upright man, yet laughed to scorn."

The following verse may be thus understood:—"A lamp is for him that is ready to totter, but is despised by him that thinketh himself safe." This was a rebuke to the self-confidence, and self-righteousness, of the three friends.

In reply to the assertion that prosperity denotes Divine approbation, Job points out that robbers, and rebels, often prosper (v. 6); that among beasts and birds, the strong prey upon the weak (v. 7); that brambles destroy the gentle flower, and sharks the timid whiting (v. 8); he asks, in verses 9 and 10, if these are not all the creatures of God's hand, and subject to His will; and the section is closed by admitting what Bildad had stated, that aged men are wise (v. 12), but his friend's words were empty (v. 11).

The argument of verses 13-25 is:—That God for some just reason hidden in Himself (v. 22), and in the exercise of His wisdom, strength, counsel and understanding visits man with adversity, or prosperity, as it pleaseth Him.

The eighteenth verse may be thus paraphrased:—He undoeth the governmental power of kings, and leadeth them, girded with a rope, into captivity.

Thus, in these verses, Job contrasts the wisdom of God with that of the aged men of verse 12, and sets this action of God before his friends as a baffling problem, pointing out in verse 20, that He destroys the opinions of the most highly-trusted persons, and the understanding of the most aged.

JOB XIII.—As already pointed out, this chapter contains three sections, corresponding to those of the prior chapter. In the first five verses Job denies that he is inferior in knowledge to his visitors; in the second section verses 6-18, he appeals to them; and in the third section, (v. 19 to end of Ch. xiv.) he appeals from them to God.

In verses 3 and 4, he declares his willingness to reason with God, but not with his visitors, for they were neither truthful nor intelligent.

He charges them with trying to vindicate God's afflictive action toward him by using the unjust assumption that he was a secretly wicked man. In verses 9, 10 and 11, he turns the argument against them, and asks: Would it be well with them if God were to enquire into their conduct, could they befool Him as if He were a man; would He not openly convict them of partiality; and ought they not to be afraid of His anger? Verse 12 should read (R.V.): "Your memorable sayings are proverbs of ashes, and your arguments bulwarks of clay." He then begs them to be silent so that he may utter his just complaint (v. 13), and exclaims that, come what may, he will risk his flesh and his life in so doing; and though God should slay him—leaving him without hope—yet would he defend his conduct before Him" (vs. 13 to 15). He urges that this fact would contribute to his deliverance, for no consciously guilty person would voluntarily come before Him (v. 16); and the section closes with a declaration that he is certain of being pronounced righteous (v. 18) if brought into court.

The appeal to God opens in verse 19 with the promise to accept the Divine verdict if God should contend successfully with him. Only, prior to this Divine decision, he makes two petitions:—First, that his body should be freed from disease; and, second, his heart freed from terror. Then, continuing the imagery of a court of justice, in verses 22 and 23, he proposes God as Prosecutor, and himself as defendant; or, reversed, he himself as plaintiff and God as Defendant; and, in verse 23, successfully challenges Him to produce against him even one transgression or one sin. The remaining five verses picture him as unjustly condemned; the face of the Judge averted from him; he himself treated as an enemy (v. 24);

broken as a leaf; chased as dry stubble (v. 25); bitter punishments ordered, in writing, against him for errors of childhood (v. 26); his feet fastened in the stocks, and so mercilessly bastinadoed upon the soles, that his whole body becomes hopelessly diseased (vs. 27 and 28).

The words in verse 14 "I take my flesh in my teeth" mean "I venture my being." They are a proverb.

Verse 15 should read: "Behold He will (probably) slay me — I wait for Him," i.e., to do so: That is to say, "there is no hope."

The word "he" in verse 28 intends Job himself, and means that he, the person to whom the feet belong, is become a dying man by reason of the terrible punishment of the bastinado."

JOB XIV.—This chapter concludes Job's appeal to God.

He passes from his own particular misery, described in the last three verses of the previous chapter, to the wretchedness of man in general, and argues that man, being sinful by nature, frail, and full of misery, in contrast to God, who is sinless, mighty and happy, it would therefore be desirable that God should leave man to himself for the few days he has to live, and not perpetually and narrowly watch him, counting his very footsteps, noting his every sin and transgression, and registering them for future judgment. He wished God to keep as far from him as possible. David, in the very next book of the Bible, earnestly desired the contrary. Job expressed the wish of the natural heart —David that of the renewed heart.

Three statements are made in the first verse in respect to man:—That he is by natural birth sinful (v. 4); that his life is short; and that it is filled with trouble.

In verse 3 Job questions the justice of bringing so sinful, and frail, and miserable a being into controversy with God, Who is so great.

The next verse should read:—"Oh! that a clean thing could come forth out of a thing unclean! But there is none such!" The argument here is, that man is a sinner, involuntarily, by natural birth, and Job longs that it were not so; but such being the fact why should God demand moral perfection from him ? And he adds (v. 5) that, seeing that the duration of a man's life is decreed beforehand by God, and that man is helpless in the face of that decree, why should not God leave him alone (v. 6), and let him enjoy his brief life in peace !

This appeal is supported (vs. 7-12) by the argument, that a tree if cut down can grow up again, but that man when he dies, passes for ever out of this life, never getting the chance, like a tree, of living his life over again.

But this fact does not deny a future life beyond the grave ; and, accordingly, verses 12 to 15 show how much was known in Job's day about the temporary life of this world and the promise of a better.

Verse 12 states :—That man does not cease to exist at death ; that he falls into an unconscious sleep (v. 21) ; and that this sleep continues till the heavens be no more. The heavens, as distinguished from the heaven, mean the present creation, and includes the earth. This distinction is observed in the Lord's Prayer, which reads thus in the original : " Our Father, Who art in the heavens . . . . Thy will be done in the earth, as in the heaven." As Father, He is equally near His children whether in heaven or earth, for the earth is included in the heavens.

The prayer, the poetry, the imagery, the love, the faith, and the intelligence of verses 13, 14 and 15, are exquisite ! Job prays that during the whole period of God's wrath against this rebellious earth he might be preserved in the unconscious slumbering of death, till " the set time " when God would surely remember him. He declares, under the form of a question, that man will surely live again after death ; and that, therefore, during the whole of the appointed time he would wait till his reviving, or resurrection, should come. Then he exclaims, " Thou shalt call, and I will answer Thee," for all that are in the graves shall hear His voice and shall come forth ; and he closes this declaration of faith by giving the reason why he was sure that God would not fail to hear him, and awaken him on the resurrection morning ; and his assurance was that God has a longing desire for the work of His own hands. That is to say, Job did not base his assurance of resurrection upon his own goodness, but upon God's works ; and whilst, no doubt, Job himself was a creation of God's hand, and therefore

precious to Him, yet the New Testament gives the full meaning of this verse 15, and reveals the eternal truth that the justification and the resurrection of sinful man is founded upon the work of God's hand in the gift and sacrifice of Christ.

Job then contrasts (vs. 16-22) his present misery with the bliss of that future life. He complains that his actions, his sins, his transgressions, his iniquities, are noted and registered by God, who destroys a man as easily as dust, stones, rocks, and mountains are destroyed. He dismisses him into death, making palid his face, and he sinks into an insensibility so profound, in the spirit world that he is unconscious of that which happens to his own children in this world, knowing not whether they be honoured or degraded. This fact destroys the Roman Catholic dogma of the Intercession of Saints ; for, if a righteous man, such as God Himself declared Job to be, would, in the spirit world, be unconscious in regard of those so near to him as his own children, what hope could strangers have of his help ?

The last verse has no reference to pain, and sorrow in the spirit-world, but is connected with the first verse of the chapter, and with verses 16 to 20, i.e., the verse has reference to life in this world, and declares, that it is full of physical pain and mental sorrow.

JOB XV.—This is Eliphaz's second address. It is not so polite as the first. As already pointed out, he claimed to be a man of science, and, as such, judged from facts seen and experienced by himself (v. 17). His argument, however, based upon these facts, that Job's afflictions were God's just punishments upon him because of his secret sins, was altogether false.

In the first three verses he condemns Job's language, and in the next three, as a scientific man, he adduces proofs of its wickedness. In verses 7-14, he condemns his conduct, and in verses 15 and 16, offers proofs of its badness ; and, finally (vs. 20-25), repeats what he had learned from Noah and his sons, of the just action of God in punishing evil men who, like Job, had enjoyed a temporary prosperity.

The accusation of verse 4 was :—That Job's doctrine, that evil men prosper, made void the fear of God, and made useless prayer to Him. It is this teaching that is referred to in verses 5 and 6.

In verse 8, the word "restrain" means "to have a monopoly of." He asked Job if he were a member of God's Privy Council, and if he retained to himself the wisdom he learnt there.

The expression "consolations of God" (v. ii) may be idiomatic for "great consolations," and, if so, the verse would then mean : Had Job such a secret source of consolatory wisdom as to make worthless the valuable consolations of his three friends !

The following two verses may read thus :—"Why do you let your feelings carry you away, and why do your eyes flash with pride, so that you fret against God, and give utterance to such statements ? " i.e., that he was "not guilty" in the Court of Heaven.

To prove that he was guilty, three arguments appear in verses 14, 15 and 16, viz :—By natural birth ; by comparison with the angels ; and by personal conduct.

Verses 17, 18 and 19, introduce the tradition mentioned in verses 20 to 35. This tradition originated with Noah and his sons when they were "alone in the earth." It states :—That an evil man may enjoy temporary prosperity, but because he defies God (v. 25), opposes Him with stiffened neck and protected shield (v. 26), and even though his physical strength were exceptional (v. 27), yet would he be cut off before his time ; the recompense of vanity be paid to him in full (v. 31 and 32 R.V.) ; and utter ruin be his doom—his accursed offspring being mischief, vanity, and deceit (v. 35).

JOB XVI and XVII.—Job here replies that his friends were miserable and not Divine consolers (v. 1-6) ; that God's action toward him was impossible to understand (vs. 7-16) ; that God Himself was a Witness to his innocency (vs. 17-21) ; that his life was necessarily brief (vs. 22 and xvii. 1); he challenges his friends to prove themselves either upright or wise (vs. 2-10) ; and declares that the hopes of happiness they promised him would be buried with him in the grave (vs. 11-16).

The friends claimed in xv. 11 to be Godlike comforters, but Job replies that far from being so, they were miserable comforters (v. 2) ; and he adds, that their words were empty (v. 3) ; that, if positions were reversed, he could heap up accusations against them, shake his head at them, propose to strengthen them, and assuage their grief with heartless talk, and the moving of his lips (vs. 4 and 5) ; and, in verse 6, points out, that speaking, or not speaking, is, in either case, valueless in such a trial as his. The argument, therefore, is :—That the teachings of human wisdom can neither strengthen the heart, nor mitigate the sufferings of a person so mysteriously afflicted as Job.

The several statements in verses 7-16 are these :—God wearied Job with suffering ; destroyed all the witnesses that he could have produced to prove his innocence, i.e., his children and his servants (v. 7) ; shrivelled up his body with a horrible disease, which seemed an evidence of his guilt (v. 8) ; rent him in His anger ; persecuted him ; gnashed upon him with His teeth ; as an enemy, sharpened His eyes upon him (v. 9) ; evil men He permitted to illtreat him (v. 10) ; the ungodly and the wicked were given power over him (v. 11) ; God Himself dashed him to the ground, and then, broken as he was, set him up for a target (v. 12), so that the archers, i.e., Job's three friends, might attack him. The one cleft his reins asunder, the second poured out his strength upon the ground (v. 13) ; and the third broke him without mercy. The cruelty of these archers was the greater, because exercised upon a man clothed in sackcloth, humiliated in the dust, weeping bitterly, and death already shadowing his eyelids (vs. 15 and 16).

The beauty and spirituality of the paragraph formed by xvi. 17-21 are striking. Conscious of innocency, Job, recalling the murder of Abel, cries to the earth, to continually demand justice for him also slain by the three archers (vs. 17 and 18); declares that in Heaven he had a Witness Who vouched for him (R.V. v. 19) ; that, in spite of the mockery of his neighbours, he poured out his tears to God (v. 20), pleading for a Mediator, who Himself the Son of Man, would plead with God on behalf of Job ! (v. 21).

The whole of the section 17 to 21 is a great prophecy, and has been fulfilled in the life, sufferings, death, and intercession of the Lord Jesus Christ.

In verses 22, and xvii. 1, Job declares : That his breath was being already consumed ; that in a short time he should go whence none returned ; and that the grave, that is the great, deep grave ("graves," in the text, because the plural of majesty), awaited him.

Before his affliction he was as popular as a tabret (v. 6), but now, men of no understanding (v. 4), mockers (v. 2), men without credit (v. 3), provoke his eyes continually (v. 2), and he has become their bye-word (v. 6). Upright men would be astonished at their conduct, and innocent men indignant at such hypocrites (v. 8); but, as for Job, he, being a righteous man, would hold on his way, in spite of their unjust scorn, and he, having clean hands, would only become the stronger because of their cruel action (v. 9).

The happiness they promised him (vs. 11-16) in offering to change his night into day, i.e., his misery into joy (v. 12), was valueless, for the light of prosperity would be quickly quenched in the darkness of the grave, his life being well nigh over, the cherished purposes of his heart broken (v.11), and the hopes they suggested buried with him in the tomb (vs. 15 and 16).

JOB XVIII. — This is Bildad's second address. He argued from tradition that Job was a wicked man.

His address contains two sections:— The first, a reproof of Job (vs. 1-4); and, second, the certain doom of the wicked (vs. 5-21).

The word " vile," (v. 3) means, probably, " stupid," because animals are deemed to be so.

Job, in chapter xvi. 9, complained that God was tearing him in His anger. Bildad says (v. 4) that Job was tearing himself in his bad temper, and asks him if he expected natural and physical laws to be convulsed in support of his pretended innocency !

The light of verse 5 means the fire upon the hearth, and the lamp of verse 6, means the light which hangs from the roof of every Arab dwelling; to extinguish either, or both of these, symbolizes death.

The word " robber " (v. 9) means " snare " (R.V.).

" The strength of his skin " (v. 13), means " his physical forces "; and " the firstborn of death," the chief, or worst, or cruellest death.

Verse 14, if the R.V. be followed, means, that " the tabernacle " is the body," and " it," " the soul," and, therefore, the whole text states : As to Job's body, it would be destroyed, and, as to his soul, it should be handed over to the king of terrors ; and the next verse adds that, as to his habitation,

or tabernacle, or tent, strangers should dwell in it.

Reading verse 20 in the margin of the R.V. makes clear the statement that everybody, i.e., east and west, should know of God's just judgments upon wicked Job.

JOB XIX. — Job, replying to Bildad, continues the figure of a Court of Justice (vs. 6. 7), and insists that, although consciously innocent, yet God, as Judge, pronounces him guilty, and that there is no response to his cries of " Violence," and " Help."

He thus expressed his own incompetency, and that of his three friends, to unravel the mystery, why God should afflict a righteous person.

The chapter contains four sections :—

Censure of his friends.	(vs. 1-5).
Complaints of God's action.	(vs. 6-20).
His faith in God as his ultimate Redeemer.	(vs. 21-27).
Warning to his friends.	(vs. 28 and 29).

The word " strange " (v. 3) means " hard " (R.V.).

The argument of verses 4 and 5 is :—Even supposing that I have unconsciously sinned, the punishment of my error only affects myself. And, in pleading my reproach, (i.e., my sufferings), as evidence of my guilt, your real purpose is to magnify yourselves as morally superior to me.

In the section verse 6 to 20, he urges the mysterious fact of God being the Author of his calamities ; and he pictures himself as confused, and defeated, and helpless, in a court of justice (vs. 6 and 7) ; as a perplexed traveller in a dark night (v. 8) ; as a dethroned king (v. 9) ; as a branchless and uprooted tree (v. 10) ; as a beseiged city (vs. 11 and 12) ; as a friendless outcast (v. 14) ; as a despised alien, in his own house (vs. 15 and 16) ; as offensive to his wife, and loathsome to his brothers and sisters (v. 17) ; as jeered at by little children (v. 18) ; as forsaken with disgust by his most intimate and affectionate friends ; and, lastly, as afflicted with a horrible disease, that tortures his entire frame.

The R.V. margin helps to make clear verse 17. Job's own children being already dead, the second line of the verse may read thus :—" I am become loathsome to the children of my mother's womb, i.e., my brothers and sisters.

Verse 22 means :—" Why do you persecute me as if you were God ; and why are you not satisfied with the sufferings of my flesh ? "

The words that Job wished to engrave for ever with lead in a rock are given in verses 25 to 27, and may be thus paraphrased :—

I know that my Redeemer liveth,
And that He shall stand at the latter day upon the earth,
And after my body hath been thus destroyed,
Yet in my (new) body, shall I see God,
Whom I shall see on my side,
Mine eyes shall behold Him, but not now as a stranger.
For that day my heart longingly waits.

These amazing truths are here introduced by Job as being matters of common knowledge to him and his friends, and prove, what is popularly denied, that God had made to primitive man a wonderfully full revelation of New Testament truth.

The last two verses may possibly mean that on that Resurrection morning, when Job's corrupted body would be clothed with glory and immortality, his three friends would be clothed with confusion, and would cry out :—" Why did we persecute him seeing the root of the matter is found in him," i.e., he was all along sincere ; and then Job solemnly adds : " Beware of the sword (of God), for dreadful are its punishments, and its wrathful judgment is certain."

JOB XX.—Zophar's second address, like his first, was based upon the theory that human merit wins Divine favour, and heaven. His language, like that of persons to-day who think as he did, was rude and violent. His statement that God visits wicked men with calamity in this life, was not altogether true. His repeating the assertion that Job's calamities proved his wickedness, was false ; and his declaration that hell, and not heaven (vs. 4, 5 and 26) would be Job's end, was a worthless figment of his own imagination (v. 3).

The word " haste " in verse 2 means " mental excitement," and this verse, joined with verse 3, means that Zophar recognised the reproof by which Job hoped to put him to shame (R.V.), but that notwith-

standing the just excitement which such a reproof caused him, he would out of the treasures of his own understanding calmly reply by pointing out to Job, that since Adam was placed upon the earth the triumph of the wicked was invariably short, and the sinner's joy momentary ; and his saying to Job " knowest thou not this " was an intimation that Job had no solid hope, as he claimed in chapter xix. 25-27, but the contrary.

This pronouncement he elaborates in verses 6-28. This section should be read as in the R.V.

The " iron weapon " (v. 24) is the " sword of God " ; and verse 25 states that God draws that sword forth from its scabbard, and drives it through the sinner's body, so that it pierces his vitals (gall), and its glittering point comes out at the other side.

Verse 29 repeats the statement of verse 5.

JOB XXI. — In reply to Zophar's repeated theory that God, in this life, rewards the good with prosperity and punishes the evil with adversity, Job points to facts in contradiction of the theory (vs. 7-16), and states that travellers can testify to the actuality of these facts (v. 29).

The chapter may be thus divided :—

An appeal to his friends. (vs. 1-6).
Facts proving the prosperity of the wicked. (vs. 7-16).
Argument of the friends recited. (vs. 17-21).
God's hidden government. (vs. 22, 26).
The false testimony of the friends. (vs. 27, 28 and 34
The true testimony of the travellers. (vs. 29-33).

Job means, in verse 2, that silence would be a greater consolation to him than the vain talk of his friends ; in verse 3, he says they can resume their mocking after he has spoken ; in verse 4 he asks, that if his complaint were addressed to man, would he not be justified if impatient ; and in verses 5 and 6, he invites them to join him in contemplating the prosperity of the wicked, and, viewing their prosperity, to be astonished and silent, and to fear and tremble.

The prosperity of the wicked occupies verses 7-16, and yet they said to God :—" Depart from us," etc., (vs. 14 and 15), although the prosperity they enjoyed was

not created by them, (" not in their hand ")
but came from God's hand.

The " counsel of the wicked " (v. 16) is
described in verses 14 and 15, and Job
exclaims :—" Far be such counsel from me !"

The sophism of Zophar's theory is set out
in verses 17-21, and, like most sophisms, was
false. The words " but yet ye say " should
be supplied at the commencement of verse 17.

Job asks his friends will they presume to
tell God how He should act,—that God Who
judges angels ! (v. 22) ; and then points
to the fact that the prosperous man (vs. 23
and 24), and the groaning slave (v. 25), are
alike laid in the grave, and the worms devour
them.

The word " breasts " should be " milk
pails " ; and the two statements in the verse
point to the wealth and the health of the
prosperous man.

The word " prince " (v. 28) implies an
" oppressing " or " tyrannical noble."

The word " tokens " (v. 29), means " testimony." This testimony by the travellers
(v. 29) is recited in verses 30-33, and is
as follows :—That the wicked is often spared
in public calamities, and escapes from misfortunes (v. 30) ; that he occupies such a
place in society that no one dares decry his
conduct to his face, or requite him the evil
which he does (v. 31) ; that he is buried with
great pomp, and a monument erected, and
kept in good repair, over his grave (v. 32) ;
that the soft earth gently covers him ; and
that he shares the common lot of all who
precede and follow him (v. 33).

There is a double complaint in verse 34,
viz :—as to their words they were worthless ;
and, as to their friendship, it was false.

JOB XXII. — In reply to Job's facts,
Eliphaz advanced the theory that man's
goodness does not add to, or man's badness
take from, God's happiness ; that therefore
God does not prosper some, and afflict others
for His own advantage ; the cause, therefore,
of such action must be found in men themselves ; and, therefore, Job's calamities
clearly proved his guilt.

Eliphaz ignored Job's facts, and tried to
prove that they did not, because they should
not, exist ; and, like some present day professors of science and philosophy, annoyed by the
introduction of inconvenient facts, he became
abusive ; and, whereas in his first two
speeches he only hinted at Job's evil conduct,

in this, his last speech, he directly accused
him of wickedness and wrong-doing (vs. 5-9).

The first four verses state the thesis that
God's happiness is independent of man's
moral conduct.

Accepting this doctrine, Eliphaz (vs. 5-9)
falsely accused Job of evils he never committed.

The word " naked " in verse 6, as almost
invariably throughout the Bible, means
" slightly clad," as, for instance, with a
loin-cloth.

Verse 8 may mean " that the rich, by
violence, seized land and lived on it "—and
history abundantly testifies to that fact—
or the verse may mean, in relation to verse
9, that Job fawned upon the rich and trampled upon the poor.

In verses 10, 11 and 12, Eliphaz insists
that God, from His lofty Throne on high
(v. 12), in just anger, because of Job's wickedness, afflicted him with snares and terrors
(v. 10), perplexity of mind, and floods of
miseries (v. 11).

Addressing Job, he says in verse 13 :—
" And yet thou sayest," etc. Here are two
statements :—First, that God cannot see what
occurs on earth, because of the thick cloud
that hides Him ; and second :—That He
walks in the circuit of heaven, that is, He
confines Himself to heaven and takes no
interest in what transpires upon earth (v. 14).
It was, however, most unjust to put such
language into Job's mouth.

The passage (vs. 15-20) relates to the two
great judgments—the past judgment of water,
and the future judgment of fire. The word
" marked " (v. 15), means, " to hold to,"
or " continue in," and Eliphaz asks Job :—
Will he persist in a course of conduct which
brought the Flood upon their forefathers, and
which will bring the future fire upon the
remnant of the ungodly (v. 20). Verse 17
defines the rebellion which justifies these two
judgments, and verse 19, the recognition by
good men of the justice of God's wrath.

The language of verse 18 is ironical ;
Eliphaz repeats, contemptuously, Job's words
in chapter xxi. 16.

The statements (vs. 21-30) were most true,
but had no application to Job, and threw no
light upon the problem that perplexed him.

Hebrew scholars point to the negative in
the original text of verse 30, and to the word
" island " as meaning " dwelling ". Eliphaz
argued :—That God would restore prosperity

to Job's dwelling, though he was not innocent, if he would wash his hands of all his evil practices.

JOB XXIII and XXIV.—Job replying to Eliphaz denied that he was a wicked man ; repeated the fact that God does not always punish evil men in this life ; and pointed to the inscrutability of God's eternal decrees as contributing to the horror and mystery of human suffering.

Verse 2 may be thus paraphrased :— Although the strike of God's hand is heavier than my groaning, yet is my plaint accounted by my friends to be rebellion !

In the section, verses 3-12, Job declares that if he could meet with God, He, unlike these three friends, would judge him right-eously and declare his innocency ; but he mourns that he cannot find Him, although God knew the rectitude of his conduct, and that he had not disobeyed His command-ments, but, on the contrary," esteemed them more than his necessary food."

The interesting fact here appears (vs. 11 and 12), that from the very beginning of human history, God had made a sufficient revelation of Himself to man, and given him a code of laws.

The immutable and eternal decrees of God form the subject of verses 13 to xxiv. 1. Here Job states that the gloom of death (v. 17) was not so full of horror to him as the in-scrutable decrees of God. As to these decrees, they were fixed, immutable, and certain of execution (v. 12) ; they were fore-ordained for Job ; and many other decrees appointing pain awaited him (v. 14) ; therefore was he terror-stricken (vs. 15, 16) ; and he asks (xxiv. 1),why does not God explain the mean-ing and operation of these mysterious laws to those who love Him. " To see His days " means to understand His dealings with man.

Once again Job (vs. 2-25) points to facts as contradicting the argument : That pros-perity is an evidence of Divine approval, and adversity of the opposite. He indicates the success of oppressors (vs. 2-12) ; of murderers (vs. 13-14) of adulterers (v. 15) ; and of house-breakers (vs. 16, 17). Verses 18 to 20 form a parenthesis in which Job ironically repeats the assertion of his friends : That such persons are swept away as leaves upon swift waters ; that their crops and vine-yards perish ; that the grave swallows them up ; and that they are forgotten. The

contrary, however, he continues is the fact (vs. 21-25) that the prosperous, wicked man is permitted by God to oppress and rob, not only the widow and fatherless (v. 21), but even the well-to-do, so that no one was sure of a livelihood (v. 22). Such men, Job insists, are exalted ; they come to the grave in a good old age as a shock of corn fully ripe ; they die a natural death (v. 24) ; and in verse 25, he challenges contradiction.

The action of the oppressors (vs. 2-12) may be thus paraphrased :—They violently seize lands and flocks (v. 2) ; they rob the poor (v. 3); they evict cottagers (v. 4), so that they and their children have to live like wild animals (v. 5) ; they compel them to cut down their corn and gather their grapes (v. 6) ; they reduce them to such a condition of misery that they have neither clothing nor shelter (vs. 7, 8) ; they pluck the child from the mother's arms and sell it into slavery : they take the clothes of the poor as a pledge (v. 9), and then compel these naked persons to carry, though hungry, sheaves of corn, and, whilst thirsty, to tread the grapes (vs. 10,11), refusing them either food or drink ; and so great is their wicked-ness that the city, as well as the land, resounds perpetually with the groans and shrieks of the oppressed (v. 12) ; and yet, says Job, " God lays not folly to them " (v. 12), that is, God punishes not all this appalling cruelty !

Those that rebel against the light and know not, that is, do not wish to know, the ways thereof, are the murderer, the adulterer, and the housebreaker (vs.13-17); to these, light is as terrifying as death to ordinary beings.

The statement " yet His eyes are upon their ways," (v. 23) i.e., God for a time watches the cruelties of oppressors without inter-ference, corresponds to the statement in verse 12, that He does not immediately punish their wicked conduct.

" They are taken out of the way as all other " (v. 24), reads in the Hebrew text, " they gather up their feet as all other," as Jacob gathered up his feet, and gave up the ghost (Gen. xlix. 33) ; that is, they die a natural death, they are cut off as the ears of corn, and they die peacefully in a ripe old age.

JOB XXV.—This was Bildad's third and last address, and, like the two previous ones, it threw no light whatever upon the problem that perplexed Job.

The address contains two sections :—

First, God, His omnipotence (v. 2), and omniscience (v. 3). Second section :—Man, his moral (vs. 4, 5) and physical corruption (v. 6).

There are two words in the Hebrew text for "worm" (v. 6.) The first means "that which is corruptible," and the second,"that which is weak."

The repetition of the question : "How can he be clean that is born of a woman" shows that the facts of the Fall were well-known to everybody in the days of Job.

JOB XXVI and XXVII. 1-10.— Job, in this reply to Bildad's third address, rebukes the worthlessness of Bildad's human reasoning (vs. 1-4) ; points to God's ways in the seen and unseen worlds as failing to explain His Nature and His Action (vs. 5-14) ; refuses to admit the justice of his three friends' accusation against him, for to do so would be to admit what was false (xxvii. 1-5) ; and, lastly, re-affirms his conscious integrity (vs. 6-10).

Man's words are empty and teach nothing ; accordingly Job asks Bildad who inspired him (v. 4).

Job (vs. 5 - 14) invites Bildad to descend with him to Sheol and view the dead confined therein ; then, in imagination standing apart, to look at the earth suspended in space (v. 7) ; then, to survey the immense ocean of water enveloping the earth in cloud-form (vs. 8, 9) ; then, the ocean disposed around the earth, and therefore appearing alternately in light and darkness as the earth revolves (v. 10) ; then, to consider the mighty laws that maintain the celestial bodies in their orbits (v. 11) ; next, the Divine power that restrains the oceans in their respective beds, controlling their proud waves (v. 12) ; and, lastly, he invites Bildad to understand, if he can, the wisdom that beautifies the heavens with stars, and particularly the great constellation Serpens.

In verse 14, Job declares that these are only parts, or outlines of His ways, " a little portion," that is, a mere whisper of them, and he asks, " who then can comprehend the thunder of His power, if unable to understand His mere whisperings ? "

The " proud " (v. 12) mean the " proud waves."

In the first five verses of chapter xxvii., Job declares that in spite of God's mysterious action toward him (v. 2), he will never

" justify " (v. 5) his three friends, that is, admit the truth of their arguments, for if he did, he would be guilty of falsehood (v. 4), because he knew that he was innocent (v. 6) ; and he closes his address by challenging Satan himself to prove him guilty, if he could (v. 7) ; and, he asks, does it ever happen that a hypocrite, when about to die (v. 8), or when in affliction (v. 9), delights himself in God, or calls upon Him (v. 10). The answer is :—The hypocrite does not do so in such circumstances, but that is just what Job was doing ; therefore he was not a hypocrite.

Job says, in verse 7, that God " stretcheth out the north over the empty place." The scientific accuracy of these words is attested by Professor Barnards who claims to have discovered that there is a vast expanse in the northern heavens without a single star in it. It is an empty place.

JOB XXVII. 11—**XXVIII.** 28.—This is Zophar's third and last address.

In this reply he again repeats his theory that God judges wicked men in this life (vs. 11-23) ; and, then contrasts their ability in discovering material wealth (xxviii. 1-11), with their inability to find or purchase wisdom (vs. 12-27) ; and then closes (v. 28), by counselling Job to abandon his wicked life, and become a worshipper of God.

The words " then answered Zophar and said," should be supplied at the beginning of verse 11.

He proudly says :—" I will teach you," etc.

Verse 15 does not suggest polygamy as existing at that time. The husbands of these widows are the oppressors of verse 13, and, accordingly, the statement " his widows" means the widow of each one of them.

Verse 18 pictures the brief character of the wicked man's prosperity. The following verse, continuing the argument, represents the rich oppressor lying down to rest, but " he," i.e., " it," that is to say, " the silver " of verse 16, fails to be gathered, so that on awakening in the morning he finds that " he," i.e., his wealth is gone ! The word " God " should not be supplied in verse 22, for the argument of verses 20-23 follows upon the statements of verses 13-19, and is, that outraged humanity bursts like a storm upon him, and chases him from his place.

The first eleven verses of chapter xxviii.

describe the miner successfully extracting gold, silver, iron, copper and precious stones from beneath the surface of the ground. He, (v. 3), the miner, lights up the dark mine, and searches out thoroughly the precious stones hid in the deepest darkness ; he breaks open a shaft away from human habitation, and swings on a rope suspended over its depths (v. 4, R.V.). Meanwhile, he ploughs the surface, in order to get bread (v. 5), whilst, underneath, he extracts gold, dust and precious stones, as effectually and cleverly as if done by fire (vs. 5, 6). Keen-eyed as is the vulture and fearless the lion, neither of them knows the underground path of the miner ; strong as is the rock, the miner pierces it ; or mighty the mountain, he cuts into its roots (v. 9) ; he runs galleries through the rocks, until he reaches the hidden wealth (v. 12) ; the subterranean streams that threaten to flood the mine, he banks up, and he successfully brings the hidden minerals to the surface.

But clever as man is in bringing to the light the wealth hidden in the darkness of the mine, he fails altogether to find out the place of wisdom (vs. 12-27) ; nor can he purchase wisdom ; and, therefore (v. 28), Zophar urges Job to acquire true wisdom by turning from the sins and oppressions by which he had amassed his wealth, and becoming a servant of God.

But Zophar's wisdom was founded on human merit. To depart from evil was what every man would do from good policy, and this injunction was a libel upon Job, for he had not lived a life of iniquity, and he was a true servant of God.

JOB XXIX.—This chapter and the two following, compose Job's final reply to the three friends. " Self " is the keynote of the reply. Chapter xxix is the " I " of prosperity, chapter xxx. the " I " of adversity, and chapter xxxi the " I " of innocency. Job had yet to learn that " self " must die, whether it be prosperous self, or afflicted self, or innocent self ; and, that he had to be brought to abhor himself, whether innocent or guilty. Entrance into the life more abundant can only be experienced when religious self is as heartily abhorred as irreligious self.

The first verse should read as in the R.V.

The language of the sixth verse is pastoral. To " wash the steps with butter " expressed the multitude of Job's cattle, and the best

olive trees growing amongst the rocks, they (the rocks) were said to pour forth rivers of oil.

The chapter from verse 7 to the end pictures Job as a mighty prince taking his seat in the place of justice, i.e., the broad place before the gate ; the young men step backwards, the aged respectfully rise ; when Job speaks, all others accept his decisions ; the oppressed whom he delivers, and the strangers to whom he gives justice, praise him ; he punishes the evil doers, and he encourages with his smile the despondent—he himself being so consciously upright that their timid fears cannot depress him (v. 24). He sat chief among them as a king, cheering the sad, and promising himself long life and a peaceful death surrounded by his children. The words " I," " king," and " me "—fill the chapter.

JOB XXX.—The first fourteen verses describe the misery Job suffered from men. Their character is described (vs. 1-8) and their conduct, (vs. 9-14). His mental and bodily sufferings are detailed in verses 15-18 ; and, his sufferings from the Hand of God, in verses 19-31.

The character of those who derided him is thus drawn : They were younger than Job ; sons of fathers more ignoble than dogs (v. 1) ; physically unfit to be even labourers (v. 2) ; half starved (v. 3) ; living on roots, etc. (v. 4) ; chased out of the villages if they attempted to enter (v. 5) ; living in caves (v. 6) ; hiding among brambles like wild beasts (v. 7) ; and driven out from society as being the children of fools and base men (v. 8).

Their conduct is thus described :—They mocked the Patriarch with ribald songs (v. 9) ; standing at a distance they spat at him (v. 10) ; because God had loosed his scourge and afflicted him, they too cast off all restraint in their persecution of him (v. 11) ; as rabble they stood at his right hand to accuse him ; they gave him no standing room in any court of justice, and laid snares for him (v. 12) ; they broke up his path added to his sufferings, though doing so brought them no personal profit (v. 13): and, like a raging flood of waters, they roared over him (v. 14).

His mental sufferings are set out in verses 15 and 16 ; and his physical in verses 17 and 18. The " garment " and " coat " of verse 18 figure these mental and physical sufferings.

The " garment," disfigured, a figure of his outward loathsome disease, clung to him with great force, and the inner coat, his tunic, i.e., his mental terrors, were as fast bound to him as the tight collar of a vest.

His sufferings from the Hand of God were dual—the silence of God to his prayer (vs. 19, 20), and, the action of God in afflicting him (v. 21).

Verse 22 pictures the Patriarch as swept along and maimed as by a storm in the Arabian desert.

The argument of verses 23-25 may be thus set out ;—In verse 23, Job declares his faith in a life beyond the grave ; in verse 24, he states that God, having made a ruin of his physical frame, will not continue to afflict him in the spirit world ; that, during the destruction of his body, he uttered a legitimate cry of anguish because of his suffering; and, in verse 25, he argues that the Divine life in him that caused him to weep and grieve for those that were in trouble and in need, was an assurance to him that the Author of that compassion would ultimately act toward him as he, moved by that Divine pity, had acted toward others.

JOB XXXI.—Just as in chapter xxix Job challenges enquiry into his conduct as a prince, so in this chapter he confidently invites enquiry into his conduct as a private person. The keynote of the chapter is :— The " I " of self justification.

Twelve sins are enumerated. Job declares his innocency in relation to them, and either points to the consequence of the commission of any one of them, or calls for a Divine judgment upon them.

In verse 35 he attaches his signature to this declaration.

The first verse is the sin of unchastity. The consequence of its commission is given in verses 2-4. The Patriarch says (v. 4), that God saw his every action ; and, if guilty of this sin, his portion and heritage from God (v. 2) would be calamity and disaster (v. 3). See R.V.

The next sin is deceit (v. 5), and its judgment is desired (v. 6).

The sin of dishonesty is suggested in verse 7, and its just punishment in verse 8. This verse should read thus :—" Yea, let the produce of my field be rooted out." (R.V.).

The sin of adultery comes next (v. 9). The seducer is pictured waiting in hiding at the husband's door till he leaves his home. This sin is described in the passage as a " heinous crime " (v. 11), destructive of society and population (v. 12), to be punished by death (v. 11), and the wife of the criminal to be reduced to slavery (v. 10).

Injustice is the sin of verse 13, and Job points out in verse 15 that a master and a servant are alike created of God, and are brothers, having been born of the one mother, Eve, (v.15) ; and, he asks (v. 14), what would be his position as a servant, if God, as his Master, entered into judgment with him ?

The sin of inhumanity occupies verses 16-21, and a just imprecation is pronounced thereon.

The expression "when I saw my help in the gate " (v. 21) means, " when I knew that the judge would (unjustly) decide in my favour." Verse 23 may read thus :—" God's wrath was ever a terror to me, and, because of His Majesty, I dared not do this evil."

The two sins of covetousness and idolatry, and their doom, are set out in verses 24-28. The New Testament says that covetousness is idolatry. The Sun was worshipped as the male principle, and the Moon as the female. The thumb of the hand was placed in the lips in adoration as suggestive of the creation of life by the junction of these two principles. Hence the reading," the hand kissed the mouth," (R.V. margin), is correct, and should be in the text. The judgment of death is denounced upon this twin sin (v. 28), for it denies the One and only True God.

Malignity, inhospitality, and hypocrisy, and their just punishment, are the sins of verses 29-34.—Malignity (vs. 29, 30), inhospitality (vs. 31, 32), and hypocrisy (v. 33). Verse 31 should read as in R.V. ; and verse 34 should read :—" Then let a great multitude, etc." Shem and Methuselah connected Job with Adam (v. 33).

Verses 35-37 pictured Job before God as Judge. He hands in, signed, the document, protesting his innocence of these sins ; and desires that his adversary would set out upon a charge sheet his accusations against him ; and, he declares, so conscious was he of his innocency, that he would wear such a document as a crown.

The twelfth sin was fraud. Verses 38 and 39 picture labourers defrauded of their wages, and verse 40 the fitting punishment of that sin.

JOB XXXII.—Elihu pre-figures Christ as

Redeemer and Mediator. He was a near relative of Abraham (v. 2, with Genesis xxii. 20, 21), His name signifies God is Jehovah. He was " the Daysman " that Job desired. His address covers six chapters. It discloses the foundation doctrines of the New Testament. He pointed out that there was no moral difference between Job and his three accusers—that they were all sinners—and that alike they all needed a Saviour. He condemned the three friends because they unjustly accused Job of hypocrisy ; and he condemned Job, because he charged God with injustice. In reply to Job, he directed him to God's greatness in Creation, and to his goodness in Revelation.

Elihu was very much younger than the others, who were as old, if not older, than Abraham at this time.

He pointed out in verse 12 the incompetency of these three false teachers ; and, in verse 14, he declared his personal qualification to answer Job, because there was no controversy between him and Job, and, because he would not speak to Job as the three friends did. He claimed inspiration (vs. 8 and 18).

The last two verses picture a court of justice—as·is so often the case in this Book. Elihu promised to execute ·impartial justice.

JOB XXXIII.—Most of the foundation doctrines of the New Testament are found in this chapter.

Job's folly and self-justification occupy verses 8-11. God's greatness in Creation, and goodness in Revelation, are brought before Job in verses 12-30. Elihu's fitness to instruct him is seen in verses 1-7, and 31-33.

The question : Does God use sickness in saving sinners or in sanctifying saints ? is answered in this chapter in the affirmative. For illustrations, see Isa. xxxviii. 17 (mar.), and 2 Cor. xii. 7.

The teaching of Elihu is as follows :

Job's double folly in protesting his own innocence(v. 9),and God's injustice(vs. 10,11), and the Divine answer: God's greatness in Creation (v. 12), and His goodness in Revelation (vs. 14-30.).

God has three methods of speaking to men:
Through dreams (vs. 14-18).
Through sickness (vs. 19-22).
Through a mediator (vs. 23-30).

This Messenger, or Interpreter, or Redeemer, is human (vs. 6-7), and is Divine (vs. 4 and 23). He shows the sinner God's upright dealings with him (v. 23) ; how He delivers him from hades, by the provision of a ransom, i.e., Christ (v. 24) ; how, as a result,· the leprous sinner is cleansed and new-born, like Naaman (v. 25) ; prayer and fellowship with God follow ; the pardoned sinner vindicates God's righteous action with him (v. 26) ; he confesses his sin and folly (v. 27) ; he testifies of the grace that saved him, and of his confident belief in his ultimate salvation (v. 28). All this is the doctrine of the Epistle to the Romans.

What has been found : " I have found a Ransom " (v. 24). What may be found : " We have found the Messias " (John i. 41). What never shall be found : The sins of the believer (Jeremiah l. 20).

JOB XXXIV.—The first fifteen verses of this chapter were spoken to the three friends, and the remaining verses to Job. The argument is, that they were all alike, sinners, and that no moral distinction existed between them. The three friends assumed themselves to be righteous and wise, and declared Job to be wicked. Job, conscious of his innocence, declared himself to be righteous, but rebelled against God's treatment of him, pronouncing it to be unjust. Thus was the rebellion of his nature against God brought to the surface and made visible, at the same time that the ignorance and malignity of the same nature in his three friends were revealed. Elihu's ministry was designed to make all four conscious of their moral ruin when brought in contact with God, and that they could only stand accepted before Him in the perfection of a Divine righteousness. In the previous chapter he had already announced to them Christ as being that righteousness.

" Ye that claim to be wise men," i.e., " Ye that profess to have knowledge " (v. 2).

The words " Ye say " may be supplied at the beginning of verse 4 ; and the word " know" may be translated " discern." The whole verse expresses the pride and assumption of the three friends in choosing right as opposed to wrong, and in being experts in goodness. As such they condemned Job as being a worker of iniquity, and the companion of wicked men (v. 8) ; and as teaching (v. 9) that it was useless to fall in with, or consent to, the will of God.

Verses 5-8 are the words of the three friends, taken up and quoted by Elihu.

In verses 10-15 Elihu vindicates God, and rebukes the three chieftains. He states that God could not possibly do wrong (v. 10) ; that His action is just to every man (v. 11) ; and that He never perverts judgment (v. 12). He asks (v. 13) if God has a superior who committed to Him the care of the earth as to a steward, or who laid upon Him the maintenance of the whole world ; and, finally (vs. 14-15), he points out the absolute frailty and insufficiency of man by stating, that if God should set His heart upon Himself, i.e., should think only of Himself, and gather unto Himself His spirit, i.e., His breath, all men would immediately cease to exist (see Gen. ii. 7, Eccles. xii. 7, Acts xvii. 28).

In verse 16 Elihu speaks to Job personally, in verses 17-33 vindicates God's action toward him, and reproves Job's refusal to accept the Divine chastisement.

Verse 23 means that God, unlike earthly judges, needs not to enquire into a man's conduct prior to bringing him into judgment, for He knows all hearts, and verse 24 adds, that He convicts of sin men mighty in moral excellence. Verse 25 asserts that without inquisition, for He knows their works, He over-turns and destroys them in the night, whilst others (v. 26) He exposes in the daytime as being evil men ; and the justice of this double action is made plain in verses 27-28.

In verses 31-33 he counsels Job to accept God's dealing with him, and to seek by prayer (v. 32) for an explanation of its mystery.

He closes by declaring that men truly wise will agree with him as to the folly of Job's words, for his answers were those of evil men (v. 36) ; and these words revealed the hidden insubjection of his will to God's will (v. 37).

JOB XXXV.—Elihu in this chapter answers an error personal to Job (vs. 2 and 3) and an error general to man (v. 9), and in verses 14-16 corrects a second error of Job's.

Job's argument (vs. 2 and 3) to which Elihu replies (vs. 4-8) was : How could his goodness profit God, or what advantage would accrue to himself if he refrained from sinning (see chs. ix. 17 and 34, xvi. 12 and 17, xxvii. 2 and 6, and xxxi.). He says that Job's goodness might profit himself, and his wickedness injure his neighbour, but that the one would not injure

God, nor the other enrich Him ; and, with Divine skill, he leaves it to Job's own heart to supply the answer to the question : Why then does God concern Himself so much about man as to chasten him ? The answer is : Because he loves him ! A father chastens his child for the child's own advantage, and not for the father's ; and the motive that originates the punishment is love.

The error of mankind is set out in verses 9-12, and is : That they cry out readily when oppressed by the arm of the mighty, i.e., of the tyrannical ; and, that although gifted by God with an intelligence higher than that of beasts and birds, yet no one enquires after God their Maker, and yet He gives songs in sorrow's night.

Elihu's argument in verses 14-16 is : Although you say I do not see Him, i.e. understand His action toward me, yet judgment is before Him, therefore take Him on trust; and do not say that He thinks lightly of evil because He does not always immediately punish sin, for in thus speaking you fill your mouth with vanity, and multiply words without knowledge.

JOB XXXVI. and XXXVII. — These chapters conclude Elihu's address, and their subject is . The greatness of God in wisdom and in power.

His wisdom is shown in His dealings with man (xxxvi. 1-25), and His power illustrated by a thunderstorm (xxxvi. 26 to xxxvii. 22).

Elihu's great argument is that God does not act by caprice, but by perfect law established upon perfect love. He argues that He designedly teaches men by affliction ; and he points out to Job (vs. 1 and 16) that had he humbly accepted the Divine chastening, and learned the lesson thereby intended, the affliction would have speedily been removed, as indeed it was in the last chapter directly he did learn his lesson.

This lesson was a bitter one for Job — as it is for all persons of perfect moral conduct. He had to learn that all his righteousnesses were as filthy rags ; he had to come to an end of himself, i.e., he had to abhor and put to death all his goodness, equally with all his badness, and to find perfection alone in Christ ; and thus to learn neither to trust himself, however morally cultured, nor any child of Adam however religiously endowed. The true Job, Jesus of Nazareth, had wit to learn that lesson, He knew it divinely. In the Book of the Psalms He continually declares that He trusted God, and no man. In His "haste" through this world He said (not "hastily") that all men were liars whether they were good men or bad men; and it was a true judgment. Hence in John ii. 24, He did not trust Himself even to the men who professed faith in Him; and the reason is given, He knew all men to be untrustworthy.

Thus Elihu's address prepared Job for that which God Himself was about to say to him in order to lead him to the designed result, that Job should not only abhor his words and his ways, but himself; and yet he was, in comparison with his fellow men, a perfect man and an upright.

The expression "God is mighty" (v. 5) introduces the subject of His providential dealing with man—and it is shown to be perfect in wisdom.

The statement "God is great" (v. 26), introduces the majesty of His power in Nature, and it is shown to be beneficial, inscrutable and super-human.

Elihu speaks on God's behalf.

" He that is perfect in knowledge is dealing with thee, O Job" (v. 4).

Though God is mighty, yet no one is too insignificant for His heart (v. 5).

The rebellious are excluded from ever-existing felicity, but the poor in heart are perpetually under His eyes; and such shall be exalted as kings upon thrones in the coming day of glory (vs. 6 and 7).

Afflictions are Divine instruments to lead men to Christ; if disobeyed, death and judgment must result (vs. 8–15).

Had Job accepted this Divine teaching he would have been removed into pleasant circumstances (v. 16); but he filled himself with the judgment of the wicked, i.e., he was governed by the spirit and the wisdom of this world, and the result was Divine wisdom was still chastening him (v. 17).

Elihu counsels him not to desire the night of death (v. 20) as Job had done (ch. iii.), and urges him to judge as iniquity and rebellion the choice of death rather than affliction (v. 21).

Elihu asks "Who teacheth like God?" (v. 22), or "Who will presume to teach God?" (v. 23), and advises Job to admire the Divine action with him; for all men who recognise even from a great distance such teaching, applaud it in song (vs. 24 and 25 R.V.).

Elihu chooses a thunderstorm as illustrative of the Divine majesty.

This passage (xxxvi. 26–xxxvii. 22) is a magnificent piece of poetry, and reveals a knowledge of science in that early age of man's history, greater than that of to-day.

The section opens with the declaration that the nature and operations of God are beyond and above human knowledge (v. 26).

He draws up the water from the ocean and distils it in rain and mist upon man for man's benefit.

No one can understand the disposition of the clouds and their relation to electricity (v. 29).

God displays the lightning upon them, and covereth the heavens with the depths of the sea (v. 30, R.V. margin).

This He does as the benevolent Despot of the nations in order that He may give man food in abundance.

He holdeth in His hand the lightning flash, commanding it where to strike (v. 32); but for man's safety he gives him a double premonition, the rumbling of the distant thunder, and the action of cattle; for these, as to-day in Sweden, know by instinct that a storm is coming, and, in refusing to leave their stalls, warn men of its approach.

The distant reverberation of the thunder terrifies the heart (v. 1).

The word "them" in verse 4 means the snow, the showers and the rain of verse 6 —the latter so heavy that it stops field labour (v. 7).

A scientific fact and a declaration appear in verses 2–7. The fact is: that rain is a form of electric action. This has not yet been discovered by modern science. The declaration is: that man should recognise the existence of God through, or by means of, the physical creation (v. 7 with Rom i. 20).

Thunderstorms are sent by God for correcting man, or for enriching the soil (v. 13). They are, therefore, sent in chastisement or in mercy.

In conclusion Elihu asks Job if he can explain the nature of lightning (v. 15); the balancings of the clouds (v. 16); why the south wind is warm (v 17); or the sky like a molten mirror (v. 18). He further challenges Job to teach men, whose understandings are darkened by the fall, what they should say to God (v. 19); and adds (v. 21), if men cannot endure to look upon lightning, how can they endure to look upon God its

Author, He who causeth His wind to blow from the north, thus dismissing the storm and restoring fair weather.

The reading of verse 22 in the R.V. is very beautiful : " Out of the north there comes a golden splendour."

Thus Elihu teaches man's inability to know God apart from revelation (v. 23) ; he declares Him to be full of righteousness and truth ; to be incapable of sending affliction without design ; and that men, be they never so wise, should fear Him, for they cannot know Him—unless He chooses to reveal Himself ; and this He has done in Christ.

JOB XXXVIII. 1-38.—Jehovah now addresses Job and His theme is Himself. Thus He made Job conscious of his littleness and ignorance. Elihu revealed the wisdom of God and the power of God. Now God reveals Himself ; and the result was that Job abhorred himself (xlii. 6). That was " the end of the Lord " i.e., the purpose designed by God, of which the apostle James speaks.

Jehovah's address presented to Job the inanimate creation (xxxviii. 1-38), and the animate creation (xxxviii. 39 to xxxix. 30), and with fine poetic irony, Job is asked what part he took in the origination of both creations, and what assistance he was lending in their maintenance.

This address, like the preceding ones, reveals, or shows, how great was the scientific knowledge common to Job and to his friends. The terms employed are human, such as " foundations " " measures " etc., etc., for if God were to express Himself in terms of exact science the cleverest men in the world would not understand one word He said. It is, therefore, intensely interesting to find in this—the oldest book in the world—the suspension of the earth in space (xxvi. 7) ; the rotundity of the earth (xxvi. 10) ; the revolution of the earth (xxxviii. 14) ; the motion of the earth within its orbit (xxxviii. 4-7) ; and the circular motion and density of the clouds (xxviii. 26). See " The Hebrew Bible and Science " (Nisbet, London).

This first section of the address speaks of God in relation to the earth, the sea, the dawn, light, darkness, snow, hail, lightning, rain, dew, frost and the heavens ; and the weakness, ignorance and insufficiency of Job are exposed in apposition to them. How foolish, therefore, for him to pretend to wisdom, and propose to rebuke the glorious Creator of these wonders?

Job (xlii. 3) confessed that he it was " who darkened counsel by words without knowledge " (v. 2).

The expression " Thou knowest " (vs. 5, 18 and 21) is ironical, and is to be understood as meaning : " Seeing that thou perfectly understandest all these things " ; similarly, verse 4 should read : " Seeing thou hast understanding."

Verse 6 is thus translated by competent Hebrew scholars : " Whereupon were its sockets sunk ? or who launched it into space like a revolving stone ? "

The boards of the Tabernacle were kept in their places by a socket having two hands. This is the same Hebrew word used in verse 6 ; and thus beautifully is expressed the restraining force that keeps the earth in its orbit, and the propulsion which causes it to continually revolve. The words " socket " and " tenon," i.e., " hand " are therefore accurate scientific terms which express the centrifugal and centripetal forces which sustain the earth in her appointed path.

The " Sons of God " (v. 7) are the angels.

Gen. i. 2 is referred to in verse 9.

The discovery of circular clay cylinders in the ruins of Babylon explains verse 14, which therefore reads : " It revolves like a clay cylinder ; and all living creatures clothe it as a garment."

As a clay cylinder revolved so that the words written on it came successively into view, so the earth revolves toward the sun, and as the light mounts up its " ends," or sides, beneficent creatures come forth to adorn the pastures, and the evil hide themselves (vs. 12-15).

The incompetency of Job to explore the depths of the ocean (v. 16), the realm of the dead (v. 17), the source of light and darkness (vs. 19-22), the snow, etc., and to control the the heavenly bodies (vs. 22-38), closes this section.

In xxxviii. 31, the " sweet influences " of the Pleiades are appealed to as a matter of common knowledge at that time. Modern astronomers know but little about them. The ancient Greeks called them the Seven Stars, and named them the " Pleiades " because their appearance indicated a favourable time for sea-voyages ; and hence the name is derived from the Greek verb to sail. The Chaldaic name means a " pivot " ; and recent astronomers claim to have discovered that the largest of these stars forms a pivot around which the solar system revolves. When it is remembered that the Sun is more than three thousand billion miles away from the Pleiades, some idea is got of the amazing " influence " of these seven stars in swinging this vast universe—the earth included—at the rate of more than 150,000,000 miles a year in an orbit so vast that one revolution occupies thousands of years to make, and yet with unvarying regularity and smoothness.

Thus this remote verse in what is generally accepted to be the oldest Book in the world, speaks of the influences of these stars as a matter of every-day knowledge ; and it is remarkable that the expression " sweet " is employed—the very word which engineers use in describing the smooth working of complex machinery.

JOB XXXVIII. 39-XL. 5. —This section contains the argument from the animate creation. As in the inanimate, so here, ten illustrations are chosen, viz. : Lions, ravens, wild goats, deer, the wild ass, the wild bull, the ostrich, the war-horse, the hawk and the eagle. The king of beasts and the king of birds open and close the list.

Job is asked if he can create and sustain in being these living creatures, and the argument is that their Creator and Sustainer must be almighty in power and perfect in wisdom, and that consequently Job was guilty of rebellion and folly in questioning the action of God toward himself.

The first five verses of chapter xl. may be thus paraphrased : In this manner Jehovah spake to Job and said, " Shall he that cavil-leth with Shaddai instruct Him ? thou that reproveth Eloah, answer me ! "

Then Job answered Jehovah and said : " Lo, I am vile ! what shall I answer thee ? Rather would I lay my hand upon my mouth. Already have I spoken too much. I cannot answer ; I will add nothing more."

This section, like the whole of the Book of Job, should be read with the assistance of the R.V. and of the Companion Bible.

Modern Science defines light to be the result of rapid vibrations in the ether. Verse 19 in chapter xxxviii asks : " Where is the *way* where light dwelleth ? " not, " Where is the place ? " As light involves motion it can only dwell in a *way*—travelling, according to science, at the rate of 186,000 miles a second.

JOB XL. 6-XLII. 6.—In Jehovah's second address to Job He asks him could he redress the miseries and injustices of mankind by striking down all wicked men, and shutting them up in perpetual prison (vs. 6-13) ; and if so, God confessed Himself ready to admit that Job could save himself, and thereby convict God of injustice (vs. 8 and 14).

He further asks Job, that if unable to control the fierce and violent amongst men, could he at least govern those among beasts ; and the hippopotamus (vs. 15-24). And the crocodile (xli. 1-34), are suggested to his power of supposed domination. But, it being evident that Job could neither create nor control such monsters, God puts the question to him, " Who then is he that can stand before Me ? " etc. (xli. 10 and 11).

Thus Job's inability to control either wicked men or wild beasts proved his incapacity to save himself (xl. 14) or to stand before God (xli. 10).

Job, convicted of his ignorance, his impotence and his sinfulness, exclaims that he it was that was hiding counsel without knowledge, and speaking words full of vanity ; and at last learns the lesson that he might have learnt without such trial, that, as a son of Adam, he was a total moral wreck, and consequently he loathed himself, though he knew himself to be innocent, just and upright.

But he did not learn this humiliating lesson so long as he confronted the Church, i.e., his three friends, but he learned it directly he entered into the sinless light of the presence of God. That light showed his comeliness to be corruption, and his righteous-nesses filthy rags.

Obscurities in this passage, for example verses 18-21, are removed by the Revised Version.

The words " Thou askedst " should be supplied at the commencement of xlii. 3 ; and Job replies in the same verse that *he* was that foolish person.

The words " Thou hast said " should be supplied in the middle of verse 4, and Job replies (vs. 5 and 6) that he will no longer dispute with God, for he has now learnt not only to loathe his words, but his thoughts and himself.

He reported that he had not abhorred himself, but, on the contrary, thought well of himself, and had held fast to his moral excellency. The discovery of the deep corruption of the heart is the most painful and humbling that a religious man can make.

So the Patriarch had to crucify all his goodness as truly as all his badness, and sit in wood ashes as a public confession that he merited death because of his sin-defiled nature. This moral principle governs the salvation of the sinner as well as the sanctification of the saint; and this inspired book reveals that God employs sickness as an instrument in both cases. See notes on chapter xxxiii. 14-24.

JOB XLII. 7-17.—Everybody had to change except God! Job had to humble himself, and to pray for God to bless these three chieftains who had so despitefully used him and persecuted him; and the three princes themselves had to confess themselves worthy of death, and to seek forgiveness from God through the precious blood of Christ, as foreshadowed in verse 8, and acceptance before God in the person of Christ; as typified in verse 9.

Jehovah turned the captivity of Job when he prayed for his friends. This loving and humble action of Job's showed how truly he had learned the lesson to find beauty and perfection in Christ alone; and, like the apostle Paul, to say, "I now know that in me dwelleth no good thing."

Job's latter end was better than his beginning. God gave him twice as much as he had before; and such is ever the result in the spiritual life. Increased spiritual wealth results from the death of self, i.e., the death of good self as well as of bad self.

Thus this book sets out the action of God in leading his children into a higher Christian experience. The subject of the book is not how God justifies a sinner, but how he sanctifies a saint; and hence none but a good man could have been chosen for the process, or profited by it. It is plain to all that a wicked man should die to self, but that a perfect man should also need to die, is not so clear. And yet this is the offence of the Cross. All that goodness and beauty which men recognise in themselves, and in others, must be nailed in death to the Cross; and the only Man that is to live must be the risen man, Christ Jesus.

True self-abhorrence comes not from self-examination, but in looking away from self to Jesus, the Perfecter as well as the Author of faith. Job was very much satisfied with himself until he saw God. "Self" is very enticing to man, especially religious self, and self-examination is an interesting occupation, and accordingly it is found very difficult to learn the lesson to crucify it; and to find that victory is enjoyed only when self is ignored and Christ adored.

Faulty as was Job in his complainings, yet had he a knowledge of Christ as a Saviour, and his heart was taught to accept the Divine way of salvation by faith. The three friends had no such knowledge of God as a Saviour; they believed in salvation by works; and hence their pious phrases sound much more pleasing to human ears than Job's rebellious groanings! But yet God was angry with them because they spake not of Him that which was right, as Job had done.

Thus, as already pointed out when commenting on chapter i, this book reveals the first step in the life of higher emotional Christian experience, and which is carried on through the Psalms, Proverbs, Ecclesiastes and Canticles. That is to say: The death of self; the risen life; the school of God; the emptiness of the world; and the fulness of Christ.

Verses 10 and 13 establish the doctrine of the immortality of the soul. To add ten children in this world to the ten in the spirit world was to double the number. It was otherwise with the animals. The prior flocks had all ceased to exist, and consequently the numbers had to be doubled in this world! Individuality does not perish. Abraham and Lazarus of Bethany were the same in death, and had the same names. Hence the Lord Jesus said: "Lazarus, come forth!"

These princes came to rob Job; the princes of Matt. ii came to enrich Christ. Both companies came from the East.

THE PSALMS AND THE MESSIAH

INTRODUCTION

On the road to Emmaus, and in the Upper Chamber, Messiah spoke to the disciples of the things in the Psalms concerning Himself Luke xxiv).

The Holy Spirit trained the writers of the Psalms ; but He was their Author (Acts i. 16, ii. 25 and 30, and Heb. iii. 7). Hence He says that no Scripture is of human origination (2 Pet. i. 20), but that all scripture is of Divine Inspiration (2 Tim. iii. 16).

The Book of the Psalms is a volume of prophecy ; its principal predictions concern the perfections, the sufferings and the succeeding glories of Messiah.

God having been dishonoured by human unbelief and disobedience, it was necessary that a man should be born who would perfectly love, trust and serve Him ; and Who would be the True Adam, Noah, Abraham, Israel, Moses, and David, etc.

God's moral glory demanded that sin should be judged ; that sinners should repent, confess and forsake sin and worship and obey Him ; and being God His nature required perfection in these emotions of the heart and will.

Such perfection was impossible to fallen man, and it was equally out of his power to provide a sacrifice that could remove his guilt and restore his relationship with God.

The Psalms reveal Christ as satisfying in these relationships all the Divine requirements. He, though Himself sinless, declares Himself in these Psalms to be the sinner ; and He expresses to God the abhorrence of sin accompanied by the repentance and sorrow which man ought to feel and express but will not and cannot. Similarly the faith, love, obedience and worship which man fails to give He perfectly renders.

Thus as the High Priest of His people He, the True Advocate, charges Himself with the guilt of their sins ; declares them to be His own ; confesses them, repents of them, declaring at the same time His own sinlessness ; and atones for them. Thus those Psalms in which the Speaker declares his sinfulness and his sinlessness become quite clear of comprehension when it is recognised Who the Speaker is.

Messiah's other offices and ministries as Son of God and Son of Man, as King and Priest, as Servant of Jehovah, as Angel of Jehovah, as the Word of God, and as the Burnt Offering the Meal Offering, the Peace Offering, the Sin Offering, and the Guilt Offering ; and as the Resurrection and the Life, are all sung of, together with the sufferings or the glories appropriate to each office.

The Gospels record the fact that He prayed ; the Psalms furnish the words of the prayer.

The Psalter is an inexhaustible source of strengtn, guidance, consolation and moral teaching to the people of God, and many valuable commentaries point out these treasurès. It may, therefore, in this aspect be justly regarded as a diary kept by the Lord when on earth in which are recorded His own experiences and the experiences proper to those in whom He dwells. But this commentary studies the Psalter in relation to the Messiah ; and in its compilation the best commentaries, together with the Hebrew text and its Greek, Latin, German, French, Italian, Spanish and English translations, have been used

Some of these Messianic experiences were entirely personal, others representative, others sympathetic, and others proper to Him as the true Israel.

The interpretation of the Book, therefore, belongs to Him as Messiah, to Israel as His people, and to the nations as His possession. Its application is to all who feel their need of a Saviour from sin and from its consequences. As stated in Romans xvi. 25, and Ephesians iii. 5, the Church, as such, does not appear in the Book.

The great opposing figures in the Book are the True and the False Messiahs. The one is termed the Man of the Earth; the other, the Blessed Man, the Lord of the whole earth. The Psalms, ignorantly called vindictive, predict the just doom of the one and of his followers; other Psalms foretell the glories of the heavenly Man and of His servants. Vengeance belongeth unto God; and He has apppointed a Man—the Messiah —who will righteously execute that vengeance; and He will asssociate with Himself His people and His angels as the executors of His wrath. The psalms mainly belong to this coming period of judgment. They predict the advent of the Day of Christ when all evil workers shall be cast out of the earth (Matt. xiii. 41). These judgment Psalms, which will be so appropriate at that time, do not belong to the present day of grace. Rightly dividing the Word of Truth (2 Tim. ii. 15.) will relieve Christian people, who, not being skilful in the Word of Righteousness (Heb. v. 13), feel distressed when reading these predictions.

The volume contains five Books corresponding to the Five Books of the Pentateuch and to the Five Books of the Apocalypse. This correspondence may be thus shewn:—

Ps. i-xli.	Genesis	Rev. i.-iii.
xlii.-lxxii.	Exodus	iv.-ix.
lxxiii.-lxxxix.	Leviticus	x.-xi.
Ps. xc.-cvi.	Numbers	Rev. xii.-xviii.
cvii.-cl.	Deuteronomy	xix.-xxii.

Only the sinless Messiah can sing the Psalms in their fulness. It deeply affects the heart to listen to Him as He sings; especially when, as the Representative and Sin-bearer of His people, He declares their sins, sorrows, sufferings and chastisements to be His own.

Many features mark the correspondence between the Psalms and the Pentateuch. They mutually set out the glories of Messiah as Creator, Redeemer, Sanctifier, Leader and Teacher, and the Divine titles attaching to Him are appropriately used in these Books. They point to the perfection of Messiah as the same yesterday, and to-day, and forever, He Who was, He who is, and He Who ever shall be.

The Psalms are appealed to in John x. 34, xv. 25, and Romans iii. 10-19, as " the Law." Genesis is similarly appealed to in 1 Corinthians xiv. 34; and Isaiah in 1 Corinthians xiv. 21.

The volume has an application to all who in any dispensation hunger and thirst after righteousness and in consequence suffer persecution. Messiah as man here suffers with his people—for how could He suffer if He were not Man? And as God He delivers them—for how could He deliver if He were not God?

Guided by Habakkuk, iii. 19, the subscriptions have been restored to their respective psalms.

THE PSALMS

BOOK I

PSALM I.—The Blessed Man of this Psalm is the Son of Man, the Messiah. The word blessed means happy. He is the Happy God of I Timothy i. II. This Psalm stands in relation to the entire Book of the Psalms as the first chapter of Genesis does to the Pentateuch ; for the Psalms concern themselves with this Blessed Man and His relationship to His people, and to His enemies.

This Man, the Lord from heaven, is here contrasted with the first man who was of the earth. This true Adam did not " walk," " stand " or " sit " (v. I), in the counsel of the ungodly, the way of sinners, or the seat of the scornful, but meditated in the law of God night and day, and was, and is, a tree of life. The Man of the Earth—the Anti-Christ—here unnamed, the Head of the wicked and of the ungodly, will, with them, be driven away and not stand in the judgment, nor in the congregation of the righteous (vs. 4 and 5). Jehovah acknowledged—had respect to—" the way " of Abel, but to " the way " of Cain He had not respect (Gen. iv. 4).

This Psalm predicts the moral glory of Messiah in His first Advent (vs. 1-3) ; the next Psalm foretells His millennial glory in His Second.

PSALM II.—The Blessed Man of Psalm i. and the Crowned King of Psalm ii. are one and the same Divine Person, i.e., the Messiah, Son of Man and Son of God. In both Psalms He stands in contrast with the first Adam as Man and King in the earth and over the earth.

The Psalm contains four sections :—In verses 1-5, the Holy Spirit speaks. In verse 6, Jehovah speaks. In verses 7-9, the Messiah speaks ; and in verses 10-12, the Holy Spirit again speaks.

The Psalm is interpreted in Acts iv. 25, Acts xiii. 33, and Hebrews v. 5. The Holy Spirit states in these passages that this is the second Psalm; that David was the channel for its communication ; and that the Messiah fulfils it.

Verse 12 should read as in the R.V. To " kiss " a prince means to do him homage (Gen. xli. 40). A subject at the present day kisses the monarch's hand when doing homage on appointment.

The Book of Genesis opens with a man in weakness—Adam—and closes with a man in power—Joseph. Thus it pre-figures the two Advents of Him Who is at once the True Adam and the True Joseph.

The Psalm predicts that though Israel and the Gentiles, with their princes and rulers, crucified God's anointed King, yet will God enthrone Him upon Zion's hill and give Him not only His ancient people for a Kingdom, but also all the nations of the earth for a possession ; and that those who seek refuge in Him shall be blessed, but that His enemies shall suffer wrath.

" Thou art my Son " is the Divine formula used in anointing Christ as Prophet (Matt. iii. 17), as Priest (Matt. xvii. 5), and as King (Heb. i. 5).

PSALM III.—The first eight Psalms form the opening section of the first Book of the Psalms. The section presents the Messiah as the Blessed Man (Psalm i) ; as the En-throned King (Psalm ii) ; it describes man's futile hatred against Him ; the experiences of the king during this time of rebellion (Psalms iii-vi) ; the king's delight in the Law of Jehovah (Psalm i) ; His trust in the wing of Jehovah (Psalm vii) ; and, finally, the rebellion subdued and the Messiah enthroned (Psalm viii).

These great themes form the subject matter of the entire Book of the Psalms.

Psalms iii-vi alternate between day and

night. The third and fifth speak of the king's outward enemies; the fourth and sixth of His inward sorrows. The third and fifth are morning Psalms. They set forth Jehovah as the Shield and Sufficiency of His Servant; the fourth and sixth are evening Psalms and each asks the question "How long?"

The Holy Spirit put the words of Psalm iii. into David's mouth the morning after his flight from Jerusalem because of Absalom's unnatural rebellion. David is here seen as a type of the Messiah rejected by His own people. Though surrounded by enemies he slept in confidence upon the mountain-side beneath Jehovah's sheltering wing; and in the assurance of faith declared that God would lift up his head and destroy his foes (vs. 3 and 7).

A false sentimentality decries the justice of verse 7. The language is figurative. To make a wild beast harmless men break its teeth; and if there are men who merit to have their teeth broken and their cheek bones smitten, why should they not suffer these just punishments and so be rendered impotent for evil?

The word "Selah" is first mentioned in this Psalm. It occurs three times. These occurrences help perhaps to suggest its meaning. Its position between verses 2 and 3 possibly denotes contrast; between verses 4 and 5, consequence; and between this Psalm and the following, connection. These three words, therefore, Contrast, Consequence, Connection, may help to open its meaning.

The Psalm, and the three following, have an application to David, to Elect Israel, and to Christ. They record David's experiences when in rejection; they predict Israel's sufferings under Anti-Christ; but their interpretation belongs to the Messiah in His First and Second Advents.

This fact helps the interpretation of the entire Book of the Psalms. Romans iii. 10-19 shows that the Psalms belong to Israel. But they belong to Israel in relation to the Messiah. The activity of His Spirit in them produces the moral fruit of their cries and tears. But the main subject is His own experiences when on earth; and His joys and sorrows alone fully exhaust them. The present Dispensation of Grace is not here in view, but the Dispensation of Righteousness whether in the past under Law or in the future under Wrath (Rev. vi. 9). Hence His Spirit calls justly for vengeance upon the workers of iniquity.

In its Messianic interpretation the Psalm touches the heart. It pictures Him in the morning looking out upon the day opening before Him; contemplating the multitude of His enemies (vs. 1 and 2); declaring His confidence in Jehovah (vs. 3 and 4); the courage resulting from that confidence (v. 6); and, finally, the prayer that these enemies of truth might be rendered impotent for evil (v. 7)

Faith records as accomplished that which it confidently expects. Hence the use of the past tense in verse 7. The particulars of this victory are recorded in John viii. 1-12. Every man, the disciples included, went to his own home. Jesus, having nowhere to lay His head, went to the Mount of Olives; spent the night there; and in the morning, anticipating what would occur during the day, sang this Psalm. On entering the Temple (John viii. 2), the scribes and Pharisees appeared with their victim, the adulteress. But Jesus covered them with shame (v. 9), i.e., He smote them on the cheek-bone, and He broke their teeth, for He delivered the woman from their power.

Guided by 2 Tim. iii. 16, and following the Hebrew text, it is suggested that the superscription "of David," with the ellipsis supplied, should read: Given to David by the Spirit; or it may simply mean "Relating to David," i.e., David Messiah.

The subscription "Neginoth," i.e., smitings, is attached to Psalms iii. v. liii. liv. lx. lxvi. and lxxv. Judging from the statements in these Psalms the word is to be understood as a figure of speech, expressing that as the smitings of the hand on the strings of a harp produce music, so the smitings of God's hand awake moral melodies—strong strokes expressing judgment, gentle strokes, chastisement.

PSALM IV.—It is the evening, and before laying Himself down to sleep upon the lonely mountain side, the rejected King of Israel reviews (v. 2) the conduct of the Scribes and Pharisees, who, themselves loving vanity and falsehood, accused Him of imposture and wickedness. The eighth chapter of John records how they defamed His glory. He calls upon God as testifying to His righteous conduct (v. 1), and acknowledges the Divine power (v. 3) that enlarged Him when in distress (John viii. 59). Contemplating His traducers, the Pharisees, at this hour already in bed, He, having none for Himself, counsels them to tremble; to commune with their own hearts; to be silent in true conversion; and to offer righteous sacrifices and not vain oblations (vs. 4 and 5). As to the sceptics, i.e., the Sadducees, and their mocking question (v. 6), He replies that the conscious presence of God satisfies the heart with a gladness which wealth, however great, cannot give (v. 7); and, finally, declares that though " in solitude " amid the shadows and dangers of the night now enwrapping Him, He will both lay Himself down in peace and sleep—sleep at once— because of the sure protection of Jehovah's wing. He did not lay Himself down in nervous fear as a disciple might, but in peace, and went immediately to sleep, for He was the Prince and Perfecter of faith (Heb. xii. 2).

The " how long " of Psalm iv. 2 respected His sufferings at the hands of man; the " how long," of Psalm vi. 3, His vicarious sufferings at the hands of God.

His glory was that He was the Son of God, the Saviour. Men turned it into shame, declaring Him to be a devil (John viii. 48-54), and that, far from saving others, He could not save Himself (Matt. xxvii. 42 and 43). His traducers loved vanity, for they willingly gratified the passions of their nature (John viii. 44), and they followed after falsehood, for their father Satan whom they willingly imitated, was a liar (v. 44).

But He whom they defamed was the Godly One whom Jehovah had set apart for Himself. Only once was there seen on earth a Man whom the Holy Spirit could declare to be absolutely " godly " (Psalm iv. 3), and " righteous " (Psalm v. 12).

PSALM V.—As the third and fifth Psalms relate to the Lord's outward enemies, so do the fourth and sixth to His inward sorrows. The third and fifth are morning Psalms. Thus, " Jehovah My Shield " (Ps. iii. 3), corresponds to " Jehovah my God " (Ps. v. 2). If threatened by enemies, He had a Shield; if needing succour and vindication, He had a God.

The word " meditation " (v. 1) connects this Psalm with the " meditation " of Psalm i. 2. He meditated in the Word of God (Ps. i), and in the ways of God (Ps. v.).

The Messiah was a True Worshipper. He prayed in private (v. 2), and in public (v. 7). He began the day with God; He spent it with God; and He closed it with God.

He knew that man would refuse Him righteous judgment (John vii. 24), but His heart reposed in the righteousness of a Judge who was sinless and who could not be influenced by evil or evil men (vs. 4-6). This relieved and consoled Him as He set out in order His petitions and confidently awaited the answers (v. 3).

The circumstances of the day here contemplated are recorded in Matthew xxi. and Luke xx. He entered Jerusalem as King (v. 2) and the Temple as God (v. 7). He was immediately opposed by the Pharisees, who watched Him that they might entangle Him in His words (Matt. xxii. 15, with Luke xx. 20, and the margin of Ps. v. 8). Their moral character is revealed in verse 9, and their falsehood, cruelty, and flattery recorded in Matthew and Luke. But God declared them guilty (v. 10, R.V.); they fell by their own counsels; and the Messiah demanded judgment against them, not because of their shameful conduct to Him, but because they were rebels against God (v. 10). The moral glory of God (v. 10) and the happiness of His people (v. 11) were His great interests. As for Himself, The Righteous One, all He desired was protection and blessing (v. 12).

Just as a harp is not the author of the music which the hand awakes upon its strings, and yet must be attuned before the musician can use it, so David, and the other inspired writers, were not the authors of these Psalms, but were attuned by sorrows and joys to be as instruments from which these songs could be drawn. Only the Messiah, as the High Priest of His people, can exhaust the language of these songs; but they have precious lessons for the heart that knows what it is to suffer shame and hatred for His Name's sake.

So as the result of His " meditation " in the Scriptures day and night (v. 1, and Ps. i. 2) He, as a man, learned that He was to enter Jerusalem; to cleanse the Temple of the Canaanite, i.e., the trafficker; to meet the hatred of the leaders of the nation; and to cause His people to rejoice.

He was King of Jerusalem and God of the Temple (v. 2), but in subjection as man He ascribed these titles to Jehovah (Matt. xxi. 5, and 12). In the morning He set out His petitions in order before God, and during the day He kept looking up for the answers ; and the Gospels record how He received them. His enemies, i.e., those who watched H...n (v. 8, margin, with Luke xx. 20), were the Pharisees, for they had no faithfulness in their mouth—they were mere professors of the Law ; the Sadducees, for their heart was an abyss of hatred (Luke xix. 47; and xx. 27-38) ; and the Herodians, for they flattered Him with their tongue while the purpose of their speech was to destroy His life (Luke xx. 19-26). In answer to His prayer (v. 11), the disciples and the children shouted for joy ; and He Himself, the Righteous One (v. 12), was so encompassed with Divine power that no man durst ask Him any question at all (Luke xx. 40).

The Pharisees, by their question of Matthew xxi. 23, claimed to be His judges ; but He was their judge.

PSALM VI.—The Messiah sang this Psalm at night. The question " How long ? " (v. 3), related to the duration of His inward sorrows from the hand of God, as the " How long ? " of Psalm iv., also sung in the night, had reference to the duration of His inward sorrows from the hand of man.

He as the High Priest and Advocate of Israel pleads in verse 1 for them. He makes Himself one with them, and prays as though He Himself merited.God's just anger and displeasure. This is the import of the word " Me " in the verse. It is here to be understood in the sense of Acts ix. 4.

" My soul is troubled " (v. 3). He repeated these words later in His Ministry when He said, " Now is my soul troubled " (John xii. 27).

" For Thy mercies' sake," (v. 4), i.e., in order to illustrate Thy mercy.

As to the unconsciousness of the grave (v. 5) Psalms xxx. 9, lxxxviii. 10-12. cxv. 17, cxviii. 17, Eccl. ix. 10, Isa. xxvi. 14, xxxviii. 18 and 19, together with New Testament Scriptures which speak of the Blessed Dead as sleeping, should be studied.

Verses 8-10 read as in the R.V. They are a prophecy. It will be fulfilled in Matt. xxv. 31-46. He will then say, " Depart from Me " (v. 8) ; and they will depart from Him (v. 10) into sore trouble, i.e., into ever-lasting punishment. They shall " turn away " (v. 10) and accordingly it says, These shall " go away," (Matt. xxv. 46.)

" Turn to Me " (v. 4) stands in contrast with " they shall turn from Me " (v. 10). This night He had a bed (v. 6), for it says, He went out to Bethany and lodged there (Matt. xxi. 17) ; but He did not sleep, for in secret He wept bitterly over the guilty City (v. 1-7) as that day He had wept aloud over it in public (Luke xix. 41). He burdened Himself both day and night with the sins and sorrows of the City He loved.

PSALM VII.—The theme of this Psalm is the suffering of the Messiah in sympathy with the elect remnant of Israel, under the persecution of the future Anti-Christ. That remnant, guided by the Spirit of Christ in them, will use this language and be strengthened by it.

The word " shiggaion " means a loud cry of anguish, and the term " words " include actions (Heb.).

The Bible does not say who Cush was except that he belonged to the tribe of Benjamin—Saul's tribe. The word means " black." Cush himself was a grandson of Noah and progenitor of the Egyptians (Gen. x. 10). Here he is introduced as a type of Anti-Christ, the future Pharaoh.

It was probably during Saul's pursuit of David that this member of Saul's tribe spoke and acted in a manner against David that furnished the opportunity to the Holy Spirit to inspire this prophecy.

That David's personal experiences and moral character were much below the language of the Psalm is evident. It therefore is prophetic of the Messiah ; for He here stands in the merciless light of the Throne of Dan. vii. 9-14, and invites scrutiny into His sinless life (vs. 3 and 4), and sinless nature (vs. 8-10).

Christ and Anti-Christ confront each other in this Psalm, as they will do in the future day described in the Book of the Revelation. Behind them appear their respective followers. The one is " The Enemy " spoken of in verses 2, 5, 12, 13, 14, 15, 16, and His followers are " the enemies " of v. 6, and " the wicked " of v. 9.

The reference in v. 6 is to Dan. vii. 9-14, when God will return on high (v. 7), i.e., to take His place on the Judgment Seat, when the nations will be gathered before Him and judgment will be given in favour of the Messiah and His servants.

The doom of the Anti-Christ is predicted in verses 12-16 ; and that His doom will be a just one (Rev. xix. 20), is evident from His moral character as portrayed in the passage.

The title "Most High" (v. 17) is here first used in the Book of the Psalms. Its first appearance in the Bible is in Gen. xiv. 18. It is one of the titles of the Messiah as Most High over all the Earth.

In these prophetic communications the great fact once more appears that the Lord Jesus Christ is never far from those who love Him ; that He sympathises with them ; that He makes their sorrows His own ; and that He will surely deliver them from their strongest foes, whether spiritual or physical. This fact has comforted and strengthened the servants of God in the past, it comforts and strengthens them in the present, and it will most signally do so in the future.

PSALM VIII.—This Psalm closes the first section of the First Book of the Psalms. The Holy Spirit in Matt. xxi. 16, 1 Cor. xv. 27, Eph. i. 22, and Heb. ii. 5-8, affirms the Messiah to be the Man of this song.

As already stated, these eight Psalms set the Messiah forth as the true Adam (i) ; as the true King (ii), but rejected and persecuted (iii-vii) ; and, finally, as Lord over all the earth (viii).

The Psalm pictures the happiness that is to fill the earth when, after the destruction of the Anti-Christ and his followers (Ps. vii), Messiah will establish His Kingdom of Righteousness and Peace ; and His right to ascend the throne is declared in His Glory as God (v. 1), as Lord of the whole earth (v. 6), as Son of Man (v. 4), and as King of Israel (v. 5). John xi. and xii. anticipate these glories : as God He raised Lazarus ; as Son of Man the Greeks sought Him ; as Lord of the whole earth He drew all to Him ; and as King of Israel He rode into Jerusalem.

His glory as Creator appears in verse 1, and as Redeemer in verse 2. The term "babes" is figurative (Matt. xi. 25). They are the Redeemed. It is also actual, for the children sang His praise (Matt. xxi. 15). The word "strength" (v. 2) by a Figure of Speech means praise. The doctrine of verse 2 is that the happy inhabitants of the millennial earth will be those who are morally described in Matt. xviii. 3 and 4.

The argument of verses 3-8, is the amazing love of Christ in coming forth from the highest glory to redeem a being so insignificant as man. That insignificance is illustrated by contrasting man with the heavens (vs. 3 and 4). But the Messiah in thus coming forth dims those glories by His Personal excellency ; and then, as the Son of Man, having them all placed beneath His feet, clothes them with a greater glory than they ever previously possessed.

His name is not now excellent in all the earth, for He is still despised and rejected by men, but on the millennial morn His name will indeed be excellent.

The mystic number seven is stamped upon this Psalm in the Hebrew Text. It there contains seventy-seven words. Its related Psalm, the one hundred and forty-fourth contains 119 words, i.e., seven times seventeen words. This remarkable Law of the number seven governs the entire Bible from Genesis to Revelation, and is one of the ten thousand proofs of Inspiration. "The Enemy" and "the Revenger" (v. 2) are titles of the Anti-Christ. The Messiah will destroy him by His "strength," and, consequently, His people will praise Him.

PSALMS IX. AND X.—These Psalms are bound together by the word Selah, and by a broken acrostic—its brokenness no doubt designed to harmonize with the "times of trouble" here predicted. They appear as one in the LXX.

Psalms ix. to xv. form the Second Section of this First Book. It is a prophecy. It predicts the advent, character, career, and doom of "the Man of the Earth" (x. 18), i.e., the Anti-Christ. This group of Psalms stands, therefore, in contrast with the first eight, which deal with the advent, character, career, and triumph of the Blessed Man (i. 1). i.e., the Messiah. The period when these prophecies shall be fulfilled is the future "time of trouble" (ix. 9 and x. 1) of which the Lord speaks in Matt. xxiv. 21. That will be the "time of Jacob's trouble," out of which he is to be delivered, and to which Jer. xxx. 7, and Dan. xii. 1, point.

The Spirit of Christ in "Jacob," when delivered out of his trouble, will sing the song of praise with which Ps. ix. opens (vs. 1 and 2), and review the night of sorrow which shall precede the deliverance (vs. 3 to 14). It is characteristic of faith to make present and real, and to give thanks for, a redemption yet to be accomplished. This principle appears in the first two verses of Ps. ix.

The expressions "at Thy presence" (v. 3) and "in Thy sight" (v. 19), refer to the visible coming of the Messiah in power and glory. The brightness of that coming will occasion the deliverance of His people Israel and the doom of Anti-Christ (2 Thess. 1).

Ps. ix. distinguishes between the Anti-Christ, the apostate Hebrews who will accept him as the true Messiah, and the nations who will march beneath Anti-Christ's banner. That wicked prince is here called " the Lawless One " (vs. 5 and 16), " the Enemy," (v. 6), " the Man " (v. 19), " the Covetous One " (x. 3)," the Man of the Earth " (x. 18), and " the Man of Violence "(xviii. 48). The apostate Hebrews are " the enemies " of verse 3, and " the wicked " of verse 17 ; and the hostile nations are " the heathen " of verses 5, 8, 11, 15, 17, 19, and 20.

Ps. ix. pictures the Messiah ascending His throne at Jerusalem (vs. 4, 7, 16, R.V.).

In verses 5 and 6 the heathen are rebuked, and the Anti-Christ destroyed, together with his cities, and their memory. This judgment will synchronize with the close of " the desolations " foretold in Dan. ix. 26. The words " O thou enemy ! the desolations (R.V. Margin) are finished for ever,"·form a parenthesis. The whole passage will, therefore, read, " Thou hast rebuked the heathen, etc., and Thou hast destroyed cities ; their memorial shall perish with them."

The apostle Paul referring to the future judgment of the nations, quoted the eighth verse of this Psalm to the Athenians (Acts xvii. 31).

Verse 12 predicts that God will permit the False Messiah to slaughter multitudes of His beloved people, but that He will avenge their deaths. He may allow their oppressors to torture and kill them, but He will not forget their cry (Rev. ii. 10, vi. 9, and xiii. 7). The Divine judgment will manifest (v. 16) that the Antichrist is but a man(v. 19), and that the nations are but men (v. 20). So the lesson is taught thatGod is to be trusted in circumstances which seem to make certain that either He is indifferent to the misery of His people, or else unable to deliver them. Ps. x. expresses the belief that there is a just and wise purpose in the temporary inaction of God's protective power in respect of His servants.

Ps. x. gives a vivid picture of the appalling sufferings thatIsrael will undergo in the future " time of trouble."

As in Ps. ix. so here the Anti-Christ is called The " Wicked " or " Lawless One " in verses 2, 3, 4, 13, and 15, and " The Covetous One " in verse 3. " The Strong Ones " (v. 10), are his followers. Their temporary prosperity and successful oppression of the Saints of the Most High are described in verses 2 to 11. These verses detail that Anti-Christ will hotly pursue the oppressed (v. 2) ; that they will be captured by him (vs. 2 and 9) ; that he will boast of the success of his plans (v. 3) ; that he will renounce and revile Jehovah (v. 3) ; that God's judgments will be willingly quite beyond his ken (v. 5) ; that in his pride he will declare that there is no God, or that if there is, He takes no interest in human affairs (v. 4) ; as to his own ways, he will find them always successful (v. 5), so that he will be enabled to despise his enemies (v. 5) ; he will promise himself exemption from adversity (v. 6) ; his mouth, his tongue and his eyes will be all employed in the oppression and destruction of the poor in spirit (vs. 7-10) ; and, finally, he will assure his own heart that, as to the past, God will forget it, and as to the future, there never will be a judgment (v. 11).

Ps. ix, 12, 17 and 18, and Ps. x. 12, when compared, prove that God does not, and will not, forget His oppressed people. " He will never see it " (v. 11), may be compared with " Thou hast seen it, for Thou wilt behold travail and grief," i.e., persecution, "in order to take the matter into Thy hand " (v. 14). Because the helpless and the fatherless know and believe this, therefore they commit themselves unto Him.

The doom of the False Messiah is the subject of verse 15, and the reign of the True Messiah the prediction of verse 16. These events will result in the disappearance out of the earth of the hostile heathen. The apparition of Messiah will so effectually destroy " the Man of the Earth " that he will be terrible no more (vs. 17-18, R.V.).

PSALM XI. — Ps. ix. and x. having portrayed the Lawless One, Ps. xi-xiv describe the lawlessness which will characterize his kingdom, and the consequent oppression and suffering of the righteous.

The picture in this Psalm of these times of trouble is very vivid. Immanuel's land is a scene of tumult, and His servants are cruelly oppressed. Timid friends urge them to flee to some high and strong refuge, as a bird to a mountain (v. 1), because already plans have been perfected by the violent for their destruction (v. 2), and all law having been abolished from the foundation and replaced by lawlessness (v. 3), righteous men, therefore, have no legal remedy and can accomplish nothing (v. 3).

To these counsels faith replies, " Jehovah is in His Holy Temple, Jehovah's Throne is in the Heavens ; He is, and shall be, my place of refuge " (vs. 1 and 4).

Messiah here speaks personally, and also representatively in sympathy with Israel. Both these experiences appear in Luke xiii. 31-35. He was personally urged to flee to " His mountain " from the meditated violence of Herod, whose conduct as chief magistrate destroyed the foundations of law, but He refused to flee and remained in sympathy with Israel to pour His heart out over Jerusalem (vs. 33 and 34).

But though seated in the heavens, yet does God narrowly watch all that occurs upon earth (v. 4), and so these very " times of trouble " subserve His purpose of testing and approving the upright (v. 5). They will stand the test ; and in the day of His coming upon the clouds of heaven to succour them, they shall behold His face (v. 7), but their enemies shall drink the cup of His wrath (v. 6).

In verse 4, Immanuel beholds His people in their affliction ; in v. 7, they behold Him in His glory (R.V.).

The doctrine of the Psalm is that God is not indifferent to the sufferings of His children ; that these sufferings are permitted for their welfare ; that evil and evil-workers will certainly be destroyed ; and that righteousness will ultimately triumph. Faith can, therefore, blindly trust Him and wait.

PSALM XII. — Violence and falsehood are Satan's two great weapons against the servants of God. The violence of the False Messiah is, accordingly, the theme of Ps. xi. and xiii, and his falsehood, the theme of Ps. xii. and xiv. The False Messiah has his book of falsehood and folly, and the True Messiah, His Book of truth and wisdom. These Princes and these Books are contrasted in these four Psalms, and violence and falsehood alternate in them.

As, therefore, the prior Psalm predicts that, under the reign of the False Messiah, violence will prevail, so this Psalm foretells that falsehood will supersede truth ; that the Bible will be displaced by human teaching ; and, as a logical result, righteous men will be persecuted.

A series of contrasts appear. The first verse contrasts with the eighth ; the second with the sixth ; the third with the seventh ; and the fourth with the fifth.

When faithfulness fails, godly men cease (v. 1), but when vile teaching becomes popular wicked men abound (v. 8).

Human teaching is vain, false, deceitful, and boastful (v. 2). God's word is pure and tested (v. 6).

This sixth verse contains four members :—

The words of Jehovah are pure words ;
  As silver tested in a furnace.
Words poured out upon the earth ; (Heb.)
  Purified seven times.

If the first and third lines, and the second and fourth, be read together, the second verse becomes the more striking in contrast with the sixth. God has made a revelation to man. That revelation is pure and begets purity. Its very words are pure words, comparable to silver seven times refined in a furnace. See notes on John xvii. 8 and 14.

Such is the Bible. Not only is it a pure revelation from God, but the very words with which it is composed are pure words, seven times purified, that is, thoroughly pure. The impure teachings of man give birth to vile actions. A true creed produces pure conduct ; a false creed, vile conduct.

The destiny of those who love and obey the Word of God is contrasted in v. 7, with the fate of those in v. 3, who accept man's teaching. These shall be " cut off," but lovers of the Bible and the Bible itself shall be preserved for ever.

The contrast between verses 4 and 5 is instructive and comforting. The teachers of violence will boast in that future day that they are their own masters ; that their lips are their own ; that their teaching originates with themselves ; that it is independent, free, and untrammelled ; and that, thanks to their tongue, it will prevail.

Over against these proud boasters and their prosperity stand the afflicted in their oppression (v. 5). But they will be upheld in their time of trouble by the promises of God's word. The fifth verse contains four members :—

Because of the oppression of the oppressed
  Because of the sighing of the needy,
Now will I arise, saith Jehovah,
  I will set each one of them in safety from
    the oppressor.

If the first and third lines and the second and fourth be read together, the great facts will appear that because of the oppression of His people, God will arise in their defence, and that he will set the needy, that is, the defenceless, in safety from their persecutors.

Such will be in that day the hope and expectation of Israel. God will arise; His enemies will be scattered; oppressions will be determined; desolations will be ended; and the False Messiah and his followers will be confounded.

PSALM XIII.—This Psalm continues to picture the sufferings of Israel during the " times of trouble " under the reign of the False Messiah.

The afflicted one in the Psalm is Israel; the Speaker is Immanuel. As the High Priest of His people, He prays for them as if He Himself were suffering the affliction. This gives great and tender meaning to the words " Me," " My," " Mine " and " I." Thus He makes His people's sorrow His own. Compare Acts ix. 4 and Col. i. 24.

The " enemy " of verses 2 and 4 is the False Messiah, and " those that trouble " (v. 4, R.V.), i.e., the adversaries, are his followers. The complaint of the Psalm is the violence of these adversaries and their Prince.

The Psalm contains two sections. The first is formed of the first four verses; the second, of the last two. It contains seven members, divided into three and four. The three members treat of the "times of trouble," and they are duplicated in sympathy with the subject. The remaining four members sing of deliverance and victory. Thus the general subject of the wretchedness and oppression of Israel, and the deliverance which they shall enjoy, are vividly depicted.

The seven members of the first section may be thus set out :—

Forgetfulness	v. 1
Darkness	v. 1
Weakness	v. 2
Remembrance	v. 3
Radiance	v. 3
Deliverance	v. 4
Past	v. 5
Future	v. 5
Future	v. 6
Past	v. 6

The first verse should read as in the R.V. The continuance of the " time of trouble " is the subject of the cry of anguish. It may be thus expressed : " How long wilt Thou continue to forget me, O Lord ? How long wilt Thou keep hiding Thy face from me ? "

The " salvation " of verse 5 means deliverance from the affliction complained of.

" Dealt bountifully " (v. 6) may be translated " compensated," and thus re-affirm, what so often appears in the Scriptures, that the overcomer will be compensated in the future state for all his sufferings as a Christ confessor in the present life; and that he will learn that perfect wisdom and infinite love permitted and over-ruled every trial.

The certainty of the faithfulness, love and power which the Messiah will show to His people in the day of His coming again, strengthens the faith of His people during the time of their waiting and suffering.

PSALM XIV.—The folly of Anti-Christ— who will be the Fool of 2 Thess. ii. 4 ; the corruption of his followers (v. 1) ; their mutual doom (v. 5) ; and Israel's final redemption (v. 7), are described and predicted in this Psalm.

The Holy Spirit in Romans iii. 10-12 repeats the testimony of this Psalm (vs. 2 and 3), as to the total depravity of man's moral nature. This is a doctrine of the Word of God which is extremely distasteful to modern society, and is vehemently denied by its popular religious teachers.

Verses 2 and 3 record God's judgment of man, and verse 4, His expostulation with man.

The Messiah is the " Righteous man " of verse 5, and the " Poor man " of verse 6. The " people " of verses 4 and 7 are those whom He redeems from out of the mass of depraved men. He draws near to men (v. 2), but they do not draw near to Him (v. 3). The climax of their depravity is that they eat up His people as they eat bread ; that they do not worship Him ; and that they mock the faith and love that make Him a refuge (v. 6).

The dark picture of the " times of trouble " (Ps. ix-xiv) here draws to a close, and the workers of iniquity and their chief (v. 4), who mocked the counsel of the Poor Man and His people (v. 6), now fear a great fear (v. 5), for the great day of Messiah's wrath shall have come and they will not be able to stand (Rev. vi. 17).

The last verse predicts and pictures the

final deliverance of the Elect of Israel. The word " salvation " appears as the plural of majesty in the Hebrew text in order to emphasize the greatness and completeness of the deliverance.

Jacob is the natural name ; Israel the spiritual. Compare " Thou art Simon ; thou shalt be Peter " (John i. 42).

For the relation of this Psalm to Psalm liii see notes on that Psalm, and notice an alternative interpretation of verse 5.

The word " there " (v. 5) should read " at that time," and the prediction is, that at that time they shall fear a great fear, i.e., at the apparition of the " Rider " of Rev. xix. 11-13.

The Pharisees, who were covetous, mocked the counsel of the " Poor man " (Luke xvi. 14) when they heard His teaching about serving God and Mammon.

PSALM XV.—The character, the enduring reign of the Messiah, and the happiness of His Kingdom in contrast with the misery of Anti-Christ's kingdom, are the themes of this Psalm. It therefore contrasts with the ninth Psalm ; and these two Psalms commence and close the second section of the First Book of the Psalms. That section, as already stated, is a prophecy describing the future Man of the Earth and the misery and violence which he will cause in it.

The Sermon on the Mount (Matt. v-vii) is an expansion of the Psalm. The King, His Kingdom, and its subjects, are the theme of both Scriptures. A comparison between the opening and closing of both will show the connection. The immovability of " the man that doeth these things " (v. 5), is illustrated by the house built upon a rock ; and the ' poor in spirit " and " pure in heart " are those described in verses 2 to 5. Thus the Psalm and the Sermon describe those who are to be citizens of the millennial kingdom.

But the great theme of the Psalm is : Who shall be entitled to reign on Mount Sion as a king over the kingdom ? i.e., Who is to be the Chief Citizen of the kingdom of Heaven when established upon earth ? The answer (vs. 2-5) describes a Man Who once lived on earth and Who has never had a moral peer. That man is Messiah. He alone satisfies the requirements of verses 2-5.

These requirements are set out in four statements, two positive and two negative. They alternate. The second and fourth verses are positive ; the third and fifth, negative. The fifth verse should commence with the words " He that sweareth to his own hurt," etc. Each member of the quatrain contains three statements—excepting the third, which contains only two. This, no doubt, is designed ; and the student should seek its meaning.

The verbs used in the quatrain imply in the Hebrew text Continuance. That is : The Chief Citizen in the Kingdom of Heaven will be a Perfect Man, Who perfectly kept, and perfectly keeps, God's perfect Law. He lives blamelessly and always did so live ; He practises righteousness, and never practised aught else ; He speaks, and always spoke truth in His heart ; He always contemns vile persons and continuously honours them that fear Jehovah ; He never did backbite with His tongue and does not do so, or injure His neighbour ; He never did, nor does receive a malicious story against another ; He always kept, and does keep His pledges ; He never practised, nor practises usury ; and He never accepted, nor accepts bribes (vs. 2-5).

Messiah was such, and is such. He alone therefore can and shall sit upon the throne of Jehovah on Mount Sion (1 Chron. xxix. 23).

But the citizens of such a kingdom must morally resemble the King. All men fail in this resemblance both by nature and by practice. Those, therefore, that would " see " and " enter " that Kingdom must by a birth from above receive a new moral nature (John iii. 3 and 5). In such persons the Messiah by His Holy Spirit lives the blameless life here portrayed.

PSALM XVI. — Ps. xvi-xli. form the Third Division of the First Book of the Psalms.

Its subject is the sufferings of Christ for, and with, Elect Israel. It sets out His perfections and experiences as a Man, as the Servant of Jehovah, as the Lamb-of God, as the Great High Priest, as the Good Shepherd Who died for the sheep, as the Great Shepherd Who lives for them, and as the Chief Shepherd Who will return to deliver them and set them in a safe and enduring pasture. The great themes, therefore, are the sufferings of Christ and the glories that are to follow; and that Atonement, Resurrection, and Advent are the bases respectively, of life, righteousness and glory.

Accordingly, in these Psalms, His equality

with God is veiled.   As a Man and a Servant He takes the place of dependence and trust. His declaration of His dependence reveals that He had a title to Divine equality; for were it not so He need not have said it. Therefore it is that He Who exclaimed " Destroy this temple and in three days I will raise it up," in this Psalm says, " Thou wilt not leave My soul in Sheol." He spoke the one as God, the other as Man.

The word " Michtam " means " engraved," i.e., written in stone. All Michtam Psalms have reference to Christ and resurrection.

The Holy Spirit in Acts ii. and xiii. declares the speaker in this Psalm to be the Messiah. The reader is, therefore, permitted to hear Him speaking to Jehovah.

The first section of the Psalm (vs. 1-3) contains a prayer for preservation (Heb. v. 7-9), and a double statement that Jehovah was His highest good and His people His greatest joy. The second and third verses may read thus :—" I said unto Jehovah, ' Thou art my Lord.' I have no good beyond and apart from Thee," i.e., Thou art my highest and only good. " As for the saints that are in the earth, they are the excellent in whom is all My delight ! " Thus the Messiah appears as a Man in His relation to God, and as a Brother in His relation to Israel. These He calls the " excellent of the earth." The False Messiah and his followers will regard them as the refuse of the earth ! What is true of the redeemed of Israel is true of God's saints in all dispensations; for His delights are with the sons of men (Prov. viii. 31).

Verses 4-6 present Him as a true worshipper; and they contrast the joys of such worshippers with the sorrows of idolators.

The " Inheritance," the " cup," the " lot," the " lines," (portion) and the " heritage " of verses 5 and 6 express the mission and characterize the ministry given to the Messiah and declared by Him to be pleasant and goodly.

His perfect dependence as a man, and that which His sinless body taught Him, are the two statements of verse 7. He, by dwelling in a human body, " learned obedience " (Heb. v. 8). He had not to learn to be obedient, for that would imply that He was a sinner by nature, but He " learned obedience." which is quite another thing.

The closing section of the Psalm occupies verses 8-11. It contemplates Him as a man about to descend into the realms of the dead. It is this section that is quoted in Acts ii. and xiii. The statements are of supreme importance. The Messiah, looking into the black mouth of death, declares He was not affrighted (v. 8); that, on the contrary, His heart was glad and His tongue (glory) rejoiced, and that His body would rest confidently in expectation of resurrection (v. 9). This confident expectation He bases upon the promise made to Him, that His soul should not be left in Sheol, nor His body in the sepulchre (v. 10), and that He would be shown a path of life out of the prison of the dead that would lead Him to the right hand of the Majesty on High, where is fulness of joy for evermore.

This is a passage of amazing interest. The Spirit of Christ, commended to the Father at the moment of death, ascended with that of the penitent thief to Paradise, His soul descended into Sheol, and His body was laid in Joseph's tomb. His spirit, contemplating His soul in Sheol, says to God, " Thou wilt not leave my soul in Hades," and looking at His body in the tomb, He cries, " Thou wilt not suffer it to see corruption." Accordingly on the third day

From the dark grave He rose,
The mansions of the dead,
From thence His mightiest foes
In glorious triumph led.
Up through the sky the Conqueror rode,
And reigns on high, the Saviour God.

PSALM XVII.—The speaker in this Psalm, as in the previous one, is the Messiah; but here in verses 7 and 11 He associates His people with Himself. The words " my " (v. 1), and " us " (v. 11) may, for example, be compared.

The keynote of the Psalm is " Hear the right " (v. 1), i.e., vindicate My righteous conduct. In the previous Psalm it was " In Thee do I put my trust " (v. 1). The Messiah appeals to God from the unjust judgment of man, and claims an affirmative sentence upon His upright conduct. Only the Messiah as Sinless Man could use the language of this appeal.

The Psalm is entitled a Prayer. Five are so entitled—xvii., lxxxvi., xc., cii., and cxlii.

The second verse may read thus :—Let sentence in My favour be pronounced by

Thee ; for Thine eyes discern upright actions.

The last member of verse 3 reads :—" My mouth does not exceed my purpose," i.e., I am sincere. This could only be true of Him Who used similar language in John xiv. 30. Satan found no imperfection in Him, and God found nothing but perfection.

The path of the Destroyer and the path of Jehovah are contrasted in verses 4 and 5, and the statement is made that preservation from the one and perseverance in the other alone are secured by allegiance to the Scriptures. This was demonstrated in the Temptation in the desert. The Destroyer (v. 4) and the Wicked, and the Enemies (v. 9) are titles proper to the future Anti-Christ and his followers. The Hebrew text distinguishes between Wicked One and wicked men.

God's " eyes " (v. 2), His " hand " (v. 7), His " wings " (v. 8), and His " face " (v. 15) are precious facts of faith, but only Israel's Shepherd perfectly measured and experienced their fulness.

In verses 7 and 14 He associates His people with Himself ; they have the same enemies. If He confides in Jehovah so do they (v. 7) ; if He trusts El-Shaddai's wings and is as the apple of His eye, they also are equally precious to God, and trust the same refuge. He describes His enemies and theirs in verses 9-12, and prays for deliverance for them as for Himself in verses 13 and 14.

A lion when greedily watching his prey sets his eyes close to the ground (vs. 11 and 12).

The word " disappoint " (v. 13) means forestall and confront, and the person to be so forestalled and confronted is Anti-Christ, who in this verse is called the Lawless One (" the wicked man "). Verses 13 and 14 should read as in the R.V. The expression " my soul," so frequently found in the Psalms, means " me ". However prosperous the men of this world may be (vs. 13 and 14) the sword and hand of God will surely reach and judge them.

The " satisfied " of verse 15 contrasts with the " satisfied " of v. 14, R.V.

Guided by the argument the fifth verse should read " My steps have held to Thy paths, My footsteps have not slipped."

The Psalm, in correspondence with the prior one, closes with the assured hope of resurrection. The statements express the highest joy of the spiritual nature. Not glory, nor the material joys of Heaven here enrapture the speaker, but the one absorbing desire to see God's face and to be like Him. This is measurably true of everyone who has the Spirit of Christ, but immeasurably true of Him Who prayed " Glorify Thou Me with Thine own Self, with the glory which I had with Thee before the world was " (John xvii. 5).

Opposition to truth, and the indulgence of selfwill in evil or ritualism, or both, make the heart insensible to the influence of the Holy Spirit (v. 10). Compare notes on Isaiah vi. 10, and Acts xxviii. 27.

PSALM XVIII.—The circumstances under which the Holy Spirit inspired David to write this prophecy are stated in the Title. It was first written in 2 Sam. xxii. and here handed to the Chief Musician for use in public worship. The variations were made, and designed by the Divine Author. David himself must have recognized that the experiences of the Psalm went far beyond his own personal deliverance from Saul (1 Peter i. 10-12).

The Holy Spirit states in Rom. xv. 9 and Heb. ii. 13, that the speaker here is the Messiah, and that the Psalm predicts the sufferings of His First Advent (vs. 20-36), the glories of His Second (vs. 37-50), and the majesty of the Resurrection which connects the two (vs. 1-19). These are the three great divisions of the prophecy.

The Messiah was sinless, and He will in righteousness destroy out of His future kingdom all the workers of iniquity (Matt. xiii. 41, Rev. xii. 12, and xix. 1-5). This explains the seemingly self-righteous language of the speaker and His exultation over the destruction of His enemies ; for they were the enemies of His people and of all goodness.

The first verse should read : " Fervently do I love Thee, O Jehovah my Strength ! " For the distinctive meanings of " rock," " fortress," and " strength " the Hebrew text should be consulted (vs. 1, 2, 17, 17, and 39).

The opening and close of the prophecy correspond. In verses 1 and 49 Jehovah is spoken to. He is loved in the one and praised in the other. In verses 2 and 50 He is spoken of. He delivers.

Zacharias (Luke i. 69) prophesied of the Messiah as the " Horn of Salvation," thus quoting verse 2 of this Psalm. He also quoted from verse 3 when using the words "We shall be saved from our enemies."

The mysterious sufferings of the Messiah when in Hades are partially unveiled in verses 4 and 16-18. See notes on Psalm lxxxviii. The "day of His calamity" (v. 18, R.V.) was the day of His supreme distress (Heb.) when He descended from the cross into the realms of the dead. The "strong enemy" (v. 17), and the "many waters" (v. 16) are figures of death and of the abode of the dead. "The large place" (v. 19) is Paradise, into which He entered after His resurrection. His spirit was already there. See notes on Psalm xvi.

Three times heaven opened to testify that God delighted in Him (v. 19).

The language of verses 20-26, could only be used by the Messiah, for He was sinless. The words "mine iniquity" (v. 23) do not mean that He had a besetting sin, nor may they be here understood as intending the iniquity of the Elect which He made His own, but they point to a form of iniquity specially planned by Satan for Him, and to which He alone could be tempted. Such for example was the Third Temptation in the Wilderness (Luke iv. 9).

The word "merciful" (v. 25) means the Merciful One. It is a very interesting word to Hebrew scholars. It is a Messianic title. He is, and will be, the full depository and witness of God's mercy—not mercy merely in relation to sinners, but favour and grace shown and enjoyed so as to become an evidence of moral perfection. It is particularly celebrated in Psalms lxxxvi. 2, and lxxxix. 19, where the Messiah is entitled God's Holy One, i.e., Merciful One—the Hebrew word for merciful and holy is the same—because all these mercies centre in Him ; hence the expression "Sure mercies of David" (Acts xiii. 34). The Resurrection demonstrated the security of these. The Messiah is also the "Upright Man" of verse 25, and the "Pure One" of verse 26. The "Perverse One" of verse 26 is the future Anti-Christ. With him God will show himself a "Wrestler" (Heb.). When Jacob was perverse the Angel of Jehovah wrestled with him (Gen. xxxii. 24) ; and when Balaam was perverse the same Angel withstood him ; (Num. xxii. 22), and when Saul of Tarsus was perverse he found it hard to kick against the ox-goads. Jacob and Saul yielded and were blessed ; Balaam persisted and was lost (Josh. xiii. 22).

Jesus was merciful, upright, and pure, and found God to be such. There was perfect correspondence between His nature and God's. So He could rest in full confidence in the just judgment of such a scrutinizing Judge. No one ever trusted the Word of God, and was deceived (v. 30). That Word, whenever tested, was always found to be true as pure gold, and trustworthy.

The Lord Jesus did not use warlike weapons. The language of verse 34 is figurative. When the Herodians, the Pharisees, the Scribes, and the Sadducees warred against Him with their bows of steel, He bent their bows and broke them ; i.e., He showed the folly of their hard questions and confounded them. In Luke iv, 30, He "broke through a troop," and in John viii. 5, He "leaped over a wall" (v. 29).

In the closing section of the Psalm (vs. 37-50), the future tense may be used throughout, as in the Hebrew text, for the language is prophetic ; but the past tense may also be used, for when sung on the millennium morn the facts will be accomplished facts.

This magnificent passage sets forth the future glory of the Messiah ; His destruction of the enemies of His people ; their restoration ; the conversion of the Gentiles ; and the establishment of the Millennial Kingdom. "The Man of Violence" (v. 48) is the False Messiah ; "His Anointed" (v. 50) the True Messiah. These are here contrasted. The superscription of the Psalm, the ellipses being supplied, may possibly be read thus : For the Chief Musician. Relating to the Servant of Jehovah. Given by the Spirit to David, who spake unto Jehovah, etc.

PSALM XIX.—The "Servant" of this Psalm is Messiah (vs. 11 and 13).

The structure of the Psalm demonstrates its unity and destroys the hypothesis that it is "a piece of patchwork."

It contains 126 words in the Hebrew text. That is : seven multiplied by eighteen. Seven is the number of completion, eight of resurrection, and ten of divinity—five being the number of grace, and five upon five expressing "grace upon grace" (John i. 16).

The Psalm is formed of four sections :—

God in Creation, v. 1-4.

God in Ordination, v. 4-6, (Col. i. 17).

God in Revelation, v. 7-10.

God in Incarnation, v. 11-14.

These subjects are still further thus arranged :—

The Heavens
    In them the sun.
The Scriptures
    In them the Servant.

In the Hebrew text the first and third members correspond and have eight lines each ; and the second and fourth members correspond, and have six lines each. The Heavens declare God's glory ; the Scriptures declare His grace. The Heavens reveal His hand ; the Scriptures reveal His heart.

The Messiah as a Servant, dependent and obedient, praises God ; admires His handiwork (vs. 1-6) ; subjects His will to the Scriptures (vs. 7, 11) ; prays to be preserved in that subjection (vs. 12 and 13) ; and confidently predicts that as a result His words and His thoughts will be acceptable to God (v. 14). This last verse is in the future tense in the Hebrew text, and reads therefore, both as a prayer and as a prediction. John viii. 28 and 29, and xvii. 8 and 14, record the fulfilment of this prophecy.

The material earth is the sphere in which the heavenly message operates, and the message itself is addressed to the inhabited " world "(v. 4). There is no limitation. All nations are embraced in this gracious revelation.

The word " line " (v. 4) means teaching. Although no voice is heard, yet the heavens and its constellations keep continually pouring forth teaching respecting the glory of God, so that all nations are without excuse (Rom. i. 19 and 20).

Modern science has discovered that the sun is enclosed in an envelope of fire, but this fact has shone in this Psalm for more than 2,000 years.

Six statements are here made respecting the Scriptures (vs. 7-9). Each statement has three members, i.e., titles, attributes, and effects. There are, therefore, six titles, six attributes, and six effects.

The titles are : Law, Testimony, Statute, Commandment, Fear, and Judgment.

The attributes are : Perfect, Sure, Righteous, Pure, Clean, and True.

The effects are : Converting the soul, Making wise the simple, Rejoicing the heart, Enlightening the eyes, Enduring for ever, and Altogether righteous.

Man says the Bible is imperfect ; the Holy Spirit says it is perfect (v. 7).

There was but one Man ever lived on earth Who could exhaustively use the words of verses 10 and 11, and He dwelt in the Scriptures, as the sun dwells in the heavens. They " warned " Him, i.e., they admonished or taught Him.

Owing to defective education scholars find it difficult to translate verses 12 and 13. The sense perhaps is : Who can find errors in the Scriptures? The answer is " No one." Rather let each search for hidden faults in himself ; and let him pray to be guarded from the influence of those who presumptuously claim to find such. So will he be saved from the great transgression of stepping outside of the Scriptures.

Thus was it with Jehovah's perfect Servant (v. 13, R.V.). He prayed that He might be kept back from association with the presumptuous ; that He might be guarded from their influence ; and clear from the great transgression of stepping outside the Scriptures, as the sun is clear of the great transgression of stepping outside its tabernacle in the heavens. Such an act on the part of the sun would wreck the universe, and such an act on the part of the Servant of Jehovah would bring eternal ruin upon angels and men.

The Hebrew verbs employed in. v. 13 are astronomical. This is one of the many proofs that the Creator of the heavens is the Author of the Scriptures.

As nothing is hid from the warmth of the sun, so from no nation is withheld the grace of the Servant (vs. 6 and 11).

Day unto day and night unto night (v. 2) mean day and night continually.

The great titles of Elohim (El) and Jehovah occur at the opening and close of the Psalm ; just as they appear at the opening and close of the Bible, and in the same relationship.

PSALM XX.—The speakers in this Psalm are the Elect Remnant of Israel (vs. 1-5, and 7-9), and the Messiah (v. 6).

They speak to Him, and He, animated by their faith and sympathy, declares His confidence in His promised resurrection. He is " the Anointed One," i.e., the Messiah of verse 6.

As in Psalm xvi. He associates Himself with the sufferings of His people, so here His people associate themselves with His sufferings. They love Him and they love His Law. Their joys and hopes are bound up with Him. They pray and confidently declare that He will be delivered in the day of His trouble (vs. 1 and 2) ; that the sacrifice of His sinless life and atoning death will be accepted (v. 3) ; that He will be raised from the dead (v. 5) ; that all His petitions will be fulfilled (v. 5) ; and that victory is assured for Him and them (v. 5). Thus the Spirit of Christ in the Remnant gives utterance to affections, to desires, and to assurances that are common to both, and proper to both. All the verbs in the Psalm, excepting in verse 8 and part of verse 6, and verse 9, are in the future tense in the Hebrew text, and thus prayer and prediction are both expressed.

The King here is the King of Psalm ii. He is both King and Jehovah (v. 9). In the next Psalm, as in Psalm ii, Jehovah and the King are associated· in judgment. God in Christ, and Christ as God, is the testimony of the Book of the Psalms.

The " name " stands for the Person. The term occurs three times in the Psalm. The Defending Name (v. 1) ; the Displayed Name (v. 5) ; the Delivering Name (v. 7).

The God of Jacob (v. 1) was the God Who met Jacob when he had nothing, and promised him everything !

The first and last verses are thus contrasted in the Hebrew text :—" Jehovah shall hear Thee (Messiah) in the day of trouble " (v. 1), and : " The King shall hear us in the day of our cry " (v. 9). His day of trouble is past ; Israel's is future. He was heard in His ·day of trouble—His First Advent— and was raised from the dead (v. 6), and set on High (v. 1). Israel will be saved out of their day of trouble and set on high in response to the cry " Save us, O Jehovah " (v. 9).

This last verse is very beautiful. Need cries " Save us, O Jehovah ! " and faith immediately adds, " The King will hear us in the day of our cry."

The day of His trouble was that envisaged in John xii. 27 ; the day of their trouble, John xiv. 1.

PSALM XXI.—This Psalm is the answer to the prayer, the faith, and the predictions of Psalm xx. Its theme is the exaltation and crowning of the Messiah as King over all the earth, and His appointment as the source and channel of blessing to all nations (vs. 1-6. with Gen xii. 2).

Putting the superscription and the subscription together—as suggested by the position of the latter in Hab. iii—the reader learns that the Psalm is a prophecy concerning David Messiah, and that it will be sung at His coronation upon Aijeleth Shahar, i.e., at " the dawn of the morning," that is, at the opening of His glorious millennial reign.

The Psalm contains two Sections. The First, verses 1-7 ; the Second, verses 8-13. Each Section has three members :—
The Messiah, strong in Jehovah's strength (v. 1).
Jehovah's action towards Him (vs. 2-5).
His reward and His merit (vs. 6 and 7).
Messiah's action toward His enemies (v. 8-10).
Their guilt and defeat (vs. 11 and 12).
The Messiah, strong in His own strength as Jehovah (v. 13).

In the first three members, Jehovah is addressed ; in the second three, Messiah is addressed.

The speaker in the Psalm is Israel (v. 13). The occasion intended in verses 1-7 is the morning of Messiah's Resurrection, and in verses 8-13 the morning of Israel's Restoration.

The strength and salvation of verse 1 signalized the Resurrection. He was raised by the power of God. What His heart desired and His lips requested (v. 2) may be learned from verses 3-7. Because of His perfect faith and obedience (Heb. v. 7, and xii. 2), He, as Man, was granted life and length of days for ever and ever (v. 4) ; on His return from the death world Jehovah came to meet Him with the blessings of goodness (v. 3) ; He clothed Him with honour and majesty (v. 5) ; He gladdened Him with the Divine favour (v. 6) ; He made Him a source of universal and perpetual blessing (v. 6 with Gen. xii. 2) ; He crowned Him with an imperishable crown (v. 3) ; and He seated Him on an immovable throne (v. 7). In all this blessing there was no evil ; there was nothing but goodness (v. 3).

The unlimited power given to Messiah (Matt. xxviii. 18), but not yet taken—for the present period of time is the kingdom and patience of Jesus Christ—He takes in verses 8-12 (Rev. xi. 17), and righteously finds out with His almighty hand the enemies and haters of His people (v. 8) ; in His just anger He thrusts them into the furnace of fire

(Matt. xiii. 42) ; and, as Jehovah, destroys them out of His kingdom (vs. 9 and 10). Their guilt is stated in verse 11, and their impotency and defeat in verse 12.

Verse 11 may read thus : They intended evil against Thee ; they planned a mischievous device ; they shall not be able to perform it.

On the millennial morn Israel will acclaim Him as King and worship Him as God (v. 13).

PSALM XXII.—Psalms xxii. xxiii. and xxiv. form a group setting out the glories of Messiah as the Good Shepherd (xxii.), as the Great Shepherd (xxiii.) ; and as the Chief Shepherd (xxiv.). Compare John x. 11 ; Heb. xiii. 20 ; and 1 Peter v. 4.

This twenty-second Psalm predicts the sufferings of Christ (vs. 1-21) and the glories that are to follow (vs. 22-31). Compare Luke xxiv. 25-27, and 1 Pet. i. 10-12. It presents a sinless Man forsaken by God. Such a fact is unique in history, and needs not, and never will need, to be repeated. That sinless Man—Himself God manifest in flesh—was made sin (2 Cor. v. 21), and, therefore, forsaken ; placed outside the promises ; and pierced with the Sword of Divine wrath (Zech xiv. 7). In that judgment God dealt infinitely with sin, and in so dealing with it in the person of His beloved Son, showed His wrath against sin, and His love for the sinner. Thus He vindicated Himself and redeemed man. God revealed Himself at Calvary.

Those who deny the fact of prophecy cannot explain away this Psalm. Its translation into Greek by the LXX proves, that it was in existence at least 300 years before Christ, and yet it contains a number of minute predictions, the actual and material fulfilment of which the New Testament records.

The Holy Spirit in Matt. xxvii. 46 states that Christ spoke this Psalm when hanging on the tree. It glorifies Him as the sin-offering ; Psalm xl glorifies Him as the burnt offering ; and Psalm lxix as the trespass offering.

The Gospels narrate the facts of the crucifixion ; this Psalm the feelings of the Crucified. Combining these Scriptures the believer recognises that he can accompany the Lord Christ a little way in His sufferings, but there soon comes a point beyond which he cannot go. What was the depth of horror to which the sinless soul of Jesus sank under the wrath of God, as the Sin Offering, is unfathomable for men or angels.

Four degrees of suffering appear in the Psalm. Suffering from the hand of God (vs. 1-6) ; suffering from the rejection of Israel (vs. 7 and 8) ; suffering from the demons who gathered round His Cross in exulting and hellish triumph (v. 12 and 13) ; and the physical suffering of crucifixion—the most painful form of death (vs. 14-18).

Had the Messiah been only man He would have put His physical sufferings first and His religious last. But to Him as the Only Begotten Son of God there was no anguish so infinite as the hiding of the Father's face. His physical sufferings were agonizing ; His mental and sensitive, from the onslaught of the bulls of Bashan, i.e., the demons, still more terrible ; the pain of His wounded heart because of the hatred of those He loved and came to save, was a still deeper depth of agony ; but an agony unspeakable was His being forsaken of God.

During His ministry on earth Christ spoke of God as His Father and resumed the title after He had triumphantly shouted " Finished," but while suffering Divine wrath as the Sin-Offering He addressed Him as God (vs. 1, 2 and 10).

Four statements (vs. 9 and 10) assert and emphasise His true and essential humanity. " Roaring " (v. 1), i.e., loud lamentation. The " night season " (v. 2) was that of the three hours of darkness. So long as He was made a Sin-offering He was not heard (v. 2) ; but sin having been atoned for, He was heard in resurrection (v. 24). Yet while thus forsaken, as His Hebrew fathers had never been (vs. 4 and 5), and while shut up in Sheol, He trusted and thus proved Himself to be the Author and Finisher of faith ; and so teaches His people to cling in confidence to God when circumstances would apparently prove that God had abandoned them.

But at the outset of His supreme agony He hastened to vindicate God as being always worthy of praise (v. 3). As dwelling between the cherubim in the Holy House He inhabited the praises of Israel.

The words " My darling " (v. 20) are usually understood to mean the Church. But Romans xvi. 25, and Eph. iii. 5, destroy this hypothesis. The term means His precious sinless body. It was unique and inexpressibly precious to God (Heb. x. 5). He prayed that it might be preserved from the Gentile dog, and that His soul might be delivered from the abyss. The term " sword" is here a figure for death. In this entire passage Messiah speaks of Himself, and in this particular verse fortifies His cry by using this expression (which was a term of affection, " My Only One ", Heb.) which God was wont to address to Him as His Only Begotten Son. The term could not be used of anyone else. The Hebrew word occurs eleven times and generally means an only son (Gen. xxii. 2 and 16, Prov. iv. 3, Jer. vi. 26, Amos viii. 10, Zech. xii. 10, Psalm xxv. 16, xxxv. 17. lxviii. 6, Judges xi. 34, and Psalm xxii. 20).

Verses 21 and 22 are to be read thus :— " Save me from the lion's mouth, for Thou wilt hear me (and deliver me) from the horns of the wild ox, and I will declare Thy name unto my brethren," etc.

The lion's mouth and the horns of the wild ox are figures of death and of him that has the power of death (Heb. ii. 14).

The word " heard " (v. 24) implies resurrection ; and on that very day He thus spoke (v. 22) to Mary Magdalene in the garden (John xx. 17) ; and, later on, praised God in the congregation (1 Cor. xv. 6). The great congregation (v. 25) is Israel ; the ends of the world (v. 27) all nations. Both shall be blessed ; for the kingdom over Israel shall be given to Messiah, and He shall be Governor among the nations (v. 28). He was " the Afflicted One " of verse 24.

In His future kingdom the meek of verse 26 shall be the prosperous and happy of verse 29. Compare Ps. xxxvi. 8, lxiii. 5, and xcii. 14. They, and all who, like them, were doomed to return to the dust because of sin, will praise Him because, in order to save them, He did not keep alive His own soul. This appears to be the sense of verse 29.

Those who believe upon this atoning Saviour shall be regarded as a new race— a generation—of which Messiah will be the Head (1 Cor. xv. 22, and Isa. liii. 10 and 11). They shall continually serve Him, they shall keep coming, and shall keep declaring unto nations yet to be born that God's Righteous One accomplished this annihilation of sin by the oblation of Himself as the Sin-offering. The last word in the Hebrew text is " accomplished, " and corresponds to the word " finished " in the Greek text of John xix. 30.

PSALM XXIII.—Only one voice sang this Psalm in perfect tune. It was the voice of Jesus. When walking through the dark valley of His earthly life Jehovah was His Shepherd. There is no suggestion of sin in the Psalm. Its great theme is not so much what Jehovah gives, or does, as what He is.

Christ is the Great Shepherd of His people, for He was raised from the dead in order to be such (Heb. xiii. 20). He is spoken of in verses 1, 2, 3, and 6, and spoken to in verses 4 and 5 ; for the heart that begins to speak of Him will quickly be found speaking to Him.

The Jehovah titles given by the Holy Spirit in the Old Testament to the Messiah appear in the Psalm. They express the fulness of His ability as a shepherd for His sheep. They are :—Jehovah Jireh (Gen. xxii. 14), verse 1 ; Jehovah Shalom (Judges vi. 24), verse 2 ; Jehovah Rophi (Ex. xv. 26), verse 3 ; Jehovah Tsidkenu (Jer. xxiii. 6), verse 3 ; Jehovah Shammah (Ezek. xlviii. 35), verse 4 ; Jehovah Nissi (Ex. xvii. 15), verse 5 ; and Jehovah Mekaddishchem (Ex. xxxi. 13), verse 5.

In the East the sheep follow the shepherd, He leads them to the best pastures and waters them at the gentlest streams. He guides them in right paths ; and when weary restores them by pouring oil upon their heads from a flask, and by giving them water to drink from a cup. These he carries for this double purpose. He is provided with a club and with a crook. With the one, he helps the sheep when in danger of slipping, or wandering, and with the other he fights their foes. He guards them from two enemies —poisonous herbs in the pasture and ravenous beasts in the rocks. They feast while he fights. The credit of his name as a shepherd is tarnished if he leads the sheep in wrong paths, or if he loses even one of them.

So the Psalm is fitly placed between the sufferings of Psalm xxii, and the glories of Psalm xxiv.

The Great Shepherd gives His sheep a conscious salvation. Each one can say " He is mine "—not " I hope He is mine." He leads them into the green pastures of " Ephesians " and the still waters of " Romans." He keeps restoring their soul ; and because His name is " Righteousness " (John xvi. 10), He leads them in paths of righteousness in the home, in the place of

daily toil, in the market, in the public
street, in the railway train and steamboat,
etc., for there is a path of righteousness
for the believer in each one of these. He
accompanies the sheep so that " the valley
of the shadow " is wealthier than the garden
of Eden, for there His companionship was
only occasional. He defends and supports
the flock, sees to the purity of their food,
refreshes them with oil for their heads and
water for their lips, loads them with goodness
and mercy every day, and, finally, brings
them safely home.

PSALM XXIV.—The Holy Spirit here
sings of the day when the Chief Shepherd
shall appear (1 Pet. v. 4). He shall enter the
city of Jerusalem with His sheep and take
His seat upon the throne of Jehovah in
Mount Sion.

The song celebrates Messiah as Creator
(v. 1 and 2), as Redeemer (vs. 3-6), and as
King of Glory (vs. 7-10). The Hebrew
Scriptures give the title " shepherd " to kings
(Isa. xliv. 28 and Zech. xiii. 7, etc.)

Two questions are proposed in the Psalm.
First: Who is this Chief Shepherd? The
answer is " Jehovah Messiah." The second
question : Who are His sheep? The answer
is : " Such as are pure in doctrine and holy
in life."

The Shepherd's right to the throne of the
whole earth, to all that is in it, and to the
obedience of its inhabitants is the double
right of creation and redemption (vs. 1-5).
Compare Rev. iv. and v.

The Shepherd's flock is morally described
in verses 4-6. Hands, heart, soul, and
tongue express purpose, conduct, language,
and feeling. These form character. " Lifting
up the soul unto vanity" and " swearing
deceitfully," i.e., swearing allegiance to a
false god, mean idolatry, and covetousness.

" The blessing " (v. 5) is the right of entry
to the King's court ; and " righteousness "
is the raiment suitable to the sinlessness of
that court. A person in foul raiment would
be miserable in a king's court, if by some
chance he had secured a title to be there.

Such persons receive the blessing from
Jehovah admitting them to His kingdom,
and a righteousness befitting them for its
purity. But this righteousness is not merited
for it is " received " (v. 5), and received from
a personal Saviour—a God of " salvation "—
the God of Jacob ; that is, the God Who

elected Jacob unto salvation when he only
merited condemnation (Gen. xxviii. 12-15,
and xlviii. 16).

The prophecy having portrayed the subjects of the Kingdom, next describes the
King Himself (vs. 7-10). Two statements
are made respecting Him : What He did
(v. 8), and What He is (v. 10). As to what
He did, He fought the battle of Calvary
as the Good Shepherd. As to Who He is, He is
Jehovah the Great Shepherd of Israel, the
King of Glory.

" Everlasting " in verses 7 and 9 should
read " ancient." The most ancient gate of
Jerusalem is the East Gate. At present
it is walled up. The Moslems have a tradition that it will never be opened until Jesus
of Nazareth returns to earth, and that He
will be the first to pass through it into the
city.

The last verse may read : Who then is He,
this glorious King ? The prompt, confident,
and assured answer is : Jesus Jehovah, He
is the glorious King !

PSALM XXV.—Psalms xxv-xli. conclude
the last section of the First Book. They
set forth the Messiah as Israel's great High
Priest. As such He leads their worship,
confesses their sins, prays for pardon, voices
their confidence and hope and faith, burdens
Himself with their sorrows and fears, and
in every respect acts as the True Priest of and
for His people. See notes on Ps. xvi.

Thus it appears that though personally
sinless, He confesses Israel's sins as His own,
asks for forgiveness for them, and yet at the
same time declares the moral perfections of
the petitioners. This is to many, confusing ;
but it is quite simple. He takes to Himself
His people's sins and He accredits to them
His own merits. He is at once Priest,
Advocate, Mediator, and Substitute.

The previous Psalms of this First Book
(xvi-xxiv), displayed His perfections as Man,
as Servant of Jehovah, as King, as the suffering Messiah, as the atoning Saviour, as the
Good Shepherd, the Great Shepherd, the
Chief Shepherd, and as Jehovah. The
introduction of the False Messiah (Ps.
ix-xv.) forms a dark back-ground to the
glories of the Chief Figure in the picture.

The Psalm in the Hebrew text is an acrostic.
There are nine such in the Five Books of
the Psalms, and eleven others in the
Old Testament. The first acrostic links

Ps. ix. and x. and is connected with Israel's national sufferings under Anti-Christ. This second acrostic deals with Israel's moral griefs voiced by the True Messiah.

In the opening of the Psalm Israel's Priest looks up to God (vs. 1 and 2), and in the close of the Psalm He prays that God will look down upon Him (vs. 18-22).

The beauty of the Psalm is matchless. The reader is deeply moved as he remembers that the speaker is the Lord Christ Himself pleading for His people. He has neither sins nor transgressions personally, but He confesses those of His people as His own (v. 7). His Spirit in Daniel (ch. ix) acted similarly.

In verse 8 sinners are taught the way of salvation; and those of them who obey become the " meek " of verse 9.

The word " covenant " now first appears in the Book of the Psalms (v. 10).

This Priest when confessing His people's iniquity as His own, asks for pardon on two grounds—the magnitude of the sin, and the name, i.e., the character of God as a pardoning God (v. 11). Man tries to belittle his sin and magnify his penitence, and pleads for pardon because the one is so small and the other so great, but the True Priest rightly estimates sin as being great, and urges its magnitude as a ground of pardon. Compare 1 Tim. i. 12-16.

Uniting verses 10 and 14, the great rule of Christian living is found, i.e., Christ and the Scriptures. They go together. The word " show " (v. 14), means " cause to know." These verses point the principle that the Scriptures unfold themselves only as they are read in communion with Him Who wrote them, and that they are God's channel for revealing Divine truth which otherwise would remain secret. Compare 1 Cor. ii. 9-12.

The Person of this Great Priest, and His sympathy with His people, shine with great beauty in verses 15-22. He, as their Head, has His eyes ever toward Jehovah, and they, as His feet, are temporarily caught in the enemy's net (v. 15). He, as God's Only One (v. 16, Heb. and LXX.) afflicts Himself with the distresses, afflictions, pains and sins of His people; their troubles enlarge His heart, i.e., make it swell with sorrow; the hatred shown to Israel He accepts as shown to Himself; and He pleads the perfectness of His faith, His integrity, and His uprightness as the argument for their redemption out of all their troubles.

Never was there a love like this ! Not merely with His lips does He officially confess His people's sins and accept their distresses as His own, and plead for forgiveness and deliverance, but with and from His heart (v. 17) He really burdens Himself, and bears and makes His own their sorrows as no earthly priest ever could or did (Matt. viii. 17).

PSALM XXVI.—Israel's great High Priest continues in this Psalm to plead for His people. He bases His petitions for them upon the perfection of His own nature and conduct (v. 1-8). He makes their soul and His a unity, and prays that it may be delivered from sinners and from men of blood, and publicly vindicated by God with the Divine favour (vs. 9-11).

Similar language is used by an advocate in a Scottish court of justice. Addressing the judge on behalf of his client, he will say, " My Lord, I did not mean to commit the crime. Give me a light sentence." Thus he makes himself one with the guilty person. But he cannot proceed to plead his own moral perfections as a just ground for mercy to the accused. This the Heavenly Advocate can do, and does.

Failure to recognise who the Speaker in this and similar Psalms is, leads to the unjust charge that David had a very high opinion of himself, and was in effect a self-righteous Pharisee.

The Psalm is rich with instruction for the people of God in all dispensations, but two facts full of consolation are specially prominent. The one is, that help is sure to be given in response to such a Pleader and to such a plea. The second is, that this Divine Priest is willing and able to live His blameless life in whoever trusts Him.

There are in the Hebrew text of the Psalm five " I haves " and seven " I shalls." Only the Messiah could thus fully describe His past, and guarantee His future action. The words " judge me " (v. 1), mean " vindicate me " ; the word " integrity " should read " blamelessness " ; and the word " therefore " should be omitted. " Reins " and " heart " (v. 2) are figures of speech for thoughts and feelings.

As the Levitical priest scrutinized both inwardly and outwardly the lamb for the daily sacrifice, so the Lamb of God (v. 2) could confidently offer Himself to the searchings of God's eye. All was perfection in Him. Every emotion of His spirit, soul and body, every thought and affection of His heart, every look, word and action were absolutely and alway sinless !

Continuance is expressed in the Hebrew text in verses 3 to 8. Verse 4 should read " I will not sit." The Divine Advocate pleads on behalf of His people that God's loving-kindness was always before His eyes ; that He habitually walked in His truth ; that He never did sit, and was resolved that He never would sit with vain persons ; that He ever hated and continued to hate evil-doers ; that He loved and always did love God's house ; and He pledges Himself never to associate with hypocrites and the lawless, but, on the contrary, to recount with loud praises God's wondrous works.

The repeated " my " of verse 9, and the repeated " me " of verse 11, are to be interpreted of Israel as personated by her Advocate.

As the Intercessor, His foot was planted upon the smooth, i.e., the righteous pavement of the Divine audience chamber, and the foot itself was as " even " as the pavement on which it stood ; for, as prefigured in the meal offering (see notes on Lev. ii.) there was an evenness in His life among men that all their hatred and treachery and snares failed to roughen. And He could therefore say " My foot has always stood, and stands, and will continually stand in an even place." See Psalm xlviii. 26.

" Congregations " (v. 12) is the plural of majesty for the great congregation.

PSALM XXVII.—Messiah in the Garden of Gethsemane (John xviii. 1-6), is the theme of the first six verses of the Psalm ; its remaining verses belong to His subsequent experiences in the hands of His captors.

On seeing in the darkness of that night the lanterns and torches and weapons of those coming to seize Him, His heart sang in the quiet confidence of an assured faith, " Jehovah is my light and my stronghold, whom shall I fear ? " ; and when, a moment later with majesty He said : " I am the I am, " they went backward and fell to the ground.

On the way to, and in, the palace of Caiaphas, and, later, on His way to the judgment hall of Pilate—abandoned and defenceless, and knowing all things that should come upon Him—He perfectly trusted, and believed that He would certainly be resurrected.

The doctrine, therefore, of the Psalm is that the Messiah is an all-sufficient High Priest for His people ; and that He can by His example, by His ministry, and by His spirit in them, carry them triumphantly through the sharpest trials, and through death itself (Heb. iv. 14 and 15, and v. 2). A priest who can help must be a priest who has suffered and won, and who, having been tempted in all points, can have compassion on the ignorant and defeated.

The perfection of His faith and love as a Man is very beautifully set out in both sections of the Psalm. The one desire of His heart to return to the glory which He had with the Father before the world was, He refused to let present terrors affect (v. 4) ; and, in the second section, He utters the touching plea, " Thou taughtest Thy people to seek Thy face, and my heart said, I will seek it ! O Jehovah, now that I am in trouble wilt Thou turn that face away from me ? " This was not a cry of unbelief, but of an affection that made God His all and His refuge (vs. 8 and 9). Jehovah had said, and was continually saying to Israel," Seek ye my face " (Deut. iv. 29 ; 1 Chron. xxviii. 9 ; Isa. xlv. 19 ; Amos v. 4.) One heart. Messiah's, promptly replied " Thy face, O Jehovah, will I seek " (v. 8).

The sense of verse 3 is : " Though wars should rise up against me, even in that event will I continue confiding."

The last member of verse 4 may read : " To consider the pleasantness of Jehovah and look upon Him with admiration in His temple."

Verses 5 and 6 reveal His unshakable confidence in His Father, and His conviction as to resurrection ; and He consequently pledges Himself to sing loud praises in the heavenly temple. These were among the joys that He set before Him, and because of which He endured the cross, despising its shame.

Verses 7 to 10 belong to the moment of His arrest ; of the abandonment of His disciples (v. 10. R.V.) ; and of His experiences when on the way to the palace of Annas and Caiaphas.

All He had on earth were His loved disciples (Mark iii. 35). As He looked upon them as they fled His heart must have been pierced with anguish, but it rested in the consciousness that Jehovah would compensate Him by gathering Him and them into

His bosom. The Hebrew verb "take up" (v. 10) is the same as "gather" (Psalm xxvi. 9).

The prayer of verse 11 contemplates the moment of His entering the palace of Caiaphas ; and verse 12, the hour when the false witnesses accused Him, and the Pharisees cruelly determined to crucify Him.

But He believed that though crucified yet would He be raised from the dead (v. 13) ; and on the way to Pilate's judgment hall He addressed the words of the last verse to His own heart.

The sense of verse 13 is : " I have always believed, I do now believe, and I will continue to believe, that I shall see the goodness of Jehovah in the land of the living."

In the Hebrew text of the Psalm there are 147 words, that is $3 \times 7 \times 7$. Thus Deity and Perfection are stamped upon the Psalm.

PSALM XXVIII.—The title of this Psalm,. together with verse 8, assure its Messianic interpretation.

Praying on behalf of His people, He asks in verses 1 and 2 for audience ; in verses 3 and 4 He makes definite petitions in favour of His people and against His and their enemies ; and in verse 5 He sets out the just ground of the judgment which He demands.

To become like them that go down into the sepulchre is to be hopeless (v. 1).

The " me " of verse 3 means Israel. The sense of the passage is : " Do not associate me in the same doom with the wicked." To this High Priest, and to His people in whom His spirit dwells, there can be no greater horror than association with evil and evil-doers.

The triple repetition of " them " in verse 4 expresses emphasis.

Reading verses 4 and 5 in the R.V., the contrast is recognised between " their works " and " the works of Jehovah," and between " the operation of their hands " and " the operation of His hands." The last sentence of verse 5 should read as in the R.V.

The great High Priest in verse 6, in the perfection of the faith of which He is the Author and Finisher, declares that His supplications have been heard although the fact is yet future.

The past, present and future appear in the statements " I have trusted," " I am helped," " I will praise."

The argument of the context proves that verse 8 is to be thus read : " Jehovah is His strength ; yea He is a stronghold of salvation to His Messiah."

The title " Anointed " declares the Trinity, for He Who anoints is God the Father, and He Who is anointed is God the Son, and the oil with which He is anointed is God the Holy Spirit.

PSALM XXIX.—The Messiah as the Sweet Psalmist of Israel here fulfils the promise given in verse 7 of the prior Psalm.

The name Jehovah occurs eighteen times—four times in the first two verses, four times in the last two, and ten times in the intervening verses.

The Divine Psalmist calls upon the angels to worship Jehovah (vs. 1 and 2) ; He recites God's power over nature (vs. 3-9) ; declares that in the beauteous temple of creation everything, animate and inanimate, proclaims His glory (v. 9) ; records that Jehovah sat as King at the Flood (v. 10) ; and predicts that the strength of verse 1, and the peace of verse 11, will be given to His people.

The doctrine of the Psalm is that Jehovah is mightier than the angels of His might (Ps. xcvii, and Heb. i) ; that He is stronger then the forces of nature ; that He is Almighty ; and that all this limitless strength is at the disposition of His weakest child. The forces against His children may be mighty, but He who loves and cares for them is mightier than they.

The Psalm is a beautiful instance of the testimony which it is the joy of the Son to bear to the Father. Other Psalms instance the testimony which it is the joy of the Spirit to bear to the Son.

The mighty angels are summoned to hear a Voice mightier than theirs ; and the majestic sanctuary of creation is commanded to ascribe all its glory and power to Jehovah. The words " the beauty of holiness " mean the beauteous temple of nature—the temple of verse 9.

When forest trees toss and wave to and fro in a great storm they are said to dance (v. 6).

" Sirion " is Mount Hermon (Deut. iii. 9), and " Kadesh " is Kadesh-Naphthali near Lebanon.

Lightning is the flaming sword pictured in verse 7. The word " divideth " has possibly a double meaning—" hewn out " and " cleaveth." The sword of flame is first fashioned, or hewn out, and then cleaves trees and shatters rocks.

Terror-stricken by the noise of the thunder animals give birth to their young, at the same time that the furious storm strips the forests of their leaves (v. 9, R.V.).

The special Hebrew word for " flood " occurs twelve times in the Hebrew Bible—eleven times in Genesis and once in this Psalm (v. 10, R.V.). The argument of the verse is that even the Flood—nature's mightiest convulsion—was controlled by this mightier Power; and that that is the mighty God Who gives His own strength and His own peace to His people (v. 11) See Phil. iv. 7 and 13 and Ps. xciii.

PSALM XXX.—The superscription states that this song is " of David," i.e., it concerns the Messiah, and that it is to be sung at the dedication of the House, that is, at the dedication of the future millennial temple.

The Hebrew people are God's House (Heb. iii. 6), for He dwelt among them, and He will dwell among them. The Tabernacle in the wilderness was His material house in the past, and the millennial temple will be His material house in the future. The one was set up when Israel was delivered from Pharaoh; the other will be dedicated directly Israel is delivered from Anti-Christ. The first was dedicated without a song. Solomon's temple was a fore-picture of the future millennial House, and it was dedicated with a song (2 Chron. v. 13), for it witnessed to the New Covenant; but the Tabernacle belonged to the First covenant, and hence there was no song—there was the sounding of trumpets. These two houses appear in the Psalm. The Tabernacle belongs to the first six verses and the future temple to the last six.

The Psalm has an application to any servant of God in any dispensation; but its interpretation belongs to Israel as a nation, and it will doubtless be sung by them and their Great High Priest in a future day, when, at the dedication of the millennial Temple, He reviews their history and leads their praise.

The structure of the Psalm may be thus presented:—

Praise to Jehovah	v. 1.
Pharaoh's oppression	vs. 2 and 3.
Song of Deliverance	vs. 4 and 5.
Establishment	vs. 6 and 7.
Anti-Christ's Oppression	vs. 7-10.
Song of Deliverance	v. 12
Establishment	v. 11.
Praise to Jehovah.	v. 12.

The first four members belong to the House in the Wilderness; the last four to the future House of the kingdom. The word " strong " (v. 7) should be the last word of verse 6: and the word " for " may be supplied at the beginning of verse 7. Verse 6 will then read: " And in my prosperity I said, I shall never be moved; for by Thy favour, O Jehovah, Thou hast made my mountain to stand strong."

Thus personal and national experience is in the Psalm imbedded in praise and prayer; and the doctrine of the Book of Job is again taught that whatever may be human experience, with its necessary admission of weakness, sin and folly, there is neither error nor change in God; and at the end, as at the beginning, praise is due to Him.

The figure of a sick man at the point of death, but brought back from the very mouth of the grave, is used to express the past and future history of the nation.

David and Israel could, with limitation, sing this song, but the ear of God waits to hear it sung in perfect tune and fulness by David's Son and Lord.

Pharaoh designed the death of the entire nation, but his purpose was defeated (vs. 1-3). Anti-Christ will design its annihilation, but his purpose (v. 7 from the words " Thou didst hide ") will be also defeated.

Verse 5 reads thus in the Hebrew text: " For a moment His anger; for a lifetime His favour. Weeping may come in to lodge at even, but singing comes to dwell in the morning." So sadness precedes gladness, and, in verses 6 and 7, gladness succeeds sadness.

A bridegroom handing his bride two rings, the one smooth and the other rough, said, " Such will be your life; but unchanging love will enwrap both."

The word " mountain " (v. 7) means " assured position." Such was Israel's when planted in Palestine. But how quickly came sorrow because of sin !

The words " to the end " (v. 12) may read

on from verse 10. Verse 11 will then be a parenthesis giving the facts for which the tongue ("glory") will sing praise.

PSALM XXXI.—The title of the Psalm defines its interpretation. The speaker is the Servant of Jehovah (v. 16) and the Righteous One (v. 18). Compare Isa. lii. 13 and Acts iii. 14, vii. 52, and xxii. 14.

The doctrine of the Psalm is that Messiah was tested in all points, yet without sin; that as Captain of His people's salvation He was perfected through suffering; that having suffered being tempted, He is able to succour them that are tempted (Heb. ii. to v.); that He was a Man of Sorrows and acquainted with grief, and was hated, despised and rejected of men (Isa. liii.).

The Psalm consists of two stanzas: The first, verses 1 to 8; the second, verses 9 to 24. Each stanza contains five members. The five members of the first stanza correspond with the five members of the second, thus:

" Let me not be put to shame " (vs. 1 and 2).

" For " (vs. 3 and 4).

" Thy hand " (v. 5).

" I trust " (v. 7).

Assurance (vs. 7 and 8).

" Let me not be put to shame " (vs. 16-18).

" For " (vs. 9-13).

" Thy hand " (v. 15).

" I trust " (v. 14).

Assurance (vs. 19-24).

The cries and the faith of the Psalm reveal the distress and the confidence of Him Who is the Author and Finisher of faith. In the first two verses He prays to be rescued from the scribes and Pharisees and Herodians who were seeking His life; and He cries for deliverance from the net which in private they prepared in order to entangle Him in His talk (v. 4). On the cross He uttered aloud the first sentence of verse 5; and, inwardly, in the next sentence, gave thanks for His redemption out of death—in the energy of faith, speaking of it as an accomplished fact already performed by Jehovah the God of truth, He was the God of truth, for He had promised to resurrect His beloved Son.

The " lying vanities " of verse 6 mean the material idols which Israel had worshipped prior to the Exile, and the ritual idols bowed down to by the Nation in Messiah's life-time.

If it were possible Immanuel was more precious to God when in adversity and trouble and danger than at any other time (vs. 7 and 8). Man refuses to recognize a companion when in adversity, but God did not so act toward His Servant. He recognized both Him and His adversities (v. 7). He was a Man of Sorrows and acquainted with grief (vs. 9 and 10). The word "iniquity" in verse 10 should read "affliction." It is the same Hebrew word as in Ps. xxxviii. 6, and is so translated by the LXX. He was a derision to His enemies and to His neighbours, and His relatives abandoned Him through fear of being put out of the synagogue (vs. 11 and 12). Compare John. vii. 5 and ix. 22. He was defamed by the majority, and the terror of death met Him, no matter to what side He turned (v. 13). Compare Matt. xi. 19 and xii. 14. Yet was His faith unbroken (v. 14); and He kept believing that His times, i.e., His fortunes, were not in man's hands but in God's (v. 15). See Luke xiii. 33. They spoke grievous things against Him saying He had a devil (John viii. 48). But He was God's " Righteous One " (v. 18) as He was God's " Servant " (v. 16).

The word " haste " (v. 22) means " flight." His experience at Nazareth illustrates this verse. He was cut off from public worship, and to save His life was obliged to hasten through His would-be murderers. When in safety He gave thanks because His cry for deliverance had been heard.

In verses 19-24 He speaks words of comfort and succour to His people; the argument being that they will surely be delivered because He Himself was delivered; and that they will not have to tread an untrodden road of suffering and shame and hatred, for it was a way already trodden by Him.

" Reproach " (v. 11) should read " derision." Only a Divine Person could be both so despised and so hated. As man he was despised, and as God He was hated. The revilings of the malefactors vividly expressed this contempt and hatred. What criminal hates and reviles his fellow-sufferer? This depth of shame and anguish was reserved for Christ.

PSALM XXXII.—The superscription states that the Psalm relates to David, i.e., to the Messiah, and that it gives instruction. (Maschil).

There are thirteen Maschil Psalms : xxxii. xlii xliv. xlv. lii. liii. liv. lv. lxxiv. lxxviii. lxxxviii. lxxxix. and cxlii. There is no Maschil Psalm in Book iv.

This Psalm is quoted by the Holy Spirit in Rom. iv. in support of the doctrine of justification by grace and not by merit.

That Gracious Spirit here instructs the listener as to the misery resulting from unconfessed sin ; the relief and conscious pardon enjoyed as the result of confession ; the peace and safety accompanying companionship with God ; and the conditions affecting that fellowship.

He teaches penitents that the great High Priest speaks in His own name and person on their behalf as if He Himself were the guilty transgressor.

What an ineffable consolation it is to have a Priest who thus makes Himself one with the repentant sinner, pleads and prays as the sinner ought to plead and pray, but cannot, and uses the very words which will be acceptable to God. Such a High Priest becomes repentant men.

Historically, this Psalm may describe the restlessness and tumult ("roaring") of David's conscience during the period between the seduction of Bathsheba and the denunciation of Nathan ; and, if this be so, it would explain David's immediate admission of guilt to the prophet (2 Sam. xii. 13).

The Psalm is prophetic. It foretells the confession of guilt which, in the coming day of her repentance, Israel will make of her two great sins of adultery in having loved idols and of murder in having slain Messiah (Acts vii. 52). Because they refuse to make this confession they have during many centuries suffered as a nation the anguish of verses 3 and 4. Yet in this Psalm the High Priest encourages them to this confession, and uses for them the language befitting it, bringing them at the same time into an intimacy with God into which conscious forgiveness leads.

The word "blessed" (vs. 1 and 2) is in the plural number in the Hebrew text. The verse may read : O the happinesses of the man etc.

"Transgression" implies rebellion against law ; "sin" points to moral failure ; and "iniquity" to corruption in the nature. The first is forgiven, that is, its punishment is unbound from off the transgressor. To forgive is to unbind. The second is covered, that is, atoned for by a blood sacrifice. The third is not imputed, on the contrary, the spotless righteousness of Christ is imputed or accounted to the repentant and believing sinner (Rom. iv.).

A full forgiveness dislodges guile from the heart (v. 2) ; for who will not declare all his debts to one who engages to discharge them, or who will hide any symptom of his malady from a physician who can cure perfectly ! The Selah of verse 4 contrasts the misery of unconfessed sin with the relief of forgiven guilt (v. 5). The Selah of this latter verse connects that forgiveness with the future salvation from wrath of which it is an earnest (vs. 6 and 7), and the last Selah unites that future safety with present holiness.

Salvation is simple, swift and sure— "I acknowledged," "Thou forgavest."

Verses 6 and 7 assure the safety of the forgiven man in the coming day of God's wrath. The term "godly" means one to whom God shows mercy. It expresses the attitude of God toward the repentant sinner, rather than the moral worthiness of the repentant sinner toward God. "In a time when Thou mayest be found" should read, "In the time of the finding out of sin." "The floods of great waters" picture the wrath of God in the day of inquisition and punishment of sin. In that day God will be the hiding-place of the forgiven sinner ; he will be compassed with singing and as safe from floods and fears (vs. 6 and 7) as Noah was when he made the Ark his hiding place.

Intimacy and love make the teaching and guiding of the eye possible in the way to the Father's home (v. 8) ; but as bit and bridle are necessary with a horse in order to keep it near to, and under the control of the owner, so must the wilful Christian be constrained.

The Holy Spirit in the last two verses instructs His pupils respecting the sorrows which will surely come upon the self-willed ("the wicked"), and the joys unspeakable and full of glory which will be the present and eternal portion of those who trust in Jehovah Messiah.

In verses 1 and 2 and 10 and 11 the Spirit speaks ; in verses 3–7, the transgressor ; and in verses 8 and 9 the Messiah.

PSALM XXXIII.—The absence of a Title unites this Psalm to the prior one, and thus connects, as in Rev. xiv, the New Song (v. 3) with redemption. This New Song is the theme of the Psalm. It is sung by the Great High Priest and the redeemed of Israel. He now leads their song of praise, as He had in the fore-going Psalm voiced their cry for pardon.

This is the first mention in the Bible of the New Song. The last mention is in Rev. xiv. Uniting these two passages together it is evident that Israel will sing this song on Mount Sion at the opening of the millennial reign of Christ, and that He will stand with them and lead the song.

The song is spoken of seven times in the Old Testament and once in the New Testament, as follows: Ps. xxxiii. 3, xl. 3, xcvi. 1, xcviii. 1, cxliv. 9, cxlix. 1, Isa. xlii. 10 and Rev. xiv. 3. It will be sung on earth by redeemed men. The New Song of Rev. v. 9 will be sung in heaven by sinless angels and cherubim. It has relation to the New Song sung on earth, and its theme is also redemption.

Ps. xxxiii consists of two stanzas, each containing four members. The first stanza is an invitation to praise Jehovah (v. 1-9); the second stanza reviews the actions of Jehovah.

The four members of the first stanza are:

Israel praises Jehovah (vs. 1-3).
Reason—His word and works (vs. 4-7).
The Gentiles fear Jehovah (v. 8).
Reason—His word and works (v. 9).

The four members of the second stanza are:

Man's relation to Jehovah (vs. 10 and 11).
Its results (vs. 13-17).
Israel's relation to Jehovah (v. 12).
Its results (vs. 18-22).

The word "rejoice" (v. 1) should read "shout for joy" and so connect this first verse with the last verse of the prior Psalm. The word "right" (v. 4) should read "faithfulness," as in the R.V. Man says that the Creation was a crime; the Creator says that it was "truth" (v. 4).

Verses 6 and 7 correspond with verses 4 and 5. The statements respect God's past and present actions. As to His past, He created the universe in truth; as to His present action, He restrains the oceans (v. 7) in faithfulness to His promise to Noah (v. 4). The "depth" means the waters that are above the earth.

The Trinity appears in verse 6 in connection with Creation—"Jehovah," "The Word," "The Spirit" (breath).

Verse 9 may read thus: He spake, and the earth came into existence; He commanded, and it stood fast, i.e., it remained suspended in space and confined to its orbit. These great facts should teach its inhabitants to worship Him and not idols imagined by them (v. 10).

The counsel and thoughts of God's heart (v. 11) are contrasted with the counsel and thoughts of man's heart (v. 10 R.V.). The former endure; the latter perish.

The statement in verse 15 reveals the Divinely-given consciousness to man of the existence of God and of His future punishment of sin.

God, knowing man perfectly, declares his great armies and navies to be in themselves useless (vs. 16 and 17), and thus exposes the consequent folly of dependence on them. He can use them as His instruments in His government of the nations. The last five verses of the Psalm contrast the safety of those who wait on, and wait for Jehovah, with the helplessness of those who trust human strength and resources.

The Hebrew word "new" (v. 3) means "unheard of before." The New Song, therefore, belongs to the life above the sun, for Eccles. i. 9 and 10 declares there is nothing new beneath it.

PSALM XXXIV—Verses 19 and 20, together with John xix. 36, make certain the relationship of this Psalm to the Messiah.

Many Psalms have the superscription "of David." The Hebrew reads "to David." If the ellipsis be supplied the superscription in all such Psalms will read, "Given by the Holy Spirit to David" or "to Asaph" or "to Hezekiah," etc. Or it may mean, "relating to David," i.e., to David Messiah.

That the Holy Spirit should give this prophecy to David immediately after his degrading conduct in Gath (1 Sam. xxi) is incomprehensible to strangers to the spiritual life. Verse 18 removes the difficulty. When the believer is mortified, ashamed, broken and contrite in spirit, and amazed that such a wretch should find pardon and deliverance, then is the soul restored and fresh revelation

given respecting a Divine David Who found
deliverance not by deceiving man but in
trusting God. The Scriptures record that a
sad fall may swiftly follow upon spiritual
revival; they also record the contrary.
These facts are enigmas to unrenewed men.

Abimelech is a title. The name of this
Abimelech was Achish.

In the Hebrew Bible the Psalm is an
acrostic, having the twenty-two letters of
the alphabet; and it is divided into two
sections, each section containing eleven letters. Verses 1-10 form the first section; verses
11-22 the second section. The theme of the
first section is Praise; the theme of the
second, Precept. The last statement of the
first section is: "They that seek Jehovah
shall not want any good thing" (Rom. viii.
28-32); the last statement of the second
section is: "None of them that trust in
Him shall be condemned." R.V. (Rom.
viii. 1).

In the first section the Messiah invites
His people to join with Him in singing
praise to God (v. 3). In the second section
He instructs them as to the felicity of His
disciples and the misery of evil-doers. These
alternate thus:

> Believers (vs. 12-15).
> Evil-doers (v. 16).
> Believers (vs. 17-20).
> Evil-doers (v. 21).
> Believers (v. 22).

The Psalm is a prophecy. It deals with
the government of God in the earth; His
permitting His people to be oppressed; His
ultimate deliverance of them; and His
destruction of their foes.

In inviting His people to unite with Him
in praising Jehovah, the Messiah encourages
them by pointing to His own experience
(vs. 4 and 6) and to the experience of others
in whom He dwells (vs. 5 and 7).

This is the first interlocutory Psalm. There
are others, such as xci. and cxlv.

The Holy Spirit quotes verse 8 in 1 Pet.
ii. 3, and verses 12-15 in 1 Pet. iii. 10-12).

Only such a faith as the Messiah had could
bless Jehovah at all times. A carnal faith
can bless God in prosperous times only.
"Humble" (v. 2) should read "oppressed."
That which they hear with joy is the
resurrection of Christ (v. 4). He was rescued
from all His fears in Sheol. He was the
Poor Man (v. 6) Whom Jehovah heard and

rescued. He was rescued out of all His
troubles (v. 6); and His people shall be
rescued out of all their troubles (v. 17).

In resurrection (v. 3) He invites His people
to unite with Him in praise; and in verse 5
He reminds them that their comrades looked
with expectation during all the time of their
oppression to Jehovah, and as a consequence,
their faces became radiant. To look at self
(Ps. lxxvii.) clothes the face with misery; to
look at man (Ps. lxxiii.) clothes it with
distraction; to look at God makes it shine
(Ps. xxxiv). So was it with Moses (2 Cor. iii.).

The Hebrew verb "to encamp" is related
to the name Maha-naim, i.e., "two camps"
(Gen. xxxii. 1-2). One was Jacob's feeble
camp; the other, the encompassing camp of
God's mighty angels (2 Kings vi. 17).

The Divine title "The Angel of Jehovah"
(v.7) only occurs here and in Ps. xxxv.5 and 6—
here for deliverance, and there for destruction. An angel delivered Peter and
destroyed Herod (Acts xii.).

The second section (v. 11) should commence thus: "Come, ye sons of men, hearken
unto Me . . . What man is he," etc.

Guided by Exod. xii. 46 and John xix. 36,
verses 19 and 20 read thus: "Many shall
be the afflictions of the Righteous One, but
Jehovah shall deliver Him out of them all.
He shall keep all His bones; not one of them
shall be broken." His people are "of His
bones" (Eph. v. 30), so not one of them shall
be broken. They are eternally safe in Him
and with Him. He was heart-broken
(Ps. lxix. 20), but not bone broken.

"Desolate" (v. 21) should read "condemned," as in the R.V.

The gift of this prophecy at such a crisis in
David's life emphasizes the truth that
salvation and inspiration are both based upon
the principle of grace and not of merit.
Moses, David, Isaiah, Peter, Paul, etc.,
illustrate the fact. It was when broken or
contrite or mortified or ashamed, and so
made conscious of their moral worthlessness,
that they could be used as spiritual channels.
Isa. vi. and Luke xxii. 32 are notable illustrations. Self-adulation could not therefore
be indulged.

PSALM XXXV.—The Lamb of God is here
seen among the wolves of Satan, and His
cries to God when surrounded by them are
recorded in this prophecy. The Messiah Himself speaks, as is clear from John xv.20-25.

The prophecy relates to His rejection and crucifixion. With Ps. xxii. it teaches that atonement is the basis of salvation and the foundation of eternal glory, and that the advent of the Messiah revealed the love of God's heart to man and the hatred of man's heart to God (John xv. 23). Righteousness judges hatred and love. The one is justly condemned (vs. 4, 8 and 26); the other adequately described (vs. 13 and 14).

Many think that this Psalm, and others of a similar character, should be removed from the Psalter. They say that no Christian person should pray so vindictively.

It would certainly be improper for David, or any other sinful man, to present such petitions to God. But in such Psalms the Petitioner is the Sinless Man Christ Jesus, and He fittingly calls for the Divine judgment upon those who hate Him; for in hating Him, they hate God and His people, and goodness, righteousness and truth. Hence, when judging the Pharisees (Matt. xxiii. 13-36) He used language of similar terrific import; and in Matt. xiii, and related prophecies, He predicts that He will destroy and cast out of His kingdom all who hate goodness and practice iniquity.

Some of these petitions for judgment are personal to Himself, and others affect His oppressed and hated people. Whilst it is not fitting for them to cry for vengeance upon their tormentors, it is most fitting for Him, in their interest, to do so.

In the Psalm His enemies unjustly accuse Him (v. 11). He calls on God to vindicate Him (vs. 23 and 24), and invites His people, in expectation of that vindication, to join Him in a song of praise (vs. 9, 10, 27 and 28)

This prophecy, with other Scriptures, strengthened His faith and made brave His heart prior to, and during, the trial in the palace of Caiaphas. This is evident from His quotation of verse 19 when on the way to the Garden of Gethsemane (John xv. 25).

" To seek after the soul " (v. 4) means to kill, and " to devise hurt " here predicts the agonizing form of death by crucifixion, for such was the death by which in their hatred they planned to " hurt " Him.

The Angel of Jehovah who pursues the haters of goodness in order to destroy them (vs. 5 and 6) is the same Angel that camps about the lovers of truth in order to deliver them (xxxiv. 7).

Every part of Christ's physical body praised God (v. 10); and every member of His mystical body unites with Him in magnifying God. Compare Deut. xxxii. 31, xxxiii. 26 and 27, 1 Sam. ii. 2, and Ps: lxxi. 19, lxxiii. 25, and lxxxix. 6.

The false witnesses of verses 11 and 20 are those of Matt. xxvi. 60 and xxvii. 40.

" To spoil the soul " (v. 12) means to put to death. His enemies rewarded Him evil for good even to the extent of killing Him. He loved them, but they hated Him (vs. 11-16), and that hatred was causeless (John xv. 25 and Rom. iii. 24). From these false accusations He appeals to the righteous judgment of God (vs. 17, 22, 23, and 24).

The petitions of verses 4-8 are also predictions—notably those of verse 8 in regard to Judas.

The words " I knew not " (v. 11) mean " I was not conscious of "; and " I knew not " (v. 15) either means " I knew them not," or the statement relates to the secrecy of the murderous plans of " the abjects." The Hebrew verb here translated " to know " has many meanings in English.

" Humbled " (v. 13) should read " afflicted," as in the R.V. " My darling " (v. 17) i.e., His body, unique, sinless. and specially prepared for Him by God (Heb. x. 5). See note on Ps. xxii. 20. This prayer was answered (Matt. xxvii. 57-60).

" The mighty people " of verse 18 R.V margin, are the people of Israel.

" Judgment " and " judge " (vs. 23 and 24) mean " vindication " and " vindicate."

When the Pharisees had Him hanging naked upon the tree, they rejoiced at His hurt, i.e., His agony (v. 26). Righteousness justly demands that their only clothing shall be shame, and their " hurt " the second death (Rev. ii. 11).

Verse 27 should read: " Let them shout for joy and be glad that favour My justification," i.e., My vindication. The verse expresses the joy of the redeemed at God's vindication of Christ in raising Him from among the dead and granting Him eternal prosperity. Christ was Jehovah's Servant.

The Messiah (v. 23) addresses Jehovah as " My God and My Lord." Thomas (John xx. 28) worshipped the Messiah saying, " My Lord and My God." These Scriptures together proclaim the Deity and Godhead of Jesus Christ.

The Great High Priest of His people (v. 28)

promises unending praise to God throughout an eternal day.

PSALM XXXVI.—The following translation of the superscription, the ellipses being supplied, is suggested :
" For the Chief Musician. Relating to the Servant of Jehovah. Given by the Holy Spirit to David." Compare the superscription of Ps. xviii.

The Saviour's atoning work, the theme of Ps. xxxv, is here applied to the sinner for whom He died (v. 1-4) ; and its moral effect in changing him into a good and happy man described (vs. 7-12).

The structure of the Psalm may be thus exhibited :

Description of the sinner,   vs. 1-4.
The saving grace of the Saviour,   vs. 5-6.
Happy state of the forgiven sinner, vs. 7-9.
His prayer to the Saviour,   vs. 10-12.

The following translation of the first two verses is proposed : " Transgression speaketh as an oracle to the self-willed man, within his heart (LXX). There is no fear of God before his eyes. For it (transgression) flatters him in his own eyes that his iniquity will never be found out and be punished."

Transgression against God's revealed law does not merely speak to his heart, but, as an enthroned oracle, speaks within it, and has an accepted dominion over it. The moral consequence is that his words are impure and false ; he ceases to be wise and to do good ; he plans, when in bed, injury to his neighbours ; he resolutely enters upon a course of evil ; and no longer shrinks from what is sinful (vs. 3 and 4).

Such a man would find no compassion on earth, but the grace that is born in the heavens and written upon the clouds, as exhibited in the prior Psalm, can pity and save just such a sinner.

Hence the second section of the Psalm (vs. 5 and 6) presents the Saviour in His fulness, lauds His loving kindness, His faithfulness, His righteousness, His judgments, His keeping power, and declares that these attributes are not for the annihilation of His creatures, but for their preservation.

The third section of the Psalm (vs. 7-9) pictures the happiness of the kingdom of love into which the Saviour introduces the sinner of verses 1-4, now pardoned and cleansed.

He finds safety (v. 7) ; abundant provision (v. 8) ; unfailing pleasures (v. 8) ; perpetuity (v. 9) ; and light (v. 9).

A place of safety without food, happiness and light, would be useless to a fugitive needing these things ; and these things without perpetuity would bring no real peace to the heart.

The prayer of the fourth section of the Psalm is a dual one—a prayer of desire (v. 10) and a prayer of apprehension (vs. 11 and 12).

The prayer of desire is : O draw out at length (marg.) Thy loving-kindness, etc., that is,—I have begun to drink of that sweet cup, O continue to give me rich draughts of it ! I have begun to experience Thy power to make me holy, O make me as holy as a pardoned sinner can be made !

The prayer of apprehension is : By nature my foot is proud and my hand is wicked. Shield me from their power. I am surrounded by men of proud feet and wicked hands. O let me not be influenced by them, for they lead and push men into that deep pit into which evildoers shall fall, out of which they will desire to rise but will not be able, for they shall be eternally thrust down into it (R.V.) ; and their ever-enduring and conscious misery will be sharpened by the knowledge that their own sin and rebellion caused them to be justly shut up in that dark prison house of death.

The word " there " (v. 12) means that place to which the proud foot and the wicked hand move and lead. The doctrine of the verse destroys the popular theory of annihilation.

PSALM XXXVII.—To the redeemed sinner of Ps. xxxvi, cleansed by the atoning blood of Ps. xxxv, the Great Shepherd now says, Fret not thyself because of the mysterious prosperity of the wicked (vs. 1-11) and because of the murderous hatred of the world (vs. 12-15 and 32) ; and He adds that such prosperity and such hatred will be short-lived, and that ever-enduring prosperity and infinite and eternal love will be enjoyed by him, if he keeps trusting the Shepherd, for He promises to most certainly deliver him and enrich him for ever (vs. 17-40).

Thus this Psalm anticipates the two principal difficulties which confuse and discourage beginners in the Christian life. That they should be hated by their fellowmen because they have become followers of

Christ, is unexpected and painful, and that evil-doers should prosper is confounding. With what perfect understanding of the poor human heart, and with what exquisite tenderness does the Messiah in this Psalm again and again say, Don't fret thyself (vs. 1, 7, and 8) ; keep trusting (v. 3) ; and delighting (v. 4) ; and committing (v. 5) ; and waiting (v. 7) ; and He keeps repeating His promises as to the speedy disappearance of the wicked (vs. 2, 9, 10, 13, 15, 17, 20, etc.). He assures him that He will hold him by His hand (v. 24) : that He will enrich him (v. 29 and 34) ; and, finally, most surely deliver Him (v. 40).

The Psalm is for the heart, and bids it contemplate the Great Shepherd as He loves and guards and vindicates His people. Contrast vs. 1-4 of the prior psalm.

The lessons taught are to wait on God and to wait for God when perplexed by the prosperity of evil-doers, and when oppressed by them ; not to become heated with vexation (vs. 1, 7, 8) ; and not to grow angry and retaliate, for Messiah will vindicate His people when slandered (v. 6), deliver them when persecuted (v. 40), and establish them as the rulers of the world (vs. 9 and 10). As to the power and prosperity of their enemies, that is only temporary (vs. 2, 9, 13, 15, 17, 20, 22, 28, 34, 36 and 38). The term " day " (v. 13) signifies punishment.

Messiah Himself, in the days of His flesh, when in the midst of His foes, perfectly learned and lived the lessons of this Psalm.

As a prophecy, it will have its fulfilment during Israel's future " time of trouble " (v. 39) when under the oppression of Anti-Christ. It has, at the same time, counsel and comfort for the people of God in any dispensation when perplexed and persecuted.

" Judgment " (v. 6) should read " vindication," and verse 11 is quoted in Matt. v. 5.

The Psalm is an acrostic in the Hebrew Bible. There are 22 stanzas, each commencing with the successive letter of the twenty-two letters of the Hebrew alphabet. Each stanza contains four lines except verses 7, 20, and 34 (in the English Bible) which have only three lines each. This is evidently designed, and is very beautiful.

PSALM XXXVIII.—The last four Psalms (xxxviii-xli) of Book I correspond to the four last Psalms of Book II (lxix-lxxii). The title : " A Psalm to bring to remembrance " common to Ps. xxxviii and lxx, helps to show the correspondence. There are many other links connecting these two groups of Psalms.

The theme of the first group is the personal and sympathetic sufferings of Messiah as Man and Priest. His sufferings as Man were personal ;   His sufferings as Priest, sympathetic and representative.

The theme of the second group is His rejection as Redeemer and His exaltation as Governor.

These groups of Psalms cause these great subjects to be brought to remembrance in order to be kept in remembrance. His atoning death and His coming glory are inseparable from a true remembrance of Him (Luke xxii. 19 and 1 Cor. xi. 26).

The Psalm contains six members :

Prayer—" Do not rebuke me."	v. 1.
Sin and its suffering.	vs. 2-10.
Man and his hatred.	vs. 11-16.
Sin and its sorrow.	vs. 17 and 18.
Man and his hatred.	vs. 19 and 20.
Prayer—" Do not forsake me."	v. 21.

The Psalm reveals the thoughts that filled the heart of Jesus up to, and upon the Cross. The statements of verse 13 link the Psalm to Ps. xxii, Isa. liii, 2 Cor. v. 21, 1 Pet. ii. 22 24, etc. It describes His sympathetic intercession for His people, justly suffering the wrath of God because of their sins ; and it records the hatred and ingratitude of those who ought to have loved Him. He came unto His own but His own received Him not. Himself sinless, He here loads Himself with the believer's sins ; makes full confession of them ; admits the justice of the Divine wrath against them ; and utters no reproach against those members of His nation who sought to destroy Him. He does not excuse or belittle sin ; nor does He murmur at the wrath of God against it. He magnifies that wrath, and reposes in the righteousness of the Judge of all the earth.

What a possession to have a Priest who can perfectly fulfil the Divine requirements, and who can furnish to His people in all dispensations a fitting vehicle of language with which to approach God in confession and prayer !

" Loathsome disease " (v. 7) should read " burning fever." Verse 10 pictures an over-loaded porter about to faint. There are three lines in verse 12 : Action (" they lay snares ") ;   speech (" they speak mischievous things ") ;   motive (" they imagine deceits "). " All the day long " i.e., " the long day " of their hatred (vs. 6 and 12).

Before men the Lamb of God was dumb (vs. 13 and 14) ; before God, He was eloquent (vs. 15 and 16).

This latter verse may perhaps, read thus : " Hear me lest they rejoice over Me ; lest if My foot slips, they magnify themselves against Me."

The great High Priest teaches that sin and its consequences are more to be feared than man and his hatreds. Sin is worse than suffering.

Jeduthan was possibly the name of the chief musician. This may be the subscription to Ps. xxxviii. See Hab. iii. 19.

PSALM XXXIX.—The theme and circumstances of the prior Psalm are here continued. Elect Israel suffers from the hand of God and from the hand of man (vs. 8 and 10) ; the pressure of the one hand, just, the pressure of the other, unjust. Their Great High Priest prays with them and for them ; furnishes their lips with the language they should use in confession, supplication and deprecation ; urges the sinlessness and perfection of His own nature as a plea on their behalf why they should be heard and delivered ; and instructs them as to their feelings and conduct toward their prosperous and persecuting enemies (vs. 1-5). They are neither to rebuke their foes nor rebel against God (v. 9). They are to trust Him though He smites them ; and, themselves lighter than vanity and but the creatures of a day, yet are they to wait for Him to deliver them from the pride of man (vs. 5-7). Thus the Great Shepherd takes His place at the head of the flock ; associates Himself with the many sons in their sorrows and sufferings, He Himself having suffered ; and leads them to glory.

So the Psalm is a development of verses 12-14 of the prior Psalm. The wicked spake " mischievous things " against Him. They said He was possessed by a demon ; that He was a glutton and a drunkard ; a boon companion of debauched men ; a blasphemer of God ; and a transgressor of the law. He calls these " my transgressions " (v. 8) i.e., the transgressions that they heaped upon Him. He, in the wonders of His grace, took upon Himself the very sin which they committed in thus falsely accusing Him, and confessed it as His own ! Although He could have confounded them with a

fitting (" good ") reply (v. 2) yet He remained dumb before them (v. 1), His heart stirred with sorrow for them (v. 2), whilst at the same time it felt the biting flame of their cruel words (v. 3). But though dumb before men He was eloquent before God (vs. 3-13) ; as Man He recalled the brevity of human life (vs. 4 and 5) ; and its vanity (v. 6) ; and He reposed on the knowledge that His life of shame and sorrow and rejection had been ordained for Him (v. 9). But that knowledge did not make Him insensible or stoical ; and accordingly He cried for relief from the pressure of that afflicting Hand (v. 10), whilst recognizing its justice (v. 11) ; and, citing His own preciousness to God, He prayed for strength to pursue this path of affliction until the day dawned when He would go hence to the glory from whence He came, and be no more afflicted (vs. 12 and 13).

The Psalm contains two stanzas. The first, verses 1-8 ; the second, verses 9-13 ; and their subject matter corresponds.

There was only one Man Who could bridle His tongue and Who did not sin with His lips, and He was the sinless Son of Man (v. 1). This sinlessness triumphed even while viewing the prosperity of the wicked and suffering their hatred and false and bitter reproaches (vs. 1 and 8).

" Good " (v. 2) means fitting or effective, that is, a fitting reply to the falsehoods of the wicked. " Frail " (v. 4) means short-lived ; and " age " (v. 5) means life-time.

When speech is uttered in relief of feeling (v. 3) the High Priest instructs His people (vs. 4-8) not to retort to the wicked but to seek from God forgiveness for their own transgressions, and for a just conception of their own nothingness and of man's emptiness. If Christian people followed this instruction they would bring glory to their Master and salvation to their calumniators.

The believer does not wait for riches but for God (vs. 6 and 7), Who is all his expectation.

" Blow " (v. 10) rather " pressure"

2 Sam. xvi . 10 illustrates verse 9.

The sense of verse 13 is : Ease the pressure of Thine afflicting Hand that I may thereby be comforted for a little, before I go hence and be no more afflicted.

PSALM XL.—The Holy Spirit in Heb. x. declares the Messiah to be the Author of this Psalm. This is a fact of the very greatest importance. It furnishes the key for the interpretation of the entire Book of the Psalms. The theme of the Psalm is His sufferings and glories as the Redeemer, High Priest and Commander of His people. As their Redeemer, He atones for their sins, having loaded Himself with them and confessed them as His own. As their Priest, He burdens Himself with their sorrows, encourages them to follow Him in His life of absolute confidence in God, teaches them to believe in promises which never fail, and furnishes them with perfect forms of confession, prayer and praise. As their Commander he engages to deliver them. (Isa. lv. 4).

The first eight verses relate to His incarnation (vs. 6 and 7), to His atoning sacrifice (v. 8), and to His glorious resurrection (v. 1-3). His life of perfect testimony appears in verses 9 and 10 (fulfilled in John xvii. 6, 8, 14) ; the hostility of man is the subject of verses 11-15 ; the felicity of His disciples is predicted in verse 16 ; and the prayer that was answered in verse 1 is found in verse 17.

The doctrine of the Psalm is Christ's perfect obedience to the will of God as the Sin-Bearer of His people, and His perfect patience in waiting on and for God to deliver Him and them out of all their afflictions. The perfection of His confidence and obedience is seen in His not shirking, or shrinking from, any trial however bitter, or in taking matters into His own hands out of the hands of God, as, for example, in sending for twelve legions of angels, or in drinking the stupefying myrrh, or in fearing to face man and preaching to Him righteousness. He sought no outlet or escape from indignities, sorrows, shame, or wrath. The Psalm points to the reward which crowned this perfect obedience (vs. 1-3).

The result of coming to do the Father's will, of delighting to do it, and of revealing God's heart to man, was to bring Him into the greatest distress on earth and to plunge Him into the horrible pit of Sheol.

The first three verses give the answer to the prayer of the last verse. Faith loves to record the answer before setting out the prayer. He was brought up out of a double Sheol, the Sheol of man's hatred (" the miry clay ") and the Sheol of God's wrath (" the horrible pit ").

The " New Song "(v. 3) is the Resurrection song. See note on Ps. xxiii. 3. On the Resurrection morn it was new in fact, but not in purpose.

The " many " who trust and worship God (v. 3), encouraged by the example of the Redeemer, are the countless multitude of the Redeemed.

The " proud " of verse 4 are the self-righteous, and those who turn aside to lies are the idolators. Their misery contrasts with the happiness of believers.

The words " our " (v. 3) and " usward " (v. 5) mark the association of the Messiah with His people.

A literal translation of the closing words of verse 5 is suggested : " None can set them in order before Thee : I will declare and speak of them ; they are more than can be numbered." Man cannot enumerate God's works or reveal His thoughts ; but Messiah can both declare them and speak of them.

The sense of verse 6 is found in Heb. x : " A body hast Thou prepared Me." God prepared a sinless body for His obedient Servant, and so perfect was His obedience, that the entire body is imaged as an ear. There is no reference to Exod. xxi. 6.

The Divine displeasure with sacrifice and offering is defined in Heb. x. as displeasure with them as types and symbols, and it does not conflict with God's infinite delight in the one great sacrifice of Calvary. The contrast, on the contrary, heightens that delight.

The four great offerings—the burnt-offering, the meal-offering, the sin-offering, and the peace-offering, four aspects of Christ's one great offering of Himself—are intended in verse 6.

The words " Lo I come " (v. 7) signalize His incarnation, and the words " I delight to do " (v. 8) His immolation. The " Book " is the Bible. In that book it was " engraved " concerning Him that He was to be born as a Man and suffer as a Sacrifice. The argument and declaration of these two verses (7 and 8) are : That incarnation and atonement were necessary because so predicted of Him and prescribed to Him in the Scriptures ; and the statement is made that He delighted to obey these prescriptions, for they were not only in The Book, but also in His heart.

Verses 9 and 10 declare how faithfully He revealed God's righteousness, faithfulness, salvation, loving kindness and truth to man when on earth. John xvii. records the fulfilment of this prediction.

The result was hatred from man, as stated in verse 12. Hence in verse 11 He cries that God should show Him tender pity and kindness and fidelity, for He met with none of these from man.

Calamities and afflictions in the sense of "evils" and "iniquities" (v. 12) result from sin. See the intensive meanings of the Hebrew words. But these sorrows and troubles did not result from Messiah's sins, for He had none, but from the sins of those whom He came to save. These griefs so bent Him down that He was not able to look up, and they enfeebled His physical powers so that His heart fainted. He said "My soul is exceeding sorrowful, even unto death." Never was there sorrow in this world comparable to His !

Sinlessness, when face to face with the wickedness that rejected the teaching of verse 10 and hung upon the tree the Teacher, justly prays the prayer of verses 14 and 15. These verses are also a prediction foretelling the doom of these haters of the Messiah, just as verse 16 predicts the salvation and felicity of His lovers. (2 Thess. 1. 6-10).

Some are poor and some are needy, but only One was, in the fullest sense, at the same time, both poor and needy.

PSALM XLI.—This Psalm closes the First or Genesis Book of the Psalms. As Genesis opens with the First Adam in blessing and closes with his children in affliction, so this First Book of the Psalms opens with the Second Man in blessing and closes with His people in affliction. The Pharaoh of Israel's first affliction prefigures the Anti-Christ of Israel's future and last affliction.

The Poor Man of xl. 17 is the Messiah ; the sick and faint man of xli. 1 represents His people.

The statements in Matt. xxv. 36 and in John xiii. 18 establish the relationship of this Psalm to Messiah and His people.

The Psalm is prophetic ; and, whilst having a general application, it mainly concerns the future sufferings of Israel under Anti-Christ —sufferings permitted by God in just punishment of their sins (v. 4). Israel is pictured as sick and faint (vs. 1, 3 and 8). The word " poor " in Hebrew means sick and faint. It is not the same word as poor in the last verse of the prior Psalm. God's future loving sympathy to the fainting Elect of Israel (v. 3) is here contrasted with man's

duplicity and heartlessness (vs. 5-8). He promises blessing to anyone who concerns himself with these sick ones (v. 1). As for these poor sufferers themselves, He promises to deliver them in their " time of trouble " ; to preserve them ; to keep them alive ; to bless them in the earth ; to defend them from their enemies; to strengthen them under trial; and to mitigate their sufferings (vs. 2 and 3). So did He preserve them alive and save them from the will of Pharaoh when he planned their destruction. It is here suggested that the " him " of verses 1-3 means Israel under affliction. Whoever " considers," i.e. ministers to this afflicted people will be blessed by God.

Messiah confesses their sin, thereby admitting the justice of their punishment (v. 4) ; He defines the conduct of their enemies as hatred against Himself, which indeed it was in its fulness and malignity (vs. 5-9) ; associating them with Himself, He prays that God would raise them up from their couch of affliction, so that He could execute a just judgment upon their oppressors (v. 10), as He did upon Pharaoh and the Egyptians ; He predicts victory for them over their enemies because God tenderly loved both Him and them (v. 11) ; and as to Himself, personally, He asserts that because of His sinlessness (" integrity ") He will be seated upon the throne of glory for ever. Thus this verse answers the question of Ps. xxiv. 3.

The Philippian jailer (Acts xvii.), when bathing the wounds and furnishing food to the sick and fainting apostles, illustrated v. 1.

The promise of blessing in the earth (v. 2) points to millennial felicity and resurrection glory.

The " Thou wilt " of verse 2 and that of verse 3, form a beautiful double interruption to the meditation and statements of the verses.

There is no conflict between the sinfulness of verse 4 and the sinlessness of verse 12. The one is priestly ; the other, personal. His association with the guilty people of His love was love indeed ! His confession of their sin (v. 4) drew out their hatred to Him (v. 5). Man is self-righteous, resents exposure, and refuses to acknowledge his sinfulness.

Evil-doers hate Him and His people. They desire the destruction of both. They treat them with falsehood, malice and slander. They speak vanity, that is, they make lying professions of sympathy, but their hearts invent malicious falsehoods and they then go forth to publish them.   Judas was the embodiment of all such treachery (vs. 5–9).

The double "me" of verse 10 means Israel ; the "I" means Messiah. Vengeance is His, and He will repay.

The tenderly loved one of verse 11 R.V. is Israel ; the Sinless One of verse 12 is Messiah.

The whole Psalm illustrates the love of Him Who makes His people so truly one with Himself that, in the coming judgment, He will say to those who "considered" them, "I was sick and ye visited Me!" (Matt. xxv. 36).

THE PSALMS

BOOK II

This Book comprises xlii-lxxii. Its theme, like that of the second book of Moses, is the redemption of a multitude of slaves and their elevation into a nation. Hence it opens with a people sunk in misery (Ps. xlii.) and closes with a King reigning in glory (Ps. lxxii).

As Book I, in correspondence with Genesis, treats of Jehovah in covenant relationship to man, so Book II, in harmony with Exodus, treats of Elohim in creative relationship to Israel. Accordingly the Divine title Jehovah occurs two hundred and seventy-nine times in Book I, and only thirty-seven times in Book II, whilst Elohim appears two hundred and sixty-two times in Book II, and only forty-eight times in Book I.

Book II is composed of three sections: Israel's affliction, Ps. xlii-xlix; her Redeemer Ps. l-lx; and her deliverance, Ps. lxi-lxxii.

The Divine title, Jah, is first mentioned in Book II of the Psalms, as it is also first mentioned in Book II of the Pentateuch.

PSALM XLII.—This Psalm gives a fore-picture of Israel when, as Lo-Ammi and out of covenant relationship with Jehovah, and suffering the oppression of Anti-Christ, she will cast herself for deliverance upon God as Elohim.

The speaker is the Messiah. He takes His place with the oppressed as Moses did; fitly voices their cry of anguish and of faith; makes God their sufficing portion in the absence of all prosperity; and expresses a thirst and affection for God and a confidence in Him such as Israel ought to express.

Thus in all circumstances whether in the land or exiled from it, whether as Ammi or Lo-Ammi, the Messiah is, and always will be, for Israel, before God, what she ought to be, so that God perpetually finds in Immanuel's cries for mercy and pardon, and in His songs of faith and praise, all that His nature and heart demand.

This is the first of the eleven Psalms for the sons of Korah—xlii-xlix, lxxxiv-lxxxviii (xlii and xliii counted as one Psalm, and lxxxvi omitted because given to David). Korah himself died under the wrath of God (Num. xvi. 31); but his children were spared (Num. xxvi. 11). These special Psalms, therefore, sing of redeeming grace.

This forty-second Psalm exhibits the perfection of the faith, and the warmth of an affection, which make God everything, when by His just judgment nothing remains but poverty, helplessness and oppression.

The scoffing question "Where is Thy God?" (v. 3) caused more pain (v. 10) to the heart of the Lord Jesus when on the Cross than the nails caused to His body. This third verse shows that this taunt was levelled at Him during His ministry as well as during His final agony. Satan, for example, in the first temptation practically said, "Where is Thy God?"; and the Pharisees in effect repeated the mocking question when they demanded of Him a sign from heaven. This very taunt will be addressed to the unhappy Sons of Israel by the Anti-Christ and his people in the coming "time of trouble" (Joel ii. 17).

The word "when" (v. 4) should be omitted and the verse should read: "These things I remember, i.e., the things set out in verses 1-3, and so "I pour out My soul in Me" in desire and prayer and sorrow mainly because of the taunt "Where is Thy God?" Then the second half of the verse reads: 'For I shall go with the multitude" etc. Thus faith in a time of great darkness believes the promise and looks forward to its realization. So did Moses in Egypt (Heb. xi. 25 and 26); and no doubt so did God's "hidden ones" during the more than two hundred years of slavery under which they groaned beneath the scourge of the Egyptians.

If the translation "I had gone," etc., be adopted as well as the translation "I shall

331

go," etc., then the verse unites the past with the future. In the past, Israel, delivered from the bondage of Pharaoh, went up in festive array to the house of God with Moses their king and priest at their head (Exod. xl. 34). As to the future, Israel shall go up to the house of the Lord on Mount Zion with songs and everlasting joy upon their heads (Isa. xxxv. 10, Heb. ii. 10, Rev. vii. 9, etc.). The Redeemer's soul shall be satisfied (Isa. liii. 11) ; but only a countless " multitude " keeping holiday will satisfy the affections of that great heart.

It is the popular interpretation that the words of verse 4 were uttered by David when fleeing from Absalom ; but the use of the future tense in the Hebrew text, and the absence of David's name in the superscription, militate against this supposition.

The faith that boldly says (vs. 5 and 11) " I shall yet praise Him," is the same that testifies in verse 4 " I shall go up to the House of God."

" The land of Jordan," etc., describes a position of exile from the land of promise, while verses 7 and 9 predict the sufferings of Israel ; but only of Messiah Himself could it be fully said that all the waves and billows of the Divine wrath went over Him.

The words " help " (v. 5) and " health " (v. 11) mean salvation. The word " countenance " is a figure of speech for the entire person. Accepting the Hebrew text, " His countenance " (v. 11) as accurate, and combining these verses, the sense of both is, that the apparition of Messiah will occasion Israel's deliverance from suffering and oppression, and that the joy of that deliverance will be seen on Israel's face.

Thus in the Psalm Messiah speaks personally and representatively, and so unites His beloved people with Himself that He makes similar language common to both.

PSALM XLIII.—This Psalm is a continuance of the prior one. The Messiah prays that God would plead the cause of His people ; deliver them from the power of a cruel nation ; and vindicate their character from the false and unjust slanders of man (v. 1). He asks why does God seemingly forget them, and why does He permit them to mourn in affliction all the time that their oppressors rejoice in prosperity (v. 2). He instructs them not to take matters into their own hands and strike at their oppressors,

but to trust " light " and " truth " to lead them into God's goodly land (v. 3) ; and, on their behalf, He promises to lead a song of praise to God upon Mount Sion (v. 4). He assures them that they will certainly be there because God is both their Redeemer and their God ; and, meanwhile, under affliction, He makes their depression and disquietude of heart His own (v. 5).

The interpretation of the prophecy belongs to the darkest hour of Jacob's future " time of trouble," but an illustration and an experience of it is furnished by Moses and was enjoyed by him. Israel suffered oppression from the Egyptians—" an ungodly nation," and from Pharaoh—" the deceitful and unjust man." God was Jacob's Strength in that time of trouble, though for upwards of two hundred years He had apparently cast them off. The pillar of fire and of truth led them to the tabernacle of Divine worship and fellowship, where with harps they sang their Redeemer's praise. In a greater and more wondrous day the Elect of Israel will sing with the Lamb of God upon Mount Sion, as predicted in verse 5 and Rev. xiv.

" Judge me " (v. 1) means " vindicate me." The " altar " (v. 4) i.e., atonement is the foundation of praise.

Only the Messiah could truly say that God was His exceeding joy, (v. 4) i.e., the perfection of a perfect joy ; and only He could worthily offer in sacrifice a promised praise ; yet in His grace He credits His people with all that is properly only His ; He makes their fears and sorrows His own ; and endows their service and worship with beauties and perfections which are proper to Himself.

PSALM XLIV.—The superscription does not say to whom the Spirit gave this Psalm. Its theme suggests that it was given to Hezekiah under the circumstances recorded in 2 Kings xviii. and xix. 2 Chron. xxxii. and Isa. xxxvi. and xxxvii. A three-fold record by the Holy Spirit of any matter marks its exceptional importance, and declares its moral import to be of special value. Hezekiah and his fellow-believers must have been animated by this revelation of the Spirit when suffering the oppression of the Assyrian and grieved by the reproaches and blasphemies of his captains (2 Kings xix. 22.)

Judah was reduced to the last extremity (vs. 9–14); Hezekiah's face was clothed with shame and his mind filled with confusion (v. 15); the Assyrian general stood before the walls of Jerusalem, Judah's last uncaptured city, taunting and blaspheming (v. 16); though sore broken and threatened with death, Judah, unlike Israel, still clung to the Law and to Jehovah, secretly in their hearts as well as publicly in their worship (v. 17–21), a proof of their fidelity to Him being that for His sake they were continually being destroyed (v. 22); they recalled His favour to their forefathers (vs. 1–3); they appealed to Him to deliver them out of their present distresses (vs. 23–26); they protested that they would not trust in their own military resources (v. 6); and they confidently declared their assurance of victory if He commanded deliverance for them (vs. 4–8). Historically, therefore, the " we " and the " us " may intend Judah, and the " I " and " my," Hezekiah.

This is the third of the thirteen Maschil Psalms and the second of the eleven Korah Psalms.

Prophetically, the Psalm is a fore-picture of the affliction of the believing remnant of Israel under the oppression of Anti-Christ, and it records the cry for deliverance which the Messiah will then make on their behalf for them. He it is Who uses the words " I " and " My " respectively, and Who associates the sufferers with Himself in the words " us " and " our " and " we." He, therefore, for Himself, and for them, can use the language of verses 17–22 in a sense much deeper than it could have been used by Hezekiah and Judah.

The Psalm contains two sections—the First (vs. 1–8), belonging to the past and future; the Second (vs. 9–26), descriptive of the present. The past reviews the victory of Joshua over the Canaanites, and the planting of Israel in their lands (vs. 1–3), and states that grace and not merit was the procuring cause of their establishment in Canaan; and the argument based upon these facts is (vs. 4–8): That the God who showed such favour to Joshua was Hezekiah's king and is Messiah's king. Let Him command deliverance for unworthy and stumbling Jacob and the sure result will be victory (vs. 5–7); and the praise will be His for ever (v. 8).

In verse 2 the word " them " which occurs twice means Israel (R.V.); and " the heathen" and " the peoples " are the Canaanites.

A beautiful instance of faith's usage of the past tense when intending the future is seen in verse 7. Prophetically it reads, " Thou shalt save us and shalt put to shame those that hate us "; but confidently it declares, " Thou hast saved us," etc. So the believer in the Lord Jesus Christ can confidently say " I am saved, for I have been saved, and I shall be saved."

The Holy Spirit quotes verse 22 in Rom. viii. 36. It records a principle and fact true of all dispensations.

Guided by Hab. iii. 19 the superscription to the Psalm states that it was handed to the Chief Musician for public use at the great Spring festival, the Passover; for the word Shoshannim, that is, lilies, possibly may, by a double figure of speech, symbolize the Spring, and, therefore, the Passover.

PSALM XLV.—The word " loves " in the superscription is probably the Hebrew plural of excellency, so that the Title may read: A Song of Supreme Love, i.e., Messiah's love for Jerusalem as a bridegroom for a bride (Isa. lxii. 5).

It is possible that the Psalm was given by inspiration to Isaiah on the occasion of the marriage of Hezekiah with Hephzibah (2 Kings xxi. 1 and Isa. lxii. 4).

The interpretation of the Psalm as Messianic is decided in Heb. i, and His Godhead affirmed.

The Psalm introduces the Deliverer prayed for in the three prior Psalms. His apparition changes everything, and throws a bright ray of sunshine upon the dark background of those Psalms. It is a precious instance of the power of a Divine faith to occupy itself with such glories when surrounded by such terrors. So, doubtless, Hezekiah and his companions sang this song of conjugal love within the walls of Jerusalem when shut in by the Assyrian host.

So will it be in the future. At the moment of Israel's greatest distress (Zech. xiv. 2, 3) Messiah will appear (vs. 3–5), will marry Jerusalem (vs. 9–15), and will destroy her oppressors. The result will be that Israel's future glory will eclipse her past splendours (vs. 16 and 17). See Rev. xix. and Ps. xlvii. 3.

The Introduction may read thus: " My heart overflows with a goodly theme. I must speak! The theme concerns the King!

My tongue is like the pen of a ready writer."

In conformity with this introduction the language of the Psalm is abrupt, as is the case when words burst from the heart.

There is no contradiction between verse 2 and Isa. liii. 2. The one statement affects His first advent ; the other, His second.

The words "because of" (v. 4) should read "on behalf of." The whole passage (vs. 3–5) describes Messiah's destruction of Anti-Christ, and all Israel's enemies (Rev. xix.)

The Deity of Christ (" O God ") and His humanity ("Thy fellows ") are asserted in verse 7. In this verse man is Christ's fellow ; in Zech. xiii. 7, God is His fellow.

Verse 8 should read as in the R.V. ; and in verse 9 " did " should read " doth."

The sense of verse 13 is : The King's daughter, i.e., the bride, is seated in splendour within her palace ; her clothing is made with tissue of gold.

In the East the bride, in her wedding dress, receives in her father's house her visitors, and then at the appointed time, accompanied by the bridesmaids, her companions, is conducted to the palace of her husband, who, attended by the most distinguished women of his court (v. 9), receives her and conducts her alone into the nuptial chamber (v. 14).

Such is the touching and beautiful figure by which Jerusalem is here portrayed. That city is the bride ; her companions are the cities of Palestine ; the daughter of Tyre and the King's daughters represent the Gentile nations. All these will be brought into relationship with the Messiah (Rom x. 12), and all will be blessed.

The song extols the fidelity and power of the Messiah as Israel's Bridegroom—to her, fidelity; to her foes, severity. Rev. xix. will fulfil the double prophecy.

PSALM XLVI.—The Bridegroom of the previous Psalm is the Mighty God of this Psalm. Encouraged by the prophetic vision of the one, Israel will in her future time of trouble (v. 1) sing this other and the two following Psalms. They form a group. The First, presents Messiah as supreme over the earth and mighty to deliver His people. The Second, sings of the effect of that supremacy in respect of the nations ; and the Third, of its results in relation to the earth and to Sion as its capital city. Although these three Psalms (xlvi–xlviii) will uphold and express the faith of Israel in the dark days that await

her, yet the siege of Jerusalem by the Assyrians in the reign of Hezekiah illustrates them, as it does Ps. xlv. It is quite possible that the Holy Spirit gave them at that time through Isaiah to Hezekiah and Jerusalem.

This Psalm (xlvi.) points to a successful defence and not to a battle. Hezekiah was in trouble (v. 1)—trouble so great as to be compared to the earth convulsed, to mountains swept into the midst of the seas, and to raging billows roaring with a force great enough to make the mountains tremble (vs. 2 and 3). The infuriated nations, and their maddened governments, are thus fitly pictured (v. 6). They threaten to overwhelm and destroy Jerusalem, just as in an earth-quake the tottering mountains and the wild seas threaten destruction to a city. A secret water channel cut through the rock by king Hezekiah, and recently discovered, supplied the city with an unfailing stream of pure water. This source of refreshment and strength could neither be seen nor touched by the enemy. He, like the wild sea, raged without, while its gentle waters flowed within (v. 4). The R.V. omits the word " shall " in this verse.

Under these circumstances Hezekiah, strengthened himself in Jehovah His God and cried out, " The Lord of Hosts is with us, the God of Jacob is our Refuge " (vs. 7 and 11).

Jerusalem was God's city. He was in her midst. Therefore she could not be captured. The word " midst " in verse 2 is to be contrasted with " midst " in verse 5. National governments will perish in the tumultuous seas of democracy, but Messiah's government will for ever firmly stand in Sion. Her deliverance will come at " the dawning of the day "(" right early " v. 5).

In verses 8 and 9 the invitation is given to issue from the city and to look upon the desolation of the Assyrian camp. It was destroyed at the dawning of the day. It was at the dawn that Pharaoh and his host were drowned in the Red Sea, and it was very early in the morning that Satan and his angels were overthrown at the Sepulchre. But this brightest dawn awaits Jerusalem in the coming day of her final deliverance.

In verse 10 the Messiah counsels His people to exercise the inactivity of faith in a time of trouble ; to leave matters entirely in His hand, for He is God ; He promises to demon-strate His almighty power on their behalf ;

and this He proceeds to set forth in the two following Psalms.

Luther's famous hymn, " Eine feste Burg ist unser Gott " illustrates the value of this Psalm to God's people in all dispensations and under all trials. He is an unseen source of spiritual strength (v. 4) and a sure Refuge (v. 1).

PSALM XLVII.—Messiah's prediction that He will be exalted among the nations (xlvi. 10), i.e., enthroned over them, is the theme of this Psalm. Hence the words " gone up " (v. 5) should read " exalted." This word is repeated in verse 9. The word " people " in verses 1, 3 and 9 should read " peoples " ; but People in the centre of verse 9 is singular, and means Israel, and should be printed with a capital P.

Jerusalem here celebrates the enthronement of Messiah as King over all the earth, and invites the nations to fear and worship and praise Him (vs. 1, 2, 5, 6, 7 and 8). Her sons declare that He will apportion them their inheritance (v. 4) ; that He will establish their dominion over the peoples, whom He will appoint to be their servants (vs. 3 and 9) ; and they invite all the nations to worship Him Whom they acclaim as their God and King (vs. 6 and 7).

Assuming that this Psalm was sung by Hezekiah and his feeble folk when shut up in Jerusalem, it is a very striking instance of faith making real things unseen (Heb. xi. 1). Sennacherib's vain-glorious record, now lodged in the British Museum, states that after having totally destroyed the Hebrew people and their country and cities, he shut up Hezekiah in Jerusalem " as a bird in a cage." But he did not know that Hezekiah sang in his cage, for he surely sang this Psalm and those which precede and follow it (xlv-xlviii). It is remarkable that the Assyrian monarch does not say that he captured the city. In his message to Jerusalem (Isa. xxxvi. 4 and 13) he styles himself the great king, the king of Assyria." But Hezekiah and his handful of followers sang of Messiah, the Great King, the King of all the Earth (v. 2) ; and they looked forward in faith to the promised day when all the mighty Gentile nations and their kings, princes and rulers, should be put by God beneath their feet (vs. 3 and 9).

But the Psalm will certainly be sung in the future time of Jacob's supreme trouble, and so furnish a striking picture of the power of a God-given faith. The Tribes in the hour of their greatest weakness and misery will sing of the morning, soon to dawn, when their king shall appear, and shall ascend His throne in Sion as Most High to reign over all the earth, and shall appoint them masters of the world, as promised in xlv. 16.

Verse 2 may read : For Jehovah Elyon is to be feared ; He is become a great king over all the earth ; or : For Jehovah Messiah is the Most High. He is to be feared. He shall become a great King over all the earth.

The sense of verse 4 may be thus expressed: He shall choose our inheritance for us, and establish the excellency of Jacob whom He loved. " The excellency of Jacob " means the supremacy of Jacob over the nations. This was involved in the birthright which he valued and which Esau despised. He was given this double promise, the inheritance of Canaan and the lordship of the nations. To him, therefore, Canaan was more precious than Egypt ; and hence his earnest injunction to Joseph to bury him in that land of promise.

Messiah being enthroned (v. 5) as Israel's God and King (v. 6), the nations are commanded to praise Him " with understanding," i.e., to recognize and accept God's purposes as to Israel's supremacy, and to bow to the authority of Messiah's throne (v. 8). Christians are commanded to sing " with the understanding " (1 Cor. xiv. 15), that is, to sing hymns that are scriptural and profitable—vehicles of spiritual worship and of mutual instruction.

The sense of the last verse may be given in this translation : The princes of the nations shall be gathered together by God to serve the People of the God of Abraham ; for the rulers of the earth belong unto God (Hos. iv. 18, R.V. margin). He shall be greatly exalted, i.e., mighty as earthly monarchs are, Messiah shall be still mightier.

PSALM XLVIII.—The triumph of Messiah over Anti-Christ and the Ten Kings (Rev. xiii. 1 and xix. 19) is the theme here as in the prior Psalm, and the destruction of the Assyrian in the days of Hezekiah continues to illustrate the statements of the Psalm.

It pictures the kings and their Chief besieging Sion (v. 4) ; their discomfiture (vs. 5-7) ; the enthronement of the Messiah at Jerusalem (vs. 1-3) ; the permanence of

His kingdom (v. 14, ; and the joy of redeemed Israel (vs. 8-13).

The faith and sighing of Psalms xlii and xliv are here satisfied. In Ps. xlii. verses 1-5, Israel longs for the day when she would accompany the multitude with songs of joy to the House of God. This longing is now gratified (vs. 9-11). In Ps. xliv. 1-8 she recalls what she had heard of God's past deliverances. Now in this Psalm (v. 8) she joyfully exclaims : " As we have heard, so have we seen." Thus the sighings and longings of the land of Jordan and of the hill Mizar are changed into the songs and rejoicings of Mount Sion.

The prophecy of Isa. lii. 13 respecting the exaltation of Messiah is here asserted in verse 1 ; and the many predictions regarding the future glory of Sion here also are reviewed by faith (vs. 2, 12 and 13).

Not only will Messiah be exalted, but His city will be also exalted. Compare Zech. xiv. 10 and Ezek. xlv. Verse 2 may accordingly read: " Beautiful in elevation, joy of the whole earth shall be Mount Sion—the sides of the north, the city of the Great King." The expression " sides of the north " is possibly a Hebraism for "supremacy." Compare Isa. xiv. 13 and 15 R.V. The reference there is to the king of Babylon's descent from greatness to impotence. So in verse 2, four statements are made regarding Sion : it will be exalted ; it will be the joy of the whole earth ; it will be supreme ; and it will be the residence of Messiah.

A picture of great poetic force is seen in verses 4-7. Anti-Christ and the Ten Kings assemble and march against Jerusalem. They meet there an unexpected power (Matt. xxiv. 30). They are amazed ; they are terror-stricken ; they flee. Their anguish is compared to that of a woman in child-birth, and their impotence to that of ships in a hurricane.

A ship of Tarshish meant an ocean-going vessel. The modern expression is a Liner. The ancient ship did not necessarily sail to Tarshish, just as many modern ships never cross the line, i.e., the equator.

In the midst of the greatest dangers faith enjoys the stillness and strength and love of the immediate presence of God (v. 9 with xlvi. 5 and 10).

God's action being ever in harmony with His character, His fame therefore extends, and will extend, to the very ends of the earth (v. 10). This is not true of earthly princes.

Full of righteousness is His right hand in favour of His people as promised, and in destruction to their foes as predicted.

The " daughters of Judah " (v. 11) are the villages round about Sion.

The enemy being defeated, the joyful inhabitants can issue from the city and walk about Sion and observe that no damage has been done to her towers, bulwarks, or palaces; and they are enjoined to recount the fact to succeeding generations (vs. 12 and 13). In the spiritual realm this also may be morally true in respect of the kingdom of God and of the individual Christian. Complete victories may be enjoyed.

The expression " unto death " (v. 14) is a figure of speech for perpetuity embracing eternity. Rev. vii. 17 confirms and fulfils the expectation of this verse.

Viewed from a certain standpoint, the royal city of David is seen on the sides of a northern hill. Some think so will it be in the millennium, and that this is what is meant in verse 2.

There need be no conflict between verse 13 and Zech. xiv. 2, for the language of the Psalm may be figurative, or it may envisage the city after its restoration by the Great King, as predicted in Ps. li. 18 and Acts xv. 16.

PSALM XLIX.—As already stated, Book II contains three groups of Psalms. This Psalm is the closing one of the first group. It reviews the doctrine of the group, that is, the affliction of Messiah's people ; the foolishness and feebleness of their oppressors ; and the glory of Israel's Redeemer. The oppressor is feeble, for he has no power against death, to which he is justly doomed because he is a sinner ; and he is foolish, for he denies that he is a sinner, and he ignores the fact of death.

The Psalm will support Israel's faith in her future suffering under the oppression of the false Messiah, just as in the past its truth sustained her when oppressed by the Assyrian. Confronted with the power and wealth of Sennacherib, she, defenceless and impoverished, could say : " Why should I fear in the days of evil ? " (v. 5) and her Lord could say to her : " Be not thou therefore afraid when one is made rich " (v. 16). Thus faith can fitly measure man in his folly and impotence however exalted he may be (vs. 12 and 20).

The speaker is the Messiah. In the first

four verses He proposes an enigma and invites all the nations of the earth to hear His solution of it. The proposal is expressed in a double quatrain.

The enigma is : Man being without understanding and without power, how can he redeem himself from the dominion of death ? The solution is : Through the death and resurrection of a Redeemer (vs. 5 and 15).

Thus the Psalm re-states the doctrine of the preceding Psalms as to man's moral ruin, and brings forward a Redeemer Whose sufficiency, as such, forms the subject matter of the succeeding group of Psalms (l–lx).

The mightiest oppressors being the hopeless slaves of folly and death, the " Why should I fear ? " of verse 5 and the " Fear not, therefore " of verse 16 are well founded.

Verses 5–11 correspond with verses 13–19. Verse 12 and verse 20 form a refrain. Each of these members contains two couplets and two quatrains. These correspond and are arranged to alternate and introvert, so that a quatrain replies to a couplet, and, in its turn, the first line of a quatrain corresponds to the third, and the second line to the fourth. Accordingly, verse 5 corresponds to verses 16–19 ; verses 6–9 correspond with verse 15. The first two lines of verse 10 correspond with verse 14 ; and verse 11 commencing " They leave their wealth to others " corresponds with verse 13. Thus the perfection in the structure of the Psalm not only enhances its beauty but emphasizes its doctrine.

" People " (v. 1) should read " peoples " ; and " together" (v. 2) should read " alike." " To open a dark saying " means to explain an enigma (v. 4).

Gen. iii. 15 is indicated in verse 5. It refers to Christ's incarnation. He thereby became vulnerable, and iniquitous man energized by Satan wounded Him. Yet, despite the horror of the fact, the rage of man and the power of death, He as the Author of a perfect faith, calmly cried " Why should I therefore fear ? "

The sense of verse 8 is : That the price of redemption from the dominion of death is so costly that the matter must be laid aside for ever. The price is so great, so impossible, as to for ever put to an end all negotiation.

Reading verse 9 immediately after verse 7 it clearly appears that immortality is what man would purchase if he could, and so be freed from corruption, i.e., death.

" He seeth " (v. 10) means : It is a visible

fact that wise men and brutish people alike die. They are equally helpless.

Verse 10 should close at the word " perish " the word " and " should be omitted, and verse 11 should begin : They leave their wealth to others, etc.

Man's folly is set out in verse 11, that although knowing he must die, yet he names himself after his lands. He wishes to persuade himself that he is to live as long as his lands last.

Verses 12 and 20 press the point that let a man be never so exalted, he, like the beasts of the field, is the helpless prey of death.

Man's folly appears the greater from the fact that succeeding generations approve the foolishness of the preceding ones (v. 13).

Death is pictured as a shepherd (v. 14 R.V.). The verse contrasts the destinies of the fools and the upright. For the upright there will be " the morning " ; for the fools, Sheol. " Their glory " (v. 17) with themselves shall consume in that eternal grave far from their stately earthly palaces.

In verse 15 the Messiah declares with confidence that God will redeem Him from the power of death, and He adds, For He shall take Me out of it.

The word " therefore " may be supplied in verse 16 so as to read, Be not thou therefore afraid, etc. By so doing the conclusion of the argument is emphasized and applied.

The doctrine of verses 18 and 19 is, that although the rich of verse 6 indulge themselves, and though society applauds them for so doing, yet shall they descend into the abyss of eternal night and there join their moral ancestors. The sense of the Hebrew text is : That the self-indulgent gratifies every appetite of his soul (v. 18), but at death his soul shall follow his moral forefathers into darkness ; and the terrible addition is made that they shall never see light. This implies existence (Jude 13). Out of that abyss of horror only one was ever delivered, and that one was the sinless Man, Christ Jesus (v. 15).

Omitting verse 12 and reading on from verse 11 to verse 13 the point is clearly recognized as to man's foolishness. He names himself from lands which he must soon leave ; and though this action proves him to be a fool yet posterity applauds his folly.

PSALM L. — The crucified and risen Messiah of the previous Psalm (vs. 5 and 15) appears as the Eternal Judge in this first

Psalm of the second group (l.-lx.) of Book II.

Psalm xlix. predicts His first advent; Psalm l. His second.

Just as in the second Book of the Pentateuch He appeared in fire upon Mount Sinai, so in the second book of the Psalms He appears in fire on Mount Sion (v. 3). Then He appeared in connection with the redemption of His people from the oppression of Pharaoh; now He will appear to redeem the same people from the oppression of Anti-Christ. The Egyptian monarch was a fore-picture of this last and most terrible monarch.

The facts of this Psalm, and the time of its fulfilment, will synchronize with Dan. vii. 13, Mark xiii. 26, Acts xvii. 31, 2 Thess. i. 7, and Rev. xix.

Immediately prior to the apparition of the Messiah, Israel will be reduced to the lowest possible depth of misery and well-nigh extinction as a nation. But at that moment her Deliverer will appear on Mount Sion with all the accompaniments of terrific majesty as at Sinai (vs. 2 and 3), and He will summon the whole earth to judgment (v. 1); He will despatch His angels to gather His saints together to Him (vs. 4 and 5); He will judge them (vs. 7-15), for judgment must begin at the House of God; then He will judge the wicked (vs. 16-21); the inhabitants of the heavens will applaud the righteousness of the judgment, declaring the Man Who judges (Acts xvii. 31) to be God (v. 6); and the Psalm closes with a warning to the wicked (v. 22) and with a message to the righteous (v. 23).

With great majesty the Psalm opens thus in the Hebrew text: " El Elohim Jehovah hath spoken," etc. The doctrine of the verse is: The God of Gods, Jehovah Messiah, summons the earth to judgment. The certainty of this judgment is so sure that it is spoken of as a present fact. The words " spoken " and " called " intend " commanded " and " summoned." The extent of this judgment from the rising of the sun to its going down is repeated in Matt. xxiv. 27.

The word " from " (v. 4) should be omitted, and the word " saving " should be supplied at the close of the verse. The sense is: He will command His angels to gather His elect to Him (Matt. xxiv. 31). The term " saints " does not express the believer's moral attitude toward God, but God's attitude toward the believer. The Hebrew word might be rendered " beloved," or " engraced " (Eph. i. 6), or " benignantly regarded." Those whom God so regards and names are those who have entered into covenant relationship with Him by a sacrifice for sin. A literal translation of the Hebrew of this passage is: " Those ratifying My covenant over a sacrifice for sin." This covenant made by sacrifice was typified in Exod. xxiv. 8, explained in Heb. ix. 20, and fulfilled in 1 Cor. v. 7. The words " made a covenant " read in Hebrew " cut a covenant." They imply the death of a victim, the placing on one side and on the other of its divided members, and the ratification of a covenant between them. The ordinance pointed forward to Calvary and is illustrated by Gen. xv. 9-21. See Bible League Quarterly, April 1925.

The word " saints " is a covering term embracing not only the elect of Israel but also the elect of the nations—all in fact who enter into covenant with God at Calvary. The Church of God does not appear in this judgment.

In judging His people (vs. 7-15) He first owns them as His, declaring before angels and men, in infinite love and faithfulness, that they are His people and that He is their God. He then reproves them, not for any defects in their outward worship, but that, like the church at Ephesus (Rev. ii), they did not give Him the first place in their hearts, nor did they call upon Him in the day of trouble (v. 15), for had they done so He would have delivered them, and by doing so, glorified Himself. Thus verse 15 may be understood when connected with this judgment; but its language is necessarily so moulded as to be an admonition and encouragement pending that coming day. The " vows " of verse 14 mean vows of thanksgiving and praise.

The judgment of the wicked (v. 16-21) exposes them as mere professors. Their lips were filled with religious language (v. 16) but their conduct was otherwise (vs. 17-20); and because God " kept silence " (vs. 3 and 21), i.e., was inactive in judging sin, they assumed that He regarded it as lightly as they themselves did; but the Messiah reproves them and ranges their sins in order before their eyes (v. 21). The language of this verse, like that of verse 15, is composed so as to warn professors of what will be said and done in that day of wrath. Such men know the Gospel, but not obeying it they will be punished with everlasting destruction (2 Thess. i. 8 and 9).

Harmonious with the character of the Psalm nothing is said as to the destiny of those who will be judged. Other scriptures deal fully with that. The one company is simply and solemnly warned of the just wrath that will " tear them in pieces " and from which there will be no escape (v. 22) ; and the other company is assured of the salvation of God (v. 23).

This last verse should perhaps read : " And to him that puts himself in His way will I show the salvation of God." Christ is God's way of salvation.

As respects the professors the judgment reviews their conduct, but as regards the saints it reviews their faith and love. This is a great principle, and should be reverently observed.

The prophet Asaph here first appears in the Book of Psalms. That he and David were prophets is declared in Matt. xiii. 35, and Acts ii. 30.

PSALM LI.—This Psalm was given by the Holy Spirit to David when, his heart broken and contrite because of his sin against God, he pleaded for pardon through the atoning blood of the Lamb of God foreshadowed in Exod. xii. (v. 7). Thus was he not only fittingly provided with a vehicle of expression in repentance and faith, but he was also used as a channel of prophetic communication.

David in his sin, repentance, and restoration, is a fore-picture of Israel ; for as he forsook the Law and was guilty of adultery and murder, so Israel despised the Covenant, turned aside to idolatry, and murdered the Messiah. Thus the scope and structure of the Psalm go far beyond David : they predict the future confession and forgiveness of Israel in the day of Messiah's apparition ; when looking upon Him Whom they pierced they shall mourn and weep (Zech. xii. and xiii. and Rev. i. 7). The first seventeen verses are personal to David ; the last two are national for Israel.

The great principle here appears that only those can be true messengers of the Gospel who have themselves a conscious experience of pardon. This principle is, in the first part of the Psalm, personally illustrated by David (v. 13) ; and in the latter part nationally illustrated by Israel (vs. 18 and 19).

These two last verses are not, as some think, a meaningless addition to the Psalm by some later writer. They both belong to the structure and prophetic scope of the Psalm. They refer to that which is spoken of in Amos ix. 11 and 12 and Acts xv. 15, 16 and 17. David's sin, confession and restoration, illustrate this future chapter in the nation's history. Their idolatry (" adultery ") and murder forgiven, they will go forth as messengers of the Gospel to win other nations to whole-hearted faith and service in and for Christ.

Amos ix. and Acts xv. predict that Israel, repentant and forgiven, will gather to Jehovah the residue of the nations that will survive the judgments of the Book of Revelation ; that Messiah will at the same time do good to Sion ; that He will build the walls of Jerusalem (Ps. xlviii. 12) ; that He will unite the nations to His people ; and that He will establish and accept their righteous and whole-hearted worship in the Holy City. This is the worship foretold in verse 19 ; and the term " they " means the redeemed nations.

As David, forgiven and restored, won transgressors to God, so Israel, forgiven and restored, will win nations to God. To-day conversion is individual ; then it will be national.

In harmony with all this the fifty-first Psalm fitly follows the fiftieth, for its theme is the repentance and sorrow which the appearing of the Messiah, depicted in Ps. l., will produce in the nation.

The acknowledgment of verses 3 and 4 is the condition of Divine forgiveness. All sin is in essence committed against God ; hence David said, " I have sinned against Jehovah." Pharaoh, Saul and others said : " I have sinned," but they did not add, " against God."

The second half of verse 4 is quoted in Rom iii. 4. It teaches the doctrine that God is justified in judging sin, and that His statement that all have sinned is true. If after the words " in Thy sight " the sentence " I confess my guilt " be supplied, the meaning and argument of the verse will be clearer.

The declaration of verse 5 is not urged in mitigation but in aggravation of guilt ; and this appears the more evident from the following verse which, with Matt. v. 28, demands purity of heart as well as of conduct.

The contrition of a true repentance is always accompanied by the confidence of a Divine sense of forgiveness. This appears in the Hebrew text, for the verbs " purge," " make," " rejoice," " open," and " build " (vs. 7, 8, 8, 15, and 18) are in the future tense, and so grammatically express not only petition but certitude. David enjoyed the consciousness that he was purged ; that he should hear joy and gladness ; that his bones would rejoice ; that his lips would be opened ; and that the walls of Jerusalem would be rebuilt.

There was no sacrifice provided under the Law for the sins of adultery and murder. David had, therefore, to seek pardon through the death of the Lamb of God, as foreshadowed in Exod. xii. That Divine way of redemption from death preceded the Law and pre-figured Calvary. Taught by the Holy Spirit, David could, however dimly, plead that sacrifice. The petition " purge me with hyssop " expressed by a figure of speech " purge me with the blood which on that night in Egypt was sprinkled on the door post with a bunch of hyssop."

Forgiveness for the past does not exhaust the fulness of pardon. There is provision for the future ; and this appears in verses 10-12. A clean heart, a willing spirit and a steadfast will are given by the Holy Spirit. A steadfast will (v. 10) which secures perseverance in the way of holiness, and a free spirit that delights in, and wishes to do God's will, are gifts given by Him to new-born men.

The Holy Spirit dwelt with Israel. Ezek. xi pictures His slow and unwilling withdrawal from Jerusalem ; Isaiah lxiii. 9-11 records His love for the nation in the past as Ezek. xxxvi. predicts His love in the future ; and chapter xliii. promises His swift return to the repentant people.

Only the consciously pardoned sinner can " sing aloud " of God's righteousness (v. 14). Unpardoned men can speak of His mercy , but their thoughts about it are unholy thoughts.

Not penances or sacraments or gifts of costly churches in expiation of past sins, are desired by God, but repentance, faith, love and an abandonment of all known sin (vs. 16 and 17).

PSALM LII.--The circumstances which occasioned the inspiration of this Psalm are recorded in ·1 Sam. xxi. and xxii. Doeg hated David and desired his destruction (v. 1). He falsely accused the High Priest and his family, who were true to David (vs. 2 and 3), and at Saul's command, willingly slaughtered them (v. 4). He is therefore a type of Anti-Christ, and David a type of Christ. The doom of the " mighty man " of boasting and mischief (v. 1) is predicted in verse 5 ; the deliverance of those he will oppress declared in verse 6 ; and the triumph of the True Mighty Man set out in verses 8 and 9.

The word " Maschil" means instruction. See note on Psalm xxxii. The three following Psalms are also Maschil Psalms. They fulfil David's promise in li. 13 to teach transgressors God's ways. Hence the doctrine of these four Psalms (lii.-lv.) is that, if sin is not confessed and forsaken, God's wrath will surely follow. Psalm li., therefore, stands in contrast to these four. In it is found confession and forgiveness ; in them persistence in evil and consequent judgment.

Only the false Messiah can satisfy the statements of the first four verses and of verse 7 ; and only the true Messiah the language of the last two verses.

" Mischief" means calamity to others ; and " mighty man " signifies a proud and cruel tyrant The abrupt introduction of God's goodness is designed in contrast to Anti-Christ's wickedness, and in explanation of God's long-suffering patience toward him, and of his abuse of it (v. 1).

The facts, therefore, set out in this first verse are : That Anti-Christ will be a powerful and merciless tyrant ; that he will boast of his success in injuring and destroying Messiah's people ; and that he will abuse the goodness of God which leads men to repentance.

Four further statements are made respecting him in verses 2-4 ; He devises mischiefs, i.e , a supreme mischief ; he loves evil more than good . falsehood rather than truth ; and he delights in devouring, i.e., murderous command.

The supreme mischief here intended will be the destruction of Messiah and His people (Dan. viii. 25 and xi. 44).

Doeg illustrates these four statements respecting Anti-Christ. He devised the destruction of David ; he loved evil rather than good ; he falsely accused Ahimelech ; and he rejoiced at Saul's murderous command authorizing him to destroy Ahimelech's entire family.

The four-fold judgment of verse 5 corresponds to the four-fold wickedness of verses 2-4 : God shall destroy him for ever ; He shall take him away ; He shall pluck him out of his dwelling-place ; and He shall root him out of the land of the living.

Anti-Christ, abusing the mercy of God in verse 1, is instructed in verse 5 to apprehend the wrath of God. But he will reject this instruction, as is evident from verses 6, 7 and 9, and as is repeatedly predicted in many other Scriptures. Israel shall witness his punishment ; will rejoice with holy laughter ; and will fear, i.e., praise and worship God, saying : " Lo that is the man," etc. (vs. 6 and 7). The word " saying " should be supplied at the close of verse 6.

Three statements are made respecting Anti-Christ in verse 7 as justifying his doom. He made not God his strength ; he trusted in the abundance of his riches ; and he strengthened himself in his wickedness.

On the other hand, in contradistinction, four characteristics describe the Messiah in verses 8 and 9 : He resembles a green olive tree ; He perfectly and eternally trusts ; He perpetually praises ; and unfalteringly waits.

That for which He praises God in the first member of verse 9 is the execution of His wrath upon Anti-Christ, threatened and predicted in verse 5   It is this Divine action which is pointed to in the word " it " necessarily supplied in the text.

The last verse contrasts with the first : Anti-Christ boasts of himself ;   Messiah praises God. Anti-Christ acclaims the success of his malignity ;   Messiah points to God's judgment upon it. Anti-Christ abuses the goodness of God ;   Messiah rejoices in it.

The Psalm was committed to the Chief Musician in reference to Mahalath, i.e., the great dancings. When David slew Goliath there was dancing, but when Messiah destroys Anti-christ there will be great dancing. Short as the Psalm is it promises a long day of laughing (v. 6), singing (v. 9), and dancing.

PSALM LIII.—This is the second Maschil Psalm of the group lii–lv.

Many regard this Psalm as a repetition of Ps. xiv. This is a mistake. The notes on that Psalm should be read and the following variations noticed : The one is placed in the " Genesis " book ; the other in fhe " Exodus." The one was for private,   the other, for

public use. " Jehovah " occurs seven times in the primitive text of the one ;   " Elohim," seven times in the other. The affliction of the oppressed is the theme of the one ; the doom of their oppressors that of the other. The one views Israel in the power of the oppressor, as in the land of Egypt, thus harmonizing with the close of Genesis ;   the other predicts her triumphant exodus from affliction and so harmonizes with the Second Book of the Pentateuch. Verse 5 in the one points to the reverential fear of the oppressed ; verse 5 in the other to the terror of the oppressor.

The two Psalms are, therefore, quite distinct. In Psalm xiv. the attention of the reader is directed to the suffering of Messiah and His servants. It is for private use. The absence of the subscription " for the Chief Musician " shows this. Its purpose is to sustain Israel's faith in her future affliction, of which that under Pharaoh was a fore-picture. In Ps. liii. " instruction " is given respecting the judgment of the oppressor and the deliverance of the oppressed. It is for public use, hence the subscription " for the Chief Musician relating to Neginoth," i.e., " smitings," that is, the smitings of God's wrath—He smote all the first-born in the land of Egypt. In both Psalms the folly of the oppressor and his followers necessarily forms the background.

The Psalm instructs the Fool and his followers respecting the judgment that must overtake them if they do not confess their abominable iniquities and seek forgiveness for them.

It is because Israel is the central figure of Ps. xiv. that the covenant title "Jehovah " is there used ;   and it is because Anti-christ is the central figure of Ps. liii. that the creation title " Elohim " is employed.

Ps. xiv. 6 pictures the Fool and his followers putting the afflicted of Israel to shame ; Ps. liii. 5 views the Messiah putting the Fool and his followers to shame.

Ps. xiv. 5 may read : There, i.e., in the furnace of affliction, they feared a Fear, i.e., God (Gen. xxxi. 42), for Jehovah is in the congregation of the Righteous One. Ps. liii. 5 may read : There, i.e., in the place of judgment, they feared a fear to whom no fear had been, for God hath scattered the bones of him, i.e., the Fool, who encamped against thee, i.e., against Sion (Zech. xiv).

This last verse points to the place and predicts the time of the destruction of the Fool and his followers.

The Fool is Anti-Christ. His folly is described in 2 Thess. ii. 4 as well as in verse 1 of this Psalm. The word "they" in this verse means his followers. The moral effect of his leadership is fitly expressed in the words "corrupt," "abominable," and "altogether filthy."

The commencement and close of both Psalms are necessarily similar for they treat of the character and judgment of Anti-Christ. But the intervening verses are, as already pointed out, dissimilar, for the subject matter of the one is the oppression suffered, and the theme of the other is the oppressors scattered.

But in both Psalms, as also in Romans I and II, God's moral judgment of man, as man, whether he be a Jew or a Gentile, is declared to be the same—all are corrupt. Thus this fundamental doctrine of the Gospel is taught under Conscience (Genesis), Law (Exodus), and Grace (Romans).

PSALM LIV.—This is the third Maschil Psalm of the series depending on li. 13. It gives instruction respecting the deliverance enjoyed by those who yield themselves unto God, and the judgment suffered by those who oppose themselves to Him. These latter are warned to confess their evil actions, as David did, and to seek forgiveness.

1 Sam. xxiii and xxvi narrate the circumstances under which the Holy Spirit gave this Psalm to David.

But it prophetically concerns the Messiah and the minority of the Jews who will in the last days believe on Him. He here prays for them, using the words "me" and "my"; and He it is Who in verse 5 as their Advocate, asks for a just punishment upon their enemies. Being Himself sinless as Man, and righteous as God, He can demand a fitting judgment. In human courts of justice the government advocate claims from the judge a just sentence upon convicted transgressors.

The "strangers" of verse 3 mean primarily the Ziphites, and the "violent men" (R.V.) Saul and his soldiers. Together they typify Anti-Christ and his supporters. They will be the great atheists of the future (v. 3).

Verse 6 should read as in the R.V.; and the ellipsis in verse 7 should be: Mine eye hath seen His judgment upon mine enemies. The past tense is here employed because the nature of faith is to sing of future promises as accomplished facts.

"Judge" (v. 1), i.e., "vindicate." The terms, "Thy name" "Thy strength" "Thy truth" illustrate the doctrine of Deut. xxxii. 35 and Rom. xii. 19, which is, that vengeance belongs to God, and that the trusting servant when tried does not take matters into his own hands, but relies on his Master to rescue him (v. 1); to vindicate him (v. 1); to punish his tormentors (v. 5); and so to verify the promise "I will recompense, saith Jehovah."

This Psalm, similar to the prior one, relates to Neginoth, i.e., to the smitings of the sword of God. These smitings contrast with the dancings of Ps. lii. The oppressors will feel the one; the oppressed will enjoy the other.

PSALM LV.—This is the closing Maschil Psalm of this series Its lesson to transgressors (li. 13) is that God hears their words (v. 3); sees their actions (vs. 9-11); marks their hypocrisies (vs. 12-14 and 21); records their breaches of faith (v. 20); and the Psalm warns them of the consequent judgment (vs. 15 and 23).

The conduct of Absalom and Ahithophel (2 Sam. xv) illustrate, but do not exhaust, the Psalm. It concerns the hatred and treachery which Messiah suffered personally in the days of His flesh; and which He now suffers, and will yet suffer, in sympathy with His people (Col. i 24).

As predicted in Dan. xi. and John v. 43, the majority of the Jews will accept Anti-Christ as the promised Messiah. He will make a covenant with them, and, with them, cruelly persecute the believing minority. But after a little time he will break the covenant and seek to destroy them all. This is the covenant referred to in verse 20; and his is the hypocrisy of verse 21.

The Gospels record the words and acts of Christ; the Psalms reveal His prayers and thoughts.

How wonderful to be permitted to hear Him speaking to God! and what a dignity to be made a partner with Him in the thoughts and emotions of His heart! His is the voice that is heard in this Psalm, His are the thoughts, and His the instruction.

The subscription of the Psalm entitles it "the dove of the distant oak-woods." Verses 2, 6, and 17 illustrate this title. "Make a noise" (v. 2) means "mourn as a dove," as does also "cry aloud" (v. 17). Compare Ezek. vii. 16 and Isa. xxxviii. 14.

Historically David is symbolized by this dove, but prophetically it means the Messiah.

The unnatural rebellion of Absalom and the treachery of Ahithophel foreshadowed the rebellion of Israel and the betrayal of Judas. The moral condition of Jerusalem when Jesus rode into it is described in verses 9-11 ; and the pain which the words and actions and hatred of its citizens caused Him is the subject of verses 1-8. This anguish reached its climax in Gethsemane (vs. 4 and 5) when He said, " My soul is exceeding sorrowful even unto death." From that stormy wind and tempest He fain would have hastened as a dove to a place of refuge in some distant wilderness (vs. 6-8).

" To divide the tongue " (v. 9) means to confuse counsel. This prayer was answered in 2 Sam. xvii. 1-14. Ahithophel and Judas both perished in a similar manner.

Violence, strife, mischief, sorrow, wickedness, deceit and guile will be the moral condition of Jerusalem at Messiah's Second Coming, as it was at His first (vs. 9-11).

The words "equal," "guide," and " acquaintance," as applied to Judas may be translated " my chosen," for Jesus elected him an apostle, " my fellow tribesman," for he was the only member of the twelve who, like the Lord, was of the tribe of Judah, and " one who has got to know Me," for he accompanied with Him for three years and a half (vs. 12-14).

Verses 15 and 23 predict the doom of Anti-Christ and his followers. Messiah, in the interest of truth and holiness, and in love for His people, desires the infliction of this judgment.

Verse 19 may be thus understood : " God, even He that sitteth as king of old, shall hear Me and afflict them, because they have not changed their conduct and, therefore, they fear not God." This verse contrasts with the prior one which should read as in the R.V. The reference in that verse is to the calmness of soul in which the Messiah was preserved when defending Himself against the scribes and Pharisees. David tasted a little of this victory in 2 Sam. xvi. 5-13.

Messiah is " the Righteous One " of verse 22. The words were addressed to Him in His first Advent by the Holy Spirit. The " burden " was the load of man's hatred, as pointed to in verses 3-21. This load He rolled upon God, and waited on Him for vindication. The message has an application to all who, because of fidelity to Him and to the Gospel, are burdened in a like sense as He was.

PSALM LVI.—This and the four following are Michtam Psalms. There are six altogether. The first is the sixteenth. It is the great resurrection Psalm. It suggests that all six relate to the resurrection of Messiah.

The meaning of the word is obscure. It possibly means " engraven in gold." Gold in the Scriptures suggests Divine power and relationship, and what is engraven expresses permanence. Christ was raised from the dead by the power of God, and resurrection is a permanent doctrine of the Gospel. The word Michtam, therefore, may be a term expressing the certitude of faith in the predicted resurrection of Christ, as does the word " Resurgam, " which in the present day is so often engraved upon Christian tombstones.

This Psalm and the two following ones are " Al-Taschith " Psalms. These words mean " do not destroy." It is impossible to decide the intention of this command, but it may have been a direction to the Chief Musician to take special care of these inspired songs.

David's experiences when far from his father's house and in exile among those who hated him (1 Sam. xxi.) occasioned the giving of this Psalm. He was inspired to write it ; but its full theme is the experiences of the Messiah when living in this world among sinners, and in the under-world among demons, far from the glory which He had with the Father before the world was. He is the Speaker, His are the petitions, and His the expressions of faith and confidence. Luke xi. records the facts which necessitated these cries of sorrow and pain and faith.

The Psalm is constructed as a double stanza, each containing three members

Prayer, vs. 1 and 2 ; Trust, v. 3 ; Praise, v. 4, and

Prayer, vs. 5-8 ; Trust, v. 9 ; Praise, vs. 10-13.

Verse 2 should read as in the margin of the R.V. The " liers in wait " were the Scribes and Pharisees of Luke xi. 54. They fought against Him daily (v. 2) ; they wrested His words (v. 5) ; they planned His death (vs. 5 and 6). The thrice-repeated " all the day long " means not only all the day but at any moment of the day (vs. 1, 2 and 5).

The expression "in God" (vs. 4, 10 and 11) may be contrasted with the term "in man." Confidence in man, and in his word, never gives occasion for praise.

The petition of verse 7 is that the proud talkers of verses 1, 2 and 5 may be humbled.

"To tell" (v. 8) means to record. In the East mourners catch their tears in a bottle and place them in the tomb with the deceased.

"This I know" (v. 9) is a most precious declaration of the perfect faith of God's beloved Son. The "vows" of verse 12 are the promised praises of Psalm xxii. 22.

The last verse accords with Ps. xvi. 10 and 11. The sense of the statement is: That God would surely deliver Messiah's soul out of the death-world and His body out of the grave. As "ear" in Ps. xl 6 intended His whole body, so "feet" here has a similar force. The word "falling" has in the Hebrew text no moral significance. It only occurs here. and in Ps. cxvi. 8 and 9. It means a thrusting down. Man proposed to thrust His dishonoured body down into the earth. God placed it in an honoured tomb, raised it in glory, and caused Him to walk in resurrection life. In incarnation He was an "ear," i.e., perfect obedience; in resurrection He was a "foot," i.e., perfect power, for His enemies will be made a footstool for His feet, and in that day of universal dominion His feet shall stand upon the Mount of Olives (Ps. cx. and Zech. xiv.).

PSALM LVII.—The Holy Spirit sustained David's faith with this Psalm when lying in the gloomy cavern into which he had fled for fear of Saul and out of which he afterwards came forth to be king of Israel (1 Sam. xxii.). Thus taught, he was enabled to say that he did not trust the cavern but the Divine Wing that sheltered him from his foe (v. 1).

In all this he was a type of his Greater Son. The Psalm foretells the hatred of men to the Messiah (v. 4); His descent into the realm of the dead (v. 3); His glorious resurrection therefrom (v. 3); and His exaltation as King of both heaven and earth (vs. 5 and 11).

The structure of the Psalm may be thus displayed:

Suffering, verse 1: Faith, verse 2; Glory, verse 3.
Suffering, verse 4; Glory, verse 5.
Suffering, verse 6; Faith, verses 7-10; Glory, verse 11.

The entire Psalm is the language of the Messiah, with the exception of verses 5 and 11, which are addressed to Him by the Holy Spirit.

The middle members of verse 1 may read: "My soul taketh refuge in Thee, and under the shadow of Thy wings will I continue to take refuge."

The words "all things" (v. 2) are not in the Hebrew text. The verse is a blank cheque. "Performeth" means perform and will perform. The blank which occurs in the text may be filled in as trials or needs demand. Had one or more been mentioned their mention might have intimated the exclusion of others; but as the verse stands it makes a provision for all needs.

Mercy and truth are personified as the heavenly messengers sent to rescue Messiah from Satan who desired to keep Him swallowed up in Sheol. His captivity there was a reproach.

A vivid picture is given in verse 4 of what the Lord suffered from men's tongues, sharp as swords, and set on fire by hatred and by hell (James iii. 6).

The Holy Spirit in verses 5 and 11 addresses Messiah as God. The imperative tense of the Hebrew verb here employed implies the certainty of the desired exaltation, and so marks the contrast with the sufferings described in verse 4. The reading: "My soul is among lions; I must lie among them," etc. (R.V. marg.) suggests that in the under-world, as in the upper, the Lord suffered from the hatred of man and demons, and that there was no distinction or difference in the vehemence of their hatred in either world. He met with universal hatred.

"I will awake the dawn" (v. 8 R.V.) predicted the song of praise which He sang to God "very early in the morning" of His resurrection: and verse 9 is a re-affirmation of His promise made in Ps. xxii. 22. See notes on Ps. lx. and cviii.

PSALM LVIII.—This fourth Michtam Psalm contrasts the righteous Judge of Israel (vs. 6, 9 and 11) with the unrighteous judges of the nations (v. 1-5).

Israel being an earthly people to whom the government of the world will be committed, and who will be responsible to God therefor, has been, and will be, hated by the nations, and the predicted Divine way of delivering her from their oppression will be by their destruction. Hence her deliverance and their judgment will synchronize. She will, therefore, with spiritual intelligence, desire and pray for their punishment. These desires and petitions are voiced for her in the Psalms by her Great High Priest.

But what will be proper to Israel in the coming day of the Lord as an earthly people with earthly promises, is not proper to the Church of God in the present day of grace. Her position and promises are heavenly. She is not to be delivered by the destruction of her persecutors, but by her being raptured to heaven from out of their midst ; and the same Holy Spirit that will instruct Israel to pray for the destruction of her enemies, teaches the Church to bless them and to seek to save them. Thus the Church and Israel belong to two differing Divine economies. Confounding these leads to confusion of thought and misinterpretation of Scripture. This Psalm belongs to the day described in Isa. lxiii. and Rev. xix. when Messiah will come in the glory of His mighty angels to execute vengeance upon the oppressors of His people (vs. 9–11).

Six statements are made respecting these unrighteous judges, and six corresponding predictions are given concerning their punishment : They sin naturally (v. 3) ; easily, (v. 3) ; willingly (v. 3) ; murderously (v. 4) ; stubbornly (v. 4) ; and they judge unrighteously (v. 2).

The six predictions respecting their just doom are : They shall be helpless (v. 6) ; powerless (v. 7) ; weaponless (v. 7) ; placeless (v. 8) ; hopeless (v. 8) ; and swiftly and thoroughly judged (v 9).

Verse 1 may read : " Are ye dumb ? Ye should decide righteously ! Ye should judge uprightly, O ye sons of men ! " This is a cry of righteous indignation uttered by Messiah on behalf of His outraged people and addressed to these unrighteous judges. They were dumb when they should have denounced wrong-doing, and when they did speak it was to deny justice to the oppressed.

The sense of verse 2 is : In heart they planned illegality and in public they dispensed injustice.

To extract the teeth of a wild animal is to make it harmless (v. 6). The language here is figurative.

Water when conserved is powerful ; when dispersed it is powerless (v. 7). The remainder of this verse reads : " When he, i.e., the

unjust judge, bends his bow to shoot his arrows, i.e., prepares a false judgment, they shall be as arrows whose points have been cut off."

A snail's trail remains for a time marked by the slime which melts from its body, but the snail itself so effectually disappears that it cannot be found.

The sense of verse 9 is : " Before your pots can feel the heat of the lighted thorns, He shall take them away as with a whirlwind, the fresh and the burning ones alike." The illustration pictures the swiftness and thoroughness of the Divine judgment upon these unrighteous judges. The judgment will be swifter than the brief time between the placing of a pot over a thorn fire and the heating of the metal, and it will be thorough as when a hurricane carries a thorn fire completely away, both the sticks already burning and those not yet on fire.

The judgment of verse 10 foretells the vengeance which Messiah the Righteous Judge will take upon these evil men. Righteous men will approve it. He, i.e. Messiah, shall wash His feet in their blood. Compare lxviii. 23. To dip the foot in oil expresses wealth (Deut. xxxiii. 24) ; to dip it in blood, power. Not only will Messiah's feet be splashed with the blood of these cruel oppressors, but also His garments as stated in Isa. lxiii. and Rev. xix. All these expressions are figurative and not actual.

The God that is to judge the earth is the Great God and Saviour Jesus Christ (Acts xvii. 31 and Titus ii. 13, R.V).

PSALM LIX.—The superscription records the time of the giving of this prophecy and the subscription reveals its theme. David's sufferings and sorrows in 1 Sam. xix attuned his heart to receive these communications from the Holy Spirit. They form the fifth Michtam Psalm. David, delivered from the murderous hatred of his encircling enemies, here typifies the deliverance of Messiah and Elect Israel from their foes. The subscription states that the prophecy relates to Shushan-eduth, i.e., to the Lily of testimony. Can. ii. 2 compares Israel to a Lily among thorns. One beauteous lily among many sharp thorns. Such is the double picture in this prophecy. Messiah when on earth was a lily among thorns. He was the faithful and true Witness. Elect Israel is also here pictured as a lily witnessing for her King, and in deadly peril of destruction from the power of the many thorns which surround her.

The words "My people" and "our shield" (v. 11) make it clear that He Who in sympathy with Israel here speaks is Messiah. David could not use such language, only Jehovah Messiah could use it, as in 2 Sam. xxii. 44, Ps. xviii. 43, and many other Scriptures. Messiah was to be called Jesus for He should save "His people" from their sins. In all their afflictions He was afflicted (Isa. lxiii); and, being Jehovah, He could perfectly enter into them. Hence He wept over Jerusalem saying, "How often would I have gathered thy children together." Then He spoke as Jehovah; but in this Psalm, as in so many others, He places Himself among the children, and uses the words "our" and "we" etc. Consequently He can righteously desire and pray for the destruction of their tormentors.

The prophecy relates to the last hours of Jacob's trouble."

Verses 13 and 16 point to this fact. The believing remnant of Israel is pictured at the last extremity shut up in Jerusalem by the nations and by certain wicked transgressors, i.e., ungodly Jews in league with them (Zech. xiv. 14). Messiah in spirit takes His place in their midst; cheers them with the assurance of deliverance; and prays for the destruction of their besiegers (v. 5). Judgment is the keynote of the Psalm.

Verses 6 and 7 morally describe the besiegers, and verses 14 and 15 may be understood as the challenge of faith declaring their impotency. The statement compares them fittingly to howling dogs. It reads: They return at evening; they howl like a dog; they go round about the city; see! they belch out cruel and biting words with their mouth, etc. In the East travellers are frequently kept awake all night by the howling and barking of savage dogs prowling round the towns. The challenge of verse 15 may be thus translated: "Let them wander up and down for food and stay all night because they are not satisfied," and so the better mark the contrast with the following verse which reads: "But in the morning will I, i.e., Israel sing," etc. The contrast is very fine. The morning dawns upon the howling and hungry dogs and upon the singing and triumphant saints.

The Divine titles Jehovah and Elohim here occur, as is invariably the case, so as to mark the distinction between God's relationship to Israel and to the nations.

The words "me," "my," "our." and "I" express this relationship of Immanuel with His people. When asking deliverance for them He prays in the first person.

Although their conduct will be blameless, as His was in the days of His flesh, yet will men hate them as they hated Him (John xv. 18 and vs. 3 and 4).

"To visit" (v. 5) means to punish. The heathen are the nations; the wicked transgressors, the unbelieving Jews. The punishment of the latter is predicted in verse 13; of the former, in verse 11. There is consequently no discord between these petitions. The one demands the judgment of dispersion upon the nations; the other, of consumption upon the transgressors. Compare Deut. xxviii. 21, Ps. civ. 35, Isa. i. 28 and x. 23 and Dan. ix. 27.

Verse 9 in sympathy with verse 17 should read—in the judgment of many competent scholars—"O my Strength! I will wait upon Thee."

The sense of verse 10 is: That the Author of the goodness shown to Israel should anticipate her, that is, place Himself between her and the enemy; and then let her see His judgment upon them. Melchisedek placing himself between Abraham and the king of Sodom so as to prevent Abraham making a moral fall, illustrates the meaning of this verse.

PSALM LX.—This vision was given to David in the midst of a life and death struggle with the Syrians, the Edomites, the Moabites and the Philistines. These nations, as stated in the superscription, lived in the countries of Syria and Mesopotamia. It animated him, and no doubt Jehoshaphat and Hezekiah and many others since. Its interpretation, however, belongs to the time of Jacob's trouble and his deliverance out of it (vs. 11 and 12).

The vision is inspiring. A little company (v. 5) true to Immanuel shelter beneath a gifted banner (v. 4) in the midst of a multitude of foes (vs. 9-12), and in a time of Divine chastening because of national apostasy (vs. 1-3). The Messiah pleads for them in His own person and name (v. 5); claims the promises made in Gen. xlix, Deut. xxxiii, Num. xxiii. and xxiv, and 2 Sam. vii. (vs. 6-10), and in reply to the query of verse 9 gives the confident answer of verses 10-12.

Helped by the context, and influenced by the Hebrew word for "banner," i.e., an ensign or standard, and by its use in the prophecies of Isaiah and Jeremiah, it is clear that the marginal reading in the R.V. is the true translation of verse 4. The banner provided a place of refuge from the power ("bow") of the enemy. Isaiah xi. 10-12 and xxxi. 9 define this banner, or ensign, as symbolizing the Messiah.

This is the sixth and last Michtam Psalm. The Speaker is the Messiah. As in other Psalms He suffers as Man with His people— for how could He suffer if He were not man ? and as God He delivers them—for how could He deliver if He were not God ? For the supposed discords between the Psalm and 2 Sam. viii, 1 Kings xi. and 1 Chron. xviii, see notes on 2 Sam. viii.

The subscription states that the Psalm relates to Neginah, i.e., smiting. Neginah is the singular of Neginoth (liv). It is suggested that the singular signifies chastisement upon the nation, and the plural wrath upon their enemies.

Verse 3 should read " Thou hast suffered Thy people to experience hard things ; Thou hast made us to drink the wine of trembling."

In the first three verses the Spirit of Christ in the faithful Remnant acknowledges the fact and the justice of God's chastisement, and confesses in verses 10-12 that their only hope is that He will return to them and deliver them. This will be their righteousness. They will accept the punishment of their iniquity, they will exhibit no spirit of rebellion, and they will not look to man for help. Messiah will be their Jehovah-Nissi (v. 4). The promises of verses 6-8 will sustain their courage and faith in that great tribulation. " Earth " (v. 2) means Palestine.

The fourth verse beams like a shaft of light in the gloom of a dark night. The little company in the midst of hatred and error draw around their " banner " ; and so should God's servants in all times and in all circumstances (Exod. xvii. 8-16).

The Messiah prays in verse 5 that God will hear Him and deliver them. This argument of petition reappears in John xvii. 24. Because He is beloved they are beloved.

In the section verses 6-8, the gift of Palestine to Israel as her home, and of the nations as her servants, is recalled. Messiah,

quoting the promise, exclaims, " I will exult in His holiness," that is, in the certainty that the promise will be kept. He confidently declares it shall be so (vs. 6-8).

So He will take possession of the whole country from Shechem to Judah. He then contrasts the dignity of Israel with the ignominy of their enemies. As to Israel, Ephraim shall be His crown and Judah His sceptre. As to the enemy, Moab shall be His foot-bath, Edom His shoe slave, and Philistia His out-runner to precede Him in the street and proclaim His passage with shouting. To provide a foot-bath and sandals and to run before the chariot of the master, were duties performed by slaves. Then the Messiah asks with exultation on behalf of His people, " Who will bring this wonderful victory to pass " ? and answers that the very God Who in righteous chastisement cast them off, is the God Who will deliver them from trouble, for human help is vain, and that He will tread down their enemies (vs. 9-12). See notes on Ps. lvii. and cviii.

The spiritual intelligence and instruction in the Psalm should be noticed. The defeat of Israel's armies is recognized as resulting from Divine chastisement and not from military incapacity. This chastisement is not rebelled against ; and deliverance from the enemy is sought not from man but from God:

PSALM LXI.—Psalms lxi. and lxxii. open and close the third and last group of Book II. The theme of the one is the king and His people in rejection ; that of the other the king and His people in reception. The subject of the entire group is Israel's redemption.

The doctrine of this, and similar Psalms, is the perfection of the faith of Messiah, as man, under every form of hatred, affliction and adversity. The sharper these became the more He trusted. His moral glory as the Servant of Jehovah shines through all. This position of dependence and suffering He voluntarily took in union with, and on behalf of, His people. Hence they are cheered and comforted in trial, and their faith sustained by these communications, for they prove that their King and Shepherd trod these dark paths before them ; that He trusted God and was delivered ; and that a like deliverance is consequently assured to them.

The Psalm expresses the griefs of a heart

at once true, sinless, and human. It may
be thus analysed :

A cry (v. 1)—Its petitions (vs. 2–4)—Its
related vows (v. 5).

A prayer (v. 1)—Its petitions (vs. 6 and 7)
—Its related vows (v. 8).

The lips are Messiah's. The alternation
in the cry (vs. 2–4) between future and past
should be noticed. " I will cry "—" Thou
hast been a shelter for Me." " I will abide
and will trust."—" Thou hast heard My
vows " (vs. 2–5). This exhibits a past
experience and a future confidence, both
equally perfect. As dependent Man He
prayed to be led to a rock shelter that was
Divine ; and as sinless Man He conceived of
no higher joy than to perpetually dwell' in
the presence of God (v. 4).

The prayer (vs. 6 and 7) may read thus :
" O prolong Thou the King's life and His
years from generation to generation !
Enthrone Him before God for ever ! O
prepare mercy and truth, let them preserve
Him. "

The vows of verses 5 and 8 are those of
Ps xxii. 22, the heritage that of Isa. liii. 10
and 11 and Heb. ii. 13. He has not yet
received the heritage, but He is trusting for
it (Heb. ii. 13) saying, " I will trust in Him."
This is a Jeduthun Psalm, as also are
xxxviii. and lxxvi. A comparison of 1 Chron.
vi. 44, xxv. 1–6, xxvi. 10, 2 Chron. v. 12,
and xxxv. 15 makes it clear that he was one
of the chief musicians ; that he was also
named Ethan ; and that he was a descendant
of Merari. Asaph was a descendant of
Gershom, and Heman of Kohath. These
were the three chief musicians. All were sons
of Aaron.

PSALM LXII.—Acts xvii. 31 and Matt.
xvi. 27 make it evident that Messiah is the
Man of verse 3 and the God of verse 12.

The Psalm contains two divisions. Man's
hatred to the Messiah occupies the first four
verses, and man's hatred to His people the
following six. The last two verses relate to
the judgment of Matt. xvi. and Acts xvii.

In the first advent the enemy tried to cast
Him down from His excellency (vs. 1–4), and
they will try to cast His people down from
their excellency immediately prior to His
future coming in power and great glory
(vs. 5–10)

The first two verses reveal the perfection
of Messiah's trust when suffering the hatred

described in verses 3 and 4 : and verses
5–8 predict the faith which His people,
animated by His spirit, will repose in God
when suffering the oppression of the men
described in verses 9 and 10. Except morally
verses 5 and 6 are not a repetition of verses
1 and 2. They are separated by a long period
of time : the one is the expression of Christ
personally when on earth ; the other, that of
Christ sympathetically in His people's time
of future trouble. He in the days of His
flesh stilled His heart and waited on God for
deliverance. He desired to wait on none other,
and He was not moved (v. 2) or cast down
(v. 4). His people will wait only upon God,
and will desire to wait upon none other, and
He will deliver them, and they shall not be
moved (v. 6). The words " I " (v. 6) and
" us " (v. 8) mark His oneness with His
people.

The words " truly " " only " and " surely "
are translations of the one Hebrew word.
It occurs six times in the Psalm. Its modern
meaning is " Whatever happens."

The term " greatly moved " (v. 2) may
mean that great efforts to move Him failed,
or it may mean that His enemies were permitted to put Him to death, but that further
than that they could do nothing. Against
His people they will not be permitted to
obtain any advantage whether temporary or
permanent.

The presence of the word " glory " in verse
7 in relation to verse 2 points to the distinction between His first coming in weakness
and His future coming in power, and marks the
distance which separates these two verses.

Verses 3 and 4 should read as in the R.V.
The picture is most vivid. A Man so feeble
as to be comparable to a bowing wall and a
tottering fence is set upon by a bloodthirsty
multitude hungering for His life and their
hearts inflamed with the very hatred of hell.
These were the men that shouted " Crucify
Him ! Crucify Him ! " If they blessed with
their mouth it was hypocrisy (Matt. xxii. 16),
for they were liars like their father the devil
(John viii. 44 and 55), and they only consulted
to cast Him down from His excellency. He
speaks to them in verse 3, and of them in
verse 4.

The loving words with which He speaks
to encourage His people (v. 8) are as
altogether priceless as the words which He,
on their behalf at the same crisis, addresses
to God (vs. 5–7).

In verse 9 He speaks of their oppressors, and in verse 10 He speaks to their oppressors ; and so, as predicted in Isa. liii., He, the Righteous One, will by His teaching turn many to righteousness.

The last two verses are rich with fact and teaching. God has once for all spoken (v. 11 with Heb. i. 2). Two facts are revealed in that revelation. First : that power belongs to Him. Second : that He will render to every man according to His work. Christ will be the Almighty and impartial Judge. But the great beauty of the passage is the parenthesis between these two statements : " Also unto Thee, O Adonai, belongeth mercy." The foes will be doomed by their works ; the redeemed saved by His grace.

PSALM LXIII.—When David was in the Wilderness of Judah exiled from the worship of the Tabernacle (v. 2) and pursued by those that sought his life (v. 9), this prophetic message was given him by the Spirit to refresh his heart and sustain his faith. It sings of the first and second Advents of David's Son and Lord. His first Advent occupies verses 1-10 ; His second, verse 11.

In His first Advent He found this world a wilderness, a dry and weary land without one stream of moral refreshment (v. 1), and His heart longed for the joys He had tasted from all eternity in His Father's bosom (v. 2 and John xvii. 5). But if He found this world to be a thirsty wilderness yet by day (v. 4) and by night (v. 6) He found God to be there a satisfying source of perfect happiness (v. 5) ; and enriched by His knowledge of God He closely followed Him (v. 8), con- sciously experiencing every moment the support of His upholding hand (v. 8), de- clared that He would seek no other shelter than Jehovah's wings (v. 7), that He would rejoice in that sure place of refuge (v. 7), and confidently predicted His future glories as King (v. 11), the exaltation of His people, and the doom of His false followers.

Only once did perfect music reach the ear of God from the Wilderness of earth. It was when Jesus sang these Psalms. Man is incapable of realizing what a refreshment such singing was to His Father's heart and ear.

The moral activities of His soul and flesh in verse 1 reveal His sinless human nature.

The statement of verse 3 is most sweet ; and the declarations that follow are an added sweetness. They testify that amid the solitude, the emptiness, and the deadly perils of the Wilderness He found God's presence and favour a cause of loud rejoicing and a portion better than life itself.

Verses 1 and 9 speak of the earth—the one, its surface; the other, its lower parts. He descended from the Father's glory to the surface of the earth and found it dry and thirsty. His enemies shall descend into the lower parts of the earth and will there find not one drop of water to cool their parched tongues (Luke xvi. 24). The bodies of these persecutors of His people, who are to Him as His own soul, shall be slain by the sword and devoured by wild beasts, whilst their souls shall descend into the under-world (vs. 9, 10).

The enthronement of Messiah as King and His consequent joy in fellowship with God ; the happiness of His true worshippers who are to enter into that joy and to shout aloud with glory ; and the eternal silence of the false professors and idolators—set out the rich contents of this last verse.

PSALM LXIV.—In Matt xxii, Luke xi, and in other similar passages, it is recorded that the leaders of the Jews composed in private crafty questions for the Lord so as to entangle Him in His teaching, and thus to be in a position to accuse Him either to the Sanhe- drim or to the Roman Government as a heretic or an insurgent, and consequently guilty of death, and that they then in public rudely and vehemently proposed these questions to Him.

In this Psalm are found His comments upon their conduct, and His appeal to God about it.

As man hated the Master so will he hate the servant ; and, accordingly, the Psalm reveals the similar persecution which His followers are sure to suffer. Christ here pleads for them in His own name, and encourages them by the certainty of the doom which is speedily to fall upon their oppressors, and by the happiness which they are to enjoy together with Him.

" Prayer " (v. 1) here reads, " sad musing." The hatred of man to Himself and to His people occasioned these sorrowful musings. " Fear of the enemy " means apprehension of the snares of verses 2, 5, and 6 purposed by the enemy.

The first member of verse 2 pictures the

enemy in secret planning the questions with which to entangle Him. The secret counsel of Matt. xxii. 15 is that here predicted. The second member views the tumultuous proposal of these questions in public—as recorded in Luke xi. 53 and 54 (R.V. marg.).

So cunning were these snares, and so successfully, as they thought, hidden, that they triumphantly ask: " Who shall see them ? " (v. 5).

" Iniquities " (v. 6) mean " iniquitous questions "—questions which they hoped would involve Him with the Jewish or Roman governments ; and the addition " they accomplish diligent search " expresses the satisfaction which they felt at planning questions so clever and crafty that they were sure to accomplish the desired purpose. Christ, Who read their thoughts and knew their hearts, gives in this verse His judgment on both. He says their heart was deep. As to those who love Him their heart is upright (v. 10 .

Encouraging themselves in their evil purpose (v. 5) they suddenly (compare v. 7) spring their questions upon Him (v. 4) secreting themselves under an assumption of moral earnestness and patriotism. The Hebrew text, illuminated by the Gospel narrative, suggests this meaning as the import of the words " in secret." These artful questions are described by the Lord as bitter words, like to poisoned arrows, and shot from a tongue whetted as a sword.

With these many arrows they tried in vain to wound Him ; but God shall without fail and suddenly (compare v. 4) wound them fatally with but one arrow (v. 7) ; and the bitter slanders of their tongues shall rise in judgment against them and cause them to perish (v. 8).

So fearful will be their doom that as in the case of Korah, Dathan and Abiram, all seeing it shall flee (v. 8) ; and all men shall fear and shall pronounce the judgment to be from God ; and will intelligently ascribe it as His (v. 9).

At the very time that this just judgment shall fall upon the enemy, He Who is both Perfect (v. 4) and Righteous (v. 10) shall be glorified together with the upright—He upon His throne, and they round about it.

PSALM LXV.—The Remnant according to the election of grace (Rom. xi. 5) here sings of the day of the establishment in Sion, and over the happy earth, of the Kingdom of God and the power of His Messiah (Rev. xii. 10) ; of the new moral birth necessary to entrance into that Kingdom (v. 4) ; of the sufferings of its subjects (v. 3) ; and of the judgment of its foes (v. 5). Israel will then perform her vow of praise (v. 1), and the converted nations will unite with her in the worship of Messiah (vs. 2 and 8).

Praise waits, not in the silence of apprehension but of confident expectation, for the promised moment of Messiah's apparition, and then will be heard the song vowed in the time of trouble ! The Gentiles are to rejoice with His people (Rom. xv. 10), so He will reign not only in Sion (v. 1) but also over the whole earth (vs. 2 and 8), and fill it with happiness (vs. 9-13).

But while awaiting this desired day the Remnant is trodden down. Iniquitous actions prevail against them (v. 3). But their hearts, contrited by the Holy Spirit, do not speak further of man's transgressions against them but only of their own transgressions against God, and faith looks forward for purging to Calvary as now it looks back to Calvary. Faith then said " Thou shalt purge " ; faith now says " Thou hast purged."

All sin being purged by the precious blood of Christ, fellowship with God in the light is possible (1 John i. 7), and the joys of that fellowship become a conscious experience (v. 4).

God, in righteous fidelity to His promises, will answer the prayer of His people for deliverance from their persecutors by terrible deeds of judgment upon these evil-doers.

As He executed terrible things in righteousness upon Pharaoh and his people in the past, so will He upon Anti-Christ and his hosts in the future, and thus ever be to His saints the God of their salvation.

Not yet is He the confidence of all the dwellers on land and of them that are afar off upon the sea, but He is worthy to be such (v. 5) ; and this He demonstrates to the dwellers on land by His being girded with power to set fast the mountains, and to those that are afar off upon the sea by His government of its mighty waves. He also can still the tumult of the peoples, and so establish universal peace. This demonstration of His power over nature and over man will compel all that dwell in the uttermost parts of the earth to worship Him (v. 8). The verb

" to fear " here means to worship. This central section of the Psalm should close with the word " tokens," and the final section commence thus : " Thou shalt make the outgoings of the morning and of the evening to rejoice," that is to say, the entire earth.

The millennial bliss pictured in verses 8-13 is entrancing. The morning and evening of every day from the one end of the heaven to the other will witness and minister joy. The river of God (v. 9), i.e., the waters which are above the earth, will discharge grateful showers (v. 10), with the result that years (v. 11) as well as days (v. 8) will be crowned with goodness. Hill and vale will wave with golden grain ; the pastures will be clothed with flocks ; and earth's happy inhabitants will be constrained to sing aloud and shout for joy. The Hebrew text here is very emphatic. It may be translated : " They shall most certainly sing."

PSALM LXVI.—In harmony with its Neginoth subscription the Psalm praises God for smiting the nations in judgment and Israel in chastisement. It will be sung by Israel and the Messiah at the opening of the millennium. She will recite His past action with her enemies (vs. 3-7) and with herself (vs. 9-12) ; she will offer the sacrifices of praise promised when in trouble (vs. 13-15) ; and she will invite all who fear God to listen to her testimony as to His faithfulness and love in the fulfilment to her of His promises of deliverance (vs. 16-20).

The Psalm is composed of two corresponding stanzas. These may be thus set out :

Exhortation, " Make a joyful noise unto God," vs. 1-2.
Declaration, God's action to His foes, v. 3.
Adoration, " All the earth shall worship Thee," v. 4.
Invitation, " Come and see," vs. 6-7.

Exhortation, " O bless our God ye nations," v. 8.
Declaration, God's action to His people, vs. 9-12.
Adoration, " I will go into Thy house," vs. 13-15.
Invitation, " Come and hear," vs. 16-20.

The " sea " and the " flood " (v. 6) are the Red Sea and the Jordan. " People " (v.8)

should read " peoples," i.e., the Gentiles. They are invited to bless " our God," i.e., Israel's God.

In spite of the unceasing efforts of Satan and man to utterly destroy Israel, her twelve tribes will appear at Mount Sion upon the millennium morn, and so demonstrate the truth of the ninth verse. They will testify that the chastisements justly laid upon them (vs. 10-12) were designed in love and executed in wisdom.

The praise promised when in trouble (v. 14) will then be offered under the leadership of the Great High Priest. On behalf of them He will use the first person singular (vs. 13-15).

" A wealthy place " (v. 12) i.e., restored Palestine.

The last three verses read thus :—

Had I regarded iniquity in my heart
Jehovah would not have heard me,
But God did indeed hear me ;
He did attend to the voice of my prayer.
Blessed be God Who did not turn away my prayer,
Nor His mercy from me.

PSALM LXVII.—According to the Scriptures God chose Israel as His agent to lead all nations to Him ; and to this end He gave her a sufficient revelation of Himself and of His salvation.

Israel refused this high honour ; but the Divine purpose has not thereby been defeated. She will be restored ; she will yet publish peace to the nations, and win all peoples to the knowledge and service of God. It is of this great fact of the future that this Psalm sings. It therefore fitly follows the preceding song. God will bless Israel ; and, as the result, all nations will fear Him.

Here appears a deep principle of the Word of God, true in all dispensations, that the spiritual welfare of those far from God is dependent upon revival and restoration of soul among the people of God.

The Psalm may be thus analysed :—

Israel restored—Effect : all nations won, verses 1 and 2.
The nations praise God
Effect : National felicity, vs. 3 and 4.
The nations praise God
Effect : National prosperity, vs. 5 and 6
Israel restored—Effect : All nations worship, verses 6 and 7.

" Us " (v. 1) means Israel. " Way " (v. 2) expresses God's character in action. The term " Thy saving health " means God's power to save. " People " (vs. 3, 4, and 6) should read " peoples." If the word " nations " (v. 2) be used right through the Psalm the distinction between them and Israel will be better observed.

Verse 4 should read : " Then shall the nations be glad," etc. The reading will show the correspondence with verse 6 : " then shall the earth yield her increase." Thus restored Israel will bring joy of heart and wealth of pocket to all the inhabitants of the earth.

The prophetic doctrine that the salvation of the world depends upon the restoration of Israel (Rom. xi. 12 and 15) is repeated in the last two verses, as it was affirmed in the first two. This repetition emphasizes its importance.

The great moral lesson is here again taught that spiritual prosperity is not to be desired for mere personal enjoyment but also for the spiritual enrichment of others.

PSALM LXVIII.—The Redeemer waited for in the previous Psalms now appears (Num. x. 35). The majesty of His person, the destruction of His foes, the deliverance and joy of His people, and their appointment as head of the nations furnish the context of the Psalm. His love to them in the Wilderness (vs. 7–10) and in Canaan (vs. 11–14) are cited as illustrating His future fellowship with them in the sanctuary (vs. 24–27) and in the government of the world (vs. 28–35) ; and all is based upon His resurrection (vs. 17 and 18), as is declared in Acts ii. and Eph. iv.

The Psalm is rich in Divine titles. Jah occurs twice. It first appears in the Second Book of the Pentateuch, and, correspondingly, it first appears in the Second Book of the Psalms. The defeat of the enemy being the great background of the Psalm, the title Elohim is found twenty-six times. The other titles are Shaddai, Jehovah, El, Adonai. At the setting forth of the Ark (Num. x. 35) the formula was : " Let Jehovah arise ! " Here it is : " Let Elohim arise ! " because here His enemies are in question, but in Num. x. His people form the subject.

This song was probably first sung at the going up of the Ark to Sion (1 Chron. xv). Its subscription, Shoshannim, suggests the Passover festival. See notes on Ps. xliv.

Two facts of peculiar sweetness are prominent. First, this Mighty God in His distant habitation, and in the sinless essence of His Being, is a Father of the fatherless and a Guardian of the widow (vs. 5 and 6) ; and second, that He restores and enriches rebellious sinners (vs. 6 and 18).

His " goings " in the Wilderness (v. 7) correspond to His goings in the Sanctuary (v. 24) ; and His subjugation of the kings of Palestine (v. 12) corresponds to His future conquest of the kings of the whole earth (v. 29). Further, the accompaniments of this double going correspond (vs. 8 and 25). In verse 8 the earth, the heavens, and, between them, Sinai. In verse 25, the singers, the players, and, between them, the damsels with timbrels. The singers and the players were men.

Verse 6 may read thus : " God bringeth the exiled home. He bringeth those that were bound with chains, even the rebellious who dwelt in a parched land." Thus Israel is described as exiled, imprisoned and rebellious.

The manna and the quails " rained " upon them from heaven, and the water flowed for them from the smitten rock (v. 9) ; and so " therein " (v. 10), i.e., in the Wilderness, God prepared of His goodness for impoverished Israel ; for apart from Him they were poor indeed.

The conquest of the kings of Canaan is recalled in verses 11–14. " Jehovah gave the word," i.e., commanded and occasioned victory. A great company of women proclaimed the fact, as is the custom in the East. Women proclaimed the destruction of Pharaoh, the death of Goliath, the Resurrection of Christ, and they will celebrate the defeat of Anti-Christ (v. 25).

The song of the women is recited in verses 12–14. The word " saying " should be supplied at the end of verse 11. Verse 13 is a figure of peace (the sheepfold) with honour (the gold and silver). The verse reads : " Ye shall lie down among the sheep-folds, and ye shall be as the wings of a dove," etc. The completeness of the victory is stated in verse 14 : " When Shaddai scattered kings in it (Canaan) it was as snow in Salmon "—that is, the kings disappeared before the Sun of Righteousness as snow before the sun of the heavens ; they were as powerless as it.

" A mountain of God," i.e., a mighty mountain, " is the mountain of Bashan—a mountain of lofty peaks " (v. 15). " Why are ye envious (of Sion) ye lofty peaks " ? (v. 16). These mountains symbolize earthly monarchies. Their jealousy of Sion is rebuked. God tells them that He has chosen that mountain as His home, and that He will never leave it.

The resurrection stanza (vs. 17-20) forms the basis of Acts ii. and Eph. iv. These two chapters establish this Psalm as Messianic. Christ having made death His captive and ascended to the right hand of God, as Man received gifts from God for men. These gifts were the Holy Spirit (Acts ii.) and inspired men (Eph. iv.). His delights were with the sons of men ; and in the exceeding riches of that grace He gives gifts even to the rebellious so that He may make His home among them—no longer rebellious but new-born.

" The issues from death " (v. 20), i.e., means of escape from death.

The righteous judgment of Israel's oppressors is foretold in verses 21-23. The sense of verse 22 is : I will bring their oppressors again even from Bashan ; I will bring them again from the very depths of the sea ! This expresses their inability to escape. The purpose of their being thus fetched back for justice is declared in verse 23 — a verse that strikes against man's unholy thoughts of the love of God.

This translation is suggested for verse 26 : " In the congregations from the fountain of Israel "—i.e., from Abraham as the father of the Twelve Tribes—" bless ye Elohim Jehovah " (Heb. Primitive text). These Twelve Tribes are all included in verse 27 between Benjamin on the extreme south and Naphtali on the extreme north. Benjamin was the least of the tribes, and the last on the jasper stone of Aaron's breast-plate, but jasper is the first stone in the foundations of the Holy City (Rev. xxi. 19).

The future supremacy of Israel over all earthly monarchs, here compared. as in Daniel, to wild beasts (v. 30 R.V.), is predicted in the last stirring stanza of the song (vs. 28-35). The kings will bring their tribute money (vs. 29-31) for the rebuilding of the Temple at Jerusalem. They will " stretch out their hands " in homage filled with gifts (v. 31), and in adoration, for Messiah will be " terrible," i.e., an object of reverential worship in that coming day of His power and glory (v. 35).

PSALM LXIX.—Eight quotations from the New Testament establish the relationship of this Psalm to the Messiah. They are John xv. 25, John ii, 17, Rom. xv. 3, 2 Cor. vi. 2, Matt. xxvii. 34, Mark. xv. 23, John xix. 29, Rom xi. 9. The voice is, therefore, that of the Man of Sorrows, excepting verses 22-28 which record the Holy Spirit's prediction of temporary wrath upon the nation because of its supreme sin in the crucifixion of their King and Redeemer (Rom. xi. 9-12).

The theme is the sufferings of Christ as the Guilt-offering. Ps. xxii predicted His sufferings as the Sin-offering, and Ps. xl as the Burnt-offering.

He, as the Guilt-offering, restored that which He took not away ; that is, He perfectly restored to God the love and obedience of which man had robbed God ; and, at the same time, He voluntarily charged Himself with man's foolishness and guiltiness, called them His own, thereby declaring Himself to be the guilty person (vs. 4 and 5 with Lev. v. 14-16).

Founded upon this Divine fact three fundamental doctrines of the Gospel are taught in the Psalm : First, that sin is the cause of man's misery and of God's wrath. Second, that Christ's atoning sacrifice is the Divinely-appointed way of salvation. Third, that the resurrection of Christ is the demonstration of God's acceptance of His person and of His work, and a pledge of the future redemption of the world. This universal restoration is sung of in verses 30-36 ; and, as predicted throughout the whole Bible, it is here declared that Sion will be the metropolis of the renewed earth.

The Psalm discovers to the reader the depth of the spiritual, mental and physical sufferings of Immanuel; His sufferings from man appear in verses 4, 7, 8, 9, 10, 11, 12, 19, 20, 21 and 26 ; His anguish in Gethsemane in verses 1, 2, 14 and 15 ; and His agony upon the Cross in verses 3, 5, 6, 16, 18, 20 and 21. So appalling was the horror of Gethsemane that to His anguished soul earth and hell must have become one ; and, accordingly, His cries in the one equally apply to the other.

The sense of verses 6 and 7 is, that God's abandonment of His beloved Son at Calvary might upset the faith of those who confide in God for deliverance from human or Satanic hatred. He prayed that they might understand that He, as the Guilt-offering, should be so forsaken.

That Mary of Nazareth had other sons besides Jesus is stated in verse 8.

"The acceptable time" (v. 13) was the morning of the resurrection, as is clear from Isa. xlix. 8 and 2 Cor. vi. 2.

The judgment (vs. 22–28) pronounced by the Spirit through David upon the haters of Messiah and His people (v. 26), is declared in Rom. xi. to be a temporary judgment, and to occasion the offer of the kingdom to the Gentiles.

The predicative judgments of Matt. xxiii are a development of verse 27.

Having been in response to His prayer set up on High (v. 29), He utters the loud praises of verses 30–36. An animal for sacrifice should be full-grown and ceremonially pure. Horns determined the one and hoofs the other (v. 31).

Sion will be appointed as the royal city, and Palestine as Immanuel's land. The children of Abraham, Isaac, and Jacob, His servants, shall inherit Canaan as promised ; and with them shall be associated all that love Messiah's name.

The Psalm throbs with unspeakable agony. It helps the reader to feel how amazing was, and is, the love that endured such depths of anguish and horror in the interest of people who only hated Him.

PSALM LXX.—The purpose of this Psalm is to animate the courage and sustain the faith of the Remnant of Jacob in their future day of trouble by remembering the sufferings of the Divine Son of David predicted in Ps. xl. and recorded in the gospels.

Just as Ps. liii. is not a meaningless repetition of Ps. xiv. (see notes on those two Psalms) so this Psalm is not a repetition of Ps. xl. 13–17). The one is placed at the end of the Genesis Book ; the other, at the end of the Exodus Book. Jehovah is the marked title in the one ; Elohim in the other. The theme of the one is the Messiah's personal sufferings in His first advent ; that of the other His sympathetic sufferings in His people immediately prior to His second advent. The first predicts the eternal punishment of His persecutors and the unending felicity of His lovers ; the second assures the like destinies to those who hate or love Him in the persons of His followers The one was committed to the Chief Musician for public use ; the other is an incentive to

remembrance to cheer fugitives hiding from their persecutors. The words "together" and "destroy" appear in the one but not in the other. Desolation is the reward of the enemy in the one ; retribution (v. 3) in the other. "Yet Jehovah thinketh upon Me" are replaced by "Make haste unto Me, O Elohim."

On comparing these differences it will be noticed how they harmonize with the change of persons and times.

The Remnant, hated and oppressed by their future enemies, will use this Psalm ; and calling to remembrance the similar hatred suffered by their Messiah, will, like Him, and animated by His Spirit in them, wait patiently for Jehovah to deliver them out of their distresses ; being assured that the Elohim Who delivered Him will deliver them.

As throughout the Psalms so here, Christ makes Himself one with the redeemed and prays for them as if for Himself.

The import of the words "Say continually let God be magnified" implies the actual and perpetual possession of the felicity promised in the verse (4).

Christ remained poor and needy to the very end, waiting patiently for Jehovah. His people will, in a like extreme poverty, wait and trust to the end. This Psalm and Ps. xl are both fitly placed at the end of their respective Books. Joseph in Genesis and Israel in Exodus illustrate them. Both suffered from the hatred of man because they were witnesses for God. Joseph in the prison waited for Jehovah and was set upon a throne. Israel in "the furnace" similarly waited and was delivered. She in her trial of cruel bondage must often have been cheered by calling to remembrance the sufferings and subsequent glories of Joseph. In her future day of deeper suffering she will nourish her faith by singing this Psalm and by calling to remembrance, as commanded by it, the facts of Ps. xl.

Retribution appears to be the sense of verse 3 in a literal translation of the Hebrew text.

Ps. xl sings of the perfection of His person ; Ps. lxx, the sufficiency of His work.

"Poor and needy," i.e., poor in spirit, needy in circumstances.

PSALM LXXI.—The previous Psalm having been given to David, this, in the absence of a title may be assumed to have been also given to him, and very possibly to have refreshed his heart during the dark days of Absalom's rebellion. It must also have refreshed the heart of his Lord when suffering man's hatred, and it will feed the faith of Israel in the future and darkest day of her history. It will be her response to Messiah's heartening message of the last two verses of Ps. xxxi. This seventy-first Psalm shows that she will keep loving Him, and trusting Him, and waiting for Him in the confidence that He will deliver her from the wicked, unrighteous, and cruel man of verse 4, i.e., Anti-Christ.

The connection between Ps. xxxi and lxxi helps to show that the similar language of the first three verses of each is not idle repetition but a most precious proof that Christ and His people are bound in the one bundle of life. The prior Psalm predicts His personal sufferings in the past; the later, His sympathetic sufferings in the present and in the future. The similarity of the three first verses of both Psalms in relation to verse 11 of this Psalm points to the fact that the servant is not greater than his Lord; and that His words are true when He said: "If they have persecuted Me they will also persecute you."

Israel here reviews God's love and care and training of her from birth to old age. She was born of Sarah. This review is thus repeated:

Youth, Maturity, Old age, verses 5–9.
Youth, Maturity, Old age, verses 17 and 18.

Conformably with the interpretation of the two Psalms, the fourth verse of Ps. xxxi. introduces the Pharisees, the Sadducees and the Herodians, and the fourth verse of Ps. lxxi. presents their true master Anti-Christ.

The future tense should be used in verses 8 and 13, and thus emphasize, by contrast, the "I wills" of verse 14 and the "shalls" of verse 15.

The expression "I know not the numbers" (v. 15) is a figure denoting infinitude. The sense of verse 16 is: "I will come with the inexhaustible narration of the mighty acts of Jehovah Elohim" (R.V.). "Very high" (v. 19) means very distinguished. The title "Holy One of Israel" (v. 22) occurs three times in the Psalms and thirty times in Isaiah.

The words "continually" and "all the day" alternate thus: continually (v. 3), continually (v. 6), all the day (v. 8); continually (v. 14), all the day (v. 15), all the day (v. 24).

Using the R.V. marginal reading verse 6 may read: "Thou hast been my Benefactor from the moment of my birth."

PSALM LXXII.—This Psalm sings of the king that is to reign in righteousness (Isa. xxxii. 1). Its title declares it to relate to Solomon, i.e., to Him of whom Solomon is a type as Prince of Peace.

As the Second Book of the Pentateuch opens with a people bound in slavery and closes with Messiah throned in majesty (Exod. xl. 34), so this Second Book of the Psalms begins with a people sunk in misery (Ps. xlii) and ends with a king reigning in glory.

Christ's millennial reign, and the universal happiness which it will secure, is the subject matter of the Psalm. The speaker is the Holy Spirit; the Person spoken to, God; and the Person spoken of, Christ. The Holy Spirit in verse 1 asks God to commit the execution of His judgments and the administration of His justice unto the true Solomon; and confidently states that the result will be the punishment of evil-doers (v. 4), the happiness of His people (vs. 2–4), and their perpetual loyalty to God's service (v. 5).

In these predictions there is no misgiving in the Divine mind as to the perfection of Messiah's government; just as in other prophecies there is no misgiving as to the perfection of His person and the efficacy of His atoning work.

The beneficence of His rule in favour of the poor and needy is pointed to eleven times in the prophecy. This contrasts with the attitude of earthly sovereigns, who, as a rule, abandon the oppressed and support the oppressor.

The words "by righteousness" (v. 3) intimate that as a result of His righteous rule the "mountains" and "hills," i.e., the great and small governments shall bring peace and not terror to the nations of the earth.

Messiah will dispense justice in favour of the poor (v. 4); and His government will be as beneficent to man as rain is to the ground (v. 6). In His days righteousness shall flourish (v. 7); and the three great families of Shem (vs. 8 and 9), Ham (v. 10), and Japheth (v. 11) will form His dominion, as predicted in Gen. ix. 26 and 27.

Accepting the word "they" as in the R.V.

and supplying the ellipses, verse 15 will read: And they, i e., the poor and needy (vs. 12-14), shall live prosperously and happily; and they in their gratitude will give Him of the gold of Sheba; they will pray to Him and for Him continually; and they will keep praising Him all the day long. All Christian people should have a liberal hand, a praying heart, and a praising tongue.

The Hebrew text favours the double translation: " Prayer also shall be made to Him and for Him." 'In Rev. v. prayer is made to Him in verses 8-10, and prayer is made for Him in verse 13.

Material prosperity will accompany moral felicity. A handful of corn cast into the ground on the top of a mountain will produce a harvest comparable to the forests of Lebanon, and dwellers in the city slums will then be as healthy as the grass of the earth (v. 16). The impoverished farmer and the sickly artizan will be alike prosperous and vigorous.

As in the other Books of the Psalms, a doxology and a double Amen close the prophecy (vs. 18 and 19).

In the epilogue (v. 20) David declares that this predicted reign will fully satisfy all his prayers. The Psalm realized will mean all prophecy materialized.

THE PSALMS

BOOK III

This Book corresponds to the Third Book of the Pentateuch. Its subject is the Sanctuary, as that of the First Book was the Blessed Man and that of the Second, Israel.

The Divine title of Leviticus is: "And He called." Only those whom God chooses to approach unto Him (lxv. 4) can worship Him; and He seeks such worshippers (John iv. 23).

Two groups of Psalms compose the Book. The first group contains Ps. lxxiii.-lxxxiii. It presents the Sanctuary in relation to man. Its prominent Divine title is Elohim. The second group contains Ps. lxxxiv.-lxxxix. Its subject is the Sanctuary in relation to Jehovah, and that title distinguishes it.

All the Psalms speak of, or refer to, the Sanctuary; those in the first group are " to Asaph " and those in the second, " to Korah "—except lxxxvi. and lxxxix.

Israel as a worshipper in her future time of trouble, is the subject of the Book rather than the Messiah and the Remnant, which is that of the first two books.

PSALM LXXIII.—The Third Book views Israel as a Nation.

The " I " and the " Me " in this Psalm are emphatic. The Revised Version should be used throughout. The Prophet, perplexed with the problem that the ungodly prosper and the children of the kingdom suffer, learns the lesson that, outside the Sanctuary, the mind is distracted and the heart fermented, but that inside all is peace. Verse 1 is the conclusion; the following verses describe the distraction. Looking in confounds; looking out confuses; looking up comforts.

Verse 1 accords with Rom. viii. 1. The accord appears if both verses are translated literally, thus: " Nothing is a condemnation," and: " Nothing but good is God to Israel."

The sense of verse 15 is, that to express publicly the statements in verses 13 and 14 would morally injure the children of God The verse contrasts with verse 28. To publicly declare God's teachings in and for the soul profits the hearers.

In respect of the problem in question the light of man's intellect resolves nothing (v. 16), but the supernatural light of the Sanctuary explains everything.

The prosperity of the foolish is as a dream or illusion; and the image that God shall despise is the illusion of which they dreamt. Their prosperity has no substance.

The last stanza of the Psalm (vs. 23-28) records the fruit of the experience. The heart learns the sufficiency of God to satisfy it both in time and eternity (v. 25). Such fruit explains the value of trial. Under such experiences flesh and heart fail (v. 26). Nature can do nothing else. It can give no victory in such conflicts. But in God the heart finds a reservoir of strength that is inexhaustible; it is a portion for ever. These verses (25 and 26) are thought by some to contrast with verses 10 and 11 which are understood to mean that God's people turn from Him to follow the prosperous of this world, the result being bitterness (v. 10) and scepticism (v. 11). But an interpretation more in harmony with the teaching of the Psalm would be, that the word " hither " means the Sanctuary into which the writer had retired under the pressure of the problem, and he states that because of the facts set out in verses 3-9, " therefore " God's people do as he himself did, repair to the Sanctuary and make the experience that the Psalmist made (vs. 23 to 28), that an abounding cup of refreshment is there poured out to them. In this interpretation the eleventh verse is the language of the ungodly.

The " Me " of the last verse, as of the second, is emphatic. The argument of the verse is three-fold. First: The experience of trust in God when He seemingly hides

Himself is desirable (Jno. xx. 29). Second : It is good to company with Him. Third : It is profitable to others to testify for Him. So Messiah chose the Twelve that, first, they should be with Him, and, then, that they should preach for Him (Mark iii. 14).

The similarity of the language of verses 23-28 with that used by the Messiah in other Psalms is a striking evidence of the government of His Spirit in those who walk with Him.

PSALM LXXIV.—The enemy in the Sanctuary is the theme of the Psalm (v. 3). It predicts the destruction of the first Temple by the Chaldeans, of the second Temple by the Romans, and, possibly, of the future third Temple by the Ten Kings, and it describes the present condition of Sion under the treading-down of the Gentiles. It is the ninth of the thirteen Maschil Psalms. It was " given to Asaph." This may .mean that Asaph was a prophet ; or the name may be a term expressive of a certain class of Psalmodic prophecy. It was confided to the Chief Musician with the injunction " Don't destroy, " i.e., Al-taschith.

The second Psalm of each Book of the Psalms treats of the malignity of the enemy. " Thy pasture " (v. 1) " Thy congregation " (v. 2) " Thine inheritance " (v. 2) " Thy Sanctuary " (v. 7) " Thy turtle-dove " (v. 19) and " Thy poor " (v. 19) are all terms of affection for Israel.

In verse 2 " rod " should read " sceptre," " this " should be omitted before Mount Sion, and the word " remember " should be repeated thus : Remember Thy congregation, etc. Remember the sceptre of Thine inheritance, etc. Remember Mount Sion, etc. God purchased Israel from Pharaoh.

A modern translation of verse 3 reads : " Hasten to the perpetual desolations, and see all that the enemy hath done wickedly in the Sanctuary "; and verse 4 : " Thine adversaries roar as lions in the midst of Thy great congregation ; they set up their signs as Divine signs." So to-day is seen, in that which professes to be the Kingdom of God, the abolition of Scriptural worship and the substitution of idolatrous symbols.

Verses 5 and 6 compare the energy of the constructors of the Temple with the energy of its demolishers.

The Lord, when foretelling the destruction of the Temple by the Romans, in substance repeated verses 7 and 8 of this Psalm. They cast it down to the ground, they did not leave one stone upon another, and history says they burned all the synagogues in Palestine. This is the first occurrence of the word synagogue in the Bible. It is Greek. The Hebrew term means meeting-house.

Israel's anguish was, is, and will be deepened by the three statements of verse 9 : No signs from God manifesting relationship, no preacher to comfort (1 Cor. xiv. 3), and none to show from Scripture how long the tribulation should last. All fails except faith ; and it, counting upon God, turns the " how long " of verse 9 into the " how long " of verse 10, and keeps presenting to the heart of God His people in their condition as poor and needy and despised and oppressed.

These two points are of singular beauty in the Psalm. First, that Israel's Advocate presses this condition of His people as a reason why they should be delivered ; and second, He identifies their interests with God. Hence His Spirit in them calls on God to arise and plead His own cause (v. 22).

The first word of verse 12 should read " yet." The succeeding verses describe the deliverances which Israel's king wrought in the earth. The Red Sea (v. 13), the destruction of Pharaoh (v. 14), the cleaving of the rock and the drying up of Jordan (v. 15), and the ordered procession of day and night and summer and winter—His power over man and nature—all evidenced His ability to save His people. " The people inhabiting the wilderness " (v. 14) mean the vultures and wild beasts. The Spirit here supplements the Exodus record by stating that the bodies of the Egyptians, dead upon the seashore, were devoured by these creatures.

This translation of verse 18 is suggested : " Remember this, that the enemy hath reproached Jehovah Messiah, and that the arrogant have blasphemed Thy name." The following verse reads as in the R.V. " O deliver not the soul of Thy turtle dove unto the Wild Beast," i.e., to Anti-christ (Rev. xiii.).

The covenant of verse 20 is that made with Abraham ; and verse 21 contrasts with Ps. vi. 10.

PSALM LXXV.—The prophetic vision of this Psalm is that prefigured in Lev. ix 22-24. Aaron, having by himself purged the people

(Heb. i. 3)—for there was no one with him when making atonement in the Sanctuary—appears, accompanied by Moses, to rule and bless the people. So Christ as Priest perfected the atonement—as typified in Lev. i.–ix.—and as King and Priest will come forth to judge His House (vs. 4–7) and the nations (v. 8).

This vision of Messiah in the Sanctuary contrasts with the enemy in the Sanctuary of Ps. lxxiv. It is a Neginoth Psalm, for it predicts the chastisement of Israel (vs. 4 and 5) and the destruction of " the wicked of the earth " (v. 8). The Ransomed utter the first verse, and Messiah Himself the remaining verses. They address Him as God. Their utterances may be thus translated : " Unto Thee O God do we give thanks, unto Thee do we give thanks ! Thy Name is near. Thy people rehearse Thy wondrous works." The expression " Thy Name is near " means His manifested apparition in His future appearing. It corresponds to the moment when Moses and Aaron appeared at the door of the Tabernacle when, according to the Rabbis, they were greeted with joyful cries by the congregation. Jesus is the Greatest Name of God, i e., God manifest in flesh.

The full meaning of the Hebrew text of verse 2 will be learned by uniting the marginal reading with the English text. The sense is, that at the time appointed by God (Acts xvii. 31) Messiah will receive, in order to judge them, the congregation that " shall be gathered before Him " by God (Matt. xxv. 32) He will then " judge uprightly," first His own house, its rulers (Matt. xxiv. 45–51), its members (xxv. 1–13), and its servants (xxv. 14–30), and, afterwards, the nations, whom with infallible justice He will so divide that there will be not as much as one sheep among the goats nor one goat among the sheep. Such will be His upright government ; and it will contrast with man's unrighteous rule.

Verse 3 predicts the termination in confusion and guilt of man's government, and the firm establishment of Messiah's rule.

Eastern women wear a protruding ornament on the forehead called a horn. As sons are born the horn is raised. Hence the expression " to lift up the horn " means to become proud. The word promotion should read, " lifting up " ; and this term should be repeated in verses 7 and 10.

The north is omitted in verse 6, possibly because " on the sides of the north " will stand the city of the Great King from whom comes lifting up. Messiah's city will be on the northern slopes of Mount Zion. He will from thence as Judge either put down or lift up (v. 7). See note on Ps. xlviii. 2.

The words " Thy wondrous works " (v. 1) may be supplied after " I will declare " (v. 9). The God of Jacob is the God of all grace ; for grace promised everything to Jacob when he deserved nothing.

PSALM LXXVI.—As the two previous Psalms spoke respectively of the enemy in the Sanctuary and of Messiah in the Sanctuary so this speaks of His destruction of the haters of the Sanctuary. Its fulfilment belongs to the days of Micah iv, Zech. xii, and xiv, Rev. xix, and other similar prophecies, when the future kings of the earth under the captaincy of Anti-Christ will with their armies encompass Sion, and, to their discomfiture, meet Messiah there, Who will judge them and deliver Israel.

God is not known to-day in Judah, but faith here sings of the time when He shall become known in Judah and when His name shall become great in Israel (vs. 1 and 2), for the destruction of the kings in that future day at Jerusalem will demonstrate that God is there, and that in very deed Sion is His dwelling-place. Messiah will there make Himself known by breaking in pieces all the weapons of the enemy (v. 3) ; and then the enemies themselves He will cast into the deep sleep of death (vs. 5, 6 and 12).

Not to find the hand (v. 5) is an idiom for helplessness. To lose one's head or one's feet is a modern corresponding figure of speech. With poetic vividness the chariot and the horse represent those using them (v. 6). Similarly a modern general might report that he had lost ten per cent. of the artillery and twenty per cent. of the horse in an action, and mean artillery men and cavalry men.

The announcement heard from heaven (v. 8) is possibly that of Ps. lxviii. 16 and cxxxii. 13 and 14 in which Mess ah announces to the world H s selection of Jerusalem as His royal city.

" The mountains of prey (v. 4) symbolize the great and violent monarchies of earth. To Daniel they appeared as furious wild beasts. Sion shall become more glorious and excellent than they because of its selection by the Great King as His residence.

The wrath of man praises God by its futility (v. 10). The second line of this verse is difficult to understand. It may mean, as in the R.V., that just as a conqueror, in order to show the completeness of his victory, wears the sword of his defeated antagonist, so Messiah in a symbolic sense will gird himself with the broken power of Anti-Christ.

The first line of verse 11 is addressed to Israel ; the second line, to the nations and their princes round about Sion. Their " presents " will be those spoken of in Isa. xviii. 7, xliii. 6, and xlix. 22, when they will bring the outcasts of Israel as a present to Jehovah. Then will be seen kings and queens and princes carrying little Hebrew children in their arms up to Jerusalem. An eastern prince or peasant to-day, as in the past, would think himself degraded were he to carry a little girl in his arms.

Dan. v. 23 and 30 illustrate the last verse of the Psalm. The superscription " to Jeduthan " is examined in the last comment on Ps. xli.

PSALM LXXVII.—Occupation of heart with others outside the Sanctuary (Ps. lxxiii) and occupation of heart with self outside the Sanctuary (Ps. lxxvii) alike produce misery, but occupation of heart with God inside the Sanctuary gives comfort and victory.

The previous Psalm speaks of Messiah's action toward the enemies of the Sanctuary, and their end ; this Psalm declares His ways with the lovers of the Sanctuary and their end.

Outside the Sanctuary, that is, out of fellowship with God, the heart is awakened to a sense of its loss, and does not merely wish for restoration but cries " with the voice," i.e., with the consciousness of real need, to Jehovah and seeks Him. The effect of this is to make the seeker sensible of his " trouble " (v. 2) so that his hand is stretched out all night in prayer ; he realises that no one but God can comfort him ; but remembering God his conscience is disturbed and his spirit faints (v. 3) ; he realizes his distance from the Sanctuary (v. 4) ; he remembers his former happiness (vs. 5 and 6) ; and, engaged with his own heart, he wonders whether he has been cast off for ever (vs. 7-9). This introspection, this occupation with self, only enfeebles the spiritual life (v. 10). But directly occupation with God in the Sanctuary is resumed, joys and victory result (vs. 10-20).

So here, as in many other Psalms, the first verse gives the spiritual result of the inward experiences narrated in the succeeding verses.

God's way in the Sanctuary (v. 13), and God's way in the sea (v. 19), stand in relation the one to the other. The former is His character ; the latter, His action Faith recognizes the one (v 13) ; nature cannot know the other (v. 19). Faith knows and trusts God, and is never stumbled at His action because it knows that He loves His people and bends all circumstances to their real advantage. But if God's ways in the sea are judged by human sense the result is as futile as searching for footsteps in water.

Verse 2 should read as in the R.V. " Complained " (v. 3) means " thought in myself "—not the complaining of irritation or anger because of trial, but the disquiet which accompanies the self-condemned heart when seeking the Lord (1. Jno. iii. 19-21). " I will talk " (v. 12) should read " I will muse." Occupation with self begets the miserable questions of verses 7-9 ; occupation with God inspires the glorious challenge of verse 13.

God's way in the Sanctuary secured the salvation of the sons of Jacob and Joseph ; His way in the sea demonstrated the preservation of the flock of Moses and Aaron. The names Jacob and Joseph and Moses and Aaron are significant. Moses and Aaron typify Christ as King and Priest. A flock thus doubly led is surely led. Jacob and Joseph express how doubly precious to God is the flock itself, because the sheep are the sons of these fathers so beloved of God.

The way of God is the action on earth of the will of God. The nature of that will is expressed in the word " Sanctuary " Its nature is holiness. There must, therefore be always a Divine harmony between His will and His action. Those who would have fellowship with Him must subject themselves to the action of His holy nature. Man must suit himself to it ; and by means of the new birth this fellowship is made possible.

PSALM LXXVIII.—The Psalm narrates how Jehovah, who is Israel's Sanctuary in Egypt, in the Desert and in the Land, was dishonoured in all three periods of the nation's history, and it predicts His election of Mount Zion for His future Sanctuary. The first part of the Psalm tells how the fathers turned away from Him in the desert, and the second part records similar action by the children in the land.

The structure of the Psalm may be thus displayed :—

The Covenant of Law	8	
Canaan	9-11	1st stanza
Egypt	12	
The Wilderness	13-39	
The Wilderness	40-42	
Egypt	43-53	2nd stanza
Canaan	54-64	
The Covenant of Grace	65-72	

Matt. xiii. 35 assures the language of the Psalm as that of the Messiah.

The term " dark sayings " means that Divine history, unlike human history, contains beneath its surface deep moral lessons. For example no moral lessons are taught by the Battle of Waterloo, but many lessons of fundamental moral importance by the battle of Exodus xvii. 8. So the facts of this psalm are " dark sayings "; they secrete spiritual teaching.

The tribe of Ephraim having been the first to introduce idolatry is accordingly selected in verse 9. Equipped with the Word of God they were faithless to it (v. 10), and hence their defeat. This principle is true to-day in the spiritual realm.

Verses 30 and 31 may read thus : " Yet did they not turn away from their lust ; for while the meat was yet in their mouths the wrath of God came upon them." The actual enjoyment of the desired food did not expel from their hearts the unbelief and rebellion which reigned there. Hence the equity of their punishment. It illustrates John iii 36, Eph. v. 6, Col. iii. 6, etc.

" They remembered " (vs. 35, 36) ; " He remembered " (v. 39). His faithful remembrance is contrasted with their faithless remembrance.

Just as the fathers carried the idolatry, rebellion and unbelief of Egypt into the Wilderness (vs. 8-39), so the children carried the idolatry, rebellion and unbelief of the Wilderness into the Land (vs. 40-64).

A comparison of verses 40-42 with verses 8-11 shows that the hearts of the children were as the hearts of the fathers. They were self-willed (verse 40 with verse 8), they

turned back (verse 41 with verse 9), they forgot (verse 42 with verse 11). Verse 41 may read : They kept turning back and tempting God and setting limits to the power and love of the Holy One of Israel.

The power, forgiveness and patience which God showed to the fathers He showed also to the children ; and accordingly verses 43-51 correspond to and develop verse 12, and verses 13-16 correspond to and develop verses 52-54.

Seven plagues are detailed in verses 44-48 and 50 and 51, and three intimated in verse 49. The order in Exodus is historic ; here it is moral. A correspondingly beautiful instance of this principle will be found in contrasting 1 Cor. x. 1-12 with the quoted episodes in the Book of Exodus.

" The beginning of their strength " (v. 51 R.V.) means the first-born. Jacob said that Reuben was the beginning of his strength

The recital of His love to the children in the Wilderness occupies three verses (52-54); the review of the same love to the fathers occupies twenty-seven verses (13-39).

" This mountain land " (v. 54 R.V. margin) i.e., Canaan.

As the fathers provoked Him in the Desert (vs. 17-20), so the children provoked Him in the land (vs. 56-58) ; and as wrath fell upon the one (v. 21), so upon the other (v. 59).

The Divine Title in verse 21 is Jehovah, in verse 59 Elohim. As in the first Book of the Bible so here, and throughout the Scriptures, these changes of title are designed. Jehovah expresses Covenant relationship ; Elohim, creation relationship. He did not forsake them in the Wilderness (Neh. ix. 17) but He did forsake them in the land (v. 60) ; and accordingly the titles are used in harmony with the facts.

The history detailed in verses 60-64 is that of 1 Sam. iv. The Ark, symbol of His " strength " and " glory," was captured by the Philistines (v. 61) ; there was a great slaughter among the people (v. 62) ; Hophni and Phinehas fell by the sword (v. 64) ; and their widows made no lamentation for, Phinehas' wife when dying bewailed the loss of the Ark more than the loss of her husband.

The last eight verses of the Psalm contrast with the first seven, and illustrate how the bringing in of a better Covenant displaces the old. Israel having failed to keep the law and thereby merit life and righteousness, grace introduces the true David.

Ephraim, a figure of merit, is displaced, and grace choses Judah in order to the introduction of the true Shepherd of whom David was the type, and in order to the establishment of the future Sanctuary.

The facts set out in the Psalm teach the fundamental doctrine that the moral nature of fallen man refuses submission to the will of God, whether that nature be tutored by the goodness or the severity of God. This fact demonstrates the necessity of a new moral birth operated by the Spirit of God.

In the structure of the Psalm rebellion and unbelief follow the revelation of law (vs. 1–39) and precede the introduction of grace (vs. 40–72). In the action of the fathers is seen the ability of fallen man to disobey, and in the action of the children his inability to obey. Thus positively and negatively by a double lesson the corruption of man's nature is demonstrated and the double declaration of Rom. viii. 7 is illustrated. He can merit wrath but cannot merit heaven.

Messiah sprang out of Judah (Heb. vii. 14). Hence the expression in the Psalm " our fathers " (v. 3), but never our " children " —always " their children " (v. 4, etc.).

PSALM LXXIX.—The enemy in the Sanctuary is the theme here, as in Ps. lxxiv. The destruction of the Temple and of the city, or their pillaging, by the Egyptians (1 Kings xiv), by the Babylonians (2 Chron. xxxvi) and by the Romans illustrate these two Psalms ; but their fulfilment is still future.

The nations (v. 1) are the Gentiles, " Our neighbours " (v. 4), the Arabs, the Edomites, the Idumeans, etc. " Shed " (v. 3) should read " poured out." It is the same word in Hebrew as " pour out " in verses 6 and 10. The judgment desired, and predicted, in verse 6 is that of Jer. x. 25 and 2 Thess. i. 7–10. In this latter Scripture judgment is predicted upon them that know not God wilfully—that is the first member of verse 6—and that wilfully obey not the Gospel —that is the second member of verse 6.

" Dwelling-place " (v. 7) means pasture. Jacob is likened to a sheep devoured by wild beasts, i.e., by the nations, and they trample upon and waste the pastures.

The second member of verse 8 reads : " Let thy tender mercies speedily come to meet us."

Grace marks the prayer of verses 8 and 9,

for its petitions are five in number : " Remember not," " speedily come to meet us," " help us, O God," " deliver us," and " purge away our sins." The Hebrew word here translated " purge away " means " cover " or " atone for " (Exod. xxix. 33).

The sense of verse 10 is that the existence of God, the God of Israel, will be convincingly demonstrated to the now mocking nations by the vengeance that will fall upon them from heaven.

The subscription is that of Ps. lix. See notes on this title in that Psalm. The spelling of the word is slightly altered, for one is singular and the other plural. Compare Ps. xliv. and lxviii.

This Psalm was given by the Spirit of Christ to the prophet Asaph. See note on Ps. l.

PSALM LXXX.—God in the Sanctuary (v. 1) is the theme of this and of the two following Psalms. Israel here cries to Him to cause them to return to that Sanctuary (vs. 3, 7 and 19), and to rebuke those that destroyed it and them (v. 16).

In the blessing of Joseph (Gen. xlix. 22–26) the figures of the shepherd and the vine whose fruitful branches run over the wall are used. Hence the nation is here called Joseph, and the Messiah is addressed as its Shepherd (vs. 1 and 8–11).

When the cloud was taken up the Tribes journeyed, and immediately after the Kohathites (bearing the Sanctuary and the Ark) Ephraim, Benjamin and Manasseh marched, and Moses cried " Rise up, O Jehovah, and let Thine enemies be scattered, and let them that hate Thee flee before Thee " (Num. x. 11–36) Accordingly, in this Psalm (v. 2) they occupy this position in relation to the Ark. These tribes were the children of Rachel.

The awe-striking flame called the Shekinah which flashed between the cherubim upon the Mercy-seat in the Sanctuary (v. 1) was the glory of God and symbolized His presence. In the opening chapters of Ezekiel that glory is seen withdrawing itself in stages, and reluctantly, but in chapter xliii. it is viewed returning at once and with alacrity. Mal. iii. 1 speaks of the same event, and this Psalm prays for it. Messiah will return (v. 14) ; He will cause His people to return (vs. 3, 7 and 19) ; He will shine forth from the Sanctuary to their relief and to the discomfiture of their oppressors ; and thus recover and replant His vine. He will then drink the new wine of the kingdom of which He spake at the Last Supper.

The prayer " Cause us to return " (Heb.) is a petition to be restored to nationhood in Palestine, and to the worship of God in the Sanctuary.

The Divine titles " O God " (v. 3), " O God of Hosts " (v. 7), and " O Lord God of Hosts" (v. 19) teach the importance of seeking to learn the lesson which the Holy Spirit designs in such variations.

The miserable state of the scattered nation during the past nineteen centuries is vividly portrayed in verses 4-6.

Israel was the vine that God brought out of Egypt (v. 8 with Isa. v). Having evicted the Canaanites He planted it in the pleasant land of Palestine. It was ravaged by the Egyptians, the Assyrians, the Babylonians, the Persians, the Greeks, and the Romans ; but it will suffer its greatest injury at the hands of the future Anti-Christ. In his days this prophecy will be fulfilled. These are the " wild beasts " of verse 13. The boar was the emblem of the Roman power. But the Messiah will shine forth from His Sanctuary. There will be the shining of His countenance and the rebuking of His countenance. The shining of His countenance will succour His people ; its rebuking will destroy their foes (v. 16). This verse should read : " They," i.e., the destroyers of the vine, " shall perish at the rebuke of Thy countenance."

" The sea " (v. 11) means the Mediterranean, and " the river," the Euphrates. Solomon was the overlord of all that country.

The intensity of the petitions in verse 14 will be felt if the words " once more " be supplied : " Once more look down from heaven ! Once more behold ! Once more visit this vine ! "

" The Man of the right hand even the Son of Man " is the Messiah (v. 17). It is possibly to this verse and prophecy that the Lord pointed when claiming for Himself the title of " Son of Man." The Hebrew word Benjamin means the son of the right hand. Jacob laid his right hand upon Ephraim, thus symbolizing the bestowment of privilege, power and authority. Christ is the true Benjamin and Ephraim. He is the Son of the Father's right hand, Whom God has made strong for Himself.

The moral results of the Messiah's entrance into the Sanctuary is seen in verse 18. They are continuance and loyalty. In the soul into which He shines there is no going back ; and whom He quickens He eternally attaches to His name.

PSALM LXXXI.—The satisfying abundance to be found in the Sanctuary is pointed to in this Psalm (vs. 10 and 16).

The identity of Jehovah and Messiah clearly appears in Matt. xxiii. 37 and Luke xix. 42. He as Israel's Shepherd is the speaker in the Psalm. In it the tender thoughts and loving purposes of His heart for His sheep find expression.

Here also appears the sad fact that just as man immediately fell from Creation blessing, so Israel immediately fell from Redemption blessing. Both Covenants were conditional ; the one upon abstinence from the knowledge of evil, the other upon abstinence from the worship of idols. Both Covenants failed because of human imperfection. But grace acting in Divine perfection avails, and will avail to recover, and more than recover, all that was lost

The Psalm contains two stanzas. The first : The call to praise (vs. 1-7) and to listen (vs. 8-10). The second : The consequences of refusal (vs. 11-16).

The Shepherd and the sheep are one. Hence the term " Our strength." This oneness He affirmed to Mary Magdalen (Jno. xx. 17).

The appellations Jacob, Israel and Joseph express grace, glory and affection.

" The time appointed," " the new moon " (v. 3, R.V.), " the feast," " the testimony " (v. 5) all intend the Passover of Exod. xii.

" I heard a language that I understood not" (v. 5). This does not mean that the Great Shepherd did not understand the Egyptian language, but that He did not acknowledge as His sheep the Egyptians. The Hebrew verb here should be translated " acknowledged," as in Ps. xxxii. 5, li. 3, Prov. iii. 6, Isa. xxxiii. 13, etc. He makes the statement in order to emphasize the separateness of Israel as His flock. They knew His voice and He knew theirs ; but He stood in no such relationship to the Egyptians, nor they to Him. This definite separation is what He in the Psalm presses upon them to recognize ; for in their recognition of it, and obedience to it, consisted their spiritual glory. Israel refused to recognize it and to practice it, and so does the Christian Church act to-day, and the result is with the Church, as it was with Israel, faithlessness and defeat.

Pots " (v. 6) should read " baskets." They may be recognized in the Egyptian paintings in the British Museum. The " trouble " of verse 7 is a covering term expressive of the trials of the Wilderness. They were designed as tests of faith ; for faith when tested grows exceedingly (1 Pet. i. 7 and 2 Thess. i. 3). " The place of thunder " was Sinai.

Verses 8-10 may be understood as having been addressed to Israel on leaving Egypt. The love which invites the wide-opened mouth (v. 10) is grieved if saint or angel be turned to for sustenance.

The moral facts disclosed in the last six verses apply to the modern professing church equally as to Israel. To be given one's own way, and to be let alone by God (Hos. iv. 17), is an appalling judgment.

The honey which the bees lodge in the rocks of Palestine is esteemed most delicious (v. 16).

The sense of the passage, and the Hebrew text, not only permit the translation of the English text but also allow a present force, thus : " Oh that my people did hearken . . . I should at once subdue their enemies . . . the haters of Jehovah should be at once compelled to submit . . . and with honey out of the rock would I satisfy thee."

The nation is called " Joseph." This is love's title. The Shepherd calls them to praise Elohim as the " God of Jacob," that is the " God of all grace." These are His Old Testament and New Testament titles.

PSALM LXXXII.—When Messiah stood in the Temple in the midst of what was the congregation of God and judged the rulers of the people, He fulfilled the first four verses of this Psalm (Matt. xxi-xxiii, John viii-x, etc.) ; for He, God, stood in the congregation of God, and judged among the gods, i.e., the magistrates or rulers. But they rejected His judgment. They willed not to know or to understand. They chose to walk on in darkness ; and, accordingly, He told them that they were the blind leading the blind. As the result of their corruption of foundation truth the whole land was moved away from righteous judgment (v. 5).

Israel was designed by God to be His representative in the earth and judge of the nations. Hence her magistrates were termed " gods " i e., representatives of God ; and to them the word of God was committed in order that they should communicate it to the nations (Exod. vii. 1, xxi. 6, xxii. 8, 9 and 28, John x. 34-35, Acts xxiii. 5). The Hebrew word for " gods " and " judges " is the same.

But Israel failed to fulfil this purpose ; and the prediction of this Psalm is that Messiah would take up this Divine purpose and perfectly fulfil it as Judge of Israel (v. 1) and of all nations (v. 8). He, being at once the Representative of God and God Himself, will administer just judgment to all (v. 8) ; but He will recognize Israel and the Sanctuary as the centre of His government (v. 1). He is, therefore, here addressed as God (v. 8).

Between these two verses the judges of Israel are judged and their incompetency and injustice exposed (v. 2-7). Their unrighteous judgment, their neglect to protect the defenceless, their ignorance, their refusal to learn, their aimless going to and fro in the the darkness, proved them to be no better than ordinary men although officially representatives and sons of God. As men they should die, and as angels (" princes ") they should fall.

The Psalm should be read in the Revised Version, and as interpreted by John x. 34-35.

The appeal of the last verse will be better felt if this reading be adopted : Arise O God ! Judge *Thou* the earth ; for Thou shalt inherit all the nations."

PSALM LXXXIII.—The apparition of the Wild Beast with the seven heads and ten horns of Rev. xiii. whose purpose as Satan's agent will be to cause the Hebrew people to cease to exist, and whose destruction in Rev. xix. is assured, with the consequent enthronement of the Messiah as Most High over all the earth, engage the faith and prayer of this Psalm.

The titles Elohim (vs. 1, 12 and 13), El (v. 1), Jehovah (vs. 16 and 18), and Most High (v. 18) express Messiah's relationships toward Israel, toward the millennium and toward the nations.

The Psalm opens with the description of Israel's peril (vs. 1-4) ; it proceeds to describe the might and malice of the enemy (vs. 5-8) ; it predicts their destruction (vs. 9-17) ; and the final and permanent victory of Messiah (v. 18).

The Ten Kings of verses 6-8 and the Seven Kingdoms of verses 9-11 correspond to, and represent the seven empires and ten kingdoms of the Books of Daniel and Revelation. What the seven empires said is recited in verse 12, and what the ten kings will say is recorded in verse 4. In the notes on the Books of Daniel and Revelation will be found suggestions as to the identity of these seven empires and ten kingdoms.

The numbers seven, ten, seventeen, and seventy are significant in Scripture. The ten-fold confederation is followed by the seven-fold destruction. Ten is ordinal perfection, and seven spiritual perfection. Seventeen is the seventh prime number. Man's rebellion and God's judgment are expressed in these numbers.

" Make a tumult " (v. 2) means " rage like the sea," as in xlvi. 3. " The hidden ones" are those who hide themselves in God as a refuge, so they become His hidden ones. The expression is full of comfort for His people, for if He hides them how can the enemy destroy them ? " Houses " (v. 12) should read " pastures," and " wheel " (v. 13), " a rolling thing." In harmony with the word " stubble " in the same verse it may mean the wild artichoke of Palestine which throws out branches of equal length and which when dry breaks off at the root and is carried by the wind as a wheel over the plains.

The enemy's purpose will be to annihilate the Hebrew nation (v. 4) and to seize their country (v. 12).

Grace will offer life and salvation to these rebels (v. 16) ; but the offer will be refused, and they will suffer an eternal doom (vs. 13-17).

The significance of the verb " to know " is " to make the experience" that the Kingdom promised in the titles Jehovah and Most High is an actuality. A corresponding " know " is found in Exod. vi. 3 This verse seems contrary to fact, for Moses' forefathers used the title Jehovah, but they had not experienced the redemption which that title promised ; Moses did.

PSALM LXXXIV.—The Captain of their salvation in leading the many sons to glory (Heb. ii. 10) here sings of the desirability of the Sanctuary (vs. 1-4) and of the rich supplies provided for the road thither (vs. -7). The " for " of verse 10 concerns the Sanctuary, and the " for " of verse 11, the road to it. This second " for " asserts the happiness of those on the way to the Sanctuary ; the first " for " the happiness of those who enter and dwell there. The doctrine of the Psalm is that the Sanctuary is a home of pure and satisfying bliss, and that the road to it is a highway of happiness though it pass through a valley of weeping (v. 6, R.V.).

In Ps. lxiii. Israel as an exile finds fulness of blessing in God Himself even in a dry and thirsty land. In this Psalm it is rather the joys of His dwelling-place, and restoration to it, that occupy the heart. Yet it is not the Sanctuary apart from God that is longed for. And the road thither is only a way of sunshine and safety if trodden with Him. The valley of weeping becomes a well to the celestial pilgrims (Num. xxi. 16). Trial enriches faith ; and strength when tested becomes reinforced strength, and begets a praying people (v. 9).

The Divine titles are significant : Jehovah Sabaoth (v. 1), Jehovah (v. 2), El (v. 2), Elohim (v. 3), Jehovah Elohim (v. 8), and, notably, the God of Jacob (v. 8).

" Amiable " (v. 8) means lovable, or desirable. " Tabernacles " is the plural of majesty, expressing the greatness and glory of the Sanctuary. Compare " His courts " (vs. 2 and 10) and " His house " (vs. 4 and 10).

The sense of verse 3 is : That as the sparrow and the swallow find love and rest in their nests so the believer finds love and rest in the Sanctuary. The first member of verse 3 is a parenthesis ; the second member follows on from verse 2. The altars pointed to are the brazen and the golden altars. These foreshadowed Christ in His atoning death for the sinner and in His risen life for the believer. The soul finds its home in a crucified and risen Saviour.

The sparrow is a common bird. Five were sold for two farthings (Luke xii. 6). They are local birds, and hence have " a house." The swallow is a bird of passage, and, therefore, has " a nest." The believer is both a sparrow and a swallow. Like the one bird he is very commonplace and has a house in this world ; like the other, he is here to-day and gone to-morrow and only has a nest. His real home is in the Sanctuary with his King and his God (v. 3).

Unceasing praise (1 Chron. ix. 33) fills the hearts and clothes the lips of those who dwell with God. This is not always so as respects earthly princes. At first they may appear attractive, but the longer they are lived with the less they are liked (v. 4).

The companionship of the Messiah on the homeward road (vs. 5-7) guarantees all needed supplies for the way (v. 11). He prays for them (v. 8) and they pray for Him (v. 9). He shall appear before God in Sion ; and His appearing there is the assurance that they also will be there (v. 7). The only feet that will be found upon that road will be the feet of those whose hearts are in that road (v. 5). To the carnal nature it is a valley of weeping (v 6 R.V.) but to the new nature an unfailing reservoir of strength and refreshment.

God's heart rests with infinite delight in His beloved Son (v.9); and " the many sons " are taught by the Spirit that that secures to them preservation upon the road and reception at its close. The Messiah Himself is to them a shield for safety and a sun for happiness. Upon the way He will minister to them grace, and in the home to which it leads, glory.

PSALM LXXXV.—The grace that gave these words of life and hope to the descendants of the rebel Korah (Num. xvi.) is the grace that saves sinners dead in sins ; and of the exceeding riches of that grace the Spirit speaks in Ephesians ii.

The Psalm contains three stanzas : Precedent (vs.1-3) ; Prayer (vs. 4-7) ; Promise (vs. 8-13). The prayer is based upon the precedents of the first three verses ; and the peace and plenty promised in verses 8 and 12 are founded on the atonement foreseen in verses 10 and 11. Thus faith binds together the past, the present and the future.

The precedents pleaded in verses 1-3 are those recorded in the Book of the Judges. These precedents and this Psalm must often have refreshed the captives by the waters of Babylon ; and they have nourished faith through the present long captivity and wrath, from the destruction of the Sanctuary by the Romans up to the present, and will nourish it up to the apparition of Messiah in glory. This is the Great Tribulation of Rev. vii. 14.

The Psalm from verse 4 acknowledges the justness of God's anger ; confesses Israel's need of salvation (vs. 4-6) ; declares God to be the only Saviour (v. 7) ; announces that salvation is a completed work and within reach of the believer (v. 9) ; that it is obtained by listening to the Word of God (v. 8, Rom. x. 8-14, Gal. iii. 2) ; that there is a power in it that saves from a turning back to sin (v. 8) and that keeps the feet in the path of righteousness (v. 13) ; affirms that only a heaven-born righteousness could undertake the justification of guilty men (v. 11) ; and that the foundation of this salvation was laid at Golgotha, where in the cross of Jesus, verse 10 was fulfilled. There truth and righteousness judged sin in the Person of Christ ; and that one and only question between God and man being settled, mercy and peace flow to sinners and the pardon and prosperity of verses 1-3 are made possible of realization and enjoyment.

Mercy fulfils the promises given by truth ; therefore it is that in the Psalms mercy always precedes truth ; and necessarily so, for man has forfeited every title to Divine favour and promise. Righteousness through the atoning death of the Lamb of God furnishes the salvation, and mercy bestows it. Thus Christ is become the believer's righteousness, so that what in judgment would have been his ruin, has in grace become his peace : righteousness and peace kiss each other. This righteousness was not wrought by man on earth—that was impossible—it descended from heaven (v. 11) ; hence it is ever enduring ; and, as a result, truth springs out of the earth, glory dwells in the land, it yields its increase, and righteousness reigns. Jehovah becomes merciful to His land and to His people (Deut. xxxii. 43).

The sense of verse 13 is that not only will righteousness precede Messiah the Prince during His future reign, but it will also accompany and follow Him wherever He goes. He will leave a trail beautiful with the lovely fruit of righteousness ; and in this respect He will contrast effectively with the past and present rulers of the earth. Those in whom He by His Spirit dwells, will express the moral glory of this same righteousness in their daily lives amongst their fellow men.

PSALM LXXXVI.—Israel's Advocate pleading their cause in the Sanctuary is the vision that here engages the heart and awakens its worship. The title of the Psalm is " A prayer of David " ; that is, an intercession by the Messiah on behalf of His people.

The argument of the prayer is that God, having by His mighty power rescued Him from those that sought His life (vs. 1-7), and also from the dominion of the lowest hell (v. 13), will surely deliver His beloved followers from their enemies and from their sufferings (vs. 14-17). He appeals to Jehovah's ear (vs. 1 and 6). In His distress He finds all His joy and comfort and hope of deliverance in God. He finds Him a sufficiency. But He expresses this faith and love and confidence—so infinitely perfect in His own case—as the Advocate of His people. The faith and love and confidence they should confess He confesses for them, thus making them true and acceptable worshippers. Personally, He was poor, needy, holy and believing (vs. 1 and 2), but as their Intercessor, He pleads for sympathy (vs. 1 and 6), deliverance (v. 2), compassion (v. 3), refreshment (v. 4), and forgiveness for them (v. 5).

God is incomparable in His nature and in His works (v. 8) ; and God is incomparable in His works and in His nature (v. 10), This is a beautiful instance of introversion.

" Jesus is the greatest Name of God " (Phil. ii. 9). See W. B. Doherty (Partridge). All nations will bow before Him (v. 9). Matt. xxv. 31-46 describes the occasion. God's Name will then be glorified by the eternal felicity of the redeemed and by the everlasting punishment of the lost. (Rev. xix. 1-9 and note on Hab. ii. 14).

In harmony with numberless instances in the Bible He here speaks in verse 13 of His resurrection as an accomplished fact ; for what God promises faith believes and declares to be present and real.

The introduction of the Virgin Mary in verse 16 emphasizes the fact that Christ became truly man ; for otherwise He could not be an Advocate for men. It was necessary that as man he should be tempted in all points (Heb. iv. 15). It was equally necessary that as an Intercessor He should be sinless ; hence He, the true David, could say what David himself could never say, " I am holy " (v. 2).

In praying for His people He uses the powerful personal plea " Be gracious unto Me," etc., etc., and the good things He asks for them (vs. 16 and 17) He claims for them by faith, and declares that He has already received them. The past tense, accordingly, is used for them in verse 17 as for Himself in verse 13

PSALM LXXXVII.—This prophetic song was probably given by the Spirit on the occasion of the bringing up of the Ark to Jerusalem (2 Sam. vi). The theme is the birth of Messiah in the hill country of Judea, and the subsequent establishment of His throne and Sanctuary in Mount Zion. The glory of Zion will not then be her beauty or wealth or military strength but the presence of Emmanuel. The consequent supremacy of Zion and of Israel over all other nations is declared.

The following translation is suggested : " His foundation is in the holy mountains, i.e., plural of majesty for Mount Zion. Jehovah loveth the gates of Zion more than all the dwellings of Jacob. Glorious things are spoken of thee, oh city of God. By those knowing Me I will cause Egypt and Babylon to remember—Philistia and Tyre with Cush —that this Man was born there. Yea as to Zion it shall be said, a Man, yea a Man was born in her ; He shall establish her —Himself the Most High. Jehovah shall record when writing the history of the nations that this Man was born there. And, every singer as well as every dancer shall say : ' All my springs of joy are in thee.' "

This prophecy was probably known to the Easterns, for the wise men came to Jerusalem saying " Where is He that is born King of the Jews ? "

" Mountains " (v. 1) may be the plural of majesty for Mount Zion, or it may mean the hill country of Judea, which was the birthplace of the Messiah. The Spanish translation reads : " His birth-place is in the holy mountains ; " and this may be the first meaning of the word " foundation."

The threshold of the Sanctuary at Zion will surpass in glory the richest chambers of all other palaces (v. 2). Among the glorious things to be spoken of that palace is, that it shall be a never failing spring of joys ; and this because it shall be the dwelling place of the Great King.

Ps. xxii. 27 helps to explain verse 4. Those that know the Messiah will cause the proud nations to remember that the King of kings was born of Israel. Rahab means Egypt. Coupled with Babylon the two names express in Hebrew " Arrogance " and " Confusion." These two terms fitly portray the nature of human government.

The three great families into which Noah's prophecy divides humanity (Gen ix 25-27) are brought together in verse 4. Shem, Ham and Japhet are represented by Israel, Egypt and Assyria. All nations are comprised in these. (Isa. xix. 25). All shall become Jehovah's servants.

The manhood and Godhead of Messiah are emphasised in verse 5. As man, Zion should be His birth-place ; as Most High, it should be His dwelling-place. Bethlehem may be accounted a suburb of Jerusalem.

The history of the nations as written by God may possibly be a delightful study during the millennium. Israel will have the chief place in that history because in her Messiah was born (v. 6).

The subscription, Mahalath-Leannoth, means "the great dancings." There were two such in Israel—the great dancing that celebrated the death of Goliath, and the great dancing that accompanied the establishment of the Ark in Zion (2. Sam. vi). David was the central figure in each. These dancings foreshadowed the First and Second Advents of David's Son and Lord. They, respectively, concern Christ's glory as Saviour of His people in atonement, and as Monarch of the world in appointment.

The themes of the three closing Psalms of this Third Book are : Incarnation (lxxxvii) ; Expectation (lxxxviii) ; and Coronation, (lxxxix).

PSALM LXXXVIII.—As Jonah was three days and three nights in the power of death, and shut up in the dark prison of the sea monster, so was the Greater than Jonah three days and three nights in the dominion of death, and shut up in the darkness of the abyss (Matt. xii. 40 and 41). And as Jonah trusted and prayed and believed for deliverance, so did the Messiah. And as the Holy Spirit has given to the world the words of Jonah's prayer, so has He given in this Psalm the words of Messiah's prayer. How amazing that the Spirit of Truth should here invite men to contemplate the eternal Son of God when shut up in the abyss, and should communicate to them the very words of the prayer which He from thence addressed to God !

Just as He trusted God during His lifetime, and when hanging on the cross, so He trusted Him when imprisoned in Sheol. Confessing that He was shut up there and could not come forth (v. 8), yet He believed that God would surely deliver Him (v. 1) ; and He looked forward in faith to the resurrection of the third morning (v. 13).

The Psalm is unique in that it does not end in a burst of sunshine, as usual, but in deepest night. It does not record suffering from the hand of man, but from the hand of God. There is faith and hope in the Psalm, but no comfort.

It is a " Maschil " Psalm. It instructs as to the mystery of Christ's experiences when under the wrath of God in the nether world. It should be read in the R.V. The structure shows a double stanza :

Prayer (vs. 1 and 2)   Prayer (vs. 9-14)
  Dissolution (vs. 3-6) Dissolution (v. 15)
    Wrath (v. 7)   Wrath (vs. 16 and 17)
      Desolation (v. 8)   Desolation (v. 18)

The " dead " (v. 10), i.e., disembodied spirits.

The last line of the Psalm may mean that in the region of horror in which He was, darkness was His only companion.

Heb. v. 7 states that He was saved out of the death-world because of His " piety," i.e., because of His reverent submission to death, as ordained for Him by God. This Psalm illustrates the " piety " which that scripture praises.

The depth of suffering disclosed in the Psalm, beyond the power of human reason to fathom, pierces the heart with a sense of the sinfulness of sin, and melts it with a consciousness of the amazing love of Him who voluntarily suffered its judgment in order to redeem those justly doomed to its eternal punishment.

PSALM LXXXIX.—The Messiah in the confidence of coronation and of the fulfilment of the sure promises made to Him as David (Isa. lv. 3, Acts xiii. 34) recites these promises (vs. 2-4), voices the lament of His people at their seeming breach (vs. 38-51), but closes the Psalm as He began it with praise to Jehovah (vs. 1 and 52). Thus during His life of sorrow, His death of shame, and His arrest in Sheol, nothing is seen in Him but perfection—perfection of faith toward God and of love toward man.

The word faithfulness occurs seven times (vs. 1, 2, 5, 8, 24, 33 and 49 R.V.). It expresses the certain fulfilment of all the promises made to Him as King and Priest of Israel.

In verses 1-4 He claims the throne as His by Divine appointment. In verses 5-7 the Holy Spirit celebrates His supremacy over the angels. They are here styled saints, i. e., holy ones and sons of the mighty, that is sons of might. Such is His relationship toward them.

His relationship toward Israel is set out in verses 8–37. His cleavage of the Red Sea (v. 9); His destruction of the Egyptians (v. 10); His mastery of nature (vs. 11–13), His moral perfections (v. 14); the happiness of His people (vs. 15–18); His appointment as their Prince (vs. 19 and 20); the assurance of victory to Him over His enemies (vs. 21–23); the promise that He should never be forsaken (vs. 24 and 25); the declaration of His Deity and of the eternal nature of the Covenant made with Him (vs. 26–29); the chastening of His children if unfaithful (vs. 30–32); the engagement that their conduct shall not affect the Covenant (vs. 33–37); His description as Priest of the degradation (v. 39), desolation (v. 40), subjection (vs. 41–43) and rejection of the nation (v. 38); His enquiry how long the Divine indignation was to last (vs. 46–49); and, finally, the complaint that His path, and that of those who walked in His steps, was one of reproach (vs. 50 and 51). Such are the statements of the Psalm; and they reveal the glory and dignity of His Person and the faithfulness and love of His heart.

The heavenly witness to the fidelity of a Divine government is the rainbow (v. 37): hence its appearance here and in Rev. iv. 3 in connection with Messiah's throne.

The sufferings intended in verses 50 and 51 are those suffered by Christ as High Priest in sympathy with the sufferings of His people. All the shame and hatred of all the most cultured and powerful nations for His people He in His faithful love as their High Priest and Advocate gathers into His own bosom, and all lies as a mighty burden upon His heart. This is an affecting pictuie of the identification of a true Advocate with the miseries and sorrows of those he represents. Christ's Spirit in the apostle Paul produced, but imperfectly, similar affections (2 Cor xi. 23–29).

All true followers of the Messiah must expect to suffer shame because of His name.

Thus fitly closes the Third Book of the Psalms, that is, the Leviticus Book. The theme in both Books is the same. The Great High Priest, having perfected atonement for His people outside the Sanctuary, entered into the Holy Place there to appear before God for them. Such is the double vision —the Sanctuary, and the Priest.

THE PSALMS

BOOK IV

PSALMS XC.–CVI.—The theme of this Book, in correspondence with the Fourth Book of Moses, is the Wilderness. Sin not only destroyed man, it also introduced suffering into nature, and changed the world from a paradise to a wilderness. The argument of the book is that, apart from the promised Messiah, there is no hope for man and for the creation. Ps. xc. is the prologue, and Ps. cvi. the epilogue. The one recalls man's fall; the other, man's recovery. The intervening Psalms form three groups: The kingdom desired (xci.–xciv.); The kingdom anticipated (xcv.–c.); The King portrayed (ci.–cv.). So Israel when passing through the Wilderness desired and anticipated Canaan, and awaited in faith the apparition there of the promised king. The keynote of the first group is xciv. 1-7; that of the second group, xcvi. 11-13; and that of the third group cii. 19-22.

Ps. xciv. contrasts with Ps. ciii. The one pictures the misery of the earth under the government of Anti-Christ; the other, its happiness under the Lord Christ.

Delivered from the kingdom of Pharaoh, Israel became a pilgrim, and set out through a wilderness for the promised land. Delivered from this present evil world, the Christian becomes a pilgrim, and hastens as through a wilderness to the Father's house on high.

PSALM XC.—The eternity of Elohim Adonai (vs. 1 and 2) is contrasted with the frailty of man (vs. 3-11); and the lesson taught by the contrast is given in verses 12-17.

The Psalm contemplates the people of God in the wilderness. Those who pass through it depending on their own strength (v. 10) find it a way of labour and sorrow; those who lean upon the Hand of Adonai find it a way of joy and rejoicing (v. 14). Even in the Wilderness the heart finds in Him its dwelling-place. Five "generations" are pointed to here: Creation (v. 2); the

Fall (v. 3); the Flood (v. 5); the Wilderness (v. 10); and the Kingdom (v. 15). The "ages" may change but Messiah remains (Heb. i. 2).

The dark background of verses 3-12 makes the doctrine of verses 13-17 the more precious to faith. The doctrine is, that the only hope for the earth and its inhabitants is in the coming of the Messiah. His advent will compensate for all the calamities of the Wilderness in this night of mystery and pain; and He will endow man with a new moral nature so that the works of his hands will be only good (v. 17). His power will be absolute, but not arbitrary (v. 11). His government will be truth and holiness (vs. 7 and 8). He will judge sins both secret and open (v. 8). The effect will be that the pride of man's heart will be broken, its self-sufficency banished, and its energies governed by wisdom (vs. 9-12).

Verse 3 should read: "Thou causest man to return to dust saying, 'Return ye children of men'" (Gen. iii. 19).

The Divine wrath intended in verses 3-11 is that of Gen. iii. 19.

Adam lived 930 years after the Fall. If he lived a few years prior to it then is he perhaps suggested in verse 4, and the argument pressed that even so long a life as 1,000 years in contrast with the eternity of God is but as a day in duration. It is may be that during the millennium human life will be prolonged to a corresponding length (Isa. lxv. 20).

The "strength" of verse 10 R.V. means the pride of self-reliance—of independency of God—as contrasted with the action of the dependency of faith. The carnal will draws on its own resources of strength and fortitude and courage and wisdom. The result is labour and sorrow. Faith finds its resources in God, and proves Him to be an inexhaustible treasury of gladness and song and victory.

"Repent" (v. 13) ought to read "have pity on."

PSALM XCI.—That Messiah is the great figure of this Psalm is decided by Matt. iv. 6.

The previous Psalm having introduced the Wilderness, and contrasted the misery and happiness of travellers in it who trust self or God, this Psalm points to the one Man Who passed through it undefiled, unhurt, and trusting and loving God in perfection. To Him the Holy Spirit speaks in verses 1, 3-8 and 10-13 ; of Him God speaks in verses 14-16 ; to the Holy Spirit the Messiah responds in verse 2 ; and to God he declares His trust in verse 9. Thus in the Psalm, Christ is the object of the Father's love and of the Spirit's ministry ; and the quickness of Messiah's ear to listen to the Spirit's voice is revealed in the impulsive declarations of verses 2 and 9. He breaks in on the promises of the Spirit with eager assurances of confiding affection and belief. How amazing that sinful men should be permitted to hear the sweet converse of the three Persons of the ineffable Trinity !

In the opening verses Messiah enters the Wilderness, and in the closing ones ascends the Throne. As He enters, the Holy Spirit assures Him (v. 1) that companionship with God will be a safe refuge from Satan's power, and from all the dangers of the way. This He sets out in verses 3-13.

In response to the statement of verse 1, i.e., that he that dwelleth by day in the secret place . . . shall abide by night under, etc. Messiah immediately makes His confession of verse 2, and repeats it to God personally in verse 9. R.V. So He passed through the Wilderness without stumbling. He trod upon the lion—the serpent (v. 13)—at Calvary ; and He will finally tread him down together with the young lion—the False Prophet—and the Dragon—Anti-Christ—as predicted in Rev. xix. At the close of His passage through the Wilderness, because of tne perfection of His love (v .14) and of His faith (v. 15), God seated Him on the Highest throne in the heavens.

The Psalm comforts and encourages the most timid believer, for it assures him that what God was to His dearly Beloved Son in His journey through the Wilderness of this world He will be to the weakest of His children. They can prove Him to be what Christ proved Him to be.

The absence of a superscription suggests that the Psalm was written by Moses ; for the previous one was written by him. If this be so, then all the Scriptures quoted in the temptation in the desert (Matt. iv.) were Mosaic.

The Messiah's path through the desert was one of dependence upon God. Satan's effort in the temptation was to move Him to independence ; but he failed. He walked a path of perfect submission, obedience and dependence, and makes good all the fruit of it (vs. 3-13) to those who walk after Him in a like dependence and faith.

Verse 9 should contain only one member, the second member belongs to verse 10. The first is the utterance of the Messiah ; the second, of the Holy Spirit. The reading is : " Thou O Jehovah art my refuge ! " This was a cry of faith and love ; and it breaks in upon the Spirit's promises to Him in verses 3-13. The second member of the verse should form the first line of the succeeding one, and may read " Because Thou hast made the Most High thy habitation there shall, " etc.

Satan when quoting verses 11 and 12 —and his quoting them showed his intelligence in recognizing that the Psalm applied to Jesus—left out the words " To keep Thee in all Thy ways " and put in the words " At any time." Thus he corrupts the Scripture.

The promise of the throne (vs. 14 and 15) is here presented as a reward because He knew and made known God's Name, i.e., His character. So at the close of His pilgrimage He could say " I have manifested Thy Name unto the men whom Thou gavest Me " (Jno. xvii. 6).

PSALM XCII.—Travellers through a wilderness soon grow weary. They need rest. So appropriately this third Wilderness Psalm sings of the Sabbath. Israel will be the singer on the morning of the sabbath day of Heb. iv. That is the Sabbath intended in the superscription. Then will be fulfilled the promise of the previous Psalm (v. 14) " I will set Him on high." For Christ is God's Sabbath. God rests with infinite repose in Him, and He invites man to share that rest with Him. This sabbath day and this rest may be enjoyed by faith throughout the entire Wilderness journey.

Israel here sings of Him and addresses Him as Jehovah (v. 1), Elyon (v. 1), and Elohim (v. 13). She praises Him for what He is to her (vs. 1-4) ; for His attributes (vs. 5-15) ; for the destruction of her enemies (vs. 6, 9 and 11) ; and for the favour shown to her and to the righteous (vs. 10-15).

When a king is both great and righteous then is his government perfect (vs. 5 and 15).

Verses 6-9 correspond to verses 12-14. The brutish man is contrasted with the righteous man, and the workers of evil with the operators of good. The doom of the one company stands over against the felicity of the other. The workers of iniquity shall be destroyed for ever ; the workers of righteousness shall flourish as the palm and cedar in the courts of their God. The one are fuel (" grass ") ; the other, fruit (" palms ").

The Christian is comparable to a palm and to a cedar. The one grows in a sandy plain, the other on a rugged mountain. The one has a tap-root that draws nourishment from beneath, the other is refreshed from above. The one is beautiful, the other strong. The Christian has a secret source of life, he receives blessing from beneath and from above ; and he is morally beautiful and strong.

Verse 8 reads : " Thou, O Jehovah, art enthroned for ever." This statement, preceded and followed by declarations as to the destruction of the wicked, makes terribly clear the doctrine that the eternity of His government necessitates the eternity of their misery ; for so long as His government lasts a rebellion and recovery by them will be impossible.

Israel in verse 10 joyfully cries, " I am being continually anointed with fresh oil," i.e., with ever renewed strength and youth (LXX.).

The sense of verses 6-10 is that unconverted men refuse to recognize the wrath that awaits them and the glory that awaits the righteous.

The words " Thy judgment," i.e., the Divine judgment of verse 9, would better supply the ellipses in verse 11 than the words " my desire." Israel's enemies are Messiah's enemies (vs. 9 and 11). They both have the same enemies. Relationship with Him involves this.

The fruit and strength of the Spirit exhibited in the Christian life is an effective testimony to the moral glory of the Lord Jesus Christ (vs. 12-15). Recognizing that moral glory Israel shouts with exultation, " He is my Rock—there is no unrighteousness in Him "!

PSALM XCIII.—Israel will doubtless sing this Psalm upon the millennial morn at the close of her weary wilderness journey.

It presents a picture of millennial glory. The angry nations (Rev xi. 18), likened to the raging waves of the storm-tossed ocean, are subdued, and the Messiah, mightier than they, is seen seated upon His throne.

The Psalm should be read as in the R.V. the word " above " being repeated before the second line of verse 4. As He stilled the raging of the Galilean sea (Jno. vi. 16) so will He still the future raging of the hostile nations and establish universal peace.

All human history, and its final settlement, is comprised in the brief compass of this poem. It sets out the majesty of the king's person (v. 1) ; the stability of His kingdom (v. 1) ; the antiquity of His throne (v. 2) ; the eternity of His Being (v. 2) ; the hostility of the nations (v. 3) ; His supremacy over them (v. 4) ; the fidelity of His promises (v. 5) ; the purity of His court (v. 5) ; and the perpetuity of His government (v. 5).

That morning of glory will demonstrate the trustworthiness of His promises. Pardoned and restored Israel will then say joyfully what in the Wilderness they said believingly, that His testimonies are very sure.

The last verse contrasts the promises and courts of earthly princes with the promises and courts of the Prince of Princes. Their promises are not sure, nor are their courts pure.

Psalms xciii. xcvii. and xcix. begin with " Jehovah reigneth " and close with a declaration respecting holiness. All will be holy when He reigns ; and everything will be characterized by holiness, as predicted in Isa. xxiii. 18, Zech. xiv 20 and 21, and Rev. iv. 8.

The Hebrew verb translated " becometh " (v. 5) is rich in its root meanings. The sense is that not only will holiness be the supreme ornament of Messiah's court, but that also, possessing consciousness, it will gladly make there its eternal home

PSALM XCIV.—The time of Jacob's trouble (Jer. xxx. 7) will conclude Israel's Wilderness journey. It is here pictured ; and the two Messiahs and their thrones confronted (vs. 2 and 20). The false Messiah, " the Lawless One " (v. 13)—" the Wilful King " (Dan. xi. 36), the " Man of Lawlessness " (2 Thess. ii. 3)— is seated on his throne of iniquity (v. 20) where, by statute, he legalizes

" mischief " (v. 21), which his followers, " the lawless " (v. 3) execute against the followers of the true Messiah (vs. 5 and 6). They cry for deliverance (v. 2), and the mighty God of " vengeance " (v. 1) reveals Himself in flaming fire (2 Thess i. 7 and 8), ascends His throne as Judge of all the earth, recompenses " tribulation " to the oppressors (v. 2) and " rest " to the oppressed (v. 13). The false Messiah is cast into the pit prepared for him (v. 13 and Rev. xix. 20), and his followers (v. 23) are cut off with the edge of the sword (Rev. xix. 21). Thus Jehovah, the God of vengeance, is declared in 2 Thess. i. to be the Lord Jesus.

Dan. xi, Rom. xi, 2 Thess. i and ii, and Rev. xix should be read in connection with this Psalm.

The confession is made that only the appearing of the Messiah can end the affliction and turn the Wilderness into an Eden ; and faith intelligently accepts the suffering as just chastening (vs. 12 and 13), and as distinguished from chastisement (v. 10)

The words " planted " and " formed " (v 9) as applied respectively to the ear and to the eye, are found by modern science to be exactly appropriate to the marvellous structure of these organs.

The " thoughts " of the natural man (v. 11) are not as those of the spiritual (v. 19). The thoughts of the latter are rich in comforts and delights ; those of the former are emptiness.

The law-learner of verse 12 contrasts with the Law-breaker of verse 13. In the great judgment day of " adversity " the one shall enjoy rest, the other be cast into the pit. As Judas had " his own place " prepared for him (Acts i. 25) so Anti-Christ has a " pit " dug for him (Rev. xix. 20).

Judgment divorced from righteousness entails oppression (v. 15). When the Son of Man returns to judge the earth then will judgment return to righteousness, and all the upright in heart will gladly follow in its train. Judgment was in Pilate ; righteousness in Christ. There was divorce and opposition ; and, as a consequence, the crime of crimes—the crucifixion of the Prince of Life

" Almost " means quickly ; and " to dwell in silence " means to die (v. 17).

The confession of verses 16-19 is that Messiah alone could protect defenceless Israel (v. 16) ; deliver her when in deadly peril (v. 17) ; hold her up when in danger of stumbling (v. 18); and comfort her when perplexed. " Thoughts " here mean perplexing thoughts.

The sense of verse 18 perhaps is : " Had I said, My foot is about to slip, then Thy mercy, O Jehovah, would have held me up." There can be no fellowship between the thrones of Christ and Anti-Christ (v. 20).

The majesty of the first verse may be felt in this translation : " O mighty God of vengeance, Jehovah, mighty God of vengeance, shine forth ! "

PSALMS XCV.—Through the night of weeping, at the close of the wilderness journey, faith will desire the millennial joy, that is to come in the morning (xci.-xciv.), will anticipate its praise (xcv.-c.), and will in advance acclaim its kingdom (ci.-cv.). Such will be the activities of Israel's heart through that night of sorrow and horror. She will contrast the earth under Anti-Christ (xciv.) with the earth under Christ (ciii.). See the Introduction to Book iv. Thus this psalm, and the five following, are priceless illustrations of the victorious power of a Divinely-given faith that will enable the lovers of Messiah in that dark night of shame, torture and death to sing praise to His Name in the sure expectation of His glorious appearing and Kingdom.

The first and last psalms of this second group correspond. In xcv. His sheep praise Him in anticipation because He is great (v. 3), in Psalm c. they praise Him because He is good (v. 5). Psalms xcvi. and xcix. sing alternately the " new song " to be sung to the Messiah when He comes for judgment and enthronement.

The Holy Spirit is the Author of this Psalm (Heb. iii. 7). He is also the Author of all the Psalms. He here calls upon Israel to worship the Messiah as God of the whole earth (vs. 3-7). He divides the Psalm into two stanzas—verses 1-7 and 8-11. The first stanza is an invitation ; the second, a warning. Their doctrine is that faith admits into the future sabbath rest of the Kingdom and unbelief excludes from it. That Kingdom will be earth's great sabbath of rest.

Creation rest, redemption rest and millennial rest are all based upon the Person and work of Christ. Faith brings into these rests ; unbelief excludes. Hence the invitation in this first stanza to come to Jesus (v. 6). He is God's rest—an ineffable rest. How wonderful is the grace that invites sinners to share God's rest! That is a rest that never can be disturbed; its wonders are developed in Hebrews iii. and iv.

The heathen believe that there is a god for the mountains, another for the plains, and another for the sea with its sands and shoals, but this song witnesses that there is but one God, and that the sea and the deepest and highest portions of the earth are His (vs. 4 and 5).

The word "hand" closes verse 7 and the first stanza, as decided by Hebrews iii. 7.

In order to feel the force and anguish of the appeal this translation of verses 8 and 9 is suggested: "Oh that ye would hear His voice to-day! Oh that ye would not harden your heart as at Meribah, and as at Massah in the wilderness, when your fathers tempted me and put me to the proof! And yet they saw My mighty works! . . . . I was grieved with that generation . . . . they shall not enter into My rest." Such is man's heart. He wills not to recognise God's ways in severity and in goodness (v. 10). Those who believe the Scriptures, and who have some little knowledge of their own hearts, have no difficulty in believing that the very people who witnessed and profited by the marvellous miracles of the wilderness, challenged God to provide a table for them in the desert, and when it was provided, declared that Pharaoh's was better, and so they appointed a captain to return into Egypt!

The Psalm, which should read as in the R.V., is pronounced by some to be a meaningless and accidental union of pieces of other psalms. This shows deplorable ignorance. It is a unity, as its structure and teaching clearly demonstrate.

Few pictures in the Bible are more affecting than that which forms the setting of these six songs (xcv.-c.). Through the land of trouble and anguish where dwell the lion, the lioness, the young lion, the adder, and the flying fiery serpent, the little band of the Hebrew believers of the future advance Zionwards—not now southwards (Is. xxx. 6); and during the last and most terrible stage of the wilderness journey, under fierce persecution, but in the confidence and courage and patience and sympathy of a divine faith, they sing of the promised appearing of the Messiah — courage in suffering persecution, patience in waiting for the morning, and sympathy in inviting all nations, (including their persecutors—symbolized by the wild beasts of the desert) to unite with them in the song.

PSALMS XCVI.—Israel having sung the previous psalm ("us" v. 1 and "we" v. 7) now invites the nations to join her in "a new song." The next psalm is the song. Similarly Psalm xcviii. is a summons to sing a new song, and Psalm xcix. is the response. The reasons why the nations should sing a new song are given in verses 4-6 and 13. This new song belongs to the day when the kingdoms of the world shall become the kingdom of Jehovah and of His Christ (Rev. xi. 15, and xii. 10.)

The doctrine of the psalm is that the advent of the Messiah into the world will make it a Paradise, and that His rule alone can banish dissension, war, misery, and injustice, and establish society in an enduring brotherhood.

Men may test the reality and credibility of this prophecy by surrendering their sinful hearts to the government of Immanuel. They will then experience a love, a peace, and a moral power that their hearts were strangers to previous to conversion.

The nations, as the next Psalm shows, will respond to Israel's invitation; and creation itself (vs. 11 and 12) will unite in the song (Rom. viii. 18-23).

The first line of verse 11 displays the name "Jehovah" as an acrostic in the Hebrew text; and the statement proclaims the great climax which is the subject of the Five Books of the Psalms.

Faith repeats the word "cometh" in verse 13 as a confession of certitude.

PSALM XCVII.—This is the new song of Ps. xcvi. not new for heaven but new for earth. It sings of a new day for humanity—a day of righteousness and peace and brotherhood It will. dawn when God causes His First-Begotten to return to the earth on the millennial morn, and commands all the angels to worship Him (Heb. i. 7). In this quotation the Holy Spirit interprets the Psalm, and declares its God to be Messiah.

"Holiness" (v. 12) will characterise that

new day, as predicted here and in Psalms xciii. and xcix. These three Psalms begin with Jehovah enthroned, and close with holiness encamped. This promised reign of peace and love and righteousness is yet future ; but in these prophecies faith makes all a present reality, and He who gives songs in the night will enable His little flock in the coming night to sing, in anticipation, its glad strains. Such is the nature of a living faith. It is divinely given ; and it is always based upon definite Bible promises.

The song pictures the gladness which will fill the world when Messiah is enthroned, His adversaries destroyed, and His people delivered. The " foundation " of that throne will be righteousness and judgment (v. 2). The great islands of verse 1 figure the nations dwelling in the continents washed by the waters of the great oceans of the world. The previous psalm summons them to sing the song. Here they respond.

The Messiah Himself told the High Priest that He would come with clouds (v. 2, Matt. xxvi. 64). The prophet Daniel and the Apostle John make a similar statement ; and the Apostle Paul adds that flaming fire will be also an accompaniment (2 Thess. i). Thus will He appear to His adversaries whom He will destroy (v. 3), and to idolators whom He will confound (v. 7). These terrible manifestations will be similar to those that made Israel and the earth tremble at Sinai (vs. 4 and 5).

The nations shall see His glory (v. 6) ; the angels (" god's " Heb. i. 7), shall worship (v. 7) ; and the redeemed of Israel rejoice because of Messiah's judgments upon idolators (v. 8).

The titles Adon (v. 5) and Elyon (v. 9) are Messianic titles in relation to the earth.

" The righteous " (v. 11) is singular and " the upright " plural. This expresses the comforting assurance that not only is ever-enduring felicity promised to the whole body of God's people, but it is assured to each member of that body however insignificant.

PSALM XCVIII.—The sweet melody and perfect harmony of the new song that will salute Jehovah Messiah on the millennial morning will have three voices, the Hebrew (vs. 1-3), the Gentile (vs. 4-6), and Nature (vs. 7 and 8). But Israel will have the leading part and a double theme, for she will sing of grace in past redemption and in present restoration.

The first summons to the nations to sing this new song (xcvi.) is based upon the grace to be shown to man and to nature ; the second summons is based upon the grace that is to be shown to Israel, and to man and nature in association with Israel.

Just as He did " marvellous things " for her in the past in Egypt with His right hand and His holy arm (v. 1), so will He make a public demonstration of His fidelity to her in His salvation of her from her future oppressors (vs. 2 and 3) ; and just as the nations witnessed with wonder the birth of the Twelve Tribes, so will they see with astonishment their restoration. These are the marvellous things, and the victory and the salvation and the righteousness and the mercy and the truth celebrated in verses 1-3.

Thus Israel is summoned to sing a new song, and the reasons why she should do so are set out in the statements following the word " for " in verse 1. The nations are summoned to sing in unison with nature because of the two facts following the word " for " in verse 9 ; these are, first. because Messiah will govern the earth with righteousness, and, second, because He will judge the nations with equity. Well may men sing at the prospect of such a rule ! for they have never enjoyed a government exhibiting righteousness and equity.

PSALM XCIX.—The little company of believing Hebrews as they press through the wilderness of trouble and anguish see in vision Rev. iv. and v., and here sing of that expected day-break when Jehovah Messiah, bearing in His hand the title-deeds of the earth (Rev. v. 5), will ascend His throne, to which are attached the cherubim uttering their cry of Holy, Holy, Holy, and when angels and men and the creation will fall in worship at His feet. This psalm and Rev. iv. and v. should be read in the R.V.

Animated by this vision, the pilgrim company joyfully shouts " Jehovah takes the Kingdom " (v. 1 with Rev. xi. 17), " He establishes His Throne in Zion ! " (v. 2). " Let all peoples worship Him ! " (vs. 3 and 9, with Zech. xiv. 16-21). Thus in this song they invite all nations to unite with Israel in worshipping Messiah the King.

The cherubim in Rev. iv. announce the Kingdom and its judgments with a thrice repeated "holy." They here appear (v. 1); and their three-fold cry is given in verses 3, 5 and 9, R.V. This triple "holy" marks the three stanzas of the psalm. The first (v. 3) states the reason why the nations should praise Messiah; the second (v. 5), why Israel should praise Him; and the third (v. 9) repeats the motive why all nations should praise Israel's God and Lord.

In the first three verses Israel invites the nations to come to Zion and worship the King; in the following five verses she invites her own Twelve Tribes also to worship at His footstool; and in the last verse she repeats the invitation to the nations, and emphasizes the important command that the place of worship is to be Zion's holy hill.

Verse 4 promises that the power of the King shall be employed on behalf of judgment, equity and righteousness. This is not true of earthly governments and monarchs.

In harmony with the rewards of Rev. xi. 18, the princes of Israel appear in verses 6-8. This is very touching and very important. The Holy Spirit recognises, and brings forward, those who in the past were true to His communications, in spite of national and ecclesiastical apostasy. Moses and Aaron represent the Law, and Samuel the Prophets, and these together figure all who loved and trusted Messiah in the past, and who were faithful to His word. These three died thousands of years ago; but true to His promise they will appear with Him in the glory of His Kingdom, and with them all whom they represent and who exercise the faith that they exercised. This is full of consolation to all who at any time trust the promises of God; and the consolation is the greater when it is noticed that verse 8 declares these great saints to have been sinners, that is, weak and erring and sinful men, and not sinless men.

Two divine principles appear in these verses. One, that God forgives confessed sin; the other, that He judges its action (Gal. vi. 7 and 8). Sin may be forgiven but its consequences must be reaped.

The structure of verses 6 and 7 should be studied. The first member of verse 6 and the first member of verse 7 correspond, and the two intervening members also correspond. Thus to Moses and Aaron and their companions He spake in the cloudy pillar; to Samuel and those with him He answered when they called.

Verses 6 and 7 have a special message for the heart. They reveal that the new-born Israel of the future will be identified with the faithful Israel of the past. The child of Ruth will be hailed as a son born to Naomi; and Mara will be forgotten!

PSALM C.—This psalm closes the second group (xcv.-xc.) of the Fourth Book, in which the little band of Wilderness pilgrims, in the confidence and joy of faith, anticipate and sing of the renewed earth, of the one flock and of the one Shepherd. (Ezek. xxxvii. 19)

This last psalm of the group corresponds with the first one, xcv. It declared Jehovah Messiah to be "great"; this proclaims Him to be "good."

Ps. xcvi. contains the central verse of the Book of the Psalms (v. 11): "Let the heavens rejoice and let the earth be glad," and the reason is given in verse 13, "because He cometh." Psalm c. sings of the consequent universal gladness. When He comes the whole earth will make a joyful noise unto Him (v. 1). Because He is not yet come a dreadful noise of weeping and quarrelling and mutual slaughter ascends continually to heaven. His Advent will put an end to the reign of sin and it visible fruit.

The Psalm is constructed with two stanzas. These correspond. They may be thus presented:

Exhortation to worship (v. 1).
　Entrance with singing (v. 2).
　　Declaration: Messiah is God, Creator and Shepherd.

Entrance with singing (v. 4).
　Exhortation to worship (v. 4).
　　Declaration: Messiah is good, merciful and faithful.

Verse 3 is the centre of the song. The two verses which precede, and the two which follow, belong, respectively, to Israel and the nations. In harmony with this distinction worship has the first and prominent importance for the one, and entrance for the other; for Israel's position was assured, but the Gentile being outside the Covenant needed the assurance of entrance, and this was given him in the promise "I am the door, by Me if any man enter in he shall be saved" (John x. 9).

So this prophecy assures the fulfilment of all the promises of the Old Testament respecting the millennial glory, and the one flock. This of course is distinct from the higher glory which is to be the heritage of the Church. Each member of that wonderful fellowship says "My churchmanship is in the heavens."

Messiah's titles and attributes are declared in verses 3 and 5. As God He is good, as Creator, merciful, and as Shepherd, faithful. It is the new creation that is intended here; and this will be recognized if this translation is accepted: "Recognize that Jehovah Messiah He is God; He made us His people and the sheep of His pasture; and we are His."

The Psalm is built with five verses containing fifteen members. Three is the number of Deity; five, of Grace. There are forty-two words in the Hebrew text, that is six multiplied by seven—six expressing human imperfection and seven Divine completion. In all this, as in the statement "He made us His people," appears the fact of election; which is the great foundation doctrine of the Gospel.

PSALM CI.—Psalms ci. to cvi. compose the third and final group of this Fourth Book. Its subject is the character and capacity of the King to Whom is to be given the kingdom. His portrait engages the affections of the travellers, during the last stage of the wilderness journey. These Psalms show how He was to be tested by suffering, whether personal or sympathetic. David who was a type of Him, was also tested by suffering. Messiah's fitness tor the throne, His sympathy with all who fear God, and His opposition to evil and evil-doers, are set out in this third group. The King pledges Himself in this first psalm of the group to reign with mercy for the righteous (v. 6), and with judgment for the wicked (vs. 3-5, and 7-8). These activities will characterize His government.

His personal perfection is the subject of the first two verses of the psalm. His love

for Jehovah, His loyalty to mercy and judgment (v. 1), His intelligent course of conduct with a perfect heart in the perfect way in which Abraham was commanded to walk and be perfect (Gen. xvii. 1); prove His personal suitability to exercise the government of the whole earth (v. 2); and His pledge to destroy the wicked, to honour the righteous, and to maintain a spotless court, reveal His moral ability to administer with executive perfection the kingdom to be committed to Him (vs. 3-8).

The parenthesis "O when wilt Thou come unto me" (v. 2) is explained by Mark xiii. 32. In sympathy with His afflicted people, and with a sorrowing world, He longs for the establishment of God's kingdom in the earth, but as man the appointed time of its institution was hidden from Him. Hence this cry of desire for its inauguration.

PSALM CII.—Interpreted by Hebrews i. 10-12 it is evident that verses 1-11 and 23 and 24, as far as the word "days," are the utterances of the Messiah as the Man of Sorrows; and that verses 12-22 and 24, from the word "They" to 28, are predictions addressed to Him as the Mighty God by the Holy Spirit.

The subject of this group (ci.-cvi.) being His suitability as King of all the earth (v. 12, R.V. margin with Heb. i.), it was necessary that He should both be the Man of Sorrows and the Mighty God. As the one, He is equipped with mercy; as the other, with judgment. He is the Afflicted One of the Superscription.

In response to His complaint (vs. 1-11) the Holy Spirit addressing Him in verse 12, and with special reference to verse 11, says: "But Thou, O Jehovah, shalt sit enthroned as King for ever." He then passes on to foretell the restoration of Israel (vs. 13 and 14); the salvation of the Gentiles (v. 15); the subjection of all the Kings of the earth (vs. 15 and 22); His apparition in glory (v. 16); and the beneficence of His reign over the new nation that is to be born (v. 18, with Matt. xxi. 43). Thus His glories (1 Pet. i. 11, R.V.) as The Great King are set over against His sufferings as the Rejected Man. Here, as in so many other Scriptures, His sufferings and His glories are brought together, and always in that order.

A striking feature of the Psalm is the

introduction of verse 23, and the first member of verse 24. They interrupt the recital of Emmanuel's glories, and appear to disjoint the Psalm. But this is designed in order to heighten the contrast between His glory as the Eternal God, the Creator of the Heavens and the earth, and His weakness and dependence as Man on the earth. Thus the beauty, the structure and the doctrine of the Psalm are emphasized and presented. The sufferings of verses 1-11 introduce His glories as Redeemer; those of verses 23 and 24, His glories as Creator. The word " days " should, therefore, close verse 24; and, supplying the title Jehovah from verse 12, the response of the Holy Spirit to Messiah's cry reads : " Thy years O Jehovah, shall endure for all generations. Of old hast Thou laid the foundation of the earth, etc."

The scribes and Pharisees, as is evident from verse 8, bound themselves by an oath similar to Acts xxiii. 12, to destroy Him. On the Mount of Transfiguration He was " lifted up," for the Voice said " This is My Beloved Son " ; and on the Mount of Condemnation He was " cast down," for He cried saying, " Why hast Thou forsaken Me (v. 10) ? "

Acts xv. 16 and 17 are based upon verses 13-16. The " way " of verse 23 was Messiah's way through the wilderness to Calvary. So, wearied with the journey, He sat as a wearied man on the well (John iv. 6).

He was less than thirty-five years of age when God delivered Him up, (Rom. viii. 32), so He was taken away in " the midst " of His days ; for the days of man's life in the wilderness are threescore years and ten (xc. 10). Yet a seed shall serve Him ; and He shall be satisfied with that heritage (v. 28 with Isa. liii. 10, 11).

PSALM CIII.—The King's engagement to rule justly (ci.), and His personal fitness for the throne (cii.) having been declared, the theme of His suitability is further developed, and His glories as Redeemer (ciii.), and as Creator (civ., proclaimed in unison with Hebrews i. and Rev. iv. and v. These latter Scriptures speak of His glories as Redeemer and Creator, but in the inverse order. In Heb. i. His glory as Creator comes first— " He made the worlds " ; and then His glory as Redeemer—" He purged our sins." Similarly, Rev. iv. 11 says, " Thou

hast created all things," and Rev. v. 9 adds, " Thou hast redeemed men." Thus His glory, first as Creator and then as Redeemer, is acclaimed. But these two Psalms celebrate His praise, first as Redeemer, and then as Creator. This is designed ; it harmonizes with the argument and structure of this Fourth Book ; for His activity as Creator here has relation to the future when He will re-create Israel as a new nation, in the sense of Eph. ii. 10 ; and that new creation is founded upon redemption.

The title declares the relationship of the Psalm to the Messiah. The Author is the Holy Spirit. He composes the words for the hearts and tongues of lovers of Immanuel, framing the language so as to be a personal and fitting expression of worship and praise.

Messiah's benefits to sinful and sorrowing men without distinction, occupy the first place in the psalm—they are six in number (vs. 1-5). Then the Spirit recalls His benefits in the past to His ancient people when oppressed in Egypt (v. 6) ; when wanderers in the desert (vs. 7-9) ; and when settled in Canaan (vs. 10-18)—an amazing story of love, patience, power and forgiveness ; and, finally, the Spirit confirms the benefits promised under Messiah's coming dominion when angels and men and nature will unite to bless Him (vs. 19-22).

His throne will be prepared in " the heavens." The term " heavens " includes the earth ; as is the case in the words " Our Father who art in the heavens " (Greek). The sense here is that the one throne will then govern both heaven and earth, and so fulfil the Lord's prayer. The distinction between heaven and earth is observed in the petition, " Thy will be done on earth as it is in heaven."

The natural intelligence can recognize Divine " acts," but only to the spiritual mind does God make known His " ways " (v. 7).

As it is impossible to bring the east and the west together so is it impossible to bring the forgiven sinner and his forgiven sins together (v. 12). The divine fact stated in this verse gives to those who believe it a peace which nothing can destroy.

PSALM CIV.—Since Messiah is Jehovah Elohim (v. 1), then is He fitted to be King over all the earth, for having made it and man and the living creatures, He is the most suitable Monarch to govern it and them. His glory as Creator is the doctrine of the Psalm ; and it harmonises with Genesis i. and ii. His personal glory (v. 1), His wisdom as Creator of the heavens (vs. 2 and 3), and His supremacy over the Angels (Heb. i. 7 and v. 4), are the subjects of the first stanza.

This conception of Deity and of creative power is not human but divine ; and the language is that of pure science. None of the great religions of the world, either ancient or modern, approach this cosmogony in sublimity and accuracy. Light here appears, as in Genesis i., as the first attribute and evidence of the Creator (v. 2). " Curtain " means tabernacle. The word occurs fifty-three times in the Bible. Of these, forty-seven relate to the Tabernacle in the Wilderness. The heavens are presented scientifically in verse 2 as a vast tent curtaining from view the angelic hosts and their glorious Creator. The higher heavens (" His chambers " vs. 3 and 13), the atmosphere (the deep, v. 6), the waters, the clouds and the winds picture the wondrous envelope within which the world that then was existed.

The apparition of the solid earth (vs. 5-9), the provision of streams of water for the living creatures (vs. 10-13), and of vegetable food (vs. 14-18), coupled with shelter (vs. 16-18), form the subject matter of the second stanza of the Psalm. His appointment of the Sun and Moon for times and seasons, and His providence toward the earth and its living creatures, including man, is celebrated in the third stanza (vs. 9-24).

The seas and their inhabitants are sung of in the fourth stanza (vs. 25-30). These creatures also depend for breath and food upon the wisdom, the power and the benevolence of their mighty Creator. The nautilus and the whale (v. 26) represent, respectively, the small and great creatures of verse 25. To the present day sailors name the nautilus a ship, and when observing the motion of a whale through the waters, shout " There she plays ! " These creatures, like man, are made of dust (v.29)."Creeping " would better read " swarming."

Earthquakes and volcanoes, so full of terror to man, are wholly subject to God(v. 32.)

The word Hallelujah first occurs here in the Bible (v. 35). It is connected, not with the salvation, but with the destruction of men. The first Hallelujah in the New Testament also celebrates the destruction of sinners (Rev. xix. 1 and 2). This is very solemn. It does not accord with modern popular religious teaching.

Verse 35 is a prediction and a prayer. Both are expressed in the form of the Hebrew verb, which reads : " Sinners shall be consumed out of the earth," and, " let sinners be consumed out of the earth." The language of the new Testament is similar, for Matt. xiii. 41 and 42, 2 Thess. i. 8 and 9, Gal. i 8 and 9 and 1 Cor. xvi. 22, together with many passages in the Revelation, are predictions and prayers fore-telling and approving the destruction of the wicked.

PSALM CV.—This Psalm reviews the grace and faithfulness of Messiah to the Patriarchs and to Israel as demonstrating His ability to rule the whole earth, and thus suggests the argument that, as He was able to deliver and maintain them, so is He competent to bless and govern all men. The following psalm continues the argument and strengthens it.

The song opens with an exhortation to praise Messiah the King (vs. 1-7), and closes with the hallelujah of verse 45. The basis of redemption is next stated to be the Covenant in promise (vs. 8-12), and the Covenant in performance (vs. 42-45). The intervening verses restate the history of the Patriarchs (vs. 13-22), and of the Nation (vs. 23-41). Verse 18 is an instance of the Law of Subsequent Narration. Joseph is the central figure of the one history ; Moses of the other. They are brought forward to illustrate the fitness of Messiah for the throne of the world. Grace in forgiving, and ability in delivering, characterized them. Israel rejected both these princes, as they did Him of Whom they were types (Acts vii).

Thus the action of Messiah with Israel is a picture and a promise of His future action with the world. The Covenant consummated at Calvary will be the basis of His millennial rule ; and the promises of that covenant will be then performed and fulfilled.

The wonders and judgments of verse 5 are, respectively, the miracles in Egypt and the laws of Sinai.

The promise of the Covenant "I will give," is stated in verse 11, and the per formance, "And He gave" in verse 44.

The Patriarchs were both kings and prophets (v. 15). Pharaoh and Abimelech were threatened with death if they touched them (Gen. xii. 17, xx. 3, and xxvi. 11).

The sense of verse 19 is, that during the two years that elapsed before Joseph's interpretation of the dreams was told to Pharaoh, the Word of God was training him. That is, Joseph kept trusting the fidelity of that Word which was the source of his interpretations. It was a very real and lengthened testing of his faith and patience that he, the interpreter, should remain in a prison and the subject of the interpretation, the butler, dwell luxuriously in a palace.

What God permits to be done the idiom of the Hebrew language declares Him to do (v. 25) ; and, governed by the same idiom, what the prophets were commissioned to announce, they are stated to have personally performed. Illustrations of this beautiful feature in Hebrew sacred literature will be found in Gen. xli. 13, Jer. i. 10, John xx. 23, Heb. xi. 7, etc.

The Holy Spirit in repeating facts frequently does so in moral and not in historic order. So is it here, and in Ps. lxxviii., 1 Cor. x., and in other parts of Scripture. Also He, with design, may omit parts of the history. Thus only eight of the ten plagues in Egypt are here reviewed (vs. 28-36).

The close connection between the plague of darkness and the compelled submission of the Egyptians (v. 28), is very striking. God sent the darkness and the Egyptians let the Hebrews go. This alludes possibly to the ninth plague ; but as a substantive statement the word darkness is to be understood as a covering term expressive of the entire period of the divine punitive action upon Pharaoh. It was indeed a time of darkness for him ; and it lasted several months.

The energy of Messiah's love is revealed in verses 37-41, and the purpose of His love in verse 45.

"Made" (v. 9), i.e., ratified by cutting a sacrifice in twain (Heb.) See Genesis xv. 9, 10, 17, and Jer. xxxiv. 18.

PSALM CVI.—The ability of the Messiah

to execute the mercy and judgment promised in Ps. ci. is illustrated in Pss. cv. and cvi. The former sings of mercy ; the latter, of judgment. This psalm closes the Fourth Book.

His fitness for the Throne of the whole earth is argued positively in Ps. cv. and negatively in Ps. cvi. His personal perfection is the theme of the one Psalm, the moral imperfection of His subjects is the theme of the other. The claim, consequently, is made by the Holy Spirit on His behalf, that having so lovingly and skilfully and powerfully shepherded such a wholly unloveable, unbelieving, treacherous, idolatrous, immoral and ungrateful a people as the Israelites, He is the only One fitted to successfully govern corrupt and sinful humanity. The conduct of Israel is a humiliating proof of the hopeless corruption of human nature, and an overwhelming demonstration of man's need of a new birth in order to fit him for the Kingdom of Heaven.

The Scriptures predict with confidence that Christ will establish a just understanding and a gracious government over man ; and that He will change the earth, at present a wilderness, into a paradise.

Ps. xciv. contrasted with Ps. ciii., sharply distinguishes the future happiness of man under the reign of Christ with the misery of man under the approaching rule of anti-Christ.

The answer to the question of verse 2 is, that no one can exhaustively analyse, understand and show the meaning and purpose of Divine actions, or adequately praise such actions. But Messiah can, and He will show forth all God's praise (Ps. ix. 14).

But a spiritual intelligence will recognise Divine action and bow in worship because of such action (v. 3). That intelligence results only from subjection of mind to the Scriptures, and from an unvarying life of righteous conduct. A conscious salvation (v. 4) enables the believer " to see," " to rejoice " and " to glory " (v. 5). Love delights in possession. Hence the terms " Thy people," " Thy chosen," Thy nation," " Thy inheritance " (vs. 4 and 5).

The nature of evil is seen in the terms " sin," " iniquity " and " wickedness " (v. 6).

Israel did not wish to understand, nor take the trouble to study the ten plagues, nor wish to remember the countless mercies of their Great Shepherd (v. 7). Forty hours took Israel out of Egypt, but forty years did not take Egypt out of Israel.

The sons of Korah escaped the judgment of verse 17, as appears from Num. xvi. 1-35, xxvi. 11, and Ps. xlii.

The sacred name of Horeb is given to Sinai (v. 19) so as to heighten the sin of representing the God of glory by a beast that ate grass (v. 20).

Solomon's prayer (1 Kings viii. 50), was answered (v. 46). Details are recorded in Daniel, Nehemiah, Esther and Ezra.

The Book closes with the expected Amen; but the repeated Amen is here changed into Hallelujah. This harmonises with the theme of the Book. Amen expresses the desire that the wilderness journey should end, and that the Kingdom should be established, and Hallelujah joyfully announces the gratification of both desires. It is, therefore, fitting that the end of the dark night of the Wilderness and the dawn of the bright day of the Kingdom should be greeted with a double Hallelujah, one at the commencement of the psalm (v. 1) and the other at its close (v. 48).

THE PSALMS

BOOK V.

PSALMS CVII.-CL.—The Fifth Book of the Psalms corresponds to the Fifth Book of the Pentateuch. The Divine title for that book is "These are the words." Israel was about to take possession of Canaan and was promised prosperity there if obedient to the Word of God, but slavery, affliction and banishment if disobedient. The message of the Fifth Book of the Psalms is similar, but the circumstances are different. Prosperity is shown to be dependent upon acceptance of the Word of God as the rule of life. But the message is not now directed to a new and untried people but to a tested, rebellious, and fallen people. Hence the message is accompanied by grace, and the accumulative effect is given in the last verse of Ps. cvii. That is, that on observing the facts set out in this Book the observer will learn that the Messiah is both loving and kind and kind and loving.

The Book sums up the teaching of the previous books and states that all blessing for man (Book i.), all blessing for Israel (Book ii.), all blessing for Sion (Book iii.), and all blessing for the earth (Book iv.) depends upon subjection to the Word of God. Hence Ps. cxix. is found in this book.

The five closing Psalms are Hallelujah Psalms, and correspond respectively to the five books of the Psalms and to the five books of the Pentateuch, and to the five books of the Apocalypse.

This Fifth Book, therefore, presents the beauteous picture of the Messiah coming as the Word of God with healing and help to those who, by disobedience to that Word, had brought themselves to ruin.

PSALM CVII.—The first Psalm of each book gives the keynote of the book. So is it here. The redeemed (v. 2) are urged to proclaim the grace that redeemed them. They are grouped into four companies: The Eastern: these are wanderers (vs. 4-9); the Western: these are prisoners (vs. 10-16); the Northern: these are fools (vs. 17-22); and the Southern: these are sailors (vs. 23-32). The four companies furnish a four-square picture of the rejector of God's Word. He is homeless, enslaved, infirm and restless. But in Christ as the Word of God there is redemption for these self-ruined rebels. His grace and power not only avail to recover them (vs. 2-32), but also to restore nature (vs. 33-38). He can make the wilderness to rejoice and blossom as the rose. Disobedience to His word not only banished man from Paradise but changed Eden into a stony desert, for such is that fair garden to-day. Romans viii. predicts redemption for the earth as well as for man. To have excluded the earth from this Psalm would have given an imperfect picture of the lovingkindness of Jehovah (v. 43).

In Luke xiii. 29, Adonai Messiah speaks of these four companies, and groups them in the same order. This is very interesting. He so grouped them there because the Holy Spirit so grouped them here. Why this order should be so designed excites the sanctified imagination. The historian possibly will discover that primitive man moved eastward and westward and northward and southward from his original home in Eden.

Verses 33, 34 and 39, emphasize the ruin that results to nature and to man from disobedience to God's law. Verses 35-38 display the happiness that crowns both nature and man when that Divine revelation becomes the rule of faith.

Princes who despise that Word are clothed with contempt (v. 40), but the poor in spirit who love that Word are set high above the reach of calamity (v. 41). These have families like flocks; those are lonely wanderers in the pathless wilderness. Israel contrasted with the princes of Pharaoh and of Egypt, Daniel and his companions in confrontation with the proud monarchs of the East, illustrate these two last verses.

The Lord Jesus at the tomb of Lazarus illustrates verse 43. He was kind, for He by His power raised Lazarus to life and restored him to his mourning sisters; He was loving, for He wept and mingled His tears with theirs. Action reveals kindness; Emotion expresses love.

PSALM CVIII.—This song is composed of portions of Pss. lvii. and lx. This is not a haphazard borrowing from two Psalms to make a third, as some, unskilful in the word of righteousness, think (Heb. v. 13), but is a beauteous medley of songs arranged by the Holy Spirit, and harmonises with this Deuteronomy Book of the Psalms; for just as the Fifth Book of the Pentateuch recalls and repeats Divine lessons and facts taught and recorded in the prior books, so is it here. Hence the dominant note in this song is sounded in the words, " God hath spoken " (v. 7). Upon this assured foundation Messiah builds all His confident expectations in regard to His future Kingdom in Israel and His dominion over the Nations (vs. 7-9). His expectation is based upon the holiness of the Word of God; for such being its moral character and value, its engagements and promises are absolutely sure of fulfilment. By the union of these two Psalms lvii. and lx. from Book II, the fundamental truth is repeated and emphasised that all blessing for Israel, for the Nations and for the Earth is based upon Messiah as the Word of God.

The holiness of God is alike shown in The keeping of His promises (v. 7) and in the chastening of His people (v. 11).

For an exposition of this Song see notes on Pss. lvii. and lx.

The stanza, verses 7-11, may be better understood if this free translation be accepted. The speaker is the Messiah. He says, God hath spoken, i.e., promised Me possession of Canaan and dominion of the earth—I will exult in His holiness, i.e., His promise is sure of fulfilment, for He is holy; consequently I will divide Shechem and measure the valley of Succoth; Gilead shall be Mine; Manasseh shall be Mine; Ephraim also shall be the mighty diadem of My head;

Judah shall be My sceptre; Moab shall be My wash-basin; I will throw My shoe to Edom; Philistia shall announce My triumph. Thus He predicts the future supremacy of Israel, and the subjugation of the Gentiles. The one shall be His ministers of state; the others, His slaves (Ps. lx.).

PSALM CIX.—The Holy Spirit is the Author of this Psalm (Acts i. 16-22). The speaker is the Messiah. He appears as the Word of God. As such He personifies love, goodness and righteousness, and is the representative Head of all who love Him as the Truth. For these He prays, and they are assured of happiness and victory. Judas, unnamed, is here the head and representative of all who rebel against Messiah as the Word of God; and who, consequently, hate all that is pure and lovely. For these there must, therefore, be the bitter fruit of rebellion. This doom they bring not only upon themselves but also upon those connected with them. This is an eternal law which operates to-day, and which was illustrated when the wives and children of Daniel's accusers perished with them in the den of lions (Dan. vi. 24). So the drunkard and the impure bring upon their wives and children the same fearful diseases which they bring upon themselves by their transgression against physical law.

The language accordingly of this Psalm is judicial and prophetic. Enemies of Messiah, the Word of God, will be judged (vs. 6 and 7); and the righteousness of their punishment and the grounds for it, are set out in verses 8-20.

The passage, verses 8-15, is prophetic. It should be read in the future tense. But it also expresses approbation. It predicts the sure consequences and fruit of hatred to the Word of God and to His people. The future will approve and fulfil this prophecy. It is foolish to object to and argue against facts. There is a modern unhealthy sentimentality against punishment. The prophetic prayers of the New Testament demanding judgment upon the opponents of the gospel are as terrible as those of the Old Testament foretelling, and approving the destruction of the opponents of truth and grace. Righteousness can have no fellowship with evil, but must from its nature judge it. Thus Christ judged the Pharisees in Matt. xxiii.; and the Apostle Paul, when opening out the doctrines of grace, predicted and approved the eternal doom of all who opposed them (Gal. i., 2 Thess. i., 1 Cor. xvi. 22). See also the prayers and praises of the Apocalypse.

The Messiah recognizes that the hatred shown to His people is shown to them because they belong to Him. It is really directed against Him. In return for the love which He and they show to men, men recompense hatred (vs. 1-5). Therefore is their punishment just (vs. 6-20). The fact that man so treated Him, and so treats those that love Him is an unanswerable proof of the unfathomable corruption of man's moral nature.

He was the poor and needy Man ; His was the wounded heart (v. 22) ; at Him they shook their heads as He hung upon the tree (v. 25) ; but God stood at His right hand, and in resurrection delivered Him from the power of those who sought to eternally destroy Him (v. 31). As to Judas, Satan stood at his right hand (v. 6), and then entered into him (Luke xxii. 3).

In Ps. cix. Jehovah stands at the right hand of The Poor Man. In Ps. cx. the Poor Man sits at the right hand of Jehovah. He was poor in spirit as well as in circumstances.

PSALM CX.—Seven quotations in the New Testament confirm the application of this Psalm to the Messiah—Matt. xxii. 44, Mark xii. 36, Luke xx. 42, Acts ii. 34, 1 Cor. xv. 25, Heb. i. 13, and x. 13. The reference in 1 Cor. xv., Matt. xxv. 31, and Rev. iii. 21, is to the Messiah's session on His own throne as distinguished from His session on His Father's throne.

The speaker is the Holy Spirit. The human instrument was David. The Person spoken of and spoken to, Messiah. The verb "said" (v. 1) is a special Hebrew word almost always used of Divine personal utterance.

The first verse covers the whole of the present period of time from Acts i. 9, to 2 Thess. i. 7. During this period the Messiah is living a life of faith (Heb. ii. 13), waiting for the fulfilment of the promise that His enemies be made a footstool for His feet.

The second verse pictures His enthronement in Sion and the committal to His hand of the sceptre of strength, emblem of His world-wide dominion.

The third verse should be divided into two and read thus : " Thy people shall, in the beauties of holiness, offer themselves as free-will offerings in the day of Thy power." And then as a distinct verse : " From the womb of the morning Thou hast the dew of Thy youth." No longer rebellious and idolatrous His people will in that day be morally arrayed in the beauteous garments of holiness.

" From the womb of the morning " (v. 3) corresponds to " From the brook in the way " (v. 7). Both statements refer to the resurrection—the one to its occasion ; the other to its continuance.

The Epistle to the Hebrews is a development of verse 4. Verses 5 and 6 predict Messiah's triumph over Anti-Christ and his followers. Anti-Christ will be the great head over many countries, his followers will be the dead bodies of verse 6. Messiah's fidelity to His people and His almighty power having been demonstrated in the past by the " dead bodies " of Exodus xiv. 30, and Isa. xxxvii. 36, will in the future be again evidenced by the " dead bodies " of Ezek. xxxix. 4 and 5, and Rev. xix. 21.

The poor and needy Man of the previous Psalm (v. 16), Who was hated for His love (v. 3), here appears exalted to God's right hand, and addressed as God ; and His people (v. 25) who were ashamed of Him in the day of his humiliation now become Amminadib in the day of His power (v. 3, and Cant. vi. 12).

During His present session in the heavens (v. 1) the "accepted time" of 2 Cor. vi. 2, continues. Verse 2 of the Psalm marks its close, and the beginning of the day of wrath so frequently predicted in the New Testament. Messiah Himself emphasized this distinction by stopping at the word " Lord " when reading Isa. lx. in the synagogue at Nazareth (Luke iv. 16-20.)

PSALM CXI.—This and the two following songs are the three Hallelujah Psalms which Israel will sing to Messiah on the day of His enthronement in Sion. They will acclaim the perfection of His works (cxi.), of His ways (cxii.), and of His Person (cxiii.) ; and this triple anthem will praise Him as the Word of God because of His fidelity to the Word of God (cxi. 5, 7, 9, and cxii. 1). The first two songs commence with " Hallelujah " and the last commences and closes with " Hallelujah."

The power of His works (vs. 2-7) and the preciousness of His words (vs. 7-10) and their united providence (2-5) and effects (9-10), express the content of the song.

The word " judgment " should close verse 7, and the words " all His commandments " begin verse 8.

A comparison of verses 8-10 with 2 Tim. iii. 15-17 will make yet clearer the glory and preciousness of the Word of God in its essence and effect. As to its essence, it is divine and, therefore, sure (v. 7), eternal (v. 8), true and upright (v. 8). As to its effect, it announces (v. 9) and makes wise to salvation (v. 10) all who submit to its power and authority. All this harmonizes with the Deuteronomy character of this Fifth Book.

Messiah's providential care of His people in the past in Egypt (v. 4), in the wilderness (v. 5) and in Canaan (v. 6) is recalled and celebrated ;   and His performance of His word is acknowledged in verses 6 and 7.

The glory of His works is stated to be the joyful study of His people (v. 2).

In the Hebrew Bible this and the following Psalm are acrostic. This shows relationship and correspondence ;   as will appear in Ps. cxii.

PSALM CXII.—The correspondence between these two acrostic psalms may be thus exhibited :

cxi. Six couplets (v. 1-6)
    One quatrain (vs. 7 and 8)
      Two triplets (vs. 9 and 10)
cxii. Six couplets (vs. 1-6)
    One quatrain (vs. 7 and 8)
      Two triplets (vs. 9 and 10)

The more closely this structure is examined the more perfect appears its correspondence and introversion. Not only does this beautiful form appear in the members of each psalm respectively, but it appears between the two psalms. For example, the two middle members of the quatrain in cxi. will be observed not only to stand in correspondence to each other, but also to correspond to the middle members of the quatrain of cxii. If this examination be pursued, further beauties will be discovered in these Psalms, both singly and jointly.

The Psalm is an expansion of the last verse of the previous one. It praises Messiah because of His ways upon earth, and because He moulds men into His own moral image. It celebrates and illustrates the fact that everyone who surrenders himself into the hands of this mighty God, and obeys Him, speedily becomes like Him. So the first three verses apply to Messiah. He is the Blessed Man of verse 1 and the Upright Man of verse 2, while the upright men of verses 4-8 are His servants. ' Upright " (v. 2) and " upright " (v. 4) are respectively singular and plural in the Hebrew text. They apply to Messiah and to His servants. Thus is the argument illustrated that He can make His servants like Himself ;   just as David moulded the timid fugitives of Adullam's cave into the mighty men of Hebron's throne (1 Sam. xxii. 2 and 2 Sam. xxiii. 8).

" Righteousness "   (vs. 3 and 9) means beneficence, as is evident from 2 Cor. ix. 9. The wealth and riches of grace in Messiah's treasury (v. 3) He pours out upon the needy (v. 9), and this beneficence He continues indefinitely. But the striking lesson of the Psalm is that His people imitate Him in this graciousness (vs. 4 and 5) ; and this lovely community of action is emphasized by the hiatus before the word " gracious " in verse 4. It may be thus supplied : He is, and they are gracious and full of compassion and generous, etc. " Lendeth " (v. 5) signifies all kinds of generous actions, because to lend is a very rare grace.

" Seed " and " generation " (v. 2) signify the spiritual sons of Messiah (Isa. liii. 10).

In the quatrain (vs. 7 and 8) the first and fourth members correspond : Evil tidings shall not put the believer in fear, for he shall see God's judgment upon his enemies ; and the two central members of the quatrain, united with the word " until," express the steadfastness of his faith during the entire period between the reception of the news and the destruction of the foes.

The true and false Messiahs and their followers are contrasted in the last two verses of the Psalm. Three statements are made respecting Messiah : He enriches, His beneficence never ends, and He triumphs.

" Wicked " in the first line of verse 10 is singular in the Hebrew text. It means The Lawless One of Dan. xi. 36 and 2 Thess. ii. 8. " Wicked " in the last line of the verse is plural in the Hebrew text and means the lawless ones, that is, the followers of the Lawless One. " Desire " should read hope or expectation.

Thus the great picture is drawn. Anti Christ and those who hope in him perish

Christ and those whose expectation is based on Him, triumph.

PSALM CXIII.—This is the last of the three Hallelujah Psalms. It differs from the two previous ones in that it begins and closes with Hallelujah.

It is also the first of the six Hallel Psalms —cxiii–cxviii. These Israel sang, and sings, at the Paschal Supper. At that supper there were, and are, four cups of wine drunk. The first three were sung, and are sung, after the second cup ; the remaining three after the fourth cup. They were sung in Matt. xxvi. 30. The Greek text here reads : " And having sung (the last Hallel Psalm—cxviii), they went forth to the Mount of Olives." That these Psalms are intended is without doubt, for they were sung, and are sung, at the Passover by all godly Israelites.

It brings these Psalms very near to the heart when it is remembered that they were sung by the Lord Himself on the night of His betrayal. Read in the atmosphere of that last supper they have an added preciousness for the believer.

This Psalm, cxiii., sung in that night of weakness, and to be sung in the coming day of power, links together Messiah's sufferings and the glories that are to follow. It invites the servants of Jehovah to praise Him. These are defined in verses 1, 7, 8 and 9. They were sunk in the lowest squalor (v. 7), were joyless (v. 9), but abounding grace looked down from heaven (v. 6) and made the servants (v. 1) princes (v. 8) and sons (v. 9).

Only those can worship God who are the servants of God. " To praise the Lord " is to bless Him for what He is in His being and essence. " To praise the name of the Lord " is to bless Him for His perfections and excellencies manifested in His actions. These issue from His essence. See note on cxxxviii. 2. " Name " (vs. 1, 2, 3) expresses character in essence and action. What Messiah is personally is, as already stated, the theme of this song.

Historically the words " from this time forth " (v. 2) relate to the occasion of His future enthronement in Sion. The duration of that kingdom is predicted in verse 2 ; its extent in verse 3 ; its universality in verse 4 ; its supremacy in verse 5 ; and its benevolence in verses 6–9.

The question of verse 5 is at all times the confident challenge of faith.

To interest Himself in the heavens (v. 6) is wonderful condescension, but to descend in His affections still lower to the earth, is amazing grace (Gen. i. 1).

The sense of the words " Who dwelleth on high " (v. 5) in the Hebrew text is, " Who has enthroned Himself on high," i.e., over the highest heavens from whence He looks down upon both heaven and earth. God enthrones Himself, for there is none greater than He.

" The barren woman " of verse 9 is Israel, as is evident from Isa. xlix. 12–21 and Gal. iv. 27.

PSALM CXIV.—The sublime poetry of this Psalm is felt by the dullest, and delighted in by the noblest minds. It links Messiah's intervention on behalf of His people Israel at the commencement of their national history (vs. 1–6) with His future intervention on their behalf at the close of the present period of their exile (vs. 7 and 8).

The argument of the Psalm is, as to the past, that if nature, represented by the Red Sea, Sinai and Jordan, trembled at the manifestation of God, how much more should the sinners of Canaan tremble before Him ? That they did so Joshua ii. and v. record ; and, as to the future, the physical convulsions of nature accompanying His second advent, predicted in Revelation, should make, and will make Israel's future adversaries to tremble. The " presence " of the Lord (v. 7) means His parousia or revelation—that is, His future coming in power and great glory. The word " Lord " in this verse is Adon.

If the question be asked, Why should men tremble before a God so kind as to deliver a multitude of slaves from their oppressor (v. 1), making them His dwelling-place and kingdom (v. 2), moving seas, mountains and rivers for their advantage (vs. 3 and 4), and, finally, turning flinty rocks to water for their thirst (v. 8), the answer is that this kindness shows affection for His ancient people, and is so much evidence that a fearful doom will fall upon all who illtreat them (Matt. xxv. 31–46).

The word " it " should not be supplied in verse 3 ; and the answer to the question of verses 5 and 6 is left to the reader. There can be but one answer—nature trembled, not at these feeble fugitives, but at Him Who led them. The name Jacob is repeated in verses 1 and 7 to emphasize that grace and not merit forms the basis of past and future deliverance for Israel.

PSALM CXV.—On the happy morning of Israel's restoration she will ascribe to the Messiah the glory of the double deliverance sung of in the previous Psalm. His mercy to her throughout her entire history, and His truth to her in fulfilling the promises of her restoration (v. 1), will be the theme of her song. Reviewing her history she will exultingly say : Why should the nations at any time have said, and how can they now say, " Where then is their God " (v. 2) ; and she will triumphantly exclaim that her God, though invisible, is in the heavens, and not a visible god of wood or stone in the earth (v. 3), and that all His dealings with her were the actings of His grace and truth. This activity of love and holiness and wisdom she will joyfully contrast with the helplessness of idols, and with the worthlessness and folly of idolatry (vs. 4-8).

Verse 8 states what has been, and is, true to fact, that the worshippers of idols become like the idols which they worship—senseless, cruel and impure. Multitudes at the present day worship idols made with their hands or with their heads. An idol is an idol whether it be made manually or mentally ; and to worship God under the similitude of metal, stone or bread is idolatry.

The House of Israel, the House of Aaron, and the worshippers of Jehovah (Acts xiii. 26) are urged to keep trusting Him Who, in the past, was so faithful, and Who throughout the now opening millennial reign will in His continued fidelity add ever multiplying blessings (vs. 9-14).

The earth has been given to Israel and to the nations (v. 16). The Church's home is above the heavens. Her portion in the earth is a cross ; Israel's is a sceptre. Hence the Church sets not her affections on things below but on things above. She is crucified to the world, and declares that it is very much better to leave it and to be with Christ far above all heavens.

The argument of verse 17 is that only living men can witness in the earth to God's love and holiness and power. They only can vindicate before men His name, that is, His character, by their testimony to the perfection of His ways with them.

" From this time forth" means, historically, from the commencement of the millennial reign (v. 18). The verse expresses Israel's confidence in the glory and success of Messiah's government.

Faith can make spiritually and morally true future divine promises, and can sing of them.

PSALM CXVI.—2 Cor. iv. 11 to v. 9 makes it clear that the Messiah is the speaker in this fourth Hallel-Psalm. The comforting message to faith in both Psalm and Epistle is that the resurrection of Christ is a pledge and assurance of the resurrection of His people ; and that as God carried Him victoriously through the sorrows of life and of death, so will He triumphantly carry those who by faith are united to Him. Hence their resurrection (v. 15) is based upon and connected with His resurrection (v. 8).

The Psalm sung by Him and the little flock on the eve of His crucifixion will be re-sung by Him in the midst of the great congregation (xxii. 25) on the morn of His coronation. This will take place in Jerusalem (v. 9) in the Courts of the Temple described by Ezekiel (xl-xlviii). As already stated, the three Hallel Psalms cxvi., cxvii., and cxviii., closed the Paschal Supper. They were sung after the fourth and last cup.

The structure of the Psalm presents an introduction (vs. 1 and 2) and two stanzas. In the former (vs. 3-11) Messiah recalls His First Advent in weakness and atonement ; in the latter He anticipates His Second Advent in power and glory (vs. 12-19), and He praises and worships Jehovah in respect of both.

This double theme appears in the introduction. He offers praise because of His deliverance out of the death-world (vs. 3 and 8) and because of the promised fulfilment of the Covenant granting Him the kingdom (vs. 14-19).

Suggested by the Latin translation this reading of verse 1 is proposed : " I am filled with delight ! for Jehovah hears," etc.

His sorrows in the death-world, and His prayer when there, are the subjects of verses 3-6, and His joyful testimony on the morning of His resurrection is the theme of verses 7-11. The " rest " intended in verse 7 is that of John xvii. 5. Having accomplished redemption, He returned to the ineffable repose of the Father's bosom. The word " soul " in verses 4 and 7 demonstrates that the Person Who prayed in Sheol is the very same Person Who praised in resurrection life and power (Acts ii. 27). He was " this same Jesus " (Acts i. 11).

Because He was " simple," i.e., sinless, He was guarded safely when in Sheol, and His feet, i.e., Himself, delivered from being perpetually thrust down, for Sheol is bottomless ; and so He was raised up out of it to walk before God in the land of the living (ys. 8 and 9). The word " falling " has here no moral significance, for how could Messiah morally stumble ? The Hebrew word means " a thrusting down."

" Haste " (v. 11) does not mean "hastily" but hasting on. He found in this world nowhere to lay His head. He hasted through it as a pilgrim making speed to the Father's House ; and as He hasted His true and deliberate judgment as to man was that all men are untrustworthy. The Holy Spirit repeats this testimony in Rom. iii. 4.

The first line of verse 10 means that because Messiah believed the resurrection promise made to Him, therefore He uttered this testimony respecting His sorrows and man's brokenness (vs. 10 and 11). Faith in Jehovah and in His Word opens the mouth in testimony, and has always her tribute of praise to offer. This faith of verse 10 is most striking, for it was exercised by Messiah when in the death-world, and is now exercised by Him in resurrection ; and it energizes His song anticipating His future reign of power and majesty.

" Thy handmaid " (v. 16). This means Israel, for Messiah was born of that nation (Rev. xii. 1–5). The resurrection of verse 15 assures the audience of verses 14 and 18.

PSALM CXVII.—Rom. xv. 11 interprets this doxology and unveils its beauty. Israel here invites the nations to unite with her in praising Messiah, and the reason is set out in the second verse. It is because of His grace and fidelity to her. The words " is great toward " should read " has prevailed over." Two statements are made. First : His grace abounded ; and, second : His fidelity endured. In that enduring fidelity He will fulfil to her the promise of the kingdom, and in His abounding grace which will prevail over all their misconduct, He will forgive their sins.

Israel from the day that she was redeemed out of Egypt to the present moment has done, and in the future will yet do, everything possible to prevent the fulfilment of the promises made to her. Idolatry, apostasy, hypocrisy, ingratitude, the murder of prophets and of the Messiah, centuries of hatred to His name and people, and the future acceptance of Anti-Christ in preference to Him (John v. 43)—all will be forgiven ; and she will invite the nations to join with her in praising a grace that as to sin forgives everything, and as to promise forgets nothing. Thus the nations will learn through His dealings with her what a God and Saviour Messiah is.

PSALM CXVIII.—Matt. xxi. 9 and 42 with xxiii. 39 show the relation of this Psalm to the Messiah. He is named in it thirty times as Jah, Elohim and Jehovah. Gen. xlix. 24, Isa. viii. 14 and xxviii. 16, Acts iv. 11, Matt. xvi. 18, 1 Cor. iii. 11, Rom. ix. 33, Ephes. ii. 20 and 1 Pet. ii. 8 should be read in connection with the Psalm.

This being the last song sung at the Pascal Supper, as stated by Hebrew historians, it gives it an added preciousness to the heart that knows the Lord to picture Him singing it immediately before setting out for Gethsemane. As the true Israel He could perfectly sing it, and as the High Priest of His people thus express His faith and her faith, and make real and bring near the joys of the morning which are predicted to follow the sorrows of that dark night and the afflictions of Jacob's long exile.

This song will be sung by Israel on the happy morning of her renewed espousals. She will invite those who in Ps. cxv. 9–11 were called to trust Jehovah now to praise Him (vs. 2–4) ; she will testify that Messiah is her one and efficient Saviour (vs. 5 and 14) ; she will acknowledge the wisdom and love which permitted her sufferings at the hands of man (vs. 6–18) ; she will approve the moral lessons of that chastening (vs. 19–21) ; she will proclaim that the once rejected Saviour is now her God and Redeemer (vs. 22 and 23) ; that her Sabbath has at last dawned (v. 24) ; that there is no blessing apart from Him (v. 25 R.V.) ; that He is the one and only gate into righteousness (v. 20) ; and that He is the promised Deliverer who comes with blessing out of the House of Jehovah.

" Thou " (v. 13) is important. It means Satan. He energized the enemies of verses 7–12. He it is who excites the Wild Beasts of Daniel and Revelation to persecute Israel.

Job illustrates this section of the Psalm. Satan was the unseen power behind the Sabeans, the Chaldeans, the tempest, the sore sickness, and all the calamities that afflicted the Patriarch. God permitted Satan thus to chasten him, but forbade him to touch his life (Job i. 12). So is it here (v. 18), Satan is permitted to chasten Israel sore, but not to destroy her. The moral effect of this divine action will be the same with Israel as it was with Job. She will enter the gates of righteousness and will praise Messiah (v. 21) ; and she will confess that she certainly would have fallen beneath the strokes of the Adversary, had not her faithful Lord and Redeemer supported her (v. 13).

The words " His vengeance " should displace the words " my desire " in verse 7.

The great note of the Song is reserved to its close. It is, that there is no restoration for Israel apart from the once rejected Messiah. She will exclaim : " Jehovah Messiah is God. He has shown us light. He is blessed. He cometh in the name of Jehovah " (vs. 26 and 27) ; and Messiah will, for His part, say, " Thou art My God, I will praise and exalt Thee " (v. 28) ; and then altogether, He with them and they with Him, they will sing the words of verse 29.

So this whole song will be sung by Messiah and Israel on the future glad morning of their espousals. The Psalm voices His oneness with them. Their name in that day shall be called " Adam " (Gen. v. 2) ; and also this is His name whereby He shall be called (Jer. xxiii. 6), and this is the name whereby she shall be called (Jer. xxxiii. 16), " Jehovah-Tsidkenu." They both shall have the one name.

The words " our eyes," verse 23 with verse 26, together with Matt. xxi. 9 and xxiii. 39, reveal the Singer of the Song, and the time when it is to be sung.

Only the faith of Him who is the Author and Finisher of faith could sing such a song of promised glory when descending into the horrors of Gethsemane and Calvary.

PSALM CXIX.—Messiah's testimony to the authority and sufficiency of the Bible as the rule of life is the theme of this Psalm.

The Psalm is an expansion of the second verse of the first Psalm. Its theme is the Word of God hidden in the heart, and obeyed in the life. Messiah is the Blessed Man Who fully satisfies its language, for He Himself is the Word of God. They only who, like Him, are subject to that Word are blessed. They thereby make their way prosperous and have good success (Deut. iv. 1–20 and Joshua. i. 7 and 8). The Psalm is found appropriately in this Fifth Book, in correspondence with the Fifth Book of the Pentateuch. The theme of both books is the Bible ; and the argument of both books is that it is an infallible counsellor in every possible need and circumstance of the heart and life.

The Psalm is an acrostic. There are twenty-two letters in the Hebrew alphabet and there are twenty-two stanzas in the Psalm. Each stanza contains eight verses. There are therefore, one hundred and seventy-six verses in all. All the first words in the eight verses of the first stanza begin with the letter A ; all the first words of the eight verses of the second stanza with the letter B ; and so on to the end of the Psalm.

In it the Bible is given ten titles corresponding to the Ten Commandments. They are, Way, Testimonies, Precepts, Commandments, Law, Judgments, Righteousness, Statutes, Word and Words—these two last harmonize with John xvii. 8 and 14.

The Psalm contemplates the celestial pilgrim walking through a squalid place on a dangerous road in the dark night and wholly dependent upon a lamp to light his way and guide his feet (2 Pet. i. 19). The lesson of the Psalm is that the lamp may be wholly trusted, and that whoever follows its light will be preserved from the squalors of the way, saved from the dangers of the path, and surely led to its desired end. This lamp is the Bible.

PSALM CXIX. 1–8.—" Undefiled " (v. 1), i.e., " perfect," as in the R.V. This is the perfection of 2 Tim. iii. 17. If, as some say, the Old Testament is morally imperfect, how can it then produce moral perfection ? But the Old Testament is morally perfect, and obedience to its teaching makes the man of God perfect.

Eight of the ten titles given in the Psalm to the Bible appear in this stanza. Two of them are found in verse 7 which reads : " the judgments of Thy righteousness." That righteousness judges what is pure and what is impure, and so instructs the disciple to walk as the Master walked.

The stanza contains two sections : A general statement (vs. 1–4), and a personal cry (vs. 5–8). The first lays down the double happiness of those who read and obey the Bible ; the second, the moral effect of such obedience. It speaks of the straight and consistent conduct of all whose public life is governed by the Holy Scriptures. Such a consistent life can never be put to shame.

The Bible and public and private worship are brought together in verse 7. True worship is dependent upon knowledge of the Word of God ; and the moral condition of the heart is decided by obedience to that Word. The sense of verse 8 is : Do not in any case take away this lamp which I am trusting, else I shall stumble in the darkness and fall.

PSALM CXIX. 9–16.—Two foundation principles of the spiritual life appear in this stanza. The first, that the Bible associates its reader with God (v. 10) ; the second, that its teachings make the life clean (v. 9) and the heart happy (v. 14). The moral result, therefore, of subjection to the authority of the Holy Scriptures is health of soul, holiness of life and happiness of heart.

Verse 11 presents the Bible as the Word of God, and verses 9 and 16 as the Words of God (Hebrew). Compare John xvii. 8 and 14.

There was only one Bible Student once on earth who could truthfully use the words of this Psalm. He was the Messiah. He could fully say " Thy Word have I hid and treasured in my heart "—just as the Ten Words were hidden and treasured in the Ark of the Covenant. That Ark was Christ. The word " hid " also means " treasured " (Hebrew).

Before the lips can fitly declare the teachings of the Scripture (v. 13) the heart must be its home (v. 11). Its words form the rule of faith (vs. 9 and 11) ; and subjection to its judgments is the secret of a life of victory.

The best book in the world is the Bible ; the best place to put it in is the heart ; and the best reason for putting it there is that it saves from sinning against God (v. 11).

PSALM CXIX. 17–24.—The first four verses of this stanza express the activities of the heart toward God excited by the study of, and obedience to, His Word ; and the second four, the contempt and hatred which such an obedience receives from man.

Man lives by every word which proceedeth out of the mouth of God. He therefore that would live a full life must love and obey the Bible (v. 17). It is only as God's word is " kept " that life, and life more abundant, can be experienced. There are wondrous things in that Word : but the eyes must be unveiled in order to see them (v. 18) ; and the reader must sit where Mary of Bethany sat.

The Bible makes its lover a stranger in this world ; but it is a satisfying companion for the lonely exile (v. 19) ; and it creates a desirable nostalgia (v. 20).

Those who are too proud to subject their wills to the teaching of the Scriptures bring a curse and not a blessing upon themselves (v. 21) ; and become the bitter persecutors of those that make them their delight (vs. 22-24).

" For " (v. 22) and " but " (v. 23) will better read " because." " Also " (v. 24) should read " nevertheless." The facts will then appear that the Bible lover is regarded by the populace with hostility and by the cultured with contempt. But this does not embitter his spirit. Unaffected by their contempt and hostility he keeps on reading, loving and delighting in the Book ; its words are his counsellors, as contrasted with the counsellors of verse 23 ; and he does not attack his enemies but takes refuge in prayer (v. 22).

PSALM CXIX 25–32.—This stanza presents the Bible as a restorative (vs. 25 and 28) and as a critic (vs. 29 and 30). It reveals the condition of heart needed to experience and profit by these facts. Such a heart hides nothing from God (vs. 26 and 32). Because the Word of God quickens (v. 25) and strengthens (v. 28) therefore the fainting pilgrim of verse 25 becomes the strong runner of verse 32. That Word is living water, it gives life and keeps alive ; and it is heavenly bread and so strengthens man's heart. To experience and enjoy these truths a teachable will (vs. 26 and 27), and active moral affections are necessary (v. 32).

The entire life inward and outward must be subjected to the searchlight of the Holy Scriptures. The continuance of such criticism must be desired (v. 26) ; and they must be accepted as the infallible judge of truth and error (vs. 29 and 30). Not the judgment of the conscience, nor of the church, nor of society, but that of God's Word should be desired and sought for and accepted.

" Stuck " (v. 31) should read " cleaveth," as in verse 25. It is the same word in the

Hebrew text. Even when lying fainting in, and so cleaving to, the dust, the true servant of Jehovah kept cleaving to His testimonies.

"To enlarge the heart" (v. 32) means to arouse its moral affections. To understand and profit by the Scriptures, contrition of heart rather than cleverness of head, is necessary.

Messiah's love for the Bible and His perfect obedience to its teachings, alone illustrate the statements of this stanza.

PSALM CXIX. 33-40.—This fifth stanza teaches that if the Bible student dissociates the Book from its Author, his eyes will be unopened (vs. 33-37), his mind uninstructed (vs. 34 and 38), his heart unaffected (vs. 34 and 36), and his feet unled (v. 35). So the eyes, the mind, the heart and the feet must be governed by the Word of God.

"Teach.me" (v. 33). This means "make me to see," and so will correspond with the companion petition "make me to go "(v. 35). The Bible is more precious than gold (v. 36). It can fill the broken heart with hope and strength. Money cannot do that. Teaching which does not harmonize with the Bible is "vanity" (v. 37). The ellipsis in verse 38 might be thus better supplied, "which instructs to Thy fear," i.e., the Scriptures, teach the true way of worshipping God.

The entrance into the promised land put an end to the reproach of Egypt that Israel was trusting a God that was not able to perform His promises. The true heart dreads such a reproach, but rests in the conviction that the divine judgments as to the fitting time and way of making good the promises are animated by perfect wisdom and infinite love (v. 39).

The affections are so disposed to inertia in the spiritual realm that the prayer for quickening in verse 37 needs repetition in verse 40.

PSALM CXIX 41-48.—The Bible proclaims a salvation (v. 41) that closes the mouth of the sceptic (v. 42) ; fills the mouth of the believer (v. 43) ; energizes a life of obedience (v. 44) ; gives breadth of view (v. 45) ; dignity of conduct (v. 46) ; satisfaction to the emotions (v. 47) ; resolution of character (v. 48) ; and provides inexhaustible food for the highest intellect and noblest mind. Thus the Scripture is competent to perfectly

furnish all who turn to it as a moral teacher (2 Tim. iii. 17).

The terms Thy mercies, Thy salvation, Thy word, Thy words, Thy judgments, Thy law, Thy testimonies, Thy precepts, Thy commandments and Thy statutes mark the unity existing between the Bible and its Author. To belittle the one is to belittle the other (vs. 41-48).

A scriptural and personal experience of conversion (v. 41) confounds opponents (v. 42) and impresses kings (v. 46). To the humblest life the Scriptures, if loved and obeyed, impart a refinement, a dignity, a grace, a power and an intelligence that secures perfection of conduct under all circumstances and in all circles. Evil will be rebuked with courage and righteousness praised. A salvation which is not according to God's Word (v. 41) is a false salvation. It can neither silence mockers nor influence kings.

The word "utterly" (v. 43) is an interesting term in Hebrew and not easy to translate. Its first occurrences are in Gen. i. 31 and vii. 19. It suggests a mouth overflowing with words of Divine truth.

Multitudes believe that a life shut in between the covers of the Bible must necessarily be a narrow one. The opposite is found by experience to be the truth (v. 45).

To "lift up the hands" (v. 48) expresses a resolute engagement, and also a prayerful desire.

A Christian needs little grace or courage to speak for the Bible to those who are beneath him socially, but to so speak to his equals or superiors and not be ashamed, is quite another matter ; and is dependent upon a life of close fellowship with God (v. 46).

PSALM CXIX. 49-56.—The Messiah here sings of what the Bible with its promises and records were to Him during His earthly pilgrimage (vs. 4-9, 52 and 54). In the darkness of this world (v. 55), its trials (v. 50) and its hatreds (v. 51), the Word of God sustained Him (v. 49), comforted Him (v. 50), animated Him (v. 50) and set Him a-singing (v. 54). Thus during His life of sorrow, trial and hatred He did not throw the Bible aside as useless or untrue but clung to it all the closer. Such is the experience also of those in whom He dwells. Like their Lord the more they read and love the Bible the more they want to read and love it.

The theme of this section is the Bible as the sustainer of the life and the comforter of the heart (vs. 50 and 52). It pictures the child of heaven amid the sorrows of earth, sustained and comforted by the Words of Life.

The proud deride the promises of the Bible, but the humble rest upon them and hold fast to them (vs. 49 and 51) ; and they prove that in the absence of all natural joys the Scriptures can fill the life with sweetness, sunshine, fulness and strength.

"Word" (v. 49) implies promises that comfort and animate. "Remember" means remember to fulfil.

The inspired records of what God has been to His people in the past, comfort His people in the present (v. 52).

Verse 53 should read : "Hot indignation hath taken hold upon me because of the lawless who forsake Thy law." The Messiah felt this hot indignation in Mark iii. 5 and vii. 6-13, Luke vii. 30-35, Luke xi. 39-54, and on other occasions. A holy anger and a just indignation become the true witness for God and for His truth. Men who take little interest in the authority and inspiration of the Scriptures rarely become heated when discussing them ; but the more they are loved the hotter will be the indignation of those who love them against those who corrupt or deny them.

The last verse reads : "This I have had that I have kept Thy precepts." That is, it was peculiar, unique and characteristic of the Messiah that although all other servants of God, without exception, failed in believing and obeying the Bible He perfectly loved and followed its precepts. Thus He alone satisfies the language of this section, as He alone illustrates the faith, loyalty and love of the other sections of the Psalm.

Contrast "Remember Thou" (v. 49) with "I have remembered" (vs. 52 and 55).

PSALM CXIX. 57-64.—Jehovah was Levi's portion (Joshua xiii. 33) but he failed to realize his wealth and walk worthy of it. Messiah was the true Levi. These verses exhibit Him as such, and reveal the loyalty and affection of His heart to the Scriptures. God was the portion of His soul ; the Bible the treasure of His heart (v. 57). His knowledge of, and union with, God did not make Him independent of the Scriptures ; but, on the contrary, because Jehovah was His

portion therefore He said that He would keep and hold fast to His Word. Some modern religious teachers declare that the Scriptures are not necessary in a life of intimate fellowship with God, but this stanza contradicts such teaching.

"Favour" (v. 58) means the conscious presence of God. Messiah's whole heart desired such communion ; and also a practical experience of the good things promised to faith in the Inspired Word (v. 58). He only desired such things as the Bible spoke of. He, as Man, had an independent will. Hence He could say, "Not My will but Thine be done." As Man, He judged His ways by the Word of God, and always set His feet in the paths pointed out by the Scriptures, and not in the paths suggested to His own will (v. 59).

Abraham (Gen. xxii. 3) hasted and delayed not to keep the commandments given to him. Yet his obedience was not always perfect. Jesus was the true Abraham.

Verse 61 should read as in the R.V. Neither suffering (v. 61) nor ease (v. 62) could weaken the affection of His heart to the Scriptures. Paul and Silas at Philippi illustrate these two verses. They were cruelly scourged by the wicked, and painfully confined in the stocks. But this treatment did not affect their belief in, nor chill their attachment to, the Scriptures of Truth, for at midnight they prayed and sang praises to God. Faith declared those sufferings to be righteous which reason felt to be pitiless.

The Bible introduces to the best society (v. 63). Such is here Messiah's joyful testimony.

As Jehovah was His portion (v. 57) so was He His praise (v. 62).

As the adversity of verse 61 failed to turn Him away from the Bible, so the prosperity of verse 64 did not weaken His fidelity to it. On the contrary, the abundance of the mercies experienced by Him intensified His love for God's statutes. How often is it otherwise with men ! Adversity on the one hand and prosperity on the other sap their loyalty to the Sacred Book.

PSALM CXIX. 65-72.—This stanza emphasizes the argument of the Psalm that the God-breathed Scriptures make men wise to salvation, teach, reprove, correct, discipline, perfect and furnish them thoroughly unto every good work (2 Tim. iii. 16 and 17).

Here is the " seven " of Divine completion. The Scriptures, because morally perfect, produce moral perfection when perfectly obeyed.

The speaker here, as always, is the Messiah. He speaks for Himself and for His people. This appears specially in verses 67 and 71. These verses illustrate His offices as the Sin-Offering and the Peace-Offering (Lev. iv. viii). He takes the sins of His people upon Himself, and transfers to them the perfections which belong to Himself. Thus He makes their defections from God's Law His own. As a true Priest and Advocate He presents Himself as the guilty one, and at the same time credits them with the perfection of the obedience which He personally rendered to the Word of God.

His testimony to the goodness of the Author of the Scriptures in His dealing (v. 65), His government (v. 66), His chastening (v. 67), His nature (v. 68), His action (vs. 69-71) and His Law (v. 72) is thus fully declared.

Chastening and discipline (v. 71) make the Bible more precious and the life more fruitful (John. xv. 2 and Heb. xii. 5-11). They are helpful Bible teachers.

The statutes of a God who fills the earth with goodness (v. 64), Who does good, and Who is good (Acts x. 38) must be themselves good (vs. 64 and 68). His actions accord with the promises and engagements of His Word (v. 65) ; and obedience to His government, as revealed in His commands, secures intelligence and a right judgment in the duties and responsibilities of life (v. 66).

" Afflicted " means " oppressed," and " went astray " means " a straying one " (v. 67). Prior to restoration Israel is here described as continually erring from God's Law. The second line of the verse reads " But now I am observing Thy Word."

The hatred of the proud makes the Bible more precious to the meek ; and helps to establish its inspiration (v. 69).

A heart " as fat as grease " is insensible and stupid. Such an heart is incompetent to judge the commandments of God (v. 70).

The Pharisees accused the Lord of breaking the commandments because He healed on the Sabbath Day. They forged that lie (v. 69) on the Devil's anvil ; but having hearts " fat as grease," they were disqualified as judges ; and He could say that far from breaking the Law He delighted in it (v. 70).

The possession of the Scriptures is greater wealth than all the treasure the world contains (v. 72).

In the Hebrew text the first letter of each verse in this stanza is a T. If the word " before " (v. 67), and the words " It is " (v. 71), be changed to " Till " and " Tis " then each verse will commence with T in English as in Hebrew.

PSALM CXIX. 73-80.—Christ's human life of dependence on God and affection for His Word shine forth in every verse of this stanza. The body that God prepared Him (Heb. x. 5) He returns thanks for (v. 73) ; and, as Man, expresses His dependence on God to interpret the Scriptures to Him.

His affection for, and reliance on the words of God, and the consequent blessing which resulted, cause those who worship God to rejoice when they look upon Him. His experience of the trustworthiness of the Scriptures enheartens His disciples ; and when by-and-by they see Him by sight they will indeed be glad ! They will then witness the glories which will be given to Him because He perfectly loved and obeyed the Law of God (v. 74).

The word " afflicted " has relation to His first advent in great humility. He was poor and needy and acquainted with grief. But far from murmuring at this design of His Father's will, or chilled in His affection for the Scriptures, He clung to them the more as being faithful to Him ; and He admired the righteousness of their judgments. In the following verse He does not pray for the removal of these afflictions, but for the enjoyment of compensating comforts; but only such comforts as accorded with God's Word. God's tender mercies, and the delights of His Law, were life itself to Jesus (v. 77). " Delight " in the Hebrew text stands in the plural number, and, therefore, means supreme delight.

The closing verses may be read in the future tense, as in Hebrew. They predict that the proud shall be put to shame ; that those who worship God shall turn to Messiah in order to learn the Divine testimonies ; and that Christ shall never be put to shame because His heart was sound in the statutes of Jehovah.

The unjust and contemptuous conduct of the proud Pharisees toward Him did not embitter His Spirit ; the only effect was to dispose Him more than ever to meditation in the Scriptures (v. 78). In such action His people should imitate Him.

His enemies accused Him "without a cause," they hated Him "without a cause" (vs. 78 and John xv. 25); but He in His love saves sinners "without a cause" (Rom. iii. 24). "Freely" and "without a cause" are the same word in the Greek text.

The initial acrostic letter in this stanza is the smallest in the Hebrew alphabet. The Messiah Himself mentions it in Matt. v. 18, A "tittle" is an ornamental mark set over a Hebrew letter.

PSALMS CXIX. 81-88.—Every test, and all tests, however sharp, to weaken the Messiah's affection for, and confidence in, the Scriptures not only failed but helped to make more manifest His faith in them and His trust in their Author.

The first four verses of the stanza concern testing at the hands of God; the second four, testing at the hands of man.

Verses 81 and 82 contain two complaints, including a resolution, followed by a question. The two sorrow-burdened cries are: "My soul fainteth for Thy salvation from trouble": and: "My eyes faint with desire for Thy Word," i.e., for the fulfilment of its promises. The resolution of faith introduced between these cries is: "I have hoped, I am hoping, and I will ever hope in Thy Word"—that is, I will persist in believing in the reality and certainty of its promises. The question is: "When wilt Thou comfort Me?"

Verses 83 and 84 contain also two complaints, enclose a resolution, and are followed by a question. These correspond to those of the two previous verses.

The first sorrowful cry is: "I am withered like a wine-skin in the smoke"; the second is: "Few are the days of Thy servant." The intervening declaration of faith is: "I do not, and will not neglect Thy statutes"; and the question is: "When wilt Thou execute judgment on My persecutors?"

The four remaining verses deal with man's efforts to prove Christ ignorant of (v. 85), or losing confidence in (v. 87), the Bible; and three of the verses contrast the deceitfulness (v. 85), the malignity (v. 86) and the hatred (v. 87) of man with the faithfulness (v. 86), the love (v. 86) and the preserving power (v. 87) of God. The last verse affirms the fact that the Scriptures were the very life of Messiah. He Himself said that man lives by every

word that comes out of the mouth of God.

Thus was Messiah's fidelity to the Law and Book of God fully tested and found perfect.

A wine-skin when hung up in the smoke becomes dry and withered (v. 83). Such was the outward appearance of the Lord Jesus under the burden of sorrow that perpetually rested on Him. This was pre-figured by the outermost covering of the Tabernacle in the Wilderness. It had no beauty that it should be desired; but it veiled beauties unspeakable and full of glory.

The words "How many" (v. 84) are a form of speech meaning "Few are," etc.

Christ as Lord could at any moment have destroyed His persecutors; but, as Man, He would not take vengeance into His own hands; for vengeance belonged unto God (v. 84).

Matt xxii. 15-40 records some of the pits that the proud digged for Him (v. 85). They professed zeal for God's Law; but He, knowing their hearts, could truthfully say "They are not after Thy Law," that is, their questions were not in harmony with the Scriptures, and they themselves were not subject to the Scriptures.

The "proud" are the self-righteous, the "wicked" are the self-willed.

"Almost" (v. 87) means "quickly." The sense of the verse is: They wish to quickly make an end of Me, etc.

PSALM CXIX. 89-96.—The Messiah here sings of the unshakeable rock, the Word of God, to which He clung, and from which all the tests of the previous stanza failed to detach Him. He declares that rock to be firm, infinite and eternal (vs. 89 and 96).

The stanza may be thus analysed:

The Word, firm and eternal (v 89).
Stronger than affection (v. 92).
Its power to revive (v. 93).
Its power to preserve (v. 94).
Stronger than oppression (v. 95).
The Word, perfect and eternal (v. 96).

Verse 89 may read: "O Jehovah, Thou art for ever; Thy Word is settled in heaven."

Amid the changes and trials of earth the eternal and unchanging Word of God is a priceless possession. Messiah Himself said that heaven and earth should pass away but His Word never, for it is settled in heaven where nothing can reach or shake it. Hence the unceasing efforts of its enemies to corrupt or destroy it have failed, and will fail.

Affliction (v. 92) and oppression (v. 95) only make it more precious (v. 92), and its Author more near (v. 94). To possess the Book is wealth untold (v. 72) ; to belong to its Author is joy unspeakable (v. 94).

" They " (v. 91) mean the heavens and the earth. They are God's servants and obey His laws .

God's law was Messiah's " delights," i.e., the supreme joy of His heart (v. 92).

The verb to perish (v. 92) has many meanings in Hebrew. Here it suggests that the Messiah's sinless body would have sunk under the pressure of severe suffering—as for example in the garden of Gethsemane—but that He was kept alive by resting on the words of the Scripture (v. 93)

" Save " (v. 94) signifies preservation through trial and opposition. " I have sought " includes " I am seeking and I will seek."

As in the previous stanza so here (v. 95) man's hatred failed to awaken in his heart any doubt as to the faithfulness of God's Word and the value of its promises (v. 90).

The last verse states that there is an end, i.e., a limit or boundary, to the extent of God's work in creation, but no boundary to His Word in revelation—it is infinite and eternal. There is no end to that commandment. This last line may read : " Spacious exceedingly is Thy commandment." Spacious as are the heavens and the earth—and even an elemental study of astronomy overwhelms the mind with the vast distances in space—yet does the Bible exceed it all in dimension.

PSALM CXIX. 97-104.—As in the previous stanza Messiah sang of the strength of God's Word so here He sings of its sweetness (vs. 97 and 102) ; and He testifies that this sweetness is filled with wisdom. Thus the lesson is taught as to the nature and effect of inspiration. Its nature is sweetness ; its effect, wisdom. Messiah here joyfully exclaims how sweet to His palate (v. 103), and how precious to His heart (v. 97), was the Law of God ; and that through its study He was wiser than His enemies (v. 98), wiser than His teachers (v. 99), and wiser than His elders (v. 100). Compare Luke ii. 46 and 47.

He also declares that that Word instructed Him as to the moral character of every course of conduct (v. 101), and taught Him so effectively that He did not swerve from any

path approved by the Divine judgment (v. 102) ; and the stanza closes with the statement that the wisdom which flows from the Scriptures destroys all desire for false teaching (v. 104).

Every servant of God should love the Bible to the extent of meditating in it all the day ; but only One Servant of Jehovah ever lived Who could truthfully make the declaration of verse 97.

PSALM CXIX. 105-112.—To Messiah the Bible was a lamp (v. 105), a guide (v. 110) and a companion (v. 111). In the first two verses He speaks of it as a light, and declares His purpose to follow it (vs. 105 and 106) ; in the last two verses He speaks of it as a heritage, i.e., a treasure, and professes His determination to obey it (vs. 111 and 112). The intervening verses describe the path which the Bible was to lighten and gladden. It was a path of affliction from God (v. 107), and of hatred from man (vs. 109 and 110). To have " the life in the hand " means to be in deadly danger. Messiah records that throughout this experience of suffering and danger the Word of God kept Him alive (v. 107) ; set Him a-singing (v. 108 with Heb. xiii. 15) ; directed Him in difficulties (v. 108) ; supported His faith (v. 109) ; and delivered Him from the snares of His enemies (v. 110). Thus the Sacred Word was a light to His feet (v. 105) and a joy to His heart (v. 111). A lamp is useless unless used ; and a treasure valueless unless drawn upon. The heart rather than the head is to be exercised in Bible study ; and the sure result will be obedient action (v. 112).

He said : " If a man love Me he will keep My word (John xiv. 23). Such a man will find that Word to be a lamp and à light, a treasure and a joy on, and in, life's pathway.

PSALM CXIX. 113-120.—This stanza may be thus analysed :

Messiah's hatred of false teaching (v. 113).
False teachers addressed concerning God (v. 115).

Uphold me } (v. 116).
        } (Isa. xli. 10 and xlii. 1).
Hold me up } (v. 117).

False teachers : God addressed concerning them (v. 118).
Messiah's horror at their doom (v. 120).

The false Bible and its authors are here

contrasted with the true Bible and its Author, and the declaration is made that the skilful efforts of these teachers to deflect the Messiah from His attachment to God's Word failed (v. 118).

" Thoughts " (v. 113) mean double thoughts (R.V. and James i. 8). The reference doubtless is to associating another god with Jehovah and thus setting up a double worship; as in the past Jehovah and the golden calf; later, Jehovah and tradition; and to-day Jesus and Mary. But to Messiah as Man, as Abraham's Seed and as the True Israel, the Law of God was supremely lovable (v. 113). That Law inspired His confidence; and its Author was His hiding-place and shield (v. 114).

The verse also condemns the opposing of human thinking ("Oh, I think otherwise ") to Bible teaching.

False teaching leads into sin; and, consequently, false teachers are evil-doers (v.115). Their efforts, however, only resulted in attaching the Messiah, if it were possible, more resolutely to the commandments of God (v. 115).

" Uphold me " (v. 116) and " hold me up " (v. 117) are noteworthy verbs in the Hebrew text. They represent God supporting the believer both from above and from beneath—carried, and at the same time held by the hand.

The following verse may be thus paraphrased (R.V): " Thou hast set at nought all them that err from Thy Statutes, for their cunning efforts to turn me from them have been in vain." Compare verse 115. Thus The Messiah gives the glory to God for the failure of these false teachers to detach Him from the Bible.

The appalling doom awaiting these teachers caused Messiah's heart to love the Sacred Book which predicts their destruction (v. 119); whilst, at the same time, His sinless flesh shuddered with horror at the nature of that judgment (v. 120).

PSALM CXIX. 121-128.—He Who was Himself the incarnate Word of God here reveals His affection for the written Word of God (v. 127). He prays for deliverance from its detractors (v. 122), and bases His claim to be delivered from them on His integrity (v. 121), His relationship to God (v. 122), and His loyalty to the Scriptures (vs. 123, 127 and 128). He being perfect, affirms in this stanza the moral perfection

of the Bible; and declares it to be His rule of life. Only the Sinless Son of David could say that He practised judgment and righteousness (v. 21).

Gen. xliii. 9, and Isa. xxxviii. 14 (R.V.) illustrate verse 122. Jehovah was the intervening surety between His Beloved Son and the proud oppressors. Christ, as Man, was defenceless; hence His prayer to God to become His security.

" Fail " (v. 123) expresses longing desire. Because He Himself was righteousness (Jno. xvi. 10) He loved the Word of righteousness.

God had only one perfect Servant upon earth. He had many servants; hence He said " My servant Abraham," " My servant Moses " etc, but of Messiah He said " My Servant." It was not necessary to add the name Jesus. Therefore He says " Behold My Servant Whom I uphold."

" To work " (v. 126) means " to intervene." Compare Matt. xv. 6 (R.V.).

In the last two verses the Messiah testified to the inspiration, moral perfection, inerrancy and authority of the Bible; and declares that its effect as a moral teacher is to beget hostility to evil. He says that all its precepts concerning all things are right.

PSALM CXIX. 129-136.—Immanuel's love for the Scriptures (v. 131), and His grief because men ignore them (v. 136), are the keynotes of this stanza. He affirms their statements to be wonderful (v. 129); that they give light and understanding (v. 130); refreshment (v. 131); guidance (v. 133); and that they bring the soul into conscious touch with their Author (vs. 132 and 135). This last experience is what the Bible aims at and secures, if it be submitted to as the rule of life and faith.

It testifies to wonders both physical and moral. The excellence of its moral wonders proves the volume to be Divine; the accuracy of its physical marvels demonstrates it to be super-human. Because its testimonies are wonderful therefore Messiah cherished them (v. 129).

" Entrance " (v. 130) signifies a doorway. An eastern peasant's house has no windows. Light enters through the door; hence to open the Scriptures means to explain them. Messiah opened the Scriptures to the disciples after His resurrection (Luke xxiv. 45); and the Apostle Paul opened them to the Thessalonians (Acts xvii. 3), and prayed that they might be opened to the Ephesians (Eph. i. 18). " Simple " means sincere.

As the thirsty traveller in the hot desert longs for water and drinks eagerly of it so Jesus felt toward the Scriptures.

Verse 133 may be thus translated : " Guide my steps by Thy Word," i.e., cause that my conduct harmonise with the Bible, " and let not any iniquitous action of man have power against me." The following verse praying for deliverance from man's evil actions proves that this is the force of the word " iniquity " in verse 133. It has no moral relation to Messiah.

His prayer for deliverance from oppression was not in order that He might have leisure to enjoy Himself, but liberty to practise the teachings of the Bible. Persecution aims at preventing the reading of that Holy Book, and seeks the destruction of those who do read it.

Reading, loving, practising and obeying God's Law bring the soul into God's presence and into the conscious enjoyment of fellowship with Him (vs. 132-135).

" Floods of tears " is the corresponding English idiom for " rivers of water " (v. 136). In the previous stanza (v. 126), Messiah mourned because men made void His Father's Law ; here He wept because they did not prize and obey it.

PSALM CXIX. . 137-144.—The Messiah in these verses sets out in order the excellencies of God's Word as righteous (v. 137), pure (v. 140), true (v. 142), and everlasting (v. 144). He pours out His grief because men forget it (v. 139), and mourns that He was despised because He did not forget it (v. 141) ; and testifies that in trouble He found it an unfailing source of joy (v. 143), and a counsellor that vivified Him (v. 144).

The righteousness of the Divine Essence and the righteousness of His testimonies, commandments, precepts, and statutes is one and the self-same righteousness (vs. 137 and 144) ; as a consequence the statements and doctrines of the Bible are dependable and free from error (v. 138).

Men make void the teaching of the Book (v. 126) ; then they cease to obey its laws (v. 136) ; and, finally, they forget it altogether (v. 139).

Messiah's testimony to the holy Word of God was that it is very pure ; and, therefore, He loved it (v. 140).

" Small " (v. 141) means insignificant.

One of the reasons why the Lord Jesus was despised was because He loved and believed the Bible. All who similarly love and believe it must expect to be also despised.

God's righteousness is everlasting, and His Word is also everlasting because it is truth (v. 142, R.V.). That Word is a fountain of happiness and a source of wisdom that keeps the heart cheerful and living in times of trial. Such is the testimony of the two closing verses.

PSALM CXIX. 145-152.—This and the following stanza correspond in theme and structure. The correspondence may be thus shown :—

Prayer	(vs. 145-149).
The Enemy—near	(vs. 150-151).
The Bible	(v. 152).

Prayer	(vs. 153-154).
The Enemy—numerous	(vs. 155-159).
The Bible	(v. 160).

The theme of these stanzas is the relationship which the Messiah establishes between prayer and the Bible in circumstances of danger and opposition.

Intelligence, variety and fulness in prayer result from daily meditation in the Word of God. As the Bible is neglected so is prayer impoverished. It is a cherished treasure for the heart (v. 145), and a ruler of the conduct (v. 146) ; and Messiah's eager prayer for deliverance from His enemies was not that He might have exemption from opposition, but that He might have liberty to enjoy and obey it.

" Prevented"(vs. 147 and 148) signifies forestalled. Messiah here states that ere darkness fell He read the Bible each evening and meditated therein, and that before morning dawned He was found upon His knees ; and He states that His reason for so acting was because He believed and confided in and counted upon its Divine promises (v. 147).

He further (v. 149) prayed that the answer to His petitions should be measured by God's lovingkindness, and that His heart should be refreshed, revived, and maintained sensitive by the judgments of the Divine Law. He desired that the Scriptures should be the instrument and channel of refreshment and vivification to His mind and faith. He prayed to be kept in between the banks of that channel. Such is the force of the term

" according to." This term occurs twice in the verse. It first measures the boundlessness of God's love, and then the boundaries of His judgment. Answers to prayer measured by that love and limited by that judgment, strengthen faith, instruct the understanding, and animate the heart.

Those who pursued Messiah in order to injure Him were murderously near to Him and far from the Bible (v. 150) ; but Jehovah was near also. His commandments were truth ; the enemies', falsehood (v. 151).

In the last verse Messiah testifies to the inspiration and antiquity of the sacred Scriptures. He declares God to be their Author ; and predicts that they will endure for ever (Matt. xxiv. 35).

PSALM CXIX. 153-160.—The structure of this stanza appears in the previous one.

Neither suffering (v. 153) nor fear (v. 157) could weaken Messiah's affection for the Bible, nor cause Him to swerve from its teaching. On the contrary He prayed that it might continually be the source of refreshment and strength to Him (vs. 154, 156, 159).

Affliction, affection, subjection and dependence appear in the petitions of the first two verses. Affliction has caused many of God's servants to forget His Law ; but it was not so with Messiah—it only deepened His affection for it. David in his affliction forgot the promises of that Law and said, " I shall one day perish by the hand of Saul " (1 Sam. xxvii. 1).

When suffering injustice most men defend themselves ; but Messiah resigned Himself to God, and said, " Plead Thou My cause and deliver me " (v. 154).

Only a sinless heart could say " I do not forget " (v. 153), " I do not swerve " (v. 157), and " Consider how I love Thy precepts " (v. 159). In David's lips such words would have been untrue, self-righteous, proud, and pharisaic ; but not so in Messiah's lips.

The prayer for " quickening " is repeated nine times in Psalm cxix.—three times in this stanza. It expresses Messiah's continual dependence as a man upon God and His Word.

Deliverance was near to this dependent Man because He loved the Bible (v. 153) ; but far from the self-reliant (the " wicked ") because they despised it (v. 155).

" I looked upon the traitors and loathed them because they kept not Thy word "

(v. 158). So ardent was His affection for the Scriptures that thus He regarded His persecutors the Scribes and Pharisees (v. 157). In contrast with their treachery to that Holy Law He could truthfully exclaim " Consider how I love it " (v. 159).

In the last verse He repeats the testimony of verse 152 ; but especially urges the inerrancy of the sacred volume. He says, Thy word is true from the first chapter of Genesis ; and all its statements are righteous, and shall stand eternally. He thus testifies to the truthfulness of the Bible as a whole, and to the truthfulness of all its parts. It is true as the Word of God, and its words are the words of God.

PSALM CXIX. 161-168.—Once only was there a Man on earth whose heart continually maintained a right attitude toward the Bible. His pure soul trembled with holy fear at its words (v. 161) and rejoiced at its teaching (v. 162). As Jehovah's Servant He fulfilled the conditions of Isa. lxvi. 2 and Deut. vi. 5 ; for not only did He love God's Holy Law v. 163) but He loved it exceedingly (v. 167) · All day long He kept praising God for the Bible (v. 164) ; He found nothing in it to offend Him, as so many do to-day (v. 165) ; and He laid bare all His conduct to its scrutiny (v. 168).

Luke xi. 53 to xii. 12 illustrates the first verse of this stanza. His heart did not tremble at the threats of the Rulers (xi. 54), but His heart did tremble at the words of God (xii. 5). A soul that neither trembles nor rejoices when reading the Bible is dead.

The Hebrews inscribe upon the first page of the Bible the words : " How dreadful is this place ! This is none other than the House of God, and this is the gate of heaven."

The more the teaching of the Bible is loved the more will falsehood be hated and abhorred (v. 163). " Seven " (v. 164) is the number of completion. It signifies unceasing praise.

A heart governed by the Sacred Writings is filled with peace (v. 165). It is not disturbed by difficulties and doubts as to their inspiration, and as to supposed moral defects in them.

Only a perfect Believer could make the statements of the last three verses. Such a Believer was Jesus of Nazareth. But the verses set up the standard which His followers should aim at ; works of obedience should follow upon faith for salvation (v. 166) ; and love for the Scriptures, with subjection of the entire life to their teaching (v. 167), should characterize all who profess to believe upon Him.

The testimony of Psalm cxix. to the inspiration, authority, infallibility, sufficiency and moral perfection of the Scriptures in the mouth of the most deeply consecrated Christian, as a personal testimony of affection and obedience, would reveal spiritual blindness, religious pride, self-righteousness and ignorance. But in the lips of the Lord Christ it is the very perfection of truth.

PSALM CXIX. 169-176.—This last stanza completes Messiah's testimony to the authority and sufficiency of the Holy Scriptures. He is presented in it as defenceless (v. 176), dependent (v. 175), sighing for deliverance (v. 174), but asking for understanding before pleading for deliverance (v. 169), promising praise (v. 171), and testimony (v. 172), protesting His affection for the Bible (v. 176) ; and, finally, desiring that all these mercies of sustainment, instruction and deliverance should be according to, i.e., in harmony with, God's Word.

" Utter " (v. 171), i.e., " bubble over with." The effect of heaven's legislation is to make earthly lips overflow with praise. Because all the teaching of the Bible is righteousness (v. 172), the instructed tongue sings (R.V.) of its perfection. So Messiah sang. This was His testimony.

Neither the deliverance of man's hand, nor the prosperity of his ways, was desired by Jesus, but God's salvation and His Word (v. 174).

The Bible instructs the mind (v. 169), relieves the heart (v. 170), animates praise (v. 171) and inspires testimony (v. 172). It helps (vs. 173 and 175), it delights (v. 174), it quickens (v. 175), and it perfects the memory (v. 176). Verses 173 and 175 should read in the future tense, as in Hebrew.

" I have wandered about as a lost sheep " . . " but I have not forgotten Thy commandments." These statements are not contradictory but complementary, To wander as a lost sheep here expresses defencelessness and loneliness, not moral defection. This is plain from Messiah's declaration that even under such circumstances He had not, and did not, forget God's commandments.

When man wanders as a lost sheep it is because He has wilfully chosen his own way (Isa. liii. 6).

PSALM CXX.—The Messiah having in the twenty-two stanzas of the previous Psalm sung of the Lamp that lightens the celestial way, in the fifteen Psalms of the Ascents sings of that way ; for it is an ascending way—it leads up to God. Thus the connection between these groups of Psalms with each other, and with the Book of Deuteronomy, is shown.

These songs are fifteen in number, and form five groups of three each. Each triplet has as its theme trouble, trust and triumph. That is, the first Psalm of each triplet is a cry of distress ; the second, a declaration of trust ; and the third, a song of triumph. Thus in each group there is an ascent from trouble through trust to triumph. Habakkuk is a song of Ascents from trouble (ch. i.) through trust (ch. ii) to triumph (ch. iii).

The central Psalm of the fifteen is entitled " For Solomon," i.e., relating to the Greater than Solomon. Seven Psalms precede and seven follow this central Psalm. The name Jehovah occurs twenty-four times in each of these two groups, and three times in the central Song. Jah occurs twice ; each time in the third Psalm of the respective two groups.

The " Ascents," " Degrees " or " Steps " are supposed to mean the steps leading up into the Temple ; or the going up of the Tribes to Jerusalem at the three annual feasts ; or connected with Hezekiah's added fifteen years, coupled with the degrees on the sun dial of Ahaz (Isa. xxxviii. and 2 Kings xx). But all these are suppositions.

The seeming inaccuracy between " Me," " My " and " our " in these songs is designed. The Composer is the Messiah ; the singers, Messiah and Israel. Hence the expression " We will sing thy songs," etc. See notes on Ps. cxxii.

The theme of this first song of the ascents is the sufferings of Messiah from the companionship of the ungodly (vs. 1 and 5), and from the torment of their slanderous tongues (v. 2). These falsehoods attested His innocency.

Verses 3 and 4 may be thus paraphrased : " What shall He—Jehovah, in response to My cry of verse 1—give unto thee, AntiChrist ? or what shall He add unto thee, thou false tongue ? He shall give Thee the sharp arrows of the strong man ; and He shall add with them coals of juniper." Such will be the doom of the False Messiah. The arrows will be sharp and such as are used by strong men ; and the fire will be that of the juniper which grows in the Syrian desert and makes an exceedingly hot flame.

Some Bible students understand verse 4 as descriptive of the pain caused by the false tongue of verse 3.

Meshech and Kedar were sons of Ishmael. They represent the Scribes and Pharisees, who were indeed of the seed of Abraham but born after the flesh.

The Lord's earthly life was a short one, yet was it so filled with sorrows that, measured by suffering, it could truthfully be recorded as a long one (v. 6).

In verse 5 Messiah mourns that He had to sojourn in Meshech and to pitch His tent among the tents of Kedar. See Hebrew text.

In His earthly life Messiah had to pitch His tent among men that hated peace. They were animated by the spirit of Anti-Christ. In the future, in fellowship with Israel, He will have to dwell with Anti-Christ himself. Verse 6 speaks of that coming Prince, and verse 7 of his followers. The true Messiah was peace, the false Messiah war ; and every time that Messiah proposed peace (v. 7) the followers of that wicked prince replied with war.

PSALM CXXI.—This is the second Psalm of the first triplet, and, consequently, its keynote is Trust. The first two verses are spoken by the Messiah. In them He expresses His determination to look for deliverance from the trouble described in the prior Psalm, not to the mountains, but to Him Who not only created them but also created the heavens. The remaining six verses are spoken by the Holy Spirit. He addresses the Messiah, and assures Him that because He trusted for help from Jehovah, therefore would Jehovah be to Him a Keeper delivering Him from every calamity (v. 7), and sheltering Him day and night (vs. 6 and 8).

In these six verses what Jehovah will not do, and what He will do, alternate. What He will not do is set out in verses 3 and 4, and what He will do, in verse 5. Again, what He will not permit is stated in verse 6, and what He will perform, in verses 7 and 8.

The terms Keep and Keeper should be read throughout the Psalm, as in the R.V.

What God was to His Beloved Son during His earthly life He is willing to be to those who trust Him as Jesus trusted Him. They also if they make Him, and not the mountains, i.e., idols—for these were set up on them—their confidence, may, and can prove that He is a very present help in time of trouble, and a Keeper Who guards to the uttermost.

Christ's servants are oft-times counted mad, but that is a desirable madness which necessitates such a Keeper on the road and assures such an asylum at the close !

PSALM CXXII.—Triumph is the scene presented in this Psalm. It celebrates the victories over the enemies of Ps. cxx. through the faith of Ps. cxxi.

Messiah is the speaker in verses 1 and 2 and 8 and 9. The Holy Spirit speaks in verses 3-7. In verses 6 and 7 He invites the nations to pray for the peace and prosperity of Jerusalem, and He composes the prayer that they should utter.

The Psalm predicts and pictures the opening of the millennial reign of Christ. Jerusalem appears as the capital of the world. The throne of Jehovah (v. 5) is seen in the Temple of Jehovah (v. 109). Israel's Twelve Tribes, redeemed, and with new hearts, are presented as worshippers (v. 4). The nations, blessed with Israel, unite in prayer for Zion (vs. 6 and 7). The Sons of Israel occupy the glorious station of brethren and companions of the Messiah (v. 8). All is sunshine and glory, and is in marked contrast to Ps. cxx. That Psalm speaks of the sufferings of Christ ; this Psalm, of the glories which are to follow.

Messiah's heart, saddened by the long centuries of Israel's unbelief, is now gladdened by their cry, " Let us go unto the House of Jehovah " (v. 1, R.V.) ; and He hastens to triumphantly exclaim, " Our feet are standing within Thy gates, O Jerusalem ! " (v. 2, R.V.) So is it ever ! Assurance of salvation quickly follows upon true repentance.

The vision belongs to the future, but faith makes present what grace promises. So Messiah exclaims that His feet and Israel's feet are already standing within the gates of Zion.

The Holy Spirit makes three statements in verses 3-5. He predicts that restored Jerusalem shall be indwelt by a united people (v. 3) ; that all Israel will testify for Christ by ascending thither (v. 4) ; and that Messiah's throne will be placed there (v. 5).

The word " compact " in Hebrew means " united." In Deut. xvi. the Tribes were commanded to repair three times a year to Jerusalem to give thanks to the Name of Jehovah. They will do so in the millennium. It will be Israel's testimony for God in the face of the world (v. 4). Supplying the ellipsis, and omitting the word " Unto," the sense of this member of verse 4 is, " A testimony ordained by God for Israel." This harmonizes with the Hebrew text. Israel will thus in the future testify for Christ as she ought to have done in the past, but did not. " Thrones for judgment " (v. 5, R.V.) means the Great Throne for judgment, the Throne of the House of David, i.e., Messiah's throne (Matt. xxv). The plural is used to express greatness and majesty. That throne will be placed in Jerusalem.

Two perfections of Messiah's heart appear in the last two verses—its sensitiveness to the voice of the Holy Spirit, and its affection for the people of God's choice. Directly the Spirit invites the nations to say, " Peace be within thee " immediately Messiah exclaims, " I will now say ' peace be within thee.' " His affection is expressed in the words " brethren " and " companions." In John xx. He anticipated the day here predicted, and calling them His brethren He said " Peace be unto you " (Jno. xx. 17 and 21) ; and He sought their prosperity by enriching them at Pentecost, not because they were so admirable, but because they were the dwelling place of God. The last word of the Psalm should read " prosperity " in harmony with the prayer for prosperity in verse 7.

The history of Hezekiah illustrates these songs of the Ascents. He was in trouble, for he was oppressed by the Assyrian, but he trusted, and triumphed. He was a type of Christ, and the Assyrian of Anti-Christ. Anti-Christ is named the Assyrian in more than one Scripture. He will oppress Israel ; and the oppressed, animated by the Spirit of Christ, will trust God for salvation, and will be triumphantly delivered.

These songs of the Ascents relate to that time of future trouble. In them Messiah identifies Himself with His oppressed people, and, as their High Priest, pleads for them, believes for them, and, as their Prince, delivers them.

This song is " for David " (Heb.) i.e., it relates to David, that is, to the true David, the Messiah.

PSALM CXXIII.—This is the first Psalm of the second triplet, and, accordingly, its keynote is trouble. Messiah speaks personally in the first verse, and, on behalf of His people, in the following three verses. Hence the " I " of verse 1, and the " our " and " us " of verses 2-4. He credits them with His own faith, and burdens Himself with their fear.

" Dwellest " (v. 1) better reads " sittest enthroned." The contrast is thus shown between the Great King of the heavens and the proud but puny king of the nations (v. 4).

In the East masters direct their servants with the hand rather than with the voice. Servants, therefore, watch the hand of their masters. God's hand directs, supplies, protects, comforts, caresses, corrects and rewards His servants.

" Mercy," signifies a pity giving deliverance (vs. 2 and 3). Messiah and His disciples suffered the contempt and the scoffing of the proud and careless Pharisees (v. 4).

PSALM CXXIV.—Messiah (v. 1), when calling to remembrance past victories (vs. 2-6) animates Israel to trust for present ones (vs. 7 and 8) ; and as faith makes actual the escape trusted for, so is it here regarded as an accomplished fact.

The enemy is compared to a raging flood (vs. 3-5), to a wild beast (v. 6), and to a fowler (v. 7). The term " proud waters " expresses arrogancy. " Stream " (v. 4), would be better translated " flood." Israel's escape from Sennacherib in the time of Hezekiah illustrates the Psalm ; but its message belongs to the future. In a vainglorious cylinder of Sennacherib's now in the British Museum, the proud monarch records that he shut up Hezekiah in Jerusalem " as a bird in a cage." But the Scriptures of truth relate that the snare of the fowler was broken and the bird escaped !

PSALM CXXV.—This song celebrates the destruction of Anti-Christ's kingdom and the establishment of Messiah's government (vs. 2 and 3). It contrasts these governments (vs. 3 and 4), and predicts the happiness promised to the citizens of the one (vs. 1, 2 and 5), and the doom awaiting the citizens of the other (v. 5). It is a triumph song.

The word "henceforth" (v. 2), defines the time of the fulfilment of the prophecy. It will be the morn of Christ's millennial reign.

Verse 3 should read thus: "The sceptre of The Lawless One (Dan. xi. 36, and 2 Thess. ii. 8), shall not remain upon the lot of the righteous," i.e., on Palestine. The verse predicts the close of Anti-Christ's reign, and of his possession of God's pleasant land.

The last line of verse 3 may mean that righteous men when maddened by injustice and oppression, are tempted to defend themselves and shed the blood of their fellow creatures—so putting forth their hands to iniquity. Or it may mean manacled subjection to iniquitous oppression. If this latter interpretation be correct, then the words point to the liberation of Israel from the tyranny of Anti-Christ. The theme of the Psalm supports this latter interpretation.

Messiah's goodness and severity appear in verses 4 and 5—His goodness to the loyal, and His severity to the disloyal citizens of His Kingdom. A path is either straight or crooked (v. 5). Those who profess to be His citizens, but who compromise with evil, will share the doom of the sons of Israel who will compromise with Anti-Christ; they will be eternally associated with the workers of iniquity.

PSALM CXXVI.—This is the first song of the third triplet. In it Israel's High Priest prays for His people's restoration to Divine relationships (v. 4). He compares their present condition to pain-burdened husbandmen in the hot southern desert sowing their scanty store of seed in a time of famine. It is a day of trouble; and He animates His people's faith by recalling the joy that their fore-fathers felt when delivered from the Assyrian (vs. 1-3 and 2 Kings xix).

"To turn again the captivity" is a figure of speech for to restore prosperity. God turned the captivity of Job (xlii. 10); and He has promised to turn the captivity of Sodom, Samaria and Jerusalem.

The meaning of verse 4 will appear if thus paraphrased: "Restore, O Jehovah, prosperity to us as the streams restore prosperity to the Southern Desert." This desert

depends upon the streams of the springtime for its prosperity. Suffering burdens that land if these streams fail. Such is the vivid picture here given of Israel's future time of suffering. But as the one bearing the seed basket certainly goes forth weeping because of suffering and hardship, so the one bearing his sheaves will surely come again rejoicing. Philip by Divine command left joyful Samaria and went down into the Southern desert, possibly lonely, depressed and tearful, but he returned rejoicing (Acts. viii).

PSALM CXXVII.—This is the central song of the ascents. It is preceded and followed by seven songs. The subscription suggests that it was given by the Spirit to Solomon, and that it relates to the greater than Solomon.

In this song faith contrasts the sufficiency of God with the insufficiency of man. Man's efforts to build a house, to defend it, and to furnish and enrich it are vain (vs. 1 and 2). In contrast God builds, furnishes, enriches and defends a house "during sleep" without human help (vs. 2-5). Thus trust is the key-note of the song.

The indefinite Article "a" should be used before house, city and watchman in verse 1.

The argument of verse 2 is that God gives to His loved-one, in sleep, treasures that men toil for early and late in vain. Thus He gave to Adam; when sleeping, a bride, to Abraham a covenant, to Jacob a promise, to Solomon wisdom, and to Daniel the substance and interpretation of the dream which the Chaldean magicians toiled in vain to discover. "His Beloved" is singular in the Hebrew text. Solomon's name was Jedediah, i.e., Beloved of Jehovah. This song is "for Solomon" i.e., relating to Solomon, that is, the true Solomon, Messiah. He is God's Beloved One; and to Him when sleeping in death He gave a "house" even sons, a seed that will satisfy Him (Isa. liii. 10 and Hebrews iii. 6). That house is built of living stones—a multitude of redeemed sinners that no man can number. (1 Pet. ii. 5, and Rev. vii. 9). It is quite true that God often gives sleep to a sleepless patient in answer to prayer; but that is not the doctrine of this second verse. Its teaching is that God gives gifts to His obedient children "when sleeping"—gifts which human energy can never win.

God is building a spiritual house of sons. These sons, loved and energized by Him, become more than conquerors (vs. 4 and 5). In Hebrew the words " house " and " son " are related ; for a son is regarded as the builder of a house, i.e., of a family.

PSALM CXXVIII.—This is the closing song of the third group. It triumphantly pictures the happiness which Israel and humanity will enjoy when Messiah is seated as King in Zion. From thence as a centre streams of blessing, and rivers of joy, will flow out to the ends of the earth. Zion will no longer be childless (vs. 3 and 6), the earth will be productive (v. 2), Israel and Jerusalem peaceful and prosperous (vs. 5 and 6), and families will be happy, united and large (vs. 1-3). Felicity will be both general (v. 1) and particular (v. 2). It is all a vivid picture of the future millennial Kingdom.

The sentence, " Jehovah shall bless thee out of Zion " (v. 5) furnishes the answer to the charge of untruthfulness made against the Psalm. It is objected that its statements are not true, for many excellent Christian people have unproductive lands or trades, sickly wives and childless homes. This is true now because Christ is still neglected and by the world disowned. Man prefers to govern himself ; and the result is misery. Christian people have to share this misery in sympathy with their fellow creatures. But when Messiah is crowned in Jerusalem the statements in this song will become true ; and its truth will be recognised by contrasting verse 2 for example with Lev. xxvi. 16, and Deuteronomy xxviii. 30-40. These words warned Israel that if they turned away from the Bible they should not enjoy the labour of their own hands, but that others would eat the crops produced by their toil. This has come to pass ; it is true to-day, and will remain true until Israel repents and turns to the Lord. This principle affects all nations.

The word " blessed " in verse 1 means " happy," and in verse 4 " prosperous." The change from the impersonal (v. 1), to the personal of verses 2 and 3, emphasizes the reality of the promised happiness under the future government of Messiah ; and the dependence of both the happiness and the prosperity upon relationship to Him.

Faith can spiritualise the material blessings of this song and make them real and present. Thus homes filled with spiritual children, lands clothed with spiritual harvests, and hearts filled with millennial peace may cause believers to taste the happiness of verse 1 and experience the prosperity of verse 4.

PSALM CXXIX.—This is the first song of the fourth triplet ; and, as in correspondence with the other groups, its theme is trouble. The first three verses recall past trial ; the last four, future trouble ; and the central verse justifies God's action in both periods. The statement (v. 4), that " Jehovah is righteous," placed in the centre of the song, vindicates His action in permitting the past and future afflictions of His people. However sharp and prolonged the trial, faith always justifies God, and is satisfied that there is a righteous reason why such suffering should be permitted. As in the case of Job, so in every similar trial the end glorifies God and secures blessing to man ; wisdom is justified of her children ; and God in His moral government vindicates Himself and disciplines His people. The fruit of trial, therefore, secures for God vindication, for man benefaction.

Messiah the composer of the Psalm, will sing it in sympathy with Israel in the future time of her oppression by Anti-Christ.

The affliction in the past was caused by the Egyptians, the Midianites, the Syrians, etc. They ploughed Israel's back and made long their furrows. The power that energised them was Satan. He also moved the High Priests and the Romans to scourge Messiah, the true Israel. The anguish of that form of torture is here vividly expressed by the terms " They ploughed," and, " They made long their furrows."

But the affliction that yet awaits the Nation will far exceed that already suffered, and the faith of the Remnant will then be sustained by the teaching of this song. Just as the enemy failed in the past, so will he fail in the future. His failure in the past is stated (vs. 1-3) ; his failure in the future is predicted (vs. 5-8). The word " let " in these latter verses also means " shall " in the Hebrew text. In reading, the future tense should be used. The doom of the enemy is predicted and desired. The destruction of the first-born in Egypt, and of the Assyrian host in the days of Hezekiah, illustrate verse 4. Jehovah in a judgment that was righteous,punished in these instances the oppressor and delivered the oppressed.

The future haters of Zion (v. 5) will be execrated by men (v. 8) and destroyed by God (v. 5).

PSALM CXXX.—The faith that waits on God (vs. 1-4), and that waits for God (vs. 5-8), animates this song. Saul was willing to wait on God but not to wait for God, and so lost the Kingdom (1 Sam. x. 8, and xiii. 8-14).

The first four verses are a cry for forgiveness from the guilt of sin ; the last four, for deliverance from the misery of sin. The last line of the Psalm is to be understood as a prayer for deliverance from the iniquities which the righteous suffer from evil men.

The Singer is Messiah. He will as Israel's High Priest in the day of her future sufferings, confess her sins, plead for forgiveness from them, and animate her to set her hope upon Jehovah, Who will surely redeem her out of the hand of her enemies.

The first word in verse 4 in the Hebrew text is " For, " and corresponds with the " for " of verse 7 ; and the double argument then clearly appears, that a cry for forgiveness of sins is to be addressed to God, for He only can forgive, and a cry for deliverance from oppression is to be made to Him, for He is mighty to save. A double lesson is at the same time taught : first, that Divine forgiveness aims at holiness as a consequence (v. 4) ; and second, that suffering is the certain companion of sanctification ; for evil hates goodness (v. 8). This song, therefore, recognises the fact of suffering, but attaches more importance to the forgiveness of sin which causes suffering, than to deliverance from suffering itself. Men are always very willing to ask God to relieve them from suffering, but very unwilling to ask Him to save them from sinning.

The depravity of all men is declared in verse 3. Verse 4 may be thus translated : " For with Thee is forgiveness to the end that Thou mayest be reverenced; and verse 6 : " My soul watcheth for Adonai more than watchers for the morning watch for the morning."

" The depths " (v. 1) relate to the depth of the affliction which Israel will suffer under the False Messiah, and which will be the just punishment of her rejection of The True Messiah.

Such will be the Divine action with Israel —forgiveness of sin, and then redemption from its misery. Mark ii. 1-12 furnishes a fore-picture of this double grace. Compare Hosea ii., and many similar prophecies.

PSALM CXXXI.—The character of Israel's future King, and the happiness of His subjects,inspire the music of this exquisite song. The King sings the first two verses, and the Holy Spirit, basing His appeal upon their truth, in verse 3 invites the nation to reposeful confidence in such a Monarch, and to enter and enjoy the Kingdom promised in the last verse of the previous Psalm. Earthly monarchs are mostly proud, selfish, ignorant, self-confident, unjust and cruel. Messiah offers a contrast to all this. The Spirit here paints Him in beauteous colours. Neither haughty nor proud, neither self-confident nor wilful, but gentle, submissive and resigned, He is subject to God's will and government as a weaned child accepts and submits to the wise and loving action of its mother in changing its food. In the East mothers wean their children at three years of age, and in the case of boys, and especially if he be the only boy, sometimes as late as six years of age. Isaac was, therefore, old enough to be murdered by Ishmael at the instigation of Hagar (Gen. xxi. 8, and Gal. iv. 29). Thus as a weaned child submits its will to that of its mother, so will Messiah, as God's perfect King, be wholly subject to God, and ruling in His fear will form a contrast to self-willed human kings.

The character of the King being such, a perfect government will, therefore, be enjoyed by His subjects, and Israel will dwell in peace.

In the previous Psalm (v. 7) the nation is encouraged to set her hope on Jehovah because He was about to redeem her (v. 8). In this Psalm (v. 8) she is invited to continue setting her hope upon Him " from henceforth and for ever," because the promised redemption shall have then become a reality.

This translation is suggested for verse 2 : " Have I not stilled and quieted myself as a child that is weaned of its mother ? Yea, I am as a weaned child."

PSALM CXXXII.—The great prophecy of Numbers x. 35 and 36 reappears in this last triplet of the Songs of the Ascents. Messiah arises, scatters His enemies (vs. 8 and 18), returns to the many thousands of Israel (v. 14), unites Judah and Ephraim (cxxxiii.), and from Zion sends forth world-wide blessing (cxxxiv.). These Psalms speak of promise, presence and provision as well as of trouble, trust and triumph. The first recalls blessing promised to Messiah. The second, blessing pictured with Messiah, and the third, blessing predicted from Messiah. Until He comes there will be only distress of nations (Luke xxi. 25); but when He comes there will be universal concord, and Zion, His city and throne, will be an inexhaustible source of happiness to Israel and to all the world. The nations will become His disciples and experience the baptism into the Name of the Father, The Son and The Holy Spirit; for they will find in Messiah, then revealed in glory, the fulness of the Godhead bodily.

The Psalm contains a prayer (vs. 1-10) and a promise (vs. 11-18); and, as always, the promise exceeds in grace the prayer. Compare for example verses 13-18 with verses 8-10, and the "shout aloud" of verse 16 with the "shout" of verse 9.

It recalls David's anxieties respecting the Ark and his zeal in bringing it up from Kirjath-jearim to Jerusalem (1 Sam vii. and 2 Sam. vi.); and it was probably given by the Holy Spirit to Hezekiah when shut up by the Assyrians in Jerusalem. That was a time of trouble, distress and disunion. The King was childless, helpless and hopeless. God's promises to David of sonship and glory had seemingly failed. It was a trial sharp enough to confound Hezekiah and Isaiah and their companions. But they trusted and were delivered, and they were assured that the virgin would surely give birth to the Son promised to David, and that to Him would be given His Father's Throne in perpetuity and power. He is the True Ark of Jehovah; and as Priest, Prophet and King nought can be found in Him but perfection. Three men were prominently associated with the Ark of Israel—Eli, the priest, Samuel the prophet and David the King. They all sinned and failed; but in Him Whom they typified there is not, nor can be, either sin or failure.

"Remember David" (v. 1) means remember to fulfil the promises made to him. "Afflictions" should read "anxieties." He was distressed because the Ark of God dwelt in a tent and he himself in a palace. Hezekiah was in much greater distress, for the Ark of God was apparently about to fall into the hands of the Assyrians. Most men's distresses concern their own fortunes and not God's interests. It was not so with David and Hezekiah.

The Ark was heard of at Ephratah, i.e., Bethlehem, and found in the field of the woods, i.e., Kirjath-jearim. The joyful shouting which accompanied its entrance into Zion fore-shadowed the shouting aloud for joy which will signalise Messiah's future entrance into His beloved city; which He will then enrich with all desirable things (v. 15). His government will be caused to prosper; He will shine forth as a lamp; His dominion will be an everlasting dominion; and His enemies will be put to shame (vs. 17, 18).

PSALM CXXXIII.—In this exquisite song faith looks forward to the happy day when the Holy Spirit will be poured out upon the whole House of Israel, and, no longer broken into two nations, they will become one family dwelling together in unity. Ezek. xxxvii. 15-28 predicts this future unity, and makes it synchronize with the Second Coming of Messiah.

Faith can sing in days of sorrow, "all will be well"; and most probably this psalm was sung by Hezekiah and the people of Jerusalem in their day of disunion and distress.

The unity predicted in the prophecy will be the creation of the Holy Spirit. He is here compared to the oil descending upon Aaron, and to the dew descending upon Zion. That oil was precious, and that dew was Hermonic. It was a sea mist precipitated upon the mountains of Hermon, and it was of all forms of dew the most valuable. The oil united Aaron and his garment, and the dew united Hermon and Zion. Hermon on the north figures Ephraim; Zion on the south, Judah. Thus Ephraim and Judah will enjoy the baptism of the Holy Spirit; for that baptism establishes unity (Eph. iv. 5). The uniformity of the flesh is not the unity of the Spirit; the one is originated by man and fails, the other is created by God and lasts.

The words "It is like" should be supplied at the beginning of verse 3 (R.V.). The same dew that descended upon Hermon descended upon Zion, and the same oil that descended upon Aaron descended upon his garment. The double figure emphasises unity.

Unity in the Hebrew Church (Ezek. xxxvii 19, and John x. 16) as well as unity in the Heavenly Church, will be effected by the Coming of the Lord.

Blessing for Zion, blessing in Zion, and blessing from Zion are the keynotes of these three songs.

Whether it was the collar, as the Hebrew suggests, or the hem of the garment does not affect the argument. The oil reached the clothing. Hence the woman had only to touch the hem of His garment and she was made whole.

PSALM CXXXIV.—This is the last of the Songs of the Ascents, and all is sunshine and blessing. It is a scene of millennial peace and glory. Messiah as Creator of the heavens and of the earth, is enthroned in Zion (v. 3), and from thence, as a source, blessing flows forth. Men will then lift their eyes to Zion (v. 2) and from thence expect the supply of all their needs.

In the first two verses the Holy Spirit invites the servants of Jehovah to praise Jehovah in the house of Jehovah. Verse 3 is the response to the invitation. In the millennial day men will bless Him, and He will bless men.

" By night " may mean at the time of the evening sacrifice ; or it may mean the praise which faith renders during the " night " that precedes the millennial dawn.

The " Thee " of verse 3 may emphasise the certitude of millennial blessing to every subject of the Kingdom irrespective of age or status or sex ; or it may intend Messiah, in which case it affirms the divine promises made to Him as the centre of blessing to Israel and to the world. The Hebrew text reads : " Jehovah shall bless Thee out of Zion."

Thus these fifteen Songs of the Ascents, grouped into five triplets, mount in each triplet from trouble through trust to triumph, and lead into the peace, the glory, the blessing and the happiness of Messiah's future Kingdom.

PSALM CXXXV.—This Psalm and the following were most probably sung by Hezekiah and the inhabitants of Jerusalem after the destruction of the Assyrian host. The King then " got to know " (v. 5) that Jehovah is indeed above all gods. Future final deliverance will confirm this knowledge.

But these Psalms are prophetic, and will be sung by redeemed Israel at the coronation of the Great King in Zion. This is made clear by verse 21, and by comparing verses 13 and 14 with Exodus iii. 15 and Deut. xxxii. 36. Exodus xiii. 15 declares God's election of Israel and His uniting the memorial of His name with her. Deut. xxxii. predicts her apostasy to idolatry, her rejection of Messiah, the Divine indignation that should justly follow, and her final restoration and pardon.

Messiah is not now dwelling in Jerusalem, but He will be dwelling there at the time which this and the following Psalm contemplate. Hence this first Psalm · commences and closes with "Hallelujah."

The worshippers of verses 1-4 comprise Priests, Levites, and People. These are the three measures of meal that the false woman corrupted with leaven (Matt. xiii). Now cleansed and pardoned, they worship Messiah as the Supreme God (v. 5), as Creator (6 and 7), as Judge of Egypt and the nations (vs. 8-11), and as the Benefactor of Israel His people (v. 12).

The impotency of idols and of everyone who trusts them (vs. 15-18) is contrasted with the almightiness of Messiah and the happiness of those who trust Him. This contrast is not borrowed from Ps. cxv. That song looks forward in faith to the time which this song celebrates. This is shown by the word " trust " (cxv. 9) and the word " bless " (cxxxv. 19). That which was true to faith in the former Psalm is here acclaimed as fact. Verse 14, should read : " For Jehovah will vindicate His people and have compassion on His Servants."

With the three groups of worshippers of verses 1-4, are associated in verses 19 and 20 the redeemed nations. They are here introduced as the fearers of Jehovah (v. 20). Compare the people, priests, Levites and fearers of God in Acts. ii. 47, iv. 36, vi. 7, xiii. 26, etc.

PSALM CXXXVI.—This Psalm is Israel's response to the call of the prior Psalm to worship and praise Messiah. It was possibly sung by Hezekiah.and his companions, and also by the returned captives from Babylon. But it will yet be sung by the tribes of Israel in the future day of their deliverance, when Messiah will appear in majesty and destroy all their adversaries.

In the first twenty-two verses His glory as

Creator and Sustainer of the heavens and the earth (Col. i. 16, 17), and His Grace and Power on behalf of His ancient people in the past, are set out. The remaining verses apply to their future deliverance from Anti-Christ—Israel's greatest enemy—and from the misery of their low estate, and that of all flesh (v. 25) under his oppression.

The title " God of heaven " (v. 26) unites the prophecies of Daniel and of Revelation, and makes certain the period to which this psalm belongs. Messiah is the God of heaven in antagonism to the kings of earth, who have oppressed, are oppressing, and will oppress the people of Immanuel. In that future day of His glory and Israel's redemption, the whole nation will praise Him for His dealings with them from the day He brought them out of Egypt to the day when He delivers them from Anti-Christ, the last and fiercest of the wild beasts of Daniel's vision and of John's Apocalypse.

That the destruction of the first-born in Egypt (v. 10) should evidence the enduring mercy of God, angers unconverted religious people. But an Egyptian mother, taught by the Holy Spirit, could while looking on the dead face of her only child, bow her head in faith and worship and say " His mercy endureth for ever." This is a secret only known to those who are born of the Spirit.

The future blessing of all nature in unison with Israel is assured in verse 25.

PSALM CXXXVII.—The captives of Israel, such as Daniel, Ezekiel, Nehemiah, Esther, Mordecai, Ezra and their companions, must often have wept by the waters of Babylonia as they remembered Zion. Their hearts were not in captivity to the wealth and honours and pleasures of Babylon, but were true to the broken walls and buried gates of distant Jerusalem.

The Psalm contains two stanzas. The first has as its theme love to Messiah and to His city (vs. 1-6). The second has as its theme hatred to the Messiah and to His city, and it predicts the just judgment which the haters must therefore suffer (vs. 7-9).

From its foundation in Gen. x. to its fall in Rev. xviii. Babylon continually appears as the hater and oppressor of Jerusalem.

These two cities are opposed. The one is God's city; the other, man's. The one figures truth; the other, falsehood. The one re-presents the Kingdom of Light ; the other, that of darkness. These cities exist to-day as principles. They will exist in the future as principles and as facts. Jerusalem as a material city will, with the spiritual principles attaching to it, become the city of Messiah the Great King, while Babylon also as a material city will, with the principles of evil attaching to it, for ever perish.

Captivity to the world paralyses both hand and tongue so that it is impossible in such an atmosphere to sing the Lord's song. Jehovah's servants may bring their harps down with them into Babylon in the belief that they will be able to sing there, but they find it impossible. The hand that should awaken on the harp-string the sacred song is the very hand that must hang the harp upon the willow ; and the tongue that was wont to sing of Messiah and of Zion, only has sufficient energy to lament. Babylon robs the Christian of his song and his testimony directly he is enslaved by it ; and tears instead of songs must be his bitter experience.

The word " there " (vs. 1, 2 and 3) emphasises this hostile environment.

The Psalm predicts the just judgment which will overtake Babylon and her children. The doom that involves the children is in principle in operation to-day, and has always been in operation. The principle is that a man in doing evil not only destroys himself but also destroys those dearest to him. This fact is illustrated in Daniel vi. 24, and is seen in the present day in the misery that the wives and children of drunkards suffer.

The two last verses are an offence to many. To connect the happiness of the man who dashes little children against stones with the happiness of the forgiven sinner of Ps. xxxii. 1, is to them impossible. And yet the language is exactly similar in the Hebrew text. " How happy is the man whose transgression is forgiven," and, "How happy is the man that dashes the little ones against the stones." The word " happy " is from a Hebrew root meaning to be upright. The happiness of a true moral relationship to God is a right happiness whether it results from receiving God's pardon or executing God's wrath. The former happiness belongs to the present day of grace ; the latter, to the future day of judgment. God's action, whether in grace or judgment, is perfect and in harmony with His being and nature, and awakens praise in every Spirit-taught heart.

That a tyrant should suffer the same misery that he inflicted on others is not injustice but justice. There is, therefore, nothing unrighteous in verses 8 and 9. But the language of these two verses is no doubt figurative. Babylon represents idolatry; her children, the idol images beloved by her. To destroy these is indeed happiness to the servants of Truth. So a great brewery may be pictured as a mother, and its tied-houses as her little ones. How happy every right-thinking man would deem himself were he legally empowered to utterly destroy them all ! Three figures here appear : The woman, the child and the Stone—the Stone of Daniel ii. 34, and Matt. xxi. 44. These represent idolatry, its fruit, and Messiah in conflict. The issue must be His triumph and their destruction.

PSALM CXXXVIII.—The praise of the first three verses of this Psalm, the predictions of the next three, and the persuasion of the last two are based upon the trustworthiness of the Word of God. The first six verses will have their fulfilment in the future day of Messiah's glory, and the last two express His faith while waiting for that glory. As Israel's High Priest He sings the song for, and with, His people.

The predictions in verses 4-6 relate to the time when all the kings of the earth—the gods of verse 1—will become subject to the words of Messiah's mouth (v. 4) ; they will applaud His ways, and great will be His glory (v. 5). He as the self-humbled One (Phil. ii. 8) will be enthroned (v. 6) ; but the Proud One (Isa. x. 13, Dan. xi. 36) will be afar off in the lake of fire (Rev. xix. 20). The followers of the Lowly One will share His glory ; the followers of the Proud One will become the companions of his doom.

On the millennial morn Israel will proclaim in song that all her expectations founded upon the promises of God will be surpassed by their performance (v. 2). God will in that day magnify His Word above all His Name. His Name means His reputation and character for faithfulness and goodness. His Word is His promise. In that future day His performance will exceed His promise. It shall be as if a penniless man owing one hundred pounds turned for help to a rich man having a reputation for benevolence. The rich man promises to pay the debt, and on the day when it is due hands the debtor a cheque for one thousand pounds. Thus the rich man would magnifiy his word above all his name.

The confidence of Messiah and His people in the trustworthiness of the promises of God is expressed in the last two verses. He and His people are one, hence He walks with them in the midst of trouble, their enemies are His enemies, and if His people are revived and delivered He accounts that as true for Himself (v. 7). He is persuaded of a perfect fulfilment of the Divine purposes relating to Himself and to them (v. 8). The most perfect work of God's hands was the sinless body which He prepared for His Beloved Son. He glorified that body on the Mount of Transfiguration, and in the day of Ascension. He did not forsake, and never will forsake, that supreme work of His hands ; as the next Psalm reveals.

PSALM CXXXIX.—The closing words of the prior Psalm introduce, as already noticed, the sinless tabernacle of clay prepared by God for His Beloved Son. This Psalm developes the subject, and sets out the moral and physical perfections of that perfect human body. The Singer is Messiah. He here exposes His whole nature, emotional and physical, as man, together with His action, His inaction, His thoughts, His words and His ways to the scrutiny of God's eye, and nothing but perfection is found. There is here absolute harmony between the Incarnate Word of God and the written Word of God. The Psalm is therefore fittingly placed in this Deuteronomy Book of the Psalms, for it reveals the perfect submission and obedience of Christ's human nature to the Word of God.

Messiah sings with joy of God's omniscience (vs. 2-5) ; of His Omnipresence (vs. 7-12) ; and of His Omnipotence (vs. 13-16). He expresses His admiration for the infinite intelligence of the love which cherishes Him (v. 6), and His abhorrence of all who oppose that love (v. 21).

" Compasseth " (v. 3) means " scrutinises." " To lay " (v. 5) signifies to lay protectingly ; and to " beset " means to guard. As man Messiah admired God's infinite intelligence and love, and rejoiced that it was impossible to get outside them

(v. 6). He lived and moved and had His being in God ; and He exulted in the knowledge that the greatest distance could not separate Him from God, nor the darkest night hide Him from His loving eye (vs. 7-12).

To " possess " and to "cover " (v. 13) here mean to collect and to knit together ; and " reins " is a comprehensive term embracing the human body both physical and emotional. The verse may be illustrated by the action of an able manufacturer in first assembling the parts of a machine and then putting them together. The mystery of the incarnation is, therefore, the subject of verses 13-16. The members of Christ's sinless body existed continually in the secrecy of the Divine Wisdom ; and when the time came they were woven together in the body of the Lord's Mother (vs. 13 and 14). The miraculous nature of that birth, and Christ's full testimony to it, form the subjects for praise in verse 14. " Fearfully " signifies miraculously, " Curiously wrought in the lowest parts of the earth " (v. 15) means skilfully made with the dust of the ground. The members of that sinless body were not imperfect but unperfect, i.e., unformed in fact but all its parts inscribed from eternity. These truths were very precious to Messiah (v. 17) ; and continued to be precious to Him when, having died as a man, He awoke in resurrection, and returned once more to the glory which He had with the Father before the world was.

These mysteries relating to His physical body are also true of His mystical body ; for just as the members of Christ's human body were registered in God's Book from eternity, and so had a continuous existence, so all the members of His mystical body have had a corresponding existence ; and just as the Divine Love and care for every several one of the precious members of Christ's human body existed from everlasting, so are they ever enduring for every several member of His mystical body.

The statement that He was made of the same material as the first Adam (v. 15), emphasizes the fact that His body was human and not angelic.

What Messiah was persuaded Jehovah would perfect (cxxxviii. 8), was the unperfect substance (v. 16) of His human and mystical body. That body was the supreme work of God's own hands (Heb. x. 5).

The sinlessness of Messiah's humanity is expressed positively and negatively in verses 19-22 and 23 and 24. He rejoices that all wicked and bloodthirsty men will be destroyed by God ; He gives a satisfactory reason for the justice of their doom (v. 20) ; He abhors them (v. 21) ; and He hates them with a perfect hatred—not a sinful hatred, but a perfect hatred (v. 22). This demands a sinless nature.

PSALM CXL.—This prophetic vision foretells the First Advent (vs. 1-8), and the Second Advent (vs. 9-13). Messiah the Afflicted One, and His followers the needy ones (v. 12), are contrasted with the False Messiah the Lawless One (v. 8), and his followers the proud ones (v. 5). The Pharisees, the Sadducees and the Herodians with their snares, nets and gins of Matt. xxii. appear in verse 5. The False Prophet is the Impious Man associated with the False Messiah in verses 1 and 8-11. The eternal destiny of both these Heads and their followers, is contrasted in verse 10 with the eternal felicity of Messiah and His followers in verse 13. Messiah when on earth suffered the hatred foretold in verses 1-5. The Gospels record the mischiefs (v. 2), the hostility (v. 2), the stinging slanders (v. 3), the cruelty (v. 4) and the snares planned in secret, and skilfully set in public (v. 5) in order to cause him to swerve from the Law of Moses (v. 4, R.V.).

His people are called to suffer similarly ; but they have the strength and consolation derived from the knowledge that He makes their afflictions His own ; that He understands them ; and that He engages to supply sufficient faith and fortitude to endure them.

The Holy Spirit quotes the third verse in Romans iii. 13 as a proof of the total depravity of fallen man's nature.

The Divine protection sheltering Messiah's head (v. 7) contrasts with the mischief that is to overwhelm the head of His enemies (v. 9).

The Lawless One of verse 8 is Anti-Christ. The False Prophet (Rev. xix. 20) is associated with him in the last member of the verse, which reads in the Hebrew text, " they shall exalt themselves." With this is contrasted in the Hebrew text the last member of verse 10, which reads, "they shall not rise again."

The future tense is used in the original text in verses 9-11. These verses predict that the evils planned by the False Messiah and the False Prophet shall fall upon their

own heads as burning coals ; that they shall
be cast into the fire of the bottomless pit ;
that they shall be eternally shut up there-in ;
that they shall have no place in the redeemed
earth ; and that the Divine wrath shall
pursue them to their destruction. Their
followers will share their doom.

The glorious predictions of verses 12 and 13
will also be fulfilled by the same faithfulness
that will judge the oppressor.

PSALM CXLI.—The address " Jehovah
Adonai," of verse 8 and the similarity of
that verse and verse 9 with verses 5 and 7 of
the prior Psalm, together with the continued
prophecy of both Psalms, establish their
relationship.

The hatred of man's heart to Messiah and
His followers (vs. 7 and 9) ; the just judgment
of these haters (v. 10) ; and the faith and
dependence of Messiah Himself in and upon
God, and His preciousness to God (vs. 1, 3,
4, 6, and 8), form the teaching of the song.

The confidence in God (v. 8), the sweetness
towards His enemies (v. 6), and the separation from evil (vs. 3 and 4) which characterised Him when on earth, characterise those
in whom He dwells ; and will appear in the
future night of Israel's final trial.

How precious the incense of Messiah's
prayer, and how acceptable the lifting up of
His hands were to God, surpass human
comprehension (v. 2).

His subjection and dependence as a man,
and His shrinking from evil, are foretold in
the petitions of verses 3 and 4. " Incline
not " means " permit not to incline."

Perhaps " their dainties " (v. 4) are intended to contrast with " their calamities "
(v. 5), and so predict that He refused their
honours (Jno. vi. 15), but sympathised with
their calamities (Luke xix. 41). Or there
may be no comparison ; and so the last
member of verse 5, would mean that He
prayed for the righteous to be delivered from
their calamities.

The spiritual nature prefers the darts of
the righteous to the dainties of the wicked ;
and finds their wounds as health-giving and
refreshing and desirable as oil upon the
head.

The iniquities of verse 4 are to be understood as doctrinal and not moral. The
reference is to the Scribes and Pharisees,
as is clear from verses 9 and 10, together with
verses 4 and 5 of the prior Psalm. Compare

Matt. vii. 23, Philippians iii. 2, etc., and the
Epistles of Timothy and Titus.

The words " in stony places " (v. 6) in
Hebrew read " the hands of the rock " and
correspond to " the hands of the snare "
of verse 9 (Heb.). The snare for the foot had
two " hands " which sprang up and seized
their prey. The judges of verse 6, were the
Scribes and Pharisees, and Messiah was the
Rock. When in Mark xii. He had overthrown
these the common people heard Him gladly ;
for to them His words were sweet. " They
shall hear," i.e., the people shall hear. So
the " hands " of the Rock over-threw those
who had planned that the " hands " of the
snare should overthrow Him. But the
Hebrew word used here shows the Rock was
an immovable Rock (Compare Matt. xvi. 18
in Ginsburg's New Testament).

The doom of the wicked is predicted in
verse 10. The future tense should be here
used, as in the Hebrew text ; and the sense
of the second member of the verse is that the
Pharisees, the Sadducees and the Herodians
were caught in their own snares, but that
Messiah passed safely through and over them.

PSALM CXLII.—Four statements appear
in the title of the Psalm : It is to instruct
(Maschil) ; it was given by the Holy Spirit
to David; it was written by him in a cavern
and it is a prayer.

David when in the cavern reviews his experiences prior to his descent into it (vs.
3-6) ; prays that he may be delivered out
of it ; and believes that his prayer will be
heard (v. 7). In all this he was a type of his
Son and Lord.

The reader is invited to contemplate
Messiah when shut up in the prison-house
of Sheol (vs. 1, 2 and 7); he is permitted to
hear Him reviewing before God His life as
Man (v. 3) ; His anguish and prayer when
hanging on the tree (vs. 4-6) ; His petition
to be delivered out of the death-world ;
His assurance that that prayer will be heard
(v. 7) ; and the subsequent joy that His
resurrection would cause to His people (v. 7).
How very wonderful that men should be
invited to look upon Him in Sheol ; and
how amazing that they should be told
what He said and felt when in that dark
prison.

To cry " with the voice " expresses deep
anguish, and the repetition of the expression
implies the deepest anguish (v. 1). In this

cry there was no rebellion, only affection and confidence.

The sense of verse 3 is : When my spirit was overwhelmed within me, then was I supported by the remembrance that Thou knewest my life of sorrow. This implies conscious sinlessness. He invited God to scrutinise His conduct from the cradle to the cross. It was a life of constant and bitter trial ; but it was a sinless life. He was daily tested by snares privily laid for Him ; but He never sinned. Men hated Him ; but He was unspeakably precious to God.

Verses 3 and 6 correspond. The one sings of comfort in affliction ; the other, of deliverance from affliction.

His absolute abandonment and loneliness when in the hands of the High Priests and of Pilate, and when nailed to the tree, are declared in verse 4 ; and in verses 5 and 6 His unfailing faith in, and dependence upon, God up to the last moment that in " the land of the living " He suffered the rage and cruelty of His persecutors, is touchingly expressed. The words " On my left hand " may be supplied after " beheld " in verse 4.

Shut up in the prison-house of Sheol into which He descended from Golgotha, He trusts and prays and believes. He cries for deliverance, and predicts the triumph which His resurrection will bring to the righteous. See notes on Ps. xvi.

This translation of verse 7, is suggested : " Bring my soul out of prison that I may thereby give occasion for praise to Thy name, and that the righteous may crown themselves because of Me, for Thou shalt deal bountifully with me ". His resurrection did cause the righteous to crown themselves with joy (Jno. xx.) ; and when the fact of the resurrection shall be manifested to the world by and by, then will there be indeed a crowning day both for Him and it !

PSALM CXLIII.—As in the two prior Psalms so here Messiah prays from out of the depths and darkness of Sheol. Those Psalms viewed Him there personally ; this Psalm, representatively (vs. 2, 9 and 12). In verse 2, He declares the righteousness of God and the unrighteousness of man, and as Jehovah's atoning Servant occupies the centre of the verse as the Daysman. Thus the commencement of the verse points to the Righteous Judge, the close of the verse to

the unrighteous sinner, and the middle of the verse—between the Judge and the accused—to the mediating Saviour.

The last verse of the Psalm reveals the same principle. As Jehovah's Servant He pleads Himself as the sufficient ground for the destruction of His people's enemies. So in the second verse He pleads for the justification of His people, and in the last verse for the destruction of their enemies. The doctrine of the former verse is acceptable, that of the latter verse repugnant to what is called the religious world.

The enemy of verses 3 and 4 is death—the last enemy that is to be destroyed. He that has the power of death is Satan. In these two verses are fore-told Messiah's death on the cross—" His life smitten down to the ground "—and His imprisonment in Sheol— " made to dwell in darkness." The extremity of horror which He suffered in the death-world is revealed in the statements that He dwelt in darkness ; that to His consciousness His imprisonment was prolonged ;   that His Spirit was overwhelmed, and His heart desolate.   This depth of anguish was deepened by the remembrance of the glory which He had with the Father before and at creation (v. 5).

The language of intense suffering, of full subjection of will, and of confident expectation of the promised resurrection, are all expressed in verses 6-11. He is pictured in the darkness of the abyss stretching out His hands in His distress (v. 6) ; His soul thirsts for God ; He cries out, Do not continue to hide Thy face from me, for I am become like the eternal prisoners of death (v. 7) ; and raise me in the morning, for I trust in Thee for this—Thy Name and righteousness are pledged thereto. He makes no attempt to deliver Himself from the horrors that overwhelm Him, but prays that the Holy Spirit may show Him the way out of the prison (v. 8) and into the land of uprightness (v. 10). Men in pain welcome death as a relief from suffering. It was not so with the Lamb of God. His atonement finished, He descended into the horrors of the abyss ; but what was His anguish there will possibly never be known by man. The fact that He did suffer there is declared in many passages of the Scriptures.

God's true servants in all dispensations may, with David use the words of this Psalm as a vehicle of prayer and faith in times of deep trial ; but only One could suffer fully the sorrows here revealed.

PSALM CXLIV.—The First Advent is here predicted in verses 1-8 ; the Second, in verses 9-15.

That the Mighty God Whose glory and power nature reveals (vs. 5 and 6) should so concern Himself about man, who is as a breath and a shadow (vs. 3 and 4), as to send His Beloved Son to redeem him, fills the heart with wonder and praise. To that gracious God David ascribed His victory over Goliath, and over all lesser foes ; and it was He Who disposed the hearts of his subjects to affection and obedience (v. 2). In all this David was a type of Messiah Who having been raised from the dead (v. 7) promises to sing a new song on mounting His millennial throne (v. 9).

The two previous Psalms, which preserve the prayer of Messiah when in the darkness of the eternal grave, are followed in this Psalm by the triumph and sunshine of the resurrection and millennial mornings. These mornings are here brought together ; as they are in so many passages in the Bible.

The multiplication of the expressions of what God was to Him as a Man make verses 1 and 2 throb with exultation and emotion. Such emotion becomes the resurrection and the millennium. In the resurrection (vs. 5-8), His then foes were defeated and He was delivered from " them " (v. 6), i.e., from the " strangers " of verse 7 ; and in the millennium He and His people will enjoy victory over their future foes and be delivered from them (vs. 9-11).

There is no meaningless repetition in verses 8 and 11. The fundamental doctrine of man's incurable corruption is declared to be the same at the time of Christ's future coming as it was at the time of His first coming. Both advents foretell man's unchanged moral condition notwithstanding two thousand intervening years of so-called culture.

Man's miserable estate at the First Advent and since (v. 4) is contrasted with his happy future estate under the Second Advent (vs. 12-15).

Verse 7 should read as in the Revised version ; and also verse 11. The word "mighty" should be supplied before " hand " ; for the word hand is the plural of majesty in the Hebrew text.

The statements of verses 12-15 are under-

stood by some as the vain boastings of the " strange children " of verse 11. The passage would then read : " Their right hand is the right hand of falsehood who say, ' our sons are as plants . . . . We are the happy people ! ' " The last line of this fifteenth verse would then read : " Nay, happy is the people whose God is Jehovah ! " See notes on Psalm viii.

The word " strange " (vs. 7 and 11) is derived from a Hebrew root signifying to know and not to know, i.e., estrangement and hostility. Messiah's enemies in His First Advent knew Him and yet refused to know Him (Jno. vii. 28), and His future appearance will be preceded by similar conduct (2 Peter iii. 1-7, etc.). Man is by nature a stranger to grace and to God—estranged from Him and hostile to Him.

The sense of the second and third members of verse 14 is that war will be abolished—there will be no more battering down of city walls, no more sorties, and no more cries of alarm in the streets. Such will be the happy result of Emmanuel's government.

PSALM CXLV.—In Psalm xxii. 25, Messiah said, " My praise shall be of Thee in the great congregation." This vow He here fulfils on ascending the throne of Jehovah at Jerusalem (1 Chron. xxix. 23). As Viceroy He acts for God the Great King, addressing Him as " My God the King " (Heb.). Before Him stands " the great congregation " composed of the princes and people of Israel, and the representatives of all nations. This mighty anthem is then sung. Messiah leads the song, and the great congregation responds. The subjoined arrangement has been suggested :—

Messiah sings : " I will extol Thee," etc., (vs. 1 and 2).

The great congregation responds : " Great is Jehovah, etc., (vs. 3 and 4).

Messiah sings : " I will speak," etc., (v. 5).

The congregation responds, " and men shall speak " etc., (v. 6).

Messiah sings : " Yea, I will declare," etc., (v. 6).

The congregation responds : " They shall abundantly " etc., (vs. 7-20).

Messiah sings : " My mouth shall speak " etc., (v. 21).

The response : " And all flesh shall bless," etc., (v. 21).

The great congregation worships Messiah as

God ; and Messiah worships God. Thus the Holy Spirit in the Psalm testifies to Christ's Deity and Humanity.

The great congregation sings without misgiving of the character, perfection and duration of the government which Messiah will administer, and of which Daniel vii. 22-27, speaks (vs. 7-20). The present and future tense may be used in these verses in all statements respecting Messiah's power as Jehovah—for example : Jehovah is the One upholding and the One Who will uphold all that are about to fall (v. 4). In the Synagogue (Luke xiii), He manifested His power to raise up all those that be bowed down ; in feeding the multitude He opened His hand and they were all satisfied (v. 16) ; and He fulfilled the desire of the dying thief and saved him (v. 19). The result of His administration shall be that all flesh shall bless His Holy Name for ever and ever (v.21), for He will cast out of His Kingdom all that offend (v. 20).

All servants of God may personally foretaste in their hearts the sweetness and power of Christ's future perfect earthly government.

PSALM CXLVI.—As the Five Books of the Psalms correspond to the Five Books of the Pentateuch, so the five closing Hallelujah Psalms also correspond. This Psalm is therefore the Genesis Psalm. It recalls the formation of man (v. 4), and the creation of the worlds (v. 6).

Each Psalm begins and ends with Hallelujah. All five are millennium Psalms. They connect the Books of Genesis and Revelation. They will be sung by the happy subjects of Christ's future Kingdom. Happiness in that Kingdom will be personal as well as communal (v. 1). It is possible that the singer will be David, raised from the dead as " the prince " of Ezekiel xliv. and xlv. He will represent the nation as he sings.

The Psalm opens and closes with the voice of a great multitude as the voice of many waters, and as the voice of mighty thunderings, shouting, " Hallelujah " ; and between these Hallelujahs the singer contrasts man and the Messiah, showing the inability of the one and the sufficiency of the Other as a Saviour. Thus : Man—faithless, powerless and mortal (vs. 3 and 4). Messiah—faithful, powerful, eternal (vs. 5-10).

The Old Testament title " God of Jacob "

corresponds to the New Testament title " God of all grace " (v. 5). He met Jacob when he deserved nothing and promised him everything. The millennial reign of Christ will prove the faithfulness of the promise.

The beauty and force of the last verse will be felt if it be thus read : " Jehovah shall reign for ever and ever. Oh Zion ! Thy God shall reign unto all generations."

PSALM CXLVII.—The Exodus character of this Psalm appears in the grace that redeemed Israel out of Egypt celebrated in verses 2 and 3 ; and in the gift of the Law at Sinai recalled in verse 19.

The structure of this millennial song has been thus shown :

Hallelujah ! (v. 1).
Messiah's goodness (vs. 1-3) ; His attributes (vs. 4 and 5) ; His discrimination (v. 6).
Messiah's goodness (v. 7, ; His attributes (vs. 8 and 9) ; His discrimination (vs. 10 and 11).
Messiah's goodness (vs. 12-14) ; His attributes (vs. 15-18); His discrimination (vs. 19 and 20).
Hallelujah ! (v. 20).

Israel's redemption from Egypt, the healing of the wounds there inflicted, and her formation into a nation, illustrate the greater deliverance now awaiting her, and which she will celebrate when the kingdoms of the earth become the Kingdoms of her Messiah.

His ability to count and name the stars, and the infinity of His understanding, assure the outcasts of Israel (v. 2) that He will not overlook or forget one of them. " He calleth His own sheep by name " (vs. 4 and 5).

The meek subject their wills to God's word ; the wicked refuse to do so. Messiah discriminates between them (v. 6).

His power over nature, and His ability to make it serve His creatures, is recognized by His people and excites their praise (vs. 7-18). In verses 10 and 11 He distinguishes between physical and spiritual strength.

His election of Israel as the depository of His Word, and as the channel of its communication to the world (vs. 19 and 20), moved both Moses and Paul to wonder and worship (Deut. iv. 8, Rom. iii. 2 and xi. 33).

PSALM CXLVIII.—This is the third of the last five Hallelujah Psalms. It corresponds to the third Book of the Pentateuch.

Worship is the subject of that Book. This Psalm pictures a place of worship and describes the worshippers. The place of worship is vast. It reaches from the depths beneath the earth (v. 7) to the heights above the heavens (v. 1). The worshippers embrace angels, men, and the entire creation, animate and inanimate. The heavens and their inhabitants praise Messiah (vs. 1-6) ; and then the earth and its inhabitants praise Him (vs. 7-13).

The last verse reveals that this Mighty God whom both the heavens and the earth are eternally to adore is Messiah the God of Israel. The heavens are to adore Him for He created them (v. 5) and He maintains them (v. 6 and Col. 1, 17) ; and the earth and all that is therein adores Him for His Name alone is excellent (v. 13). This song of millennial worship opens and closes with a Hallelujah as the noise of many waters.

The laws which govern the countless worlds revolving in space, and which confine them to their orbits, are pointed to in verse 6. " Dragons," i.e., sea monsters. They mean all kinds of fish which live in the ocean (v. 7). With the ocean are associated rain and wind (v. 8).

The phrase " the earth and the heavens " (v. 13), is noteworthy. This order is only found here and in Gen. ii. 4. It is connected with the Divine title Jehovah Elohim. This title first occurs in Gen. ii. 4 ; and as it expresses God's relationship to man as a redeeming Saviour, the earth is, therefore, made to precede the heavens.

The term " a people near unto Him " (v. 14), gives the leading thought of the Book of Leviticus (Lev. x. 3, xxi. 21 and Ps. lxv. 4).

This song pictures the happy estate of man and all living creatures under Messiah's coming reign.

PSALM CXLIX.—This is the fourth Hallelujah Psalm and corresponds to the Book of Numbers. At the close of that Book, Israel stands at the entrance of Canaan, her brows wreathed with victory over the Moabite and the Amorite. In this Psalm she stands at the entrance of the Millennial Kingdom crowned with victory over Anti-Christ and the False Prophet.

There are two stanzas in the song—Israel rejoices in Messiah (vs. 1-3), and Messiah rejoices in Israel (vs. 4-9).

The second line of verse 4 would better read in harmony with the theme of the song, " He will adorn the meek with victory " ; and " beds," or couches of glory (v. 5), here mean thrones. Eastern princes are enthroned upon cushions or divans (Esther vii. 8 and Amos vi. 4).

The future tense should be used in verses 5-9. This section foretells the efficiency, the piety and the equity of the government which Israel will exercise over the Nations of the earth. It will be efficient, for a two-edged sword will be in their hand ; it will be pious, for the high praises of God will be in their mouths ; it will be just, for it will exact vengeance ; it will be impartial, for it will bind kings ; and it will be legal, for it will execute the judgment written in the statute books of heaven.

These features are not prominent in man's government. History records the feebleness of their governments ; that the mouths of their magistrates are more usually filled with cursing than with praising ; that their administration is unjust rather than just ; that they shew partiality to the rich and great ; and that they inscribe unrighteous laws upon their statute-books.

The two-edged sword of verse 6 is that of Joshua v. 13 ; Hebrews iv. 12, and Rev. i. 16 and ii. 12 and xix. 15. It may also intend the executive governmental sword of Romans xiii. 4—now inefficiently used, but to be efficiently employed in the government of the millennial earth.

The sword of this verse is two-edged. It can reach and punish with equal effect if escape be attempted on the right hand or on the left. It has an edge for the evil-doer and for the unfaithful wielder. So Israel proved in Joshua's day ; for one edge judged the debauched Canaanite, and the other the disobedient Israelite.

The second member of verse 9 should read : " This dignity shall be to all His Saints," i.e., they shall be victorious and enthroned. In that day, as predicted by Messiah Himself, His Apostles will sit on twelve thrones judging the Twelve Tribes of Israel ; and, as foretold in the Scriptures, Israel will sit on thrones judging the nations of the earth. In the millennium the nations will be allocated by God in the earth in correspondence with, and in relation to, the boundaries of the sons of Jacob (Deut. xxxii. 8).

PSALM CL.—This is the fifth Hallelujah Psalm ; and as the last Psalm of the Fifth Book may be entitled the Deuteronomy Psalm of the Deuteronomy Book (Deut. iii. 24 and xxxii. 43). The Divine titles used are El and Jah. El is essentially the Almighty, Jah signifies the Ever-existing One, i.e., Jesus Christ the same yesterday and to-day and for ever.

The song pictures a place of worship (v. 1) ; describes the worshippers (v. 6) ; and predicts the theme (v. 2), the mode (vs. 3-5) and the extent (v. 6) of their worship.

The place of worship has two courts—the sanctuary and the firmament (v. 1), The sanctuary is earthly ; the firmament heavenly. Moses and David were commanded to construct the earthly sanctuary according to the heavenly pattern shewn to them. Nothing was left to their taste or imagination (1 Chron. xxviii. 19, Heb. viii. 5). Here both are united and form one place of worship. This song will be sung on the future happy morn when the heaven and the earth will be reconciled, and the prophecy of Jacob's ladder and of Hosea ii. fulfilled.

The theme will be double. First, what He does—His mighty acts. Second, what He is—His excellent greatness. These express His glory as Creator, as Redeemer, as the Lamb of God and as the Son of God. Compare John i. 29 and 34, John v. 32, 33 and Rev. iv. and v. The scene of worship in Revelation is heaven ; in this Psalm it is the earth in unison with heaven.

In the day when He appears everything that hath breath will praise Him. His appearance will vindicate Him. In that day it will be recognised that His government of the world with its permitted evil and injustice and suffering, was the highest wisdom and the most perfect love. Men will have nothing but praise for Him. The Book of the Psalms assures this. Its pages are wet with tears, its music broken with sighs, but its last song is a burst of satisfied rapture ; and so its five volumes fitly close with a loud Hallelujah !

Thus Messiah the Blessed Man of the first Psalm will be worshipped as the Blessed God of the last Psalm ; whilst the intervening Psalms sing of the countless perfections of His nature and of His actions as both Son of Man and Son of God.

PROVERBS

PROVERBS I.—The Hebrew word "Proverbs" is formed from the verb to "rule," or "govern." This verb first occurs in Gen. i. in the statement that the sun and the moon were to rule the day and the night with the light which shone from them as light-holders. "Proverbs" is a wisdom-holder, and its purpose is to rule with its heavenly light man's conduct in the earth.

The wisdom in this Book is not human sagacity or cleverness or ability, but the application to the smallest details of human life of the wisdom which built the heavens and the earth, and maintains them in being. This is grace indeed that God should place His wisdom at the disposition of man in order to man's happiness, and to his walking in a safe road in the midst of confusion and evil and danger.

The Book contrasts the fear of Jehovah and the folly of self-will. The former is declared to be the foundation of wisdom, and prosperity ; the latter is denounced as the cause of suffering and death.

The Book deals with God's moral government in the earth, and is a sure guide amidst life's perplexities. It undertakes to lead men safely whether they be princes or peasants ; and to direct them aright in all their concerns whether public or private.

Rejection of this wisdom is declared by the Book to open the door to corruption and violence. Such was the moral condition of the Antediluvians (Gen. vi. 11).

The Book contains six volumes. The first and last correspond, the four intervening volumes alternate. The subjoined structure exhibits this analysis :—

Volume I. The words of the wise Teacher i.-ix.
Volume II. Proverbs by Solomon x.-xix. 19.
Volume III. Proverbs for Solomon xix. 20 -xxiv.
Volume IV. Proverbs by Solomon xxv. and xxvi.
Volume V. Proverbs for Solomon xxvii.-xxix.
Volume VI. The words of Agur and of Lemuel xxx. and xxxi.

In the East a teacher addresses a pupil as his " son."

The first verse of chapter x. and the character and poetic form of the Proverbs which follow, suggest this structure.

Solomon when young was trained by the Proverbs that were taught him to fit him as a ruler of his people. When he became a king he wrote the proverbs that were given by the Holy Spirit to him. If this suggestion be true it illuminates his prayer for wisdom ; for a pupil, listening to these " words of the wise," would feel his need of the Holy Spirit to enable him to understand and obey them.

The Book opens with the double statement that fear of God (v. 7), and obedience to parents (v. 8), form the foundation of a just relationship to God and man.

The introduction to the Book contains the first six verses as far as the word " interpretation."

The remaining words of this verse form the heading of the first volume of the Book, and should be printed in copies of the Bible thus :—

" The words of the wise and their dark sayings."

These words of the wise form the first volume of the Book, that is from i. 7 to ix. 18.

" To know " " to perceive " " to receive " " to give " " to understand " (vs. 1-6) mean " in order to know " etc ; that is, these

416

Proverbs were taught to Solomon, when a prince, in order that he might become wise.

There are six words for " wisdom " in the Hebrew Bible. " Simple " (v. 4) means " unsuspecting. "

" Interpretation " (v. 6) means the point, or lesson of the Proverb.

" The fear of Jehovah " (v. 7) is the foundation of wisdom.

There are three Hebrew words for " fools " in this Book. · The Bible abounds in illustrations of verse 7.

" They " (v. 9), i.e., the " instruction " of the father, and the " law " of the mother, form the desirable chains which should encircle the neck of a child.

God in His love to man has ordained family and national government in order to man's happiness.

Verse 16 is quoted in Romans iii. There are many other quotations in the New Testament from this Book.

The argument of verses 17-19 is, that as a bird with its eyes open flies into a net spread for its destruction, so evil men rush with their eyes open into death. They destroy their own lives (v. 18) in secretly attacking the lives of others.

In Luke vii. 35, the Lord Jesus Christ says that Wisdom is justified of all her children. That is the Wisdom who here speaks to Solomon, and to all men (v. 20), and invites them to become her sons. She speaks in public (vs. 20 and 21) and pleads with the frivolous, the mockers, and the hostile (v. 22), promising them (v. 23) that if they would " turn " she would abundantly enrich them with her own spirit and with understanding. This enrichment is dependent upon the condition of conversion, and conversion is repugnant to man because it humbles him.

The terms " simple," " scorner," and " fool " (v. 22) mark progression. The man who treats wisdom with good-humoured and polite inattention presently becomes a mocker, and finally a hater.

So was it with the Pharisees and the rulers of the Synagogue. At the first they politely permitted the Lord to read the Scriptures in the Synagogue and to preach, but very soon they began to mock Him, and, finally, they hated and crucified Him (Luke xiv. 1. and xv. 2, xvi. 14, and Matthew xxvii. 20. They " watched," they " murmured," they " mocked," etc.).

Verse 26 does not mean that wisdom will actually deride her rejecters. It is the language of idiomatic argument. Such a mode of expression is quite common at the present day. The rejecters laughed and mocked at wisdom ; when therefore the calamities came upon them which wisdom predicted, their laughter and mocking turned upon themselves, and so wisdom may be justly said to deride their calamity. For example, a wise and kind and elderly physician gently points out to a young man that if he does not turn from his course of conduct he will lose his property and wreck his constitution. The young man listens politely, and smiles, and compliments the physician and says it will be all right. But at a second admonition he mocks, and a final one so enrages him that he strikes the wise counsellor a cruel blow. After some time, ruined in fortune and in health, he turns to the physician for help, but too late ; and then the laughter and the mockery is against himself.

A striking introversion appears in the Hebrew text of verses 26 and 27, and is made to appear in the R.V. :—

Calamity   (v. 26).
Fear   (v. 26).
Fear   (v. 27).
Calamity   (v. 27).

There are many instances in the Scriptures illustrative of verses 24-32, and of verse 33.

The " prosperity " of Belshazzar " destroyed " him, and Noah's obedience caused him to " dwell safely and to be quiet from fear of evil."

PROVERBS II.—The expression " My son," and the words " thee " and " thy " and " thou " are pointed to by some commentators in support of the distinction to be made between the Proverbs for Solomon and the Proverbs by Solomon.

In reading the Proverbs for Solomon it will be noticed that they are based upon the teaching of the Book of Deuteronomy, and that they especially recall its instructions for a king. In that Book, and in these Proverbs, he is warned against love of money ; counselled against fellowship with foreigners ; commanded not to multiply horses nor wives ; and enjoined to love and make a copy of the Law. All these injunctions Solomon disobeyed. It is true that in the Proverbs which were by

2D

him he extols Wisdom above horses and gold, and affirms the excellency of the Law; but it is noteworthy that he never refers to the folly of polygamy, and of marriage with foreign women, though this is specially and repeatedly denounced in the Proverbs taught to him. This entanglement with foreign women was the cause of his ruin.

Eternal life is to know God and Jesus Christ whom He sent (v. 5). This verse gives the result of the earnest quest for wisdom urged in the preceding verses.

"Hide" (v. 1) implies, lay up as in a treasury.

As verse 5 points to the beginning of the Christian life, so verses 6-11 pass on to describe its character. These verses should be read as in the R.V.

This wisdom which is from above saves from the power of sin (vs. 12-15); from the seduction of false doctrine (vs. 16-19); makes its pupil actively good (v. 20); and preserves him unto Eternal Life (v. 21).

"Froward" (vs. 12, 14, and 15) means "perverse"; i.e., "opposed to God." The word fitly describes those who throw off all moral restraints.

Religious teachers who lead people away from the Scriptures are likened in the Bible to women who are faithless to their husbands (v. 16).

"Guide" (v. 17) means "protector," "ruler" and "companion" as well as "guide." Such is the Bible conception of a husband.

The words "strange" and "stranger" (v. 16) are different in the Hebrew text. The first means "apostate"; the second, "foreign." They suggest that a faithless wife ceases to be of Israel and makes herself an alien. The heart that becomes faithless to the Lord is very soon among strangers. Not many days after the Prodigal desired the father's goods rather than the father's fellowship, he took his journey into a far country.

Verse 18 may read thus:—"She sinks men down into death—it is her house—and her paths lead to the Rephaim," i.e., the lost-spirits who are never to return to the earth (v. 19).

The "wicked" (v. 22) are the "lawless" of vs. 12-15, the "traitors" (v. 22, R.V.) are the followers of false doctrine (vs. 16-19).

PROVERBS III.—Wisdom enriches the heart (chapter iii.) as well as purifies the conduct (chapter ii.).

The heart is frequently mentioned in the Book of Proverbs rather than the head; for Divine wisdom appeals to the affections of the heart—human wisdom to the interests of the mind.

This third chapter teaches that life and wealth, in their full and worthful meaning, are not obtainable by natural sagacity but by subjection to heavenly wisdom.

This wisdom enriches (vs. 13-15) and disciplines (v. 11 and 12).

These last two verses cleave the context in sunder and appear out of place. But it is not so. Wisdom shews her love as much in rebuking as in enriching. Wealth without character, whether that wealth be material or intellectual, means moral disaster.

The fact that the verb "to add" (v. 2) is masculine in Hebrew, and the words "law" and "commandment" (v. 1) are feminine suggests that the teaching of the first two verses is, that wisdom is added as age advances and riches increase. In ordinary life men often grow silly as they grow old, and foolish as they become rich.

Pity and truth (v. 3) when bound upon the neck are visible to men, and when written upon the heart are seen by God. The joint result is good repute in the sight of God and man (v. 4), R.V.

"Direct" (v. 6) means "divide." That is, when two paths claim a decision heavenly wisdom will divide them, and instruct as to which should be chosen.

Few men obey verses 5 and 6. They address the heart that loves Jesus; that confides in Him; that refuses self-confidence; and that delights to own His government.

"Be not wise in thine own eyes" (v. 7) is quoted in Romans xi. 25, and xii. 16.

Spiritual health is dependent upon fellowship with God and separation from evil (vs. 7 and 8).

"Honour" (v. 9) signifies the giving of money. To honour parents means to support them.

It is natural to shrink from chastening, and to grow restless under chastisement (vs. 11 and 12); but Hebrews xii, Job xlii, and many other passages of the Scriptures, illustrate and prove the profit of Divine discipline.

"Peace" (vs. 2 and 17), implies "prosperity."

The happiness that wisdom carries into the heart is greater than all the treasures of earth (vs. 13-18). The words " findeth " and " getteth " (v. 13) are proper to a man eagerly searching for gold, and drawing it forth from the ground.

The excellency of wisdom is evidenced by the Creation, and by its maintenance (v. 19).

This is grace indeed that the wisdom that created, and maintains, the universe, and that distils the vapour from the sea and distributes it as dew upon the land, should be the same wisdom which delights to order, and prosper, the smallest details of a man's private and public life.

" Broken up " (v. 20) may read " divided," or " separated." The allusion is to the action of the sun in separating the vapour from the ocean and distributing it as dew upon the earth.

Health of soul and beauty of conduct distinguish wisdom's children (v. 22).

Wisdom guards from stumbling (v. 23), and delivers from fear (vs. 24 and 25), by keeping the soul in fellowship with God (v. 26).

Money due to a creditor should be promptly paid (vs. 27 and 28). This principle affects all claims of Christian sympathy, and of missionary responsibility.

" Securely " (v. 29) signifies " unsuspiciously."

There are many instances in the Holy Scriptures of a curse from God being in the house of the wicked ; and also many illustrations of a blessing from God being in the habitation of the righteous (v. 33).

Verse 34 is quoted in James iv. 6, and 1 Peter v. 5.

The wise shall " inherit " not " merit " glory, and fools, clothed with shame, shall " merit," and go into everlasting contempt (Daniel xii. 2).

PROVERBS IV.—In the first nine verses one of the " wise men " of chapter i. 6, passes on to the young Prince Solomon the counsels which he had from his father, and that counsel was to get heavenly wisdom at whatever cost ; and that that wisdom guards from evil (v. 6), promotes to honour (v. 8), and crowns with moral beauty (v. 9).

The wise man then, speaking from himself (v. 10), points the prince to the path of wisdom (v. 11), declares it to be a safe path and wide (v. 12), and a path of life and sure reward (v. 13).

Embracing wisdom (v. 8) brings to honour ; embracing folly, to dishonour (chapter v. 20).

Verse 11 may read : " I have directed thee into the way of wisdom " etc. ; and the next verse speaks of the pleasantness and smoothness of the way.

That verse should read : " When thou walkest," and " if thou runnest." To walk is obligatory ; to run is optional. Wisdom secures both. When walking, the way opens —it is not " straitened " ; if running, the feet are guarded from stumbling (Jude 24).

The path of folly (vs. 14 and 15) is contrasted with that of wisdom (vs. 11 and 12). These paths are again contrasted (vs. 16-19). The one is a path of light and goodness ; the other, a path of darkness and violence.

" Bread of wickedness " (v. 17) means wealth acquired by fraud, and " wine of violence " property seized by force.

As the tender and beauteous light of dawn grows to noon-day splendour so does the life that begins and continues in wisdom.

The repeated entreaties of verses 20-22 are necessitated by the double fact that submission to, or rejection of, wisdom is a matter of life or death, and that fallen man is most unwilling to listen to heavenly counsel.

The closing verses of the chapter concern the heart (v. 23), the mouth (v. 24), the eyes (v. 25), and the foot (conduct).

Because the heart (v. 23) is the citadel of the life it should be specially guarded. Above all guarding it must be guarded. A wise man guards his health and his property ; but, above all things, he should guard his heart as the seat of the will and the emotions.

Wisdom delivers from a loud, assertive, overbearing, and quarrelsome manner of speaking.

To make a straight furrow, to march straight, and to steer straight, the eye must be kept looking straight at a given point

The Christian looks off unto Jesus. This ensures a straight course through life. A crooked path is one of falsehood, double-dealing, cowardice, and defeat.

The second line of verse 26 should read :— " And all thy ways shall be established."

" Ponder " means to " prayerfully weigh " ; that is, not to hastily enter upon any course of conduct.

PROVERBS V. — The Foreign Woman is wisdom's enemy and rival. Wisdom's gifts are health, honour, and life. Folly's wages are disease, dishonour, and death.

Wisdom, the True Woman, pictures true religion; the Foreign Woman represents false religion.

The religion of the Bible has but few adherents ; the religion of man has countless followers.

In vivid language the chapter likens the ruin which the soul suffers from following false religious teaching to the physical ruin which follows upon debauchery.

Solomon's teacher here warns him vehemently against idolatry, polygamy, and marriage with an idolatress.

Solomon disobeyed these three injunctions.

The teaching of the Inspired Scriptures always has been, and is, unacceptable to man. False teaching (I John iv. 5), has been, and is, to him as the droppings of an honeycomb ; but the honey is poisoned and ends in death.

Wisdom and understanding are distinct the one from the other. Understanding is the discrimination which recognises wisdom. A child, not having understanding, cannot discriminate between a glass ball and a diamond. So to discern between the gaudy glass of folly and the simple beauty of wisdom, understanding is needed (v. I).

The translation of verse 6 is difficult. It, and the entire Book of Proverbs, should be read as in the Revised Version.

The verse may be contrasted with verse 21, R.V. and understood to state that the path of false teaching is rough, false, and dark.

"Sons" (v. 7, R.V.) may be the plural of majesty for "noble pupil" ; i.e., Solomon. This suggestion is supported by the immediate use of the singular "thy" and "thine" although the verbs "hear" and "depart not" are plural to agree with "sons."

"Mourn" (v. II) should read "groan." "Almost" (v. 14) should read "quickly." Departure from God's Word is quickly followed by enslavement to evil.

Israel was forbidden even to look at false worship, and wisdom (v. 8) warns against approaching idolatry's door. Obedience to this injunction will save Christian tourists from looking at the idolatrous worship of the Greek and Latin Churches.

To dally with false teaching, i.e., to come nigh her door, is dangerous. The Enemy of Truth knows that if he can introduce an idolatrous picture, or a false doctrine, into a family, he will quickly have the family in his net.

The physical suffering which follows upon vice (vs. 7-14) is a fearful picture of the wreckage wrought in the soul by false religion.

The leavening power of evil doctrine appears in the words "congregation" and "assembly" (v. 14).

Evil in a gambling-house is evil, but in a congregation it is doubly evil.

Thus was it with Solomon. He departed from the Law of God, and quickly set up idols on Mount Zion itself !

Perhaps in his old age he groaned, and repeated the words of verses 12-14.

The satisfying joys of wisdom's teaching are set out in verses 15-19.

For an Eastern farmer to turn on to the streets the precious water that should irrigate his fields, would be as insensate as it is for a man to turn from wisdom to folly.

Not only should wisdom be loved and embraced for her own sake, but she should also be cherished because her path is smoothed by a Hand that is Divine, and because an Eye that is all-seeing watches those who enter, or turn from, that path (v. 21).

"Take" (v. 22) better reads "entrap."

PROVERBS VI.—The worthfulness of wisdom is shown in this chapter upon a background of thoughtlessness (vs. 1-5), slothfulness (vs. 6-11), worthlessness (vs. 12-19), and faithlessness (vs. 20-35).

How much suffering would be escaped if the counsel of wisdom, in the first section of this chapter, were followed. The thoughtless folly of guaranteeing the debts of strangers has wrecked many a family.

"Friend" (v. I) means a neighbour who is a "stranger." Some Hebrew scholars understand this word to mean an "apostate."

The word "if" should be repeated before the two lines of verse 2.

In the East the ants gather their food in the summer.

The argument of verse II is that poverty comes as a robber, and want as a soldier. Such visitors leave a man penniless.

A "naughty person" should read a "worthless person" (v. 12), and a "froward mouth " should read a "lying mouth," and "frowardness" (v. 14) should read "deceit."

Easterns, the better to protect themselves from the detection which speech would expose them to, use signs in the Court of Justice with the eye, the hand, the mouth and the foot. Example, to raise a finger is a signal to a judge of an understood bribe. To raise two or more fingers intimates a doubling and trebling of the bribe.

This worthless and wicked man lies with his mouth, winks with his eyes, speaks with his feet, teaches with his fingers, deceives with his heart, plans injury to others, and sows discord in society.

These seven features are repeated in verses 16-19, as being abominable to God, viz: A proud look, a lying tongue, murderous hands, a deceiving heart, injury to others, and perjury and discord.

The justice of the judgment sure to fall upon such a man is declared in verse 15.

"Six things, yea seven" (v. 16) is a figure of speech arresting attention, and signifying that the list is not exhausted.

Things abominable to God are set out in chapters iii. 32, vi. 16, viii. 7, xi. 1, xii. 22, xv. 8, 9, and 26, xvi. 5, xvii. 15, 15, xx. 10, and xxviii. 9.

Declension appears in verses 17-19 thus: The eyes, the tongue, the hands, the heart, the feet, and the whole man.

Religious rather than moral evil is warned against in this fourth and last section of the chapter.

False religion is likened to a woman who is faithless to the marriage bond ; and the injury to the soul which results is compared to the ruin which comes upon society when the sanctity of marriage is violated.

The attraction of false religious teaching is illustrated in verses 24 and 25.

The "commandment" of the father and the "teaching" of the mother (v. 20) are: Above all getting get wisdom (ch. iv. vs. 5-9).

Wisdom governs the heart and adorns the neck (v. 21). It gives outward beauty of life, and inward wealth of principle.

The three Persons of the Trinity appear in verse 22. It reads : "When thou walkest she (wisdom) shall guide thee ; when thou sleepest she shall guard thee ; when thou wakest she shall talk with (teach) thee."

God the Father guides (Ps. xxxii. 8, Jer. iii. 4). God the Son guards (Ps. cxxi. 4).

God the Holy Spirit teaches (Luke xii. 12, John xiv. 26).

The following verse (23) repeats this triplet. The lamp guides, the light guards, and reproof teaches.

To hearken to these teachers is a path of life, and saves from the path of death to which the "strange woman" seduces.

As moral evil leads to poverty and death (v. 26), so spiritual evil causes spiritual poverty and death.

Such evil is to be feared as men fear fire (vs. 27-29).

Sin burns and enflames like fire ; but its flame is very vehement when violating the marriage vow.

The argument of verses 30-32 will appear clearer if the following translation be accepted: "Men do not esteem it a light matter if a thief steals to satisfy his hunger ; if he be found he shall restore sevenfold, etc., how much more he who committeth adultery, etc." If a thief be severely punished for a crime to which he is driven by necessity, how much more a man for an action prompted by passion. The injury done is irreparable, the dishonour and wound and shame (v. 33) abiding, and, the outraged husband (vs. 34 and 35) demands a vengeance that no compensation can satisfy.

This illustration vividly pictures the spiritual ruin which results from turning away from Christ to "another gospel" (Gal. i. 6).

From these four evils of thoughtlessness, slothfulness, worthlessness, and faithlessness, wisdom preserves.

PROVERBS VII.—The seducing power of false teaching is here illustrated by the figure of a treacherous wife, in the absence of her husband, alluring a youth to evil.

The words "stranger" (v. 5) and "strange" are dissimilar in the Hebrew text.

The one signifies a woman who is faithless to the marriage vow : the other a woman who is a foreigner.

The suggestion is that such a woman was never really a member of the Israel of God, for her conduct proved her to be an alien.

Such is false teaching in that which professes to be the House of God (2 Tim. ii. 20-22). She claims a legitimate position in the House, but she is, in truth, an alien, and was never anything else. She is the false woman of Zech. v. 7, and Matt. xiii. 33.

The " master of the house " (v. 19 and Luke xiii. 25) is the Messiah

" Wisdom " leads to life (v. 2) ; " falsehood," to death (v. 27).

The heart and the hand (v. 3) must both be governed by wisdom if the thoughts and the actions are to be pure from idolatry.

" Wisdom " is the only power that can save from idolatry (vs. 4 and 5).

Idolatry's victim is thoughtless (v. 7), " young " (v. 7), wanting in principle, i.e., " void of understanding " (v. 7), frequents " back streets " (v. 7 Heb.), saunters confidently and pompously (v. 8 Heb.), and prefers darkness to light (v. 9).

There is a perpetual disposition in the heart of all men to false teaching and idolatry, and they fall easy victims because they are in character as these verses describe. Men prefer the gloom of idolatry to the sunshine of truth. Hence the great temples of ancient and modern idolatry are dark, and the worshippers like the darkness.

False teaching is perpetually at work both in public and private to attract adherents, and she arrays herself attractively to that end (vs. 10-12). She is very sweet and kind (vs. 13 and 15), deeply religious (v. 14), and devoted to ceremonies and vows (v. 14). Her places of worship are temples of beauty (v. 16), of incense (v. 17), and of deep and sensuous emotion (v. 18). Everything in them appeals to, and excites, the emotions. The worship is sensual. There is a recognition of the existence of the Master of the house, and of the fact that He will return to the house, but He is far away, and there is, therefore, no danger of His presence disturbing the worship (vs. 19-20).

The path of false teaching, like the path of immorality, is downward (v. 25), and deadly (v. 22), and leads to eternal night (v. 27).

PROVERBS VIII.—If Folly—the False Woman—appeals to men (ch. vii.) so does Wisdom—the True Woman—appeal to them in this and the following chapter.

Chapters viii. and ix. may be thus analysed :

The Preacher (v. 1).
The Place of preaching (vs. 2 and 3).
The Persons preached to (vs. 4-6).
The subject of the preaching (vs. 7-9).
Its value (vs. 10 and 11).
The dignity of the Preacher (vs. 12-31).
The eternal issues involved (vs. 32-36).

The Preacher's Palace and Feast (ix. 1-3).
The Persons invited (vs. 4-6).
The Response (vs. 7-9).
The eternal issues involved (vs. 10-18).

Christ is the wisdom of God (1 Cor. i. 24), and in Him are hid all the treasures of Wisdom (Col. ii. 3). This Wisdom is active, it cries aloud, it invites men, it declares there is but one path to life, and that if it is not followed death is the consequence. That path is the fear of Jehovah, the abdication of self-will, the hatred of evil, and the detestation of arrogance and hypocrisy.

Amid the many wonders and glories of these two chapters shines forth the grace that places at the service of man the wisdom that made the heavens.

In this Book of the Proverbs there are three Hebrew words translated " fool." The word in verse 5 means dull, or stupid

Folly's mouth speaks falsehood and wickedness ; wisdom's mouth, truth and righteousness (vs. 7-9).

The value of Wisdom's teaching is above all wealth (vs. 10 and 11).

The " knowledge " of verse 12 (see R.V.) is intuitive knowledge, as distinguished from acquired knowledge.

To depart from evil may be the action of policy, but to hate evil is the effect of conversion (v. 13).

Not only kings and princes (vs. 15 and 16) but all persons without distinction of station (v. 17) may enjoy the love and sure guidance of wisdom.

Christ, as the wisdom of God, dwelt with God in eternity (vs. 22 and 30), and before the creation of man (vs. 23-29), and after the creation of man (v. 31). He was God's delight (v. 30), and men were His delight (v. 31).

He took creature form in order to create, (Col. i. 15) and human form in order to redeem. Rev. iv. hymns His glory in relation to the former, and Rev. v. His glory in relation to the latter. His is a double glory—a glory " from before the foundation of the world," and a glory " since the foundation of the world." The former glory has relation to the Church ; the latter, to Israel (Ephes. i. 4 and Rev. xiii. 8).

Verse 23, Before the earth.
Verse 24, Before the seas.
Verse 26, Before the earth.
Verse 27, When the heavens.
Verse 29, When the seas.
Verse 29, When the earth.

" Whoso findeth Me " (v. 35) ; " he that misseth Me " (v. 36 R.V. margin). See Heb. iv. 1.

PROVERBS IX.—Wisdom has her temple and sacrifices and sacred feasts (vs. 1 and 2) in contrast with Folly's idolatrous house.

This temple has seven pillars hewn out of living rock, indicating stability and abundance of room.

Wisdom sends forth her preachers (v. 3). They are young men and maidens. The Hebrew word means servants of both sexes.

Wisdom directs them where to preach (v. 3), and tells them what they are to say (vs. 4–6).

" She saith " (v. 4), that is, each one of the messengers says on behalf of wisdom : " Whoso is simple come eat of my bread," etc.

Wisdom's " wine " is mingled with spices, not with water (vs. 2 and 5 and Cant. viii. 2).

The preachers are told beforehand of the reception which they may expect (vs. 7–12). Scorners will mock them (vs. 7, 8, and 12), the violent will injure them (v. 7), but the " wise " will love them (v. 9).

The doctrine which the messengers are to preach (vs. 10–12) is : acceptance of a personal Saviour (v. 10) ; holiness of conduct (v. 10) ; usefulness of life (v. 11) ; that conversion is a personal matter which one cannot operate for another ; and that the rejecter of the Gospel message must personally suffer the consequence of his rejection (v. 12).

" Knowledge of the holy " (v. 10) means not only knowledge of the Holy One but also the spiritual ability to recognize and to practice holiness.

Length of physical life is not necessarily intended in verse 11, but rather fulness and usefulness of spiritual life.

Thus closes Wisdom's Fifth Call to the sons of men ; and Folly's Fifth Call immediately follows (vs. 13–18).

These Five Calls of Wisdom and Five Calls of Folly alternate in these first nine chapters of the Book. The First Call is Wisdom's ; the last, Folly's.

Wisdom's last cry is : " Forsake the foolish and live ! " (v. 6). It is a call to life, and life eternal. Folly's last cry is : " Stolen waters are sweet ! " (v. 17) ; but, as to her house, the dead are there, and her guests descend into the depths of hell.

Thus end " the words of the wise " to Solomon.

PROVERBS X.—The Second Book of the Proverbs consists of Proverbs by Solomon. They fall into two groups. The first : chapters x.–xv. the second : chapters xvi.–xix. 19.

The word " My son " no longer occurs, but instead are found the words " he," " him," " they."

These Proverbs are intended for all.

The wise and the self-willed are contrasted. In the first six chapters the contrast is chiefly antithetic, and concerns their lots in life in relation to their fellow-men.

The remaining three chapters are chiefly synthetic and compare the character and action of the wise and self-willed in relation to God.

Illustrations of each one of these Proverbs will be found in the Scriptures.

All the Proverbs in these nine chapters contain two lines apiece except xix. 7, which contains three lines.

The second line of verse 3 better reads : " He repels the greedy desires of the self-willed."

The second line of verse six should read : " The mouth of the lawless hideth violence."

The argument of this Proverb is that a righteous person is a fount of blessing to society, but an unrighteous person a source of injury, even though he tries to hide the fact with honeyed words

So important for society is this double fact that the Holy Spirit repeats it in verse 11.

The wise in heart accept, and submit to, Divine rules of conduct, but the wordy opponent of such rules falls suddenly and eternally (v. 8).

The connection between verses 8 and 10, is that, in the former, the prating fool is contrasted with the wise in heart ; in the latter, he is associated with the corrupter of justice, or the defamer of character.

Verse 8 : The Scientist and Divine Law— Effect, corruption.

Verse 10 : The Trader and human law— Effect, oppression.

Both are " prating fools ", one with his tongue, the other with his eye. The one corrupts divine law ; the other, human law.

" To wink with the eye " is in the East a method of signalling a bribe to a judge, or, in general society, of injuring the character of an acquaintance.

" Known " (v. 9) signifies to be found out and punished.

Hatred provokes litigation, but love has the opposite effect by its forgiveness of injuries (v. 13).

A man of principle is amenable to wisdom, but a rod is the best teacher for people void of principle (v. 13).

Wise men store up knowledge, and expand it for the advantage of society; but the teaching of fools immediately injures the public (v. 14).

Rich men are destroyed by their wealth, and poor men by their poverty (v. 15); the former, because they trust it, the latter, because they need it.

True wealth is labour, for it tends to life; but the produce of wrong-doing is in its nature evil (v. 16). A poor, but honest, shoemaker is, in relation to society, a richer man than the wealthy distiller of intoxicating drink. The one benefits, the other injures society!

Heeding correction leads to the way of life, but refusing reproof causes to err from it (v. 17).

He who hides hatred with falsehood and utters slanders is a fool, for he will certainly be found out.

The Apostle Peter was the most talkative of the Twelve, and he erred most deeply with his tongue (v. 19).

Fools not only fail to benefit many, as do the righteous, but they destroy themselves (v. 21).

Verse 22 should read as in the R.V. margin. Injuring others is the fool's pastime; wisdom is the pastime of the man of understanding (v. 23).

The whirlwind sweeps away the wicked but not the righteous; for he stands upon an everlasting foundation (v. 25). Compare Matt. vii. 24-27.

Verse 27 does not necessarily mean a long or a short life, but rather a full, in contrast to an empty one; or a happy, in contrast to an afflicted life. Compare Psalm cii. 23.

" Hope " (v. 28) in the Hebrew text means an unlikely hope, whilst " expectation " means a confident hope. The confident hope of the self-willed issues in disappointment; the unlikely hope of the child of wisdom comes to pass.

" The way of Jehovah " (v. 29), i.e., the government and providence of God, is strength to the upright, but destruction to the workers of evil.

" The mouth of the righteous buddeth with wisdom " (v. 31) as with a healthy plant, whilst that which the perverse tongue germinates will be cut down as a poisonous plant.

" The lips of the righteous know " (v. 32), i.e., recognize and utter, what is acceptable; the mouth of the self-willed poureth out all kinds of deceit and boasting.

PROVERBS XI.—The tender love of God for men, and especially for the poor, appears in these Proverbs, for if they were obeyed, injustice, dishonesty, fraud, and cruelty would cease to exist.

Four times is it stated that fraud in business is abominable in God's sight (v. 1, xvi. 11 and xx. 10 and 23). Thus is God's sympathy for the poor emphasized.

Miriam (Numbers xii. 10), Uzziah (2 Chron. xxvi. 16-21), and Nebuchadnezzar (Dan. iv. 30), illustrate the first line of verse 2, and Joseph, David, and Daniel, the second line.

" The Day of Wrath " (v. 4) is the day of God's wrath. From death, which is the judgment of that wrath, Righteousness, i.e., Christ (John xvi. 10) delivers. Riches, i.e., sacerdotal ceremonies and good works, are profitless (Mark x. 24).

" Perfect " (v. 5) means " blameless."

Daniel and his wicked accusers illustrate verse 8. Mordecai and Haman illustrate verse 10.

" Despiseth " (v. 12) means " reproacheth," and " wisdom" is " heart " in the Hebrew text. An unsympathetic man reproaches his neighbour, but a sympathetic man remains silent.

" Stranger " (v. 5) signifies " one who has forsaken truth." Such is man. Christ in His love for him became his surety: and, as a consequence, was sore broken at Calvary.

Verse 18 should read as in the R.V.

" Upright men " (v. 30) found industries that provide a living profitable to the workers and advantageous to the state. Self-seeking men act otherwise. A righteous man founds a linen factory; an unrighteous man, a distillery. The factory is a way of life, the distillery a way of death

The statements of verse 31 were operative under the First Covenant, and their operation will resume under the coming Reign of Righteousness. Because the King is now in rejection this principle is now in suspense; God, however, reserves liberty of action to Himself to apply it how and when He will.

Wise and foolish farmers illustrate verse 24. To scatter little seed ensures a poor harvest.

1 Kings xvii. 10 and 2 Kings iv. 8 accord with verse 25. "Good" and "mischief" (v. 27) i.e., the good or the injury of others. "Riches" (v. 28), i.e., sacramental and moral works of merit. Absalom illustrates verse 29.

PROVERBS XII.—The righteous man is comparable to a fruit-tree (vs. 3 and 12). He is firmly rooted, which is an advantage to himself ; and he is richly fruited, which is an advantage to others.

Verse 5 reads : " The plans of the righteous are honesty, but the plans of the wicked are deceit."

Upright men benefit society, but evil men destroy a nation (v. 6) ; or, the religious teaching of the self-willed is soul-destroying, but that of Christian men saves from eternal death.

"The purposes of the wicked" (v. 5), " the words of the wicked " (v. 6).

" He that is of a perverse heart " (v. 8) denotes an unprincipled man.

" Better to be little noticed and have a servant " etc., (v. 9). To have a servant implies honest diligence. For example, a small farmer has a servant.

A Christian sets a higher value upon the life of an animal than the wicked set upon the life of a man (v. 10).

" The net of evil men " (v. 12), denotes what is caught in it. Many envy the high dividends which merciless merchants draw from the Congo and the Amazon.

The language of evil men entraps them, but that of just men saves them from threatening trouble (v. 13).

A prudent man, when shamefully insulted, covers, i.e., disregards the insult ; but a fool immediately blazes up with anger (v. 16).

Wise words console ; bitter words stab like a sword (v. 18).

Suffering results from the plannings of deceit, but joy .from the counsellings of peace (v. 20).

" Evil " (v. 21) denotes " nothing vain." Nothing happens to the righteous by accident, or without Divine permission and purpose.

A modest man hides rather than displays his learning, but the voluble assurances of the fool proclaim his folly. Profound students of the Scriptures are usually thoughtful and silent men, but the shallow enemies of the Sacred Book are noisy and verbose (v. 23).

" Tribute " (v. 24) denotes " task-work." " More excellent than " (v. 26) implies " a good example to." The argument of the Proverb is : that a good man helps his neighbour morally whilst a bad man injures him. The one guides the neighbour aright : the other leads him astray.

The slothful does not profit by his opportunities (v. 27), but that which a diligent man gathers is true wealth.·

PROVERBS XIII.—A wise son accepts a father's correction, but a scornful son refuses to listen to his rebukes.

Gentle language " eats," i.e., obtains good, and does good as the wholesome and refreshing fruit of a tree. Treacherous language obtains violence.

Had the Apostle Paul observed verse 3, he would not have damaged his testimony, and impeded the progress of the Gospel (Acts xxiii. 1-10).

Verse 6 may read : " Righteousness, i.e., he who is right with God, guardeth the uprightness of the way," that is, the faith once for all delivered to the saints (Jude 3), " but lawlessness subverteth the sin-offering " ; that is, he who breaks away from the Bible denies the doctrine of the Atonement.

A pretence of wealth is as untruthful as a pretence of poverty (v. 7), and both these lies injure society.

A translation of verse 8 is :—·· He that heareth not rebuke becomes poor."

The R.V. translation suggests that wealth exposes a man to danger, but that poverty is a safeguard.

" Well-advised " (v. 10) denotes modest. Modesty marks the wise man ; contention the proud man.

" Vanity " (v. 11) is opposed to labour. Wealth gathered by labour benefits society, but wealth obtained by gambling is a vanity ; i.e., it is useless to the well-being of the community.

The walk to Emmaus illustrates verse 12. The heart was sick, i.e., faith was enfeebled, but when the Desire of all Nations came, the two disciples found Him to be a " Tree of Life " to their sad hearts.

Jehoiakim despised the Word (v. 13) and was destroyed (Jeremiah xxxvi. and xxii. 18 and 19) ; Josiah, his father, feared the commandment and was rewarded (2 Chron, xxxiv. 37).

Zedekiah rejecting the wise counsel of Jeremiah illustrates v. 14 (Jeremiah xxxviii. and xxxix).

Cain and Abel illustrate v. 15 (Heb. xi. 4). King Ahasuerus illustrates verse 16 (Esther iii. 10).

To obtain what is really desirable demands self-denial. But it is most distasteful to a fool to obtain anything worthful by the surrender of worthless and injurious pleasures (v. 19).

Those who joined the fellowship of the Apostles became wise, but the associates of the Pharisees perished (v. 20).

" An inheritance " (v. 22) does not necessarily mean money, but rather reputation. It is a treasured inheritance to be the grandchild of David Livingstone.

The injustice (v. 23, R.V.) that removes the small farmer in order to make room for large farms, or cattle ranches, or game-preserves, ultimately destroys the food reserves of a nation. Dutch land-owners, having dispossessed the tillers of the soil, and finding the result disastrous, are now seeking to restore them.

Hatred spares the rod ; love uses it (v. 24). God, because He is love, punishes sinners. If a child is not disciplined " betimes," i.e., before three years of age, it will never be disciplined.

PROVERBS XIV.—The force of the verbs in verse 1, is that the wise woman has builded and continues to build, her house, but that the foolish woman is pulling down, and will pull down, her house.

The foolish woman dissipates the wealth of her home by worthless entertainments ; the wise woman increaseth the wealth of her home by wise and careful housekeeping.

Right conduct results from fearing God, wrong conduct from despising Him (v. 2).

The words of a fool's mouth furnish a rod for his back ; the words of wise men become a shield to them (v. 3).

Cleaning out cattle-pens is not attractive work, but it is profitable. A clean crib and cleanness of teeth, i.e., hunger, are associates (v. 4).

An habitual liar cannot give true evidence, but an habitually truthful man gives credible testimony (v. 5).

The scornful Pharisee professed to seek wisdom and found nothing ; to the understanding Ethiopian knowledge was easy (Acts viii.). Jesus is Wisdom. He was a stumbling-stone to the Pharisee, but a stepping-stone to the Ethiopian (v. 6).

Having failed to win the worldling, the ritualist, or the Unitarian, the Christian is to withdraw from them. This command is rarely obeyed (v. 7). The Lord withdrew into silence from the High Priest and from Pilate.

Fools mock the guilt-offering, i.e., the atonement ; but among the righteous it is prized (v. 9).

A stranger, i.e., a stranger to God, can neither understand the bitterness of a sin-burdened conscience nor the joy of a forgiven heart (v. 10).

The citizen of this world has his house, but the citizen of heaven has his tent. It will flourish, but the house will perish (v. 11).

Salvation by sacraments and personal merit is, to most men, an acceptable way to eternal life ; but in reality it leads to death (v. 12).

False religion may have a joyful appearance, but it leaves the heart sorrowful and heavy (v. 13).

The backslider is filled—not satisfied—with that which he himself provides for himself ; but he who walks with God is satisfied " away from himself " ; i.e., with what is provided for him by God (v. 14).

The credulous believe everything ; but the prudent look well ahead before acting (v. 15).

Wise men draw back from impending danger, but fools rush on confidently and suffer loss (v. 16).

A hot-tempered man acts foolishly, but a cool-tempered intriguer is hated (v. 17).

Verse 24 should be read as in the R.V.

A preacher of the Gospel is a true witness, and helps men ; but a preacher of " modern thought " propagates falsehood (v. 25).

To escape eternal death and be united to life there is one sure and only way, it is to fear Jehovah ; that is, to love and serve and follow the Lord Jesus (v. 27).

A large population is true political economy (v. 28). The King of kings and Prince of Life will have a multitude of subjects that no man can number.

He that is hasty of spirit is carried away

by folly (v. 29). This is perhaps what the Hebrew text means.

"A tranquil heart" (v. 30) promotes spiritual and physical health. A heart agitated by envy and jealousy has the opposite effect.

Belshazzar illustrates the first line of verse 32, and the Apostle Paul the second line.

Wisdom rests in the heart of the wise man for use when crises arise. It only needs a crisis to manifest the folly of a fool.

PROVERBS XV.—"One grievous word stirs up anger" (v. 1, R.V.). 2 Chron. x. 13-16, 1 Sam. xx, 30-34, and Acts xv. 39 illustrate this statement. Lev. x. 16-20, Joshua xxii. 15-34, Judges viii. 1-3, and 1 Sam. xxv. 25, record the potency of a soft answer.

Wise men commend knowledge by their speech; the verbosity of fools disgusts.

Gentle language soothes and pacifies, but ill-natured words wound the spirit.

"Much treasure" (v. 6) i.e., the unsearchable riches of Christ.

The worship of the self-willed (v. 8), and the way, i.e., the conduct, of the self-willed (v. 9) are both abominable. Such was Cain's worship and conduct. Abel illustrates the prayer of the upright, and his way of righteousness (vs. 8 and 9).

Verse 10 should read as in the R.V.

The unseen world (v. 11) is all visible to God, how much more then the hearts of men !

The wise grow wiser; the fools more foolish (v. 14).

Christ is a substitute for every good thing; but nothing is a substitute for Him (v. 16).

The difficulties of the slothful arise from a want of energy, but the way of the righteous is "a raised road" i.e., the king's highway (v. 19).

"Understanding" is joy to the upright, but "folly" is joy to the fool (v. 21).

Plans will prove disappointing if the opinion of the wise and good is unsought (v. 22).

Good advice blesses the giver and the receiver (v. 23).

To the wise the way of life goes upward in order that he may depart from the way of death which goes downward (v. 24).

The "border" (v. 25), i.e., the boundary of the widow's little farm is here contrasted with the house of the proud.

The pure speak "pleasant words" (v. 26); i.e., pleasant to God.

"Avarice" troubles the miser and his family (v. 27); but he that refuseth bribes shall have a life free from care.

Caution is the fruit of wisdom; rashness, of folly (v. 28).

The light and glad tidings of the Gospel rejoice the heart and make fat the bones (v. 30).

The man that hearkens to the Gospel message shall be numbered among the wise (v. 31). That message is a "reproof," tending towards, and leading to, Life Eternal.

He that refuseth such reproof sets the lowest value on his own soul; but he that hearkens to it has an understanding heart (v. 32).

The doctrine of the Gospel is submission to Jesus Christ (v. 33). This is true humility, and it will be crowned with imperishable honour.

PROVERBS XVI.—As the Proverbs of chapters x.-xv. affect man's relationships with his fellow men, so the Proverbs of chapters xvi.-xix. concern man's relationship to God.

Man proposes but God disposes, is the doctrine of verse 1.

A man's actions may appear right to his own conscience, but God sees and condemns the emotions which prompt the actions (v. 2). Conscience is a blind guide unless enlightened by the Word of God.

When God is permitted to plan, then are the plans established (v. 3).

"Evil" (v. 4) means suffering. God has justly linked sin and suffering together.

"Purged" (v. 6) denotes "covered" or "atoned for." Mercy and truth atoned for iniquity at Calvary; and the moral effect of this great fact and doctrine is to cause men to fear God and depart from evil (v. 6).

There are many illustrations in the Scriptures of verse 9.

The Divine Judgment on Herod Agrippa (Acts xii. 21-23), illustrates verse 18.

"He that giveth heed unto the Word (of God) shall find good; and whoso trusteth in Jehovah oh how happy is he !" (v. 20).

Verse 26 should read as in the R.V.

The labouring man (v. 26) contrasts with the worthless man (v. 27), the froward man (v. 28), and the man of violence (vs. 29, 30).

A man shuts his eyes the better to plan, and compresses his lips the better to execute

(v. 30). The one action expresses purpose ; the other, determination.

An old man living a life of vice excites a special horror and repulsion (v. 31).

Men may cast lots as they will, and plan and scheme as they choose, but God disposes as He wills (v. 33).

PROVERBS XVII.—A mischief-maker believes a liar, and a liar believes a mischief-maker (v. 4).

The translation of verse 8 is not clear. The proverb may mean that the wise granting of gifts procures success in all directions. Or it may teach that the acceptance of a bribe subjects the receiver to the influence of bribes. In this case the bribe is as a precious stone ; it " prospers," i.e., it " sparkles," however turned ; and hence its owner loves to look at it and keep it.

The action of a mischief-maker (v. 11) upsets families and communities. He is less amenable to reason than a wild animal (v. 12), and the despatch of a cruel messenger against him is justifiable in the interests of society.

True wisdom nips contention in the bud so as to prevent it developing into quarrelling (v. 14).

The folly of entering into a money bond is all the greater if it is done in the presence of a remonstrating friend (v. 18).

To " exalt the gate " is to proclaim one's wealth (v. 19). In the East the door of a poor man's house is low, that of a rich man's high. Hence 2 Kings xxv. 9.

Easterns carry their money in a fold of the robe covering the breast (v. 23). A rich man in court by placing his hand in his bosom, can thus signal a bribe to a judge.

Wisdom is the visible goal of a man of understanding, but the eyes of a fool have nothing definite before them.

Lev. x. 3, Num. xvi. 4, 1 Sam. viii. 6, 1 Pet. ii. 23, illustrate verse 27. An " excellent spirit " denotes a cool and controlled will.

PROVERBS XVIII.—The recluse pleases himself and quarrels with the infinite wisdom which has designed communal christian life (v. 1).

A fool in conversation gives vent to, and reveals, the folly that is in him (v. 2).

Illustrations of all these Proverbs may be found in the Scriptures.

Verse 8 should read as in the R.V. The second line may be freely translated : " And they are greedily devoured."

Verses 10 and 11 form a contrast. The rich man's wealth is contrasted with the Name of Jehovah ; the one is a strong city, the other a strong tower ; the one is an high wall, the other a high place. But verse 10 is fact and verse 11 fiction. The histories of Asa and Hezekiah, of Job and of the Apostles, illustrate these two verses.

Goliath and Jezebel illustrate verse 12, and David, Ahasuerus, and Darius provide illustrations of verse 13.

The argument of verse 14 appears to be that a brave spirit faces difficulties, but a broken spirit can brave nothing.

Let a profession be never so crowded yet will talent make its way to the front (v. 16).

" Offended " (verse 19) should read " injured."

If the " fruit of the mouth " and the " increase of the lips " be heavenly then is there inward content ; if not, there is inward desolation (v. 20).

" It " (verse 21) means the power of the tongue. It can kill, as in the instance of the ten spies, and it can make alive, as in the preaching of the Twelve Apostles.

The word " good " appears before " wife " in some ancient Hebrew Texts. It is of course implied in the Received Text.

Verse 24 is perhaps better translated thus : " Human friends break in pieces, i.e., fail, but there is a lover who cleaveth closer than a brother."

Wise speech is like an inexhaustible spring of beneficent waters (v. 4), but hasty language causes contention and destruction (vs. 6 and 7).

PROVERBS XIX. 1-19.—These verses close the Proverbs by Solomon which form the Second Section of the Book of Proverbs.

The word " rich " should be supplied in the second line of the first verse. The statement is : that poverty with integrity is better than wealth with dishonesty.

Ignorance of moral principle, and a hasting to be rich, lead to sin (v. 2). Illustrations of this truth may be found in the Scriptures.

Self-will subverts men from a straight course ; and they are angry with God when suffering the consequence of their own action (v. 3). Israel's history is full of instances of this truth.

Verse 9 is not a needless repetition of

verse 5. The latter verse defines the punishment announced in the former; and the repetition emphasizes God's just anger against falsehood and His love for humanity, and especially for the oppressed.

The "wisdom" and "understanding" of verse 8, mean heavenly knowledge.

"Delight" (v. 10) means "luxury." As incapable as a fool is of rightly using wealth, yet more incapable is a servant of exercising government.

A forgiving spirit marks the true man of God under both the First and Second Covenants (v. 11).

Opposition to lawful government ensures just suffering, but obedience secures prosperity (v. 12).

It is in the power of man to amass and bequeath wealth, but only God can create and bestow a "prudent wife" (v. 14).

Indolence in the study of the Scriptures and in prayer causes spiritual poverty (v. 15).

He that cherishes "the commandment," i.e., the Bible, safeguards his life; but indifference to Divine teaching ("His ways") causes spiritual death.

Scholars, because of imperfect knowledge, find a difficulty in translating verse 18. It may mean that if a child be disciplined when young he will be saved from moral ruin; or it may mean that a parent, when punishing a child, must not angrily strike it so as to cause death.

Verse 19 may be thus understood: A bad-tempered man incurs fines, and if you pay them for him you must do so continually, i.e., kindness is lost on ill-natured people.

PROVERBS XIX. 20-27.—The Third

Division of the Book of the Proverbs begins here and closes at the last verse of the twenty-fourth chapter. They are Proverbs for Solomon. This is shewn by the use of the Second Person "Thou" "Thee," "Thy, etc., and by the appellation "My son."

These eight verses are a call to Solomon to hear and obey the Proverbs which follow. He failed "to hear" them, and became a horse-dealer, a world-server and an idolater.

Had Solomon listened to the counsel and instruction of wisdom he would never have become an idolater in his old age.

Plans born of self-will fail, but those received from God stand (v. 21).

A little kindness received from a poor man is better than the false promises of a rich liar.

To love and serve the Lord Jesus Christ leads to an endless life of abiding bliss; not to do so, results in everlasting misery (v. 23).

"Visited with evil" means "punished with affliction" (v. 23).

Verse 24 should read as in the R.V. Such slothfulness is true of those who will "put their hand into the dish," i.e., read a chapter of the Bible, but they will not carry the food to their lips, that is, they are too indolent to meditate on what they have read.

The simple, and much more the wise, profit by the judgment of evil (v. 25).

Had Solomon listened to wisdom he never would have hearkened to his wives, and so have become a rebel to the Word of God (v. 27).

PROVERBS XIX. 28 — XX. 30. — These

Proverbs to the end of chapter xxiv., instruct all men, but are specially applicable to a prince. This latter fact will be recognized if the reader connects each Proverb with a king who, at the same time, is the judge of his people. Thus verse 28 guards a king against accepting false evidence, and verse 29 instructs him to exercise just severity. The first two verses of chapter xx. warn him against the excitement of strong drink, and point out that the anger of a monarch should be a just anger and not one occasioned by wine.

The suitability of all these Proverbs for the guidance of a prince will be recognised if they are in this manner understood as addressed to Solomon.

Boasters can readily be found on every side, but trustworthy men must be sought for (v. 6).

A righteous king judges evil (v. 8), disclaims personal moral perfection (v. 9), and in fellowship with God, protects the poor against the injustice of fraudulent traders (v. 10).

The repetition of verses 10 and 23 in the Book of Proverbs emphasises the anger of God against injustice, and His care and compassion for the oppressed and the poor.

If the actions of a child reveal his character how much more is this true of a prince; hence he should seek from God "the hearing ear" and "the seeing eye."

Wealth is a necessity for a monarch, but wisdom is his greatest need (v. 15).

A Christian prince should shew no mercy to idolatry (v. 16).

" Bread of deceit " (v. 17) means wealth gotten by falsehood.

Princes should not make war through caprice (v. 18) ; and wealth hastily gotten does not always bring happiness (v. 21).

No one whether prince or peasant should recompense injury. Vengeance belongeth unto God (v. 22).

Verse 25 should read as in the R.V. Money should never be promised without careful inquiry as to the worthfulness of its proposed objective.

As in verse 8 so in verse 26, a wise monarch strikes at all who injure his subjects.

" The inward parts of the belly " (vs. 27 and 30) mean the hidden thoughts of the heart. Such thoughts are corrected and purified by wise discipline (v. 30, R.V.).

" Stripes that wound " i.e., effective discipline (v. 30, R.V.).

PROVERBS XXI.—In this first verse Solomon was instructed that his will should be as easily directed by God as the waters which irrigate a garden are controlled by the husbandman's foot.

In the East the husbandman opens or closes a water-channel by placing, or displacing, a sod with his foot.

Sin (verse 4) is a special word in the Hebrew text meaning " sin-offering." Connecting this verse with the preceding one, the argument may be that just as upright conduct is more acceptable to God than great donations to religion, so haughtiness, pride, and prosperity are more acceptable to the worldling than a crucified Saviour.

" Robbery " (v. 7) may read " rapacity " ; and " to do judgment " means " to act justly."

Verse 8 should read as in the R.V. Margin. The straightness of the one man is contrasted with the crookedness of the other.

The roofs of Eastern houses are flat, and in one corner there usually is a little chamber (v. 9).

The manufacturer and seller of intoxicating drink " desires evil," that is " plans injury " to his fellowmen ; and in his desire to make money destroys even his neighbour, and has no compassion on those nearest him (v. 10).

The punishment of evil instructs the ignorant, but the intelligent can be taught by knowledge (v. 11).

Upright men act justly under all circumstances (v. 15), and refuse to shield themselves from public or private hostility by secret bribes (v. 14).

Wisdom is preferable to physical force (v. 22).

He who treats his fellow-men with pride, contempt, and violence merits an opprobrious name (v. 24).

Hypocrisy is more hateful to God than infidelity (v. 27). " Mind " in this verse means " purpose." A professional man, or a trader, who attends public worship in order to get business, is guilty of a sacrifice which is an abomination to God.

The testimony of a truthful witness stands, but that of an untruthful one perishes (v. 28).

Military preparations do not secure victory. It lies in God's disposition and purpose.

The first verse of the chapter may be read using the future tense. Thus read it predicted that the heart of Israel's king, the Messiah, should be as truly subject to Jehovah as the irrigating waters are to the husbandman. As the Son of Man in His First Advent, God turned His heart whithersoever He would. So will it be in His Second Advent when He comes as King to reign.

The sense of verse 5 is : That the diligent prosper, but that every one who hastens to get rich becomes poor either financially or morally, or both.

PROVERBS XXII. 1-16.—Character is more to be coveted than wealth (v. 1).

The rich and the poor are equal before God. Thus should they be before a king (v. 2).

The prudent provide for sickness and old age. The thoughtless fail to do so, and suffer for it (v. 3, R.V.).

Verse 4 should read : The reward of humility, that is, of the fear of Jehovah, is riches, honour, and life eternal. These riches are contrasted with those of verse 1. True wealth, honour, and eternal prosperity result from loving and serving Jesus.

The perverse (v. 5), that is, those who do not love and serve Him, are rewarded with thorns and snares. Those who watch and pray escape the companionship of such men ; and, consequently, escape their miseries.

Verse 6 may read : " Hedge in a child in the way in which he ought to go " etc., just as cattle are hedged in.

As a rule wealth is hostile to moral independence (v. 7).

Haman illustrates verse 8.

Most people go through life desiring to be "getters" and are, consequently, discontented. The true christian goes through life as a giver, and is, consequently, happy (v. 9).

Ishmael illustrates verse 10.

There is never any friction between just men and just governments (v. 11).

God prospers truth but overthrows false teaching (v. 12).

Any foolish excuse is good enough for indolence.

False religions are sure to capture those who turn away from God and the Bible (v. 14).

By natural birth man is a fool, but discipline can save him from his folly (v. 15).

PROVERBS XXII. 17-29.—Verses 17-21 contain the second call of the Third Book of the Proverbs.

The call is addressed to Solomon and is uttered by Wisdom.

"Wise" (v. 17) is plural, but the word "my" points to it as being "the plural of excellence," and it signifies that the "knowledge," i.e., the teaching of wisdom, is above all human excellence.

That teaching refreshes the heart and makes skilful the lip, so that the words of Wisdom's pupil are like apples of gold in baskets of silver (v. 18).

Verse 19 may read: "These teachings I have made known to thee this day, even to thee, O Solomon, in order that thy confidence may come to be in Jehovah."

The "excellent things" (v. 20) written for Solomon ("for thee") with perfect counsel and knowledge, and in the certainty of truth (v. 21), are set out in the Proverbs which precede and follow; and they were designed to equip him to respond with words of truth to those who inquired of him.

The Queen of Sheba illustrates this.

In the five injunctions that follow, Solomon was urged not to exploit the poor (v. 22); not to company with men of hasty and overbearing temper (v. 24); not to engage in financial risks (v. 26); not to covet land to the injury of others (v. 28); but to work diligently at an honest business.

"Landmark" (v. 28) means the boundary-stone which marked the mereing of a farm.

PROVERBS XXIII. 1-18. — A prince is counselled when dining with a king (vs. 1-3), or with a millionaire (vs. 6-8), to be on his guard; for the one will seek to deceive

him (v. 3), and the other to rob him (v. 8).

"What" (v. 1) should read "who."

Verse 2 should read: "For thou wilt put a knife to thy throat" etc., i.e., ruin thyself.

Cunning men conceal their wicked plans under a covering of kind words and profuse hospitality (vs. 6 and 7); but in the end their generosity sickens and their words impoverish (v. 8).

2 Chron. xxv. 14-16, illustrates verse 9. Possibly it was in obedience to this Proverb that the true Solomon refused to speak to Herod. He also, when sitting at meat with rulers and rich men, observed the counsel of verses 1-3, and 6-8.

Verse 10 is not a meaningless repetition of chapter xxii. 28. The one refers to a foolish reversal of a parent's wise arrangement of property; the other to an unjust seizure of that which belongs to the defenceless.

Verse 11 should read: "For their Redeemer—i.e., their Kinsman—is strong, and He shall plead their cause against thee."

How touching is the grace which claims kinship with the poor, the widow, and the fatherless; and intervenes on their behalf. Such is not the action of the great men of society.

Rather than set the heart upon material wealth (v. 10), it is urged (v. 12) to covet moral wealth; and not only for oneself, but for one's children (vs. 13 and 14).

Most parents are more careful to enrich their children with gold and silver than with character and education.

The tenderness of the appeal of verses 15 and 16 affects every true heart.

The lips speak "right things" (v. 16) when the heart is "wise" (v. 15).

"An end" (v. 18) means an hereafter—an hereafter of misery for sinners (v. 17), but of recompense for those who love and follow Christ. Their "expectation" shall not be "cut off," that is, they shall not be put to shame (Rom. x. 11).

PROVERBS XXIII. 19-35.—Verses 19-25 form Wisdom's third call to Solomon in this Division of the Book of Proverbs.

The slaves of appetite (v. 20) are here contrasted with wise and honoured parents (v. 22); and the poverty and misery (v. 21) connected with the one, are set over against the moral wealth (v. 23) and joy (v. 24) of the other.

Verse 25 should read as in the R.V.

In the injunctions which now follow, man's religion is likened to a false woman (vs. 27 and 28), and worldly pleasure to a wine-cup (vs. 29-35).

" Observe " (v. 26) should read " sparkle with delight."

False religion and intoxicating pleasure make the eye to sparkle, but not with pure joy. It only lights up the eye when the " heart " (v. 26) is governed by wisdom, i.e., by Christ the Wisdom of God.

" Prey " and " transgressors " (v. 28) should read " robber " and " traitor."

Just as a " strange woman " robs men of life and makes them traitors to their wives, so False Religion makes men traitors to truth and robs them of Eternal Life. Whoso falls into her " deep ditch " and " narrow pit " (v. 27) finds it well nigh impossible to climb out.

Verse 31, vividly pictures fermentation, verse 32 its after effects, verse 33, the horrors of delirium tremens, and verses 34 and 35 the stupidity, insensibility, and brutality which it causes.

" Strange women " (v. 33) should read " strange things " i.e., snakes and serpents ; and " perverse things " (v. 33), blasphemous and wicked language. Such accompany delirium tremens.

If the injunction of verse 20 not to keep company with wine-bibbers be disregarded the result will be the degradation and brutality of verses 31-35 ; for companionship leads to imitation, and what a man's friends are he himself will be.

PROVERBS XXIV. 1-22.—Verse 1 may read : " Do not be excited because of the prosperity of evil men, neither desire to share it with them, for their heart " etc.

The enduring prosperity of verses 3 and 4, procured by heavenly wisdom, is contrasted with the temporary prosperity of verses 1 and 2, based on earthly scheming.

Seven statements are here made :

The house is builded.
It is established.
It is enriched.
The riches are precious.
They are pleasant.
They are abundant (" filled ").
They are infinite (" all ").

" *The* multitude of counsellors " (v. 6,

R.V.), is the plural of excellence meaning wisdom. It makes a man morally strong with increasing strength (v. 5) ; and gives him victory in the war with evil (v. 6). " Safety " should read " victory."

To " open the mouth in the gate " (v. 7) was the action of a city magistrate. The pupil of folly never reaches an influential position in society ; but, on the contrary, his teacher counsels him to practice injury to society (v. 8), and leads him into sin (v. 9) ; with the result that, in the end, he becomes obnoxious (v. 9), is pronounced mischievous (v. 8), and is removed from the community by imprisonment or death.

Moral strength based upon earthly wisdom fails when tested (v. 10), but Heavenly Wisdom gives a strength that does not fail (v. 5).

To plead ignorance as an excuse for neglect of duty (vs. 11 and 12) cannot deceive God ; for He reads the heart.

Not only is it the duty of a prince to deliver those who are unjustly about to be put to death, but it is an obligation resting upon every christian to rescue the perishing, and to do his utmost to save all who are on the way to eternal death. Inaction in this matter entails the judgment of verse 12.

As honey is delicious, and excites the appetite when tasted, so is wisdom (vs. 13 and 14). To those who find it there shall be an hereafter of bliss (" reward ") ; and that expectation shall not be disappointed (" cut off ").

The word " calamity " (v. 16, R.V.), governs verses 15-18.

The argument is : if calamity overtakes an honest man, do not, as a wicked man (R.V.), take advantage of the occurrence to seize his pasture and his sheepfold (v. 15) ; for this man, being honest, can recover himself again and again, whilst his oppressor will be overthrown beyond recovery (v. 16). But the honest man is not to rejoice if misfortune strikes his enemy, lest God see it and turn His anger from the enemy upon the exulting neighbour.

The seeming repetition of verse 19 (chs. xxiii. 17 and xxiv. 1, Pss. xxxvii.1, and lxxiii. 3), is not meaningless but is motived by the special infirmity of human nature.

In verse 1, the argument points to the destruction which evil men bring upon society (v. 2) ; but, in verse 19, to the destruction which they bring upon themselves (v. 20).

Verses 21 and 22 may read thus : My son,

fear thou Jehovah, even the Supreme King, and have nothing to do with them that make a difference in administering justice (i.e., between a rich man and a poor man) for their overthrow (that is, the overthrow of the unjust judge and the favoured client) shall suddenly happen; and who can estimate the depth and horror of their mutual ruin?

PROVERBS XXIV. 23-34.—The statement: "These also are sayings of the wise men" should, as in the R.V., precede these verses.

The wise men are possibly those mentioned in 1 Kings iv. 31.

The first demands impartiality in the Courts of Law (vs. 23-26); the second forbids trading without capital (v. 27); the third condemns needless accusation of a neighbour, dishonesty in business, and retaliation of injuries (vs. 28 and 29); and the last points to the ruin sure to result for want of energy in, and attention to, the earning of one's bread (vs. 30-34).

"He that saith" (v. 24) means the judge that saith, and "them" (v. 25) means those just judges that rebuke wicked litigants. Verse 26 may be thus paraphrased: He that giveth a just judgment shall be honoured.

To "kiss the lips" (v. 26) means to honour, or do homage to.

Chapter vi. 9-11, predicts the ruin verified in verses 30 and 31 of this chapter. It is not needless repetition.

PROVERBS XXV.—This, and the following chapter, compose the Fourth Book of Proverbs. They are Proverbs by Solomon, and copied by the men of Hezekiah—not imagined, or remembered, but copied from the original manuscript. This may explain the three capital letters which are found in all editions of the Hebrew Bible up to the end of 2 Kings. They are possibly the initials of King Hezekiah confirming the accuracy of his transcribers. These three letters appear in some of the manuscripts later than 2 Kings, but were, it may be assumed, copied by subsequent writers, who thought them to be a word signifying "Be strong."

If these Proverbs were practised and obeyed how much happier would the world be!

The lucidity of human law honours man, but the inscrutibility of Divine law honours God (v. 2). His glory is seen in the marvels of the universe and in creation. These are beyond human comprehension, Job xxxvi.-xxxix.

"Pictures of silver" (v. 11) should read "baskets of silver."

"Breaketh the bone" (v. 15) means overcomes obstinacy.

As fire melteth the hardest metal so does love the hardest heart (vs. 21 and 22).

The north wind produces rain, and a back-biting tongue produces an angry countenance (v. 23).

As the purest spring becomes corrupt if trampled, so do Christian men if they permit themselves to be influenced by the world (v. 26).

The Hebrew of verse 27 is too difficult for modern scholars to translate. It may mean that glory, like honey, is in itself good, but should be enjoyed in moderation.

PROVERBS XXVI.—The first twelve verses of this chapter concern the fool, the next four, the sluggard, and the remaining twelve, the hypocrite.

Snow in summer and rain in harvest are as much out of place as dignity in a fool (v. 1)

Divine wrath is as reasonable as that a sparrow hops and a swallow flies (v. 2). It will surely strike the fool however clothed with dignity he may be.

The whip is the best and only teacher for a fool (v. 3). It is useless to reason with him, for if you answer him according to his folly you will become like him, and if you do not answer him according to his folly he will think himself wise. So silence best rebukes him.

He that transacts business by the hand of a fool is as a man that cuts off his own feet; he renders himself helpless (v. 6).

The translation of verse 7 is difficult. It may mean that a fool affecting wisdom is as manifestly absurd as a lame man affecting a graceful manner of walking: or it may mean that a fool expounding a proverb exposes his folly as a lame man in walking, his lameness.

To give honour to a fool is as useless in its results as to fasten a stone tightly in a sling (v. 8).

A thorn has a point and so has a parable, but a fool is as insensible to the one as a drunkard to the other (v. 9).

Verse 10 may be thus paraphrased : A master workman does things well, but he that hires a fool hires a botcher.

However much his folly disgusts others a fool always returns to it (v. 11 and 2 Pet. ii. 22).

It is easier to teach folly than conceit (v. 12)

A door turns, but always in the same place, and a sluggard moves about but never advances (v. 14) ; he suggests any excuse for inactivity (v. 13) ; the effort to complete an action is distasteful to him (v. 15) ; and his ignorance of the fact that he is ignorant makes him so self-satisfied that he will not exert himself to acquire knowledge (v. 16).

Verses 13 and 15 are not unmeaning repetitions of chapter xxii. 13, and chapter xix. 24, as a comparison of the verses will show. They complement each other. The one adds the possibility of death from the paw of the lion, and the other explains why the sluggard is unwilling to carry the food from the dish to his mouth.

To hold a dog by the ears is very dangerous, and to let him go is more dangerous. It is sound wisdom not to meddle with him (v. 17).

A hypocritical and affected interest in a neighbour, and a meddling in his affairs (vs. 17-19), is as injurious as the tale-bearing which fastens strife (v. 20), or the contentions which excite it (v. 21).

Verse 22 is repeated in this connection from chapter xviii. 8, to emphasise man's eagerness to listen to falsehood.

Lips professing burning affection which the heart does not feel, is as worthless earth which remains worthless though adorned with silver (v. 23).

Verse 25 illustrates verse 24, and verse 26 predicts the unmasking of the hypocrisy.

Verse 27 points to Jacob who deceived with a kid and was deceived by a kid ; to David who slew with a sword and mourned his sons slain by the sword ; to Haman who prepared a gallows for Mordecai and was himself hung thereon ; and to the men who perished in the den prepared for Daniel.

The injured forgive ; but the injurer, never (v. 28).

PROVERBS XXVII.—This, and the two following chapters, are Proverbs for Solomon. This is shewn by the use of the second person " boast not thyself " ; by the address " my son " (v. 11) ; and by the special injunctions for a king and prince (xxviii. 16, and xxix. 4).

The rich fool of Luke xii. 20 boasted of the morrow (v. 1) ; but that night his soul was required of him.

" Envy " (v. 4) should read " jealousy." The ragings of a furious temper may be withstood, but not the deadly hatred of jealousy.

A love that says and does nothing (v. 5) is not as worthful as an affection that rebukes.

The labouring man is happier than the satiated millionaire (v. 7). The sailor on the deck finds the bitter wind sweeter than the wealthy but discontented passenger does the luxury of his berth.

The little bird that wanders from its nest before the appointed time, loses the care of the parent, and exposes itself to great danger (v. 8). The self-willed lose the immediate care of God, and enter the way of death.

Counsel, energised by love, is as sweet to the heart as ointment and perfume.

The tested sympathy of a neighbour is better than the untried affection of a relative (v. 10).

When men reproach the Bible as being unable to produce character they, in reality, reproach Him who wrote it. Hence the Lord Christ says : " My child, live so as to give joy to my heart, and so as to confound mine enemies (v. 11).

Verses 12 and 13 are not meaningless repetitions of xxii. 3 and xx. 16, but emphatic repetitions demanded by the context.

The danger to be avoided in verse 13 is religious rather than moral ; though it is quite true that idolatry and impurity are bound up together. There are two Hebrew words for " stranger." The one symbolizes a Hebrew who corrupted the true worship of Jehovah ; the other, a foreigner introducing idolatry. The counsel of verse 13 is that neither of these teachers was to be listened to ; and that those who went bail for them were not to be trusted.

The loud blessing of verse 14 is a curse to whom it is addressed ; for it is self-seeking and deceitful.

Verses 15 and 16 should be read as in the R.V. The argument is : that as it is impossible for the hand to control either oil or wind, so is it impossible to govern a contentious woman.

Intellectual conversation and discussion sharpen the intelligence, and the countenance reflects the fact.

Faithful service is the best road to promotion (v. 18).

Verse 19 should be read as in the R.V.
(margin). As water reflects face to face,
so the heart, man to man. This is humbling ;
for it declares that on looking into the heart
of the vilest criminal one finds his own heart
reflected. There is no difference, for all have
sinned.

Silver and gold are tested by fire, and man
is tested by praise (v. 21). Few endure the
test ; they are wise whom praise unaffects.

A man who fails under this test is comparable to the hopeless fool of verse 22.

Wealth, and even a crown, as Rehoboam
proved, can only be retained by unwearying
diligence (vs. 23-27). This principle governs
the spiritual as well as the business life.

Verse 27 may be thus read, supplying the
ellipses : " There shall be goats' milk—
Enough for thy food ;
Enough for the food of thy household ;
And enough for the maintenance of
thy maidens. "

PROVERBS XXVIII.—The Midianites fled
before Gideon (Judges vii. 22), and the Syrians
before the four leprous men (2 Kings vii.
6). A bad conscience engenders fear.

The republics of North and Central America
illustrate verse 2. Columbia has had about
thirty presidents in twenty years ; but a man
of understanding, i.e., George Washington,
founded the former on a stable foundation.

Heavy rain in the East frequently carries
both crops and soil from off the mountain
sides. Thus needy landlords have often
rack-rented their tenants to their mutual
ruin.

Forsakers of the Bible applaud the enemies
of the Bible, but lovers of the Bible oppose
and condemn them (v. 4).

Ignorance of truth results from unwillingness to learn. Ahab accused Elijah as the
author of the Divine judgment resting on
the land. Being evil he was not willing to
understand judgment (v. 5).

Wealth does not excuse sin ; and poverty
cannot affect goodness (v. 6).

Comparing this verse with xix. 1, and
remembering that the earlier proverb was by
Solomon and this latter for Solomon, it will
be recognized there is instruction and
amplification and not repetition. Perversity
in language and conduct is pointed to—
in relation to a fool in the one case and to a
millionaire in the other.

An appetite for the Holy Scriptures is, in

verse 7, contrasted with greediness for human
teaching. The latter causes shame.

Outward worship where the heart refuses
obedience to the Gospel, is an abomination
to God (v. 9).

Verse 10 is constructed with three members.
The first : the possibility of seducing the
upright. The second : the doom of the
seducer. The third : the security of the
perfect.

Belshazzar was wise in his own eyes, but
a poor man, Daniel, exposed his folly (Dan. v).

Verse 12 should read as in the R.V.

Achan covered his transgressions (Joshua
vii.), and neither he nor Israel prospered
He was found out and justly judged. Had he
voluntarily confessed his sin and forsaken it,
he would have found mercy. Many are willing
to confess their sins, but few willing to forsake
them (v. 13).

A tender conscience produces happiness ;
a hardened conscience leads to eternal
calamity (v. 14).

" Roaring " (v. 15) reads better " growl-
ing." A lion growls when devouring his
prey, and a bear prowls when seeking its
prey. Both actions express the conduct of a
wicked prince to his defenceless people.

Even if a prince (v. 16) be not personally
cruel but is deficient in character and selfish,
he becomes a great oppressor, and shortens
his days, that is, risks assassination ; but a
prince that hates self-indulgence prolongs his
days. By supplying the words " shortens
his days " to the first line of the Proverb, the
argument of the verse becomes clearer.

" Stay " (v. 17) means " sustain " or
" help ." The injunction is that no one is to
shelter, or help, a murderer ; but, on the
contrary, he is to be deemed worthy of death.

" Perverse " (v. 18) implies double-minded ;
and " shall fall at once " should read : " shall
fall in one of the two." The statement of the
verse is that a straight path leads to prosperity, but that whoever tries to walk in two
ways, i.e., deceitfully, shall fall in one of
them.

" To make haste to be rich " (v. 20) implies
the use of fraud. People bless an honest
trader, but demand the punishment of a
dishonest one.

Verse 21 should read : " To have respect
of persons is not good ; for, for one piece of
bread even a strong man will transgress.
The Hebrew word used here denotes a strong
man, and so points to the humbling fact that

it is possible to corrupt even the best of men with the smallest of bribes.

Hebrew law declared property to belong to the family (v. 24). An undutiful child might, with a shew of logic, take money, or goods, and declare it not to be theft. But Heavenly Wisdom ranks such a child with a " destroying man " i.e., with " a highwayman."

" A proud heart " (v. 25) rather means a greedy disposition ; and is here contrasted with a trusting faith. The one secures prosperity ; the other, leads to strife.

" To hide the eyes " (v. 27) means to avert attention from the misery of the poor (v. 27).

PROVERBS XXIX.—The Antedeluvians and Pharaoh illustrate verse 1.

A prince who dispenses impartial justice promotes the prosperity of a nation ; but a prince who takes bribes injures a nation (v.4).

The spies sent out by the Pharisees spread a net for Christ's steps, while flattering Him. But He exposed their hypocrisy (Luke xx. 19–26).

Wrong doing leads to trouble, but right doing to gladness (v. 6).

A righteous prince interests himself on behalf of the helpless ; but a wicked prince has no desire to acquaint himself with their needs (v. 7).

Had there been even ten wise men in Sodom the Divine wrath would have turned away ; but the city being filled with scoffers (Gen. xix. 14) they set it in a flame (v. 8).

It is useless, and a waste of time, to argue with a fool. He is insensible to either severity or ridicule (v. 9).

Jezebel in her hatred of Naboth and Elijah illustrates verse 10 (R.V.).

Verse 11 should read as in the R.V. a fool is governed by his temper ; a wise man controls and stills it.

Evil has many imitators. A lying master makes his servants to be liars ; and if he listens to falsehood his servants become wicked.

The debtor and the usurer are alike dependent upon God for life and intelligence. He, as Umpire, makes them both conscious of their ignorance and dependence ; and will judge them.

Messiah's future kingdom is described in verse 14.

Man's natural depravity and constitutional bias to evil is demonstrated in verse 15.

A flower, if left to itself, becomes beautiful ; a child, if left to himself, and undisciplined, brings shame upon his mother, no matter how high born he may be, or how pious his parents. Eli's sons illustrate the second statement of this Proverb (1 Sam. iii. 13) ; and Manasseh illustrates its first statement (2 Chron. xxxiii. 12).

Five times in these Five Books of the Proverbs the Holy Spirit counsels the wise discipline of children. Here (v. 17) is found a gracious encouragement for Christian parents who are willing to exercise that discipline.

Verse 18 should read as in the R.V. Man, left to himself without a " vision," i.e., a revelation from God, becomes utterly vile. On the other hand true happiness is linked with the Bible and its obedience.

" Answer " (v. 19) means " obey." A disobedient servant, as God continually finds, must be corrected with something sterner than mere words.

" Words " (v. 20) implies action as well as speech. The affairs of life should be discharged with due forethought and prayer.

The word " son " (v. 21) implies a masterful son. The statement therefore is, that a servant, foolishly indulged, becomes a master.

Verse 23 should read as in the R.V. Adam, (Gen. iii. 5) illustrates the first line of this Proverb, and Joseph (Gen xli. 40) illustrates the second line.

Verse 24 should read as in the R.V. Lev. v. 1 condemns the witness who, after adjuration, refused to give evidence.

1 Sam. xxvii. illustrates the first statement of verse 25, and Neh. vi. 3 and 13 illustrate the second. Nehemiah was " set on high " so that his feet were in no danger from the snares set for them.

An earthly ruler may err in dispensing favours, but Emmanuel the Prince will exercise discriminating judgment infallibly.

PROVERBS XXX.—The Sixth Book of Proverbs is composed of this and the following chapter.

The Bible does not say who Agur was but it does give his " prophecy " ; that is, his message.

Ithiel and Ucal may have been his disciples ; or this second line of verse 1 may be read as in the Revised Version Margin ; or Agur, Ithiel and Ucal may be names of Solomon.

Verses 2-9 relate to God, and verses 10-33 to man.

A right relationship to man (vs. 10-33), is dependent upon a right relationship to God (vs. 2-9).

Society is saddened by slander (v. 10); ingratitude to parents (v. 11); contempt of parents (v. 17).; self-righteousness (v. 12); pride (v. 13); violence (v. 14); covetousness (vs. 15 and 16); the denial of (v. 19) and concealment of (v. 20) evil; and misgovernment (vs. 21 to 23).

Such is society without God; and the argument of the passage (vs. 24-31) is, that amidst its disorder, wisdom (vs. 24-28) is a better defence than physical strength (vs. 29-31).

A right relationship to God confesses man's ignorance in the absence of a Divine revelation (vs. 2-3); it presents the person of the Saviour (v. 4); the infallibility of His Word (v. 5); the safety of those who confide in Him (v. 5); the judgment that awaits those who add to the revelation given in the Bible (v. 6); and the fear lest wealth should lead to independence of God, and poverty to rebellion against Him (vs. 7-9).

Verse 3 should read: "I have not been taught wisdom so as to have the knowledge of the Most Holy One."

The dogmas which the corrupt Christian Church have added to the Gospel are falsehoods: and those who added them are false teachers.

"Take the name" (v. 9) means attack the character; i.e., accuse God of injustice in permitting poverty.

The Hebrew word translated "horseleach" (v. 15) is unknown to scholars. The two daughters have the same name, i.e., "Give." They are insatiable, like the four things in verse 16.

An eagle, a serpent, a ship and a man may effect important movements without leaving any trace of them. An unfaithful wife may "wipe her mouth," i.e., remove all traces of her misconduct, and challenge condemnation (vs. 18-20).

From the throne to the kitchen (vs. 21-23) all is unrest and confusion when God is not recognized and served.

The ants, the conies, the locusts, and the lizards are feeble and defenceless, but because of wisdom they have food (v. 25), security (v. 26), government (v. 27), and dignity (v. 28).

Man is feeble and defenceless, but let him be the pupil of wisdom and he also will have food, safety, government and dignity.

Verse 28 should read: "The lizard may be captured with the hand yet is it in the palace of the King."

"Greyhound" (v. 31) should read "War horse."

The argument of verses 32 and 33 is: if feeble man in his folly has lifted up himself against God, or even indulged hard thoughts of Him, let him listen to the voice of wisdom and lay his hand upon his mouth; for otherwise there will be a result as surely as there is a result when milk is churned, the nose wrung, or anger excited.

The Talmud says that Solomon had many names. Amongst them it mentions the Son of Jakeh, Agur, and Lemuel.

If this be so then verse 1 of this chapter may be thus read: The words addressed to Agur the son of Jakeh. This is the message: The hero spake unto Ithiel even unto Ithiel and Ucal, i.e. to Solomon, saying "Surely," etc.

PROVERBS XXXI.—Verse 1 of this chapter may be read: "The words addressed to King Lemuel, i.e., to Solomon, the Divine lesson which his mother kept continually teaching him."

Solomon's teacher in chapter xxx. was a man, but no ordinary man, a hero. His teacher in chapter xxxi. was a woman, but no ordinary woman, she was his mother.

As chapter xxx. contains two sections so does chapter xxxi. In it the false woman, i.e., idolatry, is contrasted with the true woman, i.e., the Gospel.

Although this latter woman is doubtless symbolical yet does she give a very lovely picture of God's ideal of a wife: and if all women were like this woman earth would be a heaven.

Her character and excellence are set out in the chapter in a double alternation, thus making more prominent her perfection:

Her husband (vs. 10-12).

Her occupation (vs. 13-19).

Her character (v. 20).

Her household (v. 21).

Her person (v. 22).

Her husband (v. 23).
  Her occupation (vs. 24 and 25).
    Her character (v. 26).
      Her household (vs. 27 and 28).
        Her person (v. 29).

There is sufficient in the Scriptures to suggest that Bathsheba became a woman of faith and character prior to the birth of Solomon. She dedicated him to God before his birth (v. 2). He was a child of repentance and faith.

The false woman (v. 3), i.e., idolatry, leads into debauchery (v. 4), apostasy (v. 5), injustice (v. 5), neglect of duty (vs. 8 and 9), and death (v. 3).

The instruction and truth of verses 6 and 7 were recently realized by a Christian brother, the only support of his invalid sister, and very poor. The doctor said that only champagne could save her from death. To buy it was impossible. In their distress a large packet was brought in by a carrier. It contained a present of champagne sent by the brother's employer. The sister, who was ready to perish, drank the wine and recovered; and both she and her brother, who were heavy of heart, forgot their poverty and remembered their misery no more. Such is the function designed for wine by Wisdom.

The true woman, i.e., the Gospel, brings with her a double portion of love (vs. 11 and 23); of prosperity (vs. 13-19 and 24 and 25); of character, i.e., benevolence (v. 20); and wisdom and gentleness (v. 26); of enrichment for others (vs. 21 and 27); and of personal dignity (vs. 22 and 29).

This last verse is the utterance of the husband; and the two closing verses of the chapter are the Holy Spirit's conclusion, not only to the chapter itself, but to the message of all the Six Books of the Proverbs, which is: that the fear of the Lord secures abiding favour, moral beauty, public approbation (v. 30), and eternal recompense (v. 31).

This last verse may read: " The fruit of her hands shall be given her, and her works shall praise her in the gates."

Verses 10-31 form an acrostic in the Hebrew Bible, each verse beginning with a successive letter of the Hebrew alphabet

Eastern ladies of rank add to the wealth of their husbands by the sale of embroideries made by their own hands.

The word " virtuous " (v. 10) is not in Hebrew limited as in English in its meaning; it is a covering term suggesting character and ability.

" She shall rejoice in time to come " (v. 25) means she laughs at the future; that is, she makes ample provision for sickness and old age.

ECCLESIASTES

ECCLESIASTES I.—This title is the Latin form of the Greek word meaning " the Preacher." The Hebrew title is " Koheleth," i.e., the Convener, or Master and Teacher of an Assembly. It is one of Solomon's titles. It is also symbolic of Wisdom. Uniting these facts Solomon is presented as the Teacher inspired by Wisdom.

His theme is : what is the chief good ? Chapters 1-6 state what it is not, and chapters 7-12 what it is.

Verse 1 of the first chapter forms the Introduction ; and the last two verses of the last chapter, the Conclusion.

The argument of the Book is the vanity of all things " under the sun " ; and that the only satisfying and abiding happiness is in loving and serving God.

The grace which in the Six Books of the Proverbs condescends to relate heavenly Wisdom with earthly circumstances so as to guide her children (Luke vii. 35) in a sure path, in the Book of Ecclesiastes exposes the emptiness of earthly wisdom in hasting after impossible satisfaction whether sensual, industrial or philosophic.

The love that placed this Book within the Holy Scriptures is recognized and adored by every one who is born of the Spirit.

The section of the Sacred Book from Job to Canticles illustrates spiritual facts in the spiritual life, and may be thus set out :

Job	Romans vii. 18.
The Psalms	Galatians ii. 20.
Proverbs	1 Corinthians i. 30.
Ecclesiastes	1 John ii. 15-17.
Canticles	1 Peter i. 8.

The first step in the spiritual life is to abhor equally one's badness and one's goodness ; the second step is to live by the faith of the Son of God, that is, to live in the energy of the faith by which the Messiah lived ; the third step is the subjection of the will to Christ the Wisdom of God; the fourth step is deliverance from the spirit of this present evil world ; and the climax is the joy unspeakable of union and companionship with Christ.

The supposed conflict which some have pointed out between the teaching of this Book and other Books of the Bible, arises from inattention to the structure and argument of the Book. It truthfully describes the weariness and confusion which exist " under the sun " ; and it employs irony and quotation in its examination of man's helplessness to remedy this misery.

CHAPTER I

The vanity (v. 2), the brevity (v. 4), and the weariness (v. 8), of man and his labours are set out in verses 2-11 ; in verses 12-15 the personal experience of the Preacher is recorded ; and in verses 16-18 the excellency of the wisdom which is from above is contrasted with the wisdom which is of the earth.

" Vanity of vanities " (v. 2) is a Hebraism for the most utter vanity, as a " servant of servants " (Gen. ix. 25) expresses hopeless slavery, and " Holy of Holies " (Exod. xxvi.) highest sanctity.

The brevity of human life is contrasted with the age of the earth. The words " for ever " are comparative, not absolute.

The anguish of verses 5-11 is that all things move in an appointed circle, and so there is to man the dissatisfaction of recurrence. There is in reality " nothing new " (v. 10) ; that is, nothing occurs, or can occur, which can transport him into a new world, or give him new joys or new emotions. Modern inventions are only " new " in a comparative and not in an absolute sense ; and verse 11 declares that the records of the antediluvian world are as totally destroyed as shall be the records of this present world. The former were destroyed by water ; the latter shall be destroyed by fire.

The eye and the ear (v. 8) are tyrants which no man can satisfy, and which, in continually demanding novelties, thereby declare there is nothing new.

The " wisdom " of verse 13 and verses 17 and 18 is human political science. All that that science can do is to recognise the vanity of all man's efforts to turn earth into a heaven without God.

The expression " under the sun " (vs. 3 and 14) occurs twenty-nine times in this Book, and is peculiar to it. " It means " Without God in the world " (Ep. ii. 12).

Man's inability to straighten what has been made morally crooked, and to furnish what is defective (v. 15) is insisted on with truth in the entire Book.

The title " Jehovah " (v. 13) is not used in this Book because here man is viewed in relation to God as Creator and not as Redeemer.

" Exercised " (v. 13) means " humbled."

" Vexation of spirit " (v. 14) may be translated " feeding on wind " ; and " madness " (v.17), the extravagance of self-conceit.

" Grief " (v. 18) means " mortification."

The Book discusses " labour " (v. 3) as man's proposed " end " or ideal of happiness. The Book argues that, as an end, it is unsatisfying, however profitable it may be as a means.

In Ecclesiastes the heart is too large for the portion, and in Canticles the portion is too large for the heart. Those who set their affection on things that are " under the sun " feed upon wind, but those who set their affection on things that are above the sun (Col. iii. 2) enjoy a satisfying banquet.

Proverbs sets out the sufficiency of Divine Wisdom, and Ecclesiastes the insufficiency of human wisdom ; yet is that wisdom, and its opposite folly, examined and tested by a wisdom that is super-human.

ECCLESIASTES II.—The dissatisfaction and vexation of spirit which Solomon experienced in testing the insufficiency of industry, philosophy and pleasure, were the more painful because of his possession of the super-human wisdom which remained with him (v. 9) ; for the greater the capacity of enjoyment the greater the disappointment and vexation. His misery was, therefore,

greater than that of any who preceded or succeeded him, because of this unique gift of wisdom ; and if ordinary intelligence finds everything " under the sun " to be vanity, extraordinary intelligence finds it to be " vanity of vanities."

Solomon having tested the incapacity of pleasure to satisfy the heart (vs. 1-3), sought to discover what occupation could afford lasting happiness to man (v. 3). He, therefore, built palaces surrounded by paradises (vs. 4-6), hired servants, bought flocks and herds (v. 7), amassed gold and silver and precious stones (v. 8), procured the best music (v. 8), and a multitude of wives of the highest rank, but found that though he was interested for the time (v. 10), yet his share or " portion " of all his toil was vanity and vexation of spirit, and provided no profit, i.e., no satisfying happiness (v. 11).

The last line of verse 8 should read : " A princess and princesses," i.e., a Queen and many wives. Pharaoh's daughter was the Queen, and the princesses were the concubines, that is, secondary wives.

In verses 12-17 Solomon set himself " to " behold wisdom," i.e. to study philosophy, with the result that he observed that death no more respected the wise man than the fool (vs. 14 and 16). He thus discovered philosophy to be vanity.

The question (v. 12) " what can the man do " etc. : means no one could, or can, possibly compete with king Solomon in determining the vanity of things under the sun, for no one ever was, or will be, as efficiently equipped as he was for this experiment.

The knowledge that however artistic and beautiful may be the works of a clever man (v. 21), and however vast the wealth which he may amass (v. 26), yet must he leave all to his successor who may be a fool, and this saddened him. The wise man's " portion," or share, is sorrow, grief and vanity, but his foolish successor's share is the possession, without effort, of all that his father painfully toiled to bring into being. This Solomon found to be vanity and a great calamity (v. 21) ; and accordingly he gave up as desperate all hope of solid satisfaction from his toil (v. 20). His son Rehoboam was his successor, and he was a fool.

He verified that a life of honest labour (v. 24) ministers a happiness appointed by the hand of God. " Eat and drink " in this verse is to be understood as enjoyment of needful food with an appetite quickened by honest " labour " ; and the word " it " in this verse means true enjoyment.

He who thus works for his daily bread in obedience to the Divine Will (v. 26), to him God recompenses wisdom, knowledge and joy; but to the disobedient He gives the fruitless toil of amassing wealth for honest men to enjoy. This latter " travail " Solomon found to be vanity and a striving after wind.

" Labour " (v. 24) means fruitful toil, " travail " (v. 26) on the other hand means toil that only gives fatigue. Had Solomon profited by the Proverbs of the wise men, and had he listened to his father's dying words (1 Chron. xxviii. 9), he would have been spared the suffering here recorded.

God in His love has placed this Book in the Bible for the warning and instruction of His children ; and in His goodness He denies them the means of making the experiment which Solomon found so bitter.

ECCLESIASTES III.—The argument of this chapter is, that God having appointed fixed laws for the well-being of man (vs. 1-8), and having given him a consciousness of another life (v. 11), it is man's wisdom and happiness to obey these laws (vs. 12 and 13), consoling himself with the fact of their immutability and benevolence (vs. 14 and 15).

The chapter points out (vs. 16 and 17), that disobedience will meet with punishment in the future life ; and that God permits free-will to man in order to humble him, and that he may himself recognise that, in relation to this life, he has no pre-eminence over the beasts (vs. 19 and 20), for that, like them, he must die ; and that he is absolutely unable to find out what happens after death (v. 21) : the conclusion being (v. 22) that man has but one life " under the sun " ; that Supreme Wisdom has appointed labour as the law of that life ; and that the limited happiness suitable for him is to be found in obeying the decrees of that Wisdom.

The " seasons " and " times " appointed under the heavens are of Divine appointment.

Illustrations of the benevolence and wisdom of such appointments may be found in the Scriptures.

" To kill " (v. 3) means to justly condemn to death.

The point of the question in verse 9 is,

that to make the actions of the foregoing verses the chief end of life is to seek a profitless object. God has given labour to man (v. 10) as a discipline and not as an end ; accordingly He made everything beautiful in its season, and at the same time, gave to man the consciousness of " eternity " (v. 11) ; but He limited this intelligence so that man cannot review, or criticize, the whole of God's actions as they embrace the past and the future (v. 11).

" The world " (v. 11) should read : " eternity " ; this limitless period is here set in opposition to " time " (vs. 1-8).

The eating and drinking and toiling, and the enjoyment resulting therefrom(vs. 12-15), means legitimate labour as man's daily duty; but not as the end, or purpose, of his being.

The immutability and unchangeableness of God's actions and purposes (v. 14) awaken reverential fear and holy love and worship in all who are born of the Spirit. This consolation is deepened by the added statement that God will bring again that which is passed away ; or, as some translate the Hebrew text, He will vindicate those whom men have condemned because of their obedience to His laws. The principle underlying either translation is the same : viz., that man cannot thwart God's plans ; they are certain of fulfilment.

A difficulty is presented in verse 16, but answered in verse 17. The difficulty is : If God governs human affairs, why is injustice found where justice should be enthroned ? The answer is, that God permits this folly on the part of man in order to humble him ; and that He will in a future life judge him for his wrong doing. The word " there " (v. 17) means in the world beyond the grave ; that is, in the great day of future judgment.

The question in verse 21 not only declares that man is wholly unable to discover what lies beyond death, but the form of the question implies that he does not wish to know. A similar question is : " Who hath believed our report ? " (Isa. liii. 1). The answer is, no one : for none wished to believe it.

The fact of death, and the darkness that lies beyond, impenetrable by man, turn into vanity and vexation of spirit all man's efforts to make this world a satisfying portion.

ECCLESIASTES　　IV.—The　　confusion,

ignorance, and misery which result from banishing God from the world is in this chapter made more apparent by the absence of the Divine Name. It does not once appear.

" I returned and saw " means : 1 resumed my investigation ; and has special reference to chapter iii. 16 (v. 1).

" I praised " (v. 2) means I esteemed happy. The argument is that men suffer so much from the injustice of governments that it were better to be dead or never to have been born.

The repetition of the statement " they had no comforter " (v. 1) emphasizes the tender pity of God for the oppressed.

If there be no God, and no future life, then indeed it would be better never to have been born ; and when knowledge is limited to what takes place " under the sun " (v. 1) then is the congratulation of verses 2 and 3 sound philosophy.

Having studied civil government (vs. 1-3) the writer then studied commerce (vs. 4-12), and he observed that " every right work " (v. 4),that is, every successful business enterprise, excited envy, and, consequently, suffering.

He further observed that the man (v. 5) who with grasping hand, enriched himself by robbing others, was a fool ; for he ate his own flesh, that is, was eaten up with self-remorse ; and Solomon observed that one opened handful with tranquillity was better than two closed handfuls with toil and vexation (v. 6).

The Hebrew text here points out that the one hand is open and the two hands closed.

The word " another " should be supplied before " vanity " in verse 7. The verse will now read : Then I resumed my investigation and observed another vanity under the sun, i.e., the misery of the miser (v. 8). His consciousness continually asks a question which he cannot answer (v. 8).

The words " I also observed that " should be supplied at the commencement of verses 9 and 11 and 13.

The argument of verses 7-12 is that co-operation is morally and commercially better than individualism.

Verse 12 should read as in the R.V. The statement is, that it is easy to overthrow an individual, more difficult to destroy a partnership, and most difficult to break down a corporation.

The facts which Solomon verified " under the sun," and records in verses 13-16, proved

a prophecy of what would happen to himself, to his son Rehoboam, and to his servant Jeroboam.

He became the " old and foolish king," who refused to listen to the Divine admonition (1 Kings iii. 14 and ix. 3-9 and xi. 9-40) ; Jeroboam was the poor but clever youth who came out of prison and was made king ; and whilst Rehoboam, the second youth, reigned in his father's stead, and for a time was accepted of all the people, yet they did not continue " to rejoice in him " but followed Jeroboam. Thus Rehoboam, though born to the kingdom and wealth of his father, became poor ; for the king of Egypt took from him the wealth, and Jeroboam took from him the kingdom. Thus there is no stability nor satisfying happiness guaranteed even to a throne ; and the multitude who applaud a prince to-day will strike off his head to-morrow.

If the investigator limits his observations to what takes place " under the sun," then indeed is the conclusion a just one that all is vanity and a feeding upon wind.

But the Christian recognizes that God exists, that there is a future life, and that man, having been gifted with free-will, it is reasonable that God should permit him liberty of action ; and although such liberty involves suffering, yet the misery is over-ruled by God for the ultimate good of His people, and for the discipline and humbling and moral enrichment of man.

ECCLESIASTES V.—To put God first (vs. 1-7), not to be stumbled by His permission of oppression (vs. 8 and 9), and the acceptance of His Will in the gift of small or large incomes (vs. 10-20), secures the limited amount of happiness possible, and desirable, " under the sun."

" Keep thy foot " (v. 1) means be reverent, the " house of God " means the presence of God, and " to hear " means to obey. Cain offered the sacrifice of fools, i.e., dreams, vanities, and " many words " (v. 7 and Gen. iv. 8-14) ; Abel offered the worship of obedience. He silently bowed, and sought acceptance, life, and pardon through the shed blood of the spotless lamb—God's appointed way of worship. See 1 John iii. 12.

Verse 2 points to loud religious professions with the lips ; and such a multitude of words (v. 3) marks the fool as the pressure of business affairs causes a dream.

Vows, as, for example, the temperance pledge, if made to God, should be observed ; but vows that cause the flesh to sin should not be taken (v. 6). God, who reads the heart, rejects the excuse that the non-performance of an engagement was legitimate because the promise was given in error (v. 6). He will judge such conduct (v. 6).

The professors of ceremonial religion construct a worship of dreams, vanities, and many words (v. 7). True religion is a personal relationship to God—" but fear *thou* God."

The argument of verse 8 is : that if God, Who is higher than the kings of the earth, temporarily permits oppression, His child is not to be stumbled, or confused, by the fact, but approve the Divine purpose ; at the same time recognizing (v. 9) that God never intended the private ownership of land ; that such an economic system is the basal cause of poverty ; and that the profit of the land should be for the benefit of all the members of the province who co-operate to produce the profit.

A labouring man (v. 12) is really happier and richer than the millionaire (vs. 10 and 11).

Wealth acquired selfishly (v. 13) is often dissipated by adverse fortune (" evil travail "). " His hand " means his son's hand ; but the " he " of verse 15 applies to the father. And even if such wealth remains with him to the close of his life, yet does it bring to him perplexity, vexation, ill-health, and an irritable temper.

The labourer (v. 18) who accepts from God his lot in life (" his portion ") " enjoys good "; and the man to whom God " gives " wealth also " rejoices in his labour," and is contented with " his portion." He does not, like worldly men, recall with vain longings the happier days of the past, because God answers him, i.e., responds to his acceptance of his lot in life by daily putting joy in his heart. This gift of contentment is equally enjoyed by the labourer as by the man of wealth, if they alike live in the Will of God.

The entrance of God manifests the folly of man (vs. 1-7) ; and the acceptance of His Will gives a contentment to the heart which the vain hope of earthly happiness apart from Him, cannot give.

ECCLESIASTES VI.—" Common " (v. 1) should read " heavy " ; for the misery described in verses 2-7 is peculiar to the miser and not to all men.

The rich man of verse 2 is to be distinguished from the rich man of chapter v. 19. The one uses the given wealth legitimately ; the other hoards it.

" Power to eat " (v. 2) means capacity to enjoy.

The argument of verses 3-7 is : that a long life, and the possession of one hundred children, with discontent, is more to be commiserated than an abortive birth.

" Filled " (v. 3) means " satisfied."

To " have no burial " (v. 3) is in the East a great degradation.

Verses 4 and 5 should be read as in the R.V.

" This " (v. 5) refers to the still-born child ; and " the other " refers to the miser.

The word " that " should be supplied before " man " in verse 7 ; and the statement then appears that all the toil of " that man," i.e., the miser, is for " his mouth," i.e., selfish, and yet is his lust for gold never satisfied.

The word " advantage " should be supplied in verse 8 before the wise man and before the poor man ; and " to walk before the living " means to live aright. The question in this verse is asked : " What advantage has a sensible man over a fool, and what advantage has a rightly living poor man over a miser ? This is answered in verse 9 by the statement that what is before the eyes is better than what is vainly imagined by the mind. A dinner of plain food, seen by the eyes, is better than a banquet vainly imagined in the mind. This latter is vanity and a feeding on wind.

This ninth verse closes the first section of the Book of Ecclesiastes. That section examined what is not man's chief good under the sun ; what is man's chief good under the sun is now introduced in verses 10-12, and set out in the chapters that follow.

Verse 10 may be thus paraphrased : Whatsoever he be, whether rich or poor, his name was given him long ago, and is known to be Adam, i.e., a morsel of red dust.

It is manifest that such a creature is incapable of contending, i.e., disputing, with his Creator (v. 10) ; hence the fact that his use of " many words " in disputation only increases vanity and fails to better him (v. 11) ; and, finally, only the Creator can know what is good for man all the days of his life of vanity, for the Creator alone can tell a man what will happen in the world under the sun after the man is dead.

Thus man's ignorance and limitation may be recognized by his impotence to procure for himself a life of satisfying contentment, and by his inability to tell what will take place in the world after he has left it.

ECCLESIASTES VII. — " Name " (v. 1) stands for character. This is solid good, and not vanity. Character is " precious," and so is ointment ; but the one is transitory, the other eternal The fragrance of the ointment of Mark xiv. 3–9 was for a time ; but the " name " given to the woman by Christ endures for all time. The Messiah Himself is the Anointed One ; and His Name shall endure throughout all generations.

To him who has this " good name," but only to such an one, is the death-day better than the birthday, for it introduces him to a blissful and perfect life " above the sun " (Phil. i. 23).

It is easier to sin when mirthful than when sorrowful (vs. 2–4 with Job i. 4 and 5).

Gravity is better than frivolity (v. 3) ; and 2 Cor. ii. 1–10 illustrates the moral advantage to an erring heart which the grieved face of a true friend may cause (v. 5).

A fire of thorns makes a great noise but lasts a short time (v. 6).

The warning of verse 7 may be that the wise man, i.e., the Christian, is in danger of desiring, and being corrupted by, the pleasures which may be obtained by extortion and bribes, but verse 8 directs attention to the " end " of such pleasures— pointing out that they produce pride and not patience ; verse 9 counsels him not to be vexed because he may not be so fortunately placed as the fools ; whilst verse 10 warns him not to complain of his having fallen upon evil days, for such irritation shows a want of heavenly wisdom, and a questioning of the love that plans all things for man's good.

" Wisely " (v. 10) should be rendered " out of wisdom," i.e., heavenly wisdom ; and the excellence of that wisdom is set out in verses 11–14.

Verse 11 may be rendered : " For them that see the sun," i.e., for the inhabitants of this world, "wisdom is as good as riches, and more advantageous." Wisdom shields from the ills of life ; and money also shields from such ills (v. 12). But money can be lost, wisdom, never. Money shields in prosperity, and for a time ; wisdom, in adversity and for ever. It is therefore, more advantageous.

It enables the heart " to consider " God's perfect action (vs. 13 and 14).

The argument of these verses is : If God sends adversity, i.e., makes a thing crooked, who can reverse His decree and defeat His will ? Heavenly Wisdom teaches a joyful acceptance of His will if He grants prosperity, and an approbation of His will if He ordains adversity.

The words " be thankful " should be supplied after " adversity " in verse 14 ; and " consider " should commence a new sentence in correspondence with the " consider " of verse 13.

Verse 14 may then be thus rendered : " In the day of prosperity be joyful, and in the day of adversity be thankful. Consider that God hath even made, or set, the one side by side with the other, so that man shall not find any cause of complaint against Him."

It is true that " under the sun " righteous men often are poor and wicked men rich ; but " the righteous man " of verses 15–18 is to be understood as the self-righteous man.

The word " facts " might better be supplied in verse 15 ; thus : " All these facts have I verified in the days of my vanity, i.e., my vain life : There is a self-righteous man " etc.

Verses 16 and 17 may be thus understood : " Be not self-righteous at all, neither make thyself more wise than God," and " Be not wicked at all, neither be thou foolhardy against God."

The instruction of verse 18 is : Take hold of these two facts, i.e., the certain doom that will overtake the self-righteous man on the one hand, and the profligate on the other ; and learn that both extremes may be escaped from by " fearing God," that is, by accepting His way of righteousness and life.

Chapter viii. 12 should be read in connection with verse 15.

" Wisdom " (v. 19) is here heavenly wisdom ; the wisdom of verse 25 is earthly wisdom.

Heavenly wisdom is a sure defence (v. 19) ; a true moral teacher (v. 20) ; it gives a forbearing and forgiving spirit (v. 21) ; and it humbles with the consciousness that all hearts are diseased by sin, and are, in this sense, alike (v. 22).

That which is far off and exceeding deep, is heavenly wisdom (v. 24) ; and it is impossible to be found by earthly wisdom (v. 23).

Verse 25 may be thus rendered: I resumed my investigations and I determined to ascertain, etc., the cause of actions, i.e., the actions of self righteousness on the one hand, and of debauchery on the other; and to know the wickedness of folly and the extravagance of foolishness.

In verse 26 the cause of self-righteousness and of profligacy is found to be idolatry. This is symbolized by a woman. Salvation by personal merit and immorality distinguish idolatrous nations.

It is also a fact in life that nothing drives a man either to the foolishness of asceticism or to the madness of debauchery as the conduct of a false woman; for woman is man's highest conception of moral and physical beauty; and when that ideal is wrecked all is lost, and folly becomes master.

God's favour is better than life; woman's infidelity more bitter than death.

A sure escape from the snares of idolatry is " to please God " (v. 26); that is, to commit oneself by faith to the one and only Saviour (John vi. 29).

Solomon had one thousand wives. Amongst them he failed to find one true woman (v. 28). This resulted from his exercise of self-will. He chose idolatrous women, and they corrupted him. Had he sought Divine guidance in the matter, God would have given him one wife; and he would have made the experience that he who finds a God-given wife finds a good thing.

" Counting one by one " (v. 27) might be better rendered: Examining these women one by one.

Amongst his courtiers Solomon may have found one worthful man; as, for example, the prophet Ahijah (1 Kings xi. 29); but doubtless this is a prophetic utterance, and points to the only Human Being Who was perfect, the True Man, the Man Christ Jesus.

The declaration of verse 29 is, that God made Adam and Eve upright, but that they and their children introduced many inventions; the most popular of which are idolatry and polygamy. Solomon suffered from these two.

Wisdom, i.e., knowing God in Christ, gives a joy so true that it makes the house of mourning to a Christian happier than the house of mirth to the worldling (vs. 1–6); it enriches the believer with patience and intelligence (vs. 7–14); it recognizes that the self-sufficient effort to be righteous, and a life of active evil, alike end in judgment (vs. 15–18); and, finally, it pronounces the efforts of human wisdom to explain earthly phenomena to be labour in vain (vs. 23–29).

The meaning of verses 11 and 12 is, that wisdom is good and money is good, but that wisdom has this advantage over money that it can preserve life, while money, whether inherited or made, cannot.

ECCLESIASTES VIII. 1-15.—Verse 1 might better read: " Who is like the wise man? and who, like him, knoweth the interpretation of a matter? Such wisdom makes a man's face to shine, and changes the sternness of his countenance."

When Christ, Who is Wisdom, lives by His Holy Spirit in the heart, man is made intelligent, and his face, naturally discontented and gloomy, is made bright and benignant.

Verse 2 may read: " I say then: keep the King's Commandment; and do so on account of the oath of God."

This oath is that of Ps. lxxxix. 35; and although it may have an application to Solomon personally, yet verses 3–5 prove that the Messiah is intended.

Verses 3 and 4 may be thus rendered: " Be not hasty to go out of His presence, persist not in an evil purpose, because He doeth whatever pleaseth Him, and because His Word, as King, hath power, and because who may say unto Him, What doest Thou? "

To dwell in His presence is life and power; to hasten away is darkness and death.

Verses 5–7 may read thus: " Whoso keepeth the commandment (i.e., the King's) shall experience no calamity (Rom. x. 11); and a wise man's heart (i.e., the Christian) discerneth a time-limit and a judgment; for every action there shall be a time-limit and a judgment (Heb. ix. 27); therefore the misery of (the unconverted) man is heavy upon him, because he knoweth not that which shall be (i.e., his fate in that judgment) for who can tell him how it shall be? "

The Christian, though he knows there will be a day of judgment, feels no terror; but to the worldling the thought of that judgment embitters his life, and spoils his pleasure.

This bitterness is made the more bitter by the knowledge (v. 8) that he cannot avoid death, and by the fear, here declared to be well grounded, that his plans of escape from its power are useless.

" Neither shall wickedness deliver its possessors." " Wickedness " here means a way of salvation other than God's way. Human priests offer dying men a salvation which they themselves have invented, and which they sell for money; but such " wickedness " shall not deliver those who trust it. In such a way of salvation one man (the priest) ruleth over another (the dying person) to their mutual injury (v. 9).

Verse 10 should read as in the R.V. and may be thus paraphrased : And, accordingly, I saw the wicked (i.e., evil men dying in the false hope of verse 8) buried, and they came to the grave with pomp ; and I saw those that had done right (that is, the righteous) and they passed away from the holy place, and were forgotten in the city.

This verse, with the four following, are illustrated by the Lord's narrative of the rich man and Lazarus (Luke xvi. 19).

If God, and eternity, and what is above the sun, have no existence, and if death is annihilation, then is the philosophy of verse 15 sound philosophy. But the argument and teaching of the Book of Ecclesiastes is that it is folly ; for God exists, and will bring every action into judgment. When this fact was brought before Felix's mind he trembled (Acts xxiv. 25) ; and, therefore, his misery was heavy upon him (v. 6).

ECCLESIASTES VIII. 16 - IX. 10. — This section of the Book declares the inability of the ablest scientists to discover the laws which govern the mystery of life and being, and the problems of adversity and prosperity.

" Business " (v. 16) means the activities of life. They are so unceasing that they are here compared to a sleepless man. This verse should be read as in the R.V. (margin).

" Work " (v. 17) is a term expressing the whole philosophy of life. However hard an ordinary man may try to discover its nature and laws he is incapable of succeeding; and though a " wise man," i.e., an able scientist, may " think " to discover them yet is it beyond his power also.

Solomon (ix. 1) who was exceptionally gifted and placed to make this investigation, and who resolutely laid it to his heart to explore (R.V.) the matter, found that there was only one great fact that could be verified, and that is, the fact of death. This supreme evil (v. 3) strikes all, whether good or bad young or old, without pity.

" Love or hatred " (v. 1) may mean prosperity or adversity. This mystery is beyond human knowledge. The close of this verse, and the commencement of the following, should read thus : " All lies before them, i.e., before the righteous and the wise, just as before all others." That is, under the sun, the vicissitudes of life affect the good as the evil ; and therefore the good are not exempted from the supreme calamity of death.

Verse 3 would better read : " This is the greatest calamity of all," i.e., the fact of death ; and yet in spite of this fact men's hearts are filled with evil and madness so long as they live.

In the East a dog is the vilest of animals and a lion the noblest.

The last line of verse 5 may read : " Neither have they any advantage at all, for their faculty of remembering ceases to exist."

The dead lose six factors possessed by the living (vs. 5 and 6) viz. : knowledge, memory, love, hatred, envy, and " a portion under the sun," that is, life.

" God hath already accepted thy works " (v. 7) : this may be understood to mean " God has prospered thy business."

The philosophy and the declaration of verses 7-10 are : That recognizing the fact of death, and accepting it as the extinction of existence, the wisest life is one of enjoyment if God has given the means for enjoyment ; and that so long as strength is enjoyed an active life is commendable. The declaration is : yet is that life of enjoyment and activity only vanity and empty toil.

The words " so that " may be supplied at the commencement of verse 10. The verse will then read : " So that whatsoever thy hand findeth to do, do it whilst thou art able; for there is no work, nor plan, nor knowledge, nor wisdom in Sheol."

ECCLESIASTES IX. 11-X. 15. — " I returned " (v. 11) i.e., I resumed my investigations.

The first line of verse 12 should be the last line of verse 11. " His time " means the day of his death.

The argument of verse 11, thus added to, is, that because man is ignorant of how long he has to live therefore is he the helpless toy of time and chance ; and his success in life, as viewed from " under the sun," is not dependent upon swiftness, nor strength, nor cleverness.

The statement of verse 12 is : that man is suddenly ensnared by death as birds and fishes by a net. This fact reveals his ignorance and his helplessness.

The argument of verses 13-x. 15 is : that Wisdom is better than strength (v. 16) ; than weapons of war (v. 18) ; than reputation (x. 1) ; than self-assertion (v. 4) ; than coercion (v. 10); and than human science (vs. 13-15).

The declaration of verses 16 and 17 is : that, in spite of the fact that a wise man delivered the city (vs. 13-15), and advantaged it more than its generals and weapons of war, yet, as a rule, the counsel of wise men is never followed.

The Lord Jesus Christ by His wisdon. delivered man from out of the power of " the great king," i.e., Satan ; and yet is He forgotten and despised by men.

One little inconsistency in the character of a renowned Christian as effectually destroys his testimony as a dead fly the fragrance of a precious ointment. The greater the renown the greater the damage.

" The right-hand " (v. 2) is a better defence than the left, and more expert. The verses which follow depend upon this fact. The teaching is : that even in the most ordinary affairs of life, (" the walking by the way "), watchfulness, discretion, and intelligence are needed. The fool by his left-handed folly proclaims every day, in the ordinary affairs of life, that he is a fool (v. 3). But the man of discretion, the right hand man, " leaves not his place ," i.e., does not assert himself when attacked (v. 4), but by gentleness escapes worse evils (R.V. margin).

" As " (v. 5), i.e., " because of." That is : Wisdom is as much needed by kings (vs. 5-7) as by peasants (vs. 8-10). Earthly rulers promote folly and overlook ability ; and ordinary men need intelligence and care in digging a well, in taking down a fence, in squaring stones, and cutting wood, lest they injure themselves, or others.

In the East fences are made of loose stones, and serpents frequently hide in them.

The point in verse 10 is, that intelligence is better than coercion. The latter may succeed, but it costs effort and involves danger.

The argument of verse 11 is : that both a slanderer and a serpent may be skilfully avoided.

Human science (vs. 12-15) multiplies books and theories, and wearies itself in such labour. But its uselessness and ignorance are demonstrated by its inability to declare the future (v. 14).

" To go to the city " (v. 15) proverbially expresses the inability of a fool to find his way to even so conspicuous a place. Man is mentally and spiritually incapable of finding his way to the Holy City. Hence the necessity of a Divine revelation.

ECCLESIASTES X. 16-XI. 6.—The message of these verses is : that it is better to engage in honest industry (xi 1), and to practice benevolence (xi. 2 and 3), than to irritate oneself because of the wealth and debauchery of others (ch. x. 18-20), and to vainly try to find out why such inequalities and injustices are permitted by God.

" Child " (v. 16) should read as in the R.V. margin " servant," i.e., " a slave " ; that is to say, a slave to vice.

" Son of nobles " (v. 17) should read as in the R.V. margin " a free man " ; that is, free from the bondage of vice and folly. The contrast is, at base, between folly and wisdom, not between childhood and nobility.

When magistrates " eat in the morning " (v. 16) it is, in the East, an evidence of neglect of duty ; for that is the time when princes administer justice at the gate of a city. Honest princes (v. 17) " eat in due season " ; that is, they do not neglect duty in order to indulge appetite.

The fabric of government and of the state (v. 18), here compared to a neglected house, suffers serious damage when members of the government neglect duty and give themselves over to debauchery and pleasure (v. 19).

" Money answereth all things " (v. 19), i.e., " money respondeth to all things "; that is, money can procure all the luxuries needed for banquetings and revellings.

Verse 19 is, perhaps, to be understood as the drunken reply of the princely revellers to the rebuke contained in verse 18.

The argument of verse 20 and of verses 1-6 of chapter xi. is : not to denounce in a spirit of just irritation these high-placed revellers, nor to waste time and injure faith, by vainly trying to find out why God permits such wrong-doing to take place (v. 5), but rather to busy oneself in reproductive industry (v. 1), such as that of a farmer, and to share with the poor the resulting profit

(v. 2). The clouds and the trees are pointed to (v. 3) as illustrations of this life of industry and benevolence. The clouds fill themselves with water, but do not keep it for themselves, they empty it out upon the thirsty earth. A tree, whether it happens to be in the cold north or the hot south, gives its fruit and shade to others.

The Egyptian farmer throws the seed upon the Nile waters which inundate his land, the seed sinks into the soil, and a bountiful harvest results. " Evil" (v. 2) means "calamity" or "misfortune"; i.e., a famine for example. The argument of the verse is: that because a famine is possible, therefore surplus wealth should be generously distributed. Such is the Divine principle. Man argues an opposite principle. It is, that because of the possibility of future need, each one should hoard up his surplus wealth for himself. The late Thomas Crossley of Manchester said that the reason why he gave away to the poor almost all the profits from the sale of his gas-engine, was because he daily expected that someone would invent a better engine and so put an end to his power to help others.

The statement in verse 3 respecting the trees is popularly understood to mean, that as a tree falls when cut down, or blown down, and remains fallen, so will the sinner's destiny be fixed after death. This is true as regards the sinner, but the argument of the verse is: that if the lot of a tree happens to fall in the north or in the south of a land, its function is to grow and bear fruit and afford shade, and so benefit the people.

A farmer that declines to work because of the wind or the rain (v. 4) will not enjoy the full harvest that will reward the diligence of verse 6.

The Christian should apply the principles of these two verses in his work for the Lord. Difficulties should not discourage him: and he should be as energetic in purpose in the evening of his Christian life as in its morning.

It is as fruitless and as vain to waste time in trying to find out God's secret purposes in the permission of evil as to try to ascertain, how the bones of a child are formed prior to birth.

ECCLESIASTES XI. 7-XII. 8.—These verses testify that youth and mature age, however richly provided with pleasures, are bound to lead to decrepitude and death; and are, therefore, vanity of vanities if God be excluded.

" Light " (v. 7) means life and prosperity. " Darkness " (v. 8) means adversity, old age, and death.

" All that cometh is vanity " (v. 8). This is true when God is suppressed. The child expects boyhood to give a satisfying happiness; the boy expects the same from youth; and the youth from manhood. But disappointment is met at every stage of life's journey; and the experience made that all that cometh is vanity.

The verses that follow continue the argument of the emptiness of youth and maturity (v. 10) even when furnished with all means for enjoyment (v. 9); and this emptiness is embittered by the consciousness of future judgment (v. 9). The better path of turning away from pleasures which only irritate the mind, and injure the body (v. 10), and of remembering God, in and from, boyhood, and before the advent of old age and death, is set out in verses 1-7 of chapter xii.

"Or ever" (v. 1 R.V.) means "before that." " Now," i.e. " I beseech you" (Isa. i. 18. Heb.)

Verses 2-5 describe old age; verses 6 and 7, death.

Verse 2 pictures the depression and gloom which accompany old age. In youth life appears all brightness; and if there is rain, sunshine follows it. But not so in old age, clouds then return after rain, i.e., the mind loses its power of recovery and cheerfulness.

" The keepers of the house " are the arms, the " strong men," the legs, the " grinders," the teeth, " the windows," the eyes (v. 3), " The house," more than once in the Bible, figures the human body.

" The doors shall be shut to the streets," etc. That is, the mouth of the aged man is closed when masticating his food, and no sound is heard owing to the absence of teeth (v. 4).

The cry of a bird causes the aged to start; the power to distinguish melodies is lost; the nerve to climb, or even to walk, broken; the hair turns white; the lightest load becomes a burden; and appetite fails (vs. 4 and 5).

These evidences of decay precede the dissolution which occasions the processions of mourners in the streets (v. 5).

" The silver chord " is the spinal marrow (v. 6). It is " snapped asunder " (R.V.). " The golden bowl " is the head, " the pitcher," " the fountain," " the wheel " and

" the cistern " figure the heart with its organs for the circulation of the blood.

Such being the disappointments and miseries and mournful end of life, as viewed " under the sun," and independent of God, exceptional intelligence fittingly declares it all to be vanity of vanities (v. 8).

ECCLESIASTES XII. 9-14.—The eternal value of the Sacred Writings are contrasted in verses 9-12 with the worthlessness of human writings ; and in verses 13 and 14 are summed up the conclusions resulting from a study of this entire Book.

The Sacred Writings are words of delight ; of righteousness ; of truth ; stimulating as goads ; reliable as nails well fastened ; communicated through prophets ; and inspired by One Shepherd, Jehovah the Shepherd of Israel (vs. 10 and 11).

Verse 12 should be read as in R.V. margin.

Human writings, however numerous, lead nowhere, and only produce weariness. The Divine writings lead to Christ and to heaven ; they are words of delight ; and they refresh and do not weary.

Having heard all that can be said in favour of trying to secure happiness in this life by the use of material agents, the conclusion is : that it is impossible ; that the only happy life is one in fellowship with God and the Bible ; that such fellowship produces the ideal man ; and that any other life is madness, because there is a Day coming when every action, however hidden, will be brought into the unsparing light of the throne of God and judged.

God having revealed Himself to man through His commandments (v. 13), they (the commandments) can produce a perfect moral character (2. Tim. iii. 17). The last line of verse 13 should read : " This is the whole man " i.e., this produces the ideal, or perfect man.

The subject then of this Book is the folly of seeking happiness " under the sun," and that the possession of exceptional intelligence only renders more evident the folly and unhappiness of this quest. The Book gives the experience and the reasoning of man on all that happens in the visible world, and therefore he is necessarily infidel. He is compelled to confess his ignorance, for he can know nothing outside of his five senses ; and hence the solution of moral problems is beyond his capacity. But God having in grace revealed Himself in the Scriptures, and gifted man with a conscience and free-will, the happiest life, therefore, is one of obedience to God ; and this is made the more reasonable because of the judgment that is to follow death.

The sense of verse 11 appears in the following translation : " The words of the wise are as goads, and as tent-pegs well fixed are the words of the masters of assemblies. Both are given by the same Shepherd." A shepherd gives to one servant a goad for the cattle, and to another a tent-peg to fix firmly in the ground. So the Great Shepherd gives to some of the under-shepherds words which act as goads ; to others, words which stablish and strengthen.

THE SONG OF SONGS

THE SONG OF SONGS.—As in Ecclesiastes
all is emptiness, so in the Song of Songs all is
fulness. Christ and the world are contrasted.
In the one book the heart is too large for the
portion ; in the other, the portion is too
large for the heart. The relation of the two
Books is pointed out in the Introduction to
the notes on Ecclesiastes.

If in the Sacred Scriptures one book may be
spoken of as more sacred than another, then
may this song be declared to be the most
sacred of all. It is the Holy of Holies of
communion with God. Under the figure of a
bride and a bridegroom is expressed the love
of Christ to the believer, and of the believer
to Christ. There is no sin, and, therefore,
no shame. Adam and his bride, prior to the
Fall, illustrate the Song, and are types of
the Messiah and Israel. For though this
Song has an application to every believer in
his relationship to Christ, yet does its
interpretation belong to Israel. She as the
unfaithful wife of the prophecies of Jeremiah
and Ezekiel has been judged. But she is to
be new-born as a pure virgin (Hos. ii.) and,
as such, betrothed to the Divine Solomon
and become the wife of the Lamb, and reign
with Him over the millennial earth. The fulfilment of this Song belongs to that future time.

CHAPTER I-II. 7.—In verses 2-7 the
Bride speaks, and mainly of the bridegroom.
It is not necessary to mention his name,
just as Mary at the sepulchre assumed that
the supposed gardener would know whom
she meant.

" To kiss with the mouth " (v. 2) implies
betrothal. The believer (v 4) does not wish
to go to heaven alone ; but those who can
testify : " the King has brought me into
His chambers," they only can, with effect,
invite others to taste the gladness, and
rejoicing and love that are found in Christ.

All who love Him, rightly love Him, and
sincerely love Him ; He is worthy of their
love, and His love begets in them a sincere
affection towards Himself.

As to herself she confesses that she is
unlovely as the " tents of Kedar " (i.e. the
black tent of the Arab) but, through the
comeliness that has been put upon her, she
is as the curtains of Solomon. Such is the
believer in himself and in Christ.

As in chapters viii. and ix. the bride's
relatives despised her, so here in verse 6. They
made her toil in the blazing heat for them,
so that she had no time to beautify herself,
i.e., dress her own vineyard.

In verse 7 she cries out for a fellowship
sweeter than that of the companions.
Christian fellowship is sweet, but it is
" veiled " (see margin) ; the heart desires the
sweeter fellowship of the Bridegroom Himself.

He now speaks in verses 8-11, for He
declares her to be the fairest among women ;
and adds words of admiring love. He tells
her that He is to be most quickly found in
the places of daily duty.

The Bride speaks in verses 12-14. While
the King sat at His table in John xii. 1-3 the
house was filled with the odour of Mary's
spikenard (v. 12).

In the East a bag of myrrh is suspended
round the neck of a sleeper in order that its
delicious fragrance may refresh the slumberer.

" He " (v. 13) should read " it."

Henna flowers (v. 14 R.V.), and especially
those of Engedi, have a most delicious
perfume.

Such is Christ to the believer : in this night
of mystery and pain He is the bag of myrrh ;
in the day of toil and heat, the cluster of Henna
flowers.

The Bridegroom is the speaker in verse 15.
He insists on the loveliness of the Bride in
His eyes, repeating the declaration—emphasis
being laid on the word " behold " and the
word " art."

The Bride cries in response : " Behold *Thou* art fair," intimating that He only was fair, and she herself unlovely.

" The couch," or divan, or resting-place, is that desired in verse 7. In the East, at noontide, shepherds rest upon the bed of green grass beneath the shade of pleasant trees, both cedar and fir. Such is the silvan house of verses 16 and 17.

Having spoken of the beauty of her bridegroom, and of this house of the forest, she humbly adds : " As for me personally I am no better than a rose of Sharon or a lily of the valley." These were the commonest flowers of the field.

This first stanza of the Song contains two themes. The first : Communion desired (i. 2-7); the second : Communion enjoyed (i. 8-ii. 7).

The words of admiring love of the Bridegroom for the Bride are addressed by Him to her personally ; but the words of admiring love of the Bride for the Bridegroom are not addressed to Him personally, but to others.

The scene in this second portion of the stanza is the shady resting-place at noon desired in verse 7, and enjoyed in verse 16 to ii. 7.

In response to the statement of the Bride (ch. ii. 1) that she is as a common field-flower, the Bridegroom replies (v. 2) that, beautiful as the daughters of Jerusalem may be, they are in comparison with her no better than thorns, and she is, in His eyes, as a lily.

One lily but many thorns ! So it is ; and so it has always been. God's people are a little flock, comparable to one lily ; the unconverted are without number, and are comparable to many thorns.

The trees of the wood (v. 3) may be beautiful, but they are not to be compared to the apple-tree. In it is food as well as shelter. Saints are beautiful as sons, but they cannot take, in the soul, the place of the Divine Apple Tree. In union with Him there is rest (" I sat down ") ; there is joy (" with great delight ") ; there is shelter from the heat (" His shadow ") ; there is appetising food (" His fruit was sweet to my taste ") ; there is the wine of the Kingdom ; and, over all, the protecting canopy of love (v. 4).

Thus the companionship of the Bridegroom, and all that is found in Him and with Him, turns a sylvan glade into a banqueting house. Christian experience knows the truth of this ; for all that the Bridegroom is here to the Bride, Christ is to the Believer.

Verse 5 may read thus : " Strengthen me with cakes of grapes, refresh me with apples, for I am overcome with love." Grapes and apples here picture heavenly food, and only such is desired by the heart that warmly loves the Saviour.

Christian biographies abundantly testify to instances of believers being so overcome with love to Christ that they had to cry out to be strengthened when under such spiritual emotion.

The imagery of verses 6 and 7 is very lovely. After the midday meal in the glade with the Beloved, and the other shepherds, the Bride, supported by Him, (v. 4) falls asleep. After a little while He gently lays her upon the soft grass, adjuring the shepherdesses not to disturb her. She needs all the rest that she can get, and they had treated her hitherto with harshness (ch. i. 6). This shows His love for her ; and He impresses them, that just as the slightest sound would awaken the roes and the hinds of the field, so would the least movement arouse her.

Such is the nature of communion. A word, a look, a thought, suffices to break it ; and the Bride here resting in a delicious sleep upon the arm of the Beloved is a very lovely picture of Communion.

" The kisses of His mouth " are John xiii. to xvi. " He " should read " it " (v. 7 and iii. 5) as in the R.V.

SONG OF SONGS II. 8-V. 1.—The scene now changes, and a new relationship of the Bride and Bridegroom is introduced in order to give another aspect of Him in the perfection of His love. She is pictured in her home from whence He would call her to the mountains of separation (v. 17).

The strength of His love is evidenced by His speedy overcoming of all hindrances (vs. 8 and 9) ; by the ardour of His appeal (vs. 10-13) ; and by His declaration that her face was beautiful to Him and her voice sweet (v. 14).

That Christ should declare the believer's face to be comely, and his voice sweet, is amazing love. He desires, first, to see the face, and, then, to hear the voice. This is a great encouragement to prayer. He loves to see His people drawing near to Him, and He loves to hear them speaking to Him.

The last three verses are spoken by the Bride. She first says : " Catch for us the foxes, the little foxes that spoil the vineyards." Directly the Lord makes a manifestation of Himself to the soul at once there is a conscious recognition of the little sins that hinder the grapes of testimony, and there is the desire to bring Christ practically into the daily life in order to set it right.

The Bride then establishes her heart in the knowledge of her union with Him (v. 16), and of where she will be sure of fellowship with Him (v. 16) ; and then prays that at dawn of day He will return, and return quickly as a roe or a young hart, over the mountains that then separate them. These mountains of separation would then become the mountains of spices " (chapter viii. 14).

The section (ii. 8–v. 1) predicts the conversion of the Elect Remnant of Israel, her marriage with the Messiah, and the setting up of the millennial kingdom. As before stated the entire Song deals with the restoration and glory of Israel ; but this section is rich in detail in relation to that time. In ii. 8-14 Immanuel quickens Israel's affections and confidence ; assures her that the winter time of her rejection is over ; and that the inextinguishable love that wept over Jerusalem now calls to her and awaits her affection. It is all exquisitely beautiful. She replies (vs. 15-17) desiring perfect cleansing ; acknowledging a heavenly relationship ; and praying for His manifested appearing.

SONG OF SONGS III.—In vs. 1-4 the energy of the affection awakened by Him in her heart is strikingly evidenced. The comfort, luxury, and repose pictured by a couch cannot satisfy a heavenly affection —an affection that desired companionship upon the lofty summits of the mountains of separation. Indeed she would rather walk with Him at night-time in the darkened streets than find her pleasure in the love and luxury of her mother's house, into which she with great propriety at once brought Him when found. In that house are also found the daughters of Jerusalem ; for the midnight cry has aroused them : " Behold the Bridegroom cometh," and they have gone forth to meet Him. In the meantime the Bride has fallen asleep, and the Bridegroom forbids her being disturbed (v. 5, R.V.).

Whenever communion is restored and the heart brought into the joy and confidence and rest of union with Christ, it is His will that nothing should interrupt that rest.

Israel, as a nation, is the mother of the Elect Remnant ; hence verse 4 is most important as fixing the interpretation of this great love song.

Her full heart, like Mary's at the sepulchre, assumes (v. 3) that everybody is interested in her Beloved. She therefore does not mention His name to the watchmen ; and just as the angels were uninteresting to Mary, so were the watchmen to the Bride. Angels, and ministers of the Gospel, are precious gifts from God, but they can never satisfy the heart that is seeking Jesus.

The marriage day of the Great King now dawns ; and His coming on is set out with great glory in verses 6-11.

" Bed " (v. 7) should read " car of state," as in verse 9. Four pillars of silver, one at each corner, supported its curtains, the back (not bottom) was made of gold, the seat (not canopy) was covered with purple, and the floor tessellated with the affectionate and skilful work of the daughters of Jerusalem. The Great King's mother, i.e., humanity, for He is the Son of man; who in the day of His rejection crowned Him with thorns, now crowns Him with the nuptial wreath.

Thus in language of striking splendour are set forth in these verses the Deity, the Humanity, and the Royal and Bridegroom glories of the Divine Solomon

The " daughters of Jerusalem " possibly picture the Gentile Nations ; for these will in that day become daughters of Jerusalem, and will be blessed in subordination to Israel.

SONG OF SONGS IV-V.1.—The love that here minutely declares all that the Bride was in the Bridegroom's eyes, appears the more wonderful when it is remembered that He was the Great King and she but the Shulamite, earning her bread as a day-labourer in a vineyard, and scorched and blackened by the sun.

His words of admiring love pour forth as a torrent, and exhaust every lovely thing in order to express her beauty in His eyes (vs. 1-5 and 10-15). He declares that hers is the perfection of beauty (v. 7), and that a minute examination fails to discover the least imperfection in her loveliness. His heart expresses His delight in her. As already pointed out, it is a fine moral thought that the Bride never speaks of the Bridegroom's perfections to Himself, as if she was to approve Him—she speaks of Him fully, and with true affection—but He speaks fully to her herself, and assures her of His love.

This is very beautiful as expressive of the affection that subsists between Christ and the believer.

Just as the Shulamite confesses (v. 16) that all the precious fruits and spices declared by the Bridegroom to be hers, were really His, so the believer knows that the graces, the beauties, and the perfections that clothe him are all gifts from Christ, and are in truth His.

So unbelieving is the heart that the Heavenly Bridegroom has to repeat Himself and say " Behold thou *art* fair, thou *art* fair my love " (v. 1).

" Appear " (v. 1) might better read '' descending.''

Verse 2 should read as in R.V. margin. The whiteness of her teeth, their correspondence in pairs, and their full number is here finely expressed.

Her neck was not bent in slavery, nor weakened by disease, but erect, full, and beautifully proportioned as a tower, and adorned, not as with a few bucklers carried by the common soldiery, but as with a thousand princely shields.

A gazelle feeds not on but among the lilies. The best pasture is found there. It is a peaceful pasture. To feed among the thorns suggests anger and hatred. The verse not only points to the beauty of the Bride's form but to the softness and gentleness of her character.

Whether she or the Bridegroom is the speaker in verse 6 is very difficult to say ; but the probability is that she is the speaker.

" Look " (v. 8) would better read " go or " come." He invites her to leave the beautiful mountains of Lebanon and Hermon etc., and the horrid dens of the lions and the leopards and to be His life companion. It is easy to turn away from a lion's den, but not so easy to leave a beauteous mountain. Christ's call demands a forsaking of everything in order to be His.

In the East gardens are enclosed, and fountains sealed (v. 12) ; else would they be quickly destroyed by men and animals. The heart of the believer is to be guarded on every side from the intrusion of the world, and perpetually watered by the Holy Spirit, and, as such, is to be a garden for the Lord.

The Shulamite is the speaker in verse 16, and in chapter v. 1 the Bridegroom, to the end of the fourth line. The last two lines are spoken by the Bride. In verse 16 she invites Him to come into His garden, and He immediately responds saying, " I am coming into my garden," etc. She then invites all the companions of her marriage day to join in the feast ; but she is careful to reserve the first place for Him.

SONG OF SONGS V. 2—VI. 3.—Every Christian heart knows, alas, the discipline of this chapter. There can be sufficient spiritual life to hear the Shepherd's voice, but the soul is drowsy, and there is not energy enough to open the door to the Heavenly Visitant. There is, therefore, the loss of the conscious presence of the Lord, and the loss of rest (v. 6), and of power (v. 7), and of dignity (v. 7) ; and there is, also, the loss of a true testimony to Christ ; for it discredits a husband if his wife is found searching for him at night time.

The spiritual condition of a church may be pictured by verses 2-5 together with Rev. iii. 20. The door is duly fastened so as to exclude evil ; and, inside, all is beauty and order. The robe is laid aside ; the feet are washed ; the hands drop with myrrh ; but the Lord stands without, and the very order and beauty of the church occasion His exclusion. Many churches to-day could not afford to open the door to Him, for His entrance would disturb their stately ritual.

However warm and fervid may be the love of the Christian to Christ yet is it imperfect. Christ's love is a perfect love ; hence in this song there is no failure in affection on the part of the Bridegroom, but there is on the part of the Bride (vs. 2-5).

The joys and excitement of the marriage-day are now followed by the duties of the every day life. Her husband, who is a shepherd as well as a King, returns home late at night, but His sleepy bride is too indolent to open the door. He does not upbraid her, as He might, but He gently chides and disciplines her by a withdrawal. Thus the True Shepherd chides and teaches.

In the East it is an offence against public order that a young married woman should go about at night time ; and, therefore, the watchmen and the keepers of the walls punish her. Loss of communion entails loss of power and dignity ; and it can happen that a Christian, when out of communion, and feeling the consequent restlessness and misery, may expose himself to the just rebuke of the official guardians of public or private societies.

Not to the watchmen but to her companions does the Bride give the exquisitely beautiful testimony to the perfections of her lover (vs. 9–16). Her testimony is so warm and heart-filled that they desire to find Him ; and, her intelligence quickened as the result of her testimony, she can tell where He may be found (ch. vi. 2 and 3).

When testimony to Christ flows out of a warm heart, then has it an effect upon others.

" This " (v. 16) might better read " such."

In chapter ii. 16, the Bride joyfully said, " My Beloved is mine," but in vi. 3, with deeper and chastened intelligence, and no longer able to think with satisfaction of her love to Him, she says " I am my Beloved's." This marks very real progress in the spiritual life, and establishes the heart in the assurance of salvation.

SONG OF SONGS VI. 4-13.

When on the way to the gardens (vs. 2 and 11), and accompanied by her companions, the Bride suddenly meets her Husband. But He does not upbraid her, as He might justly do, but, on the contrary, overwhelms her with a torrent of burning words of love (vs. 4-10). This was both grace and deepest and tenderest affection. Prior to the failure of her love for Him, He had testified to her preciousness in His eyes (ch. iv. 1-7). Now He again speaks of her beauty, and speaks with the same passion and affection. But it is not repetition. There is a distinction. Before, He pointed rather to her perfections as peculiar to herself ; now He speaks of that which she is for Himself. He recalls her beauty, but it is in order to delight in His possession of her and to praise her in the presence of the companions. She belongs to Him ; she is His only one. Other princes may have countless wives, He has but one ; and she surpasses all others in beauty and grace.

All this illustrates the affection of Israel's Shepherd for the Elect Remnant ; and is a precious testimony to the unchanging warmth of Christ's love for the cold-hearted believer.

" Terrible " (vs. 4 and 10) might better read " majestic."

Verse 10 predicts, and pictures the glory of redeemed Israel in the crowning day that is coming by and by.

Assuming that verses 11 and 12 are spoken by the Shulamite they teach that conscious restoration of communion may be recovered in the place of daily duty ; and that the heart may be raptured away to heaven with chariots of love as Elijah's body was with chariots of fire.

As the Bride hastens away with her Bridegroom her companions call to her to return, for they would now interest themselves in her. This rapture awakens them to the importance and preciousness of the Shulamite ; for just as the despised and unknown Jacob was found to be a prince waited upon by angelic princes, so the despised Shulamite is found to have also her Mahanaim.

SONG OF SONGS—VII. 1 - VIII. 4.

Once again (vs. 1–9) the Bridegroom addresses words of admiring love to the Bride. She is altogether perfect. The minutest scrutiny can discover no blemish in her. Such was Eve to Adam in the Garden of Eden. They were the first Bride and Bridegroom. They were both naked, but they were not ashamed, for they were sinless. Such is the figure and relationship here. To the pure in mind it is sacred and precious. This section of the song helps the believer to realise how beautiful he is in the eyes of Christ ; but it fills him with humility, for he knows that his moral beauty is not his own but Christ's comeliness put upon him.

In verses vii. 10 to viii. 3 the Bride speaks. The consciousness of being her Lord's property, and the object of His affections, is declared in verse 10. This is most deep and perfect joy. Chapter ii. 16 and vi. 3 mark two precious expressions of the affection of the heart to the Lord, and the second is an advance upon the first ; but this third outpouring of a satisfied heart sets the crown upon a love that desires nothing more ; for all here is of grace.

The joy of conscious fellowship leads to Christian activity (vs. 11–13) ; and such activity is effective love (v. 12). True service, whether at home or abroad, is the natural result of the engagement of the heart's affections with Christ. It is in " the field," in " the villages " and in " the vineyards " that the believer " gives his loves " to the Beloved, i.e., his deepest affection expressed by the plural of magnitude, in the activities of service.

These verses also point forward to the time when Israel will go forth with Immanuel in the certainty and communion of His love to enjoy the fruit of the millennial earth. Then will all manner of precious fruit, new and old, appear in restored Israel to delight the heart of Him whom she at the first rejected.

" Despise " (viii. 1) would better read " reproach." The Bride does not say : " O that Thou wert my brother," but " O that Thou wert as my brother."

Verse 2 should read as in the R.V margin.

The Bridegroom speaks in verse 4, R.V., in response to the ardent affection of His Bride's love. He desires that she may rest in His love and enjoy it, as long as she will ; and that none should disturb her. Such is the value He sets upon the refreshment that the rest of communion ministers to the believer's heart.

SONG OF SONGS VIII. 5-14.—The question of verse 5 is asked by the daughters of Jerusalem ;. that is, by the nations who will be redeemed in relationship with Jerusalem.

The picture presented by verses 5-7 is most touching and gracious. The Bridegroom and the Bride are presented coming together up out of the Wilderness ; she is leaning upon Him ; and it is permitted to hear their sweet converse. Hers is the weakness and His the strength. She leans on Him. They have their backs to the wilderness and their faces towards the spice mountains. She is not alone. He accompanies her. Such is the relationship between Christ and the believer. Christ has gone down into the wilderness of this world to seek the believer and save him out of it. The believer, who is all weakness, leans upon the Beloved who is all power ; and they move forward together, having their backs to the world and their faces to the Father's Home.

The speaker in verses 5-7 is the Beloved. He first reminds the Bride of where in His grace He found her (Gen. iii.),and then gently hints at her past unfaithfulness in having given her heart and her arm to others, thus causing Him to suffer the bitter pains of a holy jealousy (v. 6) ; He urges that, for the future, her heart and arm might be sealed for Him ; and He assures her (v. 7) that His love for her was a love that, on the one hand, could not be quenched by even floods of indifference or unfaithfulness, nor, on the other hand, purchased by all the perfections of moral merit. Such is grace. It is love setting its affections upon an object wholly unworthy of such affection. The corrupt Christian Church teaches that the Divine love can be purchased by works of merit, and that God's justice and pity can be bought with a sufficiency of money and so induce Him to release His suffering children from the pains of a supposed Purgatory.

The last line of verse 7 may be understood to read : " He, and it, would utterly be contemned." That is, both the man and his money would be rejected in the effort to purchase love.

Verses 8 and 9 are spoken contemptuously by the Bride's brothers, the sons of her mother (ch. i. 6). The word " little " is not here to have the modern affectionate meaning: The argument is : that their sister was too young to marry, and that she was of no use whatever. She was neither " a. wall " nor " a door ," i.e., of no use to exclude or to admit ; that is, she was good for nothing.

The verses may be thus paraphrased : " We have a little sister and she is yet a child : what shall we do for our sister in the day when she shall be asked for in marriage ? If she be a wall," etc. That is, if she were worth anything we would furnish her with rich clothing and with jewels. " Boards of cedar " means ornamental panels of cedar.

The Bride speaks in verses 10-12. She exclaims " I am of worth, and no longer a child " (v. 10) ; and she exults in the consciousness that, though despised by her brothers, the children of their common mother, yet was she beautiful in the eyes of her Beloved.

In the East the development of the figure announces the season of marriage.

The contrast between the compulsion of. law and the compelling of love is set out in verses 11 and 12. Solomon's tenants were bound to furnish the legal rent of the vineyard hired out to them (v. 11), but love constrained the Bride to give the produce of her vineyard; whilst, at the same time, not forgetting what was justly due to the labourer.

In the enthusiasm of a whole-hearted surrender to the claims of Christian service there is a danger of.forgetting what is due to those employed by the Christian in personal and daily toil.

The speaker in verse 13 is the Bridegroom. He says : Thy companions in the vineyard hear thy voice. That is good, but speak to me, " cause me to hear it ! " Such is Christ's just plaint to-day. Many speak to their companions in testimony, and in the necessary ordering of Christian service, but they neglect private prayer and secret communion.

The song closes (v. 14) with the ardent cry of the Bride to the Bridegroom to hasten His return—to come as a roe or a young hart ; that is, to come quickly.

Thus this Book, the last of the poetic books, corresponds to, and closes like the Apocalypse, the last of the prophetic books. There the Bride says " Come ! " (Rev. xxii. 17), and the Bridegroom answers " Yes, I am coming " ;   and the Bride repeats : " Do so ! come, Lord Jesus ! "

The principal personages, and the circumstances, in the two Books are similar. The Bride, i.e., Israel, is despised and ill-treated by the sons, i.e., the Nations. She and they are children of a common mother (compare viii. 5 with Gen. iii. and Ezek. xvi.). The Bridegroom is the Messiah. The Bride's vineyard is Palestine (v. 12). The Divine Solomon's vineyard, the Gentile world. In the Apocalypse, as in the Song of Songs, the Bridegroom descends into the Wilderness, rescues His Bride from her persecutors, celebrates His marriage with her, establishes His Kingdom, and makes her His companion in His glory.

The depth and preciousness of such grace is seen in the contrast between " the mountains of spices " (v. 14) and " the tree " (v. 5) of Gen. ii. It was under that fatal tree He " found " her.

Thus the theme of this Book of exquisite beauty is, not the justification of the sinner, but the cultivation and discipline of the affections of the heart toward Him who is worthy of its supreme affection. These affections cannot be too ardent when Christ is their object. He who loves Him not knows Him not. It is impossible to exaggerate the importance of cultivating such affections. As for Him no language, however exaggerated, can express, or exhaust, the strength of His love for the believer. The minutest scrutiny reveals that He sees nothing but perfection in him, and He declares that all is lovely in His eyes. This assures the heart before Him, and satisfies its deepest longings.

ISAIAH

ISAIAH.—Isaiah was a contemporary of Jonah, Amos, Hosea, and Micah. Like Samuel, Jeremiah, and Daniel he commenced to preach at about fifteen years of age. He died at about eighty-five. Tradition states he was sawn asunder by Manasseh (Heb. xi. 37). His Book is divided by almost all commentators into two sections, but the Book divides itself into three. Each of these three is marked by an earnest call at its opening and a solemn warning at its close. The First Section contains forty-eight chapters. Its earnest call is found in i. 18, and its solemn warning in xlviii. 22. The Second Section ends with chapter lvii. Its earnest call is xlix. 1, and its solemn warning lvii. 21. The Third Section is formed of chapters lviii.-lxvi. Its earnest call is lviii. 8-14 and its solemn warning lxvi. 24.

These three Sections harmonise with the dispensational purposes of God as revealed in the Bible (Acts. xiii. and xv. 16). The first forty-eight chapters are addressed to Israel while in Covenant relationship with God. The next nine are addressed to the Nations, Israel included, during the time that Israel is " Lo-Ammi "; and the remaining chapters are addressed to Israel when brought back into relationship with God.

While, therefore, the interpretation of the First and Third Sections belongs to Israel, and the central Section to the Nations as nations, yet have the three Sections a moral application to all, for Israel is a nation ; but when in Divine relationship she becomes the " chosen people."

Prophecy is sad but sweet ; sad, because it deals with sin ; and sweet, because it reveals a Saviour from sin. All prophecy gathers round the person of Christ, and mainly concerns Israel. The Church nowhere appears in the Old Testament prophecies (Ephes. iii. 5).

The Divine Titles in xlviii. 22 and in lvii. 21 are appropriately " Jehovah " and " Elohim. " God is " Jehovah " to Israel, but " Elohim " to the Nations. This distinction in these Divine Titles appears in the first two chapters of Genesis and in the last two chapters of Revelation, and throughout the intervening Books of the Bible.

From Moses to Christ was fifteen hundred years. Were two men to start from the extremities of this period of time, and advance towards each other at a uniform pace, they would meet in Isaiah liii. 6 ; that is, they would meet in the great doctrine of the Atonement. That verse reveals the righteous platform upon which God can act in grace to fallen man.

The hypothesis of two Isaiahs was proposed by Voltaire, passed on by Payne, and accepted by some modern scholars. It attacks inspiration, for the Holy Spirit, in the New Testament, gives twenty-one quotations, ten from the former portion of the Prophecy and eleven from the latter, declaring them to be by Isaiah, whom He mentions by name. If there were two Isaiahs then has the Holy Spirit erred ; and the Scriptures are consequently unreliable as an authority, for he who errs in one point can err in many.

This effort to discredit the supernatural in prophecy is based mainly upon change of style and the use of new words. The Book itself destroys this theory, and John xii. 38-41 disproves it, for it quotes Isa. liii. 1, and vi. 9 as spoken by the one prophet.

ISAIAH I. 1-20.—To step out of Cant.viii into Isa. i. is to pass from sunshine to shadow. The love that exults in the one (viii. 4 and 13) laments in the other (vs. 2-4).

The statement of verses 5 and 6 does not describe moral character, but the severity of just but unavailing punishment. Israel refused to repent notwithstanding such punishment.

The very worship which God Himself had commanded was debased by them to an abomination in His sight. As in the days of the First Advent, ceremonial zeal was everywhere seen, but the weightier matters of the Law—justice, judgment, and mercy—disregarded.

The promise and consolation of verse 18 can only be claimed by those who obey verses 16 and 17 ; and the continued enjoyment of such consolation is affected by verses 19 and 20.

Chapters i. 21 to iv. 6 form the First Book of the First Volume of Isaiah.

ISAIAH I. 21–I. 31.—The interpretation of this prophecy belongs to Jerusalem and to the Election of Israel (vs. 25 and 27), but its application embraces the whole millennial earth. In many passages in the Bible humanity is pictured as a city, because the Divine purpose is, that all men should dwell together in righteousness, and peace, and love.

" The faithful city " (v. 21) is Jerusalem ; the term " harlot " means " idolatress," and " judgment " means justice, i.e., obedience to the Bible.

Idolatry is a murderess (v.21) ; it puts every virtue to death in the soul and in society.

The magistrates of verse 23 are compared in verse 22 to impure silver and diluted wine. They were neither worthful nor honest. " Gifts " mean " bribes."

God's love perpetually appears throughout the Bible in indignant denunciation of injustice and hardness of heart toward the widow and fatherless (v. 23).

The title " Mighty One of Israel " (v. 24) is peculiar to Isaiah. It is repeated in his later prophecies (compare xlix. 26 and lx. 16 with Gen. xlix. 24).

" I will turn my hand " (v. 25) means protection and guidance (Zech. xiii. 7) ; " upon thee " i.e., upon Jerusalem.

" Dross " and " alloy " (v. 25) do not here figure sins, but the " princes " and " companions " of verse 23. In opposition to these are promised the righteous judges and counsellors of verse 26.

" Converts " (v. 27) should read " they that return " ; i.e., the Divine Election out of Israel.

The wrath of God is as certain and perfect as the love of God. The one will be vindicated in the judgment of the transgressors of verse 28, and the other in the redemption of the converts of verse 27.

The reference in verses 29–31 is to idolatry. It is figured by " oaks " and " gardens." They were both idolatrous. The garden possibly was an imitation of the Garden of Eden, and the oak, of the Tree of Life. Satan's effort has ever been to imitate God in order to oppose Him. The word " Druid " is believed by many to be the Greek word for a tree, and especially the oak tree, beneath which that form of idolatry was practised. It had no doubt a reference to the Garden of Paradise and the Tree of Life.

But as a dried up garden and a withered oak-leaf so is the idolater (v. 30) ; and his eternal doom is pictured in the fire of verse 31 which will consume both him and his idol.

ISAIAH II. 1–21.—The interpretation of prophecy is rendered difficult by the necessity of distinguishing between that part which referred to the circumstances which were near at hand at the time of its utterance and that part which applies to the future. The future only can give a fulfilment which will satisfy and exhaust the predictions of prophecy.

Some of the prophets heard what was imparted to them by God ; others, like Isaiah, " saw " what was revealed (v. 1).

Possibly, when in a trance, the words passed before the mental vision of the prophet and were uttered by him at the moment as he read them, and recorded by a scribe, or else committed to writing by the prophet himself when released from the trance. A communication from man can be readily forgotten or partially forgotten, but when God imprints His living words upon the mind, as in the case of a prophet, they remain imprinted there.

Verses 2–4 in this chapter correspond to Micah iv. 1–3. Micah's prophecy was seventeen years later than Isaiah's. Some can only here recognize the latter prophet borrowing from the former. But this shews a want of intelligence. When God repeats a message the repetition emphasises its preciousness to Him and its importance to man. In Jer. xxxvi. 32 and in Matt. v. and Luke vi. are recorded such repetitions. They throw light upon Isa. ii. and Mic. iv. The Messiah sent this message through Isaiah to the Southern Kingdom. Seventeen years later he sent it through Micah to both the Northern and Southern Kingdoms ; that is, to a larger audience (compare Isa. ii. 1 with Mic. i. 1). This enlargement appears in Matt. v. and Luke vi. In the former, the Messiah revealed to Israel the character of the kingdom He proposed to set up upon the earth : in the latter it is repeated to the Nations.

That repetition in the New Testament shows how precious to Him, and how important to Israel and to the nations, is the establishment of such a kingdom of peace and goodness and love.

Similar features appear in the prophecies of Isaiah and Micah. Their repetition shows how eagerly the Messiah longs for the desired day of His future coming in blessing to the earth. His people should have fellowship with Him in this hope.

" Mountains " and " hills " (v. 2) are figures of speech for governments; the greater, Imperial (mountains), the lesser, Monarchical (hills). Messiah's government (" the Mountain of Jehovah's House ") shall be at the head of them, and exalted above them (R.V. margin).

" The Law " (v. 3) should read " law " ; i.e., instruction, direction, teaching.

" Judge among " (v. 4) should read " arbitrate between " and " reprove " would be better translated " decide the disputes of." Man's Courts of Arbitration are doomed to failure, but to Messiah's Court is here promised success. The result of His decisions is predicted in verse 4.

In the certainty of such success the Prophet (v. 5) calls upon his contemporaries to profit by such " light." This light is God's moral teaching. It is the teaching of the Bible. To read, believe, love, and obey that Book is to walk in the light of God.

" Therefore " (v. 6) should read " for," and after " replenished " (" filled " R.V.), should be supplied the words : " with idolatrous rites."

" To strike hands " (v. 6 R.V.) means " to contract marriage," or to form commercial partnerships. This was forbidden by the Law. The accumulation of wealth, the multiplication of horses, and the making of idols (vs. 7 and 8) were also forbidden.

The bowing down and humbling of verse 9 refer to the adoration of images ; and " the mean man " and " the great man " figure all ranks of society. While outwardly loyal to the Law (ch. i 11-15) they, like the Pharisees, were privately idolaters (Luke xvi. 14, Col. iii. 5).

The judgment of verses 12-21 had a partial fulfilment in the destruction of Jerusalem by the Babylonians, but its plenary fulfilment is described in Rev. vi. In that coming " day " when the Lord Jesus shall be revealed from Heaven in flaming fire (2 Thess. i.), He will judge every thing and every one (v. 12, R.V.) that is proud and lofty, and that is arrogant and self-sufficient. The great and haughty, comparable to cedars and oaks (v. 13), and the proud governments, likened to high mountains and lofty hills (v. 14), with their standing armies (v. 15), their navies (v. 16), and their religious works of art (v. 16), and their idols (v. 18) shall be utterly destroyed.

ISAIAH II. 22-IV. 6.—The first verse and the last verse of this message give its import, which is, the folly of dependence upon man and the wisdom of trusting Messiah. As for man (v. 22), he is the feeble creature of a moment, but the Messiah (iv. 6) is an all-sufficient and eternal refuge.

The insufficiency, helplessness, and folly of man are set out in iii. 1-iv. 1.

In the East, as to-day in the West, expensive clothing (iii. 6) is accepted as an evidence of position and ability.

" Let this ruin be under thy hand " (v. 6) means " repair the fortunes of the state."

A vicious life (v. 9) quickly shows itself upon the countenance.

The love of God for His people, and His sympathy for the poor, appear in the burning and indignant words of verses 12-15.

Where polygamy is an institution the harem governs the State (v. 12).

" To destroy or swallow up the way of thy paths " means to do away with the Bible as the rule of moral conduct. " Thy paths " denote " the paths of righteousness " designed by God for His people (Ps. xxiii. 3).

In the East in former times, and in certain countries to-day, slaves are given no clothing, except a loin-cloth, and are branded with the names of their masters. The prediction of verses 16-24 is that such should be the fate of Israel. The prophecy had a fulfilment under the Babylonian oppression.

The statement of chapter iv. 1 exhibits an excess of human folly. The number " seven " here is indefinite meaning several. Man in his weakness and need and shame will run to anyone rather than to God ; but if they do so they have to furnish their own bread and apparel. God ordained (Exod. xxi. 10) that these should be provided by the husband for the wife. How much better, therefore, to confide in God than in man.

The love, the power, the wealth, and the sufficiency of the Messiah are set out in vs. 2-6

He is "the Branch of Jehovah" (v. 2) —the Gospel of John: He is "the Man the Branch" (Zech. vi. 12)—the Gospel by Luke: He is "the Branch the King" (Jer. xxiii. 5)—the Gospel by Matthew; and He is "the Servant, the Branch" (Zech. iii. 8)—the Gospel by Mark.

"Blood" (v. 4) means bloodguiltiness. Not only is Jerusalem guilty of the blood of all her prophets and righteous men, but she is especially guilty of the blood of the Messiah—but she will be cleansed from all such guilt.

The cloud of glory at the beginning only covered the Tabernacle, but, in the future (v. 5), it will cover every dwelling-place—the cottage as well as the palace. The last line of the verse may read: "For over every home shall the glory be a bridal canopy. Such is, and shall be, Jesus for, and to His people. Thus closes the First Book of the First Volume of Isaiah.

The message of ii. 1-21 begins with grace and ends with judgment; that of ii. 22 to iv. 6 begins with judgment and ends with grace. Every true message contains both these notes.

ISAIAH V.—The vineyard is Israel (v. 7), the singer Elohim, and the Beloved, His Beloved Son (Luke xx).

The destruction of the Vineyard occupies verses 1-7, and the judgment of its husbandmen verses 8-30.

The Divine Solomon in Luke xx. refers to this vineyard and to the judgment of the husbandmen.

The disloyalty and ingratitude of the husbandmen to the Beloved Son not only illustrate the response of Israel, as a nation, to the amazing love of the Messiah, but also faithfully pictures the moral condition of the heart of many present-day Christians in response to the tender love and care of Christ.

Hebrew scholars point out (v. 7) an arresting play upon words similar in pronunciation. This might be expressed in English: "He looked for equity but behold iniquity; for right but behold might."

"Cry" (v. 7) means a cry for help because of oppression and injustice.

The husbandmen are divided into six groups and woes denounced against them in verses 8-30 as follows: The Avaricious (vs. 8-10); the Pleasure-Seekers (vs. 11-17); the Sceptics (vs. 18 and 19); the Preachers of a false gospel (v. 20); the Self-Righteous (v. 21); and Unjust Magistrates (vs. 22-24).

Big farms cause a scarcity of food, and a corresponding rise of prices. Small farms secure the opposite (vs. 8-10).

The judgment predicted in verses 25-30 had a partial fulfilment in the destruction of Jerusalem and the devastation of Palestine by the Babylonians and the Romans; but its plenary fulfilment awaits the future.

"They" (v. 30) means the hostile nations, and "them," the Israelites.

The false preachers of verse 20 of the present time substitute the "sweet" of universal salvation for the "bitter" of the wrath to come; the darkness of the Missal for the light of the Gospel; the misery of Purgatory for the felicity of Paradise; and say that to rob the thrifty is a good and not an evil action.

See note on xxvii. 2, 5.

ISAIAH VI.—Wherever sinners are found the Saviour is never far off. So is it here. They are described in chapter v. and He is immediately presented in chapter vi.

That Jehovah (v. 1) is the Lord Jesus Christ is declared by the Holy Spirit in John xii. 37-41.

Such is grace! it places Jehovah Jesus the Saviour in the midst of guilty and lost men, just as He is seen at Golgotha; for there they crucified two thieves with Him, placing Him in the midst.

The Holy Spirit in the Scriptures does not always record facts in chronological order but oftentimes in moral order. Compare, for example, 1 Cor. x. with Exodus and Numbers. It is possible that this chapter precedes the first five as to time, and that it records the conversion, new birth, and ordination of Isaiah. But it is placed here, and thus attracts the attention of the reader to the great moral fact that the Prophet, having pronounced the six preceding woes upon others, pronounces the last and greatest upon himself: crying out that he was morally a leper and justly doomed to death (v. 5).

The first four chapters, therefore, may be

viewed as forming an introduction to the entire Book.

The popular opinion that the prophet's lips were touched in order to make him an effective preacher obscures the beauty, the force, and the message of the chapter.

King Uzziah was " a man of unclean lips," that is, he was a leper (2 Kings xv. 5). His death in " a separate house " emphasized the terrible fact. Doubtless he was felt to be a very great sinner.

So long as men see themselves and their sins in the light of their own conscience, or in the judgment of society, or of the Church, they are not disquieted ; nor do they feel their need of cleansing. But when, like Isaiah, they see themselves in the Divine Light, they cry out like the Prophet that they are " undone."

" Undone " (v. 5) means justly doomed to death. See the Hebrew text.

In the light of the throne Isaiah learned that he was a moral leper ; that his people were moral lepers ; and that they altogether were as vile as king Uzziah.

If the sinless seraphim in the presence of the thrice holy Lord of Hosts had to veil both their faces and their feet, how hopeless was it for a moral leper such as Isaiah to stand in such a light !

He needed a cleansing and covering of his sin (vs. 6 and 7). The living coal from off the altar of burnt-offering, symbolizing the fire of the wrath of God and the blood of the Lamb of God, when brought in contact with his " unclean lip " removed his iniquity and expiated his sin.

There is no other way of cleansing and expiation than through the wrath of God and the atoning blood of Christ. These are revealed and glorified at Calvary. There God judged sin infinitely and eternally in the person of Christ ; and His precious blood there shed is the one and only and perfect expiation for, and covering of, sin.

As in the case of Saul of Tarsus on the road to Damascus (Acts ix.) so here, true conversion manifests itself in surrender and activity. Paul said : " What wilt Thou have me to do ? " and Isaiah said : " Here I am ; send me."

To be an effective preacher an experience of conversion is essential.

The seraphim instructed Isaiah in the due proportion to be observed between worship, conduct, and service. A pair of wings covered the face and the feet and energized the flight. The proportion was four to hide self and two for service.

The sinless king of verse 5 is to be here contrasted with the leprous king of verse 1.

No one has seen God at any time (John. i. 18) but the only begotten Son, as Jehovah, and as the Son of Man, manifested Him. Hence, in vision, Isaiah saw " Jehovah "— not " Elohim." Moses and Daniel and John also saw Him as such ; and Abraham saw Him in Angelic form. God has revealed Himself in Creation Form, in Angelic Form, and in Human Form.

By a striking idiom of the Hebrew language a prophet is said to do what he was commissioned to declare God would cause, or permit, to be done. This idiom appears in verse 10. See John xx. 23.

The just judgment of this verse is repeated seven times in the Scriptures by the Holy Spirit. This shows its deep importance for Israel—Matt. xiii. 14., Mark iv. 12, Luke viii. 10, John xii. 40, Acts xxviii. 26, 27, Rom. xi. 8. These passages make it clear that Israel did not wish to hear, or to understand, and that a judicial blindness from God justly descended upon their heart.

The answer to the question of verse 11 is found in Rom. xi. 25. It is faith alone that can ask this question. This blindness will rest on Israel's heart until the consummation of the judgment inflicted on her (vs. 11 and 12).

But God has not cast away His people for ever (v. 13)—a Remnant shall be saved ; this is beautifully set forth in this last verse thus translated : " But yet in it (the land of Palestine) shall be a tenth ; and it shall return and be swept away ; but as a terebinth and as an oak whose stock remaineth when they are felled, so the holy seed (the Remnant) shall be the life thereof."

So it came to pass ; and so it will come to pass. Israel was carried away to Assyria and Babylonia ; a tenth part returned ; it was swept away by the Romans ; but a hidden living root has been cherished by Israel's faithful God ; and the day will come when that root will spring up into a greater and fairer tree than ever it was in the past.

ISAIAH VII. 1-VIII. 10.—2 Kings xvi. and 2 Chron. xxviii. should be read in connection with this prophecy.

Ahaz here represents " the House of David " (v. 2).

The sons of Aaron having failed as a link between God and His people (1 Sam.), the family of David was chosen to maintain that relationship, and promises were made to it. It also failed. Ahaz, David's son, set the brazen altar aside and substituted for it an idolatrous altar. But God in His pity sought to save him, and not only spoke to him (v.10), but caused Isaiah, and his sons, to symbolize to him the judgment that was coming and the grace that would save a Remnant out of it. This grace would be personated in the fulness of time in the Divine Immanuel, of whom the Prophet's second son was a type.

But Ahaz refused to listen, for his heart was already given to Assyria and her idols; but, like many at the present day, he tried to hide his hostility to the Word of God behind a veil of religious zeal for the Law. (Compare verse 12 with Deuteronomy vi. 16.) "His" (v.2) i.e., Ahaz.

Supply "with fear" after "moved" in verse 2.

No doubt Ahaz had gone out to the neighbourhood of the conduit to inspect the operations in progress for the defence of the city.

Isaiah's child was to accompany him (v. 3) as a symbolic child, in order that his name might carry a message of judgment and of grace to the heart of the king.

To an energetic, warlike, and capable monarch an injunction to do nothing but believe (vs. 4 and 9) was both trying and irritating.

A blazing torch is dangerous, but the butt-end of a smoking-torch is innocuous (v. 4).

The Scripture does not say who the son of Tabeal was (v. 6), but no doubt he was a prince chosen by the kings of Samaria and Damascus to be, as king of Jerusalem, their servant.

In the East not to use a man's own name but to speak of him as "the son of Remaliah" expresses contempt.

After "Damascus" (v. 8) supply "it shall be spoiled," and after "Rezin" "he shall be slain." Supply similar words after "Samaria" (v. 9) and "Remaliah's son."

Rezin and Pekah were both killed within two years. Pekah was a murderer (2 Kings xv. 25), and he himself was murdered (2 Kings xv. 30).

Ahaz refused a sign (v. 12). Such is "the flesh." It refuses a sign when offered one, and demands a sign when refused one (Mark viii. 12).

To "weary" a man is to doubt his promises (v 13). Grace, unwearied by repeated distrust, gives signs so as to assure the doubting heart (v. 14).

Poverty should teach the child the "good" of obedience to the Word of God and the "evil" of idol worship. Abundance flows from the one; hunger from the other (v. 15).

Verse 14 should read thus: "Behold the young woman," i.e., my wife, the Prophetess, Isaiah's second wife (viii. 3) "is with child, and about to bring forth a son, and she shall call his name Immanuel."

But this child was also to be called "Maher-shalal-hash-baz" (viii. 4). Thus was he a symbol, and by his double name predicted the wrath of God that was coming and the incarnate Saviour who saves from that wrath (1. Thess. i. 10).

This child was a type of the Divine Child that was to be born of the Virgin Mary. But His mother was not only to be a "young woman" but she was also to be "a Virgin," for such is the technical term used by the Holy Spirit in speaking of her in Matt. i. 23; and such is the term employed by the LXX. in their translation of Isa. vii. 14.

Local and temporary features appear in every type, otherwise it would be no type but the thing itself.

"Butter" (v. 15) should read "sour milk" or "curds." This statement, connected with verse 22, means that the poverty of the land would be so extreme at the time that the child should be weaned, that there would be no food for him other than this spontaneous food. This verse, therefore, does not picture abundance and luxury, as is commonly understood, but extreme poverty as the result of the Assyrian invasion so soon to come

But while the child would be yet an infant the two kings abhorred by Ahaz would have ceased to live (v. 16 R.V.).

"The land" (v. 16), i.e., Northern Palestine and Syria regarded as one because their kings were confederates.

God who could read Ahaz's heart and its plans, addresses to him personally the message of verse 17. He tells him plainly that great as were the miseries suffered by the kingdom since the Disruption, they would be exceeded by those now about to come.

Those miseries are set out in verses 18-25.

"Desolate" (v. 19) should read "rugged." The hordes of the Egyptians and of the

Assyrians, comparable to flies and to bees, would settle down upon the land so thickly that not one acre would escape.

" The hired razor " (v. 20) means the king of Assyria, " the river " is the Euphrates. At the moment that razor was being hired by Ahaz to shave Samaria and Syria ; but the intimation here is that God would hire it to shave Judea.

To shave the head and the feet is to shave all ; and to shave the beard is, for an Eastern, great indignity.

A young cow and two sheep (v. 21) express poverty. The last line of the verse points to the sparcity of the inhabitants, as curds and honey point to the absence of food.

Briars and thorns should displace vines (v. 23) ; and the hunter, the husbandman (v. 24).

Verse 25 should read : "And all the hills that were digged with the mattock, none shall come thither for fear of briars and thorns, but· they shall be for the letting loose of cattle and the trampling down of sheep."

Uriah the priest (viii. 2) was Ahaz's colleague in idolatry (2 Kings xvi. 16).

His attaching his signature to the tablet predicting the birth of Isaiah's symbolic child, made the denial of the circumstances of the birth and its prediction impossible.

But the prophecies of the Scripture have in many instances not only a partial but a plenary force. Hence verses 7 and 8 point forward to the time in the future when the Assyrian, i.e., the Anti-Christ, will conquer Immanuel's land ; but he shall come to his end, and none shall help him (Dan. xi. 45).

Verses 9 and 10 relate to that future day of " Jacob's trouble." The verses should be read as in the Revised Version. The peoples are those that the Anti-Christ will lead against Jerusalem. His and their determined preparations are expressed in the repetition of the term " gird yourselves " ; but the certainty of their defeat is assured in the repetition of the prediction " ye shall be broken in pieces."

" Give ear all ye of far countries " (v. 9) is an invitation to outlying nations to witness the discomfiture of Anti-Christ and his army.

" Take counsel together " refers to the plannings of Anti-Christ and his colleagues (v. 10) ; " speak the word," i.e., " Command the assault upon Jerusalem " decided on in the Council of war. But that council shall come to nought, and that command shall be

without result ; and why ? Because of Immanuel, i.e., " God with us." His presence will discomfit and destroy the Assyrian.

The gentle waters of Shiloah (viii. 6) figured Immanuel's government ; the rough waves of the Euphrates (v. 7), that of the Assyrian monarch.

" The neck " (v. 8), Jerusalem, was the head of the Judean kingdom. The Assyrians forty years later, as here predicted, flooded the whole land and besieged Hezekiah so that he was like a man up to his neck in the water and about to be drowned. But they had to withdraw to Lachish and there Immanuel, as the Angel of Jehovah, slew 185,000 of them (xxxvii. 36). Rev. xix. 11–21 will fulfil the prophecy when Immanuel will slay a much greater multitude of the enemies of His people.

ISAIAH. VIII. 11–IX. 7.—This prophecy had a message of warning and consolation for those who heard it at the time of its utterance, but its interpretation belongs to the First and Second Advents of the Messiah, and to the long period of time between, during which Immanuel hides His face from the House of Jacob (v. 17).

Up to the end of verse 2 of chapter ix. the Prophecy concerns the First Advent and the hiding of Immanuel's face.

Verses 3–7 of chapter ix. relate to His Second Advent in power and great glory when He shall establish His kingdom over repentant Israel and the converted Nations.

" For " etc. (v. 11) would better read " Now Jehovah had spoken," etc.

" With a strong hand " i.e., " grasping me with His hand," that is, with the mighty inspiration of His Holy Spirit (1 Chron. xxviii. 19, Jer. xv. 17, Ezek. i. 3, iii. 14 and 22, and xxxvii. 1).

" Conspiracy " (v. 12) i.e., " confederation " ; it refers to the alliance that was then proposed with the Egyptians and the Assyrians and to which Ahaz and the people looked for safety. This was man's confederacy. In opposition, God's confederacy is recorded in chapter ix. 11. Man's confederacy is made in unbelief ; God's, in judgment.

The Prophet was commanded to stand aside from the confederation, and instructed not to share the people's fear but to seek for safety in trusting Immanuel, who should be to them that trusted Him a " Sanctuary," but to those who rejected Him " a Stumbling-block." (Matt. xxi. 44, Deut. xxxii. 4, 15, 18, 30, 31, and 37, Dan. ii. 34, Rom. ix. 23, 1 Pet. ii. 8).

" Many " (v. 15) means " the majority " ; and so it has come to pass : To the vast mass of the Hebrew Nation Immanuel has been, and is, a stumbling-block.

Isaiah had children and disciples and testimony and law (vs. 16-18). He, his children, and his disciples were signs and wonders to Ahaz and Jerusalem. But they figured and foreshadowed the Divine Prophet and His disciples, His spiritual children, His law, and His testimony, and so reveal the perfection of His manhood. Christ is both Son and Father (ch. ix. 6). As Son, He speaks of His " brethren," and, as Father, He speaks of His " children." Hebrews ii. 12 and 13.

The close of verse 19 should read as in the Revised Version.

When men are in fear and need direction they prefer spirit-rapping to Bible- reading, with the result that " surely there shall be no morning for them " (vs. 19 and 20 R.V.). These Hebrew despisers of the Light of the World shall pass through Immanuel's land (Palestine) in distress and darkness and hunger ; they will revile Him, their true King and God ; they will in vain look up-ward and downward for help ; above and around there shall be nothing but a darkness causing anguish ; and they shall be driven away into thick darkness (vs. 21 and 22).

Such has been Israel's experience since the betrayal and murder of the Messiah ; but greater misery and darkness await her on her return in unbelief to Palestine. Yet has there been, and will there be, a believing minority preserved by God and reserved unto salvation. This remnant will be multiplied into the nation of ix. 3 R.V. and taste the joys of the Crowning Day that is coming.

But there should be no darkness to Galilee of the Nations (ix. 1). There was anguish in that part of Palestine when the kings of Syria and Assyria smote it (1 Kings xv. 20 etc.), and repeopled it with a mixture of nations, so that the Pharisees regarded it with contempt. That was a time of darkness ; but a greater darkness, because a moral darkness, rested on Galilee and the Jordan valley when the Great Light appeared (v. 2). That Light shone in " the shadow of death " (v. 2), for the people of Israel, and the

Gentiles, and the Messiah Himself were in that shadow ; for the shadow of Calvary, with its deep darkness, shadowed His sinless spirit from Bethlehem to Golgotha.

" The sea " (v. 1) means the sea of Galilee. Most of Christ's ministry was exercised in Galilee of the Nations, because He was not only to be Israel's Redeemer, but also the World's Saviour.

Between verses 2 and 3 the present long period of Israel's exile intervenes.

Verse 3 should read as in the Revised Version.

What is future is often expressed in the Hebrew Bible as past, or present, or both ; for to God there is neither past, present nor future. His counsels are of old ; and hence, in that sense, have a past existence ; they are present, for they are sure of fulfilment ; and they are future. Hence the Past Tense occurs in verses 3 and 4, the Future in verses 5 and 7, and the Present in verse 6.

The oppressor of verse 4 is the Anti-Christ ; his doom will be accompanied by the des-truction of all military equipment (v. 5). The discomfiture of Sennacherib foreshadowed the judgment upon this future Assyrian Monarch.

The Child was born, the Son given (v. 6) ; thus is declared the Humanity and Deity of the Messiah. The Son was not born, He was given, for, as God, He was from Everlasting, but, as Man, He was born.

" Upon them " (v. 2), not " in them " as some teach. This verse, therefore, interprets John i. 9, R.V. The Greek construction of this latter verse, and the argument of the context, make evident that the birth of one particular Child, and not the entrance of children in general into the world, is the point of the verse. That Child was The Great Light, and in coming into the world He shone " upon " its moral darkness, as the material sun shines upon physical nature every morning. Both the sun of nature and the sun of Righteous-ness shine upon men without exception or distinction. But the moral darkness of the human realm refused this Light ; men loved the darkness rather than the Light—they nailed Him to the tree—and so proved that man in his natural birth does not possess the Holy Spirit. See notes on John i.

The Babe as He lay in the manger was the Divine glory as fully as when afterwards He stood upon the Mount of Transfiguration. The glory shone from out of Him and all around Him, whitening His swaddling clothes as it whitened His raiment ; but that glory was only visible to faith. In and upon those rays of glory appeared the awe-striking testimonies to His full-orbed God-head as theWonderful Counsellor, infinite in wisdom ; the Mighty God, infinite in power ; the Everlasting Father, infinite in love ; and the Prince of Peace, infinite in redemption. See notes on Luke ii.

ISAIAH IX. 8- X. 4.—The Holy Spirit here resumes the history of the Nation from chapter v.

The fivefold repetition of the lament (v. 25, ix. 12, 17, 21, and x. 4) " for all this His anger is not turned away," etc., links these chapters together.

The judgment threatened in chapter v. affected the entire nation, that of chapter ix. the Northern Division, i.e., the Ten Tribes ; here addressed as " Jacob," " Samaria," " Ephraim," and " Israel."

At the close of chapter v. the national history is interrupted in order to introduce the Messiah ; for He was to spring out of Judah, that is, out of the Southern Kingdom.

The history is resumed at ix. 8, and the judgments incurred by the Ten Tribes recited; leading up to the apparition of theAnti-Christ, who will be a member, very possibly, of the Tribe of Dan (Gen. xlix. 17 and 18, Exek. xlviii. 2, Rev. vii. 5-8 and John v. 43). This part closes at x. 32.

The last section of the prophecy (x. 33- xii. 6) presents the Messiah destroying the Anti-Christ, and establishing the kingdom of God in the Earth.

The five judgments of chapters v., ix. and x. should be read together with the five judgments of Lev. xxvi. 14, 18, 21, 24, 28.

In these Scriptures a similarity in the sins denounced, the judgments threatened, and their unavailing effect will be observed by the reader.

These judgments may be thus set out :

The Bible despised (vs. 24, 25).
Judgment threatened.
Anger not turned away.
Pride (ix. 8–12).
Judgment threatened.
Anger not turned away.
False teaching (ix. 13–17).
Judgment threatened.

Anger not turned away.
Violence (ix. 18–21).
Judgment threatened.
Anger not turned away.
Injustice (x. 1–4).
Judgment threatened.
Anger not turned away.

" The Word sent into Jacob and which fell upon Israel " is recorded in 2 Kings xv. 19. Here by a striking figure the judgment threatened, and the instrument of its execution, i.e., the king of Assyria, are united in the expression " The word sent *into* Jacob."

In pride and self-confidence Israel declared that she would soon repair the damage done by the Assyrian, and make Samaria more glorious than she had ever been (vs. 9 and 10). And they did so, for they prospered greatly, for a time, under the reign of Pekah.

The adversaries of Rezin, king of Damascus, were the Assyrians (v. 11) ; " him " and " his " mean Ephraim ; and " shall join," mean shall confederate. This was Jehovah's " confederation " in opposition to Israel's (viii. 12).

" Before " and " behind " (v. 12) mean " eastward " and " westward. "

"A stretched-out hand " denotes a hand stretched out executing judgment (v 12).

" Conversion," i.e., " turning round ensures blessing ; to refuse to turn round makes wrath certain (v. 13).

" Head and tail, branch and rush " (v. 14) depicts all ranks and conditions of society.

" Leaders " (v. 16) should read " flatterers" these are the prophets of verse 15. Like many preachers of the present day they flattered their congregations by preaching what the people liked to hear.

The reason why the fatherless and widows are not here exempted, as usual, from the threatened judgment (v. 17) is stated in the verse itself.

" Where will ye leave your glory ? " (x. 3), means " where will you deposit your wealth ? " i.e., the bribes and the property secured by unrighteous decisions in the Law Courts (vs. 1 and 2).

" The slain " (v. 4) might better read " the deadly wounded." The feebleness and misery of these unrighteous magistrates are vividly pictured by viewing them as bowing down even to prisoners, and falling before deadly wounded men.

Here ends the message predicting the coming wrath of God upon the Northern kingdom.

ISAIAH X. 5-32.—The Anti-Christ now reappears. His career and destruction, and the enthronement of his Victor, the Messiah, is the theme of this prophecy. It closes at xii. 6.

Verses 5 and 6 should read as in the Revised Version. The Assyrian is Sennacherib, the profane nation Judah, the anger and indignation, God's just wrath against Jerusalem and the Southern kingdom, the Assyrian monarch, God's rod and staff, i.e., His instrument for the chastisement of the profane nation.

But though the prophecy had an application to Sennacherib and his destruction, with the consequent deliverance of Jerusalem (2 Chron. xxxii.), its fulfilment belongs to the great Assyrian monarch of the future, and to the deliverance of the Remnant of Israel from his hand.

Verse 5 is the Divine summons to the Assyrian king. He (v. 7) believed himself to be a free agent ; but it is here shewn that he was but an instrument.

The monuments record that " the nations not a few " (v. 7) that he proposed to cut off were the Egyptians, the Libyans and the Ethiopians.

Verse 8 should read as in the Revised Version , and verse 9 might be thus phrased : " Is not Calno as much mine as Carchemish? " etc.

This prophecy was uttered during the reign of Ahaz when that wicked king, and all Judah, had turned to idols (v. 10), and about thirty years before the Assyrian Invasion. This prophecy attests the inspiration of the Bible. No political forecast, however clever, could predict with such minuteness the actions and words of a king thirty years beforehand.

" His whole work " (v. 12) means God's complete punishment of Judah.

The vainglorious language of the Assyrian king (vs. 13 and 14) corresponds with that found on the monuments. This is one of the numberless undesigned testimonies to the antiquity and truthfulness of the Book of Isaiah.

The terms " his fat ones," " his glory " (v. 16), " his thorns," " his briers " (v. 17), " his forest," and " his fruitful field " (v. 18), are all figures of speech for the Assyrian soldiery.

" The Light of Israel " (v. 17) is a Messianic Title. Such was He to Israel when He led them out of Egypt and through the Desert. Such is He here : a Light to His people (v. 17) but Fire to their foes (v. 16) ; for Israel's God is a consuming fire.

" In one day " ; and so it came to pass (2 Kings xix. 35).

The last statement of verse 18 should read as in the Revised Version margin. Here is predicted, thirty years beforehand the manner of the death which struck the Assyrian host at Lachish.

So few soldiers survived the plague that a lad could reckon them (v. 19). So was it here predicted, and so, without doubt, it happened.

The Remnant of verse 20 is here contrasted with the remnant of verse 19.

" Him " (v. 20) means the Assyrian king. Judah leant upon him (Sennacherib) in the past, and will lean upon him (Anti-Christ) in the future ; but never again, for she will lean upon the Messiah in truth, i.e., sincerely. He is Jehovah the Holy One of Israel.

He is here entitled The Mighty God (v. 21) because of His manifested power in the destruction of Anti-Christ (vs. 16-19).

Verse 22 should read as in the Revised Version (Rom. ix. 27).

" The consumption decreed " (v. 22) means the burning up of all the fruitless branches of the " vine " brought out of Egypt. " The consummation decreed " (v. 23) is the completion of the wrath predicted against Israel because of her apostasy. " The midst of all the earth " is Palestine.

" After the manner of Egypt " (v. 24) means : like as did the Egyptians in the time of Moses.

God's " indignation " and " anger " against Israel (vs. 5 and 25) shall be consummated (v. 23) on the day of Anti-Christ's destruction. These great events will synchronize.

" Scourge " (v. 26) should be printed with a capital S ; for it is here a Messianic Title. Gideon destroying Midian with a light shining from a broken earthen vessel is a type of the Messiah, who is to destroy the Assyrian with the brightness of His appearing (2 Thess. ii. 8). Gideon was the scourge raised up by the Lord of Hosts to destroy the Midian, and Messiah is the Scourge who will destroy the Assyrian ; and as He lifted up His Sceptre against Pharaoh (v. 26) so will He lift up the same Sceptre against Anti-Christ.

"After the manner of Egypt" (v. 26) contrasts with "after the manner of Egypt" (v. 24). The one pictures the might of the Messiah ; the other, the hatred of the Assyrian.

"His burden" and "his yoke" (v. 27), i.e., the burden and yoke of Anti-Christ ; "thy shoulder" and "thy neck," i.e., the neck and shoulder of Israel.

"Because of the anointing" (v. 27) better reads : "by reason of the appearing of the Anointed One," i.e., Christ. That will indeed be a "day" (v 27) of light and outshining.

In a passage of magnificent poetic prophecy (vs. 28-32) Isaiah, in a vision, describes the approach of Anti-Christ and his hosts against Jerusalem. The march of Sennacherib and his army, in the days of Hezekiah, was a foreshadowing of this greater future danger. That monarch, on reaching the Mount of Olives, shook his fist in anger (v. 32) at Mount Zion ; but hearing that the Egyptians were moving north against him, he passed on from Jerusalem to engage them in battle. But the loss of 185,000 of his men by a mysterious plague in one night at Lachish compelled him, for fear of the Egyptian army, to retreat hastily to his own land, and thus was Jerusalem delivered.

The Anti-Christ will likewise reach the Mount of Olives, but will there perish, for Messiah's feet will in that day stand upon that Mount (Zech. xiv. 4).

Aiath (v. 28) is Ai where Achan sinned.

These villages (vs. 28-32) all lie to the north of Jerusalem, Ai being the furthest off and Nob the nearest.

This whole passage should be read as in the Revised Version.

ISAIAH X. 33-XII. 6.—" The bough," " the high ones," " the haughty," " the forests," and " Lebanon " are figures descriptive of the Assyrian Monarch and his hosts and generals (vs. 33 and 34). Sennacherib himself uses these figures (2 Kings xix. 23). Such will be the end of Anti-Christ. The Mighty One, i.e., the Messiah, by Whom he will be destroyed, is described in the first five verses of the eleventh chapter.

He as " the Branch " is here contrasted with Anti-Christ as " the bough."

The Spirit of Jehovah rests permanently on Him—the Spirit in His sevenfold fulness (Zech. iii. 9 and Rev. iv. 5). This hepdad of fulness appears in the words " wisdom " " understanding," " counsel," " might," " knowledge," " reverence," " instinct " (vs. 2 and 3).

" Quick understanding " (v. 3) means scent or fragrance or delight. It suggests a disposition instinct with delight in God, and fragrant to God (Gen. viii. 21).

" Reprove " (v. 3) means " decide " ; and " reprove " (v. 4) should read " set right with equity," i.e., " administer justice on behalf of the meek."

" The earth " (v. 4) might better read " the oppressor of the land," i.e., Anti-Christ. The four members of the statement will then appear in correspondence thus :

He shall smite the oppressor of the land
    With the rod of His mouth,
    And with the breath of His lips
Shall He slay the wicked one, i.e., Anti-Christ.

Verse 5 presents Immanuel as a Priest.

Verses 3 to 5 prove that the earth will be full of violence at the time of His second advent and not of love and peace, as many foolishly imagine. He will commence His reign with righteous judgments and punishments.

The moral and physical effect of His Government is set out in verses 6-9.

" The ensign" (vs. 10 and 12) is the Messiah. He will be the centre and the attraction of millennial society.

" His rest " (v. 10), or resting place, will be Mount Zion. It will be " glorious," because covered with the glory.

" Assemble " (v. 12) should read " gather in " ; and " gather together " should read " gather out."

" The tongue of the Egyptian sea " (v. 15) means the gulf of Akabah ; the " river " is the river Euphrates ; and " in seven streams" should read " into seven streams."

In " that day " (ch. xii. 1) shall His Name be exalted. It is not exalted now, for this is man's day. In " that day " His performance of excellent things will be known in all the earth (v. 5).

Here ends the Second Book of the First Volume of Isaiah (v.-xii.). It gives the whole history of the people of Israel in its grand features up to their future establishment in blessing as the people of God, having Jehovah the Messiah in their midst.

" My Salvation, " " My Strength, " " My

Song." Such is Christ to the believer- his
life, his strength and his joy—a full Saviour
for the Christian life. " The wells of salvation "—not a cistern—for unfailing assurance,
consolation, hope and victory. The rope,
faith ; the bucket, the measure of the need.

ISAIAH XIII. 1 XIV. 2.—Here begins the
Third Book of the First Volume of Isaiah. It
closes with chapter xxvii. Its subject is : the
judgments upon the nations which Messiah
will execute when establishing His millennial
kingdom. The position of Israel in the midst
of these nations is shewn (xxii.), and their
punishment because of their hostility to Zion
predicted.

Babylon is first judged. She has been, is,
and will be the great enemy. She is Satan's
city in opposition to Jerusalem, which is
Messiah's city. She was founded by Nimrod
who was a mighty hunter of men against the
face of Jehovah (Gen. x. 9). He was a type
of the future Nimrod, the last king of Babylon,
the Anti-Christ. Perhaps he is the Anti-Christ,
for that mysterious prince is to come up out
of the abyss (Rev. xi. 7).

" Babylon " symbolizes, also, all that
which, energized by Satan, corrupts and
opposes the truth and work of God in all
dispensations. She is, as such, the religious
head and fountain of all religions approved of
man and accepted by him, and of the
philosophies of the East, both ancient and
modern, and of the corrupt Christianity of
the West. This religious system, i.e., the
symbolic Babylon, will be destroyed at the
same time as the material Babylon.

This chapter xiii. connects events which
were then comparatively near with those
that are yet future. This relationship of the
near and the future in prophecy heightens
the interest of the reader, though it tests his
discernment. The prophecy had an application to the capture of Babylon by the
Medes in the days of Daniel ; but its fulfilment belongs to the future (vs. 10-13 and
20 and Matt. xxiv. 29).

The minute predictions of this prophecy
testify, as all other prophecies, to the
inspiration of the Scriptures. At the time of
its delivery Babylon was a city of no importance, and its empire did not exist. One
hundred years later it governed the world
under Nebuchadnezzar, and after a second
hundred years it perished with Belshazzar.
Its mode of capture is foretold in verse 2 ;
and its assailants are mentioned in verse 17.

Here the Medes only appear ; in chapter
xxi. 2, the Persians and the Medes ; and in
chapter xlv. 1, the Persian only is named
(Cyrus). The order is chronological.

The chapter should be read as in the
Revised Version. The " consecrated ones,"
the " mighty men," and the " exulting
ones " are the Medes. They were chosen by
God to execute His anger (v. 3). " The
whole land " (v. 5) means Chaldea ; " the
world " (v. 11) means mankind at large in
the future.

" Cruel " (v. 9) would better read " stern ";
for there will be no mercy in that day. He
will cast out of His Kingdom all that do
iniquity (v. 9 and Matt. xiii. 41).

So great will be the destruction that a man
will be as rare as a nugget of fine gold (v. 12) ;
for everyone that does not flee (v. 15) will
perish.

Their punishment will be just ; for as they
did to others so will it be done to them
(vs. 16 and 18).

Verses 19-22 relate to the judgment
described in Rev. xvi. 6 and xviii. 1 and 2.

What may be chronologically distant is
ever " near " to faith (v. 22).

Chapter xiv. 1 predicts Zion's captivity and
restoration, and, with verse 2, foretells
Israel's future conversion and the ingathering
of the Gentiles into the Kingdom of God, in
relationship with Israel, and in subjection
to her.

ISAIAH XIV. 3-27.—The descent of the
Assyrian, the king of Babylon, the Wild
Beast (Rev. xix. 20), i.e., the Anti-Christ,
alive and without burial, into the lake of fire,
is the subject of verses 3-22 ; and the
destruction of his city, the theme of verse 23.

As frequently in prophecy, the prediction
had a temporary relation to the Assyrian
monarch in the days of Hezekiah, and to the
Babylonian king in the time of Daniel, but
its fulfilment belongs to the future ; for
these two monarchs will be united in the
person of the Anti-Christ.

" Thee " and " Thy," i.e , Israel.

Verse 6 should read as in the Revised
Version.

" Proverb " (v. 4) should read as in the
margin.

The tranquillity of verse 7 results from
the doom of the Anti-Christ. " They "
refers to the nations of verse 6.

The entrance of the Anti-Christ into

Sheol, and his reception there, is vividly pictured in verses 9-17.

In verses 18-23 Israel raises her eyes from Sheol to earth and contrasts the burial of the Anti-Christ with that of other kings. They rest in their splendid mausoleums (v. 18), but he should have no sepulchre (v. 19 R.V.), not even the stone-filled pit of the common soldier.

"Abominable branch" (v. 19), i.e., a useless sucker such as the husbandman cuts away from the root of a plant.

"Day-Star" and "Son of the morning" (v. 12) are Messianic Titles. The Anti-Christ will assume them because he will claim to be the Messiah ; and on his descent into the abyss the Rephaim will taunt him with these titles. He will claim to be God (vs. 13 and 14 with 2 Thess. ii. 4).

"The sides of the North" (v. 13) may mean Mount Zion ; upon which the future temple is to be built, and in which the future Anti-Christ is to take His seat (2 Thess. ii. 4).

The ancients believed that the throne of God was set above the North Star.

The Rephaim are possibly the giants who were drowned in the Flood ; and because of whose existence and actions the Flood, in mercy to humanity, was sent.

Verses 21 and 22 should read as in the Revised Version. The persons here addressed are primarily the Medes, but finally the future nations.

Verse 20 is sometimes cited as an argument in favour of the belief that the Anti-Christ will be an Apostate Hebrew.

"Thought" (v. 24) might better be translated "intended." "Them" and "their" (v. 25) mean Israel. Just as Mary at the sepulchre, in her love, spoke of the Lord as "Him," so Israel's Shepherd, in His love for His ancient people, often speaks of them without mentioning their name. He assumes that the reader loves them as He does

The words "in wrath" should be supplied after "sketched out" (vs. 26 and 27).

The Assyrian, as king of Babylon, i.e., the Anti-Christ, will be "broken" upon the mountains that are round about Jerusalem (v. 25).

Here and in Ezek. xxxii. and in Luke xvi., the veil is drawn aside a little and a glimpse permitted into the spirit world.

"Nephew" (v. 22) i.e., grandson— Belshazzar. Compare Daniel v. verses 2, 11, 18.

ISAIAH XIV. 28-32.—Babylon, as an immense religious system, and as the political and world opponent of the throne of David, having been, as was to be expected, first judged, the other nations hostile to Israel (xxii.) now enter the prophetic scene as follows :

Philistia (xiv.).
Moab (xv. and xvi.).
Syria (xvii.).
Egypt (xix. and xx.).
Idumea (xxi.).
Arabia (xxi.).
Tyre (xxiii.).
The earth at large (xxiv.).
The serpent, i.e., Anti-Christ (xxvii.).

The oracular utterance concerning Philistia was a call to that nation to repentance, and, at the same time, a message of encouragement to Jerusalem.

Such is prophecy, it warns the rebellious, and nourishes the faith of the believers.

"The broken rod" (v. 29) referred not only to the death of Ahaz, but also to Israel's loss of independence under Shalmaneser (2 Kings xvii. 20).

Uzziah, grandfather of Ahaz, conquered the Philistines and brought them under tribute. Hence their joy at the fracture of Judah's sceptre.

There are three personalities pointed to in verse 29, first, the serpent, second, the adder, and third, the fiery-flying serpent.

Such titles in prophetic lips would appropriately apply to Shalmaneser, to Sargon, and to Sennacherib : for these monarchs were serpents and adders to the Israelites as well as to the Philistines.

Sargon's attack upon Philistia, and upon Palestine, is recorded in chapter xx. ; and Sennacherib's campaign in chapters xxxvi.- xxxvii. They are also recorded upon the Monuments now in the British Museum.

The expression "first-born of the poor" means "the poorest of the poor," i.e., of Israel. They and the needy of Jerusalem should lie down in safety ; but Jehovah would punish Philistia with famine, and cause the residue of her inhabitants to be slain. (v. 30).

"And" (v. 30) would better read "but." "Thy" designates Philistia.

"The smoke from the north" (v. 31) is Sennacherib, the fiery-flying serpent of verse 29.

The last line of verse 31 should read: " And there shall be no straggler in his ranks" (R.V. margin).

The Assyrian host is possibly here described as a smoke because of the immense clouds of dust raised in the East by an army when marching.

This last verse will then read : " What at that time shall the ambassadors of the nations report ? "—this is what they will report.—" That Jehovah hath founded Zion, and the poor of His people flee for refuge to it."

This actually happened in the days of Zechariah after the Restoration of Jerusalem and the Temple.

But the prophecy will have its plenary fulfilment in the future happy day of Zion's strength and glory.

ISAIAH XV. AND XVI.—The land of Moab was eastward of the Lower Jordan and the Dead Sea. It was compelled by Ahab to pay an annual tribute of 10,000 lambs. The Northern Kingdom being enfeebled, or destroyed, Moab is counselled in this prophecy (xv. 1) to send the tribute to Jerusalem, and so establish relationship with God's people. The idolatry of the Moabites was exceptionally gross and obscene.

This prophecy was uttered in the year that King Ahaz died (xiv. 28, and xvi. 14), and had a primary fulfilment three years later ; but its exhaustive fulfilment awaits the future (xvi. 4 and 5).

The first and second verses may be thus more effectively read : " Surely in one night shall Ar of Moab be laid waste, and brought to nought ; surely in one night shall Kir of Moab be laid waste, and brought to nought. Bajith and Dibon are gone up to the high places to weep : Moab howleth upon Nebo and upon Medeba, etc."

" The high places " were centres of idolatrous worship ; the two most important being upon Nebo and Medeba. The prophet, in vision, sees the terror-stricken Moabites hasting up these mountains to seek help from their god Chemosh ; but in vain (xvi. 12).

As elsewhere, so here, the present tense is used for the future in order to emphasize the certain fulfilment of the prophecy.

The preacher who lives in touch with the Master, like Him delivers the Divine message of wrath with tears and not with exultation (xv. 5, xvi. 9, Luke xix. 41).

Verse 5 should read as in the Revised Version, or the words, " bellowing with fear as " may be inserted before " an heifer of three years old."

" A cry of destruction " (v. 5), may mean the cry of the fugitives reporting the destruction wrought by the Assyrians ; or the word " they " may refer to the Assyrians pursuing the fugitives and shouting for their destruction.

" Dimon " (v. 9), should read " Dibon " as in verse 2, and " lions " should read " a mighty lion," i.e., Nebuchadnezzar.

The verse predicts that under the Assyrian invasion the rivers should run with blood, but that under the later Babylonian one, the remnant of the nation would suffer greater calamities.

Jerusalem was to replace Samaria as ruler of the land of Moab (xvi. 1).

" Execute judgment " (xvi. 3), means to act wisely.

Verses 4 and 5 belong to the future. The extortioner and the oppressors allude to Anti-Christ and his soldiers. The One Who is to sit upon the throne in the Tabernacle of David is the Messiah. The outcasts of Moab in that day will belong to Him (Jer. xlviii. 47). He here speaks of them as " my outcasts," and commands Zion to shelter them from the Anti-Christ. Moab will, in that day, together with the remnant of Israel, seek in Zion a covert from the face of the spoiler, i.e., the Anti-Christ (xiv. 32).

" Hasting righteousness " (v. 5), should read as in the Revised Version. " His boastings (v. 6, R.V.) shall come to nought."

Verse 8 may read : " The Vine of Sibmah . . . . its choice plants they reached . . . . they shall be carried over the sea," i.e., the wealth of Moab should be carried away beyond the Euphrates.

Verses 9, 10 and 12, should read as in the Revised Version.

Verse 12 pictures the Moabites presenting themselves before their idol, and, like the worshippers of Baal at Carmel, wearying themselves in their fruitless cries to him.

The Philistine was to be absolutely annihilated (xiv. 30) ; but to Moab a remnant, very small and of no account, was to be left (v. 14). This remnant is to be redeemed in the latter day (Jer. xlviii. 47).

Moab had a shameful birth ; he became an idolater ; and he lived outside of God's pleasant land. Calamities and miseries marked the history of the nation. But a new birth, with glory, is here offered in relationship with Israel, and in subjection to Messiah (xvi. 1-5).

Thus Moab illustrates the sinner. His natural birth is in shame ; his manner of life impure ; his religious position outside the Kingdom of God ; and his experience suffering and misery. But a new birth, with glory, is promised him on the condition of subjection to the Lord Jesus Christ.

" In time past " (v. 13, R.V.), i.e., at a period subsequent to the judgment that was to fall within the pending three years. The reference is to the Chaldean invasion.

Grace warned Moab four times of the wrath to come, and offered salvation from it—here and in Amos i., and, about 100 years later, in Jeremiah and Ezekiel. Then the judgment fell. See notes on Jeremiah xlviii.

In these four messages is heard the voice and felt the love of Him who wept over Jerusalem. That city, like Moab, rejected both message and Messenger. The word " burden " reveals the affections of the heart that wills not the death of even one sinner.

ISAIAH XVII. 1-11.—Damascus is the oldest city in the world. It is first mentioned in Genesis xv. 2. It contains to-day about 150,000 inhabitants. It stands in one of the most beautiful and fertile plains in the world. It was, and is, the capital of Syria. Naaman the leper lived there ; and on the road thither the Apostle Paul was re-born.

Although this message was for Damascus, yet only two and a half verses, out of the eleven which comprise it, concern Damascus itself ; the other eight and a half convey a warning to Ephraim, for Jacob was trusting the King of Damascus.

Here, therefore, appears the oft repeated lesson of the Word of God, that alliance with, and dependence upon, the world involves the servant of God in ruin and loss ; and that the advantages expected are never realised (v. 11).

Just as men to-day vainly seek to restore the Apostolic church, which the just judgment of God shattered because of its sin and corruption, so the Ancients repeatedly tried to restore the Garden of Eden. Such an effort is no doubt alluded to in verse 10 In a garden a grove of trees was planted to form a place of worship, and in it was placed an image of Astarte, the Virgin-mother, whose constellation was the moon. This " Grove " no doubt originated the modern cathedral whose pillars and groined roof represent the trunks and branches of the trees forming the silvan shrine. Astarte is now worshipped as the Virgin Mary ; she is popularly represented in image and picture as standing in the hollow of the crescent moon.

As Astarte was the moon-goddess, so Baal was the sun-god. They were worshipped in conjunction as symbolising the masculine and feminine principles which produced life. Hence their worship was grossly obscene.

The future tense may be used in verses 1 and 2, as it is in the following verses.

Damascus was destroyed, but it has been rebuilt.

The fortress of Ephraim was Samaria (v. 3). It was believed to be impregnable.

The second half of verse 3 would better read as in the Revised Version : " and the Remnant of Syria shall be, etc."

" The glory of Israel " and " the glory of Jacob " (vs. 3 and 4), means that in which Israel gloried, i.e., her wealth of corn and wine and oil and cattle. The Prophet declares that the remnant of the Syrians and the remnant of the Israelites would be mutually involved in a common ruin.

This ruin is pictured in verse 2 by the substitution of sheep for men, and in verses 5 and 6 by the scanty gleanings of the harvest field and of the olive-tree.

But Divine Love promised that in that day of suffering, Israel would look away from earthly and idolatrous supports to Messiah the Holy One of Israel.

Verse 8 should read as in the Revised Version.

The misery of that day is pictured in verse 9 by the action of a woodman throwing aside branches of a felled tree as worthless for transport. The verse predicts that the land should become a desolation ; that its cities, likened to noble trees, should be thrown down ; and that nothing would be left but a few obscure villages of no value ; and that this all should take place " before the children of Israel " (R.V.), i.e., before the eyes of the wretched captives as they were being carried off into captivity.

Verses 10 and 11, may be thus freely translated : " Because thou didst forget the God of thy salvation . . . . therefore didst thou plant a pleasant garden and didst set it with foreign plants, etc." They substituted this imitation of the primal Paradise, and these foreign gods, for the worship of the true and only God in His ordained temple at Jerusalem (see R.V. margin).

Supply after "heap" (v. 11) the words " of stones."

Many professing Christians think by alliance with the world, and an accommodation of the Gospel to its false religions, to secure a harvest of international peace ; but the harvest will be a heap of stones, and not bread, and the harvest day will be a day of grief and of desperate sorrow.

ISAIAH XVII. 12 - XVIII. 7—The march of the northern nations under Sennacherib upon Jerusalem in the reign of Hezekiah, and the destruction of that army in one night (xxxvii. 36), was a temporary fulfilment of verses 12-14 ; but the accomplishment of the prediction awaits the future ; for the verses allude to the Anti-Christ and his hosts and their destruction upon the mountains of Israel (xviii. 3, Zech. xiv., Rev. xix. 11-21).

These three last verses of chapter xvii. should be read as in the Revised Version.

" He " (v. 13, R.V.), i.e., Jehovah.

The first verse of chapter xviii. should read : " Ho to the land protecting with wings, (i.e., armies) which is beyond the rivers of Cush." It is an appeal to a nation exercising a protectorate over Cush, that is, over Egypt, the Sudan, Arabia, Mesopotamia, Persia, and India, a maritime nation sending its ambassadors in swift vessels upon the sea. Such is England ; and possibly that nation is here intended.

In appearance a vessel of papyrus (v. 2). might resemble, in colour, a modern steel vessel ; or, perhaps, in future, despatch vessels may be built of papyrus and driven by electricity.

Moses was placed in a vessel of papyrus by his mother.

The second verse should read as in the Revised Version margin. The nation pointed to is Israel.

" Rivers " (v. 2), i.e., floods of armies. Palestine is the land indicated here. Her soil has been the battle ground of contending armies for more than three thousand years.

The only nation in history which can justly be described as terrible from its beginning is Israel ; for in her birth she destroyed the greatest empire and monarch of the day, that is, Egypt and Pharaoh, so that Rahab stated that the hearts of the Canaanites melted because of them. And no nation has ever been dragged away from their own land and deliberately " peeled " of their wealth but not annihilated, as has been the case with the unhappy outcasts of Jacob.

The mountains (v. 3) are those round about Jerusalem.

The action of the Messiah during the entire period of Israel's rejection, and up to " the time " of verse 7, is declared in verses 4-6. He has always had, and will have, an election out of that nation according to grace (Rom. ix. 29, and xi. 5 and 25, 26). His silence during these ages is predicted in verse 4, which may be thus read : " I will be inactive ; yet will I keep looking from my dwelling-place ; I will be to them like sunshine after rain, and like a cloud of dew in the heat of harvest." He will not cease to love, or lose sight of, His ancient people ; but, on the contrary, He will watch over His election and be to them as sunshine and dew, thus preserving them in life.

In the following verse that Election is figured as a vine whose branches are cut off prior to the grape harvest in order that it may bear more fruit.

" He " (v. 5) is the Divine Vine-Dresser, the Messiah. His instrument will be the Anti-Christ, for although the history of the vine since the day that it was brought forth out of Egypt has been a continued discipline and pruning, yet will the crisis come under the oppression of Anti-Christ immediately prior to the millennial harvest.

If Israel's faithful Redeemer likens His people to a vine, so does He liken their enemies to ravenous vultures and wild beasts (v. 6) ; and such they were, and are, and will be. During Israel's summer time of national independence she suffered much from the ravenous " vultures," i.e., the Philistines and Syrians and Assyrians ; and during her winter-time of dependence and subjection she has been preyed upon by the " wild beasts " of Babylon, Persia, Greece and Rome (Dan. vii).

" At that time " (v. 7), i.e., when the vine shall be finally pruned, Israel will offer herself as a present to the Messiah ; and, at the same time, the nations will offer her as a present to Him (lx. 9 and 10) ; and the gift will be made upon Mount Zion.

The people who will make the present will be the Gentiles; the present will be Israel, who, at the same time, will willingly present herself; the Person to Whom the present will be made will be the Lord Jesus Christ; and the place where this event will come to pass will be Mount Zion.

Some Bible expositors think that the nation alluded to in verse one is the Sudanese, i.e., the warlike peoples of the Sudan and Abyssinia; and that the appeal is to the great army which Tir-haka, King of Egypt, led against the Assyrians in support of, and to protect, the Hebrews under Hezekiah.

ISAIAH XIX. AND XX.—The theme of this prophecy is the smiting and healing of Egypt (v. 22).

The first seventeen verses of chapter xix. is past history, and the last eight verses future history.

The term " in that day " occurs six times; and should be particularly studied (vs. 16, 18, 19, 21, 23, 24). The first " in that day " (v. 16) belongs to the day of God's wrath; the remaining five occurrences of the term belong to the future day of healing. Thus there is one day of wrath, but five of grace. Five, in the Scriptures, is the number of grace. Such is God! He judges sin but delights in mercy.

Here also appears a great moral principle taught throughout the Bible: that it is only the smitten heart that experiences the Divine healing. The Samaritan woman enjoyed what the Jerusalem Pharisee rejected.

" A swift cloud " (v. 1.), i.e., the swiftly marching army of Sargon King of Assyria. Although Sargon did not know it, yet God controlled that army as a rider does his horse.

Though idols are nothing, yet they represent demons who energize the worship addressed to them (1 Cor. x. 19-21). These demons, therefore, were " moved " with terror at Jehovah's entrance into Egypt; just as they were terror-stricken at His entrance into Gadara (Mark v).

Shortly before the invasion of Sargon, civil war broke the Egyptians up into factions (v.2).

" Familiar " (v. 3), i.e., famulus, a servant, that is, a demon who is under the control of, and who obeys, a human being.

Cruel lords " (Heb.), i.e., the Assyrians. the Babylonians, the Persians, the Greeks, the Romans, and the Moslems; and, finally, " a fierce king," i.e., Anti-Christ (v. 4).

" The sea " (v. 5) is the Nile: this whole passage should read as in the Revised Version.

The cambric of ancient Egypt, as found in the tombs, is extremely fine (v. 9). Its manufacture is a lost art. It contains 540 threads to the inch. The finest cambric to-day contains about 160.

" The princes " of verses 11-13 mean the priest-princes. They were a travesty of God's kings and priests. They claimed super-human knowledge and royal descent (v. 11).

The latter part of this verse may read thus: " How say each one of you to Pharaoh, " I am, etc."

" Let them know " (v. 12), i.e.. " Let them make thee (Pharaoh) know."

This is a fine challenge! The prophets of Jehovah addressed it more than once to the prophets of Idolatry; for only God can fore-tell what will surely happen.

Zoan (v. 11) was the seat of the Egyptian Court. It was there that Moses announced the Ten Plagues.

" Pillars " (v. 10, R.V.), i.e., " chiefs "; " all that work for him," i.e., labouring men. The statement is: that the great financiers, as well as the labouring classes, would all be brought to starvation.

Man-made priests are themselves deceived, and they deceive others (vs. 13-14, and 2 Timothy iii. 13). They are the popular " corner-stones " of every nation; but they blight " every work " (v. 14), i.e., the family, the state, education, commerce, science and art, religion and morality.

" Head or tail, palm-branch or rush " (v. 15), means high or low, rich or poor.

Supply " in wrath " after " shaketh," or " shall shake " (v. 16).

The statement in verse 17, may mean that Sargon, in his march through Palestine to Egypt, would give Judah over to fire and sword, and that the report of this would strike terror into the Egyptians.

The language of Canaan, i.e., the Hebrew language (v. 18). To " swear to Jehovah " means to serve and worship Him.

The last line of this verse most probably should read: " Each one shall be called ' The city of Righteousness.' " Scholars are not, as yet, able to translate the original text.

The Five Great Cities of Ancient Egypt were cities of unrighteousness.

" An altar " and " a pillar " (v. 19), not

" altars " and " pillars " but one way of redemption, and one testimony.

This one reliable pillar is to be contrasted with the worthless pillars of verse 10 ; and the pillar of testimony will unite Egypt and Israel; for it will be placed upon the Frontier, and will testify to Jehovah.

All the statements of verses 21-25 will surely come to pass. These verses should be read as in the Revised Version.

Thus will Noah's three sons, i.e., the entire world, become servants to Jehovah ; for the human race consists of these three great families : Assyria, Israel, and Egypt, i.e., Japhet, Shem, and Ham.

Onias IV., six hundred years later, used this prophecy, when seeking permission from Ptolemy and Cleopatra to build a temple for the Hebrews in Egypt. The Egyptian King and Queen replied that Onias might do so, if it were not forbidden by the Law of Moses. As the Law did forbid the erection of any temple other than that at Jerusalem, it is evident that the Egyptians had some knowledge of the existence of the Bible.

The subsidiary prophecy of chapter xx. may not have been given at the same time as chapter xix., but it is morally united with that chapter.

Its lesson for Israel was, the bitter fruit that the servants of God must taste when the arm of flesh is leant upon, and not the Arm of God.

Sargon, the king of Assyria, was coming out of the North with a vast army. The Philistines (v. 6), and the men of Judah and Jerusalem (v. 6), were terror-stricken. They turned mutually to Egypt for succour. In this message from God they are told that the Egyptian soldiers of whom they boasted, and on whom they set their expectation (v. 5), should be carried away as naked slaves to Assyria (v. 4). .

This came to pass ; and on the Monuments in the British Museum these unhappy captives are pictured.

" Tartan " is an eastern word meaning commander-in-chief (v. 1).

Jehovah was the speaker, and Isaiah's mouth the instrument (v. 2).

" Naked " (v. 4), i.e., scantily clothed ; that is, only wearing a loin-cloth. Such is the usual clothing of a slave, or the very poor, in the east. The third verse does not necessarily imply that the Prophet was to be thus scantily clad for three years, but that it was to be a sign of a captivity that would occur within three years (xvi. 14), i.e., he walked barefoot for a three-year sign.

But so complete and abject would be the enslavement of the Egyptian warriors, that they would not be even given loin-cloths to wrap around their naked bodies (v. 4). This additional statement shows that the Prophet was not thus naked.

" Isle " (v. 6), i.e., " coastland." The reference here is to the Philistine, whilst the " we " of the last line of the verse means the men of Judah. This last " we," in the Hebrew text, is emphatic.

The reader can picture the Prophet preaching in some broad place in Jerusalem, and, with a wave of his hand toward the distant coast line of Philistia, exclaiming : " the inhabitant of *this* coastland shall say in that day (as he looks upon these naked captives). Behold, such is our expectation ! etc.," and then the Prophet adds : " and *we*, we Hebrews, how shall *we* escape ? "

The argument is, that if the mighty hosts of Egypt and Ethiopia were to be destroyed, and enslaved, by Sargon, how could either the Philistines or the men of Judah escape !

As in chapter xvii. Samaria was associated with Damascus in its doom because Israel trusted Syria and not God, so in this chapter Judah is associated with Egypt in its destruction because the people of Jerusalem trusted Egypt rather than Jehovah.

ISAIAH XXI.—There are three messages from God in this chapter : the first; to Babylon (vs. 1-10) ; the second, to Idumea (vs. 11 and 12) ; the third to Arabia (vs. 13-17).

The Babylonians were sons of Shem who had forsaken Jehovah for idols ; the Idumeans, i.e., the Edomites, sons of Esau, who had similarly apostatized ; and the Arabians were sons of Ishmael and of Keturah, distinguished for their hatred to Israel rather than for a relapse to idolatry.

" The sea," (v. 1), i.e., the Euphrates. As the Egyptians spoke of the Nile as a sea when that river overflowed its banks. so, in similar circumstances, did the Babylonians describe the Euphrates.

In the days of Isaiah, and for centuries later, the plains of the Euphrates, far from being a desert, were a Paradise. But the Prophet, in vision, saw the day when that Paradise would become, as it did, a desert; and hence the striking imagery of the words: " The oracle concerning the desert of the sea."

These words have doubtless an allusion to Revelation xvii. and xviii., where the mystical Babylon is seen in a wilderness and sitting upon many waters.

The primal occasion of the fulfilment of this prophecy was the destruction of Babylon two hundred years later by the Medes and Persians (v. 2) on the night that Belshazzar was slain (v. 5).

The prophecy should read as in the Revised Version with the assistance of the margin.

The valley of the Euphrates is scourged with violent storms from the South.

" The desert," the " terrible land " of the first verse, means the country to the north of Babylon, the home of the Medes. It was terrible because the country of these ferocious warriors.

" It " (v. 1), i.e., the hurricane of the Median invasion, comparable to, but much more terrible than, a whirlwind from the south.

Verse 2 might better read thus: " The treacherous dealer (i.e., Babylon) is dealt with treacherously, and the spoiler is spoiled. Other prophecies support this reading in predicting that Babylon should suffer the like cruelties that she caused others to suffer (xxxiii. 1 and Habakkuk ii. 8).

The command to Elam and to Media (v. 2) to go up and besiege Babylon was a Divine command.

The last line of the verse should read: " All the sighing thereof will I (Jehovah) make to cease."

The " sighing " means the sighing caused by Babylon; especially the tears that she caused Israel to shed.

In verses 3-5, the Prophet supposes himself a citizen of Babylon on the night of its capture by Cyrus.

" The night of pleasure, turned into terror " was the night of Belshazzar's feast. The poetic force of verse 5 is very fine. " Prepare the table; spread the carpets; eat, drink! Arise, ye princes, and anoint the shield! "

The picture burns before the mind. The tables are loaded with every delicacy; rich carpets provide luxurious ease; Belshazzar and his princes eat and drink.

Suddenly a terror-stricken officer bursts into the banqueting hall and shouts out: " Arise, ye princes, grasp your shields and defend yourselves! Anoint the shields! " i.e., " Stand to arms! " The leather straps of shields were oiled to prevent them breaking.

But in that night was Belshazzar the King of the Chaldeans slain.

Verses 7 and 8 should read as in the Revised Version.

" He answered " (v. 9), i.e., " Jehovah answered."

The masses of infantry and cavalry seen by the watchman, in vision, were the hosts of Media and Elam.

The repetition of the word " fallen," and the use of the present tense, emphasize the sure fulfilment of the prophecy.

The " bruised corn " of the threshing-floor (v. 10), describes Israel as oppressed by the Babylonians. God, in His tender love and pity for His people thus beaten and oppressed, uses this term of tender affection " O, my threshing, etc." He identifies Himself with these hapless slaves, and is not ashamed to call them His people.

" Duma " (v. 11), i.e., Idumea, or Edom. There is a play here upon the words; for Duma means " silence," and the prophecy foretold an eternal silence for the sons of Esau, (ch. xxxiv, Ezekiel xxxv. and Obadiah).

The anxiety of the Edomites which prompted their appeal to the Prophet, was caused by the approaching invasion of the Assyrians; but the prophecy itself was not fulfilled until five hundred years after Christ. This fact attests inspiration; for no man, however clever, could make so accurate a fore-cast of what would happen one thousand two hundred years after he was dead. The Hebrew prophets fore-told that the sons of Jacob should be scattered and the sons of Esau annihilated, and so has it come to pass. The sons of Jacob are scattered throughout the world, and number millions; but where are the sons of Esau?

Seir was the principal mountain in Idumea; and in the Bible it often indicates the whole land.

The Edomite king called to the prophet out of Seir (v. 11): " How far gone is the night? "; i.e., that then present time of anxiety and fear because of the threatened invasion of the Assyrians. The Edomites hoped that the dark danger was passing away, and that the Prophet would give them an answer of peace. But his answer was: "For Israel the morning is indeed coming; but for Edom, the night"; and yet, in the tender compassion of the Holy Spirit, he added: "If you are in earnest, and are inquiring sincerely, then turn away from your idols and come to the Light." But Edom refused the gracious invitation, and has passed away into the eternal night.

Verses 13-17 should be read as in the Revised Version margin.

There is a play here upon the word "Arabia," i.e., "sunset," as upon the word "Duma." For the sons of Ishmael there is an evening of sorrow, but not a night of eternal silence.

Dedan and Tema were descendants of Abraham.

The caravans of the Dedanites, for fear of the Assyrian, are here pictured as compelled to encamp in the thickets, and not upon the highways; and they are enjoined to give food and drink to their fugitive brethren who seek to escape from the grievousness of war.

But clever and valiant as they were they could not escape the just judgments of God (vs. 16 and 17); but they should not be wholly destroyed, for grace would leave them "a few," i.e., a remnant. This remnant are the Arabs of to-day; and they are, though few, yet free from idolatry.

ISAIAH XXII.—"The valley of vision" is Jerusalem. Just as Babylon, her great rival, is pictured in the prior chapter as "the wilderness of the sea," so Jerusalem is here named "the valley of vision." Man's city is morally, intellectually, and religiously a "desert"; God's city is a centre of visions, i.e., of Divine revelation.

These two cities are here brought together. Both are judged; but Babylon is judged first.

The introduction of Jerusalem among the nations in this Third Book of Volume I, (xiii.-xxvii.) should be particularly noted. See notes on chap. xiv.

In this Third Book is first predicted the judgment of the Gentiles; then is shown the position of Israel in the midst of them in the last days (xxii.); next, the judgment of the land (Palestine) (xxiv.); and, finally, the setting up of the millennial kingdom (xxv.-xxvii.).

Thus Palestine and Jerusalem are the centre of this universal overthrow; and although, no doubt, the judgments under Sennacherib, Nebuchadnezzar and Titus are included in the prophecy, yet is its plenary fulfilment still future.

The occasion of this prophecy is described in 2 Kings xviii., and 2 Chronicles xxix.-xxxii. To buy off the Assyrian monarch Hezekiah stripped the Temple of its treasures (v. 8), fortified the city, and secured a water supply (vs. 8, 11).

But though he himself was sincere in his repentance and faith, it is revealed in this prophecy that the people were insincere. Outwardly, they obeyed the command of the King to seek Jehovah the God of their fathers, and to humble themselves before Him, but, privately, they held fast to their sins and pleasures—Shebna, no doubt, being their leader in the very household of the King himself (vs. 15-25).

Such is, and has often been, the case in God's earthly kingdom: outward devotion to His cause, and a measure of prosperity, but inward corruption of heart, not only on the part of the members of the church, but also in the case of its highly placed ministers.

In the east when an attack is feared the people rush on to the house-tops to try and see the enemy approaching in the distance (v. 1).

The joyous tumultuous city is Jerusalem (v. 2).

Verses 2-7, should be read in the future tense, commencing thus: "Thy slain shall not be slain with the sword, etc." i.e., spiritual death shall strike Zion.

People plunged in desperate sorrow desire solitude (v. 4).

Light-armed troops carried a quiver; heavy-armed, a shield. When not in use the shields were covered with leather for protection from rust.

"Chariots" (v. 7), should read "troops"; i.e., infantry as contra-distinguished from the horsemen, i.e., the cavalry.

"He" (v. 8), i.e., Hezekiah. The allusion is to his stripping the Temple of its gold covering which had been given to the Temple by the House of Judah, i.e., by David and Solomon. His effort to buy off the Assyrians was in vain. Sennacherib took the money but besieged Jerusalem.

"The House of the Forest" (v. 8) was built by Solomon with cedar-wood from

Lebanon; hence its name (1 Kings vii. 2, and x. 17). It had now apparently become an armoury.

Hezekiah's activity in preparing the city for defence is recorded in 2 Chronicles xxxii. 1-6.

"Him" (v. 11), i.e., Jehovah. However intelligent Hezekiah's vision may have been, the people did not really lean upon God for deliverance, nor did they recognise that this chastening was from Him, that Sennacherib was His instrument, and that God had "done" and "fashioned" this trial long beforehand. Most probably this is the meaning of the verse. Hezekiah personally trusted God at the last; and yet, instead of confession and repentance, there was revelry and merry-making and scepticism! (vs. 12 and 13).

The revellers cried: "Let us eat and drink for to-morrow we shall die"; that is, "This kill-joy Isaiah says we shall die; but there is no truth in his gloomy preachings."

But they mocked the Spirit of God; hence the fearful doom of verse 14.

There was Shebna the scribe, and Shebna the controller of the king's household. These may be distinct persons; but if there was but the one Shebna, then was he outwardly true, but inwardly false.

Only the rich and great had rock-sepulchres (v. 16). "Whom hast thou here?" may mean: "what family position hast thou here?"; and "what doest thou here?" may mean: Who do you think yourself to be?

Verses 17-19, should read as in the R.V., mar. The "he" of verse 19 means Hezekiah; and "thy lord" (v. 18) also means Hezekiah.

The imagery of these verses is that of a slinger firmly placing a ball, or stone, in the leather pocket of the sling and then whirling it round and round and shooting it to a great distance. Thus should Shebna be slung out in captivity to Assyria—"a large country," i.e., a distant land.

"There shall be the chariots of thy glory"; i.e., thither (to Assyria) shall be carried thy magnificent chariots.

Eliakim is here a type of the Messiah (vs. 20-24).

In an Eastern house, a large wooden nail is firmly fastened into the wall, and on it are suspended the family ornaments.

Christ is Jehovah's sure nail fastened in a sure place; i.e., the Heavenlies; and no one who is suspended upon Him shall ever be confounded, but, on the contrary, shall be ennobled (v. 23).

Upon that nail cups of gold and silver and brass and clay may be safely hung. The little cup of clay might think to be safer if made of brass, and the brass if made of silver, and the silver if made of gold. But the gold could say: "Brothers, if the nail falls we all fall!"

The last verse refers to Shebna. Tradition says he was led into captivity tied to a horse's tail—for directly Hezekiah died his son Manasseh, and all the people, returned to idols, and the Assyrians carried them away into slavery.

God's judgments search out and strike individuals (Shebna) as surely as they strike nations.

ISAIAH XXIII.—The word "Tyre" means "a rock."

Old Tyre stood on the mainland, New Tyre stood on an island half a mile from the shore.

Both cities were founded by the Sidonians, a tribe of Canaan, and, therefore, lying under the curse (Gen. ix. 25).

The destruction of the island city predicted in this chapter occurred a hundred years later under Nebuchadnezzar.

Amos i. 9, declares the cause of its just doom.

During the seventy years of the Babylonian monarchy (v. 15) it lay desolate, but under the Persian reign it recovered its prosperity. A hundred years later it was totally destroyed by Alexander the Great.

This second destruction was fore-told by Ezekiel (xxvi.); and the city has never since been re-built.

The first seventeen verses of this chapter concern the destruction of the city by the Babylonians, and the last verse foretells its restoration and conversion. The placing of the wealth of Tyre at the disposition of David by Hiram (1 Kings v), is an imperfect picture of a perfect future.

"Ships" (v. 1), is a figure of speech for those in them.

"No house, no entering in" (v. 1), i.e., neither warehouse nor harbour; both were destroyed by the Chaldeans.

"Kittim," i.e., Cyprus. "Them," i.e., the sailors in the ships. The Prophet foretells that the crews of the ships, on the homeward voyage from Spain to Tyre, would touch at Cyprus and there get the news of the destruction of Tyre. " It," i.e., the destruction of the city, " shall be revealed (or told) to them."

" Be still " (v. 2), i.e., " be awestruck." ·

Verse 3 may be thus paraphrased : " Carried over the great waters (the Mediterranean), the corn of Sihor (Egypt), the harvest of the Nile, is her revenue " (wealth). The "merchants of Zidon " (v. 2) transported thither, across the sea, these great cargoes of Egyptian wheat, and the wheat was there exchanged for the wealth of Spain, brought by the ships from Tarshish—the modern Tartessa in the south-west of Spain. Thus Tyre became the mart of the nations.

Verse 4 may be read : " But the sea hath spoken, saying, O daughter of Zidon, the fortress of the sea, be thou ashamed, for thou shalt say : ' I no longer travail, nor bring forth sons, etc.' " The meaning is : that, as an Eastern woman is ashamed if childless, so Tyre would no longer be able to plant distant colonies, and. in this figurative sense, would have neither sons nor daughters. Tarshish was one of her daughters (v. 10) ; and she had many others.

Verse 5 should read as in the Revised Version.

" Pass ye over to Tarshish," i.e., " flee to Tarshish." The " feet " (v. 7) of Tyre were her ships. As a man flees upon his feet so the Tyreans fled upon their ships.

In answer to the question as to who had purposed the ruin of Tyre (v. 8), the solemn reply is given in verse 9 ; and this verse presents the judgment of Tyre as an earnest of the universal judgment yet to come upon the world, which will abase the pride of all human glory and cover with contempt the great ones of the earth.

Verse 10 may read thus : " Flow at liberty through thy land as a river, O daughter of Tarshish ; for there is no bond about thee any more " ; i.e., that colony being freed from the tyranny of the mother-city, could now develop itself ; as did the American colonies when freed from the oppressive legislation of London.

" He " (v. 11), i.e., Nebuchadnezzar ; to him Jehovah gave the commandment against Canaan to destroy its strongholds, of which Tyre was the greatest.

" He " (v. 12), i.e., " Jehovah "; " oppressed," i.e., dishonoured; " pass over," i.e., flee to Cyprus ; " but there also shalt thou have no rest " i e., from the pursuing Chaldees.

Verse 13 will be clear if thus read " Behold the land of the Chaldeans ! That people did not exist at the time that the Assyrian founded it, i.e., Tyre (as a port), for them that dwell in the Wilderness ; they (the Assyrians) set up its towers, they raised up its palaces ; but he (Nebuchadnezzar) shall bring it to ruin."

The argument is : Tyre boasted of its antiquity and strength (v. 7). The Prophet pointed to Assyria, a much more ancient and much stronger government, and urged that if it fell before the king of the Chaldeans how much more surely would Tyre fall !

" The days of one King " (v. 15), means the duration of the Babylonian kingdom. It lasted exactly seventy years. During these seventy years, Jerusalem was a captive and Tyre a desolation (Jer. xxv. 11).

As an abandoned woman seeks by music to attract lovers, so Tyre, after her restoration under the Persians, sought to attract merchants and commerce, and succeeded in doing so up to the time of her destruction by Alexander the Great.

In a future happy day her wealth shall be consecrated to Jehovah (v. 18). She will not treasure it up for herself but for the servants of the Messiah, in order that they may have abundant food and stately apparel.

Thus abilities and energies, debased to the service of luxury and sin, may be, under the power of conversion, consecrated to the service of the people of God.

Tyre is here justly pictured as an harlot. for she was a great centre of idolatry.

ISAIAH XXIV.—The subject matter of this chapter may be thus set out—throughout the chapter the earth means the land of Palestine :—

Land (v. 1).
  People (v. 2).
    Land (vs. 3 and 4).
      People (vs. 4-12).
Messiah enthroned in the hearts of Elect Israel in Exile (vs. 13-15).

Land (v. 16).
  People (vs. 17 and 18).
    Land (vs. 19 and 20).
      People (vs. 21 and 22).

Messiah enthroned by redeemed Israel in Zion (v. 23).

As elsewhere, so here, the present tense is used for the future to express certainty.

The first verse can therefore read : " Behold, Jehovah shall make the land (of Palestine) empty, and shall make it waste, and shall turn it upside down, and shall scatter abroad its inhabitants."

These inhabitants are divided up into six groups doubled (v. 2). Six in the Scriptures is the number of man, and expresses his imperfection, for it comes short of the perfect number seven. Man was created on the sixth day, and the number of the future super-man (xxvii.) will be 666. He is intended in verse 18 as the one who comes up out of the pit (Rev. xvii. 8). The desolation of Palestine foretold in this prophecy, and the emptying out of its people among the nations of the earth, were effected by the Romans.

The justice of this Divine action is stated in verses 5 and 6.

The " city of confusion " (v. 10), i.e., Jerusalem.

Verse 11 might perhaps be thus translated : " In the streets, instead of wine, there shall be weeping " (tears).

" It " (v. 13, R.V.), i.e., the Elect Remnant of Israel. It is here compared to a handful of olives or of grapes. " People " should read " Peoples," i.e., the Gentile nations.

" These " (vs. 14-16, R.V.), i.e., the members of the Election of Israel, shall glorify the Messiah from beyond the seas, and in the east, and in the west, and from the uttermost parts of the earth ; and during the time of their dispersion and exile they shall sing songs of praise, heard by the angels if not by men, saying : " Glory to the Righteous One," i.e., to the Messiah. Verse 15 should end here and verse 16 begin : " But I, i.e., Messiah, said, etc."

Thus will He be enthroned in their hearts.

These are His " hidden ones " spoken of in Psalm lxxxiii. 3.

" The treacherous dealers " are the members of the nation who dealt treacherously with the Law and with the Lawgiver when He appeared in flesh among them ; and, because of this treachery, the judgment of verses 17-22 follows.

The intensity of the judgment is compared in verses 19-20 to an earthquake.

" The host of the high ones on high "

(v. 21, R.V.) are the principalities of Ephesians vi. 12, and Revelation xii. 7-9, and 2 Thessalonians ii. 6-10.

In His Second Advent the Messiah will judge the heavens and their rebellious angels as well as the earth and its rebellious princes.

" In the pit " (v. 22), should read " for the pit." The " prison " is that of 1 Peter iii. 19. The " many days " i.e., the millennium ; " they shall be visited," i.e., " punished " as stated in Rev. xx. 7-15.

On the millennial morn Messiah will be enthroned on Mount Zion in the presence of His ancient and beloved people Israel ; and the glory that shone out of His Person on the Mount of Transfiguration, will shine out with such splendour upon that coming crowning day as to confound the moon and shame the sun.

The first sixteen verses precede the First Advent ; the remaining verses precede the Second Advent.

ISAIAH XXV.—Israel is the singer of this song (vs. 1-9). She will sing it on the millennial morn. It acclaims the Messiah, whom men regarded as only a man, to be God. It celebrates His might and faithfulness (v. 1)—His might in the destruction of Babylon (vs. 2 and 3), His faithfulness in defending and delivering Jerusalem (vs. 4 and 5). The scene of the song and this triumph will be Zion (vs. 6-8 and 8-10), and Moab—representative of every form of human hostility—will be judged " in his place " (vs. 10-12).

For " things," (v. 1), read " deeds." These wonderful deeds are : first, the destruction of Babylon (v. 2) ; second, the deliverance of Zion (vs. 4 and 5) ; and, third, the treading down of Moab (vs. 10-12).

Babylon is the city indicated in verse 2. Rebuilt by Anti-Christ it will head up, and express, all the opposition to the True Prince of this world from the day of its foundation by Nimrod. After its future destruction it will never be re-built.

The terms " strong people " and " terrible nations " define the Gentiles in opposition to the Hebrews. These, up to the time of Messiah's apparition, are described in verse 4 as " poor " and " needy " ; those, as strong and terrible and strangers to God and to grace (v. 5).

The term " city " in verse 3, is an expression of power and community and association.

" Strength " (v. 4), i.e., " stronghold."

Verse 5 may appear clearer if an ellipsis be thus supplied :

" As heat in a dry place enforces silence, so shalt thou bring down the noise of strangers ; as heat is lessened by the shadow of a cloud, so the song of the terrible ones shall be hushed."

The greatness of the feast of verse 6 is vividly suggested by the way the words are heaped together. This is more apparent in the Hebrew text.

" This mountain " (vs. 6, 7, and 10), i.e., Mount Zion.

Messiah's wonderful deeds at that centre are : first, His destruction of death in His First Advent (v. 8, and 1 Cor. xv. 54) ; and, second, His destruction of ignorance. In the Revised Version the eighth verse reads in the past tense, for Calvary will be a past fact at the time this song will be sung. The veil spread over all nations is the mist of ignorance on man's heart which will remain there in regard to the way of salvation and a future life till Christ comes.

" Rebuke " (v. 8), i.e., " reproach."

" This is Jehovah " (v. 9, with Phil. ii.), i.e., " this Man is Jehovah."

" The Hand of Jehovah ' (v. 10), i.e., the manifested power of Jehovah displayed in, and from, Mount Zion in government.

As a swimmer beats back the water with both hands, so will all the gathered might of the enemy be beaten down, and that in spite of the skill of the enemy's hands exercised in resistance (v. 11).

The first nine verses contain the song that is to be sung ; the last three, faith's subscription as to the certitude of its being sung.

" Thy walls " (v. 12), i.e., the walls of Babylon (v. 2). Thus Babylon and Moab are morally united in the prophecy. Babylon often appears as a political oppressor and Moab as a religious corruptor (Num. xxii.-xxiv.) ; so in this vision they picture, in unity, Anti-Christ and the False Prophet.

ISAIAH XXVI. 1-19.—The " night " of Israel's captivity and subjection (v. 9), is to be succeeded by the " day " of her restoration and glory (v. 1).

" The lofty city " (v. 5), i.e., Babylon, representative of Satan's whole power, will be destroyed, and the " strong city " (v. 1), i.e., Jerusalem, will be beautified and fortified by Jehovah its salvation.

Man's strength has no place here, but, on the contrary, it is the feeble foot of the poor and needy that shall, in that day, tread down the glory and power of the Enemy.

" The righteous nation " of verse 2 is the faithful remnant in Israel. It is the " nation " spoken of in Matthew xxi. 43, and in 1 Peter ii. 9. " Peace, peace " (v. 3). See chapter xl.

Verse 7 should read : " Thou dost make level the path of the just."

The righteous nation does not follow the judgments of its own wisdom, but walks in the way of the Divine judgments, and in the energy of true affection for the absent but expected Messiah (v. 8).

" The earth " (v. 9), means the kingdom of the Wild Beast upon which the Divine judgments are to be poured (Rev. xvi. 10) ; " the world " indicates the rest of the habitable earth.

Verse 10 foretells the present dispensation of grace, and predicts man's rejection of it ; and verses 9 and 11 point to the day of wrath that is to succeed it. Then will man learn that God is faithful to His people, and righteous in His punishment of their adversaries.

Verse 11 may be thus understood : " Lord, Thy hand is lifted up in indignation upon Thy people Israel ; yet the wicked nations do not recognize it ; but they shall see Thy zeal for Thine ancient people, and shall be ashamed ; and the fire, reserved for Thine adversaries, shall devour them."

If men will not yield to God's grace they must bow to His wrath.

As with Israel, so with believers, their salvation is ordained and accomplished by God alone (v. 12).

The " dead " and the " deceased " of verse 14, shall not rise and live in the First Resurrection, for blessed and holy are they who shall have part in it (Rev. xx. 6) ; but they shall rise in the second (Rev. xx. 14 and 15) ; and then shall they be punished and destroyed and all their memory caused to perish.

Verse 15 should read as in the Revised Version.

Verses 16-19 should also read as in the Revised Version, following the margin of verses 16 and 18.

Here the Righteous Nation laments her failure to furnish the world with spiritual children, and deplores her childlessness; but in verse 19 the Messiah comforts her with the assurance that her dead children shall arise and live, for they are blessed. This is the First Resurrection. Then in a fine outburst of poetic grandeur He calls aloud to these sleepers in the dust to awake and sing; for just as herbs seemingly dead are kept alive by the night-dew, so shall His redeemed be preserved through the long night of Death's dominion; and He fills up the cup of consolation with the added assurance: "For the Earth shall yield up the dead," i.e., the Blessed Dead, i.e., "My dead bodies" (v. 19, R.V.). He calls them His bodies! What matchless love and faithfulness! They are His property though dead and buried.

"Jah-Jehovah" (v. 4), as a compound title expresses in the highest degree the unchanging love and power of Israel's God.

ISAIAH XXVI. 20 - XXVII. 13.—This day of indignation (v. 20, and xxvii. 1), will be the day of God's wrath against, and destruction of, Leviathan, i.e., Anti-Christ.

This indignation is to be distinguished from His indignation against Israel.

"Come" not "go" (v. 20); "thy chambers" i.e., Canticles i. 4. Faith's chambers are found beneath the shadow of His wings. Compare Matthew xxiii. 37. Chambers were built at both sides of Solomon's Temple so forming wings to it. See notes on 1 Kings vi.

Just as Noah, prior to the Flood, heard the same voice saying "Come thou into the Ark," and found safety there from the destruction that came upon the world; and just as the First-born found safety in the house sprinkled by the blood of the Pascal Lamb, so will God's people find a Divine shelter in the day when Messiah comes forth out of the heavens ("His place") to punish the inhabitants of the earth (v. 21).

Then will the earth give forth the martyred dead, and they will testify to the guilt of the world and witness its just judgment (v. 21).

Anti-Christ, the future Super-man, will, as Leviathan, fulfil the prophecies concerning Pharaoh as the Dragon of the Nile, and Nebuchadnezzar as the crooked serpent of the Euphrates, and Sennacherib as the reptile of the Tigris (See notes on xiv. 29).

The day that will witness the destruction of Leviathan and his hosts will witness also the restoration of Israel as Jehovah's vineyard. (vs. 2-6).

This is the vineyard of chapter v. There it is judged; here it is blessed. These two chapters are thus connected, and should be read together. They commence and close a section of this Prophetic Volume. i.e., Books ii. and iii.

Verse 2 should be read as in the Revised Version, using the margin.

Verse 4, may be thus read: "Wrath is not now in me: should the briers and thorns be against me in battle I would march upon them, I would burn them all together."

Leviathan and his followers are the outward enemies of the Vineyard, the thorns and briers are the inward. For these there is a gracious invitation in verse 5, and a promise of assured peace to any one of them who will make the Messiah his stronghold.

As to the vineyard, its vines are to blossom and bud and to fill the face of the world with fruit; and so all Israel shall be saved; for if the song of the prior chapter is that of Judah, this song is that of all Israel (vs. 6, 9, 12 and 13).

The question of verse 7, is: "Did God chasten Israel in the same measure that He smote her oppressors?" The following verse supplies the answer. It is "No"; for though He permitted the rough wind in the day of the east wind to strike the vineyard, yet did He "debate," i.e., curb its violence; but as to the enemy he shall be smitten with an everlasting destruction.

The cleansing effect of this purging of the vine (John xv.), is declared in verse 9. In this verse the word "fruit" means "result." The result of chastening is that iniquity is purged and sin taken away. So was it with the Tribes as the result of their captivity in Babylon. They were purged from idols and idolatry. Their present and future chastening will purge them from unbelief. This is not the expiation of guilt by the atonement of Christ, but the purging of a branch already in the True Vine.

In that day Jacob shall make all the stones of the idol altar as chalk-stones that are beaten into pieces, so that the Asherim and the sun-images shall stand up no more.

"The defenced city" (v. 10), is Jerusalem

and the boughs (v. 11) her unconverted and rebellious citizens, who, though officially branches in the Vine, yet would not have the Vine-dresser to reign over them. These will justly receive neither compassion nor favour.

But the true branches, compared in verse 12 to wheat (Matt. xiii. 30), shall be gathered, grain by grain, from the Euphrates to the river of Egypt, i.e., from every quarter.

"The great trumpet" (v. 13), will be the jubilee trump summoning all Israel to the Feast of Tabernacles that will bye-and-bye be celebrated to, and with, the Messiah at Jerusalem.

Here ends the third Book of the First Volume of Isaiah.

ISAIAH XXVIII.—This Fourth Book of the First Volume of Isaiah closes with chapter xxxv. It may be regarded as one continuous prophecy. Its "Woes" are contrasted with the "Burdens" of the preceding Section. In these "woes" the Divine purpose is alternately thrown into sharp contrasts.

The first four verses of this chapter are addressed to Ephraim and Samaria, the seventh to the twenty-ninth to Judah and Jerusalem, and placed in their midst, and addressed to both, is the gracious promise of verses 5 and 6.

The whole chapter should read as in the Revised Version.

Samaria was "the proud crown" of the men of Ephraim. It stood at the head of several fertile valleys. It is compared (v. 1), to the garland of flowers which revellers placed upon their heads when feasting. But such flowers fade.

The men of Ephraim were drunkards both actually and morally. They were intoxicated with the strong wine of idolatry.

The "mighty and strong one" (v. 2) was Sennacherib. He is a type of Anti-Christ.

After "cast down" supply the words "the drunkards of Ephraim."

Figs ripen in August, but some which ripen in June are considered a great delicacy. Immediately such are plucked they are eaten (v. 4). So should Sennacherib quickly and thoroughly swallow up Samaria.

Across the gloom of this chapter is cast the bright ray of verses 5 and 6. It promises glory, beauty, intelligence, and victory to the residue of His people who make Messiah

their confidence, and not the king of Egypt (v. 15).

Messiah is the "crown of glory" of His people, and His people are His crown of glory (lxii. 3). Contrast the "crown of pride" of v. 1.

"These" (v. 7, R.V.), i.e., the men of Jerusalem (v. 14).

The magistrates were priests, the preachers were prophets. These were drunk in the pulpit ("they reel in vision"); those were tipsy on the bench ("they stumble in judgment").

Verses 9 and 10 are to be understood as the mocking words of the scornful men of Jerusalem (v. 14). They ask two questions: First: Whom does he (Isaiah) presume to teach? and, Second: Whom does he think to make to understand theology? Is it those just weaned? for he keeps on repeating, as if to infants, precept upon precept, etc. Here they evidently mimicked the Prophet; as the scornful Athenians mimicked Demosthenes. The Hebrew text makes this clear.

"For" (v. 11), i.e., "nay, verily." The Prophet, taking their taunting words out of their lips, turns them against themselves, and predicts that God, through the Assyrians, would speak to them in another tongue and in a language that would sound "jabbering" to them. The Apostle Paul in 1 Corinthians, xiv. 21, comments upon this, and in doing so calls the Old Testament "the Law."

Verse 12, may be thus paraphrased: To this people Jehovah said: This One is the rest; offer this rest to him that is weary, for this One is the refreshing (v. 16). The argument is: that the king of Egypt was proposed as a rest for the weary, but in him no refreshing would be found; for those who thought to find rest and refreshment in him, would find him to be the bed of verse 20, in which would be neither rest nor warmth.

Because they would not hear (vs. 12 and 13) therefore by a just judgment should the simplicity of the Gospel become a stumbling-block to them, resulting in captivity.

The men of Jerusalem did not use the language of verses 15 and 17 when speaking of their agreement with the king of Egypt, but the Prophet of God describes it truthfully as a mass of lies and an agreement with death. Such will be Israel's covenant with Anti-Christ.

As Zion was not itself the Corner-Stone

so the church is not the Saviour. The Corner-Stone was lain *in* Zion. He was a tested stone, tested by sin and Satan and men and God ; and he that believeth on Him shall not haste away in flight (v. 16).

Not only is the Messiah the foundation, He is also " the plummet " (v. 17), i.e., He is the standard of the righteousness that will stand in the judgment. All who stand there will be measured by this Divine line and plummet ; and those who are not found as perfect and sinless as He, will be rejected. This vital fact destroys the hope of the sacerdotalist, the moralist, and the Pharisee : lies are their refuge and hiding-place, but the hail and waters of God's wrath will sweep these refuges away.

The Assyrians, as an overflowing scourge, should pass and re-pass through the land of Palestine ; and in such a manner as that the mere report of their passage should cause terror to the hearer. and destroy all repose (vs. 18-20).

Just as God broke forth (Joshua x. 10) at Gibeon, and (2 Samuel v. 20.) at Perizim, so was He about to break forth upon His own people ; but He adds, with anguish in His tone, that thus to act against them would be for Him foreign and unwanted (v. 21) ; accordingly in verse 22 He once more entreats them to be converted, for He had purposed a universal judgment upon the entire land of Palestine.

The argument of verses 23-29 is, that, as the farmer ploughs in order to secure a harvest, and threshes in order to have bread, so God ploughed and threshed His people with a wise and beneficent purpose. The farmer does not keep on continually ploughing. He ploughs sufficiently, and then sows. Nor does he thresh corn into powder, but only till the chaff is separated from the wheat. God has given him this intelligence ; and it illustrates His loving action towards His people.

ISAIAH XXIX.—This chapter should read as in the Revised Version.

" Add ye year to year " (v. 1), means add one year of merry-making to another.

The second " and " in verse 2, should read " yet."

Ariel, i.e., the hearth of God ; that is, " the dwelling-place of God," Jerusalem.

The siege described in verses 3 and 4, occurred a few years later. The Assyrians were the besiegers ; and, as such, God's instruments in the chastisement of His people. But the verses will have their fulfilment under Anti-Christ (Zec. xiv).

The men of Jerusalem having consulted and trusted in ventriloquists and whisperers out of the ground, it was a just judgment which drove them in terrror into the holes of the earth.

" Moreover " (v. 5) should read " but " ; and " strangers " should read " enemies." As before noticed, the abrupt contrasts in this section of Isaiah arrest and excite the attention of the reader.

The destruction of the host of the Assyrians in one night, " at an instant suddenly," had a temporary fulfilment in xxxvii. 36 ; but the predictions of that verse, and of the three following, belong to the future.

The argument of verses 7 and 8 is, that just as a hungry and thirsty man is disappointed by a dream, so will Anti-Christ and his followers be disappointed in their dream of the capture of Jerusalem.

Verses 9-14 belong to the Past and to the Future. When Isaiah announced the impending sudden destruction of the Assyrian host his hearers and their religious teachers were incredulous. A deep sleep closed their eyes and " covered " their heads, and the Divine message was to them as a book which the learned could not read because it was sealed, and the ignorant could not read because they were unlearned. And yet they made a profession of serving and worshipping God, and repeated prayers which they had learned off by heart ! Consequently a judicial blindness and ignorance was sent upon them by God (v. 14). The Lord Himself quoted verse 13, in Matthew xv. 8.

Verse 9, should read : " Be ye amazed and ye shall be amazed ! blind yourselves and ye shall become blind ! "—that is, a judicial blindness should descend upon them, and they should be amazed at God's action toward them ; and so it came to pass.

But these verses also belong to the future. Because Israel shut her eyes to the work and to the person of the Messiah in His First Advent, the Book of God and its vision has ever since been covered with a veil to them, and will so remain up to the Second Advent.

This just principle has a present application and explains why the Bible is a sealed Book to the learned, and a foreign language to the unlearned ; and why " all vision," i.e., the Gospel, is without meaning to both.

The reference in verse 15 is to the secret negotiations between the rulers in Jerusalem and the king of Egypt. In effect, their action was perversity, as though they would make the clay the potter, and the piece of furniture the carpenter. So they proposed to substitute themselves for God ; to set their wisdom above His ; and to do without Him. But in the following verse the Prophet declared that God would turn things upside down, that the wild woods of Lebanon should become a fruitful field, and, contrariwise, that the fruitful field should become a wild forest.

Such has been human folly and Divine sovereignty in all ages of the world's history. Every attempt to hide from God, and act with self-will, insures defeat and sorrow.

" The deaf " (v. 18), " the blind," " the meek," " the poor " (v. 19), " the redeemed " (v. 22), are here contrasted with " the drunken " (v. 9), " the prophets and seers " (v. 10), " the learned and unlearned " (v. 11), the " lip-servers and wise and prudent " (vs. 13 and 14), and " the perverse " (v. 15)

" The day " pointed to in verses 18-24 is the day of the pouring out of the Holy Spirit. That visitation will destroy the proud, the scornful, and the evil-workers (vs. 20 and 21), but will enlighten and heal and gladden (vs. 18 and 19), and sanctify and teach the redeemed sons of Jacob (vs. 22-24).

Verse 20 can read in the future tense as well as in the present.

Verse 21, may be thus paraphrased : " They that accuse a man for a word (i.e., unjustly), and lay a snare for him that reproveth in the gate (i.e., offer a bribe to the judge), and condemn the righteous on worthless evidence.

ISAIAH XXX.—The threatened invasion of the Assyrian king struck such fear into the men of Jerusalem that they resolved to send ambassadors to Egypt, bearing rich gifts, in order to make a league with the Egyptian monarch. This was in opposition to the word of God which said : " Thou shalt make no covenant with them " (Ex. xxiii. 32). Isaiah reproached them for this ; charged them with being rebels (v. 1) ; reminded them that they should have sought guidance from God (Num. xxvii. 21) ; and

predicted that their covenant with Egypt would end in disappointment and shame.

To " cover with a covering " means to make a league. The Hebrew text reads : " Pour out a libation " ; for it was in this manner that the ancients made covenants (v. 1).

Sin leads to sin (v. 1).

" His princes " (v. 4), i.e., the Egyptian princes ; and " his ambassadors " ; i.e., those of the king of Egypt : that is, the ambassadors were of princely rank. Thus did the devil flatter the people of Jerusalem.

The Prophet (v. 6) pictures to his hearers the beasts, i.e., the strong asses and camels, laden with presents for the Egyptian King and passing through the desert which separates Palestine from Egypt.

Verse 7, should thus read : " For Egypt shall help in vain, and to no purpose : therefore have I called her ' The Proud Boaster that sitteth still ' " ; i.e., that will do nothing. And so it was, for when the crisis came Egypt sat still and did nothing (xxxvi. 6).

" A table " (v. 8), i.e., a tablet, or placard for all to read.

" For ever and ever," i.e., for " a testimony for ever."

The Prophet's auditors were both rebels and liars ; and, not being a fashionable preacher like those of to-day, he did not hesitate to tell them so. How they must have hated him ! They were rebels, for they rebelled against the Law, and they were liars, because they claimed to keep it.

Their lips did not use the words of verses 10 and 11, but their hearts did ; and God, who reads the heart, can expose its hatred and folly.

As to-day so then, these religious professors demanded sermons that would please them, and forbade anything being said about the Wrath of God and the Lake of Fire (v. 33).

" This word " (v. 12), i.e., this message from God.

" To trust in oppression and perverseness " (v. 12), i.e., to confide in the effect of the money (obtained by oppression of the poor and perverseness against the Law) despatched to Egypt.

Therefore their plan would be as certain to fail as a clay wall out of plumb is sure to fall (v. 13).

" And He (i.e., God) shall break it, (i.e.,

the Egyptian league) as thoroughly as a clay vessel is broken in such small pieces that not one shall be found large enough to take fire from the hearth or water from the cistern.

" In returning and rest " (v. 15), i.e., in turning back from the proposed embassage to Egypt and in resting in the promises of God. This should result in deliverance. So is it in all ages : To turn away from all other saviours, and to turn to the one and only Saviour, results in rest, quietness, assurance and victory.

The word " all " may be supplied in verse 17, thus : " At the battle shout of five shall ye all flee."

A pole upon the top of a mountain, or a flag-staff on a hill, is a duplicated figure expressing loneliness and depopulation.

The expected outburst of a just indignation is in verses 18 to 26 replaced by an amazing outburst of grace. This is a marvellous testimony to the thoughts and ways of God. He waits to be gracious (v. 18) ; i.e., He allows iniquity to come to a head, and shuts up all under sin in order that He may have mercy upon all (Rom. xi. 32).

To those that wait for Him (v. 18) He gives the promises of verse 19, and, in verse 20, engages to provide bread and water during days of adversity and affliction ; He will also manifest to them the Supreme Teacher (Joel. ii. 28), i.e., the Holy Spirit, Who will guide them into all truth, telling them when to turn to the right and when to the left ; and, being the Holy Spirit, His teaching will cleanse them from all idolatry (v. 22). Outward prosperity shall also be enjoyed, for the harvest shall be plentiful (v. 23) ; the beasts of burden shall eat savoury provender (v. 24) ; the barren mountains shall be clothed with verdure (v. 25) ; and all nature be resplendent with glory (v. 26).

This exhibition of amazing grace will synchronize with an exhibition of appalling judgment (v. 25). It will be a day of great slaughter and destruction of mighty men (" towers "). The annihilation of the Assyrians, and their generals (xxxvii. 36), was a type of that coming slaughter.

That day of God's wrath is described in verses 29-33 and in 2 Thess. i. 5-10. It is the day when the Messiah, the Lord Jesus, shall be revealed from heaven in flaming fire (v. 27), to punish with everlasting destruction the rebels (v. 28), and, at the same time, to recompense rest to the believers (v. 29). Messiah will then cause His glorious voice to be heard, and will strike down with His arm in indignant anger (v. 30) the Assyrian, i.e., Anti-Christ, the rod that smote His people ; and as the strokes of the Divine rod smite that wicked king, God's people will play upon tabrets and harps (v. 32), whilst the false king shall be cast into the Tophet of the lake of fire prepared of old and made ready for him, God having made it both deep and large, and set it on fire with His breath ; and there shall that wicked monarch and his followers, be tormented for ever and ever (Rev. xix. 19-21, xx. 10).

God is Israel's strong tower (Ps. lxi. 3). Anti-Christ and the False Prophet are the " towers " intended in verse 25.

ISAIAH XXXI.—The effect of the scorn and unbelief of chapter xxviii, and of the blindness of chapter xxix, is shown in chapters xxx. and xxxi. The people go " down " into Egypt, both geographically and morally, and in their fear of the Assyrians under Sennacherib they put their trust in the wisdom and cavalry of the Egyptians. They themselves had no cavalry, the Assyrians had immense squadrons of horsemen, and so had the Egyptians. It was, therefore, what the world would call sound common sense to set the Egyptian cavalry against the Assyrian. But in so doing they despised the God of their salvation, and made nothing of His promises (v. 1).

The Prophet urged (v. 2) that if the Egyptian was wise yet was the Holy One of Israel also wise ; that it was in His power to bring evil, i.e., calamity, upon them and upon the Egyptians ; and that He never went back upon His word, but always accomplished what He threatened.

" The House of the evil-doers " was Jerusalem, " the workers of iniquity " the men of Judah, and their " help " the Egyptians.

" To stretch out the hand " (v. 3), expressed punishment. " He that helped " was Egypt, and " he that was holden up," Israel.

Verses 4 and 5, are very lovely ! The one verse points to the might of the God of Israel, and the other to His love. His might is illustrated by a strong lion putting terrified shepherds to flight, and His love by the action of a bird hovering over its nest in order to protect its brood from the hawk. Thus He " passed over " the first-born in Exod. xii. so as to protect him from the destroying angel.

Verse 6 should read as in the Revised Version.

" In that day " (v. 7), and " then " (v. 8). What day? And when? The day of Israel's conversion when she will return unto Jehovah; for true conversion is marked by a turning away from all idols (v. 7), and by the destruction of everything that disputes God's Kingdom in the soul (v. 8).

The destruction of the Assyrian host in one night at Lachish is predicted in verses 8 and 9; but that did not exhaust the prediction, the prophecy will be fulfilled in the destruction of Anti-Christ and his host.

The Assyrian did not fall with the sword of a mighty man or of a mean man; he, like the future Assyrian, was " broken without hand " (Dan. viii. 25), for a plague destroyed his army.

There is no contradiction here between the statements that he fell with the sword and yet fled from it, for after the destruction o his army he fled from the sword of the king of Egypt, having heard that that monarch was advancing to attack him; and so great was his fear that he did not stay his flight at his stronghold which he had built on the Syrian frontier, but fled to Nineveh, where he was murdered by his own sons.

The survivors of Sennacherib's army became " tributaries " (v. 8, R.V.), no doubt to the Egyptians.

" Fire," i.e., a hearth, and " furnace," i.e., an oven (v. 9), are here, perhaps, to be understood as symbolizing a dwelling-place.

But they might also symbolize the great truth that God is a consuming fire, and that that fire, covering Jerusalem with its glory, will be the " ensign " which will terror-strike Anti-Christ and his princes.

Or, understanding the term " ensign " to signify a demonstration, the sense of the statement may be that the mighty God whose dwelling-place was Zion, made, in the destruction of the Assyrian host, such a demonstration (" ensign ") of His wrath as to terror-strike the princes of the heathen.

ISAIAH XXXII.—The king of verse 1, and His princes are here contrasted with the king and princes of xxx. 33, and xxxi. 8 and 9.

Righteousness and justice will characterize the government of Messiah and His deputies.

He is to judge the world as man (v. 2, and Acts xvii. 31).

Safety, life, and rest are found in Messiah (v. 2).

Verses 3 and 4 form an introversion. The first member of verse 3 corresponds to the last member of verse 4; and, consequently, the two middle members also correspond. These two middle members refer to congregations, and the two outer members to preachers.

When the King comes the preachers will see clearly and will no longer preach defectively, but will speak uprightly, i.e., scripturally. The hearers will listen and understand.

The " rash " i.e., the hasty, or weak in faith; for he that believeth shall not make haste.

The preachers and hearers of verses 5-8, are contrasted with those of verses 3 and 4. These preachers are the modern fools and churls. They are admired as " liberal " i.e., broadminded, and " bountiful," i.e., emancipated " (v. 5). But such preaching is " folly," " iniquity," " profaneness," and " error "; it is " against Jehovah," and its effect is to rob and impoverish the hearer (v. 6).

The " instruments," i.e., the arguments, or teaching of the Atheist are also evil; they impoverish and destroy the auditors with lying words, though opposed by " the needy," i.e., Christ's servants. speaking right, i.e., pleading truth.

But the true liberals, or nobleminded, shall stand continually before the King when He comes, because they preach liberal things, i.e., the Gospel.

Prior to the setting up of the millennia kingdom, and the outpouring of the Holy Spirit (vs. 15-20), there will be an outpouring of judgment (vs. 9-14), for " many days."

The " women " and " daughters " here symbolize the Hebrew people.

But no doubt this was a message to the people of that day, all of them being intended under the figure of women gathering the grape-harvest.

Verses 10-12 should read as in the Revised Version.

" Forever " (v. 14) is qualified by " until " (v. 15).

The second member of this verse may be read, " Then shall the wilderness become a fruitful field " etc., (v. 15), and " then shall judgment," etc., (v. 16). Such will be the effect of the outpouring of the Holy Spirit.

But as for the city of Babylon, and the army (" forest ") of its wilful king, the hail of God's wrath shall destroy them (v. 19) ; and, as a consequence, the sower shall go joyfully forth in security to his labour (v. 20).

" Beside all waters "—better read : " upon all waters." The Eastern farmer floods his land, sends forth his asses and his oxen to trample the submerged ground so as to break and soften it, and then casts the seed upon the waters so that they shall sink into the loosened soil ; thus he secures a most bountiful harvest. The verse does not suggest his yoking together the ox and the ass, for that was forbidden by the Law.

During the millennium seed-time and harvest will be times of happiness, and not of apprehension as now.

But the verse carries a note of encouragement to the Christian worker ere the King comes. He is to cast the seed of the word of God upon all waters, both at home and abroad, and, in doing so, will enjoy a true happiness ; but that happiness will be indeed great when the Lord of the Harvest appears to crown the faithful sower, and invites him to look upon the fruit of his labour.

Verse 1 states that " A King shall reign in righteousness," and Rom. v. 21, declares that " grace reigns through righteousness." The one reign will magnify the love of God ; the other reign, the wrath of God.

ISAIAH XXXIII.1-12.—The predictions of this prophecy will have their fulfilment in the future. Sennacherib's breach of the covenant (Dan. ix. 27), and his hostility to Hezekiah and to his servants, illustrate the hostility of Anti-Christ to Messiah and to His servants ; and the destruction of the Assyrian " without hand," i.e., without human instrumentality, is a fore-picture of the destruction of the future Assyrian monarch.

Hezekiah stripped the Temple of its wealth, and, with it made a covenant with Sennacherib. The Assyrian king took the money, broke the covenant (v. 8), and devastated the country (v. 9). All this suffering would have been escaped, and the Temple sacrilege avoided, if Hezekiah had obeyed the Bible and not followed his own counsel.

But where sin abounds grace doth much more abound, and so the varied recitals of human weakness and fear, recorded in this section of the Book of Isaiah, are continually interrupted by gracious breaks assuring the glory of Jehovah. However His people fail, He never fails ; and however much shame covers them, nothing but glory belongs to Him.

" The spoiler " and " the traitor " of verse 1, is Sennacherib. He spoiled the country (vs. 8 and 9) and he broke the covenant (v. 8).

He ceased to spoil when death spoiled him of his soldiers, and he ceased to deal treacherously when his sons murdered him.

The first " they " of verse 1 means the servants of Hezekiah, and the second " they" the sons and servants of Sennacherib.

In verse 2, the Spirit of Christ in Isaiah pleads with, and for, the sons of Israel ; hence the change of pronoun from " we " to " their." This lovely feature constantly appears in the Book of the Psalms. It is Christ before the Father's Throne identifying Himself with the children (Heb. ii. 13), and pleading with them, and for them. So might a mother appear with her children before an earthly prince, and, pleading, use the words " us " and " them " when expressing their united need, or calling special attention to that of the children as distinguished from herself.

" Arm," (v. 2), i.e., " defence."

This second verse expresses the faith and love of the remnant in Hezekiah's day, and of the remnant in the future " time of trouble."

" Tumult " (v. 3), i.e., the tumult raised by the survivors of the night of terror when the host of the Assyrians was destroyed.

This third verse should read thus : " At the noise of the tumult peoples fled ; at the lifting up of Thyself nations were scattered." On that night Jehovah did indeed lift up Himself ; hence, in verse 5, He is declared to be exalted.

Verse 4, should read as in the Revised Version.

" Your spoil," i.e., the gathered wealth of the Assyrian camp. The Israelites leaped upon " it," and gathered it as locusts leap upon and gather every green thing.

Verse 6 should read as in the Revised Version. The reference is to the Messiah as the true Hezekiah. In His times there shall be a boundless salvation; and the wealth which will distinguish Him will be His fear of Jehovah.

The "noble messengers" of verse 7 were the "ambassadors of peace" sent by Hezekiah to Sennacherib to beg him to respect the covenant; but they were refused admission to the king's presence, and had to remain "without."

Verse 9 should read as in the Revised Version.

Man now being at his extremity of misery and helplessness, grace can act (vs. 10-12), and judgment fall—grace to His people, and wrath to their foes.

"Ye" (v. 11), i.e., the Assyrians. "Breath," i.e., "spirit," that is, their spirit of cruelty and cupidity should devour them as a fire. Many to-day are devoured and consumed by a similar spirit.

"People" (v. 12) should read "peoples," i.e., the nations composing the Assyrian host of the past, and the Assyrian host of the future shall also become as chopped thorns, the fuel in the East of the limekiln. "The burnings of lime" means fuel for burning lime.

ISAIAH XXXIII. 13-14.—" Ye that are far off " (v. 13), i.e., the heathen; " ye that are near," i.e., the men of Jerusalem. These latter had had more confidence in the "might" of the king of Egypt than in that of the God of Israel. But the destruction of the Assyrian host. compelled them to acknowledge Messiah's might.

"The fire" (v. 12) which burned up the Assyrians struck terror into the hearts of the sinners and Christ-rejectors in Zion (v. 14), and they cried out: "Who among us shall dwell etc?" They felt that if God's wrath fell with such severity upon the heathen, who did not know Him, how much more fearful would be His wrath against those to whom He had revealed Himself, but only to be rejected by them. Although "in Zion" yet were they godless (R.V.), i.e., without God, and unlike God, that is, unconverted. Similarly, multitudes to-day are in that which professes to be the City of God, but their hearts are strangers to Christ.

The answer to the question of verse 14 is: that not some of the sinners in Zion would be cast into everlasting burnings, but everyone of them.

This question proves that in the time of Hezekiah the fact of the Lake of Fire, and the doctrine of eternal punishment, were matters of general knowledge.

The term "dwell with" denotes conscious existence; and "everlasting," means "ever-enduring."

Verses 15-24 portray, on the other hand, the ever enduring bliss of the true sons of the Kingdom; their moral character is described in verse 15; their place of safety and unfailing provision in verse 16; but all their happiness is that of verse 17, in the vision of Messiah the King in His beauty.

They saw Hezekiah the king in his sackcloth, but the day is coming when they will see Messiah the King in His beauty.

In Hezekiah's day the land was narrowed to a few acres around Jerusalem, but in Messiah's day it will be a far stretching land (v. 17, R.V.).

God's wrath, as exhibited with terror in the destruction of the Assyrian host, shook with terror the heart of the unconverted in Zion, but was a subject of profitable meditation for the heart of the converted (v. 18, R.V.).

The scribe, the receiver, and the computer were three Assyrian officers. They are depicted on the Nineveh sculptures in the British Museum. One recorded the spoil, another weighed it, and the third counted the towers, i.e., the captured chiefs.

The faithful when musing on the destruction of the enemy exultingly ask: "Where now are these officials?" and the reader supplies the answer.

The word "not" (verse 19) is to be understood in the sense of "never again"; and the figure of the tent (v. 20) expresses a final and perpetual security from captivity.

"Solemnities" (v. 20), better translated "festivities." The believer feasts his eyes upon the King (v. 17), and upon His Kingdom (v. 20).

The Tigris and the Euphrates and the Nile were the foundation of the wealth and strength of Assyria and Egypt, the greatest monarchies of that day; but the Messiah will be the foundation of His people's wealth and strength in the millennial day. He will be to them broad and deep streams of grace and glory. On such streams neither war-galley nor battleship shall sail (v. 21) ; for there will be war no longer, because the Messiah will be Judge, Law-giver and King (v. 22). He will be an Almighty Saviour.

The overthrow of the enemy is compared to a shipwreck (v.23), and to a ruin so complete that even cripples would become victors.

The inhabitants of Zion in that day shall no longer say : " I am sick," for all that dwell therein shall be forgiven their iniquity. When sin is abolished, sickness 'shall no more exist ; the one is the cause ; the other, the effect.

The whole of this chapter (xxxiii.) contrasts Christ and Anti-Christ. The one king is wilful (Dan. xi. 36), a spoiler, a traitor (v. 1), a devastator (v. 9), and a murderer (v. 8). The Other came not to do His own will (John v. 30), He enriches with abundance of salvation, wisdom and knowledge (v. 6); He is faithful (v. 2); He fills the land with plenty (vs. 16 and 20) ; and He abolishes sickness and death (v. 24).

ISAIAH XXXIV.—This chapter and the following form one prophecy. In it, as throughout the Bible, the evening of judgment precedes the morning of blessing. Man, and his energies, must be judged, and broken, before the Kingdom of God can be established. This principle characterises Christian experience. Before peace and joy, and power in the Holy Spirit can be enjoyed, the " flesh " must be judged ; for God can have no fellowship with evil as light can have none with darkness. Darkness must flee before light ; and hence the evening and the morning form the first day.

These two chapters correspond with Rev. xviii. and xx. These latter predict the destruction of the symbolic and the literal Babylon prior to the setting up of the reign of righteousness and peace.

" Edom " symbolizes all that is opposed to Zion (v. 5). He represents " all the nations " (v. 2). " Edom " and " Adam " is the same word ; and the " controversy " with Zion (v. 8), relates not only to the hostility of the nations to Israel, but to the age-long war of man against God.

Verse 4 points to the period predicted in 2 Peter iii. 10, and Rev. xix. 11-21.

" The sword bathed in heaven " (v. 5), is the wrath of God purposed in heaven and descending thence upon guilty man, as the fire fell out of heaven upon Sodom.

All the power of man, as symbolised by the strong animals of verse 7, shall be destroyed in that day.

The present condition of the land of Edom is a striking fulfilment of verses 9-17. Not one of these predictions will be found to be missing if " the Book of the Lord " be consulted (v. 16).

This term—" The Book of the Lord "— shows that the Bible existed, and was known, in the days of Hezekiah. At that time it would consist of the Pentateuch and the following Books, up to shortly before the accession of that king.

ISAIAH XXXV.—The word " But " might be supplied at the commencement of verse 1, in order to express the contrast between the eternal night that will sadden Idumea and the everlasting day that will gladden Judea ; for, as already stated, chapters xxxiv. and xxxv. form one prophecy.

The words " for them " should be elided (see R.V.).

The first verse may then read : " But the wilderness and the parched land shall become a gladsome place, etc." : " They " (v. 2), i.e., the happy inhabitants of that happy land.

With these exceeding great and precious promises the servants of truth are commanded to strengthen trembling and apprehensive believers (vs. 3 and 4).

The central member of verse 4 might better read : " Behold your God ! He will come to execute vengeance, yea, a vengeance of God " ; i.e., an overwhelming vengeance.

Verses 5 and 6 had a fulfilment in Messiah's First Advent ; but their moral and plenary fulfilment belong to His Second and future Advent. Christ did not work miracles in His First Advent as mere wonders, but because it was here predicted that when He came, He would work miracles of this nature. Hence His performing these particular miracles proved Him to be the predicted Messiah. But His rejection has postponed to the future the wonders and blessings of this entire chapter.

" Jackals " (v. 7, R.V.), make their home in the sandy desert. They will be banished, and their haunts turned into verdant meadows.

The latter part of verse 8, may be thus read : " the unclean shall not pass over it, for He shall be with them walking in the way; so even the simple shall not go astray therein." It shall be the way of the Lord (xl. 3, and Mal. iii. 1), and therefore not only will His companionship exclude evil and assure arrival, but it will protect from peril (v. 9).

With such a keeper on the way (v. 8), and such an asylum at the close (v. 10), it is not to be wondered at that the ransomed of the Lord should be characterised by songs, by joy, and by gladness.

"Sorrow and sighing shall flee away," that is: the bliss of the redeemed shall not, in the perfect state, be liable to be broken as was the innocent joy of Eden's Garden.

The material marvels of this prophecy figure the spiritual marvels which are effected by the New Birth.

This prophecy, and many others, teach that there must be an ever-enduring demonstration of God's wrath (xxxiv.), as of God's grace (xxxv.); and that man, as the highest created being, must be the subject of the dual demonstration.

Here ends the Fourth Book of the first Volume of Isaiah.

ISAIAH XXXVI.—In this, and the three following chapters, the Holy Spirit, for the third time, records the facts relating to Hezekiah and the kings of Assyria and Babylon. The chapters form a necessary parenthesis between the fourth and fifth Books of this the first Volume of the prophecy.

This shews the typical and moral importance of these facts.

As in chapters vii. to xii. so here, prophecy and history are brought together, thus exhibiting their correspondence; for prophecy is history foretold, and history is prophecy fulfilled.

The notes on 2 Kings xviii. to xx. and 2 Chron. xxix. to xxxii. should be read in connection with Isa. xxxvi. to xxxix.

The relation and correspondence uniting these four chapters may be thus exhibited :

The King of Assyria. His summons (xxxvi. 1 to xxxvii. 13).

    Hezekiah. His prayer (xxxvii. 14-20).
    Isaiah. His promise (xxxvii. 21-38).

The king of the abyss. His summons (xxxviii. 1).

    Hezekiah. His prayer (xxxviii 2- 3).
    Isaiah. His promise (xxxviii. 4, 22).

The King of Babylon. His present (xxxix. 1).

    Hezekiah. His pride (xxxix. 2).
    Isaiah. His prediction (xxxix. 3-8).

Trusting man rather than God exposes the Christian to the contempt of the world (vs. 5 and 6).

To destroy the fashionable materials and corrupt ceremonies of worldly religion is misunderstood by the world and accounted sacrilege (v. 7).

The Assyrian king had evidently heard of, or seen, the prophecy of x. 6-8 given by Isaiah twenty-eight years before. This is very remarkable. Its use by Rabshakeh was a clever ruse to persuade the people to obey Jehovah ; but in verse 20 Rabshakeh contradicted the statement that the Assyrian king was coming up with Jehovah. When unconverted men quote the Bible in support of their projects, or doctrines, they contradict themselves, and expose their ignorance of the Scriptures, and their hatred to God.

The coarse language of Rabshakeh in verse 12 may be thus read in English in public : " that they may die of hunger and of thirst."

If Palestine was a land of corn and wine why should the Assyrian king propose to translate Israel to a similar and no better land (v. 17)?

There are occasions when faith's most effective reply to insulting language is the dignity of silence (v. 21), and her best refuge prayer (xxxvii. 1).

ISAIAH XXXVII.—The notes on 2 Kings xix. and 2 Chron. xxxii. apply equally to this chapter.

The most minute differences in the records should be observed, and studied, for they are designedly made by the Holy Spirit.

It is true wisdom to seek the calm and strength of the presence of God when in difficulty and danger (vs. 1 and 14).

" The children are come to the birth," etc. (v. 3). This probably was a proverb. It expressed a condition of extreme peril and inability to escape from it.

" I will put a spirit in him and he shall hear a rumour " (v. 7, R.V.), i.e., I will so affect his mind that he will be alarmed at hearing of the destruction of his army (v. 36), and of the approach of the king of Ethiopia (v. 9) and so return to his own land.

" Servants " (v. 6), i.e., mere lads ; not the same word as " servants " in Hebrew (v. 5).

The boasting of verse 25 declares that in the waterless deserts he supplied his vast armies with water ; and, at the same time, he announced his intention, and his ability, on the other hand to dry up the mighty river Nile (see R.V.). In the prior verse he proudly claimed that no natural obstacle or strong nation, could oppose him.

" Formed " (v. 26), i.e., " purposed." (See chapter x. 5). Sennacherib was a helpless instrument in the hands of God ; and his success (v. 27) was wholly due to this fact.

He proposed the shocking cruelty of verse 29 for Hezekiah and his people ; but, figuratively, he was made to suffer it himself.

Verse 30, perhaps, should be translated thus : " Ye did eat last year such as grew of itself, and this second year that which sprang up of the same ; but in this third year sow ye, etc. "; that is : agriculture was impossible for the two prior years owing to the invasion of the Assyrians, but now God encouraged the Remnant of His people (v. 32) to go out of the city into the country and till the ground, for He promised that the Assyrian king should never return to injure them (vs. 33–35).

Hezekiah could not boast that the beauty, or fervour, of his prayer purchased the victory, for God told him (v. 35) that He would deliver the city, not for Hezekiah's sake, but for David's sake, i.e., for Messiah's sake.

" They " (v. 36), i.e., the Israelites, and " they," i.e., the Assyrians.

The " letter " (v. 14), in 2 Chron. xxxii. 17 " letters," i.e., the plural of magnitude indicating an arrogant, insulting and boastful letter. Compare this letter with that of xxxix. 1. Here the plural of magnitude is again used in order to express a very kind, flattering and affectionate letter.

Satan inspired these two letters ; the effect of the first was to send Hezekiah to the Lord, the effect of the second was to draw him away from the Lord. Satan is more to be watched against as a polite sympathizer than as a roaring lion.

Hezekiah was shocked at the " flesh " in Sennacherib (xxxvii. 3) but blind to it in himself (xxxix. 2).

ISAIAH XXXVIII.—For detailed comments upon this chapter the notes on 2 Kings xx. may be read.

The king's illness occurred in the fourteenth year of his reign. This is clear, for he reigned twenty-nine years, fifteen of them being subsequent to his recovery. It happened, therefore, during the time of the Assyrian invasion, and prior to the final deliverance of Jerusalem (v. 6).

Chronologically, therefore, this chapter is displaced. The Holy Spirit frequently, in the Scriptures, places facts in a moral, and not in a chronological order. This is both grace and warning. So is it here. He hastens to record the energy and victory of Hezekiah's faith over Sennacherib, and then records his insubjection to the Divine will (v. 1).

Here is instruction and warning for the Bible student. His victory over Sennacherib, the king of Assyria, was followed by a less complete victory over Death, the king of the Abyss, and that was succeeded by a total defeat by Merodach the king of Babylon.

Declension rather than progress may be observed in the history of God's people, both within and without the Bible story.

" A sign " (v. 7) should read " the sign " ; that is, the sign asked for in verse 22.

The word " steps " (v. 8), here translated " dial " and " degrees," occurs five times in the Hebrew text. Three times five is fifteen : the Five of Grace multiplied by the Three of Deity. These " Degrees " explain, perhaps, the Fifteen Songs of the Degrees (Ps. cxx. to cxxxiv.).

Hezekiah's Psalm here corresponds in form to those of the Book of the Psalms. There is first the superscription (v. 9) ; then the Psalm itself (vs. 10–20) ; and, lastly, the subscription : " to the stringed instruments."

The Psalm should read as in the Revised Version ; and the last line be translated ; " Jehovah was gracious to me, and saved me."

In verse 21 we have what Isaiah said, and in verse 22 what Hezekiah said. These utterances are to be placed between verses 6 and 7 as to time ; but they are here introduced with design, for they emphasize the physical and spiritual weakness of Hezekiah, and display them in a warning contrast to the over-confidence of his professions in verse 20.

" My songs " (v. 20). This may be the plural of magnitude for " my great and important song " ; or it may point to the Fifteen Songs of Degrees arranged by him.

Hezekiah in his conflict with Death is a type of, and a contrast to, the Messiah. He is a type of the true king of Israel in His death and resurrection. He is a contrast, for when Christ was sentenced to die He submitted, saying : " Thy will not mine be done " ; but Hezekiah was rebellious.

The sense of verse 12 is : My life is cut off as a weaver cuts off his thread.

ISAIAH XXXIX.—The notes on this chapter should be read together with those on 2 Kings xx. and 2 Chron. xxxii.

" Letters " (v. 1). Compare 2 Chron. xxxii. 17. That was a letter filled with threatening ; this, a letter filled with sympathy. That letter, as already pointed out, sent him to God ; this letter drew him from God. Satan is a past master in writing both kinds of letters ; but he is more to be watched against when writing the kind ones than the cruel ones. (See note on 2 Chron. xvii. 1, and 2 Chron. xviii. 1).

The little words " and " and " his " occur each five times in verse 2. They call attention to, and emphasize, Hezekiah's childish ostentation in directing attention to the wonders of his palace rather than to the " wonders " of God's action in retiring the shadow of the sun, and in healing the king's sickness.

Sennacherib's ambassadors set Hezekiah a-praying ; Merodach's ambassadors set him a-prating.

Isaiah was a true and brave servant of the Gospel ; he did not fear to warn even kings of the wrath of God (vs. 6 and 7).

However disproportionate to the fault committed unregenerate man may think the punishment, it came to pass ; for, a hundred and ten years later, Daniel and the three Princes were eunuchs in the palace of the king of Babylon.

But there can be no other result if man and his strength and wisdom are substituted for God. Hezekiah forgot the sharp lesson he had learned for putting his trust in the king of Egypt , and he forgot the overwhelming evidence of God's ability to shield him, by the destruction of the Assyrian host; and he forgot the wonders of his recovery and of the Ten Degrees ; and, almost immediately after, he hastened to make an alliance with the king of Babylon against the king of Assyria, with the result that he lost his treasures and his sons ; Babylon swallowed both.

This principle is in operation to-day. A Christian, who leans upon the world, finds to his sorrow and loss, that the world robs him of his spiritual wealth, and brings weakness and death and fruitlessness into his family.

Such are some of the sad experiences which follow when God leaves even a gifted and prominent servant, in order that he may know all that is in his heart (2 Chron. xxxii. 31).

Israel was carried to Babylon because of her rejection of the Law, and beyond Babylon because of her rejection of the Law-Giver (v. 6), Lev. xxvi. 33, Deut. xxviii. 64, 1 Kings xiv. 15, Amos v. 27, Mic. iv. 10, and Acts vii. 43).

2 Chron. xxxii. 26 shews that the king's repentance was sincere (v. 8).

The historic parenthesis (xxxvi–xxxix.) having closed, the fifth and last Book of the first Volume of Isaiah (xl.-xlviii.) now begins.

ISAIAH XL. 1-11.—The popular theory that this chapter is the first of a Second Book of Isaiah, or of a later prophet of similar name, shews failure in recognizing the Three Volumes into which the Prophecy divides itself. The notes introducing to chapter i. deal with this matter. See also the last note on chapter xxxix.

The main subject of the first thirty-five chapters being the sufferings of Israel under Anti-Christ, and the promised deliverance by Messiah, chapters xxxvi.-xxxix. are introduced to illustrate that deliverance by the destruction of the Assyrian and his host. Thus there was a local and immediate message for faith to rest upon ; and when the time came a demonstration of its worthfulness.

But only the future will satisfy these great predictions.

Meanwhile the connection between xxxix. 6 and 7 and xl. 1 is very important, and teaches the heart.

Grace forgave Hezekiah ; but judgment visited his folly ; and hence the captivity in Babylon. Compare Gal. vi. 7 and 8. Daniel was one of Hezekiah's " sons," i.e., great grandsons.

But in verse 1 of this chapter Israel's faithful God hastens, beforehand, to assure the Exiles, prophetically, that He will not forget nor lose sight of them. He commands His servants the prophets to comfort them with the assurance that their " warfare," i.e., slavery, would have an end ; that their iniquity would be pardoned ; and that His own hand would hand them " the double " conveying to them the pardon.

Among the Easterns a bond is executed in duplicate, and the person bound is liberated by being handed ": the double," or counterpart. He thus holds in his possession the assurance of his discharge. Israel, at Sinai, entered into a bond, failure to keep which involved death. She failed immediately, and always. But her faithful God and Saviour, in His death at Calvary, suffered her penalty, discharged the bond, and hands her " the double." Thus is she assured that her iniquity is pardoned (v. 2) ; for it is " the double " for " all her sins." See the force of this word, and its occurrences, in a Hebrew Lexicon and Concordance, and see also the subjoined note.

The content of these eleven verses may be thus displayed :

Sin gone (vs. 1 and 2).
The Redeemer : His work glorious (vs. 3–5).
The Redeemer : His Word eternal (vs. 6-8).
Messiah come (vs. 9–11).

The " voice " of verse 3 will be that of Elijah (Mal. iv. 5 and 6). His ministry will immediately precede Christ's apparition in glory. John the Baptist came in the Spirit and power of Elijah. Morally, he was Elijah to his generation, and introduced the redemption glory of the Messiah, exhibited at Calvary, and perfected in His First Advent.

The " voice " of verse 6 is that of the Holy Spirit. He instructs the prophet what to proclaim. The message is, and will ever be, a humbling one ; but its acceptance by man is a fundamental of salvation. A consciousness that the heathen are as " withered grass " (v. 6), and a conviction that " the people" (v. 7), i.e., the professed people of God, are morally as the others, that there is no difference, and that all whether good or bad, need regeneration, is a condition of the Gospel.

The love and truth that tell man of his moral ruin reveal to him, at the same time, an ever-living Saviour, whose word is infallible and eternal (v. 8).

Verse 9 should read as in the Revised Version. The preacher is to point Israel to Jesus of Nazareth, and cry : " Behold your God ! "

His title as " Adonai-Jehovah " (v. 10) expresses His claim as King of all the earth. His arm shall rule for Him, i.e., He will not need to lean on another's arm for governmental power ; and when He comes He will " reward " His people and " recompense " his enemies.

The perfection of His love as a shepherd is set out in verse 11 with exquisite beauty.

" Gather " (v. 11) might better read " take up."

" Double " (v. 2). If this Hebrew word has here the English sense then it may have a reference to Lev. xxvi. That chapter predicted the seventy years captivity in Babylon (Lev. xxvi. 34 and 2 Chron. xxxvi. 21). It foretold five periods of punishment each lasting seven " times ," i.e. years. Five times seven is thirty-five. The " double " of thirty-five is seventy. During the Captivity, Israel, therefore, received of Jehovah's hands double for all her sins, i.e., seventy years instead of the predicted thirty-five.

The theory that the duplication of words (v. 1) in the later chapters of Isaiah proves a dual authorship is destroyed by comparison of Isaiah lvii. 19 with Isa. xxvi. 3.

How often must Daniel have wept as he read xxxix. 7 and sung as he read xl. 1.

ISAIAH XL. 12-31.—The " shepherd " of verse 11 who " takes up " the lambs in His arm is, in verses 12-17, declared to be the Mighty God who " takes up " the isles as a very little thing.

" A span " is the distance from the top of the thumb to the top of the middle finger.

This great God and Saviour Jesus Christ (Titu; ii. 13, R.V.) is here contrasted with idols (vs. 18-26).

That God made a revelation of Himself to man at, and from, the beginning is clear from verse 21 and Rom. i. 19-21.

" Upon " (v. 22) would better read " above." The word " circle " shews that the ancients knew that the earth was a sphere suspended in space.

Verse 24 should read as in the Revised Version margin.

" These " (v. 26), i.e., the stars.

" Way " (v. 27), i.e., " circumstances " ; and " My judgment is passed over," i.e., " my cause is neglected by."

But the God and Shepherd of His people who numbers the stars, who names them, and who maintains each in its orbit so that not one fails nor falls (v. 26), never fails, nor wearies, in upholding the feeblest of His people (v. 28) ; nor does He ever tire of their circumstances, nor grow uninterested in their affairs. On the contrary, far from fainting in His action on their behalf, He gives power to those who do faint amongst them. The strongest men grow feeble in effort and interest, but the " Great Shepherd " never.

Man speaks of " walking," " running," and " mounting up "; God reverses the order. This accords with Christian experience The apostle Paul at first was among " the chiefest apostles " (2 Cor. xi. 5) ; later on, he was " the least of all saints " (Eph. iii. 8) ; and, at the end, he was " the chief of sinners " (1 Tim. i. 15). The Christian is safest when walking, not so safe when running, and in great danger when mounting.

The enemies of inspiration and prophecy say that this, and the following chapters, were composed by a namesake of Isaiah after the return from Babylon. But the Hebrews were purged from idolatry at that time, and it would have been absurd for a prophet to urge them to forsake what they had already abandoned. As to the assertion that words are found in these later prophecies which do not occur in the earlier Scriptures, the contrary is the fact ; as is pointed out by many learned men.

" The isles " (v. 15). The vast Continents of the world, in comparison with the little land of Palestine, were to God only " isles." It was " the glory of all lands " (Ezek. xx. 6 and 15). This to human wisdom is folly.

ISAIAH XLI.—Man's heart clings to idolatry, let him witness never so many proofs of the nothingness of idols, and of the existence of God. So Israel clung to idolatry in spite of the destruction of the host of Sennacherib, and of " the wonder done in the land," in the retrocession of the sun-shadow. Hence in this fifth book the burning exposure and denunciation of idolatry and idols from God through the lips of Isaiah.

In this chapter He invites the nations to meet Him in argument as to the truthfulness of idols (v. 1) ; He challenges them to predict the future, or explain the past (vs. 21 and 23) ; and He states that, as to the past, He chose Abraham (v. 2) ; made him victorious over the Four Kings (Gen. xiv. 9 and 15) ; elected His children (v. 4) ; and destroyed the seven idolatrous nations before them (vs. 5-7). Here is a doubled demonstration of God's power over idols.

As to the future, he predicts the coming of Cyrus (v. 25), and his destruction of the idols of Babylon. This came to pass one

hundred and thirty-seven years later.

Thus, as to the past, he raised up Abraham to forsake idolatry ; and, as to the future, He declares His purpose to raise up Cyrus to destroy it. This explains how it was that the Hebrews returned from Babylon to Jerusalem purged from idols.

" Islands " (v. 1), i.e., the inhabitants of the maritime countries. " Peoples " (R.V.), that is, the Gentile Nations. " Keep silence before me," i.e., listen to me. " Renew their strength," i.e., make the best case they can in support of idolatry, and then let them draw near and speak." " Let us (i.e., God and idolators) come near together to judgment, ' i.e., to a decision.

The one " raised ' up from the East " (v. 2) was Abraham (v. 8). He was called in righteousness to Jehovah's foot ; for God said to him : " Walk before me and be thou perfect " (Gen. xvii. 1). He made him to rule over the Four Kings ; for they became as dust to His sword, and as stubble to His bow. These Four Kings were idolaters, and, therefore, helpless before the man of God who walked in righteousness, i.e., in separation from idols (for that was the vital matter of controversy at that time) ; and one striking feature of the existence and power of God is pointed to in the statement that Abraham passed on safely in an unknown path (v. 3).

The generations chosen from the beginning (v. 4) were the children of Abraham : for they were all in their father's loins when God chose him. (Heb. vii. 10).

" I, Jehovah, the First and with the Last— I AM " (v 4). This glorious title occurs here and in xliv. 6 and xlviii. 12, and in Rev. i. 17, ii. 8, and xxii. 13—thus three times in Isaiah and three times in the Apocalypse.

The first, i.e., Abraham ; the last, i.e., Cyrus ; but both these being types of Christ, the verse refers to the Messiah. The meaning is : I was with Abraham and will be with Cyrus.

The terror of the Seven Nations of idolaters in Canaan, and their appeal to their idols for salvation from the victorious soldiers of Joshua, is vividly set out in verses 5-7. Rahab declared that the hearts of the inhabitants of the land were melting with terror (Joshua ii. 9-11). Thus again the folly of idolatry is evidenced.

In verses 8-20 the existence and love and irresistible power of the God of Israel are set out.

Not only did the statements in these verses nourish the faith of the election in Isaiah's days, and in Daniel's and Ezra's days, but they will nourish the faith of the elect of Israel in the future day of Jacob's trouble,

How often must verse 9 have cheered the hearts of Daniel and his companions ; and how must the fine scorn of the last line of verse 7, have emboldened them to despise Nebuchadnezzar's great idol, and the burning furnace.

The progression in verse 10, is most precious : " I am with thee " ; but, He comes yet nearer : " I will strengthen thee " ; and still closer : " I will help thee " ; and, finally, He throws His arms around and says " I will uphold thee."

It is the " worm Jacob " that is to become a new sharp threshing instrument having teeth, and who is to break in pieces the great nations and the lesser nations, here compared to mountains and hills (vs. 14-16).

If poor and needy Jacob should seek water where there is none, his faithful God will not forsake him (v. 17), but will open rivers on the bare heights and fountains in the sultry valleys (v. 18), so that the wilderness shall become a pool of water, and the dry land springs of water.

In that future day of blessing Palestine, now barren and stony, will become beauteous and fertile as the Garden of the Lord (v. 19) ; and the nations of the earth will recognize that these wonders will be the work of God and not of idols (v. 20).

The physical marvel of turning a stony desert into a paradise illustrates the greater spiritual marvel of the New Birth, in which, and by which, a barren life is changed, morally, into verdant land.

" Produce your cause " etc., (v. 21), i.e., state your case in favour of idolatry ; bring forth your weighty arguments, etc.

" Let them bring them forth " (v. 22), i.e., the weighty arguments of the previous verse. Here God renews the challenge of verse 1.

The challenge of verses 22 and 23 is a double one, the first of which is itself a duplicate. The idolators are challenged to produce from the past a series of connected prophesies and their fulfilments ; or, again, to point to any one unconnected prophecy and its undoubted fulfilment. This is repeated in verse 26. The second challenge is : to predict any future event.

A third challenge, distinct from the two former, is given at the close of verse 23, in the words " do good " or " do evil " (calamity) ; i.e., reward your worshippers or punish your detractors.

The answer to these three challenges is evident, and is to be supplied by the reader. It underlies verses 24 and 26. In verse 24, God addresses the idols as if they had being, and says : " Ye are nothing, and can do nothing ; he that chooseth you, (as objects of worship) becomes an abomination."

The Scripture declares an idol to be an abomination ; hence an idolater becomes an abomination, not only abominable, but, worse, an abomination ; for a man becomes morally like that which he worships, and idolatry and obscenity are one. As the false god is abomination, so the True God, the Messiah, is Righteousness ; not only righteous, but righteousness itself. Therefore He said (John xvi.) : that the Spirit should convict the world of righteousness, because He, i.e., Righteousness, went back to heaven. Righteousness was only once in the world, i.e., when He was in it.

Abraham, the idol-forsaker, having been brought forward by God, in the fore-part of the chapter, to prove the impotency of idols to punish him, or his children, in the past, Cyrus is now pointed to, in verse 25, as the idol-breaker, who should, in the future, grind to powder the princes of Babylon, the headquarters and citadel of idolatry. This prophecy was fulfiled about one hundred and forty years later. Abraham was the man from the East, Cyrus the man from the North ; both are types of the Son of Man, Who, in His Second Advent, will destroy all idols and all idolaters.

Cyrus came from the North, but he sent forth his famous proclamation of Ezra i. from the East.

Perhaps, however, this statement in the verse may mean that Cyrus should turn from worshipping the sun, which was the great god, and would become a worshipper of Jehovah, i.e., that he would turn from the sun to The Name.

Set in contrast to this prediction as to Cyrus, the challenge is repeated to the dumb idols to produce a prediction, on their part, which could be pronounced " righteous," i.e., true. " It is righteous " (v. 26), i.e., it was a true prophecy as the event proved ; thus demonstrating the idol to be trustworthy. But the verse closes with the statement that not one of the countless idols that men worshipped could " declare " anything, or " reveal " anything, or could even utter one word. They were all dumb.

Verses 27 and 29, should read as in the Revised Version. Messiah here speaks and calls to Zion to behold the fulfilment of His predictions ; their burden is glad tidings, in contrast to that of the idols which is a religion of terror.

Not only are the idols themselves dumb (v. 26), but their worshippers when challenged to defend them, are dumb also (v. 28) ; and the inability of the idols to act, as to speak, is again pointed to in verse 29.

" Them " (v. 27), i.e., the ransomed of xxxv. 10, and the virgins undefiled with idolatry of Rev. xiv. 4.

ISAIAH XLII. 1-17.—The Holy Spirit in Matt. xii. 9-23 declares the Servant of this Prophecy to be Jehovah Messiah.

God had only one perfect Servant on earth, His own well-beloved Son in whom His Soul delighted (v. 1). He speaks of Him in the Scriptures as " My Servant." When speaking of other servants it was necessary to add the name ; as, for instance, " My servant Abraham," " My servant Moses," etc. ; for these were all imperfect servants. But, as to Jesus, it was not necessary to supply His name, because He was the one Servant of Jehovah, and there never was another in this unique sense.

This Servant of Jehovah is presented in the first seven verses in the grace and humility of His First Advent, and, in verses 8-17, in the might and power of His future Second Advent.

In the humiliation and grace of His first coming it is predicted that He would not assert His rights (v. 2), nor judge His enemies (v. 3), but that, on the contrary, He would introduce the New Covenant of salvation for Israel and for the Gentiles (v. 6), and illuminate and liberate them alike through the preaching of the Gospel (v. 7).

In the might and power of His Second Coming He will destroy His enemies (v. 13), especially the bruised reed and smoking flax so long borne with and endured (v. 14). He will deliver His people (v. 16), and utterly abolish idols and idolators (v. 17).

Thus is He the great antitype of Abraham and Cyrus, who appear in the prior chapter as idol-breakers and idolater conquerors. Imperfection characterized them ; but perfection, Him. A remarkable feature attaches to all three : it is that of prophecy. They appear clothed with prophecy, and so contrast sharply with the prophetic inability of the gods preferred by man.

The use of the past tense in verse 1 and in xli. 25 is important as emphasizing the certitude of prophecy. One hundred years before Cyrus, and seven hundred years before Christ, the Holy Spirit could say, respecting the former ; " I have raised up," and, regarding the latter : " I have put." This feature in prophecy should be recognized by those who contend that the use of the past tense shows that the prophet, spoke of fulfilled history.

The sentence " I have put my spirit upon Him " reveals the Three Persons of the Trinity (v. 1). " I "—God the Father : " Him "—God the Son : " My Spirit "—God the Holy Ghost.

God had no misgivings as to the perfect obedience and successful government and conduct, of His Servant. Centuries before His birth He could, with confidence, say : " He shall bring forth judgment to the Gentiles " ; i.e., judge them and their idols, in His first coming, by the perfection of His humiliation by which He condemned them morally ; and, in His Second Coming, by the might of His majesty, when He will destroy them utterly. He who during all this long intervening period holds His peace and endures the discord of the bruised reed and the offensiveness of the smoking flax (v. 3), will then deliver His blinded people, and break and quench both reed and flax.

The statement in verse 3 is generally understood to illustrate the grace of the Saviour in repairing the bruised reed and causing to burn brightly the dimly-lighted flax, i.e., that wherever there is a little faith He will strengthen and nourish it. That is quite true, but it is not intended in this verse, for there is a limit set in the verse to the action pointed to. This limit is marked by the words : " until He send forth judgment in accordance with truth " (Matt. xii. 20).

A reed, or pipe, is a musical instrument, a wick made of flax is a light-giver. If the reed be bruised, discord, and not music, results ; if the wick smokes, instead of light, there is an offensive odour. These illustrate false worshippers. Christ, in His first advent, endures these, and, in His grace, does not immediately judge them ; but, in His Second Advent, He will shew them no mercy.

The words " fail " and " discouraged " in verse 4 contrast with " reed " and " flax " in verse 3. He did not burn offensively, nor was He a bruised reed, but, on the contrary, He was to God, in the moral glory of His life, both incense and music (see R.V. margin).

In verses 5-8 God speaks to the Messiah ; and in verses 9-12, He points to the fulfilment of " former things," i.e., prophecies, and predicts " new things," i.e., new prophecies. One of these new prophecies is set out in verses 10-12 ; another in verses 13-15 ; and yet another in verses 16 and 17. These great prophecies foretell the conversion of the Gentiles (vs. 10-12 using the future tense) ; the judgment of the enemy (vs. 13-15) ; the redemption of Israel (v. 16) ; and the abolition of idolatry and idolaters (v. 17).

The important word " then " (Matt. xii. 22) connects the miracle with the first seven verses of this chapter.

" Cry " (v. 2), i.e., claim His rights (Luke vii. 36-50, see notes).

" His voice to be heard in the street," i.e., to speak so angrily in a house that the voice would be heard outside in the street.

ISAIAH XLII. 18—XLIII. 13.—Israel's

failure in the past as God's messenger to the nations, and her consequent judgment, is the theme of verses 18 to 25, and her success, as such, in the future foretold in verses 1 to 13.

The former section may be thus analysed :

Call to hear (v. 18).
   Israel deaf and blind (vs. 19 and 20).
      The Law magnified by Messiah (v. 21).
      Judgment (v. 22).

Call to hear (v. 23).
   Jacob spoiled and robbed (v. 24).
      The Law rejected by Israel (v. 24).
      Judgment (v. 25).

To Israel God gave a perfect revelation, the Law, intending Israel to be His messenger to declare it to the Gentiles. But Israel refused the embassage, rejected the Law, and became more blind than the idolatrous nations ; hence the judgment of verse 22.

" Who is blind as he that is perfected " (v. 19), i.e., furnished with a Law of perfection. See 2 Tim. iii. 15 to 17. To His messengers God gives a perfect message. This perfect message is the Holy Scriptures. They make the man of God perfect, if obeyed ; and they perfectly furnish him for all the possibilities of life's voyage.

But God's True Messenger, the Messiah, did not fail ; He lived and preached the Law, and made the teaching great and glorious (v. 21, R.V.).

The second call (v. 23), belongs to the " after time " (A.V. margin) and is still unheeded by the sons of Israel. They would not walk in Messiah's ways, they would not listen to the Law as taught by Him, and there fell on them, in consequence, the judgment of verse 25. It rests upon them still ; they refuse to recognize (" yet he knew not ") that it is the wrath of God that burns them ; and they refuse to lay it to heart, i.e., they refuse to repent.

Set over against this impenitence, ignorance, and rebellion is displayed the grace and power and love of the Messiah (xliii. 1).

He " created," He " formed," He " redeemed," and He " called " them. This will happen in the future day of Israel's new birth (Ezek. xxxvi.).

Thus Israel re-created (v. 1), redeemed (v. 1), preserved (v. 2), restored (vs. 5 and 6), no longer blind and deaf (v. 8), shall become God's witness (vs. 10 and 12).

But the glory of this creation will belong to Israel's Saviour (v. 3), and Lover (v. 4).

Israel's past history affords striking proofs of the truthfulness of verse 2. The future will reveal yet more striking proofs of its truth.

God rewarded Cyrus with Egypt, Ethiopia and Seba as a ransom for the liberation of the Hebrew captives, and this is here pointed to as a pledge of the greater ransom of verse 4, when whole nations will be set aside in their favour.

The points of the compass in verses 5 and 6, accord with Ps. cvii. and Luke xiii. 29.

" Since " (v. 4) better expressed " ever since."

In verse 9 the nations are invited to come together, and they are challenged once more to vindicate their idols by fulfilled prophecy. But it is in vain that they will seek for witnesses.

But Messiah will bring forth His witnesses, even His servant Israel, to prove that there is no God but the God of Israel ; that He " declares," and " saves," and " shews," (vs. 11 and 12); that He is from everlasting; and that He is Almighty (v. 13).

ISAIAH XLIII, 14.—XLIV. 5.—These verses correspond to xlii. 18—xliii. 7: i.e., Israel's failure, the consequent judgment, and her final restoration.

Her failure in respect of the Law in xlii. 18-25, was moral; that in xliii. 22-28, was ceremonial.

This latter passage contradicts the statement that the Book of Leviticus was unknown to the earlier prophets, and that they, with the later prophets, belittled or ignored, the Mosaic sacrifices.

Verse 14, may be thus expanded: " I have purposed to send the Medes and Persians against Babylon, and I will bring down the Chaldeans, even all of them, as fugitives into the ships of their rejoicing: i.e. the ships of which they were so proud would be used by the conqueror to transport down the rivers of Mesopotamia the fugitive Chaldeans; or the fugitives themselves would seek to escape in these ships of which they had been so proud.

The Chaldeans were to perish as completely as the Egyptians did in the Red Sea (v. 17). The word " together " here means " at once "; and " flax " means a wick made with flax.

This whole passage should read as in the Revised Version (14-28).

" The former things " (v. 18), i.e., the destruction of the host of Sennacherib; " the things of old," i.e., the destruction of Pharaoh and the Egyptians.

The argument of verses 18-21 is: That as.in the past Israel was God's chosen instrument for exhibiting His glory in the destruction of the Egyptians and the Assyrians, so will Israel be His chosen instrument in the future for exhibiting His greater glory in the salvation of the Egyptians and the Assyrians. This will be the " new thing " (v. 19), and it will be so wonderful that, in comparison, Israel is invited not to remember the marvels of the ancient times.

The wilderness of verse 19 here intends the whole world of the future, in contrast with the wilderness of Sinai in the past.

The wild beasts of verse 20 may mean the animals described (R.V.), or may, possibly, figure the Gentile nations. These delight to represent themselves as wild beasts and birds of prey.

The recital of Israel's contempt of, and

disobedience to the. Law (22-28) is cleft in two, and seemingly disjointed and interrupted, by the declaration of verse 25. Such is the heart of God! When sin reaches its climax, as it did at Calvary, and becomes unbearable, grace puts away the sin instead of putting away the sinner!

As man, under the First Covenant, despised the spotless lamb, and its atoning blood—God's way of salvation in type—so man to-day denies and despises the Divine Way of justification and sanctification through the precious blood of Christ, the Lamb without blemish and without spot.

Israel wearied of God (v. 22), but God did not weary of Israel (v. 23).

" Small cattle " (v. 23), i.e., lambs.

" I have not caused thee to serve as a slave " (v. 23). God did not call them to slavery, but to sonship.

" Offerings " (v. 23), i.e., the Meal-offering (Lev. ii.)

" Sweet cane " (v. 24), i.e., calamus (R.V.). It was used in compounding the precious ointment.

God, because He is God, must judge sin: hence He is made to serve, and to be wearied with, sin (v. 24) in the punishing of it.

Something of the wonders of verse 25, may be thus shewn:

It is a Royal pardon: " I, even I, am
                            He that "
It is an effectual pardon: " Blotteth
                            out "
It is a personal pardon: " Thy "
It is a full pardon: " Transgressions,
                        and thy sins "
It is a purchased pardon: " For Mine
                        own sake."

This last statement reveals the foundation, and the procuring cause, of this effectual and comprehensive pardon. God finds in Himself (Christ), and not in the sinner, a righteous ground on which He can act in pardoning the guilty. This gives eternal value and enduring stability to this principle of forgiveness; for it is based, not upon the repentance and faith of the believer, but upon the Person and Work of the Redeemer.

The invitation of verse 26 is: " Produce (if you can) a righteousness which is justifying." The answer of course is: " I cannot." When man is brought to this consciousness, he listens with wonder to the glad tidings offering him a spotless righteousness in, and through, Christ.

" Thy first Father " (v. 27), i.e., Jacob.

" Thy teachers," i.e., the priests. This is made clear by the correspondence of verses 27 and 28. The first line of verse 27 corresponds with the last line of verse 28, and the second line of the one verse corresponds to the first line of the other.

The promise of xliv. 1-5 had a fulfilment at Pentecost ; but the future only will bring the fulfilment.

The " water " here is a figure of the Holy Spirit ; the " willows " a figure of the sons of Israel.

This is the promise to which the apostle Peter pointed in Acts ii. 39. It is a promise to Israel and to her children, as such, and, as other Scriptures shew, it was to overflow from Israel to all the nations of the earth. Under this promise God offered the Holy Spirit to a man and to his children. It is household salvation ; and had Israel, on the day of Pentecost, or prior to Acts xxviii. 25-28, repented and accepted the Messiah, God would have fulfilled the terms of the promise. But Israel rejected Christ, and hence this promise is set aside, and is not now in operation ; yet it will become operative when Israel repents by and by.

But God has not, therefore, ceased to act in grace to sinners ; on the contrary, He revealed to the apostle Paul a higher glory for man—hidden in Himself and not revealed in the Scriptures—that is, the Heavenly Election, the Church of God (Eph. iii. 1-6, v. 9, Phil. iii. 14), the Mystery ; but this glory is based upon the principle of individual election, and not upon that of household promise.

However, God in all dispensations reserves liberty of action to Himself ; and as, in the past, He, from time to time, responded to faith and acted outside of the then economy, so now He can, and doubtless does, elect a man and his children to the promise of these verses.

" Jeshurun " (v. 2). This is God's title of affection for Israel. It occurs three times in Deut. xxxii. 15, xxxiii. 5 and 26.

The heart of God is here revealed in that one hundred years before their just enslavement to Babylon (xlii. 24, 25), He promised to destroy Babylon and to deliver Jacob (xliii. 14). This is very lovely. So faith was furnished beforehand with a double feast.

The Christian is chosen to salvation in order, like Israel, to be a witness (Acts i. 8 and Phil. ii. 15, 16), and if he fails to testify, judgment will surely fall also upon him.

ISAIAH XLIV. 6-23.—This section corresponds with xliii. 8-14. The subject is Israel as God's witness against idolatry.

The Divine title " I am the First and I am the Last " (v. 6) occurs three times in Isaiah and three times in the Revelation.

" Shall call " (v. 7), i.e., shall command to happen. The challenge here is : that God only can command things to happen, and can declare their nature, and arrange them in order ; and that they do not, and cannot, happen independently of Him (" for Me ") ; and that these predictions concern the Ancient People, i.e., the Israelites.

The capture of Jericho illustrates this verse. God commanded it beforehand to happen ; He declared its nature—the wall should fall down ; He set it in order, for He marshalled the host in two divisions, having the Ark in the centre, and commanded thirteen circuits of the city ; and lastly, the whole action was divine—man did not co-operate.

" Them " (v. 7), i.e., the idolators. They are here challenged to declare the things that are coming, and that shall come.

" Fear ye not (xliii. 1) for I have redeemed thee."

" Fear ye not (xliv. 2) for I have chosen thee."

" Fear ye not (xliv. 8) for ye are my witnesses."

Israel's Saviour and Lover here keeps assuring His people that they are His ; that they always have been His ; that they always shall be His ; that He will never forget them ; and, that though all other nations may perish, they never shall.

" From that time " (v. 8), i.e., from the time that God appointed, that is, elected, His ancient people.

He elected them to be His witnesses to the world ; and though they failed in the past, and still fail, still they will yet be His witnesses to all nations.

" Their delectable things," i.e., the idols they delighted in.

The idolaters as witnesses to the supposed existence and power of their idols are themselves like the idols, they see not nor know ; they have neither vision nor intelligence (v. 9).

The argument of verse 11 is : Those who

make idols, and those who worship them, when invited to come together and to stand up and give evidence in favour of them, not only are unable to do so, but they are paralysed with fear, and covered with shame, when confronted with God.

The smith makes an axe for the carpenter (v. 12 R.V.) with which he can cut down a strong tree and fashion it into the figure of a handsome man (v. 13) that it may stand in the house ; and that is all that it can do, for it cannot provide food and drink for the fainting smith, or famished carpenter.

Idolatry blinds the senses so that a man will cook his food with one half of a tree and bow down and worship the other half as a God able to deliver him. He worships a god whom he himself makes ! This is the case to-day. The superstitious man makes, or buys, an image of some saint, or of the Saviour, or of the Madonna, bows down to it and calls upon it to deliver him. The Unitarian mentally fashions a god of his own creation, and worships that. Both men are so blinded that they cannot recognize the folly and vanity of their action.

"Shut" (v. 18), i.e., daubed with clay. When anyone turns from the revelation God has given of Himself in the Scriptures and bows down to idols, a judicial blindness from God descends upon Him. This is why the Lord in John ix. 6 made clay and covered the eyes of the blind man. The man pictured Israel, and the action was designed to teach the Pharisees that Jehovah Himself was in their midst, that He was judging them, and that the Hand that, in just anger, darkened their eyes, was present to give them sight.

This grace shines forth in verses 21-23.

" I have formed thee the ancient people " (vs. 7 and 21), i.e., " the everlasting Nation." The Nation of Israel is everlasting, and will remain for ever. Hers is the everlasting God (xl. 28), the everlasting covenant (lv. 3), the everlasting salvation (xlv. 17), an everlasting name (lvi. 5), her joy is everlasting (li. 11), also her light (lx. 19) ; she enjoys an everlasting excellency (lx. 15), is loved with everlasting kindness (liv. 8), and will be an everlasting sign of God's pardoning and transforming grace (lv. 13).

" Remember these things " (v. 21), and : " remember not the former things " (xliii. 18). These form a contrast, they predict that the wonders under the New Covenant will, by comparison, cause those of the Old Covenant to be forgotten.

ISAIAH XLIV. 24-XLV. 13.—The following Scriptures should be read in connection with this passage : Isa. xli. 2-6 and xlvi. 11, Jer. xxv. 12-14, and l. and li.

The passage declares God's election of Cyrus as the future deliverer of His People and restorer of His City (v. 28) ; it restates the ignorance and impotency of idols (v. 25) ; it insists upon the unity of God (v. 25 and vs. 5-7 and 12) ; it foretells the manner of the capture of Babylon (v. 1) ; the triumphant compaigns of Cyrus (v. 2) ; it names him one hundred and fifty years before he was born (v. 4) ; and it rebukes the members of the Nation of Israel who objected to God's choice of this heathen prince as His servant (vs. 10-13).

" Alone " and " by Myself " (v. 24), i.e., without the assistance of any other God.

" Maketh," " stretcheth," " spreadeth abroad," " frustrateth," and " turneth " (vs. 24 and 25). These verbal forms have a past, present and a future force, and declare that, not only has God made the Heavens and the Earth, but He maintains, and will maintain them ; and that, similarly, not only has He, in the past, demonstrated the ignorance and impotency of idols, but He continues, and will continue, the demonstration.

" The tokens of the liars," i.e., the pretended miracles of the false prophets (see Jer. l. 35).

" Diviners " i.e., " astrologers."

The knowledge of the wise men of verse 25 means the teaching of the idolatrous priests. This teaching corresponds to the present day " assured results " of modern thought.

" His servant " (v. 26), i.e., Isaiah. " The counsel of His messenger," i.e., Cyrus " Messengers " may be the plural of majesty, and, therefore, mean Cyrus. (xlvi. 11).

" The deep " (v. 27), i.e., the river Euphrates.

It was God through Cyrus who said to Jerusalem, " Thou shalt be built," etc. (v. 28).

" To loose the loins " (v. 1), i.e., to enfeeble ; as " to gird the loins " (v. 5) means to strengthen.

Herodotus, the Greek historian, says that

the river Euphrates, in passing through Babylon, was walled on either side, and that brazen gates in these walls gave entrance to the city (vs. 1 and 2). He records that on the night that Belshazzar was slain, these gates, by a strange oversight, were left open, and that the Medes, having diverted the course of the river (v. 27), the soldiers marched up its dried bed, and, entering the city through the open gates, became masters of it after a siege of two years. Belshazzar, and his government, deemed the city impregnable.

The treasures and riches of verse 3 intend the state treasures of Babylon.

The conqueror's name was Agradates, but God surnamed him Cyrus, i.e., the sun ; and, as predicted in verses 4-6, he has ever since been known by this name.

Eight names were given by Divine Prophecy before birth : Ishmael, Isaac, Solomon, Josiah, Cyrus, Immanuel, John the Baptist, and Jesus.

In verses 1-7 God speaks directly to Cyrus and tells him that He is the One and only God, the Creator of Light and Darkness, and the Author of peace and defeat (evil).

The statements in verse 8 contrast with the fire which reigned down upon Sodom from heaven, and with the destruction of Korah and his company when the earth opened her mouth and swallowed them up. In the future day of blessing the heavens will pour down righteousness, and the earth will open in salvation, and both will unite in testifying to the being and power and grace of God.

The prosperity that returned to Palestine and Jerusalem under the beneficent reign of Cyrus pictured the greater and ever-enduring prosperity that Messiah the Prince will introduce.

The woe denounced in verses 9-13 is directed against those among the Hebrews who criticized the action of God in choosing a heathen prince as the deliverer of His People. These objectors are compared to potsherds objecting to the action of the potter (v. 9) ; they are likened to a selfish boy who is angered at the birth of a brother (v. 10) ; and they are challenged to set their knowledge against that of God (v. 11), and against His creative might (v. 12) ; and the conclusion is that, in spite of the criticisms of the objectors, God raised up Cyrus, prospered him in all his campaigns, and disposed

him to release the Hebrew captives and to build Zion (v. 13).

Verse 10 is to be understood as the angry utterance of a son and heir at the birth of a brother. It illustrates the anger and jealousy of the people of Israel at the Divine action in choosing and blessing the Gentiles.

The enemies of inspiration insist, but without evidence—that this prophecy was composed after the death of Cyrus and not one hundred and fifty years before his birth. God's Word is offensive to human wisdom.

ISAIAH XLV. 14-25.—The restoration of Israel (vs. 14, 17 and 25) ; the confounding of idolaters (vs. 16 and 20) ; the revelation of the Gospel (vs. 19 and 22) ; and the salvation of the Gentiles (vs. 22 and 23) are the main predictions of this prophecy.

" Labour " (v. 14), i.e., the wealth that is produced by labour.

" Thee " (v. 14), i.e., Israel.

The Gentiles robbed the sons of Israel and carried them away in fetters of iron and brass, but they will, in the future day of restoration, come up to Jerusalem in chains of love and repentance, bringing their wealth with them, and confessing that there is but one true and living God, Jehovah Messiah, the God of Israel.

Verse 15 is difficult to understand. It may be the expression of the Gentiles ; but more probably it is to be read in connection with verse 9 as asserting, in contrast to the vanity of idols, the inscrutability of God. Just as a piece of clay cannot read the mind of the potter, so man cannot sound, or discover, the purposes of God. Man must, therefore, remain in moral and spiritual darkness unless God chooses to reveal Himself ; and this He has done in the Scriptures (v. 19).

Verse 16, the shame of idolaters ; the second half of verse 20, the ignorance of idolaters.

Verse 17, the safety of believers ; verse 25, the glory of believers.

The heaping together of the terms of verse 18 shows how much more the Scriptures know about the creation of the worlds than the professors of modern science know.

The terms " created," " formed," " made," and " established," are terms of exact science. The verse should be read as in the Revised.

Version, and the splendour of the exclamation, " He is God ! " will then be felt.

" In vain," i.e., a waste. This statement apparently conflicts with Gen. i. 2. There the English version reads : " the earth was without form and void," i.e., a ruin and a waste. But if the correct translation be made all is clear : " The earth became a ruin and a waste " (see notes on Gen. i.). How many millions of ages elapsed between the first and second verses of Gen. i. the Scriptures do not reveal ; but they hint that the earth was originally made to be inhabited ; that there was a rebellion, and the consequent judgment ; and that the darkness of that night of wrath was followed by the light and re-ordering of the world that now is.

The oracles of God are plain (v. 19), and the oath of God sure (v. 23).

The Lord quoted verse 19 to the High Priest (John xv.ii. 20), thus claiming to be Jehovah.

Heathen oracles were uttered in the secrecy of dark caverns (v. 19), but God has openly revealed Himself in the Scriptures.

" In vain " (v. 19), i.e., in a pathless waste. The statement is : that God has not left man in a trackless desert hopelessly trying to find a way to life and immortality, but has given h.m the clear light of the Holy Scriptures, as He gave Israel the light of the pillar of fire which showed them the path to the Promised Land.

Verse 20 contains an invitation and a statement : the invitation is addressed to the Remnant of Israel, and the statement is : that a false god cannot save.

In the following verse the sons of Israel are instructed to bring before the worshippers of false gods the prophecies of Isaiah concerning Cyrus and the rebuilding of Jerusalem, and the idolaters are invited to confer together and produce, if they can, predictions equally trustworthy made by their gods.

This verse will be clearer if thus read : " Tell ye (Oh Israel) and bring forth (the Prophecy of Isaiah), let them (the idolaters) confer together, then ask them who declared this prophecy one hundred and fifty years ago ? Who predicted it from that time ? " To this there could be but one answer : the only true and living God.

Truth, having in verse 21, confounded the idolaters, grace, in verse 22, offers them without exception, a sure and eternal salva-

tion in the words : " Look unto Me and ye shall be saved all the ends of the earth ; for I am God. " See note at end of next chapter and read it here.

Thus salvation in simply looking, is here set over against man's way of salvation in perpetually working in order to obtain merit ; which is the essence of idolatry.

Verse 23 is quoted in Rom. xiv. and Phil. ii., and in each place is ascribed to Christ, so asserting His Deity, that He is Jehovah, and that all men shall worship Him as God by bowing the knee to Him.

" Shall not return," i.e., shall surely be fulfilled and never revoked.

Verse 24 should read as in the Revised Version, placing the comma after " say." " Him," in this verse, means Christ, against whom the unbelieving Jews were incensed. But in that Divine Saviour all the true sons of Israel shall be justified and shall glory.

Verse 22 :

The Greatest possible Blessing.

The Greatest possible Blessing on the Easiest Terms.

The Greatest possible Blessing on the Easiest Terms for the Greatest number.

The Greatest possible Blessing on the Easiest Terms for the Greatest Number on the Best Authority.

    1. The Blessing—Salvation.
    2. The Terms —Look.
    3. The Number—All.
    4. The Authority—God.

ISAIAH XLVI.—These judgments upon idolatry by the spirit of God, through Isaiah, demonstrate the power of the Word of God, for it cleansed Israel from idol-worship, and so effected what the miracles of Egypt, the Wilderness and Canaan failed to effect. Many think, and teach, that miracles can convince of the truth of spiritual claims, but they deceive themselves. Witnessing miracles does not necessarily produce spiritual birth and give men a new moral nature (John ii. 23–iii. 3). But the Word of God effects both. Israel came out of Egypt with miracles in her eyes, and turned to idols ; she came out of Babylon with the Bible in her hands, and turned from idols. One hundred years before being carried into captivity to Babylon, her faithful Saviour and Lover gave her these prophecies, so that, during her exile, she might feed upon them, and experience the power of the Word of God to cleanse the heart and beget and sustain faith.

Such is the power of the Holy Scriptures to-day! Eighteen centuries after their completion, and during those centuries, they are found to have provided, beforehand, for every need of the spiritual life (see notes on 2 Tim. iii. 14–17).

In this chapter the sufficiency of God is contrasted with the insufficiency of idols. Men make them, and carry them, and pray to them in vain. God makes His worshippers, and carries them, and delivers them, and glorifies them (v. 13).

Bel (abreviation of Baal), was the Zeus, or Jupiter, of the Greeks and Romans. Nebo was the Egyptian Anubis, the Grecian Hermes, and the Roman Mercury (Acts xiv. 12). Most of the Babylonian kings were named after this god; as, for example, Nebuchadnezzar. A block of basalt, dug up in Babylon, and now in the British Museum, contains the names of these gods.

"Boweth down" . . . "stoopeth," i.e., fall prostrate, like Dagon (1 Sam. v. 3).

Eastern conquerors loaded the idols of the conquered upon animals, and carried them off into exile. Verse 2 should read as in the Revised Version.

Verses 1 and 2 and 6 and 7 assert the impotence of idols; and verses 5 and 8–13 the almightiness of Jehovah Messiah.

The "hearken" of verse 3 corresponds to the "hearken" of verse 12.

God has not to be made, and carried, but, on the contrary, He makes and carries from birth to old age (vs. 3 and 4); and He delivers.

Idolatry is costly (v. 6); but God enriches.

"Him" (v. 7) should in each case read "it."

"Remember, and keep remembering, this fact, and show yourselves men against idolatry." It is a call to repentance and decision. To be godly is to be manly; and the word virtue is derived from the Latin vir, a man, a hero (v. 8).

The "transgressors" of this verse, and the "stout-hearted" of verse 12, were those Hebrews who desired to retain the worship of idols together with the worship of Jehovah.

"The former things of old" (v. 9), i.e., the signs and wonders of Egypt and the Desert.

Once more (v. 10) fulfilled and unfulfilled prophecy is appealed to as proving the existence of God.

The supposed "counsel" and "pleasure" of the idol, ascertained by divination, are neither "purposed" nor "performed" (v. 11, R.V.).

"The man from a far country, the ravenous bird, that shall execute my counsel" was Cyrus. His standard was a golden eagle. This powerful bird symbolized the strength and swiftness of his military campaigns.

Man by nature is "far from righteousness" (v. 12); hence, in order to save him, God must bring near His righteousness (v. 13); it shall not be far off, and His salvation will not tarry, i.e., will not be too late.

To become possessors of this justifying and spotless righteousness men have but to "hearken."

Salvation is found alone in Zion, i.e., in Christ; and it is found in Him with eternal glory (2 Tim. ii. 10).

ISAIAH XLVII.—This chapter should be read in connection with Rev. xviii. Both Scriptures predict the future doom of the city of Babylon. This city was founded by Nimrod, the first Anti-Christ, and will be restored with great magnificence by the last Anti-Christ.

"Babylon" in the Scriptures symbolizes corruption of Divine truth, developed into the enemy of Truth.

This symbolic Babylon, as well as the material Babylon, will perish beneath the wrath of God.

The chapter presents Babylon as a proud queen degraded to the lowest form of slavery.

The second line of verse 1 should read: "sit throneless on the ground."

"Virgin" (v. 1), i.e., uncaptured, or impregnable.

In verses 2 and 3 grinding corn and fetching water express the most abject slavery. Samson, when enslaved, was compelled to grind meal. These verses should be read as in the Revised Version.

"I will accept no one" (v. 3, R.V.), i.e., "I will spare, or give quarter to, no one."

The word "saith" should be supplied as the first word of verse 4.

"The lady of kingdoms" (v. 5), better expressed, "the mistress of kingdoms."

After "ancient" (v. 6) supply "people," i.e., the people of Israel.

"These things" (v. 7) and "their latter end," i.e., God's judgment upon His ancient people in their then present captivity.

Babylon should have reasoned that if God punished His own people so severely because of idolatry, how much more severely would He punish them (the Chaldeans) because of their wickedness, and how terrible would be their end.

" I am, and there is none else beside me " (v. 8). Babylon here assumed a Divine title (xlvi. 9). The Babylonian tablets in the British Museum shew that these monarchs had the title of " King-Vicar." The same title is claimed by the Pope, and is given to him at his coronation.

It signified that the Monarch was the kingly substitute of God on earth, and, as such, had no peer. " None seeth me " (v. 10), i.e., no one can oppose, or punish me. This is to be read in connection with the title of King-Vicar (v. 8).

Verse 9 should be read as in the Revised Version.

" Evil " (v. 11), means calamity, and " mischief," ruin.

" Stand " (v. 12), i.e., " persist now in."

" Monthly prognosticators " (v. 13) claimed to foretell the future from the phases of the New Moon.

The last line of verse 14 means that these diviners were to be totally destroyed, and that the doom that should fall upon them would not be as a little fire that one could comfortably sit at, but a devouring fire of horror and death.

ISAIAH XLVIII.—This chapter closes the First Volume of Isaiah. Its gracious opening is : " Come now, and let us reason together, saith the Lord " (i. 18), and its solemn ending is :" There is no peace, saith Jehovah, to the wicked " ; i.e., the lawless in Israel. (See notes in the Introduction).

The appeals of this First Volume were addressed to Israel prior to the Captivity, while yet in relationship with God, and acknowledged by Him as His people. But the appeals were rejected ; Judah persisted in associating idols with Jehovah ; and, as a consequence, they were banished from God's Land, and became " Lo-Ammi," i,e., " not My people."

The anguish, the pathos, and the love of this last appeal in chapter xlviii. is most touching ; and the grace and wisdom that linked prophetic promises with burning entreaties, excite admiration.

The argument of the chapter is : that the Exiles would find it impossible to credit their idols with having disposed Cyrus to restore them to their own land, for here one hundred and fifty years before the birth of that prince, God predicted his advent and action.

In all this Cyrus is a type of the Messiah. He will come, and restore Israel to the Promised Land, and rebuild Jerusalem.

This continued pleading against idolatry, whilst having an application for that time, supports the statements in other Scriptures that, at the time of the end, the majority of the Hebrews will be idolaters, for they will worship the image to be set up in the Temple at Jerusalem by Anti-Christ.

The moral government of the world is one of the main questions in the Bible. Satan's method is to govern it by idols. His purpose in doing so is to secure the unhappiness of man. Israel was chosen by God to be a witness for Him against idols ; and, at the same time, to be an object lesson to the world of the happiness and prosperity resulting from direct Divine government. But Israel failed in keeping the Law which conditioned this prosperity. Influenced by Satan, they associated idols with God. At the time of the end this iniquity will re-appear ; and hence the necessity, and application, of this, and the prior chapters, to the period immediately preceding the Second Advent.

" Jacob " is the nation's natural name ; " Israel," the spiritual name (v. 1).

" The waters of Judah," i.e., plural of majesty for great fountain.

" To swear by the Name of Jehovah " is an idiom expressive of worship.

" Not in truth nor in righteousness," i.e., not sincerely, nor pure from idolatry.

Supply " citizens " after " themselves " (v. 2).

" Stay," means profess to stay (v. 2).

" The former things " (v. 3), i.e., the predicted birth of Isaac and the foretold exodus from Egypt ; " showed " (v. 3), i.e., " revealed " ; and " suddenly," i.e., " unexpectedly." Immediately prior to their deliverance from Egypt there was nothing to indicate its coming, and yet it came suddenly. So will it be by and by: The sudden apparition of the Son of Man in the clouds of Heaven will startle an unprepared world.

The argument of verses 4-8 is : That God knowing beforehand the obstinacy with which His people would cling to idols, and attribute all their good fortune to them, here announces, one hundred years in advance, what should happen in the days of Cyrus ; so making it impossible for the people to credit their idols with this happy change in their circumstances.

" It " (vs. 5 and 6), i.e., their liberation from captivity.

" See all this " (v. 6), i.e., examine this closely ; and " Will ye not declare it ? " that is, " Will you not confess that the event fits the prediction ? "

" The " new things " (v. 6) contrasted with the " former things" of verse 3 mean the prophecies respecting Cyrus and the restoration. " Not from the beginning " (v. 7), that is, " not from of old " (R.V.).

Their father Jacob was " a transgressor " from the moment of birth (v. 8).

Israel's annihilation was not escaped from because of their goodness, but because of the glory of Jehovah's name and praise (v. 9) and (v. 11).

" I refined thee, but not for silver " (v. 10), i.e., silver did not result from the process but dross." The furnace of affliction" was Egypt; typified by the furnace of Gen. xv. 17.

" It " (v. 11), i.e., the deferring of His anger. Had He not deferred His anger, and had He cut Israel off, then would His Name have been profaned, and His glory would have been given to another god.

The Messianic Title " The First and the Last " occurs here for the third time (see xli. 4 and xliv. 6).

" Spanned " (v. 13), i.e., " spread out." " They stand up together," i.e., " they stand forth at once." When the Messiah commands the Heavenly Bodies to move in their orbits they immediately obey ; preserving, at the same time, their distances and mutual relationships. (Col. 1. 17).

" Ye " (v. 14), i.e., " the sons of Israel " ; " them," i.e., the idolatrous priests ; " these things," i.e.; the predictions concerning Cyrus and the restoration ; " him " and " his," i.e., Cyrus ; " his arm shall be on the Chaldeans," i.e., he shall strike down the Chaldeans and their idols. Cyrus is the person spoken of in verses 14 and 15.

" Ye " (v. 16), i.e., Israel ; " Me," i.e., the Messiah. The invitation to " come near " breathes the tenderest love. " In secret," i.e., ambiguously. " Purposed " should be supplied after " was "; and " there am I " also implies " there was I." The Three Persons of the Trinity appear in this verse.

" Teacheth " and " leadeth " (v. 17), i.e., willing to teach and to lead.

Verses 18 and 19 should read as in the Revised Version margin.

The sons of Israel were to forsake Babylon and her idols (v. 20) ; and to testify to the ends of the earth that their deliverance was due to Jehovah Messiah, and not to any false god.

In leaving Babylon for the desert (v. 21), they were encouraged to expect the same love and care as their forefathers enjoyed at the time of the Exodus ; and that love and care would not be grudging, for the waters " gushed out " of the smitten rock.

But for those sons of Israel who determine to be lawless, and to cleave to idolatry, there is, and shall be, no peace.

The theory that chapters xl.-xlviii. were spoken by a second Isaiah in the days of Cyrus, is destroyed by the message of this section of the Book, for, as pointed out, the argument is the existence of God demonstrated by prophecy. But this demonstration would have failed if these predictions had been uttered at the time of fulfilment, and not, as was the case, more than one hundred years beforehand.

Thus this argument from prophecy, and the fact that, after the captivity, the Hebrews were purged of idolatry, together and separately, destroy the second Isaiah hypothesis.

Acts xxviii. 28, records the point of time when the first volume of Isaiah closed and the second volume opened.

ISAIAH XLIX.—Chapters xlix. to lvii. compose the Second Volume of Isaiah. Its gracious invitation is xlix. 1, and its solemn warning, lvii. 21. Its interpretation belongs to the period during which Israel is Lo-Ammi, and its Divine action is set out in Rom. ix. to xi., and in 2 Cor. vi. 2. Its theme is Israel's rejection and crucifixion of the promised Messiah, their consequent temporary disownment by God, and the offering of the Kingdom of Heaven to the Gentiles. Out of these, i.e., the Gentiles, an election is predicted during the time of Israel's blindness ; and when that blindness is healed, all the Gentiles, including that election, will be given to Israel as sons and daughters. This will fill Zion with amazement. The Church does not of course appear. See Eph. ii , iii and iv. in explanation.

The Divine Title " Elohim," and not " Jehovah," appears in lvii. 21 because this Second Volume is addressed to mankind at large—Israel being regarded as merely one of the nations. See notes on Ezek. xxii. 16 (R.V.).

The speaker in verses 1-6 is the Messiah; He invites the inhabitants of the isles, and the peoples, that is, the whole Gentile world, to listen to Him (v. 1). See last note on chapter xl.

"A polished shaft" (v. 2), i.e., "a pointed arrow."

"Israel" (v. 3), i.e., the Messiah. Israel the nation having failed to glorify God, and thereby testified that it was impossible to please God because He was a hard Master, it was necessary that a true Israel should be born (v. 1), Who would glorify God, and so vindicate His traduced Name. This true Israel was the Messiah. He here comes forth as such, not only to redeem the faithless tribes of Jacob (v. 6), but also to be the salvation of the Gentiles.

The security of His Person is predicted in His being hidden in the Divine hand and quiver, and the success of His preaching, in the terms "sword" and "pointed arrow" (v. 2).

From the Exodus to Pentecost (Acts ii. and xxviii.), He laboured and spent Himself for Israel, but in vain (v. 4); yet His "judgment," i.e., vindication, was with Jehovah, and His "work," i.e., His reward, with His God.

Verse 5 should read as in the Revised Version. The verse predicts that He will gather Israel to God; that the ability enabling Him to do so will be God's; and that, as a consequence, He Himself shall become glorious in the eyes of Jehovah.

The declaration of the whole passage is that, in spite of temporary disappointments owing to Israel's unbelief, the Messiah will ultimately, not only bring back all the tribes of Jacob to Jehovah, but in addition, and in union with them, will bring back to God the whole of rebellious humanity.

"A light thing" (v. 6), i.e., "a small matter."

The speaker in verses 7-12, is Jehovah, and the one spoken to (His Holy One), is Immanuel—despised by man and abhorred by Israel (v. 7). Such was He in His first advent; but, in His second, Kings when they see Him shall stand in awe, because of Him, and Princes fall in worship.

The "acceptable time," and "day of salvation," (verse 8) was the Resurrection Day. God heard His Holy One from out of the depths of hell, delivered Him, and accepted Him; and because of this acceptance of His Person, and His Work, and because of His present preservation as High Priest, the redemption of Israel and the Gentiles is assured. This is the argument of 2 Cor. v. 19 to vi. 2.

"The people" (v. 8), i.e., the Hebrews; "to raise up the land," i.e., to restore fertility to Canaan.

"The bound," i.e., the Hebrews; "those in darkness," i.e., the Gentiles (v. 9).

Verses 9-13 picture the Great Shepherd leading His sheep to Zion. He provides them with food in the ways and on all bare heights; He shelters them from the heat and furnishes them with water; He removes all difficulties and bridges all chasms. No matter how widely dispersed, He will gather them everyone, and with such success that both the heavens and the earth shall break forth into singing.

Verses 14-26 record Zion's temporary complaint (v. 14), and her future astonishment at seeing her sons and daughters, accompanied by the Gentiles and honourably treated by them, (vs. 21-23), returning to her.

"The land of Sinim" (v. 12), i.e., China. The four points of the compass appear in this verse; the word "far" representing the south.

The chief members of society, the Kings and Queens, shall carry the little Hebrew children as nurses carry infants. For an Eastern man to carry a female child is an indignity; but kings will, by and by, consider it an honour to carry in their arms an infant daughter of Zion.

The Mighty and Terrible One of verses 24 and 25, is Anti-Christ; his prey and lawful captives will be the sons of Israel. They will yet accept him as the true Messiah, as predicted in John v. 43; and will, consequently, be his lawful captives. The answer to the question of verse 24 is: "It is impossible." But what is impossible to man is possible with God (v. 25), He will judge and destroy Anti-Christ, and deliver the captives.

The denunciations of idolatry so frequent in the First Volume do not appear in the Second, for it deals with the first coming and rejection of the Messiah. That rejection was both by Israel and the Nations. Hence the controversy in this Volume is not with Idolatry but with man's treatment of Immanuel when He appeared amongst men for their redemption.

This section predicts that in spite of man's hatred Redeeming Love will overcome all opposition, and so all Israel shall be saved and all the Nations blessed in union with her. Such will be the result in grace of the entrance of the True Israel into the world.

As the lines graven upon the palms of the hands in birth remain, so God's faithfulness for His people remains (v. 16).

ISAIAH L.—The cause why Israel is Lo-Ammi is declared in this chapter. As a faithless wife she abandoned her heavenly Husband the Messiah. He, in love to her, came down from heaven to woo her back (v. 2), and she, aided by the Gentiles, mocked and crucified Him (v. 6). God vindicated Him in resurrection (v. 8); and those who now obey His voice no longer walk in darkness (v. 10).

Thus when pleading with men, whether as to idolatry, or as to the rejection of Christ, grace hastens to set out the love and faithfulness of Jehovah Messiah before introducing the consequences of idolatry or rejection. Such is the heart of God! He anticipated the fall of man by providing the Lamb slain before the foundation of the world.

But the heart of man is revealed in the sad and dreadful fact that the presence of this God of love was availed of in order to insult and put Him to shame and to death.

But no amount of suffering could turn back that Saviour and Lover from the accomplishment of His purpose in becoming the Sin-offering for the world that so despised and rejected Him; so He "accomplished" His decease at Jerusalem (Luke ix. 31).

Israel has been "put away" for a time, but not divorced (v. 1). The challenge here is for her sons to produce, if they can, the Bill of divorcement, or to furnish proof of the sale of Zion's children. They sold themselves; and their mother forsook the Messiah as a faithless woman her husband.

But He was not like the fickle husband or heartless father of the East, who lightly divorces his wife and sells his children to his creditors.

On the contrary, He, Who was Himself the Mighty God (vs. 2 and 3), came from heaven to earth to seek and bless her (v. 2); but no one would receive Him, or open the door to Him when He knocked (John i. 11, Acts xiii. 46, xxviii. 28).

His dignity as God, declared in verse 2, is followed by His perfection as Man, pointed to in verses 4-9.

In verse 4, He is presented as the perfect Disciple. He only spake the words that were given Him by God ("That I should know how to speak"). He asserted this seven times when on earth (John vii. 16, viii. 28, 46, 47, ch. xii. 49, xiv. 10 and 24, ch. xvii. 8). His teaching was, therefore, not merely that common to the capacity of a Rabbi of His day, as many impiously assert. Connect Matt. xi. 27.

"To sustain with words him that is weary" (v. 4, R.V.). (Connect Matt. xi, 29).

Matt. xxvi. 67, and xxvii. 26 fulfilled verse 6; and Luke ix. 31, and 51 fulfilled verse 7.

"Justifieth" (v. 8), i.e., vindicated in resurrection. Man declared the Messiah to be an impostor, and therefore hung Him on a tree. God declared Him to be His beloved Son, and so seated Him on a throne.

"Who is my adversary" (v. 8); better: "who can convict me" (John viii. 46). "They," i.e., all His accusers, shall perish like a garment under moths.

There are times of darkness in every believer's experience (v. 10); but light will surely be had if the voice of Jehovah's Servant be obeyed. Those who provide themselves with a light of their own devising, shall lie down in sorrow (v. 11). The language is ironical.

ISAIAH LI. 1-8.—The three "Hearkens" (vs. 1, 4 and 7), teach the same doctrine as Galatians iii. 2, which is, that the spiritual life begins, and is sustained by listening to, and believing, what God says, and not by resorting to self-religious efforts and carnal ceremonies.

These three "Hearkens" also accord with the Apostle Peter's First Epistle, the argument of which is, that the people of God have always been few in number and continually persecuted (see notes on that Epistle).

The content of these eight verses may be thus displayed :—

Selection : Grace (v. 1).

Illustration :   Abraham   and   Sarah, (vs. 1 and 2).

Consolation :   Comfort   and   joy, (v. 3).

Sustentation :   The   Scriptures,   (vs. 4 and 5).

Illustration :   Heavens   and   Earth, (v. 6).

Consolation :   Mankind   redeemed, (vs. 5 and 6).

Opposition : Hatred, (v. 7).

Illustration : Moth and Worm, (v. 8).

Consolation :   Fidelity   and   Victory (v. 8).

Man, being guilty, needs a spotless righteousness, and, being lost, requires a Divine Redeemer (v. 1).

Those seeking this Saviour and Righteousness are instructed, and encouraged, by the reference to Abraham and Sarah (v. 2), for they were dug out of the deep quarry of idolatry, and they were impotent, aged, and childless. Religiously, they were idolaters, " ready to perish," i.e., ripe for hell (Deut. xxvi. 5) ; and, physically, they were " dead."

But God chose them to salvation ; and His Election of persons such as these, wholly without claim or merit, opens the door of the Kingdom of God to all sinners without reservation upon the one condition of listening to, and believing what God says. Thus the doctrine of Election is the most comfortable of all the Gospel doctrines.

The interpretation of these three " Hearkens " belongs to Israel ; but an application concerns all men.

The " quarry " of verse 1 was idolatry.

The second line of verse 2, should read : " When he was but one I chose him, and I blessed him, and I multiplied him."

The promises of verse 3 will be actually fulfilled in the restoration of the tribes of Jacob, and in the restored fertility of the Land of Palestine ; but these promises also picture the perpetual bliss promised to all who listen to, and obey the Lord Jesus Christ.

The spiritual life is sustained, as well as initiated, by the principle of " hearing " (v. 4). The Divine provision for this is the Bible (v. 4). That is the " Law " which has proceeded from God ; and that is the " judgment " established to be the light of the nations (v. 4, R.V.). See 2 Peter i 19.

Christ is both " righteousness " and " salvation " (v. 5). As " salvation " He has come forth, and, as righteousness, He is come near. He is, therefore, within the reach of all sinners ; and all will surely come to Him and trust Him (v. 5, R.V.)— excepting those of verses 6 and 8, who, rejecting Him, and persecuting His people, shall be destroyed as the heavens and the earth, and perish as the moth and the worm. But eternal salvation and ever-enduring righteousness (v. 6) shall be the sure portion of those who hearken to the Shepherd's voice.

" Know " (v. 7), i.e., experience and live the life of Christian holiness.

" In whose heart is my law " (v. 7), i.e., whose will and affections are governed by the Scriptures.

Progress in the Christian life entails increasing hostility from the world (vs. 7 and 8) ; but faith does not fear these persecutors, because they, on the one hand, are but creatures of a moment, and God, on the other hand, is Eternal in His fidelity and power to deliver.

" Righteousness " (v. 8), i.e., fidelity to His promises, and " salvation," i.e., abiding victory.

Verse 5 :   " My righteousness and my salvation."

Verse 6 :   " My salvation and my righteousness."

Verse 8 :   " My righteousness and my salvation."

A confidence founded on ecclesiastical position and ceremonies, can imitate Divine faith, but gives no power over sin, and ends in ruin and the wrath of God. This solemn truth appears on comparing verses 1 and 2, with Ezek. xxxiii. 23-29.

ISAIAH LI. 9—LII. 12.—The three-fold repetition, " Awake, awake " (vs. 9, 17, lii. 1), following the three-fold repetition of " Hearken " (vs. 1, 4 and 7), is extremely beautiful. The first " Awake, awake " is a cry of faith and desire addressed to the Messiah by those who hearken unto Him, and in whose heart is His Law. The second " Awake, awake " is a different word in the Hebrew text and rather means

" Arouse." It and the " Awake, awake " of lii. 1 is Messiah's response to the cry of verse 9. This repeated " Awake, awake " gently rebukes Israel's appeal of verse 9 ; for it suggests that the need to awake applied to her and not to Him.

As with respect to the three " Hearkens " so here the interpretation belongs to Israel, and to the future ; but the great principles of the passage belong to God's people in all dispensations.

Verse 18 shews that the restoration from Babylon did not exhaust this prophecy, for Jerusalem at that time had many gifted sons to guide her. In her future day of distress she will have none. Without doubt, however, this prophecy, and many others which await fulfilment, nourished the faith and comforted the heart of the exiles of the Babylonian Captivity and Restoration.

Thus Zion had need to awake and not Jehovah Messiah, for He, and His salvation, were there (lii. 6, R.V. margin).

" Rahab (v. 9), means Egypt ; " the dragon," Pharaoh ; and " the sea " (v. 10), the Red Sea.

" Therefore " (v. 11) better, " and," followed by the supplied words : " Hast thou not promised," etc.

The reply to the cry of verses 9-11, is the response of the Messiah in li. 12, to lii. 12.

He it was that formed the heavens and the earth (v. 13) ; and He it is Who will plant the new heavens and the new earth (v. 16).

The man, the oppressor, (vs. 12 and 13), is His great antagonist, Anti-Christ. Under his oppression Israel will reach the lowest depth of misery ; but they will be delivered, for, in reply to the question : " Where is the fury of the oppressor " (v. 13), the answer is : " The captive exile shall speedily be loosed, and he shall not die in the pit, neither shall his bread fail " (v. 14, R.V.), " for I am Jehovah thy God, Who stilleth the sea when the waves thereof roar " (v. 15, R.V. and Matt. viii. 26).

The cup of wrath, justly placed in Zion's hand, will be transferred to that of the enemy (vs. 17-23) ; and she will arise from the dust and " seat herself as Queen " (lii. 2).

The name " Assyrian " (v. 4) has been generally assumed to be an error in the Hebrew text, but recent excavations have proved that the Pharaoh of the Oppression was, by race, an Assyrian. He was a type of Israel's last great oppressor, who will also be an Assyrian. In a sense every oppressor of God's people is an Assyrian, i.e., a son of Nimrod, for he was the first great hunter of God's people " against the face of Jehovah " (Gen. x. 8-12). See notes on Hos. viii. 13, and xi. 5.

" What do I here ? " (v. 5, R.V.). What He did in the past, iii. 9 and 10 states ; what He will do in the future day of verse 5 is declared in verses 5-12.

" Howl " (v. 5, R.V.), better : " Shout exultingly."

The beautiful feet (v. 7) are those of the Messiah. In verse 8 the watchmen shout (" sing ") announcing His approach, and He comes so near that they see Him " eye to eye," that is, the watchman's eye meets the eye of the Messiah. This verse is popularly misapplied to predict agreement in religious opinion amongst Christian people.

In that great day when Jehovah shall return to Zion (v. 8, R.V.), His people shall be all holy (v. 11) ; He shall go forth at their head, and will, at the same time, be their rear-guard.

They left Egypt " in haste " (v. 12), but they shall not so return to Zion.

Romans x. 15 quotes verse 7.

ISAIAH LII. 13—LIII. 12.—This prophecy predicts the sufferings of Christ in His First Advent, and the glories that shall follow in His Second (1 Pet. i. 11).

The prophecy will be fulfilled on the day in which the Tribes of Jacob shall look upon Him Whom they have pierced, and shall mourn and weep and wail because of Him (Rev. i. 7, and Zech xii. 10-14). The Tribes will remain in unbelief until they see Him. Thomas represents them in his unbelief. He was forgiven and blessed ; but richer and higher blessing will be the portion of those who, in this dispensation, have not seen and yet have believed. For all such this prophecy has an application ; but its interpretation belongs to Israel. It is her repentant sons who are intended in the words " we " and " our " and " us."

Jehovah is the speaker in verses 13-15 ; the Gospel messengers are the speakers in verses 1 and 7-10 ; the Remnant mourns in verses 2-6 ; and Jehovah once more speaks in verses 11 and 12.

The Five Books of the Pentateuch reappear in this prophecy, as may be thus shewn :

Genesis (lii. 13-15), Redemption planned.
Exodus (liii. 1-3), Advent of the Redeemer.
   Leviticus (liii. 4-6), His Atoning Work.
Numbers (liii. 7-9), Rejection of the Redeemer.
Deuteronomy (liii. 10-12), His future glories.

The last three verses of chapter lii. form a summary of chapter liii. The subjoined analysis will exhibit this :

The Messiah, (lii. 13).
   His sufferings (lii. 14).
      His glories. (lii. 15).
The Messiah (liii. 1-3).
   His sufferings (liii. 4-10).
      His glories, (liii. 10-12).

It was not necessary to mention this Servant's name, as in the case of " My servant Abraham," " My servant Moses," etc, for God never had but one perfect Servant. Verse 13 should read as in the Revised Version.

God had no misgiving as to the perfect and skilful conduct of His Servant seven hundred years before He was born. Hence He could say : " He shall deal wisely."

He then, in His love for His Beloved Son, hastens to over-leap the humiliation of His First Coming, and immediately adds : " He shall be exalted etc."

The " as " of verse 14 corresponds with the " so " of verse 15. The statement is :. that just as the Messiah astonished men by the humiliation of His First Advent, so will He astonish them by the glory of His Second. For, as in His First Coming, the basest of men mocked Him, so in His Second, the chiefest of men will stand in silent awe before Him.

Then will the rations and their kings hear and understand the Gospel.

But meanwhile in answer to the question who does believe it (liii. 1), and to whom the arm of Jehovah, i.e., Christ, is revealed ? The answer is : " No one "—excepting those chosen for His Kingdom, and those out of Israel and out of the Gentiles, whom God wills to give to His dear Son as a personal and peculiar reward for His obedience. That glorious and elect company is the Church ; but this secret is not revealed in the Old Testament Scriptures ; it was hidden in God (Eph. ii.-iv).

The Messiah grew up before Jehovah as a tender plant and as a root out of a dry ground (v. 2). To God's eye Palestine and the earth was a " dry ground." But that Eye rested with delight upon one tender plant which had a living root. It was Jesus. The beauty of this figure of speech is marred by preachers who interpret it as meaning that Christ was unattractive to men. To man indeed He had neither form nor comeliness, but to God He was as a tender plant and as a living root.

If two men, moving at the same speed, were to advance toward each other, one starting from Moses and the other from Christ, they would meet exactly in the middle of verse 5. Here is the simple doctrine of the Gospel—the death of Christ. This is the unique glory of the Gospel. All other Founders of religions base their claims upon their life and their teaching—their death was a calamity, and without significance. But Christ's death was His glory, and forms the imperishable foundation of the one and only salvation. His purpose in coming was to die. (1 Cor. xv. 1-4).

" Of " (v. 5), i.e., which procured.

Verse 8 should read as in the Revised Version. The verse means that, bound and with violence, He was taken away to death, justice being denied Him ; and that being " cut off," (Dan. ix. 26), He would have no posterity (" generation ").

In 1 Pet. ii. 22-25, the Holy Spirit quotes verses 5 and 6 as referring to the Messiah ; and in Acts viii. 32-35, He quotes verses 7 and 8 as also referring to Him.

" Jehovah hath caused to meet on Him the iniquity of us all " (v. 6).

" He made His grave " (v. 9), i.e., His grave was intended with the wicked, but He was interred in the tomb of a rich man, having fulfilled " in His deaths " the many symbolical sacrificial deaths of the book of Leviticus. The use of the plural here also expresses excellence and completion (Heb.).

Honourable burial could not be denied Him, for He was innocent, as Pilate declared (v. 9).

" It pleased Jehovah " (v. 10), i.e., it was Jehovah's purpose.

" His soul " (v. 10), i.e., Himself. Not only was Christ the Sin-offering, but He was constituted sin itself (2 Cor. v. 21).

" He shall see His seed " (v. 10). This

predicts, and declares, His Resurrection. Compare : " Who shall declare His generation ? " (v. 8).

" Justify many " (v. 11), better read : " make many righteous." By His atoning death He sets believers before the throne of God in the righteousness of God, and by His indwelling Spirit He causes them to live righteous lives.

To be appointed with the great, and to divide the spoil with the strong, is figurative language expressive of full victory, and it here means that Christ, by His death, delivers from Satan, the Strong One, mankind that was His " spoil " (v. 12).

" He poured out His soul unto death," for He said : " No man taketh it from Me, I lay it down of Myself " ; " He was numbered with the transgressors," for He was crucified betw en two malefactors ; He bare the sin of " the many," i.e., of all, for " He bare our sins in His own body on the tree " ; and He made intercession for the transgressors, for He said : " Father forgive them for they know not what they do."

In this chapter all the offerings appear : viz—The Burnt-offering (v. 11) ; the Peace-offering (v. 5) ; the Sin-offering (vs. 6, 10, 12) ; the Trespass-offering (v. 5) ; and the Meal-offering (v. 10). See notes on 1 John i.

ISAIAH LIV.—The singing of this chapter will be the moral result of the weeping of the prior one. The Tribes of the Land, having wailed because of Him, will then sing because of Him. This is a great moral principle. Before the heart can taste the joy of God's salvation there must be the recognition, and confession, of its guilt in its rejection of Christ.

The barren woman of the chapter is Israel.

Two periods of her history are pointed to : the first, as the married wife, i.e., when in official relationship with God ; and, second, when out of relationship as the " desolate " woman.

During the first period of her history she gave birth to many sons ; but, during the second period she will give birth to a countless multitude.

This is very interesting when read in connection with Psalm lxxxvii. and Gal. iv.

Christ was born of the Hebrew Church ; and, being owned as her son, all born of Him, during the time of her desolation, become her sons, and will be recognized, as

such, to her astonishment in the day when she shall be restored to relationship with Jehovah.

But this is not " the Mystery " that was revealed to the Apostle Paul, for he states that that Secret is not found in the Scriptures. The shame of Israel's youth, (v. 4), was idolatry ; the reproach of her widowhood, her present rejection.

" Maker " and " Husband " (v. 5) : Hebrew : " Makers " and " Husbands " ; i.e. the plural of majesty expressive of the excellency and glory of these relationships. The God of the whole earth shall He be called ; that is, Jesus will not be recognised as God by the world until the day of Israel's restoration. He will then appear in the clouds of heaven in power and great glory.

" Called " (v. 6), i.e., recalled.

The promise of verse 9 is that, as God assured Noah that He would never again destroy the earth with a flood, so does He promise Israel that He will never again rebuke her with His wrath.

The " mountains " and " hills " of verse 10 may be a figure of speech for empires and kingdoms, and the declaration may be : that God may withdraw His favour from these, but will never break His Covenant of Peace with Israel.

Her present condition is that of the first part of verse 11, and the remainder of the verse, with those that follow, pictures her future happiness and glory.

The Messiah Himself in John vi. 45, quoted verse 13. Accordingly the words may read : " All thy children shall become disciples of the Lord Jesus." This was not the case in His First Advent, but it will be so in His Second.

Verses 15-17 should read as in the Revised Version. The statements here are : that hostility may be shewn in the future to Israel, but it will not be purposed of God, and it shall fail ; for the smith that forges a weapon of war, and the waster, i.e., the soldier that uses it, are alike creatures of God's Hand ; and the conclusion is, that in Jehovah His people have an Almighty Defender and a Divine Righteousness.

ISAIAH LV.—LVI. 1-8.—The present Gospel Dispensation is here predicted and described ; its moral effect is pointed to in verse 13 ; and its spiritual enlargement of restored Israel is fore-told in verse 5.

Israel being during this period Lo-Ammi, the Gospel invitation is here addressed to all nations, Israel included; but only as one of the nations, not as the Election (Romans ix.-xi.).

Thirst is the one claim and only condition of the first verse.

The three " comes " here correspond to Rev. xxii. 17 ; and the four articles of purchase—water, bread (to be supplied after " eat "), wine, and milk express the plenitude of grace in the Saviour, as exhibited in the Four Gospels.

" Money " in verses 1 and 2 is a figure of speech for merit.

The nations are invited to hearken to Messiah Himself, and not to any priest or saint or Angel (vs. 2 and 3).

" Of " (verse 3), i.e., pertaining to, and " mercies," i.e., promises.

" David " here means Christ the Divine David. The following verse makes this clear. In this verse " people " should read " peoples " i.e., the Gentiles.

" And nations " (v. 5) : correctly translated " A nation." (R.V.). This nation is possibly that of Matthew xxi. 43. It is, perhaps, what is called " the Christian Church," i.e., the present kingdom of God. It does not recogni e the Hebrew Church and the Hebrew Church does not recognize it ; but there will be a mutual recognition and union in the future. This is, however, quite distinct from " the mystery," i.e., the Church of God, the Heavenly Election, the " New Man" the " One Body " of the Ephesians the Colossians and the Philippians.

" Thou " and " Thee " and " Thy " (v. 5), i.e., Israel. " Jehovah Thy God even the Holy One of Israel," i.e., the Messiah.

He glorified the Hebrew Church in that He was born of it, and He has purposed to glorify it in the future by enlarging it so as to include all the redeemed nations.

The fulness, the freeness, and the moral power of the Gospel shine out in verses 6-13.

" But " (v. 10) should rather read " until that " ; and the following verbs " watereth " " maketh " and " giveth " should be in the past tense, as in the Hebrew text. For the rain does return to the heavens, as other Scriptures declare, after having accomplished its purpose of blessing ; just as God's Word (v. 11) returns to Him, but not empty.

" Ye " and " you " (v. 12), i.e., the liber-ated captives of Jacob who shall go out and be led forth from captivity by the Leader and Commander of verse 4.

The " mountains," the " hills," and the " trees of the field " (v. 12), are figures of speech for emp'res, kingdoms, and men. They may also express even physical nature ; for the whole creation is to be brought into blessing when Jehovah returns to the Tabernacle of David that is fallen down.

Sinful man is both " a thorn " and " a brier " morally ; but the Messiah can re-create him a fir-tree and a myrtle. No church, nor sacrament, nor priest can perform this great miracle. The popular doctrine of moral evolution is destroyed by this verse, for what system of scientific culture could evolve a myrtle out of a brier ?

A sincere thirst for forgiveness of sins, and for communion with God is marked by a separation from all known sin, and by a subjection and attachment of heart and will to the Lord Jesus Christ, in whom are found salvation and righteous-ness, and who is Himself the Saviour of the New Covenant (Luke xxii. 20), and God's true Sabbath (lvi. 1-5).

A desire to be saved from the wrath to come unaccompanied by a desire to be saved from the bondage of sin, is not a true thirsting after righteousness (Matt. v. 6).

Whenever the Holy Spirit moves the heart to hunger for the knowledge of God, He leads the seeker to Christ crucified. A professed fellowship with God that ignores, or denies, the Divine Priest of the New Covenant, and the atoning and precious blood which He shed for the expiation of human guilt, is a false profession.

To associate the Virgin Mary, or any Saint or Angel, with Christ in the perfection of His person and work and offices in relation to salvation, is to pollute God's Sabbath, which is Christ. See notes on Heb. iv.

Both the First and Second Advents are intimated in lvi. 1. John the Baptist called to repentance both Jew and Gentile prior to the first revelation of Righteousness, i.e., Christ, and Elijah the Prophet will summon both Jew and Gentile to repentance prior to His second revelation.

" This " (v. 2), i.e., that observes equity and practises righteousness.

" It " (v. 2), i.e., the " revealed righteous-ness " of verse 1 assured in the Covenant of verse 4.

Both " the stranger " and " the eunuch " were excluded from the terms of the First Covenant.

Verse 3, should read as in the Revised Version. Under the New Covenant none is excluded.

The House of Prayer, the burnt-offerings, the sacrifices, the altar, and the Sabbath, (vs. 6 and 7), may all be restored in the future, and so point back to Christ and to Calvary as, prior to the First Advent, they pointed forward to them. But possibly these terms have a spiritual meaning.

" The others " (v. 8) that Adonai-Jehovah will gather to Israel may be the " other sheep " of which He Himself speaks in John x. 16 ; i.e., the saved nations. These are to be brought into the Hebrew Church and thus there will be one flock and One Shepherd. But see note on Ezek. xxxvii. 16.

The Lord's quotation of verse 7 (Matt. xxi. 13), supports the belief that there will be an actual temple in Jerusalem during His millennial reign, and therefore, the word " temple " may be here understood as having a material as well as a spiritual force.

ISAIAH LVI. 9-LVII. 21.—In the last four verses of the one chapter, and the first two of the next, Israel is compared to a flock of sheep neglected by unfaithful shepherds, who feed themselves, and persecute the godly. Such was the moral condition which caused Israel to become an outcast (v. 8).

When shepherds are unfaithful, wild beasts ravage the flocks. The beasts of verse 9, symbolize the Gentile princes who oppress the Israelites, both past, present, and future.

The introversion in verses 10-12 may be thus exhibited :—

Shepherds	Blind and ignorant
Dogs	Lazy
Dogs	Greedy
Shepherds	Ignorant and selfish.

Thus the extreme members correspond, and the inner members are related.

"Watchmen " (v. 10), mean shepherds who watched their flocks by night. " They have all turned to their own way, each one to his gain, one and all " (R.V.).

Unfaithfulness to duty often leads to gross vice (v. 12).

But in the flock there was, as there always is, a little company true of heart to the Chief Shepherd (lvii. 1 and 2). These were persecuted to death. The Hebrew words " perish " and " take away " express a violent death (Mic. vii. 2). But God may permit the death of His servants as an escape from calamities worse than death (1 Kings xiv. 13, and 2 Kings xxii. 20).

" He," (v. 2), i.e., the righteous man ; " they," i.e., the godly men.

These enter into rest and into peace from out of the storms of persecution and hatred, because they walked each one straight before him (R.V.). The path of faithfulness to God may be thorny, but it is straight, and leads to everlasting peace.

The physical features of verses 3-21 prove that this prophecy was written in Palestine, and was applicable to that country, and could not have applied to Mesopotamia, nor have been written there ; for in that land are neither valleys nor mountains nor rocks, nor smooth stones in mountain torrents, nor the ocean with its troubled wave.

In the East to be called the child of an harlot is a supreme insult (v. 3). The nation of the Hebrews, by its attachment to idolatry, especially under King Ahaz and king Manasseh, was justly so styled.

It was against those faithful to the Law that they thrust out their tongues, and it was such they mocked (v. 4).

In the valley of Tophet outside Jerusalem, children were burned to death in the heated brazen arms of the god Moloch. Moloch in Hebrew, means, " the king " (v. 9). Drums were beaten to drown their cries of agony. The Hebrew word for drum is " toph." Whence the name of the valley.

A smooth stone (v. 6), was chosen as an idol.

" Shall I endure with patience such cruelties and abominations " (v. 6).

" Bed " (v. 7), i.e., altar.

" Remembrance " (v. 8), i.e., idolatrous picture. God commanded His people to put texts of Scripture upon the walls of their rooms. The Hebrews removed these, and replaced them with idolatrous emblems ; just as to-day it is the fashion to banish from private houses Bible texts, and hang up instead pictures of the Madonna and Child, and ornament the rooms with crosses and crucifixes (Deut. vi. 9 and xi. 20).

" Thou hast enlarged thy couch" etc., (v. 8), i.e., introduced the worship of every false god.

Moloch the king (v. 9), was worshipped with ointments and perfumes.

Ambassadors were sent to distant countries (vs. 9 and 10), to secure the alliance of idolaters, and to bring back their idols and set them up in the Temple of God at Jerusalem ; and though wearied with the length of their journeys, and discouraged with the poor results, yet they kept cherishing hope in the protection of these heathen princes to defend them from the Assyrians and Egyptians, of whom they were afraid.

And yet they professed loyalty to Jehovah ; but they lied (v. 11) ; for they did not remember Him, nor heartily record His past goodness and power ; and they misused His long-continued gentleness in not punishing them.

" Declare " (v. 12), i.e., I will expose thy hypocritical righteousness, and thy useless works.

Verse 13, should be read as in the Revised Version margin ; and also verse 14. The people of this verse are those pointed to in the prior one who make Jehovah their refuge. Their homeward path will be " cast up " and " prepared " ; that is, made smooth and even.

" Covetousness " (v. 17), i.e., idolatry.

The word " now " may be supplied between " have " and " seen " (v. 18). " His ways " : that is, the repentance of the contrite and humble spirit of verse 15. So long as Israel practised idolatry there was no healing ; it is only promised to a repentance which forsakes sin.

Guidance, protection and comforts are promised (v. 18), as well as healing.

The message of perfect peace (v. 19), is a Divine Message. It is not of human origination or imagination.

" Him that is far off " (v. 19) i.e., the Gentile ; " him that is near," that is, the Hebrew.

God in His condescension to the unbelief of man's heart, repeats the promise : " I will heal him."

" When " (v. 20) should read " for." The statement is : that the sea is never at rest ; that it continually casts up mud and dirt ; and, therefore, is a true picture of the enemies of truth. To these there is, and shall be, no peace.

The Divine Title here is, " Elohim," not Jehovah " ; as in xlviii. 22.

Thus closes the Second Volume of Isaiah.

Its interpretation belongs to the period during which Israel is Lo-Ammi. Hence the title " Elohim." Like the First and Third Volume, it opens with a gracious promise (xlix. 1), and closes with a solemn warning (lvii. 21).

ISAIAH LVIII.—Here begins the Third Volume of Isaiah. Its interpretation belongs to the future when God will resume relationship with His Ancient People. Its gracious invitation is given in verse 9, and its solemn warning in lxvi. 24.

In verse 1 the God of Jacob directly addresses His People. He begins with the question of sin. This is a fundamental principle of blessing throughout the entire Scriptures. Directly relationship with God is in question, the fact of sin must be immediately dealt with ; for it is the one disturbing factor between God and man.

The religious activity of verse 2 is all outward ; and the question of verse 3 indignantly asks why God did not properly value such ritualism.

The Divine reply is given in verses 3-7. These verses should be read as in the Revised Version—using the margin in the last line of verse 3.

To fast for strife and contention, and to smite with the fist of wickedness, means to use religion as an instrument for oppression.

" Light " (v. 8), i.e., prosperity.

" The yoke " (v. 9), i.e., slavery ; the putting forth of the finger, i.e., bribery ; the speaking wickedly, i.e., perjury.

The Revised Version margin should be followed in verse 10.

The cities of Palestine, now waste for many generations, shall be rebuilt (v. 12).

" Paths to dwell in " (v. 12), that is ; paths leading home. The returning exiles of Israel are not to dwell in these paths, but in the homes to which they shall lead.

When Christ, God's True Sabbath, is honoured (v. 13), joy and victory (v. 14), result.

It is possible that in the future day of God's renewed action with Israel as a nation, the observance of the sabbath will be the main test of their professed attachment to their ancient Law.

An idle sabbath is the sabbath of an animal ; a sporting sabbath is a sabbath of the Golden Calf, when the people sat down to the sacrificial feast and spent the rest of the day amusing themselves—as is so largely the practice to-day. People attend " early communion," and give up the rest of the day to selfish excitement. A sabbath of profanity and debauchery is the Devils' Sabbath.

" The heritage of Jacob " (v. 14), i.e., Palestine.

Men when even contemplating murder will be very scrupulous in the observance of religious obligation (John. xviii. 28).

" For the mouth of the Lord hath spoken it " is a formula declaring that these statements and promises were not originated by the Prophet, but were the utterances of God Himself.

ISAIAH LIX.—The frequent references to the Levitical sacrifices in this Third Volume, as well as its topographical features, show that the Hebrew exiles will rebuild their temple and resume its services immediately after their return to Palestine and Jerusalem. They will return in unbelief (Ezek. xxxvi), and, whilst ceremonially religious, will be morally unrighteous. But there will be no idolatry ; hence in these closing chapters of Isaiah there are no appeals made urging its abandonment.

The " salvation " of this chapter (vs. 1 and 16), as that of the prior one, means deliverance from the oppression of enemies. For directly after their return to Palestine many nations will combine against them. This may be the period of Gog's invasion (Ezek. xxxviii. 39). Gog is, most probably, a future Ruler of Russia.

The first eight verses of this chapter are the Holy Spirit's declaration that sin will be the cause of Israel's misery at that future t me; and they point forward to Messiah's inactivity in delivering them.

That is a principle which applies to all periods of human history.

Verses 8-15, as far as the word " prey," is Israel's confession of her moral condition before God.

In this confession there is no admission of idol worship. On the contrary, Jehovah is recognized, but unfaithfulness in obedience to Him is confessed.

From verse 15, commencing with the words " and Jehovah saw it," and reading to the end of verse 21, there is the predicted apparition of Messiah, appearing for the deliverance of Israel, and for the taking of vengeance upon their persecutors.

Verse 4 should read as in the Revised Version.

As Adam and Eve tried to cover themselves with fig leaves, so will the children of Jacob vainly try to cover themselves with carnal works (v. 6).

Verses 7 and 8 are quoted in Rom. iii. 15-17.

The expression " innocent blood " (v. 7), occurs only once in Isaiah, but five times in Deuteronomy (ch. xix and xxi).

" Judgment " (vs. 8, 9, 11), is the same word in the Hebrew text as " justice " (v. 9). It should read " righteousness," and means righteous conduct, both on behalf of the Hebrew restored exiles and on behalf of the neighbouring nations in their relationship to them.

The last line of verse 10, should perhaps read as in the Revised Version so as to show the parallelism with the prior line ; so that the statement is : while others are prosperous we wander about as dead men.

" Our transgressions are with us " (v. 12), that is : we are conscious of them ; " and our iniquities we know them," i.e., we acknowledge them.

" Judgment " and " justice " in verse 14, should read in both cases " righteousness," as in verse 8.

" Truth faileth " (v. 15), rather, as in the Revised Version, " truth is lacking," for truth never fails.

" A prey " (v. 15) means a victim of persecution. This fact is true of all ages. The few who are faithful to the doctrinal and moral teaching of God's Word, are despised, or derided, or persecuted by religious professors, and by the world.

" Judgment " (v. 15), i.e., " righteousness " ; that is : just action toward His people on the part of the surrounding nations ; " no man," and " none to interpose " (v. 16), that is, no one to step between the persecuted and their persecutors.

" Salvation " (v. 16) means deliverance, and " righteousness " here points to Messiah's righteousness in keeping His promises to Israel.

The whole passage to the close of the chapter belongs to the future Second Advent when Messiah will appear, clothed with vengeance, to recompense tribulation to the adversaries of His Ancient People, but rest to them (2 Thess. i).

" Islands " (v. 18) ; that is, the inhabitants of maritime countries, i.e., the Gentiles.

The result of this judicial action will be that Messiah's Name will be feared from one end of the earth to the other (v. 19).

To lift up a standard against an enemy (v. 19.) means to put him to flight (A.V. margin).

"The Redeemer shall come to Zion," that is, for or on behalf of, Zion (v. 20). This is quoted in Romans xi. 26 ; where it reads : "The Redeemer shall come out of Zion." Both statements are true. In His First Advent He came "out of Zion," for He was born of her. In His Second Advent He will come "to Zion." But before He could come as Messiah to Zion to deliver her, it was necessary that He should have first come out of Zion to redeem her.

"Them" (v. 21), i.e., them that turn from transgression in Jacob (v. 20). These, for emphasis and assurance, are personally addressed in verse 21 and promised the predicted gift of the Holy Spirit, of which Pentecost was the fore-taste—a gift that should abide with them for ever.

Rom. xi. 26, with verse 20 of this chapter, present the human and Divine aspects of conversion. Believers turn away from transgression because they have been caused by God so to do ; as when a traveller learning from a signpost that he is walking in the wrong direction, turns round. He turns himself round, but it was the information on the signpost that caused him to turn round.

ISAIAH LX.—This is one of the prophecies to which the Holy Spirit points in Rom. xi. It predicts that all Israel shall be saved, and that their restoration will bring universal blessing to the nations.

The Hebrew Church, and not the Heavenly Church, is the subject of this chapter. The latter Church is not mentioned in it.

The speaker here is the Holy Spirit ; the person spoken to is Israel.

Upon her the glory of Jehovah is to arise. As a consequence she is to reflect that glory on to the nations (v. 1), who up to that future time, and at that time, will, as nations, be sunk in gross moral darkness (v. 2). This latter statement by the Holy Spirit destroys the popular belief that the world will grow morally better, and evolve of itself into the Kingdom of God.

The Light is to come upon Israel, and the brightness is to rise upon her (v. 3). It is

not to be originated by her, but is to be poured upon her.

It was not so with the True Israel on the Mount of Transfiguration. There the light and the glory and the brightness poured out from Him, for He was God.

Verses 1-7, declare the accession of the nations ; verses 8-11, their ministry ; verses 12 and 13, their subjection ; and verses 14-16, their homage.

The last six verses predict Israel's glory in that future day when all her sons will be righteous.

"Fear" (v. 5), should read "rejoice"— "tremble" (R.V.), i.e., tremble with holy joy.

The chapter presents a wondrous picture, which will surely come to pass ; for to believe, as some do, that this prophecy was fulfilled in the days of Ezra and Nehemiah, is impossible to the intelligent reader. The Eastern nations (vs. 6 and 7), and the Western (vs. 8 and 9), their kings at their head, will escort the Hebrew exiles home to Jerusalem and Palestine, and will bring enormous wealth with them. British believers indulge the hope that English ships are intended by "the ships of Tarshish."

With this wealth and these materials (vs. 13 and 17) shall be built the House of the Great King at Jerusalem (v. 7). It will be a palace of beauty and glory such as the world has never yet seen.

In its courts the kings and princes and peoples of all nations will worship Jesus of Nazareth as God (v. 6).

Foreigners were forbidden under the First Covenant to build the Temple of Jehovah at Jerusalem (Ezra. iv. 3, Lev. xxii. 25, and Neh. ii. 20, and vi. 3) ; but under the Second Covenant they shall have this ministry (v. 10).

Verses 4 and 5, picture Zion looking around her with wondering joy at her lost children coming back to her on all sides, carried by the kings and princes of the great nations. Even the little Hebrew girls will be carried by kings ; although in the East the poorest peasant thinks it a degradation to carry a female child. See xlix. 22.

"Lightened," "enlarged" (v. 5, R.V.) ; that is lightened, etc., with joy and wonder.

"The abundance of the sea," and "the wealth of the nations," i.e., the riches of the maritime and land peoples (v. 5, R.V.).

"They shall show forth the praises of

Jehovah " (v. 6), i.e., the redeemed nations of the East ; " the isles shall wait upon me " (v. 9), i.e., the redeemed nations of the West.

The last line of verse 7, should read " I will beautify my beautiful house," that is, the palace at Jerusalem which is to be built will be beautified with costly woods, precious stones, and with gold and silver and brass and iron.

So great will be the traffic to Jerusalem that its gates will never be shut, for there will be continual light there.

" For " (v. 9), i.e., " upon." (See xlii. 4, and li. 5).

The mention of day and night (v. 11) does not conflict with verses 19 and 20 ; for the latter verses do not state that the sun and the moon will, at that time, cease to exist, but that the light which will shine forth from the King's palace will as effectually obscure them as the light of day now obscures the stars.

The city of Jerusalem is the subject of verse 14, and the Land of Palestine that of verse 15. These are reversed in verse 18.

" The little one " and " the small one " (v. 22, R.V.), i.e., the little Hebrew church and nation. The figure is that of a man who has one or few sons quickly becoming a great nation. Abraham presents an illustration.

" Exactors " (v. 17), i.e. tax-gatherers (Luke iii. 13).

" For ever" (v. 21), these two words decide the controversy as to whether the fulfilment of this chapter is past or future.

ISAIAH LXI.—The subjects of the last six chapters of this Third Volume, and their correspondence, may be thus shewn :

The Messiah in grace :   His First Advent (lxi. 1-9).
Praise for present blessing (lxi. 10-11).
Prayer (lxii. 1-7).
The answer promised (lxii. 8-12).
The Messiah in wrath :   His Second Advent (lxiii. 1-6).
Praise for past blessing (lxiii. 7-14).
Prayer (lxiii. 15-lxiv 12).

The answer given (lxv. 1-lxvi. 24.)
The first nine verses of this chapter present Messiah (vs. 1-3), and His people (vs. 4-9). The speaker in verse 1 is the Messiah

Himself. This is proved by Luke iv. 16-21.

The Divine Titles here are " Adonai-Jehovah " in the first line of the verse, and " Jehovah " in the second line. (See verse 11),

" Anointed " (v. 1). As Prophet He was anointed in Matt. iii. 17 ; as Priest He was anointed in Matt. xvii. 5 ; and as King, in Ps. ii. 7, and Hebrews i. 5—the Divine formula of consecration in each case being : " Thou art My Son."

This first verse pictures men as oppressed (meek), broken-hearted, enslaved and spiritually blind.

" The acceptable year of Jehovah," i.e., the Year of Jubilee (Lev. xxv. 9). Scholars point out that the reading of this verse by the Lord in the Synagogue of Nazareth took place on the First Sabbath of the Year of Jubilee. See " The Magi," by Col. Mackinlay. (Hodder and Stoughton).

The year of acceptance contrasts with the day of vengeance (v. 2). Nearly two thousand years already intervene between this " year " and that " day " though only separated by a comma in the text. See notes on Luke iv.

The Lord, when reading these verses at Nazareth, stopped in the middle of the second line and did not go on to read of the day of vengeance. Thus He rightly divided the Word of Truth ; for the year of acceptance is the present period of grace connected with His First Coming, and the day of vengeance the future day of wrath connected with His Second Coming. Hence " He closed the Book " on reaching the Name " Jehovah."

" Beauty " (v. 3), i.e., a nuptial crown. Wood-ashes placed upon the head expressed mourning, a nuptial garland signified gladness.

The " trees " of verse 3, are the redeemed of lx. 21. As pointed out in both verses, no praise will be given to the beauteous trees but all praise will be given to their wondrous Planter.

To assure the reality of the statements in verse 4, they are repeated. Thus the first and third lines of the verse predict the rebuilding of the deserted cities, and the second and fourth lines foretell the fertility of the desolate fields.

To the proud nations of the past and present it was, and is, a degradation to be servant to a Hebrew ; but in the future it will be an honour (v. 5).

In that day of restoration the entire Hebrew nation will be a nation of priests and ministers, and will act as such in relation to God and the inhabited world.

As in verse 4, so in verse 7, the vision is repeated in order to emphasise its reality. The first and third lines of the verse predict compensation --double honour for shame and reproach; the second and fourth lines promise rejoicing.

The word "honour" may be supplied after "double." "Confusion" i.e.," reproach."

" Judgment " (v. 8), i.e., " Justice."

When men offer to God a portion of that which they have robbed from others, it is not accepted of God. Hence the handsome buildings dedicated to God by opium-merchants, alcohol-distillers, slave-owners and similar rich people are rejected by Him, but greedily accepted by His Church.

This verse shews that Levitical worship was in operation in the days of Isaiah.

" I will direct their work in truth " (v. 8). This should read : " I will, in faithfulness, recompense them," that is : to His ancient people He will recompense honour for shame, and everlasting joy for reproach.

In that day the restored sons of Jacob will be a testimony to the moral glory of the Messsiah (v. 9). This testimony should be true of Christian men to-day.

"Adonai-Jehovah" (v. 11) will introduce a government which will evoke praise. Till then all man's efforts to set up a praiseworthy rule in the earth will be fruitless. Compare the Divine Title in this last verse with the first verse in the chapter.

ISAIAH LXII.—The speaker is the Messiah ; in verses 1-9, He speaks to Israel, and in verses 10-12, to the Nations.

He is a faithful High Priest. He pleads unceasingly for His people, and is, at the same time, their righteousness and their salvation (vs. 1 and 11).

The righteousness and the glory which the nations and their kings shall see reflected in the restored Hebrew Church will be the righteousness and glory of its High Priest.

For the " New Name " (v. 2), compare Jer. xxxiii. 16, and Rev. ii. 17 and iii. 12.

This Divine Priest can transform defiled and degraded sinners into royal diadems and crowns of glory (v. 3).

Hephzi-bah, that is : My delight is in her, corresponds to " forsaken," and " Beulah," that is," married " corresponds to "desolate," i.e., " widowed."

" Thy sons " (v. 5). By changing the vowel points (which are not inspired) in the Hebrew text this word would read " Thy builders," i.e., the plural of majesty for " Thy Restorer," and thus the correspondence with the name of God in the last line would be preserved—the first and third lines picturing the bridegroom, and the second and fourth, the Messiah.

Verses 6 and 7 should read as in the Revised Version, following the margin.

Faithful watchmen upon the walls of an Eastern city keep calling out day and night all matters of interest or of danger. The figure expresses the watchful love and care of Immanuel, and those in fellowship with Him, for His oppressed people.

The Nations and their Princes (vs. 10-12) will at that time be commanded by Israel's king to go forth from their cities and facilitate the return of the Hebrew exiles to their own land.

The " people " in the second line of verse 10 are the Hebrew people, the " peoples " in the last line, the nations.

The " ensign " is to be displayed at Jerusalem so as to make clear to the nations the place to which they are to bring the exiles (v. 10). This ensign will be the apparition of Messiah on the Mount of Olives.

Zion's " salvation " is Jehovah (v. 11). He will return to her bringing both rewards and recompenses with Him—rewards for those who love Him, and recompenses for those who hate Him (2 Thess. i).

" And they " (v. 12), i.e., the " peoples " shall call " them," i.e., the Hebrews, " The Holy People, the Redeemed of Jehovah " ; " and thou," i.e., Jerusalem," shalt be called " " Sought out, A city not forsaken."

ISAIAH LXIII. 1-6.—Chapter xxxiv. and Revelation xix. 11-21 should be read in connection with this prophecy. These three Scriptures predict the future coming of the Lord Jesus Christ in power and great glory to deliver His Ancient People, and to punish their oppressors.

The prophecy pictures the Messiah as the Word of God, and as King of Kings and Lord of Lords, marching in righteous indignation and stately power, His raiment splashed with the blood of Israel's enemies, and His arm bringing deliverance to them.

The vision is popularly interpreted as descriptive of Christ as a Saviour, having

His garments dyed with His own blood. But that is the vision of chapter liii, and belongs to His First Advent in grace. This vision, as the language states, concerns vengeance, which is the opposite of grace, and it belongs to His future Second Coming in judgment.

The words "Edom" and "Bozrah" signify man and his strength. "Edom" and "Adam" both mean man.

The Messiah Himself answers the two questions of verses 1 and 2. The first answer declares His personality (v. 1); and the second answer (vs. 3-6), His action.

The "wine-press" is the wine-press of the fierceness of the wrath of Almighty God (Rev. xix. 15).

In His work as Redeemer, and as Judge, no man is associated, or can be associated, with Him (v. 3).

"Fury" (v. 3), i.e., "indignation"; but righteous indignation (v. 1).

"Mighty to save" (v. 1), i.e., mighty to deliver His oppressed people the Hebrews; and, therefore, able to deliver anyone who flees to him for refuge.

"Vengeance" concerns only a "day"; but redemption "a year" (v. 4). Compare lxi. 2.

Those who had no helper and no upholder (v. 5), are the sons of Jacob, who at the time of Messiah's Second Coming, will be suffering most cruel persecution. It will be "the time of Jacob's trouble."

"People" (v. 6), that is, "nations." This verse should read as in the Revised Version.

"I made them drunk in mine indignation" may also be translated: "I brake them in pieces." Compare li. 17, and 21-23, Ps. lxxv. 8, and Jer. xxv. 26 and 27.

The joy and peace and happiness described in chs. lix.-lxii. follow this outpouring of wrath; but, as so often appears in the Scriptures, the Holy Spirit delights to speak of blessing before predicting judgment.

The prophecy may be read in the past or in the future tense (Heb.).

This gramatical form of the Hebrew verb expresses the sure future accomplishment of a long purposed design.

ISAIAH LXIII. 7-14.—As praise for present blessings (lxi. 10 and 11) follows the First Advent (lxi. 1-9), so praise for past blessings (vs. 7-14) here follows the Second Advent.

The words "lovingkindnesses," "praises," "great goodness," "mercies," and "multitude of lovingkindnesses" (v. 7) are heaped together, and so help in making sensible the incredible love of God for Israel.

Such is also His love for everyone of any nation who loves Him.

"Children that will not deal falsely" (v. 8, R.V.); that is, children who will sincerely love and obey Him; so He became their Saviour from the bondage of Egypt.

For the first line of verse 9 there are two readings in the Hebrew Bible. These are shown in the Revised Version text and margin. Putting them together, the great fact is stated that He felt with them in their afflictions, but that they brought these upon themselves, for He did not arbitrarily send them.

"The Angel of His Presence," i.e. Messiah. "Saved" that is preserved them in the Wilderness. So through that great and terrible desert He saved them, and loved them, and pitied them, and redeemed them, and burdened Himself with them, and carried them (v. 9), and led them (v. 13), and caused them to rest in the fertile valley of the "Promised Land" (v. 14).

Their response to all this kindness, and loving-kindness, and loving-kindnesses, and multitude of loving-kindnesses, is recorded in verse 10.

"Shepherds" (v. 11, R.V.), that is, Moses and Aaron; but more probably it is the plural of majesty in order to distinguish Moses, or, as some think, indicative of "The Angel of His Presence." But as "He" in the first line means the Angel, and as He is the speaker in the verse, the word "shepherds" would therefore mean Moses the supreme shepherd, to whom the Holy Spirit was given in a special manner.

Moses was the instrument, but the Angel was the Author of the mighty deeds (v. 12).

The ordinary Eastern wilderness is so free from obstacles that a horse can travel without fear of stumbling (v. 13). Equally smooth was the pathway through the Red Sea.

The glory for all these past blessings is ascribed (v. 14) not to Israel but to Israel's Great Shepherd.

This section of the prophecy (vs. 7-14) illustrates the "comfort" of Rom. xv. 4; for if God could love and pardon so hopelessly unlovely and sinful a people as the Hebrews, then will He be merciful to all who to-day condemn themselves as equally guilty and sinful (1 Cor. xi. 31).

ISAIAH LXIII. 15-LXIV. 12.—This prayer corresponds with that of lxii. 1-7. It is constructed of two corresponding sections, and may be thus analysed :

Look down (lxiii. 15).
  Father (v. 16).
    Sin (v. 17).
      Desolation (vs. 18 and 19).
Come down (lxiv. 1-7).
  Father (v. 8).
    Sin (v. 9).
      Desolation (vs. 10-12).

The spirit of prophecy puts this prayer in the mouth of the believing remnant of Israel prior to the Second Advent. The faith and attachment and anguish of the prayer are most affecting, and are made the more so by the way in which the Holy Spirit lends Himself to the feelings of a dependent and desolate heart, recalling past blessing, expressing present distress, acknowledging sin and the justice of God's judicial blinding, but pleading for deliverance, not because of the repentance and faith of the suppliants, but because of the election of God and the immutability of His nature. In the midst of so much weakness and suffering faith clings to the knowledge that the city and the land and its Tribes are God's. He was the Potter, and the people of Israel the clay, the house that had been burnt was His house, and His glory was concerned in its restoration.

The entire prayer should be read as in the Revised Version, with the exception of verse 5, which should be read as in the Authorised Version.

The Pharisee based his expectation of heaven upon his relation to Abraham, but the spiritual Israelite bases his upon his relation to God (v. 16, and lxiv. 8). See note on Acts vii. 16.

" Thy name," i.e., nature and character, "is from everlasting." The immutability of God is the sure foundation of the confidence of faith.

Verse 17, should read : " O, Jehovah, why hast Thou suffered us to err from Thy ways ? and why hast Thou let us harden our hearts to Thy fear ? "

Thus true repentance confesses that God justly gives men over to a hardened heart when they resist His will. At the same time faith holds to it that the Tribes of Jacob were God's inheritance, and His holy people.

The descent of the Messiah upon the mountains of Judea will create a terror to the adversaries comparable to that caused by a volcanic eruption of excessive magnitude (lxiv. vs. 1-3).

The Apostle Paul (1 Cor. ii. 9) alludes to verse 4 and states that, under the Second Covenant, the wonders prepared for believers are revealed. Here faith declares that neither has eye seen, nor ear heard of, a God doing such wonders as the God of Israel did.

Whoever " waits on " this gracious God and Saviour is met with joy and righteousness (v. 5) ; and in those ways of the divine grace there is continuance, and not fickleness ; and hence the salvation of the believer is assured.

The provisions of the Gospel " prepared " under the First Covenant and " revealed " under the Second (See note on 1 Cor. ii. 9 and 10) are fore-shadowed in verse 5. If the reader begins in the middle of the verse and then moves backwards and forwards, the doctrine of a full-orbed Gospel will be found, viz :—Sin (" we have sinned ") ; Wrath (" thou wast wroth ") Revised Version ; God's way of salvation (" Thy ways ") ; Holiness (" him that worketh righteousness ") ; Happiness (" him that rejoiceth ") ; Fellowship (" Thou meetest him ") ; Perpetuity (" in those ways is continuance ") ; and Assurance (" we shall be saved ").

God's way of pardoning and justifying the sinner is opposed to man's way. First, there is the belief of His revelation respecting sin and its eternal doom, and then the acceptance of the atoning Saviour, Who said, " I am the Way." The moral effect is an activity in working righteousness ; in the possession of the joy of God's salvation ; in the sweetness of fellowship with Him ; in the comfort of knowing that there is no fickleness in His purposes of love, but continuance (Phil. i. 6) ; and lastly, in the certitude of enduring bliss.

" Unclean " (v. 6), i.e., a leper.

" Be not wroth very sore " (v. 9), that is : " continue not to be," etc., and : " do not keep on afflicting us very sore " (v. 12).

The Romans burned the Temple, and therefore those who will pray this prayer will naturally speak of the fact as having occurred in the past, for the prayer is here proleptic.

ISAIAH LXV.—This chapter, interpreted by Rom. x. 20, 21, foretells the character and wonders of the millennial kingdom, and states that it will be enjoyed by the New Israel (xxvi. 2, and lxvi. 7, 8, Matt. xxi. 43, 1 Pet. ii. 4-10). That "righteous nation" will be born of Israel, and will include the redeemed nations (Rom. ix.-xi.). The carnal Israel will be utterly destroyed.

These two Israels are contrasted in this chapter. The one rejects Christ ; the other accepts Him. It was of the carnal Israel that Stephen (Acts vii.) in Jerusalem its religious centre, and that Paul (Acts xxviii.) in Rome, its governmental centre, spoke ; and it was the doom of the same nation that Messiah Himself announced (Matt. xxi. 18-xxiii. 39).

Although carnal Israel had outwardly rejected idolatry, yet that evil spirit had returned to its garnished house bringing other spirits worse than itself, and hence Stephen charged them, as does the prophet in this chapter, with being not only Christ-rejectors but idolaters.

These two nations are contrasted in vs. 1-16. The new Israel in verse 1 ; the old Israel in vs. 2-7.

"Stand by thyself " etc. (v. 5). This is not the language, as is popularly supposed, of the Pharisee, but of the idolater, who had been initiated into the mysteries of the god. This initiation into the mysteries was always imparted (v. 4) in a cavern.

The idol's incense altar was of brick ; Jehovah's of unhewn stone, or gold (v. 4).

In an Eastern house the fire of cow-dung burns in the centre of the room, and there is no chimney. The smoke is offensive ; and if the fire burns all day there is no relief (v. 5).

Verse 7 links together into one guilty company the idolaters of the past and the Pharisees of the present. Both are Christ-rejectors. Therefore the conduct of the former will be judged in the bosom of the latter, as predicted in the last line of the verse.

But there will be an election of grace out of Jacob (vs. 8 and 9) ; and this election shall inherit the land (v. 10) ; and that grace will turn the valley of Achor, which was a scene of wrath, into a door of hope (Hos. ii. 15), whilst those that were Israel after the flesh shall perish (vs. 11-15).

"That troop " (v. 11), i.e., the god " Fortune," that is, Jupiter ; and " number," i.e.,

the goddess " Destiny," that is, Venus (see R.V.).

" The God of truth " (v. 16), that is, the God of the Amen, i.e., of Jesus Christ (2 Cor. i. 20, Rev. iii. 14).

The new heavens and new earth of verses 17-25, will not be those of Rev. xxi. 1-8. The latter will be physical ; the former, moral. The heavens will be morally renewed because of the expulsion of Satan and his angels (2 Thess. ii. 3-10, and Rev. xii. 7-9). Then will there be " peace in heaven " (Luke xix. 38), and on earth (Isa. ix. 7).

Sin will be possible during the Messianic reign, but will be immediately punished with death (v. 20). Life will be long, as at the first. Man will probably live for one thousand years. He will outlive the strongest houses that he can build (v. 22, R.V.). There will be neither premature death, nor incomplete age. A man, one hundred years old, will be accounted an infant. Those who die prematurely will be " accursed," i.e., " cut off " because of the commission of some sin. Evil will not then be patiently borne with, as during this present dispensation of grace. This immediate judgment of sin will result from the presence (v. 24) of Jehovah in the midst. His presence in the camp, as in the time of the Wilderness, will be a terror to evil doers, but a joy to the righteous.

" Thence " (v. 20), i.e., from that time forward.

Rom. viii. 19-22 is based upon the last verse of this chapter. The animal creation will enjoy the beneficence of Messiah's government ; but the Serpent, i.e., Satan, shall be made " to eat the dust." This is a fine and striking idiom expressing his perpetual impotency and degradation. Dust was never a serpent's food ; the language here is figurative (Prov. xx. 17, and Rev. xx. 1-3).

ISAIAH LXVI.—This chapter takes up and reviews all the prior chapters of the prophecy.

Messiah's First Advent, and the judgment which followed it, is the subject of the first six verses ; His Second Advent, and the judgment which will follow it, occupies the rest of the chapter.

The chapter opens by contrasting Herod's Temple with that of the Universe—the one so puny, the other so vast (vs. 1-2).

The double question of verse 1 may be

thus translated : " What manner of house is this that ye are building unto me ? " and : " What is this house ? Is it the place of my rest ? " The answer to be supplied is " No ! "

Both priests and people were very proud of Herod's temple, boasting that it took forty and six years in building. Even the disciples called the Lord's attention to its magnificence (Matt. xxiv. 1 and 2), but He told them that not one stone should be left upon another.

The Great Temple fashioned by Jehovah's hand, i.e., the heavens and the earth, is contrasted in verse 2, and the statement is made that God's true temple is the heart that trembles at His words.

The sacrifices which the Pharisees offered so zealously are declared in verse 3 to be abominable to God, as if they offered men, dogs, and swine, and their worship stated to be as offensive, as if addressed to an idol.

Man, tutored by Satan as a minister of righteousness, has succeeded in all times in corrupting the Divine revelation and ordinances. This is very apparent at the present day, so that religious services and ceremonies, which are very beautiful to man's judgment, and appeal to his religious feeling, are declared by God to be abominable.

Israel's rejection of Christ at His First Coming is recorded in verse 4, and the persecution of His disciples predicted in verse 5.

" Let Jehovah be glorified " is the ironical challenge of the Pharisees. It means : " Let Jehovah manifest His power and favour in your behalf." Compare ch. v. 19, and Matt. xxvii. 43.

The swift reply to this mocking is given in the last line of the verse : Messiah shall appear to the joy of His disciples, but to the shame of their persecutors.

The choice and delight of the Pharisees (v. 3), are contrasted with the choice and delight of the Messiah (v. 4).

The destruction of Jerusalem and of the Temple, and the doom of the nation at the hand of the Romans, are predicted in verse 6. It was a righteous judgment consequent upon their rejection of their Prince and Redeemer.

Between verses 6 and 7, the present long period of nineteen centuries occurs.

The sudden and vast enlargement of the Hebrew Church, her glory, her spiritual wealth, her consolation, and her headship over the nations, are all pictured in verses 7-14, and will accompany Messiah's Second Advent.

The judgment that will then take place is predicted in verses 14-18, commencing at the words " But His indignation," and ending with the words " For I know their works and their thoughts."

The seventeenth verse does not necessarily mean that the unconverted Hebrews will practise these idolatries, but that their opposition to Christ, and the rejection of Him in favour of a self-chosen worship, will at the end be, in principle, what it was at the beginning (Acts vii. 42, 43). See also Rev. xi i. 8.

Verse 19 speaks of the undescribed ensign that is to be displayed upon the mountains at Jerusalem—the Royal Standard of the Messiah under which all His loyal subjects, both of Israel and the nations, shall range themselves.

After having destroyed all the unbelieving Jews, the believing residue will go forth, as misssionaries, to the nations to proclaim Messiah's glory ; and they will do so with such success that entire nations will be " baptized," i.e., converted, in one day (v. 8). Then will be fulfilled the command of Matt. xxviii. 19 and 20 ; for that command applies to this time.

Tarshish means Spain and France, and England ; Pul and Lud, Africa ; Tubal and Javan, Greece and Russia and Germany ; and " the isles afar off " America and Japan, India and China, that is, all the nations of the earth.

" Swift beasts " (v. 20), should, in correspondence with chariots, read " swift carriages " ; perhaps railway trains. Railways are now being rapidly built in Syria, Mesopotamia and Palestine.

" The new heavens and the new earth " (v. 22) are those of lxv. 17.

The eternal doom of verse 24, is confirmed by the Messiah Himself in Mark ix. 48.

Thus this Third Volume of Isaiah, like the First and Second Volumes, commences with a gracious invitation (lviii. 8 and 9) and closes with a solemn warning (v. 24).

Isaiah is popularly called the Great Evangelical Prophet. This fact adds to the horror of his closing words.

JEREMIAH

JEREMIAH.—Anathoth, Jeremiah's home, was about three miles north of Jerusalem. He was converted in his boyhood during the revival of B.C. 629, and immediately began to witness for the Lord, about sixty-six years after the death of Isaiah. His ministry continued for forty years up to the destruction of Jerusalem by the Babylonians. This period corresponds to the Apostolic testimony of forty years which preceded the destruction of Jerusalem by the Romans. Most probably a similar period of forty years will precede the future destruction of Jerusalem by Anti-Christ (Zech. xiv). Jeremiah was first sent to Jerusalem (ii. 2), and then to the cities of Judah, no doubt to announce the finding of the Bible(2 Chr xxxiv 14), and to preach its doctrines(xi. 6). On returning home the people of his village (xi. 21), and of his family (xii. 6), persecuted him. He, therefore, went to Jerusalem where he met with worse persecution (xxvi. 8-11). This persecution grew more intense ; and he would have perished but for the courage of a black man (xxxviii. 6-13). After the capture of Jerusalem he was carried off by a party of rebellious Jews to Egypt, where he died. Tradition says he was martyred by the Jews in Egypt.

He appears to have been both timid and sensitive. This made him the more suitable as a messenger of wrath and judgment. Such a message is the more effective when delivered with tears. The ministry committed to Isaiah was mainly one of consolation ; that to Jeremiah, of denunciation (ch. i. 10 and 18, R.V.). He was to be " against " the court, the clergy, and the nation.

His prophecies are not placed in chronological sequence but in moral and dispensational order. Carnal readers think they should be arranged in historic sequence ; and, consequently, they think they find mistakes, as, for example, in xxvii. 1 and 12. They say that the name " Zedekiah " in this latter verse should read " Jehoiakim." This is no mistake, but the delivery to a guilty king of a message given to the prophet years beforehand. Such cases frequently occur in the Scriptures.

The variations and omissions in the Septuagint translation of this Book evidence its Alexandrian Jewish handiwork. For the prophecy denounced the Egyptian alliances of the last four kings of Judah, and it predicted Divine calamities upon the survivors of the Babylonian invasion who sought refuge in Egypt. It was not, therefore, an acceptable Book to the Hebrew scholars of that country. These men, also, modified passages in the prophecies of Isaiah which asserted the Diety of the promised Messiah. Thus they handled the Word of God deceitfully (2 Cor. iv. 2).

JEREMIAH I.—" Sanctified " (v. 5), i.e., " set apart."

" I have put my words in thy mouth " (v. 9). This explains inspiration. The mouth was Jeremiah's, the words were God's.

The Hebrew Prophet was stated to do that which he was commissioned to announce (v. 10). Compare John xx. 23.

The " almond-tree " is, in the East, the first to awake after the sleep of winter. It therefore symboli ed the nearness of the predicted event (v. 11). The " seething-pot " (v. 13) symboli ed the eruption of the Babylonians into Palestine.

" Toward " (v. 13), should read " from " (R.V.). The Prophet being in Anathoth, and looking north, was confronted by the mouth of the pot.

Verse 15 was fulfilled in xxxix. 3.

The word " against " occurs seven times in the last two verses. This emphasizes the fact that man is estranged from God (Isaiah lv. 8). Scriptural teaching is, therefore, opposed to human teaching. Doctrines which appeal to the natural heart, and which are in harmony with the "assured results" of modern thought, must therefore be false; for the natural mind is enmity against God, and is not appealed to by Divine teaching (Rom. viii. 7).

JEREMIAH II-III. 11.—This message was addressed to Judah, but as it did not flatter them it was rejected, and its rejection shews that the revival of B.C. 629 did not last (iii. 10).

The prophet's second message was directed to the Northern exiled Tribes—Israel—and comprises iii. 12-iv. 2.

These addresses sought to awaken the conscience of the people. They reveal not only the affection of the prophet for them, and his hatred for their idols, but they also shew the tender pity and love of God for his treacherous and ungrateful children. The Divine compassion and anxiety expressed in these prophecies is most touching.

To Jeremiah's sensitive heart it was a most painful burden to have to expose the hypocrisy and sins of his countrymen, and to be compelled to announce the coming wrath of God. He was truly a man of sorrows, and, therefore, a type of The Man of Sorrows.

But he was sustained in his faithful ministry—first, by the energy of the Holy Spirit in his heart, in face of the opposition and hatred of men; and, second, by the revelation of the ultimate blessing of the nation.

The espousals of the Nation (vs. 1-3) open the prophecy, and their adultery closes it (iii. 1-11).

The latter half of verse 3 should read: "all that devoured him (or wished so to do) were held guilty; calamity came upon them." The reference here is to the punishment suffered by the Amorites, and others, who sought to destroy the Israelites when on their way from Egypt to Canaan. "Vanity" means an idol (v. 5). In the Wilderness they walked after Jehovah; in Canaan they walked after Moloch, and became vain, for man becomes morally like to that which he worships.

The love and anguish that pulsate in verses 6 and 7, can be felt.

The priests, the magistrates, and the prophets (v. 8), i.e., the whole nation, apostatized from God to Baal.

The mention of the Law in this verse shews that it was well-known in Jeremiah's time,

and that the priests were its custodians (Lev. x. 11, Deut, xvii. 11, and xxxiii. 10). "Pastors" (v. 8), i.e., "magistrates."

"Plead" (v. 9), i.e., "chastise." "Children's children," i.e., your posterity. This chastisement began with the first king of Babylon, Nebuchadnezzar, and will close with the last king of Babylon, Anti-Christ.

Chittim lay to the westward, and Kedar to the eastward of Jerusalem. The challenge here was to find, if possible, either east or west, a nation that had changed its gods. Such a quest would be fruitless.

Here is found an unanswerable argument in support of the credibility of the Bible, and in refutation of the popular theory that Jehovah was a Tribal God invented by the Hebrews themselves. Had that been so they never would have forsaken Him, but would have clung to Him with the same devotion with which all nations cling to the gods and goddesses of their own creation. The devotion to the Madonna is an illustration. In Southern Europe it is no strange thing to hear the people say: "We could do without Jesus Christ; but we could never do without the Madonna."

The men of Jerusalem were morally lower than the heathen. They committed two evils (v. 13). First, they forsook Jehovah; and, second, they embraced idolatry. They exchanged a living fountain for a broken cistern. The heathen were only guilty of one evil, that is, of idolatry, for God had not revealed Himself and His Law to them.

Israel was a son, and not a slave (v. 14); but he became a slave to the Assyrians (v. 15) and to the Egyptians (v. 16). Noph and Tahapanes were Egyptian cities.

So long as God leads there is sonship, liberty and dignity, but self-will ensures slavery (v. 17).

"Sihor," i.e., the Nile; "the river," i.e., the Euphrates (v. 18). The men of Judah alternately sought help from the idols, and the idolaters, of Assyria in the north, and Egypt in the south.

The suffering that comes upon men results from their own self-will, and is not justly chargeable to God (v. 19).

Verse 20 should read: "Of old time I broke thy yoke and burst thy bonds" (i.e., the yoke of Egypt); but thou saidst: "I will not serve Thee, for upon every high hill," etc. They did not, perhaps, say this with their lips, but their action in setting up idols upon their hills expressed it very plainly.

Sin deadens and blinds the conscience (v. 23) :—" see thy way in the valley ! recognize what thou hast done ! " Here the prophet indignantly points to the valley of Hinnom, which was filled with idolatrous altars.

In verses 23-25, Judah is compared to the camel and to the ass, who, in the mating season, run hither and thither after the males, so that these need not weary themselves in searching for them. Thus Judah ran after the idols.

"Traversing" (v. 23), i.e., running to and fro. " Pleasure " (v. 24), i.e., sexual ardour. " Occasion " has the same meaning.

The animal running hither and thither in this manner in the desert wears down its hoofs and suffers thirst (v. 25). So Judah in hasting after the idols only brought suffering upon herself. Had she kept still, and not forsaken Jehovah how much happier would she have been ! But she said " No," I love strange gods, and after them will I go " ; but the result was shame to their kings, their princes, their priests, and their prophets.

The impotency of idols, and the mental degradation of idolaters, are the sad burden of verses 27 and 28.

The guilty cannot plead (v. 29), but a righteous judge can (v. 9).

Luke xi. 47, Acts vii. 52, and 1 Thess. ii. 15, confirm the statement of verse 30, that it was the sword of Judah, and not that of Jehovah, that destroyed her prophets.

God does not lead His people into lowliness and darkness but into light and fellowship (v. 31).

The last line of this verse means : We have freedom of action, and of will. We are our own masters ; we prefer the religion of Moloch to that of Jehovah !

" Wicked ones " (v. 33), i.e., wicked women. The idolatrous nations are here compared to debauched women having Judah as their teacher in vileness.

It is a sad fact that the rejecter of Biblical Truth falls to a lower moral level than those who have never heard the Gospel.

" The poor " (v. 34), i.e., " helpless." " Skirts " is to be supplied after the words " all these." The accusation is : that the evidence of Judah's guilt as the destroyer of God's servants, is so visible that it needed not to be searched for.

A revival which is not based upon conviction of sin, and the certainty of God's wrath, is a false revival (v. 35, and iii. 10).

" To place the hands upon the head " is, in the East, an expression of misery (v. 37). Confident schemes reposing upon human promises, and ignoring God, never prosper.

It was contrary to the Law of Deut. xxiv. 1-4, for a husband to take back a faithless wife, and yet Judah was invited to return (iii. 1). Did God then propose to violate His Own Law ? Rom. vii. 1-4, supplies the answer. The old Israel was to die, and a New Israel to be created ; and thus the foul harlot of this chapter shall become the spotless bride of Rev. xix. 7 and 8.

There was not a mountain in Palestine which was not defiled with an idolatrous " high place " (v. 2).

The language : " My Father," etc., (vs. 4 and 5) was insincere. This is shewn by the words which follow : " Behold thus hast thou spoken ! But thou hast practised evil, and hast persisted in thy way," that is, in idolatry.

In verses 6-11, the northern kingdom is contrasted with the southern ; and the latter is charged with deeper guilt than the former because she added treachery to apostacy. Judah professed attachment to the Law, but it was a feigned loyalty (v. 10) ; and untaught by the judgment that had fallen upon the Ten Tribes (v. 8), she secretly and openly practised idolatry.

" I saw " (v. 8) should read " she saw " ; that is " Judah saw."

JEREMIAH III. 12-IV. 2.—This second prophetic message was sent to the Ten Tribes, then and now, in captivity. It assured them that the proclamation of Cyrus embraced them as well as the exiles of Judah ; and it must have nourished the faith of those in that dispersion who feared God and loved His word. The amazing love and pity and grace of God for those captives appear in every sentence of the message.

The Ten Tribes had been carried captive into the kingdoms of the north (v. 12). This verse should read as in the Revised Version.

There are three calls to return (vs. 12, 14 and 22), and three reasons why they should return : (1) " For I am merciful " (v. 12), (2) " For I am a husband unto you " (v. 14), (3) " For I will heal your back-slidings "(v. 22).

The one condition of acceptance, viz : acknowledgment of their guilt and a sincere desire to break with sin, is in each instance repeated (vs. 13, 21, iv. 1).

This is, in all dispensations, the one fundamental condition accompanying true conversion.

" Scattered thy ways to the strangers " (v. 13), i.e., gone hither and thither after strange gods.

This thrice repeated invitation has never yet been responded to by the Ten Tribes, but it will be in the future, and then God will bring to Zion all who accept it. He will not overlook any, but will take out of a great foreign city even one Hebrew man or child, or two out of a group or family of cities, without fail (v. 14).

" In those days " (v. 16), i.e., in that future time of restoration, the Ark, which was a symbol (v. 16), will be replaced by the throne (v. 17), which will be the reality. The Ark, and the glory which shone above it, characterized the First Covenant ; the Throne, with Messiah sitting on it, will characterise the Second.

" Visit " (v. 16), better translated " miss." " Neither shall that be done any more," rather, " neither shall it be made any more."

The gathering of all nations to the throne of Jehovah at Jerusalem is yet future.

Palestine is God's pleasant land ; and will be the richest and most beautiful of all lands (v.19).

Verses 12-20 are spoken by the Messiah ; verse 21, by the returning suppliants ; the first member of verse 22 by the Messiah again ; and the rest of the chapter by the returning exiles.

It was upon the " high places " (v. 21) that idolatrous Israel sang to the idols, and these high places will witness her tears of sorrow and repentance.

No doubt many f om amcng the Northern Tribes returned with Ezra to Palestine. See Luke ii. 36.

The argument of verse 23 is : As surely as deliverance is vainly hoped for from the multitude of idols placed on the hills and mountains, so surely is salvation a certitude when sought from Jehovah. Hence the Psalmist said he would not lift up his eyes to the hills, that is to the idols on the hills, for no salvation was to be obtained from them, but he would lift up his eyes to Jehovah (Ps. cxxi. 1).

Serving God enriches and ennobles ; serving idols degrades and impoverishes (vs. 24 and 25).

The Lord Jesus Christ Himself is salvation ; hence the first verse of Ch. iv. reads (R.V.) : " If thou wilt return, O Israel, unto Me shalt thou return." True conversion means not only the acceptance of Gospel doctrine, but also a living and saving union with Christ personally.

The closing words of the prophecy may be paraphrased thus : If thou shalt put away thine abominations out of My sight, and wilt not wander from Me, and wilt worship Me, the Living God, sincerely, justly and righteously, then shall the nations bless themselves in Him (the Messiah), and in Him shall they glory

In those days the Ten Northern Tribes will unite with the Two Southern, and, beneath the government of the Messiah, will dwell as one people in the pleasant land of Palestine in abiding prosperity. (John x.16).

JEREMIAH IV. 3-31.—The appeal to the men of Judah and Jerusalem is resumed in these verses.

The eruption of the Babylonians is predicted (vs. 5-7) ; the helplessness and perplexity of the Hebrews (v. 9), and their folly in putting their trust in idols and in the Egyptians (v. 14) is declared ; and the destruction of Jerusalem foretold (v. 31).

" Fallow-ground " (v. 3) is ground that is unbroken, in a natural state, and covered with briers and weeds. It pictures the natural heart of man, which must be broken and contrite before it can receive the good seed of the kingdom. The call here was to break up their idols. This was a necessary condition of forgiveness and deliverance.

Circumcision of the heart is spoken of three times in the Old Testament—here in verse 4, and in Deut. x. 16, and xxx. 6. It is frequently met with in the New Testament (Rom. ii. 28 and 29, Col. ii. 11, Phil. iii. 3, etc.).

Verses 5 and 6 picture the Hebrews in obedience to the trump of alarm, fleeing to the defenced cities, and above all to Zion. It was specially pointed out by the " standard " set up " toward " it. " Evil," i.e., calamity.

" The lion " (v. 7), was Nebuchadnezzar. His invasion was so certain that the Prophet here speaks of him as already issued from his lair, and on his way to destroy Jerusalem.

The " heart " (v. 9), i.e., wisdom, or courage.

The statements of verse 10, are : that the false prophets preached, saying : " Ye shall have peace " ; that God permitted them to thus greatly deceive the people ; that this was a just judgment, for they refused to listen to the truth, and preferred falsehood ; and that there should be no peace but a deadly wound from the sword.

A similar deception will be permitted in the future (2 Thess. ii. 9-12). Israel, having rejected the True Messiah, will be permitted to believe " the lie " of Satan. That lie will be, that Anti-Christ is the True Messiah.

In verses 11-13 the Chaldean army is compared to a hurricane from the wilderness ; " A full wind," i.e., a wind too violent to fan corn and cleanse the threshing-floor, (see R.V. margin) but a hurricane of destruction. It should come " for Me," i.e., as God's instrument of wrath.

" Evil thoughts," that is, vain thoughts that bring calamities, i.e., dependence upon idols and upon Egyptians for deliverance from the Chaldeans (v. 14).

Verses 15-17 describe the messengers from the northern towns reporting the advance of the Chaldeans ; and, later, their investment of Jerusalem.

" Watchers " (v. 16), i.e., besiegers. As keepers of a field (v. 17) surrounded it, so should the Chaldeans surround Zion.

" This is thy wickedness " (v. 18), i.e., this is the fruit of thy idolatry : " it is bitter, it reacheth unto the heart."

Verses 23-27 vividly picture the complete ruin of Judea.

" Moved lightly " (v. 24), better, " rocked to and fro."

Verse 30 should read as in the Revised Version. Eastern women, in order to make themselves more attractive, paint their eyes so as to make them appear larger. But Zion's efforts to win the sympathy of the Babylonians were in vain, for after the capture of the city they pitilessly massacred, in the presence of their weeping relations, all the aged, the sick, the little children and everyone unable to march into captivity. Thus Zion's soul " fainted before the murderers " (v. 31, R.V.).

JEREMIAH V.—As in the Epistle of Jude, so in the Book of Jeremiah, groups of threes may be noticed. For example : " See," " know," " seek " (v. 1) ; " lion," " wolf," " leopard " (v. 6) ; " nation," " nation," " nation " (v. 15) ; " eat up," " eat up," " eat up " (v. 17).

" Ye " (v. 1), i.e., Jeremiah and the few, who, with him, were faithful to the Law.

" Swear falsely " (v. 2), i.e., " worship insincerely." The people, and their princes, professed to be true to God, saying, " Jehovah liveth " ; but their worship was false, for they associated idols with Him. But God demands truth (v. 3).

The " yoke " and " bonds " (v. 5), i.e., the Bible. They rejected the Law as a binding authority ; as corrupt Christendom does to-day.

The Chaldean (v. 6) is here likened to a lion, a wolf, and a leopard.

" When I had fed them to the full " (v. 7), i.e., given them a full revelation in the Pentateuch, they practised idolatry in response, and assembled themselves by troops in the idol's temples.

The idolatry of the East was so impure that God likens it in the Scriptures to adultery.

Verse 8 may be thus read : " They were as fed horses roaming at large, everyone sought after his neighbour's god."

In verse 10, the nation is compared to a vine in a walled vineyard (R.V.) ; and, as is a feature in the Hebrew Bible, the Prophet is said to do that which he was commanded to announce.

Verses 12 and 13 may be thus paraphrased : " They have contradicted Jehovah, and said : ' Not He ! ' neither shall calamity come upon us, neither shall we see sword nor famine ; for the prophets, (i.e., Jehovah's true prophets) are wind-bags, and the Word (of God) is not in them ; and the miseries which they threaten will come upon themselves ! "

Thus the popular preachers of that time, as at the present day, said that God never punishes sin and sinners ; that He will never cast anybody into the Lake of Fire ; and that those preachers who announce His coming wrath, belie His character and talk nonsense.

But verses 14-17, and the last line of verse 31, declare how wicked and mendacious are these popular preachers.

God's tender pity for guilty men is revealed in the sentences : " I will pardon her ' (v. 1), " but make not a full end " (v. 10), and " I will not make a full end with you " (v. 18).

The sands of the sea-shore obey God ; but His people disobey Him (vs. 22-23).

Verse 27 may be thus understood : As a cage is full of birds caught in traps, so their houses are full of riches secured by deceit.

Verse 28 should read as in the Revised Version.

" Wonderful " (v. 30), better translated : " astounding."

Chapters xxiii. 25, 26, xxix. 24-32, and Ezek. xiii. 6, illustrate verse 31.

The priests were appointed to teach the Law. They failed to do so. God then raised up the prophets to teach the people, for He loved His people. Satan, who always opposes God on His own ground, immediately sent out false prophets to oppose and confuse truth, and the priests united with them.

False teaching prospers for a time; but " the end thereof " (v. 31) will be ever-enduring darkness.

JEREMIAH VI.—The Prince of Life, whose knowledge is infallible, says (Matt. vii. 14) that few walk the Path of Life. It was so in Jeremiah's day. Many associated idols with Jehovah ; others substituted idols for Jehovah ; and the remainder observed, outwardly, Temple services, but crushed and robbed the poor and bribed the magistrates. Only a few really knew and served the Lord.

The consequence of this universal corruption and insincerity was the destruction of Jerusalem and the Temple by the Chaldeans.

This judgment is the subject of the chapter, which should be read as in the Revised Version.

The shepherds and their flocks (v. 3) were the Babylonian generals and their soldiers. These are the speakers of verses 4 and 5. In their eagerness to capture Jerusalem they fight in the burning heat of the mid-day, lament that the evening hinders their operations, and resolve to fight by night and destroy her palaces. And so it came to pass.

" Visited " (v. 6), i.e., " punished."

The " grief and wounds " (v. 7) were those inflicted on the poor by their rich oppressors. God loves the poor, and pities the oppressed ; hence their sufferings are continually before Him.

As a grape-gatherer keeps putting the grapes into his basket and causing his hand to return to the basket till he has gleaned all the grapes, so is it here predicted (v. 9) that Nebuchadnezzar would keep returning to Jerusalem till he had taken away all its inhabitants. And so it was, for the Chaldeans carried the wretched captives away at intervals (2 Chron. xxxvi.).

" It " (v. 11), i.e., the fury of Jehovah.

The judgment of verse 12 was that predicted in Deut. xxviii. 30.

When an unconverted man is disquieted (" hurt ") about death and the judgment that is to follow (Heb. xi. 27), fashionable preachers heal " the hurt " with a false peace-plaster. They assure him that there is no judgment to come, and thus they deal falsely (v. 14). But they themselves shall perish with their dupes (v. 15).

True rest and healing is to be found in " the old paths," and " the good way," that is, the Gospel as taught in the Bible (vs. 16 and 19).

God always has faithful preachers of the Gospel, but the world ever refuses to listen to them.

Because of this refusal, and the rejection of the Bible (v. 19), a great congregation of the nations is summoned (v. 18) to witness God's just wrath upon this people, i.e., upon Judah (v. 19).

When the Holy Scriptures are thrust aside, incense and burnt offerings become abominable to God (v. 20), and a darkness so deep descends upon the people that they fall and perish upon the stumbling-blocks. This is inevitable. The only Light to the feet and Lamp to the path is the Bible ; outside of its pages all is darkness.

Family and social influence are usually exercised in opposition to God and His truth (v. 21). . Hence the father and the sons, the neighbour and his friend, equally perish.

The nation of verses 22 and 23 was the Chaldean.

Yet again, in verse 26, a love which calls these idolators and oppressors " My people," cries aloud to them to repent ; but in vain.

In verses 27-30 God speaks personally to Jeremiah, and, under the figure of an assayer of metals, commands him to expose the corruption of the people, and so demonstrate that they refused to yield to truth and were morally " refuse-silver."

" Tower " and " fortress " should read " assayer " and " examiner," or scrutinizer.

As " brass and iron " (v. 28) the people were, like the one, of little value , and, like the other, very hard.

An assayer in seeking to separate dross

from silver uses lead in the process, and when the ore is very base he finds no pure metal, though the furnace be heated so as to consume the lead and burn the bellows. This verse should read as in the Authorised Version.

So was it with Israel. The furnace of affliction, though very hot, failed to separate the dross, with the result that men adjudged the nation as refuse-silver (v. 30).

The deepening hostility of man to the Bible appears in verse 10, etc. It is there a "reproach"; in viii. 9, it is "rejected"; in xvii. 15, scoffed at; and in xxiii. 36, "perverted." All these features are visible at the present day.

JEREMIAH VII-VIII. 3.—The occasion of this address is stated in chapter xxvi. The people were so incensed by it that they demanded the death of the preacher. He was no doubt alone, none having the courage to stand with him. It is an affecting scene to picture the youthful hero of truth standing outside the principal entrance into the Temple and boldly proclaiming the Word of the Lord at the risk of his life.

Most probably then, as now, there were those who counselled him to be more prudent and gentle in his efforts to do good, urging that the best way to help his hearers was to avoid all violent language, to sympathize with them in their religious practices, to make use of whatever good was in them, because there is good in every religion, and to excuse, or touch lightly, their actions which were at variance with morality and righteousness.

Had Jeremiah listened to such counsellors he would have been disobedient to truth, and to the Word of God, and he would have injured, and not helped, his hearers.

Similar false counsel might have been given to the prophet of 1 Kings xiii. when he attacked the religious worship of king Jeroboam.

The Temple was of Divine ordination. The men of Judah and Jerusalem had an idolatrous pride in it (v. 4). They believed that its presence in their city secured their national independence and safety, and that its worship could be made to harmonize with the idolatry and injustice of verses 6 and 9, and 30.

The "worship" of verse 2, was mere outward ritual, and, therefore, offensive to God.

The "lying words" of verses 4 and 8 were: that the Temple, being the Temple of Jehovah, no calamity could come upon them.

The repetition of the words "the Temple of Jehovah," like the repetition of the words "Great is Diana of the Ephesians" (Acts xix. 34), expresses the fanaticism common to all idolaters.

After the word "these" (v. 4) supply "courts," i.e., the court of the Gentiles, the court of the Hebrews, and the court of the Priests.

Before "come" (v. 10) supply "yet."

The language is that of righteous indignation, and the whole passage (9-11), may be thus read: "Will ye steal, etc., and yet come and stand before Me in this House, upon which My Name is called, and say: 'We are delivered!' and is it that ye may continue to practise these abominations?" i.e., the abominations of verses 6 and 9.

The triumphant exclamation, "We are delivered!" i.e., "saved," had reference to the temporary withdrawal of the Babylonian army from the neighbourhood of Jerusalem owing to the advance of the Egyptians (see notes on ch. xxxvii. 5-11). It was also intended as a blow in the face to Jeremiah and his foolish prophecies of impending destruction. And, further, it was hypocritical, for they assembled in the Temple professedly to praise God for their deliverance, but without any intention of forsaking their sins and their idols.

Jehovah Himself in Mark xi. 17 and Luke xix. 46, quoted verse 11, accompanying it with Isa. lvi. 7.

The prophet (vs. 12-14) pointed to the ruin of Shiloh as illustrating the wrath of God, which, when corruption enters, falls upon that which He Himself sets up; and he predicted a like destruction for the Temple.

So has it happened in the Apostolic Church. It was Divinely founded "at the first," but speedily became corrupt, and has been visited by the wrath of God, as predicted by the Apostle Paul in his letters to Timothy and Titus.

It is, therefore, both rebellion and folly to try and set up, as many do, what God has cast down.

The expulsion of the Ten Tribes should

have warned Jerusalem ; but it did not (v. 15).

" Pray not for this people " (vii. 16). To substitute the idols of man's religious will for Christ is the sin unto death of 1 John v. 16. See notes on that chapter.

Man's rebellion against God (v. 20) brings suffering upon the animal creation and blight upon the vegetable-kingdom.

The flesh of the burnt-offering was forbidden to be eaten by the worshipper (Lev. i), but that of the other offerings permitted (Lev. iv). Verse 21 means that, so far as God was concerned, the sacrifices had become hypocrisies, and they might eat them all if they liked ; God accepted none of them.

A very important fact is recorded in verses 22-24. This can be verified on reading the opening chapters of Exodus. There a simple and intimate worship was proposed by God (ch. xx.), such as the worship of Abel. The eldest son of each family (xx. 5), was to be the priest, and an altar of earth, or stone, the place of sacrifice. The Ten Commandments, and its related Statutes (xx.-xxiv.), formed their moral law. But the people refused to draw near unto God, and requested Moses to do so for them, and so the Tabernacle, and its wonderful ministry, as a condescension to their weakness, was set up.

In connection with verse 22, the following passages may be read : Lev. xxvi. 3-13, Ps. l. 8 and 9, Ps. li. 16 and 17, Isa. i. 11-17, Hos. vi. 6, Amos v. 21-24, Mic. vi. 6-8, Matt. ix. 13, xii. 7, and xxiii. 23. " I will have mercy rather than sacrifice." This reading expresses the meaning of the Hebrew text. Merciless people often, at great expense, ornament Churches.

These facts vindicate this passage from the attack of modern scholarship.

An Eastern woman cuts off her hair, and casts it away, when rejected and forsaken (v. 29).

" The generation of His wrath " (v. 29), i.e., a people sentenced to suffer His wrath.

" Fray ' (v. 33), i.e., " frighten."

When God visits a people with judicial blindness intercessory prayer becomes impossible (xi. 14, and xiv. 11, and 1 John v. 16).

The very large number of references in this chapter to the Pentateuch, as well as in the rest of Jeremiah, prove the popular acquaintance of the people at that time with the Five Books of Moses.

" At that time " (viii. 1), i.e., the sack of Jerusalem by the Chaldeans. Doubtless they rifled the tombs of the kings, the princes, the priests, and the prophets and of the inhabitants of Jerusalem in their search for valuable objects, often in the East interred with the dead.

The repetition of "and " in verses 1 and 2 is very important ; it compels the attention of the reader to be given to every fact stated, and every object described. The repetition of the word " bones " is also important. Thus, not only are the objects of their idolatrous worship designated, but also, the fact that every class of society had apostatized from Jehovah.

And yet so great should be the misery of the living in their captivity (v. 3) that they would prefer death to life.

JEREMIAH VIII. 4-IX. 9.—In this prophetic utterance the anguish of the speaker reveals the love of God to rebellious man ; and the rejection of the message prove the hatred of rebellious man to God.

Verses 4 and 5 might be thus translated : " Shall they fall and not rise up again ? Shall they return to Him, and He not return to them ? Why then is this people of Jerusalem turned back by a perpetual turning back ? They hold fast deceit, they refuse to return."

" They spoke not aright " (v. 6), i.e., their expression of repentance was insincere ; for no man questioned the character of his actions, but rushed into evil as a frenzied horse into battle.

Migratory birds have more intelligence than unconverted men. They obey the migratory instinct, and so escape famine and death. Man disobeys his conscience and the Word of God, and perishes. "They know not the judgment of the Lord," i.e., they refuse to act in obedience to that knowledge.

Verse 8, should read as in the Revised Version. The import of this verse is : That if such men were wise then the Law of God was folly ; and, second, that at that time, as to-day, many of the commentaries written upon it were filled with falsehood, and dishonoured and contradicted it.

" Rejected " (v. 9). See note on vi. 10.

Verses 11 and 12, shew that the prophet Jeremiah, like the Prophet of Nazareth, was not ashamed to repeat the words given him by God. (See notes on vi. 14 and 15)

" The time of their visitation "   12).

See Luke xix. 44. For further occurrences of this expression consult a concordance.

"Visitation" sometimes means punishment.

Israel in the Scriptures is presented as a vine, as a fig-tree, and as an olive-tree (v. 13). These express Divine relationships.

The prophet speaks in verses 14 and 15.

" Silent " in this verse expresses defensive action in a fortified city.

The Chaldeans entered the land from the north (v. 16) ; and, in verse 17, they are compared to serpents and adders, so fierce that to placate them would be impossible.

The expression " The daughter of my people " (vs. 19, 21, ix. 1 and 7) applied to this nation of idolaters, liars and oppressors, strikingly exhibits the amazing love and pity of God, and proclaims His willingness to forgive the greatest sinners, if they will but turn to Him.

But these men refused to do so (ix. 3, 6).

Verse 19 should read :   " Behold ! the voice of the cry of the daughter of my people because of (the people of) a land (i.e., Chaldea) that is very far off."

What the voice of the cry said is immediately stated : " Is not Jehovah in Zion ? is not her king in her ? " The Divine answer is : " Yes ! but why have they provoked Me to anger " etc.

"Strange vanities" (v. 19), i.e., foreign gods.

Mic. iii. 2, illustrates this verse, and shows how the people thought themselves quite secure from foreign subjugation because of the presence of the Temple of God in Jerusalem, and that, therefore, they might safely continue worshipping idols and defrauding their fellow citizens.

The prophet speaks in verses 20-22 and ix. 1, 2. Verse 20 means that every hope of deliverance from the Babylonian invasion had passed.

" Balm " (v. 22), i.e., balsam. Gilead was famous for this product. Hence it was a favourite residence for physicians (Gen. xxxvii. 25, Jer. xlvi. 11, li. 8).

In verse 22, Jerusalem is pictured as sick ; but, in ix. 1, as slain.

" A lodging place for wayfaring men " (v. 2), i.e., a public Khan, or caravanserie. These, in the East, are free to travellers ; but neither food nor bedding is provided, and they are repulsively foul. Yet the prophet preferred the physical vileness of such an inn to the moral vileness of Jerusalem.

From the last line of verse 2 to the end of verse 9, God is the speaker.

The last line of verse 2 may be thus read : " They are all idolaters, an assembly of traitors." This is a just description ; for they worshipped idols, at the same time professing loyalty to God and the Bible. Hence they were traitors.

Verse 3 might better read : " They bend their tongue as it were their bow for falsehood ; and they are grown rich in the land, but not by speaking truth ; for they proceed from evil to evil, and they refuse to recognize Me, saith Jehovah." They put God aside, and acted as if He did not exist.

" They weary themselves " (v. 5), i.e., they take laborious pains in · defrauding their relatives and neighbours (vs. 4 and 5).

And accordingly God says to Jeremiah : " Thy habitation is in the midst of deceit."

The second line in this verse means that they refused to be converted to God, because that would cost them the loss of the money gained by fraud. This is why many men at the present day refuse to yield their hearts to Christ.

Verse 7 should read : " Behold, I will melt them and try them (i.e., as metal is melted and tested in a furnace), for how else should I do because of (the conduct of) the daughter of My people."

The furnace in this instance was the seventy years captivity in Babylon.

" Visit " (v. 9), i.e., punish. Compare vs. 9, and 25.

" My soul " : an emphatic expression for " I Myself."

The mention of balsam (v. 22), shows that medicine was used by God's ancient people. Compare Isa. i. 6, and xxxviii. 21.

JEREMIAH IX. 10-26.—" Habitations " (v. 10), i.e., " pastures." Compare xxv. 30, R.V. This verse and the following is the utterance of the Messiah fore-telling the devastation that the Chaldeans would cause.

Verse 12 should perhaps be thus translated : " Who is the wise man that may understand this ? Even he it is to whom the mouth of the Lord hath spoken it (i.e., hath revealed it), in order that he may declare (i.e., explain—see Judges xiv. 12) why the land is perished," etc. The connection with the following verse (13) will be better shewn by translating the first word " Yea."

The doctrine of these verses is :   that

unrenewed men, however intelligent, are incapable of recognizing the hand of God in the private, or public, calamities that come upon them; that it needs a revelation from the Holy Spirit to awaken them to the fact that such calamities are God's just judgments; and that those who are thus enlightened are responsible to declare and explain the true nature, and the cause, of the suffering experienced.

The International War of 1914, illustrates this insensibility; for all the nations involved were guilty before God of great crimes; yet did they not recognize either their guilt, or the justness of the wrath of God in punishing them. The same insensibility appeared in the Great War of 1815.

The Word of God, and not the teaching of "the Fathers," is the only authoritative and infallible rule of faith and obedience (v. 14); for " the Fathers " can oppose truth, and, consequently, perish with their pupils (v. 16).

" Them " (v. 16), i.e., those who follow " the imagination of their own heart " (v. 14), and not the Law of God.

The third line of verse 17, should read : " Yea, send for the women skilful (in wailing) that they may come." The words of the wailing are given in verse 19.

The first word of verse 20 would better read " Yea "; for it was just that the women should share in the suffering, because they had urged their husbands to be idolaters (xliv. 9, 15-27).

So great would be the destruction of life (vs. 21 and 22), that the professional wailing-women—a profession peculiar to the East—would be insufficient in number to perform the customary services of lamentation; hence their daughters and their neighbours, would need to be impressed into the service (v. 20).

In verse 22, the proud Hebrews are compared to dung, and to grains of corn trampled into the ground by the feet of the harvestmen, and therefore worthless to be gleaned.

Men glory in their wisdom, their power and their wealth (v. 23) In a great war a nation boasts of its political sagacity, its naval and military power, and its inexhaustible financial resources. But God can shatter all these, using a poor, foolish and weak nation as His instrument. How much better, therefore, to recognize, and trust, the God of love, of judgment and of righteousness

(v. 24); for in Him are found true Wisdom, Power and Wealth.

The last two verses should read as in the Revised Version. The prediction here was, that the Cup of Wrath for the people of Judah would have this added bitterness of having to be drunk in fellowship with the neighbouring nations whom they so despised. These nations practised circumcision, as Judah did, but, like Judah they were uncircumcised in heart (v. 26). These words " in heart " are to be understood as applying, not only to the House of Israel, but to the other nations mentioned in the verse.

The dwellers in the wilderness—the Arabs—at that time publicly declared their attachment to their god by trimming the beard after a certain fashion. " Dragons " (v. 11) i.e., " jackals," and " heaps," i.e., plural of magnitude for a great heap of stones.

Verse 24 is quoted in 1 Cor. i. 31.

" To know God " (v. 24) is the foundation of all blessing, and all trust, and all holy living. One Unknown cannot be trusted at all. (John xvii. 3, Ephes. i. 17, Col. i. 9, 1 John v. 20). Not to know God is the cause of all misery and corruption (Rom. i. 28, Isa. i. 3, Luke xix. 42-44). All future glory is connected with this knowledge (Isa. xi. 9, xxxii. 4, and liv. 13). Hence the fundamental necessity of the Incarnate Word (John i. 18), and of the Inspired Word (2 Tim. iii. 15).

JEREMIAH X.—The contrast between God and idols, and the moral and physical destruction caused by idolatry, are vividly set out in this chapter.

" Way " (v. 2), i.e., " religion." "The signs of heaven," i.e., comets, eclipses, etc. The Bible liberates nations from such fears.

" Customs " (v. 3), i.e., images of wood. The second line of this verse should read as in the Revised Version margin.

" Upright," (v. 5), i.e., stiff.

Verses 6 and 7 contrast God with these blocks of wood. The first line of verse 7 may read : " Who would not worship Thee, O King of nations ? for it (worship) beseemeth Thee."

" They " (v. 8), i.e., all the wise men of the nations (v. 7); these, through idol-worship, become brutish and foolish; and, indeed, more debased morally than the beasts of the field.

" The stock is a doctrine of vanities " (v. 8), i.e., the teachings of idolatry are delusion and falsehood.

Verses 10-13 again contrast God with idols ; and verses 14-16, like verse 8, declare the stupidity of idolaters.

God is true, living and eternal, in contrast with a block of wood, which is false, dead and perishable.

Verse 11 is written in Chaldee. It provided the godly exiles with the reply that they were to make to their Babylonian captors when pointing out the impotency and folly of idols.

If verses 12 and 13 be read immediately after verse 10 the elevation and magnificence of the language will be felt.

The first line of verse 14 may mean that the skilful manufacture of idols makes the manufacturer brutish ; or it may mean that he is too brutish to recognize the absurdity of what he is doing.

The doom of the idolatrous Babylonians, and of their idols, at the hands of Cyrus, is predicted in verses 15 and 25.

" Former " (v. 16), i.e., " Maker."

Verse 17 better reads. : " Take up thy bundle from the ground, oh inhabitant of the fortress ? " (Jerusalem). That is : the unhappy captives when setting out for Babylonia would be permitted to take nothing with them but what could be carried by hand.

" That they may find it so " (v. 18), i.e., that they may experience the misery that results from rejecting God's Word in favour of the false teaching of idolatry.

In verses 19-22 Zion speaks through the mouth of the Prophet. The " shepherds " (v. 21) here mean Jehoakim and the princes.

The Babylonians entered Palestine from the north (v. 22). Zion refused to listen to the voice of God and so was compelled to listen to the voice of the Chaldean (R.V.).

Two statements are made in verse 23. First : man does not enjoy liberty of action. Second, he cannot assure himself of success. The prophet here applies these facts to Nebuchadnezzar, and, accordingly, recognizes him as God's instrument. No man is his own master, but he thinks he is.

Zion's prayer in the last two verses is: Correct me, but destroy them. This prayer has been, and is being, answered ; for the Babylonians have been utterly destroyed, but Israel is being preserved under correction (Ps. lxix. 6 and 7).

The justness of this judgment upon the Chaldeans is recorded in chapters l. and li.

JEREMIAH XI. 1-17.—This Covenant (v. 2), i.e., the Book of the Law that had been found in the Temple some years previously during the reign of King Josiah, and which originated the revival proposed by that good monarch. Directly he died the nation restored idolatry (vs. 9 and 10). This action proved the insincerity of their professed conversion, and justified the righteous judgment that fell upon them (v.11).

" Cursed " (v. 3), i.e., condemned to death. This is the function of law, it cannot give life to dead men, it condemns law-breakers to death. The Law was given to make man conscious of his moral condition as a sinner, and of his need of a Saviour. The Tabernacle and its sacrifices which accompanied the law revealed that Saviour in symbol.

God does not ask men to obey Him (v. 4) as a selfish and tyrannical master orders a slave in order to gratify his own cruel temper, but He commands man's obedience in order to man's happiness. This He demonstrated by bringing the people out of the iron furnace of Egyptian slavery, and bringing them into a land of freedom and wealth (v. 5). Disobedience to natural law entails suffering ; disobedience to spiritual law,—that is to love—ensures death.

Jeremiah was a street-preacher both in Jerusalem and in the cities of Judah (v. 6) ; he carried in his hand the Bible, caused the people to hear its words, and urged his hearers to believe and obey them.

He contrasted (v. 8) the teachings of the Bible with those of the human imagination, and declared the latter to be evil, and that the wrath predicted in the Bible would certainly strike those who accepted this religion of the imagination.

It is clear from verses 9 and 10 that king Josiah's subjects secretly decided to return to idolatry, and to set aside the Bible at the first favourable opportunity. " Went " (v. 10) should read " are gone."

The impotency of idols to protect idolaters is declared in verses 11-14. History attests this fact, for the people of Judah were overthrown by the Chaldeans, and carried captive into Babylon.

Not only does idolatry bring shame upon idolaters (v. 13), but the most popular idol of the East at that time was so shameful that a description of it is impossible.

An explanation of verse 15 is difficult because the Hebrew text is difficult. The following interpretation is suggested : Judah, notwithstanding their moral degradation, and the introduction of many idols with their obscene ceremonies into the Temple itself, is called " My beloved." The " holy flesh," i.e., the Levitical sacrifices (Hag. ii. 12), were neglected, or had lost their savour for God ; and yet though judgment was near at hand, the worshippers rejoiced because confident of deliverance by their idol.

Another reading of this text will be found in the Revised Version margin.

" The green olive-tree " was Israel, the " tumult " was the Chaldean invasion, here symbolized by a thunderstorm with lightning (v. 16). The storm destroys the tree, and the lightning sets it on fire.

Israel is compared in the Scriptures to an olive-tree, a fig-tree, and a vine. These symbolize religious, national, and spiritual privileges.

" Against themselves " (v. 17). Sin injures the sinner, for men sin to their own hurt.

JEREMIAH XI. 18-XII. 6.—Jeremiah came unto his own and his own received him not (v. 21). They resolved to kill him though he was to them as a gentle lamb (v. 19), and his only crime was that he prophesied to them in the name of the Lord. Anathoth was his native village, it belonged to the priests, and they, together with the members of the Prophet's family, joined in the plot to destroy him.

So was it with the Messiah, of whom Jeremiah is here a type. Those who first sought to murder him were the men of his own village of Nazareth (Luke iv. 16-29).

Jeremiah was guileless and unsuspecting (v. 19) ; but God revealed the conspiracy to him (v. 18).

This verse may read : " Now Jehovah gave me knowledge of it (i.e., of the plot against his life) and thus I came to know it."

The Divine revelation saved his life, and, at the same time, strengthened his faith, for it was a proof to him of God's tender care.

" Then " (v. 18), i.e., at the time that his life was in danger. " Their doings," i.e., the murderous plans of the men of Anathoth, including the prophet's own family (xii. 6).

The " tree " figured the prophet ; its " fruit," his preaching (v. 19).

The prayer of verse 20 is that proper to truth and righteousness in conflict with falsehood and evil. It corresponds to similar language in the lips of David and of the Apostle Paul (Gal. i. 8 and 1 Cor. xvi. 22).

The energy of truth in Jeremiah's soul desired to see God's vengeance upon evil and evil-doers. He would not take vengeance into his own hands, but gave place unto wrath, i.e., stepped aside so as to give room for the wrath of God to act (Rom. xii. 19). He committed his cause unto God (v. 20), his cause was God's cause, and, therefore, it was fitting that he should pray for the destruction of the enemies of that cause. It was not a personal but a ministerial prayer, and so corresponded to that of the apostle Paul, which was of the same nature.

It was very bitter to the gentle spirit of the prophet to be not only hated by his fellow-citizens, but also by his family, and to the extent that they were resolved to murder him.

Their doom, therefore, was most just (vs. 22 and 23).

Amidst his sorrows and dangers the brave young preacher hastened to vindicate God (vs. 20 and xii. 1). He judged righteously, and was Himself righteous ; but yet the prophet desired to reason with Him of His action in permitting evil to prosper.

" Very treacherously " (v. 1), i.e., why are all they happy that are out-and-out traitors ?

" Thou art near in their mouth " (v. 2). His enemies being priests, mouthed the services, but their hearts were bound to their idols and to their sins.

It was the priestly caste who sought to murder both Jeremiah and Christ.

It was because he knew that the salvation of the people, and the fertility of the land (v. 4), depended upon the destruction of the wicked, therefore he prayed for their extinction (v. 3).

" He shall not see our latter end " (v. 4 R.V) that is, the prophet's enemies were confident of a successful future for themselves and for Jerusalem, but they were determined that Jeremiah should not see their good fortune, nor share in it, for they determined to kill him.

Verses 5 and 6 are God's gentle answers to the prophet's plaint. The " footmen " represent the men of Anathoth, the " horsemen " the rulers of Jerusalem, whose hatred and blood-thirst would be far worse than Anathoth. "The land of peace" in which he thought himself secure, was his own village, "the swelling of Jordan," the wild fury he would have to face in the capital-city. The swelling of Jordan is caused by storms ; but some scholars think the term means the fierce beasts that inhabited the Jordan valley.

This comparison prepared Jeremiah for the fiercer battles that were ahead of him, it assured him of his present safety, and illustrated God's loving protection of him.

His family loudly called, i.e., urged, a multitude after him to murder him, but to his face they spoke fair words. This Divine revelation to him of the treachery of his relatives must have deeply pained his heart.

Thus the prophet was trained to feel how bitter was the pain that hurt the heart of God, when, in response to Messiah's love, sinful men met Him with hatred and murder. The hatred Jeremiah suffered was, in comparison with that which Christ suffered, as "footmen" to "horsemen" and calm to storm ; for no one was ever so much hated by his family and his fellow-citizens as was Jesus of Nazareth. (Psa. lxix. 8).

"Horses" (v. 5), i.e., horsemen.

JEREMIAH XII. 7-17.—These verses apply to Judah and Jerusalem, and are, therefore, to be distinguished from those of the previous section which relate solely to Anathoth.

Verse 7 supplies the answer to verse 1. When God, for reasons satisfactory to Himself, withdraws from active interference in the affairs of men, and leaves them to their own free-will, the result is oppression of the weak by the strong, and the robbery of the poor by the rich ; evil and violent men prosper, and good men suffer.

And yet in spite of national corruption, and religious apostacy, God here styles Israel " the dearly-loved of His soul " ; and there is a sob in the words stating that He had given her into the hand of her enemies. This amazing love is further evidenced by the words " Me " and " My " which occur fifteen times in these eleven verses.

So degraded and hostile had idolatry made them that they are compared in verses 8 and 9 to an angry lion and a fierce vulture. Such is man's moral response to God's wondrous love. And yet though Judah had become as a foul vulture, surrounded by similar birds of prey, and yet outwardly diverse from them,

because speckled, Jehovah pitied her because the other foul birds were against her, and were calling to the wild beasts to come and help to devour her.

"Hated" (v. 8), i.e., less cared for, or favoured. This Hebrew verb is not the same as the verb which means " to hate with malice," but signifies " to love less." For example, " Jacob have I loved, but Esau have I hated ; " and again : " If a man have two wives and love the one but hate the other " (Deut. xxi. 15). In this sense God " hated," temporarily, His beloved people by forsaking them, and permitting them to fall into the hands of their enemies. This " hatred " still continues, but will determine in the day of their future restoration.

" Pastors " (v. 10,) i.e., heathen princes.

" No man layeth it to heart " (v. 11) read : " Because no man layeth God's Word to heart." Refusal to follow the teachings of the Bible ensures loss and suffering.

" The sword of the Lord " (v. 12), i.e., the Chaldean army.

" They have put themselves to pain " (v. 13), i.e., they painfully toiled. Judah is here compared to a hard-working farmer whose toil is rewarded by a harvest of thorns and disappointment. The last line of the verse reveals the fierce anger of God as having caused such a miscarriage of industry, and intimates that it was a just anger.

" My evil neighbours " (v. 14). This is both truth and grace. Truth declares their moral character, but grace owns them as " neighbours." These nations whose frontiers touched Palestine, will be restored and spiritually prospered in a future day. They are Egypt, Edom, Philistia, Ammon, Moab and Syria. See chapters xlvii., xlviii., and xlix. But a necessity of their restoration must be a destruction of Babylon. Thus will the Divine purposes, prior to the founding of Babylon by Nimrod, be accomplished. The one condition of this national blessing is stated in verses 16 and 17.

All this makes clear the unchangeable love of God to His ancient people, and the unbreakable nature of His faithfulness to them. He has designed Israel as the centre of all earthly governments. This national system is now in confusion because of Israel's fall, for she is the keystone. Her restoration will be their recovery. The Lord Jesus Christ, as Man and Messiah, will unite in His person the headship of man, and the dominion of Israel.

" Pluck " (twice, v. 14). This is the same word in the Hebrew text. It means to uproot It has a bad sense in reference to the nations, but a good sense in regard to Judah, and implies her liberation from the oppression of her powerful enemies.

The future redemption of these enemies is predicted in verse 15.

" The ways of my people " (v. 16), i.e., the Divine way of salvation, revealed and committed to Israel.

" To swear by my Name " saying : " Jehovah liveth," i.e., to worship God through Jesus Christ ; for " Jesus " is God's Greatest Name.

In verse 9 Israel is pictured in the midst of the nations ; in verse 16 the nations are pictured in the midst of Israel.

The prophet was forbidden to pray for the nation (xi. 14), but not forbidden to pray for the believing Remnant, and to console them with the hopes of verses 14-17.

JEREMIAH XIII.—This message was addressed to King Jehoiachin, who was about eighteen years of age, to the Queen mother Nehushta, and to the priests and people of Jerusalem (vs. 15-18). The speaker was Emmanuel, not Jeremiah (v. 15) ; he was a mere instrument.

This was the Divine speaker of Matt. xxiii. He then repeated the predicted and righteous doom of verse 14.

He also was the speaker of Luke xix. 41. Then were seen publicly the secret tears of verse 17.

So in those two chapters appear the grace and truth that are recorded in this chapter. Both came by Jesus Christ ; and both were perfect. His wrath (v. 14) is as perfect as His love (v. 17).

In this chapter He compares Israel to a girdle (v. 11), and to a wine jar (v. 12). A girdle adorns, and wine refreshes. Such was the high double honour offered to Israel. She has temporarily lost both through disobedience. But the day will soon come when He will clothe Himself with her, and she shall become, and express, His glory ; and will also be to Him as the " new wine ' of the kingdom that will refresh His heart in that day of the restitution of all things (Luke xxii. 18).

In the East to-day, as in ancient times,

girdles are worn both by men and women. Those of the poor are made of leather, those of the rich of fine linen or silk, often richly embroidered and bejewelled. Aaron's girdle was a girdle of glory (Ex. xxviii.). The Divine Aaron girded Himself with a towel (John xiii. 4). He afterwards appeared in glory girdled with a golden girdle (Rev. i. 13). The seven angels (Rev. xv. 6) also wore golden girdles. Elijah and John the Baptist wore leather girdles (2 Kings i. 8 and Matt. iii. 4). Soldiers wore girdles upon the loins (Neh. iv. 18), they were sometimes richly ornamented, and given as rewards (2 Sam. xviii. 11).

By this touching symbol Israel was taught how Emmanuel had bound her upon His heart, and worn her as an ornament, the fine linen expressing her purity. Such was His love to her.

But her disobedience compelled Him to remove the girdle and bury it at the Euphrates ; where it became marred and worthless (v. 7).

This symbolical action foretold the captivity of seventy years in the Euphrates valley.

A similar lesson was taught by the wine jars. Love proposed to fill them all, big and little, with wine, but a just and perfect wrath dashed them to pieces.

Most Bible students confound this beauteous girdle with the unlovely loin-cloth of the East. But this would rob verse 11 of all meaning. A loin cloth is not worn for praise and glory. If all the verses in the Bible which speak of girdles be read, the beauty and force of this symbol will be recognized. Just as a girdle of fine linen would be marred by burial in the bank of a river, so should the pride of Israel be marred by her servitude at the Euphrates. To make it quite clear that it was the river bank that marred the girdle the prophet was told not to put it in water.

The chapter should be read as in the Revised Version.

Verse 19 means that the Southern cities should be besieged, and there would be none to raise the siege.

" Them that come from the north " (v. 20), i.e., the Babylonians.

In verse 20 King Jehoiachin is pictured as a shepherd responsible to an owner, and his flock are the children of Judah.

" He," i.e., Nebuchednezzar, " them," i e., his princes. The meaning of these words is : that the king by his alliance with the Chaldean monarch, had " taught " him to become his chief, and his princes to become Judah's masters.

" Iniquity " (v. 22), i.e., idolatry caused this just judgment. Nakedness and bare feet express slavery. Such should be their lot measured to them by God (v. 25).

The impurity of idol worship is vividly expressed in verse 27. The close of the verse should read as in the Revised Version. The words recall the Saviour's sob of anguish when He said : " How often would I have gathered thee ; but ye would not ! " Matt. xxiii. 37.

JEREMIAH XIV. 1–18.—Jeremiah's Tenth Prophecy begins here and ends at xv. 21. This order is moral and not chronological.

The first six verses state the occasion and circumstance of the prophecy.

This drought preceded one of the three sieges of Jerusalem by the Chaldeans. If verse 18 implies captivity then the drought would appear to have preceded the second siege, which was followed by the Seventy Years Captivity.

Bible students should distinguish between the Seventy Years " Servitude " which followed the first siege, and the Seventy Years " Captivity " which followed the second siege, and the Seventy Years " Desolations " which followed the third and last siege.

" The word of the Lord that came to Jeremiah " (v. 1). The Hebrew here is peculiar. It suggests : The message which proved to be the Word of the Lord.

Verses 2–6 should be read as in the Revised Version ; but " little ones," and " pits " (v. 3), should be changed to " servants," and " cisterns."

The prophecy commences at verse 7. Its form is a double triplet, as subjoined :

Supplication (vs. 7–9).
   Repudiation (vs. 10–12).
      Denunciation of false prophets (vs. 13–18).

Supplication (vs. 19–22).
   Repudiation (vs. xv. 1–9).
      Vindication of true prophets (vs. 10–21).

" Iniquities," " backslidings " and " sins " (v. 7) express the moral character and

worthlessness of man, however high may be his religious privileges. Hence forgiveness can only be prayed for for His Name's sake, i.e., in the Name of Jesus. That Name being Perfection, it secures a perfect pardon.

" Thus have they loved to wander ; they have not refrained their feet " (v. 10). Attention here is directed to the countless idols to which the people hastened. This feature in idolatry is very visible at the present day, special trains and steamers being perpetually engaged in bringing thousands of worshippers to renowned religious shrines.

" Visit " (v. 10), i.e., punish.

The closing verses (13–18) predicted the doom of the false prophets, and God's denunciation of them. This denunciation was announced with abundance of tears (v. 17). The True Prophet, Christ, faithfully told men of their sins, and of the wrath to come ; but He did so with sobs and tears. Every preacher controlled by His Spirit, in like manner warns men with tears (Acts xx. 31) either secret or public.

The last statement in verse 18 may mean (R.V.) that the false prophets preached about matters of which they were ignorant, just as do unconverted ministers and missionaries of the present day ; or (A.V.) it may predict the exile of the prophets to a foreign land. Scholars have not sufficient material to help them to translate the original Hebrew text.

JEREMIAH XIV. 19 - XV. 21. — The prophet's intercession (19–22), its rejection (1–9), and his vindication and the great principles connected with it (vs. 10–21), correspond with xiv. 1, 18, as already pointed out.

As a true intercessor he identifies himself with those for whom he intercedes ; hence the " us," the " we," and the " our," of his prayer.

" Vanities " (v. 22), i.e., idols. To give the sense supply " themselves " after the heavens, for the heathen believed that the heavenly bodies were conscious divinities, and gave rain in answer to prayer. In contrast with this belief Jeremiah declares that it was Jehovah the Maker of all the heavenly orbs, who gave rain ; and so He cries out : " Art not Thou He " who can dismiss the present drought (xiv. 1) by sending abundant rains ?

Moses and Samuel loved and interceded for Israel more than any of their prophets

Exod. xvii. 11, xxxii. 11, Num. xiv. 13, 1 Sam. vii. 9, viii. 6, xii. 16-23, and compare Ps. xcix. 6, and Ezek. xiv. 14, and see notes on this last verse).

" Cast them out of my sight " etc. (v. 1). The prophet is here said to do what he was commissioned to foretell, i.e., their expulsion from Palestine, and their exile in Babylonia.

Three-fourths were doomed to death, and one-fourth to slavery (v. 2).

The judgment of verse 3 was a just one, for they worshipped the gods of war, the vultures of the heavens, and the wild beasts of the earth.

Manasseh repented and died (v. 4) ; but the bitter fruits of his conduct and teaching remained, and occasioned the wrath of God eighty years later.

Repentance is a change of mind (v. 6). In relation to God, it is judicial and perfect ; in relation to man, condemnatory and remorseful.

Verse 8 should be read as in the Revised Version. " A spoiler," i.e., Nebuchadnezzar. So wholesale would be the destruction of life that a mother of seven sons would not have one left to comfort her (v. 9).

The Spirit of Christ (vs. 10-21) here expresses itself in Jeremiah. In Christ the expression is perfect ; in Jeremiah, imperfect, because the prophet was only a man, and sinful. He loved the people, bore their sorrows upon his heart, confessed their sins, suffered, in sympathy, their judgments ; and yet they hated him.

" And Jehovah said " (v. 11). This formula, as commencing a sentence, occurs only here and in xlvi. 25. It is found in Luke xi. 39, xii. 42, xviii. 6, and xxii. 31.

" Thee " (v. 11), i.e., the Remnant as represented by Jeremiah.

" Iron " (v. 12), i.e., Judah ; " the northern iron and brass," i.e., the Chaldeans. The figure expresses the impossibility of Judah defeating the Chaldeans. Northern iron was renowned for its hardness and strength.

" Thy " (v. 13), and " Thee " (v. 14), i.e., the nation as represented by Jeremiah.

The prophet (v. 15) here prays for the Remnant. In the Spirit of Christ he calls their persecutors his persecutors, and pleads that God in His long-suffering to the persecutors will not allow the persecuted to perish ; adding that in his identification of himself with the Remnant he, therefore, suffered reproach. Compare Luke xviii. 1-8, where the same principle of long-suffering to the persecutors seems to imperil the hopes of the elect (see notes on that passage).

The Bible (v. 16), was found in the eighteenth year of king Josiah, and its Divine words were the joy and rejoicing of the prophet's heart. In this verse the prophet is a marked type of Christ.

His indignation against sin (v. 17), his perpetual pain for the sinner (v. 18), his consciousness of the moral hopelessness of the nation, all mark the energy and intelligence of the Divine life and love in his soul. This verse should read as in the Revised Version.

In the last three verses the prophet is addressed as the representative of the Remnant. The Remnant was first to return to Jehovah ; second, to separate the precious from the vile ; and, third, to invite the nation to come over to them—but they were not to return to the nation. As a result the Remnant should enjoy protection and deliverance. All this Daniel and his companions found to be true ; and the Remnant in the future time of Jacob's trouble will also prove its truth.

The moral effect of the Word of God when found and read and believed and obeyed may be learned from this chapter.

It awakens the conscience (v. 16 and 2 Chron. xxxiv. 19).

It conveys a sense of pardon (v. 19).

It gives real happiness (v. 16).

It cleanses the life and conduct (v. 19).

It separates from the world (v. 19).

It gives courage for testimony (v. 20).

It ensures contempt and opposition (v. 15).

It begets hatred of sin (v. 17).

It assures of everlasting salvation (v. 21).

It fills the reader with compassion for the rebellious (v. 18), and not with contempt for them.

JEREMIAH XVI.—The marriage age among the Hebrews for men is eighteen and sometimes earlier. Jeremiah may, therefore, be assumed to have been not more than seventeen years of age when he spoke these brave and unacceptable words to the proud and angry princes, priests and people of Jerusalem.

So certain and so imminent was the coming

wrath of God that he was commanded not to marry (v. 2) not to mourn (v. 5), and not to feast (v. 8).

The reason for each prohibition is stated. For the first, the certainty of death (vs. 3 and 4) ; for the second, the Divine withdrawal of peace (v. 5), so that only a false consolation could be offered ; and, for the third, the impending cessation of even legitimate merry-making, so that to provide a feast would be a hollow mockery (v. 9).

In a time of crisis a true servant of God must become a personal witness for God, and thus will he best help his perishing fellowmen. Jeremiah's action in withdrawing from sympathizing with his fellow countrymen in either their sorrows or their joys was an announcement of the wrath to come which they were compelled to hear. But they refused to believe it, and the terrific doom denounced against them came to pass, and is still in operation.

But grace abounds amidst judgment, and therefore, the prophet was commissioned to announce the future restoration of Israel (vs. 14 and 15)—preceded, however, by effective punishment (v. 18) ; and also the gathering of all the nations into the Covenant of Grace (vs. 19–21).

" Grievous deaths " (v. 4), i.e., deadly diseases.

Relatives and friends of a bereaved family were accustomed to bring to the house of mourning food and wine with which to cheer the mourners (v. 7, R.V.), and to eat and drink in company.

Sin deadens the conscience (v. 10).

The straight and bold reply of the prophet (vs. 11–13) shews amazing courage in so young a preacher. But the courage was not personal, it was imparted.

" Ye " (v. 12) is emphatic.

" Serve " (v. 13), i.e., compelled by torture to serve. Compare Dan. iii. and vi.

As the darkness of a tunnel may be realized by contrast with the bright burst of sunshine on issuing from its mouth, so the sunshine of verses 14 and 15 reveals the darkness of verses 13, 16, 17 and 18. Great as was the suffering in Egypt, and great as was the deliverance therefrom, so much greater is Israel's present affliction, and so much more wonderful will be her future deliverance, that the wonders of the former redemption will be obscured by those of the future.

It is evident that the Restoration from Babylon did not fulfil the language of verse 15, because that verse proposes the recovery of all the children of Israel out of all the countries in which they are dispersed.

" Fishers " (v. 16), i.e., the Egyptians ; " hunters," i.e., the Chaldeans.

Verse 18 reads : " But first of all (i.e., before restoring them), I will recompense," etc. For notes on the word " double " see Isa. xl. 2. Possibly here the word " double " may have a reference to the past Tribulation in Babylon, and to the present Great Tribulation ("the Tribulation, the Great One " Rev. vii. 14), which began at the destruction of Jerusalem by the Romans, and will close at the apparition of the Son of Man.

" Carcases " (v. 18), i.e., idolatrous images (Lev. xxvi. 30).

The Restoration of Israel will ensure the salvation of the Gentiles, and they, and the sons of Israel, will cast away their idols, and learn once for all and for ever of the existence and might of Jehovah.

The absurdity of the creature forming the Creator is finely expressed in verse 20.

" Once " (v. 21), i.e., once for all.

JEREMIAH XVII.—" The sin of Judah " (v. 1), i.e., idolatry. With the iron pen it was graven upon the heart, and with the point of a diamond upon the altars. The moral condition of the heart is declared in verse 9.

" My mountain," i.e., Zion ; the " field," i.e., Judea (v. 3). " For," i.e., " because of."

The sense of verse 4 is that the men of Judah had to blame themselves for their miseries.

" Forever " (v. 4), i.e., until it had accomplished its purpose.

The people of Judah at this time proposed an alliance with the Egyptians as a protection from the Chaldeans (v. 5). The folly of trusting them, and not Jehovah, and the wisdom of trusting Jehovah and not them, is contrasted in verses 5–8 ; and (v. 9) the nature of the heart—incurably diseased with deceit—which proposed this alliance, is exposed.

" Cursed," i.e., doomed to death ; " blessed," i.e., ordained to life. Here is found a great principle which governs all periods of human history, and all religious teaching. To believe upon the Lord Jesus

Christ is to make eternal felicity a certitude ; to depend upon saints and ceremonies is to doom oneself to death. To trust in Christ and saints and ceremonies is idolatry, for it associates other gods with Christ.

" The heath " (v. 6) is insensible and fruitless. Such is the Christless man, insensible of good, fruitless in life, and a stranger to real fellowship.

The believer (vs. 7 and 8), is living and fruitful, unmoved by calamities ("heat"), and not tortured with anxiety (" careful "), when privations threaten.

" Desperately wicked " (v. 9), i.e., incurably diseased. God knows the hopeless corruption of the natural heart, and so He said to Nicodemus that no one, however cultured and moral, can either see, or enter into the Kingdom of God. There must be a new birth.

The Hebrew text of verse 11 is difficult of translation. As a bird lays its eggs on the bare sand, her effort to hatch them out frequently fails because the eggs are destroyed by other birds, or by animals. In such an event it is stated by some that the bird will sit on the eggs of another bird of any breed, and these, when hatched, forsake her. The sense of the verse is : that whoever trusts in wealth is a fool. To trust man (v. 5), to trust one's own heart (v. 9), or to trust wealth (v. 11) ensures ruin.

In verses 12-14 the wisdom of trusting Jehovah, The Hope of Israel, and the happiness which results, are contrasted with the folly and misery of confidence in human saviours.

" Our " (v. 12) is emphatic. " Sanctuary," i.e., place of sacred security ; that place is glorious, it is set on high above the reach of calamity, and is long established.

" Written in the earth," i.e., a name written in sand is soon blurred by the wind. A name " written in heaven " (Luke x. 20) abides forever. Perhaps when the Lord stooped and wrote upon the ground (John viii. 6) he wrote the names of the woman's accusers " in the earth," at the same time writing her name in heaven.

In verse 14 the prophet, pleading on behalf of the people, and as their representative, and identifying himself with them, prays that their incurably sick hearts may be healed. How could a wicked and deceitful heart be trusted ? He pleads that God, and not the Egyptian monarch, should save them from the impending danger.

But the people for whom he prayed ridiculed the Divine judgment which the prophet announced (v. 15), and, with sceptical contempt, demanded an immediate demonstration of it.

Jeremiah, like a true minister of the Gospel, did not in self-will choose to be a preacher (v. 16), nor, when bravely and faithfully announcing the coming day of judgment did he desire that day ; and he could sincerely state that the truth he preached was uttered in the conscious presence of God (R.V.).

" Be not a terror unto me " (v. 17), i.e., his only dread was that God should forsake him ; as threatened in i. 17 ; and he adds : " Thou art, and shalt be, my refuge in the coming day of wrath." Thus he appealed to God for protection and vindication ; and in verse 18 justly prays for the destruction of the enemies of truth and of God's people. God will be a terror to them.

One test of professed repentance was proposed to them (vs. 19-27)—the observance of the Sabbath. It was rejected (v. 23). And yet grace outlined a picture of glory and happiness (vs. 24-26) for them ; for God in His long-suffering, even at the last moment, opened the door of repentance to them and to their king.

The length of the captivity—seventy years—was made to correspond with the number of Sabbaths which they had defiled during the four hundred and ninety years of their history from Saul to the exile (Lev. xxvi. 34 and 35 and 2 Chron. xxxvi. 21).

" They " (v. 23), i.e., the " fathers " of v. 22.

Verse 24 should read thus : " But it shall come to pass if ye," etc—this " ye " is emphatic.

Christ is God's Sabbath. To burden that Sabbath with sacerdotalism, and its ceremonies and doctrines, is to desecrate and destroy it.

JEREMIAH XVIII.—The lesson of the potter's house is that God never mends what man mars. He creates something new. Hence the " New Man," the " new heart," the " New Israel," etc.

" The potter's house " (v. 2), evidently a particular and well-known house.

The interpretation of this symbol belongs to the " House of Israel " (v. 6). The verse beginning and closing as it does with these words decides the interpretation of the symbol; but its application is general.

God's liberty of action is absolute. There is, and can be, no moral change in Him; but the moral changes in man are recognized by Him, and He, therefore, in His sovereignty, judges, or forgives them (vs. 6-10).

The calamity that God was framing against them at this time (v. 11) was the Chaldean invasion.

Coupling verse 12 with verse 18 the words: "There is no hope" may perhaps mean: "There is no hope in *your* preaching! *you* are a kill-joy prophet! You say our hearts are evil and their religious plans evil, but we deny both charges. In spite of all that *you* are predicting, the Law shall not perish from the priest," etc. (v. 18).

Faithful preaching and miracles harden a rebellious heart. Compare Exod. viii. 19 with Rev. xvi. 9. This eighteenth verse presents a dreadful picture of blindness. Ecclesiastical influence is always greatest at the time when conscience is hardened; and unbelief and rebellion shelter themselves behind apostate forms of what God has set up, and thus men try to put to sleep the disquietude which they cannot help feeling.

The "very horrible thing" of verse 13 was Israel's forsaking Jehovah for Baal. This is the argument of verse 14, which should read: "Will a man leave the snow-water of Lebanon for the rock-water of the field (i.e., the muddy water which gathers in the rocky hollows of the field), or shall the cold waters which flow down from afar be forsaken? (i.e., forsaken for turbid and tepid waters).

In this symbol Christ is compared to the cool and pure waters which flow from the summit of Lebanon, and man's religion to the muddy waters of the trampled field.

"They," i.e., their teachers; "them," the people (v. 15). This verse should read as in the Revised Version.

The ancient path, the way cast up, i.e., the king's highway, was the Law. The by-paths picture human teachings which cover over and corrupt that Law. This verse also portrays modern Christendom.

The speaker in verses 19-23 is Christ. His Spirit in Jeremiah thus prays. It is not a prayer for the gratification of personal vengeance, such as fallen human nature would use, but the prayer of a crown-counsel justly demanding a righteous judgment upon evil-doers in the interest of truth and society. If it is right for God to punish evil-doers, then is it right to pray Him to do so; and such men having been fore-warned of the consequences to them, and to their families, no charge of injustice can be brought against God for carrying out the decrees of these righteous laws.

But this, and similar prayers in the Holy Scriptures, belong to the past dispensation of law and the future dispensation of righteousness—not to the present dispensation of grace—and they predict the certain judgment of evil and evil-doers.

JEREMIAH XIX.—The breaking in pieces of the pitcher symbolized the irrecoverable destruction of Judæa.

But just as the potter makes a new vessel with the broken pieces of the old, so will God create a New Israel. This will be the nation predicted in Matt. xxi. 43.

This judgment foretold by Jeremiah came to pass. It is foolish for some religious teachers to state that the wrath of God is a baseless imagination, for that God is only love. The Chaldean invasion, with its merciless slaughter and slavery, is an historic fact. The records in the British Museum prove it; but Jeremiah predicted it from the mouth of the Lord.

An "earthen bottle" (v. 1), i.e., a pitcher. "East-gate" (v. 2) should read "potter's gate." See Revised Version margin.

The Valley of the son of Hinnom lies beneath the western wall of Jerusalem, and turning sharply to the east, it passes beneath the southern wall and joins the valley of Kedron, which comes down from the north on the eastward of the city. It was beautiful and fertile, but because dedicated by the Jerusalem apostates to the horrible worship of the fire-god Moloch (i.e., Melek the king), it was polluted by king Josiah and made the refuse-pit of the city. Fires were kept burning there so as to prevent disease. Hence it was called "the Gehenna of fire." It was to this valley, and its worm and its fire, that the Lord pointed when preaching about hell, but added that in that dread place the worm should not die nor the fire be quenched, because that on which they feed shall never be annihilated, and so it will thereby differ from the Valley of Hinnom. See note on Mark ix. 48.

It was in this valley of sin and doom that the prophet was told to preach.

" Estranged " (v. 4), i.e., devoted to the worship of strange divinities. This verse should read as in the Revised Version which better expresses the guilt of the idolaters of Jeremiah's day.

The Spirit of God in Jeremiah, as afterwards in Christ, did not hesitate to repeat His messages ; so verses 5 and 6 repeat chapter vii. 31 and 32.

The counsel of Judah and Jerusalem (v. 7) was their plan to defeat the Chaldeans by means of the Egyptian alliance. But in that very Valley of Hinnom the folly of that plan was demonstrated by the appalling slaughter by the Chaldeans of the men who made it ; and there were they justly punished for the blood of the tortured children burned alive in sacrifice to Moloch (v. 5). Such cruelty to children never was contemplated by the loving heart of God (v. 5).

" Tophet," so-called from Toph, a drum, which was beaten to drown the agonizing cries of the burning children. They were innocent (v. 4), but their murderers were guilty, and, therefore, judged (v. 6).

To " harden the neck " in order not to hear (v. 15) means to refuse to turn the head to a speaker so as to listen to him.

Jerusalem had twelve gates (v. 2) :

The valley gate (Neh. iii. 13).
The fountain gate (Neh. ii. 14).
The sheep gate (Neh. iii. 1).
The fish gate (Neh. iii. 3).
The old gate (Neh. iii. 6).
The potter's gate (Jer. xix. 2) also called the dung gate.
The water gate (Neh. iii. 26).
The horse gate (Neh. iii. 28).
The East gate (Neh. iii.29).
The Miphkad gate (Neh. iii. 31).
The Ephraim gate (Neh. viii. 16).
The prison gate (Neh. xii. 39).

JEREMIAH XX.—Pashur, the chief officer of the Temple, perhaps fortifying himself by Deut. xxv. 3, scourged Jeremiah, as the apostle Paul afterwards was scourged, and then without any Scripture warrant, condemned him for about twenty-four hours to the torture of the stocks. That was a beam of timber with five holes in it through which the head, the hands and the feet were thrust, thus bending the body so as to cause great suffering.

Pashur means " Security on every side," Magor-missabib means " Terror on every side."

The words of verses 3–6 were not the hot-tempered utterances of the prophet, but the solemn warnings of Jehovah. Most probably Jeremiah spoke them with tears. Their fulfilment proved them to be God's words ; for, as before stated, the Chaldeans, after the capture of Jerusalem, slew a multitude of the citizens in the presence of their friends and relatives, who were then carried off into slavery.

Pashur is the first person named in this book. The first mention of the king of Babylon is found in verse 4.

" Strength " and " labours," i.e., the wealth obtained by these (R V.).

" Deceived " (v. 7), i.e., persuaded. See i. 6–10. God did not promise him exemption from suffering, but he did promise him moral victory.

" Stronger than I " (v. 7), i.e., he was compelled to preach.

The subject of his preaching is expressed in the two words " violence " and " spoil." (v. 8 with vi. 7). This oppression and robbery of the poor so deeply stirred him that he shouted aloud against it, but the only response to his outcries was that he was had in derision daily, and everyone laughed at him (vs. 7 and 8). " Because " should read " therefore."

The preacher who is thrust out by God cannot refrain from proclaiming the Word of God (v. 9).

The " for " of verse 10 follows verse 8 ; and the " defaming " and " fear " have relation to the prophet. " Denounce " and " We will denounce him," these are the words of his enemies encouraging one another, and his pretended friends, to " entice " him to a moral lapse, or a charge of heresy against the Law of Moses, and so to denounce him to the judges and have him put to death.

But faith gives the victory (v. 11) and foresees the judgment and sings (vs. 12 and 13). " Triest " (v. 12), i.e., testest. " Reins " and " heart," i.e., emotions and affections.

Jeremiah is here a type of Christ (see Luke xi. 53 and 54)

Jeremiah in this book is sometimes a type of Christ and sometimes a type of the Remnant. He typifies the one when the language is that of faith and praise, and when he pleads for vengeance in the presence of hatred against the truth and against God's people. He is a type of the other when the language is that of bitterness and despondency.

Thus in verses 14-18 is he a type of the Remnant, for this will be their experience and language in the future day of their oppression.

The words were uttered by the prophet most probably when suffering the torment of the stocks. They correspond to those of Job when he was in affliction (Job iii. 3, 10 and 11). The words " I had said " may be supplied at the commencement of verse 14, and so all that follows expresses the mental, moral, spiritual and physical suffering from which he was delivered and for which he praised the Lord (v. 13).

All this pictures and foretells the sufferings of the Remnant, their experiences, and final deliverance.

Much in this chapter corresponds to the sorrows felt by every true servant of God who witnesses for truth. He meets the bitter hatred of the official ministers of religion and their followers ; he is laughed at, and his feeble heart recoils before hostility which has neither pity nor conscience. Yet has he the consciousness of God's presence with him ; and, in pleading for the triumph of truth, he is, as a fact, praying for the destruction of the teachers of falsehood. But imperfection will appear in his words and ways.

With Christ, on the contrary, all is perfection. He felt most intensely the trials He had to undergo at the hands of man ; but these sorrows were precious stones in the foundation of grace laid for their salvation.

JEREMIAH XXI.—The prophecies of Jeremiah are not arranged in chronological, but in moral and logical order ; which is more important. Hence the attack on its inspiration by some scholars reveals injustice and ignorance. This chapter records the Divine wrath upon Jerusalem, announced on the eve of the fall of the city, and the following chapters show the justice of that wrath. Those prophecies were uttered many years prior to that of this chapter.

Pashur (v. 1). This was not the Pashur the son of Immer of chapter xx. Nineteen years separate the prophecies addressed to these two priests.

Hezekiah's mission to Isaiah (2 Kings xix). contrasts with this of Zedekiah to Jeremiah.

Man, when in trouble, can use religious language and talk of God's " wondrous works " (v. 2). and remain, like Zedekiah and the priests and princes unconverted and rebellious. The " wondrous works " intended were doubtless those in Egypt, and those in Israel's history, but perhaps in particular the destruction of the host of 2 Kings xx.

This illustrates the great Bible doctrine that man is a moral wreck, comparable to a broken vessel of pottery, and, therefore, impossible of reparation. Hence he must be re-made. This great doctrine, so unpalatable to society, is taught, positively, in the Lord's words to Nicodemus, " Ye must be born again," and, negatively, in the fact, so often recorded in the Scriptures, that miracles do not necessarily effect conversion of heart, but, on the contrary, harden men in rebellion and sin. The history of Israel, the hatred of the Pharisees to Christ, and the predictions of Rev. xvi. furnish illustrations.

Many men when preaching before a king are careful only to say what the king would like to hear. But it was not thus with this brave and faithful man of God.

God, in His love and grace, as always, offered life to these stout rebels even at the eleventh hour (vs. 8 and 9).

" His life shall be unto him for a prey," i.e., he should lose both property and liberty, but not his life. Some accepted this offer. Compare xxxviii. 2. xxxix. 18 and xlv. 5.

Those who believed, and acted on, this promise are referred to in xxxix. 9 and lii. 15.

" In the morning " (v. 12), i.e., promptly.

Even at the time that the city was being besieged by the Chaldeans the rich kept oppressing and robbing the poor (v. 12). God pities the oppressed, and His fury burns like fire against the oppressors.

The Inhabitress of the valley and Rock of the plain (v. 13 R.V. margin) was Jerusalem ; " her forest " (v. 14) was the houses of the city, which were largely built of cedar of Lebanon, and, being compacted close together, were like to the trees of a wood.

JEREMIAH XXII. 1-XXIII. 8.—In this chapter and the prior one the four kings who hastened, and presided at, the ruin of their people are contrasted with the Righteous

King who will restore and bless His people (xxiii 5 and 6).

These four kings were Jehoahaz (also called Shallum) Jehoiakim, Jehoiakin and Zedekiah.

The first two and the last were sons of good king Josiah, Jehoiakin was son of Jehoiakim, and therefore, grandson to Josiah.

Zedekiah's guilt was all the greater because he must have heard the warnings addressed to these three kings who preceded him. This excess of guilt no doubt explains his precedence in this section of the Book over the other kings.

As in the case of Zedekiah so in that of Jehoiakim, grace, even at the last moment, offered, and repeated, a promise of life and glory (vs. 1–4). Compare xvii. 25.

The king of verse 1 is Jehoiakim.

" The dead " (v. 10), i.e., King Josiah (see 2 Chron. xxxv. 24, 25 and Zech. xii. 11). "Him that goeth away," i.e., King Jehoahaz (Shallum). Dying saints are to be envied ; living sinners, to be pitied.

Uniting the scattered passages of the Scriptures the following is suggested. Two political parties divided Jerusalem at this time. The one, the Babylonian ; the other, the Egyptian. The former placed Shallum on the throne, and the injunction to weep sore for him suggests that he was a popular prince ; the other party supported Jehoiakim.

The Egyptian monarch intervened, carried Shallum to Egypt, where he died, and placed Jehoiakim on the throne. The Babylonian monarch refused, however, to recognize Jehoiakim, but approved his son Jehoiakin as chief ruler. This reconciles the seeming error as to Jehoiakin's age when he began to reign (2 Kings xxiv. 8 and 2 Chron. xxxvi. 9), for Jehoiakim reigned eleven years, portions of years being counted as years, as was the custom of the Hebrews. At the end of this period the king of Babylon slew Jehoiakim, and raised his brother Zedekiah to the kingly dignity. This was the last Hebrew monarch.

The indignant question addressed to Jehoiakim : " Shalt *thou reign* ? " (v. 15) is the key to the seeming error in the age of his son Jehoiakin. God refused to recognize this impious prince as a reigning monarch ; and therefore it is that in 2 Chron. xxxvi. his son is recorded as reigning during his father's life-time.

" Cedars " (v. 7), i.e., the king's great palace built of cedar.

Jehoiakim not only oppressed the people in order to raise the tribute due to the king of Egypt, but he robbed them by building a palace for himself with forced labour (vs 13 and 14 and 17).

" Closest " (v. 15), i.e., " strivest to excel ' (R.V.). This palace violated Lev. xix. 13, and Deut. xxiv. 14 and 15.

" Thy father " (v. 15), i.e., Josiah. He was satisfied with the simple life of eating and drinking necessary food, and only obtained fame by ruling justly (v. 15).

" To know " (v. 16), i.e., to recognize and obey.

" Innocent blood " (v. 17), that of Abijah the prophet.

It is noteworthy that 2 Kings xxiv. 6 omits the usual mention of the burial of the deceased king. Chron. xxxvi. 6 records that he was bound in fetters in order to be carried to Babylon, but it does not state that he ever reached that city. Here, and in xxxvi. 30, his miserable end is predicted, and most certainly the prophecy came to pass (v. 19). Wild beasts and vultures devoured his dead body, thrown upon one side of the highway (no doubt he died upon the march) just as they devour the carcase of an ass.

Lebanon, Bashan, and Abarim (v. 20, R.V.), i.e., Syria, Ammon and Moab. " Cry," i.e., weep.

" O Inhabitress of Lebanon " (v. 23), i.e., Jerusalem, which was largely built with cedar of Lebanon. " How gracious shalt thou be " : " how greatly to be pitied shalt thou be " (R.V.).

" Coniah " (v. 24). The Holy Spirit here cuts off from his name the first syllable signifying relationship to Jehovah so as to emphasize the dreadful fact that God had cut him off. He, and his mother Nehushta (v. 26), died in Babylonia ; and though he had descendants, not one of them ever sat upon the throne of Jerusalem (v. 30)

" The shepherds " (xxiii. 1), i.e., these four kings.

" A righteous branch " (v. 5), i.e., the Messiah. The justice and benevolence of this rule here stand in contrast to the injustice and selfishness of that of the four kings.

The beauteous title " the Branch " is given to Him four times in the Old Testament, thus fore-shadowing the Four Gospels, and the necessity that there should be four. The Branch, the King (Matt.) ; the Branch, the Servant (Mark) ; the Branch, the Man (Luke); and the Branch, Jehovah (John). (Jer.

xxiii. 5 ; Zech. iii. 8 ; Zech. vi. 12 ; Isa. iv. 2).
Verse 6. See note on xxxiii. 16:
" Ye," " You" (v. 2), emphatic. " And "
(v. 3), better, " but."

JEREMIAH XXIII. 9-40.—This is a
distinct prophecy. Its title is : " Concerning
the prophets " (R.V.).
As the previous prophecy concerned the
four kings, so this concerned their favourite
preachers.
The message to the king was one of present
grace and future wrath ; the message to the
prophets was similar (v. 22 and v. 39).
But the fashionable preachers, like the
kings, rejected the offer of grace, and perished
in the tempest of wrath.
Modern fashionable preachers who, instead
of the Word of the Lord as found in the
Bible, gratify their hearers with " the assured
results of modern thought," and proclaim
that there is no wrath to come, and who
teach what they learn from their " theological " neighbours, are exactly described in
this chapter.
The hostility of the false prophets to the
Person of the Lord, and their contempt for
His Inspired Word, broke the heart and
agitated the body of Jeremiah (v. 9).
" Adulterers " (v. 10), i.e., idolaters.
" Swearing," i.e., idol-worship. " Course,"
i.e., their teaching. "Force," i.e., their
pulpit power.
The material misery and moral corruption
which resulted from the teaching of these
prophets appear in the statement that it
did not produce rectitude (" right "), and
that it occasioned a drought.
The priests set up idols even in the Temple
(v. 11).
" Their way " (v. 12), i.e., their fashionable
religion. It should be to them as uncertain
as the way of a man walking on the slippery
edge of a precipice in the darkness.
" Evil " (v. 12), i.e., calamity ; and " visitation," i.e., punishment.
The guilt of the prophets of Jerusalem
is declared to be greater than that of the
prophets of Samaria (vs. 13 and 14).
Falsehood, and the corruption of society,
are the fruit of idolatry (v. 14).
The moral condition of a nation results
from the character of the religious teaching
given to it (v. 15).
The false prophets promised vain hopes
(" vanity, " v. 16, R.V.) ; they promised

peace and no wrath to come (v. 17) ; and they
denied inspiration (v. 18), for they scep-
tically asked : " Has Jeremiah, or anybody
else, had personal intercourse with God,
and noted down His words, and announced
them ? "   Thus many modern preachers
ridicule the inspiration of the Bible.
" The mouth of the Lord " (v. 16), i.e.,
inspiration.
" They say still," i.e., they keep on saying.
" Ye shall have peace, and no calamity
shall come upon you " (v. 17) ; i.e., God is
love, and He will never cast anybody into
hell !
The Divine answer to this infidelity is given
in verses 19-21 ; but grace couples with this
announcement of doom the loving words
of verse 22.
The second " heard " (v. 18) should read
" announced."
" In the latter days," etc., (v. 20). Years
afterwards the exiles in Babylon understood
perfectly that Jeremiah preached truth from
the mouth of the Lord, and his opponents
falsehood out of the imagination of their
own hearts.
Verse 22 makes clear that the guilt of
the teacher is greater than that of the pupil.
In the future day of Israel's restoration the
sons of Israel will understand perfectly
the justice of their present dispersion.
The impossibility of false teachers hiding
themselves and their doctrines from God
is declared in verses 23-27.
The prophet of verse 28 is God's prophet in
contrast with man's prophet of verse 25,
and the dream of verse 28 is opposed to that
of verse 25.
This verse 28 may be thus understood :
The true prophet to whom a dream is given,
shall be compelled to tell the dream ; and he
that receives a message from God is
responsible to speak it faithfully.
The false prophet is the chaff ; the true
prophet, the wheat (v. 28) ; and the Word of
God is a fire and a hammer : a fire to burn, a
hammer to break.   Thus the doctrine
preached reveals the truth or falseness of
the preacher. Preaching which leaves out,
or denies, the wrath to come, is false ; and
the preacher is false.
These prophets got their teaching from
their neighbours, and not from God (v. 30) ;
as modern preachers get theirs from
Divinity professors.
There is a play on the word " burden "

(vs. 33-40). It means a heavy load, and also a Divine message.

The question in verse 33 was asked in mockery. It may be thus understood : " What doleful sermon have you to-day, you who are always preaching about wrath and judgment ? " The answer was prompt, " What burden ? Here it is ! ' I will cast you off," saith the Lord ; and everyone that shall keep on mockingly saying, ' The burden of the Lord,' that man, and his family, shall be punished " (v. 34). In the following verse they were enjoined to reverently say : " What hath Jehovah answered ?" etc. But if they kept on saying " the burden of the Lord " when they were commanded not to say it, then they should be forgotten utterly (v. 39), but their perpetual shame should never be forgotten (v. 40).

JEREMIAH XXIV.—The Babylonian servitude was a Divine judgment because of disobedience to the Word of God. Recognition of that judgment and submission to it, shewed intelligence in the Word and spirituality of mind. Conspicuous among these contrite and intelligent captives were Daniel, Shadrach, Meshach, Abednego, Mordecai, Nehemiah, Ezra, Ezekiel and their companions. These were the good figs (v. 3).

Refusal to recognize and submit to the wrath of God, and a carnal reliance on ordinances, which, at the first ordained by God, were corrupted by man, reveal spiritual death, and, therefore, neither intelligence nor faith. Conspicuous amongst these were Zedekiah, the priests, the false prophets and the residue who remained in Jerusalem. They boasted of their official religious position as citizens of Zion, and proprietors of, and worshippers in, the Temple. They could point to its Divinely ordained ritual, and, also, to the improvements and additions which man introduces, and which he defines as " development." They also congratulated themselves on their alliance with Egypt, and they looked with contempt upon their captive but godly brethren in Babylon. These Jerusalem Hebrews were the bad figs.

The latter end of these two groups was : in the one case, chastening and restoration ; in the other, chasing and annihilation.

Thus in this chapter two principles appear : first, the importance of an intelligent submission to the judgment of God upon man's unfaithfulness to the Word of God ; and, second, that God owns such faith, and promises to it a perfect fulfilment of all His promises, for their accomplishment depends on His faithfulness, whatever may have been the unfaithfulness of the official custodians of His truth.

Fruit-baskets (v. 1) are common objects in Jerusalem to-day.

The relief which God brought to the captives in Babylon is illustrated by 2 Kings xx., and xxv. 27-30.

" For good " (v. 5, R.V.). These words connect with " acknowledge," i.e., favourably regard.

Christian people can take no credit to themselves in the matter of their conversion and salvation, for God disposes them to seek His face, and is the sole operator in their redemption (vs. 6 and 7).

The new heart is a gift from God (v. 7).

The judgment upon Zedekiah, his princes and upon the residue of Jerusalem is that predicted in Deut. xxviii. 25 and 37. Compare xxix. 17 and 18.

JEREMIAH XXV.—This chapter records the Great Prophecy of the Seventy Years Servitude in Babylon (v. 11).

It also predicts the overthrow of Babylon by the nations whom she had enslaved (v. 14).

But the prophecy goes much further than the judgment of ancient Babylon, for the principle of universal judgment (vs. 29-38) is developed, and foretold. The repetition of the judgment of verse 10 in Rev. xviii. 23, shews that the predictions of this chapter were not exhausted by the destruction of the Chaldean Empire in the days of Cyrus.

This is the more evident from the fact that judgment here begins at the House of God (1 Pet. iv. 17) ; for the judgment of evil in Jerusalem is a principle demanding the judgment of evil in the whole earth ; and the statement that Babylon is to be judged last points to the future king of Babylon, the Anti-Christ, whose doom at the apparition of the Messiah will be a climax of judgment.

The statement that the fourth year of Jehoiakim was the first year of Nebuchadnezzar is of essential importance in fixing Bible chronology (see " Romance of Bible Chronology, " Rev. Martin Anstey, B.D.).

The expression " Jeremiah the Prophet " is peculiar because of the title " Prophet " following the name (i.. 5, xx. 2, xxviii. 5, 6, 10, 11, 12, and 15, xxix. 1 and 29, xxxii. 2, xxxiv. 6, xxxvi. 8, xlv. 1, etc).

"Thirteenth year of Josiah" (v. 3). See i. 2. "The three and twentieth year," i.e., of Jeremiah's ministry, that is, eighteen years under Josiah, three months under Jehoahaz and four years under Jehoiakim.

Settlement in the land of promise was contingent upon obedience (v. 5).

"Perpetual" (v. 9), i.e., age-abiding, that means long-continued.

The sound made by the woman of the East every morning in grinding corn for the breakfast is a pleasant sound, and no Eastern house, large or small, fails of a lamp burning night and day.

"Shall serve themselves of them" (v. 14), i.e., shall make slaves of the Chaldeans.

The symbolic cup of fury (v. 15) is the cup of the wine of the fierceness of the wrath of Almighty God of Rev. xvi. That chapter should be read in connection with this prophecy, for the fulfilment of both lies in the future.

"Be moved" (v. 16), i.e., reel to and fro. "Become mad," maddened with battle-fury.

Judgment will begin at Jerusalem (v. 18) because it is the House of God (1 Pet. iv. 7), and it will end with Babylon (v. 26).

"As it is this day" (v. 18). These words were no doubt added by Jeremiah after the destruction of Jerusalem by the Chaldeans.

Verse 23 should read as in Revised Version.

Zimri (v. 25). These were, perhaps, the descendants of Zimran, a son of Abraham (Gen. xxv. 2).

"One with another" (v. 26), i.e., they were all, without exception, to drink of the cup, the effect of which would be that they would fight one with another, and injure one another (v. 32).

"All the kingdoms of the world" (v. 26) and "all the inhabitants of the earth" (vs. 29, 30) and "from one end of the earth even unto the other end of the earth" (v. 33); these statements prove that this prophecy belongs to the future.

"The city" (v. 29), i.e., Jerusalem.

"Shall roar (as a lion)" (v. 30). "Upon His habitation." should read "Against His pasture." What was "His pasture" became "their pasture" (v. 36); just as the Passover "a Feast of Jehovah" became "the Passover a feast of the Jews" (John vi. 4, vii. 2). His pasture was Israel.

"Plead" (v. 31), i.e., judge.

"A great tempest" (v. 32), i.e., a universal war. The next verse predicts the appalling slaughter that will result; and Rev. ix. 15, xiv. 17-20, and xvi. affirm that many hundreds of millions will perish in that future war.

The shepherds and princes of verses 34-36, were Zedekiah and his ministers and men of war. Their attempt to escape, foretold in verse 35, was fulfilled in 2 Kings xxv. 4-7.

"Accomplished" (v. 34), i.e., "fully come" (R.V.). When a precious, but fragile vessel falls, it breaks in pieces beyond repair. Such was Israel, a pleasant vessel, now broken, and never to be repaired. But a new Israel, a pleasant vessel never to be broken, will be made by the Heavenly Potter.

A pasture is silent when bereft of flocks (v. 37, R.V.).

When a country becomes a desolation (v. 38), the lions forsake it.

"The oppressor" (v. 38), i.e., the Chaldean. "His fierce anger," i.e., God's anger.

"Sheshach" is a cypher for "Babel" obtained by the common transposition of the letters of the Hebrew alphabet by which the last letter is put for the first, etc.

"My words written in this Book" (v. 13). Compare Dan. ix. 2. The words were God's words, and they were written in a book of the Bible, i.e., the Book of Jeremiah. Such is inspiration. See xxxvi. 18, and 1 Pet. i. 11.

JEREMIAH XXVI.—Previous chapters, specially chapter vii., record the words which Jeremiah spoke in the Court of the Temple.

As to-day so then, people were willing to attend religious services, but not to abandon their sins (vs. 2 and 3).

Shiloh, where the Tabernacle of Moses was situated up to the days of Solomon and the Temple, was a desolation in the days of Jeremiah (v. 6).

"A curse" (v. 6), i.e., not a source of moral corruption but a visible illustration of the wrath of God.

The mob is ever fickle. Led by priests they demand a preacher's death (v. 8), controlled by magistrates they protect him (v. 16); but, again influenced by others, possibly in this case by the priests, once more they clamour for his life (v. 24).

A solitary man, young and timid, bravely facing a bloodthirsty mob (v. 9), and, later on, with courage and dignity and courtesy, facing with equal courage the magistrates and death (vs. 12-15), and with great moral force pointing out to the court the illegality of its conduct should he be condemned (v. 15), and asserting the reality of his own Divine commission (v. 15)—furnishes a picture of striking grandeur.

No doubt the priests demanded his death in accordance with Deut. xviii. 20. But the fact that Jeremiah spoke in the name of Jehovah, and that time had not been given to prove his prediction false, deprived his accusers of any case against him.

" Against " (v. 12) better translated " concerning." The same Hebrew word occurs in verse 11, but there the prophet's accusers used it in its unfavourable sense of " against." Jeremiah employed it in its better sense so as to avoid needless irritation, and to imply there was still time for repentance and deliverance.

Few persons have sufficient love and grace and moral courage to preach to a bench of magistrates, as Jeremiah did on this occasion (v. 13).

In verses 16-23 two precedents were brought forward : one by Jeremiah's friends in his favour (18 and 19) ; the other by his enemies in order to secure his death (20-23).

The Prophecy of Micah is recorded in Mic. i. 1 and iii. 12, and was at this time one hundred and forty years old.

" And " (v. 20) : better translated " but." Here the enemies of the prophet eagerly intervene with their, " But there was also a man," etc.

These enemies would have carried the day against Jeremiah by their clever introduction of the king's name and action but for the influence of Ahikam, who seems to have been a high official, somewhat corresponding to a modern Home Secretary. He and his family were steadfastly friendly to the prophet.

The king of Egypt, being the overlord of Jerusalem and the placer of Jehoiakim on its throne, readily surrendered Urijah. Had that prophet shewn more courage he might have saved his life. It is disastrous for a servant of God, and unworthy, to take shelter in the shadow of Egypt rather than in the secret place of the Most High. The path of duty is usually the path of safety.

Ahikam was one of those who found the Bible (2 Kings xxii. 12). His son Gedaliah was also a good man, and friendly to Jeremiah (xxxix. 14, and xl. 6).

JEREMIAH XXVII.—The formula " In the beginning " (v. 1) occurs four times in the Bible (Gen. i. 1, Jer. xxvi. 1, and xxvii. 1, and John i. 1).

Some suppose " Jehoiakim " (v. 1) should read " Zedekiah," as in verse 12 ; but the word " also " (v. 12) opposes the supposition. The Divine message was given to Jeremiah in the reign of Jehoiakim, but publicly announced thirteen years afterwards in the reign of Zedekiah. It is not an uncommon experience for men of God to be given words years before the occasion arrives for their utterance. The truths which made Felix to tremble, the apostle Paul had, as a prophet, learned years beforehand personally and directly from the Lord Jesus Christ in the Deserts of Arabia.

The occasion for the delivery of the message (v. 3) occurred at the time of the visit of the ambassadors of the kings confederate with Judah against Chaldea. " Yokes " (v. 2) is in the plural. This shews that the symbol was literally constructed as a symbol and a vehicle of doctrine. The yokes expressed a condition of slavery, and the prophecy symbolized by them was fulfilled.

The declaration of verses 5 to 11 was such as Gentile princes could easily understand— the Being and almighty power of God (v. 5) ; His purpose in giving the Supreme Government to Nebuchadnezzar (v. 6) ; the punishment of those who should rebel against him (v. 8) ; the tranquillity of those who would submit (v. 11) ; and the future doom of Babylon itself (v. 7).

" The very time " (v. 7), i.e., the appointed end ; " many nations and great kings," i.e., the Medes and Persians under Darius and Cyrus, " shall serve themselves of him," i.e., shall enslave him.

" Why will ye die ? " (v. 13). Every word in this question beats hotly with the love of God.

Satan himself and his servants often prophesy in God's name (v. 15). Compare Matt. iv. 6, and vii. 22 and 23.

The vessels of the Lord's House had been carried away to Babylon in the reign of Jeconiah and Jehoiakim (2 Kings xxiv. 13, and 2 Chron. xxxvi. 5-7), and the remainder (v. 18) were carried away when the city was destroyed and the Temple burned (2 Chron. xxxvi. 18). These vessels were restored by Cyrus (v. 22), and brought to Jerusalem by Ezra (Ezra i. 7, and v. 13 and 14).

History testifies to the accuracy of the prediction of verse 7, for Nabonidus, in whose seventeenth year Babylon was taken by Cyrus, was grandson, by male descent, of Nebuchadnezzar. Belshazzar was a son of Nabonidus, and was associated with him in the Government of the Empire. He was king of the sacred city of the Babylon situated on the one bank of the Euphrates over against the civil city posted on the other bank, and which was captured by the Medes a considerable time before the other.

The chief subject of this, and the following chapter, is the duty of submission to the Head of the Gentiles ; and the loving promise is given that Jerusalem would not be forsaken if obedient to this command, but disobedience to it would entail judgment. Thus God cared for, and disciplined, His people.

This transference of the dominion of the earth from Israel to Nebuchadnezzar and his political successors—this committal of power in the earth to a man—is very remarkable. The term, " The Times of the Gentiles " defines its duration. The power of the magistrate in Rom. xiii. is based upon this Divine ordination ; and should be recognized and obeyed to the present day.

The beasts of the field and the fowls of the air are willed by God to this obedience, and their submission was, and is, a rebuke to Israel's insubjection.

But all this figures the power and glory of the Man who is to come, the Messiah, to whose government man, and the entire animal world and the universe, will be subjected by God.

Whenever tested by God man has always failed. To Israel was committed the Law, and, with it, the sovereignty of the earth. Had Israel kept the Law, universal happiness would have resulted. But there was disobedience and failure.

God then committed universal dominion to the first king of Babylon. All nations were commanded to obey him. He was bound by no law, other than personal responsibility to God. He was to recognize his subjection to God ; and he was to make those happy whom God had subjected to him. But he also failed, became senseless and presumptuous, ravaged the world, and oppressed the people of God. The future, and last king of Babylon will fill up the measure of his iniquity. Then will close the Seventy Great Years of the present captivity, of which the Seventy Calendar Years of Jeremiah xxv. 11, was a forepicture, and then will fall the full and final judgment. But meanwhile between this first and last King of Babylon, rule in the earth is committed by God to the representatives of the Chaldean sovereignty, and hence in Rom. xiii. the people of God are commanded to recognize, and submit to, such God-given authority.

JEREMIAH XXVIII.—The Bible is not afraid to couple places and dates with its predictions (v. 1).

Hananiah was a false prophet, as the sequel shewed.

Jeremiah's " Amen " (v. 6) is a beautiful instance of self-annihilation, for the success of Hananiah's prophecy would discredit Jeremiah and belittle his preaching. But the prosperity of the people was more to him than his own reputation. Jonah's love for Israel was also greater than his concern for himself as a prophet ; but he failed in limiting that love to Israel. See notes on the Book of Jonah.

The prophets that preceded Jeremiah and Hananiah, Isaiah, Amos, Joel, Hosea, etc., being true men of God, faithfully warned the people of coming judgments (v. 8) ; and the judgments came. Hananiah prophesied of peace (v. 9), and the truth of his prediction could only be demonstrated by a happy fulfilment; but verse 17 revealed its falsity.

Subjection to the Word of God is a light yoke ; insubjection, a heavy one (v. 13).

Satan and his ministers can preach most sweetly in the name of the Lord (vs. 10 and 11). See note on verse 15 of prior chapter.

Silence after the Word of God has been, however, first quoted (vs. 7-9, with Deut. xviii. 22) is often the best rebuke to false teaching (v. 11) ; and if the silent man of God waits on God, and for God, he will get a message that will overwhelm the popular propagator of falsehood.

Hananiah's hearers were to be cast out of Jerusalem into Babylon, but he himself was to be cast out of the earth into Sheol. He promised them deliverance within two years, but was himself struck down by death within two months (vs. 1 and 17).

JEREMIAH XXIX.—Intelligence in the ways and counsels of God, as revealed in His Word, and submission to those counsels, and a recognition of His just judgments upon unfaithfulness, together with a blameless life, and prayer for the peace of the earthly government ordained by God, bring a measure of tranquillity and prosperity to the obedient (vs. 4-7), but suffering and punishment to the disobedient (vs. 21-23).

Meanwhile faith believes, and waits for, the promised redemption (vs. 10-14), and rests in the grace upon which that redemption is based, and whose truth and beauty are the more fully revealed by the wrath and judgment which must precede its manifestation (vs. 17-19).

Elasah and Gemariah were the sons of the good men who found the Bible (v. 3). No doubt they willingly carried Jeremiah's letters to the captives.

Recognition of God's judgment upon unfaithfulness was necessary in order to explain why the Divine promise of supremacy to the throne of David seemed to be forgotten. The popular preachers (vs. 8 and 9) could point to these Bible promises, and, with a shew of spirituality and fidelity, console the people with them ; but the true prophets of Jehovah (v. 31 and xxviii. 8) recognized the temporary forfeiture of these promises because of sin, and announced the coming wrath of God, for in the spiritual as in the physical realm night precedes the day.

Daniel and his companions illustrate the intelligence and faith and obedience commanded in this chapter. They prayed for the peace of the government, they obeyed its laws, were blameless in their conduct, and waited for the hoped-for end (v. 11).

The restoration under Cyrus fulfilled the prophecy of verses 10-14. That restoration was an earnest of the yet greater one of the future.

Most of the suffering which Christian people in the past and in the present have suffered, and do suffer, results from their disobedience to the Word of God, and from their own misconduct (vs. 20-32).

The import of Shemaiah's letter from Babylon in reply to Jeremiah's was : that it was the duty before God of Zephaniah the High Priest to arrest and imprison Jeremiah, that he was a madman and a self-ordained preacher. His command that Jeremiah should be shut up in the prison was met by the Divine judgment which shut him, and his children, out of the restored Jerusalem (v. 32). Many of the exiles lived to see the restoration, and to enjoy it with their children (Neh. vii. and x.).

Gemariah was one of those who interceded with king Jehoiakim that the prophet's roll should not be burned (xxxvi. 25)

The slaves of vice and the drunkard illustrate the law that rejecters of God's commands destroy not only themselves but also their wives and children (v. 32). Compare Dan. vi. 24.

JEREMIAH XXX.-XXXI. 1. — The Divine authorship of these twenty-five verses is asserted sixteen times (vs. 1, 1, 2, 2, 3, 3, 4, 5, 8, 10, 11, 12, 17, 18, 21, xxxi. 1).

The communication was " the Word of the Lord " (v. 1) and was composed of " the words of the Lord " (v. 2).

Similar terms are employed in John xvii. 8 and 14.

The wonders of God's love and grace (vs. 3, 10, 11, 16, 17, 18) ; His fidelity to His promises (v. 9) ; the guilt of the sinner (vs. 14 and 15) ; his total depravity (v. 12) ; his inability to save himself, or to find salvation in any creature (vs. 12 and 13) : the judgment of evil, whether in the believer (v. 15) or the unbeliever (v. 23) ; and the fulness and perfection of the salvation founded on Christ (v. 9), operated by God (v. 10), and bestowed in grace (v. 17), are some of the treasures of this chapter.

Its main subject is the future restoration of the Twelve Tribes of Israel (v. 3 and xxxi. 1).

But the glory of that restoration is to be preceded by the horror of " the time of Jacob's trouble " (v. 7).

It is here predicted that the anguish and suffering of " that day " will be so great as to have no equal in human history. That is the day spoken of in Matt. xxiv. 21 and 22, and Mark xiii. 19 and 20.

Thus the great principle once more here appears that the night of wrath must precede the morn of righteousness.

God in His fore-knowledge knowing that Jeremiah would never be carried away to the captives in Babylon, commanded the compilation of these prophecies into a book, which should reach the captives of both Israel and Judah (v. 3) and nourish their faith and intelligence. Daniel was thus instructed and strengthened by reading this Inspired Volume (Dan. ix. 2).

The predictions in this chapter have not

yet been fulfilled. They belong to the "latter days." Their accomplishment will then be recognized and understood (v. 24).

"His yoke" (v. 8), i.e., that of the last king of Babylon—Anti-Christ. "Thy neck," i.e., all Israel, for the Gentiles shall then no more enslave God's beloved people.

"David their king," i.e., the Messiah (Isa. lv. 3, Ezek. xxxiv. 23, 24, and xxxvii. 24, 25 and Hos. iii. 5).

The Holy Spirit, as also the Lord Jesus, delights to repeat Himself. Hence verse 10 gathers together many gracious utterances. Compare, for example, Isa. xli. 10, xliii. 5, xliv. 2, etc.

God, being a righteous judge, the justice promised in verse 16 commands the admiration of every true moralist.

"The palace" (v. 18) will be the Temple at Jerusalem. It will be the dwelling place of the Messiah ; and it shall be inhabited in a style befitting its glory (R.V.).

"Their nobles" (v. 21) Hebrew : "his Prince," i.e., Jacob's Prince (R.V.).

He will also be Jacob's Priest (v. 21). As such He "engaged His heart," i.e., pledged His life at Calvary, in order to put away sin, open the way to God, and so enable His people, in fellowship with Himself, to approach the throne of grace, not with timidity, but with boldness. (Heb. iv. 16).

"Who is this ? " (v. 21). See Isa. lxiii. 1, and Matt. xxi. 10. Christ's appearing in grace (Matt.) ; in wrath (Isa.) ; and in restoration (Jer.).

JEREMIAH XXXI. 2-40.—The future restoration of both Israel and Judah, and the re-building of Jerusalem, is the subject of this vision.

"The sword" (v. 2), i.e., the murderous cruelty of Pharaoh.

"When I went," i.e., as the Pillar of Fire and Cloud.

"To cause him to rest," i.e., to establish Israel in Palestine.

Verse 3 should read as in the Revised Version margin. Compare Ps. xxxvi. 10 (A.V. margin). The argument is : That God having chosen to love Israel with a love from all eternity, therefore He kept exhibiting proofs of that love with unwearied affection.

"Shall eat them as common things" (v. 5). The Revised Version gives the true meaning of these words. Compare Lev.

xix. 23-25, Deut. xx. 6, and xxviii. 30. Thus under the Law the vine-owner had to wait five years before he could gather for himself the fruit of his vineyard. Consequently he might never enjoy its produce because of the insecurity of the times. But in the Restoration there will be a perfect government, and so his enjoyment of the fruit of his labour will be assured.

In Ephraim's sad past (v. 6) the watchmen summoned the people to go up to Bethel, or to Dan, to worship an idol, but in the happy future they will be summoned to go up to Zion unto Jehovah the Messiah.

"For " (v. 7), i.e., "concerning." "The chief of the nations," i.e., Israel. "Among," i.e., "concerning" (R.V.).

So certain is salvation sure to those who call upon the Lord that it can be published and praised for in advance (v. 7).

The "north country" (v. 8), i.e., Russia. To the present day this one country contains more than half the Jewish population of the world. It is plain that the same fact will obtain at the time of the Restoration.

Isa. xlix. 22 and 23, and lxvi. 19 and 20, predict the comfort and dignity in, and with, which the Exiles are to return. Hence the afflicted and the sick (v. 8). shall be tenderly cared for. But the following verse foretells that these circumstances will not inflate their hearts with pride, but that God's goodness will melt them to weeping and repentance.

"Rahel " (v. 15), i.e., Rachel. She was the mother of Joseph and Benjamin, and therefore of the two kingdoms, and the two peoples.

Ramah is a Hebrew word meaning "a high place." Here evidently a high place near Bethlehem.

Rachel wept for her children when they were carried captive to Babylon, and, again, when they were slain by Herod, and thus, to this extent, was the prophecy fulfilled, as stated in Matt. ii. 17 and 18 ; but the weeping and the promise of verses 16 and 17 belong to the future.

True conversion has God as its agent (v. 18), and is followed by repentance (v. 19).

"High heaps " (v. 21), i.e., finger-posts.

"The highway even the way by which thou wentest " (v. 21), i.e., the king's highway which Israel trod at the beginning when redeemed from Egypt.

"A woman shall compass a man " (v. 22).

This is popularly understood to predict the Birth of the Messiah of a virgin. But the context destroys this, for it predicts something that has not yet taken place, and something in connection with the future restoration of the tribes of Jacob. The woman is Israel, the Man is Messiah; " to compass" means to attach oneself with worship and loyalty, as in Ps. xxvi. 6. The prediction is that the virgin of Israel will cease to go " hither and thither after idols " (R.V.) and will seek and cleave to Immanuel. In the first creation the man attached himself to the woman, but in the New Creation the woman will attach herself to the Man.

During the captivity the proverb of verse 29 (see Ezek. xviii. 23), must often have been used, but during the millennium the principle of verse 30, will be in government.

The promise of vs. 31-34 is that of a new moral nature ; and the argument of vs. 35-37 is the impossibility of God's ceasing to love His ancient people, or of casting them away because of their past misconduct.

There is a play upon the word husband in verse 32 which is employed in Heb. viii. 9.

The word in Hebrew means both an husband and a rejecter. Adding this verse and Heb. viii. 9 together, the full import of the statement is obtained : that is, that though He loved Israel as a husband loves, yet her breach of the Covenant compelled Him to reject her.

The knowledge of God (v. 34) is the foundation of salvation. (See note on ix. 24).

Scholars find a difficulty in translating the third statement in verse 35, which repeats Isa. li. 15 and confirms it. Some understand it as stating, that God excites the sea so that its waves roar. Others, that He stilleth the sea when its waves roar, as in Luke viii. 24. But the references in the verse to Gen. i. respecting the sun, the moon, and the stars, and their obedience to their Great Creator carries the reader to Gen. i. 9 and 10, and to Job xxxviii. 11, when God divided the sea from the dry land, setting a law upon its mighty waves which they cannot disobey. Thus this third statement supports the two preceding in assuring the unchangeableness and fidelity of God's love.

The last three verses foretell the beauty of the future Jerusalem : there will be spaciousness, holiness and permanence.

JEREMIAH XXXII.—This chapter predicts the restoration of the Land ; the next chapter, the restoration of the People. Both these "words" came to Jeremiah when in the court of the prison.

He was imprisoned there the first time because he foretold the capture of the city by the Chaldeans. When the Egyptian king raised the siege he was thrown into the dungeon, and scourged, on a false accusation, but removed again to the court of the prison (xxxvii. 11-21). While there he resumed his faithful preaching, and was cast into the pit, but again removed to the prison-court (xxxviii. 1-13), and, finally, was led away in chains to Ramah and liberated (xl. 1). Prior to these imprisonments he suffered the cruelty of chapter xx.

The raising of the siege by Pharaoh-Hophra must have exposed the prophet, and his message, to public ridicule ; but the return of the Chaldeans, and the destruction of the city and Temple, vindicated the Word of the Lord.

This chapter, and the following, shew how a true faith recognizes, and approves, the wrath of God whilst announcing the grace of God. A false faith limits itself to preaching the love of God.

Verses 2-5 form a parenthesis explaining why the prophet was in prison. Verse 6 reads on directly from verse 1.

Zedekiah's eyes saw the Chaldean monarch at Riblah, they were then put out, and he was carried to Babylon where he died. Thus, as predicted by Ezekiel, he died in Babylon and yet never saw it (2 Kings xxv. 6 and 7, Ezek. xii. 13, and Jer. xliv. 3).

" Besieged " (v. 2) " was besieging."

" Until I visit him " (v. 5). See xxxiv. 4 and 5. These verses suggest Zedekiah's repentance prior to his death.

The purchase of the field at Anathoth helps to interpret Rev. v. See notes on that chapter.

The law concerning the redemption of land is found in Lev. xxv. and Ruth iv.

A deed of purchase was executed in duplicate. The original contained the terms and conditions (v. 11, R.V. margin) and was sealed on the outside. The copy only recited the fact of the purchase, and was unsealed.

" Many days " (v. 14), i.e., the seventy years of the Captivity and desolation.

This purchase demonstrated the prophet's

belief in the Divine promise of restoration (v. 15).

The Roman historian Florus states that while Rome was being besieged by Hannibal the ground on which he was encamped was purchased by a Roman who thus attested his confidence in the victory of the Roman people.

The piece of ground redeemed must have been very small for seventeen shekels is less than two pounds. But though small it was precious to God. Compared with the universe this world is but a grain of sand ; and yet it was loved and redeemed at infinite cost (Rev. v.).

" For " (v. 25) should read " whereas " or " though " (R.V.). The prophet, wondering how the promise of verse 15 could be performed in view of the facts of verse 25, had recourse to prayer (vs. 16-25) which is the grand remedy against perplexities. And yet his prayer revealed the feebleness and unbelief and ignorance of his heart.

" Hard " (v. 17), i.e., wonderful.

The conjunction of love to thousands, and of suffering to children because of their parents' sin (v. 18), is an offence to the carnal mind. It did not offend Daniel, though he suffered for Hezekiah's sin.

" The mounts " (v. 24) were structures of earth raised by besiegers so as to overtop the walls of a city.

In the reply to the prophet's prayer (vs. 26-44), the two foundation doctrines find expression, viz : the incurable depravity of human nature even in the most favourable moral conditions (vs. 30-35), and the necessity of a new spiritual birth (vs. 39 and 40).

These two doctrines deeply offend moralists.

The Hebrews, having substituted Moloch the god of fire for Jehovah, it was a just judgment which burned their houses with fire (v. 29).

Solomon who beautified Jerusalem also established idolatry in it (v. 31).

The popular belief that a good intention excuses superstitious worship is destroyed by verse 35.

The carnal mind passes easily from presumption (v. 3) to despair (v. 36).

But when man is brought to despair grace can intervene to infinitely and permanently bless him (vs. 36-41). Thus man's incurable sinfulness must be fully demonstrated in order to provide a field of action for the operations of grace.

If it be objected that God should at once have given to Israel, when leaving Egypt, the new moral nature promised in verse 39, and thus prevented the sin and suffering of dark centuries of ignorance and idolatry, the answer is : that there must have been a Divine necessity for such action ; and, further, that even to man's present intelligence it is evident that such action on the part of God respects man's will, and, at the same time, eternally prevents him from taking any credit to himself for his salvation.

If it be further objected that 6,000 years given to manifest the incurable sinfulness of human nature was an unreasonable period, the answer is : that, in contrast with an eternity of felicity, that period of time is but an hour, and that man has not yet learned his lesson.

That the promises of this vision are future is abundantly proved by verses 37-44, for these predictions have not yet come to pass.

" I will give them one heart " (v. 39), i.e., conversion ; " they shall not depart from Me " (v. 40), i.e., consecration. The conversion of the sinner, and the preservation of the saint, are both operations of the Holy Spirit.

Hebrew scholars instance verse 44 as illustrating the force and beauty of the Infinite Absolute in emphasizing the certain fulfilment of the several predictions of the verse.

JEREMIAH XXXIII.—This chapter predicts the restoration of the people ; as the prior one fore-told the restoration of the land.

The chapter contains three sections, each section being, in its turn, constructed in triplets. An analysis will exhibit this double structure :

THE PROMISE OF JEHOVAH (vs. 1-14).
THE BRANCH OF JEHOVAH (vs. 15-18).
THE FAITHFULNESS OF JEHOVAH (vs. 19-26)

THE PROMISE OF JEHOVAH

Desolated Jerusalem (vs. 1-5).
Healed (v. 6).
Restored " As at the first," (vs. 7-9).
Desolated towns (v. 10).
Gladdened (v. 11).
Restored " As at the first " (v. 11).
Desolated Land (v. 12).
Enriched (vs. 12 and 13).
Restored as promised (v. 14).
The Great Prophecy respecting the Messiah

is placed in the midst of the chapter, thus emphasising that He is the centre of all God's purposes, and that upon Him depends, and is founded, the redemption of Israel and of the human race.

The triple form of the second section of the chapter may be thus shewn :

THE BRANCH OF JEHOVAH.
As Jehovah (v. 16).
As King (v. 17).
As Priest (v. 18).

The third section :

THE FAITHFULNESS OF JEHOVAH.
Tokens, Day and Night (vs. 19 and 20).
Covenant with David (v. 21).
Tokens, Stars and Sand (v. 22).
Children of David (v. 22).
Tokens, Day and Night (vs. 23-25).
Captivity of David (v. 26).

The Epistle of Jude shews a somewhat similar structure to that of this chapter. See Notes on that Epistle.

" Maker " (v. 2) better translated " performer."

" Mighty things " (v. 3), i.e., things above human knowledge—" hidden things " i.e. the restoration of all Israel (Rom. xi. 26).

The grammatical structure of verses 4 and 5 is difficult to Western minds. The statement appears to be that the houses proposed to be demolished in order to form barricades against the Chaldeans, were destined by God to be, on the contrary, filled with the dead bodies of the Hebrew soldiers.

" Them " (v. 9). Some editions read " it," i.e., Jerusalem. As the verse begins and ends with " it," this is most likely the correct reading.

" They " (v. 9), i.e., the nations.

" Telleth " (v. 13), i.e., " counteth."

Messiah's name in xxiii. 6, is declared to be Jehovah-Tsidkenu. Verse 16 in this chapter states that this name will be given to the New Israel. The Hebrew Text reads : " This shall call to her." That is, His name shall be called upon her, as the bridegroom's name is given to a bride.

" This people " (v. 24), i.e., the doubters among the captives. The natural heart first ridicules the promises of God and then doubts them.

The last line of verse 26 reads—emphasizing the double " will "—" for I *will* cause their captivity to return, and I *will* have compassion upon them."

The sorrows and rejection of Messiah are not the subject of Jeremiah's prophecies, but rather the guilt of the nation at that time, the resulting judgments, and the grace which promised a restoration. This grace will be exercised by Messiah ; and the restoration, with all its wealth of mercy and blessing, will be based upon His Person and atoning work. The full effect of His love to guilty Israel will then be revealed ; and the energies of this grace will be according to, and measured by, the perfection of His love and counsels.

JEREMIAH XXXIV.—This chapter illustrates the worthlessness of a conversion produced by self-interest, or carnal fear.

The Chaldeans were at this time fighting against Jerusalem (v. 7). Moved by fear, and by the preaching of Jeremiah, the citizens covenanted to obey the Bible (Exodus xxi. 2) and emancipate their slaves (v. 10). But their allies, the Egyptians, (v. 11, and xxxvii. 5) having raised the siege, they brought back the slaves into bondage (v. 16).

This covenant was made in the Temple (v. 15), and its members passed between the parts of a calf cut in twain (v. 18)—thus expressing the solemnity of the covenant, and their acceptance of the sentence of death if they failed to keep it (Gen. xv. 9-17).

Because they enslaved others God justly condemned them to be themselves slaves to the Babylonians (v. 21), or to the equally just punishment of death.

Verses 1-7 detail the prophecy of xxxii. 2-5.

It is plain from v. 5 that Zedekiah, in the misery of his blindness and captivity in Babylon, experienced a true conversion. This was predicted in the words : " Thou shalt not die by the sword, but thou shalt die in peace."

God having delivered the Hebrews from slavery (v. 13), the cruelty of their action in enslaving others was thereby made the more inexcusable. " At their pleasure " (v. 16), i.e., at the option of the slave to accept liberty or not.

A distinction in guilt appears to be drawn here between those who originate evil and those who are, through weakness of character, led into evil. The former (vs. 19 and 20) were doomed to the major punishment of death ; the latter (v. 21), i.e., Zedekiah and his princes, to the minor punishment of slavery.

JEREMIAH XXXV.—The conjunction of this chapter with the prior one illustrates the moral, and not the chronological order of the Book of Jeremiah. The moral order is much more important than the chronological.

The obedience of the Rechabites to their earthly father is here contrasted with the disobedience of the Israelites to their Heavenly Father.

The Rechabites were descended from Hobab the brother-in-law of Moses. They were Kenites, and migrated with Israel to Canaan. They were not idolaters (Num. x. 29, Judges i. 16, iv. 11-17, v. 24 and 1 Sam. xv. 6.

" A man of God " (v. 4), i.e., a prophet.

An earthly father's commands may be reasonable or unreasonable (vs. 6 and 7), but God's commands are perfect in love and wisdom.

The wickedness of Israel's disobedience is emphasized by the Title " Jehovah Elohim Zabaoth, Elohim of Israel." (v. 17). The full and most solemn use of this Divine Title occurs three times in this Book (xxxv. 17, xxxviii. 17, and xliv. 7).

The last verse appears to warrant the belief that the Rechabites are still in existence, and will appear, as a distinct people, in the Millennium.

JEREMIAH XXXVI.—The king first mutilated and then burned the roll. So have men treated, and so do men still treat, the Word of God. Some mutilate it ; others burn it.

The words were the words of Jehovah, the instrument that uttered them, the mouth of Jeremiah, and that which recorded them, the pen of Baruch. This describes the fact of inspiration.

The roll contained the prophecies of twenty-three years (v. 2), and, being written, could be sent to the Ten Tribes of Israel, then in captivity, and read by the two tribes, then about to be carried into captivity (v. 2).

One of God's objects in writing the Bible was that it should be read to the people and by the people (v. 6), and that the moral effect of reading it should be amendment of life (v. 7), and, consequently, an escape from the wrath to come (v. 7).

God in His love to sinners warns them beforehand of their danger. Hence this book was prepared in the fourth year of Jehoiakim (v. 1) but published in the fifth year (v. 9).

" The fast day " (vs. 6 and 9) was, possibly, appointed to be observed because of the threatened second visit of the Chaldeans to Jerusalem. In their first visit they had made the king a prisoner, but afterwards released him, and they carried Daniel and the princes to Babylon.

The ninth month (v. 22) was December ; hence the fire in the brasier.

As Jehudi kept reading the roll, leaf by leaf, the king kept cutting them and burning them (v. 23). The intercession of Elnathan and his companions added to the king's guilt.

As to-day so then, men in high places were not afraid to oppose and dishonour the Word of God. How different was the reception given to it by Jehoiakim's father, king Josiah ! (2 Chron. xxxiv. 19).

It is useless for the enemies of the Bible to try and destroy it. They cannot dishonour it ; but they can dishonour themselves, for Jehoiakim was buried with the burial of an ass, drawn and cast forth without the walls of Jerusalem (xxii. 19).

The princes feared the Word of God (vs. 16 and 19), but the king and " his servants," i.e., his courtiers, did not fear it (v. 24).

JEREMIAH XXXVII.—The events of this chapter and chapter xxi. are closely related. The latter comes in chronologically between chapters xxxvii. and xxxviii. These were two messages from Zedekiah to Jeremiah, that of this chapter preceding that of chapter xxi. Here the issue between the Chaldeans and the Egyptians was undecided ; there the message was sent when, after the defeat of Pharaoh, the Chaldeans were again advancing against Jerusalem. Hence the conjunction of the names Zephaniah, Jehucal and Pashur in the embassies to Jeremiah. After the defeat of Pharaoh the Egyptians abandoned Zedekiah (2 Kings xxiv. 7). Zedekiah's alliance with Pharaoh was a violation of his oath to Nebuchadnezzar (2 Chron. xxxvi. 13 and Ezek. xvii. 15 and 17).

When circumstances are prosperous men can get on very well with a fashionable religion, and shut up the preachers of truth in prison ; but when adversity threatens, they seek help from the despised prisoners.

Zedekiah was like many in the present day, who in secret profess attachment to

Christ, but, afraid of their companions, do not confess Him in public.

The nobility, moral elevation, courage, wisdom and courtesy of Jeremiah in his interview with the king were admirable (vs. 17-20) ; and the prophet's bearing makes that of the king the more despicable.

" Whom " (v. 1), i.e., Zedekiah.

Zedekiah and his cabinet ministers, like many to-day, were willing that God's servants should pray for them (v. 3), but determined to continue to disobey the word of the Lord (v. 2).

The advances of the Egyptians temporarily raised the siege of Jerusalem by the Chaldeans (v. 5).

Court preachers are careful to say what kings wish to hear, but it was not so with Jeremiah (vs. 6-10).

" To separate himself " (v. 12), i.e., to inspect and take official possession of, and receive (R.V.), the lands which he had bought from his cousin (chapter xxxii). " In the midst of the people " (v. 12), i.e., openly.

" Irijah " (v. 13) was grandson of Hananiah. Perhaps this was the Hananiah of chapter xxviii. If so, this would explain Irijah's action.

As Jeremiah came to receive his own (v. 12), was arrested on a false accusation (v. 13), brought before the princes (v. 14), scourged (v. 15), and cast into the pit of the dungeon (v. 16), from whence he emerged (v. 21), so his great Antitype came unto His own, and His own received Him not, but scourged Him, crucified Him and buried Him. But there was this distinction, the Prophet purchased his inheritance with gold that perisheth ; the Saviour purchased His with the ever precious blood of Calvary.

Jeremiah's pathetic appeal not to be left to die of starvation in the dungeon (v. 20), while shewing his natural fea of death, makes his courage in testimony the more remarkable, and the result proves that honest reproof sometimes gains more favour than flattery.

" The court of the prison " (v. 21). See notes on xxxii. 2.

" A piece of bread " (v. 21), i.e., a soldier's ration, which consisted of three loaves in the time of the Romans, and was held to be sufficient food for a day, or for a meal (Luke xi. 5).

The servant of God is to be courteous (1 Pet. ii. 17 and iii. 8). Hence Jeremiah said : " My lord, O king " and Paul said . " Most noble Festus." See also Rom. xiii. 7. Neither King nor Governor merited these titles morally, but they did merit them officially.

The effect of burning the Bible is illustrated in this chapter. Hence its position in relation to the prior chapter. An enemy of the Word of God injures his family and his friends ; and the passage of time does not remove nor mitigate the injury—unless God in grace intervenes.

Jeremiah was a faithful and pitiful preacher of the Divine message. He most earnestly and affectionally warned the king of the sure wrath of God, and begged him to accept the grace of God that promised absolute safety from that wrath. But the king, like the men of to-day, chose death rather than life, as is related in the next two chapters.

JEREMIAH XXXVIII.—Jeremiah sank in the mire physically (v. 6), but Zedekiah sank in it morally (v. 22). The mire to the one was a mantle of glory ; to the other, a vesture of shame.

Although the Prophet had already been twice cruelly scourged (xx. 2, and xxxvii. 15) yet he continued to courageously preach truths which the people did not wish to hear (vs. 2 and 3), with the result that he was thrown into a cistern in which was no water, but much mire (v. 6), and left there to die of hunger (v. 9). Such was the cruelty of the haters of truth, and servants of God must not think it a strange thing if God permits such suffering to befall them.

The impotency of the King, his weakness of character, his fear of his ministers, and his inward conviction of the truth of God's word, appear in verses 5, 10, 14, 16, 19, and 24-26.

These last two verses are the last words of Zedekiah recorded in the Scriptures, and they give a truthful, but sad, picture of his character.

The courage of Ebed-Melech (vs. 7-13) stands here in contrast with the cowardice of the king. He boldly in public (v. 7) dared the anger of both princes and people, and so shamed the king (v. 10) that he obtained authority to deliver the Prophet. So dangerous was the mission that he needed thirty soldiers as a protecting guard. This word " thirty " is not a copyist's error or " three," as some suppose.

The affection and skill shewn in verses 11-13 not only honoured Ebed-Melech, but illustrated how God can use old clothes and rotten rags as instruments in His service, and teach us to do a kind action in a way that will not hurt.

The nobility and elevation of Jeremiah's character appear in this, that in his interview with the king (vs.14-26),he did not indignantly denounce the brutality of his enemies, and demand their just punishment, nor did he, in righteous anger, rebuke the king for his cowardly conduct in the matter. On the contrary he earnestly and affectionately urged the king to save his life and theirs (vs. 20-23) by obeying the Word of the Lord and surrendering to the Chaldeans.

"That made us this soul" (v. 16). This means: "may God take my life if I take thine."

The weak king, fearing lest the Chaldeans should hand him over to the Jews who had surrendered to them (v. 19), and urging that as a reason against his own surrender, Jeremiah told him that greater indignity would result from disobedience, for his own wives would point out to the Babylonian princes his moral feebleness (" thy friends have set thee on and prevailed against thee "), his political degradation (" thy feet are sank in the mire "), and that these so-called friends, having secured their own safety, would desert him (" they are turned away back ").

What the king commanded his subject Jeremiah to say, and which the Prophet, as a subject, truthfully repeated, was but a half truth. What men said was not inspired, but the record of what they said is inspired.

JEREMIAH XXXIX.—Ebed-Melech, Zedekiah, and Jeremiah illustrate the wisdom of faith, the folly of unbelief, and the reward of faithfulness. Such results always follow faith, faithlessness, and faithfulness respectively.

And yet all through his unbelief and disobedience and cowardice Zedekiah kept up an outward shew of religion. He acted as men do to-day. He was practically an unbeliever, and up to the very end thought he could defeat the Word of the Lord by breaking a passage through the south wall of the city (Ezek. xii. 1-16), and thus escaping from the Chaldeans. See notes on 1 Kings xxii. 30.

But he was defeated and captured at Jericho. That ancient city thus witnessed the last defeat of Israel, as it had witnessed their first victory.

The northern end of the city was separated from the southern by an interior wall in which was a gate called the Middle-Gate. The Chaldeans captured that portion of the city, and then took up their position (" sat in ") opposite the Middle Gate in order to force it. Zedekiah, despairing of being able to resist them, resolved to flee, but failed to escape.

Rabsaris (v. 3) and Rab-mag are titles ; the one means chief of the eunuchs, the other, chief of the Magi.

" He gave judgment upon him " (v. 5), i.e., he pronounced sentence upon him for his perjury in breaking his oath of allegiance (Ezek. xvii. 13, 2 Chron. xxxvi. 13).

The sentence was a terrible one. It was five-fold : viz :—the death of his sons, the death of his nobles, the loss of his eyesight, the loss of his liberty, and his exile to Babylon. Thus, as predicted in Ezek. xii. 13, and Jer. xxxii. 4, his eyes saw the eyes of the Babylonian monarch, but not the Babylonian capital, though he died there. Captive princes were compelled to kneel before the conqueror to throw back their heads, and look up into the monarch s eyes, who then, with the spear that was in his hand, destroyed the eyes of the miserable prisoner. Thus the sightless eyes of the Hebrew king, when closing in death in Babylon, only saw the cruel eyes of the Babylonian conqueror.

God sometimes moves heathen princes to honour faithful preachers of His Word (vs. 11-14). Jeremiah was thus honoured ; for the highest officers of the empire were commanded to attend upon him, to remove his fetters (xl. 1), and to do all that he wished.

But Jeremiah was despised, and, finally, destroyed by his own people. So Christ, despised by Israel, is to-day honoured by the Gentile.

" Peace through believing " is illustrated by Ebed-melech. He feared the vengeance of the princes of Judah (v. 17), and he feared the sword of the Chaldeans (v. 18). But this double fear was dismissed by the words " I will deliver thee," " Yea, I will surely deliver thee " (vs. 17 and 18).

This Divine promise was made to him because of his faith (" thou hast put thy trust in Me "). Thus this black man was saved ; and he knew it. Believers in the Lord Jesus Christ enjoy a similar peace and assurance.

JEREMIAH XL.—The carnal mind discovers no profit in this and the four succeeding chapters. But the Holy Spirit wrote them for the help and instruction of God's people ; and were Christian people more spiritually minded they would discover wondrous things in these records.

But on the surface the lessons may be learned that the confusion, sin, misery, and cruelty here recorded resulted from the refusal of Zedekiah to obey the Word of the Lord ; and that no matter how great the confusion and wickedness, God guards His own, for He did not permit Ishmael to murder Jeremiah ; and though Jeremiah suffered repeatedly at the hands of both his countrymen and the Chaldeans, yet was he not embittered against either but desired, and laboured for their good ; and, lastly, if men, like Gedaliah, refuse to listen to sound advice, they must suffer the consequence of their refusal, for had Gedaliah put Ishmael in prison he would have thereby saved his own life and hindered Ishmael from committing murder.

War and captivity cannot prevent the Great Shepherd from speaking to His Own (v. 1).

The clear vision of the heathen prince (vs. 2-5) contrasts with the blindness of the men of Judah.

Jeremiah was carried captive in chains (vs. 1 and 4). He was again a captive (xli. 10) ; and yet again (xliii. 5).

" Now while he was not yet gone back " (v. 5), i.e., while Jeremiah was yet hesitating to reply.

The prophet preferred poverty and obscurity with the hostile and degenerate Hebrews rather than fame and comfort amongst the admiring Chaldeans (v. 6).

The abundance of the summer-fruits (v. 12) testified to the love and compassion of God for His disobedient people.

Gedaliah should have listened to Johanan (vs. 13-16) ; had he arrested Ishmael he would have saved himself and others from calamity.

JEREMIAH XLI.—Ishmael being a member of the Royal Family (v. 1), was no doubt moved by jealousy to murder Gedaliah because he had been made Viceroy.

The hypocrisy and treachery of Ishmael (vs. 1 and 6) became him as a murderer.

The Temple of Jehovah (v. 5) existed to faith but not to sight ; for it was burned. So eighty believers, obedient to the Word of the Lord, came to worship at the place where Jehovah had set His name, and where He had commanded His people to worship Him.

Faith recognized and approved the appalling judgments that had fallen upon them and turned, not from, but to Him who had poured out those judgments, and brought Him thank offerings of the abundance which grace provided (xl. 12). Seventy of these men were permitted to perish, for theirs was the faith that overcomes. See notes on Rev. vi. o, xii. 11, xiii. 7, etc

JEREMIAH XLII.—The treachery and cruelty of Ishmael and his companions, and the hypocrisy, obstinacy, rebellion and unbelief of Johanan and the people, reveal the moral condition of the nation and the justness of the calamities which came upon them.

Ishmael illustrates the ugliness of the " flesh," and Johanan, its unbelief.

The " flesh," whether murderous or religious, is the flesh ; for that which is born of the flesh is flesh, and the carnal mind is enmity against God when making a show of religion as when shedding blood. Cain illustrates this fact, for he was just as hostile to God when worshipping at his æsthetic altar as when murdering his brother. The Holy Spirit (1 John iii. 12) says that Cain's religious works were evil.

When people are in trouble they are quite willing to pray, but unwilling to obey. Like Johanan and his friends, they secretly make their plans and then propose public prayer.

Double names were common among the Hebrews, hence Jezaniah (v. 1) had a second name Azariah (xliii. 2).

Unconverted people can use very pious and very humble language (vs. 2-6), but the humility of the natural man is as abhorrent to God as the pride of the natural man (Col. ii. 18 and 23).

" Evil " (v. 6), i.e., suffering.

The prophet waiting in silence for ten days for the mysterious inflatus of the Holy Spirit, presents a striking picture to the mind (v. 7). It was a testing time for him and for his hearers. He kept trusting and obeying ; but they rejected the grace which gave this interval for repenting of their settled purpose.

The calamities which men suffer often result from self-will. What peace and happiness would these people have enjoyed had they obeyed the Word of the Lord !

The predictions of verse 17 all came to pass. It is folly for men to deny the fact of the wrath of God (v. 18).

Human intelligence is incapable of the knowledge shewn in verses 20 and 21. The Holy Spirit revealed to the prophet the hypocrisy of the petitioners (v. 20) and their pre-determined resolve to disobey the voice of God (v. 21). " Ye have not obeyed," i.e., " you have not intended to obey."

JEREMIAH XLIII.—Unbelief toward God (v. 2) is often discourteous and unjust towards His servants (v. 3).

Tahpanes (v. 7) was a fortress on the Syrian frontier of Egypt. It was a royal palace. Petrie in 1886 discovered here a ruin called : The palace of the daughters of Judah. It was doubtless built by Pharaoh for the daughters of Zedekiah (xli. 10 and xliii. 6).

" Brick-kiln " (v. 9). The Hebrew word means " brick pavement." Petrie discovered it in 1886. Such a brick platform is seen to-day outside all great houses in Egypt. See note on 2 Sam. xii. 31.

On the brick pavement the Chaldean monarch pitched his royal pavilion. Josephus records the fact. Thus was the prophecy fulfilled to the letter.

Seated there he condemned to slavery, or to death, the captives brought before him.

" He shall also break the images in the Temple of the Sun." The Egyptians called this place On ; the Greeks, Heliopolis. Its site is about ten miles north-east of Cairo. There was a similar temple in the land of Canaan (Joshua xv. 10, Judges i. 33 and 1 Sam. vi. 9 and 19). " Beth-Shemish " means The House of the Sun.

" Baruch " (v. 3) was a noble (xxxii. 12). The message to him xlv. 1-5, suggests a reason for his being suspected of intriguing with the Chaldeans.

The people (xlii.) confessed the truthfulness of Jeremiah, but here (v. 2) declared him to be a liar. Such is man, even when cloaked with religion.

The sinking of the Egyptian great stones in the brick pavement (v. 9), and the setting of the Chaldean throne upon them (v. 10), symbolized the downfall of the Egyptian monarchy and the supremacy of the Chaldean.

God often makes one wicked nation a scourge to another (Ezek. xxix. 18-20).

" Death to death " (v. 11), i.e., to death by the plague. So the Chaldean king gave judgment : some to slavery, some to death, and the residue to perish by disease.

" He shall burn them " (v. 12), i.e., the idols of wood ; " and carry them away captives," i.e., their worshippers.

Beth-Shemesh (v. 13), i.e., the Temple of the Sun, i.e., On. Joseph's father-in-law was priest of On (Gen. xli. 50).

JEREMIAH XLIV.—This was Jeremiah's last prophecy relating to Israel. The remaining prophecies of the Book concern the Gentiles.

Although the destruction of Jerusalem and Palestine (vs. 2, 6, 22) was a fact that could not be denied, yet these obstinate unbelievers refused to recognise its cause (vs. 3, 6, 13, 23), but, on the contrary, declared their misfortunes arose from their want of devotion to the Queen of Heaven, i.e., the Great Mother of God (vs. 17-19).

Thus the Spaniards, and other nations, to-day attribute their decadence to a lack of zeal in the adoration of the Madonna.

The plaintive cry in verse 4 breathes an agony that only Divine love could feel and utter.

" Incense " (v. 3) expresses the whole range of idol-worship.

Women (v. 9), especially the wives of nobles and princes and kings, have been in the past, and are in the present, the most active introducers of idolatry. Instead of helping each other towards heaven husband and wife often ripen each other for hell (v. 19).

The change of person from the third to the second (v. 10) is designed to express how idolatry alienates from God.

" All " (v. 11), i.e., all the idolaters. These men no doubt believed that by putting aside the Bible and worshipping the Egyptian gods (v. 8), they would secure a prosperous return to their native land (v. 14), but that those who surrendered to the Chaldeans, who rejected idolatry, and who clung to the Bible, would perish. The exact opposite, however, is an historic fact.

A few should, however escape (vs. 14 and 28). These must have, like Jeremiah and Baruch, refused to burn incense to the idol. God always has, and has had, His "few" (1 Pet. iii. 20, Matt. vii. 14, Rev. iii. 4). The awakened heart cries : " Oh to be one of that few ! "

The Queen of Heaven (v. 17) was Astarte, i.e., Venus, the modern Madonna. The cakes made in her honour and eaten, were crescent-shaped ; for, like the moon, Venus also appears as a crescent from time to time to the inhabitants of the earth.

Unregenerate men are incapable of recognizing the Hand of God in calamities (v. 18).

People when doing wrong often hide themselves behind others, as these women did behind their husbands (v. 19).

" Them " (v. 21), i.e., the fathers ; " it," i.e., the incense, that is, the idolatrous worship.

It is popularly affirmed (v. 25) that a vow, however idolatrous, or contrary to nature, as for instance the vow of chastity, should be maintained by people after they have come to a knowledge of the truth and been converted to God. But such vows, having been imposed by man, and based on falsehood, possess no obligation.

The argument of the last member of verse 25 in connection with the verses that follow is : that if these people were determined to accomplish their vows, God, on His part, was resolved to perform His in their destruction.

The Mass of the Virgin Mary as the Queen of Heaven, with its sacred communion cakes, or wafers, will possibly be commanded in the Roman Church at some future Council. A Spanish Archbishop preaching 20 years ago in the cathedral at Madrid said, that the decadence of Spain was due to its want of devotion to " the Queen of Heaven."

History records the miserable end of Pharaoh-hophra at the hand of his enemies, headed by Amasis a rebel. The civil war which this man provoked facilitated the conquest of Egypt by Nebuchadnezzar.

JEREMIAH XLV.—As the Apostle Paul addressed prophetic writings to individuals as well as communities, so here Jeremiah addressed Baruch.

This message comforted Baruch eighteen years before the sack of Jerusalem.

To enjoy such consolation fellowship with a persecuted servant of God is necessary. Baruch was closely associated with Jeremiah, and so shared the shame and danger and consolation of the association (chapter xxxvi.).

Baruch was the grandson of Maaseiah, governor of Jerusalem in the reign of Josiah (2 Chron. xxxiv. 8), and brother of Seraiah chief-chamberlain (li. 59). He was, therefore, of noble family and had a high position in society.

Baruch's grief added to his sorrow was possibly his grief at the burning of the roll, and his sorrow at being suspected of treason.

Jeremiah's gentle " Thou didst say " suggested to him that he should have rejoiced rather then sighed because he was deemed worthy to suffer shame for Jehovah's name.

" Thou " (v. 5) is emphatic. When the eye keeps steadfastly fastened on God's judgments upon a guilty world (v. 4), and upon His assured promise of personal salvation (v. 5), then the heart is delivered from earthly expectations, and is, at the same time, prepared to suffer calamities in sympathy with national distress.

It often happens that a christian, who has himself failed in faith and fortitude, is used by God to encourage His servants when in similar trial. Thus Jeremiah, who himself was assailed by despondency (xii. 1-5 and xv. 10-18 and xx.), comforted Baruch with the comfort wherewith he himself was comforted of God.

Perhaps Baruch desired some political or social distinction. Only those fear the world's frowns who seek its smiles.

JEREMIAH XLVI.—This closing group of prophecies (xlvi.-li.) concerned the Ten Kingdoms of Jeremiah's day under the headship of Babylon. They also concern the Ten Kingdoms of the Books of Daniel and of the Apocalypse, under the headship of the future king of Babylon.

The Ten Kingdoms here addressed are : Egypt, Philistia, Moab, Ammon, Edom, Damascus, Kedar, Hazor, Elam and Babylon.

" Against the Gentiles " (v. 1) rather, as in Revised Version, " concerning the nations." Similarly in verse 2 " against " in each case should read " concerning."

This prophecy was delivered after the death of King Josiah in the Battle of Megiddo (2 Chron. xxxv. 20-25), and four years prior to the Battle of Karchemish on the Euphrates, where Nebuchadnezzar defeated Pharaoh Necho.

The mobilisation and march of the Egyptian army is pictured in verses 3 and 4 ; its defeat in verses 5 and 6 ; its self-confidence in verse 7-9 ; its destruction, as ordained by God, in verse 10 ; its hopelessness of recovery in verse 11 ; and the world-wide knowledge of its destruction in verse 12.

This prophecy, and that which follows, should be read as in the Revised Version.

The Egyptians, rendered effeminate by luxury, employed, as mercenary soldiers, the Ethiopians, the Abyssinians, the Libyans and the Sudims. These no doubt are those who fell upon one another (v. 16), and who said, " Arise and let us go again to our own people," etc. (vs. 16 and 17).

The conquest of Egypt by Nebuchadnezzar is foretold in verses 13-26.

' The time appointed " (v. 17) possibly means a victory promised by Pharaoh at a given date.

" He " (v. 18), i.e., Nebuchadnezzar.

" Destruction " (v. 20), i.e., Gad-fly (R.V.) ; that is, Nebuchadnezzar.

A heifer was the great god of Egypt. As is the god, so are its worshippers. In verse 21 they are pictured as timid calves (R.V.). A god that flees from a fly is a poor defence. Perhaps, therefore, verses 20 and 21 are ironical.

" They " (v. 22), i.e., the Chaldeans ; " her," i.e., Egypt.

" Her forest " (v. 23), i.e., Egypt's army. " Though it cannot be searched " : possibly this means that the Egyptians boasted that their army was as impregnable as a forest.

" They " (v. 23), i.e., the Chaldeans.

" Those that seek their lives " (v. 26), i.e., the Egyptian rebels under Amasis.

" But in the latter time it shall be inhabited as in days of old " (v. 26). This prophecy respecting Egypt yet awaits fulfilment.

Admonition as well as consolation is in the message of verses 27 and 28. It assured the safety and restoration of the captives in Babylon, and, therefore, by implication, the doom of the self-willed Exiles in Egypt (xliv.).

Thus amid the welter of warring nations God watches over and guards His people, making use of public calamities as instruments for their discipline.

A serpent (v. 22) when frightened sounds its rattle and retreats. A heifer (v. 20) afraid of a gad-fly, and a serpent afraid of a woodcutter, here picture the impotency of Egypt to protect the Judean fugitives from the Chaldeans.

JEREMIAH XLVII.—The judgments on these nations made possible the sole dominion of Babylon. Restoration was promised to those exterior to Palestine, but not to those within the territory promised to Israel. Hence the judgment was to be final upon Edom, Damascus, Philistia and Hazor. When therefore the Times of the Gentiles, i.e., of Gentile domination, are fulfilled, God will restore Egypt, Elam, Moab and Ammon. In this connection the prophecies concerning Edom (xlix. 7-22 and Obad.) should be specially studied. All this illustrates the ways of God in government. He judges nations, He chastises His people (xlvi. 27 and 28), they shall not be condemned with the world, and grace abused brings a just doom, as in the case of Edom.

Three lessons are taught by the prophecy concerning Philistia : the wrath of God upon sinners ; the inability of man to save himself, or his fellows, from that wrath (v. 4) ; and the grace of God in warning sinners of its coming so that they may repent and escape.

The Word of the Lord begins the prophecy (v. 1) ; and the sword of the Lord closes it (vs. 6 and 7).

That word announced the Chaldean invasion (vs. 2 and 3 and 4), and the terror (v. 2), the feebleness (v. 3), and the anguish (v. 5) which would result.

The definiteness and the nearness of the judgment appear in the words : " Before that Pharaoh smote Gaza." This attack upon Gaza was most probably subsequent to the Battle of Megiddo in which Josiah was slain. The " remnant " of verse 4, were those left in Philistia after its devastation by the Egyptians. These were destroyed, or carried captive, by the Babylonians.

The Philistines originally came from Caphtor (v. 4). Many scholars believe it to have been a province of Lower Egypt.

" Waters " (v. 2), i.e., the Chaldeans.

Easterns when in extreme grief pluck off their hair and cut themselves (v. 5).

In a passage of sublime poetry (vs. 6 and 7) the sword of the Lord is apostrophized, and its action vindicated.

God did not wish that even one Philistine should perish, so in His love He warned them beforehand to flee from the coming wrath. But they refused to listen and obey.

JEREMIAH XLVIII.—This prophecy anticipated by about twenty-three years the overthrow of Moab by the Babylonians. It was a just judgment (vs. 26, 27 and 29 and 30). But the grace that promised a future restoration (v. 47) expressed the love which warned the Moabites in advance, so that they might escape the coming judgment.

Such is the love and grace which warn sinners to-day, and which announce a Saviour who saves from the wrath to come (1 Thess. i. 10).

"Against Moab" (v. 1), i.e., concerning Moab.

"Praise of Moab" (v. 2), i.e., praise of her military power and courage. Heshbon was the capital city of the Amorites, and Madmen was a subordinate city of the same nation. Its citizens helped in the destruction of Moab; but the Prophet here tells them that the Chaldean sword should pursue them also and cut them down.

"Luhith" (v. 5) was on a height and Horonaim lay in a valley; hence the appropriateness of the terms "going up" and "going down."

"The heath" (v. 6), or juniper-tree, suggests loneliness and depression. It was under such a tree that Elijah cast himself down.

"The spoiler" (v. 8), "the pourer" (v. 12, R.V.), "the spoiler" (v. 32), and "he" (v. 40) mean the Chaldean army. In verse 10 it is addressed, and threatened if it does its work of destruction negligently (R.V.).

Wine when at rest retains its taste and perfume, but loses both if emptied from one vessel into another, or, wine is purified by being emptied from vessel to vessel. Hence prosperity corrupts a nation but adversity purifies it.

Moab is here likened to wine, and the Babylonian monarch to a pourer-out of wine.

"Aroer" (v. 19) was a neighbouring city. Its citizens are pictured standing by the highway and looking at the Moabite fugitives and asking them what has happened. The answer is given in verse 20; and the fugitives call to the others to howl and cry with terror, and to report the news to Arnon, because the like destruction will surely overwhelm them also.

"Drunken" (v. 26), i.e., drunken with anguish.

Not only was Moab a rebel against Jehovah (v. 26), and an impure idolater, but he also skipped for joy, and laughed with derision, when the Assyrians carried the Ten Tribes into captivity. And yet the prophet asks: "Was he found among thieves?" The answer is "No," and the suggestion is that Israel did not thievingly covet the lands of the Moabites as they did those of the Israelites.

Anger and falsehood (v. 30) never accomplish anything that is worthy.

Sibmah in Moab (v. 32) was famous for its vines; they reached to the shores of the Dead Sea. "The weeping of Jazer" may be a reference to its destruction by Joshua.

Cutting the hair, lacerating the hands, and clothing with sackcloth are Eastern expressions of mourning (v. 37).

To turn the back with shame (v. 39) is to flee in battle.

The fugitives who trusted the fortress of Heshbon perished (v. 45), for a fire, i.e., treachery, consumed them.

See notes on Isa. xv. and xvi. and xxv. 10, and Amos ii. 1, 2, and Ezek. xxv. 8, 9.

JEREMIAH XLIX.—As in the judgments of the former chapters, so in those of the nations in this chapter the grace and truth that came by Jesus Christ (John i. 17) are conspicuous, i.e., the truth announcing the justly merited wrath of God, and the grace warning the guilty of that wrath, and offering deliverance from it.

Moab and Ammon, born of shame, will yet be redeemed (v. 6, with xlviii. 47).

Ammon occupied the country eastward of Jordan and northward of Moab. It was naturally strong and fertile (v. 4). Rabbah was its capital (v. 2), and her daughter-cities were numerous (vs. 2 and 3).

When the Ten Tribes were carried into captivity Ammon took possession of the territory of Gad (v. 1, with 2 Kings xiv. 26 and Amos i. 1 and 13). Hence the question of verse 1, which should read as in the Revised Version.

Malcam, Milcom or Molech was the god of the Ammonites.

"His people" (v. 1), i.e., the worshippers of Malcam; "his cities," i.e., the cities of Gad.

"Her daughters" (v. 2), i.e., the villages around Rabbah.

" Their king " (v. 3), i.e., Malcam.

" Thy flowing valley ' (v. 4), i.e., thy valley flowing with blood. The Ammonites gloried in their great valley as being impregnable, but the prophet here foretold that it should flow with blood.

" Her treasures " (v. 4), i.e., her military resources.

" None shall gather up him that wandereth " (v. 5), i.e., no officer would remain to reorganize the disbanded soldiers.

The prophecy concerning Edom, that is Esau, and his country Idumea, should be read in the light of Hebrews xii. 16 ; where the Holy Spirit speaks of him as " a profane person." Hence his judgment, as a nation, will be as final as that of Sodom and Gomorrah (vs. 17 and 18). Compare l. 40. Similar guilt brings similar punishment.

Esau was famous for wisdom (Gen. xxxvi. 15, Job. ii, 11, Obad. 8). (v. 7).

Dedan (v. 8) was a tribe associated with Esau and descended from Abraham (Gen. xxv. 1-3, Isa. xxi. 13, Ezek. xxv. 13).

Ezekiel xxv. should be read in connection with the judgments upon Ammon and Edom. These nations assisted the Chaldeans in their attack upon Judah and exulted at her fall (2 Kings xxiv. 2, Ps. lxxxiii. and Zephaniah ii. 8 and 9).

The argument of verses 9 and 10 is that a grape-gatherer might leave a few grapes, or a house-breaker some pieces of property, but that God, in His just severity, would absolutely extinguish Edom. " He is not " (v. 10), means he shall be caused to cease to exist.

The compassionate invitation of verse 11 may be addressed to Israel, oppressed by Edom ; or it may express the extinction of all the adult males in Edom.

The first member of verse 12 applies to Israel ; the second member to Edom. If God's children must be punished for sin, how much more those who are not His children !

The present day desolation of Petra, of Bozra and her sixty cities (vs. 13-18) fulfils, and satisfies, the predictions of these verses. " He " (v. 19), i.e., the Chaldean general ; " the strong," i.e., Edom ; " him," i.e., Edom ; " her," i.e., Idumea the country of Esau ; shepherd, i.e., ruler ; " habitation " (v. 19) " habitations " (v. 20), i.e., sheepfolds with pasture.

" He " (v. 22), i.e., the Chaldean.

Damascus was the capital of Syria and here intends that whole country (v. 23).

" Sorrow on the sea " (v. 23). This may mean sorrow on the sea-shore, or anxiety restless as the sea.

" Not left " (v. 25). This should read : " become defenceless." The helplessness of Damascus is the subject of the lamentation.

" Kedar " (v. 28), i.e., the Arabians, sons of Ishmael.

Hazor a nation in the neighbourhood of the Persian Gulf ; neighbours of the Arabians.

" To dwell deep " (v. 30) possibly means to retire into the depths of the eastern deserts. These verses should read as in the Revised Version. Contrast Damascus and Hazor. The latter was to continue, but enfeebled ; the other, to perish absolutely. So has it come to pass. God's word is definite and true.

Elam was situated to the north-west of Persia (v. 34). The Elamites helped Nebuchadnezzar against Judea ; hence their punishment.

The gracious prediction of verse 39 had a partial fulfilment in Acts ii. 9, when Elamites heard the Gospel in their own tongue.

But the doom of verse 36, as well as the promise of verse 39, demand the present existence of the outcasts of Elam. The only people, other than the Jews who, to-day, are scattered in all nations, and yet do not mingle with them, are the Gipsies. Can these mysterious people be the outcasts of Elam ?

JEREMIAH L. and LI.—These chapters group together six distinct prophecies concerning Babylon and its judgment, and with each prophecy there is linked a message of consolation for Israel.

The six prophecies may, perhaps, be thus indicated :

Babylon and Israel	(l. 2-7).
Babylon and Israel	(l. 8-20).
Babylon and Israel	(l. 21-34).
Babylon and Israel	(l. 35-li. 5).
Babylon and Israel	(li. 6-19).
Babylon and Israel	(li. 20 58).

The House of David having failed as Jehovah's Viceroy, the government of the earth was committed to the Babylonian monarch and his successors. But these also failed, for they introduced idolatry and violence, and their present day heirs are no better. Judgment must, therefore, fall upon them, for God is Righteousness, and He must destroy evil as light destroys darkness. The entire period of this domination in the earth is named in the Scriptures "The Times of the Gentiles"; and its last monarch will be, as its first, a king of Babylon. These six prophecies embrace both these kings; for though mainly addressed to the monarchy that was to be destroyed by the Medes (vs. 3, 9, 41, li. v. 2, 11, 27, 28, and 56), at which time all the Hebrew Exiles were delivered from bondage, and offered restoration to their own land with Ezra, and Nehemiah, yet these prophecies contain predictions (v. 4) that the future alone can satisfy, when the government of the earth, as originally purposed by God, will be given to Israel, who will then become Jehovah's sceptre (li. 19).

As in all prophecy, so here (v. 1) the speaker is Jehovah, and the instrument through which He speaks, the mouth of Jeremiah. The words are, therefore, God's words.

The "nation from the north" (v. 3) was the Median; but a future enemy is here pointed to, as is evident from the statements of verses 4 and 5.

Israel's "shepherds," i.e., rulers, as for example Jeroboam and Ahaz, caused them to turn away from Jehovah to the idols worshipped on the mountains and hills (v. 6).

In those days idolatrous shrines were usually placed on such elevations; just as to-day thousands of hills throughout the world are crowned with shrines of the Virgin, or of Buddha.

The invitation of verse 8 was addressed to the Exiles. Their leaders are there pictured as he-goats. Those exiles who obeyed this command escaped the suffering which at that time fell upon those who disobeyed it. Compare Rev. xviii. 4 and Luke xxi. 20 and 21.

"Your mother" (v. 12), i.e., Babylon, which was chief of the confederated nations who were the "destroyers" of God's pleasant land of Palestine (v. 11). The desolation of the idolatrous land of Chaldea was, therefore, a just judgment.

"To give the hand" (v. 15) signified surrender, as "Hands up" signifies to-day.

"I have found a ransom" (Job xxxiii. 24). "We have found the Messias" (John i. 41) and "the iniquity of Israel shall be sought for and shall not be found" (v. 20). These statements declare God's provision of an atoning Saviour for guilty men, the simplicity of its appropriation, and the assured result of its possession.

"Merathaim" (v. 21) a symbolical name for Babylon meaning "doubly rebellious." This double rebellion is recorded in verses 24 and 29.

"Pekod" (v. 21), i.e., visitation, or punishment. Pekod was a province of ancient Assyria having Nineveh as its capital. Both Assyria and Chaldea oppressed the Children of Israel; and there may be a reference to this double oppression in the use of the name Merathaim.

The command of verse 21, may be understood as addressed to the Median monarch (Isa. xiii. and xiv.), or to Jeremiah who is here commanded to do what he was inspired to announce.

Babylon was God's "hammer" (v. 23) to break the nations (li. 20-23); but judgment fell upon her because she rejected the Divine revelation given to her through Daniel; and because she exceeded her instructions (Dan. v. 17-23 and Isaiah xlvii. 5, 6, and Zech. i. 15).

Cyrus laid a snare for Babylon (v. 24) by diverting the Euphrates; and by this means he captured its commercial, and larger portion, on the Eastern bank of the river, without the Western portion being aware of the fact.

The Medes and their allies are addressed in verses 26 and 27.

"Bullocks" (v. 27), i.e., princes.

Dan. v. 1-5, records the dishonour done to the Temple of Jehovah which cried aloud for vengeance (v. 28).

The success of the Medes against Babylon is predicted in verses 29-32.

Across this scene of judgment shine the bright rays of verses 33 and 34. God never loses sight of His people, even when, as is here suggested, they give up all hope of escape from their oppressors who hold them fast in slavery and refuse to let them go. But they are consoled, and their faith nourished, by the statement that their Redeemer is strong, and has mighty armies of angelic soldiers under His command, and that He will give rest to them and their land, but recompense disquiet to their oppressors (2 Thess. i. 6 and 7).

Not by mere power but by righteousness does God deliver His people ; for He pleads their cause (v. 34), the plea being the Person and Atoning Work of their High Priest and Saviour.

The fourth prophecy of this group occupies, as already pointed out, verses 35-li. 5.

The Chaldeans claimed to be wise men, they boasted especially of their astrological knowledge (v. 35), but in verse 36 they are declared to be " liars," that is, impostors who shall " dote," i.e., who shall be shewn to be foolish by the non-fulfilment of their prognostications.

The diversion of the Euphrates by Cyrus is intimated in verse 38.

The eruption of the Medes and Persians is indicated in verses 41-43 ; and their leader Cyrus is compared in verse 44 to a lion.

" The habitation of the strong " (v. 44), i.e., Babylon ; " them," i.e., its defenders ; " her," i.e., Babylon. Compare xlix. 18 and its note.

"Whoso is chosen " (v. 44, R.V.), i.e., Cyrus.

" Who will appoint Me a time ? " (v. 44), i.e., Who can give Me commands ?

" Who is the shepherd," i.e., the ruler, " that will stand before Me," that is, that can oppose Me.

" Desolate with them " (v. 45), i.e., the city was to be desolate without inhabitants, and its citizens were to be desolate without a home, for they should be dragged away into slavery and exile. There would, there-therefore, be a mutual desolation. Thus would the judgment upon Babylon and her children correspond to that upon Zion and her sons.

The reading of li. 3 should follow the Authorised Version and not the Revised Version. This is determined by the last line of the verse.

" Their land is full of guilt " (v. 5, R.V.), that is, full of desolation in consequence of their guilt. The argument is that, although the desolation of Palestine seemed to evidence Jehovah's desertion of His people, the destruction of Babylon proved the contrary, hence the importance of the word " for "

The command to flee out of Babylon (v. 6 and l. 8, and compare Rev. xviii. 4) appears to have been addressed to the nations as well as to the Exiles.

Babylon was the Head of gold (Daniel ii. 38), and the golden cup (v. 7) of dominion in the earth was committed to its princes. But they filled that pure and costly vessel with the maddening wine of idolatry. Hence the justice of their doom.

The prediction of verse 8 yet awaits ful-filment, for ancient Babylon was slowly, and not suddenly, destroyed. Restored Babylon will perish like Sodom (Rev. xvi. 19 and xvii. and xviii).

" We tried to heal Babylon " (v. 9). " We " here means God's ancient people. Their efforts failed ; as have also failed the efforts of God's present people to heal corrupt Christendom, the modern spiritual Babylon.

" Our righteousness " (v. 10), i.e., the faithfulness of God to His promises upon which the Exiles reposed, and not the righteous conduct of the Exiles themselves. The words " our righteousness " stand over against the words " her judgment," that is : to Babylon God recompensed judgment ; to Israel, righteousness. Both words, there-fore, relate to God and His action. The second member of verse 10 makes this plain ; for the activity that was to be celebrated in Zion was that of God, and not the bad conduct or the good conduct of men.

The argument of verses 11-14 is the useless-ness of a military defence of Babylon, for God had purposed, and would accomplish, her destruction.

" Many waters " (v. 13), i.e., the Euphrates which largely caused the prosperity of Babylon. Compare " the many waters " of Rev. xvii. 1.

" Measure " (v. 13) i.e., the termination or limit.

The creative power, glory, and wisdom of God (vs. 15 and 16) are contrasted with the ignorance of idolaters and with the vanity of their idols (vs. 17 and 18), and verse 19 triumphantly exclaims : " Not like these (i.e., the idols) is the Portion of Jacob (i.e., Emmanuel), for He is the Former of all things, and the Sceptre of His inheritance is Israel," etc.

The last of these six prophecies concerning Babylon (vs. 20-58) opens with a charge to Cyrus (vs. 20-23) to execute God's righteous judgment upon that guilty city because of her cruelty to Israel and to the nations (vs. 24, 34, 35, 49, and 56).

The ten terms of the commission to Cyrus (the tenfold " with thee ") reveal the justice which inflicted on Babylon miseries similar to those that she inflicted on others.

In the Bible great empires are addressed as " mountains " (v. 25).

The countries in verse 27 are the modern Armenia and Asia Minor.

" At one end " (v. 31), this would better read : " at each end " ; for thus the soldiers of Cyrus entered the city, marching along the dry bed of the Euphrates.

Lofty walls, pierced with passages, bordered the river on each side. These " passages " were defended by palisades. The reed and passages of verse 32 refer to these. " Stopped " should read " seized " or " surprised."

" Her sea " (v. 36), i.e., the Euphrates.

The drunken and boastful feast of Belchazzar is pictured in verses 38-40. Historians suggest it was celebrated in honour of the great goddess Shack, and was accompanied by grossly obscene ceremonies. The introduction of the Temple vessels (Dan. v. 2) into such an orgie of idolatry and impurity, emphasized the bold vileness of the Babylonian monarch.

They boasted like lions (v. 38), and heated themselves with wine (v. 39) ; but God intervenes with fine irony saying : " I will make their feasts, and I will make them drunken (with blood) that they may rejoice, and sleep a perpetual sleep, and not wake, saith the Lord."

The " sea " and the " waves " (v. 42), i.e., the Median armies and soldiers.

The Wall of Babylon (v. 44) was three hundred feet high, ninety feet wide, and sixty miles long. It formed a square having twenty-five huge gates of brass on each face, and two hundred and fifty towers, that is, in all, one hundred brazen gates, and one thousand towers. The Babylonians believed the city to be impregnable. They boasted of the height and strength of its walls (v. 53). History records that the inhabitants of all Chaldea retired into the city for safety on the approach of the enemy and thus their slaughter, there " in the midst of her " fulfilled the predictions of verses 47 and 49.

History also records that the first year (v. 46) a rumour reached Babylon of the Median preparations for invasion ; in the second year a rumour arrived announcing that the Medes had set out on the expedition ; and the following year, which was the third of Belshazzar, they captured the city.

Thus the Great Shepherd loved and cared for His people, so that those who read and believed the Bible were able, guided by these verses (vs. 44 and 45) written seventy years beforehand, to put themselves in safety, and prepare for their return home (vs. 50 and 51), and so be relieved from the confusion and shame which they suffered during their long exile.

" The great voice " (v. 55) and " her waves " i.e., the loud boastings of Babylon. Supply with blood " after " drunk " (v. 57).

" Shall labour " (v. 58), better translated : " shall have laboured." Immense multitudes of slaves were employed in building the mighty walls, and fashioning in the fire the brazen gates, of Babylon ; but their labour was in vain, and only secured weariness.

This result is twice emphatically declared (vs. 58 and 64). Such is the one and only and invariable result of human toil, whether religious, or physical, without God.

This volume of prophecies concerning Babylon was despatched to that city six years before the destruction of Jerusalem by the Babylonians. Thus were God's people strengthened in the time of their supreme calamity.

The sinking of the book in the Euphrates (v. 63), apart from the symbolic action, is very important as shewing that prophecies were committed to writing, and copied, so that it was not a loss to sink one of the copies in this manner.

JEREMIAH LII.—The capture of Jerusalem, and the deportation of its people, have little interest for historians, but so great interest for God that the event is narrated four times, and with considerable detail (2 Kings xxiv. 25, 2 Chron. xxxvi., Jeremiah xxxix. and Jeremiah lii.).

This repetition of the narrative, together with Luke xix. 41 and Matt. xxiii. 37, shews how deeply God loves His people, even when their conduct proves them to be wholly unworthy of being loved.

Did children act toward a father as Israel acted toward God, they would certainly extinguish all love for themselves in their father's heart. But it is impossible to exhaust the love that fills God's heart.

But, as in the case of Jerusalem, appalling chastisements must visit aggravated sinfulness (vs. 2-3).

Disobedience to the Word of God ensures hunger, defeat and slavery (vs. 4-7). Many in their spiritual history have had this sad experience.

No amount of skill, or sagacity, can defeat the purposes and judgments of God. Zedekiah and his soldiers thought to escape by making a hole in the city wall at night time; but they were defeated and captured in the very scene of Israel's first victory.

So in the Christian life defeat may dishonour a once victorious field when there is a departure from first love.

The sentence pronounced upon Zedekiah for the breach of his oath of allegiance, and for his rebellion (2 Chron. xxxvi. 13), was a terrible one. It contained five counts. The execution of his sons before his eyes; the slaughter of his princes; the loss of his eyes; his degradation to slavery; and his condemnation to penal labour for life. "The prison" (v. 11) was similar to that in which Samson was confined. It was a house of hard labour.

There is no discrepancy between verse 12, and 2 Kings xxv. 8, for "unto" and "into" are not the same thing.

For notes on verses 17 and 23, see 1 Kings vii.

These beauteous and precious vessels and pillars pictured the power and glories of Christ. As the material Babylon robbed Jerusalem of these, so "the world" robs the church, and the believer, of spiritual power and wealth when it gets the upper hand.

"Seven men" (v. 25). 2 Kings xxv. 19, records "five men." This marks accuracy and not error, for the greater includes the less, and Riblah, being many days journey from Jerusalem, two of the captives may have escaped or died during the journey.

The great captivity is that of verse 27; three lesser captivities are those of verses 28-30.

The Hebrews and the Babylonians did not reckon time in an exactly similar manner. Hence the seventh year of Nebuchnadezzar, according to the one reckoning, would be the eighth according to the other (2 Kings xxiv. 12, 14, and 16).

The numbers of the captives recorded in 2 Kings xxiv. and those recorded in this chapter, refer to different stages of the great deportation of the people as a whole; and, further, some of these numbers related to the citizens of Jerusalem, but others to the country people who had taken refuge there.

Probably two days intervened between the liberation of Jehoiachin (v. 31) and his appearance at court (2 Kings xxv. 27).

LAMENTATIONS

LAMENTATIONS.—He who in these five elegies weeps because of the destruction of Jerusalem is He who wept because of her desolation (Luke xiii. 34, and xix. 41).

He identifies Himself with the guilty city, burdens Himself with her guilt, and suffers the Divine wrath as a consequence (chs. i. 12-14 and iii. 1-21).

Again, as High Priest, He makes His people's griefs His own, and personifies their sorrows (iii. 22-66 and v.).

Each elegy contains 22 stanzas arranged as the Hebrew alphabet, except the third which has three times twenty-two. See notes on chapter iii.

LAMENTATIONS I.—The frequent use in this Book of expressions peculiar to the Pentateuch, and especially to Deuteronomy, proves how well-known those ancient books were to Jeremiah and his contemporaries.

The destruction of Jerusalem by the Chaldeans has little interest for the historian, but so much for the Spirit of Christ that He wrote these five poems!

Lovers and friends (v. 2), i.e., the Allies whom Jerusalem trusted in preference to Jehovah.

Judah's captivity was to be an exile of affliction and servitude (v. 3).

"Straits" (v. 3), i.e., narrow passages in which fugitives can be overtaken and captured. The language is figurative.

"The ways of Zion" (v. 4), i.e., the roads leading to Zion, crowded in happier days with the worshippers going up to the feasts of Jehovah.

"Her adversaries are become the head" (v. 5). Compare Deut. xxviii. 13 and 44.

Sin was the procuring cause of the city's ruin (v. 8).

To shut out eternity is to shut out the Comforter, and to fall wonderfully (v. 9).

"My affliction" (v. 9). Here the Messiah personates Jerusalem.

"I am become vile" (v. 11), i.e., in the eyes of the nations.

When the Messiah's soul was made an offering for sin upon the altar of Calvary then was fulfilled verses 12-14 ; for although these words have an application to Jerusalem, their interpretation belongs to Him.

True repentance vindicates God and condemns self (v. 18).

"The day Thou hast proclaimed" (v. 21). The terms of this proclamation are found in Jer. l. and li. which declared that the cruelty which Babylon inflicted on Jerusalem the Medes would inflict upon her (v. 22). From this fact may be learned the lesson not to rejoice when calamity falls upon an enemy.

LAMENTATIONS II.—The deep sorrow of the second Elegy was occasioned by the recognition of the fact that the wrath which overthrew the Temple was Divine wrath. Never had there been, therefore, such sorrow.

But this foreshadowed the wrath which smote the True Temple at Calvary. That was sorrow indeed, for that Temple was without blemish and undefiled, whilst the Temple at Jerusalem, which God had planned and set up, man had polluted.

It is this latter fact which gives the sad keynote of Jeremiah's ministry. God disowned that which He Himself had established, and transferred to the Gentile the dominion of the earth entrusted to Israel.

But it could not have been otherwise under the First Covenant, for its promises were based upon obedience—an obedience which the natural man cannot give ; for the carnal mind is not subject to the Law of God, neither indeed can be (Rom. viii. 7).

"The beauty of Israel" (v. 1) and "His footstool," i.e., the Temple and the Ark of the Covenant.

The noise of the Chaldean soldiers in the Temple (v. 7) is likened to the noise of a Feast-Day ; but how sad a contrast as to the occasion of it !

" To stretch out the line " (v. 8) expressed unsparing demolition, and, perhaps, mainly with the object of discovering hidden treasure.

" The law " (v. 9), i.e., the Bible. It is mostly prized where it cannot be had. In the Middle Ages £25 was given for one page of it.

" The liver " (v. 11) was regarded by the Easterns as the seat of the emotions.

The statement of verse 13 is that it was impossible to console Jerusalem by pointing to others in a like affliction, for her misery was great like the sea, and beyond human aid. Mourners are often consoled by knowing that others suffer like griefs.

As to-day so then, the fashionable preachers did not discover, i.e., unveil, the iniquity which caused Israel's captivity (v. 14).

Loss of fellowship with God means the loss of joy and moral power and perfection (v. 15).

" Cried " (v. 18), i.e., cried with anguish unto Jehovah. The word " saying " should be supplied after Jehovah.

LAMENTATIONS III.—This Third Elegy contains, like the others, twenty-two stanzas arranged as the Hebrew alphabet ; but it presents this special feature, that each stanza consists of three verses, each verse commencing with the same letter of the alphabet.

This triple formation harmonizes with the triple relationship of the Elegy to the Spirit of Christ in the Prophet personally, in the Remnant prophetically, and in Christ Himself absolutely.

The suffering here expressed, and felt, was educative with regard to Jeremiah and the Remnant, but absolute and perfect with respect to Christ.

These deep sorrows were moral teachers to the faithful in Israel, and led them to repentance and to a richer knowledge of God.

But with respect to Christ it was not so; for all was perfection in Him, but this perfection involved a depth of agony impossible for man to fathom. In the completeness of His sinless nature He identified Himself perfectly with human sin and guilt, took His place in the midst of evil, drew it all into Himself with an intelligence that was infinite, and, in the fulness of that knowledge, suffered with equal intelligence the fulness of the wrath of God. All this is beyond human knowledge.

Yet the suffering of the Messiah, of the Remnant, and of the Prophet, as unveiled in this elegy, had this in common : that the sharpest agony suffered was, that the wrath of God should fall, with repeated fury, upon that which He Himself had loved and established. It was that which caused Christ to weep aloud over Jerusalem.

The Prophet's personal sufferings in his repeated scourgings and imprisonments foreshadowed those of the Greater Prophet. He loved the people, but they hated him ; he sought their good, but they sought his life ; and what deepened the anguish was, that they were God's people, and that the Prophet, though he knew them to be such, and loved them, yet had to tell them faithfully of the wrath that was to overwhelm them.

Placed as he was in the midst of the evil, he found that when the Divine Hand had, in just judgment, broken to pieces the nation that that Hand had established, the Prophet learned (vs. 22–33) that God Himself is a sufficing portion for faith in the absence of all outward spiritual fellowships.

This is an important principle for christian people to-day, and since the day, that judgment fell upon the Church of God soon after the death of the Apostle Paul, and destroyed it as a visible and corporate witness for Christ. Repeated efforts have been made to reconstruct it. but in vain. Man has established many imitations of it, but they are only imitations. But God remains ; and in the ruin and confusion of to-day His child finds Him to be what Jeremiah found Him to be—a satisfying portion for the soul

The Spirit of Christ in the Prophet, as in the Psalmist, and in the Apostles, prayed for the vengeance of God upon the enemies of Truth (vs. 64-66).

" The man " (v. 1), in Hebrew : the great, the strong man, the hero, i.e., Israel.

" Their song " (v. 14), i.e., their mocking song. See verse 63.

Verse 19 should read as in the Revised Version.

" For " (v. 31), better read " but," so as to shew the contrast with verses 28-30.

Confession of sin, and testimony as to God's readiness to forgive and to bless (vs. 22-45), became the Prophet and become the Remnant, but are only perfect when uttered by Israel's High Priest.

The primitive text of verses 20 and 21 reads :—" Yea, verily Thou wilt remember, and Thy soul will mourn over Me. This I recall to my heart, and, therefore, I have hope."

LAMENTATIONS IV.—In this elegy and in the following the Prophet contemplates the ruin of what had been the Kingdom of God, but he makes this survey in fellowship with God as one who had found rest in God.

Three stages may be noticed in his experience as revealed in these elegies : First, his anguish and confusion that the wrath of God should fall with such fury on the Kingdom of God. Second, the relief of finding in God Himself a satisfying fount of consolation and intelligence in the midst of the ruin. Third, being now at peace in God he presents the whole affliction of the people to God, confesses their sins, and prays and believes for the creation of a New Israel.

This progress and experience and intelligence is very important, and has an application to present-day difficulties. God never repairs what He has judged. Efforts to restore the apostolic church are hopeless and impious. But God has not changed ; and His broken and scattered people find Him to be their Sanctuary in exile, as Daniel and the faithful among the exiles found Him to be. They did not erect an imitation Temple in Babylon with imitation Levitical worship. They met together to read the Bible and pray. See note on Ezek. xi. 16.

It was otherwise with the self-willed fugitives in Egypt. History records that they built a Temple and established a Biblical worship. But far from their action being recognized and applauded in the Word of God, it is wholly ignored.

Bringing God into circumstances terrorizes the sinner, but tranquillizes the saint. Such tranquillity was felt by the Prophet. The sense of the affliction saddened him with its full weight ; but he could cast that burden on the Lord, and prove that He is good to them that wait for Him and on Him (iii. 25).

" No hands stayed on her " (v. 6), i.e., her overthrow was directly from God.

" Known " (v. 8), i.e., recognized.

Jerusalem was deemed to be impregnable (v. 12) ; but the following verse states that sin was the cause of her overthrow.

" They cried " (v. 15), i.e., men cried to the citizens of Jerusalem that they should leave the city because it was polluted with blood.

The transposition of the Hebrew letters of the alphabet in verses 16 and 17, as also in chapters ii. and iii., is clearly designed, and not erroneous, as some suppose. The design may be to fasten the attention of the reader upon the cause of the suffering stated in the displaced verse. It is to be found in the transposed verse which follows.

" The nation that could not save " (v. 17) was Egypt. " They " (v. 18), i.e., the Chaldeans.

" Rejoice and be glad " (v. 21). This is ironical. The cup of God's wrath is the cup of this verse.

For Edom (v. 21) there is no promise of restoration, but, on the contrary, a disclosure of her sins ; for Zion, a full judgment, but a covering up of her sins.

LAMENTATIONS V.—As in the Psalms so in these elegies, the Spirit of God expresses His thoughts through those whom He chooses as vessels of His testimony, in circumstances exhibiting the judgment of God on that which He had Himself founded. This is one of the beauties and marvels of inspiration. The Spirit Himself furnishes a picture of His own activities in the hearts of feeble men. Such is His love for them. He hearkens to their sighs, records their fears, and registers their victories.

" To give the hand " (v. 6), i.e., to surrender and accept slavery.

The Assyrians, the Egyptians and the Chaldeans being children of Ham, were " servants " (v. 8). That they should rule over the sons of Shem was shame indeed.

" Their " (v. 12). This may mean the Chaldean's hand.

" Remainest " (v. 19), i.e., " sittest as king." Compare Ps. xxix. 10.

True conversion is a Divine and not a human action (v. 21).

The Hebrews when reading in public Ecclesiastes, Isaiah and Malachi, repeat the last verse but one so as to end the reading with comfort.

EZEKIEL

Ezekiel was contemporary with Jeremiah and Daniel. He was carried away in the second captivity (2 Kings xxiv. 10). He was a priest (i. 3). Obedient to Jeremiah xxix. 5 he dwelt in his own house (viii. 1). He was married, and his wife died in the year when the final siege of Jerusalem began.

The order of the prophecies in his book is moral and not chronological.

The structure of the Book may be thus exhibited :

The Desolation (i.-xii. 28).
 The Prophets (xiii. 1-23).
  The Elders (xiv. 1-11).
   The Nation (xiv. 12-xix. 14).
   The Elders (xx. 1-44).
   The Nation (xx. 45-xxxiii. 33).
  The Shepherds (xxxiv. 1-31).
 The Restoration (xxxv. 1-xlviii. 35).

The correspondence between "nation' and "nation" appears thus :

The Land (xiv. 12-xv. 8).
 The City (xvi. 1-63).
  The Foe (xvii. 1-24).
   The People (xviii. 1-32).
    The Captives (xix. 1-14).

The Land (xx. 45-xxii. 31).
 The City (xxiii. 1-49).
  The Foe (xxiv. 1-xxxii. 32).
   The People (xxxiii. 1-22).
    The Captives (xxxiii. 33).

The great subject of the Book is the retiring from, and the return to, the Temple at Jerusalem, of the Glory of God.

That glory is seen in vision in chapters i. and x.

It leaves slowly (x. 3, 4, 18, 19), and returns suddenly (xliii. 1-5).

Such is the way of love : it lingers when retiring, it hastens when returning.

Ezekiel prophesied for twenty-two years. His death is not recorded in Scripture. Tradition states he was one of those referred to in Heb. xi. 37, as having been stoned to death.

The throne of God seen in vision in chapters i. and x. was at that time removed from Jerusalem to the Heavens, because the government of the earth was taken from Israel and conferred upon the Gentile. Hence Daniel spake of Him as the God of the Heavens.

The Cherubim, also called Seraphim and Teraphim, which words are Chaldean, are mysterious angelic beings connected with the throne of God in relation to the earth. Their number " four " indicates this relationship. They represent animated nature : man, the animals—wild (the lion), and domestic (the ox)—and birds and fishes (the eagle). They express the intelligence, the majesty, the stability and swiftness of the glory of God in creation. Their purpose appears to be to present perpetually before the throne of God the perfection of animated creation as originally designed ; to be the executors of the wrath brought upon creation by the Fall ; and to be the guardians of the hope of a restored creation.

Hence they appear at the gate of Eden guarding the Way of Life, upon the veil of the Temple predicting the incarnation, upon the Mercy-Seat witnessing to the atonement, and in Rev. iv. leading the song in celebration of Redemption.

The Teraphim were most likely idolatrous imitations of the Cherubim, a description of whom had been handed on by Noah and his sons. Thus the worship that should have been addressed to God Himself was offered to these angelic creatures.

The winged bulls, and other grotesque creations of Chaldean idolatry, accompanied by sculptured trees and flowers, were very probably intended to represent the Garden of Eden and the Cherubim.

Ezekiel in the Book is addressed as " Son of Man " one hundred times—possibly in contradistinction to the Cherubim. Christ is declared in the New Testament to be " The Son of Man," ninety-two times.

EZEKIEL I.-II. 2.—The spiritual life commences by the revelation of Christ to the soul (Matt. xi. 27). Then occur the New Birth and Conversion. Abraham (Acts vii. 2), Isaac (Gen. xxvi. 2), Jacob (Gen. xlviii. 3), Moses (Exod. iii. 2), and Samuel, Isaiah, Jeremiah, and the apostle Paul (Acts ix. 3), all illustrate this foundation truth.

" The thirtieth year " (v. 1), i.e., of the Babylonian kingdom. This synchronizes with the discovery of the Bible in the reign of king Josiah, and the consequent revival.

" The heavens were opened " (v. 1). This is one of the compensations accompanying rejection with Christ. Ezekiel was a type of the rejected Messiah. It was when Stephen was being stoned that he saw the heavens opened ; it was during his lonely banishment on Patmos that John enjoyed a similar vision ; and it was from his Roman dungeon that Paul wrote to the Ephesians about their being seated in the heavenly places.

The captive slaves by the river Chebar were pitied by their proud brethren in Jerusalem because they were shut away from the Temple and its services. But where was the God of glory ? Not in His Temple, which He had forsaken (ch. x. 4, 18, and xi. 23), but among the despised captives in Babylonia (ch. i.).

So was it when the God of Israel came to earth. The Temple services were daily celebrated with great splendour but where were Jehovah and the glory ? He was outside of it all, and was to be found in Bethany with a little company of despised people.

Four statements relating to inspiration appear in verses 1-3. First : The heavens were opened. Second : Ezekiel saw visions from God. Third : The word of the Lord came actually to him. Fourth : The hand of the Lord came upon him. Thus of these experiences three were outward and one inward ; and thus was he enabled and com-pelled to speak the very words of God (ii. 7).

" Expressly " (v. 3), i.e., " in reality," " without doubt."

The great subject of this chapter is the Man in the Glory (v. 26).

" Infolding itself " (v. 4), i.e., a fire flashing continually, and fed of itself. This was the pillar of fire and cloud—the glory of the God of Israel—that appeared in the Desert, and in the bush (Exod. iii. 2).

" Straight feet " (v. 7), i.e., not at right angles but shaped like those of an ox. This emphasizes that the cherubim did not move by walking.

Their hands and their wings were in proportion. It is not always so with Christian people. Some are all wings and no hands, i.e., visionary and unpractical, and some are all hands and no wings, i.e., very practical but without vision.

Verse 13, should perhaps read as in the Revised Version margin, thus : " As for the likeness of the living creatures their appearance was like burning coals of fire. And there was like the appearance of a great lamp (lamps, plural of Majesty) : it went up and down among the living creatures."

This great lamp symbolized the Holy Spirit, and reveals the energy which moved the cherubim and the wheels. This lamp appears in Gen. xv. 17 (see notes on that chapter).

The wheels and the cherubim were one in intelligence and glory. The One Spirit energized both. What the wheels signify is difficult to understand.

These glorious beings were beneath the firmament (vs. 22, 23 and Gen. i. 6) ; but the throne was above the firmament (v. 26) ; and the Man on the throne was the Messiah, Jesus Christ the Lord. Associated with the throne was the rainbow (v. 28, and Rev. iv. 3). Compare Exod. xxiv. 9-18.

" I fell upon my face " (v. 28). This is the proper posture of the sinner. " I heard a voice " this is conversion, " stand upon thy feet " (ii. 1), this is life and power. " The Spirit entered into me (v. 2) and I heard Him speak." The Divine Word is carried into the soul by the Divine Spirit, Who first humbles, then exalts, and strengthens and equips and gives an intelligence and a disposition that can hear and obey the Voice of God.

The cherubim displayed the glory of the Man on the throne in His relationship to creation and redemption. Each cherub had four faces, four wings, four hands and four wheels. All was perfection and proportion. Character, emotion, action, and subjection are suggested by these endowments. Equal intelligence indwelt their entire being, and the One Spirit energized them all. Christ in the perfection and proportion of His Nature as the glory of God, revealed in His life on earth that glory in its moral splendour. This appears in the Four Gospels. In them, He is portrayed as the Lion (Matt.), the Ox or Cherub (Mark), the Man (Luke) and the Eagle (John). Thus He is the true Cherubim in their totality.

EZEKIEL II. 3 - III. 3.—Ezekiel in this Book is addressed as a son of man, and not as a son of Abraham, for Israel was now Lo-ammi. Jesus was The Son of Man. This was His title in rejection ; hence He forbade His disciples to announce Him as the Messiah, for He, as the Son of Man, was to suffer (Luke ix.).

He was rejected by His own, and, consequently, outside of Israel claimed this title of The Son of Man ; that is, the only true, real Man—the only perfect human servant of God.

The words (v. 7) which Ezekiel was to speak were to be the words of Adonai Jehovah. God was their Author (v. 4).

The title Adonai Jehovah (Heb.) is characteristic of Ezekiel's prophecies. It occurs two hundred and fourteen times. It is very rarely used in the other prophets. The title harmonizes with the action of God in Ezekiel's day. He had, in just wrath, forsaken His people, and was now acting as Adon, or Lord, of the whole earth. But yet He had not cast off His people for ever, therefore the title Jehovah is retained.

The true moral character of the prophet's auditors is declared in verses 4-6 : hard-faced, stubborn-hearted, rebellious, briers, thorns and scorpions. This description is true of modern congregations ; and when the Spirit of God, through faithful preachers, declares the fact, a few accept His testimony, and, humble and contrite, seek the Saviour ; but the majority are filled with rage.

The Book contained lamentation, mourning and woe, and yet was sweet to Ezekiel, as it was also to John (Rev. x.), for the Words of God are ever sweet to a spiritual palate. But they are bitter to the flesh

(iii. 14) ; for they judge its nature and activities, and announce the Wrath of God which is coming upon it.

Before the preacher can speak with effect to his fellow sinners he must personally experience the sweetness and bitterness of the Words of God, as given forth by the Holy Spirit in the Book of God.

EZEKIEL III. 4-27.—Ezekiel's ministry here begins. Its character should be compared with that of Jeremiah's. His ministry was exercised while God was yet in relationship with Israel, and while He yet spoke of them as " My people." Ezekiel's ministry was addressed to Israel after the rupture of the Divine relationship, and when Israel was " not My people." Jeremiah warned the nation of God's threatened abandonment of them ; Ezekiel exposed the moral conduct which caused them to be forsaken. Jeremiah predicted the rupture ; Ezekiel justified it.

Such being the circumstances it is harmonious that he should be addressed as a son of man, and that God should act under the title of Adonai-Jehovah, rather than Elohim-Jehovah.

The prophet was told beforehand that his fellow captives would refuse to accept his message from God (v. 7) ; but, at the same time, he was inspired to predict the birth and glory of the New Israel (xl.-xlviii.).

The Divine statement (v. 6)," Surely they would hearken unto thee," throws a shaft of light across the darkness of the heathen world.

" All my words " (v. 10) ; " thus saith Jehovah Adonai (v. 11) ; " The hand of the Lord " (v. 14) ; " The Word of the Lord " (v. 16) ; " The Word at My mouth " (v. 17) ; " When I say " (v. 18) ; " When I speak with thee " (v. 27) ; " I will open thy mouth and thou shalt speak to them saying : thus saith Jehovah Adonai "—all these terms affirm inspiration.

The exclamation " Blessed be the glory of the Lord from its place," or " His place," may mean that that glory awakens praise wherever it goes, and so could make even Babylonia God's " place." This would be full of comfort to Ezekiel ; for being a priest he would naturally feel that Zion was " the place " of the glory of the Lord, and therefore blessed. But every place where Jesus comes is hallowed ground.

"Then the Spirit took me up" (v. 12), i.e., laid hold of me. The statement is: that the Spirit, which energized the cherubim and the wheels, then took hold of Ezekiel to energise him; and, accordingly, in the power of the Spirit he was "lifted up" (v. 14), i.e., lifted from off his face, and led away to Tel-abib (v. 15), which was several miles further off upon the banks of the Chebar.

The bitterness and hot anger of the prophet (v. 14) may have been the righteous indignation of his enlightened heart against his fellow nationals because of their determined idolatry, to the true nature of which the vision of the glory of God had awakened him; or it might be that the heat of his spirit was caused by that alone, and that his bitterness confessed his unwillingness to be the bearer to them of a message of lamentation, mourning and woe (ii. 10).

If this be so, then it gives point and emphasis to the "but" of the declaration: "But the hand of the Lord was strong upon me"; that is, it overcame his reluctance, and sanctified his anger.

"Astonished" (v. 15), i.e., dumfounded.

The substance of his message is given in verses 17-21, and the dual character of the Christian Ministry is found in the instruction: "Hear the word at My mouth" and, "give them warning from Me." (v. 17).

But to hear the word from His mouth, the servant of the Lord must be willing to withdraw into the "plain," or "low place" (v. 22), for it is there that the Master speaks with the servant, and afresh reveals Himself in His glory to him (v. 23), and where he receives a fresh enduement of spiritual power (v. 24). "The plain," i.e., a low place reached with difficulty through obstacles (Heb.).

When under the control of that mighty Spirit, the lips are taught when to be dumb (v. 26), and when to speak (v. 27).

"They shall put bands upon thee," etc, (v. 25), i.e. their unbelief and hostility would straiten him. The apostle Paul intimates such bands in writing to the Corinthians (2 Cor. vi. 12) and to the Hebrews (Heb. v. 11).

Thus the prophet proved that, even as a slave in the idol-filled country of distraught Babylonia, when walking with the Lord in the light of His Word He shed a glory on the way.

EZEKIEL IV.—A tile was two feet long by one broad The Babylonians engraved figures and letters upon them. Many such have been dug up in the ruins of ancient Babylon.

It is thought by some that this symbolic siege of Jerusalem, expressive of the misery of that city, was not actually operated by Ezekiel but only represented in a vision.

But the captives being but children in intelligence, there is no difficulty in believing that, just as in the advanced Sunday schools of to-day children are taught religious facts by means of wooden and clay models, so the prophet taught his hearers.

The lesson taught was the misery which the inhabitants of Jerusalem were about to suffer during the third and last siege by Nebuchadnezzar, and that it was better to be a captive by the river Chebar in fellowship with the glory, than to be a rebel in the land of Judah without the glory.

What is to be understood by the two periods of three hundred and ninety years and forty years is extremely difficult to say. It is true that from the disruption of the kingdom of the ten tribes to the destruction of the Temple was three hundred and ninety years; and that the ministry of Jeremiah to the two tribes continued for forty years. It is also remarkable that the sum of these two periods, that is four hundred and thirty years, was the exact period from the promise to Abraham up to the deliverance from Egypt. It is also true that from the death of Christ to the destruction of the Temple by the Romans, and the casting away of Judah out of their land, was forty years, and that three hundred and ninety years covers the interval between Calvary and Malachi. But the posture of the prophet expressed punishment during the periods determined, and the symbolic siege of Jerusalem represented a crisis. This crisis demanded that the two periods should synchronize as to their close. It is quite true that in this chapter Jerusalem represents the one nation of Israel in its totality; but to what periods in their history these years point remains a difficulty.

"Lay the iniquity" (v. 4), and "bear the iniquity" (v. 6), i.e., the punishment of the iniquity. To lie in such a posture was painful. Ezekiel was given strength to endure it (v. 8).

The Easterns bake bread of fine flour.

Bread baked with the materials of verse 9 would be coarse.

" Twenty shekels " (v. 10), i.e., ten ounces. " The sixth part of an hin " (v. 11) i.e., a pint and a half. " Abominable " (v. 14), i.e., putrid.

" Therewith " (v. 15), i.e., " thereon " (R.V.). The Arabs having no wood make a fire with camel's dung, which they use as fuel.

For a Hebrew, and above all a priest, to have any contact with putrid animal matter was to become ceremonially unclean.

The three hundred and ninety years of judgment upon the Ten Tribes illustrate the severity of God, and the forty years of pleading with the Two Tribes through Jeremiah, the goodness of God, but both actions were resisted by the nation. Such is the human heart !

EZEKIEL V.—This second symbolic lesson is linked with the first (iv.) by the sentence " In the midst of the city " (v. 2), i.e., the city as portrayed on the tile—Jerusalem.

Verse 1 should read as in the Revised Version. The symbolic action predicted that the fire, i.e., the wrath of God in pestilence and famine (v. 12), should destroy one third of the nation ; war a second third ; and exile the remaining third ; and that of this last remnant, the majority should perish by sword and famine (vs. 2-4).

All this came to pass ; and the fulfilment of these predictions shows the folly of those religious teachers who deny the fact of the wrath of God.

" This is Jerusalem " (vs. 5-7), i.e., " Here are the facts as to Jerusalem ! " The facts are thus recited : she, as representing the nation, was placed in the centre of the nations in order to shed upon them the light of the Gospel. But she rebelled against truth more than the heathen (v. 6, R.V.), multiplied idols (v. 7), and sank morally lower than her neighbours (v. 7).

" They refused " etc. (v. 6), i.e., the Heathen refused. The reference here is, probably, to the primitive laws of God handed on to man by Noah, especially those respecting the Sabbath.

" Idols " should be supplied after " multiplied in number " in verse 7.

The laws of the surrounding nations (v. 7) were more righteous than those of Bible-rejecting Israel.

" I, even I " (v. 8). This solemn formula emphasizes the certainty of the wrath of God, just as in Isa. xliii. 25 it emphasizes the certainty of the pardoning love of God ; and it rebukes the unbelief of the natural heart which denies both these activities of the Divine Essence.

The righteous judgments, consequent upon the abominations of verse 11, which are detailed in verses 8-17, are still in operation, and will reach a crisis under the reign of Anti-Christ, when the " Indignation " against Israel will be consummated (Dan. xi. 36, and xii. 1).

Righteousness must, from its nature, be restless till evil is judged. Then it is comforted (v. 13). Such was the effect of the judgment of sin at Calvary ; and those who recognize this Gospel fact, and take refuge in the great God and Saviour Jesus Christ who was the Actor in it, taste the sweetness of the Divine comfort.

This chapter abounds in technical expressions characteristic of the Pentateuch. This is an undesigned testimony to the truthfulness of John i. 17, that the Law was a gift from God through Moses.

EZEKIEL VI.—As the prior message attacked idolatry in Jerusalem, so this message (vi. and vii.) attacked it in the land.

Idol temples were erected usually on mountains and hills, and by water-courses and in valleys (v. 3).

Just as the prophet (1 Kings xiii. 2) disdained to speak to the king and addressed himself to the idolatrous altar, so here Ezekiel addresses the idolatrous centres of worship.

He did not speak his own words but the Word that came to him from Jehovah (v. 1) ; and he delivered it in the very words given to him (v. 3).

The emphatic formula : " I, even I " (see note on v. 8), occurs in verse 3.

Verse 6 illustrates the expression " Abomination of desolation," i.e., the desolation which is the moral and material result of idolatry.

This fundamental moral principle, i.e., that desolation is produced by idolatry, may be verified in modern as well as ancient times, for to-day vast portions of the richest districts in the world are desert because of idolatry and in the case of multitudes a sad personal experience demonstrates the fact ;

for where the heart is governed by an " idol " there is inward desolation, and spiritual fruit and wealth and beauty are unknown.

" Ye shall know that I am Jehovah " (v. 7). This formula occurs in this actual form twenty-one times in Ezekiel, but only twice elsewhere (Exod. x. 2 and 1 Kings xx. 28). Varieties of it appear frequently in the Hebrew Scriptures ; as for instance in verse 14, in Exodus vi. 7, and in very many other passages.

The force of this formula is : " You shall make the experience that I am the living God (in contrast to dead idols) whose promises and judgments are realities, and not empty words."

God can be known in grace or in wrath, in salvation or in judgment. Israel proved Him by experience to be a Saviour when He redeemed them out of Egypt (Exod. x. 2), and, by experience, to be a Judge (Ezek. vi. 7) when He abandoned them to exile.

Those who will not know Him as a Saviour must know Him as a Judge (John xii. 46 and 48).

" A remnant scattered through all countries " (v. 8). This remnant exists to-day ; and of it will be born the New Israel.

" I am broken " (v. 9). This may be translated ; " I have broken." The one translation means that God's heart was broken with Israel's determined idolatry. The other that, because of that idolatry, He broke His Covenant with them. Both are true.

" I have not said in vain, etc.," (v. 10), i.e., when I said that I would send these calamities upon them, the threat was not an empty one.

In the " cultured " congregations of to-day, there is disapproval if a servant of the Truth strikes with his fist and stamps with his foot when preaching, but the Holy Spirit may command the true servant of God to do so when exposing. the hypocrisy and idolatry of christendom, just as He commanded Ezekiel to do when denouncing the abomination of the religious professors in his day (v. 11), and when announcing the sure wrath of God that was coming (vs. 12-14) as a consequence.

EZEKIEL VII.—This prophecy preceded by only a short time the third and final siege of Jerusalem. This siege resulted in the destruction of the city and the Temple, and the banishment into slavery of the few Hebrews who survived the slaughter of the inhabitants.

The prophecy asserts the justice of the Divine anger, and points to the aggravated idolatry which provoked that Wrath.

" An end, the end is come " (v. 2), i.e., " an end, the predicted end, is about to come upon the land," that is, the land of Palestine.

The words " the fruit of " may be supplied after " I will recompense upon thee " (v 3). Similar words may be supplied in verse 4 between " and " and " thine."

" An evil, an only evil " (v. 5), i.e., a calamity, one sole calamity, cometh ; i.e., the Babylonian invasion.

Verse 7, should read as in the Revised Version.

" Behold the day " (v. 10), i.e., the day of wrath.

" The rod hath blossomed " (v. 10), i.e., Nebuchadnezzar is ready to strike. For " pride hath budded," i.e., Israel's determined sin which demanded the rod.

A " rod of wickedness " (v. 11), i.e., a rod to punish wickedness : that is, by violent injustice they destroyed and impoverished each other (R.V.).

" Neither shall any strengthen himself," etc. (v. 13), i.e. no man shall be able to lengthen his life by wrong-doing. The reference in this, and the prior verse, is to the Year of Jubilee, when lands that were sold reverted to their original owners (Lev. xxv.). The prediction here was that none of these sellers and buyers would live to see the Jubilee.

Those in verse 14 who refused to obey the trumpet-call were the Hebrew soldiers.

The " multitude " (v 13), i.e., of buyers and sellers ; the " multitude " (v. 14), i.e., of soldiers.

Doves when chased by the hunter fly off to the mountains (v. 16).

" Everyone because of his iniquity " (v. 16), i.e., because of the bitter consequences of his idolatry. Repentance motived by personal suffering because of misconduct, is false repentance. True repentance is born of a sense of sin against God.

" Idols " should be supplied after " silver " and " gold " (v. 19).

" It " (v. 19), i.e., idolatry.

" His " and " He " (v. 20) should be printed with capital letters. The " ornament " pointed to was the Temple. " They " and " their," i.e., the Hebrew idolaters who set up the idols in the Temple. " I set it far from them," i.e., the Temple. They were set far from it by being exiled, and it was set far from them by being burned.

The " strangers " and " wicked " of verse 21, and the " robbers " of verse 22 were the Babylonians. They robbed and profaned the Temple.

" My face will I turn from them," i.e., God would not strike dead the Chaldean soldiers who would intrude into the Holy of Holies, as had been the case if a Hebrew, other than the High Priest, had dared to enter, but he would avert His face so as not to witness the intrusion of the Chaldean. This fact affirmed the rupture between God and Israel.

" Make a chain " (v. 23). This symbolic action predicted the captivity just as the prior one (vi. 11) foretold the invasion.

" Their holy places " (v. 24), i.e., their places of idolatrous worship.

" Mischief " (v. 26), i.e., calamity.

The prophet preached, the priest taught, and the elder counselled (v. 26).

Thus closes this first section of the Book. It belongs to the River Chebar and the captives, and predicts the judgment that should come on the whole nation. It would be a complete judgment, for it would fall on the four corners of the land (v. 2). The nation having failed in its testimony for God, the execution of the judgment was now the only testimony to the existence and nature of God. How sad that under the circumstances then present, judgment should be the only possible testimony.

EZEKIEL VIII.—Ezekiel's second prophecy begins here and closes at chapter xi. It concerns Jerusalem, and exposes the hypocrisy, abominations and violence existing there. Five years later the city and Temple were destroyed by the Chaldeans. The outward profession of fidelity to God, and to the Law, that was made by Jeremiah's hearers, emphasises, by contrast, the excessive iniquity and hypocrisy of the people (Jer. xviii. 18).

So the wrath of God fell on the guilty city ; and this chapter and the following expose the abominations which justified that wrath.

Obedient to the command of Jeremiah xxix. 28 the prophet sat in his own house (v. 1) ; and the elders among the exiles were there gathered to hear him preach. Suddenly the hand, i.e., the power, the Holy Spirit, fell upon him ! It is a striking scene.

The fiery appearance that he saw had the likeness of a man. He was the God of Israel in human semblance and accompanied by the glory ; and He it was who spoke in vision to the Prophet (vs. 2-5).

More than a year having elapsed since he shaved his head with a sharp sword, his hair had had time to grow.

Samson's hair was laid hold of by the Philistine, and he fell, Absalom's hair was caught by the oak, and he perished, Ezekiel's hair was gathered in the Hand of Him who counts the very hairs of His people's heads, and he was lifted up into the visions of God (v. 3) ! A man's hair expresses his weakness (1 Cor. xi. 14). When that weakness is laid hold of by the hand of Omnipotence then a power enters into the soul that lifts it up between earth and heaven.

Four pictures of abomination (vs. 5-17), each succeeding picture revealing a deeper depth of idolatrous iniquity, are set out in these verses.

At the north gate of the Temple, in the very entry, stood an idol upon a pedestal, wounding with jealousy the Love that shone forth in the glory (vs. 4 and 5).

A greater abomination was the chamber of Egyptian idolatry ; and here stood all the seventy members of the Hebrew Synod worshipping the loathsome reptiles portrayed on the walls (vs. 7-12). The deep pain of this scene is sharpened by the presence of Jaazaniah. His father Shaphan had taken part in Josiah's reformation (2 Kings xxii.), and two of his brothers were friendly to Jeremiah (Jer. xxvi. 24 and xxxvi. 10, 25).

A yet greater abomination was evidenced by the women weeping for Tammuz (vs. 13-15). Tammuz was the son of the Queen of Heaven. As to-day so at that time, the favourite divinity of women was the Virgin and her child. She was supposed to lose her son, and later on, to find him. The loss was celebrated by a festival of weeping, and the recovery by a festival of rejoicing. These were two of the greatest festivals of the ancient sacred year. These women were weeping in the Temple of Jehovah, not for their sins, but for Tammuz !

The final, and most appalling form of idolatrous abomination, was that of the High Priest and the chiefs of the twenty-four Courses of Aaron standing in the Holy

Place with their backs to the Most Holy Place, worshipping the sun !

Sun-worship is believed by some to be the purest form of idolatry. Here it is declared to be the most impure, for it was at that time associated with the Branch, i.e., the Asherah (v. 17).

Four times in the Hebrew Scriptures the Holy Spirit addresses the Messiah as " The Branch," that is, as the Author of Life. Satan's parody of this was the Asherah—the Greek Phallus. The ancients, in their effort to reach back to the origin of life, and worship it as a god, arrived at the lowest depth of moral and intellectual degradation by the institution of Phallic worship.

That this was the deepest depth of abomination is affirmed by the words of burning indignation : " Lo they put the branch to my nose ! " (v. 17). Or, freely translated : " Look at them ! they are thrusting the branch into my face ! "

The original Hebrew here reads " My nose," i.e., " My face," or " My nostrils " ; but the Sopherim changed this word into " their nostrils," putting the original text into the margin , and this they did from a false sense of the dignity of God.

Some worshippers put a certain kind of plant to their faces when adoring the sun, and it is thought that the reference in verse 17 is to this fact. But such an action would not call forth the hot indignation which burns in the language of the verse, or explain why this fourth picture revealed the greatest abomination.

It is most probable that the great golden image of Nebuchadnezzar was a phallis (see notes on Daniel iii.).

Idolatry blinds. The God of Glory was actually present in His Temple (v. 4)— " there," i.e., the Temple—but the priests and elders declared he was not there (v. 12). This blindness is affirmed again in the following chapter (vs 3, 9).

Such blindness exists to-day. The heart that is governed by any form of idolatry, whether material, scientific or philosophic, is insensible to fellowship with God, and cannot see His glory as revealed in the face of Jesus Christ (2 Cor. iv. 6).

EZEKIEL IX.—The last verse of the previous chapter and the first verse of this chapter should be read together, and the contrast between the " loud voice " of the idolaters (v. 18) and the " loud voice " of the God of Judgment noticed (v. 1).

This first verse should perhaps read : " Ye that have charge over the city, draw near every man with his weapon of death in his hand."

These seven beings were evidently supernatural. Six were ministers of wrath, and one of grace.

The minister of grace was clothed in linen, which material, in the Scriptures, usually symbolizes righteousness, and his ministry was to set a Divine mark upon all who judged and bewailed the abominations that were practised in city and Temple (v. 4).

Some think this white-robed minister pictured Israel's True and Great High Priest (see Rev. vii. and xiv.).

That the ministers of wrath should be six in number is mysterious. One minister of mercy and six of judgment suggests that there were six idolaters for every true worshipper. Six is also the number of man. He was created on the sixth day ; possibly on that very day he sinned and fell ; he works for six days ; his great men Goliath, Nebuchadnezzar, etc., were characterized by the number six (see notes on 1 Sam. and Dan.) ; and the great Super-man of the future will be recognized by the numbers 666.

The six ministers of wrath entered the Temple from the North gate, where was the image that provoked to jealousy (viii. 5).

All seven stood beside the brazen altar (v. 2). The number seven marks perfection. Here was the perfection of grace and truth.

At the brazen altar sin was atoned for and forgiven. The introduction of man's religion thrust this altar aside. (See notes on king Ahaz). This altar foreshadowed Calvary. From that altar the ministers of wrath and mercy went forth. The minister of grace first (v. 4), those of wrath after him (v. 5). So is it to-day, and so shall it be. The grace of God acts from Calvary, and the wrath of God will act from Calvary. Calvary is the centre of the Divine activities in grace and judgment. God's controversy with man concerns His dearly-beloved Son, and the atonement He made for sin. Man's religious efforts, energized by Satan, are continually directed to the substitution of another way of life than that provided by God at Golgotha. Thus they dishonour Christ.

When men sin against nature and righteousness they drag down into death their wives and children (v. 6). See notes on Num. xxi. and Dan. vi.

Judgment always begins at the House of God (v. 6, with 1 Pet. iv. 17). There is a throb of anguished love in the words " My Sanctuary."

The word " then " may be supplied before " Go ye forth " (v. 7).

" I was left alone " (v. 8), i.e., in vision he saw all the priests slain except himself.

The righteousness of the judgment is revealed in verse 9.

Three times is it declared that pity must not be shewn (viii. 18, ix. 5 and 10) ; but this is not the triple language of pleasure, but of agony. It is love compelled to keep reminding itself of the sad necessity of judgment.

EZEKIEL X.—The departure of the glory from the Temple is the vision of this chapter. It retires unwillingly. Its throne was the Most Holy Place " (there " viii. 4) ; it then withdrew to the threshold (ix. 3) ; then, above the threshold (vs. 1 and 4) ; then it retired to the Eastern Gate ; and, finally, to the mountain on the east side of the city (xi. 23). Thus did the God of Israel in lingering love forsake His city and Temple, not to return till ch. xliii. 2. That return lies in the future.

This vision of the Throne (v. 1) superintending the judgment (vs. 2 and 7), assured Israel that their national calamities were not accidental but providential. This great truth nourishes God's people in all ages.

Righteousness is the foundation of Divine action whether in redemption or judgment. He who in grace set the mark upon the redeemed, cast the burning fire upon the rebels (ix. 4 and x. 2). The righteousness of God in His judgment of sin at Calvary, and in His faithfulness in fulfilling His promises to the believer, is the foundation of the Christian's assurance of salvation ; and it is the righteousness of God which assures eternal condemnation to the rejecter of Christ.

The fire (v. 2) was that of i. 13.

Verses 3-5, form a parenthesis.

The detailed statement of verses 8-22 is not a meaningless repetition of chapter i. What the Holy Spirit repeats claims the deeper attention of the believer. Much instruction is here suggested. The God of Glory who appeared to the obedient captives

by the river Chebar in blessing, was the very same God of Glory who appeared in judgment to the rebels at Jerusalem. This was quite opposed to the religious thinking of the citizens of that guilty city They thought themselves blest, and the captives cursed.

Again it will be noticed that the words " As it were " and " as if," so often occurring in chapter i., are here mostly omitted ; and the face of an ox is here declared to be the face of a cherub. Such is the glory.

The prophet insists (viii. 4 and x. 20) that " the living creature " that he saw in vision at Jerusalem was the very same as that he saw at the Chebar.

" O wheel " (v. 13). This should read : " as for the wheels it was cried unto each one of them, ' Roll ! ' " that is, each wheel was commanded to revolve in order to execute the Divine purpose.

EZEKIEL XI.—Jeremiah stated that the Chaldean invasion was near at hand ; he likened it to a boiling cauldron (Jer. i. 11-16) ; and he sent a message to the captives to build houses, for that their exile would last for seventy years (Jer. xxix. 5).

The princes in Jerusalem opposed him, and ridiculed his preaching, and put him in prison. These no doubt are the five and twenty-princes of verse 1. Judging by his solemn death (v. 33), Pelatiah appears to have been the leader. Their action and influence is stated in verse 2. Their mocking words (v. 3) may be thus paraphrased : The fall of the city is not near ! *We* will build houses ; *this city* is the cauldron and *we* are the flesh ! That is : it is for us, and not for the captives to build houses ; Jerusalem is the cauldron, and not the Chaldean, and we are as safe in the city as flesh in a cauldron.

The Divine response is found in verses 7-13. The prophet takes up their own words, declares them to be the flesh in the cauldron, i.e., Jerusalem, but that God would bring them forth out of the midst of it (v. 7), judge them in the border of Israel (v. 11), and there should they be slain. And so it fell out (2 Kings xxv.) ; for the princes were carried away to Riblah and there put to death.

Instead of exulting at the death of Pelatiah (v. 13) Ezekiel wept aloud. Such is grace ; but he is comforted by the message that his real brethren and kindred were the captives in Babylon, and not the priests in Jerusalem

(v. 15) who had proudly said to the exiles, " Get you far from Jehovah, for this land is given to *us* in possession ! " And the comfort was deepened by the prophecy that though the captives had no material Temple yet God Himself would be to them a Sanctuary for the " little while " their exile was to last, i.e., for the predicted seventy years (v. 16, R.V.), that then they should return and purge Zion from every detestable thing (v. 18). This had a fulfilment in the return under Ezra and Nehemiah, and by the consequent reformation which those leaders so vigorously carried out.   (See notes on Ezra and Nehemiah).

But the prophecy, as to its fulfilment, belongs to the future (vs. 19 and 20).

Having reluctantly left the Temple the glory then forsook the city (vs. 22 and 23) ; lingering for a little, with sorrowing love, upon the Mount of Olives. But the glory returned to that Mount, veiled in the sinless flesh of the Messiah, and once more Love looked upon the beloved but rebellious city and wept over it (Luke xix. 41). A few weeks later He ascended from that Mount ; and in a yet future day, in the glory of His Second Advent, His feet shall stand upon it (Zech. xiv. 4). Then shall Israel have one heart and a new spirit.

The prophet, awakening from his trance, communicated to his hearers the things shewn to him in the vision (vs. 24, 25) and the hearts of the little flock were comforted with the wonderful revelation that Israel's God of glory was in their midst as a sanctuary —a true and pure Temple ; that He would continue so to be for the whole period of the captivity ; that He shared their exile with them ; and that He would certainly restore them to the home-land.

EZEKIEL XII.—In this object-lesson the prophet predicted the attempted escape and capture of king Zedekiah. The prophecy preceded the event by five years.

He was commanded to make a bundle as for a journey (v. 3) during the day time ; to dig a passage through the wall surrounding his house (v. 5) ; to disguise his face (v. 6) ; and, at night-time, to creep through the hole with his bundle, and make as if to go into exile.

This object-lesson was necessary because of the unbelief of the captives (vs. 2 and 9).

False prophets were promising restoration to them and victory to Zedekiah.

All, as fore-pictured, came to pass (2 Kings xxv. and Jer. xxxix). Zedekiah, disguised (v. 12) so as not to be recognized, and with a few articles for the journey, forsook the city by night through a hole made in the city wall, and fled to Jericho. But God using the Chaldean army as a net (v. 13)—he was captured and brought to Riblah ; and, his eyes having been put out, transported to Babylon where he died (v. 13).

Josephus says that this prophecy was sent to Zedekiah ; but he declaring that Jeremiah (xxiv. 8, 9), contradicted verse 13 of this chapter, it stating he should not see Babylon, and Jeremiah predicting he would be carried there, concluded to believe neither. He has many imitators at the present day, who, fancying that they find contradictions in the Bible, treat its threatenings and promises as valueless.

" My net " (v. 13), i.e., the Chaldean army which overtook the king and his troops in the plains of Jericho. Compare Hab. i. 14-16.

The few reserved from destruction (v. 16) were spared that they might vindicate God's action by informing the nations of the abominations which justified it. Dan. ix. 5-14 illustrates this prediction.

So corrupt and unbelieving is man that he turns the patience and longsuffering of God into a mocking proverb (v. 22).

But the day will surely come when the vain visions of popular preachers (v. 24) will be proved false, and the sure words of God's Book demonstrated true (vs. 23 and 25).

The unbelief of verse 27 develops into the scepticism of verse 22. The moral order is here reversed with design. This Law of Design is frequently apparent in the Scriptures. " Prolonged " (vs. 25 and 28), i.e., deferred (R.V.).

Thus the false expectations of the Captives that they would be immediately restored to their native land, and the equally false expectations of the people of Jerusalem that they would never be conquered by the Babylonians, were all destroyed by the symbolic prophecy of verses 3-7.

Ahab and Zedekiah tried, but in vain, to outwit God. Their action was the more wicked because God, in His love and pity, told them beforehand of their fate if they persisted in their folly. He did not want them to perish.

All who refuse to flee from the wrath to come must get to know God in judgment (v. 15) ; those who obey the command shall get to know Him in grace (v. 16).

EZEKIEL XIII.—As the prophecy of the prior chapter denounced false expectations, so that of this chapter denounced the authors of them

The structure of the prophecy may be thus exhibited :—

The men prophets (vs. 1 and 2).
  Their lies (vs. 2-7).
    Divine denunciation (vs. 8 and 9).
    The House—Its material (vs. 10-16).

The women prophets (v. 17)
  The House—Its furniture (vs. 18 and 19).
    Divine denunciation (vs. 20 and 21).
    Their lies (vs. 22 and 23).

" Their own spirit " (v. 3)—not the Holy Spirit. They preached what the people wished to hear, i.e., a speedy restoration to Palestine.

The preaching of the false prophet was subjective ; he preached out of his own spirit. The preaching of the true prophet was objective ; he preached from the Word of God. As to-day, so at all times, man sets inward religious emotion above outward Divine revelation, and desires a Christ without a Bible.

" Foxes " (v. 4), i.e., jackals ; they howl through the darkness of the night, and their one object is to get something for their appetite. So fashionable preachers fill the moral night of human ignorance with their noisy teachings, and their aim is personal fame and financial profit (vs. 19 and 20).

The true soldier takes his place in the breaches made in the fence of truth, and valiantly fights in the battles of the Lord (v. 5).

Verse 6 should read as in the Revised Version. The " word," i.e., the promises made by them when preaching ; but such promises are never confirmed, although such preachers claim to possess Divine authority (v. 7).

The judgment denounced against these prophets was, that on the restoration of Israel (v. 9) they should be excluded from the church and people and land of Israel, and so their names should be blotted out of the Book of Life.

The teaching of these false prophets is here compared to a fair white-washed house, such as is usual in the hot East. In appearance the house is here assumed to be strong, for it is called a wall, and is beautified with white-wash (i.e., " daubed with untempered mortar ") ; but the destruction of the house by rain, hail and storm proved it to have been made of mud, and built upon the sand as a foundation (v. 14). Such will be the end of this teaching, and these teachers. The present mud-house was built by Voltaire and Paine, and is being whitened by " modern " preachers.

As the men prophets built the house, so the women-prophets furnished it ; and what could be more fitting than that men should build and women should furnish ?

" The pillows " (v. 18) " for all joints " (R.V. margin) symbolized the teaching which gave a false rest, and which the people wished to hear ; and the ornamental coverings for the head, picture attractive and pleasing doctrines which obscure the facts of death and the judgment to come.' ' Every stature," i.e., hearers of every age.

" To make them fly " (v. 20), i.e., to make their hearers fly into their nets so that they might plunder them (v. 19).

" Will ye save the souls alive ? " etc., (v. 18), i.e., they offered life to their listeners ; they " slew " (v. 19), i.e., they mocked believers, and they " saved," that is, promised felicity to unbelievers ; they saddened the hearts of God's people with their lies (v. 22), and encouraged the unconverted in their sins by promising them heaven.

Thus the professing church and its accepted teachers of Ezekiel's day correspond to Christendom and its accepted teachers of the present day.

EZEKIEL XIV. 1-11.—The elders of " Israel "—for the whole nation is here (xii. 21-xiv. ii.) in view—like those of viii. 1, were no doubt in some difficulty, and, therefore, sought for Divine guidance.

Many people, when in trouble, ask God's servants to pray for them, as these elders desired Ezekiel to inquire of the Lord on their behalf (v. 3).

But such people, including these elders, refuse to break with their idols and their sins (v. 6).

God can have no fellowship with evil ; and He, therefore, not only refuses to answer such prayers, but He replies to them with just judgments (vs. 4 and 8).

Servants of the Lord should, like Ezekiel, courageously tell such applicants that God does not hear the prayer of the lip if iniquity is cherished in the heart (Ps. lxvi. 18).

These elders must have been deeply offended with the prophet's reception of them. To treat religious men in such a fashion would be judged by present day society as the grossest rudeness.

But the prophet immediately pointed to the inward idolatry of their hearts, and its outward evidence in their homes and lives.

To set idolatrous objects before the eyes causes moral stumbling to the feet (vs. 3, 4, and 7), whilst to set the words of God's Book before the eyes guards the feet from stumbling (Prov. iii. 21-23).

A verbal reply was refused to these elders, and a terrible response, in action, directly from the Hand of God Himself, promised (v. 8)

The last sentence of verse 4 might be thus translated: " I Jehovah will answer him according to it (i.e., the stumbling-block) and according to the multitude of his idols." That is: the judgment should be measured by the sin.

However fair the outward profession of faith in God may be, the Holy Spirit can unmask the evil lodged within the heart (v. 5).

To judge people because of that which is in their heart, and which estranges them from Christ, is a most just judgment.

But God loved and pitied these hypocrites, and the fact of this love added to the certitude and horror of the just doom that was impending over them. He cried to them to repent (v. 6), no longer to keep far from Him (v. 11), and He would receive and acknowledge them as His loved people— " My people " (v. 11).

The threatenings in this prophecy are, in substance and language, all found in Leviticus and Deuteronomy.

" I Jehovah have permitted that prophet to be deceived " (v. 9). It is most just that one who deceives others God should permit to be deceived The history of Jacob illustrates this moral principle.

This ninth verse, coupled with 1 Kings xxii. 21, Rom. i. 24, 2 Thess. ii. 11, and many other scriptures, reveals the dreadful fact of demons permitted to have power over men.

EZEKIEL XIV. 12-23.—In Jeremiah xv. 1, guilty Jerusalem was told that the intercession of Moses and Samuel (Exodus xxxii. 11-14, Num. xiv. 13-20, 1 Sam. vii. 8-12) would fail to avert her coming doom, and in this chapter it is added that the presence in the city of Noah, Daniel and Job would also fail to preserve it from destruction.

Noah's family owed their salvation to him (Gen. vi. 9 and 18 and vii. 1), Daniel's companions were similarly saved (Dan. ii. 12, 17 and 49), and Job's three friends were pardoned because of Job's intercession (Job xlii. 7-9)

The argument of verse 21 is that if these three men could not turn aside one judgment how could they turn aside four sore ones ?

Daniel is here found in very good company—Noah on one side and Job on the other. These were Patriarchs and both lived before Israel was a nation. Daniel had already been fourteen years in Babylon, and twelve years had elapsed since he interpreted Nebuchadnezzar's dream. His fame and piety were doubtless world renowned (Dan. ii. 48). The Hebrews must have been proud of him, and must have believed that God would, for His sake, shew them great favour.

Ezekiel here bears witness to Daniel ; and in his ninth chapter and second verse Daniel bears witness to Jeremiah.

" The land " (v. 13) should read " a land."

" To stretch out the hand " (v. 13) implies anger.

The four sore judgments were famine (v. 13), wild beasts (v. 15), war (v. 17) and pestilence (v. 19)

" Their own souls " (v. 14), i.e., their own-selves.

" Blood " (v. 19). This word in Hebrew expresses every kind of unnatural death.

The last two verses should be read in connection with chapter v. The remnant mentioned (v. 22) is that of the final third of chapter v. 2.

The argument here is that " the way," i.e., the idolatrous religion of these new arrivals, and their " doings," i.e., their immoral conduct, should convince Ezekiel and his companions (" You " v. 22) of the justice of God's wrath upon Jerusalem (v. 23). In this sense therefore would the prophet and his friends be " comforted," i.e., reconciled to God's action.

No doubt many of the faithful captives had

very near relations who were dear to them, and who lived in Jerusalem. That the wrath of God should fall on these must have perplexed and deeply agitated the exiles. But when they had a visible demonstration of the idolatry and impurity of these relatives, they were comforted concerning the evil that God had brought upon them.

Many christian people feel that they could not endure witnessing the future judgment of dear relatives. But that judgment will manifest the justice of their doom, and all beholding it will be " comforted."

Neither this chapter nor Jer. xv. can be quoted in support of the supposed value of the intercession of dead saints. The argument is the reverse ; for Jeremiah xv. 1 declares that Moses and Samuel, being dead, their value, as intercessors, ceased ; and that even if they were alive, their intercession would be unavailing. It is evident, therefore, that being dead they were not then " standing before God " as conscious and efficient representatives of the nation. In Ezek. xiv. the words " in it " (vs. 14, 16, 18, and 20) affirm the same principle ; that is, that the saintly intercessors must be alive. There is, moreover, in Ezekiel no suggestion of intercession, but only of residence as securing respite for the city. The ten righteous men simply residing in Sodom, whether interceding for the city or not, would have furnished a reason for its preservation. But it is evident that ten deceased righteous who had resided in Sodom could have had no intercessory value in averting its doom.

Noah was " perfect " (Gen. vi. 9), Daniel, " greatly beloved " (Dan x. 11), and Job, " unequalled in the earth " (Job i. 8).

EZEKIEL XV.—This symbolic prophecy forms a foreword to that which follows, for its subject is Jerusalem. See note on verse 4.

Israel, in the Scriptures, is symbolized as a vine, as an olive, and as a fig-tree.

The vine symbolized spiritual privilege.

The one business of the vine is to bear grapes. Otherwise it is worthless, except as fire-wood (John xv. 6), Israel was the vine brought out of Egypt whose one duty and privilege was to bear moral fruit unto God (Matt. xxi. 33-46).

The second member of verse 2 should read : " And what value has a vine-branch which has come to be among the trees of the forest ?

That is : having lost its power to bear grapes, the vine-branch is more worthless than the branches of any other tree. It is not even good for making pegs (Isa. xxii. 23-25). A Christian who does not bear fruit is more unprofitable than the worldling (Deut. xxxii. 32).

The Hebrews were inferior to all other nations except in the one respect of having had the oracles of God committed to them.

" The ends of it " (v. 4). The Assyrians burnt the northern end, the Egyptians the southern. " The midst of it," i.e, Jerusalem, was then on the eve of being burned by the Chaldeans. This last point is the subject of the following prophecy.

Before Jerusalem was burned it was useless as a moral agent, and, therefore, wholly useless when burned (v. 5).

2 Kings xxv. 9, records the fulfilment of the prediction of verse 6.

The one fire of verse 7 was the destruction of Jerusalem, when multitudes perished ; the other fire was the captivity during which the residue perished ; and thus the elect exiles were taught " to know the Lord."

The cause of their doom is declared in verse 8. They perversely fell into determined rebellion. The Hebrews were not merely sinners as the surrounding nations, they were worse, for they were apostates, transgressors and rebels. They sinned against light, for to them alone had been given the Law, i.e., the Bible.

EZEKIEL XVI. — In this prophecy the apostasy of Jerusalem is presented under the figure of an unfaithful wife. It recites her birth (vs. 3-6), her marriage (vs. 7-14), her misconduct (vs. 15-34), her punishment (vs. 35-52), and her restoration (vs. 53-63).

What is here true of Jerusalem was equally true of the nation.

" A Syrian ready to perish " was Abraham their founder. Religiously he was a Canaanite, having an Amorite for a father and a Hittite for a mother (v. 3), and possessing neither moral beauty, worthfulness, nor social position (vs. 4 and 5). Such was the squalid and foul birth of Jerusalem.

The interpretation of this prophecy belongs to that city and nation, but an application truly describes the moral condition of all men by natural birth ; for these verses give a true picture of man's essential corruption.

The grace of the Redeemer in loving such

a foul being (v. 6), in making her His Bride (v. 8), and in giving her such a priceless trousseau, surpasses all human experience.

The sinner's first need is life (v. 6), then cleansing (v. 9).

" I looked upon thee " (v. 8), " I loved thee " ; " I spread my skirt over thee," i.e., I betrothed thee. " I covered thy nakedness," i.e., I clothed thee. " I entered into a covenant with thee and thou becamest mine," i.e., I married thee.

That a mighty prince should make of an abandoned infant his queen (v. 13, R.V.) is amazing ; but what adds to the wonder of it all is, that this Divine Prince knew beforehand that His Bride would forsake Him, and ultimately betray and crucify Him.

Such affection is impossible among men, for when a man adopts a child he hopes for a recompense in the love of the child ; but who would adopt a child knowing beforehand that the child would hate and murder its benefactor ?

The love that provided such a marriage outfit as is described in verses 10-14, is a love that passeth knowledge.

Jerusalem reached this degree of beauty in the time of Solomon.

The " then " of verse 8 touches the heart. He first loved and then washed (Rev. i. 5). Such is the Divine love. The foul sinner is first loved in his foulness, and then washed from it, as the prodigal was first kissed in his rags, and then clothed with the best robe.

The two specially horrible features of the impure and cruel forms of idolatry which Jerusalem madly gave herself to are described in verses 15-34. They were impure ; for in her frenzied rage for idol-worship she specially adopted the idolatries of Egypt (v. 26) and Chaldea (v. 29), whose great feature was their obscenity ; and the cruelty of her favoured form of worship was the burning alive of little children in honour of Moloch (vs. 20 and 21).

The throbbing agony of these two last verses can be felt by the reader. Divine indignation and anguish combined in crying out to this faithless wife : " Bad as was thy conduct in forsaking Me for vile and worthless lovers, yet greater is thy guilt and cruelty in putting My children to so horrible a death."

Whilst the sin of idolatry, and not of immorality, is intended by the expressions used in these verses, yet is it true that the forms of idol-worship here struck at were marked by the grossest immorality, elevated into actions of religious devotion.

" The like things shall not come," etc, (v. 16), i.e., such a frenzied fever of debauchery has never been, and shall never again be witnessed.

That a wife should hand on to her paramours her husband's gifts and wealth is vileness indeed ! Such was Jerusalem's action to her God and King.

" Images of men " (v. 17). The Hebrew text here, as many scholars think, intimates phallus-worship.

" A sweet savour " (v. 19) " a savour of rest."

" And thus it was " (v. 19), that is : " I saw it ; it is really true, saith Adonai-Jehovah." The sense here is, How could such a shameful object of worship, made of wood, stone or metal, give " rest " to either heart or conscience ?

" Thy high place," " an eminent place " (v. 24). This special chamber for worship is fitly described in the margin of the Authorised Version. Here were these religious ceremonies of horror and shame observed.

The religion of the Philistines (v. 27) was comparatively pure, and they did not forsake their gods for those of Egypt and Chaldea ; hence they were religiously superior to the Hebrews.

The Holy Land became morally " the Land of Canaan " (v. 29) because of its adoption of the foul and ancient religion of Canaan.

Idolatry weakens the heart, i.e., the moral perceptions ; but " the Way of the Lord is strength to the upright " (Prov. x. 29).

The madness of Jerusalem's devotion to idolatry is vividly exposed in the revolting figure of verses 31-34.

This unbridled shamelessness justified the severity of her punishment (vs. 35-52). The indecency of phallic worship is, without doubt, intended in the last sentence of verse 43, which should read : " For hast thou not committed this lewdness," i.e., practiced this form of worship, " above all thine abominations ? " (See R.V. Margin).

" Thy filthiness " (v. 36), i.e., " thy brass " (R.V. margin) ; that is, the money spent by Jerusalem on the establishment and maintenance of idol-worship. Silver figured clean money ; brass, unclean.

" I will discover thy nakedness " (vs. 36,

and 37), i.e., her walls should be dismantled, and the city thus exposed to the invaders.

Idolatry destroys all moral defences (vs. 36 and 37).

" Thy lovers " (v. 36), i.e., the Assyrians and Chaldeans ; " those thou hast hated " (v. 37), i.e., the Moabites, Ammonites and the Philistines.

The doom of verse 38 is that of Lev. xx. 10 and Deut. xxii. 22. It is also pointed to in verse 40.

" I will leave thee naked and bare " (v. 39), i.e., the city should be sacked, and (v. 41) no longer able to finance idolatrous worship. See 2 Kings xxv. 9.

Jerusalem's forgetfulness (v. 43) may be contrasted with Immanuel's faithful remembrance (v. 60). The sinner may forget ; the Saviour, never.

Because Jerusalem adopted the specially loathsome form of idolatry practised by the Canaanite she, therefore, morally became her daughter (vs. 44 and 45).

Jerusalem regarded with loathing Samaria and Sodom. She felt herself, religiously, as immeasurably elevated above them (vs. 46 and 56). But she is here declared to be viler than they.

" Thy elder sister " (v. 46), i.e., thy full sister ; " thy younger sister," i.e., thy haif-sister, for Moab and Ammon, born of Sodom, were relatives of Israel by Abraham and Lot.

The Easterns face the East when marking the points of the compass (v. 46).

" Her daughters " (v. 46), i.e., the neighbouring towns.

A false religion is selfish, it neglects the poor ; the true religion of Christ is unselfish and ministers to the poor (Gal. ii. 10) (v. 49).

Financial prosperity was the cause of Sodom's moral fall : " they became haughty (i.e., against God), and committed (a certain) abomination before Me (or against My face) ; therefore I took them away when I had seen it " (Gen. xviii. 21).

" Justified " (vs. 51 and 52), i.e., were made to appear innocent by comparison with the guilt of Jerusalem, for that city was more guilty than Sodom — not positively but relatively (2 Kings xxi. 9).

The future restoration of Jerusalem, together with Samaria and Sodom, is predicted in verses 53-63.

The amazing nature of the grace that will perform this regeneration is preceded by the argument of verses 53-59, which appears to be : That Jerusalem had no more claim to forgiveness and restoration than either Sodom or Samaria, and that, therefore, her recovery was as eternally hopeless as theirs. This principle of grace reappears in Rom. xi. 32.

But a grace rich enough to forgive Jerusalem must, in its nature, be rich enough to forgive her less guilty companions, for there is no difference, all having sinned.

The fact of pardon being granted to Jerusalem brings " comfort " to Samaria and Sodom (v. 54).

But it is humbling to religious pride to be compelled to seek mercy in the company of the degraded and fallen (vs. 55 and 56), and of those formerly despised (v. 57).

The " oath " and " Covenant " (v. 59) formed the marriage bond of Sinai. Jerusalem was unfaithful to that bond ; but not so her Heavenly Lover (v. 60). On the contrary, under the New Covenant, He will make an everlasting marriage-bond with her, giving her at the same time, as bridesmaids, her sisters Sodom and Samaria (v. 61) ; and then will she learn by experience (" know ") what a wonderful husband is Immanuel ; and her boasting will be silenced, (v. 63), for His praise only will fill her mouth.

" Thy Covenant " (v. 61), " My Covenant " (v. 62), i.e., Sinai contrasted with Golgotha.

" Pacified " (v. 63), "forgiven " (R.V.). Heb. " have accepted a propitiation for thee." This propitiation was consummated at Calvary. It provides the righteous ground upon which God may meet, and forgive, the vilest sinners without injury to the righteousness which is the establishment of His throne ; for if God were to forgive sins unrighteously, He would wreck His throne, and cease to be God.

" To turn the captivity " means to restore the prosperity.

The future restoration of Sodom will mark the fulfilment of one of the most marvellous prophecies of the Bible. Compare Matthew x. 15 and xi. 24.

EZEKIEL XVII.—The punishment of king Zedekiah illustrates the heat of God's anger against falsehood, deceit, and breach of Covenants.

The predictions of this prophecy, up to verse 21, were fulfilled five years later.

The historic facts reviewed by the prophecy and recorded in the Scripture, concern

Nebuchadrezzar's second siege of Jerusalem ; the dismissal of Jehoiakim to Babylon ; the selection and elevation to the throne of his uncle Zedekiah, who took in the name of Jehovah an oath of fidelity to the Babylonian monarch ; the breach of that oath by the alliance with the Egyptians ; the consequent third and final siege and capture of the city ; its destruction and that of the Temple by fire ; and the severe punishment pronounced upon Zedekiah and his sons and his princes. These were put to death in the presence of the unhappy king ; he himself was then blinded, loaded with chains, and lodged in the prison at Babylon, where he died.

" A riddle " (v. 2), i.e., an enigma—a dark saying. It was also a parable, that is, the comparison of one thing to another.

This enigma is stated in verses 3-10 ; its solution, in verses 12-21.

" A great eagle " (v. 3), i.e., Nebuchadrezzar.

" Lebanon " (v. 3), i.e., Jerusalem, whose houses were built of cedar from Lebanon.

" The top of the cedar," i.e., the royal family. " The topmost of the young twigs," i.e., Jehoiakim. " A land of traffic," i.e. Babylonia. " A city of merchants." i e. Babylon.

" The seed of the land " (v. 5), i.e. a Hebrew of the Royal family, that is, Zedekiah. " A fruitful soil," that is, Palestine.

" A vine of low stature " (v. 6), i.e., a base kingdom enjoying a measure of prosperity Its branches were toward him, and its roots nourished by him, i.e., by Nebuchadrezzar.

Thus the kingdom of Judah ceased to be a lofty cedar enjoying independence, and became a lowly vine subject to the Gentile monarch.

This was by Divine appointment ; but Zedekiah's rebellion robbed the nation of this limited prosperity, caused its total dispersion, and put an end to the only kingdom upon earth that God had recognized as His.

" Another great eagle " (v. 7), i.e., Pharaoh-Hophra king of Egypt.

" Shall it prosper ? " (v. 9), i.e., the treaty with Egypt which proposed the prosperity of verse 8. The answer is " no " ; for he, Nebuchadrezzar (v. 9), should uproot Zedekiah and destroy his kingdom, with an effort that needed no great power nor many soldiers.

In the solution of the enigma (vs. 12-21) the evil of Zedekiah's conduct in breaking an oath made in the name of Jehovah, is vehemently asserted (vs. 13, 14, 15, 16, 16, 18, 18, 19, 19, 20).

" It might stand " (v. 14). God's loving purpose was the peace and prosperity of His people in subjection to the Gentile ; and that they should be a witness for Him. So should they have been His recognized people, and a light to lighten the Gentiles. But their rebellion lost this prosperity and that glory.

" In the place "—Babylon—" where the king " — Nebuchadnezzar—" dwelleth that made him—Zedekiah—king " etc. (v. 16).

" Make for him " (v. 17 R.V), i.e., help him. " When they," i.e., the Babylonians.

" He gave his hand " (v. 18), i.e., Zedekiah sealed the covenant with the Babylonian king.

" My net and My snare " (v. 20), i.e., the Babylonian army.

" I will plead with him there " (v. 20). This verse, with Jeremiah xxxii. 5 and xxxiv. 4, 5, suggests that in his earthly prison and physical blindness, grace gave him inward eyesight and spiritual freedom.

The kingdom predicted in verses 22-24 is that of the Messiah. The lofty top of the cedar is the Royal Family of David. Its topmost and tender twig, the Messiah (Isa. liii. 2) ; the high mountain. Zion ; " all fowl of every wing,' the kings of the nations, including the great eagles of verses 3 and 7 ; " all the trees of the field " (v. 24), the great men of the earth—these will all submit themselves to the Great King of Israel and enjoy the prosperity of His Kingdom. The high and green tree of man's proud dominion will be brought down and dried up, and the low and dry tree of despised Israel made to flourish.

The Virgin (Luke i. 52) repeated in her song the prophecy of verse 24.

The " green tree " may pre-figure Anti-Christ and the " dry tree," Messiah.

EZEKIEL XVIII.—Entrance into the kingdom promised in the closing verses of the prior chapter is declared in this chapter to depend upon personal conversion (v. 30) and the new birth (v. 31)

The miseries suffered by the people in Jerusalem because of the Babylonian war, were declared by them to be due to their fathers' sins, for that they themselves were righteous. Hence their proverb of verse 2.

repeated in verse 19, and its principle insisted on in verses 25 and 29.

That is : they charged God with injustice, for man always throws the blame upon God, as Adam did (Gen. iii. 12).

Ezekiel's message vindicated God's justice, and shewed the equity of His moral government. It based itself upon the Divine plan, afterwards revealed, by which God can righteously declare a sinner to be a justified person.

As in Ezekiel's day, so in that of his Lord's (Matt. xxiii. 32 and 34-36), the Hebrews believed themselves to be righteous, and attributed their misfortunes to the misconduct of their ancestors. Exod. xx. 5, Jer. xvi. 4, and Lam. v. 7 appeared to warrant this belief ; but Jer. xxxii. 18, 19, Deut. xxiv. 16, and the statement in Exod. xx. 5—" them that hate Me," i.e., the children hating Me—together with Matt. xxiii. 32, prove that descendants are personally not punished for the sins of their ancestors. unless they persevere in them. It is otherwise with national judgments ; but God always did and always does promise individual forgiveness to sinners who repent. His ways are therefore. equal.

The righteous principle upon which God acts in pardoning original sin and personal sins is revealed in Rom. iii. 21-26.

The actions denounced in verses 6-9 are those forbidden in the Law.

But God's love not only forbids injury to others it commands benevolence to the needy (vs. 7 and 8).

" Hath not eaten upon the mountains " (v. 6), i.e., taken part in idolatrous feasts celebrated there (1 Cor. viii. 4). This verse should read as in the Revised Version.

" He is just " (v. 9), i.e., He is a righteous man ; and declared by God to be such.

The second case here cited is that of the bad son of a good father, and the argument is, that this fact aggravates his guilt, and that the merits of his father shall not, and cannot, shield him from punishment.

The third case supposed further illustrates the impartiality of God's justice. It is that of the good son of a bad father, such as Josiah and Hezekiah, and it is stated that just as the righteous conduct of a father is not credited to an unrighteous son, so the wickedness of a father is not charged to the account of a godly son.

The repetition in detail of actions injurious to others (vs. 6-18) is an evidence of God's love to mankind, and of how His nature revolts against all injustice, and selfishness.

The spirit of Exod. xxii. 25 instructs the Christian not to enrich himself by taking advantage of a neighbour's necessities, but to lend his fellow-believer money at moderate, or no interest.

So far from God punishing a man for the sins of others, He will not even punish him for his own sins if he repents and avails himself of God's salvation, which is Christ.

" In " (v. 22)—not " by " as a reward—but in the righteousness of God imputed to the repentant sinner, then as now, because of the Divine action of Rom. iv. 25.

Self-righteous men object to God's justice, however plainly manifested, because they do not wish to recognize it. Hence the repetition of the statement : " But is it not a fact that the son is punished for the iniquity of the father ? " (vs. 19, 25 and 29). Compare Mic. ii. 7, Matt. xi. 18, 19.

The question of verse 23 is answered in verse 32.

Conversion and regeneration (vs. 30 and 31) can only be effected by the Holy Spirit. But the sinner is responsible to repent (v. 30) and to seek this new moral nature (v. 31). Directly he tries to provide himself with these he discovers his helplessness ; and, broken in spirit, and casting himself on God for salvation, the Holy Spirit reveals Christ to him, and thus works the mighty miracle of the New Birth.

EZEKIEL XIX.—The first nine verses of this Lamentation picture the nation of Israel as a lioness, and bewail the fate of her two whelps Jehoahaz (vs. 3 and 4) and Jehoiakim (vs. 5-9). The mourner is Immanuel.

The remaining five verses picture the nation as a vine, and Zedekiah as a strong rod, and bewail his end, and that of the nation.

These three princes were the sons of good king Josiah. They, with Jehoiakin, who only reigned three months, were the last kings of Israel They are here called " princes of Israel," and not princes of Judah, for they were, divinely, the legitimate kings of the whole nation.

Jerusalem was called a great lion, in a good sense (Isa. xxix. i) ; and Judah a lion's whelp, a lion, and an old lion (Gen. xlix. 9).

But Israel should not have associated with

other " lions," or nourished her " whelps" among the young princes of the neighbouring nations. for they became, like them, robbers and murderers (vs. 2 and 3).

God calls His people to separation from the world so that they may have power in testifying against it, and may thus help it, and so be a true witness for God. But the bent of the natural will is to imitate the world and be as like it as possible.

" One of her whelps " (v. 3), i.e., Jehoahaz. He was taken prisoner by Pharaoh-Necho and brought in chains to Egypt (v. 4).

When she had waited (v. 5), i.e., waited in vain for his return, she made another —Jehoiakim (v. 5)—" a young lion," that is, king.

" He knew " (v. 7), means he plundered.

" The nations " (v. 8), i.e., the Babylonians, captured him, and he died on the way to Babylon—drawn and cast forth and unburied.

In the East lions are captured by a net in a pit (v. 8).

The vine of verse 10 is that spoken of in xvii. 6 ; and " its strong rod," and " a rod of her branches " (vs. 11 and 14) was Zedekiah.

Israel, as a vine, enjoyed, under the over lordship of Babylon (v. 11), a limited prosperity (xvii. 5 and 6).

Verse 12 predicted her violent end ; and verse 14 foretold that Zedekiah's treachery would be the cause of the destruction of the city and temple by fire. It also foretold that no king should henceforth reign on the throne of Israel. But other scriptures promised that Jehovah should send the Rod of His strength out of Zion, i.e., Messiah (Ps. cx. 2 and Isa. xi. 1).

Verse 13 describes Israel's miserable state during the Seventy Years of the Captivity.

" This is a Lamentation " for Jehoahaz and Jehoiachim, whose punishment was already then a matter of accomplished history.

" This shall be for a Lamentation " for Zedekiah, whose doom was still future at the time that this lament was given by the Spirit to the prophet.

EZEKIEL XX. 1-44.—The fact of man's moral estrangement from God, and of his incurable attachment to any god rather than Jehovah, is demonstrated by five proofs from Israel's history here recited by the Holy Spirit through Ezekiel.

These five were followed by four more in Israel's later history, viz.: After the Restoration ; under the ministry of John the Baptist ; during that of the Lord Himself ; and, finally, in the period between Pentecost and Titus.

During these nine periods of appeal, and of alternating mercy and judgment, the nation persisted in worshipping any god or every god rather than the true God.

In this the nation demonstrates the hopeless moral corruption, and mental and spiritual degradation and blindness of man at large.

This fundamental doctrine is exceedingly offensive to human pride ; but it shows the necessity of a new creation, without which no man can either recognize or experience spiritual phenomena (John iii. 3, 5, and 2 Corinthians v. 17).

The five periods pointed to by Ezekiel in this prophecy during which Israel chose idols rather than God are :

In Egypt (vs. 5-9).
In the Wilderness (the fathers), (vs. 10-17)
In the Wilderness (the children), (vs. 18-26)
In the Land (vs. 27-29).
In Exile (vs. 30-38).

The seventh year (v. 1), i.e., of the prophet's captivity.

" Certain of the elders came " (v. 1). False prophets among the Exiles were at this time predicting a speedy restoration to Palestine (Jer. xxviii. 11). These Elders desired Ezekiel to preach the same comfortable doctrine, but he refused to do so, and, on the contrary, exposed the deep-seated idolatry of their hearts (v. 16), and announced an accession of the Wrath of God upon them.

To outwardly profess the worship of God (v. 1) and to inwardly love idolatry (v. 16) is gross hypocrisy. Such hypocrisy characterizes modern christendom, as it did ancient Israel.

Verses 5-8 reveal that in Egypt the Israelites were idolaters ; that God raised up prophets (v 5) to plead with them there, but in vain (vs. 7 and 8) ; and that He threatened to destroy them whilst there, and prior to the Exodus (v. 8), but for His Name's sake did not do so. See Leviticus xvii. 7, Amos v. 25, 26, Acts vii. 4, and Ezek. xxiii. 8, with Joshua xxiv. 14.

" I lifted up mine hand." This formula occurs three times (vs. 5, 5, 6). It signifies promise engaged by oath and affirmed by the Triune God.

Ezekiel speaks about Israel's sojourn in Egypt more than any other prophet. In this prophecy he mentions it seven times (vs. 5, 6, 7, 8, 8, 9, 10).

The interrogative here (v. 4) is a command in Hebrew.

Verses 12 and 20, with Deut. v. 15, suggest that, prior to the Exodus, the sabbath of Gen. ii. 3, was not observed by men, but was given by God to Israel, as He gave circumcision, as a sign of special relationship.

Verses 5-10 demonstrate that Israel did not merit so glorious a relationship; it was all due to grace.

" Live in them " (v. 11), not, " by them," for life cannot be thus merited.

The Divine Title Jehovah-Mekaddishkem (Lev. xx. 8) is here repeated (v. 12). See note on Ps. xxiii. 5.

When fathers are hardened in sin (vs. 13-17) hope has recourse to their children; but then as now these are found to possess the same corrupt nature as their parents, and, consequently to love the same sins (vs. 18-21).

" I gave them " (v. 25), i.e., " I permitted them to furnish themselves with "; and, " I permitted them to pollute themselves." These destructive religious ceremonies they adopted from their neighbours, and God did not restrain them from doing so. In His judgments are life (v. 11); in man's judgments, death (v. 26).

God commanded that their children should be passed over to Him and live. Idolatry commanded that they should be passed through to Moloch and die (vs. 26 and 31). Compare Isa. lxiii. 17.

" That they might know that I am Jehovah " (v. 26). God may be known experimentally as a Saviour or as a Destroyer. He must be " known " as the latter by everyone who refuses to know Him as the former.

To Israel He showed both goodness and severity (Rom. xi. 22); but neither action moved them from their idols, for man is by nature evil (Rom. iii-viii).

" They committed a trespass " (v. 27) Heb. " they trespassed a trespass," that is, they were guilty of a supreme trespass, i.e., they associated idols with God. This is the great sin of the Greek and Latin Churches.

This fourth period of Israel's history (vs. 27-29) was as evil and idolatrous as the three preceding ones.

" Saw " (v. 28). This has the sense of selected. " All," i.e., every.

The four " theres " (v. 28) are employed to emphasize the contrast with the one Divinely appointed place of acceptance (v. 40) i.e., Calvary, as foreshadowed by Mount Moriah. Access to God, forgiveness and righteousness, as Abel proved, can only be enjoyed through Christ's atonement; for He is, as He Himself said, the one and only Way to God.

" Bamah," that is " High-place " (v. 29), i.e., Man's preferred religion to God's Holy Mountain (v. 40). The sense of the question is: What Divine authority has the High-place? The very name " High-place " convicted these worshippers of rebellion, and not of ignorance (Deut. xii. 1-5). Patriarchal worship, and that of Elijah, was not High-place worship. The one preceded the giving of the Law; the other followed its rejection.

The fifth period of Israel's idolatrous history is the subject of verses 30-32. The Exiles polluted themselves with idolatry after the manner of their fathers. The " ye " and the " you " of these verses are emphatic; and the interrogative form is here adopted to express strong affirmation.

Ezekiel, by inspiration, refused to pray for his visitors (v. 31). They must have been very angry with him, for, instead of preaching to them the comfortable doctrines which the other prophets announced, he exposed their idolatries and hypocrisies, and predicted their eternal ruin (v. 28).

The determined bent of the Hebrew mind to worship any god rather than Jehovah, and their efforts during 3500 years to become like to other nations and be one of them (v. 32), prove the existence of God and the inspiration of the Bible. For their failure to be as other nations, in spite of all their efforts—and these efforts are still in operation—demonstrates the existence of a Will that plans the contrary, and has planned it for thousands of years; and their repeated rebellions against Jehovah, culminating in the crucifixion of the Messiah, and continuing to the present day, reveal inspiration, for no nation refuses devotion to a God of its own invention. Had the Hebrews invented the God of Israel they would have been loyal to Him.

The predictions of verses 33-44 belong to the future.

" The uplifted hand " (v. 5) promised

blessing ; the " stretched out arm " (v. 33) assured judgment.

" People " in these verses should read "peoples. "

The statements in the prophecy appear to be that, as God at the first brought Israel out of Egypt into the Wilderness (" the wilderness of the land of Egypt," v. 36) and judged them there, so will He in the future bring them out of the Egypt of the nations (v. 34) and into " the wilderness of the peoples " (v. 35), where He will plead with them (v. 36), causing His sheep—the election— to pass under His Shepherd rod of selection into the bond of the everlasting covenant (v. 37), and, at the same time, eternally judging the rebels (v. 38), who shall be refused entrance into the restored land of Israel ; and thus in that day shall the New Israel know the Lord ; and no more shall God's Holy Name be profanely associated with idols (v. 39).

The four " theres " of verses 40-43 contrast with the four " theres " of verse 28.

Redeemed Israel, in the happy day of her future glory, will recognize, and confess, all her happiness to be due to the worthfulness of the Name of Jesus, and not to any moral value in herself, for her " ways " were evil, and her " doings " corrupt.

" Go ye, serve," etc. (v. 39). The language here is ironical. The verse should read as in the Revised Version margin.

The acceptance of the worshipper (vs. 40-41), is the result of the value of the victim offered in sacrifice for sin. Hence believers are engraced in the Beloved One (Eph. i. 6), Christ ; for they have no grace in themselves.

It is ever the aim of fashionable professors of religion to accommodate that of the Bible with the great religions of ancient and modern history. This Ezekiel, like all true servants of God, refused to do (v. 32).

This exposure of the persistent attachment of Israel to idolatry justified God in His employment of the Babylonians to destroy Jerusalem and burn the Temple.

This vindication of God's judicial action is the keynote to the Book of Ezekiel.

Though the sufferings of the exiles proved the falsehood of idolatry and of its prophets and the truth of God's predicted wrath, yet they clung to their idols. Only a few of them repented and were restored with Ezra and Nehemiah to Palestine. Such is the folly and incurable rebellion of the natural heart.

EZEKIEL XX. 45-XXI. 7.—This double-vision prophecy concerned Judah and Jerusalem. Its energy was the wrath of God (45-49) ; the instrument of that energy, the sword of Nebuchadnezzar (vs. 1-7)

The prophecy forms an introduction to chapters xxi.-xxxii.

The correspondence between these two prophecies of the fire and the sword may be thus exhibited :

The Forest of the South—Judah (vs. 45 and 46).
   The Fire of Jehovah (v. 47).
     All flesh shall see (v. 48).
      The Message derided (ridicule) (v. 49).

The City of the Sanctuary—Jerusalem (vs. 1 and 2).
   The Sword of Jehovah (vs. 3 and 4).
     All flesh shall know (v. 5).
      The Message rejected (anger) (v. 7).

"Set thy face" (v. 46 and xxi 2). This action determines direction and certainty of accomplishment.

The four-fold repetition of the word " south " made absolute Judah as the scene of the approaching judgment (vs. 46 and 47).

A dense population is frequently compared in the Scripture to a forest of trees (v. 47).

The wrath of God is here symbolized as fire (v. 47); the green trees figure the righteous, the dry trees, the wicked (vs. 47 and xxi. 4).

The inclusion of the righteous with the wicked in national and universal judgments is one of the principles of God's moral government. It is important to recognise this principle. He does not promise exemption to His people from the suffering which justly follows national sin ; but He makes this great distinction that the wicked perish under such suffering, whilst the righteous are sustained in it ; and, finally in resurrection, delivered from it (Heb. xi. 35).

The accomplishment of the prediction proves the Divine origin of the prophecy (vs. 48, xxi. 5).

The ridicule of unbelief (v. 49) is often more painful than the anger of unbelief (v. 7). From what may be learned in other passages in Jeremiah and Ezekiel of the religious feeling, and condition, of the Hebrews at this time, it may be justly concluded that the interrogation : " What are you moaning about ? " (v. 7) was envenomed by anger.

" The holy places " (v. 2), i.e., the Temple (Plural of majesty). For " Thy word," read " My word."

" It shall not return any more " (v. 5), i.e., the sword should not be returned to its sheath until it had accomplished its purpose.

" The breaking of thy loins " (v. 6). The words, " the girdle of," should be supplied before " thy loins." Physical suffering may be so violent as to break a waist-belt.

" Because it cometh " . . . " behold it cometh " (v. 7), i.e., the sword of the Chaldean— the instrument of the wrath of God.

EZEKIEL XXI. 8-32.—The Divine mission of the Chaldean sword, i.e., the Babylonian army, and its success against Judah (vs. 1-27) and against Ammon (vs. 28-32), is foretold in this vision.

The prophecy preceded the destruction of Judea by five years, and of Ammon by ten years.

The minuteness of detail in these predictions years before they became history, is one of the striking facts of inspiration.

The Babylonian monarch no doubt thought himself to be a free agent ; but, long beforehand his campaign against Judah (vs. 9 and 10), his victory over Zedekiah (vs. 10-17), his recourse to divination at the parting of the high roads in northern Palestine (vs. 18-22), and his victory over the Ammonites (v. 31) was here foretold. And so it happened. Zedekiah, Israel's last king, broke his oath of allegiance (v. 23), the Chaldean king marched against him in consequence, halted in the north of Palestine at the junction of the eastern and western roads leading south, sought, by divination, a choice between them, selected the western, captured and burnt Jerusalem and its Temple, put to death all the leading citizens, struck the crown off the head of Zedekiah, and carried him captive to Babylon.

It is unseemly to make mirth, God having announced His coming wrath (v. 10).

" It contemneth," etc., (v. 10). The sense here is : the steel sword of the Chaldean would cleave in two the wooden sceptre of Judah as it would a twig from any tree.

The grace and love that here recognise idolatrous Judah as " My son," awaken wonder and worship in the heart.

God handed this sharpened sword to the Chaldean slayer in order that it might be used against the Judean wrong-doer. The Apostle Paul in Rom. xiii. states that He had handed the same sword to Nero, Nebuchadnezzar's successor, as the supreme civil magistrate recognized by God, and responsible to Him for its use against evil-doers, and for the protection of well-doers.

Verse 12 should read : " for it shall come upon My people, it shall come upon all the leaders of Israel, they shall be delivered over to the sword together with My people."

Once more the anguish of the Divine love is felt in the words " My people," as in the words " My Son " (vs. 10 and 12).

The sense of verse 13 will appear in the following translation. " There shall be a trial (between the steel sword and the wooden sceptre) and what will happen if the rod despise the sword ? It (the rod) shall be no more ! "

That is : in a test of strength between Nebuchadnezzar and Zedekiah, the latter would be defeated and his sceptre forever broken.

" For the sword shall be doubled the third time " (v. 14). This reading gives the sense, and predicts the third, and final, campaign against Jerusalem. When a well-tempered sword strikes an object it doubles but does not break. Such a sword is justly described as the sword of a great one that inflicts deadly wounds (v. 14). In the sack of Jerusalem that sword pursued its victims into their innermost chambers (v. 14).

" Wrapped up " (v. 15), i.e., sharp.

In verse 16 the sword is addressed, for " thee " in Hebrew is feminine. The sword is here promised success in whatever direction it turns.

The picture of the king of Babylon standing at the parting of the ways (vs. 19-22), is very striking. The future tense should be used in verses 21-23.

They twain, i.e., the two ways, shall come forth out of one land, i.e., Babylonia, and thou shalt choose a place at the head of the way to the city, i.e., Jerusalem (v. 19).

Two arrows, one marked Ammon and the other Jerusalem, were placed in a quiver, and whichever one the king drew was accepted as an omen. The liver of a beast, or a fowl, offered in sacrifice, was also examined, and its healthy or unhealthy condition accepted as favourable, or the reverse (v. 21).

But it, i.e., this divining of Nebuchadnezzar shall be unto them (Zedekiah and the princes) as a false divination in their sight, even to them (Zedekiah, etc.) that have sworn oaths (of allegiance to Nebuchadnezzar); but God will remember that treachery, and they shall be taken."

The iniquity, the transgression, and the sin of verse 24 was this breach of the oath of allegiance taken in the name of Jehovah. The plural of majesty is here used to emphasize that great transgression, and that great sin.

Zedekiah is the profane prince of verse 25, and his crown, the diadem of verse 26. "This shall not be the same," i.e., shall not endure. He was, in effect, the last king; he was high, but was abased; and there will be no other king until He that is low, i.e., the despised Jesus of Nazareth returns, and to Him shall the diadem be given; for it is His right. Meanwhile God overturns all efforts to give that crown to another.

The Ammonites rejoiced at the destruction of Jerusalem. That was their "reproach" (v. 28). But five years later they rebelled against the Chaldeans, who consequently invaded their country and destroyed them so effectually that they ceased to exist as a nation. They perished in their own land (vs. 30 and 32) whereas the captives of Israel whom they reproached still exist, and will be restored.

Thus the very sword that fell upon Judah fell upon Ammon.

"They" (v. 29), i.e., the false prophets of Ammon "see vanity," i.e., promised empty victory unto Ammon. These popular preachers amongst the Ammonites divined lies unto them, with the result that the dead bodies of their hearers were cast upon the headless bodies of the slain Israelites; whose day of slaughter had already come when "their iniquity," i.e., their breach of allegiance, was put an end to.

The sword having accomplished its purpose was to be caused to return into its sheath (v. 30).

EZEKIEL XXII.—The series of prophecies concerning Jerusalem which begin here, coupled with the review of Israel's moral history in chapter xx., and with the entire Book of Jeremiah, have extraordinary interest because they mark the transference of the government of the world from Israel to the Gentile; the unfailing faithfulness of God to His Covenant with Abraham; the justice of His action in the destruction of Jerusalem; and, finally, because there is revealed in these prophetic messages, on God's part, a patience, a tender care, a love, an oft-repeated forgiveness, countless interventions in grace, and heaped-up promises of mercy voiced by spirit-filled messengers, and, on man's part, a demonstration of the entire vanity of his nature, the rebellion and folly of his will, his determined attachment to evil, and the radical corruption of his heart, which neither goodness nor severity could change. Thus did this lengthened test of fallen human nature effectually prove that the carnal mind is enmity against God, that it is not subject to the Law of God, neither indeed can be.

But these prophecies reveal a future of blessing for man based, not upon his goodness, for it has been demonstrated that he has none, but founded upon, and secured by, a goodness reposing in the bosom of God—that is Christ.

The dominating key-note of chapters xxii.-xxiv. is the exposure of the moral condition of Jerusalem as a vindication of the justice of God in its destruction.

The blood-stained city was Jerusalem (v. 2), and "her abominations" are shown to have been the practice of idolatry, with its impure ceremonies, and the violation of the moral legislation of the Book of Leviticus.

The blood shed in the city (v. 3) was that of children sacrificied to Moloch, and of people murdered for the sake of gain (vs. 6, 9, 12 and 13).

"That her time may come" (v. 3), i.e., the time of her punishment. The sense in verse 4 is similar: the "days" and "years" of sinning were now about to receive their judgment, i.e., days of slaughter for Jerusalem, and years of slavery for the captives. The close of this verse may read: "therefore have I purposed to make thee a reproach," etc.

Verse 5, should read as in the Revised Version. How sad that Jerusalem, once famous and full of peace, should become infamous and full of confusion!

The kings of Israel (v. 6) used their power for violence, injustice and murder, and not for protection and peace and righteousness. The actions and conduct denounced in verses 7-12, were all sternly forbidden in the Law. There are some religious teachers who say that that Law was invented by Ezra and his companions fifty years later than the date of this prophecy!

The action threatened in verse 14 is described in verses 15 and 16. This latter verse should read as in the Revised Version. The Divine purpose was that Israel should be apart from, and throned as queen above, the nations of the earth ; but her own conduct caused her to lose that supremacy, and thus she profaned herself, by making herself a common nation.

The second of these messages to Jerusalem (vs. 17-22) had, in principle, a fulfilment five years later ; but its plenary fulfilment belongs to the future day of God's judgment of the city during the reign of the false Messiah.

The point in these verses appears to be that, in a crucible silver may be extracted from baser metals, but that in the case of Jerusalem the process only produced the dross of silver (v. 18), because all had become dross (v. 19). " Will leave " (v. 20) should read : " I will blow upon you, etc."

The third prophecy (vs. 23-31) reviews the moral condition of the city, and groups its inhabitants into four sections : preachers (vs 25 and 28), priests (v. 26), princes (v. 27), and people (v. 29). All are declared to be corrupt, neither " cleansed " nor " rained upon " (v. 24). The conscience that is not cleansed by the precious blood of Christ, and the heart that is not fertilised by the rain of the Holy Spirit, are necessarily unclean, however the outward life may be adorned with religious ceremonies.

The preachers (v. 25) were united ; they destroyed souls ; they enjoyed large salaries ; and they made many widows by urging their husbands to fight, and by promising them victory. They thus furnish a striking picture of present-day preachers accepted by the world (1 John iv 5 and 6). The preachers are mentioned first because their influence was greatest, and because the moral character of a people is determined by its creed.

The priests did not suppress the Bible, of which they were the custodians, they violated it ; i.e., they denied its inspiration and authority ; they profaned its teachings, that is, they lowered the Book to the common level of other books ; they thrust aside its teaching as to separation from evil ; and

by making the Sabbath similar to the rest of the days of the week, they degraded its Author to a position in the common multitude of gods, and thus profaned Him.

The princes (v. 27), and their private chaplains (v. 28), like the other three sections of society, had one main object in view — the amassing of wealth by fair means or foul. A wall built with untempered mortar soon falls. It fitly pictures the value of the religious teaching of men who profess to be the spokesmen of God, but whom God never sent.

The people (v. 29) oppressed and robbed others without compassion. This treatment of " the stranger " was especially wrong, for Israel's duty was to win strangers to the God of Abraham, and not by injustice to alienate them.

Neither a reformer (" the hedge ") nor an intercessor (" the gap ") was found in the guilty city to save it from destruction (vs. 30 and 31).

Jeremiah it is true was there ; but he had been taken out by God from among them, and forbidden to pray for them (Jeremiah xi. 14). Among the citizens none were found able or willing to attempt a reformation, or call the nation to prayer.

But none could accuse   as the unjust Author of their sufferings, for they were the reasonable fruits of " their own way " (v. 31).

EZEKIEL XXIII.—The idolatry of the ancients was not the senseless worship of savages but a highly developed, philosophical and cultured religion, beautified with impressive ceremonies, made awesome and mysterious by human sacrifice, and accepted by the deepest religious feelings of kings, princes, philosophers, scientists and all classes of society, both cultured and uncultured.

But God in order to make men sensible of the vileness and horror of a religion so approved by man, was obliged to use the imagery of this chapter ; for none other could express its bestiality and loathesomeness.

To charge the Bible with indelicacy in its condemnation of sin, is as just as to condemn a mirror for reflecting the loathsome marks of a repugnant disease upon a man's face. The Bible and the mirror being truth, can, neither of them, act contrary to their nature.

Aholah and Aholibah figure Samaria and Jerusalem. They were the daughters of one mother—Sarah. Aholah means " her tent " ; Aholibah, " My tent." Samaria and the Northern Kingdom set up a place of worship of their own, but Jerusalem and the Southern Kingdom were the custodians of God's place of worship—the Temple Hence as this chapter points out, the sin of Jerusalem was greater than that of Samaria ; for priests and people associated idolatry, in its most blood-stained form, with the worship of Jehovah (vs. 38 and 39).

Judgment had already destroyed Samaria and swept its people into captivity, and a similar doom was now impending over Jerusalem (vs. 31-34). She, far from taking warning by the fate of her sister, plunged deeper into the abominations of idolatry (v. 11).

There was no moral difference between these sisters. The same conduct shewed the same nature. The heart at the close was the same as at the beginning. They were the children of an idolater (Joshua xxiv. 2) ; they were idolaters while still in Egypt (Joshua xxiv. 14), and in the Wilderness (Acts vii. 42, 43) ; and, now after long years of Divine pleading and goodness and discipline, they were attached more than ever to their idols, including those brought from Egypt (vs. 8, 19, 27).

These facts, reaching a climax in this chapter, vindicate God's action in the outpouring of His wrath upon them.

The chapter reviews their conduct from Egypt (v. 3) to the final destruction of their city and the nation (v. 47).

Thus under this lengthened test of 1,000 years was demonstrated the incurable idolatry of man's fallen nature.

Idolatry continues to-day in a materialistic form in Heathendom, and in varying mental and material forms in Christendom, and will reach its climax under Antichrist.

The Assyrians were clothed with blue i.e., purple (vs. 5 and 6) ; the Babylonians, in vermilion (v. 14). These colours appear to-day on the bas-reliefs in the British Museum.

" Her mind was alienated from them " (vs. 17 and 22). Impure love usually ends in open hatred. So Israel in the end hated the Egyptians, the Assyrians, and the Baby-

lonians, and they hated her (vs. 22-26, and 28, 29).

Recalling old sins frequently leads to a resumption of them (v. 19). " In bruising " (vs. 8 and 21), i.e., in permitting to be handled.

Pekod, Shoa, and Koa (v. 23) were Eastern nations. They are all named in the Babylonian inscriptions now in the British Museum.

" Their judgments " (v. 24), i.e., the cruel punishments usual among the Babylonians. They mutilated their prisoners by cutting off their noses and ears (v. 25), they slaughtered others, or burned them alive, or, stripping them of their property and clothes, made them slaves (v. 25).

The fact that Israel was an idolater in Egypt is again recalled (vs. 3 and 27).

" Drunkenness " (v. 33), i.e., the drunkenness of anguish—an anguish so great as to cause the captives to tear their bosoms (v. 34, R.V.).

" Thy lewdness," etc. (v. 35), i.e., the punishment of thy lewdness.

The deepest depth of evil is the association of idolatry with God (vs. 38 and 39).

" Their hands " and " their heads " (v. 42), i.e., the hands and heads of Aholah and Aholibah already old in idolatry (v. 43). Old women, living lives of debauchery and loaded with jewellery, present a loathsome picture that fills the heart of the spectators with pity and horror.

" Righteous men " (v. 45), i.e., the Chaldeans.

Jerusalem suffered the just doom of an adulteress ; her walls were beaten down with stones, her houses burned with fire, and her children slain with the sword (v. 47).

This fearful doom was occasioned by their own conduct, and could not be ascribed to Divine injustice.

EZEKIEL XXIV.—The people boasted (xi. 3) that Jerusalem was a cauldron and they the food in it, and that, consequently they were quite safe. This prophecy (vs. 1-14) informed them that the cauldron was corrupt and poisonous (vs. 6 and 11), and that its contents would be consumed (vs. 4, 5 and 10).

The second prophecy of the chapter (vs. 15-27) predicted that the destruction of the city and its inhabitants would be a calamity so overwhelming as to extinguish public expression of private sorrow.

Three years later (compare xxiv. 1 with xxxiii. 21) these two prophecies were fulfilled.

Thus the lesson is taught that a church founded by God, may become corrupt; and that membership in a church is no security against the wrath of God.

"This same day" (v. 2). Thus, by prophecy, the exiles knew what the public could only have learned three months later by post, owing to the distance of Jerusalem from the river Chebar.

"Every good piece" (v. 4) "with the choice bones and the bones under it" (v. 5), i.e., both princes and common people.

"Whose scum" (v. 6), i.e., verdigris. That is, the cauldron itself was poisonous, and, as such, symbolized the moral condition of the city.

"Bring it out piece by piece, let no lot fall upon it" (v. 6). Prisoners were usually selected by lot for death or liberty, but no such chance should be enjoyed by Jerusalem.

The Law commanded (Lev. xvii. 13) that blood should be hidden in the earth. But Jerusalem's guilt was as visible, and cried as loud for judgment, as blood exposed upon the top of a rock; and God, therefore, dealt with her as a blood-stained city (vs. 6-9).

The vessel itself as well as its contents, were to be consumed by fire (vs. 10 and 11).

"The scum" pictured idolatry.

Verse 12 should read as in the Revised Version margin. Compare Luke xiii. 34.

"Neither shalt thou mourn (v. 16), i.e., mourn publicly, only secretly as in verse 23.

A son of Aaron was permitted to remove his turban as a sign of grief (Lev. x. 6; xiii. 45; and xxi. 10).

To cover the lips (Micah iii. 7), and remove the shoes, were public evidences of mourning.

"The bread of men," i.e., the food brought to the house of mourners by sympathising neighbours.

The Temple was the desire of the Hebrew's eyes, as a wife is that of her husband's (vs. 16 and 21).

The word "behind" should be supplied after "left" (v. 21). The parents were exiled, and their hearts naturally yearned for their children left behind in Jerusalem; yet public grief swallowed up private sorrow as to its outward expression (vs. 22-24).

The prophet was to be dumb to his people until the arrival three years later of the messenger announcing the capture of the city ("their strength"), the destruction of the Temple ("the desire of their eyes"), and of that whereon "they set their minds" (their children) (xxxiii. 21). (v. 25).

God took from Ezekiel his happiness and from Paul his health, thus fitting them as preachers the more fully to sympathize with suffering humanity, and at the same time, fortifying them against calling. Both men accepted the discipline.

EZEKIEL XXV.—The prophet, dumb to Israel, now speaks to seven neighbouring nations; that is, to the world at large, under the dominion of Babylon.

One lesson learned from this chapter is: not to rejoice when God punishes guilty men, for that will bring His anger upon such as do so.

Psalm lxxxiii. and the prophecy of Obadiah and Ps. cxxxvii. with Lam. iv. and Amos i. 11, should be read in connection with this prophecy.

The Ammonites, the Moabites, the Edomites, and the Philistines have perished, as nations, but the Israelites exist in millions. This fact is one of the many proving the inspiration of the Bible.

The burning of the Temple "profaned" it (v. 3).

"The men of the East" (v. 4), i.e., the Babylonians.

"Their palaces" (v. 4), i.e. pavilions.

"Stamped with the feet" (v. 6), i.e., danced with joy.

These nations were conquered by the Babylonians five years after the burning of the Temple (Josephus).

The judgment upon Edom by Israel (v. 14) is demanded by Gen. xxv. 23. Isa. lxiii. defines the time.

Thus these four nations (vs. 5, 11, 14 and 17) should get to know to their sorrow that the God of Israel exists, and that He judges sin.

EZEKIEL XXVI.—The prophecy concerning Tyre occupies this and the two following chapters.

This chapter sets out its sin (v. 2); its punishment (vs. 3-6); the executors of its doom—Nebuchadnezzar (v. 7) and Alexander (v. 12); and the effect produced on other nations by her judgment (vs. 15, 16, 18 and 21).

The "eleventh year" (v. 1), i.e., of the prophet's exile, and, therefore, one year before the fall of Jerusalem.

The month is not stated, but a comparison of Jer. xxxix. 1-7 and lii. 4-14 suggests the fifth month. It is, therefore, probable that Tyre voiced her delight at the close of the fourth month, as her nearness to Jerusalem would permit of her hearing of its fall very soon. On the first day of the following, that is of the fifth month, Ezekiel's prophecy was a swift condemnation of her joy.

"Gates" (v. 2) plural of majesty for great-gate, i.e., international mart.

"She is turned" (v. 2), i.e., "it" (her trade) "shall be turned."

The Eastern peoples brought their productions into Jerusalem and exchanged them there for Western money and goods. The destruction of Jerusalem would, therefore enrich Tyre by the transference of this traffic to her.

There were two Tyres. The older city was built upon a promontory jutting out into the sea. It was captured by Nebuchadnezzar, and its ruins thrown into the sea by Alexander. New Tyre was built upon an island at a little distance from the shore, and was captured by Alexander.

The siege of Tyre by Nebuchadnezzar lasted thirteen years (xxix. 18 and Isa. xxiii.).

Tyre is a Hebrew word, and means a rock.

People who rejoice at the bankruptcy of business rivals bring upon themselves the anger of God (v. 2) ; for heartlessness and selfishness are sins against Him.

"Many nations as waves" (v. 3). The first great wave was the Babylonian ; the last, the Grecian, for the prophecy of this chapter embraces both destructions. Nebuchadnezzar destroyed her walls ; Alexander scraped her dust (v. 4), for, in order to attack New Tyre, he built a causeway to the island through the sea with the materials of the Old Tyre, and history records that his soldiers, in order to complete the causeway, gathered the dust of Old Tyre in baskets and emptied them into the waters. To-day, as for centuries past, the site of the ancient city is a bare rock upon which fishermen dry their nets. Tourists now seek in vain for even a relic of the doomed city (v. 21).

These prophecies are a striking demonstration of the inspiration of Scripture. The demonstration is heightened by a comparison with the prophecy concerning Sidon. It was to be filled with blood—and there have been appalling massacres therein from time to time—but the city itself was to continue whilst Tyre was to disappear. Such is the fact to-day—New Tyre disappeared in 400 A.D. ; Sidon exists.

"Her daughters" (vs. 6 and 8), i.e., the neighbouring towns dependent upon Tyre.

The "he" and "his" of verses 9-11 is Nebuchadnezzar ; the "they" of verse 12 the soldiers of Alexander.

The "and" in the last line of verse 20 would be better translated "but." The argument is, that instead of the nations enriching Tyre because of the destruction of Jerusalem (v. 2), they would impoverish her (vs. 3 and 19) ; and whilst her inhabitants would be shut up with the Antediluvians in the prison-house of Sheol (v. 20), Messiah would be reigning in glory in the Land of the Living, at Jerusalem, in the midst of the redeemed sons of Israel.

Thus the close of the chapter corresponds and contrasts with its beginning. Jerusalem destroyed and its citizens in captivity, Tyre enriched and her citizens clothed with glory ; Tyre destroyed and its citizens in eternal captivity, and Jerusalem and her citizens rejoicing in the glory of Messiah's endless life and kingdom.

EZEKIEL XXVII.—In this inspired Elegy Tyre the city (vs. 3-9 and 26 and 27) is likened to a ship, and (vs. 10 and 11) to a fortress. She was both a continental and a maritime power, and her wealth was founded upon both land and water.

The prosperity of the city is set out in verses 3-26, and its total destruction in verses 26-3 .

The abruptness of the change from prosperity to ruin in the middle of verse 26, will be the more noticed if the word "but" is supplied, and the second member of the verse thus read : "but the East wind shall break thee in the midst of the seas. The past tense is here used in the Hebrew text to express the sure fulfilment of the prediction. This grammatical form frequently appears in the Hebrew prophetic Scriptures.

"The sea" (v. 3). This should read "the seas" (See Revised Version margin) : for the island opposite the port provided two entrances, so that ships could enter by the south passage in a northerly gale, or by the north passage in a southerly storm.

Thy " Borders " (v. 4), i.e., thy hull. Tyre is here compared to a ship. This whole passage (vs. 3-9) should read as in the Revised Version.

" Thy pilots " (v. 8), i.e., officers. Zidon and Arvad supplied the common sailors, but Tyre the officers.

" Occupy " (v. 9), i.e., barter.

Verses 9 and 10 describe her soldiers, as the prior verses her sailors.

" The persons of men " (v. 13), i.e., slaves. " Javan, Tubal and Meshech, " i.e., Greece and Russia.

" Togarmah " (v. 14), i.e., Armenia.

The " Dedan " of verse 15 was in Syria ; that of verse 20, in Arabia.

" Great waters " (v. 26), i.e., the Eastern and Western Oceans. This first line of verse 26 is the culminating point in the statement of prosperity.

" Ships of Tarshish " (v. 25), i.e., ocean-going vessels. Compare the expression " East India-man," or " liner." Thus a ship going to Tarshish might be a small vessel, but a " ship of Tarshish " might be continually employed navigating the Indian Ocean.

The abrupt break in verse 26 has been already noticed.

Verse 27 pictures the stately ship, richly freighted, sinking in the ocean with all on board.

" The peoples shall hiss because of thee " (v. 36). This " hiss," expressive of mental shock, corresponds to the low whistle which men give to-day on suddenly hearing of some great calamity.

" Terror " (v. 36) Hebrew " terrors," i.e., the plural of magnitude for a great subject of supreme terror.

" Thou shalt never be any more." This prediction has been fulfilled. Old Tyre was utterly destroyed in 600 B.C. and New Tyre in 400 A.D

EZEKIEL XXVIII.--The dual personality of the Demoniac (Mark v.) corresponds to the dual personality of the Prince of Tyre, except that, in this case, Satan himself, and not a subordinate, energized his victim.

As thus indwelt, and energized, the Prince of Tyre is here a fore-picture of Antichrist, and the city itself pictures the polished point

of the spear wounding the people of God. Tyre, as a fortress of the Evil One, was planted in Immanuel's Land, and, as a source of moral corruption and falsehood, visualized the Kingdom of Darkness in its perpetual antagonism to the Kingdom of Light.

The King of Tyre at this time was Ethbaal II. Ethbaal means " God Himself." He claimed to be the great god. Antichrist will declare himself to be the Supreme God (2 Thess. ii. 4).

In verses 1-10. the Prince of Tyre is addressed as a man (v. 9) ; in verses 12-17, the king of Tyre is addressed as Satan.

" Strangers " (v. 7), i.e., the Babylonians noted for their barbarity.

" Deaths " (v. 8), i.e., the appalling death. Compare Rev. xix. 20.

" But thou shalt be a man " (v. 9), i.e., thou art a mere man.

" Thou sealest up the sum," i.e., thou art the perfection of wisdom and beauty. This statement, and those which follow in verses 13-15, describe Satan prior to his fall.

" Thou hast been " (v. 13) ; better translated : " thou wast."

" Eden " (v. 13). Excepting Isa. li. 3, this is the first mention of Eden since Gen. iv. 16. To emphasize its reality the words " the Garden of God " are added. Eden itself is, therefore, pointed to, and not a mere summer-garden of the prince of Tyre. It is again spoken of in xxxi. 9, 16, 18, xxxvi. 35, and Joel ii. 3.

The precious stones detailed (v. 13) are those of Gen. ii. 11 and 12. Nine of these were found on the breast of the High Priest.

" Created " (v. 13), not begotten, therefore super-human. " Thou art " (v. 14), rather " thou wast." Satan as the anointed cherub " covered," i.e., was guardian of, the world of Gen. i, 1 ; or, perhaps, the " garden " of verse 13. See xxxi. 8.

" And I have set thee so " (v. 14), rather : " and when I appointed thee thou wast placed upon the holy mountain of God, and thou didst walk to and fro in the midst of the stones of fire."

" The mountain of God " was Eden. Most probably it was a pyramid. Hence man's religious impulse for, and veneration of, pyramids. " The stones of fire " perhaps mean the precious stones of verse 13. These, not then hidden in the ground, shone and sparkled on its surface like fire, and, it so originated the Arabian tales of valleys covered with sparkling diamonds.

"Iniquity was found in thee" (v. 15). Pride was the form of this iniquity (Luke x. 17, 18). This rebellion probably caused the catastrophe which occured between the first and second verses of Gen. i.

The idolatry, violence, and sin of Tyre were inspired and energized by Satan (v. 16) through malice because of his ejection from Eden (v. 16).

The city of Tyre is addressed in verses 18 and 19.

Thus here, as in Mark v., the master and his slave are addressed alternately.

The judgment upon Zidon (vs. 22-24) was suffering, but not extinction. Therefore she exists to-day; but her history has been one of pestilence and bloodshed.

The city was founded by a son of Canaan (Gen. x. 15). It was famous as the shrine of the Virgin Queen of Heaven and her Child. Jezebel was a daughter of the king of Zidon, and introduced this degrading form of idolatry into Israel.

The happy future of Israel (vs. 25 and 26) is contrasted with the extinction of Tyre and the judgment of Zidon.

"They that despise them" (v. 26), that is, that despised the sons of Israel; as in verse 24.

"They—the Zidonians—shall get to know (to their sorrow) that I am Adonai-Jehovah" (v. 24).

"They—the Israelites—shall get to know (to their joy) that I am Jehovah their God" (v. 26), for He will faithfully fulfil His promise o Jacob (v. 25) and will give them the land.

The Great God and Saviour Jesus Christ (Titus ii. 13 R.V.) can be known as a Judge or as a Saviour. All men must know Him as either. How much wiser to fall at His feet in contrition and faith, and so prove His grace as a Saviour, than, later, to experience His severity as a Judge.

The return of the Hebrews to Palestine is foretold in many prophecies. Some of the more striking are Deut. xxx. 3 and 4, Isa. xi. 11, 12, 13, xxvii. 12 and 13, Jer. xxxi. 8-10, xxxii. 37, Ezek. xxxiv. 13, and xxxvii. 21, and Amos ix. 14 and 15.

The ancient Greeks dedicated the Isle of Tyre to the god Hercules, i.e., the Mighty One. It is remarkable that the Hebrew word for God in this prophecy (v. 2) is "El"—The Mighty One.

EZEKIEL XXIX-XXXII. The seven prophecies of these four chapters concern Egypt. They cover the period from 588 to 572 B.C. and appear in moral and not in chronological order.

Egypt is the last world-kingdom addressed by Ezekiel. It is the first addressed by Jeremiah (xlvi.) whilst Babylon is the last (l.).

Herodotus and Josephus state that this Pharaoh—Hophra or Apries—captured Gaza (Jer. xlvii. 1), made himself master of Palestine, recovered what was lost in the battle at Carchemish (Jer. xlvi. 2), and that, because of his successes for twenty-five years, he declared that not even a god could defeat him (v. 3). But he was overthrown by Nebuchadnezzar (Jer. xliii. 10-12 and xliv. 30) and strangled by his own rebellious soldiery.

"The dragon" (v. 3), i.e., the crocodile. It was the national emblem of Egypt, as the lion is of England.

"The fish of thy rivers," etc. (v. 4), i.e., Pharaoh's adherents.

"Thou shalt not be brought together" (v. 5), i.e., his army would be broken beyond hope of recovery.

"To be at a stand" (v. 7), i.e., disjointed.

"I will bring a sword" (v. 8), i.e., the Babylonians.

Verse 10 should read as in the Revised Version.

"A base," that is, a subordinate kingdom (v. 14). Such has Egypt been from that day to the present time.

The forty years (vs. 11-14) of desolation and dispersion closed at the destruction of the Babylonian Empire by the Persians. Thus the seventy years of Israel's captivity and the forty years of Egyptian exile terminated at the same time. This may point to the future restoration of Egypt and of Israel at the same time as predicted in Isa. xix.—for Egypt is to be restored and blessed in the latter day. The independence of Jerusalem in 1917 after 2520 solar years of subjection, and of Egypt in 1922 after 2520 lunar years of servitude, support this expectation.

Zedekiah's trust in Egypt caused his destruction (Jer. xxxvii. 5-8, xliv. 30 and xlvi. 25, 26).

Verse 16 should read as in the Revised Version. Israel "looked after" the Egyptians instead of "after" Jehovah; and by so doing kept bringing their iniquity (unbelief) to God's remembrance.

The prophecy of verses 17-21 was given seventeen years later (vs. 1 and 17), but introduced here to secure the unity of the subject.

The siege of Tyre lasted thirteen years. The Babylonian king undertook it at God's command (Jer. xxv. 9). He captured the city, but secured no treasure, for the Tyrians had removed it, and most of their citizens, to other cities by sea. Carrying earth and timber for the construction of besieging forts made the soldiers' heads bald, for baskets of earth and stones were carried on the head, and peeled their shoulders, for timber was carried on the shoulder.

"They," i.e., the soldiers, wrought for Me" (v. 20). See Jer. xxv. 9.

"The horn of the house of Israel" (v. 21). Perhaps this means Zerubbabel, who may have been born in that year. The word Zerubbabel means "born in Babylon."

EZEKIEL XXX.—The great space given to Egypt in the Bible, and the number of prophecies concerning her, is largely due to the attraction which her wealth and idolatry had for Israel. They continually confided in her rather than in Jehovah.

Egypt symbolizes the world. The Christian Church leans upon it rather than upon God. Hence its religion is copied, and, when money is needed by the Church, the help of "Egypt" is sought by liquor-licensed bazaars, whist-drives, betting, horse-racing, theatrical performances, subscription-dances, smoking concerts, and similar devices. This leaning on "Egypt" destroys the spiritual life of the Church, as the covenant with Egypt destroyed the national independence of Israel.

There are two messages in this chapter. The first (vs. 1-19) probably followed that of xxix. 17 on the eve of the Babylonian monarch's march against Egypt after the capture of Tyre. The second (vs. 20-26) was communicated three months before the capture of Jerusalem by the Babylonians, and, therefore, shortly after the breaking of one of Pharaoh's arms (v. 21) in the defeat which he suffered in attempting to raise the siege of Jerusalem (see notes on Jer. xxxvii. 5 and xlvi. 2).

The formula "the Day of the Lord" (v. 3) is an idiom expressing Divine intervention in human affairs. It occurs twenty times in the Old Testament, and four times in the New. See notes on Rev.

i. 10, 1 Thess. v. 2, 2 Thess. ii. 2, and 2 Pet. iii. 10.

The intervention is necessarily punitive; for the Lord's Day terminates and judges Man's Day.

Before "time" (v. 3), supply the word "judgment."

"The sword" (v. 4), i.e., the Babylonian sword. Its slaughter was the "Day of the Lord" for Egypt.

"Her foundations" (v. 4) i.e., the Egyptian government.

"The men of the land," etc. (v. 5), i.e., "the sons of the Land of the Covenant" (R.V.), that is, the Hebrews who made the covenant denounced by Jeremiah, and who sought refuge in Egypt from the Babylonians (Jer. xlii.-xliv.). Ezekiel here unites with Jeremiah in predicting their destruction.

"From the tower of Syene" (v. 6), i.e., "from Migdol to Syene"; that is, from one end of Egypt to the other (See R.V.). Compare xxix. 10.

The predictions of verse 7 were not fulfilled for more than 1,000 years. During that lengthened period the enemies of the Bible could triumphantly point to the power and magnificence of the Egyptian cities. They were among the most splendid in the world. But 500 years after Christ the Mahomedans ruined the land; and up to a recent date, it only presented a spectacle of ruin, and her poor and squalid cities were built in the midst of the ruined cities of her former splendour, now wasted.

"In ships" (v. 9), i.e., dispatch-boats up the Nile.

"Noph" (v. 13), i.e., Memphis. The Moslems destroyed every trace of idolatry in Egypt, whether pagan or papal.

"There shall be no more a prince," etc. (v. 13). This prophecy had an immediate fulfilment, for, from the days of the Persians to the present time, the kings of Egypt have never been Egyptians by race.

"Pathros" (v. 14), i.e., Southern Egypt.

"Zoan," i.e., Tanis, a city of northern Egypt. "No," now Thebes.

"Sin" (v. 15), i.e., Pelusium in the Egyptian Delta.

"Aven and Pi-beseth" (v. 17), i.e., Heliopolis and Bubastis; where was a famous temple to the sun.

"Tehaphnehes" (v. 18) the Tahpanhes of Jeremiah xliii. 7; a city on the Syrian frontier of Egypt; the Greek Daphne.

"The yokes of Egypt " (v. 18), i.e., the oppressive rule imposed by Egypt on other nations.

"The one arm " i.e., the army of Pharaoh (v. 21) was broken at Carchemish (Jer. xlvi. 2); the other, in Egypt (v. 22), for, weakened by a revolt, he was easily overthrown by Nebuchadnezzar, and thus both his arms were broken (Ps. xxxvii. 17 and Jer. xlviii. 25).

The natural heart quickly wearies of these repeated threatenings of judgment, hence the books of Jeremiah and Ezekiel are unpopular in Christendom. But these repetitions reveal God's heart and man's heart—the one so loving, the other so evil. Love sought continually to save; rebellion refused continually to listen.

EZEKIEL XXXI.—This prophecy was uttered about two months before the fall of Jerusalem.

In it Pharaoh is compared with Sardanapalus, the last king of Assyria, and conquered by Nebuchadnezzar.

The prophet likens empires to great trees and their kings to the highest branches.

The prophecy penetrates the world of the dead, and reveals the disembodied spirits of deceased kings as no longer royal personages, but members of the general multitude of the dead (v. 14).

Thus this chapter is one of the few which unveils the mysterious spirit-world. Compare Isa. xiv. 9-27 and Ezek. xxxii. 17-32.

The answer to the question in verse 2 is : " Thou art like to Sardanapalus, the last king of Assyria."

The Assyrian Empire is here compared to a great cedar—a cedar of Lebanon, a cedar of the Garden of God. These are terms expressing magnitude, strength, and beauty. The outstanding top of the tree (v. 3) figured the Assyrian monarch ; the waters, the deep and the rivers (v. 4) pictured the nations that contributed to the wealth of the empire ; and the trees of the field symbolized the subordinate kings. These occasioned the splendour pictured in verses 5-9. Assyria outshone all other kingdoms.

"Shroud " (v. 3), i.e., foliage.

"The mighty one of the Nations " (v. 11), ." and strangers, the terrible of the nations " (v. 12), i.e., Nebuchadnezzar and the Babylonians.

"All peoples have left him " (v. 12).

Upon the defeat of Sardanapalus he was forsaken by all his allies. Pride caused his ruin (vs. 10 and 14).

"All that drink water " (v. 14), i.e., all the trees that drink water. The argument here is : that as a tree is dependent upon water, and cannot stand up in its own strength, so kings are dependent, as all other men, upon the Hand of God.

"Thou," " he " (v. 10). The change of person is poetic. Sardanapalus is first addressed personally, and then figuratively.

Some scholars think that the Hebrew word in verse 3 should read " a box-tree " instead of " the Assyrian." If that be so, then the verse would read : " Behold a box-tree (desired to be as) a cedar in Lebanon " ; i.e., Egypt, a mere box-tree, essayed to exalt itself into a cedar-tree as Assyria.

"The deep," " the floods," " the great waters " (v. 16) signify nations, and the trees, their kings—as is plain from verse 16. These kings and nations lamented the downfall of the Assyrian monarchy. Compare Rev. xviii. 15-19.

"The grave " (v. 15), " hell " (v. 16). Both these words in Hebrew are " Sheol," i.e., the abode of the dead.

It was God that cast Sardanapalus down into Sheol (v. 16).

"The pit " (v. 16), i.e., " the dungeon." or " abyss." The words " the nether-parts of the earth " (vs. 14, 16 and 18) suggest that Sheol is situated in the centre of the earth.

In that " pit " (v. 14) the greatest monarchs rank with the disembodied spirits of the generality of men.

"They " (v. 17), i.e., the kings. " With him," i.e., with Sardanapalus. Companions in misery (v. 16) derive a sad comfort from mutual suffering.

The question of verse 2 is repeated in verse 18, and the answer here is that Pharaoh was only comparable to ordinary monarchs, and that his death would be without honour. And so it fell out, for he was strangled ; and so the prophet exclaims pointing to him : " This is Pharaoh."

EZEKIEL XXXII.—The destruction of Pharaoh and his army (vs. 1-16, and their perdition (vs. 17-32), repeat the destruction and perdition of the three preceding chapters.

The repetition of facts or prophecies by the Holy Spirit marks their importance ; emphasizes the great moral lessons and principles which they teach ; and proves the incurable resistance of the natural heart to the repeated pleadings of Divine love.

The first prophecy of this chapter (vs. 1-16) links the Divine judgments on Egypt at the Exodus (vs. 6 and 7) with those then about to be executed, and with the future judgment of Antichrist and his kingdom, of which Pharaoh and Egypt are types. See notes on Rev. xvi.

This prophecy was uttered shortly after the destruction of Jerusalem (v. 1).

" Phra " in Burmese signifies king, priest, and God.

The second verse should read as in the Revised Version. Pharaoh aspired to be as a strong lion ; but he was only a crocodile.

" The seas " (v. 2), i.e., the Nile. Pharaoh, as a crocodile, is here pictured passing from his own river, the Nile, into other great rivers, and troubling and fouling them. Thus is signified his invasion of other kingdoms, and the injury done to them.

" My net " (v. 3), i.e., the Babylonians.

A sea-monster thrown upon dry land is helpless, must soon die, and his flesh is devoured by vultures and wild beasts (vs. 4 and 5).

" Thy height " (v. 5), i.e., the high heap of his slain soldiers.

The Nile valley is formed by the Eastern and Western mountains (v. 6). As in the days of Moses the waters were turned into blood, so in the days of Nebuchadnezzar the land was drenched with blood.

It is quite possible that the phenomena of verses 7 and 8 were a repetition of the Plague of Darkness (Exod. x. 21) ; but perhaps here, as elsewhere in the Scripture, the language is figurative and poetical, and intends the overthrow of the imperial and executive governments.

The neighbouring nations, hearing of the utter destruction of the Egyptians by the Babylonian sword, were filled with terror (vs. 9-12).

" My sword " (v. 10), i.e., the sword of the king of Babylon (v. 11).

" Deep " (v. 14), i.e., subside. The sense here is that owing to the absence of human and animal life during forty years, the waters of the Nile would become clear and untroubled, in contrast with verse 2.

Thus should the Egyptians know to their sorrow that God is, and that He judges evil.

The last prophecy concerning Egypt (vs. 17-32) presents in vision Pharaoh and his armies, and the armies of his allies, helpless captives, covered with shame, and shut up in the dungeon of Sheol, in company with other kings and their armies. All these, when on earth, were mighty and caused terror ; but in the world of the dead they suffer a common misery, ignominy, and helplessness.

This Scripture is one of the few which permit a momentary glance into the dreadful mystery of the spirit-world. See notes on chapter xxxi. 1-18, Luke xvi. 19-31, and 1 Pet. iii. 19, 20.

" The fifteenth day of the month " (v. 17). The word " twelfth " may be supplied before " month "from verse 1.

" Cast them down " (v. 18). The Hebrew prophets were said to do what they were commissioned to declare. See verse 20.

" The famous nations " (v. 18), i.e., Pharaoh's allies.

" Nether " (v. 18), i.e., lower. The pit, i.e., the dungeon of Sheol.

The answer to the question in verse 19 is " No one." Pharaoh thought himself greater, richer, and more cultured than any other monarch.

" Go down," i.e., into the world of the dead.

" The uncircumcised " (v. 19). This term occurs ten times in this prophecy. It expresses non-relationship to God and corresponds to the modern word " unconverted."

" Slain by the sword " (v. 20). This formula is repeated twelve times in the prophecy. It signifies Divine judgment.

" Draw her " (v. 20), i.e., drag Egypt away, and all her armies, into Sheol.

" The strong " (v. 21), i.e., the chiefest. " To him " i.e., to Pharaoh.

" Asshur " (v. 22), i.e., Assyria ; " him," i.e., Pharaoh.

" Their shame " (v. 24). On earth they were robed with honour ; in Sheol, clothed with shame.

" They " (v. 25), i.e., Assyria and Elam— " her," i.e., Egypt—" him," i.e., Pharaoh— " he," i.e., Pharaoh ; " him " (v. 26), i.e., Pharaoh.

" But they " (v. 27), i.e., the Egyptians. The preceding monarchs had honourable burial in their armour and with their swords beneath their heads. But not so Pharaoh.

He was strangled according to history.
" But their iniquities " (v. 27) and " their bones," i.e., the iniquities and the bones of the Egyptians.

" Thou " emphatic (v. 28), i.e., Pharaoh.
" My " or " His terror," (v. 32), i.e., the Babylonian, who was God's " terror." " He " i.e., Pharaoh.

Thus close these seven prophecies concerning Egypt. She sought in self-will and the pride of nature to take the place which God had given to Babylon. The mighty empire of Assyria had had to bend to God's gift of supremacy to Nebuchadnezzar ; and Pharaoh, though he owned no god but himself (xxix. 3 and 9), was no better than other monarchs in power and might. He was uncircumcised like the others ; that is, not owned of God, nor upheld by Him.

Pride, in effect, characterized Egypt, and self-will. She had been the confidence of God's people (xxix. 16), but should be so no longer ; for how could such a principle ever furnish the victories which are only given to faith ? Egypt shall have her place in the future (Isa. xix.) but never as a ruler ; and her judgment secures Israel's blessing, for the will of man in Pharaoh cannot frustrate the purpose of God in grace.

The election of Nebuchadnezzar as God's " sword " and " terror " is one of the great facts of Scripture. That sword humbled Egypt in whom Israel trusted. It humbled also all the neighbouring nations, and thus destroyed many snares which entrapped the sons of Israel. All these judgments reach forward to a future day, and will be followed by the establishment in grace of the redeemed nations in union with the New Israel (Isa. xix.) so forming the one flock of John x. 16, in the Shepherd-care of the Messiah.

EZEKIEL XXXIII.—The first prophecy of this chapter (vs. 1-20) was spoken the evening before the arrival of the messenger (v. 21) announcing the fall of Jerusalem. This intelligence liberated him from the enjoined silence of xxiv. 15-27 ; and he was now permitted to resume his ministry to the exiles.

The seeming conflict between the doctrine of this prophecy (vs. 10-20) and that of Lev. xxvi. 39 is removed when the distinction between national and individual conduct is

observed. Upon the destruction of Jerusalem, and the judgment of the nation, Israel became Lo-ammi, and a new principle of individual relationship to God was established. Thus under national judgment the door was opened to personal repentance. This is very important ; for the nation, being under judgment, a faith which rested on Divine promises to the nation was, in effect, unbelief and hardness of heart, but a faith which bowed to God's righteous judgment on the people, and which produced personal repentance, was a Divine faith. Thus the moral effect of this latter faith confirms the distinction between national and personal relationship to God. When He resumes relationship with His people, as a nation, then a faith which reckons on the promises to Israel, as a nation, will be a faith born of the Holy Spirit, and not the faith of national pride and carnal privilege.

The Law failed to give life to man, not because it was defective, but because man was defective. The principle upon which God, without abating anything of His moral claims, could yet promise forgiveness to the repentant sinner, was revealed at Calvary, and is the subject of the Epistle to the Romans.

Just as an unfaithful sentry is judged to be guilty of the death of his comrades and shot, so Ezekiel was warned of a like guilt if he were faithless as a watchman (vs. 2-9).

" A man of their coasts " (v. 2). The sense here is : the most capable, chosen out of the entire community. See Hebrew Text and Revised Version.

The notes on chapter iii. 17-21 and xviii. 20-32 should be read in connection with this chapter.

" His soul " (v. 5), i.e., himself. " Thy soul " (v. 9,) i.e., thyself.

The language of verse 10 may be sceptical or despairing. It may be sceptical, as objecting that the prophet's teaching contradicted what he had previously said (iv. 17 and xxiv. 23), and that it struck against Lev. xxvi. 39 ; or it may have been despairing, as similar to Isa. xlix. 14. But the prophet assured them that God had no pleasure in the death of the wicked, but the contrary.

" Give again that he had robbed " (v. 15). See Exod. xxii. 26, Lev. vi. 2, 4, 5, Deut. xxiv. 6, 10-13 and 17. The conversion of Zaccheus (Luke xix. 1-10) illustrates the power of the new life in Christ to fulfil the requirements of the Moral Law.

Perfect love beams in verse 11, and perfect justice in verse 20.

The second prophecy (vs. 21-33) was uttered the following morning (v. 22) on the arrival of the fugitive from Jerusalem (v. 21) six months after the destruction of the city.

The double message of this prophecy— that to the residue of the people left in the land by Nebuchadnezzar after the fall of the city (vs. 23-29), and that to the Exiles by Chebar (vs. 30-33)—reveals the unbelief, pride, blindness, self-righteousness, rebellion and self-will of the natural heart. Both companies claimed to be the people of God ; they publicly worshipped Him ; were proud of their church position ; but they lived in idolatry and moral abomination.

The fulfilment of the prophecy of verses 23-29 is recorded by Jeremiah (xl., xli., xlii., xliii., xliv.).

The argument of verse 24 is : that if a mighty nation was born of one man, Abraham, and possessed and held the Land of Palestine, how much more powerful a nation could spring out of the many sons of Abraham whom the Babylonian king had left in Judah ! The faith that said " the land is given us for an inheritance " was a proud and carnal faith. Judgment upon their iniquities, and not blessing snatched by presumption, should cause them to know the Lord. Compare Isa. li. 2, Matt. iii. 9, John viii. 39.

To " eat with the blood " (v. 25) violated Lev. xix. 26, was done in honour of an idol, and, consequently, was a double sin against the Law.

The answer to the repeated question (vs. 25 and 26) is evident, and is to be supplied by the reader.

Though proudly claiming to be children of Abraham, and, therefore, children of God (v. 24), they were idolatrous (v. 25), self-confident, violent and impure (v. 26).

" They shall fall by the sword " (v. 27). Thinking to stand by it (v. 26), by a just retribution, they fell by it ; some by the sword of Ishmael, some by the Chaldeans, and the remainder, in Egypt, by the Babylonians.

Verses 28 and 29 should read as in the Revised Version. Visitors to-day are astonished that a land so barren and stony could ever have been singularly beautiful and fertile.

The unbelief and self-will that rejected the Master (v. 24) rejected the servant (v. 31). Thus did they reject the True Servant and His Father.

" Against " (v. 30) should read " of " (R.V.) Connect the words " with their mouth they shew much love " (v. 31). The exiles were proud of their prophet Ezekiel, they admired his preaching, and crowded to hear him, but did not for a moment intend any change of conduct. Similar features present themselves to-day in the professing Christian Church.

" Come and hear " (v. 30). Curiosity, and not repentance, prompted their Church-going.

" As the people cometh " (v. 31), i.e. in crowds.

" As My people " (v. 31), i.e., professing to be My people.

" Their covetousness " (v. 31), i.e., money-getting and all forms of self-pleasing.

This (v. 33), i.e., the judgment of verse 28.

Anger against sin reveals God (v. 29)— " they shall know " ; and fulfilled prediction accredits a prophet (v. 33)—" they shall know."

The revelation of the rebellious corruption of the listener's heart (v.31) saved the prophet from the self-complacent corruption of his own heart which his popularity as a preacher (vs. 30-32) would naturally excite.

EZEKIEL XXXIV.—In this message the Holy Spirit contrasts the false shepherds (vs. 1-10) with the True Shepherd (vs. 11-16 and 23 and 24), and the false sheep (vs. 17-22) with the true sheep (vs. 25-31).

" Shepherds " in this chapter mean rulers, i.e., the four last kings of Judah.

" Fat " (v. 3). The Hebrew word here should be translated " milk " (Deut. xxxii. 14, Prov. xxvii. 27). The milk of sheep and goats was permitted by the Law.

False shepherds feed themselves (v. 2) ; the True Shepherd feeds the sheep (v. 23).

The four-fold " neither " and the " not " (v. 4) should be noticed.

" With force have ye ruled " (v. 4). This was forbidden by Lev. xxv. 43.

Matt. ix. 36, illustrates verses 5 and 6 and 8.

Not one of Israel's kings was a perfect shepherd ; the majority of them were selfish and cruel.

The action, the love, and the unselfishness

of the True Shepherd are set out in verses 11-16.

The false sheep (vs. 17-22) are characterized, as the false shepherds, by selfishness and violence (v. 21).

The true sheep, like the True Shepherd, are unselfish and gentle.

" You " (v. 18), i.e., the false sheep ; " My flock " (v. 19), i.e., the true sheep.

The Hebrew Text (v. 23) reads " A Shepherd, one." That is one pre-eminent and unique shepherd—the only one of his kind, to whom none other is comparable.

The word " David " (v. 23) means The Beloved One, i.e., the True David, the Messiah (Isa. lv. 3, 4, Jer. xxx. 9, Hosea iii. 5).

" A covenant of peace," etc. (v. 25). Thus the promise of Lev. xxvi. 6, Isa. xi. 6-9, and xxv. 9 and Hos. ii. 18, will be fulfilled under the future happy reign of the Messiah ; and then will be witnessed the gathering predicted in verses 12-15 ; and so all Israel shall be saved (Romans xi. 26).

Israel will be in that day, as originally intended by God, a blessing in the midst of the earth (v. 26).

The Messiah will then be manifested as " The Plant of Renown " (v. 29). That " Plant " will be so rich with nourishment that they who feed upon it shall be no more pinched with hunger (v. 29), and their happy condition will secure renown for the " Plant " and not for themselves. Christian people should so live as to win renown for their Lord.

" The shame of the heathen " (v. 29) . after conversion a man thinks with shame of his conduct before conversion (Rom. vi. 21).

" They " (v. 30), i.e., the heathen shall know ; " they " i.e., the House of Israel.

" Ye My flock are men " (v. 31), i.e., human beings, and not merely " sheep.'

But there is here a deeper meaning. Helpless, sinful " men " could never do such marvels, only the God who is Adonai-Jehovah.

EZEKIEL XXXV.—Edom's hatred to Israel is, in the Scriptures, not only regarded as personal but as also expressive of man's enmity against the people of God in every age. Compare xxv. 4-14, Isa. xxxiv. 5, lxiii., Jer. xlix. 17-22, Ps. lxxxiii. and cxxxvii. and Obadiah.

The ever-continuing hatred (v. 5) of Edom was a legacy from their ancestor Esau (Gen. xxvii. 41).

Mount Seir, also called Idumea, was the country of the Edomites.

They rejoiced at the Fall of Jerusalem ; its fugitives they either slaughtered, or handed over to the Babylonians to be killed (v. 5) ; and they proposed to themselves to seize both Samaria and Judah, and take the whole of Palestine in possession (v. 10).

But God here finally decides the controversy between Edom and Israel. To the one He adjudges perpetual desolation ; to the other, ever-enduring prosperity. This is the last message to Esau. All previous appeals of goodness and severity were rejected, but judgment lingered till 400 A.D.

Even in Zion's desolation Jehovah was there (v. 10) as in her prosperity He will make Himself " known among them," i.e., among His people Israel (v. 11).

When God judges His people the world rejoices, and stretches out its hand to seize their possessions ; but the world knows not that the commencement of judgment at the House of God is the precursor of the eternal doom of the enemy (1 Pet. iv. 17 and 18).

" Thou shalt know that I am Jehovah (vs. 4, 9, 12), i.e., Edom should know to her sorrow Jehovah's power to punish.

" They shall know that I am Jehovah " (v. 15), i.e., Israel shall know to her joy His power to restore.

In spite of his infidelity man must know God ; for, if he will not know Him as a Saviour, he must know Him as a Destroyer.

Four sins are judged in this message : " hatred " (v. 5) " anger " (v. 11) " envy " (v. 11) and " malice " (v. 15). Thus it may be learned how God's anger justly burns against people who rejoice at the sufferings of others, enviously covet their money, and nourish feelings of anger and hatred against them.

The Revised Version of verse 5 makes clearer the double action of Edom in murdering the Hebrew fugitives, or in delivering them up to their pursuers (Obad. 14).

In the Hebrew Text (v. 6) there is a play upon the words Edom and blood.

" These two countries " (v. 10), " these two nations," i.e., Samaria and Judah.

" It " (v. 10), i.e., all of it, the entire country. But " it " may have a reference to the blessing which Esau tried to recover from his brother, but in vain, because as in Genesis xxvii. 34 and 41, so here Jehovah was present to defeat his impious purpose.

God promised Palestine to Abraham (Gen. xvii. 8). Isaac made Jacob by Divine ordination (Gen. xxv. 23) the depository and possessor of the promise. Esau and his sons disputed the gift with perpetual hatred. Before birth (compare John ix. 2 and note) and after birth (Gen. xxv. 22, and xxvii. 34 and 41) Esau tried to murder Jacob ; and in this chapter his sons proposed to, at last, seize the land. But God was there (v. 10). They thought, as Esau did, that they could ignore or defeat Him. These are not parables, or pious poems, or fables, as prominent religious teachers affirm to-day, but historic facts recorded by the infallible Spirit of God.

For one thousand years men could mock the prophecies predicting the absolute disappearance of Edom, but not longer, for in the Third Century A.D. every word was fulfilled, and the fulfilment after so long a period is an overwhelming demonstration of the fact that the Bible is a super-human book.

The majesty and power of the words : " Whereas Jehovah was there " (v. 10) can be felt by the reader.

The suffering which people desire for others sometimes falls upon themselves (v. 11). Far from Edom securing Palestine she would be deprived of her own land, and perish for ever as a nation. Acts xv. 17 proves that " Edom " in Amos ix. 12 is a generic term for mankind at large.

Bitter words against God's people are accounted by God as spoken against Himself (vs. 12 and 13).

When the sons of the kingdom enter into joy their haters shall descend into gloom (vs. 14 and 15).

EZEKIEL XXXVI.—The double prophecy of this chapter predicts the restoration of the Land of Palestine (vs. 1-15) and of the People of Israel (vs. 16-38) ; and the fundamental moral principle is taught that inward holiness must precede outward prosperity.

There was a limited fulfilment of these prophecies at the restoration under Zerubbabel ; but their plenary fulfilment is yet future (v. 10) ; for " all of Israel " did not then return.

God chastens His people (v. 4), but destroys their enemies (v. 5) ; His people's shame is temporary (v. 6); that of their enemies perpetual (v. 7 and Dan. xii. 2).

As a wild beast swallows its prey, so the enemy is pictured as swallowing Palestine (v. 3).

The sense of the last member of verse 3 is that the heathen charged Jehovah with inability to protect His land. Compare Deut. xxviii. 37, Jer. xxiv. 9, Dan. ix. 16.

Idumea (v. 5), i.e., Edom. Edom here has a universal as well as a local meaning.

. " I have lifted up mine hand " (v. 7), i.e., I have sworn.

" O mountains of Israel " (v. 8) and " the everlasting hills " of Gen. xlix. 26 are terms expressive of the moral elevation of Israel over the physical elevation of Edom.

Fertile as Palestine was in the remote past, it will be much more fruitful in the future (v. 11). Compare Job xlii. 12.

Verse 12 should read as in the Revised Version. Compare Num. xiii. 32.

" The shame of the heathen " (vs. 6-15) ; i.e., the shame with which the heathen covered them (v. 3 and Ps. cxxiii. 3, 4) spreading the evil report that the land devoured its inhabitants (vs. 12-15). Compare Num. xiii. 32.

The restoration of the people (vs. 16-29) will synchronize with the restoration of the land.

Material prosperity (vs. 29-38) unless preceded by a spiritual regeneration (vs. 25-29) is not only useless as a moral lever but often a cause of deeper degradation. Many a family has been ruined morally by a sudden increase of wealth.

This chapter exposes the folly of well-meaning people who think that the social betterment of the masses will necessarily secure a regeneration of character. God's plan is : first, repentance and conversion, and then, social betterment.

" Their own way " (v. 17). Man's way is defiling and defiles.

The uncleanness of verse 17 (Lev. xv. 19) pictures the vileness of the sinner in God's sight. The first statement of verse 29 declares the ability of the Saviour to fully cleanse the sinner.

The argument of verses 19 and 20 is, that not only did Israel profane Jehovah's name in the land prior to the Exile, but they also profaned it among the heathen during the Exile. Their conduct was so bad as captives that the heathen pointed at them with contempt and revulsion and said : " These are the people of Jehovah," etc. They profaned God by degrading Him to companionship with the idols of the heathen, and also by their immoral conduct.

God acts in grace toward guilty men solely because of His name as Saviour, and not because of any moral excellence in them (vs. 21, 22, and 32). The sinner's only claim for life and righteousness is his sinfulness.

" I do not this " (vs. 22 and 32), i.e., the new birth of verses 24-29, and the prosperity of verses 29-38.

" Then " (vs. 25 and 36). This important word marks the time for the fulfilment of these two prophecies. Israel, as a nation, will not be won for Christ until after they have returned to Palestine (v. 24) ; and the nations will not be won to Him, nationally, until after the restoration of the People and the Land of Israel (v. 36). Efforts, therefore, at national salvation prior to that time are useless, because not in fellowship with God's revealed plans.

" I will sprinkle clean water ", (v. 25). Num. xix. illustrates this cleansing ; and Heb. ix .and x.

The exiles were cleansed from outward idolatry (v. 25), but not from all their filthiness nor from all their idols ; neither were they the subjects of the great miracle of verses 26 and 27. The statements and premises of these verses do not belong to the present dispensation, for Christian people are not relieved of the stony heart. This miracle belongs to Israel, and will take place at the time here foretold. Present-day believers have the privilege of proving the power of the Spirit of Life to " make dead " in them the stony heart, and to keep it dead (Rom. vi.).

This new moral nature will be a gift to Israel of the Sovereignty of God ; but Israel will ask for it (v. 37), for this responsibility will attach to them. Sovereign grace and human responsibility are co-existent (Phil. ii. 12 and 13).

The removal of the stony felds from Palestine and of the stony hearts from Israel will synchronize. Both miracles belong to Israel and to the future. A Christian farmer cannot claim the first miracle to-day, and, consequently, cannot claim the second.

The first clause of verse 29 should be the last clause of verse 28 ; and should read as in the Revised Version.

Regeneration, not reformation—a new heart, and not a changed heart—is essential to salvation.

" I will call for the corn " (v. 29) as a master calls a servant ; for all the productions of nature are His servants.

The effect of grace is self-judgment (v. 31).

" Like the Garden of Eden " (v. 35). Tyre and Assyria claimed to be like the Garden of Eden. But this similitude belongs only to Israel. (xxviii. 13 and xxxi. 8 and 9, and Isa. li. 3).

" I will be inquired of " (v. 37). See chapters xiv. 3 and xx. 3. Daniel possibly read this verse prior to his prayer (Dan. ix.)

At Passover, Pentecost, and Tabernacles vast flocks surrounded Jerusalem for the purposes of the feasts.

The theme of these chapters is the relationship between Jehovah and His people. Hence there are no details given respecting the First Advent. The chapters present a general picture of the last days, of the re-birth of Israel, and of her enjoyment of earthly glory and blessing. To these " earthly things," as well as those of Num. xxi., the Lord pointed Nicodemus (John iii. 12) ; for every time that Nicodemus read the Bible Jesus spoke to him. This fact affirms the deity of Christ and the inspiration of the Bible.

EZEKIEL XXXVII.—The first prophecy of this chapter (vs. 1-14) foretells the moral, national, and physical resurrection of Israel ; the second prophecy (vs. 15-28) predicts the unity of the nation, and its happy settlement in Palestine under the government of the Messiah.

The first prophecy presents the singular and beautiful feature of a prophecy in action ; thus making the Resurrection scene more vivid and sure.

The repetition of " behold " (v. 2) fastens the attention upon the two facts :—that the bones were very many and very dry.

" Ye shall live " (v. 6), i.e., " Ye shall come to life again ; so shall ye get to know that I am Jehovah." God demonstrates His existence and power by raising the dead (John v. 21, Rom. i. 3 and iv. 17 and 2 Cor. i. 9).

" There was a noise and a shaking " (v. 7) rather : " there was a voice of thunder and, behold, an earthquake."

" But there was no breath in them " (v. 8). Professors may assume all the semblances of spiritual life and yet have no life but be dead before God.

" Prophesy unto the wind " (v. 9). Compare verse 4. " Prophesy upon," or over, " these bones.".

" These slain " (v. 9), and, " I will open your graves " (v. 12). The valley was covered over with the bones of men slain by violence, and the graves were filled with the bones of the dead, but the resurrection of both to life is equal to God.

" We are cut off for our parts " (v. 11), i.e., we are clean cut off, like a withered branch from a tree.

Verse 13 better reads thus : " Ye shall know that I am Jehovah by My opening your graves, O My people, and by My causing you to come up out of your graves ; " and (v. 14) " I will put My Spirit in you, and ye shall live, and I will place you in your own land," etc.

The formula " saith Jehovah " (v. 14), is to be understood as a confirmation written at the foot of the prophecy saying : " This is Jehovah's declaration."

The commanding voice of Cyrus (v. 7) caused a political earthquake and raised the Exiles out of their captivity grave. A mightier Voice will raise the nation from its present long-continued dispersion and moral death.

The second prophecy of the chapter (vs. 15-28) predicting the future union of the Tribes, their restoration to Palestine (v. 22), and their settlement there under one Shepherd (v. 24) teaches that a Divinely wrought union is real and enduring, brings its subjects into fellowship with God, and disposes them around a Divine centre.

" His companions,"in the first part of (v.16), means Benjamin and Levi ; and in the second part of the verse means the rest of the Ten Tribes.

When God takes groups of His servants and unites them they actually become one in His hand (v. 19).

Verse 21 was chosen for the legend on the Zionist medal commemoration—the First National Federation (1896) since the days of Titus.

" David My servant " (v. 24). This may mean David-Messiah, or it may mean David himself ; as in verse 25 and xliv. 3, xlv. 16, xlvi. 2, 10 and Jer. xxx. 9.

Very probably the Lord pointed to this prophecy (vs. 21, 22, and 24) when uttering

the words of John x. 16. It so " this fold " means Judah, " the other sheep I have " being the Ten Tribes. Most Bible students understand the " other sheep " · to intend the Gentiles.

The setting of the Divine Palace in Jerusalem (vs. 26-28) will cause the heathen to know that God has especially chosen Israel for His peculiar treasure (v. 28).

" My sanctuary " and " My Tabernacle," may mean one and the same palace ; or the " sanctuary " may be the Temple on Zion; and the Tabernacle, a cloud of glory o'erspreading it as a canopy. Compare Exod. xl. 38 and Isa. iv. 4 and 5 (R.V.).

The lost hope of despair (v. 11) can be changed into the living hope of faith (1 Pet. i. 3, R.V.).

As the first restoration from Babylon was opposed by Satan (see notes on Ezra, Neh. and Daniel), so will he oppose Israel's future settlement in Palestine. The two following chapters deal with this, and foretell the agents he will employ.

This chapter destroys the Anglo-Israelite theory.

As bones, flesh, sinews and skin (v. 8) form perfect manhood, so they here symbolize fully organized and equipped nationhood. The Hebrew people will become a true and real nation, but spiritually dead. A little later they will be Spirit-born.

EZEKIEL XXXVIII.—The events foretold in this and the following chapter are the return of the sons of Israel to Palestine (v. 8 and xxxix. 25-29) ; their settlement there on a non-military basis (v. 11), and possibly under a protectorate (v. 13) ; their accumulation of wealth (v. 12) ; the invasion of the Northern and Eastern Nations prompted by cupidity (vs. 9-12) ; the protest of the Southern and Western Nations (v. 13) ; and the destruction of the invaders (vs. 18-23).

Whether this invasion will precede or follow the reign of Anti-Christ is difficult to say. But see last note on prior chapter.

It is remarkable that the Holy Spirit in Ezekiel confines Himself to the subject of the cleansing and restoration of the Land, and the resumption of the relationship between God and Israel. The Great Prophecies of Daniel and Zechariah have, therefore, no place in Ezekiel ; nor the prophecies of Isaiah predicting the First and Second

Advents of the Messiah. The manifestation of Divine government on the earth, from Israel as the centre, is the keynote in Ezekiel. Hence the repetition of the formula : " They shall know that I am Jehovah."

There are many passages of Scripture such as Mic. v., Jer. li. 20 and 21, Ezek. xxv. 14, Isa. xi. 10-14, and several chapters in Zechariah which suggest that the Messiah, having suffered as David, will reign as David, conquering His enemies, and finally, reign as Solomon, that is to say as the Prince of Peace. Anti-Christ being destroyed, Messiah will lead the armies of Israel in perpetual victory against all who dispute His government, and will establish His people in peace upon their own soil. The invasion ot Gog may, possibly, be subsequent to these events. For a suggested connection with Rev. xx. 8 see note on verse 4.

The effect of these future events will be the convincement of the world that Israel is God's people ; that He dwells amongst them ; that it was their sins that caused their banishment and long-continued suffering ; and that He had not failed either in power or in the stability of His promises (xxxix. 21-29).

Magog, Meshech, Tubal, Gomer, Togarmah were sons of Japhet and peopled the north ; Cush and Phut were sons of Ham and dwelt on the Euphrates, and the Persians settled in the East. As in Israel's early history the sons of Ham afflicted her, so will she in the future suffer from the sons of Japhet.

Learned men think " Gog " to be appellative, corresponding to the title Caesar or Pharaoh etc., and that, as prince of Rosh, Meshech and Tubal, he is a future Russian ruler. It is certainly true that the Russians greatly covet Palestine, and deeply hate the Hebrews. The word " Gog " means a cover, i.e., a protector, that is, an emperor or over-lord. See xxviii. 13.

" I will turn thee back " (v. 4). The sense here is " I will permit thee to be enticed " (xxxix. 2. R.V.). If in Rev. xx. 8 the words " as he deceived Gog of the land of Magog " be supplied, the statement there would accord with that here ; for God will permit Satan to deceive the Russian Prince.

" After many days " (v. 8), i.e., at some future time ; " thou shalt be visited," i.e., punished.

Sheba and Dedan are the Arabians. Tarshish and her colonies (" young lions ") suggest the western nations.

" Art thou he ? " (v. 17). Some think that these words identify Gog with Anti-Christ. But the statements in verses 21 and 22 and xxxix. 4 do not accord with the overthrow of Anti-Christ in Rev. xix. 17-21.

Six agents will be employed in the judgment on Gog (vs. 21 and 22). Compare xxxix. 2 (margin).

EZEKIEL XXXIX.—" Thou shalt fall upon the mountains of Israel'" (v. 4). The overthrow of Gog and of Anti-Christ (Rev. xix.) accord in many particulars but not in this ; for Anti-Christ is to be cast alive into the Lake of Fire, but Gog is to be devoured by vultures and wild beasts.

All that sympathize with him will suffer the judgment of Jehovah in their own lands (v. 6).

The certainty of these events is affirmed in verse 8.

" The cities of Israel " (v. 9), i.e., the villages bordering the battlefield ; " shall set on fire," i.e., shall use as firewood.

The military weapons of the future may be actual shields, etc., and electric bows and arrows ; or weapons corresponding to these (v. 9).

" The valley (v. 11, R.V.) shall obstruct the passengers." It will apparently traverse the high road running north and south along the coast of the Mediterranean.

" The House of Israel," " all the people of the land " (vs. 12 and 13) " shall bury them," i.e., the Execu ive Government will employ and pay the men described in verse 14 to collect human bones wherever found and bury them in the huge trench of verse 11. This operation will occupy seven months.

The animals of verse 18 symbolize the superior officers of Gog's army.

" Horses and chariots " (v. 20), i.e., cavalry horses and artillery horses.

" So fell they all by the sword " (v. 23). The Dispersions under the Assyrians and the Romans having been effected by the sword, all the Hebrews who die in exile can justly be stated to fall by the sword.

The equity of God's action with Israel in all periods of their history past, present, and future is declared in verses 22-29.

Verse 26 should read as in the Revised Version. The pardoning love of God fills the repentant heart with self-abhorrence.

So certain is the future restoration of

Israel that the past tense is here used in predicting it (vs. 28 and 29).

The vision opens and closes with a valley of dry bones, for after the vultures and wild beasts shall have finished their feast (vs. 17-20) nothing but bones will remain. But for these bones there will be no resurrection to life. So these two valleys contrast the one with the other—the one a testimony to God's faithfulness in love ; the other to His fidelity in judgment.

EZEKIEL XL. 1-46—Jerusalem the city of the Great King is the subject of Ezekiel's last vision as it is of his first.

In this last vision the City appears as the capital of the whole Land ; and the great object for both eye and heart (v. 4) is the Palace of Messiah.

The Palace of Messiah, the City of the Great King (Ps. xlviii.), and the Land promised to Abraham appear, therefore, in this millennial vision.

The scene being millennial the dimensions of each are on a corresponding scale.

The Land will extend from the Euphrates on the north to the Nile upon the south, and from the Mediterranean on the west to the Indian Ocean upon the east. The tongue of the Egyptian sea will be dried up (Isa. xi. 15) thus enlarging Arabia. The Land of Israel will, therefore, in that day, be a magnificent territory embracing a vast portion of the Ancient World.

The city will have a dimension of one hundred and forty-four square miles, befitting the future metropolis of the world.

It will be upon the north side of the very great valley of Zech. xiv. 4 and 5, thus occupying a magnificent position, and will be beautiful for situation, the joy of the whole earth. Its suburbs will form a square of sixty miles, that is, three thousand six hundred square miles.

The Palace of Messiah will occupy the centre of a reservation called " the sanctuary." This sanctuary will be a great square of a mile each side. The Palace will have a boundary wall enclosing a square of about one-fifth of a mile on each face. Within this square will be the Inner Court, a square of about six hundred and twenty-five English feet, and within this square will stand the Palace, the Court of the Palace, and the " Separate Place " all forming a rectangle of about four hundred feet by two hundred.

Finally, in the middle of the Separate Place will stand the altar twenty-five feet square on a platform about thirty feet square.

Thus the altar will be the actual centre of the millennial Sanctuary :—the Temple, or Palace, being immediately to the west of it.

Messiah will enter the Great Square of the Sanctuary by the East Gate, and pass through the Courts into the Palace. Then will be fulfilled Ezek. xliii. 4 and Matt. xxiii. 39.

The centre of the millennial earth will therefore, be an altar, testifying that all blessing is founded upon Atonement.

The date of the Fall of Jerusalem is fixed by verse 1.

" A very high mountain " (v. 2 with xvii. 22, 23 and Isa. ii. 2). Physically Mount Zion has no great elevation, but to the eye and heart of God it is " a very high mountain."

" A reed " (v. 3) represents twelve feet.

To the carnal mind these chapters have no interest, but to the spiritual mind (v. 4) they are of surpassing preciousness because written by the Holy Spirit, and because the sacred feet of Immanuel are to tread these courts and passages and gates

Attention is first directed to the wall enclosing the square in which will stand the Palace (v. 5). This wall (" building ") will be twelve feet high and twelve feet broad.

The East Gate is then the subject of verses 6-16. It will be one hundred and twenty feet high (v. 14), will contain six lodges, three on either side, and the governing figure of its dimensions, as also of those of the Sanctuary and the Oblation will be five—the number of Grace.

Through this magnificent porch the Messiah will enter ; it will then be closed and reserved for the use of the Prince, who, possibly, will be David.

All the statements about this gate—its porches, its thresholds, and its measurements teach spiritual lessons concerning the beauties and perfections of Christ as the Way, the Truth and the Life. But the spiritual vision of Christian people is not sufficiently keen to recognize them.

As Moses was shewn in the Mount the pattern of the Tabernacle, and commanded to make all things according to it (Heb. viii. 5), and as David was similarly instructed with reference to the Temple (1 Chron. xxviii. 11 and 19), so was it in the case of Ezekiel as regards the future millennial sanctuary. In the construction of these three Places of

Worship nothing was left to man's taste or imagination. Everything, even in the matter of measurements, was commanded by God.

The great Square of the Outer Court with its thirty chambers, its pavement, and its superficial measure, is specified in verses 17-19. The Hebrew word for " pavement " suggests ornamental pavement.

The Thirty Chambers will be placed all along by the three gates giving access to the Great Square. It may be assumed that ten chambers will be apportioned to each gate, five on the one side and five on the other, and that these chambers will be attached to the external walls of the gates and will look out upon the pavement. Thus each gate will be provided with six internal and ten external chambers; that is, forty-eight chambers in all.

Each gate will be constructed as an arcade 100 feet long and 50 feet broad, having an arched roof and latticed windows. The exit into the Great Square will be ornamented with two square pillars 120 feet high, and having palm-trees sculptured on them. The six internal chambers will be arranged three on each side, and will open into the Arcade.

The pavement on the external side of these arcaded gates will be lower than that of the Great Square itself (v. 18).

The distance from each gate of the Great Square to the corresponding gate of the Inner Court will be 100 cubits on every side.

The North Gate and the South Gate with their chambers, their pillars, their arches, their windows, their seven steps, and their measurements, will be exactly as the East Gate. It will be the standard of entrance, utility, strength, and beauty. Through it the King of Glory will enter.

There will be no West Gate, for the Messiah, when seated on His throne within the Palace, will face to the East ; the worshippers will enter by the North and South Gates and stand before Him ; behind Him will, perhaps, stand the Cherubim of Glory.

Thus the Outward Court and its Gates and its boundary-wall are described in verses 5-27. The wall will be 600 feet in length on each side.

The Inner Court (vs. 27-46) with its three gates South (v. 28), East (v. 32), and North (v. 35) with their eight steps, their chambers, their pillars, their porches, and their measurements, all similar to that of the East Gate of the Outer Court is then described.

This Inner Court will be six hundred feet square. It will be surrounded by a wall of which no particulars are given.

On either side of each gate there will be apparently five arched chambers at the top of the steps, fifty feet deep and ten feet wide apiece, and facing toward the Outward Court (vs. 30 and 31).

The North Gate will be peculiar in that it will be furnished with eight stone tables, three feet by three feet by two feet, four on one side of the colonnaded entry, and four on the other side. These tables will be for the offerings. In the Tabernacle of the Wilderness the sacrifices were slain on the North side of the altar (Lev. i. 11, and viii. 5).

" Within " (v. 43), i.e., inside the chambers of verse 38 were " hooks " on which possibly the portions due to the priests will be fastened.

Verse 44 appears to be elliptical. This reading is suggested : " And outside the Inner Gate were the two chambers of the singers (i.e., the priests belonging to the Inner Court), they were beside the North Gate ; the prospect of the one was toward the south, and the prospect of the other (on the east side of the Gate) was toward the north."

These two chambers will be for the priests ; the one facing south for those having charge of the Temple, the one facing north for those having charge of the altar. These will be sons of Zadok (vs. 44-46).

Such is the description of the two courts, the Outer and the Inner. The provision of noble chambers and abundant food reveals the love of God for His servants, and makes evident the happy estate of those engaged in so honourable a service. In this—the Father's earthly House—there will be many mansions ; and they are here pictured as lifted up above the earth, and built in dependence upon the House.

This revelation testifies to the interest of God in His people. He will rebuild His sanctuary among them ; and He has informed them of this fact, and of its details, as a testimony of His faithful love, and as a message to their heart and consciences. Therefore the Prophet was commanded to shew these things to the House of Israel (v. 4).

EZEKIEL. XL. 47-XLI. 26.—The Court of the Priests (v. 47), the Porch of the Palace (vs. 48 and 49), the Palace itself (xli. 1-4), its outward hall (vs. 1 and 2), and its inner hall (vs. 3 and 4), the wall of the house (v. 5), the side-chambers (vs. 5-11), the altar of wood (v. 22), and the ornamentation of the Palace and its side-chambers, are here described and measured.

" So " (v. 47) better translated " then." The " Court," i.e., the Court of the Priests ; also called the " Separate Place."

The " Porch of the Palace " (v. 48) will be twenty cubits by twenty cubits (i.e., eleven cubits, plus the gate, the posts and the pillars) ; corresponding to the dimensions of the Most Holy Place (xli. 4). This fact illustrates a great spiritual truth.

In this Palace, and its dependencies, the measurements of " foundations " and the " posts " have great importance ; for the one word expresses stability, the other, permanence. In the Bible the " posts " of a door mean the whole house as an erect structure, and they figure its strength. This is imitated in the massive stone door-posts of the Egyptian temples. If, therefore, the posts of the doors shake, the whole house shakes.

In this House of Jehovah all the foundations will be of like measure.

The massiveness and loftiness of the " posts " (xli. 1) reveal the magnificence of the Palace.

The door will be formed of two pieces, each ten feet wide. This first chamber of the Palace will be eighty feet by forty ; the Inner chamber, as already stated, forty by forty.

The Palace will occupy the top of a very high mountain (xl. 2) to be formed, no doubt, when the whole land is to be " lifted up " (Zech. xiv. 10). The mountain will form a square, its base being a mile on each face (xlii. vs. 15-20) ; the Outer Court, higher up the mountain, one thousand feet on each face ; the Inner Court, still higher, six hundred feet square ; near the summit, the Court of the Priests, two hundred feet by two hundred ; and, finally the Palace of the King, with its terraced side-chambers, covering the highest platform, one hundred feet by one hundred (Gen. xxii. 14, Isa. ii. 2. Mic. iv. 1, Ezek. xliii. 12).

This mountain of the House of Jehovah will be a spectacle of surpassing beauty, glory, and magnificence—a . fitting Central Temple of Worship for the entire world.

It is difficult to understand the arrangement of the chambers at either side of the Palace. There will apparently be thirty side-chambers constructed in three storeys ; that is, ten houses with three chambers to each house, one over the other. Five of these houses will stand on the north side of the Palace, and five on the south side. Each house will stand on a higher face of the mountain than the other ; and there will be a roadway leading upward from the lowest " gallery ," or terrace, to the highest (xli. 6 and 7). The palace itself will stand on an elevated platform (v. 8 R.V.), thus causing it to tower above even the highest side-chamber. The foundations of the side-chambers and of the Palace itself will be of similar dimensions. Between the chambers and the Palace will be a passage forty feet wide on each side (v. 10) ; and between the inner wall of each house with its three chambers, and the side wall of the Palace there will be buttresses (v. 6).

In these side houses the second storey will project over the first, and the third storey over the second. This will be quite-feasible when it is remembered that the ground will be the sloping face of a mountain. One house will stand sufficiently high above the other to permit of the passage of the winding road which will lead on both sides of the Palace to the summit of the mountain, crowned with the Most Holy Place (v. 7).

The doors of these houses will face north and south, according to their position on either side of the Palace.

This Palace, with the houses on either side, will have a frontage of one hundred and forty feet facing the Court of the Priests (v. 12). The length of these buildings will be one hundred and eighty feet.

The Palace itself will be two hundred feet long ; and the court in front of it will have a similar length (v. 13).

The three-storied houses, as the Palace itself, will be finished off with wooden wainscotting ornamented with cherubim and palm trees (vs. 16-20). Everywhere there will be massiveness, beauty, and harmony (v. 21).

Within the Palace will be the Table of Jehovah (v. 22).

In this Temple there will be no Veil nor Shewbread nor Lampstand. Messiah by His presence will abolish these. See notes on xlviii and Heb. ix.

EZEKIEL XLII. 1-14.—Verses 1-14 give further details respecting the three gates of the Inner Court. These gates will be flanked by three-storied houses similar to those attached to the Palace, excepting that the chambers narrowed instead of broadened in elevation. Perhaps the Palace-chambers suggest the enlarged vision enjoyed in communion, and the gate-chambers the humbling experience gained in service.

The chamber (v. 1) over against the Separate Place, i.e., the collection of chambers that face the north side of the court of the Priests. The length of that face will be one hundred cubits (v. 2).

At the exit of the corridor into the Inner Court will be two three-storied houses; and at the entrance of this gate from the Outer Court, will be five houses on either side having three stories of one chamber each. There will be, therefore, thirty-eight chambers altogether at this gate.

The frontage of the gate next the Outer Court will measure one hundred feet (v. 7), and the distance from these houses to the Temple area, two hundred feet (v. 8).

Thus the number "five" will dominate the measurements of the Temple, its courts, its houses, and its gates.

Verses 9-12 state that the East and South Gates and their chambers will be similar to the North Gate and its chambers.

All these three groups of chambers (vs. 13 and 14) will be for the Priests the sons of Zadok. The regulation as to their priestly garments reveals a feature of the spiritual life, that there are affections, energies and ministries which belong exclusively to the life of communion and intercession, and must, therefore, be reserved expressly for the Lord. Refreshed and enabled by this inner communion the Christian can go out to minister to the world (v. 14).

The Great Square, one mile each way, within which the Holy Mountain will stand, is measured in verses 15-20.

The sanctuaries given by inspiration to Moses and to David were built, and thus set visibly before the eyes of Israel. The sanctuary given to Ezekiel in vision is yet to be built; but its details are revealed in writing (xliii. 11) as a testimony and instruction to Israel. These details make real God's interest in His ancient people, and give substance to His promise to establish His home among them. Thus this vision is a perpetual call to repentance (xliii. 10 and 11).

EZEKIEL XLIII.—Atonement as the eternal foundation of God's relationship with man, is the keynote of this chapter.

The Palace being now ready, the Glory of Jehovah (Messiah) enters.

His reluctant departure xi. 23 contrasts here with His swift return.

The words "this is," are to be supplied before "the place of My throne," etc. (v. 7).

"Whoredom" (v. 7), i.e. idolatry; "their kings," i.e., the idols who reigned over them.

"Their threshold," "My threshold," "their post," "My post" (v. 8, R.V.), i.e., their idol-temple by the side of God's Holy House. "Threshold" and "post" signify a large public building, such as a palace or temple.

"Let them measure the pattern" (v. 10). When this Great Sanctuary is actually built a comparison of it with the Vision of Ezekiel will demonstrate the Divine Inspiration of these chapters; and, comparing this Glorious Palace with the Pagan and Papal Temples of idolatrous worship, the people will be ashamed of shrines, both ancient and modern, of which they are now so proud. Similarly, a comparison between the way of salvation and holiness patterned in the Scriptures and those invented by man, fill the contrite heart with self-condemnation (vs. 10 and 11).

The entire summit of the mountain is to be reserved for Immanuel (v. 12). A transgression of this regulation will presumably involve death.

The altar of verses 13-17 is to be distinguished from the "Table of Jehovah" (xli. 22). The table will be of wood, and will stand within the Temple; the altar will occupy the centre of the Court of the Priests, and, therefore, the centre of all the other square courts, and of the Land and of the World.

It will be twenty-four feet by twenty-four, and will stand upon a base twenty-eight feet by twenty-eight. It will be fourteen feet high. "The bottom" (v. 13), i.e., the fire-space beneath. The lower "settle," i.e., ledge. From one ledge to the other will be eight feet, the breadth of each ledge, two feet.

"The stairs" (v. 17), i.e., the ascent to the upper ledge. The "bottom," i.e., the fire-grating near the top of the altar.

All things as well as man being sin-defiled, atonement will be made for the altar (vs. 18-26). The perfection of the Atonement appears in the seven days of its action. It will need no repetition.

A comparison with Leviticus is instructive. There the burnt-offering preceded the sin-offering; here it follows (23 and 24). Then faith praised in looking forward to the sin-offering of Calvary; in the future day faith will praise looking back to Calvary. Thus the Great Sin-offering of the Lamb of God stands in the midst of the ages, and is preceded and followed by praise.

There will be no Day of Atonement in millennial worship; for the sacrifices then will recall the One All-sufficing Atonement perfected at Golgotha.

As the Levitical offerings predicted the preciousness and sufficiency of the offering-up of Christ Himself, so will the millennial sacrifices recall and testify to that Great Offering as an accomplished fact. These sacrifices will be necessary; for when Israel, and the Nations, look upon the resplendent form of Immanuel as He will appear on this Mount of Glory, they will be disposed to forget that He hung in blood and death for their sins upon the Cross of Calvary. This Great Blood-sprinkled Altar (v. 18), with its burning fire, will vividly instruct them; and it will help them to feel that they are sinners, and that the precious blood of the Lamb of God shed for tnem is the One and only and necessary atonement, and the foundation of all their millennial happiness.

" They did cleanse it with the bullock " (v. 22), i.e., with the blood of the bullock.

" The priests shall cast salt upon them " (v. 24). This ordinance does not appear in Leviticus.

" Themselves " (v. 26), read " it," i.e., the altar (R.V.).

This Palace and Throne of Jehovah shall no more be defiled by profane things (v. 7). Israel's responsibility in relation to the holiness of Immanuel's dwelling-place is declared in verses 9-11.

" Threshold " suggests access and fellowship; " post," protection and safety. If the posts of the doors stand, the house stands; if the posts fall, the house falls. Dagon was broken to pieces on the threshold; and his temple fell when Samson pulled down its posts. The threshold of Immanuel's Palace will be holiness; and the massiveness of its posts will reveal its enduring strength. Holiness will become that House for evermore; and the Enemy will never prevail against it.

EZEKIEL XLIV.—The Messiah having entered His Palace, the Inner Gate of the Eastern entry shall be shut, thus giving a memorial of the fact, and an assurance that He will never again forsake His Temple (vs. 1 and 2). See notes on xlvi.

Jehovah the God of Israel is Messiah (v. 2).

" To eat bread before the Lord " (v. 3) is, in the Scriptures, an act of worship (Gen. xxxi. 54, Exod. xviii. 12, xxiv. 11, 1 Cor. x. 18).

The prince shall enter the outer porch of the eastern gate and advance to the inner exit, but no further. He shall sit there and eat the sacrificial meal. The congregation of worshippers will take its place in front of, and outside of, the gate. The prince, having worshipped, will retire as he entered.

" Mark well " (v. 5) rather " set the heart upon." The heart, the eyes, and the ears are all to be engaged with Jehovah's House and its ordinances, laws, and statutes. On entering God's presence it is of the utmost importance that the heart should be deeply affected; and it should be as deeply exercised when going forth from the Divine Presence. See xl. 4.

Unconverted people profane a true temple of worship (v. 7) by professing to be what they are not.

Israel added this breach of the covenant to her other abominations (v. 7 R.V.). This verse makes clear that the Inner Courts of the millennial sanctuary will be reserved for those who are physically sons of Israel and spiritually sons of Abraham. They will enjoy this honourable position in Messiah's Court. The worshippers of all other nations will stand behind and around them (v. 9).

The Levites, grown weary of the Temple-service, engaged others to discharge it instead of them (v. 8). So to-day spiritually indolent Christians employ men at large or small salaries to read and study the Bible for them, and to perform their worship.

The Levites appointed to teach the Law turned from that Holy Book and taught man's way of salvation (vs. 10 and 12). In this they have many modern imitators.

As a consequence they will be confined to the Court of the Priests (v. 11) and not permitted to enter the Palace itself (v. 13). Such will be their punishment all through the millennial age.

This principle applies to all ages. There

miy be a recovery from unfaithfulness to Truth, but a life-long loss of spiritual privilege and power results.

The action of the sons of Zadok (v. 15) may have been loyalty to Solomon (1 Kings ii. 35), God's appointed king—a type of Messiah in His millennial glory ; or this verse may be an instance of the law of subsequent narration, similar to Jude 14, etc.

Messiah's Palace will be a standard of cleanliness and health to the world (v. 23). No intoxicating drink will be permitted in it (v. 21) ; its worshippers will be clean in body as in soul (vs. 15, 18 and 20). Marriage shall be had in honour, and be in the Lord (v. 22). That House will be a Court of Arbitration for all nations (v. 24), and Sabbath desecration will be forbidden.

God must have the first place in worship and service, but natural affection must not be violated (v. 25). Yet even in these lawful relationships, because of human infirmity, the cleansing of the precious blood of Christ is needed (vs. 26 and 27).

It is a good thing to be a son of Zadok, i.e., wholly surrendered in heart to the Lord ; for God gives such the best of everything (vs. 28-30). The bread of Heaven is theirs, and not any degraded food (v. 31).

Egyptian priests and Roman monks shave the head, and those of the Greek Church wear the hair long ; God's priests will follow neither fashion (v. 20).

A blessing rests on the house (v. 30) when Prov. iii. 9 and 10 and Mal. iii. 10 are obeyed.

The restoration of animal sacrifice, with its necessary suffering, appears to conflict with Isa. xi. 9, and the Epistle to the Hebrews. But it may be assumed that animal food will be a necessity during the millennium, and its provision is not morally either hurtful or destructive. Further, it may be a Divine necessity that Israel having in the past failed to observe the legislation of Leviticus, and so to testify of the one great sacrifice that was to come, must by the perfect observance of the future sacrifices witness of an atoning Saviour who has come. Thus Calvary will be shown to be the Divine centre of God's purposes of grace and wrath. It is conceivable that only by such object lessons will it be possible to interpret the Book of Leviticus to the various nations of the millennium earth, and in this way to vindicate God's action in the past and in the future.

EZEKIEL XLV.—The Mountain of the House of Jehovah will form the centre of the "Oblation." Israel will offer this Oblation to the Messiah on their re-establishment in the Promised Land. It will be a square of sixty miles by sixty ; that is, three thousand six hundred square miles. This Great Square will be sub-divided into three portions : the possession of the Levites on the north, the possession of the Priests in the centre, and the possession of the City in the south.

The possessions of the Levites and of the Priests will be equal ; i.e., sixty miles by twenty-four each, or one thousand four hundred and forty square miles. The Sanctuary will stand at the centre of the Priest's possession.

The possession of the city will measure sixty miles by twelve, or seven hundred and twenty square miles. This will be subdivided into five blocks of twelve miles by twelve each, or one hundred and forty-four square miles. The central square will be the city of Jerusalem. The adjoining squares, east and west, will be vegetable gardens for the supply of food to the city workmen (xlviii. 18, 19). The extreme squares east and west, will be for the prince.

Thus the city will be a truly magnificent one, the fitting capital of the world, covering one hundred and forty-four square miles, having vast gardens of equal dimensions on both sides, and, beyond these, the prince's private gardens and grounds of corresponding size.

The gardens of this great garden-city will, therefore, have an area of two hundred and eighty-eight square miles, and the demesne of the prince will be of similar extent.

Twenty-five thousand reeds equal sixty miles ; ten thousand reeds, twenty-four miles.

The Sanctuary, as stated in xlii. 15-20, will occupy an area of about one square mile (v. 2).

The possession of the Priests is the subject of verses 1-4. Verse 3 is not a repetition of verse 1 but is explanatory and additional.

Thus in these verses the " Holy Portion " and the " Sanctuary " alternate three times.

The possession of the Levites (v. 5) will contain the same area as that of the Priests. " Chambers," here have the sense of cities of dwelling-houses.

Verse 8 may read : " As touching the Land this shall be his possession in Israel," i.e., the prince shall have no land other than these two portions.

God's love for man, and His hatred of injustice, appear in His making His Dwelling-place among them (vs. 2 and 3), and in His Laws respecting land (v. 8), courts of justice (v. 9), excessive taxation (v. 9), evictions (v. 9), and commercial property (vs. 10-12). Thus the poor and defenceless will be cared for by Him.

A homer equals ten ephahs, i.e., about eight bushels. An omer equals the one-tenth of an ephah. There is therefore no discrepancy between verse 11 and Lev. xxvii. 16, Num. xi. 32, etc.

The contrast between the legislation of verses 18-25 and that of Leviticus emphasizes the difference between Mosaic and millennium worship. It also destroys the theory of the Exilic composition of Leviticus. Here the year begins (vs. 18-20) with the demonstration of accomplished redemption, and the provision of a pure ground of worship. Thus shall atonement be made for the house on the first day (v. 18), and for the worshippers on the seventh day (v. 20). The year will begin with the memorial of a perfected atonement for sin ; in Leviticus the year closed with an atonement pointing forward to a purgation yet to be accomplished.

The two feasts of Passover (v. 21) and Tabernacles (v. 25) will be marked by sevenfold offerings in contrast to the twofold ones of Leviticus ; and this because these offerings will testify to the perfection of the cleansing for sin fulfilled at Calvary. The character of worship in that future day, and the sense of the sufficiency of Christ's sacrifice of Himself as the sin-offering and the burnt-offering, will be perfect.

Thus these two feasts will celebrate the perfection and sufficiency of the atoning work of Christ, and, together with the Feasts of the Sabbath and the New Moon, testify to the fulfilment of God's promises to Israel in bringing them into rest, and making them to be a light to the Gentiles (Isa. lx. and lxvi.).

Under the First Covenant the Passover was a domestic and family Feast, under the New Covenant it will be a princely and national one (v. 22).

EZEKIEL XLVI.—On the Feasts of the Sabbath and the New Moon the Prince shall enter by the East Gate and worship at its extremity in front of the Palace ; but he shall not go beyond that inner door (1-2). The people shall worship standing in front of the Eastern entry of this gate.

The Prince will provide the offerings and the priest will present them (v. 2). The offerings for the Sabbath will number seven, and there will be no wine. In Leviticus they numbered four, with wine.

" As he shall be able to give " (vs. 5 and 11) " and as his hand shall attain unto " (v. 7). The Divine foundation being laid —the blood and the oil—the heart is given freedom to express its joy and its communion in the meal-offering, i.e., fellowship with God in the enjoyment of Christ, as the Bread that came down, and cometh down, from Heaven, whereof if a man eat he shall never die.

The offerings for the Feast of the New Moon (vs. 6 and 7) numbered nine without wine ; in contrast with the nineteen of Leviticus with wine.

In the National Feasts the Prince will worship with, and among, the people on the common ground of brotherhood and fellowship (vs. 9 and 10). For these Feasts he will provide the meal-offering (11). There is no such command in Leviticus.

The regulation as to entering and leaving the Temple (v. 9) harmonizes with 1 Cor. xiv. 33.

The voluntary offering of the Prince (v. 12) shall be presented at the inner door of the eastern gate ; and possibly will be for himself and for the people, or for himself only.

Under the law there was the Morning and Evening Sacrifice, but under grace there will be only the Morning Lamb (vs. 13-15) ; for to that Day there shall be no evening.

God's hatred of robbery, oppression and injustice appears in the legislation of verses 16-18 ; and His loving care for the physical needs of His servants is shown in verses 19-24.

There is a ministry to God only (v. 20) and there is a ministry to man (v. 24). In Christian service this distinction must be observed ; and the richer will be the ministry to man if that to God be given the first place.

EZEKIEL XLVII.—Not water (v. 1) but " waters " issued from the House—their source the Throne of Jehovah ; their channel the Altar of Jehovah, i.e., Calvary. Joel iii. 18, Zech. xiv. 8, Rev. xxii. 1.

These waters shall grow of themselves, and not, as in nature, by accession from side streams.

Messiah will go in by the east gate, and the waters will flow out by the same gate. Christ ascended into Heaven, and, as a result, the Holy Spirit descended from Heaven.

One thousand cubits—one-third of a mile. The waters shall be living and life-giving ; but there shall be no healing for the miry places (v. 11). Imperfection will exist during the millennium, for man will still be under trial. He will have freedom of choice. If he accepts Messiah's rule, he will enjoy the felicity pictured in verses 1-10 and in verse 12 ; but if he rejects that government, he, like Lot's wife, will be turned into salt, for grace despised, involves bitterness and death. Millennium blessing will be powerful and abiding, it will greatly surmount and almost efface evil, but not entirely ; for only in the New Heaven and New Earth will there be perfection.

The trees shall perpetually bring forth new fruit (v. 12) because nourished by waters issuing from the sanctuary. The fruit will heal as well as nourish. Such is the character of a life and ministry based upon Calvary, and energized by the Holy Spirit.

In Joshua the land was divided from south to north. In the coming Day of Restoration it will be apportioned from north to south.

Inheritance was forbidden under Law to the Gentile ; but, in the millennium, it will be fully granted.

Then will God's original purpose be effected —Palestine will first be possessed, and then the greater territory promised to Abraham secured. See notes on Joshua xxii.

EZEKIEL XLVIII.—Seven Tribes will have their possession north of the Oblation, and five Tribes south of the Oblation.

The children of Leah and Rachel will be placed near the Oblation ; those of the slave wives at a distance.

The city will be four-square, with twelve gates, three on each side. On the Messianic, i.e., the east side, will be a gate for Dan (v. 32). In Revelation Dan disappears. Why?

The city will contain one hundred and forty-four square miles. This harmonizes with the one hundred and forty-four thousand of Rev. vii.

It will be a copy of the city of Rev. xxi. and xxii.

Jehovah Shammah is one of the Divine titles of Christ in the Old Testament. See notes on Ps. xxiii.

Thus brightly will open the millennium. Rev. xx. predicts its sad close.

The Book of Ezekiel teaches that God's purposes may be deferred but cannot be defeated ; for Israel will be restored, the Palace of Jehovah certainly built in Jerusalem and memorial sacrifices offered (Isa. lvi. 7, lxvi. 20-23, Ezek. xliii., and Zech. vi. 12, 13). Christ will be enthroned on the Mountain, and national worship established.

In the inner court of that Temple there will be neither Ark, Shew-bread, Lampstand, nor Veil, for the actual presence of Messiah will abolish these. Thus Mat. xviii. 20 explains 1 Cor. v. 7, 8 ; for a Risen Lord in the midst abolishes memorials of His absence.

The Feasts of the outer court will be the Sabbath, the New Moon, Passover, and Tabernacles ; but no Pentecost, or Day of Atonement, for these cannot be repeated.

Atonement and spiritual birth will be the base of millennial blessing.

Israel's possession of the land under Joshua was founded upon the Passover (Joshua v. 10). Millennial possession of the land will be based upon that which the Passover fore-shadowed.

The variations between the priestly legislation of Leviticus and that of Ezekiel form a profitable study to a Bible student, and demonstrate the ignorance of the Priest-code theory.

Atonement will be made for, i.e., on behalf of the House (xlv. 20) ; for its righteousness will need vindication and satisfaction because the worshippers will be sinful (Lev. xxiii. 6, 17).

The Bible student, as well as the Hebrew prophet, is commanded, and invited, to behold with his eyes, to hear with his ears, and to set his heart upon all that God reveals in this Book of Ezekiel (xl. 4).

Ezekiel was a captive for twenty-five years, yet he enjoyed visions of, and from God. These empowered him ; man's visions are powerless.

The Mountain of the House of Jehovah will be both a city and a temple, because God shall dwell there. To-day a city should be a temple, and a temple a city.

Everything in Ezekiel's temple was measured by the man that had the reed and the line. Christ, the Head of the Church, the Divine Man, measures, and tests, everything in a professed temple. His instrument of measurement is the Bible.

The Christian is a temple having walls, gates, chambers, narrow windows, etc., i.e. limitations, openings, emotions and prejudices. These must be tested by the reed and the line.

In the South Chambers there was sunshine and service ; in the North Chambers, sacrifice and intercession.

The flax line, and the plumb line expressed divine principles affecting the Christian life. Amos and the plumb-line of house-breaking, must precede Haggai and the plumb-line of house-making; associated with this line are the seven spirits of God. Zerubbabel was not alone, the seven spirits of God were with him.

As in the Tabernacle of grace, and in the Temple of glory, all was perfection because all was Divine, so in this future building everything will utter His praise, and from that day the name of the city shall be " Jehovah-shammah."

This last vision (xl.-xliii.) predicts that Palestine will be the Divine centre of government in the earth ; that in the centre of that country a great platform will be formed by God sixty miles square ; that upon it will be built the millennial city of Jerusalem ; that it will cover one hundred and forty-four square miles ; that it will be a garden-city ; that in its centre, and above it, will stand Messiah's Palace ; that in its centre, and above it, will be placed the Temple of His glory ; and that in its centre will be the throne of God and the altar of burnt-offering. Thus atonement will be the centre of the future Kingdom of God on earth. Over all will be the bridal canopy of glory (Isa. iv. 5, R.V.). The whole vast structure from its platform base to its glorious summit will be, as the Garden of Eden possibly was, a pyramid.

DANIEL

Daniel was born in the land of Palestine about six hundred and fifteen years B.C., and he died in the province of Bablyon in 534 B.C. in the third year of Cyrus, King of Persia. He was, therefore, upwards of eighty years of age at the time of his death. He was carried into captivity by Nebuchadnezzar when he was a boy about ten years old. He was a Prince of the Royal House of David, and with the other princes of Judah, was made an eunuch and slave in the palace of the king of Babylon ; thus fulfilling about one hundred years later the prediction of Isa. xxxix. 7. (See notes on ch. i. 8). The name Daniel means God is my Judge.

Confronted by the minuteness of Daniel's prophecies, the enemies of inspiration have tried to prove that the book is a forgery composed shortly before Christ. But Ezek. xiv. 14 and xxviii. 3, together with several references to Daniel in the New Testament, and the testimony of the LXX., destroy their contention.

Many of these prophecies have been fulfilled, and many await fulfilment.

The unique glory of this book is, and was, that it predicted, to a day, the Crucifixion of the Messiah (ix. 25, 26). The Hebrew Church was, therefore, without excuse in its condemnation of Him as an impostor. Had not this great prophecy been given through Daniel the Nation would not have known when the Redeemer was to appear. Hence the special value of this book.

God had made Israel the centre of a system of nations, peoples and languages that arose in consequence of the judgment on Babel, and had committed the sceptre of the world to her hand (Deut. xxxii. 8). But in consequence of her persistent idolatry, He took that sceptre from her and placed it in the hands of Nebuchadnezzar and his successors, where it remains to the present day. The Book of Daniel occupies itself with the fortunes of these successive governments, and with a Remnant of Israel in subjection to them, and it closes with the substitution of the Kingdom of the Messiah, which is yet to be established upon earth, and of the universal happiness which will then result.

The prophecies of the Book cover the period of human history named by the Lord " The Times of the Gentiles," and, therefore, reaches from Nebuchadnezzar's accession to Anti-Christ's destruction—possibly a period of two thousand five hundred years.

Not only is Daniel mentioned twice by Ezekiel who was his contemporary, but he is referred to in Matt. xxiv. 15, 17 and 30, and xxvi. 64, and Mark xiii. 14 ; and the Lord Jesus Christ pointed to Dan. viii. 13, ix. 27, xi. 31 and xii. 11.

To understand, therefore, this book, it is of the utmost importance to recognize that its prophecies cover the whole period of the Divine committal of dominion in the earth to the Gentile, and that they predict the character of that dominion.

DANIEL I.—Jeremiah (xxv. 1) records this siege of Jerusalem as occurring in the fourth year of King Jehoiakim, but in this there is no discrepancy with Daniel, for he points to the setting out of the Babylonian monarch for Jerusalem, while Jeremiah relates his arrival in the following year. He was delayed by the opposition of the king of Egypt, whom he finally defeated at Carchemish on the Euphrates. The one Hebrew verb form can be equally translated " to come " and " to go." The context decides the translation. This first verse of the chapter may, therefore, read : " Nebuchadnezzar the king of Babylon set out for Jerusalem."

Part of the vessels of the house of God

(v. 2) were carried off at this time ; the residue afterwards.

" And " (v. 3) should read " even," that is, the boys chosen belonged to the royal family and to the nobility. They were most probably from twelve to fourteen years of age.

The Hebrew names of Daniel and his three companions mean, respectively :   " God is my judge," " Jehovah is gracious," " Who is as God," and " Helped of Jehovah." These names were changed (as Pharaoh changed Joseph's) to " A prince of Bel," to " Inspired of Rak," i.e., the sun, to " Who is as Aku," i.e., Venus; and to " The servant of the Fire-god."

These divinities correspond to the Trinity and the Virgin Mary—the Babylonian trinity being the ether, the earth, and fire. The moon-god was the one female divinity —the Queen of heaven—that is, Astarte —represented by the modern divinity called the Virgin.

" Daniel purposed in his heart " (v. 8) that is, resolutely determined.

To eat unbled flesh was forbidden by the Bible, and to drink the king's wine was to have fellowship with idolatry ;   for the Easterns always consecrated the wine by pouring out a libation to the idol (1 Cor. viii. 7 and 10 and x. 27 and 28). Thus these princes chose to suffer affliction with the people of God rather than to enjoy the pleasures of sinful disobedience.

They, as eunuchs and slaves, were suffering the wrath of God because of the vanity and disobedience of their royal ancestor Hezekiah (Isa. xxxix. 7). The Divine judgment which they were suffering, and which they might have denounced as inhuman and unjust, and altogether disproportionate to Hezekiah's trivial fault, they, in the energy of faith and love, used to glorify the God that smote them. This was very fine ; and is a striking direction to all Christian people to approve, as well as to patiently suffer, God's moral government of man.

God's over-ruling hand may be recognized in verse 9.

Melzar (v. 11) was the steward, or butler, who had charge of the king's meat and wine.

" Pulse " (v. 12) means vegetable food of all kinds.

" Continued " (v. 21), i.e., continued in office unto the first year of King Cyrus ; but he lived for two or three years longer, and, therefore, witnessed the commencement and

the ending of the seventy years Captivity.

The feast on the night in which Belshazzar was slain was held in honour of the moon-god, that is, the virgin.

That boys of from twelve to fifteen years of age should have possessed such spiritual intelligence, knowledge of the Scriptures, resolution of character and courage, is most remarkable.

The five following chapters contrast the Man of God and the Man of the Earth. The first was characterized by purity (ch. i.), prophecy (chs. ii., iv., v.), bravery (chs. ii. and vi.) and fidelity (chs. i. and vi.) ;   the second, by stupidity (chs. ii. and iv.), idolatry (chs. iii., v. and vi.), vanity (ch. iv.) and blasphemy (ch. v.).

DANIEL II.—The second year of Nebuchad- nezzar (v. 1) was the second of his reign as sole king, for he had reigned as co-rex with his father, and it was when sole monarch that the events of chapter i. occurred.

There is no conflict between chapter 1. 19 and chapter ii. 26, for all kings, especially Eastern monarchs, frequently forget in a few days people who had greatly interested them ; and, further, verse 26 does not suggest that the king did not recognize Daniel but that he was not aware that he could make known a dream and interpret it.

The king's action in consulting priests and mediums rather than God is one of the many proofs of the accuracy of this history, for unconverted men in their difficulties seek help in every direction other than from the Scriptures. The king, recognizing that the dream was super-natural, should have at once sent for Daniel.

There are, therefore, no difficulties in the statements of this chapter, as some people assert.

The king may have affected forgetfulness of the dream so as to test the capacity of the magi to interpret it.

" Gain the time " (v. 8), i.e., " gain time " ; either to search for a lucky day, or in the hope that the king might forget the matter.

" Dreams " (vs. 1 and 2), i.e., plural of majesty for a super-natural dream.

" Mercies " (v. 18), i.e., plural of majesty for the " great mercy " of revealing the dream.

The faith of these four princes—they were possibly about fifteen years of age at the time—in going to bed after their prayer is admirable. They were to die in the morning if Daniel failed to tell the dream. In such circumstances many Christians to-day would be too much agitated to sleep, and would organize an all night of prayer.

God gave to His beloved when sleeping (Ps. cxxvii. 2) whilst the magi laboured in vain.

Thus faith saves its exerciser and others (1 Tim. iv. 16) from oppression and from corruption.

" He changeth the times ," etc. (v. 21). This has reference to the successive empires as seen by Daniel in the vision of the night.

The king's dream predicted a succession of four monarchies—the Babylonian (B.C. 625-540), the Persian (B.C. 540-332), the Grecian (B.C. 332-32) and the Roman (B.C. 32 to a future date). The close of the Roman Empire will be featured as a confederation of ten kings having the future Anti-Christ as their chief. He will be the last and greatest Emperor. He and his government will be destroyed by the Messiah, who will be the stone unshaped by human agency (v. 34), and whose apparition will destroy all these kings simultaneously ("together" v. 35, v. 44). These verses destroy the popular belief that the Gospel will gradually conquer the world.

The empires that succeeded the Babylonian were increasingly inferior (vs. 39-43) because of the introduction of the democratic principle in association with kingly despotism. The final stage appears in verses 41-43, the iron representing imperialism, the clay, democracy.

" Broken " (v. 42), i.e., " brittle."

" The kingdom shall not be left to other people " (v. 44), that is, it will be without a successor, for it will be Messiah's.

The devolution of these ten kingdoms may result from the recent Great War (1917).

The word " answered " (v. 47) supports the conviction that Daniel refused Divine honours and directed the king away from himself to God.

Daniel did not forget his companions (v. 49), as the chief butler forgot Joseph.

" Sat in the gate of the king," i.e., was appointed Prime Minister. This expression is preserved by the Turkish executive government, which is styled The Porte, i.e., the Door.

The six substances gold, silver, brass, iron, clay and amalgam represented the six forms of human government that would rule Immanuel's land, that is to say, the Baby-lonian, the Persian, the Grecian, the Roman, the Arabian, and the Ten Kings. Five of these have passed away and the sixth is now in being, having commenced in 1917. It will be succeeded by the seventh kingdom, i.e., Messiah's, and of that kingdom there shall be no end, for it shall stand for ever.

DANIEL III.—The erection of this image (v. 1) so soon after the events of the previous chapter illustrates the darkness and incurable rebellion of the natural heart ; and proves that, apart from a new spiritual birth, no circumstances, however powerful, can teach man to know and worship God.

All monarchs recognize that to consolidate their power they must have a state religion. This is man's wisdom, otherwise religion, being the most powerful motive of the heart, becomes a dissolvent to the authority of the throne. Man naturally likes supreme power, blended by religion into one solid body around the head of the State, for this helps to obscure the appearance of authority. But the religion chosen must be one that will suit and gratify man's will. Hence idolatry. This is the great feature that characterizes the dominion of man in the earth from the first king of Babylon, Nebuchadnezzar, to its last king Anti-Christ. God is disowned by the Gentile, but acknowledged by a little group of suffering believers. These moral features will re-appear most vividly during the final and future days of Gentile government. God will allow his faithful witnesses, typified by Shadrach and his companions, to be cast into the fiery furnace so as to be tried in the place where evil exists ; but He will walk with them in the fiery trial, and He will deliver and glorify them (vs. 25 and 30), but with this distinction that He will permit their bodies to perish. (Rev. xiii. 7 and 15).

The great image (v. 1), as suggested by Rev xiii 14, is thought to have been that of a man, but its proportions militate against this assumption and suggest that it was a phallus. If so it adds to the horror and shame of this popular form of idolatry—the phallus being held to represent the life-giver.

It was marked by three sixes 666 : sixty cubits high, six cubits broad, and proclaimed by six instruments of music (vs. 1 and 7).

The Greek names of these instruments are pointed to by some as striking against the antiquity of this book, but history records a traffic between Greece and Babylonia at this time sufficient to account for any similarity of name.

The False Prophet (Rev. xiii. 13-15) will set up an image of the Anti-Christ, and men will worship the image of the last king of Babylon as they worshipped that of the first king. See notes on Rev. xiii. and xiv.

But believers, in that day, like those of this chapter, will prefer death in a temporary fire (v. 21) to torment in an eternal fire (Rev. xiv. 9-11).

The faith and intelligence of verses 16-18 awaken admiration.

Like Noah, these three believers did not come forth from trial (v. 26) until directed to do so. They intelligently recognized the Divine appointment of the king, and, therefore, were subject to him as to their bodies (ch. ii. 37).

" Changed " (v. 27) i.e., discoloured. The fire had power in itself, but it had no power upon these men, nor upon their clothes except to burn their bonds so that they walked at liberty.

" Astonied " (v. 24) i.e., terrified—a Chaldean word (see Hebrew concordance).

" Dunghill " (v. 29) that is, " a heap of mud " ; for the houses being built of clay, if thrown down, would become such.

These three believers would have no sympathy with the present-day teaching respecting comparative religions. They refused any concession. They denied that the religion of the Bible was one of a brotherhood of religions. They declared that there was but one true God, and that He alone must be acknowledged ; that truth is the full revelation of Him and can only recognize itself ; for to put it on a level with falsehood would be to deny that it was truth.

The " God of heaven " is the distinguishing title in these chapters. Messiah, as the God of the earth, had His throne at Jerusalem. Nebuchadnezzar could have had no place there. God withdrew to heaven and committed the government of the earth to the Gentile Monarch. The character of his government, and of that of his successors, has been, and is, characterized by ignorance of God, by the substitution of idols, and by the building of Babylon. Such are the debased moral characteristics of power originally established by God. Yet He watches over all, and will judge those to whom He has committed authority.

The testimony of the Three was fivefold : (1) Confession ; " God " ; (2) Possession :

" Our God " ; (3) Consecration : " Whom we serve " ; (4) Separation : " We will not serve thy great god " ; (5) Resolution : " We will not worship the golden image."

Result : Confusion of the enemy (v. 25) and Promotion of the Three.

DANIEL IV.—Just as the experiences of chapter ii. failed to change Nebuchadnezzar's heart, so did those of chapter iii., though so much greater, equally fail, and the failure is recorded in this chapter.

It is a proclamation made by the king to all nations, and it may import that at last, after this further experience (v. 34), he was born of the Holy Spirit ; for he accepted the judgment of God upon himself as being one of the basest of men (v. 17), and he blessed and praised and honoured and acknowledged the very God that smote him (vs. 34 and 37).

Once again the king when in difficulty (v. 6) turned for help to any except to God. Such is the human heart ! At last Daniel was fetched ; he should have been at once sent for.

" Gods " (v. 8) plural of majesty for " God." This is made clear by the adjective " holy " ; for the gods of the ancients were impure.

By a bold change of figure from a tree to a beast (vs. 15 and 16) the degradation of the king is described.

This degradation predicted that the entire period (" seven times ") of man's government would be characterized by brutality and folly. History proves the accuracy of this prediction ; and the recent Great War (1917) illustrates the continuing madness of kings. The insane policies of past and present governments, as for example slavery, opium, drink and militarism, abundantly prove the fulfilment of the prophecy.

The king had a beast's heart given to him for seven actual years (v. 16). These " seven times " may possibly foreshadow the two thousand five hundred and twenty years of Gentile dominion (360 x 7). If so, this long period of time is now closing, and great events connected with the nation of the Hebrews may be expected to occur.

The preservation of the root-trunk of the tree (v. 15) with the band of iron and brass and with the dew of heaven, may point to the Divine preservation of the Babylonian monarchy by means of the kingdoms of Rome and Greece as its successors, and heirs ; and the reappearance of these two kingdoms in recent history appears to support the supposition.

" A watcher even an holy one " (v. 13), i.e., an angel.

" Demand " (v. 17), i.e., mandate. " Watchers " and " holy ones," plural of majesty for the Supreme Watcher and Holy One.

The prediction of the chapter may be that after centuries of madness, human governments will come to their right mind and will acknowledge the great God and Saviour Jesus Christ.

" One hour " (v. 19), i.e., for a moment, and " astonied," i.e., awestruck.

The earnest appeal of the prophet (v. 27) was quickly forgotten (v. 29).

" In " (v. 29) should read "upon," i.e. " upon the roof of the palace." This palace has been described by historians as one of incredible splendour.

DANIEL V.—The iniquity of the Gentile comes to a head in this chapter ; and its insolence and blasphemy reveal its ignorance and weakness. The king threw down a bold challenge to Jehovah. He and the companions of his orgie drank wine out of the sacred vessels of the Temple of God, and praised the idols, six in number, of gold and silver, brass, iron, wood and stone.

The Divine response was the destruction of the king that very night, and of all his glory.

Daniel, though subject to the king, did not invite him to repentance, as he did Nebuchadnezzar, or treat him with the same respect. He announced his coming doom ; and this prefigures the judgments which will fall upon the last king of Babylon who is to be cast into the lake of fire. For Babylon has given its own character to all the governments which have succeeded it ; and however forbearing God has been, and is, with these governments, all was already lost for them even in the days of Nebuchadnezzar.

Belshazzar was the son of Nabonidus and grandson of Nebuchadnezzar. There is no textual difficulty in this history. The Hebrew word for " father " and " grandfather " is the same. It also means " ancestor." Jer. xxvii. 7 makes the matter quite clear : " All nations shall serve him (Nebuchadnezzar) and his son (Nabonidus) and his son's son (Belshazzar) until the very time of his land come."

Belshazzar was Co-Rex with Nabonidus and reigned in Babylon while his father was warring with Cyrus. The hall in which he held his drunken orgy has lately been found. It is sixty feet wide and a hundred and seventy-two feet long, and its walls are beautifully decorated.

Daniel was an aged man at this time.

" In the same hour " (v. 5), i.e., at that moment. " The part of the hand," i.e., the fingers.

" The king's countenance was changed ' (vs. 5 and 9), i.e., he turned deadly pale.

" Third ruler in the kingdom " (vs. 7 and 16)—Nabonidus and Belshazzar being the first and second.

" Astonied " (v. 9), i.e., dumbfounded.

" The Queen " (v. 10), i.e., the king's mother. Possibly she feared God, for she evidently did not join in this impious banquet ; and she was acquainted with Daniel ; and she spoke of the true and holy God (v. 11).

" Father " (vs. 2, 11 and 18), i.e., grandfather.

" Then was Daniel brought in " (v. 13). The king, true to fallen man's unchanging action, sought help from God as a last resource and not as the first ; but even then the great big pompous fool condescendingly says " I have even heard of thee " (v. 14), but he does not add that " the Spirit of the holy God is in thee," as the Queen-Mother had said, but that " the spirit of the gods " is in thee.

With magnificent dignity Daniel rejects his gifts (v. 17) ; and in words of burning power thrusts the sword of the Spirit into his heart and conscience (vs. 18 to 28).

The repetition of the word " Mene " (v. 25) announced the immediateness of the doom.

Belshazzar kept his word (v. 29) ; but there is no evidence of his repentance, nor any information as to how he was slain, only that that night he perished.

Recent excavation, and the labour of scholars, prove the importance of the Balance in the religious teaching of the ancients, but show at the same time, how its moral force was destroyed by priestly corruption and greed.

DANIEL VI.—This chapter closes the first division of the Book of Daniel. It prophetically pictures the impious climax of earthly government in Anti-Christ's setting himself in the place of God. The evolution of human rebellion is pictured by the three monarchs; Nebuchadnezzar associated idols with God ; Belshazzar substituted idols for God ; and Darius set himself up instead of God (vs. 8 and 9).

Darius was probably the Astyages of history. " Darius " means Emperor.

Daniel was upwards of eighty years of age when cast into the den of lions, and was as faithful to Truth in his old age as when a little boy. His enemies no doubt hated him because of his determined opposition to bribery and corruption, and because of his attachment to the Word of God (vs. 4 and 5).

Their statement that " all " the presidents etc. had concurred to make this interdict was not true ; for Daniel was not a partner in it.

The action of the king (vs. 8 and 17) shows how his royal authority was limited and shared with the nobles, and, therefore, inferior to that of Nebuchadnezzar.

Daniel prayed in public, and in subjection to 1 Kings viii. 47-50 (v. 10).

" Daniel regardeth not thee " (v. 13) " nor the interdict that thou hast signed." Men in all ages have established a state religion so as to make non-conformists rebels to the State, and thus legalise their destruction.

History says that this Darius was abandoned to wine and women, and was destitute of strength of character (vs. 14 and 18).

The sin and folly of Darius were deepened by his knowledge of the true God (vs. 16 and 20).

His affection for Daniel, and his confidence in him, is seen in verses 2, 14, 16, 18, 19, 20, and 26, 27.

Religious pictures always depict Daniel's mouth closed and the lion's open. Verse 22 states the contrary.

The decree ordered that Daniel should be cast into the den, and it was obeyed ; it did not order his detention there, and so he could legally leave it. Darius then had authority, as king, to cast his accusers into it ; but they had to stay there, for they were devoured by the lions. By Persian law, as history proves, their wives and children were cast into the den with them. God's law forbade this. But a great and ever present principle is here illustrated that men cannot sin without injuring others. The drunkard not only destroys himself but he destroys his wife and children.

" Or ever they came " (v. 24). That is, directly they came ; this marks the hunger of the lions : and emphasizes the

reality of the Divine power that restrained them from devouring Daniel.

Thus closes the first Book of Daniel.

DANIEL VII.—The Second Book of Daniel is mainly occupied with the history, in prophecy, of the fourth kingdom upon earth, its destruction, and the establishment in its place of that of Messiah the King.

Nebuchadnezzar saw the Four Empires as a glorious and majestic figure, and the kingdom of the Messiah as a rough mountain stone. Daniel saw these kingdoms as fierce wild beasts, and the Messiah as the Son of Man resplendent with Divine glory (vs. 13 and 14).

To Nebuchadnezzar the empires appeared contemporaneously (ch. ii. 31), they similarly appeared to Daniel (vs. 3 and 17). They are the same kingdoms ; but how differently they appear to the man of God and to the man of the earth !

The first wild beast was the Babylonian Empire. The wings with which it lifted itself up from the earth were plucked and a man's heart was given to it, and it was made to stand on its feet as a man. Thus is described the king's insanity and conversion.

The second wild beast was the Medo-Persian Empire (v. 5) ; it raised up itself on one side, that is, the Persian, and the three ribs in its mouth were the countries of Chaldæa, Lydia, and Egypt which it conquered. History records the appalling destruction of human life effected by that government.

The third wild beast was the Grecian Empire (v. 6). Its four wings predicted the rapidity of its conquests, and its four heads the subsequent division into Greece, Thrace, Syria, and Egypt.

The fourth wild beast was so terrible as not to be comparable to any known animal ; and it is with the history of this last empire that the remainder of the Book of Daniel is concerned.

This empire from the human standpoint was much superior to the preceding ones. It was the Roman Empire ; but, from the Divine standpoint, it was the most dreadful, for under it millions of God's saints perished, and by it was the Lord of Glory crucified.

Its future and ultimate form will be that of a confederation of ten kings. The great War of 1914-18 will possibly develop this feature.

Among them will appear an insignificant

prince, here pictured by the little horn, who will over-throw three of the kings ; he will have super-human knowledge, and will speak great things, for he will declare himself to be God manifest in flesh.

This will be the Anti-Christ. His title as " the little horn " is the first of the twelve titles given to him in the Scriptures The other titles are : the King of Babylon (Isa. xiv. 4) ; the Assyrian (Isa. xiv. 25) ; Lucifer (Isa. xiv. 12) ; the Prince (Dan. ix. 26) ; the fierce king (Dan. viii. 23) ; the wilful king (Dan. xi. 36) ; the king of the north (xi. 40) the man of sin (2 Thess. ii. 3) ; the son of perdition (2 Thess. ii. 3) ; the lawless one (2 Thess. ii. 8 and Rev. xiii. 18) ; and the wild beast (Rev. xiii. 1).

" Cast down "(v. 9) should read " placed." "Thrones," plural of majesty for great throne.

" Did sit " (v. 9), i.e., took His seat.

The doom of this last king and his kingdom (v. 11) is more fully described in Rev. xix.

As to the preceding wild beasts (v. 12) their dominion endured for the divinely appointed time, and, in turn, was taken away by the succeeding one. Such was their history ; and it is here introduced to make more terrible, by way of contrast, the ending of the last kingdom.

Then will be introduced the perfect government of Emmanuel (vs. 13, 14 and 27).

" The saints " (vs. 21 and 22, 27), i.e., Daniel's people (ch. xii. 1) the Hebrews.

The term " shall arise " (v. 17) is not chronological but original. It points to the origin of these governments. They arise from the earth. They do not originate in heaven, as will the kingdom of the Son of Man.

DANIEL VIII.—The pedigree and history of Anti-Christ are continued in this chapter. It shows his connection with the Third World Empire, and it is written in Hebrew because the main interest of the prophecy is the affliction that is to come upon Daniel's people from the hand of that future prince prior to his judgment by the Prince of princes (vs. 24, 25).

The future Anti-Christ, as the " little horn," will, therefore, be connected with both the Roman and Grecian Empires ; will himself be king of one of the divisions of Alexander the Great's dominion, no doubt Assyria ; will, therefore, be one of the ten kings ; and will become their emperor.

His kingdom of Assyria will be the successor to that of Seleucus and Antiochus.

In vision Daniel was carried from Shushan to the river Ulai, now the Karun river near Susa. He saw the Medo-Persian ram, the higher horn being the Persian, throwing over its opponents (vs. 3 and 4), but, in its turn, destroyed by the Grecian goat (vs. 5-7).

Ancient Persian coins represent the king wearing a ram's head of gold, and a goat was the acknowledged symbol of Greece. It appears on its ancient monuments.

The rapidity of Alexander's progress is expressed in the words " and touched not the ground " (v. 5).

He, as the notable horn upon the goat's head, having been broken, four others came up instead of it (" For it ") (v. 8), i.e., Greece, Thrace, Assyria and Egypt.

Between the eighth and ninth verses already have elapsed about two thousand three hundred years.

" Out of one of them " (v. 9), i.e., the kingdom of Seleucus ; that is, Assyria. Verse 17 shews that the prophecy from verse 9 onwards should be read in the future tense.

This " little horn " (v. 9) will win victories in the south and east and in " the pleasant land," i.e., Palestine ; will capture Jerusalem (v. 10) ; oppress the " host of heaven " i.e., the Hebrew church ; put to death some of its members and ministers (" stars ") ; and stamp upon the residue. He will attack the high priest (" prince of the host ") ; he will take away the daily sacrifice from him, and throw down his place of worship (v. 11). " By reason of transgression," i.e., because he will be accepted as Messiah by the Jews.

Verse 12 may read : " And the host (believers) shall be given up to him (to destroy), together with the daily sacrifice, because of transgression ; and he (" it ") shall cast down truth to the ground," etc.

The two saints of verse 13 are " holy ones," that is, angels. They desire, as 1 Pet. i. 12 states, to examine and understand these prophecies. Their sympathy for man, and their service to him, appear in verses 13 and 14, for the one angel asked the question for Daniel's benefit, and the other gave the answer to Daniel himself.

It is very difficult to know as yet what period of time is intended by two thousand three hundred days.

One of these angels was named Gabriel (v. 16), the other was very probably Michael ;

they are the only angels named in the Scriptures.

That the fulfilment of this prophecy is still future is most plainly stated in verses 17 and 19.

" The indignation " (v. 19), i.e., God's past, present and future indignation against Israel. To that indignation He has set an appointed limit.

" Not in his power " (v. 22), i.e., not with Alexander's power.

" The latter time " (v. 23) ,i.e., a time still future when the transgressors are come to the full, or have filled up their measure ; that is, when the nation of Israel will reach the climax of their guilt by accepting Anti-Christ instead of Christ, as predicted by the Lord Himself (John v. 43). This verse is a blow to all who believe that the world will gradually get better and develop into the kingdom of heaven.

" Fierce countenance " and " dark sentences " (v. 23), i.e., of majestic presence and super-human knowledge.

" Not by his own power " (v. 24), i.e., by Satanic power.

" The mighty and the holy people " (v. 24), i.e., the Hebrew Church—Daniel's people.

His policy will be by cunning rather than by coercion to secure peace, i.e., prosperity. He will destroy the majority of the Hebrews ; for it is easier to " destroy " professors of the truth of God by prosperity than by adversity. Finally, he will attack Messiah the Prince, but he shall be " broken " without human instrumentality.

It was reasonable that Daniel should have expected the manifested kingdom of glory of the Messiah at the close of the seventy years Captivity. So great was the disappointment when he was told that the vision belonged to far distant days (" it shall be for many days ") that he fell sick and was dumbfounded (" astonished.")

" And did the king's business " (v. 27). Those whose interests are set on heavenly things are the best executors of earthly things.

DANIEL IX.—Daniel's prayer was based upon the " Books," i.e., the Bible (Lev. xxvi., 2 Chron. xxxvi., Jer. xxv. and xxix.). He confessed Israel's sin ; acknowledged the justice of her punishment ; sought (" seek " vs. 2, 3, and 19) forgiveness ; and pleaded for the city and the nation (vs. 4–19).

The answer to the prayer (vs. 24-27) promised enduring restoration for both city and nation (v. 24), but stated that it would be preceded by a long period of desolation and suffering (v. 26) ; and that, during that period, the Messiah would come, be crucified, and not obtain the kingdom (v. 26) ; and that the false Messiah (v. 27) would be accepted of the nation, abolish the Temple Worship, and introduce in its stead an idol of supreme abomination.

The Angel Gabriel (v. 21) is here called a man. Directly Daniel began to pray he was sent forth with the answer (v. 23). His words are a direct prophecy—recalling other Angelic Prophecies of the Bible.

The study of prophecy was not for Daniel a mere intellectual entertainment but moral spiritual nourishment. (v. 23).

The Apocalypse of the Old Testament was given to Daniel who was greatly beloved (v. 23), and that of the New Testament was given to John the disciple whom Jesus loved. This should enchance the value of these books to the Christian.

The prophet's hope that the close of the seventy year's desolation would be followed by the restoration of the throne of David, was confounded by the declaration that an immense period of seven times seventy years was marked off (" determined ") by God from future chronology, and that only after that period would the six statements of verse 24 be fulfilled.

" The transgression " (v. 24), i.e., the climax of Israel's wickedness in crucifying the true Messiah and accepting the false one.

" To make an end of sins and to make reconciliation for iniquity " (v. 24), i.e., the atoning sacrifice of Calvary.

" To bring in everlasting righteousness " (v. 24), i.e., the Millennium.

" To seal up the vision and prophecy " (v. 24), i.e., to fulfil them.

" The most holy " (v. 24), i.e., the Temple.

The " commandment " of verses 23 and 25 was that predicted in Isa. xlv. 13, and recorded 2 Chron. xxvi. 32 and Ezra i. 1.

From that event to the death of Messiah the Prince was 483 years. There is a conflict here between Bible chronology and popular chronology. " The Romance of Bible Chronology " examines this discord (Marshall, London).

The period of seventy heptads is divided

into "seven weeks," "sixty two weeks" (v. 25), and "one week" (v. 27).

The seven weeks, or heptads, cover the period from Cyrus to Malachi, the sixty-two heptads, from Malachi to Calvary, and the one remaining heptad belongs to the future; for, as a judgment because of Christ's rejection, the Romans destroyed the city and the Temple (v. 26), and the Hebrews were carried away into exile, where they must remain till the final "week" is reached.

"Troublous times" (v. 25), i.e., under Ezra and Nehemiah. "Cut off but not for himself" (v. 26), i.e., crucified and have nothing, that is, not receive His Kingdom. "The people" (v. 26), i.e., the Romans. "The prince that shall come," i.e., Antichrist.

"The end thereof" etc., (v. 26), i.e., the city and Temple would be utterly ruined as with a flood.

"And unto the end," etc., (v. 26), i.e., "and after the close of the war desolations (the plural of majesty for an immense period of desolation) are determined"—that is, marked off by God. This period of time interposes between verses 26 and 27, and during it Israel is "not My people."

"He" (v. 27), i.e., Antichrist, the prince of verse 26, shall confirm a covenant with the many," i.e., the majority of the Hebrew people, for seven years; but after three years and a half he will violate it, and abolish Divine worship, and in its stead erect the abomination that maketh desolate; and it will "overspread," i.e., continue for the remaining three years and a half of Antichrist's reign, and then "the consummation" of judgment determined by God shall be poured upon the desolate people of Israel because of their past wickedness, and because of their final filling up of their cup of wrath in their acceptance of Antichrist and his worship.

The conflict between Bible and Ptolemaic chronology may be resolved by a possible Divine gap between the seven heptads and the sixty-two, as there is between the sixty-second and the last, thus: 7 heptads (gap of 82 years) 62 heptads (gap of 1900 years) and one heptad—total, 490 prophetic years.

The heptads mark off prophetic from cosmic time because affecting God's action with Israel; but the term "the times of the Gentiles" intends solar or lunar time, or both. It is remarkable that the seventy heptads are broken by the Scripture into these three portions, viz :—7, 62, and 1.

The unique glory of this prophecy is that it alone foretold the time of Messiah's appearing, and the very year of His crucifixion.

DANIEL X.-XI. 1.—" A thing was revealed," (v. 1), i.e., a communication was made.

"But the time appointed was long" (v. 1), i.e., "Even a long warfare" (R.V.)

"The first month" (v. 4), i.e., the fast of unleavened bread (Exod. xii. 18). Daniel mourned for three times seven days. Hiddekel is the modern Tigris.

The similarity of the apparition in verses 5 and 6 and in Rev. i. 13, 16, suggests that it was Immanuel Himself Who appeared to Daniel (vs. 10, 16, 18). Or these latter verses may intend the Lord, and the former, Gabriel.

In Divine communications to man there is a parallel progression between the Old Testament and the New. In the former Christ appeared visibly in angelic form, then spoke through the prophets, and, finally, through angels in an Apocalypse. In the latter He spoke in human form, then by His Spirit through the apostles and prophets (Rom. xvi. 26, and Eph. iii. 5), and, lastly, through angels in the Apocalypse.

"For thy words" (v. 12), i.e., because of thy prayer.

"The prince of the kingdom of Persia" (v. 13), i.e., the evil angel appointed by Satan to control the Persian government. Ezra iv. possibly explains the subject of this contest.

This mysterious passage appears to reveal that Satan places an agent in charge of every nation; and, if so, this may explain national hatreds and national movements. Similarly, God has His angelic agents operating in opposition to Satan's. The conflict of Eph. vi., and the battle of Revelation xii., harmonize with this supposition.

The mystery of prayer is deepened by the facts recorded in verses 12-14.

"I remained" (v. 13), i.e., "I was no longer needed" (R.V.).

"Thy people" (v. 14), i.e., Daniel's people, the Hebrews. "In the latter days," i.e., the future. "For yet the vision is for many days," i.e., belonged to the then far distant future, that is, to the time which will immediately precede the Second Advent.

The answer to the question, "Knowest

thou wherefore I come unto thee?" (v. 20) may be supplied by the angel himself: "because thou art a man greatly beloved." The rest of the verse may be thus paraphrased: Now will I return to fight with the satanic prince of Persia, and when I shall come forth (victorious over him), lo, the satanic prince of Grecia shall come (and I shall have to do battle with him on behalf of thy people).

"The Scripture of Truth" (v. 21), i.e., the Bible. All these predictions existed in the mind of God before their committal to writing by men chosen of God. Being Truth they are by nature infallible.

To Michael alone as the chief prince was committed the safe-keeping of Israel. All the world powers, and their satanic rulers, are opposed to Israel, and continually seek her destruction.

"Him" xi. 1, i.e., Darius. See ch. vi.

DANIEL XI. 2—45.—This prophecy is an expansion of that of ch. viii. 22-25. The prophet was an angel and not a man.

Up to the words "on his part" in verse 31, it is past history; and from the words, "And they shall pollute," etc., (v. 31), to the end, future history.

That a vast period of time may intervene between two statements only separated by a comma, is proved by the Lord's action in Luke iv. 19.

To the unspiritual mind this chapter is without interest, and to the sceptical and critical mind, untruthful; for it is contended that these pretended prophecies were written after the events took place.

But students of history, and of the LXX., know that these prophecies were written before they began to come to pass (v. 4), and that their most important predictions yet await fulfilment (vs. 21-45).

Further, the heart that is in fellowship with God takes an intense interest in all this history, both past and future, because it concerns God's dearly-loved people and His pleasant land. That land was devastated, and will yet again be devastated by the contending armies of Egypt and Syria, and that people suffered, and will suffer, appalling miseries at the hands of these opposing powers.

The Bible only interests itself in wars which affect Palestine and the Hebrew Church.

The great theme, therefore, of this chapter is the Antichrist, his pedigree, his exploits and his doom.

Thus the five visions of the Book of Daniel: chapters ii., vii., viii., ix., xi., all close at the same future point of time; that is to say, the advent and overthrow of Antichrist.

A similar arrangement of prophecies appears in the Book of the Revelation.

"Three kings" (v. 2), i.e., Cambyses, Darius Hystaspes, and Xerxes. He was "the fourth" from Darius the Mede.

"A mighty king" (v. 3), i.e., Alexander the Great.

"Not to his posterity" (v. 4), i.e., not to his children. On the death of Alexander his generals murdered the great king's sons and divided the empire into four kingdoms. Of these the North and South became very powerful, and absorbed the others.

"The king of the South" (v. 5), i.e., Ptolemy-Soter.

"One of his princes" (v. 5), i.e., Seleucus, king of the North. He became stronger than Ptolemy ("him") and secured a great dominion for himself.

"They" (v. 6), i.e., Ptolemy the Second the king of the south, and Antiochus the king of the North.

"The king's daughter" (v. 6), i.e., Berenice daughter of Ptolemy. She married Antiochus, who divorced his wife Laodice and disinherited her son Callinicus. But Berenice did not strengthen Antiochus, for she and her child and all her retinue were murdered by Laodice; and her father Ptolemy, who had protected her, died.

"The power of the arm" (v. 6), i.e., the power of Egypt.

"Neither shall he stand nor his arm" (v. 6), i.e., Berenice's son.

"A branch out of her roots" (v. 7), i.e., Ptolemy the Third, the brother of Berenice.

"In his estate" (v. 7), i.e., instead of his father Ptolemy the Second. He invaded Syria, defeated the king of the North, avenged the murder of his sister, and carried off immense booty to Egypt (v. 8).

Hence he was called by the grateful Egyptians "the Benefactor." He lived four years longer than the king of the North (v. 8).

"His sons" (v. 10), i.e., the sons of Antiochus, king of the North.

"One of them shall certainly come" (v. 10), i.e., Antiochus the Third; for his brother was accidentally killed at the opening of the campaign.

"Overflow and pass through" (v. 10), i.e., the land of Palestine.

"Then shall he return" (v. 10), i.e., Ptolemy.

"He shall set forth" (v. 11), i.e., Antiochus. "But the multitude shall be given into his hand," i.e., the hand of Ptolemy, who overthrew Antiochus with great slaughter at Raphia; but he by dissipation failed to profit by the victory.

"The king of the North" (v. 13), i.e., Antiochus.

"The king of the South" at this time (v. 14) was Ptolemy the Fifth. He was a boy of twelve. A rebellion, aided by the turbulent Jews resident in Egypt ("the robbers of thy people"), paralysed the Egyptian government, and helped to its defeat.

"To establish the vision" (v. 14) "But they shall fall." These turbulent Jews thought that by helping Antiochus they would bring about the fulfilment of prophecy and the independence of Judah, but the result was that they all perished at the hands of the Egyptians.

"Neither his chosen people" (v. 15), i.e., the best Egyptian troops. These were sent against Antiochus, but were totally defeated in the neighbourhood of Sidon.

"But he (Antiochus) that cometh against him" (Ptolemy V.) (v. 16).

"The glorious land," i.e., Palestine.

"And upright ones," etc., (v. 17). This should read: He will make equitable conditions with him, i.e., with Ptolemy V. that is, a treaty of peace. The conditions were that Antiochus' daughter, Cleopatra, aged eleven, should marry Ptolemy. The Holy Spirit here describes her as "the daughter of women." The term denotes beauty. She is famed as the most beautiful of women.

"Corrupting her" (v. 17). Her father ordered her to be a spy in the Egyptian court in his interest, but she sided with her husband, and defeated her father's plans by inviting the protection of the Romans.

After this marriage Antiochus the Great marshalled an immense army and with a fleet attacked Asia Minor and Greece (v. 18); but a Roman general, Lucius Scipio, defeated him, and restored the prestige of the Roman name which had suffered "re-

proach" because the Roman Senate had failed to protect Egypt and Greece. Scipio did not act in his own interest, for he refused to be bribed by the proffered release of his son who was a prisoner in the hands of Antiochus, and after his great victory he magnanimously offered the same conditions of peace as before. Thus he caused the "reproach" to turn from the Romans on to the king (v. 18).

"He shall stumble" (v. 19). In his efforts to raise the indemnity commanded by the Romans, Antiochus plundered a popular temple and the enraged worshippers killed him.

His son Seleucus (v. 20) was mainly engaged in raising money to satisfy the Roman tribute. He sent Heliodorus into the "kingdom" (Judah) to plunder the glory of the kingdom, i.e., the Temple. On his return Heliodorus poisoned his master, and thus he died neither in anger nor in battle.

Antiochus Epiphanes in his character, actions, and cruelties illustrates the closing predictions of the chapter, but does not fulfil them. Their fulfilment awaits the future Antichrist. The Lord's statement in Matt. xxiv. 15, that verse 31 is still future, confirms this conviction.

"In his estate" (v. 21), i.e., the kingdom of Syria, inclusive of the ancient Assyria and the modern Armenia. The recent War has partly developed the restoration of that kingdom.

"They" (v. 21), the neighbouring kings.

"They" (v. 22), i.e., his opponents.

"The prince of the Covenant" (v. 22), i.e., the future High Priest of Israel.

The league made with him (v. 23), i.e., the covenant of the previous verse.

"A small people" (v. 23), hence this title "a little horn."

"He" (v. 25), i.e., the king of the South.

"His army shall overflow" (v. 26), i.e., his soldiers shall desert him.

Man's plans can never postpone God's appointments (v. 27).

"The Holy Covenant" (v. 28), i.e., God's Covenant with Israel.

"The former" (v. 29), i.e., verse 25, "the latter i.e.," verse 42, that is, this middle campaign against Egypt will be unsuccessful (v. 30). This expedition will demonstrate the insincerity of the conference of verse 27.

The mention of ships in verses 30 and 40

predict the size and importance of navies in the final wars of the present period of time.

They that forsake the holy covenant (v. 30), i.e., the Jews, who will forsake the Law of Moses and assist this wilful king in polluting the future temple, and in substituting the abomination for the daily sacrifice (v. 31).

" They that understand " (v. 33), i.e., the faithful leaders and ministers of the Hebrew church.

" Many days " (v. 33), i.e., 1,260 days—the final tribulation of Matt. xxiv. 21, and Rev. xiii. 5-7.

" Fall " (v. 34), i.e., fall by the sword.

" Cleave to them with flatteries," i.e., will beset them with flatteries in order to induce them to apostatize. Satan has two weapons against faithfulness to truth, one is violence, the other is flattery.

" They shall be holpen with a little help " (v. 34). This may mean they shall obtain but little help, or, the help offered them will be false because based on flattery. Most of the faithful will perish in that future tribulation ; and all of them would perish but that those days shall be shortened (Matt. xxiv. 22). See Rev. xiii. 7.

Persecution is permitted because of its moral value ; but it never can continue one moment longer than God has decreed, however Satan and men may exert themselves to continue it.

" The king " (v. 36), i.e., the King of the North (v. 40), the Antichrist. The true Messiah did not act according to His own will (John vi. 38).

This verse (36) is quoted in 2 Thess. ii. 3, 4.

" The indignation " (v. 36), i.e., God's wrath against Israel. " Determined," that is, decreed. The just anger decreed by God against the Hebrew Church for its idolatry and rejection of Christ, will be executed, as to its fulfilment, by the false Messiah as God's instrument. This illustrates the principle of the Divine punitive activity, which constantly appears both in nature and in Scripture.

The words " The God of his Fathers " (v. 37) is thought by some to indicate that Antichrist will be a Jew, but it could equally define him as the son of professing Christians.

" The desire of women " (v. 37), i.e., the idol desired by women—that is, the Queen of Heaven, the Mother and Child, the Astarte of the Ancients, the Venus of the Greeks and Romans, the Isis and Horus of the Egyptians, and the Madonna of corrupt Christendom. The preceding and succeeding sentences in the verse dealing with divinities decide the meaning of this word " desire."

" In his estate " (v. 38), i.e., instead of God (v. 37). Antichrist will set up the god of the forces of nature,"—a strange god " (v. 39), that is, a god never before known. This suggests his discovery, and use, of some powerful secret of nature with which he will destroy his enemies and their fortresses ; and all who will acknowledge this strange god (v. 39) will he enrich (v. 38) and promote to high positions (v. 39), and divide amongst them the land of Palestine (v. 39).

" At the time of the end " (v. 40). This should be connected with " even to the time of the end " (v. 35). This latter denotes duration; the former, completion ; and these statements coupled with x. 14, and xii. 1, define and declare the futurity of these predictions.

" Push at him " (v. 40) ; that is, at the King of the North, Antichrist. " And the King of the North shall come against him," that is, against the King of the South. This verse is generally understood to mean that these two kings will attack Antichrist. But this is not so for Antichrist is the King of the North.

" The glorious land " (v. 41). See vii. 9, and verses 16 and 45.

" Tidings out of the east and out of the north " (v. 44), i.e., the destruction of his capital city, Babylon, by fire from heaven (Rev. xviii.), and the revolt of his supporters in Jerusalem.

To destroy and utterly to exterminate the Hebrews (v. 44).

" Tabernacles " (v. 45), i.e., plural of majesty for Royal pavilion. " The seas," i.e., the Mediterranean and the Dead Seas. " The glorious holy mountain," i.e., Mount Zion. Antiochus died at Tabor in Persia, therefore he is not the monarch pointed to here.

" He shall come to his end," etc., (v. 45) that is supernaturally (ii. 44, and Rev. xix. 19-21).

DANIEL XII.—The three statements in verse 1, decide the futurity of these wonderful events (v. 6).

" A time of trouble," i.e., the Great

Tribulation predicted in viii. 24, 25. Matt. xxiv. 21, etc.

" Thy people," i.e., Daniel's people, the Hebrews written in " the book " (Luke x. 20, Rev. xiii. 8, and xx. 15).

" Many of them " (v. 2), better read : " Many from among them." There are two resurrections pointed to in this verse. These are separated by a long period (Rev. xx. 3, 5, 6, John v. 28). The term " everlasting life " here first occurs in the Old Testament.

" Even to " (v. 4), i.e., " until." To " shut up the words and seal the book " may mean a direction to commit all these prophecies to writing, so as to ensure the safety and continuance of the book, in order that it may be a guide to those who will be alive at " the time of the end." The fact is that this book and its second Edition—the Apocalypse —have been preserved in spite of repeated efforts to destroy them.

" Many shall run to and fro " (v. 4) and knowledge (of evil ?) shall be increased." This may indicate a running after false teachers and false doctrines (2 Tim. iii. and iv.), and may predict the Apostasy of 2 Thess. ii. 2.

" To raise the hands " (v. 7), betokened affirmation.

" He " (v. 7), i.e., Antichrist. " The holy people " i.e., the Hebrews. Their period of suffering under him shall be a time, times and a half (v. 7), that is, three years and a half, or forty and two months, or twelve hundred and sixty days.

The two questions " How long ? " (v. 6), and " What ? " (v. 8), point to the duration of these wonders, and to the event which is to conclude the period.

The ninth verse declares that these prophecies belong to the future.

" The wise shall understand " (v. 10). Compare Matt. xxiv. 15.

Three periods are mentioned : Twelve hundred and sixty days (v. 7), twelve hundred and ninety days (v. 11), and thirteen hundred and thirty five days (v. 12). That is, 1260 + 30 + 45. These are astronomical numbers. At the time of the end the " wise " shall understand them and be helped by them.

" Waiteth " (v. 12), i.e., endureth or holds out.

" Thou shalt rest " (in death) and " stand " (in resurrection).

THE MINOR PROPHETS

HOSEA, JOEL, AMOS, OBADIAH, JONAH, MICAH, NAHUM,

HABAKKUK, ZEPHANIAH, HAGGAI, ZECHARIAH, MALACHI.

THE MINOR PROPHETS.—These are twelve in number, and in the Hebrew Bible form one Book, just as the twelve Tribes of Israel form one nation. They are called "Minor" not because less important, or less inspired, but because shorter than the prophecies of Isaiah, Jeremiah and Ezekiel.

Six of them are dated: Hosea, Amos, Micah, Zephaniah, Haggai and Zechariah. The remainder are not dated. Nine were given before the Captivity and three after it. Of the dated prophecies two contain the names of the kings of Israel, two contain kings of Judah only, and two contain kings of Persia.

The structure of the twelve books may be thus set out :—

Hosea : Like Amos, uttered in the reign of Jeroboam II and certain kings of Judah.

Joel : Undated, addressed to the Gentiles and Israel.

Amos : Like Hosea, uttered in the reign of Jeroboam II and of one king of Judah.

Obadiah : Like Habakkuk, concerns Edom.
Jonah : Like Nahum, concerns Nineveh.
Micah : Like Zephaniah, concerns Judah.
Nahum : Like Jonah, concerns Nineveh.
Habakkuk : Like Obadiah, concerns Babylon.
Zephaniah : Like Micah, concerns Judah.
Haggai ⎫
Zechariah ⎬ Uttered after the Captivity.
Malachi ⎭

Thus the twelve Books form three groups : the first, containing Three Prophets, the second, Six, and the last, Three.

HOSEA

HOSEA I.—The word Hosea means Salvation.

His prophecies covered more than sixty years (v. 1). His ministry, and probably his life, terminated at the destruction of the northern Kingdom.

The prophecy is mainly addressed to the Ten Tribes shortly before their dispersion. The nation is appealed to under the figure of an unfaithful wife, because of its devotion to idols and forsaking of Jehovah.

The word "whoredom" (v. 2) is to be read "idolatry." The prophet, who was a spiritual son of Abraham, and, perhaps, of the children of Judah, was commanded to marry a wife

belonging to the Northern kingdom, and to have children by her. Hence the symbolic language of this verse. The verb "beget" may be supplied before the word "children."

The words "departing from the Lord" (v. 2) define the symbolic language of the verse.

Jezreel (vs. 4 and 11). There is a play on this word. It means "I will scatter," and "I will sow." The former meaning is to be understood in verse 4; the latter in verse 11.

"The blood of Jezreel" means the blood shed by Jehu at Jezreel, for he exceeded his commission, was guilty of murder, sought

631

his own interests, and lapsed into idolatry. Jeroboam II was his son in the third generation. His reign was the longest in Israel, and was prosperous; but his son was the last king of the House of Jehu, for he perished in an insurrection (2 Kings x. 30, and xv. 10).

The valley of Jezreel (v. 5), i.e., the plain of Esdraelon.

"Lo-ruhamah" (v. 6) means "not pitied." Compare Rom. ix. 25 and 1 Pet. ii. 10. Other references to Hosea in the New Testament are Matt. ii. 15; ix. 13; xii. 7; and 1 Cor. xv. 55.

2 Kings xix. 35 illustrates verse 7; but the fulfilment of this verse belongs to the future (2 Thess. ii. etc).

"Lo-ammi" (v. 9), i.e., "not My people." The language of verse 10 is not that of exaggeration, for how could human language set a limit to Divine promise? This verse is quoted in Rom. ix. 25 as an illustration, not as an interpretation.

"In the place" (v. 10) means "instead of."

The restoration under Zerubbabel did not satisfy the prediction of verse 11, for it was very small, only concerned two or three of the Tribes, and did not secure national independence. The future will satisfy the prophecy, for then will God "sow" the Hebrew nation unto Himself in righteousness (ii. 23).

HOSEA II.—The appeal of verse 1 is to that little company of spiritual men which God has in all ages, and which is here distinguished by the affectionate titles of "My People," and "The Engraced." These brethren of the prophet, believing the gracious promises of the preceding verses, and energized by them, are called to plead with the nation (v. 2), and to win it back to Jehovah. Thus God invites His people into fellowship with Himself in His love toward the guilty and sinful.

Verse 2 may be thus read: "Let her, therefore, put away her idols out of her sight, and her idolatries from her heart."

The reference in verse 3 is to the Exodus from Egypt and the entrance into the wilderness.

"Played the harlot" (v. 5), i.e., practised idolatries.

"My bread" and "my water," etc. Here are in three pairs, food, clothing and luxuries.

She claimed them as hers, and as having been given to her by her idols, but God said that He gave them to her, that they were His (v. 8), and that He would take them back (v. 9).

Verse 6 had its fulfilment in the Dispersion. Then were her "paths" to her idols, whom she tried to eagerly follow after (v. 7), obstructed so that she could not overtake them, or find them.

Like the prodigal son, and multitudes of others when in misery, she said I will return to Jehovah (v. 7) for then was it well with me.

"I will return (in judgment) and take back my corn," etc., (v. 9). They were all His, and given by Him.

None of the idols could deliver her from the Assyrian (v. 10).

"Visit upon her" (v. 13), i.e., judge her.

The closing verses of the chapter predict the restoration of Israel under the covenant of Grace as opposed to that of Law. The nation is pictured as a faithless and debauched wife betrothed as a spotless bride to Immanuel. This impossibility will be effected by the miracle of the New Birth. The old impure Israel will die, and a pure virgin will appear as the new nation, and then will take place the Marriage Supper of the Lamb (Rev. xix. 7).

"Therefore" (v. 14). This word connects the second section of the chapter with the first section. After such a recital of sin and shame (vs. 1-13) a just sentence of eternal wrath would naturally be expected; but where sin abounded grace here much more abounds, and forgiveness and restoration are promised.

"I will allure," "I will bring," "I will speak," "I will give" (vs. 14 and 15).

"Comfortably" (v. 14), i.e., "to the heart."

"Into the wilderness" (v. 14) as at the first when He led her out of Egypt into the wilderness in order that there He might make known to her the riches of His love, so a man allures a maiden into marriage and then takes her to some retired spot and speaks to her heart.

The way to the vineyards is through the wilderness. Spiritual discipline precedes blessing and fits for its joys. Hence the words "from thence" (v. 15).

The valley of Achor was a vale of horror (Josh. vii. 24) but is to become for Israel

a. door of hope. Where the wrath of God justly fell the grace of God is to brightly shine. The valley of horror becomes the vale of hope. Such was Calvary—a place of horror to the suffering Saviour under the wrath of God, but a door of hope to the redeemed sinner under the grace of God.

" She shall sing " (v. 15), and, naturally, as the result of the four " I wills " of verses 14 and 15.

" Ishi " (v. 16), i.e., " My husband " " Baali " : i.e., " My master."

Wild beasts and warlike men will in the coming day of Israel's restoration be expelled from the land of Palestine, and the happy sons of Jacob will lie down safely like sheltered sheep (v. 18).

" I will betroth thee " (vs. 19 and 20). This thrice repeated promise confirms the engagement.

The betrothment will be perpetual (" for ever "), legal (" in righteousness "), well considered (" in judgment."), affectionate (" in loving kindness "), well endowed (" in mercies "), and faithful (" in faithfulness ").

" Thou shalt know the Lord " (v. 20). All evils come from not knowing Him (Isa. i. 3, Luke xix. 42 and 44).

" Jezreel " (vs. 21 and 22), (i.e., Israel); as sown by God in the land (v. 23), will cry to the corn, the wine, and the oil to supply her needs ; they will cry to the earth to fructify them ; the earth will cry to the heavens for the needed rain in order to produce the fruit ; and the heavens will cry to Jehovah to fill them with the required water, and from Him there will be no further appeal, for He is the Great First Cause ! In response to the appeal He will fill the heavens with moisture, the heavens will discharge it upon the earth, the earth will produce, as the result, the corn, the wine, and the oil, Israel will have ample provision, and thus heaven and earth will be bound together with a chain of love. Israel that was Lo-Ruhamah and Lo-Ammi (v. 23) will become Ruhamah, i.e., Pitied One, and Ammi, i.e., My People.

HOSEA III.—The symbolism of this chapter is obscure ; not in itself, but to man's infirmity of perception.

But it may be thus understood. Gomer, who was an idolatress (i. 2), proved faithless to the prophet, and fell into degraded bondage. Hosea was commanded still to love her, to redeem her from slavery, to remain faithful to her for a lengthened period, and then to fully restore her.

This illustrated God's action with Israel, and is the teaching and argument of the chapter.

" Go yet " (v. 1), i.e., notwithstanding her shameful conduct.

" Love," not " take " as in i. 2. " Take " implies take in marriage. The prophet was to renew his love for his guilty wife.

" A woman beloved of her friend " (v. 1), i.e., a wife loved by her husband, the husband being Hosea ; but Gomer had forfeited by her misconduct the right to use these honourable words of wife and husband.

" According to the love of Jehovah " (v. 1). This action of Hosea's illustrated the measure and fulness of the Divine love to the guilty nation.

" Flagons of wine " (v. 1), i.e., cakes of grapes used in idol worship (Jer. vii. 18).

The redemption price of a slave was thirty pieces of silver (Exod. xxi. 32) and so much barley. Fifteen pieces of silver and so little barley marked the worthlessness of this slave.

Gomer was to wait (" abide ") " many days " before enjoying full restoration to her position as a wife. Hosea promised that he would not prove unfaithful to her during the necessary period. The word " abide " in Hebrew signifies to dwell sequestered (Deut. xxi. 13).

Verses 4 and 5 destroy the theory that the British nation are the Ten Tribes.

This prophecy is addressed to the Ten Tribes. It predicted that they should remain for a long period of time (already 2600 years) without a government, or a Priest, or a Levitical sacrifice, and yet be free from idolatry. So has it been, and so is it to-day, and so will it continue until they return to Jehovah their God and David-Messiah their King.

They revolted from the throne of David but they will return to it " in the latter days.'

" His goodness " (v. 5), should be translated " His Gracious One," that is, the Messiah (xiv. 2, and Eph. i. 6). " David " means " Beloved." A voice from heaven said " Thou art My David " (Matt. iii. 17).

" Many days," " afterward," " the latter days." These terms define the periods of the dispersion and restoration of the Ten Tribes. They were never lost.

The conduct of Israel in defiling herself with idols, as symbolized by the action of Gomer, will appear more vile and debased if it be assumed, as some suggest, that in an excess of religious superstition the unhappy woman left her husband and dedicated herself to the hideous life of a Temple-woman (iv. 14). From that bondage Hosea redeemed her. It was a religious zeal, energized by Satan, which carried Israel into idolatry.

HOSEA IV.—All this chapter, except verse 15, is addressed to the Ten Tribes; and yet Grace calls them " My People " (vs. 6 and 8).

The evils detailed in verse 2 result from not knowing God (v. 1). " Blood touched blood," i.e., murder follows murder.

" Be taken away " (v. 3). This may be translated " shall be gathered " (i.e., into the ranks of the mourners). Creation, animate and inanimate, suffers as the result of man's sin.

Reproof was hopeless (v. 4). The priest was the judge having the power of death (Deut. xvii. 12) ; hence to strive with him was folly.

Divine judgment strikes evil both by day and night (v. 5). " Thy mother," i,e., The Ten Tribes.

" Knowledge " (v. 6), i.e., the knowledge of God. Israel as a nation was designed by God to be the priest of all nations.

" I will change their glory into shame " (v. 7). This may also read : " My glory have they changed into shame " ; that is, they substituted a Phallus for God. It, was, therefore, just to turn their glory into shame.

" They (the priests) eat up the sin (offerings) of My People " (v. 8). " Iniquity," i.e., wrong doing.

" Like people like priest " .(v. 9). They were one in guilt ; and, therefore, justly one in punishment.

They legalized concubinage (v. 10) but did not thereby increase their children.

Idol-worship, and its licentious rites (v.11), destroy the understanding, and make men insensible to their own good.

" Their stocks " (v. 12), i.e., wooden idols. " Their staff," i.e., divination rod (Ezek. xxi. 21-22). The Assyrian Monarchs are depicted on the monuments holding these in one hand. They were usually placed in a bag, and, one being drawn out, directed by its mark action or inaction in a proposed matter, or decision in taking either of two ways. The modern gypsies use the divination rod.

The spirit of idolatry (v. 12) causes to err ; the Spirit of God saves from error.

The Ten Tribes had gone from under the protection and authority of God just as Gomer had from under the protection and authority of Hosea.

The tops of mountains, of hills, and of houses (v. 13) were chosen for worship because nearer to the sun, moon and stars.

The wives and daughters (vs. 13 and 14) were guilty of actual adultery because their fathers and husbands (" themselves ") were guilty of spiritual adultery. And it was reasonable that they should, therefore, not be punished.

The unhappy women with whom these fathers and husbands dishonoured themselves were the Temple-women of ancient and modern idolatry. The violation of their bodies in honour of the god was a supreme act of worship to which they willingly dedicated themselves, or, as in India to-day, to which they were cruelly dedicated when children (Num. xxv. 1-3, R.V. and Deut. xxiii. 18).

The Ten Tribes did not wish to understand (v. 14), and, therefore, they fell and were dispersed.

The true worshippers of God are ever liable to fall ; hence they are .forbidden to visit centres of false worship (v. 15), or to have fellowship with idolaters (v. 17) who say : " Jehovah liveth," i.e., who associate God with idols.

" Ye " (v. 15), i.e., the people of Judah. Gilgal once holy (Josh. v. 10, 1 Sam. x. 8, and xv. 21), was afterwards desecrated by idol worship (ix. 15, xii. 11, Amos iv. 4, v. 5, Judges iii. 19 margin). Beth-aven, " house of vanity," or idols, once Bethel " house of God " (Gen. xxviii. 17, xxxv. 7, 1 Kings xii. 28, 29).

" Swear " (v. 15), i.e., worship, using the formula " Jehovah liveth." The association of idols with God is applauded by man to the present day.

Verse 16 reads better : " Israel is refractory as a refractory heifer," that is, one that throws the yoke off its neck.

" Jehovah will feed them," etc., (v. 16),

i.e., will scatter them in exile throughout the whole world.

It is dangerous and useless to maintain relations with a person who determines to practise a false religion, or to pursue a course of evil (v. 17).

Drunkenness leads to idolatry, impurity, and bribery (v. 18). " Sour," i.e., " causes to rebel " (Isa. vii. and xxviii. 1).

" The wind " (v. 19), i.e., the spirit of idolatry (v. 12) (see notes on Zech. v. 9) carries its votaries into bondage, and the result of their sacrifices is that they are put to shame.

HOSEA V. — VI. 3. — Neither the kings nor priests of the Northern Kingdom were legitimate, but they claimed to be kings and priests, and God met them on their own ground, and, in grace, warned them of the judgment about to fall upon them because of the idolatry established at Mizpah and Tabor (v. 1).

Verse 2 may better read thus : " And the apostates are deeply resolved to slaughter victims in sacrifice, but I will be a rebuker of them all." The term " slaughter " instead of " slay " is here used contemptuously.

The term " to know the Lord " (v. 4) in these prophecies means, in Hebrew, to know experimentally rather than intellectually.

The " Pride, " or Excellency, of Israel (v. 5) is an appellation for Jehovah (vii. 10, Amos viii. 7). The Divine testimony saves, or destroys, as it is accepted or rejected.

Profuse profession of repentance is only pride in the absence of contrition of heart, and meets with no response from God (v. 6).

The spirit of idolatry moves and energizes idolaters as the Spirit of God moves and energizes believers (v. 4).

As the illegitimate children of a treacherous wife are " strange " to her husband, so are apostates " strange " to God (v. 7).

" A month " (v. 7), i.e., a short time. Shallum reigned a month (2 Kings xv. 13). " Portions," i.e., idols (Deut. xxxii. 9. Isa. lvii. 6.)

Gibeah, Ramah and Beth-aven belonged to the Northern Kingdom, and Benjamin to the Southern (v. 8). An army invading the latter would first attack Benjamin. " After thee," i.e., " behind thee," may

mean : " look behind thee " (for the enemy is coming upon thee).

The princes of Judah, like those of Israel, removed " the bound," i.e., broke away from the Bible (Deut. xix. 14, and xxvii. 17), just as the professing churches do to-day (v. 10). " Them," i.e., Ephraim and Judah. Ahaz set aside the Bible and the Altar (2 Kings xvi. 10 to 18).

" The commandment " (v. 11), i.e., of Jeroboam (1 Kings xii. 28 and 2 Kings x. 29-31 and Micah vi. 16).

" Rottenness " (v. 12), or, a worm (mar). The word " Judah " (v. 13) should be supplied before " sent to king Jareb." Jareb was king of Assyria, and his name spells 666. The future Antichrist will be a king of Assyria, the number of his name will be 666, and Judah will send to him for healing.

The last sentence of verse 14 should read : " I will carry off, and none shall rescue." Such is the action of a lion.

" I will return to my place " (v. 15). During the present long period of the Dispersion, God has withdrawn Himself from Israel as a nation.

" In their affliction," i.e., the future Great Tribulation, or time of Jacob's Trouble (Matt. xxiv. 21).

The word " saying " should be supplied after the word " early " (v. 15). The Exiles in that future day of misery will be like the Prodigal Son who returned to his father because he was starving, and they will meet with a similar gracious reception.

The terms " two days " and " third day " may be a prophecy defining the period of all Israel's subjection, and affliction, and restoration ; that is, her subjection is to last two thousand years, and her millennial reign one thousand (vi. 2).

" To know the Lord " (v. 3), i.e., experimentally.

" Prepared " (v. 3), i.e., fixed and sure.

The latter and former rains fall in spring and October in Palestine, and cause the extraordinary fertility of that land, when not under judgment.

Thus faith can always take refuge in a God of judgment and of wrath. This is darkness to the natural man.

The incessant denunciation of the popular religion as idolatry suggests that then, as now, the people fiercely denied that they were idolaters. They repeated the formula " Jehovah liveth," i.e., the images represented

God and they worshipped Him and not them. But God called it whoredom. No wonder that they were enraged.

HOSEA VI. 4-11.—The priest having failed to maintain moral relationships between the people and God, He, in His grace, inspired the prophet to maintain those relationships. The original purpose of God was not a question of outward forms (v. 6, and Matt. ix. 13, xii. 7, and Micah vi. 8) but of moral relationship, or fellowship, with Himself in and through Christ. (See last note.) Sacrifices were consequently appointed, just as pictures are with children, to teach man his sinfulness and his need of an atoning Saviour. The prophet spoke to the heart and sought to bring it back to God. The prophecy of Hosea is important because it furnishes a moral picture of a people whom God had judged and upon whom that judgment was bound to fall. Here is found an affecting mixture, on God's part, of reproaches, of compassions, of appeals, and of reference to happier days, but all in vain.

God's love is sure as the morning (v. 3); man's goodness, fleeting as a morning cloud (v. 4). Similarly may be compared the early dew and the latter and former rain.

The Hebrew prophet was declared to do what he was commissioned to announce (v. 5).

The last sentence of verse 5, should read: " My judgment is as the light that goeth forth "; that is, it is sinless, and swift, and exposes the evil which hinders communion with God.

Mark xii. 28-34 interprets verse 6.

" Men " (v. 7), in Hebrew, Adam. " The Covenant," i.e., the prohibition respecting the forbidden fruit. His children, like their father, perpetually transgress, and deal treacherously.

Gilead (v. 8), i.e., Ramoth Gilead. It was a city of Refuge—now a city of workers of iniquity, and the road to it " polluted," i.e., " tracked with heel marks " of blood. Intentional murderers found a refuge there under the protection of its corrupt priests.

" By consent " (v. 9), Hebrew, " the shoulder "—as oxen push together with the shoulder, hence this translation. But it should read (as in the margin and in the R.V.) " Shechem," which means " shoulder." It also was a city of refuge, but its priests instead of saving men " murdered " them by making them idola-

ters, for they taught them to commit lewdness, i.e., to practise idol worship.

" He hath set " (v. 11), i.e., " He hath appointed an harvest of wrath at the time when I shall restore the captivity of my people." The great Tribulation (ch. v. 15) will immediately precede the return of the Messiah in power and great glory.

Verse 6 may read thus: " I desired compassion rather, than sacrifice," etc. The Levitical sacrifices and the priesthood of Aaron were established because Israel refused to be a kingdom of priests to God and to observe the simple patriarchal worship of Exod. xx. 22-26. This was God's original intention, and it explains Jer. vii. 22.

HOSEA VII.—The first seven verses of this chapter declare the inherent evil of man's heart, and the remaining verses the weakness, folly and rebellion which are its fruit.

This inward wickedness is compared to a heated oven, and the outward weakness to a cake not turned.

" When I would have healed Israel " (v. 1), i.e., at the commencement of the reign of Jeroboam ii. (2 Kings xiv 23-27).

The iniquity of Ephraim, comparable to a thief, was inward and discovered; the wickedness of Samaria, comparable to a public troop of robbers, was outward. Both practised falsehood, for they professed a repentance (v. 14) which was not sincere.

Evil conceived in the heart produces manifest fruits which are seen by both God and man (v. 2).

" The King " (v. 3) possibly Shallum.

Wicked kings and princes welcome religious teachers who assure them that there is no wrath to come or lake of fire. These lies make glad the hearers (v. 3).

" Adulterers " (v. 4) i.e., faithless to the Divine bond. See James iv. 4.

" Who ceaseth from raising " (v. 4) i.e., from raising the temperature by stirring the fire during the short period between kneading the dough and putting it into the oven immediately after fermentation. It is not necessary for the baker to give himself this trouble, the leaven will do its work. " The day " (v. 5): perhaps the king's birthday or his coronation day.

" Made him sick," i.e., inflamed him with bottles of wine, not merely glasses of wine. " He stretched out his hand with scorners"' i.e., he held out the wine cup to clink it against those of his boon companions, as is still the custom in drinking circles.

Their heart is compared to an oven, but with this difference : that no baker was needed to sit up all night to keep up its temperature, for it was so inflamed with wickedness that it burned in the morning as a flaming fire. Thus the sixth verse stands in relation to the fourth.

An ordinary oven bakes bread, but this oven burnt up what was put into it (v. 7). So fierce was the fire of sin in the nation that it devoured its magistrates and murdered its kings. All were slaughtered (see 2 Kings). Not one of them called upon God.

"People" (v. 8), i.e., "Peoples." A cake of dough not turned when being baked is burned on one side and not cooked on the other, and therefore useless.

"The excellency of Israel" (v. 10), i.e., the Bible (Rom. iii. 2), "testifieth to his face," i.e., warned Ephraim.

The second "and" in verse 10 would better read "but." "For all this," i.e., in spite of all this testimony.

"When" (v. 12), i.e., in whichever direction they shall go, either to Egypt or Assyria, in neither case shall they escape judgment. The word "congregation" is found many times in Exodus, Leviticus, Numbers and elsewhere. But here "their congregation" is contrasted with "the congregation of Jehovah," just as "the Passover of the Jews" (John v. 1) is contrasted with "the Passover of Jehovah" (Exod. xii.). Thus was the congregation of Jehovah degraded.

The Christian is called to separation from the world. When he disobeys this call and mixes himself among the "peoples" and "strangers" (vs. 8 and 9), i.e., strangers to grace and to God, he becomes worthless (v. 8), weak (v. 9), wilful (v. 10), and wandering (v. 11). At first he is unconscious of his loss of power and spiritual decay (v. 9), but when, like Samson, he becomes sensible of his weakness he wanders off (v. 11) to "Egypt," or to "Assyria," i.e., to man-made religions—anywhere except to God in order to find recovery and enduement (v. 10).

Spiritual declension is further marked by, first, turning away from the Lord; then, transgressing against Him; then, speaking lies respecting Him; and, lastly, rebellion against Him (v. 14). So to-day enemies of

the Gospel are frequently met who once professed to tenderly love the Lord Jesus Christ. By a natural operation of Divine law both woe and destruction must fall upon such persons (v. 13).

To sin against law is impious, but to sin against the love that says, "I have redeemed them" makes sin exceeding sinful.

They cried with the voice but not with the heart (v. 14). It was not the soft sobbing of repentance but the howling with pain of a hurt beast.

"They assemble themselves for corn and wine" (v. 14), i.e., they met in their idol temples to ask these false gods for an abundant harvest, and this at the very time that they affected loyalty to Jehovah.

"He taught and strengthened their arms" (v. 15), i.e., He helped Jeroboam II to win all his victories ; yet his response, and that of his subjects, was to imagine mischief against that gracious God, that is, they planned and kept on practising idolatry (2 Kings xiv. 24).

"A deceitful bow" (v. 16) is a bow that warps so that to shoot straight is impossible.

"For" (v. 16), i.e., "because of;" "rage" i.e., "boasting." Because of this proud language the Egyptians would deride them.

The world regards with contempt, and ridicules, professing Christians who seek its support and fellowship.

This message was evidently specially addressed to the king, the nobles, and the magistrates.

HOSEA VIII.—Menahem was king in Samaria at this time ; he purchased the support of the Assyrian at a ruinous price for the State (2 Kings xv. 19).

Uzziah was king in Jerusalem. He built fortified cities (2 Chron. xxvi. 9).

The one king trusted the Assyrians ; the other, a defenced city. Neither sought help from God. Thus there is no difference as to the "flesh" between an idolater and a nominal Christian (v. 14).

The first verse should read : "The trumpet to thy mouth !" The abruptness of the language proclaims the imminence of the Assyrian irruption (Isa. lviii. 1).

"He" (v. 1), i.e., the Assyrian monarch. "As an eagle," i.e., swift and cruel. "Against the house of the Lord," i.e., Israel, not the Temple at Jerusalem.

The cause of this irruption is stated to be their disobedience to the Bible (v. 1).

The profession (v. 2) of the knowledge of God, and of attachment to Him, was false (Matt. vii. 22, John. viii. 54, 55).

Verse 3, may read: "Israel has cast off Him that is good."

"Not by me" (v. 4), i.e., Not with my sanction. "I knew them not," i.e., "I did not recognize them."

Verse 5 should read: "He shall cast off thy calf, O Samaria." Thus the rejection of the Messiah (v. 3) received a just judgment in the rejection of the calf (v. 5).

"For from Israel was it also" (v. 6), i.e., the people invented the calf. It was broken in pieces by the Assyrians, and thus its impotency to save demonstrated.

"It' (v. 7), i.e., the corn crop.

The Assyrian "swallowed up" the Ten Tribes (v. 8), and ever since they have been thrown aside as a despised vessel. They were intended to be the masters and teachers of the Gentiles, but their own sin brought them into centuries-long degradation.

A Christian is sent into the world to bless it, but directly he ceases to live in fellowship with God he becomes useless and despised.

Lovers hire a false woman, but Israel reversed what is usual (v. 9).

The word "lovers" should be supplied after "have hired" (v. 10).

"Now" (v. 10), i.e., speedily. "Them," i.e., the nations. "They," i.e., the Ten Tribes. The further translation may read: "shall writhe in a little time under the burden of the king of princes," i.e., under the tribute imposed by the Assyrian monarch (2 Kings xv. 19, 20). Recent excavations at Nineveh show Menahem's name in the inscriptions as a vassal.

Sin brings its own punishments (v. 11).

"A strange thing" (v. 12), i.e., a matter with which they had no concern. So is the Bible treated to-day; it is accounted as outside of, and unconnected with, personal family, and political life.

"I wrote My Law." The writer was God, the pen, Moses. Moses did not originate the Law. This verse, together with Luke xxiv. 27, and many other Scriptures, declare that no inspired books were in existence prior to Moses.

If they did make a pretence of sacrificing to Jehovah, their real object was that they might furnish a feast for themselves.

"Visit" (v. 13), i.e., punish.

"They shall return to Egypt" (v. 13). "He shall not return to Egypt" (xi. 5). Deuteronomy xxviii. 36 and 68 (see notes) may explain this · seeming contradiction, that is: their captivity in Assyria would be, in its nature, Egyptian bondage (see note on Isa. lii. 4.) Or it may predict that the Ten Tribes would be carried to Assyria, and the returned Exiles to Egypt; and so it came to pass. See note on xi. 5, and Isa. lii. 4.

"The palaces thereof" (v. 14), i.e., "her fortresses"; that is, the forts that fenced the cities.

HOSEA IX.—Loss of fellowship with God (vs. 3 and 15), and of fruitfulness for God (vs. 11 and 12), result from the association of idols with God (vs. 1 and 10). When the world, which is idolatry, is permitted to share the heart with Christ, fellowship and fruit cease (John xv. 1-11).

The joy of verse 1 was no doubt occasioned by the treaty then made with the Assyrians, (see note on viii. 1), but it resulted in destruction and not prosperity (vs. 2, 5 and 6), (see note at end of chapter).

The bountiful harvest expected from their idols failed of realisation (vs. 1 and 2).

Banishment from God's land (v. 3) and from God's protecting care (v. 12) was the necessary result of the action of moral law.

Ephraim shall return to "Egypt" (v. 3) as a captive and exile. See notes on xi. 5, and the resolution of a seeming contradiction (Isa. lii. 4). See also note on viii. 13.

Worship in imitation of the Levitical model was observed, but was disowned by God and declared by him to be polluted (v. 4). Death, recalling the fact and entrance of sin, made ceremonially unclean all in contact with it, hence mourning meals were unclean (Deut. xxvi. 14). "Their bread for their soul," i.e., their daily bread was as unclean as their mourning bread.

The answer to the question in verse 5 is found in verse 6. It means that religious festivals would be impossible because the land would be denuded of its inhabitants. Egypt would gather them up for interment, and Memphis would bury them, and the pleasant places of their former homes and churches would be covered with nettles and thorns.

"The days of visitation" (v. 7), i.e., of the wrath of God (Luke xix. 44, and xxi. 22).

In that dread day Israel shall know by experience that her teachers who professed to be prophets and inspired were fools and liars. The fashionable preachers of to-day who deny the fact of the coming wrath of God, and who promise peace and happiness to every body, will be equally found liars in the coming day of the Lord.

" Hatred " (v. 7), i.e., " provocation." The sentence may read : " For great is thine iniquity and great is thy provocation." They provoked God with their idols, and this was the cause of their destruction and captivity. Idolatry inflames the heart with hatred against God's word (v. 7) and God s people (verse 8).

In verses 8, 10, 13, x. 1, and xi. 1 and xiii, 1, are found six contrasts setting out what Ephraim had been but had now become.

In the days of Joshua she was a true watchman in fellowship with Hosea's God, but she was now become a false prophet— a provocation in the house of her false god— and hence a moral snare, with the result that she sank to the horrid depths of Gibean vileness as recorded in Judges xix.

This reference to the Book of Judges shows that it was at this time a book well-known to all the people.

Grapes in the wilderness and first ripe figs (v. 10) are most refreshing and delicious to the traveller. Such was Israel to God at the first ; but they went away from Him to Baal-peor (Num. xxv. Deut. iv.) and consecrated themselves unto that shameful worship, prostitution being its highest religious action. Its moral result was that the worshippers became as abominable as the object of their worship (R.V.).

Ephraim means " fruitfulness," but a righteous judgment, because of this abominable form of worship, decreed the loss of this fruitfulness, and justly doomed to death, from the very beginnings of life, their children. There is no want of harmony between verses 11 and 12 ; they are complementary.

" Tyre " (v. 13) was beautifully situated, as was Ephraim at the beginning ; but now her fruitful birth-rate only provided victims for the murderer.

The prayer of verse 14 is a prayer of compassion. Of two evils the prophet choses the lesser. Better to be childless than to provide children for the murderer. Compare Luke xxiii. 29 and 1 Cor. vii. 26, (R.V.).

" In Gilgal " (v. 15) they dethroned Immanuel (1 Sam. viii. 7 and xi. 14, 15) and, later, they enthroned the golden calf under Jeroboam. Hence the expression " all their wickedness," i.e., their chief guilt was found there.

An outraged husband effected divorce by putting his guilty wife outside the house. God, being love, He must of necessity hate evil and judge it.

Instructed by the R.V. margin of verse 1, the joy was possibly deepened by a religious union of the Hebrew church with the idol churches of the neighboring nations. Equally great will be, no doubt, the exultation in Eastern and Western Society when a " Christian Union " will be established under the headship of the Pope.

HOSEA X.—" Empty " (v. 1), i.e., " that empties out," i.e., " productive " or " luxuriant " (R.V.). Such was Israel ; but she brought forth fruit to herself and not to God, and she used her wealth to enrich the magnificence of her idolatry.

"Their heart is divided (v. 2); now shall they be found guilty " (R.V.). Compare 1 Kings xviii. 21, 2 Kings xvii. 32, Matt. vi. 24, and James iv. 8.

" Now " (v. 3), i.e., " speedily." The natural heart is opposed to God. It sets up in self-will a king, declaring him to be a necessity, and when God removes him in wrath, they at once say : " We can do very well without him ; what use is he ! "

" They have spoken words," etc., (v. 4). 2 Kings xvii. 3 and 4 furnish the particulars. They swore allegiance to the Assyrian monarch and at the same time made a treaty with the king of Egypt. Therefore Divine wrath (v. 4) would cover the whole land as the commonest weed springing up in every furrow.

" The calves of Beth-aven " (v. 5), plural of majesty for the golden calf of Bethel. The capture of that town by the Assyrians, and the deportation of its great idol, terrified the citizens of Samaria. " The people thereof," that is, its worshippers and its priests, boasted of it and of its glory, but they should mourn because of its degradation. The word " priest " here means priests of Baal, "or black ones," because of the black robes worn by them. This no doubt was the origin of the cassock.

" King Jareb " (v. 6), i.e., Shalmaneser

" His own counsel," i.e., the calf, the setting up of which they thought to be a very clever stroke of policy (I Kings xii. 26, 28).

" Foam upon the water " looks substantial (v. 7), but the wind cuts it off in a moment

" Aven " (v. 8), i.e., Bethel. Aven means " emptiness " or " vanity." What was the house of God—Bethel—became the house of vanity, the sin of Israel. Such is corrupt Christendom to-day.

" The thorn and the thistle " (v. 8). This combination occurs only here and in Genesis iii. 18.

The mountains and hills crowned with their idols, unto which they lifted up their eyes for safety, should be appealed to, to hide them from the wrath of God. In that dread day men will prefer death to life (Luke xxiii. 30, Rev. vi. 16, and ix. 6).

The argument of verse 8 is, that when judging evil at Gibeah (Judges xix.) God enabled them to stand firm, and so the battle did not overtake them, that is, they were not defeated but on the contrary victorious, but that now the evil, which was even then in their hearts, had overcome them, and brought them defeat and slavery.

" It is my desire " (v. 10), i.e., " I am resolved to chastise them, therefore shall the nations be gathered together against them and they shall be bound in their two furrows." That is : both Judah and Israel would be carried into captivity and made to toil like oxen each in his own furrow.

A heifer likes the light work of threshing, and, because permitted to eat the corn, grows fat (v. 11). Such was the political position of Ephraim under Jeroboam the Second. The next sentence may read : " But I will place a yoke upon her fair neck, I will set a rider upon Ephraim, etc.," that is : both Judah and Ephraim would be carried into captivity and enslaved.

But grace sends a message of mercy (v. 12) which, had it been accepted, would have saved them ; but they sowed wickedness (v. 13) and, therefore, reaped iniquity and lies. Their inward trust was their " way," i.e., their false religion, and their outward confidence was their standing army. But these saviours would fail them, and Samaria would perish at the hand of Shalmaneser as certainly as Beth-Arbel did (2 Kings xvii) ; and the cruelties to be suffered by them were not to be chargeable to God but to idolatry (v. 15).

" Till " (v. 12), true repentance seeks till it finds, just as the True Shepherd seeks till He finds.

" Your great wickedness " (v. 15), Hebrew—" the evil of your evil," i.e., the Golden Calf.

" In a morning " (v. 15), i.e., in a moment.
" The king of Israel," i.e., Hoshea (2 Kings xvii.).

HOSEA XI. 1-11.—God's love and Ephraim's response are thus contrasted in verses 1-5 :

Love (v. 1).
   Ingratitude (v. 2).
Love (v. 3)
   Insensibility (v. 3)
Love (v. 4)
   Insubjection (v. 5)

Verse 1 is quoted in Matt. ii. 15. The argument is, that while yet in Egypt God owned Israel as His son, and, as such, brought him out of Egypt. To preserve his life, He sent him down into Egypt (Gen. xlvi. 3), and to establish him in Canaan He brought him up out of Egypt. Satan obstructed these plans and seemed to have won a victory. But God retired into the true Israel—His dearly beloved Son. It was therefore necessary that He, as the true Israel, should seek safety in Egypt, be God's Son there, and, as such, enter the Promised Land. In all this there was no defeat.

" They " (v. 2), i.e., the prophets ; " they," i.e., sons of Israel ; " them," i.e., the prophets. " They sacrificed," i.e., they kept sacrificing, as the prophets kept calling.

To ease the straps fastening the yoke upon an ox's neck, and to give him food, are humane actions.

2 Kings xvii. 4 reconciles Hosea viii. 13 and xi. 5. This latter statement means that Ephraim's expectation of help from the king of Egypt would be disappointed because they refused to return to God their true king. Had they turned to Him for deliverance instead of to the king of Egypt they would not have been carried into captivity to the Assyrian. That monarch brought the Ten Tribes into an Egyptian bondage ; and the Romans carried the two Tribes as slaves into Egypt itself. See note on Isa. lii. 4, and on ch. viii. 13.

" His branches " (v. 6), i.e., his villages.

" Their own counsels " (v. 6), i.e., their clever plan of playing off the king of Assyria against the king of Egypt.

" They " (v. 7), i.e., the prophets.

The agony of the love which pulsates in verse 8 touches the heart. Admah and Zeboim were the companion cities of Sodom and Gomorrah.

" Repentings " (v. 8), i.e., " compassions " (R.V.).

A covenanted salvation based upon grace can never be affected either by man's merit or demerit (v. 9).

" I will not enter into the city " (v. 9), i.e., I will not come against the city to destroy it, as I came against Admah.

Verses 10 and 11 predict the final restoration of the Ten Tribes. Jehovah will arise as a lion on their behalf. He shall summon them with a lion's roar, and the " sons " of Jacob, agitated with joy, shall come from the west and from Egypt and from Assyria, that is, from Europe, Asia, Africa and America, and they shall be securely placed in their own houses in the pleasant land of Palestine.

HOSEA XI. 12-XII. 14.—This prophecy contrasts Jacob and Ephraim—the latter, self-reliant and trusting the kings of Assyria and Egypt; the former, weak and dependent and trusting Jehovah the God of his father Isaac. So the lesson is here once more taught that God cannot give victories to the flesh, and that Jehovah's servant is strong when he is weak (2 Cor. xii. 10).

Ephraim is named four times in the prophecy (vs. xii. 1, 7, 8 and 14), and Jacob is mentioned four times (vs. 3, 4, 4, and 12). These eight passages compose the contrast.

" Faithful with the saints " (v. 12) i.e., faithful to the Holy One the Messiah (R.V.) ; for Judah nationally, in spite of her sins, was faithful to the house of David, to whose Divine Son was promised the throne.

" Wind " and " East wind " (v. 1), i.e., the treaties with the Assyrians and with the Egyptians. To these kings Ephraim daily increased lies, and the result was desolation. A Christian's dependence upon the world is really based upon falsehood, and results in spiritual desolation.

" In the womb " (v. 3), i.e., at his birth " ; " by his strength," i.e., " in his manhood " ; " he found him in Bethel," i.e., the Angel of Jehovah converted him 'when a penniless wanderer. That Angel was Jehovah the God of Hosts, and His Memorial Name shall be Jehovah, that is, Jesus the Saviour, for His Name of Renown is that He saves sinners.

The argument of verse 6 is : Imitate Jacob, turn to Jehovah, live uprightly, and keep trusting Him. Saul lost the kingdom because he would not wait for God, though willing to wait on Him.

Verse 7 should read as in the Revised Version. The Hebrew word for " merchant " and " Canaanite " is the same. With holy contempt the Spirit of God here calls Ephraim a Canaanite. Self-reliant and clever he defrauded ("oppress "), and boastfully declared that " they," i.e., the prophets, should find nothing wrong in his business activities, for his commercial prosperity demonstrated his honest dealing.

But he forgot the love that brought him out of the land of Egypt and that pledged itself to make him yet to dwell in joyful tabernacles in Canaan (v. 9).

Ahijah, Jonah, Shemaiah, Iddo, Azariah, Hanani, Jehu, Elijah, Elisha, Micaiah, Joel and Amos were some of the prophets of verse 10.

Gilead and Gilgal were become wholly idolatrous, and the idol altars were as numerous as the heaps of stones in the furrows of the fields. In a stony agricultural country such heaps are numberless.

The lowest form of servitude in the East is that of a shepherd (v. 12). This is the fourth reference to Jacob and completes the argument that weakness wins victories. His feeble hand as an infant won the birthright, as a penniless vagabond he won the kingdom, as a slave he won Rachel, and as a cripple he won a title.

The Divine Jacob, i.e. Immanuel, is the Great Anti-type ; for, by weakness, He won the birthright and the throne and the kingdom and the bride.

" A prophet " (v. 13), i.e., Moses—not a soldier, but a prophet. Nations are saved by prophets such as Whitfield, Wesley and Moody and not by military generals.

Ephraim refused to listen to the prophets and provoked Immanuel most bitterly. It is only love that can be thus provoked

" Blood " (v. 14), i.e., blood-guiltiness.

" Reproach" (v. 14), i.e., the astonishment, the proverb and the byword of Deut. xxviii. 37.

HOSEA XIII.—The subjoined structure exhibits the correspondence of verses 1 to 8, and sets out their teaching :—

Glory (v. 1).
    Sin (v. 2).
        Judgment (v. 3).
Glory (vs. 4 and 5).
    Sin (v. 6).
        Judgment (vs. 7 and 8).

Verse 1 should read as in the Revised Version. When Ephraim walked with God, as in the days of Joshua, he spake with authority and people trembled, and so he had a position of dignity and power. But he turned to idolatry and died spiritually, as Adam did when he sinned. Compare Rom. vii. 9. The Christian has moral power and dignity so long as his heart is wholly governed by Christ and free from idolatry.

"Their own understanding" (v. 2): a self-will worship (Col. ii. 23) is the principle of idolatry ; and its ritual, as at the present day, necessitates the labour of many craftsmen.

The worshippers were commanded to kiss the golden calves as an expression of adoration (v. 2). Kissing images, statues, and so-called sacred pictures and ikons, is a prominent feature of modern idolatrous worship.

The four figures of the morning cloud, the early dew, the chaff and the smoke, express brevity and worthlessness. These figures correspond to those of verses 7 and 8.

Israel's greatest glory was that Jehovah was her God and Shepherd (vs. 4 and 5). No god was associated with Him, nor any saviour nor shepherd, in the redemption out of Egypt and the preservation through the desert. "I knew thee" (v. 5), i.e., I knew thee as a shepherd knows his sheep (John x. 27).

The argument and the injunction of verses 4 and 5 are that God manifested to Israel His unity in Egypt and in the wilderness, and that, therefore, no god should be associated with Him.

"According to their pasture" (v. 6), i.e., in proportion as God prospered them so did they forget Him. In verse 2 they associated an idol with Him; in this corresponding verse 6 they forgot Him. Such is ever the moral action of the natural heart, it associates idols with God, and

then forgets Him; it degrades Him and then suppresses Him.

The four wild-beasts of verses 7 and 8 predict the military monarchies of Babylon (the lion), Persia (the bear), Greece (the leopard), and Rome (the wild-beast). The leopard is designedly displaced. Why ? Here, as in Dan. vii, the fourth monarchy, in its oppression of the people of God, is not likened to any known wild-beast but to an imaginary one of appalling ferocity and cruelty.

Verse 9 should read as in the Revised Version. The argument is, that in turning away from her true helper, Israel brought all her calamities upon herself. Some of them are detailed in verses 15 and 16.

Verse 10 should read as in the Revised Version. In answer to the question "Where is thy king ? " the reply to be supplied is " In prison " , for it was there that Shalmaneser put Hoshea.

The king given in anger (v. 11) was Jeroboam I, and the king taken away in wrath was Hoshea. Jeroboam was Ephraim's first king, and Hoshea was her last king.

Ephraim's iniquity was "bound up" by God and their sin "reserved" (hid) by Him (Deut. xxxii. 34, Job xiv. 17, xxi. 19, and Rom ii. 5). To blot out the handwriting against the sinner (Col. ii. 14) is the opposite action to binding up and reserving sin.

Helplessness and foolishness characterise the sinner in relation to the wrath to come A woman cannot escape the anguish of child-birth—she is helpless ; and a son who lingers where population increases is foolish, for he does not look ahead and recognise the certain prospect of poverty. A prudent man foreseeth the evil, but the senseless sinner lives for the moment and takes no steps to escape approaching calamity.

Verse 14 cleaves the sense of the whole passage, as Isa. xliii. 25, similarly interrupts its context. This is very beautiful. Mercy rejoices against judgment, and so Grace bursts out with the cry : " Guilty, sinful and foolish though they be, yet will I ransom them." This glorious verse is quoted in 1 Cor. xv. 55. It should read here as in the Revised Version. "Plagues" imply " victory," and " destruction " a " sting." The O.T. terms are Hebrew ; the other terms, Greek—both express the same thing.

Ephraim means " fruitfulness " (v. 15).
The " east wind " and " the wind of

Jehovah " (v. 15), i.e., the Assyrians. " He,"
i.e., Shalmaneser.

" Her God." Love pulsates in this term.
To sin against righteousness is a great evil,
but to sin against love is the evil of evils.

Israel could not charge God with the appalling cruelties of verse 16, for her misconduct
caused them (v. 9).

Just as a bird in its desire for the fruit
flies into the net set in its sight (Prov. i. 17),
so the sinner rushes into sin, notwithstanding
God's earnest warnings, and ruins himself
and his wife and children. Compare notes
on Num. xiv., Josh. vii., Dan. vi., etc. Thus
Israel suffered the doom of verse 16, though
divine love tried to save them from it by
fore-telling it.

HOSEA XIV.—The new birth which will
follow Israel's restoration to Palestine is
here predicted.

Her fall was caused by her own iniquity
(v. 1); but that did not set aside God's
faithfulness, and so grace declared Him to be
" Jehovah thy God."

Divine love provides the fitting words for
the truly repentant tongue (vs. 2 and 3).

" Take with you words,"—not sacraments
nor ceremonies—but " words." These are, a
hearty confession of sin (v. 1); a cry for
forgiveness upon the principle of grace and
not of merit (v. 2); a promise of praise (v.
2); an engagement to forsake the sins of the
past; and a testimony to the nature of
Divine Mercy (v. 3).

" Receive us graciously " (v. 2), i.e., " in
grace," as opposed to personal merit.

" The calves of our lips " (v. 2), i.e., praise
(Heb. xiii. 15).

Israel's sin (v. 3) was, trusting man (Assyria
and Egypt), and idols for salvation.

" We will not ride upon horses," i.e., " we
will not trust Egyptian cavalry " (Deut.
xvii. 16).

Israel was " fatherless " (v. 3), for she
was Lo-Ruhamah and Lo-Ammi (chs. i.
to iii.).

The Divine response of verses 4-8 exhibits
the moral result of true conversion.

" Backsliding " (v. 4), i.e., apostasy to
idolatry. Forgiveness based upon grace, and
not upon merit, can pardon the most desperate sins; hence " I will love them freely,
i.e., without a just cause. Compare notes
on John xv. 25 and Rom. iii. 24.

Redeemed Israel will be comparable to
the lily for beauty, the oak of Lebanon for
strength, and the olive for fruitfulness; and
her fragrance shall be as Lebanon itself
(vs. 5 and 6); but all this beauty, perfume,
strength and fruitfulness will be produced by
the dew of Divine grace.

The Gentile nations that dwelt, and that
were intended by God to dwell under Israel's
beneficent shadow, shall return thither; and,
as a result, they shall revive as the corn and
grow as the lily (Rom. xi. 12). Israel's
" scent," i.e., " memory," or " remembrance," shall be pleasant as the wine of
Lebanon. It was esteemed to be the best
wine.

Verse 8 may be thus displayed:

Ephraim: " What have I to do any more
with idols ! "

Immanuel: " I have heard and observed
him."

Ephraim: " I am like a green fir tree."

Immanuel: " Yes, but remember that
from Me is thy fruit found."

Verse 9 forms the epilogue to the whole
prophecy. God's way of salvation is
a stepping stone to the believer, but a
stumbling stone to the unbeliever. Christ
is a rock of defence to the one but a rock of
offence to the other.

JOEL

JOEL.—Joel preached to guilty Judah (ii. 1 and 15, iii. 1 and 6 and 20) ; Hosea, to guilty Israel. The latter preceded the former by about eighty years. Hosea's contemporaries were Jonah, Amos, Isaiah, Micah and Nahum. That is, six prophets. Their ministry preceded the Captivity of the Ten Tribes. Joel's contemporaries were Jeremiah, Habakkuk, Zephaniah, Daniel, Ezekiel, and, probably, Obadiah. That is, seven prophets. Their ministry accompanied the overthrow of the throne of David and the captivity of the Two Tribes.

The prophecy of Joel is undated for it is general. It covers the period of " The times of The Gentiles," that is, from Nebuchadnezzar to Antichrist. Hence the prophecy speaks of the Temple and its Levitical worship, but makes no mention of a king.

JOEL I.—This prophecy was not originated by Joel ; God composed it and gave it to him (v. 1), as to all the Prophets (Luke i., 70).

" Joel " means " Jehovah is God." He is stated to have been the son of Pethuel, no doubt in order to distinguish him from other men of the same name.

Most probably at the time the prophecy was given by God to Joel, the whole country was utterly devastated and ruined by a plague of locusts, and this fact was used to illustrate the Divine judgments that were about to be inflicted upon the land, and to have their climax in the dread " day of the Lord " at the close of Judah's history. This period of judgment (ch. 1), was to introduce that Great Day (ch. 11.). These judgments would be so exceptional as to be without previous experience (vs. 2 and 3).

Here is an instance, not unusual in prophetic teaching, of the Spirit of God using an event such as this plague of locusts to awaken the conscience of the people at the moment, and, at the same time, to make use of it to picture a future event of much greater moment.

The development of the locust exhibits four stages. These four stages are expressed in four Hebrew words here translated " palmer-worm," " locust," " canker-worm " and " caterpillar." The last stage is the most destructive of them all. Possibly they pre-figured the four military monarchies of Babylon, Persia, Greece and Rome which successively devastated Judah as locusts destroy a land (v. 4).

So absolute would be the destruction of food that all classes would be plunged into a common misery (vs. 5-20).

In the East a maiden's betrothed is called her husband (v. 8).

" At hand " (v. 15), i.e., " now present." Compare 2 Thess. ii. 2. The " day of the Lord " is the future day of God's wrath which will be poured out upon the nations.

" The Almighty " (v. 15), also means " The All-Bountiful." The Hebrew root is " shad," a woman's breast. This may have originated the many-breasted goddess of the Indian Pantheon. The use of this Divine Title in this passage augments its terror. Compare the term " The wrath of the Lamb " (Rev. vi. 16), and see notes on 2 Cor., vi. 18, and Phil. iv. 19.

A country devastated by locusts appears as if swept by fire (vs. 19 and 20).

Faith hides herself in the very God Who executes the judgment (v. 19).

JOEL II.—Verses 1 and 15 are explained by Num. x. 5.

The terms " Zion," " My holy mountain," and " the land," define Palestine and Jerusalem as the scene of these future events.

The expression " the day of the Lord " (v. 1), means the period in the future when the Messiah will interfere on behalf of His ancient people and deliver and restore them. That day, like the First Advent, will probably last about forty years. Its details are predicted in the Book of the Revelation. The Divine intervention in Egypt, and the deliverance of Israel therefrom by Moses is an illustration of the whole history of the future day of the Lord.

The Divine instrument in that future day to chasten Israel will be a people great and strong from the North having Antichrist as its leader (vs. 2 and 20).

That army will cause a destruction, and be as irresistible, as an army of locusts (vs. 3-11).

Faith recognises the presence of God in every judgment and cleaves to Him (v. 11). It is good to have to do with God and to recognise Him as a consuming fire. Thus David trusted Him in the judgment that smote the nation upon his numbering of the people.

Divine chastisement produces spiritual and temporal blessing (vs. 12-14) if there be a sincere repentance (v. 13). " A blessing " (v. 14), i.e., an abundant harvest.

As judgment affects all classes (ch. i. vs. 8-14), so a cry for deliverance affects them equally (vs. 15-17). The presence of children and infants (v. 16) expresses helplessness.

" Between the porch and the altar " (v. 17). Compare Ezek. viii. 16. The altar proclaims accomplished redemption ; the porch, fellowship with God. This latter can only be enjoyed as the result of the former.

" The heathen " (v. 17). This term demonstrates that the locusts symbolized men.

" The east sea " (v. 20), i.e., the Dead Sea " ; the " utmost sea," i.e., the Mediterranean.

" He hath done great things " (v. 20), i.e., he magnified himself to do great things ; for he (Antichrist) will propose to attack and defeat Immanuel Himself (Rev. xix. 19).

But Immanuel will do great things (v. 21), for He will free His land from the oppressor, make it exceedingly fruitful (vs. 22-25), and He will redeem His people (vs. 26 and 27) so effectually that they shall never be put to shame. The repetition of this promise is not tautology, as has been ignorantly supposed, but a condescension to the timidity of the heart so as to assure it.

" Afterward " (v. 28), that is, after the occurrences predicted in verses 30-32. This promise of the Spirit is put out of chronological order in order to couple it with the material blessings of verses 23-26, and to provide for Acts ii. All ranks will participate in the visitation. Pentecost was an earnest of it. The apostle Peter did not say, " Now is fulfilled that which was spoken by the Prophet Joel," but he said, " This is that which was spoken by the Prophet." Its nature and characteristics were similar.

Prior to this visible exhibition in men's bodies of the nature and powers of the Holy Spirit (" all flesh "), the judgments and the deliverance of verses 30-32 will have been experienced. In that day deliverance will be enjoyed in Mount Zion and in Jerusalem by those who call upon the Name of the Lord ; but all will not call, only the remnant whom the Lord shall call. The apostles, indicating the proximity of that day of wrath, called upon all both far and near (Acts ii. 38-40) to repent, but only those that really believed were made members of the Remnant and delivered (Acts ii. 47 and xiii. 48).

" The Name of the Lord " (v. 32), i.e., "Jesus," as proved by Acts ix. 20, 21. Rom. x. 13, and 1 Cor. i. 2. The phrase " to call upon " is only applicable to Deity.

" All flesh," i.e., Jews and Gentiles, Acts ii. 39.

The Pentecost of Acts ii. is past ; " the Day of the Lord " of 2 Thess. i. is future. The chronological displacement of verses 28 and 29 in relation to verses 30-32, harmonises with this seeming disturbance of the text.

Thus the Holy Spirit in this passage not only binds together material and spiritual wealth but foresees Pentecost.

The trumpet announcing the wrath of God (v. 1) is the same trumpet that announces the grace of God (v. 15). The Gospel tells of the lake of fire and of the redeeming blood. A gospel that omits either of these is a false gospel.

JOEL III.—This chapter should follow the preceding one without a break. In it the Spirit describes the future deliverance of Israel ; the judgment of the nations that oppressed her ; the ascension of Immanuel upon the throne of Jehovah at Jerusalem ; His vindication of His ancient people ; the destruction of the army of Antichrist ; the moral glory of Jerusalem ; its appointment as a centre of blessing to the earth ; and the future amazing fertility of the land of Palestine. Effectual and sovereign grace will be the eternal foundation upon which this recovery and glory will rest. For He chose Jerusalem from the beginning as His Throne and Israel as His heritage, and He will demonstrate these facts in the day of His power.

" Bring again the captivity" (v. 1): Hebrew idiom for restore the fortunes of.

" All nations " (v. 2), i.e., representatives of all nations.

" Valley of Jehoshaphat " (v. 2), i.e., " the valley of the judgment of Jehovah." Possibly that judgment will take place in the actual valley of Jehoshaphat.

" Plead " (v. 2), i.e., " give judgment in favour of." Notice the terms " My people," " My heritage," " My land." Hebrew boys and girls were sold to purchase lust and drunkenness, but their terrible fate was not lightly regarded by God, and He will avenge them four-fold (v. 4).

" Coasts of Palestine " (v. 4), i.e., Philistia. " What have ye to do with me," i.e., " will you dare to oppose me ? "

The mention of Tyre, Sidon, Philistia and Greece (vs. 4 and 6) supports the view that this prophecy covers the whole period of the Times of the Gentiles. The prediction concerning Egypt and Edom (v. 19) is·a further argument, for all these prophecies have been fulfilled.

" Sabeans " (v. 8), i.e., " Sheba." God uses His people as the instruments of His just wrath in the day of His wrath just as He uses His angels.

Verses 9-11 picture the assembling of the mighty army which the Antichrist is to lead against Jerusalem. Here the army is envisaged by the prophecy ; other prophecies direct attention to its commander. Thus the Holy Spirit parted prophetic facts among prophetic preachers.

" Thy mighty ones " (v. 11), i.e., the angels (Ps. ciii. 20, Isa. xiii. 3, 2 Thess. i. 7, Rev. x. 1).

" Get you down " (v. 13), i.e., " step into the winepress in order to tread it." Compare Rev. xiv. 14-20.

" Decision " (v. 14), i.e., Jehovah's decision —His concision, or judgment of the living nations ; for He will part them asunder, as He Himself afterwards declared in Matt. xxv. 31 and 32.

" The heavens and the earth shall shake " (v. 16). Earthly monarchs have no such power. But those who make Him their refuge and stronghold they shall not shake.

" Pass through " (v. 17), i.e., " pass through to destroy." Compare Ex. xii. 23.

" Roar " (v. 16), i.e., roar as a lion, or thunder.

" Drop down " (v. 18), i.e., " distil." " The valley of Shittim," i.e., the Dead Sea valley. Compare Ezek. xlvii. 1-12.

There is no contradiction as to Egypt between verse 19 and Isa. xix. The judgment here predicted is past ; the promise there fore-told is future.

" Cleanse " (v. 21), i.e., Avenge.

AMOS

AMOS.—Amos lived about a hundred years before Joel. He was a herdman and a gatherer of sycamore fruit (i. 1) and resided at Bethel (vii. 10, and 14). His was " the mighty ordination of the pierced hand " ; for he was not what would to-day be known as a clergyman. The Divine title " Adonai-Jehovah " is a feature of this prophecy (iii. 11 and v. 3). The very numerous references to the Pentateuch destroy the theory that that volume was mainly composed by Ezra after the Exile. Amos preached during the reign of Uzziah, king of Judah, and of Jeroboam II, king of Israel, shortly before the death of the latter monarch. His ministry was a short one ; probably it did not last longer than two years.

AMOS I. AND II.—" The words of Amos " (v. 1), i.e., the words of Jehovah through Amos (v. 3).

" Which he saw " (v. 1), i.e., in a vision. Man's words cannot be " seen," only God's words. Hence the apostle John said : " I turned to see the voice " (Rev. i. 12).

" The earthquake " (v. 1). This earthquake is not recorded in Scripture. Its mention here is an instance of the Law of Subsequent Narration.

" Concerning Israel " (v. 1). This defines the subject of the prophecy as being the Ten Tribes shortly prior to their captivity.

" From Zion," " from Jerusalem " (v. 2). Here was Jehovah's throne. The kings of the nations uttered their feeble voices from their governmental centres, but Jehovah roared as a lion from out of Zion.

" The habitations of the shepherds " and " the top of Carmel " (v. 2), i.e., the northern kingdom of the Ten Tribes.

" For three transgressions, yea for four " (v. 3). This is a Hebrew idiom expressive of " many." Compare Job xxxiii. 29, marg.

" They threshed Gilead " (v. 3). See 2 Kings xiii. 7. " With," i.e., " as it were with." God's anger burns against inhumanity.

" Palaces " (v. 4), i.e., fortresses. " Ben-hadad," i.e., " Child of the Sun." This was a title corresponding to Pharaoh, Caesar, etc. This was the Ben-hadad of 2 Kings xiii., not that of 2 Kings viii. The inhumanity of Hazael was predicted in 2 Kings viii. 12.

" Aven " and " Eden " were fertile valleys near Damascus. " Kir " formed the southern border of the Caspian Sea.

" To deliver them up to Edom " (v. 6), i.e., to hand over the captive Israelites to their bitterest enemies, the Edomites, as slaves. God's anger burns against treachery and slavery.

" The brotherly covenant " (v. 9). See 2 Sam. v. 11 and 1 Kings v. 1, and ix. 11-14. God's anger also burns against the treatment of treaties as " scraps of paper."

" He kept his wrath for ever " (v. 11). i.e., he kept up his grudge, see Gen. xxv, 24, etc. God's anger burns against hatred. Num. xx. 14-21 ; 2 Chron. xxviii. 17 ; Ps. cxxxvii. 7 and Obad. 10-14.

" That they might enlarge their border " (v. 13). Compare Jer. xlix. 1.

" Because he burned," etc. (ii. 1). See 2 Kings iii. 27. Or, this may confirm the tradition that the king of Moab disinterred the bones of the king of Edom and burned them into lime. God's anger burns against unnatural and cruel crimes even though their victims be as cruel and wicked as was the king of Edom.

These six nations defiled Immanuel's land, for they lived within its original boundaries, and, therefore, judgment expelled them. But Judah and Israel, the heirs of that inheritance, also defiled it, and consequently a similar judgment struck them. It is very solemn when God's professing people are condemned with the ungodly.

The distinction between the causes of the judgment respecting Judah and Israel is significant and instructive. The one was doctrinal; the other, moral. Judah claimed to be orthodox; Israel, to be progressive. Judah's sin was despising the Bible, and accepting the lies of man's religious teaching (v. 4). Such is the feature of Protestantism to-day. There is a profession of loyalty to the Bible, but it is really despised, and the religious teaching of prominent men preferred. To call these teachings "lies," as Amos did, would be denounced to-day as rude and violent language.

Israel was addressed as having some knowledge of truth (vs. 8-12), but the main charge against the Northern Kingdom was a moral one. Their conduct was in question. To have spoken to them as professing Keepers of the Law was impossible, but their conscience could not repel an accusation as to their actions. They sold the righteous and the poor into slavery for a trifle (v. 6); they crushed the head of the poor into the very dust (v. 7); they perverted justice; a man and his son debased themselves with the same unhappy victim of the idolatrous and obscene worship of Astarte; the pledged clothes, which God commanded should be restored before sunset (Exod. xxii. 26), were used as a couch of feasting before "every altar"—God having ordained but one altar; and the money which they fined those unjustly condemned in their courts, they spent on wine to be drunk at these idol banquets (v. 8).

In contrast with this sad recital, Divine Love recalls its action toward them in delivering them out of Egypt (v. 10); in totally destroying the Amorites (v. 9); and in raising up prophets and Nazarites so as to maintain relationship between God and them when the ceremonial Law had failed (v. 11).

Judgment, therefore, was inevitable; and its action (vs. 14-16) was committed shortly afterwards to the Assyrians, who slaughtered the men of Israel in thousands and carried the residue into captivity; from which they have not yet escaped.

"Naked" (v. 16), i.e., weaponless. A soldier, when running away, throws aside his armour and weapons so as the better to escape.

AMOS III.—Having addressed the several nations dwelling in the Promised Land, God now addresses the whole family of Israel redeemed from the land of Egypt. This family alone He recognised ("known") as His, and for this reason He would punish them for their iniquities (vs. 1 and 2). This is a solemn principle. Relationship to God compromises the Name of God. It is a great privilege to be a testimony for God, but that testimony must accord with the holiness of God and must not falsify His character. If the testimony becomes corrupted its professors must be judged, for God must vindicate His moral glory. Hence if calamity and suffering ("evil" v. 6) occurred they were not accidental but from God. There was a cause (vs. 3-8).

Companionship with God (v. 3) can only be enjoyed upon the basis of separation from evil.

There can be but one answer to the five parables of verses 3-6. The argument is, that there is a cause for every action.

The parent lion roars when he has captured food, and the young lion cries out of its den in response, for it knows that the parent is bringing it something to eat. But both are silent if nothing has been caught.

The second sentence of verse 5 should read as in the Revised Version. A snare does not spring up from the ground unless something has touched it.

Two great principles—one of Law, the other of Grace—appear in verses 6-8. The first: God will judge evil. The second: He forewarns those whom He is about to judge. There is a just cause why He should judge evil, but love intervenes with her warning. Hence just as trembling is caused by the lion's roar, so prophesying, by Jehovah's voice. When He speaks the prophet cannot be silent however men may demand his silence (vii. 10-17).

In verse 9 the Philistines and the Egyptians are invited to behold the great evils and oppressions in the midst of Samaria and to recognise the justice of God in sending them. This principle appears frequently in the Scriptures that the heathen are oftentimes righteous judges of the professing people of God.

Persistence in the evil of covetousness and the love of money deadens moral consciousness (v.10), e.g. professing christians enriching themselves with the violence and robbery of the slave and liquor and opium trades.

" An adversary " (v. 11), i.e., Sennacherib the Assyrian king ; he emptied the palaces filled with the spoils robbed from the poor.

So thorough would be his action that the few people left alive would only be comparable to a piece of an ear of a sheep taken out of the mouth of a lion, to prove to the owner it was killed.

" The corner of a bed," etc., (v. 12), i.e., the luxurious rich.   See R.V.

" Altars " (v. 14) plural of magnitude for the great altar erected at Bethel by Jeroboam I for the worship of the golden calf.

AMOS IV.—Bashan was a rich pastureland east of Jordan and cattle fed there became strong and turbulent.

The nobles of Samaria are here compared to them (v. 1).

The feminine and masculine genders are here used in the Hebrew text so as to distinguish the persons and the symbols.

God's love for the poor, and His indignation against oppression, is a feature of the Book of Amos.

" Masters " (v. 1), plural of majesty for Jeroboam II.   " Bring " is singular in the Hebrew text.   The nobles appealed to him to provide them with luxurious banquets furnished by money robbed from the poor.

" He " (v. 2), i.e., the Assyrian monarch. They passed a hook through the lower lip of their captives and thus led them away to slavery.   " Posterity " should read as in the Revised Version.

Not through the gates of the city of Samaria but through its broken walls they were to be led forth, and they would go quietly and in a straight line so as to mitigate the pain of their tortured lips (v. 3).

The translation of the last sentence of verse 3 is difficult but it may be thus paraphrased :   " Ye shall be cast as slaves into the palace of Sennacherib."   Thus may the contrast be expressed between their reclining as luxurious nobles in the palaces of Samaria and their grovelling as slaves in the palaces of Nineveh.

The invitations of verses 4 and 5 are ironical.   " Go to Bethel "—but not to worship Me—to transgress against Me ! They professed to be His worshippers, but they adored Him under the similitude of the golden calf—as multitudes do to-day under the similitude of images and pictures. God denounces it as idolatry.

In these verses (4 and 5), there is an imitation of the Divine worship commanded in Leviticus, yet corrupted—for leaven was forbidden (v. 5).   But it was will-worship (" for this liketh you ").   Compare Col. ii. 23.

But God's will would be as active as theirs, yet sinlessly, and, therefore, the chastisements of famine (v. 6), drought (vs. 7 and 8), blasting (v. 9), pestilence (v. 10) and fire (v. 11) fell upon them ; but impenitence was the unchanging response to each stroke—" yet hath he not returned unto Me."

As a consequence they are now warned of a supreme judgment—that is, to meet God Himself (" I will do this unto thee," v. 12).

The majesty of the judge is set forth in verse 13.   The mountains may be seen, the wind unseen, man's thought unread, day and night unchangeable and the revolution of the earth in its orbit invariable ; but all was in the power of this Dread Judge— " Jehovah Elohim Sabaioth is His Name ! "

AMOS V. 1-17.—This lamentation the prophet took up as a heavy burden over, not " against," the House of Israel (see Revised Version and Hebrew text).   The true preacher's heart is burdened with the sinner's doom ; and he pleads with him and not against him.   Elijah erred in pleading against Israel (Rom. xi. 2), and was superseded by Elisha.

The Northern Kingdom is here compared to a virgin, because never hitherto conquered. It shall never be restored (v. 2) as a separate nationality.   This prophecy destroys the Anglo-Israel hypothesis.

So great would be the destruction of her armies in the battles with the Assyrians, that battalions a thousand strong, or companies a hundred strong, that marched away from the cities to the war would only have a hundred or ten survivors respectively (v. 3).

" He that hath the Son hath life " (1 John v. 12) ; for apart from Christ there can be only death (vs. 4 and 6).

Bethel, Gilgal and Beersheba were the great centres of the worship of God under the similitude of a calf.   But that idol could not quench the fire that broke out in the house of Joseph (v. 6).

" Gilgal shall surely go into captivity " (v. 5).   There is a play on words here in the Hebrew text.   It might be rendered in English :   The Roller, rolling, shall roll away. God can have no fellowship either with falsehood in doctrine (v. 5), or evil-doing in conduct (v. 7). This latter verse denounces bribery and injustice. Justice was cast to the ground and perverted to most bitter wrong.

The greatness of God, as contrasted with the impotency of idols, is set out in verses 8 and 9.

The showers that water the earth are produced by the action of the sun upon the sea (v. 8). This supposed discovery of science was a matter of common knowledge 3000 years ago.

" The shadow of death " (v. 8), i.e., the deep darkness. This Hebrew word occurs ten times in the Book of Job, four times in the Psalms, and occasionally in other books of the Bible. Yet men who profess to be loyal Bible scholars declare it to be a modern word.

The words " Seek Him " should be supplied in verse 8 before " that calleth," etc., and at the beginning of verse 9. This latter verse should read as in the Revised Version.

But Israel's response to the pleading of verses 4-6 was the cruel wrong of verse 7 ; and her response to the loving entreaty of verses 8 and 9, the anger and hatred of verse 10.

" They " (v. 10), i.e., the judges. They hated a truthful witness, for his honesty rebuked their wickedness.

God's anger burns against exactions (" burdens ") upon the poor (v. 11), and the luxury obtained by such oppression is short-lived (v. 11), and He knows the multitude and magnitude of such cruel deeds.

" They " (v. 12), i.e., the judges. " Turn aside," i.e., pervert justice. Consequently (v. 13) prudent men suffered wrong in silence and did not prosecute those that injured them knowing it to be useless because of the corruption of the Courts of Law.

To enjoy God's companionship which Israel proudly claimed to possess (" as ye have spoken "), there must be a definite separation from evil, attachment to good, and abolition of bribes in the Courts of Justice (vs. 14 and 15).

" It may be " (v. 15). These words do not declare uncertainty respecting God's readiness to pardon, but relate to man's unwillingness to repent and be pardoned. This latter is proved by the prediction of verses 16 and 17. For they refused to seek Him, and, as a consequence, suffered the horrors of the Assyrian invasion.

" I will pass through thee, saith the Lord " (v. 17). God " passes through " for judgment and " passes over " for salvation. See Exod. xii. 12 and 13.

AMOS V. 18 — VI. 14.—A double woe is the burden of this message. The first was pronounced upon false profession (vs. 18-27) ; the second, upon false peace (ch. vi.).

They professed their readiness to welcome the establishment of Messiah's Kingdom (v. 18), but the prophet asked : " Wherefore would ye have that day ? " (R.V.). For them it would be a day of terror and gloom ; and escape would be as impossible as that of a man who, fleeing into a field to escape a lion, is met by a bear, or running into a house for safety, is stung by a serpent.

They should not escape notwithstanding their elaborate ritual accompanied by exquisite sacred music (vs. 21, 23). God refused to acknowledge them. He called them " *Your* feast days," etc. The worshippers no doubt declared these services to be beautiful and impressive ; but earnestness and good intention cannot turn falsehood into truth.

Once again burning words of indignation (v. 24) denounce the prostitution of the Courts of Justice, and the consequent oppression of the poor and innocent ; for at that time, as now, rich ceremonial religion accompanied gross corruption, oppression and debauchery.

Verses 25-27 reveal that the evil of associating idols with God had been their rule from the beginning, and now re-appeared in the Calf of Bethel—it was the resurrection of the Golden Calf. But their sin was all the blacker because of the long years of patience and love which God had shown them.

These verses may be thus paraphrased :—Did ye offer me sacrifices and offerings forty years in the wilderness, O House of Israel ? (You certainly did, outwardly). But, at the same time, ye bore aloft the tabernacle of Moloch and the image of Chiun your star god, which ye made to yourselves Therefore, etc.

They could hide these gods behind the back of Moses when marching through the wilderness, but they could not hide them from the eye of God. Even Joshua suspected them (Josh. xxiv. 14). It is easy to make an outward profession of loyalty to Christ and to enthrone idols in the heart.

Enemies of inspiration affirm that Stephen erred in saying " Babylon " and not " Damascus " (Acts vii. 43). There are two replies to this. First, Babylon is beyond Damascus; and second, Stephen did not say : " As it is written in the Book of the Prophet " but : " in the book of the Prophets," i.e., the Scriptures; and they more than once predicted a captivity beyond Babylon. So it fell out. The Ten Tribes were carried beyond Damascus, and the Two Tribes beyond Babylon.

The second woe (vi. 1-14), denounced a false peace. The first verse should read as in the Revised Version. Zion was the seat of orthodox religion ; Samaria was esteemed an impregnable military fortress. Material force and traditional religion make a grateful foundation for the natural heart, and beget a false peace.

" The chief of the nations " (v. 1), i.e., Israel.

" These kingdoms " (v. 2), i.e., the kingdoms of Israel and Judah.

The destruction of Calneh, Hamath, and Gath, and their strongly fortified borders, evidenced the folly of a false peace.

" The evil day " (v. 3), i.e., the approaching day of God's wrath. " The seat of violence," i.e., the corrupt Court of Justice. These luxurious revellers (vs. 4-6) ridiculed the prophet's announcement of the coming wrath of God ; falsely claimed their music to be like David's ; feasted upon food violently taken from the righteous ; and, like their forefathers, who sat down to eat and to drink while their brother was in the pit, they were indifferent to, and insensible of, the sufferings of God's true people, the spiritual Joseph. Therefore they should be the first to go into captivity. And so it fell out.

" Excellency " (v. 8). This may mean " pride " ; or it may mean that which had been excellent.

" The city " (v. 8), i.e., Samaria.

Pestilence should accompany captivity, or follow it, so deadly that even a large family of ten persons (v. 9) should have but one survivor (v. 10) ; and so conscious would the survivors be that it was a Divine Judgment that they would feel that they dared not use the ordinary language of religious consolation uttered at funerals.

" A man's uncle " (v. 10), i.e., a distant relative. " Him," i.e., the deceased. " And,"

i.e., " even." Pest corpses were burned. " Him that is by the sides of the house," i.e., the one survivor. This verse should read as in the Revised Version.

When God commands he executes (v. 11). " The great house," i.e., the Ten Tribes; " the little house," i.e., the Two Tribes.

" A thing of nought " (v. 13), i.e., idols. It is as great folly to trust in idols and military strength (" horns "), and to corrupt justice; and make it as bitter as gall and wormwood (v. 12), as it would be to race horses on rocks, or to try and plough there with oxen.

" A nation " (v. 14), i.e., the Assyrian " Hamath unto the river of the wilderness," i.e., all Palestine from the extreme north to the extreme south. Thus these nobles, indifferent to the affliction of Joseph, were themselves afflicted by the invader. Contrast 1 Kings viii. 65.

These two chapters, with all the others of the Book of Amos, abound with references to the Pentateuch.

AMOS VII.—The revelation of the first nine verses is : that persistence in evil after repeated forgiveness, will meet with eternal judgment.

" Grasshoppers " (v. 1), i.e., locusts. " The king's mowings." See 1 Kings iv. 7, and xviii. 5. The king taking the first crop of hay, and the locusts taking the second, nothing remained for the unhappy people.

" For he is small " (v. 2). The Psalmist said (Ps. xxv. 11), " pardon mine iniquity for it is great." When praying for personal pardon, sin should be magnified ; when pleading for pardon for a neighbour, sin should be minimised.

" It shall not be " (vs. 3 and 6), i.e., it shall not be final.

" Fire " (v. 4), i.e., drought. " To contend," i.e., against Israel. " The great deep," i.e., the deepest springs of water. " A part," i.e., the land of Gilead, which first went into captivity.

A plumb-line signified Divine judgment (2 Kings xxi. 13, Isa. xxviii. 17, xxxiv. 11. Lam. ii. 8).

The intimacy of the fellowship between Immanuel and Amos appears with peculiar sweetness in the prophet being addressed as " Amos " (v. 8). " He calleth His own sheep by name " (John x. 3).

" In the midst " (v. 8), i.e., the city of Samaria. The first destruction fell on Gilead

(v. 4) which was the frontier; the final judgment, upon Samaria the capital.

" Pass by " (v. 8), i.e., forgive. See Micah vii. 18.

" Isaac " (v. 9), i.e., the entire nation.

" I will rise against the house of Jeroboam " (v. 9). This was fulfilled in 2 Kings xv. 10.

The locust (v. 1) may symbolize Hazael's invasion (2 Kings viii. 12) ; the fire, that by Tiglath-Pileser (1 Chron. v. 26) ; and the plumb-line that by Shalmaneser (2 Kings xvii). The Northern Kingdom then perished never, as such, to be restored again.

Preaching of this character was out of place in the Chapel Royal (v. 10). A state religion negatives civil and religious liberty ; and if it is of human origination it cannot endure the testimony of truth. Not to be a member of the State Church is to be, in a degree, a rebel ; and the king being the head of the Church, no religious teaching could be permitted which was displeasing to him and to the priests that he appointed (1 Kings xii. 31, and xiii. 1-4). Amaziah was one of these man-made priests. He was not of the House of Aaron. His charge that Amos predicted the death of the king (v. 11) was a falsehood. Amos predicted the doom of the *house* of Jeroboam (v. 9).

" In the midst " (v. 10), i.e., publicly, openly.

" There eat bread and preach there " (v. 12). Amaziah thought that Amos, like himself, preached for money.

But Amos replied (vs. 14 and 15) ; " I am not a preacher of my own will, nor of the will of others ; I am a shepherd and a gatherer of sycamore fruit. That is my daily business. God has given me a message and I must deliver it " (v. 15). Prophets are not born such, nor are they self-made, nor made by others.

It is a fearful thing to oppose the Holy Spirit (vs. 16 and 17). God had not renounced His rights as the God of Israel. He called them " My people Israel " (v. 15), and, therefore, He pronounced this judgment upon Amaziah.

It contained five terms. His wife should be dishonoured in the streets of the city by the soldiers (Isa. xiii. 16, Lam. v. 11) ; his children should be slaughtered ; his property portioned off to others ; he himself should die as a slave in a foreign land ; and his nation should be carried away into hopeless captivity.

Sin ruins the sinner and those connected with him. This great moral fact adds to its horror. It is in operation to-day. Amaziah brought ruin upon his wife and children, just as Daniel's accusers involved their families in their own doom (Dan. vi. 24). See notes on that chapter.

AMOS VIII.—Amaziah's interruption disposed of, the fourth symbol follows those of the locusts, the drought and the plumb-line ; and once more the affecting intimacy of the Divine fellowship appears in the personal touch " Amos."

The basket of fruit (v. 1) declared the approaching end of summer ; the fruit was ripe, and had been already plucked from the trees. So the symbol announced the end of the kingdom ; its ripeness for judgment ; and that its citizens would be plucked out of the land.

" Pass by " (v. 2), i.e., forgive.

" Temple " (v. 3), i.e., palace. The songs were those of vi. 5, now to be turned to howls.

The dead bodies of the revellers should not be laid in stately tombs but cast forth as carrion ; and the silence of terror should replace the accustomed funeral pomp and eloquence.

God's love for the poor, and his burning anger against their oppressors, once more appear (v. 4).

Those who prefer market-days to Sabbath-days are the enemies of God and humanity, for they soon put aside equity and practise dishonesty.

By reducing the size of the ephah, by overcharging, and by falsifying the scales, they robbed the defenceless; and, plunging them into debt, they sold them into slavery for a trifle in defiance of Lev. xxv. 39.

" The Excellency of Jacob " (v. 7), i.e., God Himself. " I will not forgive " (v. 2), and, " I will never forget " (v. 7) express His pity for the oppressed and His eternal anger against the oppressors.

" For this " (v. 8), i.e., this oppression and robbery. The R.V. suggests that the earthquake of i. 1 was the Divine judgment upon all this evil.

" The sun to go down," etc. (v. 9), possibly symbolic language expressive of great calamities never before known.

" It " (v. 10), i.e., " that day " (v. 9).

When men are in prosperity they ridicule or neglect the Word of God, but when in adversity, they desire it ; but a just judgment declares " they shall not find it " (v. 12).

The most attractive persons (v. 13), if idolaters (v. 14), shall fall and never rise again.

The " god " of Dan and the " manner " of Beersheba were the golden calves set up in those centres. They were dead pieces of metal, but their sincere and earnest worshippers declared that they were living gods.

" From sea to sea " (v. 12), i.e., from the Mediterranean to the Dead Sea, that is, from the west to the south, i.e., from the gods of the Philistines to the gods of the Egyptians. " From the north," i.e., the gods of the Assyrians ; to the east, i.e., the gods of the Chaldeans. The sense of the statement is that they would vainly seek a divine message from idolatry in any part of the world.

AMOS IX.—Judgment begins at the House of God (vs. 1-4). From that judgment there will be no escape ; for the Judge is Omniscient and Irresistible.

As to the land of Palestine, He declares that He will " touch " it in wrath (vs. 5 and 6), and, afterwards, bless it in grace (vs. 11-13) ; its inhabitants would be exiled from it (vs. 7-10), and, afterwards, restored to it (vs. 14 and 15).

As a kingdom the Ten Tribes should perish for ever (v. 8) ; but not one member of the Elect Nation should perish (v. 9, Rom. xi. 26). That restored Nation will take possession of all nations and bring them to the Messiah's feet (v. 12).

" Upon " (v. 1), i.e., " beside." " The altar," that is, the altar of 1 Kings xiii. This verse should read as in the Revised Version. It predicted the total destruction of the Northern Kingdom.

" For evil and not for good " (v. 4), i.e., for adversity and not for prosperity.

The repetition of viii. 8, and ix. 5, makes absolute the threatened judgment.

" Stories " (v. 6), i.e., " chambers " (Ps. civ. 3 and 13). Astronomers, ancient and modern, use the term " Houses," and they figure the Sun as passing through these several sections of the heavens.

" His troop in the earth " (v. 6) that is,

" His vault over the earth," i.e., the visible sky which appears as a vault above the earth.

The proud boast of the Israelites that they were God's peculiar people, and that their redemption from Egypt demonstrated that they were His favourites, was a fleshly boast and is combated by verse 7. Religiously they were " as Ethiopians," (Jer. xiii. 23), and historically they could only rank as the Philistines and the Syrians whom God in His providence had also delivered from captivity, and had probably brought originally out of Egypt.

" I will destroy," " I will command," " I will sift " (vs. 8 and 9). God Himself promised to be the Actor. This is all lovely and consoling to faith ; and it secures the absolute salvation of the Elect. The smallest grain is as sure of eternal safety as the largest.

The chaff and dust which pass through the sieve are the sinners of verse 10.

" In that day " (v. 11), i.e., the future day of restoration which will follow the present night of desolation.

" The Tabernacle of David," not of Jeroboam nor of Jehu, is to be raised up.

" I will raise up," " I will close up," " I will build," " I will perform " (" doeth ") " I will bring," " I will plant " (vs. 11-15). These " I wills " of God, in grace, contrast with His " I wills " of wrath (vs. 8 and 9).

" Edom " (v. 12), i.e., " Adam " that is, mankind. Acts xv. 14-18 illuminates this promise.

The new-born Israel will take possession of all nations, and bring them as captives to Immanuel, thus fulfilling the commission of Matt. xxviii. 19. Then will nations, as nations, be " baptized " into the Name, (not into the names) of the Father, of the Son, and of the Holy Spirit ; and thus will Jehovah's Name be called upon them. That baptism will not be into water but into Christ, who is the Fulness of the God-Head.

Thus the Spirit in Amos sets out the ways of God with His people ; reviews their moral condition from the golden calf of Sinai to that of Bethel ; declares the consequent judgment ; predicts the spiritual birth of the Twelve Tribes ; and the physical transformation of their ancient home.

OBADIAH

OBADIAH.

This is the shortest Book in the Old Testament. Obadiah means "Servant of Jehovah." The predictions of the Book concern the destruction of Edom (vs. 1-16) and the restoration of Israel (vs. 17-21). The Edomites were the descendants of Esau. They cherished for the descendants of Jacob the murderous hatred of their ancestor for his brother. The Israelites were commanded on the contrary to love their fierce relatives (Deut. xxiii. 7).

Edom largely appears in the prophetic Scriptures. More than twenty predictions are there recorded respecting him. The principal are Isa. xxxiv., lxiii., Jer. xlix., Ezek. xxxv. Babylon shares with Edom this sad prominence in the Scriptures. The one symbolizes corruption of truth; the other, violence in action. These are Satan's two great weapons against the kingdom and people of God. Hence this prophecy of Obadiah concerns not only the historic Edom but rather the symbolic, for it reaches forward to the future day when man, i.e., Adam, that is Edom, headed by Anti-Christ, will attack Jerusalem and seek its total destruction (Ps. cxxxvii.). Thus that Edom will be as totally destroyed as the Edom of Obadiah's day was.

These predictions by Obadiah concerning Edom are independent of, and complementary to, those of Jer. xlix. Obadiah lived about two hundred years after Amos.

OBADIAH.—"We" (v. 1), i.e., the nations who invaded Edom. They here claim Divine inspiration for their expedition.

The Edomites boasted of their strength (v. 2), the impregnability of their country (v. 3), and their wisdom (v. 8).

"I will make thee small among the heathen," "Thou shalt be greatly despised (v. 2). The past tense is used to affirm certainty.

"The men of thy confederacy have brought thee to the border" (v. 7), i.e., Edom's allies helped to exile him.

The fact of Edom's destruction is predicted in verses 1-9; and the cause of that doom is set out in verses 10-16.

The ruin and captivity of the children of Judah and of Jerusalem (vs. 11 and 12) caused great jubilation among the sons of Esau. "Day" (v. 12), i.e., calamity

"Spoken proudly" (v. 12)—Hebrew, "enlarged thy mouth," i.e., laughed loudly with pleasure.

The heartless action of the men of Esau against their brothers of Jacob is detailed in verses 10-14; and this detail reveals God's anger and indignation.

"The day of the Lord" (v. 15), i.e., the future day of God's wrath. At this point the prophecy passes on to the future and predicts the annihilation of all the nations, as nations (v. 16), that shall seek to injure God's ancient people.

The restoration and age-enduring prosperity of the House of Jacob are the themes of verses 17-21. The entire land from the Euphrates to the river of Egypt, promised to Abraham, shall become the possession of his children.

"Any remaining" (v. 18). Two thousand four hundred years ago this prediction was written. To-day no Edomite can be found. But the symbolic Edom persists, and will persist, up to the day of the Lord (Isa. lxiii., 1-6).

"Sepharad" (v. 20) possibly Asia Minor; or it may be a term expressing the Dispersion.

"Saviours" (v. 21), i.e., deliverers, as in the Book of Judges; but above them will be Messiah the King, and His shall be the Kingdom.

654

JONAH

Matt. xii. 39-41 with 2 Kings xiv. 25-27, prove that the Book of Jonah is history and not allegory. He was the. first of the prophets after Elijah and Elisha. He was the only prophet sent to the Gentiles, and he was the only prophet who tried to conceal his message. This concealment may have been motived by chapter iv. 2. The prosperity of Nineveh meant the subjection of Israel; the destruction of Nineveh, the prosperity of Zion. Love of country and hatred of idolatry would unite to make his mission distasteful to him. Christian men are often pushed into a wrong course of action by false religious zeal and by national spirit.

Jonah belonged to the Tribe of Zebulon; his home was near the frontier, and he ought, therefore, to have had some sympathy for the nations that lived so near him.

Nineveh was founded by Nimrod (Gen. x. 11). The name signifies City of Nimis, i.e., Nimrod.

The Book is unique in that it is more concerned with the Prophet himself than with his prophecy The condition of his soul, and God's loving discipline of him, instruct and humble the reader.

The Lord's supplemental statements in Luke xi. 30 and 32 that the Ninevites knew of Jonah's entombment in the fish—for he was a " sign unto them "—and that the very men to whom he preached are to re-appear in the future day of judgment, make. conclusive the historic truth of the Book.

JONAH 1.—" The Word of the Lord " (v. 1). This statement is decisive, and claims and demonstrates the truthfulness of the entire Book. The claim is affirmed also in ii. 10, iii. 1 and 3, iv. 4, 9, 10 with i. 1, thus making in all seven declarations.

' Tarshish " (v. 3) most probably Spain. Ps. cxxxix. 7 should have instructed Jonah as to the impossibility of going from the presence of the Lord. (See notes on chapter ii. as to Jonah's knowledge of the Psalms).

To-day Christian people, like Jonah, sometimes seek by foreign travel to escape apprehended duty, and so " flee from the presence of the Lord."

There is no conscience so insensible as that of a disobedient Christian (v. 5). The sailors were praying, but Jonah was sleeping. He first went down to Joppa, then down into the ship (v. 3), and then down into the sides of the ship (v. 5).

The heathen sailors believed there were many gods, one for the sea, another for the dry land, etc. (v. 9), but Jonah declared there was but one God—the God of heaven Who made both the sea and the dry land. Hence the terror of the sailors (v. 10).

Jonah confessed his sin to man; but not, as yet, to God (vs. 9-12).

To save the ship's company, and, perhaps, to save his nation by ensuring the overthrow of Nineveh, he was willing to sacrifice his life (v. 12). In this he was a type of Christ; excepting that Christ designed to save Nineveh as well as Israel by his death.

" They took up Jonah " (v. 15), i.e., with reverence. See Gen. xlvii. 30. (Heb).

" A great fish " (v. 17):—not necessarily a whale but possibly, for the famous writer, Frank Bullen, states in his books that he often saw in the stomach of whales whole fish twelve times the size of a man.

JONAH II.—In spite of Jonah's effort to get away from God, the Holy Spirit declares (v. 1) that Jehovah was still " His God," and Jonah himself when disciplined and restored in soul could say " My God." Fellowship may be broken; relationship never. A father might justly confine a disobedient child in a room, but if the house took fire he would not leave him there to perish.

In verses 2-9 the prophet quotes nine Psalms—cxx., xlii., xxxi., lxix., cxlii., xviii., xxxi., cxvi., iii.

" I will look again to thy holy Temple " (v. 4). See I Kings viii. 38.

Jonah's acquaintance with the Psalms, and the other Scriptures, is a testimony to their antiquity and inspiration.

" Thou hast brought up " (v. 6), i.e., " Thou wilt bring up." Faith uses the past tense because certain of the fulfilment of the hope.

" For ever " (v. 6), that is, in relation to man's inability to deliver himself from such a living tomb. " Her bars," i.e., the dry land and the waters. Man cannot break through these or free himself from them if imprisoned by them.

" Lying vanities," i.e., idols; " mercy," i.e., God (Ps. lix. 17 and cxliv. 2). The fact that suffering and self-ruin result from self-will and the negation of God, had now become a matter of personal experience to the prophet, for he had forsaken God and united in travel with idolaters.

" Salvation is of Jehovah " (v. 9). This is the last lesson that proud man consents to learn ; for it teaches him that he cannot contribute to his own salvation—for what could Jonah do inside the great fish ?—and so if man is to be saved the salvation must be wholly Divine.

" Then spake Jehovah unto the fish " (v. 10). Compare verse 1.—" then prayed Jonah unto Jehovah." So great effects may follow feeble prayers.

This chapter has spiritual teaching for the believer personally ; but its main value is that it fore-pictures the experiences of Christ's soul when in hades, as also do certain Psalms, and reveals that Christ, as during His life, and upon the cross, and now upon the throne, when disembodied and in hades, trusted God even in that extremity and called Him " My God." Therefore is He the Author and Finisher of Faith.

JONAH III—Jonah was a " sign " to the Ninevites (Matt. xvi. 1-4 and Luke xi. 30) ; that is, he was a personal illustration of the wrath and the grace of God. The word " sign " makes it evident that the facts of his entombment in the fish, and his deliverance, were known to the people of Nineveh,

and hence their acceptance of his message. Nineveh will, therefore, condemn Jerusalem in the judgment, for she repented at the preaching of a (to Nineveh) dead and risen prophet, but Jerusalem refused to repent when summoned thereto by the dead and risen Messiah.

Grace delivered the mariners when they cried (i. 14), and Jonah when he cried (ii. 10), and the men of Nineveh when they cried (iii. 10).

Nineveh was about ninety miles in circumference, and, therefore, a very great city, with a population of, perhaps, one million. It might be termed a " garden city " ; for it enclosed both gardens and pastures, thus providing food for man and beast within its walls. Recent surveys, and the statements of Diodorus Siculus and of Herodotus confirm the truthfulness of verse 3.

" Three days' journey " (v. 3), i.e., in diameter. A day's journey, i.e., about twelve miles (v. 4).

" Forty days " (v. 4). This in Scripture is the number of probation and of testing and humiliation. Moses, Elijah, and Christ were thus tested. From Pentecost to the destruction of Jerusalem was a probation of forty years ; but that guilty city refused to humble itself and repent.

Grace warned Nineveh of approaching wrath. Thus both the wrath of God and the grace of God demonstrate the love of God. This is the great argument of the Epistle to the Romans.

Ancient writers record that nations when in trouble caused both man and beast to fast (v. 7).

True repentance involves separation from evil (v. 8).

Fear and a sense of guilt cause a man to repent ; love and a sense of pity, God ; for He reserves liberty of action to Himself (v. 10). Repentance with God means a change of purpose or action.

JONAH IV.—" Displeased " (v. 1), i.e., deeply grieved religiously. And, further, his reputation as a prophet was at stake.

" Better for me to die " (v. 3). See notes on Elijah (I Kings xvii. et seq.).

Man's moral consciousness demands punishment for evil, and a fleshly orthodoxy requires suppression of heterodoxy. Jonah was religiously indignant that the crimes and cruelties of Nineveh should be lightly regarded by God in this fashion and forgiven, just as a moral mind would be shocked to-day if God were so to treat the Turkish Ruler and his people. Elijah was angered because his efforts to compel Israel by suffering to return to the law failed, and, therefore, he and Jonah declared that it would be better for them to die than to live. The heart is deceitful above all things, and can use the just demands of morality and orthodoxy as instruments of sectarian and national supremacy, and of personal importance.

Jonah's knowledge of the Bible was accurate (v. 2). He could quote Ex. xxxiv. 6 and Num. xiv. 18. This knowledge occasioned his flight. No one but himself could say this.

He no doubt reasoned that a total destruction of Nineveh, manifestly Divine, would advantage his own nation religiously and politically. It would remove her oppressor, and, at the same time, convince his countrymen of the wickedness and folly of idolatry.

To Jonah's legal mind and spirit it must have been very humbling to have been compelled to announce God's forgiveness ; but God's plan was to teach Israel by the example of Nineveh how inexcusable was their own impenitence and how inevitable their ruin.

Jonah did not know that Messiah Himself was thus to apply the lesson.

The contrast between the feeling of God's heart on the repentance of Nineveh, and the feeling of Jonah's heart on the repentance of God toward Nineveh is sad and humbling.

But how gently God reasoned with him (vs. 4, 9, 10 and 11).

" The gourd " (v. 6) was the castor oil plant. It grows to a height of about ten feet, and has very large leaves. One very small worm at its root can destroy it in a few hours.

Religious emotions which are personal and not of the Holy Spirit, can be easily affected by the provision or loss of material comforts (v. 6).

" Vehement " (v. 8), i.e., continuous (Heb.) (Josh. x. 12).

" That cannot discern " (v. 11), i.e., one hundred and twenty thousand infants. The population of the city, therefore, must have been about one million.

The last two verses contain the great lesson of the Book. Jonah needed the gourd, which he had not himself made, and grieved at its destruction. God created the inhabitants and cattle of Nineveh. His love needed them ; how much greater, therefore, would be His grief in their destruction !

MICAH

Micah was a native of Morasheth a village between Jerusalem and the sea. His full name was Micaiah, i.e., "Who is like Jehovah?" He was not the Micaiah of 1 Kings xxii. 8. He prophesied at the same time as Isaiah; and, because of the moral condition of Jerusalem at the time, their preaching was necessarily similar. The moral need being the same the message was the same, the speaker in each case being the Holy Spirit (Heb. i. 1.) Sixteen passages in the two Books corresponding, shew that the prophets, like the Apostles, quoted from the inspired Scriptures. The invasion of the Assyrians (2 Chron. xxxii.) partially fulfilled the predictions of the Book; but their full accomplishment belongs to the future.

MICAH I.—Micah did not compose this Book. God is its Author. His word "came" to Micah (v. 1).

"People" (v. 2) rather "Peoples." This verse may read: "Adonai Jehovah shall be a witness against you." He, knowing men's hearts, and acquainted with every action of their lives, is a terrible witness.

Powerless man can only tread upon the dust, Jehovah can tread upon the highest mountains (v. 3). Before Him mountains should melt as wax, and valleys be cleft as water (v. 4), i.e., no obstacles should stop the Syrian army.

The transgression of Jacob was the idol worship set up at Samaria, and the sins of the high places of Judah, the idolatrous altars set up in Jerusalem (v. 5).

"Hires" (v. 7), i.e., the costly vessels donated to the idol temples. "For she gathered it," etc,. i.e., the wealth gained by idolatry should be carried off by the Assyrian idolaters.

"Naked" (v. 8), i.e., wearing only a loin-cloth.

"Wound" (v. 9), Hebrew, "wounds," i.e., plural of majesty for a final and deadly wound. So it came to pass. Samaria was utterly and finally destroyed.

Having accomplished the ruin of the Northern kingdom, the Assyrians, ten years later, entered the Southern, but got no further than the gate of Jerusalem; for the city was delivered in answer to Hezekiah's prayer (2 Chron. xxxii., Isa. xxxvii.).

The destructive and triumphant march of the Assyrian host upon Jerusalem is poetically described in verses 10-16, and a corresponding description appears in Isa. x. 28-32. The towns would call to each other for help, and Jerusalem would appeal to them all fo-assistance, but in vain.

The meaning of the names of these towns heightened the effect of the poetry. Gath may here mean "Weep-town"; Aphrah, "Dust-house"; Saphir, "Beauty-town"; Zaanan, "Aside-town"; Beth-ezel "Neigh-bour-town"; Maroth, "Bitter-town"; Lachish, "Horse-town"; Achzib, "False-hood-town"; and Mareshah, "Possession-town."

The play upon words in the Hebrew text may be thus exhibited:

Weep-town, Weep not; Dust-house, roll thyself in dust; Beauty-town, go into captivity with beauty shamed; Aside-town, respond not to the mournful appeal of Neighbour-town, for he, i.e., Sennacherib, will feed his army on you. Bitter-town shall bitterly grieve for her goods, but evil, i.e., calamity, shall only reach the gate of Jerusalem. Horse-town, bind the chariot to the swift steed (for flight). She, i.e., La-chish introduced Samaria's idolatry to Zion, therefore should she give up possessions at Moresheth to the foe. Falsehood-town should prove false as a helper, and the Assyrian should become the possessor of

Possession-town. The "glory" of Israel, i.e., the nobility, should flee for safety to the cave of Adullam

MICAH II.—The Holy Spirit in this chapter judges sin against one's neighbour, as in the first chapter He judged sin against God. These sins of idolatry and violence transgress the two Tables of the Law.

If man planned iniquity (v. 1) God, in reply, planned calamity (v. 3).

"For this time is evil" (v. 3). This should read : "For that time shall be evil," i.e., the time of the Assyrian invasion.

The Assyrian yoke would not be an easy one (v. 3) as is Immanuel's (Matt. xi. 28).

Man always blames God as the Author of the evils which his own sins cause (v. 4). God had not "changed" or broken His covenant —verses 12 and 13 prove this—but in just anger He divided the fields of Palestine to the invader.

"To cast a cord" (v. 5) means to measure a farm.

Israel refused the testimony of truth (v. 6) and, by a just judgment, it was replaced by a spirit of falsehood (vs. 6 and 11). If men will not listen to the Holy Spirit they will be condemned to listen to the unholy one.

God's words are pleasant ("do good") to those who walk in subjection to the Bible ; but they are distasteful to those who do not so walk (v. 7).

The preaching of falsehood (v. 11) has as its moral result the violence, cruelty and injustice of verses 1 and 2 and 8 and 9.

The command of verse 10 is not addressed to God's servants in a good sense but is a declaration of Divine wrath. Canaan would "destroy" them because they had polluted it (Lev. xviii. 27 and 28).

If the popular preachers announced good tidings of wine and strong drink (v. 11) God, through His true servants, proclaimed the better tidings of restoration (vs. 12 and 13). This prophecy was not fulfilled by the restoration from Babylon, for all of Jacob was not then assembled, but it will be fulfilled in the future.

"The Breaker, (the Good Shepherd), is gone forth before them," i.e., the sheep. All obstacles, removed by Him, the sheep break forth from captivity, pass through its gates, and, their King and Shepherd at their head, return to Palestine ; the Spirit adds that that Divine Breaker and Shepherd and King is Jehovah (v. 13).

MICAH III.—This message was addressed to the magistrates (v. 1). It denounced their taking of bribes (v. 11) ; their acquiring property and houses by injustice (vs. 2, 3, 9 and 10) ; and their merciless stripping of the helpless of all they possessed.

Once more this denunciation reveals God's hatred of oppression.

"To know judgment" (v. 1), i.e., to recognize what is justice, and to fearlessly administer it. It also may suggest that, as judges and having knowledge of judgment, they were bound to recognize the justice of God's judgment upon themselves (v. 4).

"They," (v. 4), i.e., these unjust magistrates.

"At that time" (v. 4), i.e., the time of the Assyrian invasion (ii. 3).

"Their doings" (v. 4). Men cannot do ill and fare well. Just as their claimants cried to them for justice, but they would not hear them, so should they, in their turn, cry to God for deliverance from the extortion of the Assyrians, but He would justly refuse to deliver them.

"Bite with their teeth," and "he that putteth not into their mouths" (v. 5), i.e., to preach for a large salary. "Cleanness of teeth" (Amos iv. 6) expresses want of food ; "biting with teeth," abundance of food.

The fashionable preacher proclaims "peace," i.e., that there is no future wrath of God, no lake of fire, and no judgment to come (v. 5). The true preacher (v. 8) denounces sin, and announces judgment. All the false preachers shall be confounded (vs. 6 and 7), they shall cover their lips, i.e., be compelled to silence, for they shall have no answer from God.

"Judge for reward" (v. 11), i.e., take bribes.

Priests were commanded to teach gratuitously (Lev. x. 11). They were supported by tithes.

Sin becomes exceedingly sinful when pride, self-indulgence and injustice base themselves on religious privilege and Divine promises (v. 11).

"The high places of the forest" (v. 12), i.e., a rough jungle-top. This prediction was fulfilled at the destruction of Jerusalem by the Romans.

The judgment on Samaria (i. 6) and on

Jerusalem (iii. 12) was similar—both a heap of stones—but the cause, dissimilar. Doctrine doomed Samaria ; conduct, Jerusalem. See notes on the Epistles to the Seven Churches from Romans to Thessalonians.

Drink-sellers often build churches with blood-money (v. 10) and make a loud profession of religion (v. 11).

MICAH IV. TO V. 1.—The Holy Spirit here through Micah repeats, and confirms, the promise of restoration made through Isaiah (ch. ii.). There could be no change, for there was no room for change, hence the message is similar, for the moral facts were the same.

" The last days " (v. 1), rather, " at the end of the days," i.e., the long period of desolation predicted in iii. 12.

" In the top of " (v. 1), rather, " at the head of." " Mountains " and " hills " symbolize empires and kingdoms. In the promised future the Hebrew nation will be supreme over all other nations.

" Judge " (v. 3), rather, " arbitrate between." The result of His arbitration and reproving will be the abolition of war (v. 3) and the establishment of universal peace and prosperity (v. 4). Man's efforts to secure this are, and will be, vain. This era of concord and plenty will be introduced by Immanuel and never till then.

Verse 5 forms a parenthesis. It means : Let other nations, if they will, trust their gods, the Remnant of Israel resolves to trust none other than Jehovah, and to trust Him for ever and ever—believing that, however long delayed, the happiness promised in verses 1-8 will surely be realized.

As " Jacob " did not become " Israel " till he was maimed, so " Jacob," as a nation, will not be restored and blessed until spiritually maimed by affliction. Then, as a strong nation, she will possess a mighty King for ever (vs. 6, 7. 8).

" Tower of the flock " (v. 8), i.e., Jerusalem. " The first dominion," i.e., the former dominion under Solomon. To assure the doubting heart· the Spirit adds : " the kingdom *shall* come to the daughter of Jerusalem."

The " Now " of verses 9, 11 and v. 1, should rather read " meanwhile." That is, during the long period preceding restoration, the Hebrew people shall suffer extreme affliction. In Micah's day the Assyrian was the oppressor that caused Israel to utter cries of anguish (v. 9), that drove them from their land, and banished them to Babylon (v. 10). This was one of the prophecies the Holy Spirit recalled in Acts vii. 43.

The nation is still in bondage in " Babylon " ; but it will be rescued and redeemed from thence (v. 10).

The " thoughts " or " plans " of Jehovah (v. 12) are His purpose to gather many nations into Palestine as sheaves into a threshing floor, and " His counsel " is to employ Israel as His instrument to judge them there (v. 13). " I will " should read " Thou shalt " (R.V.). See notes on Rev. ii. 26, 27, xvi. 16, and xix. 14, 15, and 19.

The following verse may mean : " Meanwhile thou shalt have sore affliction O daughter of affliction "—and such indeed has been, and is, Zion's experience ; or it may mean a call to Jerusalem to mobilise its forces to resist the oncoming Assyrians : or, most probably, it may mean " Prepare O Jerusalem to go into captivity."

" He (the Assyrian) hath laid siege against us," i.e., " He shall lay siege against us." This use of the past tense for the future is peculiar to Inspiration, for it certifies the fulfilment of the prediction. It occurs frequently in both the Old and New Testaments. For example : " I have finished the work which Thou gavest me to do " (John xvii. 3), and, " He saved us " (Titus iii. 5).

" The Judge of Israel," i.e., the then king. The Romans repeated this action when striking Messiah the true King; and Israel's participation in that supreme sin brought upon her the added judgment of v. 3.

MICAH V. 2-15.—As to His humanity, Christ was born in Bethlehem of Judah ; as to His Deity, He is from of old, from everlasting. The Hebrew term here expresses the very highest conception of ever-enduring existence.

The Pharisees promptly pointed Herod to this text as fixing the place of Messiah's birth.

There were two Bethlehems. The other was in Zebulun. The Spirit, to prevent mistake, distinguishes this village by giving it its Hebrew and its Aramaic name. Both names mean " House of Bread."

Zion will, in her future anguish and affliction, give birth to a New Nation (Matt. xxi. 43, and Micah v. 3). At the same time He who was born of the Virgin will be manifested as the Son of God. That New Nation will be the fitted instrument of making this manifestation to the world. Naomi, and Ruth's child, declared to be born to Naomi (Ruth iv. 17), illustrate this.

"The Remnant of His brethren," i.e., the Jewish Dispersion. These will return to the children of Israel—not to the Church revealed in Ephesians. This negatives the Anglo-Israelite theory.

"He" (v. 4), i.e., the Ruler, or Shepherd, of verse 2. His ability, as such, shall be measured by the strength of Jehovah, and His character and attributes by the Majesty of Jehovah's Name.

"They shall abide" (v. 4), i.e., His sheep shall dwell in permanent security.

"This man" (v. 5), rather, "This Ruler" (v. 2).

When the time comes the "seven shepherds and eight principal men" (v. 5) will be recognised. They will be Immanuel's generals (v. 6); but Immanuel Himself will be the Author of every victory (v. 6).

In that great day of restoration the nation of Israel will be to the world as dew (v. 7) and as a lion (v. 8); that is, they will be the channel of Divine grace toward the obedient, and the instrument of Divine wrath upon the rebels. Both energies are independent of human co-operation.

Zion's outward enemies (vs. 9 and 15) and her inward (vs. 10-14), shall in that day be all cut off. Verse 15 should read as in the Revised Version.

The promises of verses 7 and 8 and of verses 9-15 should be spiritually proved, manifested, and experienced by the Christian.

"Therefore" (v. 3). Because Israel united in smiting Messiah with a rod upon His face "therefore" has He given them up to the still-enduring night of suffering.

MICAH VI.—The great prophecies of Israel's present dispersion and future restoration being declared, the prophet by the Spirit makes in these last two chapters a moral appeal to the people, if by any means He may save some of them from an eternal doom.

In the first eight verses of the chapter the earth is summoned to listen to God's controversy with His people (vs. 1 and 2). He reviews in the presence of the mountains and hills (v. 1) His action with Israel in the past (vs. 3-5). It was an appeal that should have touched their hearts, for what greater demonstration of love and long-suffering could have been made! He redeemed them from bondage; He provided them with able shepherds (v. 4); He defended them from their enemies both human and demoniacal; and He supplied their every need all the way from Shittim to Gilgal (v. 5). In return He only asked for affection and companionship for Himself, and justness and kindness for one another (v. 8), and not for costly and inhuman sacrifices (vs. 6 and 7). See notes on Jer. vii. 22 and Hosea vi. 6, and Exod. xx. 24.

There is no conflict here with the legislation of Leviticus. That was substituted because Israel, as a nation, refused priestly position in relation to God immediately after the redemption out of Egypt (Exod. xx. 19-26). The Levitical sacrifices were lessons and means to an end, but not the end itself. That end was fellowship with God and a life of beneficence to one another, based on an all-sufficient sacrifice that God Himself would provide. See notes on Exod. xx.

"Thou," "thy," (v. 1), i.e., Israel.

"Before the mountains and hills" (v. 1), i.e., in the presence of. The mountains and hills, i.e. earthly governments, form the audience that should listen to Israel's contention and Jehovah's controversy.

"House of servants" (v. 4) "House of bondage" (R.V.).

A full stop should follow the word "him" (v. 5), and the word "remember" should be repeated before "from Shittim unto Gilgal."

"Righteousness" (v. 5), i.e., righteous actions.

The revelation recalled in verse 8, was made in Deut. x. 12. Compare Matt. xxiii. 23, Luke xi. 42, and Jas. i. 27.

The second section of the chapter occupies verses 9-16. This appeal is made to the guilty city of Jerusalem, and laments that her sins (vs. 10-12) compelled the judgments of verses 13-16, predicted in Leviticus xxvi.

Micah lived more than two hundred years before Ezra and quotes continually and minutely from the Pentateuch. Yet there are men professing to be historical experts who affirm that Ezra composed the Pentateuch!

"The city" (v. 9), i.e., Jerusalem.

The words " And the man of wisdom shall see Thy Name " should be enclosed in a bracket. " See Thy Name," i.e., recognise Thy just action in judging the city because of its evil.

The term " Name " expresses in the Bible the character of God in gracious or punitive action, in harmony with all that He has revealed Himself to be.

" Hear ye the rod," etc., (v. 9), i.e., " Hear, O Jerusalem, what punishment awaits you, and from whom." The message was not Micah's, it was God's, and, therefore, to be dreaded.

" Are there yet ? etc.," (v. 10), i.e., Do you still keep on practising these abominations of fraud and falsehood and robbing the poor ? (vs. 10-12).

" I will make thee sick " (v. 13). See Lev. xxvi. 16 and 1 Cor. xi. 30.

" Thy casting down," etc., (v. 14), i.e., Jerusalem would fall because of internal distress rather than outward attack.

" Thou shalt take hold," etc., (v. 14), i.e., upon thy money-bags filled by fraud, but shall not carry them away.

" Sweet wine " (v. 15), i.e., Thou shalt tread the vintage but shalt not drink the wine.

Omri founded Samaria and its incredible and shameless idolatry.

" That I should make thee " (v. 16), i.e., so as to compel Me.

" The reproach of My people." Relationship to God entails honour or reproach— honour if that relationship be accredited by an upright and obedient life ; reproach if not so accredited. The world respects a consistent Christian, but looks with contempt upon an inconsistent one.

The word " reproach " is always used in the Scriptures in a bad sense, it means : scorn, derision, contempt. Therefore this statement in verse 16 cannot mean that God's faithful people would deride their idolatrous brethren when punished by God. The first use of a word in the Bible generally determines its meaning. This word is first used in Joshua v. 9. The " reproach of Egypt " may be understood to mean the derision which Israel suffered from the Egyptians during her forty years of wandering in the desert ; for the Egyptians must have made merry over the aimless trekkings of these homeless fugitives.

The ingratitude of Israel was so unnatural as to make inanimate nature conscious of its enormity (vs. 1-5). This is a poetic figure of great force and beauty.

MICAH VII.—Just as a hungry man searches in vain for food in a well gleaned harvest field so the prophet searched in vain for a good man in Jerusalem (vs. 1 and 2). Corruption was universal. The word " good " has relation to kindness toward man rather than piety toward God. Nothing suitable' to their title of " The People of God " was to be found.

" The· Prince asketh and the Judge (judgeth) for a bribe " (v. 3). That is : the prince bribed the judge, and requested him to decide in his favour against the helpless poor. " The great man uttereth his mischievous desire ; so they wrap it up." That is : the rich man communicates to the judge the evil he purposes against the poor ; and " they," i.e., the rich man and the judge, concoct the matter between them.

" Thy watchmen " (v. 4), i.e., the prophets. " Thy visitation," i.e., God's wrath. " Now," i.e., In that day of coming wrath. " The day," i.e., the judgment predicted by the watchmen.

At that time of perplexity faith could not be reposed in any one (v. 5). The following verse should be read using the future tense ; for, at that time, the son shall dishonour the father, etc.

The Lord (Matt. x. 35, 36) quotes this verse, to prove that Gospel grace when rejected arouses the iniquity of the heart, and that the entrance and nearness of perfect love, i.e., Christ, exasperates into activity its hatred.

In the midst of this corruption the believer keeps looking unto Jesus, waiting for His salvation, and leaning upon Him in confident prayer (v. 7).

" When I fall " (v. 8), i.e., into affliction—not into sin. " When I sit," or, better, " though I sit."

The Prophet, energized as was Daniel (ch. ix.) by the spirit of intercession proper to the High Priest of Israel's confession (Heb. iii. 1), confesses that nation's sins as his own ; accepts the wrath of God as just ; and confidently awaits a future vindication (v. 9). This is a most touching feature of the prophetic office. " If," said Jeremiah " he be a prophet let him make intercession to Jehovah " (xxvii. 18). " He (Abraham) is a prophet," said God to Abimelech, " and he will pray for thee " (Gen. xx. 7). The Spirit of God, as Light, reveals judgment. The Spirit of God, as Love, begets intercession for, but not against, the guilty. Here Elijah failed (Rom. xi. 2), and was, therefore, removed from office and Elisha substituted in his place.

"Execute judgment for me " (v. 9), i. e. give judgment in my favour. " His righteousness," i.e., His righteous vindication of me.

" Mine enemy " (v. 10), i.e., the Babylon of iv. 11. She said " Let our eye look upon Zion ! " Zion will say : " Mine eye shall look upon her." " At that time (" now ") shall she be trodden down as the mire of the streets."

"Thy walls" (v. 11), i.e., Jerusalem. " The decree shall be far removed," better " Thy boundary shall be widely extended."

" He shall come home to thee " (v. 12), i.e., The dispersed of Israel shall return home to Jerusalem.

" The fortress " (v. 12), i.e., Egypt ; " the River," i.e., Euphrates. See R.V.

"Notwithstanding " (v. 13), i.e., " But before this." Neither in Micah's day, nor at the present day, can the Hebrews claim that their future glory will be the reward of their fidelity, for Zion's long continued desolation is the fruit of her misconduct, and restoration will only follow upon repentance.

The prayer of verse 14 is addressed to the Messiah as the Great Shepherd of His people. This rod will comfort and not smite them. His people will dwell solitary, that is, shall enjoy distinct nationality (Num. xxiii. 9) and absolute security (" the wood "), and abounding prosperity. The richest pastures were those of Carmel, Bashan and Gilead. In this prayer the future tense is implied.

Verses 15-17, is the Great Shepherd's prompt reply to the prayer.

" Him " (v. 15), i.e., the Anti-Christian leader of the hostile nations of the future. As God showed marvellous things unto Pharaoh when redeeming His people out of Egypt, so will He show marvellous things to Anti-Christ when redeeming His people out of Babylon.

Verse 17 should read as in the Revised Version.

" He will turn again " (v. 19), i.e., He will return in compassion to Jerusalem.. He turned away in wrath, He will return in pity, subduing iniquities, annihilating sins, and fulfilling His promises.

Thus the prophecy, like the Epistle to the Romans, begins with God's wrath against sin (i. 2-7) and closes with God's forgiveness of sin.

That the proud nations, especially those of Japan, China, Hindoostan, Arabia, Russia, England, Germany and America, should crawl like reptiles (v. 17) at the feet of a Jew and tremble before him, excites ridicule ; but it is here predicted. They will fear the Jew in that day, because God will manifest tokens of His Almighty power in his favour, and own the little nation of the Hebrews as His peculiar people.

NAHUM

Nahum signifies "Jehovah will avenge and comfort His people." This is the theme of the Book. It announces the destruction of Nineveh and the restoration of Zion.

Nahum and Jonah correspond. Both are undated. The one records the repentance of Nineveh; the other predicts its destruction. Nahum prophesied about a hundred years after Jonah, and a hundred years later the city was destroyed.

Nahum was a contemporary of Isaiah and Hezekiah. This appears from statements in his prophecy. The Assyrian monarchs had already conquered and exiled the Ten Tribes; had invaded Egypt and destroyed No-Ammon, i.e., "Thebes"; and Sennacherib, having ravaged Judea, was approaching Jerusalem as Nahum was uttering his message of consolation.

In answer to the prayer of Hezekiah the Assyrian host was destroyed. Its king returned with shame of face to Nineveh; and, as predicted by Nahum (i. 14), the house of his god became his grave; for he was murdered in it by his sons.

The plenary fulfilment of these prophecies belongs to the future when God will comfort His people and avenge them of their adversaries, the future Assyrian and his armies, i.e., the Anti-Christ.

NAHUM I.—The first eight verses form the introduction. It is a majestic picture of the Majesty of God (vs. 4-6); of His longsuffering (v. 3); and of His benevolence (v. 7).

"The burden of Nineveh" (v. 1), i.e., the prophecy announcing the doom of Nineveh.

Elkosh was a village in Galilee; perhaps the village of Capernaum, which means: "village of Nahum."

"God is jealous" (v. 2), that is, He has a jealous love for His people, and will allow no one to injure them, though He may employ nations as instruments to chastise them.

"Revengeth," rather, "avengeth." "Is furious," i.e., is a possessor of wrath. He avenges His people on their adversaries, and possesses wrath for their enemies (v. 2).

His longsuffering is not due to impotency, for He is great in power (v. 3). "And" should here read "But."

Bashan, Carmel and Lebanon are the most fertile districts in Palestine.

"Burned" (v. 5), i.e., "upheaved" (R.V.).

"He knoweth" (v. 7), i.e., He owns as His people. Hezekiah proved the truth of this verse, for on taking refuge in Him he was delivered and the Assyrian destroyed.

"The place thereof" (v. 8), i.e., The place from whence the trouble of verse 7 comes. In this case, Nineveh.

"Ye" (v. 9), i.e., the Assyrians. "Imagine," i.e., "plan." "An utter end," i.e., of the Assyrians and of Nineveh—so complete that the affliction then suffered by Zion should not occur a second time (v. 9).

"While" (v. 10) better translated: "though." "Folded together," i.e., though militarily equipped as an overwhelming army, impregnable as the folded thorns of the East, and drunken with pride and strength, yet should they be devoured as stubble fully dry.

Verse 11 should read as in the Revised Version. Sennacherib, or possibly Rabshakeh, is here intended; but the future Antichrist is pointed to.

"Quiet" (v. 12), i.e., "secure." "Thus," i.e., as dry stubble. "He," i.e., Jehovah. He "passed through" the Assyrian host in judgment and slew an hundred and eighty-five thousand of them, just as He "passed through' the land of Egypt and slew the firstborn. He "passed over" His people at that time to deliver them, and He " passed over " Hezekiah and Jerusalem to protect them, as He promised in Isa. xxxi. 5, saying : " As birds flying," i.e., as a great bird with out-stretched wings " so will Jehovah protect Jerusalem ; He will protect and deliver it ; He will pass over and preserve it."

Israel should be afflicted (v. 12), but only in measure ; the Assyrian, eternally.

Thus was the Assyrian yoke broken from off Hezekiah ; and the Gentile monarch found his grave in the temple of his idol, where he died, slain by his own sons (vs. 13 and 14). The word " it " i.e., the house of his great god, should be supplied after " I will make " (v. 14).

The promise of verse 13 belongs, as to its finality, to the future when the yoke of Antichrist will be broken from off the neck of Israel.

The excited messengers hasting over the mountains to Jerusalem with the glad tidings of the destruction of the Assyrian army, are pictured in verse 15 ; and they illustrate Gospel messengers announcing the glad tidings of the victory of Calvary.

" Solemn feasts " (v. 15), i.e., " joyous festivities." " Perform thy vows," i.e., sing the songs of joy promised when asking for deliverance, for " the wicked," i.e., the wicked-one, the Assyrian monarch, Antichrist, shall be utterly cut off.

A comparison of this verse with Isa. lii. 7 shews Nahum's knowledge of this already existing Scripture and so negatives the second Isaiah theory.

NAHUM II.—The siege, capture, spoliation, and annihilation of Nineveh by the Babylonians under Nabopolassar, father of Nebuchadnezzar, is here predicted and described.

Such is prophecy ! One hundred years beforehand the capture of Nineveh, and the mode of its capture, are minutely foretold.

" He that dasheth in pieces " (v. 1), i.e., Nabopolassar. He was God's battle-axe or hammer. Compare Prov. xxv. 18, Jer. li. 20.

" Thy face " (v. 1), i.e., the walls of Nineveh. The advice here offered to Nineveh is ironical.

The argument binding verses 1 and 2 together is : that as God humbled the Ten Tribes, making use of the Assyrians as His instrument, for they " emptied out " the whole land of northern Palestine, so would He not

merely humble Nineveh but would dash it to pieces. God chastises His people but utterly destroys His enemies.

Verses 3 and 4 describe the Babylonian host. " His," i.e., Nabopolassar. His soldiers were dressed in scarlet and carried red shields. These two verses should read as in the Revised Version. The language vividly describes an army marching into battle. " Fir-trees," i.e., spears made from fir-trees.

Verse 5 pictures the vain effort of the king of Nineveh and his troops to defend the city. " He," i.e., the king of Nineveh " shall recount his worthies," i.e., shall review his best troops. Supply " but "— " but they shall stumble in their march," i.e., they shall prove undisciplined. " The wall thereof," i.e., the wall of Nineveh.

" The rivers " (v. 6), i.e., the Tigris and its canals. These surrounded the city making it practically impregnable. See note on iii. 8.

History states that a flood broke down the river gates of the city and so opened it to the Babylonians. The king, Sardanapalus, seeing the city lost, collected his wives and his treasures into the palace, and setting it on fire, all perished in the flames. The Hebrew verb here translated " dissolved " may better read " become molten." Thus remarkably and minutely does the prophet describe the capture and fate of the king nearly one hundred years before Sardinapolis was born !

" Huzzab " (v. 7), i.e., Nineveh. This verse should read as in the Revised Version. It pictures the women of Nineveh setting out for captivity lamenting and beating their breasts.

" But " (v. 8). This should read " although " in answer to the " yet " of the next line. " Like a pool of water," i.e., filled with men as a pool is filled with water. " Yet they," i.e., the soldiers. " Shall they cry," i.e., their officers.

Verse 9 is addressed to the Babylonians and should read as in the Revised Version. " Glory " here signifies abundance and costliness. Many valuables have been found in the ruins of Nineveh, but no gold nor silver, showing how completely the Babylonians responded to this injunction.

" She shall become empty and void and waste," (v. 10). The three Hebrew words here are similar in sound, each having more syllables than its predecessor, thus expressing the solemnity and finality of the city's doom as being a climax.

" Where is the den of the lions ? " (v. 11). Compare i. 8. In the Hebrew the word " where " expresses wonder and awe. That so great and ancient a city, founded by Nimrod, and deemed impregnable, should so utterly disappear as to make its site uncertain, excites amazement. These three last verses should read as in the Revised Version. Compare 2 Kings xviii. 34.

" In the smoke " (v. 13) rather " into smoke " ; " And the (proud) voice of thy ambassadors shall no more be heard ! "

NAHUM III.—The cause of Nineveh's eternal doom (vs. 1, 4, 19) and the certainty of her doom (vs. 2, 3, 5, to 18) are here set out.

" Bloody " (v. 1), rather, " blood-stained." " The prey departeth not," i.e., " They ceaselessly plunder the defenceless."

The next two verses should read as in the Revised Version. They vividly describe the Babylonian army advancing to the attack— the cracking of the whips urging on the chariot horses ; the noise of the chariot wheels ; the thunder of the cavalry charging with bright sword and glittering spear ; the multitude of the slain Assyrians ; and the victors stumbling over the corpses of the vanquished.

" Whoredoms " (v. 4), i.e., " idolatries," " Harlot " i.e., " idolatress." Idolatry and its accompaniments of oppression and vice, caused the ruin of Nineveh.

Nations are bought and then sold (v. 4) by idolatry. They are redeemed and liberated by Christianity.

" I will discover thy skirts " (v. 5) and I will cast filth upon thee and set thee as a gazing stock " (v. 6). The ancients stripped a debauched woman, exposed her to the public, and she was bespattered with all kinds of filth.

Nineveh's character and doom are here so pictured.

" Populous No " (v. 8), means No-Ammon, i.e., Thebes. (v. 8). This great city, like Nineveh, was so fortified by the Nile and its canals as to be deemed impregnable, yet was it captured by the Assyrians ; and its

stupendous ruins excite to-day the astonishment of the world. The prophet here asks Nineveh was she " better " or more strongly situated than Thebes.

" Drunken " (v. 11), i.e., with the cup of God's wrath. " Hid," i.e., covered up with the sands of the desert.

The language of verse 14 is ironical and is addressed to Nineveh—as are also the three preceding verses. " The brick-kiln," rather, the " brickwork " needed to strengthen the wall of the city.

The argument of verses 15-17 is : that though the soldiers of Nineveh were as countless as the locusts, and her merchants more in number than the stars, yet should they perish as the locusts that flee before the rising sun.

" Shepherds " (v. 18), i.e., " generals." " Slumber," i.e., " sleep the sleep of death." " Dwell in the dust," i.e., " lie down in death."

" Clap the hands " (v. 19), that is, with joy at the destruction of Nineveh. " Thy wickedness," i.e., " thy cruel oppressions."

The doctrine of the prophecy of Nahum is God's faithfulness to His people ; and that however great His patience with their enemies, a day is coming when He will no longer bear with evil ; and that His wrath will be so much the more terrible because of that patience. God cannot be indifferent to the fact of sin. He judged it on behalf of His people at Calvary ; and the rejectors of that atonement must suffer His wrath and know His power in the lake of fire. That wrath is not the anger of Almighty power without intelligence, for He is a stronghold to all who flee to Him for refuge ; and He owns and recognises as His those who thus trust Him. So the eternal doom of Nineveh predicts, and certifies, the eternal doom of Anti-christ, of his city, and of all who, like him, rebel against the Lord of the heavens and of the earth.

The destruction of Thebes occurred about sixty years before Nahum, and that of Nineveh about a hundred years subsequent to him. Yet Nahum frequently refers to the Pentateuch which Germans (who claim to be historians and scholars) declare to have been written more than a hundred years after his death !

HABAKKUK

This Hebrew word means a wrestler. The prophet wrestled with God about the double problem of God's permission of violence and injustice inside the Hebrew Church, and of His using so wicked a nation as the Chaldean to chastise the Church.

This reproving of God by the prophet, and the Divine response to his complaint, form the subject of the Book ; and the sublime poem reviewing God's past action with His people, and His future deliverance of them, concludes the prophecy.

HABAKKUK I—II. 1.—This " burden "—and love felt its weight—concerned Zion and the Divine judgment upon her, actioned by the Chaldeans as God's instruments (v. 1).

The prophet's heart, jealous for God and the Law, asks (vs. 2-4) why God is silent and inactive in view of the cruelties (" iniquity ") and oppressions (" grievance "), and robbery, and violence, and strife, and contention practised by the rich in Zion against the poor owing to the slackness of law and the corrupt administration of justice.

" Slacked " (v. 4), i.e., " benumbed."
" Judgment," i.e., " justice." " Wrong judgment proceedeth," i.e. " perverted justice goeth forth."

The Apostle Paul in Acts xiii. 41, quotes verse 5. His argument was : that just as the Hebrews would not believe Habakkuk foretelling the destruction of Jerusalem by the Chaldeans, and the salvation offered to Israel, so the Hebrews did not believe Paul foretelling the destruction that then impended at the hands of the Romans and the salvation proclaimed through Christ.

Verses 5-11 record the Divine answer to the complaint of verses 2-4.

The answer is : that punishment should certainly fall upon these wicked men, and that the executors of the punishment should be the Chaldeans, a cruel and energetic people, who would mercilessly destroy both land and city and carry their inhabitants into captivity.

" Bitter and hasty " (v. 6), i.e., cruel and impetuous.

" Judgment and dignity " (v. 7), i.e., They will recognise no judge or prince superior to themselves.

" For violence " (v. 9), i.e., for destruction and not for construction.

" Their faces," etc., (v. 9), i.e., their eager faces. The east wind kills all verdure in Palestine ; the Chaldean would be equally destructive.

" Heap dust " (v. 10), i.e., erect earthmounds so as to dominate the walls of Zion.

" He shall transgress and offend " (v. 11). Nebuchadnezzar exceeded the commission given him by God (Isa. xlvii. 6), attributed his success to his military ability, and declared himself to be a god, commanding everyone to worship the golden image (Dan iii.).

Thus will it be with the future Assyrian —the Anti-christ.

In verses 12 to ii. 1. the prophet complains of the Divine action in employing for chastisement a people more wicked than the Hebrews, whom they were commissioned by God to punish. This greatly perplexed Habakkuk.

" He recalls " (v. 12) the everlastingness and the holiness of God, and His ordination and establishment of the Chaldeans to judge and correct Israel.

" We shall not die " (v. 12). The primitive text here reads : " Thou shalt not die."

The plea in verse 13 is that God is too righteous to regard wrong-doing and cruelty with indifference.

" Them that deal treacherously " (v.

13), i.e., the Chaldeans. " The wicked," i.e., the Chaldean. " The man that is more righteous than he," that is, the Israelite.

" And makest men " (v. 14), i.e., the Hebrews. " No ruler," i.e., no defender. The Chaldeans treated men as if they were fish.

" Empty " (v. 17), that is, " keep perpetually filling and emptying their net."

In verse ii. 1, the prophet waits in silence and inward watchfulness the Divine answer to his complaint.

The last line of verse 1 means : " What reponse I shall get to my complaint." The words that follow furnish the answer.

It was pain and mystery to the prophet that his unchanging God (v. 12) should be denied by the instrument He was using (v. 11) ; and that his beloved people should be trodden down by people more wicked than themselves (vs. 13-17). But faith rested in this God and called Him " my Gôd," " my Holy One," " my undying One."

The prophecy is a Song of Ascents from trouble (ch. i.), through trust (ch. ii.), to triumph (ch. iii.)—a triumph meet to be sung of by the Chief Singer on His own stringed instruments. See notes on Ps. cxx.-cxxxv.

HABAKKUK II. 2-20.—Habakkuk's double complaint why God permitted such evils in the Hebrew Church, and why He employed so wicked an instrument to punish them, here received its double answer.

As to the Church, everlasting life was promised to its believing members (v. 4), and, as to the oppressors inside the Church and the Chaldean oppressors outside, five woes (vs. 6, 9, 12, 15 and 19) were pronounced against them ; to be succeeded by an earth filled with the glory of the wrath of God (v. 14).

The prophet kept watching for an answer (v. 1), and he got it (vs. 2-20).

" Write the vision " (v. 2), i.e., that which follows, and which was revealed then to him.

" Upon tables " (v. 2), i.e., box-wood tables overspread with wax. Compare Luke i. 63.

" That he may run," etc., (v. 2). The tables were to be exposed to public view so that readers might run with the joyful tidings to others of redemption for Israel and destruction for Babylon. This verse is frequently misread so as to mean that a person running past would be able to read the tablet.

" Yet " (v. 3), i.e., " Not now." Faith waited with confidence for that which the vision promised ; and so the heart, oppressed by the feelings to which faith itself gave birth, was sustained and comforted. God, Who values faith, would certainly intervene and not tarry.

In verse 4 the righteous man and the unrighteous are contrasted. As to the unrighteous, either Israelite or Chaldean, his soul was lifted up and not upright in him, and his doom should be death. As to the righteous, his soul was humbled, for he lived by faith and should enjoy everlasting life. The one was self-relying, the other self-renouncing.

The apostle Paul quotes this verse in Rom. i. 17, Gal. iii. 11 and Heb. x. 38. In Romans he teaches that the just man's righteousness was a righteousness " from God " ; and, in Galatians, that the righteousness was obtained on the principle of faith, and not of works.

The Chaldean is the main subject of the five following woes. His lust of empire (vs. 5 and 6) ; his lust of wealth (vs. 9-11) ; his lust of magnificence (v. 12) ; his lust of vice (v. 15) ; and his attachment to idolatry, the mother of all sins (v. 19).

" Transgresseth by wine " (v. 5). Compare Daniel v. 1-4.

" All these " (v. 6), i.e., the nations and peoples of verse 5.

" How long " (v. 6). Compare Ps. vi. 3. This is the triumphant " How long " of faith. It declares that the oppressor shall enjoy his possessions but for a brief day.

" Thick clay " (v. 6) This may contemptuously mean gold and silver, which is dug out of the clay ; or oppressive treaties, enscribed on clay tablets, and made with conquered nations ; or vast buildings of brick-work.

" They," " Them " (v. 7,) i.e., these oppressed and plundered peoples of verses 6 and 8.

" Of the land," etc. (v. 8), i.e., " against the land," etc.

" An evil covetousness " (v. 9), i.e., wealth gotten by evil doing ; such as the gain derived from the sale of alcohol and opium and by gambling and the slave-trade.

" His house " (v. 9), i.e., his family. " The power of evil," i.e., the possibility of poverty. Rich men gather wealth in order to establish their families in assured affluence ; but they in reality devise shame to their children and ruin to their own souls because of the injury done to others (v. 10). Sitting in their palaces their guilty consciences hear the stones accusing them of their evil deeds, and they hear the timber confirming the accusation of the stone (v. 11). Compare Luke xix. 40.

God has ordained for the fire the great and strong cities and palaces which the nations weary themselves in building (vs. 12 and 13). Nebuchadnezzar proudly said : " Is not this great Babylon which I have builded ! " but God ordained it for the fire ; and, (v. 14) He will make a demonstration of His power in delivering His people and destroying their enemies, which will compel a world-wide recognition of the righteousness of His past ways and the equity of His judgments. This demonstration will satisfy every heart that is now distressed with the problem of evil, and oppressed by the present effects of God's permission of man's misgovernment.

As a drunkard incites others to drink and to become shameless and bestial (v. 15), so a conquering nation excites other nations to conquest and to corresponding degradation.

" The cup " (v. 16) that is, the cup of God's wrath. " Unto thee," i.e., Babylon.

" The violence of Lebanon " (v. 17), i.e., the violence against Jerusalem and the Temple—here called Lebanon because built with cedar brought from thence. " Cover," i.e., " overwhelm." " The spoiling of wild beasts shall make thee afraid " (R.V.), i.e., the nations, here pictured as wild beasts, would rend the Chaldean monarchy. This was effected by the Medes and Persians.

" Because of human blood shed by thee, and because of violence against the land," etc. Verse 8 refers to the violence suffered by the nations at the hand of the Chaldeans, but verse 17 to that suffered by Palestine and Zion.

An idol may outwardly be splendid (v. 19), but inwardly it is lifeless. " And," read " But." This verse denounces woe to those who to-day use images in worship, saying they help and instruct the people.

On the contrary Jehovah (v. 20) is the living God ; and He will demonstrate this fact so effectually that all the earth will stand hushed to silence before Him. In idolatry the idol is silent and its worshippers eloquent.

This vision was committed to writing because it belongs to the future (vs. 2 and 3).

The great prophecy of verse 14 is here repeated for the fifth and last time—Num. xiv. 21, Ps. lxxii. 19, Isa. vi. 3, xi. 9 and Hab. ii. 14. Contrary to popular opinion that glory will be the glory of His wrath. (See the context of v. 14, and the note on Zeph. iii. 8).

So the prophet learned that God has given liberty of action to man. Hence man is a responsible being. Those who abuse that liberty God will judge, whether they be citizens of Jerusalem or of Babylon.

HABAKKUK III.—This prayer of remembrance, faith and praise, was born of the vision of chapter ii.

The meaning of Shigionoth is obscure.

Verse 2 may be thus paraphrased : " Oh Jehovah, I have heard thy fame and I bowed in reverent worship. Oh Jehovah, repeat Thy doings of old in the midst of these years of affliction, in the midst of these years of sorrow, demonstrate Thy power ; in wrath remember mercy."

The poem recalls God's comings (vs. 3-5) ; His doings (vs. 6-11) ; His goings (vs. 13 and 15) ; and His doings (v. 14).

Verses 3-5 recall Sinai. The " Teman " and " Paran " indicate the desert of Sinai. There He manifested His glory, but hid His Being.

" Horns," i.e., manifestations of power issued from His hand ; but His full power, as also His Being, were hidden (v. 4).

Pestilence and lightning (v. 5) were His attendants in the judgment of Egypt. The pestilence smote the first-born, and the lightnings ran along the ground.

" Measured " (v. 6), i.e., " made to tremble." " The nations," i.e., those that opposed Israel from Egypt to Canaan. Sinai was " scattered," i.e., shattered ; and the " perpetual," i.e., primeval hills did bow.

" Cushan " (v. 7), i.e., Egypt, at the death of the first-born. " The land of Midian," i.e., the country between Egypt and Canaan.

" The rivers " (v. 8), plural of majesty for the great river, the Nile, when turned by Moses into blood. " The sea," i.e., the Red Sea when divided. Pharaoh's horses and chariots of destruction perished in it whilst Immanuel's horses and chariots of salvation triumphed with it.

" Oaths " (v. 9), plural of excellence for the great promise, confirmed with an oath, made to Abraham, and to the Tribes, for they were then in his loins. " Of " should read " to."

" Thou didst cleave the earth with rivers " (v. 9), i.e., He brought forth water out of the flinty rock for their thirst.

" The overflowing of the water " (v. 10), i.e., the Jordan. By a fine poetic figure it is pictured as lifting up its voice and hands in worship.

" Stood still " (v. 11), Hebrew : " continued shining " or "stayed," as in Joshua x. 13. " Like light Thine arrows flew, like lightning, Thy glittering spear." The reference here is to the great victory given to Joshua at Gibeon. See notes on Joshua x.

" The land " (v. 12), i.e., Palestine ; " the heathen," i.e., its inhabitants.

" The head of the house of the wicked " (v. 13), i.e., the chief king ; the " head of his villages," i.e , the lesser kings of Canaan. " The foundation unto the neck," i.e., a total overturning so as to lay bare the foundations.

" Strike through " (v. 14) better, " pierce."
" His staves,'' i.e., his own weapons.

" Me " (v. 14), i.e., Israel.

" The sea," " the heap of great waters (v. 15), i.e., the seven nations of Canaan.

" When I heard " (v. 16), i.e., the predictions of the prior chapter. On hearing Immanuel's fame in the past (v. 2) the prophet worshipped, on hearing the words of the vision revealing the future triumph of the Chaldean, he trembled and shook with grief.

A full stop should be placed after " myself," and what follows should read : " O that I might be at rest when he (the Chaldean) cometh up against the people (of God), for he will overcome them with his troops."

But if not granted this request, and he be fated to witness the devastation of the country (v. 17), yet will the prophet rejoice in the Lord, Who, as His strength, will enable him morally to walk above the trials and sorrows of the time, just as a hind walks securely upon the edge of the giddiest precipices.

Such is the triumph of faith ! It trusts God in the darkest hours and sharpest trials ; awaits His vindication of His action ; and looks forward with conviction to the sure dawning of the promised day of glory.

ZEPHANIAH

This prophet was a contemporary of Habakkuk and Jeremiah. As "Hizkiah" should read "Hezekiah" it is thought that he was a great great-grandson of that monarch. He predicts the desolation of Nineveh (ii. 13), reveals the moral condition of Jerusalem under the enforced reformation of king Josiah, and foretells the destruction of that city and the captivity of its people by Nebuchadnezzar.

Man having after the Flood established idolatry (Rom. i. 21-23), God chose the Hebrew people, revealed Himself to them and commissioned them to win the nations from idols to Him. But they forsook Him and joined themselves to idols, and, as a just judgment, the very nations whom they should have saved became the agents by whom their privileges were lost.

So long, however, as they maintained ever so imperfect a testimony for truth, God, Who is slow to anger, bore patiently with them and with the nations; and in order to recover them He sent them prophets from Samuel to John the Baptist, but in vain. Hence their present and past misery, and that of the nations. Judgment began with the Chaldeans because they, by their cruelties, exceeded the commission given to them (Jer. xxv. 9).

ZEPHANIAH I.—The Gospel in Zephaniah, as in the Epistle to the Romans (Rom. i. 18), begins with the wrath of God. All other Gospels are false.

"Stumbling blocks with the wicked" (v. 3), i.e., idols and their worshippers.

"The remnant of Baal" (v. 4); king Josiah destroyed idolatry outwardly but the people clave to it inwardly. "Chemarim," i.e., the black-robed priests of Baal here found in fellowship with the priests of Jehovah.

"Swear by the Lord" (v. 5), i.e., profess allegiance to Him.

Four companies appear in verses 5 and 6. Idolaters, uniters of Jehovah and idols, backsliders and agnostics. The wrath of God will not distinguish between these. At that day, as to-day, it was fashionable to profess and practise the fundamental unity of all religions, and so to make the religion of the Bible complementary to the great religions of the East. But there are only two religions in existence, and they are antagonistic, and the one will destroy the other. These religions are : Man's religion and God's religion.

"The day of the Lord" (v. 7), i.e., the Chaldean invasion. "A sacrifice," i.e., the guilty Jews. "His guests," i.e., the Chaldeans.

Verse 8 was fulfilled in Jeremiah xxxix. 6. "Strange," i.e., "foreign."

"Those that leap" (v. 9), i.e., the servants of the rich men who rob the houses of the poor.

Such, under the royal reformation of Josiah, was the real moral condition of Jerusalem. Violence and idolatry cried aloud for judgment.

Verses 10 and 11 describe the arrival of the Chaldean army at Jerusalem and its victorious penetration of the city from the northern Fishgate to Maktesh where the wealthy merchants had their palaces. "The hills," i.e., Ophel, Zion and Moriah, all of which were within the city.

"With candles" (v. 12), i.e., the Chaldean soldiers.

As wine becomes thick when undisturbed, so the rich become spiritually insensible through prosperity.

If Satan have half the heart he is sure to secure all; if half the heart be offered to God He will have none.

Verses 13-18 give a vivid picture of the sack of Jerusalem, and of the ruin of the whole country. Silver and gold (v. 18) may mean idols of silver and idols of gold.

ZEPHANIAH II.—The first three verses are a call to Israel to repent.

" Not desired " (v. 1), better, " not desirous of convening such a gathering."

Verse 2 may be thus paraphrased : " Before the judgment decree fall bring forth works meet for repentance, (ah, the day passeth as the chaff, i.e., the opportunity for repentance is short-lived), before the fierce anger of Jehovah come upon you, before the day of Jehovah's anger come upon you."

The third verse is addressed to King Josiah and his supporters who wrought God's judgment (1 Kings xiii. 2, 2 Kings xxiii. 17) upon the idols, to keep on seeking the Lord and seeking righteousness and meekness, for so escape might be possible for them. Compare Isaiah xxvi. 20., and the name Zephaniah, which means : " Hidden by Jehovah."

The remainder of the chapter predicts the fierce anger of God upon the Philistines on the west, the Moabites and Ammonites on the east, the Egyptians on the south (v. 12), and the Assyrians in the north.

This arrangement of west, east, south and north is unusual and peculiar.

In the Hebrew text there is a play upon the words Gaza, Ashkelon, Ashdod and Ekron.

The Philistines had a fifth city, Gath, in the days of Samuel, but it was subsequently captured by, and attached to Judah (1 Chron. xviii. 1 and 2 Kings xviii. 8). Jeremiah, Amos, and Zechariah similarly mention only four cities of the Philistines. The Cherethites and the Philistines were one and the same nation.

Their country would become the possession of the Israelites (vs. 6 and 7). This prophecy was fulfilled on the return of the Jews from the Babylonian exile.

As at that time God cleared the land of its inhabitants in order to make room for the returned captives, so may it be that now He is acting similarly in favour of the present day Zionists.

" He will famish " (v. 11), i.e., deprive the idols of their worshippers. " Everyone from his place," i.e., his own Gentile home. Compare John iv. 21.

" Ethiopians " (v. 21), i.e., Egyptians. " My sword," i.e., Nebuchednezzar (Jer. xxv. 9).

" He " (v. 13), i.e., Nebuchednezzar.

ZEPHANIAH III.—" Filthy " (v. 1) rather, " rebellious " (R.V.). " Her," i.e., Jerusalem. She was rebellious, for she " obeyed not the voice " (v. 2) ; she was idolatrous, for she polluted the Temple with idols (v. 4) ; and she was oppressing, for her princes and judges were as devouring lions and evening wolves. Thus the root of civil and religious corruption is departure from the Bible.

" Her God " (v. 2). Compare Matt. xxiii. 37. The love that throbs in these words " Her God " is pathetic. Proud and polluted as Jerusalem was, yet He said she was His, and that He was " her God."

Princes, judges, preachers and priests (vs. 3 and 4) were workers of iniquity and teachers of falsehood. " They gnaw not," etc., better translated : " They defer not till to-morrow to gnaw the bones." Ravenous wolves gnaw the bones immediately they have devoured the flesh.

Jehovah as a just Judge (v. 5) is here contrasted with the unjust judges of verse 3.

Five statements are made with respect to Him and in contrast to the ordinary Eastern judge. First : He was accessible (" in the midst"). Second : He was righteous (" He will not do iniquity "). Third : He attended the Court diligently (" every morning "). Fourth : His decisions stood the light (" His judgment "). Fifth : He was dependable and impartial (" He faileth not ").

Eastern judges, both ancient and modern, notoriously fail in all these characteristics.

Such will be the administration of justice by Immanuel in the future at Jerusalem, for law shall go forth from Zion (Isa. ii. 3).

" The unjust " (v. 5), i.e., the unrighteous judges of verse 3.

The argument of verses 6 and 7 is : That surely it was to be expected that the total destruction of the neighbouring nations (ii. 4-15) would have warned Jerusalem so that she would not compel God to cut her off, however sternly He might punish her ; but she refused to learn the lesson, and, on the contrary, set herself with the greatest eagerness to more deeply corrupt her conduct both civil and religious. " Their dwelling," i.e., Jerusalem.

" Ye " (v. 8), i.e., the little flock that received instruction, that confided in Jehovah, and that drew near to Him (v. 2).

" The day that I rise up to the prey "

(v. 8), i.e., the day of the wrath of God pointed to in the remaining members of the verse. Until that day corruption and injustice will continue; and they can only be endured by a faith that waits for that day. Compare James v. 7.

" My jealousy " (v. 8), i.e., God's jealous love for the little flock that wait upon Him. It will reveal itself in the destruction of their oppressors. This last sentence of this verse explains the word " glory " in Habakkuk, ii. 14. This latter verse is frequently quoted by popular preachers, and misinterpreted, but Zephaniah iii. 8 is never noticed.

This verse is remarkable as being the only one in the Hebrew Bible containing all the letters of the Hebrew Alphabet.

In this verse and those which follow, God reveals to the little flock that love Him His future purposes of judgment upon their foes and deliverance for themselves. Judgment on these foes does not belong to them but to Him; and all hope of reformation being lost, they are taught to wait on Him till He should rise up to banish evil and restore righteousness.

" Then " (v. 9), i.e., immediately after the judgment of verse 8. " A pure language," i.e., the reverse of the confusion of tongues caused at Babel. Perhaps this pure and universal language will be Hebrew.

Verse 10 should read as in the Revised Version margin.

The statement in the first line of verse 11, does not mean that Christian people may live sinful lives, and not be ashamed in heaven when recalling such conduct, but it means that the true servants of Immanuel will no longer be ashamed of the actions of their professed brethren, for all such insincere members will be taken away out of the midst of Zion (v. 11) and only sincere members retained there (v. 12).

These sincere believers will not oppress the poor (" iniquity "), nor follow idols (" lies "), nor profess loyalty with the tongue but not with the heart, for in their mouth will be found no guile (Rev. xiv. 4).

The Holy Spirit in verses 14-17 provides the song which happy Israel will sing in the day of her restoration, and which, through the preceding night, she can in faith sing.

" Thy judgments " (v. 15), i.e., Divine chastisements because of sin. " He hath cast out thy foes." Sins are first removed, then troubles; happiness follows holiness. See notes on Josh. xx.

" The king of Israel, Jehovah " (v. 15), i.e., the Messiah.

" Evil " (v. 15), i.e., affliction.

" Be slack " (v. 16), i.e., hang in despondency.

Verse 17 contrasts with verse 5; the latter is past; the former, future. In verse 5, He was in the midst of rebellious Jerusalem offering Himself as a righteous judge able to correct its evils; in verse 17, He will reside in redeemed Jerusalem mighty to prevent any evil. Contrast also " He " (4 times, v. 17) and " she " (4 times, v. 2).

In creation He rested in the perfection of His work (Gen. ii. 1-3); in redemption (v. 17) He will rest in the perfection of His love. Love is oft-times too deep for utterance. He will not need to chide His people then.

The corruption of the Hebrew Church (v. 18), and the consequent reproach levelled at it by the heathen, was a burden upon the hearts that lived in fellowship with God. The great feasts (Lev. xxiii.) of Jehovah had become feasts of the Jews (John v. 1), and were degraded or abandoned. So to-day, the nations justly reproach the professing Christian Church—so deeply corrupted—and the hearts of God's servants are consequently burdened.

The prophecy closes with a repeated promise of future restoration for the Hebrew Church. She will be saved and gathered (v. 19) and restored to Palestine (v. 20); all that afflict her will be undone; and she will be clothed with praise and fame in every land.

Three times the statement " Jehovah in the midst " occurs in the chapter; and the three correspond with John xix. 18, xx. 19 and Rev. vii. 17.

First: " In the midst " to cleanse (v. 5). Love brought Him into the midst of the evil of verses 1 to 9, as it did " in the midst " between the malefactors, that He might bless and save and cleanse. Second: " In the midst " (v. 15) to conquer and chase away enemies and fears, as in John xx. He can conquer and cast out of the life everything that weakens. Third: " In the midst " (v. 17) to crown with the victorious life of " fruit," " more fruit," and " much fruit " (John xv.) in this world, and with the crown of righteousness in the world to come. So He cleanses, He conquers, and He crowns

HAGGAI

The name means "My feast." He is the first of the post-exilic prophets, and is consequently separated from Zephaniah by the seventy years of the Babylonian captivity.

He was sent by God with four messages for the princes and people of Jerusalem. The first two occupy chapter i. and chapter ii. vs. 1-9 ; the third and fourth, the remainder of the prophecy.

The re-building of the Temple at Jerusalem is the theme of the Book.

It records the unwillingness of the returned Exiles to build (i. 2) ; their shame of the inferiority of the new House (ii. 3) ; and their fear of the Persian Government because they built without special permission (Ezra iv. to vi.).

In reply to their unwillingness to build His House, God rebuked them for their energy in building their own houses (i. 4) ; in respect to their feeling of shame He announced that the House would be more glorious than Solomon's (ii. 9) ; and to dismiss their fear He said He would everthrow not only the Persian throne (ii. 22) but all thrones (ii. 6 and 7).

On the part of the people there was want of interest and fear ; on the part of God, chastisement (i. 6, and ii. 16-19) and encouragement (ii. 4-9).

Deprived of almost everything symbolic and outward, Israel had Jehovah Himself (ii. 4) , and the promise that He would be as faithful to them in their present weakness as in their glorious past.

HAGGAI I.—This Darius was Darius Hystaspes Ahasuerus Artaxerxes the Persian. He reigned about fifteen years after the Cyrus who commanded the building of the city and the laying of the foundation of the Temple (Ezra i. and Isa. xlv. 13).

Zerubbabel, i.e., " born in Babylon," was of the royal house of Judah (1 Chron iii. 19, Ezra ii. 2. iii. 2), He was, therefore, grandson of Jehoiachin (1 Chron iii. 17. Neh. xii. i. Matt. i. 12), and as a son of David a type of Messiah the King (ii. 23).

If the time had not come to build Jehovah's House it therefore had not come to build their own ceiled houses (v. 4). Unbelief and fear readily accept any excuse (Ezra iv. 24).

" Ways " (v. 5), i.e., experiences. The prophet asks them to study the facts set out in verse 6.

" The house " (v. 8), i.e., the Temple. " I will take pleasure in it," i.e., however poor and faulty your effort may be I will be pleased with it (ch. ii. 7).

God first is the secret of spiritual and temporal prosperity (v. 9).

The obedient heart of verse 12 always is rewarded with the " I am with you " of verse 13.

The prophetic message was delivered on the first of the sixth month (v. i.) and obeyed in the twenty-fourth of the same month (v. 15). Such is the slowness of the heart to accept and obey the word of the Lord !

To divert money from God's work to personal use causes poverty of soul and oftentimes of pocket (v. 6).

The Persian throne, to which, because of departure from the Law, Israel was subjected, is here recognised (v. 1), whilst, at the same time, Jehovah was with His people to animate and bless them. Thus it is His will that the things of God be rendered to God, and the things of Caesar to Caesar (Mark. xii. 17).

Unbelief never fails of arguments, but always has this capital defect that it leaves God out. The religious argument was : that the time, i.e., the seventy years of captivity, was not yet expired, and, therefore, the

674

building of the Temple should wait (i. 2) ; and the civil argument was : that they had not the king's permission (Ezra iv.).

The world did not oppose the building of the ceiled houses, but it did oppose the building of God's House.

It is so to-day. The world applauds a philanthropic, or social building, but opposes soulwinning, and the adding of living stones to the spiritual temple of God.

It is easy to please God though circumstances may hinder the doing of a great thing for God ; and the glory of God, and that which glorifies Him, are precious to the heart that loves Him (i. 8).

HAGGAI II.—Haggai's second prophecy is contained in verses 1-9.

Ezra iii. 12, 13 records the grief of those who had seen the first temple (v. 3).

Though God could not, because of their conduct, manifest His power and glory as in the days of Solomon, yet He was with them in their weakness, according to His promise that He made with them when bringing them out of Egypt (vs. 4 and 5) ; hence they were not to fear the supposed anger of the Persian Monarch, but to keep on building, relying on the reality of this great promise ; and Haggai added that, as to all earthly empires, the time would come when in the course of a few years—" a little time "—compare Rev. i. 1, and Luke xviii. 8—He would, once for all and finally, overthrow all earthly governments.

" The Desire of all nations " (v. 7), i.e., the Messiah. Not only is He the Deliverer subconsciously desired of all nations, but He will bring all the desirable things desired by the nations, e.g., peace, health, abundance and happiness.

" This House " (v. 7). In Haggai Solomon's Temple, Zerubbabel's Temple, Herod's Temple, and Ezekiel's future Temple are all regarded as one House ; and so they were, and are, prophetically.

The appearing of Christ as the moral Glory of God in the Temple at His first advent, is here over-leaped and His future apparition in glory predicted. He will then " fill " the House manifestly with glory.

" The Spirit " (v. 8) points to the excellency of that glory above the mere material

ornamentation of gold and silver. The absence of these precious metals made the people ashamed of the House ; but they were assured that its last glory should be greater than its first glory (v. 9, R.V.) ; and that it should be the dwelling-place and throne of the Prince of Peace.

The third prophecy occupies verses 10-19.

Sacrifices, however holy in themselves, cannot sanctify disobedience and self-will (vs. 12-14). That which is holy cannot sanctify what is profane ; but that which is unclean defiles that which is holy. The presence of evil destroys holiness, but the presence of God excludes evil ; and when He is acknowledged, the power of His presence banishes defilement and brings blessing (v. 19).

The legislation of verses 12 and 13 is found in Lev. vi. 27 and x. 10, 11.

The people's offerings were unclean because the offerers were unholy (v. 14).

" There " (v. 14), i.e., " the altar of Ezra iii. 2.

" Upward " (v. 15), i.e., backward ; verse 18, i.e., forward.

" Since those days were " (v. 16), i.e., during all that time.

" Blasting and mildew " (v. 17), i.e., drought and excessive rain.

The answer to the question in verse 19, is, " No " ; and the argument is that though it was the month of December, the harvest was not yet gathered and saved ; and the encouragement was that from this very date, because of their obedience, chastisement would cease and blessing would commence ; and the people were urged to observe and record the fact.

The fourth and last prophecy is that of verses 20-23 given on the same day as the third prophecy.

Addressed to Zerubbabel it actually concerns Him of whom Zerubbabel was a type, the Messiah, God's chosen One, the Signet Ring on the Hand that is to overthrow all thrones ; and the vision teaches that war and fratricidal slaughter will continue up to the advent of the Great King of Israel.

Pharaoh handed his signet ring to Joseph, and Xerxes, his to Haman, as expressing a delegation of Royal Authority.

ZECHARIAH

As Zephaniah means "Hidden by Jehovah" so Zechariah means "Remembered by Jehovah." Earthly monarchs do not always remember those whom they have promised to hide ; but there need be no misgiving as to God's remembrance.

The subject of this Book is the City, as that of the prior Book was the Temple.

The first prophecy of Zechariah was uttered between Haggai's second and third messages ; and, therefore, was given sixteen years after the Restoration.

The Book not only deals with the judgment of the nations which then oppressed Israel, and with the establishment of Jerusalem, but it predicts the final and glorious restoration of Zion, and the punishment of the nations which will then oppress her.

The advent and presence of Jehovah Messiah, and the manifestation of His power at, and from, Jerusalem, has a prominent place in the prophecy.

The love that provided the Captives with the two prophets Ezekiel and Daniel; provided the returned Exiles with the two prophets Haggai and Zechariah. However sinful in the one case, or feeble in the other, God thus maintained relationship with His people, and that by a double bond.

The structure of the Book presents eight symbols (i-vi.), four prophecies (vii.-viii.) and two burdens (ix.-xiv.). This is interesting, for four is the half of eight and two is the half of four, and is evidently designed.

ZECHARIAH I.—Zechariah is thought by many to be the prophet pointed to in Matt. xxiii. 35, but more probably it was the Zechariah of 2 Chron. xxiv. 20 ; for as Genesis is the first Book of the Hebrew Bible, so 2 Chronicles is the last.

Zechariah was a priest. Few of the prophets were priests ; the majority were what are ignorantly called laymen.

"Your fathers " (v. 2), i.e., those referred to in verses 4-6.

"Turn ye " (v. 3), i.e., sincerely in your hearts, and not only outwardly in your renunciation of idolatry — described in verse 4. as " evil ways and evil doings."

"Take hold " (v. 6), i.e., " overtake." The argument is : that both preachers and hearers (v. 5) had died, but the message of the preachers being Divine was not dead (v. 6), and, therefore, the judgment predicted overtook Jerusalem, and she was carried into captivity.

The judgment bore fruit ; the Exiles turned from idols and acknowledged the justice of their punishment (v. 6) ; and now God would take knowledge of the conduct of their oppressors to whom He had committed the government of the world, but who, at ease themselves (v. 11), were indifferent to the misery and ruin of God's people.

But Jehovah cared for them (vs. 14-16), and so He sent forth His instruments (v. 10) to execute His wrath upon the Chaldeans (ii. 8)—as He sent, and will send other instruments (v. 20) to judge the past, present, and future enemies of Zion (v. 21).

" A Man " (v. 8), i.e., " the Son of Man " to Whom judgment is committed (Acts xvii. 31).

The myrtle-trees in the bottom (v. 8), symbolize the Hebrew Church in a condition of weakness. Instead of the briar of Zedekiah's day (Jer. lii.) there had now come up the myrtle of Zechariah's day. But this was the Lord s doing and it was marvellous in their eyes (Isa. lv. 13).

The Horseman that stood (vs. 8-10 and 11) among the myrtle-trees is thus mysteriously regarded as a unity with the horse on which He rode. The other horses had angelic riders, also identified with the horses on which they rode, for they " answered " (v. 11). This bears a curious resemblance to the mythical Centaurs of the Ancient Greeks.

Here the Son of Man, standing in the midst of His Church, sends forth His angels, as such resembling Himself, to execute His wrath upon the Chaldean nation.

" The Angel of Jehovah " (v. 12), i.e., the Rider on the red horse, Israel's Redeemer, hearing of the indifference of earthly governments to the desolation of Jerusalem, pleads for the promised deliverance.

The response to the plea is given in verses 13-17.

" The heathen " (v. 15), i.e., the Chaldeans. " At ease," i.e., " indifferent." " A little displeased," i.e., with Jerusalem. " They helped forward the affliction," i.e., the Chaldeans exceeded their commission to punish Jerusalem.

" A line," etc., (v. 16), i.e., Jerusalem was to be rebuilt.

" My cities " (v. 17), i.e., Zion and Jerusalem.

" Shall yet choose " (v. 17), i.e., demonstrate that I have chosen.

" Four horns " (v. 18), i.e., the Four empires of Babylon, Greece, Persia and Rome; or Syria, Assyria, Nineveh and Babylon.

Four carpenters " (v. 20), rather, four mechanics, that is Divine instruments, or agencies, raised up by God to overthrow these empires. Perhaps these represent angelic agents.

" Fray " (v. 21), Old English word for " affray," that is, to terrify.

As in Daniel and the Revelation interpreting angels explained the visions to the Prophets, so also similar help was given to Zechariah.

ZECHARIAH II.—" Went forth " (v. 3), rather : " came forward."

" This young man " (v. 4), i.e., the man of verse 1, " saying : (' Stop ! It is needless to measure it) Jerusalem shall be inhabited as a city without walls."

The Arabs build watch-fires for a protection round their camps, but Messiah will be a wall of fire to Jerusalem, and a canopy of glory in the midst of her (v. 5).

Verses 6 and 7 should read as in the Revised Version. Up to a certain point this invitation was obeyed under the reign of Cyrus, but its accomplishment awaits the future when the Hebrew Church will be in subjection to that which will be the Babylon that is to come, and when the Messiah will manifest Himself in an irresistible glory.

" After the glory " (v. 8), i.e., the glory of His judgment upon Israel, hath He (God the Father) now sent Me (God the Son) unto the nations, i.e., the great nation, the Chaldean (i. 8), to judge it.

" I will shake mine hand upon them " (v. 9) i.e., upon the Chaldeans, and they shall become a spoil to the subject nations, i.e., the Medes and Persians. History confirms this. A mere shake of His hand sufficed to overthrow the mighty Chaldean Empire.

As Rider on the red horse, His mission was to send out the angelic riders to destroy Babylon and restore Zion.

The Deity and Humanity of Messiah are here asserted, for He is the Sender in the one case, and the Sent in the other.

This overthrow of Babylon and restoration of Zion but feebly picture the future deliverance of Jerusalem ; for in that day whole nations will be converted to God, and shall become one with the Hebrew people and members of that Church ; but the special promises of supremacy and priesthood to Israel will be fulfilled, for Zion shall be His throne, Judah His portion, and Palestine His land.

" Shall know " (vs. 9 and 11), i.e., shall get to know by demonstration. Verse 9 predicts Messiah's power in the destruction of Zion's foes, and verse 11, His grace in Zion's deliverance and exaltation.

During this present period of His indignation against Israel He is silent, and the mouths of the nations are filled with proud boasting (v. 13). But the day is coming when He will come forth from His present retirement. He will then utter His voice, and that a Mighty Voice, and all nations shall stand in speechless terror before Him.

These first three visions concern Israel's outward prosperity, and the following three her inward purity. Nations as well as individuals must be cleansed from their sins and endowed with a new moral nature or else prosperity will be a hindrance instead of a help to them. Beautifying a pump will not purify the foul water that is in the well.

The man of verse 1 is understood by some to intend Messiah who is to build the city (i. 16) as well as the Temple of Jerusalem (vi. 12), but Zechariah did not recognise him to be such, as is evident from his familiar style in addressing him (v. 2) ; and, further, Messiah, being God, would not need to measure the city.

ZECHARIAH III.—The power which, in the previous chapter, restored Jerusalem is in this chapter anticipated by the grace which cleansed her. She was guilty and polluted, and how could such a city be restored? This problem is here resolved.

Joshua represented the nation. He was clothed with filthy garments. Satan claimed him as his lawful captive. Joshua was speechless ; but so was Satan ; for as Joshua's lips were closed by the fact of sin, so Satan's were closed by the fact of election (v. 2).

Had the Angel of Jehovah urged Joshua's repentance, or religious position, Satan could have effectively replied, but what argument could he find against God choosing Jerusalem? None.

As to Joshua the Angel said he had no moral value ; that he was like to a brand plucked out of the fire ; but that God had chosen to pluck him out.

Joshua was cleansed, clothed and crowned (vs. 4 and 5). He did nothing, and said nothing. The Angel of Jehovah did everything.

Such is the Divine way of salvation. It is based on election and effected by atonement. Sin is banished, but not the sinner. His vileness is removed, and he is clothed with the robes of righteousness, and crowned with life.

If Joshua the High Priest of the Hebrew Church when brought into the light of God, was found guilty and polluted, it is manifest that ordinary people are equally impure and need a spotless righteousness. This righteousness is operated by the atoning Saviour of verse 9.

" The Angel of Jehovah " (v. 1), i.e., the Lord Jesus.

" Change of raiment " (v. 4), i.e., " shining garments " in contrast to the " filthy garments " of verse 3.

" Places " (v. 7), i.e., " a place of dignity." " These that stand by," i.e., the angelic princes attending Messiah's throne.

" Men wondered at " (v. 8), i.e., men having a typical character (R.V.). Joshua and his fellow-priests pictured a wonder, that is, the Great High Priest and His fellows (Heb. i. 9). Israel will then be a kingdom of priests.

" The Branch " (v. 8), " the stone " (v. 9), i.e., Christ as the Eternal Life and as the Rock of Ages.

The absence of David's throne, and the inferiority of the Temple foundation, discouraged the returned Exiles, but the prophet encouraged them with the prediction that the Branch of David should spring forth, and that He, as the Rock of Ages and Stone of Israel (Gen. xlix. 24), would be the glorious foundation stone of the true Temple of Jehovah.

For the relation of the title " Branch " to the four Gospels see notes on Isa. iv. 2. Jer. xxiii. 5 and 6. xxxiii. 15, and Zech. vi. 12.

" Upon one stone " (v. 9), i.e. " fixed upon that one stone." " The seven eyes of Jehovah " are fastened with the satisfied delight of perfect intelligence upon the Messiah, the Stone of Israel. Hence the voice kept repeating from heaven, " This is my beloved Son in Whom I am well pleased."

The " seven eyes of Jehovah " appear in 2 Chron. xvi. 9, Zech. iii. 9, iv. 10 and Rev. v. 6. All are connected with the Messiah and Jerusalem, and the possession and government of the earth.

Messiah's " fellows " are Israel. The nation will be a nation of priests sitting before Him, i.e., enthroned with Him as priests, and the redeemed nations will be the members of the Church. They will together form the Church of the future, the only Church God has, or ever will have, upon earth. That is, and will be, the True Catholic-Church, for it will be universal. The heavenly Church, that is, the Church of the Epistle to the Ephesians, is altogether distinct. It has no connection with the earth. It is taken out of it.

Because God will engrave the graving of that Stone (v. 9) it will be perfect in excellence as in strength (Heb. x. 5).

Christ, as the Branch, supplies life and food to his people, who rest beneath its shadow ; and, as the Stone, He is to them an imperishable foundation.

" In one day " (v. 9), i.e., the day of Calvary. See notes on Jude 9 as to " the body of Moses," i.e., the Hebrew Church symbolized by Joshua in this chapter.

" In that day " (v. 10), i.e., the day of Gospel grace when the representatives of Israel (Matt. xxviii. 19), will invite the Gentile (the " neighbour,") to enter the

Hebrew Church, here figured as the vine and the fig-tree.

Man-made garments are original, but insufficient (Gen. iii. 7), natural, but unclean (Zech. iii. 3), fashionable, but worthless (Isa. lxiv. 6), and patched, but made worse (Mark ii. 21).

ZECHARIAH IV.—The lamp-stand here pictures the Hebrew Church, and the two " sons of oil " are Zerubbabel and Joshua. They represent Christ in His relation to that Church as King and Priest.

The vision reaches on to Revelation xi., for two other representative " sons of oil " appear, but with this difference, that they themselves are lamp-stands as well as olive-trees.

The message of the vision to Zerubbabel was, that not by military might, or political power, but by spiritual energy he would certainly complete the building of the Temple (v. 6).

This seven-branched lamp-stand corresponded to that in the Tabernacle.

However great the mountain, i.e., the obstacle (v. 7) opposing God's work, it can be levelled before a man of God energized by the Spirit of God.

Grace laid the foundation, i.e., the First Advent (iii. 9), and Grace will place the head-stone, i.e., the Second Advent (v. 7). Hence, the repetition of " Grace, grace." He who begins a good work perfects it (Phil. i. 6). All God's activities with man, whether as a repentant sinner or a worshiping believer, are based upon grace.

Zerubbabel only recognised and praised the grace that founded and completed the House, but Jehovah recognised the hands of Zerubbabel in the foundation, the building, and the completion of the House (v. 9). This principle reappears in the parable of the pounds (Luke xix. 16). The servant says : " Lord *Thy* pound hath gained ten pounds " ; but the Master replies, " Well done, *thou* hast been faithful."

Messiah's saving work demonstrates the character and success of His mission (v. 9, with ii. 9 and 11).

" The plummet " (v. 10) signified the completion of the Temple.

" They " (v. 10), i.e., those who had despised the meanness of the foundation (Ezra iii. 12). " Those seven," i.e., the seven lamps (v. 2) representing the eyes of the Lord.

He shares the people's joy in the completion of the work.

Those eyes (iii. 9) being all-seeing, could well provide for, and defend, Zerubbabel.

Christ is the Author and Finisher of faith ; and hence He was the Author and Finisher of this Temple. He was the Divine Zerubbabel, the Divine Son of David, the King (v. 9).

The Hebrew Church was designed to be, and will yet be, a golden lamp-stand—gold representing Divine relationship—which will enlighten the whole world—Christ, as king and Priest, ministering the Holy Spirit as the oil to nourish the light.

ZECHARIAH V.—" The flying roll " (v. 1) and " the flying ephah " (v. 9) are the sixth and seventh visions of the first section of this Book. The book was open and had two pages.

God can have no fellowship with evil ; wherever, therefore, His Word penetrates evil must withdraw. The flying roll banished the winged ephah.

The Gospel message having converted a Scottish woman, on returning home she took the large whisky-jar out of the cupboard and threw it down the mountain side. Her husband, remonstrating, she said : " the Lord has come into this house and the whisky must go out."

When God sets up his House in the land (ch. iv.) His Word enters (ch. v.) to judge and sentence all that is not in harmony with that House. Hence the dimensions of the roll and the house were equal (Exod xxvi.). The roll, thirty feet by fifteen (all multiples of five, the number of grace) was open so that it could be read. It figured the prophetic word of Lev. xxvi., Deut. xxviii. and the denunciation of Isaiah and his fellow prophets against idolatry (" swearing " v. 3) and oppression (" stealing "), i.e., the violation of the two Tables of the Law. The one " side " or page of the roll corresponded to the first table of the Law, i.e., " Thou shalt love Jehovah thy God "; the other page, to the second table, i.e., " and thy neighbour as thyself."

Law denounces death upon law-breakers. That is its function. Hence the word " curse " (v. 3), means " sentence of death " (Rom. v. 12, and Gal. iii. 10).

" The whole earth " (v. 3) ; escape was consequently impossible. " According to it " ; therefore the word of the roll was to be the judge, and not man's religious opinions.

God's judgment is personal, comprehensive, and eternal (v. 4).

An ephah is a dry measure containing three measures of meal (Matt. xiii. 33). All idolatrous systems are similar. They are here justly presented under the symbol of a debauched wom

" Their eye " (v. 6, Heb.), i.e., their evil purpose (LXX.) that is, the aim of the woman and her confederates was to " leaven " the whole nation (Matt. xiii. 3).

Verses 6-8 should be read as in the Revised Version. The ephah had a cover of lead. The angel raised the cover, called the prophet's attention to the woman inside the ephah, and said she personated wickedness. She apparently tried to come out, but the angel thrust her back, and replaced the lead weight upon the mouth of the ephah. It was then borne by two other women to Babel in the plain of Shinar, and set down there upon the original foundation laid for it by Nimrod.

God's Temple was placed at Jerusalem, and its lampstand was flanked by the two sons of oil. Satan's temple was placed at Babylon, and its light flanked by the two women of poison.

The contrast between the roll and the ephah is striking. The roll was open ; the ephah, closed. The roll moved propelled by an inner life, for the Word of God is living ; the ephah, with its three women and its leaden cover, was borne by an infernal spirit, or wind, which filled the unclean wings of the two women, for the stork was an unclean bird. The roll was righteousness, it judged evil ; the ephah was wickedness, it cherished evil, and hence it could not remain in the Holy Land. " Wind," i.e., spirit. See note on Hosea iv. 19.

This ephah was perhaps Satan's travesty of the Ark in the Tabernacle. Within the Ark was righteousness, i.e., the Tables of the Law, the manna and Aaron's rod that budded. At the ends of the Ark were the two Cherubim with wings. All was of gold and precious wood.

The ephah was also a kind of chest, its lid was of lead as opposed to the golden lid of the Ark. Within it was wickedness, and on either side of it impure women with unclean wings. The Ark was fixed ; the ephah fugitive.

The vision, perhaps, predicts that the Roman and Grecian Churches will unite, and will carry their hidden idolatrous worship—hidden to man but not to God— back to its birthplace at Babylon, where they will build a magnificent temple for its home. Contrast the woman of Rev. xii. 13-17 (see Note), and compare Rev. xvii. where, the leaden lid being removed, the harlot issues forth in all her idolatrous glory.

The ephah, not *an* ephah (v. 6, R.V.), may be the ephah of Matt. xiii. 33. It contained three measures of meal, i.e., the three classes of the Hebrew nation—the priests, the nobles and the people.

ZECHARIAH VI.—This eighth and last vision of the first section of the Book of Zechariah corresponds with the first vision.

In the one the fragrant myrtle represents the Hebrew Church ; in the other; the two mountains of brass symbolize the proud Grecian governments of Syria and Egypt— the Hebrew Church being situated in the " bottom," between these two great " mountains."

The Hebrew Church, prior to the Captivity a bramble, is now become a myrtle (Isa. lv. 13), and the Author of the miracle stands in her midst and receives the report from His swift messengers of the indifference of the nations to the sorrows and sufferings of His people (ch. i.).

The result of the report is the despatch from the valley of the chariots of His power and wrath to punish Antiochus on the north, Ptolemy in the south, and the lesser monarchs east and west. Antiochus being the greatest oppressor of Zion peculiar satisfaction is expressed (v. 8) at his punishment.

God governs immediately or mediately. He now governs mediately ; for He has committed the government of the earth to Nebuchadnezzar and his successors. This period of history He describes as " the Times of the Gentiles." But He limits the delegated authority ; and though to the historians chaos is the result, yet He uses instruments the result of whose activity is the accomplishment of His will. The end will manifest the perfection of His moral character and the fulness of His wisdom. He honours man by giving him scope for the exercise of his free will.

But the great principle is revealed that God's mediate government of the world has relation to the fortunes of the people whom He loves ; hence He stands in their midst ; and it is from that centre that the executors of His wrath in the government of the nations go forth.

The chariots of this chapter and the horsemen of chapter 1 are figures of the angels of His might. They symbolize irresistible power and superhuman activity. The chariots of 2 Kings ii. 11, vi. 17, Ps. lxviii. 17, etc., are no doubt angels ; as interpreted by 2 Thess. i. 7 and 8 and Heb. i. 7.

" Two mountains " (v. 1) Hebrew : " The two mountains," i.e., the two ultimate divisions of Alexander's empire, Syria and Egypt ; Judah lying between them, poor and helpless.

" Four chariots " (v. 1), i.e., God's four sore judgments (Ezek. xiv. 21)—the sword (the red horses), famine (the black horses), pestilence (the white horses), wild beasts (the speckled horses).

These judgments fell mainly upon the king of the north (v. 6), (as they will once again in the future), and caused to rest i.e., satisfied the Spirit of righteous anger against that nation and monarch.

The vision views the red " horses " as having already discharged their mission ; hence their non-appearance in verse 6. And so it came to pass, *for wars of any magnitude ceased under the Grecian empire, but famine and pestilence and wild beasts were universal in the later years of that dominion. All this will be repeated in the future.

The word " bay " (v. 3) should read, as in the margin, " strong." It is a covering term meaning that all the four pairs of horses were strong, that is, that the four angels of the heavens (v. 5) are mighty angels of exceptional strength. This feature of placing a covering term at the end of several statements is illustrated in Gen. xv. 13, and other Scriptures.

The sense of verse 7 may be thus expressed ; So these strong horses went forth and sought, etc. This latter verb in Hebrew suggests willingness, zeal, activity, etc., in going forth ; and the thrice-repeated " walk to and fro " heightens the sense of the whole-hearted energy of these mighty executors of Divine justice.

At the end of this time of Gentile domination, now near at hand, the Messiah will resume His immediate government of the earth. His reign is symbolized in the crowning of Joshua as king and priest (vs. 12 and 13).

Verse 10 should read as in the Revised Version.

" Joshua " (v. 11) symbolizes the Messiah with His double crown of Kingship and Priesthood. Heldai and his companions foreshadow the future exiles of Zion (v. 15) who will return thither bringing their wealth with them, and who will become builders in the Temple of which Messiah will be the Master-Builder

The Gospel of Luke presents the Messiah as the Man Whose Name is The Branch (v. 12).

" His place " (v. 12), i.e., the family of David.

" The Temple " (vs. 12, 13 and 15). This may mean the future spiritual Temple of 1 Pet. ii. 5 ; but it may also point to Ezekiel's Temple which is yet to be built.

Christ will be the true Melchisedek, King of righteousness and peace, and Priest of the Most High God (v. 13). These two offices will be combined in His One Person, with the result that the peace planned for Zion and the world will become a fact under His reign.

The great crown (" crowns," plural of excellency) (vs. 11 and 14) was made with the silver and gold brought by the Exiles as a gift to the Temple then being built ; and it was deposited in the Temple (v. 14) as a memorial of the faith and love of these believers and of their host ; also as a memorial pledging the fulfilment of the promised appearance and glorious reign and priesthood of the Man Whose name was The Branch.

" If ye will diligently obey " (v. 15). The prophets Malachi, John the Baptist, Jesus of Nazareth and the Apostles Peter and Paul testify that this condition was not fulfilled. Hence Zion's past, present and future misery. So this promise awaits a future obedience and fulfilment.

This crown and these words must have greatly animated the faith of Joshua.

It was necessary that a Temple should be built in which the Messiah at His First Advent was to appear.

" The kindness " (v. 14, R.V.), i.e., the hospitality of the son of Zephaniah to the deputies from Babylon was to be equally honoured with their gifts ; and it is not recorded that the deputies objected. Hospitality is a Christian duty and privilege.

Matt. x. 42, xxv. 35, Rom. xii. 13, 1 Tim. iii. 2, 1 Pet. iv. 9, Heb. vi. 10, etc. Thus the action of the host was as precious to God as the bounty of the visitors. Helem is a form of the name Heldai (v. 10), and hen (v. 14) means " the kindness of " Josiah. It is not a proper name.

ZECHARIAH VII.—This and the following chapter form the second section of the Book. It contains four messages.

The first message occupies verses 1-7. It was uttered on the fourth of the modern December, and was addressed to certain enquirers from Bethel (v. 2, R.V.), who had anxiously asked the priests if they were bound to keep commemorating the fasts of the fifth and the seventh months, observed during the Captivity. These Fasts commemorated, respectively, the Destruction of Jerusalem (Jer. lii.) and the murder of Gedaliah (Jer. xl. and xli.).

It is not recorded what reply the priests made, but this first message records the reply that God interposed.

It declared that these religious ceremonies were invented by themselves and not ordained by God (v. 6) ; that they were hypocritical (v. 5) ; and that had they, when in prosperity (v. 7), obeyed the Word of the Lord given through the prophets at that time, i.e., Jeremiah, Habakkuk, Zephaniah and Joel, there would have been no Captivity, and, consequently, no reason for instituting fasts.

Anxiety was not expressed about listening to, and obeying, God's commands, but great anxiety was evidenced about the observance of vows imposed on themselves by themselves.

So is it to-day. The Bible is unread, or disobeyed ; and vows, such as chastity and fasting, etc., originated by man, imposed by man, and made to man, are rigidly observed, and their breach regarded with horror.

Men are quite ready to separate themselves (v. 3) from time to time from their occupations and associations, which usually tire them, and observe what they call a Retreat, but they are not willing to separate from the sins which they like.

" The South and the plain " (v. 7), i.e., the most defenceless part of the country, was then thickly and safely inhabited.

The second message (8-14) stated that God required moral conduct rather than self-invented religious ceremonies. The force

in Hebrew of the verb " speaketh " (v. 9) is past, present and future ; as is " scattered " (v. 14).

The charge is that these men's fathers refused to obey the commands of verses 9 and 10 ; that they themselves were continuing this disobedience ; and that their children would imitate them.

So it came to pass ; and Israel's present dispersion, and the desolation of her land, attest inspiration.

" Imagine evil " (v. 10), i.e., plan injury.

" Pulled away the shoulder " (v. 11), i.e., the reference is to an ox refusing the yoke. So Zion refused the yoke of the Law and, by a just judgment, had to submit to the yoke of the Chaldean.

" Stop their ears " (v. 11). See Isaiah vi. 10 and Acts vii. 57.

" Great wrath " (v. 12), i.e., the seventy years captivity.

" A whirlwind " (v. 14), i.e., a whirlwind of anger.

" The land was desolate after them " (v. 14), i.e., the land became desolate after they had left it. Thus God ordained then, and now since the Roman overthrow, that Palestine should remain practically uninhabited, and uncultivated, so preserving it then, and now, for the return of His people.

" They " (v. 14) and " they " (v. 14), i.e., the Jews. Their own misconduct explains the desolation of their native land.

The present desolation of Palestine is predicted in verse 14.

To arouse their conscience and to strengthen their faith the formula " Thus saith Jehovah," is repeated nineteen times in the four messages of these two chapters.

ZECHARIAH VIII.—This chapter contains the third (vs. 1-17), and the fourth messages (18-23) of the second section of the Book.

Each message commences with the formula " The word of the Lord " in the first two messages, and " The word of the Lord of Hosts " in the last two (vii. 1 and 8, ch. viii. 1 and 18).

The number four is prominent in these messages. There are four of them ; they were motived by four fasts (viii. 19), and these fasts were rebuked by four ignored commands (vii. 9 and 10 and viii. 16 and 17). See notes on verses 10 and 12.

The four messages had an application

for the men who heard them, but their interpretation belongs to the future.

The four fasts commemorated the siege of Jerusalem in the tenth month (Ezek. xxiv) ; the capture of the city in the fourth month (Jer. lii.) ; the destruction of the Temple in the fifth month (Jer. lii.) ; and the murder of Gedaliah in the seventh month (Jer. xl. and xli.).

" I was jealous " (v. 2). The force of the Hebrew verb here is : " I was, I am, and I will be jealous," i.e., the jealousy of love. Hence the doom of Babylon.

" Great fury " (v. 2), i.e., the overthrow of Babylon which occasioned the Restoration of the Exiles.

There are ten prophecies concerning Zion in these two last messages (vs. 2, 3, 4, 6, 7, 9, 14, 19, 20, 23).

" Dwell " (v. 4) better, " sit." " Streets " —(Hebrew, broad open spaces), i.e., public parks with broad alleys in which the aged will sit and the boys and girls will play (v. 5).

If the restoration from Babylon was wonderful, how much more wonderful will be Israel's future restoration ! (v. 6).

If the former was marvellous in men's eyes, should the latter be marvellous in God's eyes ?

" The east country " (v. 7). From it the Ten Tribes will return. " The west country." From it the Two Tribes will return ; for they were mainly scattered thither, as the Ten were scattered to the east.

" The prophets " (v. 9), i.e., Haggai and Zechariah.

" These days " (v. 10), better, " those days " (R.V.), i.e., the days before the Temple foundation was laid.

Neglect of that duty caused the four judgments of verse 10 ; and its obedience secured the four blessings of verse 12.

" All these things " (v. 12), i.e., all these good things.

" A curse " (v. 13). Men perhaps said when quarrelling : " May you be cursed like the Jews." " A blessing." In the future men will say as the highest expression of goodwill : " May you be blessed like the Jews."

" I repented not " (v. 14), i.e., God did not alter His purpose but actually banished them for seventy years. With equal fixity of purpose He will do them good (v. 15) and restore them.

But He attached a condition, i.e., the four commands of verses 16 and 17, repeated from vii. 9 and 10. The word " oppression " defines the civic evils here condemned. " These things I hate " saith the Lord ; and so should all do that profess to love Him. His anger burns perpetually against lying, cheating, oppression and injustice, for He loves His creatures.

" Shall be cheerful feasts " (v. 19). Man, in religious self-will, invents fasts ; God appoints feasts.

These feasts might then, and ever since, have been enjoyed had the commands of verses 16 and 17 been obeyed. They were not obeyed, though man's fasts and traditions were rigidly observed. See Matt. xv. 1-20.

But grace will triumph over all man's self-will and rebellion. These four feasts will be held in the future, and Jerusalem will become the city of the Great King ; He will dwell there (v. 3) ; and the nations of the earth will proceed thither to seek His favour (vs. 20-23).

" Ten men " (v. 23), i.e., a definite number for an indefinite. See Lev. xxvi. 26 and Num. xiv. 22.

To take hold of the skirt (v. 23) is in the East a gesture of entreaty and a claim for protection (Ruth iii. 9).

" The judgment of peace " (v. 16), i.e., an administration of justice restoring concord between litigants.

ZECHARIAH IX.—The third section of this Book (ix.-xiv.) contains two " Burdens " (ix. 1, and xii. 1). These concern, first, the oppressor (ix.-xi.), and second, the oppressed (xii.-xiv.).

Thus the Book is tri-form ; and, moving backwards, exhibits multiples of two : that is, two burdens, four prophecies, and eight symbols.

Judgment having begun at the House of God (vii. and viii.), now passes on to the enemies of that House—first, the enemies within Immanuel's land (vs. 1-8), and then the enemies exterior to that land (vs. 10-15).

These enemies are, respectively, grouped under the terms the Philistine (v. 6) and the Grecian (v. 13).

Alexander the Great is the Grecian Monarch who executed the judgment on the Philistine (1-7) ; and the future Grecian prince who is to arise out of Alexander's kingdom (Dan. viii. 23), and who will be the unconscious instrument of God's wrath on the nations, will be the Antichrist (vs. 10-15).

The mention of Ephraim (v. 13) in conjunction with Judah makes it certain that this prophecy belongs to the future and not to the times of the Maccabees; for Ephraim did not then exist as a nation, but was scattered in the Dispersion.

The order of the chapter is therefore:— First: Judgment on the nations within the Promised Land by Alexander the Great (vs. 1-7). Second: The first advent (v. 8). Third: Judgment on the nations external to the Promised Land by Antichrist as the Grecian prince who shall arise out of that Empire prior to the Second Advent.

"Burden" (v. 1), i.e., a Divine utterance of judgment

"The rest thereof" (v. 1), i.e., the regions upon which the "burden" was to alight. They were Hadrach, Damascus, Hamath, Tyre and Sidon, and the cities of the Philistines (vs. 5 and 6).

The Hebrew text in verse 1, commencing at the word "when", is difficult of translation, but guided by the last sentence of verse 8 it may perhaps be thus read: "The eyes of Jehovah shall be upon man as upon all the Tribes of Israel." That is: His eyes rested on Israel for chastisement, and now were about to rest upon men for judgment.

Verse 2 should read as in the Revised Version.

"It" (v. 2), i.e., Tyre. The Tyrians boasted of their impregnable position and attributed it to their wisdom; for they built the city on an island and fortified it by a double wall a hundred and fifty feet high. They, therefore, congratulated themselves that the Grecian monarch could never conquer them. But he speedily captured the city, slew thirteen thousand of the inhabitants, crucified two thousand, and sold the remainder into slavery.

Verse 4 might read as in the Revised Version.

"It" (v. 5), i.e., the destruction of Tyre.

"Her expectation" (v. 5), i.e., Ekron's expectation that Tyre would prove impregnable, and so she herself would escape from the Greeks.

"A bastard" (v. 6), or, perhaps better, a mongrel race.

"His bloods", "his abominations" (v. 7), i.e., his idolatrous feasts and his effusion of human blood.

"As a governor" (v. 7), i.e., a mere chieftain. "As a Jebusite," i.e., a working man.

"Because of the army" (v. 8), better, "as a garrison, that none pass through or return" (R.V.).

"For now have I seen with mine eyes" (v. 8). This does not mean that only then God became aware of the affliction of His people and of the cruelty of their oppressors, but that now, after a period of longsuffering with the oppressors, He would execute upon them a just judgment—a judgment not inflicted upon hearsay but upon eyesight and personal knowledge.

Verse 9 was fulfilled in Matt. xxi.

The four Gospels here appear. He is the Righteous One, i.e., God (Gospel by John), The Saviour (Gospel by Luke), The Servant (Gospel by Mark), The Rider upon the colt (Gospel by Matthew), for Eastern monarchs so ride. He thus appears as the Prince of Peace in His first advent—not as in His second advent, mounted on a war horse as the Mighty Conqueror (Rev. xix.).

"I will cut off," etc., (v. 10). Not only will He encamp as a garrison around His House (v. 8), but He will banish war from its neighbourhood. He shall command peace to the nations, and, like the sea, they will have to obey Him; and He will then give to Abraham the whole extent of the territory promised to him—that is, from the Mediterranean Sea to the Dead Sea, and from the river Euphrates to the extreme southern end of Palestine.

"As for thee" (v. 11), i.e., "O daughter of Zion" (v. 9). "Thy covenant," i.e., God's covenant to Zion made with Abraham and secured by the precious blood of Calvary; fore-shadowed by the death of the Covenant victim of Genesis xv. 17, 18. See notes on that chapter.

"The pit," etc., (v. 11), i.e., Israel's present miserable condition.

Verse 12 should read: "Return to the stronghold ye prisoners of hope," i.e., to the stronghold of verse 8—Zion garrisoned by Immanuel: "Hope," i.e., the promise made to Abraham. A prisoner having such a hope was very far better than a prisoner without hope.

As in the case of Job so in that of Israel, God will make their latter end doubly as prosperous as their beginning (v. 12). Isa. lxi. 7, Jer. xxxi. 15-17.

At that future appointed time He will

use Judah as His bow, Ephraim as His arrow, and Zion as His sword (v. 12) ; He Himself will be their General, and will be as irresistible as an Arabian whirlwind (v. 14).

It will be the strangest army the world will have ever seen. The soldiers will be a mob of escaped prisoners without arms ; the General will be Immanuel. He alone will fight. His weapons will be thunder and lightning and tempest. They will be effective, for His unarmed followers will destroy their enemies, trample upon their weapons, shout with joy, and be enriched with booty (v. 15). In the Tabernacle the bowls were filled with wine, and costly gifts were fastened to the corners of the great brazen altar.

Trampling the now worthless sling-stones beneath their feet (v. 15) they themselves shall be as precious stones beautifying the land (v. 16 (R.V. marg.) ; and the beforetime thirsty prisoners of the pit (v. 11) shall be enthroned in splendour upon the Glorious Land and drink its new wine. Israel will then be a starry diadem in Messiah's hand, as in Isa. lxii. 3, and Rev. i. 16.

Verse 17, guided by the context, should read : " How great shall be their prosperity, and how great shall be their beauty ! "

The Divine judgment on the nations (ix.-xi.), which is the subject of the first " Burden," and the judgment upon the Hebrews (xii.-xiv.), which is that of the second, illustrate the doctrine that God judges evil in the believer and in the un-believer.

The subject matter of the first Burden is the punishment of Damascus and the Philistines (ix. 1-7) ; the first advent (vs. 8 and 9) ; the second advent; and the judgment upon the Grecian Antichrist (ix. 10-x.). In chapter xi. 1-14 the Holy Spirit returns to chapter ix. 9 and details the facts concerning the first advent, the rejection of the Good Shepherd and the consequent destruction of Jerusalem by the Romans. In the closing three verses of the chapter, the entry of Antichrist as the idle shepherd is predicted, and the Divine judgment upon him and his armies foretold.

ZECHARIAH X.—The argument of v. 1

up to the word " goats " in verse 3, is, that had Israel not turned aside to idols they would have received the early rain, and the latter rain, and would not have been carried away into captivity. The third verse should close at the word " goats " and the fourth verse begin thus : For Jehovah Sabaoth shall visit His flock, etc., and the future tense should be observed to the close of the chapter.

The argument had an application in the prophet's day ; but its interpretation belongs to the present and to the future.

" Bright clouds " (v. 1), i.e., lightning ; scientists now say that there never is rain apart from electrical discharge.

The early rain in Palestine causes the seed to germinate, and the latter rain causes it to fructify. In Christian experience the early rain of salvation must be followed by the latter rain of sanctification.

" The false shepherd " (v. 2) leads the flock into affliction ; The True Shepherd (v. 11) leads it out of affliction. See notes on xi. 16.

" The he-goats " (v. 3) in the East lead the flock.

The second member of verse 3 should read : " But the Lord of Hosts shall visit His flock, etc., and shall make them," etc.

Thus between the first member and the last member of this verse intervene more than 2500 years.

" Him " (v. 4), i.e., the House of Judah (v. 3).

" Oppressor " (v. 4) Hebrew " Ruler " (R.V. marg.).

" Nail " (v. 4), i.e., the central pole that supports the Arab's tent and on which he hangs all his precious things. See Isa. xxii. 23.

The Messiah is here described. He is the Corner Stone, He is the Tent Pole, He is the Battle Bow and He is the Ruler. Here again is a reference to the four Gospels read backwards.

An Arab tent needs a firm foundation, a strong supporting pole, an encircling defence either of fire or thorn, and a chief who can maintain discipline. Such is Christ to His people.

" Every " (v. 4) a term here implying plenitude. " Together," that is conjointly. Christ is a perfect Governor, and the four offices of this verse conjoin in Him. The words may also read " He that will exercise all rule."

" The riders on horses " (v. 5), i.e., Judah's enemies.

The introduction of Joseph and of Ephraim (vs. 6 and 7) decide the futurity of this prophecy ; for they had no existence, as such, in Zechariah's day, nor have they in the present.

" It " (v. 7), i.e., the great victory of verse 5. Ephraim's children of the future will be the victors in that great and coming day.

Verse 9 should read as in the margin of the Revised Version, thus : " And though I sow them among the peoples yet shall they remember Me in far countries ; and they shall live with their children ; and they shall return."

Three of these predictions have been, and are being fulfilled ; the fourth and last awaits an absolutely certain fulfilment. This fourfold prophecy establishes inspiration. " Hiss " (v. 8) rather " pipe " as a shepherd when calling his flock together.

Egypt and Assyria here represent all Judah's foes ; for Egypt was the first and the Assyrian, i.e., Antichrist, will be the last, but the immediate reference is to Antiochus and Ptolemy, the two mountains of brass of chapter vi. 1.

The first line of verse 11 should read : " And He (Messiah) shall pass through the sea of affliction." As Captain of His people's deliverance He will accompany them through their future affliction, as He led them through the Red Sea, and through the Jordan.

" The sea " (v. 11) and " the river." The reference here is to the Red Sea and to the Jordan.

" In the Lord " (v. 12), i.e., in God's Beloved Son.

" Walk up and down," i.e., in safety, and with dignity as conquerors.

Teraphim (v. 2) appear eight times in the Scriptures. They were idols used as oracles, and as such, were vehicles of demoniac communications, and, therefore, immediately antagonistic to the Holy Spirit.

The moral order of these prophecies sets in the foreground promises of future restoration, and then in order to prevent a misuse of these promises, the sad prophecy of national apostasy and consequent judgment is recorded in the next and following chapters.

ZECHARIAH XI.—As the opening of this First Burden predicted the conquest of Palestine by the Greeks (ix. 1-9) and the First Advent, so its conclusion (xi. 1-17) foretold the rejection of the Messiah and the destruction of Jerusalem by the Romans.

" Lebanon " (v. 1), i.e., Jerusalem, because so largely built of cedar from Lebanon (Hab. ii. 17).

The trees of verse 2 symbolize the cities destroyed by the Romans when marching on Jerusalem ; and the argument is : that if a strong city, comparable to a cedar, fell, how much more sure was the fall of a weak city like Jerusalem, comparable to a fir or cypress tree.

" The forest of the vintage " (v. 2)—i.e., " fortified forest " (R.V.)—that is, a large, strongly fortified city, its numerous houses appearing as the trees of a forest.

" The shepherds " (v. 3), i.e., the priests, " Their glory," the Temple.

" The young lions " (v. 3), i.e., the nobles. " The pride of Jordan," their lands. The Jordan valley was the favourite hunting ground of the lion.

The prophet was, in vision, to personate the Good Shepherd (4-14), and the False Shepherd (15, 16).

" Flock of the slaughter " (v. 4), i.e., Judah destined to be slaughtered by the Romans.

" Whose possessors," i.e., the nobles of verse 3. " Their own shepherds," i.e., the priests of verse 3.

" His king " (v. 6), i.e., Caesar ; for each man said : " We have no king but Caesar " (John xix. 15).

" They " (v. 6), i.e., the soldiers of Caesar.

" And " (v. 7), better : " So I fed." Judah as a flock, rejected Jesus as Israel's Shepherd, but " the poor of the flock," i.e., the disciples, gave heed to Him (v. 11) ; and at the destruction of Jerusalem knew that they had listened to the Word of the Lord. That doom fell upon the guilty city about forty years after its prediction in Matt. xxiv.

An Eastern shepherd has two staves (v. 7). The one is a club to defend the sheep ; the other, a crook to keep them together (Ps. xxiii.).

" Loathed " (v. 8), Hebrew : " Straitened," the opposite of " enlarged " (2 Cor. vi. 11, 12).

These three shepherds are unnamed, perhaps they mean the Scribes, the Pharisees and the Lawyers of Luke xi. 44-52 whom Messiah thus cut off and doomed during the brief " month " of His ministry.

Judah having rejected the Messiah He abandoned her to her foes, the Romans, by symbolically breaking the one staff (v. 10) ; and by the breaking of the other (v. 14) effectually disjointed the whole Hebrew people ; for the Romans drove them apart in all directions, and forbade them setting foot in Palestine. This disruption continues.

"Let the rest eat everyone, etc., (v. 9). Prior to, and during, the invasion of the Romans the Jews destroyed one another by faction fighting.

"The peoples" (v. 10, R.V.)—in this case the Romans to whom God had entrusted the protection of His people. That protection was withdrawn in A.D. 70.

"My price" (v. 12), better: "My hire as a shepherd"; but He would not enforce His claim. So they valued Him at thirty shekels, the price of an injured slave (Ex. xxi. 32).

"The potter" (v. 13), i.e., "the fashioner." He might have been, if working in clay, a potter (Jer. xviii.); if in stone, a mason (Ex. xxviii.); if in wood, a carpenter (2 Sam. v.); if in iron, a smith (2 Chron. xxiv.); if in gold a goldsmith (Hosea viii.); and if in silver a silversmith (Hosea xiii.). The money was cast in the Temple (v. 13); and its ultimate destination was the hands of an ordinary hand-worker.

"Foolish" (v. 15), i.e., "impious" (Ps. xiv. 1). In this verse, and the following, the False Shepherd, the future Antichrist, is described. By a just judgment Israel will be delivered into his hands because of her rejection of the True Shepherd. He came in His Father's Name and they did not receive Him; but they will receive, as He predicted, the future wicked shepherd, who is to come in his own name (John v. 43).

"Claws" (v. 16), i.e., "hoofs." The language expresses merciless ferocity.

"Idle" (v. 17), i.e., "worthless." He will abandon the flock. Antichrist will destroy it. Hence the prophecy may mean that the arm and eye of the worthless shepherd will be destroyed by the sword of the Wicked Shepherd; and this would be a most fitting punishment inflicted by a self-chosen king.

ZECHARIAH XII.—This second and closing "Burden" concerns ("for") Israel. It belongs wholly to the future, and synchronises with ix. 10-17. It may be thus divided, xii. 1-9, xii. 10-xiii. 9, and xiv.

The Burden foretells Judah's deliverance by Him Whom they rejected and pierced; their consequent conversion; and Zion's resultant glory.

"Stretcheth forth," etc., (v. 1). In Hebrew the force of these three verbs is past and present. Immanuel made and maintains all things (Col. i. 16). His power as Creator and Sustainer assures the fulfilment of His promises.

"The spirit of Man" (v. 1). Two Hebrew words are translated "spirit" in the Bible. This one is "spirit" as common to man and the animal creation; the other is an emanation from God possessed only by man, and ever existing.

In this chapter the reader is permitted to hear the Messiah speaking (1-4, 6, 9 and half 10) and also the Holy Spirit (5, 7, 8, and half 10-14).

"People" (v. 2), Revised Version "peoples." This word in verses 3 and 4, and 6 should read similarly. These peoples will form Antichrist's army in his last effort to destroy Jerusalem (Rev. xix.).

"A burdensome stone" (v. 3), i.e., a stone difficult to lift or to move. Antichrist's effort to displace it will cause his own destruction, for the stone of Daniel ii. will fall upon him from heaven.

"Cut in pieces" (v. 3), better: "sore wounded." (R.V.)—even though helped by all the nations of the earth. Man's efforts to destroy Zion deeply wounded many nations in the past, and will deeply wound many more in the future, as the Scriptures make clear.

"Astonishment" (v. 4), better, "panic"; "madness" i.e., frenzy inspired by terror. "I will open mine eyes," etc., (v. 4), i.e., "I will interfere in behalf of."

Verse 5 may perhaps be thus read, using an ellipsis: "And the chief men of Judah shall say in their heart, 'The faith of the inhabitants of Jerusalem in the Lord of Hosts their God is a strength to me."

• Verse 7 should read as in the Revised Version.

Verses 5 and 7 read together instruct the Christian. Judah recognizes, and confesses, as a source of strength, the faith of Jerusalem; and the Messiah will reward this humility of mind by rescuing Judah first, and thus will there be equality of glory to both.

"As David" (v. 8) He was Israel's greatest warrior. "As the angel of Jehovah before them," i.e., the angel that led them through the desert.

"I will seek to destroy" (v. 9), i.e., "I will certainly destroy." Such is the force of the Hebrew verb "to seek."

"And I will pour" (v. 10), read: "But I will pour." At His second advent Christ will pour fire upon Zion's adversaries, but the Holy Spirit upon her inhabitants (2 Thess. i.).

In verse 10, the Messiah speaks as far as the word " pierced," and then the Holy Spirit points to the moral effect produced by that revelation.

There will be personal mourning (v. 10), national mourning (v. 11), and domestic mourning (vs. 12-14). Every man will feel himself guilty of having pierced Immanuel.

" The mourning of Megiddon " (v. 11) was occasioned by the death of king Josiah (2 Chron. xxxv. 22-25). His reign was the one gleam of light in the gloom that covered the nation from Manasseh to the Captivity.

" The valley of Megiddon," i.e., the plain of Esdraelon.

The house of David and Nathan (v. 12) and the family of Levi and Shimei ; i.e., the princes and the priests.

Shimei was a grandson of Levi, and Nathan a son of David and elder brother of Solomon. He was the ancestor of the Virgin Mary. Her husband, Joseph, was the direct descendant of Solomon.

It may be that the Prince of Ezekiel xliv. 3, will be named Nathan, for He will be of the House of David.

Judah's repentance and conversion will not be motived by fear of punishment but by the overwhelming sense of guilt and horror affecting the heart when they recognize that their Deliverer is Jesus Whom they crucified ; and that all along, in spite of their hatred and their conduct, He kept on loving them !

The great cup of reeling (Ps. lxxv. 8, Isa. li. 21-23) of verse 2 will by a just judgment be given to Jerusalem to drink as well as to the Gentiles. This is the sense of the verse.

ZECHARIAH XIII.—The fountain of verse 1 was historically opened at Calvary but will be consciously opened to repentant Judah in the future day of her repentance ; for the fact and function of that fountain only become conscious to the awakened sinner. A true sense of sin and guilt in relationship to God, awakens the sense of the need of cleansing, and so the shed and cleasing blood of the Lamb of God becomes precious to the convicted conscience. The fear of punishment does not come in here to impair the character and depth of Judah's sorrow and repentance.

The ever-living efficacy of Christ's atoning work, and its power to cleanse the conscience and the life, is justly comparable to a fountain and not to a font. The sense of the Hebrew text is that this fountain shall be opened and shall remain open.

Of all sinners the Jerusalem sinner may be accounted the greatest. It was Jerusalem that stoned the prophets and that crucified the Messiah. Therefore great sinners may hope for pardon and cleansing in this fountain opened for the House of David.

The entrance of Christ judges sin, unmasks its true character, and arouses a moral consciousness which approves that judgment.

That entrance dominates, adjusts, disciplines, instructs and cleanses man's affections, relationships and desires. Four of these are here set out. They are man's greatest emotions : Conjugal (xii. 12) ; Communal (xii. 14) ; Devotional (xiii. 2) and Parental (xiii. 3).

Man has degraded these emotions ; God will cleanse and adjust them ; and the effect will be that man's moral consciousness will be so harmonized with God's nature, that he will not only abolish idolatry, but he will put to death his own child who tries to support it. So the redeemed in heaven, possessing a nature harmonising with God's, will applaud the Divine action in judging their impenitent relatives whatever the judgment may be. (Matt. xiii. 40-43, and Rev. xix. 1-3).

The False Prophet will re-establish idols, and, therefore, false prophets (Rev. xiii. 11-17). These idols, and their prophets, will become very popular ; for man by nature is devotional, and his nature being fallen, the devotion takes on an idolatrous form. These prophets have been, are, and will be inspired by an unholy spirit.

The most dangerous form of idolatry is that which speaks lies in the Name of the Lord (v. 3). Such is corrupt Christendom.

These false prophets (v. 4) will be effectually put to shame when they see their great leader cast into the burning flame (Rev. xix. 20) " in that day."

The question of sin and repentance here gives occasion to a historical reference to the Sin-Bearer (v. 5) ; how He was treated by man, (v. 6) : and His true character as revealed by God (v. 7). His humanity is asserted in verses 5 and 6 ; His Deity, in verse 7. As

Man He had relatives ("friends"), for He was of the Tribe of Judah; as God, He was Jehovah's Equal (v. 7).

The false prophets thrust themselves forward and claimed reverence and position; He, the greatest of the prophets, hid Himself, did not claim to be a professional prophet—that was not His mission in coming to earth—but became a bond-servant and a shepherd; made and appointed such in the Divine purpose of redemption (vs. 5, R.V. and Phil ii. 7). For man having sold himself into slavery it was necessary that Christ should take that position in order to redeem him.

It was not only sin upon the Sinless Substitute that was smitten at Calvary, but the Substitute Himself, Jehovah's equal. He Himself must die in order that man might live; for the curse that rested upon man was the doom of death because of sin. Christ's death therefore was necessary to satisfy that claim, and to vindicate and magnify Divine righteousness (v. 7)

So the Shepherd was smitten and the sheep scattered; but not finally lost, for His hand, pierced by the flock, shall cause the "little ones" to return to Zion.

Thus between the word "scattered" and the word "and" the present immense period of time intervenes.

As in astronomy a near planet and a distant fixed star appear side by side in the heavens though the one is millions of miles more distant than the other, so in the Scriptures two prophecies side by side in the text are often, as here, separated by many hundreds of years.

If, say, three million Jews presently return to Palestine they will enter a fiery furnace of affliction at the hands of Antichrist, and two millions of them will perish (v. 8), as in A.D. 70. A tenth part of the remaining million (Isa. vi. 13), will represent the "little ones" of verse 7, i.e., "the poor of the flock," of xi. 11. They will look upon Him Whom they pierced and will repent (xii. 10-14).

This "tenth part" was represented by Thomas. He, like Judah, rejected the testimony of his fellow Hebrews; but the apparition of the Messiah with His pierced hands (John xx.) banished his unbelief, and he cried out, as Judah will in a future day when they see Him, "Jehovah is my God" (v. 9), for such is the import of his confession.

The "little ones" may also figure the 500

disciples whom the risen Shepherd's hand gathered together subsequently to His resurrection and prior to His ascension.

The relationship of verse 1, to "the water of cleansing" of Num. xix. is apparent, and is emphasized in the Hebrew text by special words proper to both Scriptures.

"In that day" occurs eighteen times, (ix. 16—xiv. 21). This shows how precious that day is to Messiah's heart. In that day His victory over the enemies of His people will be great, but greater will be His moral victory over His people themselves. The Christian's true triumphs are God's triumphs over him, and God's triumphs over His people are their only true victories.

The conversion of the Apostle Paul illustrates the future conversion of Israel. He hated Jesus, but on the Damascus road he looked upon Him Whom he had pierced and mourned and wept.

ZECHARIAH XIV.—"The day" (v. 1): should be "a day" (R.V.), i.e., the unique day of verses 6 and 7.

"Thy spoil" (v. 1), i.e., that of Jerusalem

"And the residue" (v. 2), read: "But a residue." Thus "the third part" (xiii. 9) shall be further sifted, and only a tenth delivered.

"The day of battle" (v. 3), i.e., most probably that of the Red Sea, Israel's first battle, when Jehovah Messiah "went forth' and fought for them. Israel then passed through a valley between mountains of water; in this, their last battle, they will escape through a valley between mountains of rock (v. 4).

"To the valley" (v. 5), better read:—"through the valley."

"Azal" (v. 5) perhaps a name for Jerusalem; or a place that will be so named when this prophecy comes to pass.

Verse 5, should end with the words "king of Judah"; and verse 6 should begin "and Jehovah my God, shall come," etc.

"Saints" (v. 5), i.e., His mighty angels (2 Thess. i. 7).

Verses 6 and 7 are obscure. An explanation is suggested. The twenty-four hours of the day are divided between light and darkness. The splendour of Messiah's apparition will temporarily suspend this law of astronomy; but that flaming fire having accomplished its function of vengeance (2 Thess. i. 8), it will be withdrawn, and "at evening time " the ordinary light of day will re-appear.

Thus " that day " (v. 6) will be ," one day " (v. 7), i.e., a unique day, such a day as has never been seen ; but having the same characteristics, and principle, as the unique day of Joshua x. 12-14. The date of this unique day of the future is known to Jehovah Messiah as God (Matt. xxiv. 36, and Acts i. 7) but not as man.

The "living waters " (v. 8) will not be dried up by heat nor congealed by frost.

The prophecy thrice asserts that Jesus shall be King over all the earth ; and that He is Jehovah (vs. 9, 16 and 17).

" In that day " He will be the One God of the whole earth ; there will be no religious denominations (the Church of " the mistery" will be in heaven) ; all will be members of the Hebrew Church, which is, and will be, the true Catholic Church—the claim of the Roman Church to be catholic is absurd— and all men will speak the one language, for His Name shall be one (Zeph. iii. 9). No other god will be associated with Him.

" A plain " (v. 10), read : " the plain " (R.V.). The valleys will be raised, the mountains lowered, and a great plain formed, and upon that mighty platform the future city and palace of Jehovah Messiah will be built. This great platform will be the " Holy Oblation " of Ezekiel xlv. 1-5. Through it will pass the broad and noble water-way (v. 8) which will connect the Red Sea (" the former sea ") with the Mediterranean (" the hinder sea ").

So great is Immanuel's love for Jerusalem, though hated and crucified by her, that He delights to count her towers (v. 10). See Ps. xlviii. 12.

" Utter destruction " (v. 11), read : " No more curse " (R.V.)

" That have fought " (v. 12), i.e., " that shall fight."

When racial troubles (v. 13) and physical sufferings (v. 12) affect men they accuse one another as the authors of their miseries, and are blind to God's judgments. So is it to-day, and so will it be at the last siege of Jerusalem.

" At " or " against Jerusalem " (v. 14). The Hebrew word may be translated either way. The day itself will decide Judah's action. But so corrupt and evil is human nature that it is quite possible that as she fought against Him in His first advent, so will she in His second.

Man in sinning not only brings suffering upon himself (v. 12) but also upon animals (v. 15). In war thousands of them are destroyed.

" These tents " (v. 15), read : " These camps " (R.V.).

" The Feast of Tabernacles " (v. 16). This Feast was a delightful week of holiday in the month of September at the close of the year's toil. Work and slavery ceased to exist, and there was universal brotherhood and merrymaking. It was a fore-picture of the future open air and universal festival named the millennium. It may be assumed that the temperature of the earth will be so pleasant that all its happy inhabitants will live day and night in the open air. Under vines and fig trees they will entertain each other fraternally ; and the little children will play with the gentle lion and the harmless tiger. It will be a period of unspeakable rest and peace and love for a world faint with the toil and misery of six thousand years. The concord of the nations will be maintained by obedience to the command to send representatives yearly to Jerusalem to worship the King.

The sense of verse 18 is—and the seeming obscurity of the Hebrew text helps to emphasize it—that as Egypt, unlike other countries, is not dependent upon the rainfall for its food supply, its punishment will be the plague of verse 12 ; and the certainty of its infliction is specially repeated in verse 19.

" The bowls " (v. 20) were of gold and of silver, and were used in the service of the Golden Altar inside the Tabernacle, and the Brazen Altar outside (Exod. xxxvii. and xxxviii.).

" In that day " the ordinary pots of the Temple and of the household will be as readily used for Divine Service as these sacred bowls ; for everything will be holy in Immanuel's land.

" The Canaanite " (v. 21), read, " There shall be no more a trafficker in the House of the Lord " (John ii. 14-16). The sacred ministry will cease to be adopted because a salaried profession.

MALACHI

Forty-nine years after the "command-ment" of Dan. ix. 25 Malachi gave his message to Israel; and after four hundred years of probation John the Baptist confirmed the message.

Israel, like the Amorite (Gen. xv. 16), did not profit by this probation.

Malachi means "My messenger." There are five messengers in this Book: Malachi (i. 1), The true Priest (ii. 7), John the Baptist (iii. 1), Elijah (iv. 5), and Messiah (iii. 1-3).

Moral insensibility asks eight questions in the Book; i. 2, i. 6, i. 7, ii. 14; ii. 17, iii. 7, iii. 8, and iii. 13.

Malachi was a contemporary of Socrates. His prophecies are quoted by Matt. xi. 10 and xvii. 12; Mark i. 2, and ix. 11, 12, Luke i. 17, and Rom. ix. 13.

The Book reveals the corruption which invaded the Hebrew Church shortly after the Restoration. It proves, as history affirms, that reformations and revivals are short-lived. It also demonstrates the cor-ruption of the natural heart; for although God preferred Israel to Edom (i. 2-5), and had just delivered them from captivity and blessed their land with abundance (Hag. ii. 19), yet they questioned His love, treated with contempt His worship, and put aside the Book of the Law.

MALACHI I.—"Israel" (v. 1). Judah is thus addressed. Compare 2 Chron. xxi. 2 and Ezra vii. 10. These verses, with many others, disprove the Anglo-Isiael theory.

The nation was insensible to God's love (v. 2) and to their own sin (v. 6).

But God proved His love, for He chose Jacob rather than his elder brother Esau.

If a rich man, resolving to adopt a child, selects one of two brothers he is said in the Hebrew idiom to "love" the one and "hate" the other.

God again showed His love to the nation in redeeming it from captivity, and in making Palestine fruitful, while He left the Edomites in bondage, and turned their land into a desert (vs. 2-4).

"Whereas Edom saith" (v. 4) read: "But if Edom say," etc.

"The border of wickedness" (v. 4), i.e., a country, whose desolation is due to the wickedness of its inhabitants.

"The border of Israel" (v. 5). Palestine will yet be as the Garden of Eden; and its beauty and fertility will magnify Jehovah-Messiah.

The priests and the people despised the Ineffable Name by agreeing that anything was good enough for God (vs. 6-8).

"Ye say" (vs. 6, 7, 7, 12, 13), i.e., they said in action (vs. 7 and 8).

"Bread" (v. 7) a covering term for all sacrifices.

"The Table of the Lord" (vs. 7, and 12), i.e., the Brazen Altar.

Leviticus xxii. 22 and Deut xv. 21 forbade blemished sacrifices (v. 8).

"Thy governor" (v. 8), i.e., the Viceroy of Palestine appointed by the Persian monarch.

The first member of verse 9, is ironic.

"This hath been by your means," i.e., the priests were responsible for this disobedience to God's Word, for they were appointed to teach that Word (ii. 7).

Verse 10 should perhaps read as in the Revised Version. So the words may mean: that it would be morally better to close the Temple than to continue such hypocritical services. No priest would perform the small-est function without pay.

"For" (v. 11), read "But." See Acts xiii. 46. "Incense" and "a pure offering," i.e., prayer and praise based on the offering of Calvary (Heb. ix. 14, and x. 10) and presented by the Great High Priest (Heb. xiii. 15).

" Snuffed at it " (v. 13), i.e., " sniffed " ; that is " pooh-poohed."

" Dreadful " (v. 14), i.e., " revered."

MALACHI II. 1- 16.—The first nine verses form a special message to the priests, and the remaining verses of the chapter a special message to the people.

" This commandment " (v. 1), i.e., " to give glory unto My Name " (v. 2).

" Lay it to heart " (v. 2), i.e., " this commandment."

" A curse " (v. 2), read : " The curse," i.e., the curse of Deut. xxvii. and xxviii.

" Corrupt " (v. 3), read : " Rebuke " (R.V.) ; that is, the harvest should fail.

" Dung " (v. 3), i.e., the refuse of the sacrifices. This was a just judgment ; for they considered anything good enough for God, and so anything was good enough for them.

" One shall take you away with it " (v. 3), i.e., " Men shall cart you away, with the refuse, and so regard you as contemptible and base " (v. 9). A Christian, especially a Minister of the Gospel, who irreverently panders to the doctrines and actions of corrupt Christianity, is despised by society. True ministers are hated and persecuted, but they are feared and respected.

" Might be " (v. 4), i.e., " might continue." The priests were sons of Levi.

" My Covenant " (v. 5), i.e., The covenant of Exod. xxxii. 26-28, and Numbers xxv. 11.

A covenant is made by two parties. Here God and Levi. God covenanted to give him life and peace (omit the word " of "), and Levi covenanted to fear Him and reverence His Name. Verses 6 and 7 set out the character of the Covenant, and the Divine choice of Levi as a teacher of Scriptural knowledge and a messenger of the Lord of Hosts.

The priests of Malachi's day made void this covenant (v. 8), caused many to stumble in the Law by super-imposing their traditions (Matt. xv. 3-6), and they had respect of persons in administering law (v. 9).

" According as " (v. 9), i.e., " in proportion as."

So to-day appointed religious teachers cause many to stumble in the Scriptures by declaring that they are the creation of human genius and not the work of the infallible Spirit of God.

Thus these nine verses record the corruption of the Truth by the sons of Levi then living, and the following seven verses the violation of the institution of marriage by the people. Both violations resulted from disobedience to the Word of God. Compare Mark vii. 13.

" Brother " (v. 10). This is a covering term for all a wife's relatives. When a man breaks a covenant made with his wife, he breaks his pledge with her family as well as with herself, and is guilty of treachery to them all.

" The holiness of the Lord " (v. 11), i.e., the Hebrew Church, whose purity was affected by this violation of the Marriage Covenant.

" The master and the scholar " (v. 12). Hebrew : " Him that waketh and him that answereth." This is an idiom expressing unsparing and general punishment. There should be none left to be an awakener in the morning and none to be awakened—all should perish.

" Again " (v. 13), i.e., repeatedly.

" Tears, weeping, and crying out " (v. 13), i.e., the tears of the wronged wives and children.

" Wherefore " (v. 14) ? They were as insensible to natural affection as to Divine affection. The latter insensibility quickly occasions the former.

One sin leads to another still deeper. The restored Exiles (Neh. xiii. 23), contrary to the Bible (Deut. vii. 3), married heathen wives. To this evil they now added the deeper one of divorcing their Hebrew wives (v. 14).

" Did not He make one ? " (v. 15), i.e., " Did not God make only one wife for Adam ? " " Yet had He the residue or excellency of the Spirit," i.e., God being the Author of life could have given Adam many wives, and so have instituted polygamy.

" And wherefore one ? " (v. 15). The reference is to Abraham to whom God gave one wife and a godly seed by her (Isaac). If Malachi's opponents objected that Abraham had two wives, the prophet had a double reply. First, that Abraham took a second wife not to gratify passion, but to procure an heir. Second, that in so acting he grieved God and brought suffering upon himself and others. God's appointment of monogamy is here stated to have been in order to the provision of holy children (1 Chron.

vii. 14). Countless are the evils that flow from polygamy; and when a Christian man marries an unconverted wife, the children, as a rule, resist conversion and sometimes become ungodly. Thus it happens that ministers of the Gospel are disgraced bv godless sons.

" Take heed to " (v. 15), i.e., " be watchful over.

Verse 16 snould, perhaps, read as in the Revised Version. To cover his garment with violence " would, in that case, mean to illtreat one's wife, for the wife is a covering to the husband as the husband is to the wife (Gen. xx. 16). If it should read " to cover violence with his garment," then it means to excuse and hide the injury done to a divorced wife (Ps. lxxiii 6) ; for the husband instead of " covering her with his garment "—a Hebrew act of affection and relationship (Ruth. iii. 9)—covered her rival with it.

MALACHI II. 17 — III. 6. — Israel's deeds are reproved in i. 6 to ii. 16, and her words in ii. 17. Both are judged in iii. 1-6.

Creed determines conduct. This fact is ridiculed to-day. The cruelties and oppressions practised by the rich Exiles upon the defenceless and poor resulted from the scepticism exposed in verse 17. They confronted the prophet with an invitation and a challenge. The invitation was, to face facts, and so they pointed to the prosperity of the idolatrous and wicked nations around them as evidence that God approved of wickedness. The challenge was :—" produce proofs that God judges evil."

The Divine answer is given in verses iii 1-6. ·This passage predicts the First Advent, and iv. 5 and 6 the Second Advent. But the moral facts of the first cover both.

" I will send." " He shall come " (v. 1). These words, coupled with the words " Before Me," declare the Deity of Jesus of Nazareth.

" My Messenger " (v. 1), i.e., John the Baptist (Isa. xl. 3-5 and Mark i. 2, 3).

" Prepare," (v. 1), i.e., remove moral obstacles and bring to contrition of heart.

Messiah was the Messenger of the First Covenant (Exod. iii. 2-6 and Acts vii. 38) as He is the Messenger of the Second.

" Whom ye seek," " Whom ye delight in," (v. 1). The Jews at that time, and four hundred years later, eagerly desired the coming of a conquering Prince who would set them at the head of the nations, and endow them with wealth and glory ; but they did not desire a Judge Who would expose and punish their sins (vs. 2 and 5). Read Matt. xxiii.

" The Lord " (v. 1), Hebrew " Adon," i.e., The great and Universal King.

Verse 3 describes His present action. Judgment begins at the House of God, i.e., " The sons of Levi." The purifier sits watching the silver and maintaining the temperature, and directly he sees his face reflected in the metal, he stops the process.

" Offering," read " offerings " R.V. vs. 3, 4, i.e. gift offerings—not for expiation of sin. The Hebrew word used here and in i. 11 destroys the Roman Catholic theory that these verses foretell the institution of the Mass.

The reason why the Hebrews were not as totally destroyed as the Philistines and other races, was because of the unchangeableness of God's electing love. The final salvation of the Elect of Israel, as also of the Church, is not secured by their unchangeable love to God, but by His unchangeable love to them.

MALACHI III. 7-IV. 6.—Conduct and creed are here again reviewed ; but in relation to the judgment of the Second Advent.

The subject matter of the whole Malachi prophecy may be set out thus :

Conduct	i. 6 to 11, 16.
Creed	ii. 17.
First Advent	iii. 1-6.
Conduct	iii. 7-12.
Creed	iii. 13 to iv. 4.
Second Advent	iv. 5, 6.

The displacement of the Holy Scriptures as the authority and rule of life originates declension and corruption (v. 7).

The call to conversion angered Israel's pride, and the people proudly said : " Wherein shall we return " ? i.e., " We don't need conversion ! " Such was the language, in action, of the scribes and Pharisees of Christ's day, just as it is to-day.

The prophet's answer was : " Do you not rob God, and is not that a sin to be converted from ? " And when they proudly asked wherein they had robbed Him, a convicting reply was given—disobedience to Lev. xxvii. 30-33. Num. xviii. 21-32, Deut. xii. 17, etc., and xiv. 22-29.

No nation can hold together as an organized

society without taxation for public services. The most equitable system of taxation is by tithes and free gifts. Public worship, national education, courts of justice, and maintenance of the poor were thus provided for in Israel. The Bible was the authority. This foundation being displaced all fell together, with the consequence that God was dishonoured, and oppression and suffering caused

" A curse " (v. 9), Hebrew : " The curse," i.e., the curse of ii. 2 and Deut. xxviii. 20.

To rob the poor of justice and of their goods, is to rob God, for He loves and pities the poor and defenceless. No man ever yet lost by serving God with a whole heart, nor gained by serving Him with a half one.

" The devourer " (v. 11), i.e., the locust. God delights in blessing and is ready to meet the feeblest repentance with the richest bounties (vs. 10-12).

" Meat in Mine house "-(v. 10), i.e., money in the Temple Treasury for expenses.

Their deeds having been thus exposed (7-12), their words are now recalled (vs. 13-15). They stoutly said it was folly to serve God, for no profit resulted from it ; that, on the contrary, they had concluded (" we call ") that the proud were happy; that the workers of iniquity prospered (" set up ") ; and that nothing happened to those who challenged the existence of God and His judgment of evil (vs. 14 and 15). Then, as now, men boldly said " if there be a God let Him strike me dead," and because God in His pity refused the challenge, they decided that He did not exist.

But God had then, as now, those who loved and feared Him (vs. 16 and 17) ; and, because of the corruption of the Church, they met together the more frequently for fellowship and worship, and did not yield to the temptation to lessen, or discontinue, such meetings because of the moral ruin which surrounded them. The importance of the word " then " (v. 16) should not be over-looked, nor the necessity, declared by the Bible, of spiritual fellowship and united worship (Heb. x. 25). Neglect of this command, and the substitution of private personal worship in the home, or on the hillside, leads to spiritual death.

Heaven lovingly records the worship of little groups of believing people whom earth despises. What intense interest these records will excite when published in the coming millennial day ! (v. 16).

Verse 17 may be thus paraphrased : " They shall be My peculiar treasure, saith the Lord of Hosts, in the day that I have appointed." Compare iv. 1 and 3 (R.V.).

" Spare " (v. 17), Hebrew : "To be gentle towards," " to pity," " to have compassion upon."

" Ye " (v. 18), i.e., the proud sceptics and oppressors of verses 7 and 15.

These denied any distinction on the part of God between a righteous man and a wicked man, between the man that owned God and the man that denied Him ; but the day appointed by God (iii. 17 and iv. 1 and 3) will compel them to turn from their scepticism and to recognise, and' confess, that God does distinguish between His servants and His enemies.

The " then " of verse 18 is to be contrasted with the " then " of verse 16. The latter is the believer's present day of affliction ; the former, the unbeliever's future day of doom.

" The day that I shall do this " (iv. 3) better : " The day that I have appointed " ; i.e., the day of iii. 17 and iv. 1 and of 2 Thess. i.

The fact of this appointed day of eternal doom is widely denied, and even by many salaried ministers of religion.

Verse 2 should read as in the Revised Version. When calves are released from the stall into a sunny field they skip with joy. The day of Messiah's apparition in flaming fire will be a day of joy for His people. The fire will be a furnace to their enemies (v. 1 R.V.) but sun rays to themselves (v. 2).

The proud now treat as dirt beneath their feet the confessors of Messiah's Name. In the future the position will be reversed (v. 3).

The word " therefore " may be supplied after the words " Remember ye " (v. 4). The injunction is : that in view of that appointed day of wrath men should believe, obey and observe the Word of God.

But God willeth not the death of even the vilest sinners, and so He will send Elijah prior to the Second Advent, as He sent John the Baptist in the spirit and power of Elijah, prior to the First Advent, to warn sinners of the wrath to come (Luke i. 17 and iii. 7). Hence, if the nation had repented at that time, then John would have been Elijah to them. But they rejected his testimony, refused to turn to the faith of their fathers, and so the ban (" curse ") threatened upon Palestine (v. 6) has rested upon it ever since.

The purpose of John's ministry prior to the First Advent, and of Elijah's prior to the Second, was to cause the heart of the fathers Abraham, Isaac, and Jacob to come upon their descendants, and that the unbelieving heart of the descendants should turn into the believing heart of the fathers—that is to say, the stony heart of the children should be replaced by the heart of flesh of the fathers (Ezek. xxxvi. 26).

Moses and Elijah (vs. 4 and 5), as representatives of the Law and of the Prophets, are here brought together ; they re-appear in Matt. xvii. 3, and are, possibly, the two "men" of Luke xxiv. 4, and Acts i. 10, and the two "prophets" of Rev. xi. 10. If this be so, they will provide the witnesses demanded by Deut. xix. 15 and 2 Cor. xiii. 1.

MATTHEW

Four hundred years intervene between Malachi and Matthew ; and four hundred and fifty years after Ezra i. 1, as predicted in Dan. ix. 25 (483-33), the Messiah was born

In this First Gospel He is presented as the King of Israel (Jer. xxiii. 5, 6, xxxiii. 15, and Zech. ix. 9). Hence His pedigree is given from Abraham and David, and He is portrayed as The Branch, The King. In the other three Gospels He is presented as The Branch, The Servant (Mark) ; The Branch, The Man (Luke) ; and The Branch, Jehovah (John).

There were eight Herods in the days of the New Testament :—Herod the Great, (Matt. ii.1) ; Herod Philip I. (Matt. xiv. 3) ; Herod Archelaus (Matt. ii. 22) ; Herod Antipas (Luke iii. 1) ; Herod Philip II. (Luke iii. 1) ; Herod Agrippa I. (Acts xii. 1) ; Herod Agrippa II. (Acts xxv. 13), and Herod King of Chalcis.

This Gospel sets forth the Messiah's claim as king. Events in His ministry are therefore recorded and emphasized which do not appear in the other Gospels.

The four rivers of Gen. ii. 10 flowed from one source. They, possibly, foreshadowed the Four Gospels inspired by the One Holy Spirit.

Similarly the waters of Ezek. xlvii. 3-5 have a like reference. Matthew, Mark and Luke, i.e., the King, the Servant and the Man may be measurable (vs. 3 and 4) ; but the Gospel of John, i.e., God manifest in the Flesh, is a river that cannot be passed over (v. 5).

The notes on the corresponding passages in the other Gospels should in each case be read.

MATTHEW I.—" Generation " (v. 1), i.e., " Pedigree."

" Jesus Christ " (v. 1), i.e., Jehoshua, Messiah ; that is, Jehovah the Saviour, the Anointed One.

In this pedigree the names Ahaziah Joash, Amaziah and Jehoiakim are omitted according to the law of Deut. xxix. 20 ; the first three because of being the third and fourth generation of Ahab, and the remaining one because Jehoiakim was not an independent king, and because of Jeremiah xxxvi. 23. These four names were blotted out of God's Book of remembrance

Thus the three great moral periods of Israel's history contained fourteen generations each viz. : From Abraham to David ; From David to Josiah ; and from Jeconias to Joseph.

Four women appear in the Pedigree : Tamar, Rahab, Ruth and Bathsheba—a Hebrew, a Gentile ; a Gentile, a Hebrew. These women emphasize Christ's condescension in taking human nature, for two of them were Gentiles, and only one was of good character.

The Pedigree of Luke iii. 23 is that of Mary, and shows her descent from David and Adam through Nathan, Solomon's elder brother.

Matthew's Pedigree is that of Joseph as regal heir begotten of Solomon and David. Mary was daughter of Eli and cousin to Joseph. Both Joseph and Mary were of the House of David. See notes on Luke i. 27. and iii.

Jesus, therefore, united in His Person the two only claims to the Throne of Israel ; and as He still lives there can be no other claimant.

" Now " (v. 18), rather " But," in order to mark the contrast between His birth and that of the preceding births ; for they were by natural procreation, but His by spiritual procuration.

" A righteous man " (v. 19), i.e., a man who feared the Word of God and was determined to obey it. But loving his betrothed wife he resolved to avail himself of Deut. xxiv. 1 and divorce her privately and not put her to death (Deut. xxii. 23, 24).

" An Angel of Jehovah " (v. 20 R.V.).

" She shall bring forth " (v. 21), not " of thee " as in Luke i. 35, because not Joseph's son.

" He shall save " (v. 21) Greek: " He it is that shall save " ; i.e., He and none other. Hence His Name Jehovah the Saviour, i.e., Jesus.

" The Virgin " v. 23) : the Greek word here used defines the word in Isa. vii. 14 as meaning a virgin.

Thus the great titles of Jehovah, Immanuel, Messiah, God, Son of God, Son of David, and Jesus are here grouped together.

Verses 24 and 25 prove that after the birth of the Divine Child, Mary physically became Joseph's wife ; for " he took unto him his wife," " and knew her not until " (imperfect tense in the Greek text), that is, " was not accustomed to co-habit with her as his wife until." Four sons and at least two daughters were the fruit of this marriage, as appears from chapter xiii. 55, 56. These facts destroy the Roman Catholic doctrine of the perpetual virginity of Mary of Nazareth. See also the word " before " (v. 18) in the Greek text and its force in the seventeen passages where it occurs ; and also the affirmative force of " until " ; for example, Luke xiii. 35, and xv. 4. Compare Luke ii. 7—" her son, the first-born." See note on Acts i. 14.

MATTHEW II.—" Now Jesus having been born " (v. 1), i.e., about two years before the events recorded in this chapter.

" Bethlehem of Judæa." There were two Bethlehems ; the other was in Zebulon. See note on Micah v. 2.

" Wise men from the East " (v. 1). Their number is not stated, nor is their particular country, nor that they were kings, nor that they were black men. These are human imaginations.

" His Star in the East " (v. 2). Read : " We (dwelling) in the East saw His star."

Herod the king (v. 3). He was a descendant of Esau—an Edomite—and so by nature hated and resolved to murder the Son of Jacob.

" All Jerusalem " (v. 3), excepting the little flock who had two years before—a most touching picture—gathered round Elizabeth and Zacharias and Mary and Joseph and the two babes, and Simeon and Anna and others (Luke ii. 38.)

The priests knew the Bible well (vs. 4-6). Head knowledge of the Scriptures is not the same as heart knowledge. It can be used against Christ.

" Diligently " (v. 7), i.e., " Most carefully ". See note on verse 16.

" What time the star appeared " (v. 7) (Num. xxiv. 17 and Dan. ix. 25). These Eastern prophecies were most probably preserved by the Magi, and handed on from generation to generation. That this star was miraculous there can be no doubt, for that fact is affirmed by verse 9.

" When they saw the star they rejoiced with exceeding great joy " (vs. 9 and 10). This statement makes it clear that the star did not precede them in their journey to Jerusalem, as is popularly supposed, but that after they had left Jerusalem the star which they had seen in the East suddenly reappeared and led them, not to the " Manger " at Bethlehem, but to the " house " in Nazareth, where the young child, the little boy, no longer a babe, was. The Lord was presented in the Temple forty-one days after His birth (Luke ii. 21 with Lev. xii. 3, 4), and thence returned to Nazareth (Luke ii. 39). The events in this chapter, therefore, occurred later, i.e., between Luke ii. 39 and Luke ii. 40.

" Gold " (v. 11). Thus was the money needed for the flight into Egypt, supplied.

Israel as God's son (Exod. iv. 22 and 23) having failed in obedience and love, it was necessary that a true Israel should appear to vindicate God's character, and prove that He could be loved and obeyed. Hence the necessity of the departure into Egypt (vs. 12-15).

" Children " (v. 16), i.e., male children.

" From two years old "—" according to the time," etc. These words decide that two years had elapsed since the apparition of the Star in the East.

Rachel was buried at Ramah (v. 18).

But the Son of David on returning to the land of Israel (v. 22) could not approach the Throne of His Fathers, but had to take the position of a despised Nazarene.

Galilee was despised by Jerusalem, and the town of Nazareth was especially contemptible (John i. 46). It was Joseph's native place ; and there he plied his trade as a carpenter.

"Spoken by the prophets" (v. 23). They all predicted that the Messiah, in His first Advent, would be despised ; that is, He would be a Nazarene ; and so it came to pass.

MATTHEW III.—As foretold by Malachi (iii. 1 and iv. 5) John the Baptist appeared. He was the last and greatest of the prophets (xi. 7-15), and would have been reckoned Elijah, or as Elijah, had the nation repented. He was the greatest, for he went immediately before the face of Jehovah Messiah.

Sin conflicts with the government of God (v. 2). Hence the necessity for repentance, for man is a sinner.

"The Kingdom of heaven" (v. 2). Greek, "The kingdom of the heavens" ; i.e., the kingdom that is to succeed the Fourth Empire of Daniel's prophecy (see note on Dan. vii. 9, 10).

"The prophet Isaiah" (v. 3) is quoted by seven inspired writers twenty-one times in the New Testament. There was no second Isaiah.

The Syrian peasant of to-day wears a garment of woven camel's hair fastened by a leathern belt, and his food is locusts and wild honey. The locust was a clean food (Lev. xi. 22).

"All Judea" (v. 5). An idiom for a great multitude.

To baptize Gentiles was usual, but to baptize Hebrews was unknown. If a prominent pastor in the Baptist Church were to call to repentance, and to baptize extensively members of that Church, it would cause similar excitement.

People ignorantly speak of the spirit of the New Testament being different from that of the Old, but verses 7-12 overthrow this belief ; as do many other passages, notably those of the Book of the Revelation. How could God's attitude towards sin change ? The Baptist called these men children of Satan ; he declared the wrath of God was coming ; that the axe of judgment was even then lying at the root of the tree of religious pro-

fession ; and that if these moralists did not repent they would be burned up as chaff in the unquenchable fire. God fans (v. 12) the chaff ; Satan sifts the wheat (Luke xxii. 31).

Thus the doctrines of the Baptist differed fundamentally from those of the disciples of Modern Thought.

"Meet for" (v. 8), i.e., befitting.

"Is laid" (v.10) Greek : "Is lying at."

"The root." To strike off a branch is partial destruction, but to lay the axe at the root means total destruction. The tree pictures the professor of religion. His destruction will not be his extinction ; for after being cut down he will be cast into the fire. The only good trees in existence are those who confess that they are bad ; just as an honest heart is one which accepts the Divine testimony that it is incurably diseased.

The "fire" of verse 11 is the fire of acceptance, such as the cloven tongues of fire at Pentecost, and not the unquenchable fire of verse 12 which is the fire of vengeance.

"Suffer" (v. 15), i.e., permit Me to be baptized.

"It becometh us to fulfil all righteousness" (v. 15). John was commanded to baptize, and every godly Israelite was commanded to be baptized. Jesus was a godly Israelite, and was such in order to save. Hence the obedience of righteousness rested on them both in relation to this baptism. But there was this difference,—Righteousness brought Him there ; sin brought His fellow-countrymen.

"He saw" (v. 16), i.e., Jesus saw.

"This is My Son, My Beloved in Whom is all my delight." (v. 17). In Mark and Luke the formula of the utterance is given : "Thou art," etc. Here, the import : "This is," etc. But as suggested by John i. 33, it is possible that there were two utterances, one addressed to Jesus as the Spirit was descending, saying, "Thou art," etc, and the other addressed to John after the descent of the Spirit and His repose upon Jesus, saying : "This is," etc.

The three persons of the Trinity here immediately appear upon the front page of the New Testament ; the Father speaking, the Spirit descending, and the Son praying (Luke iii. 21).

"This is My Beloved Son" was the Divine formula of anointing Messiah for the office of prophet (Matt. iii. 17) ; Priest (Matt. xvii. 5) ; and King (Ps. ii. 7).

MATTHEW IV.—The First Adam was tempted in a garden; the Second, in a wilderness. "Tempted" means "Put to the test." Adam was tested in innocence; Jesus was tempted as knowing both good and evil, though in Himself sinless. He entered the Wilderness of this world's misery and evil to render in it a life of absolute obedience and dependence; and it was therefore necessary that that perfect obedience and dependence should be tested. It demanded that He should have no other will than that of His Father; and that He would accept that Will, and delight in it, no matter what might be the consequences to Himself. It was this obedience and dependence that the tempter sought to impair; and so he invited Him to use His privileges as the Son of God, and as the Messiah, and as the Son of Man, to work a miracle in His own favour, and to manifest Himself to Israel, and to take up the sovereignty of the earth promised to Him. But he failed. See note on Num. xxi. 21-35.

"If Thou be" (v. 3), or "Since Thou art." that is: "demonstrate that you believe the heavenly utterance, and so provide for your hunger." It was a subtle snare into which any other would have fallen, but with one text from the written Word (Deut. viii. 3) the Tempter was defeated. Jesus began a ministry rich in miracle by refusing to work one. He fed others, Himself He would not feed; just as He saved others, but Himself He would not save.

Had Christ so done He would have acted independently of God, and so failed in a perfect obedience and a perfect dependence; and failure would have been sin.

The context of Deut. viii. 3 recalled Israel's hunger in the Desert. They murmured when hungry; the True Israel trusted, and waited, and He too received angels' food (v. 11).

The Lord's ministry opened and closed with a triple appeal to the Word of God (Matt. iv. 4, 6 and 7, and John xvii. 8, 14 and 17).

On each occasion one text from the Bible skilfully chosen and used, sufficed to defeat the Tempter; for he knows that the Bible is the Word of God.

The order of the Temptations here is historical; in Luke it is dispensational. There is, therefore, an inner harmony, for Matthew presents Him as the Messiah coming to His Temple, and then as Son of Man reigning over the earth. But the Spirit in Luke places His relation to the earth in the foreground, and His connection with Israel in the background. There are many other instances in the Scriptures of a dispensational or moral order designedly differing from the historical. Compare 1. Cor. x.

Satan recognizes that the Psalms belong to the Messiah, and that their promises are His. Jesus did not deny this, but said that it was also written that the servant should not test God to keep His promises. The context of this second quotation concerned Israel's challenge: "Can God give us flesh?"

Malachi predicted that the Messiah would come suddenly to His Temple (Mal. iii. 1). Satan proposed that He should fulfil this prophecy by suddenly descending into the Temple court,—adding that He need not fear, for the angels were commanded to safeguard Him. In his quotation of Scripture Satan added and subtracted words, as a reference to Ps. xci. 11 and 12 shows. When the Holy Spirit quotes the Scriptures He is at liberty to vary them as He often does, for He is their Author.

Had the Lord done as Satan suggested, He would not only have made Himself an agent of Satan's will, but He would have compelled the angels to become agents also.

Had He commanded the stones to be made bread, and the angels to safeguard Him, He would have forsaken His position as a servant, for a servant does not command.

Satan now abandoned all disguise and boldly called upon Jesus to worship him. Then it was that the Lord dismissed him. This dismissal concluded the temptations, and so declares their historic order.

Satan had captured many kings by the offer of a part of the glory of earthly dominion, and he now tried by the offer of the whole to capture the heart of the Carpenter of Nazareth. But the object of that heart was God and His Will and not earth and its glory. He did not despise the Throne of the earth, but He would only have it as His Father's gift; and it was as such that He prized it. Every heart that puts God first and seeks to please Him only, is certain to escape Satan's most subtle snares; for to that heart there is given a clearness of vision that discovers these snares.

The long predicted day at last arrived and the King presented Himself to Israel (vs.

12-17). He chose the members of His Cabinet (vs. 18-22), and He taught them (chs. v. to vii.).

His apparition as the Great Light found Zebulun and Naphtali in greater affliction under the Romans than under the Assyrians (see notes on Isa. ix.) ; and the moral darkness was greater than the national misery.

The depth of this great darkness and the people sitting in it (v. 16), are contrasted with the fame of the Great Light and the people following it (vs. 24 and 25).

The might of the Great King over all physical disease (vs. 23 and 24), and over moral disease (chs. v-vii.) demonstrated Him to be the predicted Liberator of Isa. ix.

" Cast into prison " (v. 12), Greek : " Delivered up." This whole passage up to the end of the chapter, is a précis of the Lord's Ministry and not a chronological record. The commencement of His ministry synchronized with John's imprisonment.

" Leaving Nazareth " (v. 13), i.e., " Leaving on one side " (Acts xxi. 3). He was not wanted in the family home.

The Messiah's advent was signalled by the three great words : " Repent " (v. 17). " Follow " (v. 19) " Blessed " (ch. v. 3).

These four disciples (18-22) had previously met Him in Judea, whither no doubt they had gone to be baptized of John, and then had returned to their home in Capernaum.

Christ does not call lazy men to His service. The brothers Andrew and Peter were casting their net, and the other brothers James and John were mending their net. He called them to a higher fishing, as He called David to a higher feeding (Ps. lxxviii. 70-72).

The calling of the Disciples must not be confounded with the selecting of the Apostles. They were quite distinct.

" The Gospel of the Kingdom " (v. 23), i.e., the good news of the establishment upon earth of the perfect Government of Heaven.

The association in the Four Gospels of the name " Jesus" with the words " multitude," " great multitudes," " very great multitudes," and " an innumerable multitude " does not surprise the reader who has experimental knowledge of the saving grace and power and loveliness of Christ.

The four cherubim of Ezek. i. 10 and Rev. iv. 7 correspond to the four Gospels. The four standards of Num. ii. are stated by the Rabbis to have borne these figures of the Cherubim. The lion foreshadowed the Gospel of Matthew, i.e., the King, the lion of the Tribe of Judah. The ox, i.e., Mark. The man, i.e., Luke. The eagle, i.e., John— the Gospel of the Deity of Christ ; for the way of an eagle is in the air (Prov. xxx. 19).

MATTHEW V.—Two sermons, both delivered on mountains, opened and closed the Lord's public ministry. The first was upon the mountain near Capernaum (Matt. v.), and the last upon Olivet near Jerusalem (Matt. xxiv.). The theme of each was the kingdom from the heavens—its moral characteristics in the first discourse ; its fortunes and its future, in the second.

Character determines heavenly citizenship. True possession (vs. 3-12) and true profession (vs. 13-16) introduce an exposition of the Laws of the kingdom (v. 17-vii. 27).

It is quite reasonable to believe that the Lord repeated this teaching (Luke vi. 17) ; for such is the patience of the Great Teacher with dull scholars. See notes on 1 Kings vii. and Luke vi. 17, 49.

" Poor in spirit " (v. 3), i.e., conscious of moral poverty.

" They that mourn " (v. 4), i.e., grieved because of personal sinfulness. Verse 3 is experimental ; verse 4, emotional.

" The meek " (v. 5), i.e., the opposite of the self-righteous.

" Righteousness " (v. 6), i.e., both imputed and practical.

" Pure in heart " (v. 8), i.e., the purified in heart ; that is, those who have received a new moral nature in regeneration.

" For my sake " (v. 11). Many are disliked justly because of their faults of character, but only those can rejoice who are disliked because they belong to Jesus and testify for Him. Only Christ could use the phrase " For My sake," for He was God. Moses, David, Isaiah, Paul could not so speak.

If salt loses its savour it is worthless ; for its one and only property is to prevent corruption. The Christian's one mission in life is by conduct and doctrine to guard the Church from corruption. If therefore he does not shine for Jesus he is useless ; and men treat him with contempt. He is both to conserve and to shine ; he is to be conservative and diffusive.

Thus these verses (3-16) set out the moral characteristics of the citizens of the kingdom of the heavens ; and so it is apparent that the

New Birth is an absolute necessity for entrance into that kingdom.

The Laws of the kingdom are detailed in verses 17-vii. 12.

These fulfil the Law and the Prophets (17-20); they transcend the law of Moses (21-48); they excel the tradition of the Elders (vi. 1-vii. 11); and they develop and demonstrate the whole moral teaching of the Law and the Prophets (vii. 12).

"Think not" (v. 17). Emphatic: "Do not for a moment think."

"I am come" (v. 17). This phrase affirms previous existence, and "to fulfil," claims previous authorship.

"Jot or tittle" (v. 18). "Jot" is the smallest letter in the Hebrew alphabet; "tittle" is a minute ornamental finish to ancient Hebrew letters.

"Verily" (v. 18), i.e., "I solemnly declare." This is the first occurrence of this august expression. Only Deity could thus speak.

Many ancient and modern priests have been, and are disloyal to the authority of the Word of God. Such shall be judged; but the loyal shall be honoured (v. 19).

The Pharisees distinguished between "venial" and "mortal" sins. There is no such distinction in the Word of God, and hence the force of the words "He shall be called the least" means that he will not be in the kingdom at all (v.19).

The necessity of the New Birth is declared as imperative in every case (v. 20).

The five Laws relating to Murder, Adultery, Perjury, Retaliation, and Love to personal enemies (20-48), are here spiritualized and adapted to suit and govern the conduct of the citizens of the kingdom; and this is done by Him Who ordained them at the first for His earthly people.

"Heard" (v. 21), i.e., every Sabbath Day in the synagogue. "By them." Read: "To them"; that is, "by Me." "Thou shalt not kill." This should read: "Thou shalt do no murder"; for the magistrate is ordered by God to put evil doers to death (Gen. ix. 6 and Rom. xiii. 1-6).

The feeling of anger is, in essence, murder (v. 22); unless it be righteous anger (Mark iii. 5).

"Raca" and "Thou fool" (v. 22) were Hebrew expressions of murderous anger.

Not degrees of judgment but the fact of judgment, is the force of the words "in danger of" (v. 22); i.e., certain of judgment.

A brother's justly feared wrath gives occasion to the introduction of a more dread Adversary (v. 25); and those who are in the way with Him to judgment are urged to an agreement lest they suffer eternal doom (v. 26).

In this kingdom, desire, if indulged, is declared as sinful as the action (v. 22 and v. 28).

"Looketh on" (v. 28), i.e., "keeps looking on," and "keeps lusting after."

The Lord's method of teaching was symbolic and figurative (v. 30). It is better to destroy what tempts to wrong-doing, though it be as precious as an eye or a hand, than to suffer eternal torments.

Deut. xxiv. 1 was limited to unfaithfulness to the marriage bond; but the Pharisees made it cover any excuse sought by men for getting rid of their wives (v. 31). But He Who framed this Law shows its true meaning in verse 32; and so safeguards the sanctity of marriage.

Verses 34 and 37 should be read together with Lev. xix. 12, R.V. and Num. xxx, and it will then appear that oaths and vows are to be avoided in ordinary communications. God confirmed His promise with an oath (Heb. vi. 17). That cannot therefore be wrong for the child to do which the Father did. The Lord when put on his oath by the High Priest immediately answered; and the apostle Paul took vows and more than once attested before God the truthfulness of his statements (2 Cor. i. 18, 23, xi. 11, 31, Gal. i. 20, Phil. i. 8, 1 Thess. ii. 5, 10, ch. v. 27, 1 Tim. v. 21, vi. 13, 2 Tim. ii. 14, and iv. 1, and (vows) Acts xviii. 18, xxi. 23, and 1 Cor. viii. 13). Verse 37 may read: "Let your word Yes be Yes, and your No be No; for stronger assertions come from the evil nature." Thus promises, and statements, and conversation are to be entirely devoid of expletives.

The figurative language of verses 38-48 condemns a litigious spirit (38-40); a disobliging spirit (41 and 42); and a revengeful spirit (43-48).

That the language is figurative is evident from verse 39, for the Lord when smitten on the cheek (John xviii. 22 and 23) did not turn the other cheek but with dignity rebuked the assailant.

The heavenly citizen is not to be ready to

take offence (v. 39), nor prompt to go to law (v. 40), nor disobliging (v. 41), nor heartless (v. 42), nor revengeful (v. 44), but like his Father in Heaven, he is to be kind to both evil and good men ; and so, in that sense, be perfect as His Father, for his actions will correspond. See note on Deut. xix. 21.

The actions of the enemies of goodness and of righteousness are to be "hated" with a holy hatred : but personal hatred is to be met by love.

So the child is to walk in fellowship with the Father, and to imitate Him. He is, for example, to help those of his fellow-men whom God would help, and to help them in the same way. He is not, for example, to give money to a lazy man to be spent by him in vice, for the Heavenly Father says : " If any will not work neither shall he eat." (2 Thess. iii. 10).

" The mountain " (v. 1 R.V.). Compare xxviii. 16. R.V.

The eight blessings (v. 3-10) at the commencement of Christ's ministry contrast with the eight woes at its close (xxiii. 13, 36).

MATTHEW VI.-VII. 29.—Having developed the five statutes respecting Murder, Adultery, Perjury, Retaliation and Love to enemies, the Lord now adds teaching concerning the five precepts relating to Almsgiving, Prayer, Fasting, Riches and Care.

" Alms " (v. 1). This should read " righteousness," that is, religious actions. This first verse is an introduciton to the five examples which follow.

First ; Alms-giving (vs. 2-4). True Christian service is unconscious service (xxv. 37).

Second : Prayer (vs. 5-15). Those who make God's interests their own are assured that He will make their interests His.

" Vain Repetitions " (v. 7). The Hindus and the Roman Catholics believe that by repeating the same prayer hundreds of times they will be heard for their much speaking. The Lord here says (v. 8), " Be not ye like unto them " ; and He gave a model of acceptable prayer.

It contains seven petitions—three respecting God, and four respecting man. Those respecting God come first. See note on vii. 7-11.

The first two words " Our Father " destroy the doctrine of a false humility that teaches that in prayer the suppliant should take up a position as far from God as possible, addressing Him by many august titles, and that only after a very lengthened prayer the term " Father " may be used with much timidity. But to be timid when God commands boldness is to be disobedient (Heb. iv. 16).

" In Heaven " (v. 9) : Greek, " In the heavens," that is, the universe. God is not shut away in some distant region far off from His children, but is omnipresent. " Heaven " (v. 10)—here singular because distinguished from earth.

" Temptation " (v. 13), i.e., " Testing." Peter boldly challenged testing and fell. The instructed child prays that he may not be tested. The verb " To lead " is not the same word as iv. 1 but rather suggests the leading of self-confidence.

" Evil " (v. 13). This is a covering term meaning both moral evil and temporal affliction. It may also mean the Evil One.

The foundation of forgiveness is that of Eph. iv. 32. Its super-structure is that of verses 14 and 15. If the super-structure is not visible its invisibility declares the absence of the foundation, for those who have truly experienced the forgiveness of their sins for Christ's sake do forgive those who sin against them.

Third, " Fasting," (vs. 16-18). " Anoint thine head," etc., that is, dress as usual.

Fourth, " Riches " (vs. 19-24). If the eye be set upon treasures in Heaven this single purpose will make the character and life simple and straight, and the Christian will shine for Jesus.

If the eye be set upon treasures on earth the life and character of the believer will be shrouded in moral darkness. A man's aim determines his character. If that aim be not simple and heavenward but earthward and double, all the faculties and principles of his nature will become a mass of darkness. It is impossible to give a divided allegiance (v. 24). " Hate," i.e., disregard.

Fifth : " Cares " (25-vii. 11). " They toil not " (v. 28), i.e., the work of the man in growing flax ; " they spin not," i.e., the work of the woman in weaving it.

" The oven " (v. 30). In Palestine the baker's furnace is heated with grass for fuel.

" No thought " (v . 25, 31 and 34) : the Greek word means no anxious thought.

" Sufficient unto the day," etc. (v. 34). To anticipate cares is to double them.

Men covet money in order to purchase

power, position and pleasure. The Christian seeks first the Kingdom of God. Compare v. 33 with v. 20.

God may permit poverty to test His child, but fellow-believers are not to err, as Job's friends did, and believe the trial to be a judgment for secret sin (vii. 1). On the contrary self-judgment should be exercised (remembering that anything that perverts the moral vision is comparable to a mote or a beam in the eye) (vs. 3-5). Judgment, however, is to be made respecting the ungodly (v. 6), and heavenly treasure is not to be exposed to their contempt and hostility. To these the Gospel, and the ensuing wrath of God if it be rejected, are to be preached.

The antidote for care is to betake oneself to the Royal Treasury (vs. 7-11). Application there will meet with certain response. But the mode of application must follow the pattern (vi. 9-13). There God's interests come first. They occur in a descending scale from Himself to His kingdom and from His Kingdom to the earth. The four human petitions occur in an ascending scale—from daily bread to final deliverance.

Swine trample pearls under their feet, and dogs turn round and bite the donor.

Verse 12 sums up the statutes and precepts of the kingdom; but this Golden Rule does not authorise capricious benevolent action, but only what is reasonable and morally helpful, and controlled by Divine imitation (ch. v. 48).

The entrance into the kingdom (vs. 13-14) is declared to be the narrow gate of conversion; and the Lord adds that few pass in by it. This double statement is offensive to the moralist, for it declares him to be so hopelessly corrupt that he needs a moral re-creation; and it states that few are thus reborn. Every contrite heart earnestly desires to be among the " few " of verse 14.

The preachers of falsehood (vs. 15-23) are now at once introduced because they deny the need of conversion, and because they stand in contrast to the preachers of truth (vs. 13-16).

The moral fruit of these false teachers is corruption in the Church and in the world; for how can unconverted men produce conversion ? (v. 18).

Mere profession of loyalty to Christ is valueless (v. 21).

" Lord, Lord " (v. 22). The repetition of the word " Lord " expresses astonishment,

as if to say: " Are we to be disowned ? "

Miracles (v. 22) may accredit falsehood (xxiv. 24 and Rev. xiii. 13). The Word of God is to be the alone judge of doctrine.

False teachers are workers of iniquity (v. 23), however attractive their personal character may be. This judgment would to-day be called narrow, unchristian, violent and bigoted; but it is the Master's judgment.

True wisdom (vs. 24-27) at the close of this address corresponds to true happiness at its opening (ch. v. 3-12). In both passages characters are pictured.

" Beat " (v. 25), i.e., " with violence." " Beat " (v. 27), i.e., " lightly struck." See Greek text.

" Having authority " (v. 29), i.e., Divine Authority. Compare verses 21 and 22— " Many will say to Me in that day." He here declares Himself to be God the Great Judge Eternal. Hence He spake with authority; and the people felt it. None of the great prophets could use such words.

" Not as the scribes " (v. 29). They always referred to tradition, or to what some other teacher had said.

This sermon and that of Luke vi. were possibly one and the same. The Lord descended the mountain a certain distance and meeting the multitude He re-ascended a little to " a plain " or level place suitable for the purpose and there preached. Emphasis is laid in Matthew on the necessity of a new moral birth, hence the points about sin in the heart; in Luke outward actions are reviewed. The distinction between " standing " and " state " is apparent. See note on Luke vi. and 1 Kings vii. and 2 Chron. iii. The two pillars were distinct—Jachin and Boaz—but in type, a moral unity—Christ in the glorious effulgence of His being—an all-sufficient Saviour—and the gate into the Kingdom of Heaven.

MATTHEW VIII.-IX. 1—Jehovah Messiah having on the Mount exhibited the statutes of the kingdom which He proposed to set up upon the earth, descended and in the midst of the people demonstrated His power as God over disease, (2-16) over nature (24-26) and over demons (28-32), and His ability, by banishing evil, to fill the earth with happiness and destroy the works and kingdom of the Devil; but men preferred Satanic domination, and disease, and demons, and swine (v. 34).

Sin defiles (v. 2); paralyzes (v. 6); inflames (v. 14); and enslaves (v. 16).

To touch a leper defiled. But Christ's sinlessness was undefilable, and as the True Priest He came in the closest proximity to the sinner. "Thou canst"; "I will"; "Immediately cleansed"; Such is the simplicity and actuality of salvation! Only God could cleanse the leper, hence Jesus was God; but yet, as a servant, He veiled His glory, and, as a Hebrew, in subjection to Law, commanded the man to fulfil its requirements (v. 4). Thus the Law, through the activities of the priest, confirmed the miracle wrought by the Law-giver. But Immanuel's mission in His First Advent was to deal with sin and suffer its judgment at Calvary. He suppressed anything that would hinder that purpose of grace, and so forbade the man to publish the fact of his healing.

But He came not only to cleanse Israel but to liberate the Gentile, and, accordingly, the servant of the Roman officer was set free from his malady.

The intelligence of the centurion was remarkable. He argued that the soldiers had to obey him because in his person resided the authority of the Emperor, and, similarly, disease obeyed Jesus because in Him was the authority of God.

"Many" (v. 11), i.e., the Gentile nations who by-and-by will be incorporated in the Hebrew Church. The unconverted members of that Church (v. 12) shall share the doom of demons. They are pictured in the swine of verse 32.

"The even" (v. 16), i.e., after sun-down on the Sabbath. Had they been more intelligent they would have brought the demoniacs to Him at sunrise.

Man can sympathize with suffering, but the Messiah alone "took" and "bore" infirmities and diseases. The sense of Isa. liii. 4 is here expressed; for the Divine Author of the prophecy can deal as He pleases with His own words. Thus He made human sorrow His own. (Rom. xv. 1 and Gal. vi. 2); and as to sin He bore it in His own body on the tree (1 Peter ii., 24).

The nature of "the flesh" and the claim of the Lord appear in verses 19-22. The "flesh" is either too forward (v. 19) or too backward (v. 21). The Lord understood its impotency in relation to spiritual facts and rebuked it with Divine wisdom, showing that He Himself claimed to be everything or to be nothing.

Thus two moral facts appear:—the one: Christ must be everything or nothing. The other: That man's boasting of the majesty and value of his religious will is folly.

"Bury my father" (v. 21), i.e., wait till my father dies.

"Son of man" (v. 20). This is the first of the eighty-eight occurrences of this Name, and is Christ's title as having dominion in the earth —that earth which had room for foxes and birds, but not for Him. The last occurrence appears in Rev. xiv. 14. They belong to His Advents in weakness and in power.

"Let the (spiritually) dead bury their (physically) dead" (v. 22).

To follow Christ involves suffering with Him and ensures the hatred of Satan (v. 24); for the storm designed to destroy Him would have destroyed them. This principle operates to-day.

"Rebuked" (v. 26). Compare Mal. ii. 3 (Heb.) and iii. 11.

"Oh ye of little faith" (v. 26). This rebuke occurs four times—combating care (vi. 30); fear (viii. 26); doubt (xiv 31); and reasoning (xvi. 8).

"Two" (v. 28). Mark and Luke only speak of one; just as they only speak of one blind man at Jericho and one colt at the entry to Jerusalem. This shows design, not discrepancy. The prophecies immediately preceding Matthew predicted the advent of Christ as King of Israel and Prince of Judah. The Holy Spirit in this first Gospel therefore, records the historic facts that there were two demoniacs, and two blind men, and two animals, for these represented Israel and Judah. No such duality was needed in the other Gospels.

"Jesus" (v. 29) should be here omitted. These demons were more intelligent than the disciples of modern religious thought. They declared the God-Head of Jesus; that He has appointed a time for judgment; that the judgment involves torment; and that He will command it. Many preachers to-day deny that Jesus could, or would torment any creature. So dreadful is hell that the demons preferred to indwell swine than to be banished thither. The entry of the demons into them shows that the misery of these two men was not a question of disease or of passion, but of wicked spirits.

Men can beseech Christ to leave them, and—fearful fact—He hears their prayer (ix. 1).

Only in death, but not in life, had He

where to " lay " His head, for He " laid " His head and yielded up His spirit. Compare in the Greek Testament Matt. viii. 20 and John xix. 30.

" His own city " (ix. 1), i.e., Capernaum (iv. 13).

MATTHEW IX. 2-38.—This chapter discloses the character of Messiah's ministry; the prior one, the dignity of His Person. In them He reveals Himself as Jehovah visiting Israel and the world, in grace and power; healing all manner of disease (v. 35); for giving iniquity (v. 2); electing sinners to salvation (vs. 9-13); proposing gladness to a sad world (14-17); and so manifesting Himself as the God of Ps. ciii Who first forgiveth iniquity and then healeth disease (vs. 2 and 6). In chapter viii He appears as the God of Ps. xciii ruling the mighty waves of the sea.

But the power which healed in chapter ix is the same power which will torment in chapter viii. (v. 29).

The people, however, only saw a miracle-working man (v. 8), and their religious leaders (v. 34) denounced Him as a Satanic agent. Jesus, unchilled by the blindness of the one and the hostility of the other, persisted in His mission of love (vs. 35-38). But man did not want God in their midst, even though He was there in grace—a grace that while on the way to raise to life the dead maiden, (figure of Israel to-day, v. 19) healed whoever touched Him (v. 20).

So the chapter pictures not only the grace and power of Immanuel but the sin and misery of Israel, and man, as morally paralyzed (v. 9); dead (v. 18); diseased (v. 20); blind (v. 27); and dumb (v. 32).

" Their faith " (v. 2), i.e., the faith of the sick man and his four friends (Mark ii. 3).

" Thy sins are forgiven thee " (R.V.), and " Arise and walk." See Ps. ciii. 3.

" The house " (v. 10), i.e., Matthew's house (Luke v. 29). Matthew modestly hides this fact; as also that his name was Levi, and that he had provided " a great feast," for his visitors.

There is no Saviour for the self-righteous (v. 13).

" Go ye (to Hosea vi. 6) and learn " etc. (v. 13).

" I will have mercy rather than sacrifice." Sacrifice was the means, mercy the end; sacrifice the road, mercy the goal. " Mercy " is a term expressing God-likeness. " Sacrifice," i.e., free-will-offerings. A slave-owner will work and flog his slaves to death, and out of his ill-gotten wealth build in sacrifice a church to God.

The life and liberty of the Gospel destroy the wine-skins of ritualism (14-17).

" Then shall they fast " (v. 15)—not from the use of necessary food, but from the gladness of personal fellowship. Compare Mark xvi. 14, Isa. lx. 1, 2, and 20.

" Give place " (v. 24), i.e., " go out of the room."

Jesus was truly man (v. 36), for when He " saw " He pitied.

A Roman tax-collector bought for an annual sum of money the privilege of enforcing the assessments. They were, therefore, hated and despised by the people—whom they often defrauded. Matthew was, accordingly, his own master, and at liberty to leave his post at any time without injuring the public finances. He must have lost heavily by following Jesus so instantaneously. His conversion, and that of his fellow-collector, Zacchaeus, must have pleased those whose taxes were, in the one case, unpaid, and, in the other, overpaid (Luke xix. 8).

MATTHEW X.—" Pray ye " (ix. 38); " He called " (v. 1). Thus prayer and action inter-act; but prayer precedes action.

" He gave them power " (v. 1), and commanded them saying, " Preach " (v. 7). Preaching may be scriptural and eloquent, but if not energized by Divinely-given power, it accomplishes nothing against the forces of evil.

The mighty ordination of the Pierced Hand equips the preacher to overthrow evils, and heals sorrows (v. 1). A spiritual ministry has these characteristics.

Christ did not only work miracles Himself, He gave power to others to do likewise (v. 1). This determines Deity, and assures the future kingdom on the earth of Love and Righteousness—man healed of all disease and Satan cast out (Rev. xx.). Accordingly in Heb. vi. miracles are called " the powers of the world to come," i.e., the millennial world.

The call to Discipleship and the call to Apostleship (v. 2) should not be confounded. Verse 1 : " Disciples " ; Verse 2 : " Apostles." The Election to the one precedes that to the other. A Disciple is a pupil; an Apostle is a messenger ; but an apostle can never leave the Spirit's School but must remain a learner to the end.

The twelve were sent forth in couples (Mark vi. 7) ; hence the word " two" may be supplied (in English) after the word "first" (v. 2). This word does not here mean "chief," as many think.

The first two, therefore, were Peter and his brother Andrew ; the second two, James and his brother John ; the third two, Philip and his friend Bartholomew (i.e., Nathaniel, John i. 45 and xxi. 2) ; the fourth couple, Thomas and Matthew, the fifth, James and his brother Thaddeus, i.e., Judas ; and the last couple, Simon the Zealot and Judas Iscariot.

The number twelve corresponds to the Tribes of Israel. Their division into couples harmonizes with Gen. ii. 18 and vi. 19. The association of brothers recognizes the Divine Institution of the family ; and, lastly, friendship is here ennobled and sanctified.

Eleven of these men were Galileans ; one, Judas Iscariot, was a Judean. Iscariot most probably means " of Kerioth " (Josh. xv. 25) a town in Judea.

James and Judas were sons of Alphæus i.e., Cleopas. He was married to a " sister " (i.e. relative) of the Virgin Mary. These brothers were, therefore, first cousins to the Lord. Judas is thought probably to be the writer of the Epistle; but its verse 17 conflicts with the supposition. He was more probably brother to the Lord.

The name Simon appears twice, and also the names James and Judas.

James the brother of John was the first to suffer martyrdom (Acts xii. 2) ; and John himself was possibly the last.

All true missionaries are sent forth by Christ Himself (v. 5).

These instructions are divided into three sections by the words "Verily I say unto you" (vs. 15, 23, and 42).

The first section (5-15) applied to the mission then about to be entered upon.

The second section (16-23) contemplated the period between Pentecost and the destruction of Jerusalem.

The third section (24-42) covers the present period of Gospel Ministry.

A recognition of these sections explains the limitation of verses 5 and 6, the miraculous powers of verse 8, and the seeming improvidence of verses 9 and 10.

It also throws light upon the persecutions and accompanying promise of verses 17-21, and upon the incompletion of service and the coming in judgment of verse 23.

The one Gospel and its moral effect and consequences, apply to all three periods ; and, therefore, the doom of verse 15 contrasts with the reward of verse 42.

" Rather " (v. 6), i.e., only.

The word " two " is to be understood before shoes and staves. They were to go just as they were—without additional coats, shoes or staves. Hence the one staff of Mark vi. 8.

Immanuel being then on the earth they were to depend entirely on Him for everything. In Luke xxii. 35-37 this ordinance was abrogated because Immanuel was rejected.

To neglect or reject the Gospel message is declared (v. 15) by the Eternal Judge Himself to insure a more terrific doom then that which will fall upon the loathsome Sodomite. Few believe this doctrine ; but Christ is its Author.

" I " (v. 16). This " I " is emphatic. " Behold " this word directs attention to the singular action of the Good Shepherd in *sending* His sheep into the midst of wolves.

He here warns them (v. 17) to distrust men, for they are wolves by nature (v. 16); they are cruel (v. 17) ; they are unnatural (v. 21) ; and they hate goodness (v. 22). This moral description of man is denied by modern popular preachers, and arouses their anger.

The wisdom of the serpent avoids danger, and the simplicity of the dove escapes it. A combination of the two saves Christian people from courting persecution on the one hand, and from human planning to avoid it on the other.

Persecution by the Church (v. 17) has been, and is, always followed by that by the State (v. 18).

These kings were the successors of Nebuchadnezzar, and the Hebrew church was put in subjection under them as a just judgment for its corruption. This principle rules still in Christendom.

" A testimony unto them " (v. 18) (R.V.). That is, their being hailed before these princes would provide them with opportunities for preaching to them. Thus Paul preached before Felix, Festus, Agrippa and Nero who otherwise would not have heard the Gospel.

" The Spirit " (v. 20). His descent at Pentecost is here predicted.

Judas Iscariot at the moment listening to Jesus, and himself an apostle, was to be the first to fulfil the prophecy of verse 21.

A true testimony to Christ's Name ensures man's hatred (v. 22).

" Endureth " (v. 22), i.e., bravely faces suffering.

" Saved " (v. 22), i.e., delivered from the Divine doom that overthrew Jerusalem.

So it fell out. Some were martyred (Luke xxi. 16), and some lived to see, and escape from, the destruction of the Holy City. That Coming of the Son of Man closed the Pentecostal age, and, consequently its miracles.

The instructions of this third section (24-42) cover all periods of Gospel testimony.

Ancient religions were based upon mysteries withheld from the public. The Gospel has no such mysteries (vs. 26 and 27). All its truths are to be publicly proclaimed. In the East the house-top is the usual place for public proclamation.

The objection that such action might entail death is met by the three " Fear nots " of verses 26, 28 and 31. All that the Master whispered into their ear they were to make known everywhere and to everyone.

Man " kills " the body ; God " destroys " it. To destroy is not to annihilate. The plagues " destroyed " the land of Egypt, that is, stripped it of every desirable thing. Men deny the fact of hell. Christ here affirms it, and says that both soul and body will exist in that place of torment.

" Without your Father " (v. 29), i.e., without His knowledge, or will.

To men of goodwill Christ brought peace (Luke ii. 14), but to evil-doers, a sword (v. 34). His entrance into the world, as into a family, manifests the hidden evil of the heart, as light manifests impurity in a dungeon (vs. 35 and 36). See note on Luke xii. 51.

The tenderest human affection must be subordinate to Christ. If not, it will expel Him.

Crosses were placed at the doors of Roman Courts of Justice, and convicted prisoners on passing out to execution, had to take up their cross and carry it to the place of death. Christ's followers are here pictured (v. 38) following Him to death, each one bearing his or her cross. This destroys the popular notion that the word " cross " in this verse means a trial, such as ill-health or poverty, etc.

He who thus lays down his life, whether in spirit or in fact, in fellowship with Christ, shall " find " it in the Eternal world ; but he who refuses this surrender shall lose the life which is life indeed (v. 39).

" A prophet " (v. 41), i.e., the Gospel preacher. " In the name of a prophet," i.e., in the character of a prophet, that is, because he is a preacher, and " in the name of a disciple " (v. 42), i.e., because he is a disciple. This promise assures to the supporters of Gospel preachers rewards corresponding to those that the preachers themselves will receive.

These commandments clearly foretell disappointment and failure. The king and His Kingdom would be surely rejected. The next chapter gives the secret of the " rest " of an exulting faith in the midst of the apparent ruin.

MATTHEW XI.—This chapter marks a climax. The people refused to repent or to believe (vs. 16 and 17) ; their leaders declared Jesus to be Satan (x. 25) ; and, greatest blow of all, His beloved Fore-runner doubted His Messiahship (v. 3). But this seeming failure of His mission did not confound the Lord, for He was bearing the easy yoke and the light burden (v. 30) of the Father's Will (v. 26), and in that Will He exulted (v. 25). Surrounded by ruin, He triumphantly declared that all things were delivered unto Him, and that He dwelt in a realm of mutual knowledge in the God-head that was the perfection of bliss, and that nothing could affect. He rested in Isa. xlix.

John must have wondered if Jesus were the King of Israel why did He not set up His Kingdom and deliver His Fore-runner from prison ? He had no doubt as to His being a prophet, for only a prophet could answer the question of verse 3. The Divine answer referred him to Isa. xxxv. 5 and 6 and lxi. 1. These were the particular miracles, and this the particular preaching, which should accredit His Person. His claim was not that He worked miracles, but that He worked certain predicted miracles, and preached in a certain predicted manner.

Thus He appealed to the Scriptures, and having quoted their testimony to Himself He then gave His testimony to John, declaring him to be blessed and all others who found nothing to stumble at in His (Christ's) Person, or teachings or actions. Many were offended at the lowly exterior of the Great King. But God manifest in flesh had not come to display the pomp of Royalty but to forgive the sins and to heal the diseases of humanity. This mission was more Divine and glorious than a seizure of the Throne of David, though that might have liberated John. A carnal heart could not understand Immanuel descending to the depths of human sin and misery, loading Himself with men's burdens and sorrows, and offering up Himself as a sacrifice in expiation of their sins. But such action revealed the heart of God as no Imperial splendour could possibly have done.

Verse 10 affirms the God-head of Jesus of Nazareth.

" Least " (v. 11), i.e., Christ Himself. He was " less," or younger than John. See John i. 27 and 30. John proclaimed the kingdom ; Christ possessed it ; so Jesus was greater than John though later in point of time, and esteemed " less " by Israel to this day.

" Suffereth violence " (v. 12), i.e., is being vigorously proclaimed and the energetic lay hold upon it with energy. see Luke xvi. 16. John and his disciples, and Jesus and His disciples vigorously announced the Advent of the Kingdom, but the heads of the Church would not enter it themselves, and those that would enter they hindered (xxiii. 13). Hence people had to force their way through these opposers in order to enter the kingdom.

Had the nation received John he would have represented Elijah to them, and would have been reckoned by God as Elijah. " Is " i.e., represents (v. 14). " It," i.e., " him " (v. 14).

" Let him hear " (v. 15), i.e., he will be held responsible to hear. This solemn injunction occurs fourteen times in the N.T.

In the East children play in public at weddings and funerals, and are disappointed and displeased if the onlookers do not dance or lament. Israel refused to mourn with the Baptist, or to rejoice with the Beloved (vs. 16-19).

The Christ-rejecter is morally lower than the idolaters of Tyre and Sidon, or the citizens of Sodom (vs. 20-24).

Capernaum had the unique dignity of being the Lord's dwelling-place. It was the most favoured spot on earth. Nazareth was the family home ; but there was no room for Him there, for his family did not believe upon Him (John vii. 5), and reckoned Him to be a lunatic (Mark iii. 21). But He, as Wisdom, was vindicated by His children (v. 19). See notes on Luke vii. 35-50.

" Answered " (v. 25). A Hebraism for to begin to speak, or to resume speaking.

God's action in hiding spiritual facts from the philosophic and the sharp-witted, was no stumbling block to Jesus, but, on the contrary, caused Him exultation (vs. 25 and 26).

Salvation is not a matter of education but of revelation (v. 27). All the elaborate machinery of man's religious ceremonial, and all his self-determination to be a christian are useless, for only those to whom the Son wills to reveal the Father possess a saving knowledge of God, and He wills to reveal Himself to the sinful and guilty. See John iv. 26 and xiv. 9.

Many think that the " rest " of verse 28 has relation to sin, and that the " rest " of verse 29 has relation to service. They say all who are consciously laden with guilt, and labour hard to remove it, can secure rest by coming to Jesus.

This is most true, but the invitation here is to the burdened and disappointed labourers of chap x and not to sinners laden with guilt. Verse 1 with Isa. xlix 4, and verses 28-30 with Isa. xlix. 5-12, give the teaching and import of this whole chapter. The weary worker is invited to rest where Jesus rested.

The anxious and depressed Christian worker by accepting the easy yoke of the Divine Will and so imitating Christ, will work in harmony with that Will, and, consequently, enjoy the promised rest of verse 29. To this rest He calls all His servants—that is, to the yoke of full submission to the Father's will—willing to be meek and lowly in heart—willing not to be self-willed and proud but to occupy the lowest place and to accept seeming failure as a true donation of all things (v. 27). Nothing can overthrow the servant who takes that place ; it is the place of perfect rest to the heart.

In the perfection of His faith in the Father's love, and of His submission to the Father's Will, standing amid the ruins of His mission and believing Isa. xlix. 5-12 He could say : " All things are delivered unto Me " (v. 27)

It is the privilege of the servant when confronted with apparent failure, to imitate the faith and triumph of his Master.

In fulfilment of Isa. l. 4, He eases the burden of service beneath the yoke of submission. He, as a disciple, learned of Jehovah Elohim and then says to the Christian labourer "learn of Me." The Divine yoke of service was easy to Him, and is easy to those who join Him under it.

MATTHEW XII.—Rejected by the nation as Messiah the King, He now presented Himself to them as Elohim the Creator of the Sabbath (vs. 1-14), and as Jehovah the Redeemer (vs. 22-37) and Saviour (vs. 38-50). of men.

The first action that revealed the nature of His Person and of His authority to open and to close dispensations, was His defence of His disciples for plucking the ears of corn on the Sabbath day. They were permitted to do so by Deut. xxiii. 25. But His defence was that if David the king when rejected ate the shewbread, the Son of David when in a similar case might enjoy a similar privilege ; and further, that if the requirements (Num. xxviii. 9) of the Temple worship profaned the Sabbath, He had rights greater than the Temple (vs. 3-6).

"Have ye not read"? (v. 3). This question was asked by the Lord on six occasions : Matt. xii. 3, xii. 5, xix. 4, xxi. 16, xxi. 42, and xxii. 31 and 32. These questions recalled six books and ten passages. Gen. i. 27, Exod. iii. 6, Lev. xxiv. 6-9, Num. xxviii 9 and 10, 1 Sam. xxi. 6, Ps. viii. 2, and Ps. cxviii. 22.

A greater Temple (v. 6) ; a greater Prophet (v. 41) ; and a greater King (v. 42) ; i.e., God Himself.

" I will have mercy " etc. (v. 7). See notes on ix. 13 and Hos. vi. 6.

The Sabbath was a token of the Covenant between Jehovah and the nation (Ezek. xx. 12-20). Hence the Son of Man had power over it. If His dominion over the Sabbath was denied, then was the Covenant destroyed.

The grace and power that provided food on the Sabbath day furnished also healing (vs. 9-13) ; but His love only excited their hatred (v. 14). Yet their hatred could not restrain the founts of grace that perpetually welled up in His heart (v 15). He healed everyone ; but, as predicted by Isa. (xlii. 1-4), He hid Himself, and would not even allow the fame of His miracles to hinder His purpose of offering up Himself as a sacrifice for sin. The day would come when He would reign (" shew judgment over the Gentiles "). Meanwhile He would not demand His rights (v. 19) but endure the discordance of the bruised reed and the offensiveness of the smoking flax, i.e., the unbelief and rebellion of Israel, but only up to the day that He would bring forth judgment unto victory. In that day will the bruised reed be broken and the smoking flax quenched.

It is impossible to produce melody with a bruised reed, and the smell of a smoking wick is unendurable. Such was Israel ; and such is man. Grace endures these for a time ; but judgment is certain to fall upon them. The popular interpretation of this verse as symbolizing a feeble believer is contradicted by the context.

The people were pictured in the unhappy man of verse 22 ; and though they cried out " Can this be the Son of David ? " (v. 23) yet they failed to recognize Immanuel.

The Pharisees here (v. 24) declared their belief in an organized kingdom of demons, having Satan as its chief. The Lord affirmed the truth of their belief, but very gently rebuked and destroyed their cruel attack upon Himself.

The Pharisees and their disciples claimed to cast out demons (v. 27). Perhaps here, however, under the term " children " the Lord intended the Apostles ; for they are to judge the Twelve Tribes of Israel (xix. 28).

The argument of verse 30 is : that the presence of Immanuel tested everything and everybody. All sin against Him as Man was pardonable (v. 32) ; but sin against Him as God eternally unpardonable, for it was sin against the Holy Spirit (Mark iii. 29, 30, R.V.).

" Generation of Vipers " (v. 34), i.e., offspring of Satan the great Viper. This is the plural of magnitude.

Men's words reveal their thoughts and character. In the Day of Judgment it will, therefore, be impossible and useless for them to plead that attacks upon the deity of Christ were " idle " words. God will not think so in that day.

" This world " (v. 32), i.e., the dispensation of Law. " The world to come," i.e., the dispensation of Grace. " World," here means " age " or " dispensation." Verse 35 reads as in the Revised Version.

Words reveal invisible thought. Jesus, as the Word of God, revealed the invisible Gou.

" Certain of the scribes " (v. 38), i.e., distinct from those of verse 24 ; but just as unbelieving and guilty, as appears from the Lord's language to them (v. 39). See Luke xi. 15 and 16.

The suggestion of these scribes was that the expulsion of demons was only an infernal sign, and they demanded a heavenly one to demonstrate Divine authority (Luke xi. 16).

" Adulterous " (v. 39), i.e., unfaithful and treacherous in relation to God. " Generation," i.e., " Nation " viewed morally. They abandoned the Word of God for the traditions and thoughts of men.

The heathen, represented by the men of Nineveh and the Queen of Sheba, believed the Word of the Lord, proclaimed by a prophet and by a king, but Israel refused to believe that word at the mouth of Him Who was Greater than Jonah and Greater than Solomon ; as He was also Greater than the Temple (vs. 6, 41 and 42).

If the story of Jonah is only a parable, as many say, and not historically true, then is the story of the Queen of Sheba also untrue ; but the Lord here puts them on the same historic basis ; and He insisted repeatedly that He only spake Truth because He only said what God told Him to say. See notes on the Book of Jonah and on Luke xi. 29.

The " three days and three nights " of verse 40 is idiom; " the third day " is actual. It occurs ten times. But these occurrences should read " The fourth day " if Matt. xii. 40 is literal and not idiom. But being an idiom it means any part of three days and three nights. So one complete day and night (24 hours) and the parts of two nights (36 hours in all) satisfy both the idiom and the history. In British law a man sentenced to three days imprisonment on Monday night leaves the prison at 6.5 on Wednesday morning. See note on page 8.

" When the unclean spirit " (v. 43), i.e., the spirit of idolatry, whose house (" my house," v. 44) was Israel. This spirit had left the nation on its return from the seventy years captivity. Had it been expelled, as in verse 29, it could never have returned (v. 44).

" Dry places " (v. 43), i.e., waterless places, and therefore without inhabitants or living beings.

Impure spirits may have once had bodies ; and hence their eagerness to re-embody themselves in men, or even in swine (Mark v.).

On returning he found his old home garnished with ritualism, but empty. See notes on Malachi.

" More wicked than himself " (v. 45). Idolatry is wickedness, but somewhat clumsy, and stupid, but a false Gospel is neither clumsy nor stupid, and is more wicked than idolatry (1 Cor. ii. 4 and Gal. i. 8). Judah will reach the lowest depth of moral and religious degradation immediately prior to the Second Advent ; for energized by the unclean spirit of verse 43, assisted by the seven other spirits, she will reach the " last state " of verse 45.

The Lord's first prediction of His resurrection is recorded in John ii. 19 ; His second prediction is here found in verse 40.

" Stood without " (v. 46). They came to capture and confine Him—thus in spirit uniting with the Pharisees (v. 14) who planned to destroy Him. Such is man, and such is the flesh ! See note on Luke ii. 34, 35.

But Jesus knew their purpose, and publicly breaking the bond that existed between Him and them after the flesh, He pointed to His Disciples and owned them as His nearest relatives in a family transcending any earthly one. This Word, like a sword, must have pierced Mary's heart. See notes on Luke xi. 27, 28.

" He stretched forth His hand " (v. 49) ; graphic language ; evidently that of an eyewitness.

Natural relationship has influence in earthly governments (1 Kings ii. 20), but no influence in Messiah's Government (v. 48 John ii. 4). This fact destroys the doctrine of the intercession of the Virgin.

MATTHEW XIII.—The seven parables of this chapter make public the mysteries, i.e., the secrets concerning the kingdom of Heaven.

They record and explain the evident failure of the effort begun by John the Baptist and carried on by the Lord and the Apostles to set up a Heavenly Kingdom upon earth.

Four of the parables were spoken by the sea-shore (v. 1). They predicted the outward failure of this spiritual kingdom. The remaining three were spoken in the house (v. 36). They foretold the hidden success of this moral kingdom ; and reveal that that success is based upon the Divine fact of Election.

Some understand verse 52 to be an eighth parable ; but the verse does not say so.

Compare " Another " (v. 24) ; " Another " (v. 31) ; " Another " (v. 33) ; and " Again " (v. 44) ; " Again " (v. 45) ; and " Again " (v. 47).

The mystery, or secret, of the first parable is, that only one fourth of the expended effort succeeded, and three-fourths failed. Subsequent history demonstrates the accuracy of this prophecy.

Whoever hears is responsible to hear, i.e. to obey, and will be so judged (v. 9).

A gift unused, whether moral, physical or material, sooner or later is lost ; but on the contrary if used develops.

" They see not," " they hear not," " they understand not " (vs. 13-15). That is, they did not wish to see or hear or understand; and hence by a just judgment they lost this triple moral ability. They with deliberation closed their eyes (v. 15). They would not turn to Him ; had they done so He would most certainly have healed them morally (v. 15). See Isa. vi. 9, Mark iv. 12, Luke viii. 10, John xii. 40, and Acts xxviii. 26.

Contrasted with these were the many who " desired " to see, and to hear and to understand (vs. 16 and 17).

Satan is compared by the Lord to a vulture (vs. 4 and 19).

" Anon " (v. 20) " by and by " (v. 21), i.e., "immediately." There is the one word for both in the Greek text.

" The good ground " (v. 23), i.e., prepared ground—ground ploughed up by the Spirit of conviction because of sin. The heart is incurably diseased (Jer. xvii. 9 R.V.) ; but it becomes good, that is, honest when it accepts this testimony (Luke viii. 15).

The Parable of the Tares (24-30 and 37-43) conflicts with modern religious thought. It asserts the existence of the Devil (v. 39) ; declares him to be a moral father and, as such, to have children (v. 38) ; that these children are human beings (v. 41) ; that after death they will be cast into the furnace of conscious suffering (v. 42) ; that evolution is a myth, for no system of cultivation can develop wheat out of tares ; and that people may be so morally perfect as to be indis-

tinguishable from Christians and yet be the seed of the serpent.

Such is Christ's own teaching, and it moves the contrite heart to trembling and weeping.

The Parable of the Mustard Seed (vs. 31 and 32) and of the leaven (v. 33) are popularly understood to predict the prosperity of the Church. The text declares their relation to the Kingdom, and not to the Church. The latter was a secret, and first revealed to the Apostle Paul (Eph. iii. 3-6). The parables foretell the outward failure, and the inward corruption of God's moral kingdom upon earth—introduced by the Son of Man, and the Apostles, in consequence of the rejection of the actual kingdom by Israel. This moral kingdom would become outwardly big like an abnormal mustard tree, but the Devil, symbolized by the fowls of the air (v. 19), would make his home in it, at the same time that idolatry, symbolized by the woman, would corrupt it internally. Thus in conduct and in doctrine the failure of what is called Christianity is here revealed beforehand. See last note.

Leaven is invariably presented in Scripture as a symbol of evil, and frequently a woman as an agent of idolatry. The meal was pure. The leaven introduced an element into it which produced corruption. Christendom to-day is wholly corrupted ; for it is impossible to find anywhere in the world anything which professes to be the kingdom of God and which is pure either in membership, conduct or doctrine.

A mustard bush that becomes a tree is abnormal.

The quotation of verse 35 is from Ps. lxxviii. 2. The ordinary reader of that Psalm would not recognize its Messianic character. The shaft of light from this verse 35 illuminates the entire Book of the Psalms.

The four parables addressed outside the house to the multitudes foretelling the outward failure of the kingdom are followed by the three to the Disciples inside the house, revealing and predicting the unseen success of the Divine scheme of Election. The treasure was elected out of the field (v. 44) ; the goodly pearl out of many pearls (v. 46) ; and the good fish severed out from amongst the bad (v. 48).

Election is based upon grace. Neither human merit nor demerit can affect it as a principle. It, therefore, baffles all the power of evil and of the Evil One.

Many Bible students suppose the treasure to symbolize the Church, the pearl, Israel and the good fish, the redeemed nations. But the Master says that the interpretation of all three belongs to the Kingdom of Heaven.

The correspondences between the parables support the belief that all of them relate to the earth during the period between the First and Second Advents.

The eternal destiny of the tares and of the wicked (vs. 30 42 and 50) as one of conscious misery is here revealed by God Himself.

The instructed Christian teacher (v. 52) can enrich others out of his store of Divine Truth. That Truth as to time is old, i.e., eternal; as to experience, power and character perpetually new.

It is generally accepted that the Lord visited Nazareth twice (vs. 54-58); but a comparison of all the records points to one only visit. On reaching the town He had no public and believing reception as elsewhere, nor did the multitudes press around Him for healing . Prior to the Sabbath He healed a few (v. 58), and it may be assumed, in private. The unbelief and hostility of His family and fellow-townsmen reached a climax on that day as the result of His preaching. They sought to destroy Him (Luke iv. 28).

That a carpenter, the son of a carpenter, whom they had all known for thirty years, and whose mother and brothers and sisters they knew, should claim to be Jehovah Messiah the promised King of Israel, and should say such things about the prophets Elijah and Elisha was an offence to them (v. 57). But they could not deny His wisdom nor His miracles; and their statements about His Person, and His parents and His brothers and sisters, provide irrefutable evidence of His actual humanity.

The sower's wealth (v. 18) was external; the householder's (v. 52), internal. The one gathered treasure; the other distributed it.

These parables, perhaps, cover the whole period between Pentecost and the Second Advent while the kingdom is in mystery. After the Second Advent the kingdom will come in power.

The tares may predict the Apostolic Age; the mustard tree, the Constantine Age; and the leaven the Medieval and Present Age.

The seven years of famine were assured to Pharaoh by a double dream, one from the animal and one from the vegetable world, but both predicting the one fact. So the three parables of the treasure, the pearl, and the good fish may, possibly, assure the salvation and preservation of the redeemed.

The redeemed—a term here including Israel, the Church, and the Saved Nations—form Immanuel's treasure (Mal.iii. 17). To redeem these from among men, that is, from out of the " field " and the " sea " of humanity, He sold all that He had (Phil. ii. 5-8). Amazing love !

In the parable of the sower triple failure was caused by the ground; in the three following parables, by Satanic agency, i.e., the tares, the fowls, and the woman.

The number " three " is prominent in these parables. Between the first and the seventh there are two sets of three each. There were three kinds of faulty ground; there were three Satanic agents; there were three degrees of fruit-bearing; there were three measures of meal; and there were three groups of the redeemed—the treasure, the pearl and the fish.

This triple form helps to emphasize the relationship between these parables and the Epistle of Jude.

The word " whosoever " (xii. 50) may be taken as the keynote to these parables. It marks the change in the Lord's attitude and teaching. Rejected by the nation He turns to the individual. The kingdom in power being refused, it is here introduced in mystery.

The tares and the leaven illustrate Satan's activities in imitation and corruption. See notes on Luke xiii. 10, 21.

MATTHEW XIV.—That true witnesses like John the Baptist and James the Apostle (Acts xii. 2) should be permitted to perish, and others delivered (Acts xii. 7) is inscrutable to human intelligence.

This Herod was a son of the Herod who slew the infants of Bethlehem, and was, consequently a descendant of Esau.

His wife was a daughter of Aretas the king of Arabia; but he dishonoured her by his connection with Herodias, who was his sister-in-law and niece. Her daughter was Salome. King Aretas, to avenge his daughter who had fled to him, attacked Herod, and would have destroyed him but for the intervention of the Romans.

Herod was courteously called " King " (v. 9) but officially " tetrarch " (v. 1). This is a compound Greek word meaning ruler of a fourth. Were Viceroys placed over the four Provinces of Ireland each one would be a tetrarch.

Urged by the ambitious Herodias Herod went to Rome with her and begged the Emperor to make him a king officially. But the Emperor hearing of his mal-administration, banished him to Lyons in France, from whence he went to Spain, and, it is supposed, died there.

The Baptist was a prisoner for more than a year prior to his death in the gloomy castle of Machærus on the shores of the Dead Sea. There in a dark dungeon he was slain to gratify the hatred of an abominable woman.

Herod's conscience was guilty (v. 2), it was cowardly (v. 5), and it was degraded (v. 7). Supposed faithfulness to an oath impelled him to a crime. The conscience is defiled and needs to be purged (Heb. ix. 14), not only from sinful passions, but also from dead religious works. Yet many moral teachers proudly say that the conscience is an inward spiritual light which if obeyed and followed will guide to heaven !

"A desert place apart" (v. 13), and Jesus "saw and was moved with compassion" (v. 14). Both these sentences affirm the real humanity of the Lord Jesus Christ. Deep emotion demands solitude, and the sight of need awakes compassion. He sought no doubt a place where He could give vent to the sorrow that burdened His heart because of the cruel murder of His beloved forerunner ; but in the perfection of His nature He deferred the indulgence of His grief in order to teach and heal and feed the multitude.

He crossed the lake at its northern extremity for the eastern shore. The people ran round by land and met Him as He went forth out of the ship (v. 14).

"Evening" (v 15), probably about three o'clock. "Evening" (v. 23), i.e., six o'clock.

The Church says : "Send the multitude away" (v. 15). The Great Shepherd says : "They need not depart" (v. 16).

"Hither to me" (v. 18). This is the secret of spiritual ability to feed the hungry.

"The Disciples" (v. 19) had to keep constantly going to Jesus for fresh supplies for the need of the multitude. They had no resources of their own. They were dependent upon Him. This law of the ministerial life ensures blessing to the Disciple.

The proximity of Pentecost (John vi.) originated this multitude. See notes on Mark vi.

"Constrained" (v. 22). The multitude proposed to make Him a king ; and, possibly, the Disciples thought that the favourable moment had come for the inauguration of the kingdom. Hence the necessity for this constraint.

The word also suggests that the anguish which filled the Lord's heart demanded relief and could no longer be restrained ; so He constrained them to leave. This is the second miracle of the chapter—the multitudes went away.

He was there alone (v. 23). It is an awesome picture. The Lord of glory enwrapt by the shadows of the night, alone on the mountain side, bewailing the death of the Baptist.

But His heart did not forget the storm-tossed Disciples (vs. 24 and 25). The lake here is six miles wide. The fourth watch of the night was three o'clock in the morning. In nine hours they had only rowed three miles ! And now they were about to perish ; but He at the last moment delivered them. The wind ceased, there was a great calm, and immediately they reached land (John vi.).

Such is the moral life without and with Jesus. Without Him, three miles in nine hours, and then the abyss ; with Him, three miles in nine seconds, and then the sunlit shore !

Had Peter kept his eyes on Jesus (v. 30) he would not have begun to sink. But however foolish man may be if he cries "Lord, save me" he is sure of an immediate salvation.

If the hem of His garment (v. 36) is so rich with blessing how rich must be His hand and heart !

Death was threatened by hunger (v. 15) ; by accident (v. 24) ; and by disease (v. 35), but Divine power in Jesus conquered all.

MATTHEW XV.—Once more Jesus revealed Himself as the Jehovah of Ps. ciii. He judged on behalf of the oppressed (vs. 4 and 5 and Ps. ciii. 6) and in favour of defrauded parents ; He delivered the child's life from destruction (v. 28 and Ps. ciii. 4) ; He healed all their diseases (v. 30 and Ps. ciii. 3) ; and He filled their mouth with good things (v. 37 and Ps. ciii. 5), for they did all eat and were filled.

"Then" (v. 1). This important word illustrates the truth of verse 19. Their hearts, filled with evil reasonings, and unaffected by the beauty and love and grace and tenderness recorded in xiv. 36, these religious teachers rudely intruded themselves and their ceremonial trivialities and traditions into this scene. of amazing miracle and of Divine Power. Such is the natural heart !

This washing of the hands was religious and not sanitary. (See Mark vii. 3, 4).

" Honour " (v. 4), i.e., provide for.

" Let him die the death " (v. 4), i.e., he shall surely be put to death (Exod. xx. and xxi.).

" It is a gift " (v. 5), i.e., dedicated to the Temple.

The money justly due by God's command for the maintenance of the aged parents was at the instigation of the avaricious priests, into whose pockets it ultimately came, devoted to religion.

" Teaching for doctrines " (v. 9), i.e., teaching as Divine doctrine, and, therefore, obligatory.

Multitudes in corrupt Christendom when attending religious ceremonies sprinkle themselves with what is called holy water, a ceremony commanded by men, and their consciences would torment them if they failed to obey this command ; and then, disobeying God's commandment " Remember the Sabbath Day to keep it holy," spend the rest of the day horse-racing, hurling, foot-balling, gambling, drinking and telling impure stories. Verse 9 declares their worship to be vain.

" Ye say " (v. 5) ; " He said " (v. 10).

" Let them alone " (v. 14), i.e., take no notice of them. Truth often offends (v. 12) ; but the servant of Truth must not permit himself to be influenced by the enemies of Truth. Rough truth is better than polished falsehood, and though sometimes rough is never rude.

" Declare " (v. 15), i.e., explain. This request demonstrates the ignorance of the natural heart even of a disciple.

" Evil thoughts " (v. 19), i.e., reasonings ; as for example verses 5 and 6. These religious reasonings are here declared to be " evil " ; and they issue out of the deep abyss of corruption from whence proceed the black catalogue detailed in verse 19. Before coming out of the heart these sins had of necessity their home in the heart. See notes on Mark vii. 18, 23.

Christ as a Minister of the circumcision for the Truth of God to fulfil the promises made to the fathers, refused to answer the Gentile petition addressed to Him as Son of David, but when the woman took the place of a " dog," thus admitting she had no claim, and threw herself on His grace as Lord, He at once responded ; for the Scripture said that He was so to act that the Gentiles also might glorify God for His mercy (Rom. xv. 8-12).

" Send her away " (v. 23), i.e., grant her request.

Obedience must dominate pity (v. 24). As man He was " sent " ; and was, therefore, a servant. Hence the silence of verse 23. As God He had liberty of action, and, in grace, He could respond to the need which faith presented to that grace ; otherwise He would have denied His own character and nature as God. Her plea " Lord, help me " (v. 25), was better than her first one ; but she did not get blessing till she· added : " I am a dog." This was the same ground the publican took when he said, " Be propitiated to me the sinner."

If deliverance from the power of sin and Satan be a crumb what must the loaf be ! (v. 27).

" To fill " (v. 33), i.e., to satisfy.

MATTHEW XVI. 1-20.—These verses close the first half of Matthew's Gospel. Its subject is : The king presented. The second half of the Gospel has as its subject : The king rejected.

Three forms of unbelief recorded in these twenty verses characteristically close this first section of the Book.

The first form of unbelief demanded a sign from heaven (vs. 1-4), i.e., the hostility of the natural heart.

The second form revealed blindness and inattention to Divine testimony by miracles to the Person and Nature of Christ (vs. 5-12), i.e., the stupidity of the natural heart.

The third form manifested itself in popular indifference, indolence or mere curiosity respecting the Messiah Himself (vs. 13 and 14), i.e., the frivolity of the natural heart.

Thus here as everywhere the entry of the Lord Jesus reveals and tests the natural heart and its thoughts and professions. Where there is no sense of sin and need the heart is uninterested ; but when that need is felt there can be no rest apart from Christ. Curiosity excites a carnal interest, but Faith has wants and only finds them satisfied in the Person and work of Him Who is Lamb of God and Son of God.

" A sign from heaven " (v. 1). See note on xii. 38.

" The signs of the times " (v. 3), i.e., the great sign of the great time. The time was foretold in Daniel ix. 25, and Christ Himself was the sign. Natural intelligence can observe and study natural phenomena. Only super-human intelligence can recognize spiritual facts recorded in the Bible. Hence the necessity of a spiritual birth in order to " see " the kingdom of God.

The " sign " of the prophet Jonah was his typical death and resurrection. These symbolized the actual death and resurrection of a greater than Jonah.

" Adulterous " (v. 4), i.e., faithless and treacherous.

" Leaven " (vs. 6, 11 and 12), i.e., corrupt teaching.

The Lord's numerous miracles were not wrought at random. He noted their minutest details such as numbers, baskets, loaves, etc., and His people should do likewise. This proves that His miracles were all designed. The insensibility of the Disciples to the Lord's actions (vs. 9 and 10) and to His teaching (v. 6), is a humiliating proof of the darkness of man's heart to moral realities.

" Oh ye of little faith " (v. 8). Compare " great is thy faith " (xv. 28). The heathen woman, who only met Christ once, understood His figurative language and said : " I *am* a dog." The Disciples, after two years teaching, failed to understand the figurative word " leaven ." Her faith was consequently great, and theirs was little.

In John i. 41 and 42 Simon confessed (v. 16) Jesus as the Son of David ; here as Son of the living God. There he was promised a new name : " Thou shalt be Peter ; " here that new name was bestowed (v. 18). Only a direct revelation from God (v. 17) could have enlightened Peter as to the fact that Jesus Himself was the Son of the living God. As such He is the living Rock on which the redeemed as living stones are builded ; for *other* foundation can no man lay (1. Cor. iii. 11). This verse destroys the theory that Peter is the Church's foundation. He himself denies it in his first Epistle. That Epistle is based on Matthew xvi., and his second Epistle on Matt. xvii.

Peter is petros, that is, a stone that may

be thrown here or there ; petra on the contrary means a mighty immovable mass of rock—the God head of Christ.

" The gates of hell " (v. 18), i.e., the power of death. The reference here is to resurrection and not to infallibility in doctrine, as asserted by the Latin Church. Christ being the Living God and His people living stones, Peter being one of them, they could not be held captive in the mansions of the dead. On the third day He, as the true Samson, rose and carried away the gates of hell. They could not prevail against that Rock (" it " v. 18). He prevailed against them ; and when He arose all His people arose in and with Him (1 Thess. iv. 14).

The Apostle Peter in Acts ii. opened the Gospel kingdom to the Hebrews, and in Acts x. to the nations. The figurative word " keys " symbolized these actions.

The Hebrew prophets were said to do what they were commissioned to announce (Jer. i. 10). Simon Peter was a Hebrew prophet, and so similar language was addressed to him (v. 19) ; and his companions being Hebrew prophets a corresponding commission was given to them (xviii. 18) ; and all the disciples, including women, becoming thereby Hebrew prophets, the commission was enlarged to include them all (John xx. 21-23).

The nation having definitely rejected their king, the apostles were forbidden from that moment to continue announcing that Jesus was the Messiah (v. 20).

He who said " Thou art Simon, thou shalt be Peter " (John i. 42) had previously said, " Thy name shall be no more Jacob but Israel " (see notes on Gen. xxxii. 24 -32).

But " Israel," that is, " God's Prince " determines strength, whilst Petros that is, " a stone," suggests weakness. Only twice did the Lord call him Peter and these occasions were in connection with Simon's denial of his Master (Mark xvi. 7 and Luke xxii. 34).

" My church." (v.) 18 (see notes on Acts ix.), i.e., the Kingdom of verse 10.

MATTHEW XVI. 21 — XVII. 27. — This section of the Book, recording the rejection of the King, opens with the first prediction by the King Himself of His death (v. 21), and, associated with it, His glory (xvii. 1-5).

His sufferings, and the glories that should

follow, are always associated in Scripture (I Pet. i. II, iv. I3, and v. I, etc.).

Nine passages in this Gospel foretell the crucifixion : xvi. 2I, xvii. I2, xvii. 22, xx. I7, and xx. 28, xxvi. 20, 28, 3I, 45. Each statement has an additional feature.

The poor human heart likes position and glory, and is quite willing to exalt the Messiah even to heaven, but it shrinks from self-mortification and shame and hatred and persecution and death. The term "the cross" means all this (vs. 2I-25). If anyone wishes to go after Jesus he must consent to share His reproach and die with Him. At the door of the Roman Court of Justice, crosses were piled, and the condemned on leaving, took up a cross and carried it to the place of execution. The believer must follow Christ in that path. It is the only path ; there is no other ; and if anyone would be His disciple he must enter it, for it is the path the Master took. See note on x. 38.

Those who take up that cross lose their life in relation to this world, but find it in the next ; those who refuse, safeguard their life in this world, but suffer eternal loss in the next. This great truth will be demonstrated in the judgment of verse 27. Every man will then be recompensed according to his " doing " or action (v. 27, R.V. margin). Those who in action took up the cross will be rewarded with " life " ; the others will lose " life."

Meanwhile, the glory of that judgment was promised in vision to Peter, and James, and John (xvii. I-9).

The " six days " of verse I are exclusive ; the " about eight days " of Luke ix. 28 are inclusive. Both statements agree.

The glory did not shine upon Jesus, but shone out from Him through His raiment.

Moses and Elijah represented the Law and the Prophets, and the dead and raptured Saints.

They spake with Him of His atoning death (Luke ix. 3I). This doctrine is the great theme of Heaven (Rev. i. 5, v. 6 and 9, vii. I4, etc.). This reveals the import of the word " must " of xvi. 2I. Why " must " ? Because predicted. Therefore, the Scriptures are from God ; for such language would be inapplicable to human forecasts.

God will not have even the greatest saints associated with His Beloved Son in worship or teaching (vs. 4 and 5). Peter's proposal has been adopted by the Roman Church

and men are accordingly commanded to listen to that Church as an authoritative teacher, and to associate lesser divinities with Christ. But Moses and Elijah were at once withdrawn, and the Divine Voice said : " Hear Him," and Him alone.

No sooner did Simon receive his new name than he demonstrated his personal weakness. In xvi. 22 and 23, he intruded himself as a stumbling block in connection with the cross, and in xvii. 4, as a belittler of the glory. The carnal nature can become Satan, that is, an adversary. It understands neither the cross nor the glory ; and it refuses to die to the world (xvi. 24). A Christian who is not dead to the world is an " offence," i.e., a stumbling stone, to all who try to walk the path of shame and death with Christ. Simon was rebuked on the summit of the mountain (v. 5) and Satan was rebuked at its base (v. I8).

Had he been received, John the Baptist would have been Elijah to Jerusalem at that time (vs. I0-I3).

If Christ manifested His Deity in glory on the summit of the mountain, Satan manifested his power and cruelty at its foot (vs. I4-2I).

The tribute money (vs. 24-27) was that commanded in Exod. xxx. II-I6, for the upkeep of the Temple. Christ, as the Son, was therefore free. In His grace He lifted Peter into fellowship with Himself, as being also a son, and hence the sweet words are recorded, " Me and thee." Contrast Peter's association with Satan (xvi. 23).

The tribute was half a shekel ; the stater found in the fish's mouth was a shekel, and hence sufficient to pay the tax for both.

" Prevented " (v.25), i.e., anticipated.

" Strangers," i.e., not of the Royal family.

MATTHEW XVIII.— This is called the children's chapter, for they are mentioned seven times (vs. 2, 3, 4, 5, 6, I0, I4).

The word " child " may be here understood both actually and figuratively.

Putting together the statements of the first three Evangelists, the Lord having descended from the Mount of Transfiguration and healed the boy, set out for Capernaum, on the way told the Disciples for the third time of His death, and, leaving them behind, either through desire for solitude, or to give them opportunity to think and speak together of that death, He went on before to the village and entered Simon's house.

He entering shortly afterwards, Jesus spoke with him about the Tribute money ; and the rest of the Disciples arriving, He asked them what they had disputed about by the way. They were too much ashamed to answer ; for they had soon forgotten the sorrow of xvii. 23, and had begun to dispute among themselves which of them should be greatest. What a sad proof of the indifference and selfishness of the natural heart ! Again, on the very eve of the Lord's agony and cruci-fixion, this same petty question excited them (Luke xxii. 24). Perhaps it was motived by the words spoken to Peter in xvi. 19, and by the selection of him and James and John to witness the Transfiguration.

The Lord then gently reminded them of the subject of their disputation, and they thereupon asked Him : " Who then *is* the greatest in the Kingdom of Heaven ? " (v. 1, R.V.). They left the decision to Him. He accepted it, and decided it by calling the little child—probably one of Peter's children—and told them that to enter His Kingdom, and to gain distinction therein, it is necessary to be new-born, to become a little child with its simplicity, dependence, and absence of ambition. Only One did perfectly humble Himself as a little child (v. 4), and He assuredly will be the Greatest in the Kingdom of Heaven.

Here, as in all His preaching on this sub-ject, He first insisted on the necessity of a new moral creation.

In an earthly Kingdom promotion is gained by ambition, self-reliance, the assertion of self-importance, emulation, and disregard to the interests of others.

This is not the spirit of the Kingdom of Heaven. That spirit is lowliness. In this condition there is fellowship with God ; and then it is easy to be meek and humble, and to say no to self ; for he who tastes the sweet-ness of that fellowship does not seek great-ness upon earth.

This chapter supposes Christ rejected, absent from earth, and temporarily refraining from claiming His rights (xvii. 25-27) until God shall vindicate them.

In His absence the children of His King-dom are distinguished by simplicity (v. 4), care for others' spiritual welfare (vs. 6 and 7), denial of self (vs. 8 and 9), and endless forgiveness (vs. 15-22).

" Offend " (v. 6), i.e., cause to sin. " Millstone," i.e., a great millstone turned by an animal.

" Hand," " foot," and " eye " (vs. 8 and 9) may here figure power, pleasure, and wealth, or things as precious as these. It is better to enter eternal life having lost these in this world, than having gained them to be cast into everlasting fire.

The double " for " (vs. 10 and 11) explain why a believer is not to be despised. 1. Because his angelic servant (Heb. i.14) has always access in Heaven's highest court, and if the servant has this privilege, how much more the master ! and 2. Because the Son of Man Himself came to save the believer ; though he was, it is true, lost, i.e., morally worthless.

The sinful condition of a child and its need of the Atonement is affirmed in verse 11. But here the word " seek " (Luke xix. 10) is omitted, for the salvation of a child, as dis-tinguished from an adult, is the primary thought.

Jesus must often have repeated His para-bles (12-14) ; but here the object is to show how reluctant the Good Shepherd is to lose a sheep. In Luke, the object is to show His determination to find it.

They should have a similar affection for one another ; and, furthermore, a spirit of endless forgiveness for one another. Thus in this gentle and captivating way did He rebuke their ambition for supremacy.

" Alone " (v. 15) and so to eternally bury the trespass.

In verses 18-20 the prophetic commission given to Peter (xvi. 19) was extended to the rest of the Apostles (See note on John xx. 22, 23)

" Two " (v. 20): union cannot exist with less than two. But these two if met in and unto His name, possess the power and au-thority for discipline which the Roman Church in vain claims. The mystery of united worship is not here the subject, but only discipline. See notes on Ezek: xlviii. ; and 1 Cor. v. 7.

Israel, repeatedly forgiven their mighty debt (Luke xxiii. 34, and Acts iii. 26), refused to forgive their Gentile fellow-servant (Acts xxii. 23), and as a consequence are now in the hands of the tormentors (v. 34) till the punishment of their iniquity is accomplished.

MATTHEW XIX. 1-26. The Lord's de-parture from Galilee (v. 1, with Mark x. 1, and Luke ix. 51) is more fully described in the two following Gospels. It was His fare-well to the scene of His miracles and ministry.

He now set out for Jerusalem in order to give His life a ransom for many; and on the journey thither through the countries eastward of the Jordan the events which took place are here, with design, much abbreviated.

The multitudes trusted Him; the Pharisees tempted Him (vs. 2 and 3).

Their snare is somewhat obscure to-day. Possibly it was : That had the Lord said that divorce was wrong, they would have charged Him with nullifying Deut. xxiv. 1; but if He had replied that divorce for every cause was lawful they would have convicted Him of contradicting Gen. ii. 24.

The Saviour confounded them by a double answer. First, that the "uncleanness" of Deut. xxiv. 1 only meant adultery in the Divine intention; and, second, that Moses, as a civil governor, and at the end, and not at the beginning of the Forty Years' residence in the desert, permitted, but did not command, a wider application of this law, temporarily, because of the hardness of their hearts.

The Creator himself speaks in verses 4-6. He says that at the beginning of the Creation, He made them male and female. This statement destroys the theory of man's evolution from a fish. In verse 5 He testifies that God was the Speaker in Gen. ii. 24, i.e., He Himself was the Creator of man, and the Founder of marriage. (See note on Gen. ii. 24).

The objection of the Disciples to the Lord's teaching (vs. 10-12) was: that if marriage be such a bond then is it a snare rather than a blessing, and better to be altogether avoided. The Divine reply permitted liberty of action; pointed out three classes to whom the legislation did not apply, because of the accident of birth, or because of the action of others, or because of personal resolve, and suggested that he who could accept celibacy should accept it. Hence the Apostle Paul argued that his condition as a celibate was not sinful, as his opponents at Corinth contended, but that, on the contrary, the highest forms of Evangelistic effort in the Power of the Holy Spirit were only attainable by non-marriage.

The word " then " (v. 13) is very important. A number of women, accompanied by their children, some of them being infants (Luke xviii. 15), hearing this teaching as to the sanctity of marriage, and enlightened by it, at once brought their children to Jesus.

Their intelligence was higher than that of the Disciples, who tried to prevent this action. But Jesus was much displeased (Mark x. 14) and declared that infants and little children should not be prevented from coming to Him, for the Kingdom of Heaven belonged to them, and they belonged to it. Such is the force of the words: " Of such is the Kingdom of Heaven." Accordingly He took them up into His arms and blessed them. It is a lovely picture! Jesus is the Kingdom of Heaven, so He belonged to the children, and the children belonged to Him; and this fact was demonstrated by their nestling in the kingdom of His arms.

How quickly the Disciples forgot the teaching of xviii. 1-14!

A child has little or no value in the kingdom of the world but immeasurable value in the Kingdom of God.

" Men " (v. 13) and " Money " (v. 22) are two great obstacles in coming to Jesus, and hinder entrance into the Kingdom of God.

Putting together the facts as stated by the three Evangelists, this man (v. 16) was young, noble, wealthy, strong (for he could run and kneel), courteous, educated and religious. Most men would esteem him to be perfectly happy. But he was conscious that he had not " life," and he desired to get it, and asked what should he do. Christ as a Minister unto the circumcision under the first Covenant replied that a perfect obedience to the Law would be rewarded with everlasting life. The young nobleman affirmed that he had rendered that obedience and yet was conscious that something was lacking. He was blind. Jesus put His finger on the two great commandments of the Law and said : " If you love your neighbour as yourself, then share your wealth with him; and if you love Jehovah your God with all your heart, then follow Me, for One only is good, that is God, and I am He." But he turned away!

The moral effect of salvation by works, and salvation by faith is seen in the action of the Philippian gaoler in contrast with this nobleman (Acts xvi. 33 and 34). The rich ruler, seeking salvation by personal moral merit, refused to share his money with others; the gaoler obtaining salvation upon the opposite principle of faith, at once actively expended on others everything he could.

The Gospel makes men mad, sad or glad. Naaman went away in a rage; the rich ruler went away sorrowful ; but Zacchæus received Christ joyfully.

The Law is spiritual and tests the motives of the heart. It says : " Go," " sell," " come," " follow " (v. 21). With difficulty shall a rich man enter into the Kingdom of God ; for self and the world have no place in it. The Disciples were astonished that a highly moral man, such as this ruler, should be impossible in that Kingdom. They did not understand that there is no good in man ; and they quite forgot the declaration of Ps. xiv. (Rom. iii.).

Entrance into the Kingdom of God by man, as man, however cultivated and moral, is here declared by the Infallible Judge to be impossible (v. 26). It is impossible to make a negro white, or to change a leopard's spots, because that which they exhibit externally is in their nature ; but God can do it, for with Him all things are possible. So then what cannot be obtained by merit may be received by gift ; for the gift of God is eternal life.

It is impossible for a camel to go through the eye of a needle, and it is equally impossible for the most deeply religious man to enter Heaven on the principle of merit.

At sundown the great gate of an Eastern city is closed, but a much smaller gate, called the Needle's Eye, is kept open for a little while. Through it, with difficulty, a camel may be pushed ; but he must be first unloaded. It may be to this that the Lord referred.

MATTHEW XIX. 27 to XX. 34.—It is as hard for the poor man to leave his little house as for the rich noble to forsake his great palace (v. 27).

In the regeneration, i.e., the Millennium (Acts iii. 19-21), the Twelve Apostles will sit on these Twelve Thrones (v. 28), and thus exchange a little fishing boat for a Kingdom.

But the terms " Me " and " My sake " (vs. 28 and 29) determine that the motive of true surrender is affection for Christ Himself. The reward is an encouragement in service or in suffering, after the great decision has been made to follow Him for His own sake.

He forsook home and mother and brothers and sisters, and received an hundred-fold (xii. 49).

The prediction of verses xix. 30 and xx. 16 introduced and closed the Parable of the Labourers in the Vineyard, and forearmed the Apostles against pride and self-gratulation ; for there will be a higher glory than that of the millennial kingdom, the glory that is to be the portion of the Church, high above all principality and power in the heavenlies. Israel was " first " and the Church is " last " in relation to time, but in respect of position the last shall be first. This higher glory was that which the Apostle Paul, who was " last " (1 Cor. xv. 8), earnestly desired in Phil. iii. 14.

" Early in the morning " (v.1). The Apostles were then called.

" The third hour " (v. 3), i.e., those called at Pentecost and following days (Acts ii. 15).

" The sixth and ninth hour " (v. 5) : the calling of Cornelius and the Gentiles (Acts x. 3 and 9).

" The eleventh hour " (v. 6) : The conversion of St. Paul and his colleagues.

This " eleventh hour " will probably have its plenary fulfilment shortly before the future events foretold in the Apocalypse.

The great principles of grace, election, and the sovereignty of God are affirmed in this Parable of the Vineyard. No one could enter it in self-will. All were dependent upon the grace that invited them, and that chose them as labourers, and none could justly murmur at the sovereignty that willed that grace should give to the last what justice paid to the first.

" I will give " (v. 14), i.e., I will to give.

" Evil " (v. 15), i.e., Stingy, or envious, " Good," i.e., generous.

So " the many," i.e., all were called (v. 16), but from amongst them a few were chosen, i.e., the eleventh-hour labourers. David had many followers, but only thirty and seven chosen men of valour (2 Sam. xxiii. 39).

The fourth prediction of the Crucifixion (vs. 17-19) failed, like that of xvii. 22, 23, to displace in the heart of the Disciples self-interest and self-importance (v. 21). Unless the Holy Spirit enlightens the heart, the clearest spiritual teaching has neither meaning nor power. This fact humbles man's pride.

Salome was the wife of Zebedee and mother of James and John (v. 20). They enlisted their mother's influence in their petition ; but in vain.

They did, indeed, drink of His cup and suffer His baptism, for James was beheaded (Acts xii. 2), and John was exiled to Patmos (Rev. i. 9).

The unity of Jesus and the Father, and His wondrous self-renunciation as Son of God, shine forth in His answer (v. 23). Positions in the Kingdom of the Son were planned by the Father ; and the Son, in the Unity of the God-head, would only give such positions to those to whom the Father had determined to grant them. He, as the Son, could indeed lead His followers to suffering and death, but the first places in His Kingdom He would only bestow on those whom the Father had chosen for such positions.

His gentle rebuke of the Disciples (vs. 24-28) explains the spirit of Service, the perfection of which was seen in Himself (v. 28).

One of these blind men was named Bartimæus (Mark x. 46). Here, in keeping with the purpose of Matthew's Gospel, both the blind men are mentioned ; for they represent the Hebrew nation in its two divisions of Israel and Judah ; and their receiving sight illustrates and predicts the light that will shine upon the nation in the future day, when the Son of David shall go up to Jerusalem.

For the supposed difficulties in the details of this miracle, see notes on Luke xviii.

MATTHEW XXI.—The last six days of the Lord's earthly life begin here (v. 1).

The colt being accompanied by its mother proved it to be a colt, and both animals satisfied the prediction of Zechariah ix. and of Isa. lxii. 11. This is a composite quotation.

It is quite probable that the Lord rode upon both animals—at first upon the ass, and then upon the colt.

Verse 7 should read as in the R.V.

This was Messiah's official presentation of Himself to Israel as the Great King, the Son of David. On this day, the sixty-ninth week of Daniel's prediction was completed (Dan. ix. 27).

The action of verse 12 was repeated on the following day.

The word "began" in Mark xi. 15, and Luke xix, 45 suggest this and so removes the supposed confusion in the three records. It is to be remembered that events in the Gospels have primarily a moral sequence. The reformation "began" on the first day and concluded on the second.

The quotation of verse 16 is from the eighth Psalm.

Luke xxi. 37 with verse 18 reveal the Lord's poverty. He passed the night in the open air and had nothing for breakfast.

"The fig-tree" (v. 19) represented Israel as nationally privileged (Judges ix. 10) and yet to be restored (Rom. xi. 2, 26).

"For ever" (v. 19), i.e., during the whole time of Israel's present dispersion. "Presently," i.e., immediately. It then began to wither ; and the following morning the fact appeared (Mark xi. 20), for it was dried up from the roots.

In the East, a successful teacher who can remove difficulties is entitled a rooter up of mountains (v. 21). The Apostles by their praying and preaching and faith removed the great mountains of Hebrew tradition and exclusive salvation, and cast them into the "sea" of the Gentiles.

The chief priests assumed to be judges (v. 23), but their inability to answer the Lord's question (v. 25) proved them incapable to be such. It also exposed their hypocrisy and hatred, for they were bound to receive Jesus as the Messiah if they admitted that John was His predicted forerunner.

Verse 37 answered the question of verse 23.

The son who said, "I will not" but afterwards repented (v. 29), represented the outcasts of verse 31 ; and the son who said, "I go, sir," and went not, represented the priests and the Pharisees ; for the one believed Him and repented, and the others not (v. 32).

The husbandmen (v. 35) also represented the Scribes and Pharisees. They must immediately have recognised this parable as that of Isa. v. and that it applied to themselves, for they were angry (Mark xii.-12).

This parable asserts the doctrines of the Trinity (v. 37) ; the Incarnation (v. 38) the Crucifixion ; Eternal punishment (vs. 41-44), and the Resurrection and Second Advent of the Lord Jesus (v. 42).

It also affirms the immeasurable distance between the Prophets and Jesus ; for they were only servants and men ; He was the Son, and God.

The parable also refutes the doctrine that a creed is unimportant, and moral culture all-important, for these husbandmen were not condemned because of the absence of fruit, but because of their treatment of Christ.

"They say" (v. 41), i.e., those in the multitude who sympathised with Jesus (v. 46). He accepted and repeated their judgment

{Mark xii. 9). Such is often the experience of a modern street-preacher.

In this parable, as elsewhere (xxiii. 34), Christ claimed to be God Himself.

The parable was addressed to the people in the hearing of the Priests and Pharisees (Luke xx. 9).

The fruit of the fig-tree, as of the vineyard, was to be His. If not, then both were destroyed.

This is the first parable that predicted His Crucifixion; and it quickly followed the shouts of "Hosanna." They were willing to shout, but not to submit; and He knew, and here foretold, that they would soon shout "Crucify Him." They had to render to Caesar the things that were Caesar's, for their own misconduct had made them Caesar's subjects, but had they been willing to render to Christ the things that were His, He would have delivered them from the Roman yoke, and from the dominion of sin.

The sudden change of Figure from a vineyard to a stone (vs. 33 and 42), and other abrupt changes of Figures, is common to the Scriptures. See, for example, 1 Cor. iii. 9. Gen. xxxvii. 3, 4, 13, 14, and 20, and 2 Chron. xxxvi. 15, illustrate this parable; as does also the story of Naboth's vineyard, for the High Priest imitated Jezebel in the employment of false witnesses.

That the crowd was sympathetic is evident from verse 46.

Verse 13 fulfilled Mal. iii. 8; and the Lord uttered a composite quotation from Isa. lvi. 7 and Jer. vii. 11, when emphasising the fact.

See notes on Ps. v.

The Parable of xxi. 33, declares the rejection of the person of Christ; the Parable of xxii. 2-14, the work of Christ. The first Parable expresses responsibility; the second, privilege.

MATTHEW XXII.—The Parable of verse 1-14 teaches the great doctrines of the love of God, the wrath of God, the Deity of Christ, the need of His justifying righteousness, and the eternal doom of the self-righteous.

Love invites "the many," that is, all, provides a wedding garment free for everyone, welcomes sinners into Heaven's highest joys, and—most wonderful of all—regards those justly expelled as "the many" and the residue as "the few"; for Love is not willing that even one should perish.

Wrath is demonstrated in the doom of the man not having "the wedding garment"; and it is the same doom as that of the men who murdered the servants and the son of the householder (xxi. 41).

In the East wedding garments are provided for all the guests whether they be princes or paupers; and anyone who refuses to accept one, grossly insults the host.

This man deemed his own garment good enough for the feast; and it suited very well until the King came in, then was he exposed and cast out.

The few who are chosen, as well as called, are those who humbly accept Christ as their righteousness; the many who are called, but not chosen, are the self-righteous.

The Parable of the prior chapter (vs. 43-46) declares Christ's Sonship; this affirms His Kingship and Godhead. As the Son He has the bride, as the King He comes in to see the guests, and as God He has power to cast into hell. He is at once the King and the King's Son (Ps. lxxii. 1). In the prior parable He demands something from men; in this, He gives everything to them.

The Gospel message meets with indifference or hostility (vs. 5 and 6).

"His armies" (v. 7), i.e., the Romans. "Their city," i.e., Jerusalem; once His city, now theirs; just as "My Father's House," became their House (xxiii. 38).

Collective judgment (v. 7); individual judgment (v. 13). (See Zeph. i. 7, 8, and Isa. lxi. 10).

The Herodians, the Sadducees, and the Pharisees tried to entrap Him in some statement that would give Him into the power of either the civil or religious authorities. But they failed.

The Nation was parted into these three groups. The Herodians supported Herod and his government. They might be termed royalists. The Sadducees denied the inspiration of the Bible. They were rationalists. The Pharisees accepted the Bible as the Word of God, but added tradition and ceremonies to it. They were ritualists. All, however, whether royalists rationalists, or ritualists, were confounded by the Wisdom that spake as never man spake.

Had He said it was not lawful to pay tribute, they would at once have denounced Him to the Government. Had He said it was lawful, He would have denied His claim as Messiah, the King of Israel. By simply asking for a penny He left them under the yoke which they were obliged to confess they had themselves accepted ; and by inviting them to render to Him, as God, the things that were God's, He offered to release them from that yoke, as also from the greater yoke of their sins ; and He would have done so, had they obeyed Him.

In His turn He then confounded them with the question as to the Messiah being David's Son, and David's Lord, i.e., the great mystery of Christ's Humanity and Deity.

"I am," etc. (v. 32). Here the doctrine of the resurrection is based upon the little word "am."

All are sure to err who do not know the Scriptures (v. 29).

Thus, as predicted in Pss. cxl. and cxli., the Herodians and the Sadducees and the Pharisees, tried to entangle Him in His teaching, with their snares, their nets, and their gins. The snare was hidden in the path, so as to entrap the foot (vs. 34-40), the net was to imprison the hands (vs. 16-22), and the gin, or noose, was to catch the head (vs. 23-33). But in Him intellect (the head), action (the hand), and conduct (the foot), were perfect in their harmony with the mind and being of God. His hand rendered the tribute money, His intellect unveiled the Spirit world, and His teaching magnified the Word of God. The snare hidden for His foot by the Pharisees (vs. 34-40), perhaps was that (suggested by His teaching, as it appeared to them, in His parables, and in His direction to the rich young ruler to distribute his property to the poor), He would have replied that the great commandment of the Law was to love your neighbour as yourself. But in response to the question, He promptly said, "Thou shalt love Jehovah thy God," etc., and then He convicted them—for they hated the Gentile—by adding "and thy neighbour." These two commandments were similar, for they had the one keynote—love.

MATTHEW XXIII. — The Jesus of this chapter is not the Jesus of the modern novel and of the fashionable pulpit, for this Jesus denounced eight woes upon the clergy of the Hebrew Church, and in terrific language condemned them to the damnation of hell (v. 33).

The first twelve verses are addressed to the disciples and the multitude ; the remainder, to the Scribes and Pharisees.

"Sit in Moses' seat" (v. 2), i.e., are the official custodians and teachers of the Bible. But they shut up the Kingdom of Heaven (Luke xi. 52), they took away the key, i.e., the Bible, for they withheld it from the laity, and they nullified it with their own traditions (v. 13).

"He is a debtor" (v. 16) and "he is guilty" (v. 18), i.e., a debtor ; that is, he is bound to fulfil his oath.

"The Temple and Him that dwelleth therein" (v. 21). He called it "My House" at the opening of His ministry (John ii. 14-21) and He was dwelling in it when preaching to the Pharisees. At the same moment He was sitting on the Throne of God in Heaven (v. 22). So also His Spirit was in Paradise with the redeemed thief, and His soul was at the same moment in hell with the demons. (Ps. xvi.)

"Judgment, mercy and faith" (v. 23), i.e., just conduct, pity, and faithfulness.

A gnat and a camel were both ceremonially unclean (v. 24) ; the former was one of the smallest and the latter the largest living creature in Palestine. The Pharisee, to avoid any possible defilement, poured all potables through fine gauze, but was guilty of extortion and incontinence (v. 25). Thus he strained out a gnat, but swallowed down a camel.

"Behold, I send" (v. 34), i.e., "I am about to send." Jesus here assumes and affirms His Godhead. He sent His messengers forth on the day of Pentecost. The Book of the Acts records the persecutions and deaths they suffered from the hands of the men who here declared they would not have been guilty of the similar conduct of their fathers. But the hatred that motived the murder of Abel and all the Prophets, reached its climax with the murder of the Messiah and His Apostles ; hence the just judgment of verse 35.

There were two Zechariah's—2 Chron. xxiv. 20, and Zech. i. It is uncertain which Zechariah was intended by the Lord, but as 2 Chron. is the last book in the Hebrew Bible it may be assumed to be the Zechariah of that book.

The outburst of verse 37 is most affecting. The God of Israel stands in His temple. He suddenly turns from these blind and impure hypocrites, and the sinless anger that burns on His face and in His eyes melts into anguish and pity, as, it may be assumed, spreading out His arms, He looks down and upon the city spread before and beneath Him, and cries out, " O Jerusalem, Jerusalem how often would I have gathered thee ! " Then, once more addressing the Pharisees, He said, " Behold your House is left unto you desolate," and He went out and departed from the Temple."

Men only saw a simple man leaving the Temple, but the angels saw the God of Glory and the Glory of God forsaking it. The glory of God dwelt in Solomon's Temple, but the God of Glory Himself in the Second Temple, as predicted by Haggai. See notes on Mark xiii. 1.

MATTHEW XXIV. 1-44.—Jesus, the God of Israel, having forsaken His House, it became morally leprous—as all becomes that He forsakes—and in harmony with Lev. xiv. 45 He predicted that not one stone of it should be left upon another.

This chapter should be read together with Mark xiii. and Luke xxi. The three records are independent and complementary.

The spokesman of the disciples of verse 1 is pointed to in Mark xiii. 1 ; and the four spokesmen of the disciples of verse 3 appear in Mark xiii. 3.

There are two Greek words used for the term " end " in this chapter. One is that of verse 3 ; the other, in verses 6, 13, and 14. This latter means the actual end ; the former, the concurrence of the events which lead up to the end.

Three great signs will herald the Second Advent : the false Messiah (v. 5) ; the abomination of desolation (v. 15) ; and, lastly, the Parousia itself (v. 30).

All the prophecies of the chapter concern the Hebrew Church and not the Christian Church. This is plain from the terms used in verses 15, 16, 20 and 30. That is to say, Daniel's people (v. 15), the Land of Judea (v. 16), the Sabbath day (v. 20), the Twelve Tribes of Israel (v. 30), and the Holy Place (v. 15).

" Yet " (v. 16), i.e., immediately.

" The end " (v. 14), i.e., the near destruction of Jerusalem and its future deliverance. Many prophecies have a near and a distant fulfilment. See Rev. vi. (Compare Mark xiii. 13, and Luke xxi. 24).

Prior to that event the glad tidings concerning the kingdom were preached to all the Tribes of Israel " as a witness " to all the nations of the Roman earth. The distant fulfilment of this prophecy is seen in the Seven Seals of Rev. vi. and viii. See notes on those chapters.

But the two Tribes at Jerusalem rejected the King and the Kingdom (Acts vii.), and the Ten Tribes at Rome (Acts xxviii.) made a similar decision, and hence the Divine judgment of verse 14 and Luke xxi. (vs. 20-24).

But those of the Jews who believed upon the true Messiah were delivered out of that judgment, as promised in verse 13.

Between verses 14 and 15 more than nineteen centuries have already passed away. The same period of time intervenes between verses 13 and 14 of Mark xiii., and between verses 24 and 25 of Luke xxi.

The great idol of verse 15 is that of Daniel xii. 11, and Rev. xiii. 14. It will occasion God's desolating judgment.

" The Holy Place " (v. 15), i.e., the future Temple that is to be built in Jerusalem. Whoever reads the Bible at that future point of time—and especially the Books of Daniel and Revelation—will " understand " i.e., will attentively observe and recognize those events as being the fulfilment of these prophecies.

" Woe unto them " (v. 19) that is : " Alas for them."

The tender care which the true Messiah takes of them that are His appears in verse 20. In the midst of these terrific events He is concerned as to whether it will be wintry weather at the time of their flight !

The great tribulation of verse 21 will be the future time of Jacob's trouble (Isa. xvii. 14, Jer. xiv. 8, xxx. 7, Dan. xii. 1).

" No flesh " (v. 22), i.e., the Hebrew nation. This will be Satan's last great effort to totally destroy that people. But the elect of Israel can neither be destroyed nor deceived (vs. 22 and 24).

As prior to the destruction of Jerusalem false Messiahs appeared (v. 5), so immediately prior to the Second Advent the great false Messiah and the great false prophet (v. 24) will deceive the nations ; and the latter will work the mighty miracles predicted here, and in Rev. xiii. See notes on Rev. vi.

Just as the Lord's miracles proved Him to be the True Messiah, so the future miracles of verse 24 will prove Antichrist to be the false Messiah.

The coming of the Son of Man to deliver His ancient people will not be secret, but world-wide (vs. 27-31.)

It will be a coming in judgment upon corruption as sure, swift, and unerring as the descent of vultures upon a carcase. Then all the apostate Jews and the rebellious Gentiles will be cast out of His Kingdom into the outer darkness.

The " Tribes of the earth " (v. 30), i.e., the Twelve Tribes of the land, as predicted in Zech. xii. 10.

" His elect " (v. 31); i.e., the election of Israel and the nations.

Three trees, the fig, the olive, and the vine, represent the nation of Israel nationally, spiritually, and dispensationally as a witness for God in the earth (v. 32). Israel's present claim to nationhood, and to Palestine as their political home is, therefore, a sure sign of their approaching Summer, i.e., the millennium.

" This generation " (v. 34), i.e., the Hebrew people, shall continue as a people, but in unbelief, up to the Second Advent. See Deut. xxxii. 5 and 20.

Verse 34 demonstrates inspiration, and verse 35 deity. " Be fulfilled "—Greek, " begin to take place ". The verbs " to be " and " to fulfil " are distinct in Greek. Both are found in Luke xxi. 24 and 32.

As the men of Noah's day were insensible to the signs and prophecies predicting the coming flood, so will men be blind to the signs announcing the coming of the Son of Man (vs. 37-42).

In that day the wrath of God will infallibly discriminate between those who are His and those who are not. The latter shall be left to judgment, and the former received into and enjoy the Kingdom. The connection of this judgment with the rapture of 1 Thess. iv. is suggested by the use of the one Greek verb for " take " and " receive " (John xiv. 3).

MATTHEW XXIV. 45-XXV. 46.—The four judgments of the Servants, the Virgins, the Traders, and the Nations will immediately succeed the Second Advent. Judgment will begin at the House of God, and close with the living nations.

" The faithful servant " (v. 45) will be rewarded, and " the evil servant " (v. 48) punished. Thus there will be a special judg-

ment for all those whom the Lord during His long absence shall call to the ministry of the Gospel.

If the heart surrenders the hope of the Lord's coming (v. 48) it will not be long till the conduct be that of verse 49.

" Cut asunder " (v. 51), i.e., expelled from the household, and, further, doomed to the eternal punishment of the hypocrites. This verse destroys the annihilation theory.

The foolish virgins figure professors of spiritual life ; the wise virgins, possessors, for they have the oil of the Holy Spirit with their vessels in their lamps.

" Gone out " (v. 8), should read " going out." A wick will burn brightly for a short time, but not having oil, will go out.

In a crisis it is impossible to get spiritual energy from others (v. 9).

" I know you not " (v. 12). Christ only recognises those who are born of His Spirit, for if any man have not the Spirit of Christ he is none of His (Rom. viii. 9).

The judgment of the traders (vs. 14-30) teaches the great lesson of responsibility. Faithfulness receives the like reward however diverse may be the capacity or gift of the servant (vs. 21 and 23). The slothful servant shall suffer punishment not because of evil committed, but of duty neglected. To merit the fearful doom of v. 30 it only needs inactivity (Heb. ii. 3).

The duty of the Christian as a virgin is to wait, and as a servant to work.

The argument of verse 26 is : that if the master be such as the slothful servant declared, there was, therefore, the more reason why the servant should have bestirred himself, and, at the very least, have lodged the money on deposit in a bank (v. 27) so as to bear interest.

The judgment of the nations (31-46) is by many understood to be the final judgment of Rev. xx. 11, but this judgment precedes the millennium ; the other, succeeds it : the one is a judgment of the living nations ; the other, the judgment of the resurrected dead.

Nor is it the judgment of the Church, for the Church is an election out of all nations, nor is it the judgment of Israel, for they were not to be reckoned among the nations (Num. xxiii. 9). Also the reward here is " from the foundation of the world " (v. 34), whilst the Church was chosen from " before the foundation of the world."

This judgment will take place at Jerusalem where Jehovah Messiah will set up His Glorious Throne (v. 31), and where He will be attended by all His angels. See notes on Joel iii.

Christ's millennial reign will be introduced by three general judgments—The judgment of Israel (xxiv. 27-44); the judgment of Christendom (xxiv. 45-xxv. 30); and the judgment of the living nations (31-46).

Jesus of Nazareth here declares Himself to be the King of Israel (v. 40), and the Mighty God; for He will reward with everlasting life, and doom to everlasting death.

Such action is only proper and possible to Deity.

"My brethren" (v. 40), i.e., the elect Tribes of Israel. The judgment of that day will be based upon the one test as to what was the conduct of people to them.

"Nations" (v. 32) is a neuter noun in Greek and "them" a masculine pronoun; therefore it defines individuals.

Five personalities appear in this judgment: The King; the angels; the Hebrews; the Sheep; and the Goats.

True Christian ministry is unconscious (v. 37).

To persecute the lowliest of Christ's brethren is to persecute Christ Himself (Acts ix. 5); and to minister to such is to minister to Him. Thus He makes Himself One with His people.

The condemned "go away" into everenduring punishment (v. 46). They go voluntarily—they are not driven—they recognise the justice of their doom.

The same term that declares the eternal felicity of the one company is the same term which declares the eternal misery of the other.

MATTHEW XXVI.—The prediction of verse 2 evidences the calmness and love of Deity; for if Jesus were not God the quiet majesty of this prediction would be impossible.

The Chiefs of the Hebrew Church, which was a Divine institution, consulted to "kill" Jesus as men would consult to kill a wild beast.

If all the passages concerning the household at Bethany be put together it may, perhaps, be concluded that Martha was the wife of Simon the leper, Lazarus and Mary being consequently, brother-in-law and sister-in-law to Simon. The house was evidently a large one, and Simon, therefore, would have been in comfortable circumstances; but being a leper, and, therefore, compelled to live in seclusion, Martha was the head of the household. There was consequently but one anointing, and it was by Mary, as stated in John xii. 3. Her action denoted affection and intelligence. Having heard that He was to die, she purchased a costly spikenard to assist in the embalming of His body; but instructed by the resurrection of Lazarus, hearing that Jesus was Himself the resurrection and the life, learning that He was to rise on the third day, and recognising that embalmment would be needless, she poured it upon His living body and so testified her belief in the resurrection. She was the only disciple that believed and understood the Lord's teaching as to His death and resurrection. None of the other disciples seem to have understood what He said to them upon that matter until after Pentecost.

Mary anointed both the Lord's feet and His head (v. 7 and John xii. 3). The Lord described it as the anointing of His "body" (v. 12). It was the only anointing for burial that sinless body received.

It was Judas Iscariot who originated the complaint as to the waste of the ointment (v. 8 and John xii. 4).

Opponents of inspiration deny the fact of prediction. They affirm that all the prophecies in the Bible were made after the events happened. But they cannot deny the fact of the prophecy of verse 13. It was made nearly two thousand years ago, and no one can question its fulfilment to-day.

"Thirty pieces of silver" (v. 15) equalled about £4, and was the price of a slave made useless, or killed, by accident (Exod. xxi. 32). Such was the "goodly" price that He was prized at of them (Zech. xi. 13)!

The passover was eaten between the evenings, that is, between six p.m. of one day and six p.m. of the next. So the Lord ate His last Passover after six o'clock on the evening prior to His Crucifixion. Thus He commemorated the Passover and He became the Passover on the self-same day. Whether that day was Thursday or Friday is debated by scholars. But the Passover Friday being a Sabbath—a High Day—the Crucifixion possibly took place, therefore, on Thursday.

The Lord made seven efforts to win Judas Iscariot from his fearful purpose; but in vain (John xiii. 11 and 18, Matt. xxvi. 21, 23, 24, 25, and John xiii. 27).

The Eleven addressed Him as "Lord" (v. 22)—Judas, as "Master," or "Rabbi" (v. 25). He asked "Is it I?" last of all lest his silence should expose him; and his question and the Lord's reply must have been exchanged so that the others did not hear. See "Life and Times of the Messiah" by Dr. Edersheim.

"Thou hast said" (v. 25) is the most emphatic form of "Yes!"

"As they were eating" (v. 26). This statement, with Mark xiv. 22 and John xiii. 2, R. V., contradict the popular belief, mainly derived from the corrupt Eastern Church, that Christ instituted a Supper after, and distinct from, the Paschal Supper. Luke xxii. 15 and 20 further oppose this belief; for this passage speaks of two cups, and declares that both were given at the Passover meal.

The Lord, as was the habit of the host at the Passover during the meal, handed His guests bread and wine, and declared that these gifts represented the greater gifts of His body and His blood which He was about to sacrifice for them, and upon which the New Covenant would be based. On this simple action the Mass, and its imitations, have been founded! See notes on 1 Cor. xi.

"When they had sung" (v. 30). See notes on Ps. cxiii.

"New" (v. 29); i.e., "in a new manner," that is, spiritually.

They would forsake Him (v. 31) but He would never forsake them (v. 32), for He promised after His resurrection to meet them in the well-remembered Galilean homeland. This was a very remarkable promise. It related to His Father's Kingdom of verse 29; and had that Kingdom been accepted during the Pentecostal Dispensation of the Book of the Acts, then that Galilean relationship would have been fully established.

They were now about to enter a trial where the Lord alone could stand; and had Peter, therefore, made greater protestations they would only have resulted in a deeper fall.

As the Mount of Transfiguration demonstrated the Deity of Christ, so did the Garden of Gethsemane His Humanity.

On both occasions the three Disciples fell asleep! Such is the insensibility of fallen humanity to both the sufferings and the glories of the Lord Jesus Christ!

As a man He hungered for human fellowship (vs. 36, 37, 38, 40, 43, 45 and 46). But it was denied Him (vs. 40, 42 and 45); and, therefore, angelic sympathy had to be supplied (Luke xxii. 43).

What was the nature of the agony which appalled the mind and tortured the body of Jesus in Gethsemane it is, perhaps, impossible for man to know. That a sinless Being should have any contact with sin (John viii. 46); and, further, should be loaded with sin (1 Pet. ii. 24); and, most dreadful of all, should be constituted sin (John iii. 14 and 2 Cor. v. 21), must have been unspeakable agony. Hebrews v. 7 (R.V. margin), and several of the Psalms, support the belief that the horror of being forsaken by God (Ps. xxii. 1) and cast into hell was so great that He could not, as a man, have endured it but for added angelic strength (Luke xxii. 43 and 44); yet was there no antagonism between His independent will and the will of the Father.

Love is always ready and skilful to excuse weakness (v. 41), as, for example, the lateness of the hour, and the fact that they were sleeping for sorrow (Luke xxii. 45). But had they loved Him deeply they would not have slept either in the Garden or on the Mount.

"Sleep on now," etc. (v. 45). This may be understood as an interrogative exclamation, i.e.,: "Do you sleep on now," etc?" "Rise, let us be going", that is, to meet Judas and his band—not to run away.

"Wherefore art thou come?" (v. 50). This may read: "Do that for which thou art come."

The carnal nature can never act aright. It is always too courageous or too cowardly, too wise or too foolish, too forward or too backward, too talkative or too silent. Peter struck off the ear of Malchus the High Priest's servant and then ran away, and, later on, said: "I know not the Man." (John xviii. 10). The Lord at once asked a moment's liberty from His captors and stretching out His hand touched the ear and healed it (Luke xxii. 51). All who in self-will "take" the sword are here rebuked (v. 52). The magistrate to whom God gives a sword, is responsible to use it against evil-doers; that is "its place" (Rom. xiii. 4).

Christ did not command the sword to be thrown away but to be preserved in its proper place.

A legion numbered six thousand men (v. 53). There would, therefore, be seventy-two thousand angels to defend the Lord and the eleven apostles. "Presently" means immediately. The word "must" (v. 54) affirms the Divine inspiration of the Scriptures; for had they been composed by men there would have been no necessity compelling their fulfilment.

During the last day of His life and the first of His resurrection the Lord Jesus quoted thirty passages of Scripture; and several more are pointed to by the Holy Spirit when recording the occurrences of those days. Bible in hand He descended into, and rose out of, the tomb.

The palace or court of the High Priest no doubt was constructed in the usual way. A gated porch admitted to a central courtyard, on one side of which was the palace of Annas, and on the other side the palace of Caiaphas. Opposite the porch a raised columned pavement formed an audience chamber. Here Christ would stand as a prisoner before the High Priest, and thus Peter was enabled to see Him and He to see Peter (Luke xxii. 61). This midnight examination was preliminary to that of the following morning when the whole council assembled for a public trial (xxvii. 1).

The night was cold and they made a fire in the courtyard (John xviii. 18). There in the company of servants Peter tried to warm himself. But how different was that 'fire of coals" to the "fire of coals" of John xxi. 9! At Satan's "fire of coals" Peter sat with servants, and got no real warmth; and it was night in nature and in his soul; and three times he denied the Lord. At Immanuel's "fire of coals" there was warmth, and goodly company, and food, and sunshine in nature and in his soul, and three times he confessed the Lord. These two coal fires are burning to-day.

After his first denial Peter withdrew into the porch from whence he could still see Jesus and Jesus could still see him, and there he denied Him yet twice more—the second time with a solemn oath, and the third time not only with a solemn oath, but with the invocation of a malediction upon himself if the oath were false!

The popular opinion is that Peter in his fear relapsed into the profane language that he was accustomed to use as a fisherman prior to his conversion. But all the evidence about him in the sacred records points to his having been a devout Hebrew, believing in, and awaiting the advent of the Messiah. He was no doubt a follower of John the Baptist (John i. 35-42). See also Acts x. 14. To have used vulgar oaths and curses would have been sad indeed, but to do as he did, that is, to take a solemn oath such as men do in a court of justice, and then to call upon God to curse him if the oath were false—was a sin of appalling magnitude and depth. It might be termed spiritual suicide.

But the Lord's look upheld his faith, just as the Saviour's first look had brought him into the faith (John i. 42). On these two looks Peter's spiritual fortunes were founded.

He had been told that Satan had been given permission to sift them all as wheat (Luke xxii. 31). God fans (Matt. iii. 12) to get rid of the chaff; Satan sifts to get rid of the wheat. But Peter had been given the promise that in answer to the High Priest's prayer, his faith should not fail, and that prayer contemplated the moment when, in the dark night outside the court, and whilst Peter was weeping bitterly, Satan doubtless whispered to him: "Thou hast committed spiritual suicide, now thou art mine!" Had his faith then failed he would possibly, like Judas, have destroyed himself.

In Palestine the cock crows twice—once at midnight and again at daybreak. There is, therefore, no conflict between Mark xiv. 30 and Luke xxii. 34. Hence Mark says "This night" and Luke "This day." During the night the cock would crow twice, but at break of day, once only. Luke records with emphasis what happened at daybreak; and hence the accuracy of the record. "The cock-crowing" in the Bible means that which occurs at daybreak. "Cock-crowing," without the definite article, means in the Scriptures, either or both.

The witness of verse 61 was false, for Jesus did not say "I am able to destroy the temple," but "if ye destroy this temple," etc., (John ii. 19). See Ps. xxxv. ii.

"I adjure thee" (v. 63), i.e., "I put thee on thy oath." Christ immediately answered, for he recognised the Divine sanction and authority of an oath; and His recognition of the nature and meaning of an oath shows that the command of ch. v. 34 relates to needless oaths in ordinary life.

" Thou hast said " (v. 64), i.e., " You have exactly stated the fact : I am the Messiah, the Son of God ; " and then He added, " and, later on, I will come as Son of Man upon the clouds of heaven " (Dan. vii. 13).

MATTHEW XXVII.—The morning session was that of the entire Sanhedrim ; it followed the unofficial night meeting in the high priest's house (xxvi. 57).

The field bought by the priests (v. 7) would in Hebrew law be said to have been purchased by Judas (Acts i, 18).

The prophecy " spoken " through Jeremiah, as here stated by the Holy Spirit (v. 9), was repeated, and recorded, by that same Spirit in Zech. xi. 12. See notes on that chapter.

The words " The price of Him that was valued, whom they of the children of Israel did value " are to be understood as a parenthesis.

A similar explanatory parenthesis, had the price been twenty pieces of silver instead of thirty, might have been thus interjected : " And they took the twenty pieces of silver (the price of him whom his brethren sold into Egypt) and they gave them " etc ; Or, the verse might read : " They took the thirty pieces of silver (the price given in Israel for an injured servant) and they gave them," etc. Note the difference in exchange.

" Thou sayest " (v. 11), i.e., " I am the King of the Jews."

" Barabbas " (v. 16) means the son of Abba. He is here contrasted with the true Son of Abba. The latter had God for His Father ; the former, Satan ; and Israel preferred the former (v. 21)!

The malediction they invoked upon themselves and upon their children (v. 25) rests upon them still, and was, and is, a malediction of appalling horror and suffering.

No one was ever hated so much as Christ. He was hated by princes both civil and ecclesiastical, e.g. by Pilate, Herod and the two High Priests ; He was hated by the mob; He was hated by the soldiers ; and He was hated by the malefactors. Criminals when tortured do not revile a fellow-sufferer. This depth of bitterness was reserved for Immanuel. He was tested in all points.

Alexander and Rufus were the sons of Simon (v. 32, Mark xv. 21, Rom. xvi. 13).

Sour wine (" vinegar ") was apparently offered five times to the Lord : once certainly in mockery (Luke xxiii. 36), once in curiosity (v. 48), and it may be hoped on the other three occasions, in pity, for it was the habit for compassionate people to offer a stupefying drink of sour wine mixed with myrrh or gall to criminals on the way to execution, so as to deaden their agonies. Jesus refused to drink it (v. 34).

The five occasions were : on the way to Calvary (Mark xv. 23) ; on arrival there (Matt. xxvii. 33) ; later on, after crucifixion by the soldiers—(probably at their own meal) (Luke xxiii. 36) ; later still (Matt. xxvii. 48); and for the last and fifth time in response to the Lord's cry (John xix. 29).

The accusation was written in three languages, Hebrew, Greek and Latin; hence the three inscriptions and translations recorded in the Gospels. These several superscriptions display accuracy and not, as some think, discrepancy ; for the amount of space required for the writing in each language would be the same though the translation into other languages would be necessarily different.

The Hebrew Church demanded the death of Jesus because He claimed to be God and equal with God (v. 43, John v. 18, xix. 7 and Lev. xxiv. 16.

" The sixth hour " and " the ninth hour " (v. 45) i.e., twelve o'clock and three o'clock.

Christ in His death-agony on the cross (v. 46) affirmed the Divine inspiration of the Bible.

There were seven " words " from the cross : Luke xxiii. 34 ; Luke xxiii. 43 ; John xix. 26, 27 ; Matt. xvii. 46 ; John xix. 28 ; John xix. 30 ; and Luke xxiii. 46.

The Incarnation did not rend the veil (v. 51) ; nor did the Lord's sinless life of perfect moral beauty ; nor His anguish in Gethsemane ; nor His agony on the cross. These never could have rent that veil ; for the curse resting on the sinner being the sentence of death, Jesus must actually die in order to redeem the sinner from that curse by suffering it Himself on behalf of, and for the benefit of, the sinner. Hence the veil did not rend, so permitting the sinner to approach to God, and God to come forth in grace to the sinner, until Christ had actually died. The trangressor of Leviticus iv. 27 was not loosed from the sentence of death till the sin offering was slain and all its blood—the demonstration of its actual death—poured out at the base of the altar;

nor was the manslayer of Joshua xx. liberated from the sword of the avenger of blood until the death of the High Priest.

The Mother of Zebedee's children was Salome (v. 56).

Jesus was honourably and reverently buried, not by the Eleven, for they had forsaken Him, but by two, up till then, secret disciples ; Joseph of Arimathæa and Nicodemus (v. 57 and John xix. 39).

" The other Mary " (v. 61), i.e., Mary the mother of James and Joses (v. 56).

" Error " (v. 64), i.e., deception, or imposture. The priests did not say what the first deception was.

" Ye have a watch " (v. 65), i.e., " you may have a watch ; that is, four soldiers.

Christ witnessed the good confession that is, He testified to Truth (1 Tim. vi. 13). To the High Priest He declared He was God (xxvi. 64), and to Pilate He declared He was the King of Israel (xxvii. 11).

The presence of Jesus manifested, and manifests still, the evil in man's heart. It revealed the hatred to God of the priests, the people, the Gentiles, the soldiers and the malefactors.

He refused the stupefying drink because it was necessary that He should feel fully the effects of sin and its judgment.

His sufferings on the cross are immeasurable to human intelligence ; but the abyss of horror into which He descended under the wrath of God was far more terrible and inscrutable. The floods lifted up their voices ; and none may fathom His suffering at the bottom of that abyss into which He descended in order to save men from going there. Where sin had brought man, love brought Him ; but His apprehension of being cut off from, and forsaken by, God, that is, His consciousness of hell and its horror, was infinitely beyond that of ordinary men. No one but He could fully feel or fathom such a doom.

It is a wonderful fact that the one righteous Man that ever lived should at the close of His life of perfect obedience and moral perfection, have declared that He was forsaken of God. But here faith triumphed, for though forsaken on the cross, and shut up in the pit, He still trusted. Made sin, and that in the presence of God, with no veil to hide its defilement, and no mercy to cover or forgive it, He suffered, and believed, and triumphed, as none other could have

done. The " Fathers," in their distress cried and were delivered, but He cried in vain to God Who forsook Him though He trusted Him.

His triumphant shout " Finished " showed that His death was not due to exhaustion but to self-surrender. It was not suicide, for He did not " take " His life as a man does who can not restore it, but He laid it down of Himself because He had power to take it again, and in so doing perfected a sacrifice for the expiation of man's guilt.

He predicted that if lifted up from the earth He would draw all men unto Him— all men without distinction, not all men without exception—so the centurion who had charge of His crucifixion testified : " Truly, this was the Son of God." He was the first Gentile to render this testimony of faith.

As the Roman soldiers were used by God, (with Joseph and Nicodemus, John xix. 31-42) to certify the actual death of the Lord (Mark xv. 45), so were they employed to honour and protect from indignity His dead body (xxvii. 62-66). Thus these soldiers were His guard of honour until angels came to take their place.

The testimony of the Centurion is conclusive of the fact that Jesus really died, for his evidence was official, impartial, and independent.

Unbelief has no faith in itself, and therefore the priests requested Pilate to guard the sepulchre lest there should be the resurrection which they disbelieved but dreaded.

The Lord's ministry began and ended with a Satanic " if Thou be the Son of God." (iv. 3 and xxvii. 40). The first was immediate ; the second, mediate. But He refused to act independently of God and demonstrate His Godhead by freeing Himself, as man, from the pain of hunger, or from the anguish of death. To act independently is to sin. He fed others, Himself He would not feed ; He saved others, Himself He would not save.

MATTHEW XXVIII.—" The other Mary " (v. 1), i.e., the mother of James and Joses (xxvii. 56).

" Was " (v. 2), i.e., " Had been." " An angel of Jehovah " (R.V.)—not " *the* Angel of Jehovah, for He is Jesus.

The stone was rolled away and the angel sat on it ; not that such an action was necessary, but as a demonstration to the soldiers of the triumph of resurrection. "The end of the Sabbath" (v. 1), i.e., "after the close of the Sabbath," or close of the week. See Luke xviii. 12, 1 Cor. xvi. 1.

"Come," "see," "go," "tell," (vs. 6 and 7). A dead and risen Saviour is the life and substance of the Gospel (1 Cor. xv. 1-4). Women were the first preachers sent forth to proclaim these great doctrines (vs. 7 and 8).

The difficulties and discrepancies which some find in the records of the Four Evangelists respecting the events on the resurrection day, do not really exist, for details not being needed, are not given. Not only can the statements be pieced together, but it is to be remembered that the Lord, in resurrection, was no longer confined to an ordinary human body of flesh and blood but had a resurrection body of flesh and bone, and what the powers of that body were (Luke xxiv. 39) is not known, only it is stated that He was the "same Jesus" (Acts. i. 11), though passing through locked doors (John xx. 19) and assuming "another form." (Mark xvi. 12).

The report of the soldiers (v. 11) respecting the great earthquake and the apparition of an angel of Jehovah, hardened the hearts of the Sanhedrim instead of terrifying them, and they heavily bribed ("large money") the men to circulate the lie of verse 13, and promised to screen them from military punishment for negligence by bribing ("persuade") Pilate.

The events of the day may be thus outlined: Before day-break the angel rolled back the stone from the door of the sepulchre, the terrified soldiers left the garden by one exit as the women (Luke xxiii. 55, xxiv. 10—four of them are named) entered by another. Mary Magdalene directly she saw the empty tomb, hastened to where John and Peter lodged, presumedly near by, told them that the Lord's body had been stolen, and returned with them to the garden as the other women were leaving it by a different path for the Upper Room, which it may be assumed was at another and distant part of the city. The apostles finding the tomb empty believed with Mary that the body had been taken away, and went home much perplexed (Luke xxvi. 12). Directly they left, the Lord showed Himself to Mary, then to the women as they were appoaching the Upper Room, then to Peter, then to the Emmaus dis-

ciples, and lastly to all in the evening meeting. The apparition of John xx. 11-17 must only have occupied a few moments thus permitting the appearance to the women as they were on their way to the Apostles (Matt. xxviii. 8) at the very time that the soldier deputation was on its way to the High Priests (Matt. xxviii. 11). See also the notes on the narratives in the several Gospels.

The Eleven Disciples (v. 16) were accompanied by more than five hundred brethren (1 Cor. xv. 6). "The mountain" not "a mountain." It was some of this multitude that doubted, for by this time the Eleven were persuaded of the reality of His Resurrection.

These were the "poor of the flock" (Zech. xi.) to whom in distant Galilee and far from Jerusalem the Great Shepherd connected Himself, and whom He commissioned to proclaim His rights as King and the Laws of His Kingdom throughout the whole earth. He assured them of the donation of all power given to Him both in heaven and in earth, and promised to be with them unto the consummation of the age. That consummation would have then come if Israel had repented; but the Two Tribes in Jerusalem sent Stephen (Acts vii.) to say: "We will not have this Man to reign over us," and the Ten Tribes in Rome, the capital of the Dispersion, committed a similar message to Paul (Acts. xxviii). Hence this commission is now in abeyance, but will be resumed, and obeyed, when Divine relations are once more resumed with Israel.

There were three Commissions. The first was given in Jerusalem (John xx. 22 and 23); the second "as they sat at meat" (Mark xvi. 14-18)—this was to the Eleven; and the third on the mountain in Galilee. These commissions should not be confounded. See notes on Mark xvi. and John xx. and Luke xxiv. 36-49.

There is no Ascension in this Gospel, for all in it relates to the King and to the Kingdom which He proposed to set up upon the earth; and so He promised to be with them until the predicted hour came of the establishment of the kingdom. The interpretation of this commission belongs, therefore, to the Hebrew Church, represented by the Apostles and the five hundred brethren. The Church of God—the "secret" revealed in Ephesians—does not here appear, for its home is heavenly, and its commission is, to take out from both

Hebrews and Gentiles an election to heavenly glory.

There is also no Ascension in John xxi. See notes on that chapter.

" Teach " (v. 19), i.e., " disciple." " Baptizing," i.e., indoctrinating.   Here is the Lord's accustomed use of figurative language.   There is no reference to water ; but modern disciples misunderstand Him, as did those of Mark viii. 14-21.

If He meant that nations, as such, were to be baptized into water, then should infants be baptized, for an infant is a member of a nation.   See note on Mark xvi. 16.

" Them " (v. 19), i.e., the nations, not individuals out of the nations, as some think (see Greek text).

" The name " (v. 19) not " the names." This defines the Unity of the Trinity.   See notes on Isa. xlviii. 16.

Israel was baptized " into " Moses (1 Cor. x. 2, R.V. margin) and so became " the Body of Moses " (Jude 9) but no water touched them or their children.

The apostle Paul says (1 Cor. i. 17, see note there) that Christ did not commission or command him to baptize with water.   It is, therefore, plain that the Lord used the word " baptizing," in verse 19 in a figurative sense.

" The mountain " (v. 16, R.V.).   See Ch. v. 1, R.V.

MARK

In this second Gospel the Holy Spirit portrays Jesus as the Servant of Jehovah (Zec. iii. 8). Hence the similitude of the ox of service (Rev. iv. 7 and Prov. xiv. 4). In harmony with this the Greek word translated " immediately " " straightway " ".forthwith " " anon," etc., and which occurs eighty times in the New Testament, is found forty times in this book. On the other hand the title " Lord " does not once appear in the Greek text. Parables and long discourses are almost entirely absent, for a servant does not teach. Omissions and additions distinguish this Gospel from the others, and necessarily because of the purpose before the mind of the Holy Spirit in inspiring it. Failure to recognise this purpose originates the supposed discrepancies and contradictions in relation to the other three Books. Though that purpose is to picture the Perfect Servant, yet through that service from time to time gleams the glory of His Godhead.

The additions which distinguish this Gospel from the others are subjoined. The omissions are, mainly, that here is no genealogy,for in a servant men seek a character and not a pedigree ; here is no miraculous birth or reference to childhood at Nazareth, as in Luke, or to His pre-existence and Deity,as in John ; there is no sermon on the Mount, for that became a king and not a servant ; no claim to authority, as for example,. in the parable of the tares, for the command to the reapers is omitted; here is no sentence passed upon Jerusalem, or woes denounced upon the Pharisees ; no Bridegroom as in Matt. xxv. ; no Lord judging between faithful and unfaithful servants, and no king separating the nations to the right and left hand. If parables and discourses are recorded, titles and actions are omitted. In Gethsemane there is nothing said about twelve legions of angels ; on the cross there is no promise of the kingdom to the dying thief ; and prior to His Ascension there is no statement as to His having all power in heaven and in earth. He simply dismisses the disciples to service and goes forth working with them as a servant (xvi. 20). The apostles are here regarded rather as companions than servants ; they never call Him Lord in this Gospel ; and in His miracles this title is suppressed.

The golden texts relating to this Book are : " Behold I will bring forth My Servant, the Branch "(Zech. iii.. 8), and " He went about doing good " (Acts x. 38).

The additions peculiar to this Evangelist appear in the following passages :. Chapters i. 31, 35-38, 41, iii. 5, 20, 21, iv. 26-29, 33, 36, v. 36, vi. 3-6 and 31, vii. 24, 32 and 34, viii. 22, 23, 33, ix. 22, 27, 36, x. 16, 21, 23, xv. 20, 22, xvi. 7.

All these additions harmonize with the Spirit's design in here portraying Jehovah's Servant. They demonstrate perfection and not inaccuracy, as some ignorantly declare.

MARK I.—See notes on Matt. i.-ix.

Verse 1 may read : " The beginning of the good news concerning Jesus, the Messiah, the Son of God."

Thus the Holy Spirit before setting out His perfections as a Servant testifies to His Kingship and Deity.

Repentance (v. 4) is the foundation of moral intelligence. Those who refuse to submit to it can neither understand Him nor the Book He wrote.

The dignity of Christ's Person (v. 7) is here declared, for John, who bowed before no earthly king, bowed before this Servant, declaring he was not fit even to untie His sandals.

" He was with the wild beasts " (v. 13). This is peculiar to Mark.

Two baptisms (v. 8) are here contrasted. Eph. iv. 5 states that there is now but one. That must necessarily be the major baptism of The Spirit. Therefore baptism with water has ceased.

Christ silenced and rejected the testimony of demons though it was true (vs. 25 and 34, iii. 12, and Luke iv. 35 and 41). The apostle Paul imitated Him (Acts xvi. 18). The argument that the " Tongues Movement " must be of God because its agents preach the Gospel is, therefore, no argument.

"And taught " (v. 21), i.e., began teaching. This means that He made it His habit thus to act on the Sabbath days.

This first Sabbath must have been very exhausting (vs. 21-34), and yet the next morning He rose before dawn in order to pray (v. 35).

Do Ministers of the Gospel act thus on Monday mornings ?

This Servant made healing subordinate to preaching. He left Capernaum. Had He stayed there He would have established Himself as a Healer of Diseases. But He came to earth to preach and to die ; and He allowed nothing to hinder Him in this double purpose (vs. 38 and 39).

The title " Lord " is omitted in verse 40. See introduction.

How simple is the Gospel ! " Make me clean." " Be thou clean." " He was cleansed."

Had the cleansed leper gone up to Jerusalem and shown himself to the High Priest (v. 44), it would have been a testimony to the priest that Jesus was Jehovah ; for God only could heal leprosy.

Jesus was always accessible even to the vilest. He went further—He touched the leper ; for the sinless nature of Christ was undefilable. The leper did not doubt His power, but his dejected heart questioned if this Mighty Prophet would care for such a wretch as he. But he had to do with Love and Deity and Authority. Only God could say " I will." Here was undefilable purity in power, and a love that came down from the highest heaven to minister to and touch the most loathsome sinner on earth.

MARK II.—See notes on Matt. ix.

The four friends (v. 3) might be named Sympathy, Pertinacity, Unity, and Capacity. This man suffered from two diseases, one in his soul and the other in his body. Christ first healed the more dreadful one. As God He could see the man's sins. Being physically paralysed it was impossible for the sick man by personal effort to merit earthly blessing or win his daily bread ; so man being morally paralysed cannot perform religious actions and thus merit forgiveness of sins and eternal life.

Eastern houses being flat-roofed and furnished with an external staircase, it was possible to mount upon the roof and break it.

The power of this salvation was demonstrated by the action of the man in carrying his bed (v. 12). He was made master of that which had mastered him.

The new wine of the Gospel (v. 22) is better than the old wine of the Law ; but man prefers the latter, for his pride demands salvation by merit.

The Son of Man as Lord of the Sabbath (vs. 23-38), could not submit to the authority of men who in their ignorance opposed His ordinances to His goodness. The scribes being fleshly men did not understand the Sabbath. They limited God's goodness and refused the new wine of the Kingdom. (See notes on Matt. xii.).

MARK III.—See notes on Matt. x. and xii. and Luke vi.

He was grieved as well as angered (v. 5). This is peculiar to Mark.

He withdrew Himself (v. 7). He only courted danger when necessary.

" Sons " (v. 17). A Hebraism expressing origin, destination or character (Job v. 7, Isa. xxi. 10, John xvii. 12, Eph. ii. 2.).

Verse 19 should close at the word " Him."

" They went into a house " (v. 19), i.e., they returned home, that is, to Peter's house in Capernaum. Possibly He spent some days on the Mountain before returning home.

" His friends " (v. 21), i.e., His mother and brothers and sisters, as stated in verse 32.

Their disparagement of Him (v. 21) was judged by His setting aside of them (vs. 33-35).

They pronounced Him a lunatic (v. 21), and the Scribes declared Him a demoniac (v. 22). Thus the natural heart judged the Lord of Glory !

It is several miles from Nazareth to Capernaum. Verse 21 records His mother and His brothers and sisters starting from

Nazareth in order to seize Him; verse 31 records their arrival at Capernaum. They stayed outside the house in the street so as to lay hold on Him when He would come out.

It was not surprising that their carnal hearts should have so judged Him, for His conduct must have appeared insane to them. He attacked the clergy, He sat with sinners, He defended His disciples when they ate with unwashed hands, and when they plucked corn on the Sabbath Day, and He preached to the extent that He had not time to eat. His behaviour was eccentric. See notes on Acts i. 14.

But He was founding a Heavenly family, a spiritual home, in which natural kinship, as such, had no place. Not that He denied the honour due to a parent, for He commanded it, nor the affection justly claimed by brothers and sisters, but He taught that these relationships had no authority in the spiritual realm of which He, as God, was supreme. Natural claims must be there denied.

Hence He chose the Twelve (v. 14) that they should be " with Him," and that they should go forth to preach. Fellowship with Him must precede preaching about Him. Trained by that wonderful companionship they would become " mighty men "; as did the broken and discontented who companied with David in the hold (1 Sam. xxii.).

MARK IV.—See notes on Matt. viii. and xiii. and Luke viii.

Preaching is more important than healing (v. 1). Had He stayed upon the shore the diseased could have touched Him and been healed. But His business as a Servant was to deal with sin rather than with its effects.

Judicial blindness and deafness justly befall those who do not wish to see and hear (v. 12).

The secrets of Divine teaching (vs. 11 and 21-23) are not to be privately enjoyed but to be imparted as a lamp imparts its light. Christians are responsible to preach the Gospel. If they fail to do so their inaction will not defeat God. He will make it known to all nations (v. 22); and all will be held responsible to hear it (v. 23).

In proportion to the diligence given to Bible Study so will spiritual intelligence be measured to the student (v. 24). Spiritual gifts, if exercised, will be developed; if not, they will be lost (v. 25).

The action of this true Servant, and of the under servants, and the fortunes of the Gospel Kingdom between the First and Second Advents are set out in this chapter. The history of that service, the responsibility of its agents, their quietness and faith in danger, and the storms which must exercise that faith are here foreshadowed.

The consciousness of Jesus as to the success and non-success of His preaching appears in the Parable of the Sower; but only success is predicted in the beauteous Parable of the Man and the seed (v. 26). He sows, He reaps, and between these actions He waits. This is His present attitude. He is absent; He does not outwardly interpose. The seed is left to itself to accomplish its purpose. During His absence the labourers are responsible to work in the field.

The Master, however, forearms them against disappointment and confusion. Whilst the inner Kingdom of God (vs. 26-29) would be, and continue, pure, the outward professing Kingdom (vs. 30-32) would become a great earthly institution having great branches, and would become the home of Satan and his angels; and so it has come to pass.

"Even as He was" (v. 36), i.e., so exhausted that on boarding the ship He fell asleep. This is peculiar to Mark.

There was no danger for the disciples, for He was with them and had said " Let us pass over unto the other side " (v. 35). But unbelief is folly, for how could the Servant of Jehovah, and His disciples, and His work be sunk in a lake by an accidental storm! His people are in the same boat with Him, and they cannot perish because He cannot perish; but being His companions and fellow-labourers they must expect storms of opposition for they are sure to come (Ps. xciii. R.V.). He reproved the disciples both before and after stilling the storm. The records are complementary, not contradictory.

MARK V.—See notes on Matt. viii. and Luke viii.

Unchilled by unbelief, opposition and hatred, the Lord continued to show by works of goodness and mercy that Jehovah Who had compassion on His people had visited them. He manifested this great fact in His action toward a man, a woman and a child. It is interesting that such is the order in the chapter, for it is usual thus to group men, women and children.

The man represents desperate sinners indwelt by a thousand furious passions ; the woman, anxious inquirers who, conscious that they are hopelessly lost, seek salvation ; the child, the mass of ordinary moral people who are spiritually dead.

Society restrains criminals (v. 4) ; Jesus rescues them (v. 8), and gives them a new moral nature (vs. 15 and 18-20).

A corrupt Church sells at a high price worthless sacramental remedies to people seeking peace (v. 26) ; but the touch of faith secures true and gratuitous healing (v. 29).

The child was not an active agent of any form of wrong-doing. She was dead—insensible to the grief of her parents and unconscious of the presence of Jesus. Such is the moral condition of thousands. Their parents and friends know that they are spiritually dead, but they themselves are unconscious of the fact ; and they neither see nor hear the Lord Jesus Christ Who is not far from any one of them.

Many decry sudden conversion, but the one Greek word, here translated " forthwith " (v. 13) and " straightway " (vs. 29 and 42) is used in these three miracles ; and is the strongest Greek term for immediate action.

" What have I to do with thee " (v. 7) ? This Hebraism occurs in both Old and New Testaments. It determines deep separation, and distance, and denial of authority. See 2 Sam. xvi. 10, xix. 22, 1 Kings xvii. 18, 2 Kings iii. 13, Matt. viii. 29, Mark i. 24, Luke iv. 34 and John ii. 4.

The man was commanded to go into the Gospel field (v. 19) ; the woman, to go into peace (v. 34) ; and the child to go into dinner (v. 43).

These three commands in reverse order apply to all who have experienced the saving grace·and power of Christ. The Bible must be their food ; assurance of salvation their experience ; and preaching the Gospel their employment.

All Christians, honourably earning their bread, should regard preaching the Gospel as their main business.

" In peace " (v. 34) ; Better, " into peace."

" Be not afraid " (v. 36). This is peculiar to Mark.

Of the three prayers : that of the demons (v. 12) and that of the Gadarenes (v. 17) were answered, but that of the healed man (v. 19) refused. " No," is often the most

gracious answer to the believer's prayer. Compare 2 Cor. xii. 9.

MARK VI.—See notes on Matthew x., xiv., Luke ix. and John vi.

Unbelief shuts heaven out of men and men out of heaven (vs. 1-4) ; but where need was (v. 5), His pity, never chilled or tired, worked. The few sick folk profited by a love that overleaps every obstacle because it never seeks itself.

Verse 6, is peculiar to Mark ; as are also the words " two and two " in verse 7. This form of distributive numeral is found in Aeschylus and Sophocles, and in recently discovered Papyri.

" Observed " (v. 20). This probably means" protected "from Herodias' murderous anger (v. 19).

" Did many things " (v. 20). This may mean " was perplexed what tò do ; and, yet, heard him gladly." See Matt. xiv. 5 and Luke ix. 7.

The words " heard him gladly " are peculiar to Mark.

Only women of a certain character danced in public. Herodias and her daughter in their hatred for the Baptist thus degraded themselves and Herod ; and he valued the life of the greatest. of the Prophets as only worth a shameful dance.

" Green " (v. 39). This is peculiar to Mark and is the testimony of an eye-witness. It is also an undesigned evidence of the truthfulness of Scripture, for Passover falls in spring-time and hence the grass was green.

The Lord was not a Benefactor distributing charity but a King entertaining His friends at table, for " companies " (v. 39) means dining-parties of hundreds and fifties (v. 40).

" Brake " and " gave " (v. 41). The former is the Greek Aorist ; the latter, the imperfect tense. The former was instantaneous ; the latter, continuous. The miracle, therefore, took place between the breaking and the giving. Each Disciple soon exhausted his supply and so had to return to Jesus for more, and was never disappointed.

Jehovah of Psalm cxxxii. here revealed Himself. He satisfied the poor with bread (v. 42). He walked upon the sea (v. 48) ; He hushed the storm (v. 51) ; and He brought health to all (v. 56). It was but to touch Him and be healed.

The spiritual blindness of verse 52, **was**

most probably caused by their political unity with the world in its carnal enthusiasm and purpose (John vi. 15). Nothing dulls spirituality like the religious enthusiasm of the carnal nature acting in fellowship with the religious world.

MARK VII.—See notes on Matthew xv. and xvi. and Luke ix.

The state (Herod) put to death the preacher of righteousness (Matt. xiv. 10) and the church (the scribes) corrupted the Word of Righteousness (vs. 1-13).

The scribes washed cups and pots but not their hearts. The ceremonial washing of their hands could not remove the guilt that stained them.

Jesus exposed their hearts (vs. 21 and 22), and then revealed the heart of God (vs. 25-30).

" He could not be hid " (v. 24). This is peculiar to Mark.

" An evil eye " (v. 22), i.e., envy. The omission of the "ands " in these verses (vs. 21-23) carries the attention of the reader forward to the climax—" all these evil things come from within and defile the man." This statement by Him Who is the Truth, destroys the belief that the natural heart is good, and makes foolish modern efforts to improve human nature. The assumption that only what goes into the heart defiles it is here denied ; and the necessity of the creation of a new heart declared. Luke xiv. 12-24 illustrates the use and non-use of " and." It is evident that what comes out of the heart must exist in the heart.

In verses 6, 10 and 13, the Lord declares the Bible, as written by Moses and Isaiah, to be " The Word of God." Compare Rom. ix. 6, x. 17, and 2 Cor. iv. 2. This is why it " cannot be broken " because it is the Word of God; man's word can be broken, whether written or spoken, but not God's Word (John x. 35).

Verse 19 (R.V.) and Acts x. 15, destroy the Seventh Day Adventist teaching that it is sinful to eat bacon.

MARK VIII.—See notes on. Matt. xv. and xvi. and Luke ix.

The insensibility of the natural heart appears in verse 4. The disciples apparently learned nothing from the previous feeding of the multitude. This blindness is recorded in vi. 52. and viii. 16. How grieved and disappointed Jesus must have been to have had such dull pupils ! His nine questions (17-20) led up to the pained exclamation : " How is it that ye do not understand ? "

Compassion, power and judgment formed the base of the miracle (peculiar to Mark) of the healing of the blind man of Bethsaida.

He took the blind man by the hand (v. 23). Gently guiding him, warning him of obstacles, and leading him some distance, would win the man's confidence and affection. It is a lovely picture.

Bethsaida witnessed His mighty miracles but refused to repent (Matt. xi. 20 and 21). Judgment was pronounced upon it ; and, therefore, the Lord refused to work this miracle in the town. He led the blind man away from it, and forbade him, when healed, even to enter into it (v. 26, R.V.).

When men resist the Holy Spirit, He by a just judgment, abandons them to wrath.

Many blind men were healed. Six are personally mentioned. The two men of Matt. ix. 27 ; blind Bartimæus and his companion of Matt. xx. 29 ; the man born blind, John ix. ; and the blind man of Mark viii. 22.

Unbelief is the mother of many evils, and it has a mysterious power. Because of it Jesus could not perform many miracles at Nazareth ; and before healing the blind man of this chapter, He has to lead him away from the unbelieving Bethsaida.

In healing this man, and the man born blind of John ix., He repeated His creative action of Genesis ii. 7. In John ix. He took clay and animated it with the honeyed dew of His sweet lips, so creating new eyes.

But in the case of this blind man (v. 22), His own hands of sinless clay sufficed ; for it may be assumed that this man became blind, whilst the other was born blind. See note on Lev. xv. 8.

But here the unbelief of Bethsaida seems to have affected the blind man, for his healing was not instantaneous. He, in truth, represented the blindness of heart which darkened the spiritual vision of the disciples, and which was so difficult to banish.

It is useless to give evidence to unbelief (v. 11). Had he given the most overwhelming proofs of His Messiahship they would not have believed upon Him, and for the reason that faith waits for repentance and the sense of sin against God, for the need of pardon, and for a desire to escape from its defilement. Hence He threw the responsibility upon themselves, and called to them to repent and believe the Gospel. His whole mission rested upon this moral foundation ; and the satisfactory evidence that He gave of His Deity could only be perceived by those who had moral eyesight. The demonstration that the Scribes demanded had no value ; it would not have affected the heart and produced repentance. See notes on Matt. xii. 40, and Luke xi. 23.

Disciples must observe, reflect upon, and seek to understand spiritual lessons (vs. 14-21).

The Pharisees were unbelieving (v. 11), and the disciples unreflecting (v. 18).

They were anxious about bread (v. 14) ; but they had never seen Him concerned about food.

The leaven of Herod is the fellowship of the church and the world ; the leaven of the Pharisees is sacramental salvation.

Intimacy usually destroys hero-worship, for defects in the hero's character are discovered. It was not so with Christ (v. 29). He grew greater to His desciples as time went by. Compare John i. 40-42. Those who cannot say " Thou art the Messiah the Son of the living God " do not know God.

It is characteristic of this Gospel of the Servant that it records only the words " Thou art the Messiah."

The conditions of discipleship (vs. 34-38) are three : First : the attitude of the disciple to himself—let him deny himself. Second : the attitude of the disciple to the world—and take up his cross. Third : the attitude of the disciple to Christ—and follow Me.

There is a difference between " come after " and " follow " (v. 34), Judas Iscariot went after Him but did not follow Him. To follow demands affection and repentance and loyalty of heart.

" If any man willeth to come after Me " (v. 34). This suggests the alternative ; that is to say, to save one's life, i.e., not to follow Jesus.

MARK IX.—See notes on Matt. xvi. and xvii. and on Luke ix.

" By the hand " (v. 27). This is peculiar to Mark.

" Afraid to ask Him " (v. 32). Afraid possibly of again showing their ignorance, or, perhaps, afraid of knowing the worst ; for they still hoped for an immediate Kingdom of outward glory.

Why did not John speak in vi. 30 of their action in forbidding this man (v. 38) ? Perhaps he felt uneasy in his mind. Now moved by the teaching of verses 33-37 he had to confess it all. The Lord rebuked him (v. 39) ; and added that it were better for him to be drowned in the sea than by such action to cause one of His little ones to stumble (v. 42).

" The hand," " the foot," and " the eye " (vs. 43-48) may figure the wealth and position gained by power, self-will, and covetousness. Better to suffer the loss of these things in this life and enter into the life eternal than having won them to perish for ever.

Three times here the Lord affirms the fact of the lake of fire, and the conscious suffering of those cast into it.

The Gehenna outside Jerusalem was not eternal. Its fire was quenched and its worm died because the corruption on which they fed ceased to exist. But the terrible words " their worm " reveal the eternal existence of the moral corruption that is " to go into hell " (v. 43). The belief of this doctrine will not make insane those who sit where Mary sat (Luke x. 39).

All followers of Christ, including John and the man whom he rebuked (v. 38), will be salted with fire (v. 49), i.e., tested by trial ; but it is the Master who will test them ; they are not to test one another. On the contrary, each Disciple is to have salt in himself (v. 50), i.e., to judge self ; and the result would be peace and not the disputation of verse 34.

Further, all sacrifice of service as of worship (Lev. ii. 13) should be seasoned with salt (v. 49), i.e., judged by the health-giving, purifying, and preservative Word of God.

Fire and salt are symbols of purifying and preservative judgment (vs. 33-50). For the Christian the fire is chastening in its action and only consumes the flesh (1 Cor. xi. 31 and 32). The fire of 1 Cor. iii. 15 affects doctrine and not conduct. This fire destroys the theory of purgatory. For the non-Christian the fire is eternal and destroys both soul and body in hell (Matt. x. 28). See notes on 1 Cor. iii.

Salt expresses fellowship and affection. It signifies an inward sweetening and preservative energy binding the heart to Christ and to His service—an energy of holiness that judges everything contrary to His nature and will. Hence Christians are the salt of the earth because living in fellowship with Him, and judging evil in themselves, they purify society. If they who are of Christ fail in this testimony where shall anything be found to restore this energy in them? The salt will have lost its savour and what can season it?

The declaration "He that is not with Me is against Me" (Matt. xii. 30) seems to conflict with the words "He that is not against us is on our part" (v. 40). But they coalesce when it is recognised that Christ was the Divine Object and He brought things to an issue. The world was against Him; if a man was not, he was for Him, for there was no middle position.

The Lord rebuked ecclesiastical intolerance (vs. 39-42). The apostles applied the modern test known as the Historic Episcopate. If ever such a test were true it was then when the Head of the Church and His Apostles were on earth. No church organisation can lay claim to a monopoly of the Spirit and power of the Bishop of Souls.

MARK X.—See Matt. xviii. and xix. and xx.

"He was much displeased" (v. 14); and "He took them up in His arms" (v. 16); and "Jesus loved Him" (v. 21). These statements are peculiar to Mark.

"They were amazed; and as they followed they were afraid" (v. 32). This is complementary to the other Evangelists. As the Lord passed before them to Jerusalem and to Calvary, some physical manifestation of terror in His Person must have frightened the Disciples. What follows in the text (vs. 32-34) makes it plain that the anguish that expressed itself in His body was the fore-taste of Golgotha and the wrath of God.

Notwithstanding the rebuke of ix. 35. James and John thirsted for, and demanded, pre-eminence (vs. 35-45). They were gently told that prizes in a competition, or positions in a government, are not promised beforehand by an umpire or a servant, but given to those who win them by effort or capacity. They are "prepared" for such (v. 40).

The sons of Zebedee wanted to be first and the Ten were unwilling to be last! Such was the energy of the carnal nature in all Twelve.

Jesus as the Servant of Jehovah came to be the Servant of all (v. 44) and to give His life to save "many" (v. 45). Atonement is the great central doctrine of the Word of God. The Lord Jesus here says this was His one purpose in coming to earth.

The young ruler was too rich to follow Jesus "in the way" (v. 17); the Disciples were too cowardly to follow Jesus "in the way" (v. 32); it remained for the poor blind beggar to use his new-found sight to follow Jesus "in the way" (v. 52). See notes on Luke xviii.

The words "From the beginning of the Creation God made them male and female" (v. 6), determine that there could have been no creation of man before Adam. This statement of the Lord's destroys, for those who fear Him, the theory of Evolution.

He Who created tons of bread and hundreds of fish in a few moments out of nothing when feeding the multitudes, could with equal power and wisdom create the Universe in a few days out of nothing that appears (Heb. xi. 3)

MARK XI.—See notes on Matt. xxi. and Luke xix. and John xii.

"Have faith in God" (v. 22); rather, have the faith that is of God, i.e., a Divine faith. Such a faith judges profession (the fig-tree, v. 20); removes difficulties (the mountain, v. 23); and forgives injuries (a sinner, v. 25). See notes on Luke xvii. 6.

"The time of figs was not yet" (v. 13), i.e., the fig-harvest had not commenced; there should have been fruit.

MARK XII.—See notes on Matt. xxi. and xxii., Luke xx.

Among the Pharisees there was great profession of love to God but little practice of love to man (vs. 29-34). To-day there is great evidence of love to man, i.e., philanthropy, social schemes, hospitals and such like, but little evidence of love to God.

Jesus says (v. 36) that the Holy Spirit inspired David to write Psalm cx.; and He seven times declared that He did not speak from Himself but as commanded by God. Some modern critics contradict Him and say He was mistaken as to the authorship of the Psalm; therefore God was mistaken! Christ by His refusals (vs. 13-27) demonstrated that He was the Power of God and the Wisdom of God (1 Cor. i. 24).

He refused to work a miracle at the commencement of a ministry rich in miracles (Matt. iv. 4). He fed others, Himself He would not feed, just as He saved others, but Himself He would not save. His wisdom detected the snare, and His power broke it.

He refused to answer prayer (Mark v. 18), but He refused in the interest of others (vs. 53-56). Wisdom refused the petition, and power clothed the petitioner and made him a successful soul-winner (vi. 53).

He refused to answer questions. The Churchman (Matt. xxi. 23); the Scientist (Luke xiii. 23); and the Politician (Matt. xxii. 16). His wisdom detected in each of these cases the net laid for His feet, and His power destroyed it.

He refused the wine drugged with myrrh (Mark xv. 22). His wisdom recognised the Divine necessity which forbade any alleviation of His suffering as a Sin-Offering, and His power made Him an Overcomer.

MARK XIII.—See notes on Matt. xxiv. and Luke xxii.

He left the temple and the city (Matt. xxiii. 39 and xxiv. 1). When leaving the first temple He did so reluctantly and in stages, and withdrew to the Mount of Olives, and the prophet saw Him as the God of Glory (Ezek. ix. 3, x. 4 and 19, and xi. 23). When men saw Him leaving the second Temple and withdrawing to the Mount of Olives, they saw in Him neither beauty nor glory, but only a man, the Carpenter of Nazareth!

As Man, Jesus knew not the hour of His Coming; as God He knew that men did not know it, and that angels were equally ignorant; hence His knowledge exceeded both human and angelic intelligence. His words therefore determine both His Humanity and His Deity.

All in Him was perfection—perfect ignorance and perfect knowledge. Yet the Greek text might be translated: " neither the Son but as The Father." Compare Isaiah ix. 6, and John xiv. 9.

" Watch therefore " (v. 35). These four watches were so arranged by the Romans.

He predicted that His Coming would be preceded by religious movements (v. 6); political movements (vs. 7 and 8); and physical movements (v. 8).

He warned them against religious deception (vs. 5 and 6), and spiritual failure (9-13) and against negligence (v. 23). The last day was hidden that all days might be observed.

He gave, as men say, a sad interpretation of the future. His forecast was very dark. Deception, conflict, suffering, family division and universal hatred! Such will be the experience of His people during His absence.

MARK XIV.—See notes on Matt. xxvi. and Luke xxii.

Christ revealed by His Presence the love that was in Mary's heart and the treachery in Iscariot's (vs. 3-11). To a nature like that of Judas goodness becomes more and more repugnant. Mary is for all time a type of the true disciple (v. 9). Many scholars deny the fact of prophecy. But here is one they cannot contradict, for it is true to-day in its fulfilment.

Obedient to the Divine purpose, Christ must die as a sacrifice for sin, but that necessity did not excuse the free agent who brought it about (v. 21). " Good for that man " etc. Judas concurred with this for he went and hanged himself.

Jesus was accustomed to use symbolic language and figures of speech (vs. 22-24). " Is " here means " represents."

Salvation is a gift. Hence the word " take " (v. 22).

" A certain young man " (v. 51). The language suggests that he was the rich young ruler.

Christ either deceived men by a conscious fraud, or He deceived Himself, or He was God (vs. 61 and 62). It is impossible to get out of this dilemma.

" They all condemned Him to be guilty of death " (v. 64). Thus was fulfilled the prophecy of viii. 31. " They all forsook Him and fled " (v. 50). Not being allowed to fight (v. 47) they fled. Such is nature!

" Not during the feast " (v. 2, R.V.).

MARK XV.—See notes on Matt. xxvii. and Luke xxiii.

The priests were insincere (vs. 6-15). They accused Christ as being an insurrectionist and yet demanded Barabbas who had made insurrection!

" Why hast Thou forsaken Me? " (v. 34). Some religious teachers deny that He was forsaken by God. They say He was permitted to think so. They also teach that He was not personally judged, for God only judged man's sin which was upon Him. Were these doctrines true then is man for ever lost ; for the sentence of death rested on man personally because of his sinful nature and because of his sinful actions. If Christ, therefore, would redeem him from this doom He must suffer it Himself, must load Himself with the sinners' sins and, Himself sinless, be constituted sin itself (2 Cor. v. 21 and Gal. iii. 13).

Because of sin and sins (Rom. i.-viii.) God justly doomed to perpetual banishment from His Presence, i.e., to death, guilty man (Rom. v. 12). To deliver man Christ became the sin-offering. As such He bore their sins in His own body on the tree (1 Pet. ii. 24). He abolished sin by the sacrifice of Himself (Heb. ix. 26). He suffered the wrath of God due to disobedience (Eph. v. 6) ; and the sword of that wrath awoke not only against the sins that were laid upon Him, but against Himself as being the Sinner, and yet the Fellow of Jehovah (Zech. xiii. 7) ; and, therefore, He was accursed of God personally (Gal. iii. 10), i.e., condemned to death, the mysterious death of separation from God and seclusion in hell. But He could not be holden of the abyss for He was sinless and He was God, so He carried away its gates, as Samson the gates of Gaza.

Herein lies the mystery of Christ as the Burnt-Offering and the Sin-Offering of Lev. i. and iv. Never was He more perfect and more precious to the heart of God—more truly a sweet savour than when hanging on the tree; and yet, at the same moment, was He accursed as being the impersonation of sin itself. Hence He Himself declared (John iii. 14) that the serpent on the pole, the similitude of the deadly stinging serpent, pre-figured Himself.

" The third hour " (v. 25), John xix. 14 says " the sixth hour." The one was Hebrew time, the other Roman.

MARK XVI.—See notes on Matt. xxviii and Luke xxiv.

There is no conflict between verse 7 and viii. 38, 39. A temporary defection through panic is not the same as a calculated and sustained abandonment of Christ.

The first preachers of a risen Saviour were women. No other speakers are mentioned as addressing the Church on that first Sunday morning. Many, misunderstanding the language of 1 Cor. xiv. 34, and 1 Tim. ii. 11, 12 (see notes on these passages) believe that the Scriptures forbid a woman to preach the Gospel.

The repeated unbelief of the Apostles in the Resurrection (vs. 11-13) destroys the theory that they invented the Resurrection.

Mary Magdalene, and not Mary the Lord's Mother, was the first woman or person whom He greeted on leaving the sepulchre (v. 9).

Unbelief is sinful (v. 16).

The baptism of verse 16 is generally under stood as baptism into, or with water. But this is an instance of Christ's usage of figurative language. This " baptism " must be that of John iii. 5 and Titus iii. 5, i.e., the inward renewing baptism of the Holy Spirit without which an intellectual belief in Christ is valueless (see notes on John ii. 23 and 24).

Further, if baptism in this verse means water baptism then is salvation impossible without it ; and, therefore, the penitent thief is not in Paradise ; and the many thousands who, through the ages, have truly believed and not been baptized are perished.

But if water baptism were fundamental to salvation or essential to obedience, the Apostle Paul could not possibly have rejoiced that he saved so few or made so few obedient (1 Cor. i. 14-17).

And, further, if baptism were a necessity of salvation God would have so ordered the climate of the earth that it would have been possible of performance in all countries, and at all seasons of the year. But in the Arctic and Antarctic regions, and in the vast deserts of Arabia and Central Asia and Africa, immersion in water is impossible.

If the ellipses be supplied the verse will become clearer to the reader : " He that believeth on Me, and is baptized by Me (John i. 33) shall be saved."

If water baptism saves then all persons so baptized will be saved, which is absurd. What proves too much proves nothing.

The baptism intended is Christ's own baptism of John i. 33, illustrated by Eph. i. 13 (R.V.). Simon Magus believed and was baptized (in water) and not saved (Acts viii. 13).

The signs proper to the Pentecostal age and its testimony to Israel, God's earthly people, had their fulfilment (vs. 17 and 18). The Acts of the Apostles records the evidence

But these signs accrediting the Messiah, were rejected, so the King sent His armies and burnt up their city and Temple ; and that Dispensation, like all those preceding, ended in the wrath of God.

His present purpose while awaiting Israel's conversion is the election to a Kingdom far above all heavens. This purpose, hidden in Himself and never revealed in the Scriptures until the Epistles to the Ephesians, Colossians and Philippians are reached, is not associated in those Epistles with physical miracles, but with a higher experience of suffering and shame, and weakness, and death, and glory. So the miraculous manna and water of the Desert ceased at Jordan.

It is, however, quite true that signs and not sins should follow them that believe ; but these " signs " are the excellent virtues set out in Ephesians iv.-vi.

The physical signs of verses 17 and 18 were necessary at the beginning as demonstrating the grace that went beyond the narrow bounds of the Hebrew Church and flowed out to all the world through that Church. Hence at that time the meaning and value of speaking with tongues. This gift, and that of others, belong, therefore, to the childhood of the Gospel, and were temporary (1 Cor. xiii. 8-11).

So in reading the Gospel of Mark the reader exclaims : The Being Who fashioned this Book, and all the other Books of the Bible, fashioned me ! for the Book understands me, and speaks to my head and to my heart

LUKE

In this third Gospel the Holy Spirit invites the reader to behold the Man whose name is the Branch (Zech. vi. 12).

Here, therefore, He is specially presented as the Friend of publicans and sinners ; the Saviour of Zacchæus and the penitent thief ; and the Narrator of the parable of the Prodigal son, and of the story of the Good Samaritan.

Here also are many references to women such as Elizabeth, Anna, the widow of Nain, the penitent of vii. 37, the women of viii. 2, the daughters of Jerusalem of xxiii. 27, Martha and Mary, and Mary Magdalene.

Here also, as the second Adam, He is presented as dependent upon God in prayer and as offering to Him praise.

Six miracles are peculiar to the Gospel of Luke :

The draught of fishes (v. 4).
The widow's son at Nain (vii. 11).
The infirm woman (xiii. 11).
The man with the dropsy (xiv. 1).
The ten lepers (xviii. 11).
The healing of Malchus (xxii. 50).

Eleven parables are also peculiar to this Gospel :

The Two Debtors (vii. 41).
The Good Samaritan (x. 30).
The Importunate Friend (xi. 5).
The Rich Fool (xii. 16).
The Barren Fig-tree (xiii. 6).
The Lost Piece of Silver (xv. 8).
The Prodigal Son (xv. 11).
The Unjust Steward (xvi. 1).
Dives and Lazarus (xvi. 19)
The Importunate Widow (xviii. 1).
The Pharisee and Publican (xviii. 9).

As the Son of Man the Lord here appears as the centre of a moral system much vaster than that He filled as Israel's Messiah. He here stands forth as the Saviour of the world. Not His titles nor His official glories engage the Spirit's thought so much as simply Himself as He was, a man on the earth, walking in sinless fellowship with God.

Nothing is known about Luke other than what appears in Colossians iv. 14, 2 Tim. iv. 11 and Philemon 24.

But it is interesting that God should have chosen and trained a physician to testify to, and to medically record, the miraculous birth of Jesus, and to narrate the special discourses, actions, parables and miracles which harmonize with His nature as man.

The Divine design in this Gospel in grouping incidents together out of their chronological order so as to emphasize spiritual principles, is one of the most striking peculiarities of the Book.

LUKE I.—The Gospel is a narrative concerning facts fully established (v. 1, R.V.). It is built upon facts about the Lord Jesus Christ.

True preachers of the Gospel are both witnesses and ministers (v. 2).

Perfect understanding of all the facts " from above " (v. 3) affirms inspiration.

" In order " (v. 3), i.e., in an orderly design—not in chronological order.

" Instructed " (v. 4), i.e., orally. " Certainty " can only be based upon inspired Scripture and never upon tradition.

Accordingly Luke in an orderly way first records the Lord's relationship to Israel, for salvation is of the Jews (John iv. 22), and then His moral mission and glory as Saviour of the world.

When nature is feeble and broken and dead it is then possible for God to act in power (v. 7).

" The right side " (v. 11). This was the propitious side. Compare Matt. xxv. 33, Mark xvi. 5, John xxi. 6.

Angels are prominent during the Lord's earthly ministry and in connection with His death and resurrection. Their presence proves that the Messiah was not an angel, but the Lord of angels.

John (v. 13), i.e., " beloved of Jehovah." " Great in the sight of Jehovah " (v. 15). This is true greatness.

The Holy Spirit can regenerate infants (v.15).

" The fathers " had hearts of obedience and wisdom, i.e., Abraham, Isaac, Jacob, Joseph, Moses and Joshua (v. 17).

The children, i.e., the men of John's day, were unbelieving and unrighteous. The effect of John's ministry was to give them hearts like their fathers'.

To Zechariah (v. 18) the promise seemed to come too late ; to Mary (v. 34), too early. He doubted the fact ; she only inquired as to the method.

Unbelief is exceedingly sinful (v. 18). Zechariah asked a sign and he got a painful one. He was made deaf and dumb (vs. 20 and 62).

" He could not speak unto them " (v. 22), i.e., pronounce the blessing of Num. vi. 24.

Mary was of the House of David (vs. 27, 32 and 69).

" Highly favoured " (v. 28), i.e., much engraced (Ephes. i. 6). Not " full of grace " as so fitted to bestow it upon others, as the Latin Church teaches, but one who, herself meritless, had received signal grace from God ; for of the countless millions of women born into the world she was chosen to be the Mother of the Lord. God, not Mary, was full of grace.

Grace is favour to the unworthy ; patience is favour to the obstinate ; mercy is favour to the miserable ; and pity is favour to the poor.

" Found favour with God " (v. 30). The true translation is : " received grace from God." The sweetness and plenitude of the grace was not in Mary but in God. She was the unworthy object of that grace.

The Greek tense implies the word forthwith before " conceive " (v. 31). This announcement was made to Mary on the 25th of December, and on that day the Lord was conceived. The Holy Child was born on the following 29th of September Competent expositors make this clear.

The Four Angelic Statements about the Wondrous Child (vs. 31-33) correspond to the Four Gospels.

A Son :   Behold the Man (Luke).
Jesus :   Behold My Servant (Mark).
The Highest :   Behold your God (John).
He shall reign :   Behold thy King (Matt.).

Mary asked for no sign, but the angel graciously helped her faith by telling her of her cousin Elizabeth (v. 36). The value of Christian fellowship is learned from verses 39 to 56.

Jesus was Jehovah (v. 76) ; and His descent to earth was not mainly to establish a perfect government but to deal with sins and their remission (v. 77).

Jesus was truly a human being. He was physically born of a woman, and after the natural period of gestation. But the Child was not the seed of a man but of a woman mysteriously energized by the Holy Spirit.

The Holy Spirit's great revelation in this Third Gospel is : that a Child should be conceived and born. Mary could not understand this ; but she did not doubt it although outside the order of nature.

She was willing to be the mother of the Great King, but not the disciple of the despised Nazarene. The sword pierced her heart and revealed and judged its carnal thoughts. She shared these in common with Israel (ch. ii. 34, 35). Yet she looked upon Him whom she pierced (John xix. 25) and believed and joined the disciples (Acts i. 14). In this she personates the nation. It was the Lord's mother (Rev. xii) ; and it will look upon Him as the Crucified One and believe (Rev. i. 7). See note on Acts i. 14.

LUKE II.—A Physician of good repute (Col. iv. 14) here records that the God of Glory was born a babe and grew to boyhood. and manhood (vs. 7, 42 and 52). This is most important.

He also certifies that the Birth took place in a public inn crowded with people—so possible of public verification—and not in secret.

Never was there such a wondrous Birth for it was God manifest in flesh. See note on Isa. ix. 1-7.

It fulfilled Genesis xlix. 10. See notes on that verse, and the importance of the word " first " (v. 2). Historians now discover that there were two " taxings," and that the first was made when Cyrenius was governor of Syria.

" Taxing " means taking a census. Con trast 2 Sam. xxiv.

The Roman Emperor and Joseph and Mary little thought that this Census was ordered of God so as to fulfil not only the prediction of Genesis xlix., but also that of Micah v. 2, and so secure the birth of the Holy Child at Bethlehem. Thus God manifested His wisdom.

The Throne of Jehovah Messiah was at Jerusalem. It was at this moment in the power of Augustus Caesar because Israel had refused to walk in the Law of the Lord. Yet in grace and love He came to deliver them.

Sinless angels and not sinful men first praised Him on coming to earth, and yet the angels needed no forgiveness.

When God manifest in flesh came to earth there was no room for Him there. So much the more wonderful and perfect is the love that brought Him thither. He began His life in a manger, ended it on a cross, and all along His ministerial way had not where to lay His head !

His Birth was not trumpeted forth in lordly guise to priests and princes and the great ones of the earth, but to obscure shepherds—the lowest caste in Society at that time.

The Babe was not to become a King and a Saviour. He was born both. He was a Saviour ; He was Christ ; He was Jehovah (v. 11).

" A manger " (vs. 7, 12 and 16) should read " the manger," i.e., the manger which belonged to the shepherds, for it is not stated that they had to search for it. There must have been many mangers in Bethlehem.

Just as with Mary Magdalene so with the shepherds ; angels had little interest for them in comparison with Jesus. They hastened to Bethlehem (v. 15).

God's glory in Creation was high ; in Revelation, higher ; but in Redemption, highest (v. 14). His power was seen in Creation ; His Righteousness, in Law ; but— highest attribute—His Love, in Atonement.

The shepherds " returned " from His Birth with praise (v. 20) ; the Disciples " returned " from His Resurrection (xxiv. 33) with glowing hearts ; and the whole company of the believers " returned " from His Ascension with great joy (xxiv. 52).

God's delights (v. 14) are with the sons of men ; therefore He became a Man ; and He became, and is, their peace. So man could learn all of God in a Man—that is, in the Man Christ Jesus. See Col. i. 13-19.

His Name was called Jesus. The word means Saviour. He might have chosen a loftier title, for the highest titles are His, but He passed them all by and selected a Name which speaks of deliverance for a lost world.

Jesus was made of a woman under the Law (Gal. iv. 4). This fact is emphasized by His circumcision. The Law is mentioned five times in this chapter, oftener than in the rest of the Book, and so confirms the statement in Galatians. To save man, justly doomed to death by the Law, it was necessary that Christ should be born under the Law.

The Virgin Mary was not sinless. This is evidenced by verses 21-23 in conjunction with Leviticus xii. 1-6.

Judgment having condemned to death all the first-born in Egypt, including the first-born of Israel, the latter were forfeited to God (Ex. xiii. 2, Num. xviii. 15). The Levites were accepted as their representatives (Num. iii. 12). All the first-born were, however, to be presented to the Lord in token of His rightful claim to them (Num. iii. 44 and xviii. 15).

The poverty of Joseph and Mary appears in their lowly offering of two pigeons.

" The Consolation of Israel " (v. 25). This is a Messianic Title.

He, as predicted (Mal. iii. 1), came suddenly to His Temple (v. 27), but not with pomp and circumstance as the Hebrew Church expected, but as a Babe, with working class parents, and received by an obscure company of Simeons and Annas—His hidden ones—the poor of the flock.

Simeon had not to ask Mary who the Child was, and enquire as to the wonders of His Birth. He recognized Him at once by inspiration as Jehovah's Anointed, and said : " Mine eyes have seen Thy salvation." He personally possessed that salvation, for he took Him into his arms (v. 28), and that possession conquered death and banished all its terror (v. 29).

Seven children were named before their birth — Ishmael, Isaac, Solomon, Josiah, Cyrus, John the Baptist and Jesus. But only One was the Salvation of Jehovah.

That Salvation (v. 34) should occasion the fall and rising again of many, i.e., their stumbling and restoration. He should be despised and rejected—a sign spoken against. So it proved. Men who have agreed in nothing else have agreed in hating Christ.

As light reveals the contents of a room so the entrance of Christ reveals what is in man's heart, and its thoughts. They are vain (v. 35).

Mary's heart being carnal had to come under the rays of this great light, and her soul had to feel the piercing of the Divine Sword. She (ch. i. 38) was willing to be the honoured mother of the King of Israel (i. 32), but unwilling to be the despised disciple of the hated Nazarene (Mark. iii. 21, 31). Natural grief must have pained her heart at Calvary, but this dread sword was to pierce her soul. The popular belief on this subject is manifestly mistaken. See note on Acts i. 14.

She was indeed blessed as the chosen vessel of the Incarnation, but women who follow Jesus are more blessed (Luke xi. 27).

The prophetess Anna was a hundred and three years of age. As Simeon represented the Two Tribes, so she, being of the Tribe of Asher, represented the Ten.

Christ as the manifested Glory of His people Israel will not appear such until the fulness of the Gentiles is come in. Hence the Gentiles precede Israel in verse 32 (Isa. xxv. 7).

" She spake of Him to all (v. 38) that looked for redemption." The modern Church would have forbidden her to do so.

Thus two witnesses, the one a man and the other a woman, testified to the fulfilment of Malachi iii. 1. They both loved the Courts of Jehovah's House, and He met them there.

The Holy Spirit only gives one glimpse of Christ between birth and manhood (vs. 41-52). A Hebrew boy of twelve corresponded in stature and mind to a European boy of sixteen. At that age He was recognized as a Church member, and, in a sense, independent of His parents.

" Went " (v. 41), i.e., were accustomed to go ; for they were godly people and encouraged each other to walk in the way of the Lord. The Law commanded this ascent to Jerusalem at Passover (Deut. xvi. 1).

The Lord as a youth did not dispute with the doctors (v. 46), but asked questions of them, and listened to their answers. They also asked Him questions (v. 47).

" Wist ye not " (v. 49), i.e., " How is it ye do not understand ? " They should have understood for they had had seven testimonies as to who He was. These were Matt. i. 20, Luke i. 26, Luke i. 43, Luke ii. 9, Luke ii. 29, Luke ii. 36, Matt. ii. 1. He was their God and Creator ; and so Mary should not have spoken to Him as she did. Hence His exclamation : " How is it that ye sought Me ? " and in opposition to Mary's words, " Thy father," He responds, " I must be about My Father's business."

He was conscious of Who He was ; and just as that consciousness caused Him in John xiii. 1 to wash the feet of the disciples, so it here caused Him to return with His reputed parents to Nazareth, and to become subject to them. Joseph was legally His father according to Hebrew Law. (iii. 23).

So all was perfection in Him, perfection as a child, and perfection as a man.

His first recorded words are : " I must be about My Father's business " and His last recorded words were " It is finished." Compare His first and last ministerial words (Matt. iv. 4, 7, 10, and John xvii. 8, 14, 17) and note the triple character of the comparison.

The theory that Jesus became the Son of God at His baptism by the reception of the Holy Spirit, is destroyed by His consciousness in verse 49.

LUKE III.—See notes on Matt. iii. and Mark vi.

In character with the presentation in this book of Jesus as a man among men, the political and historic statements of verses 1 and 2 are most important and valuable. All these men were infamous. The earth was given into the hands of the wicked, and the peoples were like their rulers.

But God did not cease relations with His people. This relationship was maintained by communications through the prophets. The Forerunner was sent ; and the usual formula re-appears, i.e., " The word of God came unto John " (v. 2). Such a formula is never used in connection with Jesus, for He was The Word of God.

The questions and answers of verses 10-14 are peculiar to this Evangelist.

" We, what shall we do " (vs. 10, 12, 14), i.e., to evidence true repentance and so enjoy remission of sins (v. 3). The Baptist rebuked selfishness (v. 11), extortion (v. 13), and violence (v. 14).

John did not command the tax-gatherers and the soldiers to abandon their calling.

Neither is unlawful in the sight of God. See notes on Rom. xiii.

The Holy Spirit (v. 16) as a spirit.energizes for service, and as a fire,purifies for service.

Servants of the Gospel must not be confounded if they are condemned to die in prisons (vs. 19 and 20).

The introduction of John's imprisonment here, and the displacement of the second temptation (iv. 5), illustrate the import of the word " order " in i. 1.

The people and prayer are introduced into v. 21 to accentuate the nature of Christ as Man. He prayed as being dependent,and He moved among the people as being related.

" Thirty years of age " (v. 23). At this age a priest entered on his Office (Num. iv. 3).

" As was supposed " (v. 23). This should be translated : " being by legal adoption." See note further on.

Joseph was the son of Jacob (Matt. i. 16) by birth and the son of Heli by marriage.

There are many instances in the Scriptures of this double relationship. It was ordained in Num. xxxvi. The man who married the daughter of a father having no son,became the son of that father and inherited his property. Hezron (1 Chron. ii. 21-23), and others in the Old Testament, illustrate this law. He married the daughter of Machir, and his sons were reckoned to belong to Machir. Hence by birth Hezron was of the tribe of Judah ; by marriage, of the Tribe of Manasseh.

In obedience, therefore, to the law of Num. xxxvi. Mary married her cousin Joseph ; and, accordingly, Joseph had two fathers, one by nature, the other by law.

Thus was Jesus, as Man, descended from Adam the first man. See " Outlines of Prophetic Truth," by Robert Brown.

The heaven opened upon Jesus as a man (vs. 21 and 22). In the perfection of His Manhood,He prayed. He was God's object upon earth from out of the opened heaven, as He was Stephen's object from earth in the opened heaven.

Righteousness brought Him where sin brought the people, i.e., to John's baptism. He did not love at a distance. He came by grace into the very place where sin had brought His fellows ; and in order to save them,and lead them out from death into life, He entered in by the door. He recognised and acknowledged the porter (Law), and to Him the porter opened (John x. 3).

The introduction of Cainan (Canaan, Heb.) in verse 36 is widely accepted as an error in transcription, but a conjunction of Gen. ix.24 and Luke iii. 36, illustrated by other Scriptures, points to accuracy in the sacred text.

Cainan was Ham's youngest son (x. 6), and the sense of ix. 24 is that Noah got to know what that " youngest son " had done to him. The import of the whole passage is not the sin of Noah, but the act of Cainan ; what that act was is not necessary to the history. It may have been that by Satanic inspiration he discovered how to manufacture intoxicating drink and with it seduced his grandfather ; or, that finding Noah drunk he, to degrade him still further, stripped him of his mantle. The malediction was not denounced upon Ham, he did nothing, but on his youngest son (a white man); and so important is he, and his conduct, that he is mentioned six times in the paragraph (vs. 18, 22, 24, 25, 26, 27), and his doom being triplicated (vs. 25, 26, 27), three sixes appear, i.e., the mystic number 666. Whatever Cainan's action was, it was sufficient for Satan's purpose. Ham is here a minor figure. The Hebrew text permits the translation ; " Now Ham was the father of Cainan (ix. 18) . . . and Noah got to know what his (i.e., Ham's) youngest son had done unto him " (x. 6, 24).

The deep schemes of Satan (Rev. ii. 24) were planned either to prevent the birth of the Messiah, or to bring it about by Satanic co-operation and thus destroy its redemptive nature. The precedence given to Shem (v. 32) disclosed him as the depository of the promise of iii. 15. It was necessary, therefore, to repeat, in his case, the action of vi. 2 from which Noah was " perfect,"i.e., without blemish in his pedigree. He found an agent in Cainan. He first introduced him into the family of Shem by a marriage with a daughter of Arphaxad which secured a legal right of inheritance similar to Joseph's marriage with Mary (v. 23) which made him the heir of Heli ; and, second, he influenced Cainan so as to bring upon him the doom of ix. 25, as he energized Jehoiakim (Jer. xxxvi. 30) in order to make impossible the promise to David (Ps. cxxxii. 11). Thus by this double action with Cainan as his instrument, he made him,as Jehoiakim was, the depository of the promise, as Luke shows, and then impelled him to an action in order to make impossible the performance of the promise. If it be objected that Cainan's assumed marriage with Arphaxad's daughter is not recorded in the pedigree, it can be replied that neither is Joseph's with Heli's daughter. The omissions denote harmony and not discrepancy.

It is of course quite true that just as Satan in his opposition to God and to His Christ overthrew with an " apple " (Cant. viii. 5) the divinely-appointed Head of " the world " that then was. so did he with a grape over- throw the Head of " the world " that now is. It is suggested that that was a minor purpose, but that the major was the Cainanite scheme.

Cainan, therefore, having a legal title, took possession, under Satanic impulse, of Pales- tine and Sion ; for it is possible that the Adversary fore-knew that both were pur- posed by God for Messiah. This supposition would, therefore, help to explain Abraham's and Isaac's divine instinct in guarding against marriage with Cainan (Gen. xxiv. 3 and xxviii. 1) ; and also, would shed light upon the command to Israel to utterly destroy the Cainanites (Deut. xii. 1 and 3).

The cunning and malignity of Satan in his opposition to Christ is seen in the murder of Abel, the act of Cainan, the retardation in the births of Isaac and Jacob, the introduc- tion of Pharaoh, of Abimelech (twice), and of Hagar, the attempted murder of Isaac by Ishmael, of Jacob by Esau, both before and after his birth, by the misconduct of Judah and David, and by the massacres of Pharaoh. Athaliah, Haman and Herod, and in the expulsion of Jehoiakim's descendants from the throne of Jehovah at Jerusalem.

That Cainan could be a son of Arphaxad, i.e., his heir, and at the same time a son of Ham, is illustrated more than once in the Scriptures and has been already pointed out. For example Jair was " the son of " Manasseh, but was begotten by Judah, Attai was " the son of " Sheshan, but was born of Jarha; Moses was " the son of " Pharaoh's daughter but was born of Amram; Hiram was of the tribe of Naphtali, but also of the tribe of Dan; and Joseph, Mary's husband, was " the son of " Jacob and also the son of Heli. He as a son by descent from Jehoiakim could not sit on the throne of David, but as the son-in-law and heir of Heli by his marriage with Mary, divinely legalized by Num. xxvii. and xxxvi., he could by the execution of a deed adopt Mary's child as his son and vest in him all his titles to the kingdom ; and this he did, as is shown in the force of the word νομίζω (Luke iii. 23).

Mary was by descent a daughter of David (Luke i. 27 and 32), and, consequently, was born of Heli (iii. 23), and " perfect (Gen. vi. 9) in her generations from Shem through Sala and Nathan, Solomon's elder brother. Her child, therefore, as born of her and legally adopted by Joseph, united in His person both the Davidic and Adamic claims to the throne of the world ; and He, by His resurrection, is, and remains, its only legal Sovereign. This pure descent through Nathan and Sala, defeated Satan's efforts to make impossible through Cainan and Jehoiakim the advent of the Redeemer promised in Gen. iii. 15.

Putting all these facts together, it is urged that the insertion of Cainan's name in the pedigree of Luke iii. is not an error, but a moral and historical necessity, and as im- portant and necessary as the inclusion of Jehoiakim's name in the pedigree of Matt. i. ; and so it will appear that Gen. ix. 24 illumines and interprets Luke iii. 36, and that this seeming inaccuracy is an instance of the Law of Subsequent Narration.

Some learned people believe that Canaan and Cainan are different men, but their reasonings lie outside of the Sacred Text.

LUKE IV.—See notes on Matt. iv. and Mark i.

Jesus as Man did not, like Simon Peter (xxii. 33), seek temptation. He was " led " into it by the Spirit (v. 1). Compare the words of Mark i. 12," the Spirit driveth Him."

The first and last recorded utterances of the author of ancient and modern " thought " are, " Hath God said? " (Gen. iii.) and " It is written " (Luke iv). Man was to test God's Word, vocal or written; first, to disprove it, and, last, to prove it; but, in either case, in unison with Satan.

After the temptation, He journeyed to Capernaum passing by Nazareth; and having taught and wrought there, He re- traced His steps and visited Nazareth. He never re-visited it. The particulars of this visit are related by Luke only.

" Where He had been brought up " (v. 16). This is one of the many sentences in this Gospel which are peculiar to it, and which, harmonious with its purpose, make vivid the fact that Jesus was a man.

" As His custom was " (v. 16), i.e., wherever He went.

" The Spirit of Jehovah is upon Me " (v. 18). These words affirm the fact of the Trinity.

He did not come to work mighty miracles

and to dispossess the Romans, but to deal with sin and deliver its captives.

" The acceptable year" (v. 19). See notes on 2 Cor. vi. 2, Dan. xi. 2, Dan xii. 2, Isa. lxi. 1, Luke iv. 19, and John v. 29. The Lord stopped in the middle of the verse because the day of vengeance is yet future. So a comma here already means nearly two thousand years. The " acceptable time " is " a year; " the judgment time but a " day." Such is the heart of God !

He amazed the people by stating that He fulfilled this prophecy that day.

But His words only excited a temporary admiration. Jealous because He did not work miracles there as at Capernaum, and furious at His teaching, they set about to murder Him. His own village was the first to seek His death.

But no demonstration of human hatred could dry up the founts of compassion that in infinite wealth perpetually welled up in His breast. He returned to the lake-shore, and as He went all the power of the enemy, and all the sad outward effects of sin, disappeared before Him.

" Modern thought " belittles preaching and exalts ceremony. The Eternal Son of God was wholly a preacher ; and this fact, and the opposition of Satan to preaching, demonstrate its importance.

Men bitterly dislike the doctrine of the Sovereignty of God, and this, because it strikes at their importance and the majesty of the human will. It was this doctrine that enraged the auditory at Nazareth.

LUKE V.—See notes on Matt. viii. and ix. and Mark i. and ii.

This third call of the twelve (vs. 1-11) is peculiar to Luke. The first call was that of John i. 35; and the second that of Matt. iv. 18 Yet they proposed to return to their fishing (John xxi. 1). Such is the insensibility of the carnal nature to the Divine Voice, and such is its incurable propensity to earthly things ! Pentecost, however, made them victorious over their natural inclination.

Christ had the same power over the fish of the sea as He had over the frogs, and flies, and lice and locusts of Egypt.

Modern churches are empty because men's thoughts and not God's words are offered to the people. Scriptural preaching attracts the hungry of heart (v. 1).

The Great Head of the Church calls active and not lazy men into His service—men who when not fishing (Matt. iv. 18) are busy washing their nets.

The people were wholly engaged with the Preacher and His teaching, and not with the little ship and its rigging.

Every Christian should be as fully surrendered to Christ as was this little ship ; and Jesus should so effectively speak in and through him, that society would be engaged with the preaching and not with the preacher. But there must be a definite line of separation between him and them if he would really help them (v. 3).

Lessons are slowly and gently taught in the school of God. Simon was first asked to push out a little from the land. He obeyed. There was no danger in that. He was then asked to launch out into the deep where human aid cannot reach, where man can sink, and where he is wholly cast upon God for both safety and sustenance, but where the big fish can be caught.

Simon was then invited to throw out his nets. This was contrary to science, for fish are usually caught there in the night-time. But nc was willing to learn this lesson also in the school of faith, and happy was his experience ! He found that, if willing to accompany Jesus out into the deep, the Lord could bring a mass of provision to the ship side, more than the ship could carry. So on reaching land he and his companions let everything go and followed Jesus.

The effect of this training was not to give Simon high thoughts of himself but low thoughts (vs. 8 and 9), for such is ever the effect of a manifestation of Divine power and grace upon the conscience of fallen man.

It also revealed the hidden unbelief of Simon's heart, for without doubt when casting the nets he said to himself " we shall catch nothing."

The Lord Jesus never rebuked His Disciples for manifesting or expressing too lofty conceptions of Him ; on the contrary, their confession of His Deity and Godhead was grateful to His Spirit.

This whole incident is peculiar to Luke.

" I will," (v. 13). Only God could say " I will " and thus heal leprosy.

" He prayed " (v. 16). Such was His perfection as a man born under the Law and dependent upon God. Thus His Deity appears in verse 13 and His Humanity in verse 16.

If the Divine Evangelist felt the need of prayer and spiritual retirement in the midst of successful ministry, how much more do His servants. He also prayed at His Baptism and at His Transfiguration.

A Roman tax farmer paid beforehand the required amount for the whole year. Matthew, therefore (v. 28), impoverished only himself by at once following Jesus, and he benefited the tax-payers.

Many titles in the Scriptures express Christ's affection for His people, but that of " Bridegroom " (v. 34) is the most tender and wonderful of them all.

Verse 36 may be thus paraphrased : " No one having rent a piece from a new garment, putteth it upon an old ; for in that case he will both rend the new, and the new piece will not match with the old."

Man prefers the old wine of ordinances rather than the new wine of the · Gospel (v. 39).

LUKE VI.—See notes on Matt. v.-xii. and Mark ii. and iii.

The mystery of prayer (v. 12) confounds human intelligence. It is possible to believe what cannot be understood. The sunbeam weds the dewdrop, and the fruit of the union is the gentle primrose. This can be believed but not understood.

Perhaps this mysterious night of prayer was mainly caused by the Scripture compelling Jesus, as a man, to chose for an Apostle Judas, whom He knew to be a devil.

" In the plain " (v. 17). This famous sermon was preached on a mountain (Matt. v.) and now, perhaps, repeated with alterations, omissions, and additions in the plain. He must often have repeated His messages. Compare Luke xv. 4 with Matt. xviii. 12 and Isa. xxviii. 10 ; but see note on Matt. vii. 29.

The comparison of this sermon with that preached upon the Mount, accentuates the purpose of the Holy Spirit in revealing Christ as King in the one record, and as Man in the other.

" The blind " (v. 39), i.e., false religious teachers. The argument of verse 40 is that those who listen to these false teachers will become as perfectly deluded as their masters, for pupils cannot see more clearly than their teachers. See note on Matt. xv. 14 and its striking context. They become as their masters. Hence the disciples of Romanism,

Mormonism, Christian Science, etc., become as wholly deluded as their teachers.

The fruit of the Spirit is the product of the teaching of the Spirit. Modern teaching denies this, and claims that self-sacrifice, kindness, good temper and benevolence spring out of human nature, and have no relation fundamentally to religious belief. There can be an imitation of the fruit of the Spirit, as a paper rose may be so like a real one as to be indistinguishable from it. But a bee will make no mistake ! The only power that will make men really love one another is the doctrine of the Bible which says : " Walk in love as Christ also loved us." Teaching love on any other principle is vain.

No sermon should conclude without a personal application to the consciences of the hearers (vs. 46-49).

The Sermon on the Mount and the Sermon on the Plain (see note on Matt. vii. 29) correspond to the two massive pillars, Jachin and Boaz. See notes on I Kings vii. 21. These sermons, like these pillars, exhibited the purity and power of the Messiah's kingdom. There were seeming differences in the pillars (see notes on I Kings vii.), as there were seeming differences in the sermons. Both are designed by the Holy Spirit. These pillars formed the entrance to God's house. Such is Christ. He is the one and only way. As Jachin, He sets the believer before God in sinless purity ; as Boaz, He saves him from committing sins. The Christian's standing and the Christian's state—and these must not be confounded—are thus secured in Him. He is a full Saviour.

LUKE VII.—See notes on Matt. viii. and xi.

Many people came to Jesus. One came for a son, another for a daughter, another for himself or herself, but here is the only instance of a master coming for a slave ; and this master was a Gentile—a Roman centurion (v. 2). When the servant fell sick he did not turn him out of doors, as some masters do, but he hastened to the Great Physician on his behalf.

The historic displacement of this miracle is another illustration of the moral import of the word " order " in i. 3. The reader should seek for the lessons intended by this arrangement. See notes on xviii. 35.

Matthew says the centurion came personally, Luke here states that he came by deputation. Both statements are true ; for his messengers represented him, and also the word "him" (v. 9) supports the belief that the centurion followed his messengers, and, in his anxiety for his servant, repeated the message he had given them to deliver.

There were two occasions when Jesus marvelled thus, evidencing His perfect manhood. He marvelled at unbelief (Mark vi. 6), and He marvelled at faith (v. 9). He did not marvel at the beautiful buildings of the Temple (xxi. 5)

The mighty miracle at the gate of Nain is only recorded by Luke.

When the Lord saw her He had compassion on her (v. 13). This affirms His humanity.

"I say unto thee, Arise" (v. 14). This declares His Deity. The Prince of Peace is stronger than the King of Terrors; and Death is not so mighty as the sinner's Friend.

"Offended" (v. 23), i.e., finds anything to stumble at in Me.

Miracles, as miracles, did not accredit Jesus to be the promised Messiah. What did accredit Him was that He worked those predicted of Him in the Scriptures (Isa. xxix. 18; xxxv. 4-6 and lx. 1-3). The False Prophet will work amazing miracles (Rev. xiii. 13).

"Justified God" (v. 29). This is a Hebraism. God declared them to be sinners; and, therefore, those who submitted to the baptism of repentance confessed that that judgment was just.

"Against" (v. 30), i.e., as to.

Wisdom's children (vs. 31-35) mourned under law and danced under grace, and so justified Wisdom; i.e., by their action declared Wisdom's moral perfection and intelligence.

One of Wisdom's children (vs. 36-50) is here introduced and is contrasted with the Pharisee, who was an enemy of Wisdom. This incident is peculiar to Luke.

The Pharisee invited the Lord to his table in order evidently to belittle and insult Him, for he refused Him the customary courtesies of a host to a guest (vs. 44-46), and allowed Him to find a place for Himself as best He could. The Lord did not resent this studied insult; He gently took a place, probably at the door, and waited for the honour that cometh from above. It was quickly sent. The glory of Christ's Person, and the majesty of His Deity, were both demonstrated, and Wisdom's child—the woman—justified her Lord.

Her tears gushed involuntarily, and she kept repeatedly kissing His feet and wiping them with the hairs of her head.

"This man if He were a prophet" (v. 39). These words reveal the unbelief of Simon's heart.

The parable of the two debtors is an exquisite illustration of how gently Jesus rebuked and instructed His haters and despisers.

"For" (v. 47). i.e., "on this account." That this is the force of the word is clear from what follows, and from the point of the parable. She loved much because she was forgiven much. When she first met the Lord Jesus and believed upon Him for the forgiveness of her sins is not recorded; but she may have been the woman of John viii. 3-11, introduced here not in chronological order, but in moral order.

During her ministry the Lord apparently took no notice of her affection, her service and her worship; but when the proper moment arrived, she learned that He had seen all and overlooked nothing. All was precious to Him and before the entire company He minutely described all her devotion to His person.

So is it now. His servants minister to Him in numberless ways when ministering to those who are His; but there is no evidence from Heaven that their actions are recognized. But in the Day of the Lord all will be by Him declared to the wonder of His people and the admiration of the Universe.

God's will is, that the guiltiest who believe upon the son of His Love should enjoy assurance of salvation and the conscious forgiveness of sin (v. 48).

Jesus did not say to the woman "Thy love hath saved thee," or "thy tears have saved thee," but, "thy faith hath saved thee."

"Go in peace" (v. 50). This should read "Go into peace."

LUKE VIII.—See notes on the corresponding passages in Matt. viii., xii., and xiii., and Mark iii., iv., and v.

His love unchilled by unbelief and hatred, He visited every city and village (v. 1) with the glad tidings of the Gospel.

Man magnifies sacraments and ceremonies and belittles preaching. God magnifies preaching. It pleases Him by the foolishness of preaching to save men. Christ preached incessantly (v. 1), and so did the Apostle Paul and the Twelve and the Seventy. Satan does not fear ceremonies, but he greatly fears preaching. Women are prominent and honourably mentioned in the Book of Luke (vs. 2 and 3). Some of these women were wealthy, and they used their money to minister to the Lord's necessities. His were the cattle on a thousand hills, and He could with a few loaves feed thousands. But He did not feed Himself. He depended for sustenance on these women. Thus He proved that He was a man like His fellow-men ; and, at the same time, He tested their fidelity to, and affection for, Himself. True disciples now as then minister to Him ; mere professors do not.

" Susanna " (v. 3) is only mentioned here. Nothing whatever is known of her, and yet is her name known throughout the whole world because it is recorded in this verse. Here, as elsewhere, women worked and men talked.

These verses (1-3) are peculiar to Luke.

Mary Magdalene was delivered from Satanic dominion, but there is nothing whatever in the Scriptures to support the common belief that she had been a woman of abandoned life:

It must have been difficult for these women to face the scorn and contempt of the Chiefs of the Hebrew Church ; yet they were faithful to the end. It was not a woman who sold the Lord for thirty pieces of silver. It was not women who forsook Him and fled, nor was it a woman who thrice denied that she knew Him ; but it was women who wailed and lamented when He was led forth to be crucified, it was women who stood to the last by His Cross, and it was women who were the first to visit His Tomb on the Resurrection morning.

The quotation from Isa. vi. 9 and 10 (v. 10) is six times repeated in the New Testament :—Matt. xiii. 14 and 15, Mark iv. 12, John xii. 40, Acts xxviii. 26, Rom. xi. 8 and here. This shows its importance.

" An honest and good heart " (v. 15). Jeremiah xvii. 9 says that the heart is incurably diseased. The heart that accepts this testimony is an honest and a good heart.

" Is " (v. 11), i.e., " represents." So in xxii. 19 " this is My body " means " this represents My body."

" Then cometh the Devil " (v. 12). Here the Lord Jesus, as on many other occasions, declared the existence, personality and agency of Satan.

" Keep " (v. 15), i.e., " hold fast." See note on 2 Thess. ii. 6, Heb. iii. 6 and x. 23.

" Seemeth " (v. 18), i.e., " thinketh."

As man He fell asleep (v. 23) ; as God He rebuked the storm (v. 24).

To be weary of Christian activity is sinful, but to be wearied in Christian activity is not sinful. The Lord was weary and fell asleep.

" Torment me not " (v. 28). Devils believe in a judgment and a hell. Men do not.

Matthew mentions two demoniacs, Mark and Luke but one. If there were two then there was certainly one. He is here individualized as being both probably the fiercer of the two and better known ; and also because he alone asked to be allowed to remain with the Lord, and he became an effective preacher. The other presented no such peculiar interest, and is, therefore, not mentioned by Mark and Luke.

The Gadarenes took no interest in the salvation of a fellow-creature from Satan's power, but they viewed the loss of their property with deep concern (v. 37). They have many successors to-day. The deliverance of people from the power of the drink demon excites no Stock Exchange, but the destruction of a distillery by fire causes much excitement. Similarly little interest is taken in the African, but much concern in the rubber trade.

The young ruler was commanded to follow Christ (Mark x. 21) ; the leper was forbidden to speak of Christ (Mark i. 43) ; but the demoniac (v. 39) was ordered to publish how great things Jesus had done unto him.

Three persons of rank at Capernaum proved the Lord's power to heal : the nobleman (John iv. 46) ; the centurion (Luke vii. 2) ; and the Ruler of the synagogue (v. 41).

Lev. xv. 19 declared this woman (v. 43) to be ceremonially unclean. Perhaps this knowledge occasioned her fear (v. 47).

Love descends rather than ascends. Hence parents love their children more than children their parents (v. 49). So God loves man, but man does not love God. With one exception (Mark i. 30), the Gospels do not record children coming to Jesus on behalf of their parents, but cases of parents coming to Him on behalf of their children, are frequent.

The little maid was physically dead to her parents, but only " asleep " to Jesus (v. 52).

Christ did not impose Himself or the evidences of His Deity upon scoffers (vs. 53

and 54) ; and as it was when He was upon earth, so is it now.

" Her spirit came again " (v. 55). This fact demonstrates the separate existence of the spirit as independent of the body. Where the spirit of the child was after it had left her body, the Bible very wisely does not say.

As eating food certified the reality of the Lord's Resurrection (xxiv. 41-43), so was it in the case of this child (v. 55).

Jesus sought neither publicity nor admiration (v. 56). His appeal was to the heart and to the conscience. His mission was to bring people to repentance and to the forgiveness of sins. Apart from this consciousness of sin against God, and the need of pardon, there can be no understanding of the person and work of the Lord Jesus Christ.

To work great miracles and yet seek to hide them, is foreign to human nature. Men love admiration and publicity ; and shallow streams make the most noise.

LUKE IX.—See notes on the corresponding passages in Matt. viii., x., xiv., xvii., and xviii., Mark iii., vi., and ix., and John vi.

He called ; He gave power ; and He sent them to preach (vs. 1 and 2).

The great business of the true Christian is preaching.

Jesus must be God, for God alone can give power.

There is no such thing as Apostolical succession. The Twelve Apostles are the chiefs of the Hebrew Church. Their office, as such, was isolated and peculiar ; and they still hold it. They have no successors and never will have any. Ministry in the Church of the Heavenly Election, is a spiritual succession of the ministry of Paul and Timothy and Titus and Sosthenes and Silvanus and others.

The church revealed in the Epistle to the Ephesians had eight Apostles.

Resurrection was commonly believed among the Jews (v. 7). The contrary assertion is wholly untenable. See xx. 27.

" Daily " (v. 23). This word is peculiar to Luke. It, with the word " all," teaches that no person is excused and no day excepted. Hence the Apostle said " I die daily " ; for he daily bore the shame and hatred that result from following Jesus.

There are three glories in the world of light (v. 26) : The glory of the Father ; the glory of the Son of Man : and the glory of the angels.

To a Hebrew like Peter (v. 33) Moses and Elijah were clothed with glory, and so he was overjoyed to see Jesus introduced into a glory equal to theirs. But the voice out of the cloud rebuked his folly.

The presence of Moses and Elijah on the Mount affirm the eternal safety of true believers. Moses had been already fifteen hundred years in the spirit world and Elijah nine hundred years. The one had died, the other not ; but the one had no advantage over the other in the Transfiguration.

The light shone out from the Lord's body through His raiment and not upon Him. This is the force of the unusual word translated " glistering " (v. 29).

If saints in glory delight to speak of Christ's atoning death, how much more ought sinners on earth (v. 31). The doctrine of the atonement is the theology of heaven (v. 31). In that glory Elijah learned the lesson which he failed to learn on earth—see notes on 1 Kings xvii., 2 Kings ii—that salvation is by grace and not by Law. Christ redeems men from the curse of the law by suffering Himself in atonement that curse, i.e., the wrath of God.

" As He prayed " (vs. 18 and 29). This is peculiar to Luke.

Christ's death did not merely happen. He " accomplished " it (v. 13). Therefore He was God.

" Hear Him " (v. 25). See Deut. xviii. 15 and Acts iii. 23.

" He is mine only child " (v. 38). These words are peculiar to Luke ; as are verses 51, 56.

Zeal without knowledge, and failure to rightly divide the Word of Truth, cause well-meaning men to greatly err (v. 54).

This incident, and John being surnamed " a son of thunder," show that his natural temperament was very different from what it afterwards became. The transforming power of grace may be observed in him. Three times he sinned against the spirit of the Gospel (Matt. xx. 21, Luke ix. 49, 54).

The present Dispensation is that of the kingdom and patience of Jesus Christ (Rev. i. 9) ; and the Holy Spirit as a fire sanctifies men. The kingdom and power of Jesus Christ (Rev. xii. 10) is yet future, and then fire will come down from Heaven and consume men (Rev. xx. 9).

The Apostle John at a later period in his life (Acts viii. 25) preached the Gospel, and in a very different spirit, in many villages of the Samaritans.

The natural heart is either too forward (v. 51) or too backward (v. 59) or too un-decided (v. 61). This latter verse and the following are peculiar to Luke.

Attachment to Christ and to His service must be unconditional.

LUKE X. 1-37.—All this chapter is peculiar to Luke.

Christian labourers are to go forth praying that workers may be sent forth, and not in the proud and self-confident spirit which thinks that it can sufficiently occupy the whole field of missionary effort.

" Send forth " (v. 2). Rather " thrust forth."

No shepherd sends his sheep amongst wolves (v. 3), but this Shepherd can, because almighty to save.

Shoes were distinct from sandals (v. 4). They were more luxurious. These preachers were only to wear sandals.

Salutations in the East (v. 4) are foolishly elaborate and prolonged. They waste time. The seventy were to be courteous, but they were to make haste.

Many ministers of the Gospel waste precious hours and days in slavery to the laws of modern society. They attend dinner-parties, pay morning calls and assist at fashionable gatherings, when they ought to be doing their Master's work in seeking and saving the lost.

" The labourer is worthy of his hire " (v. 7). This is the only quotation in the Epistles from the Gospel (1 Tim. v. 18), and it is stated to be " Scripture."

True Christian ministers are gentle as lambs (v. 3) ; their work is perilous, for they must face wolves ; they are simple (v. 4) ; and easily contented (vs. 7 and 8).

Though the earth and its inhabitants are polluted (v. 11), yet grace descended from Heaven to redeem both (v. 11).

Black as were the sins of Sodom and Tyre and Sidon, yet is the sin of rejecting the Gospel the greatest of all sins (v. 14.)

Great is the dignity of the Gospel Messen-ger (v. 16). The messenger may be a poor man, or a woman, or a child.

Uniting verse 18 with 1 Tim. iii. 6 the admonition appears to be : " Beware of the pride which results from being puffed up with success " (v. 17).

It is possible to preach the Gospel faith-fully and work miracles as Judas Iscariot did, and yet be a stranger to grace (v. 20). Gift, as in the case of Balaam, may be possessed without grace ; but grace alone saves.

Only twice is it recorded that Jesus rejoiced. The first occasion was that of Matt. xi. 25, and the second, that of this chapter (vs. 21-22).

The conversion of souls was the cause of the Lord's joy, and the sovereignty of God in saving sinners was the secret of His exulta-tion. He gloried in the just judgment that hid salvation from those that were " wise in their own eyes and prudent in their own sight " (Isa. v. 21) and revealed it unto babes. The self-righteous are judicially blinded, but to the repenting sinner light is granted.

The doctrine of the Sovereignty of God is most offensive to moralists, for it belittles man and the majesty of his will. But that it is a fundamental doctrine of the Bible, is absolutely certain ; and that it is a fact, is equally sure, for why is England a Christian country and China buried in idolatry ?

The God-head of Christ, and His equality with the Father, are asserted in verse 22.

" Will " (v. 22), i.e., wills. Salvation is not a matter of education but of revelation. See Notes on Matt. xi. 27.

" Tempted " (v. 25), i.e., tested His knowledge of the law. A lawyer in the Hebrew Church was a man who devoted Himself to the study of the Law of Moses.

This lawyer should have said merit and not " inherit " (v. 25). Inheritance is by birth.

Eternal life is man's greatest interest, and no more tremendous question could be asked than that of this verse.

In His reply the Lord immediately points to the Bible as an infallible authority (v. 26).

In the lawyer's answer is revealed the clear knowledge of God and of Truth which men at that time possessed in Jerusalem. It was knowledge immeasurably in advance of that of the East, and of Greece and Rome.

Men may have a very great religious know-ledge and yet presume to criticise the Lord Jesus Christ.

Three times Jesus was questioned as to how salvation might be obtained : e.g. the young

Ruler (Mark x. 17) ; Matt. xxii. 36 ; and here (v. 25).

"Willing" (v. 29), i.e., wishing. This statement discovers the character of the lawyer. He was self-righteous. He was determined to win Heaven by religious self-efforts.

Selfishness is the commanding force in human nature (vs. 31 and 32).

Compassionate feelings without practical actions are worthless.

Travellers carry oil with them as a rule in the East. So did Jacob. (Gen. xxviii. 18).

The true Christian is never heartless. He helps the needy and does not too closely enquire into their antecedents. His help is not momentarily emotional (v. 34), but is also sustained (v. 35).

In the East a wound is cleansed with grape-juice and healed with oil.

The parables of the Good Samaritan and of the Prodigal Son are peculiar to Luke. Grace is the theme of one and Love of the other. Grace seeks misery and Love desires company—so the Father's arm was thrown around the child's neck as he exclaimed : "Let us eat and be merry!" Grace goes forth alone ; Love returns accompanied. Man chose the death-road and the thieves. Unbelief and disobedience at once stripped him of his innocence and wounded him to death with the poison dagger of sin. It is possible that the thieves of verse 30 were two in number, and that they reappear in xxiii. 39. Disobedience was the penitent one.

It was impossible for the priest and the Levite to succour the meritless misery of the traveller ; for under the First Covenant the sinner had to co-operate with God in order to recovery. Such co-operation demanded outlay and activity. This man could contribute neither. Under the First Covenant the question was : "What can man do for God ?" Under the Second Covenant the question is : "What has God done for man ?" The answer to the first question is : "Nothing!" The answer to the second is : "Everything!"

The Samaritan provided a full salvation for the lost man. He cured him ; he carried him ; and he cared for him. He made glad his heart with wine, and caused his face to shine with oil. These are the most potent medicines in the East. The Holy Spirit through the apostle Paul commands the one ;

and, through the apostle James, the other. The man now cured was not told to make his way home as best he could, but was carried by the same living power which carried his deliverer. Christ imparts His own nature to the believer (Eph. i. 13). An inn is a temporary home. It and its Host are the church and the Holy Spirit. The "two pence" are the Old and New Testaments —a sufficient provision up to the return of the Divine Samaritan. When leaving, He confided His people to the Holy Spirit and to the Scriptures (John xiv. 15 and Acts xx. 32). When He returns He will "receive" his people from the Holy Spirit—not one missing.

LUKE X. 38- XI. 28.—The Divine design in grouping incidents in order to set out great spiritual principles is illustrated in this section.

The supreme importance of Bible Study (vs. 38-42) ; the necessity of prayer (1-13) ; power for testimony (v. 14) ; the unbelief and hostility of the world (vs. 15-20) ; the worthlessness of reformation apart from the New Birth (vs. 21-26); the impossibility of neutrality in the war between Christ and Satan (v. 23) ; and the insufficiency of knowing Christ after the flesh (vs. 27 and 28 with 2 Cor. v. 16) are here all brought together to reveal the spiritual nature of the Christian life.

Thus the section opens with the action of one woman and closes with the exclamation of another ; and the lesson is taught that the closest physical relationship to Jesus, though it be that of a mother, does not and cannot secure spiritual life.

In the Christian life the daily study of the Word of God must have the first place. All other duties must give way to it (vs. 38-42).

Sitting at Jesus' feet is a safe refuge from assaults upon the authority and inspiration of the Scriptures.

"Also" (v. 39). This word shows that Mary took a fitting share in the household duties.

Had Martha realised that Jesus was Jehovah she never would have spoken so petulantly to Him (v. 40).

"As He was praying" (v. 1). This is peculiar to Luke and is the sixth of seven such occasions.

The Disciples asked to be taught how to pray (v. 1), but it is not recorded that they ever asked to be taught how to preach.

He had already taught them (Matt. vi. 9) ;
but the heart is so dull of hearing that He had
to teach them the same lesson many times.
It was well for the Disciples that they had
so patient a Teacher !

The prayer contains three divisions :—the
first, God's interests (v. 2) ; the second,
the believers' wants (v. 3) ; and third, his
daily dangers (v. 4). See notes on Matt. vi. 9.

The parable of the three loaves (v. 5) is
peculiar to Luke.

Three loaves was the daily bread ration
for a Roman soldier. The loaf was very small.

The argument of the Parable is, that if a
sufficiency for daily need can by importunity
be obtained from an unwilling source, how
much more certainly from a willing Giver.

See notes on Matt. vii. 7 for verses 9-13.

" The Holy Spirit " (v. 13). The Greek
text reads " holy spirit," i.e., spiritual gifts.

There are five contrasts in this passage ;
an earthly father with an Heavenly ; good
gifts with spiritual gifts ; a stone with bread ;
a serpent with a fish ; and a scorpion with an
egg.

The similarity in colour and shape between
a Syrian loaf and a stone, and between a
fish and a serpent, and between a coiled-up
scorpion and an egg, has often been noticed.

Satan too often succeeds in imposing
silence in prayer and testimony upon God's
people (v. 14). But Jesus would have them to
speak. His power alone can energise them to
do so ; and that power is always at their
disposal.

The declaration of verse 23 interrupts the
argument respecting Satan's Kingdom (vs.
15-26) as opposed to Christ's, and is here
introduced to show that there can be no
neutrality in that war ; for in such a campaign everything takes its true place and
must be either of the Devil or of Christ.
Moreover, if the reformed soul were merely
garnished and empty, and not inhabited by
the Stronger One, the wicked spirit would
return with others more wicked, and the last
state of that man or that Church or that
nation would be worse than the first.

" The strong man " (v. 21), i.e., Satan ;
the Stronger (v. 22), i.e., Christ. In connection with this whole passage (vs. 15-26)
the notes on Matt. xii. 24-43 should be read.

This woman (v. 27), like the man of xiv. 15,
thought—and no doubt the listeners on both
occasions shared the belief—that the exclamation was befitting and truly religious.

But here as there the Lord rebuked the
exclamation ; for it was of the flesh (see note
on xiv. 15).

The Lord was teaching the most solemn
truths about the terrors of the mysterious
spirit world, and this woman rudely interrupted with her carnal thoughts. The Lord
gently reproved her, pointing out that the
natural man and natural relationships cannot
be recognised in the kingdom of spiritual
realities ; and that Mary who sat at His feet
and heard His word was absolutely blessed,
but that Mary of Nazareth unless she took
the same position, was not blessed in spite
of her physical relationship to Him.

This appears to be the force, as decided
by the context, of the peculiar Greek word
here translated " rather." It is only found
in three other places and is variously rendered
Rom. ix. 20., x. 18, and Phil. iii. 8.

See notes on xii. 13, xiii. 1, xiii. 23 and xiv.
15.

So the section sets out the excellence of
Bible study (x. 38, 42) ; the importance of
prayer (xi. 1-13) ; the necessity of testimony
(v. 14); the certainty of opposition to it
(v. 15-26) ; and the rudeness and blindness of
the natural heart (v. 27, 28). The Mary
who sat at Jesus' feet was blessed " rather
than " the Mary at whose feet Jesus when
a child sat. In the spiritual realm spiritual
relationship is everything, and the most
tender physical relationship nothing. See
the force of the words " rather than " in the
Greek Text.

This declaration by the Lord Jesus dis-
pleases mediæval and modern thought, but
the Christian believes it because the Master
made it.

LUKE XI. 29-54.—The Ninevites and the
Queen of Sheba believed without even the
working of one miracle, but the greater than
Jonah and Solomon was rejected though He
had wrought many miracles. See notes on
Matt. xii. 38.

In these verses (29-32) the Lord Jesus
testifies to the truthfulness of the Scriptures
respecting the Queen of the South and Jonah
and the men of Nineveh ; and, further, He
affirms the fact of the Resurrection and the
judgment to come, declaring that all those
persons will rise from the dead. This supplemental statement establishes the historic
truth of the book of Jonah.

Jonah was a sign to the Ninevites (v. 30)

They must therefore have heard of his deliverance from the great fish. He was entombed in the monster for three days and three nights ; and so was a type of Him who was three days and three nights in the heart of the earth.

Nineveh was given forty days in which to repent ; Jerusalem was given forty years. Repentance in the one case averted the judgment, unbelief in the other determined the destruction.

Christ was the Light of the world (v. 33). He did not hide that light ; it shone fully on every man. But few accepted it, for the majority were so wilfully blind that they remained unilluminated. See notes on Matt. v. 15 and Matt. vi. 22.

There are two factors here : the Gospel (v. 33),and the moral condition of those who heard it (vs. 34-36).

What a lamp is to a room the eye is to the body. If the lamp be broken the room is full of darkness, and if the "eye " be diseased the body is full of darkness. The Light is the Gospel and the lamp is the eye, i.e., the heart. If it be morally healthy it receives and diffuses the light so that the whole body is illuminated ; but if the eye, i.e., the heart, be diseased it cannot receive the light, and consequently the whole body is full of darkness. In the one case.the whole moral nature is illuminated with truth ; in the other case, there is moral darkness. Where the true light shines fully into the heart there remains no darkness in it ; when it does not shine there is nothing but darkness.

Those who are thus illuminated become lamps whose brilliance shines upon others to give them light. This is the meaning of verse 36.

The light (v. 35) which the Pharisees claimed to have within them was darkness. " Single " (v. 34) i.e., healthy. " Evil," i.e., diseased, " full of light " i.e., illuminated.

" To dine " (v. 37) i.e., to breakfast. The Pharisees attended the Synagogue every morning, and then returned home to breakfast.

The Lord Jesus accepted such invitations, but spoke so faithfully to both hosts and guests on such occasions that He was, without doubt, never invited again. His servants should imitate Him.

" Fools " (v. 40), i.e., unreasoning men. See notes on Matt. xxiii., where this denunciation was repeated in public.

But rather give alms, etc. (v. 41). The Greek here reads : But rather give the things that are within as alms. That is the heart, the will, the affections, and then all other actions proceeding from a heart truly given to God,will be acceptable to Him ; for otherwise such actions will be " dead works." Thus the Lord perpetually taught the necessity of the New Birth.

" Judgment and the love of God " (v. 42), i.e., justice and the love required by God (x. 27).

In Matt. xxiii. He compared the Pharisees to " whited sepulchres " and on this occasion to unseen graves. There is a remarkable difference. Some cunningly concealed their inward corruption so that men were not aware of it ; others gilded a false profession with a semblance of religion. But they were both alike ; for they were both corrupt—the whited sepulchres and the concealed graves were totally depraved.

" Reproachest " (v. 45), i.e., insultest.

" Touch " (v. 46), i.e., gently touch, as a physician gently feels the pulse of a patient. Luke was a physician—and His Gospel abounds with medical terms.

It is easier to admire dead saints than to identify oneself with living ones (vs. 47 and 48).

A man's life is the best proof of his opinions. It is hypocritical to pretend to admire dead saints and to make no effort to walk in their steps.

" The Wisdom of God " (v. 49), i.e., Christ (1 Cor. i. 24). The prophets and apostles He sent are those mentioned in Matt. xxiii. 34, Ephes. ii. 20 and iii. 5.

" The key of knowledge " (v. 52). In Matt. xxiii. 13 He denounced them for shutting up the Kingdom of Heaven ; here He charged them with taking possession of the key. Such is the action of those who forbid the Bible to the common people. The Hebrew Church substituted the Talmud for the Scriptures ; the Roman Church, the Missal, which it calls " The Key of Heaven.'

" To provoke " (v. 53). This peculiar Greek verb is only here found in the New Testament. It conveys the idea of an angry schoolmaster overwhelming a pupil with questions, so as to force the scholar to give wrong answers.

LUKE XII.—It is sweet to the Christian heart to read of Jesus and " multitudes " and " great multitudes " and " a very great multitude " and " an innumerable multitude " (v. 1) for these statements show how attractive He was to the common people. In heaven " a great multitude that no man can number " will surround with praise His Throne (Rev. vii. 9).

The Messiah and His testimony having both been rejected by Israel, the Lord here (vs. 1-12, 22-53) commits that testimony to the Disciples, and promises them the power of the Holy Spirit to enable them to render it (v. 12). He tells them that their attitude during His absence is to be that of service (v. 8) and expectation (v. 36). They were not to fear opposition (v. 4), nor to trust in themselves (v. 22), they were to be open, and to be, and say in public, what they were and said in private, for hypocrisy is a useless cloak (vs. 1-3). The greater fear of God would banish the lesser fear of man ; for man can only touch the body, but God can reach the soul and cast it into hell (vs. 4 and 5). That mighty God loved the very hairs of their head and would provide for all their need (vs. 6 and 7). If they confessed Him before men, however painful that testimony might be, He would confess them before angels ; but if they disowned Him before men He would disown then before angels (vs. 8 and 9). The testimony committed to them ' was so supreme and eternal, that whoever blasphemed it blasphemed the Holy Spirit and should never be forgiven (v. 10). But that Spirit of wisdom and power should not fail them when summoned before the princes of this world (vs. 11 and 12).

Thus he impressed their conscience and encouraged their heart. Whatever might be their trials He would protect them, for He had counted the hairs of their heads ; in heaven He would acknowledge their faithfulness before the angels ; and their mission was so important that its rejection would be more fatal than the rejection of Christ Himself (v. 10).

The distinction between soul and body, and the separate existence of the soul after death, and the misery of both in hell, are here affirmed by the Lord Jesus Himself (vs. 4 and 5). These Divine statements destroy the doctrine of annihilation ; as do also the statements in the last two verses of the chapter.

Fear is wholesome for Christians ; and every soul that is spiritually alive trembles at the Word of God

The corresponding passages in Matt. x. and the notes thereon should be read. It is evident that the Lord frequently repeated Himself, slightly altering His words so as to suit the several occasions.

The insensibility and rudeness of the natural heart is here exhibited (v. 13), as in xi. 27 and xiv. 15. See note on xiii. 1.

Had the Lord interfered in civil government He would have placed Himself in the power of His enemies. That was not His place. He dealt with souls, and directed men's attention to another life that lies beyond the grave. At the same time, as with the two other interrupters (xi. and xiv.), he at once unmasked the heart of the interrupter (v. 15), and in His parable of the rich man raised the question, what became of his soul ? This " fool," i.e., this unreasoning man talked of himself what he should do, and of his fruits and his barns and his goods. He knew he had a soul, and that he would live only for a time, but not forever. But he had to leave his fruits ungathered, his corn unreaped, his barns unbuilt, and his soul unsaved. His temporal prosperity was due not to his cleverness but to the " ground " which God in His grace caused to bring forth plentifully (v. 16).

" Be required " (v. 20). This should read " They shall require," i.e., the agents of the Divine justice. These could not be resisted ; and so he had to go. He ill-treated his own soul, and lived and died a beggar.

This message (vs. 13-21) was given to the people.

Returning to His disciples (vs. 21-53) He told them not to be anxious about either clothes or food. He undertook to provide for these ; and with them they were to be content (1. Tim. vi. 8). They were to trust the love of a Father Whose heart was interested in them, Who knew their needs (v. 30), and Who would not only satisfy these needs but would give them a kingdom (v. 32). So they were to work for Him and wait for Him and He would bring them to the Father's House and make them sit down, and He in His turn would gird Himself to serve them (v. 37) ; for love delights to serve. He came to earth to minister, and He returned to Heaven to minister, and His is the love that will never weary of ministering.

" More " (v. 23), i.e., more excellent, as in Hebrews xi. 4.

" No thought " (vs. 22, 25), i.e., anxious thought. " Ravens " (v. 24). They were unclean birds, but they are specially mentioned in Ps. cxlvii. 9 and Job xxxviii. 41 as objects of God's care, and they were His ministers to Elijah's need (1 Kings xvii. 6).

"Doubtful" (v. 29), i.e., "excited." See notes on Matt. vi. 25.

The words "little flock" (v. 32) are expressed in the Greek Text by a double diminutive, so affectingly expressing the Great Shepherd's tender care for His sheep.

"The Kingdom" (v. 32). They were expecting immediately an earthly kingdom and foremost positions in it, but He pointed them to another and more glorious kingdom; and He enthused them by that knowledge to sit loose to the treasures of earth and be givers rather than getters (v. 33). The language of this verse is figurative, This is clear from the words "provide yourselves bags" for it is evident that Christian people are not here commanded to carry material bags.

Working and waiting should characterize the Christian (vs. 35-40). Verse 37 is peculiar to Luke.

"Unto us" (v. 41), i.e., unto the Twelve as distinguished from the general body of the disciples. The Lord in His answer distinguishes between stewards and servants, although stewards are themselves servants. Stewards here represent Ministers in the Christian Church (1 Cor. iv. 1). Their duty is to rule and to feed the household (v. 42).

The Church soon ceased to wait for His coming (v. 45); and it was that and not the so-called conversion of the Emperor Constantine, which opened the door to unconverted ministers, corrupt doctrines, and persecutions of those who were faithful to the Scriptures.

The false servant (v. 45) will have his eternal portion with the unbelievers (v. 46).

Some base an argument in favour of the non-eternity of punishment upon verses 47 and 48; but verse 46 destroys the argument.

Others support the doctrine of purgatory upon them, but purgatory is said to be purgative and not punitive; hence these verses do not apply.

The great doctrine of the whole passage concerns the judgment of false and true servants, and is a solemn testimony that the giving up of the expectation of the Lord's coming caused the ruin and corruption of the Church.

It was predicted in Ps. lxxviii. 2 that the Messiah would in teaching make use of parables and dark sayings. Both are employed in verses 49 and 59. Verse 49 is "a dark saying." It is obscure to the most intelligent Christians. Some think the "fire" is that of Pentecost. Others think that it is the fire of persecution. The context supports this latter belief. The apostles expected to enter immediately into an earthly kingdom of great splendour under the kingship of their Master. But He told them that the effect of His presence upon earth would be His own death and their entrance upon a life of suffering. His object in coming to earth was to be distinguished from the effect of His coming. His object was to bring peace, but the effect was fire and sword (v. 49 with Matt. x. 34). This effect was caused through the corruption of man's nature; for the presence of Jesus brought to the surface the evil of the human heart. The depth of that evil and the hatred of the heart for God were manifested in the Cross (v. 50); and, later on, and at the present moment, against those who believed on Him Who died there (vs. 52 and 53). He predicted that that hatred would cause a mother to destroy her own child for no other reason but that of her daughter's confession of faith in Christ. This dreadful state of inconceivable evil and hatred was foretold in Mic. vii. 1-7.

The expression "straitened" (v. 50) may have a double meaning. It is translated "pressed" in Acts xviii. 5, and in this sense it may mean the ever present painful consciousness in the Lord's heart, of the fearful baptism of Golgotha which awaited Him. This anguish reached its climax in Gethsemane. Thus He Himself felt the "fire" and "sword" of human hatred which was the effect of His appearance among men, though His object in coming was to bless and save them.

Or the expression may have the force of 2 Cor. v. 14 and its import in that case would be that His burning desire to accomplish redemption, continually constrained Him; for He could not till after He had made an atonement for sin, give full liberty to the love which dwelt in unfathomable depths in His bosom, to flow out to the guilty and lost.

"Already kindled" (v. 49), i.e., against Christ Himself.

"A baptism" (v. 50). This is one of the nine baptisms of the New Testament.

"Five" (v. 52). Statisticians say that the average membership of a family is five.

The necessity of distinguishing between object and effect, is further pointed out in the notes on John ix. 39 and xii. 47.

In verses 54-59 He turns for the second time to the people (see notes on Matt. xvi. 2), and warns them of approaching judgment. He bases this warning upon two factors, signs (v. 56), and their own moral consciousness (v. 57). He accused them of wilful blindness to the prophecies of Daniel (ix. 24 and 25) which defined the actual appearing of the Messiah ; and this blindness was the more inexcusable because of their intelligence in observing the weather. But the truth was they were not honest in their enquiries, and in their profession of faith in the promised Messiah. He could read their hearts ; and so He justly called them hypocrites (v. 56).

Not only was their judgment of Him unjust (v. 57), but they were unrighteous in their judgment of any moral question.

" This time " (v. 56), i.e., the time predicted in Dan. ix. 25.

But their moral blindness would not save them from the power of their righteous adversary the Law, who would surely bring them before the Judge, and their doom would be terrible and eternal.

By Roman Law once litigants entered the Court an agreement was forbidden ; hence the wisdom of settling a dispute on the way to the Court. The adversary here is the Law of Moses ; the Judge is the Son of Man ; the prison is hell. The sinner is urged to seek deliverance from the claim of the Law while yet there is time.

In Matt. v. 25 this illustration is used to enforce the duty of forgiveness ; here it is used to enforce the necessity of salvation. Thus the Lord employed the one illustration to teach two lessons.

As the condition of release laid down in verse 59 is impossible to the sinner, for he could never discharge his indebtedness to a perfect obedience to God's Law, so is it manifest that this verse destroys the theory of annihilation. The meaning of the language is : " Thou shalt never depart at all." If the prisoner must remain in prison until he pays the very last mite, and it is manifest that that is impossible, it is clear that future punishment is eternal. This fact, and the argument of the verse, destroy the Romish doctrine of Purgatory, for purgatory is a temporary prison.

LUKE XIII.—The matter contained in the first seventeen verses is peculiar to Luke.

The Lord Jesus having come to earth to save men's souls, utilized every interruption to address the heart and conscience of the interrupters (vs. 1-8). He told his informants that the judgment of which He had just been speaking (xii. 58 and 59) would be universal (vs. 3 and 5) ; that the Galileans and the eighteen of Siloam were not exceptional sinners ; He urged them to personal repentance ; and under the figure of a fruitless fig-tree, warned them of the sure destruction that awaited them (vs. 6-8). See notes on xi. 27, xii. 13, xiii. 23 and xiv. 15.

The fig-tree was planted in a vineyard (v. 6) thus associating the fig with the vine. The fig-tree symbolised Israel's national privilege, see Judges ix. 8-12 and Jer. xxiv. 3 and Hosea ix. 10 and Matt. xxi. 19.

" A certain man " (v. 6). This formula occurs frequently in Luke, and accords with his presentation of Christ as the Son of man.

The Owner of the vineyard pictures God ; the Dresser, Jesus ; the three years, His Ministry (v. 9) ; the fourth year (v. 8), the Acts of the Apostles ; and the cutting down of the tree, the destruction of Jerusalem by the Romans.

" Cumbereth " (v. 7). The popular belief that an unconverted person who leads a moral life does no harm to humanity, is a man-made delusion. All who are not Spirit-born, and who do not bear spiritual fruit, however fair may be their lives, comparable to the leaves of a fig-tree, shall surely perish.

" He called her " (v. 12). This miracle, like that of Nain, was unsolicited. On entering the Synagogue His loving eye was attracted to this poor woman, and not to the beauty of the building or the rich clothing of the wealthy who may have been present. Such is the God of the Bible !

There are many crooked persons in modern religious assemblies, crooked in their tempers and dispositions, but Jesus can make them straight.

This glorious demonstration of grace, pity and power, proving that Jesus was the Messiah, brought out the hostility and corruption of the ruler's heart (vs. 14 and 15). So is it still. The nearer Christ comes to the Pharisee, and the greater demonstration He makes of His grace towards the victims of sin and Satan, the more violent is the anger excited.

"Then" (v. 18). This word is very important. The Greek word makes this clear. The Revised Version translates it "therefore." It connects the two parables which follow with the two facts which precede respecting the bound woman and the blind ruler. The parables were given to explain how it could be that Satan's power and teaching could have such a place in that which professed to be the Kingdom of God, i.e. the Synagogue. That Kingdom, begun with one man, Abraham, and committed to men the sons of Jacob, had become a great worldly system in which Satan made his home, just as the unclean vultures in the air nested in the boughs of the abnormal mustard tree, so that in the very synagogue itself he could bind a woman for eighteen years, and she could in nowise lift up herself. At the same time he had by his agent, so leavened the mind of the Ruler of the Synagogue with traditional corruption, that his soul was hopelessly blinded.

This little word "then" makes it plain that the popular interpretation of these parables as predicting the triumph of the Gospel is mistaken.

The "I" of verses 18 and 20 is most solemn. It is God Himself revealing His judgment about that which professed to be His kingdom.

Just as the Hebrew Church became thoroughly leavened with sacerdotal evil, so has the Christian Church. See notes on Matt. xiii. 31-33.

The Lord ignored this man and his question (v. 23), but seized the opportunity suggested by the question, to address an earnest appeal to all standing around Him, to let nothing prevent them pressing through the narrow door of conversion which alone gave entrance into the true Kingdom of God ; for directly the Master of that house shut the door they should vainly seek to enter (vs. 25-28). When that door is shut, multitudes will repent too late, and believe too late, and sorrow for sin too late, and begin to pray too late. Earth is the only place in creation where there is infidelity. There is no unbelief in hell. These verses (24-28) destroy the theory of repentance and salvation after death. See notes on Matt. vii. 13 and 23.

Men may ask religious questions and so flatter themselves that they are religious ;

and, further, they may have an ecclesiastical relation to Christ (v. 26), and yet be shut out from heaven.

"Whence." (vs. 25 and 27) not "Who." Christ only saves those who are given to Him of the Father. He knows from "whence" they come (John vi. 37, xvii. 6 and Heb. ii. 13). All others are workers of iniquity (v. 27).

"There" (v. 28) Greek. "In that place." To be shut out from heaven is to be shut into hell with its hopeless weeping of remorse and its hopeless gnashing of despair. Here, as everywhere, Christ's teaching conflicts with modern thought.

The geographic order of verse 29 corresponds with Ps. cvii. 3. (See notes on that Psalm). It is a curious fact that the Gospel began in the East, then spread to the West, then northward to the Scandinavian and Germanic nations, and finally to Africa. But just as the redeemed from Africa will possibly have precedence over those from the East, so will the Church of the Election be preferred to the Church of the Hebrews.

"The same day" (v. 31) rather "at that moment." "Will," i.e., intends. These Pharisees pretended to be friendly, but their object was to stop Jesus in His work and silence His preaching. But the Lord read their hearts, and dismissed them to their master with a dignified and befitting message. Herod was a "fox" both crafty and cruel. He murdered John the Baptist. Jesus compared Himself to a "hen' (v. 34). He was faithful and loving. And if He compared Himself to a lowly fowl, it was not discourteous to compare Herod to the nobler fox. Many great families are proud to have that animal on their armourial bearings. Yet it judged Herod justly.

Moreover if the Hebrew prophets (compare Zeph. iii. 3. and Ezek. xxii. 27) were inspired by the Holy Spirit so to rebuke kings and princes, how much more was it the duty of the Prince of the Prophets to do so.

The Lord was at this time in Galilee. It belonged to Herod's jurisdiction (xxiii. 7). He was on his way out of Perea, East of Jordan, and journeying towards Jerusalem (v. 22).

His message to Herod (v. 22) was not that He must preach the Gospel, for that would have had no interest for Herod, but that He must work miracles. That would affect Herod, and might touch His heart and conscience and so lead him to conversion.

He further told him that He would remain yet three days in his dominions actively engaged in these works of pity and power, and that then He should be " perfected," i.e., have finished, and that Herod had no power over Him either to take His life or stop His ministry.

But these days pointed to the three days that were to end in Jerusalem and Calvary where His ministry would be " perfected " in the cross ; and so just as He died, with loud and triumphant voice He shouted the one word " Finished " (John xix. 30 and Mark xv. 37).

" Walk " (v. 33). Compare in the Revised Version : " And He went on His way " (v. 22) with " I must go on My Way " (v. 33) that is His way through Herod's country. This was predicted of Him in the Scriptures ; and hence the word " must."

Jerusalem was the slaughter-house of the prophets (vs. 33 and 34). With the exception of John the Baptist, and perhaps a few others, all had been slain there.

This cry of anguish and of love (v. 34) was repeated when later He came in sight of the city (Matt. iii. 27).

The mystery of the human will and its power appear in the words (v. 34) " I would, but ye would not," The statement is even stronger in the Greek text. It is : " I willed but ye willed not."

Your House (v. 35), i.e., the Temple. It had been His (xix. 46 and John ii. 16).

" Desolate " (v. 35) a great desolation fills the house and the heart that Christ forsakes.

But His love and grace could not give them up though they hated and slew Him. So He promised to return (v. 35), and predicted that they would acclaim Him and receive Him as Jehovah. That day is yet future.

" Until " (v. 35). Compare Matt. i. 25, and notice there the imperfect tense in the Greek for " knew." This word " affirms " the performance of the action temporarily deferred.

LUKE XIV.—Self-interest is one of the strongest emotions of the natural heart. The Lord rebuked it in verses 5, 8, 14, 18 and 26.

" Before Him " (v. 2). These words, coupled with " They watched Him." (v. 1), suggest that this man was not a guest but was brought there purposely by the Pharisees in order to accuse Jesus of Sabbath-breaking if He healed him. But the Lord judged the hypocrisy which broke the Sabbath when their own interests were involved, and at the same time He vindicated the rights of grace in connection with that which was the seal of the First Covenant.

" He marked " etc. (v. 7), i.e., He noticed how they were picking out the best seats.

If he accepted invitations to lunch it was in order that He might preach the Gospel. His followers should imitate Him. On this occasion He preached first to the guests (vs. 7-11), and then to the host (vs. 12-14). Such faithfulness has either of two results : the conversion of the host and his guests, or the cessation of invitations.

With great delicacy, so as not to appear too personal the Lord alludes to a wedding feast (v. 8) and not to a lunch (v. 1).

" The chief rooms " (vs. 7, 8, 9 and 10), i.e., the best seats. See Prov. xxv. 6, 7.

The Lord evidently frequently repeated striking statements such as that of verse 11. It is three times recorded. Here, and in xviii. 14, and in Matt. xxiii. 12.

Hospitality to relatives and neighbours is not forbidden (v. 12), but the self-interest which seeks a recompense for so doing, and which is insensible to the just needs of the helpless, is condemned.

A literal and carnal interpretation of these verses (13 and 14) has often led to abuses, and caused much moral injury to society. The helpless and afflicted are to be succoured. As to all others the Divine command is : " If any man will not work neither shall he eat " (2 Thess. iii. 10).

The importance of noticing the omission or the repetition of the little word " and ", is illustrated by comparing verses 13 and 21. The word is omitted in verse 13 so as to carry the attention of the reader on to the climax " and thou shalt be blessed " (v. 14). It is repeated in verse 21 so as to fix the attention upon the several classes invited, so exhibiting the all embracing boundlessness of grace.

There will be two resurrections, that of the just and the unjust (v. 14 with John v. 28, Rev. xx. 6 and 12). The resurrection of the just will be the first resurrection. That of the evil, or the unjust, will take place at least a thousand years later. He who accepts Christ and His teaching, will have part in the first resurrection. The rapture of 1 Thess.

iv. is distinct from these two resurrections.

The parable of the Great Supper (vs. 15-24) exposed the unbelief and hatred of the heart of the guest who uttered the seemingly pious exclamation of verse 15. See notes on chapters xi. 27, and xii. 13. What this man really meant was : " It will be God's fault if I am not in heaven," i.e., he brought forward the doctrine of predestination. The Lord replied that he had been invited there but had refused the invitation, and had given his own interests more importance.

" A great supper " (v. 16). From a corresponding parable (Matt. xxii. 2) the guests were invited to this great supper to meet the King's Son. Their contemptuous treatment of the invitation warranted the righteous anger of verse 21 and of Matt. xxii. 7.

There are three great suppers recorded in Scripture : Luke xiv. 16, Rev. xix. 9, and xix. 17.

The three excuses (vs. 18-20) correspond to the three fruitless hearers in the Parable of the Sower. Compare 1 Cor. vii. 29.

Affection and a noble interest often cause and justify anger. Infidels applaud themselves that they do not get angry like their Christian opponents, when discussing the nature and claims of the Lord Jesus Christ. But an infidel would immediately be enraged if his disputant suggested that they should placidly discuss the moral character of the infidel's wife or mother.

The excuses were insincere ; for men do not buy lands and animals without first seeing and testing them ; and young married people like nothing better than an invitation to dinner (vs. 18 -20).

So Israel rejected the invitation to meet their Messiah and feast with Him. As a consequence the invitation was withdrawn (v. 24) and given to the Remnant (v. 21) and to the Gentiles (v. 23). To reject the Gospel message is to insure exclusion from heaven.

Verses 1-24 are peculiar to Luke.

The nearest affections are the strongest ; but no affection however strong must be permitted to compete with, or displace, Christ (vs. 26 and 27). See notes on Matt. x. 37.

" To hate " (v. 26), i.e., to love less. So the true believer loves his life in a less degree than his Lord (v. 27). The nearer anything is to the heart, the more dangerous it is ; and cost what it may, Christ must be followed, even to death itself. For the world hates

Him ; and all that binds us to it must be subjected to His interests. The cost must be counted, for salvation, eternal life, heaven are all in question. There is but one way to the life that is life indeed, and that is to share Christ's rejection and walk His path of shame and death. Better not to start than to become a backslider and useless (vs. 34 and 35).

In modern preaching there is almost a total absence of the teaching of verses 26-35 ; and the result is seen in the multitude of temporary conversions.

"His servant " (v. 17), i.e., Peter (Acts ii.-vii.) " Go into the streets," etc. (v. 21), Peter's second ministry (Acts x.-xii). " Another servant " (v. 23), i.e., Paul (Acts xiii.-xxviii.).

LUKE XV.—The moral effect of preaching grace (xiv. 21 and 23) and truth (xiv. 25-35) is seen in the " great multitudes " of xiv. 25, and in " all the publicans and sinners " of xv. 1. If these doctrines were preached to-day they would have the same attractive power. The point of these three parables is God's joy over repenting sinners. They unveil the sentiments of His heart, and not those of the repentant sinner, as is usually taught.

He did not sit still in heaven pitying sinners, just as the shepherd, the woman and the father did not idly bewail the lost sheep, the lost silver and the lost son. The word " found " (v. 24) reveals the Divine activities in secret in the conscience and heart of the prodigal. Christ left the starry crown of heaven for the thorny crown of earth in the activity of the love that seeks the lost till it is found.

The shepherd rejoiced, the woman rejoiced and the father rejoiced. Such is the joy of God when sinners come to Jesus. This grace is a grace that seeks and a grace that receives. The first two parables describe the former ; the third parable, the latter. Grace convicts the conscience but attracts the heart (vs. 17-20). The measure of that grace is the measure of the love that begets it (vs. 20-24). The son's reception and position were decided by the energy of that love, and not by the measure of the son's repentance.

The father's position decided that of the son. All was measured by the sentiments, not of the prodigal's heart, but of the father's heart.

The stupidity of the sinner, his insensibility

and his depravity are expressed in the three parables.

If the doubling of the dream to Pharaoh (Gen. xli. 32) assured its certitude how much more does the trebling of this parable make certain the attitude of God's heart to lost man.

" Murmured " (v. 2), i.e., kept discontentedly muttering.

" Sinners " (vs. 1 and 2), Jesus was a Friend of sinners (vii. 34), a Receiver of sinners (xv. 2), and the Guest of sinners (xix. 7).

" Them " (v. 3) and " you " (vs. 7 and 10), i.e., the Pharisees. These words determine the application of the parables. They were addressed to the Pharisees, and exposed and judged them as ignorant, self-righteous, jealous, enemies of grace and of God, and wicked. See note on xvi. 14-18.

The entire God-head,—Father, Son and Holy Spirit—is equally interested in the salvation of sinful man.

The proportions of one in a hundred, and one in ten, and one in two, is very striking.

This Third Gospel emphasizes God's love to sinners. See xv. 1, xviii. 10, xix. 7 and xxiii. 34. It was to redeem sinners that Jesus came to earth. He gloried in the fact, and was not ashamed of it.

The Parable of the lost sheep is also found in Matt. xviii. 12. There it expresses the Love that seeks ; here, the Joy that finds.

" Just persons " (vs. 7 and 29), i.e., the Pharisees who accounted themselves such. See xvi. 15 and xviii. 9.

" The presence " (v. 10), i.e., God Himself. This is the point. It is God who rejoices. It does not say " the angels rejoice," though that may be inferred.

The prodigal lost much ,but he did not lose either his father's love or his own sonship.

" Give me " (v. 12). The son fell while yet in the father's house. He fell from the moment he desired the father's goods without the father's company ; and it only needed a few days to find him in the far country (v. 13). Backsliding begins in the heart, and very soon places the feet with the swine.

" He began to be in want " (v. 14). Contrast " they began to be merry " (v. 24).

" Joined himself " (v. 15). This might be translated " forced himself " upon an unwilling employer.

His only occupation was—to a Jew—the degrading one of a swine-herd, and his only food the husks that they did eat. No man

gave to him ; for in the Devil's country nothing is given, everything must be bought ; and bought at a terrible price.

" He came to himself " (v. 15), and then he came to his father (v. 20). Such is the action of the Holy Spirit first upon the conscience and then upon the heart.

" A great way off, saw, had compassion, ran, fell on his neck, kissed him, and said to the servants, bring " etc. (vs. 20 and 22). All these activities express the grace and love that welcome true repentance.

Grace ran to kiss the prodigal in his rags, and righteousness hasted to dress him in its robes ; for he could not sit in his rags at the father's board. The robe was that of 2 Cor. v. 21.

The prodigal had not to provide the best robe, the ring, the sandals and the fatted calf. They were provided for him, and they declared his son-ship ; for servants were not thus arrayed and feasted.

The ten " ands " of verses 22-24 should be noticed as fastening attention upon the several things that love provided, and said, in the reception of the prodigal. There were no reproaches, rebukes nor reproofs for the past, nor irritating admonitions for the future, because the father and his joy is the subject of the story more than the moral condition of the son.

The elder brother pictured the Pharisee. He neither understood nor shared in the father's joy. On the contrary he was covetous, and (see notes on 2 Kings v.) refused to sympathize, although his father entreated him to do so (v. 28). Self-righteous, he claimed to have given a perfect obedience. But his desire to make merry with his friends, showed that morally he was as much lost to his father as his brother was. His bitter words " Thou never gavest me a kid," and " Thy son, who hath devoured thy living with harlots ". showed the hatred of his heart to his father and to his brother. But the father gently replied, " Child, all that I have is thine " (v. 31) and " Thy brother is found." Such is God, and such is the Pharisee !

John xiv. 6 and Luke xv. 20 are not contradictory but complementary. The one reveals the way to the Father's house ; the other, assures the reception there. The one discloses the activities of the mind of God in redemption ; the other, the emotions of the heart of God in reception.

Further, Christ as " the way " is symbolized

in the robe, the ring, the sandals, and the fatted calf, for He is righteousness (2 Cor. v. 21) eternal life (John xi. 25), sonship (John i. 12) and peace (1 Cor. v. 7, 8). The death of the sinless calf was a necessity ere the feast could be enjoyed. Had the prodigal refused this raiment and claimed the right to enter the Father's house in his rags and nakedness he, like Cain, would have been rejected. But his was true repentance, and so it accepted these gifts assuring purity, perpetuity, position, and provision. These three parables therefore, destroy the argument that no Atoning and Mediating Saviour is needed between God and the sinner, and they rest on the unseen foundation of 1 John i. 7.

LUKE XVI.—Here are two messages :— the first to the publican (vs. 1-13) ; the second to the Pharisee (14-31).

The son (xv. 13) and the steward (xvi. 1) represent the publican. The one wasted his father's goods ; the other, his master's.

The elder brother and the rich man represent the Pharisee.

The son and the steward sought homes in their conscious need ; the elder brother and the rich man gave no thought to the future.

The result for the publican was the merry-making of the father's house ; that for the Pharisee, the torments of the lake of fire.

Chapter xv. was addressed to the Pharisees in the hearing of the Disciples ; chapter xvi., to the disciples in the hearing of the Pharisees.

The word of the Lord is a two-edged sword. The Parable of the Steward may, therefore, judge the Pharisee as well as the publican. If so, then the Elder Brother, the Unjust Steward, and the Rich Man all portray the Pharisee in his three relationships to God, as a son, as a steward, and as a subject. As a son, he was loveless, for he had no affection for either his father or brother ; as a steward, he was faithless, for the Word of God, the true riches, were intrusted to him and he corrupted it ; and as a subject, he was lawless, for he refused to observe the great commandments of the Law. Thus chapter xv. revealed his heart, and chapter xvi. his conduct and his end.

" Agent " better expresses the meaning of the word " steward ' (v. 1). As a land-agent he had most probably, as was at that time and to-day the case, permission to grant abatements of rent. Hence the landlord was

not angry at his action (v. 8) but commended its sagacity.

But he made these abatements in his own interest and not in that of the landlord, which was a wrong thing to do.

The Lord's first comment on the parable was that worldly men are more alive to their earthly interests than Christian men are to their heavenly ones (v. 8). Next, He counselled these tax-gatherers to use aright and not unjustly their financial stewardship ; for they were in reality responsible to God, and in that relation it was not a temporary home that was in question but an eternal. He added that fidelity is a principle affecting little as well as big transactions (vs. 10-12) ; and He closed by pointing out the impossibility of serving two masters.

" Mammon " (v. 9), i.e., riches. " The love of money is a root of all forms of evil " (1 Tim. vi. 10). Hence the expression " mammon of unrighteousness." The expression " The unjust steward " (v. 8) might better read " Steward of unrighteousness," i.e., finance agent.

The words " friends " and " they " (v. 9) have no personal force. They only signify " that ye may be received."

Friends are to be made by means of that which usually is an instrument of unrighteousness, i.e., Christian people are to do good with money, to spend it on others and not on themselves, and so will their enjoyment of heaven be the greater.

Unfaithfulness in temporal wealth unfits for the stewardship of true riches (v. 11). So was it with Israel. The precious things of Rom. ix. 4 and 5 were committed to them, and became their own (" your own," v. 12) ; but they proved unworthy of these riches (v. 11), for they loved money and tried to serve God and mammon.

Thus the Lord pierced the heart of the publican with these searching words.

The Pharisees (xv. 1) murmured at Him in their character as the elder brother. Here (v. 14), in that of the rich man, they derided Him.

The enemies of inspiration say that verses 16-18 have no meaning here and must have been introduced by some copyist. Thus they display their ignorance.

The argument is this. The Pharisee justified himself before men, (v. 15 and xviii. 11), but God read his heart. He professed to admire the prophets, for he whitened their sepulchres, and to be a rigid observer of the Law. But John was one of the prophets, he was included amongst them, he was the greatest of them, and though all kinds of men (" every man " v. 16) obeyed him and pressed into the kingdom proclaimed by him, the Pharisee alone refused to listen and repent. Thus he treated the prophets.

As to the Law it commanded : " Thou shalt not covet," and " Thou shalt not commit adultery." Both these commandments the Pharisee disobeyed ; for he put away his wife and was secretly covetous and immoral. See notes on John viii. 1-12. This is why when exposed by the Lord, the Pharisees derided Him.

To wear a cloak of religion and to amass money and gratify passion is highly esteemed amongst men (v. 15) ; " for men will praise thee when thou doest well to thyself ;" but it is abomination in the sight of God.

But it was useless for the Pharisees to hope to escape the judgment of the Law (v. 17), and accordingly the great Law-Giver Himself drew aside the veil which hides the abyss of eternal judgment and revealed the doom of the self-righteous and self-indulgent (vs. 19-31) transgressor.

No one ever spoke so plainly about hell as the Lord Jesus. Men in high positions in the Christian Church are not afraid to say that His statements about it are untrue.

But here much may be learned :—Its locality: it is a " place " (v. 28). Its reality : the very man that fared sumptuously now suffers miserably—he is represented as having eyes, ears, a mouth, a tongue and a tortured body. Its intelligence : He remembers his past life, he recognises Abraham and Lazarus, and is acquainted with Moses and the prophets. Its torment: this is asserted four times (vs. 23, 24, 25, 28). Its eternity : the rich man asks that Lazarus might be sent to his five brothers. He did not ask this grace for himself, for he knew that he was eternally entombed. It is easy to step into hell, but impossible to step out.

The " great gulf " (v. 26) is the hindrance implied in John vii. 34.

There are no unbelievers in hell, nor is there any salvation there. The rich man repented, but too late ; and his concern lest his brothers should perish shows how effectually his conscience was aroused. But he remained a prisoner in that dread dungeon. Many believe in salvation after death. The Lord Jesus here destroys that doctrine. There is no salvation in the lower world if the testimony of the Scriptures to the conscience be rejected in this present world.

The Scriptures contain all that is necessary to salvation. A returned spirit could add nothing to them ; and a man who will not listen to the Bible would not listen to a multitude if raised from the dead (v. 31).

A few days later the Lord did raise a man named Lazarus from the grave and the Pharisees went about to put him to death.

LUKE XVII.—The Lord here again turns to His disciples, tells them that it is inevitable that occasions of moral stumbling must test the faith and sincerity of the little ones, i.e. believers (Matt. xviii. 6), and says that it were better for those stumbling blocks, i.e. the Pharisees, or any to-day who have the Pharisee spirit, to have great millstones hung around their necks and to be thrown with violence into the sea, for that would be a lesser doom than to be cast into the lake of fire and suffer its torments in companionship with the rich man.

" The little ones " (v. 2) represented the sinners who were coming to Jesus ; the Pharisees were the stumbling-blocks who hindered them, for while professing to rigidly obey the Law of Moses they were both covetous and licentious ; and such conduct in religious men is a stumbling-block to those seeking salvation.

" Impossible " (v. 1), i.e., inevitable. " Offences," i.e., causes of moral stumbling. " Millstone "(v. 2),Greek, a great millstone. " Cast," i.e., hurled with violence. " Offend," i.e., be a cause of moral stumbling.

The Lord then warned the disciples (vs. 3 and 4) not to think only of the sins of the Pharisees, but of their own also, and especially of the sin of an unforgiving spirit. A repentant brother was to be forgiven seven times " in a day " ; and when Peter asked Him (Matt. xviii. 21) on another occasion if he were to stop at seven times Jesus said, No, not " until seventy times seven," i.e., four hundred and ninety. This is an important number in the history of God's moral government of sinning Israel. It means endless forgiving. Seven times " in one day " (v. 4) distinguishes this occasion from that of Matt. xviii. 21.

Only twice prior to Pentecost do we read of the apostles asking the Lord, as a body, for spiritual energy, Here they asked Him to increase their faith (v. 5) ; on another occasion they begged to be taught how to pray. It is true also that in Matt. xvii. 19 it was probably the apostles who said, " Why could not we cast him out ? "

The searching doctrine of verses 1-4 made the apostles conscious that something higher than fallen human nature alone could obey such teaching. The Lord replied (v. 6) that faith was a power so real that its smallest provision could remove the greatest moral obstacles. Here He instanced as an illustration a tree ; in Matt. xvii. a mountain, i.e., the Mount of Transfiguration. The removal of trees and mountains were proverbial figures of speech among the Jews at that time, expressing the overcoming of great difficulties.

Then in order to fore-warn the apostles against flattering themselves that they would be entitled to admiration if they lived without injuring others, if they practised perpetual forgiveness, and if they worked wonderful miracles, He now adds that having fulfilled all these conditions, they would be no better than unprofitable servants (vs. 7-10), that is, they would in no way have benefited their Master. This is a fatal blow to the doctrine of salvation by works. The disciple is to say, " I am an unprofitable servant." The Master will say, " Well done, good and faithful servant " (Matt. xxv. 21).

Verse 7 should read as in the Revised Version, and thus mark the contrast between " straightway " and " afterward."

A common misery destroys caste. Leprosy associated these Jews with the Samaritan (vs. 12 and 16).

Conscious need begets real prayer. Superstition and sacerdotalism " say prayers."

Salvation follows upon obedience (v. 14).

Men are more ready to pray than to praise. (v. 18). Thankfulness is a rare grace, and a public confession of Christ's saving power is unusual, and is discouraged in the modern church.

" The midst " (v. 11), i.e., between. The Lord was travelling eastwards to the Jordan and to Jericho (xviii. 35).

" Afar off " (v. 12) as required by Lev. xiii. 45, 46.

" The priests " (v. 14) as commanded in Lev. xiii. and xiv. and Deut. xxiv. 8. This command assured cleansing ; for only a cleansed leper was to show himself to the priests. It was as much as to say, " You are clean." They knew they were unclean ; but they believed Christ's word, went away with the conviction that it was true, and were immediately healed on the way.

Their appearing before the priests as cleansed lepers would demonstrate that Jesus was both Messiah and Jehovah, for God alone could heal leprosy after this manner. Compare the " I will " of ch. v. 13.

The command to the Samaritan to show himself to the priest destroyed his national faith in Mount Gerizim, and enjoined him to join the Hebrew Church, for in that Dispensation salvation was of the Jews (John iv. 22).

In reply to the question of the Pharisees (v. 20) the Lord answered that the kingdom of God was at that moment in their midst, for He was the kingdom of God (v. 21). God had an undisputed kingdom nowhere else in the world except in the heart and will of Jesus of Nazareth, and certainly not in the heart of the hostile Pharisee who hated Him.

" Observation " (v. 20), i.e., carnal observation. This Greek term implies hostile observation. It appears again and again in the words " They watched Him " (vi. 7 ; xiv. 1 ; xx. 20 and Mark iii. 2 ; Acts ix. 24, Gal. iv. 10). See notes on Rev. vi. 10.

But if the Pharisees were carnal and hostile the disciples (v. 22) were spiritual and loving. How often in the years that followed the Ascension must they have longed to live again one of the happy days of the old fellowship in Galilee ! (v. 22). This hunger of heart would tempt them to believe reports as to His reappearing in one locality or another (v. 23) ; but they were not to be led astray, for He would come like the lightning (v. 24).

His Second Advent would contrast with His First. 2 Thess. i. describes it. It will not be local, obscure and with great humility, but universal, powerful and glorious (v. 24). The glories of that day will have a relation to, and will be the result of, His atoning sufferings at Calvary (v. 25). It will find the world as indifferent and corrupt as in the days of Noah and of Lot (vs. 26-30). As the keen eye of the vulture (v. 37) detects a carcase, so will Divine judgment detect corruption. It will discriminate in that day between two men in a bed (v. 34) and two women at a millstone. The one will be left for judgment ; the other received into the kingdom. All who, like Lot's wife, have their hearts in

Sodom, though, like her, they make a profession of having left it, will perish (v. 32), as well as those who put any interest, even life itself, above the claims of righteousness (vs. 31, 33). There is here a reference to I Thess. iv. 17. See Matt. xxiv. 40.

This will not be the judgment of the dead but of the living—people in bed, or at the mill or on the house-tops, or in the fields· This principle of judgment demonstrated itself in the destruction of Jerusalem ; but its consummation belongs to the future.

The doctrine of verses 23-37 strikes against the expectation of many that the world will grow morally better and ultimately become the Kingdom of God. But here the Lord gives a fearful picture of the state of the world and the professing Church at the time of His Second Coming.

More than once Jesus pointed to Noah and the state of society in his day (Matt. xxiv. 37)· as pre-figuring the condition of the nations when He shall appear.

The kind of men and women that will be spared to enter the kingdom are presented in the two parables that follow.

LUKE · XVIII. 1-30.—During the long period prior to His coming (v. 8) His own Elect (v. 7), represented by the widow (v. 3) and the publican (v. 13), would be despised (v. 11) and denied justice (v. 4). Prayer was to be their refuge (v. 1). Importunity (v. 5) and humility (v. 13) would characterize its energy. For prayer is the resource of faith, however much faith may be tested. But when He comes will He find this praying faith upon the earth ? The answer to that question is left to man's responsibility. But the question itself suggests that it will not be found " on *the earth*," but only in the little oppressed company of the Elect. There He will find it ; and it will not be disappointed or confounded.

Election is the foundation of salvation. It is a truth which awakens worship and praise in the heart of the Christian. Except God had chosen believers they would never have called upon and chosen Him. Unless He had chosen them because of some satisfactory purpose found in Himself, without respect to any goodness of theirs, they must have eternally perished, for there was nothing in them to make them worthy of His choice. Men may mock at and misunderstand election, but the believer who knows his own

heart will ever bless God for this great fundamental doctrine of the Gospel.

The moral evidence of election is connected with faith in Christ and conformity to His image (Rom. viii. 29, 30). The Apostle Paul was satisfied that the Thessalonians were elect, because their faith and hope and love were manifested in action (I Thess. i. 3 and 4).

If an unjust judge can be moved to do justice, how much more certain is it that God can be moved to vindicate and deliver those who are so precious to Him that He says they are as the apple of His eye ?

" Always " (v. 1), i.e., on all occasions. " Not to faint," i.e., not to lose heart.

These two parables are peculiar to Luke. The first parable is also unique, in that the explanation is put first.

" Avenge " (v. 3), i.e., give judgment in my favour. Compare Rom. xii. 19, 2 Cor. x. 6, Rev. vi. 10 and xix. 2.

" Came " (v. 3), rather, kept coming.

" Them " (v. 7), i.e., the oppressors of His people, to whom He shows long-suffering in order to move them to repentance. In the case of the Amorite this long-suffering continued for four hundred years, but in vain (Gen. xv. 13 and 16) ; in the present dispensation that long-suffering has already lasted nineteen hundred years, and as predicted here and in other prophecies, it will be also in vain. "Bear long." This Greek verb commonly means delay in punishing evil men (Pearce).

" Them " (v. 8), i.e., the Elect. " Speedily", i.e., in a speedy manner. See note on Rev. i. 1. Speedy deliverance for the oppressed is thus reconciled with long forbearance toward the oppressor. The oppression of Egypt was long ; its plagues followed each other speedily. Compare Rev. x. 6.

The question of verse 8 shows the uselessness of expecting the conversion of the world before Christ comes, and makes evident the foolishness of supposing that all people are good at heart in spite of their outward conduct, and so will all ultimately be in heaven. The unbelief of man in respect to both Advents is shown in Isa. liii. and 2 Pet. iii.

The Pharisee was blind to his own sinfulness. Hence he asked for nothing and got nothing. He fasted twice in the week, God only having commanded one annual fast (Lev. xvi. 29 and Num. xxix. 7). In the days of Zech. viii. 19 three more had been added by man, and at the time of the First Advent two fasts a week were commanded by the Rabbis. He gave tithes of all he possessed, the Divine Law only prescribing corn, wine and cattle. (Deut. xiv. 22, 23.)

" Afar off " (v. 13) as being a moral leper. " Smote," i.e., kept smiting. " Be merciful," i.e., be Thyself a propitiation (Rom. iii. 25; Heb. ii. 17 and ix. 5). " A sinner,"—in the Greek text " the sinner," i.e., the only one sinner in the world, or the greatest sinner in the world.

Every afternoon at three o'clock the evening lamb was offered up as a propitiation for the sins of that day. The publican pleaded forgiveness and acceptance because of the merit of that atoning blood. It foreshadowed the atoning death of the Lamb of God, who was Himself the propitiation, i.e. the mercy-seat.

" Justified " (v. 14), i.e., declared a righteous man. " The other " not justified. There are no degrees in justification. The verse does not mean that the Pharisee was partly justified and the publican fully, but it means that the one was wholly justified and the other not at all. See note on Rom. iii. 24.

" Everyone that exalteth himself," etc. (v. 14). The Lord evidently repeated this frequently (Matt. xxiii. 12). Pharaoh, Nebuchadnezzar, Herod and many others in the Bible, illustrate this principle.

Thus these two parables are like apples of gold in a basket of silver (Prov. xxv. 11. R.V.)—the basket of silver being the Coming of the Lord, which is the subject of the context.

For notes on verses 15-30 see Matt. xix. and Mark x.

Had man originated these two parables, he would have set them in an opposite order. But the order in the Scripture is Divine. First, the fruit of faith is shown, then its root. Experience is not thus. First, the sinner has faith in a God who justifies, and then in a God who vindicates.

The importunate widow (v. 3) and the importunate beggar (v. 35) had to overcome opposition. But how great the contrast between the judge and the Physician!

LUKE XVIII. 31-XIX. 10.—The chronological order in the conversion of Zacchæus and the healing of Bartimæus is here reversed by the Holy Spirit for many reasons. Two of these may be at once recognised—one, the principle that the first shall be last and the last first; the other, to contrast the mental blindness of the Twelve (v. 34 R.V.) with the physical blindness of the beggar (v. 35).

" Was come nigh " (v. 35) not " was coming nigh," i.e., " was in the vicinity of." There is, therefore, no disagreement with either Matthew or Mark. This Evangelist records the occasion on which the miracle was performed; the others point to the spot and the time.

But if it be insisted that the form of the Greek verb " to come nigh " might, by some grammatical ingenuity, be made to mean " was approaching " yet would this change not establish any discrepancy. For then the facts would read thus: " When Jesus was coming to Jericho blind Bartimæus was sitting by the highwayside begging." That is to say, as Jesus was approaching the city on the one side Bartimæus was sitting in his usual place on the other side, unconscious that the wonderful Saviour was drawing near and would presently heal him.

A legitimate rendering of xix. 1, partly supported by the Revised Version, helps to remove any supposed difficulty. " Now Jesus had entered and was passing through Jericho." This is an instance—so often to be recognised throughout the entire Bible of the Holy Spirit recording facts out of their chronological order. It is also a most notable illustration of the spiritual import of the words " in order " (i. 3)

The blind beggar is here preferred before the rich tax-collector. He was last but is put first. He was told " to rise " but Zacchæus to " come down." Thus rich and poor meet on the one level as sinners before God.

Had the Twelve learned the lesson taught them by the healing of the blind beggar, they would have prayed as he did, and Jesus would have given them spiritual sight.

The salvation of Zacchæus is one of the most striking in the Gospels. It was personal: " Zacchæus." It was pressing: " make haste." It was humbling: " Come down." It was immediate: " To-day." It was abiding: " I must abide." It was social: " At thy house."

The moral effect of the conversion was seen in Zacchæus taking his stand along with Jesus in public, and in declaring that from that moment the half of his goods he gave to the poor, and that he restored fourfold all overcharges of taxation.

Roman law required a fourfold restitution, but Levitical law only demanded the principal and one-fifth part added (Num. v. 7). But he imposed upon himself the severe measure of Exod. xxii. 1. Thus he judged himself; and true repentance acts as he did. He felt that he could not begin too soon to obey the promptings of the new life that had come into his heart. Faith that does not purify the heart and life is not a Divine faith; and grace that cannot be seen like light and tasted like salt is vain. See note on 2 Cor. iv. 1.

The conversion of Zacchæus illustrates xviii. 27.

The Deity and Kingship of Jesus appear in the words " Zacchæus, I must abide at thy house " (v. 5). He had not to ask, " Who is that man in the tree ? " for, being God, He knew him just as He saw and knew Nathanial under a similar sycamore, i.e., fig-tree. Also He did not ask for a lodging, but, as a king, He commanded entertainment.

Salvation by works buttons up the pocket (xviii. 22, 23); salvation by grace unbuttons it (v. 8). Most men give away some money in charity in their wills when they can no longer keep it.

Salvation cleanses the sinner's house as well as the sinner's heart (v. 9). Therefore the house was such as Jesus might enter; and so He disposed of the Pharisaic objection of verse 7.

Jesus was not ashamed to sup with sinners, for His purpose in coming to earth was to seek and to save them.

LUKE XIX. 11-48.—" These things " (v. 11, i.e., the testimony of Zacchæus to Jesus as King of Israel, and of Bartimæus to Him as Son of David; Christ accepted both titles. He did not rebuke them for so acclaiming Him.

Recognising this, His disciples thought that on entering His royal city He would at once establish His Kingdom, but the Lord by the Parable of the Pounds taught them that that day was yet far distant. This Parable is peculiar to Luke.

It was usual at that time for a prince or nobleman to proceed to Rome, there to receive a kingdom from Caesar and then to return and govern it. History records that Archelaus the son of Herod had just done so. The frame-work of the Parable was, therefore, familiar to the people who heard it.

So Jesus as the " Nobleman " (v. 12) went to a far country, i.e., to heaven, there to be invested with royalty (Ps. ii. 6), to receive the Kingdom of the earth, and then to return and exercise His government with great authority (Rev. xi. 15).

On His return He first judges His servants, (v. 15), for judgment must begin at the house of God (1 Pet. iv. 17), and then He judges the rebels (v. 27). Behold, therefore, His goodness and His severity—His goodness to the faithful servants; His severity to the others. False preachers proclaim His goodness, but deny His severity (Rom. xi. 22).

" Ten servants," i.e. all his servants. See note on Zech. viii. 23.

Each servant received a similar deposit, i.e., the Gospel (1 Tim. i. 11, 12, vi. 20 R.V., Margin; 2 Tim. i. 12, R.V., Margin); or some spiritual gift common to all.

If the deposit, i.e., the Pound, signifies the Gospel message, then the faithful servants were successful soul-winners, whilst the indolent servant was satisfied to keep the message to himself and not to use it in the extension of his Lord's Kingdom. That Kingdom is extended by soul-winning. Beyond degradation and deprivation, there is nothing said as to the punishment of the wicked servant (vs. 22-26).

Although similar in character, this Parable is not the same as that of the Talents (Matt. xxv. 14). It was addressed to the disciples later on in that last week of the Lord's ministry. The two Parables may be contrasted. That of the Talents presents the sovereignty of the Master; that of the Pounds, the responsibility of the servants. The latter, therefore, contemplates the joy of the servant; the former, the joy of his Lord.

Thus what is gained spiritually in this world will be not lost but enlarged in the world to come (vs. 24-26).

The servant truthfully and modestly says, " Lord, Thy pound hath gained ten pounds " (v. 16). The Master in His grace replies, " Well done " (v. 17, R.V.), " because thou hast been faithful." The servant gives all the credit to the Master's pound, and the Master declares the success to be due to the servant's faithfulness. So shall every (faithful) man have his own praise from God in the coming day of the Lord's return (1 Cor. iv. 5). Then shall the " very little " be rewarded with very much, i.e., " ten cities " (v. 17).

So there will be ten servants, and ten pounds, and ten cities. " Ten " is a Hebrew numeral signifying an indefinite number.

The wicked servant was a liar (v. 21); but his Master met him on his own ground and said: "If it be true, as you say, that I am austere and hard, then that should have impelled you to the more diligence in the handling of the deposit committed to you" (vs. 22 and 23).

The exclamation: "Lord, *he* hath ten pounds!" (v. 25) was most probably that of the people; for the Lord told the story so vividly that His hearers could not help this cry of surprise.

As to His enemies (v. 27), the Lord will command them to be slain before Him, i.e., to be gathered out by the angels of His wrath and cast into the furnace of fire (Matt. xiii. 41 and 42).

However small a man's gift may be (v. 17) he is as responsible as if it were very great. All that is required in a steward is faithfulness (1 Cor. iv. 2). The reward given to faithfulness in the Coming Crowning Day will be so great as to surprise those who see it (v. 25).

Hard thoughts of God (v. 21) are characteristic of unconverted people. They first misrepresent Him, and then try and excuse themselves for not serving Him.

The indolent servant, the foolish virgins (Matt. xxv. 12), and the unrighteous (Matt. xxv. 41), were judged, not because of what they did, but because of what they failed to do. The words, "Be sure your sin will find you out" (Num. xxxii. 23), were uttered as a warning against failure in right doing. Preachers usually quote these words in reference to secret sins, but this is not their original meaning.

The pound given to each servant may represent the Bible. All were alike responsible for its use. All Christian workers and teachers justly ascribe any success to that Sacred Book and not to themselves. The heart is compared to a treasury (vi. 45) or bank. Money is put into a Bank for two purposes —security and profit. The Word of God should be treasured in the heart and put out to Gospel interest with the lips. Those who selfishly wrap it up and do not share it with others, or circulate it, are dangerously like the "wicked servant" of this Parable.

For notes on verses 28 to 48 see Matt. xxi. and Mark xi.

The prophecy of Zechariah demanded this public presentation of Jesus as the King of Israel (35-40). The publicity of this entrance at a time when Jerusalem was crowded because of the Passover, the publicity of His trial and the publicity of His death, were most important as establishing beyond confutation the fact of His claim and the fact of His Crucifixion. Had He been stoned in some popular tumult, or secretly murdered like John the Baptist, unbelievers might have denied that He ever died at all. But there is no fact in history so undeniable as the Crucifixion. That death was the corner stone and crowning act of His ministry. It was a death for sinners in order to atone for their sins. That death was the life of the world, and it was witnessed by a multitude of people.

Jesus wept aloud over Jerusalem (v. 41). At the grave of Lazarus (John xi. 35) He shed silent tears. See the Greek Text.

This outcry of sorrow (42-44) is peculiar to Luke. As Man He wept, as God He spoke.

His compassion here appeared most vividly. He knew, as God, the cruelty, the self-righteousness, the rebellion, the pride, the hypocrisy and the sins of that people. He knew the horrible death that six days later they would cause Him to die. And yet He wept over them!

" If thou hadst known " (v. 42) or : " Oh, that thou hadst known." Compare Isa. xlviii. 18. Christ loves and pities His enemies, but only believers will be saved. Being God He predicted the doom of the unbelievers. Ignorance will not in the Day of Judgment excuse sin. When men might know truth, but refuse to know it, a just judgment blinds them (v. 42), and they perish.

" Thine enemies " (v. 43), i.e., the Romans. " A trench," rather " a rampart." In three days the Romans surrounded Jerusalem with a stone wall, so making escape impossible. The inhabitants were kept in on every side. Thus was fulfilled this prophecy uttered forty years before the event.

" Thy visitation " (v. 44). God visits sinners either in grace or in wrath. Great will be the doom of those who steel their hearts against a visitation of grace.

" Cast out " (v. 45). This was the second cleansing of the Temple. The first was that of John ii. 14. Both were effected by miraculous power; and in each case the Lord supported His conduct by quoting Scripture. See note on Matt. xxi. 12.

" Taught " (v. 47). Christ showed by His action that a house of praying (v. 46) should be equally a house of preaching (v. 47).

" The people all hung upon Him " (v. 48, R.V.); but a few days later they all hanged Him (Acts v. 30).

Before peace can be established on earth (ii. 14) it had to be established in heaven (v. 38); for the just claims of Divine righteousness against sin and sinners had to be met and vindicated and satisfied by the atoning work of Christ at Calvary.

LUKE XX.-XXI. 4.—See notes on Matt. xxi. xxiii. Mark xi. and xii. and Ps. v.

" They answered that they did not know " (v..7, R.V.). Lying is one of the commonest sins in the world. Gehazi and Ananias have more followers than Peter and Paul.

John's testimony (v. 4) provided the authority which the priests demanded.(v. 2).

" Whosoever shall fall upon that Stone shall be broken " (v. 18), i.e., at the First Advent when the nation was " broken " by the Romans.

" But on whomsoever it shall fall it will grind him to powder," i.e., at the Second Advent (Dan. ii. 35).

The terrible message of Matt. xxiii. is here compressed into two verses, 46 and 47. This illustrates inspiration. The Spirit wrote the First Gospel for the Hebrew Church, and, therefore, freely exposed its hypocrisy. He wrote the Third Gospel for the world, and, therefore, made prominent Christ's attitude towards sinners. Hence Luke only mentions the sinner of vii. 37, the Prodigal Son, Zacchæus, and the dying thief. The narrative of His grace to these occupies much space ; His denunciation of the Pharisees, two verses.

If this widow (v. 2) were one of those whose whole substance had been devoured by the hypocritical Scribes (v. 47), then her action in giving her last farthing to the Temple was very interesting. For she might well have argued that all religion was false because of the action of its professors toward her.

Not only did she give more in proportion to her means than any one of the rich men, but she gave more than all of them put together ; for they gave of their superfluity, but she of her poverty.

LUKE XXI. 5-38.—See notes on Matt. xxiv. and xxv. and Mark xiii.

LUKE XXII.—See notes on Matt. xxvi and Mark xiv.

" The Passover must be killed " (v. 7). Compare 1 Cor. v. 7 and 1 Cor. xv. 3. Jesus, God's Passover, must be killed because the Scriptures predicted it, and because only His atoning death could expiate man's sin. All Four Gospels record at great length His death, while only two briefly record His birth. Modern popular theology reverses this, it magnifies His birth, and be-littles His death.

" My blood " (v. 20). Lev. iii. 17 and vii. 26 forbade the eating of blood. Jesus and the Apostles being godly Jews would have refused to drink of such a cup. Hence the language here is figurative. Verses 19 and 20 are not in some MSS. See notes on 1 Cor. xi.

" As it was determined " (v. 22). God's fore-knowledge does not destroy man's responsibility. He wills in the sense of permission, but not necessarily in approbation.

Verses 24-38 are peculiar to Luke.

" A strife " (v. 24) ; in ix. 46 it was a reasoning. Thus one carnal thought leads to another and worse one.

It is possible, judging from Peter's permitted fall, that he desired to be the greatest.

The reference in verse 27 is to the Lord's action in washing their feet.

The section 31-38 took place between the Upper Room and the Garden of Gethsemane. Compare Mark xiv. 26-32.

" My temptations " (v. 28). He was the Man of Sorrows. His whole life was a series of trials, and griefs, and hatreds, and sufferings.

Though He fore-knew that they would all forsake Him, yet in His most wonderful and tender love He praised their fidelity and courage (v. 28), and promised them a recompense out of all proportion to their service (vs. 29 and 30). The glory of the Royal Table and of the Kingly Throne should effectually destroy the petty ambition of being chief and greatest.

They were very poor servants ; but no servants ever had such an admiring, compassionate and tender Master.

The Twelve Tribes (v. 30). These are mentioned four times in the New Testament : here and in Matt. xix. 28. Acts xxvi. 7 and James i..1. They still exist.

" Simon, Simon," (v. 31). This was the

same voice that said " Abraham, Abraham "
(Gen. xxii. 11).

" Satan hath desired to have you " (v. 31),
i.e., " Satan hath obtained *you all* by
asking." Satan sifts to get rid of the corn ;
God winnows to get rid of the chaff (Matt. iii.
12, 1 Pet. v. 8, 9).

" I have prayed for *thee*, Simon " (v. 32),
" that thy faith fail not," i.e., suffer an
eclipse. Satan's attack is always delivered
against faith, for if that fails all fails. So
he said to Eve, " Hath God said ? " and then
when that doubt had done its work he boldly
added, " You shall not surely die."

" I have prayed for thee " (v. 2). The
safety and perseverance of the believer are
secured by the prayer of the Intercessor.
Because He lives, faith cannot fail.

The appointed time contemplated in this
prayer was not the moment of Peter's denial,
but the dark moment of despair when he
went out and wept bitterly. Then Satan
must have whispered to him : " Thou hast
committed spiritual suicide ; now art thou
mine " ; but the Lord's look (v. 51) was the
means that upheld his faith, and so Christ's
prayer was answered.

" When thou art converted " (v. 32), i.e.,
" When thou hast turned thyself back to
Me, strengthen thy brothers "—not thy
servants, but thy brothers. This terrible
fall, and the glory promised in verses 29 and
30, must have combined to cure him of any
desire for supremacy.

Only here (v. 34) is it recorded that the
Lord addressed Simon as Peter. It was no
doubt designed in order to remind him of his
weakness. The word means a stone which
can be shifted in any direction. A church
built on that stone must fall. See notes on
Matt. xxvi. and Mark xiv.

" The purse," " the scrip," " the sword,"
and " the garment " (v. 36) are proverbial
and symbolical expressions. They mean
that during Christ's absence they were to
work for their daily bread and accept the
protection of an ordered government. The
term " sword " means the power of the
magistrate (Rom. xiii. 4).

Hence the Apostle Paul earned from time
to time his daily bread as a tent-maker,
and accepted and claimed the protection
of " the sword " in Acts xxi. 39 and xxv.
11. and Acts xvi. 37.

When the Lord was with them (v. 35) as
king He demonstrated His ability to supply
all their needs, but during the time of His
rejection they were to be rejected with Him.

" It is enough " (v. 38). The force of these
words may be that, recognising their hopeless
inability to understand Him, He terminated
the matter knowing that after Pentecost
they would understand.

" He kneeled down and prayed " (v. 41).
This is what the Lord did before He was
executed. His servants should imitate Him.

" This cup " (v. 42). The ancients assigned
to each guest at a feast a cup the wine in
which, by its quality, expressed the respect
given to the recipient. So the word " cup "
came to signify a portion either of pleasure
or of pain.

The Lord's agony in Gethsemane cannot
have been that which is proper to a mere
man, for multitudes of martyrs have gone
joyfully and courageously to the most fearful
deaths. Heb. v. 7 shows that the wrath of
God that was to judge Him as if He, and He
alone, were the only sinner that ever existed,
caused that agony. So His death was not
just a great example of resignation and self-
sacrifice, as multitudes vainly think.

The fact that Luke was a physician makes
most vivid the deep anguish of that agony
(v. 44).

" An angel " (v. 43). This being the
Gospel of the Man Christ Jesus, this statement, peculiar to Luke, is harmonious. The
angels also ministered to Him in the Temptation (Mark. i. 13).

" Sleeping for sorrow " (v. 45). Luke is
the only Evangelist who mentions this cause
of the Disciples being asleep.

" And healed him " (v. 51). This miracle
was exceptional. It was the healing of a
wound caused by violence ; it was worked on
an enemy ; it was unasked for ; there was no
faith expressed ; and no thankfulness.

Four downward steps that led to Peter's
fall were : (1) self-confidence ; (2) neglect
of prayer (v. 46) ; (3) vacillation,—he first
fought and then fled ; and (4) fellowship
with the world (v. 55).

Thus great back-slidings originate from
little side slippings.

Putting the several records together, it is
clear that the Lord was examined twice.
First, an informal night examination in the
palace of Annas and Caiaphas, and second,
a formal morning examination before Caia-
pas and the Sanhedrin. Peter's denial
occurred in their palace ; and it was most

reasonable that Caiaphas should repeat the same questions that Annas had previously put to the Lord.

If He had asked them questions (v. 68) that would have demonstrated His Messiahship they would not have answered them nor let Him go. This is the last occasion on which He called Himself " The Son of Man " (v. 69).

LUKE XXIII.—See notes on Matt. xxvii. and Mark xv.

" No fault " (v. 14) : Pilate, his wife, Herod, Judas Iscariot, the dying thief, and the centurion all testified to Christ's innocence. This is very valuable ; for had He been guilty of even one sin He could not have atoned for sin.

Verses 6-12 are peculiar to Luke.

" Unto Him " (v. 15), i.e., by Him.

" Cried " (v. 21), i.e., kept shouting.

Verses 27-31 are peculiar to Luke.

No woman is mentioned in the Gospels as having spoken against the Lord, or as having a share in His death. On the contrary He was anointed by a woman for His burial ; women were last at His grave and first at His sepulchre ; they ministered to His wants ; they bewailed and lamented Him ; Pilate's wife interceded for Him ; He first appeared to a woman after His resurrection ; and of a woman He was born.

The women of Jerusalem (v. 28) are to be distinguished from those from Galilee (v. 55).

" A green tree " (v. 31), i.e., the Lord. " The dry tree," i.e., the corrupt Hebrew Church.

The Gentiles, represented by Pilate and the soldiers, were indifferent and contemptuous to Christ, but the Jews regarded Him with bitter hatred. This is made plain in this third Gospel because it was written for the nations.

" Calvary " (v. 33) is Latin for the Hebrew word Golgotha ; both mean a skull.

" Father, forgive them " (v. 34). This is the last of the Lord's eight recorded prayers. The prayer surely included His Hebrew enemies as well as the Roman soldiers. Compare Acts iii. 17 and 1 Cor. ii. 8.

" He saved others " (v. 35). The insult that reproached Him for not saving Himself was replied to by Him in saving the thief. This was the purpose of His First Advent —not to set up an outward kingdom, but to save the vilest of sinners and bring them to Paradise.

The conversion of the thief (vs. 39-43) is peculiar to Luke. It is one of the most remarkable conversions in the Bible. The Holy Spirit in one flash of light revealed Christ to him and taught him of the Lord's future kingdom of glory, though at the moment He was hanging in shame and agony on the tree. The thief did not ask for any physical relief to his pain, but only for a remembrance in the future kingdom. They were in the same condemnation—he justly, but the Lord only as a sinner by imputation—and he prayed that they might be together in the same glory. So the precious blood, then flowing for his sins, cleansed him so effectually that it made him at that moment as fit to enter Paradise as Christ Himself. They both had the one title for entrance there (Heb. ix. 12 and x. 19).

The Divine nature of the thief's repentance was evidenced by six steps. (1) His concern about his companion (v. 40). (2) His confession of his own sinfulness (v. 41). (3) His confession of Christ's innocence (v. 41). (4) His faith in Christ's power and willingness to save him,—he called Him Lord, and declared his belief that He had a kingdom (v. 42). (5) He prayed to Him (v. 42). (6) He asked for no great thing but only to be remembered ; this was humility.

This short prayer embodied a great creed : (1) He believed his soul lived after death ; (2) that the world to come will be one of felicity or misery ; (3) that a crucified Jew was the Lord of Glory ; (4) that His future kingdom was better than this present world ; (5) that Christ intended to have pardoned sinners in that kingdom ; (6) that He would receive into it the truly penitent ; (7) that the key of that kingdom was hanging at Christ's girdle though He Himself was hanging naked on the tree ; and (8) that resting his soul for eternal salvation upon this dying Saviour, he had that kingdom assured to him. His intelligence exceeded that of all the Apostles prior to Pentecost.

Near the cross of the dying thief stood the Apostle John, the Virgin Mary, her sister, Mary the wife of Cleophas, Mary Magdalene and John's own mother, but to none of these exalted saints did the malefactor turn for help. He turned from them and prayed direct to Jesus, with nothing and nobody between his sin-stained soul and the sin-atoning Saviour. He did not cry " Oh, Holy mother of God !—Refuge of sinners, pray for

me ! I put my whole trust and confidence
in the power of thy intercession." Nor did
he appeal to her sister as being the holy aunt
of God, nor to John as being the beloved
Apostle of God. Had he trusted any one
of these great saints he must have perished,
for salvation is in Christ and in none other.
He is the one and only refuge of sinners (Acts
iv. 12):

The morning of that day the malefactor
walked the stone-floor of his dark dungeon
in a tumult of horror, and the evening of that
day he walked the golden street of the City
of Light in a tumult of joy !

"To-day " (v. 43). What speed ! " With
Me." What company ! " In Paradise."
What felicity !

Many think that as the Lord's soul went
that day into hell the expression " To-day "
intended the present " day " of grace which
precedes the coming " day " of the Kingdom.
But the Lord's spirit went to heaven ; for,
as man, He committed it to His Father
(v. 46). From thence He viewed His soul
in hell and His body in the tomb, and
confidently awaited the resurrection (Ps. xvi.
10 and 11.

The darkness over all the earth (v. 44)
i.e., over the land of Palestine, was miraculous
and not an eclipse, for the Passover was
always kept at the full moon when there cannot be an eclipse. This darkness was so deep
that it darkened the light of the sun (v. 45).

The loud triumphant shout (v. 46) was the
one Word, as in the Greek text, " Finished ! "
This mighty shout contradicts those who say
that He died a natural death from weakness.
It shews, on the contrary, that His death was
His own act ; " He offered Himself " (Heb.
ix. 14) ; He laid down His life and He took
it again. Such an action is not suicide.

" He gave up the ghost " (v. 46). The
Greek term here is different from Acts v. 10,
and from that used in the Greek translation
of the Old Testament in the five passages
where it is found. None of the Evangelists
say that Jesus " died " in the sense of being
the helpless victim of infirmity.

There were physical signs and wonders at
Sinai and also at Calvary (vs. 44-49 and
Matt. xxvii. 51-54). These signs solemnized
the beholders of the Crucifixion, and silenced
their railing and mocking.

The several actions detailed in verses
50-56 demonstrate the actual physical death
of Jesus.

LUKE XXIV.—See notes on Matt. xxviii.,
Mark xvii. and John xx. and xxi.

" Two men " (v. 4), i.e., possibly Moses and
Elijah. See Acts i. 10. They are prominent
in this Gospel.

" Lord Jesus " (v. 3). This is the first
occurrence of this full expression. It is His
resurrection Title, and occurs, about forty
times in the Epistles.

" The living " (v. 5). Better : " The
Living One."

" Must " (v. 7), because predicted in the
Scriptures.

" They remembered " (v. 8). Recollection
is more important than information.

" They told all these things," etc. (v. 9).
Women were the first preachers of the
Resurrection.

" Idle tales " (v. 11). The refusal of the
Apostles to believe the Lord's own statements, frequently repeated, that He would
rise from the dead, and their refusal to believe
the testimony of these five or six witnesses,
and of the Emmaus disciples (Mark xvi. 12
and 13), and their persistence in preaching
it everywhere after Pentecost, prove that
the resurrection was a fact, for if not a fact,
how could they confidently affirm to be true
that which they had steadfastly refused to
believe ?

" Peter " (v. 12) " arose," " ran,"
" stooped," " beheld," " departed," " wondered," but did not believe ; he was accompanied by John (John xx. 3). But the linen
clothes laid by themselves should have
convinced him that the Lord's body had not
been stolen. Read : " Now Peter had
arisen."

Verses 13-53 are peculiar to this Evangelist.
He Who walked on the road to Emmaus
was " this same Jesus " (Acts i. 11) but
" in another form " (Mark xvi. 12). It is
impossible to realize what were the powers of
the Lord's body after the Resurrection.
Compare John xx. 19.

Like Joseph's action with his brothers, so
the Lord did not discover Himself to these
two disciples until He had brought them into
a fitting condition of soul.

" Oh fools " (v. 25), i.e., " Oh men without
understanding ! " (v. 45).

" Ought not " (v. 26), i.e., was it not
necessary because predicted . This
emphasises the word " all " in verse 25.
They had confined their Bible reading to that
which the Scriptures promised respecting

the Messiah's glory and kingdom, but they had been blind to the multitude of types and prophecies fore-telling His sufferings as an atoning Saviour.

" Beginning at Moses," etc. (vs. 27 and 44). These are the three divisions of the Hebrew Bible. The Lord here makes two declarations respecting it : first, that it is the supreme authority as to Faith and Doctrine because inspired ; and second, its subject is the sufferings and glories of Christ—His sufferings as Sin-Bearer and His glories as Sin-Purger (Heb. i. 3, Phil ii. 5-11).

It may truly be said that Christ went into death Bible in hand, and that He came out from among the dead Bible in hand. He insisted that it predicted His death and resurrection in relation to sin and its judgment. So, immediately prior to His death and immediately subsequent to His resurrection, He made more than thirty quotations from the Inspired Word.

" He made as though," etc. (v. 28), i.e., He was simply going on—leaving them as naturally as He had joined them ; there was neither dissimilation nor deception.

" He took bread and blessed it " (v. 30). The Roman Catholic Church, and almost all people influenced by it, regard this meal as a celebration of what they call "The Lord's Supper." But it cannot be so, for there was no supper on this occasion, and the food was evidently left untasted on the table, for the disciples hurried back to Jerusalem. They rose up " the same hour " (v, 33), i.e., at that very moment.

Neither their testimony nor that of Simon Peter (vs. 33-35 with Mark xvi. 13), convinced the Disciples of the fact of the resurrection ; and, therefore, when the Lord Himself appeared (vs. 37-40) they were terrified and thought they saw a spirit !

The last time He saw them they were basely forsaking Him in the Garden, but His first words to them in resurrection were : " Peace be unto you ! " Amazing grace !

This grace was further demonstrated in His condescension to their doubts and reasonings (v. 38), by His invitation to handle Him (1 John i. 1), and by asking them for something to eat (vs. 41-43).

" They believed not for joy and were wondering " (v. 41). Such is man's poor heart. One day he believes not for sorrow, and the next he believes not for joy ! But He did not ask them to believe anything that was contrary to their senses. That which professes to be His Church demands, under pain of eternal damnation, belief in the fact of transubstantiation,—a belief which is contrary to the senses. There is much in revelation which is above fallen human reason ; but that is another matter.

If the apparition of a spirit terrifies and affrights men (v. 37) how great will be their terror at the apparition of the dread Judge of all spirits !

" Opened " (v. 45). The Bible is the only book in existence that can close itself to the reader. He Who wrote it can alone open it.

" Preaching " (v. 47) and " power " (v. 49) express the business and reveal the equipment of all followers of Christ both men, women and children.

" Beginning at Jerusalem " (v. 47). If the Jerusalem sinner can be saved then may all sinners be saved.

Bethany, with its hallowed and tender associations, was linked to heaven on the ascension day (v. 50).

His legacies in parting were the Holy Spirit and the Bible. The Spirit teaches through the Scriptures. These divorced, lead, on the one hand to mysticism, and on the other hand, to formalism. The Spirit teaches by and not without, or contrary to, the Holy Scriptures,

" Behold I send," etc. (v. 49). Only a Person can be sent, therefore the Holy Spirit is a Person, and Jesus is God and equal with the Father. All the three Persons of the Divine Trinity appear in this verse.

When last seen He had His hands outstretched in blessing. So Israel's High Priest, having made atonement, lifted up his hands and blessed the people. A beauteous figure of Him that was to come. Lev. ix. 22, 23.

" He was parted from them " (v. 51). He hastened to the cross (xii. 50) in order to atone for His people's sins, but He did not hasten to the glory, for He was reluctant to leave His beloved sheep.

In all, there are twelve appearances recorded of Him after He arose from the dead :

1. To Mary Magdalene (John xx. 14).

2. To the women (Matt. xxviii. 9).

3. To Simon Peter (Luke xxiv. 34).

4. To the two Disciples (Luke xxiv. 13).

5. To all the Disciples (John xx. 19).

6. To the Disciples a second time (John xx. 26. and 1. Cor. xv. 5).

7. To the seven Apostles (John xxi. 1).

8. To the Eleven (Matt. xxviii. 16).

9. To above five hundred brethren (1 Cor. xv. 6).

10. To James (1 Cor. xv. 7).

11. To all the Apostles (Luke xxiv. 51).

12. To Paul (1 Cor. xv. 8).

JOHN

The Holy Spirit in the three prior Books cried: "Behold your King!" (Matthew), "Behold your Prophet!" (Mark), and "Behold your Priest!" (Luke), but in this fourth Book He cries: "Behold your God!" (Isa. xl. 9); for His purpose in this Gospel is to present the Lord Jesus as God.

Thus this Gospel is necessarily distinct from the other three. They present His perfect humanity, and are called Synoptic because of this common purpose.

This fundamental distinction between the first three Gospels and the fourth demands the many differences in literary style, and in other features peculiar to this book.

This is why such matters as the Temptation in the Wilderness and the agony in the Garden, etc., are omitted because out of harmony with the purpose of the book.

For a similar reason the Transfiguration is omitted; for that concerned His physical glory, whilst the great subject of this fourth book is His moral glory.

In this Gospel His Person is presented rather than His actions; and Jerusalem is the centre rather than Galilee, as in the other three.

Words, and terms, and incidents revealing His attributes as God are peculiar, therefore, to John, as distinguished from the other Evangelists. Hence they form a group apart by themselves. In them the Lord is presented as "praying" to the Father; in this Gospel as "speaking" to Him. In the Synoptic Books, His praying on eight occasions is recorded, but not once is He so presented in John's Gospel—a different Greek word is used signifying familiarity and equality. Moreover in this Gospel alone He "lays down" His life—no one takes it from Him (John x. 17).

In the other Gospels miracles are called "powers" and "wonders," in John they are always called "signs" (Greek). There are eight of these "signs." They had a Divine order, as appears from ii. 11 and iv. 54. They were all designed to manifest forth His personal glory. Compare ii. 11 with xxi. 14.

These "signs" correspond thus; The marriage in Cana (ii. 1) and the draught of fishes (xxi. 1), i.e., the 1st and the 8th.

The ruler's son (iv. 46) and the sister's brother (xi. 1), i.e., the 2nd and the 7th.

The impotent man (v. 1) and the man born blind (ix. 1), i.e., the 3rd and the 6th.

The feeding of the Five Thousand (vi. 1) and the walking on the sea (vi. 15), i.e., the 4th and the 5th.

In the Synoptic Gospels Israel is Ammi; in the Fourth Gospel, Lo-Ammi. It was written after the destruction of Jerusalem and the Temple. (See notes on ii. 4.)

JOHN I. 1-28.—As speech reveals mind so Jesus as the Word reveals God. But to reveal God He must Himself be God, for only God could reveal God. His God-head is, therefore, the great theme of this Gospel (v. 1). The Book deals mainly with His Personality —what He is in Himself. He was ever-existing ("was"), He had a personal existence for He was with God; but He was not another Being, for He was Himself God. In His existence eternal, in His Person distinct, in His Nature Divine, so that His Personality was not of time, for prior to Creation He was with God (xvii. 5, Heb. i. 2, and Col. i. 17). Thus He existed before the world began to exist; and this existence—being a conscious personal one as distinct from the Father— necessitated His Personal Glory as Son of God; and so, being God, that relationship was in its nature eternal. "The same" (v. 2), i.e., this very Person, was in eternity with God. The Holy Spirit emphasises this in order to declare His eternal relationship as the Son with the Father.

The Word is a Person. Hence the term "Him" (vs. 3 and 4) and not "it."

All things came into being through Him, and without Him not one single thing came into being. This denies the theory of the eternity of matter which was held by all the thinking men of the ancient world, and is to-day affirmed by some scientists.

An absolute distinction, therefore, exists between Jesus and Creation. It came into being through Him. He did not begin to exist. Creation does not exist in Him—Life exists in Him (v. 4), and this brought Him into relation with an especial part of Creation —Man with whom was all His delight.

This Life was the Light of men, enlightening man as to God and holiness and wisdom and happiness. "The Light" (v. 5) shone in the moral darkness of this world. The darkness remained darkness, for it did not apprehend, i.e. receive, the Light. Blinded man made another god of the darkness.

Such are the relations of Jesus as the Word of God with Creation and with man.

Thus the Spirit, over-stepping all that intervened, presents Jesus on the earth as Him Who existed before the world was, and witnesses to Him, through John the Baptist (vs. 7 and 8), as shining not for the Hebrew Church only but for all men.

He was the True Light Who coming into the world enlightens all men without distinction (v. 9, R.V.).

He came as the Heir (Matt. xxi. 38) unto His own possessions (vs. 10 and 11), but His own servants did not receive Him; on the contrary, they killed Him.

But as many as did receive Him these became by His power and authority children of God (v. 12). To believe upon Him is to receive Him.

Men become God's children not by natural birth-(blood) nor by personal resolution (flesh) nor by priestly action (will), but by faith in Christ Jesus (Gal. iii. 26).

Verse 9 is collective; verse 12, individual.

In this Gospel the Greek word for "son" is mainly restricted to Christ, and the Greek term for "children" applied to believers. Jesus is the Son of God; He is never said in the Scriptures to have become such. The term "begotten" relates to resurrection.

"And the Word became flesh" (v. 14), i.e., clothed Himself with humanity and dwelt amongst men as in a tabernacle of flesh, full of grace and truth. So the word "flesh" declares His humanity and the word "full" His Deity, for only God is full of grace and truth; and the glory in which He was seen was that of an only Son with the Father, the one sole object of the Father's delight.

Such are the two glories displayed in these opening verses—His glory as the Word Who was with God in eternity, and His glory on earth as the only Son of the Father.

Those who were born not of Man's will but of God's will (v. 13), received Him; but it was the grace that filled Him that led them to receive Him.

Thus is seen not only what the Word was, but what He became.

There is no pedigree in this Gospel, for how could Deity have a pedigree? In Mark there is also no pedigree, for a servant needs none; he only needs a character.

He "became flesh," and His moral glory was the very image of God. Man departed from God and lost His image. So the Image of God came to dwell in man in order that man might dwell in God.

There are many distinctive words peculiar to this Evangelist, such as "light," "life," "love," "truth," "flesh," "witness," "world," "know," etc., and "the Father," "My Father," (156 times), but never "Our Father," and the reason for this is evident.

John the Baptist was the greatest of all the prophets, for to him was given the peculiar honour of being the fore-runner of the Messiah, and the witnesser to His Person and Work. He was a man sent from God (v. 6), and was a burning and shining "lamp" (v. 35, R.V.). Jesus was a Man sent from God (v. 30), Himself God (1 Tim. ii. 5). He was not a mere lamp;—He was the Light (viii. 12). John was "a voice"; Jesus was "The Word." A voice is sound; the Word, substance. The Word abides; the voice passes away.

John's testimony in the first three Gospels mainly concerned Christ's earthly relationships, but in this Gospel, His heavenly relationships. He testified to the eternity of His Being (v. 15); the fulness of His Deity (v. 34); and the sufficiency of His atonement (v. 29). The Lord Jesus declared that his testimony was true (ch. v. 32).

"Preferred" (v. 15), i.e., existed. See verses 27 and 30.

"Grace for grace" (v. 16), i.e., grace upon grace—the provisions of His love heaped one upon another in the supply of His people's needs. Not truth upon truth, but grace upon grace; for truth is simple and declarative, while grace is manifold (1 Pet. iv. 10) and executive.

The Law was "given," but grace and

truth " came " (v. 17). The Law manifested man—full of wickedness ; the Son manifested God—full of goodness. The Law demands from man the righteousness which he cannot furnish ; Grace gives to man the righteousness which he needs. Christ is both grace and truth ; for if grace were not in Him He would not be the truth ; and He " gives " grace and glory.

" Which is " (v. 18), i.e., Who exists, and ever existed. This is one of the many statements in the Scriptures asserting the eternal sonship of Christ.

" Declared " (v. 18), i.e., revealed, or unveiled.

" Record " (v. 19), i.e., witness.

" That prophet " (v. 21), i.e., the Prophet of Deut. xviii. 18 and Acts iii. 22, 23.

" Why baptizest Thou then ? " (v. 25), i.e., why do you attach disciples to yourself ? John replied that he only baptized with water, (v. 26), and that it was but a temporary symbol of the true, abiding, and effectual baptism of One who would baptize with the Holy Spirit (v. 33).

Verse 23 may read : " I am [he of whom it is written] the voice of one crying in the wilderness," etc.

Verse 9 does not concern the entrance of children into the world but the entrance of one particular Child. He was the Great Light in His birth, and, as such, shone " upon "—not within—every man. If this latter were true there would be no need for the New Birth. See notes on Isa. ix. 1-7.

The shepherds saw a babe ; the Magi, a child ; the Scribes, a boy ; the Nazarites, a carpenter ; and the Greeks, a street-preacher But Isaiah saw His glory (John xii. 21 with 41), as did aged Simeon (Luke ii. 32), and all whose eyes were opened by faith. He was the God of glory and the Great Light when in the manger as when on the Mount (Matt. xvii. 2), and the shepherds and the magi worshipped Him as such.

JOHN I. 29-II. 11.—" The next day " (v.29); " again the next day " (v. 35) ; " and on that third day " (ch. ii. 1. Greek) " the day following " (v. 43). These three days, and their events, form the subject of this section of the Gospel by John.

The " wine " of the first day was good, (v. 29), that of the second day (v. 36) better, but that of the third day (ch. ii. 10) was the best wine.

The first day—the Lamb of God in redemption (v. 29) ; the second day—the Son of God in resurrection (v. 34 and Ps. ii.) ; the third day—the Glory of God in manifestation (ii. 11).

The wine of the first day is the joy of forgiveness through Him ; the wine of the second day is the joy of meditation on Him ; and the wine of the third day will be the joy of sinless union with Him.

Deep is the joy caused by the knowledge of forgiveness of sins through the sacrifice that He perfected as the Lamb of God on the altar of Calvary ; deeper is the joy that results from a knowledge of what He is in Himself—the unsearchable riches of grace and love and pity and power dwelling in Him in infinite fulness and displaying themselves in His offices and ministries ; but deepest will be the joy resulting from fellowship with Him and likeness to Him in His future glory. In that third day the believer will exclaim : " Lord, the wine of the first day was good ; that of the second was better ; but thou hast kept the best wine until now ! "

" Coming unto Him " (v. 29), probably after the Temptation.

" Taketh away " : Greek, " takes up and bears away " (Lev. iv. and 2 Cor. v. 21).

" A man existing before me " (v. 30). This testimony affirms the actual Humanity and the essential Deity of Jesus of Nazareth.

" I knew Him not " (v. 31). This statement seems to conflict with Matt. iii. 14. There is no conflict. The Baptist had been told by God (v. 33), that one day a Man would present himself for baptism upon Whom would descend and abide the Holy Spirit, thus declaring Him to be God manifest in the flesh. When Jesus came amongst other men John knew Him as his cousin, and, perhaps, as Son of David, but certainly as a man of exceptional sanctity of life. So quite naturally he said that it were more befitting for Jesus to baptize him. The language in Matt. iii. 14, goes no further then this. Taught, however, by the Holy Spirit the Baptist declared what must have filled him with amazement, that his cousin was Jehovah, and that he was His Forerunner.

So he testified that He was the Lamb of God and the Son of God ; and the Lord Jesus said that this testimony to Atonement and Deity was true (ch. v. 32).

" No man can say that Jesus is Jehovah

but by the Holy Spirit" (1 Cor. xii. 3). Therefore neither the Baptist nor Simon Peter (compare v. 41 and Matt. xvi. 17) could recognise Jesus as Jehovah till thus illuminated; though they might recognise Him as the Messiah of Jewish expectation, and "after the flesh" (2 Cor. v. 16).

John was standing, and fastening his gaze upon his cousin as He walked, he exclaimed to himself, aloud, with awe and wonder: "Behold the Lamb of God!" The prior day (v. 29) he drew attention to the value of His work, but this day to the dignity of His Person. Thus the Baptist preached the Gospel, and presented an atoning God and Saviour to perishing men.

"Two Disciples" (v. 37), Andrew, and, no doubt, John.

"What seek ye" (v. 38). These are the Lord's first words in this Gospel. His second words were "come and see" (v. 39).

"The tenth hour" (v. 39), i.e., four p.m.

Andrew was a soul-winner—a sign of true conversion. He had to look for and then to bring (vs. 41 and 42) his brother Simon to Jesus.

"Jesus beheld him" (v. 42). That look saved Peter, and the "look" of Luke xxii. 61, secured him.

Jesus said: "Thou art Simon, thou shalt be Peter." This ability to change men fundamentally and characteristically—or rather to re-create men—abides still; as many prove to their joy.

The basis of God's first relationship to the earth was that of innocence. Sin destroyed that foundation. The Lamb of God— the Lamb Whom God alone could furnish— took away the sin of the world, and in doing so established a new foundation, the eternal basis of God's present relations with both heaven and earth.

These men (vs. 35-42) only recognised Jesus as the Messiah. Their knowledge of Him was imperfect; but His knowledge of them was perfect.

The morning of "the third day" (vs. 43 and ii. 1) was occupied by the calling of Philip and Nathanael, and its evening by the marriage feast. The first great day of the millennial kingdom, which itself will be the "third day," will present like features.

Andrew found Simon (v. 41), Philip found Nathanael (v. 45), and, between these, Jesus found Philip (v. 43).

So is it to-day, some are won to the Kingdom by human instrumentality, others by direct Divine action.

Philip made many mistakes in his testimony to Nathanael, but his heart was true, and so he won his friend for Jesus. This is an encouragement to all who seek to be soul-winners.

Nathanael, as suggested by verses 48-51, was an intelligent Bible student, and, no doubt, a disciple of John the Baptist, for all godly and guileless Israelites had been baptized by him. In effect he must have said to Philip (v. 46):—there is no such person as Jesus the son of Joseph, and no such place as Nazareth mentioned in either Moses or the Prophets. Philip could not solve these difficulties, but he could show Nathanael how to get rid of them, and so he said: "Come and see" (v. 46).

Nathanael was surprised that Jesus knew him (v. 48); and then, overwhelmed by the Lord's added words (v. 48), he exclaimed: "Thou art the Son of God; Thou art the King of Israel!"

This confession reveals what must have been the exercises and emotions of Nathanael's heart, when sitting under the fig-tree.

Having believed upon such slender evidence, greater things were promised to him (v. 51). He should learn in the future "third day" that the whole of Heaven's interest is set upon Jesus as the Son of Man; and that He, as such, will be the Divine link uniting Heaven with earth, and making both one in bliss and blessing. At the moment, like Jacob who typified Him (see note on Gen. xxviii. 12), He was an outcast, but all the angels were busied in ministering to Him. This will be manifested in "the third day" of His glory (ii. 11).

So here the Spirit groups His titles as the Word, as the Life, as the Light, as the Only-Begotten, as the Messiah, as the Prophet, as the Lamb of God, as the Man, as the Son of God, as Jesus, as the king of Israel, and as the Son of Man.

The Lord's solemn "Verily, verily" occurs twenty-five times in this Gospel.

Thus the Lord commenced His ministry by winning five young men in four and twenty hours.

Faith may be feeble and intelligence defective (v. 45), yet the reception of Jesus is the reception of all that He is. This is a fact of the greatest interest and consolation. At the dawn of the Christian life He may be believed upon as a Saviour that forgives sins, and delivers from the wrath to come ; but in response to that limited faith He gives Himself to the believer in all His plenitude as God and Saviour.

Two great principles appear in verses 38 and 43—The Centre 'and the Path. There is but one Centre of gathering in the world— Christ. No prophet or servant of God could claim, or ever did claim, to be such. Christ is the One Divine Centre around which His people gather. He accepted this place. The world was under sentence of death and without God. The Election was to be taken out of 'it and gathered around Him Who was the object of God's perfect affection. Next, He pointed out the path in which the redeemed were to walk—" Follow Me." Man needed no path in Eden, for all was innocence ; but in a world of sin there can be no rest ; so Christ gives a Divinely ordered path out of it. In Heaven there will be no path. It will be a realm of perfect peace and rest because there will be no sin there.

" On that third day " there was a marriage feast, and the poor water of man's provision was changed into the rich wine of God's providing. All that man had to do was to fill the water pots with water up to the brim— changing the water into wine belonged to Immanuel. This is a fact of great encouargement to ministers of the Gospel.

So the Millennial Kingdom will be the Father's house of wine ; and the joy of that house will be the joy and love of an eternal marriage feast.

Four hundred and fifty years had now elapsed since the last public miracle of the Old Testament. It was that of Daniel vi.

" Was there " (v. 1), i.e., was already there ; occupying a position distinct from Jesus and His Disciples (v. 2), who were only at the moment invited to the marriage. (See Greek tense). Mary never identified herself with Jesus and His Disciples until Acts i. 14.

Many point to this incident in support of the doctrine of the value of the intercession of the Virgin. The facts here recorded destroy that doctrine. It is evident (v. 5) that the servants had engaged Mary to pray for them. She did so, and was met with the rebuke " What have I to do with thee " (v. 4). This formula occurs eight times in the Scriptures—2 Sam. xvi.

10, xix. 22, 1 Kings xvii. 18, 2 Kings iii. 13, Matt. viii. 29, Mark i. 24, Luke iv. 34, and here verse 4. An examination of these passages proves that the answer is " Nothing." In every instance the contrast is between the carnal nature, which is sinful, and the Holy Spirit. The Spiritual Kingdom has no contact with the carnal. There is an impassable abyss between them. There could, therefore, be no union between the sinless nature of Christ and the sinful nature of Mary. Nor could He admit her authority. This is declared in the words " mine hour is not yet come." That is, " The moment for me to act will be revealed by My Father, and His voice is the only one that I hearken to." (See notes on 1 Kings xvii. 18).

Mary with great intelligence recognised her error, stepped at once aside from between these needy people and the Almighty Giver of every good and perfect gift, telling the servants to turn from her to Him, and when she was out of the way, He spoke directly to them, and, in a moment, the water was wine ! So long as she stood between Jesus and these needy sinners there was no wine !

" This beginning of signs " (v. 11, R.V.). This statement destroys the traditional miracles said to have been wrought by the boy Jesus.

Mary here represents Israel. The Messiah was born of that nation, but because of unbelief she became Lo-Ammi, and hence He refused to recognise her. But in xix. 26, He committed her, as again represented by His mother, to the Apostles as personated by John, who was to tarry till He came (xxi. 23) ; and the Apocalypse reveals John still in connection with Israel (xii. 1-5) ; and she is finally pictured as a glorious city, set upon twelve foundations, bearing the names of the Twelve Apostles of the Lamb. But the Apostle Paul's name will not be there. No longer Lo-Ammi but Ammi, she will be recognised by Jesus as His mother. It was when Mary looked upon Him as pierced that she fully believed ; and she in this symbolizes the nation when it will look upon Him as pierced, and will repent (see concluding note in the Introduction).

Whether these men learned the lesson permanently that the Lord Jesus is to be appealed to directly and not through an intermediary, is more than doubtful, for to this day man has not learned it, and so millions pray to the virgin, although she is dead. The fellowship prayer of believers is quite another matter.

Thus this Gospel opens by presenting the Son of God moving along the path to the Father's house and gathering around Him as He moves a company of redeemed sinners. The Book closes by presenting the same group, upon the same path, and journeying together to the same home. There is no separation.

JOHN II. 12-22. "Not many days" (v. 12) for "the Passover was at hand" (v. 13). It had been Jehovah's Passover but corruption had proceeded apace and it was now "the Jews' passover."

This was the Lord's first cleansing of the Temple (vs. 14-16). The second and last cleansing was that of Matt. xxi. 12. Here He was a Son over His Father's House; in Luke ii. 46 He was a Son in His Father's House. It ceased to be such on His leaving it (Matt. xxiii. 38 and xxiv. 1).

"It was written" (v. 17). Compare vi. 31, 45, viii. 17, x. 34, and xii. 14.

The quotation was from Psalm lxix. See chs. xv. 25, xix. 28, Acts i. 20, Rom. xi. 9 and 10 and xv. 3. Messiah is the Author and the Subject of the Book of the Psalms.

The words "that Thou art the Messiah," may be supplied after the word "us" in verse 18.

His enemies remembered His words (v. 19) and perverted them; His disciples remembered them and profited by them (v. 22).

"The Scripture" (v. 22). This term occurs twelve times in this Book: Here; v. 39; vii. 38 and 42; x. 35; xiii. 18; xvii. 12; xix. 24, 28, 36 and 37; and xx. 9.

Compare "believed on Him" (v. 11) with "They believed the Scripture and the word which Jesus had said (v. 22). A divine faith is based upon the Scriptures.

Chapter ii.: The kingdom.
Chapter iii: Its door.

JOHN II. 23-III. 21. Entrance into the human family is by natural birth, and into the Divine family by spiritual birth. As it is impossible to enter the human family except by birth, so is it impossible to enter the Divine family. This is the great doctrine of this section.

Many seeing the miracles (v. 23) believed upon him. This was "a reasonable faith," based upon evidence, and involving no consciousness of sin and its eternal doom. It was consequently a worthless faith. Jesus as God, knew that, and did not, therefore, believe in them. The terms "believed" (v. 23) and "commit" (v. 24) are translations of the one Greek word; and the repetition of the word "man" is important. There should be no break between ii. 25 and iii. 1.

For He knew all "men", and needed not that any should testify of "man," for He knew what was in "man;" there was a "man" of the Pharisees—one of the men who seeing the miracles was convinced by them; but he and the other carnal believers, remained in a moral night; and so appropriately by night he came to have a religious interview with Jesus.

Christ's knowledge as God was universal (v. 24) and individual (vs. 25 and iii. 1). This attribute is only true of God (Jer. xvii. 10 and xx. 12). His omniscience (v. 24), His omnipotence (vi. 6), His omnipresence (Matt. xviii. 20) prove that He is God.

Man demands a reasonable faith, based on evidence and scientific demonstration. The way of life preached to Nicodemus must, therefore, be unacceptable to them (v. 14), for how could looking at a piece of brass heal disease? Brass contains no healing properties discoverable by science. And how could a look to the Saviour on Calvary's tree effect a new birth? Both are impossible to the fallen intelligence of sinful man.

Christ at once raised the moral question with Nicodemus. He immediately stopped a religious discussion by telling this most religious man and professed believer (vs. 1 and 10) that he was so sinful, so hopelessly corrupt and fallen, as to be incapable of reformation, and so darkened morally that he could neither recognise nor experience spiritual phenomena (vs. 3 and 5) unless born from above. This fundamental truth is obnoxious to man, for it humbles him.

The Lord here unveiled what man really is. He is a sinner, having responsibility but no life. He is lost, and must seek life and pardon outside of himself, that is, in Christ, Who meets his failure in responsibility and gives him eternal life.

An evidential faith (v. 23) has no power to conquer man's will or alter his nature. These persons when their faith was tested, either forsook him (vi. 66), or shouted "Crucify Him" (xix. 15). He fore-knew all this ; but that did not chill His love, for the strength of that love was in itself.

"A master of Israel" (v. 10) Greek: "The (famous) teacher of Israel."

"We speak" (v. 11). Compare "we know" (v. 2).

"Ye receive not" (v. 11), i.e., Ye believe not. Compare i. 12.

"I told you earthly things" (v. 12), i.e., Jesus spoke to him every time he read the Scriptures, but Nicodemus was so blind that he did not see nor believe its lessons. Its earthly types and events had no spiritual meaning for his heart or conscience. So is it with multitudes of professing Christian people to-day.

He had thus spoken to Nicodemus from heaven ; and He was the One and only Teacher Who could reveal heavenly truth, for He came from heaven,and He dwelt there.

Enoch and Elijah did not ascend up to heaven ; they were "taken up." Only Deity could ascend up.

The Lord then (v. 14) recalled one of the "earthly things"; and opened its spiritual message. He likened Nicodemus to the dying Israelite, teaching him that the look of faith to a crucified Messiah—not the look of admiration at a Miracle-Worker—would bring healing and life to his sinful soul, as the look of faith at the brazen serpent brought health and life to the dying Israelite. So soon as the consciously guilty sinner thus entrusts himself to a crucified and atoning Saviour, the Holy Spirit operates the great miracle of the New Birth, and the life then received is an everlasting life.

"Whosoever should not perish" (vs. 15 and 16), therefore all are perishing whether moral or immoral.

The object of Christ's mission was to save (v. 17), but the issue to those who reject Him must and can only be condemnation (v. 18).

"The light "—" the darkness" (v. 19).

The Lord then dismissed Nicodemus with a keen thrust of the sharp sword, saying to him that evil-doers chose the darkness, so why did he, a Pharisee, come by night ?

Many believe they are "born from above" and become members of the family of God at the moment of baptism. They base this belief upon the word "born of water" (v. 5). But Jesus spoke of this water to the Samaritan woman and He invited her to drink it (iv. 10). It is spiritual, living

water—the Word of God (1 Pet. i. 23). This living word brings a new life into the soul. Baptism never does nor can do that. Nicodemus had often read of this in Ezekiel xxxvi.; but to him it was only an "earthly thing."

So the whole of this section brings forward the fundamental fact of sin ; its doom ; the hopeless moral condition of the sinner ; the one and only door of salvation through a crucified and atoning Saviour ; the necessity of the New Birth ; and the fact that that birth takes place when the sinner entrusts himself to Jesus as a Saviour.

"Kingdom of God" (vs. 3 and 5). This is the only time this expression occurs in this Gospel.

"Hath ascended" (v. 13): the fact assumed because certain—a Hebraism.

"Must" (v. 14), because of sin—for only Christ's death could expiate it—and because predicted. The word therefore affirms inspiration, for prophecy, if human, carries no necessity of fulfilment. Hence Christ "must" be lifted up (v. 14), and man "must" be born again (v. 3).

Nicodemus began with a self-sufficient "we know" (v. 2), but he had in a moment to confess that he knew nothing (vs. 4 and 9). The Samaritan said "I know." Jesus said "If thou knewest."

John's baptism and Christ's miracles were doubtless amongst the "earthly" things (vs. 12 and 31) of which, and through which, Christ spoke to Nicodemus, for they were visible and physical, and, therefore, of the earth. But though he submitted to the one and admired the other, he had not believed as a conscious sinner upon a sin-atoning Saviour ; and any other faith than this is not a saving faith producing a new moral birth.

The absence of the article in verse 5, before the nouns "water" and "spirit" shows that one thing only is meant ; and this is made clear in verses 6 and 8 where, the Spirit alone is mentioned. This declaration by the Lord destroys the human doctrine of baptismal regeneration.

John iii. 16 should be read with 1 John iii. 16. See notes on that chapter.

JOHN III. 22-36. "Much water" (v. 23), should read "many springs."

"Purifying" (v. 25), i.e., baptism.

John baptizing on the one hand and Jesus baptizing on the other, enabled the Pharisees (iv. 1), through their spokesman (v. 25), prompted no doubt by Satan, to raise a dissension as to the moral and religious value of these two baptisms. The Pharisees by hinting that they were in rivalry, could excuse themselves from submitting to either. But John enrolled disciples in order to pass them on to Jesus, for he declared that he was not the Messiah, that he was only the friend of the Divine Bridegroom, that he rejoiced greatly at hearing of His fame (v. 29); and was satisfied that all his disciples were leaving him and going to Jesus (v. 30). This was one of the noblest and most affecting utterances that ever came from the lips of man.

" Receive " (v. 27), i.e., assume nothing successfully unless it were given him from heaven.

The Messiah was from heaven (v. 31); He spoke of what He had there seen and heard (v. 32); His words were the words of God (v. 34); and He was indwelt by the fulness of the Godhead.

" Yet no man " (v. 32), i.e., the Hebrew Church did not believe Him ; but every individual who did believe Him set his seal to this (v. 33, R.V.), that all that God had predicted concerning Him was true; and that the Father loved Him (v. 35); and, because of that, had given all things into His hand (Matt. xi. 27).

The consequences of all this for man were eternal. Whoever believed on that Saviour obtained the life that is everlasting; he who rejected Him brought upon himself a wrath that is ever abiding (v. 36). Thus John the Baptist preached the Gospel. He told men of the love of God and of the wrath of God. He pointed to the blood of Christ for their sins or the lake of fire in their sins (Matt iii. 7, 10, 12, and ch. i. 29).—and Christ said his testimony was true, (John v. 32); and he declared that simple trust in that Saviour made absolute eternal felicity (v. 36.)

His doctrine, therefore, conflicts with the theory that there neither was, nor is, anything between God and sinners which needed to be removed by the death of Christ.

There are two Greek words for " wrath," one signifying temporary wrath and the other, permanent wrath. The latter is the word used here.

Jesus left Judea at once and so put an end to the controversy (iv. 3).

JOHN IV. Jehovah and Jesus were not two Persons but One. The first title— Lord, i.e. Jehovah, reveals His absolute Deity ; the second, His perfect Humanity. The term " knew " declares His omniscience. Compare ii. 25.

" He left Judea " (v. 3). See last note on prior chapter.

The scene at Sychar's well is one of the most amazing in human history. The dread Judge of quick and dead and one of the vilest of sinners are met together. But He is there not to condemn her but to seek and to save her. The Mighty God, the Everlasting Father, the Prince of Peace, was sitting weary by a well and thirsty, but had no means even to quench His thirst. He, as man, was dependent on an outcast woman for a little water. His grace and love, rejected by Israel, now pour out their fulness upon an impure Samaritan—for love is pained unless enabled to act. The flood-gates of grace lifted themselves up to bless the misery which love pitied. Man's heart, withered with self-righteousness, cannot understand this. Thus sinners respond to the grace which Pharisees proudly refuse ; for grace flows in the deep channels dug by sin and misery.

So these two isolated hearts met—His, isolated by holiness, for He was separate from sinners, hers, by sin, for she was separate from society—and this encounter of holiness and sinfulness resulted in the salvation of the sinner, for Jesus is " the Saviour " (v. 42).

He was the pattern Soul-winner. With Divine skill He led this defiled woman by five steps into the Kingdom of God. These steps were : Contact (v. 7) ; Interest (v. 10) ; Conscience (v. 16) ; Holiness (v. 24) ; Revelation (v. 26).

He disarmed suspicion, opposition and hostility, and won sympathy and confidence and faith, by asking for a drink of water. This was the point of contact. It touched her nature as a woman—for it was the appeal of need—and to that appeal a woman's nature responds. This tender word " woman " occurs thirteen times in this incident. The number thirteen is a happy one for believers. At the thirteenth circuit the walls of Jericho fell down, and " in the thirteenth year " Abraham won his great victory.

To arouse interest in the heart should be the object of a preacher ; and to offer a gift deepens that interest. To be relieved from thirst and from the toil and suffering of fetching water in the fierce heat of the Syrian sun, excited the woman's heart. Ashamed to come with the other women in the cool of the morning to draw water, she was obliged to come alone in the burning heat of the mid-day sun. As with Nicodemus so with the Samaritan, the Lord hastened to raise the question of sin in the conscience. Nicodemus was highly moral and the Samaritan grossly immoral yet was there no difference between them ;—both were sinners needing cleansing and salvation. But how different was the Lord's method with each of them ! The moralist was at once met with the abrupt words " You must be born again," but to the sinner He said : " Give me to drink ! "

A profession of faith in Christ which ignores the question of sin, the holiness of God, the spirituality of worship as distinct from sacerdotal ceremonies, the need of pardon, and the condition of trust in an atoning and revealed Saviour—such a profession is worthless.

As to-day so then the sinner tried by a proposed religious discussion about churches to put aside the matter of her shameless life, but Jesus gently and courteously explained to her that the true way of salvation had been revealed to the Hebrew Church (v. 22) ; and that the true place of worship was the heart and not either Geriazim or Jerusalem, for God is Spirit and Truth. Worship, therefore, must be spiritual, and must be in subjection to the Word of God.

The Holy Spirit seeks pupils (xvi. 13-15) ; the Father seeks worshippers (v. 23) ; and the Son seeks sinners (Luke xix. 10).

The woman now (v. 25) arrives at the point :—A Redeemer is promised ; everything will depend upon Him ; " He will tell us all things " ; and He will be the Saviour (v. 42). Jesus said to her " I am He ! "—and she was saved in and by that revelation (Matt. xi. 27) ; for intelligence in Divine things comes by conscience and revelation and not by intellect.

For the names of the five " husbands " See notes on 2 Kings xvii. The God of " our father Jacob " was the sixth—but not in truth in her case.

Thus the Holy Spirit as the Living Water quickens the sinner (Nicodemus) and indwells the believer (The Samaritan). The water that flows from the Smitten Rock becomes when drunk an internal fountain perpetually springing up in a life that is everlasting. Such was the life into which Nicodemus and the Samaritan entered. Merit in the one case did not admit into that life, and demerit in the other did not exclude from it.

There are different Greek words for the " well " of verse 6 and the " well " of verse 14. The latter means a spring or fountain ; the former, a dug-out well.

" Marvelled " (v. 27). The Talmud forbade a Rabbi to speak to a woman much more to a Samaritan ; and certainly not to a woman of such moral character.

The Disciples wondered that He talked with her—they should rather have wondered that He talked with them ! But they were too insensible to their own sinfulness.

The action of the woman in leaving her water-pot (v. 28) and becoming an unconscious preacher (v. 29), demonstrates the death of self, and the occupation of the heart with Jesus and His grace and goodness. So overwhelming was her consciousness of His Person and His action that it, in a sense, annihilated the consciousness of her own sinfulness. Christ Himself filled all her world. So a woman became the first preacher of the Gospel to the Gentile nations ; and so effective was her preaching that it caused a revival. She became a vessel to receive and then to minister the gift of life.

The disciples went into Sychar for food and they got it ; the woman went for souls and she got them. People usually get what they go for.

The insensibility of the disciples to spiritual realities is again evidenced in verses 31-38. His " meat " and His " harvest " were the Samaritans who at that moment were leaving the city and coming to Him and believing on Him (vs. 30 and 39). As they pressed in a great crowd along the road from the city to the well, they were to the Lord's heart—saddened by the unbelief and rejection of Israel—a white harvest (v. 35).

" Sent," " entered " (v. 38) are Hebraisms for " I purpose to send," and " ye shall enter " ; for so sure of fulfilment was their Apostolate and its success, that all is here contemplated as accomplished fact. This is the language of faith ; and it is peculiar to the Bible.

" Other men " (v. 38), i.e., the Hebrew Prophets, including John the Baptist.

" Many believed " (vs. 39 and 41). This is a unique instance in the Gospels of a true moral revival on a large scale produced by preaching apart from miracles. The Preachers were the Samaritan and the Messiah. Her ministry was the more remarkable because, apparently, she was unordained. She went without being sent. She was a volunteer preacher. But the Holy Spirit often ordains, and equips and sends forth without outward appointment; and so her action was a beautiful instance of the energy of the Spirit in making men and women unintentional preachers.

As the " Saviour of the World " (v. 42)—not as the Messiah of Israel—the Samaritans could believe upon Him for life and righteousness, and be received and blessed.

" After," i.e., the two days of verse 40 (v. 43, R.V.).

" His own country " (v. 44). As Son of David His own country was Judea. " The poor of the flock "—a few despised Galileans—were the " wages " (v. 36) which the Father's will planned for Him.

The Galileans believed because they saw His miracles (v. 45), and the nobleman, because He verified His word (v. 53); but feeble as their faith might be, He, obedient to His Father's will, acted in grace and power whenever He met faith however poor.

But the feeble faith of these people is here contrasted with the richer faith of the Samaritans who believed upon Him without any demonstration of miraculous action.

Such was the condition of Israel—little faith and no joy; but in these first two " signs " He brought back the boy from the very mouth of death, and He filled the house at Cana with joy by turning the water into wine. All this is symbolic of His future action in regard to Israel when at the point of extinction (Zech. xiv. and Rev. xix.). Meanwhile He is passing through " Samaria," and, without outward miraculous signs, reaps a harvest of elect souls for Himself.

" Ye " (v. 48), i.e., " Ye Jews " in contrast with the Samaritans.

The Lord's seemingly rough answer to the nobleman's request, similar to that addressed to Nicodemus (iii. 3), was designed to test and deepen his faith; for Jesus knew his heart and its unbelief and its demand for signs and wonders. So, strengthened by this rebuke, the cry of anguish burst from him : " Lord, come down ere my child die ! "

and he went away trusting the word : " Thy son liveth." And yet so feeble was his faith even when deepened and strengthened, that he immediately questioned the servants so as to verify the relation between the promised word and the accomplished fact.

" The seventh hour " (v. 52), i.e., one p.m. This second sign corresponds to the seventh (xi. 43).

The well at Sychar in 1869 was a hundred and five feet deep, and had fifteen feet of water in it.

See notes on viii. 2-11 and xx. 17.

JOHN V.   " A feast of the Jews " (v. 1); " A feast of the Jews " (vi. 4); and " a feast of the Jews " (vii. 2); so the Sabbath, the Passover and the Tabernacles as forms and witnesses were fulfilled when He appeared Who ordained them. Man degraded them so that they became " feasts of the Jews "; and their impotency to give life is here contrasted with Him Who is the Life. Men cling to forms and festivals all the more strongly when lacking the life which they symbolized under the first covenant of works, and use these forms to fight against Him of Whom they witnessed.

" Bethesda " (v. 2), i.e., The house of mercy.

Earthly princes on entering a city resort to the houses of the great and rich, but the feet of the Prince of princes immediately turned to the abode of misery and suffering, the fruits of sin.

The healing of the impotent man contrasts the quickening power of Christ with the powerlessness of the Law. It demanded strength on the part of the sinner in order to obtain the life it promised. But man is without strength (Rom. v. 6), and so what the Law could not do because of the weakness of that upon, and through, which it was to act, i.e., the carnal nature of man, Christ as sent by God effected, for He brought with Him the power to accomplish that which grace willed. A single word from Him sufficed. Strength was given, and the fact demonstrated by the man carrying his bed.

Love no doubt selected this man as being the most miserable, needy and helpless in all that sad company; and wisdom chose him as a vessel of instruction to the nation. For as Israel, because of her sin, was helplessly shut up in the desert for eight and thirty years, so was this man for a similar period imprisoned because of his sin; and as he vainly, because impotent, sought life in the pool of Bethesda, so Israel vainly sought life in the Law; for in both cases strength was required on the part of the person who sought what was promised through the disposition and ordination of angels (Acts vii. 53 and Gal. iii. 19).

For God had not left Himself altogether without testimony to His love for His people under that dispensation. An evidence of blessing still remained. An angel imparted healing to the pool from time to time, but strength was needed to profit by this angelic ministry, and this man was without strength.

"The same day was a Sabbath" (v. 9, Greek)—and what a Sabbath of rest and relief and joy for the man!

What follows proves that the Lord presented this sign of His Messiahship to the nation intentionally on the Sabbath that they might learn that He Himself was the True Sabbath in which God rested. God's Creation Sabbath was wrecked by sin, for how could love rest in misery? But to test man's obedience, and to awaken him to a consciousness of his impotency to profit by a rest the enjoyment of which demanded strength on the part of man, the Sabbath was given as a token of the Covenant between Israel and Jehovah. But man's disobedience again destroyed it. That Sabbath was the close of the first Creation; the Christian Sabbath—the resurrection day—opens the New Creation. The Christian rests not in the first Creation but in the second, and, therefore, observes the first day in. the week because it is God's Redemption Rest (Heb. iv.); and, Christ being that Sabbath. it is a rest that cannot be disturbed. See ch. xx.

But God is never defeated, and so the great Sabbath Day of one thousand years will be the seventh day of the First Creation upon whose fourth day the Sun of Righteousness first appeared (Gen. i. 14-18), in Whom also that future seventh day is secured.

The statement therefore, "My Father worketh until now and I work" (v. 17), is deeply affecting, for it declares that neither He nor The Father could find their Sabbath in the midst of the sad fruits of sin (Mal. ii. 17). Theirs was a Love incessant in its activities toward fallen and disobedient man, and therefore was He found at the pool of Bethesda.

Jesus did not disclaim the charge that He made Himself equal with God (v. 18) On the contrary, in words of lofty solemnity He affirmed it. He claimed absolute equality with God the Father; He declared that He did the same things and in the same manner; and willed as the Father willed. He asserted the personal distinctions in the Godhead, their unity of nature, and oneness of interest and action. He claimed that He Himself was God, for He raised from the dead and imparted life to whomsoever He willed (v. 21). He said that all judgment and administration rested in His hands, and that all men should worship Him as God (vs. 22 and 23). He announced that He gave eternal life to whoever believed on Him as sent by God (v. 24), and that the eternal destiny of all men would be decided by Him (vs. 28 and 29), so that if they would not receive Him as Life-giver they would be rejected by Him as Doom-utterer.

So there were not two Gods, but one God manifested in flesh; for there could not be two Beings both Supreme and both Omnipotent. Hence the Son did nothing apart from the Father ("from Himself," v. 19, Greek), either in action or in teaching (John xiv. 10).

"Not lawful" (v. 10). A carnal interpretation of Jeremiah xvii. 21.

"In the Temple" (v. 14), perhaps to return thanks (Ps. lxvi. 13, 14).

"Sin no more" (v. 14). Israel's thirty-eight years in the desert was the fruit of sin. They sinned yet more, and a worse punishment has come upon them.

Three times in this Gospel the Jews sought to murder Jesus (v. 16, viii. 59 and x. 31).

"Whom He wills" (v. 21). Salvation is not of him that willeth, but of God that sheweth mercy. The persons whom the Son wills to save are those in verse 24 who believe the Father's testimony concerning Him. These because they simply believe, apart from works, at once become possessors of a life that is eternal; and are assured that they shall never come into judgment.

He that refuses to worship Jesus as God refuses to worship God (v. 23). The three attempts of the Pharisees to murder Jesus were all connected with His claim to Deity.

"The dead" (v. 25), i.e., the unconverted. As Son of God He saves and imparts life; as Son of Man He exercises and executes judgment (vs. 27 and 29).

"Greater works" (v. 20), i.e., the marvels of verses 28 and 29. See notes on Isa. lxi. 1, Dan. xii. 2, and Luke iv. 19.

"Of mine own self" (v. 30), Greek: "from mine own self." See verse 19. The "do nothing" of this verse and the "know nothing" of Mark xiii. 32 declare the perfect Humanity of Christ. All as respects Him was perfection. He had His own will (v. 30 and Luke xxii. 42) and His distinct Person in the Godhead, but no interest of His own apart from the Father. Hence His judgment was righteous, for as He heard He judged. The word "judge" has here a large meaning involving judicial pronouncement, moral criticism, government, administration, etc.

"Of myself" (v. 31), i.e., "concerning myself." "Not true," i.e., not legal and manifestly convincing. See Deut. xix. 15 and John viii. 14. The verse means: If I alone testified concerning my equality with God (v. 18) my testimony would not be decisive. He did not mean it would not be trustworthy and truthful.

Obedient therefore to Deut. xix. 15 He appealed to five witnesses in support of His Godhead: i.e. John (vs. 32-35); the miracles (v. 36); the Father (vs. 37 and 38); the Scriptures (v. 39; and Moses (v. 46).

Verse 34 means He was not dependent upon human testimony, but in pitiful condescension to their unbelief, He used it that they might be saved.

John was a burning and shining "lamp" (v. 35), and they were willing for a brief period to listen to him, but when they saw whither his preaching tended, i.e., to Jesus as Son of God and Lamb of God, they turned away.

The miracles of Jesus, as miracles (v. 36), were not conclusive of His claim to Deity, but the manner in which He performed them, and the nature of them, as predicted in the Scriptures, were conclusive. No prophet nor apostle ever said, or could say, with power and majesty: "I will; be thou clean!"

Never having seen God or heard His voice (v. 37) the Pharisees were incompetent to judge whether Jesus was or was not equal with God; and their rejection of Jesus (v. 38) demonstrated not only ignorance of God but hostility to Him.

"The Scriptures testify of Me" (v. 39), and, "Moses wrote of Me" (v. 46). The Pharisees boasted of the Scriptures and of Moses, but rejected and crucified Him of whom both the one and the other spoke.

"Ye will not" (v. 40): "Ye cannot" (v. 44). These statements reveal the total moral wreckage of fallen man's will and nature.

"Another shall come" (v. 14), i.e., the Antichrist. He will better suit the heart of man which seeks honour from man (vs. 41 and 44). God does not minister to the pride of man, nor modify truth so as to please it and feed it.

"The love of God" (v. 42), i.e., love toward God.

The unity of Christ and the Scriptures is here shewn (v. 47). Their statements and His words agree in concord and equality; and of necessity, for He is the Author of the Bible.

The Scriptures will accuse (Rev. xx. 12), and Jesus, as Son of Man, will condemn (v. 27).

JOHN VI. See notes on Matt. xiv., Mark vi. and Luke viii. and ix.

As in the prior chapter (v.) Jesus is presented as the true Sabbath, and in the following chapter (vii.) as the true Feast of Tabernacles, so here He is manifested as the true Passover (v. 4).

He is here also prophetically revealed as Prophet (v. 14), as Priest (v. 15), and as King (v. 15).

Having as the true Paschal Lamb (v. 11) and the true Manna (v. 33) given His flesh for the life not only of Israel but of the world, and as Prophet asserted His superiority to Moses (v. 32), and postponed His Kingship (v. 15), He as Priest (v. 15) ascended the mountain, and from thence silently watched His Disciples, i.e., the believing Remnant of Israel, passing through the dark stormy night of their present affliction, and then descended to rescue them (v. 19) and bring them quickly (Rev. i. 1) to the land of their future millennial rest (v. 21).

During this lengthened period, subsequent to His giving His flesh, He becomes the Object of faith (v. 40) for all whom the Father gives come to Him (v. 37).

In Incarnation He is the Bread of Life (v. 33); in Immolation (v. 38), the Passover; and in Resurrection, the Object of faith (v. 40).

In the prior chapter He appears as the

Son of God equal with God and quickening whom He will. This is salvation from the Divine standpoint. In this chapter He appears as the Object of faith, the Son of Man (v 53) to Whom sinners come (v. 35) and on Whom they lay hold by faith.

Thus He fulfilled the Passover of which He was a Type (vs. 53-58), and the related Feast of Unleavened bread.

His glory as King of Israel could not be based upon the carnal will of man (v. 15), but upon the Divine will of Him that sent Him (v. 39).

Meanwhile He receives all that the Father gives to Him (v. 37), and receives them because given of the Father, be they Israelites, Gentiles, Pharisees, scoffers, harlots, or even the very castaways of the Devil. He knew they would not come to Him if the Father had not sent them. The whole mass ("all that") was certain of reception because given by the Father, and every individual in that vast multitude ("and him") was equally assured of a welcome.

The Father (vs. 38-40) willed the salvation of them all, and revealed a way of life that the simplest could understand. Whoever, notwithstanding his moral condition, looked upon Jesus and believed upon Him, immediately received a life that was everlasting, and was given the pledge—which carried with it absolute assurance—of resurrection into eternal felicity at the last day. Just as shipwrecked men looking at a lifeboat entrust themselves to it for salvation and are surely brought to land, so guilty sinners looking upon the Lord Jesus, and committing themselves by faith to Him, enter into a. position of safety, and are made certain of being brought to the resurrection shore.

For of all whom the Father gives to the Son He will lose none (v.39)—He will assuredly save them to the very end—and His "I will" (v. 40) banishes all incertitude.

Thus the Divine and human sides of salvation are presented: the one, in the words, "all that The Father giveth"; the other, in the words, "him that cometh." The door is opened wide so that all may come ; and the fact is stated that the Divine purpose in Redemption cannot be defeated.

These two aspects of salvation are repeated in the words : "This is the will of Him that sent Me" (v. 40); and in the words : "Everyone that believeth on Him."

Comparing verses 5-7 with the other Evangelists, it is quite clear that the Lord on seeing the multitudes coming to Him tested Philip's faith (v. 6) ; that the preachings and healings occurred between verses 7 and 8 ; and that then, on the Disciples coming to Him with the request that He would dismiss the multitudes, He again tested their faith.

The miracle occurred not far from Bethsaida where was Philip's home. Perhaps this is why he was asked to provide bread.

In this fourth sign, as also in the fifth, the presence of words and statements not found in the other Gospels, is complementary and disproves collusion.

" Seeking for Jesus " (v. 24)—not to be saved from their sins, but to be filled with bread (v. 26).

The Lord did not answer their question of verse 25, for His mission was a moral rather than an intellectual one. They had seen the disciples leave in the only boat alone, and they were puzzled to know how He had reached the other side before them.

Verse 27 means :   " Rather labour for that meat which endureth," etc. : " Give," not " sell."

It offends the self-righteous to tell them that without faith it is impossible to please God (Heb. xi. 6), and that, therefore, the great work that God requires is faith in His Beloved Son Whom He sent. Otherwise works, however pious, are " dead works."

Upon this the people, forgetting the great sign He had given them the previous day, and the miracles that He had just wrought (Matt. xiv. 14), replied that Moses had accredited himself as sent from God by giving them the manna (vs. 30 and 31), as stated in Psalm lxxviii., and that he had fed upwards of three millions of people therewith for forty years. The Rabbis taught that the former Redeemer, Moses, caused manna to descend from heaven for them, and that the latter Redeemer, Messiah, would perform a similar miracle.

Jesus answered them that Moses did not give them that bread, and added : " I am the Bread of Life "—those who ate of the manna died in the wilderness, but " He that cometh to Me shall never die."

There are eight " I am's " in this Gospel. " I am the Bread of Life " (vi. 35, 41, 48, 51)," I am the Light of the World " (viii. 12,) " I AM " (Jehovah) (viii. 58), " I am the

Door " (x. 7), " I am the Good Shepherd "
(x. 11), " I am the Resurrection and the
Life " (xi. 25), " I am the Way " (xiv. 6),and
" I am the True Vine " (xv. 1).

"At the last day " (vs. 39 and 40, 44, 54,
xi. 24 and xii. 48)—an expression found only
in this Gospel.

" Murmured " (vs. 41 and 43), i.e., were
muttering one to another. But the Lord
knew what they were saying, and, therefore,
told them that only those who were taught
by the Spirit, through the Scriptures (vs.
44 and 45), could recognise Who He really
was ; and that no one came to Him, or could
come to Him as a Saviour, unless predisposed
thereto by God (vs. 44 and 65) ; and that
this disposition was not of man's will or
nature, but a gift from God (v. 65) ; and that
all so influenced by the Spirit were sure to
come, and would most certainly come unto
Him (v: 45).

God draws sinners to Christ by a spiritual
operation consonant to their moral nature
and enlightening their rational conviction,
and He effects this through the Scriptures
as written in the Prophets (Isa. liv. 13, Jer.
xxxi. 33 and 34, etc.). Jesus based all His
teaching, and especially His " hard sayings,"
upon the Bible. It externally illuminates
and the Holy Spirit internally reveals. All
thus enlightened and Divinely drawn, come
without fail to Christ and cannot possibly
perish ; and He of necessity receives them
because they are sent to Him by the Father
(v. 37).

But between those thus enlightened and
the Only Begotten One of the Father, there
is the immeasurable distance that separates
Deity from humanity (v. 46).

As the Bread of Life, Christ gives life
to the believer (v. 47), and He sustains that
life (vs. 48-50). Men ate the manna in the
wilderness and died ; but whosoever eats
of the Living Bread shall never die.

" My flesh " (v. 51), i.e., Myself. The
Lord now pointed them to His atoning death
as that which alone could give life to the
world ; for the separation of the blood from
the flesh (v. 54) is death, and thus He became
the Bread of Life. That this death was not
a natural one is evidenced by the words
" I will give " (vs. 27, 32, 34, 51, 51 and 52).

In reply to the impossibility of eating
His flesh (v. 52) the Lord, instead of softening
or modifying this seemingly harsh doctrine,
intensified it by declaring it indispensable

to salvation (v. 53), stating that only those
who thus eat and drink as a definite action
(aorist tense), and continue thus eating
and drinking (present tense), have spiritual
life (vs. 53-57). So Christ Himself, in the
virtue of His sacrificial death, is the Eternal
Life ; and only those who appropriate this
atoning Saviour in their hearts by faith possess
eternal life ; and four times He promises
to raise up such at the last day (vs. 39, 40,
44 and 54). A comparison of verses 47 and
48 with verses 53 and 54 shows that believing
on Christ is the same thing as eating and
drinking Him. Such figurative speech was
quite familiar to the Hebrews of that time,
as is shown by the Talmud, and by a reference
to Exodus xxiv. 11, Deut. viii. 3, Jer. xv.
16, Ezek. ii. 8, etc.

This whole passage has no relation to
the Last Supper, and its corruption—the
mass—for the Lord's auditory in the Synagogue could not possibly have understood
Him if He spoke of what men call the Eucha-
rist. Further, He explained (v. 63) that His
words were spiritual and living and not
fleshly and material ; and added that as
He lived by The Father (v. 57), so he that
ate His flesh lived by Him ; consequently
the sense in which the believer partakes and
lives upon Christ is similar to that existing
between Christ and the Father, and in
that " eating " there cannot possibly be any
material food.

Death, therefore, is the believer's life. He
Who knew no sin put away by death the
sin that death brought in ; and He as the
Sin-Offering becomes the Meal-offering upon
which the believer feeds. Expiation being
complete and infinite, the enjoyment of
Christ as the Meal-Offering is assured. The
only disturbing factor between the soul
and God, i.e., sin, being infinitely and
eternally removed, nothing remains but a
feast ; and that feast sustains, as the Meal-
Offering, the life received through the Sin-
Offering. But it is impossible to know and
enjoy Christ as the Bread of Life in the
Meal-Offering until He is believed upon as
the Atoning Saviour in the Sin-Offering,
giving His priceless Life in expiation of
man's sin.

Had He not so died He must have abode
alone (xii. 24), for a meal-offering without
a blood-offering would have been a Cain
offering. But faith in His death being
established, a risen and living Saviour can

be feasted upon. A dead Christ does not exist; and, therefore, transubstantiation and consubstantiation are human follies. The Holy Spirit unites to a glorified Christ; and as He did not live an independent life apart from the Father, so the believer does not live an independent life apart from Christ (v. 57).

Thus He preached in the Synagogue (v. 59), and that which followed (vs. 60-71) no doubt took place in the street after the conclusion of the service.

"Many" (v. 60), i.e., the majority. "An hard saying," i.e., "an insufferable saying, who can submit to listen to it?" Thus they muttered one to the other. But Jesus, knowing what they were saying, pointed out (vs. 61-63) that if His death was a stumbling-block to them, how much more would be His Resurrection? But would not that prove the reality and value of His death, and the depth of their unbelief?

But it mattered little to these men in what sense He spoke, for they did not believe (v. 64); and Jesus knew that from the beginning (ii. 23, 24); and He reminded them of what He had already said (v. 44), that no one could believe upon Him unless so disposed by God.

This doctrine finally alienated them (v. 66); and it still alienates multitudes, for it humiliates man's pride, and annihilates his self-importance and self-righteousness.

Their defection, however, must have deeply pained the Lord's heart, for He turned to the Twelve, now first mentioned in this Gospel, with the pathetic words, throbbing with love's anxieties, " Will ye also go away? "; and for the second time—Matt. xvi. 16 being the first occasion—Simon Peter confesses Who He is; but in more emphatic language, saying: " We have believed, and have got to know—have learned by experience—that Thou art The Messiah, the Son of the Living God."

It is possible that Simon and the rest were confounded and perplexed by this " hard " teaching, and the thought may have occurred to them: " Shall we follow the majority and give up our hope? " But then arose the awful question: " To whom shall we go? " " where shall we find words of eternal life? "; and so Peter fortified himself and his faithful brethren by saying, " We have believed and are sure." So there are times when faith is tried by speculative

difficulties and its foundation seems to become a swaying platform. At such times it is felt that to turn away from the Lord Jesus is to face darkness, desolation and death, and so recoiling from this the heart falls back on " we have believed and have proved by experience," and a recovery of faith and an unspeakable relief is enjoyed.

This confession of Simon's must have been as balm to the saddened and wounded heart of the Lord.

But to save Peter and his companions from self-confidence and self-satisfaction, and from their belief in their moral superiority to the faithless disciples who went back, He said to them: " It was I that chose you. You did not chose Me." (xv. 16), and " one of you is a devil " (v. 70).

JOHN VII.-VIII. 1—As the prior chapter presents Jesus as the Anti-type Passover shedding His blood, i.e., laying down His life to deliver man from death, and as the Anti-type Feast of Unleavened Bread upon Whom faith feeds during His absence on high, so this chapter presents Him, whilst awaiting to fulfil the hope of the Feast of Tabernacles, sending forth the Holy Spirit to nourish and bless those who should believe upon Him, and to make them channels of blessing to others (vs. 8 and 39).

Hence the reader is brought from Passover to Tabernacles without any direct mention of Pentecost, for the gift of the Holy Spirit provides a continuous Pentecost for those who find life in Christ. It is true that there will be a future physical Pentecost, as predicted by Joel, and of which Acts ii. was a foretaste, as there will be a future Feast of Tabernacles, but this chapter designedly passes over this predicted Feast.

As to the Feast of Tabernacles, He said that His time for fulfilling it was not yet come (v. 8), i.e., had not yet been fulfilled; but pending that future fulfilment He would at the time appointed of the Father (v. 6) accomplish His sacrificial death; and till that time came it was impossible for His enemies to kill Him, though they nine times sought it in this chapter (vs. 1, 7, 11, 13, 19, 23, 25, 30, 44).

So at that time (v. 6) Jesus will show Himself to the world, will set Israel in possession of all their promised blessing, and begin the Feast of Tabernacles which is to endure for a thousand years. Meanwhile, having gone away (vs. 33 and 34), He gives the Holy Spirit to believers (v. 39).

It was on the eighth day of the Feast (v. 37)—a rest beyond the Sabbath rest of this world, a new scene of glory, the commencement of another period—that this great gift was promised which was to be as a river, not only refreshing those through whom it flowed, but also to refresh others; the Risen Lord Himself being its inexhaustible Source (vs. 37 and 38).

But the Lord's family, sunk in unbelief, understood none of these things (v. 5), and so would have had Him show Himself to the world (v. 4) in order to convince and win it. But He pointed out to them that the world hated Him (v. 7), because He testified concerning it that its works were evil; it could not hate them, because they did not thus testify against it. Between Him and the world there was deadly war; and hence its religious leaders were perpetually conspiring to kill Him.

Had his mother and brothers and sisters come as moral lepers for cleansing from their sins they would have learned Who and What He was, for knowledge of spiritual realities only reaches the soul through a sin-convicted heart, and not through a religious intellect. See verse 17 and its note, and Acts 1. 14.

"The Jews" (v. 1), i.e., the Judeans, or men of Judea. These were the religious leaders of the nation, and are to be distinguished from the multitude of the people (v. 31).

The Feast of Tabernacles (v. 2). This is the only direct reference to this Feast in the New Testament. Once "a feast of Jehovah" it had now become "a feast of the Jews."

His family did not believe in Him (v. 5), as predicted in Psalm lxix. 8—" I am become an alien unto my mother's children."

"Where is He" (v. 11)? It was now a year and a half since His last visit (v. 1).

"The midst of the feast" (v. 14 with v. 10), i.e., the fourth or fifth day of the eight during which it lasted. Possibly His action was designed to let the stir about Him subside, and so dispose the people to listen to His teaching rather than to be excited about His person.

"Having never learned" (v. 15). This is a valuable testimony against ancient and modern assertions that Christ's knowledge of religious matters was derived from human sources. The Sermon on the Mount is a fatal blow to that theory.

"A man of letters" at that time was a theological expert in either of the great schools of theology in Jerusalem. Compare Acts iv. 13.

"My teaching" (v. 16). This is the first of seven declarations that the doctrines that Jesus taught, and the words used in teaching them, were God's doctrines and God's words. See viii. 28, 47; xii. 49; xiv. 10, 24; and xvii. 8.

"Will do" (v. 17), i.e., "is willing to do." "Shall know," i.e., get to know by experience. See note on verse 5.

"Of Myself" (v. 17), i.e., "from Myself." "None of you" (v. 19), i.e., the Judean theologians (v. 15).

"None of you keepeth the Law" (v. 19), for they were seeking to kill Him although the Law forbade murder.

"The people" (v. 20), as contradistinguished from the Judeans. They were unaware of the murderous conspiracy of these latter; but in their blindness they could only account for His superhuman knowledge and power as evidencing demon possession.

Jesus, disregarding them and their question, "answered" (v. 21), i.e., continued to speak to the Judeans, recalled the miracle of ch. v. 1, which still offended them, and pointed out that if circumcision, which physically benefits a man in a minor degree, was lawful on the Sabbath Day, how much more an action which benefited his entire body (v. 23)? So He demanded of them righteous judgment and not prejudiced and objective injustice (v. 24).

Here is a seeming conflict between two laws—the law of the Sabbath, and the law commanding circumcision on the eighth day. Circumcision had priority, for it was of Abraham (v. 22) and handed on by Moses. Also, it was lawful to do good on the Sabbath Day; and medical science applauds circumcision.

"Know" (vs. 27-29), i.e., to know by intuition as distinguished from to get to know by experience (v. 17).

"Whence He is" (v. 27), i.e., from Nazareth. The Rabbis taught that the Messiah would come from Bethlehem, and then be hidden no one knew where. Compare 2 Chron. xxii. 11, and xxiii. 11.

"Cried" (v. 28), i.e., "shouted out." "Ye both know Me," etc. (v. 28).

Probably the meaning is : Ye know Me as Jesus of Nazareth ; and yet you do not know Me, for you do not know Him that sent Me ; but I am from Him and He did send Me.

"No man laid hands on Him" (v. 30). Their impotence was equal to their malignity.

The gift of the Holy Spirit (v. 39) followed upon His Ascension (vs. 33 and 34).

"I am" (v. 34). The formula of eternal existence. See note on vi. 35.

The dispersed among the Gentiles (v. 35), i.e., the Dispersion—mentioned three times ; here, 1 Pet. i. 1, and James i. 1.

Verse 37 should read as in the Revised Version.

This Eighth day, the great day of the feast, was a Sabbath. It was a day of ecstatic joy, of loud jubilation, and of sounding of trumpets. The priest, as on the prior days of the feast, passed in solemn procession through the streets from the Pool of Siloam, bearing in a golden vessel water which he poured out upon the Altar in front of the Temple while the rejoicing people sang : "With joy shall ye draw water out of the wells of salvation" (Isa. xii. 3). It was at this supreme moment that Jesus stood, no doubt in some elevated position, and shouted out ("cried") : "If any man thirst, let him come unto Me and drink" (Isa. lv. 1).

This great proclamation, made in the streets to the whole world, compels the hearer to choose between two alternatives ; either to say with Caiaphas "He is guilty of death" ; or to exclaim with Thomas, "My Lord and My God."

To believe on Him (v. 38) is to drink of Him (v. 37).

The quotation in verse 38 refers to the Messiah and not to the believer. Christ is the eternal and inexhaustible source of all spiritual blessing (Isa. xii. 3, lv. 1, lviii. 11, Ezek. xlvii. 1, Joel iii. 18, Zech. xiii. 1, and xiv. 8.).

"Should receive" (v. 39). The believer receives the living water which flows from the inner man of Christ the Giver.

"Glorified" (v. 39), i.e., "ascended." Compare John xvi. 7, Ps. lxviii. 18, Acts ii. 33.

The contrast here is between the lifeless water, quickly exhausted, which a mortal priest carried in a golden vessel, and the life-giving water flowing in eternal and inexhaustible fulness from out of the divine and human affections of the Great High Priest ; and the lesson to be learned is : that ceremonies, however magnificent, venerable and scriptural, can never satisfy the deep thirst of the soul. That thirst can only be satisfied by personal union with the Lord Jesus by faith. For He is the Smitten Rock who in resurrection power sends forth a stream of life to dying men and to a thirsty world.

The appeal of the people to the Bible (v. 42) is a valuable testimony to the authority of scripture as an infallible judge.

The proud question of verse 48 in effect set the church above the Scriptures ; and this misplacement continues to the present day.

Verse 49 may be thus paraphrased : "But this ignorant rabble, unlearned in the Law, are a cursed set !" Carnal religion makes people use very rude language when angered by conflict with spiritual religion.

Feeble and timid as was the plea of Nicodemus, yet was it precious to the Lord ; and so it is here honourably recorded by the Holy Spirit.

Scorn, contempt, and anger prejudice blind men, even though they be experts in Bible literature (v. 52). These Pharisees forgot the Messianic prophecy of Isa. ix. 2.

Every man, including the disciples, went unto his own home, but Jesus went to the Mount of Olives. See note on Luke xxi. 37. He had no home until He went back to heaven from whence He came. See notes on Psalms iii. and v.

JOHN VIII. 2-59.—The Holy Spirit in this and the following chapter returns to the subject of Christ's personal glories as the Word of God, the Light of the World and the Eternal Life, and records His rejection in all these relationships.

These personal glories accordingly appear in verses 2-11 when contrasted with Luke vii. 37-50. The subject there is the woman and her assurance of pardon, her love and her ministry ; but in John viii. 2-11 the theme is the Lord in His triple glory as The Word, the Light and the Life. Hence there is nothing said about the woman beyond the triple declaration : "Neither do I condemn thee" ; "go to thy home" ; and, "sin no more"

As the Word of God He wrote with His finger upon the ground ; as The Light of the World He exposed the hypocrites who, equally impure, accused the woman ; and as The Life He said " Neither do I condemn Thee,"—for He had come to earth to bear her condemnation, and to lay down His Life to save sinners such as she.

His action in stooping twice and writing with His finger on the stone at His feet—for the Temple Court was paved—recalled His action (Exod. xxxi. 18) in stooping down from heaven to Mount Sinai and writing with His finger upon the stone tables of the Law. Once more that Almighty God, now manifested in the flesh, stooped earthwards, and once more that finger wrote upon stones ; but not now that which condemned to death, but that which ordained to life. How the heart wishes that the Spirit had willed to record what was written !

The woman's guilt was undeniable. But why did they not bring forward the equally guilty man ? The law commanded that both should be stoned. The spirit of human Law is to punish the woman and protect the man.

The Pharisees having been defeated as to benefitting a man's body on the Sabbath day (vii. 23), brought forward this woman in the hope of confounding Jesus ; for if He condemned her He was not a Saviour—the Law did that—and if He let her go He despised and disallowed the Law. But how foolish of man to try and be clever when dealing with God ? His action in writing on the ground should have opened their eyes as to Who He was. He did not excuse or deny the woman's guilt, or the fact that the Law justly doomed her to death, but He announced that only those could accuse her and execute the sentence of the Law who were themselves innocent of the sin for which she was condemned. The words " without sin " (v. 7) do not mean " sinless," but they mean " without her sin." How could accusers guilty of the same sin as the accused carry out the sentence of a sinless law ? Accordingly these impure hypocrites, by slinking away, convicted themselves (v. 9), and so were themselves found out " in the very act " (v. 4) of which they triumphantly accused their victim. Confused, they separated from one another, each caring for character rather than conscience, he who had the most reputation to save being the first to retire.

How could men who were themselves sentenced by the Law to be stoned to death for adultery, stone another for the same sin ?

As older in guilt they must themselves be first stoned, and then how could they, being stoned to death, stone the woman ? This is why David could not stone Amnon, for he himself had been guilty of the same sin, and should have been himself put to death. He was, in Law, a dead man, and so incapable of exercising the sentence of the Law on another.

The Lord wrote twice on the stones at His feet. He wrote twice at Sinai. One table related to God ; the other, to man as to obedience and responsibility. So here possibly, on the first stone at His feet, He wrote, " God sent not His Son into the world to condemn the world, but that the world through Him might be saved " ; and on the second stone the words, " He that believeth on the Son hath everlasting life, and cometh not into condemnation." His action and His words suggest these writings.

So they turned away from Him Who had convicted them. They could not stay in the merciless beams of that Light and try to hide their guilt and shame (see notes on Ps. iii.). How much wiser it would have been for them, like the woman, to have remained in the Light; to have confessed their sin, and then they also would have heard the gracious words : " Neither do I condemn."

For she remained there standing " in the midst " (vs. 3 and 9)—and not lying on the floor, as represented in foolish religious pictures—and called Him Lord. She made Him her salvation ; and He Who read her heart must have known that she believed upon Him. And so He justified her, for He refused to condemn her ; and " there is no condemnation to them that are in Christ Jesus " (Rom. viii. 1).

In this fourth Gospel there are three sinful women brought into the presence of Jesus. For the first (iv.) the message was No Reprobation ; for the second (viii.), No Condemnation ; and for the third (xx. 17), No Separation.

" Then " (v. 12), i.e. because of this occurrence.

" Again " (vs. 12 and 21). He had already spoken to them of these matters (vii. 33, 34, and viii. 2, 9).

How the words " He that followeth Me shall not walk in darkness, but shall have the light of life,"—words spoken as He moved away from the Temple, inviting men to follow Him (v. 12)—must have sounded as the sweetest music in the heart of the woman as she returned to her home, assuring her of fellowship, care, love, guidance, holiness, life and heaven !

" Of thyself," i.e., " concerning Thyself " (v. 13). " Not true," i.e., " not legal " ; for the Law demanded a double testimony.

The Lord's reply was a double one ; first, that the command had no application to Him because of His origin and His destination ; and, second, because of their incompetence to recognise Who He was (v. 14). But in condescension to their ignorance He added that He had a second witness, the Father (v. 18). They judged according to the flesh (v. 15) ; He judged no one (compare v. 11), for His present mission to earth was not to judge, but to save ; and He added that even if He did judge, His judgment would be in harmony with Divine Law, for it would be the judgment of God (v. 16).

By-and-by He will come to judge, but at that moment He was the Light so that none should walk in darkness. History records that in the Treasury where He was preaching (v. 20) stood two colossal golden lamp stands on which hung a multitude of lamps that were lit during the Feast of Tabernacles, and around these the people danced with great rejoicing. But just as the water in the golden bowl carried by the high priest (vii. 37) could give no life to the soul, so those golden lamps could give no light to the heart.

" Then said Jesus again " (v. 21). See vii. 33, 34.

" Your sin " (v. 21, R.V.). What sin ? That of verse 7. How could these impure men dwell with the Lord Jesus in a pure fellowship ?

" From beneath " (v. 23), i.e., the earth. " From above," i.e., heaven.

" Your sins " (v. 24). Unbelief is the mother of all sins.

" I am " (v. 24). See Deuteronomy xxxii. 39, Isa. xliii. 10 and 13, xlvi. 4, xlviii. 12. Compare vi. 20.

" Even that which I said from the beginning " (v. 25), i.e., that He was the Light of the World (v. 12) ; and in that Light He judged concerning them, and His judgment was infallible, for all that He said was Divine because from God (v. 26).

When they should look upon Him Whom they were about to pierce (Zech. xii. 10 and Rev. i. 7), they would then get to know (v.

28) that He was indeed Jehovah. Here is an amazing statement: that a naked man hanging upon a cross demonstrated God manifest in flesh, and proved Christ's claim to be Jehovah! The triumphant word " finished " disclosed His Godhead.

Meanwhile they thought He was " alone " (v. 29 with verse 16), but He had the joy and strength of a fellowship that they knew not of.

" Many believed on Him " (v. 30), i.e., as the expected Messiah Who would restore the Davidic Throne. Such a faith, being carnal, and ignoring the facts of the Fall, of sin, and of its eternal judgment, was worthless, and the Lord at once, as the Light of the World, unmasked it (vs. 31-47) by telling these professed believers that they were morally bond-slaves of sin (v. 34) and children of the Devil (v. 44), although, physically, children of Abraham (v. 37) and, ecclesiastically, members of the Church (v. 35).

So here, as in ii. 23—iii. 21 (see notes), He urged the necessity of the New Birth— for how could children of the Devil be children of the Kingdom ?—and taught that that birth takes place when faith is reposed in Him as the Saviour from the doom of sin, from the defilement of sin and from the dominion of sin.

Such was the faith of the adulteress (v. 11), but not of " the believers " of verses 30 and 31, as is proved by verses 45 and 46. These professors began by accepting His claim as Messiah (v. 30) and ended by taking up stones to murder Him in rejection of His claim as Jehovah (58 and 59). Had they continued in the path of Messianic Faith on which they momentarily entered, He would have led them, as He led others, into the faith that saves ; and then they would have become His real disciples, for they would have got experimentally to know Him Who is The Truth (v. 32) ; and He would have freed them from the dominion of sin, as from its doom and defilement ; and, further, He would have made them sons in the Father's House (vs. 35 and 36).

Here, therefore, are contrasted salvation and sonship in the Kingdom of God, with slavery and sonship in the Kingdom of Satan (vs. 34 and 44).

Piqued by these words, these " believers " hotly replied that they were never in bondage to any man. This was not true politically for they had been in bondage to the Egyptians, the Assyrians, the Babylonians, the Persians, the Greeks, and they were at that moment in bondage to the Romans.

"Whosoever committeth sin" (v. 34), i.e., practiseth sinful habits.

The servant may be dismissed from the house; the son never (v. 35).

"Ye are Abraham's seed" (v. 37)—"If ye were Abraham's children" (v. 39). They were Abraham's children physically, but not morally; for, if morally, they would not have sought to kill Jesus (vs. 37 and 40); but they had the same moral nature as their father the Devil (vs. 38, 41 and 44).

"A Man" (v. 40). Here once only did the Lord speak of Himself as a man, and He did so to mark the contrast between Him and the "man-slayer" of verse 44. "Murderer" is man-slayer in the Greek text. Jesus is a man-saver; Satan, a man-slayer.

"We have one Father" (v. 41). This proud claim is made still by those who are morally the children of Satan. The test of true sonship is the attitude of the heart toward Jesus (v. 42). If He is loved and His Book obeyed (v. 43), then is true sonship manifest.

His Will in coming to earth was not independent of, but in harmony with, the Will that sent Him.

To understand the subject taught is to understand the words in which it is taught, otherwise they are unintelligible (v. 43). His "Word," i.e., that which He taught, was truth; His "speech"—the words used in preaching it. The one was the subject; the other the form. So they could not get to understand the words because they did not intuitively believe and accept the revelation made in, and by the words. A man destitute by birth of the musical sense listening to a lecture on music, would find the words unintelligible.

"Your father the Devil" (v. 44). Here the Lord Jesus asserts the personality of Satan, and the impurity and malignity of his nature. He was the man-slayer of Adam; he continually speaks "the lie," for in so doing he speaks out of his own nature and possessions; he abode not in the truth, and so continues to abide in the lie, and to be continuously active as Satan. So all falsehood, impurity and murder originate out of his nature (" of his own ").

"Ye will do" (v. 44), i.e., "Ye willingly do," because possessing the same nature.

"And " (v. 45). Read : " So because I tell you the truth," etc., not, "although I tell you the truth," etc, but "because"; for being the children of falsehood (v. 44) how could they accept and obey truth?

The Lord then proceeded, as the Eternal Life, to declare the sinlessness of His Nature (v. 46); the dignity of His Person (v. 54); and the eternity of His Being (v. 58).

He could convict them of sin (v. 9), but though He challenged them, they could not convict Him (v. 46).

"Say we not well" (v. 48). See vii. 20. They felt His superhuman knowledge, but declared that He was demonized. Had He been less true they would have accepted Him.

"*The* Devil" (v. 44); "*a* devil" (v. 48). Jesus with calm dignity said, "I have not a devil." His beloved servant Paul also with dignity said, "I am not mad, most noble Festus" (Acts xxvi. 25). Jesus did not add, "I am not a Samaritan," for possibly the woman of Samaria, and her fellow believers, would have been chilled by this denial of relationship had it reached them.

"There is One that seeketh and judgeth" (v. 50), i.e., God Who sought His glory and judged Him worthy of glory. He "judged," i.e., vindicated Jesus.

"He shall never see death" (v. 51), i.e., He shall by no means see eternal death. This declaration, already made in v. 24, vi. 40, chs. iii. and iv., etc., and repeated in xi. 26, is the strongest statement of this glorious truth, and is here appropriately found, for He was here presenting Himself as The Eternal Life. But these false believers altered the statement into the declaration " he shall never taste of death" (v. 52), i.e., physical death.

"Rejoiced to see My day" (v. 56), i.e., the day of Gen. xvii. 17. Abraham laughed with joy; Sara, in unbelief.

The Jews regarded fifty as the completion of manhood.

And now (v. 58) Jesus made the supreme declaration that He was Jehovah, saying, Before Abraham was brought into being I was eternally existent. Abraham "was," but "I am"—not that He came into existence before Abraham did, but that He never came into being because always existing.

Because, therefore, of this claim to Godhead these carnal believers proceeded to stone Him to death. Three times His life was thus attempted, and each time because He claimed to be God (chs. v. 18, viii. 58 and x. 30.)

Thus His glories as the Word that was with God and was God, as the Light of the World, and as the Life of men declared in the first chapter of this Book, are repeated and illustrated in this chapter, for as The Word He claimed to be God ; as the Light He exposed falsehood ; and as The Life He saved the woman and promised to save equally all who obeyed Him.

What an amazing revelation (v. 58) ! A Man despised, rejected, poor, ill-treated and hated, was God Himself ! He was there, come down from heaven, and standing in their midst. Amazing fact for those who loved Him and for those who hated Him. And He was there as a Saviour. As such He was both hidden and manifested—hidden as to His glory, manifested as to His Person.

As the Word of God He wrote thrice with the finger of God—at Sinai (Exod. xxxi.) at Babylon (Dan. v.) ; and at Jerusalem, (John viii.)

Here is seen the Lamb of God among the wolves of Satan ; and their rage provided the occasion for these three great declarations as to the sinlessness of His nature (v. 46) ; the dignity of His person (v. 54) ; and the eternity of His Being (v. 58). See notes on Pss. iii., iv., v. and vi.

JOHN IX. 1-38.—The Light that justified the adulteress and exposed and confounded her accusers (viii.), now enlightened the blind man and put to shame his haters (ix.) ; and, having brought these lost sheep into the fold (x.), that same Light revealed their safety, and the grace and truth of their Shepherd. So grace saved them, and truth enlightened them.

This woman and this man symbolized Israel—as a church adulterous, and as a nation blind. But He Who is Israel's Light and Salvation will reveal Himself to her (ix. 37) and will say " neither do I condemn thee " (viii. 11).

So chapter viii. introduces the Light, and in chapter ix. eyes are opened to see it.

The hatred which compelled Jesus to hide Himself and to pass by (viii. 59) did not chill His love or discourage His heart, and so as He passed by He healed the blind man (vs. 1-7).

The man was blind from birth ; and so was Israel morally, and so are all men. Jesus gave him sight. He produced in him that which he had not previously. He was darkness, but now became light in the Lord because enlightened by the Lord. That Inward Light was not his by natural birth but entered into him physically (v. 7) and morally (v. 37), on contact with Him Who is the Light of the World.

As a figure the Lord's action (v. 6) expressed the presentation to the eyes of men, morally blind, of Christ in a body of lowly clay, animated by Divine breath. The clay symbolized His humanity, and, the moisture of His lips, the life that animated it (compare Mark vii. 33).

But just as the man saw nothing after the clay had been put upon his eyes, so men are blind to the Person and Work of Christ though He places Himself right before their very eyes. Their eyes become the more completely closed ; as was the case with this man although the Hand that put the clay upon his eyes was there ; but he could not see it. Still it is upon this action and presentation that the Holy Spirit (v. 7) operates. He makes Christ known as the Sent One from the Father, He Himself having been Sent from both the Father and the Son.

Thus in a future happy day the Holy Spirit will unveil Israel's eyes and the nation will see Jesus the Light and Life of men.

The Lord's answer (v. 3) disposed of the question by stating the man's blindness was designed in order to provide, by its removal, an evidence of Christ's Deity. See notes at the end of the chapter.

It would not be unrighteous for God to determine before birth to punish a man for a sin which God in His fore-knowledge knew he would commit. This may appear to man's fallen sense of justice, unrighteous. But this principle of Divine justice, in foreknowledge, was demonstrated at Calvary, for God there punished sins which are only being committed to-day.

" The works of God " (v. 3), i.e., the great work of God in love, wisdom and power toward man. The Bible form of magnitude and excellency is here used.

" I must work while it is day " (v. 4). The presence of Jesus on earth made it " day " ; and the word " must " revealed that He had a precise work to do on earth, and that every particular of it was arranged for Him, each action having its precise time and place, and all limited to a determined number of years.

"Siloam" (v. 7) compare Isaiah viii. 6. The Euphrates figures human power and pride ; Siloam, the enlightening Spirit of the God of Israel in His power and gentleness in Zion.

"He is a prophet" (v. 17)—"and he worshipped Him" (v. 38). Thus the Light led the man on to recognise and worship as God (v. 38) the "man called Jesus" (v..11),and later to confess Him as a prophet (v. 17)—a Man, a Prophet, the Son of God.

The courageous testimony of this man to these priests and rulers of the Church is inspiring, and contrasts with the cowardice of his parents (vs. 20-23).

Transported with rage (v. 34), the rulers had him thrown out into the street ; and then, no doubt, proceeded to excommunicate him from the Church (v. 22). But they themselves in their anger, admitted that he was born blind (v. 34), which they had laboured to disprove (v. 18). But Jesus (see Isa. lxvi. 5) appeared to this man's joy (vs. 35-38) and to the confusion and shame of those that hated him (vs. 39-41 and ch. x.).

As to the question in verse 2, Esau sinned before he was born, for in the body of his mother he tried to murder Jacob (Gen. xxv. 22) ; and John the Baptist, on the other hand, confessed Christ before he was born, for he leaped with joy when brought into relation with Him (Luke i. 44). See notes on Ezek. xxxv.

The man's willingness to be healed in Christ's way, although it seemed so opposed to nature, and not, like Naaman the Syrian, in a way of his own, is noteworthy, and evidences the work of the Spirit in his heart.

JOHN IX. 39-X. 42.—Having appeared to the blind man's joy, the Lord proceeded to confound and put to shame those who cast him out, by declaring them to be spiritually blind and wilfully sinful (vs. 39-41), and that they were false shepherds, thieves, robbers and hirelings (vs. 1 and 12). He, at the same time, deepened the man's joy, and that of the woman (viii. 2-11), by telling them that they were sheep of the true fold ; that He was the Good Shepherd giving His life for them ; that He endowed them with eternal life ; that they should never

perish ; and that nothing and no one could pluck them out of His hand (vs. 14, 15 and 28).

"For judgment I am come into this world" (v. 39). This does not conflict with xii. 47—that refers to the object of His coming—but its effect was to give sight to those born blind, and to judicially blind those who, full of their own wisdom and righteousness, claimed to be light-givers. They judged the man as born in sins (v. 34). The True Light declared he was not blind because of sin (ix. 3), but that the Pharisee's moral blindness was caused by sin ; and it was a sin that remained (v. 41). They wilfully shut their eyes to the abundant proofs of Christ's Messiahship. Hence their guilt. Had they been unconsciously blind, they would have had no sin.

They claimed to be shepherds. Jesus contrasted Himself with them. He was the Good Shepherd. He came in by the door into the sheep-fold, and He was Himself at the same time the door for the sheep.

The sheepfold was the Abrahamic Covenant, and the flock was the House of Israel ; as declared in Isa. xl. 11, Ezek. xxiv. 33, xxxvii. 24, Zech. xiii. 7 and other Scriptures.

The True Shepherd came in by the door (v. 2). That is, He submitted to all the conditions ordained by Him who built the sheepfold. These conditions were given through Moses. Accordingly He was born of a woman under the Law, was circumcised, and fulfilled all that the Law demanded of the Messiah and predicted concerning Him. He was Jehovah's Perfect Servant, living by every word that proceeded out of the mouth of God, continually doing those things that pleased Him; and, consequently, on presenting Himself at the door of the Hebrew Church the doorkeeper (v. 3), i.e., the Law, immediately admitted Him, and the sheep recognised His voice. Thus He had access given to Him and to His sheep in spite of the Pharisees and Priests.

Out from under the condemnation of the Law He led His sheep—He Himself going before them to Calvary (v. 4). The sheep followed Him, for their safety consisted in knowing the one Voice which was life to them.

Further, He was the door for the sheep. He was their authority for going out and their means for entering in. The sheepfold which had been to them a prison He turned into a refuge ; so they went in for safety and went out for pasture. The sheep enjoyed safety, liberty and food.

" His own sheep " (v. 3). He is owner as well as shepherd of the sheep, and has, therefore, so to speak, a double love for them.

" Of " (v. 7) means " for." " Thieves etc," (v. 8). See verse 1.

" I am the door " (v. 9). The Church is not the door to Christ, as the Roman Catholic priests teach, but Christ is the door to the Church. And how simple is salvation ! He promises eternal life to all who base their claim for entrance upon Him alone.

The Good Shepherd died for the sheep (v. 11) ; the Great Shepherd lives for the sheep (Heb. xiii. 20) ; and the Chief Shepherd comes for the sheep (1 Pet. v. 4). See notes on Psalms xxii.-xxiv.

" Know " (v. 4). The Greek word means know intuitively—know by spiritual birth and not by religious education. " Know " in v. 14 means know experimentally.

The equality of knowledge claimed in verse 15 is an assertion of deity ; for here Jesus claims to be as omniscient as God.

" I lay down My life " (vs. 15, 17 and 18). This was not suicide, as agnostics state, for His life was His own as Creator, and He had the power of taking it again, and He was conscious of that power. A creature's life is not his own. He can destroy it, but he cannot resume it. Christ's death was wholly voluntary (v. 18). He did not die from weakness, as Socinians assert.

His death revealed more than only love for His sheep, it had a special value for God's heart (v. 17). His laying down His life and His taking it again was in itself pleasing to the Father, apart altogether from its value for the sheep. Man cannot furnish motives in order to attract God's love ; the Divine Son alone can do so For His death is a manifestation of the reality of God's love for the sinner, and a vindication of the justice of God's judgment upon sin. Hence His death glorified God. But in thus laying down His life voluntarily He did not step out of the path of obedience, for He died as commanded (v. 18). Thus love, obedience and dependence shine as golden rays from His cross.

" Other sheep " (v. 16). These are usually assumed to be the Gentiles ; but Ezekiel xxxvii. 15-28 suggests that they may be the Ten Tribes.

" The Feast of the Dedication " (v. 22). This Feast was appointed by Judas Maccabæus on his recovery of Jerusalem and the Temple from the Greeks, B.C. 164. It was held on the twenty-fifth of December in each year.

" Solomon's porch " (v. 23) faced the east. It therefore would catch the morning sun and make it pleasant and warm on a winter's day.

" Make us to doubt " (v. 24), i.e., hold us in suspense.

" I told you " (v.25). He did so repeatedly ; as for instance in viii. 58. Actions speak louder than words ; so He appealed to His miracles.

But they did not believe because they were not of His sheep (v. 26). A double characteristic belonged to these—they heard His voice and they followed Him. He on His part gave them eternal life and assured them of perpetual safety —for they were held in His hand and in His Father's hand. The false shepherds might pluck the blind man out of the outward fold (ix. 34), but they could never pluck him out of the Good Shepherd's hand. What words these must have been for the blind man and for the pardoned woman ! For as the events of chapters viii.-x. occurred on the one day, and as it was natural and reasonable that these lost sheep, now found, should keep close to Jesus to hear what He was saying, they could not have failed to hear and rejoice at this wonderful teaching ; and indeed for them possibly it was primarily intended.

The sheep are characterized by hearing and following. Only those, therefore, who exhibit these characteristics are sheep, and, consequently entitled to the consolation of the engagement that they shall never perish. People who profess to be believers but who do not daily hear the Shepherd's voice and follow Him, cannot claim the assurance of salvation which the Shepherd here gives.

" My hand " and " My Father's hand " (v. 29), are one hand.

" Are one " (v. 30). In the Greek text " we are " is plural and " one " is neuter singular. So " we are " affirms distinction of Person, and " one," unity of nature and purpose. Thus these simple words destroy the teaching of those who deny the distinction of Persons in the Godhead, and of those who question the Deity of Christ, and of those who oppose verbal inspiration.

The argument of verses 32-38 is a double one based on the Scriptures and the miracles. If the Scriptures termed " gods " magistrates appointed by the Word of God and prophets energized by the Word of God— persons to whom the Word of God merely " came,"—must not He Whom the Father had set apart for a special purpose and sent into the world, and Who executed the benevolent works of The Father—must not He be The Son of God in a unique sense, so that He was in the Father and the Father was in Him. To men " the Word of the Lord came," and that was true of even the greatest prophets, but this formula is never used in connection with Jesus, for He was the Word of God in all its infinitude. Further, His works of benevolence proved His claims ; for how could a demon do good works ; and how could God accredit by them the person and doctrines of a blasphemer ? His miracles were good works, i.e., works of benevolence, and the Scriptures approved His teachings, therefore the chiefs of the Hebrew Church were bound to accept Him as Messiah. But they wilfully refused to do so ; and being themselves evil and therefore hating goodness, they twice attempted to murder Him (vs. 31 and 39).

" From My Father " (v. 32)—" The works of My Father " (v. 37). All Christ's miracles were wrought by Him as commanded by God.

" The Scripture cannot be broken " (v. 35). These words proclaim the inspiration and infallibility of the Bible.

" Your law " (v. 34), i.e., Ps. lxxxii. Compare 1 Cor. iv. 34 with Gen. iii. 16. The entire Bible is the Law.

He left them, and remained away until the following April. During this interval the events of chapter xi. occurred. In this wilderness beyond Jordan those who had been baptized of John came to Him (v. 41) and believed upon Him (v. 42) ; and this faith, recognising the fact of sin and the need of pardon, was no doubt a true faith, and different therefore from the carnal faith of ii. 23 and viii. 30.

" The wolf scattereth the sheep " (v. 12). This prophecy has been fulfilled. Hence the groups into which Christians are divided. But the Great Shepherd watches over His Sheep and raises up under-shepherds in each group to minister to them. Their eternal safety is linked with His divine glory (vs. 27-30).

JOHN XI.—The impotent man (y.), the blind man (ix.) and Lazarus (xi.) picture Israel as morally impotent, blind and dead. Of these three demonstrations of Christ's Deity the last was the greatest. The sick may be healed, but there is no remedy for death. Death convicts man as being a sinner and conducts him to judgment, for, because of sin, it is appointed unto man once to die, and after this the judgment. So Jesus waited for sin to do its utmost as to the body, and then went to manifest His Divine glory in raising it to life. although already corrupt. The disciples feared the Jews (v. 8) ; but He, obedient to the Father's will, had no fear. It was " day " to Him (v. 9).

Such is His present action in respect to Israel. The nation is dead. But He loves it (v. 3) in its two divisions, represented by Martha and Mary (vs. 5 and 51 and 52). Soon the " two days " will end, and He will raise the nation into millennial life. (Hos. vi. 2).

His action in waiting seemed to contradict his profession of affection (vs. 5 and 6) ; and His statement that the sickness was not unto death was apparently contradicted by death actually occurring. But resurrection resolved both difficulties. The purpose of the sickness was not to demonstrate the power of sin and death, but to furnish an occasion for the glory of God, i.e., a manifestation of His glorious power in resurrection, and that the Son of God might be glorified thereby, i.e. through it.

As in the physical, so in the spiritual realm, light enters a man from without. Hence there is no spiritual light in an unconverted man (vs. 9 and 10). The Divine words : " There is no light in him " destroy the doctrine of the " Inner Light " as possessed by man in natural birth.

" Lazarus is dead "—" let us go unto him " (vs. 14 and 15). " Jehovah will judge, i.e., deliver, His people when He seeth that their power is gone." He waits till then (Deut. xxxii. 36).

" Fifteen furlongs " (v. 18), i.e., about two miles.

No one ever died in the presence of Jesus ; not even the two thieves (v. 21).

Martha believed that Jesus could heal the sick, and that there would be a future resurrection. These facts were valueless in the presence of death. But Jesus was there ; and He was not only the resurrection but also the Life. Man being dead, resurrection comes first. Christ by His death abolished sin, death, judgment and all that belongs to the life that man had lost. He went under all the power of the enemy and came up from it in the power of a new life in resurrection; and He becomes that life to the redeemed, for He communicates it to them. They are in a wholly new state, the old life, and all the wrath attaching to it, being behind them forever.

All this power of resurrection and of life is lodged in His Person; and the resurrection of Lazarus demonstrated the fact. He raised Himself from the dead (ii. 19), and God raised Him from the dead (Acts iii. 15); hence He raised Lazarus, for He is God; but this resurrection was exercised in obedience to, and dependence on, the Father (vs. 41 and 42).

Resurrection is the end of death; and consequently death has no more to do with the redeemed. It has done all it can do. It is finished. The redeemed live in the life that put an end to it. For them the old life, and its death and judgment, no longer exist.

Martha could believe that Jesus was the Messiah (v. 27); but the teachings of verses 23-26 were too deep for her, and so she felt that Mary, who was accustomed to sit at His feet, would understand (v. 28).

" Yet shall he live " (v. 25). This is 1 Thess. iv. 16. " Shall never die " (v. 26). This is 1 Thess. iv. 17.

" She fell down at His feet " (v. 32) where she had been wont to sit.

" He groaned " (v. 33), literally, groaned with indignation; most probably because of the malice of Satan in bringing such sorrow upon man.

" Was troubled " (v. 33) possibly because this rock tomb brought His approaching death and entombment visibly before His heart.

" Jesus wept " (v. 35) tears of silent sorrow in contrast with the loud wailing of verse 33 when weeping over Jerusalem.

The Jews of verse 36 were sympathetic; those of verse 37 unbelieving and hostile; and it was that unbelief that doubtless deepened the " groaning " of verse 38. " And " (v. 37) should read " but." These groups appear again in verses 45 and 46.

What human power can do (vs. 39 and 44) man is responsible to do.

Corruption, whether physical or moral, is no obstacle to Him who is the resurrection (v. 39).

" The glory of God " (v. 40), i.e., God's glorious power manifested in resurrection.

" Hast heard " (v. 41). This suggests that the prayer was heard and answered before the Lord left the Jordan.

Excepting ch. xvii., this is the longest prayer recorded of the Lord. Fifteen times He used the term " Father " in prayer.

There was a double miracle (v. 44)—the resurrection of the dead body, and its moving though tightly bound up in the grave clothes.

The argument of verse 48 was: that if the people enthroned Jesus as the promised Messiah, the Romans would suppress the revolt with such severity that the nation would cease to exist. Caiphas therefore said, not knowing that he was for the moment a prophet, that it was for their interest to put this one man to death and so save the nation.

The council consisted of seventy members and the High Priest—in imitation of Moses and the Seventy Elders (Num. xi. 24). The Jews at that time believed that the High Priest, when speaking officially, was inspired. God here used Caiphas as He had used Balaam.

" Ye know nothing at all " (v. 49), i.e., you do not realize how serious the matter is.

" That nation " (v. 51), i.e., Judah, Benjamin, and Levi. " The children scattered abroad," i.e., the Dispersion. Lev. xxvi. 33, Deut. xxviii. 64, Jer. ix. 16. Ezek. xii. 15, and xx. 15, etc.

The death of Jesus, proposed and commanded by the High Priest, was resolved upon from that fearful moment; for the raising of Lazarus had brought their malignity to a head.

The entrance and actions of Jesus awaken affection or arouse hatred (vs. 36, 37, 45 and 46).

Ephraim (v. 54) lay about fifteen miles from Jerusalem on the way to Jericho.

JOHN XII.—See notes on Matt. xxi. and xxvi., Mark xi. 14 and Luke xix.

" There they made Him a supper " (v. 2)— Compare " There they crucified Him " (Luke xxiii. 33); and " There ye shall see Him " (Matt. xxviii. 7).

Harmonious with the purpose of this Gospel in setting forth the Deity of the Lord

Jesus, only the anointing of His feet is recorded. See notes on Matt. xxvi.

To Mary of Bethany He had a value transcending all else. The faith that thus regards Him and knows His love which passeth knowledge, is a sweet odour, and it fills all the house. Man misjudged her; He vindicated her and understood her. That was all she wanted. She, unconsciously, erected to herself an eternal monument as lasting as the Gospel, and linked with it. Thus the facts of His earthly history constitute the substance of the Gospel; and His prediction of the enduring remembrance of Mary's action demonstrates His judicial supremacy in the government of the world. At His feet she probably learnt that on the third day He would rise again, and so the spikenard she had prepared for His dead body she now poured " beforehand" on His living body. It was a testimony to His resurrection, and she knew she had no other opportunity. She was not found at the empty sepulchre. She was too intelligent to be there.

This supper took place on Saturday evening, and the entrance into Jerusalem upon the following Sunday morning—the Sunday that preceded His crucifixion.

Martha served, Lazarus communed, and Mary worshipped. These spiritual activities should be true of every believer.

Lazarus (vs. 2, 9 and 10), i.e., communion, confession, cross-bearing. When the " much people" came to see Lazarus (v. 9) He was not ashamed to be found sitting with Jesus; nor did he run away with fear to hide and so escape death. His testimony though he did not utter a word, won many to Jesus (v. 11).

" Knew " (v. 9), i.e., got to know.

" These things were written of Him " (v. 16). He is the one great theme of the Scriptures.

" Many of the Jews " (v. 11); " much people " (v. 12); " the people that was with Him when He raised Lazarus " (v. 17); the people also that had heard of this miracle (v. 18); and " the world is gone after Him " (v. 19)—adding all these together there must have been a vast multitude that accompanied and witnessed the entrance of Jesus into Jerusalem.

This public entrance, associated with the supreme miracle of the raising of Lazarus, compelled priests and people to a decison. They decided to crucify Him. But they could have " prevailed nothing " (v. 19) had He not voluntarily surrendered Himself.

The Persians at the birth of the Messiah came from the East saying, "Where is he ? " (Matt. ii. 2) and at the death of the Messiah, the Greeks came from the West saying : " We would see Jesus " (v. 21). In the ancient world the Persians and the Greeks were the most intellectual—the former were famous for religion and astronomy; the latter, for philosophy and art.

" The hour is come " (v. 23). It was a foretaste of the glory and kingdom promised to Him by the Father. He came as King to Zion, His own received Him with shouts of Hosanna ; and the Gentiles, represented by these Greeks (v. 20), pressed forward to do Him homage.

But the formula " is come " was prophetic as well as illustrative ; for in prophecy the present tense is frequently used to emphasize certainty. So the sentence may read : " The hour shall come " ; and that which was then happening fore-shadowed its certain arrival. The Messiah will be King in Zion, and all the Gentiles shall flow together to His Name.

But His atoning death was a preliminary necessity (vs. 24 and 32 and 33). Not one single person could be delivered from the doom of death if Christ had not by His death atoned for sin the wages of death. The corn of wheat (v. 24) must die. Otherwise He would abide alone.

The principle of self renunciation for the enrichment of others must characterize the servant also (vs. 25 and 26).

" Where I am " (v. 26)—" Where I am " (xvii. 24), i.e., " crucified together " and " glorified together " (Gal. ii. 20 and Rom. viii. 17).

As Son of God He raised Lazarus ; as Son of David He rode into Jerusalem ; as Son of Man He died.

" Now is My soul troubled—Father, save Me from this hour " (v. 27). The agony of horror that death had for Jesus disproves the assertion that His death was that which all men must suffer Multitudes whether martyrs or sceptics have faced death and suffered it under cruel torments without flinching, and often with sacred or profane songs. But Christ shrank from it because it was an atoning death beneath the wrath of God, and so in it there was an element of horror impossible for man to understand.

" I have glorified it," i.e., at the resurrection of Lazarus, " and will glorify it again," i.e., at the resurrection of Christ.

In the cross of Calvary the world was judged, its prince, i.e., Satan cast out, and sinners saved (vs. 31 and 32, Heb. ii. 14).

" Lifted up," (v. 32), i.e., crucified. " All men," i.e., without distinction—not all without exception—for all who reject Him shall perish in the last day (v. 48).

" If " (v. 32), i.e., " because." Had He not died none would have been saved, but because He did die the atoning death of the cross, therefore all kinds of men are drawn to Him.

Men try to excuse their unwillingness to obey a moral appeal to the conscience by raising some Bible difficulty (v. 34). Jesus had said that He was the Messiah, and that He was about to be crucified. His hearers objected that the Bible said the Messiah was to abide for ever, e.g., Ps. lxxxix. 29, Isa. ix. 7, etc. But the Lord as the Light of the world refused to answer their question. He exposed the unbelief and hatred of their hearts (vs. 35, 36) ; and warned them that their day was nearly gone and that the eternal darkness was coming. Thus truth and love united in seeking their salvation ; and yet He had to hide Himself from them ! Such is the heart of man !

In verses 37-50 the Holy Spirit reviews and summarises the ministry of Christ when on earth. He first records His miracles (v. 37) ; then the dignity of His Person (vs. 38-46) ; and, lastly, His teaching (vs. 47-50).

The dignity of His Person as God is declared in verses 41, 44, and 45. When Isaiah in vision (vi.) saw Jehovah sitting upon a throne high and lifted up, etc., he saw Him who was revealed in time as Jesus of Nazareth (v. 41). Jesus Himself said that whoever believed upon Him believed upon God (v. 44), whoever saw Him saw God (v. 45), and that He was The Light. and, therefore, God (v. 46). See note on Ezek ; i. 26.

The double quotation from Isa. liii. and vi. destroys the " Two Isaiah " theory. See notes on Isaiah (Introduction).

Man wilfully shut his eyes to the message of the miracles. The word " therefore " (v. 39) proves that the unbelief of verse 38 was wilful, and, accordingly, by a just judgment, a judicial blindness has darkened their hearts to the present hour (v. 40).

" The Arm of the Lord," i.e., the Messiah.

The prophecy of Isa. vi., 9 and 10, is quoted in Matt. xiii. 14, here in John xii. 40, Acts xxviii. 26 and 27 and Romans xi. 8. It is also quoted in Mark iv. 12 and Luke viii. 10. Thus the Bible does not fear to repeat this doctrine which is so offensive to the self-righteous.

A few did believe upon Him (v. 42), but they were ashamed and afraid to confess their faith. Afterwards two of them, Nicodemus and Joseph of Arimathea, identified themselves with Him when dead. It requires more faith and courage to associate with a living saint than with a dead one.

As to His doctrine, He declared that its substance, and the words used in its proclamation, were all of Divine origin (vs. 49 and 50). He thus here destroys the theory that He was only a Jew of His day and honestly taught what He had learned from His human teachers. But He spoke of Jonah and the great fish as historic facts. He here says, " I have not spoken from Myself." His constant claim was that what He taught, and His very words, were from the Father (iii. 34, vii. 16-18, viii. 28-47, xiv. 10-24, and xvii. 8-14). If, therefore, He erred, God erred. See Weymouth on vs. 48-50.

The Gospel which He preached from the Father was Life Everlasting if received (v. 50), and eternal judgment if rejected (v. 48).

" I came not to judge " (v. 47), but to save. This was the object of His coming. Chapter ix. 39 was the effect.

" The Last Day " (v. 48). This is the sixth and last occurrence of this expression in John. See vi. 39, 40, 44, and 54, and xi. 24.

" What I should say " (v. 49), i.e., the Gospel. " What I should speak," i.e., the words to be used in preaching the Gospel.

" His commandment, etc.," (v. 50), i.e. the effect of it is eternal life.

The sense of verse 27 is : " shall I say, Save me from this hour ?—no, for to die am I come unto this hour ; I will say, Father, glorify Thy Name."

The three courts of the Tabernacle may now be recognised : Chapters i.-xii., the Outer Court. This was open to all. The Lamb of God in atonement is the great object. Chapter xiii. introduces the laver as necessary to entrance into the Holy Place, i.e. into chapters xiv.-xvi. Here the Lampstand—the Holy Spirit—prayer—and the Altar of Incense.

appear. Finally, chapter xvii., the High Priest is seen alone in the Most Holy Place.

JOHN XIII, 1-32.—See notes on Matthew xxvi., Mark xiv., and Luke xxii.

The Lord's lowly action in washing as a slave the feet of the Disciples, Judas included, was performed in the consciousness of His essential Deity, and because of His Godhead. See note on Luke ii. 42-52.

Nothing is more amazing than the fact of God assuming Manhood in order to serve man. Man could only be saved through the self-humiliation of Christ (v. 8)—"If I wash thee not," etc. Such is sin ; its cleansing demanded such a humiliation !

"Unto the end " (v. 1). This is not so much an expression of time as of degree. He loved them to the uttermost, to any extent, and to any depth, even to becoming a slave and washing their feet, and the next day, suffering the shameful death of a slave.

Two things were before His heart as He girded Himself (v. 4) :—first, His conscious Deity (v. 3) ; and second, the heartless conduct of Judas (v. 2). But neither the glory of the Divine relationship, which had given all things into His hands, nor the anguish of a treachery that delivered Him into sinners' hands, chilled the love which bound His heart to the Disciples, or caused it to forget their needs or their sorrows.

He was about to leave them (v. 1) and to resume the glory which He had with the Father before the world was, and so He would fit them to walk with Him in the life of communion; and to walk those Courts they needed cleansed feet. They had been "bathed" once and for all (v. 10), like Aaron's sons at their first consecration. That washing was not repeated. They were "clean every whit " (v. 10). But for this heavenly life of communion and service they needed cleansed feet, as Aaron's sons did every time they entered the Tabernacle.

His companions on earth they were also in spirit to be His companions in heaven ; and hence He "began to wash their feet " (v. 5). He is washing His people's feet still with the washing of water by the Word. Its teaching, applied by the Spirit to the heart and conscience, instructs the believer as to all that defiles, and, by separating him from it, cleanses him. In Luke xii. 37 He promises that He will in the glory act as a servant to those that love Him. There He will minister heaven's highest joys to the satisfying of His people's happiness.

Satan suggested the betrayal to the heart of Judas (v. 2), and the suggestion being entertained, he then took possession of him (v. 27).

"Supper being ended " (v. 2) rather, "Supper having been served." Washing preceded a meal (Luke vii. 44).

"Now " (v. 2), better "already."

"His garments " (v. 4), i.e., His outer garments. When these were removed, leaving only the inner tunic, the person was said to be naked.

The basin and the water in it figure the Bible and its contents.

"The flesh " cannot understand spiritual realities. It is either too backward (v. 6), or too forward (v. 9), or too courageous (v. 37), or too cowardly (v. 38). It is incapable of ever being right ; and it is impossible of improvement. Hence it must "die."

"No part with Me " (v. 8). Peter's warm heart shrank from such a doom, for he loved Jesus. There was too much of "Peter" for intimacy (v. 23) ; but not for service and martyrdom (v. 36).

"Clean every whit " (v. 10). Such is the effect of the precious blood that cleanseth from all sin (Heb. ix. and x.). That one infinite Sacrifice needs no repetition. So he that is "bathed " (v. 10) in that bath needs not save to "wash" his feet.

"Ye are not all clean " (v. 11). These words prove that Judas had never been so cleansed, though his feet had been washed.

They called Him "Master and Lord " (v. 13). To-day He is, alas, often irreverently called "Jesus " and not "Lord Jesus."

"Ye should do as I have done " (v. 15). Compare "this do in remembrance of Me " (Luke xxii. 19). The professing Church misinterprets the one command and neglects the other. It should recognise that both commands are spiritual and not material, are both equally imperative, and that both were to be imitated. He "washed "and He "gave." They were to "remember " Him, in order to imitate Him. They were to serve others and to die for others (1 John iii. 16). All here is spiritual and heavenly, for where He enters symbols disappear.

"I am " (v. 19), i.e., I am the Person spoken of in Psalm xli. (v. 18). For verses 18-30 see notes on Matthew xxvi.

The instruction in verse 20 appears to be (Matt. x. 40), that however they might be hated and betrayed, as He the Master was, yet like Him their mission was Divine.

"He was troubled in spirit" (v. 21)— "When he was gone out Jesus said: "Now is the Son of Man glorified" (v. 31). So long as Judas was present the Lord's heart was restrained from fully expanding itself to those He loved.

John was near enough to Jesus to receive communications from Him (vs. 23-26). He was not thus near in order to receive them; he was there because he loved Jesus. It was the spirit of Mary who sat at His feet. It is thus that His people may still learn of Him.

Anxiety prompted the question; so when anxious thoughts arise they can be stilled in the heart that keeps near the Lord for His own sake.

"Then Satan entered into him" (v. 27, R.V.). "Jesus therefore said" (v. 27, R.V.). These two words "then" and "therefore" are most important.

"It was night" (v. 30). Dark as was the night upon Judas' head there was a blacker night in his heart. All was darkness in his soul. Doubtless he expected and believed that the Lord would deliver Himself as usual; but to him the thoughts of God were hidden thoughts. Yet he could bear witness to the innocence of Christ, as did the thief on the cross. Death and destruction can hear the fame of Wisdom, but only God knows Him (Job xxviii. 22).

Christ glorified God in death, and God glorified Him in resurrection (vs. 31 and 32). God dealt with Job in discipline, but with Christ in justice; for He, on the cross, became sin, and there made a glorious exhibition of the attributes of God in justice, majesty, truth and love. All were vindicated and thus was God glorified. At Calvary infinite wrath against sin and infinite love toward the sinner were demonstrated. God was dishonoured in the first man, but infinitely glorified in the second; and, consequently, He straightway glorified Him in raising Him from the dead.

The Son of Man on the cross was glorified in a much more admirable way than He will be by the millennial glories attaching to that title; for on the cross, as the Son of Man, He perfectly displayed all the moral glory of God. He was there tested to the uttermost as to His ability to sustain that

glory, but He fully succeeded in so doing. When made sin, and at the same time the One Great Offering for sin, He sacrificed Himself in order to fully glorify God. Thus He established the foundations of the New Heavens and the New Earth; and, having satisfied all the claims of righteousness and of violated law against man, He has thrown wide open to all men the doors into that Kingdom.

JOHN XIII. 33—XIV. 31.—The traitor having gone out (v. 30) and the basis of heavenly relationships established in the Death and Resurrection of Christ, and the glories expressed in them (v. 32), the Lord then began His farewell to the disciples, by leading them as "little children" (v. 33) into direct communication with the Father. He told them He was about to leave them, but that He would come back for them (xiv. 3, 18 and 28); that during the interval He would not leave them in orphanage (v. 18), but would provide them a Comforter, the Holy Spirit (v. 16); and that He Himself and the Father would dwell spiritually with them (v. 23) in a conscious fellowship far exceeding that which they had enjoyed when He was visibly present with them.

The love that pervaded this farewell, beginning with the words "Little children" (v. 33), was deep and tender beyond the possibility of human comprehension.

The Mohammedan priest, when helping Henry Martyn in the translation into Persian of these chapters, exclaimed: "How He loved those men!"

"A little while" (v. 33), i.e., six weeks. "Ye shall seek Me" (v. 33). He knew they would, and the thought was a precious balm to His wounded heart.

"The Jews" (v. 33). The Lord thus speaks of them only here and in iv. 22 and xviii. 20 and 36.

During His absence—deprived of His visible and personal love—brotherly love was, in a sense, to take His place. It was not a new commandment in point of time (Lev. xix. 18), but in point of degree and of family relationship. Under Law the disciple was to love his neighbour as himself; under Grace, more than himself, for he was to love as Christ loved (v. 34). He loved His enemies, and not merely His neighbours, more than Himself, for He gave His Life for them; and so Christian men should give their lives for their brethren (1 John iii. 16). They were to love one another as He had loved them, overlooking their faults and pitying their weakness. Thus were they to support each other.

"Whither I go thou canst not follow" (v. 36). As the passage through Jordan had to be made by the Ark alone, so Christ had to pass through the waters of Golgotha by Himself; and through those waters Peter could not accompany Him. Afterwards he too would be crucified; but, like Israel, he would pass through the river dry-shod.

"Lord, whither goest Thou?" (v. 36 and xiv. 5). There is no conflict here with xvi. 5, for this latter statement shows that the Disciples, as was ever characteristic of their incredible deadness to their Master's spiritual teaching, thought that He proposed to go to some other country; and as they did not know which, they did not, therefore, know the way thither. Besides, they were so occupied with themselves and buried in the sorrow which separation from Him would cause, that they could think of nothing else but their own loss and danger. But dull and blind and selfish as they were He kept on loving them, and so He talked of their joys and their sorrows, setting aside the deeper joys and sorrows that were His (xvi. 6 and 20-22).

Immediately upon predicting Peter's shameful denial He said: "Let not your heart be troubled, believe in God, believe also in Me," i.e., repose the same trust and confidence in My forgiving love and Almighty power and care as you repose in God. What a commanding claim to equality with God!

What balm to Peter's troubled heart these words must have been at daybreak when weeping bitterly he lay broken-hearted in the depths.

The Master's heart was "troubled" (xiii. 21), but He put His own trouble aside and told them not to be troubled (xiv. 1 and 27), for that He would never cease to care for them, and though He must leave them He would be busied preparing mansions for them. There would be room for them all. And then He would come for them and have them there with Himself. Angels were not to prepare these mansions, nor were angels to come to fetch them home to them. His own hands would prepare the mansions, and He Himself would come to bring them

home, for in His Father's house were many mansions (see note on Ezek. xli. 6).

Meanwhile there was no necessity why they should be troubled, for His gift to them of the Holy Spirit would assure them a Companion Who was both a Comforter and an Upholder, and Who, being All-loving and Almighty, would provide for all their needs and so relieve them from anxiety.

There were four interruptions, but these helped to bring out precious truths: Simon Peter (v. 36); Thomas (xiv. 5); Philip (v. 8); and Judas, not Iscariot (v. 22).

Three times He comforted them with the assurance of His promised return (vs. 3, 18 and 28). Their hopes did not rise higher than earthly glory with the promised Messiah in His Kingdom over Israel. But in this farewell He drew their hearts to a higher glory, that is, a heavenly.

He told them that they knew whither He was going and the way; for He was going to the Father, and they had seen the Father in Him, and they knew the Way, for He was the Way (vs. 5-11). Verse 6 should read as in the Revised Version.

"If ye had known Me" (v. 7), i.e., "If ye had learned to know Me spiritually and experimentally, ye should have got to know that I and the Father are One."

"So long time" (v. 9). Philip was one of the first of the apostles (i. 43).

The argument of verse 10 is: That the words that He spake were not from Himself, but from the Father Who dwelt in Him. He spake them. And, similarly, the miracles He performed were not performed from Himself, but from the Father. He performed them.

"Greater works" (v. 12). The Acts of the Apostles record these greater works, performed in a greater world. The Lord's ministry was confined to Palestine; the Apostles went "everywhere," "throughout the whole world" (Acts viii. 4 and Rom. i. 8).

He put them in immediate connection with the Father (vs. 13 and 14). Their access to Him was to be most intimate, and the answers to their petitions should be based upon the Father's glory in the Son, and only limited by the Almighty resources expressed in the words "Ask in My Name," i.e., in harmony with Christ's character and will (xiv. 13, 14, xv. 16, xvi. 23, 24, 26).

If they loved Him (v. 15) it was to be shown not merely in sorrow because of His departure, but in the keeping of His commandments (vs. 21, 23). Obedience was to be the condition of fellowship.

He Himself could only abide with them for " a little time " (xiii. 33), but the Holy Spirit should abide with them perpetually (v. 16).

" But ye know Him," i.e., " but ye shall get to know Him ; for He dwells and shall dwell with you, and shall be in you " (v. 17). He dwelt with them at the moment in the person of Christ ; for the Holy Spirit, as well as the Father (v. 9), tabernacled fully in Jesus.

As in Hebrew so here, and frequently in the New Testament, the present tense is used for the future in order to express continuance and certainty. So verse 17 with verse 9 reveal the Three Persons of the Trinity.

At Pentecost they learned to know experi mentally the Holy Spirit. Till then they had not known Him in that sense. Compare Acts xix. 2.

Companionship ("He shall dwell with you") and Indwelling ("and shall be in you"). These great realities assure gladness and victory to the believer.

" I will come to you " (v. 18)—and " at that day (v. 20) ye shall get to know that I am in My Father and ye in Me and I in you."

" That day " here primarily meant the Pentecostal Dispensation, but it also means the future day of perfected knowledge and consummated bliss. At Pentecost He came to them in the Person of the Holy Spirit ; in the yet future day He will come in His Own Person.

" A little while " (v. 19), i.e., about thirty hours. The last time the world saw Him was when He was being entombed.

As Christ subsists in God, so the believer subsists in Christ and Christ-in him (v. 20). This is a great mystery full of the deepest awe.

Their love to Him was to show itself in cherishing and obeying His commandments, and they would, as a consequence, consciously enjoy inward manifestations of His indwelling by the Spirit (vs. 21 and 23). To Judas, not Iscariot, He explained that His manifestation of Himself was to the heart it was inward and spiritual, so that the heart would consciously enjoy His abiding in it. The word " abode " (v. 23) is the same as " mansion " in verse 2.

All therefore who truly love Him, love the Bible, and obey its teaching.

The love of verses 21-23 is not here the activity of the love of God in grace to sinners, but the activity of a Father's love for His children ; and hence the conscious enjoyment and manifestation of that love is dependent upon obedience. Naughty children are loved, but are not caressed. If the Spirit be grieved the divine manifestations to the heart cease to be consciously enjoyed, communion is interrupted, and the Spirit has to deal with the conscience in conviction rather than with the heart in manifestation. Thus communion and obedience are interrelated.

" In My Name " (v. 26). " Name " in the Scriptures expresses authority and character. The Holy Spirit represents Christ on earth, and displays His moral glories in the consecrated lives of those whom He indwells in ungrieved power.

The personality of the Holy Spirit appears in this farewell in the terms : " teaching," " reminding," " testifying," " coming," " convincing," " guiding," " speaking," " hearing," " prophesying," " taking " and " bringing."

His legacy of peace (v. 27) was not only the peace for heart and conscience secured by the Blood of His Cross (Col. i. 20), but His own peace in which He lived when on earth as a man. That was a peace that the world could neither touch nor reach nor destroy. In that peace He Himself walked as a Man in fellowship with the Father.

Earthly legacies are limited and frequently do not materialize, but this legacy is unlimited and real.

So He speaks of " My peace " (v. 27), " My love " (xv. 9), " My joy " (xv. 11), and " My glory " (xvii. 22), and these are in the bequest.

In His wondrous grace He reckoned upon their affection for Him, and it was a precious thought to Him that they would rejoice in His glory and joy (v. 28).

" My Father is greater than I " (v. 28). A son is not inferior to his father as to his essential being, but only as to office. Hence the claim that this statement denies the Perfect Deity of Christ is not only unfounded, but the statement itself affirms the contrary. The holiest saint, when dying, would not dare to use such language, and, if he did, he would inexpressibly shock all who heard him.

" If " (v. 29), i.e., His Death and Resurrection, more particularly the latter, which they had found so difficult to believe.

" Hereafter," i.e., " no longer."

If the prince of the world, i.e., Satan, could find nothing in his rival the Messiah to which to appeal, why then should Jesus die, for death was in the power of Satan ? (Heb. ii. 14). It was because the Father had commanded the Son to offer up Himself as a sacrifice for sin in order to its expiation, and by so dying the Son manifested to the world His love and obedience to the Father.

" Even so I do " (v. 31), i.e., as thus commanded so I am about to do ; and the very next day He did it.

" Arise, let us go hence " (v. 31). Chapter xviii. 1 makes quite clear that this " arise " was figurative and not physical. It expressed haste to accomplish the Father's will.

JOHN XV. 1—XVI. 4.—The relationship of this chapter to the prior one is very important. The personal glory of Christ as the True Priest is the theme of the one chapter, and His personal glory as the True Vine, the subject of the other. Israel had been elected both priest and vine (Hosea iv. 6, and Isa. v.), but lost both glories through disobedience. But God had His True 'Priest and His True Vine in reserve.

Again, the one chapter concerns the gift of the Holy Spirit to man ; the other chapter, His activities in man.

In the prior chapter believers as priests live a life of fellowship with Christ in heavenly places ; in the following chapter they live a life of testimony and beneficence as vine branches in earthly places. The one chapter is the Epistle to the Ephesians ; the other, the Epistle to the Philippians. The one is the indwelling of the Spirit in the believer within the vail ; the other, the outward working of the Spirit in the believer outside the camp.

" Fruit " (v. 2). " More fruit " (v. 2). " Much fruit " (v. 5).

" His Word " (v. 3) cleansed the vine by removing the fruitless branch. The effect therefore of His teaching was to remove Judas Iscariot and the untrue disciples who walked no more with Him. So speaking to the Eleven, He could say, " Ye are clean." i.e., purged branches.

Fruit is the evidence of vital union with Christ. It glorified the Father, and manifested true discipleship.

The life of the believer as a vine branch is one of dependence (v. 4) and obedience (v. 7).

A vine branch has only one purpose, and that is to bear fruit. Otherwise it is useless (v. 6).

Union with Christ (vs. 1-8) leads to Communion with God (vs. 9-17) and Disunion with the world (v. 18—xvi. 4).

That only is fruit which the Holy Spirit produces in the life of the Christian. All else are " dead works." A life of habitual practical nearness of heart to Christ, of love to His Person and subjection to 'His Word (vs. 9 and 10), is the secret of a life of fruit-bearing and of joy (vs. 8 and 11).

His commandments (v. 10) are the expression of what He is ; and those who keep them consciously enjoy His love.

" He taketh away " (v. 2). This may also read " He raiseth." A vine-dresser frequently supports a branch on a forked stick in order to its bearing fruit. But the argument of the passage supports the English text.

Cleansing is not the same as chastening. The fruitful Christian is cleansed, if necessary, by trial, or by sickness, in order to the production of more fruit and much fruit. The unfruitful Christian is chastened.

Fruit is the exhibition in Christian conduct of the Spirit and example of the Lord Jesus Christ, so that from the conduct of the disciple the world may learn what the Master was like. His Spirit in the believer produces the fruit of the Spirit (Gal. v. 22).

" Continue ye in My love " (v. 9), not : " continue ye to love Me," but : " continue ye in the enjoyment of My love, measured by the Father's love to Me." His enjoyment of the Father's love (v. 10) resulted from His life of dependence and obedience as a man on earth in the path of service.

" Ye shall ask what ye will " (v. 7) — and : " ye shall ask of the Father " (v. 16). Answers to prayer are affected by the condition of fruit-bearing.

" In My name " (v. 16). The argument here is : that as the Father loves the Son, so He loves those whom the Son has chosen ; and, therefore, He will answer their prayer ; for how could He withhold anything from them in such a case ?

The theme from verse 12 to xvi. 4, is the exercise of mutual love in a realm of Divine love environed by hatred.

The world would hate them because it hated Him ; but they were to live in an atmosphere of love one to another, and unaffected by this environment of hate. They were to love one another as He loved them. See note on xiii. 34.

But the sphere or realm of love into which He had brought them was the wondrous love subsisting between the Father and the Son— a love of affection based upon relationship. The believer is lifted into the enjoyment and dignity of the very kingdom of love, in which God and Christ mutually exist and subsist. Such knowledge is too wonderful for the poor human heart.

This commandment of verses 12 and 17, and of xiii. 34, He calls " My commandment " —His own special commandment to His dearly loved disciples.

In the East the disciple chooses the master, but Jesus reversed this order (v. 16). He chooses His disciples and ordains them to go forth and bring forth fruit, and fruit that should remain. So these disciples went forth to a life of fruit-bearing ; and the multitude of Christian people in the world to-day testifies that their fruit remains.

" He chose them out of the world " (v. 19). While yet in the world they were given to Him of the Father (xvii. 6). While yet in the world they belonged to Jesus though they did not know it.

" Remember the word " (v. 20), i.e., the word of xiii. 16.

" No cloak " (v. 22), i.e., no excuse. His preaching (v. 22), and His miracles (v. 24), both plainly revealed who He was. He was God—Love itself in human form—and they turned from Him in detestation, and in their hatred to Him crucified Him. Such is man's heart ! Hating Him they hated God (v. 23) ; and they hated Him without any reason (v. 25). See Psalms xxxv. 19, lxix. 4, cix. 3, cxix. 161, Rom. iii. 24, and Rev. xxii. 17. " Freely " and " without a cause " are the same Greek word.

" They had not had sin " (vs. 22 and 24), i.e., the supreme sin of rejecting Christ (xvi. 9).

The loved ministry and office of the Holy Spirit is to testify of Christ (v. 26). The Spirit proceeds from the Father, and is sent by the Son.

In fellowship with the Holy Spirit they were to return love for the hatred that surrounded them ; and they were to unite with the Spirit in witnessing for Christ. Only those who know Him and live in communion with Him can testify of Him (v. 27)

They were not to be stumbled or con founded because hated and ill-treated by the chiefs and members of the Hebrew church. Their action resulted from not knowing God in Christ. That church was of Divine ordination, and intended as a light to the world, but its knowledge of God was carnal ; and carnal men can be very zealous for religious truth, and use it as an authority for persecuting those who have a true and spiritual knowledge of God.

JOHN XVI. 5-33. —The Mission and Ministry of the Holy Spirit depended upon the return of Christ to the Father (vs. 5 and 16). The disciples were, therefore, not to mourn, for the Spirit would be their Comfor ter (v. 7) and Teacher (vs. 13-15). While comforting them He would convict the world of the supreme sin of rejecting Christ (vs. 8 and 9) ; of righteousness, for Jesus was righteousness, and declared so to be by the resurrection ; and of judgment, for the Prince of this world being judged at Calvary all His subjects, therefore, were judged ; for on that solemn day the Prince of Death associated the whole world with himself— Jew and Gentile, priest and people, kings, governors, princes, soldiers, subjects and even malefactors in his enterprise of hatred against the Prince of Life. The Serpent and his seed were then judged ; and the execution of the judgment will take effect in Revelation xix.

Righteousness was, accordingly, only once in the world. He returned to heaven and has never been seen on earth since (v. 10). Man's last view of Him was when He was being laid in the tomb.

Such is the Ministry of the Holy Spirit. He convicts men of sin, He convinces them of a spotless righteousness in the presence of God for them, and He warns them of the judgment that they must suffer if His testimony is resisted.

" I go My Way " (v. 5). " Sorrow hath filled your heart " (v. 6) ; here faith and nature are contrasted. Faith in Him looked at the future into which God was about to lead Him through death. Nature in them occupied with its own interests and with that which it loses, made the Disciples so insensible to His sorrows and to His joys that they had not sufficient activity of affection to ask Him " whither goest Thou ? " See note on

xiii. 36. Had they thought of Him and not of themselves, they would have asked Him. But in His matchless love and comprehension He excused them.

" Expedient " (v. 7), i.e., " profitable."

" I will send Him " (v. 7). His promise was fulfilled at Pentecost.

" Righteousness " (v. 10). The Ascension declared Him to be Righteousness Whom man declared to be a sinner and an impostor. He was God fully revealed in love ; but man would not have Him. Man hated Him. The more He manifested His Deity and Goodness, the more He was hated and opposed. Appalling fact that when perfect Goodness appeared on earth in sinless flesh, He excited man's detestation.

Satan is called the Prince of this world in xii. 31., xiv. 30, and xvi. 11.

The office and Ministry of the Holy Spirit is to glorify Christ (v. 14). He does not speak of and from Himself (v. 13), but He unveils to the believer's heart the glorious perfections, ministries, offices, graces, and fulness of the Lord Jesus Christ. He guides into all truth—hence the inspiration of the Gospels and the Epistles—and He shows things to come—hence the Apocalypse. All the attributes of God belong to Christ (v. 15) ; and it is the Spirit's joy to declare and reveal these attributes.

Such being the nature and the limits of the Spirit's ministry, all pretended revelations of the Spirit which do not throw light upon the Person of Christ as the Incarnate Word, and upon the Bible as the Written Word, are vain ; and such pretended revelations are from the Spirit of evil and lead men into darkness, bondage and death.

In the words " All things that the Father hath are Mine," The Lord Jesus claims absolute community with God. Here is a wonderful glimpse into the inner relations of the Godhead.

So the Holy Spirit communicates heavenly facts to earthly pilgrims. The Disciples had seen the moral glory of Christ on earth ; the Holy Spirit would unfold to them His Divine glories in that which belonged to Him as Jehovah's Fellow.

Historically, the prediction of verses 16, 19, 20 and 22 was fulfilled by His entombment and resurrection, but a larger fulfilment yet awaits consummation ; for the " little while " of His present absence, with its sorrow, is to be succeeded by the Day (vs. 23 and 26) of His return. Meanwhile He is with the Father (v. 16) ; and He places His people in direct relations with the Father (v. 23), assuring them of the Father s love for them (v. 27) ; and He gives them His own Name as the Authority through which all needed supplies should reach them. But He pointed out that it would not be necessary for Him to urge the Father to grant their petitions, for neither He nor they would appeal to an unwilling ear (v. 26).

" In My Name " (vs. 23, 24 and 26). All blessing from the Father comes in His Name. It is in His Name that the Holy Spirit has been sent by the Father. The Father hath committed all things unto Him. " In His Name " means in harmony with His being and will, and in furtherance of His glory.

" In that day ye shall ask Me nothing " (v. 23). " In that day ye shall ask in My Name " (v. 26), i.e., He placed them in direct relationship with The Father as enjoying the same access as He Himself enjoyed. And, further, the Holy Spirit would be so effective a Teacher (1 John ii. 27) that He would answer all their questions, if profitable.

Putting aside His own sorrows and joys, He in this night of betrayal speaks of their sorrows and joys (v. 22). When He meets His people by-and-by His joy will be immeasurably beyond theirs, but here in His grace He speaks of their joy in that day. Such is the perfect and unselfish love of that sinless bosom.

Fulness of joy is dependent upon boldness and constancy in prayer (v. 24).

His Disciples were like children (vs. 29 and 30). They hastened to assure Him of their intelligence and of their faith. But Jesus sorrowfully tells them that they will return every man of them to his own home and forsake Him in His hour of greatest need. As a Perfect and Sinless Man, He was exquisitely sensitive to sympathy ; and yet He loved them, though they denied Him that human fellowship which His heart craved.

" These things " (v. 33), i.e., all that He had said during His farewell.

" Reprove " (v. 8) means convict and refute. Acts ii. 37 and vii. 54 furnish illustrations. His action on the heart awakens faith or fury.

JOHN XVII.—This is the longest of the Lord's prayers in the Gospel records; and the only one stated to have been made with the disciples.

It contains seven petitions—two respecting the Lord Himself and five respecting His people.

Those respecting Him are given in verses 1 and 5; those respecting His people are found in verses 11, 15, 17, 21, and 24.

The prayer views the Lord as resuming His position in glory as Jehovah's Fellow (Zech. xiii. 7)—bringing up with Him into that Divine glory His nature as Man. It regards the disciples as taking His place on earth, and, as under the Father's guardianship, continuing His work of manifesting the character of God in love and judgment in a world of hatred and sin, and saving men out of it.

The prayer puts the disciples into an immediate relationship with the Father; commits them to His love and care; asks that they may be loved as He Himself was loved; and reveals His own indwelling in them by the Holy Spirit, so equipping them for the effectual accomplishment of their ministry. This efficiency is expressed in the three last mighty words " I in them."

The Lord apparently did not kneel. As He reclined at the supper table, He lifted up His eyes and prayed (v. 1).

His first petition was for the promised glory of power over all flesh so as to be the channel of giving eternal life (v. 2). But He would not have this glory except to glorify the Father (v. 1); and He would exercise the ability of giving life in favour only of those chosen by the Father and given to Him (v. 2).

This double glory had been promised to Him by the Father because of His obedience unto death.

Only here (v. 3) does the Lord speak of Himself as " Jesus Christ "; and He associates Himself as such with God, and so claims Deity and Equality; for the Knowledge of God and a creature could not be eternal life.

" I have glorified," " I have finished," " I have manifested," " I have given," " When I was in the world," " Now come I to Thee " and " Where I am." These statements characterize the prayer. It was, in spirit, offered in the heavenlies (Heb. ix. 11) after the accomplishment of His Death and Resurrection and Ascension.

In His Second petition (v. 5), the Lord asks that in return for His fulfilled ministry upon earth (v. 4) He should be glorified as man with the glory which is eternally His as God. He asked to be reinvested with His pre-existent glory, not however simply as before, but now in human nature.

He next (vs. 6-13) puts His Disciples into relationship with the Father, munitioned by the words He had given them, and that they might enjoy as witness-bearers in the world, the joy of which He knew the fulness in His path of service and testimony upon earth (v. 13).

In verses 14-21, He prays for them in respect of their relationship to the world. Such was their double relationship, first, with the Father, and second, with the world.

The disciples were dull, insensible and full of faults, and yet the grace that loved them spoke of them in the admiring words of verses 6-8.

" I pray not for the world " (v. 9), i.e., not then. See Psalm ii.

" The men Thou gavest Me out of the world " (v. 6). While yet in the world and ignorant of Jesus they belonged to Him because given to Him by the Father. Seven times in this prayer He speaks of His people as having been given to Him (vs. 2, 6, 6, 9, 11, 12, 24).

A man can say " All mine are Thine " (v. 10), but only Jesus could say " All Thine are Mine." This is a claim of perfect equality with God.

Wonderful is the grace that reveals these desires, and the privileges that flow from His care for His loved people. Here is heard the Son conversing with the Father respecting their common love for sinful men; and here the very heart of the Great Shepherd is laid open. It was so natural and easy to Him to rest His eyes one moment upon the loved disciples and then lift them to heaven to ask precious things for them.

In relation to them He could say : " I have glorified Thee; now glorify Me " (vs. 4 and 5). Here is equality of nature and subjection of love. He did not say " I will glorify Myself."

" Out of the world " (v. 6); " Not of the world " (v. 16): " Into the world " (v. 18). A ship is useless unless in the sea, but perishes if the sea gets into it.

" Father " (v. 1) · " Holy Father " (v. 11); " Righteous Father " (v. 25). The first title embraces both Christ and His people ; the second, expresses the mingled energy of affection and holiness capable of enabling them to live a life of sanctification and testimony in a world given over to evil ; and the third, concerns the distinction that God as a righteous Father will make between those in whom Christ dwells (v. 26) and the world which rejects Him.

The first prayer for the disciples was that they might be kept (v. 11) ; the second prayer asked for protection from the evil one (v. 15) ; the third (v. 17), that their knowledge of the Scriptures should result in separation from all evil (v. 17) ; the fourth (v. 18-21) related to oneness with Christ and God in soul-winning—not in church unity, as is popularly supposed (contrast Gen. iii. 22), and the fifth and last (v. 24) concerned their eternal home.

There are three unities desired in the prayer. First, unity in communion, in the Fellowship of Christ with the Father—" One as we are " (v. 11). Second, unity in purpose with the Father and the Son in the salvation of sinners (vs. 18 and 21)—".One in us." Third, unity in glory (v. 22)—" As We are One."

The Father sent the Son into the world to save the world, and the Son sent His disciples into the same world for the same purpose (v. 18). This is the " glory " of v. 22, and this unity in purpose will help the world to " believe " (v. 21) ; and the unity in glory will cause the world to " know " that God loved Christ and loved His people as He loved their Head (v. 23).

Everyone was to be a soul-winner—clothed with the moral glory of v. 22, animated with the love of v. 20, and unchilled by the failure of v. 25. Compare 2 Cor. v. 18 and the glory of the gospel ambassador which is His and which He gives to His disciples (v. 22).

The prayer of verse 24 is remarkable : First, for its style : " Father I will " ; next, for its subjects : " those whom Thou hast given Me " ; then, for its requests : " that they may be with Me where I am," and "that they may behold My glory;" and, finally, for its argument : " for Thou lovedst Me."

No saint however exalted dared to say in prayer " I will." Christ loved His erring disciples so deeply that [He entreated that He might never be separated from them ; and prayed that having witnessed His shame they might be brought to behold His glory.

" I have declared and will continue declaring Thy Name " (v. 26). As on earth it was His joy to reveal to His disciples the Father's character with its unutterable wealth of love and holiness, so in the glory He continues this ministry in order that His people may consciously enjoy, and know that they possess, the very same love that Christ on earth as a man enjoyed and knew that He possessed—only that in His case the knowledge was infinite. This community of conscience and testimony should have as a result the moral demonstration to the world of " I in them."

The love that desired reunion with the Father in glory (vs. 1 and 5) equally desired the fellowship of His loved disciples in glory (v. 24), and His entrance into that glory after having finished the work of their redemption (v. 4), guaranteed their presence there (v. 2). His being there was their title to be there.

All that was the Son's was the Father's (v. 10), and all that was the Father's was the Son's, and; amazing fact, these dull and unintelligent disciples were the joint object of this mutual affection within the eternal love of the Father and the Son.

Such was the foundation of this wondrous prayer. He prayed for the disciples because they belonged to the Father. Therefore He must pray for them ; and the Father must be interested in them because Christ was glorified in them.

The disciples lost the companionship of Christ visibly, but it was to find themselves put in Christ's own relationship with the Father, enjoying all that He enjoyed in that blest fellowship on earth.

It was in the power of the enjoyment of this relationship to the Father that the disciples were enabled to maintain their relationship to the world in love and testimony ; and the rule of that spiritual life was to be the Word, i.e., the Scriptures.

That Word was to come first, and then their mission was to follow. The Word would make it intelligent and effective. The Word was, and is, opposed to the world. Were they of the world, they could not be sent into it ; but they had been taken out of the world.

" I sanctify Myself " (v. 19), i.e., He set Himself apart as a glorified Man in the glory to be the one channel of truth for the enduement and enrichment of His people, and for their intelligent persistence in separation from the world and its evil. He is a perfect illustration in glory of separation to God, and His people should be a similar illustration upon earth; and if they would but yield themselves unto Him He would, by His Holy Spirit, willingly and efficiently live His life of separation in them (v. 26).

In the day of His appearing the world will know (v. 23) that His people have been loved by God, as their Redeemer was loved; and meanwhile it is the privilege of His people to know that God does love them as He loved Christ.

The prayer corresponds with 1 Kings viii. The Aaronic priesthood is absent in each, for in each the Petitioner is both king and priest. The petitions in each are seven in number. In each they fall into two groups —two general and five personal. The first two in 1 Kings: God and Solomon. The first two here: God and the Divine Solomon. Both prayers were based upon Calvary (1 Kings viii. 5, John xviii. 4) and the glory (1 Kings viii. 11, John xvii. 5)—and between Calvary and the glory. (See 2 Chron. vii. 1, with 1 Kings viii. 11 where the glory is anticipated in the record).

JOHN XVIII.—See notes on Matt. xxvi., Mark xiv., and Luke xxii.

The Godhead of Christ being the distinctive feature of this Gospel, His apprehensions of the cross; His agony in the garden; His cry "Why has Thou forsaken Me?"; the darkness of the cross; the commendation of His Spirit to God; and other features characteristic of His manhood are here omitted; whilst His Deity, expressed in His farewell to the Eleven; the effect of His "I am" upon His enemies (v. 6); and His triumphant cry "Finished," etc., are made prominent.

This record, therefore, brings out His personal glory as Son of God abolishing sin, and destroying him who had its power.

It was full moon; but treachery and hatred distrusted its pure and gentle light, and, therefore, His enemies brought their torches and lanterns.

Three times Jesus said "I am" (vs. 5, 6 and 8), and, as predicted in Psalm xxvii, they went backward and fell to the ground.

As they approached Him with their lanterns His heart sang: "Jehovah is My Light

and My salvation, whom shall I fear?" See notes on Psalm xxvii.

Annas to whom they at once brought Jesus sent Him immediately to Caiaphas (vs. 13 and 14).

"In secret . . . nothing" (v. 20), i.e., nothing against Moses or Caesar.

It is clear from a comparison of the Four Gospels that both these High Priests occupied the one palace.

"The Hall of Judgment" (v. 28), i.e., Pilate's court of Justice—upon this occasion a court of injustice.

Conscience without the cleansing of the Holy Spirit through the Scriptures, is a false teacher (v. 28); it needs to be purged (Heb. ix. 14).

They had no case against Him, so they could not answer Pilate's question (vs. 29 and 30).

"What death" (v. 32), i.e., what manner of death—i.e., crucifixion.

Partly because they feared the multitude and partly because their hatred thought a death by stoning too painless, they determined to bring Him into the power of the Roman Governor; for against him the people could do nothing, and so the priests could secure the punishment of crucifixion.

Before the High Priest Jesus declared that He was the Son of God, and before the Roman Governor He claimed to be the King of the Jews (vs. 33 and 37).

The word "My" occurs four times in verse 36—thrice in relation to His Kingdom and once in relation to His servants.

"It is as you say—I am a king" (v. 37). "Now is My Kingdom," i.e., My Messianic Kingdom, "not from hence," i.e., not of human origination or appointment. By and by it would be of Divine institution (Rev. xii. 10). His present kingdom is the moral kingdom of truth (v. 37). There is but One Teacher in that Kingdom, and every Spirit-taught heart listens to that Voice.

In Pilate's day discussions about truth were interminable. No doubt he was tired of them and did not want to start a fresh discussion; and so, having asked the question he did not wait for a reply (v. 38).

They chose a robber; and ever since they have been mercilessly robbed.

Comparing xiii. 36-38 with Matt. xxvi. 33-35, Mark xiv. 26-31 (noting the words "he spoke the more vehemently") and

Luke xxii. 31-34 (noting the words " I tell thee Peter," i.e., I tell you again) it would appear that the Lord twice warned Peter of his denial—once at the supper-table and then again on the way to Gethsemane.

JOHN XIX.—See notes on Matt. xxvii., Mark, xv., and Luke xxiii.

In reading of the Crucifixion the believer can accompany the Lord part of the way, but there comes a point beyond which he cannot go, and perhaps never will be able to go, and that point was when the sinless soul of Jesus entered into the horrors of the wrath of God. The unseen darkness of that abyss was faintly figured by the created darkness which enwrapt the cross and the land.

" Behold the Man " (v. 5) and " Behold your King " (v. 14).

" Whence art Thou " (v. 9)? This was Pilate's fifth question. See xviii. 33, 35, 37, 38: Pilate evidently was agitated with superstitious fears. This question expressed his apprehension that his prisoner was super-human.

The word " me " (v. 10) is emphatic.

" From above " (v. 11), i.e., by God's pre-determination.

" He that delivered Me unto thee " (v. 11), i.e., Caiaphas. Judas delivered Jesus to Caiaphas, and Caiaphas delivered Him to Pilate. Pilate was guilty of the sin of refusing justice to his innocent prisoner, but Caiaphas was guilty of the greater sin of the death of Christ, for he sinned against a Bible knowledge to which Pilate was a stranger.

" Gabbatha " (v. 13). The meaning of this word is, uncertain.

" The sixth hour " (v. 14), i.e., nine a.m. The word " about " is important, i.e., it was coming on to nine o'clock Roman Time.

" I find no crime in Him " (v. 4)—" Then delivered he Him to be crucified " (v. 16). Thus, as predicted in Isaiah liii. 8, He was taken from judgment, i.e., He was refused justice.

Jesus watched the soldiers parting His garments and casting lots for His vesture ; and He heard what they were saying to one another, and He thought of and possibly prayed the whole of Psalm xxii.

The minuteness of this prediction and its detailed fulfilment 750 years later by Roman soldiers, is one of the many overwhelming proofs of inspiration. How little these soldiers thought that in sharing the Lord's clothing, and making an exception of the tunic, and casting lots for it, they were fulfilling a prophecy centuries old !

A tunic woven from the top throughout had exceptional value and distinguished a Rabbi ; just as ministers of religion to-day wear a distinctive dress.

He was mocked by those that passed by (Psalm xxii. 7, Matt. xxvii. 39 and 40) ; He was mocked by the chief priests, the Scribes, and the elders, saying " Himself He cannot save " ; He was mocked by the soldiers (Luke xxiii. 36) ; and He was mocked by the malefactors (Matt. xxvii. 44).

Salome, John's mother, was also there (v. 25). Why the name is here omitted is strange (Matt. xxvii. 56). Both John's parents were alive so that his home (v. 27) was their house.

John vii. 3-5 explains the need of the provision of verse 26.

The perfection and affection of a true humanity, and the calm power of a true Godhead, appear in the exquisite picture of verses 25-27.

After the resurrection Mary and her children became disciples (Acts i. 14). Mary, a figure of Israel, only fully believed on Him when she saw Him pierced for her sins.

" He bowed His head " (v. 30). Till that moment He had evidently kept it erect.

" He gave up the ghost " (v. 31). This in the Greek text is quite another word from " expired." In John the Holy Spirit emphasizes the voluntary nature of His death. In Luke, His filial trust is emphasized ; in John, His Divine Competency. The special word here found is never used in this way in the Bible, except in this passage in reference to Christ.

Verses 33-35 and 38-42 are fundamentally valuable as affirming beyond controversy the actual death of Jesus Christ. The added testimony of the centurion (see notes on Matt. xxvii.) is also most valuable. For the doom to which the sinner is justly sentenced was death under the wrath of God, and if Christ did not really die and suffer that wrath, then the Divine sentence has not been satisfied and the sinner is not released.

" Forthwith came there out blood and water " (v. 34). Thus the streams of life from Christ a lifeless victim flowed.

" The Scripture fulfilled " (v. 36)—" The Scripture saith " (v. 37). Here the distinction between fulfilled and unfulfilled prophecy is shown.

Joseph was a secret disciple and Nicodemus a midnight disciple, but God used them to honour the dead body of His Beloved Son. Up to the moment of His death, shame and suffering were appointed to Him. But from the moment He died, honour and glory were destined to Him, so angels, soldiers and counsellors honoured and guarded His sacred body.

And yet as to these two, it has often been the case in history that men honoured dead saints with whom, when living, they were ashamed to associate. To follow Christ in His path of shame, and to daily compromise oneself on His account, is a very different thing from association with His cause upon some great occasion which does not in itself demand this shame and loss.

" The body of Jesus " (v. 38) ; Again, " The body of Jesus " (v. 38) ; Again, " The body of Jesus " (v. 40), but in verse 42, " There laid they Jesus "—not " the body of Jesus " ; for it was not a corpse although dead, it was " Jesus " Who lay in that rock tomb. Such language could not be used of a mere man. It could only be true of Him Who was ever-living.

So He rode upon a colt upon which man had never ridden, and He reposed in a tomb wherein man had never yet lain.

JOHN XX.—In this Fourth Gospel the Holy Spirit records four appearings of the Lord after He rose from the dead, and these appearings banished four great enemies of the human heart, i.e., sorrow, fear, doubt and care ; for Mary was weeping (v. 11), the disciples were trembling (v. 19), Thomas was doubting (v. 25), and the apostles were despairing (xxi. 3). But in each case the appearing of Jesus sufficed to dismiss the enemy, and to fill his place with joy, courage, faith and contentment. Many other priceless effects also resulted from these appearings— and these were not the only ones—but the Spirit with design mentions no others. See notes on Rev. xx.

Adding the four records together it may be understood that at about five o'clock in the morning a group of women, including Mary Magdalene, went to the sepulchre and found the stone rolled away. Mary immediately returned to the city, found Peter and John, and told them that the Lord's

body had been removed. They set out for the garden followed by her. On reaching the tomb they shared her belief as to the removal. Meanwhile the other women had gone on to the door of the sepulchre and seen the vision of angels, and set out for the city to bring the disciples word. Presumably the disciples were lodged in different localities owing to the crowded state of Jerusalem at the Passover.

Peter and John returned to their lodging but Mary remained in the garden, and to her—not to His mother—the Lord first appeared ; and she then hastened back with the glad news.

Directly after His appearing to Mary, He showed Himself to the other women as they were still on their way in search of the disciples ; then He appeared to Peter ; and, later on, to the two disciples at Emmaus.

Still collating the four evangelists, and especially Mark xvi. 10-14, it is clear that they all assembled in the evening, and Mary, the other women, and Peter, and the two from Emmaus, affirmed the resurrection of the Lord and of His having appeared to them ; but the disciples would not believe them. Then Jesus Himself appeared, and having breathed peace upon them by the Holy Spirit, upbraided them for their unbelief and hardness of heart because they believed not them which had seen Him.

" The other disciple did outrun Peter " (v. 4), for Peter's heart and conscience were weighted with his denial. The popular belief that Peter was an old man is absurd and baseless.

" And believed " (v. 8), i.e., what Mary reported (v. 2) ; for as yet they knew not the Scripture that He must rise again, and so unbelief sent them home (v. 10).

But a deeper love kept Mary at the sepulchre, and a deeper misery. She pictures the Hebrew Church. Cleansed from the evil spirit of idolatry, the Church returned from Babylon swept and garnished, but empty ; and seven other spirits more wicked took possession of it. But they will be cast out and that Church brought into the glory of verse 17.

" Two angels one at the head, the other at the feet where the body of Jesus had lain " (v. 12). This was the true mercy-seat, and the angels represented the cherubim. The angels sat but the cherubim had stood, for expiation was now accomplished (Exod. xxv.

19), Luke i. 19, Rev. viii. 2). Most probably these angels were princes; for the dignity and importance of the resurrection demanded the ministry of the highest angels. Compare Daniel ix. 21, x. 21, xii. 1, Luke i. 19 and 26.

" She turned herself back " (v. 14), better : " She was caused to turn back." Perhaps she noticed the angels looking behind her, and it was that that caused her to turn round. To a wounded heart seeking Christ Himself angels, however glorious, have no interest. This fact demonstrates the idolatry and the folly of modern angel adoration.

" Touch Me not " (v. 17). Better : " Grasp Me not, for I am not yet ascended." Like the other women her companions who held Him by the feet (Matt. xxviii. 9), she seized Him so as not again to lose Him.

But He revealed the amazing fact to her that now, as the result of expiation and resurrection, she was brought into an intimacy and a unity of life and affection which were Divine and eternal. He Who had spoken of them as " My disciples " (xv. 8) and " My friends " (xv. 14) and " My servants " (xviii. 36) now raised them to the highest dignity by speaking of them as " My brethren "—for He and they were now all of one nature. Hence, he was not ashamed to call them brethren. See note on Heb. ii. 11. Never, however, in the Scripture do His brethren speak of Him, or to Him, as " Brother Jesus."

The difficulties supposed to exist as to the angelic visions on the resurrection morning, disappear when it is remembered that angels can become visible and invisible, e.g., Num. xxii. 31, 2 Kings vi. 17, etc.

Prior to His atoning work and to the settlement and removal of sin, this fellowship was impossible, for " except a corn of wheat die it remaineth alone." Sinless as the Son of God, He could not bring a sinner into the same relationship to God ; but having as the God-Man annihilated sin, He can bring the cleansed, redeemed, regenerated and adopted believer into this position of glory. See notes on viii. 2-11.

" Peace be unto you " (v. 19) " and again He said, Peace be unto you " (v. 21). Having shown them the proofs of His atonement and resurrection (v. 20), and that He was the same Jesus, He set them in this perfect peace ; for He had made peace for all who should receive the testimony of the grace

that made it ; and so from the bosom of that peace He sent them forth energized by the Holy Spirit to announce the forgiveness of sins to the world that had hated, rejected and crucified Him.

Into Adam He breathed the breath of life, and now upon His sons and daughters He breathed the Holy Spirit. This Spirit was to be their Guard and their Teacher for the mission to which He sent them. He Himself, as sent by the Father, had received the same Spirit, but without measure.

The Hebrew Prophet was stated to personally perform that which he was commissioned to declare (v. 23). Ignorance of this Hebraism originated the huge edifice of auricular confession and priestly absolution. Compare Gen. xli. 13, Jeremiah i. etc.

" Hands and side " (v. 20). Luke says " hands and feet." All three were pierced.

Christ was the first-fruits of the resurrection harvest. About the time that He showed Himself to the women the High Priest was waving the sheaf of the first fruits in the temple (Lev. xxiii. 10, 11).

Thomas is mentioned three times, i.e., xi. 16, xiv. 5, and xx. 24.

" After eight days again " (v. 26). This verse, with verse 19, sufficiently authorizes the observance of the first day of the week as the Christian Sabbath. For it must be presumed that the disciples met every day for Christian fellowship and worship during the week intervening between these two " first days." But the Lord distinguished these days by only appearing then in their midst.

Thomas here pre-figures the unbelieving Hebrew nation who will not believe until they look upon Him Whom they have pierced. In rebuking him the Lord gave a precious promised blessing to those who having not seen Him love Him.

Christ accepted Divine worship from Thomas who confessed Him as both Jehovah and Elohim, the Mighty and one God of Genesis i. and ii. Had Jesus been only conscious of humanity He would have rebuked Thomas ; but He accepted these titles and this worship ; and the words of verse 29 disprove the assertion that Thomas' exclamation was only that common to man when greatly surprised—such an expression of astonishment as " Oh ! my God."

Many other miracles Jesus most surely

performed but they are not written in this Book, for its object is to make prominent the eternal life which all who believe in Him, apart from miracles and material vision, receive ; and that faith accepts the testimony of the Scripture that Jesus of Nazareth is the Messiah officially and the Son of God essentially ; and that whosoever believes in Him shall live eternally in ever-enduring bliss.

JOHN XXI.—These seven apostles when the morning dawned were tired, dejected, friendless and foodless. They were filled with care, anxiety and perplexity. It was a desperate position ; but this fourth appearance of the Lord dismissed their care, and provided them with an abundant breakfast, and with the fellowship of Him Who brought with Himself all heaven in its fulness and the cattle on a thousand hills for their sustenance. Thus these Four Apparitions banished four enemies, i.e., Sorrow, Fear, Doubt and Care.

He does not now appear to visible eyesight but manifests Himself to the spiritual consciousness ; and such appearings have the same moral power that they then had.

The spiritual life originates in a manifestation of the Lord Jesus Christ to the soul (Matt. xi. 27), and that life is sustained by a repetition of such manifestations (v. 1) ; and these manifestations are not confined to houses of prayer and worship but may be enjoyed in the ordinary places of daily toil, e.g., by the sea of Tiberias.

" Showed " (v. 1). Better : " manifested " —and not only Himself but also His power. He loves to manifest Himself " again " and " again " to His disciples.

" I go a-fishing." " We also go with Thee." (v. 3). They went forth without prayer, " and that night they caught nothing." A Christian ministry originating in the energy of the carnal will, and which secures the co-operation of others by its effect and sympathy, is sunless and fruitless ; but when under the governance of the Head of the Church is full of sunshine and rich in fruit (vs. 4 to 6).

" Naked " (v. 7), i.e., only clothed with his tunic.

Two hundred cubits, i.e., about one hundred yards.

" Dragging with difficulty " (v. 8)—" drew with ease " (v. 11). See the Greek text. A moment or two at the feet of Jesus put such strength into Peter's arm that he could do with ease what the others failed to do with difficulty.

" A fish and one loaf of bread " (vs. 9-13). See Greek text. This was the second miracle of that morning. It recalled the feeding of the five thousand and of the four thousand, and of the barrel of meal and the cruse of oil. (1 Kings xvii. 16).

" The disciples knew not that it was Jesus " (v. 4). A self-willed ministry in the energy of nature blinds the spiritual vision.

" The net full of fishes " (v. 11) corresponds to the water-pots full of wine (ii. 6). This was the eighth sign which manifested the glory of His Godhead.

The Gospel net breaks (Luke v. 6), but the Election net (v. 11) never.

Some of the fishes might have been bigger than others, but they were all " great fish " ; and they were numbered. The broken numbers of Scripture are full of meaning for the heart of the believer. The sons of Levi, the mighty men of David and the great fish of this chapter record broken numbers. Had it said a hundred and fifty fish the statement would have suggested an estimate, but an hundred and fifty and three records individuality. All His sheep are named and numbered.

" Dine " (v. 12), better : " breakfast."

Just as the defeated Elijah (1 Kings xix.) went many days in the strength of the miraculous breakfast provided for him, so the discouraged Peter went many days in the strength of this miraculous breakfast, and went to heaven on a cross of glory (v. 19) as Elijah went to heaven in a whirlwind of fire.

Had the Lord sternly asked Peter, " Lovest thou Me " at the moment when Peter reached the beach hungry, wet, weary and dejected, he would not have had either the moral or physical energy to say " Yes."

But when he had been well rested and warmed, and had had an abundant and delicious breakfast, then it was his love was challenged. Such is the exquisite skill and ineffable grace which marked the Lord's treatment of His erring servant ; and His skill and grace are just the same to-day.

The first question was : " Lovest thou Me more than these men love Me ? " as thou didst declare (Mark xiv. 29). Peter answered " I have an affection for Thee."

Note the differing terms in the Greek text for "love."

The second question omitted the words "more than these," i.e., "Do you love Me at all?" Peter answered, "I have an affection for Thee."

The third question employed Peter's feebler term and said," Have you got even as much as an affection for Me?" The Lord's use of this word, and His putting the question three times in the evident remembrance of the three denials, probed Peter's heart to the very depths and he cried out with anguish: "Lord, Thou knowest all things, Thou knowest that I have an affection for Thee." He was too heart-broken and miserable to use the stronger term.

But the Lord only wounded his heart in order to train and fit him for the high honour of shepherding that which was most precious to Himself, i.e., the sheep of chapter x.—the Hebrew Church—for Peter was the Apostle of the circumcision (Gal. ii. 7), and to the nations that are to be blest in that relationship. The sheet let down from heaven, and Cornelius, are figures of the nature and sphere of his ministry. It had to do with the earth, with Israel, with the Kingdom and the millennium. The ministry committed to the Apostle Paul, and his companions, was altogether different, as the notes on the Epistle to the Ephesians point out.

The "thou" of "Lovest thou Me" (vs. 15, 16 and 17) is emphatic.

The prediction (v. 18) of Peter's faithfulness unto death not only comforted and strengthened his pierced heart, but prevented the other disciples from scornfully reminding him of his cowardice.

"My lambs," "My sheep." These words express the tender affection of the Great Shepherd; and they instructed Peter as to how he was to love and cherish them.

"Young" (v. 18), better: "Younger," i.e., "when a lad." This word does not at all support the popular belief that Peter was at this time an aged man. See xx. 4.

Peter was always addressed by the Lord as "Simon" except in Luke xxii. 34. See note on that verse.

"Verily, Verily" (v. 18). This is the twenty-fifth and last occurrence of this double Amen.

"Follow Me" (v. 19). Compare its first occurrence in i. 37.

This Gospel opens with Christ on the way to the Father and unaccompanied. It closes with Him on the same way, but now accompanied by the redeemed. There is no mention of incarnation nor ascension; and consequently no separation.

Peter (v. 18) represents the church, whether earthly or heavenly, crucified with Christ, and John (v. 23), the church living on earth up to the Coming of Christ. Each believer should in this sense be a Peter and a John.

Peter evidently had an especial affection for John so he asked: "What will happen to this man?" The Lord's reply: "If I will," etc., expressed His absolute disposal of human life, and revealed His God-head; for how could a man, or a Super-man, make such a claim!

"Follow thou Me" (v. 22). "Thou" here is emphatic.

The prediction of verse 22 was fulfilled; for John lived to see the end of the Pentecostal dispensation, and the Coming of the Lord in judgment upon the nation. He also saw in a spiritual trance (Rev. i. 10) the "Day of the Lord," i.e., His future appearing in power and great glory.

All this chapter is a prophetic picture of the coming millennial kingdom. The dawn of that morning, which is to follow the fruitless toil of this present night, will reveal Messiah; and at His command the apostles will bring the one hundred and fifty-three nations of the earth to His feet without fail; for in that day of His power there shall be nothing defective or marred. It will be then seen that He Himself had gathered a Portion for Himself—symbolized by the fire, the bread, and the fish—and to that Portion the multitude of the nations will be added, and they will all become His sheep. But, as already stated, the apostle Paul and the Church of the heavenly Election of course do not appear here.

It is said that there are one hundred and fifty-three kinds of fish in the sea of Galilee; and probably there are one hundred and fifty and three nations in the sea of humanity.

The Books of Hebrews—Revelation follow Acts xxviii. They resume the Messiah's relationship with Israel and with the Pentecostal Church of the Covenant made with David. See notes on Acts vii., xv. and xxviii.

As in the Acts of the Apostles so in Revelation ii. and iii., the several assemblies are representative of that church.

But the great theme of the Gospel by

John is not the glory of any church but the personal glory of the Lord Jesus. His Person, and the eternal life that is in Him, form the foundation of faith ; and however human testimony to His sufficiency and preciousness may fail, He Himself remains in all His perfection and faithfulness as the sustainer of faith.

So John presents God to us in Him, and Paul presents us in Him to God

" The world," i.e., humanity. " Contain," i.e., " receive " (v. 25). The statement here is not primarily that the physical world could not support on its surface the number of books that could be written about the Lord Jesus Christ, but that human intelligence in its totality is incapable of receiving, and accepting, all that could be written about Him. The subject is inexhaustible. Already millions of volumes have been written, and countless millions more may be written, and were the world to last for millions of years the day could never come that would exhaust the Gospel story. Christ is infinite, the earth finite ; hence the supposition of the verse is most reasonable.

" Come and dine"—' Lovest thou Me ? "

The Gospel invites to a feast. Many accept its gifts but do not love the Giver. Hence the question. True conversion is to love Him.

" Feed My sheep "—" Follow thou Me."

The Christian is saved to serve. Feeding others successfully depends on frequent " dining," i.e., communion. Each disciple had to keep going to Jesus for food for the multitude. Personal obedience in following is more important than curiosity in knowing what this or that man may do.

ACTS

ACTS I.—In the Four Gospels the Messiah was presented by God to Israel in the humility of His Incarnation, and in this Fifth Gospel He was presented to them by the Holy Spirit in the glory of His Resurrection. Israel rejected both presentations—the Two Tribes at Jerusalem, the centre of Jewry (vii.), and the Ten Tribes at Rome, the centre of the Dispersion (xxviii.). As a just judgment the King sent His armies, i.e., the Romans, and destroyed those murderers and burned up their city (Matt. xxii. 7).

This Book, therefore, records the offer of the kingdom to Israel, and not, as is popularly believed, the formation of the church revealed in the Epistle to the Ephesians. See notes on that Epistle.

The establishment on earth of the Kingdom of God under the Messiah was the Hope of Israel. The administration of that Kingdom was promised to Israel, and membership in it thrown open to all nations. This Divine plan will yet be accomplished.

The kingdom being earthly and having earthly promises, it was necessary that the Holy Spirit should accredit it to Israel by miracles, and gifts of healings, and of tongues; but Israel having rejected the testimony (i. Cor. xiv. 21 and 22) these manifestations ceased—for they do not harmonize with the life of the heavenly places where all is spiritual—and so Israel became Lo-Ammi, and still remains so.

Twelve Apostles, Discipleship, Baptism, Breaking of Bread and many other words characteristic of the Gospel of the Kingdom are naturally prominent in this Book; for, as stated, its subject is the Restoration of the Kingdom to Israel (v. 6).

" The former treatise " (v. 1), i.e., the Gospel of Luke.

" Began to do and teach " (v. 1). He is doing and teaching still.

" The Holy Spirit " (v. 2). He is the Speaker and Actor in this Book.

" Witnesses unto Me " (v. 8). This involves shame and often death, but to witness to a church and its ceremonies may not involve either. The Gospel is to be preached to all centuries and not " adapted," as is popularly demanded to-day.

Three circles of testimony were commanded:—Orthodox Jerusalem, unorthodox Samaria, and the Heathen (v. 8). These three circles are represented to-day by Protestantism (including the Greek Church), Romanism, and Heathenism.

" While they beheld " (v. 9)—" While they looked steadfastly " (v. 10). These statements are important because affirming His actual ascension testified to by eye-witnesses. Only a cloud hides Him from His people.

" Two men " (v. 10). The Law required two witnesses to establish a matter. So two men appeared at the Transfiguration, and two men at the Resurrection, and two men at the Ascension, and, most probably, two men at the Crucifixion. These two men were possibly Moses and Elijah.

" Where abode " (v. 13) not " where lodged." It was a room used as a meeting-house. It must have been a large room to hold one hundred and twenty people.

The Holy Spirit appears four times in the chapter:

1. The Commandment of the Holy Spirit (v. 2, R.V.).
2. The Cleansing of the Holy Spirit (v. 5).
3. The Enduement of the Holy Spirit (v. 8).
4. The Teaching of the Holy Spirit (v. 16).

The commandment was that of John xx. 22, to preach forgiveness of sins—The prophet was said to do what he was commissioned to proclaim—See Jer. i. 10.

The cleansing was by "fire" from fear and unbelief, etc. These hinder effective preaching.

The enduement was a moral dynamic force that overthrew the kingdom of Satan in the heart of man.

The teaching was through the Scripture—the mouth was David's—the speaker, the Holy Spirit.

The inbreathing of the Holy Spirit (John xx. 22), and the Bible lessons taught during the Forty Days of the Lord's post-resurrection life (Luke xxiv. 45), instructed Peter to obey the commands of Psalms xli. 9, lxix. 25, and cix. 8, and so, in harmony with the Law of Moses, they cast lots ; and Matthias was numbered by God with the Eleven Apostles. See 1 Cor. xv. 5.

Verses 18 and 19 form a parenthesis, so verse 20 follows immediately on verse 17.

Fields being difficult to obtain in the neighbourhood of great cities, the one' that Judas intended to purchase with the blood-money was no doubt the same that the High Priest actually got possession of ; for Judas defiled it with his own blood, the rope with which he hanged himself having evidently snapped. Thus he *caused* it to be purchased. But see note on Matt. xxvii. 7.

" Let his habitation," etc. (v. 20). This is both a prayer and a prediction ; for it may read in the Hebrew Text : " his habitation shall be desolate," etc.

" The Lord Jesus " (v. 21). This is His resurrection title; and, as such, now constantly appears.

Verses 21 and 22 state the main qualification for apostleship to Israel.

The language of the prayer of verses 24 and 25 makes it clear that the prayer was addressed to the Lord Jesus, and was, therefore, a testimony to His Godhead.

" His own place " (v. 25), i.e., the lake of fire. It was his own place before he went there, ready and prepared for him.

The statement in verse 14, and the grace of the Holy Spirit in making it, bring deep and sweet relief to the Christian heart. At last Mary and her children take their place publicly among the disciples. Had they made this great decision at the beginning, how much happier they would have been ! Excepting 1 Cor ix, 5, Gal. i. 19, and iv. 4, and, perhaps, Acts xv. 13, and

the Epistle of Jude they do not again appear in the apostolic writings. It is humbling to religious self-esteem to learn that the Lord's daily intimate family life of perfect love and exquisite moral beauty for many years in the home at Nazareth, and later, His miracles and teaching, failed to win His brothers and sisters to believe on Him ; and their unbelief makes more convincing the truth of the incurable corruption of the natural heart (Jer. xvii. 9). But they did not believe on Him (John vii. 5). It is clear that the Virgin was willing to be the mother of the King of Israel (Luke i. 32-38), but unwilling to be a disciple of the despised Nazarene (Mark iii. 21, 31-35, and Luke xi. 27, 28). The terrible sword of Luke ii. 34, 35, revealed the thoughts of many hearts, and of her heart (Heb. iv. 12). The pain she felt when viewing the crucifixion belonged to the realm of nature, but the double prediction of Luke ii. belonged to the realm of judgment. She herself illustrated Luke ii. 34. She fell (Mark iii.) ; she rose again (Acts i.). Corrupt Christianity has composed a different history of the Virgin—and the natural heart prefers it—but the Christian believes only what the infallible Spirit of God records.

ACTS II.—The popular belief that this chapter records the birth of the church revealed to the apostle Paul is erroneous. Pentecost was an earnest of the promise made through the Prophet Joel to the Hebrew Church. To that church, and to all in any nation who called upon its Lord, were promised the Holy Spirit and deliverance from judgment. Jerusalem (Joel ii. 32) was the Divine Centre of that salvation. This great prediction yet awaits fulfilment. See notes on Joel ii.

The Hebrew Church was re-born at Pentecost. It then became the " New Nation " that should bring forth the fruit of the kingdom. It was the " church " predicted in Matthew xvi. 18, and there described as the Kingdom of Heaven. The keys of that Kingdom were committed to Peter. With one key he opened the Kingdom to the Hebrews in Acts ii., and with the other key to the Gentiles in Acts x. The miraculous gift of the Holy Spirit accredited in a similar manner both occasions, for the spiritual demonstration at Caesarea was similar to that at Jerusalem.

The Hebrew Church was established as the kingdom of God upon earth, and was thrown open to all from among the nations that called upon the Name of the Lord. Being earthly it was distinguished by outward forms and miraculous gifts. The Pauline Church, on the other hand, was hidden in God, never revealed in the Scriptures, and was taken out of the earth and established in the heavens, where its worship is wholly spiritual and independent of material ceremonies such as baptism and the Paschal Supper and miracles.

It is of the utmost importance to recognise the distinction between the Hebrew Church and its earthly blessing and glory, and the Election Church with its heavenly blessing and glory.

On reading, therefore, the prophecy in Joel it will be clearly recognised that Pentecost belongs to the Hebrew people, and to all who by faith in Jesus Christ associate themselves with that people. Its centre is, and will be, Jerusalem, and it awaits the completion of this prophecy.

The sealing of the Holy Spirit (Eph. i. 13, R.V., Titus iii. 5), i.e., regeneration, is different from the out-pouring of the Holy Spirit (v. 4) which is restoration, and, therefore, accompanied by miraculous demonstrations such as tongues, miracles, etc.

Hebrews and proselytes, all devout men (v. 5), were assembled from many nations (vs. 9-11) at Jerusalem for the Feast of Pentecost. These represented the Hebrew Church as it will be in the future. The Pentecostal Dispensation closed in xxviii. 25-28, but will be resumed when God returns to the Tabernacle of David which is fallen down (xv. 16, Amos ix. 11).

" The third hour " (v. 15), i.e., nine a.m. " This is that which was spoken " (v. 16). Not " Now is fulfilled." That which took place was an earnest and illustration of that which is yet to be.

The great visitation was first to affect the Hebrew Church (vs. 17-18), and then whosoever in any nation called on the name of the Lord (v. 21). All such were promised deliverance in the terrible Day of the Lord. Here is a principle that operates to-day, that is, that God hears and responds to a cry for salvation forced from the heart by fear.

" David speaketh concerning Him " (v. 25).

See Psalm xvi. " I " (i.e., the Messiah " foresaw Jehovah alway before My face," etc· The language expresses Christ's confidence in view of His death and resurrection. His flesh rested in the rock tomb, in the hope of incorruption, and His soul. in Sheol, believed for " the ways of life," i.e., for resurrection, and for the certitude of Ascension, i.e., the joy of Jehovah's countenance. This Messianic passage throws a flood of light, as to interpretation, upon the whole Book of the Psalms. Compare verses 29-33 and 34-36.

Two conditions prior to the forgiveness of sins were necessary in the Pentecostal Church, i.e., repentance and water baptism (v. 38). Had a professed believer refused either of these conditions, or both, he could not have claimed the promise of the Holy Spirit and the forgiveness of sins. Some modern churches, misunderstanding the nature of the Pentecostal Church and seeking a defective imitation of it, teach that baptism in water is necessary to salvation, but they only baptize those who declare that they have already received the remission of their sins and the Holy Spirit. This is a reversal of the Petrine procedure.

" The promise " (v. 39), i.e., The Holy Spirit as promised in Joel. " You and your children," i.e., the Hebrews. " All that are afar off," i.e., the Gentiles. On fulfilling the double condition of verse 38, they also received the Holy Spirit (xi. 17), but with this remarkable difference, that the Gentile believers were baptized with the Holy Spirit prior to, and not after, their baptism with water (x. 44, 47).

" Untoward " (v. 40), i.e., perverse, crooked. " Three thousand souls " (v. 41). It being impossible for this number to have been baptized by the apostles on that one afternoon it must be accepted that all the hundred and twenty (i. 15), including women, assisted; and, further, there being only one small brook at Jerusalem—the Kedron—which at this time of the year contained very little water—immersion was impossible. It may, however, have been possible at Bethesda and Siloam.

" The Apostle's doctrine " (v. 42), i.e., that Jesus of Nazareth was the promised Messiah, as stated in verses 22-36.

" And fellowship," as described in verses 44-46, i.e., community of goods and property.

" Breaking of bread," as described in verse 46.

" And in the prayers " (R.V.), as in verse 46, i.e., the daily liturgical Temple Service at 3 p.m. (iii. 1).

The ecclesiastical structure which many have erected upon verse 42, and which they call the Christian Church, and some " The Assembly," is based upon the belief that this fellowship was distinct from, and in opposition to, the Hebrew Church. But the argument and teaching of the whole passage is opposed to this ; for what is here pointed out is that there was no breach with the Hebrew Church, but on the contrary a designed and intelligent unity with it ; and that the Apostolic company was careful to keep inside it and worship daily in the Temple. For it was to that Church, and to Gentiles who united with it, that the promise of the Spirit was given. The Epistle to the Ephesians describes quite another church in which everything is heavenly and its worship spiritual and not material.

" Such as should be saved " (v. 47), i.e., those that were being saved (R.V.).

For notes on " breaking bread," see chapter xx. 7 and i. Cor. xi.

Verse 3 should read as in the Revised Version. The tongues were not " cloven " ; they were distributed.

The first harvest fore-shadowed Christ's ascension (Lev. xxiii. 10) ; the second, the Spirit's testimony to it (Lev. xxiii. 15). The harvest is nature's testimony to resurrection. Pentecost is the Spirit's testimony.

ACTS III.—" The hour of prayer " (v. 1). See ii. 42 and 46 and the corresponding notes.

" By the right hand " (v. 7)—as His Master had done with Peter's mother-in-law (Mark i. 31).

" His feet and ankle bones " (v. 7). This is the language of a physician.

" His Servant Jesus " (v. 13, R.V.). The word " Servant " here, and in verse 26, is used in the high sense in which the Holy Spirit in Isaiah applies it always to Messiah (Isa. xlii. 1, xlix. 6, lii. 13, and liii. 11).

" And killed the Author of Life " (v. 15). What a glorious paradox ! and how piercing to the consciences of Jerusalem sinners.

" Through ignorance ye did it " (v. 17). Here the Holy Spirit responds to the prayer ; " Father, forgive them for they know not what they do." Guilty as they were of the supreme ten-thousand-talents-sin of having

put the King's Son to death, the king remits the sin, and sends a message of mercy, calling them to repentance.

" God showed " (v. 18)—" God spoke " (v. 21). These solemn statements declare the inspiration of the Scriptures. The words, the statements, the doctrines were God's words, God's statements, and God's doctrines.

" When " (v. 19). Better, as in the Revised Version, " so that." " The times of refreshing," i.e., the millennial kingdom, awaits the repentance of the Jews. Till then the King remains in the heavens.

The twenty-first verse destroys the claim of the Romish priest that he brings Christ down from heaven every time that he consecrates the wafer.

" That Christ should suffer " (v. 18) Here the apostle Peter preached the doctrine of a suffering Messiah against which doctrine he had protested (Matt. xvi. 22). The Bible readings (Luke xxiv. 45) between resurrection and ascension, and the Pentecostal illumination, wrought this great change.

The Blesser—God (v. 26) ; the Bearer of the blessing—Jesus ; the objects of the blessing, " you first," i.e., His murderers ; and the nature of the blessing, a definite separation from everything sinful.

The Apostolic Gospel was based upon the Bible. Its authority was decisive and infallible. Upon this basis was placed a personal testimony. Man's moral ruin as a sinner, and the certitude of the wrath of God upon sin and sinners, were enforced. The note dominating all was the Person and Work of the Lord Jesus Christ, and that belief in Him secured eternal life, and necessitated a definite break with sin and sinning.

As in 1 Cor. xv. 1-8 so here the facts and doctrines of the Gospel were based upon the infallible Word of God. It decided everything. From it there was no appeal. Then human testimony was added to assure man's doubting heart. But the testimony of the Bible came first and was decisive. A school of modern thought reverses this so as to place man above the Bible.

Many claim to-day to be the successors of the Apostles, but if they preached these Apostolic doctrines they would lose their ecclesiastical appointments.

ACTS IV. 1-31.—Satan used the Pharisees to oppose Christ in atonement, and the Sadducees to oppose Him in resurrection.

Both were his instruments. The one were self-righteous and sought eternal life through personal moral merit; the others were self-thinkers and denied the fact of resurrection, and hence they became prominent as opposing the Gospel (vs. 1-3 and ch. v. 17).

The section from iv. 1 to v. 16 may be termed a "great" section. It records great conversions (iv. 4 and v. 14); great opposition (iv. 6 and v. 17); great boldness (v. 13); great faith (v. 24); great Bible intelligence (v. 25); great expectation (v. 30.); great unity (v. 32); great power (v. 33); great grace (v. 33); great sacrifice (v. 34); great fear (vs. 5 and 11); great miracles (v. 16); and great love (v. 34).

"Filled with the Holy Spirit" (v. 8). This formula is used in every instance in this Book in relation to special Satanic opposition. It is a very solemn afflatus, and those who without reflection speak of the filling of the Spirit should remember this relationship to Satanic rage, and to bold aggressive action entailing possible persecution and death. Compare verses 29 and 31. Those, therefore, who keep inside safe Christian conventions and do not venture outside to face Satan in aggressive Gospel preaching, should not expect this special filling of the Spirit. See note on Eph. v. 18.

The Apostle boldly told these clergy (vs. 5 and 6) that they needed to be saved, and he shut them up to salvation in the One Person whom they had set at naught (v. 11) and crucified (v. 10), but whom God had raised from the dead and appointed the Head of the corner. Thus he contrasted their treatment of the Messiah and God's treatment of Him.

"Unlearned and ignorant" (v. 13), i.e., unordained and not holding a College theological degree.

"The impotent man" (vs. 10 and 14) was very brave. Risking hatred, excommunication and death, he boldly identified himself with the Apostles, and voluntarily took his stand with them in court.

"This Name" (v. 17), i.e., Christ. The term "Name" as expressive of the Person continually occurs in this Book.

"We cannot but speak" (v. 20). There are two groups of Christians: Those who "cannot speak" and those who "cannot but speak.' The little word "but" distinguishes between these groups. The one group is so inflamed with love to Christ that

they cannot "but" speak; the other is so wanting in love to Him that they cannot speak.

"Because of the people" (v. 21). Those who derive their authority from the mob are governed by the mob.

"Their own company" (v. 23), i.e., in contrast with the company described in verses 5 and 6.

They did not pray for protection from persecution or deliverance from possible death, but for courage to keep on preaching (v. 29), and for a continuance of the Divine endorsement of their testimony (v. 30).

Verse 25 states that the second Psalm was written by David. This is an instance of the Law of Subsequent Narration.

These verses state that the Messiah is the Person spoken of in the second Psalm; and thus a flood of light is thrown upon the entire Book of the Psalms.

"Child" (vs. 27 and 30), rather "Servant," as in the Book of Isaiah.

His Hand performed what His Counsel determined (v. 28).

The Pharisees and Sadducees' though hating each other, as they still do, united in their greater hatred to the Lord Jesus; and having, as they thought, got rid of Him, were confounded and angered at finding Him re-appearing in His confessors (v. 13).

ACTS IV. 32—V. 16.—Had the nation accepted the Apostle's testimony to Christ He would have at once returned and established universally the socialism figured in verses 32-37. But persisting in their rejection of Him, this community of goods and principle and practice of brotherhood, await His Coming. By their refusal they brought suffering not only upon themselves but upon the believers, for not long afterwards the Christians at Antioch had to send money to Jerusalem for the relief of the brethren there (xi. 29).

The one and self-same Holy Spirit that was a spirit of life to the impotent man (iii. 7), was a spirit of death to Ananias and Sapphira. If electricity be obeyed, it is a beneficent force; if disobeyed, a deadly force. The presence of God in the camp meant death to the carnal nature, for God is intolerant of evil. Hence the terrible judgments of the Wilderness and of the Acts of the Apostles. When because of disobedience both in the days of Moses and Peter. He withdrew from the " camp," these judgments ceased, and their cessation proved His departure. So, greater sins afterwards committed under the First Covenant and under the Second, were unjudged outwardly ; but their judgment will come.

Where the Mighty Spirit of God works, His operation is sure to manifest the evil and opposition of the carnal nature (vs. 3 and 9). His power manifested itself outside the church in grace to the helpless, diseased and sinful, and inside the church in judgment upon falsehood and evil.

He will have holiness in His house ; and it is a fearful thing to sin against Him. Many to-day in that which professes to be His church, affect, like Ananias and Sapphira, a devotion which is false.

"They were all filled with the Holy Spirit " (iv. 31)—"Why hath Satan filled thine heart ? " (v. 3). A terrible possibility is here suggested ; for doubtless Ananias and Sapphira attended that great prayer-meeting and, consequently, experienced that filling.

"The Holy Spirit " (v. 3) "God " (v. 4). These statements affirm the personality and God-head of the Holy Spirit.

Ananias and his wife laid their deceitful money at the Apostle's feet (v. 2) and judgment swiftly laid their deceitful selves there (vs. 5 and 10).

"Solomon's porch " (v. 12). This fact is recorded to make it clear that the whole church (v. 11) was Davidic ; and hence the miracles of verses 15 and 16.

"Beds and couches " (v. 15). The rich lay on beds and the poor on couches, i.e., mattresses.

ACTS V. 17-42.—Two powers and their instruments are here seen in opposition—the Holy Spirit, with the apostles and angels as His instruments (vs. 18 and 19), and the Evil Spirit with the Priests and Sadducees as his instruments. For wherever the Holy Spirit manifests His power there Satan manifests his.

"Indignation " (v. 17), rather "envy ", or "jealousy." The Priests were envious of the influence which the Apostles were winning over the people, so they lodged all the Apostles in the prison in which common criminals were confined.

"An angel of the Lord " (v. 19) not "The angel of Jehovah."

"The words of this Life " (v. 20), i.e., words announcing eternal life to dying men.

"They doubted " (v. 24), i.e., " were much perplexed " (R.V.)

"They feared the people " (v. 26) ; but they did not fear Him Who manifested His power in opening their prison, for their hearts and consciences were hardened with hatred against Him and His followers.

"Ye have filled Jerusalem with your doctrine " (v. 28). This was a fine testimony to the success of their preaching.

"This man's blood " (v. 28). They prayed that His blood might be on them and on their children (Matt. xxvii. 25), but now they sought to avoid their own imprecation.

"We must obey God " (v. 29 R.V.). In this brave reply there was neither pride nor self-will. There was faithfulness, subjection to truth, and intelligence in the Scriptures.

"A Prince and a Saviour to Israel " (v. 31). These titles express Royalty and Atonement. Not only is the Lord Jesus the medium of forgiveness and life, but He is the dispenser of both. He gives, not sells, repentance and forgiveness. Forgiveness of sins means release from the eternal punishment of sins, and repentance expresses and involves a moral revulsion against sin and a determined breach with it. Repentance is a Divine gift as forgiveness is a Divine gift.

The fact that the priests had not received the Holy Spirit, proved that they were rebels to the God of Israel (v. 32).

"They were cut to the heart " (v. 33). Truth pierces the heart (ii. 37) or saws the heart. The Greek verbs are different in these verses. The piercing of the heart causes contrition ; the sawing of the heart, rage and murder ; hence they took counsel to slay them. Had their hearts been pierced they would have repented and believed.

Neutrality in relation to the Gospel is hostility to Christ ; as He Himself said (Luke xi. 23).

Their scourging the Apostles—a cruel and brutal punishment (v. 40)—was cowardly and unjust. But hatred to Christ drives men to the lowest depths of moral degradation.

The first sharp stroke of persecution —bitter and painful to the flesh—caused rejoicing to the spirit. Shame is glory if suffered for the Name (v. 41, R.V.).

Boldly, and properly disregarding their illegal judges, they kept on preaching that Jesus was the promised Messiah (v. 42, R.V.). This was the Gospel of the Pentecostal Dispensation committed to the Twelve. Paul's Gospel ("my Gospel," Rom. ii. 16) had another purpose and called to a higher glory.

ACTS VI.—There was leaven in the Pentecostal Church. It was introduced by Satan. It showed itself in deceit (ch. v. 2) and partiality (vi. 1). But the power of the Holy Spirit was present to expose and deal with the evil. If the Pentecostal and Apostolic Church, filled with the Holy Spirit and enriched with miraculous gifts, contained leaven, it is not to be wondered at that the Christian Church to-day is enfeebled by evil.

The first contention in the Pentecostal Church was about the maintenance of widows ; and it needed no fewer than seven practical business men filled with the Holy Spirit to compose the matter. Both Hebrews and Hellenists were Jews (v. 1, R.V. margin) ; but the Hebrews regarded the Hellenists as their inferiors.

This contention and its settlement shows (1) how easily disputes may arise even among people who are filled with the Holy Spirit ; (2) how quickly they may be composed if grace and intelligence be used ; (3) how effective moderation and readiness to yield are in such misunderstandings, for all the seven men have Greek names, and they were undoubtedly appointed by the "Hebrews" who were in the majority ; and (4) how free the Apostles were from the lust of power, for they handed the matter to the congregation for settlement. The selection of these officers rested with the people, and their appointment with the Apostles.

The Law of Leviticus commanded that widows should be supported. The Law of love now continues the obligation.

" The daily ministration " (v. 1), i.e., the daily donation of money or food from the common purse.

" Neglected " (v. 1), i.e., overlooked, or slighted.

" Reason " (v. 2), i.e., not pleasing to us (R.V. margin).

" The Word of God " (v. 2), i.e., the preaching of the Gospel. " Serve tables," i.e., attend to business matters. Gospel preaching is more important than Social Schemes.

Prayer is more important than preaching and should come first (v. 4).

Six of these officers were Hellenists and one Nicolas a Gentile (v. 5).

" The Word of God increased " (v. 7), i.e., conversions multiplied.

The Libertines (v. 9) were Hebrew slaves who had been freed by the Romans.

Possibly Saul of Tarsus was amongst them of Cilicia (v. 9), but not amongst those of verses 11 and 13.

As Jezebel employed false witnesses to accuse Naboth of speaking against God and against the government, so false witnesses were suborned to accuse Stephen of blaspheming God, Moses and the Temple (vs. 11 and 14).

Stephen's undoubted testimony that Jesus of Nazareth was God would be regarded by these men as blasphemy against God.

It is remarkable that the Holy Spirit selected a Hellenist and not an Apostle, to be the first martyr. In this He acted independently of Apostolic authority.

ACTS VII.—This chapter is very important. It records the last offer of the King and the kingdom to Judah and his companions Benjamin and Levi (Ezekiel xxxvii. 16). See note on chapter xxviii.

The offer was made through the Hellenist Stephen and not through the chief Apostle Peter, and the offer was made at Jerusalem which was the city of the great king and the ecclesiastical centre of the nation. Peter had declared that if they repented the King would return immediately, introduce the times of refreshing, and restore all things. These three Tribes rejected this testimony, and as a consequence the Holy Spirit, through the mouth of Stephen, pronounced judgment upon them. But this was not an official breach on the part of God, for that would have been made through the Apostles. It was made later, and took place when the judgment was executed in the destruction of the city and the Temple by the Romans. But the judgment was the result of their action in sending Stephen to say " We will not have this Man to reign over us " (Luke xix. 14, 27).

Stephen made no defence but on the contrary accused his judges of hypocrisy. He declared that their devotion to the Law and to the Temple was hypocritical, for they continually resisted Him Who gave the Law and Whose House was the Temple. To boast of the Temple and eject its Indweller was wilful blindness and idolatry ; and he charged them with being at heart idolaters from the very beginning of their national history, although professing obedience to the Law. He pointed out that they had sold Joseph and thrust Moses from them ; and that as to the Temple they were not entitled to pride themselves respecting it, for they had always resisted the Holy Spirit who built it and slain those whom He sent, their wickedness culminating in their being now the betrayers and murderers of Messiah Himself.

In his review of the national history he began with Abraham and recalled the glory of the grace that chose that idolater. It was the glory of that grace that gave meaning to the magnificent appellation " The God of Glory." It was not an outward physical glory but the glory of absolutely free grace ; for Abraham was a Syrian ready to perish (Deut. xxvi. 5).

Prior to the Flood the earth was filled with violence ; subsequent to the Flood, with idolatry. Electing grace chose one of these idolaters, Abraham. Then Law was given to make Abraham's sons conscious that they were sinners and needed a Saviour. The Prophets followed in patient grace ; and, finally, the Son was sent. He was crucified ; but in grace He sent the Holy Spirit. He, through Peter, pleaded with them for repentance, and, upon their refusal He reviewed their history by the mouth of Stephen and so judged them. Officially, in connection with the Twelve, He manifested His power and glory in the tongues of fire on earth ; and, in connection with Stephen, His power and glory in heaven. Thus heaven and earth united in testifying that Jesus of Nazareth was the God of glory Who appeared to Abraham. Therefore it is that in verse 2 is found the expression : " The God of Glory," and in verse 55 : " The Glory of God."

" Stephen was filled with the Holy Spirit " (v. 55) ; his judges continually resisted the Holy Spirit.

" Four hundred years " (v. 6), i.e., from the birth of Isaac. See Notes on Gen. xv. and Gal. iii.

" Seventy-five souls " (v. 14). These were Jacob's " kindred " ; those mentioned in Genesis were his actual children. See Notes on Gen. xlvi.

Stephen's first accusation was : That moved with envy they had sold Joseph, but that God had raised him up to be a Saviour to the whole nation.

Three explanations may be given of the supposed conflict between verse 16 and Gen. xxiii. The first is : That the Holy Spirit here states that Abraham bought a tomb from the sons of Hamor at Shechem, and no one can produce evidence to the contrary. Jacob on returning to Palestine, bought a field, and most probably the tomb was situated in it.

The second explanation is : That when Jacob bought this field it was an Abrahamic purchase. This use of the family name, " Abraham " appears in Isaiah xxix. 22, and lxiii. 16.

The third explanation is : That Stephen, speaking in Hebrew, was enabled to make two statements, which his hearers knew to be accurate, in one sentence. He said that the bodies of their fathers, Jacob and Joseph, were carried up out of Egypt into Canaan, the one body being interred in the sepulchre at Hebron which Abraham bought, the other body in the field at Shechem which Jacob bought. Verse 16 may be, therefore, elliptical.

Stephen was accused of blaspheming God (no doubt because he said that Jesus was God) ; of setting aside the Law ; and of be littling the Temple. But he retorted that his judges blasphemed God by the substitution of idols (verses 41-43) , that they thrust Moses aside (v. 39), and refused to obey the Law (v. 53) ; and that their professed devotion to the Temple was hypocritical for that they had ejected its Indweller.

As illustrating their blindness and hypocrisy he pointed to their treatment of Joseph (v. 9), and of Moses (v. 27). Of Moses he spoke most nobly, saying that personally he was divinely beautiful (v. 20) ; intellectually, he was highly cultured (v. 22) ; and potentially he was mighty in speech and action. Thus he rebutted the charge of having spoken against Moses (vii. 11).

In bringing these two great deliverers forward, his argument was that they were types of the Messiah, for just as God exalted Joseph whom they had sold, and extolled Moses whom they had thrust aside, and made them to be Saviours to Israel, so God had exalted Jesus to be a Prince, like Joseph, and a Saviour, like Moses ; and He was willing to deliver Israel from a greater bondage by giving them repentance and remission of sins. But they had treated Him as they had treated Joseph and Moses.

"The Angel of Jehovah" (v. 30) said : "I am the God of thy Fathers," etc. (v. 32). "Then saith Jehovah" (v. 33).

The answer to the question in verse 42 is that though outwardly they offered sacrifices to God, yet in secret they worshipped idols (vs. 41 and 43 and Joshua xxiv. 15).

There is no conflict between verse 43 and Amos v. 25. The Ten Tribes were carried away by the Assyrians beyond Damascus, as predicted by Amos, and the Two Tribes by the Chaldeans beyond Babylon, as foretold by Moses. Hence the words : "The Book of the Prophets," i.e., the prophetic books, i.e., The Bible. Stephen did not say : "As it is written in the Book of the Prophet Amos."

The sin which banished the Ten Tribes beyond Damascus, and the Two Tribes beyond Babylon, originated in each case at the very start of their history (v. 40).

Thus Stephen laid bare the full measure of their guilt. Nothing now remained but their final banishment. They had rejected all Three Persons of the Trinity, by despising the Law, rejecting the Prophets, and crucifying the Messiah. Man was judged and his nature revealed in the conduct of Israel, for Israel not only sinned, but being under the special care and love of God, sinned against that care and that love. They slew Christ in His humility, and now rejected Him in His glory.

The Three Persons of the Trinity appear in verse 55.

"The heavens opened" (v. 56) that earth might see Jesus there in His glory as God, just as the heavens had opened to see Jesus in His humiliation on earth as Man. Stephen saw an Object in the opened heavens ; but Christ saw no Object there when on earth ; on the contrary, the heavens looked down upon Him as the Object of its approbation and worship. By and by the heavens will open (Rev. xiv. 14), and He, as Son of Man, will come forth. This shows the connection between the Book of Acts and the Revelation. So He is the Object seen in heaven when it opens.

"The Son of Man" (v. 56). This is the only time that He is so styled after His ascension, except in Rev. i. 13, and xiv. 14, for the history of the Apostolic Church, interrupted at the close of this Book, is resumed in Rev. i.

As a consequence of seeing Him in heaven, Stephen resembled Him upon earth, and hence the words : "receive my spirit," and then with "a loud voice" : "Lord, lay not this sin to their charge." But it does not say that Christ "fell asleep." This formula is never used in relation to Him. He breathed out His Spirit, and He laid down His life in order to take it again.

"Cut to the heart" (v. 54) not "pierced." See v. 33.

"The witnesses" (v. 58), i.e., the false witnesses of vi. 13. In order to stone Stephen they put off their outward garments. It was the duty of a witness to execute the condemned (Deut. xvii. 7).

In verse 59 the title, "Lord Jesus," would be better supplied than "God." Here Stephen rendered Divine worship to Jesus Christ in the most sublime form, and in the most solemn moment of his life.

Stephen saw the Lord Jesus standing, and ready to receive his spirit ; and not only his spirit, but those of His believing people until the moment of resurrection. This is an illuminating and comforting fact respecting the blessed dead.

The entry of the Apostle Paul (v. 58) upon the scene is dramatic and characteristic.

This chapter is, therefore, one of the most important in the Bible. A clear grasp of its meaning, significance, and position is necessary to a right understanding of God's relationship to Israel, and of His action with the nation at that time, in offering them the King and the Kingdom. Had they accepted the offer, the Pentecostal Church would have continued and filled the whole earth, under the government of Christ and the Twelve Apostles. But the national rejection of the glorified Messiah closed the Pentecostal Dispensation, occasioned the destruction of the Temple, and postponed Divine relationships with Israel until Rev. i. 10.

The heaven now is opened, and the veil being rent, the Great High Priest is seen as the Son of Man in the glory. All is open to the believer—the glory and He Who entered into it with His own blood on behalf of His people. He stands in heaven their Great High Priest, and bears their names upon His breast. As King He is seated ; as Priest He stands—though as to the perfection of His atonement He sat down. Israel did not know till the High Priest came out on the Great Day of Atonement, that his work was accepted for the nation ; but his reappearance assured them. So will it be by and bye. When they see Him coming out of the heavens with His pierced hands and feet, they will learn that His atoning work availed for their justification.

But for believers to-day it is otherwise, for the Holy Spirit has come out from the glory to reveal the perfections of Him Who is in the glory, and to assure their hearts of the fact of the acceptance of His atonement and the power and sufficiency of His mediation.

It is remarkable that the only two men, prior to Rev. i., who saw the Man in the glory were both Hellenists and not of The Twelve—Stephen and Saul.

Ezekiel was addressed as "son of man " ; but the title " The Son of Man " belongs exclusively to the Messiah. It reveals Him as the representative Man, the long-promised and predicted Man, the seed of the woman.

" When his father was dead " (v. 4). This shows that Abraham's father formed the hindrance to Abraham's complete obedience. See notes on Gen. xi. 31 to xii. 4.

ACTS VIII.—" Consenting " (v. 1). The Greek word expresses hearty approval.

The Master commanded them to go everywhere preaching the glad tidings ; but they remained in a great group at Jerusalem, and it needed a persecution to scatter them.

Yet Jerusalem remained the Apostolic centre (vs. 1 and 14), for the promise of Joel belonged to Israel as the Hebrew Church, and the Twelve Apostles were its head, and Jerusalem its seat. This important fact is unrecognised by most commentators. The Apostle Paul was not one of the Twelve. See 1 Cor. xv. 5.

The word " preaching " occurs seven times in this chapter (vs. 4, 5, 12, 25, 25, 35, 40). Satan dreads preaching, but has no controversy with either ritualism or philanthropy ; for it pleases God through the foolishness of preaching to save them who believe—the Gospel being His power unto salvation, and the preachers being not sinless

angels, but pardoned rebels. Such is the simplicity of the Divine plan for recovering humanity from the dominion of sin and Satan.

" Philip " (v. 5), not the Apostle but the comrade of Stephen (vi. 5)—a Hellenist.

" Hearing and seeing " (v. 6) i.e., hearing what he said and seeing what he did.

" Bewitched " (v. 9), i.e., " amazed," R.V.

" Then Simon " (v. 13), i.e., when he saw which way the people were going, made a profession of faith in Christ—but only a profession, as verses 18-24 clearly prove. " He was baptized " (v. 13). This fact disproves the theory of baptismal regeneration.

In verse 14 Peter is not the Pope of the Apostles, but their servant and agent. This fact destroys the claim of the Papacy.

" The Holy Spirit " (vs. 15-17), i.e., the outward, physical, visible, and miraculous reception of the Holy Spirit, as on the day of Pentecost.

This gift, promised in Joel and mediated through the Twelve, makes more vivid the character and earthly position of the Pentecostal Church.

The term " simony," i.e., the purchase of offices in the church, is so called from the action of Simon in verse 18.

No doubt Simon proposed to make a great deal of money by selling this miraculous gift to others, who, like himself, desired to possess this mysterious power.

Peter said : " May you perish, and may your money perish with you ! " (v. 20), i.e., he predicted that Simon would perish, and he prayed that the prediction might come true. This is one of the imprecatory prayers of the New Testament. See Notes on Gal. i. 8 and 9, and 1 Cor. xvi. 22, etc.

The contrast between David and Simon marks the difference between true and false conversion (v. 24). When David was charged with his sin, he cried out : " I have sinned against Jehovah." The first thought in his heart was God, and the grief and damage occasioned to Him, and not the injury done to Uriah, his wife and the nation, nor the punishment that he himself would certainly suffer. Simon's first thought was himself, and his only desire was to escape from punishment. He did not know God. See Mark xvi. 16.

Simon's prayer to Peter to intercede for him met with no response. It was the petition of ignorance and superstition. Multitudes since then, and at the present day, have vainly applied to Peter for the supposed efficacy of his powerful intercession.

" They returned to Jerusalem and (on the way) preached the Gospel to many villages of the Samaritans " (v. 25, R.V.)— including possibly the one that John wanted to destroy (Luke ix. 54).

The simplicity of the Ethiopian pleasantly contrasts with the duplicity of the magician (vs. 19 and 34).

" The Angel of Jehovah " (v. 26). This should read : " An angel of Jehovah " (R.V.). " The Angel of Jehovah " is the Lord Jesus.

Philip's energy and obedience shew how truly he was under the control of the Holy Spirit. He at once left Samaria, where he was the most important person in a great revival, and willingly went to preach the gospel to one man in a desert.

Candace is a title like Caesar or Pharaoh.

This prince had worshipped, but was returning home not knowing the Lord Jesus Christ. Many to-day are in a like case. It is possible that he was a Jew or a proselyte. See chap. ii. 8-11.

He was " reading aloud " (Greek, vs. 28 and 30). It is interesting to learn here that the Bible was known in Upper Egypt, of which country Candace was Queen ; and, as the educated classes in Egypt spoke Greek, and as the Bible had been translated into that language 300 years before Christ, it may be assumed that it was the Greek text of Isaiah that the Treasurer was reading ; and as Greek was the most universal language at that time, and Philip, being a Hellenist, was most likely acquainted with it, it was possible for him and the Ethiopian to converse as they did.

An angel (v. 26) told Philip to take this journey, but it was the Holy Spirit Himself (v. 29) who told Philip to preach to the traveller. These facts shew the importance and solemnity of preaching ; an angel may be charged with directions as to a journey, but the Holy Spirit Himself immediately acts in soul-winning.

The question of verse 30 was not rude but kind ; and the invitation to Philip (v. 31) shews it was so recognised.

Verse 35 decides the meaning and application of Isa. liii.

" His judgment was taken away " (v. 33), i.e., He was refused justice. "Who shall declare His generation? " i.e., He would

apparently have no successors or followers.

The acceptance of Christ as Lord, and the washing away of sins, were signified by baptism (v. 38).

The Ethiopian (v. 39) went on his way rejoicing, and Philip (v. 40) went on his way preaching.

The conversion of this Ethiopian prince is an instance of how prayer may be answered after one thousand years. Compare verse 27 with 2 Chron. vi. 32.

ACTS IX. 1-31.—There are two Divine purposes revealed in the New Testament. The one is the " kingdom," the other is the " Mystery." The Mystery is the heavenly Church ; the Kingdom, the earthly. To this latter belong the Hebrews and the Nations ; to the other, an Election separated from the Hebrews and the Nations. The one Church will be set up upon the earth and will be there the Kingdom of God. The other Church is eternally seated with Christ in the highest heavens far above all principalities and powers in a glory of unutterable splendour. The glad tidings concerning the one Church were revealed from all ages (Rom. i. 2) ; the glories of the other were never revealed (Rom. xvi. 25). The ministry of the Kingdom was committed to the Twelve, Peter being the chief, and that of the Mystery to the Eight, Paul being their chief.

These Eight were Paul (Gal. i. 1.), Barnabas (Acts xiv. 4 and 14), Apollos (1 Cor. iv. 6 and 9), Sosthenes (1 Cor. i. 1, iv. 9). Silvanus and Timotheus (1 Thess. i. 1, 6 and 9, ii. 4 and 6), Andronicus and Junia (Rom xvi. 7). Those who wrote the Epistles were necessarily Apostles and inspired.

To the apostle Paul was committed a stewardship in respect of both the Kingdom and the Mystery ; and hence in his conversion facts appear characteristic of both ; but his ministry of the Mystery was the higher and greater stewardship. For that he was taken out of, and separated from, both Jews and Gentiles and became a citizen of heaven (xxvi. 17 and Rom. i. 1).

The characteristics of the Gospel of the glory (vs. 3, xxii. 6, 11 xxvi. 13, Rom. viii. 18, 2 Cor. iii. 7, 9-18, iv. 17 and Eph. i. 16, 17 and 18, Phil. iv. 19, Col. i. 27 and iii. 4, 1 Thess. ii. 12, 2 Thess. ii. 14, 2 Tim. ii. 10, etc.), and of the heavenly Election—chosen in

Christ as Son of God—and the mystery of the oneness between the Head and the members, appear in verses 3, 4 and 20.

The characteristics of the Gospel of the Kingdom are seen in the mission of Ananias, a devout Jew; his laying his hands upon Paul in order to the reception of the Holy Spirit (vs. 10 and 17); the baptism in water in order to the forgiveness of sins (xxii. 12-16); his introduction by Ananias to the believing Jews and proselytes at Damascus; and in his testifying in the synagague that Jesus was indeed the Messiah (vs. 20 and 22).

The subject of the Acts of the Apostles is the " Kingdom " with its outward accompaniments of baptism, breaking of bread, physical reception of the Holy Spirit and His gifts of healings and of tongues.

The subject of the apostle Paul's Epistles to the Seven Churches is the " Mystery " and its unseen spiritual realities and endowments.

Confounding these two Divine purposes of the " Kingdom " and the " Mystery," has produced the confusion which began ere the apostle Paul was dead, and continues to the present day.

" Threatenings and slaughter " (v. 1). Compare xxii. 4 and xxvi. 10, 11 and 1 Tim. i. 13.

" Women " (v. 2). This is recorded as an aggravated feature of his cruelty (viii. 3 and xxii. 4).

" A light from heaven " (v. 3). In that light he saw the Lord Jesus, as is plain from verses 5 and 17 and Gal. i. 15, 1 Cor. ix. i and xv. 7.

" Saul, Saul " (v. 4). The same voice that said " Abraham, Abraham," " Samuel, Samuel," " Martha, Martha," " Simon, Simon."

The God of glory manifested Himself to Paul on the Damascus road both outwardly and inwardly; as is clear by comparing verse 17 with Gal. i. 15.

The simplicity of Ananias' words and of the Lord's replies is most touching, and reveals the nature of the relationship between them, for He spoke to Ananias as a man speaks to his friend.

But He did not say, " Ananias, Ananias," just as in John xx. 16, He did not say, " Mary, Mary." Intimacy and fellowship appear in the simple " Ananias."

How much the heart wants to know about this beloved man !

" Hearing a voice " (v. 7), " in the Hebrew tongue " (xxvi. 14). " They heard not the voice " (xxii. 9). They heard the sound but not the words that were spoken. Compare John xii. 29.

The street called " straight " (v. 11). It still exists.

" Thy saints " (v. 13). These words declare the God-head of Christ.

" The children of Israel " (v. 15). These are put last, for Paul's great ministry was to the Church.

" The Lord, even Jesus " (v. 17). Therefore every time the title " Lord " here appears it means Jesus.

" That call on Thy Name " (v. 14), i.e., that address Divine worship to Jesus Christ. Compare 1 Cor. i. 2.

" A chosen vessel " (v. 15). Compare Rom. ix. 21, 23, 2 Cor. iv. 7, 2 Tim. ii. 20 and 21.

" Christ " (v. 20). This should read " Jesus." See Revised Version.

So Saul made a terrible discovery that overwhelmed his mind and heart and broke up the whole man for ever. He found that, zealous as he was for the Law, yet was he fighting against God and destroying His people. But grace in its sovereignty elected him as a chosen vessel, and sent him out to preach the Gospel of the glory. That grace united him to a glorified Christ in the eternal glories of the highest heavens. Hence he preached that Jesus was the Son of God. This was the first time that this was done. Peter had already proclaimed Him as the exalted Messiah, but Paul testified to his personal glory as Son of God. Upon this title the church is founded. Matt. xvi. 18, does not conflict with Eph. iii. 5, as the words " other ages " and " now " plainly show.

" After that many days " (v. 23), i.e., three years (Gal. iii. 1). After this first testimony at Damascus, Saul retired to Arabia for three years; and there the Lord Jesus so minutely related to him His whole life from His birth to His ascension that the apostles were unable to supplement it (Gal. i and ii.). But more wonderful than this, He revealed to him the Mystery (Rom. xvi. 25) till then hidden in God and never made known to the sons of men, i.e., the Church—the " new man " of Ephesians ii. 15. See notes on these passages.

After the three years Saul returned to Damascus and resumed his testimony there.

This period of time, therefore, is to be understood between verses 22 and 23.

His escape (v. 25) is re-told by himself in 2 Cor. xi. 32.

Verse 27 with verse 17 makes it quite clear that the apostle saw the Lord Jesus on the Damascus road, and it was He that spoke to him.

This conversion may justly be regarded as the greatest in history.

The omission from the narrative here of the period spent in Arabia is designed, and harmonizes with the character of this Book, for in it the " Kingdom " occupies the foreground and the " Mystery " the background. In the Church Epistles the reverse is found—the Mystery occupies the fore-ground and the Kingdom the background.

ACTS IX. 32—XI. 18.—The history of which Peter is the central figure—interrupted by the conversion of Paul—is here resumed, and its " Kingdom " character emphasized by the introduction of Aeneas, Dorcas and Cornelius. These represent the helpless, dead, and ignorant world into which the Messiah proposed, through His chief apostle, to introduce health, life, and salvation. The impotency of science, benevolence and observance stand brth upon the record. Science could not heal Aeneas, and benevolence could not give life to Dorcas, and religious observance failed to secure salvation for Cornelius. Science, benevolence, and observance are excellent in themselves, but they cannot give healing, liie and light to the soul. But Christ can give these, and He only can ; and personal contact with Him secures them.

Tabitha and Dorcas (v. 36). Both these names mean " gazelle." One is Greek, the other Chaldean.

All had not the gift of working miracles (v. 38), nor could those who had that gift exercise it in their own will.

There are two figures of speech in verse 39. " All the widows," i.e., many widows ; " The coats and garments which Dorcas made," i.e., specimens of them.

Peter put them all forth so that all the glory of the miracle might belong to the Lord Jesus, and none of it shared by the widows and the garments—just as in Joshua iii. a mile intervened between the Ark and Israel. See notes on that chapter.

" Peter kneeled down " (v. 40). It is never recorded that Christ knelt when performing a miracle.

The many details here given (vs. 40-42) attest its truthfulness.

The baptism of Cornelius is popularly understood to signalize the entry of the Gentiles into the Christian Church, but its character, and the employment and authority of Peter, and the meaning of the vision of the great vessel, and the many prophecies promising blessing to the Gentiles in union with Israel, all make it clear that it was entrance into the Hebrew Church, i.e., the Kingdom of God upon earth, and not into the Christian Church of Eph. ii. 15.

This officer (vs. 1 and 2) and his devout servant (v. 7), together with Luke iii. 14 and other Scriptures in harmony with them, prove that the Christian may be a soldier and a policeman.

Notwithstanding his moral worthfulness and religious culture and earnestness, Cornelius was an unsaved sinner (v. 43), and was told by the angel that he must listen to words whereby he should be saved (xi. 14). Therefore prior to hearing and believing the Gospel he was unsaved.

" What thou oughtest to do " (v. 6). These words made it clear to Cornelius that all his " doing " had no saving power.

The great vessel of white linen corresponded to the Ark of Noah. It, like the Ark, provided salvation for all nations, and not just for one nation, and without any moral distinction. Some animals were more beautiful and more useful than others, and many were ceremonially unclean, but the representatives of all were found in these two great vessels. So will it be in the earthly kingdom. All the nations, including Israel, will be shepherded in the one fold. This was a hard lesson for Peter and the Twelve to learn. But Christ is " Lord of all " (v. 36) and the Gospel is for " whosoever " (v. 43). Peter had proclaimed the election of the Gentiles to salvation in chapter ii. 21 and 39, but he was so dull and prejudiced that this vision had to be given to him to make him realize the fact.

" The ninth hour " (v. 3), i.e., three p.m.—the time of the evening sacrifice. This statement, with others in the chapter, make it clear that Cornelius and his friends were Jewish proselytes and acquainted with the Scripture and the life and death of the Lord Jesus Christ (v. 37).

"Common" (v. 14), i.e., not sacred.
"Unclean" i.e., ceremonially unclean.

This vision had to be repeated three times (v. 16); for after Pentecost, as well as before, Peter was extraordinarily slow in learning spiritual lessons.

"Certain brethren" (v. 23). There were six in number (xi. 12).

"And worshipped him" (v. 25). The Greeks and Romans rendered Divine worship to gods; and they believed that these from time to time indwelt men.

Servants rarely speak with enthusiasm of their master's piety (v. 22).

"In every nation" (v. 35)—not "In every religion" as corruptors of truth assert.

"The word" (vs. 36 and 44), i.e., the message of salvation through Jesus Christ.

"Anointed" (v. 38), i.e., "at His baptism." This was His anointing as Messiah.

Peter set Him before the company as a Judge (v. 42) or a Saviour (v. 43). This same choice confronts men to-day. Those who refuse to accept Him as a Saviour must meet Him as a Judge. Peter's auditors made the better choice; and, consequently, received the remission of sins and the Holy Spirit.

"Remission" of sins (v. 43), i.e., remission of the dread sentence of eternal death which is the just punishment of sins.

"All the prophet's" (v. 43)—beginning with Abel. Those who cannot find this witness in "all the prophets" are spiritually blind. The words "sin," "atonement," "forgiveness," "whosoever," "believeth" cover the pages of the Hebrew Scriptures.

"Heard" (v. 44), i.e., accepted and believed the message of salvation preached by Peter; and consequently upon believing they were sealed with the Holy Spirit (Eph. i. 13, R.V.).

The question in Galatians iii. 2 is here answered. Cornelius did not receive the Holy Spirit on the principle of works, but on the opposing principle of faith. See notes on Gal. iii.

Notwithstanding all the teaching they had received from the Lord, and from the Holy Spirit through the Scriptures, Peter and his companions were amazed (v. 45, R.V.) that the Holy Spirit should indwell Gentiles.

This was the miraculous power of the Holy Spirit demonstrating itself in the gift of tongues (v. 46). This must not be confounded with the moral power of the same Spirit—though both energies may synchronize—as they undoubtedly did in the Pentecostal Dispensation.

Peter's actions (vs. 47 and 48) were governmental and official. As custodian of the key he opened the door of the Kingdom to the nations, and he commanded these believers to be baptized into the Name of Jesus the Messiah (R.V.).

Baptism was symbolical and harmonized with that Dispensation. It had a double significance. It expressed attachment to the Messiah as a disciple, and it symbolized the washing away of their sins (xxii. 16).

Similarly all Israel, women and children included, were baptized into Moses in the Red Sea (1 Cor. x. 2)—although the water did not actually touch them—and in that baptism became his disciples and his "body" (Jude 9, see note there). It and the Petrine baptism correspond.

Had Cornelius and his friends refused to believe on the Lord Jesus Christ (v. 43), and declared that they preferred to trust for salvation to their own prayer-saying and almsgiving, they would have received neither the remission of sins nor the gift of the Holy Spirit.

The action of the Holy Spirit (x. 44) following upon belief in Christ, contrasted with the religious activities recorded in verses 2, 4, 22, and 30, confirms the fundamental doctrine that entrance into the Kingdom of God is not through works of righteousness, but through faith in Jesus Christ (Titus iii. 5 and 7).

Most probably some of the Twelve were among those who condemned Peter's action (xi. 2).

"Lord Jesus Christ" (v. 17). This is the first occurrence of this great title. It expresses Trinity in Unity—Jehovah—Jesus —and the Anointing Spirit.

So important was this matter of the reception of the Gentile nations into the Messianic Church, that the Holy Spirit records the facts twice.

"Repentance unto life" (v. 18), i.e., such as issues in life. Compare "repentance unto salvation" 2 Cor. vii. 10.

Cornelius owed all to grace. It reigned at every stage in his conversion.

ACTS XI. 19-30.—This passage makes it quite clear that Jerusalem was the centre of the Messianic Church. The Assemblies were Christian Synagogues governed on the model of the Jewish synagogue, but embracing Gentiles.

Everything here takes place in connection with Jerusalem (vs. 22. 27 and 30). The links binding these Christian synagogues to Jerusalem are shewn by the mission of the Prophets from Jerusalem, and by the sending of relief to Jerusalem. That city was the religious metropolis of the Kingdom of Heaven. There was no setting up of a religious system apart from, or in opposition to, the Temple, but rather the dawning of the day predicted by the Prophets when the Gentiles were to rejoice with Messiah's people. The following chapter further shews the position of Jerusalem.

Phenice (v. 19), i.e., Phoenicia.

" And " (v. 20). This should read " but " (R.V.) in order to mark the contrast between the action of those who only preached to the Jews and those who preached to the heathen as well.

Antioch on the Orontes (v. 19) was one of the greatest cities of that day, and was to a large extent the meeting-place of East and West. It is not to be confounded with Antioch in Pisidia.

" The grace of God " (v. 23), i.e., the fruits of that grace, as in verse 21.

" Good " (v. 24), i.e., large-minded and sympathetic.

Evidently feeling the need of skilful help Barnabas fetched Saul from Tarsus.

Antioch is immortalized as the birthplace of the term " christian " (v. 26). The word is Roman rather than Grecian, and means a follower of the Messiah. It was not, perhaps, at first used in contempt. It occurs three times in the New Testament—Acts xi. 26 Acts xxvi. 28, and 1 Pet. iv. 16. The Jews contemptuously called the disciples " Nazarenes " (Acts xxiv. 5)

A " dearth " (v. 28). This took place in A.D. 41, and its mention here is a valuable testimony to the historic value of this book.

ACTS XII.—Herod the king (v. 1). He was grandson of Herod the Great who murdered the babes of Bethlehem.

This James (v. 2) was one of the three, with Peter and John, who enjoyed the innermost intimacy with the Lord.

His murder is simply stated. Had man inspired this record there would here appear much excited language. And yet beneath the words what a deep of anguish and sympathy may be felt.

The Romans divided the night into four watches ; so sixteen soldiers were appointed to safe-guard Peter, four soldiers for each watch—one at each gate (v. 10) and two chained to the prisoner (v. 6). These four soldiers were relieved at the end of the respective watches. Peter's release must, therefore, have taken place during the last watch (v. 18), i.e., between 3 and 6 a.m.

Intending to bring him forth to the people (v. 4), i.e., for execution.

Easter (v. 4), i.e., Passover and the Feast of Unleavened Bread. A public execution would not have been acceptable during the Feast.

" The iron gate opened of its own accord " (v. 10). This statement is ridiculed by a science falsely so called.

" The angel of Jehovah " (vs. 7 and 23). This should read " An angel of Jehovah," as in the Revised Version.

" Mary " (v. 12) was the sister of Barnabas (Col. iv. 10) who was a person of substance (Acts iv. 37). Her son John Mark accompanied his uncle Barnabas in his first and second missionary journeys (xii. 5 and xv. 39). He was, perhaps, a son in the Gospel to Peter (1 Pet. v. 13).

Mary's house must have been a large one, for many attended the prayer meeting held in it (v. 12).

It must have been an all-night prayer-meeting, and perhaps then, as so often now, the prayer was very vehement (v. 5), but not very profitable for it weakened faith (v. 15). Faith in John xxi. 18 (" when thou shalt be old ") would have put them all asleep in bed. Contrast Peter in v. 6. See notes on Dan. ii.

Many great men in sacred and secular history are forgotten because their names are unknown, but Rhoda is immortal (v. 13). The Holy Spirit records her name, for the Great Shepherd calleth His own sheep by name. A little girl's testimony, though she may be only a servant maid, may confound the unbelief of a congregation (v. 15). Rhoda could not have given this testimony if at that time, as now, women were forbidden to speak in prayer-meetings.

The sheep know not only the Shepherd's

voice, but sometimes also that of the under-shepherd (v. 14).

"It is his angel" (v. 15), i.e., his disembodied spirit.

The priests thought they had made, by means of the Roman soldiers, their prisoner secure, as they had made the sepulchre sure (Matt. xxvii. 66).

Faith has her gifts and compensations, for Peter was sleeping peacefully (v. 6) although it was proposed in the morning to put him to death.

"A light shined in the prison" (v. 7). It was so that night physically, and many prisoners for the Truth have since then found it to be true spiritually.

"James" (v. 17). He presided at the council in chapter xv; and, possibly, was the author of the Epistle.

"Examined" (v. 19), i.e., "tortured." Failing to obtain any information, Herod commanded the unhappy soldiers to be put to death; for such was the practice of the day if a prisoner escaped. On the prior occasion (v. 20.) Peter was commanded to at once resume his public preaching, but now he apparently withdrew into privacy (vs. 17 and 19).

James was left to perish (v. 2) but Peter was delivered (v. 10). This is one of the mysteries of God's moral government. Faith approves of both actions.

"Highly displeased" (v. 20), i.e., "intended war," but the people of Tyre and Sidon desired peace for economic reasons.

The angel smote Peter (v. 7) and the result was life and liberty. He smote Herod and the result was disease and death.

So Herod having proposed an ignominious death for Peter, himself suffered one much more ignominious. His word perished but God's Word grew and multiplied (vs. 23 and 24).

"Their ministry" (v. 25), i.e., that of xi. 29 and 30.

ACTS XIII.—Very few recognise the significance of the facts stated in the first four verses of this chapter. An Authority—The Holy Spirit—at Antioch, independent of the Twelve Apostles at Jerusalem, selects another group of Apostles, eight in number, as appears later on, of whom the first two were Paul and Barnabas as His agents for calling out of the world an Election—the calling-on-high-of-God in Christ Jesus (Phil. iii. 14)—the Divine purpose revealed to

the apostle Paul and called by him "The Mystery." This special Election being based upon the Son of God in the glory, the manner of Paul's conversion harmonized with that glory, and prepared him for this special ministry. He never knew Christ after the flesh, as the Twelve Apostles did. He only knew Him in the glory; and his ambition was to be eternally associated with Him in that glory.

This Divine purpose was, therefore, independent from that committed to the Twelve. Their centre was Jerusalem, and their business was to bring the Tribes of Israel to the feet of the Messiah, and to baptize all the Gentiles into the Hebrew Church. That accomplished, the Messiah would set up His Kingdom on the earth, and the apostles, as the Twelve Princes of the House of Israel, would reign upon their promised thrones (Matt. xix. 28). Hence the Twelve were the source of authority in that ministry, and the apostle Paul recognised their authority within the bounds of their commission. Jerusalem was its centre during the Pentecostal Dispensation, and will be its centre when that Divine purpose shall be resumed and accomplished.

The Governmental number 12, therefore, characterizes the kingdom; the number 8, the Church.

The calling out of that Church from the world here opens: and the source and energy of that ministry was the Holy Spirit. Antioch, a city of the world, was its starting point and not Jerusalem, the capital city of the Kingdom of God upon earth. In that Kingdom, Jews and Gentiles were recognized as such. the Jew having precedence; in the heavenly Election there is neither Jew nor Gentile; there is a redemption out from among men.

The apostle Paul intelligently recognized these two Divine purposes and acted accordingly. As before stated the one purpose—the Kingdom—occupies the foreground in the Acts of the Apostles, and, therefore, Paul went first to the Jew and the synagogue.

The Church (v. 1), i.e., the group of believers that formed the Christian fellowship in Antioch.

"Prophets and teachers" (v. 1); not Apostles and Elders.

Manaen or Menahem, the name of one of the kings of Israel. He was foster brother to the Herod who murdered John the

Baptist. Susanna's husband was Herod's steward (Luke viii. 3), and possibly the courtier of John iv. 46 was attached to Herod's palace. This unhappy king, therefore, was surrounded by disciples of the Lord Jesus ; and yet how dreadful his end contrasted with that of his foster-brother !

Ministry to the servants is in effect ministry to the Master (v. 2).

" The Holy Spirit said " (v. 2). He was the source of their apostolate ; and He energized them (v. 4). See Romans i. 1. He is a Person, He speaks, He sends.

" Elymas " (v. 6) was a Magus. The Magi of Matt. ii. 1 were true men ; but Elymas was a false Magus.

Paulus is a Latin name and means " little."

The believers at Antioch laid their hands on these two apostles. To-day, the procedure is reversed, for those who claim to be successors of the apostles lay their hands on the believers.

Elymas personates the Hebrew nation. It opposed the Gospel and for a season darkness blinds their moral vision. It is remarkable that this was the moment chosen by the Holy Spirit to introduce Saul's new name. It may be termed his Church Name. Simon's new name Cephas was his Kingdom Name.

Thus is introduced the Apostle Paul, and this was his first missionary journey.

" They sat down " (v. 14), i.e., on a special seat, thus intimating, as was the custom in the Synagogue, that they were willing to speak, if invited.

" Ye that fear God " (v. 16), i.e., the Grecian proselytes.

" Four hundred and fifty years " (v. 20). The captivity years are here excluded.

The particulars set out in verses 24 and 25 were given to Paul by the Lord Jesus in Arabia.

" When they," i.e., the Rulers of verse 27 ; " they took Him down," i.e., Nicodemus and Joseph.

" Mercies " (v. 34), i.e., promises made to David.

" All that believe " (v. 39) not all who are baptised, and confirmed, and who partake of the Mass, and live a life of carnal holiness, but all who simply repose in faith their sin-stained souls upon an atoning and ascended Saviour.

" Justified," i.e., declared innocent. Here is the great problem of the Gospel message. How can a righteous God declare guilty men innocent (Rom. iv. 5). The Epistle to the Romans resolves the problem.

Let never so great a list of sins be presented to the believer as having been committed by him, he can, whilst sorrowfully confessing them and turning in shame from them, write the Divine words across them " Justified from all things."

A comparison of Peter's first sermon with Paul's first sermon shews that the one object of both was the Lord Jesus ; the one subject, the forgiveness of sins ; the one authority, the Bible ; and the one warning the wrath of God—and a personal testimony was added.

If those who claim to be their successors would preach the same doctrine, direct men's attention to the one Saviour, and add a personal testimony of His saving power, the moral Kingdom of God would be a present day reality.

With the Apostles all was based upon the Holy Scriptures as an infallible authority (vs. 17-41).

Warning men of the wrath of God is condemned by modern thought, but approved by Apostolic action (vs. 40 and 41).

" Persuaded " (v. 43), i.e., " urged " (R.V.)

" It was necessary " (v. 46) because so predicted in the Scriptures (Isa. xlix. 6).

" Ordained " i.e., disposed by God (v. 48). Personal salvation is not a matter of man's resolution but of God's ordination.

The filling of the Holy Spirit in this outward and physical sense as recorded in this Book, was always connected with Satanic opposition.

ACTS XIV.—" Long time therefore " i.e., at Iconium (v. 3)—" And there they abode long time " i.e., at Antioch (v. 28). This latter period was probably three years, and the missionary journey itself two years. That is, five years in all.

" Therefore " (v. 3). Because in spite of the opposition the Gospel was having so much success.

" In the Lord " (v. 3). This reveals the secret of the success of their ministry.

" The word of His grace " (v. 3). This is an exquisite title for the message of salvation. That message, though grace be its key-note, causes dissension, and disrupts families, communities, and nations (v. 4).

" They fled " (v. 6). So long as they only encountered opposition they persisted with their preaching, but when threatened with injury and death they went to other cities, as the Lord had commanded.

" The same heard Paul speaking " (v. 9, R.V.). So the Apostle must have been preaching in the open air.

Tradition describes Barnabas as a man of majestic presence (v. 12) ; perhaps it was because of this the people judged him to be Jupiter.

" Which was before their city " (v. 13), i.e., " whose temple was before the city " (R.V.).

The Greeks and Romans adorned with garlands of flowers the animals offered in sacrifice (v. 13).

" Like passions " (v. 15), i.e., a similar human nature,—and sadly proved in the contention of xv. 36-39.

" These vanities " (v. 15), i.e., idols and their sacrifices.

Although God permitted men the exercise of self-will (v. 16), He did not leave them without witness (v. 17) ; and hence they are without excuse (Rom. i. 20).

" To fill the heart with food " (v. 17). This is a very beautiful figure of speech expressing the gladness which the heart feels when the body enjoys sufficiency of food.

The fact that man's moral and intellectual nature is fallen, appears in the conduct of these cultured Greeks who stoned to-day the man they worshipped yesterday (v. 19).

The fact that Paul was able to start the next day for Derbe, which city lay many miles distant from Lystra, proves that his recovery was miraculous. The companions of George Fox and of John Wesley had somewhat similar experiences.

But the Apostles were not cowards, for they returned again to Lystra and to Iconium and to Antioch in Pisidia.

It is most important to notice that Paul and Barnabas were " Apostles " though they did not belong to the Twelve, nor were appointed by them, but were wholly independent of them (vs. 4 and 14).

But Paul's sufferings at Lystra were more than compensated for by the conversion of his beloved child Timotheus ; for if xiv. 21, xvi. 1-3 and 2 Tim. iii. 10, 11 be put together it will be clear that Timothy's conversion must have occurred during Paul's first visit to Lystra.

" Ordained " (v. 23), i.e., by a show of hands on the part of the disciples. They chose their presbyters, and the apostles Paul and Barnabas accepted and recognised their choice. All this shows that these companies of disciples organised themselves on the model of the synagogue.

" All that God had done, and how He had opened the door," etc., (v. 27). Here, and in the following chapter God is stated fifteen times to have been the Worker in this first missionary journey.

The catch-words Synagogue, Jews, Gentiles, signs and wonders, Kingdom of God, disciples, etc., reveal the Messianic character of this first great journey ; and, at the same time, the facts that the preachers were not of the Twelve and were yet styled " apostles," and that they were chosen and sent forth by the Holy Spirit Who was the source of their authority, reveal the operation of the Spirit in gathering an Election for the heavenlies, i.e., the Church.

Thus these two great Divine purposes may here be seen in simultaneous operation ; only that the Messianic Church and Kingdom occupy the foreground ; the other purpose but dimly appears.

The word " disciple " is not found in the Church Epistles.

ACTS XV.—The declaration made by the apostle James in verses 15-18 illuminates this chapter and makes quite clear that its interpretation belongs to the Messianic " kingdom " entrusted to Peter and not to the " church " revealed to the apostle Paul. See notes on Matt. xvi. 18, etc.

Jerusalem was the royal and ecclesiastical centre in the earth of the Messianic kingdom. It was the House of Israel under the new Covenant. That Covenant promised and secured circumcision of the heart instead of circumcision of the flesh, and inward moral cleansing instead of outward and ceremonial purifying. Israel was to enjoy a new spiritual birth and to experience God's Law written in the heart and not in stone.

But this Covenant was designed not only for Israel's glory but also for the salvation of all nations ; and their salvation was to follow immediately upon the rebuilding of the Tabernacle of David that was fallen down.

These facts understood, the apostle James's decision becomes quite clear. He argued that the day predicted by the Prophets had arrived; the New°Covenant was in force; Zion was being rebuilt. The New Covenant secured the righteousness which the Law under the First Covenant aimed at, and within its wide boundaries all the Gentiles were embraced. Therefore it was not necessary to salvation to observe the outward laws given through Moses.

Recognition of the distinction between this church of the New Covenant and the Church which is Christ's body seated with Him in the Heavenlies, explains this seemingly contradictory action of the apostle Paul in circumcising Timothy and refusing to circumcise Titus; as also the apparent conflict between his teaching and his conduct; for he earnestly contended that Christians were freed from the commandments of the Levitical law and yet he declared himself to be a Hebrew of the Hebrews, and a Pharisee; he took the vow of a Nazarite; recognised the place and authority of the Twelve Apostles; worshipped at the Temple; and offered sacrifices.

There was no inconsistency. There was intelligence, for he recognised that these two Divine Purposes—the Kingdom and the Church—were both in operation; the one having its centre at Jerusalem in the earth, the other its home in Christ above all Heavens.

Galatians i. and ii. should be read in connection with this chapter. See notes on those chapters.

At Antioch the order of the names is Paul and Barnabas (v. 2); at Jerusalem, Barnabas and Paul (v. 25). This harmonises with the dispensational import of the chapter.

"Peter" (v. 7). This is the last mention of him in this book.

"A good while ago" (v. 7), i.e., about fifteen years. "The Gentiles," i.e., Cornelius and his household.

"The hearts" (vs. 8 and 9). Purity of the heart and not ceremonial washing of the body, is what God requires, and what this new Covenant provided.

The gift of the Holy Spirit in equal abundance and manifestation proved that God made no distinction between Jews and Gentiles, but that they were to form one family in the Hebrew church. "Tongues" illustrated this unity and equality.

"Tempt" (v. 10), i.e. provoke.

"A yoke" (v. 10), i.e., the vain effort to obtain righteousness by works of Law. This hopeless yoke contrasts with the glorious operation of salvation by grace (v. 11). That principle recognises all men, whether Jews or Gentiles, as morally helpless and lost, and assures them of life and righteousness through faith in the Lord Jesus Christ.

This great resurrection title Lord Jesus Christ occurs four times in this book—xi. 17, xv. 11, xvi. 31 and xx. 21.

This was Paul's third visit to Jerusalem. He took Titus with him; and the events related in Gal. ii. 1-10 took place on this occasion.

The democratic government of the Pentacostal church appears in verses 2, 12, 22 and 23.

The apostle James evidently presided at this discussion, and closed it with his pronouncement (vs. 13 and 19).

"Agree" (v. 15), i.e., symphonize. The word figures a circle of musicians each member playing an independent and exquisite melody, and, all the melodies sounding together, producing a magnificent harmony.

"The residue of men, even all the Gentiles upon whom my name shall be called, saith Jehovah, who is now doing the things made known, i.e., predicted from the beginning of the world."

"Are turned" (v. 19). This should read "are turning."

The sanctity of marriage, the sacredness of life, and the holiness of God (vs. 20 and 29) were legislated for by the assembly at Jerusalem on this great occasion.

This legislation struck at the three great sins of heathendom—idolatry, impurity, and murder. In these sins the ancient Greeks revelled and gloried.

The argument of verse 21 was doubtless double. First—there was no danger of Moses being set aside, for he was read every Sabbath day throughout the intellectual world; and, second—the Levitical law being so constantly kept before the public, therefore it was the more necessary that the Gentile believers should be careful not to shock the prejudices of the Jews.

"Silas" (v. 22), i.e., the apostle Silvanus.

"Confirmed" (v. 32), i.e., in the doctrine that circumcision was not necessary to salvation, but that the teaching of the Holy Spirit was obligatory for sanctification.

The sharp contention between the two great apostles Paul and Barnabas proves how easily the most exalted servants of God may lose their tempers in connection with Christian work.

Putting the passages together it is clear from the Greek text that John Mark through cowardice forsook the apostles on their first journey. Barnabas being his uncle, and a man of large sympathy and easily influenced (Gal. ii. 13), wished John to be forgiven and taken with them, but Paul was inexorable; and it would appear from the farewell which the church gave him and Silas, that the brethren approved his action (v. 40).

It was at this time also that Paul sharply rebuked Peter for his inconsistent conduct at Antioch (Gal. ii. 14).

ACTS XVI.—The distinction between the Divine purposes respecting the Kingdom and the Church, is illustrated in this chapter by the independent action of the Holy Spirit on the one hand, and by household baptism on the other.

The Holy Spirit having, without reference to the Twelve at Jerusalem, and independently of them, elected as Apostles for the Church Paul, Barnabas, Silas and now Timothy (v. 3) sent them forth forbidding them (vs. 6 and 7) to preach in certain places, and commanding them to preach in others. The Twelve were commanded to preach to all nations (Matt. xxviii). This action of the Holy Spirit did not, therefore conflict with that commission, for it was the execution of another purpose equally Divine, i.e., the gathering out from among the nations of an Election for the Heavenlies.

Household baptism harmonised with, and was characteristic of, the promise of the Kingdom made to Abraham and to his children. This promise was illustrated at the first Passover (Ex. xii.) and confirmed by the promise of Joel ii. In Exod. xii. the lamb was slain for the household. It was household salvation. Infants are members of an household. Each blood-sprinkled house was a kingdom of God upon earth. The head of the household whether a woman (Acts xvi. 15) or a man (Acts xvi. 33), sprinkled the blood upon the door-posts on behalf of the first-born whether he were an adult or an infant. All Israel was a family and represented the Kingdom of God upon earth. Hence the wives and children were baptized into Moses as well as the men (1 Cor. x.).

The Twelve at Jerusalem, as the Executive of the earthly Kingdom, set up the King's standard, announcing He was about to appear, called upon all to range themselves beneath it, and threatened destruction to those who refused. Every man, therefore, who took shelter under that standard naturally brought his wife and children with him so that they should be in safety from the King's wrath. This Gospel was preached to the Jew first and also to the Gentile. But it closed in Acts xxviii.; and then, without distinction of Jew or Gentile, the Gospel of the grace of God, especially committed to the apostle Paul and called by him "my Gospel" (Gal. i. ii. and Rom. ii. 16), came into the foreground and still occupies it.

The apostle Paul and his seven brother apostles had, therefore, for a time a double ministry; and this explains the inconsistency which seemed sometimes to appear between their conduct and their doctrine.

Timothy was Paul's son in the Gospel (1 Tim. i. 2). His attachment to St. Paul, and his own value as an apostle, appear in 1 Cor. iv. 17, xvi. 10, 11, Phil. ii. 19-23, 1 Thess. iii. 1-6, and 2 Tim. iii. 10, 11. The apostle circumcised him so as to make him a more efficient agent in saving others (v. 3); but he refused to circumcise Titus because false teachers declared circumcision to be necessary to salvation. There was no inconsistency in the apostle's action.

"We endeavoured" (v. 10). At this point—Troas (v. 8)—the evangelist Luke joined the party. He was a preacher (" us ") as well as a physician (v. 10).

Two days later the Gospel messengers brought the Gospel message into Europe (v. 11). This is of great interest to European believers.

The first meeting was a prayer-meeting (v. 13). It was held every Sabbath day, and apparently attended by women only. The first persons in Europe to hear and believe the Gospel were women. This has an added interest for European Christian women.

"Wont to be made," i.e., a permitted place of prayer. There was evidently no synagogue at Philippi.

The Holy Spirit gently opened Lydia's heart; and she evidenced her conversion by courageously opening her house (v. 15). It needed an earthquake to open the gaoler's heart (v. 26). He also opened his house, and so proved the reality of his conversion (v. 34).

"As we went to prayer" (v. 16), i.e., "as we were accustomed to go to prayer, a certain damsel was accustomed to meet us and follow us, and this she did many days" (vs. 16-18).

Her testimony was true; but the apostle Paul refused to accept it — just as His Master had refused — for acceptance would have established fellowship with Satan.

Her master's accusation was hypocritical (vs. 20 and 21), for though it was indeed true that Philippi was a Roman city under Roman law, and that law tolerated existing religions but forbade new ones, yet they would have had no objection to any religion preached by Paul and his companions provided it did not affect their pockets.

Roman law forbade Roman citizens to be scourged if uncondemned (vs. 22-24 and 37-39). Hence the terror of the magistrates at what they had done.

"Their clothes" (v. 22), i.e., the clothes of Paul and Silas. In 1 Thess. ii. 2, he recalls this shameful treatment.

Scourging under Roman Law was a most brutal and cruel punishment. Many died under its torture. Paul and Silas must have been given super-human strength to have endured it. They had then to suffer the added torture of the stocks in the inner prison, which usually was a noisome and wet dungeon without any light, and the stocks were frequently so placed that the unhappy prisoner's shoulders lay on the wet stone floor, and his feet, drawn as far apart as possible, fastened high up to the wall.

Paul and Silas must have been faint and sick for many hours and unable, possibly, even to think. But at midnight they began both to pray and sing. The Greek Text suggests that bursts of song broke out as they prayed from time to time—as frequently happens to-day in spiritual prayer-meetings. So vigorous was their singing that in spite of the thick walls and ponderous doors, of the dungeon, the other prisoners heard them.

Thrice the apostle Paul endured the torture of scourging (2 Cor. xi. 25).

He giveth songs in the night (Job. xxxv. 10) and also earthquakes (v. 26).

The gaoler treated Paul with great brutality (v. 24), but Paul treated him with great humanity (v. 28).

The testimony of the damsel (v. 17) and the preaching of the apostles, must have become common knowledge, for many weeks had evidently gone by since their arrival, so that the gaoler's question as to what he was to do to be saved was most natural (v. 30). He was told that salvation was conditional upon belief in the Lord Jesus Christ; that there was no other condition; and that offered salvation included his family (v. 31).

Now, willing to hear, the Gospel was preached to him and to all that were in his household.

The word "house" in verse 31, means family—in verses 32 and 34, "household." This distinction appears in the Greek text. "All his" were baptized because they were his (v. 33).

The moral effect of salvation by faith in contra-distinction to salvation by works, may be recognised by contrasting the conduct of the gaoler and that of the rich young ruler (Mark x. 22). When Christ, as a Minister of the circumcision under the First Covenant, offered him salvation on the principle of works he withdrew, buttoning up his pockets, but the gaoler accepting salvation on the principle of faith, opened his purse and his house to the shamefully entreated preachers of the Word of God.

Silas was a Roman citizen (vs. 37 and 38). The apostles' conduct (vs. 37-40) was wise and dignified, and calculated to recommend the Gospel message.

ACTS XVII.—"Thessalonica" (v. 1), is the modern Salonica.

"Christ" (v. 3) R.V. "The Christ," i.e., the Messiah. This appellative appears twice in the verse. The appellative "The Christ" is characteristic of the Messianic Church; the substantive title "Christ", of the Heavenly Church. Hence the term "the Christ" occurs frequently in the Acts and rarely in the Epistles, and the reverse is the case with regard to the title "Christ." Christian preachers should, therefore, very rarely use the appellative "The Christ." To do so shows a want of intelligence in the Scriptures.

Only some Jews believed (v. 4) but a great multitude of the Greeks. The two Epistles to the Thessalonians accentuate this fact. This shows independence of Jerusalem and of the Hebrew Church.

Paul and Silas lodged in the house of Jason (vs. 5 and 7); hence the assault upon that house, and the effort to bring out the apostles to the people.

"These have turned the world upside down" (v. 6). This would be most desirable, for the world is wrong side up.

"They" (v. 9), i.e., the magistrates, here called the "rulers of the city"—literally the Politarchs. This title has been recently found in an inscription on an ancient arch in the city of Salonica.

"These were more noble" (v. 11), i.e., these Jews. "Therefore many believed." Sincere study of the Bible leads to faith in Christ.

Three points here appear (vs. 2, 11 and 12). First: people no less than ministers are entitled to search the Scriptures. Second: they are to exercise private judgment as to whether the teaching they receive from the ministers is scriptural. Third: no faith is living that does not result from personal conviction based upon the Scriptures.

"To go as it were to the sea," i.e., "to go as far as to the sea" (v. 14, R.V.).

Timothy, judging from 1 Thess. iii. 1 and 2, joined Paul at Athens, was sent thence to Thessalonica, and then rejoined Paul at Corinth (xviii. 5).

Connecting verse 17 and verses 2 and 3, it is to be understood that in the synagogue at Athens Paul reasoned that Jesus was the Messiah and proved it from the Scriptures, but that in the market-place he used other arguments with the Grecian disputants. Some of these latter arguments appear in his address on Mars Hill; and more matter probably would appear but that evidently he was interrupted by the scoffers and not permitted to finish what he would have said.

The Epicureans (v. 18) taught that pleasure was the chief aim in life; the Stoics contended that a passionless acceptance of natural law was the highest wisdom; and that such law was inexorable and merciless.

The Areopagus (v. 19) was the supreme court in Athens.

The Athenians were the most highly cultivated and artistic people in the ancient world, and their art and philosophy are to-day regarded as standards in the greatest centres of learning. But they did not know God, and hence in speaking to them, the apostle had to come down to the lowest step in the ladder of truth. He set forth the unity of God; His glory as Creator; man's relationship to Him; God's just right as Creator to judge His creatures; His manifestation of Himself in Christ; the resurrection of Christ; and the delegation of future judgment to Him as Son of Man. In effect he preached Jesus (v. 18) as being God. No doubt he would have developed his theme and definitely preached of sin and salvation but that he was not permitted, as already suggested.

He pointed to three days: The Day of Ignorance; The Day of Repentance; and the Day of Judgment; and his hearers divided themselves into three groups — Scoffers—Procrastinators—and Believers (vs. 32 to 34).

"Too superstitious" (v. 22) should read "Very religious." "Devotions" (v. 23), i.e., objects of devotion. "Ignorantly worship," rather, "worship in ignorance" (R.V.). "One blood" (v. 26), i.e., "one man." This statement, with many similar in the Scriptures, destroys the theory of a multiform creation of men. The earth's "appointed seasons" (v. 26, R.V.). "Winked at" (v. 30), i.e., "overlooked."

ACTS XVIII.—That the Church of God— "The Mystery"—is not the official subject of these chapters is clear from the use of the words "Disciples," "Jews," "Synagogue," "Baptism," "Kingdom," "Miracles," "Tongues," "Demons," "Vows," "Jerusalem," "Feasts," "Sacrifices," "Breaking of Bread," etc. All these are in this Book of the Acts grouped around its message and keynote, i.e., that Jesus was the Messiah (vs. 5, 28) promised to Israel.

In effect two Kingdoms are here contrasted: The Kingdom of God and the Kingdom of Satan. The one was a moral realm of liberty and holiness; the other, of slavery and wickedness. Under the term "Kingdom of God" can be placed all the moral activities of God in relation both to the Messianic Church and to the Church which is His Body.

"Persuaded" (v. 4), i.e., did his utmost to persuade both Jews and Greeks that Jesus was the promised Messiah (v. 5).

The arrival of the Apostles Silas and Timothy animated Paul to greater energy and vehemence in this testimony.

"From henceforth" (v. 6), i.e., so far as Corinth was concerned.

"One that worshipped God" (v. 7), i.e., a Greek proselyte. He and many others were baptized into the Messianic Church. Paul's main ministry being a spiritual one connected with the Heavenly Church, which commission did not include physical and outward symbolic ceremonies such as baptism (see note on 1 Cor. i. 17), rejoiced that he only baptized at Corinth Crispus and Gaius and the household of Stephanas (1 Cor. i. 14-16).

During their residence in Corinth the apostles Paul and Silas and Timothy wrote their two Epistles to the Thessalonians.

"I have much people in this city" (v. 10). This statement affirms the fact of election. Although the Corinthians were sunken in the most abominable impurities, yet God had much people among them—these people being unconscious of the fact prior to their salvation.

"Be not afraid". (v. 9). These words are often found in the Scriptures as having been spoken to timid or desponding servants—notably to the women (Matt. xxviii. 10) on the Resurrection morning.

"Gallio" (v. 12) was brother to the famous philosopher Seneca the tutor of Nero. Nero murdered them both. Seneca, writing of his brother, describes him as loving and lovable.

"The Law" (v. 13), i.e., Hebrew Law— "your law" (v. 15).

It may be understood that Crispus having believed (v. 8) was deposed from his position in the Synagogue; that Sosthenes was put in his place; and that he appeared before Gallio to accuse Paul. If so he deserved the beating he got (v. 17).

"He had a vow" (v. 18), i.e., the vow of a temporary Nazarite. See notes on Num vi. and Acts xxi. 24. The period engaged in the vow expired at the time of reaching Cenchrea.

"He himself entered" (v. 19). The Greek text means that in passing he paid a visit to the Synagogue, and then, leaving Priscilla and Aquila at Ephesus, he hurried on to Jerusalem to keep the Feast—probably Pentecost. He revisited Ephesus as he had promised (xix. 1).

"And gone up" (v. 22), i.e., to Jerusalem.

His third missionary journey is briefly described in verse 23. Timothy, Erastus, Gaius and Aristarchus were apparently his companions (xix. 22 and 29; 2 Cor. i. 1), and from 2 Cor. it may be presumed Titus also.

Thus it can be learned that Satan uses various weapons in opposition to the Gospel. At Philippi it was money; at Athens, philosophy; at Thessalonica, religion; and at Corinth, vice.

The fifth Apostle chosen by the Holy Spirit as an agent in relation to the heavenly Election was Apollos (v. 24). He now appears for the first time. It is noteworthy that the Eight Church Apostles were either Hellenists or Gentiles. Apollos as an Alexandrian was peculiarly fitted for the ministry of the Mystery. It was beyond doubt that secret purpose of God that Priscilla and Aquila explained to him (v. 26). The expressions "The way of the Lord" (v. 25, R.V.) and "The way of God" (v. 26) support this belief. The one term relates to the Divine promises made to Israel; the other, the Divine purposes respecting the Church. Paul needed no such human instruction, for he had learned everything personally from the Lord in Arabia.

As in the Revised Version, Priscilla is here given the precedence above her husband (v. 26), and this implies that she it was who mainly taught Apollos. It is instructive to read of a woman teaching an Apostle.

"He mightily convinced," i.e., he overwhelmed with argument, and continued to do so (v. 28), proving from the Scriptures that Jesus was the Messiah, and so he bore down all opposition.

Some Christian people condemn disputation when preaching the Gospel of love. The Holy Spirit here commends it (v. 28), and, in Jude 3, commands it.

Paul's action in verse 6 and in xix. 9, was based upon Isa. xlix, and was approved by the resulting success.

ACTS XIX.—"The upper coasts (v. 1), i.e., the hill country of Asia Minor.

The twelve disciples (vs. 1-7) were Hebrews, and, as such, submitted to John's baptism as a preparation for the baptism of the Holy Spirit which John promised them, and which they were expecting to receive. But they had not heard of the fulfilment of the promise. That is the meaning of their words as recorded in the second verse. On being baptized into the Name of the Lord Jesus they received the Pentecostal Baptism in its miraculous form upon their bodies, for they spake with tongues and prophesied.

The sealing of the Holy Spirit (Eph. i. 13) i.e., the regeneration of the Holy Spirit (Titus iii. 5) which takes place at conversion, is not to be confounded with the miraculous out-pouring of the Holy Spirit upon the flesh of believers which is so remarkable a feature of the Acts of the Apostles, and which was promised to the Hebrew Church (Joel ii.).

Prophesying, speaking with tongues, working miracles, and casting out demons (vs. 6 and 12) were gifts to that Church, but they are not promised to the Church of Col. i. 24. A higher and purely spiritual ministry and testimony belong to it, whilst, of course, God reserves liberty of action to Himself to do as He pleases in His moral government of man. Speakers at Conventions misunderstand and misapply this second verse, to the confusion and injury of their hearers.

"Jesus I recognise, and Paul I know" (v. 15). Different Greek verbs mark this important distinction.

The evil spirit knew a great antagonist of Satan's kingdom like Paul, but as to these obscure Jews he cried: "Who are you?" Only two of the seven brothers attempted this exorcism (v. 16, R.V.).

When God enters in power, devils flee, sinners tremble (vs. 12 and 17), and the conscience of believers is awakened and judged (vs. 19 and 20).

Fifty thousand pieces of silver have a present value of about £5,000.

During this period at Ephesus, Paul must have paid a second visit to Corinth, seeing that the one next recorded (xx. 2 and 3) is twice called his third visit (2 Cor. xii. 14 and xiii. 1). 2 Cor. i. 15 and 16 might seem to disprove this but need not, Ephesus and Corinth being near each other.

At this time also he and Sosthenes his "brother" apostle (1 Cor. i. 1) who now appears, wrote the first Epistle to the Corinthians. Perhaps at this time also Paul wrote his personal epistle to the Galatians.

As is stated in 1 Cor. xvi. 9, a great door and effectual was opened to him at Ephesus.

The vast field of Gospel ministry which Paul proposed to himself appears in verses 21 and 22.

The Temple of Diana, or Artemis, at Ephesus was reckoned as one of the wonders of the world. It was built in 550 B.C. of pure white marble and rebuilt in 356 B.C. with still greater splendour. It was adorned with one hundred and twenty-seven columns sixty feet in height, and each the gift of a king. It contained incredible wealth. The goddess had the form of a many breasted woman, emblematic of the abundance of nature, and was believed to have fallen from heaven. Silver models for sale were made of this Temple, and of the goddess, and were believed to bring prosperity to houses in which they were placed. Ephesus was devoted to this divinity; and however people might speak lightly of other divinities no one dared to disparage Diana (See note on 2 Cor. vi. 18).

Similarly to-day models are made of the Virgin Mary and her supposed house at Loretto, and are believed to convey spiritual grace; and in Spain however blasphemy against God might be tolerated by the mob, an attack upon the Virgin of Saragossa would be promptly punished with death. A corresponding devotion to the Virgin exists in all Roman Catholic lands.

Money and religion powerfully move the carnal heart, but when united they excite men to measureless violence (vs. 25-28).

The common people believed these images to be gods; the more intelligent used them as aids to devotion. It is exactly so in the Churches of Greece and Rome.

Aristarchus and Gaius are mentioned in xx. 4 and xxvii. 2, Rom. xvi. 23, 1 Cor. i. 14 and perhaps in 3 John i.

If it was in the house of Aquila and Priscilla that he found refuge (1 Cor. xvi. 9) that would explain Romans xvi. 3, where he says that to shield him they laid down their own necks, i.e., they risked their lives.

"The chief officers of Asia" (v. 31, R.V.). These were noble citizens selected to preside over the games celebrated in the month of May. It was an office of great honour, and much coveted.

The Alexander of verse 33 was probably the coppersmith of 2 Tim. iv. 14. As a Jew, hostile to the Gospel, he would hate Paul, and as a coppersmith, he would sympathize with the craftsmen. No doubt his object was to explain that the Jews were not to be blamed in any way, but only Paul and his followers.

" The town-clerk " (v. 35) rather resembled a Lord Mayor of the present day.

The Roman government insisted on public order, and punished with merciless severity magistrates who neglected it ; hence the danger spoken of in verse 40.

The statement made in verse 37 that the Gospel preachers did not insult the religion of the people, is an example to be followed by missionaries and ministers. At the same time the apostle did not compromise truth, as is evident from verse 26.

ACTS XX.—Paul now departed after Pentecost (1 Cor. xvi. 8) to go into Macedonia as planned (xix. 21), and revisited Troas (2 Cor. ii. 12) where he found an open door for the Gospel. From thence he went into Macedonia—no doubt to Philippi (2 Cor. xi. 9 with Phil. iv. 15). Here he met Luke and Titus (2 Cor. vii. 5, 6, 7 and 13), and from here he and his brother apostle Timothy wrote what is known as the Second Epistle to the Corinthians. It must have been at this time that he went " round about unto Illyricum " (Rom. xv. 19). Then, as further purposed in xix. 21, he visited Achaia and there abode three months (v. 2), no doubt in the city of Corinth and the neighbourhood. Here he wrote the Epistle to the Romans. The hostility of the Jews preventing a straight journey to Jerusalem, he changed his plans and went back through Macedonia and so to Troas via Philippi. His several companions who met him at Troas were most probably delegates proceeding to Jerusalem with the money from the various assemblies, subscribed for the poor saints in that city. Tychicus and Trophimus (v. 4) appeared to have particularly attached themselves to Paul (Eph. vi. 21, 22, Col. iv. 7, 8, Acts xxi. 29, and 2 Tim. iv. 12 and 20).

" To break bread " (v. 7) was a Hebraism for to dine in company (Deut. xxvi 14, Job xlii. 11, Jer. xvi. 7, Ezek. xxiv. 17, Hos. ix. 4, Isa. lviii. 7, Matt. xiv. 19, xv. 36, Luke xxiv. 30, 35, Acts xxvii. 33-36). The belief entertained by some that it was the Mass, and by others that it was what is now called the Lord's Supper, is without foundation. See note on Exod. xxiv. 11.

The Roman road from Troas to Assos (v. 13) was about twenty miles—the distance by sea round Cape Lectum is forty miles.

The address to the elders of Ephesus (18-35)

destroys the figment of the Historic Episcopate. Paul had no successor. He did not commend the Ephesian brethren to Timothy, or to the Twelve, or to a Church organisation, or to a body of tradition. He commended them to God and to the Bible (v. 32), assuring them that such a provision amply sufficed for all their spiritual necessities whether as a Church or as individuals. All official resource he set aside. The terms elder, bishop and overseer all indicate the one office. Such was the simple organisation of the Church at Ephesus.

The apostle's ministry was energetic (" from the first day ") ; incessant (" at all seasons ") ; loyal (" serving the Lord ") ; not self-willed (" with all humility of mind ") ; affectionate (" with many tears ") ; tested (" with bonds and afflictions " verses 19 and 23) ; honest (" I kept back nothing that was profitable ") ; thorough (" publicly and from house to house ") ; evangelical (" repentance " and " faith ") ; wholehearted (" I count not my life dear unto myself ") ; instructive (" all the counsel of God ") ; admonitory (" I cease not to warn everyone ") ; and disinterested (v. 33).

" None of these things move me " (v. 24). Jacob cried out " All these things are against me " (Gen. xlii. 36). He looked at " the things " ; Paul looked through the things at God.

" The Kingdom of God " (v. 25). " The Counsel of God " (v. 27). The one concerned the dominion of the Messiah over the nations ; the other, the purpose of God in taking an election out of the nations. This purpose of glory and of grace is revealed in the Epistle to the Ephesians.

" The flock in which the Holy Spirit hath made you elders " (v. 28, R.V.).

" Grievous wolves " from the outside (v. 29) and " perverse teachers " from the inside (v. 30) form the historic apostolic succession.

" Take heed to yourselves and to the flock (v. 28). Personal is here put before pastoral care.

The words " It is more blessed to give than to receive " (v. 35) are not found in the Four Gospels. Paul learned them from the Lord Jesus Himself. This is a beautiful instance of the Law of Subsequent Mention.

So far as is known the apostle never saw these Ephesian brethren again.

He was undoubtedly of a most affectionate

nature, as is clear from verses 1, 19, 25, 31, 34, 35, 36, and 37.

They should have sorrowed most of all for the words which he spoke in verse 30. Had they done so they would not all have turned away from him and his teaching in less than five years (2 Tim. i. 15). Excessive demonstrations of affection are not to be trusted.

ACTS XXI.—Many think that the apostle erred in persisting to visit Jerusalem, and they support their conviction by pointing out that at this juncture the record of his evangelistic labours ceases. They find it also difficult to understand how the author of the epistle to the Galatians could take the vow of the Nazarite and offer the sacrifices (vs. 25-27) of Numbers vi. 13-20.

But both this difficulty and this conviction disappear when the Book of the Acts is intelligently interpreted, and its relation to Messiah's earthly kingdom recognised, and when the approbation of xxiii. 11 is remembered.

Paul was a chosen vessel (ix. 15) to offer that kingdom to Israel, as well as to proclaim it among the Gentiles. The final and official offer to the Twelve Tribes at Jerusalem, and at Rome, by the greatest of the apostles, and its rejection, is the subject of chapters xxi.-xxviii. This final offer was a Divine necessity; and, therefore, the apostle felt bound to go up to Jerusalem and afterwards to Rome. He was best fitted for this ministry, for of all the apostles he most resembled the Master. He was willing to die for his people, and to be accursed, if only they might be blessed. Like the Master they shouted "Away with him" (v. 36) and handed him over to the Gentiles to be slain, and at their hands he died. He was a child of the promises made to the Fathers, a Hebrew of the Hebrews, a Pharisee, and as a godly Israelite he offered the sacrifices of Numbers vi. in commemoration of the Great Sacrifice which, prior to it, they fore-shadowed. They were a Divine institution, and they pointed forward and backward to Christ with equal significance (See notes on Ezek. xl.-xliv.). It is true that personally he was quite willing to surrender all his privileges as a Hebrew in favour of the greater glories of the calling on high of God in Christ Jesus (Phil. iii.); but that desire did not release him from his appointment as a prophet to Israel (ix. 15).

Gotten (v. 1). Greek : gotten with difficulty i.e., torn from them.

The predictions as to what would happen to him if he persisted in going up to Jerusalem (vs. 4 and 11), were doubtless designed to test his resolution to obey the inward voice which bound him to go. So Elijah tested Elisha.

The wives and the children joined in the solemn worship of verse 5. This is a sweet picture.

Philip the Evangelist, last seen in viii. 40, now appears (v. 8), and his four gifted daughters. Paul who in his anxiety to reach Jerusalem could not give even one day to Ephesus (xx. 16), here stayed many days (v. 10), and no doubt in order to profit by the ministry of these women.

"Besought him" (with tears) (v. 12)—see next verse.

"Carriages" (v. 15), i.e., luggage.

"An old disciple" (v. 16), i.e., an early disciple

At Jerusalem Paul recognised the authority of the Twelve (vs. 19-26), and did so intelligently. See note on page 850.

"Be at charges with them" (v. 24), i.e., defray the expenses of the sacrifices. Each one had to offer a burnt-offering, a sin-offering a peace offering, a meal-offering, a drink offering and unleavened bread as commanded by God in Num. vi. (see notes on that chapter), so it was a somewhat costly matter, and among the Jews it was esteemed a very great proof of fidelity to the law to pay for such sacrifices. A Nazarite bound himself for a period or for life. Paul and his companions had taken this vow for a given period of time; and as commanded by the law they hastened to offer the prescribed sacrifices appointed for the termination of the vow. These sacrifices struck at self-righteousness, for the Nazarites in offering them declared themselves to be lost and guilty sinners, notwithstanding their religious resolution and conduct. They publicly confessed that sin attached even to their holy things, and that they themselves needed cleansing and forgiveness.

This was Paul's fifth visit to Jerusalem. It concluded his third missionary tour; and, so far as recorded, his last. But between his first and second imprisonment at Rome he must have made a very extended tour; and doubtless being entirely in connection with the Church of God, it naturally finds no place in the Book of the Acts.

In connection with this fifth visit see the note on Rom. xv. 31.

" Drew him " (v. 30). Greek : " dragged him."

" Chief Captain of the band " (v. 31), i.e., the commander of the Roman garrison of one thousand men. They were lodged in the castle of Antonia. It overlooked and commanded the great court of the Temple. It was the duty of this officer to prevent rioting.

" Bound with two chains " (v. 33)—no doubt as Peter was bound to two soldiers (xii. 6).

A flight of stairs led from the Temple Courtyard up to the entrance to the barracks (v. 35).

The four thousand assassins (v. 38) are mentioned by Josephus.

Tarsus was famous for philosophy and learning, and was regarded by many as equal in culture to Athens and Alexandria.

ACTS. XXII.—This chapter and the following record the final offer of the King and the Kingdom to the Two Tribes at Jerusalem and their rejection of both.

The greatest of the apostles was not ashamed to tell the simple yet wonder-filled story of his conversion to this great crowd, and again (xxvi.) to the Royal Court and its brilliant personages ; nor was he ashamed to preach the Gospel of love and peace under the protection of soldiers. See note on Rom. xiii. 4.

The apostle adds the words " of Nazareth " (v. 8) to make it quite clear of whom he was speaking.

The Hebrew language (v. 2). The fact that Paul was a Jew (v. 3) ; the introduction of Gamaliel (v. 3) ; " of the Law " (v. 3) ; of the high priests and the elders (v. 5) ; of Ananias and his reputation amongst the Jews (v. 12) ; of the God of Abraham, Isaac, and Jacob (v. 14) ; and of the Temple, was all designed and intended by the Holy Spirit to make this offer of the kingdom official to Israel, as promised in the Scriptures.

" They heard not the voice of Him that spake to me " (v. 9), i.e., they did not hear what the voice said, they only heard the sound (ix. 7). " Sound " and " voice " are the same word in Greek.

" Thy testimony concerning Me " (v. 18). So Paul, like all true preachers, presented Christ to them as the only Saviour, and stated that calling on His Name secured the washing away of their sins (v. 16).

He would no doubt have obeyed the command to leave Jerusalem quickly (v. 18) but for the unforeseen action of the Jews of Asia (xxi. 27). The language of xxii. 21 supports this supposition.

The word " Gentiles " (v. 21) lashed their pride and prejudice into fury, although their own prophets largely predicted that Messiah should reign over the Gentiles.

To throw dust into the air (v. 23) expressed that the accused merited death.

" Examined " (vs. 24 and 29), i.e., " tortured."

Paul did not shrink from torture when it was directly connected with the Name of Jesus, but he quietly and with much dignity avoided it when ordered by official ignorance.

In the providence of God Paul was both a Jew (v. 3) and a Roman (v. 25).

It was contrary to Roman law to torture a Roman and uncondemned.

The commandant was a Greek (xxiii. 26) and bought his Roman citizenship at a great price. Such was the case under the Emperor Claudius ; but, later on, it was bought for next to nothing.

He commanded the chief priests and all their counsel to appear, and they admitted their subjection to the Roman government by obeying the command.

ACTS XXIII.—The accusation against Paul being that he was a traitor to the Law and to the nation, he began his defence most properly by stating that, as to such a charge, he had a good conscience before God. He declared his integrity and his loyalty in those relationships. He did not mean that he was sinless. It was, therefore, a violation of law on the part of the high-priest to order him to be struck on the mouth, i.e., to be forbidden to speak.

The contrast between this Ananias and the Ananias of xxii. 12, is very striking.

God did smite him (v. 3) for he perished not long after in the Jewish war at the hand of an assassin.

It was very difficult at that time for a visitor to Jerusalem, as Paul was, to know who was high-priest, for the Romans made and unmade them at their pleasure, in addition to those made and unmade by the Sanhedrin.

As a lawyer Paul was stung by the insult

illegally ordered by the judge; but if he was for a moment thrown off his guard (Christ never was), nothing can surpass the grace and the frankness with which he expressed his sorrow; and so the manner in which he atoned for his error honored Christ.

The apostle's declaration that he was a Pharisee and the son of a Pharisee was not just a clever stroke in order to produce dissension in the counsel, but it was a noble declaration in connection with the claims of the Messiah as risen from the dead, and, consequently, King of Israel. Had he withdrawn his membership from the religious society of the Pharisees, his action would have been a blow at the scriptural doctrine of the resurrection of the dead.

The words " let us not fight against God " (v. 9), are not found in the Revised Version. It is most probable that the uproar drowned the remainder of the sentence, or prevented and broke off this conclusion.

The " must " of verse 11 together with the " must " of xviii. 21, and the statement that Paul was " bound " to go up to Jerusalem, all make clear the Divine purpose in chosing Paul as the messenger to Israel both in Jerusalem and in Rome (chs. xxiii. and xxviii).

The depth of infamy to which the religion of the carnal heart can sink cultured and religious people, is seen in the collusion of the chief ministers of the Hebrew Church with the assassins (vs. 12-15).

God always has His instruments ready at the right moment (v. 16).

The commandant's action in taking the lad by the hand (v. 19), throws a pleasing light on the character of that officer, and suggests that the lad was but a boy.

Four hundred and seventy men was not excessive (v. 23), for the Romans sternly opposed rioting, and already they had had frequent proofs of the turbulence of the Jews. Roman officers who permitted rioting, and who failed to protect Roman citizens, were usually put to death.

Claudius was a Latin name—no doubt assumed when citizenship was purchased—and Lysias a Greek name (v. 26).

As is the case with state servants in all ages, the commandant credited himself with becoming intelligence (v. 27). The commandment to the accusers to appear (v. 30) was given no doubt before the letter reached Felix.

The soldiers started at nine p.m., the third hour of the night (v. 23), and marched all night and part of the next day to Antipatris. As the distance was forty miles they must have marched without stopping for fifteen hours. Modern soldiers could rarely equal this. Here the infantry halted and returned to Jerusalem, while the cavalry marched the remaining twenty-six miles to Cæsarea and handed over Paul to the Viceroy.

So the apostle recognised soldiers as God servants, and profited by their protection (xxi. 39, xxiii. 11, and Rom xiii. 2, 3).

ACTS XXIV.—Roman Law and the Latin language being usual in the Vice-Regal courts, advocates such as Tertullus were frequently employed by the Jews. Such men practised in the provincial Courts of Law before proceeding to the great cities of the empire.

All his charges laid against Paul were false except the accusation that he was a Nazarene. This was not a crime in Roman Law.

The followers of Jesus were called " Christians " by the Gentiles, and " Nazarenes " by the Jews.

" Whom " (v. 8), i.e., Lysias.

The dignity and truthfulness of Paul's language contrast markedly with the false and flattering address of Tertullus.

The apostle believed everything written in the Bible (v. 14). Many modern religious teachers claim to be much more intelligent, and, accordingly, believe little written in the Bible.

Drusilla was a daughter of the Herod of Acts xii. 1 and 23, and a sister of the Herod Agrippa of Acts xxvi.

She and Felix were both historically infamous persons. No doubt they intended to entertain their curiosity by sending for Paul, but he made Felix tremble with the terrors of the world to come.

The injustice that kept Paul imprisoned for two whole years, and left him in prison, must have been bitter to an upright lawyer such as Paul was; but it provided him with a lengthened rest cure, and no doubt this was why it was permitted by God.

ACTS XXV.—Little is known of Festus. He died a few years after the events of this chapter.

The hatred of the priests to Paul, and

their resolve to murder him (v. 3), still burned fiercely though two years had gone by (xxiv. 27).

Recognising the hopelessness of getting justice from Festus (v. 9), Paul was constrained to appeal to Caesar, and by so doing co-operated with the Divine purpose that in that city he should utter the judgment of xxviii. 23-28. See notes on that chapter.

Agrippa and his sister Bernice were the children of Herod Agrippa I. The pomp of their visit to Cæsarea contrasts with the horrible death of their father in the same city.

" Superstition " (v. 19), i.e., religion.

" One Jesus, Who was dead, Whom Paul insists is alive " (v. 19). This shows that the death and resurrection of Christ was the great subject of Paul's preaching, but that it was altogether insignificant and without interest to the Roman Governor.

" Augustus " (v. 21), i.e., " The Augustus," that is, " The Emperor " (R.V.). This title, with that of " lord " (v. 26), attests the historic accuracy of this Book, for the title " Augustus " was first conferred by the Roman Senate not long before this, and Nero, the then emperor, accepted the title " lord " which his predecessors refused.

It was predicted that the apostles should have the opportunity of preaching before kings and rulers (Luke xxi. 12 and 13). Hence Paul's appearance before this distinguished company (v. 23).

But what a contrast he presented to them ! He, morally, so noble, and they so ignoble.

ACTS XXVI.—Paul addressed Agrippa as a fellow member of the Hebrew Church, and as, therefore, accepting the Holy Scriptures as a Divinely inspired and infallible authority (vs. 3, 6, 19, 22, 23 and 27), and as believing in the coming of the promised Messiah. He was not ashamed to once again tell the story of his conversion ; and he used it as a sword to pierce the heart and conscience of the king, of his sister, and of all the exalted persons with them—all of whom were living lives of abomination though professing forms of religion.

The apostle protested his loyalty to the Hebrew Church (vs. 4-7) and to its true Head (vs. 13-20, 22, and 23).

The appeal of verse 8 was majestic in

its power and certain to remain embedded in the minds of the hearers.

The apostle did not trouble to refute the charge of sedition. He confined himself to the one great subject of salvation.

In verses 14-18 Paul condensed into one embracing sentence various messages given to him by the Lord Jesus so as to present at one view the nature of the commission given to him, and so help Agrippa to understand it.

He pointed out that man is blind, enslaved, impure, morally poverty-stricken and unholy, but that he can receive sight, liberty, forgiveness, true wealth and holiness upon the principle of faith in Christ (v. 18).

His enemies said he should have been disobedient to the heavenly vision, he most earnestly declared he was not disobedient to it (v. 19) ; and he pressed upon the King personally—" Oh, King Agrippa "—that he should repent and be converted and live a clean life (v. 20) ; and that it was through the atoning death of the Messiah and His glorious resurrection (v. 23) that salvation should reach the Hebrew people and the Gentile nations.

The whole of this address, but especially its close, is one of the most noble and elevated pieces of oratory in existence. Never did the King and that great company hear or read language so majestic.

The dignity of the apostle's reply to Festus cannot be surpassed for self-possession, courtesy and nobility.

Festus as a heathen could not understand, as Agrippa could, the great argument that the atoning death and resurrection of the Messiah fulfilled the predictions of the prophets (vs. 22 and 23) and were necessary in order to the salvation of sinful men.

It is doubtful how the Greek of verse 28 should be understood, whether Agrippa was really moved and said sincerely, " You almost persuade me to be a Christian " ; or that seeking to hide his emotion from his godless court, he said with affected carelessness : " You think you can easily make me a Christian ! "

The dramatic majesty of Paul's words, and his action in lifting up his manacled hands, form a picture of arresting grandeur.

But they did not want to hear any more, and so they rose, and thus closed the audience and silenced the brave confessor.

This chapter should be read in the Revised

Version. " Compelled " (v. 11), i.e., " strove" (R.V.) that is, " did my utmost to make them blaspheme " (but failed).

Thus he tried by torture to suppress heresy. He was the first Grand Inquisitor.

If Agrippa and his courtiers hoped to entertain themselves with the new religious views of this Jewish reformer, as they would account him, they were quickly undeceived, for the brave preacher immediately raised moral and eternal issues, and presented Christ to them as a Saviour from their sins (xxv. 22).

ACTS XXVII.—Fellowship with God gives courage to the heart whether facing kings or tempests, though both be energized by Satan in order to destroy the Christian; and it clothes the person and the mind with a dignity which confounds the enemies of the. Gospel.

Hence the apostle Paul forms an heroic figure on the wave-swept deck of the storm-tossed ship, and he became a minister to the mental, spiritual, and physical needs of its terrified passengers and crew. The companionship of God can accomplish similar effects to-day if His people would prove its power.

" We " (v. 1). Luke now rejoined the apostle.

" Augustus' Band " (v. 1), i.e., the Imperial cohort. A cohort was composed of 200 men.

This chapter, like the preceding one, should be read as in the Revised Version.

" Aristarchus " (v. 2). See Acts xix. 29; xx. 4; Col. iv. 10: and Philemon 24. " The Fast " (v. 9), i.e., that of the great Day of Atonement held at the close of September (Lev. xvi. 29).

" Long abstinence " (v. 21), i.e., from regular meals.

" Must " (v. 24). This is an important word, as will appear in the notes on chapter xxviii., for there was a Divine necessity that the kingdom should be offered to the Ten Tribes of the Dispersion at Rome, the capital of the Gentile world.

While the terror-stricken passengers and crew were vainly trying to battle with the tempest, Paul was pleading in prayer that they might all be given to him (v. 24).

The statements " Whose I am," " Whom I serve," and " I believe God " (vs. 23 and 25) form a noble confession of faith.

" Except these abide in the ship ye cannot be saved " (v. 31). This does not contradict the assurance given in verse 24. The one was a Divine pledge; the other, an indispensable condition of escape. Divine agency and human instrumentality are both found within the will of God.

" Nothing " (v. 33). The Greek word used here shews that it means they had eaten no regular meal.

Ships at that time were steered by two large rudders. They were fastened while the vessel was at anchor, and loosened when the ship began to sail (v. 40).

When prisoners escaped Roman law condemned their guard to death (v. 42). Hence the soldiers' counsel.

ACTS XXVIII.—The majority of scholars agree that Melita is the modern Malta.

This chapter recording the last offer of the Kingdom to Israel, the miracle of verse 4, and those of verses 8 and 9, being characteristic of that dispensation, harmonize with its import. Excepting a reference to them in 1 Corinthians miracles now pass from view.

Castor and Pollux were the favourite divinities of Mediterranean seamen at that time. St. Antony is their popular divinity to-day.

" The Three Taverns " (v. 15) were about thirty miles from Rome, and the Forum of Appius about forty.

Paul's affectionate nature appears in the statement of verse 15 that when he saw these Christian brethren he was encouraged.

The wisdom and grace of his address to the prominent Jews of Rome (vs. 17-20) are admirable.

" The Hope of Israel " (v. 20) is a Messianic title. Compare Jer. xiv. 8 and xvii. 13.

The one infallible authority that all the apostles appealed to as declaring that Jesus of Nazareth was the promised Messiah, was the Old Testament, i.e., the Bible, and true servants of God in all subsequent centuries have acted and do act similarly (v. 23).

" The Kingdom of God " (v. 23). Paul explained that this was the Kingdom proposed to be set up on earth; that it was not to be confined to Palestine and the Hebrew people, but was to embrace the whole world and all nations, and that its King was to be Jesus of Nazareth.

There are three important terms that

should not be confounded: "The kingdom of God" (v. 23); "the salvation of God", (v. 28); and "the high-calling of God" (Phil. iii. 14). The first is the subject of the Book of the Acts; the second is the theme of the epistle to the Romans; and the third is revealed in the epistle to the Ephesians.

Seven times the Holy Spirit records the Divine judgment of verses 26 and 27, thus emphasizing its extreme importance, for it signalises the closing of the door of the Kingdom to Israel consequent upon their rejection of it. See Isa. vi. 9, Matt. xiii. 14, Mark iv. 12, Luke viii. 10, John xii. 40, Acts xxviii. 26, and Rom. xi. 8. This last passage predicts Israel's future repentance and acceptance of the King and His Kingdom.

The language of verse 28 is very clear. The "salvation of God" was to be "sent" to the Gentiles, but the "Kingdom of God" was not to be "given" to them, for it was promised to Israel.

Thus the command "to the Jew first" (Acts iii. 26 and Rom. i. 16) was obeyed and fulfilled, and so is not now obligatory; for all are now regarded as sinners without distinction, and the Gospel is to be preached to them as such.

So Israel's action occasioned the sending of the Gospel to the Gentiles, and that enriched them partially (Rom. xi. 11); but Israel's repentance will occasion the incorporation of all the Gentile nations with the Kingdom of God, and then will be manifested the true Catholic Church. The Church of God is apart from, and will be above, this earthly Church.

"Two whole years" (v. 30). God refreshed His beloved and precious servant with a five years' rest (xxiv. 27), and at the same time taught him the humbling lesson that the success of the Gospel message did not wholly depend upon him.

During these years of imprisonment he wrote his main Epistles, and carried upon his heart the care of all the churches. This multiple ministry was exercised in Rome, the capital of the then-known world. These facts destroy the platform on which the Vatican Church is built.

The subject of this Book being the offer of the Kingdom to Israel and their rejection of it, and not, as it is unfortunately called "The Acts of the Apostles," it necessarily closes here. But the activities of the Twelve Apostles did not terminate, nor did the activities of Paul and his companions, but they are not recorded because not needed. Hence certain catch-words such as "disciples," and operations such as miracles, recede from view, and the reader is brought on to "the salvation of God" in Romans, and "the Church of God" in Ephesians. (See notes on those Epistles.) Romans, 1 and 2 Corinthians and Galatians are parenthetical between Acts and Ephesians. Romans lays the moral foundation upon which God constructs His purposes of grace in regard to Israel, the nations, and the Church, while Corinthians and Galatians deal respectively with declension from that basis in conduct and in doctrine. (See notes on those Epistles).

In passing, therefore, immediately from Acts to Ephesians, the reader advances from the "Kingdom" to the "Church."

"Well spake the Holy Spirit by Isaiah" (v. 25). The instrument was Isaiah, the speaker was the Holy Spirit. There was but one Isaiah, as is proved beyond contradiction by John xii. 37-41. The New Testament specifies eight of the men employed as agents by the Spirit:—Moses, David, Elijah, Isaiah, Joel, Hosea, Jeremiah and Daniel.

Verse 28 marks the passage from the first section of Isaiah to the second section. See notes on Isaiah xlviii, and on the Introduction to Isaiah.

At the opening of this Book (ch. vii.) the Kingdom was offered to the Jews of the Homeland at Jerusalem, the capital of the Hebrew world, and at the close of the Book (ch. xxviii.) to the Jews of the Dispersion at Rome, the capital of the Gentile world. The offer was rejected, and a just judgment destroyed their City and Temple, and scattered them among all nations. Divine relations were broken; and will continue so up to the pre-determined time of Acts xv. 16. That judgment closed the Pentecostal era.

The Apostle Paul had a triple ministry—to Israel (Acts ix. 15); to the Gentiles (Rom. ix. 13); and to the Church (Col. i. 25-27). He was an Israelite (Rom. xi. 1); and there is, therefore, no conflict between his teaching in Galatians and his action in offering the sacrifices of Num. vi. 13, 21 (Acts xxi. 23-26). Those sacrifices pointed backward as well as forward to Calvary. They were Divinely ordained. The Epistle to the Hebrews illustrates his ministry to the Jews; the Epistle to the Romans, his ministry to the Nations; and the Epistle to the Ephesians, his ministry to the Church.

ROMANS

The Second Volume of the New Testament now opens with the Apostle Paul's letters to the seven churches of Rome, Corinth, Galatia, Ephesus, Philippi, Colosse, and Thessalonica. They may be thus analysed:

Rome, The Gospel.
    Corinth—reproof.
    Galatia—correction.
Ephesus. The Mystery.
    Philippians—reproof.
    Colossians—correction.
Thessalonians. The Return.

After the Lord's return there cannot possibly be any need for "reproof" or "correction" (2 Tim iii. 16). Hence no church Epistles follow Thessalonians.

Reproof concerned departure from moral teaching and correction applied to departure from doctrinal teaching in respect of the Epistles to Rome and Ephesus.

The subject of the Epistle to the Romans is that God declares righteous the guilty sinner who believes upon the atoning Saviour, whether that sinner be a degraded heathen, a cultured Greek, or a Hebrew moralist.

The content of the Epistle may be thus set out :—

The Gospel, revealed before, never hidden, i. 1-6.
Salutations, etc., i. 7-15.
    Doctrinal ; Justification i. 16-v. 11. and Sanctification v. 12-viii. 39.
    Dispensational, ix.-xi.
    Practical, xii. 1-xv. 7.
    Dispensational, xv. 8-13.
Salutations, etc. xv. 14-xvi. 24.
The Mystery, hidden before, now revealed xvi. 25-27.

The Correspondence between the opening and closing Salutations, etc., can be thus displayed :—

Salutation i. 1-7.
    Paul's prayer for them i. 8-10.
    His journey to them i. 10-13.
    His Ministry i. 14-15.
    His Ministry xv. 14-21.
    His journey to them, xv. 22-29.
    Their prayer for him, xv. 30-33.
Salutations xvi. 1-24.

The doctrine of the Epistle answers the ancient question (Job. ix. 2)—"How can man be just with God?"—by stating that the Gospel reveals a righteousness from God (i. 17) for those who merit the wrath of God (i. 18).

The doctrine of the Epistle distinguishes also between "sins" and "sin," i.e., man's sinful nature (chs. v. 12-viii. 39) and the works of that nature (chs. i. 16-v. 11) ; and it reveals in relation to that nature and its works, the sufficiency of God's activities in justification and sanctification.

This distinction between "sins" (i. 16-v. 11) and "sin" (v. 12-viii. 39), i.e., between the corrupt tree and its evil fruit, provides the key to the whole teaching of the Epistle.

Christ as the believer's justification and sanctification releases him from the doom of sins and from the dominion of sin. Justification has to do with the believers "standing" and sanctification with the believer's "state." These should not be confounded. It is the entry of the new nature in regeneration which originates the never-ceasing conflict between the "flesh" and the "spirit" of Galatians v.

This is the first in position of the Epistles of St. Paul to the Seven Churches of Rome, Corinth, Galatia, Ephesus, Philippi, Colosse, and Thessalonica. It is remarkable that this order appears in all the ancient MSS. of the New Testament. See notes on the First Epistle to the Thessalonians.

ROMANS I. 1-17.—This letter, like that to the Ephesians, was personal (v. 1). No other apostle was associated with Paul; and designedly not, for the theme of the one was the personal ministry committed to Paul (i. 1, and ii. 16) and the theme of the other the "mystery" revealed to him.

The Epistles were inspired and were clothed with apostolic authority. Those associated with Paul in writing them were consequently apostles.

The three statements of verse 1, emphasize the apostle's independency of the Twelve at Jerusalem. He was chosen by the Holy Spirit. He was not their servant, nor was he chosen by them to be an apostle, or ordained by them to preach the Gospel.

The formula "of God" in this Epistle is very important, e.g. the Gospel of God (v. 1), the Son of God (v. 4), the will of God (v. 10), the power of God (v. 16), the righteousness of God (v. 17), the wrath of God (v. 18), etc., etc.

The glad tidings of God are all about His Beloved Son (vs. 1 and 3).

He is at once presented in the perfection of his Manhood (v. 3) and of His Godhead (v. 4).

As to His Manhood He was "made" man (v. 3), but as to His Godhead that was powerfully proved by the resurrection (v. 4). His Divine Sonship always existed and had not to be "made," only to be declared.

The formulae "according to the flesh" (v. 3) and "according to the spirit" (v. 4) define His human and divine natures.

"Declared" . . . . "with power" (v. 4), i.e., overwhelmingly proved to be the Son of God.

"Grace" (v. 5). This was the apostle Paul's great theme and his, so to say, trademark (2 Thess. iii. 17). His was the apostleship of grace "among" all nations, i.e., to gather out of them an election for heaven on the principle of faith as opposed to works, and "for His name," i.e., for association with Christ above the highest heavens for the praise of His glory (Eph. i. 12).

"Called" (vs. 1 and 6 and 7), i.e., chosen or elected. Paul was elected an apostle; the Romans were elected saints.

He prayed not only for them but also for the Ephesians (i. 15), the Philippians (i. 3), the Colossians (i. 3), and the Thessalonians (i. 2).

It is needful and profitable for believers to hear the Gospel (v. 15).

"The Jew first" (v. 16). See note on Acts xxviii. 28.

The Gospel reveals a righteousness from God on the principle of faith as opposed to merit, and this righteousness is to be received by faith, for the just, i.e., the justified, live before God on that principle (v. 17).

"From faith to faith" (v. 17). "From faith" i.e., justification by faith as opposed to works. "To faith," i.e., justification accepted by faith. So "from faith" relates to God as the provider and "to faith" relates to man as the receiver. The one offers life on the faith principle; the other accepts the gift on the same principle.

Having presented the Saviour in His fulness, the writer now describes those whom He came to save, and groups them into three companies respectively responsible to Reason (i. 19-32), to Philosophy (ii. 1-16), and to Revelation (ii. 17-29).

ROMANS I. 18 to **II.** 29.—The Gospel reveals a righteousness from God on the principle of faith, as opposed to merit, for those who are justly exposed to the wrath of God (vs. 17 and 18) not only because they are without righteousness, but because they are wholly unrighteous and corrupt; and all humanity is here declared to be sunken in this corruption.

The heathen world (19-32), then as now, debased the gift of reason, degraded God to a "creeping thing," and conduct being determined by creed, they gave themselves up to vile affections. Twenty-four of these are particularized, all of them together proving fallen human nature to be sunken into an appalling abyss of moral putridity. This true picture of sinful man is fiercely denied by modern thinkers, as energized by the evil author of ancient and modern thought.

The Greeks and Romans who were the disciples of philosophy, condemned the heathen (ii. 1-16). One of the greatest of the Grecian philosophers was Socrates, and one of the most celebrated of the Roman was the Emperor Marcus Aurelius. But these cultured nations disobeyed and degraded and corrupted the wisdom which they had, for whilst applauding virtue they practised vice, and taught that man being impotent to do what was right was not to be condemned if he practised what was wrong.

To the Hebrew people (vs. 17-29) was granted by Divine election the most precious of all gifts—Revelation. Since man is a creature it was reasonable that his Creator should have made a revelation of Himself to him. But just as the Rationalists and the Philosophers degraded the light given to them, so Israel corrupted the Law, and became proud and self-righteous (17-29).

Thus all men are by voluntary action subject to the wrath of God; and the Holy Spirit places this terrible truth in the forefront of the Gospel in order that the doctrine of Justification by Faith might be based upon the fact of universal guilt and condemnation, and so open wide the door of boundless salvation. For the Gospel can only be truly preached, or embraced, as being the good news of life and pardon to all who are lost beyond recovery. See notes on Lev. xiv. as illustrating Rom. i. to viii., and compare I Cor. vi. 9-11.

So the first foundation doctrine of the Gospel which the apostle preached (v. 15) announced the wrath of God (v. 18). This dogma angers self-righteous man.

ROMANS III.—The first twenty verses of this chapter declare that all mankind whether enlightened by Reason, Philosophy, or Revelation, are, without distinction, equally guilty before God; and the conclusion is stated that no one is righteous.

This conclusion is rejected and denied by modern theology, and many prominent religious teachers are not afraid to contradict the Holy Spirit and to charge Him with saying what is not true. These teachers point to well-known sceptics and agnostics of blameless life and noble character, and they say that to class such men with those described in chapters i. 29-32 and iii. 10-18 is an outrage. But God reads the heart, and all who claim to be wiser than He proclaim their own folly.

One piece of ground under the coercion of culture may be full of flowers, and the next piece full of weeds because left to nature. But the ground in both cases is similar, and equally in the power of a principle of evil hidden in the soil which originates thorns and brambles. So is it in human society. No man is righteous as to his nature. All are unrighteous, and, therefore, subject to the wrath of God. Man's greatest need consequently is a righteousness in which God can discover no flaw. That is the righteousness which the Gospel offers; and it offers it on the principle of faith in an atoning Saviour.

" The oracles of God " (v. 2). This is the Holy Spirit's title for the Old Testament. He here declares its authority, and states that its utterances were the utterances of God. Many who profess to be Christian ministers boldly deny this, and declare the sacred Book to be the oracles of man.

The greatest glory of the Hebrew Church is here affirmed to be the possession of the Bible. Sacerdotalists esteem its greatest glory to have been the Temple and the Priesthood. But Inspiration points to the Scriptures and to nothing else (v. 2).

The unbelief which rejected the Bible (v. 3) by no means nullified its truthfulness or the faithfulness of its Divine Author. On the contrary unbelief only proved man to be a liar (v. 4).

The import of verses 4-8 is :—God in the Bible declares man to be a " liar " (v. 4) and " unrighteous " (v. 5). Man's words and ways demonstrate the truth of this Divine statement. Therefore the more untruthful and the more unholy men are, the more do they demonstrate the truthfulness and holiness of God. Two objections are consequently proposed. First: Is it not unrighteous for God to punish man for proving the righteousness of God (v. 5)? The answer to this is conclusive. It is that God shall judge the world (v. 6). The second objection is :—If man's falsehood makes God's truth to abound (v. 7) then man brings the greatest glory to God by continuously committing the greatest sins, and, consequently, it would not be just that God should judge him as a sinner (v. 7). To this objection no answer is given. The dogmatic statement is simply made that all persons who reason and act thus shall suffer a just judgment (v. 8).

" The deeds of the Law " (v. 20). This should read " By works of law," i.e., by personal religious efforts and ceremonies to obtain moral perfection.

The terrible declaration of verse 20 that not one member of the human family, however good and beautiful morally, can procure by meritorious efforts a righteousness that God will accept, and the added statement that the Law of Moses was given not to enable man to furnish himself with this needed righteousness, but to make him conscious that he was a sinner, and therefore unrighteous—this terrible pronouncement destroys all hope of salvation by works.

Verses 21-26 may be thus freely translated :—" But now, apart from law, a righteousness from God has been manifested, being borne witness to by the Law and the Prophets, even the righteousness of God, which is through faith in Jesus Christ unto all those who believe, for there is no distinction, for all have sinned, and come short of the glory of God ; being declared righteous without a cause by His grace through the redemption which is by Christ Jesus, whom God fore-ordained to be a mercy-seat through faith in His blood for the display of His righteous action in putting upon one side, through the forbearance of God, the sins committed aforetime—for a display of His righteousness at this present time that He might be shewn to be righteous and the declarer of the righteousness of him who believes in Jesus."

" Without the law " (v. 21). This should read—" apart from law," i.e., from works of merit.

The testimony of the Law to the Divine principle of justification by faith is that of Genesis xv. 6 ; and the testimony of the Prophets is that of Habakkuk ii. 4. The term " the Law " in the New Testament frequently means the Old Testament, i.e., the Hebrew Bible consisting of the Law, the Prophets, and the Psalms (Luke xxiv. 44). The testimony of the Psalms to justification by faith is that of xxxii. 1 and 2.

Whoever believes in Christ becomes in Him the righteousness of God (v. 22).

All having sinned, and no one possessing any merit, the principle of justification by faith is universal in its application (v. 23).

" Freely " (v. 24). Greek : " Without a cause." Without a cause (John xv. 25) men hated Christ ; and without a cause He loves them.

God's justification of a sinner is an action of His grace based upon, and because of, the redemption that is in Christ Jesus. It is only because of Christ's atoning sacrifice that God can not only pardon but justify sinners (vs. 24 and 25).

All sins committed by the people of God prior to, and up to, the one great sacrifice of Calvary were put upon one side by God in His forbearance and then judged there ; and all sins committed since Calvary were equally judged there. Thus Calvary stands at the centre of human history.

" That He might be just," i.e., in judging Christ as a sinner on the cross and in pouring upon Him all His wrath, and, therefore, justify, i.e., declare righteous, the guilty sinner who believes upon that Saviour (v. 26).

Salvation by works of merit permits of self-gratulation, but salvation by faith excludes boasting (v. 27).

The conclusion (v. 28) is that God declares the believer to be a righteous person apart from and independently of personal moral merit ; and this principle of grace not only embraces all men whether Hebrew or Greek (vs. 29 and 30) but establishes the moral teaching of the Old Testament (v. 31).

Thus in this short passage (vs. 19-28) the Gospel, i.e., that God declares righteous the believer in Jesus, is Divinely stated. Verse 19 declares all men guilty ; verse 20, that it is impossible by religious effort or moral culture or by priestly ceremonies to obtain a righteousness that God will accept; verse 21 reveals a Divine righteousness independent of human effort ; verse 22 assures that righteousness to all who plead the person and the atoning sacrifice of Christ, and assures it so effectually that all such persons become the righteousness of God (2. Cor. v. 21) ; and verse 25 sets forth the righteous foundation upon which the doctrine of justification is set up, i.e., the Atonement.

Justification, therefore, is not a religious emotion felt by the repentant sinner, nor an experience and degree of sanctity reached by him, but it is the action of God declaring him to be a righteous person.

It is of the utmost importance to learn that justification is the action of a judge declaring an accused person to be righteous according to law, and, therefore, blameless. For such a person there is no condemnation.

Verses 10-18 illustrate a composite quotation thrown into two classes—the general and the particular. The general (vs. 10-12) taken from Ecclesiastes and the Psalms. These references declare the universality of sin. The particular (vs. 13-18) taken from the Psalms and Isaiah. These illustrate the manifestations of sin in particular cases. In these quotations the reasoning is from the general to the particular and not from the particular to the general; which is so popular but false in logic and fatal in argument.

The expression " the righteousness of God," in its personal sense, may be defined as God's activity in harmony ·with all that He has committed Himself to in revelation. For example, He has committed Himself to eternally judge the unbeliever and to eternally save the believer. His so acting is His righteousness.

" A righteousness from God " is the righteousness of God reckoned to the believer.

ROMANS IV.—Having stated (iii. 31) that the Old Testament teaches that God justifies the sinner on the faith principle as opposed to the merit principle, the Holy Spirit now brings forward Abraham (vs. 1-5) and David (vs. 6-8) as illustrating this truth. Both these men were " ungodly " by nature (v. 5), and both had a Divine righteousness reckoned to them, not because of any meritorious actions that they performed, but because they believed God and made Him their salvation.

Abraham and David were progenitors of the promised Messiah, and, as such, they held a unique place in the faith and veneration of the Hebrew people. If, therefore, they had no personal righteousness, and were sinners by nature, i.e., " ungodly," it was evident that all members of the Hebrew Church and nation were in a similar moral condition before God; and if these eminent men were justified by faith, apart from works, then all men must be similarly justified.

Abraham was a Gentile, " a Syrian ready to perish " (Deut. xxvi. 5) and an idolater (Josh. xxiv. 2 and 3) when grace chose him and promised a Redeemer through him (Gen. xv. 6); and because he believed what God said to him, his faith was reckoned to him for righteousness, and God justified him, i.e., declared him to be a righteous man,

Abraham's faith was more than" a reasonable faith," for reason, nature and science all combined to deny the possibility of a child being born to him and to Sarah (vs. 17-22).

The assertion of those who teach justification by works that Abraham's faith was in itself a work of merit, contradicts the entire argument of the chapter, for it contrasts justification by faith with justification by works and denies the possibility of the latter.

The doctrine of verse 5 stumbles and offends the carnal religious mind. It declares that whoever does no works but believes upon a God that declares sinful men righteous, to such a believer God reckons his faith for. righteousness, that he from that moment is justified, and, consequently, stands in a righteousness before God in which a flaw can never be found.

David supports this testimony in Psalm xxxii. by speaking of the happiness of the man to whom righteousness is reckoned apart from works. The man is described as " ungodly," for he has iniquities which need forgiveness and sins which require atonement (v. 7). Such a man has no righteousness of his own. David sings of what God was in grace to such a man, and not of what the man was to God. His happiness was that God did not impute to him the sins he had committed, but covered and forgave them. His blessedness was not based upon any personal righteousness which he had in himself before God, but it was based upon the activity of God in providing him with a Divine righteousness, which being of God, and from God, was infinitely acceptable to God. David describes God as the Justifier, and man as the passive believer.

The force of the Hebrew term " to cover " (v. 7) is dual. It implies atonement and justification. Atonement does not mean " at-one-ment " but means expiation of guilt by a blood-sacrifice which covers it.

The argument of verses 9-12 is that Abraham was declared by God to be a righteous man while he was yet uncircumcised, i.e., outside of the Covenant within which the Hebrew Church afterwards stood in its unique relation to God.

Had the promise of heir-ship of the world been based on the principle of law, i.e., of merit, that would have set Abraham aside, for the inheritance was given him by promise, and, therefore, on the principle of faith. Faith does not fulfil a promise made to it, but believes it; and that faith was reckoned to Abraham for righteousness. This principle consequently opened wide the door of grace to all men.

" Through the law " (v. 13), i.e., in virtue of obedience to the law. " Through the righteousness of faith " i.e., in virtue of faith in a Divine promise. The contrast here is between law-keeping versus promise-believing; and the argument is: that the promise was assured to the latter, but not to the former, otherwise (v. 14) the whole Divine method of justification by faith, apart from works, would be subverted.

The effect of law (v. 15) is condemnation; the action of grace (v. 16), justification.

The character of Abraham's faith was that he believed in a God that could bring life out of death, and who could declare that to exist which as yet had no being (v. 17). Where no ground for reason or hope existed, he believed in hope against hope, i.e., he confidently expected when no ground for hope appeared. He gave no attention to those physical obstacles both in himself and in Sarah which rendered the promise hopeless, but he firmly believed in the ability of God to fulfil His promise, and no difficulties shook him. His faith rested upon a God of creation and of resurrection; and these facts are recorded, not as mere history, but as illustrations for all time of God's method of justification by faith. Men are commanded by the Gospel to exercise a similar faith (vs. 24 and 25), i.e., faith in a God Who judged sin in Christ, and then raised Him from the dead. In thus believing God, faith embraces the whole extent of His redemptive work. By believing in such a God the believer accepts the testimony of Scripture that He delivered up His Beloved Son for the expiation of the believer's offences, and raised Him from out of the death-world in order to the justifying of the believer's person. The activity of God in grace, through righteousness, is here declared in abolishing sins, in declaring innocent the sinner, and in vindicating righteousness (v. 25).

Abraham's faith, being marvellous, cannot have been of, and from himself, but must have been a Divine gift in grace (Eph. ii. 8), and, therefore, not in itself a justifying work.

" So " (v. 18), i.e., as numerous as the stars.

" He gave glory to God " (v. 20) by firmly believing that what He had promised He was able to perform (v. 21).

The conclusion of the argument is that God declares the guilty righteous on the principle of faith as opposed to works; and that He never saved men on any other principle.

The doctrine of justification by works generates religious pride—that of justification by faith produces contrition and humility. In the matter of justification faith and works are opposite and irreconcilable—as opposed as grace and debt. Since God declares ungodly men righteous (v. 5), works cannot in any sense furnish a ground for justification, and hence the first step towards salvation on the part of a sinner is to humble himself and accept the Divine pronouncement that he is " ungodly." Then the second and concluding step is to repose faith in Him Who justifies the ungodly. Nothing gives more glory to God than simply believing Him. Justification is not a change in character but a declaration by God as to the believer's standing before Him. It is objective. Sanctification affects character and is subjective.

ROMANS V. 1-11.—This section of the Epistle sets out the effects of the great foundation doctrine of justification by faith, and two words may express these effects :— Delight (vs. 1, 2, 5 and 11) and Discipline (vs. 3 and 4).

The Christian can rejoice in justification, peace, access, the present enjoyment of the love of God, a spotless righteousness, an assured salvation from the wrath to come, a guaranteed preservation, and an unspeakable joy in God Himself (vs. 1, 2, 5, 9, 10 and 11).

The grace wherein the believer stands (v. 2) is that he is set before the throne of God in a righteousness that is spotless, in a life that is endless, and in a dignity that is glorious.

All the sins of the believer are cancelled by God in the death of Christ ; God has consequently no sins to impute to the believer. That matter has been eternally settled by Christ's sufficing atonement ; and His resurrection attests the fact. There is, therefore, no longer any question as to the believer's sins between him and God. That question was the one and only disturbing factor in relation to God, and Christ removed it according to the requirements of Divine righteousness. He bore infinitely all the wrath of God due to sin and its fruit, and satisfied and vindicated all the claims of the Throne of God against man as a sinner.

This great salvation is, therefore, founded upon eternal righteousness, and is the result of the Divine activity operating in grace.

Peace is the result of justification and is, consequently, distinct from it. Faith enjoys this peace, and glories not only in salvation and all that it embraces, but in its Divine Author God Himself.

Job illustrates the discipline of verses 3 and 4. He exercised patience and so had the experience, or proof, that the issue of the Divine action is that God is full of pity and of tender mercy (Jas. v. 11), so that he could boast of the tribulations which had disciplined him, and rejoice in the hope that made him not ashamed.

" The love of God " (v. 5) is God's love to the believer enjoyed in the heart by the Holy Spirit—Who is here first mentioned in this Epistle.

The nature of that love is declared in verses 6-10. Man can sacrifice himself when he thinks he has an adequate motive, as is evidenced in war, but the unique character of God's love is displayed in the fact that Christ died for men when there was no motive to move Him so to do, but every reason to the contrary ; for man is morally impotent (v. 6), and actively ungodly (v. 6), sinful (v. 8), and hostile (v. 10). It was God's own heart that prompted Him to pity and redeem lost men. He could not possibly have found in them any adequate reason or moral worthfulness to justify His action ; and this is clear from the declaration as to man's impotency, ungodliness, sinfulness, and hostility.

No non-christian would lay down his life for a Nero. The extraordinary character of God's love is seen in that Christ died for the temporal and eternal welfare of men who hated Him, and were much worse than Nero.

Men have endured every form of suffering and death without a murmur because they deemed it unworthy to cry out against unavoidable ill. But this stoicism has nothing in common with the Christian grace of patience, which is the brave endurance of ill because sent by God in His love and wisdom in order to the moral progress of the believer.

Present peace and future safety are announced in verse 9. " Now justified " assures the one and, " We shall be saved " makes absolute the other. These are based, not upon the pious emotion or personal moral merit of a religious man, but upon Christ's Person and atoning sacrifice. This Divine foundation is displayed in the words " His blood," and " Through Him." Notice also the expression, " Christ died " set over against man's fourfold demerit.

Modern Theology denies Christ's atonement and God's wrath. Both these foundation truths of the Gospel are here declared to be fundamental. Those who believe there is no wrath to fear, naturally seek no Saviour, and so cut themselves off from the salvation that is in Christ alone.

Christ's obedience unto death (Phil. ii. 8)— and that death was a sin-offering (1 Cor. xv. 3)—is the central truth of the Gospel. The effort to get rid of this foundation truth, or to minimise it, or to substitute the Incarnation for it, is one of the saddest features of what is proudly termed " Modern Thought." The expiatory sacrifice of Christ is the one and only and eternal ground on which God can act in declaring ungodly men righteous. Gal. iii. 21, and many similar Divine declarations, reveal the hopelessness of standing before God in a righteousness which He will accept upon any other principle than that of faith in a crucified Sinbearer.

Christ's perfect obedience to the Law of God formed His own righteousness and gave virtue to His sacrifice—for a sacrifice for sin must have neither spot nor blemish. But it was not the spotlessness of the Lamb which made the atonement, but its out-poured blood, i.e., its surrendered life, for the blood is the life. The judgment pronounced upon sin being death, that claim could only be vindicated and discharged by the suffering of death. Christ suffered that penalty, and, in consequence, saves the believer from it.

If Christ's obedience during His life was man's obedience, then man stands as He stood, and, consequently, there was no reason why He should die. In that case there was no penalty, for if man fulfilled in Him all righteousness there was no occasion for judgment. But the Scripture declares that He died for sinners, so that it is His death that provides a spotless righteousness for sinners who believe in Him ; and it was His obedience in life which gave efficacy to His suffering in death.

The first great section of this Epistle ends here. As stated, sins and justification form its theme. An intelligent grasp of this teaching is necessary to a knowledge of the Gospel, i.e., the principle upon which God can declare guilty men righteous. The second section of the Epistle starts from verse 12 and reaches to the end of chapter viii. Its theme is sanctification. So the first section sets out Christ's work for the believer, and the second section Christ's work in the believer. The first section declares God's action in relation to " sins," and the second section His action in relation to " sin," i.e., to that which is the root of sins. The first section shows God's activity in declaring the sinner righteous, and the second section, His action in making him righteous. The first is justification ; the second, sanctification.

What then is justification ? It is the action of a judge declaring a prisoner innocent. The accused says nothing and does nothing. The judge is the sole actor—he justifies the man, i.e., he declares him righteous.

ROMANS V. 12-21.—This section of the Epistle narrates the facts as to the entrance of sin and death by one man Adam, and the introduction of life and sanctification by the Second Man, the Lord from Heaven.

These two great Federal Heads of their respective sons are here contrasted ; and the old nature and the new nature exhibited in opposition.

" Sin " is a term expressive of the old nature—" the flesh," " the carnal mind," etc.

" Spirit," when used, expresses the new nature—" the spiritual mind," " the inward man," and " the spirit of Christ." i.e., the Christ-like disposition and nature.

The moral effect of the death and resurrection of the Second Man is here explained, and its subjective import declared.

The argument of verses 12 and 18 is that the one disobedience of the first man assured death for all men, and the one obedience of the second Man secured life for all men. That is, all the sons of the First Adam by reason of their relationship to him and because they possess his sinful nature, stand in death, and all the sons of the Second Adam in virtue of their relationship to Him, and because they possess His spirit, stand in life.

Verses 13-17 form a parenthesis in which the doctrine of verse 12 is developed.

The subject is sin and its reproductive energy. One command was given to Adam. He disobeyed it. Many commands were given to Moses. They were all disobeyed. So the trespass abounded, i.e., the principle of evil which caused one trespass in Adam caused countless trespasses under Law, and so manifested sin's abounding fertility. A fact of science illustrates the matter. A germ when acted on by a certain temperature produces one deadly microbe, but on the temperature being raised, it produces millions. Such was the moral effect that followed the introduction of Law. The nature of the principle of evil (termed " sin ") and its venomous energy, were made apparent to man's consciousness and to history.

" Imputed " (v. 13). This is a different Greek word from that used in iv. 22 and 24 and 2 Cor. v. 19, and might better be translated " reckoned."

" Many " (v. 15), i.e., " the many " that is, all the sons of Adam.

" The many " (v. 15), i.e., all the sons of God by the One Man Jesus Christ.

" The free gift," i.e., justification securing eternal life (v. 18).

One offence entailed condemnation (v. 16), but justification from countless offences is a free gift.

" Much more " (v. 15), i.e., if the many are justly condemned for the sin of one, it is much more agreeable to the principle of grace that " the many " should be benefited by the merit of One ; and hence the one offence is contrasted with the many offences, and the resulting condemnation in the one case contrasted with the gift of justification in the other case. The condemnation in Adam was for one sin, but the justification in Christ is an absolution not only from all sins but from the original germ of sin lodged in the nature of every child of Adam. Thus grace abounds in the abundance of the gift of righteousness—a gift not only rich in character but rich in detail, for it leaves no one sin uncancelled, and, notwithstanding countless offences, sets the believer before God in a righteousness that is spotless.

Death and life are here contrasted (v. 14 and 17) ; but while it says " death reigned " over man it does not say that life reigns over the believer, for that would invest life with tyranny, but it says that the believer reigns in life, and thus the environment of freedom and liberty is preserved. This life is legally secured by the life and death of Christ (v. 17).

Christ's one righteous act of obedience was His obedience unto death (Phil. ii. 8) ; but this was the climax for His whole mission to earth was one great act of obedience.

" The many " therefore, who are born of Adam, and consequently possess his sinful nature, are hopelessly lost, for they cannot undo the fact of their birth, and the many who are born of the Second Adam and, consequently, possess His nature, are absolutely saved, for that nature cannot sin.

The doctrine of universal salvation based on 1 Cor. xv. 22 is untrue, for it is only the " all " who are " in Christ " who shall be made alive.

Sin reigns unto death, grace reigns unto life—but it reigns " through righteousness," i.e., because of God's righteous judgment of sin at Calvary executed in the Person of His Son Jesus Christ.

ROMANS VI.—The doctrines of grace—especially that which declares justification to be by faith apart from works—excites the enmity of the natural heart, and this enmity expresses itself to-day, as it has from the first, by the outcry of verse 1. Here human reasoning conflicts with divine teaching. The latter declares that man is absolutely ruined by sin and wholly unable to restore himself to God's favour ; the former teaches that man is not wholly ruined, that he can by self-culture merit God's favour and secure his own happiness.

The objection is plausible : If the sinner is justified without works, and if grace abounds above sin, may not sins be multiplied and practised in order to the more abundant display of grace ? This objection comes spontaneously from the carnal heart of man. The answer of this chapter is : How can a dead man sin ? And : How can a man live in that to which he has died ?

To believe in Christ implies association with Him in His death and resurrection. His death is styled in verse 3 His baptism. He was baptized into death, and all His members were associated with Him in that baptism ; and His death and resurrection being inseparable in their purpose and efficacy, union with Him in the one carries with it participation in the other (see v. 5).

He died to sin. He has done with it forever. The believer died in Him, and this great fact when believed (v. 8) and reckoned to be true (v. 11) and practically obeyed (v. 13), becomes a moral experience in the activities of a life of holiness and consecration.

The vast majority of mankind accepts the human doctrine of salvation by merit ; a very small minority believes the divine doctrine of salvation by grace. As the Lord Jesus Himself said, few tread that narrow way. It is abhorrent to human pride.

Sacerdotal theology believes the baptism of verses 3-5 to be the immersion of the physical body in material water, but this destroys the meaning of the passage. If it means baptism with water then all persons so baptized will be most certainly saved because united with Christ in His life beyond death and judgment. But what proves too much proves nothing, and, consequently, the baptism of the passage must be Christ's death symbolized under the word baptism.

Further : To be baptized into water cannot mean to be baptized into Christ, as many think, for when is a believer baptized into Christ ? Undeniably at the moment of the New Birth. This is proved by Eph. i. 13, R.V. and Titus iii. 5, 6. And who is the Baptizer ? The Holy Spirit. What purpose therefore could baptism into water serve ? See note on 1 Cor. i. 14.

Verse 3 should read as in the Revised Version. This is the baptism of Matt. xx. 22 and Mark x. 38.

" The glory of the Father " (v. 4), i.e., the glorious power of the Father. Verse 5, see verse 3.

" The old man," i.e., the invisible principle of evil lodged in man as a son of the first Adam ; " the body of sin," i.e., the visible activities of that evil principle.

" Freed " (v. 7), i.e., legally discharged. Death frees a slave from the power of his master.

" We died with Christ " (v. 8, R.V.). This great divine fact is to be believed, reckoned to be true, and, as a consequence, the members of the body are to be yielded to God as weapons of righteousness.

These three words " believe " (v. 8), " reckon " (v. 11), and " yield " (v. 13) express three energies of the Christian mind which secure and make real a life of Scriptural sanctification.

Sin as a principle of evil dwells in the Christian's mortal body ; but it is not to reign there (v. 12). If sanctification were based upon the principle of law-obedience, (v. 14), i.e., upon works, it would be impossible to escape from the lawful dominion of sin, because a perfect obedience to divine law on the part of man is impossible, but being based upon the opposite principle of grace, liberation from the power and dominion of sin, as a master, is secured and may be enjoyed experimentally. Under law sin has a dominion, but it has no dominion under grace. These are two totally independent realms.

"Dead" (v. 11), i.e., "dead persons." "Alive," i.e., "living persons."

The second objection of the religious carnal mind to the doctrines of grace is that of verse 14. The term "No punishment" may express this objection as the term "no shame" may express that of verse 1. That is: professing Christians may without shame indulge all manner of sins in order to demonstrate the forgiving nature of grace (v. 1); or they may live sinful lives, for, not being under law, but under grace, they are assured against punishment (v. 14).

The answer to the first objection is that a dead man does not sin, and the answer to the second is : that whoever lives a life of sinning, no matter how orthodox his profession of faith may be, is the servant of sin, and must accept its wages, and these are " shame " (v. 21) and " death " (v. 23).

Two masters are here contrasted—sin and righteousness (v. 16). A man must be the servant of either, for no man can serve two masters.

Verse 17 should read as in the Revised Version.

The formula " form of doctrine " is very important. It declares the Christian faith to have been once for all delivered to the Church as fixed and complete, and, therefore, neither needing nor accepting additions. Into that form, as into a mould, the Roman believers were poured or " delivered," and the two sides of that mould being justification and sanctification, it was manifest that anyone leading a sinful life had not been poured into the mould. For as the subject of i. to v. 11 is God declaring a sinner righteous, i.e., justification, so the theme of v. 12 to viii. 39 is God making the believer righteous, i.e., sanctification. " Neither present," or " yield," (v. 13), i.e., " do not keep yielding " your members unto sin, but yield them once for all to God."

" The manner of men " (v. 19), i.e., the Apostle descends for illustration to earthly facts because of the feebleness of the spiritual intelligence of those to whom he was writing. Servants of iniquity lead a life of uncleanness, but servants of righteousness, a life of sanctification (v. 19). So long, therefore, as a man is the servant of the one he is not bound to obey the other (v. 20). The one service is shameful and ends in death (v. 21) ; the other is pure and ends in life (v. 22). This life is consciously eternal and this death is also consciously eternal, the one being set over against the other. To be dead is horrible. To be consciously dead is more horrible. To be conscious that one is dead eternally, and to be eternally conscious of the fact, is most horrible.

The sinner earns his wages, but the believer does not earn eternal life. It is a free gift (v. 23, R.V.) from God ; and its channel is Christ and His atoning work.

God reckons the believer in Christ to have died with Him. The believer is to reckon this to be true. He is, therefore, dead to sin, to self, and to the world, and cannot, therefore, live in that to which he has died. He is associated with Christ in His death, and so freed from the dominion of sin, and he is associated with Christ in His risen life and consequently become the bond-slave of righteousness. In the death and resurrection of Christ he is liberated from the one master, sin, in order to be handed over to the other master, righteousness. It is in that risen life that the believer really knows Christ, and experimentally proves His power to sanctify him wholly.

ROMANS VII. 1-6.—These verses conclude the section from ch. v. 12. It reveals the Divine method of sanctification, and sets out its impossibility under the bondage of law and its certainty under the freedom of grace.

The argument here is : that just as death is the only force that can liberate from the claims of sin, so is it the only force that can liberate from the claims of law.

The illustration, corresponding to that of the master and slave in the prior chapter, is that of the husband and wife. The marriage contract can only be dissolved by death. Here it is the wife who dies—not the husband, the great point being that death alone can dissolve the bond.

There are two husbands—the Law and Christ. Union with the one is bondage and brings forth " fruit unto death " (v. 5) ;

Union with the other is freedom and brings forth fruit unto God (v. 4).

The Law does not die neither is its Divine authority affected. On the contrary its righteous requirements are satisfied by the fruit brought forth under grace to God.

" I speak to men that know law " (v. 1, R.V. margin). The Romans were law-makers, and their laws are operative to-day throughout the world.

" The body of Christ," i.e., the death of Christ. In the vehicle of His body He died to the law (v. 4).

" In the flesh " (v. 5), i.e., when uncon-verted.

" The motions of sins which were by the law " (v. 5), i.e., the emotions which the law declared to be sinful.

Verse 6 should read as in the Revised Version.

Service in the letter means seeking salva-tion by works, i.e., in union with the first husband. Service in the Spirit means enjoyment of salvation in union with the second husband.

Thus the believer learns that association with Christ in His death liberates him from Death as a King (ch. v.) ; from Sin as a Master (ch. vi.) ; and from Law as a Husband (ch. vii.).

Chapter v. : Sin on a person, i.e., con-demnation. Chapter vi. : Sin over a person, i.e., domination. Chapter vii. : Sin in a person, i.e., desperation.

The only power that can deliver from these is not Law, but Grace ; and the mode of liberation is death, i.e., the judicial death of the believer at Calvary.

Death, Sin and Law triumphed over Christ at Calvary ; but their dominion over Him ended directly He was dead. In that death the believer died ; and, consequently, their authority ended there for him also, so that he is no longer in their dominion. Risen with Christ—united to Him the new husband—a life of liberty and sanctification is enjoyed in the life and energy of the Holy Spirit.

ROMANS VII. 7-25.—Just as two objec-tions (vi. 1 and 15) to the fact of deliverance from the mastership of Sin are met, so two objections to the truth of liberation from the dominion of Law are now disposed of (vs. 7 and 13).

The first objection is : that Law must in itself be evil since a result of its action upon man is fruit unto death (v. 5). The answer is that, on the contrary, the Law is holy (v. 12).

The second objection is : Granting that the Law is good in itself, yet it becomes evil to men because of its effects in them (v. 13). The reply to this is that its moral effect in them is beneficent, for its action reveals to them how evil they are.

An illustration may make this plain. A piece of ground is barren. The sun rises and shines upon it. Very quickly it is covered with weeds. The sun, therefore, must be maleficent in itself. Science replies that the sun is good in itself. But it is objected the sun which is good in itself becomes evil to the ground, as the weeds make manifest. To this science replies that the sun does not become evil to the piece of ground, but that the effect of its action is to reveal the evil that is in the ground and not in the sun.

God's moral Law is holy and just and good. Man's fallen nature is evil. The effect of Law acting on that nature mani-fests not only the fact of the disease, but the exceeding malignity of the disease. Sin, i.e., the principle of evil lodged in fallen man, is manifested as exceedingly sinful (v. 13), and so made evident to man's own consciousness.

Man did not know that to covet is to sin (v. 7) until the Law said," Thou shalt not covet " ; and the moral effect of the commandment manifested the depth of covetousness hidden in man's nature (v. 8), and not only covetousness, but insensibility, for in the absence of law Sin is dead—not dead in relation to God, but dead to the sensibility of corrupt man (v. 8).

Thus prior to the coming of Law, man believes himself to be " alive," i.e., righteous (v. 9), but the entrance of Law makes him conscious that he is dead and that sin is alive. Its malignity and strength spring to life in his consciousness, and he learns that he is, in relation to God, a dead man. Thus the commandment which was designed to give life, if obeyed, introduces death because disobeyed (v. 10) ; and it is sin which, using the commandment as a point of attack, seduces man to do the very thing which the commandment forbade, and so slays him (v. 11).

The fall of Adam illustrates verse 11. One only commandment was given to him. Sin profited by that, used it as a point of attack, i.e., took occasion by it (v. 8), deceived Adam and so slew him ; for in that hour he died morally.

Sin as an evil principle in man's nature makes use of Law to provoke men to the practice of sins that the Law forbids, and so plunges the soul into a conflict that, apart from Law, could not take place. But Law originates this conflict, and by making the sinner responsible, deposits the sentence of death in his conscience. The result is death in the conscience without any deliverance for the heart from the power of coveting.

Law as a barrier to the will excites it ; and the consciousness of sin thereby awakened, produces in the presence of God a conscience under sentence of death. Thus the commandment ordained unto life becomes in fact the instrument of death. " This do, and thou shalt live " became death to man because his sinful nature refused to obey ; and in so refusing his own conscience condemned him to death.

Thus the Law was holy and each of its commandments just and good, but it condemned to death all who failed to render to it a perfect obedience.

Such is the effect of Divine Law upon man's carnal nature ; and the rest of the chapter (vs. 14-25) illustrates the doctrine by showing how fruitless is the effort of the " old man " to live as the "new man." This emphasizes the absolute necessity of regeneration ; for it is impossible for an unconverted man, however moral and highly cultured, to live the Christian life. He is carnal, sold under sin, and all his righteousnesses are as filthy rags in the sight of God.

The " I " of this passage is the " I " of generic argument. The Apostle imagines himself as having lived prior to, and subsequent to, Moses, and as being the contemporary of the philosophers of all ages who applauded virtue but practised vice. For, though the Law of conscience, in which they delighted, summoned them to a life of virtue, yet a different Law in their nature compelled them to a life of vice (vs. 22 and 23).

The points here are that these two Laws of Sin and Conscience dwell in all men, that men are the helpless captives of the Law of Sin, and that they cannot liberate themselves from it by the moral purity demanded by conscience because that purity is impossible to them.

But there is One, and One only Deliverer— the Lord Jesus Christ ; for in response to the anguished cry," Who shall deliver me ? " the answer is : that God can, and that the vehicle of the deliverance is through the work and person of Jesus Christ the Lord.

The conclusion of the argument from verse 14 to 24 is : that man's conscience applauds the Law of God, but that his nature serves the Law of Sin. The formula " I myself " of this passage is generic.

The controversy therefore whether the Apostle Paul speaks in these verses of himself as a regenerate or an unregenerate man does not arise, for the fact here stated is true of all men whether Christian or non-Christian. All possess a conscience and all possess a carnal nature. The difference is that the Christian (v. 25) enjoys a new life (viii. 2) which liberates him from the power of his sinful nature.

" Allow " (v. 15) read " approve."

" I was alive " (v. 9), i.e., " I thought myself to be alive."

Thus the three mighty Princes, Death, Sin, and Law lose their authority over all who by faith become associated with Christ in His death and resurrection. With Him they enter a new realm of life and righteousness ; and, energized by the Holy Spirit (viii. 2), they live a life of true sanctification.

At Christ's birth the three Eastern Princes worshipped, and at His death these other Three Princes triumphed. But they perished in their triumph whilst the Magi live.

If the believer makes " death " his refuge he is safe from the domination of sin. For what can Satan do with a dead man ?

ROMANS VIII—As the subject of chapter iii. is God declaring the sinner righteous, so the theme of this chapter is God making the sinner holy. The former chapter deals with Christ's work for the sinner, i.e., justification ; the latter chapter, Christ's work in the sinner, i.e., sanctification.

The chapter opens with " No condemnation " and closes with " No separation."

The subject of ch. v. 12-21, is " condemnation " for all who are in Adam ; the theme of this chapter is " no condemnation " for all who are in Christ. The special Greek word used for " condemnation " occurs only in ch. v. 16 and 18 and viii. 1. It therefore links these two passages.

The first verse of the chapter completes

the teaching of vii. 24 and the first half of verse 25.

An Egyptian punishment at that time was to fasten a criminal to a corpse, and the attachment continued till death. It was a terrible bond, and the more so because the man bound knew that the bond would result in death. This was possibly before the apostle's mind when writing verse 24. Such a helpless and hopeless prisoner, held in a bond so loathsome and fatal, would cry out with anguish : " Who can deliver me from this dead body ? "

This is the moral condition of all who are in Adam.

Christ took this very position at Calvary, and died in consequence. But being God He rose from among the dead and ascended above the highest heavens, having by His death destroyed death (Heb. ii. 14), abolished sin (Heb. ix. 26), and exhausted the curse of the Law (Gal. iii. 13).

The glad tidings of the Gospel consist in the declaration that all who by faith are in Christ died and rose with Him, and, consequently, there is no person, and no thing, that can condemn them. For Christ there is now no condemnation. He suffered its fulness infinitely at Calvary. But He suffered that condemnation there on behalf of, and for the benefit of, all who believe upon Him. Hence there is no condemnation for them. They are in a new position entirely beyond and above the reach of everything to which condemnation attaches. Where Christ and His members now stand there can be no question of sin or of wrath or of condemnation or of imputation. All such questions were settled before He ascended thither ; and He is on the Throne of God, His Person and Work accepted, because these questions were settled. And the glorious truth that liberates the believer's heart is that he is there in that glory with Christ where nothing that condemns can reach him.

But this is not only a new position in the Second Adam as contrasted with the old position in the first Adam, but it is also a new life—a life of power and holiness and victory. The Christian faith is not a scheme of salvation intellectually accepted, but a life of power and holiness experimentally enjoyed.

Immanuel's destruction of sin at Calvary may become to faith a moral reality now, as it will become in the New Heavens and in the New Earth a physical fact : for in them righteousness alone will dwell.

The believer is dead, for he was crucified with Christ. He, therefore, as a partner with Christ, enjoys all the advantages of the partnership acquired by Christ before he was brought into it (v. 3). This is not necessarily an experience, it is a Divine operation apprehended and enjoyed by faith.

But the believer is conscious that his carnal nature is not dead, but that between it and the new spiritual nature he received at conversion (Eph. i. 13, R.V.) there is a deadly warfare.

If the carnal nature were actually dead it would not be necessary to urge Christian people not to make provision to gratify its appetites (Rom. xiii. 14).

This great moral fact of the existence of these two natures in the believer is the theme of this chapter, and it teaches that the Christian may enjoy, through the victorious energy of the new nature within him, a moral experience so liberating that the fact of indwelling sin may become to him only a matter of belief—because the Word of God asserts its existence—but not a painful fact of consciousness.

Most Christian people have the opposite and sad experience. They are painfully conscious of this principle of evil lodged in their nature, whilst the existence of the new nature within them is a matter of belief because declared in the Scriptures.

Thus verse 2 of this chapter forms its keynote. It asserts the existence of these two natures in the believer ; but declares that the new spiritual nature liberates from the old carnal nature.

So the subject of the chapter is not the forgiveness of sins and justification from them, but liberation from the power of sin in order to a life of sanctification.

The chapter may be thus analysed :

First section : Verses 1-4.

Justification (v. 1) and sanctification (v. 4).

Second section : Verses 5-14.

Flesh and Spirit and their conflict.

Third section : Verses 15-27.

Sonship (vs. 16, 17) and sympathy (vs. 18-28).

Fourth section : Verses 29-39.

Love and purpose.

Verse 1 should read as in the Revised Version.

" The spirit of life " (v. 2), i.e., the spiritual nature imparted to the believer. That nature operates with the regularity of a law just as the principle of sin operates as a law in its sphere. The one spirit issues in life ; the other, in death.

The law could not make a man holy (v. 3), not because of its impotency, but because of the impotency of man on whom it acted. If a railway engine were built of paper, steam would be powerless to move it, not because of any weakness in the power of steam, but because of the weakness of the material of which the engine was built.

But God does what the Law could not do, i.e., pardon the transgressor and give him a new nature, for He first in the sinless flesh of His Beloved Son destroyed sin, condemning it to death, and then by the impartation of the Divine nature to the believer causes him by faultless conduct to satisfy all the righteous requirements of the Law (v. 4).

These righteous requirements cannot be satisfied by anyone who walks " after the flesh," i.e., who is controlled by the principle of sin in the flesh, but only by him who is controlled by the spirit.

In this whole passage the word " spirit " signifies the spiritual nature upon which the Holy Spirit acts. In verse 16 the Holy Spirit Himself as a person speaks and witnesses to the spiritual nature which all who are born of God possess.

There are two wills contrasted in verses 5-8—the will of the carnal nature and the will of God. The carnal will being independent of God's will is, consequently, hostile to it, and cannot be otherwise. Therefore all who are governed by the carnal will cannot, so long as they are thus governed, please God, let them be never so religious, moral, cultivated or noble. It is not that God takes no pleasure in noble actions performed by unconverted men, but that He cannot take pleasure in and accept religious worship and meritorious actions designed to purchase His favour which are prompted by the carnal mind. Hence He rejected Cains' worship and offerings.

All who are controlled by the carnal will set their affections upon gratifying it. The opposite is true in the case of those controlled by the Divine will (v. 5). The one control ends in death ; the other, in life (v. 6). If anyone is not controlled by the nature of Christ it is evident that he does not belong to Him (v. 9). This terrible truth destroys what is termed sacramental salvation, as well as salvation by works, for the one and only question here raised is that of the possession of a new spiritual nature, and that nature no church nor meritorious action can give. Only by a personal living faith in Christ does a man become a child of God (Gal. iii. 26).

" The body is dead " (v. 10), i.e., mortal because sinful ; but the spirit is immortal because sinless.

But the mortal body will be raised and made immortal by Him Who raised up Christ from among the dead ; and this because Christ's spirit dwells in the believer (v. 11).

Every claim, therefore, of sin as a master is at an end (v. 12) in God's great scheme of holiness.

But if the believer does not kill sin, sin will kill him (v. 13). He cannot kill sin but he has received a power that can make dead all the passions of sin in the body, and only those that are being thus led by the Spirit of God are the sons of God (v. 14) ; and this fact does not bring back the believer under the bondage of the Law where He was perpetually oppressed with doubts and fears as to whether or not he was righteous before God, but it brings him into the high and glorious position of a child who, possessing his father's nature, spontaneously cries out Abba, i.e., Father.

As already set out the keywords of this third section of the chapter (vs. 15-27) are sonship (vs. 16 and 17) and sympathy (vs. 18-28), i.e., " children " and " pain." The key-words of the first section (vs. 1-4) are " justification " (v. 1) and " sanctification " (v. 4) i.e., condemnation and righteousness, and those of the second section (vs. 5-14) are " flesh " and " spirit," and the conflict between them.

In verse 16 the Holy Spirit appears (see R.V.) and witnesses to the believer that he is both a child and an heir.

But the Holy Spirit also binds the heart of the believer in sympathy with the suffering creation and with all its pain and misery. Christ felt that sympathy ; and anyone who believes himself to be a Christian but does not so suffer with Christ deceives himself, for only those who suffer thus in sympathy with the suffering creation, and in this sense with Christ will be glorified with Him (v. 17).

" The sufferings of this present time " here mean (v. 18) the misery and ruin into which man and the creation are fallen because of man's sin. The future time for which man and the creation hope (vs. 18, 19, 23, 24 and 25) is the promised day of the restitution of all things when the redeemed and the creation will be delivered from the bondage of mortality and brought into the freedom of immortality. The glory of that future time will bear no relation to the misery of this present time (v. 18).

" Creature " (vs. 19-22) should read " creation," as in the Revised Version, and the words " waiteth I say " (from v. 19) supplied before " in hope because etc."

This passage personates creation ; and, perhaps, creation is personated by the cherubim. Those mysterious beings seem to connect creation with the throne of God. They appear in Genesis at the beginning of the Bible, in Ezekiel at the middle of the Bible, and in the Apocalypse at the end of the Bible. They were also represented in the Tabernacle, which was a pattern of heavenly things.

The link which unites the believer with the suffering creation is his body. Because of sin it is subjected to pain, decay, and death. This connection with the creation brings into conscious suffering the heart that is indwelt by the love of Christ. It is the suffering of sympathy. The sense of the pain and evil that encompass the Christian oppresses him ; and the more conscious he is of the indwelling warmth and liberty and power of the Divine nature, which is love, the more is he sensible of the weight of the misery introduced into the creation by sin.

Thus the believer is united to the creation by the body and to heaven by the Spirit ; and the sympathy which he feels for the suffering creation is a Divine sympathy.

When God searches such a heart (v. 27) He does not find there a selfish burden of misery that causes the heart to groan, but the unselfish affections of the new nature ; and its sighings being of the Holy Spirit must be as sweet music to the ear of God.

" Vanity " (v. 20), i.e., death. " Not willingly," i.e., not of its own will. This verse and the following should read as in the Revised Version. God because of man's sin subjected the creation to death ; but He did so in hope, for He looked forward to its recovery when man should be redeemed.

Creation also shares this hope and waits for it (vs. 19-21).

" The bondage of corruption " (v. 21), i.e., mortality. " The liberty of the glory," i.e., immortality. Compare the possible immortality of the sinful body.—Gen. iii., 22.

" Waiting for the adoption " (v. 23), i.e., the manifestation in redeemed bodies on the resurrection morning of believers as sons of God.

" Hope " (v. 24), i.e., absolute conviction and assured expectation. That hope saves from depression and animates the heart. It is the hope of verses 19 and 23.

" Infirmity " (v. 26, R.V.), i.e., ignorance as to how to pray and what to pray for. What a refreshment to know that the Holy Spirit prays within the heart making intercession in harmony with the will of God (v. 27) ; and though the Christian does not know what to pray for, he does know (v. 28) that all things work together for his good. And how fortifying also to know that when God searches the heart, saddened with the sense of the misery that afflicts creation, He finds there not the emotions of the carnal will but the affections of the spiritual nature.

Verses 19-21 may be thus read : " For the earnest expectation of the creation waiteth . . . . in hope because the creation itself also," etc., etc.

The keywords of the fourth and last section of the chapter (vs. 28-39) are " love " and " purpose " (v. 28), i.e., the activities of God's heart and God's hand in choosing and fitting " the many brethren " (v. 29) to partake of the sinless, immortal, and glorified Humanity of His Beloved Son, and to be His companions in the highest heavens.

These " many brethren " He fore-knew in His love and fore-ordained and conformed in His purpose ; for His fore-knowledge reposes in His love, and His fore-ordination in His purpose. Because He loved them He fore-knew them and therefore, in His purpose He fore-ordained and conformed them, and consequently, they were called, justified, and glorified. The first three, i.e., fore-knew, fore-ordained and conformed, occupy the affections of His heart ; the last three, i.e., called, justified and glorified, engage the activities of His hand ; and this last activity of His purpose is so certain of accomplishment that it is here stated as a present fact.

How amazing is the thought that God

has fore-ordained men sunk in the loathsome depths of ch. i. 21-32 to possess, eternally, bodies of glory similar to Christ's body of glory as seen on the Mount of Transfiguration and in Rev i. 13-15 ; and how certain is its accomplishment ! for its certitude is not based upon man's moral excellency but upon the two eternal and immovable pillars of God's love and God's purpose, i.e., His fore-knowledge and His fore-ordination.

These things being so, if God be for the Elect who can be against them so as to injure them ? (v. 31). And the Election need not be anxious, for God being for them fills the heart with a rest and a peace that shuts out all anxiety as to anything that could trouble it ; for how could the heart and the hand that gave what was most precious to them (v. 32) fail in bounty, liberality and protection to those whom He fore-knew ?

The climax of the Epistle is now reached (v. 33) and the Apostle triumphantly challenges anyone to lay anything to the charge of God's elect. This glorious word here first occurs in the Epistle. The expiatory character of Christ's death is affirmed in verse 34, and the meaning of justification in verse 33, for the challenge : Who shall bring a charge against God's elect ? i.e., who shall pronounce those guilty whom God pronounces righteous, makes clear its significance.

" Shall God who justifies ? " " Shall Christ who died ? " supply triumphant answers to the challenge.

The love of verse 35 is Christ's love to the " brethren " of verse 29, and their love to Him. Both affections survive every test (v. 36).

The challenge is—what power can separate them from His love, or compel them to cease loving Him ? and the power of men (vs. 35 and 37), of angels (v. 38), of demons (v. 39) and of any created thing is considered and dismissed as unable to do so.

The foe's armoury contains seven weapons (v. 35)—the whole of his resources ; but however these weapons may disfigure, deform, degrade, or destroy the believer, Christ will still love and prize him. Joseph was just as dear to that love when lying in the dungeon as when seated on the throne. It is possible to separate from human love, but not from Christ's love. A man may love his betrothed very deeply, but if by the power of an enemy her beauty and her wealth be destroyed, his love for her can die.

And His people love Him and believe in the fidelity of His love to them (v. 37) ; for trials do but assure the heart which knows His love that nothing can separate from it ; and they know well that being called, justified, and glorified no link is wanting in the golden chain that binds them to His heart. That chain begins in the immeasurable past and reaches into the immeasurable future. It stretches from one Eternity to the other. Love and purpose planned that they should have the one and same portion with Himself. This faith makes them more than conquerors over " all these things," i.e., these trials. Joseph, Daniel, etc. are examples. See notes on the three women of John iv.,viii and xx.

Let the enemy search death and life and the present and the future ; let him mount to the greatest heights or descend to the lowest depths ; let him turn to all created things, and to men, angels, and demons, and he will fail to find any power that can separate the redeemed from the love of God which is in Christ Jesus the Lord.

As in the Lord's farewell to His disciples eight activities of the Holy Spirit are found (John xiv. 16, 17, 26, xv. 26, xvi. 8, 13, 13, 14) so in this chapter eight corresponding activities appear. He quickens (v. 2) ; sanctifies (v. 4) ; witnesses (v. 16) ; sympathizes (v. 23) ; animates (v. 24) ; teaches (v. 26) ; intercedes (v. 27) ; and conforms (v. 29 with 2 Cor. iii. 18, and Phil. iii. 21).

ROMANS IX. 1-29—The Apostle Paul was accused of being disloyal to the Hebrew Church and to the promises made to it through the Fathers. The doctrine of justification by faith, apart from works, common to all men whether Hebrews or not (i.-viii.), seemed to set aside those promises. The problem, therefore, was to reconcile the doctrine of the grace of God in justification with the special privileges granted to Israel. The resolution of the problem is found in the doctrine of the Sovereignty of God in Election and Restoration.

The Gospel is immovably and eternally founded upon these two great divine facts of the grace of God in justification (i.-viii.), and the sovereignty of God in Election (ix.-xi.). These latter three chapters form, therefore, the second great section of the Epistle.

The Apostle begins by affirming his deep love for Israel. Far from despising them he loved them as much as Moses did (v. 3, with Exod. xxxii. 32). He points out all the privileges belonging to them (vs. 4 and 5), and argues that the sovereignty of God admits the Gentiles to these privileges and thereby enriches their glories instead of nullifying them.

This section of the Epistle is, therefore, dispensational, as the first section was doctrinal.

It begins with Paul's sorrow as to Israel's failure (ix. 1-5), and it closes with Paul's joy as to Israel's future (xi. 33-36) ; and between this opening and this close is set out God's purpose respecting " some " (a remnant ix. 6-29), and His purpose respecting " all " (xi. 1-32), whilst between these purposes he records Israel's rejection of the Messiah in spite of the prophets (ix. 30-33), in spite of the Law (x. 1-13) and in spite of the Gospel (x. 14-21).

Paul did not hesitate to take an oath when it was necessary to do so (v. 1).

The contrast between verses 3 and 5 is between Paul a man and sinful, and Christ God over all and blessed for ever, but both Israelites as concerning the flesh.

" The adoption " (v. 4) i.e. sonship in God's earthly family; the glory, i.e., the Shechinah ; " the covenants," i.e., those given to Abraham, Isaac and Jacob ; " the law " as given at Horeb ; the service of God as detailed in Leviticus ; " the promises" as recorded in the Scripture ; " the fathers," i.e., Abraham, Isaac, and Jacob ; and the glorious climax—the Messiah, God blessed for ever !

In the double recital of Israel's glories the Bible is placed as the commencing (iii. 2) and the Messiah as the ultimate glory. (ix. 5).

" The Word of God " (v. 6), i.e., the promise to Abraham. " None effect," i.e., " had come to naught." The argument that this promise had not failed is declared in verses 6-8, for it is pointed out that this promise did not contemplate the children born of Abraham's body, but those born of Abraham's faith—" the children of the promise " —i.e., all who should exercise the same faith as Abraham did in God Who brings life out of death and Who is the God of Resurrection. Such a faith is above reason.

So the promise concerned some and not all.

The words some, any, and all are keywords for chapters ix.,x., and xi. Thus : " Not all " i.e., some (ix. 6) ; " whosoever," i.e., any (x. 13) ; and " all " (xi. 32).

Isaac and Jacob illustrate the doctrine of the Sovereignty of God in Election. Man complains of this doctrine, as he does of the doctrine of grace in justification.

God did not chose Ishmael nor any of the sons of Keturah, but only Isaac (vs. 7 and 9) ; and if the Jews urged that they were not the sons of Sarah, the apostle replied by pointing to Jacob. He and Esau were twin brothers, born of the one mother, and yet God chose Jacob prior to birth, and before his conduct in doing either good or evil could determine God's choice in acceptance or rejection.

The election of Isaac and of Jacob establishes, therefore, the Sovereignty of God.

But the proof of the fact of God's Sovereignty is declared in verses 7, 9, 12, and 13, to be the Scriptures ; and such an authority puts an end to all controversy (v. 16).

" Hated " (v. 13) a Hebraism for not chosen. Of two lads who apply for a situation a merchant accepts one and rejects the other, i.e., he " loves " the one he accepts, and he " hates " the one he rejects.

Two objections to the doctrine of Election are now brought forward :—first : That it is inconsistent with the righteousness of God ; and second : That it conflicts with the responsibility of man and is unjust (v. 19).

The answer to the first is simple and overwhelming. All men being justly doomed to die it is not unrighteous on the part of God to save some of them (v. 15)—and the Scripture justifies this by pointing to Exodus xxxiii. 19. All Israel, as guilty of idolatry, justly merited death. But there was one door of escape, and only one—the Sovereignty of God. If He had dealt with them in righteousness all must have perished ; but He employed His Sovereignty in order to have mercy on them. No action of theirs (v. 16) could have purchased mercy. It was sovereign grace that forgave them.

Isaac and Joseph illustrate, respectively, the determination of man's will and the energy of his nature ; and both are found in opposition to God (v. 16).

Isaac, though he knew the will of God (v. 12), wilfully determined to bless Esau, and he " trembled exceedingly " when defeated. He "loved" Esau and "hated" Jacob. Joseph when he saw his aged father placing his right hand upon the younger boy's head, moved by the energy of nature, "ran" to prevent the action. He also was defeated. And so in spite of man's willing and running God's Election stands.

If guilty Israel (v. 15) illustrates the sovereignty of God in mercy, guilty Pharaoh illustrates His Sovereignty in wrath. Pharaoh said "Who is Jehovah that I should serve Him?" He was the enemy of God and of His people. He proudly exalted himself against God and treated His claims with contempt, so being in this state God used him as an example of His wrath. But here also, as in His action toward Israel, the Sovereignty of God designs the blessing of man, for He showed His power in Pharaoh in order that the earth might know His glorious name ; and all blessing comes from knowing God, and misery results from not knowing Him. Further, it was God's Sovereignty in mercy that hardened Pharaoh's heart, for the Divine action that hardened the monarch's heart was the sovereign mercy that successively removed the plagues that righteously judged him. As the opposite effects of heat and cold harden iron into steel so the Divine actions of punishment and mercy hardened Pharaoh.

"The Scripture saith unto Pharaoh" (v. 17) i.e., God, as recorded in the Scripture, said to Pharaoh (Ex. ix. 16).

This formula "The Scripture saith," and "the Scripture preached" (Gal. iii. 8), asserts the inspiration of the Bible. What God says, the Scripture says, and what the Scripture says, God says.

The second objection (v. 19) is : That it is unjust to punish the sinner, for he cannot resist God's will if God exerts it as He did in the case of Jacob, whom He chose to salvation irrespective of his conduct.

The reply is double. First : It is foolish and irreverent for the creature to judge the Creator. If the creature were sinless he might, perhaps, claim liberty of criticism, but being sinful he can make no such claim. Is not God entitled to the same liberty of action as the potter? And this the more so as humanity being a lump of sinful clay only merits dishonour. And, therefore, it is not unjust on the part of God to fashion part of it into vessels of mercy—all being by nature self-fitted to destruction, not "afore-

prepared." The distinction in the language between verses 22 and 23 should be observed.

The second reply is (v. 22) : If there be a Divine necessity, as undoubtedly there is, that God should demonstrate the power of His wrath as well as the riches of His mercy, it is reasonable that "vessels" should exist as vehicles of that wrath and mercy.

The Apostle now reaches the point he is aiming at (vs. 24-29), i.e., that vessels of mercy are chosen equally from among the Jews and from among the Gentiles (vs. 24-26); and that the non-elect of the children of Israel are vessels of wrath justly punished in righteousness (vs. 27-29).

A man is not guilty because having been born of consumptive parents he is consumptive, but he is guilty of self-destruction if he refuses to be healed by an assured remedy.

God's sovereignty, therefore, is the first of all rights, the foundation of all justice, and the fundamental of all morality. Is God to judge man, or man to judge God?

This sovereignty expresses itself in power, patience, and preparation—power in willing, patience in long-suffering, and preparation in mercy.

This doctrine, therefore, is a most comfortable doctrine of the Gospel. For if God elects men to salvation, as He did Jacob before his birth, for a just reason hidden in Himself, then the vilest sinner may be saved. Further, the sovereignty of God is benevolent toward man for it hastens to fashion the vessels of mercy with its own hands (v. 23), but it lingers to punish the vessels of wrath fitted—not by Him but by sin and self-will—to destruction. So it was because God was sovereign He elected Gentiles as well as Jews, in the exuberant riches of His moral glory, unto millennial glory.

And the Scriptures vindicate this action (Hosea ii. 23, and i. 10). Peter, who writes to Hebrews, only quotes chapter ii. where Israel becomes once more the people of God, but Paul adds the quotation from chapter i. where certain persons shall be called "Sons of the living God." These sons he argues include Gentiles.

As to Israel, though numberless as the sand of the sea, yet only a portion should be saved ; for in righteousness the others would be cut off. "Finish the work," i.e., "cease to plead," and "cut it short," i.e., destroy all but a small part. "Upon the earth," i.e.

Palestine. See notes on Isa. i. 9 and x. 22.

Thus once more the Scripture is appealed to as divinely vindicating the righteousness of God's activities in mercy and in wrath.

An election out from among the Gentiles is first mentioned in this chapter in verse 24. Had Israel's rejection being total, God's promise to Abraham would have fallen to the ground, for the substitution of the Gentiles instead of the Hebrews would not have satisfied the terms of the promise, but a remnant from out of Israel being preserved, to it the promises are made good—but only on the principle of Election by grace—and thus God's word is fulfilled.

The doctrine, therefore, of the sovereignty of God in Election based on grace, reconciles the "no difference" between Jew and Gentile of chapters i. to viii., and the promise to Abraham of ix. 3-6 which appeared to establish a difference. That promise only applied to an Election. Man complains of election as unjust. But all men being sinful and justly doomed to death, it is not unjust on the part of God to engrace some of them; and His liberty of action in sovereignty is benevolent, as evidenced by His activity and long-suffering. Further, the election of Jacob prior to his birth proves the impartiality of Election. So on this principle of grace any man may be saved, and this fact is now brought out in the "whosoever" of the next chapter, which should begin at verse 30 of chapter ix.

God according to His own purpose and grace in Christ Jesus before the world began, elects sinners, as He elected Jacob, to the salvation which is in Christ Jesus with eternal glory (2 Tim. i. 9); and His action toward Israel and the Gentiles proves that the last shall be first and the first last (Matt. xx. 16); and that earnestness in religion is fatal as a ground of confidence before God, if it be the earnestness of the carnal will which rejects God's way of salvation by faith in favour of salvation by works.

Chapter ix. belongs to the past, chapter x. to the present, and chapter xi. to the future, and they correspond to the three Books of Isaiah.

ROMANS IX.-30—X.-21—As the key-word of the prior chapter is the word "some" so in this chapter the keyword is "whoso-ever" and the argument is that God cannot be blamed for His action toward the vessels of wrath, i.e., unbelieving Israel, for He thrice offered them life and righteousness under the Prophets (ix. 30-33), under the Law (x. 1-13), and under the Gospel (x. 14-21), but they rejected all three offers.

In their self-will and carnal activity (ix. 16) God's Corner-Stone became Israel's stumbling-stone.

There are four members in the passage 30-33. The first and the fourth correspond, and the second and the third. Thus: no running or willing in the believer (v. 30) and, therefore, no stumbling (v. 33); and no believing in the runner or willer (vs. 31 and 32) and, as a consequence, stumbling (vs. 32-33).

"As it were" (v. 32), i.e., as if righteousness were attainable by works.

The Gentiles did not follow, therefore they were not runners. They believed, therefore they were not self-willers. Israel "followed" in carnal activity, and in self-will sought righteousness by works.

But to all Israel, without distinction whether elect or non-elect, the prophets announced that whosoever believed upon the Rock laid in Zion should not be put to shame.

The Law (x. 1-13) testified to justification by faith apart from works both negatively (v. 5) and positively (vs. 5-11). Negatively, for righteousness on the principle of Law-obedience was impossible of attainment owing to man's incapacity to give such an obedience, and positively, as declared in Deuteronomy xxx. 12-14; for that message of grace was based upon Israel's failure under Law, and was given especially for the time of her captivity when Law-observance would be impossible.

The Apostle Paul declares in a parenthesis (v. 8) that that was the same doctrine that he preached—" the Word of Faith "—i.e., justification on the faith-principle as opposed to the works-principle.

The word "whosoever" (vs. 11 and 13) uttered by Isaiah (xxviii. 16) and Joel (ii. 32) made it evident to the Hebrew people that life and righteousness were offered to faith and not to merit or to privilege, for it was manifest that the word "whosoever" embraced the entire world without distinction. This word makes certain that just as there is "no difference" between men as justly sentenced to death because sinful (iii. 22), so is there "no difference" between men as to their petition for life, for the One Lord is Lord of all, and is infinitely kind unto all who call upon Him whether Hebrew or Greek (v. 12).

Intellectual matters interest the head, moral issues, the heart (v. 10). Multitudes to-day, like the Hebrews of old, refuse to believe on Christ because of the moral issues involved. Man believes with the heart when he is morally interested. His affections are engaged, and they are drawn to the object upon whom he believes and not upon the fact of his believing. He is not concerned with the state of his affections, however important that matter is, but with the truth of that which is presented to him for acceptance.

Israel's "going about" and "not submitting themselves" (v. 3) illustrate the willing and running of ix. 16; and the contrary principle of believing (v. 4) illustrates ix. 30.

"Christ is the end of the Law," etc., (v. 4), i.e., the righteousness demanded by the Law is embodied in Christ. Whoever, therefore, believes upon Him possesses that righteousness.

Israel's rejection of God's gift of righteousness in Christ is predicted and declared in verses 14-21. They heard the Gospel, for preachers Divinely sent announced it to them (vs. 14 and 15), but they did not obey it (v. 16). It was a message from God; and if they had listened to it and believed it (v. 17) they would have become partakers of the peace and the good things it proffered. They all heard it for it was proclaimed throughout the whole world (v. 18). This throws an interesting light upon the diffusion of the Scriptures throughout the whole known world, prior to, and at the time of, the First Advent.

"Did not Israel know?" (v. 19), i.e., know that the Gospel would be preached to the Gentiles, that they would listen to it, but that the Hebrews would reject it. The answer is they did know, and two witnesses, Moses and Isaiah, prove it. For Moses (Deut. xxxii. 21) predicted the acceptance of the Gospel by the Gentiles. But Isaiah (lxv. 1) went further, for not only did he foretell Gentile obedience to the Gospel, but he predicted Israel's rejection of it, and that they would be disobedient and fault-finding although through a long day of grace Immanuel Himself, in exquisite pity and patient love, would keep stretching out His hands to them.

Thus the majority of Israel by their self-will and unbelief fashioned themselves into vessels of wrath, for they rejected Christ as announced by the Prophets, by the Law, and by the Gospel.

In this chapter, as in the prior one, the entire argument and its dogmatic statements are based upon the Divine and conclusive foundation of the inspired Scriptures.

The Gospel is thus set out in the chapter :—

Its provisions : life (v. 13) and righteousness (v. 4).

Its simplicity : within reach (hand), well-known (mouth), easily understood (heart) (v.8).

Its conditions : faith and submission (v. 9).

Its freeness : "Whosoever" (v. 11).

ROMANS XI.—The theme of this chapter is grace saving nations—Israel included—who, by unbelief, forfeited all right to Divine blessing, just as in the prior chapter the theme was grace saving individuals equally meritless and guilty.

Three arguments are brought forward to prove that God has not cast Israel away for ever—first : The fact of Paul's own salvation (v. 1); second : Salvation was sent to the Gentiles in order to incite Israel to seek and find it (v. 11); third : The nation shall yet be saved, for Immanuel the Deliverer shall come out of Zion, forgive their sins, and cleanse them from all their unbelief.

Israel was the olive-tree (v. 17), Abraham was its root, and the Messiah its Creator and Nourisher. This tree stood on the earth and the promises were its sap. They were earthly promises involving government and priesthood. The tribes of Israel were its branches. Their union with the olive-tree was maintained on the principle of faith and not of works. The nation failed. They were unbelieving and the majority were, consequently, cut off. Another "nation," known to God and chosen from among the Gentiles, was grafted into the olive-tree (Matt. xxi. 43). But this new "nation" was grafted in upon the same principle of standing by faith, and warned that if it sinned it should also be cut off. That wild olive-tree is not the Church. It has its position in the heavenlies, and is distinct from both the Hebrew Church and the Gentile Church. If, therefore, the unbelief of a part of the

Hebrew Church (v. 25) occasioned the reception into Divine favour of a " nation " from among the Gentiles, much more shall Israel's repentance and restoration effectuate the salvation of all the nations of the Gentile world.

In the contemplation of these great purposes of sovereign grace the Apostle concludes the subject of these three chapters (ix., x., xi.) by a triumphant outburst of admiration (v. 33) and of adoration (v. 36), and mainly because of the riches of the grace expressed in the climax of the whole argument (v. 32), which is: that God having tested both the Hebrew and the Gentile nations, and both having broken down under the test, He shut them·up in unbelief so that, being manifestly without merit, and having by demonstration forfeited all claims and all rights to Divine favour, He might in the unsearchable riches of His grace, have mercy upon them all !

And so will it come to pass. The guilty Hebrews and the faithless Gentiles will, as nations, receive mercy from God on the principle of sovereign grace and will form one olive-tree in the millennial earth.

The chapter does not discuss the eternal safety of a member of the mystic body of Christ united to Christ in the heavenlies, but of nations as branches in the olive-tree of Divine blessing planted in the earth—a totally different subject. Thus in these chapters ix., x., xi., the Holy Spirit reconciles sovereign grace shown to sinners, whether Jew or Gentile, with the especial privileges of the people of Israel. Under law they lost everything ; under grace they recover everything ; and the great fact is emphasized that they and the nations will " all " be blessed together upon the one principle of salvation by grace and not by works.

" Against Israel " (v. 2). Elijah should have pleaded for Israel and not against Israel. See notes on 1 Kings xvii.-xix.

" A remnant " (v. 5), i.e., of Israel. The nation exists to the present day in spite of countless efforts by Satan to destroy it ; and God always has in the nation His " seven thousand." But they are unseen—they are God's " hidden ones. "

Two principles of salvation are contrasted in verse 6—man's merit and God's grace. These principles are opposed. They cannot be combined. Salvation must rest wholly on the one or on the other.

As in the prior chapters so here, all the arguments and statements are based upon the Scriptures (vs. 8, 9 and 26).

Israel did not wish to see or to hear, and a judicial blindness and deafness and insensibility hold them in darkness to the present day (vs. 7-10). This is a fundamental principle of God's government, and it operates in all ages, and its activity cannot be denied.

" Their table " (v. 9), i.e., their special privileges. Israel rested carnally in these, and they became a snare to them.

The apostle magnified his office as apostle to the Gentiles in order to awaken to emulation his fellow Hebrews and so save some of them. He did not magnify himself (v. 13).

It is contrary to nature to graft a wild plant on to a fruit tree.

The branches were not broken off in order that the Gentiles might be grafted in. They were broken off by unbelief ; and God to move Israel to jealousy engrafted the Gentiles temporally into this national position of blessing and privilege (vs. 17-24).

" In part " (v. 25), i.e., for a time—not eternally.

" Enemies " (v. 28), i.e., God accounted them as such. " For your sakes," i.e., by His turning in grace to the Gentiles. He loved them ; but He doubly loved Israel.

" Without repentance " (v. 29), i.e., God having purposed to bless a nation, no demerit on its part can cause Him to change His mind.

" Ye " (v. 30), i.e., Gentiles. " Your mercy " (v. 31), i.e., the mercy shown to the Gentile. " They also," i.e., Israel. The sovereign mercy that engraced the meritless Gentile will also engrace the meritless Israel.

ROMANS XII.-XV. 13. — The principle of grace having been established as the basis of salvation (i.-viii.), the Spirit in this section of the Epistle describes the character and conduct of those who have been born into that kingdom of grace.

Accordingly Christian conduct is set out in seven paragraphs ; and this number marks completion. These paragraphs deal with the believer's relation :

To God—Consecration (xii. 1 and 2).

The Church—Communication (xii. 3-8).

Fellow-believers—Affection (xii. 9-13).

Enemies—Benediction (xii. 14-21).

The State—Subjection, (xiii. 1-7).

Society—Consideration (xiii. 8-14).

Weak brethren—Compassion (xiv to xv. 7).

The first evidence of real Christian life is consecration to God and transformation from the world. This is not an outside mechanical action, but an inward perpetual renewing of the mind seeking for, discerning, and doing the will of God.

Communications in public ministry in the church should not go beyond the faith (v. 3) and the grace (v. 6) apportioned for the exercise of the ministration, whatever its character might be.

"One body in Christ" (v. 5). This is the first mention of the Heavenly Church in the Bible. See notes on Ephesians.

Ministry in the assembly should be diligent, simple, prayerful, and sympathetic.

"Not slothful in business" (v. 11), i.e., in the activity of affection one to another (vs. 10 and 13).

"Condescend to men of low estate" (v. 16), i.e., company rather with humble people than with those of high position. The natural desire of the heart is toward companionship with titled people.

"If it be possible" (v. 18)—sometimes it is impossible owing to the conduct of others.

"Give place unto wrath" (v. 19), i.e., leave the ground free for God to execute wrath, if the enemy persists in his enmity. But just as fire melts the hardest metal, so kindness the hardest heart ; and the Christian is to act on that principle. A Chinese emperor pardoned a large number of rebels, and when his counsellors objected, saying he had promised to destroy all his enemies, he replied : " Have I not done so ? These men are now my friends. They are no longer enemies ! "

Government in the earth is of Divine ordination (xiii. 1). The magistrate is a minister of God. The sword in his hand is a Divine instrument for the punishment of evildoers. He is responsible so to use it ; and, consequently, all Christian people are responsible to aid him in the discharge of this duty. It is, therefore, lawful for a Christian to be a policeman and a soldier ; and, further, it is his duty to be such if the magistrate so commands. But if the magistrate uses the sword not against evil-doers, but against the innocent, then the servants of God are not bound to obey him. The question whether the persons to be punished are innocent or guilty is always a difficult one. The government is responsible for its answer rather than the private soldier or police officer.

No form of government is here attacked or recommended. Authority is recognized as from God. Nero was the authority in Paul's day. Whoever resisted him resisted the ordinance of God and merited punishment for themselves (v. 2). No one who does good need fear a government. On the contrary, such people are commended by the authorities (v. 3).

" Wrath," i.e., the wrath of the magistrate. " Conscience," i.e., recognition of God's ordination in government (v. 5).

" Love " (v. 8). This is a debt that never can be repaid. Love fufils law (v. 10), for love could never injure its fellow-men by doing any of the evils forbidden in verse 9. " For this " (v. 9), i.e., the law of love. " And this" (v. 11. R.V.) i.e., the second reason —the coming of the Lord.

" Cast off " (v. 12), i.e., as a garment.

" Honestly " (v. 13), i.e., " nicely dressed." The clothing is the Lord Jesus Christ (v. 14)— so fully covering the Christian that Christ alone is seen.

" Make not provision for the flesh," i.e. for the carnal nature (v. 14). This injunction proves the fact of sin in the Christian, for he could not make provision for gratifying the appetites of that which did not exist. Mark vii. 21-23 says that these appetites have their roots in the heart.

Gentleness and forbearance with weak brethren is the subject of the fifth and last paragraph. " Compassion " is suggested as its keyword (xiv.-xv. 7).

" The weak in faith " (v. 1, R.V.), i.e., those defective in Christian intelligence were to be received into the fellowship at Rome, not for the purpose of forcing them by contentions and disputes to decide to give up their scruples about the uncleanness of certain foods (v. 2) and the sacredness of certain days (v. 5), but that they might be loved and cherished and pitied and borne with as weak brethren, and so strengthened and built up in Christian character (v. 19).

The Law forbade certain kinds of food as ceremonially unclean, and idolatry consecrated certain foods to its gods. Hence the action of Daniel and the other princes (Dan. i. 8). Paul had been persuaded—and to a Hebrew of the Hebrews as he was, it must have demanded much persuasion—by the Lord Jesus (v. 14) that the ceremonial law was fulfilled in Christ, that an idol was an illusion (i Cor. viii.), and that to the believer seated in and with Christ in the heavenlies, all foods are clean and all days are sacred. Those who accepted this teaching were the strong in faith, and enjoyed with Paul a delightful liberation from the bondage in which the weak in faith were held. But the Apostle, whilst urging sympathy and for-bearance in relation to them, did not fail to make it quite clear that their faith was defective in intelligence, and that there was a higher Christian experience intended for them in the Gospel. See note on Mark vii. 19.

Meanwhile they were not to judge one another, for they were all bond-slaves of Jesus Christ, whether living or dying (vs. 7-9), and after death were to stand at Christ's judgment seat (v. 10); and each one would there have to give an account of himself, and not of his neighbour, to God.

The Deity of Christ is frequently asserted in these verses. Compare xiv. 3 with xv. 7; and compare " Lord " and " God " in xiv. 6; and the statements of verses 8 and 9; and of 10, 11 and 12; and of 17 and 18.

But God only held up those and made them to stand (v. 4) whose abstinence or non-abstinence from food, or whose observ-ance or non-observance of the Sabbath-Day, had relation to Him, for this action or in-action, having God as its motive, put all the disputants on the same level before Him.

The teaching therefore of verse 6 regarding the Sabbath Day destroys the arguments of the Seventh Day Adventists.

Christ's absolute ownership of the believer, both spirit and soul and body, is a most precious fact for the heart of the Christian (vs. 7-9).

" Thou " (v. 10), i.e., the abstainer from meat. " Thou," i.e., the eater of meat.

" Bow " (v. 11), i.e., worship. " Confess," i.e., " sing praise." In this quotation from Isa. xlv. 23, the Holy Spirit declares Jesus to be both Jehovah and Elohim.

" But judge this rather " (v. 13), i.e., but come to this judgment, or Christian decision, not to do anything to cause a fellow-believer to fall morally.

It is of vital import not to violate the conscience (v. 14). To the conscience that esteems that to be unclean in the Levitical sense, which under the Gospel is really not so, to that conscience it becomes unclean. So the believer's liberty of action (vs. 15-23) is affected, and he must not by eating idol-offered meat (v. 15) grieve or wound the conscience of his brother; for to do so would not be walking in love toward him, but, on the contrary, set on a road which leads to destruction a man whom Christ died to save.

" Your good " (v. 16), i.e., the liberty which is found to be so good, but which because of the injury it does to another, is pointed to by óthers as evil.

" The Kingdom of God " (v. 17), i.e., the Gospel fellowship. In that fellowship the Holy Spirit by His energy and government actuates righteousness, peace and joy, i.e., uprightness in conduct, concord in brother-hood, and joy in experience. The Apostle says that these are the great matters in the Church, and not eating food and drinking wine. Corrupt Christianity declares the contrary, for it says that the most important spiritual exercise of a Christian congregation is the eating of bread and drinking of wine in what is known as the Mass in the Eastern and Western Churches, and as the Lord's Supper or Breaking of Bread in the Reformed Churches. Eating and drinking are not essen-tial in Christian Fellowship, but righteous-ness, peace and joy are absolutely funda-mental.

The question of the eternal safety of the believer is not raised in verses 15 and 20, but the dread principle is laid down that the wilful violation of conscience sets the violator upon a road that leads to ruin.

He that in the Christian fellowship obeys verse 17 in such actions serves Christ, pleases God, and compels the approval of men even though they may hate and persecute him (v. 18).

The Christian is to build up (v. 19) and not to throw down (v. 20) his fellow Christian; for every believer is the work of God.

All foods are pure (v. 20), but they become evil agents if they cause moral stumbling in others (vs. 20 and 21). See Mark vii. 19.

" Happy is he," etc., (v. 22), i.e., the man is to be congratulated who never does any-thing that his conscience condemns.

He that puts a difference between foods is condemned by· his conscience if he eats what he believes to be " unclean," because his action is not based upon faith (v. 23). Faith is dependence on God. Every action which displaces in the conscience that dependence is an independent action ; and all such independence is sinful.

" Pleasing self "(xv. i) ruins Christian fellowship. Others must be pleased, provided it tends to edification (v. 2). Christ pleased not Himself " (v. 3), for had He done so He might have avoided the hatred of man's heart to God. That He was so hated is a testimony to His Deity, for only God could be thus hated by man.

" God " (v. 5) is the Author of the patience and consolation lodged in the Scriptures to nourish the hope of believers. They are to imitate Christ (v. 5, margin) by receiving one another to the glory of God as Christ received them to that same glory (v. 7). He received them that they might be exhibitors of God's moral glory and so glorify Him (v. 6).

The argument of verses 7-13 supports the command " Receive ye " of xiv. 1. The argument is : that just as Christ as a Minister in the Hebrew Church, received the Gentiles into that Fellowship, so weak believers should be received into Christian Fellowship. And, further, that the right to fellowship was not agreement on petty points of observance, but on the fact of reception by Christ, and of recognition of Him as the Head and the Centre of the fellowship.

This is most important, and this argument of the apostle shows how essential to right Christian conduct, both in the Church and in the world, is intelligence in dispensational doctrine, i.e., the activities of the Divine Purpose in the various periods of human history, as revealed in the Scriptures. " Now I say " (v. 8), i.e., " Now what I have said " (ix. x. xi.). " I repeat that Jesus Christ," etc.

" The truth of God " (v. 8) i.e., the fidelity of God to His promises made to the Hebrew Church. The Hebrew claim was based on the fidelity of God as promised ; the Gentile hope was based on the mercy of God (v. 9) as prophesied. In verse 8 Christ is seen as the centre of the believing Hebrew Fellowship, and in verse 9, as the centre of the believing Heathen Fellowship, whilst in verses 10 and 11 He is presented as the Centre of a vast fellowship formed of the Hebrews and Heathen now united. " Ye people," (v. 11), i.e., " Ye Hebrew people." So Isaiah predicted that

there should be one Hebrew Root upon which all the Gentiles would hang their hopes. Therefore the apostle prays (v. 13) that God, the Author of such hopes, might fill the Roman brethren with all joy and peace in believing.

Of course the vast Christian fellowship of verses 8-12 is an earthly fellowship, and the future will witness its manifestation. The Heavenly fellowship revealed in Ephesians is quite another matter.

The carnal conscience is either careless or ceremonial. It was, therefore, easier for a Gentile to break away from his religious traditions than for a Hebrew. To the latter, consequently, much forbearance was due.

So the keywords of these seven paragraphs —Consecration, Communication, Affection, Benediction, Subjection, Consideration and Compassion—set out moral principles obedience to which would secure an ideal society.

The membership of the Gentile believers in the Hebrew Church (8-12) is based upon Scriptures taken from the Law of Moses, the Prophets and the Psalms (Luke xxiv. 44). The Hebrew Bible was, and is thus composed.

Paul's conduct illustrates the principle of xv. 1, as recorded in Acts xvi. 3, xxi. 23, etc. He knew and taught that all symbols were fulfilled in Christ, including baptism, circumcision, the Paschal Supper, and the Sabbath Day, etc. (see notes on Rom. xiv. 6. Col. ii. 9, 17, 1 Cor. v. 7, etc.), but in the interest of " the weak " he observed or did not observe them, provided foundation gospel truth was not involved (Gal. ii. 3). Intelligent Christian people enjoy the like liberty to-day, and therefore lovingly unite with "weak" brethren in baptism and the breaking of bread because these latter believe that these symbols are still to be retained and are essential to salvation or obedience.

ROMANS XV. 14—XVI. 27. — This section closes the Epistle. It is full of personal matters, of affection, and of greetings. Its correspondence with the first section of the epistle is very striking.

" Boldly " (v. 15), i.e., frankly ; for it needed boldness to declare man's hopeless depravity ; to teach justification and sanctfication in Christ apart from works ; and to prove that the Gentiles were branches in the Olive-tree of Divine privilege, and consequently, members of the Hebrew Church.

In verse 16 the apostle as a priest (Num. viii. 11) pictures himself offering up the Gentiles as a pure sacrifice acceptable to God because sanctified by the Holy Spirit: the Jews regarded the Gentiles as " unclean."

Paul gloried in his appointment as a preacher to the Gentiles (16-21). With him preaching was a higher service than working miracles, for (v. 18) he places preaching first (" word ") and the deeds, signs, and wonders next. Verses 18 and 19 should read as in the Revised Version.

The love of the Apostle for the believers at Rome appears in verses 23 and 24, and for those at Jerusalem in verses 25-28. His minuteness in disclosing his plans shows how nothing is too small for a heart that loves when that love is God's love.

So verses 16-24 describe his ministry as a dispenser of the Word of God, and verses 25-28 his ministry as a dispenser of the charity of the Church.

So busy was he preaching the Gospel (v. 22) that he had been again and again prevented from pushing on to Rome, " but having no more place in these parts," i.e., no more engagements in and about Corinth he planned to visit Rome via Jerusalem (v. 25), and he was sure (v. 29) that he would reach them richly endowed with Christian blessing for them. Such is faith. He would reach them not as a spiritual pauper, but with a well-filled purse of Christian blessing for their enjoyment and enrichment.

" If first I be somewhat filled with your company " (v. 24), i.e., " but before going on to Spain I will give myself a good long time of fellowship with you."

" Partakers " (v. 27), i.e., admitted to partnership in the Hebrew Church.

" Sealed to them this fruit " (v. 28) i.e., made sure that the poor saints at Jerusalem got the money.

Four subjects for prayer are detailed in verses 30-32, and their foundation and principle of energy declared. The foundation: Christ's interests; the energy: the love of the Spirit moving their hearts with sympathy (v. 5).

The four subjects are: that he might be delivered from hostile Jews at Jerusalem; that the money gift might be given in a right way and right spirit so as to be acceptable and not insulting; that he might reach Rome with joy; and that he

might there be refreshed with the believers.

The Acts of the Apostles records the answers to these prayers; but not just as the Apostle would have wished.

" Strived " (v. 20); " labour " (2 Cor. v. 9); " study " (1 Thess. iv. 11). One Greek verb meaning to make it a point of honour, or ambition, is represented by these three English words " strive," " labour," " study." This Greek verb only occurs in these three passages in the New Testament. Chronologically, Thessalonians comes first, then Corinthians and lastly Romans. This is important, for it shows how highly Paul estimated preaching the Gospel, and how he kept at it up to the very last. So he made it a point of honour and ambition as a citizen to be quiet, as a Christian to be well-pleasing, and as a preacher to be energetic.

Twenty-eight names appear in xvi. 1-16— twenty men and eight women. It is interesting that the first name is that of a woman, and that she was a minister of the Church at Cenchrea which was the port of Corinth. Ministry in the primitive Church was not confined to men.

Most probably it was at Ephesus (Acts xviii.) that Priscilla and Aquila risked their lives to save Paul. Priscilla, except when they are first mentioned, is always put first. No doubt she was a much more gifted minister than her husband.

Three groups of believers appear at this time in Rome:—the first (vs. 3-5) enjoyed the ministry of Priscilla and Aquila, in whose house the group met; the second (v. 14) was ministered to by the five brethren mentioned there; the third (v. 15) was served by the five leaders there recorded, three of whom were women. It is interesting that in these two latter groups five leaders respectively appear. The words " with them " (vs. 14 and 15) make it clear that the five respectively mentioned were leaders, or ministers, or bishops, or overseers, or elders. These titles are synonymous.

All these friends the Apostle must have met from time to time in his missionary journeys in the East. Some of them were his own relatives, e.g. Andronicus, Junia (v. 7), Herodion (v. 11), Lucius, Jason and Sosipater (v. 21).

Andronicus and Junia were not only apostles, they were more, they were notable apostles—not of the Hebrew Church, but of the Heavenly Church.

" Approved " (v. 10), i.e., a veteran in the faith.

Persis was a woman (v. 12). Rufus (v. 13) may have been the son of Simon of Cyrene (Mark xv. 21).

Five times the Holy Spirit commands Christians to salute one another with a fraternal kiss (Rom. xvi. 16, 1 Cor. xvi. 20, 2 Cor. xiii. 12, 1 Thess. v. 26, and 1 Peter v. 14). The Greek word for one another being masculine, the social customs of the time, and primitive Church history make it clear that this form of Christian greeting was confined to men with men and women with women.

The false preachers of verse 17, if avoided would have no hearers and thus be brought to silence.

" Your obedience " (v. 19), i.e., obedience to the doctrine of verse 17. This verse should read as in the Revised Version.

The principle of simplicity concerning evil was contrary to the teaching of heathen philosophers, who recommended acquaintance with evil—thus defiling themselves—in order to avoid it. Fellowship with God secures the wisdom which is good, and assures the simplicity which is lovely.

As the God of peace the Lord Christ (v. 18, R.V.) makes war against Satan, and will bruise him (v. 20). Here is a seeming contradiction—the Prince of Peace going forth to war ! The effect would be the discomfiture of those causing divisions (v. 17), and the establishment of fraternal peace in the Church at Rome ; and if this verse 20 was a prophecy, it must have been shortly afterwards fulfilled.

Where dissension is introduced the necessity of the grace of the Lord Jesus Christ is especially needed (v.20).

In verses 21-23 Paul's companions send their greetings to the brethren at Rome. Tertius would not be left out. He sends his salutation. So he was not an indifferent person just employed by the Apostle as his secretary, but a beloved brother whose heart was in the matter. This is interesting as showing what instruments the Holy Spirit employed even in a mediate writing of the Scriptures.

All these persons are mentioned in either the Acts, or the Epistles, or both. Gaius was no doubt the hospitable well-beloved of 3 John, 5 and 6. He was evidently not only very hospitable, but rich. Quartus had nothing distinctive like the others to mark his importance, so he is described as simply " the brother." He may have been a slave ; but yet he is coupled with Erastus who held the high position of city treasurer. His salutation is sent as well as that of the others.

In verses 25-27 the Apostle gathers together into a brief postscript of commanding grandeur all the wonderful teaching of the entire Epistle, with the addition of a reference to the great secret hidden from all times, first revealed to him, and then to all nations through his prophetic writings, of which the Epistle to the Ephesians is the principal.

" My Gospel " (v. 25), i.e., the glad tidings concerning the secret revealed to him.

" The preaching of Jesus Christ," i.e., salvation for all nations through Him on the principle of faith-obedience (as opposed to works) as commanded by the everlasting God. So Paul had a double ministry,—that of the Gospel, and that of " My Gospel," i.e., the Gospel of the Mystery.

Thus the Epistle begins with the Gospel, always revealed, never hidden, and closes with Paul's Gospel, always hidden, never revealed, This " mystery," i.e., secret, is the theme of the Epistle to the Ephesians.

Romans corresponds to Egypt and redemption; Corinthians and Galatians, to the Wilderness and weakness ; Ephesians, Philippians and Colossians, to Canaan and unfaithfulness, and Thessalonians to the true Solomon and glory.

1 CORINTHIANS

The Apostles Paul and Sosthenes (i. 1) wrote this letter at Philippi some time after Paul's first visit to Corinth (Acts xviii.).

Its keynote is " reproof " (2 Tim. iii. 16), because of departure from the moral teaching of the Epistle to the Romans.

Corinth was notorious for vice, as Athens was famous for philosophy.

The appeal of the letter is to the conscience rather than to the intellect.

1 CORINTHIANS I,—Having saluted them (vs. 2 and 3) and praised them because of their wealth of ministerial gifts (vs. 4-7) he reproves them for their divisions (vs. 10-17); for their desire for miraculous powers (v. 22); and for their pursuit of carnal skill in preaching (vs. 18-31).

" The will of God " (v. 1). Many at Corinth questioned Paul's Apostleship because he was not one of the Twelve (ix. 1-23). Hence his insistence that he was elected an Apostle by God (2 Cor. i. 1).

" And Sosthenes my brother Apostle " (vs. 23 and iv. 1 and 9). See notes on Eph. iii. 5 and 1 Thess. ii. 6.

A Judge when speaking officially from the Bench speaks of his companion judge as " my brother."

" All " (v. 2). The letter was intended for all believers as well as for the Corinthians. It was, therefore, a circular letter.

There are more quotations from the Old Testament in 1 and 2 Cor. and Galatians than in any other Books in the New Testament.

Six titles are given to the Lord Jesus Christ in verses 1-9. These reveal His glory, and rebuked the sectaries who boasted of Paul and Apollos, etc.

The grand substantive name " Christ," as distinguished from " The Christ," i.e., the Messiah, characterizes the Church Epistles.

The gifts which enriched the Corinthians confirmed the testimony respecting Christ, for they accredited His Person, His salvation, His position in the heavens, and that He gave gifts to men.

The crown and top-stone of their " knowledge (v. 5) was that they were waiting for the coming of the Lord (v. 7).

They confirmed the testimony of Christ, and He engaged Himself to confirm them up to the day of His Coming (vs. 6 and 8).

The assurance that they would be so confirmed was the fidelity of God Who had called them into the fellowship of His Son v. 9).

Without further preface the Apostle hastens to his first reproof, and does not hesitate to say who had informed him of the contentions at Corinth (v. 11).

The man who said " I am of Christ " (v. 12) was as much a sectarian as the man who said " I am of Paul," for he degraded the Lord to the level of a party leader.

Baptism " into the name of Paul " expressed attachment to Paul as a disciple.

Baptism is not necessary to salvation as many believe and teach, for, if so, then the Apostle thanked God that he saved so few ; nor is it essential to obedience, as others urge, for in that case the Apostle thanked God that he made so few obedient.

The argument that a master and not the servant is responsible for consequences (v. 15) is met (v. 17) by the statement that baptism was not in Paul's commission. It was a characteristic of the Pentecostal testimony to Israel, and foreign to the heavenly position of the Church.

" The preaching of the Cross " (v. 18), i.e., the doctrine of the Atonement. This verse should read as in the Revised Version.

The answer to the questions in verse 20 is

—" nowhere." " The wise," i.e., the Grecian philosopher. " The scribe," i.e., the Hebrew lawyer.

God by leaving man to his own wisdom (v. 21) demonstrated man's folly ; for he not only was incapable of knowing God, but he degraded Him to the level of a " creeping thing " (Rom. i.) in ancient times, and in modern days to a piece of bread which he first adores and then devours ; and, further, by offering him life on the principle of believing in opposition to the principle of merit, God demonstrated man's moral and intellectual corruption.

" The foolishness of preaching " (v. 21), i.e., the exceeding simplicity of a proclamation.

The Jews demanded that the religion of Jesus Christ should be accredited by physical wonders, and the Greeks, that it should be demonstrated by commanding arguments presented with intellectual splendour (v. 22). Both found it difficult to accept as God a dead man hanging on a cross, for such Christ was to them.

But to those whom God had elected to salvation both from among the Jews and Greeks, Christ was the great miracle of God and the great philosophy of God (v. 24)—the power of God in destroying sin and death, man's greatest foes, and the wisdom of God in devising a plan of salvation which pardoned guilty men and at the same time vindicated and glorified the justice of God.

The fact that the group of Christians at Corinth was composed mostly of poor men, and that they were " called " to the Gospel by men that were not noble (vs. 26-28), was a further demonstration of God's judgment of man's assumed importance and wisdom.

The Countess of Huntingdon based her hope for salvation on the letter M, for verse 26 does not read : " Not any noble," but " not many noble."

" Foolish, weak, base and despised " (vs. 27 and 28) contrast with " wisdom, righteousness, sanctification and redemption " (v. 30).

" Things which are not," i.e., which have no value in man's opinion (v. 28). Peter and John before the counsel (Acts iv. 13) did not possess a theological education. Their judges did. They enjoyed " things that are "; the Apostles, " things which are not " ; and yet they brought their judges to nought.

All the riches of salvation are lodged in Christ (v. 30). The believer, therefore, cannot boast of anything in himself, but he can glory of all that he possesses in the Lord Jesus.

I CORINTHIANS II.—As to-day so in Paul's day people demanded that the Gospel should be preached in " terms of modern thought " embellished with scholastic learning, convincing logic, forensic reasoning and cultured eloquence. The Apostle refused, declared such culture to be the wisdom of this world, and said that preaching according to the Divine wisdom was preaching in the power of the Holy Spirit, and that that was the only power which effected the moral result of the new birth (vs. 1-5).

" The mystery of God " (v. 1, R.V.), i.e., the Divine secret of the Church as revealed in Ephesians. It could not be revealed to the Corinthians because of their feeble spiritual condition (iii. 1-4).

The theme of Apostolic preaching was the Divine Person and atoning work of the great God and Saviour Jesus Christ (v. 2).

" Perfect " (v. 6), i.e., of full age, or the initiated.

The secret hidden in God, ordained before the world, was the glory to which the Church is destined. Compare verses 1, 7, and the Epistle to the Ephesians.

" Crucified the Lord of Glory " (v. 8). These words affirm the Deity and Humanity of Christ.

The Old Testament—the Father for man ; the Gospels—the Son with man ; the Epistles —the Holy Spirit in man.

" Things prepared " (v. 9) under the Old Covenant ; " things revealed " (v. 10) under the New Covenant. See note on Isa. lxiv. 4 and 5.

The personality and God-head of the Holy Spirit are declared in verses 10-13 ; for God-head cannot be separated from the Spirit of God as manhood cannot be separated from the spirit of man.

" Comparing spiritual things with spiritual," i.e., communicating spiritual truths to spiritual men through a spiritual medium, i.e., the Holy Spirit.

All who have not been born again of the Holy Spirit are " natural men " (v. 14). They cannot recognise nor experience spiritual phenomena. They are foolishness unto them (v. 14). Spirit-born people (v. 15) can discern all things, but their actions and their motives cannot be understood by the unconverted. The true Christian life is unintelligible to human wisdom, just as God's mind and ways are beyond natural wisdom (v. 16).

" As it is written " (v. 9). Here the Holy Spirit gives the sense rather than the words of the quotation. He, as the Divine Author, is at liberty to alter the arrangement of the words, and to add to them. So what He says universally in Isaiah He here says particularly in 1 Corinthians.

I CORINTHIANS III.—" And I, brethren " (v. 1), rather, " So I, brethren."

The proof that they were like men of the world, i.e., carnal men, is shown in verses 3 and 4. They acted and spoke in the same way that men of the world act and speak.

" Are one " (v. 8), i.e., have the same aim.

The figure of verses 6-8 is that of husbandry; the figure of verses 10-17 is that of building.

The Divine foundation laid by God is Jesus Christ (v. 11). Paul as a skilful master-builder in fellowship with God, laid the Gospel foundation (v. 10). On that foundation preachers can build up doctrines either precious, worthless, or destructive (vs. 12 and 17). Their converts will correspond. A day of testing will come; what is worthless will be burned up, but the preacher himself will be brought through the judgment. Doctrines which destroy foundation truth (v. 17), and the preachers of such doctrines, will be destroyed together in another judgment.

These verses overturn and do not affirm, as some say, the doctrine of purgatory This fire lasts only for a day. It is future, not present; it is destructive, not purificative; it destroys doctrines and not persons; it causes loss and not gain.

God's spiritual temple is formed of living stones (Eph. ii. 20-22 and 1 Pet. ii. 5). In that temple the Holy Spirit dwells. It is holy; and its stones, i.e., new-born sinners, are also holy (v. 17).

" A fool " (v. 18), i.e., in the estimation of the world (v. 19).

The quotation from Job, v. 13 proves the inspiration of that Book.

It was foolish for a man to appropriate only one apostle, for they all belonged to him (v. 22), and much more, for all things were his because he was Christ's and Christ is God's.

" With God " (v. 19), i.e., God judges the wisdom of this world to be foolishness.

I CORINTHIANS IV.—All Christian people should regard themselves and regard each other as simply servants and stewards (v. 1).

As to stewards, what is most required by a master is faithfulness (v. 2). Servants are not to judge one another (v. 3), nor to judge themselves, for though a servant may know nothing against himself, yet that does not prove him to be without blame (v. 4). The master only is entitled to judge (v. 5). Servants, therefore, must not exercise premature judgment upon each other but wait till the Master comes, and He will bring to light hidden actions and secret motives, and then every servant shall receive the praise due to him, if he merits praise.

" A figure " (v. 6), i.e., the apostle figures himself and Apollos as servants and stewards so that the Corinthians might learn to treat them as such—for so God's servants are described in the Written Word—and thus none of them would boast of Paul as better than Apollos, nor of Apollos as superior to Paul.

Individual saints distinguished by miraculous gifts are addressed personally (v. 7) and reminded that no one can boast of that which he merely receives. A man can only boast of that which he creates.

In verses 8-13 a contrast is drawn between the gifted and popular believers at Corinth, reigning as kings upon their thrones, and Paul and his brother apostles Sosthenes, Apollos, Timotheus, etc., clothed with shame and treated as refuse.

Paul longed (v. 8) that Christ's Kingdom were really come and that they did reign as kings; for in that case he and his companions would reign with them. Here is felt the throb of a noble heart wounded in its affections.

In the ancient amphitheatre the greatest criminals appointed to death were brought forth last as a spectacle to gratify the brutal passions of the multitude on seeing them torn to pieces by wild beasts (v. 9).

The language of verses 8 and 10 is ironical.

He besought them to imitate him in walking so closely with the Lord Jesus Christ that they would meet with the same contempt and hatred which men showed to Christ (v. 16); and, therefore, he sent Timotheus to them to remind them of his Christian manner of life taught by him in every church (v. 17).

Some boasted that his sending Timothy showed that he would not come himself, and so was, as some asserted, fickle of purpose. But he said, " Come to you I will, and that shortly " (v. 19). " Know," i.e., get to know and expose.

God's moral kingdom (v. 20) is not an assemblage of words but a life of spiritual realities lived in the power of the Holy Spirit.

Conscience is not an infallible guide (v. 4). There is but one infallible guide—the Word of God.

" A rod " (v. 21), i.e., the punitive power to hand men over to Satan for the destruction of their flesh by sickness or death (v. 5). This power ceased with the Apostolic Age. Many to-day pretend to this power, as claiming to be in the apostolic succession, but they cannot punish any one with any form of physical sickness.

1 CORINTHIANS V.—Roman and Grecian law legalized polygamy. One of the leaders in the Church at Corinth, claiming that Gospel liberty emancipated from national and civil law, took one of his father's wives into his home, and his action was applauded (vs. 1-20) by the Assembly. This action was not, on the surface, motived by animal passion but by false religious philosophy; but this only made his conduct, example and teaching the more deadly to the spiritual life and the more destructive to the Gospel.

This chapter, therefore, uncovers something of the evil and folly of the natural heart even in a Christian; and also illustrates the depths of Satan in cunningly persuading Christian men that grossly immoral conduct is exalted Christian liberty

The apostle sternly reproved this man, and commanded that he should be handed over to Satan for the destruction of his flesh.

God uses Satan as an instrument of discipline (v. 5). Such he became to Job (Job. ii. 4-7) to Paul, (2 Cor. xii. 7) and to Peter (Luke xxii. 31).

This terrible power of committal unto Satan was peculiar to that time; for God was then in the camp, and His presence there judged evil, and was death to the flesh. Such was He to the Hebrew Church also at the first; but when because of persistence in evil, He left the camp, men found they could sin with impunity. So when corruption entered the Christian Church power left it; and it is now consequently weak and fallen, and its professing members can sin without fear of physical pain.

One false teacher in the Christian fellowship, or one evil member, can corrupt the entire company. The Divine principle of action in such a case is expulsion (v. 13).

The companionship of professing Christians who do not walk with God in separation from the world is more dangerous to the believer than necessary contact with unconverted people (vs. 9-12).

Judgment characterized the primitive church in respect of doctrine or conduct; compromise governs the modern church. The one principle is divine; the other, human.

2 Cor. ii. 6-8 records the happy effect of this threatened discipline.

Verse 1 should read as in the Revised Version.

The true Christian repents of his own sins and mourns because of the sins of others (v. 2).

Verse 7 establishes the principle of typical teaching, for it states that the Paschal lamb of Exod. xii. foreshadowed the Lamb of God of the New Testament.

Leaven is invariably in the Scriptures a figure of false doctrine or of evil generally. See notes on Matt. xiii. 33. In Leviticus leaven was permitted when the offering represented the offerer, because he was sinful, but it was forbidden when the offering represented Christ. for he was sinless (Lev. vii. 12 and 13).

The Christian feast of love, joy and peace, cost the Lord Jesus shame and tears and blood (vs. 7 and 8). It was to be observed after a heavenly and spiritual manner and not as a supper with material bread. See notes on Ezek. xlviii.

True Christian liberty is liberty to live a life of holiness (v. 8), and that liberty was purchased at the expense of Christ's priceless life.

1 CORINTHIANS VI.—The sixth and seventh reproofs now follow—the first, against litigation (vs. 1-11); the second, against fornication (vs. 12-20).

Not only were they blameworthy in citing one another before the civil judges (v. 1), but they were altogether at fault in going to law one with another (v. 7). They should rather suffer injustice (v. 7). But far from shewing such Christian acceptance of wrong, they themselves did wrong (v. 8), forgetting that wrong-doers shall not inherit the Kingdom of God (v. 9). And he pressed the point that they were to cherish no illusion as to this, for none of the characters pointed to in verses 9 and 10 should ever dwell with God.

In these seven reproofs (i.-vii.), the apostle takes the highest ground. Here he recalls the two amazing facts that believers are to govern the world (v. 2)—and more wonderful still—to govern angels! (v. 3).

Verse 4 is ironical, as verse 5 proves.

At that day, as to-day, men professing the Christian faith taught that all physical passions and appetites (v. 12) were as lawful as eating and drinking, and were to be as freely gratified. Hence free love was a legitimate passion (v. 13). But the Apostle called it fornication, and commanded that it should be fled from (v. 18); and, always placing the matter on the highest level, he asks with horror, are Christ's members to be taken away from Him and made the members of an harlot? (v. 15). Whoever so acted became one flesh with her (v. 16); but the true Christian becomes one spirit with the Lord (v. 17). Every other sin whatsoever is external to the body, but this particular sin is against one's own body (v. 18).

As in the prior rebuke, so here two amazing statements are made, one that the Lord exists for the believer's body (v. 13)—He ministers to it, He cherishes it, and He will raise it from the grave (v. 14); and the other, that the believer's body is a sanctuary of the Holy Spirit (v. 19).

The Christian is not his own, he has been bought with a price—not with silver and gold, but with the precious blood of Christ; he is, therefore, a slave, and his body has been redeemed not for the purpose of practising impurity but by saintly conduct for glorifying God (v. 20, R.V.).

Verses 9 and 11, interpret Lev. xiii. and xiv. The lepers and their exclusion from the camp of God are viewed in verses 9 and 10, and their triple cleansing in verse 11, which, accordingly, should read as in the Revised Version margin. See notes on Lev. xiv. 1-20, and compare the triple cleansing of Rom. i. to viii.

1 CORINTHIANS VII.—The Apostle now begins to reply to the questions asked in the letter to him from the Corinthians (v. 1), but not until he had first given them his seven rebukes. They said nothing in their letter about these seven faults for which he reproved them. Such is the natural heart! It eagerly discusses social, ecclesiastical, and even doctrinal questions, but is blind to personal moral faults.

In this chapter the Apostle replies to questions respecting marriage, divorce, giving in marriage, and the duty of a slave in respect to freedom.

Guided by ix. 1-6 it is deducible that Paul's opponents at Corinth argued that he could not be an Apostle because he was unmarried. To be a celibate was to be a rebel against God's marriage laws. Therefore Paul was a rebel, and celibacy was an unholy and immoral condition. The Apostle replies (v. 1) that it is not sinful but " good " for a man to be unmarried, but he added (v. 2) that because of the prevalency of fornication at Corinth it was better that all the members of the Church there should be married and so present to that profligate city a testimony of family affection and purity.

The married were not to defraud (v. 5) one another of the " benevolence " of verse 3.

Satan often tempts with distressing doubts the heart that aims at too much and fails; and he also tempts because of deficiency in self-control (v. 5).

The intimate fellowship that Paul enjoyed with the Lord Jesus appears in verse 6. He was permitted, but not commanded, to write thus.

God indeed ordained marriage before man sinned, and so whoever opposes it must suffer the judgment of God. But sin marred everything of nature. A power altogether above nature, i.e., the power of the Holy Spirit, can lift the creature above nature; and to a very few is granted the gift (v. 7) of walking in that power. The Apostle wished that because of the then existing distress (vs. 26, 28 and 29) and the approaching trials connected with the Divine judgments upon Israel and Jerusalem, that all men in the Church at Corinth had received the same gift of continency as had been given to him.

Here (vs. 6, 10, 25, and 40) is to be distinguished the difference between spiritual thoughts and inspiration. The ignorance of " Modern Thought " confounds these. The Apostle gives his opinion as a spiritual man— his mind animated and guided by the Holy Spirit—but contrasts that opinion with inspiration, and with what the Lord said.

So in his Epistles everything is inspired except when otherwise stated (v. 12). It is clear, therefore, that the Apostle knew he was inspired when writing his Epistles. He affirms their inspiration ; he says they were to be received as emanating from the Lord Himself.

Grecian and Roman law permitted a woman to divorce her husband (vs. 10 and 13).

Under the Law (Ezra x. 3) the heathen wife and her children were ceremonially " un-clean;" and, therefore, ejected from the earthly family of God. But under grace it was not so (v. 14). Had Israel's repentance permitted the visible establishment of the Messianic Kingdom on earth, the believing husband could have brought in his heathen wife and their children. They would not have been treated as " unclean."

" Uncircumcised " (v. 18), i.e., by a surgical operation.

The words " is everything " should be supplied at the end of verse 19.

A slave was to live in the power of being Christ's freed man ; and that power would deliver him from depression of heart because he was a slave. But if he could obtain his freedom he should do so, for thus he would be liberated from the capricious government of a heathen master and be free to wholly serve the Lord. But all, whether bond or free, were to be most concerned with their relation toward God (v. 24).

" Virgins " (v. 25), i.e., unmarried people, whether men or women. Compare Rev. xiv. 4.

Divine love operating in the soul of the Apostle desired to shield them from trouble, i.e., from family cares (v. 28).

Here may be felt the very throbbings of the heart of God. Everything that affects His people is of commanding interest to Him. Nothing is too small for that wonderful love. He would have His children free from cares (v. 32, R.V.) ; and His children's ambition should be to please Him (v. 32).

A father should give his daughter in marriage if she so wished ; her will was to override his, she was to be permitted to marry her suitor (v. 36). But if she had no will in the matter, and if his means permitted him to support her, then, owing to the then present circumstances, he would show more love to her as his child if he kept her with him (v. 37). Thus God thinks of young women and courtship and marriage ; and His principle in such legislation is affection.

The Corinthians boasted of their spiritual knowledge. The Apostle meets them with gentle irony on their own ground (v. 40) saying, " I think that I also have the Spirit of God," thus conveying the reproof that he was conscious of having an intelligence which they only claimed.

The contrast between the purity, refinement, sympathy, respect and liberty of these marriage laws, and the impurity, grossness, cruelty and slavery of those of the Koran and of the Vedas, is most striking.

1 CORINTHIANS VIII.—Having answered their questions about marriage and slavery, the Apostle now replies to those regarding the eating of food offered to idols ; and his reply is contained in chapters viii. to xi. The denial of self, and love to others, form the keynote of his reply.

For the sake of others Paul denied himself the enjoyment of flesh food (viii.), the sweet companionship of a wife (ix.), and the relief of a salary (ix.), and said that he kept under his body lest while inviting others to the Christian race he himself should fail of a prize ; and he pointed to the fate of Israel in the desert (x.) as a warning to all who gratified their appetite for special food without consideration for the spiritual welfare of others. He reasoned with these Corinthians that there should be no connection whatsoever between the religious feasts of the heathen and the weekly fellowship supper of the Christians ; he urged that at that meal self should be denied and the food shared with the hungry ; and he recalled how the Lord thus acted the last time that He supped with his disciples (xi.).

Knowledge, i.e., such knowledge as all have (v. 1), puffs up with selfishness and grieves the Holy Spirit, but love builds up in unselfishness and pleases God.

Animals were offered at that time in sacrifice to idols, and the flesh was eaten at feasts in the Temples, or in private houses, or offered for sale in the public market. The Law (Num. xxv. 2) and the Twelve Apostles (Acts xv.) forbade the eating of such meat ; but the fuller church revelation given to Paul liberated him, and all who listened to his teaching, from these ordinances. To him an idol had no being (v. 4) ; and, therefore, meat was not profaned if offered to an idol, i.e., to an illusion, but remained for him God's pure gift.

But to "weak" brethren the idol did exist ; and, therefore, if they ate of meat consecrated to it they violated their conscience, and by doing so put themselves upon a road that led to moral and spiritual ruin. Because of this, therefore, the Apostle denied himself the enjoyment of such meat (v. 13).

Knowledge is imperfect (v. 2) ; but God will acknowledge as His those who love Him, however imperfect their knowledge (v. 3). He will not say to these " I never knew you."

Though an idol has no being, yet all who worship idols worship devils, for demons introduced such worship to man (x. 20).

The sun, moon, and stars in heaven, and deified kings, heroes, and beasts on earth are those pointed to in verse 5.

The words of verse 8 are evidently taken from the letter Paul received from Corinth. They urged that the believer's " standing " before God is not affected by what he eats or does not eat, for meat does not commend the believer to God. The Apostle admitted the truth of this, but begged them to take heed lest this knowledge, if given liberty of action, should stumble others. The Apostle could eat meat in an idol's temple because he knew that idols and idolatries and temples were all illusions, but he would not do so lest his indulgence of self should cause the moral destruction of his brother for whose salvation Christ gave His very life. Some of the Christians at Corinth tempted their brethren to their condemnation instead of denying themselves in order to their salvation.

So love decided this question, and denied self lest, so far as it depended on the believer himself, his action in eating might lead another to moral ruin. God would indeed guard His " weak " child, but that would in no wise diminish the sin of him who led his brother to sin against his conscience.

I **CORINTHIANS IX.** 1-23—As Christ's

freed-man and as an apostle, Paul was entitled to marry (v. 5) and to receive a salary from the church (vs. 4, 6-15), but he denied himself these privileges that he might benefit others and by all means save some (vs. 19-23). The fact that he was an apostle, and, therefore, possessed the highest claim to consider what was due to his rank, but did not do so, is pressed by him in support of his appeal to the Corinthians to live for others and not for themselves.

Paul saw the Lord corporeally and not only in a vision (v. 1, xv. 8, Acts ix. 7 and 17).

" Power to eat and to drink " (v. 4), i.e., without having to labour (v. 6).

The Christian's wife should be a sister in the faith (v. 5).

He who ordained the law of Deut. xxv. 4 is the same as He who ordained that of Luke x. 7, (vs. 9 and 14). This is a testimony that Jesus and Jehovah is the one God.

The Apostle took a salary from other churches (2 Cor. xi. 8), but not from the Corinthians lest, in their case, he should hinder the Gospel of Christ (vs. 12 and 15).

God cares for oxen (v. 9) and for His people too (v. 10).

In verses 16 and 17 Paul recalls the parable of the talents, and points to the reward assured to him if faithful, but to the certain judgment awaiting him if he should hide the Gospel talent committed to him.

" Abuse not my power " (v. 18), i.e., use not to the full his privilege in claiming maintenance.

All Christian people should be governed by the noble passion of soul-winning (vs. 19-23).

In verse 23 the Gospel is personified. The verse should read as in the Revised Version.

I **CORINTHIANS IX. 24—X.** 14—Close to Corinth on the Isthmian Plain annual athletic games were held and were famous throughout the world. A competitor had to produce three certificates : one to attest birth as a Greek ; a second to prove that he had been ten months in training ; and the third to certify that he was free from all legal claims. Failure in any one of these respects resulted in being " cast away," i.e., forbidden to compete.

The Apostle pictures himself (v. 27) as urging others to engage in the contests and yet being himself disqualified.

His argument is that those who strove in these games, whether as runners (v. 24), wrestlers (v. 25), or boxers (v. 26), denied themselves pleasant foods so as to obtain the mastery, and that if a corruptible crown was worth such self-denial, how much more an incorruptible !

The crown which Paul longed for (1 Thess. ii. 19) was the winning of men to Christ. In that contest he ran not uncertainly but with assurance ; and he did not aimlessly fight the air, but hit hard and straight at his own body and held it in subjection, lest it should hinder him from winning his desired diadem (v. 27).

Israel refused to deny self and demanded the flesh-pots of Egypt, and so became " a castaway " in the desert (x. 1-11).

" Moreover " (v. 1) : this should read "for," thus shewing the connection with the word " castaway."

The greatest baptismal scene of the Scriptures is that of verse 2. It necessarily included a multitude of infants ; and though it was a true baptism yet no water touched any of the baptized. All were baptized " into " Moses, and thereby became his " body " (Jude 9).

The five " alls " in verses 1-4 emphasize the five downward moral steps of verses 6-10—the argument being that the very persons who enjoyed these five privileges were the very same who five times so deeply sinned.

The subject of this section of the Epistle (viii.-xi.) being the denial of self in the eating of meat offered to idols, the Apostle points to the fact (vs. 6, 7, 9, and 10) that food gratification largely caused the downfall of Israel.

The order of those examples is here moral ; in Exodus, chronological. This is designed. The five successive steps are downward, and they may be recognised to-day.

The first .step in the experience of the backslider (v. 6) is a distaste for the Bible and a desire for novels and theatres (Num. xi. 4-6).

The next step is the substitution in the heart of a worldly religion for Christ—for the heart must have a religion; so when Christ is dethroned there, an idol is of necessity enthroned. (Exod. xxxii. 6). See notes on that chapter (v. 7).

The third step always follows the second in this moral sphere. It is fellowship with the world. That is, spiritual adultery, for the world is Christ's great rival for the affections of the heart, and when the rival is preferred the marriage bond is defiled (Num. xxv. 1-9). Twenty-four thousand perished at that sad time, and here the Holy Spirit adds the terrible fact that 23,000 of them perished on one day alone (v. 8).

Infidelity is the fourth step (v. 9). Compare Psalm lxxviii. 18 and Numbers xxi. 6.

The first three downward steps lead surely to scepticism, which is the fourth step.

The fifth and last step is a resolution to throw Christ and the Bible aside and to go back altogether to the world (v. 10). Israel said, "let us make a captain and return to Egypt" (Num. xiv. 4).

The believer's responsibility is to take heed lest he fall (v. 12), and to keep trusting the faithfulness of that God who will not permit his child to be tested beyond his strength, but will furnish *the* appropriate way of escape in every time of temptation. See Greek Text.

1 **CORINTHIANS X. 15—XI. 1.**—The Christian principle of denying self, especially in the matter of eating and drinking, is here applied to public (v. 16) and private (v. 27) meals. The Christian is taught that he is a member of a fellowship (v. 17), and, therefore responsible for the spiritual health of his brothers and sisters (vs. 24 and 32). All food was allowable (v. 23) because of Divine creation (v. 26), but self-gratification was to be denied in favour of communal edification (v. 23).

Idolaters at that time, and previously (Exod. xxxii. 6), observed fellowship feasts in honour of their idols. The Apostle said that these idols had no existence, and that the dedication of food to them neither sanctified nor profaned it. But he declared (v. 20 and Deut xxxii. 17) that Satan was behind the idolatry, and that the nations worshipped demons and not God This Apostolic declaration is contradicted by " modern thought," which asserts that the heathen when adoring their idols adore God.

The Christians at that time had also their fellowship feast. It was enjoyed on the first day of each week, and history records that the food consisted of meat and roast fowls and bread and wine, and other edibles. Christ was assumed to be the Host and those who attended were His guests ; so it was called " the Lord's Table "; the other was called " the table of devils " (v. 21), i.e.,

Satan's table, for he is the prince of the demons.

The Apostle argues that to gratify the appetite at both tables meant the association of demons with the Messiah. It placed them on an equality. Such action provoked Jehovah to jealousy, and of the result of conflict with Him and His superior strength there could be no question (v. 22). Holy jealousy is an activity of Divine love.

The bread which they broke, and the cup for which they gave thanks (vs. 16 and 17), are covering terms expressive of all the food that was upon the table. They symbolized the common spiritual life which animated all the guests, and the common brotherhood into which they were born.

But there was fellowship with Christ as well as with one another. The meal expressed a participation with Him, as foreshadowed by the participation of the worshipper in the Wilderness with the altar (v. 18). And just as in that case the death of the Peace-offering was necessary in order to the feast, so the fellowship meal at Corinth was based upon, and only possible because of, the out-pouring of Christ's precious blood. Thus the meal was a participation in the body and blood of the Lord, and outwardly expressed in shadow the inward reality of John vi. 51-65.

The fact contrasted sharply with the Table of Demons, for none of them had sacrificed himself in order to provide a feast for his worshippers. But Christ did so, and in doing so denied Himself; and upon this fact the Apostle based his powerful appeal that they should imitate Him (xi. 1). See note on 1 John iii. 16.

For conscience sake (vs. 25 and 28), i.e., the conscience of the vendor (v. 25), and the conscience of the host or fellow-guest (v. 28).

At the Passover Feast the third cup was termed "the cup of blessing." The employment of this term (v. 16), and the reference to the Passover itself (xi. 23), emphasized the Messianic and temporary character of this fellowship supper. It was earthly and not heavenly; and had relationship to the Lord's return to the earth (xi. 26).

The first Passover illustrates verses 16 and 17. It was a family feast. They all came together into one place. It was a communion of the blood, i.e., the life of the lamb—for they owed their common life to the death of the lamb—and it was a communion of the body of the lamb, for its flesh furnished the food of which they all partook in common. So they had fellowship with the lamb (Christ) and with one another; and anyone who acted in an unworthy manner, i.e., by selfish indulgence, sinned against that fellowship.

The Table of Demons having ceased to exist as a public religious observance, the Christian Fellowship meal therefore lost its counter-significance and testimony and use.

The majority of Christian people believe that the Lord instituted a sacred supper—apart from the Passover—on the night of the betrayal, and that the observance of that supper is obligatory upon His people until He come again.

But the Scripture says that "as they were eating" the Paschal Supper (Mark xiv. 22, R.V.) He handed them the bread and wine. This was always done at the Passover by whoever presided. Nowhere in the Scriptures is it said that Christ instituted a supper.

Many to-day try to imitate this communion supper. But an imitation has neither power nor meaning; and to-day it emphasizes division and not communion. Daniel and his companions did not try to set up in Babylon an imitation of the Temple at Jerusalem. They made God Himself their Sanctuary (Ezek. xi. 16, R.V.), and read the Scriptures (Daniel ix. 2), and prayed together (Daniel ii. 17 and 18).

The Church is now in captivity. The sheep are scattered (John x. 12). A supper illustrating and symbolizing communion is therefore impossible; but God remains, and His scattered children find in Him an unfailing source of fellowship and blessing.

"The communion" (v. 16). This should read "a communion" (R.V.).

"Followers," i.e., imitators (xi. 1., R.V.).

Paul denied self, and in conduct imitated and obeyed his Master's symbolic action and command at the Paschal Supper, for he gave his body and blood for others (1 John iii. 16), and he pressed the Corinthians to imitate him in his imitation of Christ.

1 CORINTHIANS XI. 2-34.—Here, together with chapters xii. and xiv., is found

a picture of the Corinthian fellowship supper. Had it been baptized in the love of chapter xiii., it would have been a scene of great moral beauty and wonder. But the facts, as disclosed here, mingle sadness with interest.

It was a fellowship meal—rich and poor, masters and servants, men and women and children all dined together. The Lord the Messiah was the unseen Host. The table was His. The guests were His, and were, therefore, on an equality before Him. During the meal and after it they sang hymns; they united in prayer; they read and expounded the Scriptures; they prophesied; and they spoke in various languages both human and angelic. Women ministered as well as men, but they, as to government, had not the same authority. They had to practise the denial of self. The men also had to exercise the same denial by recognizing their subjection to the Host, of whose spotless Humanity the Head was God (vs. 3-16).

The rebellion of these wives against the authority of their husbands (v. 3, and 1 Tim. ii. 11, 12); the selfish gluttony of others (v. 21); and the intrusion of caste (vs. 18 and 22) proved that the Lord's conduct at the last supper that He ate in denying Himself necessary food and handing it to others, and so considering them and not Himself, was not imitated at Corinth, but that a contrary principle prevailed. This the Apostle rebukes; and he commanded that those with large appetites should satisfy them at home (v. 34). If all did so, then the communion would be as truly expressed when they came together without the eating of a material supper. The important principle was that each one should discern the "body" (v. 29), i.e., their fellow-christians, for, if not, they sinned against the Head of the body (v. 27).

The Apostle praised them that they remembered and observed His teachings (v. 2); but He judged their practices (v. 17).

The head of the wife is the husband (v. 3); and women were to submit to the custom of that day (v. 6) in the public acknowledgment of it. This custom does not obtain to-day; but the principle remains. Christian women, therefore, are at liberty to preach and pray in public unveiled, but they are not at liberty to claim governmental equality in the Church, or authority over their husbands (see note on 1 Tim. ii. 12).

At that time women of bad character were shaven. Hence for a woman to appear in public unveiled covered her with shame (vs. 5 and 6).

God originated at the Creation the relationship of husband and wife (v. 12) and of child and parent (v. 11).

Because of the angels (v. 10, R.V.). This is, as yet, impossible of explanation. It is suggested that angels veil their faces before God, and that women should imitate them. Or, that angels are spectators (iv. 9) of the Christian Assemblies, and that this fact should determine believers to maintain order in their meetings. Or, that angels recognise their subjection to man, and so effectively veil themselves that though always present yet are they never seen (Heb. i. 14 and Matt. xviii. 10).

In the East the woman veiled herself (Gen. xxiv. 65) in modesty and subjection and as expressive of fidelity to her husband (Gen. xx. 16). The head of a suspected wife was uncovered (Num. v. 18), indicating her having withdrawn from the power and government of her husband. At that time, therefore, for a woman to veil herself shewed that she accepted of her own will that subjection to her husband which nature taught her by adorning her with long hair (vs. 14 and 15).

"First of all" (v. 18), i.e., as to their conduct at the fellowship supper. His second subject of condemnation (xii. 1) respected their misuse at that meal of the spiritual gifts with which they had been enriched by God.

"Divisions" (v. 18) and "heresies" (v. 19), i.e., as suggested by verses 20 and 21—distinctions made between the rich and the poor. This made it impossible to really eat a communal meal which could justly be called the Lord's supper, for at His table, and because of His presence, all the guests were dwarfed into equality—all became brethren.

The language of verses 21 to 29 destroy the meaning and teaching based upon this fraternal meal by the Protestant, the Greek, and the Roman Churches. If it had the supernatural and awe-inspiring significance which they all in common, to a greater or less degree, believe that it has, the Apostle could never sum up his commands respecting it (v. 33), by telling them that when they met together to eat it they were "to tarry for one another"; and that anyone that was too hungry to do so (v. 34), and was a householder (v. 22), was to dine at home. A general acceptance of this direction would, therefore, have led to an observance of this fellowship feast in a spiritual manner without material food, as is the habit in the Salvation Army and in the Society of Friends, and as legislated for in the Visitation of the sick in the Church of England Prayer Book.

At this Corinthian fellowship supper the rich ate and drank to repletion and refused to share their abundance with their brethren who were mostly slaves and who were compelled to sit by and hunger (vs. 21 and 22). Not so acted the Lord, said the Apostle (v. 23), for He at His last fellowship supper gave the food to His brethren, declaring that it symbolized the giving of Himself—His very flesh and blood—for them. This indeed was self-denial; and here is the climax of the Apostle's argument. To sacrifice self and self interest for the profit of others is to effectually shew forth the Lord's death till He come, for it is an exhibition of the great principle which animated that death.

So the words to be noted are; " Everyone taketh," but He said " Take ye "—. . . . . " this do " (vs. 21, 24), Jesus " gave " (Luke xxii. 19), 1 John iii. 16 explains the meaning of the Lord's words and action.

To emphasize the argument the Apostle reminds them that it was on the night of the betrayal when all should forsake Him that it was with such men that He supped, and it was for such men that He died. They did not merit such love. So ought the Christian to act towards even the most unworthy.

" Is " i.e., " represents " (v. 24).

" The cup " (v. 25). The Passover supper was closed by the host handing to the guests the final cup. There were not two suppers that night, as people suppose. (See Mark xiv. 22, R.V.). This cup symbolized the New Covenant based upon the Atonement (" in My blood.") " This cup is the new covenant." Can sacerdotalists explain how a cup becomes transubstantiated into a covenant?

" Unworthily " (v. 27), i.e., in an unworthy manner—" not discerning the body " (v. 29, R.V.), i.e., ignoring the fact that they were members of a brotherhood—a body—that the

Lord had purchased for Himself at the price of His own precious blood. To eat one's own supper (v. 21), and not share it with the hungry, was to ignore the brotherhood, and so sin against the body and blood of the Lord (v. 27). This angered Him (vs. 29-32), for He recognised the table as His. No such punitive power appears to-day in connection with the tables which almost all sections of Christianity have set up in imitation of the table at Corinth; and, consequently, it is plain that Christ does not recognise any one of them. But there are multitudes of true Christians who are unable without the use of material bread and wine to sup with the Lord and remember Him in His death and passion. These Paul would gently describe as " weak brethren," and he would deny himself and unite with them, because he believed and taught that those who like himself were " strong," i.e., brought by the Spirit into the teaching of Ephesians and Hebrews, ought to bear the infirmity of the " weak " and not to please themselves. So he would eat with them.

At the Passover Israel showed forth the death of the Paschal Lamb and confessed that they owed their redemption to its blood.

The true Paschal Lamb having been slain, the Apostle Paul, and all like him who were Jews inwardly (Rom. ii. 29), observed the feast after a heavenly manner, for the presence of the Risen Lord in the midst abolishes all memorials of His absence.

Verse 26 should read " Show ye," as in the margin and not " ye do show." The argument of the entire passage, as already pointed out, makes this reading clear. Associate " Shine ye " (Phil. ii. 15 margin.)

Had the Messiah commanded water baptism and the breaking of bread as universally and perpetually obligatory, as most people believe, then would He have created a universal climate to make both possible; but they are impossible in vast regions of the earth. They can, however, be everywhere spiritually observed, as taught in chapter v. 7, and as intended in John i. 33, and vi. 48-58, and 1 John iii. 16.

At the Passover the Lord acted as a servant. He washed the disciple's feet, and He handed them the bread and wine saying, " Ye should do as I have done," and " this do in remembrance of Me "—i.e., " give your lives for others as I am giving Mine for you."

1 **CORINTHIANS XII.** 1-27 — Having "first of all" (xi. 18) rebuked their un-Christlike and selfish conduct at the communal supper-table, the Apostle now, in the second place, reproved their selfish action in respect of the "gifts" which the Holy Spirit had given them for the profit of all (vii. 7). They selfishly misused both the material and spiritual gifts of God. Chapter xi. records the former, and chapters xii. and xiv. the latter.

Selfishness in the physical realm is deplorable but in the spiritual realm it is destructive. Convention-goers have to watch against this latter sin. The gratification of physical self is degrading; the gratification of religious self is dishonouring. Such is man's heart. He will use even spiritual gifts as instruments of personal indulgence, and as a platform for personal importance.

This chapter states that there is only One Divine Spirit (1-11); that He has a treasury of gifts; that He gives these gifts to men; but not all to one man but distributively to many men; that each one is to use his "gift" not for his own gratification or glory but for communal profit (v. 7), and this because the Christian assembly is comparable unto the human body (vs. 12-27). As therefore the members in the body mutually aid one another and do not desire selfish isolation and function, so the members of the Body of Christ should recognise their mutual relationship and dependence.

The Greeks and Romans believed there were many divine spirits, but these in reality were Satanic agents who were permitted at that time to incarnate themselves, and the inspired utterances of their afflicted victims were accepted by the heathen as divine messages. These "spirits" carried the Gentiles away unto the worship of idols, which themselves were dumb—but the demons who energized idolatry were not dumb (v. 2).

The utterances of the One Divine Spirit could easily be recognised, for He testified always of Christ, declaring Him to be Jehovah (v. 3).

Satan changes his methods. In Paul's day his plan was opposition to truth; to-day it is corruption of truth. So Satan imitates God in dispensational purpose and activity. When God spoke through Apostles, Prophets, and Teachers, Satan spoke through his human agents, and now that God speaks to men through the Holy Scriptures Satan speaks to them through his unholy scriptures. Hence the multitudes of books now produced, professedly in support of the Bible, but in reality in opposition to it. Confusion and corruption are his weapons; and Romanism, Unitarianism, Mormonism, and a science falsely so called demonstrate his activity and cunning.

Whether " a spirit " cursed or blessed the Name of Jesus (v. 3) his testimony was to be refused So the Lord when on earth refused to permit the demons to speak, though they spoke truth; and the Apostles acted similarly at Philippi (Acts xvi. 16-18).

"Withal" (v. 7), i.e., for the profit of all.

"Faith" (v. 9), i.e., such as David's in battling with Goliath or in removing mountains (xiii. 2).

"Christ" (v. 12) should read "The Christ," i.e., the body of believers with Christ as Head.

The baptism of verse 13 is that of the Spirit and not of water, as is clear from the use of the term "to drink," i.e., to receive. The Samaritan woman was invited thus to drink; and at the Feast of Tabernacles (John vii. 39) men were told that to believe on Him was to drink, i.e., to receive His Spirit.

In the living and effectual baptism of the One Spirit believers are baptized into one spiritual and living body (Eph. iv. 3, 6).

Christ is the Head, the lowly believer is the foot, and yet, amazing fact, the Head cannot say to the foot " I have no need of thee " (v. 21)!

" Be honoured " (v. 26), i.e., " be nourished."

" In particular " (v. 27), i.e., "severally."

Corinthians is the wilderness; Ephesians is the land. The Pillar of Fire which was an outward manifestation in the wilderness became a hidden glory in the Temple. So the outward miraculous physical manifestations of Corinthians become hidden spiritual realities in Ephesians.

Further, in Corinthians is seen the spiritual Temple of God set up on the earth. Hence its activities are earthly, physical and outward. In Ephesians a spiritual Temple is seen located in the heavens, and its activities are spiritual, unseen and inward. "All in all" (v. 6), i.e., all these gifts in all these members of the Church.

1 CORINTHIANS XII. 28—XIV. 1—A comparison of verses 28-30 with Eph. iv. 8-16 shows the distinction between that which was set up on earth and that which was in the heavens. There are no miracles, or gifts of healing, or tongues in Ephesians. There is ministry eventuating in maturity. Demonstrations of power upon man's flesh belong to the earth and to the promised Messianic Kingdom.

In these verses (28-30) the Apostle descends from the apostolate to tongues. They are put at the bottom of the list. In xiii. 1 and 2 he ascends from tongues to knowledge and faith. This shows his estimation of the relative value of that testimony. These signs and miracles may disappear, and they have, but the care of the Great Shepherd in ministry has not ceased. Apostles and prophets have been superseded by the Scriptures: and the Holy Spirit bestows the gifts of Evangelists, Pastors and Teachers for the exercise of that ministry and care. These were the "greater gifts" (xii. 31, R.V.) that they were to earnestly desire: but they were to be enwrapped in an energy—which was the very nature of God Himself—i.e., love as the "way" of life.

The argument is: that wonderful as a "way" is that is enriched by miracles and healings and tongues, a walk with God in the energy of the nature of God—that is, love—is much more wonderful, and very much more to be desired. Love is conformity to the nature of God—the expression of what He is. It acts in benevolence to others; it is the opposite of selfishness. It has its source within. It is not moved fundamentally by circumstances. Its strength is independent of outward things — even of the objects which it blesses. Thus it can bless men in circumstances which usually produce irritation or jealousy. It acts according to its own nature, for love is its own motive. It feeds others, not itself; hence the first eight qualities of love (vs. 4-5) express renunciation of self. Where love is reality is; it never changes; it is always itself. Miracles, like childhood, pass away, but love never. A man may possess all "gifts" but if destitute of this Divine Nature he is a stranger to God and to grace. For gift is not grace. Balaam had the gift of prophecy but he was an enemy of truth. It is a deep mystery that men may have and exercise spiritual gifts and miraculous powers, and die even under torture for religion, and yet be unconverted.

Miracles, healings, and tongues characterized childhood, but love and preaching (xiv. 1) characterize manhood. Love saw nothing in these miraculous powers but instruments to be used for the good of others and not for the gratification of self, or for the promotion of self-importance. The great thing that love aims at is the profit of others. Hence the importance of preaching, for it edifies, encourages and comforts (xiv. 3). But in Corinth, as to-day in Christendom, men exercised spiritual gifts for their own selfish enjoyment or in order to attract the admiration of the church.

If everywhere in chap'er xiii. the name Christ be substituted for charity, the Divine nature of love will be recognised.

"A more excellent way" (v. 31). The ministry of miracle was an excellent way, but the ministry of love was a more excellent way.

1 CORINTHIANS XIV 2-40—The power of speaking human and angelic languages is the subject of verses 2-25.

It is a deep mystery that the Holy Spirit did not withdraw this power from those who used it unworthily.

Some understood the language, or languages, which they had the power to utter. These spoke with intelligence. Others did not understand, and so they spoke without intelligence and were condemned by the Apostle. The spiritual profit of the listeners and not the exercise in themselves of these gifts, was to be the supreme interest. Self was to be suppressed. Isaiah xxviii. explains the meaning and purpose of tongues (vs. 21 and 22), and, possibly, explains why the gift was not at once with-drawn when misused. The Holy Spirit foretold in Isaiah that the advent of the Messiah as King of Israel and of the whole earth, would be accredited by this gift, and harmoniously, for men of all languages were to serve Him and sing to His Name. This prophecy was fulfilled in Jerusalem (Acts ii.), in Cæsarea (Acts x.), in Ephesus (Acts xix.), and in Corinth. It was a testimony to the Twelve Tribes of Israel.

But the prophecy fore-told that the testimony would be rejected, and that prediction was fulfilled in Acts vii. as affecting the Two Tribes, and Acts xxviii. as affecting the

Ten Tribes. As a consequence the judgment fell, Jerusalem was destroyed, the Temple burned, and the nation scattered throughout the whole earth. Of necessity, therefore, the testimony of tongues ceased. It lost its meaning and purpose; and as God now has no official relationships with Israel, such a testimony is meaningless, and those who try to imitate it are ignorant of the ways of God on earth.

So a man was not to edify himself but to edify others (v. 4). He was to utter words easy to be understood (vs. 9, 12).

Intelligent preaching in the power of the Holy Spirit pierces the heart and produces conversion and testimony.

" How is it then?" (v. 26). Compare verse 15, i.e., " what actually happens, brethren," or " what ought to be your action, brethren?" This verse (26) should read as in the Revised Version.

It must have been a very wonderful fellowship. Every member helped vocally. What a contrast with present day congregations! One had a solo, another a sermon, another a revelation, another a tongue, another an interpretation of the tongue. This was not rebuked; but it was commanded to be organized. The utterances were to be in succession so as to secure order and edification (vs. 26 and 27). In the absence of an interpreter the " tongues " were to be silent (v. 28). The " others " (v. 29, R.V.) were to judge whether the prophets spoke from the Spirit of God or not. If while a prophet was speaking the Spirit gave a revelation to a listener, the speaker was to sit down so that the other might communicate the revelation. Or the direction might mean that the receiver of the revelation should wait till the prophet had ceased speaking before communicating it to the church. This latter supposition is supported by verses 31, 32 and 33.

The women were not to converse during these communications but to be obedient to order; and if they had any questions they should ask them of their own husbands at home, for it was indecorous at that time for a woman to speak to any man but her own husband, and Genesis iii. 16, legislated as to marital subjection. Women in the East at that time, as still to-day, disturbed the congregation by conversing among themselves, or by asking questions.

The majority of Christian people under-

stand this injunction prohibits women from praying, singing or preaching in the Church Assembly. But the Holy Spirit had promised to equip women for public ministry (Joel ii. 28). The promise was demonstrated in Acts ii. and xxi. 9, and 1 Cor. xi. 3-16 legislated for the manner in which women were to exercise this ministry; and the Scriptures cannot contradict themselves.

This promised effusion of the Holy Spirit will have its fulfilment in the future; and as these Apostolic ordinances will not then conflict with that promise so they do not conflict to-day. See note on 1 Tim. ii. 8-15.

The Gospel message did not originate at Corinth, nor did it reach Corinth only (v. 36); hence the Corinthians were not entitled to set themselves up as legislators in the matter of Church order.

In verse 37, Paul declares that he wrote by inspiration, and that he knew that he did so. See notes on Romans xvi. 26 and 2 Pet. iii. 16. and 1 Cor. ii. 13. This is of supreme importance; and the Apostle added that everyone who claims to be enlightened by the Holy Spirit will recognise these commandments as being inspired and authoritative. But if any man willed to be ignorant and to deny their inspiration, the Apostle left him to his ignorance, and refused to dispute with him (v. 38).

Speaking in tongues was not to be forbidden, nor healing with aprons (Acts xix. 12), but preaching was more to be desired and coveted; and as that desire developed so would lesser ministries cease.

1 CORINTHIANS XV. — Having rebuked the selfishness of their conduct both in eating and preaching, the Apostle now reproves their error in doctrine as to the resurrection of the body, for it was the resurrection of the body that was in question. And it was a fundamental question. It attacked the very foundation of the Christian faith. For if the body be not raised then was Christ's body not raised. Then was the resurrection not a fact. And if the resurrection never occurred then the redemption of man which Christ came to accomplish He failed to perform, for His resurrection was the demonstration of the perfection and efficacy of His atonement. If Christ were not risen, sin was not put away; the Gospel was not true; the Corinthians had

believed in a fable ; the Apostles were false witnesses ; Christians were of all men most miserable ; and their loved ones who had fallen asleep had eternally perished.

Verse 1 should read as in the Revised Version, " I declare " or " make known," i.e., " I repeat in what words I preached the glad tidings to you " (v. 2, R.V.). Many to-day speak contemptuously of a creed. These verses (1-11) prove the fundamental necessity of one.

" Saved " (v. 2) means are being saved and shall be saved.

To believe in vain means to believe in a vanity. But the Gospel is not a vanity—it is a certainty (v. 2). To receive the grace of God in vain (2 Cor. vi. 1) means to fail to show to others the grace shewn to oneself.

The Apostle here (vs. 1-4) defines and declares the Gospel. If the question be asked : ' What is the Gospel ? " the answer is found in verses 3 and 4, i.e., the Atonement and Resurrection of the Lord Jesus Christ. These doctrines are the two great foundation stones of the Gospel, and if either of them be denied then the Gospel ceases to exist. For if Christ did not die as an atoning sacrifice for sins, then sin has never been put away, nor God's eternal claims satisfied, and, consequently, there is no deliverance from its power and doom. And if the Resurrection be denied, then Christ failed to accomplish what He purposed to perform, for He came to put away sin by the sacrifice of Himself as a Sin-offering (Heb. ix. 26).

These two great foundation doctrines are based upon the Scriptures of the Old Testament ; and those writings being from God their testimony silenced all discussion and controversy.

The Apostle adduces the Scriptures and more than five hundred human witnesses as establishing the resurrection. But he subordinates human testimony to the witness of the Bible. The latter was conclusive because divinely inspired.

Modern religious teaching reverses this order. It puts human testimony first and Bible testimony second, and for two reasons —to gratify man's high opinion of himself, and to belittle God's Word. See final notes on Acts iii.

The Apostle always aimed at a moral as well as a mental effect in his writings (vs. 8-10). Hence he magnified the grace that saved him—a persecutor, an abortion, a man not worthy to be the least of the Apostles, and yet that grace energized him so effectually that he accomplished more than all the apostles put together. In Romans xi. 13 and in 2 Cor. vi. 4, he magnified not himself but the ministry which grace committed to him.

" The Twelve " (v. 5). This statement makes it clear that Paul was not one of the Twelve Apostles, and that Matthias was from the beginning one of the Twelve. See notes on John xx, and Acts. i. 16, 21, 22.

" I or they " (v. 11), i.e., the Apostle Paul and the Twelve Apostles. They all preached the one Gospel of the Atonement and Resurrection of Jesus Christ.

" All the Apostles " (v. 7). The term here possibly includes many others besides the Twelve.

The second section of the chapter (vs. 12-19) points out that the resurrection of Christ being an established fact (v. 12), it is unreasonable to deny the resurrection of dead persons ; and that (v. 13) if there be no general resurrection, which is the consequent, there can be no resurrection of Christ which is the antecedent ; and if He be not risen (v. 14) the Gospel is a fable and the Corinthians were reposing faith in a fallacy ; and, lastly, the Apostles were false witnesses in declaring that God had raised up Christ (v. 15).

The unity of Christ as the Head with believers as His mystical body (vs. 16-19) places His resurrection and theirs on the same footing. What is not true of them is not true of Him. His resurrection and theirs stand or fall together. His non-resurrection (v. 17) would nullify or frustrate their faith, for it would prove the failure of His purpose to take them out of their sins, and consequently liberate them from the eternal doom attaching to them. The word " vain " (v. 14) means empty ; the word " vain " (v. 17) means an overthrow or frustration.

The term " death " is used in regard to Christ : He actually suffered death in its damnatory sense, for He descended into hell ; but the term " sleep " is used in relation to those to whom He communicates His own life. These having His life await the hour when He will awaken them by the virtue of His Spirit that dwells in them.

The resurrection of Christ establishes, therefore, the emancipating fact that the believer in Him is no longer in his sins (v. 17), i.e., in a realm of judgment and death because of sin. To believe this great truth fills the soul with assurance and victory.

But it is not only the fact of the resurrection of the dead in general that is here affirmed, but the resurrection of certain persons out from among the dead in virtue of their living union with Christ as a Man. He, as a Man, went down into death to deliver man from the power of death; and God in taking Him up from among the dead made a public exhibition in man of complete victory over all the power of the enemy. Death could not hold Him; so He, as Man, arose from among all the other dead—thus declaring deliverance and redemption—and became the first-fruits of all who sleep. Had Christ not won this victory His people must always have remained in the dark prison house of death. But they are associated with Him in resurrection. Like Him they come out not only from death but from among the dead. They are one—if they do not rise then He never rose. If resurrection be denied to them it is denied to him. But His resurrection is established; and, therefore, the believer's faith does not rest on a fable, nor can it be overthrown nor its redemption results frustrated.

God will indeed by His power bring men out of death when He commits all judgment to the Son. But that will not be a victory over death in sinless human nature. By man came death, and by Man resurrection. His was a glorious victory that brings those who believe upon Him out of the state where sin and its consequences reign, and into a realm into which neither death nor judgment can enter. If these doctrines are fables then those who believe them are of all men most to be pitied (v. 19).

Before continuing the argument in verse 29, the Apostle in a parenthesis (vs. 20-28) contrasts the two families of the first and second Adams (v. 22)—the one communicating death to all that are "in" him, the other communicating life to all that are "in" Him. Union with the first Adam results from natural birth; union with the Second Adam commences in spiritual birth. The Apostle recalled the time when neither he nor the Ephesians were "in" Christ (Rom. xvi. 7, and Eph. ii. 13). To possess the life that is in Christ there must be living union with Him by faith, for it is only by faith in Him that the children of the first Adam can become the children of the Second (Gal. iii. 26).

But this life could not have been communicated to them if Christ had not died and risen again. The corn of wheat, perfect in itself (John xii. 24), would have remained alone. But He died for His people's sins; and, their sins forgiven, purged and abolished, He communicated life to them.

The terms "order" and "end" (vs. 23 and 24) are military terms. There are three companies. The first: Christ as First-fruits. The second: Those who shall be His at His coming. The third, i.e., the end or last or rear company; those who will appear in the dread day of Rev. xx. 12.

The mediatorial reign of Christ as King over all the earth is that spoken of in verses 24-28. Psalms ii., viii., xlv., and cx., with many other Scriptures, predict that reign. Christ as the glorified Man, is now seated in the Father's Throne waiting till His enemies be placed as a foot-stool for His feet. He will then rise up from His Father's Throne, ascend His own Mediatorial and Kingly Throne, and there reign until·He has overthrown every power, including death, which disputes the supremacy of God. He will then hand that perfected kingdom with Himself as Son of God in His Humanity—His Title by merit distinct from His Sonship with God in being and essence—and, retaining His Manhood, He will in that Manhood eternally exist in perfect union and obedience with God, just as He existed upon earth in His First Advent in the same perfection of Being and obedience. These communications establish the heart of the believer in a peace that is unshakeable and in a joy that is unspeakable, because Christ's eternal Manhood secures the eternal existence and bliss of all human beings who are united to Him as human beings.

The Apostle's basing of his argument on the two words "all" and "until" of Pss. viii. and cx. is a proof of verbal inspiration.

It is strange that men won to the faith by the inspired preaching of the greatest of the Apostles, could deny the foundation doctrine of resurrection; and, further, that they could still claim to be Christians. And it is also strange that the Apostle who ordered the expulsion of the incestuous man, should not have ordered the expulsion of these false teachers; for corruption of doctrine is more serious than corruption of morals, for it opens the door to all evils (vs. 33, 34).

The parenthesis (vs. 20-28) being disposed of, the argument interrupted in verse 19 is resumed in verse 29 and continued to verse 34, and contains a statement and a question.

The statement is that men who expose themselves to suffering, contempt and hatred because of faith in a fable, are to be pitied above all men (v. 19); and the question is (v. 29): where will preachers of this faith turn for recompense (v. 32) from the baptism of much deeper suffering into which they baptize themselves as preachers for the supposed benefit in another world of people who will remain dead for ever?

Baptism for, or on behalf of the dead, is thought by some to mean the practice of baptising living persons on behalf of others who died without baptism. But this practice arose after Paul's death; and, further, it is inconceivable that the Apostle could have used even as an ad hominem argument such an action of pagan superstition. But the context makes it clear that the Apostle intends the baptism of suffering which Gospel ministers must accept in seeking to rescue and save the perishing. So Christ spoke of His baptism of suffering on behalf of lost humanity which He underwent at Calvary (Luke xii. 50).

The words "baptized," "die" and "beasts" (vs. 29, 31 and 32) are figurative; and this is made the more sure by the statement that the Apostle stood in hourly jeopardy of his life (v. 30); that he died daily (v. 31); and that the rejoicing of the Corinthians had been purchased by such suffering, for he was the author of that joy, seeing he had begotten them in the Gospel. In 2 Cor. i. 5-10 and iv. 7-12 and vi. 4-10 he describes, in detail, this baptism which he endured on behalf of his converts for their eternal advantage, and many of these were already dead. But would it not have been the height of folly to suffer such afflictions and to risk his life every day in Ephesus at the hands of men comparable to wild beasts, if all his converts were to remain eternally dead? Great as would be the folly of the believer of such a false Gospel still greater would be the folly of its preacher, because of the deeper baptism of misery which he would have to submit to.

"Else" (v. 29), i.e., otherwise; that is, "if the dead rise not."

Verse 29 may be thus paraphrased: "If the dead rise not, what shall they do who are being daily baptized into misery on behalf of them?" "If the dead rise not at all, why then are they being baptized for them?" i.e., why expose themselves to such suffering?

The Apostle then points out that the denial of the foundation doctrine of resurrection opens the door to grave moral declension (vs. 33 and 34). Deceit, evil companionship, corruption of manners, unrighteousness, sin, ignorance of God and shame result. The Corinthians boasted of their religious knowledge, but it was not knowledge of God nor His ways nor His teaching. That knowledge brings glory; carnal knowledge, shame.

If a man persuades himself that he shall die like a beast he soon will live like one (v. 33).

The "how" of verse 35 is related to the "how" of verse 12.

"Thou fool" (v. 36), i.e., "oh foolish man." The Greek text here reads "That which thou thyself sowest is not quickened except it die." So nature teaches that to have a harvest there must be a prior death. The "bare grain" figures a dead body. The grain dies in the ground and a most wonderful resurrection follows. So is it, and so will it be in respect to man.

"Celestial bodies" (v. 40), i.e., the angels.

In the section verses 35-49, the apostle speaks of "they also that are heavenly" (v. 48), i.e., those to whom Christ has communicated His eternal life. The first Adam communicates natural, i.e., human life; the last Adam, spiritual life. The last Adam can impart eternal life to others, for He possesses immortality. Although a man, He has life in Himself, and so He quickens whom He will (John v. 21). To Him, the Head spiritually of the new race, God gave to have life in Himself (John v. 26). God imparts eternal life to the believer, but this life is in His Son (1 John v. 11). It is a fallen Adam who is the father of a race born after his image, i.e., fallen, guilty, sinful, and mortal. It is the risen Adam, the Lord from Heaven, Who is the Head of a spiritual race. They bear His image; and He communicates to them eternal life.

The secret revealed in verse 51 is the great subject of this last section of the chapter (51-58). Human reason never could have discovered this secret. The power that will raise the sleeping saints will change the living believers, and altogether, in bodies of glory (Phil iii. 21), they will be caught up into the clouds to meet the Lord in the air and so ever be with Him (1 Thess. iv. 17). The time of this rapture is to synchronize with " the last trump " (v. 52), i.e., " the Trump of God " (1 Thess. iv. 16). That trump first sounded in human history in Exod. xix. 16. Some think that this is the trump of the seventh angel (Rev. xi. 15) ; and that, therefore, at that moment of time the rapture of the Church will occur. Others point out that as the Church has nothing to do with earthly prophecies " the last trump " is simply a military expression corresponding to " the last post " of a modern army, and merely signifies the home-call at the close of the day.

Apart from the atonement and Priesthood of the Lord Jesus Christ there neither is, nor can be, a victory over sin, which is the sting of death.

Just as the denial of the resurrection energizes evil (vs. 32-34), so belief in this doctrine energizes true Christian living and service (v. 58).

" Steadfast " (v. 58), i.e., not turning away from the faith of the resurrection through inward doubt ; " immoveable," i.e., not turned aside from that doctrine by the reasonings of others. Conviction as to the fact of resurrection, and to the fact that Christian activity will certainly be rewarded, animate the believer to a life of unceasing self-denial for the temporal and eternal welfare of his fellow creatures.

1   **CORINTHIANS XVI.**—The sudden step from the vast mysteries and wondrous marvels of chapter xv. to the small daily interests and duties of the Christian's everyday life, makes vivid the wonders of the power and the tenderness of the love perpetually in exercise in ministering to and protecting the feeblest member of the flock of God. So that power and love at once here legislate for the daily bread of hungry people (vs. 1-4).

This gathering of money for the poor saints at Jerusalem (vs. 1 and 3) occupies a considerable portion of St. Paul's Epistles and of the Acts of the Apostles, e.g., Acts xi. 29, 30 ; xxiv. 17 ; 1 Cor. xvi. 1-4, 2 Cor. viii. 4, and ix. 1 and 12, and Gal. ii. 10. In this last passage the words " the poor " mean their poor, i.e., the poor saints at Jerusalem.

Systematic giving is the Divine method (v. 2) of making provision for Church needs.

Christian people should manage their money affairs, especially those affecting the Church of God, with scrupulous care so as to make impossible any accusation either of negligence or dishonesty (vs. 3 and 4).

The Apostle did winter with them as here proposed (vs. 5-7).

He wrote this letter from Ephesus (vs. 8 and 9).

Doubtless Timothy's youthfulness (1 Tim. iv. 12) made him nervous when meeting the clever men of Corinth (vs. 10 and 11).

Paul might have been jealous of Apollos (i. 12) ; but far from being so he repeatedly urged him (v. 12) to return to Corinth ; but Apollos, dominated by similar love and wisdom, resolutely refused to go.

" Things done " under the dominion of love are well done (v. 14).

All who give themselves to the ministry of the Word of God at home or abroad, should be recognised, honoured and listened to (vs. 15 and 16).

Love thinks no evil but, on the contrary, believes in, and counts upon, the affection of others. Hence the Apostle says that the money given to him by the three brethren from Corinth (v. 17) not only refreshed him but refreshed the Corinthians (v. 18)—that is, in his affection for them he was sure that they would be glad to hear of his receiving this relief.

At that period churches often met in private houses (v. 19).

" An holy kiss " (v. 20). See notes on Romans xvi. 16.

Paul's salutation (vs. 21-24) proves his consciousness of the verbal inspiration of his letter, and its consequent fundamental importance. The term " grace " (in his own handwriting) was his trade-mark, and reveals the authorship of the Epistle to the Hebrews (Heb. xiii. 25 with 2 Thess. iii. 17, 18).

It is, therefore, clear that the Apostle wrote by dictation as well as by inspiration.

The Old Covenant and New Covenant imprecatory prayers form a salutary and solemn Bible lesson. For the latter see Acts viii. 20, 1 Cor. xvi. 22, Gal. i. 8, 9, Rev. viii. 13, xviii. 20, xix. 1-5, xxii. 18, 19, and other Scriptures.

The sense of the imprecation of verse 22 is : " If any man love not the Lord Jesus

Christ he shall be accursed at the coming of the Lord, and may he be accursed." The prayer is a prediction with approbation. The debauched, the unholy and the impenitent will be most certainly accursed in that day (Matt. xxv. 41); but all in addition, however moral and cultured and religious, who do not really love Christ will be involved in the same eternal doom; and all who possess a spiritual nature in harmony with the Divine nature approve that threatened judgment.

But the Apostle's love enclosed all however humble who did truly love the Lord Jesus Christ (v. 24).

2 CORINTHIANS

Titus was sent to Corinth with the First Epistle and directed to return to Troas where Paul planned to meet him. His non-arrival at Troas made the Apostle so anxious about the condition of the Corinthians that he crossed over to Macedonia where he met Titus, who gladdened him with the news that his letter had produced the happiest results. The Apostle then wrote his second letter, which, like the first, dealt with departure from the moral teaching of the Epistle to the Romans.

To those who were faithful to the truth, he addressed words of the deepest affection, and to those who were unfaithful, words of restrained severity. Both these features appear in the Epistle. See note on i. 14.

The simplicity, the grandeur, the affection, the severity, the humility, the intell gence and the authority of the Epistle, form a literature that is supernatural, and which has never been, and can never be, equalled by the ablest writers.

2 CORINTHIANS I. 1-22 — In the first eleven verses the Apostle's heart expresses the joy felt in the midst of fierce persecutions by the report that Titus brought him of the spiritual condition of his beloved children at Corinth — who themselves also were suffering persecution for the name of Jesus.

And yet in the midst of those persecutions they could applaud the teacher who advocated incest—a sin unknown amongst the heathen, and that brought such dishonour to the Name because of which they were suffering affliction! Such is man's natural heart! Paul hearing of their repentance assured himself that they also would enjoy the same comfort from God that he himself did. So grace in the heart of the Apostle laid hold of what there was of good among the Corinthians in the expectation that evil would

surely be judged—for grace does not discredit good because of the presence of evil. This shows how real was Paul's fellowship with Christ.

Christ's followers are not promised exemption from suffering, but they are assured of consolation in suffering.

Like a brave and true soldier the Apostle writes first of mercies and comfort (vs. 3 and 4) before mentioning sufferings and afflictions (vs. 5 and 6).

" And Timothy a brother " (v. 1), i.e., my brother Apostle. They wrote this joint apostolic letter from Philippi.

They only can truly comfort others who themselves have suffered and been comforted (v. 4).

'. The sufferings of Christ " (v. 5), i.e., persecutions because of fidelity to Him. He always responds with abounding consolations.

" Salvation " (v. 6), i.e., deliverance from persecution. The consolation with which Christ fortifies the believer, enables him to endure the persecutions. The Apostle and the Corinthians were joint partakers in these common persecutions, and were, therefore, joint partakers in the common consolation (v. 7). Verse 6 should read as in the Revised Version.

" Our trouble " (v. 8)—" So great a death " (v. 10), i.e., the riot at Ephesus. So narrow was the Apostle's escape from death that he had the sentence of death in himself, that is, he had the feelings of a man sentenced to death. But God saved him on that occasion (v. 10) ; and Paul was sure that he would enjoy further similar salvations ; and so would also the Corinthians (v. 6), they helping by prayer so that this " gift " of deliverance (v. 11) would be bestowed, not only upon the Apostle, but upon them also, for those who pray for others to be delivered from trial share the joy of the deliverance.

The mystery and ministry of prayer (v. 11), are incomprehensible to human reason. God was Almighty, and Paul was very precious to Him. Why then should the Apostle need to be helped by the prayers of the Corinthians? But the ministry of prayer, and of its resulting thanksgiving, trains and disciplines the Christian's heart, enlarges his affections and sympathies, and awakens and energizes him in the activities and victories of the Christian life.

In the second group of verses (12-22) the Apostle explains why he did not visit them as he had planned to do. It was because of their moral condition (ii. 1-3).

His action with them was sincere, disinterested and affectionate (v. 12). He wrote nothing to them but what they had already received and read and acknowledged to be true (v. 13); but only a " part " of them acknowledged and recognized his sincerity (v. 14). These rejoiced in Paul as he looked forward to rejoicing in them at the coming of the Lord.

So in this confidence in their affection (v. 15) he planned to visit Corinth; from thence to pass into Macedonia; then to return to Corinth; and from there to set out for Judea—so giving them a double " benefit." Visits paid in fellowship with God bring spiritual benefit; and if the fellowship be maintained, the benefit will be repeated. All Christian people should live this life of power and communion, and thus benefit one another when paying visits.

The Apostle was not guilty of fickleness of purpose because he changed his plans. He was not like men of the world who say " Yes, Yes," but in action say " No, No " (v. 17); but just as God is faithful (v. 18) to His " yea " so was the Apostle. And then, as always with Paul, he lifted small everyday matters into the highest realm of spiritual environment. His argument was—how could he act with fickleness when he proclaimed a God that is faithful to His promises; and he reminds them that, let the promises of God be never so many, yet are they all reliable for they are all deposited in the Son of God, Jesus Christ. He is the great " Yes " of these promises. The promises under the first Covenant were deposited in man and depended for realisation upon his obedience. There was of

course complete failure; but the promises of the New Covenant are all given to Christ, and their realisation depends upon Him. There can, therefore, be no failure, for He is the " Amen " as well as the " Yea," i.e., He is the Performer as well as the Promiser and all His action in relation to these promises has for its aim the glory of God, and the objects of those promises, the beings in whom they will be exhibited, are redeemed men (" by us," v. 20). It was only in pardoned sinners that this demonstration of the grace and faithfulness of God and of His Son Jesus Christ could have been made.

To these engraced objects of His love He gives His Holy Spirit as a pledge, an earnest, of the eternal glory, splendour, dominion and bliss that they are to possess, in order that they may enjoy, while still in this world, in their hearts, foretastes of the felicity which they then shall have; and all such persons He " seals " for Himself as His own by that very Spirit which He gives them.

2 CORINTHIANS I. 23—III. 6.—God can read the soul and its thoughts, and Paul did not hesitate to summon Him as a witness to testify that he did not fail to keep his promise to visit Corinth through fickleness of purpose but through the unwillingness of his affection to cause them pain—for owing to their moral state he would have been compelled to visit them with " a rod " (1 Cor. iv. 21)—but he hastens to add (v. 24) that he did not wish to lord it over their faith (as the Roman Church does) for in that they stood personally responsible to God, but he greatly desired to be helpers of their joy and that they should be helpers of his joy—the Greek text here suggests mutual joy.

It is clear from verse 23 that it is not wrong for Christian people to take oaths in confirmation of testimony.

So he resolved not to pay them a painful visit (v. 1), and, therefore, he wrote to them instead (v. 9) ordering them to expel the evil-doer and so demonstrate their obedience to his authority as an Apostle. But having heard from Titus of the repentance of the man who made both Paul and the Corinthians sad (v. 2), he commands them to forgive him and to receive him back into Christian fellowship (vs. 6-8). Otherwise he might be lost to the faith by overmuch sorrow (v. 7) and so fall into a **Satanic** snare (v. 11). For Satan by his wiles seduces Christian ministers to clothe immorality with sanctity, and then when they awake to their error, he tricks them into the belief, as in the case of Judas, that they have sinned too deeply to be forgiven, and thus he overthrows their faith.

Wrong-doers should not be rebuked proudly and scornfully but with sorrow (v. 3), with anguish and many bitter tears (v. 4) ; and with an abounding love that thinks the best of people (v. 3), and which continually flows toward them (v. 4).

The Apostle does not name the evil teacher but only speaks of him impersonally (vs. 2 and 5-8).

The statement in verse 5 appears to mean that the evil teaching of the wrong-doer did not grieve Paul only but also the Corinthians ; and so he generously disclaimed any intention of charging them with sympathy with the evil. On the contrary he recognises them as partners, i.e. as having " part " with him in the sorrow.

" In the Person of Christ " (v. 10), i.e., as Christ's Apostolic representative invested by Him with punitive power.

The simple matter of a journey from Troas to Philippi (vs. 12 and 13) was, as always with Paul, lifted up into the highest realm of the Divine purposes and activities. As a proof of his deep affection for the Corinthians, he left a delightful field of Gospel success at Troas, and hastened to Macedonia to meet Titus and hear news of them (vii. 6 and 7). The principle here appears that shepherding the sheep is more important than preaching the Gospel.

But it was painful to him to discontinue preaching at Troas, and to leave people who were willing to listen to, and to obey the Gospel. He, however, comforted himself with the knowledge that continually and everywhere he was being led in triumph by God in Christ ; that he was Christ's willing captive; that both he and his message were a sweet savour of Christ to God ; that he was a faithful preacher of the Gospel—not adulterating it as many did— and that though incompetent in himself to originate any spiritual matter, yet he had been made fully competent by God for the ministry of His Word (vs. ii. 14 to iii. 6).

The scene before the Apostle's mind (vs. 14-16) was evidently that of a Roman triumph. The advent and the presence of the victorious general were announced by slaves scattering sweet odours all along the historic way that ended at the Capitol. The victor was followed by a multitude of captives, some destined to life, others to death. On reaching the Capitol those doomed to death were slain ; those assured of life, liberated. The glory of the conqueror was published by the condemnation of the one group and by the liberation of the other.

The odour of the incense was a savour of death to the captives condemned to death, and of life to the captives ordained to life. The glory of Christ is the subject and purpose of the Gospel. It announces everlasting destruction to those who refuse to obey it (2 Thess i. 8 and 9) but eternal salvation to those who accept it (1 Thess. v. 9). A Gospel that excludes either of these doctrines is a false Gospel—it is not a sweet savour of Christ to God—and it does not glorify, but, on the contrary, it dishonours Him.

So the Apostle here pictures himself at one and the same time as a slave scattering the sweet incense of the Gospel, as a willing captive ordained to life, and as a loyal soldier sharing the Great Conqueror's Triumph. In his hands the perfume of the Gospel was pure (v. 17).

The Gospel and its messenger are so truly one that they jointly are a sweet savour of Christ unto God (v. 15).

The question " Who is competent for such a ministry " (v. 16) is answered in iii. 5 by the statement that this competency is of God ; and the Apostle claims this endowment. He did not need, as other preachers did, including Apollos (Acts xviii. 27), letters of commendation, for the Corinthians themselves were his letters of commendation ; and he affectionately adds that that letter was written in his heart, and that it was written in such large letters that it was known and read of all men. That is, the Corinthians made so public a profession of Christ that they were a large-type letter written by Christ. But the Apostle's ministry (v. 3) had won them to Christ, therefore they by their Christian life and testimony commended him as a true preacher of the Gospel. He spoke of Christ sincerely, without adulterating the truth, as being sent by God, and as labouring in the continual consciousness of the presence of God (ii. 17).

Not upon dead cold stone but on the

living affections of warm hearts, Christ wrote that letter with the Spirit of the Living God (iii. 3).

Verse 5 of chapter iii. follows verse 16 of chapter ii. and claims the sufficiency needed to be a competent preacher and incense-bearer. Paul was confident that in the sight of God he possessed that competency through Christ, though personally absolutely incompetent.

The First and Second Covenants are contrasted in verse 6. The First Covenant, that of the " Letter," i.e., the Law, condemned to death because of man's inability to keep it. The Second Covenant, that of the Spirit, proclaims life because of Christ's ability to give it. The " Letter " killeth—that demonstrates its authority, its inspiration and its power — for were the letter of Scripture human writing it could not kill ; the highest human literature has no such power.

2 CORINTHIANS III. 7—IV. 12.—Verses 7-18 form a parenthesis descriptive of the Gospel. At iv. 1, the Apostle resumes the subject of his ministry — its Divine commission ; its Apostolic authority ; its affection ; its suffering ; its self-sacrifice ; and its profit to the Corinthians. This section closes at vii. 16.

The ministry announcing death, i.e., " the Letter," that is, the Law, came with glory— a glory so great that man could not look upon it, for it judged him, making him conscious that he was a sinner—but the ministry announcing life has so much more excellent a glory that it eclipses the glory of the former. The Law demanded righteousness ; the Gospel provides righteousness. The Law bartered righteousness for obedience, and as that obedience was impossible to man, it was unobtainable by him ; hence his condemnation to death. The Gospel provides man with a spotless righteousness as a free gift ; hence the Gospel is the ministry of life. Man being guilty, his greatest need is righteousness. So the one was the ministration of condemnation ; the other, the ministration of righteousness. Both were " with glory," for they both express God's moral glory demonstrated in judgment and in grace. Both demonstrations were Divinely necessary to the manifestation of that glory.

The end of the Law (v. 13) is Christ (Rom x. 4) ; but Israel refused to look stedfastly to that end, and still refuses. The veil that was then before their eyes is now upon their hearts as they listen to the reading aloud of the Scriptures every Sabbath day in the Synagogue (vs. 14 and 15). But just as a flower when uncovered turns to the sun so will the heart of Israel turn to the Sun of Righteousness when the veil is removed from off it (v. 16).

" The things which remain " (v. 11), i.e., the glories attaching to the Person and redeeming work of Christ provide a hope (v. 12) which needs not to be veiled, but, on the contrary, proclaimed without reserve. The Apostle could, therefore, say he had fully preached the Gospel of Christ and kept back nothing that was profitable (Acts xx. 20 and Rom. xv. 19, Col. 1. 25 margin).

" The Lord is that Spirit " (v. 17), i.e., the Spirit of verse 6. In the life and under the domination of that Spirit there is no bondage (v. 17) but, on the contrary, progress from one degree of moral glory to another (v. 18), for where the Spirit is Lord there is liberty.

The bronze mirrors of that day reflected the light that shone upon them. The believer to-day receives morally on his unveiled face the glory as Moses received it. The glory of the Lord Jesus—the Spirit— reflects that glory into the moral darkness of society ; and the Light being the Living Light of the Spirit has power to transform and to change. Thus the believer as he walks in fellowship with the Lord and keeps his eyes fastened on Him becomes unceasingly more and more like Him (iii. 18) ; and, at the same time, as he contemplates the numberless glories promised by his Divine Companion, and their exceeding weight, he is braced to bravely endure the hardships of the Gospel ministry (iv. 18). Thus iii. 18 and iv. 18 are connected.

The face of Moses reflected as a mirror the glory that shone upon it in the Mount of God, and was seen by man when he came down from the Mount. The minister of the Gospel should, in spirit, dwell in the Mount of God ; and so when he comes forth to preach men will feel, and see upon his face and in his conduct, the effects of that communion.

The face of Moses did not shine the first time that he came down from the Mount. It was when Israel had sinned and when God had made all His " goodness " to pass before him that then his face reflected the glory. And yet Israel could not bear this reflection, partial as it was, for it judged the secrets of their hearts although that glory proclaimed the Name of Jehovah as being merciful and gracious; for Christ is the end of the Law. The glory on the face of Moses caused terror—it " killed "—for it made man conscious of his guilt and therefore of his inability to stand in the presence of a Holy God. But the glory on the face of Jesus the Man on high gives life, for it is the proof that all the sins of those who behold it are blotted out. Moses said: " I will go up; *peradventure* I shall make atonement." But Jesus first made a perfect atonement and then went up. Therefore the believer gazes upon His face with joy; for the surpassing glory of that face declares that the beholder's sins are no more.

Resuming (iv. 1) the subject of his office as a minister of the Gospel of the glory of God in the face of Jesus Christ, the Apostle points out that, before receiving this ministry, the mercy which it proclaims must be received—that is, that the preacher must have first himself consciously accepted as a sinner God's pardoning mercy in Christ before he can announce it to others; and he adds that the doctrine of a risen Saviour makes the preacher victorious over all the fear of death, and over all the sufferings possible of infliction upon the " earthen vessel " in which the gospel treasure is carried (vs. 7-12 and 16-18).

" The Word of God " (ii. 17 and iv. 2). It would be impossible to adulterate, or to wrest, what has no form. Hence the Bible is the Word of God (2 Pet. iii. 16).

" Manifestation," i.e., a full clear statement of the Way of Salvation. Such a statement reaches man's conscience and receives God's approval.

But however clearly the Gospel may be preached it is veiled to them that are perishing; and Satan as the god of this world spreads that veil (vs. 3 and 4) lest the bright sunshine of the Gospel of the glory of Christ— Who is in nature and essence One with God— should shine upon them.

The Apostle was not guilty of that blindness (v. 5), for he preached Jesus as being Jehovah. Hence he was a true preacher. He was also a true servant, for (v. 6) he gave to others the Gospel knowledge which he had himself received on the road to Damascus, and which Abraham and Stephen had received, i.e., that Jesus is the God of glory and the glory of God.

So the glory of God was fully revealed in the face of Jesus Christ—it was unveiled— and the Apostle Paul as a true minister of that glory proclaimed it to the world without a veil in his clear and full preaching. He announced the glory of God in the Person of Christ. To point to any other Saviour would have been to put aside and declare worthless what Christ had done. But that work brings the vilest of men into the very glory of God, placing them there in a righteousness in which it is impossible to find a flaw.

As in Gideon's day the earthern vessel carried the light which conquered the foe and brought deliverance, so God has committed the Gospel message, not to mighty angels with celestial bodies, but to feeble men with earthen bodies. But His power enwraps the earthen vessel, so that though it be troubled, perplexed, persecuted, and struck down it cannot be destroyed. The preacher is immortal till his work is done. The Apostle not only carried as a principle in his soul the dying and the resurrection life of Jesus, but he also consciously experienced them in his body; for Satan and men were continually trying to destroy him and possibly may have killed him more than once—as at Lystra (Acts xiv. 19) and when he was a night and a day in the deep (2 Cor. xi. 25). So it was made plain to men that the power which kept him alive was not human but Divine (v. 7).

Willingly because constrained by the love of Christ (v. 14), he suffered the anguish of these perpetual " deaths " in order that the Corinthians might have life (v. 12); and in so doing he followed in the steps of Him Who died that men might live (v. 5).

2 CORINTHIANS IV. 13—V. 21—The preacher and his message occupy a large portion of this letter because popular teachers at Corinth were corrupting the Gospel, and their followers were denying that Paul was either an Apostle or a preacher.

Paul's reply may be thus set out :—

The Preacher of the Gospel: what enables him, ii. 14-iii. 6.

The Gospel preached by him: iii. 7-18.

The Preacher of the Gospel: what animates him, iv. 1 to v. 10.

The Gospel preached by him: v. 11-21.

The Preacher of the Gospel: what approves him, vi. 1-10.

Thus iv. 14 to v. 10 is one section having as its argument faith in the resurrection and in a future reward as that which animates the Gospel preacher.

The Spirit of faith (vs. 13, 14) in the fact and hope of resurrection, which animated the Apostle in the endurance of these sufferings, was the same Spirit that animated the Messiah in His sufferings for truth (See notes on Ps. cxvi.). Believing and speaking belong one to the other. The Apostle was certain that he and his Corinthian converts would be raised from the dead and would stand together in the presence chamber of the King (v. 14), and, therefore, like the Messiah, he testified because he believed. He knew that He Who raised up Jesus from among the dead would surely raise him up also. The distinction between Christ's sufferings for truth at the hands of man, and His sufferings in Atonement at the hands of God, must ever be preserved. Paul could share the former with Him, but not the latter.

Like his Master he suffered all " these things " for their sakes (v. 15) that grace might abound to them, and that they might have a life of joy and thanksgiving ; but all the glory of such grace should be wholly given to God and nothing attributed to him.

The glory of the things unseen upon which he fastened his eyes, so dwarfed the sufferings endured, that to him they were light and but for a moment (vs. 17, 18).

He who lives a life of faith and not of sight (v. 7) will be able to say " I know " (vs. 1-6) and " I am always confident " (vs. 6 and 8), for faith makes Divine facts real, and illumines the mind with certitude.

Satan and men might do their best to destroy the clay-tent (v. 4) in which Paul lived, but that did not trouble him ; for he knew he had, not a " tent " but an " house," a building from God, not made with hands, eternal, in the heavens.

But he did not desire to be disembodied, but, on the contrary, to be alive at the coming of the Lord, so that his mortal body might be clothed upon by his immortal body, and so mortality be swallowed up of life. He groaned in his mortal body for it was burdened with pain and mortality, but he knew that the faithful God who wrought his house for him (v. 1) wrought him for it (v. 5), and as an earnest and

pledge of the double fact, had given him His Holy Spirit. A body indwelt of that Spirit must of necessity rise from among the dead. God had fashioned him for this glory—the Resurrection Glory of Christ. Paul was God's workmanship, and the indwelling of the Spirit secured his enjoyment of the fact. So he was full of confidence; and his ambition (v. 9), whether in the body or out of the body, was to be an acceptable preacher to Him. All Christians should be " workers " (vi. 1) ; and as such they will appear before the judgment seat of Christ (v. 10) where their work—but not their sins for they were eternally abolished at Calvary—will be tested, and if found comparable to gold, silver, and precious stones (1 Cor. iii. 12) it will be declared " good," but if found to be wood, hay, and stubble it will be condemned as " worthless."

The Greek verb here translated " labour " (v. 9) occurs only three times in the New Testament. See Rom. xv. 20, (" strive ") and 1 Thess. iv. 11, (" study "). It means to be ambitious, or to make it a point of honour. Placing them in chronological order they express the ambition of inoffensive honest independence (1 Thess. iv. 11)—the ambition of pleasing Christ (2 Cor. v. 9), and the ambition of preaching the Gospel in the regions beyond (Rom. xv. 20). So Paul's enthusiasm as a missionary remained with him to the very end, and grew stronger rather than weaker.

Once again (vs. 11-21) the Apostle states the Gospel which he preached. The catchwords are :—" Terror " (v. 11), " Love " (v. 14), " Sin " (v. 21) and " Righteousness " (v. 21), and the moral effect of the Gospel he declares to be the " death " of the carnal nature (v. 15) and of its wisdom (v. 16). The four verbs " persuade " (v. 11), " beseech," " pray " (v. 20) and " entreat " (vi. 1, R.V.) express the Spirit and methods of the true Gospel preacher.

The Apostle did not receive the grace of God in vain, i.e., to no purpose (vi. 1). He no longer lived unto himself (v. 15), but, his heart filled with pity and love for perishing men, he showed to them the grace that had been shown to himself, and did his best to persuade them to flee from the wrath to come (v. 11). He preached the true Gospel of the wrath of God and His love in Christ ; and, as in Romans i. 18, he in faithfulness to truth first announced the coming wrath, and then proclaimed the virtue of the atoning blood (Rom. iii. 25).

Modern religious thought denies the wrath of God and does not believe in conversions motived by fear of that wrath. But the human race would have utterly perished had not one man been " moved with fear " (Heb. xi. 7) when he heard of the approaching judgment of the flood.

The Apostle knew that the purity of his doctrine and of his motives were manifest to God, and he hoped that they were manifest also to the Corinthian conscience (v. 11). He did not again commend himself to them but gave material to those in Corinth who were loyal to the Gospel that they might boast of him in opposition to those with whom carnal endowments were everything and sincerity of heart nothing (v. 12). If he appeared to have been mad it was for God's glory, but if now accounted to be in his right mind it was for their benefit (v. 13), for the love of Christ over-mastered him (v. 14) : and knowing that Christ's death proved all men to be " dead," he as a fellow worker with Him (vi. 1), besought men to be reconciled to God (v. 20).

Christ indeed died to save men from the doom of their sins, but that death also meant that they should no longer live unto themselves ; i.e., His salvation is a salvation from sin and self (v. 15).

The believer is " a new creation " (v. 17), and, as such, he is brought into a realm in which all things are judged and measured and viewed in the life and light of the Holy Spirit. Prior to spiritual birth the believer was in a realm in which everything was judged by the wisdom of the carnal mind. That wisdom knows Christ " after the flesh " i.e., as the greatest religious Teacher, Moral Philosopher, and World Benefactor that ever lived, and, perhaps, also as the promised Messiah and Regenerator of Society. Man is also judged in the light of the same wisdom and declared to be an emanation of God, and, as such, having a glorious history, is perpetually advancing to an ever higher level of moral and mental splendour. These are the " old things " that pass away where the New Birth is a reality (vs. 16 and 17).

The Gospel announces that God because of the Person and work of His Beloved Son, is reconciled to sinful man (v. 18) ; and He commits the proclamation of these glad tidings, not to sinless angels, but to redeemed sinners. So the Apostle was to announce (v. 19) the fact of this reconciliation, and that its proclamation had been committed to him as an ambassador. He therefore besought men to be reconciled to God ; and he told them that because the sinless Saviour (v. 21) was made to personate sin itself, and because He had offered up Himself as a sin-offering of infinite value, God was thereby reconciled, His justice vindicated, all the claims of His throne satisfied, and a spotless righteousness provided for guilty men. In that righteousness no flaw can be found. He has gone in to the very holiest, and has been accepted before the Throne of God. Christ is the Righteousness of God (John xvi. 10). In that righteousness God stands, and in that same righteousness the believer stands. God and the believer stand in the one and self-same righteousness. So the believer can say, " I have a righteousness in which no flaw can be found ; it has preceded me into heaven and has been accepted there." This great fact contradicts the human doctrine of purgatory—for believers only are said to go to purgatory—but the believer's righteousness is the righteousness of God, and how could a supposed purgatory make that righteousness more pure ?

The word " men " should be supplied in verse 20 instead of the word " you," for the Apostle was writing to persons who had already accepted the message of reconciliation.

2 CORINTHIANS VI.—VII. 1.—The first ten verses of this chapter set out what approves a true messenger of the true Gospel ; and it is remarkable that Paul points to riots (v. 5) occasioned by the action of the preacher in preaching as being one of the evidences accrediting him as an ambassador for Christ. Many persons to-day argue the opposite.

His appeal to the Corinthians (v. 1) not to receive the grace of God uselessly, but to become Christian workers, and, avoiding (v. 3) everything that might stumble men, to seek to save them, is based upon his claim to be in this great mission of love a fellow labourer with Christ (Acts xv. 4 and 1 Cor. iii. 9).

The Apostle points out (v. 2) that all Christians should engage in this activity of grace, for it was a time, or day of grace in which God was accepting sinners and saving them. It was a day of salvation because of the death and resurrection of the Lord Jesus Christ. This is the force of the quotation from Isa. xlix. 8, where God is heard speaking to His Beloved Son on the morning of the resurrection. He succoured Him out of the abyss, and accepted Him and His atoning work—for the resurrection demonstrated that acceptance. The fruit of that succour and acceptance is for man's enjoyment; and, consequently, the present dispensation is for him a day of grace and acceptance; and all those who have experienced this grace should seek to make it known to others though it be at the cost of the shame and suffering described in verses 4-10. See note on 1 Cor. xv. 2.

The remaining section of the chapter to vii. 1 carries on the subject of not receiving the grace of God in vain, i.e., to no purpose; for grace saves (vs. 4-10); sweetens (vs. 11-13); and separates (vs. 14-vii. 1). It seeks to save others; it fills the heart with the sweetness of Christian love; and it separates to a life of holy fellowship with God. It animates to association with Christian workers and separation from world-servers—not isolation from perishing sinners but separation from defiling connections.

The Apostle had a large heart (v. 12). So large that there was room in it for all at Corinth (v. 11). Therefore he spoke to them without reserve, for such is the nature of love (v. 11); and as children requite with love the love of their parents, so he bade them —for they were his children in the Gospel— to make room in their affections for him (v. 13, and vii. 2 and 3).

Controlled by this love they were to be the companions of the despised and hated Gospellers (vs. 4-10) and not the associates of unbelievers (vs. 14 and 15).

There are two fellowships, and only two, and all men belong either to the one or to the other. No one can belong to both and claim to be a Christian, for God only recognises as His children those who walk in fellowship with Him. These fellowships are in opposition. The one is fellowship with God; the other, fellowship with the world. The world is the assemblage of all unconverted people.

Christians are the companions of the living God. He dwells with them and walks about among them. Therefore they must have no fellowship with the world, and only on this condition will God recognise them as His sons and daughters (vs. 16-18). God will not have worldlings in His family. He will not recognise those whose affections are in the world. The world rejected and crucified His Beloved Son, and whoever will be the friend of the world must be the enemy of God. If such separation threatens starvation, the believer need not fear for He with Whom he walks is Jehovah Shaddai (v. 18) and being Almighty can, therefore, furnish him with daily bread as He furnished Elijah.

This glorious title "Jehovah Shaddai" occurs only here and six times in the Revelation—seven times in all in the N.T.

The Hebrew word shad means a woman's breast. The title Shaddai suggests love and unfailing benevolence. Satan had his travesty. Diana of the Ephesians (Acts xix.) was a many-breasted divinity.

Holiness becomes the sons and daughters of the Lord God Almighty (vii. 1). This holiness is both inward in the mind and outward in the body; for some sins are physical and some mental. Sanctification is progressive; hence the word "perfecting." Justification is an accomplished fact and lies wholly in the activity of God. Christ is indeed the believer's sanctification as well as his justification. The believer cannot grow in justification, but he is commanded to grow in sanctification and in grace and in knowledge.

The Christian is useless unless he is in the world, but if he lets the world into him he perishes—just as a ship is useless unless in the sea, but if the sea enters into it, it sinks. An angel could serve God in the world, but he would not associate himself with its idolatries and its sins. To do so would be an abdication of his position and character. To yoke oneself with those who have never been born of the Spirit, is to be bound with persons who can only have worldly motives; and hence it is impossible to draw the plough in a furrow common to both.

"As God hath said" (v. 16) not: "For God hath said" because the quotations (Lev. xxvi. 12, Isa. lii. 11, Jer. xxxi. 1) belong to Israel—but they reveal the principle of fellowship with God and of membership in His family.

There are two ways of holiness—man's way and God's way. The latter appears in the words "holiness in the fear of God"

(vii. 1) i.e., the holiness revealed in the Scriptures. That is an effective holiness, and recognised by God. Man's way of holiness has neither power nor sanctity in securing purity of heart (Heb. xiii. 9) or victory over sin (Col. ii. 20-23). See notes on those Scriptures.

Thus ends this description of the source, the character, the proving and the victory of the Gospel ministry lodged in an earthen vessel.

" Greatness of heart " (v. 11) does not easily express its feelings, for it thinks of others and not of itself. But with artless courage, if necessity so demands, it declares its affections. Fellowship with Christ gives this largeness of heart and this unaffected simplicity and warmth in the utterance of its affections.

2 CORINTHIANS VII.   2—16 — The Apostle now descends from the loftiest heights of the Gospel and its ministry to the lower but very sweet level of human interests and affections. He writes of his love for his converts at Corinth ; his anxieties about them ; his apprehensions as to their spiritual condition ; his joy at hearing of their faithfulness to truth ; his hope that they will contribute liberally to the fund for the poor saints at Jerusalem ; and such like matters.

" Receive us " (v. 2). Better : " Make room for us in your heart." Compare note on vi. 11 and 12. In these affections the heart of the true minister of the Gospel is revealed. He loved them so fervently that he had them all inclosed in his heart and wished to die and to live with them (v. 3). Both in Troas and in Macedonia his love for them permitted him no rest because of anxiety as to their spiritual condition (vs. 5 and 6). Love has its joys as well as its fears (vs. 4, 6, 7, 9, 13). He rejoiced at their earnest desire to carry out his commands ; their grief because of the misconduct committed amongst them ; their zeal against evil through affection for him (v. 7) ; their carefulness in searching out the evil ; their separation from it ; their indignation against the evildoer ; their fear of the anger of God ; their desire for restoration ; their zeal for holiness ; and their exacting of punishment (v. 11)— all filled him with an overflowing joy which was still further increased by union with the joy of Titus (v. 13, R.V.).

" His cause that did the wrong " (v. 12), i.e., the incestuous person. " His cause that suffered wrong " i.e., the outraged husband, who was at the same time the father of the incestous person.

To themselves he spoke without reserve and sternly. Behind their backs he boasted of them (v. 14). All Christian people should obey this principle.

The distinction between the writer and inspiration appears in verse 8. He knew that his first letter was inspired. Its words were " the commandments of the Lord." But as a feeble, anxious and affectionate man he trembled lest the effect of the communications should estrange the Corinthians from him, and should cause them pain. In that first letter he marked the distinction between what was his opinion and what were the commandments of the Lord, and in this second letter he confesses the agitation which that distinction caused himself. This is an interesting instance of the difference between the individuality of the Prophet and the message of the Holy Spirit given to him (see note on 1 Pet. i. 10-12, and 2 Pet. i. 20). The distinction between repentance and remorse (v. 10) is illustrated by Simon Peter and Judas Iscariot. Repentance was life to the one ; remorse, death to the other.

2 CORINTHIANS VIII.—The grace that is not received in vain (vi. 1) delights to minister to the needs of the necessitous ; and hence it is that in this and the following chapter, money thus used is called a " grace," and those who give it are declared to be themselves recipients of the grace of God (v. 1). Thus the giver of such grace is regarded as a receiver. To give and to receive is the one verb in Hebrew.

The famine predicted by Agabus (Acts xi. 28) appears to have particularly affected the believers in Judea (v. 29), and Paul when at Jerusalem (Gal ii. 10) promised that he would help to get money for them. Hence his activity in the matter in these two chapters ; and his prayer (Rom. xv. 25-27) that the money so collected might be acceptable to the Judean saints (v. 31).

It was in the fulfilling of this promise (Acts xxiv. 17) that the Apostle met with violence at Jerusalem and imprisonment in Rome ; and it was in that prison that he wrote the Epistles to the Ephesians, the Philippians, the Colossians, Philemon, and, perhaps, to the Hebrews. How small a matter may have so great a consequence !

But nothing is really small in Christian life and ministry ; and this appears in chapters viii. 9 and ix. 8, which blaze with Divine splendour from out of the midst of these simple arrangements affecting a collection of money for poor believers ! Christ is here set forth as the highest pattern of the grace that gives ; and the ability of God to furnish all grace at all times and in all abundance, is revealed as the basis of Christian bountifulness.

Christian liberality does not originate in the giver but is the effect of a bestowment of Divine grace enabling the giver to be a channel of that grace to others (v. 1).

There is a delightful contrast in terms in verses 2 and 3—abounding joy from abounding affliction, and overflowing liberality from deepest poverty. Such is Divine book-keeping. Twenty wealthy men may have put £1000 apiece into the Treasury chest on the day that the widow put in her farthing. But the Scripture says that she gave more than all the others put together. Thus out of her deep poverty her liberality abounded above theirs.

The Apostle pointed to the liberality of the Macedonians in order to spur the Corinthians to equal generosity.

" Not as we hoped " (v. 5), i.e., beyond our hopes. The surrender of self to the Lord involves the surrender of the purse. It is God Who makes the heart willing to such a surrender.

A year before Titus had begun at Corinth to make up this fund (v. 6) and now the Apostle was sending him back (vs. 18 and ix. 3) in advance of himself (ix. 4) so that the promised sum might be ready (ix. 5) and that the Apostle would not be compelled to demand it. " Covetousness," i.e., extortion (R.V.).

Promises are good but performances are better (v. 11).

Paul arranged (vs. 16-24) that the purse of money for Judea should not be entrusted to him alone but that he should have companions in the trust, so as to avoid the possibility of a suspicion or accusation of mal-administration and personal profit.

Who Titus' companions were is not stated but they are supposed to be Luke and Trophimus.

2 CORINTHIANS IX.

— The ancients used the past tense in letter writing because to the receiver the contents of the letter would be past (v. 3).

Facts in the spiritual realm harmonize with those in the physical (v. 6). Many a farmer has a poor crop because he sows sparingly, and many a Christian suffers inward poverty because of outward illiberality. God loves a cheerful giver ; but few people believe it.

" His righteousness " (v. 9), i.e., his liberality. " It remaineth for ever," that is, God does not tire, as men do, of giving largely and continuously. He gives a crop to the farmer (v. 10) sufficient to feed him and his family, and to provide seed for the next season, and to help the necessitous and the poor.

Christian benevolence not only supplies the wants of the needy (v. 12) but also motives a great thanksgiving chorus to God from the hearts and lips of the needy.

It also fortifies the faith of the Christian recipients, for it is a demonstration to them of the reality of the Gospel and its moral power in the heart of the believer.

It also awakens and deepens Christian love (v. 14), for the recipients of the bounty feel an affection for the donors and desire to meet them and to know them.

Man's gifts are measurable in language but God's great gift of His Son—the best thing in heaven for the worst thing on earth—is unspeakable.

2 CORINTHIANS X.

— The Epistle proper closes at the last verse of the previous chapter, but the Apostle in his anxious love for his converts at Corinth adds a personal postscript (x.-xiii.)—marked by the words " I," " Me," and " My "—to enforce his Apostleship, to expose the self-made and false apostles who were corrupting the faith of the converts, and to save them from the destructive teaching of these ministers of Satan (xi. 13-15).

The postscript throbs with entreaty and severity—both vehemently expressed because of the vehemence of Paul's love for his children in the Gospel.

It may be gathered from the postscript itself that these false apostles were Hebrews (xi. 22) ; that they were of commanding presence and gifted with eloquence (x. 10) ; that they were highly cultivated (x. 5) ; that they were personally attractive, for they had a large following in the church (xi. 18) ; that they preached without payment (xi. 12) ; and that they announced an " ethical Gospel " (xi. 15).

" Confidence " (v. 2), i.e., Apostolic punitive authority.

" Walk in the flesh " (v. 3), i.e., are men physically.

" Strongholds " (v. 4), i.e., philosophic strongholds (v. 5).

Verse 6 should read as in the Revised Version. Paul in his affection for them assumes their obedience.

" Authority " (v. 8), i.e., his power to inflict sickness or death. The power was real, for when exercised, as in the case of Elymas, it was effective ; and so the Apostle did not fear to be put to shame as he would have been if nothing followed upon his imprecation (xi. 15).

The words " measure," " rule " and " line " (vs. 13-16) are geographical expressions expressive of the respective missionary regions apportioned by God to the Apostles. Land was measured by lines and rule. Apparently Asia Minor and Europe were apportioned to the Apostle Paul as his missionary field of Gospel service. Peter seems to have been given Palestine and Mesopotamia (Gal. ii. 8 and 9 and 1 Pet. v. 13). " Dare not " (v. 12). This is irony.

The argumemt of verses 13-16 is that Corinth was within the field of labour apportioned to the Apostle ; that he was the first to preach the Gospel there ; that God had delegated punitive power to him in relation to Corinth ; and that, therefore, he was authorized to act toward them as he did both by letter and by visitation. He added (vs. 15 and 16) that it was their duty to help him to occupy all the ground apportioned to him as a missionary and so not to tempt him to enter another missionary district ; he pointed out that no preacher, no matter how successful, should boast of his ability or of his success as a missionary ; and that Christians have only one legitimate subject of boasting, and that is the Lord Jesus Himself and the perfections of His Person and work. Further, that self-commendation does not prove Divine ordination, but that where spiritual results follow they demonstrate that the preacher enjoys the commendation of the Master.

The statements in verses 3 and 4 confute those who teach that it is the duty of the Church and of Christian princes to defend the faith by torture and death.

2 CORINTHIANS XI. 1—29—To most men it is pleasant to speak of themselves and of their doings ; to the Apostle Paul it was painful. Yet the anxiety of his love for the Corinthians compelled him to this humiliation. His love for them was a true affection, for it was charged with anxiety for their spiritual welfare. So he begged them to listen to him (v. 1) while he acted like a fool in speaking of himself.

His love for them was a jealous love (v. 2) ; but he was not jealous of their affection for himself, but of their affection for Christ.

Satan is to be dreaded as a lion ; more to be dreaded as a serpent (v. 3) ; and most to be dreaded as an angel (v. 14).

If these self-introduced teachers (v. 4) announced another Saviour it was reasonable to listen to them, but not reasonable when their mission was to corrupt the teaching concerning Christ which they had received from Paul.

" The very chiefest apostles " (v. 5) i.e., not the Twelve Apostles, but these self-made and very pre-eminent apostles (R.V margin). The language is ironic.

Paul was not defective in knowledge both sacred and secular ; and he reminds his converts that he had made that fact thoroughly manifest amongst them by his teaching in all the realms of the Christian faith (v. 6).

" God knoweth " (v. 11), i.e., " God knows that I love you dearly."

The meaning of verse 12 is that Paul determined to continue his practice of preaching the Gospel at Corinth without payment so as to prevent the false Apostles making the point against him that they preached gratuitously and that he did not ; and so they could hint that his object in preaching was to get their money.

In verses 13-15 Paul says that these preachers of " an ethical Gospel" were sham apostles, deceitful workers, servants of the devil and doomed to the lake of fire. Such language shocks modern religious feeling ; but the shock proves the existence of the immense gulf lying between the teaching of the Apostles and of those who profess to be their successors.

" I say again " (v. 16), i.e., " to return

to what I was saying in verse 1:" that is, "don't think I am foolish in speaking of myself; but if you do think me foolish, yet listen to me as you do to my detractors."

"After the Lord" (v. 17), i.e., not as commanded but permitted; and I speak as a fool in his foolish boasting speaks when applauding himself.

Verse 19 is ironical. Claiming to be wise they listened with good-humoured conscious superiority to fools.

"Suffer" (v. 20), i.e., accept or tolerate. "Devour," i.e., devour your property. "Take," i.e., lives at your expense. "Exalt himself," i.e., claims priestly and divinely appointed authority. "Smite," either with a hand or a foot. The Romish priest enslaves, amasses property, lives at the people's expense, claims super-human authority, declaring that he has power to compel God to descend from heaven as often as he wills and to become a piece of bread, and he frequently uses personal violence in the maintenance of his sacerdotal assump· tions, e.g., the Holy Inquisition.

"Reproach," i.e., in self-disparagement (v. 21, R.V.). This means that when with them, far from acting with such priestly arrogance, he had lived among them as an ordinary feeble man.

However in verses 21-29 he challenges these false teachers to prove their fidelity to the Gospel and to suffering humanity, by a similar or a superior record of devotion, of affliction and of national privilege.

So real was his love for all his converts (vs. 28 and 29) that he consciously felt their weakness, and burned with shame or indignation when anyone was injured or caused to sin.

2 CORINTHIANS XI. 30 — XII. 10.
—Men boast of their strength (v. 30) but he boasted of his weakness; and appealed (v. 31) to God as to the truthfulness of the statement.

Compelled by fidelity to the Gospel, and by affection for the Corinthians, to establish his Apostolic superiority to his opponents who had introduced themselves into the Church at Corinth, he contrasts his being let down in a basket (xi. 33) and his being lifted up in a vision (xii. 2). The one happened to a man in the flesh; the other, to "a man in Christ." Of the former man (xi. 30) he would boast—for how small and contemptible was great Saul of Tarsus crouching terror-

stricken in a basket! Of the other man (xii. 5) he could boast, for he was "a man in Christ" having no conscious physical being (vs. 2 and 3), enjoying an experience of which a man in the flesh could not boast, for it was an exertion of Divine power in which man had no part. Self and everything that could exalt him as man were forgotten. He, as a man, had no share in a power which raptured him into Paradise. It was "a man in Christ" that was so raptured. Of such a man he could boast; but of himself he would not boast except in his infirmities.

"I knew" (v. 2). "I know" (R.V.).

If he wished to boast (v. 6) he could do so truthfully, for he had very much to boast about.

But he was an earthen vessel (v. 7) and nothing can amend the carnal nature—not even a rapture into Paradise. So to save him from falling he was empaled upon a stake. The Holy Spirit has not revealed what that stake was, so it is not necessary to know, but what it is necessary to learn is its moral purpose in saving the Apostle from destruction. To be in Paradise, as out of the body, does not minister to pride, but to have been there can be a subject of carnal boasting. Paul would have been exalted in his own eyes, and would have boasted of the fact that he alone had had such an experience. And had he been taken up into a fourth heaven that would only have increased the danger of a deeper fall. The presence of God alone can silence the carnal nature. So soon as that presence is ·removed nature boasts of the experience enjoyed. Therefore corrupt nature must be bridled; and such was the ministry of the stake in the Apostle's flesh. He says it was "given" to him (v. 7)—given by God although it was "a messenger of Satan."

Prevention and humiliation are both Divine instruments. Paul was saved from falling by prevention; Peter was permitted to fall in order to humiliation. There was no difference between them; they were both indwelt by a corrupt nature incapable of amendment. This is one of the most bitter and humbling lessons for the human heart. It is painful but salutary for the Christian to have an experimental sense of the principle of evil which indwells him. But a greater power also inhabits the temple of his body, and its victorious warfare is a profitable exercise for the heart.

If the Apostle Paul needed so humbling and painful an experience of what the carnal nature is, it is evident that all Christians need it; and it is plain that whatever weakens and belittles and humiliates that proud and wilful nature should be regarded by the believer as most worthful (xi. 30-33).

The distinction between the sinless nature of Christ and the sinful nature of Paul is seen in that Christ needed no stake in his flesh on descending from the Mount of Transfiguration. Facing Satan at the foot of the Mount He was the same Person Who shone in the glory of God on the top of the Mount. The scenes were different, but He was alike perfect in both. All was evenness in Him—the fine flour of the meal-offering. On such chords as Paul the Divine Hand can awaken exquisite music; but Christ is all the music itself.

" Rest " (v. 9), i.e., envelop. The earthen vessel was weak, but it was wrapped around by almighty power.

" Sufficient ". (v. 9), i.e., sufficient to keep Paul standing every time that Satan struck a blow. That is: every time he received a buffet there was a sufficiency of grace immediately given to meet the blow—not a moment too soon, and not a moment too late, or not too little or not too much.

" My strength is made perfect in weakness " (v. 9); and, " I take pleasure in infirmities " (v. 10). These are amazing statements ! The one is the result of the other.

The lesson of verses 1-9 is that the higher the Christian experience the sharper must be the " thorn," i.e., the physical infirmity (Gal. iv. 13) needed to guard the believer from falling. This apostolic teaching overthrows the doctrine that " full salvation " secures perfect physical health.

2 CORINTHIANS XII. 11—XIII. 14.—
The Apostle once more (v. 11) returns—and for the last time—to the subject of his credentials as a true Apostle. They might esteem him to be " nothing," but he was, on the contrary, in nothing behind those very pre-eminent and self-made apostles of whom they were so proud.

Verse 12 may read : " The signs of a true apostle were," etc. Paul does not say " I wrought," but " were wrought among you in all patience, by signs," etc. These miraculous signs have not been transmitted to others, neither has the Apostleship. The silence

of fourteen Epistles as to miracles, evidences the superiority of doctrine to miracle; and the passing allusions to miracles in seven Epistles, whilst proving their occurrence, evidence their unimportance in contrast with doctrine, and proves that they were facts known to all, and, therefore, needing no extraordinary relation. This is a stronger proof of their reality than if they were kept in the fore-ground by much excited writing. In the Bible miracle is inseparable from history; to deny the one is to deny the other. To account for the existence of Christianity in the world is much more difficult than to deny the fact of miracle.

" I seek not yours, but you " (v. 14). False apostles could never feel or show such affection as this.

The duty of parents to provide for their children has here (v. 14) Scriptural authority.

To spend ; to spend gladly ; to spend very gladly ; to be spent ; to love more abundantly though to be the less loved—such a depth of affection is impossible to fallen man (v. 15). Its existence proves the fact and power of the New Birth, and was an overwhelming testimony to the Apostle's claims.

After the word " nevertheless " (v. 16) the words " you say " should be provided so as to give the sense. Paul with indignation (vs. 17 and 18) exclaims : " Did I get money from you either directly or through Titus and his companions ? " The accusation was that his refusing money was a trick, for that he extracted it through second parties.

How very painful must it have been to a noble heart like that of Paul's to have been compelled to discuss the motives which govern the false and selfish hearts of unconverted men ! But love must bear such things ; it must think for others, though it cannot think with them.

" Spirit " and " steps " (v. 18), i.e., the inward motives and the outward actions.

The Apostle did not excuse himself to the Corinthians as though they were his judges (v. 19). He walked before God in fellowship with Christ. The closing sentence of this verse might perhaps, better read : " But we write all these things, etc.," and so concord with xiii. 10 : " Therefore I write these things," etc.

That the assembly at Corinth could have been guilty of the eleven terrible faults and sins set out in verses 20 and 21 is inconceivable. But all Scripture, both of the Old and New Testaments, invariably testifies that man immediately corrupts whatever God commits to him.

The contrast between the first and last verses of this chapter (xii.) is humbling and salutary: A man in the purity of paradise (v. 2), and a man in the putridity of Corinth ; and yet Corinth claimed association with Paradise !

The circumstances of the second visit (xii. 2) are not recorded, and are, therefore, not necessary.

" I will not spare " (v. 2), i.e., he would strike with sickness, or death, every member of the fellowship that by the testimony of two or three witnesses should be found guilty.

" Heretofore have sinned " (v. 2), i.e., continue to cleave to their old sins.

The Apostle knew he was inspired (v. 3). He knew that Christ spoke through his lips. This fact destroys the statement that Scripture nowhere asserts that its writers were unconscious of infallible inspiration.

" Which " (v. 3), i.e., " Who "—that is, Christ. Christ spoke in and through the Apostle ; He was not weak to the Corinthians but mighty among them ; though crucified through weakness, yet He was energized by the living power of God. Paul (v. 4) was weak in fellowship with Him, but was energized by the same living power ; and he bade the Corinthians beware of it (v. 2.)

In verse 5 he overwhelmed them by pointing out that if he were a reprobate Apostle, then were they reprobate Christians, for they were all his converts. He challenged them to examine themselves as to whether they were really Christians or not. They of course would promptly and proudly reply that they were, and so their confidence about themselves would admit and establish Paul's claim to be a true Apostle.

The general belief that this verse (5) commands introspection on the part of christians is quite mistaken.

In his self-denial and self-annihilation (v. 7) Paul was indifferent as to what they thought of him so long as they advanced in Christian character, so he kept praying for them, and added that his Apostolic punitive power could not be used against the truth but for the truth (v. 8). If they were free from blame, that power could not be used, and that they should be free from fault, was his loving prayer and desire. He did not wish (v. 10) to use that power. Man would like to use it in order to exalt and advantage himself. Compare Acts viii. 18.

Here ends this personal postscript (vs. 11-14). He had written what his heart, governed by the Holy Spirit, impelled him to say. He had poured out the love and anxieties of that heart upon them, and now, evidently wearied with the effort, he abruptly closes with these brief salutations.

GALATIANS

In the Epistle to the Romans the Holy Spirit defines and declares the Gospel. Its two great foundation doctrines are there declared to be justification and sanctification. To attack either is to destroy the Gospel. The Word of God (2 Tim. iii. 16) " reproves " and " corrects." It " reproved " the Corinthians for practically denying the doctrine of sanctification, and it " corrected" the Galations for corrupting the doctrine of justification. The evil in Galatia was doctrinal ; the evil in Achaia, moral.

So the Epistle to the Galatians restates the foundation doctrine of justification by faith ; it declares those who teach salvation by faith and by sacraments to be false teachers ; and it predicts and approves their eternal punishment (i. 8 and 9).

This imprecation is here doubled ; and, like the other imprecations of the New Testament, corresponds in spirit and in certainty to those of the Old Testament.

The Galatians were Celts, and no people in corrupt Christendom more eagerly accepted the teachings of sacramental salvation than they ; and this characterises them to the present hour.

GALATIANS I.—God in His love has given man the Gospel and suited it to his needs. Satan in opposition degrades it to the level of man's corrupt nature and proud will, and fashions it into a religion that suits man, as man, in the flesh. The Gospel condemns man, as man, to death, and so puts an end to him and all his religion, and it reveals " a new man " born of the Spirit and not of nature. The impotency of man to serve and please and obey God was made manifest under the Law. Satan's aim during the present day of grace, is to unite the religion of the flesh with that of the Spirit ; and the impossibility and wickedness of that union are plainly set out in this Epistle.

Christ gave Himself up for a sin-offering in order to take His people out of the world (v. 4). In His cross man and his religion and the world are judged. Every effort of man, therefore, as a man by natural birth, to make himself religiously acceptable to God is rebellion, and only an energy of the " evil world " out of which Christ redeems.

The Acts of the Apostles record Paul's visits to the Churches in the province of Galatia, and the large numbers he there won to Christ ; and in this letter he records their enthusiastic reception of him (iv. 15). But certain teachers had obtruded themselves into these Churches who attacked both the doctrine and the ordination of the Apostle, and introduced the ancient and modern Gospel of salvation by faith and sacraments. The Apostle, therefore, in this letter associates no other apostle with himself, as in other letters (v. 1), and insists again and again (vs. 1, 10, 11, 12 and 13-24) that he did not receive, or learn, the Gospel from man —whether Apostles (v. 19) or believers (v. 22)—but directly and personally from the Lord Jesus Christ Himself (v. 12).

The Galatians, being Celts, emotional and fickle, warm-hearted and simple-minded, at once welcomed the new teachers, and forsook him who had won them to the truth (v. 6).

" Who raised Him from the dead " (v. 1). The Twelve Apostles knew Christ in incarnation and resurrection ; Paul knew Him only in resurrection, and that fact strengthened his claim as a Divinely appointed Apostle apart from, and independent of, the Twelve.

In this declaration of the faith in Christ Jesus he associated " all the brethren which are with me " (v. 2) so as to show the Galatians that he was not alone in his doctrine.

There are no commendations as in the opening of other Epistles, but at once an abrupt exclamation of amazement (v. 6) that his converts were so quickly turning unto a perverted Gospel (v. 7). Satan's aim is not so much to deny the Gospel as to corrupt it.

The vehemence and abruptness of the language of the letter, and the fact that he wrote it with his own hand (vi. 11), revealed the anguish of his heart, and affirm the fundamental import of an orthodox creed.

" As we said before " (v. 9), i.e., " I repeat what I have just said."

" Let him be accursed " (vs. 8 and 9). This is a prediction and a prayer—" he shall be accursed of God, and may he be."

The Gospel is divinely perfect. To add anything to it is to destroy it ; for that is to deny its perfection.

A man-pleaser is not a Christ-server. " After man " (v. 11), i.e., invented by man, and approved by man.

" Persuade " (v. 10), i.e., aim at winning the favour of men.

Salvation is by revelation and not by education (v. 12) or evolution. See note on Matt. xi. 27, and xiii. 29 and 40.

Two arguments, the first negative (vs. 13 and 14), the second positive (15-24) prove that Paul did not invent his Gospel, or receive it from others, but was Divinely enlightened and commissioned to preach it.

The negative argument (vs. 13 and 14) urged, how could he have invented what he had hated and the believers of which he had persecuted to death ?

The positive argument insisted that his knowledge of the Gospel was wholly independent of the Twelve Apostles and their disciples—that man had nothing to do with it—and that he received it personally and directly from God.

" My equals," i.e., in age (v. 14).

The great foundation doctrine of election appears in verses 15 and 16. Paul was chosen before his birth ; and, therefore, personal merit, or demerit, could not have affected that election ; and, later on, God was pleased of His own volition to reveal Christ to him (v. 16).

His independence of the Twelve Apostles, and of all Christian people then existing, is insisted upon in verses 16-24 ; and in verse 20 he solemnly adds that the statements he then was making in writing were true, and that

he asserted their truth in the presence of God ; and he points out that his salvation and his commission were not based upon any moral excellence in him, but upon God's grace to him (v. 15).

The argument of verses 15 and 16 is the key doctrine of the Epistle. Both these births were operated by God without the Apostles' co-operation. Salvation is of electing grace apart from human merit, or will or action ; for how can a man co-operate with God in his natural birth, or will its action ? Equally impotent is he in respect of his spiritual birth. All is of grace and Divine power.

GALATIANS II.—This chapter should read as in the Revised Version. The " three years " of i. 18 and the " fourteen years " of ii. 1 contrast with the " fifteen days " of i. 18, and so emphasize the independence of Paul in relation to the Twelve and his non-indebtedness to them in the matter of doctrine. Also, had he gone up to Jerusalem earlier, the proofs of his independent ministry would not have existed. All these years he had laboured fruitfully without having any ordination from the hands of the Twelve ; and they had accordingly to recognise his Apostleship as being Divinely commissioned, for the proofs were there and God had set His seal upon them. The Twelve were compelled to acknowledge his position and authority, and also the intelligence of his ministry—an intelligence which surpassed theirs.

This visit to Jerusalem (v. 1) was that recorded in Acts xv. ; and two facts here appear. First : that he went up to Jerusalem by " revelation " (v. 2), and not in obedience to an authoritative order from the Twelve— he did not recognize their authority over him. Second : Previous to the public meeting he privately told the leading Apostles what were the doctrines he preached, and the effects produced, lest they should think that he had run or was running in vain—he had no such apprehension himself—and in order that they might be able to intelligently guide the public discussion. Their decision was that the Gentile believers were not bound to observe the Law of Moses. As to the Hebrew believers, they made no pronouncement.

But teachers visited the Galatian churches, and taught that all must join the Hebrew

Church and observe the Law of Moses if they would be saved. It was these teachers and their teaching that Paul denounced.

Two principles were in opposition : Salvation by works and salvation by faith. The one principle directed men to great activity in going about to establish their own righteousness (Rom x. 3, and Titus iii. 5) ; the other, forbade all carnal religious effort and commanded faith in a Saviour Who had accomplished everything necessary for man's redemption.

The world applauds the first principle ; and whatever the world applauds, influences and pleases man, for it gives a certain glory to him. But that glory obscures Christ's glory and falsifies the Gospel. Peter, (v. 11) allowed the opinions of others to influence him, and by his action overturned the truth. Paul lived in the light and power of the Gospel of which a glorified Christ is the centre, and being both firm and ardent as well as clearsighted, he did not spare Peter, but rebuked him in the presence of all.

The weakness and poverty of man are seen in Peter's conduct. A man is weak in proportion to his importance before men. When he accepts the position of being nothing he is independent of public opinion and can do everything. A Christian exercises an evil influence over the world in the degree in which it influences him ; and the evil is increased if the Christian has a reputation for godliness. It is a great snare for the heart to seek to maintain a reputation amongst men ; and when this is a motive, the esteem, even though just in itself, becomes an agency for evil. So Peter drew away all the Hebrew Christians, and even Barnabas with him, into his dissimulation.

The Apostles could not teach Paul anything respecting Christ and the Gospel that he had not already learned from the Lord Jesus Himself (v. 6).

Peter was appointed an Apostle to the Hebrew Church (v. 7). He resided habitually at Jerusalem where he ministered to the Two Tribes, and later on at Babylon (1 Pet. v. 13), from which centre he ministered to the Ten Tribes of the Dispersion (1 Pet. i. 1).

" The poor " (v. 10), i.e., " their poor "— the poor saints at Jerusalem. The Epistles to the Romans and Corinthians record Paul's activity in the fulfilment of this engagement. He was zealous for good works, but denied justification by them.

The words, " knowing that a man is not justified by the works of the Law, but by faith in Jesus Christ," form a parenthesis. Omitting the parenthesis the Apostle says : " We, i.e., you and I, Peter, who are Jews by natural birth, even we—you and I—have believed in Christ Jesus in order that we might be declared righteous upon the principle of faith in Him and not on the principle of legal works."

The argument of verses 17 and 18 is : Man is guilty and needs a spotless righteousness. This righteousness can be obtained, not through law-keeping, but through Christbelieving. A professor of the doctrine of salvation by faith who preaches salvation by works, re-erects the legal structure which he himself cast down and so proves himself to be a transgressor in having thrown it down. But Christ told him to throw it down, and so Christ taught him to do what was sinful, therefore Christ is a minister of sin ! " God forbid " exclaims the Apostle. The Law is divinely perfect ; man is hopelessly impotent, hence it is useless for him to seek righteousness by the Law. Christ Who is the righteousness envisaged by the Law, becomes such to whosoever believes upon Him ; and thus He glorifies the Law and redeems the sinner.

Man delights to return to those things which gratify the flesh. He eagerly accepts whatever appeals to him. Hence the popularity of " ordinances." But to rest upon them is to rest upon the " flesh." There are none in the Epistles to the Ephesians and to the Hebrews ; for these Epistles are heavenly, where Christ is, and He is everything to the believer and to the worshipper. If Christ be everything then is there neither room nor necessity for ordinances. Those who occupy themselves with these find in them a fatal sustenance. Their effect is to veil the Person and the perfections of the Great High Priest.

But man likes to have some credit and some position. He likes that which he can see and handle. He refuses to be treated as vile and incapable of good, and is angered that he and his religious efforts should be condemned to annihilation. He will willingly practise efforts to annihilate himself, for that ministers to his own importance ; but to accept the absolute judgment of death upon his nature, his religious energies and his moral virtues, and to be commanded to be silent, and, as a dead sinner, to trust the life-giving Saviour and to find in Him all that is needful for righteousness and worship, is distasteful and repelling. But this is the doctrine of verses 19 and 20. Saul died and a new man, Paul, was born ; and the life that energized him was vitalised and sustained by faith in the Son of God, in contra-distinction with the supposed religious life energized by the principle of salvation by works. If righteousness came upon that principle (v. 21) then Christ's death was needless.

GALATIANS III. 1-22—The Apostle Paul preached the Atonement, and with such vividness that his hearers could see Jesus Christ crucified among them. Only a minority of modern preachers follow his example.

Romans viii. 9, states that if any man have not the Spirit of Christ he is none of His. The reception of the Holy Spirit is, therefore, the great fundamental of salvation. Membership of a particular church, or attainment in moral conduct—both of which are possible apart from the Holy Spirit—do not secure a righteousness that God will accept, or a title to heaven. The one and only and all important matter is the possession of the Spirit of Christ ; and how may that Spirit be received (v. 2) ?

There are two methods : One, man's way ; the other, God's way. Man's way is : the activity of sacraments and good works ; God's way is : the passivity of listening and believing. These two methods are opposed ; and the answer to the question of verse 2 is : that the Spirit is not received by legal works but by listening faith.

This question in verse 2 destroys the foundation upon which the churches of Greece and Rome stand.

The key-words of verses 1 to 14 are "works" and "faith" ; and those of verses 15-22 are "law" and "promise." These words set forth the opposing principles of salvation by merit and salvation by grace.

Many who profess to have received the Spirit state that the spiritual life they have can only be maintained by frequent partaking of the Paschal Supper. That is to say, having begun in the Spirit they seek perfection by the flesh (v. 3). See notes on prior chapter.

"Suffered" (v. 4), i.e., from their persecutors. The confession of the doctrine of salvation by faith apart from works (Rom. iv. 5) entails persecution ; the confession of the opposing doctrine entails no persecution but approbation. The Apostle in his affection for the Galatian believers hoped that they would hold fast to the truth, or return to it, and so their sufferings would not have been needless.

God did not give His Holy Spirit to them, and manifest his miraculous power amongst them, upon the principle of law-obedience (v. 5) but on the contrary principle of faith-acceptance (Eph. i. 13).

When God told Abraham that his children should exceed the stars in multitude (v. 6), Abraham though an aged man—a "dead" man—believed Him ; and God consequently declared him to be a righteous man. Abraham's faith was not a reasonable one ; it was superior to reason (Rom. iv. 16-22).

Who can condemn a man whom God declares to be righteous, i.e., whom He justifies ?

The Bible though it did not exist at the time preached the Gospel to Abraham (v. 8).

The Law assured righteousness to all who perfectly obeyed it (v. 10), but condemned to death all who failed to give it that perfect obedience. Such an obedience was impossible to man, for he is morally imperfect, and moral imperfection cannot possibly render moral perfection. Christ (v. 13) redeems the believer from that doom because He suffered it Himself on the believer's behalf; and thus at Calvary affirmed the authority of that Law and vindicated its justice and goodness.

The quotation (v. 11) from Habakkuk ii. 4 assumes the infallible authority of the Scriptures.

The Law has nothing to do with faith (v. 12) for it teaches that he who practises its requirements lives by doing them. Christ in His life perfectly obeyed all its commands, and in His death discharged all its claims ; and the merits of both His life and death are all credited to the believer in Him as though the believer himself had performed them.

"The promise" (v. 14) is that of the Spirit (vs. 2, 3, 16, 17, 18, 18, 19, 21, and 22).

The blessing of Abraham, i.e., the blessing of the Spirit promised to Abraham.

Verse 16 should read as in the Revised Version. The distinction between Gen. xii. and xxii. must be recognised. That of Gen. xii. was made to Abraham ; that of

Genesis xxii. to his "seed," that is, to Christ. After Christ, pre-figured by Isaac, had been offered up in sacrifice and raised from the dead, the promise of chapter xii. was confirmed to Abraham; and it is on this confirmation that the whole argument of this chapter depends. The promise being confirmed, the introduction of the Law could neither disannul or add to it (v. 15).

"After the manner of men" (v. 15), i.e., to use a human illustration.

The purpose of the Law (v. 19) was to make men conscious of the evil which dwelt in their nature. It was necessary that this consciousness should be awakened. The Law not only manifested the presence of evil in human nature but also revealed its power, for it at once urged man to disobey God's revealed will. The Law was, therefore, introduced between the promise and its fulfilment in order that man's true moral condition might be manifested; but its glory was beneath that and subsequent to that of the promise, for it was ordained by angels in the hand of a human mediator, i.e., Moses (v. 19).

If it be objected that there must be two Gods, One Who gave the Promise and the other Who commanded the Law, the reply is that it was the one God Who gave both (v. 20), and that He did not give the one in order to destroy the other (v. 21), but that He might through the Law conclude all men under sin and thus clear the way for bestowing upon them the promise of the Spirit (v. 22) on the principle of faith in Jesus Christ.

The sense of verse 20 will, perhaps, be clearer if read thus:—" Now a mediator is not of one party but two; but God is One," i.e., there must be two parties where there is a mediator. Hence Moses was a mediator between God and Israel. But when God gave the promise to Abraham there was but one party, for God caused Abraham to fall into a deep sleep. So God was the One party to this covenant. It is, therefore, unconditional, and stands for ever.

GALATIANS III. 23 IV. 9—" Faith " (v. 23). This should read " the faith."

The ancients entrusted their sons when children to a moral guardian who restrained and educated them until they were of an age appointed by the parent. Such was the Law to Israel during the infancy of the nation.

The Law restrained them morally and taught them their need of Christ; and the nation remained under that guardianship until He came. His Advent necessitated the dismissal of the guardian. So the Law was Israel's tutor up to and unto the First Advent (vs. 23-26).

The key-words of this section of the Epistle are " slave " and " son "; those of the section that follows (iv. 8—v. 1) are " slavery " and " freedom."

The restraint to which Israel was subjected under Law was necessary to make them feel their need of the righteousness which Christ brought with Him for them, and for all nations this lesson was designed; for God's action toward Israel was a mirror in which all the nations were intended to see revealed the great truths of sin and the need of justification.

" Baptized into Christ " (v. 27)—not baptized into water, for the baptism here is that of the One Spirit in which baptism all become one, and that baptism demonstrated that there was no moral difference between Hebrew and Gentile. In the spiritual realm to which that baptism is the introduction, all destinction of race and religious privilege and sex disappear. Under the Law the male sex had great privileges, but " in Christ " sex relation ceases—all become " one new man " (Eph. ii. 15). Israel was baptized into Moses at the Red Sea (1 Cor. x. 2) but not into the water of the sea. Noah enjoyed a similar baptism at the Flood. He was baptized into Christ, but not into the water. The Ark, the Type of Christ, suffered that baptism (1 Pet. iii. 21). It is the ante-type baptism (Luke xii. 50) that saves, i.e., the baptism of Calvary —See Greek Text.

" The elements of the world," (v. 3), i.e., the first principles (Heb. vi. 1), that is, childhood's lessons respecting creation and revelation prior to Christ.

" God sent forth His Son " (v. 4). It was God Who acted. The Law required man to act. This requirement demonstrated man's impotency. The Son of God requires nothing from man other than his confidence.

Sin and death came in by the woman, so Christ came in also by the woman. Law claimed man as a sinner. Christ, therefore, was made under the Law. Under this double grace He took man's position—Himself without sin, being in the midst of evil, and having the knowledge of both good and evil. He redeemed them from that slavery and raised them into the position of sons of God ; and indwelt by His own Spirit of Sonship (v. 6), they possessed a nature which instinctively addressed God as Father. Such is the conscious relationship into which they were brought. No more slaves they became sons and heirs.

"The fulness of the time" (v. 4) as predicted in Daniel ix. 25. The prophecy was fulfilled to the very day—four hundred and eighty-three years—and it instructed Anna and Simeon and their fellow-believers to visit the Temple every day in order to see Him. Their faith and intelligence in the Scriptures were rewarded. They saw Him.

GALATIANS IV. 8—V. 1—The tutorship of Law in the case of Israel, and of Conscience in that of the Gentiles, was designed with its rudimentary lessons to lead them to Christ as shadows lead to the substance. When, therefore, the substance is reached and sonship established, to go back to "the rudiments," i.e., to symbols and sacraments, (v. 9), is not progress but ignorance. The rudiments are "weak"—they give no power over sin ; they are "beggarly" —for they do not possess the unsearchable riches of Christ.

In verses 8 and 10 idolatry and ritualism are united and presented as having the same source and operating upon the same principle. Man misuses God's gifts and corrupts His truths. The Law which taught man that he was a sinner and needed righteousness, was used by man as an instrument to establish his own righteousness through a carnal observance of its outward requirements. The idolater similarly debased conscience and became the willing slave to gods who only existed in his imagination.

These "days," etc. (v. 10) were shadows used by God to teach His ancient people of the realities which they would find in Christ, and only thus have they any value. He knew how to employ these figures in connection with a Law that tested man in the flesh and that demonstrated man's inability to serve God. To go back, therefore, to these shadows made for man in the flesh now that God had proved the impossibility of man by them acquiring merit before Him, and now that the substance of the shadow was come, was to go back to the position of men in the flesh, and as men in the flesh to seek a carnal righteousness. It was a going back to the principles of idolatry ; for the heathen observed days and months and seasons and years for the very same reason that the Pharisee did, i.e., to establish his own righteousness. It perplexed the Apostle (vs. 11 and 20) that the Galatian believers should wish to go back to paganism ; for that, in effect, would be the import of their action if they went back to Judaism under the guidance of their false teachers (v. 17).

"Be as I am" (v. 12), i.e., free from all the bondage of salvation by works and sacraments.

Verse 12 should close with the words "I am as ye are" and verse 13 begin : "In no respect did you behave unkindly to me, for you know, etc."

"My temptation" (v. 14) R.V.), i.e., the repulsive malady from which the Apostle was suffering, and which must have been a test of faith to the Galatians, for it was confounding that one who healed others could not heal himself. (See notes on 2 Cor. xii.).

To pluck out the eyes (v. 15) was an idiom expressive of an extreme affection that would surrender what was most precious for the benefit of another.

"They zealously court you, but not honourably" (v. 17), i.e., the false teachers. They shut the Gentile believers out of the Hebrew Church so as to make them pay court in their turn to those who excluded them. It was very right and good to be courted honourably whether Paul was with them or absent from them (v. 18), for they were his own little children whom he most tenderly loved. He did not dishonourably pay court to them, but he travailed in birth for them that Christ might be fully formed in them. Moses said : "Have I conceived all this people that I should carry them in my bosom ?" But Paul was ready to travail in birth with them a second time.

"To change my voice" (v. 20), i.e., as a mother, adapting the tone of her voice when looking at the child, feels by instinct whether to be gentle or severe.

"Hear" (v. 21), i.e., "listen to and learn from."

Hagar the slave-girl and Sarah the freewoman symbolized Sinai and the New Jerusalem.

Allegory is a compound Greek word and is a figure of speech in which spiritual facts are presented in physical terms ; as, for example, when a pretty and sweet-tempered child is spoken of as a rose-bud, a lower organism is employed to describe an higher.

The Arabic name for Mount Sinai is Hagar. In the East children of a slave woman were slaves.

Sacerdotalism, like Hagar, brings forth children for bondage. The Gospel, like Sarah, gives birth to sons of freedom.

" These two Covenants " (v. 24), i.e., works and grace.

The quotation (v. 27) from Isaiah liv. celebrates the joy of the earthly Jerusalem at the beginning of the millennium. It is here quoted to show that she will have more children during the time of her desolation than when in official relations with the Divine husband ; for many more are her children under the Gospel than under Law. Such are the ways of God on earth. All Christians are reckoned as her children, for the Gospel came forth from her. Such was the promise ; and she is founded upon that promise. The Church is not of promise. It was a council hid in God and never promised in the Scriptures. But into this high secret the Apostle does not here enter for the Galatians, like the Corinthians, were incapable of understanding it ; and so are the vast majority of Christian people to-day. See notes on Isa. liv.

" Persecuted " (v. 29), i.e., " tried to kill." See notes on Gen. xxi.

Liberty and bondage are the key-words of this section of the Epistle (iv. 8 to v. 1).

GALATIANS V. 2-26.—Justification by Law-obedience (v. 4) is in this section contrasted with righteousness by faith-acceptance (v. 5). The words " justified by law " contrast therefore with "righteousness by faith." The power energizing the one is man's will ; that energizing the other is the Holy Spirit.

He reveals the hoped for glory (v. 5), and faith builds on that hope. Righteousness is the foundation. Righteousness is not waited for,—it is already possessed,—but faith waits for the hope connected with it. This faith is energized by love, for it is a life of moral realities.

"Christ is become of no effect " (v. 4). The translation should be, " Ye have been loosed from Christ." The Greek verb is that of Rom. vii. 2, " loosed from her husband."

" Fallen from grace " (v. 4) contrast Rom. v. 2, " standing in grace." Grace and legal righteousness cannot co-exist. Christ in His circumcision undertook to perfectly obey all law, and, in His baptism, to fulfil all righteousness ; not in order to obtain merit for Himself, for He was sinless, but for those who should believe upon Him, and to whom all His moral perfection, ceremonial observance and law-obedience are reckoned.

Salvation by works requires a perfect obedience (v. 3). Such an obedience is impossible to imperfect man ; hence the hopelessness of salvation by works.

The natural mind loves outward ceremonies, and so Satan ministers to that desire by imposing on the sacrificial work of Christ a super-structure of outward sacraments and religious ceremonies and prayers and fastings controlled by man-made priests. Thus the confused human heart seeks to secure moral perfection but in effect destroys the Gospel.

In verses 5 and 6 are found " faith," " hope," and " love."

Faith is the medium of justification and love is the evidence of justification. It fulfils the law, it is operative. But a little legalism (v. 9) corrupts the whole Gospel ; and such is Satan's aim.

The " Him " of verse 8 is God. He had elected them to salvation on the principle of faith. The opposite persuasion of salvation by works therefore did not come from Him.

The Apostle predicted the judgment that would strike down the false teacher, and, at the same time, he expressed the confidence which he had in the Lord that the Galatians would stand fast in the truth. It is so human to notice the Apostle's uneasiness when he thought of them as feeble men, and his confidence when he thought of them as in the Lord. Greater here was his agitation than in Corinth. Moral questions grieved him there, but here the foundations of the Gospel were in question ; and the glories attaching to the Person and work of Christ were supremely precious to the Apostle's heart.

The doctrine of the Atonement (v. 11) is offensive to the self-righteous mind, for it declares that man is morally lost, wicked and hopeless, helpless and dead, and that he can only be recovered by being re-created. This re-creation takes place when he believes upon Christ as an atoning Saviour. Man denies that he is altogether lost, and he claims that he can add something to the sacrifice that Christ infinitely accomplished for him at Calvary. Such an addition destroys the Gospel, for it denies the infinite perfection of Christ's sacrifice. If that sacrifice was infinite, then is there no room for human additions to it in order to add to its perfection.

To preach Christ and good works— proudly named "The ethical Gospel"— does not involve persecution; but to preach the true Gospel does involve persecution (v. 11).

"Cut off" (v. 12), i.e., circumcise themselves off.

"An occasion to the flesh" (v. 13), i.e., to minister to self. The Gospel does not liberate a man to a life of laziness and self-indulgence but to an unceasing ministry of loving service to humanity.

The key-words of the section (16-26 are "flesh" and "Spirit." The works of the flesh are manifold and often mutually quarrel-some, and they are more in number than the fruit of the Spirit. The "fruit," not the "fruits," of the Spirit is a unity and always harmonious. The richer vocabulary for sins than for graces is a proof of human corruption; seventeen works of the flesh are detailed, but only nine manifestations of the Spirit.

"The flesh" is a term expressing human nature as estranged from God.

The verb "fulfil" (v. 16) proves the existence of this corrupt nature in the believer. It declares the consciousness of corrupt desires, and the enjoyment of victory through the power of the indwelling Holy Spirit.

"Ye shall not fulfil" (v. 16)—"Ye may not do" (v. 17, R.V.). These statements promise victory over all the power of the carnal nature—a victory which cannot be secured by legal efforts of self repression (v. 18).

"Wrath" (v. 20), i.e., bad temper — "Seditions," i.e., divisions.

All who are really Christ's (v. 24) crucify this indwelling principle of evil, and in the power of the Holy Spirit wage incessant warfare against it. Those who are only Christians mentally, know nothing of this warfare.

Verse 25 should read as in the Revised Version. It declares both life and holiness to be the work of the One Holy Spirit. He operates salvation and He operates sanctifi-cation. Both are realized on the principle of faith. Many know that they have received spiritual life through faith, but they think they can only secure sanctification by works. This is a great error. It never brings victory. Believing in Christ for sanctifi-cation as well as for justification introduces into a life of power and victory. It is impos-sible for a cripple by personal efforts and resolutions to climb a steep mountain to the summit of which runs a steam-coach. If in faith he commits himself to it he will make the experience of a power which can bring him to the highest point.

As righteousness is not founded on law-obedience so holiness is not secured by carnal efforts to reach that obedience. Holiness is only produced by the energy of the Divine life in the soul, and not by the activity of the human will in the body. See note on Col ii. 23.

There is no difficulty in judging between the works of the fallen nature and the fruit of the Spirit. They are manifest.

The strength for holiness is lodged in the new nature. The Law does not give the Spirit. Pretensions to law-observance pro-duce pride, provocation, and envying (v. 26).

GALATIANS VI.—The antagonisms of this chapter are expressed in the key words "something" and "nothing" (vs. 1-10) and "Christ" and the "world" (vs. 11-18).

"If a man be overtaken in a fault" (v. 1), means even if a Christian man be found out in any fault.

"Restore" (v. 1), i.e., seek to restore, not to judge. "In the spirit of meekness" —not in the spirit of harshness. "Con-sidering thyself"—the most spiritual may fall at any moment if tempted with sufficient skill, and if unshielded by God.

This first verse is rich and remarkable both inwardly and outwardly. As to its form it contains five figures of speech.

If a man thinks himself to be "something" he will not carry burdens (vs. 2-5). The burdens of verse 2 are burdens which can be transferred to others, or shared by others, such as poverty, sorrow, etc. The burdens of verse 5 mean loads that cannot be transferred, such as duty etc : The Greek words here are different.

If a Christian tests his life and service by comparison with that of others, he will deceive himself with baseless self-congratulations, but if he tests his activities in the light of the presence and Word of God, he will be saved from such pride and folly, and will be refreshed with a legitimate gladness.

The burden of the personal support of, the minister of the Gospel is to be borne by the believers of the Gospel (v. 6).

He who refuses to minister to others and pleases himself in a life of sacramental enjoyment or fleshly indulgence, must reap corruption (v. 8). This principle is illustrated in the history of the Christian Church. Almost from the beginning the Church turned away from the spiritual teaching of the Apostle Paul to the sacramental teaching of the formalists, and so the sad harvest of corruption quickly appeared, and continues to the present day.

A man reaps much more than he sows. If he repents grace forgives the sin, but does not prevent the harvest. So David's transgression was pardoned, but the sword never departed from his house ; and his last days contrast sadly with his first.

A man can " deceive " himself (v. 3) but he cannot " mock God " (v. 7).

If the Galatians wished to bear burdens, the Apostle begged them to bear the burdens of others and not the legal burdens which the false teachers placed upon them. And if they desired to be under a law, he proposed to them the law of Christ and urged them to fulfil that, i.e., to love one another (John xiii. 54 and xv. 12 and Rom. xv. 3).

God never wearies in well-doing (v. 9) ; but Christian people, as a rule, grow weary because they cannot immediately reap the fruit of their benevolence.

The needs of believers are to have precedence over those of unbelievers (v. 10).

Because the foundations of the Gospel were attacked, and the glory of the Person and work of the Lord Jesus Christ obscured, therefore the Apostle wrote this letter with his own hand ; and the large hand-writing was occasioned either by the chain which fastened him to his soldier-guard, or else because of defective eyesight (iv. 15). The statement (v. 11) shows the importance the Apostle attached to his writings, and his consciousness that they were inspired and authoritative.

In verses 12-15 he sums up all the import of his letter. Those who desired to display their zeal for outward ceremonies, sought to make them necessary to salvation, but their real object was to please self and escape persecution. They gloried in these ceremonies applied to men's bodies, the Apostle gloried, on the contrary, in the cross upon which the religious world of sacraments and shadows and outward ceremonies had been crucified, and upon which cross he himself had been crucified, so that he was dead to them and they were dead to him. Outward physical sacraments and ceremonies are unimportant (v. 15). What is important is the New Birth. Most certainly the irreligious world has been judged and ended in the cross of Christ, but so also has the religious world ; and it is the abolition of that world which is the subject of this Epistle. If Paul gloried in anything physical, it was not in the sign of circumcision but in the marks of man's brutality, which in the triumph of faith he called the " marks of Jesus " (v. 17).

In contrast with his other Epistles Paul does not here send a general salutation, but only to those who walked " according to this rule " (v. 16), i.e., the abolition of all shadows and sacraments as necessary to salvation.

Masters branded the bodies of their slaves with marks showing proprietorship. The Apostle's body was horribly disfigured by the deep wounds caused by the many scourgings he had suffered. When groaning under the agony Satan may have whispered to him " There is no God ; and if there is, He has no power to deliver you ; in any case it is evident He does not love you." But as each burning lash tore the Apostle's flesh, triumphant faith said "Another mark of Jesus " ; and that this triumphant grace is available for all, even for the feeblest Christian, is declared in the words : " The grace of our Lord Jesus Christ be with your spirit, brothers " (v. 18).

Here ends what may be termed the Romans group of Epistles. The keywords of this Epistle are :

Gospel versus Another Gospel (i. and ii.).
Works v. Faith (iii. 1-14).
Law v. Promise (iii. 15-22).
Slave v. Son (iii. 23 to iv. 7).
Bondage v. Liberty (iv. 8 to v. 15).
Flesh v. Spirit (v. 16-26).
Something v. Nothing (vi. 1-10).
Christ v. World (vi. 11-18).

EPHESIANS

This Epistle was written from the Apostle Paul's prison in Rome, and is manifestly encyclical (ii. 11, iv. 17), and intended for all "the faithful in Christ Jesus" (i. 1). The word "faithful" does not merely mean believers, but those who faithfully were maintaining the faith they had received. Paul's Gospel had already been established for some years and was being hotly attacked. Only to the faithful and intelligent could the doctrine of this Epistle be communicated.

For its great subject is "the mystery" referred to in Rom. xvi. 25. It had been kept secret since the world began; not made known to the sons of men (iii. 5); hidden in God (iii. 9); never revealed in the Scriptures, but communicated to the Apostle by Christ Himself (iii. 3). This great mystery, i.e., "secret," is that of the "new man" (ii. 15), i.e., the Church, the mystical Christ, far above all heavens, "the one body" of which Christ is the Head, and an election taken out of the earth and separated from it, the members. This "new man" must not be confounded with the earthly kingdom which is to be composed of all people, as foretold in the Scriptures (Gen. xii. 3, Rom. xv. 8-12) in union with and under the head-ship of Israel.

This Epistle, therefore, is the great Church Epistle in which is revealed the secret purpose hidden in God from before all time, of associating with Christ, and engracing in Him, far above all heavens, a special redemption out of the earth to be His companions forever in that inconceivable glory. To be one of that company was the Apostle Paul's ambition; and to share its unspeakable glory he willingly surrendered all lesser blessings and privileges (Phil. iii. 7-14). Great will be the glory of the kingdom of the heavens as set up upon the earth—the true Catholic i.e., universal Church, but immeasurably greater will be the glory of the Church

of the "calling on high," not only from out of, and above the earth and above the heavens, but above all heavens. This is the theme of the Epistle.

The Romans group (Romans, Corinthians, Galatians) is here followed by the Ephesians group (Ephesians, Philippians, Colossians). The subject of the first group is the Gospel with its two foundation doctrines of justification and sanctification. Conduct at Corinth attacked sanctification and doctrine in Galatia denied justification. The great theme of the Ephesian group is the Headship and unity of "the one body." Conduct at Philippi denied its unity, and doctrine at Colosse attacked its Headship.

The matter of the Epistle is doctrinal: The believer's standing (i. 3-iii. 21), and the believer's state (iv.-vi. 20). These must never be confounded.

The "purpose" of God concerning Christ Personal (i. 3-14), and His "purpose" concerning Christ mystical (iii. 1-13), should be recognised and kept distinct.

The "counsel" of God (Acts xx. 27) concerns Christ's Headship over creation and His rule in His earthly Kingdom; the "purpose" of God belongs to Christ's Headship of the "one new man"—the body called on high above all heavens.

The formula "God and Father" in this Epistle is important. He is the God of Christ as Man and the Father of Christ as the Son of His love. The nature of God is revealed in the one title; relationship in the other. Members of the heavenly election are brought into this fellowship. The God and Father of the Lord Jesus Christ is their God and Father. He invites them to enjoy His purposes concerning the glories of His Beloved Son; and in this Epistle He makes known to the believer the highest of these glories.

In Ephesians the believer is presented

as being in Christ; in Colossians Christ is viewed as being in the believer.

The Epistle opens with God, His thoughts and purposes, and His activities in the election and the elevation to the highest glory of those whom He loved from before the foundation of the world. Redemption is viewed from the Divine stand-point, not from the human.

This Epistle being clearly encyclical, and being the great Epistle revealing the Divine purpose respecting the Church, is no doubt the one that was sent on " from " Laodicea (Col iv. 16).

EPHESIANS I.—The revelation of the Church having been made to the Apostle Paul personally he associates no one with him in communicating it to the faithful in Christ Jesus (v. 1).

Everything here is Divine—" The will of God " (v. 1); " grace and peace from God " (v. 2); His will (v. 5); " His grace " (v. 7); His blood; His will (v. 9); His pleasure (v. 9); His purpose (v. 11); His counsel (v. 11); His glory (v. 12); His calling (v. 18); His inheritance (v. 18); His power (v. 19); His right hand (v. 20).

From out of the darkness of his dungeon the Apostle looked into the heavenly places. They are mentioned five times in the Epistle (v. 3, 20, ii. 6, iii. 10, vi. 12).

The Three Princes and Daniel and Stephen and Paul and John enjoyed visions of heaven when suffering the cruelties of earth. A prison may be the vestibule of heaven.

From this prison bursts the triumphant word "blessed" (v. 3). All is glory and victory. Believers are blessed; they are blessed with all blessings; the blessings are spiritual; they belong to the heavenly places; and they are secured in Christ.

Seven of these blessings are detailed: viz: chosen (v. 4); predestined (v. 5); accepted (v. 6); redeemed (v. 7); instructed (v. 9); sealed (v. 13); and enriched (v. 14).

The Church is a company of sons (v. 5) engraced in the Beloved One (v. 6). God embraces them as sons because they are in His dearly Beloved Son. His atonement (v. 7) procured them redemption, and the measure of the forgiveness they enjoy is the measure of the unsearchable riches of His grace. If those riches can be measured so may the forgiveness be measured. The redemption is an actual possession, consciously enjoyed, and based not upon anything in the believer or anything performed by the believer, but wholly, solely, and only upon the atoning sacrifice of Calvary.

Christ is to be supreme over things heavenly and things earthly. God is the Author and Christ is the Object of these glories. His " counsel " concerned creation, for He said " Let us make "; His " purpose " concerns the Church, planned in His own heart before Creation.

In the activity of His nature and purpose He planned to surround His Beloved Son with sons Whom He could fully love and delight in. He could not delight in them unless they were conformed to the image of His Son. So they are before Him in the sphere of a love that is Divine; and they are in that sphere as holy and without blame (v. 4).

In verse 4 His purpose as God is seen; in verse 5 His activity as Father. Angels are His servants; believers are His sons. Had God one perfect object of His love? The Church is blessed in that object. Its members were sinners saved according to the riches of His grace, and made saints according to the glory of that grace (vs. 6 and 7).

This grace makes the sons depositories of the Father's secret plans (v. 9). This is an amazing privilege. They are interested in the future glories of Christ, and in the purposes of God respecting those glories. They are to be Christ's companions in the heavenly glories, and His associates in the administration of the earthly glories (vs. 9, 10, 11).

The Church is His inheritance (v. 11).

Verse 13 should read as in the Revised Version. It illustrates Mark xvi. 16.

The Church is the purchased possession (v. 14)—purchased for Him and purchased for the heavenly inheritance. No adversary can defeat this purpose of grace (v. 14).

Thus God's purpose is the foundation of all blessing. No sinfulness on man's part hinders its operations, and no merit on man's part originated it. The blessings flow from God to man just as in Leviticus the order proceeds from the burnt-offering to the sin-offering, and in the Tabernacle the description begins with the Ark and ends with the outer court. Man approached these wonders in the reverse order.

So the believer learns that before the

stars were created he was known and loved in Christ and assured of an eternal union with Christ in an unspeakable splendour of power and glory far above all heavens. This doctrine declares the eternity of the Son of God (v. 4).

When a sinner believes upon the Lord Jesus Christ he is sealed with the Holy Spirit (v. 13, R.V.). This is the baptism of Titus iii. 5, 6.

The catch-words of the prayer (15-23) are "the hope of His calling," and "the glory of His inheritance"—" Hope " and " glory " —" calling " and " inheritance."

The prayer contains four petitions : His knowledge (v. 17) ; His calling (v. 18) ; His inheritance (v. 18) ; and His power (v. 19),i.e., Person, position, pageantry and power. The prayer first draws the affections of the heart to Him Who is here presented as the God of glory in the glory of God, i.e., Jesus Christ in the plenitude of His God-head, the Author of all this grace. Then it views the position " on high " (Phil. iii. 14) to which the Church is elected ; then the splendour belonging to that position ; and, lastly, the prayer reposes in faith and triumph upon the great truth that the mighty power that raised Christ from among the dead and set Him above all heavens is the same power that will rapture the Church to the same place and the same glory.

The Church is His body, and, as such, is the fulness or completion, or complement of the Head. He is over all things (v. 22) ; and the Church as His body is, therefore, over all things—united with One Who in Himself fills all things.

The glory of His inheritance is in the saints (v. 18) ; that is, He will possess that glory in them just as He possessed the land of Canaan in the Twelve Tribes. Canaan was promised to Him as the Son of Abraham ; and the glory of the inheritance became His when Joshua conquered it. He is also heir to the Heavenly glory, and that glory will become His when the Church takes possession of it. He will possess it in them.

Without the Head the body would be incomplete. The Church will complete His glory in that wondrous realm far above all heavens which He is to fill fully. This is the "mystery "—the great secret—hidden in God and never revealed in the Scriptures until this Epistle is reached. It may, therefore, be justly stated to be the most wondrous

Book in the Bible. To be a member of that glorious company—Christ's own body—and, as such, sharing in Him and with Him His exaltation above all worlds, was the Apostle Paul's ambition ; and for it he willingly surrendered the glories attaching to the earthly kingdom promised to the Hebrew Church.

EPHESIANS II.—As chapter i. revealed the purposes and activities of God in chosing companions for His Beloved Son in the glory far above all heavens, so this chapter describes who those companions are. In verse 2 they are stated to be morally an habitation of the Devil but now created (v. 22) an habitation of God, and the creative power (v. 5) that accomplishes this marvel is declared to be grace. Amazing thought ! That a Mary Magdalene and a crucified thief should be the companions in glory of the Son of God.

These objects of the Divine election are declared (v. 1) to be " dead," that is, without any inward conscious moral movement toward God. Such He quickens in and with Christ. God does everything. It is a new creation. This chapter and Gen. i. correspond. The one reveals God's activity in physical creation ; the other, His activity in moral creation. As the earth was sunken in the deep darkness, and dead in the great deep without life or power of movement, so is human nature morally before God. It is here a declaration (v. 3) respecting man's nature—the source of the evil described in verses 2 and 3. Creation did not cease on the sixth day, it still continues (v. 10).

The Apostle Paul prior to his conversion lived a blameless life of religious rectitude ; the Ephesians prior to their conversion wallowed in an appalling abyss of idolatry and obscenity. Yet the Apostle says that there was no moral difference between him and them. They were all alike corrupt by nature, they were all alike dead in sins, sons of disobedience, led by the spirit of Satan and under the wrath of God (vs. 1-3). These are facts revealed by the Holy Spirit Who is infallible ; but they are facts that man denies, and the assertion of which enrages him.

Such are the beings whom God in the exceeding riches of His grace, loved and quickened with Christ and raised with Christ, and has made to sit together with Christ in the heavenlies. He is the sole Worker. To give such companions to His Son, it was necessary that He should make them morally as white as snow, and this He effected through the atoning work of Christ Jesus (v. 7).

All is of grace. Even the faith that saves is the gift of God (v. 8). Would anyone say that saving faith is of man? To say so would destroy the argument of the whole passage. All here is of God. He is the Operator as well as the Source of the operations. It is a creation — a creation of faith as well as of works. God takes up a sinner in whom is not one moral movement towards Himself for He says that " there is none that seeketh after God," and makes him the subject of a new creation; and in the energy of that new creation the new creature walks in good works prepared by God for his feet. He has not to make the road; it is made for him, and smoothly made, as only God can make it, and he has but to walk upon it.

There was a Divine necessity that the exceeding riches of grace in the heart of God should be manifested; and hence He chose a special election out from among the willing slaves of sin and Satan, in order that by raising them to the highest heights of glory, and associating them there with His own Beloved Son, He might thus make a demonstration adequate to the wealth of the grace that abounds in Himself.

In that new creation both Gentiles and Jews are included (vs. 11-22): The latter were ceremonially near; the others far off. They were alienated (v. 12), that is, they had been themselves at one time near, but not wishing to retain God in their knowledge (Rom. i. 28), they had become alienated. Just as Aaron was " made nigh " in the blood of the sin-offering and by the blood— the one being the element, the other the instrument—so both Jews and Gentiles are made nigh, Christ Himself being their common peace, making both one, having broken down the middle wall of partition and in His death in human nature abolished the cause of the enmity between them, i.e., the ceremonial law (v. 15). But all this He did in this relationship in order that He might create (v. 15, R.V). out of them both a " new man "—a new creation—so making peace between them, and that in one body He might present them both unto God having in His cross slain the enmity

that existed between God and them because of sin.

The great argument here is that in that new creation there are neither Jews nor Gentiles. Such distinctions do not exist there, nor could they. In Christ's baptism into death at Calvary all Jewish believers die, and cease therefore to be Jews, and, likewise, all Gentile believers die and cease to be Gentiles. They rise with Christ, and as one body—a new man—they are brought into a new creation—separated from the earth and placed in and with Christ in the heavenlies. There He as the Head and they as the members form the Church.

This purpose of God respecting the Church in the heavenlies and His counsel concerning Israel and the nations in the earth, do not conflict. All His promises made in the Scriptures to the Hebrew Church will most surely be fulfilled in the earth. The nations will be blessed with Israel, as Israel. The distinction between Israel and the nations will be maintained; for Israel will be set at the head of the nations; and all together they will become the Kingdom and the power of Christ. But the Church's home and hopes are heavenly.

The reconciliation of verse 16 was not the reconciliation of Jew and Gentile, but the reconciliation to God of an election out of both incorporated into one new man.

The City, the House, and the Temple are presented in verses 19-22. Believers of the election are members of the heavenly City, sons in the House, and stones in the Temple. But all is heavenly. These are the three heavens into which Paul was raptured (2 Cor. xii.). The lower heaven is the City; the higher, the House; the highest, the Temple. Moses and David were commanded to set up on earth a copy of that which was in the heavens. So there was the Court, the House, and the Temple, i.e., the most holy place. Zion is the earthly city of God. There shall be the palace of the Great King and the Temple of Jehovah. The redeemed nations, with Israel, will be citizens of that City, sons in that House, and living stones in that Temple. These are the two temples of verse 21 (R.V.). Christ is the cornerstone of both. The foundation of the one is the twelve Apostles and the Old Testament prophets; the foundation of the other, the eight Apostles and the New Testament Prophets. See note on Rev. xxi. 14.

Both buildings are fitly framed; both grow unto an holy Temple; and both are the habitation of God.

Some commentators understand that the House represents Christendom, and that it is to be distinguished from the Church.

So the chapter opens with men as an habitation of Satan (v. 2) and closes with these same now become an habitation of God (v.22), and verses 4 to 10 in the middle of the chapter reveal how this amazing miracle was effected.

EPHESIANS III.—Having by way of parenthesis described in chapter ii. those who are to be the companions of God's Beloved Son in the heavenlies, the Apostle now continues the communications made in chapter i. but with this distinction: that chapter presents Christ Personal: this chapter (iii.) presents Christ Mystical, i.e., Christ and the Church as the one Body, He the Head, and believers the members. Chapter i. sets out the " Mystery of God "—His great secret concerning the glory of Christ; chapter iii. the " Mystery of Christ " (v. 4)— His great secret concerning the companions of Christ. The prior chapter reveals what He has made Christ to be to His Church; the latter chapter, what He has made His Church to be in Christ.

Thus the " Purpose of God " is distinguished from the " Counsel of God." The latter has to do with the glories of the Son of Man in creation and in His dominion in the earth. Purpose has to do with the prior creation of the Church, and concerns the glories peculiar to Christ as the Son of God in union with the Church in the heavens.

In harmony with this distinction, Acts xx. 25-27 deals with dominion in the earth as " the Counsel of God," and with that only; for it is outside the subject of that Book to introduce the " Purpose of God " with respect to the Church. This distinction constitutes the difference between Paul *preaching* " according to the Scriptures " and his *teaching* according to the revelation. The Gospel was always revealed in the Scriptures; the Mystery was never revealed (Rom. i. 2, and xvi. 25) in them.

It is perfectly clear that God's purpose with respect to Christ Mystical was a great secret hidden in Himself and never revealed until made known to the Apostle Paul. He through his prophetic writings (Rom..xvi. 26)

and his apostolic companions (Eph. iii. 5) communicated the secret to all nations (v. 9)

The subject of verses 1-13 is this secret concerning Christ Mystical, i.e., what God in His eternal purpose has made the Church to be in Christ and to Christ.

This secret is not to be confounded with Christ's Headship over Israel and the Nations. That was never " hid in God " and only " now revealed " (vs. 5 and 9). See Col. i. 26. The Scriptures repeatedly reveal the association of the Nations with Israel in the Kingdom that is to be set up upon the earth; but it is promised that in that Kingdom Israel will be a special and dominant people. In the Church all earthly distinctions are lost. They would have no meaning in the heavenlies.

The Apostle Paul had a double ministry: first, to announce the Gospel of the grace of God to the Gentiles, and, second, to enlighten believers about the secret respecting the Church (Col. i. 23-27).

The first lesson to be learned is that revealed in the Epistle to the Romans, i.e., the principle upon which God declares an unrighteous man to be righteous. The second lesson is that taught in the Epistle to the Ephesians, i.e., an election of believers in Christ, united to Him in the heavenlies, and to be His glorified companions through the eternal ages.

Paul's imprisonment (v. 1) was occasioned by his preaching the Gospel to the Gentiles.

" Dispensation " (v. 2), i.e., stewardship. To him was committed by grace the communication of the Mystery (v. 3).

" Afore " (v. 3), i.e., in chapter i. 3-10. These " few words " when read show the Apostle's intelligent knowledge of the Mystery (v. 4).

The word " now " (verse 5) proves that the Apostles and Prophets of the Mystery were those of the New Testament and distinct from the Twelve.

That the Gentiles should be fellow-heirs with Israel in the earthly Kingdom promised in the Scriptures, was no secret; therefore what verse 6 reveals must be distinguished from the revelations made to Abraham and to the Old Testament Prophets.

" The promise in Christ " of this verse was made to Him by God before the worlds were framed, and it was that an election out of the world should become the members of His Body and sharers in the glories and promises made to Him—that they should be joint heirs, joint-bodied and joint partakers in the promise. This does not mean that the Gentiles, as such, should be joined to a body already in existence, i.e., to the Hebrew Church, but that redeemed men should be taken out from amongst both Jews and Gentiles and be joint-bodied with Christ, and so become " a new man."

This is the great secret—Christ Mystical, One Body, the Church, He being the Head.

The ministry of this Mystery was a gift to the Apostle Paul, not because of any merit in him, for it was a gift of grace (v. 7) ; and that same grace furnished him with spiritual power adequate to the discharge of the ministry. Gift, grace, and power, are the important words in this verse.

Verse 8 treats of this grace given to the Apostle to preach the Gospel among the nations. Compare Col. i. 23-27.

" Men " (v. 9), i.e., believers ; for they only could understand the mystery hid in God.

The creation of the world in verse 9 is brought into relationship with the creation of the Church (v. 10). The creation of the world demonstrated the wisdom of God ; the creation of the Church demonstrates, and will demonstrate to the angelic hosts, the manifold wisdom of God.

" Fellowship " (v. 9), Greek : " Stewardship."

The Apostle's imprisonment did not dishonour believers, but the contrary ; and, therefore, they were not to be down-hearted (v. 13).

"The whole family" (v. 15). Greek, "every family." Israel contained twelve families. All owed their origin to Jacob. They bare his name, and were named by him. The heavenly families are distinct.

The two prayers of this Epistle (i. 15-23, and iii. 14-19) are related. They are prayers of the Holy Spirit through the Apostle Paul. Both are based upon the fact stated in i. 3, and upon the Divine titles of " God " and " Father " assuring that fact. God is the God of Christ as Son of Man and the Father of Christ as Son of God. These two titles of " God " and " Father " are brought together in the verse. In the two prayers they are separated. The first prayer (i. 17) is addressed to " the God of our Lord Jesus Christ " ; the second prayer (iii. 14) is addressed to " the Father of our Lord Jesus Christ." This is designed ; for the first prayer is based upon the purpose of God which He " purposed in Himself " (i. 9) respecting Christ's personal glory as Man above all things in earth and in the heavens, and the second prayer is animated by His " purpose in Christ Jesus " (iii. 11) respecting His eternal glory as Head of the Church. The two prayers, therefore, are founded upon Christ Personal and Christ Mystical.

The subject of the first prayer is Power—the Power that set Christ in the heavenlies and appointed Him to be the Head to the Church, raised by the same power and set in and with Christ over all things as His Body. The subject of the second prayer is Love—Love that makes comprehensible what is incomprehensible (iii. 17-19).

The believer in Christ is the atmosphere of the first prayer ; Christ in the believer is the atmosphere of the second prayer.

There is a profound moral difference between the mind viewing the truth concerning the Mystery objectively and the heart feeling it subjectively. Therefore it is that the Apostle's heart breaks out into these two prayers.

God has His heavenly families and His earthly families (v. 15) just as He has His heavenly and earthly temples (ii. 21).

If His strength can be measured so can the riches of His glory be measured, for they are equally boundless (v. 16).

Christ does not dwell in the heart by sacraments but by faith (v. 17).

A cube has length, breadth and depth. Christ's love has breadth, length, depth, and height—for it is boundless and it is everlasting. It descended to the depths of hell in order to redeem man, and it carried him up when redeemed above all heavens. " Filled into all the fulness of God " (v. 19). A tiny cup may be filled into all the fulness of the ocean.

The Doxology of verses 20 and 21 divides the doctrinal and experimental portions of the Epistle. The first concerns the believer's standing in the heavenlies ; the second his state on the earth.

The measure of God's ability to do is the measure of His power to perform (v.20) The ability of God secures the moral perfection of the believer. Compare Phil. i. 6 and 2 Cor. ix. 8.

Verse 21 should read as in the Revised

Version. The eternal glory of God as God and Father, will be made visible throughout all ages " in the Church and in Christ Jesus." This is an amazing statement! Christ and the Church as One Body will be the vehicle of that eternal demonstration.

The heart affected by the wonderful revelations of this first half of the Epistle (i., ii., iii.), finds utterance of necessity, and overflows in prayer (14-19) and praise (20-21). Thus are the two sections of the Epistle parted and yet united.

The Eight Apostles of the Church (v. 5) are :

Barnabas Acts xiv. 4 and 14.
Andronicus Rom. xvi. 7.
Junia do.
Apollos 1 Cor. iv. 6 and 9.
Sosthenes 1 Cor. i. 1 and iv. 9.
Paul Gal. i. 1.
Silas i Thess. i.1, 6 and 9 and ii. 4 and 6
Timothy do. do.

EPHESIANS IV—Calling (i.-iii.) and Conduct (iv.-vi.) are the Key-notes of the respective portions of this Epistle. The one is motived by the other, just as a child alters his conduct when he becomes conscious that he is called to a throne. The moral conduct of a man on earth is affected by the knowledge that he is chosen by God to be a companion of Christ in His glory in the heavenlies.

So this section of the Epistle describes the believer's conduct both among believers and among unbelievers.

The Apostle was Nero's prisoner ; but faith declared him to be the Lord's prisoner (v. 1). Thus faith looks behind and above the actualities of earthly facts however confounding and painful.

"Vocation" (v. 1), i.e., the calling on high in Christ Jesus. Unless that calling be recognised it is impossible to walk worthy of it. The more its height is recognised the lowlier will become the mind and disposition of the recogniser (v. 2).

"The unity of the Spirit" (v. 3) secures the unity of the Body—the Church. That unity is a fact. Each member of the Body is to recognise the fact and to order his conduct thereby, doing nothing to militate against that unity—not in carnal irritability but in the bond of peace.

This unity is marked by one Spirit, one Lord, one Father and one Hope, one Faith and one Baptism. This is the unity of the Spirit and not the uniformity of the flesh. This latter may be seen in the Church of Rome ; the former is aimed at, however imperfectly, in the Society of Friends.

There are not two Spirits or two Lords or two Gods, and there are not two Hopes or two Faiths or two Baptisms.

All here is in the spiritual realm. The one Lord, the one Revelation and the one Baptism are all on the same spiritual plane. The subject of the passage is the unity of the Spirit. So this one and unifying baptism is objective, spiritual, and divine ; as are also the one Lord and the one Revelation. Many assume the baptism here to be the baptism into water. But that baptism is physical and subjective—it has to do with discipleship in the earth, and is limited and local, for climate makes it universally impossible ; but this one baptism is that of the Spirit baptizing both Jew and Gentile into one body. There are not two baptisms. There were two in John i., but that into water ceased and that of the Holy Spirit abides.

The one Father rules over all, acts through all, and dwells in all (v. 6).

What mighty bonds of unity ! The Spirit of God, the Lordship of Christ, and the Divine Fatherhood. Faith introduces into this unity ; and no one can be a Christian who is a stranger to it.

"The measure of the gift of Christ" (v. 7), that is to say, as Christ sees fit to bestow.

The quotation from Psalm lxviii. (v. 9) concerns Christ exalted as Man far above all heavens (v. 10) and giving men as gifts to man (vs. 11-16). Having become man in order to redeem man, and ascended as the glorified Man, He in His glorified humanity received gifts for men and distributed them among men. These gifts were themselves men (v. 11) ; and their ministry was for the winning of men to Christ ; and then, having won them, to build them up in Christ until they reached perfect Christian manhood (v. 13). The miraculous gifts of Pentecost and Corinth were distinct. They had to do with Israel and the earthly kingdom. See notes on 1 Cor. xii.-xiv.

The Apostles of verse 11 were not the Twelve Apostles. Those were given prior to the Lord's resurrection ; these, subsequent to it.

" As the truth is in Jesus " (v. 21), not " as it is in Jesus," as people say—implying there is truth which is not in Him, which is impossible.

" Given themselves over " (v. 19). " God gave them over " (Rom. i. 26). This action was a just judgment upon man's self-will.

" The old man," i.e., the carnal nature (v. 22) is to be " put off," not improved.

" Be ye angry," but beware of sinning; and do not let the sun set upon your irritation; and do not leave room for the Devil to act (vs. 26 and 27).

The Divine principle is that every man should earn his bread by honest labour (v. 28) producing what is good for his fellow creatures. A Christian man should, therefore, neither be a tobacco manufacturer nor maker of intoxicating drink. God here engages to provide work for everyone who will work and is able to work. He will reward his energy with a sufficiency for the workman's maintenance of himself and his family, and with a surplus for the maintenance of those who can not work. Those who can work and will not, should be permitted to starve.

" Clamour " (v. 31)—loud insulting language.

Mutual forgiveness costs little or nothing (v. 32). Divine forgiveness costs everything. " For Christ's sake " (v. 32). Because of what Christ is, and because of His atoning work, God can, as the righteous God, pardon guilty sinners for Christ's sake; and this principle of grace operates independently of merit or demerit on the sinner's part. Hence the pardon is infinite and eternal because founded on a base that is infinite and eternal.

EPHESIANS V. 1-17.—God forgives people who merit no forgiveness (iv. 32). His children are to imitate Him (v. 1, R.V.).

They are to act lovingly (v. 2) and their loving conduct is to be measured by Christ's, and is to be carried to the same length (v. 2).

The meal-offering and the sin-sacrifice fore-shadowed the Person and the Atonement of Christ. The meal offering was bloodless—but the meal was crushed; the other demanded the shedding of the victim's blood. It was all poured out at the base of the altar, thus demonstrating an actual death for sin. Christ's atoning death

was an odour of a sweet savour to God. as was Noah's which pre-figured it: But the doctrine of the Atonement is offensive to man. What is repugnant to man is precious to God.

" Jesting " (v. 4), i.e., impure jesting.

The Holy Spirit says that no unclean person shall have any inheritance in the Kingdom of Christ and of God (v. 5.) Popular religious teachers of the present day are not afraid to contradict the Holy Spirit and to say that unclean persons if they die in battle, will certainly inherit the Kingdom of Christ and of God.

The association of the titles Christ and God affirm the Deity of Jesus of Nazareth.

The wrath of God (v. 6) will surely judge all who refuse to be converted, but many modern preachers deceive the unconverted with vain words telling them that there is no future punishment and no lake of fire. They say that " hell " is figurative language. If so, then by a parity of reasoning, " heaven" is also figurative language.

" Sometimes " (v. 8); better, " at a former time." The natural man is not only dark and ignorant but he is darkness itself. Not only is he in the darkness, but the darkness is in him. The Holy Spirit here contradicts and destroys the doctrine of the Inner Light.

When the dark and ignorant sinner believes upon Him Who is the Light of the world, he then, but not till then, becomes a son of the Light. He enters into the light and the light enters into him. When a man is in the darkness the darkness is in him. All is dark. When a man is in the light the light is in him and all is light.

" The fruit of the light " (v. 9, R.V.) contrasts with the works of darkness (vs 3 to 5).

The sons of light put to the proof what is acceptable unto the Lord (v. 10). The first queston of the new heart is : " Will this be acceptable to the Lord ? " and thus the light is thrown upon language, thoughts, dress, house-hold furniture, pleasures, business and every department of life. All is put to the proof under the searchlight of the Word of God.

The natural man is insensible and lies among the dead (v. 14). Aroused by grace to his condition, he cries for light and Christ shines upon him (Isa. lx. 1). Light is in the Lord (v. 8) and nowhere else. When Christ shines upon a man that man becomes a light to others (vs. 11-3). He reproves their dark works, and he shows them the way to holiness and salvation (v. 13). He shines for Jesus. So will it be with Israel— Christ will shine upon her, and she will arise and shine unto the nations and so bring them to His feet. See notes on Isa. lx.

The function of light is to make manifest what before was hidden. Thus Jesus as the Light of the world, made manifest the hypocrisy of the Pharisees, and the unbelief and insincerity of those who professed to be His disciples. He exposed, for example, the unbelief or worthlessness of seemingly pious expressions such as: " Blessed is he who shall eat bread in the Kingdom of God," and " Blessed is the mother that bare thee." To know Christ after the flesh— even so intimately as to be the mother of His flesh—has no saving value ; to hear the Word of God and believe it alone secures blessing ; and failure to eat bread in the Kingdom of God will be due to man's indifference and not to God's forgetfulness. See notes on Luke xiv. 15 and Luke xi. 27.

Because the days are evil, the sons of light should make the most of every day by shining in the darkness, and by buying up every opportunity of doing good (v. 16, R.V. margin).

Intelligence as to the will of the Lord is obtained by daily Bible study and prayer (v 17).

EPHESIANS V. 18—VI. 9.—The filling of the Spirit is the subject of this section of the Epistle ; and it is humbling to learn that the discharge of Christian fellowship, and of natural and social relationships, are for the Christian impossible without that filling.

The moral filling with the Spirit should be distinguished from His miraculous filling. The latter is subordinate. It is the action of the Spirit on the flesh of man ; and it characterizes the earthly kingdom of the Messiah. It belongs to 1 Cor. xii.-xiv. See notes on those chapters.

The elevation of the everyday duties of the Christian life into the spiritual realm is a higher demonstration of the Spirit's power than is an exhibition of His extraordinary gifts.

There should be a comma after the word " Spirit " in verse 18, and a semi-colon after the word " yourselves " in verse 19, and the comma after the word " songs " should be removed.

The being filled with the Spirit is evidenced by speaking, singing, thanksgiving and submitting. It is notable, that the energy of the Spirit first expresses itself in mutual testimony. In the Scriptures " speaking " almost invariably follows " filling " as the first expression of Spiritual visitation. All the passages which speak of the filling of the Spirit should be studied, and this fact will be noticed.

Apart from this filling with the Spirit wives (v. 22), husbands (v. 25), children (vi. 1) fathers (v. 4), servants (v. 5), and masters (v. 9) cannot act toward one another as God commands.

The argument that husbands should love their wives as Christ loves the Church, does not state that the Church is the wife or that Christ is the husband, but that as Christ loves His body (the Church) so a husband ought to love his body (his wife).

The baptism of " water " (v. 26) is defined as that of the Word. As water cleanses the body so the Word of God cleanses the conduct. The verse that follows (27) makes it clear that this baptism is spiritual and not physical.

" This secret is great—I mean the secret concerning Christ and the Church " (v. 32). The union of a man with his wife was not a secret—it was revealed in Genesis ii. 24.

The argument of vi. 3, is not that obedient children are assured of long life on the earth but that God in promising such physical blessing to Israel showed the exceptional importance of this commandment.

EPHESIANS VI. 1c—24.—As the Epistle began with all spiritual blessings in the heavenlies, so it closes with all spiritual enemies in the same position. That is the sphere of Church warfare. Divine provision is fully made for its victorious discharge. This spiritual warfare demands the whole armour of God (vs. 11 and 13). Having overcome all his enemies (v. 13), the Christian is not to doff his armour and lay aside his sword, but to keep standing (v. 14) and preaching (v. 15) and sheltering (v. 16) and hoping (v. 17) and reading the Bible (v. 17) and watching and praying (v. 18).

The moral darkness of this world is ruled from the heavenlies by evil spirits. So far as they are given liberty of action by God they occasion wars, tempests, pestilences, famines, earthquakes and all physical and doctrinal disturbances which afflict mankind. The opening of the Book of Job, certain statements in the Book of Daniel (ix. 13), the storms recorded in the Gospels, and the Lord's teaching (Mark xiii. 8) that the whole period of His absence would be marked by such calamities, throw light upon the activities and powers of these wicked spirits.

The mystery of the Gospel " (v. 19), i.e., the glad tidings respecting the secret. To communicate that secret required great boldness, for its glory belittled the glories of Gentile philosophy and Hebrew privilege.

In these closing verses (19-24) the two themes of the Epistle—" calling " and " conduct "(vs.19 and 24)—reappear together with the double title of " God " and " Father " (v. 23).

The Holy Spirit is mentioned ten times in the Epistle : The sealing of the Spirit at conversion (i. 13) ; Access by the Spirit in worship (ii. 18) ; the believer a temple of the Spirit (ii. 22) ; the teaching of the Spirit (iii. 4) ; the might of the Spirit in the inner man (iii. 16) ; the unity of the Spirit (iv. 3) ; the grieving of the Spirit (iv. 7) ; the filling of the Spirit (v. 18) ; the Sword of the Spirit (vi. 17) ; and praying in the Spirit (vi. 18).

The word " Spirit " (v. 9) should read " light."

The Kingdom of God is composed of all, from Adam onward, who are born of the Spirit of God. Its sphere is the world. Its King and High Priest is Christ. The term " the Kingdom and patience of Jesus Christ " expresses its present form of moral government ; and the term "the Kingdom and power of Jesus Christ " will express its future form of material government. when He, as the Heir of the world (Rom. iv. 13), will claim the Kingdom. Hence the scene in Rev. v. Israel's position in this Kingdom is, and will be, one of exceptional splendour. All nations will be given to her as sons. Palestine will be the centre of that earthly glory. The city of Rev. xxi. will be the capital ; and the names of Israel's Tribes and Apostles, not those of Paul and his companions, will be graven upon it. This Divine counsel was always revealed in the Scriptures and never hidden.

What then was the glory of " the secret hidden in God " and " never revealed," to share in which the Apostle Paul surrendered all the amazing glory of the dominion promised to Israel ? It was the " Election on High " of Phil. iii. 14. The Epistle to Ephesians reveals it. It is that God has purposed from before all eternity to associate with Christ in a realm of inconceivable glory, not only above Rev. xxi. 2, and the earth, and the heavens, and all heavens, but " far above all heavens," a unique and glorious company out of the Redeemed from all ages, in order that through them He might make known to the angelic hosts the fulness of Christ Who filleth all in all. That wonderful company forms " the Church "—" The Body "—" the New Man " of which He is the Head and they are the members ; and it was membership in that Election that the Apostle eagerly desired, and participation in its glory that he so earnestly sought.

All these, the mightiest princes of His highest Court, will be His Companions ; they will be seated with Him in His throne in the super-celestial glory ; and they will accompany Him in the activities of His government over all worlds.

PHILIPPIANS

The Apostle from his prison in Rome reproves the Philippians for conduct inconsistent with the unity of the Body. See introduction to the Epistle to the Ephesians. Yet their attachment to the Apostle himself was sincere for they sent him money by the hand of Epaphroditus so as to soften the rigours of his imprisonment (i. 5, and ii. 25, iv. 14 and 2 Cor. xi. 8 and 9).

This Epistle corresponds therefore with 1 and 2 Corinthians for it deals with defect in conduct; and the repeated command " Be ye followers of Me " occurs twice in 1 Cor. iv. 16 and xi. 1 and in Phil iii. 17 and iv. 9.

The respective keynotes of the four chapters may be thus set out :—

The believer's purpose (i. 21).
The believer's pattern (ii. 5).
The believer's prize (iii. 14).
The believer's provision (iv. 19).

Four examples of self-sacrifice for the welfare of the Body are :—
The example of Christ (i. 27-ii. 18).
The example of Timothy (ii. 19-24).
The example of Epaphroditus (ii. 25-30).
The example of Paul (iii. 1 to iv. 9).

PHILIPPIANS I. 1—26.—Paul and Timothy here write as servants of Jesus Christ, not as apostles, for reproof and not revelation is the purpose of the Epistle (v 1).

The frequent occurrence of the word " all " is intentional because the unity of the Body is the Keynote of the Epistle.

This is the first letter of the Apostle which mentions Bishops and Deacons, and which addresses them separately. Presbyter expressed the rank; Bishop, the duty. At that time there were many bishops in one church, now there are many churches under one bishop. Departure from, and corruption of, truth early manifested itself in Christendom.

Every time that the Philippians were mentioned by anyone the Apostle praised God for them (v. 3) ; and every time he prayed for them he prayed with joy because of their fellowship in the Gospel (v. 5) and their suffering in the Gospel (v. 7) and their discernment in the Gospel (v. 10).

Their fellowship in the Gospel consisted in gifts of money (see introduction). They did not weary in this well-doing, as is usual among men, but continued in it ; and the arrival of Epaphroditus with their gifts proved that this form of fellowship was as wholehearted toward Paul as a prisoner as toward him as a preacher.

True conversion is begun by God in the soul, and is, therefore, sure of completion (v. 6).

The fact that the Philippians had the Apostle in their heart, and that they shared in the grace which made him a defender of, and sufferer for, the Gospel, was the ground of his confidence (v. 6) that God had indeed made them His own.

Love without intelligence and discernment (v. 9) is ineffective in testing what claims to be " excellent " (v. 10) but what may in reality be a false Gospel ; and such intelligence and discernment are also necessary to test conduct (vs. 10 and 11).

Verses 1-11 form the introduction to the Epistle. The next section (12-26) reveals the Apostle's concern for the spiritual welfare of the Philippians.

Satan's efforts to hinder the Gospel often further it (vs. 12 and 13). Not only the members of the Praetorian guard who had custody of Paul, but the whole Praetorium itself, and all its judges and officials and courtiers, are to be understood as included in verse 13. (See articles by Professors Mommsen and Ramsay).

Persecution frequently makes timid Christians courageous confessors (v. 14).

The Apostle Paul had a great soul. He sang songs of joy in gloomy dungeons (v. 4), and he exulted when Christ was preached though the motive might be jealousy, or faction, or a desire to embitter his imprisonment (vs. 15 and 16). Third-rate preachers took advantage of Paul's eclipse in the prison and gratified their jealousy of him by pressing to the front ; and others, more hostile, when preaching Christ denounced His servant as a heretic and impostor. But this mighty man was indifferent to it all. Christ filled all the vision of his great soul, and he was quite satisfied and happy that the servant should be denounced and the Master announced.

"Salvation " (v. 19), i.e.. liberation from prison.

" This " (v. 19), i.e., their prayer for his liberation and the supply of Christ's Spirit of submission and grace to himself. Such were the two factors that would secure his liberation—Christ's disposition supplied to him and the Church's prayer made for him.

He confidently expected that when brought before the judges he would not be put to shame, but, on the contrary would be emboldened to testify for Christ and enabled to magnify. Him whether condemned to death or acquitted (v. 20). To him to live was Christ and to die was gain (v. 21), for it was to be with Christ which was very far better (v. 23) ; but if acquitted (v. 22) he was sure of the fruit of his labour, for that fruit was Christ—he had no other object in life than to help forward His interests ; and he was quite willing to abide in the flesh, for it would promote their progress and joy in the faith (v. 25), and give them a double benefit —his liberation from captivity, and his promised visit to them.

PHILIPPIANS I. 27 - II 13. — The love of the Head for the members of His Body is the subject of this paragraph. Recognition of that sympathy draws the members together so that they stand fast in one spirit with one mind striving together for the faith of the Gospel (v. 27), and thus as members of the one Body endeavour to keep the unity of the Spirit.

A salvation from God is evidenced by persecution (v. 28) ; and persecution is to be recognized as a gift granted to those who are Christ's true followers (v. 29). The Philippians suffered a similar persecution to that which Paul suffered when among them

in Philippi, and which, at the time of writing, he was suffering in Rome (v. 30).

The "if " of ii. 1. is not the "if " of doubt but the "if " of argument. Seeing that the consolation, the comfort, the fellowship, the tender affections and the mercies treasured in Christ are boundless, there is, therefore, a satisfying provision made to secure for His members unity of purpose and affection and accord and sympathy (v. 2) and to ensure the dethronement of self and self-esteeming and self-gratification (v. 3). Occupation with personal advantage gives place to occupation with the advantage of others when the heart enters and lives in the atmosphere of verse 1 interpreted by verses 6-8.

These verses with 9-11 declare the Deity of the Lord Jesus Christ. See note on Isa. xlv. 23.

Christ's self-humiliation proved His Deity, for this renunciation would have had no value if Christ were not God. He became man ; but in contrast with the first man He did not grasp at equality with God by robbery, on the contrary He emptied Himself of all His outward glory of the form of God and revealed Himself to the world in the form of a slave. Adam, by robbery, sought to exalt himself to the dishonouring of God ; the Second Adam humbled Himself to the honouring of God (v. 11). The first Adam exalted himself and was humbled ; the Second Adam humbled Himself and was exalted.

Christ subsisting in the form of God, i.e. the visible glories shining forth from His Divine essence as God, is here set in contrast with His assuming "the form of a servant," which in its turn declares the existence of His human nature. Thus the "form of God" declares His Deity, and the "form of a servant," His humanity. He did not hold fast and bring down to earth the visible demonstration of His Deity—for such is the import of the word "robbery"—although it shone out for a moment on the Mount of Transfiguration—but emptied Himself of that outward glory in order to become man and by His death on the tree secure the eternal advantage of His members. He thought not on His own glory but on the glory of others. (v. 4).

The antithesis here is not between His being on an equality with God and His emptying Himself—for He never emptied Himself of His God-head—but the contrast is between His being in the form of God and in the form of a servant. Equality with God declares His Being ; the form of God expresses the manifestations of that Being. It was of the outward demonstrations of His Deity that He emptied Himself.

The seven downward steps of His great renunciation (vs. 6-8) are here followed by the seven upward steps of His glorious ascension (9-11). 1. His renunciation (v. 6). 2. Emptied Himself. 3. Took a servant's form. 4. Became in man's likeness. 5. Humbled Himself. 6. Bowed to death. 7. And what a death ! The death of the cross !

The seven upward steps of His exaltation are : 1. God highly exalted Him. 2. Granted Him the Name which is above every name. 3. Universal dominion. 4. Over Beings in heaven. 5. And Beings on earth. 6. And Beings under the earth. 7. And Divine glory. All tongues will confess by and by that Jesus of Nazareth is Jehovah ; and such confession will honour and not dishonour God.

He took the form of a servant at the time when He assumed humanity, as it is said " being made in the likeness of men." His subjection to the Law (Luke ii. 21 and Gal. v. 4) , and to His parents (Luke ii. 5) ; His position as a carpenter (Mark vi. 3) ; His sale for the price of a slave (Exod. xxi. 32) ; His death the death of a slave ; and His dependence as a Servant on God (Isa. xlix. 3 and 7) , all illustrate His form as a servant. This proves : 1. He was in the form of a servant directly He became man. 2. He was in the form of God before He was in the form of a servant. 3. He as truly subsisted in the Divine nature as in human nature, for He was as much in the form of God as in the form of a servant, and was so truly in the form of God as to be on an equality with God. He, therefore, could have been none other than God (Isa. xlvi. 5 and Zech. xiii. 7).

Salvation must be possessed before it can be worked out, just as a farm must be possessed before it can be developed. The moralist and the sacerdotalist work in order to get salvation ; the Christian works because he already possesses it—it is his own ; and he does not pursue the religious activities of self-will, but is moved by the Divine will ; and that will accomplishes what it purposes (vs. 12 and 13).

As God He was infinitely above all possible exaltation, but as man He was " highly exalted."

Had He been born in time like ordinary men, He would have had nothing to empty Himself of, and He could not have " taken " the form of a slave. Only God could " empty Himself." These statements, therefore, affirm His Godhead.

A comparison of Isa. xlv 22, 23 with Phil. ii. 10 makes it absolute that the Lord Jesus is Jehovah, for to the One God, and there is none else, every knee shall bow.

PHILIPPIANS II. 14-30.—The example of Timothy (vs. 14-24) and that of Epaphroditus (25-30) reveal the Spirit of Christ in self-sacrifice. They endeavoured to keep the unity of the Spirit as being members of the One Body. " Murmurings and disputings " (v. 14) break that unity. Epaphroditus must have told the Apostle of these contentions. Abraham said to Lot : " We be brethren, let there be no strife between me and thee," and the Spirit says the Canaanite and the Perizzite dwelled then in the land (Gen. xiii. 7). The one was a crooked and the other a perverse nation. Christians are to be light-holders in the moral darkness of the world, holding forth the word of life, i.e., preaching the Gospel by Christian conduct and by Scriptural teaching.

The Apostle compares the self-sacrifice and energy of the Philippians with his own (v. 17), magnifying theirs and minimizing his. They were both laying down their lives for the sake of the Gospel ; but their action he regards as the great sacrifice, and his as only the drink-offering poured out upon it. Under this beauteous figure of speech he speaks of his possible approaching death as a martyr. 2 Tim. iv. 6 and Lev. xxiii. 13.

True conversion implies sacrifice and service—the sacrifice of self and self-interests for the salvation of others, and willing service in confessing Christ and preaching the glad tidings concerning Him.

To seek one's own advantage is to sin against the unity of the Body (v. 21).

" Your messenger " (v. 25). He brought the gifts of the Philippians to the Apostle at Rome. Though an exceptional Christian he nearly died from illness contracted in his service to the Body (v. 27). Why was he not miraculously healed ? Because miraculous healing belonged to the Hebrew Church and to earth ; Epaphroditus belonged to the

Christian Church and to heaven (v. 30). He counted on the love of the Philippians for him (v. 26) and was distressed because they heard of his illness. As a son, knowing the love of his mother, hastens to inform her of his recovery in order to tranquillize her heart, so he hastened to assure them of his restoration to health.

Their faith and Paul's was all one thing (vs. 17 and 18). Their common sacrifice and service was well-pleasing to God and the supreme proof of that service, i.e., his death or theirs, could but occasion the most sacred mutual joy. Man might only see suffering and defeat, but faith viewed things in the light of God.

But though he had such confidence in Christ with respect to them, yet his watchful care sent Timothy to them ; just as in 1 John ii. the beloved Apostle, while saying that his children needed not that any should teach them, yet at the same time instructed them with all tenderness and foresight.

Here (ii.) is revealed a realm of consolation, comfort, loving fellowship, tender affections, mercies, mutual sympathy, and boundless affection, Christ's love for His people, their love for Him, the Apostle's affection for the Philippians and their affection for the Apostle, the mutual love of Paul, Timothy and Epaphroditus—the last named's concern lest the Philippians should be grieved—all furnish a picture of mutual sympathy and solicitude that is very beautiful. God's own tender love breaks out in the chapter on every side, forming a precious and beautiful chain, and developing the graciousness of Christian life in His servants. This graciousness, this solicitude, this consideration for others flowed from the grace of Him Who humbled Himself from the Throne to the Cross.

PHILIPPIANS. III.-IV. 1—The fourth example, Paul's, corresponds to the first, Christ's. He was like His Master as to the number, but not as to the nature of that which he surrendered.

His supposed gains (v. 7) were :
1. Circumcised the eighth day.
2. Of the stock of Israel.
3. Of the Tribe of Benjamin.
4. A Hebrew of the Hebrews.
5. A Pharisee.
6. A persecutor.
7. Self-righteous.

The seven gains he desired were :
1. To win Christ.
2. And be found in Him.
3. True righteousness.
4. The excellent knowledge of Him.
5. The power of His resurrection.
6. The fellowship of His sufferings.
7. The out-resurrection from among the dead.

Such were the Apostle's seven descensions and his seven ascensions.

As a Jew he believed in resurrection, for Job, Daniel, Isaiah and others declared the fact, but what he coveted was to be a subject of a special and peculiar resurrection, here pointed to by a Greek word which occurs nowhere else in the Scriptures. It was the resurrection of 1 Thess. iv., and peculiar to the Church.

" To rejoice in the Lord " (v. 1) means that He should have the first place. This was the strength of the Apostle. It was worth while to him either to live or die (i. 21 and 22), for living or dying Christ had the first place in his heart. He thought only of Him and of the interests of His Church. Such a single purpose destroyed selfishness and ennobled his life with light and peace and love and courage.

" Dogs " (v. 2) See Rev. xxi. 8, xxii. 15, Matt. vii. 6, Titus i. 15 and 16, Deut. x xiii. 18, Ps. lix. 6, 14 and 15 and 2 Pet. ii. 22. These dogs were ministers in the Church, but the Apostle declared them to be evil-workers and enemies of the Gospel, and destined to perdition (vs. 18 and 19). Because the Person and work of the Man in the Glory was in question, the Apostle used this language of these teachers and their doctrines. Such language would be condemned at the present day as violent and contrary to Christian love ; but such a judgment reveals the extent of modern departure from truth.

" Concision " (v. 2), i.e., a mere cutting of the flesh such as idolaters practised and God forbade (Lev. xxi. 5 and 1 Kings xviii. 28). The Divine ordinance of circumcision was degraded by these false teachers to concision. Believers are the true circumcision (v. 3) who worship God by the Holy Spirit. Such worship excludes all carnal ceremonies.

In Paul's teaching as to circumcision there is a striking chronological gradation. Acts xiii. 39 implies its impotency to justify ; Gal. iii. 3 points out its inefficiency to sanctify ; Rom. ii. 28, 29, declares it to be a shadow; Col. ii. 11 and iii. 11 reveals its relation to true circumcision; and here, last of all, Phil. iii. 2 declares it to be a mere flesh-cutting.

It was not sins that Paul surrendered in order to win Christ, but righteousnesses.Christ died not only to expiate and abolish Paul's sins, but also to expiate and abolish his righteousnesses. See notes on Job.

To know Christ is the most excellent knowledge.

The double keynote of Paul's life is found in the declarations: "not having mine own righteousness" (v. 9), and: "not seeking mine own profit" (1 Cor. x. 33).

The righteousness which is from God is offered to the sinner in Christ, and secured by him by faith as opposed to works.

Verses 10 and 21 concern the power of His resurrection—enjoyed and manifested morally (v. 10) and by and by physically (v. 21). As believers will in the resurrection exhibit the physical glory of Christ, so should they in daily conduct exhibit His moral glory. To believe a Divine fact, and to be energized and governed by a Divine fact, is not the same thing.

"The fellowship of His sufferings" (v. 10), i.e., to share in Christ's sufferings in His people.

"Perfect" (v. 12), i.e., perfected in the realisation of the calling-on-high of the out-resurrection—viz., verses 8-11.

For that position of glory (v. 14) Christ laid hold of the Apostle (v. 12); and Paul earnestly desired that he might so lay hold of the fact of such a destiny that its moral energy might govern his life—animating him to keep the unity of the Body and the unity of the Spirit.

The Church's glorious position above the highest heavens, is the prize of verse 14. The Apostle eagerly desired to be one of Christ's companions in that supreme glory. He felt that to look back meant to go back (v. 13). The earthly kingdom and its gifts and Pentecostal powers promised to the Hebrew Church, were glorious, but Paul turned from them all being desirous of the higher glories attaching to the Man in the glory.

Those who had received this revelation and were "perfected" in the belief of it (v. 15), he urged to hold to that revelation; but if they had not as yet reached it, God was willing to reveal it to them; but so far as they had

advanced in the truth they were to mutually walk in it.

Paul used stern language when exposing and denouncing false gospellers,but he wept as he wrote (v. 18). Gal. i. 8, 9, and 2 Kings v. 27.

"Conversation" (v. 20), i.e., citizenship. Roman citizenship was greatly coveted at that time. The true churchman's citizenship is in the heavens.

The out-resurrection (vs. 20 and 21) is that of 1 Thess. iv. The believer's body of humiliation will in a moment be fashioned like unto Christ's body of glory by that Almighty Power which can subdue everything to Himself.

Paul had seen Christ in the glory, and that glory had dimmed for him all the glamour and glitter of earth; it dethroned self and self-righteousness; it effected a radical change in his whole moral being; he ceased to be the centre of his own importance; and another, worthy of being so, became the centre of his life—a Divine Person, a Man in the glory.

So the chapter begins: "Rejoice in the Lord" and closes: "Stand fast in the Lord."

To stand fast in the Lord (iv. 1) in a time of almost universal departure from God is difficult, and also painful, for it necessitates solitude. But all is easy when the heart is set upon Christ seen in glory. Communion with Him gives light and certainty; it more than compensates for friendships which must be lost. This life of fidelity to the Word of God and of separation from evil, is displayed by the Holy Spirit in this Epistle. He gives very plainly its example, its principle, its character and its strength.

PHILIPPIANS IV. 2—23.—This closing section of the Epistle magnifies the grace which victoriously dominates circumstances (vs. 4, 6, 7, 9, 11, 12, 13 and 19).

Christian activity may exceed spirituality, and entrap believers into a subjection to self-will which issues in dissension (v. 2).

The first converts at Philippi were women; Most likely Euodias and Syntyche were amongst those who resorted to the riverside where prayer was wont to be made (Acts xvi.); and being early converted would naturally become preachers (v. 3).

"Yoke-fellow" (v. 3), i.e., Epaphroditus.

"Whose names are in the Book of Life" (v. 3). This dogmatic statement, and that of Luke x. 20, evidence inspiration. Citizenship in heaven (iii. 20) belonged to those whose names were registered there as citizens (Exod. xxxii. 32, Ps. lxix. 28, Ezek. xiii. 9, Dan. xii. 1, Rev. xx. 12 and xxi. 27). The free cities of the ancients had a roll book containing the names of those who possessed the right of citizenship. Only those who are written in the Lamb's Book of Life will enter the great city, the holy Jerusalem (Rev. xxi. 27).

Fidelity to Christ enlarges affection for fellow-servants in the Gospel and delights in all that His grace does through them ; and it remembers that that grace has a place for each loved servant (v. 3).

If the Apostle wept over many (iii. 18) yet he always rejoiced in the Lord (v. 4), for in Him nothing alters. It was not indifference that caused him to rejoice always, but it was an unfailing spring of joy which becomes more abundant in distress. The heart that drinks daily and deeply of that spring, will warmly and unfailingly love others and be concerned in their welfare. As Christ never changes this fount never changes ; and the joy which the Christian feels and manifests is a testimony to the existence of that source of joy. Four years in prison chained to a soldier, failed to destroy that source for Paul or to hinder him from urging others more at ease than himself to drink of its fulness.

"Moderation " (v. 5), i.e., willingness to give up one's own way—not to insist on one's rights.

" The Lord is at hand," i.e., standing close by.

"Careful " (v. 6), i.e., anxious or over-anxious. Anxieties as well as passions cannot stay when the Lord has His place at one's hand. Events do not disturb Him, so He is the believer's confidence and refuge. They shake neither His throne nor His heart ; they only accomplish His purposes. He loves His people, and they are the objects of His tender care. He listens to their petitions and they are sure of the answer, be it what it may. Prayer is request based upon Divine promise. Supplication is a petition addressed to the mercy of God. A man prays for the forgiveness of his sins, for that is promised ;

he supplicates for the recovery of his child for that lies in the mercy and counsels of God. The Apostle does not say that all asked for will be received, but he does say that the peace of God will garrison the heart (v. 7). This is faith ; the heart does not keep the peace of God, but the peace of God keeps the heart when all burdens are cast upon Him whose peace nothing can disturb. How match less the grace that uses even anxiety as a means of ministering this marvellous peace if the anxiety is brought to God. So in anxieties the believer may have the peace of God, and in his ordinary life of Christian testimony (v. 8), he may have the God of peace (v. 9). Paul in his painful prison at Philippi rejoiced in the Lord, and at midnight sang praises to Him.

"Lovely " (v. 8), i.e., morally lovable. Piety and morality are twins ; piety is love toward God ; morality, love toward man.

"Instructed " (v. 12), i.e., initiated. Paul needed Christ's strength to uphold him when he had plenty of money as when he had none (vs. 11 and 13).

The elevation and refinement of verses 10-19 are exquisite. The indefinable word "gentleman " expresses the delicacy of feeling revealed in this matchless passage. God and the Philippians and the Gospel and Epaphroditus and Christian fruit abounding to others, all are in the fore-front, and the Apostle himself and his necessities in the background.

Verse 19 is a note upon the Bank of Faith. "My God "—the Name of the Banker. "Shall supply "—the promise to pay. "All your need "—the value of the note. "Accord ing to His riches "—the capital of the Bank. "In glory "—the address of the Bank. "By Christ Jesus "—the signature at foot without which the note is worthless.

It is remarkable that the word "sin " does not occur in this Epistle, nor the word "flesh "—except to say that the Apostle had no confidence in it.

"In respect of want " (v. 11), i.e., through fear of privation.

COLOSSIANS

This is the third Epistle of the Ephesians group. See introduction to the Epistles to the Romans and to the Ephesians. In it the Apostle corrects the Colossians because of teaching which denied the supremacy and all sufficiency of Christ as the Head of the Body, the Church.

The Epistle attacks and destroys man's way of holiness by lacerations, adoration of angels, performances of sacraments and self-willed efforts of the carnal nature to improve and sanctify "the flesh" which God has condemned to death. The Epistle points out God's way of holiness as opposed to man's way.

The correspondence between this Epistle and that to the Galatians is most marked. Both correct doctrine and error, and both manifest the fear and anxiety of the Apostle.

The Church finds her full life in her Head. When this is recognised the uselessness and mischievousness of carnal ceremonies which appeal to the natural heart, are recognised. All that is needed for a complete Christian life of worship, service and intellectual spiritual progress, is found in Christ. All riches and all perfection are found in Him for the enrichment of His members and for their maintenance in the full practical enjoyment of fellowship with Him.

Ephesians reveals the believer in Christ in the Heavenlies ; Colossians, Christ in the believer on the earth. In the Ephesians, the Church is the fulness of Him that filleth all in all ; in the Colossians, all the fulness of the Godhead dwells in Christ, and the believer is complete in Him. In Ephesians, the Holy Spirit is mentioned ten times ; in Colossians, only once. See notes on iii. 8-10. In Ephesians, believers are addressed as saints and faithful ; in Colossians, as saints and faithful brethren, for in this latter Epistle they are viewed as dwelling upon earth al-though belonging to heaven, and being on earth they were in danger of departing from their Head Who is in heaven, and consequently of losing sight of their heavenly hope and destiny and unity.

This hope announced to them in the Gospel was the hope of glory. It was heavenly. It meant association with Christ above all heavens. Conscious union with Him there can only be enjoyed by faith. Into that sphere and element and realm sacraments and ordinances cannot enter. He is an object which delivers the heart from all such bondage. They hide Him from the heart, for they are human and earthly.

In this life of spiritual fellowship there is a principle of intelligence which is continually progressive. It is the knowledge of God Himself in the plenitude of His fulness embodied in Christ. Wisdom and spiritual understanding can only act in the soul that is spiritually active. In this life human direction is fatal to spiritual progress. The Holy Scriptures form the means used by the Spirit for the life of spiritual intelligence and growth (John xvii. 17). Thus the Christian walks worthy of God Who called him to glory (1 Thess. ii. 12), and worthy of Christ (Col. i. 10), and worthy of the Holy Spirit Who is the Agent of the Divine Election (Eph. iv. 1).

In Ephesians, Colossians and Hebrews the location and nature of Christian worship are revealed. All is heavenly. A table and bread and wine are meaningless and impossible there. Where Christ, "the Head," enters symbols withdraw, and the eye and heart are engaged with spiritual realities and not with carnal shadows.

COLOSSIANS I. 1-23—The three Church Epistles of Ephesians, Philippians and Colossians were written from a Roman prison.

The hope of heavenly glory announced in the Gospel (v. 23) is the subject of the sevenfold giving of thanks in this Epistle. Thus :—

(1). Thanks for the Hope (vs. 3 and 5).

(2). Thanks that the Christian is fitted for the Hope (v. 12).

(3). Thanks for that which fits him for the Hope (ii. 7).

(4). Thanks for the fellowship of the Hope (iii. 15).

(5). Thanks for the communications of the Hope (iii. 16).

(6). Thanks for the confession of the Hope (iii. 17).

(7). Thanks for the holy apprehensions and sweet expectations of the Hope (iv. 2).

The word " also " (v. 7) should be elided. Epaphras had taught them the Gospel. The Apostle here commends him and accredits him.

The measure of the strength at the disposition of the believer (v. 11) is the measure of the glorious power of the risen Son of God. That moral power does not in God's present ways upon earth manifest itself in amazing miracles, but in the acceptance of persecution with patience, long-suffering and joyfulness.

The believer does not pray to be made fit for heaven (v. 12), but he praises God that He has made him fit for heaven, and that He has delivered him from the power of darkness (v. 13) and carried him over into the Kingdom of His beloved Son, in Whom he has as a present possession redemption and forgiveness (v. 14). All these are possessions not sought for by sacraments but consciously enjoyed by faith.

The personal glory and supremacy and sufficiency of Christ as the Head of the Body, the Church, are set out in verses 15-23. His essential glory as the Son of God in eternity, and His acquired glory as the Son of God in time, are here both affirmed. The one declares His Deity ; the other, His Humanity. He is, and always has been, the image of the invisible God, and that in a sense impossible to Adam ; for in Christ it pleased the Godhead to dwell in fulness (v. 19 and ii. 3 and 9). There is a distinction between image and likeness. The latter implies resemblance; the former, counterpart and derivation. As First-born before every creature He existed before anything was created ; for by Him were all things created, and He is not only their Creator but their Conserver (v. 17). Thus His glory as God, as Creator and as Preservator, are set out in verses 15-17. He is the Head of creation, and to be such took creation form in order to create.

A fugitive glance into the unseen angelic world is permitted in verse 16. The angels are ordered under governments. All these were created by Him and are subject to Him.

Christ's glory as Head of the Body the Church, is the subject of i. 18 to ii. 23.

His supremacy in this relationship is declared in the statements that He is the Beginning and the First-born from among the dead—the Creator of the Church and the Conqueror of the power i.e., death, that held the Church captive. Thus His glory is manifested in the same nature in the assumption of which He humbled Himself in order to the redemption of the Church. He took a special place in the power of resurrection, not in Creation, but in the Empire of death, in order to redeem His members.

By His atoning death (v. 20) it pleased God to reconcile both heaven and earth to Himself, for sin had estranged both ; and so efficacious is that atonement that it places men before His Throne holy and unblameable and unreprovable, men who by nature were alienated and by conduct were wicked (v. 21). Of this glorious Gospel the Apostle Paul was made a minister ; and it was commanded by the Master Himself (Matt. xxviii. 19) to be preached to all nations without distinction.

But the Colossians were in danger of being moved away from the hope proclaimed in the Gospel, and this danger filled the Apostle's heart with anxiety (v. 23).

The redemption, deliverance, translation and thanksgiving of vs. 12-14 are illustrated by the two passovers and the two baptisms of Exod. xii. and xiv. and Joshua iii. and v. as interpreted by 1 Cor. v. 7 and x. 2. The second passover was a giving of thanks for actual possession of the land promised. In the first baptism Moses shook off the powers and principalities of Egypt (Col. ii. 15), and in the second baptism Joshua rose into the heavenlies with his people.

COLOSSIANS I. 24.—II. 7.—The preaching of Christ as the image of the invisible God (v. 15), as the Head of creation (vs. 16 and 17), and as the Head of the Church (v. 18), exposed the Apostle to persecution and suffering (v. 24). But he rejoiced in these sufferings, for they secured the happiness of the Colossians. They were sufferings proper to Christ Mystical, not to Christ Mediatorial. The sufferings of His members are felt by Him as Head of the Body. Hence He said to Saul of Tarsus : " Why persecutest thou Me ? "

Paul had a double ministry—the ministry of the Gospel (v. 23) and the ministry of the mystery (v. 25). The Acts of the Apostles concerns the one ; the Epistles to the Seven Churches concern the other, i.e., to Rome, Corinth, Galatia, Ephesus, Philippi, Colosse and Thessalonica.

" The mystery " fulfils the Word of God (vs. 25, 26). This statement as to the completion of the Divine revelation is of fundamental importance. It declares the plenary and exclusive authority of the Bible. That revelation exists as a totality and so excludes all that man seeks to introduce under the plea of tradition.

If Paul and His Divine Master had preached salvation by sacraments, the offence of the cross would have ceased and they would not have been persecuted. For that system associates man, as man, morally and religiously with God. But a teaching which declares all men, whether moral or immoral, to be sentenced to death, and to be incapable of procuring holiness by self-efforts and ordinances, and to be dependent upon grace alone for life and righteousness—is a teaching which the natural will of man cannot endure. To have himself and his religious activities declared worthless before God is unbearable. Such preaching aroused the hatred of both Jew and Gentile ; and that hatred continues to the present day.

Christ's double pre-eminence over creation and over the Church, His double reconciliation of things in heaven and things on earth, and Paul's double ministry to all men and to the Assembly, are set out in verses 15-27. They lift the reader into a region into which man's ceremonial religion cannot enter.

" The mystery " (vs. 26, 27 and ii. 2) is the secret, i.e., the Church—the great secret hidden in God and never revealed in the Scriptures. It is here preached in verse 26, explained in verse 27, and recognised and believed in ii. 2.

To recognise and believe this great secret liberates the believer from the teachings and ordinances of ceremonial religion. It is the hope of glory (v. 27), i.e., association in Christ and with Christ in His personal glory above all heavens.

That the Colossians might grasp, and understand, and believe this liberating hope, caused the Apostle to wrestle earnestly for them in prayer (v. 29 and ii. 1 and 2).

If all the treasures of the spiritual realm are lodged in Christ (v. 3), then are men shut up to Him as a Teacher, and all other philosophers and philosophies are not only useless but mischievous (vs. 4-7).

Christ was not only the object (v. 28) ever before the Apostle's heart, but He was the power (v. 29) that energized him in his conflict (ii. 1) to bring men to Christ and to recognize their moral perfection in Him.

In Him they were to walk (v. 6), in Him they were rooted, in Him they were built up, by faith in Him they were established, in Him they were complete (v. 10).

Confidence in the sure accomplishment of the Divine purposes does not make the heart insensible to the necessities and the difficulties that shadow the Christian's path. So the Apostle laboured and wrestled and was filled with anxieties for his beloved friends in Laodicea and Colosse that they might be assured of, and fully realize their union with their glorious Head in Whom they were to find all wisdom. They were not to seek perfection elsewhere. The foolish philosophies of men were not to entice them.

COLOSSIANS II. 8-23.—The teaching of this section may be thus exhibited :—

Caution. " Let no man deceive you " (v. 8).

Christ the Head : The believer complete in Him (v. 10).
Symbols therefore abolished (v. 14).

Caution. " Let no man judge you " (v. 16).

Christ the Head : The believer nourished by Him (v. 19).
Ordinances therefore valueless (v. 20).

Verses 4, 8, and 16, and 18, reveal the anxiety of the Apostle for the Colossians.

" Spoil " (v. 8), i.e., make you his prey. " Rudiments " (v. 8), i.e., religious rites. This Greek word confirms the connection between Galatians and Colossians. It occurs only in these two of the seven Epistles. These Epistles, as pointed out, deal with errors in doctrine. It occurs twice in each Epistle (Gal. iv. iii. 9 and Col. ii. 8, 20). The word expresses the rites of idolatry and of Judaism. In Gal. iv. 8 the Holy Spirit says to the heathen Galatians, " While ye knew not God ye did bond-service to them which are no gods, but now having known God ye turn again to the weak and beggarly ceremonies (of Judaism) whereto ye desire again to do bond-service. Ye observe days, etc. " In this passage Paganism and Judaism are put on the one level; for the rudiments which God had ordained as shadows of good things to come, the Hebrews had degraded into the idolatry of self-righteousness.

The word " Godhead " (v. 9) is here distinct in the Greek from Rom. i. 20. There it is divinity as to character, but here it is Godhead as to essence. Christ is the completion and the fulness of Deity, and in Him the believer is complete. The argument of the passage is that Christ is God, and therefore supreme over all angels (vs. 10 and 18) ; and that in Him the believer is complete. Christ is his circumcision, Christ is his baptism, Christ is his resurrection, and he is associated with Christ high above all angels, whether they be malignant or benevolent (v. 15).

The baptism of verse 12 is Christ's baptism at Calvary, just as the circumcision of verse 11 is also that of Calvary. That circumcision cut off the whole body of the " old man " and put an end to it judicially before God. The Law cut off a portion of the physical man as a shadow of the true moral circumcision which Calvary would effect.

To suppose the baptism of verse 12 to be the immersion of the flesh of man in water, is to oppose the argument of the entire passage, and to degrade its meaning from spiritual realities to carnal shadows.

The faith that grasps these realities originates from God (v. 12). He produces it and He bestows it.

In the East a bond is cancelled by being nailed to a post. Conscience and revelation were a bond that doomed both Gentile and Jew to death. Christ satisfied its requirement, took it out of the way and cancelled it.

At the same time He deprived of all their power the malevolent angels (v. 15) and so delivered the Christian from the possibilities of their hostility. Believers, therefore, need not dread them as malevolent, nor need they seek the aid of those who are benevolent. They are set high above them all in Christ ; and hence to pray to the angels would be a deplorable descent from sunshine to darkness.

The Levitical rudiments " (v. 16) were shadows (v. 17) pointing forward to Christ Who is the substance. The substance being come, the shadows cease. A hungry man looks with interest and hope at the photograph of a loaf of bread, but on receiving the loaf itself he discards the photograph.

The worshipping of angels (v. 18) may not here perhaps mean the adoration of angels, but a descent to angelic worship. The angels are servants ; Christians are sons. For sons to worship as angels worship, and to voluntarily humiliate themselves to the level of angelic worship, is to deny the relationship of the Head and the members (v. 19).

If the Divine fact be believed that the believer is complete in the Head (v. 10) and is perfectly nourished by the Head (v. 19), then the abolition and uselessness of ordinances will be recognised, for how could completion and perfection require anything to add to what is already perfect and complete ?

Each member of the Body finds in its Head an absolutely perfect provision for the fullest Christian life of fellowship, holiness, victory, testimony and progress. In Him the believer finds the substance of all ordinances and sacraments.

The human command " touch not," etc. had reference to the eating of meats. The Roman Church enforces this command on Wednesdays and Fridays. Verse 22 says that food is a material substance intended to be used and ordained to perish. But what have such commandments to do with people who died with Christ ? (v. 20). How foolish to impose commandments upon dead people How meaningless to baptize a dead man And why should people who are dead act as if they were living (v. 20), and so become subject to the doctrines of men ! Such action indeed has a show of wisdom in a self-willed worship and a carnal humility and a punishing of the body—all of which is powerless to conquer the passions of the flesh (v. 23

Greek). This is man's way of holiness. Selfwill worship is abhorrent to God. He destroyed Nadab and Abihu because of it (Lev. x.), and Uzziah (2 Chron. xxvi.) ; and Saul because of it lost the kingdom (1 Sam. xiii.).

An angelic worship, with ceremonialism and fleshly humility and asceticism and laceration of the body is appreciated and understood by the natural man. Society loudly applauds such evidences of sanctity. It is abhorrent to God, for it is a fruit of the pride and ignorance and rebellion of the carnal mind ; and the Holy Spirit says (v 23) that it is powerless to overcome the passions of man's lower nature (See note on Heb. xiii. 9).

The death-warrant which was against the first-born by the Divine ordinance, was cancelled by the blood of the Paschal Lamb sprinkled upon the door. This illustrates verse 14 ; and the baptism of Moses in which he shook off the power of Pharaoh, illustrates verse 15. In the Red Sea Israel was baptized into Moses as the leader and commander of the people (Isa. lv. 4), and at the Jordan, into Joshua as the captain of their salvation leading the many sons to glory. Both these baptisms were fulfilled in the baptism of Christ's death and resurrection. The repeated " third day " of Joshua i. 11, iii: 2 and 7 is important. On that third day God magnified Joshua. Moses having died, Joshua rose (Josh. i. 2). The two passovers and the two baptisms of Exod. xii. and xiv., and of Josh. iii. and v. correspond to the two books of Ephesians and of Colossians. See notes on Exod. xiii. Josh. i. iii. and v. and Col. i. 12-14.

COLOSSIANS III. 1—17.—" If " (v. 1). This is not the " if " of doubt but the " if " of argument.

" Dead with Christ " (ii. 20)—Peace ; " Risen with Christ" (iii. 1)—Power ; " Hidden with Christ " (v. 3)—Preservation. A dead man is beyond judgment for Christ is beyond judgment. Hence the believer has a peace that nothing can destroy. Resurrection means power and victory. Noah was hidden in the Ark. It could not perish so he could not perish. His preservation was entirely a question of the power of the Ark to save him from perishing.

The argument of the entire passage (ii. 8-iii. 4) is : what have ordinances to do with people who died with Christ ? and : How can they possibly find a place in the realm into which those are brought who are risen with Christ ?

Those who believe the great fact of the union of the members with the Head, and the perfection and nourishment furnished them by the Head, do not set their affections on things on the earth, i.e., on ordinances and sacraments and all the religious rites of man's invention, but they set their affection on things above where none of these things have any meaning, and where they could not exist or be practised.

So this great proof of the Headship of Christ delivers the believer from bondage to ordinances (ii. 20) ; and from gross sins (iii. 5) ; and from common sins (vs. 8 and 9).

" Mortify " (v. 5), i.e., " put to death." The believer's members are upon the earth though his life and affection are in heaven. He is to believe that he has died. When the Christian believes this it becomes a moral reality in his experience ; and he finds a power which puts his passions to death and keeps them dead. This is God's way of holiness and it is effective. Man's way of holiness (ii. 23) is ineffective.

The old·self (v. 9) is put off as a single and definite action at the time of conversion and a new self (v. 10) is put on. The Greek forms of the verbs used in this chapter are helpful and instructive as marking the difference between definite action and continued action.

The new self is living and is continually being moulded into ever enlarging knowledge so as to become morally like Him who created it ; and in that new creation there is neither circumcision nor uncircumcision but Christ is everything, and He is everything in everyone.

Those who died with Christ are justified in Him, and, consequently, need no ordinances to add to that justification, for it is Divine, infinite, and complete ; and those who are risen with Christ are sanctified in Him, and they need no ordinances to perfect their sanctification. It also is Divine, infinite and perfect.

Spiritual life with its activities characterizes this Epistle ; the Holy Spirit Himself, the Author and Giver of that life, characterizes the Epistle to the Ephesians (see notes on that Epistle). This is harmonious ;

for Divine action is the subject of that Epistle whilst resultant Christian conduct is the theme of Colossians. In Ephesians the believer is seated in the heavenlies; in Colossians he is a witness on the earth. See the Introduction.

So Divine life operating in the new nature produces moral fruit furnishing a most precious testimony to Him, and of Him, Who is the eternal life, and who came into the world that all men through Him might live.

Because the believer is elect, holy and beloved (v. 12) he puts on, therefore, the moral excellencies which characterize Christ.

Love is the perfect bond (v. 14) which binds together in sympathy and fellowship the members of the One Body (v. 15). It is this bond of perfectness which gives a Divine character to the social activities of this passage, and which marks the difference between the new nature and amiable human nature. Amiable nature makes little of evil; Divine love judges it. To the carnal intelligence nature is often confounded with grace, but here, as everywhere, Christ is the touch-stone. Where He is loved and His approval sought, where He reveals Himself to the heart and the heart walks with Him and communes with Him and seeks only His favour, then He is truly known; and in such a fellowship there will be no confounding of that which is of mere amiable nature and that which is of the Divinely implanted new nature.

" Rule " (v. 15), i.e., " arbitrate." In a fellowship there is always the possibility of contentions. The peace of God is the best arbitrator to secure a settlement of them.

" One Body " (v. 15), i.e., the Church— " the new man " in the heavens.

In verse 16 the semi-colon should be placed after the word " another." The Christian who lives in close touch with the Lord is a speaking and singing Christian. All who have life in Christ should be so skilled in His Word as to be able to teach and admonish one another. The Church has fallen so low that the vast mass of its members are dumb, and are satisfied that one man only in each congregation should teach and admonish.

" Intelligence " (v. 16) and " affection " (v. 17) should characterize the believer. This intelligence in the Scriptures, and this affection for Christ and His interests, express

the activity of the Divine life in the soul. This affectionate consciousness of relationship with the Lord Jesus governs every detail of the daily life. All is performed in that consciousness. Nothing is done without Him. The heart being governed by His love, the whole life and all its duties come naturally under that government. It is natural to even eat and drink in His Name. There is the sweet sense of His presence. It is an atmosphere in which the ordinary duties of the daily life are simply and happily discharged. Compare " even as He " in 1 John ii. 6. These words judge tobacco-smoking, and many other popular forms of self-pleasing.

Verses 12-14 describe Spirit-wrought garments; Gen. iii. 21, God-given garments; and Gen. iii. 7, man-made garments. Compare Zech. iii., and see last note there. With the leaf-garment God had nothing to do, and with the coats of skins man had nothing to do.

COLOSSIANS III. 18—IV. 1 — In the Apostle's day an ordinary household consisted of the father, the mother, the children and the slaves. The latter were regarded as members of the family (see notes on the Epistle to Philemon).

Where the head of the household was a kind and upright man the family life was reasonably happy; but when, as was largely the case, the householder was violent, selfish and cruel, and had moreover the legal right of putting to death without cause his wife, his children and his slaves, it resulted that the wife was turbulent, the children disobedient and the slaves false and lazy.

The picture here presented of a Christian household is very lovely. Affection being natural to a wife, subjection is commanded— " Thy desire shall be to thy husband." Children were to be obedient; fathers, gentle in order that their children might not become morose and sullen, and seek outside the home the affections and pleasures which ought to be found in it. Three verses are given to the slaves, and in them they are four times reminded of their honourable relationship to the Lord, and of the fact that they were His freed-men. Verse 22 should read as in the Revised Version. The Lord Christ makes no distinction between masters and servants (v. 25). Masters were reminded that they were His bond-slaves (iv. 1).

The whole principle of action is the presence of Christ as Lord, and relationship to Him as bond-servant. Wives, husbands, children, fathers, slaves and masters were all set in the light of His presence ; and that great fact. was to govern their mutual conduct. The practical recognition of this relationship destroyed slavery. The Apostles did not attack slavery and so cause a social revolution, but they preached a doctrine which they knew would put an end to it as an institution.

The family is of Divine ordination. Its relationships are of God and judgment will fall on whosoever despises them. Sin has marred everything, but that which sin has marred is not itself sin. And so a family beneath the government of Christ as Lord, is a realm in which not only is God's appointment recognised and obeyed, but it is a sphere in which are found affection, mutual help, self-denial and sympathy in difficulty and sorrow, and a charm which innocence itself could not have presented. A sign of the apostasy of the last days will be the absence of natural affection. Whoever fears God will respect family relationship, for He founded it. If love, which is the bond of perfectness unites the members of the household, then is there a lovely display of the life of Christ.

The poor slave was assured that he belonged to Christ and that he would certainly receive his reward if he served his earthly master heartily (v. 23), for with God there is no respect of persons.

COLOSSIANS IV. 2-18—Verse 2 should read as in the Revised Version. The mystery of Christ (v. 3) is the great secret of Christ mystical—the new Man in the heavens— the Church. The preaching of this secret was vehemently opposed by the Hebrew Church, and so a door of utterance was difficult to find.

God divides society into those that are within and those that are without. Those within are His own ; those without belong to the world. This distinction is plainly marked. but love hastens to buy up every opportunity of winning those that are without and of bringing them into the joy of fellowship with God, and is careful to say or do nothing (v. 6) that would militate against their salvation.

Onesimus belonged to Colosse, and was a slave in the family of Philemon (v. 9). See notes on the Epistle to Philemon.

Aristarchus was a Macedonian (v. 10), he was with Paul during the riot at Ephesus (Acts xix.) and he accompanied him to Rome (Acts xxvii.).

Mark (v. 10) was nephew to Barnabas, and like his uncle was a native of Cyprus. His readiness to go with his uncle to his native country was a natural emotion, but when asked to face the difficulties and dangers of the wild mountainous country of Asia Minor, he turned back to his mother at Jerusalem. Her house was a centre of Christian fellowship. But grace recovered his courage, and so he stepped bravely to the Apostle's side in his Roman prison, and later on (2 Tim. iv. 11) Paul valued and desired his help.

These three, Aristarchus, Marcus and Justus were the only Hebrews who are named as working loyally with the Apostle and who were a comfort to him.

Most probably Epaphras was the first who preached the Gospel at Colosse, Laodicea and Hierapolis (vs. 12 and 13 and ch. i. 7). Hence his zeal in prayer for them. These three cities were close together and were destroyed by an earthquake in A.D. 62.

Demas (v. 14) a little later forsook the Apostle having loved this present world (2 Tim. iv. 10).

In the synagogue and in the Church there were readers and listeners (v. 16 with Rev. i. 3). Thus the New Testament writings were put on a level with the Old Testament (Deut. xxxi. 11.).

The Epistle to be sent on from Laodicea (v. 16) was probably the encyclical letter popularly called the Epistle to the Ephesians.

" Archippus " (v. 17) was a son of Philemon. The Apostle appears apprehensive as to his faithfulness. He had no such anxiety with respect to his slave Onesimus (v. 9). Thus the slave and the master are brought together.

" Remember my bonds " (v. 18). This doubtless was to account for his bad handwriting, for a chain fastened his right wrist to the left hand of his military guard.

1 THESSALONIANS

This is the last in order, but the first in time, of the Epistles to the Seven Churches to which the Apostle wrote. It is remarkable that in the more than two thousand ancient manuscripts of the New Testament the order of the Epistles from Romans to Thessalonians is always the same. Other Books vary in order, but these never. Their import may be again exhibited. See Romans i.

Romans : The Gospel—Justification and sanctification.

Corinthians : Failure as to practical sanctification.

Galatians : Denial of the doctrine of justification.

Ephesians : The Church—Its Head and its members.

Philippians : Failure as to the unity of the members.

Colossians : Denial of the Supremacy of the Head.

Thessalonians : The Rapture of the Body into the air.

No Epistles follow Thessalonians because perfection will succeed to the Rapture. There cannot then be either failure or false doctrine.

Thus Romans, Ephesians and Thessalonians contain " doctrine " and " instruction," and the remaining four, " reproof " and " correction " (2 Tim. iii. 16).

Ephesians is the central Epistle of the Seven. It corresponds to the central upright of the seven branched lamp-stand of the Tabernacle. The frequent division into four and three also here appears. The Gospel, the Church, and the Rapture forming the three major factors of the Septad.

I THESSALONIANS I.—The great theme of this Epistle, and of that which follows, is the coming of the Lord Jesus for His Church.

The Epistle is full of doctrine, but there is neither reproof nor correction. There are a few exhortations, but there is no blame, only praise for the faith and hope and love of the believers, here specially spoken of as a Church. It was a model church. It had received all the teaching of the Apostle and was fully established in the truth of the Gospel and of the Mystery. Consequently there is nothing in either Epistle about water baptism or the Paschal supper.

Only in these two Epistles is the company of believers said to be " in God the Father," i.e., planted in this relationship—a realm of love and power and peace.

In this relationship the coming of the Lord is not a mere formal doctrine, but a living hope that warms the affections. They were converted in order to wait for Him ; and His Coming would console them for the loss of loved ones, and satisfy all their longings for moral perfection and knowledge.

The three great principles of faith, hope and love formed the basis of their spiritual life and were the powerful and Divine motives of that life (v. 3).

Silas and Timothy (v. 1) were apostles (ii. 6).

Noah's building of the Ark was a work of faith (Heb. xi. 7) ; it was a labour of love, for he loved Him Who commanded him to build, and it was to be the refuge of his wife and children ; and there was the patience of hope, for he waited one hundred and twenty years. He waited patiently also for the cessation of the Flood.

Further, verse 8 illustrates the work of faith ; verse 9, the service of love, and verse 10 the patience of hope.

The whole Christian life is enclosed within verses 4-10. Its origin is declared in verse 4, and its consummation in verse 10.

The believer is loved and elected of God from all eternity. His existence began in the will and love of God, and all the attributes and emotions of God being eternal, the believer has had, therefore, an eternal existence in the past in the mind of God, as he will have an eternal existence in the future in the presence of God. His brief existence in time is comprised within verses 5-9. He hears the Gospel (v. 5); he becomes a follower of the Lord, thus evidencing true conversion (v. 6); his life is an ensample to his fellow Christians (v. 7); he boldly preaches the Word of the Lord (v. 8); he separates from all evil (v. 9); and in verse 10 he is caught up in the clouds to meet the Lord in the air and so returns to that Divine bosom from whence he issued.

Verse 4 means that the believer is loved and chosen by God.

"Much assurance" (v. 5). Assurance of salvation is the Divine ideal, but man condemns such confidence.

"What manner of men" (v. 5). The three Apostles commended their preaching by their conduct.

Following and imitating the Lord is a sure sign of true conversion (v. 6). The joy of the Holy Spirit is usually fully felt under persecution, as appears in the Acts of the Apostles.

The Christian is not only to be a moral ensample to the unconverted, but also to the converted (v. 7).

The Apostles had not to speak about the faith of the Thessalonians, for their courageous preaching of the Gospel demonstrated its life and vigour.

The energy of the Christian life in the Thessalonians (v. 9) proved how successful was the preaching among them of Paul and Silas and Timothy. In grace as in nature, if the parent is strong and healthy the children will be strong also. So here the spiritual fruit at Thessalonica testified to the character of the labourers.

The daily attitude of the Christian heart is watching for the Lord's return (v. 10).

The doctrine that Jesus delivers from the wrath to come is hotly opposed by many professed Christian ministers (v. 10). They declare the doctrine to be dishonouring to God and degrading to man. They deny that the wrath of God is coming; that man is a sinner; that Christ by the sacrifice of Himself atoned for sin; and that He saves from the coming judgment those who trust Him. But to the repentant sinner awakened by the Holy Spirit. the declaration that Jesus delivers from the wrath to come is life and peace.

1 THESSALONIANS II.—The cruel treatment suffered at Philippi (v. 2, and Acts xvii.) did not so terrify them as to make them afraid to preach the Gospel at Thessalonica and risk similar treatment there. Men who acted thus could not be accused of deceit or immorality or guile (v. 3). God having tested them (v. 4) entrusted them with the Gospel; and they preached it so as to please Him and not men. Nor did they preach for money (v. 5), or use their authority as Apostles to demand maintenance (v. 6), but, on the contrary, they supported themselves by hard toil (v. 9). They loved these converts as a nurse her children (v. 7) and were willing to lay down their lives for them. And as a father counsels his sons, so the Apostles pleaded with them to walk worthy of God (vs. 11 and 12).

The correspondence between i. 2-10 and ii. 13-16 may be thus set out :—

Thanksgiving: Reception of the Gospel in the power of God (i. 2-5).
The effect of the Gospel thus received (i. 6-9).
Believing Thessalonians wait for God's Son (v. 10), and will be
Delivered from the wrath to come (v. 10).

Thanksgiving: Reception of the Gospel in the power of God (ii. 13).
The effect of the Gospel thus received (v. 14).
Unbelieving Jews killed God's Son (vs. 15 and 16), and will be
Delivered to the wrath to come (v. 16).

When the Gospel is received as God's Word and not man's invention, it is effectual in the moral realm (v. 13), it produces holy living (v. 14), and is not overthrown by persecution.

"To fill up" (v. 16), i.e., to keep filling up. "The wrath" (v. 16), see Deut. xxxii. 20-42. This predicted wrath was so sure to come that the Apostle said "It is come"; for even then God was preparing the Romans for the judgments which fell upon the Jews some years later.

All three Apostles longed to see their Thessalonian converts (v. 17), and Paul at any rate twice tried to visit them, but Satan was permitted to stop his way. But the Apostle's heart (v. 17) rested in the sure hope and joy of meeting them at the Parousia, and Satan could not hinder that meeting. To see them in that day of glory, and to be with them, would be both glory and joy to these three Apostles; and the greater joy of being for ever with the Lord would enrich and not destroy the lesser joy of being for ever with them.

The word Parousia occurs seven times in these two Epistles; and as usual the number seven is divided into four and three, for it occurs four times in the first Epistle (ii. 19, iii. 13, iv. 15 and v. 23) and three times in the second (ii. 1, 8, 9).

The Parousia animates the heart; believers wait for it (i. 10); it assures the communion of saints and the reward of labour (ii. 19); it satisfies longings after holiness (iii. 13); it comforts in sorrow (iv. 13) and it enriches prayer (v. 23).

I THESSALONIANS. III.—From Thessalonica the Apostles went to Berea (Acts xviii.). Silas and Timothy stayed there and Paul went on to Athens. Hearing of the hot persecution at Thessalonica and fearing lest the converts there might be unnerved by their sufferings, he asked Timothy to return to that city and encourage the brethren. Timothy at once faced the danger and returned. Meanwhile Paul went on to Corinth, whither Timothy followed him and brought the glad news of the faith and courage of the Thessalonians. The news filled Paul's heart with a lively joy (vs. 1-9).

" Forbear " (vs. 1 and 5), i.e., " endure the suspense."

" Ye know " (vs. 3 and 4), i.e., " ye know well." The Apostles predicted the persecution (v. 3), and the fulfilment of the prophecy (v. 4) established the knowledge of the Thessalonians.

Life was life indeed to these Apostles if their converts stood fast in the Lord (v. 8).

" Night and day " (v. 10). See ii. 9, and Gen. i. Man says " day and night," which is not scientific. God says " night and day : " man looks forward to a dark night; God looks forward to a bright day.

Self-will would have brought the Apostle at once to Thessalonica (v. 11), but faith, love and obedience waited for the guiding of the Master's hand. Eight years elapsed before he

was permitted to visit them. Missionary claims in Corinth, Jerusalem, Asia Minor, Ephesus and Macedonia hindered an earlier visit.

The unity of the Father and the Son in verse 11, and in 2 Thess. ii. 16 and 17, is marked by the verb being in the singular number.

The prayers of these two Epistles (vs. 10-13 and ch. v. 23, and 2 Thess. i. 11, and ii. 16, and iii. 5 and 16) instruct how to pray and what to pray for.

The responsibility of the believer (v. 12) and the ability of the Redeemer (v. 13) are here brought together and contrasted. The believer is to love his fellow-believers and all men, including his persecutors, and the Redeemer will establish him unblameable in holiness before God the Father. That is His work (Rev. xiv. 5). Then, but not till then, the believer's longing for holiness will be satisfied. In that Parousia He will appear with His holy ones. They are His— they belong to Him; and because of that union they stand in the relationship of sons to the Father.

" Your faith," verses 2, 5, 6, 7, and 10. Compare " My faith," Rev. ii. 13.

I THESSALONIANS. IV. 1-12 —The sanctity of marriage (vs. 1-8); the ministry of brotherly love (vs. 9 and 10); and the earning of one's daily bread (vs. 11-12) are the themes of this passage.

Its content may be thus set out :—

Walking before God (v. 1).
   The commandments given (v. 2).
      The Will of God: Sanctification (vs. 3-5).
      The brethren not to be defrauded (v. 6).
      The Will of God: Sanctification (vs. 7 and 8).
      The brethren to be loved (vs. 9 and 10).
   The commandments given (v. 11).
Walking before men (v. 12).

" By the Lord Jesus " (vs. 1 and 2), i.e., by His authority.

It seems strange to modern minds that the injunction of verse 3 should have been necessary to a Church so perfect as that of Thessalonica. But it will not appear strange when it is remembered that from childhood people in that city were brought up to believe that there was nothing sinful in free love. In fact there was no such thing as marriage. Sexual enjoyment was held to be as natural and as reasonable and as sinless as eating and drinking. Here, as always in the Bible, the whole matter is brought into immediate connection with God, and the argument is : how can people indwelt by the Holy Spirit (v. 8) be guilty of such action ?

The degradation of woman characterizes all forms of human religion. The Bible clothes her with sanctification and honour (v. 4). That sacred Book is woman's best friend.

" To possess his vessel " (v. 4), i.e., to get for himself a wife—but not through the impulse of mere passion (v. 5), but in conscious relationship with God and His Will and His calling (vs. 3, 5, and 7).

" In any matter " (v. 6). This should read " in this matter," i.e., in the matter of defrauding a brother of his wife. God will avenge all such conduct (v. 6), for He calls His people unto holiness (v. 7) ; and whoever despises that call despises not man but God ; and He gives His Holy Spirit that there may be progress in holiness (vs. 8, 1 and 10, and iii. 12). " Given " (v. 8) should read giveth.

The words " abound " (iii. 12), (iv. 1) and " increase " (iv. 10) and the word " giveth " (v. 8) support the doctrine of progressive holiness as to the believer's state. In his standing in Christ before God he has a holiness so perfect that it cannot be added to. " Study " (v. 11), i.e., " make it a point of ambition." Compare 2 Cor. v. 9 and Romans xv. 20. The one Greek word is here found for the three English verbs " to strive " " to study " and " to labour." They incite the believer to make it a point of ambition to be quiet in his relationships with the state and with society ; to be well-pleasing in regard to the Lord ; and to be energetic in the preaching of the Gospel. Chronologically the three commands stand in this order.

The Divine ordination is that man should earn his daily bread (v. 11), and that if he works diligently he will get it and have lack of nothing (v. 12). Compare 2 Thess. iii. 10-12 and Ephesians iv. 28. Only those who are unable to work or to find work, should receive maintenance. Were these Divine directions obeyed, the immense multitude of able-bodied idlers who are supported by modern charity, would be disbanded and compelled by necessity to earn their bread.

" We " (v. 1), i.e., the Apostles Paul, Silas and Timothy " I " (v. 9), i.e., the Apostle Paul. " We " (v. 10), i.e., the Apostles Paul, Silas and Timothy.

" Defraud " (v. 6), i.e., " deprive by violence." Prior to the French Revolution, to the American Civil War, in the Near East, and to the Great War of 1914-1918 the rich, without pity or shame, frequently seized the brides of poor men and after some days restored them to their husbands, or sometimes never restored them.

1 THESSALONIANS IV. 13—V. 11.—The subject of this passage is the Coming of the Lord. Two stages will mark that coming :—first : the ascension of the dead and living members of the Church to meet the Lord in the air (iv. 13-18) ; second : the descent of the Lord with all His saints in judgment upon the earth (ch. v. 1-11). Whether these two stages will take place on the one day, or whether an interval, long or short, will intervene, does not appear to be revealed in the Scriptures.

The Thessalonians thought that deceased believers would not share in the ascension to meet the Lord in the air. The Apostles here corrected this error (vs. 13-17).

The fact that God brought Christ again from among the dead is a pledge and assurance that He will with Him also bring all His members (v. 14).

" By the Word of the Lord " (iv. 15), i.e., by a revelation from the Lord.

" Prevent " (v. 15), i.e., have any advantage over, or precede.

" Sleep in Jesus " (v. 14), i.e., be put to sleep by Jesus and in Jesus. A mother puts her child to sleep, and she puts it to sleep in her own arms. So the Lord and His loved members. See the Greek text.

" A shout," " the voice " and " the trump " (v. 16) must have each its separate relation to the living and dead saints ; but light is still wanting on this matter. A shout is a military term commanding the assemblage of troops ; the archangel is the Lord, and the trump suggests victory (1 Cor. xv. 52).

As to the time of the Lord's appearing (ch. v. 1), it is determined not by a given date but by a definite moral condition of what is termed "the religious world" (v. 3). The sons of light (v. 8) believe He will come; and they love Him who has promised to come; and they have a confident hope of the deliverance it will bring to them.

God has not appointed believers to wrath (v. 9) but He has so appointed all unbelievers. No one, therefore, need be in any doubt upon the subject. If a man is an unbeliever he is ordained to wrath; if he is a believer he is appointed to salvation. The Gospel invites all unbelievers to become believers; and if they do so, then they will enjoy the certitude that they are appointed to salvation.

The death of the believer (iv. 13-15 and v. 10) does not in any sense put him further off from the Lord Jesus than when he was alive. Compare the words so full of meaning to the heart: "together with them" (iv. 17) and: "together with Him" (v. 10).

The word "comfort"—iv. 18, v. 11, and 2 Thess. ii. 17—unites these passages, and suggests that there will be no interval between the two stages of the Lord's Second Coming. He will descend from the highest heaven, meet his raptured Church in the air, and, continuing His descent, reach the earth and stand upon the Mount of Olives (Zech. xiv.). Then will occur the judgment of 2 Thess. i.

It is noteworthy that affection for the Person of the Lord is that which in this Epistle makes His promised coming so precious to the Christian. To meet Him—to be with Him—rather than the rest and victory and glory then to be enjoyed by the believer, is what is here set before the heart. The joy of being with fellow-believers is emphasized, but it is not given the first place.

The doctrine of the Lord's coming and the Rapture of the Church destroys the Purgatory hypothesis; for if the multitudes of the living saints are to be raptured to heaven and glorified in the twinkling of an eye, it would be unjust to subject the multitude of the dead saints to the supposed torments of a purgatory.

Israel might have entered the Promised Land a few weeks after the redemption out of Egypt, but unbelief deferred the entrance for many years. So has the Church by her corruption and unbelief delayed the Lord's Return. He could have come at once, for by His power He could have created all His members in a day.

The words "we which are alive" do not necessarily mean that Paul and Silas and Timothy believed that they personally would be alive at the Coming, but they simply mean that believers who are alive at the time shall be raptured with the blessed dead. The Apostles knew that they would all die violent deaths, for He had told them so (John xv., xvi.) and consequently they would not live to see the Rapture. This is evident from 2 Thess. ii. 3 and 5. The "comfort" (v. 18 and ch. v. 11) ministered by the "revelation" (v. 15) was not that these saints should be living when the Lord came, but that "sleeping" saints should lose nothing of the glory and bliss of that coming because they happened to have died.

1 THESSALONIANS. V. 12-28. — Gift and not office reveals the Christian minister; and those who have spiritual vision will "know," i.e. recognise and respect such ministers (v. 12).

Fraternal peace is always difficult to secure in a community (v. 13). Believers are to be at peace among themselves and to show affectionate esteem for those who are manifestly over them in the Lord, as proved by their work and labour (vs. 12 and 13). Where self-will is made dead, and communion with God steadfastly maintained, this submission to leaders and gentleness to fellow members are secured. All depends on the conscious enjoyment of the presence of God.

"Unruly" (v. 14), i.e., those who did not work for their daily bread (2 Thess. iii. 11).

"Ever follow that which is good" (v. 15), i.e., take every opportunity of doing good; and in order to rejoice evermore prayer must be unceasing, and thanks given in every circumstance. All three are in the will of God (vs. 16-18).

Believers are to "rejoice in the Lord," and "in the Holy Spirit," and "in hope," and in being "counted worthy to suffer shame," and in "falling into divers temptations."

It is possible to quench the Spirit in a Christian fellowship (v. 19) by despising utterances (v. 20) communicated by poor members, or by the uneducated, or by women or children. But all utterances (v. 21) were to be tested, that which was good held fast, and that which had even the appearance of evil doctrine (v. 22) declined.

It was natural in thinking of the Church

Assembly and its ministry, that the heart of the Apostle should turn to God Who is Himself the God of Peace (v. 23). In that Divine peace the Apostle rested. In God all is peace, and yet He is incessantly active in blessing His people and in judging evil. He gives rest, His own rest, so that in a life of incessant activity the Christian may live in a deep peace that nothing can disturb. God is never called the God of joy. Peace is more deep and more perfect than joy. In it the heart finds satisfaction for all which it desires.

God calls His people (v. 24) to the full sanctification of verse 23; and He will so effectually accomplish it that at the Parousia the saints will appear blameless.

Sin can defile the spirit and also the soul and also the body (v. 23).

Great as were these three mighty Apostles they felt their need of prayer (v. 25).

"An holy kiss" (v. 26). See notes on Romans xvi. 16.

The corrupt Christian Church forbids the Bible being read by all. But the Holy Spirit (v. 27) here sternly commands it to be given to them. The language of this verse makes it certain that the Apostle knew that he wrote by inspiration.

2 THESSALONIANS

2 THESSALONIANS. I.—If these two Epistles be read together it will appear that the teachers who confused and mistaught the Thessalonians were Jewish believers. Their hopes were set upon the return of the Messiah to the earth and the setting up of His Kingdom at Jerusalem. Those who had fallen asleep would consequently miss that Kingdom. Paul having in the First Epistle used the word " we " (iv. 17), these teachers could argue that he and Silas and Timothy (2 Thess. ii. 2) expected that event in their life-time; therefore it must be near at hand, and that of necessity the " Day of the Lord " had already begun (ii. 2). That day, as predicted in Isa. xiii., Joel ii., Amos v., etc. was to be a day of darkness and unparalleled terror, to be immediately succeeded by the appearing of the Messiah in His glory. The sufferings that the Thessalonians were enduring at the time supported such teaching. But these views were all earthly, and accordingly the principal aim of these two Epistles was to recall the Thessalonians to hold fast the heavenly hope which the Apostle had taught them. They were " called on high " to a glory greater than that of Zion. He reminded them that the " Day of the Lord "—the present day is man's day and it is darkness—was to be preceded by the appearing of the Anti-Christ (ii. 3) and the False Prophet (ii. 9), and that, prior to their destruction at some unrevealed point of time, the Thessalonian believers both living and dead would be caught away from the earth and its kingdoms and glories into the clouds, to meet the Lord in the air, there to be with Him, and from thence to descend with Him and with all His saints to execute the judgment of the Great Day. The Thessalonians appear to have lost the hope of this rapture; for, while in the First Epistle their faith and hope and love (i. 3) are applauded, in the Second only their faith and love are praised (i. 3).

" We are bound to thank God " because it was an answer to the prayer of 1 Thess. iii. 12 and the entreaty of iv. 10.

" Your patience and faith " (v. 4). Their poor hearts and their false teachers would demand the visible intervention on earth of the Lord to rescue them from their tormentors, but the Apostolic doctrine of the Rapture formed a sure basis for both faith and patience. Faith believes He will come, and patience waits for His coming.

God's action in allowing His people to be persecuted, and in permitting the existence of their persecutors, had a double purpose—first: to test the fitness of His people for government (v. 5); and second: to manifest the fitness of their persecutors for judgment (v. 9). The being " counted worthy " of verses 5 and 11 does not support the doctrine of salvation by merit, for here it is not a question of salvation but of participation in government; and also it was not a question of the making themselves worthy, but of God counting them to be so. It was a question of sharing in " this calling."

God has long patience, but at the appointed time He will recompense tribulation to the troublers of His people (v. 6), whilst to His troubled people He will recompense rest together with Paul and Silas and Timothy (v. 7), and the occasion of this just award will be at the Apocalypse of the Lord Jesus. This statement suggests that the Rapture of the Church and its appearing with Christ in His glory, are closely related.

The heathen " know not God," i.e., they do not wish to know Him, and the Hebrews "obey not the Gospel" (v.8). These two groups are here primarily pointed to; but all men come under either or both of these descriptions. Multitudes have no saving knowledge of God, and although they know the Gospel they refuse to obey it. An engine driver who would refuse to obey the red light, would justly merit the sure death that would follow his disobedience.

The punishment of the rebels and persecutors will be everlasting destruction (v. 9)—not everlasting annihilation, for these terms destroy one another. God is a consuming fire, and the Lord Jesus Christ is God; hence the statements of verses 8 and 9. The impenitent will be driven away from His presence into everlasting banishment.

Until that desired day dawns, the followers of the Lord Christ are to expect nothing but persecution from the world.

"All that believe" (v. 10). Until the Rapture the promised glory is only true to faith, and the Thessalonians were exercising that faith. Then will they see what they took in faith from the testimony of the Apostles.

In that day Christ will be the glory of His people and they will in their turn be His glory (Isa. xxviii. 5, and lxii. 3, and John xxi. 19, Gal. i. 24, and 1 Pet. iv. 14). In that day the members and the Head will share so similar a glory that He will be admired in them. On earth the members are responsible to live such Christ-like lives that He will be admired in them morally.

"The grace of our God and the Lord Jesus Christ" (v. 12). The presence in the Greek text of but one article to both, marks the essential Oneness of God and Christ.

Thus at the outset the Apostles established their hearts upon the "righteous judgment" (v. 5) which condemned their oppressors to destruction (v. 9); and "the good pleasure" (v. 11) which tested by persecution their fitness for the heavenly calling (v. 5); and which energized their faith to endure with patience their present sufferings (v. 11).

That the servants of the Lord Jesus Christ should be abandoned to persecution and that their persecutors should be permitted to oppress them, is not the result of blind chance but the operation of the righteous judgment of God—a judgment which manifests the fitness of the one company for position and dignity in His Kingdom, and the fitness of the other company for eternal banishment from that Kingdom.

2 THESSALONIANS II.—Having at once quieted their hearts as to their present sufferings, the Apostle now proceeds to prove to them that "the Day of the Lord" R.V. with its terrors and judgments had not then set in. He had told them in his First Epistle (ch. v. 4) that they should be raptured to Heaven prior to those judgments, and that when the

Lord Jesus Christ appeared to execute them they would appear with Him (iii. 13 and Col. iii. 4). So they were shaken in mind and troubled (v. 2); for if the Day of the Lord had set in, the Apostle's teaching about the hope of the Rapture was false, and if he erred on so important a matter, what security had they that his Gospel was infallible?

But Paul reminds them of what he was accustomed to tell them when with them (v. 5) of certain events which must happen before the Day of the Lord opens. The first event will be the Apostasy when both the Hebrew Church and Christendom will reject the God of the Bible and will accept the Anti christ as the true Messiah (v. 3).

He then describes this wicked Prince (v. 8). He is now held fast in the abyss (v. 6, and Rev. xvii. 8), but in his appointed time he will be revealed (v. 8) as the Man of Sin and will go into perdition (v. 3). He will sit in the Temple of God at Jerusalem declaring himself to be God; and the Second Wild Beast, the False Prophet that shall come up out of the earth (v. 9, and Rev. xiii. 11), will support the pretension by miracles in imitation of those predicted of the Messiah and performed by Him. He will imitate also Elijah's supreme demonstration of Deity, for he will bring down fire from heaven (Rev. xiii. 13). The result will be that the world will believe "the lie" (v. 11), i.e., Satan's great lie that this man from the abyss is Christ; and so all those who will not believe the truth but take pleasure in unrighteousness, will by a just judgment be permitted to believe Satan's lie and perish (v. 12).

"Even him" (v. 9). Read: Together with him, i.e., the False Prophet of Rev. xiii. who will come up out of the earth. The Son of Perdition, Antichrist, will come up out of the abyss.

So these great facts are very simple and the appointed time of their occurrence very near. The facts are that "the abyss" holds fast a man who lived. He will ascend out of the abyss by Satanic power; and in his hatred of God and rejection of His laws, he will as the Lawless King be the full development of fallen man. Satan will energize him. He will be the last great earthly monarch. The Hebrew Church will accept him as the true Messiah, and he will, as such, seat himself in the Temple which they will build at

Jerusalem, and demand and receive worship as God. The False Prophet by stupendous miracles will support his claim. But the Lord Jesus having previously raptured His people into the air, will appear with them and destroy this Wicked Prince and his Prophet and all their followers. That day of wrath will be "the Day of the Lord." It will banish this present night of mystery and pain.

The words "chosen," "sanctification," "called," and "glory" reveal the Divine purposes and activities in the selection and assembling of Christ's mystical members (vs. 13 and 14); and the words "our Gospel" and "belief of the Truth" express the means on the human side by which these Divine purposes were and shall be accomplished.

So to be endowed with and to share the glory of their Lord (v. 14) was what they were to expect, and not the terrors of the Day of the Lord. In former days they waited for God's Son from heaven (1 Thess. i. 10), but false teaching had shaken and troubled them with respect to their gathering together unto Him (vs. 1 and 2).

This secret counsel of iniquity (v. 7) already works unseen, for Satan occupies a position in the heavens (v. 7) from whence he operates on earth as a spiritual potentiality in antagonism to the Holy Spirit. But he will be ejected out of the Middle Heavens (v. 7, and Rev. xii. 7-9) and then will he call up out of the abyss the Wicked Prince that is to come. (Rev. xiii. 1. R.V.)

So having set out these facts the Apostles encouraged their converts to "stand fast" (v. 15), and only to receive as traditions what they had been taught by Apostolic lips or letters. This injunction destroys the Romish theory of tradition.

For the third time this beloved Church is comforted with respect to the Lord's Coming (1 Thess. iv. 18, v. 11, and 2 Thess. ii. 17).

The popular belief that the Holy Spirit on earth restrains the apparition of the false Messiah is destroyed by the fact of His operation and energy in Revelation xi.

To understand these Apostolic communications the distinction between the "gathering together unto Him" (v. 1) and "the Day of the Lord" (v. 2, R.V.) should be recognised. The one has relation to the Rapture of the Church; the other concerns the coming of the Lord together with the Church in judgment to the earth.

"What witholdeth" (v. 6), i.e., "that which holds fast." "That" is neuter, and "hold-fast" is a transitive verb, hence it means to hold fast something or somebody. This verb is frequently translated as "to keep" or "to hold fast," as for instance 1 Thess. v. 21, Heb. iii. 6 and x. 23, etc. The reference is to the abyss which holds fast the "Man of Sin" until the time appointed for his revelation.

"He who now letteth" (v. 7), i.e., "he who now holds fast." The Greek verb is the same as in verse 6. The verb here is the masculine participle so that in verse 6 it is something (neuter) which holds the Man of Sin fast, while in verse 7 someone is holding fast to something. The reference is to Satan who is holding fast to his present position in the heavens until he be taken out of the midst (v. 7, R.V., and Rev. xii.). Directly that Satan is cast out of the middle heavens he will stand upon the sand of the sea (Rev. xiii. i, R.V.), i.e., upon the ocean of humanity, and will call up out of the abyss the Man of Sin.

Meanwhile the attitude of the Church is to be one of comfort and of unceasing occupation in preaching and working (v. 17).

2 THESSALONIANS. III.—Popular theology teaches that Christ will come when the world becomes good; Scripture teaches that He will come when evil reaches its maximum (Dan. viii. 23). Man is not under probation, as popular preachers assert. He once was; but now he is a total moral wreck; and it is as such that the Gospel presents to him a Saviour.

The Thessalonians being a model Church and instructed in the Pauline Gospel, did not question the doctrine of the resurrection. They waited for it. They did not turn again to the weak and beggarly elements of the sacramental religions of this world, for the glories of the world to come filled their vision (Gal.). They did not mind earthly things for they were occupied with heavenly things (Phil.). They were not seduced by the teachings of a false philosophy and of symbols, for their hearts rested in glorious facts and realities (Col.). They had neither to be reproved nor corrected, for they were busy in serving the living and true God, and they were waiting for His Son from heaven. They were one in faith and hope and love, sound in doctrine and diligent in

Service. Such was the spontaneous out-working of the inworking truth which they had received respecting the character and hope of the Church seated in the heavenlies.

The Apostles asked prayer (v. 1), that pending the Day of the Lord the Word of the Lord might spread rapidly, and that its moral glories might be displayed in other places as in Thessalonica. They further needed prayer because all men are not trustworthy (v. 2) ; but his heart rested in the knowledge that the Lord is trustworthy, and that He will establish and guard His people (v. 3).

The ministry of the Holy Spirit (v. 5) is to instruct and enable the heart to love all men—even persecutors—as God loves them, and to be intelligent associates of Christ in His patient waiting (Heb. ii. 13) until His enemies be made the footstool of His feet.

He is waiting now (Heb. x. 12 and 13), and His people are waiting with Him. As He is so are they in this world.

The disorderly person (vs. 6-12) was the professing Christian who did not work for his daily bread. Paul and Silas and Timothy, though they had Apostolic authority (v. 9) to claim maintenance from the Thessalonian Church, worked hard night and day (v. 8) to support themselves and to set an example to others (v. 7).

It is easy to start in well-doing but it is hard to continue in it (v. 13).

The Apostle knew that this letter was the word of the Lord and inspired (v. 13), and that, therefore, obedience to it was obligatory.

Where the consciousness of the Lords presence is enjoyed by a community, there will be in every sense communal peace (v. 16).

To guard against forgery (ii. 2) the Apostle added to each Epistle his trade-mark in his own hand-writing (vs. 17 and 18). The trade-mark is the salutation of verse 18, omitting the Amen. The words " so I write " mean : " This is the form of my salutation, and this is my handwriting."

His letters to the Thessalonians being his first, and being conscious that they would be followed by others equally inspired addressed to other churches, it was reasonable and needful that he should guarantee their authenticity by a token.

TIMOTHY, TITUS AND PHILEMON

These personal letters form a group by themselves. They are prophetic. They foretell failure of rule in the Church (1 Timothy and Titus); entrance of ruin into the Church (2 Timothy); and abolition of slavery in the world (Philemon).

In 1 Timothy God is presented as the Saviour-God in relation to the world. This title reveals a principle that guides His people in all that concerns their intercourse with men. All men are the objects of God's grace. He desires to be their Saviour (2 Cor. v.).

Rule in the Church is the theme of this first letter. It and the other personal letters were written not long before the death of the Apostle.

1 TIMOTHY I.—Timothy is first mentioned in Acts xvi. 1. His mother was a Jewess named Eunice, his father a Greek (2 Tim. i. 5). He was probably converted at Lystra during Paul's first visit (Acts xiv); and most probably his mother and grandmother were won to Christ at the same time. In order that he might be an Apostle to the Hebrews as well as to the Greeks, he became a member of the Hebrew Church by circumcision, and joined the Apostle Paul in his preaching, first among the Jews, and then among the Gentiles. He is mentioned several times in the Scriptures (Acts, Romans, Corinthians, Colossians, Philippians, Philemon, Hebrews). The last message to him is in 2 Timothy iv. 21. Paul left him at Ephesus to contend with, and suppress, false teaching in that Church. Tradition records that he suffered martyrdom.

"Mercy" (v. 2). This word expresses God's tenderness for the bodies of His servants. Hence it does not appear in the letters addressed to Churches. Grace is for the guilty—mercy for the miserable.

As the Apostle predicted in Acts xx. 30, from amongst the elders at Ephesus men arose speaking perverse things (v. 3). Timothy was to rebuke and silence such teachers. See notes on Acts xx. 38 and 2 Tim i. 15.

"Genealogies" (v. 4). Possibly this means endless incarnations, which is a favourite doctrine in the East. The false genealogies of verse 4 contrast with the true genealogy of love (v. 5). The genealogy of love is : First, unfeigned faith, then a good conscience, then a pure heart, and then love—but love can only result when preceded by true faith, a good conscience, and a pure heart.

"Fables" (v. 4), "vain jangling" (v. 6). Compare iv. 7, vi. 4, 20, 2 Tim ii. 14, ii. 23, iv. 4, Titus i. 14, iii. 9, etc. God speaks to the heart; and those who really love Him are sound in the faith and guided by the Spirit. Speculative questions do not touch the conscience; nor do they bring the student into the conscious presence of God. Fellowship with Him is the moral fruit and glory of the Gospel. The imaginings of the human mind are fables (v. 4), but the Law (v. 8) is truth and light. See notes on 2 Tim. iii. 14, 16, 23.

"The end of the commandment" (v. 5), i.e., the ideal aimed at by the commandment is love; for the Gospel reveals the nature of God and brings the believer into that nature. It was in the warmth of that love that Timothy was to stand steadfast for the infallibility of truth (v. 19).

To walk in fellowship with God the conscience must be good and the heart pure (v. 5). The loss of a good conscience, because it interrupts this communion, opens the door to all forms of false teaching, and ultimately to immorality (v. 9), and blasphemy (v. 20).

"Lawfully" (v. 8), i.e., to use the Law as Divinely intended as a sword to pierce man's conscience and convict him of his need of a

Saviour. To use it unlawfully is to propose its observance as a ground of personal righteousness before God. This is impossible to broken humanity.

" The Law " (v. 9)—better read : " law," i.e., the application of law is to the unrighteous and not to the righteous (vs. 9 and 10).

The glory of the Gospel is its moral glory (v. 11).

" Faithful " (v. 12), i.e., trustworthy. " Enabled "—the ability and energy for the ministry of the Trust were supplied by the Master.

" Ignorantly " (v. 13). Had Paul wilfully resisted light he would not have obtained mercy. (Acts xxvi. 19). The aboundings of grace (v. 14) exceeded toward him as the " foremost " of sinners (vs. 13-16). That grace supplied him abundantly with faith and love (v. 14).

Christ Jesus did not come into the world to save the self-righteous, but the consciously sinful (v. 15). Believing on Him secures life everlasting (v. 16). This verse asserts His pre-existence.

" The only God " (v. 17, R.V.). Shortly after the Apostle's death the fables of verse 4 developed into the Gnostic teaching of many minor gods, of which Christ was one.

" The good warfare " (v. 18, R.V.).

" Concerning the faith " (v. 19, R.V.). These men were no doubt those of 2 Tim. ii. 17, iv. 14 and Acts xix. 33. Compare 1 Cor. v. 5. Shipwreck of the faith entails shipwreck of the character. Immorality follows infidelity.

1 TIMOTHY II.—This chapter contains two sections—the Prayer-Meeting (vs. 1-10) and the Home (vs. 11-15). The Apostle enjoins intelligence in the one and government in the other.

In the Prayer Meeting the prayer was to be full and instructed (v. 1)—supplications appealing to the mercy of God ; prayers claiming the promises of God ; intercessions in submission to the purposes of God ; and thanksgivings for the goodness of God.

A father may supplicate God for the recovery of his sick child, for that matter lies in the mercy of God, but he can pray to God, i.e., make request to and claim from God the forgiveness of his own sins, for God has promised in His Word to forgive all who so call upon Him. God purposed to destroy Sodom and to restore Israel, so Abraham interceded for the one and Daniel for the other. God's goodness in healing and helping His people in all times of need, calls for thanksgiving.

The character of the prayer to be offered (v. 1) is followed by a description of the persons (v. 2) who are to be remembered in prayer. Rulers are specially pointed to. They are Divinely appointed (Rom. xiii.), and they need prayer. But all men (v. 4) are to be brought to the Throne of Grace.

The place of prayer was to be anywhere and everywhere (v. 8)—not solely in the Temple at Jerusalem, as many then thought and taught. Compare Mal. i. 11—" in every place." These teachers also desired to confine prayer to members of the Hebrew Church, and condemned intercession for the heathen kings and princes of the day.

The persons to offer prayer in the meeting are described in verses 8-10. They were to be consistent Christian men and women. The men were to put aside the sins of impurity, quarrelling, and scepticism (v. 8) which are peculiar to men as men ; and the women were to lay aside the passion for extravagant clothing which so affects them ; and thus men and women " in like manner " were to publicly pray.

Verse 9 may be thus paraphrased : I will, therefore, that in like manner also the women pray everywhere, and that they adorn themselves, etc., Thus the ellipses may be supplied

" God our Saviour " (v. 3) —a Divine Title peculiar to this Epistle.

" Will have " (v. 4). There are two Greek verbs one expressing desire, the other determination. The former is used here. God desires that all men should be saved. If He determined to save all men then all men must and will be saved. Salvation is universal but conditional. All men who accept the conditions of repentance toward God and faith in the Lord Jesus Christ will be saved ; those who refuse these conditions will be lost. God is willing to save all men without distinction, whether Hebrew or Heathen, but not without exception ; that would entail universalism.

There is but One Mediator as there is but One God. This is the distinctive doctrine of the Gospel. These two facts characterize the Mediator—His humanity (v. 5) and His redemption(v. 6).

Guilty man needs a Mediator. The

Mediator must be God so as to fully know what God's righteousness demands, and He must be man in order to represent man, to bear the sin of man, and to suffer as man the wrath due to man. He came down from heaven into the lowest depths in order that the most wretched and fallen should know and feel that God in His love had come near to them in order to lift them out of their misery, and that there was no degree of wretchedness and sin and sorrow into which He did not enter and which He would not relieve. What He was on earth He is still in heaven. Nothing can equal the tenderness, the understanding, the sympathy, the experience of necessity of His heart. He shared in all the sorrows of humanity, and was wounded, oppressed and afflicted in sympathy with man. No one has come so low, no one so near to weak and broken men. He cleanses their conscience, He heals their broken heart, He energizes them to live lives of beauty and value. To give these glories to another would be to degrade Him and to rob man. He is not merely a Mediator between God and Israel, but between God and men (v. 5). His heart of love is ever burdened with the sins and needs of mankind at large.

At the appointed time (v. 6) He came as a Ransom to redeem them all. This great fact is to be witnessed, or testified to, by the ransomed (v. 6). For this testimony Paul was ordained (v. 7) in order to preach " the faith " and " the truth " (v. 7), i.e., the Gospel. It is true, and it is to be accepted by faith.

" Shamefacedness and sobriety," i.e., shamefastness and self-restraint—a face that need not be put to shame. " Broidered hair," i.e., plaited with gold, silver, and precious stones. Sobriety or self-restraint here has relation to self-denial in the matter of costly clothing.

Government in the family (vs. 11-15) as ordained by God does not accord with modern thought. The father, the mother, and the children (vs. 12 and 15) here appear. The husband was to rule, the wife was to recognise and accept this Divine ordination, and if husband and wife were faithful to each other and loved each other with a pure affection tempered by habitual self-restraint (v. 15), then the wife would be succoured in her hour of greatest peril and pain ; and, by inference, the children born

of such love and faithfulness would be blessed children.

" Learn in silence " (v. 11) is a Hebrew figure of speech meaning to be submissive. See Job. xxix. 21. Josh. x. 12. m., Ps. xxxvii. 7.m., and Ps. lxii. 1, and Hab. ii. 20, 1 Thess. iv. 11, 2 Thess iii. 12, etc. These verses make it quite clear that the word " silence " does not mean dumbness, but acceptance of authority and quietness as opposed to contention and disturbance. So a married woman (v. 12) was not to teach or to claim authority over her husband but to be in subordination. Many misunderstand this command, they divorce it from its context, which is the family, and they carry it into the prayer-meeting (vs. 1-10), and argue that a woman is forbidden to preach or pray —she is not to teach men—not even her dying husband how to escape from the wrath to come ! This is a popular error. What God here says is that a wife is not to govern her husband nor to teach other women to govern their husbands.

Eve was Adam's help-mate, i.e., his equal, but having been thoroughly deceived she became involved in the transgression and lost that equality (v. 14). Her husband was not deceived. He sinned with his eyes open ; but it was through love of her. Undeceived he followed her, weak through his affection, and chose fellowship with her in death rather than fellowship with God in life. The second Adam, not through weakness, followed his deceived and guilty bride in order to redeem her by taking her sins upon Himself and so delivering her from the transgression and its doom into which she fell.

Further, the condemnation to pain and sorrow—a mark of Divine judgment—furnishes to His tender and understanding love an occasion for help and sympathy and blessing if the woman and her husband live together in the holiness of sanctified wedlock. The terms " faith," " love " and " holiness with self-restraint " have reference to the married relationship and not, as usually supposed, to the ordinary Christian life in relation to God. So the children born of this pure affection and not of mere emotion, will be blessed children.

The doctrine that pain and death never come from God is overthrown by the judgment of Gen. iii. 16.

1 TIMOTHY. III.—The Holy Spirit here

describes the men and women fitted for ministry in the Church as presbyters and deacons.

The word " man " in verse 1 in the Greek text reads " anyone."

The government of the Christian Assembly imitated that of the Synagogue. In it the presbyters ruled and the deacons, or ministers, were their assistants.

The word " deacon " means servant or minister. The Diaconate was a covering term embracing all forms of ministry in the Church. Christ in this sense was a Deacon. The Apostles were deacons also ; and women (v. 11) were members of the Diaconate both as presbyters and ministers.

Presbyters and deacons alike preached the Gospel to Hebrew and heathen, and ministered the Word of God to the faithful ; but rule was vested in the men and women presbyters.

The word " episcopos " at that time was a commercial term. It meant the manager of a shop, the chief clerk of an office, or the director of a public company, etc. It had not the religious meaning of to-day. It meant bishop, ruler, presbyter or elder. All these terms are equal.

It was natural at that time that those who wished to be apostles, teachers, or evangelists should be highly esteemed, whilst to be merely a ruler or a servant in the Assembly, was not deemed so honourable. Paul here says (v. 1) that those who eagerly desired to be bishops or deacons coveted a noble work. But it was necessary that they should have a certain reputation both within and without the Church before appointment (vs. 5 and 7).

The Roman and Ritualistic Churches forbid marriage for Christian ministers, but verses 2-5 reveal God's thoughts. Corrupt Christendom reveals man's thoughts.

" Not a novice " (v. 6), i.e., not a young convert. Satan was condemned because of the sin of pride. That was " the condemnation of the Devil "—" the snare of the Devil " (v. 7) is the appointment of unconverted ministers in the Church. Into that snare the early Church quickly fell ; and the resulting corruption planned by Satan quickly followed.

" Likewise " (v. 8), i.e., those who eagerly desired the office of a deacon or minister. The popular belief that deacons only concerned themselves with the business matters of the Church is erroneous, as is clear from verses 9 and 13, for they were to steadfastly preach the Gospel, but with an uncondemning conscience.

Verse 11 should read as in the Revised Version. " Even so " i.e., " in like manner " (ii. 9) ; that is, women who eagerly desired to be elders and ministers desired a noble work. Pliny in his famous letter to the Emperor Trajan said that the two ministers of the church in his city were young women.

Stephen and Philip illustrate verse 13. They purchased to themselves a good standing among the believers and great Gospel boldness among the unbelievers.

Verse 15 should read as in the Revised Version. The subject is the character and behaviour of ministers in the Assembly in which God dwells.

The church is not the truth, it is the pillar and support of the truth. A pillar does not teach. It is the truth that teaches. The Church exalts Christ as the Ark was exalted at the passage of the Jordan. See notes on Josh. iii. When an earthly monarch engraves his laws upon a pillar, the attention of the people is not addressed to the pillar but to the laws displayed on it.

It is the common belief that the Church as the House of God is planted on the earth. The Hebrew Church is so planted ; but the Assembly of the Living God is founded in the heavens.

Confessedly the wondrous mystery of the Divinely-revealed Gospel is great (v. 16). God was manifested in flesh ; vindicated by the Spirit at His baptism, by His miracles, and in His atoning death ; seen by the angels who had not up till then seen God ; preached unto the nations ; the world in part believed on Him ; and Heaven received Him.

The clauses in verse 16 are parallel ; each two form a pair, heaven and earth being in opposition ; viz :—Flesh and Spirit—Angels and Gentiles—World and Glory ; and there is a correspondence between the first and the last clause—" manifested in flesh " ; " received up in glory." The argument here being conduct, the atonement does not appear. The subject is the manifestation of *godliness* in human flesh. It was attested by the Spirit; seen by angels ; believed by men ; and approved by heaven.

Possibly Timothy is intended in verse 15 as the chief pillar and upholder of the truth. Compare Gal. ii. 9, Rev. iii. 12. His behaviour in the assembly is the theme of the verse.

1 **TIMOTHY IV.**—This prophecy (vs. 1-3) began to be fulfilled shortly after the death of the Apostles, and it is still in course of fulfilment. It relates to the "mystery of iniquity" (2 Thess. ii. 6) which stands opposed to "the mystery of godliness" (1 Tim. iii. 16).

"Latter times" (v. 1), i.e., the times immediately succeeding the death of the Apostles. "The last days" (2 Tim. iii. 1) immediately precede the Coming of the Lord.

"Some," not all, shall depart from the faith (v. 1). To depart from the faith there must have been a profession of the faith. A profession of Christ is not necessarily a possession of Christ. To give heed to the teachings of demons evidences mere profession; for he that is born of God does not so sin (1 John iii. 9).

"A seared conscience" (v. 2) means an insensible conscience. "A branded conscience" is a conscience enslaved by sensuality. The latter, perhaps, is here meant.

"Hypocrisy" (v. 2), i.e., a pretending to a higher degree of sanctity by forbidding to marry and to abstain from food. The Greek, Roman and Ritualistic churches illustrate the inspiration of this prophecy. Food is sanctified by the Word of God (v. 5). See Gen. i., Mark vii. 19, Acts x. 15, etc. In all ages men have sought a spurious spirituality by doing violence to these natural laws.

"Know" (v. 3), i.e., "fully know." These false teachers claimed a spiritual knowledge superior to the Bible. The Apostle here attacks this assumption and destroys this carnal sanctity. See notes on Colossians ii. 23 and Hebrews xiii. 9. This spurious holiness attacks God Himself, for it declares to be evil what He declares to be good, in which case He is an imperfect moral being; and it is a short and easy step in advance to declare Him an evil being.

"*The* faith" and "*the* good teaching" (v. 6, R.V.). "Attained," i.e., which you have followed and which you still follow.

"Bodily exercise" (v. 8), i.e., the physical discipline of abstinence from marriage and food. It only affects the body; it relates to time, and may have a little medical profit. But godliness, i.e., true spiritual discipline, is immeasurably superior. It far exceeds carnal discipline, and is fully profitable in both the present and the future life.

The "faithful saying" of verse 9 is set out in verse 10, and it is: that because God is potentially the Saviour of all men and effectually the Saviour of those amongst them who believe, therefore Paul and Timothy laboured and toiled (R.V.) in preaching the Gospel; for it pleases God through the preaching of the Gospel to save men. Timothy, perhaps, had a leaning to this outward carnal self-discipline—see ch. v. 23—but that is man's way of holiness and it obscures and nullifies God's way. Man seeks to improve the "flesh"; God puts it to "death" as being impossible of reformation (Rom. vi)..

"Reading" (v. 13), i.e., reading the Scripture aloud in the congregation.

"Through prophecy" (v. 14) the Apostle learned by inspiration that Timothy would be a gifted servant of the Truth. The gift in question was given him at the moment that Paul placed his hands upon him (2 Tim. i. 6). The presbyters added their concurrence (v. 14) either then or later on.

"Save thyself and them that hear thee" (v. 16), i.e., from the false doctrines of verses 1-3. "Continue in them," i.e., in the practice of all that is set out in verses 12-15. Whole-heartedly walking with God in the light of His Word saves from departure from the truth, and nourishes a profitable Christian life visible to all (v. 15).

"Meditate" (v. 15). Food only profits when digested, and Bible-study only has power in the soul and life when meditated upon in dependence on the Holy Spirit. The Christian minister's preaching will be of no avail unless a gracious Christian conduct accredits it.

1 **TIMOTHY V.**—"Rebuke not an elder" (v. 1). Greek—"Rebuke not sharply an old man."

"Honour" (v. 3), i.e., support, that is, place upon the Church's widows' pension list. But only widows that were penniless and without relatives were to be thus provided for. All other widows were to be supported by their relatives (v. 4). "Nephews" means grandchildren. True Christian widows, like Anna (Luke ii. 36 and 37), wholeheartedly burdened themselves with the needs of God's people (v. 5). That ministry was their one great and absorbing interest, as was evidenced by their lives of supplication and prayer, not for themselves, but for others. They prayed for the brethren "night and day." Satan accuses them " day and night " (Rev. xii. 10) ; for Satan's " day " is the believer's " night," and Satan's " night " will be the believer's " day ." A pleasure-loving widow (v. 6) is spiritually dead while living.

" Blameless " (v. 7). This word has relation both to the widows (vs. 5 and 6), and to their relatives (vs. 4 and 8). The Christian faith is a faith of love, sympathy, and self-denial, therefore to act unfeelingly toward poor relatives is to deny the faith.

Many think that a new subject begins at verse 9, and that the legislation which follows concerns women presbyters. A widow was not to be taken, i.e., elected into the number of the presbyters unless she satisfied the eight requirements set out in verses 9 and 10. It is thought that they pledged themselves (v. 12) to give their whole time and attention to their work as bishops. Younger widows were not to be elected to this office (vs. 11 and 12), because, by a remarriage to which they would naturally be tempted, they would put aside their " first " or prior engagement to ministry in the Church. But it is now impossible to say what is meant by " the number " (v. 9). At that time public opinion among the Greeks and Romans and Hebrews, condemned second marriages on the part of religious teachers. The Apostle perhaps counsels deference to this feeling so as not to injure the progress of the Gospel.

Election to office in the Church was decided by a show of hands on the part of the believers ; and the persons elected, both men and women, were then presented to the Apostles for ordination.

In support of the argument that there is a distinction between the widows of verse 3 and those of verse 9—the former meaning ordinary widows, the latter, female bishops—it may be urged that the legislation respecting the latter would be harsh in respect of the age limit if applied to the former, for it is possible for a widow of forty years of age to be destitute of both income and relatives ; and, further, the term " widow " in verse 3 may be understood to include elderly unmarried women, if such existed at that time in the Church, equally destitute but euphemistically called widows, as to-day in many countries such persons are given the status of matrons and politely addressed as such.

" Elders " (v. 17), i.e., men and women bishops or presbyters. They formed two classes, ruling elders and preaching elders ; the latter were not only to be maintained by the Church, but they were to especially receive the additional honour of affection and obedience due to all that ruled well, for the Scripture said (v. 18) : " Thou shalt not muzzle the ox while he is treading out the corn " (Deut. xxv. 4) ; and, " The labourer is worthy of his reward " (Matt. x. 10 and Luke x. 7). The Holy Spirit in stating this latter quotation to be Scripture, declares the inspiration of the Gospels by Matthew and Luke.

The position of a minister in the Church exposed him or her to the jealous attacks of ungifted members of the fellowship (v. 19).

" Them " (v. 20), i.e., " bishops." " That others," read : " that the others," i.e., the other bishops.

" The elect angels " (v. 21), i.e., the angels of His might who are appointed beforehand to accompany Him in His future judgment, and to be the executants of His will either in gathering together His people from the four winds of heaven (Mark xiii. 27) for entrance into His Kingdom, or for assembling the rebels to cast them into the lake of fire (Matt. xiii. 42). The mention here of these officers of the Divine government deepens the solemn effect which that double action must have had upon Timothy's mind.

"Preferring" (v.21). Read : " pre-judging," that is, judging an accusation against a bishop before hearing the evidence." Partiality " means respecting of persons in judgment.

The Greek word for " man " and "men " in verse 22 is generic and not individual. It includes women ministers as well as men ministers. If Timothy hastily ordained unworthy persons chosen by the Church and presented to him for appointment, he made himself responsible for the sins into which they might fall and which he was commanded to rebuke (v. 20). He was to keep himself pure. " Thyself " is emphatic in the Greek text.

Verse 23 is a parenthesis. It reveals the tender love of the Spirit expressing itself in the warm and affectionate sympathy of the Apostle for his beloved child Timothy. Wine was a temptation to bishops (iii. 3 and 11). Timothy was a total abstainer, and the injunction to keep himself pure from other bishop's sins would confirm him in this rigid abstinence. But the Spirit interjects this parenthesis in His pity for Timothy's feeble health ; and, whilst acknowledging how carefully he had kept himself from exciting his passions by the use of wine, he directs him to drink a little as a medicine because of his often infirmities. In the East the two most powerful remedies for illness are oil and wine. The Apostle Paul enjoined the one, the Apostle James the other, and the Good Samaritan used both.

Verse 24 follows, and is connected with verse 22. Both open and secret sins will be dealt with in the judgment (v. 24) ; and open and secret good works will be there equally recognised and rewarded. Timothy's responsibility was limited to sins that were open and manifest.

The direction in verse 23 establishes the principle of the value and use of medicine in illness—a little medicine for aggravated disease ; and the Apostle James points out that the medicine should be used prayerfully (James v. 14).

Neither Paul, Timothy, Gaius, Epaphroditus, nor Trophimus were healed by faith, God having provided a better and higher glory for them and for the Church.

The legislation of these chapters support the claim that Timothy was an Apostle.

1 **TIMOTHY VI.**—The communications of the Holy Spirit in this chapter respect the conduct of Christian servants to their masters (vs. 1 and 2) ; the contrast between the health-giving words of the Lord Jesus Christ (v. 3) and the poison-filled words of perverse men (vs. 4, 5, and 20) ; the actions of those who make themselves rich (vs. 9 and 10) and those to whom God entrusts riches (vs. 17-19) ; and, lastly, the comparison between Timothy as a confessor of the truth (vs. 11-14) and Christ (v. 13), Whom God will manifest in glory (v. 15) in that very city where He made the good confession—the argument and stimulus for Timothy being that, as Christ because of His good confession will be so glorified by God (vs. 15 and 16), so Timothy, if likewise faithful, will be made one of the companions of that glory.

" The yoke " (v. 1), i.e., the yoke of slavery. Dishonest service on the part of a professing Christian servant brings discredit upon God and His doctrine.

" Despise " (v. 2), i.e., " be wanting in respect for." Christian servants are to be especially faithful to Christian masters,

because the masters are " believing and beloved "—believing in Christ and beloved by Him. It is difficult to say what is meant by " partakers of the benefit." Most likely it means that as Christian masters and Christian servants are partners in the great salvation, therefore the masters were to receive fitting respect and affection.

The Apostle's words (v. 3) were those of the Lord Jesus Christ. This is a striking testimony to inspiration, and to Paul's consciousness that his words were inspired. God's word aims at, and produces, moral fruit ; man's word addresses the intellect, inflates pride, and generates the evil fruit detailed in verses 4 and 5. These teachers were ministers in the Apostolic Church ; and they have never failed of successors from that time to the present day.

" Gain is godliness" (v. 5), should read godliness is a means of gain. The order of the words is reversed, godliness being put last for emphasis. When it is accompanied by contentment it is indeed great gain.

" They that will be rich " (v. 9), i.e., who are determined at all costs to amass wealth. They do not merely expose themselves to temptation, from which they should pray to be delivered, but they actually fall into it. The statements of this verse and of verse 10 burn as a fiery flame. Verse 10 should read : " The love of money is a root of all kinds of evil " . . . it seduces (" erred ") from the faith." It is the love of money which is here condemned. A legacy might seduce to idolatry (Judges xvii. 3) ; let not, therefore, the Christian disappointed of a legacy grieve, but praise God for a possible snare escaped.

" Man of God " (v. 11), i.e., God's man. He was in the world on the part of God. He was to represent Him, and to exhibit in his conduct the moral beauties of uprightness, godliness, fidelity to his word, etc. : for these were the things which in him as God's man presented God to the world and glorified Him. This involves conflict (v. 12) because of the presence of the enemy. The man of God must contend for the faith of God ; and the knowledge that he is chosen for the life that is eternal, animates him to give his whole being to the interests of that life. Timothy in the presence of many witnesses, had pledged himself to this mighty warfare, and engaged to keep fast hold on the life that is life indeed (vs. 12 and 19).

Christ, as God's man, and faithful to the

truth and to the life that is eternal (v. 13), witnessed to the truth. He in bearing witness to the truth attested the truthfulness of the whole of Christianity. His was " the good confession " (R.V.).

" The commandment " (v. 14, R.V.), i.e., the Gospel as commanded by God and given forth by the Holy Spirit. Timothy was not to add to it or corrupt it ; and the Gospel is to remain unchanged up to the appearing of the Lord Jesus Christ.

The inaccessible majesty of God (vs. 15 and 16) is here presented as nowhere else in the Bible ; and it harmonizes with the character of this Epistle.

Wealthy believers (v. 17) are not commanded to abandon their wealth, but to employ it as stewards for the advantage of their fellow-believers, and for the enrichment of the life that is life indeed (v. 19, R.V.).

" That which is committed to thy trust " (v. 20). Rather : " The deposit," i.e., the truth of the Gospel, which is opposed by a knowledge which pretends to penetrate into Divine realities as though they were subject to human science and investigation.

The language of this whole letter reveals anxiety lest Timothy should withdraw from the field of battle.

II TIMOTHY — So far as is known this is the last letter that the Apostle Paul wrote before being put to death. This adds an emotional interest to its Divine inspiration. It views the Church in ruins, and instructs the man of God as to his personal conduct in the midst of the ruin.

The keyword " Truth " (ii. 18, 25, iii. 7 and 8, and iv. 4) characterises the letter ; and the three downward stages of departure from the truth are exhibited in ii. 18, iii. 8, and iv. 4 ; i.e., erring from the truth, then resisting the truth, and, finally, turning away from the truth. These three prophecies have come true.

The first letter to Timothy predicts and fore-pictures " the latter times " ; the second letter, " the last days," i.e., the days preceding the Coming of the Lord.

It is apparent from both letters that the Apostle Paul was anxious about Timothy's courage and endurance and faithfulness in the presence of so much unfaithfulness, opposition, and corruption ; and this is not altogether to be wondered at owing to Timothy's youth and feeble health. Hence the significance of the word " hardship " which occurs four times in the R.V. (i. 8, ii. 3 and 9, and finally, iv. 5).

The title " Lord " occurs fourteen times : i. 8, 16, 18, 18 ; ii. 7, 14, 19, 22, 24 ; iii. 11 ; iv .8, 14, 17, 18. It characterizes the Epistle, for in the " last days " the Deity and Lordship of Christ will be denied.

II TIMOTHY I.—About to lose his life the Apostle declares himself a herald of life (v. 1). He was a messenger to announce to death-doomed men the Divine promise of life eternal offered to men in Christ Jesus. Only in that Saviour is life to be found, and only in Him is it offered to sinful men. This great promise of an ever-enduring life would nerve Timothy to fortitude in facing hardship and in preaching truth.

" From my forefathers," i.e., " as did my forefathers." It is noteworthy and important that both Paul and Timothy (vs. 3 and 5) had a spiritual ancestry, so in their cases the hearts of the children returned to the faith of their forefathers, for they believed on the Messiah (Mal. iv. 6, Luke i. 17, and Rom. xi. 23, 24, and 28). The use of the past tense in verse 5 implies that Lois and Eunice were now dead.

" Stir up " (v. 6) Greek : " Stir into flame." The special gift here intended must have been in connection with Church government, and that in verse 14 in relation to Gospel preaching. But only an Apostle could confer this gift by the putting on of his hands ; the presbyters could only express their concurrence (1 Tim. iv. 14). The Apostles being dead, such miraculous action is now impossible. The gift conferred (v. 6) carried with it a spirit of courage, power, love, and sound judgment (v. 7). That being so, Timothy was not to be ashamed of the Gospel (v. 8), nor of those who were suffering shame because of faithfulness to it ; on the contrary, he was to be a courageous partner in Gospel hardships, and there would be supplied to him the limitless power of God to enable him to discharge these requirements. The energy ministered would be " according to " the power of God. That would be the measure of the supply. If that power could be measured, then must Timothy's action and testimony be limited.

Paul had urged Timothy to come to him in his prison , and to come soon (iv. 21). He evidently was somewhat apprehensive lest

Timothy should be both ashamed and afraid to do so ; and therefore there was somewhat of a spur (vs. 16 and 17) suggested by his reference to Onesiphorus.

The glory of election, of free grace (v. 9), and the majesty of the Author of both election and grace (v. 10) are here set out with Divine clarity. God, for some satisfactory reason only discoverable to Himself, saved both Paul and Timothy before the world began, and then, in time, called them. The call was to a life of holiness, but not based upon, or measured by their moral worthfulness, but according to the immeasurable fulness of the Divine purpose and grace lodged in Christ Jesus. This purpose and grace having been formed countless ages before Paul and Timothy were born, could not be affected by either merit or demerit on their part ; and, therefore it was not according to works. The appearing of the Messiah manifested this purpose in grace ; and that Almighty Saviour in His atoning death annihilated death and enlightened darkened man respecting life and incorruptibility. The ancients had a dim sense of the existence of the soul after death, but of the resurrection of the body and incorruption they knew nothing. " Immortality " should here read " incorruptibility."

Paul was not ashamed of being cast into a felon's prison (v. 12), and he here hints that his beloved child is not to be on his part ashamed if he also should suffer like indignity and hardship. If God had saved them before the world began, and had called them to a life of holiness and testimony, He would surely accomplish the lesser wonder of equipping them to bravely endure the shame and suffering connected with the preaching of the truth. These hardships did not embitter the affections and heart of the Apostle (vs. 4 and 18), for he remembers the tears of his dearly-loved and faithful child, Timothy (v. 4), and he desires mercy for his former lover Onesiphorus (v. 18). When all is prosperous ministerial work is easy in spite of opposition, but when converts forsake their Gospel parents, it is not easy to maintain both faith and love and courage. But truth held in fellowship with God so establishes the believer, that the experience is made that Christ can satisfy and strengthen the hungry heart that is denied every affection and comfort and sympathy and fellowship and help that it naturally craves. How

precious—how satisfying—to possess that which is eternal and which is founded on the purpose and grace of God! This is a sure and immovable rock-refuge for the soul against which all waves break in vain.

" I have trusted," " I am persuaded," " I have committed " (v. 12). Happy they who can express themselves with such definiteness and assurance. The Apostle does not say, " I know Him in Whom I have trusted," but, " I know Whom I have trusted." To Him he had committed not only himself but his work ; and although outwardly his ministry was a failure (v. 15), yet he was persuaded that He Whom he trusted would guard both up to " that day."

The form, or pattern, of healthful words (v. 13), i.e., the Bible and the Apostolic teaching—(" words heard of me "). Faith in Christ Jesus and love for Him make the Bible precious. Without these it is practically a sealed Book to human wisdom. Moses was commanded to set up the Tabernacle "according to the pattern " given to him in the Mount ; Solomon was commanded to build the Temple according to the pattern given to him (1 Chron. xxviii. 11, 12) ; and Timothy was commanded to build the spiritual Temple according to the pattern given to him (v. 13). Nothing was left to the religious taste or pious imaginings of these builders. All three were bound to the pattern. This Divine command (v. 13) destroys the human additions of " tradition " and " development." Ministerial work which accords with the " pattern " is gold, silver, or precious stone. What does not accord is wood, hay, and stubble. What the Apostles taught is given to the Church in their writings, and nothing is to be believed which they did not teach. See notes on 1. John iv. 1-6.

The power to keep and to preach the truth committed to the preacher is Divinely provided. It is the Holy Spirit dwelling in the preacher. It is possible to be a preacher, and to be destitute of the Holy Spirit.

It is very bitter and painful in the darkness of a dungeon awaiting a violent death to be forsaken by one's own converts, and especially by converts at one time so intelligent and affectionate as the Ephesians (vs. 15 and 18, and Acts xx. 37). But the Apostle knowing Whom he had trusted, was not embittered, and so he did not pray for judgment upon the leaders of this defection, Phygellus, Hermogenes, and Onesiphorus, but, on the contrary, he desired mercy for them. He does not say that they turned away from the Gospel, but that they had turned away from him (v. 15), and that would imply that they had put aside his teaching respecting the heavenly calling of the Church, and had joined the majority in being satisfied with the earthly glories connected with Israel. For notes on verses 16-18 see iv. 19.

2 TIMOTHY II.—" Therefore " (v. 1), because all had forsaken Paul and his teaching (i. 15) " therefore " Timothy was to stand fast, and not in the spirit of stubbornness, reserve and pride which in such circumstances often harden the human will, but, on the contrary, in the energy of the grace that is in Christ Jesus. Verses 24 and 25 illustrate the nature and activities of that grace. He was not to despise the faithless, but to show them the grace of His Divine Master.

The " many witnesses " of verse 2 could confirm Timothy himself and could certify others that the doctrine he taught was beyond all question Apostolic, for he had received it from Paul himself. This is important. He was to communicate that truth to trusty men—men competent to teach others. There are two facts to be marked here. One : The uncertainty of oral tradition. Second : The presence of authority in the truth itself and not in those who communicated it. Thus the supposed claim that the Church is an authoritative teacher is shown to be baseless. Timothy himself was not an authority. He was only an instrument for the communication of the truth, and his successors were to be so likewise. The many witnesses served as a guarantee of that which he had heard from Paul, and so hindered the introduction of anything false, or what he might himself think. He was to pass on only what he had heard from Apostolic lips. It was Divinely revealed truth he was to communicate, and nothing else. That Divine teaching the Holy Spirit has given to man in the inspired writings. This fact shuts out tradition and establishes the Divine authority of the sacred Scriptures.

The Christian is a soldier (v. 3) a wrestler (v. 5) and a farmer (v. 6). As a soldier his one purpose is to please his Captain. It is a time of war, so he stands aside from many legitimate interests and pleasures so as to conserve his full strength for the battlefield. As a wrestler he observes the rules of the arena. For the Christian wrestler these rules are the Scriptures. As a farmer he first labours, for otherwise he will never partake of the fruits—that is, he in this present life sows the seed of the harvest which he will enjoy by and by. Timothy was to deeply ponder these facts, encouraged by the promise : " The Lord shall give thee understanding in all things " (v. 7 R.V.).

The true soldier, wrestler and husbandman was the Lord Jesus, and the Apostle points to Him and says to his beloved child so as to enhearten him : " Remember Jesus Christ of the Seed of David raised from the dead ! " The argument is : Christ, as a man, acquitted Himself without fault in this triple service and is now a glorified Man in the heavens. So Timothy, though a man, would also be rewarded if faithful (v. 8 R.V.). The atonement is not introduced here. It is impossible for man to enter into that sacrifice. Christ by Himself purged man's sin (Heb. i. 3).

As the elect are absolutely certain of entrance into eternal glory (v. 10) it might be urged that the Apostle was foolish to expose himself to such needless suffering. But he says that it was this consciousness that animated his mind and sustained his courage in preaching the gospel (v. 8) in order that they might be saved. The servant of God courageously faces a hostile mob fortified by the feeling that God has elect persons in that angry multitude whom He will save through the efforts of the preacher ; for the Divine method of saving men is through the foolishness of preaching.

This is a faithful saying : " If we died with Him we shall also live with Him   if we endure with Him we shall also reign with Him ; if we deny Him He also will deny us ; if we become faithless He continues faithful, for He cannot prove false to Himself."

Young men are by nature readily attracted by what claims to be new and intellectual. It is evident that the Apostle was anxious in this regard with respect to Timothy (vs. 14, 15, 16, 17, 23). See notes on 1 Tim. i. 4. Contrast the fact of the resurrection in verses 8 and 18. False teachers, perhaps basing their arguments on Paul's own writings, as for instance Ephes. ii. 1, asserted that there was no physical resurrection either in the case of Christ or of the believer. Resurrection they urged was entirely a spiritual conception.

3 P,

The true workman seeks God's approbation only (v. 15). A servant divides the bread among the children (Luke xii. 42). So the Christian minister rightly divides the truth and does not give to the dogs what is meant for the sons.

There is progress in false teaching, but it is progress away from God and from moral likeness to Him (v. 16).

The firm foundation of God (v. 17 R.V.) bears the double signature that He recognises, and will recognise, those that are His (Num. xvi. 5) ; and that those who profess to be His, accredit their profession by departure from evil. The ancients engraved inscriptions upon foundation stones.

The servants of " a great house " are given bread upon a bread-board made of wood or earthenware ; the master, upon a salver made of gold or silver. The believer is not to purge others but to purge himself, so that he may become a vessel unto honour reserved for the Master's use and not for common use. " Dishonour " i:e., common use (v. 20).

The best way to fight some sins is to flee from them (v. 22). Uprightness, good faith and love are to be followed after, and peace with them that call upon the Lord out of a pure heart. There should be no comma after the word " peace." It is not possible to follow peace with all men—that is to be sought after, but not at the expense of holiness (Heb. xii. 14 and James iii. 17). To unite the Name of Christ and evil is to blaspheme that Name (vs. 19 and 22). He only recognises those who call upon Him out of a pure heart ; and His people are only to associate themselves with those who in action manifest themselves as possessing a pure heart.

False doctrine genders quarrels (v. 23). The true servant is not to quarrel. He is to patiently suffer ill treatment, and, with all gentleness, keep on preaching (v. 24) in the hope that God will touch the heart of the opposers (v. 25) ; that He will give them repentance ; and (v. 26) that, being taken alive by Him, they may awake out of the snare of the Devil and live to do God's will. This last verse is difficult of translation, but by placing the last two verses together, and by observing the argument, it is plain that the persons whom the preacher seeks to reach are in a Satanic snare, and that before they perish, and while still alive, they are,

through the preaching of the truth, Divinely rescued, and rescued in order that they should live to do the will of God.

2 TIMOTHY III.—The teaching and conduct of the Apostle Paul (vs. 10-12) are here contrasted with the teaching and conduct of the false apostles who wrecked the testimony of the Christian Church (vs. 1-9).

The prophecy of verses 1-9 has come to pass and now only awaits (v. 9) its last phase. See Rev. xvii.

Men have always manifested the characteristics of verses 2-4, but the peculiar force of this prophecy is that it predicted that such conduct would accompany " a form of godliness " (v. 5)—not *the* form. This is a prominent feature of " the last days." Christianity is professed, but its power denied. The necessity and the fact of the new birth are derided. Such moral facts and false teachings prove that the professing Church has now reached these "last days " ; and they also demonstrate the inspiration of this prophecy

In the First Epistle, which concerns rule in the Church, Timothy was commanded to oppose and silence false teachers, but in this later Epistle, which predicts the ruin of the Church, he was commanded to turn away from such.

A comparison of verses 2-5 with Rom. i. 19-32 evidences that the nature of man under Paganism and Christianity is the same ; except that Christianity imposes an outward restraint so as to hide certain sins from the public view. Paganism was the corruption of primitive truth and Christendom is the corruption of New Testament truth. Man's mental and moral degradation under the former was reproduced under the latter with the addition of hypocrisy. Verse 4 does not mean a lesser love for God and a greater for pleasure but the total displacement of the higher love by the lower.

" Silly " (v. 6). Old English for " simple," i.e., thoughtless. " Divers lusts," i.e., desirous of new doctrines. " Ever learning," i.e., always wanting to learn something new. " Laden with sins," i.e., the conviction that they had a burden of sin. Women are more conscious of this burden than men are. They are, therefore, much more religious, and continually on the search for ceremonies and doctrines to still the conscience.

The Law of Subsequent Narration is

illustrated in verse 8. The Holy Spirit deferred information as to the number and names of these magicians (Exod. vii. 11) until A.D. 67.

" Persecution " (v. 12). The marvel of the Christian religion in relation to other religions proves its Divine origin, for it condemns all other religions however ancient; it mortifies self and its passions; it teaches impossible doctrines such as the resurrection; and it promises persecutions to those that embrace it.

The evolution and progression of evil in the Christian Church predicted in verse 13 destroy the popular doctrine of the upward glorious march of humanity. See note on Dan. viii. 23. God permits, and will permit, these false religious teachers to mislead others and to be themselves misled, but only up to the point of time predicted in verse 9. That day is yet future.

But in the midst of these " last days " of difficulty and peril the Christian is not left without a guide and a Divine safeguard on which he may wholly rely to preserve him from being misled. That safeguard is the Bible (vs. 14-17) Timothy is reminded of the Holy Scriptures themselves (v. 15) and of those who had introduced them to him (v. 14). Such teachers he could trust; but what they taught him was based upon the Word of God and not upon the vain imaginations of man. The Holy Spirit states that no part of Scripture is of human origination (2 Pet. i. 20, 21) but that every part is of Divine inspiration (v. 16). These statements decide the Divine origin of the entire Scripture. See note on 2 Pet. iii. 16.

The Holy Scriptures reveal the mind and will of God. It is not only that they contain the Word of God but that they are the Word of God. They are the one and only and Divine authority. With them the Lord silenced Satan. The Spirit chose men whom He had Himself fashioned as His channels of communication; hence Paul was His servant to the Church to complete the Word of God (Col. i. 25). These men were not the Truth; they only communicated the Truth. Verse 16 does not say that they were the authors of inspiration, but that the Scriptures themselves are inspired; and that they are able not only to perfectly inform man as to salvation to be enjoyed by reposing faith upon the Lord Jesus Christ (v. 15), but to perfectly fit him out morally for the dis-

charge of all the duties of the Christian life. If the Scriptures were produced by imperfect men how could they effect moral perfection? Imperfection cannot produce perfection.

The expression " thoroughly furnished " (v. 17) is a Greek maritime term used in relation to the fitting out of a ship for a long voyage. All that may be necessary for the voyage is provided beforehand so that there is a perfect provision made for the necessities of the crew. Such a provision for the voyage of life the Christian finds in the Holy Scriptures. There are degrees of revelation in them, but not of inspiration. All that God saw necessary to be there He has put there, so that they are a complete and sufficient rule, and need no oral tradition to add to their perfection, or to more fully equip them to produce perfection in those who love and obey them.

So Timothy, like the elders at Ephesus (Acts xx. 32), was cast upon the Scriptures as an infallible and sufficient rule and guide of personal Christian conduct in the midst of ecclesiastical corruption and the triumph of moral evil. This is God's precious provision for the nourishment and enlightenment of His children in this present night of confusion, sin and error (2 Peter i. 19) in that which professes to be the Church of God. There will be no recovery. Evil will leaven the three measures of meal; and the final judgment of corrupt Christendom will result as foretold in Rev. xvii.

Three illustrations of the Law of no " ands " occur in this chapter—verses 1-5; verses 10 and 11; and verses 16 and 17. In the first the reader is hurried on to the climax: " From such turn away "; in the second to the climax: " But out of them all the Lord delivered me "; and in the third to the climax: " That the man of God may be perfect, etc." See note on Luke xiv. 13.

The importance of this last passage, (v. 16) is emphasized by the perfection of its structure:

God's divinely-inspired Word.
  Its profit to God's man.
    Teaching what is true.
      Condemning what is false.
    Teaching what is right.
  God's divinely-fitted man.
His profit in God's Word.

Thus may be seen at a glance the sufficiency of God and His Word for the spiritual life of the believer in a time of departure from the truth and the cessation of Church fellowship and testimony. This helps to mark the distinction between these two Epistles. In the first the man of God was instructed as to his conduct in the Church in its corporate capacity prior to its ruin. In the second, his conduct as an individual is enforced. In chapter i all are stated to have turned away from Apostolic teaching (v. 15), and the words " I," " thou " and " thee " are prominent. In chapter ii. error enters (vs. 18 and 19) and " everyone " that is loyal departs from iniquity. In chapter iii. the descent is accentuated—truth is resisted (v. 8), and the individual believer is cast upon the God-breathed Scriptures. In chapter iv. the climax is reached—truth is abandoned and " fables " enthroned in its place (v. 4). The immediate injunction follows : " But watch *thou* in all things."

Thus in the second Epistle by the repetition of the pronouns, the conduct of the Christian as God's man in the midst of ecclesiastical and moral evil is emphasized.

The Scriptures edify—they are profitable ; but this is not all—they are inspired. Compare 2 Pet. iii. 16 and the important word " other."

All Scripture is given by inspiration of God (v. 16). That this is the proper translation, is proved by eight similarly constructed passages, i.e., Rom. vii. 12, 1 Cor. xi. 30, 2 Cor. x. 10, 1 Tim. i. 15, 1 Tim. ii. 3, 1 Tim. iv. 4, 1 Tim. iv. 9 and Heb. iv. 13. The Revised Version correctly translates these eight as in the Authorized Version, but arbitrarily alters 2 Tim. iii. 16. But if this construction be applied to the eight other passages, which would have been consistent, its falseness at once appears. The grammatical form of the Greek word for " God-inspired " further condemns the translation of the Revised Version. However the Revisers place the correct translation in the margin.

The Bible defines its own terms. If all the passages in which the term " Scripture " occurs be read it will be recognised that the expression is, in the Bible, confined to and always means, the Word and Words of God.

Christ's testimony (R.V) to the verbal inspiration of the Sacred Writings is frequent, e.g., John vii. 16, viii. 28 and 47, xii. 49, xiv. 10, and 24, xvii. 8, and, notably, Matt. xxii. 32.where the doctrine of the resurrection is based upon one word. Similarly the Apostles Paul and Peter give a like witness in Gal. iii. 16, 2 Tim. iii. 16. 2 Pet. i. 20, and iii. 16, etc., and Gen. xvii. records verbal inspiration (v. 3), syllabic inspiration (v. 5), and letter inspiration (v. 15).

2 TIMOTHY IV—Because of corruption within the Church and of opposition without it, Timothy was to be the more energetic in preaching the Gospel to the world (v. 5) and sound doctrine to the church (vs. 2-4). He, and also the Apostle Paul, might have argued that all their efforts as preachers having apparently failed, it would be reasonable for them to cease from all further activity. But the contrary was the case. Because of seeming failure, and in spite of it, the Apostle urged his beloved child to keep on preaching so long as he had breath with which to preach ; and he points him to the " day " of the Master's appearing (vs. 1 and 8), and to the crown of righteousness which will be the reward of all who love that appearing, and who have acquitted themselves well as Christian workers in spite of countless difficulties and disappointments. The words " in season and out of season " (v. 2) have reference to Timothy and not to his hearers, As a preacher he was not to consider himself, but in spite of heat and cold, and circumstances seasonable or unseasonable as affecting himself whether in the moral or physical realm, he was to continue unceasingly active in the ministry of the Gospel inside and outside the Church.

The prophecy of verse 3 has come to pass. The professing Church, as here predicted, has displaced the Bible and substituted fables for it.

Paul encourages Timothy to complete his ministry (v. 5) by the fact that he himself had fulfilled the ministry committed to him (vs. 6-8). He could confidently say in the light of the judgment of verse 8 that he had fought *the* good fight, he had finished *the* course, and had safeguarded *the* faith. That faith was now given in Divine fulness to Timothy in the Scriptures (iii. 15-17), and he in his time was to guard it—not corrupting it or adding ought to it.

The lonely prisoner from out of the chilly gloom of his dark dungeon urges Timothy to hasten to him (vs. 9, 11, 13, and 21). Although living enwrapt in the power of the Holy Spirit yet his poor human heart hungered for human fellowship. All in Asia had forsaken him ; Demas had also forsaken him (v. 10) ; and at his first defence (v. 16) no one had the courage to stand by him. All forsook him. Yet his faithful Lord did not forsake him. He stood by him and streng-thened him to preach the Gospel to the Roman Emperor, to his court, and, through them, to all the Gentiles ; and so he was delivered —not out of the mouth of Nero—but out of the mouth of Satan (Ps. xxii. 21). Satan's expectation must have been the hope that Paul through fear of death would deny or compromise truth.

Demas and Mark (vs. 10 and 11) here stand in contrast. The latter, once cowardly (Acts xiii. 13), now bravely faces death ; the former, once courageous (Col. iv. 14, Phil. 24) now abandons the Apostle. It is encouraging and affecting to have this testimony to Mark's usefulness to the Apostle in the midst of his loneliness and sorrows.

The approach of winter and Paul's poverty (v. 21) necessitated the return of the cloak left at Troas (v. 13) ; but the heart, faithful to Him who had chosen him, esteemed the books and the parchments as more important.

The difference of language in verses 14 and 16 is instructive. As to the copper-smith the Apostle says, " The Lord shall reward him according to his works " ; but as to the timid brethren in verse 21 he prays that they may be forgiven for their cowardice.

Although he knew he was to die, yet he did not cease to look for the day of the Lord's appearing (v. 8). He loved that appearing because he loved Him Who was to appear.

He was confident that He Who had de-livered him out of the mouth of the lion at his first defence would certainly continue to deliver him from every evil plan (v. 18) that that lion might scheme ; and he was equally confident that his dear and faithful Lord would preserve him unto His Heavenly Kingdom. This confidence and intelligence on the eve of his execution is a most precious testimony to the reality of the bliss and victory that lie beyond death.

Erastus was chamberlain, i.e., treasurer of the city of Corinth (Rom. xvi. 23).

The miraculous healing of disease accredited the Messiah to the Hebrew Church, and, consequently, ceased when that Church rejected Him and the Pentecostal testimony. Hence Trophimus (v. 20) and Timothy and Epaphroditus and Gaius and Paul and others

had to suffer the illnesses common to fallen man ; and this has its value as establishing sympathy between the believer and his suffer-ing and afflicted fellow-creatures, and in teaching that victory in suffering is a higher spiritual experience than exemption from it.

The doctrine of prayers for the dead is largely based on ch. i. 16-18. In Greek "house" is masculine (v. 16). Therefore " him " (v. 18) should read " it." The passage will then read : " The Lord grant mercy to the house of Onesiphorus. . . . The Lord grant to it to find mercy," etc. The intervening words form a parenthesis. Putting therefore i. 16-18 and iv. 19 together it may reasonably be suggested that Onesiphorus was the only Christian in his family ; that touched by the memory of his affection shown before he forsook him, the Apostle specially prayed for the conversion of the family, and sent a courteous greeting to them so as to influence them in favour of the Gospel. Thus he worked as well as prayed. To base the doctrine of prayers for the dead on these passages is futile, for they show that both Onesiphorus and his family were all living at the time the Apostle wrote to Timothy. Further, the " mercy " was not petitioned for a lengthened period, such as purgatory, but for one definite " day " (i. 18). The subject of the prayer was not Onesiphorus but his family ; and the context is desertion and not death, for all were turning away from the Apostle (i. 15).

TITUS

This letter was probably written in Macedonia by the Apostle Paul prior to his second imprisonment and death. Its subject is government in the Church ; for God is not the Author of confusion, but of order. The government was to be exercised by persons chosen by the Church members and then appointed to office by Titus as Paul's delegate, the Apostle having to leave Crete before the settlement of this matter (i. 5). These persons were called elders and bishops, the one title expressing the dignity of the office, the other, its duties (vs. 5 and 7). The procedure in the choosing and appoint-ment of elders was no doubt similar to that of Acts vi. 3-6. There was evidently a Jewish colony in Crete (i. 10 and 14), and Acts ii. 11 states that Cretan Jews were present in Jerusalem at Pentecost.

As in the letters to Timothy, so here the

promise of life is prominent ; and the title of " God our Saviour " characteristic.

There is not in this letter the same intimacy of affection as in Timothy. Titus was a beloved child in the Gospel, but Paul does not open his heart to him in the same way as he did to Timothy. In Timothy doctrine has a large place ; in Titus, rule.

Rule in the Church is committed to elders (i. 5) and in the State to magistrates (iii. 1) ; and obedience to both governments is based upon the Gospel and its moral teachings (ii. 11-14, iv. 3-8).

TITUS I.—The statements in verses 1-3 are that Paul was divinely appointed to minister to the faith of the elect, and to bring to the knowledge of the nations the truth concerning eternal life, purposed and promised by God before the world began, and in time declared to man through the preaching of the Apostle. The Apostle had, therefore, a double ministry, one to the Church and the other to the world.

Man not existing before the world began, it must have been to Christ that God promised an " election " in a life that should be endless. Believers, therefore, are not elect because they have faith, but they have faith because they are elect, for faith is the gift of God. That election, and that free gift of faith, were not confined to Israel but common to all men (v. 4)

The religions of the heathen were impure, but the Gospel is " after godliness " (v. 1) ; it demands a life of self-denial and separation from all forms of evil.

Paul was a Jew and Titus a Gentile, but they stood together in a faith common to both (v. 4).

God cannot lie (v.2), man is by nature a liar (v. 12). See note on Ps. cxvi. 11. The impossibility that God should lie, and especially that He should lie to His dearly Beloved Son Who was the Depository of this promise (Prov. viii. 30 and 31, Luke ii. 14 and Ps. xl. 6-8), secures the eternal safety of the elect. How wonderful that they should be the objects of the Divine communications in the past eternities, and that Paul and Titus, and all included in the common faith, engaged the thoughts of God before all the ages ! This promise made in eternity (v. 2) He manifested in time for "His word " (v. 3), means the promise of verse 2. These communications of the Spirit

are for the heart more than for the head.

" The faithful word " (v. 9), i.e., the Bible. " Faithful children " (v. 6), i.e., children who were believers, and not open to the accusation of being disobedient to their parents at home or troublesome abroad.

" Subvert " (v. 11). False teachers are the Devil's levers for upsetting families.

" A prophet of their own " (Epimenides, 600 B.C.) (v. 12), not " a prophet of the Lord." The statement may read : " The Cretans are alway liars, dangerous animals, lazy gluttons." The Holy Spirit says (v. 13) " This witness is true."

" All things " (v. 15), i.e., " all meats." One company of false teachers in Crete advocated gluttony and another commanded abstinence from certain foods as being impure. The Apostle overthrew both by teaching the necessity of a pure heart and a clean conscience. God claims the heart. The man whose heart is defiled does not need to go out of himself to find what is impure, but though making a profession of faith (v. 15), in his actions he denies Christ and is in fact detestable, disobedient, and useless for any good work.

TITUS II.—" Thou " (v. 1) is emphatic, and " sound doctrine " means teaching which is scriptural and which is healthy for the soul.

Rule in the Church, and the conduct of its members (vs.1-10), based upon grace and its moral energies (vs. 11-15), are the subjects of this chapter.

" As becometh holiness " (v. 3), i.e., as becometh consecrated women. " Teachers of good things." This does not conflict with I Tim. ii. 12, for that prohibition was against wives teaching and practising authority over their husbands.

" Keepers at home " (v. 5) Greek : " Keepers of the home," i.e., efficient housekeepers. " Good," better translated " generous," for an efficient housekeeper is disposed to be niggardly.

Uncorrupt doctrine (v. 7) means teaching which is wholly and solely scriptural.

The freedom of the Gospel and its brotherhood conflicted with the institution of slavery, and ultimately abolished it (vs 9-10) ; but meanwhile slaves were commanded to be subject to those who owned them ; for in no rank of society was there more danger of the equality of Christians being misunderstood than in that of slaves. Hence the large legislation affecting them (I Cor. vii. 20, 24, Eph. vi. 5, Col. iii. 22 I Tim. vi. 1, I Pet. ii. 18, etc.). So great a portion of inspired Scripture being given to slaves ennobles them, and reveals how warmly God loved them, and how largely they engaged his thoughts. The most amazing revelations from God before which great kings and mighty scientists stand dumb and stupid, are in the Scriptures connected with slaves and revealed to them.

The best testimony to the doctrines of the Gospel is to adorn them by a Christ-like life. Carnal men are ready to die for the Gospel, but only spiritual men can live it. God would have His truth adorned even by slaves, whom the world at that time regarded as no better than beasts of burden, and whom some at the present day believe to have no souls, if they are Negroes, and whom it is lawful to shoot as vermin are shot.

True liberty and true equality reign in a Divinely governed and consistent Christian Church. Its moral order secures both. Satan's aim is to introduce disorder and thus disrupt the fellowship and destroy its testimony. But if the precious proprieties ordained by God are not maintained, liberty perishes and carnal tyranny replaces Christian freedom.

The Holy Spirit recognises every relationship which God has formed. Age and youth, husband and wife, child and parent, servant and master all have their own proprieties and ministries to maintain toward each other in the sweetness and power of the grace that at its appearing brought health and healing to all men.

So the conduct of Christian people amongst themselves in the Church (vs. 2-10), and their conduct among their fellow-citizens in the State, are both based upon the great doctrines of Christianity (vs. 11-15 and iii. 3-8).

Grace appeared—not to a particular people but to all men—and it did not bring them nutriment for their passions, but nourishment for their souls. It did not demand righteousness from men, but brought righteousness to them. They needed righteousness. And so grace overleaped every obstacle in order to reach every man and to

discipline him (v. 12), so that in relation to himself he should be sober, in relation to his neighbour, righteous, and in relation to God, pious.

Grace has appeared (v. 11) ; glory will appear (v. 13). Grace disciplines the believer as to his conduct while waiting for the glory which in its turn is to crown him.

Verse 13 reads thus in the Greek text : " Looking with constant expectation for the blessed hope, that is to say (" even "), the appearing of the glory of our great God and Saviour Jesus Christ " (R.V.).

There is but one Greek article to " God " and " Saviour " which shows that both titles are predicated of one and the same Person. Also, the word " appearing " is never by Paul predicated to God as Father but is invariably applied to Christ. Also, in the context (v. 14) the reference is to Christ alone. Also, the term " Great God " as applied to Christ accords with the context which speaks of His Divine glory. He also is " the True God," as declared in I John. v. 20. Compare 2 Peter i., I R.V.

" A peculiar people " (v. 14), i.e., a people for His own possession. Consistent conduct and Bible preaching disarm contempt (v. 15).

TITUS III.—The conduct of the Christian as a subject of the state is governed by the same principle as motives his conduct as a member of the Church. He is to be obedient to the government and to show to his fellow-citizens, however hostile, immoral, debased or degraded, the same grace that God showed to him, remembering that he himself possesses the same corrupt nature as they, and that in that nature the seeds of all vile passions lie (v. 3). This governing principle of public conduct is foreign to, and opposed to, human nature. Self-interest, ambition, love of ease or of money or of position animate the ordinary members of society. The Christian's conduct is regulated by his relationship to God as the Saviour God —the especial title of these three Epistles. He recognises that that which makes him different from others is not any merit in himself or any personal or moral superiority. He is even as they. Grace makes the difference, and it teaches him to be as kind and merciful to others as God was to himself. The sense of what he once was, and of the evil of the nature which dwells in him and of the pitiful action of God towards him, combine to govern his conduct towards others.

The Christian is to cheerfully obey the government and to willingly volunteer to support it in "every good work" (v. 1). This is his duty, for the magistrate is a Divinely appointed officer (Rom. xiii.) to punish evil doers and protect society. When therefore the magistrate calls for volunteers to arrest and bring to justice evil-doers, it is the duty of the Christian to assist him. It is the legitimate employment of force; and force implies putting to death.

But the Christian in his own private life (v. 2), and in his relationship to all men however hostile and abominable, is to be gentle towards those that attack him, and, generally to pursue a course of peace and benevolence; for the principle of grace excludes all violence of thought, language or action.

The Apostle could truthfully say that he lived in all good conscience towards God from his childhood, for prior to his conversion, he was blind to the corruption of his moral nature as now described in verse 3. The seeds of all these sins were in his heart; but as a sincere Pharisee he was unconscious of the fact. As a Jew he hated Titus as a Gentile, and in his spiritual blindness he thought that hatred to be just. And Titus as a Gentile hated him. They both lived in malice and envy. Both were filled with hate, and they mutually hated each other. How amazing that God should have had compassion on such men. But such is grace. The Saviour God (v. 4) appeared to them in kindness and love and in the boundlessness of His mercy "saved" them (v. 5), not because of any meritorious works performed by them, but because of His grace (v. 7) operating through Jesus Christ (v. 6). He appeared to them (v. 4); He saved them; He washed them; He renewed them (v. 5); He justified them; and eternally enriched them (v. 7).

How arresting and illuminating are the three great words: "He saved us" (v. 5). Paul could say: "Ah, Titus, He saved you and He saved me; He has saved both of us, and we know it; and we rejoice because we are saved!"

"The washing of regeneration" (v. 5). This should read "The laver of regenera-tion." The reference here is to the laver at the door of the Tabernacle, in the Wilderness. In it the priests were baptized, i.e., washed, for to baptize means to wash, the water being poured upon them. This symbolized the New Birth. The most effectual way of cleansing from sin is by putting to death. In the New Birth of regeneration the believer in Christ is put to death. He was baptized into death with Christ at Calvary and He rises into a new life with Christ in resurrection. This is an effectual break with sin. It is an effective washing—not the application of material water to the outward flesh, which accomplishes nothing, but the effectual action of the Holy Spirit within the soul which accomplishes everything. That Spirit not only regenerates but renews (v. 5) and in doing so sustains richly (v. 6 m.) the spiritual life which He imparts, thus preserving the believer unto his eternal inheritance (v. 7).

"Justified" (v. 7), i.e., declared righteous. See notes on Rom. iii.

"Regeneration" (v. 5). This word only occurs here and in Matt. xix. 28. By placing the two passages together, the force and fulness of the word appear.

"Shed" (v. 6). Better: "Poured." To wash, i.e., to baptize, was performed by pouring water upon a person. Elisha baptized the hands of Elijah. This verse 5 is almost universally understood to mean water baptism. But the Apostle does not speak of the washing of water, which is material, but of the washing of regeneration which is spiritual, and quite a different thing.

The "according to" or measure of the believer's hope is that he is heir to a felicity that is eternal (v. 7).

The simplicity of the Gospel (vs. 5-7) contrasts with the folly and darkness of man's vain religious thoughts (v. 9).

"Heretic" (v. 10), i.e., a leader or member of a carnal faction. After a second warning such a person was to be avoided (R.V. margin). It would be well if all Christian people observed this direction.

Christian congregations need pastors and teachers (v. 12). Titus was not to leave the Cretan Church until either Artemas or Tychicus arrived. The latter is spoken of in Eph. vi. 21 and 2 Tim. iv. 12. He must have been an effective minister.

Nothing is too good for whole-hearted ministers of the Gospel (v. 13). In a sense

Apollos was a rival (1 Cor. i.), but Paul wished him to get every help in his ministry.

Verse 14 may be thus translated : " Let our people also learn to follow as a good example honest trades for necessary wants, so that they may not live useless lives." Tobacco is not a necessity. A Christian who devotes his life to manufacturing tobacco lives a useless and possibly injurious life in relation to his fellow-creatures. A Christian, therefore should not either sell or smoke tobacco. This same principle applies to the manufacture of beer and whisky. The Master by trade was a carpenter. It was an honest trade for the provision of a necessary want. Happy the Christian who when dying can reflect that his business life as well as his Christian life benefitted his fellow-men !

PHILEMON

Philemon was a convert of St. Paul and was evidently a wealthy man. He lived at Colosse. He had a house large enough to receive the Church ; and he had slaves, among whom was Onesimus. He ran away, having most probably robbed his Master (vs. 11 and 13), and reached Rome. There he met the Apostle Paul having, it may be assumed, got some post in the public service that brought him into contact with him as a prisoner (v. 10), and was won by him to Christ. Onesimus, whose name in the Greek tongue means " profitable," must have been a man of some energy and talent (vs. 11 and 13) both as a friend and as a minister of the Gospel. The Apostle would have willingly retained him as a colleague, but with a fine sense of what was due to his master, to law, to public opinion and to the Gospel, he sent him back to Philemon entreating that he might be received as Paul himself (vs. 12 and 17), and that he might be given his freedom (v. 21). The Apostle's promised visit (v. 22) was an assurance to Onesimus of his master's hoped-for forgiveness. His action in running away merited, at that time, death. He and Tychicus brought, with this letter, the one written to the Colossian Church (Col. iv. 7-9).

A Christian family in the Apostolic age is here pictured. The master of the house, Philemon, his wife, Apphia, their son, Archippus and the slave, Onesimus.

THE LETTER TO PHILEMON

The greeting of verses 1 to 3 was sent to the Church and the remainder of the letter addressed to Philemon. This is marked by the words " you " (v. 3) and " thee " (v. 4).

This is the letter of a gentleman ; and it is the most gentlemanly letter in existence. As always when grace animates the heart, it commences with commendation (vs. 4-7).

" Archippus " (v. 2) may be assumed to have been a son to Philemon and Apphia, and a minister in the Colossian Church (Col. iv. 17) as well as a fellow evangelist with Paul himself.

" The communication of thy faith " (v. 6), i.e., the benevolent actions of Philemon to others, the fruit of the living faith that was in his heart. The Apostle prayed that these might not be restricted, but that he might fully recognise and practise every good thing unto the glory of Christ (v. 6 R.V. margin), and to the benefit of Onesimus.

The conduct of Onesimus would naturally arouse the anger of the " flesh " in Philemon ; and Satan would not fail to help to cause it to do so. Paul recognised this, and, therefore, he mentions his Apostolic authority, which demanded obedience, only in order to abandon it (vs. 8 and 21), and he beseeches his friend to receive and pardon the runaway —to receive him as himself (v. 12) and to forgive him for his sake (v. 17).

" In Christ " (v. 8), i.e., the element in which Paul's Apostolic authority was exercised.

There is a play upon the meaning of the word Onesimus in verse 11.

" Whom I have sent again," i.e., " whom I am sending back again." Compare verse 21, " I wrote unto thee," i.e., " I am writing unto thee." The ancients in writing letters used the tense which, in time, would affect the reader and not the sender.

" Mine own bowels " (v. 12), i.e., " My very heart." Onesimus was no ordinary person thus to win the warm affection of such a man as the Apostle Paul.

" Thy benefit " (v. 14), i.e., " thy kind action."

" Departed." Greek : " was parted from thee." This was the Apostle's gentle way of saying " he ran away "—no doubt so expressed to soften Philemon's just anger. It was a good thing for the Christian Church

to-day that Onesimus ran away, for otherwise the Church would have lost the comfort
and instruction of this exquisite letter.

" Not now as a slave but much more than a
slave, a brother beloved . . . both in the
flesh and in the Lord " (v. 16).

" A partner " (v. 17), i.e., Paul and
Philemon were partners in the life which is
eternal.

" I Paul am writing this with mine own
hand," etc (v. 19). He always employed a
secretary except when writing to Philemon
and to the Galatian Church. A tumult of
anxiety in the latter instance, and a tumult
of affection in the former, produced these
letters written by " his own hand."

The closing words of the letter plainly
reveal the writer's belief that Philemon would
forgive his slave ; free him ; and not expect
compensation from the Apostle for any loss
occasioned by him.

The principle of grace which forgave the
runaway slave, forgave also the fugitive
Prince (2 Sam. ix.). " For Paul's sake "
and " for Jonathan's sake " as a principle
of forgiveness, is based upon Ephesians
iv. 32—" God for Christ's sake hath forgiven
you."

The Apostle made no direct attack upon
slavery as an institution—that would have
thrown the world into confusion—for he
knew the Gospel would destroy it in time.

HEBREWS

The Author of this letter was the Holy Spirit. The Hebrew whom He trained to write it was the Apostle Paul. This is proved by xiii. 25 which was his token in every Epistle that he wrote. See note on 2 Thess. iii. 17, and compare 1 Pet. i. 1, and 2 Pet. i. 1, iii. 15. The omission of his name was necessary because of the argument and statement in ch. i. 1 and 2. The Apostle (iii. 1) who here speaks was the Messiah, who as the Son, made a full revelation of God to the Hebrew Church.

The argument of the letter is that the First Covenant was indeed divine but was only a shadow of the promised Second Covenant ; and that being so, if the shadow was divine how much more must the substance be !

So here the Holy Spirit teaches that all the divinely given shadows and types and symbols and figures are satisfied in Christ Who is their substance, and He leaves nothing before the heart of the worshipper but the glorious form of the Great High Priest Who is passed into the heavens. In Him the worshipper finds his Priest, his Altar, his Sacrifice, his Baptism, his Pascal Supper, his Circumcision and his place of worship. The Epistle to the Romans is a Court of Justice. The Epistle to the Hebrews, a Temple of Worship.

Contrast rather than comparison is prominent in the Epistle. It is addressed to the many thousands of the Jews who believed that Jesus was the Messiah, and who were all zealous in keeping the Law and in not forsaking circumcision or the customs (Acts xxi. 20). To understand the purpose and teaching of the Epistle this fact must be clearly grasped. The interpretation belongs to them ; an application belongs to all Christian people. These were the Hebrew believers of John ii. 23, 24, vi. 60-71, vii. 31, viii. 30-32.

The letter aimed at leading the Hebrews who believed in Jesus as the Messiah to recognise that He fulfilled, and consequently abrogated, all the types and shadows of the Law ; and that in the true Messianic fellowship and worship, all material and visible elements were put aside and only that which was spiritual and unseen enjoyed. This was very important, not only as being the mind of God, but also because the Temple and its sacramental worship were about to be destroyed by God at the hands of the Romans (viii. 13). This letter prepared these Hebrew believers for that event, and taught them that worship was not destroyed, for in Christ they would find a Temple and a spiritual worship that nothing could destroy —it was the substance ; the former only the shadow. See note on Ezek. xi. 16, R.V.

The Epistle covers the period from Pentecost to the destruction of Jerusalem. That city is the centre of the Acts, and is the Camp of Hebrews xiii. 13.

The Camp cannot be the world for God walked in the midst of it (Deut. xxiii. 14). All there was Divine. Yet the Hebrew believers were called to come out from it and to enter into the despised fellowship of the Lord Jesus, for here they had no continuing city. Jerusalem had become the barren figtree, and was now ripe for judgment. She had rejected her last " year " of signs and wonders and divers miracles and gifts (ii. 4). The Camp, the Anti-type of Israel in the Wilderness, began on the Day of Pentecost. God then manifested His presence in it by blessing believers and judging professors. But the Messiah being rejected, He left the camp, all tokens of His presence there ceased, the Hebrew Remnant was called to go out with Him, and wrath fell upon Jerusalem. While the Camp continued the Gentiles were brought into it by the washing of the flesh in water. It was a ceremonial purification proper to that period.

The Camp had its glory; but this Epistle invited the Hebrew believers to go on to better glories. It taught them that Christ was better than angels (i.); better than Moses (iii.); better than Joshua (iv.); better than Aaron (vii.); and better than the Law (x.). It directed them to a better covenant (vii. 22); better promises (viii. 6); a better substance (x. 34); a better hope (vii. 19); a better sacrifice (ix. 23); a better country (xi. 16); a better resurrection (xi. 35); and a better thing (xi. 40).

The Holy Spirit is mentioned seven times. His personality (ii. 4); His inspiration (iii. 7); His impartation (vi. 4); His teaching (ix. 8); His Deity (ix. 14); His testimony (x. 15); and His grace (x. 29).

The word " promise " occurs seventeen times.

HEBREWS I.—In the Son (v. 2 R.V.) God made a full revelation of Himself to man. Prior to His advent He spoke partially through the Hebrew Prophets, but now perfectly in Christ. A king speaks by, not in, his ambassador, but God speaks in the Son, for He is the last and highest manifestation of Deity—the fulness of the Godhead bodily (Col. ii. 9).

The Spirit hastens over His glories as Heir of all things, as Maker of all worlds, as Upholder of all things, as Revealer of all deity to emphasize His highest glory as the Sinpurger seated on the throne of God, and the argument is: that that purification of sin must have been effectual and perfect in contrast with the imperfection of the Levitical purification, for how could the Sin-purger take His seat on that throne if sin still attached to Him? Therefore the sin with which He loaded Himself on the tree He must have absolutely purged away before sitting down upon the throne. This great truth fills the heart of the believer with a peace that nothing can overthrow.

The argument of the chapter involves the excellency of the Messiah above the angels, and eight quotations from the Scriptures are used to prove it. He has a more excellent name than they (v. 4), i.e., the Name of Son—they are only servants (v. 14).

Christ is the Eternal Son of God as to His Being (v. 3), but as Man He earned the title by His obedience. " Thou art my Son " appears to be the Divine formula for the anointing of Christ as Prophet (Matt. iii. 17),

as priest (Matt. xvii. 5), and as King (Ps. ii. 7). His glories in eternity as Son of God are set out in verses 2 and 3, and His glories as Son of God in time in verses 3-13. The word " being " (v. 3) declares His pre-existent and Eternal Being, and the words " been made " (v. 4) affirm His manhood in time. He always had Sonship as God, but by inheritance (v. 4) He obtained it as Man.

The answer to the questions in verses 5-13 is, that God never spoke such words to an angel, however exalted, but only to His Son the Messiah. The " fellows " of verse 9 are redeemed men. He in Incarnation became man's fellow. In His Godhead He is Jehovah's fellow (Zech. xiii. 7). Marvellous link between God and His people!

The Godhead of Jesus is declared by the Holy Spirit in verses 3, 8 and 10; but the special beauty and wonder of this truth is based here upon Psalms that contain the most complete expressions in Scripture of the consciousness which Jesus had of His weakness as man, of His dependence on Jehovah, and of the certitude that He was to be cut off in the midst of His days. But here may be seen the perfection of faith in Him who was the Author and Finisher of faith, for how could a Messiah who was to be cut off redeem Israel?

So the chapter sets out His suitability as occupant of the throne of God.

HEBREWS II.—The structure of these two first chapters may be thus shown:
  i. God speaks in His Son.
      The Son—God—better than the Angels.
  ii. God speaks in His Son.
      The Son—Man—lower than the angels.

Chapter ii. 1-4 therefore reads on from chapter i. 1-3, and chapter ii. 5 reads on from chapter i. 14.

The Son of God is the great subject of the Epistle; and His suitability to sit upon the throne of God—having made purification for sin and satisfied and done away with all outward and visible symbols—is declared.

Because God in His Son is the speaker (i. 1-3) therefore the more earnest heed should be given to the things which He says lest the hearer drift away from them (v. 1). If the judgment of sin under a law given through angels stood fast (v. 2), how could the greater judgment under grace, pronounced by God Himself, be escaped from? That great salvation was announced by the Lord, confirmed by His Apostles, and accredited by the miracles of the Pentecostal era (vs. 3 and 4). But Israel rejected all three testimonies, they therefore ceased and Israel is become Lo-Ammi until the day, yet future, when the Messiah will return to the Tabernacle of David that is fallen down (Acts xv. 16).

The position and ministry of angels interrupted at i. 14 is now resumed at ii. 5 but only to put them aside in order to present the Messiah as Man, lower than the angels for the suffering of death, now crowned with glory and honour, and so satisfying the statements of Ps. viii. The purpose of the Spirit in verses 5-18 is to declare the actual humanity of Christ.

" The world to come " (v. 5), i.e., the millennial world when the Messiah, as Man, will set man over the works of God's hands and put all things in subjection under his feet, thus fulfilling Ps. viii. His title as Son of Man defines Him as the ideal man, and therefore in Him, as Man, all will be subjected in the millennial world, to man. Man boasts of the present world but believers speak of the world to come, i.e., the millennium.

Writing to Hebrews it was not necessary to mention the eighth Psalm or its writer, but, courteously recognising their intelligence, to say " One in a certain place," etc. (v. 6). This Psalm is not yet fulfilled (v. 8) but its fulfilment is assured by the exaltation of Jesus, as Man, into the glory of God (v. 9). Made lower than the angels in order to the suffering of death, for only as man could He die, He actually tasted death in a realistic consciousness proper only to Him, for the purpose of redeeming man; and that redemption was not motived by the moral beauty of man, but by the grace of God. Such a descent, such a subjection beneath angels, and such a death did not dishonour Him (v. 10) but " became " Him—glorified Him for Whom all things exist and by Whom all things exist; for thus God perfected His Beloved Son, as the Captain, or File-Leader of the many sons to be surely brought by Him unto glory. Moral perfection is not here intended but a perfect equipment as Man in order to discharge the office of Captain of Salvation. He undertook the cause of the sons whom God purposed to

bring to glory, and it was therefore necessary that He should enter into the circumstances in which they were found, suffer their penal consequences, and so deliver them. Such a subjection into man's nature honoured God and " became " Him; so the Captain of Salvation was made perfect through sufferings—the perfection of suffering—even the death of the cross—was His. As the Sin-offering He died (v. 9), as the Meal-offering He suffered (v. 10). Such an oblation being infinite, it is consequently suitable and sufficient for the salvation of every man without distinction—not without exception—for its saving virtue only affects those who believe upon Him (v. 11).

" See " (v. 8) and " see " (v. 9). These are different Greek verbs. The latter implies the deliberate regarding of something that the beholder tries to see.

" The Sanctifier and they who are sanctified, " (v. 11) i.e., Christ and the many sons are all a unity in human nature. This is the great argument of the entire passage. Most commentators, supporting themselves upon John xx. 17, understand the words " are all of one " as meaning " are all of one Father." But did it mean this He could not possibly have been ashamed to call them brethren. He could not do otherwise. But guided by the argument of the chapter it appears more reasonable to believe that the unity intended is His association with humanity. Such an association might well cause Him shame, for " the many sons " with whom He became One were by nature sinful—He Himself being sinless—and had been redeemed from the lowest depths of vice and shame.

But He does not call every man His brother, He is such only to the sanctified (v. 11). He and they appear before God in the nature and position of men. He sanctifies them, they are sanctified, and on this account He is not ashamed to call them His brothers.

This relationship is developed in the Scriptures which follow (vs. 12 and 13). He is One in a company of brothers; He is a Worshipper in the midst of worshippers (v. 12); He is a Believer surrounded by believers; and a Son accompanied by sons (v. 13).

Further, His unity with them is declared (v. 14) in His sharing their nature. Because they are made of flesh and blood He also Himself " in a somewhat similar manner "

(Greek)—for His birth was miraculous and His nature sinless—also became flesh and blood, and in that sinless flesh by dying He stripped Satan of his power and delivered the sons from their slavery to terror.

The force of " verily " here (v. 16) is " you know very well that the Messiah did not assume angelic nature but became a Hebrew." This fact does not exclude His unity with the Gentiles, but the letter being written to Hebrews by a Hebrew; His unity with them, as the descendants of Abraham, is made prominent.

This relationship to Abraham introduces the subject of priesthood, and He is at once declared (v. 17) to be both a compassionate and a faithful High Priest—faithful in things pertaining to God, and compassionate in matters affecting the people. For being a man who felt the pain of trial and temptation (v. 18), He is able instantly to succour (Greek) all exposed to similar suffering.

Moved by a profound love for man, the Son of God—become the Son of Man—humbled Himself to all the circumstances of man in order to deliver him, and was fully equipped to redeem and bring to glory His brothers, the many sons ; and, as a Priest, having made propitiation, He presents them before God in all the beauty and perfection of His own person and work.

" He suffered being tempted " (v. 18). He never yielded. Men do not suffer when tempted for they take pleasure in the things wherein they are tempted. The spiritual nature suffers. Christ trod this path of suffering. He was tested by God, tempted by Satan, and tried by man. His human heart felt all the agony of it. If the Christian in his coarse and fallen nature feels the pain of temptation, what must have been the pain suffered by the sinless nature of Jesus ! He was truly a Man of sorrows—He suffered being tempted.

His humiliation is pointed to in this chapter as a four-fold necessity—to glorify God (v. 10) ; to despoil Satan (v. 14) ; to accomplish propitiation (v. 17) ; and to succour the tempted.

Propitiation was not antecedent to God's love but God's love planned propitiation.

This High Priest (v. 17) is declared in these two chapters to be God, Son of God, Son of Man, Heir of all things, Creator of the worlds, Sin-purger, Captain of Salvation, Apostle, and Son over His own House.

Verse 14 overthrows the Gnostic and Christian Science doctrine that Christ had no physical human body, and that He never died in that body.

Verse 13 may be thus paraphrased ; " As for me I will company with those who are putting their trust in Thee." He as a believer is living a life of faith in the heavenlies, awaiting with His fellow-believers the fulfilment of the promises.

The " many sons " need a Captain (v. 10) because they are weak, and a Priest (v. 17) because they are sinful.

The family of God is here treated of. Christ is the Head of the family, and, consequently, its Priest.

HEBREWS III.—Moses, Aaron and Joshua were the three great princes of the Hebrew nation. Joshua is hinted at (ii. 10), Aaron is also intimated (ii. 17), but Moses is named (iii. 2) for he was the greatest of all the Hebrews, and he is named in order to show his inferiority to the Messiah Who is both the Apostle and High Priest of the Hebrew Church (v. 1). As Apostle He reveals God to them, and as High Priest He presents them to God. The verb " consider " has · an astronomical force. It expresses the fixed attention with which a beautiful constellation in the midnight sky is observed. " Profession " should read " confession," for God gave the nation that Apostle and High Priest, and faith confesses to His Name. Aaron appeared before the people bearing the name of Jehovah upon his forehead, and he appeared before God bearing the names of the Twelve Tribes upon his breast.

The words " Apostle " and " High Priest " are to be understood after the words " Him that appointed Him " (v. 2). The argument here is (vs. 2-6) : that Moses was only a servant in God's house, i.e., in the Hebrew Church, but that Christ is a Son over the house ; and it is His own house—Whose house are we, i.e., we Hebrews if we hold fast (vs. 6 and 14). Compare John ii. 23, 24 ; vi. 60-71 ; vii. 31 and viii. 30-32. See note on verse 14.

Jesus being God built all things ; therefore He built the House of Israel.

Moses as a servant handed to Israel the Law. It was a testimony of the " better things " that were to be subsequently announced (v. 5).

The Holy Spirit was the Author of Ps. xcv. He was the speaker, David was simply the repeater (v. 7). Compare the many passages where a similar statement is made. These all overthrow the theory that David and others originated the Psalms.

"To-day" (vs. 7, 13 and 15), i.e., the day of God's patience during the forty years from Egypt to Canaan, and the corresponding forty years from Pentecost to the destruction of Jerusalem.

"Proved me" (v. 9), i.e., "put me to the proof" whether I was able and willing to help them—secretly believing both to be impossible.

"Forty years" (vs. 9 and 17). As God patiently pleaded with Israel at the first by miracles and signs and wonders, so at the end (vs. 6 and 14) He again, and also with miracles (ii. 4), pleaded for a like period, i.e., from Pentecost to the Judgment. During both periods the nation hardened its heart; the rejecters all perished, and the miracles ceased. "They" (v. 11), Greek: "These very persons". They did not continue steadfast unto, the end. (Compare John viii. 31) and lost the "rest" (v. 18), just as their unbelieving forefathers lost the land.

These Hebrews who accepted Jesus of Nazareth as the promised Messiah, were in the same danger of turning back from that living God as were those of John vi. 66 (v. 12).

That "To-day" (v. 13) was then very near its close. This was God's last prophetic message to His ancient people. It was written just before the Apostle's violent death, and just as the Romans as God's instruments of judgment were being prepared to march against Jerusalem. That day of God's patience then closed for Israel as a nation; but grace reigned embracing both Jews and Gentiles, gathering out of them a people to Messiah's Name; and this action still continues. In addition to this "counsel" of God there operates also the "purpose" of God in taking out of the nations an Election, i.e., the Church revealed in Ephesians

Sin deceives (v. 13)—Eve was the first to be deceived by it.

Verse 14 may be thus. paraphrased: "For we shall be made partakers with Christ (in His millennial kingdom) if we hold" etc. The aim of the Epistle was to bring on those Hebrews who accepted Jesus as the Messiah and were at the same time zealous

of the Law—to bring them on to the end, i.e., to true conversion, to the New Birth, into a spiritual Canaan—the "rest" of verse 18. They were invited to share that rest with Christ immediately, (Matt. xi. 28-30) and at His appearing to share also His millennial rest.

Verse 16 should read as in the Revised Version. There are three interrogatives (vs. 16, 17 and 18). The first contemplates Israel coming out of Egypt; the second, her conduct in the Wilderness; and the third, her judgment at the end. The answer to the first question (v. 16) is that all did provoke —the exception of Joshua and Caleb did not contradict the national fact. The answer to the second interrogative (v. 17) is that all who sinned perished; and the answer to the third interrogative (v. 18) is that all the unbelievers lost the promised land of blessing through unbelief—it shut them out.

Just as at the beginning the people murmured because they were not at once and without difficulty established in Canaan, so at the close they turned away because the Messiah did not at once expel the Romans and restore the throne of David. At each period the nation desired material rather than moral wealth.

HEBREWS IV.—God's three "rests" are now presented. His creation rest (v. 4); His Canaan rest (v. 6); and His redemption rest (v. 1). The first two are fore-pictures of the . third. It is emphatically "His rest" (v. 1), and they who believe enter into it (v. 3). It is Christ—the True Sabbath— God's rest; and that repose can never fail nor be disturbed. Into that rest—His own rest—God invites sinners to enter. Unbelief shuts out from that rest (v. 6) and belief admits to it (v. 3). The Apostle besought these Messianic Hebrews to be on their guard lest through unbelief they should come short of entering it (v. 1), just as, through unbelief, their fore-fathers came short of the promised Canaan rest. They went a certain distance and then perished. They did not continue to the end (iii. 6 and 14).

The great Sabbath rest of this chapter that "remains," i.e., that is now provided for the people of God, i.e., for the Hebrew people—is not heaven, nor the Millennium, as is popularly understood, but is the great redemption rest of Luke vii. 50. This is the argument of verses 1-11. These Hebrews were urged to give all diligence ("labour" v. 11) to enter into that rest. That rest intends real conversion, the New Birth, conscious salvation and peace with God through the Lord Jesus Christ, as set out in Rom. iii.-viii. Just as their forefathers did not, through unbelief, enter into God's Canaan rest, so these Hebrews were warned that they also would surely perish if they did not enter into God's redemption rest in Christ. To accept Jesus as the promised Messiah did not necessarily mean the great moral change of the New Birth; but that birth, typified by the passage of the Jordan, was necessary, and it only followed faith in Christ as an atoning Saviour (i. 3).

"A promise being left" (v. 1). "There remaineth therefore" (v. 9), i.e., He still leaves a promise, and there still remains a rest. This Gospel rest, and the kingdom connected with it, "remained" from Pentecost to the destruction of Jerusalem. It was nationally rejected through unbelief, and lost. But just as the children (Neh. ix.) entered Canaan, so will the future children be engraced with the faith of their believing fathers (Mal. iv. 6) and will look upon Him with faith who loved them and washed them from their sins in His own blood (Rev. i. 5).

The glad tidings preached in the Wilderness promised the milk and honey of Canaan; the glad tidings preached during the Pentecostal era announced forgiveness of sins and the gift of the Holy Spirit (v. 2).

"Mixed with faith" (v. 2). This does not mean that the glad tidings were profitless to them because they did not add faith as they listened. It is most true that salvation results from listening and believing, but the argument of this verse is (see margin) that there were two companies, the company of the believers and the company of the unbelievers, and because these latter were not one in faith with the former, therefore, they failed to enter Canaan.

God rested in a finished creation (v. 4) but in Ps. xcv. (v. 5) He proposes another and a future rest and calls it "My rest"; and that cannot have been His Canaan rest, for in the ninety-fifth Psalm written long after Joshua was dead (v. 8) He still points to it. It is the "rest" of verse 9—the eternal rest that God has in Christ, and into which the Hebrews were invited to enter.

"A certain day" (v. 7), i.e., the day of the Pentecostal era. After the close of that day individual Hebrews of course had the Gospel preached to them, but as sinners and not as Hebrews; for in the present Gospel of the heavenly election there is neither Jew nor Greek—only saved sinners.

The doctrine of verse 10 is: that the Messiah entered into His rest having ceased from His own great work of redemption —for He cried "It is finished"—just as God, having finished His great work of creation, entered into His rest. "Works" is here to be understood as the plural of majesty for "work." This letter was no doubt written in Hebrew. Creation was one perfect work, and so was redemption.

The popular view that this verse (10) treats of the sinner ceasing from his dead works and finding rest in Christ, is destroyed by the argument of the whole passage, and also by remembering that the works that God ceased from were good works, whilst the works of self-righteousness that the sinner ceases from are "evil works," (1 John iii. 12) and therefore they cannot be compared.

The Hebrews are warned that the ninety-fifth Psalm is the Word of God—a death-dealing sword from whose double edge nothing escapes (v. 12). And what is true of the ninety-fifth Psalm is true of the whole Bible. It is living and effective. It is living, for it is the Word of the living God (iii. 12); and effective, for when He said "They shall not enter" their carcases fell in the Wilderness (ii. 17).

The identity of the living Word with the living God is further pressed in the words "Him with Whom we have to do" (v. 13), for these words predicate what the Word of God (v. 12) predicates.

That Word is a perfect instrument for exposing and judging the most secret emotions of the heart and nature. Hence the ninety-fifth Psalm speaks of the heart and ch. iii. 12 also speaks of it; and the Psalm divides between the soul and spirit, for it recalls the appetite that cried out for flesh in the Wilderness and the spirit which underlay that unbelieving cry. That great sword reaches to the interior of the most remote joint and to the very marrow of man's fallen will and nature. To the believer this is exceedingly precious for He rejoices in that which infallibly exposes and judges the deepest emotions of his being.

But this two-edged and piercing sword is

held by the hand that was pierced at Calvary (vs. 14-16)—the hand of the Great High Priest that has passed through the heavens. The heart of that Priest is not insensible to the sorrows and needs and infirmities and temptations of those for whom he acts, for He personally, as Man, suffered all forms of temptation, but never sinned.

To come timidly to the Throne of grace is to disobey God for He commands His people to come boldly (v. 16). Man condemns this boldness and applauds his own commanded fearfulness.

The Christian does not wish for sympathy with the sin that is in him. He detests it —he desires it to be slain with the two-edged sword—to have no mercy shown to it.

This is the purpose and action of the sword. But he does desire sympathy for his weakness and difficulties and temptations, and this sympathy he finds in all perfection in the Great High Priest who wields the sword. These Divine provisions of the sword and the Priest encourage him to hold fast his confession in spite of the difficulties that beset his path.

There is an ever-present danger of coming short of the glory of God (Rom. iii. 23), of the grace of God (Heb. xii. 15), and of the rest of God (Heb. iv. 1).

HEBREWS V. 1—10.—The Great High Priest is the subject of IV. 14 - viii. 1. From v. 11 to vi. 20 is a parenthesis. Two conditions are first laid down regarding a priest : 1. He must be a man (v. 1) ; 2. He must be appointed by God (v. 4). The argument of this section shows that Christ satisfied these two conditions. As man Christ did not appoint Himself High Priest (v. 5). His Sonship and His Priesthood are inter-connected (vs. 5 and 6). As the Son of God, in time, He was so saluted at His incarnation (Ps. ii.),and at His ascension He was saluted as a Priest for ever (Ps. cx.) ; for He could not be a priest on earth (v. 6 and viii. 4).

To be fully equipped as a Priest it was necessary that He should during His life-time on earth (v. 7) feel to the utmost possible degree as man the fear and horror of death. It was impossible that He could be exempted from a conciousness of any form or degree of the suffering afflicting men. Yet He never sin - ned while feeling the anguish, the terror, the pain and the horror of death. He prayed to be saved " out of death " (R.V. margin) and was heard because of His perfect submission to the suffering of that supreme · horror. That prayer must have been offered more than once (Mark x. 32-34, John xi. 33 and xii. 27 and Luke xxii. 44). It was answered in resurrection.

As a Son it was necessary that as a Priest He should, through suffering, learn obedience —not learn to be obedient, for that would prove Him to be a sinner—but being sinless He learned obedience in order to have compassion on the ignorant and to sympathize with the feeble. Thus being perfected or fully equipped as a Priest (v. 9), He, because of His eternal Priesthood (v. 10), endows with eternal salvation all who believe upon Him (v. 9). Because His Priesthood ever endures, the salvation He obtains for those who obey Him ever endures. This is the argument that unites verse 10 to verse 9. Aaron (v. 4) was called of God to a temporary priesthood. Christ (v. 10) was called of God to an eternal Priesthood.

HEBREWS V. 11—VI. 20—This parenthesis blames the dulness of those to whom the letter is addressed. As pointed out in the Introduction they were Hebrews who believed that Jesus of Nazareth was the promised Messiah, and that, though crucified, He was living and was about to return to Jerusalem to restore the throne of David and introduce the millennial world. They were at the same time zealous observers of the Law of Moses. But it was possible to take this position sincerely and yet not be Christians in the sense of Rom. iii. viii. Vital Christianity demanded the raising of the moral question respecting sin ; the atoning character of Christ's death ; the necessity of the New Birth ; and of faith in Him as a Saviour from the wrath to come. It was to all this that the Apostle would bring these Hebrews.

So he rebukes them (vs. 11-14) ; and he warns them (vi. 4-8) ; and he encourages them (vs. 9-20).

There is no greater hindrance in the path-way to true conversion than attachment to a traditional religion consisting in ordinances. It sets up a barrier between the soul and God. The heart—easily deceived—rests in these religious ceremonies ; and the spiritual intelligence is so impaired as to be unable to discern between good doctrine and evil doctrine (v. 14). This was the more deadly for these Hebrews because the forms and symbols to which they were attached were of Divine ordination.

They were urged to go on from the infancy of John the Baptist's ministry (vi. 1 and 2) and from the childhood of Pentecostal miracles (vs. 4-5) to full manhood (" perfection "), i.e., to real conversion. John the Baptist preached the rudiments of the teaching respecting the Messiah—that is repentance, faith, ceremonial washings, and, in obedience to Leviticus, of laying their sinful hands on the head of the sacrificial lamb; and in calling upon his hearers to escape from the wrath to come, he preached the resurrection of the dead and eternal judgment. The importation of what is called Christian baptism and confirmation into verse 2 is an illustration of the ignorance of v. 12.

" If God permit " (v. 3). The Apostle was in prison and might be liberated or put to death. If liberated he was resolved that, as for him, he would not stand still and remain a child, but press on to preach and experience full manhood in Christ.

The language of verses 4 and 5 describes Pentecostal experience. It gave the Hebrew people a " taste " of the powers of the world to come, i.e., the millennial kingdom that was offered by the Apostle Peter to the nation (ii. 4). These powers, and the public manifestation of the gifts of the Holy Spirit, were an earnest of the good Word of God, which would be perfected in the promised kingdom. Ananias and others, like Balaam, were made partakers of these gifts and so tasted the good things promised by the word of God. But this did not necessarily involve the New Birth.

So the argument of verses 6-8 is that if, having come so far as to acknowledge a crucified Jesus as Messiah, they turned back from these realities to Mosaic rudiments, it would be impossible that they should restart at John's baptism and once again advance to Christ's salvation, for they had abandoned that one road, and there was for them no other way of life and blessing. They were comparable to land which had received every possible blessing from God and in response produced thorns and briers. The only fitting end for such ground was judgment (v. 8).

This interpretation belongs to Hebrews who act in this way, but an application of the principle affects all who forsake the realities of spiritual experience for the rudiments of sacramental shadows.

The land having received blessing from God produced thorns and briers as before. There was no New Birth, no new creation. That which is born of the flesh remains flesh. To taste the goodness of God's Word —i.e., the sweetness of the Gospel message— is not the same thing as being quickened by it (1 Pet. i. 23). The message may be even received with joy and yet have no living root (Matt. xiii. 20, 21). Fruit supposes life; and this fruit appears in verse 10. Here is the earth which bringeth forth herbs of blessing for man because of having received blessing from God (v. 7). These herbs were proofs of life; and this introduces the third section of the parenthesis in which true living Hebrews are encouraged to go on to full salvation in Christ in whom is found eternal life (17-20).

Like Mary of Nazareth these Hebrews were willing to believe in a Messiah Who was about to sit on the Throne of David and establish the millennium. But just as the sword of iv. 12 had to pierce her heart revealing its sinfulness and bringing her as a sinner to the cross for eternal salvation, so these Hebrew believers needed a like experience; for it alone issues in true conversion.

These are they who are addressed (vs. 9 and 10). They had advanced to " the better things " even the things " nigh to salvation " (Greek). " Nigh to salvation " contrasts with " nigh unto cursing " (v. 8). . These Hebrews had tasted the good things of the Baptist's ministry (vs. 1 and 2) and of the Pentecostal era (vs. 4 and 5) and had gone on to the better things of perfection in Christ (v. 1). Their action (v. 10) proved this, and it was sure of Divine recognition. The possible reference here is to the money which they gave the Apostle Paul for the poor saints at Jerusalem (Rom. xv. 26, 2 Cor. viii. 1, and ix. 2). In that proof of love to His Name Gentile believers had a share.

But the Apostle longed that everyone of them should labour (v. 11), i.e., show the same diligence to go forward and enter into the Divine rest of redemption, and he encouraged them to do so by pointing to the certitude and stability of that salvation (vs. 13-20). It was to be a life of faith.

Abraham had to rest on promises which he did not possess. As fore-runner Jesus assures eternal salvation to all who trust Him. He, as such, personally guarantees the fulfilment of the promises to all guilty and broken hearts that seek refuge in Him (v. 18), and lay hold upon Him as a Hope and Anchor which neither breaks nor drags, and which is cast within the veil. This anchor unites earth to heaven.

The oath of God's grace (v. 17) is as eternal as the oath of God's wrath (iii. 11). A Gospel which excludes either of these oaths is a false Gospel.

In the birth of Isaac, Abraham, in type, obtained the promise (v. 15). He is still patiently awaiting its plenary fulfilment.

If necessary for confirmation an oath is lawful (vs. 13-18). The command "Swear not at all, but let yes be yes and no, no" affects ordinary intercourse between Christian people who are "heirs of promise" and "heirs of glory."

"Two immutable things" (v. 18), i.e., God's promise and God's oath.

"The better things" of this Epistle are immutable. Eternity is stamped upon them : Eternal salvation (v. 9) ; Eternal redemption (ix. 12) ; Eternal judgment (vi. 2) ; Eternal spirit (ix. 14) ; everlasting covenant (xiii. 20) ; "consecrated for evermore" (vii. 28) ; "Priest for ever" (vii. 21) ; "Their sins will I remember no more" (x. 17) ; "no more offering for sin" (x. 18) ; "perfected for ever" (x. 14) ; "no more conscience of sins" (x. 2) ; and "eternal inheritance" (ix. 15).

HEBREWS VII.—The mysterious figure of Melchisedec is now returned to in order to set forth the superiority of his person and priesthood to Aaron. These two priests are here contrasted, as also are the systems founded on the respective priesthood of each.

He may have been Shem. Abraham was a hundred and fifty when Shem died. That would be about fifty years after this scene with Melchisedec. Or Melchisedec may have been a patriarchal king and priest such as Job ; or he may have been Christ in angelic form as in Gen. xxxii. 24, Joshua v. 13, Judges xiii. etc., and Gen. xviii. This last supposition is based upon the statements made in verse 3 and verse 8.

But the argument of verse 3 may be that whereas Aaron had to produce a pedigree establishing his parentage before being consecrated high priest (Ezra ii. 62), and as he could only hold office from thirty to fifty (Num. iv. 3), he was inferior to Melchisedec who needed to produce no evidence of parentage and who retained his priesthood so long as he lived. Further, the use of the present tense in the words " abideth " and " liveth " (vs. 3 and 8) is a frequent form in the Scriptures expressing continuity of argument or doctrine but not necessarily of person or action. Melchisedec was assimilated, or likened, to the Son of God, and in that sense he still lives.

The argument of verses 1-11 is, that if Levi when in the loins of his fore-father Abraham paid tithes to Melchisedec then was he inferior to him.

In Melchisedec righteousness and peace kissed each other—peace based upon righteousness. Melchisedec was not only righteous, he was righteousness itself. As Priest of the Most High God and as Prince of Peace Christ will fulfil Zech. vi. 13.

The title "The Most High God" only occurs here in the New Testament and in Mark v. 7 and Acts xvi. 17. The title overthrows idols.

" Here " (v. 8), i.e., in the Aaronic priesthood . " There," i.e., in the Melchisedec priesthood.

The word " order " is a term expressing Divine arrangement.

Christ did not, like Aaron, pay tithes in Abraham for He never was in the loins of an earthly father. His mother was a daughter of Abraham.

" Another priest " (v. 11), i.e., a different priest—one of a different order (Greek).

A change of priesthood necessitates a change also of the law, i.e., of the principle of restoration to God (v. 12). The Aaronic Priesthood presents many priests and many sacrifices. On them as a principle or Law of Life was based the First Covenant—salvation by works. That priesthood could not possibly make perfect the conscience of the worshipper as to the guilt of sin and its removal (vi. 1, vii. 11 and 19 and x. 1 and 2). The Melchisedec Priesthood presents One Priest and One Sacrifice. On them is founded the Second Covenant—Salvation by grace. This Sacrifice being infinite, and the Priest ever-living, secures perfection of conscience before God as to the forgiveness of sins.

The double . argument supporting the

change of Priesthood contained in verses 13-17 is : first, Christ's membership of the Tribe of Judah (vs. 13 and 14) ; and second, the testimony of Ps. cx. 17.

The words " carnal commandment " and " endless life " stand in contrast. The First Covenant was a commandment addressed to carnal man ; the Second Covenant, a life in man both powerful and endless. The Commandment (v. 18) was not weak and unprofitable in itself, but because of that on which it had to act. A powerful engine in a weak ship is useless because the ship breaks up under its vibrations.

" Nigh unto God " (v. 19). The purpose of redemption is to bring man near to God.

Christ's superiority to Aaron is further evidenced by His appointment as Priest having being made with an oath (v. 20). This shews the meaning and sanctity and value of an oath. This is the third oath of the Epistle—the Oath of Imprecation (iii. 11) the Oath of Consolation (vi. 18) and the Oath of Consecration (vii. 20). These oaths establish immutability.

Christ being an ever-living High Priest He can save out to the very end those who place themselves in His hands (v. 25).

Man's principle of life and righteousness is : many priests and many sacrifices daily offered up. God's way of salvation is : One Priest and One Sacrifice—A Sacrifice so infinite and satisfactory that it needs no repetition.

Christ as High Priest intercedes only for those who come unto God by Him (v. 25). He does not intercede for the unbelieving world (John xvii. 9).

As Fore-runner (vi. 20) He guarantees the fulfilment of the promises (v. 12) to the heirs of promise (v. 17) ; and as the Surety of a better Covenant (vii. 22) He establishes their perpetuity.

Three essentials belonged to priesthood : Appointment, Sanctification and Consecration. These appear in type in the Book of Leviticus. In the Messiah Sonship and Priesthood are united. God's original purpose lodged priesthood in the first-born. The Levitical priesthood was a temporary institution. On Aaron's appointment as high priest he was first baptized and then anointed (Lev. viii.). His sons were not anointed until after a sin-offering had been made for them. So Christ was baptized and then anointed (Matt. iii. 16 and 17). He needed

no sin-offering. Consecration is the completion of sanctification. He sanctified Himself (John xvii. 17)—" I sanctify Myself in order that they may be truly sanctified." This was the final act in His consecration as High Priest of His people. Hence He is not ashamed to call them brethren (ii. 11) for they and He are one, just as Aaron and his sons were one. His priestly garments which the Spirit put upon Him are described in Luke iv. 18. They were the Holy garments.

" Sanctify " and " consecrate " are priestly words (Exod. xxviii. and Lev. viii.). The one is the completion of the other (v. 9, vii. 28 and x. 14). Sanctification means separation wholly to God—consecration means " a filled hand " ; and when the hand is full it needs no more. Hence the word " perfection " in respect of Christ's Priesthood in this Epistle. Having accomplished the one great satisfying oblation for sin, Christ passed through the heavens and entered upon His ministry there as a perfected High Priest ; and there He remains. Aaron entered the Most Holy Place, but only once a year and then withdrew immediately. Christ entered the Heavenly sanctuary and sat down. There was no seat for Aaron in the earthly tabernacle, for his ministry could never settle the question of sin and its judgment.

Abraham was the greatest of the patriarchs, but Melchisedec was greater than he. In blessing Abraham he brought forth bread and wine. These signified the fulness of creation blessing in heaven and earth. Corn springs from the earth; the Grape hangs down from above. Melchisedec represented the Most High God possessor of heaven and earth. At the Last Supper the True Melchisedec brought forth bread and wine and spake of the kingdom of millennial blessing which they signify (Matt. xxvi. 29, Mark xiv., Luke xxii. 15 and Rom. viii. 21).

Two great statements now appear—the nature of the sacrifice and where it entered. No such sacrifice as this was ever seen in the universe before, nor could be seen. It was the offering for sin of Him Who was both God and Man in One Person. This sacrifice did not, like the Aaronic, enter into an earthly sanctuary, but into Heaven itself. This great sacrifice resulting in the blessing and restoration of the fallen creation, was purposed by God from before the foundation of the world, as appears from Job xxviii. and many other Scriptures.

At the Last Passover Christ as Melchisedec signified, in the first cup, the deliverance of creation ; and as the Passover Lamb He signified in the last cup, the deliverance of His people. Both these deliverances are secured by His offering up Himself. See notes on Rev. iv. and v.

Melchisedec suddenly appears after the slaughter of the kings. Up till then he was hidden. The true Melchisedec is now hidden but will appear in blessing after the destruction of the kings of Revelation xix. As King of righteousness He will judge the wicked, and as King of peace He will bless the earth. Peace does not displace righteousness but is based upon it. These are all millennial glories reserved for Israel and the redeemed nations ; but the Church being one with Him will share all His glories whether heavenly or earthly.

HEBREWS VIII.—The two priests having been contrasted in the prior chapter, the two covenants, the two sanctuaries, the two mediators, the two ministers and the better promises and their foundation are now set out, and the superiority of those founded upon the Messiah as High Priest declared.

" The sum " (v. 1), i.e., the chief point. " Such ", i.e., so unspeakably glorious a High Priest.

Moses pitched the earthly tabernacle, but God formed the true Tabernacle (v. 2 and ix. 11).

" This man " (v. 3), i.e., " This High Priest." A priest must have a sacrifice to offer. Christ offered Himself (vii. 27). This was His one great and all embracing sacrifice, satisfying all the types of the Old Covenant and abolishing all its offerings for sin.

The Old Covenant was a shadow (v. 5) of heavenly things. Christ is their substance (v. 6). A photograph is the shadow of a mansion, but a legatee would not be satisfied with the photograph. He would go on to take possession of the mansion of which it was the shadow. These Hebrew believers were zealous of the Law—that is, satisfied with a shadow of heavenly things. This letter urged them to lay hold upon these heavenly realities themselves.

" The Better Covenant " (v. 6) is that of verse 10, and the better promises are those of verses 10-12.

The word " new " (v. 8) establishes the verbal inspiration of the Scriptures, for on that one word occurring once (Jer. xxxi.) is based the whole of the argument of this chapter.

Three blessings are contained in the better Covenant : Sanctification (v. 10) ; a knowledge of God (v. 11) ; and forgiveness of sins (v. 12). The last blessing forms the foundation upon which the other two are placed. Forgiveness of sins, knowledge of the Saviour, and the impartation of a new moral nature are the order in which experience places them.

" All shall know me " (v. 11), i.e., all Israel —" and so all Israel shall be saved " (Rom. xi.), " and there shall be no more the Canaanite in the house of the Lord " (Zech. xiv. 21).

" Ready to vanish away " (v. 13). Soon after the writing of this letter the Temple at Jerusalem was burnt down, and with it the ministry of the Old Covenant perished for ever.

These two Covenants were made with Israel. A Covenant is a principle of relationship between man on the earth and God. Such is Israel's glory as an earthly people. The First Covenant was established with them at Sinai ; the Second was established with Christ.

The Gospel is a Covenant, a revelation of the salvation of God. The Church enjoys all the fulness of the New Covenant, and much more. The foundation of her blessings are based upon the same foundation upon which is founded the New Covenant. It will be fulfilled to Israel in the millennium.

HEBREWS IX. and X.

CHAPTER IX.—The Two Covenants having been introduced and contrasted, the imperfection of the atonement for sin under the first is in these two chapters contrasted with the perfection of the atonement under the second, and the unrelieved conscience of the worshipper under the one set over against the perfected conscience of the worshipper under the other—that is, a conscience perfectly relieved from a sense of guilt in the presence of God. The Scriptures proving these contrasts are quoted, and a warning (x. 26-31) added as to the judgment certain to fall upon those Hebrews who rejected this second Covenant and the atoning sacrifice that ratified it.

" Then verily." (v. 1). Greek : "Accordingly then "—in resumption of viii. 5.

"A worldly sanctuary" (v. 1), i.e., a sanctuary of this world in contrast with the heavenly sanctuary of viii. 2. This Tabernacle was formed of two tents, the first described in verse 2 with its furniture, the second in verses 3-5 with its furniture. The Tabernacle pictured Israel under the First Covenant having no assurance as to the forgiveness of sins and no access to God. Only the priests had the right of entrance into the first tent, and the high priest alone once a year for a few moments into the second tent. Such was the relationship of the nation with God. They could not draw near to Him or stand in His presence. The First Covenant in its highest and nearest access to God placed a priesthood between God and the people, and the second tent, the holiest of all, characterized the inadequacy of that access.

The golden altar of incense (v. 4) *on the annual day of atonement* became of necessity part of the furniture of the second tent. It was placed against the vail so that when Aaron passed through the vail he must have closed it behind him so as to shut it in and enable him to use its incense (see notes on Exod. xl.). When the vail was rent, all the furniture of the outer tent became furniture of the inner ; and thus all these types were brought together and unified.

The cherubim (v. 5) were mysterious beings connected with Eden at the beginning and with the Throne of the Lamb at the close of Bible History, and possibly represented the universe. See note on Gen. iii. 24.

" The Holy Spirit this signifying " (v. 8). He explains the types He ordained in Leviticus. Inspiration is a fact to be recognised and not a theory to be interpreted.*

The conscience of the worshipper is a reflection of the sacrifice. An imperfect sacrifice necessitates an imperfect conscience. A perfect sacrifice gives a perfected conscience (x. 1 and 2).

" Carnal ordinances " (v. 10), i.e., religious ceremonies which touched man's body but went no further. They were as powerless as modern " sacraments."

" The good things to come " (v. 11)—not primarily the good things of the coming millennial kingdom, but " the good things "

* See Mark xii. 36, Matt. xv. 4, Heb. iii. 7, ix. 8 x. 15, Acts i. 16, iii. 18, xxviii. 25, etc.

of a perfected conscience, assurance of salvation, and access to God—the good things, in fine, of the New Covenant.

" This building " (v. 11), i.e., the Tabernacle, represented at the moment by the Temple.

" The purifying of the flesh " (v. 13), i.e., the ceremonial purification of the worshipper's body.

" Offered Himself " (v. 14). Compare vii. 27 and the note on viii. 3.

The Mediator of the New Testament (v.15), i.e., the Negotiator of the New Covenant —a covenant securing those that are " called."

" The redemption of the transgressions " (v. 15), i.e., in order to redeem from judgment those guilty of transgressions against the first covenant.

All here is eternal (vs. 12, 14 and 15) —eternal redemption, eternal spirit, eternal inheritance.

Because of the fact of sin no covenant could be made between God and men which ignored sin. Hence both covenants were based upon atonement—the one typically, the other actually (vs. 16-23). But whereas the blood that ratified the first covenant was only the blood of calves and of goats, that which ratified the second and gave to it its eternal validity, was the precious blood of Christ (v. 23). Apart from the death of a sacrificial victim, a covenant proposing the establishment of relations between God and men has no value (v. 17). Christ was. both the testator and the victim of the New Covenant (vs. 16 and 17). The Greek of these two verses is somewhat difficult to translate. See Luke xxii. 10 and note on Gen. xv. 17.

Christ appeared to put away sin (v. 26) ; He appears to silence sin (v. 24) ; and He will appear without sin (v. 28). He saves from the penalty, the power and the presence of sin. His one offering of Himself once offered has made an eternal settlement of the question of sin and abolished it for ever. The appointment of death to man because of sin, and the doom that lies beyond death, were both endured in grace by Him on behalf of " the many " i.e., " they which are called " (v. 15). These look for Him, and to them He will appear (Rev. i. 5-7). When He returns He will have nothing to do with sin for He abolished it for His people. For. them He will appear, not for judgment but unto salvation.

The extent and value of Christ's atoning sacrifice of Himself is, therefore, the glorious theme of these chapters. Three results appear : access to God ; purification of the conscience ; and eternal redemption. These provide fellowship with God in a righteousness in which no flaw can be found, and in a redemption possessing eternal value. All is eternal because Divine. The worshipper has a perfected conscience. This is much more than an innocent conscience. That is unconsciousness of evil and of God's holiness. A perfected conscience knows God and dwells in His presence with joy because of a consciousness of the value of the precious blood that cleanses from all sin.

The key words of verses 11-14 are " priest " (v. 11) ; " blood " (v. 12) ; and " serve " (v. 14), i.e., presentation, purification and dedication. The moral effect of Christ's presentation of Himself in the preciousness and power of His atonement before God on behalf of those interested in that atonement, is that they joyfully dedicate themselves to a life of serving God.

Christ entered into the holy place through a greater and more perfect tent (v. 11). The Tabernacle was a copy of the Three Heavens. The outer court corresponded to the earth, the first tent to the firmament—the visible heaven—the second tent to the unseen heaven—the " third heaven." These three heavens are viewed in the words : " Our Father Who art in the heavens " (Greek). See note on Matt. vi. 6-9. Israel's high priest passed from the outer court through the first tent into the second on the Great Day of Atonement. So Christ ascended from the earth, passed through the heavens, and entered into the Holy Place.

The ashes of the red heifer (see note on Num. xix.) ceremonially cleansed the body (v. 13), the atoning blood of Christ cleanses the conscience (v. 14). The one was outward and carnal and a shadow, the other inward, spiritual and substantial. The conscience is defiled not only by gross sins but by dead religious works. It needs to be cleansed ; and only one moral power can cleanse it, and that is—the atoning value of Christ's precious blood revealed to the conscience by the Holy Spirit through the Scriptures. The doctrine of this verse destroys the belief of many that the conscience is a perfect moral monitor, and that it will surely lead a man to God if obeyed and followed.

"The end of the ages," (v. 26, R.V.), i.e.,

the consummation of the ages of innocence, conscience and law. God allowed these ages to pass, and thus fully demonstrated that man is corrupt in nature and hostile in will. This demonstration of man's hopeless corruption magnifies, as a black background, the grace and efficacy of Christ's sacrifice of Himself. He appeared to load Himself with the fulness of that corruption ; to suffer its doom ; to remove it ; and to redeem its slaves. So effectual was His atonement that He blotted sin out of the heavens and the earth, making so complete an end of it as to cause as if it never had existed (v. 26). Thus when He appears the second time He will appear " apart from sin "—not only as respects His own sinless Person—but as respects the redeemed. He put an end to their sins in His first manifestation. Not only did He bear their sins in His own body on the tree, but by personating sin itself He put it away. Thus He destroyed at Calvary both the root and the fruit of sin. Accordingly the words " without sin " (v. 28) contrast with the words " The sins of the many."

These communications of the Holy Spirit respecting Immanuel's grace and His work affect the heart that loves Him ; but it is particularly His work that the Spirit emphasizes here in its glorious sufficiency and efficiency in contrast with the insufficiency and inefficiency of Aaron's work. Aaron called sins to remembrance year by year. He entered into a holy place every year with the same repeated sacrifices. Christ did not enter into a holy place made with hands (v. 24) to offer repeated sacrifices, but to present Himself in the perfection of His one great sacrifice—so sufficing and effectual that it needs no repetition, as the sacerdotalists teach—and that one sacrifice sets " the many " whom He represents before God in a righteousness in which no flaw can be found. He made an atonement for all, but He only bore the sins of " the many " (v. 28). The position, therefore, of this High Priest and of the worshipper before the Throne of God in the most Holy Place, is a testimony to the perfection of His atonement. Three Greek verbs are here translated by the one verb " to appear " (vs. 24, 26 and 28). They mean to present, to manifest, and to be seen. As Prophet He was manifested ; as Priest He presents Himself ; and as King He will be seen.

The sense of verses ix. 16-18 is that a

sacrificial death makes valid a covenant. For a covenant is of force over dead victims or sacrifices. It has no validity so long as the appointed sacrifice which makes it is alive. Therefore the first covenant was dedicated with the blood of sacrificial victims, and the second covenant with the blood of the Lamb of God.

" Better sacrifices " (v. 23), i.e., one better and greater sacrifice, for Christ offered only one sacrifice. This is the plural of Majesty.

" The end of the ages " (v. 26). See note on Gen. iii. 1. Each age begins in blessing and ends in wrath. This is history as recorded by the infallible Spirit of God and not human imagination or interpretation.

HEBREWS IX. and X. continued.

CHAPTER X.—Having contrasted the many priests and the many sacrifices of the First Covenant with the one Priest and the one Sacrifice of the Second, the Holy Spirit now sets before the reader the perfection which clothes the worshipper as the result of the perfection which indwells the sacrifice. The worshipper is " sanctified once for all " (v. 10) and " perfected for ever " (v. 14)—that is, set apart for God and perfected in a Divine righteousness before Him.

The Law was only a shadow of " the good things to come " ; the Gospel provides the good things themselves (v. 1).

" Perfect " (v. 1) : that is, as to the conscience in respect of the guilt of sin.

" No more conscience of sins " (v. 2)—not " no more consciousness of sin." The subject here is the perfect peace of conscience resulting from the perfection of the offering presented to God. Because the offering, being the Body of Christ, was infinite in its atoning efficacy, therefore the worshipper enjoys a perfected conscience, that is, perfect peace of conscience—the sense of guilt is removed directly the value of the offering in expiation is known. As before pointed out, the conscience of the worshipper is a reflection of the value of the offering. If the offering is perfect the conscience is perfected ; if the offering is imperfect the conscience is imperfect.

" Thy will, O God " (vs. 7 and 9), i.e., God's will that Christ should offer Himself in atonement for the sins of the world. This is clear from verse 10. The effort to prove

from this passage that an atonement for sin is not necessary, and that trying to do what is supposed by man's fallen intellect to be the will of God, is the way of salvation, is futile. God ordained the sacrifices and offerings of Leviticus as shadows of the great substance offering of Calvary. He found no abiding pleasure in them, but He does find an eternal joy in the Body He prepared for His Beloved Son (v. 5), in which Body Christ was to make the great Offering (v. 10) purposed by the will of God before the world began. It is awe-striking to be permitted in Ps. xl. to hear the Father and the Son in the past eternities planning the Atonement. The sacrifice of dumb and irrational creatures is here contrasted with the intelligent obedience of Christ's sacrifice of Himself.

The repetition of the quotation (vs. 8 and 9) is designed to emphasize the two statements in the Scripture quoted—the " above " or first statement, and the subjoined or second statement (" Then "). The first statement is that the offerings of the Old Covenant were temporary and ineffective ; the second statement, that Christ's one offering is eternal and satisfactory. So the first is taken away in order to the establishment of the second. Through that one offering of the Body of Jesus Christ once for all, the worshipper is sanctified for ever and perfected for ever (vs. 10-14).

Many priests daily stood offering perpetually and uselessly the same sacrifices (v. 12). This Priest offered one sacrifice for sins for ever, and then sat down, thus demonstrating its sufficiency as a perfect atonement. Nothing needs to be added to it. It glorifies God. It satisfies all the claims of His righteousness against the sinner. It leaves no question unanswered. It perfectly satisfies God, and, therefore, eternally saves the believer ; for if God is satisfied with what Christ did for the sinner, then is the vilest sinner who pleads that sacrifice of necessity eternally saved because of the eternal perfection of the sacrifice.

The Hebrew " An ear hast thou formed for me " (Ps. xl.) is here accurately translated by the Holy Spirit " A body hast Thou prepared Me." He was the one and perfectly obedient Servant—only listening to one Voice, and only speaking the words that He was given to speak (see notes on John viii. and xvii.). He was, so to say, simply an ear. This figure of speech vividly pictures

Him as the Perfect Servant whose ear was opened morning by morning (Isa. l.).

The bond servant in Exod. xxi. engaged to serve perpetually his master, his wife and his children; and his pierced ear witnessed to his affection. Ps. xl. and Heb. x. 5 may, perhaps, point to this, for Christ in love to God, to Israel and to her children, took the form of a servant and suffered the painful death of the tree.

In order to perform the will of God perfectly (v. 7) Jesus must Himself of necessity be God; for to do all that will demanded perfection of knowledge. All God's will cannot be accomplished twice. Were it possible to do so it would be a proof of the inadequacy of the first effort; and so of both.

Those whom He calls He sanctifies, that is, He sets apart for Himself. This is an operation of God's will and not of man's. This sanctification is effected by the one great offering. Such was its cost. God took the unclean Hebrews from amongst the nations and set them apart for Himself. The blood of the Paschal Lamb effected this consecration. Faith can joyfully exclaim: " Christ our Passover is sacrificed for us, therefore let us keep the feast " (1 Cor. v. 7).

This offering is " once for all." It admits of no repetition. The sanctification it secures is eternal. It consecrates to God for ever because of its eternal and unchanging value. He Who made this perfect offering is seated in the heavens; and He is Himself there the righteousness of God. That is a righteousness suited to the Throne of God. If never can ever vary or fail. In that righteousness the worshipper stands.

The communication and certitude of this expiation of sin is assured by the Holy Spirit (v. 15). All here is Divine. The will of God (v. 9); the work of Christ (v. 10); the witness of the Spirit (v. 15). God is the source of this great salvation, Christ the means, and the Holy Spirit the evidence.

The guilty conscience that seeks peace with God is shut up to this evidence. There is no other witness. The Spirit has recorded His evidence in the Scriptures, and outside of them there is no other testimony for faith to rest upon. So the certainty that God will never remember the sins and iniquities of the believer in Jesus, is founded on the unchanging will of God, the perfect work of Christ, and the sure witness of the Holy Spirit.

The Church of Rome claims reverence and admiration for its bloodless repetition of the Sacrifice of Calvary. There are four difficulties which destroy this claim. If Christ offered Himself at the Last Supper, as that Church teaches, then He offered Himself a second time on the cross. There were, therefore, two offerings of Himself. But the Holy Spirit (v. 10) said He offered Himself but once. There cannot, therefore, be a repetition of this sacrifice. Further, where there is no effusion of blood there is no remission of sin (ix. 22); and, lastly, the church contradicts itself in declaring that the wine is the actual poured out blood of Christ and yet is the offering bloodless!

The quotation from Jer. xxxi. is here repeated (v. 16). It was first cited (viii. 8) to set aside the Old Covenant; here it is used to prove the perfection of the New Covenant. The words " He adds " should be supplied at the beginning of verse 17, as in the Revised Version.

Those who proudly seek to enter into the presence of God in any other way than by the blood of Jesus (v. 19)—a newly slain and living, i.e., resurrection way (v. 20), and through Him as the Great Priest (v. 21), will surely be judged as Cain and Korah were judged.

Christ as High Priest deals with infirmity; as Advocate He restores communion (1 John ii.). Power and enjoyment rest upon this double ministry. Man condemns the full assurance of salvation (v. 22), but such an assurance magnifies the offering upon which it is based, and an absence of assurance discredits the perfection of that offering.

The sons of Aaron were sprinkled with blood and washed with water (v. 22). These carnal shadows of the First Covenant were figures of the spiritual realities of the Second. The sprinkling and the washing of this verse must therefore, be wholly spiritual—the conscience cleansed by a consciousness of the value of the blood of Christ, and the conduct cleansed by obedience to the Word of Christ applied by the Holy Spirit. See note on Titus iii. 5, 6, and 8. The popular belief that water baptism is here intended destroys the argument of the passage; and as there is no such thing in the world as " pure " water, a true baptism is impossible if that be here meant.

Because He is unwaveringly faithful (v. 23)

therefore He should be unwaveringly confessed.

" Consider " (v. 24), i.e., take an interest in, be full of sympathy for, encourage in order to provoke unto love, etc.

To unite in public worship (v. 25) exposed to persecution and possible death ; and still does so in some lands. There is, therefore, a temptation to be a secret disciple. But this snare may be broken by setting the eye upon the approaching day (2 Thess. ii. 1) ; that is, the " day " of Christ's appearing in power and great glory. When that hope is real, courage is given to hold fast the confession of faith without faltering. The similar Greek word, only found here (v. 25) and in 2 Thess. ii. 1, appears to designedly connect these two passages. If so, then the gathering together of believers for Christian fellowship is an earnest of the gathering together to Him at His appearing.

To avoid, through cowardice, a public confession of the faith of Christ (v. 23) in fellowship with the public assembly of His people (v. 25), might eventuate in the apostasy of verses 26-29. Further, this public confession is related to the approaching " day " of 2 Thess. i. In that day the courageous will be recompensed with rest ; the cowardly, with wrath (Rev. xxi. 8). Luke-warmness in open identification with the confessors of faith in Christ leads to a Laodicean condition of soul and possibly to a denial of Christ.

Having told these Hebrews of the good things to be enjoyed by them if they advanced to the perfection of the New Covenant and its New Birth, he now warns them of " the fearful things " awaiting them if they retreated (vs. 26-31).

The wilful sin of verse 26 is described in verse 29. It is to treat with contempt the New Covenant of grace founded on the precious blood of the Son of God and testified to by the Holy Spirit. To reject that one sacrifice for sins, to account the blood of the Son of God that of a common man ("an unholy thing"),entailed certain and eternal judgment; for there was no other sacrifice in reserve (v. 26). Many Hebrews who for a time professed themselves disciples of Christ may have been guilty of this wilful sin.

" If we sin " (v. 26), i.e., if we Hebrew professors sin there remains no more in reserve a sacrifice for sins but an undefined fearful expectation of judgment (v. 27).

"The knowledge of the truth " (v. 26). Knowledge of spiritual things is not spiritual knowledge.

" Without mercy " (v. 28). Greek : " mercies," i.e., without the least mercy. " Under " : that is, upon the evidence of. " Sorer punishment " (v. 29). The punishment of the First Covenant was physical and temporal ; that of the Second, spiritual and eternal.

Every member of the Hebrew Church was sanctified officially and nationally, i.e., set apart by God as a possession for Himself (v. 29). This sanctification was founded on the blood of the Covenant both in type and in fulfilment.

" His people " (v. 30), i.e., His Hebrew people.

The Apostle now turns to those Hebrews who were advancing to full salvation, and who by their conduct evidenced the fact. These were the " good ground " of Matt. xiii. They were not the shallow ground hearers that in time of testing fell away, for they endured great afflictions (vs. 32 and 33), or the thorny ground hearers, for they took joyfully the spoiling of their goods (v. 34). They knew that they had for themselves property in heaven that was both better and eternal. These two words characterize this Epistle. The certainty and magnitude of such a reward (v. 35) animate the believer to perseverance.

The " Christian Scientist " teaches that the blood of Jesus was no better than the blood of a common man (v. 29). Many of these persons formerly professed to be sanctified by that blood. For " Christian Science " there is, therefore, a future fearful doom.

Once more the hope of His coming (vs. 27 and 37) is set before these Hebrew believers as an animating and certain expectation. He Who cherishes that hope finds in it a moral power that makes real a life of victory. See note on Hab. ii. 3 and 4. Christ is the subject of Habakkuk's vision. Not the beginning but the perseverance of God's righteous man, as opposed to declension and apostasy, is the force of the quotation here. As the righteous man receives life by faith so by faith he continues to live ; but if he draws back God has no pleasure in him. The Holy Spirit in Habakkuk states the cause of his drawing back—pride. Here the Spirit states the effect—his soul is not upright in him. He who is not right in his own soul is not right with God; God has no pleasure in him. See note on Hab. ii. 4.

The Apostle says: " But we believing Hebrews are not among those of verse 29 who are drawing back unto perdition, but we are the companions of them that through faith are advancing to full salvation."

The Hebrew people were by election and promise God's people. They were sanctified by the Blood of the Covenant, and those who confessed Jesus to be the Messiah are con templated in verse 29 as belonging to that people. But the foundation truth is declared in verse 38 that those who are really justified are those who exercise a living and continuing faith; and the action of this faith is set out in the next chapter and its Author and Finisher (xii.2) acclaimed.

Christ by His own blood entered in once for all into the Holy Place (ix. 12)—" having therefore, brethren, boldness to enter into the holiest by the blood of Jesus " (x. 19). This is the wonderful revelation of these two chapters. Christ as High Priest and the believer have the one title to heaven. That one title is the precious blood. His title is the believer's title and the believer's title is His Title.

" Sins every year " (v. 3)—" sins no more " (v. 17). These statements contrast the Two Covenants. They express the impotency of the one and the sufficiency of the other.

Verse 34 should read as in the Revised Version.

The first half of the Epistle—i. to x.—ends here. Its subject is: " Accepted in Him." The second half—xi. to xiii.—now begins. Its subject is: " Rejected with Him."

" Are sanctified " (v. 10); " are being sanctified " (v. 14). The one is perfect; the other, progressive.

HEBREWS XI.-XII. 2.—Having proved from the Scriptures that the " rest " and " the good things" of the New Covenant are secured and held by faith, the Holy Spirit now illustrates the activities of faith. Verse 1 is not a definition of faith but a declaration of its action. It makes promises present and real and unseen things visible. So the promises respecting Canaan were real to Abraham and to Isaac, Jacob and Joseph though they were wanderers, and all died without getting them (v. 13). Similarly Abel saw the Lamb of God that takes away the sin of the world; Enoch saw his Divine companion (v. 6);

Noah saw the coming Flood; Abraham saw the city which hath the foundations; Moses saw Him Who is invisible; women saw " a better resurrection," and they all saw the " better thing " which God provided for them (v. 40).

The action, energy, activity and pattern of faith are set forth in the chapter thus:

The path of faith (1-7).
The patience of faith (8-22).
The power of faith (23-40).
The pattern of faith (xii. 1, 2).

The subject of the chapter being the activity of faith Adam and Eve are passed over, for their faith was passive and receptive. God clothed them, not with wool, but with coats of skins. This necessitated death. To atone means to clothe or cover. They humbled themselves and accepted this Divine covering. Abel learned this lesson.

A tree is visible, but the gases of which it is made do not appear.

By faith Abel—by faith Enoch—by faith Noah. See notes on Gen. iv. v, and vi.—ix. These three patriarchs illustrate Worship, Walk and Witness; and, Salvation, Consecration and Condemnation. This is faith in action upon the path of faith

" His gifts " (v. 4), i.e., His great and acceptable gift, thus expressed by the plural of excellency. It was a lamb. Here was a lamb for one man; in Exodus xii. a lamb for a family; in Lev. xvi. a lamb for a nation; and in John i. a lamb for the whole world.

The human race owes it existence to the fact that one man was " moved with fear " (v. 7). Fear as a factor in salvation is decried at the present day, and only love declared to be the true Gospel. Enoch predicted the wrath of God, i.e., the Flood (Jude 14). Society tittered; Noah trembled.

Abraham and his sons are still awaiting in the patience of faith the promises made to them. They are not dead, for God is not ashamed to be called their God. It does not say that He was not ashamed, but that He is not ashamed. He is not the God of the dead but of the living (vs. 8-22). See notes on Gen. xii. 1. and Mark xii. 26, 27.

" He obtained the promise " (vi. 15)— " He received not the promises " (xi. 13). He received the promise but not the things promised. He will receive them. Chapters vi. 15 and xi. 17 and Gen. xxii. are here brought together.

" These all died " (v. 13). Enoch is excepted in verse 5.

" A better country " (v. 16). This Epistle speaks of better persons, of better places and of better things.

Isaac's action in blessing Jacob, and Jacob's in blessing Ephraim, illustrate Rom. ix. 16. Isaac willed to bless Esau and Joseph ran to set Jacob's hands aright, but neither could defeat the purpose of God in election.

" The top of his staff " (v. 21). See note on Gen. xlvii. 31.

The power of faith in victory is witnessed to in verses 23-35 ; and its power in suffering in verses 36-38.

Sarah's unbelief (v. 11) and Moses' cowardice (v. 27) are here forgiven and forgotten and only their faith and courage recalled.

Moses chose the slave-driver's lash (v. 25) rather than Egypt's crown (v. 26). Thus he forsook the throne of Egypt (v. 27), and in so doing braved the anger of the king who must have been much incensed that a royal prince should degrade the imperial throne and family by such a decision. Or it may be that the reference here is to his courage in not fearing the threat of Exod. x. 28, 29. Or to the courage of his faith in Exod. xiv. 10-14 when the children of Israel were " sore afraid," and (v. 10) Moses said " Fear ye not " (v. 13) " Jehovah shall fight for you " (v. 14). He had no fear at this great crisis for he saw Him Who is invisible.

The blood of Christ is precious to faith (v. 28), but the doctrine of the atonement is offensive to the self-righteous moralist.

The Red Sea (v. 29), the walls of Jericho (v. 30) and Rahab (v. 31). See Notes on Exod. xiv. and Joshua ii.-vi.

Wrought righteousness (v. 33, i.e., executed justice ; as, for example, in the case of Agag.

" Escaped the edge of the sword " (v. 34). The faith that escaped the sword was as precious to God as the faith that braved the sword or that broke it ; and the faith that awaited a future resurrection was as Divine as the faith that received an immediate resurrection (v. 35).

All these elders (vs. 2 and 39), because of their faith, were approved by God ; but He did not give them " the promise," for He fore-saw " a better thing " for them and for the Hebrews of Paul's day (" us all ") so that, apart from them, they should not enjoy the perfection of the better resurrection (vs. 40 and 35).

Thus faith has its own objects. These are supplied by God. They govern the heart and the whole life. They leave no room for other motives and affections which would divide the heart ; and as a result a life of liberty, dignity, power and testimony, follows.

Providence placed Moses in the court of Pharaoh, but faith caused him to forsake it. Thus faith as a motive produced the effect which providence prepared. Providence governs circumstances ; faith governs conduct.

The faith that did not fear the wrath of Pharaoh (v. 27) feared the wrath of God (v. 28). By the sprinkling of the blood Moses acknowledged that he was as much the object of the just judgment of God as was Pharaoh himself. There was no moral difference between them. Both were sinners. Neither of them was innocent Both stood under the sentence of death ; and, being guilty, both merited it.

The Red Sea was a temple to Israel but a tomb to Egypt. The faith that sprinkled the blood, and the unbelief that refused its shelter, fixed this great gulf between them.

Moses balanced the best of the world with the shame of Christ and deliberately chose the latter. He saw its future wealth (vs. 1 and 26 R.V.).

" The Egyptians were drowned " (v. 29) " The earth swallowed them " (Exod. xv. 12). They sank in the sands and in the waves of the sea. See Rev. xii. 15.

"Mindful"(v.15), means if they had longed for it, or desired to return to it. See verse 16. This illustrates the import of the verb "to remember " (1 Cor. xi. 24), i.e., not a mere recalling to mind but an imitative action motived by remembrance — such action in Corinth being the denial of self in ministering to the needs of others. See notes on 1 Cor. viii.-xiv.

HEBREWS XII.—" Witnesses " (v .1)—not spectators, but witnesses to the power and activity of faith. The figure is that of a race-course ; these are the competitors and not the spectators. They bear witness to faith ; and their actions furnish the evidence. But attention (v. 2) is directed unto the Prince and Perfecter of faith—not of " our faith "—that would be a poor thing—but of faith itself. The elders witnessed to faith in one or other of its activities, but Jesus ran the entire course of faith from the beginning to the end and furnished a perfect testimony. The elders had travelled a part of the path and triumphed over some difficulties, but He had been subjected to every trial. He was sheltered from none. The elders trusted in God and were delivered; He was a worm and no man, and was forsaken. But as Prince and Perfecter of faith He won the victory by submission, and sat down in a glory magnified in proportion to the depth of His abasement and obedience. Reward is never the motive of faith, but ever its encouragement.

"The sin" (v. 1), i.e., unbelief. It besets and entangles the feet and so hinders the runner. When looking at Him (v. 2) nothing is easier than to lay aside a weight; when not looking at Him nothing is harder. If the runner's heart is set upon the prize he will readily throw away even a bag of gold, for it is a weight.

"Author" (v. 2). This Greek word is translated "Prince" in Acts iii. 15 and "Captain" (Heb. ii. 10). It means Prince, Leader, Author, Originator, Beginner, etc. As such Jesus ran the whole path of faith. He exercised its patience, for "He endured"; He demonstrated its power, for "He despised the shame"; and He proved its victory, for He sat down on the Throne of God.

Unlike Him these disciples of His to whom Paul was writing had not faced death (v.4) and they had forgotten the Scripture (v. 5). Christ never forgot it; and He actually died.

An earthly father (v. 9) chastens his son as seems fit to his imperfect judgment; but the Heavenly Father disciplines with infallible judgment and perfect love. Death (v. 4) frees from sin; discipline saves from sinning. God chastens those whom He loves. The fruitful branch is purged that it may bring forth more fruit; the self-willed child is chastened in order to the production of the peaceable fruit of righteousness. Love chastens, but not without a motive; and so the child must not be discouraged.

Until the will is won there is warfare, but when won there is peace (v. 11); and the fruit of that peace is upright conduct. But this only results for them who are exercised by the chastisement.

All men are not sons; as popular theology teaches (v. 8).

Nobility of character (v. 10), as well as uprightness of conduct (v. 11), result from Divine chastening. Recognition of this action of grace and wisdom empowers the hands and makes strong the knees (v. 12) of the witness-bearers to faith.

All who follow the Lord fully (v. 13) smooth the path of faith to feeble brethren; but those who do not follow fully, roughen the path for others' feet and create spiritual cripples.

Every effort must be made to live peacefully with all men, but not at the expense of holiness. Christ's name must not be associated with evil. Only the pure in heart shall see God (v. 14, Matt. v. 8, Eph. v. 5). Failure to diligently show to others the grace that one has himself received, is to fail from that grace (v. 15 and 2 Cor. vi. 1 and 3) and to prepare the ground for a root of bitterness which will surely defile "the many" (R.V. and Deut. xxix. 18). When grace governs the heart and life then peace and holiness flourish and bitterness withers.

To sell eternal and spiritual riches for temporal and physical gratification is profanity and impurity. Esau, with tears, tried to get his father to repent, i.e., to change his mind and give him the inheritance, but in vain (v. 17). The Holy Spirit here says with terrible severity that Esau was a "profane person."

Once more (18-29) the Two Covenants are contrasted; and for the fourth time (v. 25) a warning of mingled goodness and sternness is addressed to the readers of the Epistle.

The seven outward and visible signs of the Old Covenant (vs. 18-19) are contrasted with the seven inward and spiritual realities of the New (vs. 22-24). The first are :—the mountain, the fire, the blackness, the darkness, the tempest, the sound of the trumpet, and "the words," i.e., the Ten Commandments—the Law. It doomed to death.

The second are :— the city, the angels, the first-born, the Judge, the righteous, the Mediator, and the blood that speaks peace and life.

The ellipses in the quotation from Exod. xix. 13 may be thus supplied : "and if so much as a man or a beast touch the mountain—if a man, he shall be stoned—if a beast, he shall be thrust through with a dart" (v. 20).

An illustration of the Law of Subsequent Mention is given in verse 21.

" Ye are come, and ye shall come " (v. 22). Both statements are here intended. The present tense is true to faith; the future, to fact. The establishment of heavenly glory in the millennial earth is the subject (vs. 22-24).

" Made perfect " (v. 23). Compare xi. 35 and 40. This is the perfection promised to those who believe to the end. It will be enjoyed in the First Resurrection. The righteous, now in the spiritual world, still await this perfection.

The blood of Abel's lamb spake good things, the blood of God's Lamb " better things." The use of the masculine and neuter articles in the Greek Text help to make this comparison quite clear. The relation between two things of the same kind —Abel's sacrifice and Christ's sacrifice—is more natural than between two things different both in kind and result, viz., Christ's sacrifice and Abel's own blood which was not a sacrifice at all. The argument of the Epistle and of this passage is further evidence, for it illustrates the superiority of Christ's one sacrifice of the New Covenant to the Old Testament sacrifices of which Abel's is the first recorded and which was Divinely declared to be acceptable. The popular interpretation that Abel's blood cries for vengeance and Christ's for mercy, opposes the point of the argument.

The glory, the wonders, and the splendour of the heaven (vs. 22-24) from whence Messiah speaks (v. 25) add to the majesty of His voice and makes certain the doom of all who turn away from it. To refuse Moses who spake on earth was to perish; how much surer, therefore, the judgment of those who refuse Christ who speaks from heaven.

He has promised to burn up once and for all the present heavens and earth (2 Pet. iii. 7 and 10)—for they may be shaken—and to found a kingdom which cannot be shaken. For the believer this is a promise (v. 26); for the unbeliever it is a terror.

The believer's God (v. 29) is love; but He is also a consuming fire.

As Moses (Deut. xxx. 19) set before the Hebrews life and death and intreated them to choose life, so Paul pleaded with these their children. He urged them to advance from a national belief in Jesus as the Messiah to a moral belief in Him as the Saviour in Whom alone was eternal life, and He warned them that if they refused to so believe upon Him, they would choose death and not life. The

downward course of these death-choosers is thus marked in the Epistle:

Salvation neglecters (ii. 3).
Heart hardeners (iii. 8).
Grace corruptors (vi. 7).
Christ forsakers (x. 38).
Christ opposers (x. 29).
Christ despisers (xii. 16).
Christ rejecters (xii. 25).

Thus a salvation neglecter may become a Christ rejecter.

All types and shadows having been put aside as fulfilled in the substance—Christ—He, as the Great High Priest, is set before the heart as a Priest for sin, for infirmity and for worship, and is, as such, competent (for He is Divine), ever-living, compassionate, sinless and human. By Him therefore—but only by Him—the Christian sacrifice of praise is offered to God continually (xiii. 15).

HEBREWS XIII.—Gentleness to all men (xii. 14) and love to fellow-believers (v. 1) are to be earnestly practised by the Christian.

Abraham, Lot and Manoah entertained angels unawares (v. 2).

" Remember prisoners " (v. 3), " remember martyrs " (v. 7) and " obey ministers " (v. 17).

Prisoners at that time, and in some lands to-day, were dependent on their friends for food. They starved to death if they got none. So these Hebrew believers were to remember these Christ-confessors and to send them food. They were also to think of those in adversity, for they themselves, as human beings, were liable to similar affliction.

Verse 4 should read as in the Revised Version; and also verse 5. Filthy lucre and filthy lust are close companions. See note on Neh. ix. 31.

" I will never let go thine hand," i.e., withdraw My presence, nor forsake thee, i.e., refuse My help. Therefore the believer may confidently say: " Jehovah is My Helper. I will not fear. What shall man do unto me ? " (v. 6). See note on Deut. iv. 31.

They were to remember, in order to imitate, those who first preached the Gospel to them and who had died as martyrs of the faith (v. 7, R.V.). The attempt to base prayers to the dead on this verse falls to the ground.

Because perfection and completion of doctrine are found in Christ Who is the same yesterday and to-day and for ever (v. 8), therefore divers and strange doctrines are to be ignored by those who love Him.

God's method of morally establishing the heart is grace; man's method is "meats" (v. 9), i.e., outward, sensual, physical ceremonies and carnal ordinances. Many say that such ceremonies and exercises appeal to them and help them. If that is so then the Holy Spirit is in error in saying they are profitless. Religious emotion is a very different thing from spiritual endowment. The latter enriches the spiritual life; the former impoverishes it. True spiritual life exists only in the realm of grace. In that realm Christ is all, and self—even religious self—is made dead and kept dead.

"We (Hebrews) have an altar" (v. 10). At the moment the Apostle was writing it was still standing in front of the Temple at Jerusalem and on it was still annually sacrificed the sin-offering (v. 11). Of that offering none were permitted to eat (Lev. vi. 30). The altar was shortly afterwards destroyed by the Romans. To suppose this altar to be what is to-day called the Lord's Table is strange, for all partake of that table; but no one partook of the altar of the sin-offering, and this prohibition is the argument of verses 10-12. The victim personating sin was wholly burned without the camp, and thus was symbolized God's wrath against sin. But its blood was brought into the immediate presence of God as being most precious to Him.

So Christ suffered the wrath of God without the gate and entered into the presence of God within the vail (v. 12).

These Hebrew believers were urged to go forth unto Him outside "the camp" i.e., Jerusalem and the law of Moses, and bear His reproach. For note upon "the camp," see the Introduction.

The sacrifices now acceptable to God are those of praise addressed to Messiah's Name (v. 15), and benevolence exercised towards all in need (v. 16).

To refuse to listen to and obey the Gospel (v. 17) causes not only grief to the preacher but eternal ruin to the hearer.

Verse 18 should read as in the Revised Version. When before the high priest (Acts xxiii. 1) the Apostle said he had a good conscience. He here again repeats the statement, and denies that he had in any way acted dishonestly in respect of the law of Moses.

In virtue of (" through ") His blood, i.e., His atoning sacrifice as the Good Shepherd. He is the Great Shepherd of the sheep. He could not be such had He not, as the Good Shepherd, shed His blood for the sheep and so established the everlasting Covenant.

Paul's suppression of himself and his Apostolic authority, and his urging affection and submission to the Twelve Apostles (vs. 7 and 17), and his humbly asking only prayer for himself, were all calculated to disarm the prejudices of those to whom he wrote (v. 22).

The sufficiency of Christ as a Saviour appears in the offices which He fills in this Epistle. These are the holy garments of His heavenly priesthood:

Chapter i.: The Sin-purger.
Chapter ii.: The Captain of Salvation.
Chapter iii.: The Son over His own house.
Chapter v.: The great High Priest.
Chapter vi.: The Fore-Runner.
Chapter viii.: The Mediator.
Chapter xii.: The Prince and Perfecter of faith.
Chapter xiii.: The Great Shepherd.

In these several ministries He meets His people's need as:

Sinful, feeble, children needing food and love, infirm worshippers, apprehensive pilgrims, incompetent covenanters, defective believers and defenceless and foolish followers.

All in Him is perfection—perfection of cleansing and victory and the supply of love and food for the children; perfection in worship, and as a Fore-runner in making sure the road and certain the entrance for His people; perfection as the Negotiator of the everlasting Covenant, so making its permanence absolute; perfection in the provision of the faith in which and by which the righteous live; and perfection in the care and guardianship of His foolish and defenceless flock.

Pending His return fellowship with Christ can only be enjoyed outside the camp and inside the veil. Corrupt Christianity is the present-day " camp."

The structure, language, and argument of the Epistle, together with the personal note apparent in x. 34, and xiii. 18-25—especially " the token " in v. 25 (2 Thess.iii.17)—support the conviction that Paul was the prophet through whom the Holy Spirit made this last appeal to Israel on the eve of the destruction of Jerusalem by the Romans.

JAMES

The person inspired by the Holy Spirit to write this letter was most probably the James of Acts xii. 17, xv. 13, xxi. 18 and Gal. ii. 9, but the Scriptures do not make the matter certain. This James may have been the Lord's brother (Gal. i. 19). The apostle James was put to death by Herod (Acts xii. 2). James the son of Alpheus, and James the son of Cleophas, were one and the same, for Cleophas is Hebrew and Alpheus is Greek.

The letter is addressed to the Twelve Tribes of Israel. Its interpretation, therefore, belongs to the Hebrew Church, but its message affects all who profess to be disciples of the Nazarene.

The closing Books of the Bible—Hebrews to Revelation—relate to the future, and will uphold the faith of the elect members of the Hebrew people and of the Gentiles who will love and confess the true Messiah, and brave the persecutions of the future false Messiah. These Books specially belong to them, and will be understood by them.

The Epistle to the Hebrews reveals the excellence of a Divine and saving faith; this Epistle fitly follows in warning professors against a carnal and worthless faith.

JAMES I.—The faith exposed in this letter was possibly like that professed by the believers of John ii. 23, vii. 31, Acts xxi. 20, and Hebrews vi and x.

The Epistle is an appeal to the conscience, and not an exposition of the foundation doctrines of the Gospel.

It addresses the entire Hebrew nation as a nation of unbelievers, but recognises in the midst of it a little company, oppressed and suffering, who exercised true faith in the Lord Jesus Christ. These believers, being still Hebrews, observed the Law; and their fellow nationals might, therefore, without any vital moral change, make a similar pro-fession of faith in Christ as the True Messiah To these, in the latter day, the new birth of verse 18 will be as incomprehensible as it was to the Hebrews to whom James wrote.

The nation in the Epistle is officially viewed as the people of God; and, as such, the privileges of the New Covenant belonged to them.

The temptations of verses 2-12 in which these believers were to rejoice (v. 2), and which made them blessed (v. 12), were not temptations to sin, but testings of faith. The exercise of heart and conscience caused by such testings were more valuable than gold and silver (vs. 10 and 11).

" Perfect work " (v. 4), i.e., full effect. Patience under trial secures perfect discipline.

Trials are very perplexing, and much wisdom is needed to bear them victoriously. Abraham in Genesis xxii. is an illustration. But in asking for this wisdom there must be no uncertainty, for a heart that is double-minded (v. 8), that is, that partly leans upon God (v. 5), and partly upon a rich man (v. 7), receives nothing (v. 7).

The Gospel places all men on the same level (vs. 9 and 10). The beggar, Bartimæus, was told to rise, and the rich Zacchæus to come down, and both were made to stand side by side before Jesus.

The two main tests of faith are patience and obedience. Christ was the Perfect Believer. In Him these two features are seen in perfection. As a man He was thoroughly tested and found perfect. True faith is always tested so as to make it stronger and richer. It leans wholly upon God, and seeks dependence nowhere else. The heart is single and not double. It is foolish to depend on the rich, for they vanish away like the flower of the field. The riches of faith that endure eternally are here contrasted with the riches that perish in a day.

God gives liberally and without upbraiding

(v. 5). Such was His action with Solomon. He gave him much more than he asked for, and did not upbraid him though He knew how he would forsake that wisdom.

"The crown of life" (v. 12). Compare "The crown of righteousness" (2 Tim. iv. 8). These crowns are for all who love Him.

The temptations of verses 13-15 are temptations to sin. These temptations do not come from God but from the appetites of fallen man's sinful nature (vs. 14 and 15). There must be no mistake on this point. Sinless gifts and boons come from God and not sinful seductions. He is not the God of evils (v. 13, marg.) but the Father of lights, i.e., of sinless blessings. Evil is darkness; light is goodness.

God's greatest boon is the New Birth (v.18). The cause of that boon is not the goodness of the receiver but the will of the Giver. This New Birth is operated by the Holy Spirit through the Gospel message—The Word —and by the same Word the imparted Divine life is preserved (v. 21). The reality and moral power of this new life is only visible to men in the conduct of those who profess to have received it (vs. 22-27).

There are many contrasts here:—Death (v. 15), and Life (v. 12).; "Sin when finished" and "perfect gift" (v.17), etc.:"First fruits" (v. 18). See notes on Lev. xxiii. and 1 Cor. xv. The sheaf of first fruits was presented to God on the morrow after the Sabbath. It represented the great harvest that rose out of its earthen grave. So Christ as the first fruits of all the blessed dead, rose on the morrow after the Sabbath. The resurrection, therefore, of all who believe upon Him is assured, for God will bring them with Him (1 Thess. iv). Israel also is a first fruits of the nations, and her moral resurrection (Rom. ix-xi) will assure that of the nations. The believing remnant of Israel (v. 18) will be "a kind" of first fruits of Israel.

When under trial from God, or under temptation to evil from man, the wisdom of verse 5 will discipline the heart to be swift to hear, slow to murmur, and slow to rebel; for the anger and irritation of the natural heart do not produce anything that God accepts as righteous (vs. 19 and 20). The heart that humbles itself before God's Word (v. 21), without questioning or murmuring, and that obeys its teaching (vs. 22-25) is a heart that enjoys the sweetness of liberty (v. 25); for there is no life so free

as the life proper to the New Nature. Hence the Psalmist cries joyfully: "I will walk at liberty for I keep thy precepts"—but to the carnal nature such a life is bondage. Liberty to do the will of God is the freedom that the New Nature delights in.

The tongue is a certain index to the state of the heart (v. 26). A faith that does not bridle the tongue is a dead faith.

As a man may behold his natural face in a mirror so a reader may perceive his moral image in God's Word, and, turning away, quickly forget the painful sight. A mirror which faithfully reflects the physical deformities of a face cannot justly be condemned. On the contrary, its truthfulness must be praised. So it is unjust to charge the Bible with immorality because it faithfully exposes the moral deformities of human nature.

Separation from sin, and sympathy with suffering (v. 27) reveal the presence of a Divine faith in the heart. The disciple is like his Lord, for these two moral activities shone forth perfectly in Him.

The New Covenant is a law of liberty, for it begets a new nature, and so frees the believer from the bondage of the old and carnal nature. This new nature desires nothing better than to do the will of God. Its tastes and appetites are heavenly and spiritual. Not only is there liberty from the doom of the Old Covenant, but the new-born soul is set free to taste the joys of the New Covenant. Thus was it with Christ. His liberty was found in doing the will of God; and if He could have been prevented from doing that will, He would have lost His liberty. The liberty of the New Man is liberty to do the will of God; and, accordingly, the Gospel in its moral excellence is the law of liberty.

JAMES II.—The Holy Spirit here condemns a profession of faith in Christ which distinguished between the rich and poor (vs. 1-13), and which was barren of good works (vs. 14-26).

The Lord Jesus Christ is the God of glory Who appeared to Abraham (vs. 1 and 21); and in the light of that glory the distinction between rich and poor disappears.

The letter being addressed to the Hebrew people, the word "Assembly" (v. 2) should read "Synagogue," as in the Margin.

The spirit of the world courts the rich

and despises the poor ; the Spirit of Christ honours both alike. Rich and poor are here viewed as classes and not as persons. It does not, therefore, mean that all poor men are Christians and all rich men are not.

The supreme law is that of verse 8 (Lev. xix. 18). To make a distinction between rich and poor violates this law, and this violation is sin (v. 9). Such action breaks the whole law, though not the whole of the law. To break one link in a chain is to destroy the chain (v. 10).

" Do not kill " (v. 11), i.e., " do not commit murder." The magistrate is commanded by God to kill evil-doers with a sword which God places in his hand for that purpose (Rom. xiii. 3 and ·4) ; and all who despised Moses' law were killed by God's command without mercy (Heb. x. 28).

All who profess to believe the Gospel which offers liberty from sinning, and who yet live a life of sinning, will be judged by the Gospel (v. 12) ; and that judgment will decree a sorer punishment than the judgment of the law of bondage (Heb. x. 29). To sin against love is much more terrible than to sin against law. " For he shall have judgment without mercy that hath shewed no mercy ; and mercy applauds that judgment." This is the import of the term " against."

When, as a result of reading this passage, a Christian ceases to have respect to persons, then does he illustrate the meaning of Eph. v. 26. The application of this Scripture to his conduct cleanses it.

Verse 14 should read as in the R.V. : " Can *that* faith save him ? " The answer is " No ; for it is a dead faith." The argument of the whole passage (vs. 14-26) is : that life demonstrates its unseen existence by visible fruit. The life of a tree cannot be seen, but it is easy to distinguish its presence or absence for foliage demonstrates the existence or non-existence of life. But which comes first—life or fruit ? Abraham's works declared him to be justified, and made plain that his faith was sincere, i.e., perfect (v. 21 and 22).

The justification by works of this Epistle is justification before man by furnishing to him that which he can see. God needs no such evidence, for He can read the heart and see if it is animated by a living faith. . The source of justification is grace ; the ground, atonement ; the means, faith ; and the evidence,

works. The Epistle to the Romans deals with the first three ; the Epistle of James with the last.

The profession of a lifeless faith is profitless. If a man " say " he has faith (v. 18). This is the key to this part of the Epistle. He " says " he has it, but where is the proof of it ? Works are the only proof. Nobody can see faith, but anybody can see its evidence. If the fruit is there, then assuredly the root is there. The profession of a Christian doctrine may be faultless—the faith may be as real as that of the demons (v. 19)—but if there is no union of the soul with God by means of the New Birth, then there is nothing there but death. A benevolence which only proffers words (v. 16) is as dead as a faith which only proffers professions. Faith can only be evidenced by action (v. 18) ; but such action is not simply the movement of a kindly nature, proper to man as a creature,. but, on the contrary, it may be action against nature, as in the two illustrations cited here of Abraham and Rahab. For the one put his son to death (in intention), and the other betrayed her country. These were not the fruits of an amiable nature, or actions such as man would call good works. But neither of them could have acted as they did if they had not had a living faith in their hearts. Everything was against them both naturally. Abraham sacrificed his only son for God, and Rahab believed her country to be doomed before Israel had gained one victory.

In grace, as in nature, life precedes fruit, so the faith that saved Abraham preceded the sacrifice of Isaac by 40 years.

JAMES III.—As in i. 26, so in this part of the letter the tongue is declared to be the index to the heart, revealing its relation to a dead or living faith. Language discloses the thoughts of a man, and makes it clear whether he is governed by self-will or by God's will. Where there is Divine life it displays itself, not only in language, but in action ; and in both the modesty of true wisdom is seen (v. 13). The wisdom that accompanies bitterness and contention arises out of the carnal nature of fallen man (v. 15).

" Masters " (v. 1), i.e., teachers who put themselves forward to be the moral masters of others. Such persons will receive severer judgment, for all teachers stumble in many things (v. 2). Those who do not stumble in word are fully-matured Christian men; for to control the tongue secures the control of the whole body.

A horse is moved by his will; a ship, by the wind. The one power is inward, the other, outward. Man is like a horse and a ship. He is moved hither and thither by his inward will or by outward influences. Just as the tiny bit, and small rudder, can move these great bodies in one direction or another, so man's entire body can be moved by the tongue; and not only that, but it, though so small, can move masses of men, and so inflame them that it will set their entire nature on fire and excite them to terrible deeds (vs. 3-6).

Man can subjugate all kinds of living creatures (v. 7), but no man can subjugate the tongue (v. 8).

Everyone who claims to be wise and intelligent (v. 13) can prove it by Christian conduct, and by the modest action of true wisdom (v. 13). Vanity can easily be fed in teaching others. Envy and strife are born of that vanity. Such a wisdom is not to be boasted of (v. 14). The Gospel teaches men to be gentle and holy. To profess to believe the Gospel and not to be gentle and holy·is to give the lie to the Gospel.

The wisdom that comes from above has three characteristics: it is pure; it is peaceable, gentle, and sympathetic; and it is active, sincere, and impartial in benevolence (v. 17). Purity, absence of self-will, and activity in goodness reveal the presence of true wisdom in the heart. The action of this wisdom is from within, and is not the result of outward circumstances which influence the natural emotions and move men occasionally to acts of kindness.

The sons of peace sow peace, and the fruit of the harvest is uprightness of conduct (v. 18). The sons of contention sow strife, and its harvest is tumult and every evil work (v. 16).

The righteousness that is born of peace rebukes, and does not excuse sin, and it is the physician rather than the executioner of sinners.

JAMES IV.—Pleasing self is here declared to be sinful (v. 17). This self-pleasing may take a positive form (v. 13) or a negative (v. 17). It may also express itself in violence (v. 1 to 3), or in worldliness (v. 4). It originates in the corruption of the human spirit (v. 5), and is a favourite weapon of

Satan's (v. 7). It can be conquered by grace (v. 6). Grace gives birth to self-denial (vs. 8-12), and can subjugate the tongue (v. 11).

Quarrels are not caused by outward circumstances, but by inward passions (v. 1). If men were sinless there would be no contentions or wars. War characterises the carnal nature; peace, the new nature.

Envy involves murder (v. 2). David and Ahab are illustrations.

God calls men to pray, and not to quarrel (v. 2). His promises are addressed to those who pray, not to those who fight. If men prayed, there would be no fighting. If it be replied that they do pray, and that nothing results, the answer is that their prayer is animated by the passion for self-pleasing (v. 3).

Christ and the world are rivals for the human heart (v. 4). The heart that gives itself to Him is married to Him; but if it turns its affections to His rival, it breaks its marriage faith and is an " adulteress." This verse should read as in the R.V.

" Whosoever will be " etc., (v. 4), i.e., is resolved to be a friend of the world is the enemy of God.

The natural heart loves the world, covets its friendship, and is made passionate with envy. Envy is a power that all the efforts of human culture cannot overcome. A new nature alone, implanted by grace (v. 6), can conquer it. But man refuses a victory upon these terms, for he is proud (v. 6), insubject (v. 7), hostile (v. 8), and impure.

To be the friend of the world is to be the enemy of God (v. 4).

The Scripture teaches that man is indwelt since the Fall by a corrupt spirit dominated by envy (v. 5). Some understand the word " spirit " in this verse to mean the Holy Spirit, but the argument of the passage, as well as the language of the verse, forbid this interpretation; for mighty as is this corrupt spirit, grace is mightier (v. 6); but grace is not for the proud but for the contrite in heart. Conversion is submission to God.

" He will flee " (v. 7), better, " he shall flee." It is a promise. He is not willing to flee; he must flee. But God is willing to draw nigh (v. 8).

The heart that is governed by the Holy Spirit reveals that government in the actions described in verses 6-10 in the midst of a people professing to be the people of God, as·

the Hebrews did ; but in reality they were unbelieving and self-pleasing.

God wants His people to do all the self-humbling (v. 10) and leave Him nothing but the uplifting. He does not like to humble His children. He loves to exalt them. Here the subject is growth in grace ; in 1 Pet. v. 6, it is submission to God's moral government in the earth.

Every child has his own place in the Father's heart. To speak evil of one whose value is so great is to speak evil of the counsel that gives each its place. Besides, to love one's neighbour as one's self forbids such evil-speaking. Evil-speaking also judges the Law, and makes a man to be not a doer of the Law, but a judge. But only One is both Law-giver and Judge ; and He only is able to save and to destroy (vs. 11 and 12, R.V.). This is the last mention of the Law in the New Testament.

In verses 13-17 self-will and self-pleasing appear as motives antagonizing the command to love one's neighbour as one's self. The action is both negative and positive. Not to chose to do what is known to be right to do, is to sin negatively (v. 17) ; and to determine to give one's self wholly to money-making (v. 13) so as to have no time to do good to others, is to sin against this commandment positively. Knowledge without practice is presumptuous sin.

JAMES V.—Here is pictured the condition of Jerusalem immediately before its destruction at the hands of the Romans. These conditions will reappear prior to His coming in His Personal power and glory. The mass of the people was unbelieving, but in their midst was a little flock who loved Messiah's name, and believed upon Him. These were oppressed and hated by their rich brethren who robbed them. (v. 4) and persecuted them (v. 6). As then, so in the future this remnant of the Nation were not to take matters into their own hands, but patiently enduring their sufferings (v. 7), were to await the Coming of the Lord in judgment. He was then drawing nigh (v. 8) and standing before the door (v. 9). He came, the rich oppressors were judged, and the believing and persecuted Remnant delivered. So will it be once more in the near future ; and in those coming days these verses will uphold and fortify the faith of the future Remnant as they upheld and fortified the faith of the Remnant at that now distant time.

" Go to now " (v. 1), i.e., " listen . . . howl for your miseries that are coming upon you . . . your riches are about to be destroyed." In the East money is largely invested in costly clothing laid up in chests, and at the mercy of moths (v. 2).

" In the last days " (v. 3, R.V.). Compare Luke xii. 16-21. These were the last days of God's patience for Israel. To heap treasure in such days was to deny the fact and imminence of the predicted judgment.

The sense of verse 3 illustrated by Rom. ii. 5 may possibly be : " Ye have treasured up wrath for the last days."

" In a day of slaughter " (v. 5 R.V.). As an ox greedily eats the rich herbage on the very day that it is to be slaughtered, so the senseless rich indulged their passions at that time on the very eve of the coming judgment. These conditions will be repeated in the future (v. 3).

Sacred and secular history concur in declaring that the rich as a class oppress the poor (vs. 4-6).

" Kept back by fraud " (v. 4). See Deut. xxiv. 14, 15. The rich ought to give to the poor. Not to do so is sin. A still greater sin is to rob the poor.

" Jehovah Sabaoth " (v. 4). This great title of the Lord Jesus Christ in the Old Testament here only appears in the New In Rom. ix. 29, it is a quotation. It is a precious title for the defenceless poor who believe upon the Messiah, for it assures them that His are all the hosts of heaven, and that they are at His command to guard and avenge His oppressed people.

The Holy Spirit in v. 7 sets the Coming of the Lord as the term of the condition both of the unbelieving rich oppressors in Israel and of the poor believing Remnant. The rich heaped up treasures, but they found themselves " in the last days." The poor groaned in oppression, but the Coming of the Lord drew near, and deliverance would not be delayed. But as the farmer has long patience for the harvest, so the servant for the Master's Coming. Thus patience characterizes the life of faith. (See notes on Heb. xi.). The rich are not happy, but those who endure affliction for Messiah's sake they only are happy (v. 11). This expectation of the Coming of the Lord fortified their faith and nourished patient endurance under persecution and injustice.

The early rain falls in November; the latter rain, in April.

The unjust judgment of fellow Christians are sometimes more painful than the hatreds of unbelievers (v. 9). A spirit of discontent and murmuring against fellow-believers who are more favoured in their outward circumstances, and the misjudgments which generally accompany this discontent, must be guarded against, otherwise they come under the condemnation of the Eternal Judge Who is standing at the door.

" The end of the Lord " (v. 11), i.e., the issue of God's discipline of Job. His feelings were full of pity; His actions, full of mercy. This verse proves that Job really lived.

When robbed (v. 4) persecuted (v. 6), or misjudged (v. 9) the sufferer is liable to be carried away by anger, and, in the self-will of nature, to use oaths which are only sanctioned by Scripture in the moral realm (Exod. xx. 7 R.V. margin, Lev. xix. 12, Deut. vi. 13 and x. 20). When the High Priest put the Lord on His oath (Matt. xxvi. 63) Jesus immediately accepted the oath as administered to Him, and no longer remaining silent, at once responded. This proves that Matt. v. 34 does not apply to judicial oaths.

The Apostle Paul frequently took oaths (2 Cor. xii. 19., Gal. i. 20, 1 Tim. v. 21, etc.), and the Epistle to the Hebrews is based upon God's three great oaths. See note on Heb. vii. 20.

It is painful in fairs and markets, as also in private life, to hear people emphasizing their statements by irreverent and unnecessary oaths (v. 12). If afflicted, or merry, or sick (vs. 13 and 14), prayer, praise and medicinal remedies are to be employed, and not violent language. The two great medicines of the East are wine and oil. They should be used with prayer. St. Paul recommended the one; St. James the other; and the Good Samaritan used both. This principle sanctions the prayerful use of medicine in the healing of disease. The action and teaching of the Church of Rome in extreme unction has no authority here. Its priests anoint only when certified that death is sure. The Hebrew elders anointed for, and believed in a restoration to health. " To raise up " (v. 15) does not mean to raise up to heaven, as the Roman priests say, but to raise up to health. " To save " and " to make whole " (Matt. ix. 21, 22) are the same verb in the Greek text. The sins of verse 15, and the faults of verse 16, are plainly those committed against fellow-believers and not secret sins committed only against God. Hence the command to mutual forgiveness and mutual prayer. Sickness and pain may often be Divine chastisements for un-Christlike conduct. Charity and grace and truth should be in full exercise with regard to mutual faults, so that even such faults would be an occasion for the activities of love and mutual confidence. The forgiveness of verse 15 is clearly that of the offended person forgiving the offender. Here is a beautiful picture of Divine principles animating and governing Christian people.

" Let him pray " (v. 13). Personal prayer. " Let them pray " (v. 14). United prayer. The prayer of faith (v. 15). Believing prayer " Pray one for another " (v. 16). Mutual prayer. " Effectual fervent prayer " (v. 16). Operative prayer. " He prayed earnestly " (v. 17). Earnest prayer. " He prayed again " (v. 18). Continued prayer.

He who wins back a wanderer from truth wins his soul as well as his person, and spreads the veil of love over the multitude of sins. So love vanquishes sin—such is its nature and power.

1 PETER

This letter was addressed to the members of the Divine Election out of the Dispersion sojourning in Asia Minor, and was written shortly before the Coming of the Lord in wrath upon Jerusalem, as predicted in Matt. xxiv. 2 and Luke xix. 44. James, as pointed out, wrote to all the Tribes at the same period of time; for God still maintained relations with Israel and acknowledged them as His people and the Temple as His House (John i. 11 and ii. 16). These relations were broken when the judgment fell; but they will be resumed in the near future, and the believing Remnant of the nation in that future day will be fortified by these letters, for the moral conditions then will resemble those of the days in which the Apostles wrote.

The believing members of the Dispersion were confounded and discouraged because they were so few in number and so fiercely persecuted. The Apostle animated them by reminding them that though the Messiah Himself preached by His Spirit in Noah for a hundred and twenty years (iii. 19) heralding the approaching judgment, yet the whole world disbelieved Him, and only eight persons were saved in the baptism of the Ark. As to their sufferings, they as servants were appointed to share their Master's rejection and to feel the bitter hatred of the world. The Coming of the Lord was to be their hope then (iv. 7), as it will be to their suffering brethren of the future (i. 7 and 13).

1 PETER I.—The elect sojourners of the Dispersion (v. 1) owed their salvation to God's purpose, Christ's atonement and the Holy Spirit's operation.

God's fore-knowledge and fore-ordination are one and the same (v. 20 and Acts ii. 23, and Rom. xi. 2). He ordained these elect Hebrews unto obedience and sprinkling of the blood of Jesus Christ, as in Exod. xii. The elect on that night were saved by obeying the command to sprinkle the blood of the Paschal Lamb upon the doors of their houses.

The resurrection of Jesus Christ provides " a living hope " (v. 3). Such was the resurrection to Peter after his terrible fall. Had there been no resurrection there would have been for him no restoration. The word " living " characterizes Peter's Epistles as " faith " and " love," Paul and John's respectively.

The inheritance (v. 4) is reserved in heaven but it is to be brought down from thence, and manifested and established upon earth. It has been promised to Israel. They are guarded for it (v. 5) as surely as it is reserved for them. This is true for believers in general.

The assurance of this inheritance causes " great joy " (v. 6); but knowing and loving Jesus causes a " joy unspeakable " (v. 8).

The key words to this letter are " trial " (v. 6) and " suffering " (v. 11).

The trial of faith is more precious than gold, and the trial proves it to be so (v. 7); and He at His future appearing will praise and honour and glorify the faith of His confessors. See notes on Heb. xi.

The salvation of the soul is a present reality to faith (v. 9); the redemption of the body is the future hope of faith.

That the Messiah should suffer puzzled the Prophets (vs. 10-12). They spoke by inspiration but could not understand the utterances of the Spirit through them. They were, however, told by the Spirit that their prophecies belonged to the future. The Holy Spirit, through the prophets of the New Testament, completed and explained these great prophecies. This statement affirms the inspiration of the Apostles.

The interpretation of verses 7 and 13 belong to the future, but the principle contained in them is a living hope for all time.

Both His salvation (v. 5) and His judgment are ready to be revealed (iv. 5).

Verse 17 should read as in the Revised Version. The judgment here is that of a Father in the government of His children during the life-time of their sojourning. They, as children, reverence Him as a Father, and also because He redeemed them at such a cost (vs. 18 and 19).

Faith in God can only be exercised through Christ (v. 21). He that does not believe in that Divine Saviour does not believe in God (1 John. ii. 23), for he that hath not the Son hath not the Father. A faith and a hope that are " living " are founded on God Himself and not merely in statements about God.

Children of the One Father, redeemed by the One Saviour, and sanctified by the One Spirit, stand in a tender relationship to one another as brothers and sisters (v. 22), and, therefore, love one another fervently. They are born of the ever-living Word of God ; and that Word is the Gospel message that was preached to these people by Peter and his companions. Man, in contrast, is as perishable grass ; and his outstanding teachers in religion, philosophy and science are as the flowers of the grass. All wither and perish.

Men can only believe in God by believing in the Lamb of God. It is not by means of the Creation that they believe, for that cannot give rest to the conscience. Nor by means of providence, for that leaves the ways of God upon earth in profound darkness. Nor by means of the Law, for that fills the conscience with terror. It is only by means of Jesus, the Lamb of God who redeemed them to God.

The Scripture almost always links with the sufferings of Christ the " glories " that should follow (v. 11, R.V.). Compare Luke xxiv. 26. His glories—as His riches— are unsearchable ; but these glories are those won by Him because of His obedience unto death.

The obedience that appropriates the atonement of Christ (v. 2) makes the cleansed heart the living organ of unfeigned love to others (v. 22).

1 PETER II.—1-10.—The unfeigned love of i. 22 expels out of the heart the evil tempers of verse 1. They are once for all laid aside (Greek). These passions form a genealogy of sin as opposed to the genealogy of love. See 2 Peter i. 5-7. Malice begets guile, and guile hypocrises, etc.

The Holy Spirit operates the New Birth in the soul of the believer (i. 23) and nourishes that life (v. 2), and the vehicle of these operations is the Word, i.e., the Bible. To desire the Word there must be life, for the child must be born before it desires food. The attachment of the affections of the heart to the Lord Jesus Christ (v. 3.) only occurs where the New Birth is a reality. He and His Word form a unity. They are both precious to the renewed heart, for the Word reveals Him and His fulness to the soul. He is the God of all grace, full of grace, acting in grace, and seated upon a throne of grace. To Him and not to Sinai, the new-born come (v. 4) and to His Word ; for it reveals the grace that dwells in Him, and it sustains the life that it communicates. To taste that He is gracious whets the appetite for the Word and seats the believer where Mary sat. Israel cast aside as worthless that Living stone, but to God He was chosen and precious. The word " living " was real to Peter's heart, for the Father had revealed to him that Jesus was the Son of " the living God " (Matt. xvi. 16).

The reference in verse 5 is to the material Temple at Jerusalem with its carnal priest-hood, and animal sacrifices. These believers of the Dispersion were living stones in a spiritual temple, a holy priesthood offering up spiritual sacrifices. They were members of the Messianic church (Matt. xvi. 18)— not the church revealed in the Epistle to the Ephesians, for that was hidden and not revealed until made known to Paul.

The Spirit groups (6-10) His previous utterances in Psalm cxviii., Is. xxviii., and Hos. ii.—repeating His language of Exodus xix.—and applies them to this Rem-nant ; for in their believing eyes this Stone was precious, for faith sees as God sees. But to unbelief He was an offence. It stumbled at the Word, and to that fall the nation was appointed. The nation was not appointed to sin nor to condemnation, but its rebellious members, because unbelieving, were destined to fall upon that which was to faith the prec-ious Stone of Salvation. This great moral fact cannot be disputed. If Christ be not a stepping-stone to faith He must be a stumbling-stone to unbelief.

The nation rejected Him, but God had spiritual blessings for those members of it who believed upon Him. They could not, at the moment, enjoy on earth the Kingdom promised to the nation, but they could taste and enjoy the sweetness of relationship with God as a people accepted of Him. They were a holy nation—the nation to whom the Kingdom of God was to be given (Matt. xxi. 42-44)—who would exhibit the spiritual fruit of that Kingdom. They were the New Nation brought out of Egypt in grace, and brought into fellowship with God upon a new principle (Hos. ii.). Israel, after the flesh, had utterly failed in every respect and forfeited everything, but this new-born Israel, built up a living house upon the Living Stone, possessed the Kingdom and all its promised glories upon the principle of grace; and upon that principle all was secured to them. It was all grace, but grace through righteousness, for the Messiah Himself had suffered the judgment due to the guilty nation, and in His atoning death magnified the justice of God.

As a purchased people they were to shew forth not their own praises but the praises of Him who had called them out of darkness. They were in darkness and darkness was in them before He called them out of it. This fact disproves the doctrine that the Inner Light is possessed by natural birth.

In the first chapter the Hebrew believer appears as a pilgrim despised and persecuted (vs. 6 and 7), but in the second chapter, as a priest holy (v. 5) and royal (v. 9). Inside the veil in the presence of God, a holy priest; outside the camp in the presence of man, a royal priest.

This double priesthood is common to the Messiah and His people. On high, He is a Holy Priest as Aaron: on earth, He is a Royal Priest as Melchisedec. This double glory is true also of the elect nation. Its sweet privilege is to be brought as near as possible to God and to offer—sure of being accepted—spiritual sacrifices, for they are offered through Christ. This part of its life is the most excellent and is the source of its Royal priesthood on earth, for these spiritual sacrifices are those which the heart instructed by the Holy Spirit offers to God through Jesus Christ. The priesthood of Aaron and of his sons typified this ministry.

The glory of the second priesthood (v. 9) is to exhibit on earth the virtues of the Great High Priest Himself. Its description is seen in Exod. xix. i.e., Chosen, Royal and Holy. The royal priest reproduces Christ morally, in the world. The one priesthood is His heavenly life; the other, His earthly.

I PETER II. 11-III. 7—God has established three governments on earth: that of the magistrate (vs. 11-17); that of the master (vs. 18-25); and that of the husband (iii. 1-7). These governments were designed for man's happiness. They are resented by man—especially at the present time—and the result is confusion and misery.

The attitude of the Christian to the State, and his conduct in the world, is the subject of verses 11-17. As to his attitude, he is a stranger and a pilgrim. He is not of this world but has to pass through it. He is to be blameless in his conduct and submissive to the government. Pleasing self will injure his soul (v. 11); but a godly daily life will glorify God and silence the ignorant accusations (v. 15) of foolish men preferred against him in the magistrates' courts (v. 12).

At that time Christians were doubly accused as promoting revolution against the government and as practising obscene rites in their secret religious assemblies. But such charges being investigated by the magistrate and found baseless, and, on the contrary, evidence of good conduct being given, their accusers were put to silence (v. 15) and the Messiah's name magnified (v. 12). Acts xviii. 12 furnishes an illustration.

"The day of visitation" usually in Scripture means the day of God's visitation to judgment. It may mean that here; but it is more probable, if verses 12-15 be read together, that the word "visitation" here means magisterial investigation. If so, the passage may be thus read: "Whereas they (your accusers) accuse you as evil-doers, they (the magistrates) may on the evidence of your good works which will be placed before them, pronounce you innocent; and their verdict will, in effect, glorify God and nullify the ignorant accusations of malicious and foolish accusers."

"Maliciousness" (v. 16), i.e., evil habits. "Froward" (v. 18), i.e., harsh and unreasonable.

"Hereunto were ye called" (v. 21), i.e

elected by God to act toward revilers as Christ acted (v. 23).

The sheep returns to the shepherd (v. 25) ; the sow to the mire (2 Pet. ii. 22). The respective verbs are active and passive. The sow returns of its own will ; the sheep is caused to return.

" Plaiting the hair " (iii. 3), i.e., with golden and silver thread. The ostentatious wearing of gold and of costly clothes is unbecoming in a stranger and a pilgrim. " The hidden man of the heart " (v. 4) means the " new man " hidden in the heart—but manifested in the life by a meek and quiet spirit. Sarah called Abraham " lord," i.e., she recognised and submitted to his Divinely-given authority ; and all wives are her daughters as long as they so act and live the Christian life courageously, whatever may be the threats of their ungodly husbands. They are not to be panic-stricken with fear but to persist in goodness. Compare verse 14 and Phil. i. 28.

Christian husbands and wives (v. 7) are alike " vessels " fashioned by the Divine hand. The wife is the weaker vessel ; but she is to be honoured because she is a vessel, and also because she is a fellow-heir of the gracious gift of eternal life. The husband is to remember that he himself is a weak vessel ; that he needs to pray ; that he is to pray with his wife ; and that such prayer will not be answered if he disobeys the commands given him. As in the East the birth of children was, and is, regarded as an evidence of Divine favour, it is possible that that is hinted at here.

"Called" (i. 15, ii. 21, iii. 9),"chosen" (ii. 9) and " faithful " (i. 7) are words of glory for the Christ-confessor (Rev. xvii. 14).

The duty of the Christian to support the magistrate when using his Divinely-given sword for the punishment of evil-doers, is taught in verses 13-15 and Romans xiii. 1-6.

Such are the three governments that God has appointed on the earth. Men are responsible to recognise and to observe them. God permits freedom of will to man, with the result that disobedience to these commands has produced misery ; but this misery is chargeable to man and not to God. The heart that fears God has no other fear (v. 6) ; and this is the secret of its boldness and peace in confessing Christ, and in submitting to these governments.

1 PETER III. 8-22.—Christian conduct (vs. 8-12) ; human hatred (vs. 13-17) ; and Divine comfort (vs. 18-22) are the three lessons of this passage.

The nature of the " one mind "—one disposition—(v. 8) is defined in the sentences that follow, i.e., mutual compassion, mutual affection, etc., (vs. 8 and 9). The heirs of blessing should be distributors of blessings ; and those who desire a full and happy life (v. 10) will secure it by observing the injunctions set out in verses 10-12.

Jesus was a follower of that which is good (v. 13), yet men harmed, hated and crucified Him, not because of His goodness, but because He was God. So His disciples are not to be terrified or troubled with doubts if, although followers of that which is good, they find that men harm them and hate them. Man does not hate benevolence in itself, but if it is coupled with the Name of Christ it arouses his murderous anger. He applauds good conduct,but bitterly hates good conduct " in Christ " (v. 16). Yet he who suffers for righteousness' sake is to be envied (v. 14). Verse 15 should read as in the Revised Version. Where Christ has the lordship of the heart, neither fear nor doubt can find a lodgment ; and such a man can with modesty and caution explain to a questioner what is the nature of the hope that animates him to endure both suffering and death. " Fear " may here be understood to mean both reverence and caution—reverence because of the solemnity of the subject, and caution lest in the earnestness of discussion anything might be said which would give an opponent occasion to accuse the Christian to the civil magistrate. A bad conscience may be brought to God for pardon and mercy, but only a good conscience can stand without fear before an enemy (v. 16).

A double mystery confronts the Christian disciple. First, the mystery of suffering. Second, that God wills it sometimes (v. 17). This double mystery is sharpened by the fact that this permitted suffering may be because of well-doing and not because of evil-doing. See notes on the Book of Job.

The Divine comfort of verses 18-22 is conveyed in the statements that Christ Himself suffered ; that His preaching had so poor a response ; and that hated and rejected by earth, He was yet enthroned in heaven. Along this path of suffering and testimony and glory His followers are called to travel.

Three popular doctrines pretend to be founded on this passage—the doctrine of salvation after death; the doctrine of salvation through purgatory; and the doctrine of salvation by baptism. The term " spirit " overthrows all three.

The moral conditions and circumstances at the time the Apostle wrote corresponded to those in the days of Noah. Christ was not present corporeally, but by His Spirit He was pleading with men to escape from the wrath to come. The world disbelieved, a few believed and entered into an immediate and conscious salvation, but had to endure the scoffs and hatred of the unbelieving. But the Spirit of that unseen Saviour in them enabled them to witness as He enabled Noah. A prison awaited the unbelievers of that day, and the long suffering of God lingered then in compassion over man as it was now lingering over Israel on the eve of the destruction of Jerusalem. This comparison is confirmed by the words " My spirit shall not always strive with man . . . . yet his days shall be a hundred and twenty years " (Gen. vi. 3), and by the word, " the Spirit of Christ was in them " (1 Pet. i. 11). Now it would be an extraordinary thing that Christ should strive in testimony with the Antediluvians only after their death! They were in prison because they did not obey His Spirit pleading with them in Noah (2 Pet. ii. 4-9).

The sense of the passage therefore is, that during a hundred and twenty years while the Ark was being built, the Spirit of God in Noah warned men of the coming flood. Only eight believed; the rest disbelieved, and, as a consequence, were shut up in the prison of the abyss. The believers were sheltered in the refuge of the Ark, and were saved through the waters of the judgment in the baptism of the Ark. It suffered the judgment, passed through it, and rose out of it into a new earth. In the antitype baptism (v. 21 Greek) the believer is saved in the " baptism " of Christ at Golgotha, of which the baptism of the Ark was a type. Christ at Calvary was baptized into the wrath of God.• All the waves and billows of that wrath passed over Him (Ps. xlii. 7 and Jonah. ii. 3) and on the third day He arose. In that baptism the believer is baptized and saved, and in that resurrection the believer is raised and brought into a new world. So the sinner is saved by the baptism and resurrection of Jesus Christ (v. 21). He is not saved by the washing away of bodily defilement with material water, but by a sincere inward acceptance before God of this " baptized " and risen Saviour.

Salvation by water-baptism is not taught here, nor anywhere else in the Holy Scriptures; nor is after-death salvation; and as to the claim that verse 19 affirms the existence of purgatory, it is manifestly untrue, for verse 20 declares that these prisoners were infidels, and the Roman Church teaches that such at death pass into the realm of eternal damnation and have no benefit of purgatory. Therefore purgatory, even if it existed, has no place in this passage of Scripture.

That they should be so few in number and be so cruelly persecuted, discouraged and perplexed these believers of the Dispersion. The Apostle points out that God's people were always few in number and were always persecuted. For example Abel and Noah.

1 PETER IV.—The first six verses carry on the subject of suffering because of the Name of Christ; and the added argument here is, that suffering is better than sinning. To be exempted from suffering is desirable, but to be saved from sinning is much more desirable. This great truth lights up with fortitude and glory the darkest hours of pain and suffering.

To " suffer in the flesh " means to be put to death (v. 1). To arm oneself with the same mind is to reckon oneself to be dead (Rom. vi. 11). Death is an effective breach with sinning; for how can a dead man practise sinful passions (v. 2)? A living man. raised with Christ, lives to do the will of God.

" Us " (v. 3), i.e., " we Hebrews." At that time, and at many other periods of their history, the Hebrews tried to be as like the Gentiles as they could. To-day, as then, those who by a life of separation from sin testify against it (v. 4) are evil spoken of; but these evil speakers will have to account for their conduct to Him that is ready to judge the living and the dead (v. 5).

The sense of verse 6 is that the murder of God's servants was not accidental, or because the Devil was stronger than God, but because God had a purpose—hidden from His people but satisfactory to Himself—in permitting such cruelty. This permission manifested both the malignity of man's nature against God, and the triumph of faith in God. The blessed martyrs (the " dead ") were judged by men to be unfit for human society, and were consequently killed, but they were judged by God to be worthy of heaven's society and consequently glorified (Rom. viii.). Cain and Abel illustrate the verse. The Gospel was preached to them. Abel believed it. Cain judged him as to his flesh, i.e., he killed him, but Abel lives according to God.

" The end of all things,"—the destruction of Jerusalem—was then at hand (v. 7). The imminence of that judgment sobered the mind, restraining it from passionate outcries against persecution. and it disposed the heart to prayer.

The Apostle now passes from the outward circumstances of the little company of believers to its inner and mutual affections and ministries. (vs. 8-11). Fervent love was to rule their hearts, and mutual love to veil their faults, as Shem and Japhet cast a garment over their drunken father. The doctrine that a man can cover his own sins by " charity " is not taught here, for then the Greek middle voice would be used; but it is a quotation from Prov.x. 12.

Gifts follow grace (vs. 9-11). Those who could entertain were to do so without grudging ; those who preached were to keep within the living word of God as revealed in the Scriptures (v. 11 with Acts vii. 38, Rom. iii. 2, Heb. v. 12) ; those who were enabled by God to minister to the physical necessities of the brethren were to do so after a Divine manner ; so that these many-folded graces should be practised in a way that would give all the glory to God through Jesus Christ.

The Apostle now returns to the fiery trial of persecution which was then testing them (v. 12 R.V.). Satan controlled these persecutions (v. 8). But they were universal and not peculiar to the Hebrew believers in Asia Minor. Besides, God had a purpose in permitting them. Persecution purifies the Church and energizes Christian testimony. See note on verse 6. Trials do not " happen." They are designed by wisdom and operated by love. Job proved this. The world is the Christian's greatest enemy. Persecution cuts off from the world and breaks its snare.

To share Christ's sufferings (v. 13) is a cause of joy, but to share His glories will be to taste an exceeding joy. Moses esteemed His reproach greater riches than the treasures in Egypt (Heb. xi. 26), and consequently the spirit of glory and not of shame—the very Spirit of God—rested upon him, as it did upon Stephen visibly (Acts vi. 15). What man esteems to be shame faith cherishes as glory.

Believers were first nick-named Christians at Antioch (Acts xi. 26). History records that the witty people of that city were famous for inventing nick-names. The word occurs three times in the Scripture—here and in Acts xi. 26 and xxvi. 27 and 28. The Jews called them Nazarenes, the Scripture called them " brethren," " disciples," and " saints." To be so like Christ as to be called a Christian is to cause glory to God (v. 16).

Israel was the House of God. Judgment was about to fall upon it. The Romans were the instruments of that judgment. The Apostle, and those to whom he wrote, were members of that House. Hence the word " us " (v. 17). That House, as a house, knew the Gospel but did not obey it ; and, consequently, it was judged. The righteous members of the nation (v. 18) would with difficulty be saved out of the judgment—and so it proved—but as for the rest, multitudes perished by the sword, by famine, by pestilence, by banishment into slavery, and the residue were driven forth into all lands and forbidden under a threat of death to set foot in Palestine. Lot was a righteous man and he was saved with difficulty out of Sodom. Israel was saved with difficulty out of Egypt, and out of the wilderness. The righteous do not save themselves—they must be saved by a Saviour.

The argument of verse 18 is, that if in order to escape persecution they joined the ungodly and the sinners they would share their doom. There was but one thing to do (v. 19), they were to commit themselves to Him Who had created them and so knew and felt their sufferings ; He was a faithful Creator—faithful to His promises to them ; and it was His pierced hand which planned all for them according to His will. Thus had their Master acted (ii. 23). All the power of the God of all grace (v. 10) is engaged to carry the Christian safely through all the difficulties of the pilgrim way. That grace is sufficient for all the temptations and trials and sorrows and needs and dangers of the road.

Because God is holy His House must be holy also, else it must be judged (Ezek. ix. 6). Grace does not change the nature of God. Everything must be conformed to that nature or banished from His presence. Hence the necessity of the New Birth. Without it none can enter the family of God.

A shipmaster sees and understands the warning message of the lighthouse ; but if he does not obey it, he perishes. To hear and understand the Gospel is not salvation. The Gospel must be obeyed ; that is, there must be a definite surrender of the heart to the Lord Jesus Christ and faith in His precious blood as the atonement for sin.

The persecuted follower of Christ is not to commit himself to God in a passive quietism but " in well-doing." He is to be unceasingly active in doing good to his persecutors, and to all men.

1 **PETER V.**—The great figures here are those of the Chief Shepherd (v. 4) and the Roaring Lion (v. 8). The lesser figures are those of the under-shepherds and the flock. The under-shepherds are divided into seniors (v. 1) and juniors (v. 5). The Hebrew synagogue was governed by junior and senior shepherds, presided over by a chief shepherd. The Christian assembly adopted this system of government.

" Therefore " (v. 1, R.V.), i.e., because of the gracious provision of iv. 19. An Apostle to the Hebrew Church had to be a witness of the Crucifixion. Peter must, therefore, have been amongst those who stood " afar off " and witnessed it (Luke xxiii. 49). He here humbly claims to be only an under-shepherd, but hints at his higher dignity as an Apostle. Compare Acts i. 21, 22 ; ii. 32 ; x. 39. The sufferings are present ; the glories future—they shall be revealed.

Paul and his companion apostles having a special ministry (see notes on Ephesians) were outside of the requirements of Acts i. 21, 22.

" Feed " (v. 2), i.e., tend as a shepherd. This ministry occupies the interval between the sufferings and the glory. During that interval hope sustains the heart. The ground of that hope was to be confessed with modesty and caution (iii. 15). The Roman Church forbids this. It commands that its dogmas be received with unreasoning credulity.

The heart of the Apostle rested where the Lord placed it. He had said " tend my sheep" and " pasture my lambs." This He said only after He had led him to the humiliating confession that it needed the eye of God to see that His terror-stricken disciple really loved Him. It was when convinced of his utter weakness that the Chief Shepherd entrusted to him that which was dearest to Himself.

All in this chapter, as indeed in the whole Epistle, is Hebrew in character. Israel is God's House, Jerusalem the place of His throne and the moral centre of the earth. The Chief Shepherd will appear in glory, reward the under-shepherds with crowns, and establish the flock in the choicest places of the earth.

Already corruption had invaded the Gospel ministry. Men became pastors for the sake of a salary (v. 2 with Titus i. 7). Compare 2 Cor. xi. 8.

The flock belonged to God (v. 2). It was among, not beneath, the under-shepherds. It was God's great heritage (" heritages "). They were not lords over God's heritage, but only ensamples. Man has reversed all this.

" A crown "—not a diadem, for that only is given to a king—but a garland of victory (v. 4). Earthly garlands wither, but the crowns of glory for the under-shepherds are incorruptible.

All the sheep, including the pastors, were to be willing slaves to one another (v. 5,R.V.). They were to tightly fasten round them the humble working tunic of the slave, and to fasten it so firmly that it would not be loosened. Thus the Lord girt Himself with a towel on the night of the betrayal (John xiii.). There is an abundant provision of grace to enable the proudest heart to descend to this lowly service.

What a wonderful heart is the heart of God ! He does not wish to humble His children, so He begs them to humble themselves and only leave to Him the joy of exalting them ; and that He certainly will do at the fitting time.

God invites His people's confidence and offers to carry all their cares (v. 7). But how foolishly they act ! They cast away their confidence and carry all their cares.

But the depositing of all anxiety upon Him does not release from the necessity of self-control and vigilance, for Satan, as a roaring lion persecuting the people of God, is to be vigilantly watched. As a roaring lion he persecutes ; as an angel of light he deceives (Gen. iii. 1). He is more to be dreaded as an angel than as a lion.

" Steadfast in the faith " (v. 9), i.e., willing to suffer torture and death rather than deny the faith. Their afflictions were not confined to Asia Minor but were universal; for Satan as a roaring lion goes to and fro in the earth (Job i. 7).

In verse 10 the eternity of the glory is contrasted with the brevity of the suffering. Grace can make the feeblest Christian a full grown man, firm, courageous and immovable in the presence of torture and of death. But all the glory of this dominating grace must be for the Master and not for the servant (v. 11).

If verse 12 be coupled with 2 Pet. iii. 15, 16 and Acts xxi. 20 and 21, and if the notes on Galatians and 1 Corinthians be read, Peter's testimony to Silas as a faithful preacher of the true grace of God will be recognised as most significant and humble. Peter was the head of the Hebrew Church —he was the Apostle of the Circumcision. That Church regarded Paul and his companions Silas and Timothy, with much suspicion. Their teaching was declared unorthodox ; it was, therefore, a precious testimony on Peter's part to account Silas to be a faithful preacher of the true Gospel (v. 12 R.V.) ; and Peter adds : " stand fast in that true grace ! "

Whether the Apostle meant his wife (v. 13, R.V.) or the Christian synagogue at Babylon, or at Rome, or at Jerusalem is difficult to say. The argument of the Epistle, insisting that the Divine wrath was about to fall upon Jerusalem because it had morally become Babylon (compare Rev. xi. 8),inclines to the belief that that guilty city was here thus named and intended. The fact that Peter was the head of the Hebrew Church would make his residence at Jerusalem the more probable.

" A kiss of love " (v. 14). See note on Rom. xvi. 16.

The benediction of peace is limited to all that " are in Christ."

2 PETER

This letter was addressed to the same persons as the first letter (iii. 1) ; and also to the believing Gentiles who had attached themselves to them.

In it the Apostle continued to feed the flock, as commanded by the Chief Shepherd (John xxi.) ; and this obligation he more than once recalls (vs. 12, 13, 15, iii. 1, 2).

The main purpose of the letter was to warn the sheep against false shepherds ; but before giving these warnings he urged them to make their own calling and election sure—not sure in the heart of God, but sure to their cwn hearts—by so walking in faith and love as not to stumble (vs. 5-7 and 10). The Scripture was the divine and unfailing lamp (vs. 19-21) that would illuminate their path to the promised Kingdom (v. 11) ; and the great hope of their hearts was the promised appearing of the Messiah in power and glory (iii. 4, 9, 10, 12, 13, and 14). The instability of all that unbelief rested upon (iii. 4) i.e., the dissolution of the heavens and the earth (iii. 10)—was an additional warning inducing to holiness of conduct.

2 PETER I.—Faith is not bought, it is "obtained" (v. 1), and is the gift of grace operating as the result of God's righteousness vindicated and glorified at Calvary through Jesus Christ (Eph. ii. 4-9).

Faith is precious (v. 1) ; its trial is precious (1 Pet. i. 7) ; Christ is precious (1 Pet. ii. 4) ; His blood is precious (1 Pet. i. 19) ; and His promises are precious (2 Pet. i. 4).

The faith that saved a dying thief was the same that saved an Apostle, for its object in each case was the same (v. 1, Luke xxiii. 42 and Jude 3).

The Divine Titles given to Jesus in this chapter are : " Jesus Christ " (v. 1) ; " Our God and Saviour Jesus Christ " (v. 1, R.V.) : " Jesus our Lord " (v. 2) ; " Our Lord Jesus Christ " (vs. 8,. 14 and 16) ; and " Our Lord and Saviour Jesus Christ " (v. 11).

Life must precede godliness (v. 3). That life is " given " through a personal knowledge of the Giver ; and He by His Divine power provides everything necessary to sustain that life and its Christian manifestations. As moral glory and nobility of character characterized Him, so must they characterize those who live by Him. Not only does He give life (v. 3), but He gives also exceeding great and precious promises (v. 4). Glory, valour and divine promises are the objects of the heart that is under the dominion of His nature, and the power of that Divine nature saves from the corruption that is in the world (v. 4). These promises assure the glory to which the road leads ; and they assure the valour needed for the battles of the road itself. The Kingdom will be obtained then (v. 11) ; faith is " obtained " now (v. 1). It is nourished by the grace and peace which are multiplied through the full knowledge of God (v. 2, Greek). Grace and peace (v. 2) and fruit (v. 8) multiply as knowledge of Him deepens.

Only the possession of the Divine nature can deliver from moral corruption ; but it is not enough to have escaped evil, there must be victory (vs. 5-7) and fruit (v. 8) ; for if growth is lacking (v. 9) death results ; but if there is spiritual progress, assurance of salvation (v. 10) is enjoyed on the way and an abundant entrance experienced at the close (v. 11).

" Add in your faith valour " (v. 5, R.V.)— and for this very reason (" beside this ") that everything necessary to life and godliness has been provided. To valour were to be added knowledge, self-control, patience, godliness, love to fellow Christians, and love to all men—enemies and persecutors included. So the first and last links in the golden chain are faith and love. Love governs all and directs all. It is the nature of God. Faith is God's gift, and therefore it is not added to anything. It is the source out of which all virtues spring, and love is the point to which all virtues move. Hence "whatsoever is not of faith is sin" (Rom. xiv. 23); and "the end of the commandment is love" (I Tim. i. 5).

Whoever lacks "these things" (vs. 5-7) cannot see the glories that lie ahead, and forgets the happy day when Jesus washed his sins away (v. 9). His forgetfulness is evidenced by his returning to them.

The Apostle knew that there would be no Apostolic succession (vs. 13 and 15). Therefore he wrote these two Epistles. Like the Apostle Paul (Acts xx. 30-32) he handed them the Bible as the rule of Faith, and told them that false Apostles would succeed him.

As predicted (John xxi. 18) the agonizing death of crucifixion awaited him, but he went forward to meet it with the dignity and courage that faith gives. Man was not to destroy his body—he calmly says he himself was to put it off (v. 14). He could have escaped martyrdom.

The Gospel is based upon the testimony of the Apostles and the authority of the Scriptures (vs. 16-21); the latter is more permanent (v. 19) than the former. The Apostle was diligent (v. 15 Greek) to obey the command "Feed my Sheep"; and his testimony, and that of all the Apostles, was inspired of the Holy Spirit.

"He received honour and glory" (v. 17). Christ was then appointed as Priest, for the subject spoken of on the Mount was the atonement which He should accomplish at Jerusalem (Luke ix. 31). Compare Exod. xxviii. 2 for the priestly garments of honour and glory.

The words "in your hearts" (v. 19) should follow the verb "take heed." The Bible is a lamp. The world is morally dark and squalid, and will remain so until the Lord comes and the Day dawns. The words "private interpretation" should read "human origination," for that is the sense of the passage. The question is: where did the Holy Scriptures originate? The answer is: not in the will of man but in the Spirit of God. The Holy Spirit here declares that no

Scripture is of human origination, and in 2 Tim. iii. 16 He adds that all Scripture is of Divine inspiration.

2 PETER II.—The relation between this chapter and the previous one may be thus shown:

Teachers of Truth	The Apostles i. 16-18.
	The Scriptures i. 19-21.
Moral effect	Purity i. 3, 4.
Issue	Heaven i. 11.
Teachers of Falsehood	False Prophets ii. 1.
	Doctrines of destruction ii. 1.
Moral effect	Impurity ii. 2.
Issue	Hell ii. 17.

The Apostles and Prophets, inspired of the Holy Spirit, were teachers of Truth. The false prophets were teachers of falsehood. These introduced their heresies of destruction (Greek) so secretly that it is not easy to point out the exact date of the birth of their teachings. The principal doctrine they denied was that of the Atonement (v. 1). Christ purchased humanity with His precious blood; but only those who accept and plead that sacrifice enjoy its benefits; those who deny it bring upon themselves swift destruction. All who perish "destroy themselves" by their rebellion and unbelief; but the judgment is Divine (v. 5).

Infidelity and immorality are partners (v. 2). Those who profess to walk in the way of truth but deny its doctrines and practise the sins it condemns, cause truth to be evil spoken of.

God is fully awake to the actions of such false teachers, and He has not lost time in pronouncing their appointed doom (v. 3). The swiftness and certainty of their judgment is illustrated by the fate of the angels, the Antediluvians, and the Sodomites (vs. 4-6). The angels are cast into dungeons of darkness (v. 4 Greek) and there await judgment. The Antediluvians and the Sodomites are also reserved in the same prison-house unto the judgment of the great day (v. 9). But the righteous shall, like Noah and Lot, be delivered (v. 9).

"Now" (v. 3), i.e., threatened of old. See Jude 4 and 14.

The persons described in verses 10-22 were ministers in the Apostolic Church. At that early age gross corruption, both in doctrine and conduct, invaded the church; and after the death of the Apostles men were shut up to God and to the Word of His grace, i.e., the Bible.

But this chapter, as the whole Epistle, is a prophecy of the condition of the Hebrew Church immediately prior to the Lord's Second Coming.

"Dignities" (v. 10). Compare Jude 8-10. False teachers, as a class, are ordained to destruction. Members of this class on repentance and faith in the Lord Jesus Christ, can thereby become ordained to salvation (v. 3).

Verse 5 should read as in the Revised Version.

"Cursed children" (v. 14), i.e., professors who shall be sentenced to death (Matt. xxv. 41).

A dumb animal rebuked an inspired prophet (v. 16). Modern popular theology denies this, and so accuses the Holy Spirit of falsehood. It also characterizes the language of this chapter as violent and bigoted—declaring all men to be good at heart and to be the children of God. It denies the existence of these dungeons of darkness (v. 4); of a reservation to a future judgment (v. 9); of the malediction of verse 14; and of the eternal darkness of verse 17.

"Clean escaped" (v. 18), should be "just about to escape." A knowledge of the Gospel (v. 20) may be enjoyed without the occurrence of the New Birth (v. 22). The dog remains a dog though he may have turned for a time from his vomit, and the sow remains a sow though washed. Their nature is unchanged, and their willing return to what their nature craves, proves it. See note on 1 Pet. ii. 25.

Sinners destroy themselves (v. 1) and God destroys them (v. 5). The redeemed will ascribe their salvation wholly to God's free and sovereign grace, and the lost will ascribe their condemnation wholly to themselves; for the justice that brought the flood upon the ungodly was the righteousness that would have saved them as well as Noah had they believed the tidings of salvation.

2 PETER III.—The false teachers who, in the previous chapter, denied the Atonement (ii. 1) in this chapter denied the facts of the Deluge and the Second Coming (vs. 3-6). The Holy Spirit describes these ministers as " scoffers " (v. 3). The language of this, and the prior chapter, would be condemned in the modern popular pulpit as contrary to Christian love.

This letter was addressed to the same persons as the first letter (v. 1).

The word "Beloved" occurs four times and is a key-word: "Beloved, be mindful" (v. 2); "Beloved, be not ignorant" (v. 8); "Beloved, be diligent" (v. 14); and "Beloved, beware" (v. 17).

The commandment spoken by the Apostles, and the Word spoken before them by the Prophets, were equally inspired, for the one Spirit of Christ which was in them spake through them (v. 2).

How did Peter know what would happen in "the last days" (v. 3); and how did he know the conditions of "the world that then was" (v. 6); and how did he know the conditions of the world that is to be (vs. 7, 10, 12, and 13); and how did he know the Divine measurements of time (v. 8); and how did he know that all the Pauline Epistles were inspired (v. 16)? There is but one answer —Inspiration—for all these matters are as wholly outside the realm of human consciousness, intelligence, reason, and investigation as are the conditions present in the angelic and sidereal worlds.

Judgment fell upon these false teachers at the Coming of the Lord in wrath upon Jerusalem, and judgment will fall upon similar scoffing teachers at His future Coming (v. 3), for the moral conditions will be similar at both periods. Many ministers of the Gospel deny that there ever was a Flood. They are materialists and declare that all things continue as they were from the beginning of the Creation (v. 4). The language of this passage makes it plain that these are religious teachers having a knowledge of the Scriptures; and the term "the fathers" further shows that the Hebrew Church is particularly intended. It was to that Church the Apostle wrote, and these predictions mainly belong to it. These scoffers recognised Creation but denied revelation. Their ignorance was wilful (v. 5)—the world that then was perished, but was not, therefore, annihilated (v. 6).

There are two arguments based on verse 8. One; that a Divine promise is as certain of fulfilment in a thousand years as in one day —a human promise is weakened or destroyed by time. The second: that the Divine activity is unique so that God can spread over a thousand years, or execute in a single day any purpose of His mind or action of His hand. "This one thing" (v. 8), i.e., this fact of chief importance was to be recognised.

God " wills," i.e., purposes, and He " wills," i.e., is willing. Two different Greek verbs distinguish these activities of His mind (v. 9).

God is willing to save the scoffers (v. 9) of verse 3. He desires to save everybody if only they would come to repentance. The Greek verb here " come " implies certain reception.

The term " the Day of the Lord " in this passage is a covering term embracing the millennium and introducing the eternal state (Rev. xx.-xxii.). The prediction here is the dissolution of the material universe which man declares eternal (v. 4) and the substitution of a new heavens and a new earth. In these righteousness will " dwell " (v. 13) ; in the millennium righteousness will " reign " (Rev. xx. 6).

" Hasting unto " (v. 12), i.e., eagerly looking for and desiring (R.V.). That " day " is fixed and cannot be hastened. It is in the eternal state that all the promises of God will be finally accomplished. It is at the close of the millennium that the present universe is to be dissolved.

During the period of God's long-suffering with man's unbelief and rebellion, the Church is being gathered out (v. 15). This " mystery " was revealed to the Apostle Paul (see notes on the Epistle to the Ephesians), and he was inspired in communicating the revelation. In these writings the Spirit recorded the vacillation of Peter himself (Gal. ii. 11). Peter then and now humbled himself before the Spirit and salutes Paul as his " beloved brother." Two great statements of fundamental importance are made in verse 16 :—first : that " all " Paul's Epistles are inspired ; second : that they are as fully inspired as the " other " Scriptures. The statement is based upon the two words "all " and " other." Verbal inspiration is here asserted. If either of these words were omitted the assertion would have no authoritative foundation. There are no degrees in inspiration. It is a fact or it is not. They who sit where Mary sat have no views about inspiration. They recognise and believe the fact. They know it is the Shepherd's voice whether He speaks to them in Leviticus or John or Ecclesiastes, or Isaiah, or Canticles, or Revelation, or any other Book of the Bible. All are equally precious to those who know and love that Voice. It is true that one Book may be intended as milk for babes and another as strong meat for men, but all are equally inspired, for the speaker is the Shepherd.

The Apostle Peter knew that all the Pauline Epistles were inspired and had, therefore, equal authority with the rest of the Scriptures, and he here wrote this statement by inspiration. He could not have possibly learned the fact in any other way.

Instead of being led away with the erroneous teachings of wicked men holding office in the Church (v. 17), the lovers of the Scriptures are through them to grow in grace and in the knowledge of the Lord and Saviour Jesus Christ.

1 JOHN

The Gospel of John is objective; the Epistle, subjective. The message of the latter is the humanity of Christ ; that of the former, His Deity. Ere the Apostles were dead the actual physical human body of the Lord Jesus was denied to have really existed. It was declared to have been visible but not real. His Deity was also denied.

Prophetically the Epistle belongs to the future. Its interpretation concerns Hebrew believers during the period immediately prior to the Coming of the Lord (ii. 18, 28, iii. 2 and iv. 3).

The Epistle contains two sections. The first : the children in the bosom of the Father—Christ and the children having the same title. The second : the children in the world—Christ and the children having the same power, i.e., the Spirit. As in the bosom of the Father, the children are sinless —for how could sin be embosomed there ? As in the world, they are sinful and perpetually need the efficacy of the blood and the advocacy of the Paraclete.

The word " if " occurs twenty-one times in the Epistle. Four times in the form " ἐι " and seventeen times in the form " ἐάν." "ἐι " means a fact ; " ἐάν " a probability verified by experience.

The term " as He " is to be noted in this Epistle.

1 JOHN I.-II. 6—." That which was " —not " began to be " — but " was " essentially (Greek), i.e., a living and life-giving Word, Jesus Christ. Here is a demonstration of verbal inspiration. The gradation of " heard," " seen," " looked upon," and " handled," is noteworthy. The eternal Sonship of Jesus of Nazareth is here affirmed ; and the unity of the Father and the Son is declared in the statement that fellowship with either means fellowship with both (v. 3). Fulness of joy in both teacher and pupil (v. 4) depends upon this fellowship with the Father and with the Son ; and that fellowship is the subject of this first paragraph of the Epistle.

Light is righteousness, sin is darkness. To live a sinful life and at the same time to profess (v. 6) to have fellowship with God, is to act a lie. That fellowship can only be enjoyed as a man walks in the light as God is in the light. The reference in verse 7 is to Aaron, as representative of Israel, having fellowship with God in the Most Holy Place. There was the Light, the sinner and the blood. The Light flashing from between the cherubim above the blood-sprinkled Mercy-Seat revealed the sinfulness of Aaron, and at the same time revealed the preciousness of the blood sprinkled upon and before the Mercy-Seat. That blood was all the time he was there cleansing him in type, from all sin ; that is, it had an ever-present efficacy. Hence in verse 7 the force of the word " cleanseth " —not " has cleansed " nor " will cleanse."— has no reference to time but to efficacy, as when it is said that a medicine cures a disease. The fellowship " one with another " means fellowship of the believer with God in the Light, just as Aaron had fellowship with God in the Light. It is only in the Light, and in virtue of the efficacy of the atoning blood of Christ, that fellowship with God can be enjoyed. All who declare that they have fellowship with God and yet deny the Deity and the Atonement of Christ are self-deceived and are liars (v. 6), for they are walking in the darkness.

Christ is the Life (v. 2). That Life in its infinite preciousness is manifested in the Person of Jesus. The believer contemplating all His perfections, His obedience, His purity, His grace, His tenderness, His patience, His holiness, His love, His sinlessness, can say :

"That is my Life!" The Life was manifested, therefore it is no longer necessary to grope after it in the darkness of the natural heart in order to find it, nor to labour fruitlessly at religious ceremonies in order to obtain it. It is revealed—it is in Jesus—whoever possesses Him possesses that Life and Light.

He Who is the Light and the Life reveals God (v. 5). This knowledge is of priceless value for it searches the heart. It also declares the Deity of Christ, for only Deity could reveal Deity. That Light judges everything, and is the rule of faith to those who walk in it. The moral rule of the Christian's will is God Himself as revealed in Christ and the Scriptures.

There are seven "ifs" in this paragraph of the Epistle and they are divided into three and four—three declarative of condemnation, and four revealing salvation. "If we say we have no sin" (v. 8)—degradation of human nature; "if we say we have not sinned" (v. 10)—defilement of human conduct; "if we say we have fellowship with Him" (v. 6)—darkness of the human mind. The four "ifs" revealing salvation are— Justification (v. 9); Sanctification (v. 7); Preservation (ii. 1); and Consummation (ii. 3)—"to know that we know," and "to know as we are known," unites the knowledge of heaven and earth.

"No sin" (v. 8), i.e., no sinful nature. As to "our sins" (v. 9) He is faithful and just to forgive them. His faithfulness is involved because He promised to forgive; and His righteousness is in question for it would be unjust to punish sin a second time—the penalty of the believers' sins having been already borne at Calvary. The Spirit reveals these truths in order that the believer may not sin (ii. 1); but if he does sin he has an Advocate who is the Righteous One and at the same time the Mercy-Seat, His Work, His Person and His Action all unite in maintaining the believer in the enjoyment of conscious fellowship with God. As a Priest He deals with the guilt of sin; as an Advocate, with the restoration of the soul. Sin interrupts communion; the Advocate restores it. The efficacy of His action is guaranteed by the righteousness of His Person and the value of His propitiation, and these are unchangeable. Before Peter sinned He prayed for him; when he sinned He looked on him; and when he repented He restored him—and restored him so effectually that Peter was able to strengthen his brother Apostles. So efficacious is that Mercy-Seat as a propitiation for sins, that did all men approach Him for forgiveness of sins then all men would be pardoned. The atoning sacrifice of Christ furnishes an ample provision for the redemption of all men, but its benefit is only appropriated by those who believe.

He Whose life is moved and governed by the Scriptures knows that he knows Him (v. 3)—not that he comprehends Him, but that he knows Him. Whoever professes to know Him and yet does not subject his heart and mind to the Bible, i.e., "His commandments"—is a liar and self-deceived (v. 4). He Who is governed by the Bible in him is the love of God perfected; that is, His love aims at the believer being saved and knowing it, and living a life of victory over sin and of conscious communion. That love plans and provides this life of assurance, enjoyment and holiness, and is perfected where these aims are realized (v. 5). Subjection to the Scriptures (v. 5) and Christ-like conduct (v. 6) are tests of profession; where these are absent spiritual life is absent.

The first step in the life of walking in the light (i. 7) is the confession of sin; the second step (ii. 1) is the forsaking of sin.

The Holy Spirit is the Paraclete within the believer (Rom. viii. 26 and John xiv. 16) on earth, and Christ is the Paraclete for the believer in heaven (ii. 1). His righteousness is both the foundation and the energy of His advocacy, for if He failed He would cease to be righteous. His advocacy is limited to believers—for they only avail themselves of it—but His propitiation extends to wherever sinful men exist. Substitution is only true in respect of His people, but propitiation is universal. These should not be confounded.

The believer is to walk as He walked (v. 6). He is sanctified unto the obedience of Jesus Christ. He obeys on the same principles as those on which Jesus obeyed. It is the obedience of a life to which it is natural and delightful to do the will of God. A child submits to the will of the parent, but Christ did not obey in that way. He came to do the will of God. Obedience was His mode of being and the law of His being. This great inward principle, that is, the Divine nature operating in the believer, motives and characterizes his life. Only those who possess that new nature can understand this principle of obedience. All who are destitute of a spiritual birth are outside of, and ignorant of, this realm of love and light. It is a common life—common to Christ and to the believer (ii. 8).

"We make Him a liar" (i. 10), i.e., contradict God. Compare ch. v. 10.

I JOHN II. 7-29.—The old commandment and the new commandment are the one commandment (v. 7), and the word "love" is the commandment (John xiii. 34). This energy was true in Him, for He was the True Light then shining, and it was true in them because the darkness was passing away (v. 8, R.V.) Whoever professed to be in the light and was energized by hate, was in the darkness even though the light was shining all about him (v. 9), for love and hatred cannot dominate the heart at the same time. He that loved dwelt in the light and was not a moral stumbling-block to others (v. 10). To walk in the light is to be governed by love; to walk in the darkness is to be governed by hatred (v. 11).

The foundation consciousness enjoyed by the Sons of God is that their sins are forgiven for Christ's sake (v. 12 with Eph. iv. 32). Here is the fundamental Divine principle of grace and acceptance; and neither merit nor demerit can affect it. God forgives sin not because of any merit in the sinner, but because of the infinite merit of the Saviour.

In verses 13-27 the sons are segregated into "fathers," "young men" and "babes." The babes know the Father; the young men overcome the Wicked One; and the fathers know Him that is from the beginning. To know Him in Himself and for Himself, apart from His gifts—though they are priceless and precious—is the highest knowledge.

In the East a letter is written as read by the receiver. Hence the past tense is used. Here (vs. 13 and 14) East and West come together; for in verse 13 the writer says "I am writing" and then in verse 14, contemplating the receiver, he says "I have written." In verses 14-27 he developes the messages of verse 13; but as to the "fathers" he cannot develop the supreme experience of knowing Christ, so he repeats it. It is otherwise with the young men. They were strong, the Word of God abode in them. They wielded the sword of the Spirit and so defeated Satan. But the tendency of youth is toward the world (vs. 15-17). The ardour

of nature, the vigour of health unite to draw the heart in that direction. There must be total separation from all that appeals to the natural heart and will (v. 16). For the world is opposed to God, and the heart that loves the world is a stranger to the love of God (v. 15). The term "overcome" (v. 13) is characteristic of the Apostle John. It was His Master's (John xvi. 33); it occurs sixteen times in the Apocalypse; six times in this First Epistle; and only three times in the rest of the New Testament. The Father and the world, the Spirit and the Flesh, Christ and the Devil are here put respectively in opposition. These agents are viewed in their source and moral nature and as Authors of principles that act in and characterize those subject to them.

The "babes" are now addressed and are warned with tender affection to beware of teachers that sought to seduce them from the truth (v. 26). It was "the last time" (v. 18) because Christ had already been manifested, and until He had come the Advent of an Antichrist was impossible. But directly He came an Anti-Christian opposition at once appeared; and it will have its climax in the Antichrist. All the period, therefore, from the First to the Second Advents may, in this sense, truly be called "The last time." This, and the following Epistles, belong prophetically to "the last hour" of "the last time" (v. 18, R.V.). These teachers might believe all that a Hebrew believed as revealed in the Scriptures, and yet deny that Jesus was the Messiah. To do so was to deny both the Father and the Son (v. 23, R.V.). Antichrist will declare that he himself is the Messiah (2 Thess. ii.). The foundation of Christianity is that Jesus of Nazareth is the Messiah. All who claim to worship God and yet deny the Godhead of Jesus Christ, deny both the Father and the Son, for to deny the Son is to deny the Father.

These Anti christs came out from among the Christians (v. 19), but all professors are not Christians (v. 19). Their presence, however, in the Christian fellowship tended to shake the faith of the babes. The Apostle strengthens their faith by reminding them of the Spirit that dwelt in their hearts (vs. 20 and 27) and of the Scriptures that rested in their hands (v. 24). These two Divine safeguards—the Holy Spirit and the Holy Scriptures—preserve from error, and teach young converts to recognise and reject false teaching (vs. 20 and 27). What these babes heard "from the beginning" (v. 24) was later on written by Divine inspiration, and together with the Old Testament formed the truth, the Word of God. The Roman Catholic plea of "Development" is overthrown by the words "that which is from the beginning," for the safeguard here pointed to is, that and only that which was heard from the beginning; and the sheep listen to nothing else, for they know the Shepherd's voice.

Young converts as indwelt by the Holy Spirit and taught by the Holy Scriptures, not only know what is the truth but they are able to detect a lie as being opposed to the truth (v. 21). They are furnished with a Divine equipment capable of causing them to know "all things" (vs. 20 and 27). In themselves they have no such competency —the ability only resides in the anointing.

Verse 22 should read as in the Revised Version; and, also, verse 23.

Safeguarded by the Holy Spirit and by the Holy Scripture the babes were assured of the enjoyment of the promise of verse 25. The words "abide in Him" (v. 27) should read as an imperative.

In verse 28 the Apostle resumes his address to all the children, as in verse 12. Their Christian conduct was to be such that neither they nor their Apostolic teacher should be put to shame at Messiah's appearing.

Righteousness is not natural to man (v. 29). If, therefore, anyone manifested the righteousness *which appeared in Christ* —and the knowledge of Him as "The Righteous One" provided such discernment —such a person was born of God, for similar fruit demonstrates similarity of nature. Abel was a "doer" of righteousness (iii. 12) in that he humbled himself to God's way of life and acceptance through the death of the Lamb of God. See notes on chapter iii. and Gen. iii.

"Last hour" (v. 18, R.V.), i.e., the then last hour of God's patience over Jerusalem --but all appeals were in vain, so the king sent forth His armies (the Romans) and destroyed those murderers (of His Son) and burnt up their city (Matt. xxii. 7).

I JOHN III.—"Called" (v. 1), i.e., elected to be, and recognized as sons by God. With Him "to call" is to cause to be sons; and believers are such (R.V.). The world does not recognise nor acknowledge believers as sons of God; just as they did not recognise nor acknowledge Christ to be the Son of God.

The term "manifested" occurs three times in the Greek Text (vs. 5, 2, and 8) and responds to three cries of the heart. First: the cry for liberation from sins and their eternal doom. Answer: He was manifested to take away sins, and as He could not possibly fail in what He came to do the believer learns with wonder and joy that his sins are taken away for ever (v. 5). Second: the cry of the renewed heart to be sinless. This cry will be satisfied when He shall be manifested, for His people shall be like Him (v. 2). Third: the cry of anguish and perplexity of the heart awakened to the misery, injustice, cruelty and suffering in the world. The answer is found in verse 8. They are "the works of the Devil" and the Son of God was manifested to destroy them, and will do so.

Whoever has the hope set on Him (v. 3) of seeing Him as He is, seeks to be as like Him now as possible. He purifies himself. Christ does not need to purify Himself, for He was, and is, ever sinless; and sin is a violation of law (v. 4). The Christian cannot practise what Christ came to take away and to destroy (vs. 5 and 8), hence Joseph said: "How *can* I do this great wickedness" (Gen. xxxix. 9). Sin dwells and reigns in man; it dwells but does not reign in a believer. His heart, like the magnetic needle, may be disturbed by a temporary attraction, but it hastens to its resting-point, which it always re-seeks.

Whoever is truly born of God does not live a life of sinning (v. 6) for he is dominated by the Divine nature received at conversion, and that nature cannot sin because it is Divine (v. 9). To "commit sin," i.e., to practise sinning and to live a sinful life, is foreign to true conversion. Whoever lives in sins has never been born of God (v. 6). He that "does righteousness" (v. 7)—as Abel did (v. 12)—is righteous as He is righteous. Christ defines and standardizes what is righteousness. Whoever lives a life of habitual sinning (v. 8) is the moral child of the Evil One—though he may be a very religious man like Cain (v. 12)—and is energized by the Spirit of Satan. There is no middle class between children of God and children of the Devil. Abel was a child of God and Cain a child of the Devil. To "do righteousness " (v. 7) is to act as Abel did (v. 12). He humbled himself and accepted God's way of righteousness. To "commit sin " is to act as Cain did. His religious works were evil (v. 12). He was a religious man but not a righteous man. His worship would have secured the admiration of "modern thought" but the Holy Spirit here says it was evil. He rejected the Divine Way of Righteousness and thus shewed that he was "out of" the Evil One (v. 12). Popular modern preachers teach that both religions were equally good ; but God did not think so, for He accepted the one and rejected the other. He also here states that there is a Devil ; and that morally he has children ; and that these children may be very religious. See notes on Matt. xiii. 36. Satan has two ways of salvation : one by sacraments, and the other by ethics. Christ's Atonement—possessing infinite moral value— condemns and destroys both these false ways of seeking acceptance with God. Christ is the measure of the believer's acceptance ; and, therefore, that acceptance is perfect, full, and eternal. In that righteousness no one can find a flaw ; and it needs neither ecclesiastical ceremonies nor human merits to add to its perfection.

Having declared that righteousness characterizes the children of God as contrasted with the children of the Devil (vs. 1-12), the Apostle now points to love as another characteristic of the Divine family (vs. 13-24); for just as Christ is the measure of righteousness so is He the measure of love. What love is can only be learned at Calvary (v. 16). It would be a marvel if the world did not hate the believer (v. 13). The term "world" means the unconverted. Abel's "world" was Cain (v. 12). The believer is conscious that he has Divine life because he loves his Christian brothers ; and Divine "life" and "love" are synonymous terms. To "abide in death" (v. 14) means to be spiritually dead, i.e., never to have been born again.

If the Christian practises the sympathy of verses 17 and 18 he can walk before God with an assured heart (v. 19) ; but if his heart condemns him in this matter he cannot enjoy this Divine fellowship for he knows that God knows much more than he does, and is, therefore, fully acquainted with all his selfishness (v. 20). An uncondemning heart (v. 21) has confidence in the presence of God, and receives from God (v. 22) because His commandments are obeyed and the things

that please Him are practised. His "commandments" are comprised in the one great "commandment" (v. 23) : Believe the Lord Jesus Christ and thou shalt be saved ! " and to do the things that are pleasing in His sight is to love one another (v. 23). So obedience and love demonstrate the presence of the new nature in the believer (v. 24) ; and the Spirit makes the fact of this indwelling conscious to the believer. The fact is true to faith ; the enjoyment of the fact is conscious to obedience.

" Of God " (v. 10) ; " of that Wicked One " (v. 12) ; " of the Truth " (v. 19). These mean born of God ; born of the Wicked One ; and born of the Truth.

The Christian is to preach John iii. 16 and practise 1 John iii. 16. The first verse is more popular than the second, for the one speaks of what the believer gets ; the other, of what he should give ; and it interprets the meaning of the words " this do in remembrance of Me." See notes on 1 Cor. xi.

1 JOHN IV. 1-6—The mention of the Holy Spirit and those whom He inspires (iii. 24) gives occasion for this parenthesis which instructs with respect to the Evil Spirit and those whom he inspires. The Apostle provides two tests which decide whether a teacher in the Christian fellowship spoke by Divine or by Satanic influence. The two tests are : the confession of Jesus the Messiah having come in flesh (v. 2) ; and second : subjection to Apostolic doctrine, (v. 6).

Christ come in flesh, i.e., in actual physical and perfect humanity involves atonement and resurrection ; for in order to die as the sin-offering He must become man, for God could not die ; and that His atoning death should have a demonstration of Divine acceptance He must be raised from the dead, otherwise His oblation failed in its purpose and did not satisfy the claims of righteousness. The Docetae of that time, like the Christian Scientists of to-day, distinguished between Jesus and the Messiah. They taught that the Messiah was an Illusion, a Power, that influenced Jesus of Nazareth. The Messiah, therefore, had no proper actual humanity.

What the Apostles taught was by the Holy Spirit committed to writing, and all teachers of truth (v. 6) teach what they taught.

These two tests, i.e., presenting Christ as a personal Saviour, and subjection to the Holy Scriptures as the Divine fount of doctrine, reveal the true minister of the Gospel.

To confess Jesus Christ having " come in flesh " is more than the intellectual acceptance of the doctrine of the Incarnation. It is a confession to Him and of Him personally that involves conversion and the New Birth ; and a presentation of Him to guilty men as the only Saviour of man.

The term " spirit " (v. 1) means a religious teacher who claims to speak by inspiration. There were many false teachers already in the Church at that early date (v. 1).

The sense of verse 3 is : that Antichrist will deny that Jesus was the Messiah "come in flesh"; that he himself will claim to be the promised Messiah ; and that already the spirit that will energize Antichrist operated in the Apostolic age.

The " them " of verse 4 means the false prophets of verse 1.

In verses 2 and 14 the perfect tense is used in the Greek text implying not only a past historical fact but a present moral continuance of the fact and its effects upon the human heart. The statement that the Messiah " came in flesh " affirms His previous existence before He came. To deny the reality of His flesh, i.e., His manhood, is to deny His love and His Deity. Everyone that is of the truth hears His voice (John xviii. 37).

These verses show that it is the duty of the Christian to be what is contemptuously called " a heresy-hunter."

The sacrifice of the Mass denies the full and proper humanity of Christ, for a human body cannot be broken into millions of pieces as in the Mass and yet be a human body.

Christ as the fulness of the Levitical Offerings appears here, but most plainly in chapter i, where the order is the same, beginning with God's glory (the Burnt-Offering) and ending with man's need (the Sin-Offering). Thus : the Burnt-Offering—that which might be only looked upon and handled, but not eaten (ch. i. 1-3) ; then the Meal-Offering and the Peace-Offering (vs. 5-7) ; and lastly the Sin and Trespass Offerings (vs. 8-10).

1 JOHN IV. 7-21—The main subject of the Epistle resumes here. This is shown by recalling the commandment of iii. 23—" This is His commandment that ye love one another "—" Beloved, let us love one another " (v. 7).

The three tests of true conversion, i.e., obedience, love, and the indwelling of the Holy Spirit, are now developed. In order to know what love is, and in order to feel and to express that love, the nature that loves must be possessed. God is love. It is His nature. He is its source. He is essentially love and not merely loving. It is not said : " Love is God," but : " God is love " ; therefore a man who does not love does not know God and never knew Him (Greek). Love is the nature of God ; and by virtue of the New Birth the believer becomes a partaker of that nature, and his actions exhibit the affections of that nature. Thus he knows God, and begins to know what love is in its fulness. By fixing his attention on the perfection of God's love as exhibited at Calvary(vs. 9 and 10), the believer is saved on the one hand from mysticism and on the other hand from doubt. Mysticism occupies itself with its love for God, and doubt occupies itself with God's love to it.

But it is a knowledge of the perfection of God's love as exhibited in the gift of Christ (v. 9) and in His atoning sacrifice for sins (v. 10), and it is occupation with that love, which perfects love in the heart of the believer A child who knows the perfection of its father's love to it, confides fully in him without terror, and in that sense has a perfect love for its father (v. 18).

God's love is perfected " towards " believers as sinners (vs. 9 and 10) ; it is perfected " in " them as sons (v. 12) ; and it is perfected " with " them as servants (v. 17). Hence the three terms : " towards us " ; " in us " (v. 12) and " with us " (v. 17, margin).

In the section (vs. 9-19) the great doctrines of Life (v. 9 " that we might live through Him ") ; of Peace (v. 10 " He is the propitiation for our sins ") ; of Power (v. 13 " He hath given us of His Spirit ") ; and of Boldness (v. 17, margin " love made perfect with us "), are developed.

Christ as He stands before the Throne of God in the glory represents the believer while yet in the world. All that He is in the sinless perfection of His nature is the property of the believer, who can, therefore, say : " Thus I stand before God ! "

To find love, i.e., God, attention must not be directed inwardly—as some say—for God loves man without finding any love whatever in man (v. 19), but attention must be directed outwardly to Christ as the propitiation for sins (vs. 9 and 10).

No man has seen God at any time, but when as the result of the New Birth he partakes of the nature of God, then the unseen God dwells in him and he knows Him.

The Apostle (vs. 14 and 16) saw Christ —as sent from God—the Saviour of the world (John iv. 42) ; he recognized that love, and confided in it (v. 16) ; and, consequently, that perfect love dismissed terror from his heart (v. 18).

If a man professes to love God but is dominated by a nature that hates, he is self-deceived (v. 20) ; for the Divine commandment is that whoever professes to love God must also love his brother (v. 21).

This love is not known by the poor results of its action in man but by its perfect action in God ; and that perfection manifested itself at Calvary. This perfect love is a fact, and it manifested itself outside of man in order to the salvation of man. The believer knows it by the gift of God's Son, and he enjoys it by the gift of God's Spirit. It is at Calvary that he learns what love is (v. 10) ; and that when he had no love for God, God loved him perfectly though he was far from Him and dead in sins. Man has no love for God ; his pretension to possess it is self-deception. He cannot find it by searching within himself, but he can know it as manifested in the atoning sacrifice of Christ. He gave the Life which loves and made propitiation for sins.

Those who really possess this Divine nature love because they are loved. It is especially a fraternal love ; it loves fellow-believers more intimately than the nearest relatives who are unconverted. It binds the heart with a stronger bond to persons never seen than to the dearest companions of childhood: It is a new nature, a realm outside of natural human affection—a realm of Divine love—of fellowship with God and with all who know Him. There is in truth no love outside that realm.

1 JOHN V.—Because a "brother" (iv. 21) is born of God therefore everyone that is born of God and consequently loves God loves the brother so divinely born. Love for fellow Christians evidences true love for God ; and this love is active toward all believers whether agreeable or disagreeable, because the motive is the fact that they are born of God. To love those that are pleasant is not, at base, divine love. The test of true love for the brethren (v. 2) is a love for God that keeps His commandments. Unless He is loved they are not loved as born of Him. They may be loved as companions or as friends, but not as the children of God if God Himself be not loved. If He has not His true place in the heart that which bears the name of love shuts Him out. Obedience to His commandments proves love for Himself. To actively love those who do not keep His commandments whilst professing to be His children, is not to love them as children. To unite in disobedience under the pretext of brotherly love with those who profess to be the children of God, is not to love them as children of God, and is not to love God and keep His commandments. True brotherly love is to love all the children of God within the realm of the commandments of God. To encourage disobedience to God is not true brotherly love but carnal love.

The commandments to love are not grievous to love (v. 3). The little girl who was commiserated because of the heavy baby she carried exclaimed brightly : " Oh, but he is my brother ! " The great obstacle to this love and its obedience is the world (vs. 4 and 5); but the faith that is born of God overcomes the world ; the faith that is born of reason is overcome by the world. The faith that is born of God believes upon Jesus as the Son of God (v. 5).

Only those who are born of God divinely believe that Jesus is the Messiah (v. 1). The Christian Scientists deny the identity of Jesus with the Messiah. They teach that the Messiah, as a Spirit, descended upon Jesus Who was only a man. They, therefore, are not born of God. Continually in this Epistle the Holy Spirit employs the titles God and Christ interchangeably and predicates the same things indiscriminately of both. Hence to believe in Jesus is to believe in God and to be born of Him.

" Whatsoever " (v. 4), i.e., the whole body of the regenerate (John iii. 6 and vi. 37 and 39).

The faith that believes that Jesus is the Son of God (vs. 4 and 5) defeats the teaching of the world which denies His Deity. Whoever is truly born of God does not commit that sin (v. 18). The " supreme sin " of this Epistle is the denying of the essential humanity and eternal Deity of Jesus of Nazareth. That denial is a sin unto death (v. 16). See note on Jer. vii.

The eternal life (v. 11) is not in the first Adam but in the Second; and because it is in Him it is eternally secured to all who believe upon Him. Man as born of Adam does not possess it and cannot acquire it. The effect of the Law was to demonstrate both facts.

Three witnesses testify to the fact that eternal life is in the Son. The three witnesses are the Spirit, the Water and the Blood. These three agree in the one testimony. That to which they bear witness is the gift of eternal life to man; and that that life is in the second Adam. The water and the blood flowed from the pierced side of Jesus. They provide expiation and purification. They doubly testify to the humanity (v. 6) and to the Deity (v. 5) of the Lamb of God. The Spirit bears witness to the life-giving water (John iii. and iv.) and to the sin-cleansing blood (v. 6). They provide life and peace (Col. i. 20); and the Spirit floods the soul with love (Rom. v. 5). See notes on Lev. xiv.

The water witnessed to His full and proper humanity (John xix, 34), the blood witnessed to the nature of His atoning death (John xix. 34), and the Spirit witnessed to the Deity of His person (Mat. xxvii. 54 and Luke xxiii. 42, and 44).

The believer's sins are, therefore, fully expiated and He enjoys a perfect purification before God. That which was impure no longer exists, for the old man is crucified with, and dead with Christ; that which exists as born of God is perfectly pure. Only death could provide this expiation and purification; and the out-flow of water and blood from the Redeemer's side demonstrated the actuality of death. The pouring of all the blood of the sacrificial lamb at the base of the altar declared the actual death of the lamb, and fore-shadowed the actual death of the Lamb of God at Calvary beneath the wrath of God.

The popular belief that man can be his own saviour by sacrificing his life for others, whether on or off the battle-field, is overthrown by the doctrine of verse 12.

The Spirit did not write these things in order that believers might doubt their possession of eternal life, but that they might be assured of it (v. 13, R.V.). It is impossible to pray with confidence (v. 14) if there be uncertainty upon this fundamental point. Prayer, according to God's will, is an activity growing out of the consciousness of the sweet relationship of a child and a father. Such an intimacy involves harmoniousness of will and only asks for what accords with that will. Faith, as in Hannah's case (1 Sam. i. 18), claims the answer before the fulfilment (v. 15).

To " request " is to demand; to pray is to intreat. Sickness and death when God is in the Camp are punishments for rebellion in doctrine or conduct (1 Cor. xi. 30); and there are sins, like that of Ananias and Sapphira, which are unto death. No " request " should be made for them (v. 16, R.V.). Jesus " requested " for He was Jehovah's fellow. He did not intercede for the sin-hardened world (John xvii. 9), for it sinned unto death, but He made request for the Roman soldiers, for they knew not what they did. Compare James v. 13-20.

Satan cannot tempt that which is born of God (v. 18). He finds nothing in the new man to entice.

Verses 19-21 form a summary of the whole Epistle. The believer possesses a divine nature, the object of his heart is Christ, and all outside of Him is idolatry.

2 JOHN

It is thought by many that this "Elect Lady" signifies a church, but the import of the letter, and the personal address of the Third Epistle, and the use of the word "mercy" in the greeting, confirm the belief that this Epistle was also personal. Both are precious specimens of private letters in the Apostolic age.

The Greek word "lady" is Kyria It is the Hebrew "Martha."

Very important features appear in this brief letter. The ordination of a preacher was not to be questioned, but what he preached was to be judged; and a woman was capable of exercising this judgment and was responsible to do so. The First Epistle taught her (iv. 1-6) how to exercise that judgment. See notes on 1 John iv.

This Elect Lady was evidently a woman of wealth, a mother of children, and had a house large enough to entertain travelling preachers. She was to shut her door against whoever did not hold the Apostolic teaching respecting Christ. She was not even to "salute them" so as not to form any association with them, however attractive and amiable they might personally be. Such action to-day would be condemned as unchristian, narrow and bigoted.

But the semblance of love which ignores truth, or accommodates itself to that which is not true, is not love according to God. The test of true love is the maintenance of truth. The Holy Spirit fills the heart with the love of God (Rom. v. 5). He is the Spirit of Truth and His office is to glorify Christ. It is impossible, therefore, that a love which condones teaching that dishonours Christ can be of the Holy Spirit.

True Christian love is based upon truth (v. 1), and is exercised in the interests of truth (v. 2), and it is only in the realm of truth and love that grace, mercy and peace can be enjoyed (v. 3). They who love in the truth also love because of the truth.

"Commandment" (v. 4). This is a covering term for the Gospel as delivered by the Lord Jesus from the Father to the Apostles (v. 5). The nature of that Gospel is love; for that is the nature of its Author. The standard of truth is, therefore, the Holy Scripture as the Word or Commandment of God. That some of this lady's children were converted to God and walked in the truth of God (v. 4), caused intense joy to the Apostle.

What does not accept the inspiration and authority of the Scriptures of Truth is not Christian love (v. 6).

Every preacher who does not proclaim Jesus to be the Messiah manifested in actual human nature, is a deceiver and an Antichrist. See notes on 1 John iv. 3. Whoever denies Christ's proper human nature, and that He came in such a nature, denies the possibility of the incarnation; whoever denies that He has come, denies its actuality. Antichrist will deny both, declaring himself to be the promised Messiah.

Verse 8 should read as in the Revised Version margin. Good deeds are the fruit of good doctrine (v. 8), evil deeds, the fruit of evil doctrine (v. 11). Cain and Abel present an illustration (1 John iii. 12). This fundamental principle is of vital importance, especially in the present day when a Scriptural creed is denounced as being opposed to religious liberty. But it is a basic fact that character is moulded by belief.

"Transgresseth" (v. 9). The Greek means "goes beyond" the teaching respecting Christ. As to-day, so at that time, "Advanced Thought" had many followers. All however who reject a Divine and atoning Saviour reject God. Only they who accept the teaching of the Holy Spirit respecting the Person and Work of the Lord Jesus Christ know God and possess Him. All who reject His Godhead and atonement have a god of their own imagination; and that god is an idol.

Such teachers are not to be received into Christian families (vs. 10 and 11).

" If there come " (v. 10). The Greek verb is here in the indicative mood intimating that such do actually come and are sure to come. True love shuts the door against such religious teachers, as teachers. Love should minister to them if in affliction or sickness, but it was not to help them in their propaganda of error.

The distinction between " you " and " thee " is to be noted in the Epistle.

3 JOHN

As the previous letter was written to a wealthy woman telling her to shut her door against preachers of a false Gospel, so this letter was written to a wealthy man telling him to open his door to preachers of the true Gospel.

Three men are named : Gaius, Diotrephes and Demetrius. Gaius was evidently a man of substance and one of a small circle of friends who were true to the Scriptures, faithful to the Apostle John, and despised by the local church. Diotrephes was the ruler of that church, probably by self-appointment and popular election. He and the church rejected the authority of the Apostle (v. 9) ; refused to receive preachers accredited by him ; and excommunicated those who did receive them (v. 10). Demetrius was an evangelist (vs. 7, 8 and 12), commended by the Apostle and many others, and accredited as a preacher of the truth by the spiritual results of his ministry (v. 12).

The letter shows to what a head false doctrine and evil conduct had come at that early age ; and it is a vivid picture of the present condition of the modern church. Corruption in doctrine, rejection of Apostolic teaching, ecclesiastical assumption, and a little group of personal friends faithful to the Word of God, active sympathizers with and supporters of evangelistic work, unrecognized by the Church, and actively opposed by its leaders.

The Apostle prayed "above all things" that Gaius might be as healthy in body as he was in soul. This suggests that he was not strong physically (v. 2) The prayer conflicts with the teaching which states that full physical health accompanies full spiritual health.

"The truth that is in thee" (v. 3), i.e., Gaius' fidelity to the truth evidenced by his hospitality to its messengers (vs. 5 and 6).

Verse 5 should read as in the Revised Version.

The fact that these itinerant preachers refused to accept money from the Gentiles ; the import of the repeated word "we" ; the force of the expression "and not for ours only" (1 John ii. 2) ; and the distinction marked by the word "Gentiles" support the belief that these itinerant preachers were Hebrew disciples.

To give hospitality to the preacher of the Gospel is to be a fellow-helper with the truth (v. 8).

The Apostle wrote to the church to receive these preachers, but the church, led by Diotrephes, refused to do so, and excised those who did (vs. 9 and 10). Most probably the church was composed of Gentile believers.

The word "beloved" occurs four times (vs. 1, 2, 5, and 11) and reveals Gaius as a believer (v. 1) ; as a sufferer (v. 2) ; as a worker (v. 5) ; and as a doer of good (v. 11). See notes on 2 Pet. iii. and Jude.

A good report of the truth itself (v. 12) is evidenced when spiritual fruit accompanies ministry.

Demetrius knew that the Apostle John only commended true men (v. 12).

The little group of friends faithful to Apostolic teaching was so small that they could be greeted by name.

Insistence on the Truth as the test for the last days in receiving, or not receiving preachers, is very remarkable. The question of authority to preach is not even hinted at. What was preached was the fundamental matter and question. Further, it is instructive to observe that Gaius persevered in his independent action in spite of the condemnation of the church and its government. The authority of the preacher lay altogether in his fidelity to truth. The Apostle pointed to no authority which sanctioned his mission, the absence of which would prove it to be false or unauthorised. The Apostle himself had no other way to judge of the authority of these preachers. There was, therefore, no other than the truth itself, for had there been any other authority it would have been vested in the Apostle. So he did not instruct Gaius or Kyria to examine their papers but to test their doctrines. If they brought the truth they were to be received, if they did not bring the truth, the doors were to be closed against them.

JUDE

The apostasy of the last days prior to the Coming of the Lord will be, as predicted in the New Testament, both doctrinal and moral. This Epistle develops the history of that Apostasy, and reveals its root—both doctrinal and moral—in the self-will of Cain. His followers, like himself, doctrinally went out from the presence of Jehovah (Gen. iv. 16 with 1 John. ii. 19), and then privily creeping back into the visible church, like Lamech (Gen. iv. 19-24), returned to corrupt it morally.

The Epistle foretells that there will be no arrest to these double Apostasies, and it predicts their continuance up to the appearing in judgment of the Lord Jesus with the angels of His might (2 Thess. i.). This prophecy and fact conflict with the belief that Christendom will be recovered from its present corruption; that the Gospel will conquer and purify the nations; that God's moral government will be established thereby in the earth; that that is what is meant by the Coming of the Lord; and that His personal visible return is not a doctrine of the Scriptures.

2 Peter and this Epistle envisage the same period of time—the former views its sin; the latter, its apostasy. Both Epistles trace these doctrinal and moral rebellions to their root in the self-will of man.

The arrangement of the Epistle in triplets and quartettes is remarkable. The former are :

Chosen, loved, kept (v. 1 R.V.).
Mercy, peace, love (v. 2).
Ungodly, distorters, deniers (v. 4).
The People, the Angels, the Sodomites (vs. 5-7).
Defile, despise, revile (v. 8).
Cain, Balaam, Korah (v. 11).
Hidden rocks, false shepherds, waterless clouds (v. 12).

Fruitless trees, raging waves, wandering stars (v. 13).
Murmurers, complainers, boasters (v. 16).
Separatists, sensualists, carnalists (v. 19).
Convince, save, pity (vs. 22 and 23 Weymouth).
Before all time, now, evermore (v. 25 R.V.).

The quartettes are :—
Beloved, beloved, beloved, beloved (vs. 1 R.V. 3, 17, 20).
Saves, destroys, reserves, sets forth (vs. 5, 6 and 7).
Ungodly, ungodly, ungodly, ungodly (v. 15).
Building, praying, keeping, looking (vs. 20, 21).
Glory, majesty, dominion, power (v. 25).

Judas was a brother of the Lord Jesus Christ after the flesh but His bond-servant after the Spirit (v. 1). See note on Matt. xiii. 55.

Christ keeps His own for God (John xvii. 12), and God keeps His own for Christ (Jude i., R.V.) and thus the prayer of John xvii. 11 has an assured answer.

Mercy, peace and love (v. 2) correspond with chosen, loved and kept (v. 1 R.V.).

The "beloved" of verse 1 (R.V.) establishes the position of the believer; that of verse 3 commands him to be a contender for the faith; that of verse 17 urges him to the study of prophecy; and that of verse 20 animates him to a life of conscious enjoyment of God's love, and to an expectation of Christ's Coming. See notes on 2 Pet. iii. and 3 John.

The sense of verse 3 is : that as Jude was thinking of writing a letter explanatory of the way of salvation, such probably as the Epistle to the Romans, news reached him of such a nature as to cause him to put that project aside and hasten to write this letter urging believers to contend earnestly for the faith once for all entrusted to them. It was a fully revealed faith, needing no additions, repelling all corruptions, and infallibly declared in the Apostolic writings.

"Ordained" (v. 4), i.e., fore-written in 1 Tim. iv. 1, 2 Tim. iii. 1, and in 2 Pet. ii., iii. Such false teachers are ordained to judgment; they are ungodly; and they distort grace and deny Christ. If any of them, however, repented, even for such there was mercy and pardon—they might be snatched out of the very fire (v. 23). "Of old," i.e., by Enoch (v. 14).

"Once" (v. 5), i.e., already familiar to you.

"In like manner" and "likewise" (vs. 7 and 8), i.e., in self-will like the Israelites, the angels and the Sodomites. Self-will is the root of wickedness, as is taught in the Book of Proverbs.

Verses 4 and 25 declare Jesus of Nazareth to be the One and only and eternal God: The oldest manuscripts and versions read "Jesus" in verse 5 as having saved the people out of the land of Egypt and afterwards as having destroyed the unbelievers. He saves (v. 5); He destroys (v. 5); He reserves (v. 6); He sets forth (v. 7).

"Strange flesh" (v. 7), i.e., unnatural vice. Yet Ezek. xvi. 53-55 predicts the restoration of Sodom. "Sodom" may, however, mean Jerusalem.

"The Body of Moses" (v .9) means the Hebrew Church, as "the Body of Christ" (Eph. i. 23) means the Christian Church. Israel was baptized "into" Moses in the judgment of the Red Sea (1 Cor. x. 2) and thus in that baptism became his body. The Church was united with Christ in the baptism of Calvary and so became His body(Rom. vi.). The dispute with Satan was that of Zech. iii. This is clear from the expressions "Jehovah rebuke thee"; "the garments spotted by the flesh"; and "saved with fear pulling them out of the fire." Joshua in his spotted garments represented the Hebrew people, i.e., "the Body of Moses" recently plucked out of the Babylon fire. See notes on Zech. iii. The Hebrew name Michael means "like unto God." Compare Heb. vii. 3. It is Messiah's title as Head of the angelic princes. In the Hebrew text of Dan x. 13 He is styled the First of the chief princes; in Dan. xii. 1, the Great Prince; in 1 Thess. iv. 16 the Archangel; in Jude ix. Michael the Archangel; and in Rev. xii. He appears as the Great Captain of the angelic hosts battling with Satan. Here these antagonists once more appear disputing about "the body of Moses" —now represented by the woman of verse 1. Satan's object was, and is, and will continue to be the total destruction of the Hebrew people. Mark xiii. 20.

"Woe unto them" (v. 11). The imprecatory prayers of the New Testament, and their related praises, are much more terrible than those of the Old Testament. For example: Acts viii. 20, Rom. iii. 8, Gal. i. 8, 1 Cor. xvi. 22, Rev. vi. 10, viii. 13, xi. 5 and 6, xvi. 5-7, xviii. 20, xix. 1-5, xxii. 11, 18 and 19.

The way of Cain was man's way of life and righteousness as opposed to God's way (see notes on Gen. iv.); the error of Balaam was hiring himself out as a prophet; and the gain-saying of Korah was his rebellion against Aaron as God's appointed priest. (See note on Num. xvi.). This was, in principle, a denial of the High Priesthood of Christ. He was dissatisfied at being only a minister, and claimed to be a sacrificing priest. He has many successors in corrupt Christendom; for all who are officially ministers, but claim to be sacrificing priests, are, in principle, partakers in his rebellion.

"Spots" (v. 12) should read "hidden rocks" as in the Revised Version. The entire verse should read as in that version.

The prophecy of Enoch (v. 14) is an illustration of the Law of Subsequent Narration. The Holy Spirit introduces it here, and states that Enoch prophesied "to these" false teachers (R.V.) who corrupted truth in his day, who corrupt it ever since, and who will corrupt it in the future days of which this Epistle treats. The spurious "Book of Enoch" was, no doubt, based upon this verse.

False teachers ever pay court to the great and rich for the sake of the advantage which they hope to thereby gain for themselves.

The earliest prophecies concern Christ's Second Coming in glory rather than His First Coming in humiliation. Prophets used the past tense because the fulfilment of their predictions was certain.

This prophecy (v. 15) is the oldest specimen in existence of Hebrew poetic parallelism. Lamech's poem was perhaps composed in mockery of Enoch. The one announced coming judgment; the other denied there will be any judgment. All opposition to truth and its confessors is "against Him" (v. 15).

Jude does not say "Remember the words of us the Apostles," but, "Remember the words of the Apostles" for Jude was not an Apostle. These words are found in Acts xx. 29, 1 Tim. iv. 1, 2 Tim. iii. 1, 2 Pet. iii. 2.

"Mockers" (v. 18). This special Greek word is only used here and in 2 Pet. iii. 3.

"Separate" (v. 19), i.e., arrogantly set themselves up as leaders of the Church. Verses 17-19 illustrate the importance of the study of prophecy in relation to the life of holiness.

The verbs "building," "praying," "keeping," and "looking" (vs. 20, 21) form the four sides of an impregnable moral fortress. To "keep in the love of God" means to keep in the conscious enjoyment of that love as revealed by Him in Christ. It is God's love to the believer and not the believer's love to God.

There are three groups reviewed in verses 22 and 23 R.V. The first group was to be reasoned with; the second, energetically saved; and the third, pitied as being beyond human help. This compassion was to be accompanied by fear on the part of the Christian lest he himself should fall. With these last there was to be no association whatever, even in such outward and necessary things as a garment illustrates. A garment is a necessity, but if it had even one spot of leprosy upon it, it was to be hated and destroyed (see notes on Lev. xiii.-xv.). Gold and brass are necessary and valuable metals, but Moses destroyed the gold of which the calf was made, and Hezekiah the brass of the brazen serpent. Both metals were "spotted by the flesh" because connected with idolatry. The brazen serpent, like the Paschal Supper, was of Divine appointment, but both having become idolatrous should alike be judged. See notes on Deut. xx.

"Now unto Him" (v. 24). This should rather read "But unto Him" so as to emphasize the contrast between the love of the believer to Christ and the hatred of the unbeliever against Him. Only those who are loyal to Him and prove His power to keep them from stumbling on the highway of verses 20 and 21—only these are able to save others (v. 23).

Verse 25 should read as in the Revised Version. It declares the eternal Godhead of Jesus Christ.

Thus this Epistle guides the Christian as to his conduct in the midst of the corruption of Christendom; reminds him of the infinite provision provided for him in the Scriptures as his counsellor; and animates him with the promise and assurance that his Lord will never fail him but will guard him even from stumbling.

NOTE ON REVELATION i. 1.

This verse is the key to the entire Apocalypse, and forms the link with Dan. xii. 1 and 13. The fact that no such swift succession of judgments have occurred at any period during the past nineteen centuries, proves that the whole prophecy belongs to the future. (See page 1027.)

REVELATION

Israel's Redeemer appeared to Daniel (x. 5 and 6) and unveiled to him (v. 14) what should befall the Hebrew people in "the latter days," and in Rev. i. 13 He appeared to John and revealed, or unveiled, to him a development of the events affecting Daniel's city and people at the time when the Fourth Kingdom should appear in its final form as ten confederated kingdoms under the rule of Antichrist. Hence this Book is called "the Revelation," or unveiling, which the Messiah, as Son of Man, made to John in continuation of that previously made by Him to Daniel. Daniel predicted the coming and character of Antichrist: The Revelation unveils what will take place during the government of that prince and oppressor.

The entire Book is, therefore, a Hebrew prophecy. Its imagery, its language, its promises, its glories and its judgments have Jerusalem and Palestine as their centre. The Book thinks in Hebrew, and was most probably originally written in that language. It belongs to the Hebrew Church of the Acts of the Apostles. That Church embraces all the Gentiles who believe on Jesus as the Messiah "come in flesh" (1 John and 2 John). The Church revealed to the Apostle Paul does not, therefore, once appear in the Book, just as it never once appears in the Book of Isaiah.

The repeated statements in Daniel (vii. 18, 22, 27, viii. 10, 11, 19, 23, 24, ix, 24-27, x. 14, xi. 41, xii. 1-3 and 13) that the events predicted of all four Empires up to the very end concern the Hebrew Church, throw a flood of light upon the Book of Revelation, and help the reader to interpret it. The Book is largely, therefore, a development of Dan. xi. 36, and details the deeds that will be done by God in His judgments, first upon Israel as His house, and then upon her oppressors. These oppressors will be led by the last great Emperor, guided and energized by Satan

In this Book the word "heaven" is always used in the singular number in contra-distinction to the "earth." It closes the great controversy between heaven and earth which began in Genesis. This is one of the many links that bind the first and last Books of the Bible together.

The Messiah's visible appearing in judgment is the great climax of the Book.

The three Hebrew Books of Matthew, Hebrews and Revelation are rich with quotations from the Hebrew Scriptures. Matthew contains 92, Hebrews 102, and Revelation 285. The title "Son of Man" is proper to the Book. It is never once used in St. Paul's Epistles to the seven Churches. It occurs 84 times in the New Testament outside those Epistles. Its first occurrence is Matt. viii. 20, where it is said: "The Son of Man hath not where to lay His head," and the last is in Rev. xiv. 14 where the Son of Man is seen having on His head a golden crown.

The title "The Almighty" occurs 9 times in the Book and only once elsewhere in the New Testament. See note on 2 Cor. vi. 18, and then only as a quotation. It is expressed in Hebrew by two titles, viz., Jehovah Sabaoth, i.e., the Lord of Hosts, and El Shaddai, i.e., God All-Bountiful. The respective contexts suggest that El Shaddai should be read in 2 Cor. vi. 18 and Rev. i. 8, iv. 8, xi. 17, and xix. 22, and Jehovah Sabaoth in Rev. xv. 3; xvi. 7, 14, and xix. 6, 15.

All the titles given to Christ in the Book are significant, and are drawn from the Old Testament. They are: the Son of Man, the Almighty, Jehovah Elohim, the First and the Last, He that cometh, the Living One, etc.

The term "The Day of the Lord" (i. 9) means "the day" of God's wrath. This is the subject of the Book. Into that "day'

John was carried by the Spirit, as in iv. 2. The other Hebrew prophets such as Isaiah, Zechariah, Daniel, etc., were similarly carried by the Spirit into that same future Day of the Lord. The term does not mean Sunday.

Daniel and Revelation are identical. Dan. xii. 7 and Rev. x. 6 illustrate this fact. Both Books relate to the time when the Living One shall come to deliver Daniel's people and to destroy their oppressors. See final note on Rev. xviii.

The subject of the whole Book is the visible appearing of the Messiah in power and glory to execute this double purpose. Hence the expression " The Day of the Lord " furnishes the key to the Book. It is a Hebrew prophecy respecting the Hebrew people ; and it unveils their future deliverance and glory.

The expression " He that hath ears," etc., occurs 14 times—6 times in the Gospels and 8 times in the Revelation. Compare Mal. iv. 5. It signifies responsibility. He to whom the message comes must obey it.

The vision of " The Man " in Daniel x. and Rev. i. helps to show the unity of these Books.

The seven synagogues of chapters ii. and iii. belong to the past and to the future. They are assemblies of Hebrew believers in Jesus as the promised Messiah. They represent Israel as the House of God. Judgment, therefore, begins at that House ; for judgment will characterize the Day of the Lord. The seven golden lamp-stands picture the nation in Dispersion but divinely recognised. The one golden lamp-stand of the Tabernacle marked the unity of the nation when in the land.

The Four Gospels unveil the First Advent ; Revelation unveils the Second.

The letters to the seven synagogues were to be bound in " a book " i.e., the Book of the Revelation (i. 11), and the entire book was to be sent to each Assembly;

The language of chapters ii. and iii—with certain characteristic terms and expressions—makes it clear that the Hebrew and not the " Mystery " Church is here addressed. The latter Church does not once appear in this Book. The arguments in support of this statement will be briefly found in " The Apocalypse " by E. W. Bullinger, D.D.

The content of the Book may be thus set out :

Introduction i.
  Daniel's people on the earth ii. iii.

  Heaven iv. v.
    Earth vi.-vii. 8.
  Heaven vii. 9-viii. 6.
    Earth viii. 7-xi. 14.
  Heaven xi. 15-19.
    Earth xi. 19
  Heaven xii. 1-12.
    Earth xii. 13-xiii. 18
  Heaven xiv. 1-5.
    Earth xiv. 6-20.
  Heaven xv. 1-8.
    Earth xvi. 1-xviii. 24.
  Heaven xix. 1-16.
    Earth xix. 17-xx. 15.

  Daniel's people on the new earth xxi.

Conclusion xxii.

The Introduction and the Conclusion correspond. Each consists of four pairs of four members each.

The seven pairs of visions predict the results on earth of occurrences or utterances in heaven.

As predicted in Rom. xi., all Daniel's people who share his faith shall be saved, and their salvation will be the riches of the Gentiles ; for all nations are to be given to that people and to their Messiah, and will be, consequently, redeemed and blessed.

Daniel foretold the First Advent (ix. 26) and the Second (ii. 44). The rejection and crucifixion of Messiah was to be the sad feature of the First, and the deliverance of Israel from the Anti-Messiah the glad hope of the Second. John in his Gospel supplies the details respecting the one prophecy, (see i. 2) and in the Revelation the particulars respecting the other (i. 19). The terms " Word of God " and " testimony of Jesus Christ " (vs. 2 and 9) unite his two Books.

As the circumstances of the First Advent occupied about seventy years, so by analogy those of the Second may be expected to occupy a like period.

Seven benedictions are recorded in the Book : i. 3, xiv. 13, xvi. 15, xix. 9, xx. 6, xxii. 7 and xxii. 14.

The four main Bible divisions are :

The Old Testament—The King promised.
The Gospels and the Acts—The King rejected.
The Epistles—The King hidden.
The Apocalypse—The King revealed.

During the period that the King is hidden the Church occupies the Divine activities.

The relation of the Five Books of the Apocalypse to the Five Books of the Psalter and the Five Books of the Pentateuch may be thus recognised :

Pentateuch	Psalms	Apocalypse
Genesis	i.-xli.	i.-iii.
Exodus	xlii.-lxxii.	iv.-ix.
Leviticus	lxxiii.-lxxxix.	x.-xi.
Numbers	xc.-cvi.	xii.-xviii.
Deuteronomy	cvii.-cl.	xix.-xxii.

The theme in the Three Books of the Pentateuch, the Psalter and the Apocalypse is the same, i.e., a Prince and a Saviour appearing for man's redemption and sin's retribution ; and the election of Israel as the depository of this revelation and their consequent supremacy over all nations. As stated in Rom. xvi. 25 and Eph. iii. 5 the Church does not appear in any one of these Three Books. They have priceless teaching for the Church ; but they belong to Israel.

Genesis records the election and declension of the House of God, i.e., the Hebrew people (Heb. iii. 6). This is the theme of Rev. i.-iii. Judgment begins at that House. Exodus tells of the redemption of the oppressed and of retribution upon the oppressor. Such is the double theme of Rev. iv.-ix. The Paschal Lamb and His precious blood with which He purchased the land and the people, are features of this Second Book. Leviticus deals with worship and witnessing. The Tabernacle was the place of worship, and also the tent of testimony. These features appear in Rev. x.-xi. The Temple is mentioned four times, and is that which Moses was commanded to copy (Heb. viii. 5). The two witnesses and the worshippers complete the picture. Numbers records wandering and war. These are the subjects of Rev. xii.-xviii. Deuteronomy has as its Divine title " These are the words " ; and it predicts at its close the happiness of Messiah's kingdom (xxxiii. 26-29). In Rev. xix.-xxii. Messiah appears as " The Word of God " and establishes His Kingdom of felicity and glory in the restored earth.

The actual prophecy occupies chapter ii. 1 to chapter xxii. 5. The opening and closing words of the book are therefore chapter i., and chapter xxii. 6-21. This locates the words " Write the things which thou hast seen."

The first and last occurrence of the word " love " in the Bible are Gen. xxii. 2 and Rev. i. 5, and the theme of both is atonement.

REVELATION I.—This unveiling of the future was given by God to the Messiah as Man that He should communicate it unto His servants, i.e., Daniel's people ; and the Messiah, as with Daniel, employed an angel to make it known to John. The word " signified " (compare John xii. 33, etc.) has not here the symbolic force which some give it ; and the word " shortly " means " swiftly " in the sense of Luke xviii. 8, (see note). The sense is that the events of " the Day of the Lord," here unveiled, will succeed each other swiftly as the plagues of the Day of the Lord in Egypt. The events being Divinely ordained they " must " come to pass. [See note on p. 1024.]

John's testimony that Jesus the Messiah is the Word of God, and that he actually saw Him and the things that He did, is recorded in his Gospel and in his Epistles. Compare John i. 14, xxi. 24, and 1 John i. 1, 2, and 3.

To read, to keep in memory, and to obey the words of this prophecy, though they will not be understood until " the time " in view becomes " at hand," i.e., contemporary history, bring special promised blessing to the student ; yet multitudes of Christian people make light of this promise for they neglect this book. The entire Book is a prophecy ; and, as already stated, concerns the Messiah and the Hebrew Church.

The sense of the statement " the time is at hand," is to be understood as an assurance that the time will surely come when all the events of this prophecy will take place.

The Seven Assemblies, or Synagogues, represent the Hebrew Church of the Apostle's day, and the Seven Angels represent its government. Prior to the destruction of Jerusalem Israel, as a nation, rejected the Messiah, but a multitude of both priests and people believed upon Him. These formed synagogues and outlived the destruction of the city and Temple ; but in exile. These assemblies of believing Israelites formed, officially, the Hebrew Church. But just as the nation rejected the Messiah, so the Church forsook Him. It became corrupt ; and, as the House of God, was judged. This judgment is the subject of chapters ii. and iii. Judgment begins at the House of God ; and such is the position of these chapters in the prophecy. Judgment swept this Church away as it swept the Temple away. But both are to be restored, and will become the great golden lamp-stand.

As stated in the Introduction these Seven Assemblies do not represent the Christian Church. That view runs counter to the principle that Scripture interprets itself. Revelation teaches how to understand the times, not the times how to interpret the Revelation. The number seven expresses totality ; it is written on the face of the Hebrew Scriptures.

The Divine titles of this chapter are given indiscriminately to God and to Christ. He is the One Who is and Who was and Who is to come (v 4). With the three titles of verse 5 compare Isa. lv. 4, Col. i. 18, Ps. lxxxix. 27 and 37. Rev. xix. 16 and Ps. ii. 2 and Dan. viii. 25.

"Unto Him that loveth us" (v. 5, R.V.), for He says to Israel : " I have loved thee with an everlasting love " ; and He has purposed that that people shall be a royal priesthood to God and His Father. Compare Exod. xix. 6 and I Pet. ii. 5 and 9 He washed because He loved. Not the reverse. So the Apocalypse opens with the blood of Christ for sin, and closes (xxi. 8) with the lake of fire in sin. There is no middle position. The sinner must make his choice.

"Behold He cometh with clouds " (v. 7), i.e., in judgment, and they especially that pierced Him shall see Him ; for it will be a personal coming, and all the Twelve Tribes of the land shall mourn in respect of Him, as Joseph's brethren in like manner the second time mourned. " Even so ' is Greek, " Amen " is Hebrew. Both mean the same. Compare Matt. xxiv. 30, xxvi. 64, Mark xiv. 62 and Dan. vii. 13 and 14. This mourning is described in Zech. xii. 10-12, and is there declared to take place in " The Day of the Lord." This fixes the meaning of Rev. i. 10.

The title " Alpha and Omega " is explained in verse 17 and in xxii. 13. See Exod. iii. 14, Isa. xli. 4, xliii. 10, xliv. 6-8, xlviii. 12 and Rev. xxi. 6. " The Lord God " (v. 8, R.V.), i.e., the Jehovah Elohim of Gen. ii.

" I John " (v. 9) Compare " I Daniel " (Dan. vii. 28, ix. 2 and x. 2). " Also," i.e., I am an Apostle as well as a brother and companion in the tribulation and kingdom and patience which are in Jesus. This is the true reading. The kingdom was theirs in Him, but they had to wait for it, and, while waiting, suffer tribulation because of it.

Paul was placed in Arabia in order to receive the revelation made to him there, and John was placed in Patmos for a similar purpose. It is quite possible also that he was banished there because of his fidelity to the Gospel.

The sense of verse 10 is that the Apostle was carried in a spiritual trance into the future Day of the Lord (see Introduction and iv. 2, xvii. 3 and xxi. 10). All that he saw and heard when in the trance became therefore to him contemporary history.

The entire prophecy (v. 11) was to be written in a book and sent to the Hebrew Church as represented by this Heptad of synagogues. It is an error to suppose that these seven letters were sent separately to these seven assemblies.

" To see the voice " (v. 12), i.e., of Him that was speaking.

The Temple at Jerusalem was the great golden lamp-stand. It was near destruction, and this heptad of lamp-stands outside the land and placed among the heathen formed the Divinely recognized testimony to the Messiah. Like the Temple they were judged and removed. But there will be a restoration. The gold symbolizes Divine relationship and appointment. The voice was as of a trumpet, for judgment is the subject of the scene and of the entire Book. The assemblies form a camp and the Messiah is pictured walking amidst them just as He walked in the midst of the camp in Deut. xxiii. 14, and He appears clothed as the Divine Aaron and in aspect as the Ancient of Days (Dan. vii. 9). His voice was as the noise made by the waves of the sea upon the shore (v. 15). His feet as of burning brass symbolized judgment, as also did the sharp two-edged sword that proceeded out of His mouth. These are all Old Testament similes. Compare Dan. vii. 9, Ezek. i. 24 and 26, viii. 2, xliii. 2, Isa. xlix. 2, Matt. xxiv. 50 and 51, Luke xii. 46, xix. 27, 2 Thess. ii. 8, and Rev. ii. 12 and 16 : xiv. 2, xix. 15 and 21. His countenance shone as the sun in its strength, so, though the lamp-stands were removed, the light remained in its Divine power and fulness. The light is not the Church, as many think. It is only a lampstand. The stars appeared probably as a star-studded crown in His hand (Isa. lxii. 3) and symbolized Israel (Zech. ix. 16).

This great voice summoned with authority John's attention and he turned aside to see it, as Moses turned aside to see the bush, and both prophets saw the One Messiah, as God the consuming fire indwelling Israel, and yet was not that Church consumed. Here He appears as Son of Man, for such is His relation to the Hebrew Church. He is also the Ancient of Days. and is Jehovah. His eyes, His feet, His countenance and the sword of His mouth were all as fire, for He here appears as the Righteous Judge. John, like Daniel and Isaiah, fell at His feet as dead (v. 17), but the Messiah claimed to be the Redeemer as well as the One and only God, the First and the Last (Isa. xli. 4, xliii. 10, xliv. 6, xlviii. 11, 12), "the Living One" (Joshua iii. 10), He Who indeed became dead but returned to life for evermore, the Conqueror of death and the grave ; thus as Man obtaining the victory over all that man was subjected to by sin and which fills him with terror (Heb. ii. 14 and 15).

Most commentators apply the command of verse 19 to the whole period from Pentecost to the Second Advent. But verse 10 confines it to the future Day of the Lord (see note on that verse). And as the prophetic past tense in Hebrew is used when predicting the certitude of future events, and as the verb "to be" often signifies "to represent," the Greek text may read thus : "Write the things thou shalt see and the things they represent, even things which shall be soon." John was told what the things he saw represented, and that they all belonged to the near future. Verse 1 expresses necessity, "must come to pass" ; verse 19, sequence, things soon to come to pass. So the Apostle wrote all that he saw, and he added what they represented (v. 20). Thus verse 20 illustrates verse 19.

Directly the Messiah appears as risen from the dead (v. 5) the song of praise bursts forth and salutes Him as the Atoning Saviour. Atonement is the basis of worship.

REVELATION II.—Failure and its cause is the subject of the message to the seven groups of Hebrew Christians viewed as a camp in its totality. This chapter and the succeeding may, perhaps, be a prophetic picture of the Hebrew Church at the opening of the future "Day of the Lord," when Divine relations will have been re-established

with that Church, as promised in Acts xv. 16 and 17.

The groups are divided into three and four. In the first three promise follows injunction ; in the last four the order is reversed.

The Judge does not pass along a line of assemblies but walks in the midst of them (v. 1). The reference here is to Deut. xxiii. 14 and Lev. vi. 12. He holds firmly the seven stars in His right hand and addresses these "angels," i.e., the government of the Synagogue. The assembly (James ii. 2 and v. 14) met and was governed as a Synagogue (v. 9 and iii. 9). These were not private communications to an ecclesiastic, but public messages to the churches (v. 7).

The judgment upon Ephesus was that they no longer loved Him as they did at the first (v. 4). Service and orthodoxy had displaced Him (vs. 2 and 3). It was a fall from a great height (v. 5). There cannot be a true testimony where He has not the first place in the heart. See note on Acts xx. 38 and 2 Tim. i. 15.

This judgment is preceded and followed by praise (vs. 2, 3 and 6). Nicolaus is the Greek name of Balaam. The Nicolaitanes raised fornication to a religious ceremony and made it the highest act of worship.

"He that hath an ear" (v. 7), i.e., all to whom the Word of God comes are responsible to hear and obey it ; and such will be judged accordingly.

When Satan fails to entice the Christian back to the world he plans to interest him in doctrine, or service, or both, so that these take the place in his heart that Christ Himself should occupy.

Sins and not sinners should be hated (v. 6).

The promises to the overcomer mount as the defection of the church descends. The ascent is from the Tree of Life (ii. 7) to the Throne of the Messiah (iii. 21). Life is the first necessity and must precede kingship. The intervening steps mark the upward path of ever increasing glory.

These promises to the Hebrew Church of the past and of the future respecting fidelity in testimony are based upon action, and should not be confounded with the promises of life and forgiveness made in the Gospel to guilty sinners.

Christ as God is the First and the Last ; as Man He became dead and returned to life (v. 8).

"The synagogue of Satan" (v. 9) "the

throne of Satan " (v. 13) and " the depths of Satan " (v. 24)—these statements help to make clear that the great protagonists in this Book are Satan and Emmanuel. This conflict unites this latest Book of the Bible with the oldest (Job) and so finishes the Mystery of God (Rev. x. 7).

The claim to be Jews (v. 9 and ii. 9) and therefore members of the synagogue of Emmanuel, proves these assemblies to be composed of Hebrews.

Christ does not entice men to follow Him by promising them ease and pleasure, but plainly tells them that they shall have pain and death. When Garibaldi in 1860 offered similar terms to the Italian youth they flocked in thousands to his standard.

The ten day tribulation is usually understood to mean the ten persecutions under Rome Pagan. But the argument here is the brevity of the trial. The term " ten days " is a Bible expression for a very short period. Compare Gen. xxiv. 55, Num. xi. 19.

" That ye may be tried " (v. 10), i.e., cast into prison in order to be tortured to death.

The temporary pain of the first death is here contrasted with the enduring pain of the second death (vs. 10 and 11). Smyrna was to make its choice. If it feared the hurt of the first death then must it suffer the unspeakable hurt of the second. Here the distinction between the judgment of a church and the justification of a believer must be observed.

To animate them to be faithful unto death He tells them that He Himself was tortured to death (v. 8) but returned to life ; and that He will reward the victors with a crown of life. So the glory of that crown attracts, and the horror of the second death terrifies.

Pergamos was the seat of the ancient mysteries (v. 13). It contained a Temple of world-wide fame and of great magnificence, devoted to the worship of the serpent as the god of healing. He was named Esculapius. Its votaries boasted of the " deep things " of these sacred mysteries. But the Spirit of God speaks of them as the depths of Satan (v. 24).

Pergamos, like Ephesus, had in its ministry the disciples of Balaam, i.e., Nicolaus. Verse 15 should read : " So *thou* also hast them that hold the doctrine of the Nicolaitanes in like manner " (R.V.). This verse proves that this doctrine was that of Balaam, i.e., the grossest impurity practised as expressive of the

purest form of divine worship. It reached its highest development under Jezebel (v. 20).

The " hidden manna " (v. 17) is here set in opposition to the public banquet which accompanied idolatry ; and the white stone contrasts with the nameless obscenity of the Pergamos worship. The Brook Cherith (1 Kings xvii. 4) and Jezebel's table (1 Kings xviii. 19) illustrate this contrast.

Isaiah xlii. 2 promises Israel a new name which the mouth of the Lord shall name. Compare Isa. lxv. 16.

In the East a white stone in a court of justice signified " not guilty," a black stone the opposite (Acts xxii. 20). It was also a token of nobility. An overcomer in the Grecian games received a white stone. It guaranteed him a life pension from his native city. Among the ancients men parted a white stone, wrote their names upon the two pieces and exchanged them, and so vowed perpetual friendship. The white stone, therefore, of this chapter may express : Salvation, Elevation, Sustentation and Affection.

God's fiercest anger burns against idolatry because God is love and idolatry is hatred. It is the mother of all abominations and of all suffering. When God is displaced in the heart then an idol occupies His throne, and the entire man becomes the victim and agent of evil, and the principle of evil is hatred.

Thyatira heads the last four of these seven groups. The development of idolatry is here seen. The eyes of fire (v. 18) read the thoughts and the affections (v. 23) and the feet of blazing brass break the earthen vessels to shivers (v. 27). All is judgment. In the midst of the corruption a little group held fast to love and service and faith and patience ; and their energy was progressive ; it marked increasing devotedness ; they toiled harder at the end than they did at the beginning.

As " Son of God " He speaks to Thyatira (v. 18). As " Son of Man " (i. 13) He speaks to all the Assemblies as a unity. His eyes of flame detect evil and evil doers and His feet tread down the wicked (Isa. lxiii. 1-6, xli. 25 xiv. 25, Mal. iv. 3, Dan. viii. 7 and 10 and, Rev. xix. 13-15).

Toleration was the sin of Thyatira. A false charity let " Jezebel " alone (v. 20). Loyalty to Christ demanded that these teachers should have been opposed and not tolerated.

" Balaam " was outside the Hebrew Church ; " Jezebel " inside. Three of the Assemblies were warned with regard to this evil—Ephesus (v. 6), Pergamos (v. 14) and Sardis (v. 4). The historic Jezebel was cast out of a window ; the ecclesiastic Jezebel will be cast into a bed (v. 22)—a bed of anguish and death. As Jehu destroyed the one when painting her face and adorning herself so Antichrist will destroy the other at the moment of her greatest beauty and splendour (xvii. 3).

" None other burden " (v. 24), i.e., other than the duty of opposing " Jezebel " teaching (v. 20). (Compare Acts xv. 28, 29). The truth already held was not to be modified but firmly maintained up to the coming of the Judge (v. 25). Those who thus stood fast to the end practising His works (" My works " v. 26) as contrasted with Jezebel's deeds (v. 22), to them He promised a dominion of despotic power harmonizing with His own (v. 27, Ps. ii. 7-9), and, further, He would privilege them to participate in the first stage of His Advent as the Morning Star. So in the first stage of His First Advent the Baptist's parents and Simeon and Anna and others of that little company, were permitted to greet Him as the Dayspring, i.e., the Day-star from on high. Thirty years later the people that sat in darkness—the fishermen of Galilee—saw " The Great Light." Compare Num. xxiv. 17 and Rev. xxii. 16, and note on 2 Pet. i. 19.

" I have this against thee " (v. 20, R.V.), i.e., this terrible fact.

The contrast between the disciples of Jezebel (v. 23) and " the rest," i.e., the little remnant who held fast to Jesus, is emphasized by the terms " her works " (v. 23 R.V.) and " My works " (v. 26), and between the " I will give " of verse 23 and the " I will give " of verse 28. " Everyone of you," i.e., the followers of Jezebel should be rewarded according to their works, but " the rest of you," i.e., the followers of Jesus, should be rewarded according to their works because they were " His works." See notes on Ps. ii.

In Ephesus there was much truth, but little love ; in Thyatira much love, but little truth.

" The reins and hearts " (v. 23), i.e., the desires and the thoughts. The desire to know evil sank man into " the depths " of Satan. Gen. iii.

" He that hath an ear " is now placed after and not before the promises to the overcomer, because from now on individuals are addressed rather than assemblies, and the 3 of Divine relationship becomes the 4 of human responsibility.

REVELATION III. The possession of the Seven Spirits of God and of the Seven Stars declares omnipotence and omniscience.

" Thou livest but art dead " (v. 1). Compare 1 Tim. v. 6.

" How thou hast received," not " what thou hast received." Compare 1 Thess. i. 5.

The promise of ii. 28 contrasts with the threat of iii. 3.

The term " defiled " (v. 4) suggests idolatry. Few enter the strait gate (Matt. vii. 14), and few defile not their garments. The unspeakable glory of walking with Him in white thrills the heart that loves Him ; and makes it thirst to be one of these blessed "few."

Those who joined themselves to David in the day of his rejection (1 Sam. xxii. 2) he confessed in the day of his kingdom and power (2 Sam. xxiii.) ; but some names were blotted out on the eve of Solomon's reign of peace and glory—Joab and Ahithophel and Abiathar, etc. Messiah's Book of Life is spoken of in Luke x. 20, Dan. xii. 1, Rev. xvii. 8, xiii. 8 and xxi. 27.

The titles claimed by Messiah in verse 7 express relationship to Israel. He is the Holy One of Israel. He is the True God—the Very God— as distinguished from false gods, and He is the true Eliakim of Isa. xxii. 22. The reference to the Synagogue, to the Jews (v. 9), to the Temple (v. 12), to the open door (v. 8), to the dwellers upon the earth (v. 10), and to the promise of verse 9—all characterize the Hebrew Church. Jotham " entered not " into the Temple (2 Chron. xxvii. 2) ; Ahaz " shut up " the doors of the Temple (2 Chron.xxviii. 24) but Hezekiah—type of Messiah—" opened " the doors of the Temple (2 Chron. xxix. 3).

The promise of verse 9 is that predicted in Isa. xlv. 14, xlix. 22 and 23, l. 14 and lvi. 1-5 and 14.

" The word of My patience' (v. 10), i.e., My command to endure. See i. 9, ii. 2 and 19, xiii. 10 and xiv. 12. The patient endurance of suffering for His Word's sake is intended. Chapter xii. 14 illustrates the promise of exemption in verse 10.

The possessor of little strength (v. 8) will

be made a pillar of strength and glory in the Temple of God (v. 12). In Christ is seen the perfection of a faith that waits. On earth He waited patiently for Jehovah (Ps. xl. 1). Faith has a double character—it overcomes and waits. See notes on Heb. xi. The church at Philadelphia patiently endured the shame of His Name, for His approbation was sufficient. That was the test of faith. They were content with His Word and satisfied with His praise. His promise to come (v. 11) animated their hearts and taught them that only that coming can set the world right. Despised by those who claimed successional ecclesiastical authority (v. 9) they were promised the position of pillars in the very Temple of God ; and the Name of the Great High Priest Himself should be written upon them. The fourfold repetition of the word " My " makes absolute and real the association with Him in glory (v. 12) of those who confess Him in shame (vs. 8 and 9).

" A little strength " (v. 8) ensures an open door. Compare 1 Cor. xvi. 9 with 2 Cor. iv. 7-12. The promise of verse 10 does not necessarily mean exemption from persecution but rather deliverance out of persecution (see Greek text).

The pillar is to bear three names (v. 12). The name of Messiah, the name of the city and the name of God. These three names form the one name " Jehovah-Shammah." This is to be the name of the New Jerusalem which is to come down out of heaven (Ezek. xlviii. 35). To write, or brand, a name on a person declared the person so branded to be the absolute property of his owner. Such is the blissful servitude of the Christian (see note on Gal. vi. 17).

Want of heart characterizes Laodicea (v. 16). If interests which chill the warmth of first love (ii. 4) be not overcome, the end will certainly be no love at all, as in Laodicea. That church could get on very well without Christ, just as Israel could without Moses. (See notes on Exod. xxxii. 6 and 1 Cor. x. 7) So complete was the banishment of the Great High Priest that He had to use the sorrowful words " If any one " (v. 20). Such an one should sup with Him whilst the assembly would be spued out of His mouth (v. 1). There is no prospect here of repentance on the part of the church, or restoration. There is Divine rejection. Historically this was the judgment of the Pentecostal Church even before John's death. Prophetically it predicts

a similar judgment upon the future Messianic Church at the opening of " the Day of the Lord."

" Amen " is a Hebrew word expressive of life and unchanging faithfulness (v. 14). It is one of the titles of the Messiah. It expresses what is immediately added : " Faithful and true." See Isa. lxv. 16, 2 Cor. i. 20., Rom. xv. 8, Rev. i. 5 and xix. 11 and Ps. lxxxix. 3 7. Christ is not only the Way. He is also the Amen, i.e., the Truth. Hence He so often says : " Amen, Amen I say unto you." As the faithful and true witness He judges evil and exposes the true condition of the soul ; and as the Amen He is unchangeably faithful to those who respond to His knock and open the door to Him (v. 20). He is the Author of Creation, He is also the Author of regeneration—able to save and re-create any of the wretched and miserable and poor and blind and naked that hear His voice. For their poverty He has gold, for their blindness eye salve, for their nakedness white raiment.

It is easy to quench man's love for Him but impossible to quench His love for man (v. 19) ; so sickness, calamities and suffering may be proofs of the reality and tenacity of His love.

The popular picture of Christ standing at the door as a suppliant and crowned with thorns is very false. He stands as the Judge, and His portrait is that of i. 13-16—a portrait so terrible that John fell at His feet as dead. He is the Judge ; He is also the Saviour. Whoever answers His call as Judge will sup with Him as Saviour—will at once enjoy a feast of love and peace and conscious salvation in this life, and a position with Him in His throne (v. 21) in the coming kingdom. He has two thrones : His Messianic Throne and His Father's Throne. The overcomer will also have two thrones : his own (ii. 27) and the Messiah's (iii. 21). Such is the promise to the repentant Laodicean : a supper table here and a throne of glory hereafter.

The promises to the overcomers may be grouped and related thus : Restoration (ii. 7) ; Security (ii. 11) ; Nobility and maintenance (ii. 17) ; Dominion (ii. 26) ; Victory and Confession—the millennial " V.C. "—(iii. 5) ; Priesthood (iii. 12) ; and Kingship (iii. 21).

Here is an ascent of glory ; and every golden step exceeds in splendour as the overcomer mounts the shining way.

The related Book of Daniel pictures some overcomers. Daniel was an Ephesian overcomer. He overcame all that tends to chill the first warm love of the heart to Jesus. When a boy he refused to touch idolatry (i. 8) and when an old man (vii,)he bravely faced a horrible death rather than cease to pray to Him. His " first love " was never left. His three companions were Smyrna overcomers (iii.). They preferred the hurt of the first death in the fiery furnace to the hurt of the second death in "the lake of fire" (xxi. 8). These four princes triumphed also over all the wiles of the enemy from Pergamos to Laodicea : and the promise to their leader (xii. 13) may surely be understood as given to them also.

The Pentecostal Church was composed of Hebrews who believed that Jesus of Nazareth was the promised Messiah, and all Gentiles who held the same belief became members of that church. Its rise and progress are recorded in the Acts of the Apostles, and its declension and judgment in the second and third chapters of the Revelation. But just as many prophecies, as for example Joel ii., have a near and a distant fulfilment, so has this prophecy. Its near fulfilment occurred possibly before the death of the Apostle John, and its distant fulfilment awaits the future.

The structure of Revelation accords with Gen. i. 1 ; shows the relationship between heaven and earth ; and may be thus displayed :

Introduction.   i. 1-9.
Heaven. Israel's Great High Priest i. 10-20.
Earth.   The Seven Assemblies ii. and iii.
Heaven. The Messiah as Creator and
         Redeemer iv. and v.
Earth.   The Six Seals, and the 144,000
         vi. 1-vii. 8.
Heaven. The great multitude, and the
         Seventh Seal vii. 9-viii. 6.
Earth.   The Six Trumpets viii. 7-11-14.
Heaven. The Seventh Trumpet xi. 15-19.
Earth.   The Earthquake xi. 19.
Heaven. The Woman the child and the
         Dragon xii. 1-12.
Earth.   The Dragon and the Wild Beasts
         xii. 13-xiii: 18.
Heaven. The Lamb and the 144,000
         xiv. 1-5.
Earth.   The Six Angels xiv. 6-20.
Heaven. The Seven Vials xv. 1-8.
Earth.   The Seven Vials xvi. 1-xviii. 24.

Heaven. The Marriage of the Lamb
         xix. 1-16.
Earth.   The final Five Judgments xix
         1 7-xx. 1 5.
Heaven. The New Heavens xxi. 1-8.
Earth.   The New Earth xxi. 9-xxii. 5.
Conclusion. xxii. 6-21.

Thus each vision in Heaven is preparatory to its related vision on earth. The one explains the other.

REVELATION IV.-V.—Chapter iv: The Messiah having as Israel's Great High Priest commissioned John as Prophet (i.) and judged His own House (ii. and iii.), appears in these two chapters (iv. and v.) as Creator (iv) and Redeemer (v.), and prepares to come forth from His Throne of Judgment (iv: 5) as the Lamb of God, not now to.take away the sins of the world but to execute judgment in the world. Hence the expression " The wrath of the Lamb " (vi. 16). He who was seen in " the midst " of the lamp-stands (i. 13) is now seen in " the midst " of the Throne (v. 6). In both He appears as a Judge exercising judgment. He judges His House because it failed to exhibit His moral glory to the world ; and He judges the world because it rejected the testimony given to it in grace. Only in Him is found perfection as the Receiver and Revealer of the Word of God.

But if He is about to judge the world He does so from a Throne encircled with a rainbow like unto an emerald ; for He is the gracious God who made the Covenant of Peace with Noah (Gen. ix. 13) ; and its colour (green) emphasized its relationship with the green earth, and symbolized rest.

The door lay open in heaven (v. 1) in order that John might enter. The voice was Messiah's which spoke to him at the first (i. 10). " Things which *must* be " because predicted by God through the Hebrew prophets, especially Daniel.

The Throne of verses 2, 3 and 6 is that spoken of in Ps. ciii. 19 and in Pss. ix., x., and xi. and cxlix. 5-9, and in Dan. vii. 9 and 10

The five openings of the Heaven in this Book are significant (iv. 1, xi. 19, xv. 5, xix. 11 and xxi. 1). To admit John only, a door sufficed. To give exit to the Messiah and His hosts the entire Heaven was opened (xix. 11).

The Throne was encircled by countless myriads of angels (v. 11). Inside the circle of the angels were placed the twenty-four thrones of the princes; inside them the four living creatures, and in the centre of them all the Throne itself. The Scriptures never describe the Person of God (v. 2).

" In the Spirit " (v. 2), i.e., carried into heaven in a spiritual trance. Compare i. 10 and Ezek. xxxvii. 1.

Princes crowned with gold and robed in white because both Kings and Priests (iv. 4 and v. 8) sat on their thrones in association with the great Throne. These were not men, as universally supposed, but mysterious Beings. The Hebrew word "elder" here means ruler or governor, i.e., a prince. Twelve, and its multiples, is the Bible number of government. Compare 1 Chron. xxiv. 5, xxiii. 3 and 4, xxvii. 1-15 and 25-31, Isa. xxvii. 2 and Jer. xix. 1. That these princes were not men is clear from chs. v. 9, 10 (R.V.), vii. 11 and 13, xi. 16, xiv. 3 and xix. 4. They always appear in association with the Throne and with the living creatures, and apart from redeemed men.

The lightnings, the thunders, the voices, the seven torches of fire, and the sea of glass all determine the character of the Throne. It was a Throne of judgment.

The four living-creatures were the cherubim —cherubim in government (Gen. iii. 24), seraphim (Isa. vi. 2) in worship. They formed the four sides of the Throne. The expression "full of eyes" (vs. 6 and 8) suggests perfection of intelligence, as their six wings (Isa. vi. 2) symbolize character, service and worship. They represented the four species of living-creatures in the ordered earth—a man, an ox, a lion and an eagle. The ancients lowered their worship from God to these beings, and tried to picture them in the huge statues that have been discovered at Nineveh. But they were the products of creative wisdom and symbolized the intelligence, the strength, the power and the vision which belong to God as Creator.

The cherubim first appear in Gen. iii. 24 as guardians of the Tree of Life. They next appear in the vail of the Tabernacle and on the golden Mercy-Seat. These two objects symbolized the Messiah as Creator and Redeemer, and they correspond to Rev. iv. and v. Creation is beautiful, but it is a vail; redemption is wonderful, it reveals what is behind the vail and is more glorious than the vail. The cherubim appear again in 1 Kings vi. and vii. (see notes) in the

Psalms, in Isaiah, in Ezekiel, and finally in Revelation xix. 4. The word in Hebrew signifies fulness of knowledge. As cherubim they are connected with creation and government; as seraphim, with redemption and worship. Both these characters are united in the expression "living-creature" (Ezek. x. 20). They are not angels, for they are distinguished from them in vs. 8 and 11. They are not men as is clear from vs. 9 and 10 (R.V.). They are attached to the Throne of God and are never seen apart from it. It is impossible for the human intellect to visualize them or to declare what they are. Their connection with the Throne is a pledge of the restoration of the whole Creation. See notes on all the passages here quoted.

The worship of the living creatures and the crowned princes is addressed to the Triune God as Creator. Hence the "Holy, Holy, Holy"; the three titles "Jehovah, Elohim, Shaddai"; the three statements "was, is and is to come"; the ascriptions "glory and honour and thanks" (v.9) and "glory, honour and power" (v. 11)—all mark Trinity in Unity.

This is the first of the seventeen heavenly utterances of this Book. It declares and establishes the holiness of God in connection with His government of the earth. Hence the petition "hallowed, or holy, be Thy Name Thy will be done on earth." Pss. xciii., xcvii and xcix. speak proleptically of the coming reign of holiness. The three Psalms which precede these commence with a command to sing, and the command will be obeyed when "The Lord reigneth." Each of these three Psalms begins with the words: "The Lord reigneth" and ends with a reference to Messiah's holiness; because only in the millennium will He truly reign. But in the Revelation the proclamation of holiness precedes the advent of the kingdom because holiness must judge all that is evil before the earth can be made to sing.

The princes remained seated on their thrones while the lightnings, thunderings and voices proceeded from the great Throne, but every time that the cherubim celebrated the glory of Messiah as Creator they forsook their thrones and cast their crowns before the Throne—more blessed in owning His glory than in possessing their own.

Chapter v.—The glory of Jehovah Messiah as Creator having been declared (iv.), His higher glory as Redeemer is now proclaimed.

The first heavenly utterance asserted the holiness of His Nature (iv. 8) ; the second, the efficacy of His atonement (v. 9). Three times the one is declared (iv.8), and three times the other (v. 6, 9 and 12). The importance of this thrice repeated word " slain " is emphasized by its repetition. Atonement is the great doctrine of heaven. See note on Luke ix. 31.

The vision of the chapter is the action of the Messiah, symbolized by a Lamb as having been slain in sacrifice, claiming and taking possession of the scroll which declared Him to be the Redeemer, i.e., Goel, of the land and people of Israel. Ruth iv. and Jer. xxxii. explain the vision. Boaz, as kinsman, redeemed both Ruth and the piece of ground. He did so in grace, for neither merited redemption. Jeremiah bought a piece of ground, and a sealed scroll recited the purchase and declared him to be the owner. No person other than Jeremiah could, therefore, claim ownership of the land ; and he only as owner could break the seals on the document establishing his right as owner. The action of both Boaz and Jeremiah was Messianic in type. He, as Israel's Redeemer, Goel, Kinsman, at the expense of His own precious blood redeemed the land of Palestine and the people of Israel—Daniel's people— from the hand of the violated Law to which both were forfeited ; and a scroll was engrossed and sealed declaring the purchase and the name of the Purchaser. The necessity and importance of the price of the redemption is pressed in the triple declaration that the Divine Purchaser was slain in sacrifice. But though this purchase primarily affected Israel and Palestine, its operation affects the whole world and all mankind ; for, as the Scriptures abundantly declare, the salvation of Israel guarantees the salvation of all nations, so that the great purchase deed of this chapter embraces the whole world.

The view that this roll was one of judgment, comparable to that of Ezek. ii. 10, is contradicted by the language and argument of the chapter, both of which are declarative of redemption (v. 9).

Verse 1 should read thus and be so punctuated, " I saw . . . a scroll written within, and on the back close sealed with seven seals." It was a legal document in the form of a roll and secured on the outside by seven seals. These seals could only be broken by the legal owner of the document.

The great question being the redemption of Daniel's and of John's people, both wept bitterly because no redemption was visible (v. 4, Dan. x. 2). It is evident from John's distress that he understood the nature of the scroll, and what the absence of a claimant involved. On being invited to see a Lion he looked and saw a Lamb. These expressed price and power ; for if the price be paid and there be no power to take possession and evict the usurper, the payment is in vain And if, on the contrary, power be used in eviction without the previous payment of redemption, the action would be unrighteous. For the redemption of a forfeited inheritance both price and power are necessary. Thus the first redemption song sings of price ; the second, of power (vs. 9 and 12). So John saw Him in heaven as the Lamb of God as he saw Him at the first on earth (John i. 36).

Neither the cherubim, the princes, nor the angels could redeem, for they were not kinsmen of lost man. Only the Son of Man, of the Tribe of Judah, and the Root of David was " next of kin " to fallen men. He prevailed as the slain Lamb in His First Advent, and He will prevail as the crowned Lion in His Second Advent. It is of this latter that the Book of Revelation treats.

Rob heaven of the doctrine of the Atonement and of the person of the slain Lamb and it becomes a place of tears and bitter weeping (v.4). Christ crucified is the centre of heavenly glory.

" The midst of the Throne " (v. 6). Compare iv. 6 and Ps. xcix. 1. The thrones of earthly monarchs are supported by sculptured lions—dead pieces of stone. The Throne of God is established upon the wondrous Cherubim—living creatures of ineffable glory. " Jehovah is throned upon the cherubim." Ps. xcix. 1 (Hebrew).

The " horns " and " eyes " of the slain Lamb symbolize perfection of power and knowledge. With these attributes He is now about to come forth to remove the iniquity of the land of Israel " in one day." (Zech. iii. 9 and iv. 10).

The action of verse 7 corresponds with Dan. vii. 9-14.

The prayers of verse 8 are those of Luke xviii. 7 and 8 ; of the Psalms, ignorantly called imprecatory ; and of Rev. vi. 10, xi. 18 and xix. 2. They are prayers by God's earthly people calling for vengeance upon their enemies. God's heavenly people—the Church

—testify of the grace of God to a guilty world during a period of grace, and so they are forbidden to pray for vengeance upon their persecutors. But Israel is otherwise commanded. The claim that this verse 8 teaches the efficacy of prayers to the dead is baseless, for these are not prayers for salvation but for condemnation.

As already said the first heavenly utterance (iv. 8) proclaimed the holiness of Messiah's nature; the second (v. 9), the infinite value of His sacrifice. In this latter utterance the crowned princes unite with the living creatures. It is a new song—the new song of Ps. xcviii., its theme being redemption. Six times in this first vision "in Heaven" these voices are heard; for all Heaven unites in singing the glories of Jehovah Messiah as Creator and as Redeemer. Verses 9 and 10 should read as in the Revised Version.

Daniel's people had been once redeemed from Egypt by the blood of the Paschal Lamb (Exod. xv. 13), they are now about to be redeemed from the four quarters of the earth —kindred, tongue, people, nation—this time to reign over the whole earth and not merely in the land of Palestine. The number 4 in the Scriptures marks earthly order, hence these four divisions of the human family.

The anthem of the angels, the cherubim and the princes contained seven terms because its theme was redemption; that of the creatures (13) contained four because its theme was creation; both songs were completed by the " Amen " of the Cherubim and the adoration of the four and twenty tzkainim i.e., princes.

The subjoined plan shows the connection between the Seals, the Trumpets, and the Cups—the Seventh Seal expands into the Seven Trumpets, and the Seventh Trumpet into the Seven Cups:

1st Seal, 2nd Seal, 3rd Seal, 4th Seal, 5th Seal, 6th Seal,
_____

                    Seventh Seal

1st, 2nd, 3rd, 4th, 5th, 6th, 7th Trumpet

                              1, 2, 3, 4, 5, 6, 7th Cup

Descent of Messiah

REVELATION VI.—The predictions of this chapter harmonize with those of Matt. xxiv., as the subjoined parallel shows ·

THE SEALS

Matthew xxiv.				Revelation vi.
4, 5	1	The False Messiah		1, 2
6, 7	2	Wars		3, 4
7	3	Famine		5, 6
7	4	Pestilence		7, 8
8-28	5	Persecution		9-11
29-30	6	Physical signs		12-17

It is, therefore, quite clear from this comparison that the rider on the white horse (v. 21) symbolizes the False Messiah. ·He will head up all false Messiahs (Matt. xxiv. 5), just as the False Prophet (Rev. xiii. 11) will head up all false prophets (Matt. xxiv. 24).

This False Messiah at once appears as the opponent of the True Messiah directly the latter rises up to take the inheritance. He will claim it; for Satan, either personally or through an agent. always opposes, and from the very first opposed, every Divine movement in regard to man and the earth.

The subject now is Messiah rising up from His Father's Throne in order to resume relations with Israel, and to claim the land of His possession. The Adversary, Satan, immediately is seen in the activity of his enmity producing a counter-claimant.

The first living creature shouts with a voice of thunder: "Go!" for Satanic agents cannot act without Divine permission. The words "and see" should be omitted. That the Greek verb should be translated "go" and not "come" (v. 1 R.V.) is clear from the responsive words "he went" (v. 2). This permission to go forth will be given at the moment pointed to in 2 Thess. ii. 6.

Antichrist will present himself to the world as the Prince of Peace, and, therefore, riding a white horse; and he will bear a crown and a bow, the insignia of imperial power He will go forth resolving to conquer; and he will succeed, for he will overcome (xiii. 7).

But the double effect of his rule is pictured in verses 3-11—for the world, bloodshed (v. 4), famine (v. 5), and pestilence (v. 8), and for Messiah's people, persecution (v. 9).

The Seven Seals, as is usual in Scripture with the number seven, are parted into four and three—the four horses (compare Zech. vi.) and the three judgments—the martyrs (see note on 1 Pet. iv. 6), the nations (v. 15), and the two Wild Beasts (xix. 20).

The Sixth Seal is separated off from the seventh in order to permit of the introduction of the synchronous judgments of the trumpets and the vials (see note on viii. 1). The six seals furnish a preliminary summary of the judgments which cover the entire period up to the seventh. The seventh seal includes the seven trumpets and the seven vials. The "earthquake" is one of the key-words connecting the sixth seal with the sixth trumpet (xi. 13) and the seventh vial (xvi. 17), and both with the seventh seal (viii. 5).

It is very probable that as the First Advent covered a period of about seventy years, so also will the second. In His First Advent He " came out of " Bethlehem (Mic. v. 2) to those watching for Him, and thirty-three years later He " came unto " Jerusalem publicly (Zech. ix. 9) ; 37 years later the doom fell.

As stated, Antichrist will be followed and accompanied by war, famine and pestilence. Men will rend each other to pieces. They will eat their food by weight (Ezek. iv.). A measure of corn was a slave's ration and cost the one-eighth of a penny, as recorded by Greek historians. In this famine, therefore, corn will be eight times its usual price. In the time of Trajan twenty measures of wheat were bought for one penny. " Death " (v. 8) here means " pestilence " (R.V. margin) for it as the cause produced death as the effect.

Daniel's people who bravely hold fast to the Word of God and to their testimony respecting the True Messiah will suffer martyrdom at the hands of the False Messiah (vs. 2 and 9). This will be " the time of Jacob's trouble "—the climax of " the Great Tribulation." These martyrs cry aloud for judgment upon their persecutors (v. 10). This is the cry of Luke xviii. 7 and 8 and of the judgment Psalms. It is not the cry of the Church of God during the present period of the grace of God. Luke xvii. 20 to xviii. 8 helps in the interpretation of this fifth seal.

The Pharisees demanded when the kingdom of God should come. Jesus answered it would not appear to carnal verification ; that He Himself the true kingdom of God stood in their midst—then in grace—but soon to stand in judgment (24-37) ; and that at that time Israel as a widow (xviii. 3) would cry aloud for vengeance upon her adversary ; and He promised that her prayer for vengeance would be granted and her persecutors destroyed (v. 7). This is the cry of Rev. vi. 10. It is addressed to the Messiah as Sovereign Lord, the Holy and True God. Such is the import of the titles here used.

Robes of victory (xix. 14) were given to the martyrs as evidence that the " little season " (v. 11) would soon end, and that they were now being already arrayed for the day of vengeance.

Two interesting questions are here touched. The souls of the martyrs are pictured as consciously in heaven, their dead bodies being on earth (see note on 1 Pet. iv. 6) ; they are stated to be interested in what is going on upon the earth ; and it is intimated that the number of the martyrs from Abel onward is a definite number as decreed by God.

The Cherubim, expressing the activities of God's providential ways on earth, gave permission to the four riders to go forth. The position in heaven of the victims of the First Rider shows that God all through these judgments was really thinking of His saints, and so they come here into prominence before other visions are developed. Their position at the base of the altar of devotion—not of atonement—expresses their action in having sacrificed their lives as a seal to their testimony. They walk with Him in white for they are worthy; for the white robes are a recognition of their righteous and brave conduct in suffering martyrdom (xix. 8).

The Sixth Seal provides a test for all Apocalyptic interpretation. The reader of Matt. xxiv. 29 with Rev. vi. 12-17 learns that they speak of the same event ; and, further, that the light shed by Matt. xxiv. on the entire Book of the Apocalypse makes it absolutely clear that Jerusalem and the Hebrew people are the subjects of that Book. (See notes on Matt. xxiii. and xxiv.).

The great earthquake of verse 12 is that of xvi. 18, of Haggai ii. 6, 7 and 22, of Zech. xiv. 4 and of many other passages. It will without doubt be confined to the prophetic earth as enclosed between the river of Egypt and the river Euphrates. The heavens above that area will roll asunder so as to give exit to the True Messiah and His armies (xix. 11). The word "island" may here perhaps be understood of the coast-lands of the Mediterranean. The intervening territory will be elevated so as to form an immense plain, the centre of which will be allocated to "the holy oblation" of Ezek. xlv. Possibly this earthquake will restore the garden of Eden to its former position before it perished in the Flood.

"The kings of the earth," i.e., the successors of those of Acts iv. 26. While the martyrs, robed in white, triumph in heaven (v. 11) their persecutors tremble on earth (v. 16). The action of the Lamb (ch. v. 9) sets heaven shouting and earth shuddering (vi. 16). The opening of this seal marks the time spoken of in Pss. ii. 2, lxviii. 4, xcvii. 5, Isa. xxiv. 19-23, xxxiv. 12, Nah. i. 5, Haggai ii. 6 and 22, Heb. xii. 26. Thus it is shown that these judgments do not arise from chance but from Divine decree, and that they will take place at the time Divinely purposed. The answer to the question : "Who shall be able to stand ?" is given in the next chapter.

Israel is the olive tree and the vine of prophecy. Hence the prohibition not to injure the oil and the wine (v. 6) may mean that Daniel's people are to be shielded from famine at this future period just as their fore-fathers in the land of Goschen were exempted from the plagues of that day.

REVELATION VII.—In answer to the question of vi. 17, the first fruits of Israel (3-8 and xiv. 1-5) are seen standing upon Mount Zion, and the first fruits of the Nations appear standing before the Throne (v. 9). These two redeemed companies are related ; for, as predicted, the restoration and salvation of the Gentiles depend upon that of the Hebrews. See Notes on Ps. lxvii., Isa. xlix. and lii, and many similar Scriptures together with Rom. ix.-xi.

Rev. iv. and vii. accord with 1 Kings i.-vii. The Beloved of Jehovah (Jedidiah) and Prince of Peace (Solomon) was set upon his father's throne in spite of the opposition of his enemies. After a period of patient waiting he rose up to take possession of his own throne ; and, after the destruction of his enemies, established his glorious kingdom

in all the land. He then built the Temple, and, apart from it, a great tri-form palace of extraordinary magnificence. The central court was the Throne room, the palace on one side the King's own house, and that on the other side, the house of Pharaoh's daughter. These outside palaces were mutually related to the central one, were dependent upon it, and so related to one another. The King was in the midst. This is what appears in Rev. iv.-vii. The great King is seen in the midst. On one side His own House ("Solomon's House")—the 144,000 out of all the tribes of Israel—for the King is a Hebrew. On the other side the countless multitude out of all nations ("The House of Pharaoh's daughter"). The multitude out of the Tribes can be numbered, but not that out of the nations ; for if the casting away of Israel occasioned the salvation of some of the Gentiles, how limitless will be the blessing that will reach them through a restored Israel ! Thus these two companies of Rev. vii. are presented in their proper relationship to the Great King and to each other. But Israel comes first : afterwards the Gentiles.

In chapter vii. 3-8 the 144,000 are armed for the moral conflict with the False Messiah. As to their bodies, they perish in the battle ; but in chapter xiv. 1-5 they appear triumphant upon the Mount Zion having gotten the victory of xii. 11 and xvii. 14. The seal in their foreheads (vii. 3) was that of xiv. 1 promised to them in iii. 12. Dan and Ephraim are not found amongst these over-comers, for Deut. xxix. 18-21 declared that any Tribe that introduced idolatry into Israel should have its name blotted out from under heaven. These two Tribes were guilty of the introduction of that sin. Joseph is substituted for Ephraim and Levi for Dan.

The formula "after this" has not a time sense but a relationship significance ; as when it is said "in connection with these things." The Apostle relates the great out-lines of the vision and then goes back from time to time to fill in details and declare their relationships to each other and to the vision itself.

"The four winds" (v. i). Compare Dan. vii. 2. "Holding" i.e., controlling. These angels did not then take their stand on the four corners of the earth, but attention is now drawn to the fact that they were there all the time waiting for the command for action. So close is the relationship between God and creation that it grieves Him to "hurt" it; so it is here presented as a sentient being.

The followers of the False Messiah will receive his mark in their foreheads (xiii. 16) and the followers of the True Messiah will bear His mark in theirs (v. 3). Compare Ezek. ix. 3, 4. He Who in the days of Ahab and Jezebel reserved seven thousand for Himself will in the days of Antichrist and the False Prophet reserve 144,000. Of these not one shall perish in the war; just as in Num. xxxi. none perished in the battle with Midian (vs. 48 and 49). In that battle one thousand fought out of each Tribe; in this battle twelve thousand will fight out of each Tribe.

Redemption being the theme, all Heaven makes a seven-fold ascription of praise to the Atoning Lamb (v. 12). The redeemed themselves ascribe their salvation to God and the Lamb, i.e., to the Great God and Saviour Jesus Christ (v. 10). See Titus ii. 13 R.V. and 2 Peter i. 1 R.V.

The position and question of the crowned prince of verse 13 present him as apart from this great company of pardoned sinners. See note on iv. 4.

This multitude came out of "The Great Tribulation" (v. 14), and they washed their sins away, not in the tears of penitence or the waters of baptism, but in the atoning blood of the Lamb of God.

The beatitude of this multitude (vs. 15-17) corresponds to that promised to Israel. Compare Isa. xlix. 8-10, xxv. 8, lxv. 19 and Rev. xxi. 3 and 4. This marks relationship, as did the porch that extended from Solomon's house on the one side of the central palace to the house of Pharaoh's daughter on the other.

REVELATION VIII.—The breaking of the Seventh Seal occasioned the trumpets of judgment (v. 2) and the cups of wrath (xv. 6). These express the activities of the true Messiah in answer to prayer (v. 3). The prior chapters told of His claiming the inheritance promised to Abraham, and of the riding forth of the false Messiah to oppose the claim. War, famine, and pestilence as a consequence afflict the nations of the world, and persecution destroys the people of God. Such are the activities of the False Messiah. On

breaking the Sixth Seal, the True Messiah begins to put forth His power, and to prepare the platform for the exhibition of His anger in the trumpets and vials attached to the Seventh Seal. But He first offers the vengeance prayers (v. 3).

An "hour" is a Hebrew idiom for a brief space of time. Compare Dan. iv. 19 (R.V.) and v. 5. Matt. xxvi. 40, Rev. xvii. 12. xviii. 10. Occasionally it means a longer, but definite period (John iv. 21). Half an hour, therefore, signifies a very brief period. It was sufficient for the angel here (v. 3) to present the prayers and incense, as it was for the High Priest in the Temple on earth, which was a copy of that in the heavens. See Heb. viii. 5, ix. 23-24, 1 Chron. xxviii. 11, 13, 19. While the High Priest was thus engaged the whole congregation waited in silent worship. It was the silence of adoration and expectation. (See notes on Ps. lxv.) As in this Book the Lord Jesus appears as Creator and Redeemer and Shepherd and Messiah and Prince, etc., so, perhaps, in this verse 3 He appears as the great High Priest; and His action, as such, caused the Trumpets and vials to strike the oppressors of His people.

The prayers are vengeance prayers and sweet to God. The Divine response is immediate (v. 5), for manifestations of Divine power are seen on earth just as they were seen at Sinai. What the language of these prayers for vengeance is, will be found in the Psalms; as, for instance lxxxiii.-cxli., etc. The present day of grace having closed, and the time of the wrath of the Lamb begun, petitions for judgment on the persecutors of the saints and enemies of righteousness now begin to have their appropriate place and fulfilment. These Spirit-taught prayers, and their Divine responses, anger what is proudly termed "modern religious thought."

The claim that these verses support the doctrine of prayers to departed saints is baseless, for these prayers were not offered to saints; and, further, they were prayers for destruction and not for salvation.

The Lamb opened the Seals, but angels sounded the trumpets, and proclaimed war as commanded by the law (Num. x. 9). Jericho fell when the Seven Trumpets sounded seven times on the seventh day. A similar scene to verse 5 is found in Ezek. x., and is predicted in Ps. xviii. The reproach of **Ps. lxxix.**

11-12 is now to be rewarded "seven-fold" in answer to the petitions of verse 3. Physical marvels result, as was promised in Exod. xxxiv. 10, Deut. xxviii. 10, Isa. xi. 15-16.

The trumpet and vial judgments are continuous once they begin ; but the description of them is interrupted x.-xv. and xvii. -xviii.) in order to give information showing the necessity for them.

The judgments of the Seven Trumpets may be actual or symbolic. The historical interpretation of this Book accepts the latter view. But the fall of the Roman Empire, and the centuries of war which followed, fail to satisfy the statements of the vision. The plagues of Egypt were actual, and six of these trumpet plagues resemble them. When the hour strikes for their infliction, the "wise" (Dan. xii. 10) will recognise them, and be instructed by them.

Each judgment only affects a third part of the earth (viii. 7) and a third part of men (ix. 18). This suggests the compassion of God, and is possibly explained by Ezek. v. and Zech. xiii. The judgment of fire upon the sea may be an allusion to Jer. li. 25 and Amos vii. 4.

The eagle (v. 13 R.V.) may be the fourth of the cherubim. He cries "Alas ! alas ! alas ! " and so voices the pity of God even for the most wicked of men.

Assyria (Armenia) is to be first judged and then blessed as "a third" with Israel and Egypt (Isa. xix. 24). Antichrist will be the King of the North (Dan. xi. 40), i.e., the King of Assyria (Isa. x. 5 and xiv. 25, etc.). That land will be his "seat" and "kingdom" (Rev. xvi. 10). The term "third" may, therefore, in this vision of the trumpets mean that these judgments will only strike Assyria as at first the plagues only struck Egypt. The wrath of God judged Egypt at the beginning, then Palestine, and, finally, in the future will judge Assyria. The judgment on Palestine is now possibly ended and that on Assyria about to begin.

God once spoke through the mouth of an ass (Num. xxii. 28). Why not then of an eagle ?

REVELATION IX. This "star" had fallen from Heaven (v. 1, R.V.). It was a person as the word "him" denotes. The bottomless pit is the abyss of Luke viii. 31 and Rev. xx. 1, i.e., the dread prison house of the demons. This "star" was Satan (see

note on Luke x. 18)—but he could not open the prison house without Divine permission. The key was "given" to him. This impotency of the demons is consolatory to Christians.

The eruption of the demons out of the abyss and the suffering that they are to cause to those who have not the seal of God on their foreheads (v. 4) when compared with Jer. iv. 23-28, make it clear that this judgment is to fall upon the sinners in Zion. The following woe will fall upon "men" in general (v. 18), i.e., the Gentiles.

As the locusts of Joel ii. symbolized the Chaldean host, so these "locusts" (v. 3) symbolize the demonic host. They will not be visible, but they will be the carriers of the plague (v. 20) which will afflict the unbelieving Hebrews. Locusts destroy vegetation (v. 4) and do not hurt men. These demons will hurt men and will not injure vegetation. Their licence, and the duration of their activity, will both be limited (v. 5).

The description of the "locusts" (vs. 7-10) suggest that they are a kind of infernal cherubim. Satan, the Destroyer— "Abaddon" and "Apollyon"—is their King. This does not mean that he is here seen marching at their head. It means they are his subjects and belong to his kingdom. Ordinary locusts have no king (Prov. xxx. 27). Compare Exod. x. 14. Five months, from May to September, is the limit of a plague of locusts. The words "like" and "as" occur nine times.

The plague will not produce repentance but only a desire for death (v. 6). Nor will the following plague cause men to turn from their idolatries and impurities (vs. 20 and 21). Suffering and misery are impotent to effect the New Birth.

Evil is shut up and chained in the abyss (2 Pet. ii. 4 and Jude 6). It will be punished in the lake of fire (xix. 20 and xx 10 and 15 and xxi. 8).

The association of the golden altar (v. 13 and viii. 3) makes clear the connection between the sixth trumpet and the vengeance prayers. The number "four" (v. 13), the "Euphrates" (v. 14), and the word "men" (vs. 18 and 20) distinguish this plague as striking others than the Hebrews. The four angels (v. 14) are fallen angels imprisoned at the Euphrates for the execution of this judgment at the moment decreed by God

(v. 15). The Greek text shows that these periods determine a point of time—the appointed hour of the appointed day of the appointed month, of the appointed year. Not only are the fallen angels reserved unto judgment but they are reserved for judgment, i.e., to be the executors of God's wrath. The Book of Daniel together with this verse 14, and other Scriptures, suggest that both good and evil angels have fixed localities appointed to them, and are in that sense "bound."

The horsemen number 200,000,000 (v. 16). This is twice stated. They are not human but super-human. God's servants will recognise this plague at the time of its infliction, and will profit by the knowledge.

The Euphrates is associated with the judgments of the future Day of the Lord. See Jer. iv. 13 and 29 (R.V.) and xlvi. 4-10 (R.V.).

Idolatry (v. 20), licence (v. 21), and sorcery (v. 21), i.e., trafficking with the dead, will reach in the future an excess never known in the past. All will lead up to the worship of the Wild-Beast.

As an eruption of demons will be permitted in connection with the Second Advent to chasten Israel (v. 2), so was an eruption, but much more limited, permitted in connection with the First Advent (Luke viii. 31, etc.); but at that time, as again in the future, they were not and will not be allowed to kill men but only to hurt them (Mark ix. 26). Both eruptions proceeded from the one abyss (v. 2 with Luke viii. 31).

REVELATION X.—The open scroll in the angel's hand (v. 2) was a prophetic commission connected with the title-deed of chapter v. and committed to the Apostle John (v. 11). This commission is introduced here because the Ten Kings and their Head, Antichrist, are about to appear in the great vision (xii.- xix.). The Word of God is sweet to the spirit but bitter to the flesh (v. 9). David found it sweet when it struck down Dagon (1 Sam. v.) but bitter when it struck himself (2 Sam. vi. 8, 9). So was it sweet to John to announce the coming judgments upon the kings and the nations who oppressed his fellow Hebrews, but bitter because it also judged the Hebrew people. To read the promises is sweet to the spirit, but to experience the chastening of will which conditions the promises, is bitter to the flesh.

An angel—a mighty one—the Creator (Ps. xcv. 5) robed with a cloud, a token of Divine dignity, crowned with "the rainbow" (R.V.). of chapter iv. 3, His face and His feet as fire, evidently was the Angel of Jehovah—the Messiah. As the Divine Joshua He makes His what He sets His foot upon (Joshua i. 3); and as the Lion of the Tribe of Judah, He utters His voice against all the opposing inhabitants of the land (Jer. xxv. 30) who array themselves against Him and His people (Joel iii. 16). As legal possessor of the inheritance He now takes possession of the "parcel of ground" (Ruth iv. 3). He is here seen coming down out of Heaven (v. 1) and His great opponent is seen ascending out of the abyss (xi. 7). The conflict now increases in intensity—the two Messiahs, with their hosts, prepare themselves for the battle; and permission is given to Satan to place in the field all the power of his demonic kingdom together with many peoples, nations tongues and kings (v. 11).

Directly the Angel of Jehovah with a mighty voice claims the inheritance (v. 3), seven thunders—a full heavenly testimony—approve the claim. What the thunders said (John xii. 29) John was not permitted to record. A similar prohibition was given to Daniel (Dan. viii. 26 and xii. 4-9). John was afterwards told not to seal up the prophecy of this Book (xxii. 10).

The reference to creation (v. 6) establishes the Messiah's claim as Creator, as verse 3 does His claim as Redeemer to the possession of the inheritance. The time was now come to take possession; hence the statement "there shall be delay no longer" (R.V. margin). See Dan. xii. 7.

The mystery—the secret—of verse 7 does not mean the secret of the Church, for that was never declared to the Prophets (Eph. iii. 5), but is the Divine secret respecting the duration of the times of the Gentiles (Rom. xi. 25) and of the judgment decreed upon Israel because of the cutting off of Messiah (Dan. ix. 26, 27). See xvi. 17.

Three factors appear in verse 7: Glad tidings (R.V.); the prophets; and the secret. The glad tidings were that the Messiah would surely redeem Zion; the messengers were the Old Testament prophets; and the secret was, and still is, when the promised restoration would take place. The Deliverer promised deliverance, but did not reveal the time of its occurrence. The

3U

"mystery of God" contrasts with the "mystery of iniquity" (2 Thess ii. 7).

The eating of the book corresponds to Ezek. ii. 9 and iii. 3 and 14. To eat and digest the contents of a book is idiomatic language ; and is still in use.

"Before" (v. 11), i.e., "concerning." Chapters xi. to xviii. contain the messages concerning these kings and peoples.

The open book and the firmly planted foot declare definite purposes respecting well-known territory ; and the statement as to delay marks definiteness of time.

REVELATION XI. 1-14.—The Temple will be rebuilt in Jerusalem, for Antichrist will enthrone himself in it, thus declaring himself to be both God and Christ ; and prior to the Second Advent, as prior to the First, a little company will meet there, and daily watch for the promised Deliverer (Luke ii. 25-38). Perhaps the sense of verse 1 is that these will be sheltered from the fury of the Wild Beast and his Gentile hosts (vs. 2-7). The faith of these worshippers will be sustained by the testimony of the two witnesses. (vs. 3-14). The names of these witnesses are not revealed. It is useless, therefore, to speculate as to who they will be. It is true that Elijah is to reappear at this epoch, and to win by his preaching a multitude of the Hebrew people to the same faith as converted and animated their fathers (Mal. iv. 5, 6).

The testimony of the two witnesses is to continue for the same time as the Lord's own testimony when on earth, i.e., three years and a half, that is forty and two months or 1260 days (vs. 2-3). It is, therefore, to be understood that they will preach every day during that period of time.

Just as after the restoration from Babylon God had His two witnesses (Zech. iv. 3, 11, 14), so in the future restoration of the Hebrew people He will have similar witnesses comparable to olive trees and lamp-stands (v. 3). As lamp-stands they will hold up the light or testimony for the True Messiah in face of the fury of the false Messiah ; and the Holy Spirit, symbolized in the olive trees, will feed the sacred flame. The Lord of the whole land (Zech. iv. 14, with v. 4. R.V.) will make them invulnerable, and equip them with terror-striking powers, as He did Moses, till their testimony shall be finished (v. 7). He will then permit the Wild Beast to kill them (v. 7). This is the second appearance of

Antichrist in this Book. His first appearance was in vi. 2. He appears thirteen times in this Prophecy, and occupies thirty-one verses.

The language, the imagery of the vision, the distinction it draws between the Hebrews and the Gentiles, and its statements concerning Jerusalem (vs. 1-2), prove that it does not concern the Church of God but that it deals with the near future when God will resume relationships with Israel.

Four facts are declared respecting these witnesses : their commission (vs. 3-6) ; their sufferings (vs. 7-10) ; their reward (vs. 11-12) ; and their avengement (v. 13).

Their death by the hands of Antichrist shows that he will be on earth at this time. So this chapter anticipates chapter xiii.

The great city as here stated (v. 8) will be Jerusalem. Then will be fulfilled Ps. lxxix. etc. Jerusalem is called "the great city" (v. 8), and the "beloved city" (xx. 9), and the "Holy City" (xxi. 11), and "that great City" (xxi. 10). Compare Neh. vii. 3, 4, Jer. v. 1, xxii. 5, 7, 9, 2 Chron. xxxii. 6. She is likened to "Sodom" in Isa. i. 9-10, iii. 8, 9, Jer. xxiii. 14, and is called "Egypt" in Ezek. xxiii. 3, 4, 8, 19.

Verse 9 intends representatives of the Gentiles, whilst verse 10 points to the unbelieving Hebrews then dwelling in the land.

The triumphing of the wicked over the two witnesses will be short (Job xx. 5), for as "their Lord" (v. 8, R.V.) rose from the dead and ascended to heaven, so will they (vs. 11, 12). At His resurrection there was an earthquake (Matt. xxvii. 51), and so will there be at theirs ; and it will destroy a tenth part of the city of Jerusalem (v. 13) and justly avenge their murder.

These two witnesses appear as suddenly in this book as does Elijah in 1 Kings. They will certainly come as here foretold ; and these facts concerning them will surely take place.

As in Elijah's day 7000 overcomers were reserved by God to Himself, so in this future day will 7000 opposers of His Anointed be destroyed (v. 13).

Under the judgments of the seals, the trumpets, and the cups of wrath, the earth will quake five times (vi. 12, viii. 5, xi. 13, xi. 19, and xvi. 18).

REVELATION XI. 15 19—The seventh seal, the seventh trumpet, which is the third woe, and the seventh cup of wrath, form the content of this brief passage.

The main subject of this Book, i.e., the sovereignty of the world, now appears, by anticipation, at the close (v. 15) as at the beginning (iv. and v.). As Creator and Redeemer of the world, the Messiah claims the sovereignty, and great voices in heaven (v. 15), and the four and twenty crowned monarchs (v. 16), and the Ark of the Covenant (v. 19), and demonstrations of the Divine power on earth (v. 19) approve the claim, whilst the judgments of the seals, the trumpets and the cups on the Pretender disprove his claim.

" The kingdoms of this world" (v. 15) should read " The sovereignty of this world." That sovereignty (v. 15) and its institution and its administration (vs. 17 and 18) are here introduced in anticipation. The Ark containing God's Covenant with His Anointed (v. 19) is here disclosed as a demonstration not only of God's faithfulness to this Covenant made with the Messiah promising Him the ends of the earth for His possession, as well as the House of Israel, but also as evidence that the sovereignty of the world was really His. This Ark in the Heavenly Temple was a pledge of God's Covenant with Christ, as the Ark in its earthly counterpart was a pledge of God's Covenant with Israel.

The words " and are to come " (v. 17) should be omitted (R.V.) because He is now viewed by anticipation as come. The three great titles Jehovah, Elohim, and Shaddai, are here used by the Crowned princes as by the Cherubim in iv. 8.

The anger of the nations and Messiah's anger (v. 18) are the subjects of the second Psalm. The dead here are the blessed dead of xx. 4. They were judged by man to be worthy of death (1 Pet. iv. 6), but they shall be judged by the Messiah to be worthy of His kingdom. The Greek verb " to judge " has both an approbatory and a condemnatory force. The former is to be understood here in the sense of vindication. This will be the first resurrection (xx. 6). The rest of the dead will not be raised until the millennial reign closes (xx. 5). The subject of verse 18 is the vindication and reward of all, both small and great, who have been, and shall be, faithful to the true Messiah, and the destruction of their oppressors. He will "judge" His people but "destroy" their oppressors. This destruction will be that of xix. 21.

The effect on earth (v. 19) of the seventh angel's trumpet corresponds with the effects under the seventh seal and the seventh cup.

Man says "great and small" (Esther i. 20) God says "small and great" (Gen. xix. 11, 1 Sam. v. 9, Ps. cxv. 13, Acts xxvi. 22, Rev. xi. 18, xiii. 16, xix. 5 and 18 and xx. 12, etc.).

REVELATION XII. 1-12.—The woman and the serpent here reappear as in Gen. iii. His purpose then was to destroy God's rest in Messiah as Creator, and here to destroy His rest in Christ as Redeemer. The woman (v. 1) signifies Israel, as is plain from Gen. xxxvii. 9 and 10, Isa. lx. 20, Rom. ix. 4, 5, 8, 2 Tim. ii. 8. Satan knew it was the Child of the woman (Gen. iii. 15) that should crush his head, and, later on, that He was to be born of the Hebrew nation. Both the woman and the serpent are here declared to be "signs," not wonders (vs. 1 and 3). The serpent was a " sign " but the woman was " a great sign " because of the Child to which she was to give birth. The serpent is represented standing before her (v. 4, R.V.). His colour denotes his ferocity. His seven " heads," here crowned, signify the seven Empires that he energized to destroy the people of Israel and so prevent the birth of the Messiah. These Empires are Egypt, Syria, Assyria, Babylon, Persia, Greece and Rome. These powers in turn—notably the Egyptian and the Persian—almost succeeded in annihilating the Hebrew people. The ten horns represent the ten kings of chapter xvii. 3, 7, 12, 16 and xiii. 1. In this last reference the crowns are seen to have been transferred from the seven heads to the ten horns, for the ten kings of Daniel's prophecy will be the successors of Nebuchednezzar and will reign over the lands which the Four Empires governed.

So Satan from the first sought to make impossible the birth of the promised Redeemer. His action explains the corruption that necessitated the destruction of the human race in the Flood ; the hindered birth of Isaac ; the murderous animosity of Ishmael and Esau ; the edict of Pharaoh ; the rebellions in the Wilderness ; the idolatry of Solomon ; the murder of the Royal family by Athaliah ; the curse upon Jehoiachim ; and the slaughter of the Bethlehem children by Herod, etc.

It is clear from verse 4 that he seduced one

third of the angelic host—here, and in other Scriptures, called the "stars" of heaven. Their fall to earth is anticipated in this verse and narrated in verse 9.

The ministry, crucifixion and resurrection of Christ are passed over in verse 5 not being necessary to the subject, and His ascension only mentioned.

Between verses 5 and 6 the present interval, of about two thousand years intervenes, and Israel's preservation in the Wilderness, anticipated in verse 6, is described in verses 14-17. Her protected life there will last for three years and a half (v. 6). This is the "short" time of verse 12.

The war in heaven is future (v. 7). Satan and his hosts now occupy the lower heavens (Eph. vi. 12) and he will hold fast to that position until ejected (2 Thess. ii. 6). This verse 7, therefore, describes the action of Michael the Prince of Israel in ejecting him and his armies from his present position. The dragon does not attack Michael, Michael attacks him. The triumphant voice of verse 10 connects the fall of Satan with the manifestation of the power of God's Messiah, for Satan's defeat in the heavens assures the defeat of his Messiah upon the earth (xiii. 1). The death of Christ, and His people's testimony to the preciousness of that death—a testimony which they will seal with their blood—will defeat Satan and his Messiah upon earth, as Michael and his angels will defeat him in the heavens. Both victories will be based on the one foundation of the Atonement. It is, and will be, the great doctrine of heaven and of earth.

The visions of chapters xii.-xv. form the central subject of the whole Book and are a parenthesis. This parenthesis is a notable example of prophetic form by which earlier events are narrated later. This parenthesis xii.-xv. records events which will take place before chapter vi. and are parallel with chapters vi.-xi. These latter chapters give the outer view of prophetic history; chapters xii.-xv., the inner view.

The only title to inheritance, whether in heaven or on earth, is the blood of the Lamb (v. 11).

The word "and" occurs forty-four times in this chapter. See note on Luke xiv. 13 and 21.

REVELATION XII. 13—XIII. 1-18.—After

Satan's expulsion from the heavens (xii. 9, 2 Thess. ii. 7) he will persecute the confessors of Jesus as the Messiah (vs. 13 and 17), just as after the Lord's ascension he persecuted similar believers (xii. 6 and the Acts of the Apostles). But as God carried His people out of Egypt on " eagles' wings " (Exod. xix. 4) so will He miraculously deliver these believers of the future, (compare Ps. xxxv. 1-5, Zeph. ii. 3, Matt. xxiv. 15-28, Mark xiii. 14-23, and see note on Zech. v 7) while out of the nation, as such, is nourished in safety (v.14, Dan. vii. 25, xii. 7) an election chosen for martyrdom (v. 17, xiii. 7). These are the martyrs of vi. 9, xx. 4. The expression "cast out of his mouth" may mean that the serpent will command a mysterious agency, either physical or demonic (xvi. 13) to destroy the Hebrew people, and that an earthquake will nullify his efforts. Compare Exod. xv. 12, Isa. xi. 15 and 16, lix. 19. " The commandments of God" are the Old Testament, and " the testimony that Jesus is the Messiah " (v. 17) is the New Testament.

The dragon (xiii. 1, R.V.) stands upon the sifting sand of the tumultuous sea of humanity (xvii. 15 and Dan. vii. 2) and calls up out of the warring nations the Wild Beast, i.e., Antichrist. This is the third of his seventeen appearances in this Book (vi. 2, xi. 7, xiii. 1). He accepts the kingdoms of the world which the True Messiah refused (Luke iv. 5), and, therefore, here appears having the seven heads and ten horns of the dragon. The horns are now crowned, for the ten kings of Daniel's prophecy will at this time be reigning monarchs, Antichrist being their chief (xvii. 12). The Wild Beast will be the fourth beast of Dan. vii., and will exercise the power of the Grecian, the Persian, and the Babylonian kingdoms, signified by (v. 2) the leopard, the bear, and the lion. The future will reveal the meaning of verse 3. His reign as risen from the dead—for he is to ascend out of the bottomless pit (xi. 7)—will only last three years and a half (v. 5).

The sense of verse 10 is destiny. Compare Jer. xv. 2, xliii. 11, Ezek. v. 2 and 12, Zech. xi. 9. This idiom has a double force—one, the certainty of the martyrdom of the "saints," i.e., of Daniel's people; and, second, the eternal doom of their persecutors. This explains the reference here to patient endurance of torture and martyrdom by the saints, and their faith in God's promised vindication of them, and the punishment of their tormentors.

At this crisis is heard for the last time the solemn words that all who hear these revelations of the Spirit will be held responsible to believe and obey them (v. 9).

He who to the prophet when in a spiritual trance appears in the horrible form of a wild-beast, will appear to men as a prince of noble countenance and superhuman knowledge. (See note on Dan. viii. 23). He will be so attractive that he will be universally accepted as the promised Prince of Peace and restorer of humanity. He will claim to be God, and the world will accept the claim and worship him ; except those whose names are written in the Book of Life.

The Beast as it had been slain (v. 3) will be Satan's counterfeit of " the Lamb as it had been slain " (ch. v. 6). Further details respecting this First Beast will be found in the notes on xvii. 8-12.

Messiah having, either in Person or by deputy, planted His feet upon the sea and upon the earth (x. 2) as King and Prophet, this action will compel Satan to plant by deputy his feet upon both sea and land. But as he could not combine these offices in one person he will be compelled to choose two agents, and hence he will call the First Beast out of the sea and the Second out of the land (v. 11). The earth may mean the land of Palestine—the land of prophets and prophecy ; the sea may suggest the Gentile nations—the realm of kings and kingdoms. Man must have rule and religion notwithstanding the efforts of anarchists and sceptics, and so Satan will provide him with these two Wild Beasts, and they will produce a system of government and of religion which will be heartily welcomed by the world and by the majority of the Hebrew people.

As the Lord in Matt. xxiv. warned the Hebrew Church of the Advent of the False Messiah, so did He predict the appearance of the False Prophet, who no doubt will pretend to be the promised Elijah, and his fire miracles will support the pretention (v. 13). The second Wild Beast will appear as a lamb with its two horns of testimony, but it will speak like the dragon. Its double testimony will be false, and its teaching will be subtle, crafty and deceitful as was the serpent's (Gen. iii. 1, xlix. 17, and 2 Cor. xi. 3). The Dragon will be the Anti-God ; the Wild Beast

will be the Antichrist ; and the False Prophet will be the Anti-Holy Spirit. These three will form the infernal trinity. All the Scriptures which speak of these Wild Beasts speak of them without exception as individuals.

This False Prophet appears four times— xiii. 11, xvi. 13, xix. 20 and xx. 10. He will be the great Priest of the future. The worship he will introduce will be based on the resurrection of the first Wild Beast (vs. 3 and 4) and he will accredit this worship by great miracles. Man is superstitious. He demands miracles, but not truth. Miracles in themselves are no proof of Divine origination and approbation. Christ was accredited not by miracles, as such, but by the performance of a predicted class of miracles; and they operated in support of the truth of God's Word rather than of the Divine power of Christ. Hence they are generally called " signs." This is clear from Matt. xi.1-6. Miracles are common place. They were wrought by Johannes and Jambres and by multitudes of their successors. The astounding miracles that will be wrought by the False Prophet (v. 13) will establish his infernal origin and not his Divine appointment. The words " before him " (v. 12) mean in the presence of the first Wild Beast.

As Nebuchednezzar made his great image, so will the first Wild Beast have his great image ; but it will be much greater, for it will speak and will strike dead all who refuse to worship it (vs. 14 and 15). Seven passages predict the erection of this image— xiii. 15, xiv. 9 and 11, xv. 2, xvi. 2, xix. 20 and xx. 4. Ps. lxxiii. 20 foretells its destruction—" Oh Jehovah, in the city Thou shalt tread down their Image " (R.V. margin). This image will be set up at Jerusalem without doubt. All the world will worship the Image, and will receive its mark in their hands or foreheads. No one will be allowed to live otherwise (vs. 16 and 17), but the overcomers of chapters ii. and iii. and xiv. 1, xv. 2 and xx. 4, will refuse to be branded, and will suffer torture and death in consequence. Of these a few will survive to the end and be saved from martyrdom (Matt. xxiv. 13 and Ps. lxxix. 11).

To calculate the " number " of the Wild Beast (v. 18) is possible but difficult. This is suggested by the language of the verse. But when the time comes Daniel's faithful compatriots will recognise it. Meanwhile it is interesting to observe that the name of the Assyrian King—Antichrist will be king of Assyria—Jareb (Hos. v. 13), and the Hebrew King Jakim, i., Jehoiachim, the Jehovah prefix being omitted—are one and the same name and both count 666. This is man's number. Six is to man what the hall-mark is to silver. He was created on the sixth day. Man's great men have been so stamped. Goliath was six cubits in height, his spear's head weighed six shekels and he had six pieces of armour. Nebuchednezzar's Image was sixty cubits high, six cubits wide, and six instruments of music commanded its worship. 666 has a remarkable property, being the sum of all the numbers which make up the square of 6. It was also the mystic symbol of the Pagan mysteries. In Greek letters it is formed by the introduction of the serpent shaped letter between the first and the last letters of the word Christos, and thus the False and not the True Messiah can be mystically represented in number (χξς).

REVELATION XIV. 1-5.—The 144,000 called and chosen and faithful (xvii. 14) who were sealed in chapter vii. to go forth and war against the False Messiah and lose their lives in the battle (xii. 11 and xiii. 7), are here seen standing in triumph with their great Captain of Salvation,not one missing of the victorious host. This will be a greater victory than that of Num. xxxi. (see notes on Rev. vii.), for those combatants were "defiled with women" i.e., corrupted with idolatry, but these overcomers were not so "defiled." As to idolatry, and all its abominations which are to reach their climax in that future day, they will come out of the conflict "virgins" (v. 4) and "without blemish" (v. 5), and as a reward they will form the body-guard of Messiah during His millennial reign (v. 4). Impure as has been, and is idolatry, its full development of abomination will appear in the future when the Great Harlot will be seen seated on the Wild Beast (xvii. 3) and exercising a dominion over the kings of the earth (xvii. 18). Coupled with the unspeakable impurity of this system will be the world-wide acceptance of Satan's great "lie" (v. 5), i.e.. that Antichrist is the true Messiah (2 Thess. ii. 11).

These harpers (v. 2) will sing and will accompany the song with their harps. Such is the force of the Greek text. They will sing " as it were " a new song because such a conflict as this never had been fought before ; and only those who go through it will be entitled to sing of it (v. 3).

These will be a first-fruits (v. 4) of the harvest of verse 15 ; as in chapter vii. they are of the great multitude that no man can number.

Ephraim and Dan of necessity will not appear among these called and chosen and faithful, for they defiled themselves with " women," i.e., early lapsed into idolatry.

They whom God seals beforehand for the battle (vii.) are absolutely sure of victory. Not one of them can perish (xiv.).

The Throne, the Living Creatures, and the Princes will understand and appreciate this New Song, for though its subject will be new yet its theme will be the judgments with which these heavenly powers are associated.

" The lie " (v. 5, R.V. with 2 Thess. ii. 11) which all other lips will profess will not be found in the mouths of these true soldiers of Jesus Christ. From that crowning act of apostasy they will be without blemish.

These had followed the Lamb in His path of suffering and death, and now they are to follow Him in His path of glory and triumph.

REVELATION XIV. 6-20—This passage anticipates the outpouring of the seven last plagues. It views the ground and the people that will be tormented by the plagues (6-11) ; it shows the necessity for them (v. 8) ; and it briefly describes the judgment that will immediately follow them (vs. 14-20).

The great conflict of the future will at this point of time reach its climax. Men will have to decide between the worship of the true and of the false Messiah (vs. 6 and 9). Those who elect—whether from among the Hebrews or the Gentiles—to worship the True Messiah will be cast by the False Messiah into a burning fiery furnace whose torment will last for a few moments ; those who decide to worship the False Messiah and his image will be cast by the True Messiah (v. 10) into " the furnace of fire " whose torment shall last for ever and ever. This time of dread decision will distinguish true believers (v. 12) from mere professors. Only the former will bravely suffer the temporal torment of Antichrist's fiery furnace. They will keep the commandments of God and the faith respecting Jesus as being the True Messiah. As a consequence they will perish in the flame, animated by the words of verse 13. This verse has an application no doubt for all ages, but its interpretation belongs to these martyrs of the future. They will be blessed ; they will be liberated from their sufferings (" labours ") ; and their brave deeds will not be forgotten, but will accompany them to the land of triumph and of song. On the contrary the worshippers of the false Messiah will in this life have no rest day nor night, and in the life to come unceasing torment (v. 11). The words " worship " and " receiveth " in the Greek text determine the meaning as applicable to time. Thus was it in Egypt. Under the plagues the Egyptians had no rest day nor night; and in the sea they suffered an eternal doom.

The worship of Antichrist and the worship of Christ being in opposition, the glad tidings preached at the beginning by Him as Creator (v. 6) occupies the fore-front of the vision ; for evil will at this time have reached such a climax that the elementary facts of creation will be recalled. They were a Gospel for they declared that man did not create himself, nor was he created by some malignant Spirit, but by the God of love, afterwards revealed in redemption as the great God and Saviour Jesus Christ. The message commanded those " settled in the land " i.e., the Hebrews (v. 6), and, also, all nations to fear God and give glory to Him, and not to Antichrist. It announced that the very " hour " of the judgment had struck (v. 7) ; that only they who worshipped this Mighty Creator should escape ; and the third angel (v. 9) added that all others should suffer the wrath of God (v. 10). Such will be the Gospel preached during the Coming Day of the Lord. It will announce the actual " hour," i.e., the beginning of the judgment. The Gospel preached during this present period of mercy and long-suffering is the Gospel of the grace of God. It warns sinners to flee from the wrath to come, and not, as here, that the wrath has come.

This is the first mention of Babylon in this Book (v. 8). Her judgment (xvii. and xviii.) is here anticipated because she will be the great city of the false Messiah, the place of his throne and the centre of his religion. That religion will be the full grown fruit of the idolatry introduced by Nimrod. All nations have drunk of the maddening wine of that system of abomination.

The predictions of verses 10 and 11 are repugnant to " modern thought " but they are true, and will most certainly come to pass. The false worshipper will be " tormented "—a term expressing consciousness and personality—it does not say he will be annihilated.

Evil having reached a climax, judgment immediately follows (vs. 14-20). The Messiah is here presented as Son of Man (v. 14), for God has appointed a day in which He will judge men by that Man Whom He has ordained, for the Father has committed all judgment unto the Son because He is the Son of Man. As in nature so here, the vintage follows the harvest. They are predicted in Joel iii and Matt. xiii. At the bidding of the Son of Man the angels will harvest all workers of iniquity and cast them into the furnace of fire, and will assemble the vintage for judgment. The harvest symbolizes the Gentiles ; the vintage, the Hebrews —the vine that God brought out of Egypt.

The Messiah is here crowned with the stephanos of victory—not the diadem of monarchy. The sharp sickle denotes judgment. The word " thrust " (v. 15) should read " send." Here it is to be understood that He hands the sickle to the executant angel, as in verse 17. All is judgment. The sickles are sharp. A fiery angel (v. 18) carries the message ; the cloud is white, denoting righteousness ; the scene of the judgment is the earth (vs. 15, 16 and 18), and the place of the vintage will be Jerusalem (v. 20 with Joel iii. 12). The figurative language of verse 20 expresses the fullest destruction. Compare the terms " rivers of blood " and " miles of ruins."

The denunciation of the angel (vs. 9-11) and the consolation of the angel (vs. 12 and 13) will nourish the faith and brace the heart of Daniel's people at that time. This double proclamation makes it plain that it will be in reply to an opposite proclamation made by Antichrist. So it will be better to die than to apostatize ; and as this period of horror will only last three years and a half, the sufferings of these brave confessors of Christ will be short-lived.

The first mention of the Son of Man is Matt. viii. 20. He had not then where to lay His head. The last time the title is used is in this verse 14. His head is now crowned with gold, as promised in Ps. xxi 3.

REVELATION XV. The vision of the outpouring of the seven cups of God's wrath upon the Wild Beast (xvi.), the False Bride (xvii.) and Great Babylon (xviii.)—Satan's travesty of the Lamb of God. Israel and Jerusalem, is the most terrible of all the visions of this Book. It is immediately followed by the descent of the Messiah upon the earth. These plagues will fulfil the covenant of marvels which God made with Israel in Exod. xxxiv. 10. Their resemblance to His marvels in the field of Zoan and in the land of Ham can be at once recognised. They will complete the wrath of God, for they will be executed at the time when transgressors are come to the full (Dan. viii. 23). Seven is the figure of completion in the Scriptures.

Before the throne of Jehovah in the Temple at Jerusalem there was "a sea." It was contained in a vast vessel of polished brass, and no doubt represented on earth the heavenly pattern here seen (v. 2). This great sea of transparent fire possibly figures the righteousness of God and the wrath of God.

At, not on, this sea of fire another company of redeemed Hebrews whose bodies perished under Antichrist, but whose victorious souls defeated him, sing, not of their bravery and fidelity, but of the perfections and glories of the Lamb as Jehovah, Elohim, Shaddai, King of nations, and Lord Most Holy, the only Lord. These are all Old Testament titles. It is the Song of the Lamb.

Thus under the seals a redeemed multitude is safely sheltered (vii. 9); under the trumpets a further company, equally blest, is enthroned on Mount Zion (xiv.); and now under the vials a third company is gathered home (xv.). These companies are respectively seen in heaven by anticipation before the judgments are poured out upon the earth, so as to emphasize the faithful love of God assuring His people beforehand of the absolute safety of their souls whatever may be the fate of their bodies at the hands of wicked men (Isa. xxvi. 20). All these three companies speak only of the Lamb and His glories, and not of their own courageous conduct. But that is not forgotten by Him, for the Spirit says that their brave deeds will accompany them to the Throne (xiv. 13).

The "Song of Moses" (v. 3) is that of Deut. xxxii. The "Song of the Lamb" is given in this verse. It is the fulfilment of the predictions of the Song of Moses. A comparison may indeed be made between this celestial sea and the Egyptian sea of Exod. xv., but the song sung that day was the "Song of Moses and the children of Israel." "The Song of Moses" was that of Deut. xxxii. (See notes on that chapter).

The emphatic words Heaven, Temple, Testimony, Living Creatures, golden cups, golden girdles, the wrath of God and the smoke of His glory—all are designed to make absolute the Divine origin of these seven last plagues. Old Testament terms are heaped together, and very many passages from the Prophets and the Psalms are quoted directly and indirectly. The seven angels connect the Throne with the judgments, and the Living Creatures appear because the earth, as the sphere of the judgments, is about to be purified by them and Paradise restored.

Here is the end of the long parenthesis and of the series of episodes commencing in chapter xii. 1. The seventh trumpet, last mentioned in xi. 15-19 and there briefly outlined, is now to be described under the outpouring of the seven cups of the wrath of God.

The gold of the girdle and of the cup mark Divine relationship (vs. 6 and 7).

REVELATION XVI.—Excepting chapter xix. 11 this is the most important of all the visions that are to affect the earth. More space is apportioned to it than to any other. It completes "the mystery of God" (see Note on x. 7), and its subject is, as already stated, the Great Wine-press (xvi.); the Great Harlot (xvii.); and the Great City (xviii.). Eleven times the word "great" is found in this chapter—more often than in any other chapter in the New Testament. See Acts iv.

Having completed the parenthesis of chapters xii.-xv., the history of the Book now resumes and foretells that these last judgments will fall upon the Wild Beast, his kingdom and his worshippers so that they will have no rest day nor night.

There is a similarity between these judgments and those of the trumpets, but they were limited whilst these are general.

God promised Israel that in the end of His indignation against them He would deliver them from an oppressor more terrible than Pharaoh, and would strike their oppressor with judgments more appalling than those which fell upon the Egyptian tyrant. This promise, so often recalled in the Prophets and in the Psalms, will be at this time fulfilled ; and the similarity of these plagues to those of Egypt is consequently most striking. (See Exod. xxxiv. 10, etc.).

The earth, the sea and the rivers are here no doubt to be limited to the kingdom of the Wild Beast (v. 10) and are not to be understood of the entire earth. The plagues themselves will possibly be actual and material. They are possible to faith though not to reason. Similar plagues have occurred more than once in past Bible history. Compare Exod. ix., Job ii., 1 Sam. v., Num. xii., Deut. xxviii., Lev. xxvi., etc. But as these plagues were seen in vision they may be symbolic of exceptional suffering and misery both personal and national.

The "Great Voice" of verses 1 and 17 may be assumed to be that of Messiah Himself.

The sufferers are the Wild Beast and his worshippers ; and the language of verse 11 suggests that the judgments will be cumulative rather than consecutive.

"Soul" (v. 3), i.e., creature.

The expressions "angel of the waters," and "the angel having power over fire" (xiv. 18), show that angels have their spheres of duty ; that the operations of nature do not result from blind chance ; and that He Who made natural law has capable agents to attend upon their execution.

So incurably corrupt is man's heart that the fiercest judgments fail to affect its religion (v. 9) or its conduct (v. 11). The angel of xiv. 6 will cry to them to fear God and give Him glory but the message will meet with defiance.

The throne of the Wild Beast (v. 10) is that spoken of in ii. 13 and xiii. 2. The darkness here predicted will possibly be as real as that of Exod. x. 21, Joel ii. 1, 2, and 31, Mark xiii. 24, 25, etc.

The great climax of this vast prophecy now approaches, and the Rider on the white horse of vi. 2, crowned and armed, is about to meet in battle the Rider on the white horse of xix. 11, on whose head will be the many crowns, and out of whose mouth will issue a sharp sword.

Time will tell whether the Euphrates is here actual or symbolic (v. 12). The servants of God, with this Scripture in their hand, will recognise the Divine action. The expression "Kings of the East" is difficult of interpretation. Isa. xl. 3, Matt. iii. 3, Luke i. 76, Ezek. xliii. 2, Matt. xxiv. 27 and other Scriptures connect the East with the Messiah and His people. They, as kings, will accompany Him, the King of Kings, from the way of the East to claim His Throne in Zion. In this sense the drying up of the Euphrates may correspond with the drying up of the Red Sea. Compare Isa. x. 26, xi. 11 and 15 and Zech. x. 9-11. Or, on the other hand, the Kings of the East may be among the Kings pointed to in verse 14. But if that be so, it would appear strange that the angel of verse 12 should assist the demons of verse 14 in their Satanic war against the Messiah and His army (xix. 19). Or the expression may be the plural of majesty for "The Great King," i.e., Antichrist who is to arise out of the East (Dan. viii.).

This plague of the frogs corresponds with Exod. viii. 1-14, only it will be much more terrible, for these "frogs" will be demons. The battle of verse 16 will be that of xix. 19 and Zech. xiv. at Jerusalem.

The sixth vial judgment should be compared with the sixth trumpet judgment (ix. 13).

At this solemn moment (v. 15) the voice of Messiah Himself is heard animating and warning His soldiers. "Garments" here symbolize conduct. When it does not accord with profession the "nakedness" of that profession is seen by all and the unwatchful Christian is covered with shame.

"He" (v. 16) should read "They" (R.V.).

The mighty voice that shouted "Finished" from the Cross now shouts "Finished" from the Throne (v. 17). At the Cross the Divine purpose in grace was finished ; here the Divine purpose in wrath.

The manifestations of Divine power on earth under the seventh cup will be those under the seventh seal and the seventh trumpet (xi. 19, viii. 5). "The great city" here (v. 19) is Jerusalem. The destruction of Babylon introduces the details given in chapters xvii. and xviii. This judgment will be poured out into the air ; it will be comprehensive embracing both the heavens and the earth, i.e., "Babylon" and the cities.

In vi. 14 "mountains" and "islands" were moved. Here they flee (v. 20). After the millennium the whole earth and heaven will be driven away and no place be found for them. What is here meant by "islands" and "mountains" may be figurative.

History, and the newspapers of to-day record hail stones of extraordinary weight. The plague of hail in Egypt was real (Exod. ix.).

REVELATION XVII. and XVIII.—This is the most conspicuous prophecy of the Book. It describes the destruction of the religion and of the city founded by Nimrod. In the Revelation, the True Messiah and His city Jerusalem contrast with the False Messiah and his city Babylon. These two cities represent true and false religion, and are symbolized by the True and the False Women. The one is the Bride; the other, the Harlot. All the idolatries, both ancient and modern, originate in Babylon. She is the Great Harlot and they are her daughters. This vast system of falsehood and abomination is Satanic. Its purpose through all the ages has been to lead men to worship the serpent as the true God of love. This purpose will be accomplished in the near future, as predicted in this and many other prophecies. Satan will become incarnate in the False Messiah, and men will worship him as God. Under the ancient mysteries, and in the East to-day, this Satanic worship was addressed to the Phallus, and this is one of the reasons why the Scriptures so frequently speak of it as an abomination; for although it was philosophically held to honour the Creator and to promote the population of the earth, yet its effect was to depopulate whole countries and produce desolation. This was probably the hateful form of idolatry commanded by Nebuchadnezzar; and it will possibly reappear and be perfected by his successor Antichrist. That God's fiery indignation should fall with fury upon such wickedness is reasonable, and it will receive the acclamations of both heaven and earth.

"In the Spirit" (v. 3), i.e., in a spiritual trance. "The Scarlet Beast" (v. 3), i.e., Antichrist. He, as the last monarch will represent the six great empires that precede him, all of whom were energized by Satan to persecute and seek to destroy Daniel's people. These kingdoms are:—Egypt, Assyria, Babylon, Persia, Greece, and Rome. Antichrist himself will be the seventh. (see note on 1 Sam. xvi. 10) and he also will be the eighth (v. 11). As seventh Head he will be

mortal; will be slain with a sword; will descend into the bottomless pit; will re-ascend (v. 8); and will become the eighth and superhuman head of the Great Beast. The ten horns upon the seven heads (v. 7) are the ten toes of Daniel's image. They will appear in the near future.

So the seven "Heads" represent seven "Mountains" (v. 9) and these "mountains" represent seven empires (v. 10). Five of these are fallen, i.e., Egypt, Assyria, Babylon, Persia, and Greece. One still exists, and will exist at the point of time here contemplated in verse 10, i.e., the Roman. The seventh, i.e., Antichrist, is not yet come. When he comes he will, as a mortal, only reign a "short space," i.e., three years and a half, and then, raised from the dead, he will reign for a further similar period, at the close of which he will lead his armies to the great battle of xvi. 14 and xix. 19 when he will be cast alive into the lake of fire (xix. 20) and thus go into perdition (xvii. 8).

The "Woman" is here pictured supported by the Wild Beast and the ten kings, and from her throne she reigns over all the kings of the earth (vs. 3 and 18). But the Wild Beast and the ten kings (v. 16, R.V.) will destroy this great system of idolatry, and, as other prophecies declare, will substitute the worship of Antichrist himself. It is, therefore, reasonable to expect that in the near future a confederation of Governments covering the prophetic earth will establish a form of idolatrous worship that will be popular (vs. 2-4) and yet murderous to God's people (v. 6). But after a time the kings will destroy that worship (v. 16). Its centre and throne will be placed at Babylon (Zech. v.).

The word "Mystery" (v. 5) should be printed in ordinary small type and should read "A secret symbol," and that secret symbol is expressed in the words "Babylon the Great," etc. That is; the woman symbolizes the great Babylonian system of idolatry which has reigned, does reign, and will reign over the kings of the earth.

When John saw this woman he was overwhelmed with amazement, for it is plain that he had a consciousness that she claimed to represent the Messianic Church; and such indeed will be the final phase of what is called Christendom.

This Wild Beast and his confederates will make war with the Lamb (v. 14 with xvi. 14 and xix. 19), but the Lamb and His soldiers

—for such is the sense of the words "with Him"—shall be victorious over them. These soldiers are "called," for no one can make himself a soldier of Jesus Christ; and "chosen," for the Great Captain will only use picked troops in this final battle; and they will be "faithful," i.e. dependable.

The two chapters should be read together with Jer. li., Isa. xiii. and xlvii. Their prophecies connect the destruction of the Babylon of the past (Dan. v. 30 and Jer. li. 31, R.V.) with the Babylon of the future (compare xviii. 4 with Jer. li., 45, etc. and Jer. li. 48 with Rev. xix. 1-7).

Just as the silversmiths at Ephesus were enriched by the magnificence and popularity of the worship of the great goddess Diana, so the monarchs (xviii. 9), the merchants (v. 11), and the mariners (v. 17) of the future will be enriched by the magnificence of the religion of Babylon and by the vast system of idolatry that is to be enthroned there; for the trade of Babylon, like that of Ephesus, will include the sale of useless and idolatrous luxuries (vs. 11-19).

The Great Harlot of chapter xvii. having been destroyed (v. 16), the worship of Antichrist, of devils, and of every unclean spirit will be substituted (xviii. 2), and will continue till the city itself is destroyed and its monarch cast into the burning fire (xix. 20).

"Partakers of her sins" (v. 4), i.e., of the punishment of her sins.

Ps. cxxxvii. 8 and 9 and Rev. xviii. 6-8 will be fulfilled in the Divine doom of this debauched mother and her children. See notes on Ps. cxxxvii.

"The kings of the earth" (v. 9) are to be distinguished from the ten kings of xvii. 16.

The importance of the word "and" is emphasized by the Holy Spirit in verses 12 and 13. See note on Luke xiv. 13, 14 and 21.

Ancient Babylon gradually decayed, but this Babylon will be totally destroyed "in one hour."

That man should worship a Virgin is reasonable for she is the purest and the most beautiful god that he can see. Satan's aim all through human history has been to exploit this emotion, with the result that the Babylon of the past and the Babylon of the future will be the development of the worship of woman into a religion of revolting obscenity. Many useful books have been written on this subject, and they should be studied.

The prayers of Daniel's people for vengeance on their oppressors (vi., 10, viii. 3), will be followed by their praises (xviii. 20).

If xiii. 7, xviii. 24 and Jer. li. 47-49 be read together it will be quite clear that the martyrs of xviii. 24 are "the slain of Israel."

The reader of the Apocalypse must continually remember that the subject of the Book is "the Day of the Lord" (i. 10); and that that "Day" is the day—so often predicted in the Prophets—when the Messiah "will rise up to the prey" (Zeph. iii. 8) and will gather the nations together (Rev. xvi. 16) to pour upon them His wrath and to take vengeance upon them because of their oppression of His people. The interpretation, therefore, of the entire Book belongs to Israel—chapters ii. and iii. presenting her as the House of God with which judgment first begins, and continues all the time that the events of chaps. vi. to xix. are taking place. Thus chapters ii.-xix. concern, and fulfil, that "day" of visitation and wrath. Harmonious with this the prophetic field in the Book limits itself to Jerusalem as the centre, and to the lands contiguous to Palestine as the theatre, of these great events.

REVELATION XIX.—XX. 3. The people of the earth will cry "Alas, alas" (xviii. 10) but the people of Heaven will shout their fourfold "Hallelujah" (xix. 1, 3, 4 and 6) at the destruction of Babylon.

This (vs. 1-16) is the last of the visions seen in Heaven; and it records the final heavenly utterances and actions which close the prophecy.

If the messages to the seven assemblies be included there are twenty-four heavenly utterances in the Book. Six occur in chapters iv. and v. and four in chapter xix. In these are recorded the utterances of the Living Creatures. In the first, they praise Messiah that He is about to execute vengeance; in the last, they praise Him because He has done so. Only, on these two occasions, and in these two visions, are their voices heard.

In verses 1 and 6 is heard the voice of the great multitude. In verse 1 they rejoice over the destruction of the Harlot, and in verse 6 they rejoice because of the blessing and glory of the true wife. They utter a second "Hallelujah" (v. 3) because the judgment of verse 2 (which occasions the first Hallelujah) will be eternal (xiv. 8-11 and xviii. 21).

The word Hallelujah is a compound Hebrew word and means "Praise ye Jehovah." It occurs twenty-eight times in the Bible— twenty-four times in the Old Testament and four times in the New. Its first occurrence in the Old Testament (Ps. civ. 35) corresponds with its final occurrence in the New Testament (Rev. xix. 1). It calls for praise to God in both passages because of His destruction of sinners out of the earth. What earth laments over (xviii. 10) Heaven rejoices over (xix. 1). Heaven's moral judgment of sin and sinners is different from earth's. The reason why the great multitude shout "Hallelujah" is because Babylon is judged, and the reason why they repeat the "Hallelujah" is because the judgment is irrevocable and eternal. The cry of vi. 10 is now answered and the blood of the martyrs avenged.

The last time the Princes and the Living Creatures appear is in verse 4. Directly the Throne is set for judgment they are seen (iv.). Now that the judgment is accomplished they withdraw—adding their significant "Amen; Hallelujah"—so expressing their admiration for, and joy in, the judgments of God.

The "voice" of verse 5 is that of Ps. civ. 1, 33-35 and xxii. 22-28. See Matt. v. 10 and 12.

The eternal portion of the False Woman will be the lake of fire (v. 3) whilst that of the True Woman will be the Throne of glory (v. 9). That this woman symbolizes Israel is clear from Isa. liv. 5-8 and lxii. 4 and 5, Jer. iii. 14 and Hosea. ii. 16-19. Then will be fulfilled the marriage of Isa. iv. 5 when Messiah having purged Zion will spread above her the glory of the "Chuppah," i.e., the bridal canopy mentioned in Ps. xix. 5, Joel ii. 16, and Isa. lxii.

The pure and spotless raiment of the Wife (v. 8) contrasts with the purple and scarlet clothing of the Harlot (xvii. 4). The one was "arrayed" in the gaudy raiment that befitted her, and the other was "arrayed" in the spotless clothing suitable to her. This contrast helps to define the raiment as expressing reward—the fine linen represents, or rewards, the righteousness of saints. The Greek word expresses righteous actions, and the context suggests righteous awards.

If the happiness of those invited to be guests at the marriage supper will be so great, how great will be that of Israel as the Wife of the Lamb!

The word "worship" occurs twenty-four times in this Book. When followed by the Accusative Case it means to do homage as to a king; when followed by the Dative Case it means to give Divine worship. That the Apostle John should have twice so acted is a proof of the incurable religious blindness of the natural mind, and of its idolatrous bent.

The loved ministry of the Holy Spirit is to testify to Christ and of Christ. Hence the Spirit of prophecy is testimony concerning the Person and atoning work and glories of the Messiah as set out in this prophecy and in all prophecies. (v. 10).

The greatest heights of heavenly joy predicted in this Book are those of chapters iv. and v. and chapter xix. The one mighty anthem hails the atoning Lamb of God as He appears in the glory of His grace (iv. and v); the other greets Him in the display of His wrath. The Living Creatures and the Crowned Princes appear for the first and last times in these two great celebrations of praise. In all there are fourteen anthems in the Apocalypse. The four Halleluias of the New Testament appear in this passage.

The white robes of righteousness before the Throne (vii. 9) must not be confounded with the white robes of reward for faithfulness exhibited before man. The one is the ground of justification; the other, the evidence.

Falsehood and violence characterize the Harlot and her daughters in all ages; truth and gentleness reveal the Bride.

The final prophetic hour is now reached (v. 11) and the True Messiah appears in all His power and glory—faithful to His promises and true to His judgments. He contrasts with the False Messiah of vi. 2. He was neither faithful nor true. He will go forth to conquer for himself, and will accordingly make war in unrighteousness. But this Rider will come forth for judgment, and will wage righteous war and fulfil the prophecy of Ps. xlv. 3-6 and of Zech. ix. In this latter prophecy His First Coming in humility (v. 9) and His Second Coming in glory (v. 10) are both foretold.

The glorious majesty of His Deity and of His Messiahship are set out in verses 12 and 13. Faith knew Him as faithful and true: and His appearing now in judgment will be a demonstration of His faithfulness and truth. Though thus revealed, He has a glory no man can penetrate into. That Name of glory is written so that it is not to be unknown but yet it will be unknowable; for no one knows the Son but the Father. In His humiliation that glory was hidden from man in the unsounded depths of His Person, but it was written there and read by the Father. When revealed in glory that Name will remain unsearchable to man. His revealed Name was the Word of God, for He revealed God in His grace and power so as to make Him known, and so the believer can say "I know Him."

His vesture is dyed with the blood of His enemies (v. 13 with Isa. lxiii. 1) for He here appears as the Avenger of His people. The raiment of the mighty hosts that follow Him will not be so stained for He will tread the wine-press alone; to them will remain only the triumph, and as His chosen, called, and faithful ones they will share that triumph with Him. His was the vengeance of Idumea. They will be later His instruments in smiting the nations (v. 15, Mic. iv., Zech. x. 3-10. Now will be fulfilled the prophecy of Luke xix. 27 and of Jude 14 and 15.

The Divine titles of Elohim, Jehovah, Shaddai, the Lamb, the Word of God, and King of Kings and Lord of Lords are here heaped together and given to Him. All judgment is committed unto Him, just as all creation was formed by Him and all redemption accomplished by Him. "By the breath of His lips" i.e., the sword that proceeds out of His mouth (vs. 15 and 21), He shall slay the wicked as predicted. The language of this passage is doubtless symbolic, but yet it must be remembered that Elijah and Elisha both saw horses of fire round about them in the heavens.

Now will be fulfilled the faithfulness and truth of Ps. xlv. and of Isa. xxv. Israel's Bridegroom will gird His sword upon His thigh and ride forth to deliver His Bride, to destroy her foes, to establish His Throne and to celebrate the Marriage Supper. The faith that trusted Him through the long intervening years will now acclaim Him as the Faithful and True Bridegroom (see notes on Ps. xlv.).

Essentially (His thigh) and by investiture (His vesture) He is King of Kings and Lord of Lords (v. 16). Hence the title is written both upon His person and His raiment.

The judgment of the Wild Beasts (v. 20) of their followers (v. 21), and of Satan (xx. 3) now follow. The impotency of the False

Messiah immediately appears, for how could he reach an angel standing in the sun (v. 7)? "Foul demons" (xvi. 14) gathered these armies together but a holy angel summons the fowls of the heaven to devour them, for they are but men, and hence the word "flesh" is repeated five times in verse 18. These armies will be composed of both volunteers and conscripts; and they will be furnished by nations both small and great. This will be "the Great Supper" (v. 17, R.V.). It contrasts with "the Marriage Supper" (v. 9). Both are now preceded by the Gospel Supper (Luke xiv. 17).

The battle planned at Armageddon now takes place at Jerusalem (v. 19). The Wild Beasts are cast alive into the lake of fire and their armies are slain; and as they refused burial to Emmanuel's followers (xi. 9) so will burial be refused to them. As the angels whom Satan corrupted are bound in the abyss with "chains" (2 Pet. ii. 4 and Jude 6), so will Satan himself be bound (xx. 2), not with a chain of iron or of steel but with what the Holy Spirit here describes as "a great chain." These communications of the Spirit make it plain that Satan, and the two Wild Beasts, and the members of their armies are persons and not moral abstractions. The bottomless pit —the abyss—is to be distinguished from the lake of fire (xix. 20 and xx. 10 and 14). The four designations Dragon, Serpent, Devil, and Adversary are here used to assure absolute personality. Within the terrible word "must" (v. 3) lies a Divine secret that doubtless will be revealed at the time of Satan's eternal doom (v. 10).

Just as God used the Chaldeans to judge Jerusalem and then judged the Chaldeans themselves (Isa. xlvii.), so will He use the ten kings to judge Babylon (Rev. xvii. 16) and then will He judge the kings themselves (xix. 21). To be cast into the lake of fire (xix. 20) does not imply annihilation, for one thousand years later the False Messiah and his companion are seen there (xx. 10). If the abyss is such a place of horror that the legion of devils besought the Lord not to dismiss them thither (Mark v. 12), how terrible must be the horror of the lake of fire!

REVELATION XX. 4—XXI. 8—The field of prophetic vision in the Apocalypse is confined, in the main, to the final conflict between the False and the True. Messiahs and their respective followers during the period of the future "Day of the Lord." In harmony with this only the overcomers (vs. 4 and 6) appear in the First Resurrection (v. 5). The judgment of the Church (2 Cor.vi. 10) and of the living nations (Matt. xxv. 31), together with other predicted actions of theDivine purposes, are not mentioned as not being necessary to the theme. The subject is the doom of the False Messiah (xix. 20), the triumph of the True Messiah (v. 4), the destruction of the followers of the one (xix.21), and the blessedness of the followers of the other (v. 6). The "overcomers" of verse 4 are those who appear in this Book from chapter ii. onwards, and the "blessed" of verse 6 include all the holy dead from Abel who shall rise at this resurrection of the just. This is the former of the two resurrections of John v. 29; the latter is the resurrection of xx. 12. See Introduction.

"They" (v. 4), i.e., those that had been beheaded because they had not worshipped the Wild Beast, etc. The words "I saw" should not be introduced before "the souls of them," etc. Man could destroy their bodies but not their souls. Accordingly they appear in resurrection. The expression "the souls of them that were beheaded" may simply read: "those that had been beheaded." These are the thrones of Dan. vii. 9, 21, 22 (see note), and they will be placed around the Throne of the Messiah. Matt. xix. 28, Luke xxii. 30, The True Messiah will come not only to make war in. righteousness but also to judge in uprightness. The promise made in vi. 11 is now fulfilled in xx. 4; and it includes not only the martyrs but all who had refused to worship the Wild Beast. So those who lose their lives for His sake will refind them in resurrection, and those who through cowardice secure their lives will lose them (Matt. x. 39). This "first," i.e., of the two resurrections of this chapter (v. 12)—for the rapture of the Church (Col. iii. 4) will precede both of these—will last a thousand years. Righteousness will "reign" during that millennium, but it will "dwell" in the New earth (xxi. 1). These terms "reign" and "dwell" must not be confounded (2 Pet. iii. 13).

The condition of the impenitent dead (v. 5) while awaiting the final resurrection (v. 12), is not revealed in Scripture. Outside the Bible no one knows anything about death and judgment. But a child skilled in the Holy Scriptures may know all that can be known on these subjects

This first resurrection is that to which both prophecies and Psalms point, and it will satisfy those predictions (Luke xiv. 14, John v. 29, Acts xxiv. 15, xxvi. 6-8, Dan. xii. 2, John xi. 24, Heb. xi. 35, etc.); and the promise that Israel shall reign on the earth as a kingdom of priests will then be fulfilled. (Rev. i. 6 and v. 10 (R.V.), Isa. lxi. 6, Exod. xix. 6, etc.).

Continually in this Book God and Christ are presented as One in the Unity of the Godhead (v. 6).

It being necessary that man's moral impotency should be fully demonstrated and tested, Satan will be loosed from his prison (v.7), and, as at the first so at the last, seduce men. The creation Sabbath witnessed the first seduction, and the millennial Sabbath will witness the last. In this, as in many other features, the first and last Books of the Bible correspond. Satan's final rebellion is here confronted with his first; and man's final rebellion with his first. So incurably diseased is the natural heart (Jer. xvii. 19) that a thousand years of perfect happiness and absolutely just government, together with exemption from all forms of suffering, will fail to win man's heart to God; and he will at the close choose Satan and the depthless miseries of his government rather than Emmanuel and righteousness.

The counsel of God as revealed in the Scriptures decreed an exhaustive test of man as a moral creature in order to demonstrate his inability to stand in his own strength, and thus illustrate the great lesson of the Bible that, apart from Christ, no creature and no created thing can stand. He created all things; and only in Him do, and can all things continue to exist. Hence man was tested under Innocence, Conscience, Law, Grace and will be tested in the future under Righteousness. Rev. xx. foretells that he will fail under it as he failed under the four prior tests. This final test explains the word "must" of Rev. xx. 3.

"Gog and Magog" (v. 8) is a Hebrew term expressive of multitude and magnitude. It here embraces all nations—"four quarters of the earth." This is not the Gog and Magog of Ezek. xxxviii. and xxxix., for xxxix. 25 says that "at that time," as the result of that battle, the captivity of Jacob will be restored ; but this assemblage of the nations (v. 8) will take place at the close of the millennium. This is conclusive.

The beloved city, Jerusalem (v. 9), and those faithful to Emmanuel encamped around it, will be the object of Satan's vengeance. Apparently at the close of the millennium the Messiah will retire into the heavens and leave man to this final trial ; and as in past ages, so in this future one, a little company of believers will become the object of human hatred energized by Satan. But God having declared that there shall be war no more, fire from Heaven will devour the rebels, and Satan their leader will be cast into the lake of endless torment.

The subjoined Divine Plan of the Ages (Eph. iii. 11, R.V. margin) helps to interpret these prophecies :

The First Heavens and the First Earth (Gen. i. 1).
  Satan's First Rebellion (Gen. i. 2).
    The Earth Restored (Gen. i. 2 and ii. 25).
      Satan's Entry (Gen. iii.).
        Mankind the object of Divine Love (Gen. iv.-xi.).
        Israel Called and Blessed (Gen. xii.—Malachi).
        The First Advent (The Gospels).
        The Church taken out (Eph.).
        The Church taken up (Thess).
        The Second Advent (Rev.).
        Israel Recalled (Rom. xi.).
        Mankind the object of Divine Love (Rom. xv.).
      Satan Bound (Rev. xx. 3).
    The Earth Restored (Rev. xx.).
  Satan's Final Rebellion (Rev. xx.).
The New Heavens and the New Earth (Rev. xxi.).

Satan fell through pride (Luke x. 17-20, 1 Tim. iii. 6 and 7). It is reasonable to believe that his fall occasioned the ruin of the Primal Creation, for Isa. xlv. 18 states that it was created not a waste, and Gen . i. 2 declares it became a waste. There must, therefore, have been a terrible convulsion ; and more than one passage of Scripture suggests Satan as the cause of it (Isa. xiv. etc.).

That dead people are to stand (v. 12) is one of the most appalling statements of prophecy. In that dread judgment will reappear those who will suffer death during the millennium because of sin (Isa. lxv. 20), and the dead of xix. 21, and all the impenitent from Cain onwards. None will be able to question the justice of their doom, for their own actions will decide their eternal destiny (v. 12) ; and the presence of the Book of Life will be a testimony to the fact that they rejected an eternal salvation offered to them during their lifetime. Whether devoured by the fish of the sea or the worms of the land (v. 13), they shall rise from their graves and shall be " shaken out " of death and the grave into the lake of fire. See Greek text. Not one shall by any possibility find a hiding place. Only those whose names are written in the Book of Life shall escape the eternal horror of the second death (v. 15). Grace and not merit inscribes names in that Book (Luke x. 20, Phil. iv. 3 Exod. xxxii. 32, Dan. xii. 1, Heb. xii. 23).

" I saw," " I saw," " I heard " (xxi. 1-3). These repetitions displace imagination and assert reality. This " new earth " (v. 1) will not be sunken in the dark sea of Gen. i. 2 for there will be no more sea. See notes on Isa. li. and lxv. and 2 Pet. iii.

" And He said " (v. 5) " and He said," (v. 5), " and He said " (v. 6). These repetitions assure reality and fulfilment. The heavens and the earth will be revived, but death and the grave never. They will never have any power again, for death—the last enemy—is to be destroyed. There will no longer be a mediatorial kingdom. The Lamb is not now seen in the vision. God is all in all. Man is His dwelling-place. It will be a paradise which nothing can pollute (v. 4). See 1 Cor. xv. 28.

The mighty declaration " Finished " heard in the morn of creation, and at Calvary, and now here repeated for the last time, closes all prophecy (v. 6). He Who as the Alpha created the primal heavens will as the Omega establish the New Heavens, and so once more in His love He invites all who thirst for eternal life to accept it from Him as a gift (v. 6). He assures them that if they bravely overcome (v. 7) they shall inherit the joys set out in verses 3 and 4, but that if through fear they shrink back (v. 8) their eternal portion must be the lake of fire. This together with xxii.17, is the last message of grace and love and warning to perishing men. It is of arresting solemnity that the "fearful," i.e., the cowardly, are here placed with murderers, and idolaters, etc.

The establishment of this sinless and deathless world of bliss and love, and this last double message of invitation and of warning, closes the Bible history of God's redemption of man.

Here the prophecy ends. In verse 9, the reader is brought back to the millennium.

There are eight apparitions of Messiah in this Book, viz.: i. 13; iv. 3 and 11; v. 6; vii. 9; xiv. 1; xiv. 14; xix. 11; and xxi. 6. The first and last correspond, i.e., the judgment of the House of God and the judgment of the world. This harmonizes with the character of the book as a book of judgment. Hence it opens with the judgment of Calvary (i. 7) and closes with that of the Lake of Fire (xxi. 8).

The four appearings of The Man in the Glory of John xx. and xxi. (see notes on John xx.) and His eight appearings in the Apocalypse, reveal the majesty of His Person (Rev.) and the might of His power (John). The proportion in the numbers illustrates how man's need (4) is doubly provided for by Christ's fulness (8).

REVELATION XXI. 9.—XXII. 5.—The reader is now brought back to view the Holy City which is to illumine the millennial Earth and afterwards the New Earth. This is the city which "has the foundations" which the Old Testament Saints looked for (Heb. xi. 10, Isa. lx. etc.). Its relationship to Messiah (v. 9 and Ezek. xlviii. 35); its name (v. 10); its gates (v. 12); its glory (v. 23); its purity (v. 27); its government (xxii. 3); and its citizens (vs. 3 and 4) are all connected with the promises made to Israel and with the establishment upon earth of the Throne and home of Jehovah Messiah. This city contrasts with Babylon, and this Bride with the Harlot.

The city will be 1,500 miles square (v. 16). It appears as a pyramid—its top stone 1,500 miles above its base. This vast mountain will be made of transparent gold. It will be Eden restored. Eden was possibly a pyramid. The Tower of Babel was a pyramid and was man's effort to restore Eden, and to construct a home which would be at once a city and a Temple. The Pyramids of Egypt and of Mexico and other lands, evidence this

thirst of fallen man for a happiness which he lost. A broad street paved with gold will border the base of the mountain on each of its four sides. Through the middle of that street the River of Life will flow, and on its banks the Tree of Life will grow. A wall about 250 feet high and having twelve gates, three on each face, will encompass the city. Its twelve foundations will bear the names of the Twelve Apostles of the Hebrew Church and its gates those of the twelve tribes of Israel. See note on Eph. iii. 5.

There will be no Temple therein (v. 22) for the city itself will be the Temple of God; and so it will satisfy the desire of man in all ages to have a city which at the same time will be a Temple.

Statements such as verses 12, 24, 26 are millennial, and others such as xxi. 2, are eternal. The city will, therefore, be the Throne and Palace of God during both ages; and will consequently not pass away in the destruction of the present universe (2 Pet. iii. 10 and Heb. xii. 28, xiii. 14). The controversy as to the relation of this city to the millennium or to the New Earth need not, therefore, arise.

The correspondence between these two last chapters and the two first chapters of the Bible proves that they have the one Divine Author. Paradise reappears, and the Tree of Life, and Elohim preparing a sinless earth, and Jehovah Elohim placing man in it (xxi. 2 and xxii. 5). As Creator He is Elohim; as Redeemer, Jehovah Elohim. See Gen. i. and ii.

They only which are written in the Book of Life shall enter into the city (xxi. 27 R.V.).

If it be objected that a gold pyramid 1,500 miles square and 1,500 miles high is inconceivable, the answer is that this earth is 8,000 miles high and 24,000 miles in circumference and yet is conceivable. The Christian believes much that he cannot understand. To the Red Indian who knew that an ounce of iron cannot float it was inconceivable that a great canoe of iron carrying 10,000 people and propelled by blazing fires inside, should not only float but travel for thousands of miles across the ocean.

Paradise is always presented in Scripture as a definite place. It was planted in Gen. ii.; lost in Gen. iii.; reappears in Luke xxiii. 43; visited in 2 Cor. xii. 2-4; promised in Rev. ii, 7; and regained in Rev. xxii. 1-5 and 14 and 17. Its first inhabitants hid themselves from the face of God. Its future occupants shall see the face of God (v. 4).

The dimensions of the city are here given according to a human scale of measurement as when on a map a vast continent is reduced to a few inches (v. 17).

The number 7 appears in connection with the government of Jerusalem. The Amoritic, the Davidic, the Post-exilic, the Herodic, the Islamic, the Antichristic, and the Messianic.

REVELATION XXII. 6-21.—The certain accomplishment of the prophecies of this Book is three times declared (xix. 9, xxi. 5, xxii. 6). In the Introduction and Conclusion it is three times affirmed that these are Divine predictions and not mere human imaginations (i. 1, xxii. 6 and xxii. 16). At the opening and close of the Book a blessing is pronounced on its readers and observers (i. 3 and xxii. 7).

The Holy Spirit is the Author of the Book. If He is not, then is the Book worthless.

The Conclusion of the Book (xxii. 6-21) corresponds to its Introduction (i. 1-20). This may be thus shown :

The angel testifies.
  The things testified.
    Benediction.
      Advent.
John testifies.
  The things testified.
    Ascription.
      Advent.
John testifies.
  The things testified.
    Advent.
      Salutation.
Jesus testifies.
  The things testified.
    Advent.
      Interpretation.
Conclusion (xxii. 6 21).
The angel testifies.
  The things testified.
    Advent.
      Benediction.
The angel testifies.
  The things testified.
    Advent.
      Benediction.
The angel testifies.
  The things testified.
    Advent—the Morning Star.
      Benediction.
Jesus testifies.
  The things testified.
    Advent.
      Benediction.

These four witnesses and the things witnessed, assure the nearness of the Advent and the blessing reserved for all who love and watch for it.

These structures, together with the terms " shew " (v. 6), " wash " (v. 14 R.V.), " churches "(v. 16), and the titles " Root and Offspring of David " and " Bright and Morning Star," and the Benediction (v. 7), emphasize the unity of the Book, and militate against the popular partitioning off of the first three chapters.

The Revised Version reading of verse 6 emphasizes the fact of Inspiration.

" Shortly " (v. 6), i.e., swiftly. " Quickly " (v. 7), i.e., suddenly. That is, directly the period of time comes, defined in this Book as " the Day of the Lord " (i. 10), these great events will swiftly succeed each other and will close with a sudden apparition of the Messiah.

In harmony with the form of Hebrew prophecy the angel uttered personally what he was commissioned to report (v. 7).

John affirms that he both saw and heard what he here records (v. 8). The incurable enslavement of the human heart to idolatry notwithstanding Ch. i. 12-18, here again appears (xix. 10 and xxii. 8). If the wisest monarch that ever lived, and who also was an inspired prophet, and if the most beloved of the Apostles were by nature idolaters, how needful is it for all Christian people to watch against the smallest beginnings of this evil in the shape of crosses, crucifixes, pictures, images, etc.

Daniel was told that Divine purposes had to intervene prior to the commencement of the prophecies shown to him (Dan. xii. 9 and 13) ; but John was assured that the time was at hand (v. 10), that is, that this future period of human history was " at hand," i.e., next in order for fulfilment.

The lesson of verses 11 and 12 appears to be that the suddenness of the apparition of the Great Judge will make repentance and conversion impossible. Every man will be rewarded according to his conduct ; and the eternal destiny of each will be fixed either as holiness or vileness. Verse 11 may therefore read : " He that is unrighteous he shall remain unrighteous," etc. The Deity of the Judge, declared in i. 8, is here (v. 13) reaffirmed. There could be no more decisive and conclusive assertion of absolute Godhead and Deity than the claim to be "the Alpha and the Omega." See Isa. xliii. 10 and 11, and xliv. 6.

The sense of "I come quickly," is : I will come suddenly, i.e., in a moment, unexpectedly.

Verse 14 should read as in the Revised Version, and is connected with i. 5 and vii. 14. The redeemed prior to conversion were sin-stained and altogether unfit to enter in through the gates into the city, and had no right to the Tree of Life. Such was the moral condition of Abel as he stood outside the gates of Paradise. But he washed his robes in the Blood of the Lamb of God in type and symbol. He found salvation in the great Priest of the Atonement. Cain on the other hand loved and practised a lie (v. 15), and proved himself to be a murderer and in spirit an idolater. His religious worship was evil (1 John iii. 12).

The Messiah assures John (v. 16) that the angel was His messenger. He calls Himself "Jesus" but John addresses Him as "Lord Jesus" (v. 20) ; and all Christians should be similarly reverent.

The churches (v. 16) are primarily those of chapters ii. and iii. ; and the titles "Root and Offspring of David" and "Bright and Morning Star" and "Bride," define the interpretation of these prophecies as Hebrew property.

The Spirit and the Bride, and the hearer of these prophecies, and he that thirsts for their fulfilment, all cry out "Come, Lord Jesus" ; and those who dare not meet Him—no matter how guilty and sinful—are invited to take as a free gift and undeserved the water of life (v. 17) and so have a right to the Tree of Life (v. 14), and in their turn be enabled to unite in the cry "Come, Lord Jesus."

The sufficiency of the Holy Scriptures as a full and final revelation from God, is here asserted in verses 18 and 19 by the Lord Jesus Himself ; and the doom of eternal judgment is denounced upon all who shall add to or subtract from them. Whilst "this Book" means the Apocalypse, the warning applies to all Scripture as given by inspiration of God.

"Once more the Messiah speaks, and for the last time His voice is heard saying "Surely I will come suddenly" ; and faith and love respond saying, "So be it ! do come, Lord Jesus."

The Bride of Gen. iii expelled man from the world that then was, but the Bride of Rev. xxii. invites men to enter the world that will be. Genesis is the Book of beginnings ; Revelation the Book of endings. The benediction of restored Paradise and its Tree of Life and Water of Life correspond to the First Paradise, but far exceed its primal conditions.

The eternal permanence of restored Paradise is assured by the title Alpha and Omega, for that declares that the Messiah is the One and only God and that there will never be another. The world sees and can see nothing of these coming glories, but to faith the dawn is there, and Christ is the Morning Star—and more, the Bright and Morning Star to all who love His appearing. His promise to come is the delight and joy of the heart that watches for Him. The world will never know Him as the Bright and Morning Star. All on earth is failure and corruption ; but the promise of His Coming sustains the faith and strengthens the courage of His people ; and animates them to urge whosoever will to take the water of life freely.

So the Book closes with a salutation of grace (v. 21) leaving the promise to come as the last message from the Lord Jesus to the believer's heart ; and on this sweet note the prophecy ends.

The office of the Messiah as Saviour is repeated again and again throughout the prophecy. He is the Lamb that was slain, and His blood washes from sin and alone makes fit for entrance into the eternal city.

The great theme of the New Testament at its opening is, the First Advent, and its great theme at the close is, the Second Advent.

The first and last "I wills" of the Bible move the heart, for they affect its most intimate and tender relationship, i.e., marriage. The first is "I will make him a help meet for him" (Gen. ii. 18) and the last is, "I will show thee the Bride the Lamb's wife" (Rev. xxi. 9).

The Holy Spirit declares that no Scripture is of human origination (2 Pet. i. 20) but that on the contrary all Scripture is of Divine inspiration (2 Tim. iii. 16) ; and those who sit where Mary sat (Luke x. 39) know that this double testimony is true.

Τῷ δὲ βασιλεῖ τῶν αἰώνων ἀφθάρτῳ, ἀοράτῳ μόνῳ θεῷ τιμὴ καὶ δόξα εἰς τοὺς αἰῶνας τῶν αἰώνων.

NOTE TO THE READER

Because of the unfamiliarity of most of us today with the Roman numeral system used throughout this book, the following conversion table may offer welcome assistance to many readers:

i	1	xxii	22
ii	2	xxiii	23
iii	3	xxiv	24
iv	4	xxv	25
v	5	xxvi	26
vi	6	xxvii	27
vii	7	xxviii	28
viii	8	xxix	29
ix	9	xxx	30
x	10	xl	40
xi	11	l	50
xii	12	lx	60
xiii	13	lxx	70
xiv	14	lxxx	80
xv	15	xc	90
xvi	16	c	100
xvii	17	cx	110
xviii	18	cxx	120
xvix	19	cxxx	130
xx	20	cxl	140
xxi	21	cl	150